W9-CAS-558

1977 BRITANNICA BOOK OF THE YEAR

ENCYCLOPÆDIA BRITANNICA, INC.

Chicago, Toronto, London, Geneva, Sydney, Tokyo, Manila, Seoul

Library of Congress Catalog Card Number: 38–12082
International Standard Book Number: 0–85229–325–9
International Standard Serial Number: 0068–1156

BRITANNICA BOOK OF THE YEAR

(Trademark Reg. U.S. Pat. Off.)
Printed in U.S.A.

THE UNIVERSITY OF CHICAGO

The Britannica Book of the Year is published with the editorial advice of the faculties of the University of Chicago.

Contents

Feature Articles

People of the Year

Chronology of Events

Book of the Year

Special Reports

SALGADO—GAMMA/LIAISON

The Aftermath of Angola

by Basil Davidson

Much changed in central and southern Africa during 1976, and with dramatic speed. What happened then, in all present likelihood, marked the ending of a long phase in modern history and the onset of another and very different one.

Late in March 1976 there came the final defeat of a number of attempts to prevent the victory in Angola of a radical or "root and branch" nationalism led by the 20-year-old Popular Movement for the Liberation of Angola (MPLA) under its veteran chairman, poet and former physician Agostinho Neto. But this was only one of a series of comparable events and sets of consequences that had begun exploding all around this vast subcontinental region in 1974, impelling new developments whose limits could not yet be marked.

By the summer of 1976 the situation was such that critical but previously fixed positions in subcontinental politics had become blurred, uncertain, and liable to shift or even disappear. The further unfolding of all this would obviously reach out into the future. Yet the history of 1975–76 already appeared to have ensured an early end to white minority rule in Zimbabwe (Rhodesia), made South Africa's continued administration of Namibia (South West Africa) more than problematical, brought to Africans even within South Africa itself a fresh and vivid hope of progress against the apartheid system of racist rule, and signaled, in close relation with these trends, a major and most public setback for the pro-minority policies of the West, notably those associated with U.S. Secretary of State Henry Kissinger. Whatever the precise future of these territories might be, things would never be the same again.

How and why has all this come about? We are now in midstream of events that still have far to go; and if their general course and direction seem broadly set, their pace and actual destinations have yet to become known. So an attempt to answer this question may best begin with singling out and considering the historical "turning points" or moments of decisive change that have occurred in the past three years. These are not hard to find.

Portuguese Africa Liberated. The first of these "turning points" began in Lisbon on April 25, 1974. This was the revolt of young officers of the Portuguese armed forces, chiefly in the Army and assembled clandestinely in the Armed Forces Movement. Impelled by defeat in Portugal's colonial wars as well as by a growing disgust at the nature of these wars, their action overthrew Portugal's 48-year-old dictatorship and, under the slogan of "Decolonization and Democratization," led very quickly to the full success of the nationalist liberation movements in the Portuguese African colonies.

In West Africa, by the middle of September 1974, the African Party for the Independence of Guinea-Bissau and Cape Verde (PAIGC) achieved the complete independence of Guinea-Bissau and went on to establish a second sovereign republic in the Cape Verde Islands in July 1975. Its closely associated companion movement in Mozambique, the Mozambique Liberation Front (Frelimo), reached the same destination in June 1975. Their likewise closely linked companion in Angola, MPLA (whose founding members had included the late Amílcar Cabral, initiator of the PAIGC), had to face internal rivalry and bloodshed together with actual or imminent foreign intervention. But by September 1975 it had managed to assert its control over some 12 of Angola's administrative districts and was poised to secure the rest. Rounding off the destruction of Portugal's African empire, the islands of São Tomé and Príncipe in the Gulf of Guinea became independent in July 1975.

The Challenge of Radical Nationalism. This collapse of the Portuguese colonial system had consequences far outside the territories concerned. The balance of power in central Africa immediately shifted, to the especial detriment of the U.S.-favoured Pres. Mobutu Sese Seko of Zaire (ex-Belgian Congo), and a comparable shift threatened in the southern region where minority rule had until now appeared so safe as to be able to continue for many years into the future. In losing Angola and Mozambique to a coherent and radical nationalism, the minority regimes were at once deprived of their two great "flank guards" on the northwest and northeast. Beyond this, the successes of the liberation movements also changed the regional balance of influence between a new type of nationalism, aiming at domestic revolutions, and the old-style reformist nationalism of the 1960s. Hitherto it had been this reformist nationalism, now increasingly attacked by the younger generation (and about half of all African populations are under 20 years old), that had held the balance; now it was the nationalism of the liberation movements. Successful in their own territories, the ideas for which these movements stood were on the march elsewhere as well.

These ideas encompassed two governing principles of policy. One of them was that independence, to be worth its name, must be able to displace the attitudes and structures of colonial rule by new ones that should be genuinely indigenous, and therefore capable of self-development. This, it was held, also had to mean an end to projections of external capitalist supremacy, such as had appeared during colonial times, in favour of an increasingly noncapitalist

---

Author and historian Basil Davidson, winner of the Haile Selassie African Research Award, 1970, has written extensively on African affairs. His books include The African Awakening *(1955)*, Which Way Africa? *(1964)*, Africa in History: Themes and Outlines *(1968)*, The African Genius *(1969), and* In the Eye of the Storm: Angola's People *(1972)*.

ALON REININGER—CONTACT

U.S. Secretary of State Henry Kissinger and South African Prime Minister B. J. Vorster met in Zürich in September. Observers thought that Kissinger put pressure on Vorster that led to Rhodesia's acceptance of the principle of majority rule (by blacks) in two years' time.

or anticapitalist mode of progress. Any other policy, in this view, would confirm an exterior, if indirect, economic and cultural control. The second principle, flowing from the first, was one of military nonalignment in world affairs. While many of the leaders of these movements were of Marxist persuasion, it was strongly argued that the movements themselves were neither Communist nor inherently anti-Western: on the contrary, all their leaders repeatedly called for friendship with the West.

The West Seeks Stalemate. Kissinger and other Western statesmen thought otherwise. They had long since concluded that any far-reaching form of anticolonial change in this subcontinental region must be adverse to Western interests. They had accordingly buttressed the Portuguese dictatorship with large quantities of finance, arms, and diplomatic support all through the long colonial wars that Portugal had waged against the liberation movements. So sure was Kissinger that the dictatorship would win that he had given his approval to a basic policy document of 1970, *National Security Memorandum 39* of the U.S. government, which forecast that white minority regimes were there to stay and that U.S. policy must be predicated on this assumption. In the embroilments of 1975 the West, therefore, continued to treat the MPLA in Angola as an enemy, just as it had formerly treated Frelimo and the PAIGC as enemies. Portugal's defeat thus became a defeat for the West, leaving the U.S.S.R. to score an easy advantage by using its support for these liberation movements as an immediate means of widening the African area of nonalignment and "noncapitalism." In the case of Angola, the Soviet Union had the additional satisfaction of aiding in the defeat of China's chosen friends there.

The West rapidly accepted the success of the movements in Guinea-Bissau and Mozambique, there being no usable alternative. But in the case of Angola, the richest of the territories, it still appeared possible to prevent the MPLA from coming to power. Efforts had long been made in that direction, principally through the agency of President Mobutu. The same efforts were continued in 1975 on an altogether larger scale, eventually involving the agency of Pres. Kenneth Kaunda of Zambia as well. In the end it was only the hostility of Congress, which sensed possible involvement in "a second Vietnam," that prevented the U.S. government from continuing to channel money to Mobutu for use against the MPLA in Angola. In the event, neither of the anti-MPLA contenders, the National Front for the Liberation of Angola (FNLA) of Holden Roberto, based on Zaire, and the National Union for the Total Independence of Angola (UNITA) of Jonas Savimbi, based on Zambia, was able to dominate the MPLA, which was now receiving much larger quantities of aid from the Soviet Union, Yugoslavia, and some other Communist countries. By September the MPLA had secured all but a handful of districts. With independence due on November 11, the MPLA was set to win.

South Africa's Gamble. What further intervention might even now prevent this? The answer was in fact already on the scene. Early in August 1975 the South African government had sent military units into southernmost Angola to occupy dams on the Cunene River and destroy guerrilla base camps of the Namibian liberation movement, the South West Africa People's Organization (SWAPO). This minor invasion in a remote and sparsely populated area could make no difference to the outcome on November 11. On October 23, however, the spearhead of an armoured force of the South African Army, eventually numbering perhaps 6,000 men, thrust northward over the Namibian frontier and began advancing toward the MPLA stronghold of Luanda, Angola's capital.

With FNLA and UNITA bands and European mercenaries

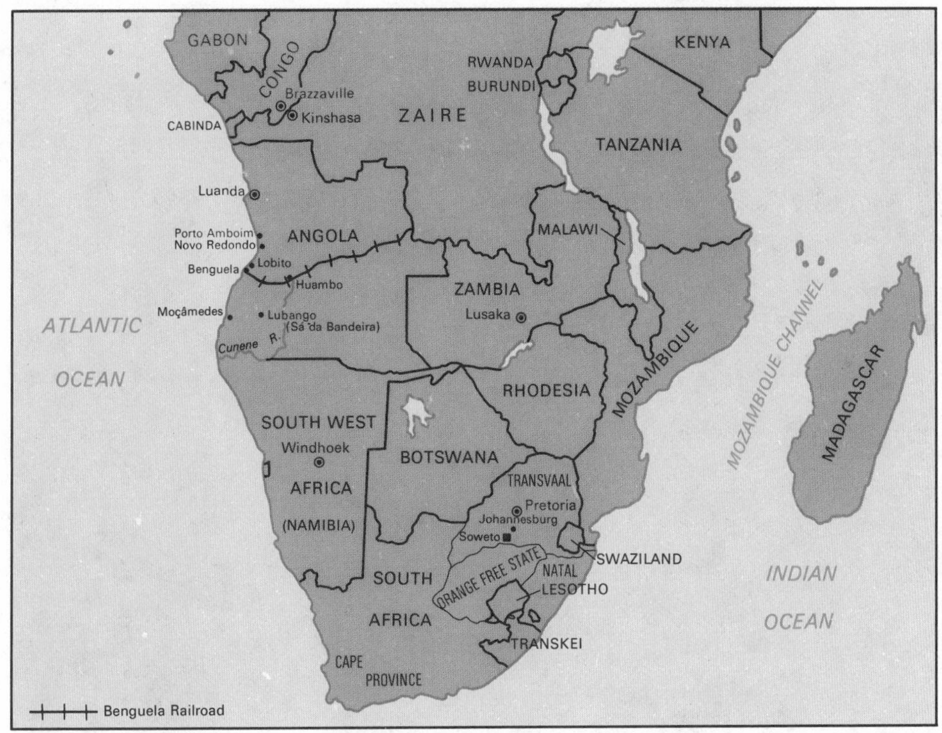

The collapse of Portugal's colonial system weakened the flanks of the two remaining white-dominated states, South Africa and Rhodesia. On the east, Mozambique sheltered guerrillas from Rhodesia. On the west, Angola became a haven for nationalists from South West Africa (Namibia), still administered by South Africa. To the north were the other black "frontline" states of Tanzania, Zambia, and Botswana.

to occupy the towns it took, this force rapidly swept aside weak MPLA garrisons in Moçâmedes, Sá da Bandeira, Benguela, Lobito, and Novo Redondo. North of the last-named seaport, some 650 km from the Namibian frontier, the invaders ran out of steam short of Porto Amboim and were stopped by units of the MPLA army. By this time, these MPLA units were reinforced with Cuban troops who had begun to reach Angola in strength on November 5, at MPLA invitation.

Here, for a while, stalemate supervened. Other MPLA forces, meanwhile, continued to defend Luanda against a joint FNLA-Zaire-mercenary force sent in from Zaire and equipped to some extent with Chinese weaponry, Peking now having appeared as an active supporter of Mobutu and the FNLA against the Soviet-supported MPLA. These FNLA and mercenary units were shattered and driven out of Angola during January 1976. Things then changed in the south. Large Cuban reinforcements—in a total Cuban involvement variously put at between 10,000 and 15,000 troops, but probably around 13,000 with an actual military commitment considerably less—arrived to stiffen MPLA offensive capacity with artillery of Soviet origin.

By late February it had become clear that this joint force was too powerful for South Africa's invasion force unless Pretoria should send large additions to its strength. Denied such reinforcements, and beginning to be badly mauled, the invaders now went back the way they had come. On March 27 the last of South Africa's units retreated into Namibia. Pretoria's choice had lain between the acceptance of an MPLA regime in Angola and commitment to a major war; bitterly enough, though no doubt wisely, Pretoria refused the second choice. White South Africa had thus embarked on the military gamble which it had refrained from making a year earlier in Mozambique, and the gamble had failed.

Pressure on Rhodesia Intensified. Yet the momentum of these remarkable events, including as they did this signal defeat for South Africa's enormously expensive Army, was not so easily brought to a halt. The next point of change and tension came without delay in Rhodesia (Zimbabwe), South Africa's principal client and frontier state, where a small white minority continued to rule by its own version of apartheid in defiance of the British Crown. Up to that time, on the African side, policy with regard to Zimbabwe had been periodically settled by an informal "presidents' council" of the black "front-line" states. The "council" consisted initially of Pres. Julius Nyerere (*see* BIOGRAPHY) of Tanzania and President Kaunda, sometimes with the presence of President Mobutu and latterly with the regular membership of Pres. Sir Seretse Khama of Botswana.

This "council" had generally striven to forge unity among exiled Zimbabwean politicians, though with little success, in the interests of a constitutional settlement whereby the white minority should transfer its political power, gradually and if necessary partially, into African hands. Their prospect was one of a slow African advance within the continuing structures of white minority control. But with Portugal's collapse this kind of solution came under increasing criticism. Pres. Samora Machel of Mozambique joined the "council" while Mobutu, the declared enemy of the liberation movements and of any radical solution, found himself excluded from it. Machel believed that a resolute political movement using the instrument of guerrilla war could now become as sovereign in Zimbabwe as Frelimo had become in Mozambique, and that nothing less should be its aim. To that end his government declared full support for UN sanctions against the illegal minority regime of Ian Smith—its illegality deriving from a unilateral declaration of independence from

SALGADO—GAMMA/LIAISON

Mozambique soldiers patrol the Rhodesian border in March 1976. Their purpose was to see that the border remained closed to traffic and to rebuff any armed attack from Rhodesia. Their new country was born in the collapse of Portugal's colonial system.

Britain in November 1965—and opened Mozambique's territory to training and base camps for Zimbabwean guerrilla fighters.

By this time Nyerere was seeing things in the same light as Machel. Together they outweighed the still very hesitant Kaunda, whose preference was for a gradualist compromise, and the necessarily hampered Khama, whose country was more or less surrounded by South Africa. With MPLA success in Angola, President Neto joined this group of policymakers, bringing with him the same ideas that were espoused by Machel and Nyerere. Meanwhile Zimbabwean guerrillas stepped up their war in Rhodesia, made some important advances there, and caused the Smith regime to declare a state of emergency while stretching its mobilization of white and black troops to the probable limits of the possible.

Now running hard to overtake events, the principal statesmen of the West came quickly to the only choice that remained open to them save renewed frustration. This was to get rid of minority rule, at least in the extreme and direct form represented by the Smith regime, before the last chance for a gradualist compromise should vanish. It would be wrong to say that Western policy underwent a change at this point, for it continued to hold that Western interests must demand the preservation at least of the basic economic system that had been built by white-settler domination in Rhodesia and, beyond that, must try to ensure that new pressures on white South Africa stay within manageable limits. But some shifts of emphasis were now seen as unavoidable.

The Kissinger Initiative. It was evident, for example, that the West would be wise to put intolerable pressures on the Smith regime so as to make it go away, while at the same time achieving some clear progress toward Namibian independence and, if feasible, some relaxation of apartheid severities within South Africa itself. For these purposes, Secretary of State Kissinger held an initial meeting in Bavaria, West Germany, late in June 1976, with South African Prime Minister B. J. Vorster.

Little was released about this evidently difficult encounter, but further negotiations became necessary and were resumed at a second meeting between the two men, this time in Zürich, Switz., early in September. Vorster's position was a delicate one. He remained a staunch believer in white supremacy, whether for South Africa or Rhodesia. As a shrewd and practiced politician, however, he was well aware that he might have to sacrifice the Smith regime in the interests of his own. His own electorate made that a difficult operation. But his own electorate was now badly shaken by storms of African protest in the Transvaal and elsewhere (*see* below), and Kissinger applied unanswerable arguments. Either Pretoria show itself ready to withdraw its crucial economic support for the Smith regime and thus destroy it, or a guerrilla war would radicalize the Zimbabwean situation in the manner of Angola and Mozambique.

The outcome of this second meeting became public three weeks later. Then it was seen that the intolerable pressures had been applied and had worked. After meeting Kissinger in Pretoria on September 19, Smith told his electorate that majority rule would have to come in two years' time. In Smith's version of the agreement he had made with Kissinger (Vorster assenting in silence), there would be an immediate conference under British chairmanship. A council of state would then frame a majority-rule constitution. International sanctions would be called off, and so would the guerrilla war. Though without U.S. or British consent to this interpretation, Smith presented these and other proposals as a "package deal" not open to negotiation on its components, his evident aim being to secure a "fallback" position of compromise with minority rule.

The "front-line" presidents and the various sections of the Zimbabwean nationalist movement at once reacted against Smith's attempt to impose preconditions; they would, they affirmed, accept none. The conference, for them, was one between the British and the Africans; its task was to discuss every aspect of a rapid but complete transfer of power to the majority. Against this background, a conference under the chairmanship of a British diplomat, Ivor Richard, duly assembled in Geneva at the end of October. Prolonged for many weeks, discussions ran repeatedly aground on the actual date for independence and other issues. But the real ground of contention lay in African determination to secure a genuine majority rule against the Smith regime's maneuvers in favour of some form of continued white minority control.

South West Africa. The Namibian case was in some ways less complex, but no easier to resolve. Although repeatedly condemned as illegal by the UN, South Africa's administration of the country remained as intact as ever. Yet Pretoria had accepted that moves must be made in the direction of African autonomy, or at least the semblance of such moves. Plans to modify direct South African rule into indirect forms were already in play. In September 1975 Pretoria had organized a political conference (with all political parties banned in Namibia) by which the territory would eventually be splintered into "tribal" states on the Bantustan model; as in South Africa, continued white control would not be in question. The lost gamble in Angola now hastened matters. In March 1976 Pretoria reconvened its conference of nominees. On August 18 Pretoria announced that Namibia was to be given an interim state government composed of approved "tribal" and local white individuals, and that formal "independence" would follow at the end of 1978.

This proved too little and too late to win any African or other international recognition. To begin with, it excluded from participation the majority Namibian nationalist organization, SWAPO, as well as the smaller African political groupings. The U.S., Britain, and West Germany had already rejected South African requests that they accept the validity of the conference proposals, and the UN and the Organization of African Unity roundly condemned what the UN Council for Namibia (set up to assist Namibia toward and after independence) described as a "maneuver" designed to prolong white minority control. While Kissinger sought to persuade Vorster to accept SWAPO as a necessary negotiating partner, it now appeared that only much stronger Western pressure on Pretoria could achieve a genuine Namibian sovereignty. All the same, the position from an African standpoint was notably stronger than it had been a year or so earlier.

White Rhodesians had few friends in 1976. Below, a white settler near the frontier is guarded by reservists against raids by black guerrillas. In some areas buildings were burned and buses blown up by mines. On the other side of the border, Mozambique troops rallied to cheer Pres. Samora Machel when he announced in March that he was closing the border with Rhodesia. "Our country has been attacked," he declared, "and our people are being massacred." (The sign says "Down with imperialism.")

MICHAEL EVANS—CONTACT

SALGADO—GAMMA/LIAISON

CAMERAPIX—KEYSTONE

In order to counter the guerrilla movement, Rhodesia established "protected villages." Here a black guard checks the identity cards of returning villagers. They were also searched to prevent them from smuggling weapons into the village.

Protest Erupts in South Africa. These various developments deepened white South Africa's political isolation from the rest of the world and even from its major economic partners in the West. And at about this point, midway through 1976, still another twist was added to the drama of eruptive change, once again to Pretoria's disadvantage. This was provoked by the enforcement of an apartheid order to the effect that African schools must adopt the language of the ruling minority, Afrikaans, as a medium of instruction for some subjects. There followed huge demonstrations of protest of a size and vigour scarcely seen before. Beginning in June, these protests occurred initially in the Transvaal African township of Soweto near Johannesburg, and were answered by police bullets in circumstances of widening defiance and disorder. The South African authorities admitted that their police had killed 176 Africans in Soweto, but African sources put the total of dead at about twice that number.

While antiapartheid protests around Johannesburg spread from one town to another and ranged from well-organized strikes to outbursts of violence, comparable demonstrations appeared elsewhere, eventually in several of the chief towns of Cape Province. In the weeks that followed many hundreds more were shot by the police, although exact figures are in dispute. It was remarked by observers that these demonstrations were not only massive and determined, with unarmed youths and women literally advancing against police rifles, but were also joined by people of the Coloured (mixed origin) community of the Cape and even, here and there, by a handful of whites. Almost overnight the hitherto voiceless masses were now most vocally upon the scene.

With his police force shooting into crowds of angrily defiant Africans, Vorster had to meet Kissinger and defend the stability of his regime. It cannot have been easy for him, and the order for compulsory Afrikaans was quietly withdrawn. This was clearly not the end of apartheid or anything like it. But what the demonstrations had shown the world was that even the "white fortress" was no longer invulnerable. These demonstrations sounded a sharp political note, especially that of the long-banned and persecuted African National Congress of South Africa; and the meaning of the music could scarcely be mistaken. If minority rule could be ended in the Portuguese colonies, and now prospectively in Zimbabwe and even in Namibia, why not also in South Africa?

South Africa's Response. There was just as obviously a long and painful way to go. Apart from a few minor gestures to the critics of apartheid, the leaders of South Africa clung firmly to their established policies. These were chiefly two, the one military and the other administrative. They spent more on armaments. Having pushed up their military budget every year since the mid-1960s, they raised it again from the equivalent of U.S. $1,322,-000,000 in 1975 to $1,494,000,000 in 1976. Already making sophisticated weapons on license from British, French, and

DE LA PORTE—GAMMA/LIAISON

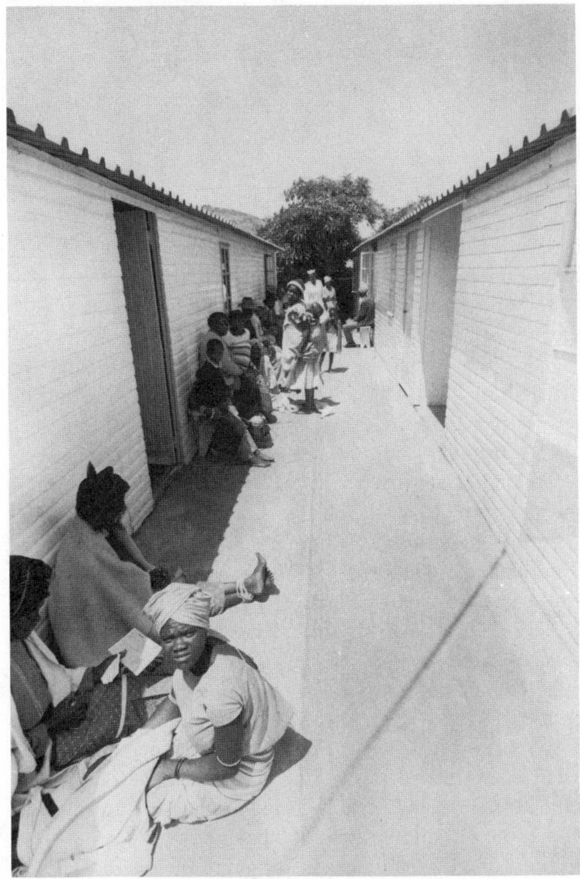

A hospital in Transkei, a new black state established by South Africa. The hospital was founded by missionaries in 1932.

other Western companies, they continued to buy abroad what they could not manufacture at home.

Currently, the most important of these overseas purchases were from France, which, as before, placed no obstacle against the sale of arms to South Africa. On order in 1976 were 32 Mirage F-1 AZ fighter aircraft and French naval matériel. South African factories were meanwhile filling orders for 30 Impala interceptor-support fighters and 37 Kudu transports.

While thus preparing for a major war, since no other kind of war could justify or explain the size and type of its already enormous armoury, Pretoria continued its efforts to take the steam out of political discontent among the mass of nonwhites who, in 1974, numbered about 21 million, compared with 4.2 million whites. This involved a long-prepared project to reshape the native reserves, covering less than 15% of the whole territory, into a cluster of "tribal" states with internal autonomy, the so-called Bantustans. The ruling Afrikaner National Party had never in the past envisaged these as independent states, but now, striving for cosmetic effect, the claim was duly made. The largest of the Bantustans, the Transkei (a group of native reserves since 1913), became "independent" on Oct. 26, 1976. No member of the international community gave any sign of being willing to recognize this "independence," since all the evidence indicated that the government of the Transkei, or that of any other Bantustan, would remain under Pretoria's close control.

How little this administrative devolution could in fact reduce the pressures of discontent, even if there were to be real devolution of power, was indicated by the population statistics. When all the Bantustans were launched, they would contain about seven million Africans on the 1970 figures. But eight million other Africans would remain outside these "tribal" states and live exactly as before. They would continue to be noncitizens subject to the full rigours of apartheid. And the June–October demonstrations had confirmed, once again, that the greatest pressures of discontent came not from the rural areas, from the native reserves, but from the towns and zones of white employment and direct race discrimination.

Such policies might have looked adequate before 1974, even if they already presumed years of internal strife and, in the end, a major war against the "white fortress." They wore a different look in the aftermath of Angola. More and more qualified persons in South Africa, white as well as black, were now saying that an unrelaxed apartheid could only tear the country apart. Outside South Africa, even Kissinger had begun talking a very different language from before. "The Americans," President Nyerere told a press conference in Bissau on September 20, shortly after his first meeting with Kissinger, "say that they support those who want majority rule in South Africa, and that they will try to bring this about as soon as possible."

Pointers to the Future. Could or would the apartheid system set about dismantling itself to any meaningful extent? Given white South Africa's attitudes anchored in an extreme racism, there was nothing to make one think so. If not, however, then to what extent would Western pressures on the Smith regime become, and for much the same reasons, an unavoidable prelude to eventual Western pressures on white South Africa: whether to protect the West's position in the rest of Africa or to conserve the West's substantial interests in South Africa itself? How far was Kissinger sincere in what he said to Nyerere? How far, in the wake of Angola, could he afford not to be sincere? Or again, with Pres. Jimmy Carter at the helm, how far would U.S. policy readjust to these realities?

Such questions had apparently acquired a stiff underpinning of realism. Aside from the shifting balance of power and influence, there was the fact that Western economic interests in black Africa had grown steadily in recent years. Nigeria, for example, was now the U.S.'s largest non-Arab (though not non-Organization of Petroleum Exporting Countries) oil supplier, and Angola could become another. At a different level, there was the relative certainty that a continued Western preference for white South Africa at all points of crucial decision, as in the past, must now enable the Soviet Union to reap other political and diplomatic gains of the kind scored in Angola. At a lesser but still important level, along with sentiment in the U.S. Congress against more foreign crusading, there was the growth of humanitarian condemnation of the apartheid system among groups and individuals who could not be written off as radicals. The year ended in uncertainty. Large social and political forces were obviously on the move toward far-reaching change. Perhaps that march might slacken its pace for a while, but the balance of the evidence agreed that it would certainly continue.

The Coming of Metricated Man

by Herbert Greenberg

With the passage of the Metric Conversion Act of 1975, the 94th Congress and the president of the United States committed Americans to one of the most far-reaching—and expensive—adventures ever undertaken in the country's history.

The debate about metric had been going on for nearly two centuries before this momentous decision was taken by America's leaders. The metric system originated in France in the 1790s, during the early years of the Revolution. France had supported the American colonies during their own revolution against Britain, and during the first decades of the 19th century there was considerable sentiment in the United States in favour of adopting the new, un-British system. But tradition prevailed until 1968, when Congress directed the secretary of commerce to undertake a "U.S. Metric Study."

Its report was transmitted to Congress in 1971; entitled "A Metric America, A Decision Whose Time Has Come," it was an unqualified recommendation that the country go metric. Congress acted in 1975, and Pres. Gerald Ford signed the bill with the remark that the main impetus for the legislation had come from the private sector. The implication was that ordinary people, like you and me, had at last seen the light. There is some doubt, however, whether ordinary people had much to say about it, or whether they would have wanted metric if they had known what they were in for.

What are the main arguments that have been proposed in favour of the international metric system (SI, for Système International)? And how well do those arguments stand up to examination?

Basically, there are four arguments in favour of metric. The first is that metric is a more rational and convenient system, and more appropriate for the ordinary activities of everyday life. The second is that the metric system is easier to teach and easier to learn, and that its adoption will produce significant savings in educational time and money. The third is that there are major computational advantages of metric over customary units. And finally, it is said that by switching to metric the U.S. will join the rest of the world in an inevitable progress toward greater international communication and understanding.

Is Metric More Convenient? Metric units may be more rational than customary units, but are they more convenient? Ask for justification of metric and one is told that humans have ten fingers and ten toes, that most countries use a decimal number system and a decimal monetary system, and that it is untidy to suffer from such inconveniences as the fact that there are 5,280 feet to a mile. But these arguments seem to miss the point.

Perhaps the most basic objection to metric units is that they come in the wrong sizes for people. When we are engaged in the ordinary measurements of everyday life, the metric precision of hundredths (*centi*) or thousandths (*milli*) is seldom required, while the halves and quarters of the customary units, when absent, are sorely missed.

To appreciate the inconvenience that metric entails, imagine what it would be like if the only coins one had were the "decidollar" (1/10 of a dollar—the dime) and the "centidollar" (1/100 of a dollar—the penny). No nickel. No quarter. No half-dollar.

Yet it is precisely this kind of inconvenience that metric measurements impose. A cubic centimetre, the metric building block of volume or capacity, is much too small to be useful (except in a chemistry lab), besides being hard to say and spell. It doesn't get easier when one knows that a cubic centimetre is a millilitre, that is, one-thousandth of a litre. Who in the home would ever want to divide a litre (about a quart) into 1,000 parts anyway?

The same difficulty exists for units of length. The SI units commonly used are the metre (about a yard), the centimetre (one-hundredth of a metre), and the kilometre (one thousand metres). The millimetre (one-thousandth of a metre) is admittedly for machinists. But even the centimetre is not convenient for humans. It's too small. Two and a half centimetres is not quite an inch. A person who is 5 feet 10 inches tall turns into 178 centimetres—a large number and certainly no easier to say or remember because it is the same as 1.78 metres. The metre is not useful for most home measurements. It's too large.

The most useful people-size measurement of all, the foot, disappears. The nearest thing to it is the decimetre (one-tenth of a metre—less than four inches), and this unit is not commonly used in the SI system.

The kilometre is a unit of a useful size for measuring large distances. But so is the mile, which is easier to say and spell. Nature regards neither as sacred. It is approximately 3,000 miles from New York to San Francisco, the Earth is approximately 8,000 miles in diameter, and the Sun is approximately 93 million miles away. It doesn't get easier in kilometres; one just gets larger numbers.

Temperature next. The scale Americans are used to is called Fahrenheit. Markings of temperature in Fahrenheit are on the stove, in the car, on the fever thermometer, outside the window, on the living room thermostat.

Metric temperatures are measured on the Celsius scale, which used to be called centigrade. On this scale, water freezes at 0° and boils at 100°. One of the big selling points of metric is that this is a lot simpler to remember than the Fahrenheit equivalents of 32° (for freezing) and 212° (for boiling). Perhaps for chemistry exams; but the gain doesn't

---

Herbert Greenberg is professor and past chairman of the department of mathematics at the University of Denver. His specialties are applied mathematics, numerical analysis, computing, and mathematical education.

seem to amount to much when we remember that in countries situated in the temperate zones of the Earth, like the United States, the temperature largely ranges between 0° and 100° *Fahrenheit.* When it's 0° it's *cold,* when it's 100° it's *hot,* and everything else lies pretty much in between. The corresponding temperatures in Celsius are about −18° and 38°, not exactly catchy numbers to remember.

Another human dimension of the discredited customary units becomes apparent when one measures body temperature. Normal body temperature is 98.6° on the Fahrenheit scale. Not a very convenient number, to be sure. But look at it this way: normal body temperature is just under 100° Fahrenheit. Over 100° call the doctor, under 100° wait and see. Normal body temperature on the Celsius scale is 37°—a nondescript, hard-to-remember number if there ever was one.

The situation, as far as ordinary humans are concerned, gets even worse when one asks for the metric unit of weight. Alas, there is no metric unit of weight, or at least none that will be taught to schoolchildren or used by ordinary people.

"What about the kilogram or gram?" one may ask. "Aren't these units of weight?" The answer, sadly, is no. Neither the kilogram nor the gram is a unit of weight. Both are units of *mass.*

In SI one measures the mass of an object rather than its weight. Why? Because mass is the more basic physical unit. The mass of an object doesn't change from place to place in the universe. Weight does, being a measure of the gravitational attraction present. So astronauts always have the same *mass* whether they are on the Earth, on the Moon, or in orbit. But they only weigh one-sixth their Earth weight on the Moon and are weightless in orbit.

To be frank, it is simply absurd to insist on a concept like mass because of its invariance from place to place in the universe, when our concerns about weight never get any farther from home than the neighbourhood store and the gym! And even if one gets used to thinking like a physicist, the units of mass are still inconvenient for ordinary use. From gram to kilogram is a huge jump, with nothing useful—like the ounce—in between.

The pedantry of metric measurement is also apparent when we deal with smaller amounts of substances, used by people most commonly in medicines. Take, for example, the vitamin pill. In metric terms we do not say that we are taking a half-gram pill of vitamin C, nor does the label on the bottle tell us that. No, each pill is 500 milligrams. And since a milligram is one-thousandth of a gram, each pill contains 500/1,000 of a gram—which, as everyone should know, is just one-half. One-half gram is three syllables to say, 500 milligrams is six. Which conveys meaning more readily? Which is easier to spell? Unfortunately, fractions like one-half, one-third, one-fourth are considered to be "unmetric."

Is Metric Easier to Learn? Proponents of metric are unanimous in maintaining that the metric system is easier to teach and to learn. The U.S. educational establishment is especially vociferous on this point, going so far—as reported in a U.S. Metric Study Interim Report (1971)—as to claim that savings of substantial amounts of time spent teaching arithmetic, and as much as $500 million a year in educational costs, would result from the adoption of metric. But aside from the fact that there is absolutely no hard evidence to support these claims, there are also good reasons for thinking the claims are not true. The main reason is that there are serious psychological obstacles to learning the metric system, especially for English-speaking people.

If a number of objects are assigned code names, the more similar the names are (in the absence of other clues), the more difficult it is for the human mind to learn to associate the names with the objects. There is a mathematical basis for this psychological fact. "Information theory" tells us that, to reduce errors in communication, we must make the words of a code as dissimilar as possible.

One further mathematical point. Information theory also tells us that, for maximum efficiency of communication, symbols should be as short as possible. Why only three digits to a telephone area code? Since each digit can be any of the ten numbers 0 to 9, the area codes can range theoretically from 000 to 999, so a total of 1,000 different areas can be labeled. That is more than enough to blanket the Bell System. More than three digits would be redundant and would add to the memory and system burden.

Now back to metrics. Listed in the left-hand column below are the most-used units of length, area, capacity, and weight of the customary system. In the right-hand column are an equal number of most-used units in the metric system.

inch	millimetre
foot	centimetre
yard	metre
mile	kilometre
acre	hectare
ounce	millilitre
cup	centilitre
pint	decilitre
quart	litre
ounce (weight)	gram
pound	kilogram

The first thing that becomes obvious is that the English words are much *shorter* than the metric ones. Next, except in one case (the word ounce has two meanings), the English words are *dissimilar* to each other, while many similarities exist among the metric terms. Both the short word length and the dissimilarity are distinct advantages of the customary system for communication. And, of course, the English words are easier to say and spell.

There is a pattern to the metric terms, which is the basis for the claim that they are preferable to the customary terms. The metric terms for length all end in "metre" and differ only in prefix. The same holds true for the metric terms for capacity, where the ending is "litre," and for mass, where the ending is "gram." The prefixes are the same in each case, those most used being *milli* (= one-thousandth), *centi* (= one-hundredth), *deci* (= one-tenth), and *kilo* (= one thousand).

Superficially, the pattern in metric names seems to give them an advantage over the totally unrelated words of the customary system. The catch is that for English-speaking people, especially children but probably for the majority of adults as well, the prefixes *milli, centi, deci,* and *kilo* can only be considered as nonsense syllables. So to remember the association between these syllables and the sizes of things—or, more precisely (where computation is required), the collection of multiples 1/1,000, 1/100, 1/10 and 1,000 which they represent—must be an exercise in pure memory and a difficult one at that.

Proponents of the metric system often ridicule the rods, furlongs, square perches, poles, chains, cords, fathoms, cables, nautical miles, leagues, pecks, gills, drams, hogsheads, and barleycorns of the customary system. Yet these are specialized units, which most people never use or have to learn, but which make good sense and are familiar and appropriate to (and even beloved by) the sailor, horse trainer, farmer, or whoever lives with them. But if one thinks customary units are a laugh, get a load of the metric prefixes—*tera, giga, mega, kilo, hecto, deka, deci, centi, milli, micro, nano, pico, femto,* and *atto.* The only things missing are chico, harpo, zeppo, and groucho.

Also, psychologically, one should not forget the intimate connections that exist between customary units and the dimensions of the human body. This is not only significant for learning, it is also important for the way we view ourselves and our relation to the universe or, more humanly, the relation of the universe to us. But the entire metric system is independent of any human dimension. Is it really a disadvantage for the human mind, and isn't it significant to the human spirit, that the adult foot is about a foot in length, that the first joint of the thumb is about an inch in length, that a man's stride is about a yard?

Does Metric Simplify Computation? Turning from pedagogy to arithmetic, what about the claim that metric units will simplify computation?

It is easier to divide by 1,000 to go from metres to kilometres, one is told as a typical example, than to divide by 5,280 to get from feet to miles. If one merely compares two division problems this may be true. The rule for dividing by 1,000—move the decimal three places to the left—is, for some, simpler than the rule for long division. But both rules have to be learned anyway, and in fact division problems as such are seldom encountered! Only in classrooms and textbooks are we asked to divide one number by another. What we encounter in daily life are problem *situations;* what is significant is the ability to reduce such problems to mathematical computation. This is called *problem solving,* and at the level we are discussing it requires knowing what operation to use. Do you add, subtract, multiply, or divide to get the answer? A mere change of units does not simplify that problem at all.

Moreover, in everyday problem situations, *exact* answers are seldom required, only *estimates.* We usually round numbers to the nearest ten, hundred, thousand, million, or billion before we compute, regardless of the system of measurements we are using. For example, it would be absurd to use an "exact" figure for the mileage between Chicago and Denver and an "exact" airspeed of a plane to compute the "exact" time required to fly a jet between the two cities. Instead, we estimate the distance at 1,000 miles, the air speed at 500 miles per hour, and divide 500 into 1,000 to come up with an estimate of two hours' flying time. Newer schoolbooks recognize this and devote considerable attention to estimation, approximation, and rounding. The importance of emphasizing these skills becomes even more evident when it is realized that inexpensive handheld electronic calculators are now available to do exact computation, whereas the human mind is uniquely suited for the reasoning that underlies estimation.

In 1975 the National Assessment of Educational Progress published a report on problem-solving competence of U.S. children and adults in several age groups. Simple word problems were posed that required translation into one-step arithmetical problems. On the average, these problems were missed by about one out of three adults and two out of three 13-year-olds. But, interestingly enough, it was found that only a very small percentage of those who set up the problems correctly (that is, knew *what* to do) were then unable to do the computations (that is, failed to know *how* to do it). This suggests strongly that the arithmetic itself is not where the trouble lies.

Indeed, the developing disputes and difficulties over the curriculum and teaching of metric reminds many of the situation during the 1960s that surrounded the imposition of the "new math" on teachers, students, and parents. The cost to the United States of the "new math" has not yet been tallied, but it was undoubtedly high. Estimates range from tens to hundreds of millions of dollars, to say nothing of the subsequent violent backlash against *any* innovation in math teaching.

Would a Metric U.S. Join the Rest of the World? The argument here, of course, is familiar. By switching to metric, the United States will join the progressive, enlightened rest of the world, leaving only presumably backward nations like Liberia, Yemen, and Burma as holdouts. Even the United Kingdom, that last bastion of tradition, has given up the English or customary system of units. Of course, the U.K. no longer had the power to resist.

It may be that even the United States, with its secure geographic position and its enormous wealth and power, was unable to resist. Certainly the world of American business has felt that way. Hearings held prior to the passage of the 1975 act revealed that the larger the business and the more international its scope, the more fervently it supported metrication. The disadvantages of the metric as compared with the customary system of units—and I think they are clear—may seem to pale when compared with the disadvantages of continuing to use two different systems in a world that grows smaller every day.

In the last analysis, it is a matter of the majority having won. The majority of nations, large and small, have adopted the metric system over the last two centuries, and now the richest and strongest nation must join the rest.

I have no quarrel with the idea that the majority should rule. There isn't any other principle that works, so long as persons and nations disagree. But in this case I wish the majority had joined the minority.

Just think what we've lost—besides having to pay a bill (if you're a U.S. taxpayer) that, it is estimated, may go as high as $100 billion before the conversion is finished. No more giving an inch, or fathoming the deep. No more proverbs like "An ounce of prevention is worth a pound of cure." No more coffee cups to measure out our lives. As the language changes, so will we change, from variegated human being to universal metricated man.

Mexican Mythology and Modern Society

by José López Portillo

Limestone sculpture symbolizing Quetzalcóatl's rebirth. Transformed into the morning star, he emerges from the jaws of a serpent, illustrating the symbolic permanence of Quetzalcóatl in the heavens. From the ancient city of Uxmal, Maya culture, seventh century AD.

COURTESY, JOSÉ LÓPEZ PORTILLO

From the dawn of time, man has re-created in mythology his eager quest to find the answer to the fundamental mystery of his being. The world's mythologies, the source of almost all religions and customs, reveal to us that men everywhere entertain similar longings, although they may be manifested in different forms. At the same time, these differences bear witness to the unlimited diversity of man's imagination and to the creative potential of humankind. Man has used mythology to symbolize the possibility of discovering his origins and the forces that influence his existence. Thus he created, through allegory, norms and patterns of behaviour that in the course of time evolved into moral codes.

In the mysterious and fascinating world of mythology, gods and heroes bestow on man his life and his reason, but above all they preside over his destiny. It is here that the deepest roots of culture are born, in the comforting illusion that man is protected by higher powers who will save him from brute and unfeeling nature. Within the mythological realm all things are possible; as in a dream, everything occurs in uncertain places where instinct and conscience—that restless duality which sets men apart from the rest of creation—are balanced.

Four thousand years ago, the early peoples of Meso-America produced a mythological complex that foreshadowed one of the most splendid cultures of history. Throughout a rich and imaginative cultural process, the mythology of ancient Mexico finally became one of its people's fundamental expressions and an inseparable element in its great achievements. A special being brightens the mythical world of Meso-America. It is representative of primal strength, an entity associated with creation and life; with the aspiration to elevate human nature to the altar of perfection, to transform reality, through knowledge and work. This being is Quetzalcóatl.

The Plumed Serpent. Quetzalcóatl is an entity that embodies two irreconcilable beings: Quetzal, the bird, and Cóatl, the serpent. It is the result of the metamorphosis of the serpent which, after dragging its inferiority along the earth, is transformed into the spirit of the plumed Quetzal. Thus, this transmuted being embodies humanity's ideal of rising above itself, overcoming its baser instincts, and achieving the excellence of which it is capable.

The origin of Quetzalcóatl may be gleaned from the same historical horizon that gave birth to the Meso-Amer-

---

José López Portillo was elected president of Mexico on July 4, 1976, and inaugurated on December 1. A lawyer and for many years professor of political science at the National University of Mexico, he later entered government service, becoming secretary for finance in the administration of Pres. Luis Echeverría Álvarez.

CARL FRANK—BLACK STAR

Representations of the plumed serpent Quetzalcóatl appear in the ruins of the ancient city of Teotihuacán, north of Mexico City.

COURTESY, JOSÉ LÓPEZ PORTILLO

The plumed serpent Quetzalcóatl (Cóatl: serpent; Quetzal: bird), symbol of spiritual elevation and cultural creativity—of human nature rising from the earth to the realm of the spirit.

ican cultures. It emerged with the historical identity of those peoples, it is as old as they are, and it developed with them. From a simple totem—the serpent appears engraved on the pottery of the Pre-Classical period, when agriculture was being discovered and the peoples settled along the lakeshores—it evolved into a divine entity through a process of mythical maturing. In the course of that process it intermingled with the symbol of the water deity, giving rise to a great symbolic synthesis that bespeaks a mature and complex cultural concept. From that moment, as if preordained, the representation of the plumed serpent appears on the friezes and altars of the great temples, on the ceramics, and in the codes of all the cultures from Casas Grandes in the north to the impenetrable jungles of El Darién.

This mythical entity was an intimate part of daily life, education, religion, and government. At the same time, it possessed a diverse nature: it was a principal deity of the pre-Hispanic cosmogony, a teacher and priest which lent its name to generations of priests, an initiator and exemplar of moral codes, and a wise and austere ruler, living promise of a future state of justice and prosperity.

The Gifts of the God. The manuscripts tell how Quetzalcóatl, as a god, was present, together with other primordial deities, during the interminable darkness when, gathered around the campfire, they first thought of placing the Sun, and then the Moon, and finally the stars in the heavens. They next thought of peopling the Earth with men, and in order to bring about man's creation they sacrificed themselves by plunging into the fire. From this comes the custom of calling men the *macehuales,* which means "those merited through penitence." Another version tells how Quetzalcóatl sprinkled his own blood upon the ancient bones of those who had lived in previous worlds, thus imparting life to man.

As the god of the winds, Quetzalcóatl foretold the rains and the time to sow. He was credited with the discovery of maize (corn) and with teaching men how to cultivate it. He bestowed music and the arts upon men in order to cheer their lives during their sojourn on Earth.

God of inner light, of the knowledge that brightens men's paths, Quetzalcóatl was eternally at war against darkness and the gods of the netherworld. He practiced penitence and preached the subjection of natural impulses through asceticism. Nevertheless, one fatal day, misled by the deceitful words of his enemies, he allowed himself to become intoxicated, fell into temptation, and revealed his weakness. Repentant, he later looked upon his countenance, deformed by time and penance, ordered his palace set afire, and departed sorrowfully toward the coast. According to the Tellers of Sahagún:

Quetzalcóatl portrayed as God of the Wind with a bird's beak and wearing the Venus symbol in his conical headdress from which emerges a flowering bone (symbol of the creation of life) out of which the bird of spirituality drinks. On his shield is the cross of Quetzalcóatl, representing the balance between opposing forces and the dialectical harmony of opposites. On his breast is a shell-shaped box from which the winds emerge, a symbol of natural evolution. From the Magliabecchi Codex, Mixtec culture, eighth century AD.

COURTESY, JOSÉ LÓPEZ PORTILLO

COURTESY, JOSÉ LÓPEZ PORTILLO

The mythical personage Quetzalcóatl, idealized as the "tall, bearded man who would dictate the philosophies of an inward perfection." Reverse of a pyrite mirror, Totonac culture, seventh century AD.

When to the divine sea's edge
He arrived, upon the luminous
Border of the ocean, he stopped and wept.
His adornments he donned, one by one;
The plumed mantle of Quetzal
His Turquoise mask,
And once again in splendor himself
Set aflame.
And it is said that when consumed
His ashes rose anew,
And other birds were seen
Birds of lovely plumes
That rose and flew on High.
When his ashes stopped burning
Quetzalcóatl's heart begins to rise.
They look upon him, they say,
Lifted up to Heaven
Wherein he entered.
The Ancients tell that he was transformed
Into the morning star
And may be seen at dawn.
That is why he is called
"He who masters the Dawn"
And it is said from thence
He began to reign.

Thus the fall and the rise of the hero are accomplished. Through purification, he recovers his lost virtue and turns into a sign of brightness, a light that returns each day out of the darkness of night. The deeper meaning of the allegory, the spiritual pilgrimage whereby excellence is achieved through penitence, informed the character and world view of the Meso-Americans and these qualities, in turn, were reflected in the grandeur of their art and the orderliness of their daily lives.

For centuries the cult of Quetzalcóatl was presided over by priests who were called by his name. Thus Quetzalcóatl was called the wise teacher of the young, as well as the ancient priest of the heavenly observatory and instructor to countless generations of builders and artificers. His abode, the calmecac (the "temple of wisdom" where boys were instructed in the priestly arts), was the crucible and fountain of knowledge. There the ancient Mexican acquired his identity. There he first learned admiration for his people, pride in work well done, and love for things beautiful and for all that justifies man.

The manuscripts also mention an exemplary ruler named Quetzalcóatl. Scholars have speculated endlessly on the legend of the white, bearded man/god who, according to the annals, ruled over the Toltec city of Tula-Xicocotitlán. The dates of his birth and the names of his parents are uncertain, but he was renowned for his wisdom and for his earnest desire to transform and improve his people. Under his tutelage, they experienced a renaissance of science and the arts, becoming famous as men who put heart and soul into their work.

We have evoked Quetzalcóatl in the Omeyocan ("place two," the mythical site of dialectical dualism) as a focus of consciousness when he cried out the words of the Chilam Balam (Book VIII): "'Am I someone?' wonders Man in his spirit. 'Am I the one who I am?' he wonders in the midst of Earth." In the midst, in the heavens too, he is an eagle and a serpent; sprung from two, wind and darkness, in the Yohali-Ehécatl, he is the origin of light and feather.

As in the case of Quetzalcóatl, this legendary god's enemies conspired to seduce him with earthly pleasures and, following in Quetzalcóatl's footsteps of repentance and sacrifice, he abandoned Tula and vanished. But before his disappearance he promised to return and once again lead his people on the path of wisdom. The tradition of that promise was so strong among the peoples of Meso-America that the unfortunate Aztec ruler Montezuma practically handed over his empire to the Castillians in the belief that Hernán Cortés was the god come back again.

A New Nation. Just as all myths blend disparate symbolic elements and assume unpredictable guises, the myth of Quetzalcóatl is entangled with historical data, so that the mythical allegories intermingle confusedly with references to priests and rulers. Nevertheless, it is evident that the extraordinary cultural development of the pre-Hispanic cities can only be understood in terms of the intense dedication to work and to excellence—to vocation—that constitutes the heart of Quetzalcóatl's epic.

Earthenware jug in the shape of a snail adorned with serpentine motifs which suggest the spiral movement of organic evolution and the creation of life. Maya culture, seventh century AD, Villahermosa Museum, Tabasco, Mexico.

COURTESY, JOSÉ LÓPEZ PORTILLO

IHRT—STERN/BLACK STAR

Teotihuacán, the city of the gods. "The deeper meaning of the allegory, the spiritual pilgrimage whereby excellence is achieved through penitence . . . [was] reflected in the grandeur of their art and the orderliness of their daily lives."

To inquire whether and in what manner Quetzalcóatl's teachings have reached beyond the Conquest is to ask how pre-Hispanic culture as a whole affected the formation of present-day Mexico. Pre-Columbian culture is one of the two great roots of modern Mexico; the other is the Spanish, with its valuable Occidental heritage. Mexico was born in the traumatic collision of these two cultures, with their widely varying technologies and world views. The birth and infancy of the nation were difficult, not least because, in both societies, the bulk of the common people had suffered centuries of oppression and misery. But in the end a new culture appeared.

To this culture, ancient Mexico contributed its vital experience, its impulse toward perfection, both individual and collective. Officially, traces of pre-Hispanic civilization were obliterated by the Spanish conquerors, but it lived on among the people. Thus, the old religion remained, cloaked under the appearance of the new doctrine, oftentimes strangely coincident with the rituals of Christianity. So it was that the essence of Quetzalcóatl's example and teaching survived and became integrated into the habits and customs of colonial life and, later, into the life of the independent nation, so deeply rooted a part of our national being that it cannot be excised.

To find how Quetzalcóatl's aspiration toward perfection has affected our history, our contemporary life, our nationhood, we must first look back to our beginnings as a nation. Nationality springs from the fact of birth. To belong to a nation is to be born of a certain blood, to be born on a certain soil. From this blood and this soil emanate the identity of a people, their culture, their language, and their common history, the pride of triumph and the sorrow of defeat. Over 150 years ago, we Mexicans decided to acquire our own lawful, sovereign identity before history. Rooted in a territory full of contrasts, we took as our vocation *mestizaje,* the blending of the two races coexisting on that territory into a superior synthesis.

Like Quetzalcóatl, we have eagerly sought within ourselves the meaning of our existence, our mode of life, our legal structure, the perpetual vocation for justice that bolsters the will of a people who were often abused and never satisfactorily treated but nevertheless remained true to themselves. In large part, the history of Mexico has been an effort to overcome colonialism and its consequences, but it was not until the triumph of the Revolution that the nation achieved the right to determine its own destiny through its own counsel, subject to its own views, and in accordance with its own will.

Thus each new Mexican generation finds itself deeply committed, to the nation's history and to its future. Each new generation must revitalize the institutions inherited from its predecessors, renewing them constantly so that they can better serve the country's purposes. This sense of history, of the commitment bequeathed by each generation to the next, finds an echo in the dedication of the ancient Mexicans to the discovery, through each succeeding generation, of the reason for their existence.

The Legacy of Quetzalcóatl. A nation can become great only if it gives due importance to the individual. One of the fundamental teachings of the allegory of the plumed serpent is that man, through self-discovery and the discipline of self-knowledge, can learn to recognize and interpret the evidence of the natural order and to reshape it through his own efforts. It is precisely here that the myth of Quetzalcóatl reproduces the human adventure, the individual or collective experience of beings who are destined to act in history and who thus bear the responsibility for understanding and transforming the world. And it is here that we can find parallels between the pre-Hispanic myth and some fundamental concerns of today's Mexicans, although, in truth, the deepest meanings of the myth apply to all mankind.

Three coincident points between the meaning of the Quetzalcóatl myth and the experience of present-day Mexico stand out: awareness of the dynamism of human events; awareness of the dialectical synthesis of opposites; and a sense of harmony.

THE DYNAMISM OF HISTORY. Society may be conceived as a structure in process of becoming, as permanence amid change and flow. If change were total, the result would be chaos and not even the memory of society would remain; we would be ignorant of our very existence. But though everything changes, something remains to provide that sense of continuity we call history.

Many philosophers have questioned whether this fluidity has any meaning. In their symbolism, the ancient Mexicans represented movement by a hieroglyph called *mahuiollin* and associated it with Quetzalcóatl to indicate that such historical dynamics have a meaning and a destiny. Another ancient symbol, "the jewel box of the wind," drawn as a seashell upon Quetzalcóatl's chest, identifies this movement with the upward spiraling of the shell toward perfection.

For the ancient Mexicans as well as for those of the present day, the human event has a clear purpose: to excel. Each human being has the fundamental right to desire and to search for perfection. That is why Quetzalcóatl, the serpent that dons the quetzal's plumage, symbolizes man's superiority, his eagerness for wisdom, and his need to achieve eminence. Today the meaning embodied in this ancient symbol is admitted by one and all: the purpose of development is to become a fully realized human being, a person of dignity, and society is responsible for creating the conditions whereby man may contribute effectively to the task of building a better world.

And the only way to contribute to the building of a better world is through labour. Here again, modern Mexicans concur with the teachings of Quetzalcóatl, who preached dedication and the necessity of striving toward the creation of transcendent works. Today, as yesterday, man is able to build his own future, and Mexico's creative effort has been inspired by the magnificent reminders of its past. The Toltecs became skilled craftsmen, excellent builders, and great artists because of their high regard for

A view of the ancient Mayan city of Chichén Itzá in Mexico's state of Yucatán, as seen by the archaeologist Frederick Catterwood in 1844. At left is a stone carving of the plumed serpent. The structure in the background covered with vegetation is known as the Castillo or castle. It probably was built in the ninth century AD.

COURTESY, JOSÉ LÓPEZ PORTILLO

the productive effort and creativity that make men brothers to the gods. We have been inspired by their example to wish for a better life. From them we learn that we can achieve that better life only by working together, by gladly accepting the task before us.

Finally, just as we Mexicans believe work to be a fundamental right, we also feel that song, dance, and laughter are ends in themselves. If we join together work, heart, and intellect, we have the full definition of a human being. Today, as yesterday, man has the possibility of building his own future. Mexico, though, has managed to draw inspiration, for its creative effort, from the magnificent achievements of its past.

THE SYNTHESIS OF OPPOSITES. As a nation, Mexico emerged from the fusion of two races. Our earliest desire was to find a face, an identity, that would reconcile the opposites contributed by our two cultural roots.

For our flag, we chose an emblem of synthesis: the union of the high-flying eagle, symbolizing the heavens, and a serpent symbolizing the earth, perfection, that which exists as a possibility. Thus is represented the synthesis to which we aspire in our eagerness for perfection: the integration of all essences, for through our nationalism throbs the very synthesis of all humanity. Eagle and serpent, Quetzalcóatl represents the same principle, combining, in a creative tension, an awareness of reality with the upward flight of the spirit toward perfection.

We may apply this sense of synthesis to the vision we have for our country. Our objective is to discover whether, in the contradictions of our society, we can find kindred identities that may help us achieve common objectives: to become integrated into a unity, but without losing our own individual characteristics; and so to contribute to the enrichment of the human experience.

A society is known in history through its national identity, and that which identifies, and consequently unites, is to be found in its origins—the will to identify ourselves, to be kin, to be Mexicans, to recognize ourselves wholly as men and therefore worthy to participate in the universal values. Identity is achieved through a process of integration, embodied in our vocation of *mestizaje,* which demands respect for our two roots. This is becoming a reality in our national life; its fulfillment is our destiny.

A SENSE OF HARMONY. The synthesis of opposites, the impulse of the quiescent toward life, the movement to join that which is scattered, the order of creation—all are found in Quetzalcóatl, as is indicated by the hieroglyph in the form of a cross which represents the beginning of harmony. The vertical axis joins heaven and earth and the horizontal, love and pain. Quest for harmony in the union of opposites, in a union that may be different from each of its components but that embodies the best of their aspiration—Quetzalcóatl represents this and, in addition, the sense of the possible whereby great ideals are converted into great realities.

Our times seem marked by imbalance and inequality. Desire for harmony corresponds not only to the spirit's aspiration but to man's imperative need for justice. That is why, faced by dehumanizing ideologies and technologies, our social democracy, our nationalistic Revolution, proposes the equilibrium of a balanced science and ecology, well-thought-out and enriched by a social humanitarianism that gives equal weight to individual and collective values—for the individual is the means through which the collective achieves consciousness, satisfaction, pain or joy. Quetzalcóatl means harmony in the synthesis of opposites, in the unity of what can be different but desires to follow only one path. His name, too, conjures up the sense of reality that is needed if great ideals are to be transformed into full-blown realities. The serpent is a symbol of wisdom on Earth, of the slime that is gathered by human experience in its quest to be useful. This experience has been transformed by its upward momentum; it will take man to a true fulfillment.

Mexico's political constitution, which synthesizes the best of the aspirations and purposes of our history, points out that democracy is not only a juridical system or a political regime but a way of life, something so vital that it is renewed daily through the constant pursuit of the economic, social, and cultural improvement of the people. Such is the great purpose of democracy in our country: to effect man's full vocation toward the realization of his being. Such is also the ultimate meaning of Quetzalcóatl's message, so profoundly ours within the history and tradition of Mexico.

FRANCISCO URIBE

The murals of José Clemente Orozco in the Hospicio Cabañas in Guadalajara, Mexico, mingle the dreams and thoughts of the past with present reality and the illumination of the spirit. "Today, as yesterday, man is able to build his own future, and Mexico's creative effort has been inspired by the magnificent reminders of its past."

PEOPLE OF THE YEAR

BIOGRAPHY

The following is a selected list of men and women who influenced events significantly in 1976.

Ahrweiler, Hélène

A woman president of the Sorbonne? *Incroyable, Messieurs!* But after 700 years Hélène Ahrweiler was elected to that post.

A Frenchwoman by marriage, she was born Helene Glykatzi in Athens on Aug. 29, 1916. She spent part of her career as a historian and archaeologist there, moving to France in 1950. She is considered an outstanding expert on the Byzantine Empire, the subject to which she devoted her doctoral thesis and on which she subsequently wrote several other works. In 1967 she became head of the department of history at the Sorbonne, and in 1970 one of the university's vice-presidents. Elected president on Feb. 12, 1976, she found herself presiding over 30,000 students, 700 professors, and up to 2,000 guest lecturers.

Petite, speaking with a marked Greek accent, Mme Ahrweiler gives an impression of fragility and grace that hides great strength and determination, the qualities that won her the confidence and the votes of her colleagues, most of whom were men. Although a member of the most powerful university teachers' union (SNES-Sup), she has resisted union pressure in choosing members of the university councils and commissions.

(PIERRE VIANSSON-PONTÉ)

Amalrik, Andrey Alekseyevich

On July 15, 1976, Andrey Amalrik, author of the *samizdat* ("published abroad") pamphlet *Will the Soviet Union Survive Until 1984?* and one of the most celebrated Soviet dissident intellectuals of the past decade, arrived in Amsterdam by air from Moscow. He and his wife had been deprived of Soviet citizenship and expelled from the U.S.S.R., as had Aleksandr Solzhenitsyn two years previously. Since 1965 Amalrik had spent some six years in labour camps and in recent years had been subjected to harassment by the KGB—the Soviet political police.

Amalrik told reporters at Schiphol Airport that he was sad at being banished from his country and hoped to be able to return one day. In a later interview on BBC television he said that he had always felt hostile to many aspects of the Soviet system, mainly because of the lies and deceit that formed its very basis, but he would not say that there

KEYSTONE

was nothing good in the Soviet Union. He had wanted to stay but was faced with the choice of leaving or going to prison.

Amalrik was born in Moscow in 1938, the son of a historian and great-grandson of a French industrialist who settled in Russia in the mid-19th century. He studied history at Moscow University but was expelled in 1963 because, in a paper entitled *The Varangians and the Kievan Rus,* he opposed Soviet historians who denied the Norse origin of the Rurik dynasty. He became a playwright but in 1965 was arrested because the KGB said that one of his plays (none of which was ever performed in a Soviet theatre) was "pornographic." He was deported to Siberia but his three-year sentence was quashed by the Supreme Court of the U.S.S.R. Returning to Moscow in 1966 he was employed by the Novosti Press Agency. In 1968, when he and his wife took part in a demonstration against arms deliveries to Nigeria during the Biafran war, he lost his job and became a postman.

The typescript of his *Will the Soviet Union Survive Until 1984?* was brought to The Netherlands by Karel van het Reve, professor of Russian literature at the University of Leyden and in 1967–68 Moscow correspondent of a Dutch newspaper. It was published in Amsterdam by the Aleksandr Herzen Foundation in 1969. Amalrik was arrested in May 1970 and sentenced to three years' detention at a labour camp for "disseminating falsehoods derogatory to the Soviet state and its social system." In July 1973 he was sentenced to another three years; he was released in May 1975.

(K. M. SMOGORZEWSKI)

Anderson, Sparky

Joe Morgan, the National League's most valuable player for the second consecutive year in 1976, looked at major league baseball's best team and pointed out its most valuable man without hesitation. He selected a prematurely white-haired fellow who did not have a single hit in 1976, Sparky Anderson. "Team discipline is the key to this team and there's the guy who makes it all possible," Morgan said of Anderson, manager of the Cincinnati Reds.

The Reds won their second straight baseball championship in 1976, becoming the first team ever to win the league play-offs in three straight games and follow with four consecutive wins in the World Series. "I'm glad the best team is a bunch of great guys who don't always have to be different," Anderson said, making an obvious contrast to the individualistic Oakland A's, Series winners from 1972 through 1974.

George Lee Anderson, born Feb. 22, 1934, in Bridgewater, S.D., became the youngest major league manager when the Reds hired him Oct. 9, 1969. His team won 102 games and the National League pennant the next season, and in Anderson's seven years the Reds have won five divisional titles, four league pennants, and the World Series in 1975 and 1976. His 683–443 record gave him a .607 winning percentage, the best in National League history.

When the 1976 Reds quickly disposed of the Philadelphia Phillies in the league play-offs and the New York Yankees in the World Series, many considered them one of the best teams in baseball history. Their 210 stolen bases and 141 home runs led the league, an unusual combination of power and speed, and their .280 batting average and 857 runs were tops in baseball.

Anderson batted .218 in 152 games with the 1959 Phillies, the only time he played in the major leagues. In ten seasons as a minor league infielder, he batted .263 and hit only 19 home runs. He became a minor league manager in 1964, and his teams fin-

ished lower than second place only once after 1965. Perhaps remembering his own days as a substitute, Anderson was careful to use all of the players as much as possible.
(KEVIN M. LAMB)

Andreotti, Giulio

One of the leaders of Italy's ruling Christian Democratic Party for decades, Giulio Andreotti in 1976 formed his third government (the 39th in the history of the Italian republic) following the June 20–21 general elections. It was a one-party government, voted in by the Chamber of Deputies and the Senate only by virtue of the abstention of the Communist Party, Italy's second largest political force. The new government's survival depended, in fact, upon the Communists' tacit support. With that support, Andreotti was able to introduce, early in October, a package of austerity measures necessitated by the country's worsening economic situation.

Andreotti was born in Rome on Jan. 14, 1919, took a degree in law at the University of Rome, and was president of the Catholic students' federation. A member of the Constituent Assembly elected in June 1946, he was given an appointment as undersecretary by Premier Alcide De Gasperi and retained that post until 1953. He chose to be left out when Giuseppe Pella formed a centre-right government with the Liberal Party in 1953, but was interior minister in Amintore Fanfani's first government the following year. He was later in charge of finances (1955–58), treasury (1958–59), defense (1959–66), and industry and commerce (1966–68). His first government, a one-party attempt in 1972, lasted only four months. The crisis that followed ended after 21 days when Andreotti himself was able to form his second government, this time in a coalition with the Liberals and Social Democrats. From 1974 he held office as minister for defense and later for the budget.

Long active in journalism, Andreotti was a co-founder of his party's daily newspaper, *Il Popolo*. He was a writer of repute and author of, among other works, *De Gasperi e il suo tempo* ("De Gasperi and His Time"). His main quality was described as the capacity to be politically mobile, but throughout his career he remained essentially a party man. "Power destroys," somebody once said to him. "Power destroys those who haven't got it," he replied. (FABIO GALVANO)

KEYSTONE

Armstrong, Anne

When Anne Armstrong was mentioned as a possible Republican vice-presidential candidate for the 1976 elections, it was the first time in U.S. political history that a major party seriously considered giving its vice-presidential nomination to a woman. But being first is not unusual for Anne Legendre Armstrong. In February 1976 she became the first woman to be U.S. ambassador to Great Britain. Pres. Gerald Ford's appointment of Mrs. Armstrong to the prestigious diplomatic post was not merely a token act to please the women's movement; it was done because of her proven capabilities as an administrator and her demonstrated skill in dealing with difficult political problems. Both Republicans and Democrats praised the appointment.

WIDE WORLD

Born Dec. 27, 1927, in New Orleans, La., Mrs. Armstrong earned Phi Beta Kappa honours at Vassar College in Poughkeepsie, N.Y. She became active in Texas Republican politics after raising her family on the 50,000-ac ranch her husband Tobin operates near the town of Armstrong, Texas. She served as the state party's vice-chairman, as national committeewoman, and was the first woman to be elected a co-chairman of the Republican national committee. In 1972, she became the first woman to deliver a keynote address at a major party's national convention and the first woman to be named a counselor to the president.

The counselor post was one of Cabinet rank and brought Mrs. Armstrong to Washington as a top-level adviser in the Nixon administration's second term. She was the White House liaison to Spanish-speaking voters, women, and youth groups, and served on delegations to the 1974 World Food Conference in Rome and the 1975 International Women's Year Conference in Mexico City. In Washington, she was a leader in support of the Equal Rights Amendment.

During the dark days of Watergate, she was the Nixon administration's link to Republican Party leaders across the country and did her best to rally them in support of their embattled president. Inside the White House, Mrs. Armstrong advocated full disclosure of the circumstances surrounding Watergate.

In the aftermath of Watergate, Mrs. Armstrong remained in the White House to assist Pres. Gerald Ford through the difficult transition period and attempted to help cut the disastrous Republican losses in the 1974 elections. She "retired" briefly to the Texas ranch, until Ford named her ambassador to Great Britain. The British press dubbed her "Auntie Sam," and she quickly became a popular and respected ambassador.
(HAL BRUNO)

Assad, Hafez al-

In 1976 Syria's president, Gen. Hafez al-Assad, defied the opposition of all the Arab states except Jordan in his massive intervention in Lebanon to end the civil war there and prevent partition of the country. Having cut off military aid to the Palestinian and leftist forces, he formed a de facto alliance with the Lebanese rightists and aroused the strong enmity of most elements in the Palestine Liberation Organization. Despite the Arabs' decision to replace the Syrians in Lebanon with a peacekeeping force, Assad remained heavily committed in Lebanon and was thought to have ambitions to establish a Syrian-Jordanian-Lebanese federation under Syrian leadership.

Hafez al-Assad was born in the Lataki province of Syria in 1928 to a poor family of Alawites, a minority Islamic sect. He graduated from the Homs Military Academy in 1955 as a pilot officer and was sent to the U.S.S.R. in 1958 for training in night warfare. He was later promoted to squadron leader but was dismissed from the armed forces in 1961 because of his opposition to Syria's secession from the union with Egypt. He then devoted his activities to the Baath Party, which he had joined as a student in indignation against social conditions in Syria, and became one of the key figures in the party's military wing when it took power in 1963. In 1964 he was made commander in chief of the Air Force, and in February 1966 he became minister of defense after the radical Baathists' overthrow of the moderate international Baath leadership in Syria. In 1969–70 he was involved in a power struggle with the party's civilian wing that came to a head after Syria's unsuccessful intervention (to which he was opposed) in the Jordanian civil war. When the civilian Baathists refused co-operation, he formed his own government and in March 1971 was elected president for a seven-year term by 99.2% of the votes cast in a national plebiscite.

As president, Assad liberalized the government in several ways and reduced Syria's isolation by improving relations with other Arab countries (although remaining hostile toward the rival Baathist regime in Iraq). His new alliance with Egypt culminated in their close collaboration in the October 1973 war against Israel, but differences over the cease-fire and the subsequent U.S.-sponsored disengagement agreements with Israel soon arose. Late in 1976 there was a rapprochement, with talk of a renewed political federation on the lines of the defunct United Arab Republic. (PETER MANSFIELD)

Ayckbourn, Alan

Britain's most prolific author and most successful exporter of stage comedies, Alan Ayckbourn, rarely allowed a year to go by without writing something new. In 1976 *Just Between Ourselves* had its world premiere at the Library Theatre in Scarborough, North Yorkshire, temporary home of the Theatre-in-the-Round Company; Ayckbourn had been the company's resident dramatist for ten years and artistic director since 1975. During 1976 he also had a mixed bill of five short plays with related themes, called *Confusions,* running in London.

COLIN DAVEY—CAMERA PRESS/FRANZ E. FURST

In 1975 Ayckbourn had four plays running concurrently in London's West End: the trilogy of *The Norman Conquests,* due to open on Broadway in 1977; and *Absurd Person Singular,* which won the 1973 *Evening Standard* best comedy award, was a Broadway hit in 1974, and had been staged throughout Western Europe and also in Eastern Europe. *The Norman Conquests* won the *Evening Standard* and *Plays and Players* best play awards for 1974, when Ayckbourn was also voted playwright of the year by the Variety Club of Great Britain.

Born April 12, 1939, in London, Ayckbourn had worked in the theatre since leaving Haileybury School. He began as an actor and stage manager in the provinces and joined the late Stephen Joseph's Theatre-in-the-Round Company while it was still a touring group. The company put down roots in Scarborough in 1964, and from there Ayckbourn wrote many of his best-known plays, including *Mr. Whatnot* (1963), *How the Other Half Loves* (1970), *Time and Time Again* (1972), *Absent Friends* (1974), and the musical *Jeeves* (1975). The last-named was written with Andrew Lloyd Webber, composer of *Jesus Christ Superstar,* but it failed. A new, unperformed play called *Bedroom Farce* went into rehearsal in the winter of 1976 and was due to open at London's new National Theatre in the following spring, 19 years after Ayckbourn's first play, *The Square Cat* (1958).

Married, with two sons, Ayckbourn lived in Scarborough, where most of his plays, best described as bitter comedies poking fun at the bourgeois way of life, were tried out. He directed all his new plays there himself, as well as those of younger writers he sought to encourage. He also wrote plays for television and for children.

(OSSIA TRILLING)

Barre, Raymond

Following Jacques Chirac's enforced resignation, Raymond Barre replaced him as France's premier on Aug. 25, 1976. A longstanding friend of Pres. Valéry Giscard d'Estaing, who had appointed him minister of foreign trade in January, Barre belonged to no political party but supported the presidential majority.

Now minister of finance and economic affairs as well as premier, Barre faced the immediate task of halting inflation and stabilizing the franc. In short order, he introduced a comprehensive plan, based on such austerity measures as price control in some sectors, wage restraint, and credit restrictions, which, however, met with a mixed reception. At the same time he showed that as head of government he was determined to exercise full responsibility in political matters. Here his problem was to extend the parliamentary and electoral majority toward the centre-left in order to win the legislative elections scheduled for 1978.

Born at Saint-Denis-de-la-Réunion, Réunion, on April 12, 1924, Barre was an *agrégé* in law and one of France's leading economists. His distinguished teaching career, from 1963 as professor at the Institute for Political Sciences in Paris, involved some participation in political affairs in an advisory capacity. During 1959–62 he headed the ministerial cabinet of J.-M. Jeanneney, minister of trade and later of industry. In 1967 he became vice-president of the European Commission, in charge of economic and financial affairs. In that capacity he was responsible for advising Gen. Charles de Gaulle in 1968 against a devaluation of the franc, contrary to the weight of expert opinion. He left the Commission in 1972 and was appointed a director of the Banque de France by Pres. Georges Pompidou.

ANDANSON—SYGMA

Barre was a pragmatist, tending to be didactic. But he surprised public opinion by the clarity of his speeches, political circles by the forcefulness of his attitudes and decisions, and even ministers by the inflexibility with which he pursued his aims and overrode objections, including on occasion those of President Giscard d'Estaing himself. (PIERRE VIANSSON-PONTÉ)

Bennett, Michael

"To commit suicide in Buffalo is redundant," according to one of the characters in *A Chorus Line.* But Michael Bennett, who conceived, choreographed, directed, and coproduced that musical, went on from Buffalo to become "Broadway's wonderboy," in the words of the editor of *Dance Magazine,* and, according to the *New York Times,* "the youngest, richest, most acclaimed, Italian-Jewish, Buffalo (N.Y.)-born, director-choreographer-producer" in show business. *A Chorus Line* swept the Tony awards and won a Pulitzer Prize in 1976.

CHRISTOPHER LITTLE—CAMERA 5

Born in Buffalo on April 8, 1943, Bennett began dancing there at the age of three, then went on to study ballet, tap, jazz, and modern dance. He began teaching when he became a teenager and dropped out of high school before his senior year to join the Broadway chorus line of *Subways Are for Sleeping.* At 19 he was teaching jazz dance at June Taylor's school. He met his best friend and constant collaborator, Robert Avian, in the *West Side Story* rumble scene, went on to choreograph *Promises, Promises* and *Seesaw* and win two Tonys for *Follies* in 1972.

All this first-hand experience inspired *A Chorus Line,* which is part revue, part musical drama, and something more original than either. A dancer's show, it depicts the process of creating a Broadway musical's dance company and describes the lives of the dancers.

After Bennett conceived the show, impresario Joseph Papp sponsored a series of workshops at which the prospective cast discussed their lives. The taped conversations provided the raw material that writers James Kirkwood and Nicholas Dante worked into a cogent script that the workshop participants, in turn, performed. As rehearsals proceeded, Bennett encouraged the performers to bring more of their own experiences to the developing play. Hence, when it reached the stage of the Shubert Theater, packed houses witnessed a dramatization of the life of a real Broadway "Chorus Line." Later the script was deliberately altered each time a new member joined the cast and every time a new touring company was born. At one point Bennett was rehearsing three companies simultaneously.

Universal Pictures paid $5.5 million for the film rights, matching the record price paid for a Broadway musical. The deal called for Bennett to choreograph the Hollywood production and to make three more films of his own choosing. Among the many honours he received was *Dance Magazine*'s annual award. (PHILIP KOPPER)

Bergman, Ingmar

"It is possible that my professional work may be so strongly linked with my environment and my language that I will not manage a readjustment now in the 58th year of my life." So wrote Ingmar Bergman, the internationally famous Swedish filmmaker, in a farewell letter published during 1976 by a Stockholm newspaper. He had decided to leave his native land for good because of a frightening experience with Sweden's tax authorities that had led to a nervous breakdown. Bergman and the government had disagreed over his tax liability for certain foreign income from his films. Early in 1976 he had been accused of tax evasion, arrested during a rehearsal, and dragged away for questioning. The criminal charges were later dropped, and Sweden's prime minister publicly appealed to Bergman to stay. But he departed just the same; his loss and the ham-fisted techniques of Sweden's tax collectors became political issues in the 1976 election campaign that saw the defeat of the Social Democrats who had governed Sweden since 1932.

Ernst Ingmar Bergman was born in Uppsala on July 14, 1918. The son of a Lutheran pastor, he had been preoccupied for many years with religious questions. Events in his private life, including his many marriages and divorces, inspired some of his work. Bergman admits that he has often contemplated suicide. Some of his films have depicted persons who did not know whether they were sane or not. A complete filmmaker, he writes his own screenplays, chooses a cast, and directs the entire production. He hires the same associates—actors, actresses, cinematographers—for one film after another. Bergman the artist is taken as seriously by the public as any novelist, painter, or composer.

Bergman had begun his career in the theatre, as an actor, director, and playwright, while attending Stockholm University during the early '40s. In 1945 he wrote and directed *Crisis,* his first film. Many more films followed during the late '40s. *Secrets of Women* and *Monika* (both 1952) mark the beginning of his mature work. He achieved international recognition with *Smiles of a Summer Night* (1955), the first Bergman film to be shown widely outside Sweden. He followed it with *The Seventh Seal* (1956), a medieval morality, and *Wild Strawberries* (1957), a meditation on old age. Both were international successes. His

JIM MC HUGH—SYGMA

reputation was at its peak during the early '60s when he produced a trilogy, *Through a Glass Darkly* (1961), *Winter Light* (1962), and *The Silence* (1963), which many consider his best work. These films deal with the borderline between sanity and madness and between human contact and total withdrawal. In 1976 his adaptation of Mozart's opera *The Magic Flute* was widely praised.
(VICTOR M. CASSIDY)

Bernhard of Lippe-Biesterfeld, Prince of The Netherlands

Among the varied ramifications of the Lockheed Aircraft Corp. bribery affair no revelations were more devastating in effect than those implicating Prince Bernhard, the consort of Queen Juliana of The Netherlands. Not only was the prince himself disgraced and humiliated but a political and constitutional crisis jeopardizing the monarchy arose, while the Dutch people were disillusioned by the ignominious downfall of the man they had adopted first as a popular symbol of wartime resistance, then as a figurehead for Dutch economic enterprise. (*See* NETHERLANDS, THE.)

KARSH OF OTTAWA—CAMERA PRESS

The 240-page report of the three-man commission appointed to investigate Prince Bernhard's activities found that in 1960–62 Lockheed, through its intermediary Fred Meuser, had paid $1 million into the secret Swiss bank account of Col. A. E. Panchulidze, a former member of the tsarist Imperial Guard and a friend of Bernhard's mother. The colonel died in 1968 but the commission concluded that the money was intended for Bernhard and that it had reached him. In 1968, said the commission, Lockheed made a further payment in the form of a check for $100,000 made out to "Victor van Baarn" and deposited in Switzerland. The payee's name was fictitious but Baarn was the name of the village in which the Dutch royal palace of Soestdijk stands. Perhaps even more damaging to Bernhard's reputation was the evidence that he had actively solicited payment for promoting Dutch purchases of Lockheed aircraft. In a letter to Parliament Bernhard admitted that his relations with Lockheed had "developed along the wrong lines" and that he accepted the consequences.

Prince Bernhard was born at Jena, Thuringia (now in East Germany), on June 29, 1911, the son of Prince Bernhard Casimir and nephew of Leopold IV, the last reigning prince of Lippe-Biesterfeld. He was educated at the universities of Lausanne, Munich, and Berlin, where he studied political science. Following the majority of German princelings after 1933, he joined the Reiter-SS Corps. In 1936, while working for the German chemical concern IG Farbenindustrie in Paris, he met Crown Princess (later Queen) Juliana, and in January 1937 they were married. Bernhard, who took Dutch citizenship and received the title of prince of The Netherlands, served with the Dutch forces opposing the German invasion in 1940 and afterward, based in England, became a pilot and flew with the Royal Air Force.
(K. M. SMOGORZEWSKI)

Bjelke-Petersen, Johannes

Premier of Australia's conservative "deep north" state, Queensland, Johannes Bjelke-Petersen attacked both the federal Liberal government and the Labor Party opposition on a variety of issues during 1976. Despite continuous rebukes from Australia's foreign minister, Andrew Peacock, for expressing his views on sensitive foreign policy issues, Bjelke-Petersen continued to do so. He focused on what he considered the government's weak-kneed policy in dealing with Communists in East (formerly Portuguese) Timor, attacking Prime Minister Malcolm Fraser for prevarication and for not reassuring Indonesia publicly that Australia approved of its takeover of East Timor.

He also attacked Fraser over what he regarded as the Liberal Party's excessively environmentalist concern with the problems of mineral exploitation and for failing the islanders in Torres Strait when Australia and Papua New Guinea adjusted their maritime border. Bjelke-Petersen's opposition to any concession in the state boundaries of Queensland, which until June 1976 reached almost to the coast of Papua New Guinea, led him to say that Papua New Guinea—a nation smaller than Queensland—had been "able to put it all over Canberra," even though it had no legal or moral claim to any part of the Torres Strait, except for its desire to lay hands on oil supposed to occur in that part of Queensland and Australia.

Shrugging off criticism that he was exceeding his power by not consulting the Cabinet on the issue, Bjelke-Petersen fruitlessly pursued his campaign against the former Labor Party government by investigating the background to Gough Whitlam's attempt to obtain an A$400 million loan from Arab sources. No evidence of graft and forgery involving senior members of the Whitlam ministry was found.

Born Jan. 13, 1911, at Dannevirke, New Zealand, the son of a Danish immigrant, Bjelke-Petersen made his home at Kingaroy, the heart of Queensland's peanut-growing industry. He was Country Party representative in the Queensland Legislative Assembly for Nanango from 1947 to 1950 and afterward for Barambah. He served as Queensland's minister for works and housing from 1963 until 1968, when he became state premier.
(A. R. G. GRIFFITHS)

Black, Shirley Temple

"I'm pleased to be the first woman in 200 years to hold this job," said Shirley Temple Black when the Senate confirmed her appointment as the U.S. State Department's chief of protocol in June 1976. And through the rest of the year the former child movie star worked her customary 14-hour day as the person in charge of visiting foreign dignitaries. It is the chief of protocol who welcomes them to the U.S., arranges and sometimes escorts their U.S. tours, introduces them at White House social functions in their honour, and generally determines what is and is not proper to do or say with visiting heads of state.

Born April 23, 1928, in Santa Monica, Calif., Shirley Temple was a child movie star, Academy Award winner, and international celebrity by the age of six. Her film career ended when she became a teenager,

PENNY TWEEDIE—CAMERA PRESS/FRANZ E. FURST

and after an early Hollywood marriage, one child, and a divorce, she faded from public view and became a licensed interior decorator. In 1950 she married Charles Black, a businessman and marine biologist; they have two children.

Mrs. Black returned to public life in 1967 as a Republican candidate for Congress from her California district near San Francisco. She lost that election, but it marked the start of a new career in politics and diplomacy. She raised $1 million for the Republican Party in the 1968 election and a year later was named a delegate to the UN General Assembly by Pres. Richard Nixon. In 1973 she was a member of the executive committee of the UN Commission to UNESCO.

By then, Mrs. Black had demonstrated that her involvement in politics and diplomacy was serious, and convinced even her severest critics that she had the ability to go with her celebrity status. Pres. Gerald Ford then nominated her to be U.S. ambassador to Ghana. In that post, she worked long hours, visiting villages in the countryside, learning Ghanaian languages and culture, championing women's rights, and opposing racial separation in Africa. She was honoured by being named a deputy chief of a Ghanaian tribe.

Her work in Ghana and her international fame led to Mrs. Black's appointment as chief of protocol. When they arrived in Washington, visiting heads of state often recalled having seen her childhood films, and Mrs. Black used that opening to take firm charge of their U.S. tour. Early reviews indicated that she handled the job with skill and developed into a knowledgeable diplomat, always making sure that it was the foreign visitor—not the legendary Shirley Temple—who was in the spotlight.

(HAL BRUNO)

Bond, Alan

Australia's sailing magnate promised to enter a yacht made of aluminum in the next America's Cup series. The races, to be sailed off Newport, R.I., in September 1977, would be the colourful millionaire's second attempt to defeat the Americans. At a news conference on September 30, Bond unveiled his latest challenger, tentatively called "Southern Cross II." Designed by Australian Bob Miller and his Dutch-born partner, Johan Valentijn, the new 12-metre yacht is shorter, lower, and will carry more sail than her predecessor.

Executive chairman of the Bond Corporation, Amalgamated Industries, West Australian Land Holdings, Robe River, and other companies, Alan Bond has been one of Australia's most successful business tycoons. Born in 1938, he started as a signwriter in 1952 and formed his own company, Nu Signs, in 1957. His empire grew until by the mid-1970s he was seldom out of the newspapers with his wide-ranging deals.

In the 1974 America's Cup races, his "Southern Cross" lost four straight races to the U.S. "Courageous."

Bond said he and his associates were putting up half the funds needed to mount the 1977 challenge, and expected to raise the rest (about $434,000) from public contributions. He had already sold another former challenger, "Gretel II" (purchased after the 1970 series), to a syndicate of yachtsmen who hoped to race it against Bond in the pre-Cup series at Newport. Bond's new ship would also have to defeat Swedish and French contenders in the pre-Cup series to determine who would contest the U.S. defender.

(A. R. G. GRIFFITHS)

Borg, Björn

Though no longer a teenage idol, Björn Borg did not let this affect his tennis in 1976. The Swedish prodigy with the flowing blond hair celebrated his 20th year by winning the Wimbledon tournament and the World Championship Tennis (WCT) title. He finished second in the U.S. Open, spoiling his bid to become the first to win the sport's modern Triple Crown.

Borg also won the U.S. professional championships for the third consecutive year. He opened his season by losing the U.S. professional indoor tournament in February to Jimmy Connors, the man who later defeated him in the U.S. Open. After losing matches in Palm Springs, Calif., and Hawaii in March to Connors and Arthur Ashe, respectively, Borg won the WCT title in Dallas, Texas, in May. He defeated Argentina's Guillermo Vilas 1–6, 6–1, 7–5, 6–1.

In the French Open in June, Borg tried for a third successive title. He lost to Adriano Panatta in the quarterfinals, but the defeat may have been a blessing. It gave him an extra week to prepare for Wimbledon, where Borg was sensational. He became the first man to capture the title without losing a set (he won 21 in a row) since Chuck McKinley of the United States in 1963. He defeated Romania's Ilie Nastase 6–4, 6–2, 9–7 in the finals and said, "I have never played better."

ALAIN NOGUES—SYGMA

At the U.S. Open in September, Borg said, "I want this more than anything." But Connors denied him victory in a 3-hour 10-minute duel, 6–4, 3–6, 7–6, 6–4. "I've always been unlucky against him," Borg said. "I hit the ball hard the same as Connors. And he likes that."

Born June 6, 1956, in Södertalje, Sweden, Borg was given a tennis racket at age nine and played the Swedish junior circuit until there were no more Swedish juniors to beat. He joined the professional circuit at age 14 and won the Italian Open at 17 and the French Open at 18. In 1975 he helped lead Sweden to its first Davis Cup, and in late 1976 he broke the hearts of thousands of girls by announcing his engagement to Romania's Mariana Simionescu.

(J. TIMOTHY WEIGEL)

Brooks, Gwendolyn (Elizabeth)

"She wrote about being black before it was considered beautiful," a *Houston Post* reporter said. "She does not write violent militaristic poems," but she does record black emotions, something she has been doing since she was 16. In 1950 Gwendolyn Brooks became the first black woman to win a Pulitzer Prize, and 26 years later she was the first of her race and sex to be elected to the National Institute of Arts and Letters.

WIDE WORLD

From the time Brooks began publishing, the catholic appeal of her poems won her numerous honours, long before the establishments that awarded them dabbled in what militants call "tokenism." *Mademoiselle* magazine named her one of its ten Women of the Year in 1945. The following year she won an award from the American Academy of Arts and Letters and the first of two consecutive Guggenheim fellowships. She is a member of the Society of Midland Authors. In 1968 she was named poet laureate of Illinois, and as Carl Sandburg's successor, she promptly offered an annual prize for young black writers of prose and poetry.

Brooks was born in Topeka, Kan., on June 7, 1917, and was raised in Chicago, where she attended Englewood High School and graduated from Wilson Junior College in 1936. Three years later she married Henry Blakely, a writer, and the couple had two children. She contributed poems to the *Chicago Defender,* was a reviewer for the *Chicago Sun-Times,* and taught at Columbia College in Chicago.

A frequent speaker on college campuses, she is known for remaining apart from vocal movements. According to the *Post*: "She understands why women's liberationists would identify with her poetry, but she does not identify with that movement. . . . 'I think we should not get embroiled in women's liberation. It is a dividing faction; we don't need any more dividing factions. . . . I favor black women and men getting married and having children. Why not?' "

In her work she celebrates the lives of ordinary blacks in Northern cities. Her books of poetry include *A Street in Bronzeville, Annie Allen, The Bean Eaters, Selected Poems, In the Mecca,* and *Riot.* She also wrote *Maud Martha,* a novel, and a children's book, *Bronzeville Boys and Girls.*

(PHILIP KOPPER)

Callaghan, (Leonard) James

When James Callaghan succeeded Harold Wilson as prime minister of the United Kingdom in April 1976, he was indisputably the most senior and the most experienced member of the Labour government. An MP since 1945, he had been a junior minister in Clement Attlee's government during 1947–51. In Wilson's first government he was chancellor of the Exchequer (1964–67) and home secretary (1967–70), and in the second Wilson government foreign secretary from 1974, these three offices being considered the premier offices of state.

In the election for party leader his status as an elder statesman told against him to some extent, for he was regarded as the safe, conventional choice. In the first ballot he was edged into second place among six contenders by the more radical Michael Foot, but he went into the lead in the second ballot and in the final ballot had a clear majority over Foot of 176 to 137.

Callaghan's special strength lay in his instinctive understanding of the Labour rank and file and his knowledge of the workings of the party machine. A member of the party executive since 1957, he had established strong ties with the trade-union movement and had opposed the Wilson government's abortive attempt to impose legislative controls over trade-union activities in 1969. At that point he was dropped from Wilson's unofficial inner cabinet, but he made a strong comeback as foreign secretary when he adroitly managed the renegotiation of terms for British membership in the European Economic Community.

LES WILSON—CAMERA PRESS

A robust mix of bluntness and jollying along had earned him the nickname of "Sunny Jim." As prime minister he at once set about telling the nation the harsh truth of its economic situation. "No one owes Britain a living," he said. He was prepared to take a line that was unpopular with the intellectual left, and in October called for a much harder view of the purpose of education in fitting people for jobs in an industrial society.

Born in Portsmouth on March 12, 1912, Callaghan knew what poverty was like. His father died when he was nine and he went to work as a clerk straight from school—unlike his Oxford-educated predecessors in the Labour leadership, Attlee, Hugh Gaitskell, and Wilson.

(HARFORD THOMAS)

Callaghan, Morley

Called by Edmund Wilson in *The New Yorker* "the most unjustly neglected writer in the English language," Morley Callaghan has happily collected anecdotes about people in faraway places who have discovered him. A productive writer, he has 18 books to his credit, the latest being *Too Close to the Sun* (1976). With the publication in 1976 of his play *Exit the Witch* (in *Exile,* a literary journal edited by his son Barry), Callaghan became known as a playwright as well as a writer of novels and short stories. His play is a study of a patriarchal relationship, reflecting his belief that the family provides the truest social picture.

PICTORIAL PARADE

Born in Toronto in 1903, Callaghan began his writing career as a reporter on the *Toronto Daily Star* while still a student at the University of Toronto. Graduating from Osgoode Hall Law School, Toronto, in 1928, he turned to a career in writing instead of law because of the success of his first novel, *Strange Fugitive* (1928). He married Loretto Florence Dee in 1929, and they spent their honeymoon in Paris, associating with such people as F. Scott Fitzgerald and Ernest Hemingway, an old friend from the days on the *Toronto Daily Star.*

The 1930s proved to be Callaghan's most prolific period, during which he published five novels and many of the short stories that helped to establish his reputation. During World War II and the postwar years, he wrote scripts for the National Film Board of Canada and was a regular contributor to the *New World Magazine.* From 1943 to 1951 he became well known to the Canadian public as a radio figure. He was the chairman of the Canadian Broadcasting Corporation program "Citizen's Forum" (1943–47) and was also a regular guest on the CBC television program "Fighting Words" from 1950.

Another creative period for Callaghan was 1950–62. During this time he published one of his favourite pieces of writing, *A Passion in Rome,* which grew from a journalistic assignment he had in the Eternal City in 1958.

A Fine and Private Place (1975) is the story of an author who wants to be recognized, especially in his own country. Callaghan insisted that it was not autobiographical. He had, in fact, begun to gain recognition as an author in Canada in the 1950s. *The Loved and the Lost* (1951) won the Governor-General's Award for fiction, and his novella, *The Man with the Coat,* won the Maclean's Magazine Award (1955).

(DIANE LOIS WAY)

Carter, Jimmy

"Every man is an exception," wrote the philosopher Søren Kierkegaard. That observation is a favourite of the newly elected president of the United States. Appropriately, it is nearly the only generalization that can safely be made about James Earl Carter, Jr., who, after an extraordinary four-year quest for the nation's highest office, achieved that goal while flying in the face of almost all the conventional wisdom about U.S. politics in the 20th century.

Jimmy Carter—he steadfastly refused any other name, even suing in two states to have the ballots changed to his nickname rather than his proper name—began his presidential campaign with no national political experience. Indeed, he was virtually unknown outside his native South. A former one-term governor of Georgia, he began in 1972 an incredibly methodical, well-conceived assault on the established leadership of the Democratic Party. Traveling almost constantly for the last two years of his campaign, Carter demonstrated both an uncanny sense of the national political mood and a determination and self-confidence that dwarfed the ambition and energy of his other national rivals.

In the first presidential campaign since the Watergate scandals drove Richard Nixon from office in 1974, Carter set himself apart from other Democrats by appealing to a sort of political fundamentalism of trust and truth. He recognized that traditional liberal promises of more social spending were being discounted heavily in the political market and instead stressed conservative values such as efficiency and the reorganization of the federal bureaucracy. His own "born-again" Baptist faith and his experience as a prosperous peanut grower and processor supported those political claims.

Carter campaigned through the primaries as an outsider, ready to cleanse Washington of both its immorality and its ineptitude. Early victories in the Iowa caucuses and then in the New Hampshire primary gave him the aura of a winner. His defeat of George Wallace in Florida earned him the gratitude of black voters and a solid hold on the South. His nomination at the Democratic national convention in July had been assured a month earlier by a victory in Ohio,

CHARLES M. RAFSHOON—PICTORIAL PARADE

demonstrating an ability to win in the northern industrial states.

After his nomination, Carter chose Sen. Walter Mondale (*q.v.*) as his running mate. The choice was a shrewd one, adding a liberal and Washington "insider" to the party's ticket. At this point, Carter's surefootedness vanished. He ran a lacklustre campaign through the fall against Pres. Gerald Ford (*q.v.*) and in the process was credited with dissipating one of the largest leads ever held by a presidential candidate. But he did succeed in defeating Ford, by nearly two million votes. His victory was based on the votes of the "Old South," and Carter was the first president from that region since before the Civil War.

Carter was born Oct. 1, 1924, in Plains, Ga. After attending Georgia Tech. he was graduated from the U.S. Naval Academy. He remained in the Navy until 1953, becoming a specialist in nuclear engineering. After returning to Plains he served as state senator from 1962 to 1966 and as governor from 1971 to 1974. (JOHN F. STACKS)

Chéreau, Patrice

The Bayreuth Festival was 100 years old and Patrice Chéreau only 30 when he staged Richard Wagner's *Ring* cycle in the summer of 1976. Though he had directed only two operatic works before, he came highly recommended to Wolfgang Wagner, the composer's grandson, who runs the festival in Bayreuth, West Germany. Pierre Boulez had agreed to conduct, and when other plans fell through Wagner hired the young French director on Boulez' advice. Boulez' "aural approach seemed to demand a new visual one too," the grandson believed.

A new look was what he got. As one critic wrote, Chéreau "broke away entirely from the symbolic representations that have become de rigueur . . . ever since the revolutionary ideas of the Wagner brothers—Wolfgang and the [late] Wieland—revived Bayreuth in the early '50s." In *Siegfried* a dragon moved its paws and wings; the *Rheingold* forest was made of real trees; a rainbow pointed to Valhalla; and *Die Walküre* rode live horses.

Even such things might have been forgiven, but not the hydroelectric dam site in the opening scene of *Das Rheingold,* or Valhalla's New Yorkish skyline which was "enthusiastically destroyed" at the end. Some patrons booed the supernumeraries, who were not conventional "spear carriers" but toted modern rifles instead. Others were shocked when the Rhinemaidens were depicted as prostitutes. Evidently the audience disagreed with Chéreau's implication, as critically interpreted, that "the basic issues of the days of Nibelheim and Valhalla remain basic issues in our own day." Evidently they preferred Wagner's dictum: "Any intelligent person knows that if we are to be in tune with Mozart, it is not the work that should be adapted to our age but we who should adapt ourselves to the age of *Don Giovanni.*"

RAJAK OHANIAN—RAPHO/PHOTO RESEARCHERS

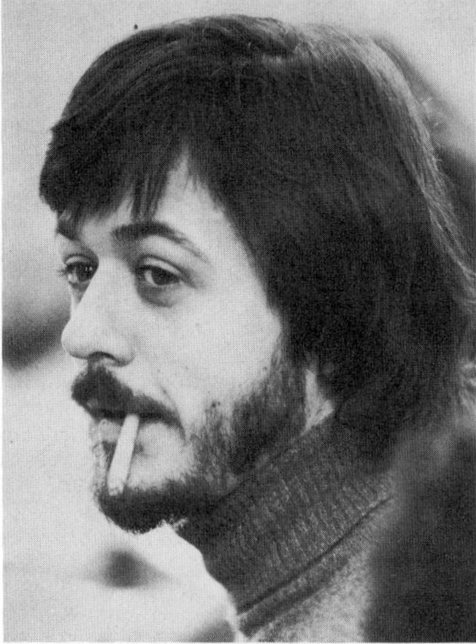

Boulez' conducting got higher marks, but Chéreau's spectacle stunned "the very heart of Wagnerland where every note is supposed to be pure and sacred, where every one of Der Meister's stage instructions is supposed to be taken literally." At a press conference after the first complete cycle, one German critic berated Chéreau for tampering with the mysteries and inexplicable motives Wagner ascribed to his characters. The director replied, "I don't believe in [those] miracles . . . I am interested only in the human psyche and emotions. Those are much more important than myths." (PHILIP KOPPER)

Clark, Joe

KEYSTONE

When he won the leadership of Canada's Progressive Conservative Party in February, 36-year-old Joe Clark became the youngest man ever to lead a major political party in Canada.

Joseph Charles Clark was born in High River, Alta., on June 5, 1939, the son of a newspaper publisher. He studied at the University of Alberta and taught political science there from 1965 to 1967. But politics was more than an academic matter for Clark. At 16 he had sat in the gallery of the House of Commons in Ottawa, watching Liberal Prime Minister Louis St. Laurent beat back opposition critics. From then on, Clark sided with the Progressive Conservatives. At 20 he became private secretary to the leader of the Alberta Conservatives, W. J. C. Kirby. He became national president of the Progressive Conservative Student Federation and was active in the struggle to oust John Diefenbaker as leader of the Progressive Conservatives in 1965. Two years later he ran the victorious campaign of Peter Lougheed for leadership of the opposition in Alberta. From 1967 to 1970 he was executive assistant to Robert Stanfield, leader of the Progressive Conservatives in Parliament. Clark was elected to Parliament himself in 1972.

The young unknown from the West was not yet in line for the leadership of his party. His victory came after several other contenders at the convention in February had been eliminated on the first three ballots. Clark presented himself as a middle-of-the-roader who could bridge the divisions between the party's right and left wings. He also had the advantage of being able to speak French, a useful asset at a time when Canadian politics is split between French and English sectors. He said, "I intend to make [the Conservatives] an open, active party, a home for all Canadians." Should he succeed in that, he might very well become Canada's next prime minister. (DIANE LOIS WAY)

Comaneci, Nadia

The most acclaimed athlete of the 1976 Olympic Games was a slim, poker-faced 14-year-old from Romania, Nadia Comaneci. Her superb performances in the gymnastics arena merited all the superlatives used by the sportswriters to hail a new superstar. Comaneci caught the eye, but she was only one outstanding member of an inspired Romanian gymnastics team that challenged the Soviet Union's long domination of the sport.

Nadia Comaneci was born in 1962 at Gheorghe Gheorghiu-Dej, a new industrial centre in eastern Romania. Among its sports organizations was a flourishing gymnastics squad, coached by Bela Karolyi, who was reported to have chosen the young Comaneci for gymnastics training as much for her uncomplaining toughness as for her latent ability. It was said that she never cried. Certainly her coolness and composure remained unshaken by the pressures of Olympic competition; the boldness of her routines and her massive self-confidence, even when somersaulting on a beam 10 cm wide, showed how well she had absorbed the lessons during her rigorous training schedule. Her performance lifted gymnastics to new peaks of excellence, in which grace was matched by discipline. The control of her apparently frail body seemed effortless; her technique was unsurpassed. In the individual events Comaneci won three gold medals and a bronze, while her near-faultless consistency helped the Romanian women to the silver medal in the team event.

The highlights of Comaneci's display came in the beam and uneven bars exercises,

CHRIS SMITH—CAMERA PRESS/FRANZ E. FURST

for in both she scored a perfect mark of 10. This was the first time a gymnast had accomplished this feat in the Olympics.

Comaneci made her debut in competition in 1969. In 1975 she won four titles at the European championships. What summits of achievement were left for her to conquer after Montreal? Some enforced adjustments in technique seemed likely, for it was reported that, following the Games, she experienced weight problems associated with the onset of puberty. However, this youngest-ever Olympic individual gymnastics champion seemed likely to dominate the sport for several years. (BRIAN WILLIAMS)

Craxi, Bettino

The dramatic setback suffered by the Italian Socialist Party in the general elections of June 20 and 21, 1976, resulted in the resignation of party secretary Francesco De Martino and his replacement by Benedetto (generally known as "Bettino") Craxi, a comparative newcomer to the Italian parliamentary scene.

Born in Milan on Feb. 24, 1934, Craxi joined the Socialist movement when still a student, and for many years his political activity was based locally in Milan. Belonging to the more advanced wing of the Socialist Party, he always appeared to favour the practical rather than the ideological way of solving problems. His pragmatism proved invaluable to his party in the climate of economic and social unrest so evident in a large industrial city. Craxi first entered the Chamber of Deputies in 1968 and became a member of the defense committee. By now assistant party secretary, he became a member of the foreign affairs committee after his reelection in 1972.

In 1973, after the coup in Chile that overthrew Pres. Salvador Allende and brought the Pinochet regime to power, Craxi went to Chile as a member of a Socialist International delegation, consisting of a representative from each of the Socialist parties in The Netherlands, France, Austria, Sweden, and Italy. This group was among the few to shed some light on the details of the coup and to collect valuable information needed for a diagnosis of the situation. Craxi carried out a similar mission in Portugal following that country's revolution in 1974.

Craxi was a personal friend of the French and Portuguese Socialist leaders François Mitterrand and Mário Soares. He described himself as "a reformist Socialist, open to modern liberal ideas." An attentive student of economics and the history of socialism, Craxi headed the European Institute for Social Studies, which issued, among other publications, a magazine called *Listy,* to which prominent refugees from Czechoslovakia contributed. (FABIO GALVANO)

Crombie, David

In July 1974 *Time* magazine named Mayor David Crombie of Toronto one of the likely leaders of the world of the future. At the time he was only in his first term as mayor. In December 1976 he was elected to his third term by a landslide, making him at least the political master of Toronto and one of the most successful mayors of that city since the turn of the century.

Crombie was born in Swansea, Ont. (now a part of Toronto), on April 24, 1936. After receiving a degree in economics from the University of Western Ontario and doing postgraduate work at the University of Toronto, he lectured on political science and urban affairs at York University and Ryerson Polytechnic Institute in Toronto. From 1966 to 1971 he was director of student services at Ryerson. He ran unsuccessfully for alderman in 1964, to protest the city's plan to allow a high-rise building in the tree-lined middle-class neighbourhood where he lived with his wife, Shirley, and their three children. In 1966 he helped form the Civic Action League, a reform organization. He was elected alderman in 1969.

In public life Crombie built a reputation as a peacemaker between pro- and antidevelopment groups, a reputation that helped him in his successful run for mayor in 1972. His hope was to preserve the core of the city as a place to live. His platform, both as alderman and as mayor, was to maintain the character of neighbourhoods. He sought to do this by preserving older buildings, maintaining stiff controls on the height, density, and style of new buildings, replacing private autos with mass transit, and providing pedestrian malls where shoppers could stroll freely.

CANADIAN PRESS

By the start of his third term as mayor, Crombie was known to urban audiences in cities and towns across Canada and the United States where he was invited to speak on his ideas. He had become the champion of the city dweller—that overgoverned, underrepresented, and increasingly marginal citizen. This struck a response as far away as New Zealand, where a taped interview with him was repeated twice on television. (DIANE LOIS WAY)

Crosland, (Charles) Anthony Raven

Appointed foreign secretary in the reconstruction of the U.K. Labour government in April 1976, Anthony Crosland would probably have preferred to be chancellor of the Exchequer. A leading theoretician of the British version of social democracy, he had previously held Cabinet posts primarily concerned with domestic affairs. He had been secretary of state for education (1965–67), president of the Board of Trade (1967–69), secretary of state for local government and regional planning (1969–70), and secretary of state for the environment from 1974.

CENTRAL PRESS/MILLER SERVICES

In his first months at the Foreign Office, Crosland traveled a great deal, visiting China, Japan, and the U.S. as well as Britain's European neighbours. In his first diplomatic confrontation he showed a certain practical decisiveness in conceding some British interests to settle the "cod war" with Iceland over fishing limits. He went on to take a tough line over British inshore fishing rights in negotiations for a 200-mi limit for the European Community as a whole. But given Britain's much diminished status in the world, Crosland could not expect to make powerful individual initiatives, and in the negotiations over Rhodesia the diplomatic initiative was taken up by the U.S.

Crosland was born on Aug. 29, 1918, of a successful professional family of the upper middle class. He made a distinguished academic record at Oxford and might have settled down there as an economics don, but he had been involved in Labour politics since his schooldays, and in 1950 he became a member of Parliament.

Crosland established a reputation as a political thinker, philosopher, and writer with his book *The Future of Socialism* (1956). He continued to develop his thinking in books and pamphlets, most recently in a Fabian Society Tract on *Social Democracy in Europe* (1975), in which he argued that a mixed economy is essential to democracy and that state collectivism is

incompatible with liberty. His qualities as a thinker and as a Cabinet minister did not win him the rank and file support he needed to make a bid for the party leadership, and he ran last in the first ballot for a new leader when Harold Wilson retired in March 1976.
(HARFORD THOMAS)

Dole, Robert Joseph

The narrowness of U.S. Pres. Gerald Ford's victory over conservative Ronald Reagan (*q.v.*) in the fight for the 1976 Republican presidential nomination apparently convinced the Ford strategists of the need to mollify the party's right wing. The selection of conservative Kansas senator Robert J. Dole, 53, as Ford's vice-presidential running mate was designed to serve that purpose.

Dole was well suited for the role. He was born July 22, 1923, in a two-room farmhouse in Russell, Kan., and had earned a high rating with conservatives during his terms in the U.S. House of Representatives and in the Senate. He entered the Senate in 1969, the same year Richard Nixon entered the White House, and immediately became one of the president's strongest congressional supporters, especially over the war in Vietnam. The senator himself had been a war hero in World War II. While leading a charge on a German machine gun position, he was severely wounded, leaving his right arm useless.

His strong support for Nixon led the president to name him Republican national chairman in 1971. From that position, Dole supported Nixon on Watergate, but he soon ran afoul of the White House loyalists by suggesting that they were isolating the president. Nixon fired Dole in 1972, and the senator managed to keep enough distance between himself and Watergate to gain re-election to the Senate in 1974.

In the Senate, Dole earned a reputation for a slashing tongue as well as an often pleasing ability to laugh at himself. He used both qualities in his vice-presidential campaign, perhaps to excess. As he and his opponent, fellow senator Walter F. Mondale, prepared for the first televised vice-presidential debate in U.S. history, Dole was wisecracking that he was a bit nervous, but that "liberals never get nervous, they just vote yes." During the debate, he blamed the Democrats for the deaths of 1.6 million Americans in wars conducted during their administrations. The debate ended with Mondale labeling Dole a "hatchet man."

The description seemed to stick. Though there is no official vote count for vice-president, opinion polls gave Mondale a huge lead over Dole, who came to be regarded as either insufficiently serious or too bitter in his partisan attacks. Many, even within his own party, blamed him for Ford's defeat.
(JOHN F. STACKS)

Eanes, António dos Santos Ramalho

On June 27, 1976, Gen. António dos Santos Ramalho Eanes was elected president of Portugal under the new constitution promulgated on April 2. His campaign for the presidency was fought against the background of vicious infighting and political maneuvering among the military and supporting civilian parties that had followed the November 1975 attempted coup. General Eanes' platform was grounded on the need to carry out the work of institutionalizing democracy while promoting the economy. He was regarded as the man who could, with the power vested in him through the

ALAIN DEJEAN—SYGMA

constitution, reconcile the three major political parties to a realistic approach to the country's problems.

General Eanes was born on Jan. 25, 1935, the son of a small builder from Castelo Branco, near the Spanish frontier. He graduated from army school in 1956 and rose smoothly through the ranks, fighting in the colonial wars in Africa as well as serving in Macau and Portuguese India. He was among the organizers of the first of the "captains' movements," which fought for pay and prestige and formed the basis for the Armed Forces Movement (AFM), which took power on April 25, 1974. After the revolution, General Eanes was recalled to Portugal and appointed, through Gen. António de Spínola, as the AFM representative on the Portuguese television network, where he continued until the abortive Spínolista countercoup of March 11, 1975.

He was exonerated from any part in the coup and sent to reorganize and purge the Army's 5th Division, which had displayed serious antigovernment tendencies. At that time he became associated with "the nine," a group of officers who stood out against Premier Vasco dos Santos Gonçalves' nationalization program. The actions of "the nine" led to polarization in the Army and an attempted left-wing coup on November 25, 1975. General Eanes organized the resistance to the coup and was rewarded by being appointed army chief of staff. He defined himself as a "professional soldier," but recognized the need for a stable society and law and order if he was to carry out his functions as president.
(MICHAEL WOOLLER)

Erving, Julius

The ultimate tribute to the basketball talent of Julius Erving is that he became widely acclaimed as one of the most spectacular players in history without the benefit of national exposure. From nursery schools to federal courts, he is known as "the fabulous Dr. J," yet he operated for years in such American Basketball Association cities as Richmond, Va., San Antonio, Texas, and Louisville, Ky., largely ignored by television. Then came the merger with the older National Basketball Association before the start of the 1976–77 season.

Erving, who passed up his senior year at the University of Massachusetts to join the ABA Virginia Squires in 1971, did things with a basketball that never had been seen before. His repertoire of slam dunks, midair fakes, and magical ball-handling kept him in what seemed to be a perpetual storm of controversy over his services.

A court ruled his Virginia contract void in 1972, and he signed a contract with the Atlanta Hawks of the NBA. The NBA decided, however, that playing rights to Erving belonged to the Milwaukee Bucks, who had originally drafted him. Erving returned to Virginia and was purchased in 1973 by the New York Nets of the ABA for a reported $4 million. There he found happiness until the merger. When Nets' owner Roy Boe could not come up with the money to renegotiate Erving's seven-year $1.9 million contract, Erving was sold to the Philadelphia 76ers in a $6.5 million deal.

Born Feb. 22, 1950, in Roosevelt, N.Y., Erving learned to play basketball on that city's playgrounds. He grew to 6 ft 7 in, but it was his coordination and jumping ability that made him outstanding. He had a five-year ABA scoring average of 28.5 points a game and 12 rebounds a game and helped draw crowds that kept the league alive. In the ABA's last year, he led the Nets to the championship, led the league in scoring, and ranked high in rebounding, shooting accuracy, blocked shots, assists, and steals.

KEN REGAN—CAMERA 5

When Erving was purchased by Philadelphia, the 76ers sold $48,000 worth of season tickets the next day. The 76ers, who paid the Nets $3 million for him, contracted to pay Erving approximately $600,000 a year for six years, making him basketball's highest-paid player. (J. TIMOTHY WEIGEL)

Fälldin, Thorbjörn

Following general elections in September 1976, Thorbjörn Fälldin became Sweden's first nonsocialist prime minister in four decades. Leader of the Centre Party, the nation's second biggest, he staked his entire political career on impassioned opposition to the further development of nuclear power in Sweden. "Mankind has intruded into an area where it does not belong," he said. "Retreat we must." He accused the minority Social Democratic government of endangering the lives of future generations by embarking upon an ambitious nuclear power program. In place of nuclear power, he called for a massive national effort to conserve energy and considerably larger capital investments in alternative energy sources

CHRISTIAN SIMONPIETRI—SYGMA

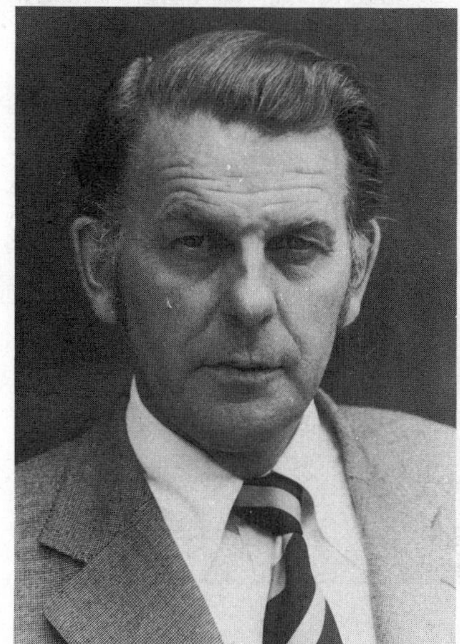

such as solar, geothermal, and wind power. Apparently the nuclear issue tipped the balance in the close elections, although opposition to high taxes and a spreading bureaucracy was also a factor. Fälldin's coalition partners in his government included the Liberal and Conservative parties.

Born April 24, 1926, in Högsjö, northern Sweden, Fälldin, largely self-educated, passed his examination for leaving school in 1945. Active within the Centre Party (formerly the Agrarian Party) from his youth, he became its leader in 1971. He rapidly transformed and enlarged it by adopting a pro-environment and antinuclear profile that had considerable appeal. First elected to the Riksdag (Parliament) in 1958, he lost his seat in 1964 but regained it in 1967. He served on several standing committees in Parliament and was a deputy member of the Nordic Council. He was serving on the National Conservation Board when he met Hannes Alfvén, Sweden's Nobel Prize-winning plasma physicist. Alfvén told him of growing scientific skepticism as to whether the problem of how to dispose of deadly radioactive nuclear wastes could ever be solved. Probing deeper into the problem, Fälldin said he became convinced that the Swedish government should reject nuclear power.

Fälldin owned a hilltop farm near Ramvik in Ångermanland, northern Sweden, where he and his family raised sheep and grew potatoes. He maintained a public image of the politician with rural virtues and common-sense judgment which served him well during the election campaign.

(ROGER NYE CHOATE)

Fidrych, Mark

Mark "The Bird" Fidrych is a pitcher who won 19 games as a rookie for the Detroit Tigers in 1976. Many pitchers have won 19 games, but none has talked to the baseball or smoothed the dirt on the mound with his hands like a kid playing in a sandbox.

Fidrych, whose 6-ft 3-in, 175-lb body and flighty personality have been compared to Big Bird of TV's "Sesame Street," played like a kid all summer. His delightfully naive antics helped fill stadiums throughout the American League. His fastball helped him finish second in voting for the Cy Young Award as the league's best pitcher, and he was named rookie of the year. His 19–9 record with a 2.34 earned run average, 97 strikeouts, and only 53 walks spoke for itself.

Fidrych spoke to the ball, he said, to help his concentration. "I've always done the same things," he explained. "Most of it is unprintable. But the gist of it is, 'Come on now, curve . . . we got to curve.' Or if my pitches are getting above the knees too much, 'Get down, get down and stay down.' Or if I need a strike, 'Come on now, get over. You need a strike on the outside corner.' "

Sometimes the act was as effective as the fastball. "How can you hit a baseball when you're almost laughing?" asked Cleveland's Rico Carty. Fidrych smooths the mound to avoid striding in the opposing pitcher's footstep. He cheers teammates for good plays and consoles them after bad ones.

Fidrych did it all for baseball's minimum salary of $16,500. "This is the most I've ever made in my life," he said. "What happens if I get a raise? It might go to my head and I might start losing. I don't need an agent. All this publicity is really a weird trip, but I'll take it. The only other job I could be doing is working in a gas station back home."

BENYAS-KAUFMAN—BLACK STAR

Born Aug. 14, 1954, in Worcester, Mass., Fidrych was Detroit's tenth-round draft choice in 1974 when he graduated from high school in Northboro, Mass. He developed so quickly in the minor leagues he was invited to spring training, where he spit tobacco juice all over the front of his uniform because he "wanted the guys to know I chew."

(J. TIMOTHY WEIGEL)

Filipacchi, Daniel

In 1976 Daniel Filipacchi, an ex-staff man, became the owner and editor of *Paris-Match,* the largest illustrated weekly magazine in France. He had joined the periodical in 1948 at the age of 20 (he was born in Paris on Jan. 12, 1928) as a photographer. That was the time when it was being relaunched by Jean Prouvost, an industrial magnate in the press and the woolen industry who had owned it before World War II. Filipacchi left *Paris-Match* 12 years later, in 1960, to set up and manage a number of publications for young people, including *Salut les Copains* and *Mademoiselle Age Tendre,* as well as jazz, skiing, and photography magazines. Then he took over *Lui,* the French equivalent of *Playboy,* and later several cultural and entertainment periodicals, as well as a record-publishing firm.

Prouvost, finding himself obliged to sell off some of his publishing ventures in 1975 to save his industrial concerns, handed over *Le Figaro* to Robert Hersant (*q.v.*) but in August 1976 refused to sell *Paris-Match* to his former photographer. It thus proved necessary to set up the fiction of a sale to the Hachette Publishing group. A few weeks later, Hachette resold its holdings in the magazine to Filipacchi, who thus finally became its owner and editor.

The magazine was in considerable difficulties, having lost about half of its readership over the past ten years. Filipacchi's first actions were to announce a reduction of about 25% in the 173-strong staff and to cut back stringently on expenses in the hope of saving the last great illustrated magazine in the French national press.

(PIERRE VIANSSON-PONTÉ)

Flindt, Flemming

One of the best breeding grounds for male dancers is Copenhagen, where the Royal Danish Ballet preserves Europe's oldest ballet traditions. There, dancers have always been most respected citizens, so it was not surprising that Flemming Flindt, born Sept. 30, 1936, the son of a well-known Copenhagen restaurateur, became aware of his destiny at an early age. Encouraged by his parents, he had his first dancing classes at eight; two years later he joined the Royal Danish Ballet School, where he came under the influence of its director, Harald Lander. Observers at his graduation class in 1953 were astounded at his mature technique, perfect placing, and sense of line.

Joining the company in 1955, he was soon dancing major roles. Considered to have potential equal to that of Erik Bruhn, who had left Denmark to dance elsewhere, Flindt realized that he, too, should work abroad in order to reach international standards. He went to London where he was auditioned by Anton Dolin and accepted as a principal of the London Festival Ballet in 1956. In his four years with the company he gained a great reputation, initially helped by a Eurovision presentation of Lander's *Études* during the 1956 wedding celebrations of Prince Rainier III of Monaco and Grace Kelly. In 1960 Flindt became a star of the Paris Opéra Ballet and while there created, originally for Danish television, a ballet based on Eugène Ionesco's play *The Lesson;* it was performed on the stage at the Paris Opéra-Comique in 1963 and taken into the Royal Danish repertory the following year. Ionesco then wrote a scenario especially for Flindt—*The Young Man Must Marry.*

His international reputation established, Flindt returned to Denmark and became director of the Royal Danish Ballet in 1966. The existing Danish repertory was mainly devoted to the 19th-century works of Auguste Bournonville. Flindt knew that it was vital to preserve these classics but saw that the company must also move with modern trends. He enlarged the repertory with works by famous international choreographers as well as creating several himself, the most successful being *The Three Musketeers, The Miraculous Mandarin,* and the full-evening *The Triumph of Death* (again inspired by Ionesco), and also reproduced the Danish and Russian classics. His wife, Vivi (née Gelker), is a principal dancer in the company and has appeared in many of her husband's ballets.

(PETER WILLIAMS)

Ford, Gerald Rudolph

For more than a year, Gerald Ford struggled to prevent his name from becoming forever associated with two descriptive words—accidental president. Yet, when the close election of 1976 was over, Jerry Ford, 13-term congressman from Grand Rapids, Mich., had failed to achieve on his own the office he inherited from Richard Nixon as a result of the Watergate scandals. Ford was defeated narrowly by a once-obscure former Georgia governor, Jimmy Carter (*q.v.*).

Ford had, however, earned more than a historical footnote. In the two years he served in the White House, he had, by all accounts, restored public confidence in the presidency itself. Although public criticism and doubt followed his pardon of Nixon, Ford himself was seen as a thoroughly honest and decent man. So strong was this perception, in fact, that a much-publicized investigation by the federal special prosecutor into allegations of Ford's misuse of campaign funds—an investigation that produced nothing—did not appear to significantly damage his candidacy.

Ford had never sought the presidency before being picked by Nixon as the successor to Spiro Agnew. His highest public ambition had been to become speaker of the House of Representatives. But once installed in the White House, he fought hard to be chosen to serve a full four-year term. Despite the advantages of his incumbency, Ford had major political problems. He had presided over the worst economic recession since World War II, and that had followed the worst bout of inflation since the Civil War. He had been unable, largely because of the opposition of a Democratic Congress, to fashion a national energy policy. The final collapse of the U.S. presence in Vietnam occurred early in his tenure.

Ford held the White House without any real national political constituency and thus faced a desperate struggle even within his own party to secure the nomination. Through months of primary elections and state party conventions, Ford fought with former California governor Ronald Reagan (*q.v.*). Finally, at the most dramatic Republican convention since Dwight Eisenhower was selected in 1952, Ford edged out his conservative rival. He immediately selected conservative Sen. Robert Dole (*q.v.*) from Kansas as his running mate.

WIDE WORLD

Ford began the election race far behind in the opinion polls but waged a skillful campaign, mostly from the White House. The large lead Carter enjoyed in the summer months led Ford to challenge the Democrat to a series of debates, an unprecedented move for an incumbent president. While Ford seemed to win the first of their three confrontations, Carter appeared to have the edge in the second and third. In the end, Ford won more states than did his Democratic rival and a switch of a few thousand votes in two states would have given him the election. (JOHN F. STACKS)

Gandhi, Sanjay

Until June 1975 Sanjay Gandhi, younger son of India's prime minister Indira Gandhi, was an automobile engineer busy implementing a project to produce small cars. Some prototypes of his Maruti ("wind god") car were already on the road when Mrs. Gandhi declared a state of emergency, which resulted in dramatic changes in Indian politics. Young Sanjay was catapulted into the political arena and found himself drawn close to his mother, who was facing the most serious challenge yet to her position as prime minister. The mother-son combination soon became the dominant factor on the Indian scene.

Gandhi first entered public life in December 1975 when he became a member of the Executive Committee of the All-India Congress Party's youth wing. In November 1976 he was chosen as the youth wing's national leader. Bespectacled and of moderate height, he talked little in public, admitting that he was not used to making speeches. Nevertheless, he continued to impress many wherever he went. During frequent visits to India's remote towns and villages he preached the policies of the government and the youth congress. He coined the slogan "Work more, talk less," which became the favourite motto in government offices throughout the country. He also framed his own five-point program calling for abolition of the dowry system and the caste system, rigorous practice of family planning, planting of trees, and encouragement of adult literacy.

He insisted that he had no ideology except the uplift of the poor and the weak. He was not in favour of large-scale nationalization of companies and would rather let public sector firms compete with private ones on an equal footing and let the former die a natural death if they failed. While his political ambitions remained unstated, Indian officialdom as well as the masses began looking to him as an important leader.

Born Dec. 14, 1946, Sanjay Gandhi had his early education in Indian public schools. He spent some time in the late 1960s at the Rolls-Royce factory in Derby, England, taking a course in auto mechanics. Returning home, he started work on his plans for manufacturing a small car. He had already established the factory in the suburbs of Delhi when the political emergency changed his life. (GOVINDAN UNNY)

Giscard d'Estaing, Valéry

After two years as president of France, Valéry Giscard d'Estaing could see threatening storms brewing on the political horizon. In 1976 France was undergoing a delayed but quite severe economic and monetary crisis; the left-wing opposition, led jointly by the Socialists and the Communists, took the lead in the opinion polls and in several by-elections; and to make matters worse the presidential majority itself split between the liberal "Giscardians" or centrists and the Gaullists of the Union des Démocrates pour la République (UDR; re-formed, as from December 5, as the Rassemblement pour la République).

LEON HERSCHTRITT—CAMERA PRESS/FRANZ E. FURST

Giscard's first move to stem the tide was to force the resignation of Premier Jacques Chirac, the UDR leader, and replace him with an economic technocrat and academic, Raymond Barre (*q.v.*). Barre immediately launched measures to deal with the country's economic difficulties, in the belief that this would be the key to victory in forthcoming electoral battles: the municipal elections of 1977 and the parliamentary elections currently scheduled for 1978. Giscard also published a book, *Démocratie française*—an immediate best-seller—in which he set out the basis of his political beliefs and described the main lines of his policies and those of his government in coming years.

Giscard had been narrowly elected in 1974 with less than 51% of the vote. Since then he had lost a little in popularity and prestige. If this worried him, he did not show it. Putting increasing stress on the almost monarchical character of his presidential role, he extended the number of his official receptions and official journeys in France and abroad, repeatedly expressing confidence in the outcome of the approaching elections and of the struggle against inflation.

Born in Koblenz, Germany, on Feb. 2, 1926, Giscard came from a patrician background, his family owning land at Estaing in the Auvergne. After a brilliant academic career he became an inspector of finances in 1954 and was elected *député* for Puy-de-Dôme in 1956. Secretary of state at the Ministry of Finance from 1959, he was minister of finance during 1962–66 and 1969–74. (PIERRE VIANSSON-PONTÉ)

Goldsmith, Sir James Michael

Sir James Goldsmith (better known as Jimmy Goldsmith) had never disguised his interest in making money. Still in his early 40s, he was one of the young tycoons who made their fortunes in the 1960s. Indeed, he was almost the last survivor of Britain's 1960s generation of City whiz kids. When the 1974 crash came, Goldsmith had a good slice of his money in the real wealth of companies making and selling things while others were going down in a whirlpool of worthless paper.

By an ironic twist, Goldsmith was summoned to the rescue of the man who was thought to be master financial wizard of them all, Jim Slater (*q.v.*), and took over as chairman of the desperately troubled Slater, Walker Securities Ltd. in October 1975. He came into the news with more than usual prominence when, early in 1976, he launched a series of libel actions and other legal proceedings against the satirical magazine *Private Eye.* Some of these actions were still proceeding at year's end.

Goldsmith started out rich, having family connections with the European banking families of Rothschild, Lambert (of Belgium), and Oppenheim (Germany). Born on Feb. 26, 1933, he had a French mother, was brought up in France, became bilingual, and went to Eton College. A substantial part of the Goldsmith empire was to be found in France, in food, property, hotels, and finance within the group called Générale Occidentale SA, of which Goldsmith was chairman.

In the U.K. Goldsmith began to move into the food business in the 1960s, buying up well-known food manufacturers and retail chains and consolidating them into a group named Cavenham Foods Ltd.; its controlling company was called Anglo-Continental Investment & Finance Co. Ltd., and Goldsmith was chairman of both. In November 1976 he was one of the bidders for the *Observer,* the ailing 185-year-old Sunday newspaper that was eventually acquired by Atlantic Richfield Co. (*See* PUBLISHING.)

Goldsmith received his knighthood in Prime Minister Harold Wilson's controversial personal retirement honours list of April 1976, which was criticized, especially by the left wing of the Labour Party, for its inclusion of big-business personalities.

(HARFORD THOMAS)

Grogan, Steve

The New England Patriots told the football world how much they thought of Steve Grogan on April 5, 1976, when they traded quarterback Jim Plunkett to the San Francisco 49ers for four high draft choices and reserve quarterback Tom Owen. The message was that Grogan, a second-year player, would be their next quarterback. They even turned down chances to trade Plunkett for more experienced "name" quarterbacks.

When Plunkett was the first college player drafted in 1971, he was thought to be the future saviour of the chronically inept Patriots. But he never saved them. He was often injured and wanted to be traded during their 3–11 1975 season, when the Patriots decided a brighter future lay with Grogan.

Grogan did what the more publicized Plunkett could not do. The Patriots shocked the National Football League with an 11–3 record in 1976, their first winning season since 1966, and they made the play-offs for the first time since 1963 before losing a 24–21 heartbreaker to Oakland. Although he did not have Plunkett's ability to throw long passes, Grogan had the discipline to do anything necessary to help New England score. He resisted the temptation to throw long passes, concentrating instead on establishing the team's running game even if it meant running himself. Grogan set an NFL record for a quarterback by running for 12 touchdowns.

The Patriots were still considered a league doormat when they played powerful Miami in their second game, but Grogan passed for three touchdowns and ran for another in their 30–14 victory. The next week, against defending NFL champion Pittsburgh, New England overcame a 20–9 third-quarter deficit and won 30–27 with Grogan passing for two touchdowns and running for one. Then the following week New England became the only team to beat Oakland in the regular season, doing so by the convincing score of 48–17 with Grogan passing for three touchdowns and running for two.

Born July 24, 1953, in San Antonio, Texas, Grogan became Kansas State University's third best all-time passer with 166 completions in 371 attempts for 2,213 yd and 12 touchdowns. His 1976 statistics, misleadingly poor because his best plays were in the most important situations, were 145 of 302 (48%) for 1,903 yd, 18 touchdowns passing, and 58 carries for 406 yd running.

(KEVIN M. LAMB)

Guthrie, Janet

A former physicist who worked as a research engineer, Janet Guthrie passed the first series of tests for the U.S. scientist-astronaut program, flew a plane solo at 16, edited a book on genetics, and has driven race cars for 13 years. But in 1976 she accomplished much more than all that. She became accepted. In the exclusive male fraternity of automobile racing, she became a "good ol' girl."

Until 1976 Guthrie's race experience was mostly on road courses such as Sebring and Watkins Glen. When car owner Rolla Vollstedt announced that he would help sponsor her in an attempt to qualify for the Indianapolis 500 in May, the plan was labeled a publicity stunt. "If it were possible for women drivers to do well against men in racing, I would love it," said veteran driver Bobby Unser. "It won't happen."

At Indianapolis, Vollstedt's car was a lemon, and Guthrie was unable to qualify in it for the 500. Owner-driver A. J. Foyt loaned her his backup car at the last moment, and she turned in a fast lap of 180.796 mph before Foyt and his crew decided against letting her try to qualify in it. "I just gave her a ride to see if she's capable," said Foyt. "I wanted to find out myself. I found out she is. Very much."

Before Indianapolis, Guthrie drove Vollstedt's car in the Trentonian 200 in her United States Auto Club (USAC) debut. "Janet and gentlemen, start your engines," the promoter said. "I would have been happier," she said, "to hear 'Championship drivers, start your engines.'" She placed 15th.

After Indianapolis, Guthrie was invited to run at the World 600 in Charlotte, N.C. She finished 15th, winning a trophy for working her way up from 27th.

Born March 7, 1938, Guthrie earned a B.S. degree in physics from Michigan State and worked six years at Republic Aviation on Long Island, N.Y. In 1965 she was among four women who passed the first series of tests for the U.S. scientist-astronaut program, but was later eliminated when Ph.D. degrees became a requirement. After working for Sperry Rand Corp. as a technical editor for five years, she started racing full time in 1973.

(J. TIMOTHY WEIGEL)

WIDE WORLD

Healey, Denis Winston

Since March 1974 Denis Healey, as U.K. chancellor of the Exchequer, had been the principal strategist in Britain's long struggle for economic recovery. In 1976 he was at the centre of the battle to save the pound. A big, burly man, he impressed by the power of his intellect, his determination to persist in courses he believed were right, and sometimes by his brutal rudeness in debate.

SELWYN TAIT—SYGMA

His single-minded attention to economic policy made him a late and rather reluctant starter in the contest to succeed Harold Wilson as prime minister. Having once entered, however, he declined to drop out after finishing fifth among six in the first ballot. "I am not a quitter," he said, and stayed on to the second ballot, which placed him number three.

Born in Mottingham, Kent, on Aug. 30, 1917, Healey grew up in Bradford, Yorkshire, and had a brilliant academic career at Oxford. Immediately after World War II he moved into Labour Party politics full-time with a job in the party secretariat. He was head of its international department for seven years before becoming an MP in 1952. The Foreign Office seemed his natural destination, but as it turned out he was minister of defense for six years (1964–70), then chancellor when Labour returned to power in 1974. He remained at the Treasury after James Callaghan became prime minister in April 1976.

Healey pushed through tough, even harsh, measures in successive budgets, but he was criticized in some quarters for unduly optimistic forecasts of British economic recovery and for failing to stem the slide in the exchange value of the pound (although this was due mainly to causes outside the control of the British authorities). He was largely instrumental in persuading the trade unions to accept limits on wage increases, and he fought through the case for public expenditure cuts in party committees and at the party conference. "I am not in politics to be loved," he said. His latest budgetary package, delivered Dec. 15, 1976, imposed wide-ranging public expenditure cuts to help meet the International Monetary Fund's conditions for a vital £2,400 million loan.

(HARFORD THOMAS)

Henze, Hans Werner

The world premiere at Covent Garden, London, on July 12, 1976, of Hans Werner Henze's *We Come to the River* (libretto by playwright Edward Bond) marked the composer's first major essay in the operatic field for ten years. Since *The Bassarids* was staged at the Salzburg Festival in 1966, Henze's work had been almost wholly influenced by his new-found Marxist affiliations, brought about by his emigration from West Germany to Italy and his contact with the Italian intellectuals of the "new left."

Born at Gütersloh, Westphalia, July 1, 1926, he had been brought up during the traumatic era of the Third Reich and had been drafted into the German Army at the end of World War II, in spite of a nature that rebelled totally against all that the Nazis stood for. Nevertheless, he managed to become trained as a musician and after the war had jobs in various North German theatres while continuing to study, particularly with Wolfgang Fortner and at Heidelberg. This upbringing bore fruit between 1947 and 1951 in the shape of symphonies, concertos, and ballet music, but his first major success came in 1952 with his opera *Boulevard Solitude* (an updating of the *Manon Lescaut* story). *König Hirsch* (1956), *Elegy for Young Lovers* (1961), and *The Bassarids* established Henze as undoubtedly the leading opera composer of the day after Benjamin Britten, and one who could be generally appreciated for the beauty and clarity of his music.

Then came the crisis in Henze's career and an apparent turning away from orthodox opera. *The Raft of the Medusa* (1968), an "oratorio volgare e militare," and the music-theatre piece *El Cimarron,* about a runaway Cuban slave, were the visible results of his change in direction; so were various concert pieces such as *Essay on Pigs* (1969), *Voices* (1974), and *Tristan* (1974). *We Come to the River* proved a summation of this work, employing his brilliantly sophisticated technique and dramatic sense to create, in his and Bond's words, "the image and consciousness of the working class."

The work was predictably controversial, creating a small uproar at its German premiere at the (West) Berlin Festival in September, part of which was devoted to a celebration of Henze's 50th birthday. What was not in doubt was Henze's high place in the musical firmament in the second half of the century.

(ALAN BLYTH)

Hersant, Robert Joseph Émile

In 1976 France found it had a press lord named Robert Hersant. A self-made man whose career as a publisher began in 1945 with a weekly motoring magazine, he had since specialized in buying up publishing enterprises that had run into difficulties. Within a few years he had founded or acquired several dozen specialized journals and local weeklies, eventually taking control of a handful of sometimes quite sizable regional dailies such as *Paris-Normandie* (Rouen), *Nord-Matin* (Lille), *Centre-Presse* (Limoges), *L'Éclair de l'Ouest* (Nantes), and *Le Berry Républicain* (Bourges), among others. Then, in 1975, came his acquisition of the leading national morning newspaper, *Le Figaro,* and in 1976 a considerable holding in the leading popular evening newspaper, *France-Soir.* This concentration of ownership in the French newspaper industry aroused active opposition from journalists and printing unions and brought references to "Citizen Hersant" and a "dictatorship of opinion."

A deputy for the Oise since 1956, Hersant belonged to the Centre Démocratie et Progrès (CDP), or centrist reform party, and was a member of the presidential majority in Parliament. However, he claimed to be apolitical insofar as his newspapers were concerned, pointing out that he published socialist as well as Gaullist and right-wing papers, and that in this matter he was a businessman interested only in making profits. Nonetheless, his links with Jacques Chirac (premier until August 1976 and after that an opponent of the Giscardian Independent Republicans and leader of the Gaullists), as well as the wide ramifications of his publishing empire, aroused the indignation of the opposition and disturbed a section of the majority party. This did not seem to worry Hersant, who continued his march toward what was interpreted by some as a rationalization of the French press—hard hit by the economic crisis—and by others as the construction of a machine to drug public opinion.

Hersant was born at Vertou, Loire-Inférieure (now Loire-Atlantique), on Jan. 31, 1920, the son of a sea captain, and went to school at Rouen and Le Havre. He was mayor of Ravenel (1953–59) and of Liancourt from 1967. Elected originally as a Radical-Socialist deputy (1956), in 1968 he was adopted by Progrès et Démocratie Moderne (later CDP), which he formally joined in 1972. He was active in the various French newspaper and periodical owners' associations.

(PIERRE VIANSSON-PONTÉ)

Hua Kuo-feng

The death in 1976 of the two men who had come to symbolize the Chinese revolution—Premier Chou En-lai in January and Chairman Mao Tse-tung in September—touched off climactic changes in Chinese politics. The man who displayed unexpected ability in coping with the crisis and emerged on top of the heap—for the time being at any rate—was an unknown party functionary, Hua Kuo-feng. In February Hua was named acting premier. Two months later he became premier, following the disgrace of Teng Hsiao-p'ing, the man Chou En-lai had picked for the job. In October Hua was declared chairman of the Communist Party, thus succeeding Mao.

CAMERA PRESS

So little was known about Hua that only in October did Communist sources, even then unofficially, venture to mention his age—56. He was at first widely reported as a Hunanese from Mao's own district of Hsiang-t'an. After foreign reports suggested a family link between Mao and Hua, semiofficial references to the new chairman began specifying that he was born to a poor peasant family in Shansi Province. The limited information on Hua's record suggested, however, that he had always been extraordinarily close to Mao. During the Cultural Revolution of the late 1960s he had clashed with Hunan's military leaders and been saved by Mao who transferred him to Peking. In 1974 there had been a poster campaign against him by the radicals then in the ascendance. Again Mao plucked him out of harm's way.

Hua has been credited with considerable administrative ability. In the early days he was particularly concerned with irrigation and water conservancy projects in Hsiang-t'an. By 1955 he was secretary of the party's district committee. Elected to the Central Committee at the ninth party congress in 1969, in 1973 he was named a member of the Politburo and in 1975 became minister of public security.

(T. J. S. GEORGE)

Hume, George Basil Cardinal

In 1976 George Hume—Basil was added when he joined the Benedictine Abbey of Ampleforth—became the first monk to be named archbishop of Westminster since the restoration of the Roman Catholic hierarchy in England in 1850. Installed as archbishop on March 25, he was made a cardinal on May 24. The appointment came after intense and inaccurate press speculation and was a surprise—on reflection, a welcome surprise, for Cardinal Hume brought to Westminster the Benedictine tradition of spirituality which combines deep inner serenity with a keen sense of the need for adaptation. In September he announced the reorganization of the Westminster archdiocese: the aim was to encourage smaller, more human groupings, and to release the cardinal from day-to-day administration.

Cardinal Hume was born in Newcastle upon Tyne on March 2, 1923, the son of Sir William Hume, a heart specialist, and a French mother. After education at Ampleforth College, he entered the Abbey in 1941, and later studied history at Oxford and theology at Fribourg in Switzerland. From then on his life was identified with that of Ampleforth, where he taught modern languages to the boys and theology to the junior monks until, in April 1963, he was elected abbot, a post he held until he moved to Westminster.

At Ampleforth his ecumenical spirit was already evident in his friendship with Donald Coggan, archbishop of York and later of Canterbury. He also encouraged boys of the Serbian and Russian Orthodox churches to go to Ampleforth as an ecumenical experiment. It was entirely in character that, on the day of his installation, he should lead the monks of Ampleforth to Westminster Abbey where, for the first time since the Reformation, they sang vespers.

Cardinal Hume was a reconciler and wont to move cautiously, but that did not mean he was afraid to speak out. In the first few

THE PRESS ASSOCIATION LTD.

months of his administration he wrote a letter about allegations of torture in Brazil to the visiting president of that country and a letter to *The Times* denouncing a projected film on the sex life of Jesus. He became a familiar figure on television, emerging from probing interrogation not only unscathed but with his reputation for shrewd gentleness enhanced. (PETER HEBBLETHWAITE)

Hunt, James

The Grand Prix automobile racing drivers' world championship of 1976 went to James Hunt by a single point (69 to 68) over his season's rival on the circuits, Niki Lauda (*q.v.*). Hunt won the title in a final dramatic race in rain and mist in Japan, in which he came in third and Lauda retired. A determined and dedicated racing driver, Hunt quickly won the admiration of followers of this dangerous and exacting sport. Good looks also gave him plenty of female supporters, although his marriage to Susan Miller came to grief, and she later married actor Richard Burton.

Born on Aug. 29, 1947, Hunt was educated at Wellington College and was destined for a medical career. His school days were occupied largely with sporting pursuits, of which squash and tennis were his favourites. He showed little interest in cars until the age of 17 when he attended a motor race. He then abandoned any idea of becoming a physician, and after trying his hand with a Mini-Cooper, acquired a Russell-Alexis Ford before he was 21. With this car he began racing in Formula Ford events. This brought him to the notice of Lotus, which sponsored his entry into Formula Three (F3) racing in 1969. In 1970 he joined the Lotus Grand Prix team. A long series of crashes followed, but Hunt did win the F3 race in France and later drove an F3 March. He then joined up with Lord Alexander Hesketh and drove his March and Hesketh Formula One (Grand Prix) cars.

From then on his fame as a racing driver advanced rapidly. In 1973 his best performance was to place second in the U.S. Grand Prix at Watkins Glen, N.Y., in a March 731. In 1974 the new Hesketh 308 had innumerable troubles, but Hunt managed three third places in championship races. His first victory was achieved in 1975 in the Dutch Grand Prix, and he also finished second in the Argentine, French, and Austrian Grands Prix. In 1976, a season marred by protests about minor technicalities of the McLaren cars he was now driving, Hunt won six Grand Prix races to take the championship. He was named Britain's Sportsman of the Year by the Sports Writers' Association in Britain. (WILLIAM C. BODDY)

Hussein bin Onn, Datuk

Following the death in January 1976 of Tun Abdul Razak (*see* OBITUARIES), Datuk Hussein bin Onn became prime minister of Malaysia. At the moment of succession Datuk Hussein, whose own state of health had been poor, appeared to be overwhelmed by the prospect of high office. Yet, if he at first seemed to be a political lamb, he soon gave the lie to this impression. At a critical juncture in Malaysia's short history, when a revival of racial tensions was matched by the revival of Communist insurgency, he showed himself to be a man of courage in acting against corrupt Malay politicians. He thereby provided assurance to the non-Malays that as prime minister he would be guided by the rule of law and not communal loyalty. His political philosophy, which appeared to derive from the influence and example of his father, former leader of the United Malays National Organization (UMNO), found expression in the Third Malaysia Plan, which he announced in July and which stressed the intention to improve the quality of life of all Malaysians.

Datuk Hussein was born in Johor Baharu, Malaya, in 1922. He was trained as a soldier in India and served during World War II with the British Indian Army. He returned to Malaya in 1945 and on demobilization joined the Malay Administrative Service. He resigned to go into politics with his father, the late Dato Onn bin Jaafar, and in 1950 served as UMNO's national youth leader and secretary-general. Leaving the party when his father's multiracial philosophy was rejected, he went to London, where he studied law and qualified as a barrister.

Datuk Hussein did not return to political life until 1968, when Tun Razak persuaded him to rejoin UMNO. He entered Parliament in 1969 and in the following year was appointed minister of education. In 1973 he was chosen as deputy prime minister following the death of Ismail bin Dato Abdul Rahman. (MICHAEL LEIFER)

Ingrao, Pietro

Elected speaker of the Italian Chamber of Deputies following the general election of June 20, 1976, Pietro Ingrao was the first Communist Party official to accede to that high position. He secured 488 votes in the 630-seat Chamber. His selection for the position by the Communist leadership was interpreted as an attempt by party chief Enrico Berlinguer to remove from direct political involvement one of the strongest critics of his proposed *compromesso storico,* or parliamentary compromise between Christian Democrats and Communists.

WIDE WORLD

On the other hand, the choice might reflect the high esteem in which Ingrao's public capacity and his stern commitment to the Italian constitution were generally held. In an interview he said: "As president of the Chamber, it is my task and duty to help guarantee the functioning and development of the democratic regime set out in the constitution of my country . . . I see no contradiction between the task . . . and my political faith as a Communist."

Born on March 30, 1915, in the small town of Lenola, near Rome, Ingrao was a university graduate in law and philosophy. While a student he had his first contacts with the clandestine Communist movements, and he became a party member in 1940. To avoid arrest he escaped to the southern region of Calabria, where he founded the first local Communist group. On July 25, 1943, upon Mussolini's fall, Ingrao came into the open and addressed a mass meeting in Milan. From that day to the end of World War II he worked as a journalist for the Communist paper *L'Unità,* which was then printed secretly. In 1947 he became the paper's editor in chief, a position he held for ten years.

Considered one of the strongest supporters of former Italian Communist chief Palmiro Togliatti, Ingrao nevertheless dissented at times from the party's official line. He was, for instance, a critic of Stalinism and could be regarded as one of the inspirers of "national Communism" and "democratic centralism" theories. He entered the party's Central Committee in 1956. First elected to Parliament in 1948, he became chairman of the Communist group in the Chamber after the 1968 general elections. (FABIO GALVANO)

Jenkins, Roy Harris

After 28 years in Parliament and 8 years as a Cabinet minister in Labour governments, at the end of 1976 Roy Jenkins left British politics to become president of the Commission of the European Community, beginning in January 1977. Awarded the Charlemagne Prize and the Robert Schuman Prize for services to European unity in 1972, Jenkins for many years had been leader of the pro-European group in the Labour Party.

His experience and ability made him a possible choice as a future prime minister, but he had antagonized the left wing of the party by his unwavering support for the European idea. In 1972, when Labour was in opposition, he had resigned from the deputy leadership rather than be associated with party decisions hostile to British membership in the EEC.

In the late 1960s Jenkins was the most powerful of the younger ministers in the Cabinet. He had proved a liberal-minded reforming home secretary in 1965–67. As chancellor of the Exchequer from 1967 to 1970, he had shown remarkable effectiveness in coping with the financial crisis of 1967–68 and had succeeded in swinging the British balance of payments into surplus—a rare occurrence.

Born Nov. 11, 1920, at Abersychan, Wales, the son of a miners' union official and La-

CENTRAL PRESS/PICTORIAL PARADE

bour MP, he entered Parliament at the age of 27. During the 13 years from 1951, when Labour was out of office, he made a name for himself as a political biographer, and at one time considered giving up politics for writing. Oxford-educated, he held honorary degrees from Yale, Harvard, and other U.S. and British universities.

By temperament Jenkins was a reformer and a gradualist, with a philosophical streak. As a private MP he was responsible for two important measures of law reform, on libel and on obscenity. As the controversy over devolution of power to Scotland and Wales developed, he said that he found himself increasingly sympathetic toward the philosophy of devolution—an issue that he might find relevant to the constitutional future of the European Community, now at a crucial stage in its development. (HARFORD THOMAS)

Jhabvala, Ruth Prawer

"Every writer is lonely but I don't think there's greater loneliness than being an English writer in India," said Ruth Prawer Jhabvala in an interview. "Very few people there have read what I wrote and they certainly haven't liked it." Notwithstanding this loneliness and indifference, she was the author of eight novels and four volumes of short stories that had brought her wide acclaim in the West as one of the finest contemporary novelists writing in English. She won the Booker Prize for fiction in 1975 for her novel *Heat and Dust* which explores one of her favourite themes, the effect of India on an outsider; and in 1976 her fourth volume of stories, *How I Became a Holy Mother,* appeared.

Ruth Prawer Jhabvala is an acute observer of different European reactions to India. Some of her characters, like Douglas in *Heat and Dust,* remain patronizing and detached. Others, like Clarissa in *A Backward Place* (1965), or the three European girls in *A New Dominion* (1972), become so intent on merging with Hindu civilization that they risk a complete loss of personality. The author herself believes firmly in the need to maintain an independence of spirit when confronted with an alien culture. Although she writes almost exclusively about India, she does so from within the European literary tradition, the tradition of Chekhov and Jane Austen. Her style is marked by precision, economy, and a fine sense of irony.

Born in Cologne, Germany, on May 7, 1927, of Polish parents, Ruth Prawer went to live in England in 1939. She took a degree in English literature at the University of London. In 1951 she married an Indian architect and moved to India. Her earlier novels include *To Whom She Will* (1955), *The Nature of Passion* (1956), *Esmond in India* (1958), and *The Householder* (1960), which has been filmed. She has also written television plays and, in collaboration with the director James Ivory, the scripts for several films including *Shakespeare Wallah* and, most recently, *Autobiography of a Princess.* (YOLANTA MAY)

Jones, Bert

Defensive linemen were the largest people Baltimore Colt quarterback Bert Jones stood up to during the National Football League season, but the toughest was Robert Irsay, his team's owner. When Irsay fired Colt coach Ted Marchibroda after the team's 2–4 exhibition season, Jones said that he would leave the Colts at the end of the season if Marchibroda were not rehired. Irsay relented, and Jones's stand helped the Colts continue to improve in 1976 after going from 2–12 in 1974 to 10–4 in 1975, Marchibroda's rookie season. They finished with an 11–3 record in 1976 and averaged nearly 30 points a game before losing to Pittsburgh 40–14 in the play-offs.

After his confrontation with Irsay, the matter of dazzling the league and winning a second straight divisional title was comparatively routine for Jones. He completed 207 of 343 passes (60.4%) for 3,104 yd and 24 touchdowns, and his passing rating was second in the league to that of Ken Stabler, who had the best since the rating system was devised. "Bert can unload one 70 yards away any time he likes and hit a dime," said his favourite receiver, Roger Carr.

Jones had been largely responsible for the Colts' turnabout in 1975, when he was their most valuable player. He threw only four interceptions in the last ten games of that season, despite having three cracked ribs for most of that time.

Jones was born Sept. 7, 1951, and 2½ months later his father, Dub, tied a National Football League record by scoring six touchdowns in one game for the Cleveland Browns. Bert made the Joneses the only father-son combination in the NFL record book in 1974 when he completed 17 consecutive passes. Even as a boy in Ruston, La., where he was born and raised, Bert showed his strong arm by flinging rocks.

After setting 20 school records at Louisiana State University, Jones was the Colts' first draft choice in 1973 and the second player taken in the NFL draft. Scouts figured that it would take more than three years for him to become a consistent quarterback, but he sped up the process by turning his bachelor apartment into a quarterbacking classroom. He mounted a screen on one wall and made a film projector a permanent fixture, studying the techniques of other quarterbacks for hours at a time. (KEVIN M. LAMB)

Jumblatt, Kamal

In 1976 the veteran Lebanese politician Kamal Jumblatt achieved new prominence as the leader of the left-wing forces in alliance with the Palestinians in the Lebanese civil war. He made visits to Cairo and Paris to seek support and sympathy for his cause, and he bitterly denounced Syrian intervention in the war.

A.F.P./PICTORIAL PARADE

Scion, and now head, of one of the two leading Druze clans in Lebanon, Jumblatt was born in 1919. He studied sociology and law at Beirut and at the Sorbonne in Paris. In his youth he supported the pro-French National Bloc, but in 1943 he switched his support to those seeking Lebanese independence, led by Bishara al-Khuri, who became the first president of independent Lebanon. Soon after becoming minister of national economy in 1947, however, he turned against Khuri and in 1949 founded the Progressive Socialist Party, which advocated extensive social reforms and the secularization of Lebanese communal politics.

As an example he distributed some Jumblatt lands in the Shuf Mountain area to the farmers there. His party became increasingly radical in the 1950s, supporting Gamal Abd-al-Nasser and Arab socialism while retaining its political base among the Druze population in the Shuf. In 1952 he joined with Camille Chamoun to force Khuri's resignation, but in the 1958 quasi-civil war he was one of the leaders of the opposition to President Chamoun.

A member of Parliament from 1947 to 1957, and again from 1964, Jumblatt held several Cabinet posts after 1958 and became minister of the interior in 1969. In this capacity he legalized the Baathist and Communist parties in Lebanon and voiced enthusiastic support for the Palestinian guerrillas and their activities against Israel while at the same time trying to control their behaviour in Lebanon. This brought him into conflict with heads of the Army and the secret services and with former president Fuad Chehab who backed them. In the 1970 presidential elections his and his supporters' votes were decisive in securing the election by one vote of Pres. Suleiman Franjieh over the Chehabist Elias Sarkis (*q.v.*). As the situation steadily deteriorated into the civil war which began in earnest in the spring of 1975, Jumblatt became the acknowledged political spokesman for the combined forces of socialists, Baathists, Nasserists, and Communists allied with the Palestinian guerrillas. (PETER MANSFIELD)

Keating, Tom

Late in Britain's blistering 1976 summer the intriguing story broke of how Tom Keating had "set up" the art world, asserting to Geraldine Norman, salesroom cor-

Tom Keating

respondent of *The Times,* that he had faked drawings reputed to be by the English 19th-century painter Samuel Palmer. He also claimed to have produced during the last 25 years around 2,000 pastiches of the work of about 100 artists and in late October named five specific "Constable" drawings as his own. He said that his motive was not personal gain, although at a 1970 auction a London gallery paid £9,400 for one of his "Palmers" ("Sepham Barn"). Usually his works seemed to have been given away or abandoned, sold by other people to junk shops, and eventually "discovered." He alleged that occasionally shady dealers had commissioned him to paint pastiches, but paid him little for them.

Keating, perhaps embittered by the chronic poverty of his childhood and imbued with socialist dislike of middlemen, seemed likely to succeed in his declared intention of embarrassing the art establishment. If his claim was true, many experts must have been deceived; even if it were to be proved false, much alarm had been engendered. Although the British Antique Dealers Association set up a committee to investigate the original 13 suspect "Palmers," owners in general were slow to put their pictures to the test; even police investigation was delayed because the police could not act until they had received complaints. Meanwhile, Keating was collaborating with Geraldine Norman in the production of a book about his life and work; rapid identification of any pastiches hitherto accepted as originals would depend on how specific he was willing or able to be about them. He maintained that he had deliberately made his pictures ultimately recognizable for what they were, writing his name in lead paint under oils, and for drawings using paper not of the imitated artist's period.

Keating was born at Forest Hill in south London on March 1, 1917, one of the many children of a house decorator. A naval stoker during World War II, he received a grant to study commercial and later fine art at Goldsmiths' College, University of London. Thereafter he made a tenuous living as a restorer of paintings, thus becoming familiar with the styles of many artists.

(STEPHANIE MULLINS)

Keneally, Thomas Michael

Australian novelist Thomas Keneally became something of a cult figure in 1976, appearing in the feature film *The Devil's Playground,* the only Australian film to be selected for Director's Fortnight at the Cannes Film Festival. In the film Keneally played a priest who supervised boys during a retreat. Round-faced and jolly, the priest chatted genially with the other priests in a teachers' common room and then went off to deliver the boys a hell-fire sermon. Keneally himself left St. Patrick's College, Manly, a Roman Catholic seminary, shortly before ordination, and later taught in a Roman Catholic boys' school in Sydney.

In 1976 Thomas Keneally worked on his new novel and moved to New York, where he established a new home. *Season in Purgatory,* published during the year, was set on an Adriatic island during World War II, and concerned the experiences of a young English surgeon tending wounded Yugoslav partisans under the worst imaginable conditions. His previous novel, *Gossip from the Forest,* runner-up for Britain's prestigious Booker Prize in 1975, had as its central theme the World War I Armistice, signed in a railway carriage in Compiègne in Normandy in November 1918. Critics observed that Keneally described in detail and atmosphere the meeting of Marshal Foch, Admiral Wemyss, and Matthias Erzberger, but failed to provide new interpretations.

Thomas Keneally, born in 1935, became one of Australia's most prolific modern novelists, and his books won him a series of prizes and fellowships. His earliest successful novels, such as *The Place at Whitton* (1964) and *Three Cheers for the Paraclete* (1968), re-created the pungent atmosphere of boyhood in Catholic institutions in the Australian bush. Other books included *The Fear* (1965), *Bring Larks and Heroes* (1967), *Halloran's Little Boat* (1969), *Childermas* (1969), *The Survivor* (1969), *The Dutiful Daughter* (1971), *The Chant of Jimmie Blacksmith* (1972), and *Blood Red, Sister Rose* (1974), dealing with themes ranging from cannibalism among Arctic explorers to Joan of Arc.

(A. R. G. GRIFFITHS)

Kennedy, Betty

After the death of her husband Gerhard in December 1975, Betty Kennedy felt that she must write something concerning his death and dying. The result was *Gerhard, A Love Story* (1976), written in only four days, which is an account of Gerhard Kennedy's last few months of life and his preparation of both himself and his family for his death. Betty Kennedy saw family life as the base which gave support, and her life with her husband and four children had always taken first place in her life.

In her marriage to Gerhard, there always seemed to be enough room for each of them to do what he or she wanted. Gerhard had several careers, ranging from the fashion industry to being a promoter of air-supported enclosures for warehouse, industrial, and recreational uses. Betty Kennedy became one of the most famous faces in Canada as a regular panelist from 1962 on the Canadian Broadcasting Corporation television program "Front Page Challenge." As the host of an interview program on a Toronto radio station from 1959, she became perhaps the best-known woman in Toronto broadcasting. Together with her husband, she began Kennedy Horizons Ltd., a company that produces educational films. Betty Kennedy served as a member of the Toronto Hospital Planning Council and of the University of Toronto Governing Council. The premier of Ontario in 1975 appointed her a member of an advisory body to review government spending.

Born in Ottawa, Ont., in January 1926, the former Betty Styran began her career as a journalist on the *Ottawa Citizen* in 1942. In 1945 she moved to Montreal and became a fashion coordinator, editing and publishing a trade journal. It was there that she met and married Gerhard Kennedy, who was in Montreal to open a branch of his family's firm which manufactured and marketed sports clothes. When the Kennedys moved to Calgary, Alta., in 1951, Gerhard acted as a representative for a distillery and Betty began her career in broadcasting with the radio discussion show "State Your Case." After spending three years in Ottawa in an unsuccessful attempt to launch a national wildlife conservation foundation, the Kennedy family moved to Toronto in 1959 where Betty became the public affairs director for radio station CFRB.

In 1974 Betty Kennedy became a member of the board of directors of Simpsons Ltd., a Canadian department store chain. In October 1976 she married the chairman of that board, G. Allan Burton.

(DIANE LOIS WAY)

Khorana, Har Gobind

What achievements might a scientist willingly accept in trade for 10 or 20 years of his life? An efficient way to manufacture such vital biological products as insulin and hemoglobin? A technique to correct genetic defects? A step along the path toward a cure for cancer? In 1976 organic chemist and Nobel laureate Har Gobind Khorana laid claim to the potential for all of these accomplishments and more when he and his research team from the Massachusetts Institute of Technology announced their success in synthesizing a gene that was able to function within a living cell.

Born in Raipur, Punjab, India, on Jan. 9, 1922, Khorana first won wide recognition as a researcher at the University of British Columbia in the 1950s for his syntheses of several kinds of proteins, called coenzymes, that play a crucial role in human metabolism. Later, at the University of Wisconsin, he helped decipher the genetic code by re-creating through synthetic techniques each of the three-letter "words," or triplets of DNA nucleotides, that serve in combination as instructions for the natural protein-synthesizing mechanism of the cell. For this latter work he shared with two other scientists the 1968 Nobel Prize in Physiology or Medicine.

To Khorana, however, this historic research was but the groundwork for an even more ambitious endeavour—the synthesis of an entire functional gene. By 1970, after five years of intense labour, his research team had succeeded in constructing a molecule of yeast DNA from chemically synthesized fragments joined with enzymes to

WIDE WORLD

Har Gobind Khorana

STANLEY TRETICK—MAGNUM

form a double-stranded helix 77 nucleotides long. But the gene was not functional, nor was a larger 126-nucleotide bacterial gene that Khorana synthesized three years later at MIT. Total success moved within reach only when Khorana cleared yet another formidable hurdle—the determination and synthesis of additional stretches of nucleotides, known as the promoter and terminator, that constitute the start and stop signals for the larger gene. Once completely assembled, the 207-nucleotide molecule was inserted into a mutated strain of bacterial virus that depended for its infectiousness on the proper functioning of the gene. That the virus thrived was the ultimate triumph, for it was proof that the gene worked as well as its natural counterpart.

Accepting the admiration of the scientific community with characteristic modesty, Khorana maintained that his successes were not goals in themselves but stages in the refinement of a technique that would allow calculated changes in a gene to be made and the results observed. In this way it might be possible to clarify the nature of genetic diseases and of the rampant mechanisms of malignant cells. Artificial genes could also be used to endow bacteria, yeast, and other rapidly proliferating organisms with the ability to make valuable proteins normally obtainable at great expense only from higher organisms.

(CHARLES M. CEGIELSKI)

Kim Il Sung

Over the years North Korea had stayed in the limelight mostly by rattling the sabre against the South. Through much of the exercise, it had succeeded in projecting the image of a strong and monolithic party leadership presided over by an unchallenged "great and beloved leader," Pres. Kim Il Sung. That image was rudely dented in 1976 with news of an unprecedented power struggle in Pyongyang.

Despite expensive worldwide publicity campaigns that suggested otherwise, Kim appeared mortal after all; a cancerous tumour in his neck was getting worse. His search for a reliable successor seemed to have been confined to the family. Starting in 1973 he had tried to project his son Kim Chong Il as a national figure, but it now appeared that his wife, Kim Sung Ae, and younger brother Kim Yong Ju were actively opposing that choice.

It was a portentous development for Kim, who had been the object of a relentless personality cult for three decades. Born Kim Song Chu near Pyongyang on April 15, 1912, he had risen to prominence as an anti-Japanese resistance leader. Guerrilla leaders who fought by his side in Manchuria and northeast China later shored up his power base in Korea. Kim was handpicked for leadership by the Soviets who had occupied northern Korea during World War II. As leader of the Communist Party (later the Korean Workers' Party), he proclaimed the Democratic People's Republic of Korea in 1948. His attempt at forceful reunification of Korea in 1950 was foiled by UN intervention. He was named president of North Korea in 1972.

KEYSTONE

In later years, Kim proved expert at steering clear of big-brother entanglements, but evidently he could not build up a cadre of acceptable national leaders. The violent border clash with U.S. guards in August 1976 rocked the leadership, and more serious trouble apparently followed the bizarre events in October that identified some North Korean embassies as smuggling centres for duty-free goods and drugs. Tokyo even buzzed with rumours of Kim's arrest. This turned out to be incorrect, but there was little doubt that Kim, master of his country for a generation, had reached a watershed.

(T. J. S. GEORGE)

Kissinger, Henry Alfred

With the election of 1976, the era of Henry Kissinger as the master craftsman of United States foreign policy came to a dramatic and somewhat bitter end. Criticism of Kissinger reached an intense level during the presidential election campaign, severely limiting his diplomatic maneuverability on the world stage. Ironically, the worst sniping came from within Pres. Gerald Ford's own party. After years of defending Kissinger and claiming his triumphs as their own, many Republicans turned on their secretary of state, and some even urged that he be replaced before the campaign began.

In challenging Ford for the Republican nomination, Ronald Reagan (*q.v.*) zeroed in on Kissinger's policy of détente with the Soviet Union, charging that the U.S. had conceded too much and received too little in exchange. Reagan attacked the Ford administration's willingness to negotiate a new Panama Canal treaty as a sign of weakness and called for the continuation of U.S. sovereignty in the Canal Zone. Reagan's criticisms helped him come back from his early primary losses, and his attacks on Kissinger continued until the Republican convention.

Criticism of Kissinger from the Democrats focused on his involvement in White House wiretapping during the Nixon administration and his alleged penchant for conducting "secret diplomacy." Though it once had deferred to Kissinger's judgment, Congress firmly rejected the Ford administration's request for funds to aid anti-Communist forces in Angola.

But for a brief period in the spring, Kissinger showed some of his old form as he engaged in "shuttle diplomacy" in southern Africa. After years of neglecting the area and supporting the status quo, Kissinger suddenly reversed direction by proclaiming "unrelenting opposition" to white minority rule in Rhodesia. He pledged U.S. support of racial justice in Africa and wrung major concessions from the ruling white regimes of Rhodesia and South Africa. Even here, however, the agreements he had put together appeared in danger of collapse at year's end.

It was inevitable that President-elect Jimmy Carter would replace Kissinger as secretary of state, though a group of Democratic senators urged that he be retained. Carter indicated he would choose his own man and selected Cyrus R. Vance.

Kissinger was born in Fürth in what is now West Germany on May 27, 1923. He became a U.S. citizen after fleeing Nazi Germany with his family in 1938. He taught government at Harvard University and in 1968 was named assistant for national security affairs to then President-elect Richard Nixon; he was named secretary of state in 1973.

(HAL BRUNO)

Kodama, Yoshio

Dressed in a World War II kamikaze uniform with a white band around his head, a 29-year-old Japanese movie actor aboard a small rented airplane crash-dived into the Tokyo residence of Yoshio Kodama in March 1976. This was done apparently in protest against Kodama, who had served as a secret agent of Lockheed Aircraft Corp. in Japan. The pilot was killed on the spot, while Kodama, who had been ill in bed, escaped without injury.

Kodama had wielded strong influence among top Japanese politicians, but he fell from power following the disclosure in February 1976 that he had received payments of $7 million from Lockheed for his contribution to the firm as a secret agent. Sen. Frank Church (Dem., Idaho), head of the U.S. Senate Subcommittee on Multinational Corporations, referred to Kodama by saying that the most disturbing fact that the panel had come upon was the employment of Yoshio Kodama, "a prominent leader of the ultra-right-wing militarist faction in Japan."

Kodama's relationship with Lockheed began in 1958 when the Japanese government was beginning to rebuild its Air Self-Defense Force (ASDF). At about that time Lockheed opened its Tokyo office for the sale of the F-104 Starfighter, and Kodama was chosen as a secret agent of the company because of his influence among Japanese politicians. The Japanese government had already decided to choose the Grumman F-11 as the ASDF's next main fighter plane, but Kodama pressed the government to overturn its decision in favour of the Starfighter.

Born in 1911 in Fukushima Prefecture, about 230 km (140 mi) N of Tokyo, Kodama moved to Tokyo at the age of 17. The next year he joined a right-wing political group. During World War II he organized the "Kodama Agency" in Shanghai at the request of the Japanese Imperial Navy and played an active role in obtaining intelligence and military materials. He was imprisoned as a war criminal in December 1945 but was never brought to trial. On his return from China to Japan after the war, Kodama carried with him a vast amount of cash, diamonds, and platinum, which was said to have been used to help finance the establishment of the Liberal Party, a predecessor of the present ruling Liberal-Democratic Party.

(YOSHINOBU EMOTO)

Larkin, Philip Arthur

As a poet Philip Larkin was perhaps most admired by those who like to see poets as capable craftsmen, respectably occupied like other clerical workers. Self-restraint and regrets for what might have been were the themes of his austere poems. Their quiet desperation might well be shared by other apparently contented administrators. The sharp, slangy expletives that occasionally erupt in them sound like executives swearing in a hotel bar. The FVS Foundation of Hamburg, West Germany, awarding Philip Larkin its 1976 Shakespeare Prize (for outstanding contributions to European culture), described him as the most important English lyric poet of his generation.

Larkin's first collection, *The North Ship* (1945), was strongly influenced by Yeats. He developed a more congenial style after reading Thomas Hardy; but he did not publish a new collection until *The Less Deceived* in 1955, although meanwhile he produced two admired novels, *Jill* (1946) and *A Girl in Winter* (1947). The poets who were gathered together in "The Movement," in 1956, saw him as the prime exemplar of the "neutral tone" they favoured. His fondness for jazz records, which he reviewed in the *Daily Telegraph* from 1961 to 1971, was a symbol of their hostility to traditional snobberies. His rejection of bardic or Delphic flamboyance was a strong, negative response to the exuberance of Robert Graves and Dylan Thomas. Larkin's refusal to show off was a form of mid-20th-century dandyism. It did not conceal his undoubted power, tenderness, and skill. The critic Clive James wrote of him: "The sole encouragement offered by Philip Larkin's poetry is the existence of the poetry itself, arguing with its own beauty against the anguish it professes." His most recent collection was *High Windows* (1974).

Larkin was born on Aug. 9, 1922, in Coventry, Warwickshire, the son of the city treasurer. He went to school there, took an arts degree at St. John's College, Oxford, in 1943 and became a librarian in Belfast, Northern Ireland. His health prevented military service, and a stammer inhibited him from teaching. From 1955 on he was in charge of the Brynmor Jones Library at the University of Hull, Humberside, and he rarely left this environment. He was a fellow of the Royal Society of Literature. In 1973 he edited the *Oxford Book of Twentieth-Century Verse,* a successor to Yeats's selection. Among other awards, in 1965 he received the Queen's Gold Medal for Poetry.

(D. A. N. JONES)

Lasser, Louise

Some lives seem to be guided by a star. Louise Lasser's television career skyrocketed in a kitchen. Not so long ago she played a dippy housewife in a commercial. The housewife's flu-racked husband thanks her for a dose of patent medicine with "you're a good wife." She replies, "I know, I know." In 1976 she became a household word in the unlaundered soap opera "Mary Hartman, Mary Hartman."

The five-times-weekly series is the unlikely product of Norman Lear, who produced "All in the Family" and a half dozen other hits. Turned down by the major networks, Lear finally sold "MH 2" to a syndicate of more than 100 independent stations. Part soap opera, part a parody of soap opera, it enraptured millions and offended thousands with its deadpan discussion of sexual problems, madness, and other "adult" subjects. Louise Lasser became what *Vogue* called a "Soaperstar."

Born in New York City about 1940 (her age is her secret), she was the daughter of the celebrated tax expert S. Jay Lasser and was raised in luxury's lap. She dropped out of Brandeis University to become an actress, bowing on Broadway as Barbra Streisand's replacement in *I Can Get It for You Wholesale* in 1962.

Her path crossed that of Woody Allen, who was not yet the celebrated writer and comedy film maker. "She promptly bought him a new trenchcoat and they lived together for the next five years," according to one account. Their marriage, solemnized on Groundhog Day, lasted four years. Allen, who is still her friend, calls her "brighter than I am, funnier than I am."

Louise Lasser is a skilled actress and a brilliant, if temperamental, woman who has survived 15 years of psychoanalysis. "It's just very tough to be a human being," she says. "When people in their work and their art touch the children in us, they are using the one thing we all have in common: we were all once short."

In her current role she plays "the under-

FRANK EDWARDS—FOTOS INTERNATIONAL/PICTORIAL PARADE

side of the person that I am in my own life . . . a survivor in a world that may not be worth surviving in." As Mary Hartman she takes TV commercials seriously. She's held hostage by a mass murderer. Her husband is selectively impotent, *i.e.,* only in her direction. Her promiscuous sister works briefly in a massage parlour. Her grandfather is known to police in their fictional Ohio town as "the Fernwood flasher." When her father disappears, her mother is bumblingly wooed by a lonely detective. The high school basketball coach drowns in a bowl of Mary's chicken soup. Her best friend is maimed in a collision with a station wagon full of nuns.

Having become a celebrity in a soap opera that's stronger than mirth and dirtier than life, Lasser believes that "it's more real than realism." As if to prove this, she made headlines in an incident that could have come out of an "MH 2" script. When a Beverly Hills boutique wouldn't accept her credit card, she made a scene and refused to leave. Police were called, routinely searched her, and charged her with the illegal possession of cocaine. "If I died tomorrow on the way to work," she says, "the exact death could be used to explain why I'm gone."

(PHILIP KOPPER)

Lauda, Niki

Son of a wealthy Austrian family, Niki Lauda set his sights on becoming Grand Prix automobile-racing world champion driver. Getting no support from his parents, he arranged a £35,000 bank loan and arrived in England in 1971 to drive for the March team. He was promoted to Formula One in 1972 but had a disastrous year with the unsuccessful March 721X car. A telephone call from Louis Stanley transferred Lauda to the British Racing Motor team for the 1973 season. As co-driver with Clay Regazzoni and Jean-Pierre Beltoise, the Austrian had a firm contract with Marlboro and performed well at Monaco and in the catastrophic British Grand Prix at Silverstone, where he momentarily ran even with race-leading Ronnie Peterson. A Ferrari talent-spotter reported on Lauda's driving ability to Enzo Ferrari at Modena, Italy, and when Regazzoni agreed to share Ferrari responsibilities with him, Lauda was signed on by the famous Italian team.

Driving for Ferrari, he experienced setbacks in 1974, including a puncture when in the lead in the British Grand Prix at

Brands Hatch and a crash at the Nürburgring in the German Grand Prix when attempting to out-brake another driver. But he rose to the top in 1975 after being in pole position in nine of his races, as he had been in 1974, and became one of the youngest drivers to gain the coveted world championship. At the age of 26 (he was born on Feb. 22, 1949) the English-speaking Austrian clinched the title before a delirious Italian crowd by finishing third in the Italian Grand Prix at Monza, won for Ferrari by co-driver Regazzoni.

In 1976 Lauda was heading for the world championship again when he had a bad accident at the Nürburgring during the German Grand Prix. This put him in the hospital on the danger list, with serious burns and lung injuries. But in a very short time the driver who was expected to be out of racing for the rest of the season was back for the final rounds of the championship, in which James Hunt (*q.v.*) of Britain, driving for Marlboro McLaren, was beginning to challenge him. In the contest to decide the championship, in Japan, Lauda declared the rain conditions too dangerous and did not finish the race, leaving the 1976 world driver's championship to Hunt, by 69 points to 68.

(WILLIAM C. BODDY)

Leach, Reggie

For an athlete who was dumped by two National Hockey League teams before he was 25, Reggie Leach proved he belonged on skates in the 1975–76 season. All the Philadelphia Flyers' forward did was have the greatest season any scorer ever enjoyed in NHL history, a record 80 goals, including 19 in the Stanley Cup play-offs. His 61 regular-season goals made him only the second player in league history to reach 60. In the play-off finals against Montreal, Leach was voted the Conn Smythe Trophy, only the third player on a losing team ever to be honoured as most valuable player in the series.

"It was just one of those years where everything went right," he said. "Everything I shot at the net seemed to go in for me. It scares me. They'll probably expect me to do the same thing this year."

Despite the records, Leach was criticized for his defensive shortcomings and was sometimes overlooked on his own line, which included centre Bobby Clarke and left wing Bill Barber. The trio set an NHL record of 141 goals, with Clarke contributing 30 and Barber 50. Both were first-team All-Stars while Leach was relegated to second team.

Leach, born April 23, 1950, in Riverton, Man., is part Cree Indian. He played junior hockey at Flin Flon, Man., with Clarke. In 1970, the Boston Bruins made Leach their top pick in the junior amateur draft. He scored only two goals for the Bruins in his first year before being traded to California, where he scored 23 one year and 22 the next. When the Flyers asked Clarke about his old friend, Clarke said, "Take him and he'll score 40 goals in a bad year." Leach scored 45 in 1974–75 before his record season.

Leach is not the flamboyant, talkative type. "I was a disturber when I was young," he said. "Quit school, did this, did that. I was crazy. You name it, I tried it. I liked the game and was pretty good but I lived in a tough town, Riverton. The best thing that ever happened to me was leaving there for Flin Flon, where I got to play with Clarke and started thinking about a pro career."

(J. TIMOTHY WEIGEL)

Lefebvre, Monsignor Marcel

Few inside or outside the Roman Catholic Church had heard of Archbishop Marcel Lefebvre until, in 1976, he became widely known as the spokesman of a traditionalist movement that regarded Pope Paul VI as a dangerous heretic and a crypto-Protestant. The immediate occasion of the conflict was the Tridentine mass, the form of eucharistic service, in Latin, that was authorized by the 16th-century Council of Trent. After Vatican Council II (1962–65) it was replaced by more varied services in the vernacular. Lefebvre, however, continued to celebrate the banned Tridentine mass, and the high point of his resistance came on August 29, when 6,000 traditionalists gathered for a mass in a Lille, France, sports stadium. The threat of schism was real. Subsequently Lefebvre met Pope Paul and, without in any way abandoning his positions, moderated his language.

Observers might be forgiven for thinking that the unedifying quarrel could easily have been resolved with a little more tolerance on all sides. But for Msgr. Lefebvre the defense of the Tridentine mass was a symbolic battle in his campaign against the contemporary church. In his *Profession of Faith* (November 1974), he declared: "We refuse and have always refused to follow the Rome of neo-modernist and neo-Protestant leanings." Lefebvre was particularly worried by what he considered to be a too generously accommodating attitude to Marxists and Freemasons. His true spiritual home was the traditionalist French right wing typified by Charles Maurras' *L'Action française*. Not content with denouncing the Vatican in speeches and statements, in 1971 he had founded a seminary at Ecône in Switzerland in order to instill his values into future priests. Several times ordered to close it down, he did nothing and as a result was "suspended" on July 24, 1976.

Lefebvre was born at Tourcoing, northeastern France, on Nov. 29, 1905. Ordained in 1929, he was a Holy Ghost missionary in West Africa, becoming the first archbishop of Dakar, Senegal, in 1948 and later superior general of his congregation. In this capacity he was present at Vatican II where he was an articulate member of the small minority who resisted change. In particular, he opposed the decree on religious liberty and, ironically in view of subsequent happenings, insisted that the pope should not yield any of his authority to the world's bishops.

(PETER HEBBLETHWAITE)

Lévesque, René

Gen. Charles de Gaulle's famous "Vive le Québec libre!" of 1967 echoed jubilantly throughout Canada's mainly French-speaking province of Quebec in 1976. In the November 15 election to the provincial National Assembly René Lévesque's separatist Parti Québécois secured 69 of the 110 seats, ousting Robert Bourassa's Liberal Party government in a dramatic upset. Sworn in as Quebec's new premier on November 26, Lévesque shortly afterward reaffirmed that political independence for the province from the rest of Canada remained his party's firm objective. He anticipated that a referendum on the question would be held within three to five years' time.

René Lévesque was born at New Carlisle, Bonaventure County, Quebec, on Aug. 24, 1924. He went to school in Gaspésie and afterward to Laval University, Quebec City. Already a part-time journalist while still a student, he broke off his law studies to serve in Europe (1944–45) as a reporter and correspondent attached to the U.S. forces. Back in Quebec after the war, in 1946 he joined the international service of the Canadian Broadcasting Corporation, became a war correspondent in Korea (1952), and from 1956 to 1959 was commentator on the popular TV program "Point de mire."

Lévesque entered politics in 1960 and in that year was elected to the Quebec National Assembly as a Liberal member for Gouin, joining Jean Lesage's government as minister of public works and hydraulic resources (1960–61). He then held the newly created portfolio of natural resources (1961–66), and in 1966, during the last months of the Lesage government, he was minister of family and social welfare. Meanwhile he had been reelected in the constituency of Laurier in the 1962 and 1966 legislative elections.

In October 1967 Lévesque left the Liberal Party and founded, with others, the Souveraineté-Association, which the following year combined with other separatist groups to form the Parti Québécois, with Lévesque as its first president. Unsuccessful in the 1970 and 1973 elections, he returned to journalism, writing daily political articles in the *Journal de Montréal* and the *Journal de Québec*.

(J. E. DAVIS)

López Portillo, José

It was a hot summer day on the Gulf of Mexico. He looked out at the sea of faces raised to him and uttered the same brief speech he had already made to hundreds of similar crowds all over Mexico's 31 states. He thanked them for coming, promised to

LONDON DAILY EXPRESS/PICTORIAL PARADE

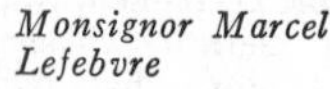

Monsignor Marcel Lefebvre

CAMERA PRESS/PHOTO TRENDS

carry out the country's laws when he was elected, and departed for the next town.

José López Portillo, 56, who on Dec. 1, 1976, became president of Mexico and chief of state for 60 million Mexicans for a six-year term, ran unopposed in the July election. No candidate of the Partido Revolucionario Institucional (PRI) had lost an election for president, governor of a state, or federal senator since 1929. (The small opposition Partido Acción Nacional did not even field a candidate for president this time.) But the PRI candidate always campaigns as if the devil himself were running against him.

López Portillo came from an excellent political background. His father took part in the revolution of 1910. López was a law professor for many years and a teacher of political science at the National University. As a late-blooming member of the PRI he did not attain Cabinet rank until less than three years before the party nominated him for the presidency. As minister of finance he seemed anything but a politician eager to ingratiate himself with the public. Mexicans think of him as tough. This attribute was most in evidence when it became his duty to impose some unpopular taxes.

Those who follow Mexican affairs wondered for a time whether the long-expected devaluation of the peso would be ordered by outgoing Pres. Luis Echeverría Álvarez or whether he would hand that embarrassment along to his successor. In the end, Echeverría attached his own name to the first devaluation of the peso in 22 years (down from eight U.S. cents to about four cents at the end of October). Echeverría also, in November, decreed implementation of a land reform that led to serious disorders even as López was being inaugurated and was still in dispute at year's end.

López Portillo announced that he would follow a policy of austerity and discipline to stabilize the economy. He hoped the flow of foreign capital and tourists would return to former levels and that exports, made more competitive by the devaluation, would bring in more dollars.

Though he speaks in the soft, didactic style of the professor, López Portillo is a muscular six-footer who runs a mile every day, swims, and punches the bag. He is married to the former Carmen Romano and they have three children: José, 21; Carmen, 17; and Paulina, 14.

(JEREMIAH A. O'LEARY, JR.)

Lowry, Sir Robert Lynd Erskine

The lord chief justice of Northern Ireland, Sir Robert Lowry, found himself in a key political role when he was appointed chairman of the constitutional convention elected in May 1975 to devise a new constitution for Northern Ireland. A brilliant lawyer, he had become lord chief justice in 1971 at the age of 52, and unlike his lawyer father, who had been an Ulster Unionist MP and a Northern Ireland attorney general, he had stayed out of politics. His political independence was a necessary qualification for the post of convention chairman.

Though he came from a family background that could be called Ulster Protestant establishment, he won the respect of both sides in Northern Ireland's sectarian conflict by his fairness and firmness, by the clarity and grip of a good legal mind, and by his personal charm, even temper, and simple good manners in a situation where these qualities were often absent. That the convention proved abortive was no fault of his. Indeed, he had been able to show that there was a willingness among reasonable men and women in Northern Ireland to work together. He had been notably effective in private discussions behind the scenes.

Born on Jan. 30, 1919, he was brought up in Belfast, went to Cambridge, where he took a double first in classics, and then into the Army, serving in Northern Ireland regiments during World War II. On his return to Northern Ireland he turned to the law, becoming a High Court judge in 1964. As a judge, he was remembered for his firmness in refusing to take evidence obtained under duress in cases against Irish Republican Army terrorists. In the social life of Northern Ireland he was well known in the world of show jumping and was a past chairman of the Show Jumping Association of Ireland. Sir Robert was knighted in 1971. He was a member of the Privy Council from 1974 and of the Privy Council (Northern Ireland) from 1971.

(HARFORD THOMAS)

McCormack, Ellen

Scarcely anyone in political circles took it seriously when Ellen McCormack, a 49-year-old housewife, announced that she would run for president of the United States as the candidate of the Pro-Life Action Committee. But before the 1976 election was over, her name had been placed in nomination at the Democratic National Convention and the antiabortion cause she represented had become the campaign's most difficult and emotional issue.

WIDE WORLD

The wife of John McCormack, a New York City deputy police inspector; the mother of four; and the grandmother of two, Mrs. McCormack had been active in her own Roman Catholic parish in Merrick, Long Island, but did not become involved in the "pro-life" movement until 1970. Her first political experience was as a Conservative Party volunteer in the 1974 New York senate race.

Professional politicians were surprised when her supporters quickly raised $5,000 from each of 20 different states, making Mrs. McCormack's campaign eligible for federal matching funds. She actively campaigned in 18 Democratic primaries, winning as much as 9% of the vote in Vermont and an impressive 3% in the crucial Pennsylvania contest. Twenty-two delegates voted for her nomination at the Democratic convention.

But more important than percentages was the effect of Mrs. McCormack's candidacy on the rest of the campaign. Other candidates found themselves compelled to take a stand on an explosive issue many would have preferred to avoid. Long after Mrs. McCormack stopped running, the right-to-life movement continued to stage emotional demonstrations. Democratic candidate Jimmy Carter was their special target because, though he personally opposed abortion on demand, he did not (as they did) favour amending the Constitution to prohibit it.

It was difficult to measure the net result of the abortion issue, since the right-to-life movement also produced a strong counterreaction from pro-abortion forces. One thing was certain, however; Ellen McCormack, the housewife from Merrick, had had her own personal impact on the 1976 election. No one would laugh if she ever decided to run for office again.

(HAL BRUNO)

McKee, Fran

"She always pretty much made up her own mind. It never entered her head that she couldn't do anything." Thus Fran McKee's mother described her daughter as a child. And Fran McKee made a career of doing things that no woman had ever done before. In 1976 she was appointed the first woman line rear admiral in the United States Navy. Staff officers are limited to such activities as supply, law, and medicine, but there is no restriction upon the type of duty that a line admiral can perform. Admiral McKee said that she was "euphoric" about her promotion and she called it a "great step forward for women."

Fran McKee's naval career had begun rather casually more than 25 years earlier. She was born on Sept. 13, 1926, in Florence, Ala., but her father worked for a railway company and the family moved often. In 1950 McKee received a B.S. in chemistry from the University of Alabama. She planned to enter medical school, but the Korean War had just begun and McKee "wanted to do something" for the country. Friends recommended the Navy so she signed up, intending to stay for two years.

After completing Officer Training School, McKee became an administrative aide to the chief of naval research in Washington,

D.C., where she found herself meeting the scientists who had written her college textbooks. McKee soon concluded that the Navy "was a great place to make one's mark." She rose through the ranks in personnel, training, and educational administration and in 1973 was the first woman ever chosen to command an activity of the Naval Security Group. Three years earlier, she had been one of the first two women officers selected to attend the Naval War College.

Over 25 years McKee lived in eight cities, including Rota, Spain, and Port Lyautey, Morocco. She thrived on this nomadic life. "There are just so many exciting places," she said. She once raced her sports car, but now drove it in road rallies. Raising tropical fish, listening to music, and reading historical novels were other spare-time activities.

A patriot of the best sort and, in her quiet way, a feminist, Fran McKee felt strongly that "women have just as much responsibility as men to support our institutions and traditions." Women now could do what they wished with their lives—pursue a career, raise a family, or both: "The nice thing is, we are now able to make a choice." (VICTOR M. CASSIDY)

Manley, Michael

In 1976 Michael Manley, 53, prime minister of Jamaica and president of the People's National Party, was a man sitting on a political and economic volcano. The husky former Royal Canadian Air Force pilot and one-time BBC newsman declared a state of emergency in June because of rioting, shootings, and tension in the capital city of Kingston. Some of the turbulence was due to the rivalry between Manley's party and the opposition Jamaica Labour Party, but the real roots of the island's problems were over-population, unemployment, and declining receipts from sugar, bauxite, and tourism.

The Jamaican crisis was important to the nearby U.S. because there was heavy American investment in the five major aluminum companies. The U.S. imported 60% of its supply from Jamaica. When Manley won election in 1972, Jamaica was riding a wave of prosperity and Manley was regarded as friendly to the U.S. In the face of the challenge from the JLP and its leader, tough, pro-U.S. Edward Seaga, Manley took a turn to the left. He negotiated with the foreign bauxite companies for purchase of 51% control and imposed special taxes on bauxite and alumina. His diplomatic and cultural flirtation with Marxist Cuba, only 90 mi away, caused the opposition to charge Manley with trying to turn Jamaica into a Cuban-style Communist state. Manley and his ministers contended that their government was a non-Communist "democratic socialist" state.

The election on December 15 brought a landslide affirmation for Manley. His People's National Party won a whopping majority in Parliament. His first act afterward was to issue an appeal for national unity, warning Jamaicans that the days of "frills and soft options" were over.

An attractive but temperamental man whose father was a Jamaican national hero, Manley is married to former radio and television personality Beverly Anderson. He has two daughters and a son by previous marriages. An inveterate reader and music lover, he owns a record library containing more than 1,000 albums.

(JEREMIAH A. O'LEARY, JR.)

Maori Kiki, Sir Albert

In 1976 Papua New Guinea's minister for foreign relations and trade, Sir Albert Maori Kiki, outlined new directions in a more self-confident foreign policy. One of the problems following independence in 1975 was that the relics and images of a colonial past still existed, especially in the minds of foreign nations who tended to think of Papua New Guinea as an appendage of Indonesia or Australia. The Swiss ambassador in Indonesia, for example, held additional accreditation to Papua New Guinea, but Sir Albert was adamant that foreign diplomats in Australia would not be able to have similar accreditation. He said that if countries wanted to be represented in Papua New Guinea, their diplomats could not come from Canberra: "We have to get away from this colonial tie."

One of Sir Albert's major achievements was the solution of a crucial foreign relations problem with Australia over the future of some islands in the Torres Strait. These islands—Boigu, Dauan, and Saibai—were designated Australian even though they were only a stone's throw from the Papua New Guinea mainland. Sir Albert and the Australian foreign minister, Andrew Peacock, arrived at a compromise agreement on the maritime border question. The new border between Australia and Papua New Guinea ran south of the islands, but the islands themselves remained Australian and their people Australian citizens.

Albert Maori Kiki was born in Orokolo village, Gulf District, in 1931. He was educated at a mission school at Sogeri and at a medical school in Fiji. He worked as a patrol and welfare officer, was founder of Papua New Guinea's first labour union, president of the Port Moresby Council of Trade Unions, and served as a member of the National Education Board. He left a promising career in public service to found the Pangu Pati (the independence party). Maori Kiki organized the Pangu Pati's election campaign in 1968 and helped to devise the slogan "One name, one country, one people." He was himself unsuccessful in the election, but subsequently under his guidance the emerging nation developed sound lines of foreign and defense policy.

(A. R. G. GRIFFITHS)

Matanzima, Kaiser Daliwonga

On Oct. 25, 1976, Paramount Chief Kaiser Matanzima became prime minister of the Transkei republic, the first African homeland, or Bantustan, to be given its independence by the Republic of South Africa. Although his small country, the home of about two million Xhosas, failed to gain international recognition, Chief Matanzima remained convinced that black and white South Africans would succeed in ending what he described as the "unjust society" only by accepting independent black states as precursors to a multiracial federation. He was a strong upholder of Xhosa nationalism, which he saw as an important element in black nationalism; at the same time, however, he strongly defended the idea of a wide multiracial society.

KEYSTONE

Born June 15, 1915, at Qamata in the Transkei, the son of the chief of the emigrant Tembus, Matanzima was educated first in the Lovedale Missionary Institute and later at Fort Hare University, the nursery of black nationalism in South Africa. He abandoned his law studies in 1955 to devote himself to the interests of his tribe, and became chief in his father's place in 1958. Three years later he was elected chairman of the Transkei Territorial Authority, which later became the Transkei Parliament. He became chief minister in 1963, when Transkei was established as the first partially self-governing Bantustan.

Matanzima had built up his power through political skill and by using tough methods against his opposition. Although often described as a "collaborator" with the South African apartheid system, he was in fact a staunch critic of racist policies. His tactics in choosing to take Transkei into a kind of independence were vigorously criticized by other prominent homeland leaders, such as the KwaZulu spokesman, Chief Gatswa Buthelezi, and by radical nationalists and white liberals. But he remained convinced that his policies would do more to transform South Africa than those advocated by his critics. (COLIN LEGUM)

Mehta, Zubin

The Los Angeles Philharmonic Orchestra was on tour in London. Zubin Mehta had just finished conducting a work by the U.S. composer Charles Ives. The applause began, and someone in the audience shouted, "Not bad for colonials!" In a body, the orchestra's trombone section arose and answered these cries by playing "Rule Britannia." Such exuberant behaviour is not common in the concert hall—except when Mehta is conducting. Praised as a genius by some and criticized as theatrical and eccentric by others, the flamboyant Mehta bores no one.

In 1978 Mehta would replace Pierre Boulez as musical director of the New York Philharmonic Orchestra, the latest move in a career that had taken him around the world several times. He was born April 29, 1936, in Bombay, India, to a family of Parsis, descendants of Zoroastrian Persians who emigrated to India during the 8th century. The Parsis have been interested in Western music since the early 1930s. Mehta's father helped found the Bombay String Quartet and the Bombay Symphony Orchestra, and Zubin was surrounded by Western music as a child.

Mehta was still not fully committed to music as an adolescent, and he entered college with the intention of becoming a physician. But one day, when he was told to dissect a lizard, he rebelled, quit school, and soon left India for Vienna, where he enrolled in the Akademie für Musik und darstellende Kunst. In Vienna he acquired a fondness for the "Vienna sound," which he characterized as "rich, round, and velvety." Mehta's special interest is in the late Romantic and early modern composers.

In 1958 Mehta won first prize in the Liverpool International Conductor's Competition and became associate conductor

CAMERA PRESS/MILLER SERVICES

of the Royal Liverpool Philharmonic for a year. His reputation grew swiftly as he made guest appearances all over the world, and in 1961 he was appointed musical director of the Montreal Symphony. That same year Mehta had guest conducted a well-received concert with the Los Angeles Philharmonic. He was offered more appearances, but Georg Solti, the newly appointed musical director in Los Angeles, was not consulted. In a fit of anger Solti quit, and Mehta got his job. For the next several years, Mehta commuted between Montreal and Los Angeles. He greatly improved the Montreal orchestra and was credited with building the Los Angeles Philharmonic into a first-rate ensemble. (VICTOR M. CASSIDY)

Mondale, Walter Frederick

Candidates for the vice-presidency of the United States are usually chosen for their ability to appeal to constituencies not attracted to the candidate at the top of the party's ticket. Minnesota Sen. Walter "Fritz" Mondale, Jimmy Carter's running mate in 1976, was no exception. He was from the North, was seen as more liberal than Carter, and had served 12 years in the

LAWRENCE FRANK—PHOTO RESEARCHERS

U.S. Senate to balance Carter's lack of experience in the federal government.

The net effect of such ticket-balancing is usually just some mild reassurance to some voters. But Mondale proved to be much more than that. Many political experts, including Carter's own campaign staff, believed that the Minnesota senator was a critical element in the Democratic victory. By election day, polls showed Mondale was preferred as vice-president by a margin of 51%, compared with 33% for Republican candidate Sen. Robert Dole (*q.v.*). "He gave us two or three extra points," observed Carter campaign manager Hamilton Jordan. In an election that Carter won by only three percentage points, Mondale was indeed important.

Born Jan. 5, 1928, in Ceylon, Minn., the son of a Methodist minister, Mondale rose in national politics by a curious route: having been appointed to every public job he held. In 1960, after practicing law in Minnesota, he was appointed state attorney general; and in 1964, when his mentor, Sen. Hubert Humphrey, was named to run for vice-president with Lyndon Johnson, Mondale was appointed to fill Humphrey's term in the Senate. After both appointments, Mondale ran on his own and won reelection.

Considered one of the most capable members of the Senate, Mondale was frequently mentioned as a possible presidential candidate himself. In 1974, he put out an exploratory bid for the 1976 presidential nomination. But less than a year later, after 200,000 mi of travel, he withdrew.

Mondale was left largely on his own during the 1976 campaign and, with a well-organized effort and an impressive showing in the first debate between vice-presidential nominees in U.S. history, further impressed Carter. Although vice-presidents are usually relegated to passive ceremonial and political roles, it seemed likely that Mondale would play an important part in the Carter administration. (JOHN F. STACKS)

Moon, The Reverend Sun Myung

In a period when exotic religious cults were growing with remarkable speed in the U.S., the Rev. Sun Myung Moon was proving to be the most successful of the new religious entrepreneurs. The Reverend Moon founded his Unification Church in Korea in 1954 and began full-scale missionary operations in the U.S. in 1973. Starting with a few hundred followers, he built his U.S. membership to more than 10,000 in three years. Worldwide, the Unification Church claimed between 500,000 and two million members, mostly in Korea and Japan.

In his book *Divine Principle,* the Reverend Moon sets forth his autobiography and theology. Born on Jan. 6, 1920, in Jung Joo, (North) Korea, he claims to have been clairvoyant as a child. When he was 16, he writes, Christ appeared to him in a vision and commanded him to "carry out my unfinished task." Moon's theology was subsequently revealed to him by Abraham, Buddha, and Moses. Moon believes that God has chosen him to save mankind from Satanism, and he sees the Communists as Satan's representatives in the world today.

Moon began to preach his doctrines in Korea in 1946. Two years later he was excommunicated by the Presbyterian Church, and shortly thereafter he was imprisoned by the North Korean authorities, for reasons that are not entirely clear. In 1950 he escaped—or was released—and fled to South Korea, where he founded what was to become the Unification Church. Combining his religious activities with a business career, he built his Korean enterprises, which in-

HIROJI KUBOTA—MAGNUM

cluded factories producing armaments, paint, machinery, and ginseng tea, into an empire said to be worth $30 million. His assets in Japan were estimated at $20 million, and after moving to the U.S., he spent millions of dollars on real estate.

A typical American Moonie, as the press called his converts, was single and young and was probably introduced to the Unification Church at a campus meeting. The conversion process usually began with a weekend session at a recruiting centre and continued with an intensive weeklong workshop. A full-time church member was required to give all possessions to the church. Thereafter, he or she lived communally with other members under strict discipline and spent long days recruiting, raising funds, and praying.

The parents of some members charged that Moon's intensive conversion techniques amounted to brainwashing, and some used physical force to remove their sons and daughters from Moon's living centres. But Moon replied that anyone could leave his church at will. He produced testimony from parents who were happy to have their children in the Unification Church. Moon also said that his converts were old enough to think for themselves. (VICTOR M. CASSIDY)

Morris, Joe

On Oct. 14, 1976, Canada experienced its first nationwide general strike called for political reasons. Its aims were to end the wage and price controls imposed by the Canadian government in 1975 and to force the government to give the labour unions an equal voice with government and business in economic decision-making. More than one million workers participated. The organization leading the strike was the Canadian Labour Congress, a federation of 115 Canadian unions with a total membership of 2.3 million workers. President of the CLC was a former logger named Joe Morris, who was able to unite the movement behind him and to get the affiliated unions to grant him authority they would not have considered granting even one year earlier.

The son of a British trade unionist, Joseph

Morris was born on June 14, 1913, in Lancashire, England. He emigrated to Canada in his youth. While working as a logger in the British Columbia forest products industry, he became involved in labour union activities. In 1936 he helped to organize a local of the International Woodworkers of America (IWA) on Vancouver Island. A secessionist movement within the local was thwarted in 1948, and Morris was elected president. At that time he also joined the staff of the international IWA. By 1953 he was president of the IWA District Council, a position he held until 1962, when he was made executive vice-president of the Canadian Labour Congress. As president of the CLC since 1974, he rallied the labour movement in a common cause as never before, making the CLC a political movement.

CANADIAN PRESS

Morris considered himself a true internationalist. He contended that unions must become truly international in order to deal with multinational corporations. In 1966 he had become a member of the workers' delegation to the International Labour Organization, a UN agency drawing representation from government, management, and labour. In 1976 he served as chairman of the ILO workers' delegation and as a member of the new executive board, and was called the one man in the ILO with the political awareness to deal with issues raised by employers, labour unions, and governments.

In Canada Morris used his abilities in an advisory capacity to the federal government as a member of the Economic Council of Canada. He was appointed in 1974 to this body, which is made up of leaders of industry, labour, finance, and the general public. (DIANE LOIS WAY)

Moynihan, Daniel Patrick

Typically, it was a year of turmoil and several incarnations for Daniel Patrick Moynihan, beginning with his role as the embattled U.S. ambassador to the United Nations and ending with his election as U.S. senator from New York. In between, he resigned his UN post, lectured at colleges and universities, campaigned for Sen. Henry Jackson's ill-fated presidential bid, and won his own five-way primary fight for the Democratic Senate nomination in New York.

Moynihan had almost quit the UN in late 1975, when his continued denunciation of the third world nations brought widespread criticism from other UN diplomats and, Moynihan thought, from U.S. Secretary of State Henry Kissinger (*q.v.*). In one speech, Moynihan termed the UN "the scene of acts we regard as abominations." His rhetoric may have been undiplomatic, but it had the support of U.S. public opinion and Pres. Gerald Ford gave Moynihan a personal vote of confidence that kept him on the job a bit longer.

Moynihan abruptly resigned early in 1976, on grounds that he was not being supported by the Ford administration and was being undermined by Kissinger. This time, the president let him go and Moynihan immediately plunged into Senator Jackson's presidential primary campaign.

Despite a previous pledge not to run for office if he left the UN, Moynihan began his own quest for the New York Senate seat soon after Jackson's presidential campaign folded.

He first had to win a bruising Democratic primary fight involving himself, Rep. Bella Abzug, former U.S. attorney general Ramsey Clark, New York City Council President Paul O'Dwyer, and businessman Abraham Hirschfeld. Moynihan won, despite the opposition of many liberal Democrats and Puerto Rican and black voters, who could not forgive him for once advocating "benign neglect" of race problems when he served as an urban affairs adviser to Pres. Richard Nixon.

Throughout the primary campaign, Moynihan described himself as "a man of the centre," and he stuck to that theme in the fall election battle against the incumbent senator, James Buckley, a Conservative-Republican. Moynihan won the election by 500,000 votes.

For the 49-year-old Moynihan, born March 16, 1927, in Tulsa, Okla., it was another achievement in a brilliant career that began with a poverty-stricken childhood in New York City's "Hell's Kitchen." A graduate of Tufts University, Medford, Mass., he taught government at Harvard and served in advisory roles under four different presidents—John Kennedy, Lyndon Johnson, Nixon, and Ford. (HAL BRUNO)

Muldoon, Robert David

The rise of New Zealand's fifth prime minister in four years seemed irresistible. Senior partner in a firm of accountants, Robert Muldoon won the National Party leadership during the only term it had been in opposition during his 15 years in Parliament, then turned a 25-seat deficit to a 23-seat winning margin at the general elections of November 1975.

A former finance minister, Muldoon had based his campaign on his credentials for rescuing the economy, but at the end of his first year in office that was still a prospect. His greater impact was in New Zealand's relations with Africa; forthright expression of personal support for New Zealand sports contacts with South Africa added fuel to the flames when African countries withdrew from the Montreal Olympics rather than compete against New Zealand athletes.

Muldoon's forthrightness had provoked personal attacks against him at the general elections, when his opponents warned that he would develop a dictatorship based on character assassination. The chunky, impatient free enterpriser had won the party leadership in July 1974 from the more passive Sir John Marshall, who had led the party to defeat in 1972. Many who con-

CAMERA PRESS/FRANZ FURST

ceded that the National Party needed more forcefulness than Marshall was likely to provide were slow to approve the coup by which Muldoon came to the leadership, making the 1975 election result all the more sensational.

Rob Muldoon was born in Auckland on Sept. 25, 1921, grandson of a Liverpool-Irish Methodist lay missionary who came to New Zealand in the 1880s. While serving with the Army in New Caledonia, Egypt, and Italy during World War II, he began to study cost accounting, and he continued this in London after his discharge. In 1946 he was the first winner outside Britain of the Leverhulme Prize of the London Institute of Cost and Management Accountants. He built a successful career in accountancy before entering politics.

Member of Parliament for Tamaki from 1960, Muldoon was undersecretary to the minister of finance (1963–66) and became finance minister himself in 1967. In 1972 he became deputy leader of the National Party, and during February–November of that year was deputy prime minister.

(JOHN A. KELLEHER)

Nicholls, Sir Douglas Ralph

There was wide acclaim and almost no opposition when Sir Douglas Nicholls was named as the first Aboriginal to hold viceregal office in Australia. But soon Sir Douglas, whose life's work was the reconciliation of black and white Australians, was distressed to find himself at the centre of controversy following Queen Elizabeth II's approval of his appointment as governor of South Australia. Sir Douglas, who spent his first nights in Melbourne sleeping on a bed of cabbage leaves at the Victorian market, was immediately affronted by questions from a Melbourne television reporter that he considered offensive. During the interview Sir Douglas called a reporter a "racist" for asking Lady Nicholls how she felt about fitting in with Adelaide's garden party set. He threatened to call the police to evict the reporter and demanded in vain that the interview not be broadcast. He then found himself at the centre of a rapidly developing row when some claimed that he would not be able to do the governor's job because he would not understand the papers he would have to sign. Aboriginals demonstrated outside the television station, but the controversy ended when Sir Douglas accepted an apology, remarking sadly that

AUSTRALIAN INFORMATION SERVICE

GUILIANI—SYGMA

"ratbags get in on a thing like this. Now they are the racists—yes I mean the Aboriginals."

Asked how, as an Aboriginal and a Christian, he could reconcile his living in luxury and lavish surroundings at Government House with his own people's plight, Sir Douglas replied that he expected criticism from his own people, "but what can I do? It's a social problem. It's not my responsibility. There are plenty of organizations working in the field." He added that he would not be a rubber stamp governor, and would refuse to give assent to legislation that he believed was not in the best interests of the people of South Australia.

Born Dec. 9, 1906, at Cummeragunja in New South Wales, Nicholls attended school there and became one of Australia's best-known Aboriginal sportsmen, being especially expert as a runner and playing league football (rugby) for Fitzroy. He served as an adviser to the Victorian Ministry of Aboriginal Affairs, a director of the Aborigines Advancement League, and a pastor of the Churches of Christ Aboriginal Mission. He was knighted in 1972. (A. R. G. GRIFFITHS)

Nyerere, Julius Kambarage

When U.S. Secretary of State Henry Kissinger embarked on his African diplomatic mission in 1976, the first leader he sought out was Pres. Julius Nyerere of Tanzania. Nyerere was the influential chairman of the "front-line presidents," so-called not only because their countries (Tanzania, Mozambique, Zambia, Angola, and Botswana) border closest on Rhodesia and South Africa but also because they were most actively committed to the struggle for majority rule in the area. One of the architects of the modern Pan-Africanist movement and of the Organization of African Unity, Nyerere's stand on principle had on occasion brought him into conflict with other African leaders. Examples included his support for the right of the Ibos to establish their short-lived Biafran Republic and his bitter opposition to his neighbour Pres. Idi Amin of Uganda, whom he denounced as "a murderer."

Nyerere announced during the year that he would not run for reelection when his present term expired in 1982. The decision was typical of the man, who, when he became president, chose to be known by the honorific title of Mwalimu, a Swahili word meaning teacher. A moralist who strongly believed in upholding principles, he held that leaders should teach by their exemplary behaviour. As the founder of his nation he remained committed to the idea of creating an egalitarian socialist society based on the concept of self-reliance. He described himself as a non-Marxist socialist who believed in achieving revolutionary change through democratic methods.

Born in March 1922 in Butiama, Musoma district, Nyerere became a staunch Roman Catholic. After studying at Makerere College (Uganda) he graduated from the University of Edinburgh (Scotland) and returned home to teach at the St. Francis School, Dar es Salaam, in 1952. From his early school days he was a rebel against the colonial system and a pioneer of the black nationalist movement. Chief minister of Tanganyika in 1960 and prime minister when the country gained its independence in 1961, he became president in 1962 and continued in office when Zanzibar joined Tanganyika to form Tanzania in 1964.

(COLIN LEGUM)

Obasanjo, Olusegun

Lieut. Gen. Olusegun Obasanjo became head of state of Nigeria on Feb. 13, 1976, when Brig. Murtala Ramat Mohammed (*see* OBITUARIES) was killed in an abortive coup. A former chief of staff of the Nigerian armed forces, General Obasanjo was an engineer with a distinguished military career. He enlisted as a soldier at the age of 21, and after training at the Mons Officer Cadet School in England he became a lieutenant in 1959. He subsequently obtained further military training at the Indian Staff College, the Royal Military College of Science, Shrivenham, England (where he won a citation as the best Commonwealth student ever to attend the school), and at the Royal College of Defence Studies in London, where he wrote a dissertation on British aid to Nigeria.

Obasanjo served with the Nigerian unit of the UN forces in the Congo in 1960, and won his spurs as a fighting soldier in 1969 during Nigeria's civil war as commander of the 3rd Marine Commando Division. After the civil war he took command of the Engineering Corps and served for a time in a ministerial capacity as federal commissioner for works and housing. As chief of staff of the armed forces, he became the de facto prime minister after the July 1975 coup that deposed Gen. Yakubu Gowon and brought Brigadier Mohammed to power.

Born on March 5, 1937, in Abeokuta, Obasanjo was a Yoruba but insisted on describing himself as a Nigerian. He was a Baptist, a teetotaler, and a nonsmoker. For recreation he played squash, table tennis, and billiards. A soft-spoken, thoughtful soldier, he enjoyed a considerable reputation as a leader of impeccable integrity and quiet modesty. (COLIN LEGUM)

Oh, Sadaharu

Throughout the Orient, Sadaharu Oh has been known for years as the "Babe Ruth of Japan." On the afternoon of Oct. 11, 1976, the first baseman of Tokyo's Yomiuri Giants justified the title before 50,000 hometown fans in Korakuen Stadium. The crowd arrived in high spirits, but intense anticipation gradually gave way to sullen disappointment as Oh was walked the first four times at bat. Then it happened. Oh got a pitch he could hit and sent his 48th home run of the season sailing out of the ball park. Pandemonium broke loose as Oh leaped into the air and circled the bases. The handsome left-hander had just surpassed Babe Ruth's lifetime total of 714 home runs. Sportswriters on both sides of the Pacific had long predicted that moment and were equally sure that the 5-ft 10-in Oh would not only out-homer Hank Aaron (755) but would raise his home run total to 800 or more before retiring. Whatever Oh's final figure, he was sure to become the greatest power hitter of all time—anywhere.

Just how good is Sadaharu Oh? In 1974 the touring New York Mets had a chance to see for themselves. In one game against the Mets, Oh grounded out to first, got a clean hit with the bases loaded, then clouted a grand slam home run to win the game. Most Mets readily agreed that Oh could hit 35 or more home runs a season playing in the U.S. Actually the more closely Oh's record is scrutinized the more impressive it becomes. During his 18 years with the Giants, he has averaged 39.8 homers per season playing the 130-game Japanese schedule. Ruth's average was 32.5 over 22 years, and Aaron's 32.8 over 23 years. And the playing season for each had 24 to 32 more games. Moreover, none of Oh's numerous home runs during championship games is included in his official career total. In the process of rewriting the record book, Oh has also hit four home runs in a single game; has homered in seven straight games; has set a Japanese season record of 55 home runs (1964); and has led the Giants to 13 Central League pennants and 11 Japan Series championships. In 1973 he won the triple crown of batting with a .355 average, 51 home runs, and 114 runs batted in.

Sadaharu Oh, a citizen of Nationalist China (Taiwan), was born in Tokyo on May 20, 1940, the son of a Chinese restaurant owner and a Japanese mother, both of whom were born in Taiwan. His pitching and long-ball hitting in high school so impressed professional scouts that the Yomiuri Giants signed the promising teenager to a contract in 1959. At the plate Oh uses an unorthodox "flamingo stance." Raising his right foot off the ground, he balances all 170 lb on his rear leg before moving into a pitch. With an annual income estimated at about $350,000 (including commercial endorsements), Oh is able to support his wife and three daughters quite comfortably. If anyone thinks that the 36-year-old superstar is already over the hill, he hasn't been reading the sports page. In 1976 Oh hit 49 home runs (plus 3 more in the Japan Series), batted in 123 runs, and for the eighth time was named the Central League's most valuable player. (ARTHUR LATHAM)

Olympic Champions: *see* pages 59–61 for illustrations of selected Olympic winners.

Orr, Bobby

In 1976 hockey's most publicized power play came in June, when the sport's "natural resource" moved from Boston to Chicago. Bobby Orr, after failing to reach agreement with the Bruins, signed a five-year, $3 million contract with the Black Hawks.

"He's the greatest hockey player who ever lived. He could play for me on one knee," said Black Hawk president Bill Wirtz.

Orr, who revolutionized hockey by becoming the highest scoring defenseman in history, admitted he was "not the same player I once was" after a fifth operation on his left knee stopped his 1975–76 season in Boston at ten games.

The Bruins, convinced that Orr could not last another year, allowed his contract to expire, and Chicago won what was described as hockey's "Battle of Wounded Knee." After much argument over compensation to the Bruins, there were lawsuits and counter-lawsuits filed and dropped. The Black Hawks claimed that the Bruins were entitled to nothing, and the Bruins insisted that the deal might not be complete for years.

KEN REGAN—CAMERA 5

Orr proved that he could still play hockey in September by starring in the Canada Cup of Hockey. Playing for the victorious Team Canada, he was especially impressive in contests against the Soviet Union and Czechoslovakia.

As expected, he missed games early in the National Hockey League season while undergoing examinations of his knee. Speculation mounted over how long he could continue to play.

With 16 individual awards, Orr was hockey's most decorated player. He was the only defenseman ever to score more than 100 points in a season and the only defenseman to lead the league in scoring. He was the only player to score 100 points for six straight seasons and the only one to register more than 100 assists in a season.

Boston discovered Orr 12 years after he was born, March 20, 1948, in Parry Sound, Ont. He joined the Bruins at 18 and helped the team to the play-offs eight seasons in a row following his rookie year. During that time Boston won two Stanley Cups. His first operation was in 1967 on his right knee. Five followed on the left knee, all for cartilage damage. (J. TIMOTHY WEIGEL)

Parker, Alan

Bugsy Malone, written and directed by Alan Parker, was the British cinema's unlikeliest success story of 1976. Combining pastiche of both gangster movies and the Hollywood musicals of the 1930s, the film

LESLIE BAKER—CAMERA PRESS

had a cast whose average age was 12 years. Custard pies and "splurge guns" emitting what looked like cascades of whipped cream replaced the bombs and tommy guns of adult-size Prohibition-era mobsters, and the cars that whined or roared around Bugsy's underworld were powered by pedals. Initially rejected by the Cannes Film Festival, *Bugsy Malone* turned out to be the most popular film on show there. It went on to enjoy an impressive box-office success.

For Alan Parker it was the culmination of a personal success story. Born Alan William Parker on St. Valentine's Day, 1944, he was the child of working people living in Islington, North London, and his accent still proudly proclaimed his origins. He left school at 19 to be post boy in an advertising agency, but soon graduated to writing copy. At 24 he was directing commercials, and in 1970 he established his own production company.

His previous film work anticipated both the style and the preoccupations of *Bugsy Malone.* Many of the 600 or more commercials he had made were nostalgic parody or pastiche of old films, and they evinced a characteristically vivacious camera style. Parker's interest in children, especially when they are assuming adult poses, was already evident in his 1971 story and screenplay for *Melody,* the first film produced by David Puttnam, the producer of *Bugsy Malone,* and again in *The Evacuees,* the story of two Jewish boys evacuated from London during World War II, which Parker directed for television in 1974. This was his first feature-length film as a director; previously, in 1973, he had directed three fiction shorts. Writing of how *Bugsy* came into being, he explained: "I wrote it because my own kids kept nagging me that going to the pictures wasn't as special as I kept telling them it ought to be."

(DAVID ROBINSON)

Payton, Walter

One Chicago Bear lineman was grabbing Walter Payton by the waist and holding him three feet off the ground. Another was stealing the football as a souvenir, which would have delayed the game except that the crowd was too noisy for the contest to continue anyway. Chicago's fans and linemen were celebrating Payton's 1,000th rushing yard of the 1976 season. "One grand for our man," shouted offensive guard Noah Jackson, the man who stole the football.

Payton let his linemen do the celebrating for him all season. They were given the football to spike on the ground every time Payton scored, which was often. That ritual is normally reserved for scorers, not unheralded blockers.

Deeply religious, Payton gave full credit to the line and the Lord whenever he had one of his routinely spectacular games. He repeatedly said, "I feel guilty about not getting more yards behind the holes those linemen make for me." He had developed his closeness with offensive linemen in college, when he insisted on taking one of them with him whenever he was interviewed.

Payton finished the season with 1,390 yd, replacing Gale Sayers as the best single-season runner in Bear history and gaining 100 yd in seven different games. He lost the league rushing title to O. J. Simpson on the season's last day but led the National Conference despite several injuries.

Payton was the youngest Bear in 1976 even though it was his second professional season. After finishing Columbia (Miss.) High School early, he became involved in special education while waiting for the next college year to begin. During 1976 he worked on his master's degree in education of hearing-impaired children and had an off-season television job in Jackson, Miss.

Payton was born in Columbia, Miss., on July 25, 1954. He intended to register at the University of Kansas when he stopped on the way to visit his brother, Edward, at Jackson (Miss.) State. Edward, then a senior, challenged Walter to stick around and see who could be better at Jackson State. Payton did, and set a college record with 464 points in four seasons. The Bears chose him in the first round of the 1975 college draft, and as a rookie he led the league in kickoff returns.

(KEVIN M. LAMB)

Poveda Burbano, Alfredo

After the bloodless coup d'etat on Jan. 11, 1976, in which the regime of Pres. Guillermo Rodríguez Lara was overthrown, Vice-Adm. Alfredo Poveda Burbano headed the military government of Ecuador. Poveda was chief of the Armed Forces Joint Command and commander of the Navy when the leaders of all the military branches decided to end Rodríguez' rule. The junta cited Ecuador's battered economy when it took power without violence and with a simple declaration of martial law, courteously delaying the coup long enough to let Rodríguez attend the wedding of his daughter.

Nominally, the junta that took over was a triumvirate, but Poveda quickly established his primacy as presiding officer and spokesman for the new government. In Ecuador's long history of military rule, it has been unusual for a navy officer to run the country, and it was equally rare for a man from the sierra, the Andean high country, to find his career and be popular in the coastal city of Guayaquil.

The junta promised to restore democratic rule to Ecuador within two years. Poveda said the objective would be to organize the civilian population into "functional" groups representing labour, business, the church, and other interests. Meanwhile, he said he would strengthen and revitalize private and public institutions.

Poveda was born Jan. 24, 1926, in Ambato, Tungurahua Province, in the high sierra. He attended both the Ecuadorean and Argentine naval academies and the Royal Navy Gunnery School at Plymouth, England. He also studied at the Brazilian Naval War College and a U.S. naval mine warfare school. As a result, he speaks both English and Portuguese.

In 1973 he was named minister of government and police, a position of power second only to the presidency in Ecuador. He thus was seen as the natural leader when the armed forces chiefs decided that it was necessary to depose Rodríguez. Poveda's mountain background, plus his close ties with the coastal region, probably cemented his role as the first among equals as president of the Supreme Council of Government.

(JEREMIAH A. O'LEARY, JR.)

Ramgoolam, Sir Seewoosagur

Few men could be less alike than Uganda's explosive president, Gen. Idi Amin, and his successor as chairman of the Organization of African Unity (OAU) for 1976–77, Sir Seewoosagur Ramgoolam, prime minister of Mauritius. A gentle, subtle politician with strong Gandhian pacifist views, the 76-year-old Mauritian leader had headed his government since 1967, continuing in late 1976 as head of a coalition government even though his Independence Party won only 28 of 70 parliamentary seats in the December elections. This was a considerable feat in an island community riven by communal and racial tensions among Indians, Creoles, and French, as well as being sharply divided between militant right-wing and left-wing political movements. His style of leadership was always to conciliate—seemingly an ideal quality for the first non-African chairman of the OAU in a year when that body was split (by the Angolan issue) as never before. A lifelong member of the Fabian Society, he had close affiliations with the British Labour Party.

Ramgoolam was born in Belle Rive, Mauritius, on Sept. 18, 1900, the son of a Hindi scholar who was also a sugar estate overseer. He studied medicine at University College Hospital, London, in the 1920s, and practiced as a doctor from 1935 to 1967. He first entered politics as a member of the Mauritius Legislative Council in 1940 and as the founder of the island's Labour Party. In 1968 he became prime minister when his country gained its independence.

Short and stocky, with thick white hair and heavy horn-rimmed spectacles, "Ram" closely resembled a kindly family doctor. His interests included art, literature, and travel. Ramgoolam was knighted in 1965 and became a member of the British Privy Council from 1971.

(COLIN LEGUM)

Ray, Elizabeth

In a city shaken by the Watergate scandals of 1974, the sex scandal that loomed in Washington, D.C., in the late spring of 1976 seemed at first to be of little importance. The confession of a rather pathetic Capitol Hill secretary, 33-year-old Elizabeth Ray, that Rep. Wayne Hays (Dem., Ohio) had kept her on his official payroll only for her sexual favours hardly amounted to a constitutional crisis. Yet the affair drove the powerful and autocratic Hays from office and added, though perhaps only marginally, to the distrust of Washington that coloured the politics of 1976.

M. BRENNAN—SYGMA

Born in Marshall, N.C., Ray claimed she was paid $14,000 a year by Hays but that her only duties were twice-weekly sexual liaisons with the 65-year-old legislator. After initially denying the charges, Hays admitted his sexual indiscretions, but he continued to claim that the government payroll had not been misused since Ray did some clerical work.

The revelations titillated Washington, and Ray became the object of media attention. Offered $25,000 to pose nude for one men's magazine, she declined, accepting instead a $250 fee for similar photos in a magazine she considered more tasteful—*Playboy*. She continued to be seen around Washington, often in revealing costumes and accompanied by a nurse hired to help her cope with the pressure of sudden notoriety. A fictionalized account of her escapades was rushed into print and had high initial sales.

Hays meanwhile was besieged by demands that he resign his chairmanships of two important committees. He quickly let go his control of the Democratic Congressional Campaign Committee, held on somewhat longer to the powerful House Administration Committee chairmanship, but soon was forced out of that spot as well. Finally, on August 13, Hays announced his retirement from Congress, largely to avoid further legal investigations of the matter. Ray too ended her career on Capitol Hill, turning instead to the stage, but her debut at a small theatre in Illinois was panned by critics.

(JOHN F. STACKS)

Reagan, Ronald

The energetic, activist heart of the Republican Party has for years belonged to its most conservative faction. But after its fling with Barry Goldwater, and the consequent electoral disaster of 1964, the party had been wary of sending a right-wing ideologue into battle for the nation's highest office. In 1976, however, the GOP came within 60 delegate votes of doing it again.

The new object of the conservatives' affections was Ronald Reagan, who was born in Tampico, Ill., on Feb. 6, 1911, and went on to a movie career in which he characteristically played the leading man's best friend. Once a liberal Democrat and head of the screen actors' union, he entered politics as a right-wing Republican and became governor of California in 1967. Even before his successful tenure as governor ended in 1975, Reagan had eyed a chance to become president, and in 1976, with the nation's first unelected president in office, he thought he saw it.

He began his campaign with the kind of doctrinaire promises that had ruined Goldwater. Late in 1975 he promised that, if elected, he would turn $90 billion in federal programs in such fields as education and health back to the states, and he spent much of early 1976 explaining that idea away. Thereafter, he stuck to safer themes, such as criticizing détente. Throughout the primary season, Reagan and Gerald Ford (*q.v.*) traded victories, and when it ended neither man was assured of the nomination. The contest turned into a nearly vote-by-vote campaign aimed at the large group of uncommitted delegates.

Reagan's manager was John Sears, a bright young former Nixon operative who mounted what was, by comparison with the Ford effort, a brilliant campaign against the long odds of unseating an incumbent president. Yet by mid-July Reagan seemed locked into second place. Sears decided to try a long shot. He approached liberal Sen. Richard Schweiker of Pennsylvania and asked him to be Reagan's vice-presidential running mate. Schweiker accepted, but even before the convention it was clear that the gambit had alienated some ideological purists while failing to add hoped-for delegates from Northern states.

TONY KORODY—SYGMA

After his loss, Reagan contended that he thought of himself as a "nonpolitician." The Schweiker maneuver hurt that claim, but Reagan obviously still held the loyalties of many GOP conservatives. He seemed likely to continue as an important voice on the right, through his newspaper column and daily radio program, and to be a contender for leadership of the defeated Republican Party.

(JOHN F. STACKS)

Rowland, Roland

Little was heard of "Tiny" Rowland (the nickname was a tribute to his imposing height and heavy build) until he was in his middle 40s. A farmer in Rhodesia, he was invited in 1961 to take over the management of the small London and Rhodesian Mining and Land Company, later to be known as Lonrho Ltd. By the end of the decade he was one of Rhodesia's most successful and colourful business entrepreneurs, while Lonrho, under his management, had become an international conglomerate of some 400 companies operating in Africa and more recently in the Middle East.

In the process of this hectic expansion the company acquired a controversial reputation in South Africa, in Rhodesia, and in the U.K. and in 1973 became the subject of a U.K. Department of Trade inquiry. The department's report, published in July 1976, was critical of Lonrho's methods of operation and of certain of its directors for neglecting to exercise proper control of the executive. It opined that Rowland's achievement would be all the greater if he would "allow his enthusiasms to operate within the ordinary processes of company management."

Rowland's flamboyant and aggressive personal style led some of the Lonrho directors in 1973 to demand his dismissal. He immediately challenged this in the High Court; though he lost the case seeking an injunction to set aside his dismissal, he won enough time to secure a ballot of shareholders who voted six to one in his favour. The publicity given in 1973 to Rowland's style of life and to the lavish payments to the Lonrho chairman, Lord Duncan-Sandys, provoked Edward Heath, then Conservative prime minister, to a much-quoted comment on "the unacceptable face of capitalism."

Little is known about Rowland's early life. He seems to have been born in India on Nov. 17, 1918, of German parents who went to Britain before World War II, and he emigrated to Rhodesia in 1947.

(HARFORD THOMAS)

Sagan, Carl

"Sagan desperately wants to find life someplace, anyplace—on Mars, on Titan, in the solar system or outside it . . . everything he has done has had this one underlying purpose." Thus did a professional colleague characterize Carl Sagan, a Cornell University astronomer who by 1976 had earned a reputation as one of the most controversial and colourful space scientists in the United States. Sagan concurred with his colleague's estimate, stating his belief that the most important question facing mankind today is whether there is life, intelligent or not, elsewhere in the universe. As a member of the Viking-lander imaging team, which analyzed the photographs sent back to the Earth from Mars by Vikings 1 and 2, he found himself in 1976 in the long-desired role of looking for evidence of extraterrestrial life.

JEFF ALBERTSON—STOCK, BOSTON

Sagan was born Nov. 9, 1934, in New York City. He became interested in astronomy as a boy and once remarked, "I didn't make a decision to pursue astronomy; rather, it just grabbed me, and I had no thought of escaping." After receiving bachelor's, master's, and doctor's degrees from the University of Chicago, he served from 1962 to 1968 as lecturer and then assistant professor of astronomy at Harvard University and as astrophysicist at the Smithsonian Astrophysical Observatory in Cambridge, Mass. In 1968 he joined the Cornell University astronomy faculty, where in 1976 he was the David Duncan professor of astronomy and space sciences and director of the Laboratory for Planetary Studies.

Sagan and others have proposed the existence of several hundred billion planets in our galaxy with environments suitable for the development of intelligent civilizations capable of transmitting messages by radio. In the belief that some of these may be trying to contact the Earth, Sagan in 1975 spent a week at the Arecibo radio telescope listening for any such signals. He did not hear them and said afterward, "I know a week is a short time, and the likelihood of success was small, but still I found myself depressed."

Sagan's ability to articulate his ideas so that they are interesting and meaningful to laymen caused him to be in great demand for lectures and television appearances. To those who criticized such activity, he responded that the kind of science he likes to do requires money—the public's money—and someone has to take the scientists' case to the people.

(DAVID R. CALHOUN)

Saint Laurent, Yves Henri Donat Mathieu

In the late 1940s women everywhere, weary of wartime shortages and uniforms, swept their closets bare to make room for Christian Dior's extravagantly romantic New Look. Nothing quite like it had happened since. Perhaps because of a faltering economy, perhaps because of the women's movement, women had tended to resist sudden style changes, and the younger ones had even shown a lamentable preference for durable jeans and overalls. But the clothing industry and its attendant groupies—the fashion writers and the women who make a career of chic—had never ceased to hope.

It may have been that hope that inspired the staid *New York Times* to use the term "revolutionary" in describing Yves Saint Laurent's fall 1976 collection and to report it on the front page. "It's the intensity of his approach that gives his collection such an impact," the *Times* declared. Saint Laurent, who had popularized man-tailored, pin-striped suits for women, had abruptly abandoned that style to show peasant-type dresses clearly derived from the traditional costume of pre-Revolutionary Russia. But the peasant look was just a starting point for Saint Laurent. To produce his rich gowns he used taffeta, chiffon, and gold lamé—fabrics no genuine farm girl had ever seen.

Any man who did not like the new Saint Laurent look might be well advised to brace himself for several years of suffering. Haute couture, dependent on a relatively small number of wealthy women, was no longer the financial mainstay of the French fashion industry, and the House of Saint Laurent was busy producing thousands of ready-to-wear copies to be sold at Saint Laurent's boutiques throughout the world. Furthermore, Saint Laurent was one of the most copied of designers, and by year's end inexpensive peasant-look dresses were appearing in shopping centres and discount stores. Whether they would actually replace the pants suits and sportswear look clothes recently in favour remained to be seen.

JACQUES VIOLET—CAMERA PRESS/PHOTO TRENDS

Born Aug. 1, 1936, in Oran, Algeria, Saint Laurent won first prize in a fashion-drawing competition at the age of 17. This distinction brought him an introduction to Dior, with whom he worked closely until Dior's death in 1957. He succeeded the Master as head of the House of Dior and scored an international triumph with his trapeze line. Three years later, Saint Laurent established his own house, and from that moment on his reputation as one of the most original and daring fashion designers increased each year.

(VICTOR M. CASSIDY)

Sampson, Will

It is difficult to be an eloquent deaf-mute, but Will Sampson achieved it when he played Chief Bromden in *One Flew over the Cuckoo's Nest* (1975). He portrayed an inmate of a mental hospital who defied the system by pretending to be a deaf-mute. Pauline Kael, in *The New Yorker,* stated that Sampson brought "so much charm, irony, and physical dignity to the role of the resurrected catatonic that this movie achieves [author Ken Kesey's] mythic goal."

Sampson, a full-blooded Creek Indian who detests the stereotypes by which motion pictures usually portray native Americans, broke the traditional patterns in which Indians were used as "livestock" (his term). Besides Chief Bromden, a complex character who cannot be classed as either a noble savage or a murderous one, Sampson had played Ten Bears, the proud chief of the Comanches, in Clint Eastwood's *The Outlaw Josey Wales;* Crazy Horse, the great Sioux warrior, in J. Lee Thompson's *The White Buffalo* (with Charles Bronson); and William Halsey, the highly educated interpreter for the Sioux chief Sitting Bull,

WIDE WORLD

in Robert Altman's *Buffalo Bill and the Indians or Sitting Bull's History Lesson* (with Paul Newman).

Notwithstanding his personal success in films, Sampson remains aware of the damage done by white prejudice and the painful problems of many other native Americans. He gives occasional talks on Indians at schools and prisons and contributes to Red Wind, a California organization that helps alcoholics.

The 42-year-old, 6-ft 5-in Sampson came to acting by accident—he considered himself a painter first. His paintings of Western and cowboy subjects have been exhibited all over the West, including the Amon Carter Museum in Fort Worth, Texas, as well as at the Smithsonian and at the Library of Congress in Washington. The self-taught painter also did a huge mural for the International Petroleum Exposition in Tulsa, Okla.

Sampson was born in Okmulgee, Okla., and grew up around ranching. He left school at 14 and began working in a rodeo. He was also an oil field and construction worker, a telephone lineman, and a lumberjack. He got the part in *Cuckoo's Nest* when a rodeo announcer recommended him for an audition to a casting scout. He said he accepted the role because acting still left him time for painting. And Sampson sees parallels between the two activities, viewing them both as media through which the artist tries to convey his understanding to the audience.
(JOAN NATALIE REIBSTEIN)

Sarkis, Elias

A technocrat turned politician, Elias Sarkis was elected president of Lebanon on May 8, 1976, by Parliament in the most difficult possible circumstances, in the middle of a civil war. Although the constitution had been specially amended so that his election could be brought forward four months, he was unable to take office until September 23 because of Pres. Suleiman Franjieh's refusal to withdraw. His election was supported by the Lebanese rightists and by Syria but opposed by the left. However, Sarkis succeeded in establishing his independence as a compromise leader at the Arab summit meetings in Saudi Arabia and Egypt in October and won the grudging acceptance of the left. It was decided that the Arab peacekeeping force in Lebanon should be under his control.

Born in the village of Ash Shabaniyah in the al Matn region of Mount Lebanon on July 20, 1924, Sarkis was not a member of any of Lebanon's leading political families. He worked his way through school and college and obtained his law degree from Beirut's Jesuit Université Saint Joseph in 1948. He was appointed judge at the Audit Office in 1953. His intellect and administrative ability brought him to the attention of Gen. Fuad Chehab, who, on becoming president in 1958 after that year's quasi-civil war, appointed him to one of the new reform committees. The next year Sarkis became the president's legal adviser, a post he continued to hold under Chehab's successor, Charles Hélou.

In 1967 Hélou appointed Sarkis governor of the Central Bank, where he was responsible for the reorganization of the banking system after the collapse of the Intra Bank and for helping restore confidence in Beirut as a major financial centre. In the 1970 presidential elections he was the Chehabist candidate and widely expected to win, but the unpopular increase in the power of the military intelligence under Chehab led to his defeat, by one vote, by the supporters of Kamal Jumblatt (*q.v.*). Sarkis remained as governor of the Central Bank, and although he was opposed by the leftist forces in the 1976 presidential elections, the fact that he was a technocrat who did not belong to any of Lebanon's traditional political clans gave him some advantage in his desire to appear as a moderate capable of reuniting the country. (PETER MANSFIELD)

Schorr, Daniel

For television newsman Daniel Schorr, it was a clear and simple proposition: He had acquired a copy of a congressional committee's report on the Central Intelligence Agency, which the committee had voted to withhold from publication. Schorr believed that the report should be made public, and when his own television network, CBS, did not accept the material he gave it to New York's *Village Voice* newspaper, which printed it and touched off a year of controversy.

DENNIS BRACK—BLACK STAR

Most Washington reporters agreed with Schorr that the report should not have been suppressed once it got into a journalist's hands; but some questioned the professional ethics of giving it to a news organization other than his own, even though he was not paid by the *Village Voice*. At Schorr's request, the paper had made a donation to the Reporters Committee for Freedom of the Press.

Schorr, a controversial but respected newsman, was born in New York City on Aug. 31, 1916. He graduated from the City College of New York and worked for various news agencies before joining CBS in 1953. He served in West Germany, the U.S.S.R., and other overseas posts and was considered a tough investigative reporter when covering the U.S. Congress. The network supported Schorr's right to make the report public, but suspended him from his congressional beat when it became known that he had given it to the *Village Voice*.

Congressional and administration officials were furious and determined to find Schorr's source for the report. After several months of delay, the U.S. House of Representatives appropriated $150,000 for an investigation by its Ethics Committee, which interviewed about 400 witnesses over a period of five months. The committee was stymied when Schorr stood on his First Amendment rights and refused to reveal his source, even when subpoenaed and threatened with a possible contempt of Congress citation.

Schorr conceded that the House Intelligence Committee had a right to keep the report secret if it could, but it did not have the right to prevent him from publishing it once he had obtained a copy. The Ethics Committee finally limited itself to calling Schorr's action "reprehensible," admitting that it could not find the leak. When the investigation ended, Schorr resigned from CBS and said that he would become involved in lecturing and in writing a book.
(HAL BRUNO)

Shoemaker, William Lee

He had already become the winningest jockey in horse racing history in 1970, and so it was with some nonchalance that William Lee Shoemaker greeted the 7,000th triumph of his career at age 44 on March 14, 1976. "I knew it was bound to happen sooner or later. I think everyone else was anticipating this one more than I was," he said, after bringing Royal Derby II from behind in the fifth race at Santa Anita racetrack in Arcadia, Calif.

Few racing experts believe anyone will match Shoemaker's record. Only one man before him ever had 5,000 winners, Johnny Longden, whose mark of 6,032 was broken by Shoemaker on Sept. 7, 1970.

Royal Derby II was the 29,203rd mount of Shoemaker's 27-year career. In addition to 7,000 victories, he had 4,598 second-places finishes and 3,603 thirds at the time of the milestone. Thus, in an astounding 52% of his rides he finished "in the money."

Shoemaker's mounts won more than $58 million, of which the jockey gets at least

PETER BORSARI—CAMERA 5

10%. Thus, he earned close to $6 million, and probably more, making him one of the richest athletes in the world. Mention retirement, however, and he says, "What else would I do?"

Two months after his 7,000th winner, Shoemaker was informed by sports physician Robert Kerlan that he was in better physical shape than many of the Los Angeles Rams of the National Football League. "When he told me that, wow, it was mentally an upper," said Shoemaker. "Where I was riding four or five times a day before the test, I'm back to six or seven races a day." Shoemaker, who prefers the nickname "Bill" to "Willie," is 4 ft 11 in tall and weighs less than 100 lb.

Born Aug. 19, 1931, in Fabens, Texas, Shoemaker began his career in 1949, becoming national riding champion five times and leading money-winning jockey ten times. Among his top achievements were three victories in the Kentucky Derby, two in the Preakness, and five in the Belmont Stakes.

Shoemaker suffered serious injuries in 1968 and 1969. A broken pelvis caused many to predict his career was finished at age 37, but he was back in action three months later. (J. TIMOTHY WEIGEL)

Shomron, Dan

During the evening of July 4, 1976, Israel's defense minister, Shimon Peres, called a press conference at short notice and opened it with the words: "Good evening. May I introduce, on my right the IDF [Israel Defense Force] chief of staff, Major-General Gur; on my left is Brigadier-General Dan Shomron who commanded the Entebbe [Uganda] operation during last night. When his force left the State of Israel yesterday afternoon it left behind a country in deep distress. When he returned this morning he found a proud country, for that night his IDF force had displayed some of the most

NACHUM GUTMAN—KEYSTONE

memorable qualities of the IDF: wise planning, daring execution, the element of surprise, and heroic performance. It was a supreme test for the commander's capability, for his planning and performance." The defense minister could have added that Shomron had left Israel on Saturday a man unknown except in intimate Army circles and returned on Sunday as an officer whose name had become a worldwide byword for courage and daring.

Dan Shomron was born in 1937, during the "Arab troubles," in kibbutz Ashdot Yaacov. At the age of 19 he was a junior paratroop officer in the capture of the Mitla Pass during the Suez War of 1956. In the Six-Day War of 1967 he led the commando unit that was the first to reach the Suez Canal in the northern sector. He then took command of a much-coveted commando battalion, the successor to the famed 89th that had been Moshe Dayan's unit 20 years earlier.

Within the IDF, Shomron became known for his raids into Arab territories, in Jordan against terrorists and into Egypt during the war of attrition in 1969. In 1971 he was appointed commander of an armoured brigade that excelled during the most difficult days of the Yom Kippur War (1973). As commander, from 1974, of the Infantry-Paratroop Combined Operations Unit, he was largely responsible for organizing the force that was able to carry out the Entebbe operation at short notice.

Within six weeks of Entebbe, on Aug. 29, 1976, Shomron was appointed to a new, senior post that was not officially identified. The Israelis would have to wait for the next surprise that would again bring Dan Shomron into public focus in his latest command position. (*See* DEFENSE; ISRAEL; UGANDA.) (JON KIMCHE)

Simplot, Jack Richard

"Big potato boys playing chicken," said William Bagley, chairman of the Commodity Futures Trading Commission, in the spring of 1976. Two powerful groups of speculators had been struggling for weeks in the potato futures market. Prices had fluctuated wildly. In late May, Jack Richard Simplot and his trading partner, P. J. Taggares, had defaulted. They were unable to fulfill contracts to deliver 50 million lb of Maine potatoes worth $4 million. It was probably the largest default in the history of the U.S. commodities market. As of late 1976, government regulatory authorities had yet to resolve the situation.

Jack Richard Simplot and his market rivals had been trading in commodity futures—agreements made by farmers to deliver specified amounts of a commodity at some future date. At the beginning of each growing season, a potato farmer may contract to deliver his entire crop to a broker at a certain price. The farmer receives cash to pay his operating expenses and has a buyer for his crop. The broker then sells the potato future to a speculator. The speculator hopes that the market price of potatoes will rise during the course of the season. If it does, his profit will be the difference between the price paid to the farmer and the market price for potatoes at harvest time.

Jack Simplot probably knows as much about potatoes as anyone in the U.S. Born Jan. 4, 1909, in Dubuque, Iowa, he quit school as a boy of 14 and started to work sorting potatoes for an Idaho broker. He saved his money and soon was growing potatoes himself. In 1943 he founded J. R. Simplot and Co., which over three decades grew into one of the largest privately held industrial empires in the country. Simplot grew and processed potatoes, raised livestock, manufactured chemicals, and mined iron. The sales of his firms totaled roughly $600 million per year.

Simplot and Taggares bought potato futures in 1975 believing that the market would rise. The prediction was correct. Prices went up spectacularly and they agreed to deliver 50 million lb of Maine potatoes to another group of speculators in May 1976, realizing a huge paper profit. The other speculators bought from Simplot and Taggares because they believed that prices would rise even more. But Simplot and Taggares correctly anticipated that the market would fall. By the spring of 1976, they thought, they could purchase potatoes at low cost, fulfill their legal obligation, and pocket the profit. But when May arrived, they were unable to buy Maine potatoes at any price. No one would sell to them. Their rivals were trying to force up the price of potatoes in order to lessen or to eliminate their paper losses. Simplot and Taggares had no choice but to default. (VICTOR M. CASSIDY)

Slater, James Derrick

Jim Slater, Britain's prototype whiz-kid financial tycoon of the boom years of the 1960s and early 1970s, was the most notable victim of the great crash of 1974–75. In the 12 years from its founding in 1964, the value of Slater, Walker Securities Ltd. rocketed to an estimated £600 million in 1972, only to crash to around £6 million by September 1976. (Peter Walker, a Conservative Cabinet minister in the Edward Heath government, had been Slater's partner from 1964 to 1970, hence the parent company's name.)

Born in Brighton, England, on March 13, 1929, Slater was trained as an accountant, moved into industry, and had become deputy sales director of Leyland Motor Corp. Ltd. by the time he decided to launch out on his own. In the beginning Slater, Walker specialized in taking over poorly run companies, putting in more energetic management, and selling off underused assets (known as asset-stripping). By the end of the 1960s it was branching out into banking and financial services, and in the early 1970s its takeover activities extended overseas to Australia, the Far East, Asia, Europe, and the U.S.

When the 1974 recession set in, the firm was hopelessly overextended, with loans it could not recall and assets of declining value in shares and property, many bought with loans at high rates of interest. Because of the extent of its banking activities, the Bank of England had to come to the rescue in 1975, and in October 1975 Slater resigned his chairmanship, which was taken over by Sir James Goldsmith (*q.v.*).

The affairs of Slater, Walker were then examined by accountants on behalf of the company, and by the Department of Trade. The accountants' report, published on Sept. 14, 1976, shattered Slater's legendary reputation as a financial wizard (although the investment management branch was found to be competently run). At this stage Slater said that he himself owed £1 million. Meanwhile he was faced with court proceedings for alleged breaches of the U.K. Companies Act, and the government of Singapore was seeking his extradition to answer charges concerning the management of the Singapore company Haw Par Brothers International, in which Slater, Walker secured an interest in 1972. (HARFORD THOMAS)

Smith, Ian Douglas

On Sept. 24, 1976, Rhodesian Prime Minister Ian Smith broadcast the terms of his "package deal" with U.S. Secretary of State Henry Kissinger. Black leaders immediately rejected the proposed two-year transition to majority rule, and few observers welcomed it as the solution urgently needed to secure Rhodesia's future.

Smith's record of negotiated settlement was uninspiring. He had met with various British government officials and African nationalist leaders, but his views against black majority rule helped prevent any agreement on power sharing. After Smith's inconclusive talks with African nationalist leader Joshua Nkomo early in 1976, increasing pressure from South Africa, Britain, and, finally, the U.S. led to a Rhodesian constitutional conference in Geneva. When talks formally opened on October 28, Smith's rejection of any modification of his "deal" with Kissinger created an immediate impasse. A week later, irritated by the lack of progress, he returned to Rhodesia, leaving his delegation in charge of deputies. He rejoined the conference on December 8, but no settlement was reached by the year's end.

Rhodesia's internal situation was most difficult. In May, faced with an escalating guerrilla war, Smith put approximately 25,000 Territorial Force reservists on "continuous" call-up and launched a new "antiguerrilla initiative." This, plus the extension of the national service period from one year to 18 months, increased the pressure on an economy already strained by Mozambique's sanctions, declining tourism, and rising emigration. Smith, however, dismissed a pessimistic view of Rhodesia's future as scaremongering and continued his waiting game.

DARQUENNES—SYGMA

Born on April 8, 1919, at Selukwe, Southern Rhodesia, Smith was educated at Chaplin School, Gwelo, and Rhodes University in South Africa. He served with the Royal Air Force during World War II. A farmer, he entered politics in 1948 as a member of the Southern Rhodesian Legislative Assembly. In 1961 he was a founding member of the Rhodesian Front, becoming its president in 1965. Beginning in 1962 he held various ministerial appointments, and in April 1964 he became prime minister of Rhodesia, which unilaterally declared its independence from Britain in November 1965. (NICOLA SMITH)

Steel, David Martin Scott

On July 7, 1976, David Steel was elected leader of the British Liberal Party in a ballot of party constituencies. He had entered Parliament at the age of 27 when he won a by-election at Roxburgh, Selkirk, and Peebles in 1965. Since 1970 he had been Liberal chief whip or parliamentary party manager—a job more onerous than might appear at first glance in that it involved handling the small group of highly individualistic Liberal MP's.

CAMERA PRESS

Steel took over in a difficult situation. For many months the party had been racked by bitter internal disputes that led to the resignation of Jeremy Thorpe from the leadership. A quiet, calm, but determined man, Steel quickly put his stamp of authority on the Liberal Party by insisting that Liberals must be prepared to join in a coalition government "if the conditions are right." Encouraged by the support of the party assembly, he began to canvass the need for a coalition government.

Born March 31, 1938, at Kirkcaldy, Scotland, Steel went to school in Nairobi, Kenya, where his parents were then living. His Scottish roots were deep, his father being a moderator of the General Assembly of the Church of Scotland. His involvement in Liberal politics went back to his later school and university days in Edinburgh. His first job was as assistant secretary to the Scottish Liberal Party. As a BBC television reporter in Scotland for a short time before becoming an MP, he learned some of the professionalism that later made him an effective broadcaster.

Steel soon made his mark in the House of Commons, securing the passage of a private member's bill for the liberalization of the law concerning abortion. As president of the Anti-Apartheid Movement in Great Britain from 1966 to 1969, he was prominent in another area of basic liberal principle. He kept his family home in his Scottish constituency, living in Ettrick Bridge, a small village 40 mi S of Edinburgh, and had clearly thought-out views on constitutional devolution for Scotland. (HARFORD THOMAS)

Stevens, John Paul

The American Bar Association had called him "practical, not always bound by the conventional wisdom, analytic, very smart, moderate, imaginative, elegant, aggressive, a little brisk, hard to categorize." On Dec. 19, 1975, John Paul Stevens was sworn in as associate justice of the U.S. Supreme Court, the 101st justice to serve on that court and the first appointed by Pres. Gerald Ford. Justice Stevens, generally regarded as a moderate or a moderate conservative, filled the vacancy left by the retirement of Justice William O. Douglas, a noted liberal.

Unlike several Supreme Court nominees of the previous administration, Stevens generated little opposition except among feminist groups such as the National Organization for Women, which criticized his record on women's and minorities' rights and his failure to support the proposed Equal Rights Amendment. He was given the highest possible evaluation by the American Bar Association committee that assessed his record.

Stevens was born in Chicago on April 20, 1920, into a prominent family, graduated from the University of Chicago in 1941, and soon thereafter joined the Navy. During World War II he served as an intelligence officer. After the war he attended Northwestern University School of Law, graduating first in his class.

In 1948 Stevens clerked for Associate Justice of the Supreme Court Wiley B. Rutledge. Returning to Chicago, he joined a local law firm where he gained experience in antitrust law. In 1951 and 1952 he was associate counsel of the House Judiciary Committee's subcommittee on monopoly power; from 1953 to 1955 he served on the Attorney General's National Committee to Study Antitrust Laws. In 1969 he also served as general counsel to an Illinois commission to investigate judicial corruption.

Through his longtime friend Charles Percy, Republican senator from Illinois, Stevens came to the attention of Pres. Richard Nixon, who appointed him judge of the 7th Circuit Court of Appeals in 1970. In 1975 Stevens' name appeared on a list of possible nominees to the Supreme Court drawn up by Attorney General Edward Levi.

The justice's opinions showed a great respect for precedent and a reluctance to stretch beyond the facts and law of a particular case to expand the court's interpretation of the Constitution. He was said to be tough on defendants in criminal cases but insistent that the police and the courts follow proper procedure, especially in regard to search and seizure. He occasionally sided with the liberals on the court, although more often he held to a centrist or conservative position. (JOAN NATALIE REIBSTEIN)

Suárez González, Adolfo

The appointment on July 3, 1976, of Adolfo Suárez González as premier in Spain's second government under King Juan Carlos I provoked widespread and mixed reaction. Outside Spain and among liberal and opposition circles at home the feeling was one of surprise mixed with disappointment, but it was one of delight among some Spanish rightists. It seemed to them that Suárez' position in the previous government (secretary-general of the National Movement—Franco's reformed Falange), coupled with his sympathy toward the powerful Catholic organization Opus Dei, comprised a guarantee of his loyalty to the Francoist past. In addition, the refusal of Manuel Fraga Iribarne and José María de Areilza, two of the most liberal members of the last Cabinet, to join the new government reinforced the impression that democracy in Spain had suffered a setback.

Adolfo Suárez, the youngest Spanish premier of the century, was born Sept. 25, 1932, in Cebreros, near Avila (Castilla). He graduated in law from Salamanca University and held various small posts in the provinces, most of them within the National Movement. Later he worked with the national radio and television network and became responsible for the first television channel. After serving as civil governor and provincial head of the National Movement in Segovia during 1968–69, he moved back to radio and television as director general.

In March 1975 he was appointed deputy secretary-general of the National Movement and in December became secretary-general, with Cabinet rank. Also in 1975, he was founder-member and later president of the Unión del Pueblo Español, a mildly reformist political association within the National Movement. In June 1976 he strongly defended in the Cortes the new law legalizing political parties.

Suárez' Cabinet consisted mostly of technocrats in their 40s and 50s with little political experience. However, the government published a new and more liberal draft of the Political Reform Bill, which was approved by the Cortes on November 18 and by 94% of the voters in a referendum on December 15. (FRANÇOISE LOTERY)

Tabarly, Eric Marcel Guy

Sailing alone across the Atlantic is no easy task at any time, but to do it after a storm has knocked out the electric system and you've lost your automatic steering equipment calls for more than human toughness. In June 1976 French yachtsman Eric Tabarly won the Single-Handed Transatlantic Race by sailing his "Pen Duick VI"—a 22.5-m ketch that normally would carry a crew of 15 or so—across the North Atlantic through some of the worst weather in recent years. He arrived in Newport, R.I., seven hours ahead of his closest competitor, just 23 days, 20 hours, and 12 minutes after leaving Plymouth, England.

Eric Tabarly was born in Nantes, France, on July 24, 1931. From childhood, sailing was the dominant passion in his life. When in 1953 his father gave him a single-masted boat built in England in 1898, Tabarly molded a plastic hull around the old timbers and renamed it "Pen Duick," the Breton name for a small black-headed bird. This, the first of its line, was to sail successfully for many years with its 19th-century rigging.

Meanwhile Tabarly had joined the French fleet air arm and gone on to naval training college. He was a sublieutenant at the time of the 1964 transatlantic race and was given four months' leave to compete. Sailing "Pen Duick II," a 13.6-m plywood-hulled ketch built to his own design, he arrived victorious at Newport on June 19, 1964, after 27 days 3 hours 56 minutes at sea, beating the record holder, Sir Francis Chichester. In 1967, with "Pen Duick III" (17.45 m), his wins included the Fastnet and Sydney–Hobart races. He was forced to abandon the 1968 transatlantic race after his giant

KEYSTONE

trimaran "Pen Duick IV" was rammed by a cargo vessel. In 1969, with "Pen Duick V," he won the San Francisco–Tokyo single-handed race. "Pen Duick VI" was designed for the first round-the-world race (1973), which he was forced to abandon after a series of misfortunes. As of 1976, Tabarly, now a lieutenant commander, was assigned to the French armed forces' sports and physical education service. (PIERRE GUTELLE)

Tanaka, Kakuei

At about 6:30 AM on July 27, 1976, a black sedan carrying two prosecutors of the Tokyo district prosecutor's office slipped through the entrance into the spacious front yard of former Japanese prime minister Kakuei Tanaka. More than two hours later, Tanaka, once the nation's most powerful politician, was arrested in connection with the "Lockheed affair."

Tanaka was indicted on August 16 on suspicion of having accepted 500 million yen in bribes from the Lockheed Aircraft Corp. According to the indictment, Tanaka, then prime minister, was asked in 1972 by executives of Marubeni Corp., Lockheed's sales agent in Japan, to exercise his influence upon All Nippon Airways to buy Lockheed's L-1011 Tristar airbuses. It was charged that, after the ANA did decide to buy the Tristars, Tanaka received money in four installments from the Marubeni Corp.

Born May 4, 1918, in Niigata Prefecture, Tanaka was the only son among the six children of a poor cattle dealer. Having learned that his family could not afford to send him to secondary school, at 15 he left home alone for Tokyo. There he attended technical school at night while working as a construction clerk. Upon graduation, he set up his own construction firm. During World War II he was able to enlarge his business, thanks to big contracts with the Army.

In 1947 Tanaka was elected as a member of the House of Representatives (the lower house of the Diet). He later held a number of Cabinet posts, and in 1972 he was chosen as the chairman of the Liberal-Democratic Party, which had governed Japan since World War II. He became the nation's prime minister that same year, the first to hold that office who had not graduated from Tokyo University.

SVEN SIMON/KATHERINE YOUNG

Immediately after he became prime minister, Tanaka visited China to establish diplomatic relations between the two nations. A public opinion poll conducted after his visit to China showed that he had 60% support, highest figure among postwar leaders. But his popularity did not last, mainly as a result of a decline in the nation's economic growth. An exposé of shady financial dealings in an influential Japanese monthly, indicating that Tanaka had profited illegally from his office, caused him to resign as prime minister in December 1974.

At his resignation, Tanaka said, "I am to be blamed for the fact that my personal affairs invited misunderstanding among the public." (YOSHINOBU EMOTO)

Tarjan, James

He has a long beard. He thinks all day of knights, kings, queens, and castles. No, he is not Don Quixote. And he is certainly not mad. He is James Tarjan, who in 1976 became the first U.S. chess player in 12 years to attain the title of international grand master, the highest permanent honour the chess world bestows. There were 100 grand masters in the world in 1976. Of these, 12, including Tarjan, were American.

Tarjan's rise was swift. He was born in Pomona, Calif., on Feb. 22, 1952, and learned the game from his father and brother, watching over their shoulders as they played. He entered his first tournament when he was 12 years old and a year later won first place in the American Open for players under 14. In 1967 Tarjan became a master. Four years later he earned his senior master's rating.

While he studied in secondary school and at the University of California at Berkeley, he played in many tournaments both at home and overseas. In November of 1975 he entered and won a tournament at Subotica, Yugos., where he defeated several grand masters. In a 16-player tournament at Skopje, Yugos., held February 29–March 18, 1976, Tarjan shared fourth and fifth places. His success in these tourneys qualified him for the title of international grand master, according to the rules of the Fédération Internationale des Échecs, the ruling body of world chess. (VICTOR M. CASSIDY)

Thomas, Lowell

"So long until tomorrow" was the famous tag line. This time it was just, "So long." On May 14, 1976, he made his last broadcast of "Lowell Thomas and the News," ending the longest continuous run in the history of network radio broadcasting. In the course of that time the voice of Lowell Thomas had probably been heard by more people than any other person's in history. Thomas gave his first broadcast on station KDKA in Pittsburgh in 1925. For many years he had also been the voice of Movietone News. In addition he was known for his television broadcasts, for his role in the development of Cinerama, as a world traveler, and as the author of more than 50 books.

Lowell Thomas was born on April 6, 1892, in Woodington, Ohio, but his family moved to Cripple Creek, Colo., in 1900. Thomas received his B.S. degree from the University of Northern Indiana and went on to study at the University of Denver, Kent College of Law, and Princeton University. In 1915 he gave the first of what were to become famous illustrated travelogues, describing a trip to Alaska. He began touring with his lectures, speaking first before small groups and later at such prestigious locations as the Smithsonian Institution.

Thomas came to the attention of Pres. Woodrow Wilson, who appointed him to head a civilian commission on the history of World War I. On his travels he met Gen. Edmund Allenby and T. E. Lawrence, giving him material for motion-picture-illustrated lectures entitled "With Allenby in Palestine" and "With Lawrence in Arabia." In 1924 he published his first and probably most famous book—*With Lawrence in Arabia.*

Thomas made his national radio debut on Sept. 29, 1930, on the Columbia Broadcasting System's Monday through Friday evening news program. He moved to the National Broadcasting Company in 1932 but returned in 1947 to CBS, where he remained. His television career began in 1939, when he started broadcasting the news for NBC.

Thomas visited every continent and nearly every country in the world. One of his most famous trips was a 1949 visit to the once-forbidden city of Lhasa in Tibet, at the invitation of the Dalai Lama. Many of his books dealt with his various travels or with great adventures or great adventurers. They included *Beyond the Khyber Pass* (1925), *India: Land of the Black Pagoda* (1930), *The Untold Story of Exploration* (1936), *Adventures Among Immortals* (1937), *With Allenby in the Holy Land* (1938), *Back to Mandalay* (1951), and *Lowell Thomas' Book of the High Mountains* (1964).

(JOAN NATALIE REIBSTEIN)

Thorn, Gaston

Prime minister of one of the world's smallest countries, Gaston Thorn was often in the foreground of the international political scene during 1975–76. As head of government and foreign minister of Luxembourg he was included in all the councils of Europe. In September 1975 he was elected president of the 30th UN General Assembly; from Jan. 1, 1976, for the first half of the year, he was president of the European Council of heads of government of the nine EEC member states and also of the EEC Council of Ministers; and in March 1976 he was elected president of the newly formed Federation of Liberal and Democratic Parties within the European Community. Multilingual, living at the crossroads of the Germanic and Latin civilizations in Europe, he is a firm believer in the need for European unity.

Thorn was born in Luxembourg on Sept. 3, 1928, the son of a railway engineer, and raised in France. The family returned to Luxembourg at the outbreak of World War II and in 1943, during the German occupation, Gaston was sent to Germany for "corrective training" after organizing a demonstration against compulsory antiaircraft drill at school. After the war he studied in Switzerland and at the Sorbonne.

It is said that Thorn was launched in politics without his knowledge by his wife, who agreed on his behalf that he would run for the Luxembourg town council in 1957. But politics was in his blood (a Thorn had headed the Luxembourg Liberal Party early in the century), and two years later he became a member of Parliament and soon afterward of the European Parliament in Strasbourg. His political skill was rapidly recognized, and at 33 he became chairman of Luxembourg's Liberal (Democratic) Party. He at once set out to remodel the party's rather conservative program, giving it a more pragmatic, left-of-centre orientation. Following the 1968 general election he became foreign minister and minister for trade in the Christian Socialist-Liberal coalition. His personal popularity—he was as much at ease among soccer fans as with his fellow statesmen—contributed to the Liberal success in the May 1974 election, which ended 50 years of Christian Socialist domination in Luxembourg politics, and he was asked to head the new coalition.

(JAN R. ENGELS)

Tindemans, Léo

Toward the end of 1974 Léo Tindemans, prime minister of Belgium, was invited by his fellow heads of government in the European Economic Community to draw up a report on the future of European unity. He made a fact-finding tour of the capitals of the nine EEC countries and presented his report in December 1975, but as 1976 drew to a close he found to his chagrin that his colleagues had made little headway in studying his proposals for greater integration. There was compensation, however, in the award to Tindemans of the 1976 Charlemagne Prize for services to European unity.

On the domestic front, Tindemans' government of Social Christians and Liberals, later joined by the Rassemblement Wallon (Walloon federalist party), faced serious problems from the start. To begin with, although Tindemans secured the Walloons' support in exchange for a promise to grant greater autonomy to the regions with devolution of powers, they proved erratic partners in the coalition. Then, with unemployment and inflation continually rising, Tindemans' attempts to curb rising production costs by temporarily suspending the automatic wage indexation ran into strong trade-union opposition. He nevertheless succeeded in obtaining parliamentary approval for an economic recovery program embodying wage restraints. His warning that sacrifices were inevitable was clearly understood by Belgians, as indicated by the results of the October 1976 municipal elections, which were favourable for his Social Christian Party.

Born in Zwijndrecht, Antwerp Province, on April 16, 1922, Tindemans took a master's degree in economics and began a career in journalism. Joining the Social Christian political study centre, he became the party's national secretary in 1958 and a member of Parliament three years later. He was always strongly interested in foreign and particularly European affairs, and his appointment as secretary-general of the European Union of Christian Democrats en-

A.F.P./PICTORIAL PARADE

abled him to establish close contacts with the leading European political figures. In 1968 he became minister of community relations under Gaston Eyskens, and in the brief second Eyskens government (1972) he was minister of agriculture. As leader of the Social Christians, he became deputy prime minister when Edmond Leburton's tripartite coalition took office in January 1973, and he took office as prime minister in April 1974.

(JAN R. ENGELS)

Trudeau, Garry

Many observers of the 1976 election campaigns felt that Virginia Slade was the one candidate most likely to win. She was the liberated black law student running for Congress in Garry Trudeau's satirical comic strip "Doonesbury."

At a time when many newspapers had been forced to drop or reduce the size of their comic strips, "Doonesbury" was a remarkable success. Its creator, Garry Trudeau, seemed able to express the flavour of social and political life in the 1970s with just the degree of bite that appealed to large numbers of readers, especially among the young. "Doonesbury" was appearing in some 400 U.S. newspapers, and nearly a million of Trudeau's several books (the latest being *The Doonesbury Chronicles*) had been sold. The artist's achievement was recognized by his receipt in May 1975 of the Pulitzer Prize for cartooning. This marked the first time the prize had been given to a non-editorial-page cartoonist.

Trudeau's characters had been both real and fictional. Presidents Nixon and Ford, Attorney General John Mitchell, *Rolling Stone* writer Hunter Thompson, and other national figures had all done stints in "Doonesbury" panels. But perhaps Trudeau's most popular character was Ms. Joanie Caucus, a runaway housewife turned law student. The cartoonist claimed he received so much mail addressed to her that his mailman thought he was living with her.

Garretson Beekman Trudeau was born in New York City in 1948 but grew up in Saranac Lake, N.Y. He attended St. Paul's School in Concord, N.H., and entered Yale in 1966. Soon thereafter he drew his first comic strip. He became the editor of the campus humour magazine and an occasional writer for the Yale *Daily News.* In 1968 he began doing a strip called "Bull Tales" for the campus paper, poking fun at Yale notables and introducing Michael J. Doonesbury, an armchair liberal who later became the strip's central character.

After graduating from college, Trudeau entered the Yale School of Art. About the same time he signed up with the new Universal Press Syndicate for a national comic strip, with the name "Bull Tales" changed to "Doonesbury" to avoid offending readers. "Doonesbury" first appeared in October 1970 in 28 newspapers, including the *Washington Post.*

"Doonesbury" nevertheless managed to offend some people. Probably the largest flap arose over a cartoon that appeared in May 1973, in which "Doonesbury" 's militant radical declared John Mitchell "guilty, guilty, guilty" in the Watergate scandal. The decision of several newspapers in refusing to run that episode met with strong reader protest. Several million people clearly believed that "Doonesbury" was right on target. (JOAN NATALIE REIBSTEIN)

Ustinov, Dmitry Fedorovich

Appointed Soviet minister of defense on April 29, 1976, following the death of Marshal Andrey Grechko (*see* OBITUARIES), Dmitry Ustinov was the first civilian to hold that office since Leon Trotsky in 1918 (excluding Marshal N. A. Bulganin, minister of defense during 1953–55, who was also essentially a civilian). Simultaneously with his appointment Ustinov was named general of the army and three months later marshal of the Soviet Union.

Although no professional soldier, Ustinov was an expert in the field of armaments production, and as such was no doubt preferred by Communist Party General Secretary Leonid Brezhnev to either of the two obvious military candidates, Marshal Grechko's deputies Gen. Viktor G. Kulikov, chief of the general staff, and Marshal Ivan I. Yakubovsky (*see* OBITUARIES), commander in chief of the Warsaw Pact forces. The appointment could be seen as an assertion of party and civilian authority over the armed forces, so favouring a continuation of détente policy. One of Marshal Ustinov's first official duties was to head the Soviet military delegation at the September 1976 maneuvers of the Northern Group of the Warsaw Pact forces, held in western Poland.

NOVOSTI

Dmitry Ustinov was born in Samara (now Kuybyshev) in 1908, the son of a worker. After graduating in 1934 from the Institute of Military Engineering in Leningrad, he worked first as a construction engineer, then as director of an armaments factory. In 1941 Stalin appointed him people's commissar of armaments. He kept this post after World War II and after Stalin's death continued to serve as minister of armaments (the designation commissar having been abolished in 1946) in Georgy M. Malenkov's Council of Ministers (March 1953–February 1955), retaining the same portfolio under Bulganin (February 1955–March 1958). When Nikita S. Khrushchev replaced Bulganin as chairman of the Council of Ministers, he appointed two first vice-chairmen: Aleksey N. Kosygin and Ustinov, the latter continuing as minister of defense industries. When, after Khrushchev's downfall in October 1964, Brezhnev became first secretary of the party's Central Committee, Ustinov remained in the government. In 1965 he was made an alternate member of the Politburo—the supreme policymaking body —and a secretary of the Central Committee in charge of defense industries. At the 25th party congress in March 1976 he was elected a full member of the Politburo. (K. M. SMOGORZEWSKI)

Vidal, Gore

While millions observed the U.S. Bicentennial with something close to reverence, Gore Vidal earned upward of $1 million from an irreverent historical novel about the nation's Centennial. A man of many words, Vidal scorned the celebration, saying "I should think a year of mourning would be highly salutary—for our lost innocence, our eroding liberties, our vanishing resources, our ruined environment."

Time magazine quipped that the author of *1876* had bit "the land that feeds him," characterizing him as "a cinder in the public eye" for three decades. But like many who twitted the literary gadfly for his often perverse opinions, *Time* granted that the novelist-playwright-essayist-homosexual apologist-scenarist-television commentator-politician managed to persevere with undeniable style and diversion. The book was "as funny as it is unsettling . . . an ornate 200th birthday card inscribed with a poison pen." *1876* was the fictional memoir of Aaron Burr's illegitimate son, an impoverished office seeker who saw U.S. Senate seats sold for $200,000 and West Point appointments for $5,000. Vidal described the chicanery with a straight face, part of his public pose as a jade.

He was born Eugene Luther Vidal, Jr., on Oct. 3, 1925, in Cadet Hospital at West Point, N.Y., delivered by a future surgeon general of the U.S. His father, an athlete and aviator, moved the family to the home of Vidal's grandfather, Sen. Thomas Gore of Oklahoma, a blind legislator to whom young Vidal often read aloud. When the boy was ten his parents were divorced. His mother quickly remarried and he went to live with his stepfather—who later became stepfather to Jacqueline Bouvier Kennedy. After graduating from Phillips Exeter Academy, in New Hampshire, he enlisted in the Army and spent part of World War II in the Aleutians.

His first novel, *Williwaw* (1946), written in the Army, won rave reviews. He vied with Truman Capote for the postwar title of literary boy wonder. Two years later he published a quietly homosexual novel, *The City and the Pillar,* and was banished by the literary establishment. For a while he published detective stories under a pen name, Edgar Box, then wrote TV and movie scripts. He had two Broadway hits before riding into Washington on the Kennedy coattails, a camp follower in Camelot who subsequently had a falling out with Robert Kennedy.

Among his later books were *Washington, D.C.* (1967), *Myra Breckinridge* (1968), and *Burr* (1973). The latter offered a new look at the Founding Fathers and set the stage for *1876. Julian* (1964), a historical novel about a 4th-century Roman emperor, led him to Italy where he continued to spend most of his time. Said Vidal: "I have the face now of one of the later, briefer emperors." (PHILIP KOPPER)

Videla, Jorge Rafaél

After a long-planned, bloodless coup on the night of March 23, 1976, which overthrew the almost nonfunctioning government of Pres. Isabel Perón, Lieut. Gen. Jorge Rafaél Videla became the 39th president of Argentina. Videla, who had long resisted injecting the military into politics, finally moved when it seemed to him that the unbridled terrorism and economic ineptness of the Peronist government could no longer be endured. Indeed, Videla, as army commander, stayed his hand for so long that he became known as the "Reluctant Dragon." But when he and the other armed forces chiefs decided Argentina could no longer be allowed to drift, he moved swiftly and with precision. He gave the Army control of the struggle against the guerrillas of the left and right who had taken several thousand lives in Argentina during the past several years. In October he narrowly escaped assassination when a reviewing stand blew up at the military headquarters, the Campo de Mayo, moments after he had left.

Once regarded as a follower rather than a leader, Videla proved to be strong and competent. He got along well with the other junta leaders, Adm. Emilio Massera and Air Force Chief Orlando Agosti, but there was no question that Videla wielded supreme authority.

Videla was a sworn anti-Communist and a tough-minded infantry soldier who was credited with deeply ingrained Roman Catholic moralist views. His personal integrity was unquestioned, and he was described in Argentina as a "man from another time" who loathed corruption and would not tolerate it in his government.

Born on Aug. 2, 1925, in Mercedes, about 75 mi from Buenos Aires, Videla was the son of an infantry colonel. A tall, lanky man with a prominent nose and mustache and a personable but shy manner, he was exceedingly polite but had difficulty with small talk and would not abide off-colour stories. One of his closest advisers was Msgr. Adolfo Tortolo, the Army's chief chaplain. (JEREMIAH A. O'LEARY, JR.)

Vorster, Balthazar Johannes

South Africa's prime minister, B. J. Vorster, marked the tenth year of his accession to power in 1976 with a remarkable diplomatic partnership with U.S. Secretary of State Henry Kissinger that apparently persuaded the Rhodesian leader, Ian Smith (*q.v.*), to accept black rule for his country. But Vorster remained adamantly opposed to any such future for South Africa; he insisted that apartheid (racial separation) would remain no matter what modifications might be made to cope with the increasingly militant aspirations of black South Africans.

GODFREY ARGENT—CAMERA PRESS/FRANZ E. FURST

Vorster was a man in the tradition of Afrikaner leaders who believed both in the political supremacy of Afrikaans-speaking South Africans and in rigid segregation between the races. He was, however, quite capable of adopting flexible attitudes when the occasion demanded and was quick to understand the consequences of the collapse of the Portuguese colonial empire in 1974. Vorster offered cooperation with neighbouring African leaders in trying to achieve a peaceful settlement of the simmering crises in Rhodesia and Namibia. But this initiative was lost when he sent South African forces into southern Angola in an unsuccessful campaign to oppose Soviet and Cuban support for the Popular Movement for the Liberation of Angola. Later, however, he became Kissinger's enthusiastic partner, working with other African leaders to defuse violence in southern Africa.

Vorster was born at Jamestown, Cape Province, on Dec. 13, 1915, and studied law at the University of Stellenbosch, the cradle of Afrikaner nationalism, where he showed early promise as a student leader. His legal career was interrupted by his internment during World War II by Field Marshal J. C. Smuts's government because of his active opposition to the Allies' war effort. He entered Parliament in 1953 and was made a junior minister five weeks later, finally achieving full Cabinet rank in 1961 as minister of justice. When Prime Minister Hendrik Verwoerd was murdered in 1966, the National Party turned to Vorster as the toughest leader in their ranks to guide them through the difficult years ahead.

(COLIN LEGUM)

Ward, Barbara (Lady Jackson)

With her books *Only One Earth,* written in collaboration with René Dubos for the UN Conference on the Human Environment held in Stockholm in 1972, and *The Home of Man,* written for the UN Conference on Human Settlements (Habitat), held in Vancouver, B.C., in 1976 (*see* ENVIRONMENT: *Special Report*), Barbara Ward became perhaps the world's best known voice in the great debates of the 1970s on environment and development. Her status as something of an international guru was recognized when, in June 1976, she was given a life peerage in Britain's House of Lords. (Her appellation of Lady Jackson derived from her marriage to Sir Robert Jackson, an undersecretary-general of the UN.)

The founder-president of the International Institute for Environment and Development, with headquarters in London, Barbara Ward was a woman of immense energy that belied her frail appearance. She was not only a prolific writer of books but a busy lecturer and broadcaster, a great traveler (at one time regularly spending four months of every year abroad), and an adroit activist behind the scenes. She had learned how to exploit the potential of nongovernmental organizations (NGO's) to influence governments, notably at the UN world conferences which provided a forum where NGO's could be heard.

Born in England on May 23, 1914, Barbara Ward might well have become a university teacher. On leaving Oxford she spent a few years as an extramural university lecturer, but then switched to journalism and was soon an assistant editor on *The Economist*. After her marriage in 1950 she lived at different times in India, Pakistan, and Ghana, gaining a first-hand view of development in the third world that prompted the first of a series of books on this theme. In the 1960s she began to spend more time in the U.S., which was some years ahead of Europe in its concern over industrial pollution. Brought up a Roman Catholic, she was appointed to the pope's Commission for Justice and Peace in 1967 and in 1971 was the first woman ever to address a Vatican Assembly.

(HARFORD THOMAS)

Wertmüller, Lina

Arcangela Felice Assunta Wertmüller von Elgg Spanol von Braucich-Job is an enigma. Born in Rome "somewhere between 1812 and 1928, I'll never tell precisely," she was the socialist great-great-granddaughter of a Swiss aristocrat who fled Zürich after a duel and the renegade daughter of a distinguished lawyer whose wife sent him packing after 50 years of marriage. Possessed of "boiling blood" herself, as a schoolgirl she once set fire to a teacher's robes. In 1957 she graduated from the Academy of Theatre in Rome, worked in the avant-garde theatre and with a puppet theatre that staged Kafka for children, and then became Federico Fellini's protégée (having met the director through a childhood friend who married his leading actor, Marcello Mastroianni). By 1976 she had made more than half a dozen films, been named best director at the Cannes Film Festival, become the toast of American movie audiences, and signed a multifilm Hollywood contract.

CAREN GOLDEN—PICTORIAL PARADE

Among the films of Lina Wertmüller, as she was better known, are *Love and Anarchy, The Seduction of Mimi, Swept Away,* and *Seven Beauties.* They were wildly applauded in the U.S.—one earned more than $100,000 in two weeks—though critics disagreed as to what they were about, let alone what they meant. "Wertmüller's films are a torrent of paradox," wrote one. "Opposites always go together. Her villains or, rather, those who embody noxious ideas, are touched with some splendor or at least some humanity." Similarly, her heroes were tainted with madness or the macabre. If she had a single message it lay in such seeming contradictions. "It is not the bad guys who make society what it is," she told an American interviewer. "It is us. We have to keep clear that society is us, the result of our choices."

Her effect rested in part on her ability to be constantly complex—to present many compelling conundrums at once, while mixing metaphors, mores, and morals. *Swept Away,* for example, involved a Communist deckhand and a haughty yacht mistress. Adrift in a dinghy, the millionairess scorns him; marooned on an island, he beats her; they fall madly in love, but after they are rescued she goes her way again. Was the film about sex or politics? Viewers disagreed. *Newsweek*'s critic saw it as "a kind of witty and slapdash Marxist comedy that owes as much to Groucho as to Karl."

(PHILIP KOPPER)

Williams, Shirley Vivien Teresa Brittain

With the departure of Roy Jenkins (*q.v.*) to Brussels as president-designate of the Commission of the European Community, Shirley Williams found herself the nominal leader of the moderate social democrat wing of the British Labour Party. She did not enter the contest for the party leadership when Harold Wilson resigned in March 1976, but in October she was persuaded, somewhat against her will, to run against Michael Foot, a left-wing radical, as deputy leader. She lost by 166 votes to 128, and while it could not be said that this left her as number three in the party hierarchy, it established her as a serious contender for the leadership in a few years' time.

In the September reconstruction of the James Callaghan government she became secretary of state for education and science, a step up from secretary of state for prices

KEYSTONE

and consumer protection, the post that brought her into the Cabinet in 1974 and into the centre of political attention at a time of rampant inflation. There she gained a reputation for her relaxed, informal style, and a capacity to argue with persuasive common sense.

In 1975 the referendum on British membership in the EEC also brought her into the limelight, both as a committed European and as a woman of resolute principle, for she said she would leave the government if Britain were to leave the Community. She demonstrated her political toughness at the 1976 Labour conference by defending public expenditure cuts, a highly sensitive issue.

Born July 27, 1930, Shirley Williams was brought up in an intensely political family. Her father, Sir George Catlin, and her mother, the writer Vera Brittain, were both prominent in left-wing politics in the 1930s. At Oxford she was the first woman chairman of the university Labour Club. Before entering Parliament in 1964 she had been general secretary of the influential Fabian Society. She was familiar with academic life, both her father and her husband, Bernard Williams (from whom she was now divorced), having been university professors.

(HARFORD THOMAS)

Wilson, Sir (James) Harold

On March 16, 1976, five days after his 60th birthday, Harold Wilson announced his resignation as prime minister of the United Kingdom. He had decided as long ago as July 1974 to retire, preferably in the autumn of 1975, but his involvement in the counter-inflationary program had obliged him to defer the date. He told the queen in December 1975 that he would give up office in March 1976. But to the public the announcement came as a stunning surprise, for it had been a well-kept secret, and Wilson was in good health.

The reasons he gave for withdrawing from active politics (though he remained a member of Parliament) were the length of his time in office, the need to find a new party leader before the next general election, and the fear that he might come to lack freshness of response to rapidly changing situations. He had been prime minister for eight years, longer than any other British prime minister in peacetime in the 20th century. For almost 30 of his 31 years as an MP he had sat on one or the other front bench.

TERRY KIRK—CAMERA PRESS/FRANZ E. FURST

Born March 11, 1916, in Huddersfield, West Yorkshire, Wilson won a scholarship to Oxford University, where he became a lecturer in economics before going into the civil service during World War II and then into Parliament in 1945. He became president of the Board of Trade in Clement Attlee's Labour government in 1947, at the age of 31, and was elected leader of the Labour Party in 1963 following the death of Hugh Gaitskell.

Wilson showed no loss of energy after his retirement. During April 7–June 13 he wrote a book called *The Governance of Britain,* based on his own long experience in office, which was published in October. This remarkable ability to write books at top speed had been demonstrated earlier, when his lengthy memoirs of the Labour government of 1964–70 appeared in 1971. By a nice touch of irony, there was another compulsive writer in the Wilson Cabinet, Richard Crossman (d. 1974), the second volume of whose memoirs also appeared in October 1976 with a highly critical view of Wilson's performance as prime minister.

On his retirement, Wilson was created a Knight of the Garter, an honour in the personal gift of the queen. In October he was appointed to head an inquiry into the role and functioning of British financial institutions.

(HARFORD THOMAS)

Winkler, Henry

"Live fast, die young, and leave a good-looking corpse." Such was the philosophy of Arthur Fonzarelli, a character in "Happy Days," a U.S. television comedy series depicting high-school student life during the 1950s. Fonzarelli, or "The Fonz," as everyone called him, was a high-school dropout who wore a leather jacket, rode a motorcycle, and combed his greasy black hair into a ducktail. One of his favourite expressions was "Aaaayyy!"

"The Fonz" was largely the creation of Henry Winkler, the actor who portrayed him. Winkler was astonished by his success and worried that he might be typecast forever as a likable clod in a leather jacket. His personal history could hardly be more different. Winkler's Jewish parents fled Hitler's Germany during the 1930s and came to the U.S., where his father became president of an international lumber firm. Henry was born in New York City on Oct. 30, 1945. His mother and father, who hoped that their only son might someday become a diplomat, sent him to excellent schools. As a student, Henry dressed neatly and rarely misbehaved. He admitted that a person like "The Fonz" would have frightened him when he was an adolescent.

An interest in acting that began during his early teens intensified while Winkler was earning his B.A. from Emerson College in Boston. He then enrolled at Yale School of Drama where he earned his M.A. He appeared in some 60 plays with the Yale Repertory Company over the next five years. A stint of radio and television work in New York City followed. In September 1973 he moved to California to appear in a film. Two months later he successfully auditioned for the role of Arthur Fonzarelli in "Happy Days." The scriptwriters had originally envisioned Fonzarelli as a pleasant and rather uninteresting fellow who wore a cloth coat and casual shoes. Winkler suggested black boots, a leather jacket, a ducktail haircut, and the motorcycle. The director of "Happy Days" liked Winkler's ideas and his portrayal of "The Fonz." So did the television audience. A series that was once a modest success became a hit. And Henry Winkler became its star.

(VICTOR M. CASSIDY)

Worth, Irene

Irene Worth, Broadway's best actress in 1976, gave her Tony award-winning performance in a short-run revival of Tennessee Williams' *Sweet Bird of Youth.* In it, she said, she found "the C Major track" of total loyalty to the author's composition. If the metaphor seemed unlikely for a dramatic actress, it was appropriate for this performer. *Washington Post* critic Richard L. Coe once said "her voice must be one of the finest on the English-speaking stage." Furthermore, she is a dedicated advocate of interdisciplinary arts. She would like to mix artistic media by seeking out ways to work with such diverse creators as dancer Merce Cunningham and composer-conductor Pierre Boulez. "I think all the arts should stimulate each other," she told an interviewer. "The movies have changed everything for the stage actor. We have to find the kind of urgency . . . and documentary truth that you can get with a hand-held camera, and . . . to get it every night."

DONALD COOPER

The remark contains a clue to her success, which has always depended on well-practiced skill as well as talent. This was one reason for her notable devotion to repertory theatre, acquired long before the repertory movement swept the U.S. in the 1960s. Worth was born June 23, 1916, in either Nebraska or California (reports differ). After taking an education degree at UCLA, she taught school for several years. Turning to the stage, she made her professional debut with a road show in 1942, then appeared on Broadway a year later with Victor Jory. Seeking classical training and experience, she went to London in 1944.

Within five years her star had risen so high that she appeared in the premiere of T. S. Eliot's *The Cocktail Party* at the Edinburgh Festival, then returned to Broadway for the New York production. She worked frequently with the Old Vic Repertory Company and the Royal Shakespeare Company, touring South Africa with the former and Eastern Europe with the latter's production of *King Lear.* In 1953 she appeared in the first production of the Stratford (Ont.) Shakespeare Company with Alec Guinness. She received her first Tony award for her performance in Edward Albee's *Tiny Alice.*

(PHILIP KOPPER)

OLYMPIC CHAMPIONS

GERRY CRANHAM

Lasse Viren of Finland repeated his 1972 victories, thus becoming the first man to win both the 5,000-m and 10,000-m events in successive Olympiads.

WIDE WORLD

Shun Fujimoto, performing on the rings with a fractured knee, ended his routine with a solid landing after a triple somersault and twist; his skill and courage helped secure a team victory for Japan.

LONDON DAILY EXPRESS/PICTORIAL PARADE

Soviet gymnast Nikolay Andrianov displayed amazing virtuosity in capturing seven Olympic medals: four gold, two silver, and one bronze.

WIDE WORLD

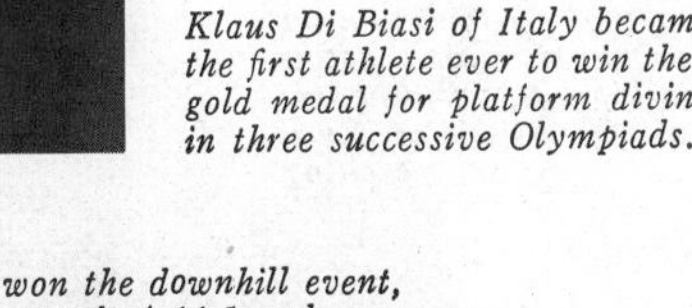

Klaus Di Biasi of Italy became the first athlete ever to win the gold medal for platform diving in three successive Olympiads.

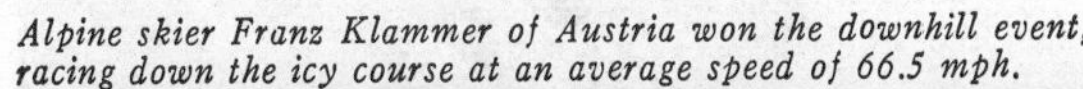

Alpine skier Franz Klammer of Austria won the downhill event, racing down the icy course at an average speed of 66.5 mph.

KATHERINE YOUNG

Nelli Kim captured three gold medals and a silver to become the Soviet Union's brightest new gymnastic star.

SYNDICATION INTERNATIONAL/PHOTO TRENDS

WIDE WORLD

Dorothy Hamill of the U.S. excelled in both the compulsory and freestyle events to win the gold medal in women's figure skating.

SVEN SIMON/KATHERINE YOUNG

Rosi Mittermaier of West Germany won gold medals in the slalom and downhill and narrowly missed an unprecedented grand slam, losing the giant slalom by just 12-hundredths of a second.

CAMERA PRESS/FRANZ E. FURST

Teófilo Stevenson of Cuba became the first boxer ever to defend successfully an Olympic heavyweight championship.

SVEN SIMON/KATHERINE YOUNG

Competing in her fourth Olympics, Irena Szewinska of Poland established a new world record in winning the 400-m dash.

GERRY CRANHAM—PHOTO RESEARCHERS

Perennial record-breaker Vasily Alekseyev of the Soviet Union set a new Olympic mark for superheavyweights with a prodigious combined lift of 440 kg (978 lb).

John Curry of England won the men's Olympic figure skating championship with a routine that was as artistic as it was exciting.

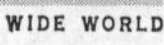

WIDE WORLD

KEYSTONE

World record holder Guy Drut of France won an Olympic gold medal by finishing first in the 110-m hurdles.

WIDE WORLD

Nadia Comaneci, a 14-year-old Romanian gymnast, made Olympic history in the process of winning three gold medals and one silver: she received seven perfect scores of 10.0.

CENTRAL PRESS/PICTORIAL PARADE

The nearly invincible women swimmers from East Germany were led by world champion Kornelia Ender, who captured four gold medals.

CANADIAN PRESS

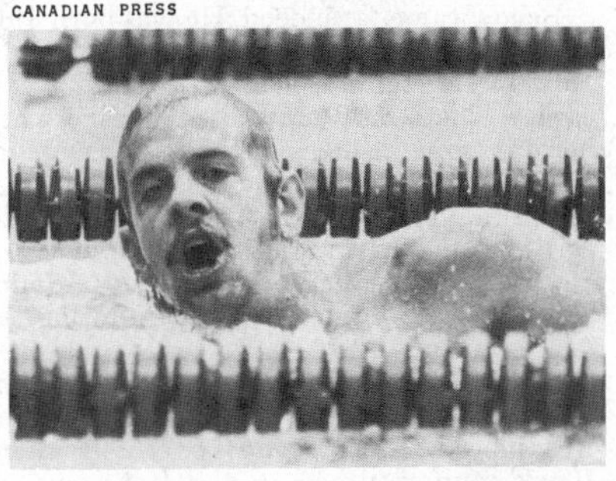

John Naber of the U.S. set world records in the 100-m and 200-m backstroke and was awarded four gold medals and one silver.

Edwin Moses of the U.S. shattered the world record as he swept to victory in the 400-m hurdles.

DEPARDON/UZAN—GAMMA/LIAISON

Alberto Juantorena of Cuba set a world record in the 800-m run and finished first in the finals of the 400-m dash.

SVEN SIMON/KATHERINE YOUNG

U.S. superstar Bruce Jenner set a world record of 8,618 points in capturing the grueling two-day decathlon.

GERRY CRANHAM

NOBEL PRIZES

For the first time since their inception in 1901, all of the Nobel Prizes for the year were awarded to citizens of a single nation, the United States. A contributing factor to this unique happening was the small number of recipients—only two prizes were shared and the Prize for Peace was withheld for the 20th time.

The U.S. monopoly was presumably the result of coincidence rather than intent. The nominees' nationalities were to have no bearing on the final choices of the Nobel award committees. Moreover, some observers speculated that the selection of Milton Friedman to receive the Prize for Economics was really a Hobson's choice. Established by the Bank of Sweden in 1968, this ancillary award had already been given to most of the living original thinkers in economics, a field that experienced few real breakthroughs in any generation. Also not surprising was the choice for the Prize for Literature; it went to Saul Bellow, a novelist who had been a favoured candidate in the two previous years.

More important than the citizenship of the science laureates was what their cited projects had in common; all involved pure research with no predetermined applications. As a *New York Times* editorial expressed it, the science selections "might almost have been designed to provide an answer and rebuke to those with more power than vision who fail to understand that basic research yields the richest dividends. . . . What the Nobel Prize committee seems to be telling the financiers and directors of research is that in the long run nothing is more practical than basic studies whose ultimate implications none can foresee."

In the heat of his unsuccessful election campaign, U.S. Pres. Gerald Ford tried to make some sort of political hay out of "the clean sweep," as many papers had dubbed it. His Democratic opponent, Jimmy Carter, had charged that American prestige was declining around the world under Republican administrations, and Ford said the Nobel selections "surely put to rest" such insinuations. This comment, in turn, provoked ten U.S. Nobel laureates to point out that "Nobel Prizes usually reflect work done over long periods of time. This year's prizes do not, therefore, reflect this year's strengths. Indeed, Mr. Ford's budgets have not been such as to encourage the growth of American science. The current appropriation for the National Science Foundation, corrected for inflation, is actually 10% lower than it was in the year when Mr. Ford took office. . . . His partisanship was unfortunate and his implicit claims inaccurate." In 1976 each prize, awarded on December 10, the 80th anniversary of Alfred Nobel's death, carried an honorarium of $160,000.

Prize for Literature

Celebrated for his "exuberant ideas, flashing irony, hilarious comedy and burning compassion," novelist Saul Bellow finally won the 1976 Prize for Literature. Bellow had been nominated previously at least twice in succession, in 1974 when the prize was shared by two Swedish novelists and in 1975 when it went to an Italian poet. Receiving the news gracefully, he said, "The child in me is delighted. The adult in me is skeptical."

Weeks later in a conversation with Joseph Epstein, editor of Phi Beta Kappa's journal *American Scholar,* Bellow reflected, "Last year, after a momentary feeling of disappointment, I felt rather relieved that [Eugenio] Montale won the prize. As I said, I have gotten a great deal of recognition, and I like to think I wouldn't have minded if I had been passed over. Perhaps this is the calm hindsight of a winner speaking, perhaps not. One of the things one fails to realize till one has won it is that the Nobel Prize for Literature has many extraliterary aspects. Winning it makes you an eminent person; it gives you certain kinds of power. I have never had much taste for the power that goes with eminence."

In another context he noted that "Nobel Prizes are rarely good for Americans, at least not writers. Sinclair Lewis and John Steinbeck hardly had a sober time afterward. Hemingway quit writing." Steinbeck's fate, in particular, saddened Bellow. The two had been friends and the 1962 winner had inscribed a copy of his Nobel address to "Saul Bellow. You're next." Bellow's selection in 1976 brings the number of American laureates in literature to seven, including William Faulkner, Pearl Buck, and Eugene O'Neill. "There is no literary life I want to live," Bellow said. "I'm just an old-fashioned writer," who hoped the prize would neither go to his head nor falsely symbolize some unattainable achievement. "All I started to do was show up my brothers. I didn't have to go this far."

Bellow came far indeed. He was born July 10, 1915, in Lachine, Que., where his parents, Russian immigrants, had settled two years earlier. The family moved to Chicago when he was nine. Entering the University of Chicago, he found it "too dense" and transferred to Northwestern University where he earned honours in anthropology in 1937. He worked on the Works Progress Administration (WPA) Writers' Project during the depression of the 1930s, served in the merchant marine, helped edit the two-volume index (the *Syntopicon*) to Encyclopædia Britannica's *Great Books of the Western World,* and returned to the University of Chicago as a professor of literature. He was the only man to have won the National Book Award three times; in 1976 he also won the Pulitzer Prize.

"If Saul Bellow didn't exist, someone exactly like him would have had to have been invented," wrote John Leonard in the *New York Times,* ". . . a very special sort of novelist, a highbrow with muscles, to tell the story of the Jewish romance with America." The Swedish Academy, which awarded the prize, cited him "for the human understanding and subtle analysis of contemporary culture." When he began writing, "the anti-hero of the present was already on the way and Bellow became one of those who took care of him. . . ." He made the antihero a man "who keeps on trying to find a foothold during his wanderings in our tottering world, one who can never relinquish his faith that the value of life depends on its dignity, not its success."

Regarding the importance of literature, Bellow said, "When it is going well a novel affords the highest kind of truth; a good writer can lay claim to a disinterestedness that is as great as that of a pure scientist—when he is going well. In its complicated, possibly even mysterious way, the novel is an instrument for delving into human truths. . . . Now more than ever, it seems to me, it becomes the writer's job to remind people of their common stock of emotion, of their common humanity, of the fact, if you will, that they have souls."

Occasional playwright and frequent essayist, he was known most widely for his eight novels: *Dangling Man* (1944), *The Victim* (1947), *The Adventures of Augie March* (1953), *Seize the Day* (1956), *Henderson, the Rain King* (1959), *Herzog* (1964), *Mr. Sammler's Planet* (1970), and *Humboldt's Gift* (1975). In 1976 he published *To Jerusalem and Back,* the memoir of a personal journey to Israel.

Prize for Chemistry

William Nunn Lipscomb, Jr., winner of the 1976 Prize for Chemistry, was "one of the extraordinary scientific innovators of our time," according to an article in the journal *Science.* Working with boranes, which are compounds of boron and hydrogen, he made fundamental discoveries about how molecules are held together. The long-known chemistry of hydrocarbons, compounds of carbon and hydrogen, suggested one concept of bonding, wherein each pair of atoms is linked by a pair of electrons. Explaining the stability of boranes in this fashion, however, was a frustrating problem because they lack sufficient electrons. Lipscomb demonstrated how a pair of electrons could be shared by three atoms, a theory that served to describe successfully even the most complex borane structures known as well as many other analogous molecular structures.

WIDE WORLD

William Nunn Lipscomb, Jr.

Lipscomb became interested in borane chemistry at the California Institute of Technology where he earned his doctorate in 1946 and studied with Linus Pauling, eventual two-time Nobel laureate. A year later, at the University of Minnesota, Lipscomb adopted a technique that Pauling had borrowed from physics: the use of X-ray diffraction for elucidating molecular structures. The difficulty of the work was compounded by the unstable, volatile nature of the boranes, which forced the use of vacuum-line handling and low temperatures.

At first he encountered a bewildering pattern of three-dimensional geometrical structures that belied the tidy, predictable order found in chain hydrocarbons. Realizing that classical theory could never accommodate the boranes, he pressed on to develop "a vast and diverse chemistry [of] cage-like molecules hardly imaginable a few years ago." At the foundation of Lipscomb's theories was the idea that two boron atoms could be linked to a hydrogen atom by one pair of electrons. As *Science*'s contributor commented, "This concept was the key to the development of a topological theory of bonding in the boranes which not only provided a plausible explanation of the known structures but, more importantly, made possible the prediction of new compounds. . . .

"By the early 1960s the boranes were the largest known family of molecular hydrides other than the hydrocarbons, [and] nearly all the general theory developed to deal with these compounds had come from Lipscomb and his associates. . . . The boranes, once viewed as molecular mavericks, have in fact provided the key to conceptually link a whole vast array of cluster-type molecules for which classical Lewis bond descriptions fail." In terms of practical applications, Lipscomb's work led to the synthesis of a variety of materials, ranging from compounds of extreme thermal and chemical stability to ones of use experimentally in radiation therapy of brain tumours.

Born in Cleveland, Ohio, Dec. 9, 1919, Lipscomb took his undergraduate degree at the University of Kentucky, an affiliation that earned him the nickname "Colonel." During World War II he worked in the U.S. Office of Scientific Research and Development, then resumed his studies at Cal Tech. After more than a decade at Minnesota, he moved on to Harvard University's Gibbs Laboratory where he became Abbott and William James Lawrence professor of chemistry.

Lipscomb maintained a reputation for running a loose and lively experimental ship and for approaching the work with a rare degree of wit. He quoted Lewis Carroll in his elegant papers, belonged to the Baker Street Irregulars (a society devoted to the fictional detective Sherlock Holmes), and rose at 6 AM daily to practice the clarinet, which he played with near-professional skill in chamber groups.

Prize for Physics

Burton Richter and Samuel C. C. Ting shared the 1976 Prize for Physics for independently discovering a subatomic particle that they respectively named "psi" and "J." Called by one Nobel judge "the greatest discovery ever in the field of elementary particles," it had no immediate applications, as Richter himself candidly admitted. "The significance is that we have learned something more about the structure of the universe" by gaining a clearer understanding of its smallest components.

Many new, interrelated elementary particles have been discovered in the past 15 years, the Royal Swedish Academy of Sciences observed, but "the new [psi/J] particle is something separate and new and it has formed the beginning of a new family of its own. . . .

"Is there anything further in these particles, thought to be the smallest building blocks of matter?" the Academy asked. "For centuries physicists and chemists have devoted much of their efforts to a search for the smallest components of matter. The limit of the smallest has slowly been moved from atoms . . . to what are known as elementary particles. For some years now the physicists have had to move this limit downward, and the signs are that the elementary particles, too, consist of yet smaller units, quarks." It was first theorized that the search might end with three basic types of quarks, "but to understand the structure of the new psi particle, a fourth quark is very likely," one with a special property arbitrarily called charm.

The *Washington Post* described the significance of the breakthrough with a certain elegance of brevity. "While it's making them work harder, the finding of the psi or J particle has simplified things for high-energy physicists. It says there are hundreds of subatomic particles but only a few fundamental entities that make up the cosmos, not dozens and dozens as has been supposed."

Working independently at opposite ends of the continent, Richter and Ting used dissimilar exploratory methods. Heading large teams of investigators, each spent years planning his experiments and amassing the necessary equipment. Then, curiously, they both discovered the same particle within weeks of each other and jointly announced the news in 1974. Another interesting aspect of this prize was its presentation for work barely two years old, a fact justified perhaps by the scientific community's consensus on its revolutionary importance.

WIDE WORLD

Burton Richter

Richter, who was born in Brooklyn, N.Y., March 22, 1931, received his doctorate from the Massachusetts Institute of Technology (MIT). Determined to investigate the behaviour of matter and energy at their most fundamental levels, he began work at Stanford University, where he built the world's first pair of electron storage rings, in which intense beams of particles could be made to collide with each other. In the 1960s he designed the Stanford Positron-Electron Accelerating Ring (SPEAR), a larger device that drove particles of matter and antimatter together at many times the energy of the older storage rings. It was anticipated that such energetic collisions might create heavy, motionless, very unstable particles, yet the massive particle that did result at one specific collision energy had a lifetime 1,000 times longer than expected—on the order of a hundredth of a billionth of a billionth of a second. Theorized to be formed of two charmed quarks, it was this entity that Richter dubbed psi.

Working on Long Island, N.Y., Ting used the Brookhaven National Laboratory's Alternating Gradient Synchrotron, a machine some 200 m in diameter. With it he fired streams of protons at a stationary beryllium target and observed the decaying particles that resulted. Gathering fruitful data was like "hearing a cricket close to a jumbo jet," according to the Royal Swedish Academy of Sciences. Sorting through the subatomic debris, Ting observed evidence of the same heavy particle, which he called J.

WIDE WORLD

Samuel C. C. Ting

Ting was born in Ann Arbor, Mich., Jan. 26, 1936, while his father was studying at the University of Michigan. He returned with his family to mainland China, then moved to Taiwan and finally to the U.S. as a student in 1956. He earned three degrees at the University of Michigan, including a doctorate, in six years.

Subsequently he worked at the European Organization for Nuclear Research (CERN) in Geneva and taught physics at Columbia University in New York City. A professor at MIT since 1967, by 1976 he was directing three research groups, at Brookhaven, CERN, and Hamburg, West Germany. He frequently worked seven 16-hour days a week at CERN and commuted home to Lexington, Mass., to visit his wife and daughters every other weekend.

Prize for Physiology or Medicine

Primitive people sent D. Carleton Gajdusek and Baruch S. Blumberg down independent investigative paths that led to the 1976 Nobel Prize for Physiology or Medicine. The two versatile physicians had something else in common: both were cited for medical research that at its inception had no obvious practical application.

In 1955 Gajdusek began work at the Walter and Eliza Hall Institute for Medical Research in Melbourne, Australia. He learned from a medical patrol officer that the Fore people, an aboriginal tribe in New Guinea, were being decimated by a disease they called kuru, meaning trembling. He went out to study the Fore and the fatal disease that seemed unique to them.

Quickly learning their language, the scientist traded axes and tobacco for the bodies of kuru victims. Inside a bamboo-walled field laboratory he performed autopsies; outside he studied the tribe's culture. Gajdusek postulated that kuru was an infectious neurological disease transmitted through the ritual eating of human brains, part of the tribal funeral custom in which survivors hoped to assure the deceased's immortality while acquiring his virtues. But the disease was odd; infected persons did not become ill immediately, often not for years.

In 1958 he joined the U.S. National Institutes of Health (NIH) outside Washington, D.C., and studied the matter further. Working with Clarence J. Gibbs, Jr., he implanted filtered brain material from kuru victims into the brains of healthy chimpanzees. Months later the animals exhibited neurogenic symptoms associated with kuru. The investigators concluded that the disease was transmitted by a slow-acting virus, perhaps one that lies dormant for long periods.

Following this pivotal discovery, slow viruses became implicated as causes of such puzzling nervous disorders as multiple sclerosis, Parkinson's disease, and a rare form of senility known as Creutzfeldt-Jakob disease. Gajdusek said the next order of virological business was to understand how the minute kuru virus actually works after its long dormancy.

A glance at the laureate's résumé suggested that he might look very far afield and come up with solid connections. Cited for work in virology, he was also a recognized expert in anthropology, comparative child behaviour, pediatrics, genetics, immunology, and neurology. He spoke seven European and Middle Eastern languages and several tribal ones.

Born in Yonkers, N.Y., Sept. 9, 1923, to Hungarian immigrants, Gajdusek graduated summa cum laude from the University of Rochester (N.Y.) when he was 19. He earned his medical degree at Harvard University three years later, then did postdoctoral work at the California Institute of Technology and Harvard before serving as a visiting investigator at the Pasteur Institute in the Iranian capital of Teheran. In the course of his travels, Gajdusek, a bachelor, adopted 16 sons in various parts of the South Pacific. Regarding the Nobel honorarium, he said, "I'll use the money to put the boys through college."

Another globetrotter, Blumberg worked variously in Africa, India, the Arctic, and the Pacific islands to understand why certain ethnic groups contracted certain ailments and others did not. "In a lot of these places I would be the only outsider except for some anthropologist. So naturally I got interested in anthropology and such questions as how social behaviors influence susceptibility to disease."

While studying samples of blood serum from thousands of persons, he discovered that the blood of an Australian Aborigine—and of an unevenly distributed fraction of the world population—contained a protein also found in the blood of hepatitis victims.

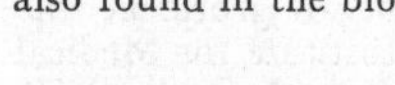

D. Carleton Gajdusek

WIDE WORLD

WIDE WORLD

Baruch S. Blumberg

Naming it the "Australia antigen," he learned that it was part of the virus that caused hepatitis B infection, a serious form of the liver disease that in chronic cases was suspected of leading to cancer.

Early application of his work led naturally to an antigen test for hepatitis B virus. Widely used in blood banks, the test sharply reduced the once tragically common transmittal of the virus via blood transfusions. A later result was the development of an experimental hepatitis vaccine.

Blumberg was born July 28, 1925, in New York City. He studied at Union College in Schenectady, N.Y., received his medical degree from Columbia University's College of Physicians and Surgeons and a doctorate in biochemistry from the University of Oxford in 1957. Like Gajdusek, Blumberg performed part of his work at NIH. As of 1976 he was associate director of the Institute for Cancer Research in Philadelphia and a professor of anthropology at the University of Pennsylvania.

The father of four joked, "I'm especially pleased that someone from Philadelphia won [a Nobel]. It's appropriate in the bicentennial year and makes up in part for the Phillies not making it to the World Series."

Prize for Economics

Milton Friedman, winner of the 1976 Prize for Economics, was a fiscal conservative and controversial dean of the so-called Chicago school of economists. The *New York Times* described him as "perhaps the foremost American exponent of the monetarist school of economics, which maintains that the economic cycle is determined more by money supply and interest rates than by fiscal policy. His philosophy is generally associated with a 'laissez-faire' or hands-off policy in regard to business and trade." In these respects he was at odds with the followers of John Maynard Keynes, who had held sway among academics and governments for many years.

The Royal Swedish Academy of Sciences stated that "Friedman was a pioneer in the well-founded reaction to the earlier post-Keynesian one-sidedness. And he succeeded —mainly thanks to his independence and brilliance—in initiating a very lively and fruitful scientific debate. . . . In fact, the macroeconometric models of today differ greatly from those of a couple of decades ago as far as the monetary factors go—and this is very much thanks to Friedman. The widespread debate on Friedman's theories also led to a review of monetary policies pursued by local banks, in the first place in the United States. It is very rare for an economist to wield such influence, . . . not only on the direction of scientific research but also on actual policy."

Friedman was cited for "his achievements in the fields of consumption analysis, monetary history and theory and for his demonstration of the complexity of stabilization policy." His selection followed an unusually heated debate among the Nobel award committee, which centred particularly around allegations that Friedman had advised the military junta in Chile—to the horror of its moral opponents. Friedman's colleagues and supporters strongly rejected these stories as mere "myths." Such arguments aside, much of Friedman's work was seen as apolitical. He apparently did not change his economic tune to harmonize with any politician; rather, he broke with politicians when they ignored his views.

Friedman's impact on the science of economics was undeniable. One observer wrote that his "most important overall contribution has doubtless been his success in reviving respect for the market as an allocator of resources and promoter of economic efficiency. A great deal of recent work in regulatory theory—and the push in Washington for deregulation—is the result of his work." Another notable effect was the U.S. Federal Reserve Board's apparent new inclination to follow Friedman's "fixed-throttle" policy, which called for steadily increasing the money supply by 3–5% per year in order to support noninflationary economic growth.

Friedman was born in Brooklyn, N.Y., on July 31, 1912, and grew up in Rahway, N.J., the son of immigrant parents. He worked his way through Rutgers University where he was a student of Arthur Burns, who later became chairman of the Federal Reserve Board; Friedman took advanced degrees at the University of Chicago and Columbia University. Former president of the American Economic Association, he went to the University of Chicago in 1946, where he later occupied the Paul Snowden Russell Distinguished Services chair.

Paul A. Samuelson, a previous laureate, frequent professional adversary, and fellow *Newsweek* columnist, called Friedman "an economist's economist." When he learned of his selection, Friedman said "it is not the pinnacle of my career" and that he cared more for the opinion of his peers than for that of the people on the Nobel selection committee. (PHILIP KOPPER)

Milton Friedman

WIDE WORLD

OBITUARIES

The following is a selected list of prominent men and women who died during 1976.

Aalto, (Hugo) Alvar Henrik, Finnish architect (b. Kuortane, Fin., Feb. 3, 1898—d. Helsinki, Fin., May 11, 1976), had an influence on modern architecture that ranks with that of Walter Gropius, Ludwig Mies van der Rohe, and Le Corbusier. But Aalto differed from such pioneers of the "international style" in his individualistic, "organic" approach, which in its finest expressions was characterized by deep affinity with Finnish landscape and culture. After graduating from the Helsinki University of Technology in 1921, he established his reputation with three major commissions: The Turun Sanomat newspaper offices in Turku (1930); the tuberculosis sanatorium at Paimio (1933); and the Municipal Library at Viipuri (1930–35; destroyed 1940). He also designed the Baker House dormitory at the Massachusetts Institute of Technology, where he was research professor from 1946 to 1948. Though he also built in France, West Germany, and other countries, the finest examples of his mature style are in Finland. Such creations as the Säynätsalo town hall group (1950–52) illustrate his awareness of individual settings and his use of regional materials. Aalto also designed furniture, often using laminated and bent birchwood. Among many awards and honours, he received gold medals from the Royal Institute of British Architects (1957) and the American Institute of Architects (1963).

WIDE WORLD

Abramsky, Yehezkiel, Jewish rabbi and renowned legal scholar (b. Grodno, Russia, March 1886—d. Jerusalem, Israel, Sept. 18, 1976), wrote 28 books of commentary on the *Tosefta,* a collection of oral traditions related to Jewish law. Rabbi at Smolevitch and later at Slutzk (1924–28), he was arrested in Moscow (1930) and sentenced without trial to five years of penal servitude in Siberia on suspicion of informing a U.S. delegation about alleged lack of religious freedom in the Soviet Union. He was released in 1931 and expelled from the U.S.S.R. as a result of international pressure. He went to Britain and was rabbi of the Machzike Hadath congregation in East London, and in 1935 became head of the London Beth Din (court of the chief rabbi). He retired to Israel in 1951.

Albers, Josef, German-born artist (b. Bottrop, Germany, March 19, 1888—d. New Haven, Conn., March 25, 1976), was a painter, poet, and influential art teacher and theoretician, important as an innovator of such art styles as Colour Field painting and Op art. In 1920 he became a student at the newly formed Bauhaus, soon to become the most important school of design in Germany. After 1923, when he became a teacher at the Bauhaus, Albers rejected all art based on self-expression and emotion in favour of art based on purely intellectual calculation. He created a style characterized by the reiteration of abstract rectilinear patterns and the use of highly saturated primary colours along with white and black. In 1933, when the Nazis closed the Bauhaus, he went to North Carolina where he organized the fine-arts curriculum at Black Mountain College and taught there until 1949. The following year, he began an eight-year tenure as chairman of the art department of Yale University. In his series of engraved plastic "Transformations of a Scheme" (1948–52), and in the series of drawings "Structural Constellations" (1953–58), he created complex linear designs, each subject to a variety of spatial interpretations. His paintings, on the other hand, explored colour relationships. "Homage to the Square" (begun in 1949) consists of superimposed squares of colour so calculated that the colour of each square appears to alter the sizes, hues, and apparent spatial relationships of the others. Like his paintings, his poems play with various modes of reality, but they have a sense of lyricism and gentle irony. They were published in *Poems and Drawings* (1958).

Anda, Geza, Hungarian-born pianist (b. Budapest, Hung., Nov. 19, 1921—d. Zürich, Switz., June 13, 1976), was best known for his interpretations of Mozart, all of whose concerti he recorded with the Salzburg Mozarteum; the second movement of the Concerto in C Major K 467 was chosen for the film *Elvira Madigan* and became a best-seller. He was a pupil of Erno Dohnanyi at the Budapest Academy of Music and made his debut in 1939 playing Brahms's Concerto No. 2 in B Flat Major with the Amsterdam Concertgebouw. Anda, who emigrated to Switzerland in 1943 and took Swiss citizenship in 1955, popularized Bela Bartok's concerti, all of which he recorded. In 1969 he became an honorary member of the Royal Academy of Music in London and played with the English Chamber Orchestra and the Northern Sinfonia.

Armstrong, Anthony (Anthony Armstrong Willis), British author and playwright (b. Jan. 2, 1897—d. Haslemere, England, Feb. 10, 1976), was a frequent contributor (1924–33) to the humorous magazine *Punch.* While wartime editor of the Royal Air Force's training memorandum *Tee Emm,* he created the fictitious blunderer Pilot Officer Prune. He also wrote humorous books as well as plays for radio and stage. *Ten Minute Alibi* (1933) and *The Strange Case of Mr. Pelham* (1957) were among those made into films. Armstrong was made an Officer of the British Empire in 1944.

Bachauer, Gina (Mrs. Alec Sherman), Greek-born pianist (b. Athens, Greece, May 21, 1913—d. Athens, Aug. 22, 1976), was a forceful, intellectual performer, supremely able to interpret such works of masculine power as Beethoven's "Emperor" concerto. She went from the Athens Conservatory to Paris where she was taught by Alfred Cortot and worked with Sergey Rachmaninoff. She launched an international career after winning a gold medal in Vienna in 1933. During World War II she gave over 600 concerts for Allied forces in the Middle East. Four years after moving to Britain, she married (1951) the conductor Alec Sherman, and commenced annual tours in the U.S.

Baddeley, Angela (Madeline Angela Clinton-Baddeley), British actress (b. London, England, July 4, 1904—d. Essex, England, Feb. 22, 1976), known to older theatregoers as a versatile classical player, achieved new fame and gained wider recognition as Mrs. Bridges, a grumpy, but lovable cook in the television series "Upstairs, Downstairs." Her long career included roles in *Night Must Fall* (1935), *Dear Octopus* (1938), *The Light of Heart* (1940), *Love for Love* (1943), and *The Cherry Orchard* (1965). When she became ill she was starring in a London production of the musical *A Little Night Music.*

Baker, Sir Stanley, Welsh film actor (b. Rhondda Valley, South Wales, Feb. 28, 1928—d. Málaga, Spain, June 28, 1976), was a handsome actor of spirit and intelligence who gained success in strong masculine roles, notably under Joseph Losey's direction in *Blind Date, The Criminal, Eve,* and *Accident.* He made his screen debut in *Undercover* (1943) and spent two years with the Birmingham Repertory Company before acting in *The Cruel Sea, The Red Beret, Sea Fury, Hell Is a City,* and *The Guns of Navarone.* Having formed his own company in the 1960s, he made and played in *Zulu* and *Sands of Kalahari.* Baker, who was knighted in 1976, became a director of Harlech Television in 1968.

Beaumont, Cyril William, British balletomane (b. Lambeth, London, England, Nov. 1, 1891—d. London, May 24, 1976), a noted critic and scholar of classical ballet and the author of *The Complete Book of Ballets* (1937), wrote prolifically on all aspects of ballet and other dance forms. For others who shared Beaumont's love of dance, his London bookstore (1910–65) was a house of treasures beyond compare. While editor (1924–70) of the magazine *Dance Journal,* he wrote about such dancers as Pavlova, Nijinsky, and Fonteyn, and called upon his impressive array of background knowledge in discussing such ballets as *Giselle* and *Swan Lake.* Beaumont Press (1917–31) issued not only dance manuals produced in collaboration with Enrico Cecchetti but the works of many renowned contemporary novelists and poets. Beaumont's memoirs, entitled *Bookseller at the Ballet,* were published in 1974.

Berkeley, Busby (William Berkeley Enos), U.S. choreographer (b. Los Angeles, Calif., Nov. 29, 1895—d. Palm Springs, Calif., March 14, 1976), added to the glamour of Hollywood with a series of highly imaginative and extravagantly produced musicals. Berkeley was able to create a dazzling kaleidoscope of constantly developing patterns by filming (sometimes directly overhead, or even from the bottom of a huge swimming pool) as 100 or more women performed in unison. Besides the *Gold Diggers* films of the 1930s, he was responsible for such other musicals as *Forty-second Street, Footlight Parade, Ziegfeld Girl, Broadway Serenade,* and *For Me and My Gal.*

Blair, David (David Butterfield), British ballet dancer (b. Halifax, England, July 27, 1932—d. London, England, April 1, 1976), who became a principal dancer at 18, created many roles for the Sadler's Wells Theatre Ballet (1947–53) and the Royal Ballet at Covent Garden (1953–73), but his position as the Royal Ballet's leading male dancer suffered a partial eclipse with the arrival of Rudolf Nureyev in 1962. Blair gave memorable performances dancing the lead roles in John Cranko's *Pineapple Poll, Harlequin in April,* and *The Prince of the Pagodas* and in Sir Frederick Ashton's *La Fille Mal Gardée.* During the 1960s he worked as producer with several U.S. ballet companies, notably the American Ballet Theatre in New York. From 1973 he worked with the Royal Academy of Dancing and in 1964 was made a Commander of the Order of the British Empire.

Bodnaras, Emil, Romanian Communist leader (b. Iaslovats, Moldavia, Rom. [later Moldavian S.S.R.], Feb. 10, 1904—d. Bucharest, Rom., Jan. 24, 1976), played a major part in the overthrow of Gen. Ion Antonescu's dictatorship in 1944 and in the post-World War II Communist succession to the monarchy. He was a member of the party Politburo from 1945 until his death, minister of defense from 1947 until 1955, and held other high posts in party and government leadership, including the vice-presidency of the State Council from 1967. Of German-Ukrainian parentage, Bodnaras became a career army officer in 1927 and defected to the U.S.S.R. in 1932. In 1934, on a secret mission to Romania, he was arrested and imprisoned until 1942. On his release he went back to the U.S.S.R., finally returning home at the time of the 1944 coup and Romania's armistice with the Allies. Despite his close Soviet links, Bodnaras was a firm supporter of Pres. Nicolae Ceausescu's pursuance of the independent line adopted by the Romanian Communists in 1964.

BOOK OF THE YEAR

Bosco, Henri Fernand Joseph Marius, French novelist and poet (b. Avignon, France, Nov. 16, 1888—d. Nice, France, May 4, 1976), won the French Academy's prize for literature in 1968. Many of his stories were set in his native Provence and showed deeply primitive life-patterns hidden beneath the veneer of modern society. Bosco, who was educated as a language teacher, was professor of comparative literatures at the French Institute in Naples from 1920 to 1930. His more than 30 books include *Pierre Lampédouze* (1931), *Hyacinthe* (1941), and *L'Antiquaire* (1954). *Le Renard dans l'île* (1956; *Fox in the Island,* 1958) and *Barboche* (1957; Eng. trans., 1959) were among those translated into English.

Bradwell, Thomas Edward Neil Driberg, Baron, British journalist and politician (b. Crowborough, Sussex, England, May 22, 1905—d. London, England, Aug. 12, 1976), served on Lord Beaverbrook's *Daily Express* from 1928 to 1943, for ten years as its original "William Hickey" columnist. As a member of Parliament for Maldon, Essex (1942–55), and for Barking (1959–74), he generally associated himself with the leftwing of the Labour Party. During World War II and in Korea he was a war correspondent and became a frequent lecturer and broadcaster. Driberg never left the back benches of Parliament, though he belonged to the Labour Party National Executive Committee (1949–72) and was its chairman (1957–58). He was made a life peer in 1974. As an active Anglican interested in liturgical reform, he also served (1968) on the Churches' Commission on International Affairs at Uppsala, Sweden. His books include a critical biography of Beaverbrook and *Guy Burgess: A Portrait with Background,* both published in 1956.

Brecon, David Vivian Penrose Lewis, 1st Baron, Welsh parliamentarian (b. Aug. 14, 1905—d. Llanfeigan, Wales, Oct. 10, 1976), was U.K. minister of state for Welsh affairs (1957–64) in Harold Macmillan's Conservative government and as such was Wales's first direct representative in Parliament. In 1973 he was appointed a member of the British delegation to the European Parliament at Strasbourg, France. Brecon, who was made a peer in 1957, developed the family quarrying business and became chairman of the Joint Industrial Council for the Quarrying Industry and a director of what was then Television Wales and West Ltd.

Britten, (Edward) Benjamin Britten, Baron, English composer (b. Lowestoft, Suffolk, England, Nov. 22, 1913—d. Aldeburgh, Suffolk, Dec. 4, 1976), was recognized at home and abroad as England's foremost operatic composer since Henry Purcell. He excelled in the display of human voice and instruments together and in his settings of the English language: in opera, sacred music-drama, choral symphony and pageant, and in works for children's voices. Deeply rooted as his inspiration was in the earlier traditions of English music, he was alert to all that 20th-century music had to offer, and this made him, especially from the mid-1960s onward, one of the most contemporary of composers. He was also an outstanding pianist and conductor.

Britten composed as a child; at 12 he began studies under Frank Bridge and attended the Royal College of Music, London. He composed at first for the radio, cinema, and theatre (music for plays by W. H. Auden). During 1939–42 he was in the U.S., where he wrote *Sinfonia da Requiem,* his only major orchestral symphony, and his first opera, *Paul Bunyan,* to Auden's text. Back in England he undertook concert tours with the singer Peter Pears, who became his lifelong companion, and composed the *Hymn to St. Cecilia,* with Auden's words, and *Serenade.*

It was, however, his opera *Peter Grimes* (1945, libretto after George Crabbe's *The Borough*) that brought him to world notice. It was succeeded by *The Rape of Lucretia* (1946) and *Albert Herring* (1947), both chamber operas; *Billy Budd* (1951); *Gloriana* (1953); and *The Turn of the Screw* (1954, based on Henry James's story), a chamber opera. During this period Britten formed the English Opera Group and in 1948 launched the Aldeburgh Festival. Later major operas included *Death in Venice* (1973, based on Thomas Mann's story).

Britten's choral music and church entertainments included *Curlew River* (1964), which owed something to Japanese Nō drama as well as to medieval church drama, and the church "parables" *The Burning Fiery Furnace* (1966) and *The Prodigal Son* (1968). Among song cycles were *The Holy Sonnets of John Donne* (1945) and *Songs and Proverbs of William Blake* (1965). *War Requiem,* his masterpiece for choir and orchestra, was based textually on the Latin requiem mass and poems by Wilfred Owen; other choral works included *Spring Symphony* (1949) and *Voices for Today* (1965), written for the 20th anniversary of the UN.

Britten's works for children were especially notable: *Let's Make an Opera* (1949), in which an audience mostly of children joins in with a cast mostly of children; *Noye's Fludde* (1958), a church pageant opera for children's orchestra; and *The Golden Vanity* (1967), for boys' voices and piano. Britten was created a Companion of Honour (1953), was awarded the Order of Merit (1965), and was made a life peer (1976).

Buchan, Alastair Francis, British diplomatic and strategic theorist (b. London, England, Sept. 9, 1918—d. Oxford, England, Feb. 3, 1976), was a seminal thinker about the strategic consequences of nuclear weapons. He was the son of John Buchan, 1st Baron Tweedsmuir, a former governor-general of Canada. Buchan was educated at Eton College and Christ Church, Oxford, and became a staff officer in the Canadian Army during World War II. From 1948 to 1951 he was assistant editor of *The Economist,* then became Washington correspondent (1951–55) and a diplomatic and defense correspondent (1955–58) in London on *The Observer.* He next directed the Institute for Strategic Studies (1958–69), was commandant of the Royal College of Defence Studies in London (1970–71), and in 1972 was appointed Montague Burton professor of international relations at the University of Oxford. His writings include *War in Modern Society* (1966) and *Life of Walter Bagehot* (1959).

Bultmann, Rudolf (Karl), German theologian (b. Wiefelstede, Oldenburg, Germany, Aug. 20, 1884—d. Marburg, West Germany, July 30, 1976),

COURTESY, JAMES M. ROBINSON

was regarded as one of the most important, and most controversial, New Testament scholars of the 20th century. Educated at the universities of Tübingen, Berlin, and Marburg, he taught at the universities of Breslau (1916–20) and Giessen (1920–21) before joining the University of Marburg (1921), where he remained until his retirement in 1951. Bultmann, who was greatly influenced at Marburg by the Existentialist philosopher Martin Heidegger, profoundly influenced the course of New Testament studies by his efforts to demythologize the New Testament in order to discover its true message. He also made important contributions to philosophy and systematic theology. Among his principal works were *History of the Synoptic Tradition* (1921; Eng. trans., 1963), *Jesus and the Word* (1926; Eng. trans., 1934), and *Theology of the New Testament* (1948–53; Eng. trans., 1952, 1955).

Burra, Edward, British painter (b. London, England, 1905—d. Sussex, England, Oct. 22, 1976), achieved recognition and acclaim as a surrealist who, however, belonged to no particular school

MAURICE AMBLER—CAMERA PRESS

or movement. After studying in London he worked in Paris and southern France painting bizarre, underworld scenes peopled by figures that often resembled automatons. His first one-man exhibition was held in 1929. His later work was much affected by the Spanish Civil War and World War II. A retrospective exhibition was held in London's Tate Gallery in 1973.

Butler, Sir Mervyn Andrew Haldane, British army general (b. Toronto, Ont., July 1, 1913—d. England, Jan. 3, 1976), commanded the British parachute brigade that took part in the Anglo-French-Israeli attack on Suez in 1956. Divisional commander in the British Army of the Rhine (BAOR) from 1962 to 1964, he held staff appointments during 1964–67, then returned to the BAOR as corps commander (1968–70). He was appointed commandant of the Royal College of Defence Studies in 1972 but retired for health reasons the following year. Colonel commandant of the Parachute Regiment from 1967, he was knighted in 1968.

Calder, Alexander, U.S. sculptor (b. Lawnton [now part of Philadelphia], Pa., July 22, 1898—

LONDON DAILY EXPRESS/PICTORIAL PARADE

d. New York, N.Y., Nov. 11, 1976), originated the mobile, a type of kinetic sculpture that moves with the aid of air currents and its own delicate balance. After graduating (1919) as an engineer from Stevens Institute of Technology, Hoboken, N.J., Calder studied art in New York and was for some time a commercial artist. In 1926 he went to Paris, where he met such avant-garde artists as Joan Miró and Piet Mondrian. In 1931 he began to make motor-driven sculptures, a form he abandoned in 1932 in favour of mobiles. While often lacking in specific reference, his mobiles and stationary metal sculptures (stabiles) recall movements, shapes, and structures in nature. Calder's inventiveness also produced a mercury fountain, stage sets, and many commissions for architectural sculpture. His work can be seen all over the U.S. as well as in Europe, Japan, Australia, and South America.

Casey, Richard Gardiner Casey, Baron, Australian statesman (b. Brisbane, Australia, Aug. 29, 1890—d. Melbourne, Australia, June 17, 1976), was Australian minister for external affairs (1951–60) and governor-general of Australia (1965–69). He studied engineering at the universities of Melbourne and Cambridge, and worked as a mining engineer in Australia until 1924, when he joined the Department of External Affairs and was sent to London. There he attended the Imperial Conference of 1930. After returning to Australia, Casey represented Corio, Victoria, in Parliament (1931–40) as a member of the United Australia Party, became treasurer in J. A. Lyons' government in 1935, and attended the Imperial and London conferences in 1937 and 1939. In 1940 he was appointed Australia's first minister to the U.S. and established close relations with Pres. Franklin D. Roosevelt. Persuaded by British Prime Minister Winston Churchill, the Australian government permitted Casey to join the War Cabinet as British minister of state in the Middle East in 1942 and then

COURTESY, AUSTRALIAN INFORMATION SERVICE

to go to India to govern famine-stricken Bengal (1944–45).

Casey later served Australia's Liberal-Country Party government as minister of works and housing (1949–51) and of national development (1950–51) in charge of the Snowy Mountains hydroelectric project. In 1951 he was made minister for external affairs; shortly afterward the ANZUS Treaty, for mutual Pacific area defense, was signed by Australia, New Zealand, and the U.S. At the 1959 Washington, D.C., conference on the future of Antarctica he was able to secure acceptance of existing territorial claims, including Australia's extensive stake. Casey was made the first Australian life peer in 1960. He published a number of books, including his diaries as foreign minister.

Cassin, René-Samuel, French jurist (b. Bayonne, France, Oct. 5, 1887—d. Paris, France, Feb. 20, 1976), was the principal author of the United Nations' Universal Declaration of Human Rights (1948) and the recipient of the Nobel Prize for Peace in 1968. As an acknowledged authority on international law he served at the League of Nations from 1924 to 1938, then joined Gen. Charles de Gaulle in Britain as a prominent member of his government-in-exile during World War II. Cassin subsequently held high legal and administrative offices in France, was a delegate to the United Nations and a founder of UNESCO, president of the UN's Human Rights Commission (1955–57), and president of the European Court of Human Rights (1965–68).

Chou En-lai, Chinese statesman (b. Huaian, Kiangsu Province, China, 1898—d. Peking, China, Jan. 8, 1976), was the architect under Mao Tse-tung of Communist China's foreign policy. A descendant of an old Mandarin family, Chou attended Japanese universities for two years before returning to China in 1919. He was then sent by Mao to study in Paris, where he became a Communist organizer and met the Vietnamese revolutionary Ho Chi Minh. Having returned to China in 1924, he was appointed by Mao to the political department of the Whampoa Military Academy where Chiang Kai-shek was training a new generation of military leaders. In 1927, the year Chiang Kai-shek turned definitively

ROBERT COHEN—AGIP/PICTORIAL PARADE

against the Communists, Chou was elected to the Politburo of the party and between 1928 and 1931 traveled to Moscow and worked in the Communist underground in Shanghai. During the epic Long March of the Communists to Shensi Province in 1934–35, he was political commissar of the Red Army.

During World War II Chou served as commissar for foreign affairs of the Yen-an Communist government that agreed to support Chiang's Nationalists against the Japanese invaders. As head of liaison, Chou accompanied Mao to the 1945 Chungking talks with Chiang and again participated in talks in 1946 with U.S. Gen. George C. Marshall that failed to establish a Communist-Nationalist coalition in China. On Oct. 1, 1949, when the People's Republic of China came into existence, Chou was named premier and retained the post until he died. On Feb. 14, 1950, Chou signed in Moscow a 30-year Chinese-Soviet treaty of alliance and in 1954 headed the Chinese delegation at the conference on Korea and Indochina in Geneva. At the 1955 Afro-Asian conference that convened in Bandung, Indon., he offered support to Asian neutrals. Between 1956 and 1964 Chou traveled widely throughout Europe, Asia, and Africa and proclaimed the latter continent "ripe for revolution." Though Chou visited Moscow in November 1964, fundamental differences between the U.S.S.R. and China were not resolved. During the Great Proletarian Cultural Revolution (1965–69), Chou was, quite typically, an advocate of moderation. In October 1971 Chou learned from

U.S. special envoy Henry Kissinger that Pres. Richard Nixon had decided to withdraw from Vietnam. The historic meeting between Mao and Nixon that took place in Peking in February 1972 was, to a great extent, arranged and implemented by Chou En-lai.

Christie, Dame Agatha (Mary Clarissa) (LADY MALLOWAN), British detective novelist and playwright (b. Torquay, England, Sept. 15, 1890—d. Wallingford, England, Jan. 12, 1976), whose books sold more than 400 million copies and were

SNOWDON—CAMERA PRESS

translated into 103 languages, was one of the world's most widely read authors. Though her first detective hero was the eccentric Belgian Hercule Poirot, she later preferred to write of the elderly and inquisitive spinster Jane Marple, first introduced in *Murder at the Vicarage* (1930). During World War I Christie became a qualified pharmacist, thus acquiring knowledge of poisons utilized in her first Poirot story, *The Mysterious Affair at Styles* (1920). After her first major success, *The Murder of Roger Ackroyd* (1926), she produced some 75 other novels, including *Murder on the Orient Express* (1934) and nondetective stories under the pseudonym Mary Westmacott. Her plays include *Ten Little Niggers* (1943; U.S. title *Ten Little Indians*) and *The Mousetrap* (1952). At the time of her death the latter had run continuously for nearly 24 years in London. Christie frequently traveled with her archaeologist husband, Sir Max Mallowan, in the Middle East, a setting she used for some of her stories. *Curtain,* in which Poirot meets his end, appeared in 1975, and her last book, *Sleeping Murder,* a Jane Marple story, in 1976; both had been written several years earlier but had been withheld from publication.

Chu Teh, Chinese military leader (b. I-Lung, Szechwan, China, Dec. 18, 1886—d. Peking, China, July 6, 1976), was founder of the Chinese Communist Army. The son of a landlord, he was reckless and adventurous in youth and gravitated toward military life. After graduating from the Yunnan Military Academy, he rose rapidly and by 1916 was a brigadier general. In the early 1920s he went to Germany where he met Chou En-lai and was persuaded to join the Chinese Communist Party. He studied in Moscow before returning to China in 1926 where he joined the Kuomintang. In 1927 he commanded an officers' training school at Nan-ch'ang. In the same year, Chiang Kai-shek and the Kuomintang turned against the Communists. Chu organized a revolt among Kuomintang troops in Kiangsi and in 1928 joined forces with Mao Tse-tung. Thus began a military partnership that was to revolutionize China. In 1931 Mao appointed Chu commander in chief of the Red Army. Defeated by Chiang, the Communist forces under Chu began the Long March (1934–35) to Yen-an in northern Shensi. On Aug. 10, 1945, Chu's army moved into Manchuria to accept the surrender of the Japanese and to cooperate with the Soviet armies. In 1946 Chiang launched an all-out offensive against Chu's armies in the north, but the Communists rolled back the huge Kuomintang forces in a final and decisive victory. On Oct. 1, 1949, the People's Republic of China was established and Chu became one of the six vice-chairmen of the new government and commander in chief of its armed forces. In 1954 he was elected vice-chairman of the Central People's Government Council, which made him, in effect, Mao's successor. In 1959 he was relieved of this position and lost his place on the Standing Committee of the Politburo, but was reinstated in 1967. In 1975 he became chairman of the Permanent Standing Committee of the National People's Congress (nominal chief of state).

Clarke, David, British archaeologist (b. Nov. 3, 1937—d. Great Chesterford, England, June 28, 1976), was a leading exponent of the "new archaeology," which emphasized quantitative data-handling techniques in prehistoric archaeology. Clarke turned to archaeology from physics and chemistry and chose it as a field for scientific interpretation. Cambridge University granted him a lectureship just before his death; the importance of his work, notably expressed in *Analytical Archaeology* (1968), was acknowledged by U.S. archaeologists and institutions.

Cobb, Lee J. (Leo Jacoby), U.S. actor (b. New York, N.Y., Dec. 8, 1911—d. Woodland Hills, Calif., Feb. 11, 1976), was widely regarded as one of the most accomplished character actors of his day. Though usually cast in supporting roles, Cobb more often than not provided some of the most memorable moments of the production. One of his greatest triumphs, both critically and personally, was his stage portrayal (1949) of Willy Loman, the lead in Arthur Miller's *Death of a Salesman.* In 1969 he also received enthusiastic acclaim as King Lear in his first Shakespearean role. Cobb's numerous other credits included *On the Waterfront, Twelve Angry Men, Anna and the King of Siam, The Brothers Karamazov, Boomerang!,* and the television series "The Virginian."

Cogley, John, U.S. journalist (b. Chicago, Ill., March 16, 1916—d. Santa Barbara, Calif., March 29, 1976), was a Roman Catholic lay theologian who reported regularly on modern Catholic issues, many of which came into sharp focus during the second Vatican Council (1962–65). He took a degree in theology at the University of Fribourg, Switz., and worked with Dorothy Day's Catholic Worker movement during the Depression. After World War II he edited *Today,* a national Catholic youth magazine, then became executive editor (1949) of the weekly journal of opinion, *The Commonweal.* In 1955 Cogley joined the Fund for the Republic in Santa Barbara and produced *Report on Blacklisting* (2 vol., 1956), a hotly discussed exposé of the radio, television, and motion-picture industries and their sanctions against real or suspected political leftists. After two years as religion editor for the *New York Times* (1965–67), he rejoined his former colleagues in Santa Barbara at the (since 1959) Center for the Study of Democratic Institutions and became founding editor of *Center Magazine.* His book *Catholic America* appeared in 1973. That same year, having already given up a weekly syndicated column because of personal differences with the Catholic Church over such matters as birth control, Cogley transferred to the Episcopal Church and was ordained a deacon.

Collins, Sir William Alexander Roy, British publisher (b. Glasgow, Scotland, May 23, 1900—d. Tonbridge, Kent, England, Sept. 21, 1976), fifth in line in the Scottish family business of William Collins Sons and Co., Ltd., maintained its high traditions and added a distinguished general list to its trade in stationery, printing, and Bibles. At first he published mainly middlebrow adventure stories, the work of such authors as Hammond Innes and Alistair MacLean. His interest in natural history stimulated production of the unrivaled Collins Guides on geology and flora and fauna, and he started the New Naturalist Series. He also introduced to British readers the novels of contemporary Russian writers such as Boris Pasternak and Aleksandr Solzhenitsyn. He died just before the launching of his spectacularly successful *Good News Bible.*

Constable, William George, British art historian (b. Derby, England, Oct. 27, 1887—d. Boston, Mass., Feb. 3, 1976), was curator of paintings at the Boston Museum of Fine Arts (1938–57). Previously he had been assistant director (1929–31) of the National Gallery, London; director (1932–38) of the newly founded Courtauld Institute of Art at the University of London; and Slade professor of fine arts at the University of Cambridge (1935–37). He compiled many catalogs of art collections and exhibitions and in 1953 published a definitive study of the 18th-century English artist Richard Wilson. He was a contributor to *Encyclopædia Britannica.*

Cosío Villegas, Daniel, Mexican intellectual (b. Mexico City, Mexico, July 23, 1898—d. Mexico City, March 10, 1976), was a prolific and highly respected author, whose more than 300 books and articles include *Historia moderna de México* (1955–72). His writings on the administration of Pres. Luis Echeverría Álvarez were the first critique of a government still in office. After studying law in Mexico and economics at U.S. universities, Cosío taught in Mexico, founded the Economic Culture Fund publishing house, and was an adviser to various technical bodies, including the UN Economic and Social Council.

Costello, John Aloysius, Irish lawyer and politician (b. Dublin, Ireland, June 20, 1891—d. Dublin, Jan. 5, 1976), was Taoiseach (prime minister) of the Irish republic during 1948–51 and 1954–57. In the interim, and from 1957 to 1959, he was opposition leader in the Dail Eireann (Irish parliament). A graduate of University College, Dublin, he was called to the Irish bar in 1914. From 1922 he was assistant to the new Irish Free State's attorney general and was himself attorney general from 1926 to 1932, when the (Republican) Fianna Fail under Eamon de Valera ousted the Fine Gael (United Ireland) government of William T. Cosgrave. In 1933 Costello was elected to the Dail as a Fine Gael representative, and 15 years later was chosen to lead the coalition that replaced the de Valera government. The following year (1949) he took Ireland out of the Commonwealth, hoping thereby to defuse Republican extremism, which thereafter centred increasingly on partition. In 1951 the Roman Catholic hierarchy's opposition to his government's proposals for state maternity services resulted in its fall. Costello's second administration ended as a result of dissension within the coalition over renewed Irish Republican Army activity. He then returned to his law practice, but remained a member of the Dail until 1959.

Cuisenaire, Émile-Georges, Belgian educator (b. Quaregnon, Belgium, Sept. 7, 1891—d. Thuin, Hainaut, Belgium, Jan. 1, 1976), invented a practical method of teaching arithmetic to children by means of rectangular rods or tally sticks of various lengths and different colours, each representing a number from one to ten. The feasibility of teaching children to count by associating numbers and colours gained international acceptance after the publication of *Nombres en couleur* (1951).

Cunningham, Imogen, U.S. photographer (b. Portland, Ore., April 12, 1883—d. San Francisco, Calif., June 24, 1976), was widely acclaimed for her portraits and for her exquisite photographs of plants and flowers. Her professional career began at the turn of the century when she worked in the studio of Edward S. Curtis, famous for his photographic documentation of the American Indians. After studying photographic chemistry in Dresden, Germany, she opened a portrait studio in Seattle, Wash., and soon established a national reputation. Although her commercial work was straightforward, she also continued to produce soft-focused, allegorical prints, such as "The Woods Beyond the World" (*c.* 1912). After her marriage she moved with her family to San Francisco. On the recommendation of Edward Weston ten of her plant photographs were included in the "Film und Foto" exhibition (1929), sponsored by the Deutscher Werkbund, an association of German designers and architects. In 1932 Cunningham joined the association of West Coast photographers known as Group f.64. Like other members of the group, Cunningham rejected the soft-focused, sentimental photography then still popular in favour of sharply focused prints, such as "Two Callas" (*c.* 1929), that conveyed a sensuous delight in nature. After the breakup of Group f.64, Cunningham ran a portrait gallery and taught at the San Francisco Art Institute. Many of her late prints continued the tradition of Group f.64 of not manipulating the image after the photograph has been taken. Others, however, showed significant image manipulation and betrayed the persistence of Romanticism in her work.

Daetwyler, Max, Swiss pacifist (b. Unterentfelden, Aargau, Switz., Sept. 7, 1886—d. Zumikon, Switz., Jan. 26, 1976), began a personal crusade against war during military service in 1914, and over a period of 60 years visited many countries in the hope of bringing his cause to the attention of their leaders. On two occasions he marched from New York City to the White House and in 1958 he demonstrated in Red Square in Moscow. He undertook hunger strikes and suffered internment and imprisonment for his beliefs. White-bearded and often bearing a white flag, he was a familiar figure in the streets of Zürich.

Daley, Richard J(oseph), U.S. politician (b. Chicago, Ill., May 15, 1902—d. Chicago, Dec. 20, 1976), became one of the nation's best-known Democratic politicians during his long tenure (1955–76) as mayor of the country's second largest city. As a young man he worked in the stockyards and attended law classes at night before being admitted to the bar in 1933. He began his career in politics as an Illinois state representative and senator (1936–46), then became state director of revenue (1948–50) and clerk of Cook County (1950–55). In 1955 he was elected to the first of six consecutive four-year terms as mayor of Chicago. Apparently convinced that he could not carry out his plans for the city without complete and absolute control, he set to work to strengthen the local Democratic political organization, which was highly efficient in "getting out the vote" on election days and was often denounced as corrupt. Numerous large construction projects, both public and private, transformed the face of Chicago during Daley's administration, but only token progress was made on such social issues as racial desegregation. Daley was perhaps never a more controversial figure than during the violent demonstrations that occurred at the Democratic national convention in Chicago in 1968 and when he ordered the police to shoot

PICTORIAL PARADE

to maim looters and to shoot to kill arsonists after the assassination of Martin Luther King, Jr. Though several of Daley's closest political cronies were convicted and imprisoned for graft or other crimes, similar charges were never leveled at Daley himself.

Dalnoki-Veres, Lajos, Hungarian army officer (b. Sepsiszentgyorgy, Hungary, Oct. 4, 1889—d. London, England, March 29, 1976), was a patriot swept away from his country on a tide of changing fortunes. Descended from a Szekler Calvinist military family, he fought in World War I, and after 1920 joined the Hungarian Army. After serving as military attaché in Vienna during the 1930s, he returned to Budapest convinced that Austria's union with Germany would entangle Hungary in Hitler's strategic plans. During the German-Hungarian offensive against the Soviet Union in October 1944 Dalnoki, then a commanding general, was ordered by the Hungarian regent Miklos Horthy to surrender to the Soviet forces. Before he was able to do so, however, he was arrested by the Germans and imprisoned in Germany. After World War II he returned to Hungary to organize the patriotic underground "Hungarian Community," but in 1947 was sentenced to life imprisonment. Freed by the Hungarian rising of October 1956, he reached England, where he became president of the Hungarian League of Freedom Fighters. He wrote a history (1920–45) of the Hungarian Army, which was published (1972) in Hungarian in Munich, West Germany.

Dam, (Carl Peter) Henrik, Danish biochemist (b. Copenhagen, Denmark, Feb. 21, 1895—d. Copenhagen, April 18?, 1976), was awarded, jointly with Edward A. Doisy of the U.S., the 1943 Nobel Prize for Physiology or Medicine for the discovery of the antihemorrhagic vitamin K (Koagulations-

WIDE WORLD

Vitamin). In 1939 Dam and Doisy, working independently, isolated the vitamin from alfalfa (lucerne). A graduate of the Copenhagen Polytechnic Institute (1920) and of the University of Copenhagen (1934), Dam taught in Copenhagen until 1939. In 1940 he went to the U.S. and became senior research associate at the University of Rochester, N.Y. (1942–45). After returning to Denmark in 1946, he was professor of biochemistry and nutrition at the Polytechnic Institute until 1965 and headed the biochemical division of the Danish Fat Research Institute from 1956 to 1963. His many publications included papers on cholesterol metabolism, lipids, and gallstone formation.

D'Arcy, The Rev. Martin Cyril, British Roman Catholic priest (b. Bath, England, June 15, 1888—d. London, England, Nov. 20, 1976), was a Jesuit intellectual whose writings, lectures, and broadcasts influenced many in Britain and the U.S. D'Arcy entered the Society of Jesus at the age of 18 and from Stonyhurst College went to Pope's Hall, Oxford, in 1912, where he took a first in humanities. After his ordination in 1921, he was assigned to Farm Street Church, London. He moved to Campion Hall (formerly Pope's Hall) in 1927 and became its master in 1932; from 1945 to 1950 he was Jesuit provincial superior. Among his more than 20 books were *The Nature of Belief* (1931) and *The Mind and Heart of Love* (1945).

Davies, Rupert, Welsh actor (b. Liverpool, England, 1917—d. London, England, Nov. 22, 1976), won the television actor of the year award in 1961 for his portrayal of Georges Simenon's detective character Maigret, appearing in 52 episodes. In a television serialization of Tolstoy's *War and Peace* he played Count Rostov and appeared in such films as *The Spy Who Came in from the Cold.* He was also an excellent stage actor who graduated from the Young Vic and the Birmingham Repertory to the Old Vic and the West End.

d'Avigdor-Goldsmid, Sir Henry Joseph, 2nd Baronet, British bullion broker and parliamentarian (b. Tonbridge, Kent, England, June 10, 1909—d. London, England, Dec. 11, 1976), Conservative member of Parliament for Walsall South (1955–74), became chairman of the Select Committee on Public Expenditure in 1972. His expertise in financial matters was also recognized by appointments to select committees on nationalized industries, corporation tax, and public expenditure. He became chairman of Bank Leumi in 1961 and held the same post with the Anglo-Israel Bank.

Dehn, Paul, British scriptwriter, critic, and poet (b. Manchester, England, Nov. 5, 1912—d. London, England, Sept. 30, 1976), was particularly successful with his screenplays, which included *The Planet of the Apes* series, the adaptation (1974) of Agatha Christie's *Murder on the Orient Express,* and Franco Zeffirelli's version of *The Taming of the Shrew.* A journalist who quickly specialized in film criticism, he became a member of the distinguished BBC Sunday program "The Critics." He wrote (with the composer James Bernard) the script for *Seven Days to Noon,* as well as libretti for Lennox Berkeley's *A Dinner Engagement* and *Castaway* and for William Walton's *The Bear.* He also published four volumes of poetry.

De La Warr, Herbrand Edward Dundonald Brassey Sackville, 9th Earl, British political figure (b. June 20, 1900—d. London, England, Jan. 28, 1976), was responsible as postmaster general (1951–55) for legislation that authorized commercial television in Britain. A Labour peer who later joined the Conservatives, De La Warr held minor appointments in the Labour governments of 1924 and 1929–31 and served in all the National governments of the 1930s. He served in the Cabinet (1937–38) as lord privy seal, then left the government after a term as president of the Board of Education (1938–40). When he stepped down as chairman of the National Labour Party (1931–43), he became director of Home Flax Production (1943–49).

Deutsch, John James, Canadian economist (b. Quinton, Sask., Feb. 26, 1911—d. Kingston, Ont., March 18, 1976), had a multifaceted career as an educator, government official, and high-level economic adviser. He graduated from Queen's University in Ontario in 1934 and later served his alma mater as chief administrator and professor of economics. Deutsch joined the newly founded Bank of Canada in 1936 as research assistant and held a multitude of other posts before becoming first chairman of the Economic Council of Canada in 1963. He was named director of the Canadian Imperial Bank of Commerce in 1967 and a member of the Canada Council in 1974.

Döpfner, Julius Cardinal, German prelate of the Roman Catholic Church (b. Hausen, Bavaria, Germany, Aug. 26, 1913—d. Munich, West Germany, July 24, 1976), archbishop of Munich from 1961 and president of the West German episcopal conference from 1965, played an important role in the second Vatican Council as one of its four moderators. He studied in Rome, was ordained in 1939, and at 35 became bishop of Würzburg (1948–57), then of Berlin (1957–61). He was created cardinal in 1958 by Pope John XXIII and was later named by Pope Paul VI as vice-president, together with John Cardinal Heenan, of the Vatican commission on contraception. Cardinal Döpfner, a reformist of liberal tendencies, attracted criticism in 1969 when his friend and assistant, Bishop Matthias Defregger, was found to have been implicated in a war crime in Italy in 1944 while serving in the German Army.

Dowling, Eddie (JOSEPH NELSON GOUCHER), U.S. theatre virtuoso (b. Woonsocket, R.I., Dec. 9, 1894—d. Smithfield, R.I., Feb. 18, 1976), was already an established actor, playwright, singer, songwriter, director, and prize-winning producer on Broadway when, in 1945, he rejected a sure-fire commercial success to co-produce, co-direct, narrate, and play in Tennessee Williams' *The Glass Menagerie.* The production made theatrical history and turned the obscure Williams into a celebrity. Up to the time of his retirement in the 1960s, Dowling continued to display his remarkable versatility.

Edwards, Sir Ronald Stanley, British industrialist and academic (b. London, England, May 1, 1910—d. London, Jan. 18, 1976), was chairman (1968–75) and then president of the Beecham multinational pharmaceuticals group before the government took over British Leyland and named him chairman of the U.K.'s largest auto manufacturer. He was also professor of economics, with special reference to industrial organization, at the London School of Economics (LSE), the University of London, from 1949. Edwards, who began work at 15 and obtained a commerce degree by means of a correspondence course, taught at the LSE from 1935, and after war work with the Ministry of Aircraft Production (1940–45) returned to the LSE as Sir Ernest Cassel reader in commerce (1946–49). He was deputy chairman (1957–61) and chairman (1962–68) of the Electricity Council (the central state body responsible for electricity supply), a member of numerous academic boards and governmental committees of inquiry, and published several works on industrial research and business organization. He was knighted in 1963.

Elazar, David, Israeli army commander (b. Sarajevo, Yugos., 1925—d. near Tel Aviv, Israel, April 14, 1976), was accused by a commission of inquiry of bad judgment and lack of preparedness in the fourth Arab-Israeli war that started on Oct. 6, 1973. When Elazar resigned on April 2, 1974, he noted that the commission apparently chose to ignore his role in Israel's spectacular recovery and that Israeli forces crossed the Suez Canal under his command. Elazar migrated to Palestine in 1940, studied at the Hebrew University in Jerusalem, and served in the Haganah, the Jewish illegal army. After fighting in the War of Independence (May 1948—January 1949) he was commissioned in the Israeli Army. During the second Arab-Israeli war (October–November 1956) he commanded a brigade in the Sinai Peninsula; in 1961 he headed the Armoured Corps, and in 1965 the Northern Command. In the third Arab-Israeli war (the so-called Six-Day War of June 1967) troops under Elazar's command conquered the Golan Heights against strong Syrian defenses. Four years later he became chief of general staff and commander in chief of the Israeli Army with the rank of lieutenant general.

Ernst, Max, German-born painter and sculptor (b. Brühl, Germany, April 2, 1891—d. Paris, France, April 1, 1976), was a leading figure of the Surrealist movement and a pioneer of Dadaism in Germany. His mature work was foreshadowed in childhood paintings that contained fantastic and dream-inspired images; years later, while studying psychiatry at the University of Bonn, he became fascinated by the paintings of the mentally ill. After meeting with such artists as August Macke and Jean Arp he dropped his studies and became a full-time painter. After producing "The Elephant of the Célèbes" (1921) under the banner of the Cologne Dadaists, he moved to Paris (1922), where he was a member of the Surrealists from their formation in 1924 until 1938. Paintings of this period, including "The Barbarians March Westwards" (1935), showed an increasingly apocalyptic strain. After

A.F.P./PICTORIAL PARADE

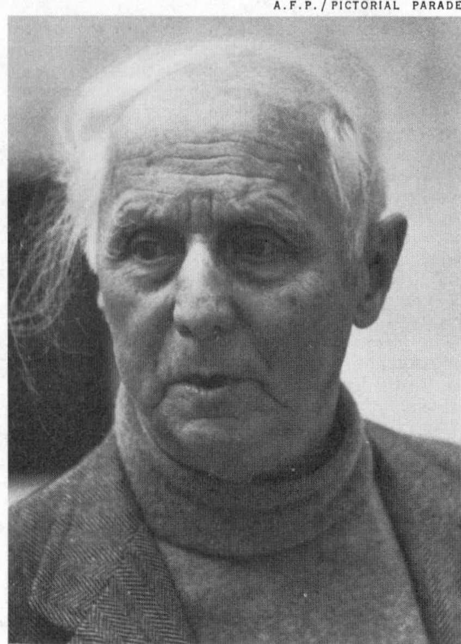

the fall of France (1940) he spent the remainder of World War II in the U.S., became a citizen in 1948, but returned to France the following year and in 1958 acquired French citizenship. Ernst received wide acclaim only after winning grand prize at the Venice Biennale (1954); during the early 1960s retrospective exhibitions were held in New York City, Paris, London, and other European and U.S. cities.

Evans, Dame Edith, English actress (b. London, England, Feb. 8, 1888—d. Kilndown, Kent, England, Oct. 14, 1976), brought rare interpretive gifts to almost every part she played, but was most widely acclaimed for her Shakespearean roles and her acting in Restoration comedy. Evans was a milliner's apprentice and drama student when she was discovered in 1912 by the producer William Poel. In time she undertook a Shakespeare tour with Ellen Terry (1918) and achieved her first popular triumph as Mrs. Millamant in Congreve's *The Way of the World* (1924). The name of Evans later became all but inseparable from such Shakespearean women as Portia, Rosalind, and the nurse in *Romeo and Juliet.* Other outstanding performances included Lady Bracknell in Wilde's *The Importance of Being Earnest* (1939), Mrs. Malaprop in Sheridan's *The Rivals* (1945), Helen Lancaster in *Waters of the Moon*

MIRRORPIC/PHOTO TRENDS

(1951), and Countess Rosmarin Ostenburg in *The Dark Is Light Enough* (1954). During her film career, Evans portrayed a deluded pensioner in *The Whisperers* and received the best actress award at the Berlin International Film Festival (1967). Her last stage performance was a zestful one-woman show in 1974.

Ewald, Marina, German educationist (b. Berlin, Germany, 1888—d. Salem, West Germany, Sept. 14, 1976), was associated with Kurt Hahn in the foundation (1920) of his renowned school at Salem, the principles of which were later followed at Gordonstoun School in Scotland. When the rise of the Nazis obliged Hahn to go to Britain, she ran Salem and its branch schools until they were taken over by the Nazis, then resumed control after World War II. From 1956 she administered a traveling scholarship for sixth-form pupils of European schools.

Farley, James Aloysius, U.S. political strategist (b. Grassy Point, N.Y., May 30, 1888—d. New York, N.Y., June 9, 1976), was a major political figure during the first two presidential terms of Franklin D. Roosevelt. Though never elected to any office higher than that of New York state assemblyman, Farley had great patronage at his disposal as U.S. postmaster general (1933–40) and exercised political power across the entire nation as chairman (1932–40) of the Democratic National Committee. He accompanied Roosevelt during the latter's first two presidential campaigns, winning friends and securing votes for the Democrats with an astonishing display of memory for names and faces. When Roosevelt announced his intention to run for a third term in 1940, Farley parted company. During the following years he continued to attend Democratic national conventions as a delegate and held the positions of chairman of the Coca-Cola Export Co. and, later, president of Coca-Cola International Corp. until his retirement in 1973.

JACK MANNING—THE NEW YORK TIMES

Feather, Victor Grayson Hardie Feather, Baron, British trade unionist (b. Bradford, England, April 10, 1908—d. London, England, July 28, 1976), led the Trades Union Congress (TUC) in its confrontations with governments over industrial relations legislation between 1969 and 1973. He joined the TUC staff in 1937, became assistant secretary (1947–60), assistant general secretary (1960–69), and finally general secretary. The main issues during his leadership of the TUC were the legislative proposals of the Labour government set out in its 1969 White Paper *In Place of Strife,* which had to be scrapped, and the following Conservative government's Industrial Relations Act of 1971, union opposition to which brought the government down and cost Edward Heath the leadership of the Conservative Party. Feather was made a life peer in 1974. On retiring in 1973 he became president of the European Trade Union Confederation, a governor of the British Broadcasting Corporation and the National Institute of Economic and Social Research, and (1974) a member of the Arts Council. In 1975 he led a campaign to enlist trade union support for Britain to remain in the European Economic Community.

Fielden, Sir Edward Hedley, British air vice-marshal (b. Bracknell, Berkshire, England, Dec. 4, 1903—d. Edinburgh, Scotland, Nov. 8, 1976), had charge of aircraft flights of the British royal family; he was flight captain for King George VI (1936–52) and for Queen Elizabeth II (1952–62), after which he became air equerry to the queen (1962–69) and was promoted to air vice-marshal. From Malvern College, Fielden entered the Royal Air Force and undertook meteorological flights in all weathers. His association with the royal family (broken only by service in World War II) began when Edward, prince of Wales, chose him as his pilot in 1929.

Fierlinger, Zdenek, Czechoslovak politician (b. Olomouc, Moravia, Austria-Hungary, July 1, 1891—d. Prague, Czechoslovakia, May 2, 1976), was Socialist prime minister (1945–46) and president of the National Assembly (1953–64). After fighting for Czechoslovak independence during World War I, he held diplomatic posts in many capitals, including Moscow (1936–39 and 1941–45). In 1948 he united his Social Democratic Party with the Communists, retaining high office and serving as chairman of the Committee for Czechoslovak-Soviet Friendship. He resigned the latter post after the Soviet invasion of Czechoslovakia in 1968.

Frumkin, Aleksandr Naumovich, Soviet electrochemist (b. Kishinev, Moldavia, Oct. 24, 1895—d. Tula, U.S.S.R., May 27, 1976), was from 1958 director of the Institute of Electrochemistry at the Soviet Academy of Sciences in Moscow; he earlier served as director (1939–49) of the Academy's Institute of Physical Chemistry. A winner of many awards, including the Lenin (1931) and Stalin (1941) prizes, he specialized in surface phenomena and evolved theories of kinetics in electrochemical reactions (1929) and the quantitative influence of an electrical field upon molecular adsorption. Frumkin was at the Karpov Institute of Physical Chemistry in Moscow from 1922 to 1946 and in 1930 was named to the chair of electrochemistry at Moscow University.

Gabin, Jean (JEAN-ALEXIS MONCORGÉ), French film actor (b. Paris, France, May 17, 1904—d. Paris, Nov. 15, 1976), was among France's best-loved film actors for almost 40 years, usually evoking sympathy in roles portraying workers, criminals, or the unfortunate. At 19 he joined the Folies-Bergère. He first appeared in film in 1930 and soon built an international reputation in such films as *Maria Chapdelaine* (1934), *La Bandéra* (1935), *La Belle équipe* (1936), *Les Bas-fonds* (1936), *Pépé le Moko* (1936), and the masterpieces *La Bête humaine* (1938;

KEYSTONE

adapted from Zola by Jean Renoir), *Quai des brumes* (1938; *Port of Shadows*), and *Le Jour se lève* (1939; *Daybreak*). After an indifferent stint in Hollywood, Gabin returned home in 1943 to serve in the Free French forces during World War II. He then adapted himself to maturer parts, playing an old peasant in *Le Plaisir* (1952) and an aging gangster in *Touchez pas au Grisbi* (1953).

Gallico, Paul William, U.S. writer (b. New York, N.Y., July 26, 1897—d. Monte Carlo, Monaco, July 15, 1976), was a gifted sportswriter whose literary talents also extended to short stories, tales for children, novels, animal stories, war reports, and film scripts. After graduating from Columbia University in New York, he was hired by the *New York Daily News* as a movie critic. He was soon switched to the sports department, where he became the sports editor and a widely read columnist (1924–36). A fine athlete who admired authentic champions, Gallico created his own news stories by getting knocked out in less than two minutes by Jack Dempsey, by swimming against Johnny Weismuller, and by challenging Bobby Jones on the golf links. While sports editor of the *Daily News* he also organized the first Golden Gloves boxing tournament. From 1950 Gallico lived outside the U.S. His writings include *The Snow Goose,* a sentimental novelette that became immensely popular; *The Poseidon Adventure,* which initiated a long series of disaster films after its success as a movie; and *Farewell to Sport.*

Geiger-Torel, Herman, German-born opera director (b. Frankfurt am Main, Germany, July 13, 1907—d. Toronto, Ont., Oct. 6, 1976), began directing symphony orchestras at age 16 but, with encouragement from his pianist-composer mother, turned to opera and made it a career. He attended Goethe University in Frankfurt and was assistant to Lothar Wallerstein at the prestigious Salzburg Festival in 1930. From 1930 to 1937 he directed operas in the major houses of Germany, Austria, Czechoslovakia, and Switzerland. After ten years as a stage director in Argentina, Brazil, and Uruguay he accepted (1948) a three-month assignment in Toronto to teach opera music and to direct a fledgling opera school at the Royal Conservatory of Music. He remained for 27 years, gradually transforming the Canadian Opera Company (established in 1950) from a student organization into a highly trained group of performers. As stage director and producer, and from 1959 also as general manager, Geiger-Torel recruited young talent that he molded into a close-knit ensemble of professional singers, coaches, managers, conductors, and stage directors. Having staged 69 productions for the Canadian Opera Company, he retired in 1975.

Getty, J(ean) Paul, U.S. oil tycoon (b. Minneapolis, Minn., Dec. 15, 1892—d. outside London, England, June 6, 1976), amassed vast personal wealth from oil investments and from substantial interests in some 200 other concerns. Estimates of his total holdings, which were concentrated in the Getty Oil Co., ranged between $2 billion and $4 billion. His art collection alone was valued at several hundred million dollars. Getty's father, a Minneapolis lawyer, laid the foundation of the family fortune by successfully wildcatting for oil in Oklahoma. At 21 young Getty began to buy and sell oil leases and within two years was a millionaire. He continued to invest in oil stock during the Depression and eventually cajoled his widowed mother into relinquishing control of George F. Getty Inc. (Her husband had refused to sell their son more than one-third interest in protest against his first three marriages.) By 1937 Getty had acquired control of Mission Corp., which held large shares in Tidewater Oil Co. and Skelly Oil, but his most important coup came in 1949 when he secured Saudi Arabia's half-interest rights to the Neutral Zone, which the Saudis shared with Kuwait.

Getty, who married five times, lived the last 25 years of his life outside the U.S. In 1973 he refused to pay $16 million to Italian kidnappers for the release of his grandson, arguing that compliance would simply make tempting targets of his other grandchildren. The young man was eventually released after his father made a reduced payment.

WIDE WORLD

Gilligan, Arthur Edward Robert, English cricketer (b. Dec. 23, 1894—d. Pulborough, West Sussex, Sept. 5, 1976), was one of the fastest bowlers of his time, a superb fielder at mid off, a quick-hitting batsman, and an inspiring leader who captained England at cricket in Australia (1924–25) and in India and Ceylon (1926–27). He also captained Sussex, and was president of the Marylebone Cricket Club during 1967–68.

Gold, Ernest, British meteorologist (b. Warwickshire, England, 1881—d. London, England, Jan. 30, 1976), who played an important part in the formation of international meteorological services, was with Britain's Meteorological Office from 1910 to 1947. While Schuster reader in dynamical meteorology (1907–10) at the University of Cambridge, he provided an explanation of the puzzling phenomenon that, whereas the temperature of the Earth's troposphere (lower atmosphere) decreases with altitude, that of the stratosphere (upper atmosphere) is relatively constant. Gold was president of the International Commission for Synoptic Weather Information (1919–47) and a fellow of the Royal Society from 1918.

Goulart, João, former president of Brazil (b. São Borja, Brazil, March 1, 1918—d. Corrientes Province, Argentina, Dec. 6, 1976), was a political protégé of Getúlio Vargas, who ruled Brazil as a virtual dictator from 1930 to 1945. On the strength of his earlier social programs, Vargas was returned to power in 1950 and named (1953) Goulart minister of labour, industry, and commerce. After Vargas committed suicide (1954) amid reports of government scandals, Goulart assumed leadership of the Labour Party and was elected (1955) vice-president in the administration of Juscelino Kubitschek. He was elected to the same office under Pres. Jânio Quadros, who suddenly resigned in August 1961. Though Goulart was ratified as president, his term (1961–64) was beset with ever increasing opposition from landlords, businessmen, and the military, all of whom resented his left-wing political policies. With inflation out of control and foreign investment declining, Goulart faced economic and political chaos. A military coup put an end to civilian rule in April 1964. Goulart went into exile in Uruguay for some nine years, then moved to Argentina.

Grechko, Andrey Antonovich, marshal of the Soviet Union (b. Golodayevka [later Kuybyshevo], Rostov region, Russia, Oct. 17, 1903—d. Moscow, U.S.S.R., April 26, 1976), Soviet minister of defense, was a career soldier who graduated from the Frunze Military Academy in 1936 and from the General Staff Academy in 1941. During the Soviet-Finnish War (1939–40) he was chief of staff of a cavalry division and in World War II successively commanded five different armies, recapturing the Black Sea city of Novorossiysk in 1943. He was given command of the Soviet forces in East Germany in 1953, was promoted to the rank of marshal in 1955, and in 1957 became first deputy minister of defense. In 1960 he was named commander in chief of the Warsaw Pact forces and in April 1967 minister of defense. Grechko, who became a full member of the Politburo in 1973, was an opponent of détente diplomacy and reduction of armaments.

Gubbins, Sir Colin McVean, British general (b. Tokyo, Japan, July 2, 1896—d. Isle of Harris, Scotland, Feb. 11, 1976), director of operations (1940–43) and executive head (1943–46) of the Special Operations Executive, the British equivalent of the U.S. Office of Strategic Services, was responsible for organizing and supporting resistance movements in German-occupied countries during World War II. The Special Operations Executive was also active in Southeast Asia against the Japanese and supported Marshal Tito in Yugoslavia. Gubbins was knighted in 1946 and decorated by all the principal Allied powers except the Soviet Union.

Haddow, Sir Alexander, British pathologist (b. Fife, Scotland, Jan. 18, 1907—d. Chalfont St. Giles, England, Jan. 21, 1976), a leading authority in the field of cancer research, was professor of experimental pathology at the University of London (1946–72) and director of the Chester Beatty Research Institute of the Institute of Cancer Research, Royal Cancer Hospital, London (1946–69). A graduate of the University of Edinburgh, he joined the Research Institute in 1936 and was among those whose experiments demonstrated conclusively that certain hydrocarbons in coal tar can cause cancer. He was also among the first to recognize the possibility of treating cancer effectively through chemotherapy. Haddow, who served as president of the International Union Against Cancer (1962–66), became a fellow of the Royal Society in 1958 and was knighted in 1966.

Harrisson, Tom, British ethnologist (b. England, Sept. 26, 1911—d. near Bangkok, Thailand, Jan. 18, 1976), was at the time of his death senior research associate in anthropology at Cornell University, Ithaca, N.Y., enthusiastically involved in the institution's Southeast Asian Program; he was also visiting professor and director of the Mass-Observation Archive at the University of Sussex in England and emeritus curator of the Sarawak Museum in Malaysia, of which he was government ethnologist and curator from 1947 to 1966. After expeditions to Arctic Lapland and Borneo, Harrisson spent two years among cannibals in the New Hebrides, whose society he described in *Savage Civilisation* (1937). In 1936 he opened up a new area of investigation when he co-founded Mass-Observation; the project developed into a study of the British people, especially under the stresses of World War II. In 1944 he parachuted into Borneo to organize guerrilla resistance to the occupying Japanese forces and prepare the people for the impending Allied invasion; he later described these experiences in his book *World Within: A Borneo Story* (1959). Harrisson, whose writings included a number of books and numerous articles for scientific journals, was also a noted ornithologist and, according to longtime colleagues, a raconteur par excellence.

Hart, Philip Aloysius, U.S. politician (b. Bryn Mawr, Pa., Dec. 10, 1912—d. Mackinac Island, Mich., Dec. 26, 1976), was elected to the U.S. Senate in 1958 as a Democrat from Michigan and during three successive six-year terms came to be known among his colleagues as "the conscience of the Senate." Though soft-spoken and unobtrusive, Hart was a potent force in shaping legislation to protect the rights of ordinary people. He sponsored, among other bills, the Drug Safety Act (1962), the Truth-in-Packaging Act (1965), and the Truth-in-Lending Act (1966), as well as the Motor Vehicle Information and Cost Saving Act (1972). He was also floor manager for the Voting Rights Act (1965, extended 1970) and for the civil rights open housing bill of 1968. In Michigan, school busing for purposes of desegregation became an explosive political issue, but Hart consistently opposed legislation to curb it. Knowing full well that Michigan was the home of numerous hunters, he nonetheless urged more stringent gun controls. Even though the U.S. auto industry was concentrated in his home state, Hart favoured antipollution laws and safety standards for cars. On these, and countless other issues, Hart's votes were accepted as expressions of sincere convictions.

Harvey, Len, British boxer (b. Cornwall, England, July 11, 1907—d. London, England, Nov. 28, 1976), at various times between 1929 and 1942 held the British welterweight, middleweight, light-heavyweight, and heavyweight championships; in 1942 he lost a bid to become world light-heavyweight title holder when he injured his back and was defeated by Freddie Mills of Great Britain. The Cornishman twice earlier challenged unsuccessfully for world crowns, going 15 rounds against middleweight Marcel Phil of France in 1932 and 15 rounds against light-heavyweight John Henry Lewis of the U.S. in 1936.

Heidegger, Martin, German philosopher (b. Messkirch, Baden, Germany, Sept. 26, 1889—d. Messkirch, West Germany, May 26, 1976), profoundly influenced atheistic existentialists and also such theologians as Rudolf Bultmann (*q.v.*). A serious student of the pre-Socratic philosophers Heraclitus and Parmenides, he also owed much to the 19th-century Danish philosopher Søren Kierkegaard. In his major work, *Sein und Zeit* (1927; Eng. trans. *Being and Time,* 1962), Heidegger examined—in a practical rather than a theoretical context—the meaning of being and

DE TOVARNICKY—L'EXPRESS/CAMERA PRESS

based metaphysical assertions on the literal meanings of the roots of Greek and German words. He left Freiburg University in 1923 to become professor of philosophy at Marburg, but he returned to Freiburg in 1928 where he was appointed rector five years later. Among his works available in English are *Kant and the Problem of Metaphysics* (1929), *What Is Philosophy?* (1956), *The Question of Being* (1958), and *On the Way to Language* (1971).

Heinemann, Gustav, West German politician (b. Schwelm, Germany, July 23, 1899—d. Essen, West Germany, July 7, 1976), president of the Federal Republic of Germany from 1969 to 1974, was previously Christian Democratic minister of the interior (1949–50) under Konrad Adenauer, then Social Democratic minister of justice (1966–69) in the "grand coalition" led by Kurt Georg Kiesinger. He changed parties over the issue of West German rearmament, to which he was determinedly opposed. While president he sought to make the office less remote and took a special interest in young people, the handicapped, foreign workers, and artists. His few state visits abroad were mainly to countries that had suffered under the Nazis. As an active member of the German Confessional Church, Heinemann steadfastly opposed the Nazis under the Third Reich.

Heisenberg, Werner Karl, German physicist (b. Duisburg, Germany, Dec. 5, 1901—d. Munich, West Germany, Feb. 1, 1976), revolutionized modern physics by discovering (1925) a way to formulate quantum mechanics in terms of mathematical matrices. Two years later he published his uncertainty (or indeterminacy) principle, namely, that the position and the velocity of an object cannot both be measured exactly at the same time. Indeed, the very concept of exact position and exact velocity taken together has no meaning in nature. The principle is vital to an understanding of subatomic particles because of the intimate connection between such particles and waves.

CAMERA PRESS

Heisenberg, who was awarded the Nobel Prize for Physics in 1932, received his Ph.D. from the University of Munich at the age of 22, then studied under Max Born in Göttingen and Niels Bohr in Copenhagen. From 1927 to 1941 he was professor of theoretical physics at the University of Leipzig and later director (1941–45) of the Kaiser Wilhelm Institute for Physics in Berlin. After World War II, as founder and director of the Max Planck Institute for Physics and Astrophysics, he continued to study a wide range of topics and became widely respected as a philosopher of science through such books as *Philosophic Problems of Nuclear Science* and *Physics and Beyond.*

Hory, Elmyr de, Hungarian painter (b. 1906—d. Ibiza, Balearic Islands, Spain, December 1976), was an extraordinarily skillful imitator of the works of Picasso and other modern painters, many copies of which were sold as authentic masterpieces. A Hungarian-Jewish refugee who settled in Ibiza in 1960, Hory was arrested for forgery in 1974, but he persistently denied having been involved in any criminal activities. Shortly after he was informed that he would be extradited to France to stand trial, he died from an overdose of sleeping pills. Clifford Irving made Hory the subject of his book *Fake!* (1969) and Orson Welles did the same in the movie *Question Mark* (1973).

Hughes, Howard (Robard), Jr., U.S. business tycoon (b. Houston, Texas, Dec. 24, 1905—d. en route to the U.S. from Acapulco, Mexico, April 5, 1976), was one of modern America's most bizarre and fascinating personalities. After his parents died, Hughes, then 18, took over personal control of the Hughes Tool Co., which manufactured and leased rock and oil drills and was worth about $700,000. During the next half-century Hughes became a daring entrepreneur and a billionaire. He produced motion pictures and became sole owner of RKO studios. He owned hotels, Nevada gambling casinos, airlines, television networks, and precious-metal mines. And he manufactured helicopters, missiles, and highly

WIDE WORLD

sophisticated space equipment for the U.S. government.

As early as the 1930s Hughes gave evidence of a complicated personality. Though he apparently enjoyed being seen in the company of beautiful women and savoured his role as a glamorous pilot who twice won the Harmon Trophy for setting world speed records in planes he designed and built himself, he frequently negotiated huge business deals at strange hours in out-of-the-way places. One grandiose Hughes venture was dubbed the "Spruce Goose," an immense wooden-framed aircraft intended to transport U.S. troops to Europe during World War II. Hughes flew it just once for one mile at an altitude of 70 ft.

In the 1950s, some years after he was disfigured and almost killed in a plane crash, Hughes went into seclusion. Abruptly moving his headquarters from one country to another (Bahamas, Nicaragua, Canada, England, Mexico), he arrived at each new destination unnoticed, took elaborate precautions to ensure absolute privacy in a luxury hotel, and was rarely seen by anyone except his five male aides. Often working for days without sleep in a black-curtained room, he sometimes subsisted on a diet of fudge and cakes carefully cut into perfect squares.

Toward the end of his life, Hughes again became a feature news item. A fraudulent biography, purportedly compiled by Clifford Irving during a series of secret meetings with Hughes, resulted in jail sentences for the author and his wife. And in 1975 it was disclosed that the strangely constructed "Glomar Explorer" had not been built by Hughes to retrieve ore from the ocean floor—the vessel had been commissioned for a secret mission by the U.S. Central Intelligence Agency.

Hughes married at least three times but left no immediate relatives. He reportedly intended to leave the bulk of his wealth, managed by the Summa Corp., to the Howard Hughes Medical Institute in Miami, but the disposition of his estate was expected to involve years of legal battles. Dozens of wills were produced, but all appeared to be forgeries.

Hughes, Richard Arthur Warren, British author (b. Weybridge, Surrey, England, April 19, 1900—d. Talsarnau, Gwynedd, Wales, April 28, 1976), was best known as the author of *A High Wind in Jamaica* (1929; U.S. title, *The Innocent Voyage*), a tale of piracy and the capacity that young children have for evil; and of *In Hazard* (1938), another maritime novel. His most ambitious project was entitled *The Human Predicament,* a trilogy of historical novels covering the years between the two World Wars. Only two volumes were completed, *The Fox in the Attic* (1961) and *The Wooden Shepherdess* (1973). Hughes also wrote poetry, children's books, radio dramas, and two stage plays, *The Sisters' Tragedy* (1922) and *A Comedy of Good and Evil* (1924).

Ingersoll, Royal Eason, U.S. admiral (b. Washington, D.C., June 20, 1883—d. Bethesda, Md., May 20, 1976), graduated from the U.S. Naval Academy in 1905, then steadily advanced in rank while serving aboard ship and at desk jobs ashore. On Jan. 1, 1942, some three weeks after the U.S. entered World War II, he was given command of the U.S. Atlantic Fleet as a vice-admiral. For the next three years he was responsible for the defense of the U.S. East Coast and for the transportation of troops and supplies across the submarine-infested Atlantic. Late in 1944 Ingersoll was reassigned to the Pacific area as commander of the Western Sea Frontier and was named deputy commander of the U.S. Fleet and deputy chief of naval operations. After receiving a Distinguished Service Medal, he retired as an admiral in 1946.

Islam, Kazi Nazrul, Bengali poet (b. Churulia, Burdwan district, Bengal [now India], May 24, 1899—d. Dacca, Bangladesh, Aug. 29, 1976), was a highly gifted poet who used his literary talents to stir his fellow countrymen into action against the British; but more significantly, his 3,000 poems, many clamouring for revolution, provided the subcontinent with some of its finest 20th-century literature. Though poverty brought an end to Islam's formal education at about age 15, he taught himself Arabic, Persian, and Sanskrit and acquired a thorough understanding of Indian religions and philosophies. His poetic imagery and allusions also bore witness to a more than ordinary acquaintance with Christian literature. Seeking support for Indian independence, Islam urged the young to tear apart "even the Sun, the Moon, and the planets" if that was the only way to freedom. Such incendiary talk stirred the country and guaranteed a prison cell for Islam. Even in confinement he poured out his heart in poems and song, and many of those he set to music were sung across the land. Islam also took up his pen to denounce class differences, disdain for others, and self-righteous attitudes. Some of his finest writings on such themes form a collection called *Samyabad* ("Egalitarianism").

James, Sid (SIDNEY BALMORAL JAMES), British comedian (b. Johannesburg, South Africa, May 8, 1913—d. Sunderland, England, April 26, 1976), whose battered features and gravelly Cockney voice distinguished an original comic talent, was the son of a South African vaudeville team. After arriving in England in 1946, he worked in repertory and played character parts in such films as *The Lavender Hill Mob* (1951), *Trapeze* (1956), and various *Carry on . . .* productions. He also acted in the stage play *Guys and Dolls* (1954), but his wide popularity was most firmly established through television. He appeared in "Hancock's Half Hour," in his own comedy series "Citizen James," and in the series "Bless This House" (1971–76).

SYNDICATION INTERNATIONAL/PHOTO TRENDS

Johnson, Eyvind, Swedish novelist (b. Boden, Sweden, July 29, 1900—d. Stockholm, Sweden, Aug. 25, 1976), shared the 1974 Nobel Prize for Literature with his compatriot Harry Martinson. Johnson's massive novels, though of the Swedish proletarian school, ranged from exposures of capitalism in *Bobinack* (1932) to a tetralogy of grim sub-Arctic logging labour in *Romanen om Olof* ("Novel of Olof," 1934–37); he also examined neutrality in *Krilon* (1941–43) and totalitarianism in *Hans nådes dagar* ("The Days of His Grace," 1960), set in the Dark Ages. His more experimental *Strändernas Svall* (1946; Eng. trans., *Return to Ithaca,* 1952) was inspired by James Joyce. Johnson served as a link to the Norwegian underground during World War II.

Jouve, Pierre Jean, French poet and novelist (b. Arras, France, Oct. 11, 1887—d. Paris, France, Jan. 8, 1976), combined Christian and Freudian imagery to explore inner conflicts of spirituality and carnality. After his conversion to Roman Catholicism in the mid-1920s, Jouve shook off the early influence of the Symbolists and the Unanimistes of the Abbaye group and produced his most characteristic works, which blended mysticism and eroticism. These elements appear in the poems of *Les Noces* (1931), *Sueur de Sang* (1935), and *Matière céleste* (1937), and in the novels *Paulina 1880* (1925), *Le Monde désert* (1927), and *La Scène capitale* (1935). During World War II he wrote poems supporting the Resistance (*La Vierge de Paris;* 1946). Jouve was also a music critic who wrote important works on Mozart and Alban Berg, and was a translator of Shakespeare. He was awarded the French Academy's Grand Prix de Poésie in 1966.

Kampmann, Viggo, Danish statesman (b. Copenhagen, Denmark, July 21, 1910—d. Copenhagen, June 3, 1976), was an able finance minister who served as prime minister of Denmark from 1960 to 1962. A member of the Social Democratic Party, he worked in the Danish taxation department before joining the Cabinet as finance minister briefly in 1950 and again from 1953 to 1960. He then replaced H. C. Hansen as prime minister on the latter's death, but was compelled to resign the premiership two years later because of ill health.

Kempe, Rudolf, German conductor (b. Niederpoyritz, Germany, June 14, 1910—d. Zürich, Switz., May 11, 1976), was musical director (1961–70) and principal conductor (1970–75) of Britain's Royal Philharmonic Orchestra. Kempe was noted for his interpretations of the works of Richard Wagner and Richard Strauss and in the 1960s was responsible for historic productions of Wagner's *Der Ring des Nibelungen* and *Lohengrin* at Bayreuth. Kempe, an oboist, became repetiteur and later conductor (1936) at the Leipzig Opera House. After opting to remain in Germany and serving in the Army during World War II, he conducted at Weimar (1948) and Dresden (1949) before becoming musical director of the Bavarian State Opera (1952). In September 1975 he was appointed principal conductor of the BBC Symphony Orchestra.

WIDE WORLD

Kerner, Otto, U.S. lawyer and politician (b. Chicago, Ill., Aug. 15, 1908—d. Chicago, May 9, 1976), was U.S. attorney for the Northern District of Illinois before entering politics as a Democrat. In 1954 he was elected a Cook County judge and six years later won the governorship of Illinois in an impressive victory. Kerner's reputation as governor was so far above reproach that Pres. Lyndon B. Johnson asked him to serve as chairman of the President's National Advisory Commission on Civil Disorders. The Kerner Report, published in February 1968, pointed to "white racism" as a major cause of the 1967 urban riots. In 1968 Kerner relinquished the governorship to accept an appointment to the U.S. Court of Appeals. In December 1972 the country was shocked to learn that Kerner had been indicted for pushing through legislation, while governor, that favoured racetrack owner Marjorie Everett. In exchange, Kerner had been allowed to buy stock in her Thoroughbred Enterprises at below-market value. He was convicted and served seven months of a three-year sentence before being paroled, terminally ill with cancer.

Kethly, Anna, Hungarian politician (b. Budapest, Hungary, Nov. 16, 1889—d. Blankenberge, Belgium, September 1976), was a minister of state in Imre Nagy's brief government in Hungary before its overthrow in 1956 by Soviet forces; she then became president of the Hungarian Social Democratic Party-in-exile. In 1922 she was the first woman Socialist to be elected to the Hungarian Parliament, later evaded capture by the German Gestapo, and became vice-president of the National Assembly in 1945. She resigned in 1948 on the forced union of her party with the Communists, and was imprisoned till 1954.

Kindersley, Hugh Kenyon Molesworth Kindersley, 2nd Baron, British merchant banker (b. May 7, 1899—d. Tonbridge, Kent, England, Oct. 6, 1976), was managing director (1927–64) and chairman (1953–64) of Lazard Brothers and Company Ltd., of which his father had been chairman before him. Serving in the firm from 1919, he became governor of Royal Exchange Assurance (1955–69) and then first chairman of Guardian Royal Exchange Assurance. During his career Kindersley was also a director of the Bank of London and South America (1938–60) and chairman of Rolls-Royce Ltd. (1956–68), and served as a director of the Bank of England (1947–67).

Klijnstra, Gerrit Dirk Ale, Dutch industrialist (b. Amersfoort, Neth., Jan. 5, 1912—d. Rotterdam, Neth., Dec. 18, 1976), became a director of the international concern Unilever in 1955 and later served as its chairman (1971–74). He was made a director of Imperial Chemical Industries, another giant corporation, in 1973. From the Delft College of Technology he joined Unilever in The Netherlands as a chemical engineer in 1938. He rebuilt factories in the Netherlands East Indies after World War II, then moved to London (1954), where he became technical director with world responsibility.

Kopanski, Stanislaw, Polish army officer (b. St. Petersburg, Russia, May 19, 1895—d. London, England, March 23, 1976), commanded Polish forces in the Allied cause in North Africa and Italy in World War II. At the outbreak of World War II Kopanski served on the Polish general staff, escaped to France, and was sent by Gen. W. Sikorski, commanding a new Polish Army, to Syria to lead the Polish Carpathian brigade. After the fall of France the brigade served in British Palestine and North Africa and later became the nucleus of the Polish Army Corps, which distinguished itself in Italy. Shortly before his death in 1943, Sikorski appointed Kopanski chief of staff of the Polish military headquarters in London. In May 1946 Kopanski became inspector general of the Polish Resettlement Corps, demobilizing more than 200,000 Polish troops in the West.

Kubitschek de Oliveira, Juscelino, former president of Brazil (b. Diamantina, Brazil, Sept. 12, 1902—d. near Rio de Janeiro, Brazil, Aug. 22, 1976), was responsible for the construction of Brasília, the nation's new ultramodern capital that sits on a plateau 600 mi from Rio. Kubitschek's hope that the transfer would open up the interior of the country to new development was being more fully realized with each passing year. As president (1956–60) he also pushed forward rapid industrial development, strove to stabilize prices by increasing food production, and initiated numerous public works projects to improve transportation. His greatest problem was persistent inflation. Kubitschek, who graduated from medical college with honours in 1927, entered politics in the 1930s and advanced steadily toward the presidency through lower elective offices. He was killed in an auto accident along the São Paulo-Rio de Janeiro highway.

Kuhlman, Kathryn, U.S. evangelist (b. Concordia, Mo., *c.* 1915—d. Tulsa, Okla., Feb. 20, 1976), used radio, television, and coast-to-coast prayer meetings to establish her credibility as an instrument of divine faith healing. Although certain medics testified that some cures were authentic, critics and skeptics viewed such cases as nothing more than obvious examples of self-deception.

GARY SETTLE—THE NEW YORK TIMES

Kuhlman was baptized a Baptist at 14, began preaching at 16, and was ordained by a nondenominational group now called the Evangelical Church Alliance. A $430,000 lawsuit filed by a former administrator brought Kuhlman unfavourable publicity; it was finally settled out of court several months before she underwent open-heart surgery and died.

Lavon, Pinhas, Israeli politician (b. Kopyczynce, Eastern Galicia, Austria-Hungary [now Kopychintsy, Ukraine, U.S.S.R.], July 12, 1904—d. Tel Aviv, Israel, Jan. 24, 1976), was educated at Lwow [now Lvov] University and joined the Zionists in 1924. He settled in Palestine in 1929, and became (1935) secretary of David Ben-Gurion's Israeli Labour Party (Mapai) and a member of its executive committee (1942). After the proclamation of the state of Israel, Lavon was elected (1949) to the Knesset (Parliament), becoming at the same time secretary-general of the Histadrut, or general federation of labour. He was named minister of agriculture in 1950 in Ben-Gurion's Cabinet and in January 1954 became minister of defense under Prime Minister Moshe Sharett. Shortly thereafter Lavon was accused of involvement in a miscarried bomb plot intended to embroil the U.S. and Britain with Egypt at the time British troops were about to leave the country. Although three inquiries cleared him, Lavon had to resign from the government (February 1955) but returned to his Histadrut post. In September 1961, supported by testimony of a former agent, Lavon accused a group of officers—all Ben-Gurion appointees—of having attempted to frame him in 1954. Ben-Gurion, who had returned to power in the summer of 1955, rejected a new inquiry into the "Lavon affair" and resigned the premiership, asserting that he would not return to office so long as Lavon remained as secretary-general of the Histadrut. Mapai's Central Committee then voted to oust Lavon.

Lawther, Sir William, British labour leader (b. Choppington, Northumberland, England, 1889—d. North Shields, Tyne and Wear, England, Feb. 1, 1976), was president of the Mineworkers' Federation (1939–45) and of its successor, the National Union of Mineworkers (1945–54), and a staunch supporter of the moderates in the Labour Party. One of his most cherished goals, nationalization of the mines, was achieved in 1947. Lawther was knighted in 1949.

Lehmann, Lotte, Prussian-born singer (b. Perleberg, Prussia, Feb. 27, 1888—d. Santa Barbara, Calif., Aug. 26, 1976), was one of the most illustrious operatic sopranos and lieder singers of her time, particularly renowned for her renditions of the songs of Robert Schumann and in the roles of Leonore in Beethoven's opera *Fidelio* and of the Marschallin in Richard Strauss's *Der Rosenkavalier*. Lehmann received her early training in Berlin and made her first major operatic appearance in Hamburg as Freia in Wagner's *Das Rheingold* in 1910. She went to the

KEYSTONE

Vienna State Opera in 1914 and became closely associated with pre-World War II Viennese culture. There Richard Strauss, who later composed for her the title role in *Arabella* (1933), chose her for roles in several of his operas. Lehmann also appeared successfully on English stages from 1913 and in the U.S. from 1930. At the Metropolitan Opera in New York City, where she made her debut in January 1934, she sang chiefly Wagnerian roles. From 1938 she lived in the U.S., becoming a citizen and continuing an active career both as a teacher and as a leading performer until her retirement in 1961.

Leighton, Margaret, British actress (b. Barnt Green, Worcestershire, England, Feb. 26, 1922—d. Chichester, England, Jan. 14, 1976), began her career with Sir Barry Jackson's Birmingham Repertory Theatre, and later joined the Old Vic company at the New Theatre, London (1944–47), where her many roles included Regan opposite Laurence Olivier as King Lear. She then played a trio of parts in James Bridie's *A Sleeping Clergyman,* acting with Robert Donat, with whom she later worked in the film of Terence Rattigan's *The Winslow Boy*. After being Stratford-upon-Avon's leading lady and playing

CENTRAL PRESS

Beatrice to John Gielgud's Benedick, she went to New York, where she won two Antoinette Perry (Tony) awards for best actress, in Rattigan's *Separate Tables* (1956) and Tennessee Williams' *The Night of the Iguana* (1962). She also received a British Society of Film and Television Arts best supporting actress award for her performance in Joseph Losey's film *The Go-Between* (1971).

Lin Yutang (LIN YÜ-T'ANG), Chinese author (b. Lun-ch'i, Fukien Province, China, Oct. 10, 1895—d. Hong Kong, March 26, 1976), was a prolific and versatile writer who expressed himself with equal grace in both Chinese and English. His output included novels, humorous and satirical essays, historical and philosophical works, plays, short stories, translations, and a Chinese-English dictionary. After teaching English in China, Lin obtained an M.A. degree from Harvard University and a Ph.D. in philology (1923) from Leipzig University in Germany. On his return to China, he wrote for Chinese literary magazines, edited English-language journals, and taught. In an effort to introduce Western-style journalism to China, he founded (1932) "Analects Fortnightly," the country's first magazine of humour. Lin's popularity in the West derived from such writings as *My Country and My People* (1935), *The Importance of Living* (1937), *Moment in Peking* (1939), *The Wisdom of China and India* (1942), *Chinatown Family* (1948), *Widow, Nun and Courtesan* (1951), and *Lady Wu* (1956).

Lisagor, Peter Irvin, U.S. journalist (b. Keystone, W.Va., Aug. 5, 1915—d. Arlington, Va., Dec. 10, 1976), graduated from the University of Michigan in 1939, then joined the *Chicago Daily News* as a sportswriter. He was hired away by United Press in 1941 as a reporter on general assignment but soon after entered the Army and toward the end of World War II was managing editor of *Stars and Stripes* in London (1944–45) and its editor in Paris (1945). By 1946 Lisagor was back with the *Chicago Daily News* reporting general news. While attending Harvard University on a fellowship (1948–49) he began to concentrate also on international affairs. The *Daily News* transferred him to the nation's capital as a foreign policy specialist and in 1959 named him chief of its Washington, D.C., bureau. Lisagor quickly emerged as one of the country's finest and most respected journalists. He accompanied every president from Dwight D. Eisenhower to Gerald Ford on both domestic and international trips and became well-known to the general public as a columnist and through regular television appearances on *Meet the Press* and *Washington Week in Review*.

Livesey, Roger, British actor (b. Barry, Wales, June 25, 1906—d. London, England, Feb. 5, 1976), made his acting debut at age 11 on a London stage, then developed into a character actor of note, often playing opposite his wife, Ursula Jeans. Important stage roles included the part of Matey in James Barrie's *Dear Brutus* and the title role in George Bernard Shaw's *Captain Brassbound's Conversion*. Livesey appeared in such films as *The Life and Death of Colonel Blimp* and *The League of Gentlemen* and gained a wide following on British television as the duke of St. Bungay in "The Pallisers."

Lommer, Stig, Danish comedian, revue producer, and artist (b. Copenhagen, Denmark, June 19, 1907—d. Copenhagen, June 28, 1976), established his own tradition of small-scale but lavish revues of comedy and satire that featured the "Lommer girls." In the mid-1920s he began a diversified career as a comic actor, newspaper caricaturist and illustrator, and producer of revues. He founded the celebrated Hornbæk Revues at his own theatre in 1935 and after World War II put on revues at a succession of Copenhagen theatres, two of which he owned.

Lowry, Laurence Stephen, British painter (b. Manchester, England, Nov. 1, 1887—d. Mottram in Longdendale, Cheshire, England, Feb. 23, 1976), made the drab scenes of industrial northern England the chief object of his artistic talents. An only child and a bachelor, he chose to people his bleak paintings with kindred souls—those who appeared to share his pervasive sense of loneliness. He was trained at the Manchester Municipal College of Art and was virtually unknown before his one-man exhibition (1939) at the Lefevre Gallery in London. The Tate Gallery held a major exhibition in London in 1967 and the Royal Academy, to which Lowry was elected in 1962, held a retrospective in 1976.

Lysenko, Trofim Denisovich, Soviet plant geneticist (b. Karlovka, Poltava Province, Ukraine, Russia, Sept. 29, 1898—d. Kiev, Ukraine, U.S.S.R., Nov. 20, 1976), the son of a peasant, persuaded both Stalin and Khrushchev that environment could cause hereditary changes in plants, a view that lent support to Marxist theory. After dominating much of Soviet science for many years, Lysenko was denounced as a charlatan. His refusal to permit research along lines that did not meet his approval also caused severe setbacks in Soviet work in biology and genetics. After graduating in 1925 from the Kiev Agricultural Institute, he worked at experimental selection stations and in 1929 was appointed senior specialist at

NOVOSTI

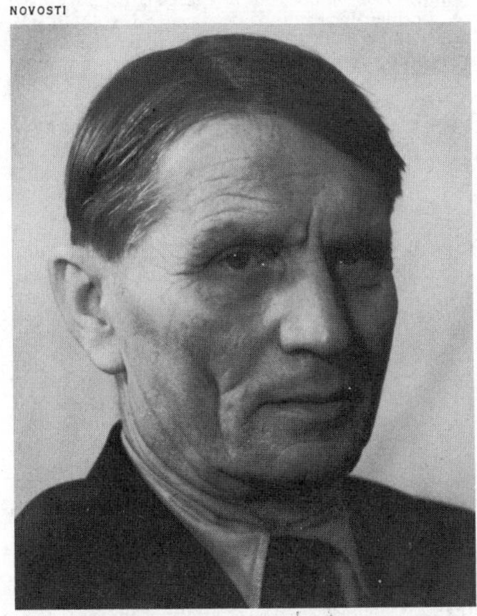

the department of physiology of the Ukrainian Institute of Selection and Genetics. In 1936 he became director of the All-Union Institute of Selection and Genetics in Odessa, and in 1938, with Stalin's backing, was made president of the Lenin All-Union Academy of Agricultural Sciences. From this position of power he was able to discredit scientists who doubted his "discoveries," notably Nikolay I. Vavilov, who died in exile in Siberia in 1942. After an eclipse following Stalin's death (1953), Lysenko again rose to a position of influence under Khrushchev, who was intent on improving Soviet harvests. With Khrushchev's removal from power in 1964, Lysenko disappeared from public view.

McAuley, James Phillip, Australian poet (b. Lakemba, New South Wales, Oct. 12, 1917—d. Melbourne, Victoria, Oct. 15, 1976), achieved notoriety in the 1940s when, with Harold Stewart, he perpetrated a literary hoax by producing and gaining acclaim for verse attributed to Ern Malley, an imaginary writer. The verse, in effect, ridiculed the pretentiousness and deliberate obscurity of some 20th-century poetry by constructing nonsensical sentences out of words and phrases that had no logical relationship. A professor of English at the University of Tasmania from 1961, McAuley published several collections of poetry, one of which was entitled *A Vision of Ceremony* (1956).

MacInnes, Colin, British author (b. London, England, Aug. 20, 1914—d. Folkestone, England, April 22, 1976), first gained wide public recognition for novels dealing with the problems of teenagers and blacks in London. His perceptions were sympathetically and convincingly set forth in the trilogy *City of Spades* (1957), *Absolute Beginners* (1959), and *Mr. Love and Justice* (1960). Other London books were *Sweet Saturday Night* (1967), about music halls, and *Three Years to Play* (1970), set in Shakespeare's time. *June in Her Spring* (1952) and *All Day Saturday* (1966) featured Australia, where MacInnes was educated, while *Out of the Garden* (1974) concerned Ulster gun-running. He also wrote *Loving Them Both* (1974), on bisexuals, and contributed to the magazines *Gay News* and *New Society*.

MacLeod of MacLeod, Dame Flora, Scottish Highland clan chief (b. London, England, Feb. 3, 1878—d. Ytham Lodge, Grampian, Scotland, Nov. 4, 1976), devoted her life to promoting the Clan MacLeod. From her ancestral Dunvegan Castle on the Isle of Skye she traveled as far as Australia and the U.S. and Canada for clan gatherings. She also worked at home to advance the prosperity of the Highlands, sitting on the Inverness-shire County Council between 1932 and 1952. Dame Flora, whose biography was published in 1974, was succeeded by her daughter's son, John Wolrige-Gordon.

MacMillan, H(arvey) R(eginald), Canadian lumber tycoon (b. Newmarket, Ont., Sept. 9, 1885—d. Vancouver, B.C., Feb. 9, 1976), amassed a sizable fortune harvesting trees and exporting lumber to worldwide markets. The company that he founded in 1919 (which was later merged to become MacMillan Bloedel Ltd.) was known for its efficient methods and advocacy of planned reforestation. During World War II MacMillan served as president of Wartime Merchant Shipping Ltd. and as timber controller for the Department of Munitions and Supply. Educational institutions were the chief beneficiaries of his philanthropy, notably the University of British Columbia, which on one occasion received more than $8 million.

Macmillan, Norman, British air pilot and author (b. Glasgow, Scotland, Aug. 9, 1892—d. Treliske, Cornwall, England, Aug. 5, 1976), made many pioneer flights including the first from Britain to Sweden (1923). After serving (1916–18) in the Royal Flying Corps, he became an Air Ministry test pilot and later chief test pilot for the Fairey Aviation Company (1923–30) and the Armstrong Siddeley Development Company (1930–33). He served in the Royal Air Force during World War II and last flew operationally during the subsequent Malayan emergency, retiring from the RAF Volunteer Reserve in 1958 with the rank of wing commander. His writings include *The Art of Flying* (1928), *The RAF in the World War* (4 vol., 1942–50), an official history, and such lighter books as *Best Flying Stories* (1941).

Malraux, André Georges, French novelist and interpreter of art (b. Paris, France, Nov. 3, 1901—d. Paris, Nov. 23, 1976), was the author of *La Condition humaine* (1933; *Man's Fate*), one of the great novels of the 20th century, about nascent Communism in China in the 1920s. Malraux, who showed an early interest in the arts and a longing for adventure, went to Indochina in 1923 and became involved in the revolutionary movement there and later in China. In the late 1920s and 1930s he made archaeological investigations in Indochina, Afghanistan, Iran, and Arabia. Malraux fought against Fascism in the Spanish Civil War and in World War II became an officer in the French Resistance. In

KEYSTONE

1945 he became an active supporter of Gen. Charles de Gaulle, who in 1958 appointed him minister of cultural affairs, a post he held for ten years. Malraux's experiences during the Spanish Civil War were related in *L'Espoir* (1937; *Man's Hope*). Among his books on art were *Les Voix du silence* (1951; *The Voices of Silence*), sounding a note of universal humanism, and *Le Musée imaginaire de la sculpture mondiale* (1952–54; *Museum Without Walls*). Malraux wrote about de Gaulle in *Les Chênes qu'on abât* (1971; *The Fallen Oaks*) and published two volumes of an autobiography, *Antimémoires* (1967) and *La Corde et les souris* (1976).

Mannheim, Lucie, German-born actress (b. Berlin, Germany, April 30, 1905—d. Braunlage, West Germany, July 28, 1976), joined the Berlin Volksbühne at age 14 and was a leading actress (1924–33) at the Berlin Staatstheater, playing Shakespeare, Ibsen, Chekhov, Gerhart Hauptmann, and Shaw as well as musical comedy. She left Germany for England in 1935 and during World War II often broadcast to Germany on the BBC European Service. She returned to the German stage after the war, and in 1959 received the Grand Cross of the German Order of Merit. Her services to the theatre were further acknowledged in 1963 when she was made Berlin State Actress.

Mao Tse-tung, Chinese revolutionary leader (b. Shaoshan, Hunan Province, China, Dec. 26, 1893—d. Peking, China, Sept. 9, 1976), was a rich peasant's son, who led the revolution that established China as one of the world's most important and powerful Communist nations. Mao was intellectually restless by nature, profoundly dissatisfied with Chinese society, and distrustful of Western liberalism. After graduating from college (1918) in Ch'ang-sha, he became a librarian at Peking University, where he founded a Marxist student circle and encouraged Chou En-lai (*q.v.*) to accept a scholarship in Paris while he remained in China. In 1921 Mao helped to found the Chinese Communist Party (CCP). When the party formed an alliance with Sun Yat-sen's more popular Kuomintang (KMT), Mao also joined the KMT and served on its central executive committee. Sun Yat-sen died in March 1925 and Chiang Kai-shek succeeded him as head of the KMT. In April 1927 Chiang began to purge both the KMT and the Army of Communist infiltration, thereby effectively severing relations with Moscow. Mao reacted by reorganizing the 50,000-strong CCP, deeply convinced that the power of the CCP resided in the peasant masses rather than in the industrial proletariat. Mao then initiated peasant revolution in the southern provinces of Hunan, Kiangsi, and Fukien from which a Chi-

SYGMACHINE

nese Red Army was recruited. In 1930 Chiang launched a campaign against the Red-dominated provinces and by October 1934 drove the Communists out of southern Kiangsi. Then began the epic Long March to Shensi Province in northern China by the Red Army commanded by Chu Teh (*q.v.*), with Mao as its chief political commissar and Chou as deputy.

The Sino-Japanese War that began in July 1937 brought Chiang into an uneasy alliance not only with the U.S.S.R. but also with Mao. In 1941, however, Soviet aid to China ceased abruptly when Stalin concluded a pact with Japan. After the collapse of Japan in August 1945 Mao met Chiang but the two leaders parted company without agreement, never to meet again. During the civil war that followed, the Red Army moved relentlessly south, winning victory after victory over Chiang's demoralized troops. On Oct. 1, 1949, as Chiang and his Nationalist followers fled to the island of Taiwan, Mao proclaimed the People's Republic of China with himself as chairman of the Republic and of the CCP. When Mao visited Moscow (his first trip abroad) in December 1949, Stalin canceled a 1945 treaty he had made with Chiang, and soon after signed a 30-year Sino-Soviet treaty. During the Korean War Mao sent a Chinese army to North Korea that effectively stalemated the UN forces.

In the process of turning China into a socialist state, Mao purged landlords and collectivized the land. In 1956, in an effort to attract intellectuals to his cause, he welcomed criticism with his policy of "letting a hundred flowers bloom." When the criticism became sharper than expected, Mao announced: "All who help to build socialism belong to the people and all who resist it are enemies." In November 1957 Mao revisited Moscow, alarmed by the ever increasing number of U.S. advisers in South Vietnam. In 1958, to accelerate industrialization, he launched the Great Leap Forward to produce more and better goods in a faster and more economical way. Nikita S. Khrushchev, Stalin's successor, warned Mao that he could expect Soviet help only in case of direct U.S. aggression. Nevertheless, China began an unsuccessful bombardment of two offshore islands held by Nationalists, as a preliminary to liberating Taiwan. Disagreement between Mao and Khrushchev (continued with Leonid I. Brezhnev after 1964) erupted in April 1960 when the Chinese attacked "revisionists," and in July and August some 10,000 Soviet military and industrial advisers left China.

The Great Proletarian Cultural Revolution, started by Mao and Lin Piao on Aug. 29, 1966, was aimed at removing higher officials with pro-Soviet sympathies. The Sino-Soviet conflict remained tense after U.S. Pres. Richard Nixon's visit to Peking in 1972, which renewed U.S. contacts with China after more than 20 years.

Mao's writings and speeches, summarized in his renowned "Little Red Book," shaped Chinese Communism, which he saw as expressing the aspirations of the masses. As he neared the end of his life, Mao became enfeebled. Chiang Ch'ing, his third wife and leader of the hard-line radicals, was accused of trying to seize power after her husband's death and became the object of a bitter campaign of vilification.

Martinon, Jean, French conductor (b. Lyon, France, Jan. 10, 1910—d. Paris, France, March 1, 1976), was an accomplished violinist and prize-winning composer before he gained fame as conductor and interpreter of early 20th-century French music. During a 1945 tour he was asked to lead an orchestra (its repertory included some of Martinon's compositions) when the conductor became ill. Martinon, who studied at the Lyon and Paris conservatories, later directed the Lamoureux Orchestra of Paris (1951–57), the Israeli Philharmonic (1958–59), and was associate director of the London Philharmonic (1954–56) before becoming music director (1960–65) for the city of Düsseldorf, West Germany. In 1963 he replaced Fritz Reiner as director of the renowned Chicago Symphony Orchestra. Though an object of bitter controversy, he remained in Chicago until 1968. He then took charge of the National Orchestra of French Radio and Television (1968–73).

Mehl, Robert Franklin, U.S. metallurgist (b. Lancaster, Pa., March 30, 1898—d. Pittsburgh, Pa., Jan. 29, 1976), studied at Franklin and Marshall College in Pennsylvania and Princeton and Harvard universities before eventually moving to the Carnegie Institute of Technology (now Carnegie-Mellon University, Pittsburgh) as first director of the Metals Research Laboratory (1932). Mehl was largely responsible for valuable contributions to metallurgy in the fields of diffusion, phase transformations, and precipitation hardening. He and his colleagues also elucidated fundamental principles involved in the heat treatment of steels. In his honour an annual gold medal is awarded by the American Institute of Mining, Metallurgical and Petroleum Engineers.

Meinhof, Ulrike, West German terrorist (b. Oldenburg, Lower Saxony, Germany, Oct. 7, 1934—d. Stuttgart, West Germany, May 9 or 10, 1976), was co-leader of the Baader-Meinhof gang, whose urban guerrilla activities led to illiberal changes in West German criminal law. The daughter of well-to-do parents, she became known during the 1960s as a radical left-wing journalist. Involved in the 1968 student riots in West Berlin, she met Andreas Baader shortly before his imprisonment for arson, and helped to free him in a 1970 prison raid. Together they established a group calling itself the Red Army Faction, which received training in terrorism from the Palestinians. Charged with five murders and innumerable other crimes, Meinhof was arrested in 1972. Guards at Stuttgart's Stammheim prison found her hanging from the window of her cell with a makeshift rope around her neck.

Mercer, Johnny, U.S. songwriter (b. Savannah, Ga., Nov. 18, 1909—d. Bel Air, Calif., June 25, 1976), had an instinctive feel for musical moods and matching lyrics that inspired scores of popular songs and brought him four Academy Awards, even though he never learned to read a score. His ability to work in easy harmony with others was a factor in some of his biggest hits, including all four Oscar-winning songs: "On the Atchison, Topeka and Santa Fe" (1946, with Harry Warren), "In the Cool, Cool, Cool of the Evening" (1951, with Hoagy Carmichael), "Moon River" (1961, with Henry Mancini), and "Days of Wine and Roses" (1962, also with Mancini). Mercer, who also sang part-time and composed for Hollywood films, included among his sparkling array of credits such longtime favourites as "Jeepers Creepers," "Goody Goody," "That Old Black Magic," "I'm an Old Cowhand," "Lazybones," "Too Marvelous for Words," and "You Must Have Been a Beautiful Baby."

Mielziner, Jo, U.S. set designer (b. Paris, France, March 19, 1901—d. New York, N.Y., March 15, 1976), was a highly imaginative and versatile designer who considerably enriched the American theatre with sets for over 300 dramas, musicals, ballets, and operas. Mielziner, whose talent helped create moods ranging from sombre to semirealistic to carefree, won five Tony and five Donaldson awards and received an Academy Award for colour art direction in the movie *Picnic*. His long list of credits includes *South Pacific, Death of a Salesman, The King and I, Can-Can, Cat on a Hot Tin Roof,* the opera *Don Giovanni,* and the ballet *Slaughter on Tenth Avenue.*

Miles, Frederick George, British aircraft designer (b. March 22, 1903—d. Worthing, Sussex, England, Aug. 15, 1976), produced, with the support of Rolls-Royce, Ltd., the Miles Magister, which remained the Royal Air Force's standard trainer throughout World War II, and the Miles Master fighter-trainer. His firm also produced a small four-engined plane and a cargo plane with detachable body that could be loaded onto a truck. After financial difficulty overtook his company, Miles became involved in the development of electronics and plastics.

Miller, Ruby, British actress (b. London, England, July 14, 1889—d. Chichester, England, April 2, 1976), began her career at the Gaiety Theatre in London in 1903, advanced from the chorus line of the much-fêted "Gaiety Girls" to leading lady, and appeared in such shows as *A Little Bit of Fluff* (1915) and the long-running (600 performances) *Going Up* (1918). Later she went into management and wrote plays. In her memoirs she recalled the time when a Russian grand duke drank champagne from her slipper—the supreme accolade for an Edwardian lady of the chorus.

Minkowski, Rudolph Leo Bernhardt, German-born astronomer (b. Strassburg, Germany [now Strasbourg, France], May 28, 1895—d. Berkeley, Calif., Jan. 4, 1976), obtained a Ph.D. in physics (1921) from the University of Breslau, then joined the faculty of the University of Hamburg. In 1935, after migrating to the U.S., he commenced a highly successful career in astrophysical research at the Mt. Wilson and Palomar observatories in southern California. Minkowski's spectroscopic observations of individual supernovae in external galaxies led to the classification of two principal types and his intensive study of remnants of supernovae in the Earth's galaxy led to an identification of the central star of the Crab Nebula. In 1960 he discovered the largest red shift for a normal galaxy. Other studies focused on planetary nebulae and on sources of X-rays and radio waves. Minkowski also supervised the compilation of a series of photographs, the *Palomar Observatory Sky Atlas,* published by the National Geographic Society (1954); it has been of immense practical value to students of astronomy.

Mitchell, Martha, U.S. personality (b. Pine Bluff, Ark., Sept. 2, 1919—d. New York, N.Y., May 31, 1976), was the vivacious, outspoken, politically conservative wife of a successful New York lawyer, but she did not become widely known until after her husband, John N. Mitchell, became U.S. attorney general in 1969 and later national campaign manager for Pres. Richard M. Nixon. When the full pattern of the Watergate scandal began to emerge in 1973, Mrs. Mitchell, suspecting her husband's involvement but fearful that he would be made a scapegoat for the misdeeds of others, made headlines with a series of bizarre late-night phone calls to the press. Her unsolicited comments about Nixon's involvement in Watergate, faithfully reported but not totally believed, so infuriated her husband that the couple's personal relationship was damaged beyond repair. They separated permanently in the fall of 1973. Mrs. Mitchell died of bone-marrow cancer 17 months after her husband and three other former government officials were convicted in a federal court.

Mohammed, Murtala Ramat, Nigerian military leader (b. Kano, Nigeria, Nov. 8, 1938—d. Ikoyi Island, Nigeria, Feb. 13, 1976), became head of state on July 29, 1975, after the peaceful coup that removed Gen. Yakubu Gowon from power. A Muslim Hausa from the north, Mohammed first came to prominence during the July 1966 coup that established Gowon, and he fought in the civil war (1967–70) against the secessionist Eastern Region (Biafra). As head of state he vigorously combated corruption but could not stem wage inflation. He was shot while in his limousine at the outset of an abortive military coup staged by a small group of self-styled "young revolutionaries."

Monnington, Sir (Walter) Thomas, British painter (b. London, England, Oct. 2, 1902—d. Tunbridge Wells, England, Jan. 7, 1976), was a pupil of Henry Tonks at the Slade School of Art in London and taught there from 1949 to 1967. He first exhibited at the Royal Academy in 1931, becoming an associate that year and a full academician in 1938. Monnington was a sensitive draftsman and painter of both portraits and landscapes and excelled at mural paintings, a notable example of which is the conference room ceiling in the Council House at Bristol. As president of the Royal Academy from 1966 he was responsible for such notable events as the Bicentenary and Bauhaus exhibitions of 1968. He was knighted in 1967.

Monod, Jacques-Lucien, French biochemist (b. Paris, France, Feb. 9, 1910—d. Cannes, France, May 31, 1976), shared, with François Jacob and André Lwoff, the 1965 Nobel Prize for Physiology or Medicine for discovering a new class of genes that regulate other genes. After graduating from the University of Paris (1931), he taught in its zoology department before moving (1945) to the Pasteur Institute. He became head of cellular biochemistry there in 1954, and professor in the faculty of sciences at the University of Paris in 1959. In 1967 he was appointed professor of molecular biology at the Collège de France and in 1971 was named director general of the Pasteur Institute in Paris. In his book *Le hasard et la nécessité* (1970; *Chance and Necessity,* 1971), which became a best-seller, he concluded that matter and life are merely different arrangements of the same atoms, and that man is the simple product of chance—an accident in the universe.

CAMERA PRESS

Montgomery of Alamein, Bernard Law Montgomery, 1st Viscount, British field marshal (b. London, England, Nov. 17, 1887—d. near Alton, Hampshire, England, March 24, 1976), in World War II defeated the German Army at el-Alamein in Egypt and led the British and Canadian forces to victory in Europe. His father, an Ulsterman, went to Tasmania in 1888 and became bishop of Tasmania the following year. After Bernard returned to England, he studied at St. Paul's School in London, was commissioned in the Warwickshire Regiment in 1908, and then served in India till 1913. In World War I he was badly wounded at Ypres, Belgium, was awarded the Distinguished Service Order, and by the age of 30 was a lieutenant colonel. He later became a directing member of the Staff College, Camberley, before taking command of his old regiment's 1st Battalion overseas (1931–34).

COURTESY, IMPERIAL WAR MUSEUM

Following steady promotions and the outbreak of World War II, Montgomery was given responsibility for the South Eastern Command in England. When Gen. W. H. E. Gott was killed in Egypt, Montgomery took command of the British 8th Army. He reorganized the forces, which had retreated into Egypt, then won a historic victory over Gen. Erwin Rommel's army at el-Alamein in November 1942. Within a few days Montgomery was rewarded with the rank of full general. The ensuing pursuit of Rommel's Afrika Korps and the linkup with Allied forces attacking from Algeria ended with a German surrender in Tunisia on May 7, 1943. Montgomery next took part in the invasion of Sicily and the early fighting in Italy before being summoned to England to command the 21st Army Group during the invasion of Europe. After the landings on June 6, 1944, he led his troops across northern France, Belgium, and The Netherlands into Germany. On May 4, 1945, near Lüneburg, Montgomery received the surrender of all German forces in northwest Germany. After the war he was appointed commander in chief of the British Army of the Rhine and British military governor, and joined the Allied Control Council of Germany. Montgomery became a field marshal in 1944, and in 1946 was successively named a viscount, chief of the Imperial General Staff, and a Knight of the Garter. In 1948 he was appointed chairman of the Western Union Commanders-in-Chief Committee and from 1951 to 1958 served as deputy supreme commander at NATO. Never reticent about expressing his personal opinions, Montgomery reiterated his sharp wartime criticism of Dwight D. Eisenhower's command in his *Memoirs* (1958).

Morand, Paul, French diplomat and author (b. Paris, France, March 13, 1888—d. Paris, July 23, 1976), was a writer of vision and style who wrote about the world as he saw it, evoking in particular the "lost generation" of the 1920s. Educated at the universities of Paris and Oxford, he entered the diplomatic service in 1912 and held posts in London, Rome, Madrid, and other capitals. Morand, a member of the French Academy from 1968, wrote novels, short stories, memoirs, history, and essays. Among his better known early fiction were *Ouvert la nuit* (1922; *Open All Night,* 1923), *Fermé la nuit* (1923; *Closed All Night,* 1924), and *Lewis et Irène* (1924; Eng. trans., 1925). His last book, *L'Allure de Chanel,* about the couturière Coco Chanel, appeared in 1976.

Morison, Samuel Eliot, U.S. historian (b. Boston, Mass., July 9, 1887—d. Boston, May 15, 1976), found time during a 40-year teaching career at Harvard University to re-create in vivid prose some of the greatest maritime stories of recent times. Combining a rare gift for narrative with meticulous scholarship, he stepped back into history to relive the adventures of such stirring figures as Magellan, Columbus, Sir Francis Drake, and John Paul Jones. He also chronicled the exploits of the U.S. Navy during World War II. To give authenticity to his writing, Morison undertook numerous voyages himself, sailed the ocean routes followed by Columbus, and during wartime served on 12 ships as a commissioned officer in the Naval Reserve. His writings include: *Maritime History of Massachusetts* (1921); *The European Discovery of America* (2 vol., 1924); *Admiral of the Ocean Sea* (1942), a biography of Columbus that won a Pulitzer Prize; *John Paul Jones* (1959), which also received a Pulitzer; *The Oxford History of the American People* (1965), Morison's "legacy" to his country; and the monumental *History of U.S. Naval Operations in World War II* (15 vol., 1947–62).

Napoli, Mario, Italian archaeologist (b. 1915?—d. Salerno, Italy, April 1976), was best known for his work at the site of the Greek colony of Paestum near Salerno in southern Italy. There he discovered (1966) the first Greek frescoes ever found outside Greece itself. Among his notable discoveries was a tomb with wall paintings, described in his book *La Tomba del Tuffatore* (1970).

Naughton, Charlie (CHARLES JOHN NAUGHTON), British comedian (b. Glasgow, Scotland, April 21, 1886—d. London, England. Feb. 11, 1976), was a member of the much-loved Crazy Gang, which for more than 30 years delighted London variety audiences—including, on occasion, the royal family. Naughton first joined with Jimmy Gold to form a music-hall dance team, then in the early 1930s formed the Crazy Gang with Bud Flanagan, Jimmy Nervo, Chesney Allen, Teddy Knox, and "Monsewer" Eddie Gray. The Gang gave its last performance in 1962.

Nevers, Ernest ("Ernie") Alonzo, U.S. football player (b. Willow River, Minn., June 11, 1903—d. San Rafael, Calif., May 3, 1976), was named by the Football Writers Association of America as the greatest college fullback to play between 1919 and 1969. The 1925 Rose Bowl game provided one measure of his greatness. Walking abnormally on two tightly taped ankles (both fractured the previous year), he gained more yards for Stanford in defeat than the famed "Four Horsemen" gained for Notre Dame in victory (27–10). Besides playing professional football—his six touchdowns and four conversions for the Chicago Cardinals in a 1929 game against the Chicago Bears is still a National Football League record—he pitched for the St. Louis Browns baseball team (1926–28). In 1927 he

UPI COMPIX

added his bit to the Babe Ruth legend by being charged with two of the Babe's record 60 home-runs. After retiring from sports, Nevers became a businessman in San Francisco.

Nicoll, (John Ramsay) Allardyce, British historian (b. June 28, 1894—d. London, England, April 17, 1976), was educated in Scotland and taught English at East London College (now Queen Mary College) of London University before transferring to Yale University in Connecticut as professor (1933–42) of the history of drama and dramatic criticism. He then served at the British embassy in Washington, D.C. (1942–45). After returning to England he was professor of English language and literature at the University of Birmingham (1945–61) and director of the Shakespeare Institute at Stratford-upon-Avon (1951–61). Nicoll's major work was the definitive six-volume *A History of English Drama, 1660–1900* (1952–59), supplemented (1973) by *English Drama, 1900–1930.* His numerous other books include *Studies in Shakespeare* (1927), *Masks, Mimes and Miracles* (1931), *World Drama* (1949), *The Elizabethans* (1956), and *English Drama: A Modern Viewpoint* (1968).

Novomesky, Ladislav, Slovak poet (b. Budapest, Hung., Dec. 27, 1904—d. Bratislava, Czech., Sept. 4, 1976), was a notable Communist poet whose books included *Sunday* (1927), *Rhomboid* (1932), and *The Open Window* (1935). He joined the Communist Party in his youth, took part in the 1944 Slovak uprising against the Germans, and was elected to the Central Committee of the party and to Parliament. He was purged in 1954 but was readmitted to the party in 1964 and again held office.

Oldfield, William Albert Stanley, Australian cricketer (b. Sydney, New South Wales, Sept. 9, 1896—d. Sydney, Aug. 10, 1976), kept wicket for Australia from 1920 to 1936, achieving the superb record of playing in 54 test matches and dismissing 130 batsmen (52 by stumping). He set a standard of Australian test wicketkeeping that successors have tried to emulate. In the Sheffield Shield matches he played for New South Wales.

Onsager, Lars, Norwegian-born chemist (b. Kristiania [now Oslo], Norway, Nov. 27, 1903—d. Coral Gables, Fla., Oct. 5, 1976), was awarded the 1968 Nobel Prize for Chemistry for "the discovery of the reciprocal relations bearing his name which are fundamental for the thermodynamics of irreversible processes." Onsager's early work in statistical mechanics attracted the attention of the Dutch chemist Peter Debye, under whose direction Onsager studied (1926–28) at the Swiss Federal Institute of Technology in Zürich. He then went to the U.S. and taught at Johns Hopkins University in Maryland and Brown University in Rhode Island. He received his Ph.D. (1935) from Yale University, where he became (1945) professor of theoretical chemistry. His explanation of the movement of ions in solution as related to turbulences and fluid densities had an important effect on the development of physical chemistry and has been described as providing the fourth law of thermodynamics.

Panagoulis, Alexandros, Greek politician (b. Athens, Greece, July 2, 1939—d. Athens, May 1, 1976), made an abortive attempt (Aug. 13, 1968) to assassinate the military dictator Georgios Papadopoulos and became a popular hero and a symbol of resistance to the regime during his subsequent imprisonment and torture. Having had his death sentence commuted as a result of international pressure, Panagoulis was freed under a general amnesty in August 1973 and remained in Italy until the junta fell in July 1974. As a Centre Union Party parliamentary deputy, he worked to bring to justice those guilty of crimes under the junta. He died in an automobile accident that members of the opposition claimed was a planned political assassination.

Patman, (John William) Wright, U.S. politician (b. Patman's Switch, Texas, Aug. 6, 1893—d. Bethesda, Md., March 7, 1976), was a 24-term Democratic congressman from Texas, who in 1963 became the powerful and controversial chairman of the Committee on Banking, Currency, and Housing in the U.S. House of Representatives. In his relentless battle to curb the influence of "big money interests," Patman often resorted to ruses to promote or kill proposed legislation, and was roundly condemned by his colleagues for doing so. Before being ousted as chairman in 1975, Patman compiled a record that included several successes: he helped secure a bonus for veterans of World War I; he co-authored legislation that protected small businesses against unfair chain-store competition; he pushed through the Employment Act of 1946, which established the Council of Economic Advisers and the Congressional Joint Economic Committee and made "maximum employment, production, and purchasing power" a national goal; and he formulated legislation that created federal credit unions and the Small Business Administration.

Paul of Yugoslavia, Prince, former regent of Yugoslavia (b. St. Petersburg [now Leningrad], Russia, April 15, 1893—d. Paris, France, Sept. 14, 1976), was the son of Prince Arsen Karageorgevich, younger brother of King Peter I of Serbia, and a man of culture. He read history at Christ Church, Oxford, and when his first cousin King Alexander was murdered in 1934 became regent during the minority of King Peter II. He was overthrown and exiled in March 1941, shortly before the German Army overran his country.

Penfield, Wilder Graves, U.S.-born neurologist (b. Spokane, Wash., Jan. 26, 1891—d. Montreal, Que., April 5, 1976), made important contributions to medical science with research on epilepsy and cerebral nerve cells. Using electric probes as stimulants, he was able to map the cerebral cortex and show a dependent relationship between specific areas of the brain and such functions of man as memory, speech, and physical movement. Applying this knowledge to corrective surgery, he was able to cure or alleviate epilepsy in a large number of cases. In 1934 Penfield both became a Canadian citizen and founded the Montreal Neurological Institute with a $1.2 million grant from the Rockefeller Foundation. With Penfield as its director (until his retirement in 1960), the institute became one of the finest centres for brain surgery in the world.

Piatigorsky, Gregor, Russian-born cellist (b. Yekaterinoslav, Russia, April 17, 1903—d. Los Angeles, Calif., Aug. 6, 1976), was a Romantic by nature but always in control of his interpretations. His renditions of such pieces as Richard Strauss's "Don Quixote" and the cello concerto of Antonin Dvorak fulfilled his own definition of a virtuoso: one who shows how good the music really is. While still in his early teens, Piatigorsky became first cellist with the Imperial Opera orchestra in Moscow, but in 1921 he fled the Soviet Union by swimming across a river to Poland, his precious cello held high above the water. In later life Piatigorsky habitually walked on stage holding his Stradivarius high in the air, apparently in memory of that event. After performing with the Warsaw Opera orchestra, he moved to Berlin, eventually becoming first cellist and soloist with the Berlin Philharmonic Orchestra under the direction of Wilhelm Furtwängler. His U.S. debut (1929) was followed by some 20 years of touring, during which he appeared with virtually every major symphony orchestra and conductor in the world. After 1949 he combined teaching at the University of Southern California with less frequent public appearances, but during the 1960s he and violinist Jascha Heifetz formed part of a select group that gave occasional chamber recitals. Piatigorsky, a delightful raconteur, displayed his talent for storytelling in *Cellist* (1965), his autobiography.

KATHERINE YOUNG

Polanyi, Michael, Hungarian-born chemist and philosopher (b. Budapest, Hungary, March 12, 1891—d. Oxford, England, Feb. 22, 1976), made important contributions in thermodynamics, X-ray analysis, and reaction kinetics before turning to problems of political theory. After obtaining degrees in medicine (1913) and chemistry (1917) from the University of Budapest, he became a leading scientist at the Kaiser Wilhelm Institute in Berlin (1925–33), but resigned in protest against the Nazis. He then taught physical chemistry in England at the University of Manchester, where he later (1948–58) became professor of social studies. Polanyi, who co-founded two international organizations to promote academic freedom and was severely critical of Soviet repression of intellectuals, became a fellow of the Royal Society in 1944. His writings include *The Logic of Liberty* (1951), *The Study of Man* (1959), and *Beyond Nihilism* (1960).

Pollard, (Henry) Graham, British author and bibliographer (b. March 7, 1903—d. Oxford, England, Nov. 15, 1976), was a preeminent bibliographical scholar, who joined with John Carter to expose the bibliographical frauds of T. J. Wise in their celebrated *An Enquiry into the Nature of Certain Nineteenth Century Pamphlets* (1934). Their exposé was based to a great extent on a revolutionary chemical and microscopic examination of paper and typography. Pollard attended University College, London, and Jesus College, Oxford, before entering the world of antiquarian bookselling and bibliography.

Pons, Lily (ALICE JOSÉPHINE PONS), French-born singer (b. Draguignan, France, April 12, 1904?—d. Dallas, Texas, Feb. 13, 1976), was a coloratura soprano whose international popularity derived almost as much from her charming personality and glamorous image as from her remarkable

PICTORIAL PARADE

voice. Her bel canto parts included the title roles in *Lakmé* and *Lucia di Lammermoor,* Gilda in *Rigoletto,* and Rosina in *Il Barbiere de Siviglia.* After studying piano at the Paris Conservatory, Pons spent years training her voice under the tutelage of Alberti di Gorostiaga. Following an uneventful debut in Alsace (1928), she auditioned with the Metropolitan Opera Company of New York City and became an overnight sensation with her first appearance in 1931 singing the role of Lucia. Pons was a reigning diva at the Met for 25 years and drew record crowds in many parts of the world. Her second husband was the conductor André Kostelanetz, with whom she made a number of successful tours. Her last public performance was at a New York Philharmonic Promenade concert in May 1972 with Kostelanetz, from whom she was divorced in 1958, conducting.

Potter, Simeon, British philologist (b. London, England, Jan. 19, 1898—d. East Molesey, England, Aug. 6, 1976), Baines professor of English language and philology at the University of Liverpool (1945–65), was the author of enjoyable and significant textbooks on the English language, notably *Our Language* (1950), *Language in the Modern World* (1960), and *Changing English* (1969). Educated at Kilburn Grammar School, London, and at the universities of London and Oxford, he lectured at the Masaryk University, Brno, Czech. (1924–31), taking his doctorate (1931) at the Charles University, Prague, before returning to England to lecture at the University of Southampton (1931–45). Potter wrote the article "English Language" in the 15th edition of *Encyclopædia Britannica.*

Pradel, Louis, French administrator (b. Lyon, France, Dec. 5, 1906—d. Lyon, Nov. 27, 1976), was mayor of Lyon for nearly 20 years, succeeding the colourful Édouard Herriot in 1957. He worked tirelessly to make his city a centre of European business and cultural activity, tearing down slums and personally inspecting the construction of such things as a congress hall, a commercial centre, a concert hall, expressways, an underground railway, housing, schools, and sports grounds.

Queneau, Raymond, French novelist, poet, and encyclopaedist (b. Le Havre, France, Feb. 21, 1903—d. Paris, France, Oct. 25, 1976), was a multifaceted creative genius, whose work influenced French prose, poetry, and cinema. A graduate of the Sorbonne in Paris, he joined the publishing house of Gallimard and became (1955) editor of the *Encyclopédie de la Pléiade,* where his scholarship had full play. His succession of brilliant comic novels included *Le Chiendent* (1933, his first), *Chêne et chien* (1937; *The Bark Tree,* 1968), *Un Rude Hiver* (1939), *Pierrot mon ami* (1943), and *Journal intime de Sally Mara* (1951). Queneau was a polymath also interested in language and experiment. *Exercices de style* (1947) described in a series of stylistic parodies a man on a bus fastening a button. In *Zazie dans le métro* (1959), made into a film by Louis Malle, he told of a working girl of free-ranging, slangy conversation. Queneau's poetry, which extended to songs for cabarets, included *Bucoliques* (1947), *Petite Cosmogonie portative* (1950), and *Cent milles milliards de poèmes* (1962), an exercise in poem-making. The avant-garde writer and film director Alain Robbe-Grillet acknowledged an indebtedness to Queneau, who became a member of the Académie Goncourt in 1951.

Radok, Alfred, Czech theatrical director (b. Tyn nad Vltavou, Bohemia, Dec. 7, 1914—d. Vienna, Austria, April 26[?], 1976), staged notable productions in many European capitals, including John Osborne's *The Entertainer,* Maksim Gorky's *The Last Ones,* and García Lorca's *Donna Bernarda's House.* From 1938 he worked at the Burian Theatre in Prague and at the Plzen (Pilsen) City Theatre. After imprisonment (1943–45) during World War II, he directed opera at the Prague Theatre of May 5, working with the stage designer Josef Svoboda, with whom in the 1950s he developed Laterna Magica, a mixed-media form of entertainment. Radok directed at both the Prague City and Czech National theatres. Following the Soviet invasion of Czechoslovakia (1968) he moved to Sweden, where he became a director at the Göteborg People's Theatre.

Radziwill, Prince Stanislaw, Polish nobleman (b. Szpanow, Volhynia, Poland, July 21, 1914—d. Essex, England, June 27, 1976), was an 18th-generation descendant of a famous Polish-Lithuanian family. He had been a deputy provincial governor in Ukrainian Poland before he fought as a cavalry officer at the outbreak of World War II and escaped to Paris. He served the Polish government-in-exile in the West at the International Red Cross Committee at Geneva and after the war went into business in London. In England Prince Stanislaw helped to organize the Sikorski Historical Institute and a Polish school near Henley-on-Thames, where he also founded St. Anna's Church in memory of his mother. The prince's third wife was Caroline Lee Bouvier, sister of Mrs. Jacqueline Kennedy Onassis.

Razak bin Hussein, Tun Abdul, Malaysian politician (b. Pekan, Pahang State, Federated Malay States, March 11, 1922—d. London, England, Jan. 14, 1976), was a key figure in gaining his country's independence from Britain in 1957 and from 1970 was prime minister, foreign minister, and defense minister of Malaysia. As deputy to Tunku Abdul Rahman, first prime minister of independent Malaya (Malaysia from 1963), he was largely responsible for the country's significant achievements in rural and national development. Appointed head of the National Operations Council set up with emergency powers in 1969, he steered the country through that year's violent racial disturbances. Razak was a lawyer by training, joined the civil service in 1950, and entered politics in 1955 when the first general elections were held. He served as minister of education (1955–57), as deputy prime minister and minister of defense (1957–70), as prime minister during Tunku Abdul Rahman's temporary retirement in 1959, as minister of rural development (1959–69), and as minister of home affairs (1969). As prime minister he pursued a policy of nonalignment, in furtherance of which he established relations with China in 1974.

Reed, Sir Carol, British film director (b. London, England, Dec. 30, 1906—d. London, April 25, 1976), made his most outstanding films in the 1940s: *Odd Man Out* (1947) and Graham Greene's *The Fallen Idol* (1948) and *The Third Man* (1949). After acquiring acting experience, he became stage director (1927) for Edgar Wallace and then went to Ealing Studios (1932) under Basil Dean. He directed his first film in 1934 and counted among his credits *The Stars Look Down* (1939), *Night Train to Munich* (1940), *Kipps* (1941), *Outcast of the Islands* (1951), *Our Man in Havana* (1959), *The Agony and the Ecstasy* (1965), and *Kidnapped* (1972). Reed, who won an Academy Award for his musical *Oliver!* (1968), was knighted in 1952.

Richter, Hans, German-born artist and filmmaker (b. Berlin, Germany, 1888—d. Locarno, Switz., Feb. 1, 1976), was absorbed most of his life with the nihilism of Dada, the spirit of which he explained in *Dada: Art and Anti-art* (1964). Without ever totally neglecting his painting, he concentrated on films after 1921, when he produced the first abstract animation, *Rhythm 21.* His best-known movie, *Dreams That Money Can Buy* (1947), dramatized the artistic vision of six Dadaist associates. After migrating to the U.S. in 1941, Richter became associated with the City College of New York, where he directed the Institute of Film Techniques from 1943 until his retirement in 1956.

Roberts, Cecil Edric Mornington, British writer (b. Nottingham, England, May 18, 1892—d. Rome, Italy, Dec. 20, 1976), was the author of such best-selling novels as *Sails of Sunset* (1924), *Spears Against Us* (1932), *Pilgrim Cottage* (1933), and *Victoria Four-Thirty* (1937). He was a war correspondent during World War I and editor of the *Nottingham Journal* (1920–25) as well as a lecturer and traveler. He also published poems and five volumes of autobiography. He was awarded the Italian Gold Medal in 1966.

Roberts, the Most Rev. Thomas D'Esterre, British prelate of the Roman Catholic Church (b. Le Havre, France, March 7, 1893—d. London, England, Feb. 28, 1976), was a Jesuit schoolmaster in Liverpool when he was appointed archbishop of Bombay in 1937. For the next 13 years he was a dedicated pastor in India, showing special concern for the poor, the prostitutes, and seamen. He resigned in 1950, having persuaded Pope Pius XII to appoint an Indian in his place. After his return to England, his nonconformist views on such matters as contraception and the church's marriage regulations frequently set him in conflict with John Cardinal Heenan and other members of the hierarchy.

Robeson, Paul, U.S. singer and outspoken critic of racial injustice (b. Princeton, N.J., April 9, 1898—d. Philadelphia, Pa., Jan. 23, 1976), was the son of a runaway slave and a man endowed with extraordinary talents. While attending Rutgers College in New Jersey on an academic scholarship, he was twice named to the All-America football team, received a Phi Beta Kappa key in his junior year, and was designated class valedictorian (1919). He then obtained a law degree (1923) from Columbia University before becoming a celebrated dramatic bass-baritone on the stage and in motion pictures. After playwright Eugene O'Neill saw Robeson perform with the Provincetown Players in Greenwich Village, he gave the actor a part in *All God's Chillun Got Wings* (1924), then the lead in *The Emperor Jones* (1924). Robeson's charismatic stage presence as Brutus Jones created a sensation in New York and in London (1925). Soon he was thrilling audiences in the musical *Show Boat* with "Ol' Man River," which Jerome Kern had composed for Robeson's resonant voice. The actor's greatest dramatic triumph came in *Othello,* first staged in London (1930). Revived in 1943, it set an all-time record run for Shakespearean plays on Broadway with 295 performances.

EB INC.

Robeson's remarkable career, however, was severely damaged when, after visiting the Soviet Union, he became involved with left-wing groups and publicly espoused the cause of "scientific socialism." Following World War II many Americans began to resent his repeated glowing endorsements of the Soviet political system and one Robeson concert was disrupted by violence. When concert halls were denied him, his annual income dwindled to almost nothing. In 1950 the U.S. government revoked Robeson's passport when he refused, on legal grounds, to sign an affidavit disclaiming membership in the Communist Party. Two years later he received the Stalin Peace Prize. By 1958, however, Robeson was able to return to the stage and his first U.S. concert in 11 years was greeted in Carnegie Hall with thunderous applause. That same year he renewed his overseas tours after a ruling of the Supreme Court restored his passport. In ill health, he returned to the U.S. in 1963 to spend his remaining years with his family and a few close friends.

Robinson, Sir Edward Stanley Gotch, British numismatist (b. Bristol, England, 1887—d. London, England, June 13, 1976), was probably the world's leading authority on ancient Greek coinage. He joined the Department of Coins and Medals at the British Museum in 1912 and became keeper of the department (1949–52). He enriched the national collection with gifts of Greek coins and advanced the study of Greek and Roman coinage through his writings. During 1938–58 he was reader in numismatics at Oxford University and honorary curator of Greek coins at the Ashmolean Museum, Oxford, to which he contributed his own coin collection in 1964. Calouste Gulbenkian, owner of a magnificent series of Greek coins, was but one of many who valued Robinson as an adviser. Robinson, who was knighted in 1972, began rewriting B. V. Head's 1911 edition of the *Historia Numorum* (on Greek coinage), but the huge task was never completed.

Rothfels, Hans, German historian (b. Kassel, Germany, April 12, 1891—d. Tübingen, West Germany, June 22, 1976), who specialized in the Bismarck and Nazi periods, was acclaimed for his book *The German Opposition to Hitler* (1948). He was professor of modern history at Königsberg, East Prussia, till forced out of his post by the Nazis in 1934. He became a research fellow (1939) at St. John's College, Oxford, guest professor (1940) at Brown University in Rhode Island, and professor (1946) of modern history at the University of Chicago. In 1951 he transferred to the University of Tübingen.

Russell, Rosalind, U.S. actress (b. Waterbury, Conn., June 4, 1912?—d. Beverly Hills, Calif., Nov. 28, 1976), won four Academy Award nominations and countless fans by giving free rein to her natural wit and effervescent personality. She made her professional debut on the Broadway stage, then moved to Hollywood where she attained stardom in *The Women* (1939), which pitted Russell against Paulette Goddard in a memorable hair-pulling, clothes-tearing battle. Among the many other career-girl comedies that featured her were *His Girl Friday* (1940), a remake of the Ben Hecht-Charles MacArthur play *The Front Page* with the lead character changed from a man to a woman, *No Time for Comedy* (1940), and *My Sister Eileen* (1942). In 1953 Russell returned to Broadway to star in *Wonderful Town.* Though she compared her singing to gargling, no one seemed to care; tickets sold by the thousands. In 1956, before arthritis ended her career, Russell played the lead in *Auntie Mame* on Broadway (and later in the movie). Her performance may have so identified the madcap role with the actress herself that future Auntie Mames had best beware.

KEYSTONE

Ruzicka, Leopold (Stephen), Swiss chemist (b. Vukovar, Croatia [now in Yugoslavia], Sept. 13, 1887—d. Zürich, Switz., Sept. 1976), was joint recipient of the 1939 Nobel Prize for Chemistry for his work on ringed molecules and terpenes. In 1917 he became a citizen of Switzerland, where he was already lecturing at the Swiss Federal Institute of Technology in Zürich. In 1926 he was made professor of organic chemistry at the University of Utrecht, Neth., but three years later he returned to Zürich to become professor of chemistry. Ruzicka's research on natural odoriferous compounds led to his discovering the unusual molecular structures of muscone and civetone, important to the perfume industry. In these molecules, carbon atoms are linked in rings larger than had been thought capable of existence. He also discovered the molecular structure of testosterone and other male sex hormones and succeeded in synthesizing them.

Ryle, Gilbert, British philosopher (b. Brighton, England, Aug. 19, 1900—d. Whitby, North Yorkshire, England, Oct. 6, 1976), was Waynflete professor of metaphysical philosophy at the University of Oxford (1945–68) and one of Britain's most influential modern philosophers. Educated at Brighton College and Queen's College, Oxford, he was tutor in philosophy at Christ Church (1924–45) and later, as professor, a fellow of Magdalen College. His first book, *The Concept of Mind* (1949), is considered a modern classic. A basic tenet of Ryle's philosophy was that misuse of language is to blame for conceptual (mental) confusion; in other words, most philosophical problems arise because of the confusion between logical concepts and the language used to express them. Almost as important as Ryle's own writings was his editorship from 1948 to 1971 of the influential philosophical journal *Mind.*

Sachs, Emil Solomon, South African trade unionist (b. Dvinsk, Latvia, Russia, Nov. 3, 1903—d. London, England, July 30, 1976), migrated to South Africa (1913), where he studied law and economics at Witwatersrand University and became (1928) general secretary of the Garment Workers' Union. The Nationalist government forced him to resign the position in 1952 under the Suppression of Communism Act, even though he had been expelled from the South African Communist Party in 1931. Following his resignation, Sachs left for Britain, where he wrote *Rebel's Daughters* (1957) and a number of other books on the growth of the South African Garment Workers' Union. *The South Africa Treason Trial* appeared in 1958.

Schmidt-Rottluff, Karl, German Expressionist artist (b. Rottluff, near Chemnitz (now Karl-Marx-Stadt), Germany, Dec. 1, 1884—d. West Berlin, August 1976), was a founder-member in 1905 of Die Brücke ("The Bridge"), a group of German artists who moved away from Impressionism to Expressionism by juxtaposing flat areas of colour emotively ("Self-Portrait with Monocle"; 1910). In 1911 Schmidt-Rottluff moved from Dresden to Berlin. Influenced by Negro art, he produced prints ("Head of Christ," woodcut, 1918) and carvings of rough simplicity. After 1933 his works were not allowed in public galleries. After World War II he taught at the Schmidt-Rottluff Academy of Fine Arts in West Berlin.

Seydlitz-Kurzbach, Walther von, German general (b. 1889—d. Bremen, West Germany, April 28, 1976), was second in command to Gen. Friedrich Paulus at the Battle of Stalingrad during World War II; in 1940 he commanded an infantry division during the invasion of France. At Stalingrad, when the German Army was clearly outflanked by the Soviet forces, von Seydlitz—in defiance of Hitler's orders—vainly urged Paulus to retreat. After their surrender (February 1943), he at first supported Soviet-sponsored anti-Nazi movements but was later reimprisoned by the Soviets (1950-53) before being finally allowed to settle in West Germany.

Shepard, Ernest Howard, British artist and book illustrator (b. London, England, Dec. 10, 1879—d. Lodsworth, Sussex, England, March 24, 1976), provided the first and best-known visual images of the characters in A. A. Milne's Winnie-the-Pooh books (1924–28). Earlier classics for which his illustrations became definitive were Richard Jefferies' *Bevis: The Story of a Boy* and Kenneth Grahame's *The Golden Age, Dream Days,* and *The Wind in the Willows.* Shepard, who studied at the Royal Academy Schools in London and first exhibited in 1901, was also a long-time contributor of humorous drawings to the weekly magazine *Punch.* His illustrated *Drawn from Memory* (1957) and *Drawn from Life* (1962) were autobiographical.

Shimada, Shigetaro, Japanese admiral (b. Tokyo, Japan, 1883—d. Tokyo, June 7, 1976), graduated from the Japanese Naval College in 1904 before serving as naval attaché at the Japanese embassy in Rome. He then held several ship commands and was successively named commander in chief of the Japanese second fleet, the Kure naval station, and the Yokosuka naval station. In 1940, when Japan was at war with China, he was promoted to the rank of admiral. Shimada held the influential post of minister of the navy in Tojo's Cabinet when Japanese planes attacked Pearl Harbor on Dec. 7, 1941. In February 1944, with the tide of the Pacific war turning against Japan, Shimada became chief of the naval general staff. After the war the International Military Tribunal for the Far East tried and convicted (1948) Shimada as a war criminal and sentenced him to life imprisonment. He was paroled in 1955 suffering from ill health.

Shtemenko, Sergey Matveyevich, Soviet general (b. Uryupinsk, near Tsaritsyn [now Volgograd], Russia, 1907—d. Moscow, U.S.S.R., April 23, 1976), was promoted rapidly by Stalin as a first-rate staff officer, becoming deputy chief (1943) and chief (1949) of the general staff. He was elected a candidate member of the Communist Party's Central Committee in 1952 and also became deputy minister of the armed forces. In January 1953 an alleged Jewish "doctors' plot" to murder prominent leaders loyal to Stalin included General Shtemenko as a purported victim. Appointed chief of staff in East Germany in February 1953, he was recalled by Khrushchev and demoted to the rank of lieutenant general but still occupied important posts. After Khrushchev's fall in 1964 Shtemenko was given back his rank of army general and regained his post of deputy chief of general staff. In August 1968 he was appointed chief of staff of the Warsaw Pact forces under Marshal I. I. Yakubovsky, and in that capacity coordinated the invasion of Czechoslovakia.

Sim, Alastair, Scottish actor (b. Edinburgh, Scotland, Oct. 9, 1900—d. London, England, Aug. 19, 1976), was a tall, droll, precise-voiced comedian, whose considerable talents often found a felicitous medium in such James Bridie plays as *Mr. Bolfrey* and *Dr. Angelus.* During a career that lasted more than 40 years, Sim starred in movies, on television, and on the stage and showed the breadth of his talent by also giving impressive dramatic performances that extended to Shakespeare's Shylock and Charles Dickens' Scrooge. In 1950 Sim was voted Britain's most popular film star and in 1953 was named a Commander of the Order of the British Empire.

Slonimski, Antoni, Polish writer (b. Warsaw, Poland, Oct. 15, 1895—d. near Warsaw, July 4, 1976), the "grand old man" of Polish literature,

WIDE WORLD

wrote plays, articles, essays, and a novel, but was especially celebrated for his poetry. *Sonnets,* his first published work, appeared in 1913. After Poland regained independence in 1918, Slonimski became one of the most influential Polish writers of his time and remained so until his death. At the onset of World War II he went to France and then to England, where he edited *New Poland;* after the war he helped found UNESCO. Having returned to Poland, he became a leading spokesman of the Polish writers' demands for cultural freedom and a fighter for humanitarian causes. He was also president of the Polish Writers' Union (1956–59).

Smith, Gerald L(yman) K(enneth), U.S. self-styled rabble-rouser (b. Pardeeville, Wis., Feb. 27, 1898—d. Glendale, Calif., April 15, 1976), was a fundamentalist preacher who became a national figure as a right-wing extremist. After moving (1928) to Shreveport, La., he became an enthusiastic supporter of Gov. Huey P. Long's legislation to "soak the rich" and offered himself as a spokesman for Long's Share-Our-Wealth clubs. Following the assassination of (then U.S. senator) Long in 1935, Smith became a virulent critic of Jews, Catholics, Communists, blacks, labour unions, and Pres. Franklin D. Roosevelt. To provide a forum for his views, he founded such organizations as the National Christian Crusade (1947) and acquired a printing press to publish, among other things, his monthly *The Cross and the Flag* (since 1942). In recent years Smith attacked the U.S. Congress as "impotent, insipid and cowardly" and called for the impeachment of the Supreme Court for its "pro-criminal, pro-Communist, pro-pornographic" decisions.

Speaight, Robert William, British actor and author (b. Jan. 14, 1904—d. Benenden, Kent, England, Nov. 4, 1976), developed fine acting skills to complement his excellent voice, all of which he used to great advantage in Shakespearean roles and in his portrayal of Becket in T. S. Eliot's *Murder in the Cathedral* (1935 and many revivals). In the BBC radio production of Dorothy Sayers' *The Man Born to Be King* (1941–42), he was the voice of Christ. Speaight also wrote four novels and biographies of Thomas Becket (1938), Hilaire Belloc (1957), Teilhard de Chardin (1967), and others.

Spence, Sir Basil Urwin, Scottish architect (b. Bombay, India, Aug. 13, 1907—d. Eye, Suffolk, England, Nov. 19, 1976), was most widely known as the architect of the new cathedral at Coventry, replacing the edifice destroyed in World War II. He was educated at George Watson's College, Edinburgh, and at the schools of architecture at London and Edinburgh universities. Spence's design for a new Coventry cathedral won a competition in 1951 for its combination of spatial simplicity and rich decoration—stained glass by John Piper and a tapestry by Graham Sutherland—and for the moving inclusion of the burned-out shell of the old cathedral. Spence also designed the British embassy in Rome (completed 1971), the Household Cavalry Barracks at Knightsbridge (1970), numerous university buildings (especially at Sussex), and large country houses. He was knighted in 1960 and awarded the Order of Merit in 1962.

JORGE LEWINSKI

Starkie, Walter Fitzwilliam, Irish scholar and musician (b. Aug. 9, 1894—d. Madrid, Spain, Nov. 2, 1976), was best known as an authority and defender of European Gypsies whom he accompanied on travels over southeastern Europe, Italy, and Spain and commemorated in such books as *Raggle Taggle* (1933), *Don Gypsy* (1936), *In Sara's Tents* (1954), and *Scholars and Gypsies* (1962). He took special delight in playing the violin as the Gypsies entertained themselves and others. Starkie attended Trinity College, Dublin, and trained in music at the Royal Irish Academy of Music. He was a professor of Spanish and lecturer in Italian literature at Dublin University (1926–47), was named first director of the British Institute in Madrid in 1940, and lectured widely.

Stoneley, Robert, British geophysicist (b. Clacton, Essex, England, May 14, 1894—d. Cambridge, England, Feb. 2, 1976), used seismological data to demonstrate that the theoretical deformation of the Earth by tidal forces is only about one-half of that indicated by observation of tides alone. He also discovered that the depth of the Earth's crust is only about one-third of that previously thought. He held appointments at Sheffield (1920–23), Leeds (1923–34), and Cambridge (1934–61) universities, and was president of the International Association of Seismology and Physics of the Earth's Interior (1946–51) and honorary director of its *International Seismological Summary* (1957–63).

Stopford, the Right Rev. Robert Wright, Anglican clergyman (b. Liverpool, England, Feb. 20, 1901—d. Newbury, Berkshire, England, Aug. 13, 1976), bishop of London (1961–73), was prominent in formulating the Church of England's educational policies. He was ordained in 1932 while senior history master at Oundle School and was principal of Trinity College (1935–41), Kandy, Ceylon (now Sri Lanka), and of Achimota College (1941–45), Gold Coast (now Ghana). After returning to England he became moderator of the Church Training Colleges (1947–55), secretary of the Church Assembly Schools Council (1952–55), suffragan bishop of Fulham (1955–56), and bishop of Peterborough (1956–61). He also served as vicar-general of the episcopal church in Jerusalem and the Middle East (1974–75) and was bishop of Bermuda at the time of his death.

Strand, Paul, U.S. photographer (b. New York, N.Y., Oct. 16, 1890—d. Oregeval, France, March 31, 1976), was a master of realism who turned away from the soft-focus romanticism of his contemporaries to produce photos that were artistic without necessarily being beautiful. Because his chief concern was "something outside himself" rather than "inner states of being," he refused to doctor negatives to create effects that the camera itself did not record. Such photos as "The Blind Beggar Woman" (1915), "Picket Fence" (1915), and "The Family" (1953) were proof of his success. Strand also photographed the beauties of nature and from the mid-1930s was involved in motion pictures. Notable accomplishments included *Redes* ("Nets"; English title, *The Wave*), a remarkable 1935 study of Mexican fishermen on strike.

Tchernicheva, Lubov Pavlovna, Russian-born ballerina (b. St. Petersburg [now Leningrad], Russia, Sept. 17, 1890—d. London, England, March 1, 1976), was, with her husband Sergey Grigoriev, a member of Sergey Diaghilev's Ballet Russe throughout its existence (1909–29) and afterward helped Colonel de Basil's company (1932–52) preserve some of the Diaghilev traditions. She danced her first solos in 1913 during a South American tour and became ballet mistress in 1926. Memorable performances included the title role (1937) in David Lichine's *Francesca da Rimini*. After 1952 she worked with British ballet companies and made her last stage appearance (1959) in Milan, Italy, portraying Lady Capulet in John Cranko's *Romeo and Juliet*.

UPI COMPIX

Teyte, Maggie (DAME MARGARET COTTINGHAM), English soprano singer (b. Wolverhampton, Staffordshire, England, April 17, 1888—d. London, England, May 26, 1976), made her name singing the songs of Fauré, Berlioz, and Ernest Chausson and in the lead role of Debussy's *Pelléas et Mélisande.* Trained in Paris by Jean de Reszke, she joined the Opéra Comique and subsequently sang in England and in the U.S. She joined the British National Opera Company in 1922 and the Covent Garden Opera in 1930; her last performance, a recital, was in 1955. Teyte, a chevalier of the Legion of Honour (1957) and a dame of the British Empire (1958), described her career in *Star on the Door* (1958).

Thadden-Trieglaff, Reinhold von, German Lutheran layman (b. Möhringen, East Prussia, Aug. 13, 1891—d. Fulda, West Germany, Oct. 10, 1976), was founder and president from 1949 of the German Evangelical Church's *Kirchentag* (Laymen's Church Congress) movement to increase contact between church and laity. After finishing his university education, he undertook social work in Berlin and opposed National Socialism (Nazism) by helping to write the 1934 Barmen Declaration of the German Confessing Church. During World War II in Belgium he was placed in charge of the German-occupied district of Louvain but refused to arrest and execute 30 hostages; for this act of courage he was made an honorary citizen of Louvain in 1947. The following year he became a member of the Central Committee of the World Council of Churches.

Thomas, Sir (James William) Tudor, British ophthalmic surgeon (b. Breckonshire, Wales, May 23, 1893—d. Cardiff, Wales, Jan. 23, 1976), was a pioneer in the technique of corneal grafting. Trained at Cardiff Medical School in Wales and at Middlesex Hospital in London, he early specialized in ophthalmology and became associate surgeon in charge of the corneal plastic department at the Central London Ophthalmic Hospital (1935–40). He then returned to Wales as ophthalmic surgeon to the Cardiff Royal Infirmary. He was president of the British Medical Association (1953–54) and of the Ophthalmological Society of the United Kingdom (1966–68), and master of the Oxford Ophthalmological Congress (1956–58). He was knighted in 1956.

Thomson of Fleet, Roy Herbert Thomson, 1st Baron, Canadian-born newspaper proprietor (b. Toronto, Ont., June 5, 1894—d. London, England, Aug. 4, 1976), was joint-chairman with his son Kenneth of the Thomson Organisation, Ltd., which owns *The Times* of London and the *Sunday Times* newspapers; he was likewise chairman of both The Scotsman Publications, Ltd., and Thomson Newspapers, Ltd., Canada, and had substantial television interests. Early in life Thomson worked as a clerk and salesman, later failed as a prairie farmer and supplier of motor parts, then sold radios successfully and built his own radio station at North Bay, Ont., which brought in advertising revenue and helped to sell sets. In 1933 Thomson opened a second station at Timmins, 200 mi farther north. In 1934 he took over an ailing Timmins weekly newspaper and made it a daily; two other radio stations were added, and by 1944 four more; that year he acquired four newspapers. He moved back to Toronto, and his chain of newspapers grew to include some in the U.S., where, in 1960, he purchased the Brush Moore group.

In 1952 Thomson was defeated as a Conservative candidate for election to Canada's federal Parliament, but in the same year he was invited to buy *The Scotsman* newspaper and went to Edinburgh to run it. Seeing its potential, he also took up the franchise of Scottish television. He left the Canadian side of his business to his son's management but, regarding Canada as his base, continued to expand there into television. In 1959 he acquired the Kemsley group of newspapers, the largest in Britain, which included the *Sunday Times,* to which he added (1962) Britain's first colour magazine supplement. In 1963 he became a British citizen, set up the Thomson Foundation, and in 1964 was created a baron. In 1967 he made his most outstanding newspaper purchase, *The Times* of London. Lord Thomson strove to give the newspaper needed financial stability and injected £5 million into it. In 1972, in his last big venture, he formed a consortium with Occidental and Getty Oil to acquire a North Sea oil concession. Thomson was a man who put pure business and money first but tempered his acquisitiveness with exceptional frankness and honesty. He was also exceptional in the freedom he allowed his editors.

Thorndike, Dame (Agnes) Sybil, British actress (b. Gainsborough, Lincolnshire, England, Oct. 24, 1882—d. London, England, June 9, 1976), was acclaimed Britain's foremost actress since Ellen Terry. After injuring her wrist, she turned from music to acting and in 1908 married the actor and Socialist Lewis Casson. The Cassons lived and worked together till he died in 1969 at the age of 93. During World War I, while Lewis was in the Army, Sybil became a Shakespearean actress under Lilian Baylis at the Old Vic and showed signs of future greatness in tragic roles. After the war the Cassons ventured into actor-management with presentations of *The Trojan Women* and *Medea,* classical tragedies by Euripides. In 1924, in G. B. Shaw's *Saint Joan,* Sybil Thorndike scored a triumph that she later repeated in Paris, South Africa, and Australia. In 1931 she was made a dame of the British Empire. During World War II the Cassons acted in government-sponsored Old Vic tours, and from 1954 to 1962, undiminished in vigour, they toured many countries to act and give dramatic and poetry recitals. In 1969 Thorndike opened the Thorndike Theatre outside London and in 1970 was made a Companion of Honour. In addition to their stage work, the Cassons actively supported many humanitarian and left-wing causes.

FREDDIE FEEST—CAMERA PRESS/PHOTO TRENDS

Tobey, Mark, U.S. artist (b. Centerville, Wis., Dec. 11, 1890—d. Basel, Switz., April 24, 1976), made his living early in life as an illustrator, but after a visit to the Orient in 1934 he developed "white writing," a technique based on Chinese calligraphy. In such paintings as "Transit" (1948), one form flows from the other in much the same way as rapidly written Chinese characters flow from a writing brush. Tobey, who held the post of artist in residence (1931–38) at Dartington Hall in South Devon, England, was a religious man who viewed his abstract works as visual representations of the music of the universe that permeates nature. Among his awards was first prize at the 29th Venice Biennale (1958). The largest collection of his paintings is in the Seattle (Wash.) Art Museum.

Tubb, Carrie (MRS. CAROLINE ELIZABETH OLIVEIRA), English dramatic soprano (b. London, England, May 17, 1876—d. London, Sept. 20, 1976), made her career on the concert stage, specializing in oratorio and the works of Wagner. She studied at London's Guildhall School of Music and in 1910 sang several operatic roles at Covent Garden. Later, she was regularly heard at Sir Henry Wood's Promenade Concerts. After retiring from singing about 1930, she taught at the Guildhall School for almost 30 years.

Turin, Duccio, Italian architect (b. near Turin, Italy, April 1, 1926—d. Italy, July 29, 1976), became the first professor of building (1965) at the University of London, and in 1974 deputy director general of the UN Conference on Human Settlements (Habitat), held in Vancouver, B.C., in 1976. He qualified in South America as an architect, and later turned also to economics. After working for the French government, he joined the UN Economic Commission, first in Europe and then in Africa, where he was based in Addis Ababa, Ethiopia. From there he went to University College, London, to occupy the chair of building set up to encourage a closer understanding between architects and the building industry.

Ullmann, Stephen, Hungarian-born philologist and linguist (b. Budapest, Austria-Hungary, June 13, 1914—d. Oxford, England, Jan. 10, 1976), obtained a doctorate in modern languages from the University of Budapest before moving to England (1939), where he worked for the British Broadcasting Corporation's monitoring service (1940–46). He then taught Romance philology and general linguistics at the University of Glasgow (1946–53) and Romance philology and French at the University of Leeds (1953–68). He became professor of Romance languages at Oxford University in 1968, was editor of *Archivum Linguisticum* (1949–64), and served as president of both the Philological Society (1970–75) and the Modern Language Association (1973). Ullmann's scholarly reputation was firmly established through such books as *The Principles of Semantics* (1951), *Précis de sémantique française* (1952), *Style in the French Novel* (1957), *The Image in the Modern French Novel* (1960), *Semantics: An Introduction to the Science of Meaning* (1962), *Meaning and Style* (1973), and *Words and Their Meanings* (1974).

Uttley, Alison, British author (b. Cromford, Derbyshire, England, Dec. 17, 1884—d. High Wycombe, Buckinghamshire, England, May 7, 1976), was best known for *The Country Child* (1931) and other tales of late Victorian rural life, and for a vast output of books for young children, featuring such characters as Little Grey Rabbit, Sam Pig, and Brown Mouse. Though a physicist, she turned to writing after her husband's early death (1930). Among other books she wrote *Ambush of Young Days* (1937), *Country Hoard* (1943), and *A Traveller in Time* (1939).

Visconti, Luchino, Italian director (b. Milan, Italy, Nov. 2, 1906—d. Rome, Italy, March 17, 1976), revolutionized post-World War II filmmaking with realistic portrayals of human struggles for survival in modern society. His first film, *Ossessione* (1942), marked Visconti as the father of Neorealism and foreshadowed the later works of Roberto Rossellini, Vittorio De Sica, Federico Fellini, and Michelangelo Antonioni. In 1948 Visconti's *La terra trema* won the Grand Prize at the Venice Film Festival for its documentary-like study of Sicilian fishermen. Among other notable films were *Senso* (1953), *Rocco and His Brothers* (1960), *The Leopard* (1964), and *Morte a Venezia* (1971; *Death in Venice*). Visconti was equally impressive on the stage, directing the plays of Jean Anouilh, Jean Cocteau, Jean-Paul Sartre, Arthur Miller, Tennessee Williams, and Erskine Caldwell. His operas included outstanding productions of *La Traviata* (1955) in Milan and *Don Carlos* (1958) in London.

ROBERT COHEN—AGIP/PICTORIAL PARADE

Vogüé, Comte Robert-Jean de, French champagne producer (b. Menetou-Salon, France, Aug. 3, 1896—d. Paris, France, Oct. 17, 1976), joined the champagne firm of Moët et Chandon as managing director in 1930 and became chairman in 1967, after the firm became a public company in 1962. A son of Louis, marquis de Vogüé, and the princesse d'Arenberg, he married Ghislaine d'Eudeville, a descendant of Claude Moët, who founded the business in 1743. Vogüé personally advocated a greater degree of worker participation that became law in 1959. After 1962 the company expanded, uniting in 1971 with Jas. Hennessy et Cie to form Moët-Hennessy, of which he was the first president. It also bought an interest in Parfums Christian Dior, and founded M & H Vineyards at Napa Valley in California. He was a Commander of the Legion of Honour and had been awarded several medals for his role in the Resistance.

Walkley, Sir William Gaston, New Zealand oil magnate (b. Wellington, New Zealand, Nov. 1, 1896—d. Sydney, New South Wales, April 12, 1976), pioneered full-scale oil exploration in Australia and was founder and managing director (1939–67) of Ampol Petroleum Ltd. and its associate company, Ampol Exploration Ltd. He was educated in Wellington and was a chartered accountant in New Zealand (1925–35). Walkley, who was also an enthusiastic patron of football, sailing, and Australian journalism, was knighted in 1967.

Weigle, Luther Allan, U.S. biblical scholar (b. Littlestown, Pa., Sept. 11, 1880—d. New Haven,

Conn., Sept. 2, 1976), long-time dean (1928–49) of the Yale University Divinity School, was appointed chairman in 1929 of a committee of 22 scholars who, with the help of others, eventually produced the Revised Standard Version of the Bible. Millions of copies were sold after publication, the New Testament first appearing in 1946, the Old Testament in 1952. The new translation, sponsored by the National Council of Churches (which Weigle helped organize), was meant to replace the American Standard Version (1901), which was in turn a revision of the Authorized (King James) Version, published in 1611.

Wheeler, Sir (Robert Eric) Mortimer, British archaeologist (b. Edinburgh, Scotland, Sept. 10, 1890—d. Leatherhead, England, July 22, 1976), was well known as a popularizer of his science, particularly on television. His principal interests were Great Britain, continental Europe, India, Pakistan, and Africa. During his career he was

KEYSTONE

secretary of the British Academy (1949–68), director (1940–44 and 1949–54) and president (1954–59) of the Society of Antiquarians (and recipient of its gold medal in 1944), and trustee of the British Museum (1954–59 and 1963–73). He became professor of ancient history to the Royal Academy in 1965, and was a fellow of University College, University of London, from 1922 until his death. Wheeler, who was knighted in 1952 and made a Companion of Honour in 1967, became a fellow of the Royal Society in 1968.

Whipple, George Hoyt, U.S. pathologist (b. Ashland, N.H., Aug. 28, 1878—d. Rochester, N.Y., Feb. 1, 1976), shared the 1934 Nobel Prize for Physiology or Medicine with George R. Minor and William P. Murphy. Whipple's independent research with anemic dogs matched the findings of Minor and Murphy and established the fact that pernicious anemia can be controlled by a diet containing liver. This discovery signaled a major advance in the treatment of noninfectious diseases even though many years passed before the vitamin B_{12} in liver was identified as the extrinsic factor responsible for restoring the blood to a healthy state. Whipple studied and taught at Johns Hopkins University and was director of the Hooper Foundation for medical research in California before moving (1921–55) to the University of Rochester in New York.

White, Minor, U.S. photographer (b. Minneapolis, Minn., July 9, 1908—d. Boston, Mass., June 24, 1976), was one of the most creative and influential photographers of his day. White's creativity began to express itself early in his career as an employee of the Works Progress Administration. In 1945 his style acquired definitive form when he learned from Edward Weston the value of realism and tonal beauty in prints, and from Alfred Stieglitz the expressive potential of the sequence (photos presented as a unit) and the equivalent (an image viewed as a visual metaphor). Both in his photographs and in his writing, White became the foremost exponent of the sequence and

ARTHUR GRACE—THE NEW YORK TIMES

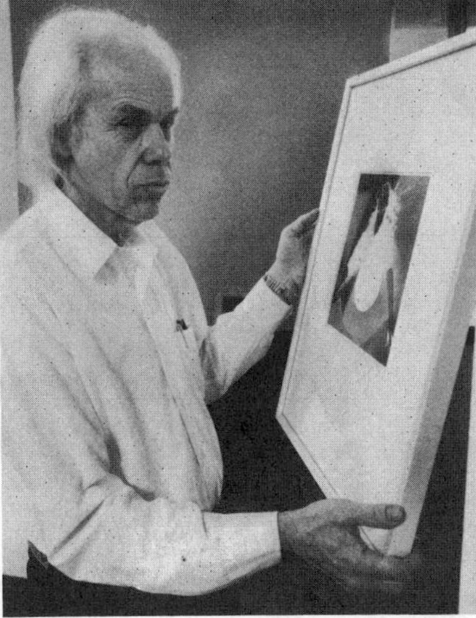

the equivalent. In 1946 White moved to San Francisco, where he worked closely with Ansel Adams and learned to previsualize how the scene or object would appear in the final print. The next year White succeeded Adams as director of the photography department of the California School of Fine Arts, where, during the course of his teaching, he developed a method of reading photographs called space analysis. He wrote extensively on his theories of photography as the editor of *Aperture,* which he founded in 1952, and *Image,* which he edited from 1953 to 1957. White was also a leading abstract photographer, often giving mystical interpretations to his photographs. His already great position of influence was further enhanced in 1965, when he was made professor of creative photography at the Massachusetts Institute of Technology.

Wildt, Rupert, German-born astrophysicist (b. Munich, Germany, June 25, 1905—d. Orleans, Mass., Jan. 9, 1976), completed his doctoral studies at the University of Berlin (1927) and worked at the university observatories in Bonn and Göttingen before moving to the U.S. in 1935. The greater part of his professional career was spent at Yale University (1946–73). Wildt was credited with two major discoveries regarding planetary and solar atmospheres. In 1938 he theorized that the masses of Jupiter and Saturn consist mainly of compressed hydrogen and therefore have low densities. The following year he concluded that the negative hydrogen ion is the essential radiation-absorbing element in the solar atmosphere. Both theories were later confirmed. In 1966 Wildt received the Eddington Gold Medal of Britain's Royal Astronomical Society.

Yakubovsky, Ivan Ignatyevich, Soviet marshal (b. Zaytsevo, Mogilev Province, Belorussia, Jan. 7, 1912—d. Moscow, U.S.S.R., Nov. 30, 1976), became commander in chief of the Warsaw Pact forces in 1967. In 1932 he entered the Military College of Minsk and during World War II commanded troops in the defense of Moscow, Stalingrad, and Kursk. He also led an armoured corps that participated in the capture of Berlin and twice won his country's highest military decoration for bravery. Having graduated from the general staff academy in 1948, he commanded a division and later the armoured forces of the Carpathian military district. Yakubovsky served as deputy commander in chief of Soviet forces in East Germany (1957–60) before being named commander in chief (1962–65). He became a member of the Central Committee of the Communist Party in 1961 and was promoted to the rank of marshal in 1967, the year he assumed responsibility for the Warsaw Pact forces.

Younger, Sir Kenneth Gilmour, British politician and expert in international relations (b. Dec. 15, 1908—d. London, England, May 19, 1976), was director of the Royal Institute of International Affairs (Chatham House) from 1959 to 1971, during which time he sought to change Britain's pattern of post-imperial relationships. He expounded a policy of participation in new international organizations in *Changing Perspectives in British Foreign Policy* (1964). The second son of a viscount, he was Labour MP for the fishing borough of Grimsby (1945–59) and held junior positions at the home and foreign offices (1947–51) before joining Chatham House in 1953. Younger, who was knighted in 1972, was chairman of both the Howard League for Penal Reform (1960–73) and the Committee of Inquiry on Privacy (1970–72).

Zinkeisen, Anna Katrina, British painter (b. Kilcreggan, Dunbartonshire, Scotland, Aug. 28, 1906—d. London, England, Sept. 23, 1976), employed her wide-ranging skill in a variety of fields that included portraiture, murals (notably for the Cunard liners "Queen Mary" and "Queen Elizabeth"), flower painting, book illustration, posters, and ceramics. Her illustrations in the field of medicine included those wounded in the London "blitz" and Sir Archibald McIndoe's plastic-surgery patients at East Grinstead in 1944. Among those who sat for her were McIndoe and Prince Philip. Zinkeisen won a scholarship to the Royal Academy Schools at 15, and first exhibited at the Royal Academy at 18.

Zukor, Adolph, Hungarian-born motion-picture magnate (b. Ricse, Hungary, Jan. 7, 1873—d. Los Angeles, Calif., June 10, 1976), was a nearly penniless orphan of 16 when he arrived in New York City and took a job sweeping floors in a fur shop. Three years later (1892) he opened a successful fur business with Morris Kohn in Chicago, then moved it to New York where, in 1903, they started the Automatic Vaudeville Co., a penny arcade. With financial backing from Marcus Loew (later head of Metro-Goldwyn-Mayer), Zukor was soon offering music and short films to arcade customers in several major East Coast cities. Zukor then advanced to make-do nickelodeon theatres with longer pictures and in 1912, having split with Loew, presented the first feature-length (40 minutes) movie ever shown in the U.S.: *Queen Elizabeth,* a French-made feature starring Sarah Bernhardt. Its success on tour led to the formation of the Famous Players Co. and provided Zukor with the necessary money and incentive to form Paramount Pictures Corp. after merging with Jesse L. Lasky's Feature Play Co. and lesser concerns. Essentially a businessman with only minor interest in the actual creation of films, Zukor generally steered clear of Hollywood. One of his most far-reaching decisions was to guarantee distribution of the films Paramount produced by buying up a chain of movie houses across the country. He became board chairman of Paramount in 1935 and did not retire until ten years before his death at age 103.

WIDE WORLD

CHRONOLOGY OF EVENTS

JANUARY

1 *China's Cultural Revolution defended*

Peking published two new poems by Chairman Mao Tse-tung and an editorial defending the results of the Cultural Revolution. It appeared to be an effort by the aged Mao to ensure that his revolutionary policies would continue after his death. One of the poems mocked Soviet "goulash Communism"; the editorial included criticism of the Soviet emphasis on economic efficiency. "Stability and unity do not mean writing off the class struggle," said the editorial.

5 *Violence in Northern Ireland*

In a new wave of violence, ten Protestant workmen were shot to death near Belfast, where five Roman Catholics had been killed the previous night. Their deaths raised the number of persons killed in fighting between Catholic and Protestant extremists to 16 in the first five days of 1976. The British government ordered more troops into the country.

8 *International monetary reform*

Finance ministers of countries belonging to the International Monetary Fund agreed in Kingston, Jamaica, to a reform of the international monetary system. The new arrangement would permit the values of currencies to "float" in the world market according to supply and demand. The agreement also would increase the amounts of currency countries can borrow from the IMF.

India suspends constitutional rights

The Indian government suspended basic rights guaranteed by the constitution: freedom of speech, freedom of assembly, freedom to form associations and labour unions, the right to move freely and to live in any part of the country, the right to own property, and the right to pursue any profession, trade, or business. India's ruling Congress Party also agreed to postpone parliamentary elections for at least a year, to continue indefinitely the state of emergency proclaimed in 1975, and to amend the constitution so as to give Prime Minister Indira Gandhi more power in relation to the judiciary. Voicing his opposition, one member of Parliament said, "The role of Parliament has been eroded and there is a danger that it will be eroded still further."

15 *Vatican statement on sex*

The Roman Catholic Church reiterated its condemnation of sex outside marriage and stated that homosexuality cannot be condoned under any circumstances. The Sacred Congregation for the Doctrine of the Faith stressed continuation of the church's traditional stand on sexual ethics.

18 *Steelers defeat Cowboys in Super Bowl*

The tenth annual Super Bowl in Miami for the championship of the National Football League was won by Pittsburgh 21–17 over Dallas.

The Soviet Union reported a poor grain crop in 1975. Here combines are at work in Krasnoyarsk.

TASS / SOVFOTO

19 *Carter emerges from the pack*

Former governor Jimmy Carter of Georgia emerged as a leading contender for the Democratic presidential nomination after winning 27.6% of the vote in Iowa's precinct caucuses.

Cambodians relocated

The Cambodian government was reportedly continuing its massive relocation of hundreds of thousands of its people, mainly to sparsely settled areas in the northwest. The forced migration began in October 1975.

22 *Cease-fire in Lebanon*

A political and military agreement was underwritten by Syria to end the fighting in Lebanon. The agreement granted some Muslim demands for a greater share in political power; the Christian minority had previously dominated the government.

24 *U.S. treaty with Spain*

The U.S. and Spain signed a five-year Treaty of Friendship and Cooperation—the first formal treaty between the two countries since the Spanish Civil War. It gave the U.S. continued use of naval facilities at Rota on the Mediterranean coast and of air bases at Torrejón, Saragossa, and Morón. Spain was to get $1.2 billion in credits and grants for military, technical, and cultural assistance.

25 *House committee reports on intelligence agencies*

Federal intelligence agencies in the U.S. operate in such secrecy as to be "beyond the scrutiny" of Congress, according to an unpublished report of the House Select Committee on Intelligence. The report, which was leaked to the press, cited a number of irregularities on the part of the agencies in question, which included the Federal Bureau of Investigation, the Central Intelligence Agency, and the National Security Agency.

26 *Economists predict gradual recovery*

Pres. Gerald Ford's Council of Economic Advisers said it would be several years before the inflationary trend of recent years was overcome in the U.S. In its annual report it called for a gradual recovery from the 1973–75 recession. "What we need is a durable recovery," it said, "not a boom that carries the seeds of renewed instability in prices, incomes, and employment." It predicted that unemployment in 1976 would average 7.7% and that prices would continue to rise by 6%.

27 *Congress rejects aid to Angola*

Despite a last-minute plea from Pres. Gerald Ford, the House of Representatives voted to cut off all U.S. assistance to the two Western-supported factions in Angola. The administration had expressed grave concern over massive Soviet military assistance to the Popular Movement for the Liberation of Angola.

28 *OPEC to provide loans for less developed countries*

The Organization of Petroleum Exporting Countries agreed to make interest-free loans to less developed countries from a fund of $800 million in 1976.

30 *Stock market bullish*

The New York Stock Exchange concluded the busiest month in its history. A total of 635,850,000 shares were traded in January. Turnover on January 30 was a record 38,510,000 shares. The previous record month was May 1975, when 457,410,000 shares were traded. The Dow Jones average of industrial stock prices rose more than 122 points in January, ending at 975.28.

Supreme Court rules on election law

The U.S. Supreme Court ruled that no limits may be imposed on spending by candidates for federal office. This had been a major provision of the 1974 election reform law. But the court upheld the law's provisions for public financing of presidential campaigns, limits on contributions to campaigns for federal office, and strict reporting of contributions and expenditures. The court's ruling against limits on spending did not extend to presidential candidates who accept public funds in their campaigns—which included all the major candidates in 1976. The court held that campaign spending is "speech" and is thus protected by the First Amendment to the Constitution. It also required Congress to reshape the Federal Election Commission set up under the law.

31 *Soviet five-year plan report*

The Soviet Union's agricultural output dropped 6% in 1975. Its grain harvest was the worst in a decade, according to the final economic figures for 1975 released by the Central Statistical Board. The five-year plan that ended in 1975 had called for industrial growth of 42 to 46%, while actual growth over the five years was 37.2%. The underfulfillment was attributed to a failure of productivity to grow as fast as planned. The grain harvest in 1975 came to 140 million tons, less than two-thirds of the planned 215.7 million tons. The Soviet Union had to buy about 25 million tons of grain abroad, mostly from the U.S., Canada, and Australia, and to cut the size of its livestock herds.

FEBRUARY

2 *Repression in India*

The government of India arrested hundreds of members of the opposition Dravidian Progressive Federation party.

Elliot Richardson becomes commerce secretary

Elliot L. Richardson was sworn in as U.S. secretary of commerce, his fourth Cabinet post in six years. He said: "I may be at this very moment entering the Guinness Book of Records as the most sworn-in of Americans."

Moynihan resigns

Daniel P. Moynihan resigned as U.S. representative to the United Nations. He charged that many officials of the State Department had not supported his policies at the UN. He had strongly criticized Middle Eastern and African governments for their antidemocratic stands. He denied emphatically charges that he was resigning to run for political office.

3 *Kissinger defends arms control agreements with U.S.S.R.*

U.S. Secretary of State Henry Kissinger said in San Francisco that the arms control agreements reached with the Soviet Union since 1963 had brought some restraint in Soviet-U.S. nuclear rivalry. An even more important advance would be made, he said, "if the 1974 Vladivostok accord leads to a new agreement."

Plyushch attacks Soviet political repression

Leonid I. Plyushch, a Soviet mathematician who left the U.S.S.R. in January, said he had been kept in a mental hospital for 2½ years because of his political beliefs. He said there were 60 other "political patients" in the hospital. He had been arrested in 1972 after publishing articles in a number of clandestine publications and had been interned in the institution until January 1975.

4 *UNESCO fails to eradicate illiteracy*

The United Nations Educational, Scientific and Cultural Organization said it is failing in its efforts to end illiteracy. It estimated that there were now 800 million illiterates in the world, compared with 735 million in 1965. However, its ten-year program had been concentrated on only 11 countries—Algeria, Ecuador, Ethiopia, Guinea, India, Iran, Madagascar, Mali, Sudan, Syria, and Tanzania.

Earthquake in Guatemala

An earthquake killed 23,000 people in Guatemala and injured more than 75,000. Over half a million were rendered homeless in the worst disaster in the history of Central America.

Young victims of the earthquake that shook Guatemala in February.

JEAN-PIERRE LAFFONT—SYGMA

Trial of Patricia Hearst begins

Lawyers made their opening statements in the bank robbery trial of U.S. newspaper heiress Patricia Hearst. The issue was whether she had joined her kidnappers in the robbery willingly or had been coerced.

Concorde on trial

U.S. Transportation Secretary William T. Coleman, Jr., ruled that the French-British Concorde supersonic airliner would be allowed to fly to Washington and New York on a 16-month trial basis.

Lockheed scandal breaks

The Lockheed Aircraft Corp. paid $7.1 million in bribes to a right-wing Japanese militarist to promote sale of a commercial jetliner, according to company documents released by a U.S. Senate subcommittee. Other countries in which Lockheed reportedly bribed officials included Italy, Turkey, Mexico, Colombia, and The Netherlands, where a commission was formed to investigate charges that Prince Bernhard received $1.1 million from Lockheed to promote the sale of its aircraft to the Dutch armed forces.

4–15 *XII Winter Olympics*

The XII Winter Olympic Games were held in Innsbruck, Austria. A total of 1,054 athletes from 37 nations competed.

5 *Doctors protest malpractice insurance rates*

Doctors in southern California ended a 35-day work slowdown protesting a 327% increase in the cost of malpractice insurance. About three-quarters of the 4,400 doctors in the Los Angeles County area participated.

7 *Hua Kuo-feng named premier of China*

Peking announced that Hua Kuo-feng, a relatively unknown sixth-ranking deputy premier, had been appointed acting premier to fill the vacancy created by the death of Chou En-lai on January 8.

9–11 *MPLA wins in Angola*

Soviet-supplied Angolan forces led by Cuban troops seized the central Angolan town of Huambo, headquarters of a government established by two Western-supported nationalist factions. The Organization of African Unity announced that it was recognizing the Angolan government formed by the victorious Popular Movement for the Liberation of Angola.

16–24 *Kissinger tours Latin America*

U.S. Secretary of State Henry Kissinger visited Venezuela, Peru, Brazil, Colombia, Costa Rica, and Guatemala. In Brazil he signed an agreement calling for semiannual consultations between the governments of the two countries on foreign policy matters—the first such agreement by the U.S. with any Latin-American government.

ADN-ZB / EASTFOTO

Residents of Huambo in Angola welcome forces of the Popular Movement for the Liberation of Angola.

17 *U.S. intelligence agencies reformed*

Pres. Gerald Ford announced a reorganization of U.S. intelligence agencies, the most sweeping reform since 1947.

19 *British socialism retrenches*

Britain's Labour government decided to make large cuts in planned public spending, amounting to $3.6 billion in 1977–78 and $6 billion in 1978–79.

Iceland severs ties with Britain

Iceland broke diplomatic relations with Great Britain in a dispute over the amount of cod that British fishing boats could take from Icelandic waters. This followed clashes between Icelandic gunboats and British trawlers.

21 *Nixon goes to China*

Former U.S. president Richard M. Nixon arrived in Peking to begin an eight-day visit to China at the invitation of the Chinese government. He was greeted by Acting Premier Hua Kuo-feng.

Israel withdraws in Sinai

Israel pulled its forces back to new positions in the Sinai desert under terms of the Israeli-Egyptian troop disengagement agreement. United Nations forces moved into the buffer zone. Three American surveillance stations were opened at the Mitla and Giddi passes.

23 *Daniel Schorr suspended*

CBS News suspended TV news correspondent Daniel Schorr pending a congressional investigation for leaking the secret House Select Committee on Intelligence report on intelligence agencies.

23–24 *Southeast Asian summit meeting*

The first meeting of leaders of the Association of Southeast Asian Nations was held in Bali, Indonesia. The leaders of Malaysia, Indonesia, Thailand, Singapore, and the Philippines agreed to set up a secretariat and high council in Jakarta.

24 *Soviet political leaders meet*

At the 25th congress of the Soviet Communist Party in Moscow, party leader Leonid I. Brezhnev said the Soviet Union would continue to favour détente with the U.S. but would not abandon the struggle against capitalism.

Ford wins New Hampshire presidential primary

Pres. Gerald Ford won the New Hampshire GOP presidential primary, receiving 51% of the votes to Ronald Reagan's 49%. Among the Democrats, former Georgia governor Jimmy Carter received 30%, Rep. Morris Udall of Arizona 24%, and Sen. Birch Bayh of Indiana 16%.

25 *Microwaves in Moscow*

Soviet officials admitted beaming microwaves at the U.S. embassy in Moscow in order to disable U.S. electronic eavesdropping devices.

26 *Military rule to end in Portugal*

Portuguese military and political leaders signed an agreement to end military rule and establish a freely elected government. Legislative elections were scheduled to be held in April.

27 *Dissension in Moscow*

The leader of Italy's Communist Party took a strongly independent line at the 25th Soviet party congress in Moscow. Enrico Berlinguer told the delegates that Italian Communists favoured cooperation with capitalism. The congress was boycotted by the leader of the French Communist Party, who had criticized the Soviet Union for suppressing political dissidents.

28 *Ford denounces Castro*

U.S. Pres. Gerald Ford called Cuba's Prime Minister Fidel Castro an "international outlaw" for sending "12,000 soldiers to intervene in a civil war in Angola" on behalf of the Soviet-backed MPLA.

29 *Arab oil countries promise to finance Egypt's debt*

Egypt's Pres. Anwar as-Sadat returned from a tour of the oil-producing Arab countries of the Persian Gulf with pledges of $750 million in grants. Saudi Arabia and Kuwait each promised to give $300 million, and the United Arab Emirates $150 million. Bahrain and Qatar were expected to raise the total sum to around $1 billion. It was reported that those countries would also help Egypt pay back its $4 billion debt to the Soviet Union.

MARCH

2 *Jackson wins Massachusetts presidential primary*

Sen. Henry Jackson of Washington won 23% of the Democratic votes in the Massachusetts presidential primary. Other leading Democrats were Rep. Morris Udall of Arizona (18%), Gov. George Wallace of Alabama (17%), and former Georgia governor Jimmy Carter (14%). In the Republican primary, Pres. Gerald Ford won 62% of the votes and former California governor Ronald Reagan 35%.

3 *Mozambique prepares to fight*

Mozambique closed its borders with Rhodesia and mobilized its armed forces against what it said was aggression by Rhodesia. The closing of the border cut off Rhodesia's access to the sea. The British government announced its support for Mozambique's move.

5 *Turkish commander implicated in Lockheed scandal*

Gen. Emin Alpkaya, commander of the Turkish Air Force, resigned after allegations that he had received a bribe from the Lockheed Aircraft Corp.

Spain moves toward democracy

The Spanish government announced that it would soon allow free political parties—but not those of terrorists, anarchists, separatists, or Communists.

6 *South Vietnam charts economic course*

The foreign minister of South Vietnam, Mrs. Nguyen Thi Binh, said in Moscow that South Vietnam's economy will be arranged in a five-tier system, allowing considerable private enterprise to coexist with socialized industry.

Examining the crater made by a meteorite in northeastern China.

KEYSTONE

7 *Australian leader censured*

The leadership of Australia's Labor Party censured former Labor prime minister Gough Whitlam for proposing to accept a contribution of $630,000 from Iraq's governing Baath Party.

8 *Early man redated*

Two scientists reported the discovery of remains of early man dating back as far as 3,750,000 years ago. This was said to indicate that *Australopithecus*, once considered to be an ancestor of man, was actually a contemporary of early man that became extinct.

Meteorites fall in China

More than 100 stony meteorites fell near Kirin in northeastern China, representing perhaps the largest stony meteorite fall in recorded history. The largest fragment found weighed an estimated 3,900 pounds.

9 *Ford wins Florida primary*

Pres. Gerald Ford defeated former California governor Ronald Reagan in the Florida Republican presidential preference primary, winning 53% of the votes. Among Democrats the leading candidates were former Georgia governor Jimmy Carter (34%), Alabama Gov. George Wallace (31%), and Sen. Henry Jackson of Washington (24%).

10 *South Korean dissidents arrested*

Eleven critics of the South Korean government of Pres. Park Chung Hee were arrested and charged with agitating to overthrow the government. One of those arrested was the opposition party's most recent presidential candidate.

Nixon testifies on wiretapping

In a written deposition taken on January 15 and released on March 10, former U.S.

president Richard M. Nixon testified that he ordered the FBI to tap the telephones of national security aides and newsmen in 1969, and that Secretary of State Henry Kissinger selected those who were to be tapped.

11 *Dow Jones passes 1,000*

The Dow Jones industrial stock average closed above the 1,000 mark in trading on the New York Stock Exchange.

Military coup in Lebanon

The commander of the Beirut military garrison, Brig. Gen. Abdel Aziz al-Ahdab, declared himself to be the military governor of Lebanon.

Nigeria executes rebels

The government of Nigeria executed the former defense minister and 29 others who had taken part in an attempted coup on February 13 in which the head of government, Brig. Murtala Ramat Mohammed, was assassinated.

14 *Egypt abrogates treaty with Soviets*

Pres. Anwar as-Sadat announced that the Egyptian government was abrogating its 1971 treaty of friendship and cooperation with the Soviet Union. Moscow replied that Sadat had been pursuing an "unfriendly policy" toward the Soviet Union for some time.

16 *U.S. cancels meetings with U.S.S.R.*

State Department officials said that because of the Soviet part in the civil war in Angola, the U.S. would not participate in scheduled meetings of Soviet-U.S. joint commissions.

British prime minister resigns

Harold Wilson announced that he would resign as prime minister of Great Britain as soon as the Labour Party members of the House of Commons could choose a successor.

Carter wins Illinois presidential primary

Former governor Jimmy Carter of Georgia won 48% of the votes in the Illinois Democratic presidential primary. Gov. George Wallace of Alabama was second with 28%, Sargent Shriver got 16%, and Fred Harris 8%. In the Republican primary, Pres. Gerald Ford received 59% of the votes to 40% for Ronald Reagan, former governor of California.

Soviet agriculture chief replaced

The Soviet minister of agriculture, Dmitry S. Polyansky, lost his job as a consequence of the poor grain harvest of 1975, lowest in a decade. He had previously been dropped from the Politburo of the Communist Party.

ALAIN DEJEAN—SYGMA

Harold Wilson waves goodbye after resigning as prime minister of Great Britain.

19 *Rhodesian talks fail*

Prime Minister Ian D. Smith of Rhodesia and Joshua Nkomo, leader of a black nationalist group, broke off negotiations on the question of eventual majority rule in the country and its timing.

Meg and Tony separate

After 16 years of marriage, Princess Margaret of Britain and her husband, Lord Snowdon, announced that they were separating but no divorce was planned.

20 *Thailand orders U.S. forces out*

Thailand ordered the U.S. to remove its military forces in four months, except for 270 military aid advisers.

Patricia Hearst guilty

Newspaper heiress Patricia Hearst was convicted in the federal district court in San Francisco of armed robbery and use of a gun to commit a felony.

22 *Britain offers assistance in Rhodesia*

Britain offered its help in ending the Rhodesian crisis provided the Rhodesian government would accept majority rule and agree to hold democratic elections in the near future.

Kissinger warns Cuba

U.S. Secretary of State Henry Kissinger warned Cuba that the U.S. "will not accept further Cuban military interventions abroad" such as the intervention of Cuban troops in Angola.

23 *Reagan wins North Carolina primary*

Former California governor Ronald Reagan upset Pres. Gerald Ford in the North Carolina Republican presidential preference primary, receiving 52% of the votes to Ford's 46%. Among the Democrats, former Georgia governor Jimmy Carter received 54% of the votes, Gov. George Wallace of Alabama 35%.

Roman Catholic Church reported losing strength in U.S.

The National Opinion Research Center reported that a survey showed the Roman Catholic Church in the U.S. had suffered substantial losses in religious devotion and nearly $1 billion in annual church income because of its ban on artificial means of birth control.

24 *Argentine president overthrown*

María Estela Martínez de Perón, president of Argentina since July 1974, was deposed and arrested by the commanders of the three branches of Argentina's armed forces. She was flown under guard to Neuquén Province.

27 *South African troops leave Angola*

South Africa withdrew the last of its forces from southern Angola, where it had maintained a buffer zone during the Angolan civil war.

29 *Argentina gets new government*

Lieut. Gen. Jorge Rafaél Videla took the oath of office as Argentina's new president. He named a Cabinet of two civilians and six military officers. Videla pledged to carry out a "national reorganization" aimed at creating a strong state.

Rhodesian war is foreseen

Pres. Kenneth Kaunda of Zambia said the breakdown of talks between Rhodesia's white government and black nationalists would engulf the country in war.

30 *Israeli Arabs call general strike*

Arab citizens in Israel held a general strike to protest a government plan to appropriate Arab land for a housing development in Galilee.

31 *Court rules Karen Ann Quinlan can die*

The New Jersey Supreme Court ruled unanimously that the father of Karen Ann Quinlan could request that she be removed from the mechanical respirator that had kept her alive for nearly a year.

APRIL

5 *Callaghan becomes prime minister*

Foreign Secretary James Callaghan became the new prime minister of Great Britain, succeeding Harold Wilson, who resigned.

Antiradical demonstrations in Peking

Violent demonstrations took place in Peking and other Chinese cities, apparently in opposition to the "antirightist" campaign begun by Chinese radicals after the death of Premier Chou En-lai.

6 *Ford wins Wisconsin primary*

Pres. Gerald Ford won the Wisconsin Republican presidential primary with 55% of the votes against former California governor Ronald Reagan. Among the Democrats, former Georgia governor Jimmy Carter received 37% of the votes, Rep. Morris Udall of Arizona 36%, Gov. George Wallace of Alabama 13%, and Sen. Henry Jackson of Washington 7%.

Jackson wins New York primary

Sen. Henry Jackson of Washington won the New York Democratic delegate primary with 38% of the convention delegates. Rep. Morris Udall of Arizona got 25%, and former governor Jimmy Carter of Georgia 13%, while 24% of the delegates were uncommitted.

Election posters cover a wall in Lisbon.

ALAIN DEJEAN—SYGMA

ALAIN NOGUES—SYGMA

French students gather under the Eiffel Tower in Paris during the April demonstrations.

7 *Hua becomes Chinese premier*

Moving against public demonstrations, the Chinese leadership hurriedly named Hua Kuo-feng premier of China and first vice-chairman of the Chinese Communist Party. It also dismissed Teng Hsiao-ping, once expected to become premier, from all his posts, allowing him to retain his party membership "to see how he will behave himself in the future."

12 *Congress approves immunization program*

Congress appropriated $135 million for a national immunization program against an anticipated outbreak of swine influenza.

13 *Foes of Israel grow stronger in West Bank*

Local elections in the Israeli-occupied West Bank of the Jordan River brought to power large numbers of Palestinian nationalists and Arab radicals.

15 *French students protest curriculum changes*

Tens of thousands of students demonstrated in Paris to protest changes in university curricula aimed at bringing education closer to job requirements.

India renews ties with China

India announced that it would send an ambassador to Peking, easing a hostility of 15 years. Relations deteriorated in the late 1950s because of a border dispute that led to a brief war in 1962.

16 *India stiffens birth control policy*

The Indian government announced a new, more rigorous policy aimed at slowing the country's rapid population growth.

21 *Queen Elizabeth turns 50*

Britain's Queen Elizabeth II celebrated her 50th birthday.

25 *Vietnamese elect joint assembly*

Voters in North and South Vietnam elected a joint National Assembly that was expected to seal the reunification of the two Vietnams into one country.

Socialists win in Portugal

Socialists won 106 of the 263 seats in Portugal's elections for a National Assembly, giving them the power to form a government. The centrist Popular Democrats won 71 seats, the conservative Centre Democratic Social Party won 41, the Communists 40, and the far-left Popular Democratic Union 1.

27 *Kissinger announces new African policy*

U.S. Secretary of State Henry Kissinger said in Zambia that the U.S. would work to force the government of Rhodesia to institute majority rule. Prime Minister Ian D. Smith of Rhodesia replied that the U.S. had "fallen into a trap."

Pope appoints new cardinals

The Vatican announced the appointment of 21 new cardinals, including one American. The names of two of the cardinals were not announced.

Carter triumphs in Pennsylvania

Former Georgia governor Jimmy Carter won a smashing victory in the Democratic presidential primary in Pennsylvania, receiving 37% of the votes as against 25% for Sen. Henry Jackson of Washington, 19% for Rep. Morris Udall of Arizona, and 11% for Gov. George Wallace of Alabama. It was Carter's seventh victory in the first nine primaries of 1976.

28 *Report on government intelligence issued*

The Senate Select Committee on Intelligence declared that the Federal Bureau of Investigation and other national intelligence agencies had violated the constitutional rights of hundreds of thousands of U.S. citizens by investigating their political activities.

MAY

4 *UN debates Israeli occupation*

The United Nations Security Council debated a resolution condemning Israel's occupation policies in the West Bank and Gaza Strip. There were 21 Israeli settlements in the West Bank territory, which was taken from Jordan in the 1967 war. On May 9 the Israeli Cabinet voted to remove ultranationalist settlers from an army base near Nablus, but it stressed that it would continue establishing settlements in selected areas of the West Bank.

6 *Earthquake hits Italy*

An earthquake killed an estimated 1,000 people in northeastern Italy and destroyed many buildings. The quake, measured at 6.5 on the Richter scale, was felt as far away as Poland.

U.S. proposes world resources bank

U.S. Secretary of State Henry Kissinger proposed the creation of a world resources bank at the United Nations Conference on Trade and Development meeting in Nairobi, Kenya.

7 *Cambodian soldiers executed*

Cambodian refugees in Thailand reported that about 300 officers and soldiers of the former Cambodian army who had been captured in the 1975 civil warfare had been executed in January. Other large-scale executions in Cambodia had previously been reported.

8 *Lebanon picks new president*

The Lebanese Parliament elected a new president of the country, but this failed to end the civil war. The president-elect, Elias Sarkis, held consultations with leaders of both sides, to no avail.

FBI director apologizes

Clarence M. Kelley, director of the Federal Bureau of Investigation, apologized to the public for some of the FBI's activities during J. Edgar Hoover's 48-year term as director. According to reports by the Senate Select Committee on Intelligence, the abuses and excesses included the persecution of civil rights leader Martin Luther King, Jr., harassment of political groups such as the Black Panthers, and illegal wiretaps.

10 *British Liberal Party leader resigns*

Jeremy Thorpe, leader of Britain's Liberal Party, resigned, charging the press with spreading false reports concerning an alleged homosexual affair.

11 *Reagan and Ford split primaries*

Ronald Reagan beat Pres. Gerald Ford in the Nebraska Republican presidential primary. The former California governor got 55% of the votes. Ford won in West Virginia with 57% of the votes.

Church and Carter win

Sen. Frank Church of Idaho won the Nebraska Democratic presidential primary, with 39% of the votes as against 38% for former Georgia governor Jimmy Carter. Carter won the Connecticut primary, getting 33% of the vote to 31% for Rep. Morris Udall of Arizona and 18% for Sen. Henry Jackson of Washington. Carter said that he expected to get the nomination of the Democratic convention "on the first ballot."

13–19 *Fighting intensifies in Lebanon*

Fighting between Muslim and Christian forces in Lebanon reached a new peak, with hundreds of casualties.

14 *India and Pakistan agree*

India and Pakistan agreed to resume in July diplomatic relations that were broken off in 1971 during the India-Pakistan war. Transportation services between the two countries also were to be restored.

Much of the town of Venzone, Italy, was destroyed in the May earthquake.

U.S.A.F./AUTHENTICATED NEWS INTERNATIONAL

17–22 *French president visits U.S.*

French Pres. Valéry Giscard d'Estaing paid an official state visit to the United States in honour of the U.S. Bicentennial. He traveled on the new supersonic Concorde jet developed through French-British collaboration.

18 *Carter wins Michigan, loses Maryland*

Former Georgia governor Jimmy Carter barely won the Michigan Democratic presidential primary, getting 44% of the votes to 43% for Arizona Rep. Morris Udall. Alabama Gov. George Wallace got 7%. Carter lost in Maryland to California Gov. Edmund G. Brown, Jr., who got 49% of the votes to Carter's 37%. Udall got 5% and Wallace 4%.

Ford wins in Michigan and Maryland

Pres. Gerald Ford won the Michigan Republican presidential primary with 65% of the votes to 34% for former California governor Ronald Reagan. Ford also defeated Reagan in Maryland, 58 to 42%.

19 *Senate establishes committee on intelligence*

After extensive hearings on the functioning of U.S. intelligence agencies, the U.S. Senate voted to establish a permanent Select Committee on Intelligence charged with overseeing the activities of the Central Intelligence Agency.

21 *NATO warns of Soviet strength*

The foreign ministers of the North Atlantic Treaty Organization warned that the Soviet Union was increasing its military strength in Central Europe.

24 *Concorde service begins*

Supersonic Concorde jets began regular flights from London and Paris to Dulles International Airport near Washington, D.C. The transatlantic runs took a little less than four hours. The service was established on a 16-month trial basis.

UPI COMPIX

An Arab gunner in Lebanon uses an antiaircraft gun as makeshift artillery in the civil war.

25 *Candidates split primaries*

Jimmy Carter won Democratic presidential primaries in Arkansas, Kentucky, and Tennessee. But the former Georgia governor lost the Oregon and Idaho primaries to Sen. Frank Church of Idaho and the Nevada primary to Gov. Edmund G. Brown, Jr., of California. Pres. Gerald Ford defeated Ronald Reagan in Republican presidential primaries in Oregon, Kentucky, and Tennessee. He lost to the former California governor in Arkansas, Nevada, and Idaho.

28 *Nuclear testing treaty signed*

The U.S. and the Soviet Union signed a five-year treaty limiting the size of underground nuclear explosions for peaceful purposes and providing for U.S. on-site inspection of Soviet tests. The accord paved the way for ratification of a companion treaty limiting underground nuclear weapons tests to the level of 150 kilotons agreed to by Pres. Richard Nixon in 1974. The signing took place two weeks after the U.S. had postponed it indefinitely without giving a reason. The postponement was thought to have been in response to presidential candidate Ronald Reagan's criticisms of Ford in the primary campaign.

31 *Syria sends troops into Lebanon*

Syrian troops moved into Lebanon on a large scale in an effort to end the civil war. Palestinian forces in Lebanon opposed the Syrian move.

JUNE

1 *Candidates split primaries*

Pres. Gerald Ford won the Rhode Island Republican presidential primary but lost in Montana and South Dakota to former governor Ronald Reagan of California. On the Democratic side, former Georgia governor Jimmy Carter won in South Dakota but lost in Rhode Island to Gov. Edmund G. Brown, Jr., of California and in Montana to Sen. Frank Church of Idaho. Carter now had 905 delegates of the 1,505 needed for the nomination.

3 *Congressional sex scandal develops*

Rep. Wayne L. Hays of Ohio came under fire from congressional colleagues after charges were made that he had placed his mistress, Elizabeth Ray, on the payroll of a House committee.

Quebec farmers protest

About 5,000 Quebec dairy farmers rioted on Parliament Hill in Ottawa. They were protesting against reductions in milk quotas and other farm subsidies.

5 *Man-made flood strikes Idaho*

A new dam on the Teton River in Idaho burst, resulting in a flood that killed 11 persons and left 30,000 homeless. Environmentalists and geologists had warned that the site was on particularly porous ground in an earthquake zone, though the sudden failure had not been predicted.

JUNE

UPI COMPIX

This is all that was left of Idaho's Teton Dam after it collapsed June 5.

6 *Celtics win NBA title*

The Boston Celtics defeated the Phoenix Suns, 87–80, to capture their 13th National Basketball Association championship, four games to two.

7 *Chile accused of police terror*

Chile's military government was accused of "arbitrary jailings, persecutions, and torture" by a commission of the Organization of American States.

British pound gets help

The British pound, which fell to an all-time low of around $1.70 on June 4, rallied after the government obtained a standby credit of $5.3 billion from a number of foreign countries including the U.S.

8 *Carter assured of Democratic nomination*

Jimmy Carter won the Ohio Democratic presidential primary, practically assuring himself of nomination on the first ballot at the party convention in July. In California, Carter lost to Gov. Edmund G. Brown, Jr., and he also lost in New Jersey where delegates committed to him received only 28% of the votes. But his Ohio victory was enough to start a stampede to him by party leaders.

Ford and Reagan split primaries

Pres. Gerald Ford won the Ohio and New Jersey Republican presidential primaries but lost to his opponent Ronald Reagan in California. As the primaries ended, neither candidate could be certain of the Republican nomination in August.

Mexico acts against opium growers

Mexico announced that it had destroyed most of the opium poppy fields in the country, which had been a major source of heroin entering the U.S.

Kissinger criticizes Chile

U.S. Secretary of State Henry Kissinger, in an address before a meeting of American foreign ministers in Santiago, Chile, criticized violations of human rights by the government of Chile: "A government that tramples on the rights of its citizens denies the purpose of its existence."

9 *Spain legalizes political parties*

The Spanish Cortes (parliament) approved a bill to legalize political parties, forbidden since the end of the Civil War in 1939. However, the government would still have the power to reject a party that it disapproves of. Rightists in the Cortes argued that the bill was unconstitutional.

10 *Rhodesian troops face guerrillas*

The Rhodesian government said guerrilla warfare on its frontier with Mozambique had taken the lives of 39 government troops and 291 black nationalist insurgents since January 1.

Arab peacekeeping force planned for Lebanon

Syria and 19 other Arab League countries agreed in Cairo to put a token peacekeeping force drawn from several Arab countries into Lebanon to replace the 10,000 to 12,000 Syrian troops currently there. Syria had been criticized in Arab circles for intervening in Lebanon.

15 *Chairman Mao no longer receiving visitors*

The Chinese government announced that Chairman Mao Tse-tung was no longer receiving foreign leaders who visited China. The decision was said to have been made by the Communist Party's Central Committee, which had evidently been convened for a special meeting.

16 *U.S. ambassador to Lebanon killed*

The U.S. ambassador to Lebanon, Francis E. Meloy, Jr., and his economic counselor, Robert O. Waring, were shot to death together with their embassy chauffeur while crossing the "green line" or no-man's-land in Beirut to engage in negotiations between Christian and Muslim factions.

16–19 *Blacks riot in South Africa*

A demonstration by 10,000 black students in Soweto, near Johannesburg, South Africa, turned into a riot that spread to a number of black townships and to two universities, leaving at least 175 persons dead and more than 1,000 injured. The immediate cause was a requirement that some part of all instruction in black schools be given in Afrikaans, the language of the majority of the white ruling class.

Enrico Berlinguer leads Italy's Communists.

NOGUES—SYGMA

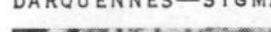

U.S. to arm Kenya and Zaire

The U.S. agreed to sell 12 F-5 jet fighter planes to Kenya and various items of military equipment to Zaire. The purpose was to offset Soviet military aid to the neighbouring states of Uganda, Somalia, and Angola.

18 *Kuhn opposes million-dollar player sales*

U.S. Baseball Commissioner Bowie Kuhn ordered the New York Yankees and the Boston Red Sox to return three star players they had bought from Charles Finley, owner of the Oakland Athletics, for $3.5 million. While the sales broke no rules, Kuhn said they were "inconsistent with the best interests of baseball."

19 *Ethiopia calls off Eritrean campaign*

The Ethiopian government called a halt to the mobilization of tens of thousands of Christian peasants on the borders of its Muslim province of Eritrea. It said it was negotiating with the guerrillas in Eritrea who were seeking independence.

20 *U.S. nationals withdrawn from Beirut*

The U.S. evacuated 263 Americans and other foreign nationals from Beirut by ship. But more than 90% of the Americans in the Lebanese capital preferred to stay on, some of them hoping to leave by road for Damascus in Syria.

20–21 *Communists gain in Italy but fail to win power*

In Italian parliamentary elections the Communist Party made impressive gains but the Christian Democrats, who had governed Italy for 30 years, kept their share of the popular vote. The result appeared to be an intensification of Italy's political crisis. The Christian Democrats won 263 of the 630 seats in the Chamber of Deputies and the Communists 228; a majority required 316 seats.

23 *U.S. denies Angola entry to UN*

The U.S. vetoed Angola's application to join the United Nations because of the continued presence of Cuban troops in the country. The Ford administration had requested Angola to defer its application, hoping to keep the matter from becoming an issue at the Republican national convention in August.

23–24 *Kissinger and Vorster meet*

U.S. Secretary of State Henry Kissinger and South African Prime Minister B. J. Vorster met in West Germany's Bavarian towns of Bodenmais and Grafenau to discuss the political situation in southern Africa. Among the subjects they talked about were South Africa's policy of apartheid (racial separation) and Rhodesia's white minority government.

DARQUENNES—SYGMA

Armed with grenades and automatic weapons, these Rhodesian reservists watch for black guerrillas.

25 *Polish workers protest food price increases*

The announcement of large increases in food prices in Poland led to strikes in several parts of the country. Railroad tracks were torn up near Warsaw. The government promptly dropped the proposal. It was the third time in 20 years that Polish workers had struck over living conditions. Other protests had occurred in 1956 and 1970.

27 *Portuguese choose General Eanes*

In their first free presidential election in half a century, Portuguese voters chose Gen. António Ramalho Eanes, 41-year-old army chief of staff. Eanes, a moderate socialist, received 61.5% of the vote.

27–28 *Economic summit held in Puerto Rico*

A summit meeting of the leaders of seven major industrial nations was held at Dorado Beach, near San Juan, Puerto Rico. They pledged to aim at sustained economic growth but to go slow on expansion that might lead to inflation. The countries represented were the U.S., Canada, the United Kingdom, France, West Germany, Italy, and Japan.

29–30 *Communists hold summit in East Berlin*

Communist leaders from 29 European countries met in East Berlin. The gathering included President Tito of Yugoslavia, General Secretary Leonid I. Brezhnev of the U.S.S.R., leaders of the Italian, Spanish, and French Communist parties, and the leaders of Eastern European parties. They endorsed the independence of each national party in seeking its own road to socialism—a break from the former predominance of the Soviet party. Several delegates spoke against that predominance, including those from Italy and Yugoslavia. The sharpest attack came from the leader of Spain's outlawed Communist Party, who said: "For years Moscow was our Rome. Today we have grown up."

JULY

2 *Death penalty held constitutional*

The U.S. Supreme Court held, 7 to 2, that the death penalty in and of itself does not violate the Constitution's ban on "cruel and unusual punishment." It upheld capital punishment statutes in Georgia, Texas, and Florida, but struck down those of North Carolina and Louisiana.

Vietnam is reunified

North and South Vietnam became one country again, with Hanoi as the capital. The country had been divided by the 1954 Geneva Agreement following the French defeat at Dien Bien Phu. The southern part was ruled by a government in Saigon until its collapse in April 1975.

3 *Pacific Islanders demand independence*

Two separatist groups from the U.S.-administered Marshall and Palau islands in the Western Pacific appeared before the UN Trusteeship Council demanding "independence now."

3–4 *Israelis rescue hostages in Uganda*

An Israeli commando unit flew 2,500 miles to Entebbe airport, Uganda, where hijackers were holding a French jetliner and nearly 100 Israeli hostages. The commandos killed 7 of the 10 hijackers, as well as 20 Uganda soldiers, and returned to Israel with 91 passengers and 12 crew members of the hijacked plane.

4 *Mexicans elect López Portillo*

José López Portillo, nominee of the ruling Partido Revolucionario Institucional, was elected president of Mexico.

U.S. Bicentennial observed

The U.S. celebrated its Bicentennial with pageantry, prayer, games, parades, picnics, and fireworks. In New York City millions watched an armada of tall-masted sailing ships from 31 countries pass in review on the Hudson River.

5 *Italian Communist gets key post*

The Communist Party of Italy won its most important political post as Pietro Ingrao was elected speaker of the Chamber of Deputies.

6 *South Africa drops required use of Afrikaans in schools*

The government of South Africa revoked a law requiring that schools in black townships use the Afrikaans language in teaching some subjects. The issue had touched off several days of rioting in June in the Johannesburg and Pretoria areas that caused the deaths of at least 175 persons.

6–11 *Queen Elizabeth II visits the U.S.*

Queen Elizabeth II of Great Britain visited the U.S. to join in the celebration of the 200th anniversary of the country's independence. She visited Philadelphia; Washington, D.C.; Charlottesville, Va.; New York City; New Haven, Conn.; Providence, R.I.; Newport, R.I.; and Boston.

7 *HEW father-son ruling overruled*

Pres. Gerald Ford ordered the Department of Health, Education, and Welfare to suspend at once a ruling that prohibited father-son or mother-daughter school events. The HEW's Office for Civil Rights had held that such events violated a law barring discrimination on the basis of sex in schools receiving federal funds.

8 *Nixon disbarred in New York State*

Former U.S. president Richard M. Nixon was ordered disbarred by a New York court for obstructing "the due administration of justice" during his presidency.

Indonesia launches satellite

Indonesia entered the space age by launching a communications satellite from Cape Canaveral in the U.S. The spacecraft, named "Palapa," was to be in permanent orbit over the 3,000-mile-long archipelago, linking Earth stations in 40 Indonesian cities with telephone and television signals. The only other countries with domestic satellite systems were the U.S., Canada, and the Soviet Union.

10 *Angola executes mercenaries*

Four mercenary soldiers, three British and one American, were executed by firing squad in Angola. Nine others had been sentenced to prison terms ranging from 16 to 30 years. They had taken part in the civil warfare that preceded the establishment of the new Angolan state. U.S. Pres. Gerald Ford and Britain's Queen Elizabeth had asked for mercy.

10–12 *U.S. shows support for Kenya*

The U.S. sent a warship and Navy patrol plane to Kenya to show support for that country in its dispute with neighbouring Uganda. Kenya had been accused by Pres. Idi Amin of Uganda of cooperating with Israel in its raid on Entebbe airport the night of July 3–4.

Israeli commandos like these carried out the surprise raid in Uganda.

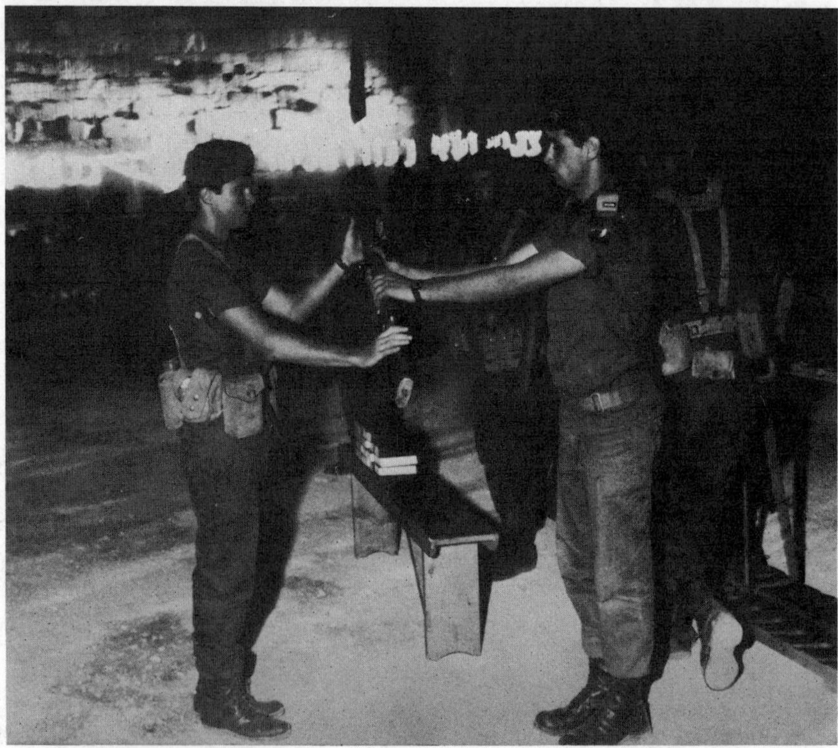

ALAIN TAIEB—SYGMA

12–15 *Jimmy Carter nominated for president*

Jimmy Carter, 51, was awarded the presidential nomination by an unusually united Democratic Party at Madison Square Garden in New York City. The former Georgia governor was the first presidential nominee of a major political party to hail from the Deep South since Zachary Taylor in 1848. He chose as his running mate Sen. Walter F. Mondale of Minnesota, 48, a liberal and a protégé of Sen. Hubert Humphrey of Minnesota.

15–17 *Busload of children kidnapped*

Twenty-six schoolchildren and their bus driver were abducted in central California and imprisoned in a buried truck. After 15 hours they dug themselves out. Three suspects were later arrested.

17 *Olympic Games begin*

The XXI Olympiad was opened in Montreal by Queen Elizabeth II of Great Britain, but the occasion was marred by politics. Athletes from Taiwan were prevented by Canadian Prime Minister Pierre Trudeau from participation under their official designation, which had been accepted by the International Olympic Committee. And the governments of 31 third world countries, most of them in Africa, forced their athletes to withdraw because of the presence of athletes from New Zealand, whose rugby team had toured South Africa.

PICTORIAL PARADE

Bicentennial fireworks in Washington, D.C., lasted an hour and drew nearly a million observers.

20 *U.S. leaves Thailand*

The last U.S. serviceman left Thailand. The Thai foreign minister said the U.S. troops had been stationed in Thailand to press the war in Vietnam, and with the war over the government had requested them to withdraw.

Viking reaches Mars

The U.S. Viking I robot craft landed on Mars after a voyage of nearly half a billion miles that took 11 months. It sent back colour photographs showing a windswept, rocky plain, and later prepared to sample the soil for chemical and biological analysis by means of automated apparatus on board. Another Viking craft was expected to reach Mars in a few weeks.

21 *British ambassador killed in Dublin*

Christopher T. E. Ewart-Biggs, the British ambassador to Ireland, was killed by a land mine that was set off under his car as he left his official residence in Dublin. The explosion, which blew a crater ten feet deep in the road, also killed the ambassador's secretary. Two other passengers, the top British civil servant in Ulster (Northern Ireland) and the ambassador's chauffeur, were seriously injured. In London, Prime Minister James Callaghan described the perpetrators as the common enemy of the Irish and British people.

26 *Nitrogen found in Martian atmosphere*

Viking project scientists announced that the first tests of the atmosphere on Mars revealed 95% carbon dioxide, 2 to 3% nitrogen, 1 to 2% argon-40, and 0.3% oxygen. "It doesn't show that there's [any life] there, but it shows that there's a chance," said one scientist.

Reagan chooses his running mate

Hotly pursuing the Republican nomination for president, Ronald Reagan announced that Sen. Richard S. Schweiker of Pennsylvania would be his choice as candidate for vice-president if he received the nomination. Schweiker, 50, was considered one of the most liberal and pro-labour Republicans in Congress. The surprising and unprecedented move was seen as an effort to win delegates from Northern states away from Pres. Gerald Ford.

27 *Former Japanese prime minister implicated in Lockheed scandal*

Kakuei Tanaka, who was prime minister of Japan from 1972 to 1974, was arrested and jailed in connection with the Lockheed Aircraft payoff scandal. He was accused of taking bribes of $1.7 million from Lockheed while in office. Tanaka was a member of the ruling Liberal-Democratic Party.

Americans evacuated from Beirut

The U.S. Navy evacuated 308 Americans and other foreigners from the Muslim section of Beirut, Lebanon, under the protection of the Palestine Liberation Army and the Al Fatah guerrilla group. They were taken to Athens.

28 *Britain breaks relations with Uganda*

The British government broke diplomatic relations with the African state of Uganda, a member of the Commonwealth. The break followed four years of growing tension between the two countries, heightened by Israel's July 3–4 raid on Entebbe airport. Uganda Pres. Idi Amin said the break was further evidence of British involvement in the planning of the Israeli raid.

Earthquakes strike northeast China

Two major earthquakes, which occurred 16 hours apart and measured 8.2 and 7.9 on the Richter scale, struck northeast China. T'ang-shan, an industrial city of about one million persons, was virtually destroyed. Extensive damage was also reported in Peking and Tientsin. Though no official casualty figures were announced by the Chinese government, a report filtering out of China put the death toll at about 700,000 and was generally accepted as reliable.

AUGUST

1 *Vacationers drown in Colorado flood*

A flash flood on July 31 along the Big Thompson Canyon, 50 miles north of Denver, took many lives. The flood was caused by heavy rain that turned the Big Thompson River into a torrent, drowning motorists, fishermen, campers, and residents who lived on its banks.

1–8 *International Eucharistic Congress draws Catholics*

The 41st International Eucharistic Congress met in Philadelphia. Nearly one million Roman Catholics took part in the conference, celebrating the central position of the Eucharist (Lord's Supper) in the life of the church. The first such congress was held in Lille, France, in 1881.

2 *"Legionnaires' disease" strikes in Pennsylvania*

A mysterious flu-like disease was found to be causing illness and deaths among people who had attended a Pennsylvania state American Legion convention in Philadelphia July 21–24. A total of 180 cases, including 29 deaths, were later reported. Scientists were unable to identify the cause.

4–12 *New rioting in South Africa*

South African police fired on crowds of youths in the black township of Soweto, near Johannesburg. The rioters were trying to keep workers from commuting to their jobs in the city. The rioting subsequently spread to dozens of other locations, including Cape Town, where 27 persons were killed in two days.

6 *Vietnam expands diplomatic ties*

The government of unified Vietnam completed its diplomatic ties with the non-Communist countries of Southeast Asia by reaching an agreement with Thailand.

7 *Iran plans new military purchases from U.S.*

The U.S. and Iranian governments announced that Iran would spend $10 billion for military purchases from the United States in the years 1975–80. Secretary of State Henry Kissinger said that the U.S. wanted a powerful Iran in the Middle East.

Idi Amin pledges peace

After several years of hostility, Pres. Idi Amin of Uganda and Pres. Jomo Kenyatta of Kenya signed peace documents that pledged them to resume normal relations.

SYGMA

North Korean soldiers attack U.S. and South Korean soldiers at Panmunjom.

8 *Rhodesia destroys guerrilla base*

The government of Rhodesia said that its raiding forces had killed more than 300 black nationalist guerrillas at their base camp in neighbouring Mozambique. The raid was in retaliation for a mortar bomb attack on a Rhodesian army base in which four soldiers were killed. Other sources put the number killed at 675 or more.

11 *FBI reorganized*

A major reorganization of the Federal Bureau of Investigation was announced by its director, Clarence M. Kelley. The changes were instituted after disclosures were made that the FBI had engaged in illegal and abusive practices against various radical groups. Kelley said that the bureau's domestic intelligence investigations were being transferred to the general investigative division.

12 *Lebanese capture Palestinian camp*

The Palestinian refugee camp of Tall Zaatar in Lebanon fell to right-wing Christian forces after a 52-day siege. It was the last Muslim enclave in the Christian-dominated area of Beirut.

16–17 *Earthquakes strike China, Philippines*

An earthquake struck China's Szechwan Province, about 800 miles southwest of the area devastated by the previous quakes of July 28. Another severe quake shook the island of Mindanao in the Philippines, producing tidal waves that killed more than 8,000 people and left 175,000 homeless.

16–20 *Nonaligned leaders meet in Colombo*

Leaders of 85 nonaligned nations met in Colombo, Sri Lanka. It was the fifth meeting of the 20-year-old movement since the Bandung Conference of 1955. Where in earlier years the meetings had been concerned with problems of colonialism and the cold war, this time the major emphasis was on "economic imperialism." The final communiqué called on the world's rich countries to give better economic terms to the less developed countries.

18–19 *Ford wins Republican nomination*

Pres. Gerald Ford won the presidential nomination of the Republican Party on the first ballot at the party's convention in Kansas City, Mo., getting 57 votes more than the 1,130 needed. He chose Sen. Robert Dole of Kansas as his vice-presidential running mate.

18–21 *Soldiers clash at Panmunjom*

North Korean soldiers attacked a group of U.S. and South Korean soldiers in the demilitarized zone, killing two U.S. officers with axes and clubs and wounding nine enlisted men. The U.S. and South Korean soldiers had been pruning a tree at Panmunjom. In response, the U.S. sent flights of planes over South Korea and cut down the tree that had been the centre of the dispute.

23 *Australian leaders flee demonstrators*

Prime Minister Malcolm Fraser and Governor-General Sir John Kerr were forced to take refuge from violent student demonstrators. Fraser was surrounded by brick-throwing students, Aboriginals, and migrant workers at Monash University in Melbourne who were protesting cuts in educational and health allowances. Kerr was trapped inside an office at the University of Sydney by students throwing eggs and tomatoes.

23–25 *Unrest continues in South Africa*

Blacks in Soweto clashed with each other over attempts by militants to keep the township's labour force from commuting to work in Johannesburg. Twenty-one blacks were reported dead as bands of Zulu vigilantes roamed the streets attacking demonstrators. Fourteen others were killed by police.

25 *France gets new premier*

Jacques Chirac resigned as premier of France and was replaced by Raymond Barre, the foreign trade minister. Chirac, a Gaullist leader, had disagreed with the political strategy of Pres. Valéry Giscard d'Estaing.

26 *Prince Bernhard disgraced*

Prince Bernhard of The Netherlands, the husband of Queen Juliana, resigned most of his military and business posts after a Dutch government commission criticized his "unacceptable" relationship with the Lockheed Aircraft Corp. He had been charged with accepting bribes of $1.1 million, but the commission said only that his conduct had been "extremely imprudent."

27 *Scientists synthesize a gene*

A group of scientists at the Massachusetts Institute of Technology announced that they had constructed the first complete synthetic gene—the basic unit of heredity—and had implanted it in a living bacterial cell.

31 *Roman Catholic bishops criticize Carter's abortion stand*

Jimmy Carter met with six Roman Catholic bishops, but a spokesman for the bishops said that they remained "disappointed" with his position on abortion. Carter had refused to support a constitutional amendment to forbid abortion, though he stated that he was personally opposed to abortion.

SEPTEMBER

1 *Hays resigns congressional seat*

Rep. Wayne L. Hays, Democrat of Ohio, resigned from the House. Once a powerful figure known as "the mayor of Capitol Hill," Hays had been accused of keeping his mistress on the congressional payroll although she did no work.

3 *Viking 2 lands on Mars*

The Viking 2 spacecraft lander settled down on the edge of the Martian polar cap in a region named Utopia Plains. It sent back photographs of a landscape strewn with boulders.

4–6 *Kissinger and Vorster meet in Zürich*

Secretary of State Henry Kissinger and Prime Minister B. J. Vorster of South Africa met for a new series of talks in Zürich. Both stated afterward that "progress" had been made. Kissinger set about preparing for a round of visits to southern African leaders.

6 *Soviet pilot defects with plane*

A Soviet MiG-25 jet was flown to Japan by a pilot seeking refuge in the U.S. The twin-engine plane, believed to be the Soviet Union's most advanced fighter, was considered a valuable prize by U.S. military intelligence authorities. Pres. Gerald Ford later granted the pilot asylum. After a long delay, the plane was shipped back to the U.S.S.R. in pieces.

Vietnamese identify missing pilots

The Vietnamese embassy in Paris identified 12 missing U.S. pilots as having been killed in action in the years 1965–68. The U.S. government replied that the list included "only a small portion of the many hundreds" of cases of missing men, and urged a full accounting.

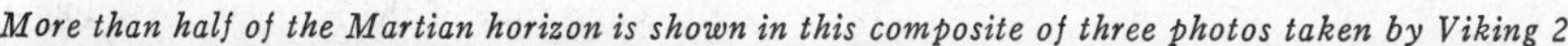

More than half of the Martian horizon is shown in this composite of three photos taken by Viking 2.

COURTESY, NASA

9 *Mao Tse-tung dies in Peking*

The leader of the Chinese Communist revolution, who founded the People's Republic of China in 1949, died at the age of 82. There was no indication of who would succeed Mao as chairman of the Communist Party. Observers expected an intense struggle for power.

9–15 *Unrest continues in South Africa*

Strikes and demonstrations by blacks and Coloureds in the Johannesburg and Cape Town areas of South Africa led to the deaths of at least 33 persons.

10 *Air crash kills 176 persons*

The worst midair disaster in history occurred when a Yugoslav DC-9 and a British Airways Trident collided over northern Yugoslavia, killing all 176 persons aboard.

10–12 *Hijackers use fake weapons*

Croatian terrorists hijacked a New York-to-Chicago jet and flew to Paris. They ordered propaganda leaflets to be dropped from the air over several cities. After surrendering, they revealed that their weapons were not real.

11 *Syria ignores Brezhnev appeal*

Soviet leader Leonid I. Brezhnev appealed to Syria's President Hafez al-Assad for the withdrawal of Syrian troops from Lebanon. Assad rejected the Soviet appeal, and the Syrian troops continued their efforts to crush Palestinian guerrillas in Lebanon.

12 *Mexico devalues the peso*

Mexico established a new value for its currency at 19.9 pesos to the U.S. dollar. Until

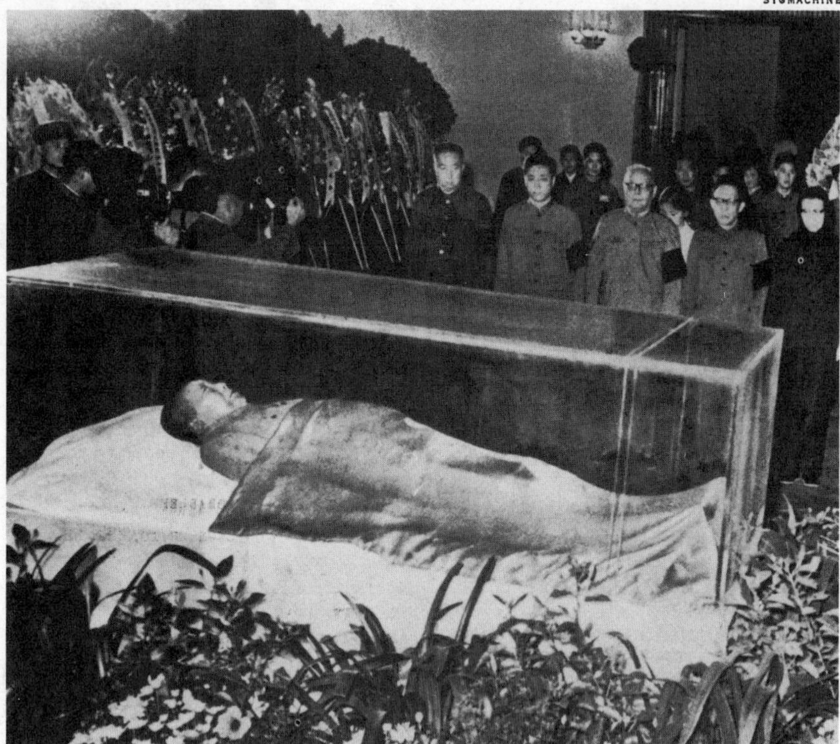
SYGMACHINE

The body of Mao Tse-tung, leader of the Chinese Communist revolution, lies in state in Peking.

August 31 the peso had been worth 8 U.S. cents; its new value was about 5 cents.

14 *Peking rebuffs Moscow on Mao's death*

The government of the People's Republic of China rejected messages of condolence on the death of Mao Tse-tung from the Communist parties of the Soviet Union and its Eastern European allies. A spokesman in Peking said, "We have no party-to-party relations with them."

14–24 *Kissinger persuades Rhodesian leader*

Secretary of State Henry Kissinger visited the African countries of Tanzania, Zambia, South Africa, Zaire, and Kenya. His aim was to persuade African leaders to compromise their differences over white-ruled Rhodesia and South West Africa (Namibia). On September 24 Rhodesian Prime Minister Ian Smith told his people in a broadcast message that after conferring with Kissinger in Pretoria he and his government had accepted Kissinger's proposal for the establishment of an immediate biracial government and for black majority rule within two years.

15 *India fights population growth*

India's Ministry of Health and Family Planning announced that sterilizations had tripled in the last year as a result of the government's drive to slow the growth of population. India was the world's second most populous country.

Newsman defies Congress

Television news reporter Daniel Schorr refused to tell a U.S. congressional committee how he obtained the Pike committee report on intelligence activities, citing his rights under the First Amendment. The committee did not hold him in contempt.

16 *Episcopalians to ordain women*

The Episcopal Church approved the ordination of women to be priests and bishops. The House of Deputies voted to concur with a resolution of the House of Bishops that the ordination requirements apply equally to women and men.

20 *Sweden's socialists turned out*

Sweden's Social Democratic Party was narrowly defeated in parliamentary elections after more than 40 years in power. It had been opposed by a coalition of the Conservative, Liberal, and Centre parties emphasizing the issues of high taxes and bureaucracy. They said, however, that they would not try to dismantle Sweden's welfare state. Thorbjörn Fälldin, the Centre Party leader, was named to succeed Olof Palme as prime minister.

Carter admits lust for women

A *Playboy* magazine interview with Jimmy Carter resulted in controversy when he was quoted as having said that he had "looked on a lot of women with lust." His remarks were made in the course of a discussion of his Baptist religious beliefs.

21 *Chilean exile assassinated in Washington*

A former Chilean Cabinet minister, Orlando Letelier, was killed in Washington, D.C., by a bomb placed in his car. Letelier had been ambassador, interior minister, foreign minister, and defense minister in the government of Salvador Allende Gossens, overthrown in 1973. An associate, Ronni Karpen Moffitt, was also killed.

22 *Government bans use of red dye in food*

The U.S. Food and Drug Administration banned the use of Red No. 4 dye and carbon black in foods. Red No. 4, the colouring agent in maraschino cherries, was thought to have a possible association with bladder polyps.

23 *Ford and Carter hold first debate*

The first debate between Pres. Gerald Ford and his Democratic challenger, Jimmy Carter, took place at the old Walnut Street Theater in Philadelphia, before a national TV audience estimated at around 90 million. The subject of the debate was domestic affairs. A Gallup Poll taken afterward found that 38% of those asked thought Ford had won, while 25% thought Carter had won and 29% called it a draw.

24 *Patricia Hearst sentenced to prison*

A federal judge sentenced Patricia Hearst to seven years in prison on charges of armed robbery and the use of a firearm to commit a felony. The sentence was more severe than most observers expected. On March 20 a jury had declared the newspaper heiress guilty of taking part in a San Francisco robbery.

26 *Guerrillas raid Damascus hotel*

Four pro-Palestinian guerrillas seized a hotel in Damascus and held 90 people hostage. Syrian troops overpowered them in a bloody battle in which one of the guerrillas and four of the hostages were killed. The three surviving guerrillas were hanged the next day opposite the hotel.

28 *British pound hits new low*

The British pound fell to a low of $1.64 in the foreign-exchange market. This was about two-thirds of what it had been worth at the end of 1971. The drop reflected fears that the Labour government would be unable to stem Britain's double-digit inflation.

30 *California recognizes right to die*

California became the first U.S. state to give terminally ill persons the right to authorize the withdrawal of life-sustaining procedures when death is believed to be imminent. The authorization has to be in writing and signed by the patient in the presence of two witnesses.

OCTOBER

3 *Helmut Schmidt squeaks through*

West Germany's Social Democratic Party kept a narrow hold on power. It won 214 seats in the Bundestag (lower house of Parliament) while its ally, the Free Democratic Party, won 39 seats, giving them a slim majority over the opposition Christian Democratic Union and its Bavarian sister party, the Christian Social Union (243 seats).

4 *Earl Butz resigns*

U.S. Secretary of Agriculture Earl Butz was forced to resign in the wake of a report that he had made an obscene remark about blacks. Butz apologized for his "gross indiscretion."

5 *Auto workers end Ford strike*

The United Auto Workers reached a path-breaking agreement with the Ford Motor Co. after a four-week strike. The new contract, which provided 13 additional days off a year, was hailed by union leaders as a step toward a four-day working week.

6 *Ford and Carter hold second debate*

The second television debate between Pres. Gerald Ford and his Democratic challenger, Jimmy Carter, took place in San Francisco at the Palace of Fine Arts. The general subject of the debate was foreign affairs and defense matters and most observers thought Carter "won" by a slim margin.

Military seize power in Thailand

The government of Thailand fell to a military coup after three years of democratic regimes. "We set our sights too high," said a leader of the coup.

7 *British borrowers to pay 15%*

The British government raised the Bank of England's minimum lending rate to 15% in a move to slow inflation.

8 *Mao's body embalmed*

The body of China's revolutionary leader Mao Tse-tung will be kept in a crystal sarcophagus and displayed to the public, the Chinese government said.

Presidential debaters Jimmy Carter (left) and Gerald Ford face their interrogators.

UPI COMPIX

9 *New ICBM on the drawing boards*

The U.S. Air Force was reported to be developing a new intercontinental ballistic missile that would be twice as heavy as present ICBM's. It would have several times the payload, carry many more warheads, and be much more accurate.

12 *Hua named to succeed Mao*

China's Premier Hua Kuo-feng was chosen to succeed Mao Tse-tung as chairman of the Communist Party of China. He kept his posts of premier and chairman of the party's powerful Military Commission.

Chinese "radicals" arrested

Mao Tse-tung's widow, Chiang Ch'ing, and other radical leaders were reported to have been arrested. The Shanghai-based group was accused of plotting a military takeover. Others named were Wang Hung-wen, Chang Ch'un-ch'iao, and Yao Wen-yüan.

Watergate convictions upheld

A federal appeals court upheld the Watergate conspiracy convictions of three aides to former president Richard Nixon—John N. Mitchell, H. R. Haldeman, and John D. Ehrlichman. They were convicted in 1975 of conspiring to cover up the 1972 break-in at the headquarters of the Democratic National Committee.

13 *King Tut's ancestor identified*

Scientists at the University of Michigan announced that they had identified the mummy of King Tutankhamen's grandmother, who lived from 1397 to 1360 BC. They X-rayed her skull and analyzed samples of her hair in order to make the determination.

15 *Dole and Mondale debate*

Vice-presidential candidates Sen. Robert Dole and Sen. Walter F. Mondale met in a nationally televised debate in Houston. Republican Dole said Democrat Mondale was "the Senate's most liberal member," and his opponent replied that Dole had "richly earned his reputation as a hatchet man here tonight."

17–18 *Arab leaders agree on cease-fire in Lebanon*

Six leaders of Arab countries, meeting in Riyadh, Saudi Arabia, agreed on a cease-fire for Lebanon. They were the presidents of Egypt, Syria, and Lebanon, the leader of the Palestine Liberation Organization, and the rulers of Saudi Arabia and Kuwait.

19 *U.S. economy slows down*

The recovery of the U.S. economy slowed in the third quarter of 1976, according to the U.S. Department of Commerce. Ford administration spokesmen called it a "pause" and predicted that the upswing would get under way again.

21 *Nobel prizes to Americans*

Americans won all five Nobel prizes for 1976. The winner in literature was novelist Saul Bellow. The prize for medicine was awarded jointly to Baruch S. Blumberg and D. Carleton Gajdusek, and the economics prize went to Milton Friedman. Burton Richter and Samuel C. C. Ting shared the physics prize, and William N. Lipscomb won the award for chemistry.

Cincinnati wins World Series

The Cincinnati Reds won the fourth and final game of the World Series against the New York Yankees. They were the first National League baseball team in 54 years to win two consecutive Series.

22 *Ford, Carter hold third debate*

In their third and final debate, at the College of William and Mary in Williamsburg, Va., Pres. Gerald Ford and his opponent, Jimmy Carter, discussed a wide array of issues, both domestic and foreign.

24 *Chinese hail Hua*

Three days of celebrations over the downfall of the "gang of four" (Chiang, Wang, Chang, and Yao) ended in a mass rally in Peking at which Hua Kuo-feng was hailed as the new chairman of China's Communist Party. The rally was televised throughout China.

25–26 *Arab League meets in Cairo*

An Arab League summit conference in Cairo approved the arrangements for a cease-fire in Lebanon and an Arab peacekeeping force that had been agreed to at a meeting of six Arab leaders in Riyadh, Saudi Arabia, October 17–18.

AUTHENTICATED NEWS INTERNATIONAL

Scientists identified this mummy as Queen Tiy, grandmother of King Tutankhamen.

26 *Transkei acquires statehood*

The republic of Transkei was given its independence by South Africa. The first of South Africa's black homelands to gain independence, it was not recognized by other nations because of general disapproval of South Africa's policy of separate development of blacks and whites.

27 *Mexican peso drops again*

The Mexican government allowed the peso to float again and it fell to 26.50 to the dollar. Since September 12 it had been pegged at 19.90 to the dollar.

28 *Rhodesians confer in Geneva*

The Geneva conference on Rhodesia opened in the Palais des Nations. It was attended by representatives of the government of Rhodesia and four black nationalist delegations, under a British chairman. Its purpose was to work out a temporary biracial government that would lead to black majority rule.

Student demonstrators taken captive at Bangkok's Thammasat University after troops occupied the campus on October 6.

SYGMA

NOVEMBER

1 *Former leader of Sinn Fein slain*

An elaborate funeral was held in Belfast, Northern Ireland, for Maire Drumm, a former officer of the Provisional Sinn Fein, the political wing of the Provisional Irish Republican Army. She was shot dead by gunmen as she lay in a Belfast hospital where she was being treated.

2 *Carter wins presidency*

Jimmy Carter was elected president of the United States with an electoral vote of 297 to Gerald Ford's 240. (One elector cast his vote for Ronald Reagan.) A strong factor in Carter's victory was support from the black voters of the South. About 53% of those eligible to vote went to the polls.

Indian government gets more power

India's lower house of Parliament approved the Constitution (44th Amendment) Act amending the country's constitution to give the government more power. Opponents of the move charged the amendments would "open the floodgate to regimentation and dictatorship."

KEYSTONE

Guests shout "Banzai!" as Hirohito observes his 50th anniversary as emperor.

5 *India postpones elections*

The lower house of the Indian Parliament voted to postpone national elections for another year. It was the second postponement since the government of Prime Minister Indira Gandhi declared a state of emergency 16 months earlier.

10 *Syrian troops enter Beirut*

Syrian military forces entered Beirut, the capital of Lebanon, without encountering resistance. They acted under the aegis of the Arab League, as part of a multinational Arab peacekeeping force—though the other countries sent no sizable contingents.

Hirohito has a golden jubilee

Emperor Hirohito of Japan celebrated the 50th anniversary of his reign. But many members of Parliament boycotted the event, and there were protest demonstrations by antimonarchists.

11 *U.S. to sell grain to East Germany*

East Germany agreed to buy 1.5 million to 2 million metric tons of grain a year from the U.S. until 1980. Under the agreement East German ships were to be allowed to dock at U.S. ports for the first time since diplomatic relations were established in 1974.

Security Council deplores Israel's occupation policies

The UN Security Council unanimously deplored the establishment of Israeli settlements in the occupied Arab territories and Israel's annexation of eastern Jerusalem.

12 *Chrysler to build new army tank*

The Chrysler Corp. will build the new U.S. main battle tank, called the Abrams, according to U.S. Army spokesmen. It will have essentially the same guns, track, and engine as West Germany's Leopard 2.

14 *Jimmy Carter's church integrated*

The congregation of the Plains Baptist Church in Plains, Ga., voted after much discussion to drop its 11-year-old-ban on attendance by blacks. The ban had been opposed by Jimmy Carter when it was first introduced, but he had not been able to persuade the congregation at that time.

15 *Separatists win in Quebec*

Elections in Canada's province of Quebec brought a smashing victory for the Parti Québécois, which seeks to eventually separate Quebec from Canada.

17 *London marchers protest plan to cut government spending*

About 40,000 people marched to the House of Commons in London to protest the Labour government's proposal to cut public spending.

19 *Patricia Hearst released on bail*

Newspaper heiress Patricia Hearst, who had been convicted earlier in the year of bank robbery, was released from prison after her family posted $1,250,000 bail pending the appeal of her conviction.

21 *Communist bloc bars congressional investigators*

A U.S. congressional fact-finding commission ended its tour of Europe after being barred from all Communist countries except Yugoslavia. It had sought to check on compliance with the 1975 security and cooperation pact signed in Helsinki.

22 *Carter meets with Ford*

Pres.-elect Jimmy Carter visited the White House and talked with Pres. Gerald Ford on the transition to a new administration.

Jubilation in Montreal: Supporters of Quebec separatism celebrate their party's victory in the provincial elections.

CANADIAN PRESS

Pres. Gerald Ford (left) shows Pres.-elect Jimmy Carter around the Executive Mansion in Washington, D.C.

24 *Human rights abuses scored by Scranton at the UN*

William Scranton, U.S. ambassador to the UN, decried abuses of human rights: "The only universality that one can honestly associate with the Universal Declaration of Human Rights is universal lip service."

Quake hits eastern Turkey

An earthquake in eastern Turkey took an estimated 4,000 lives. The devastation was followed by blizzards that hampered relief efforts in the mountain villages.

28 *Amy Carter to attend public school*

Mrs. Rosalynn Carter announced that her nine-year-old daughter, Amy, would attend a predominantly black public school near the White House in Washington, D. C.

Australia devalues its currency

Australia devalued its dollar by a peacetime record 17.5%, making it equal to U.S. $1.0174.

30 *Utah convict wins plea for execution*

The Utah Board of Pardons granted the plea of Gary Mark Gilmore that he be executed by a firing squad rather than face life imprisonment. Organizations opposed to capital punishment said they would try to obtain a stay of execution.

DECEMBER

1 *Poland slows economic growth*

Polish political leaders announced a slowdown in the planned rate of economic growth. Edward Gierek, leader of the Communist Party, said that the need to continue importing grain and meat at greatly increased prices had forced the government to cut back on funds for investment. In June an attempt to pay for the imports by charging higher prices to consumers had led to rioting.

López Portillo inaugurated in Mexico

José López Portillo was sworn in as the president of Mexico, succeeding Luis Echeverría Álvarez. López Portillo appealed for political unity and economic austerity to enable the country to overcome its current crisis.

3 *Cyrus Vance to succeed Kissinger*

Pres.-elect Jimmy Carter announced that Cyrus R. Vance, who had been deputy secretary of defense and a diplomatic troubleshooter in the Johnson administration, would be his secretary of state. Carter also said he planned to move "aggressively" to get the deadlocked negotiations with the U.S.S.R. for a second strategic arms limitation treaty "off dead center."

5 *Japanese elections strengthen the opposition*

The conservative Liberal-Democrats, who had ruled Japan for 21 years, suffered a setback. An election held in the aftermath of the Lockheed bribery scandal gave them only 249 of 511 seats in the House of Representatives (lower house of Parliament). Moderate opposition parties increased their representation.

Mexico's Pres. José López Portillo (left), with outgoing Pres. Luis Echeverría Álvarez.

Chirac rallies his followers in France

Former French premier Jacques Chirac was elected president of a new antileftist party. Called the Rassemblement pour la République, it replaced the former Gaullist party, which was dissolved.

7 *Supreme Court rules on pregnancy sick pay*

The U.S. Supreme Court ruled 6 to 3 that federal civil rights law did not require company disability plans to provide pregnancy or childbirth benefits. Justice William H. Rehnquist, for the majority, said that failure to do so did not constitute discrimination. Women's rights advocates were strongly critical.

Waldheim to continue as UN secretary-general

Kurt Waldheim of Austria won approval of the UN Security Council for a second five-year term as secretary-general of the United Nations, defeating Luis Echeverría Álvarez, former president of Mexico.

DANIEL STAPLES—BLACK STAR

Millions of gallons of oil were lost when this tanker ran aground off Nantucket.

9 *NATO countries rule out ban on nuclear strike*

Foreign ministers of the North Atlantic Treaty Organization rejected a proposal from the Warsaw Pact alliance in Eastern Europe that the two opposing military alliances agree not to initiate the use of nuclear weapons and to freeze membership in the alliances. U.S. Secretary of State Henry Kissinger said in a speech to the meeting that it would be dangerous to specify in advance when the West might choose to move from conventional to nuclear weapons in the face of an attack.

Congress to investigate charges of bribery by South Korean agents

Democrats in the U.S. House of Representatives voted unanimously to investigate charges that South Korean agents had sought to bribe members of Congress.

14 *Geneva conference on Rhodesia adjourns*

The deadlocked Geneva conference on how to achieve majority rule in Rhodesia was adjourned until January. Rhodesian Prime Minister Ian Smith said that he would negotiate with various black delegations during the recess. Britain's Ivor Richard, the presiding officer, said he would use the interval to visit Rhodesia and neighbouring countries in an effort to persuade the parties to move toward agreement.

15 *Congressmen say no U.S. prisoners left in Indochina*

A committee of the U.S. House of Representatives concluded that no Americans were still being held prisoner as a result of the war in Indochina. "There comes a time when you have to make sad statements," said a member.

Britain tightens its belt again

The British government announced a series of measures designed to overcome its financial crisis. These included cuts in government spending, increases in excise taxes, and a $3.9 billion loan from the International Monetary Fund. The chancellor of the Exchequer said that the British economy would grow by only 2% in 1977 and that the rate of inflation would continue at about 15%. He was criticized by opponents on both the left and the right.

Spanish voters open way for parliamentary democracy

Spain's voters gave overwhelming approval in a national referendum to the holding of free parliamentary elections in the spring. The new Cortes would have power to rewrite the laws of the Franco era. About 80% of those eligible voted, and about 95% were in favour of the political reform bill. However, many people in the Basque provinces and Catalonia, where separatism is strong, did not vote.

16 *Swine flu program suspended*

The swine flu inoculation program was suspended because scientists said they could not be sure that it was not linked to an outbreak of a paralytic illness called the Guillain-Barré syndrome.

17 *OPEC splits on price increase*

The Organization of Petroleum Exporting Countries, meeting in Qatar, divided over the question of prices to be charged in the next six months. Saudi Arabia and the United Arab Emirates decided to raise their price by 5%, while the other 11 member countries said they would raise their prices by 10% (and by another 5% after July 1, 1977). Initially the Saudi representative had called for a six-month freeze on prices. He said he expected the West to show "appreciation," presumably in political ways. Iraq's oil minister accused the Saudis of acting "in the service of imperialism and Zionism."

20 *Old literary manuscripts found in Britain*

A treasure chest of 19th-century literary papers, including manuscripts by Byron and Shelley, was discovered in a bank vault in London.

21 *Oil tanker spills cargo in North Atlantic*

The Liberian-registered tanker "Argo Merchant" split in half after running aground near Nantucket Island and released 7.5 million gal of crude oil into the North Atlantic. The oil slick endangered commercial fishing grounds to the northeast and beaches to the west.

24 *Fukuda named Japanese premier*

Takeo Fukuda was elected prime minister of Japan, succeeding Takeo Miki, who resigned. Fukuda had already replaced Miki as leader of the Liberal-Democrats, long the governing party of Japan.

31 *Unrest reported in China*

Armed conflicts were reported to have broken out in parts of China, including the Pao-ting area south of Peking, Fukien Province opposite Taiwan, and the western province of Szechwan. Chairman Hua Kuo-feng on December 24 called for a purge of party members and local government organizations in order to get rid of those who had collaborated with Chiang Ch'ing's "gang of four."

Aerial Sports

The year for aerial sports was highlighted by two daring attempts to achieve the first transatlantic balloon crossing and by the first 1,000-mi glider flight.

Ballooning. In October, fully aware of six previous fatalities, Ed Yost of Sioux Falls, S.D., piloted his two-ton "Silver Fox" helium balloon more than 2,000 mi from Milbridge, Maine, to a point 750 mi short of the Portuguese coast. The 57-year-old balloon designer, who spent an estimated $100,000 of his own money on the project, was forced to ditch his craft when winds unexpectedly turned northerly and drove him toward the South Atlantic. Before being rescued by a West German freighter, he stayed aloft for more than 106 hr, thereby breaking the endurance record of 87 hr set in 1913 by H. Kaulen of Germany.

German-born balloonist Karl Thomas made the 13th attempted crossing in June but with less success. His red, white, and blue "Spirit of '76" balloon reached a point 550 mi SE of New York City before it was driven downward by a violent storm. Thomas, forced to leap from his gondola some 200 ft above the waves when his life raft inadvertently ejected, was rescued by a Soviet merchant ship. A duration record of 2 hr 49 min for 400–600-cu m balloons was claimed in May by S. Peter Owens of Canada.

Gliding above Chicago's Gold Coast, a competitor in the International Free Flight Delta Glider championships is pulled by a tow rope from a boat on Lake Michigan. It was part of Chicago's Lakefront Festival in August.

WALTER KALE © CHICAGO TRIBUNE

WIDE WORLD

Karl Thomas sought to pilot his balloon from New Jersey to Paris, but had to abandon it in mid-ocean.

Gliding. Britain and Australia wrested the open and standard world soaring championships from the U.S. and West Germany in 1976, but Karl Striedieck of Port Matilda, Pa., claimed a world record with a 1,004-mi, 13.5-hr, out-and-return flight.

The world soaring championships, which took place in Räyskälä, Fin., were plagued by rain. George Lee of Britain defeated 38 other pilots to win the open class competition with 4,594 points in an AS-W 17 sailplane. Ingo Renner of Australia, flying a PIK-20B, beat 45 pilots to win the standard class with 4,056 points. Poland won both second and third place in the open class; in standard class Sweden took second and Britain third. There was, however, considerable controversy over the U.S. representation. George Moffat, one of the world's foremost sailplane pilots and the defending open class champion, had an off day during a qualifying competition in the U.S. and was not allowed to compete in the world championships. The Fédération Aéronautique Internationale was pressured to seed incumbent world champions in the next world competition.

Karl Striedieck of Pennsylvania made a record 1,004-mi flight in May on an out-and-return course over the Allegheny Mountains, and Hans Werner Grosse of West Germany set a 646-mi distance record for a sailplane flight over a triangular course at Waikerie, Australia. Other record flights included Friedrich Kensche's 45.8-mph average speed in a

CENTRAL PRESS/PICTORIAL PARADE

British pilots flew these American-built Pitts S-1S special biplanes at the world aerobatics contest near Kiev, U.S.S.R., in July and August. The Soviet Union took first place, Czechoslovakia second, and the United Kingdom third.

motorglider over a 60-mi course in France and a 62.1-mph motorglider flight over a 300-mi course in The Netherlands. Kurt Heimann made a 372.8-mi out-and-return motorglider flight in West Germany in April.

In the first world hang gliding championships, held in September at Kossen, Austria, the Class 1, Class 2, and Class 3 contests were won, respectively, by Austria, New Zealand, and Australia. Trip Mellinger and Gene Blythe of the U.S. claimed a hang gliding distance record of 47.29 mi in California.

Parachuting. At the world parachuting championships in Rome in September, the Soviet team took the overall title for men and the U.S. the overall for women. The Soviets also won overall titles in individual competitions for both men and women, but the U.S. won both the men's and the women's titles for team accuracy. The individual accuracy championship for men went to France and that for women to the U.S. The women's style title was won by East Germany and the men's by the U.S.S.R.

The U.S. Army's Golden Knights parachuting team set a world record in Kissimmee, Fla., for accurate night jumps onto a disk target by making three consecutive dead-centre landings and one just 0.04 m off target. Chuck Collingwood of the U.S. established a world individual daytime accuracy record with 33 dead centres and a night record with 37. Cheryl Stearns of Scottsdale, Ariz., set an accuracy record for women with 19 dead centres. The extraordinary performance of the U.S. also included a record 33-man star formation (free-falling through the air with hands joined) and a 19-woman star. U.S. women also set two ten-woman star speed records.

Powered Aircraft. Flying a Learjet 36, golfer Arnold Palmer established a round-the-world business jet flight record with co-pilots James Bir and L. L. Purkey. Their 22,984-mi flight took 57 hr 25 min. In addition, Jack Chrysler of the U.S. set world speed records for light and business piston aircraft.

The 1976 all-woman Powder Puff Derby transcontinental air race was won by Trish Jarish of Irvine, Calif. Flying solo, she averaged 209.7 mph over the 2,926-mi course. The 29-year-old Derby was terminated, largely because of cost and air traffic congestion. (MICHAEL D. KILIAN)

[452.B.4.d]

ENCYCLOPÆDIA BRITANNICA FILMS. *Ski Flying* (1975).

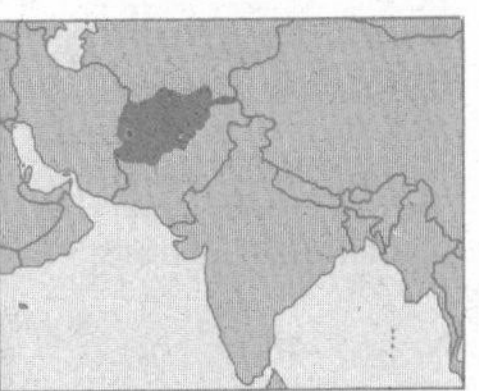

Afghanistan

A republic in central Asia, Afghanistan is bordered by the U.S.S.R., China, Pakistan, and Iran. Area: 252,000 sq mi (652,000 sq km). Pop. (1976 est.): 19,796,000, including (1963 est.) Pashtoon 59%; Tadzhik 29%; Uzbek 5%; Hazara 3%. Cap. and largest city: Kabul (pop., 1974 est., 352,700). Language: Dari Persian and Pashto. Religion: Muslim. President in 1976, Sardar Mohammad Daud Khan.

The most important alteration in Afghanistan's external relations during 1976 was a marked relaxation of the previously mounting tension with Pakistan, largely due to persuasion by Pres. Nikolay V. Podgorny of the Soviet Union and the shah of Iran.

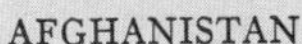

AFGHANISTAN

Education. (1973) Primary, pupils 621,437, teachers 16,293; secondary, pupils 160,458, teachers 7,376; vocational, pupils 4,729, teachers 445; teacher training, students 5,332, teachers 426; higher, students 9,399, teaching staff 1,264.

Finance. Monetary unit: afghani, with (Sept. 20, 1976) a free official rate of 49.30 afghanis to U.S. $1 (85 afghanis = £1 sterling). Gold, SDR's, and foreign exchange (June 1976) U.S. $106,530,000. Budget (1974–75 est.): revenue 10,252,000,000 afghanis; expenditure 9.8 billion afghanis. Money supply (March 1976) 13,020,000,000 afghanis.

Foreign Trade. (1974–75) Imports U.S. $276 million; exports U.S. $210 million. Import sources (1973–74): U.S.S.R. 21%; Japan 17%; U.S. 12%; India 10%; West Germany 6%. Export destinations (1972–73): U.S.S.R. 29%; India 24%; U.K. 16%; West Germany 6%. Main exports: fruits and nuts 40%; cotton 15%; natural gas 13%; carpets 9%; karakul (persian lamb) skins 6%.

Transport and Communications. Roads (1973) 17,973 km. Motor vehicles in use (1971): passenger 38,400; commercial (including buses) 26,100. Air traffic (1974): 260 million passenger-km; freight 13.5 million net ton-km. Telephones (Dec. 1974) 23,000. Radio receivers (Dec. 1973) *c.* 450,000.

Agriculture. Production (in 000; metric tons; 1975): corn *c.* 800; wheat *c.* 3,000; rice *c.* 450; barley *c.* 400; cotton, lint *c.* 43; wool, clean *c.* 14. Livestock (in 000; 1974): cattle *c.* 3,550; sheep *c.* 17,000; karakul sheep (1971) *c.* 6,800; horses *c.* 411; asses *c.* 1,251; goats *c.* 2,300; camels *c.* 300.

Industry. Production (in 000; metric tons; 1974–75): coal 187; natural gas (cu m) 2,946,000; cotton fabrics (m) 68,100; rayon fabrics (m) 20,865; cement 144; electricity (kw-hr) 527,200.

Aden:
see Yemen, People's Democratic Republic of

Advertising:
see Industrial Review

Aerospace Industry:
see Defense; Industrial Review; Space Exploration; Transportation

Afars and Issas:
see Dependent States

CZECHOSLOVAK NEWS AGENCY/EASTFOTO

Nut merchants quietly tend their wares at the market in Kabul. Most of the people of Afghanistan are farmers and nomads.

Thus, when floods and earthquakes devastated the provinces of Herat, Helmand, and Qandahar in April, Pakistan sent a message of sympathy and contributed substantially to relief operations. By mutual consent, both countries refrained from hostile propaganda. Prime Minister Zulfikar Ali Bhutto of Pakistan accepted an invitation to visit Kabul in June. There, both countries undertook to follow principles of respect for territorial integrity and noninterference in internal affairs set forth by the 1955 Bandung Conference of Asian and African nations. Talks were continued in Islamabad when President Daud Khan paid a return visit.

Domestically, Daud Khan pursued schemes of economic development and agricultural improvements with substantial aid from China, the U.S.S.R., Iran, and Kuwait, partly in the form of long-term loans and partly in technical aid. An attempted coup at the end of November, instigated by discontented retired officers and led by a retired general, Mir Ahmed Shah, was discovered and some 50 persons were arrested. (L. F. RUSHBROOK WILLIAMS)

[978.C.2]

African Affairs

Three African countries changed their dependency status during 1976. The Seychelles, a British colony, became independent in June. The Western (Spanish) Sahara was partitioned and absorbed by two of its neighbours, Morocco and Mauritania; this change was violently resisted by the Algerian-backed Popular Front for the Liberation of Saguia el Hamra and Rio de Oro (Polisario Front), which declared the independent state of the Saharan Arab Democratic Republic on February 27–28. The Republic of Transkei was proclaimed as an independent state by South Africa in October, but its independence failed to obtain any international recognition. France promised independence to its last possession on mainland Africa, Afars and Issas (Djibouti), after a referendum early in 1977. Negotiations for the independence of the rebel British colony of Rhodesia and for the former international trust territory of Namibia (South West Africa) were inconclusive.

Most African countries continued to experience serious economic difficulties. These were due largely to the world recession and inflationary pressures.

The Organization of African Unity. The organization of 48 African member states passed through a particularly difficult time in 1976 because of the conflicts over Angola, the Western Sahara, and Djibouti. The OAU failed in its policy to prevent a civil war from breaking out in Angola and to prevent international involvement in the fighting. A serious international crisis developed when the U.S.S.R. and Cuba intervened militarily on the side of the Popular Movement for the Liberation of Angola (MPLA), and the South African Army entered on the side of the National Front for the Liberation of Angola (FNLA) and the National Union for the Total Independence of Angola (UNITA). The two latter movements also had U.S. financial backing. The OAU emergency summit meeting to discuss Angola in Addis Ababa, Ethiopia, in January resulted in a deadlock, with half its members supporting recognition of the MPLA as the legal regime and the other half insisting on the right of all three rival movements to share equally in the independence government. But South Africa's intervention against the MPLA led to a two-thirds majority of African states backing the MPLA's Agostinho Neto as the legal head of state. The Angolan conflict marked the first occasion when Communist nations intervened militarily in an African domestic dispute, and when the South African Army crossed its frontiers into an independent African country.

The 13th annual summit conference of the African heads of state was held in Port Louis, Mauritius, in July. The two most seriously divisive issues were the Western Sahara and Djibouti. Algeria had won some support for Polisario's resistance to the takeover of the Western Sahara when the Ministerial Council of the OAU had met in Addis Ababa in February, and when it met again in Mauritius in June before the OAU summit; this brought a threat of boycotting the Mauritius summit from both Morocco and Mauritania, a threat which Morocco carried out. The conference eventually passed a disingenuously worded resolution that left matters as they stood. In the case of Djibouti, Ethiopia and Somalia remained strongly divided over how to ensure that the promised referendum on independence should be conducted, with each side fearing that the outcome might jeopardize its interests in the area. Both these unresolved problems were left in the hands of the chairman of the OAU for 1976–77, Sir Seewoosagur Ramgoolam, the prime minister of Mauritius (*see* BIOGRAPHY).

Southern Africa. The international crisis over Angola had two major consequences. The first was a decision by the so-called "front-line" African presidents (of Tanzania, Zambia, Mozambique, and Botswana, later including Angola) on February 7–8 to break off their negotiations with South Africa's prime minister, B. J. Vorster (*see* BIOGRAPHY), for a peaceful settlement of the problems of Rhodesia and Namibia; the second was a decision by the U.S. to become actively involved in trying to deescalate the violence in southern Africa and to stem further military intervention by the U.S.S.R. and Cuba. U.S. Secretary of State Henry Kissinger embarked on one of his notable diplomatic shuttles after announcing strong U.S. support for majority rule in Rhodesia and South West Africa and progress toward the ending of apartheid in South Africa in a major policy statement delivered in Lusaka, Zambia, in April. His initiative was backed by Britain and had the support of the front-line presidents as well as of Vorster. Faced with this formidable opposition, the Rhodesian leader, Ian Smith (*see* BIOGRAPHY), agreed in September, after meetings with Kissinger and Vorster, to accept the principle of majority rule within two years for his country. Britain invited white and black Rhodesian leaders, including the guerrilla commanders of the Zimbabwe People's Army (ZIPA), to a conference in Geneva in October to implement the Anglo-American proposals accepted by Smith. The Soviet Union and Cuba strongly opposed the conference, arguing that it was an "imperialist trick" to deny the military victory which they felt was in ZIPA's grasp.

The conference opened on October 28 under the chairmanship of Ivor Richard, Britain's permanent representative to the UN, and adjourned on December 14 with the parties still deadlocked. Smith insisted on sticking to the terms of his understanding with Kissinger, which called for a mixed black and white transitional government headed by a council with a white chairman. This was rejected by all the black nationalist leaders at the conference, who included, in addition to Robert Mugabe of ZIPA, Joshua Nkomo, Bishop Abel Muzorewa, and the Rev. Ndabaningi Sithole, but they were unable to reach a common negotiating position among themselves. Britain's offer to provide a commissioner to oversee the transition appeared to be unacceptable to both sides. Richard announced Jan. 17, 1977, as the target date for resumption of the conference, and at year's end he began a tour of Zambia, Rhodesia, South Africa, Botswana, Mozambique, and Tanzania in an effort to end the stalemate.

Kissinger was less successful in arranging for negotiations on Namibia, which had been entrusted as a mandate to South Africa after World War I. Although he won Vorster's agreement to include the South West Africa People's Organization (SWAPO) in negotiations, this failed to persuade all the Namibian leaders to come to a conference. As a result, violence continued to grow along the dangerous frontier with Angola. South Africa promised Namibia its independence by the end of 1978 with a possibility of advancement to December 1977, but on terms unacceptable to SWAPO.

SVEN SIMON—KATHERINE YOUNG

Rhodesian soldiers look across the border into Mozambique, where guerrillas of the Zimbabwe People's Army have taken refuge.

South Africa expressed willingness to accept internal changes, especially after urban black violence had erupted in Soweto in June and spread to other black urban and rural areas, as well as to Coloured residential areas in Cape Province; but no substantial progress was made during the year to defuse the serious threat of violent disorder in the continent's richest and most heavily industrialized country. The Vorster regime continued to pin its faith on the success of its policy of granting independence to nine black Bantustans, or African homelands (of which the Transkei was the first to receive independence from the republic in October), as the only way of resolving the country's racial conflicts.

Wars and Coups. Africa's series of little wars continued to threaten to escalate into larger conflicts, especially after Angola. The challenges to the Rhode-

G. BUTHAUD—NORMA/KATHERINE YOUNG

Chinese Vice-Premier Sun Chien, flanked on the left by Pres. Kenneth Kaunda of Zambia and on the right by Pres. Julius Nyerere of Tanzania, inaugurated the new Tanzam railway in July. Built with Chinese help, it links Zambia with the Tanzanian port of Dar es Salaam on the Indian Ocean.

sian regime by ZIPA (operating from bases in Mozambique and Tanzania) and to the Namibian regime by SWAPO (operating from bases in Zambia and Angola) both grew sharper. These movements enjoyed the full support of the OAU as well as of the Soviet bloc, China, and some Western European countries.

The situation in the Horn of Africa continued to deteriorate ominously as the Ethiopian military regime failed not only to make any progress against the tenacious secessionist war waged by the Eritrean Liberation Front (ELF) and its Marxist wing, the Eritrean Popular Liberation Front (EPLF), but also failed to control the growing armed insurrections in many other regions. The expected French withdrawal from Djibouti during 1977 heightened the tensions between Ethiopia and Somalia over their rival interests in the strategic Red Sea port. The U.S. continued to act as Ethiopia's main supplier of arms, but relations between the two countries worsened during the year. The U.S.S.R., still the main supplier of arms to Somalia, became more seriously engaged in developing a closer alliance with Ethiopia. The Arab countries displayed growing concern about the deteriorating security position in the Horn.

The Chad regime failed to make progress in overcoming the decade-long resistance by the Chad National Liberation Front (Frolinat), whose forces operated along the border with Libya. An attempted military invasion of the Sudan from Libya almost succeeded in July. The attack, though mounted from Libyan soil, was staged by opposition Sudanese forces and by elements identified as black mercenaries.

An attempted military coup in Nigeria was quickly put down in February but only after Nigeria's head of state, Gen. Murtala Ramat Mohammed (*see* OBITUARIES), was killed. He was succeeded by Lieut. Gen. Olusegun Obasanjo (*see* BIOGRAPHY). Other unsuccessful coup attempts took place in Ethiopia, Chad, the Comoros, Niger, and Uganda. The only successful military coup occurred in Burundi, where Pres. Michel Micombero was overthrown in November.

Intra-African Relations. Uganda and Kenya, normally friendly neighbours, came close to war in February when General Amin laid claim to large areas in western Kenya, as well as in the Sudan. Pres. Jomo Kenyatta of Kenya forced a retraction from Amin after applying severe economic pressures on his landlocked neighbour by insisting on cash payments for fuel and other imports. Relations remained troubled between President Neto's regime in Angola and two of his neighbours, Zambia and Zaire; both had vigorously defended the right of his two rival movements to a share in the government of independence. Angola's relations were partly restored with Zambia, which recognized the Angolan government in April, but those with Zaire remained uneasy even though Zaire had recognized Neto's government at the end of February. Relations between Ethiopia and Somalia continued to worsen (*see* above).

Libya's president, Col. Muammar al-Qaddafi, kept Libya in a state of continuous conflict with four of its neighbours—Egypt, Sudan, Tunisia, and Chad. He supported Algeria in its angry dispute with Morocco and Mauritania over the Western Sahara.

The most serious dispute on the continent, however, continued to be between black Africa and the white-ruled states of South Africa, Rhodesia, and Namibia. In this conflict the African states were largely united.

In spite of these many conflicts and difficulties there were signs of growing cooperation between neighbouring states and within regions. The most significant development was the restoring of good relations between the two wealthiest West African countries, Nigeria and the Ivory Coast, as demonstrated in the petroleum sales agreement reached between them in January. Their governments pledged to work closely together to develop the 15-nation Economic Community of West African States, which had been launched in 1975. Set against this was Gabon's withdrawal in September from the Common African and Mauritian Organization.

The East African Community continued to hold together despite the differences between Kenya, Uganda, and Tanzania. A significant new grouping developed during the year among Tanzania, Mozambique, and Zambia. In September the Economic Community of the Countries of the Great Lakes was formally established by the heads of state of Burundi, Rwanda, and Zaire. Another step toward closer cooperation was taken with the establishment of an African Parliamentary Union based in Abidjan (Ivory Coast). It was to serve as a link between the African states and the European Economic Community (EEC).

External Relations. Africa continued to have strained relations with the industrialized nations, especially those of Western Europe and North America, over demands for a "new international economic order." The serious differences between the two sides were revealed at the crucial fourth UN Conference on Trade and Development (UNCTAD IV) meetings held in Nairobi in May, and at the North-South Dialogue, conducted at the Conference on International Economic Cooperation in Paris during the year. The third Franco-African conference of heads of government was held in Paris and Versailles in May. France agreed to contribute 10% of the capital to a proposed African Solidarity Fund; the French Central Fund for Economic Cooperation would have an expanded role; and France would participate in the African Development Fund, set up in 1972.

Although the African countries, all members of the Group of 77, succeeded in winning some concessions at the Nairobi meeting, their dissatisfactions were strongly expressed at the summit of the nonaligned nations in Colombo, Sri Lanka, in August. The Colombo political and economic declarations were sharply critical of Western policies. Despite these

L. GIMENEZ—UPI COMPIX

Guerrillas guard their prisoners in Western (Spanish) Sahara. Calling themselves soldiers of the Saharan Arab Democratic Republic, they skirmished with the armies of Mauritania and Morocco. The Spanish withdrew from the former colony in February, ceding the territory to the two African countries, but the guerrillas had other ideas.

criticisms, however, most African governments showed a ready willingness to cooperate with the United States in regard to Kissinger's initiative in southern Africa, and the policies of some countries, such as Egypt and Sudan, continued to favour closer cooperation with the West. Similar trends were reflected in African relations with the EEC.

The majority of African countries continued to adopt a critical stand toward Israel over the Palestinian question. Although a number of African governments undoubtedly admired Israel's daring act in rescuing the victims of the hijacked plane at Entebbe airport in Uganda (*see* DEFENSE), they nevertheless collectively condemned this act of intervention on African soil. While most African countries took a pro-Arab stand on the Middle East, Afro-Arab economic relations remained uneasy. An attempt to settle their differences was made at an Afro-Arab ministerial conference in Dakar, Senegal, in April. The final declaration at the conference stressed the wish to promote cooperation based on the principles of noninterference in internal affairs, equality between nations, sovereignty over national resources, and respect of mutual interests.

Relations with the Communist world were anxiously debated following the Soviet/Cuban military intervention in Angola in defiance of the OAU's virtually unanimous opposition to external intervention of any kind in the local power struggle; however, after South Africa's military intervention, criticisms of the Communist role became more blunted. But the front-line presidents decided to try to prevent the recurrence of international involvement in the struggle over Rhodesia. A particular concern of African leaders was the heightened Soviet-Chinese rivalry for influence in the continent. Some African leaders believed that the Soviet intervention was not directed primarily toward eroding the Western position but had more to do with Moscow's interest in undermining the Chinese, who had supported the MPLA's two rivals.

Economy. Africa's economy continued to perform poorly during 1976, and was particularly hard hit by the world's inflationary cycle and by the burden of higher energy costs. With an average growth rate of only about 2.8% a year, the majority of African countries were hardly able to keep up with their annual population growth, let alone grow richer. The World Bank's annual report for 1976 observed that the least-developed countries (which included a majority of African nations) had relatively few policy options open to them when attempting to deal with the consequences of the sharp cutback in imports by industrial countries, the fall in most commodity prices, and the higher prices of manufactured goods. These countries also were not able to attract sufficient capital from abroad to sustain their growth. Many were forced to recognize the need for economic and fiscal reforms. As a result, their burden of external debt continued to increase, and their ability to pay service charges was reduced. The total external public debt of the 34 African countries south of the Sahara (excluding South Africa) totaled $15,957,300,000 at the end of 1974; their service payments as a percentage of exports of goods and nonfactor services (those not used in the process of production) stood at 7%, as compared with 2.3% at the end of 1972.

The first benefits of the Lomé Treaty between the EEC and the African, Caribbean, and Pacific (ACP) countries, which had been signed in 1975 and went into effect in April 1976, were registered during the year when the Export Earnings Stabilization System (Stabex) was implemented. It was designed to help countries largely dependent on their commodity exports by guaranteeing them against both drops in production caused by climatic circumstances and declines in sales due to fluctuations in the world market. The 12 commodities protected in this way were peanuts, cocoa, coffee, cotton, coconuts, palm nut and kernel, hides, wood, bananas, tea, sisal, and iron ore. The contributions paid varied in size depending on the loss suffered, the importance of the product in terms of a country's exports, and the EEC's share in the country's total exports.

CAMERAPIX/KEYSTONE

"Islands of prosperity in oceans of poverty" were the words one speaker used to describe the world economy at the UN Conference on Trade and Development in May. It met at the Kenyatta Conference Centre in Nairobi, Kenya.

The Economic Commission for Africa (ECA) published a five-year plan for socioeconomic development in the continent. The plan was based on Africa's need to achieve both greater economic self-reliance and a self-supporting ability to grow and diversify. Among the proposals for industry were plans to create African-owned multinational corporations, long-term agreements to supply raw materials, and development of surface transport, but the main emphasis was on the growth of the rural sector. (COLIN LEGUM)

See also Dependent States; articles on the various political units.

[971.D.6; 978 D–E]

ENCYCLOPÆDIA BRITANNICA FILMS. *Boy of Botswana* (1970); *City Boy of the Ivory Coast* (1970); *A Family of Liberia* (1970); *Two Boys of Ethiopia* (1970); *Youth Builds a Nation in Tanzania* (1970); *Africa: Living in Two Worlds* (1971); *Elephant* (1971); *Giraffe* (1971); *Lion* (1971); *Zebra* (1971); *Cheetah* (1972); *Silent Safari* (1972); *The Pygmies: People of the Forest* (1975); *The Pygmies of the Ituri Forest* (1975).

Agriculture and Food Supplies

Food supplies were again generally ample throughout the world for the second year in a row. The Soviet Union's dramatic recovery from its disastrous 1975 harvest (*see* Special Report) was the single largest change in the world agricultural situation and had a substantial effect on the level of both world and developed country agricultural output, and upon the level of world trade and prices for agricultural products. Crops were damaged by drought in both Europe and Australia, requiring adjustments in livestock industries there, but the food supply was not endangered. The less developed countries generally shared in the gains, but they were not able to match the remarkable advances made in 1975. Only in South Asia, of the less developed regions, did per capita food production fall, but even there the food situation was generally good because of plentiful supplies from 1975's bountiful crops.

A substantial buildup in world grain stocks appeared in prospect in 1977, the first since poor crops in 1972 and 1974 led to stocks being drawn down to near-minimum working levels. The traditional exporting countries—most notably the United States and Canada—continued to hold the largest share, but other countries, including the U.S.S.R., also appeared to increase their holdings. Wheat stocks appeared likely to reach the highest levels since the early 1970s, but coarse grain stocks were also expected to increase somewhat.

World food security was not generally a front-page issue in 1976. With food supplies ample, food aid was a less pressing issue than in earlier years. Little or no progress was achieved in establishing a world grain reserve system as key nations differed over the scope and details of such a system. A central question was what effect a new administration in Washington in 1977 would have on the impasse. Both the U.S. Agriculture and Consumer Protection Act of 1973 (the major legislation applicable to domestic agriculture) and the authorization for the Agricultural Trade and Development Assistance Act of 1954 (Public Law [PL] 480, the major legislation applicable to food aid for the less developed countries) were scheduled to expire in 1977.

There was important, although uneven, progress in coping with matters affecting longer-term agricultural development in 1976. The possibility and consequences of greater weather variability in the future were beginning to be recognized and studied. Agricultural development assistance increased sharply between 1973 and 1975, both in total and as a share of official development assistance, although there was some sign of slowing in 1976, and the oil-exporting and less developed countries could not yet reach an agreement on establishment of the new International Agricultural Development Fund. Progress was being made in agricultural research in the less developed countries, but much more remained to be done.

AGRICULTURE AND FOOD PRODUCTION

Production Indexes. World agricultural output (excluding China) increased about 3% in 1976, according to preliminary estimates (in December) contained in indexes prepared by the Economic Research Service (ERS) of the U.S. Department of Agriculture (USDA). Limited crop and weather reports suggested that China would probably do well to maintain its 1975 level of agricultural output.

Overall agricultural gains by both the developed and less developed countries also were around 3%. The U.S.S.R.'s strong recovery from the disastrous 1975 drought generated a more than 15% rise in its agricultural output which provided the single largest impetus to agricultural growth in the developed countries. That, together with the spurt in Canadian output, outweighed production declines in Western Europe, Oceania, and Japan as well as the little-changed U.S. and Eastern European output. The European and Oceanic declines were primarily the result of severe droughts. In the less developed nations, all regions shared in the production increases, particularly the countries of eastern and western Asia. Increases were smallest in southern Asia, where the largest gains had been recorded in 1975.

The ERS indexes also indicated that world food production (excluding China) may have increased a little faster than overall agricultural production in 1976. The director general of the UN Food and Agriculture Organization (FAO) announced a preliminary estimate of a 2 to 3% increase in food production (including China) to a meeting of the FAO Council at the end of November. While food production rose about equally rapidly in both the less developed countries (LDC's) and developed countries, the much faster population growth rates in the LDC's—2.5%, compared with 1% in the developed countries—meant that their rate of increase in food output was less than one-third that of the developed countries on a per capita basis. Although the nearly 1% per capita increase for the LDC's was far less than the extraordinary 6% recovery in 1975 from their poor performance in 1974, it was still above the 0.4% annual trend increase from 1960 to 1975. Eastern Asia led the rise in per capita

Table I. Indexes of Agricultural and Food Production
Average 1961–65 equals 100

	Total agricultural production					Total food production					Per capita food production				
Region or country	1972	1973	1974	1975	1976*	1972	1973	1974	1975	1976*	1972	1973	1974	1975	1976*
Developed countries	124	131	129	127	131	125	133	131	129	134	115	121	118	115	119
United States	122	124	118	127	128	127	130	124	135	136	115	117	110	120	120
Canada	120	124	112	126	138	122	124	112	128	141	106	106	95	106	115
Western Europe	120	122	127	123	120	120	122	127	123	120	112	114	118	114	112
European Community	119	122	125	120	116	119	122	125	120	116	112	114	116	111	107
Eastern Europe	132	135	139	136	136	132	136	140	137	136	124	127	130	126	125
U.S.S.R.	129	155	145	129	150	128	155	144	127	149	117	140	129	112	131
Japan	110	110	110	115	109	110	110	111	115	108	100	99	98	101	94
Oceania	115	116	119	123	118	122	127	126	133	128	104	106	104	108	102
South Africa	142	119	148	137	136	150	125	157	144	143	118	95	117	105	102
Less developed countries	126	131	134	140	144	125	133	131	129	134	101	103	103	107	108
East Asia	135	148	152	158	166	132	145	150	159	166	106	113	114	118	120
Indonesia	129	142	149	151	153	130	146	154	156	157	105	116	119	118	116
Philippines	133	142	145	159	171	134	143	146	161	173	103	107	106	113	118
South Asia	119	130	124	137	138	119	131	124	139	139	97	105	97	107	105
Bangladesh	101	116	110	122	125	100	118	115	127	129	80	93	88	95	94
India	119	129	122	138	138	119	130	121	139	139	98	105	96	108	106
Pakistan	155	159	163	157	161	152	161	164	163	168	117	121	119	115	115
West Asia	139	129	141	150	158	137	127	138	150	158	107	96	102	107	110
Africa	123	119	125	125	129	122	118	125	127	132	97	92	95	93	94
Egypt	119	120	118	119	124	122	124	125	132	138	98	97	96	99	101
Ethiopia	114	111	115	107	111	113	111	113	105	109	92	88	87	79	80
Nigeria	119	112	119	121	125	119	113	119	121	125	95	88	90	89	89
Latin America	125	129	139	140	145	131	136	145	150	158	102	104	107	108	111
Mexico	132	140	140	148	146	142	151	148	165	162	104	107	102	110	104
Argentina	104	114	123	123	130	107	118	126	126	135	95	103	109	108	114
Brazil	133	131	149	150	154	140	144	160	164	181	109	109	118	117	126
World	124	131	131	132	136	126	133	132	134	139	110	115	113	113	115

*Preliminary
Source: U.S. Department of Agriculture, Economic Research Service.

food output among the LDC's—largely because of good crops in the Philippines and Malaysia—followed by Latin America, western Asia, and Africa.

Southern Asia—which contains the largest number of people near the bare subsistence level—matched the previous year's level of total food production but could not maintain 1975's recovery in per capita output; the per capita index there fell from 107 to 105 (1961–65 = 100). India weighed most heavily in the regional per capita decline, but Sri Lanka's output fell most sharply, because of an early tapering off of the monsoon rains. Pakistan held its own.

Fertilizers and Pesticides. The food production shortfalls of 1972 and 1974 led to greatly increased demand for fertilizers by farmers attempting to expand production rapidly. The fertilizer industry could not increase its output rapidly enough because overexpansion of the industry in the 1960s had discouraged investment in new productive capacity. Fertilizer prices climbed to record levels, spurred also by panic and speculative buying. Although fertilizer use continued to grow in the centrally planned countries in 1974–75, sharply reduced consumption in the United States, France, and India resulted in the first decline in fertilizer consumption since World War II. The resulting growth in inventories, particularly in many LDC's which had imported fertilizer at higher prices than their farmers could afford, helped reduce the demand for fertilizer traded on the world market and contributed to a sharp decline in such prices in 1975, to the relatively moderate levels of 1973.

World fertilizer prices leveled off in 1976, and then strengthened a little in response to substantial increases in demand in the United States and to a smaller increase in Europe and South America. But inventories remained high in several fertilizer-importing countries, particularly in Asia. Prices there remained high, dampening consumption; many governments would neither reduce prices to farmers for expensive fertilizers purchased earlier nor permit the importation of fertilizers at lower world market prices until the high-priced inventories were worked off. The problem was intensified in countries where recent ample crops had reduced the prices received by farmers for their crops. The world fertilizer market was expected to continue fairly stable into 1977.

New fertilizer-producing facilities were beginning to come on stream, particularly in the LDC's. While it is difficult to estimate the exact timing of new plant additions, fertilizer capacity was expected to grow at least as fast as demand in the next few years. The FAO/UN Industrial Development Organization (UNIDO)/World Bank Fertilizers Working Group projected that nitrogen capacity would grow over 17% between mid-1976 and mid-1978, and all three nutrients (nitrogen, phosphate, and potash) were expected to exceed consumption through the late 1970s.

Pesticides, according to FAO, remained scarce in 1975, but became more plentiful in 1976. The improvement resulted partly from new production facilities becoming operational earlier than expected. Pesticide prices leveled off at relatively high 1975 levels which served to curtail demand, particularly in the LDC's. Their share of world pesticide production was estimated by FAO at less than 10%.

Grains. Forecasts (in mid-December) of a record world grain harvest in 1976/77—based on estimates of crops already harvested in the Northern Hemisphere and preharvest reports for the Southern Hemisphere—indicated the first substantial rebuilding of world grain stocks in three to four years. World grain production (wheat, milled rice, and coarse grains) was forecast at 1,321,000,000 metric tons, 100 million tons above 1975/76 and well above the 16-year trend. Record harvested area—up some 1.5%—and near-record yields were responsible.

ADN-ZB / EASTFOTO

New combine harvesters in an East German grain field. East Germany has been importing grain from the West in recent years.

The 79 million-ton recovery in the Soviet Union from an extraordinarily poor 1975/76 crop was largely responsible. Substantial production increases in Canada and the United States about offset smaller crops in Europe and Australia. Variations were expected to be small in the other developed countries. The less developed market economies as a group increased output faster than their average 2.5% population growth, although gains were largely concentrated in South America (Argentina, Brazil, Paraguay, and Uruguay) and in North Africa and the Middle East (Algeria, Morocco, Turkey, Iran, and Iraq). Only marginal increases or decreases were expected for the other less developed market economies that had experienced generally favourable crops in 1975/76. Limited crop and weather reports from China suggested a somewhat smaller grain harvest than in the previous year.

The increases in wheat and coarse grain production about equaled each other in quantity, but the rate of increase for wheat (15%) was almost twice that for coarse grain. Among the coarse grains, barley output seemed likely to increase the most, with progressively smaller increases for rye, corn (maize), oats, and sorghum. Rice production, however, was expected to fall a little, although the level of production for wheat,

Table II. World Production and Trade of Principal Grains (In 000 metric tons)

	Wheat			Barley			Oats			Rye			Corn (Maize)			Rice		
	Production 1961–65 average	Production 1975	Imports— Exports+ 1972–75 average	Production 1961–65 average	Production 1975	Imports— Exports+ 1972–75 average	Production 1961–65 average	Production 1975	Imports— Exports+ 1972–75 average	Production 1961–65 average	Production 1975	Imports— Exports+ 1972–75 average	Production 1961–65 average	Production 1975	Imports— Exports+ 1972–75 average	Production 1961–65 average	Production 1975	Imports— Exports+ 1972–75 average
World total	254,525	354,930	−62,163* +64,653*	99,686	154,031	−12,739* +12,586*	47,813	47,976	−1,623* +1,717*	33,833	24,560	−1,292* +1,296*	216,108	321,440	−44,622* +45,299*	253,213	342,592	−9,206* +9,194*
EUROPE																		
Austria	704	c.945	−24	563	1,006	−48 +2*	322	306	−14	393	347	—	197	981	−54 +1*	—	—	−50* +1*
Belgium	826	703	−1,303† +309*†	485	635	−1,065† +231*†	389	c.263	−54† +8*†	120	c.20	−9*† +7*†	2	c.27	−1,473† +270†	—	—	−69† +26*†
Bulgaria	2,213	c.3,100	−27* +295*	694	c.1,500	−85* +18*	141	c.60	—	58	c.20	−3*	1,601	c.2,000	−143* +142*	37	c.70	−4*
Czechoslovakia	1,779	c.4,500	−812	1,556	c.2,900	−106 +48*	792	c.650	+8*	897	c.650	−15* +52*	474	c.600	−374*	—	—	−c.70*
Denmark	535	541	−13 +149*	3,506	5,194	−118 +398	713	379	−22 +8	380	182	−7* +8*	—	—	−232 +1*	—	—	−13* +3*
Finland	448	559	−14 +88*	400	1,155	−13* +24*	828	1,423	+58*	141	69	−20	—	—	−99	—	—	−14* +1*
France	12,495	15,041	−306 +6,610	6,594	c.9,727	−8* +3,684	2,583	c.1,947	+168	367	c.307	−2* +61	2,760	c.8,143	−347 +3,322	120	c.39	−146 +3
Germany, East	1,357	c.2,900	−1,645*	1,291	c.3,000	−486‡	850	c.800	—	1,741	c.1,800	—	3	c.30§	−516‡	—	—	−52*
Germany, West	4,607	7,013	−2,115 +608*	3,462	6,971	−1,495 +413	2,185	3,445	−390 +33	3,031	2,125	−59 +182	55	531	−3,288 +216	—	—	−155 +35*
Greece	1,765	2,078	−63* +4*	248	c.924	−41* +1*	143	c.100	—	19	c.6	—	241	c.537	−593	88	c.94	−5* +4*
Hungary	2,020	4,084	−14* +743*	970	c.735	−360* +75*	108	96	−38*	271	c.171	−34* +20*	3,350	c.7,100	−39* +535*	36	55	−12* +4*
Ireland	343	212	−197 +9*	575	886	−73 +31*	357	159	−14	1	c.1	—	—	—	−259	—	—	−3*
Italy	8,857	9,620	−1,868 +33	276	610	−1,139 +14*	545	506	−156 +4*	87	37	−5*	3,633	c.5,290	−4,646 +10	612	931	−16* +373
Netherlands, The	606	528	−1,800 +748	390	336	−279 +189	421	158	−49 +74	312	63	−35 +27	c.1	10§	−4,001 +1,086*	—	—	−92 +31*
Norway	19	62§	−334	440	445	−126	126	259	−1* +17*	3	4	−70	—	—	−88 +1*	—	—	−7*
Poland	2,988	c.5,530	−1,540	1,368	c.3,940	−1,122 +78	2,641	c.3,230	−68* +19*	7,466	c.6,810	−37* +194*	20	14§	−623	—	—	−65
Portugal	562	646	−278	61	c.85	−52*	87	122	—	177	155	−27*	617	509	−959	167	141	−22* +1*
Romania	4,321	c.5,000	−18* +660‡	415	c.800	−100* +1*	154	c.80	—	95	c.30	−18*	5,853	c.7,000	−237* +300*	40	c.58	−50‡
Spain	4,365	4,354	−11* +90*	1,959	6,877	−36 +22*	447	619	+5*	385	247	—	1,101	1,848	−3,346 +1*	386	c.384	+50
Sweden	909	1,476	−15 +532	1,167	1,956	−39* +161*	1,304	1,360	−30* +222	142	324	−2* +96	—	—	−71	—	—	−17*
Switzerland	355	320	−371	102	c.180	−528	40	c.63	−160	52	c.32	−33	14	119§	−259	—	—	−19*
U.S.S.R.	64,207	c.65,000	−8,667* +4,457*	20,318	c.35,000	−1,600* +500*	6,052	c.11,000	−c.200* +29*	15,093	c.9,000	−700*	13,122	c.8,000	−4,300* +473*	390	c.2,000	−209* +100*
United Kingdom	3,520	4,435	−3,617 +8*	6,668	8,436	−586 +388	1,531	802	−22 +19*	21	19	−36* +1*	—	—	−3,209 +13*	—	—	−134 +2*
Yugoslavia	3,599	4,396	−384* +1*	557	703	−27* +45*	343	368	−11*	169	98	—	5,618	9,390	−181* +160	23	31§	−20*
ASIA																		
Bangladesh	37	111§	−1,677*	16	15§	—	—	—	—	—	—	—	4	c.2§	—	15,034	c.18,500	−327
Burma	38	38§	—	—	—	—	—	—	—	—	—	—	58	85§	+8	7,786	c.8,700	+320
China	c.22,200	c.41,000	−c.5,700*	14,700	c.21,000	−c.300*	c.1,690	c.3,000	—	—	—	—	c.22,720	c.33,000	−c.2,400*	c.83,200	c.114,000	+c.2,900*
India	11,193	c.25,800	−3,556 +223*	2,590	c.2,900	—	—	—	—	—	—	—	4,593	c.5,500	−3* +1*	52,733	c.70,500	−234 +25*
Indonesia	—	—	−568*	—	—	—	—	—	—	—	—	−2*	2,804	c.3,500	+150*	12,393	23,100	−1,181*
Iran	2,873	5,483	−985*	792	1,438	−65‡	—	—	—	—	—	—	16	c.30§	−112*	851	1,386	−100* +3*
Iraq	849	c.860	−350 +57*	851	c.400	+12*	—	—	—	—	—	—	2	c.19§	−4*	138	c.200	−26*
Japan	1,332	c.241	−5,391	1,380	221	−1,335	145	28	−156	2	c.1§	−101	96	c.30§	−7,308	16,444	17,101	−32 +344*
Korea, South	277	150	−1,780	1,419	2,225	−456	—	—	—	37	15	—	26	c.60§	−462*	4,809	6,485	−482* +1*
Malaysia	—	—	−378* +2*	—	—	−4*	—	—	−3*	—	—	—	8	c.9§	−188*	1,140	c.1,900	−300* +22*
Pakistan	4,152	7,299	−1,174	118	137	+38*	—	—	—	—	—	—	513	904	−4*	1,824	3,657	−20* +560
Philippines	—	—	−553	—	—	−5*	—	—	−4*	—	—	−3*	1,305	c.2,650	−117*	3,957	6,258	−319* +4*
Syria	1,093	c.1,500	−132 +134*	649	597	−11* +14*	2	2§	—	—	—	—	7	19§	−2* +2*	1	—	−65*
Thailand	—	—	−81*	—	—	—	—	—	—	—	—	—	816	c.3,000	−3* +1,931	11,267	c.15,000	+1,248
Turkey	8,585	c.14,750	−425 +197*	3,447	4,300	−6* +15*	495	400	—	734	700	+4*	950	c.1,100	—	222	238§	−25*
AFRICA																		
Algeria	1,254	c.652	−1,379*	476	307	−49* +22*	28	c.28	+2*	—	—	—	4	c.5§	−34*	7	c.5§	−9*
Egypt	1,459	2,033	−1,952	137	118	—	—	—	—	—	—	—	1,913	c.2,600	−240	1,845	c.2,450	+249
Ethiopia	663	c.618	−20*	1,323	c.700	−c.2*	5	c.5§	—	—	—	—	743	c.1,077	−14*	—	—	−1*
Kenya	122	c.160	−52* +32*	15	c.22	+1*	2	c.4§	—	—	—	—	1,110	c.1,600	+102*	14	c.33§	−1* +2*
Morocco	1,336	c.1,267	−854	1,316	c.1,187	−21*	18	c.20	—	2	2§	—	352	420	−18*	20	c.18§	—
Nigeria	16	c.6§	−349*	—	—	—	—	—	—	—	—	—	1,040	c.1,000	−2*	205	c.368	−2*
South Africa	840	1,815	−12* +230*	37	5§	−8*	117	110	−10*	11	5	−2*	5,229	9,516	−2* +2,463	2	c.3§	−86 +4*
NORTH AND SOUTH AMERICA																		
Canada	15,364	17,100	+11,873	3,860	c.9,500	+3,352	6,075	4,440	−5* +144	319	522	−1* +191	1,073	c.3,600	−818 +14*	—	—	−75*
Mexico	1,549	c.3,000	−778* +15*	175	c.260	−60* +7*	76	c.77	−9*	—	—	—	7,369	c.9,300	−1,307 +113	314	414	−37* +9*
United States	33,040	58,074	−27 +30,337‖	8,676	8,340	−294 +1,267	13,848	9,535	−22 +412	828	454	−2* +263	95,561	146,487	−34 +29,740‖	3,084	5,789	−10* +1,883
Argentina	7,541	8,200	−141* +2,026	679	594	+93	676	414	+135*	422	280	+52	4,984	7,700	+4,141	193	350	+36*
Brazil	574	1,500	−2,396	26	c.26§	−26	20	c.42	−25	17	c.19	−1*	10,112	16,491	−2* +630	6,123	7,674	−7* +24
Chile	1,082	1,003	−708	74	121	+13*	89	131	—	7	12	—	204	329	−156*	85	c.40§	−31*
Colombia	118	86§	−349	106	c.130	−47‡	—	—	−8*	—	—	—	826	c.847	−70*	576	1,614	+24*
Peru	150	150	−699	185	c.170	−24	4	c.1§	−1*	1	c.1	—	490	c.625	−197*	324	500	−32* +22*
Uruguay	465	497	−92* +25*	30	c.50§	+7*	66	58	−1*	—	—	—	148	157	−3*	67	189	+58*
Venezuela	1	c.1	−585	—	—	—	—	—	−11	—	—	—	477	686	−192*	136	c.369	−1* +14*
OCEANIA																		
Australia	8,222	11,700	+6,681	978	2,965	+1,298	1,172	1,200	+219	11	c.10	−1*	169	139	−1* +17*	136	386	+163
New Zealand	248	203	−76 +10*	98	334	−7* +17*	34	65	—	—	—	—	16	132§	+3*	—	—	−6*

Note: (—) indicates quantity nil or negligible. (c.) indicates provisional or estimated. *1972–74 average. †Belgium-Luxembourg economic union. ‡1972–73 average. §1974. ‖Including foreign aid shipments. Sources: FAO *Monthly Bulletin of Agricultural Economics and Statistics*; FAO *Production Yearbook 1974*; FAO *Trade Yearbook 1974*.

(M. C. MacDONALD)

coarse grains, and rice would still be above the 16-year trend—and well above it for wheat.

World grain consumption was expected to increase much less rapidly than production, reaching 1,277,000,000 tons in 1976/77. This would be 60 million above the depressed 1975/76 level but well below the 16-year trend. The increase in consumption would account for only about three-fifths of the forecast increase in production. Both total and per capita nonfeed consumption of grain—mostly for food, but also for industry, seed, and waste—were expected to reach an all-time high well above trend, but livestock feeding was expected to be only marginally above 1975/76 and only 85% of the 1972/73 and 1973/74 highs. By far the largest livestock feeding increases were in the Soviet Union, and others were likely to be concentrated in parts of Western Europe because of drought damage to forage, fodder, and grain crops, and in the United States and Canada because of their buildup in grain stocks.

Reductions in both the volume and value of world grain trade were likely in 1976/77. Smaller purchases by 1975's importers could reduce world wheat and coarse grain trade by more than 10 million tons. The good Soviet grain crop was likely to lower its imports as much as 15 million to 20 million tons, down to the minimums provided for in long-term agreements and in short-term agreements signed earlier in the year. Good crops or large carry-in stocks were likely to cut the imports of many less developed countries. South Asian grain imports could fall 5 million tons, and the net imports of the less developed countries as a group could fall to a six-year low of 25 million. The only major grain import increases expected were in Western Europe to compensate for drought damage to forage, fodder, and grain crops. Rice production shortfalls in several less developed Asian countries could result in marginal increases in rice trade which would be negligible in comparison to wheat and coarse grains. While world import demand for grain was estimated to be off 7%, the combined export availabilities of the five major exporters—the United States, Canada, Australia, Argentina, and South Africa—were forecast up as much as 10%. As much as 20 million tons would probably be added to stocks held by those five exporters and Thailand, with the largest shares held by the United States and Canada.

Total carry-over stocks at the end of 1976/77 might increase as much as one-third over carry-in levels, to about 13% of world grain consumption from the approximately 10% level of the previous three years. Most of the stock increases were likely to be concentrated in the Soviet Union, the United States, and Canada, with only a small part of the buildup in other importing or low-income countries. Reports of storage losses in excess of 8 to 10% in many of the less developed countries following the buildup of stocks from the bumper harvests of 1975/76 indicated that even such small increases would strain their capacity, and that any further buildup would require investment in new facilities. Over 90% of the stock buildup was expected to be wheat, while coarse grains would probably increase only marginally, and rice would probably fall by several million tons.

Record production, dampened growth in consumption, lower trade levels, and stock buildups had all acted to reduce wheat and coarse grain prices—the former most sharply. The domestic prices of countries such as the U.S. that were tied directly to the international market had also declined. Further declines could be dampened by the resulting greater attractiveness of grain—including wheat—for livestock feeding. Market conditions still suggested international wheat prices at 80 to 90% of their 1975/76 level and corn at 85 to 95%. Rice prices strengthened in the last quarter of 1976 as the effects of prospective reductions in rice supplies in several Asian countries were felt.

Table III. World Carry-over Stocks of Grain
In 000,000 metric tons

Region or country	1960/61–1962/63	1969/70–1971/72	1972/73	1973/74	1974/75	Preliminary 1975/76	Forecast 1976/77
Developed countries	143.4	126.9	87.7	77.6	74.6	78.5	94.0
United States	103.1	67.2	48.2	31.2	27.2	36.5	47.4
Canada	17.4	27.4	15.8	16.3	13.6	12.2	19.2
European Economic Community	14.2	12.2	12.1	13.8	17.1	12.1	11.2
Other Western Europe	3.9	4.8	4.8	5.8	6.9	6.4	6.2
Japan	2.6	7.3	4.1	4.6	4.8	6.0	5.3
Oceania	1.2	6.0	1.5	3.1	2.8	4.0	3.5
South Africa	1.0	2.0	1.2	2.8	2.2	1.3	1.2
Centrally planned economies	7.9	14.6	12.6	25.8	18.7	10.3	28.4
Eastern Europe	2.9	3.6	2.6	2.8	3.7	3.3	3.8
U.S.S.R.	5.0	11.0	10.0	23.0	15.0	7.0	24.6
China	—	—	—	—	—	—	—
Less developed countries	16.9	30.6	27.8	28.9	29.3	38.4	41.3
Central America	0.8	0.8	0.6	1.2	1.4	1.8	1.4
Venezuela	0.3	0.4	0.3	0.3	0.3	0.3	0.3
Brazil	2.2	2.3	1.1	0.9	1.0	2.1	2.6
Argentina	0.8	1.3	1.2	2.3	2.2	1.9	2.9
Other South America	0.3	0.9	0.9	1.0	0.9	1.0	1.0
North Africa/Middle East	2.1	3.3	4.8	3.1	4.7	6.4	8.2
Central Africa	—	0.1	0.2	0.2	0.1	0.1	0.1
East Africa	—	0.6	0.8	0.4	0.5	0.5	0.4
East Asia	0.9	4.0	3.3	5.2	5.8	5.8	6.5
Southeast Asia	0.4	1.3	1.4	1.5	1.6	1.3	1.1
South Asia	9.1	15.6	13.2	12.8	10.8	17.2	16.8
Rest of world	—	—	—	—	—	—	—
World total	166.4	173.0	127.4	132.0	122.3	122.1	171.3

Note: World total is taken from the December 1976 issue of the *Foreign Agricultural Circular on Grains* and may not match country and regional totals due to rounding and variations in country and commodity coverage. Stock data are based on aggregates of a number of different local marketing years and should not be construed as representing world stock levels at any fixed point in time. Stock data are not available for all countries and exclude China and parts of Eastern Europe; the world totals have been adjusted to reflect estimated year-to-year changes in U.S.S.R. stocks but do not include stocks accumulated prior to 1960/61.

Source: U.S. Department of Agriculture, Economic Research Service, *World Agricultural Situation* (December 1976).

Starchy Roots. This commodity is often neglected in discussions of the world food situation. Data are hard to obtain since most of the commodity is consumed where produced, it does not figure in world trade, and it is of low nutritional value relative to its bulk. Nevertheless, starchy roots, like pulses, are an indispensable source of food for millions of people in the less developed countries. Output, according to FAO, apparently increased in Africa in 1975. The bacterial blight that had affected cassava in Zaire, Africa's largest producer, began to recede. Research on disease-resistant varieties, especially in Nigeria and Zaire, had led to expectations of higher yields, mostly through reduction of post-harvest loss, but the introduction of new varieties was still very limited.

Protein Meal and Fats and Oils. World production of high-protein meal in 1977 (roughly corresponding to the 1976/77 oilseed marketing year) was forecast (in December) at 72 million tons (soybean meal equivalent), 2 million tons below 1976. An 18% reduction in the 1976 U.S. soybean crop was largely responsible. Together with a nearly one-million-ton decline in the Canadian 1976 rapeseed harvest, it more than offset a prospective 17% rise in the 1977 Brazilian soybean harvest to some 13 million tons, sharp recovery in the 1976 U.S. cottonseed harvest, and an expected sharp increase in Argentine soybean output. The 1976 Soviet sunflower crop might total only 5 million to 5.5 million tons. The 1976 Indian peanut (groundnut) harvest at 7 million tons was about unchanged from the 1975 record, and Peruvian 1976 fish-meal output, at 950,000 tons, was projected a little above 1975.

Meal disappearance in 1976 was estimated to have risen to 73 million tons, nearly 7 million tons above depressed 1975 levels, largely because of stronger demand for meal in response to economic recovery in the developed countries. Although demand for high-protein meals continued strong, some reduction in 1977 consumption might be expected, especially in the United States because of higher prices. Sufficient supplies appeared on hand to satisfy 1977 global requirements, assuming a substantial drawdown in U.S. soybean stocks and larger exports from non-U.S. sources, but meal prices were expected to continue significantly above those of 1975.

Production of vegetable, animal, and marine fats and oils for 1977 was forecast at 48 million tons, only a little below the 1976 record. Production of edible vegetable oils (excluding palm) was projected to decline a little to 25 million tons, while palm oils were expected to increase a little to another record, 7.1 million tons, in 1977. Output would be affected by the same developments affecting meals in 1976 Northern Hemisphere and 1977 Southern Hemisphere crops. Since world vegetable oil disappearance was projected to increase by about 1.3 million tons in 1977, supplies should be relatively tight and prices higher in 1977. Some drawdown in stocks appeared likely, most probably in U.S. soybeans and oil.

Meat. Meat production was up in all of the major meat-importing areas, except in Western Europe. Western European policies aimed at maintaining cattle prices led to growth in intervention beef stocks from 220,000 tons in May to 312,000 tons in September. The world's largest beef importer in 1973, Europe was again expected to be a small net exporter of beef in 1976. Although total Japanese meat production increased a little in 1976, beef and veal output fell 14%, and Japanese net meat imports were expected to increase to 40,000 tons, mostly beef and veal and pork.

U.S. meat production was expected to reach 22.9 million tons (up 7.8%); beef and veal (up 7.5%) weighed most heavily in the increase, but poultry production increased the most (12%). Slaughter of nonfed steers and heifers was well below 1975, reflecting cheaper animal feed. The reduction in U.S. cattle numbers appeared to be the strongest since the mid-1920s and followed financial losses by cattlemen over a 2½-year period. Although net U.S. meat imports were expected to decline again in 1976, beef imports were rising.

This 100-acre plot at the Missouri Agricultural Experiment Station at Columbia is a laboratory in which scientists study the soybean. Subjects investigated include plant diseases, nutrient uptake, and weed control.

AGRICULTURAL RESEARCH MAGAZINE

Much of the increase in beef imports into the United States came from Canada, where beef and veal production was forecast up 4% and where imports of cheaper manufacturing beef from Australia and New Zealand were up sharply, freeing Canadian beef for export. On October 9, the United States imposed quotas on imports of fresh, chilled, or frozen beef, veal, mutton, and goat meat. With shipments to the United States slowed, Canada found it necessary to stem the influx of Oceanic beef by imposing a global quota on beef and veal.

In the major meat-exporting areas—Australia, New Zealand, Central America, Argentina, and Uruguay—beef and veal production was expected to rise about 10%, by 640,000 tons in 1976. The traditional commercial markets—United States, Canada, Western Europe, and Japan—were expected to take about 150,000 tons of the increase. About 200,000 tons were expected to be consumed domestically or held as stocks, leaving about 300,000 tons for possible export to nontraditional markets—the most important in 1976 being the U.S.S.R. Although there was speculation that Soviet purchases would total between 400,000 and 600,000 tons, known purchases totaled only 160,000 tons through November. Additional sales before 1977 appeared unlikely because of foreign exchange difficulties.

Dairy. The pickup in milk production that began in mid-1975 continued into early 1976 because of slightly increased cow numbers and higher yields per cow that reflected cheaper or more plentiful feed supplies. But severe drought in 1976 affecting parts of Western Europe and southern Australia contributed to a marginal decline in cow numbers and halted the surge in output.

Most increases in production were in the United States (up 4%) and New Zealand (up 10%), while major declines were expected in Canada, the U.S.S.R., Poland, and Australia (down 12%). In the countries of the European Economic Community (EEC), where production had been encouraged by a 7.5% increase in the target price, the gain was estimated (in December) at 1 to 1.5%.

Demand for dairy products continued restrained in most of the developed market economies, and surplus milk continued to be converted into butter and nonfat dry milk (NFDM), which are storable and eligible for domestic price support programs in several countries. Total private and government stocks of NFDM had trebled since 1973 to over 2 million tons and now accounted for more than half of world NFDM production. EEC intervention stocks, 63% of all stocks, totaled 1.3 million tons in November despite the initiation in April of a scheme aimed at inducing feed manufacturers to incorporate 400,000 tons of NFDM in livestock rations. The program was ended October 31 after only three-fourths of the amount had been delivered. A new program, to operate through January 1977, offered a 10 cents per pound subsidy for feed use of NFDM. Both programs competed with soybean use. As of December, the EEC Council of Agricultural Ministers' decision on a proposed dairy reform program to gradually reduce the EEC's costly dairy surpluses continued to be postponed.

According to FAO, the developed and centrally planned economies fed nearly 8 million tons of milk products (milk powder equivalent) annually, almost 20% of world milk production, to livestock in the early 1970s. Such use was heavily concentrated in Western Europe, the U.S.S.R., and Eastern Europe.

While use continued steady in the centrally planned economies, it had been decreasing at an accelerating rate in Western Europe because of the substitution of vegetable and fish protein in feed.

The existence of large NFDM stocks had favoured increased food-aid shipments by the EEC and other producing countries. However, those—like FAO—who favoured greater use of such stocks for food aid or food reserves also recognized some obstacles. Their use as food aid would impose additional costs on donor countries and would require reasonable continuity of supplies because nutrition and dairy development projects need considerable planning time and ample funding, and must operate for several years if they are to have a lasting effect. This would imply modification of policies in surplus-producing countries aimed primarily at maintaining farm income, which have yielded unwanted and costly NFDM stocks. Such matters, including the possibility of adding commodities other than grains to those considered for food reserves, were discussed at meetings in 1976 of FAO's newly established Committee on Food Aid Policies and Programs.

Sugar. Prospects of ample supplies in 1976/77 pulled sugar prices down from the record levels of the previous two seasons to about 8 cents per pound (stowed at greater Caribbean ports), about the level of 1972. Prices had been stable from October 1975 through July 1976, partly buoyed up by weakened Western European crop prospects resulting from drought, but declined thereafter on news of rainfall there beneficial to sugar beets and of bumper cane harvests in several Southern Hemisphere countries. Other price-dampening factors were the consequent ending of Brazilian export prohibitions, a larger Soviet beet harvest that reduced the need for non-Cuban sugar imports, and competition from high-fructose corn syrup as a sugar substitute.

World sugar production in 1976/77, estimated in December at a record 87 million tons (raw value), was expected to exceed consumption (up 2 million tons from 1975/76) by 4 million tons, raising carry-over stocks by an equal amount to about 20 million tons. Beet sugar accounted for about one-third of increased output, mostly from the sharp recovery in the Soviet crop; the U.S.S.R. planned to increase sugar production to 12.2 million tons by 1980, about 2.6 million above its record output and about equal to projected domestic use. Cane sugar production was expected to rise about 7%, to 53 million tons, based on Southern Hemisphere crops just harvested; Brazil hit a record 7.5 million tons and planned to reach 10 million by 1980 through a modernization program.

The expiration of the International Sugar Agreement, the U.S. Sugar Act, and the Commonwealth Sugar Agreement before the beginning of 1975 had resulted in a big rise in freely traded sugar to perhaps 15 million tons. Of that amount, some 5 million tons were thought to be covered under long-term arrangements involving some ten exporting countries and a like number of importers. Most of the arrangements would run through 1980. The largest contracts were those between U.S. firms and the Philippines. Under a five-year contract Australia was to supply Japan with 3 million tons at a specified price, but the rest were tied in some way to prevailing prices.

The status of these arrangements could have an important influence on the nature of negotiations for a new International Sugar Agreement which were to open under the auspices of the United Nations Conference on Trade and Development (UNCTAD) in Geneva in April 1977. The results of a preparatory meeting held in October suggested that the conference would give particular attention to buffer stock schemes, an export quota system backed by an intervention stock scheme, or an export quota system backed by minimum stock provisions. The U.S. approach to these negotiations would be influenced by the outcome of a U.S. International Trade Commission investigation, expected to be completed before the conference opened, to determine if increased sugar imports had harmed the U.S. sugar industry. The U.S. import tariff had already been raised in September to 1.875 cents per pound from the preferential rate of 0.625 cents.

JONATHAN KANDELL—THE NEW YORK TIMES

Zebu bulls from India graze on this farm in Paraná, Brazil, where jungles grew a few years ago. The state of Paraná in southern Brazil is becoming one of South America's breadbaskets.

Although sugar prices had been below the cost of production recently in many producing countries, the annual 2 million-ton increase in consumption—enough to require 30 new mills a year—was creating strong interest in expanding mill facilities, particularly in the less developed countries. Mexico, Madagascar, Ivory Coast, Tunisia, Nigeria, Syria, Sudan, Tanzania, Panama, Venezuela, and Indonesia were all contemplating substantial building programs.

Coffee. The July 1975 Brazilian frost reduced that country's 1976/77 coffee harvest by 13.5 million bags (of 60 kilos each) below the 23 million harvested in 1975/76. World green coffee output in 1976/77 was estimated (in December) at 62.8 million bags, down 10.7 million. Coffee prices continued to rise. The average International Coffee Organization composite price for green coffee reached $1.64 per pound in October, while that for Brazilian coffee landed in New York (Santos No. 4) was $1.83 per pound in November, both almost double that of a year earlier. A one-pound can

Table IV. World Grain Supply and Demand
In kilograms per capita

Year	Supply			Demand		
	Carry-in stock	Production	Supplies	Consumption	Feed use	Nonfeed use
1960/61–1962/63	56.6	278.5	335.1	278.3	72.0	206.3
1969/70–1971/72	51.6	309.7	361.3	311.9	92.7	219.2
1973/74	33.6	327.6	361.2	323.5	94.5	229.0
1974/75	34.0	309.3	343.3	310.7	82.6	228.1
1975/76	31.0	308.6	339.6	305.4	82.9	222.5
1976/77	31.7	327.8*	359.5*	317.5	82.5	235.0
1977/78	41.2*	—	—	—	—	—

*Forecast.
Source: U.S. Department of Agriculture, Economic Research Service, *World Agricultural Situation* (December 1976).

of roasted coffee cost $2.19 in September at the U.S. wholesale level, compared with $1.46 in January. Consumers had not yet felt the full impact of the Brazilian frost since retail prices lag behind wholesale. Little relief could be expected in the next two years because of the slow maturing of the coffee trees that replaced those killed by the frost. World consumption of green coffee could be down 6% in 1976/77.

The new International Coffee Agreement (ICA) went into force on October 1, through the assent of 40 exporting and 20 importing countries. Similar agreements reached in 1962 and 1968 also sought to defend a floor price for coffee during periods of surplus, but no provision was made for controlling excessive plantings of coffee trees (and thus future surpluses) during periods of scarcity. The new agreement offered producers greater incentives to maintain stable production capacity during times of scarcity by creating the expectation that market prices and long-term earnings would remain fairly stable even during periods of surplus. To protect producers from severe price fluctuations, the ICA would impose a system of adjustable export quotas whenever prices dropped below a minimum trigger range determined each year by the ICA's governing body, the International Coffee Council. Since green coffee prices were expected to remain relatively high over the next few years, export quotas were not likely to come into effect before late 1979 at the earliest, corresponding to the end of the three-year period when members must indicate their willingness to continue under the six-year ICA.

Cocoa. World supply and demand for cocoa were roughly in balance in 1975/76, but sizable stock drawdowns were likely in 1977 because of an expected (in December) 7% decline in production of cocoa beans in 1976/77 to 1,410,000 tons. This, together with the movement of some currency traders into commodities as a hedge against the declining value of the British pound, helped push Accra cocoa bean prices (New York spot) to as high as $1.54 per pound in November, more than double the price a year earlier. World cocoa bean grindings were estimated to be well above 1975's 1,440,000 tons, but were likely to be lower in 1977 because of high prices and greater reliance on substitutes and extenders.

The International Cocoa Agreement (ICA) expired on Sept. 30, 1976, without its economic provisions ever being tested; cocoa bean prices remained above the specified 29.5–38.5 cents per pound range for the entire duration of the three-year agreement. The new ICA, negotiated in the fall of 1975 before the price rises, became effective on Oct. 1, 1976. Many producer-members now considered the new ICA's 39–55 cents per pound range too low, and discussions were likely to be held by members during 1977 with the aim of raising the price range. The United States was not a member of the ICA.

N. SEMENOV—TASS/SOVFOTO

Out to the fields in Angola. These workers from the Textang factory harvest sugar cane on their Sundays off.

ADN-ZB/EASTFOTO

Young cattle being fattened in mountain pastures in East Germany.

Tea. World tea production (in October) was expected to be up less than 2%, to 1,290,000 tons, in 1976. Record crops were being harvested in India and Kenya, while output was likely to fall in Sri Lanka and Mozambique. Supply and demand were roughly in balance in 1976, as in 1975. High coffee prices were expected to give a boost to tea consumption. Prices rose sharply at the London auction during January–July 1976 for the same reasons—related to the decline in the British pound—that influenced cocoa prices. Prices reached an average of 97.1 pence per kilo (U.S. 77 cents per pound) in July 1976, compared with an average of 62.4 pence per kilo (U.S. 63 cents per pound) in 1975.

Economic provisions of a draft long-term international agreement were to be examined at the fourth session of FAO's Intergovernmental Group on Tea. The FAO Secretariat was to prepare a draft based on a proposal by the United Kingdom for a standby quota scheme. An exporter subgroup proposed that an emergency session be called if the London auction price should fall 10% below the April 1976 average of 72.3 pence per kilo.

Cotton. World cotton production in 1976/77 was forecast (in December) to be only 58.8 million bales (of 480 lb net each), up only 7% from the previous year's poor crop. Higher cotton prices relative to

Table V. Food Supply: Calories Per Capita, Per Day

	Total				Vegetable products				Animal products			
	Average 1961–65	1972	1973	1974	Average 1961–65	1972	1973	1974	Average 1961–65	1972	1973	1974
EUROPE												
Albania	2,354	2,479	2,507	2,523	1,997	2,143	2,169	2,182	357	335	338	341
Germany, West	3,624	3,429	3,450	3,432	2,047	2,088	2,128	2,086	1,217	1,342	1,323	1,346
Hungary	3,246	3,491	3,530	3,560	2,207	2,264	2,291	2,306	1,040	1,227	1,239	1,254
Malta	2,723	3,156	3,002	3,081	2,140	2,429	2,314	2,358	584	728	689	723
Norway	3,107	3,213	3,203	3,213	2,128	2,160	2,141	2,098	979	1,053	1,061	1,115
Switzerland	3,521	3,541	3,626	3,439	2,384	2,328	2,392	2,217	1,138	1,213	1,234	1,221
U.S.S.R.	3,276	3,422	3,488	3,540	2,548	2,506	2,537	2,535	728	917	951	1,005
ASIA												
Afghanistan	2,108	1,964	2,015	2.022	1,971	1,843	1,892	1,900	137	121	122	122
Bangladesh	1,973	1,902	1,915	2,024	1,891	1,826	1,839	1,948	82	77	76	76
Bhutan	2,005	2,070	2,073	2,078	1,972	2,036	2,040	2,045	33	33	33	33
Burma	1,952	2,018	2,167	2,223	1,838	1,908	2,050	2,106	114	110	117	116
Cambodia	2,173	2,201	2,190	1,894	2,040	2,082	2,077	1,785	133	119	113	109
Hong Kong	2,468	2,608	2,657	2,533	1,964	1,946	1,992	1,887	504	662	664	646
India	2,055	2,053	1,886	1,976	1,952	1,947	1,779	1,867	103	106	108	109
Indonesia	1,926	1,905	2,058	2,126	1,881	1,853	2,007	2,074	45	52	51	52
Iran	1,891	2,284	2,326	2,368	1,692	2,089	2,124	2,165	198	196	202	204
Korea, South	2,159	2,729	2,678	2,630	2,081	2,585	2,530	2,463	78	145	148	167
Laos	1,901	2,049	2,090	2,090	1,769	1,886	1,927	1,926	132	163	164	164
Malaysia												
Sabah	2,490	2,758	2,778	2,840	2,241	2,449	2,447	2,511	250	309	331	329
Sarawak	2,437	2,511	2,510	2,522	2,277	2,325	2,306	2,305	160	186	204	217
W. Malaysia	2,436	2,467	2,538	2,574	2,149	2,208	2,263	2,284	287	259	275	290
Maldives	1,679	1,783	1,821	1,827	1,490	1,595	1,607	1,609	189	188	214	218
Mongolia	2,372	2,464	2,492	2,475	1,180	1,448	1,543	1,483	1,192	1,016	950	992
Pakistan	1,847	2,165	2,114	2,146	1,644	1,961	1,909	1,938	203	204	205	208
Philippines	1,915	1,941	1,979	1,971	1,716	1,743	1,772	1,761	199	199	208	210
Singapore	2,416	2,806	2,850	2,819	2,000	2,200	2,214	2,197	416	606	636	621
Sri Lanka	2,169	2,024	2,081	2,019	2,065	2,006	2,000	1,934	103	88	82	85
Sudan	1,875	2,101	2,036	2,074	1,593	1,776	1,716	1,756	281	324	319	318
Syria	2,415	2,502	2,491	2,597	2,151	2,261	2,231	2,318	265	241	260	279
Thailand	2,135	2,270	2,318	2,382	1,986	2,088	2,144	2,209	150	181	174	173
Turkey	2,772	2,814	2,831	2,849	2,462	2,531	2,547	2,548	310	283	284	302
Vietnam, North	2,112	2,388	2,423	2,406	1,969	2,192	2,231	2,213	143	196	192	193
AFRICA												
Algeria	1,898	2,024	2,055	2,138	1,711	1,820	1,858	1,913	187	204	196	225
Angola	1,859	1,986	1,985	2,021	1,715	1,818	1,821	1,858	144	168	164	164
Egypt	2,607	2,650	2,613	2,637	2,468	2,498	2,463	2,483	139	153	150	154
Ethiopia	2,095	2,154	2,084	1,914	1,908	1,994	1,926	1,776	188	160	157	138
Ghana	2,030	2,304	2,286	2,318	1,929	2,161	2,164	2,192	101	143	122	126
Kenya	2,282	2,159	2,144	2,117	2,046	1,965	1,966	1,935	236	194	178	182
Madagascar	2,377	2,376	2,319	2,386	2,179	2,175	2,136	2,195	198	201	183	191
Mali	2,027	1,753	1,750	1,774	1,874	1,624	1,640	1,661	153	130	110	113
Morocco	2,250	2,582	2,584	2,611	2,089	2,404	2,408	2,440	161	178	176	171
Mozambique	2,007	1,967	2,026	1,975	1,938	1,890	1,949	1,901	69	77	77	74
Nigeria	2,155	2,119	2,015	2,085	2,097	2,061	1,962	2,031	58	58	54	54
South Africa	2,803	2,861	2,850	2,886	2,338	2,398	2,384	2,421	465	463	466	466
Tanzania	1,869	1,898	1,976	2,003	1,685	1,706	1,791	1,813	184	192	185	190
Tunisia	1,985	2,356	2,337	2,440	1,832	2,160	2,130	2,212	153	195	207	227
Uganda	2,071	2,208	2,120	2,096	1,935	2,061	1,982	1,958	136	147	138	138
Upper Volta	1,943	1,673	1,651	1,859	1,877	1,611	1,603	1,813	66	63	48	46
Zaire	1,926	1,815	1,844	1,885	1,857	1,745	1,775	1,815	69	70	70	69
LATIN AMERICA												
Argentina	3,247	3,247	3,186	3,408	2,291	2,339	2,253	2,418	956	908	934	990
Bahamas, The	2,291	2,423	2,416	2,428	1,483	1,469	1,478	1,473	808	954	937	955
Barbados	2,684	3,218	3,153	3,251	2,152	2,433	2,382	2,452	532	785	771	799
Belize	2,277	2,429	2,438	2,471	1,648	1,781	1,773	1,826	629	648	665	645
Bolivia	1,638	1,879	1,852	1,849	1,397	1,594	1,581	1,575	241	285	270	274
Brazil	2,420	2,546	2,560	2,516	2,086	2,198	2,221	2,186	335	348	339	331
Chile	2,578	2,806	2,583	2,825	2,146	2,355	2,174	2,328	432	450	409	496
Colombia	2,142	2,166	2,144	2,183	1,766	1,830	1,819	1,832	376	336	325	351
Costa Rica	2,200	2,518	2,483	2,537	1,862	2,113	2,072	2,127	339	405	411	411
Cuba	2,431	2,745	2,740	2,712	1,982	2,208	2,177	2,146	449	537	563	566
Dominican Republic	1,940	2,116	2,145	2,213	1,706	1,847	1,873	1,944	234	269	272	269
Ecuador	1,895	2,057	2,080	2,123	1,589	1,714	1,731	1,778	306	343	349	345
El Salvador	1,819	1,877	1,865	1,914	1,581	1,676	1,661	1,712	237	201	204	202
Guatemala	1,956	1,989	1,984	1,994	1,759	1,795	1,793	1,803	197	194	190	192
Guyana	2,375	2,278	2,410	2,351	2,065	1,984	2,109	2,063	310	294	302	287
Haiti	1,974	2,034	2,026	2,026	1,851	1,907	1,899	1,900	123	126	126	126
Honduras	1,937	2,072	2,042	2,041	1,709	1,825	1,800	1,809	227	247	242	233
Jamaica	2,065	2,725	2,535	2,664	1,736	2,235	2,117	2,215	329	491	418	449
Mexico	2,570	2,647	2,704	2,727	2,284	2,316	2,378	2,394	285	331	325	333
Nicaragua	2,244	2,410	2,351	2,390	1,892	2,046	1,991	2,023	352	364	360	366
Panama	2,342	2,293	2,283	2,421	1,971	1,887	1,884	2,021	370	406	399	400
Paraguay	2,521	2,744	2,703	2,723	1,961	2,244	2,273	2,244	560	500	429	479
Peru	2,255	2,302	2,322	2,360	1,908	1,925	1,965	2,004	347	376	357	355
Surinam	2,117	2,391	2,375	2,376	1,865	2,104	2,120	2,122	252	286	255	254
Trinidad and Tobago	2,436	2,587	2,477	2,530	2,018	2,136	2,045	2,105	418	451	432	426
Uruguay	2,938	2,874	2,979	3,080	1,714	1,864	1,964	2,009	1,224	1,010	1,014	1,072
Venezuela	2,225	2,381	2,390	2,427	1,809	1,950	1,933	1,957	416	431	456	470
NORTH AMERICA*												
Canada†	3,080	3,190§	...	...	1,749	1,723§	...	...	1,331	1,467§	...	...
United States†	3,138	3,320	3,300	3,350	1,867	1,992	1,980	2,010	1,271	1,328	1,320	1,340
OCEANIA												
Australia	3,256	3,383	3,324	3,310	1,897	2,035	2,025	2,057	1,359	1,348	1,299	1,252
New Zealand	3,517	3,488	3,465	3,551	1,783	1,782	1,767	1,821	1,734	1,706	1,698	1,730

*Excluding Latin America. †Data not comparable to remainder of table; national sources utilized. §1970.

Note: Food supplies represent the amount of food available for human consumption at kitchen level, including plate waste and refuse given to domestic animals. Per capita net food supplies were compiled by dividing the data on total supplies by population data; in almost all cases these were midyear estimates obtained from the UN Population Division. Caloric values were calculated by applying food composition factors selected from regional or international tables, adjusted to take into account nonedible parts of food.

Source: FAO *Monthly Bulletin of Agricultural Economics and Statistics* (April 1976 and July/August 1976).

alternative crops had resulted in a 4% expansion in area—to a level still much less than that of 1974/75—but yields did not recover as much as expected because of deteriorating weather late in 1976; official policies favouring food crops had also moderated production increases. The United States, the U.S.S.R., Brazil, and Sudan were responsible for 90% of the increased output.

Consumption, at 61.9 million bales, was forecast about 1.3 million below 1975/76 because of limited supplies, higher prices, and greater use of man-made fibres. Almost half the decline was expected to be in the United States and the rest in other non-Communist countries. Although trade volume was expected to be nearly one million bales smaller than the previous year's 17.5 million because of a sharp reduction in export availabilities of non-Communist countries other than the U.S., stocks were expected to fall about 3 million bales, to around 21 million by July 1977. It was anticipated that U.S. exports should be up sharply to about 4.5 million bales, and that Soviet exports, which had been expanding in recent years, could reach 4 million. Turkish and Mexican shipments were expected to be lower.

The continuing pressure on cotton supplies was reflected in the average price of U.S. SM $1\frac{1}{16}''$ cotton of 87.56 cents per pound (cif Northern Europe) in November, one-third above a year earlier.

Wool. World wool production in 1975 (including the 1975/76 season in the Southern Hemisphere) was about 2.6 million tons (greasy basis), essentially unchanged from 1974. Small gains in the U.S.S.R., New Zealand, South Africa, and Uruguay were offset by declines in Australia, Argentina, the United States, and Spain. The wool textile industry continued depressed into 1976, and revival in demand for wool was seen to depend upon a quickened pace of economic activity in importing countries.

Jute. UNCTAD sponsored a preparatory conference on jute and jute products in Geneva in October as part of work envisioned under a resolution establishing an Integrated Program for Commodities, adopted at the UNCTAD session in Nairobi in May. The Geneva conference called for a study of measures that might produce an improved market situation for jute and allied fibres that were meeting increasing competition from synthetic substitutes. The jute-producing nations wanted to establish a buffer stock for jute and jute products forming part of an international action program for those commodities. A second preparatory conference was to be held no later than April 1977.

Tobacco. World tobacco production in 1976 was about the same as 1975's nearly 12,000,000,000 lb (farm-sales weight). Smaller crops in the United States (down 6%) because of 5% reduced acreage, Brazil (down 13%) because of heavy rains, India, Rhodesia, and Canada were offset by a 3% rise in the combined output of other countries. Although world output had been above trend the previous two years, consumption continued to grow 2–3% annually, and stocks could be drawn down somewhat in 1977. U.S. auction prices for flue-cured tobacco in 1976 averaged 11% over 1975. Cigarette production was estimated up 2% in 1976, 7% in the United States and 1% in the rest of the world.

FOOD SECURITY ISSUES

Food Aid. Commitments of food aid increased in 1975/76 to 9.3 million tons, a little short of the 10 million-ton annual goal set by the World Food Conference, but generally ample food supplies made food aid a less pressing issue in 1976.

The World Food Council (WFC), in its June meeting, drew attention to other considerations by endorsing several recommendations, including the acceptance and implementation of forward planning of food aid. It noted that only Canada and Sweden had so far implemented forward planning and welcomed announced EEC intentions for medium-term indicative planning of its food aid through both bilateral and multilateral channels.

The WFC also endorsed the channeling of more food aid through the World Food Program and contributions in cash as well as kind, the purchasing of commodities for aid from less developed countries at competitive prices, the examination of targets for non-cereal products, and special attention to the least developed and most seriously affected countries in the allocation of food aid.

In this connection, a December 1975 amendment of U.S. food aid legislation (PL 480) required that at least 75% of all concessional credit sales (Title I, the

KEYSTONE

The drought in Great Britain drained this reservoir at Pitsford of its water, leaving the cracked earth baking in a May sun.

major part of U.S. food aid) go to countries with per capita gross national products of under $300 which are also unable to meet their immediate food requirements out of domestic production or commercial imports. The potential for competition between differing concepts of food aid and other domestic agricultural and national policy goals was illustrated by a U.S. agricultural official's statement in November that "Congress has badly crippled PL 480 as an effective tool for developing export markets for U.S. farm products" by amending the law. He noted that the need for food assistance had been dramatically reduced by good crops in South Asia where the United States generally had shipped large quantities of PL 480 food, and that the United States was unable to respond to greater import needs in North Africa and the Middle East because countries there had per capita GNP's in excess of $300. He expressed doubts that the original U.S. goal of nearly 2 million tons could be met in fiscal 1977 (Oct. 1, 1976–Sept. 30, 1977) because of the restrictions. The authorization for PL 480 was to expire in 1977.

Grain Reserves. Much discussion produced little visible progress in 1976 toward establishing the international system of nationally held grain reserves envisaged in the International Undertaking of World Food Security. Some 70 countries—including the United States, but not the U.S.S.R. or China—representing about 95% of world cereal exports, 50% of imports, and 60% of production had subscribed to its broad principles since their endorsement by the World Food Conference in December 1974. The Undertaking in very broad terms affirmed the common responsibility of the international community for adequate policies on world food, called for the adoption of national stockholding policies and the establishment of national stock targets—the amount and method of their holding by individual nations to be nationally determined—that would maintain minimum stocks for the world as a whole to ensure continuity of supplies for both domestic and foreign requirements growing out of crop failure or natural disaster, and called for consultation and sharing of information on such matters.

Substantive discussions on grain reserve issues had been carried on within the International Wheat Council, the consultative organ of the International Wheat Agreement (IWA) that was recently extended to June 1978, since February 1975; one advantage of this forum was that the U.S.S.R. participated. The current IWA had no economic provisions, but many members were interested in incorporating such provisions, although views differed as to whether or how they should be linked to grain reserves.

The scope of the IWA negotiations had been at issue from the start. The U.S. proposals made in September 1975 on reserve levels were based on the relatively narrow goal of meeting potential production shortfalls; the United States favoured a new IWA with reserve provisions, but not linked to the control of grain prices. Other countries, including many of the less developed countries, argued that greater emphasis should be given to the aim of market stabilization. The position of the LDC's reflected their broader drive for the centralized restructuring of commodity trade to favour their economic position embodied in the UNCTAD Integrated Program for Commodities. The European Commission, which earlier had wanted to discuss reserves in the context of the multilateral trade negotiations, appeared sensitive to arrangements that might affect its common agricultural policy. In practice, differences over the scope of the IWA meant the advocacy of quantitative reserve triggers by countries like the United States, as against price triggers, or some combination of quantity and price triggers, favoured by others.

A related question has been the desired level and composition of world grain stocks. A reserve created primarily to meet food production shortfalls and emergency food needs presumably would consist largely of wheat and would be smaller than a reserve designed primarily to reduce price fluctuations. The latter would also probably have a larger coarse grain component because the demand for feed grains usually varies much more than the demand for food grain since feed demand is derived from the much more volatile demand for livestock products. Thus the United States proposed, in September 1975, targets of 25 million tons for wheat and 5 million for rice beyond working stock levels. Although about 100 million tons for all grains was used as a crude estimate of working stocks (excluding those held by the U.S.S.R. and China, which they do not reveal), no agreement had been reached as to their definition and level. In April the Group of 77 (a loose grouping of less developed countries often numbering more than the name implies) proposed at the first meeting of FAO's Committee on World Food Security that a safe minimum level for all grains was 17 to 18% of world consumption. This percentage originated in the FAO Secretariat but had not been officially accepted by the FAO Council or other official bodies concerned with grain reserves. Based on grain consumption in recent years, this could amount to around 200 million to 230 million tons. This compares with the forecast carryover of all grains of 171 million tons (13% of consumption) for 1976/77, the 125 million-ton average (10%) for 1973/74 and 1975/76, and the 173 million-ton average (15%) for 1969/70 and 1971/72.

In view of the complexity and slowness of grain reserve discussions, the Secretariat of the WFC at its meeting in June argued that a more practical method of dealing with the stocks issue was to take a disaggregated approach, breaking down global stock policy into more manageable components and seeking support from different groups of countries in relation to their own interests in each component. The Secretariat's proposals included the establishment of an international reserve for emergencies with an initial target of at least 500,000 tons to which potential donors would be invited to contribute; the earmarking in advance of part of their national stocks for emergencies, preferably 25% above the donor's annual food aid program; and the establishment of a 15 million–20 million-ton food-security reserve to protect against well-defined exigencies and abnormal fluctuations in grain prices. Of these three specific proposals, the WFC agreed at that time only to endorse the emergency reserve.

The world had proved unable to reach agreement on most of the major grain reserve issues during recent years when short supplies and high prices made the acquisition of stocks rather impracticable. Would it do so now when supplies were more ample and prices lower, but when dire predictions of famine no longer occupied the front pages of newspapers around the world? A related question was how a new administration in Washington would react to world food security issues and how it would relate them to domestic agricultural policy issues in an economic climate in which grain prices could be the lowest and the potential for surpluses the greatest since the early 1970s. Would it choose to move away from a heavily free-market policy orientation to a more interventionist one, and what bearing might that have on the implementation of world grain reserves?

DEVELOPMENTS AFFECTING THE LONGER RUN

The food shortages of 1972 and 1974 generated widespread warnings that the world was rapidly losing the ability to feed itself, that the Malthusian spectre was not just knocking on the door but smashing through it. More recently, a sober consensus appeared to be growing—based on studies from such diverse sources as FAO, the International Food Policy Research Institute, the ERS, and Iowa State University—that world food problems were manageable to the extent that governments and individuals were willing to act upon them to buy the time in which to bring population under control. The Malthusian argument appeared to be taking a new form, ranging on opposite sides those with optimistic or pessimistic views of the efficacy and adaptability of technology and of the individual and collective ability of human societies to organize themselves for a sustained attack on hunger.

All the above studies foresaw a substantial increase in the food import requirements of the less developed countries in the next decade or so if they did not generate substantial increases in their own domestic agricultural production. Although the developed countries probably have the physical ability to meet that deficit for some time to come, serious doubts existed about how such large quantities of food could be shipped and financed. A substantial increase in food production by the less developed countries themselves, aided by the developed countries, appeared to be the only viable solution. FAO estimated that this would require a 4% annual increase in food production, compared with the trend rate of 3% and population growth of 2.5%.

Accomplishment of this task would require adaptation to possibly greater weather variability in the future; transfer of resources to the less developed countries; development, adaptation, and transfer of technologies; and the modification of agricultural and other economic policies, particularly those that reduce the incentives to food production in the less developed countries. The latter category of actions was probably the most important and the most difficult to accomplish.

Weather and Climate. Several issues concerning weather and climatic change received increasing attention from both scientists and the public during 1976 because of their implications for world food production and world food policies. They revolved around questions of whether the Earth's atmosphere was cooling or warming, the possibility of greater weather variability in the future, and the likely effect on agriculture of such developments.

Little research has been done on the effects of climatic change on agriculture. Scientists at a conference in Italy in June 1975 discussed the consequences for North American agriculture of a total drop of 1° C over the next 20 years—the probable maximum. They noted that their comments constituted "extrapolation from limited data and informed conjecture rather than formal conclusions." They suggested that a southward shift in cropping patterns would be likely, with substitution of earlier maturing varieties in some areas, but that possible reductions in northern yields would probably be more than offset by increased yields farther south. If cooler temperatures brought increased precipitation, net yields might increase further.

But if cooling were accompanied by greater weather variation, the net effect on yields could not be estimated without postulating the nature of the variations. Greater variations would complicate the breeding and selection of suitable crop varieties. The scientists noted that strategies "designed to optimize the resistance of crops to a wide range of climatic conditions may smooth the variations in crop yields from year to year but will probably result in a reduction in total yield over a period of years."

Some scientists believe that the temperature might rise 1° C or more over the next few decades because of the effects of more carbon dioxide in the atmosphere resulting from the increasing rate of fossil fuel use. This would probably shift some circulation belts and change temperature and precipitation distribution patterns. But apparently no studies have attempted to evaluate the effects on agriculture.

Some effort has been made to systematically describe climatic scenarios, such as one presented at a conference in Toronto in November 1975 on the 1933–37 U.S. droughts. The Institute of Ecology (TIE) went a step further by examining the effect of climatic fluctuations on major North American food crops in relation to four scenarios, which include those droughts, based on the assumption of 1975 cropping patterns and 1973 technology. TIE's calculations suggest that a repeat of the 1933–37 scenario would result in a 15 to 20% reduction in the overall yield for wheat, sorghum, soybeans, and corn. But the consequences in the U.S. Great Plains—the area most seriously affected in the 1930s—although serious, would apparently be less damaging than in the 1930s because of improved technology, such as supplemental irrigation and greater use of drought-resistant grains such as sorghum.

These issues and others were reviewed in a paper presented at the National Agricultural Outlook Conference in November by Department of Agriculture economist Joseph Willett, who directed the ERS study *The World Food Situation and Prospects to 1985*. He noted that, whatever the outcome of the controversies on cooling and warming, there appeared to be a growing consensus that "the climate of major crop-growing areas is likely to become more variable than it has been during the last few decades, with resultant larger year-to-year fluctuations in agricultural output." He acknowledged that increased weather variability over an extended period of time would have major implications for U.S. policies on a number of issues, including the world food gap and grain reserves. For instance, ERS analyses of grain reserve requirements have assumed that deviations in world grain production from weather occur randomly and that the variability in future grain production will be the same as in recent decades. But if grain production variability increases in the future, "then a larger level of grain reserves would be required to meet the same degree of confidence in coverage of consumption needs."

In recognition of the importance of such issues, the USDA joined in a research project with the National Defense University and the National Oceanic and Atmospheric Administration to better define and evaluate the best judgments available on the probabilities of climatic change and weather variability, the resultant effects on U.S. and world food production and on related matters affecting national policy to the year 2000 and the policy options available for coping with such changes.

Agricultural Development Assistance. Official development aid to agriculture began picking up in the early 1970s, began to show impressive gains in 1973, and increased quite rapidly in 1974 and 1975. Between 1973 and 1975, such assistance—broadly defined to include rural infrastructure, agro-industries, fertilizer production, and regional river basin projects—more than doubled from about $2.3 billion in 1973 to about $5.6 billion in 1975, according to preliminary data presented by the FAO Secretariat to the November FAO Council meeting. Increased lending by multilateral agencies accounted for at least half the increase, and by the Organization of Petroleum Exporting Countries (OPEC) for at least a quarter. Bilateral developed country donors accounted for most of the remaining increases, but controversies over the method for calculating flows obscured the relative roles of the bilateral and multilateral donors. OPEC official commitments rose the most dramatically, from $44 million in 1973 to $200 million in 1974 and $931 million in 1975, with about half of those commitments to countries in the Near East. Fertilizer industry projects received nearly half the 1975 OPEC total, and irrigation projects 13%. Such assistance only partly compensated the less developed countries for substantial increases in their petroleum import bills from higher oil prices.

The World Bank was the single largest source of official agricultural development funds; its commitments increased from $436 million in fiscal 1972 to $1,858,000,000 in 1975, but dropped back to $1,628,000,000 in fiscal 1976. Some $418 million was granted on soft terms through the associated International Development Association, the replenishment of whose lending capacity would be an important issue in 1977. The various regional development banks and the FAO/UN Development Program (UNDP) also increased substantially the amounts and shares of funds devoted to agriculture.

As 1976 ended, the International Fund for Agricultural Development proposed by the 1974 World Food Conference had not yet been formally established. The expected signing of the fund agreement in June had to be postponed because of failure to reach the $1 billion target which was conditional for the pledges of many countries. Pledges announced in September totaled some $965 million. They included $400 million from the OPEC $800 million Special Fund (for interest-free, long-term loans), $20 million by Iran, $200 million by the United States, and the $345 million balance almost entirely from other developed country donors. Several pledges were contingent upon the achievement of "rough parity" between the traditional developed donors and the OPEC countries, with some differences arising over the interpretation of "parity." Thus further negotiations seemed in prospect.

Agricultural Research. Most solutions to world food problems have a critical technological component that assumes the creation of new technologies or the more innovative application of existing technologies. Much of the optimism about technological solutions is based on a view of research not as a discontinuous series of unpredictable flashes striking individual minds, but as an investment process that generates results in some rough proportion to the resources devoted to it.

AGERPRES BUCHAREST/EASTFOTO

Hothouses near Bucharest, Romania, grow cucumbers, tomatoes, peppers, lettuce, onions, and beans.

Until very recently, little time and attention were devoted to developing the agricultural technological capacity of less developed countries. FAO notes that such countries' share of agricultural machinery and fertilizer use is only about 25%, and of pesticides as little as 10%, even though they farm 70% of the world's arable land. Students of the "green revolution" have noted that its new wheat and rice varieties were made possible by intensive research over many years, but that an emphasis on industrial and export crops resulted in food crops being neglected in the less developed countries. It was not until the mid-1960s, with the establishment of international research centres in the Philippines and Mexico, that research was sharply focused on food crops.

Thus the continuing expansion of such centres and programs under the leadership of the Consultative Group on International Agricultural Research (CGIAR) —jointly sponsored by FAO, the World Bank, and UNDP—has been a welcome development. During CGIAR's first six years of existence, the number of centres and programs supported had grown from 4 to 12. They were primarily concerned with increasing food crop production in the less developed countries and had programs on the major food crops and farming systems in all of the major ecological zones of the less developed world. They also researched animal production systems, diseases of livestock, and conservation of plant genetic resources. Financial assistance to the group had increased fivefold in the six years, and a $14 million increase in pledges, to $78 million, was announced for 1977 in October.

While the work of such international centres is of critical importance, of even greater importance is the development of local research and extension facilities without which the discoveries of the international groups are unlikely to reach the fields.

(RICHARD M. KENNEDY)

See also Environment; Fisheries; Food Processing; Gardening; Industrial Review: *Alcoholic Beverages; Textiles; Tobacco.*

[451.B.1.c; 534.E; 731; 10/37.C]

ENCYCLOPÆDIA BRITANNICA FILMS. *Problems of Conservation: Soil* (1969); *Problems of Conservation: Our Natural Resources* (1970); *The Farmer in a Changing America* (1973); *What Makes Rain?* (1975).

Aircraft:
see Aerial Sports; Defense; Industrial Review; Transportation

Air Forces:
see Defense

THE SOVIET GRAIN DISASTER OF 1975

By D. Gale Johnson

The soft underbelly of the Soviet Union runs through the grain-growing areas of the Ukraine, Kazakhstan, and western Siberia. Sixty years after the Communists took power in a predominantly agricultural country, they are still struggling to enforce their will upon the recalcitrant earth. In 1975 they suffered a major disaster. The grain crop that year was the smallest in a decade—29% smaller than in the previous year and 37% below the bumper crop of 1973.

First Consequences. Weighing in at about 140 million metric tons instead of the 215.7 million tons that had been planned, the short grain harvest forced the U.S.S.R. to step up its imports from capitalist countries such as the U.S., Canada, and Australia. Altogether it had to import about 27 million tons of foreign grain in the year ending July 1, 1976. The Soviet Union also canceled a large part of its export commitments to the countries of Eastern Europe. These exports had been averaging more than five million tons in recent years.

The grain fiasco had other consequences, which eventually became evident on the Soviet dinner plate. The amount of grain available for feeding livestock dropped off—probably from about 107 million tons in 1974–75 to 85 million tons in 1975–76. This led to a reduction in hogs of 16% and in poultry of 12% on state and collective farms. During the first five months of 1976 meat production on state and collective farms was 7% less than during the same period in 1975. Milk production was reduced by 8% and egg production by 4%. Since meat production had been growing at an annual rate of approximately 5%, milk by 3%, and eggs by more than 6%, the reductions in 1976 represent declines of approximately a tenth from what would have been produced with an average grain crop in 1975.

A Dry Season. The immediate cause of the poor grain crop was a dry and generally hot spring and summer throughout the major grain-growing areas of the Soviet Union. The Soviet Union covers such a large geographic area that, in most years, if one part of the country has adverse weather another important producing area will have either average or better-than-average weather. But in 1975 crops were poor in each of the three major grain-producing republics. The Kazakh S.S.R., where the grain area had been greatly expanded during the New Lands Program of the 1950s, produced less than half as much grain as in an average year. The Russian S.F.S.R.'s grain crop suffered a reduction in output, compared with the average, of more than a third. The crop in the Ukraine was 34 million tons, also a reduction of about a third from the average.

Total production of wheat, the major grain, was 66 million tons, compared with 84 million tons in 1974 and 110 million tons in 1973. The winter wheat crop, which is sown in the fall and harvested in late spring or early summer, was almost 18% smaller in 1975 than the year before. The adverse weather conditions had an even greater effect on the spring-sown grains, including spring wheat, oats, barley, and corn (maize).

D. Gale Johnson, Eliakim Hastings Moore distinguished service professor of economics and provost, the University of Chicago, is the author of World Agriculture in Disarray *(1973) and* World Food Problems and Prospects *(1975).*

Needed: More Fallow. While the immediate cause of the poor grain crop was adverse weather, other and more permanent factors played a role. A large part of the grain is produced in areas with limited rainfall. In regions of North America comparable to the grain-growing areas of Kazakhstan, western Siberia, and the Ukraine, farmers do not attempt to obtain a crop from every acre every year. Instead, much of the land is left fallow for a year and tilled or cultivated to eliminate weeds and to accumulate moisture. In the Prairie Provinces of Canada and in large parts of the Great Plains in the United States, from a third to half of both fall- and winter-sown grains are seeded on fallow land. This practice has two important effects: it increases the average yield per acre actually seeded, and it reduces year-to-year variability in grain production.

In the Soviet Union relatively little land is fallowed. In recent years the amount of land fallowed has been about 14 million ha out of a total grain-producing area of 127 million ha. Given the climatic conditions that prevail over much of this area, the low percentage of fallow goes far toward explaining the large yearly fluctuations in grain production.

Why do Soviet farms utilize fallow to such a limited extent? Their agricultural scientists know as well as the agricultural scientists of North America the value of fallow in reducing production variability. The most probable reasons are the pressures put upon farms each year to achieve production goals and the promulgation in Moscow of the plans for the amount of land to be sown in local areas and on individual farms. The pressure to continuously expand output, and the penalties that are imposed for failure to do so, have apparently prevented the use of fallow as an important method of stabilizing production. It is true that output on a given geographic area is somewhat lower with fallow than with continuous cropping. However, the difference in the Soviet case might be quite small. When weather conditions there are relatively favourable during the growing season and a large crop is produced, the available evidence indicates that the amount of waste during harvesting, immediately after the harvest, and in storage is very large. With more stable output it would be possible to save a larger percentage of the crop.

Soviet Meat Consumption. Even if the 1975 Soviet grain crop had not been so small, the Soviet Union would have been an important grain importer for the next several years. At the beginning of the 1970s policymakers in the Soviet Union apparently made the decision to expand livestock production more rapidly than their own expected feed resources would permit. This decision became apparent when the U.S.S.R. imported eight million tons of grain, more than half of which was feed grains, in 1971–72, following the then second-largest grain crop on record. In 1972–73 the increase in Soviet net grain imports exceeded the decrease in grain production between 1971 and 1972 by a total of six million tons.

The effort to expand meat production by a substantial amount reflects the relatively low level of per capita consumption in the Soviet Union. At 58 kg per capita in 1975, consumption is a little more than half that in the United States. Perhaps more significant is the fact that per capita meat consumption in the Soviet Union is below that of Poland, Czechoslovakia, East Germany, Romania, and Hungary.

Grain Agreement with the U.S. A major development in the relationship between the United States and the Soviet Union was the signing of a five-year grain-supply agreement that took effect on Oct. 1, 1976. The Soviet Union committed itself to purchase a minimum of 6 million tons of wheat and corn from

Soviet Union Grain Production

In 000,000 metric tons

Year	Production	Year	Production	Year	Production
1960	126	1966	171	1971	181
1961	131	1967	148	1972	168
1962	140	1968	170	1973	222
1963	108	1969	162	1974	196
1964	152	1970	187	1975	140
1965	121				

TASS / SOVFOTO

Trucks delivering grain to a bread factory in Kazakhstan, U.S.S.R.

the United States each year. In turn, the United States agreed not to restrict Soviet imports to less than 6 million tons unless the U.S. grain supply should fall below 225 million tons. The Soviets can purchase an additional 2 million tons of wheat and corn annually without consultation with the U.S. government if the U.S. grain supply is not less than 225 million tons. Purchases in excess of 8 million tons require consultation.

The agreement does not limit imports of grains other than wheat and corn or imports of soybeans. Nor does the agreement in any way control or influence exports of grain by the Soviet Union except that grain actually imported from the U.S. cannot be reexported.

The primary objective of the agreement was to assure a steadier market for U.S. grains in the Soviet Union. In the past, Soviet grain imports have varied widely from year to year. This surprise element has made it difficult for the private firms that handle U.S. grain exports to deal with the Soviet importers. Surprise has been possible because the Soviet Union withholds information about the prospective size of its grain crop, the amount of grain in storage, and other data that are available from most countries.

The import quantities specified in the agreement do not directly indicate the total amount of grain that the Soviet Union expects to import. Since 1971 approximately 55% of all Soviet grain imports have been from the United States. The U.S.S.R. will almost certainly continue to import grain from Canada and Australia. In any case, it is unlikely to want to become fully dependent upon the United States for its grain import needs. Thus one may reasonably infer that the Soviet Union may be planning to import from 11 million to 15 million tons annually over the next five years. In turn, it may export approximately 5 million tons to the countries of Eastern Europe and to Cuba as it has done in the past.

One response of the Soviet Union to its changed situation has been to build more storage space. The effort to expand livestock production has increased its vulnerability to large crop shortfalls. When it had poor grain crops in 1963 and 1965, the lack of adequate grain reserves required drastic reductions in the livestock herd.

Outlook for the Future. The five-year plan for 1976–80 for livestock production is somewhat pessimistic. Under the plan ended in 1975 meat production was to increase by 23%, milk production by 15%, and egg production by 30%. Actual production gains were 21% for meat, 9% for milk, and 40% for eggs —a very good performance. In the new plan meat and milk production are scheduled to increase by about 7–10% and egg production by approximately 15%. The previous plan projected a rise in grain production of 16%, significantly less than the increase in livestock production. In the new plan grain production is planned to rise by 18–21%, significantly more than the increase in livestock production.

If the plan for grain production were realized, the livestock goals and the feed supply would be brought much more nearly in balance than they have been during the past five years. The requirement for imports, if the grain plan were realized, should be significantly less than during 1971–75. During this period gross grain imports averaged 15 million tons, offset by 4 million tons of exports, for net annual imports of 11 million tons. Since data have not yet been presented on many of the details of the new plan, especially with respect to feed supplies other than grain, it is not possible to tell if the objective is to reduce *net* grain imports to zero by 1980.

However, it will be no easy matter to increase grain production by 18–21% in five years unless weather factors are relatively favourable. The grain production goal for 1976–80 is an average annual production of 215 million to 220 million tons. The Soviet Union has had only one grain crop in excess of 200 million tons—222 million tons in 1973. If grain production averages 205 million to 210 million tons, representing a good performance, net grain imports could average somewhat more than 10 million tons.

Average Soviet net grain imports of 10 million tons for the rest of the decade could be fitted rather easily into the international grain market. With world grain exports now averaging 150 million tons, Soviet grain imports would not be a major factor. This assumes that the variability of Soviet grain imports will be much smaller than during the past five years. Only time will tell if increased storage capacity and the U.S.-U.S.S.R. grain agreement will result in less erratic Soviet import behaviour.

Albania

A people's republic in the western Balkan Peninsula, Albania is on the Adriatic Sea, bordered by Greece and Yugoslavia. Area: 11,100 sq mi (28,748 sq km). Pop. (1976 est.): 2,549,000. Cap. and largest city: Tirana (pop., 1973 est., 182,500). Language: Albanian. Religion: officially atheist; historically Muslim, Orthodox, and Roman Catholic communities. First secretary of the Albanian (Communist) Party of Labour in 1976, Enver Hoxha; president of the Presidium of the People's Assembly, Haxhi Leshi; chairman of the Council of Ministers (premier), Mehmet Shehu.

On Jan. 21, 1976, the People's Assembly adopted a new constitution, which had been prepared by a 51-member committee under Hoxha and replaced the old constitution of March 1946. "Socialist People's Republic of Albania" became the official name of the country. The Party of Labour was designated as the sole directing political power, and its first secretary as commander in chief of the armed forces. Private property was abolished. Equal rights would be enjoyed by both sexes. Citizens would not be taxed. Religious foundations were eliminated.

Hoxha disclosed on April 29 the discovery of a "revisionist" plot to sabotage the construction of socialism and destroy Sino-Albanian friendship. Ministerial reshuffles were carried out in April, May, and also in November, shortly after the seventh party congress. In his opening speech to the congress, Hoxha, who was reelected first secretary, indicated that in the future less reliance might be placed on China. He also announced discovery of a conspiracy among senior officials. In January the U.S.S.R.'s third offer to resume diplomatic relations, broken off by Moscow in 1961, was again officially ignored.

(K. M. SMOGORZEWSKI)

[972.B.3]

ALBANIA

Education. (1971–72) Primary, pupils 518,002, teachers 20,555; secondary, pupils 23,229, teachers 1,318; vocational and teacher training, pupils 62,212, teachers 1,712; higher (including Tirana University), students 28,668, teaching staff 1,153.

Finance. Monetary unit: lek, with (Sept. 20, 1976) a commercial exchange rate of 5.80 leks to U.S. $1 (10.10 leks = £1 sterling). Budget (1971 est.): revenue 5,750,000,000 leks; expenditure 5,463,000,000 leks.

Foreign Trade. (1964) Imports 490.6 million leks; exports 299,620,000 leks. Import sources: China 63%; Czechoslovakia 10%; Poland 8%. Export destinations: China 40%; Czechoslovakia 19%; East Germany 10%; Poland 10%. Main exports: fuels, minerals, and metals (including bitumen, crude oil, chrome ore, iron ore, and copper) 54%; foodstuffs (including vegetables, wine, and fruit) 23%; raw materials (including tobacco and wool) 17%.

Transport and Communications. Roads (1969) 4,827 km. Motor vehicles in use (1970): passenger *c.* 3,500; commercial (including buses) *c.* 11,200. Railways: (1972) 302 km; traffic (1971) 291.4 million passenger-km, freight 187.6 million net ton-km. Shipping (1975): merchant vessels 100 gross tons and over 20; gross tonnage 57,368. Shipping traffic (1973): goods loaded *c.* 2.6 million metric tons, unloaded *c.* 720,000 metric tons. Telephones (Dec. 1963) 10,150. Radio receivers (Dec. 1973) 172,000. Television receivers (Dec. 1973) 4,000.

Agriculture. Production (in 000; metric tons; 1974): corn *c.* 276; wheat *c.* 273; oats *c.* 28; potatoes *c.* 104; sugar, raw value *c.* 19; olives *c.* 47; grapes *c.* 65; tobacco *c.* 14; cotton, lint *c.* 5. Livestock (in 000; Dec. 1974): sheep *c.* 1,165; cattle *c.* 400; pigs *c.* 117; goats (1973) *c.* 674; poultry *c.* 2,176.

Industry. Production (in 000; metric tons; 1974): crude oil *c.* 2,200; lignite *c.* 850; petroleum products *c.* 1,655; chrome ore (oxide content) 286; iron ore (1970) *c.* 540; copper ore (metal content) *c.* 7; cement *c.* 360; electricity (kw-hr) *c.* 1,700,000.

Albania, the smallest of the Communist countries, began a program of industrialization over 25 years ago. Photo shows a hydroelectric project at Fierze.

EASTFOTO

Algeria

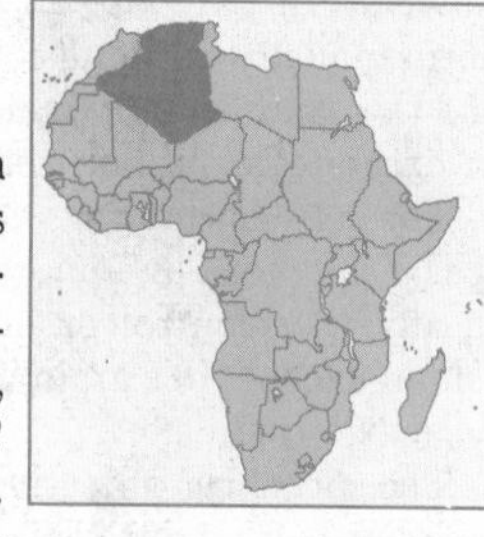

A republic on the north coast of Africa, Algeria is bounded by Morocco, Western (Spanish) Sahara, Mauritania, Mali, Niger, Libya, and Tunisia. Area: 896,592 sq mi (2,322,164 sq km). Pop. (1975) est.): 16,776,000. Cap. and largest city: Algiers (1975 UN est., 1,179,000). Language: Arabic, Berber, French. Religion: Muslim. President in 1976, Col. Houari Boumédienne.

President Boumédienne in 1976 carried through much of the political reform program that he had promised. The sole permitted political organization, the National Liberation Front (FLN), prepared a draft national charter, and in May Boumédienne initiated a "national debate" in which the charter was discussed, often contentiously, at a reputed 200,000 meetings throughout the country. The charter was eventually approved by referendum on June 27, and its concepts were embodied in a revised constitution, also overwhelmingly approved in a referendum on November 19. Algeria remained a one-party, socialist, Islamic state; the president was directly elected, and the National Assembly was revived. Boumédienne, the sole candidate nominated for the presidency by the FLN, received a sweeping vote of confidence on December 10. Elections to the National Assembly were to be held early in 1977.

There were signs that the much-vaunted industrial and agricultural revolutions were slowing down, due to managerial, technical, and financial problems. A "plague of bureaucracy" had been denounced during the debate on the national charter, and officialdom was blamed for the inefficiency of the agrarian reform program and for some of the shortcomings in the implementation of industrial projects. The program of construction of oil, gas, and petrochemical plants encountered technical difficulties, and heavy debt service commitments loomed. However, this did not limit Algeria's ability to raise fresh funds in the Eurodollar market or inhibit foreign financiers from providing new loans. Agreements were concluded for the supply of liquefied natural gas to the U.S., France, and Belgium.

In its foreign relations Algeria's main preoccupation was to honour its promise of self-determination to the Saharan nationalists, the Polisario Front. The Front and its offshoot, the government-in-exile of the Saharan Arab Democratic Republic, were given full recognition on March 6, and Algerian troops were in action against the Moroccan Army and provided arms and logistic support to the Polisario guerrillas. Morocco and Mauritania broke off diplomatic relations with Algeria on March 7. Moroccan residents in Algeria were expelled, trade was curtailed, and transport facilities were reduced.

Relations with France suffered from the twin problems of an increasing trade imbalance and the tensions connected with the large Algerian work force in France. The trade deficit, in France's favour, quadrupled, while the periodic outbursts of violence against Algerian migrants hampered attempts by both sides to start a new page in their close, if tortuous, relations. (PETER KILNER)

[978.D.2.d]

ALGERIA

Education. (1974–75) Primary, pupils 2,435,365, teachers 60,179; secondary, pupils 406,565, teachers 15,340; vocational, pupils 15,499, teachers 589; teacher training, students 7,955, teachers 727; higher (including 4 universities), students 35,887, teaching staff 4,041.

Finance. Monetary unit: dinar, with (Sept. 20, 1976) a free rate of 4.20 dinars to U.S. $1 (7.25 dinars = £1 sterling). Gold, SDR's, and foreign exchange (June 1976) U.S. $1,501,000,000. Budget (1975 est.) balanced at 13,169,000,000 dinars. Money supply (Dec. 1975) 30,547,000,000 dinars.

Foreign Trade. (1975) Imports *c.* 22,630,000,000 dinars; exports 16,615,000,000 dinars. Import sources (1974): France 28%; West Germany 14%; U.S. 10%; Italy 8%; Spain 5%. Export destinations (1974): U.S. 25%; West Germany 22%; France 18%; Italy 7%; Spain 5%. Main exports: crude oil 84%; petroleum products 5%.

Transport and Communications. Roads (1974) 78,408 km. Motor vehicles in use (1974): passenger 180,000; commercial (including buses) 95,000. Railways (1974): 3,951 km; traffic 1,058,000,000 passenger-km, freight 1,901,000,000 net ton-km. Air traffic (1974): 997 million passenger-km; freight 6.4 million net ton-km. Shipping (1975): merchant vessels 100 gross tons and over 78; gross tonnage 246,432. Shipping traffic (1974): goods loaded 44,824,000 metric tons, unloaded 9,447,000 metric tons. Telephones (Dec. 1974) 230,000. Radio receivers (Dec. 1973) 725,000. Television receivers (Dec. 1973) 260,000.

Agriculture. Production (in 000; metric tons; 1975): wheat *c.* 652; barley 307; oats *c.* 28; potatoes *c.* 327; tomatoes *c.* 136; onions *c.* 75; dates (1974) *c.* 177; figs (1974) *c.* 58; oranges (1974) *c.* 385; mandarin oranges and tangerines (1974) *c.* 133; watermelons (1974) *c.* 206; olives *c.* 170; wine (1974) *c.* 740; tobacco *c.* 3. Livestock (in 000; Nov. 1973): sheep *c.* 8,100; goats *c.* 2,400; cattle *c.* 1,029; asses *c.* 315; horses *c.* 150; camels *c.* 190.

Industry. Production (in 000; metric tons; 1974): iron ore (53–55% metal content) 3,800; phosphate rock (1973) 608; crude oil (1975) 45,050; natural gas (cu m) 5,620,000; electricity (excluding most industrial production; kw-hr) 2,630,000.

ADN-ZB/EASTFOTO

Algeria's government is stressing cooperative agriculture. These peasants are feeding sheep at a cooperative in Tiaret Province.

Andorra

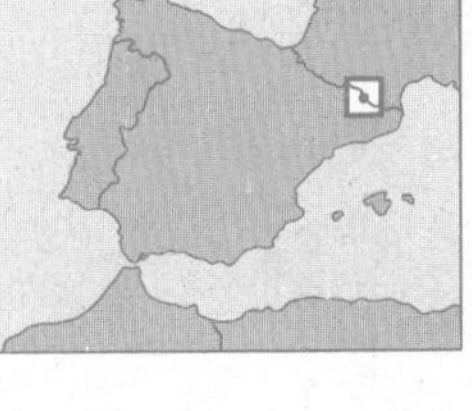

An independent co-principality of Europe, Andorra is in the Pyrenees Mountains between Spain and France. Area: 179 sq mi (464 sq km). Pop. (1975 est.): 26,600. Cap.: Andorra la Vella (commune pop., 1975 est., 10,900). Language: Catalan (official), French, Spanish. Religion: predominantly Roman Catholic. Co-princes: the president of the French Republic and the bishop of Urgel, Spain, represented by their *veguers* (provosts) and *batlles* (prosecutors). An elected Council General of 24 members elects the first syndic; in 1976, Julià Reig-Ribó.

In the election for 12 of the 24 seats on the Council General, held on Dec. 12, 1975, the Conservatives, the majority party, obtained only 2 seats; 6 went to the candidates of the Democracy and Progress group and 4 to moderates. Julià Reig-Ribó, a Conservative, was reelected first syndic for another three years. In November the Council General proposed imposition of an income tax and asked representatives of the co-regents to a special meeting to approve it. Also in November the principality's first formal political party, the Andorran Democratic Association, was established, pledged to support freedom of speech and association and respect for minorities.

From April 18, 1976, Andorrans accused of crime

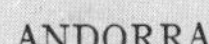

ANDORRA

Education. (1974–75) Primary, pupils 3,779, teachers 146; secondary, pupils 1,626, teachers 120.

Finance and Trade. Monetary units: French franc and Spanish peseta. Foreign trade (1975): imports from France Fr 357,046,000 (U.S. $83,297,000), from Spain 2,797,688,000 pesetas (U.S. $48,734,000); exports to France Fr 15,601,000 (U.S. $3,640,000), to Spain 97,016,000 pesetas (U.S. $1,690,000). Tourism (1974) *c.* 3 million visitors.

Communications. Radio receivers (Dec. 1973) 6,100. Television receivers (Dec. 1969) 1,700.

Agriculture. Production: cereals, potatoes, tobacco, wool. Livestock (in 000; 1974): sheep *c.* 25; cattle *c.* 3; horses *c.* 1.

Alcoholic Beverages: *see* Industrial Review

Alcoholism: *see* Drug Abuse

American Literature: *see* Literature

might be defended orally by a lawyer instead of presenting a defense in writing, as had been done for the last seven centuries. What little crime occurred was mostly petty, but with better communications and an influx of foreigners, police force numbers had been raised between 1960 and 1976 from 5 to 37.

Mme Anne-Aymone Giscard d'Estaing, wife of the French president, represented her husband in his capacity as co-prince at the celebration of Andorra's national day on Sept. 6, 1976. She said that he hoped personally to attend the celebrations in 1977 of the 700th anniversary of the charter confirming the independence of the valleys. (K. M. SMOGORZEWSKI)

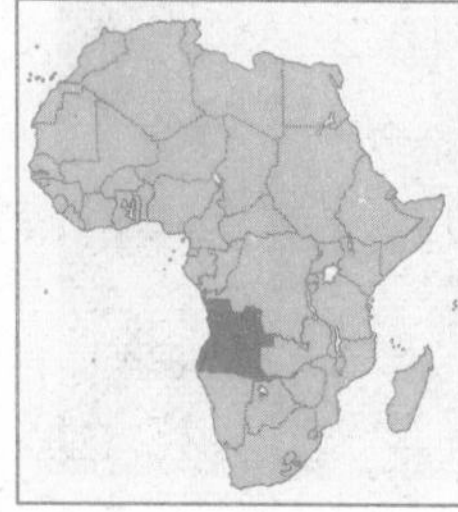

Angola

Located on the west coast of southern Africa, Angola is bounded by Zaire, Zambia, South West Africa (Namibia), and the Atlantic Ocean. The small exclave of Cabinda, a district of Angola, is bounded by the Congo and Zaire. Area: 481,350 sq mi (1,246,700 sq km). Pop. (1976 est.): 6,761,000. Cap. and largest city: Luanda (pop., 1970, 480,600). Language: Bantu languages (predominant), Portuguese (official), and some Khoisan dialects. Religion: traditional beliefs about 50%; Roman Catholicism about 38%; Protestantism 12%. President in 1976, Agostinho Neto; premier, Lopo do Nascimento.

A meeting of the Organization of African Unity (OAU) in January 1976 failed to produce a unified policy for Angola; 22 nations, led by Nigeria, voted for recognition of the Soviet-backed Popular Movement for the Liberation of Angola (MPLA) while 22 supported the idea of a government of national unity that would include all the factions fighting for control of the country. The MPLA forces, spearheaded by Cuban troops, gradually gained the upper hand, however, and this, coupled with the revulsion caused by South African armed support of the National Union for the Total Independence of Angola (UNITA), finally tipped the balance of African opinion. On February 11 the OAU recognized the Angolan People's Republic under the MPLA government as its 47th member.

The decision of the U.S. House of Representatives on January 27 to resist administration pressures and refuse to send further aid to either the National Front for the Liberation of Angola (FNLA) or UNITA was a bitter blow to South Africa as well as to the Angolan opponents of the MPLA. The South African troops gradually retreated southward, withdrawing completely on March 27. This was followed almost immediately by UN condemnation of South African aggression in Angola. Under continuing pressure from Cuban and MPLA troops, the FNLA and UNITA forces resorted to guerrilla action in the north and south, respectively, and savage fighting was reported in November.

As early as February 17 France preempted the European Economic Community's decision by recognizing the Angolan People's Republic unilaterally. Sweden also spoke out in favour of the new government, and Swedish companies were among the first to open up trade links with it; other countries were slower, Zambia agreeing to an exchange of ambassadors only in September. On December 1 Angola was admitted to the UN; the U.S., which had vetoed Angola's application in the Security Council in June, continued to oppose admission until Cuban troops were withdrawn, but abstained on the final vote. Cuban Prime Minister Fidel Castro had promised in May that a gradual withdrawal would take place, but reinforcements continued to arrive, made necessary by the signs of a resurgence of guerrilla activity late in the year.

The government was experiencing difficulty in recruiting labour to revive the country's coffee and sugar exports. A law was passed against economic sabotage, defined as any act of opposition to the program of economic revival. The takeover of Portuguese-owned firms was begun, and on May 19 diplomatic relations with Portugal were broken off. Thousands of Angolans had fled into South West Africa (Namibia) early in the year, but a UN humanitarian commission found that large-scale external assistance was needed for

Angolan armed forces paraded in Luanda in February to mark the second anniversary of the founding of the People's Liberation Armed Forces.

ADN-ZB / EASTFOTO

ANGOLA

Education. (1972–73) Primary, pupils 536,599, teachers 13,230; secondary, pupils 59,209, teachers 3,060; vocational, pupils 15,511, teachers 1,107; teacher training, students 334, teachers 47; higher, students 2,942, teaching staff 274.

Finance and Trade. Monetary unit: Angola escudo, with (Sept. 20, 1976) a free rate of 31.10 escudos to U.S. $1 (53.60 escudos = £1 sterling). Budget (1973 est.): revenue 13,707,000,000 escudos; expenditure 13,107,000,000 escudos. Foreign trade (1974): imports 15,836,000,000 escudos; exports 30,996,000,000 escudos. Import sources (1973): Portugal 26%; West Germany 13%; U.S. 10%; U.K. 8%; France 7%; South Africa 6%; Japan 6%. Export destinations: U.S. 28%; Portugal 25%; Canada 10%; Japan 9%; West Germany 5%. Main exports: crude oil 29%; coffee 26%; diamonds 10%; iron ore 6%.

Transport and Communications. Roads (1974) 72,323 km. Motor vehicles in use (1973): passenger 127,271; commercial 24,123. Railways: (1973) 2,966 km; traffic (1974) *c.* 403 million passenger-km, freight 5,460,000,000 net ton-km. Ships entered: (1972) vessels totaling 9,910,000 net registered tons; goods loaded (1973) 15,847,000 metric tons, unloaded 2,065,000 metric tons. Telephones (Jan. 1974) 38,000. Radio licenses (Dec. 1973) 115,000.

Agriculture. Production (in 000; metric tons; 1975): corn *c.* 450; millet *c.* 80; cassava (1974) *c.* 1,640; sweet potatoes (1974) *c.* 165; dry beans *c.* 70; sugar, raw value *c.* 80; bananas (1974) *c.* 320; palm kernels *c.* 12; palm oil *c.* 40; coffee *c.* 72; cotton, lint *c.* 11; sisal *c.* 70; fish catch (1974) *c.* 470. Livestock (in 000; Dec. 1973): cattle *c.* 2,900; sheep *c.* 195; goats *c.* 890; pigs *c.* 350.

Industry. Production (in 000; metric tons; 1974): cement 760; iron ore (60–65% metal content) 4,980; manganese ore (metal content; 1973) 1.9; diamonds (metric carats) *c.* 2,100; crude oil (1975) 8,400; salt (1973) 97; fish meal 63; electricity (81% hydroelectric; kw-hr) *c.* 1,050,000.

refugees still inside the country. Thirteen captured white mercenaries, most of them British, were tried and sentenced in Luanda in June; four were executed later, despite international appeals for clemency. Neto visited Moscow in October, where he signed a 20-year treaty of friendship between Angola and the U.S.S.R.

(KENNETH INGHAM)

[978.E.8.b.iv]

Antarctica

During 1976 Poland and West Germany for the first time sponsored research activities in the seas adjacent to Antarctica, and the first private expedition from Italy reestablished a camp and conducted research projects. The ten nations that maintained bases on the continent continued their programs, and two of them, Argentina and the U.S.S.R., established new bases.

International Research Projects. International cooperative efforts continued. A three-nation oceanographic study was carried out in the Drake Passage in early 1976; a U.S. marine biology program was conducted off the French research vessel "Marion Dufresne"; and the long-standing U.S.-New Zealand efforts in the McMurdo Sound area continued. Argentina and the U.S. continued their joint activities on the research vessel "Islas Orcadas," and plans were made for extended cruises to the South Atlantic section of the Antarctic Ocean in late 1976 and early 1977. The exchange scientist program between the U.S. and U.S.S.R. entered its 20th year with a U.S. scientist spending the winter at Vostok Station while a Soviet meteorologist worked at McMurdo Station.

The increased interest in the future of Antarctica was reflected by three international gatherings held during 1976. A symposium on Marine Living Resources of the Southern Oceans was held to discuss the present state of knowledge and to outline a plan for future research on the largely untapped but potentially valuable fisheries resource of the seas surrounding the continent. A special preparatory meeting of the 12 Antarctic Treaty nations was held in Paris during early July to discuss treaty questions relating to the exploration and exploitation of the mineral resources of the continent and adjacent continental shelf areas. The Scientific Committee on Antarctic Research held its 14th meeting in Mendoza, Arg., in late October. Of major concern to this group was the question of the environmental problems that might be associated with development of the continent.

Scientific Programs. The ten nations with permanent stations on Antarctica continued their research activities. The U.S.S.R. established a new summer base, Druzhnaya, on the edge of the Filchner Ice Shelf, and began geologic and geophysical studies of the mountain areas in the vicinity. No other major starts of scientific programs took place in 1976. The Dry Valley Drilling Project, a combined effort of the U.S.-U.S.S.R.-Japan, completed the drilling phase by obtaining sediment cores from the floor of McMurdo Sound. U.S. scientific activities were considerably reduced because of limited aircraft capability and funding problems.

ARGENTINA. A new base, San Martín, was opened by Argentina during the year, and plans were announced to move General Belgrano Station from its present position on the Filchner Ice Shelf to Bertrab Nunatak on the Luitpold Coast of the Weddell Sea. The move was scheduled to be completed in 1977. The research ship "Islas Orcadas" continued its hydrographic and oceanographic studies and in 1976 embarked on an ambitious effort, in cooperation with the U.S., to complete the circumantarctic survey in the South Atlantic section of the Antarctic Ocean.

COURTESY, MINISTRY OF DEFENCE, GREAT BRITAIN

Passing Antarctica's ice-covered mountains, a British patrol vessel heads for the open sea. The United Kingdom is one of 11 nations that conduct scientific research on the Antarctic continent and in the surrounding waters.

AUSTRALIA. The establishment of an automatic geophysical observatory on the Amery Ice Shelf, an inland traverse from Casey Station toward Vostok, and aerial mapping in Enderby Land were the major efforts conducted by the Australians during the year. The charter supply ships "Nella Dan" and "Thala Dan" carried out the resupply of the station and Macquarie Island. Women wintered with the Australians for the first time.

CHILE. In addition to the continuing year-round meteorological programs, Chile joined with the U.S. and U.S.S.R. in oceanographic studies in the Drake Passage. Chilean biologists worked in the Antarctic Peninsula area; glaciological studies were initiated; and geologists continued their mapping efforts. Exchange scientists worked at the U.S. Palmer Station and on board the U.S. research vessel "Hero."

FRANCE. The planned drilling effort at Dome C was delayed because U.S. aircraft were not available to transport the drill. Instead, a glaciological traverse was conducted from Dumont d'Urville inland for 270 km (165 mi). Samples for geochemical analysis were collected, and at the end of the traverse the party visited the site where a U.S. LC-130 crashed in 1971.

JAPAN. Syowa Station continued to be the single Japanese station on Antarctica. Upper atmospheric studies, geophysics, and meteorology were the major year-round science programs carried out there. Oceanographic and marine biology experiments were carried out from the ship "Fuji." Japan continued to participate in the Dry Valley Drilling Project, along with New Zealand and the U.S., in the McMurdo Sound area.

NEW ZEALAND. Work in the McMurdo Sound area by New Zealand scientists was reduced in scale during the year as a result of the limited support available from the U.S. An extended traverse in the Skelton Glacier area by a group of geologists found areas of fairly recent volcanic activity and a mineralized zone near Teall Island. The Mt. Erebus lava lake was again visited by a party that spent eight days at the

Anglican Communion: *see* Religion

Angling: *see* Hunting and Fishing

summit of the volcano on Ross Island. Studies of the parasites that plague the Weddell seals continued.

SOUTH AFRICA. Major activities in meteorology and upper atmospheric physics continued at the SANAE (South African National Antarctic Expedition) base. Programs in geology were suspended until helicopter support could be provided. Base glaciological studies continued on the network established on the glaciers in the vicinity of SANAE. Oceanographic studies were carried out on the voyages between South Africa and SANAE.

POLAND. Two vessels from Poland constituted the first Polish Marine Research Antarctic Expedition. They operated in the vicinity of the Antarctic Peninsula during the early part of 1976 to examine the krill concentration in that area as a potential for industrial fisheries. Late in the year Poland announced plans to construct a permanent base at a site on the Antarctic Peninsula during the 1976–77 austral summer. This would be the first base constructed by a nation that was not one of those involved in the International Geophysical Year (1957–58).

ITALY. A private Italian expedition visited the Antarctic Peninsula early in 1976, establishing a camp on King George Island near Admiralty Bay. Scientific work included biology and geology, using sediment cores obtained from Admiralty Bay from the ship "Rig Mate." A mountaineering team climbed seven peaks, four on Wiencke Island and three on Livingston Island.

UNITED KINGDOM. The six stations operated by the U.K. carried out a variety of research programs during the year. In addition, the Twin Otter aircraft supported field parties in the Antarctic Peninsula. In cooperation with the U.S., a satellite positioning program was carried out from Siple Station. Systematic mapping and topographic survey work continued.

U.S.S.R. The establishment of the Druzhnaya summer base was one of the major projects of the Soviet Antarctic Expedition in 1976. About 1,200 tons of supplies were placed at the site, and 20 buildings were constructed. Helicopters were used to carry geological field parties to the Pensacola Mountains and the Shackleton ranges. Oceanographic and geophysical studies were carried out in the Weddell Sea, and plans called for a major effort in geology and geophysics during the next five years.

UNITED STATES. The decreased air support capability resulting from the loss of two LC-130 aircraft at Dome C coupled with a budgetary problem had a major effect on the U.S. programs during 1976. The Ross Ice Shelf Project was postponed for a year, and all field party activities requiring heavy air support were canceled. The Dry Valley Drilling Project was the major effort in the McMurdo Sound area early in the season.

The loss of a third LC-130, again at Dome C, caused further reduction in the programs. The remaining two aircraft were scheduled to resupply South Pole Station, and tentative plans were made to close Siple Station if resupply there could not be accomplished. Later, an outbreak of hepatitis among Siple Station personnel made the closing necessary. The station was reopened late in the year, however, and all equipment for upper atmospheric studies was reactivated.

At Dome C a major effort to recover the downed aircraft was begun. By late January 1976, two of the three had been repaired and were flown out to New Zealand for further repairs. (ROBERT H. RUTFORD)

Anthropology

Out of the political turmoil of the 1960s there emerged, for some anthropologists, a serious professional interest in Marxist literature and the application of ideas drawn from this literature to contemporary issues. There also emerged a dramatic appreciation of the ways by which ideas and images themselves can apparently move people to action. One manifestation of current theoretical activity in these areas was found in the arguments between those who professed a cultural materialist strategy, as developed by Marvin Harris of Columbia University, and the structural Marxists, of whom Maurice Godelier of the Collège de France and Marshall Sahlins of the University of Chicago seemed representative.

Both cultural materialists and structural Marxists address the relationship between material and mental resources in cultural dynamics. They disagree fundamentally, however, over the primacy of Marx's analytical use of Hegelian dialectic and over the role of French structuralism as exemplified by the writings of Claude Lévi-Strauss. The cultural materialists reject dialectical analysis and seek to explain sociocultural phenomena by reference to techno-environmental and techno-economic systems. For them, social relationships, which develop as systems of allocating resources, are merely obscured or masked by ideology. By contrast, the structural Marxists rely on dialectical analysis and find much that is of use in Lévi-Strauss's theories. One source of debate occurs when the structural Marxists endeavour to demonstrate that the "objectivity" of the cultural materialist is, in effect, a product of a Western capitalist ideological system. They seem to deny any a priori, universal, ecological base and argue that the cultural "base"—the productive system together with the forms of consumption and the system of distribution and exchange —must be established through a posteriori analysis of a given culture. Developments of these ideas and a clear sense of the issues involved were set forth in *Marxist Analyses and Social Anthropology,* edited by Maurice Bloch (1975); in Bridget O'Laughlin's article "Marxist Approaches in Anthropology" in the *Annual Review of Anthropology* (1975); and in Allen H. Berger's article (with replies by many Marxists) "Structural and Eclectic Revisions of Marxist Strategy: A Cultural Materialist Critique" in *Current Anthropology* (1976; vol. 17, no. 2). A Marxist journal of anthropology, *Dialectical Anthropology,* began publication.

An area of continuing, often muddled, debate relates to the use of the terms "etic anthropology" and "emic anthropology" by some cultural materialists. The original formulation of etics and emics for cultural analysis was undertaken by the linguist Kenneth L. Pike of the University of Michigan, who coined them as analogues to phonetics and phonemics in descriptive linguistics. According to Harris, writing in the 1976 *Annual Review of Anthropology,* "If behavioral events are described in terms of categories and relationships that arise from the observer's strategic criteria of similarity, difference, and significance, they are etic; if they are described in terms of criteria elicited from an informant, they are emic." Scholars of many persuasions continued to argue that emic systems merely group etic data and that Western science itself must be understood as a cultural (emic) system

PHOTOS, UPI COMPIX

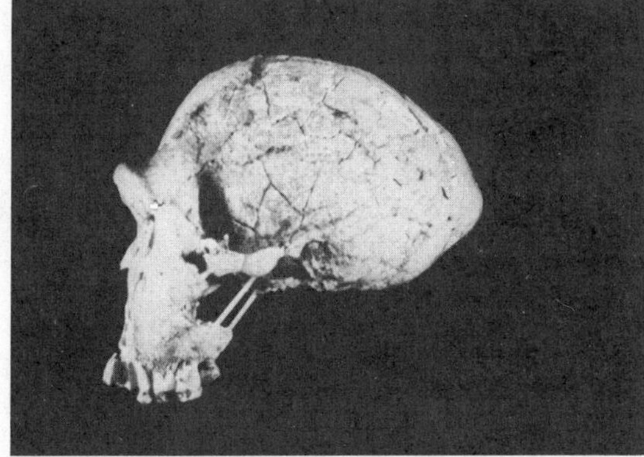

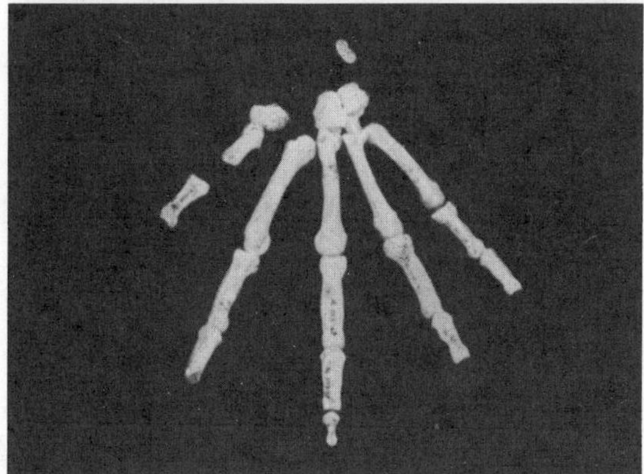

(Above) A 1.5 million-year-old skull of Homo erectus, a forerunner of Homo sapiens, found in Kenya. (Below) Fossil hand bones dated at 3.5 million years, found in Ethiopia.

in constant need of demystification. This issue was fairly old in cultural anthropology and had ramified from the professional journals into textbooks and popular literature.

Many anthropologists seemed to be working with constructs compatible with those of either the structural Marxists or the cultural materialists, if each is stripped of its near-cultist ideology. Alexander Alland, for example, called for a "structural ecology" merging these perspectives with known processes of nonhuman adaptation. This approach, as set out in the 1975 *Annual Review of Anthropology*, "must start from the double premise that human behavioral systems are the outcome of an adaptational process similar in most respects to the adaptational process that occurs in other species, but with the restriction that human brain hardware shapes response patterns according to internal structural rules." In a similar vein, the president of the American Anthropological Association for 1976–77, Richard N. Adams, published *Energy and Structure* (1975), which focuses upon energy and its control as the base for the exercise of power.

In the area of scientific and humanistic study of symbols, anthropological activity was flourishing. Victor Turner of the University of Chicago continued to integrate observations on both pragmatic action (*e.g.*, revolution, sacrifice, pilgrimage) and symbolic action by focusing on situations where people are moving between positions in a social, economic, or political structure. In such situations, a social and psychological state of "betwixt and between" inevitably occurs. Personal, shared reconsideration of structure taking place in this state may lead to activities oriented toward restructuring the given system. Symbols, according to Turner, are the "instrumentalities"—the "triggers of social action"—which are used by human actors to move others in social arenas characterized by oscillation between emotionally charged action and iconoclastic ideology.

Another symbolic analyst, Edmund Leach of Cambridge University, was considered by many to be the foremost spokesman for British structuralism. In his *Culture and Communication: The Logic by Which Symbols Are Connected* (1976), Leach established his position regarding the complementarity of empiricism and rationalism within anthropology: "that one is a transformation of the other." In his view, symbols make up a system of communication, "The key point [being] . . . that the 'meaning' depends upon *transformations* from one mode into the other and back again." Leach's exposition is close to that of Mary Douglas of University College, London, and presents a valuable introduction to this mode of symbolic analysis.

In apparent opposition to Leach's position was a book published a year earlier in the same series, *Rethinking Symbolism* by Dan Sperber of the Université de Paris X (Nanterre). For Sperber, symbolism is emphatically not a means of encoding information; it is a way by which humans organize encoded or partially encoded information that they do not understand. Individual improvisation in such an organizational process is based on what Sperber calls implicit knowledge—knowledge that is normally tacit but is made explicit by some intracultural exegetes. Symbolic processing, like language, is based on unconscious mechanisms, but they do not constitute a system of cultural communication analogous to "grammar." Symbolic processing of knowledge occurs in the course of mental activity involving an imperfect juxtaposition of shared information with individual knowledge;

JENS BJERRE—NORDISK PRESSEFOTO/PICTORIAL PARADE

Stone Age people still exist in the jungles of New Guinea. This man is selling a stone tool to a visitor from Europe.

"... cultural symbolism focuses the attention of the members of a single society in the same directions, determines parallel evocational fields that are structured in the same way, but leaves the individual free to effect an evocation in them as he likes."

Another domain of contemporary theoretical endeavour was found under such rubrics as "exchange theory," "transactionism," and sometimes "network analysis." Two books published in this area in 1976 were *Rational Choice and Social Exchange* by Anthony Heath and *Transaction and Meaning: Directions in the Anthropology of Exchange and Symbolic Behavior,* edited by Bruce Kapferer. Some found promise here of a synthesis between materialist and mentalist approaches to cultural phenomena. When one considers human exchange behaviour in the context of the environment, which may be characterized by competing economies, social organization is understood as a process of resource allocation, in line with materialist theory. If one focuses on the cognitive and symbolic structuring and restructuring of resource-allocation systems by human actors-transactors, there is no slighting of mentalist dynamics.

In 1976 the anthropological profession remained concerned but ineffectual vis-à-vis the plight of small nonstate societies and the worldwide suppression of movements of ethnic self-assertion. These processes were well documented by John H. Bodley in his *Victims of Progress* (1975). Most of the efforts in behalf of the peoples who have been the traditional subjects of anthropological research were being undertaken by such organizations as Akwesasne Notes and Indígena in the U.S., the International Work Group for Indigenous Affairs in Denmark, Unidad Indígena in Colombia, Arbeitsgruppe für Nordamerikanische Indianer in West Germany, and the Canadian Native Struggles Support Group. A directory of such organizations, prepared by Joseph G. Jorgensen and Richard B. Lee, appeared in the MSS Modular Publication *The New Native Resistance: Indigenous Peoples' Struggles and the Responsibilities of Scholars* (1974). Anthropologists Miguel Chase Sardi and Mauricio Schwartzman were jailed in Paraguay for participating with Paraguayan Indians in the Marandú applied research project.

In the U.S. the president of the American Anthropological Association for 1975–76, Walter Goldschmidt, reported an "emerging crisis" caused by a sharp decline in academic positions open to anthropologists, together with a lack of interest on the part of anthropologists in employment in government and industry. A possible trend toward involving anthropologists directly in public issues was suggested by two books published in 1976, *Anthropology and the Public Interest: Fieldwork and Theory,* edited by Peggy Reeves Sanday, and *The Sorcerer's Apprentice: An Anthropology of Public Policy* by Cyril S. Belshaw. It seemed paradoxical that the anthropological organizations which had generated so much public interest in the need to serve the interests of research subjects were now devoting their energy to seeking employment opportunities in agencies far removed from the research subjects' needs. It was doubly paradoxical that, just as anthropology was reaching the point where its theory and method could effectively address public issues, opportunities for the employment of new professionals became alarmingly sparse. (NORMAN E. WHITTEN, JR.)

See also Archaeology.

[431; 432; 10/36.B]

Arabia:
see Bahrain; Kuwait; Middle Eastern Affairs; Oman; Qatar; Saudi Arabia; United Arab Emirates; Yemen, People's Democratic Republic of; Yemen Arab Republic

Arabic Literature:
see Literature

Archaeology

Eastern Hemisphere. The 1975–76 archaeological year was an active one in many parts of the Old World. One find of some 15,000 clay tablets, inscribed in cuneiform and dating to about 2400 BC, was made in northern Syria. It was anticipated that the texts, when fully read and interpreted, would necessitate some drastic revisions in our understanding of ancient Near Eastern history. As usual, the year had its share of inflated claims of priorities for materials found in regions of new archaeological activity—claims that were often bolstered by undisciplined interpretations by journalists.

Archaeologists participated in several of the formalized visits made by academic groups to China. While the tours seemed to have been carefully organized to create such an impression, it was clear that much archaeological investigation was being carried on. At present, however, there appeared to be little interest there in general cultural history or in archaeological events outside of China.

The "monuments versus the environment" issue was becoming increasingly serious. The Greek government decided to move the 2,400-year-old Erechtheum (with a porch roof supported by caryatids) off the Acropolis and into a museum and to replace it with a marble copy, all because of the air pollution in Athens. Next came word of the resignation of 14 of the 18 members of the Greek Archeological Council because the government had granted permission for the building of a shipyard, steel mill, and cement plant on the bay at Pylos, the site of Homeric Nestor's capital.

Along with the increase in destructive clandestine excavations for the illicit antiquities market had come a rise in thefts from museum collections. Egypt passed a new law forbidding any dealing in antiquities. In May the archaeological museum at Gordion in Turkey was broken into and 41 items from an 8th-century BC royal burial were stolen.

PLEISTOCENE PREHISTORY. While very ancient "man-ape" fossil bones continued to be found in the Plio-Pleistocene beds of sub-Saharan Africa, there was not much recent news of the recovery of associated tools or living sites. The find of a skull fragment of a later (500,000 years ago) *Homo erectus* in association with primitive stone chopper and flake tools was reported from near Halle in East Germany. A French expedition accepted the invitation of the Central African Republic to undertake a survey and establish a chronological sequence; materials ranging from Acheulean to recent age were collected, and rock paintings and engravings as well as megaliths were located.

From two sites near Cape Town, South Africa, Richard G. Klein of the University of Chicago found evidence that Middle Stone Age (*c.* 125,000 to 40,000 years ago) African hunters may have begun such effective hunting of giant buffalo as to have brought about its eventual disappearance. Detailed studies, made by Arlette Leroi-Gourhan and Ralph Solecki, of fossil pollen in the soil about a burial in the Neanderthal levels of the Shanidar cave in northeastern Iraq provided evidence that bunches of flowers were placed with the dead. Some of the pollen was of plants with edible or medicinal properties, and the circumstances suggested something of belief in a hereafter.

THE NEAR EAST. In Egypt the temple of the goddess Isis at Philae was being dismantled, the last of the monuments scheduled for removal from the flood pool of the Aswan High Dam. The foundations of a new temple, identified as the first known to have been associated with the monotheist pharaoh Akhenaton, were recovered at Thebes. At Luxor the University of Chicago Oriental Institute's staff completed its recording of the reliefs of the pharaoh Seti I on the Amon temple and also began work on a detailed archaeological map. Geologists, studying aerial photographs, reported the probability that an ancient Suez canal existed some 4,000 years ago.

It was reported that over a hundred excavations had taken place in Israel within the last year; most of them were salvage operations before modern building activities began, but several dozen preplanned excavations were also involved. At Kuntillet Ajrud, in the Sinai, an 800 BC fortress of Jehoshaphat was cleared and yielded both Hebrew and Phoenician inscriptions. Work on Jerusalem's walls resulted in the identification of a tower described by Josephus, and four Babylonian lance points were found at a 15-m depth. Elisha Linder, Israel's leading marine historian, began the examination of the seaside fortress and earlier structures at Acre.

Syria had become a remarkably active focus of archaeological activity in recent years, and Paolo Matthiae's University of Rome excavations at Tell Mardikh south of Aleppo yielded what could prove to be one of the great historical finds of the century. In 1975 an archive of 15,000 cuneiform tablets, in a west Semitic language akin to Hebrew but dating back to the 3rd millennium, was recovered at Mardikh. The texts give the ancient name of the site as Ebla, mention many other place-names and personalities—some biblical—and show widespread trading and commercial contacts. New U.S., Belgian, British, Dutch, and German excavations were also started, with one British team working at ancient Kadesh.

A variety of activities were taking place in Iraq, with foreign (including Polish and Soviet) as well as Iraqi archaeologists involved. The Iraqis returned to Babylon to resume clearances there—the site had not been worked substantially since the pre-World War I German expedition. An ancient well on Nimrud, once an Assyrian capital, yielded a fine series of ivory carvings. A number of foreign and domestic teams were also at work in Iran, but detailed news of results had not yet been reported. Ezat Negahban of the University of Teheran cleared a series of early 5th-millennium BC wall paintings in well-preserved buildings at Tepe Zageh near Kazvin.

Machteld Mellink's yearly summary of news from Turkey in the *American Journal of Archaeology* was longer than usual and filled with details of new work by both Turkish and foreign colleagues. At Ikiztepe, on the Black Sea coast, Bahadir Alkim continued his excavations in this heretofore untouched region, with its Old Hittite, Assyrian, and Balkan evidences of trade. Alba Palmieri's University of Rome excavations at Malatya-Arslantepe yielded a fine series of radiocarbon age determinations from the Early Bronze Age levels. The determinations, when recalibrated, showed that materials of the Protoliterate or Amouq G horizon date to well before 3000 BC.

THE GRECO-ROMAN REGIONS. S. Milisauskas described the exposure of an early farming village, with long mud-daubed wooden houses, of the 5th millennium BC in Poland. Pottery of the Linear style and a variety of ground-stone artifacts appeared. In Belgium, a fortified village of the Michelsberg (*c.* 3250 BC) type was excavated. Second-millennium BC chariot burials were found in the Ural Mountain region of the U.S.S.R.

In Greece itself a sunken ship, said to contain 3rd-millennium BC Cycladic pottery, was located near the island of Hydra. New Canadian excavations began on the Minoan site of Kommos in Crete, and the British resumed work, after many years, on the Minoan and

AGENCIA EFE/PHOTO TRENDS

Digging down through 80 metres of debris, archaeologists have uncovered remains of the ancient Iberian settlement of Segóbriga in Spain.

Ruins of the ancient city of Ebla in Syria have yielded thousands of clay tablets, bringing to light a powerful civilization that flourished between 2400 and 2250 BC.

Mycenean remains at Phylokopi on Melos. Greek archaeologists continued their clearance of the Minoan-Mycenean settlement on Thera-Santorini, which was buried, Pompeii-like, around 1500 BC. An Irish scholar considered it likely that the major volcanic eruption (and associated quakes) on Thera did indeed end the Minoan power on Crete.

Of the Classical period proper, it was reported that the foundation stones of a building in the southwest corner of the Athenian Agora may have been those of Socrates' prison. A rustic sanctuary of Hermes and Aphrodite was cleared in Crete, yielding a bronze statuette of Hermes, and part of a sculptured pediment was found on Corfu. News of the year's results from Italy had not yet been reported, but there were the usual number of occurrences of Greco-Roman finds throughout the Mediterranean coastlands and in transalpine Europe.

In North Africa various foreign teams responded to an appeal to salvage the remains of ancient Carthage, which were being covered by the modern city of Tunis. An American Schools of Oriental Research staff, directed by Lawrence Stager, exposed portions of both the Roman and Punic docks and also encountered numerous jars containing the charred remains of human infants.

ASIA AND AFRICA. While considerable interest in Chinese archaeology was aroused by the great traveling exhibition from the People's Republic, there was little news of the year's activities there. A Yunmeng county tomb yielded a thousand inscribed bamboo strips recording Ch'in dynasty (221 to 206 BC) laws. The texts refer, among other things, to acts concerning farmland, currency, and the appointment and dismissal of officials. A Han dynasty (206 BC to AD 220) general's tomb included a map painted in colours on cloth showing some 80 villages.

Authoritative opinions were voiced disputing claims that the discovery of bronze metallurgy from a period "more than 5,500 years" ago in Thailand suggests an earlier start for "civilization" there than in the Near East.

David Lubell and his colleagues reported in *Science* on new work on Capsian shell mounds in Algeria. Much attention was given to analyses of the ancient environmental evidence suggested by the plant and animal remains in the mounds of the snail-eating Capsians.

In sub-Saharan Africa, P. S. Garlake excavated a *zimbabwe* (massive stone building)-type site, Manekweni, in southern Mozambique, the first such site known in the coastal lowlands and some 300 mi from the Great Zimbabwe itself (on the granite plateau of Rhodesia). Radiocarbon determinations ranged from AD 1100 to 1600. A shard of Chinese blue-and-white porcelain (16th to 17th century AD) was found, along with local pottery, iron, copper, and other artifacts. It is now known that these *zimbabwes* were the court centres of Shona chiefdoms, and that two Portuguese missionaries were received in one of them in AD 1560.

(ROBERT J. BRAIDWOOD)

Western Hemisphere. Fieldwork associated with historic preservation and environmental protection legislation dominated U.S. archaeology during 1976, giving rise to major criticisms that such fieldwork frequently lacked sound research goals and encouraged a split between scholarly and applied subfields. Because a certification program was believed necessary to ensure adequate training of archaeologists working in applied programs, the Society of Professional Archaeologists was formally incorporated in April 1976, with the maintenance of a registry of professional archaeologists as its major function.

No major new research trends developed during the year, but advances in established fields were reported. With respect to dating methods, for example, Irving Friedman and William Long of the U.S. Geological Survey, Denver, Colo., reported refinements in the obsidian hydration dating method, whereby hydration rates for obsidian may be calculated if the ground temperature of the discovery site can be determined and if the refractive index of the obsidian can be calculated. A potential method for dating chipped-stone artifacts was reported by R. E. Taylor, University of

California, Riverside, who demonstrated a correlation between age and the amount of fluorine diffusion within chipped-stone samples.

FAR NORTH. Extensive interdisciplinary investigations were conducted in the greater Old Crow region of the northern Yukon by several Canadian teams. R. E. Morlan, Archaeological Survey of Canada, and Owen Hughes, Geological Survey of Canada, coordinated research into the area's environmental history, while William N. Irving, University of Toronto, directed archaeological and ecological studies. The work was designed to shed light on the earliest human occupation of the easternmost portion of Beringia, the broad expanse of land, extending from eastern Siberia into northwestern Canada, that was created during the last major glacial epoch when lowered sea levels exposed the floor of the Bering Strait. Its emergence allowed humans to enter North America during the period 25,000 to 30,000 years ago.

In eastern Canada M. P. Plumet, Université de Québec à Montréal, reported survey and excavations on Akpatok Island in Ungava Bay. Both Dorset and Thule occupations, radiocarbon dated at 230 BC and AD 1480, respectively, were documented. Winfield Henn, University of Oregon, reported that investigations carried out in the Ugashik River region of southwestern Alaska had revealed two complexes previously unrecognized in the area: an earlier assemblage (*c.* 6000 BC) with microblade cores and burins and a later assemblage (*c.* 3000 BC) with side-notched points.

WESTERN UNITED STATES. Throughout the U.S. an unprecedented amount of archaeological survey and minor excavation was conducted to satisfy the requirements of environmental legislation. In California, for example, field crews from California State College, Sonoma, intensively surveyed more than 50 sq mi in conjunction with the development of geothermal energy sources. In the Southwest much work was sponsored by an array of federal agencies, as well as by private organizations. Frank J. Broilo and Charles A. Reher, University of New Mexico, completed a survey of 68 sq mi for the Coal Gasification Project in northwestern New Mexico. More than 700 sites were recorded.

In other research not associated with environmental concerns, Louis J. Tartaglia, University of California, Los Angeles, reported a comparative study of fishhooks found in southern California coastal sites. The gorge fishhook was a shallow-water implement restricted to predatory fish that swallowed their prey; the circular fishhook was adapted for bottom-dwelling fish that nibbled or explored the bait; and compound fishhooks were trolling devices used to catch striking fish in open water. The discovery of bone tools in Paleo-Indian Folsom and Clovis contexts at the Lubbock Lake site in northern Texas was reported by Eileen Johnson of Texas Tech University. The bone implements, associated with food-processing or bison-kill areas, presumably were made on the spot and discarded after use. George C. Frison, University of Wyoming, reported evidence that the North American bison gradually decreased in size from Paleo-Indian times (*c.* 8000 BC), reaching its present size between 4500 and 2500 BC.

EASTERN UNITED STATES. In 1864 a pendant carved from a fossil whelk shell with an incised drawing of a woolly mammoth was discovered near Holly Oak, Del. Because the precise find location could not be determined, and because the find was made in the same year as the discovery of a similar drawing on a mammoth tusk in France, dispute arose concerning the authenticity of the Holly Oak find and it fell into obscurity. In an article in *Science,* John C. Kraft, University of Delaware, and Ronald A. Thomas, Delaware state Division of Historical and Cultural Affairs, concluded that the pendant, if authentic, could have been incised between 8000 and 4000 BC, since an association of humans and mastodon and mammoth could be demonstrated for that time period. It was also possible that the pendant was extremely ancient and had been deposited in alluvial sediments over 40,000 years old.

MESOAMERICA. Problems associated with the origin and development of Mesoamerican states continued to receive attention. Kent V. Flannery, University of Michigan, and Richard E. Blanton, Hunter College of the City University of New York, pointed out that population growth, hereditary ranking, redistribution of goods, irrigation, and small, local petty states were all present in the valley of Oaxaca in Mexico prior to the emergence of the Zapotec state at Monte Albán (*c.* 500 BC). Stephen A. Kowalewski, University of Arizona, and Dudley M. Varner, California State University, Fresno, reported that the Early Classic in the valley of Oaxaca was characterized by low population growth and greater centralization of population than earlier periods. Payson D. Sheets, University of Colorado, proposed that the most likely explanation for the abrupt emergence of the Maya Protoclassic (*c.* AD 200) was a sudden migration from the Maya Highlands into the Lowlands, probably because of a devastating volcanic eruption.

COURTESY, JOHN A. GRAHAM AND ROBERT F. HEIZER, UNIVERSITY OF CALIFORNIA, BERKELEY

Early Mayan artifacts are still being discovered. This stela or stone slab was recently found at Abaj Takalik in Guatemala. Two costumed figures are shown facing the central panel, on which the bars and dots represent numbers. The left-hand column bears a date corresponding to AD 126.

Central America. Of particular interest for researchers in Central America was a meeting at the Universidad Nacional in Costa Rica at which North American, European, and Central American archaeologists attempted to define the frontiers between the Mesoamerican, Central American, and northern South American culture areas. In the Mesoamerican frontier zone of northwestern Costa Rica, Frederick W. Lange, Beloit (Wis.) College, reported a shift from interior valley occupation, characteristic of the Middle Polychrome period (AD 800–1200), to intensive coastal occupation during the Late Polychrome period (AD 1200–1500). Paul F. Healy, Rutgers University, New Brunswick, N.J., also conducted investigations at the Mesoamerican frontier, in the department of Colón in northeastern Honduras. Little archaeological work had been carried out in the region, now known to have had a lengthy prehistoric occupation.

In the Central American culture area of eastern Nicaragua, Richard W. Magnus, Yale University, investigated interrelations between the central and the Atlantic coastal zones. Although little interaction appeared to have taken place between the highland interior and the lowlands, there was extensive interchange within the lowlands. Anthony J. Ranere, Temple University (Philadelphia), and Olga F. Linares, Smithsonian Tropical Research Institute, conducted new investigations at the important early site of Monagrillo at Parita Bay in central Panama, first reported upon in 1954.

South America. The growing importance of locally trained and based professionals throughout South America was exemplified by the policy recently adopted in Bolivia. Research permits were now issued by the newly formed Instituto Nacional de Arqueología, and budgets had to include equal funds for Bolivian co-investigators.

Igor Chmyz, Universidade Federal do Paraná, reported excavation of a Preceramic site in southeast Brazil near Paranaguá. Although marine resources were available, no evidence of their utilization was found. Hunting tools, however, were abundant. Extensive survey and excavation along the Cabo Polonio region on the Atlantic coast of Uruguay were reported by Adhemar Bosch, Centro de Estudios Arqueológicos. Many of the 36 sites that were discovered yielded artifacts related to the Sambaquí culture (*c.* 2500 BC) of southern Brazil, and it was possible that some undated stone tools were even more ancient. In Argentina, Amalia Sanguinetti de Bórmida, Instituto de Antropología, Universidad Nacional de Buenos Aires, reported excavation of the Las Buitreras I cave on a high terrace on the Río Gallegos in Patagonia. The lowest cultural level of the cave produced remains of the extinct ground sloth *Mylodon darwini,* apparently associated with stone flakes.

Excavation of a high-elevation (4,420 m; 14,500 ft) rock shelter at Telarmachay in Peru was reported by Danièle Lavallée, Institut Français d'Études Andines. Occupation of the site began in the Preceramic period and continued into the Formative, when its use was probably seasonal, from November through June. Another high-elevation (3,170 m; 10,400 ft) site, La Chimba near Mt. Cayambe in the northern highlands of Ecuador, was reported by Alan Osborn and Stephen Athens, University of New Mexico, who worked in cooperation with the Instituto Otavelaño de Antropología. The stratified site produced evidence of trade in manioc, maize, obsidian, and marine shell; the earliest materials were radiocarbon dated at AD 730. Clinton R. Edwards, University of Wisconsin, Milwaukee, reviewing evidence related to pre-Columbian maritime trade in Peru, concluded that Peruvian maritime trade was probably peripheral to the more highly developed maritime tradition of pre-Columbian Ecuador. (DAVID A. FREDRICKSON)

See also Anthropology.

[723.G.8.c; 10/41.B.2.a.ii]

Encyclopædia Britannica Films. *Sentinels of Silence (Ruins of Ancient Mexico)* (1973); *The Big Dig* (1973); *Archeological Dating: Retracing Time* (1975); *Mesa Verde: Mystery of the Silent Cities* (1975).

Archery:
see Target Sports

Architecture

Because architectural projects take a relatively long time to come to fruition, it is difficult to appreciate major changes in thinking at short range. It may easily be 20 years between the first brief for a project and its completion as a realized workable building or complex of buildings. Even in quickly completed projects it is seldom that the whole period will be less than one year. Therefore, in reviewing the works of a year in architecture one must try to look backward and ahead more perhaps than in other fields in order to get a true perspective and to judge accurately significant trends of the period under review.

Design Trends and Awards. It seemed clear in 1976 that a major change was taking place in architecture. In comparing the work of the 1960s with that of the 1970s, critics noted that the buildings reflected many changes that were taking place in society at large. The 1960s brought forth much idealism and formalism. There were vast projects for institutions, commerce, and housing. Lip service was paid to the importance of planning and of siting buildings well in

From the concrete minaret of this recently built mosque in Riyadh, the capital of Saudi Arabia, the muezzin calls the faithful to worship five times a day.

TREVOR DANNATT & PARTNERS, LONDON

relation to their surroundings. Only in the 1970s, however, has concern with the environment together with a new seriousness (perhaps brought on by world economic problems) resulted in a new outlook by architects. They are taking greater account of such considerations as what ordinary people want in the way of housing, conserving energy in building, using solar energy for heating space and water, and, perhaps most important of all, "recycling" entire buildings and areas by means of restoration and rehabilitation. In all these areas the attention of architects in applying traditional solutions to new problems resulted in successful projects that emphasized social and human needs over purely formalistic sculptural considerations.

The editor of the British periodical *Architectural Review* suggested some of the changes that were occurring in his preview of the year 1976, in which he stated: "Modern architecture, as we have been experiencing it, has gone into hiding. Gone . . . are those massive rectilinear packages; the towers, the slabs and . . . the too-big urban footstools. Gone . . . are those self-assertive, diagrammatic buildings which made a point of having nothing to do with the neighbours. Gone is the will to assert, the will to shock. This disappearance, be it noticed, is not caused by any great change in the accommodation asked for: clients are still calling for immodest cubes of space which could as easily be thrown into the shapes and be given this city-bursting character. But by and large architects are deploying them differently and are putting a more sociable face on them. . . ."

Architectural Review saw 1976 as a period of transition requiring a rethinking of the architectural aesthetic and a reevaluating of the accepted ideals. The economic recession of the past few years was certainly a major factor in establishing the need to rethink. Much of architecture is regarded as a luxury, and, when money is tight, expensive finishes, costly materials, and inefficient use of valuable city-centre space are less easily tolerated than in more prosperous years. Building activity had certainly declined after 1973, but in 1976 it seemed that the economy was at last on the upswing and that the recession had bottomed out. In April *Architectural Record* stated that the general outlook as far as building was concerned had improved, and its editors saw an early increase in housing activity and an improvement in commercial work. Institutional work was, however, still declining because of the combined effects of inflation and recession, which had led to considerable tightening of budgets both in the U.S. and elsewhere. One effect of the slump in work in Western countries was to encourage architects to seek work elsewhere, particularly in the oil-rich Middle East (*see* below).

In Canada the architectural profession was singled out for specific restraints by the Canadian government's anti-inflation program. Firms were only allowed to increase their fees by an amount necessary to cover cost increases that had occurred prior to Oct. 13, 1975. Services for which remuneration was based on the value of the transaction in question were to be cut by an overall 1% of the rate in effect on the October date. Salaries were also controlled as were prices and profits made by contractors.

In the always controversial field of public housing it was announced that the Greater London Council (GLC), the largest housing authority in Britain, was entirely reshaping its housing policy. The GLC completely abandoned much-criticized high-rise housing, which had, in fact, been out of favour for some years. Very high densities, even in low-rise projects, were also rejected. In the future, densities were to be kept to between 70 and 100 persons per acre, and apartment buildings would be a maximum of three stories high. Families with small children were no longer to be accommodated in apartment buildings but in houses two to three stories high and with gardens. In all, it was agreed that public housing should in the future look more like that in the private sector, and it was hoped that this would help to break down social barriers between the two.

For its 1976 Honor Awards the American Institute of Architects selected ten buildings, six of them new and four adapted for reuse. The latter included the Marcus House at Bedford, N.Y., by Myron Goldfinger; the Old Boston City Hall, by Anderson Notter Associates; Butler Square in Minneapolis, Minn., by Miller, Hanson, Westerbeck, Bell, Inc.; and Whig Hall at Princeton, N.J., by Gwathmey Siegel Architects. The new structures were the R. Crosby Kemper Jr. Memorial Arena in Kansas City, Mo., by C. F. Murphy Associates; a dormitory and student union at Purchase, N.Y., by Gwathmey Siegel Architects; the Columbus (Ind.) Occupational Health Center by Hardy Holzman Pfeiffer Associates; the Waterside apartments in New York City by Davis, Brody & Associates; the Center for Creative Studies in Detroit by William Kessler & Associates; and a single-family house in Harbor Springs, Mich., by Richard Meier & Associates.

Winners of the Royal Institute of British Architects (RIBA) awards for 1976 were: Bowen Dann Davies in association with R. W. Harvey for Cefndy Hostel for 24 mentally handicapped adults, at Rhyl, Wales; E. W. Stanley (Leeds City Council) for a public housing development at Potternewton Gardens, Leeds; Cam-

The award-winning Douglas House in Harbor Springs, Michigan. Made of wood, steel, and glass, it sits on a bluff overlooking Lake Michigan.

EZRA STOLLER © ESTO

bridge Design for the Agnew House nursing home, Cambridge; Darbourne & Darke for the Eddington Street Children's Day Centre, Finsbury Park, London; Julian Bicknell (Royal College of Art Project Office) for The Old Gaol, Abingdon, Oxfordshire—a former prison converted into a sports and cultural centre; Building Design Partnership for the ICI Petrochemicals Division Headquarters at Wilton, Cleveland, England; Darbourne & Darke for the Wychavon District Council housing redevelopment at Pershore, Hereford and Worcester; Skidmore, Owings & Merrill in association with Yorke Rosenberg Mardall for the W. D. & H. O. Wills Hartcliffe Estate cigarette factory and main office near Bristol, Avon.

The RIBA awarded its Gold Medal for 1976 to the architectural historian and critic Sir John Summerson. In France the Academy of Architecture gave its Gold Medal to architect and designer Marcel Breuer.

The death of Finnish architect Alvar Aalto (*see* OBITUARIES) at the age of 78 saddened all those interested in modern architecture and again brought home to them that the survivors of Aalto's generation of pioneers were now the grand old men of architecture.

The Middle East. The oil-rich nations of the Middle East continued to provide fine opportunities for Western architects in 1976. There was a continuing demand for new public institutional and commercial buildings, and this together with ample funds promised some fine architecture. Architects working in the Middle East had, however, to solve many problems, principal among which were those created by the intractable climate and lack of industrial resources. The desert heat, though perhaps the most obvious climatic factor, was not necessarily the most troublesome; air-conditioning systems developed for other hot areas could often be used to advantage. More troublesome were the high desert winds that can carry huge quantities of sand, which in turn seeps in through openings. Almost all materials, particularly steel, had to be imported, and this was also true of skilled labour for building. Eventually, the Middle Eastern countries would be able to produce much of what the building industry required, but as yet this capability was some years off.

Britain's new National Theatre on London's South Bank. Opened in 1976, it contains three separate theatres: the Lyttleton, Cottesloe, and Olivier.

DENYS LASDUN & PARTNERS

The search for a contemporary architecture appropriate to the Middle East also posed a challenge. The *Architectural Review* devoted its May issue to the city of Isfahan in Iran, the magazine's editors believing that the West has much still to learn from the East. As the magazine pointed out, it would be a pity if the ancient cultural traditions of the Islamic world were to be swamped by those of the West and its traditional values destroyed. In architecture, for example, there is much to be said for retaining the traditional courtyard plan rather than replacing it with European-type solid blocks. Also, architects designing buildings appropriate to Middle Eastern culture must look further than pointed arches and minarets for inspiration.

The shah of Iran broke ground at the end of 1975 for a new township, to be known as Shahestan Pahlavi. This large new urban development, forming part of Teheran, was planned by the U.K.-based firm Llewelyn-Davies International. Shahestan Pahlavi would include government, commercial, and residential buildings as well as a cultural centre containing an opera house, museum, royal library, and various halls of assembly. A central plaza to be known as Shah and Nation Square together with other parks provided assurance that a large area of the new development would remain as open space. The new town was part of a scheme to decentralize and decongest the downtown Teheran area. The projected population of Shahestan Pahlavi was in the region of 40,000 to 50,000, and the total investment over the next ten years was estimated at $3.7 billion. Such an expensive and ambitious scheme again underlined the great opportunities for architects and planners to be found in the Middle East.

At Dhahran in Saudi Arabia the University of Petroleum and Minerals was taking shape on a 1,300-ac site. The architects for the project were Caudill Rowlett Scott, a U.S. firm. The project was seen as an attempt by the Saudi Arabians to create outstanding architecture under extremely difficult conditions. One requirement was that the buildings incorporate the best of traditional Arabian design. This was achieved by the use of square columns and arcades, low-rise massing, and sand-coloured exterior concrete. The solid walls would keep out the relentless sun and were splayed at the tops to deflect wind-borne sand; pointed arches were used decoratively. As in other Middle Eastern projects, problems were encountered with the limited labour and materials available, and most components had to be imported from the U.S.

In Iran the Shiraz Technical Institute, designed by U.S. architects Hugh Stubbins & Associates, was to be the first facility in that country that would provide instruction in industrial science and technology at a post-secondary school level. The design consisted of a central spine of classrooms, offices, and laboratories connected by a series of cross axes to outlying support functions. The reinforced-concrete structure was designed to withstand the frequent earthquakes that occur in the area.

Also in Iran, designs were revealed for a new and lavish Sheraton hotel for Teheran. Designed by Welton Becket Associates, the hotel, which would cost $40 million, would be 41 stories high and have 587 rooms. A revolving rooftop restaurant was also planned.

The British firm The Architects Collaborative (TAC) designed a 14-story luxury hotel for Sharjah in the United Arab Emirates. The 330-room hotel would overlook the Persian Gulf. The structure was in the shape of a truncated pyramid, and the interior featured a central garden atrium, an idea that had been successfully embodied in a number of U.S. hotels in the last few years.

The Arabian American Oil Co. (Aramco) began construction on a new outpatient clinic at al-Hasa Oasis near Hofuf in Saudi Arabia. The clinic was designed to be capable of handling 100,000 patients annually. Architects were the New York firm Haines Lundberg Waehler. An octagonal building 185 ft in diameter housed a central screening area with specialist facilities located in radiating wings. A colour-key system for signs would enable patients unused to clinics of this type to find their way around the various areas. The project included staff facilities and apartments that formed a separate residential unit. This unit was built following traditional local design with buildings ranged around private courtyards protected from wind and desert sun. The structures were of concrete slab construction for ease of building and maintenance.

Another new medical facility in the Middle East was to be the Imperial Medical Centre in Teheran, designed by the Los Angeles firm William L. Pereira Associates in collaboration with the Iranian firm LEEV. The centre included a 700-bed hospital.

British-designed projects in the Middle East included a new Government Centre in Taif, Saudi Arabia, designed by Sir Leslie Martin and David Owens. The horizontality of the project was emphasized by galleries linking the low blocks. The group of buildings was intended as summer headquarters for the government. Also in Saudi Arabia, Trevor Dannatt & Partners designed a mosque for Riyadh. The design consisted essentially of two interlocking U-shapes forming a simple square block to contrast with the tall minaret.

Kuwait designated 1976 "The Year of Construction" and declared its intention of spending much of its estimated $10 billion oil revenues on construction, especially of medical, educational, and industrial facilities. In London the Central Mosque in Regent's Park, designed by Sir Frederick Gibberd & Partners, neared completion during the year.

Cultural and Educational Buildings. A site was finally selected for the John F. Kennedy Memorial Library after ten years of discussion between Harvard University and the citizens of Cambridge, Mass. The library would be built on the Boston campus of the University of Massachusetts. Architects I. M. Pei & Partners, who had already produced two abortive schemes, were asked to design a building for the new site. The library would accommodate the presidential archives as well as a Kennedy Museum. The building was expected to stimulate the redevelopment of the whole general neighbourhood, which was somewhat run-down. In order to persuade the John F. Kennedy Library Corporation to select the Boston location, the university commissioned Hugh Stubbins & Associates to complete a feasibility study and design a building for the site. They produced a structure consisting of a long truss canopy extending over Boston Harbor and supported by six enormous cylindrical columns, two of which were sunk in the harbour. A feature of the design was a large cylindrical rotunda to provide exhibition space.

KEYSTONE

The controversial new Home Office building in London. It cost the British government £17.5 million.

At the St. Louis (Mo.) Art Museum construction began on a long-term building plan to provide additional gallery space, educational facilities, and administration areas. Architects Hardy Holzman Pfeiffer Associates designed a vast new court that would enclose the original 1904 colonnade by Cass Gilbert. The entire building project would cost an estimated $13.5 million. The first phase of construction was scheduled to be completed in the spring of 1977.

The Australian government honoured the centenary of the birth of U.S. architect Walter Burley Griffin, who designed Canberra. A memorial pavilion was to be built atop Mt. Ainslie overlooking the Australian capital. Winners of the competition for the design were Cope & Lippincott of Philadelphia. The winning entry consisted of a pair of parallel slabs that frame the view along the central axis of Griffin's city. The structure, of reinforced concrete, was unveiled on November 24, the 100th anniversary of Griffin's birth.

Those seeking a memorial to mark the silver jubilee of Queen Elizabeth II of Britain found that suitable monuments are difficult to conceive these days. Projects were described by *The Times* of London as "awful but accurate comments on the state of British architecture." The first prize was shared between Derek Walker & Associates for their proposal for carving the gravel pits near Heathrow Airport into the shape of the queen's profile and Howell, Killick Partridge & Amis who produced an innocuous idea for a Jubilee

Hill in Hyde Park to be planted with trees and shrubs. One design consisted of a white figure of a corgi dog (the queen's favourite breed) to be carved on the chalk Downs.

In Boston, Mass., a red, white, and blue striped air-pressurized pavilion occupied the South Plaza of the Prudential Center during the bicentennial year. Designed by Cambridge Seven Associates, Inc., the pavilion housed an information centre for visitors together with a 300-seat multimedia theatre. The pavilion consisted of a 162-ft-long, vinyl-coated, fibreglass air-pressurized roof supported at each end by 8-ft-deep double steel arch trusses.

Two recent buildings by the U.S. firm of Mitchell/Giurgola attracted attention. The Casa Thomas Jefferson was a binational cultural centre for Brasília, the capital of Brazil. Built by the U.S. Information Agency, the centre housed classrooms, offices, and libraries. The Columbus East High School in Columbus, Ind., a three-level structure of concrete and glass, was a fine addition to that town's living museum of first-class modern architecture.

At the University of Jodhpur, India, new botany and zoology laboratories were designed by Uttam C. Jain, using local stone and standard fenestration between masonry piers to harmonize with the same architect's earlier campus buildings. This was the first stage of a formal design that would ultimately consist of six buildings separated by courtyards and ranged around a landscaped central square.

The Brazos Valley Art Center in Bryan-College Station, Texas, was a new regional arts facility demonstrating principles of energy conservation. It would be the first public building in Texas to use solar energy. The design, by the Texas A & M University College of Architecture and Environmental Design, consisted of aluminum tetrahedrons, truncated tetrahedrons, dymaxions, and truncated octahedrons. The centre covered 70,000 sq ft and was designed to accommodate musical programs, dance studios, and an art gallery.

Commercial and Municipal Buildings. The Montreal Olympic Games held in the summer of 1976 required a considerable amount of new building. The project was plagued from its inception by cost overruns, labour troubles, and public outcry against both cost and design quality. Expenditure by the city, originally estimated at a modest $250 million, eventually neared $1 billion. Architect for the main stadium was Roger Taillibert of France. The Olympic Village, made up of two pyramid-shaped blocks, was designed by Roger D'Astous and Luc Durand to house the competing athletes and after the Games was to be converted into apartments.

A high-rise tennis facility in New York City was projected in response to the national tennis craze. The New York Sports Center was to be built in midtown Manhattan and would house 24 tennis courts, 7 squash courts, and other sports facilities. It would be equivalent in height to a 45-story building. Designed by Brodsky, Hopf, & Adler, architects and engineers, the building featured bands of reflective glass set at inverted angles at the ceiling line of the tennis courts.

In Kansas City the Republican Party convention was held at the new R. Crosby Kemper Jr. Memorial Arena, designed by C. F. Murphy Associates. The structure, seen on television by millions of viewers, was dominated by three exposed triangular roof trusses, each 27 ft deep. The arena enclosure itself was clad in metal panels. Flexibility was one of the main requirements of the design, and the arena could accommodate up to 16,000 people for ice hockey and 18,000 for basketball. It could also be adapted for horse shows, track and field events, concerts, and trade shows. Inside, the exposed structural components were painted bright yellow.

A new office development on London's Victoria Street attracted critical acclaim. Designed by Elsom Pack & Roberts for Chelwood Properties Ltd. on a site adjoining Westminster Cathedral, the development represented a breakaway from the common office "slab." Consisting of two parts with a piazza between, the new building framed the 19th-century cathedral. It was built of crystalline cubes in whose windows the cathedral could be seen reflected, and both old and new buildings gained by their juxtaposition. Accommodations included 450,000 sq ft of office space together with 34 commercial units, 11 apartments, and basement parking for 300 cars. The development, of brown glass and gray granite, also featured a colonnade over the pavement to shelter walkers to and from Victoria Station.

An office building in Sydney, Australia, by architect Harry Seidler featured stepped terraces or balconies, a formula used with success in the past for apartment complexes. The boredom of high-rise slabs was avoided, and the variation in height from seven stories down to three complied with city zoning regulations.

The prizewinning Occupational Health Center in Columbus, Indiana, designed by Hardy Holzman Pfeiffer Associates, has an exterior of black reflecting glass and corrugated steel.

NORMAN MC GRATH

TONY HOWARTH—WOODFIN CAMP

An old Minneapolis warehouse has been turned into an office-and-retail-store complex, now called Butler Square. The interior was opened up to create an atrium.

An unusual feature of new offices in Johannesburg, South Africa, for IBM was the circular tower projecting from one corner of the rectangular block that housed the service core. The block had a facing of high-quality brown tiles. Architects were Arup Associates with Abramowitch, Sacks, Moss, Sack, Feldman & Associates.

Two new commercial buildings by Kevin Roche and John Dinkeloo were given critical acclaim. The Richardson-Merrell corporate headquarters building near Wilton, Conn., was the head office of a pharmaceutical company and occupied a 57-ac rural site. The design was understated, with the parking areas cleverly arranged below ground and on the roof in order to avoid the all-too-common effect of a building entirely surrounded by a huge parking lot. Construction was of reddish-brown steel with vast areas of glass. An old mansion standing on the site was incorporated into the design.

By contrast, the Worcester County Bank Building, Worcester, Mass., was a 24-story twin-tower construction of steel sheathed with reflective mirror glass. The towers were connected by a service core and managed to harmonize with the low-scale downtown area. A notable feature was the greenhouse-style banking hall two stories high. (SANDRA MILLIKIN)

See also Engineering Projects; Historic Preservation; Industrial Review: *Building and Construction.*

[625.A.1–5; 626.C]

Arctic Regions

Oil, gas, and mining development continued to dominate the news during the year, although there was increasing interest in social and political affairs on the part of all the circumpolar nations.

Experts predicted that the Alaskan Brooks Range and North Slope would become one of the world's great mineral-producing areas. Several significant copper deposits already had been located, and further discoveries were expected in what geologists thought might be a belt of heavy mineralization running along the southern flank of the mountains.

The U.S. Bureau of Mines authorized a $250,000 study of the strip mining of coal resources along the coast of northwestern Alaska. North Slope coal resources were estimated to contain possibly 199,000,000,000 tons of coal, out of an estimated one trillion tons in the entire state—almost 2,000 years' supply at current U.S. coal production rates. The University of Alaska estimated that almost 130,000,000,000 tons of coal could be mined under existing technology. The study was designed to provide basic information rather than to lead to specific mining operations.

Persistent welding flaws were discovered on the trans-Alaska pipeline. Faulty welding, mismanaged quality control, and supervisory problems were thought to be so pervasive that they could delay the pipeline's completion, endanger its safety, and add hundreds of millions of dollars to the ultimate cost. An audit by Alyeska Pipeline Service Co., the builders of the pipeline, admitted the existence of up to 4,000 problem welds, which could cost about $10,000 each to remedy. About 2,000 welders were reported working on the pipeline; their average wage, including overtime, was estimated at about $65,000 per year.

Meanwhile, the Alcan Pipeline Co. filed formal application with the U.S. Federal Power Commission for authorization to construct and operate a 731-mi, 42-in-diameter natural gas pipeline and related facilities from Prudhoe Bay to the Alaska-Yukon border. In August an application for the Canadian portion of the line was filed before the Canadian National Energy Board. The pipeline was part of a proposed transportation system through Alaska and Canada designed to carry an average daily volume of 2,400,000,000 cu ft of natural gas to U.S. markets. Estimated total capital cost was between $5 billion and $8 billion. The sponsors believed the Alaska Highway route pipeline project could deliver gas to the lower 48 states about two years ahead of the much larger and probably more expensive joint Canadian-U.S. pipeline along the Mackenzie River valley proposed by Canadian Arctic Gas Pipelines Ltd.

Petro-Canada, a newly formed, government-controlled petroleum company, announced plans to undertake a major exploration project in Canada's High Arctic during the next few years, in cooperation with private industry. Petro-Canada held 45% of the shares of Panarctic Oils Ltd., the major and most successful oil and gas exploration company in the Canadian Arctic Islands.

Panarctic's Bent Horn oil discovery on Cameron Island in the High Arctic late in 1975 was considered a good contender in the race to bring into being the first Arctic commercial oil find in Canada. Panarctic's president predicted that success at this site could mean that frontier oil might be available in southern Canada by mid-1979. The company's plan for bringing the oil and gas south envisaged a pipeline and icebreaker/tanker transportation system to the east coast.

Despite U.S. intervention and strong opposition from Canadian environmentalists, native groups, and parliamentary critics, the Canadian government decided to allow offshore oil drilling in the Beaufort Sea. Drilling activities in this area had been opposed because of the fear that severe ice conditions might delay cleanup operations for periods of as much as a year on any oil well blowout that might occur. The Indian affairs and northern development minister, Judd Buchanan, said that "the government had to weigh pressing national energy requirements, the potentially rich oil and gas resources underlying the Beaufort Sea, and the substantial financial commitment made by Dome Petroleum, against the environmental risks and the concerns expressed by native groups and the U.S." Buchanan promised that special precautions would be taken to reduce environmental risks to an "absolute minimum." These special precautions would include a shortened drilling season of up to eight weeks; a $50 million insurance policy to pay for cleanup and damages in the event of an accident; and continuous monitoring of the drilling operations by ship-based government inspectors possessing pertinent experience and the authority to shut down the operation if necessary. Late in September Dome Petroleum Ltd. struck what was described as possibly an excellent natural gas reservoir 10,000 ft below the floor of the Beaufort Sea from a drillship located about 40 mi N of Tuktoyaktuk, Northwest Territories. At the same time a second well was abandoned after an uncontrollable seepage of fresh water through the drilling shaft damaged special equipment used to prevent and control oil blowouts.

Like a flying thermometer, this helicopter with heat-sensing equipment patrols the Alaska pipeline to monitor the heat-proofing equipment in its vertical supports. The purpose is to keep the frozen tundra from melting.

WIDE WORLD

In November the voters of Alaska chose Willow, about 70 mi N of Anchorage, as the site of the state capital. The present capital, Juneau, had been a hub of activity during the gold rush days, but it was now far from the state's population centres and could be reached only by air or water.

The Alaska Native Land Claims Settlement Act passed by the U.S. Congress in 1971 was snarled in legal and administrative delays that could hold up transfers of land to native corporations for years. This would impede development plans already under way on native lands and drain the cash resources of village and regional corporations to pay attorney and consultant fees associated with the litigation.

In northern Canada a number of important benchmarks were attained during the year concerning the issue of native land rights. Debate continued over the 1975 Dene Declaration by the Indian Brotherhood and the Métis Association of the Northwest Territories, which requested increased autonomy and related economic and cultural rights within an area representing about 450,000 sq mi of the Northwest Territories.

Eskimos from all the northern nations met for the first Innuit Circumpolar Conference at Barrow, Alaska, at the end of November. Participants discussed the possibilities of a "sixth" Arctic nation, besides the five circumpolar states, and of negotiating an Arctic seabed treaty under the auspices of the UN.

The Canadian Armed Forces reported early in June the presence of Soviet aircraft, prefabricated huts, and more than 100 personnel on an ice island $3\frac{1}{2}$ mi long within Canada's northern territory and located about 500 mi S of the Pole. The stations were providing information on the ocean bottom and atmosphere to the Arctic and Antarctic Scientific Research Institute in Leningrad. While Canada claimed sovereignty from the Yukon to the North Pole, this claim had not yet been recognized by the U.S.S.R. and certain other countries.

The Soviet northern sea route fleet was strengthened by the addition of the new 492-ft, nuclear-powered icebreaker "Arktika," a somewhat larger vessel than its nuclear predecessor the "Lenin." During the year the "Lenin" was involved in an unusual experiment, setting out from Murmansk three months before the usual opening of the Arctic shipping season in June to convoy a freighter to a new gas field on the Yamal Peninsula, in Siberia, which was inaccessible from the land. Development of the Siberian gas fields was critically important as they were expected to contribute about a third of Soviet gas production by 1980.

In October the "J. E. Bernier," a Canadian Coast Guard icebreaker based in Quebec City, completed the first clockwise voyage around North America by a Canadian vessel in a single navigation season. The "Bernier" sailed on May 14 from Quebec City for Victoria, B.C., via the Panama Canal, to carry out duties in the western Arctic and returned via the northwest passage—a 19,000-mi voyage.

A 305-ft barge built especially for the Prudhoe Bay sealift, capable of cutting a 105-ft swath through ice for tugs and other barges to follow, was expected to revolutionize Arctic sealift procedures. Conventional icebreakers have too much draft for the shallow Arctic shipping lanes, where tugs and barges work to best advantage.

Three government research ships worked off the

Alaskan coast during the summer seeking to determine what would happen to oil spills in icy waters. Information gathered by the three ships of the U.S. National Oceanic and Atmospheric Administration working in the Gulf of Alaska, the Bering Sea, and the Chukchi Sea was expected to be useful in deciding where the oil industry could drill and in writing regulations for offshore drilling. (KENNETH DE LA BARRE)

Arena Sports

Bullfighting. The bullfighting scene in Spain seemed to undergo a crisis during 1976. The total number of corridas (bullfights) decreased significantly and even the bulls appeared to be less attractive, less powerful, and less aggressive. In general it seemed that a restructuring of operations was called for and that persons in charge of individual events would have to modernize their approach to restore lost vitality to the ancient spectacle. On the positive side, attendance continued at a reasonably high level, with over 90% of all seats sold, many to tourists. In Portugal four bullfighters deliberately violated a 1799 law by killing a bull during a tourada. Though the men were arrested, aficionados proclaimed them heroes and a government official supported their causes by drafting a bill that would rescind the ban.

For Mexico, as well as for Spain, a most important event was the resumption of exchange relations, which made it possible once again for matadors from both countries to fight on the same program. Curro Rivera, Manolo Martínez, and Eloy Cavazos, who fought 64, 58, and 56 corridas, respectively, by the end of September, were the most active of the 60 Mexican matadors. The six new bullrings that opened in various parts of the country helped provide needed opportunities for the novilleros, the less experienced bullfighters, whose careers were seriously handicapped by the unexpected closing in March of the Plaza Mexico, largest bullring in the world. There were 45 such aspirants to the *doctorarse* (doctorate) registered with the bullfighters' association and 130 others trying to qualify. Some 1,150 fighting bulls were killed in about 200 corridas before late September.

Colombia celebrated its five major traditional fairs with a total of 32 corridas during December 1975 and January 1976. Outstanding matadors were Enrique Calvo ("El Cali"), Jorge Herrera, and Pepe Cáceres. Occasional corridas were held throughout the year featuring Mexican and Spanish bullfighters and imported bulls. Important Colombian breeding ranches included Piedrahita, Ambolo, and Pueblito Español.

In Venezuela's six major bullrings, 27 corridas were fought during the course of seven festivals. Matadors Carlos Málaga ("El Sol"), Rafaél Ponzo, and Jorge Jiménez were among the most popular. But it was Málaga who broke with tradition and generated heated discussions with his spectacular and unconventional arrival in the arena. He entered the bullring by parachuting from a plane, dressed in a "suit of lights."

Peru's most important taurine festival, El Señor de los Milagros, was held in Lima. It consisted of 12 bullfights, with animals supplied by the eight principal ranches of the country. The Escapulario de Oro trophy was won by Niño de la Capea. The award for the best of the ten currently functioning ranches went to Yencala. Rafaél Puga and Paco Chávez continued to uphold their country's honour.

Ecuador was best represented by Edgar Peñaherrera, a matador of worldwide reputation, and by Armando Conde. The trophy awarded at Quito's great fair, Nuestro Señor Jesús del Gran Poder, was won by Mariano Ramos of Mexico. He symbolically cut off the ears and tail of a bull from the Lizardi Sánchez ranch, and spared the bull's life because of its bravery.

JOHN P. FOSTER

Tom Ferguson wrestles a steer during a rodeo in Ellensburg, Washington. He won nearly $88,000 in the regular 1976 season.

Attempts to bring "bloodless" bullfighting to the U.S. failed again; a series of spectacles scheduled for Long Beach, Calif., was stopped at the last minute by the American Society for the Prevention of Cruelty to Animals.

(RAFAÉL CAMPOS DE ESPAÑA; LEE BURNETT)

[452.B.4.h.viii]

Rodeo. Tom Ferguson set a single regular season money record of $87,908 in 1976 in the course of winning the Professional Rodeo Cowboys Association (PRCA) all-around championship, which goes to the biggest money winner in two or more events, and the PRCA championship in steer wrestling ($49,000). Counting bonus awards and earnings during the year-end world championships, the 29-year-old cowboy from Miami, Okla., became the first rodeo performer to surpass the $100,000-a-year mark with a grand total of $114,663, including bonuses.

Other PRCA champions included Monty Henson of Mesquite, Texas, in saddle bronc riding ($34,000); Joe Alexander of Cora, Wyo., in bareback bronc riding ($48,000); Don Gay of Mesquite, in bull riding ($33,000); Leo Camarillo of Oakdale, Calif., in team roping ($30,000); and Roy Cooper of Durant, Okla., in calf roping ($37,000).

The PRCA decided that world titles would no longer go automatically to the year's biggest money winners. Instead, world championships would be determined by ten go-rounds in each of six events during a December rodeo in Oklahoma City. Ferguson became the all-around champion after winning $9,005 in calf roping and steer wrestling. Henson and Mel Hyland of Salmon Arm, B.C., shared the saddle bronc title and received $4,473 each. Gay was tops in bull riding and got $5,496. Cooper, who took the calf roping title, earned $5,789. Chris Le Doux of Kaycee, Wyo., was first in bareback and pocketed $4,912. Steer wrestling champion Rick Bradley of Burk Burnett, Texas, received $5,496. The team roping title was shared by Californians Ronnie Rasco of Lakeside and Bucky Bradford of Sylmar, each of whom got $4,512. Connie

Areas: *see* Populations and Areas; *see also the individual country articles*

UPI COMPIX

Annette Pollard of Bassett, Nebraska, rides a bucking bronc bareback at an all-girl rodeo in Pueblo West, Colorado.

Combs of Comanche, Okla., won the girls' barrel racing championship and took home $3,665.

Because steer roping requires a large outdoor arena, it was featured in only 12 PRCA rodeos during the year. At the national finals in September Marvin Cantrell of Nara Visa, N.M., became the PRCA champion with winnings totaling $10,223; Charles Good of Elida, N.M., was declared world champion after winning $3,063 during the finals. The PRCA sanctioned nearly 600 rodeos in 1976, with record prize money amounting to nearly $7 million. (RANDALL E. WITTE)

[452.B.4.h.xxiii]

Argentina

The federal republic of Argentina occupies the southeastern section of South America and is bounded by Bolivia, Paraguay, Brazil, Uruguay, Chile, and the Atlantic Ocean. It is the second-largest Latin-American country, after Brazil, with an area of 1,072,200 sq mi (2,776,900 sq km). Pop. (1975 est.): 25,384,000. Cap. and largest city: Buenos Aires (pop., 1975 est., 2,977,000). Language: Spanish. Religion: mainly Roman Catholic. Presidents in 1976, María Estela Martínez de Perón and, from March 29, Lieut. Gen. Jorge Rafaél Videla.

At the beginning of 1976, the Justicialist Party was split into factions of varying degrees of "verticalism," or subservience to President Martínez de Perón as leader of the movement. The president's attempt, at a meeting on February 10, to reach some agreement with the party's labour factions failed. Organized labour, always considered the backbone of the Peronist movement, was no longer willing to be so completely submissive to the official party leadership, especially in view of the growing calls for Mrs. Perón's resignation. These calls came from many sectors, including factions of her own party and other former allies of the Justicialist Liberation Front, which was becoming a complete dead letter as a political group. This was considered to be the result of a series of political blunders which some commentators ascribed to the executive's decision to hang on to power at all costs and others to a planned campaign to provoke a coup d'etat by the armed forces.

Finally, following months of political violence and the inability of Mrs. Perón's government to deal with the economic consequences of inflation running at an annual rate of over 600%, the armed forces took power on March 24. Mrs. Perón was removed and replaced by a military junta formed by the three commanders in chief of the armed forces: Lieut. Gen. Jorge Videla (Army; *see* BIOGRAPHY); Adm. Emilio Eduardo Massera (Navy); and Brig. Gen. Orlando Ramón Agosti (Air Force). General Videla was chosen by the junta to be president of the nation, and sworn in on March 29. Congress was dissolved, the Supreme Court and other top officers in government were removed, and all political activities connected with trade unions, political parties, and producers' associations were banned. Congress was replaced by the Legislative Advisory Commission, headed by Rear Adm. Antonio Vañek and composed of three senior officers from each of the armed forces. On March 25 it was announced that the present members of the junta would remain in power for three years, but the junta as an institution would continue in office for a term as yet undefined. In May charges were brought against Mrs. Perón, her adviser José López Rega, and his daughter and son-in-law, and in October, following an investigation of Mrs. Perón's use of public funds, formal indictments were issued charging fraud and administrative irresponsibility.

Argentina's new president in 1976 was Lieut. Gen. Jorge Rafaél Videla. He had been commander in chief of the Army before leading the coup of March 24. His troops called him "the bone."

DIEGO GOLDBERG/SYGMA

ARGENTINA

Education. (1975) Primary, pupils 3,579,304, teachers 195,997; secondary, pupils 454,194, teachers 62,334; vocational, pupils 788,864, teachers 99,525; higher, students 596,736, teaching staff 45,204.

Finance. Monetary unit: peso, with (Sept. 20, 1976) an official commercial rate of 140 pesos to U.S. $1 (free rate of 240.62 pesos = £1 sterling). Gold, SDR's, and foreign exchange (March 1976) U.S. $421 million. Budget (1975 actual): revenue 51,520,000,000 pesos; expenditure 211,450,000,000 pesos. Gross national product (1973) 377,370,000,000 pesos. Money supply (March 1976) 459,850,000,000 pesos. Cost of living (Buenos Aires; 1970 = 100; March 1976) 4,210.

Foreign Trade. (1974) Imports 32,327,000,000 pesos; exports 35,767,000,000 pesos. Import sources: U.S. 17%; West Germany 11%; Japan 11%; Brazil 8%; Libya 7%; Italy 6%; Chile 5%. Export destinations: Italy 14%; Brazil 9%; U.S. 9%; The Netherlands 7%; U.S.S.R. 5%; Chile 5%; U.K. 5%. Main exports: corn 16%; meat 11%; wheat 7%.

Transport and Communications. Roads (1974) 309,086 km. Motor vehicles in use (1974): passenger 2,160,000; commercial (including buses) 966,000. Railways: (1973) 40,210 km; traffic (1974) 13,177,000,000 passenger-km, freight 12,324,000,000 net ton-km. Air traffic (1974): 4,080,000,000 passenger-km; freight 106.5 million net ton-km. Shipping (1975): merchant vessels 100 gross tons and over 374; gross tonnage 1,447,165. Shipping traffic (1973): goods loaded 14,133,000 metric tons, unloaded 9,841,000 metric tons. Telephones (Dec. 1974) 2,374,000. Radio receivers (Dec. 1971) 10 million. Television receivers (Dec. 1973) 3,950,000.

Agriculture. Production (in 000; metric tons; 1975): wheat 8,200; corn 7,700; sorghum 5,030; barley 594; oats 414; rice 350; potatoes 1,349; sugar, raw value 1,361; linseed 372; soybeans 485; sunflower seed *c.* 732; cotton, lint 118; tomatoes *c.* 532; oranges (1974) 774; lemons 317; apples (1974) 786; wine *c.* 2,600; tobacco 111; beef and veal (1974) *c.* 2,250; cheese *c.* 225; wool 83; quebracho extract (1973) 90. Livestock (in 000; June 1975): cattle *c.* 58,000; sheep *c.* 39,000; pigs *c.* 5,500; goats (1974) *c.* 5,268; horses (1974) *c.* 2,700; chickens *c.* 31,700.

Industry. Fuel and power (in 000; metric tons; 1975): crude oil 20,200; natural gas (cu m) 7,690,000; coal (1974) 626; electricity (kw-hr; 1974) *c.* 27,990,000. Production (in 000; metric tons; 1974): cement 5,220; crude steel (1975) 2,226; cotton yarn 89; nylon, etc., yarn and fibres 47; passenger cars (including assembly; units) 214; commercial vehicles (including assembly; units) 55.

In his first broadcast, the new president emphasized that the events of March marked the initiation of a new "historic cycle" of national reorganization, directed by the armed forces. Although the actual take-over of power by the armed forces was bloodless and, in general, well received by the population, violence soon began. Hours after General Videla was sworn in as president, gunmen assassinated the chief of operations of the federal police, Guillermo Pavón. Political violence by both the right and left killed more than 1,000 people in 1976 and was responsible for 1,700 deaths during Mrs. Perón's 21 months in office. The new government stated that one of its main goals was the eradication of terrorism and subversion; as a first step, the death penalty for terrorists was established in June. Despite this, the extremist organizations remained active.

The armed forces claimed that guerrilla activity in the province of Tucumán was practically under control and that the extremists had suffered so many casualties that they were no longer in a position to mount operations against military installations, as in the past. The death in July of the Marxist leader Mario Roberto Santucho, head of the People's Revolutionary Army (ERP)—one of the most important of the guerrilla organizations as well as one of the oldest—with some of his lieutenants was a blow to extremism. The terrorists therefore concentrated their attacks on individuals, the attacks receiving wide coverage in the press. Victims included the chairman of the 1978 World Cup soccer organizing committee and officers of the armed forces and police. Other victims, probably of the rightist death squads, included two distinguished Uruguayan exiles, Senators Zelmar Michelini and Héctor Gutiérrez Ruiz, and a Bolivian ex-president, Juan José Torres, all living in exile in Buenos Aires; and, later, also in Buenos Aires, three Roman Catholic priests and two ordinands. On October 2 General Videla narrowly escaped an assassination attempt.

The internal situation prevented the new government from developing an international policy, although contacts with Bolivia, Chile, Paraguay, and Uruguay were made.

The gross domestic product (GDP) fell in real terms by 1.4% in 1975, with construction (−9%), mining (−4.3%), commerce (−4%), and transport and communications (−4%) showing the greatest declines. Industry recorded a decline of 3.6%, and positive growth rates were registered only in the textile and leather industry (4.4%) and in the nonmetallic minerals sector (0.5%). The agricultural product fell by 1.2%. Consumption, on the other hand, rose by 3.3% in 1975. With exports ($3 billion) 17.5% down from 1974 and imports ($4 billion) 1.8% up, 1975 showed a trade deficit of $1 billion. There was a net outflow on capital movements and a balance of payments deficit of $791 million ($51.3 million in 1974), reflecting deterioration in trade and also repayment of loans contracted to alleviate a foreign exchange crisis in 1972. The recovery program announced on April 2 by the new government achieved some success in the first half of 1976, with a trade surplus of $400 million, as against a $700 million deficit a year earlier.

A financial mission visited the U.S. and several Western European nations to seek some $1.2 billion from the International Monetary Fund and private commercial banks to help the nation meet its 1976 public foreign debt obligations. Gross international reserves reached a total of $1.4 billion. Net reserves of about $500 million and a deficit in the balance of payments of not more than $437 million were expected at the end of 1976. On March 31, 1976, the total foreign debt principal stood at $8,948,000,000, more than half in the public sector.

An accelerating rate of inflation continued until the end of March 1976, when the annual rate of inflation had risen to 566.3%. As a result of the recovery program, however, this rate began to decline (475.8% in July), and a rate of 350% was forecast for the year.

Tax reforms were designed to increase revenues by 100 billion pesos in 1976 and, by rationalization within the public sector, to reduce the treasury deficit to 480 billion pesos (5.6% of estimated GDP, against 12.6% in 1975). (JAIME R. DUHART)

[974.F.1]

Art and Art Exhibitions

Trends in Art. There was no dominant direction in the visual arts in 1976, but innumerable trends, ranging from Conceptualism to Photo-Realism, simultaneously vied for public attention. The current art world was characterized by catholicity of taste and an ability to embrace any kind of artistic expression provided it was aesthetically and formally meritorious, relevant, and salable. Innovation yielded to refinement, and the art forms, styles, and movements of the mid-1970s were essentially continuations and expansions of developments that originated in the 1960s.

Perhaps the most characteristic aspect of art in

Armies: *see* Defense

Art: *see* Architecture; Art and Art Exhibitions; Art Sales; Dance; Literature; Museums; Theatre

Lorenzo Vaccaro's "America" (1692–95), in silver with gold, diamonds, and emeralds, was part of a Spanish loan exhibition at the National Gallery marking the U.S. Bicentennial.

AUTHENTICATED NEWS INTERNATIONAL

1976 was an emphasis on content rather than form. One of the trends of the mid-'70s, for example, was Auto-Art, sometimes called Autobiographical Art, Self-Transformational Imagery, or Conceptual Self-Portraiture. Although descended from the Conceptualists of the late '60s, such auto-artists as John Baldessari, Laurie Anderson, Julia Heyward, Urs Lüthi, Eleanor Antin, and Stephen Loeb were all more personal and less intellectual in approach.

Social consciousness movements of the '60s and '70s also engendered a more personal art that stresses content. Internationally there continued to be attempts at establishing and defining women's art or homosexual art. In the U.S. blacks and Latinos continued to explore what they considered to be ethnically relevant in form, subject matter, and aesthetic viewpoint. Artists in the less developed nations were correspondingly concerned with the creation of an indigenous imagery reflective of their particular artistic traditions and national history.

Another indication of mid-'70s personalism was that New York, London, and Paris were no longer the focal centres of creative activity, although they remained the commercial centres for the exhibiting and selling of art. Increasingly, artists were avoiding the intensely competitive atmosphere of these world art capitals, preferring to reside in communities or environments where their individualism would not be eroded or threatened by the pressures of fashion. Aesthetic and stylistic cohesiveness tended to be regional, so that critics spoke of a Southern California aesthetic, a Midwest expression, Texas art, Catalan imagery, or the Minas Gerais school.

In the development of 20th-century art, form and subject were first abstracted and then nonobjectified. During the 1950s the materials of a work of art and its process of creation became the subject. With the advent of Conceptualism in the 1960s, only the art concept or aesthetic idea was seen as having relevance, not the physical or visual manifestation of that concept. Conceptualism, therefore, is antiobject, or nonobject, and is regarded more as an attitude than as a style or a movement. It relies upon the written word in the form of proposals and directions and is documented, if visually materialized, with photographs, drawings, video, film, or written descriptions. Christo, Joseph Kosuth, Douglas Huebler, and Lawrence Weiner were among the most acclaimed Conceptualists of the mid-'70s.

Another art trend, Contemporary Primitivism, espoused an aesthetic of natural purity. Such artists as Rafael Ferrer, Alan Shields, Ree Morton, Charles Simonds, and Judson Fine all used unprocessed materials to produce an art that is expressively counter to the rational and formalist tendencies of 1960s "cool" art. Their works were especially prompted by an antagonism to technology and by a concern for ecological reform.

Related to the "happenings" of the '60s was the Performance Art of the '70s, theatrical in presentation or form and sculptural in concept. The artist or performers present an internalized commentary between their bodies and the environment. This kinetic imagery, however, is both personal and general, for it is self-referential in content but usually ritualistic in form. Performance Art was centred in the U.S., England, and West Germany, and among the major figures were Vito Acconci, Dennis Oppenheim, Chris Burden, Scott Burton, Jim Self, Josef Bueys, William Wegman, and Gilbert and George.

Akin to both Contemporary Primitivism and Conceptualism was Land Art, or Earthworks. Michael Heizer, Robert Smithson, Walter De Maria, and Richard Serra all created large outdoor sculptures using the materials of the environment as their structural components. These sculptural forms could be either ephemeral or permanent in nature. Whether temporary or enduring, however, they were nonobjects because their monumentality of scale made it difficult to perceive the work at a single point in time and space, as well as because of their interdependent relationships to the local topography.

One of the most significant trends of the 1970s was the increasing interest in landscape painting. During most of the 20th century it was the urbanscape that preoccupied the painter, for most artists preferred the congestion and pressures of city life to the openness and serenity of country living. In recent years, however, ecological concerns and the socioeconomic difficulties of urban existence had driven many artists away from the metropolis.

Interest in landscape art was given a dramatic impetus by the U.S. Department of the Interior, which had commissioned 45 American artists to paint some aspect of the nation's countryside. Each painter was given $2,000, a government car, and a per diem expense account for traveling. To ensure geographic distribution of both painters and subject matter, three realist painters were appointed as regional advisers: Wayne Thiebaud for the West, Philip Pearlstein for the East, and Ellen Lanyon for the Midwest. The result was a panorama of the U.S. from Hawaii to New England, as well as a survey of the varying styles of contemporary realism by its best American representatives. Among the participating artists were Richard Estes, Alex Katz, Joseph Raffael, Jack Beal,

Alfred Leslie, Ralston Crawford, Edwin Dickinson, and Fairfield Porter.

The Minimal and Hard Edge Art of the '60s persisted into the mid-'70s. Artists like Brice Marden and David Novros were as insistently nonimagist as their aesthetic mentor, the late Mark Rothko. Such major Minimalist sculptors of the previous decade as Donald Judd and Anthony Caro continued to be in the mainstream of the art world. Public art also continued to flourish, especially in the monumental sculptures of Mark Di Suvero.

(ROBERT J. LOESCHER)

[628.B.6.d]

Exhibitions. The occasion of the U.S. Bicentennial in 1976 afforded an opportunity for many museums and galleries to organize exhibitions on an American theme. Such exhibitions were not limited to the U.S. but could be found in many parts of the world.

"American Art 1750–1800 Towards Independence" was a joint venture of the Yale University Art Gallery, New Haven, Conn., and the Victoria and Albert Museum in London. Funded from American sources, the exhibition was instituted by The Pilgrims of Great Britain, a British society that aimed to foster Anglo-American friendship. The many paintings, drawings, prints, and decorative objects on show illustrated the change in style from the Rococo of the mid-18th century to the severe Neoclassicism of *c.* 1800. The objects selected were always the best possible examples of their type, and visitors were able to compare the sophistication of city-made objects, such as chairs and cabinets, with the comparative simplicity of country-wrought examples.

The 240 objects in the exhibition, lent by 67 public and private collections, illustrated the range and diversity of 18th-century American culture and the way in which European ideas were transformed by American artists and craftsmen. Also part of the exhibition were a slide show, "The Look of American Arts: 1750–1800," illustrating the relationship of American to English art objects, and a 30-minute film, "The Look of America: 1750–1800," which gave a sense of the visual quality of the American environment in the second half of the 18th century. The show was seen in New Haven in April and May and in London from July to September.

A show with an unusual point of view was "The European Vision of America," a compilation of nearly 350 works from public and private collections in more than a dozen European countries as well as in Canada and the U.S. Originally conceived by the Museum of Art, Cleveland, Ohio, it was seen at that institution as well as at the National Gallery of Art, Washington, D.C., and the Grand Palais, Paris. There were no works by American artists. The earliest item was a woodcut of 1493 depicting the landing of Columbus.

The Art Museum, Worcester, Mass., held three major bicentennial exhibitions. The second, "The Early Republic: Consolidation of Revolutionary Goals," covered the dramatic half-century of American history from the signing of the Declaration of Independence to 1826, a year that saw the deaths of John Adams and Thomas Jefferson. Many pictures in the show illustrated scenes of important political and military events. "The 1776 Exhibition" at the National Maritime Museum, Greenwich, England, from April to October was chiefly concerned with details of the American Revolution. Designed to attract the general public, it included such exhibits as reconstructions of a tavern, a coffeehouse, a battlefield, and an admiral's cabin. There were also waxworks figures and 18th-century portraits.

AUTHENTICATED NEWS INTERNATIONAL

"200 Years of American Sculpture" gave visitors an encyclopaedic survey of the sculptor's art at the Whitney Museum of American Art in New York City during the U.S. Bicentennial.

German artist Hans Schult covered Venice's San Marco Square with 15,000 kilograms (33,000 pounds) of newspapers to "bring people to examine today's environmental phenomena more intensively."

ANSA/PHOTO TRENDS

"The French and the American War of Independence," mounted by the Musée des Beaux-Arts, Rennes, France, was designed to illustrate the part played by the French monarchy in the American struggle against Britain. It included 350 items from public and private collections. The exhibition was divided into three sections: the first described the philosophy prevalent at that time; the second was devoted to the battles and the peace of 1783; and the third showed how the American Revolution influenced the French Revolution.

"Three Hundred Years of American Art," a major exhibition of painting and sculpture at the Chrysler Museum at Norfolk, Va., included important contemporary works as well as items from the 18th and 19th centuries. The more than 300 works were selected from the museum's collection and were displayed in the new wing of the museum, which opened on March 1.

At the Art Museum, Cincinnati, Ohio, "Art of the First Americans" included over 1,000 objects of American Indian art assembled entirely from the museum's own collection. A photographic exhibition at the Institute of Contemporary Arts in London, "Destination America," focused on the wave of immigration to America from Europe that occurred in the late 19th and early 20th centuries.

The other major event that occasioned a number of linked exhibitions was the World of Islam Festival held in London in the spring. The largest exhibition associated with the festival was "The Arts of Islam," organized by the Arts Council and held at the Hayward Gallery in the early summer. This was a comprehensive display which attempted to show the art of a civilization that ranged in time from the 7th to the 19th century and stretched geographically from Spain and Morocco in the west to Central Asia and the Indian subcontinent in the east. Certainly there had been no exhibition on this subject comparable in scale or quality since the Islamic exhibition held in Munich, Germany, in 1910.

The organizers assembled objects from all over the world, many of which had rarely been seen by the public. Sadly, there were no items from the Topkapi Palace Museum, Istanbul, since the Turkish government prohibited the loan of works of art for exhibition. Nevertheless, it was amazing how many delicate and valuable items were lent. The aim of the exhibition was to show the essence of Islamic art to a public largely unfamiliar with that culture. Four recurring motifs—calligraphy, the arabesque, the figure, and geometry—were singled out and shown as they appeared in textiles, glass, ivory, metalwork, ceramics, wood, stucco, marble, and arts of the book.

Several supporting exhibitions were held at the British Museum. There was a small show of "Paintings from the Muslim Courts of India," a subject not covered by the Hayward exhibition. Another small exhibition, focused on the city of Isfahan, was entitled "Isfahan, City of Light and Life." Perhaps the most appealing of these exhibitions was "The Qur'ān," which displayed exquisite examples of Islamic calligraphy of the 9th to the 16th century.

The Science Museum in London mounted a fascinating and enjoyable show entitled "The Science and Technology of Islam." Visitors were reminded that skills such as navigation, cartography, surveying, architecture, astronomy, and transportation were all highly developed at an early date in the Islamic world. The show included manuscripts, practical pieces, and reconstructions of mechanical devices. A complex water clock 11 ft high was reconstructed from a 13th-century manuscript.

At the Victoria and Albert Museum there was an exhibition of Persian metalwork, the first show of its kind ever seen in Britain. Persian narrative paintings were the subject of an exhibition of miniatures at the Museum of Fine Arts, Springfield, Mass. The lavish decorative examples of painting and calligraphy ranged in date from the 9th to the 17th century. Many other shows were devoted to Islamic subjects, and commercial galleries also organized thematic shows to coincide with the large exhibitions and to take advantage of public interest in the subject.

Certainly one of winter's most popular exhibitions in London was the Tate Gallery's large show marking the bicentenary of the birth of the English painter John Constable. This vast exhibition, consisting of 340 works by Constable, his friends and followers, was the largest and most comprehensive display of his works ever assembled. In keeping with the biographical theme, exhibits were hung in chronological order with brief biographical summaries for each year.

To commemorate the 400th anniversary of the death of Titian, the National Gallery in London mounted a small exhibition of portraits by that artist. Because of the difficulty of transporting and insuring such works, only ten portraits were on display, all but one of them from the National Gallery's own collection or from private collections in Britain. Such a show could not be comprehensive, but it afforded the viewer an opportunity to study and compare the portraits in depth, free from the exhaustion that so often afflicts the visitor to marathon retrospectives.

The work of the 20th-century French painter Robert Delaunay, leader of the movement known as Orphism, was the subject of a major exhibition at the Orangerie, Paris, which later traveled to the Kunsthalle, Baden-Baden, West Germany. On view were 124 paintings and drawings, many of which were in private collections and thus virtually unknown to the general public. Included was an almost complete series of Delaunay's "La Tour Eiffel" pictures.

An exhibition of Old Master drawings at the Los Angeles County Museum of Art in the summer included some fine examples from Queen Elizabeth II's collection at Windsor. This was the first major U.S. museum presentation of old master drawings to include examples from all the European schools. The show provided a comprehensive survey of the history and development of European master drawings from the 14th to the end of the 18th century. The 237 drawings on show included works by Leonardo da Vinci, Raphael, Rembrandt, Rubens, and Goya. A show of 100 French drawings from the Fitzwilliam Museum, Cambridge, England, seen in Paris at the François Heim Gallery and also in Lille and Strasbourg, covered the period from the 16th to the 19th century.

The Petit Palais, Paris, held an exhibition of 214 very rare icons from Bulgaria. The icons, which came from museums, churches, and monasteries, dated from the 9th to the 19th century. Their presentation was enhanced by the inclusion of contemporary objects, among them sculptures, fabrics, altar crosses, and reliquaries. The exhibition was also shown in Moscow. The British Museum showed "Thracian Treasures from Bulgaria" in the winter. Many powerful individual items of gold and silver found in Thracian tombs were to be seen; most showed some influence of Greek and Persian art.

The most extensive exhibition of ecclesiastical vestments ever mounted in the U.S. was seen in the winter at the Art Institute of Chicago. Nearly 2,000 objects were shown, including copes, dalmatics, and chasubles as well as such related items as chalice covers, gloves, stoles, and burses. Covering nearly 1,000 years from the 11th to the 20th century, the show, drawn from collections in Europe, Mexico, and the U.S., provided a comprehensive survey of the history of ecclesiastical garments in the Western church.

An exhibition of works by Clyfford Still at the San Francisco Museum of Art was built around a group of 28 paintings given to the museum by the artist. An ingenious hanging system using hinged walls enabled a third of the paintings to be on permanent display while the remainder were readily accessible to scholars.

An entertaining show entitled "Just What Is It . . . ? Pop Art in England 1947–63" was seen at the Kunstverein, Hamburg, West Germany, and also at the Städtische Galerie im Lenbachhaus, Munich, and the York City Art Gallery, England. Covering the period 1947 to 1963, it was organized in West Germany and brought to York by the Arts Council. The varied aspects of Pop Art were evident in works by such artists as Eduardo Paolozzi, Richard Hamilton, Joe Tilson, Peter Blake, David Hockney, and R. B. Kitaj.

A small exhibition devoted to the life of the 18th-century English eccentric William Beckford was shown at Salisbury and Bath, England. Beckford's importance was as a patron, collector, and connoisseur, and he was well known as the builder of Fonthill Abbey. The charming show included paintings, engravings, drawings, letters, furniture, decorative objects, books, maps, and sculpture.

A major exhibition of Peruvian colonial paintings, "The Cuzco Circle," was shown in the summer at the Center for Inter-American Relations Art Gallery in New York City. Many of the 17th- and 18th-century paintings from this little-known school were presented for the first time. The works of these Peruvian artists showed mixed Flemish, Italian, and Spanish influences fused with native Indian traditions. The show was seen at several U.S. museums. A touring exhibition organized by the Arts Council of Great Britain was devoted to "Peruvian Ground Drawings," those mysterious large-scale incisions that had given rise to speculation that beings from outer space once visited South America.

A major exhibition at the Museum of Modern Art, New York City, was "Fauvism and Its Affinities," which reexamined and reassessed this important modern art movement. The show concentrated on the period from 1905 to 1907 and included works by Derain, Vlaminck, Dufy, and Braque as well as by Matisse, the leading Fauve artist. The show traveled to San Francisco and Fort Worth, Texas. A retrospective exhibition devoted to the work of Hannah Höch (b. 1889), one of the last survivors of the Dada movement, was seen at the Nationalgalerie, Berlin. It included paintings, collages, assemblages, and photomontages covering the period 1916–70. A retrospective exhibition of the Surrealist painter André Masson (b. 1896) was mounted at the Museum of Modern Art,

COMMONWEALTH INSTITUTE, LONDON

Wooden writing boards of the Hausa people, Nigeria.

WIDE WORLD

Christo's "Running Fence": a 24-mile construction of nylon, hung on steel posts, ran from the sea north of San Francisco to Petaluma, California. The artist called his two-week exhibit "process art in action."

New York City, and a retrospective of L. S. Lowry (*see* OBITUARIES), a reticent British painter of simplified landscapes of the urban north of England, was held at the Royal Academy of Arts, London.

"Symbolism in Europe," covering the years 1860–1910, included 267 items devoted to this intriguing subject. In all, 88 artists were represented. The exhibition was seen in Paris; Baden-Baden, West Germany; Rotterdam, Neth.; and Brussels. The big winter exhibition at the Royal Academy, London, "The Golden Age of Spanish Painting," included paintings by Murillo, Velázquez, and El Greco.

Two autumn exhibitions in London were "Art in Seventeenth Century Holland" at the National Gallery, which included sculpture, furniture, china, and silver as well as paintings, and the Arts Council's exhibition at the Hayward Gallery, "Sacred Circles: 2,000 Years of North American Indian Art," in which artifacts of powerful design—masks, sculpture, textiles, and work in leather, beads, and quills—were impressively displayed. Also in the autumn, the Victoria and Albert Museum held an exhibition devoted to an exhibition—a look back 25 years at the Festival of Britain exhibition of 1951.

Two of the most popular contemporary artists were the subjects of large autumn shows in New York City. "The Two Worlds of Andrew Wyeth: Kuerners and Olsons" at the Metropolitan Museum of Art was personally organized by the museum's director, Thomas Hoving. The Kuerner and Olson farms at Chadd's Ford, Pa., and Cushing, Me., had supplied Wyeth with many of his favourite subjects. Alexander Calder (*see* OBITUARIES) lived long enough to assist in the preparation of "Calder's World" at the Whitney Museum of American Art.

(SANDRA MILLIKIN)

See also Art Sales; Museums; Photography.

[613.D.1.b]

ENCYCLOPÆDIA BRITANNICA FILMS. *The Louvre* (edited version, 1966); *Henry Moore—The Sculptor* (1969); *Siqueiros—"El Maestro"* (1969); *Richard Hunt—Sculptor* (1970); *Interpretations* (1970); *Paul Kane Goes West* (1972); *Textiles and Ornamental Arts of India* (1973); *Indian Art of the Pueblos* (1975).

Art Sales

Market Trends. In terms of the U.S. dollar, prices in the art market during the 1975–76 season were fairly stable; in sterling terms they rose strongly; and reckoned in Swiss francs, they fell uncomfortably. This, of course, had nothing to do with the art market, but it made its trends difficult to interpret. The concept of auction record prices had become confused—auction records in what currency?

The fact that London had long been the leading entrepôt of the art market made the weakness of sterling a particularly significant factor. On one hand, non-British vendors were less willing to consign goods for sale in London. This led to a greater dispersion of major sales, including an increase in the number and importance of foreign sales held by Christie's and Sotheby's themselves, a notable improvement in the standard of sales in Paris, and more important sales run by local auctioneers in West Germany and Switzerland. On the other hand, it brought foreign buyers flocking to London in search of bargains; this tended to result in their bidding far more than would be justified by the fall in the sterling exchange rate.

Another symptom of Britain's economic difficulties was the introduction of the buyers' premium by Christie's and Sotheby's in London in the autumn of 1975. It required purchasers to pay an extra 10% over and above the auction price. This led to a confusing divergence in practice at different centres. (*See* Table.)

Tom Keating (*see* BIOGRAPHY), an artist and a restorer of paintings, set the cat among the pigeons of the art world by claiming to have produced as many as 2,000 imitations of well-known painters, in particular of the English landscape painter Samuel Palmer (1805–81). His assertions led to a train of examinations and inquiries in the latter half of 1976.

Works of Art. Yet another result of Britain's economic malaise was the acceleration of sales from great old family collections. Christie's profited particularly from this on account of its traditional links with the British aristocracy. The highest auction price of the year was the £1.1 million paid for an exquisite "Crucifixion" panel by the 13th-century Sienese artist Duccio di Buoninsegna. It was sold by the widow of the earl of Crawford and Balcarres, having been purchased by his ancestor Lord Lindsay at Christie's in 1863 for 250 guineas. The sale on July 2 at Christie's was made even more poignant by the fact that the auctioneer was Patrick Lindsay, Lady Crawford's son.

In October 1975 Christie's dispersed the contents of Swinton House in Yorkshire, netting £255,575 toward the £1 million death duty of Lord Swinton. A private

Buyers' Premium at Leading Auction Centres

Saleroom	Premium
Christie's, King St., London	10%
Christie's, South Kensington, London	none
Sotheby's, London	10%
Sotheby Parke Bernet, New York	none
Sotheby Mak van Waay, Amsterdam	16%
Sotheby's and Christie's, Switzerland	
Swiss private collectors	14%
Foreigners and dealers	8%
Paris	11%*
Phillips, London	none
Bonham's, London	10%

*Average of sliding scale.

sale to the nation had been negotiated for the most important family portraits, but the auction included a vast Landseer at £10,395 and a Rococo German bureau-cabinet by Kilian Bender of Mainz at £30,030. In January 1976 the contents of Stonor Park in Berkshire were dispersed by Phillips on behalf of Lord Camoys for £152,845, including a fine set of four English Gothic Revival chairs at £6,000.

Among the properties sold by Sotheby's for Eva, countess of Rosebery, was an unfinished group portrait of the Tiepolo family by Giovanni Domenico Tiepolo; it brought £110,000 (a new record for this artist) in March 1976. Sotheby's also received the superb Gathorne-Hardy collection of Old Master drawings for sale; again, private sales to the nation were negotiated for some of the prize items, but a drawing by Andrea Mantegna of a bird on a branch pecking at some berries realized £60,500, the highest auction price on record for an Old Master drawing. A pencil study of a male nude by Michelangelo brought £46,200, and a sheet of Parmigianino studies £41,800. The Italian drawings were sold in London and the northern European drawings at Mak van Waay in Amsterdam, including an Albrecht Dürer "Holy Family" at 145,000 guilders.

In May Christie's dispersed the contents of Malahide Castle, near Dublin, for a total of £529,173, including a fine Louis XIV commode by A.-C. Boulle at £31,500. The season was highlighted with the sale in June and July of a group of paintings from the duke of Sutherland's historic collection, most of which had previously been on loan to English museums. They included a painting of Dutch fishing boats in a gale by J. M. W. Turner, known as "The Bridgwater Sea Piece," at £374,000; it had remained in the family since it was commissioned from the artist about 1800. There was also a "Virgin and Child" by Sir Anthony Van Dyck at £220,000 (subsequently acquired by the Fitzwilliam Museum, Cambridge, for £231,000, partly raised by public subscription) and a G. P. Pannini "Interior of an Imaginary Picture Gallery" at £187,000. All were auction record prices for the artists.

While those aristocratic dispersals provided the high points of the British season, a new pattern of international sales began to crystallize. Christie's Geneva sales, which had long shared with New York the monopoly in major jewel dispersals, began to establish a clear preeminence in the handling of the finest historic silver. In November 1975 a pair of magnificent Louis XV jardinieres with boar's head finials and hoof feet by Thomas Germain comfortably surpassed all previous auction prices at SFr 2 million; they were depicted in two still-life paintings by Claude-François Desportes and were said to have been brought out of Portugal after the 1974 revolution. In April 1976 Christie's nearly matched this when it sold a pair of Germain tureens in Geneva for SFr 1.8 million.

Meanwhile, in Monte Carlo, Sotheby's was developing a specialty in furnishings and works of art suited to millionaire tastes. Sotheby's had held its first Monaco sales in the previous season and now consolidated its position. In June 1976 it sold Madame de Pompadour's microscope for Fr 350,000, one of the highest prices on record for a scientific instrument. The same sales included an Adam Weisweiler secretaire (bought in Paris in 1784 by the Grand Duchess Maria Feodorovna, wife of the future tsar Paul I) at Fr 1.5 million.

Paris, the traditional home of such luxuries, succeeded in disputing the preeminence of Sotheby's Monte Carlo sales. In November 1975 a set of Louis XV seat furniture by Nicolas Heurtault yielded Fr 620,000, and in June 1976 a magnificent 292-piece *famille rose* dinner service commissioned from China by the Asteguieta family of Spain brought Fr 1.5 million; three tureens modeled in the form of a cock, a goose, and a boar's head were the star pieces of the service. The same sale included a series of 15 Don Quixote tapestries woven at the Gobelins factory and based on cartoons by Charles-Antoine Coypel about the year 1717, at Fr 1.4 million.

The annual sale held in June by Kornfeld und Klipstein of Bern, Switz., proved as usual the high point of the year in the modern graphics field, with a single, rare Picasso etching, "Minotauromachie" of 1935, bringing SFr 237,000 and Edvard Munch's colour lithograph "Das Kranke Mädchen" SFr 122,000. The auctioneers in 1976 complained bitterly of their difficulties in the face of the strength of the Swiss franc as against other currencies. Sales in Paris and London indeed ran them close. Ader in Paris sold a collection of 178 Jacques Villon prints for Fr 840,-

THE NEW YORK TIMES

This multipaneled work once hung around the dining room of French master Henri Matisse. Called "The Swimming Pool," the 16-metre (54-foot) collage was acquired by New York's Museum of Modern Art in 1976.

000, while in July Christie's in London nearly matched its Picasso price with an early impression of "Le Répas Frugal" at £60,500.

Sotheby's periodic sales in Hong Kong were becoming increasingly important occasions for the Chinese ceramics market. In November 1975 a Shun-Yao flowerpot with a pale lavender-blue glaze tripled predictions to fetch £41,800, while in May 1976 a Chia-ching engraved blue-ground dragon bowl brought £56,100. Sales in London and New York, however, continued slightly to outclass Hong Kong. In December 1975 Sotheby's in London sold a 16½-in 14th-century underglaze red bowl for £137,500, and in March 1976 Parke Bernet in New York sold a Chia-ching polychrome *kuan,* or vase, for $260,000.

Sotheby Mak van Waay in Amsterdam demonstrated on two occasions that the highest prices for Dutch art were currently being paid in The Netherlands. The first occasion was the November 1975 sale of the Houthakker collection of Dutch drawings, which included Rembrandt's "Jacob Blessing the Sons of Joseph" at 40,000 guilders and a river landscape by Roeland Roghman at 32,000 guilders. The second was the B. de Geus van den Heuvel sale of Dutch paintings of the 17th to 20th centuries; records were consistently and repeatedly broken, with an Adriaen van Ostade "Interior of an Inn" at 660,000 guilders among the 17th-century pictures, Isaak Ouwater's "View in Amsterdam" at 210,000 guilders for the 18th century, and Georg Breitner's Impressionist "View in Amsterdam" at 240,000 guilders for the 19th.

Meanwhile, in the U.S. the series of sales held by Parke Bernet of paintings and works of art from the Geraldine Rockefeller Dodge collection repeatedly underlined the fact that Americans had never truly forgotten their collecting enthusiasms of the turn of the century. The sales included in October 1975 an auction record for an A.-L. Barye bronze, an allegorical group of "Peace," at $13,000; also in October a 9-ft bronze American Indian "The Passing of the Buffalo" by Cyrus Edwin Dallin at $150,000; in November a marble bust of Benjamin Franklin by J.-A. Houdon at $310,000, followed by new auction records for J.-F. Millet, T. Rousseau, and Isidore-Jules Bonheur; in February 1976 a new record for a Gérôme sculpture; and in May, for Rosa Bonheur.

London's Tate Gallery aroused a storm of controversy when it exhibited this work consisting of 120 firebricks, purchased from American sculptor Carl Andre.

THE GUARDIAN, LONDON AND MANCHESTER

For the second consecutive season the most expensive sector of the art market, Impressionist and modern pictures, was repeatedly in difficulties. Many pictures failed to find buyers when put up for auction. Nevertheless, outstanding works recorded outstanding prices. In March 1976 Paul Gauguin's "Nature Morte à l'Estampe Japonaise" sold for $1.4 million in New York, and in June 1976 Vincent Van Gogh's "L'Heure du Midi" brought £528,000 in London.

Other outstanding prices of the year included an Italianate landscape by Richard Wilson at £165,000; George Stubbs's "The Duke of Grafton's Stallion, Mares and Foals" at £187,000; Jean-Honoré Fragonard's "Le Songe du Mendiant" at Fr 2.3 million; James Peale's "Washington and His Generals at Yorktown" at £198,000 (a record for a U.S. painting); and J.-L. Agasse's painting of two leopards in a landscape at £154,000 (a record for a Swiss painting).

Book Sales. An unspectacular but steady increase in book prices took place during the 1975–76 season. There were some areas where the increase was particularly notable. Foremost, perhaps, was the sharply increased premium that collectors were prepared to pay for a particularly fine edition. There was also an unusual increase in value for illustrated books. This trend, perhaps primarily decorator-oriented, embraced both natural history and topographical books.

The final part of the Arpad Plesch library, sold in March, included A. Seba's *Thesaurus,* a superb 18th-century natural-history compilation including 449 coloured plates of birds, beasts, snakes, and other natural curiosities at £8,800. *London as it is,* the set of 26 coloured lithographs of 1842 by Thomas Shotter Boys, brought £4,180 in May.

A trend more strictly related to the traditional world of books was the strong increase of interest in manuscript material, letters, and historical documents of the post-medieval period. While a favourite of collectors at the turn of the century, this era had come to be somewhat overlooked in later years.

The autograph manuscript of Lord Byron's poem *Beppo—A Venetian Story* proved a highlight of the season when it brought £55,000 in June 1976. The same sale contained four handwritten pages from a love story by Napoleon at £11,000 and an autograph manuscript of Charles Lamb's famous essay "The Praise of Chimney-Sweepers—A May Day Effusion" at £6,600.

At the beginning of the season Sotheby's rearranged its book department, transferring responsibility for the post-1830 period to its separate sales room in Chancery Lane. Books of this period were more easily available and less expensive; the new sales room recorded a marked increase in collecting interest, particularly for children's books, English illustrated books, and topographical works.

Sotheby's also pioneered sales in new areas such as literary ephemera and science fiction. Thirty volumes of *The Autocar* magazine dating between 1898 and 1913 brought £1,012 in February, while a large collection of science fiction was sold for £2,232 in May.

The sale of 38 manuscripts from the collection of works of Jewish interest formed by the late David

KEYSTONE

Rembrandt's portrait of his mistress, Hendrickje Stoffels, was recently acquired by the National Gallery in London.

Solomon Sassoon was held by Sotheby's at Zürich, Switz., in November 1975. Efforts to sell the library en bloc to a single institution had failed on account of its enormous value. The first dispersal included the Damascus Pentateuch, one of the oldest Hebrew manuscripts of a portion of the Bible, at SFr 1.1 million. A manuscript of the Mishna with commentaries in the hand of Maimonides, the great medieval Jewish philosopher, was sold for SFr 1.2 million. These were the highest prices that had ever been recorded at auction for any book or manuscript.

In July 1976 this record was broken, but by a manuscript of important art-historical interest. Sotheby's in London sold a previously unknown 16th-century illuminated Flemish *Hours of the Virgin* for £407,000. It dated from about 1510 and contained 84 miniatures from Europe's leading workshop of the period; the manuscript was arguably finer than the famous Grimani *Breviary* from the same workshop. Other major prices of the season included a 14th-century German illuminated *Bestiary* at £66,000 in November, a 16th-century manuscript of Ferdowsi's *Shah-nameh*, or *Book of Kings*, with 53 miniatures at £99,000 in December, and a similar manuscript of the same period with 29 miniatures at £82,500 in April.

Three collections sold during the season provided special interest for serious book collectors. In October 1975 Sotheby's offered books from the earl of Rosebery's library; most had been purchased at the Hamilton Palace sale and had originally belonged to William Beckford. These were heavily annotated by Beckford himself. In March 1976 Sotheby's dispersed the collection formed by A. N. L. Munby, librarian of King's College, Cambridge, from 1947 to 1974, and an unrivaled expert on the history of book collecting. The third collection was that of John Carter, the eminent bibliophile who made history in the 1930s with his exposure of the Thomas Wise literary forgeries.

(GERALDINE NORMAN)

[613.B.3]

Astronomy

The year of the triennial meeting of the International Astronomical Union, 1976 was dotted with discoveries by observational astronomers and marked by frustration for theoretical astrophysicists. With the exception of the startling discovery of cosmic X-ray bursts, the year was mainly one of broadening and deepening knowledge of diverse astronomical systems.

Quasars and Cosmology. Debate over the distance to extragalactic objects and the nature of the large-scale structure of the universe continued unabated in 1976. Despite the impressive successes of the "big bang," or expanding universe, picture, the failure of astrophysicists to achieve a generally acceptable understanding of the nature of quasars, active galaxies, and galactic nuclei allowed the very concept of an expanding universe to come under attack.

In the 1920s, Edwin P. Hubble found that the more distant a galaxy was from the Earth the greater was its red shift (shift toward longer wavelengths of its optical spectral features). He interpreted the red shift as a Doppler shift, caused by the difference in speed between our galaxy and extragalactic objects, and on this basis developed his theory of the expansion of the universe. The program begun by Hubble continued in 1976 at the Hale Observatories, where Allan Sandage and G. A. Tammann in an extensive series of papers reported the successful verification of the original Hubble distance-red shift relation to distances of at least one-tenth the "radius of the universe."

Nonetheless, Halton C. Arp, Geoffrey R. Burbidge, and others continued to point out apparent discrepancies with the simple big-bang interpretation. Their arguments centred on several types of observations: quasars in the directions of galaxies of much lower red shift (with or without luminous filaments connecting them), associations between galaxies of very different red shifts, and the overall distributions of quasars and galaxies over the sky. For example, several years ago Arp reported the discovery of a luminous "bridge" connecting the galaxy NGC 7603 and its smaller companion. Merle F. Walker and co-workers then used an electronographic image converter to confirm the existence of the "bridge." Though they attributed the "bridge" to chance superposition, the nature of such associations remained unclear.

Recent 21-cm radio observations tend to support the cosmological origin of quasar red shifts, or at least suggest that the quasars are farther away than galaxies. Studying the quasar 3C 286, Arthur M. Wolfe, John J. Broderick, James J. Condon, and Kenneth J. Johnston showed that the 21-cm absorption line seen in its radio spectrum was probably produced by a gas cloud associated with an intervening galaxy at a distance of about 17,000,000,000 light-years. This put the quasar at 22,000,000,000 light-years.

If quasars are at the distances indicated by their red shifts, they can be used to test the laws of physics. For differing physical and cosmological reasons, Fred Hoyle, P. A. M. Dirac, Robert H. Dicke, and others proposed that the laws of physics vary with time. In particular, they suggested that some of the "constants" of nature, such as the speed of light c, the gravitational coupling constant G, the charge on the electron e or its mass m, the mass M or magnetic moment g of the proton, Planck's constant h, and the

Earth Perihelion and Aphelion, 1977

January 3	Perihelion, 91,401,000 mi (147,096,000 km) from the Sun
July 5	Aphelion, 94,505,000 mi (152,092,000 km) from the Sun

Equinoxes and Solstices, 1977

March 20	Vernal equinox, 17:43*
June 21	Summer solstice, 12:14*
Sept. 23	Autumnal equinox, 3:30*
Dec. 21	Winter solstice, 23:24*

Eclipses, 1977

April 4	Moon, partial (begins 2:06†), visible W part of Africa and Europe, Atlantic O., S. America, part of Antarctica, N. America except the NW part, E part of Pacific O.
April 18	Sun, annular (begins 7:33†), visible extreme E part of S. America, Africa except N and W part, extreme S part of Asia, part of Antarctica, S parts of Atlantic and Indian O.
Sept. 27	Moon, penumbral (begins 6:19†), visible extreme W part of Africa, N. America, S. America, Atlantic O., part of Arctic regions, most of Pacific O., and part of Antarctica
Oct. 12	Sun, total (begins 17:48†), visible N. America except N and NE part of Canada, NW part of S. America, extreme NE part of Asia, N part of Pacific O.

*Universal time.
†Ephemeris time.
Source: *The American Ephemeris and Nautical Almanac for the year 1977* (Washington, D.C.; 1975).

Association Football: *see* Football

Astronautics: *see* Space Exploration

COURTESY, THE HALE OBSERVATORIES

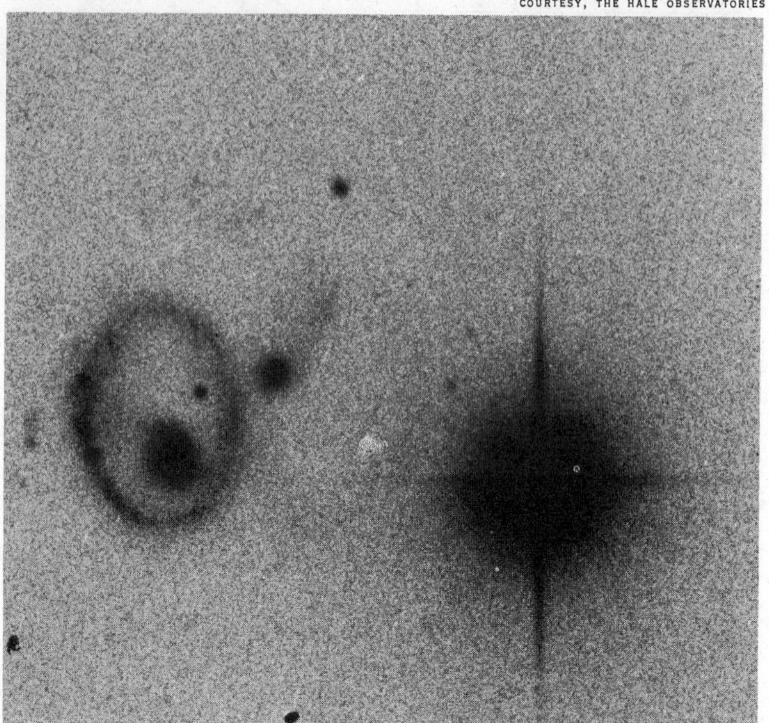

Optical photograph of the ring galaxy II Hz 4 taken at the Palomar Mountain Observatory in California. The galaxy may have originated from a collision between a normal spiral galaxy and a more compact galaxy.

fine-structure constant $\alpha(2\pi e^2/hc)$, might not have the same value in distant objects as they have locally. In two experiments, astronomers set severe new upper limits on the allowed variations of these constants.

The first test was made possible by the discoveries of the BL-Lac-type quasistellar object AO 0235+164. Optical magnesium lines were found to have a red shift z=0.52392(±0.00010) by E. Margaret Burbidge and co-workers observing at Kitt Peak National Observatory. Morton S. Roberts, Robert L. Brown, and Arthur Wolfe then obtained a 21-cm hydrogen line red shift of z=0.52385(±0.00001), consistent with the optical red shift to 1 part in 10,000. The optical and radio lines arise from emission mechanisms that depend differently on the fundamental constants. Assuming that the red shift accurately indicates the distance, the light has traveled over 7,000,000,000 years. This allows a limit to be placed on any variation in α of less than 1 part per 100,000,000,000 years and in $\alpha^2 gm/M$ of less than 2 parts per 100 trillion years.

In a separate experiment, William A. Baum and R. F. Nielsen, using a 72-in reflecting telescope and a special photomultiplier tube that allowed direct determination of the energy distribution of photoelectrons, studied light from distant galaxies centred on a narrow wavelength band measuring about 5234 angstroms. They found that "old" photons from distant galaxies have the same energy as "young" photons of the same wavelength from nearby galaxies. This directly implies the constancy of the quantity hc.

Neutron Stars and Pulsars. More than 40 years ago Fritz Zwicky and Walter Baade of the California Institute of Technology and, independently, Lev Landau of the Soviet Union predicted the existence of neutron stars. These are objects having roughly the mass of the Sun, compressed to a ball perhaps five miles in diameter and having the density of the nucleus of an atom. When pulsars (pulsating radio stars) were discovered in 1967, they were almost immediately identified as rapidly rotating neutron stars. Such objects are also believed to be responsible for X-ray emission from many of the 100 or so known discrete galactic X-ray sources, at least four of which are known to pulsate with periods of a few seconds. Not until the past year, however, have even the grossest properties of these objects, their masses, radii, or temperatures, been determined.

The discovery of several neutron stars in binary systems allowed their masses to be deduced from orbital mechanics. The first such mass determined, that of the neutron star in the pulsating X-ray source Hercules X-1, was found by John Middleditch and Jerry Nelson to be equivalent to about 1.4 solar masses. Later, three other neutron stars in binary X-ray sources, Vela X-1, Centaurus X-3, and SMC X-1, were all found to have masses in the range of 1–2 solar masses. Perhaps even more exciting, the neutron star in the binary pulsar system discovered by Russell A. Hulse and Joseph H. Taylor was shown to undergo a predicted orbital motion that allowed an estimate of its mass to be made, also in the range of 1–2 solar masses.

A group of X-ray astronomers from Columbia University headed by Robert Novick reported the first measurement of the surface temperature of a neutron star. The measurement was made possible by the first lunar occultation of the Crab Nebula pulsar since its discovery, which allowed the X-ray emission from the pulsar to be distinguished from that arising from the surrounding nebula. The lack of an observable flux of X-rays between pulses placed a limit of less than five million degrees Kelvin for the surface temperature of the object. After combining this figure with model calculations of the cooling of neutron stars, the authors concluded that the interior of the object must be superfluid.

Shortly after the discovery of regular pulses from pulsars, astronomers detected a gradual steady slowdown in the arrival rate of the pulses from each source. This was attributed to energy loss by the pulsars, which required them to rotate more slowly. Several times, however, the Crab and Vela pulsars were observed to begin suddenly to pulse faster, or "glitch." This was attributed to "starquakes," in which the star suddenly readjusted its shape for its slower rotation period. During the year two radio astronomers from Cornell University, Gordon E. Gullahorn and John M. Rankin, detected a sudden "anti-glitch" in the pulsar PSR 0823+26, producing a slowdown in pulse frequency and also a sudden "phase jump," in which the pulses began one day to arrive earlier than expected.

Cosmic X-ray Bursts. The accidental discovery of giant short-duration bursts of X-rays from the sky was perhaps the most exciting event in astronomy during 1976. Working with the Astronomical Netherlands Satellite, a group at Harvard College Observatory headed by Jonathan Grindlay and Herbert Gursky, along with their Dutch colleagues John Heise, A. C. Brinkman, and Johan Schrijver, observed bursts of X-rays from the direction of the globular cluster NGC 6624. These bursts reached high intensity in less than a second and then faded over a 10-second period. This star cluster, about 30,000 light-years from the Earth, contains approximately one million stars. It also contains a relatively steady X-ray source, 3U 1820-30. The X-ray intensity of this source increased by a factor of at least 30 during the bursts, the equivalent of turning on and off about one million solar luminosities of X-rays in ten seconds.

The existence of this spectacular and wholly unexpected object was soon confirmed by other X-ray satellite groups, including the Massachusetts Institute of Technology SAS-3, Los Alamos Vela 5, and the British Ariel V satellites. Shortly thereafter, the MIT group, led by Walter Lewin and George Clark, discovered about a dozen more X-ray "bursters." Several of them displayed a duration of several hours between bursts. Perhaps the most intriguing of these objects, discovered by Lewin and colleagues, is the "rapidly repetitive X-ray burster." Sometimes bursting with intervals of several seconds and at other times waiting minutes between bursts, this object demonstrated a pattern reminiscent of that produced by a relaxation oscillator such as a neon light bulb: the larger the burst, the longer it takes for the next burst to appear.

The great excitement about these objects initially concerned their association with globular clusters. Several of the dozen or so presently known sources seem to lie within globular clusters. Globular clusters, however, are generally thought to contain only old, inactive stars. Why, then, should they show great activity? The immediate suggestion of Gursky, Grindlay, and others was that the clusters contained giant black holes at their centres. These could then accrete surrounding gaseous material that would radiate X-rays before being swallowed up by the hole. An alternative model, suggested by Lewin, Willem Baan, and others, is that the burst results from the unstable flow of gas onto magnetized neutron stars.

Sun. During the year two independent groups using different observational techniques made the surprising discovery that the Sun is slowly oscillating. Henry A. Hill and collaborators, using a telescope especially designed to study the Sun, found it to be pulsating (changing its shape) at about 20 discrete periods ranging from about 7 to 70 minutes. The size of these motions is quite small, the largest having an amplitude of less than six miles, only 1 part in 100,000 of the Sun's diameter. Soviet astronomers at the Crimean Astrophysical Observatory headed by Andrei B. Severny, using a modified solar magnetograph to measure velocities at the solar surface, observed remarkably stable fluctuations with a period of 160 minutes. They also observed pulsations with a mean amplitude of about 6 mi, moving at the incredibly small velocity of about 6 ft/sec (a factor of 10,000 smaller than the relative Earth-Sun velocity).

By an extensive use of historical sources, John A. Eddy of the High Altitude Observatory at Boulder, Colo., confirmed the existence of and extended knowledge of the so-called Maunder Minimum. This is a period between 1645 and 1715 cited by E. W. Maunder as a time of anomalously few sunspots. By reexamining data that have come to light since Maunder's time, including radiocarbon dating of the Earth's past, terrestrial climate variations, occurrences of auroras, and further direct reports of sunspots, Eddy not only strengthened the case for unusual (and not understood) long-period variations in solar activity but also further underscored the nature of solar-terrestrial relations.

Solar System. Undoubtedly the greatest excitement in planetary exploration took place during the year with the successful landings on Mars of the U.S. Viking 1 and 2 landers. The significance of the photographs returned from the planet and of the data on those physical properties that were studied were not yet realized at the year's end. (*See* SPACE EXPLORATION.)

Between the time of the discovery of the fifth satellite of Jupiter in 1892 by Edward Barnard and the most recent discovery of the 13th in 1974 by Charles T. Kowal, the satellites have been referred to officially only by numbers. In 1976, however, the International Astronomical Union voted to assign them names. They are: V Amalthea, VI Himalia, VII Elara, VIII Pasiphae, IX Sinope, X Lysithea, XI Carme, XII Ananke, and XIII Leda.

Comet West provided during the year one of the most spectacular cometary shows of the century. At its maximum on February 26, it was about eight times brighter than the brightest star in the sky, Sirius. By March 8 it had developed a tail that stretched nearly 30° across the sky and its head was still brighter than Jupiter. It was one of the rare comets visible to the naked eye in full daylight. Even more unusual, between February 22 and March 5, astronomers watched the comet split into four pieces. Only two comets, both in the 19th century, had been previously observed to

The world's largest and most powerful optical telescope started operation at the Astrophysical Observatory of the U.S.S.R. in the Caucasus. Under the immense dome weighing nearly 1,000 tons, the telescope itself has a reflector 6 metres (236 inches) in diameter.

LEFT, THE TIMES, LONDON; RIGHT, KEYSTONE

PHOTOS, COURTESY, NAVAL RESEARCH LABORATORY

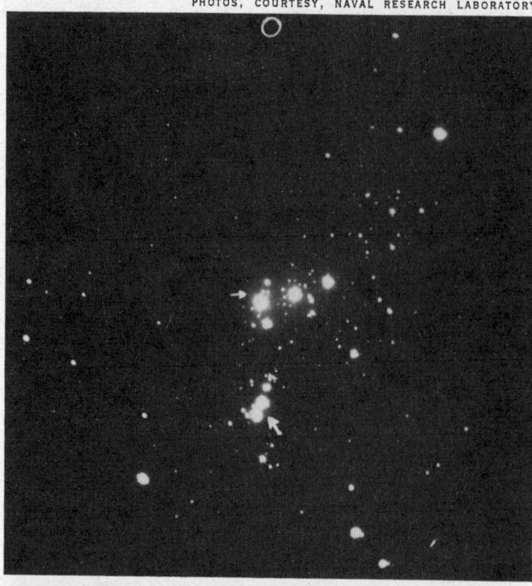

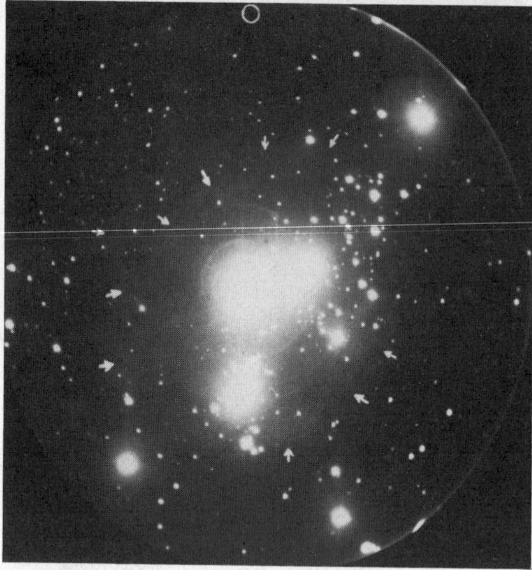

Two photographs of Orion in far ultraviolet light. The 30-second exposure at top shows the Orion nebula and a nebula near Zeta Orionis (two arrows). A 100-second exposure, below, gives details of Barnard's Loop where there is much interstellar dust. Betelgeuse, bright to the naked eye, is invisible in ultraviolet light (though circled in the upper part of each photo).

disintegrate into more pieces. Presumably it was this breakup, exposing the volatile interior material, that gave rise to such a bright cometary tail.

Instrumentation and Techniques. Though detailed and spectacular photographs of Mercury, Mars, and Jupiter have been obtained during the past few years by unmanned space probes, no global optical photographs have been obtained of the surface of Venus. Its cloud-enshrouded surface makes optical photography of its large-scale features impossible. Radio frequency radiation in the radar range, however, can penetrate the dense cloud cover to probe the surface features. Using the upgraded Arecibo radio telescope, Donald B. Campbell and R. B. Dyce (Arecibo Observatory) and Gordon H. Pettengill (MIT) were able to obtain a rather detailed radar surface-reflectivity image of Venus.

After nearly ten years of construction, the large Soviet RATAN 600 radio telescope was completed. Approximately 600 m in diameter, it is said to be capable of operating at wavelengths between 8 mm and the 21-cm neutral hydrogen line. (KENNETH BRECHER)

See also Earth Sciences; Space Exploration.
[131.A.1–3; 131.E; 132.A–C; 133.A–C; 723.E.1.b]

ENCYCLOPÆDIA BRITANNICA FILMS. *Controversy over the Moon* (1971); *The Moon: A Giant Step in Geology* (1976).

Athletics:
see Sporting Record; *articles on the various sports*

Australia

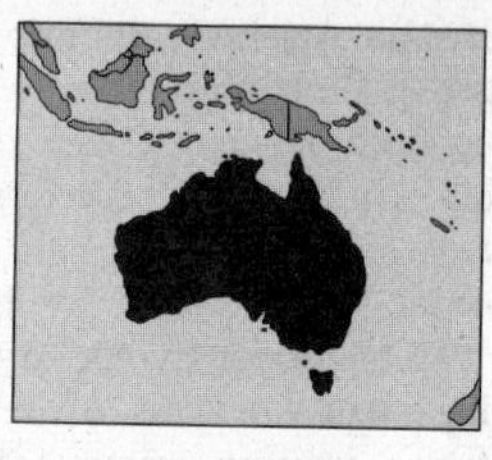

A federal parliamentary state and a member of the Commonwealth of Nations, Australia occupies the smallest continent and, with the island state of Tasmania, is the sixth largest country in the world. Area: 2,967,900 sq mi (7,686,850 sq km). Pop. (1976 est.): 13,600,800. Cap.: Canberra (metro. pop., 1976 est., 198,700). Largest city: Sydney (metro. pop., 1974, 2,898,300). Language: English. Religion (1971): Church of England 31%; Roman Catholic 27%; Methodist 8.6%; Presbyterian 8.1%. Queen, Elizabeth II; governor-general in 1976, Sir John Kerr; prime minister, Malcolm Fraser.

Domestic Affairs. The new prime minister, Malcolm Fraser, maintained a low profile in 1976, and the major political debate was on the role of the governor-general, Sir John Kerr, in dismissing the Gough Whitlam government in November 1975. (*See* Special Report.) Feeling ran high in the Parliament of Australia in February 1976 when Kerr arrived to open the new session. Labor Party members boycotted him, refusing to meet him, as was customary, in the Parliamentary Library or to attend and hear the speech from the throne. Announcing the new government's priorities, Kerr said that the Fraser government was determined to obtain jobs for all Australians and to defeat inflation. The former Liberal Party leader, Billy Snedden, was elected speaker and heard from the speaker's chair Whitlam's complaints on behalf of the defeated and reduced Labor Party. Whitlam described his dismissal as a "coup d'etat" and claimed that Queen Elizabeth II had said that if her representative in Australia wished to abuse his powers there was nothing she could do about it. Demonstrations against Kerr continued throughout the year.

In February the minister for posts and telecommunications, R. V. Garland, resigned from Fraser's government on the eve of being charged with bribery. The charge that he paid a A$500 bribe to an independent candidate in return for support in the Senate election was heard in the Canberra court of petty sessions in March; Garland was not convicted.

The reorganization of Medibank, the Australian national health scheme, was a controversial issue. A first step in the new Medibank involved the reviving of the private health funds. The second phase involved setting up within the Medibank system a stream of hospital health coverage parallel to that offered by the private funds. Under the revised law, announced on May 20, Australians were given alternatives in providing insurance coverage against illness. They could stay in the government scheme and pay a 2.5% tax levy, buy a "Medibank package" to cover their families for A$350 annually, or take out private health insurance. There was considerable public hostility toward the dismantling of the national health scheme that had been established by the Labor Party. When the government decided to provide its own intermediate and private ward coverage in direct competition with the private health funds, the private funds also were critical of the government.

The Australian Council of Trade Unions (ACTU) tried to organize Australia's first national strike over the decision to modify Medibank. Public transport, air services, power supplies, and mail were disrupted by the strike, which took place in July. Opinions varied over the effect and justness of the Medibank strike. The Australian treasurer, Phillip Lynch, described it as an arrogant and mindless attempt to blackmail the community and the government. Industrial disruption on a national scale would seriously disadvantage trade-union members, said Lynch, by reducing the prospect of jobs for the unemployed. When the strike was over both sides claimed victory.

The queen's birthday honours list contained a knighthood for the senior federal vice-president of the Australian Labor Party, Sir John Egerton. Egerton, a trade-union leader from Queensland, was subsequently the object of an attack that was designed to force his resignation from the Labor Party for accepting a knighthood from "the tainted hands of Sir John Kerr and Mr. Fraser."

Fraser's "new federalism" policy faced attacks by the three state Labor premiers, in New South Wales, Tasmania, and South Australia. Less expected was opposition from the Liberal-National Country Party premiers of Western Australia and Queensland, who criticized the government's policy on mineral development and uranium exports. Johannes Bjelke-Petersen, the Queensland premier, went so far as to say that the policy of Labor's former minister of minerals and energy, Reginald F. X. Connor, was still largely being implemented by the bureaucrats in Canberra, who ought to resign and let mineral development and exportation remain in the hands of those who knew what they wanted and were prepared to accomplish it.

The government decided to spend A$12 billion on defense over the next five years. Most of the money was to go to salaries, but the defense minister, D. James Killen, outlined the major new areas of equipment expenditure. These involved purchase of a replacement for Australia's front-line fighter aircraft, the Mirage, and the provision of a new class of patrol boats for the Navy.

Foreign Affairs. Relations with the Soviet Union, Japan, China, and East Timor were the focus of Australian foreign-policy makers in 1976. Fraser overshadowed the minister for foreign affairs, Andrew Peacock, with most of the definitive policy statements and initiatives coming from the prime minister.

In June Fraser made what he described as a realistic assessment of the state of the world. During a 52-minute speech he told Parliament that, while maintaining its own independence and national perspective and sovereignty, Australia would make sure that the ANZUS treaty between Australia, New Zealand, and the United States did not fall into disrepair and disrepute. Although acknowledging that the Soviet Union was unquestionably committed to the avoidance of nuclear war, Fraser said that its actions were all too often inconsistent with the aim of reducing world tension. He said that Soviet leaders now had a strategic and political reach—a capacity to influence and even intervene—well beyond the periphery of the established zones of security interest. He added that they had demonstrated the will to exploit that capacity wherever the opportunity offered.

Détente, said Fraser, meant not only the search for security from nuclear war but a general overall relaxation of military and political tensions. However, in the past decade the Soviet Union had expanded its armed forces by a million men, and the size of the Soviet Navy had grown while that of the U.S. had declined. The U.S., concluded Fraser, was the only power that could balance the might of the Soviet Union, and hence Australia supported the development of U.S. "logistic facilities" at Diego Garcia so that

COURTESY, AUSTRALIAN INFORMATION SERVICE

A drilling platform being towed to Australia's Bass Strait oil fields, 50 miles off the southeastern coast of Victoria.

AUSTRALIA

Education. (1975) Primary, pupils 1,819,358, teachers 78,390; secondary, vocational, and teacher training, pupils 1,099,922, teachers 74,041; higher (1972), students 175,732, teaching staff 19,920.

Finance. Monetary unit: Australian dollar, with (Sept. 20, 1976) a free rate of A$0.80 to U.S. $1 (A$1.38 = £1 sterling). Gold, SDR's, and foreign exchange (June 1976) U.S. $2,992,000,000. Budget (1975–76 est.) balanced at A$21,915,000,000. Gross national product (1974–75) A$58,420,000,000. Money supply (March 1976) A$9,994,000,000. Cost of living (1970 = 100; Jan.–March 1976) 177.

Foreign Trade. (1975) Imports A$8,491,200,000; exports A$9,052,300,000. Import sources: U.S. 20%; Japan 18%; U.K. 15%; West Germany 7%. Export destinations: Japan 29%; U.S. 10%; New Zealand 5%; U.K. 5%. Main exports: wheat 12%; wool 9%; coal 8%; iron ore 8%.

Transport and Communications. Roads (1972) 863,897 km (including 208,198 km paved roads). Motor vehicles in use (1974): passenger 4,769,200; commercial (including buses) 1,130,800. Railways: (government; 1974) 40,406 km; freight traffic (1974–75) 29,000,000,000 net ton-km. Air traffic (1975): 17,770,000,000 passenger-km; freight 362,573,000 net ton-km. Shipping (1975): merchant vessels 100 gross tons and over 419; gross tonnage 1,205,248. Shipping traffic (1975): goods loaded 158,043,000 metric tons, unloaded 23,737,000 metric tons. Telephones (June 1974) 5 million. Radio licenses (June 1974) 2,851,000. Television licenses (June 1974) 3,022,000.

Agriculture. Production (in 000; metric tons; 1975): wheat 11,700; barley 2,965; oats 1,200; corn 139; rice 386; potatoes 699; sugar, raw value 2,933; tomatoes *c.* 180; apples (1974) 340; oranges (1974) *c.* 320; wine (1974) *c.* 202; wool, clean 449; milk 6,650; butter 161; beef and veal 1,507; mutton and lamb 525. Livestock (in 000; March 1975): sheep 153,070; cattle 33,066; pigs 2,273; horses (1974) *c.* 446; chickens *c.* 44,000.

Industry. Fuel and power (in 000; metric tons; 1975): coal 67,094; lignite 28,180; crude oil 20,160; natural gas (cu m) 5,028,000; manufactured gas (including some natural gas; cu m) 9,500,000; electricity (kw-hr) 74,117,000. Production (in 000; metric tons; 1975): iron ore (65% metal content) 97,674; bauxite 21,010; pig iron 7,476; crude steel 7,845; aluminum 214; copper 162; lead (1974–75) 170; tin 5.3; zinc 193; nickel concentrates (metal content; 1973–74) 42; sulfuric acid 1,151; cement 5,017; newsprint 202; cotton yarn 25; wool yarn 20; gold (troy oz; 1973–74) 523; silver (troy oz; 1973–74) 22,231; passenger cars (including assembly; units) 351. Dwelling units completed (1975) 131,000.

the balance necessary to stability in the Indian Ocean could be maintained.

In a departure from traditional conservative policy, Fraser sought to find common ground with the government of China, starting from the premise that China was bound to be concerned by the new Soviet role on China's northern and southern frontiers. Both the prime minister and the foreign minister visited China, and it became apparent that the Soviet Union was displeased by Fraser's attack on its foreign policy.

Fraser, like Whitlam before him, visited Japan on the way to China. In Japan he held talks with the Japanese prime minister, Takeo Miki, and with other senior members of the Japanese government, besides consulting leading members of the Japanese business community. The talks in Japan, noted Fraser, were in the firm tradition of regular consultation and were the result of Australia's strong trade ties with Japan. Strengthening and deepening the bonds between Australia and Japan were among the government's foremost foreign policy objectives, said Fraser, and accordingly, on June 16, both national leaders signed a Basic Treaty of Friendship and Cooperation. Japan was Australia's major trading partner in 1976, and Australia was second only to the U.S. as an importer of Japanese goods.

The visit to China afforded Fraser his first opportunity to meet senior Chinese leaders and to discuss with them matters of mutual interest. These included the Soviet military buildup, and the Soviets obviously expected to hear more attacks on their policies from Fraser when he was in Peking. On June 20 Soviet and other Eastern-bloc diplomatic representatives in Peking boycotted the Chinese welcome of Fraser. They were absent from the diplomatic reception at the airport and the banquet in the Great Hall of the People. The Chinese premier, Hua Kuo-feng, delighted at finding an unexpected ally, took the opportunity to abuse the absent Soviets. The Australian prime minister made a more moderate speech and afterward described the Soviet snub as "fruitless, puzzling, and slightly childish."

Relations with Indonesia proved difficult. In February 1976, in his first speech as foreign minister, Peacock made it clear that Australia did not condone the use of force by Indonesia and also stressed that Australia had carefully avoided favouring any of the parties in the formerly Portuguese territory of East Timor or endorsing their claims. The government believed that there ought to be a cessation of hostilities, a resumption of international humanitarian aid, preferably through the return to East Timor of the Red Cross, a withdrawal of Indonesian forces, and a genuine act of self-determination. The East Timor question remained in the news when the Australian Journalists' Association pressed the government for action following the deaths of five newsmen who had been killed while covering the fighting in East Timor the previous year. The government pressed publicly, privately, and on a government-to-government basis for Indonesian cooperation in clearing up the circumstances surrounding the deaths, but the conflicting accounts were never satisfactorily explained.

For the dispute with Papua New Guinea over the Torres Strait Islands Boigu, Dauan, and Saibai, *see* COMMONWEALTH OF NATIONS.

The Economy. The problems of inflation, unemployment, and balance of payments were exacerbated by drought conditions and low prices for Australia's primary products during 1976. The government's strategy of cutting back on government expenditure and trying to focus its hopes for economic recovery on the private sector did not seem to be noticeably effective. Unemployment reached record heights. Seasonally adjusted figures showed that the unemployed numbered 315,257 in July, or 6.2% of the

Bulk cargoes will be carried in this freighter being built in Australia's state shipyards at Newcastle, New South Wales.

DAVID AUSTEN—KEYSTONE

work force. Treasurer Lynch attributed the increase to the continued push for pay rises led by the left-wing unions. The ACTU president, Robert J. Hawke, retorted that any independent economist would be able to demonstrate that what was lacking was an increase in consumer expenditure. For months the government resisted devaluation as a solution for falling exports on the ground that it was likely to worsen inflation and so increase unemployment, but on November 28, with official reserves at the lowest level since mid-1971, Lynch announced that as of the following day the Australian dollar would be devalued by 17½%.

Australia's largest company, Broken Hill Proprietary Co. Ltd., announced in August that it was buying into a huge gas and oil project in Western Australia. BHP bought into the A$2 billion northwest shelf development by purchasing the shares of the U.K.-based Burmah group for A$68.5 million.

The minister for primary industry, Ian Sinclair, tried to raise the incomes of Australia's drought-affected farmers in July 1976 by announcing a planned increase of 14% in wool prices, to be phased in over the next two years. The minimum price for 21-micron wool in the 1976–77 selling season was to be set at 275 (Australian) cents per kilogram, as compared with 250 cents for the 1975–76 season.

The government tried to use the Conciliation and Arbitration Commission in its fight against wage increases as a cause of inflation, and in this respect the tactic was successful. In 1975 the trade unions had agreed to moderate their wage demands if the commission would permit quarterly wage increases in line with the cost of living. The commission's decision for the first quarter of 1976 favoured the unions (*see* below), but in the next two it granted less than the increase in the consumer price index. In the third judgment it delivered an attack on the trade unions that culminated in a threat to abandon the degree of wage indexation so far achieved if the unions did not moderate their extra-court demands. For the unions, ACTU president Hawke said that the commission could have one more chance to deliver the goods, for if full cost-of-living indexation was not granted in the last quarter of 1976, the unions would also abandon their wage demand truce.

The specifics were as follows. In the first quarter of 1976, Fraser's government opposed the automatic 6.8% wage increase due to Australian salary and wage earners as a result of increases in the consumer price index. However, the Conciliation and Arbitration Commission ruled that the government had not made a sufficiently good case and awarded the maximum amount under the guidelines, as the trade unions and the Labor state governments had requested. In the second quarter the government's submission was successful, and the Arbitration Commission introduced plateau indexation. This involved payment of the appropriate percentage wage increases to the average wage and a flat rate of A$3.50 a week to all persons earning more than the average. In the third quarter the president of the Arbitration Commission, Sir John Moore, said that the commission believed that the Australian economy was still suffering from two evil influences: the unacceptably high level of inflation and the unacceptably high level of unemployment. The commission's bench therefore decided to proceed cautiously in order to avoid, if possible, any action that might prolong the hardship to which a large section of the community had been exposed.

WIDE WORLD

Margaret Thatcher, Britain's Conservative Party leader, tries her hand at drilling during a visit to the Broken Hill North Mine near Sydney.

Since the consumer price index increased by 2.5% in the June quarter, the ACTU, the Council of Government Employee Organizations, and the Australian Council of Salaried and Professional Associations asked the bench to increase all award wages and salaries by that amount. However, the bench decided to increase only the lowest wage in the metal industry, A$98 a week, by 2.5% and to increase wages and salaries of over A$166 a week by 1.5%. Wages between A$98 and A$166 a week were raised a flat A$2.50. Indexation was frail, warned the bench, and it was essential for each union member to evaluate the effect any stoppage, ban, or limitation might have on the viability of full indexation in any quarter.

The Fraser government introduced its first budget on August 17. It contained very few changes, apart from staff ceiling reductions in the Commonwealth Public Service and Statutory Bodies. The chief feature of the budget was the new taxation concessions for mining and petroleum exploration companies. Petroleum exploration expenditure was made tax-deductible against income from any source. The first stage of company tax indexation was implemented by allowing companies to adjust the value of their inventories to offset the effect of inflation, and tax concessions to businessmen were introduced. The budget provided for outlays of A$24,321,000,000 in 1976–77, an increase of 11.3% over the previous year, and predicted a deficit of A$1,879,000,000.

The budget's effect was diminished by the controversy that sprang up almost immediately afterward over the government's decision to allow the Australian National Line to buy four new ships worth A$40 million from Japanese shipyards. These contracts were at the expense of Australian shipwrights at Newcastle and Whyalla, and the resulting unemployment was only one criticism of the government's policy. The Labor spokesman on the subject, Mich Young, pointed out that to reduce the national capacity to construct ships would have strategic implications that were especially important considering Australia's vulnerable seacoast, and the labour movement said that any such ships built in Japan would be blacklisted at Australian ports. (A. R. G. GRIFFITHS)

See also Dependent States.

[977.B.2]

AUSTRALIA'S NEW POLITICAL BALANCE

By Geoffrey Sawer

One of the most extraordinary events in Australia's political history occurred on Nov. 11, 1975. A prime minister with a parliamentary majority was sacked by the queen's governor-general. Parliament was dissolved and a general election called. The outgoing prime minister, Gough Whitlam, declared bitterly: "Well may we say God save the Queen, because nothing will save the governor-general."

As it turned out, nothing could save Gough Whitlam. Australians voted overwhelmingly for his opponent in the election a month later. What had appeared to be a constitutional crisis turned out to be only a crisis for Whitlam's Australian Labor Party (ALP). The opposing coalition of the Liberal and National Country parties (LCP) won majorities of 55 seats in the House of Representatives and 6 in the Senate. This was the first Commonwealth government since 1961 with a clear and probably accident-proof majority of direct supporters in both houses.

Fraser's Strategy. The challenge to the ALP had been developing throughout 1975. It reached a crisis in October when the opposition leader, Malcolm Fraser of the LCP, announced his decision to block the passage of budget appropriation bills in the Senate in order to force Whitlam to call a general election. The LCP had acquired a bare majority in the upper house by the death of a Labor senator.

The action was technically legal, but there was some dispute as to its political morality. Australia's written constitution requires that money bills be approved by both houses of Parliament. This enables an opposition majority in the Senate to block a money bill even though it has been approved by a government majority in the House of Representatives. Hitherto no Senate majority had taken advantage of this constitutional device. The LCP leadership justified its action by charging that the Labor government had conducted its affairs so badly that it had no right to govern.

Fraser's strategy was based on an observed swing away from Labor in the preceding year. Even though Labor had a majority in the lower house, it was clear from by-elections for parliamentary vacancies, from state elections, and from opinion polls that public support had been swinging toward the Liberal and National Country parties. The smashing Labor defeat on Dec. 13, 1975, was the outcome of this trend.

The Labor Party had gone to the country on the constitutional issue. It argued that the government should not have been dismissed for failure to secure supply when it had funds enough for another two weeks. Furthermore, it declared, the governor-general was not justified in dismissing ministers who had the confidence of the lower house and had not done anything illegal. But the ALP did not succeed in making this the chief issue in the election. Instead, the LCP coalition kept the public's attention focused on economic problems. It blamed the Whitlam government for the fact that inflation had increased from a rate of 3% in 1972 to 17% in 1975, while unemployment had risen from 2% of the labour force to 5%.

Geoffrey Sawer, professor emeritus of the faculty of law, Australian National University, is the author of Law in Society *(1965) and* Modern Federalism *(2nd ed. 1976).*

Moderate Conservatism. How did the new government interpret its mandate? Prime Minister Fraser set forth a policy of moderate conservatism. It aimed first and foremost to reduce the rate of inflation. The Whitlam government had made moves in this direction, but the Fraser government pressed the fight on inflation so strongly that it became, in effect, a new policy. Promises were made to retain many innovations of the former administration, such as the Medibank system under which the government pays doctors and pharmacists, higher pensions indexed to the cost of living, programs for the advancement of the Aboriginals, and subsidies for education. But the overriding commitment was to economy and to a reversal of the trend of the previous government toward expanding the public sector at the expense of the private sector. Recognizing that this would take time, the prime minister did not promise any sudden turnaround. He did undertake to reduce taxes and to adjust income tax rates to the price level so that inflation would not keep on moving taxpayers into higher tax brackets. There was to be some tax relief for business. He also promised to reduce the government deficit and to keep a lid on the money supply.

In practice, the Fraser government pursued deflation vigorously and even, in some respects, ruthlessly. It cut sharply into the number of civil service jobs. It also cut back on welfare and employment projects for Aboriginals, on grounds of waste and inefficiency.

The "New Federalism." On another front, the Fraser regime attempted a radical departure from the policy of the Whitlam government. Since 1942 there had been a trend under governments of all parties toward lodging more power in the federal government at the expense of the states. This came about largely through an increase in federal authority in fiscal matters. To the monopoly of customs and excise duties given it under the constitution, the federal government had added powers of borrowing by a constitutional amendment of 1928. In 1942 a deft use of wartime financial powers had enabled the federal government to force the states from the field of income taxation, and this monopoly had been upheld by a High Court decision in 1957. The Whitlam Labor government had been committed to extending federal powers still further, largely by making conditional grants of funds to the states for specific programs that were subject to federal supervision.

Outgoing leader: Gough Whitlam (left), dismissed as Australia's prime minister on Nov. 11, 1975, watches as the official secretary to the governor-general reads the proclamation dissolving Parliament.

COURTESY, AUSTRALIAN INFORMATION SERVICE

COURTESY, AUSTRALIAN INFORMATION SERVICE

Incoming leader: Malcolm Fraser (centre) succeeded Whitlam as Australia's prime minister. It was a triumph for his aggressive leadership of the conservative opposition in Parliament.

The program of the Fraser government, announced in June, was to give the states more taxing authority and more discretion in the use of the funds. There was no suggestion of simply handing back to them the income tax powers they had enjoyed before 1942. They were to be given a fixed proportion of all income tax revenue, and were to be allowed to impose personal income taxes in addition to the federal tax—or to give their residents a rebate on the federal income tax out of their own state treasuries, within limits permitted by the federal government. The state governments, even those controlled by the LCP, were not enthusiastic about this scheme, though they were prepared to try it. Another element in the "New Federalism" was a reduction in the number of conditional grants to the states, either by converting them to unconditional grants or by phasing them out. The latter alternative was in line with the economy drive, and left the states with the responsibility of abandoning the programs or of finding the money to run them.

The antisocialist bent of the Fraser government expressed itself in many small ways, such as selling off some of the federal interests in business and industry acquired under Whitlam. However, the Whitlam government had not engaged in any considerable exercises in state socialism. The most striking reversal under Fraser was the decision to allow "private" (but mostly cooperative) health insurance funds to compete with the government-supported Medibank scheme; but even this underwent a change that allowed Medibank to offer a full range of types of cover instead of providing only for public-ward, salaried-doctor hospital treatment. In other respects, the Fraser government disappointed its more hard-line supporters. For example, it continued the Whitlam-created Prices Justification Tribunal set up to restrain (more by publicity than by direct legal intervention) price increases by big business. The Fraser government also retained a Pipelines Authority to provide a continent-wide distribution of natural gas (and oil, if enough is found). And though it modified the Whitlam-created restrictions on mining developments and the participation in them of foreign capital, nevertheless it kept the legal structure of restraint and used it to an extent that was much resented by the LCP premiers of Queensland and Western Australia, who wanted the federal government to get out of that sphere. The Fraser government even proposed to extend federal control over corporation law and the securities industry; this had been attempted but not achieved under Whitlam.

A key to the Fraser regime's outlook lay perhaps in the character of its leader. Fraser is a man of the country, son of a wealthy grazier. His policy had in it an element of 19th-century Disraeli-style conservatism with its distrust of urban capitalism. This was combined with the Australian Country Party's style of social radicalism, suspicious of finance capitalism in general and favourable to government intervention in behalf of the farmer and the pastoralist.

Foreign Policy. When it looked abroad, the Fraser government also saw things through its own eyes. It did not simply abandon the "nonaligned" stance, toward which Whitlam had worked, in favour of the blunt cold-war line of previous Liberal-Country regimes. Fraser journeyed to Peking in an effort to cultivate good relations with Mao's China, following the initiative taken by Whitlam in recognizing Peking and withdrawing recognition of Taiwan. He was less mellow with the U.S.S.R., however. Where Whitlam had played down the Soviet presence in the Indian Ocean and sought to keep out of great-power maneuverings, Fraser attacked Soviet expansionism as dramatized in the Indian Ocean competition between the great powers and supported the U.S. in its effort to develop a naval base at Diego Garcia. While supporting the ANZUS pact with the U.S. (as Whitlam had done), Fraser did not fear to embarrass his allies by criticizing "détente," at least as he considered it was being misused by the U.S.S.R. Thus, where Labor had sought friendly relations with Communist and third-world countries as part of a somewhat idealistic peace policy, Fraser, in a spirit of international *Realpolitik,* sought to manipulate the balance of power by exploiting differences between Communist and third-world countries. Nevertheless, in July he dispatched his deputy prime minister to Moscow in order to promote trade relations, uttering some soothing words to ease his reception.

An Early Appraisal. By September 1976 the Fraser government had achieved significant economies. It had reduced taxes while at the same time cutting the budget deficit to half what it had been a year earlier. The inflation rate had declined to 12 from 17%, with further improvement expected in coming months. Business profits had risen, and the balance of trade was in surplus. On the other hand, industrial production, sales, and business confidence remained relatively low; unemployment, after dipping, had increased again to nearly 5% of the work force and seemed likely to rise higher. The trade unions, led by the talented Robert Hawke, were marshaling their forces against the Fraser policies. Small groups of Labor supporters continued to engage in violent demonstrations against Governor-General Sir John Kerr to protest the way in which the Whitlam government had been removed from office. Some decline in the Fraser government's popularity could be seen in state elections and public opinion polls. In sum, the Fraser government's position was by no means impregnable. Its future depended partly on whether the economic front opened up and partly on its flexibility in devising new policies if the economic situation grew worse.

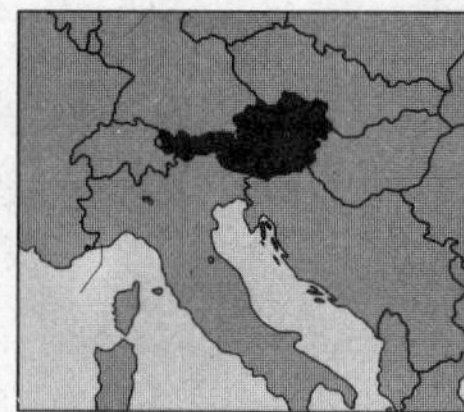

Austria

A republic of central Europe, Austria is bounded by West Germany, Czechoslovakia, Hungary, Yugoslavia, Italy, Switzerland, and Liechtenstein. Area: 32,380 sq mi (83,860 sq km). Pop. (1976 est.): 7,511,900. Cap. and largest city: Vienna (pop., 1975 est., 1,603,900). Language: German. Religion (1971): Roman Catholic 87%. President in 1976, Rudolf Kirchschläger; chancellor, Bruno Kreisky.

Austria's policy of active neutrality, particularly toward its neighbours, was evident in February 1976 when Kreisky visited Czechoslovakia and agreement was reached on relaxation of cross-frontier travel formalities, economic cooperation, and cultural exchanges. Relations with Yugoslavia developed less satisfactorily. Despite a successful meeting between Kreisky and President Tito early in the year, incidents during succeeding months brought exchanges of official notes over the question of rights for Austria's minorities and a vigorous campaign against Austria in the Yugoslav press. The immediate occasion for this was the Austrian Parliament's unanimous approval in July of a law designed to protect minority groups and providing for a special census to determine the number of persons speaking Slovene and other minority languages. This, according to Austria's viewpoint, would comply with paragraph 7 of the Austrian state treaty and provide a lasting solution of the minorities question. The minority leaders, however, labeled the legislation a tool of German national extremism. Both before and during the census, demonstrations and acts of violence took place in southern Carinthia.

In March Kreisky led a delegation of the Socialist International on a fact-finding mission to the Middle East, following which he supported proposals that the Palestine Liberation Organization (PLO) be recognized as sole representative of the Palestinians. However, negotiations over the establishment of a PLO international bureau in Vienna came to nothing. In May, on Kreisky's initiative, a first conference of European and Latin-American Social Democratic party leaders was held in Caracas, Venezuela, at which suggestions for a new "Marshall Plan" to aid less developed countries were discussed.

Following the terrorist attack in December 1975 on the Viennese headquarters of the Organization of Petroleum Exporting Countries, when OPEC ministers attending a meeting were taken hostage and later released in Algeria, it was expected that the headquarters would be removed to another country. This did not occur, however, and OPEC acquired other premises in Vienna.

In the fall of 1975 Austria had entered its worst recession since the end of World War II, with falling production, investment, and exports, rising unemployment, and introduction of short-time working. However, thanks to an undiminished level of tourism and expansionary measures in the public sector, the slump was shallower and of shorter duration than in other industrial countries, and the Austrian economy was one of the first to show an upward swing early in 1976. An austerity budget for 1977, following the deficit-spending budgets of 1975–76 and proposing higher taxes, increased charges by public undertakings, and withdrawal of subsidies, would call for sacrifices by Austrians, but public reaction was confined to a demonstration in July by Carinthian farmers.

In October 1976 the retirement of three ministers brought the following changes in Chancellor Bruno Kreisky's Cabinet: Hannes Androsch succeeded Rudolf Häuser as vice-chancellor, while retaining his post of finance minister; Willibald Pahr succeeded Erich Bielka as foreign minister; Günther Haiden succeeded Oskar Weihs as minister of agriculture and forestry; Gerhard Weissenberg succeeded Rudolf Häuser as minister of social welfare; and Albin Schober followed Haiden as undersecretary of state for agriculture and forestry.

On August 1 Vienna's Imperial Bridge, built in 1936, collapsed into the Danube, killing at least one person and causing prolonged blockage of river and road traffic and damage estimated at 1 billion schillings. Personnel and administrative changes in city government followed, with a view to lessening the likelihood of similar catastrophes in the future.

In February the Tirolean capital, Innsbruck, was host to the XII Winter Olympic Games, attended by competitors from 37 nations and by 60,000 spectators; security arrangements were handled by a police force of 2,500. (*See* WINTER SPORTS: *Special Report.*) (ELFRIEDE DIRNBACHER)

[972.B.2.a]

AUSTRIA

Education. (1973–74) Primary (grades 1–4 only), pupils 540,732; secondary, pupils 607,033; primary and secondary, teachers 61,093; vocational, pupils 261,981, teachers 14,006; teacher training, students 5,445, teachers 511; higher (including 4 main universities), students 84,349, teaching staff (excluding teachers' colleges) 10,607.

Finance. Monetary unit: schilling, with (Sept. 20, 1976) a free rate of 17.53 schillings to U.S. $1 (30.20 schillings = £1 sterling). Gold, SDR's, and foreign exchange (June 1976) U.S. $4,027,000,000. Budget (1975 est.): revenue 168.1 billion schillings; expenditure 184.4 billion schillings. Gross national product (1974) 616.8 billion schillings. Money supply (Feb. 1976) 126,480,000,000 schillings. Cost of living (1970 = 100; June 1976) 153.

Foreign Trade. (1975) Imports 163,340,000,000 schillings; exports 130,870,000,000 schillings. Import sources: EEC 62% (West Germany 40%, Italy 8%); Switzerland 7%. Export destinations: EEC 44% (West Germany 22%, Italy 8%, U.K. 6%); Switzerland 8%; Yugoslavia 5%. Main exports: machinery 22%; iron and steel 15%; textile yarns and fabrics 11%; paper and board 7%; timber 5%; chemicals 9%. Tourism (1974): visitors 10,886,000; gross receipts U.S. $2,289,000,000.

Transport and Communications. Roads (1974) 102,692 km (including 651 km expressways). Motor vehicles in use (1974): passenger 1,636,000: commercial 152,000. Railways (1974): state 5,864 km, private 636 km.; traffic 6,790,000,000 passenger-km, freight 11,237,000,000 net ton-km. Air traffic (1975): 677.5 million passenger-km; freight 8,168,000 net ton-km. Navigable inland waterways in regular use (1974) 358 km. Telephones (Dec. 1974) 1,987,000. Radio licenses (Dec. 1974) 2,151,000. Television licenses (Dec. 1974) 1,770,000.

Agriculture. Production (in 000; metric tons; 1975): wheat *c.* 945; barley 1,006; rye 347; oats 306; corn 981; potatoes 1,579; sugar, raw value *c.* 500; apples (1974) *c.* 287; wine (1974) 240; meat *c.* 546; timber (cu m; 1974) 11,656. Livestock (in 000; Dec. 1974): cattle 2,581; sheep 154; pigs 3,517; chickens 12,250.

Industry. Fuel and power (in 000; metric tons; 1975): lignite 3,380; crude oil 2,037; natural gas (cu m) 2,359,000; electricity (kw-hr) 35,207,000 (67% hydroelectric in 1974); manufactured gas (cu m) 1,225,000. Production (in 000; metric tons; 1975): iron ore (30% metal content) 3,883; pig iron 3,056; crude steel 4,503; magnesite (1974) 1,449; aluminum 117; copper 27; lead 10; zinc 16; cement 5,678; paper (1974) 1,414; fertilizers (nutrient content; 1974–75) nitrogenous 226, phosphate 156; cotton yarn 16; woven cotton fabric 14; rayon, etc., filaments and fibres (1974) 103.

Automobile Industry:
see Industrial Review; Transportation

Automobile Racing:
see Motor Sports

Aviation:
see Defense; Transportation

Backgammon:
see Board Games

Badminton:
see Racket Games

Bahamas, The

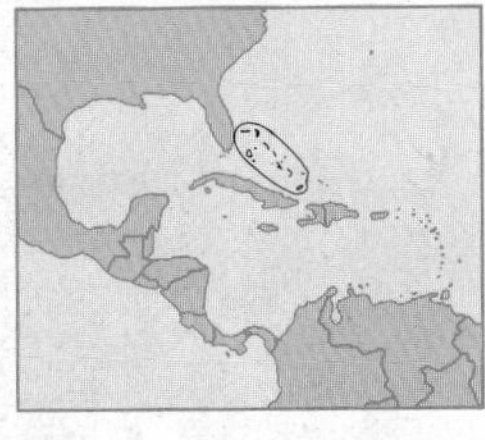

A member of the Commonwealth of Nations, The Bahamas comprise an archipelago of about 700 islands in the North Atlantic Ocean just southeast of the United States. Area: 5,382 sq mi (13,939 sq km). Pop. (1976 est.): 208,000. Cap. and largest city: Nassau (urban area pop., 1970, 101,500). Language: English (official). Religion (1970): Baptist 28.8%; Anglican 22.7%; Roman Catholic 22.5%; Methodist 7.3%; Saints of God and Church of God 6%; others and no religion 12.7%. Queen, Elizabeth II; governor-general in 1976, Sir Milo B. Butler; prime minister, Lynden O. Pindling.

In 1976 the term widely current in The Bahamas was "stability," not "destabilization" as elsewhere in the Caribbean. The political scene was calm, and the economy had survived the worldwide recession well. Inflation was down from double figures to 4.03% by midyear, and the internal monetary assets rose from B$211.2 million in 1974 to B$237.2 million at the end of 1975.

The bahamianization program—aimed at giving Bahamians 60% ownership of businesses in the country—showed progress, particularly at staffing levels in the tourism and banking sectors. In October 1975 Prime Minister Pindling had announced the government's intention to achieve economic independence within the next ten years. A part of the program was the introduction in early 1976 of taxes on non-Bahamian-owned companies to raise an additional B$10 million revenue. Of principal concern were the quadrupling of annual registration fees for non-Bahamian companies to B$1,000 and an increase in annual immigration permits for key financial personnel from B$500 to between B$3,000 and B$5,000. Despite initial concern about the effect these measures would have on The Bahamas' competitive position as an offshore financial centre, only limited repercussions were reported by mid-1976. On the debit side, unemployment rose from 8.6% in 1973 to 21.2% in 1975.

The first American to be executed in The Bahamas in 15 years, Michaiah Shobek of Milwaukee, Wis., was hanged in October for the murder of a U.S. tourist.

(SHEILA PATTERSON)

[974.B.2.d]

BAHAMAS, THE

Education. (1975–76) Primary, pupils 34,941, teachers 549; secondary, pupils 25,069, teachers 565; vocational (1971–72), pupils 427, teachers 60; teacher training, students 534, teachers 32; higher (at universities overseas; 1973–74), students 690.

Finance and Trade. Monetary unit: Bahamian dollar, with (Sept. 20, 1976) an official rate of B$1 to U.S. $1 (B$1.72 = £1 sterling). Budget (1975 est.): revenue B$134 million; expenditure B$131 million. Cost of living (1970 = 100; April 1976) 152. Foreign trade (1975): imports B$1,565,600,000; exports B$3,415,900,000. Import sources (1974): Saudi Arabia 26%; Nigeria 17%; Iran 15%; U.S. 12%; Libya 8%; Gabon 5%. Export destinations: U.S. 83%; Puerto Rico 8%. Main exports (1974): petroleum products 65%; crude oil 26%. Tourism (1974): visitors 1,316,000; gross receipts U.S. $328 million.

Transport and Communications. Shipping (1975): merchant vessels 100 gross tons and over 119; gross tonnage 189,890. Telephones (Dec. 1974) 55,000. Radio receivers (Dec. 1973) 85,000. Television receivers (Dec. 1964) *c.* 4,500.

Bahrain

An independent monarchy (emirate), Bahrain consists of a group of islands in the Persian Gulf, lying between the Qatar Peninsula and Saudi Arabia. Total area: 256 sq mi (662 sq km). Pop. (1976 est.): 256,600. Cap.: Manama (pop., 1976 est., 105,400). Language: Arabic (official), Persian. Religion (1971): Muslim 95.7%; Christian 3%; others 1.3%. Emir in 1976, Isa ibn Sulman al-Khalifah; prime minister, Khalifah ibn Sulman al-Khalifah.

Bahrain continued to prosper as a business and communications centre for the Gulf area. In January 1976 the Bahraini dinar was made interchangeable with the United Arab Emirates (U.A.E.) currency. A project was launched during the year to join Bahrain to the Saudi mainland by way of a $300 million causeway to be financed by Saudi Arabia. On January 21 the Concorde supersonic airliner made its first regular commercial flight to Bahrain. Two French companies were given contracts to enlarge the severely congested port of Mina Sulman.

BAHRAIN

Education. (1974–75) Primary, pupils 43,409; secondary, pupils 15,949; primary and secondary, teachers 2,808; vocational, pupils 1,599, teachers 70; higher, students 689, teaching staff 67.

Finance and Trade. Monetary unit: Bahrain dinar, with (Sept. 20, 1976) an official rate of 0.39 dinar to U.S. $1 (free rate of 0.68 dinar = £1 sterling). Budget (1975–76 est.) balanced at 134,240,000 dinars. Foreign trade (1975): imports U.S. $1,189,400,000; exports U.S. $1,107,000,000. Import sources: Saudi Arabia 52%; U.K. 9%; U.S. 8%; Japan 6%. Export destinations: U.S. 23%; Japan 15%; Australia 9%; Saudi Arabia 7%; Singapore 7%; United Arab Emirates 5%. Main exports: petroleum products 81%; aluminum (1974) 7%.

Industry. Production (in 000; metric tons): crude oil (1975) 3,065; petroleum products (1974) 12,213.

In February a record budget for 1976 was announced; revenues, at $464 million, were 35% above 1975, and expenditure was up 47% to $487 million. A ruler's decree established a Bahrain National Oil Co. (Banaco) with capital of $250 million. Banaco took over the government's 60% share in the Bahrain

British Airways now flies its supersonic Concorde to Bahrain, covering the 3,500 miles from London in less than four hours.

ALAIN NOGUES—SYGMA

Petroleum Co. (Bapco), but the 40% share in Bapco owned by Caltex Petroleum Corp. of the U.S. and its ownership of the refinery near Awali were not immediately affected. Inflation caused some social discontent. Strikes for higher wages and against restrictions on trade unionism, as well as hunger strikes by political prisoners detained since the dissolution of the National Assembly in August 1975, were reported from non-Bahraini sources. (PETER MANSFIELD)

[978.B.4.b]

Bangladesh

An independent republic and member of the Commonwealth of Nations, Bangladesh is bordered by India on the west, north, and east, by Burma in the southeast, and by the Bay of Bengal in the south. Area: 55,126 sq mi (142,776 sq km). Pop. (1974 est.): 74,990,800. Cap. and largest city: Dacca (pop., 1974, 1,311,000). Language: Bengali. Religion: Muslim 80%, with Hindu, Christian, and Buddhist minorities. President in 1976, Abu Sadat Mohammed Sayem.

A hopeful turn in the economy of Bangladesh in 1976 enabled the martial law regime to set the country on a path of comparative peace after the turmoil of three coups and countercoups. The 1975–76 crop year brought a record harvest; public order improved; better administrative arrangements were set up; and a divided Army was stabilized. Nonetheless, the country's strong man and deputy chief martial law administrator, Maj. Gen. Ziaur Rahman, stated in June that what had been achieved was modest in comparison with the challenges the country faced.

BANGLADESH

Education. (1973–74) Primary, pupils 7,750,000, teachers 155,023; secondary, pupils 1,955,200, teachers 80,500; vocational, pupils 1,663, teachers 331; teacher training (1972–73), students 6,700, teachers 580; higher (1972–73), students 28,613, teaching staff 1,568.

Finance. Monetary unit: taka, with (Sept. 20, 1976) a free rate of 15.50 taka to U.S. $1 (official rate of 26.70 taka = £1 sterling). Gold, SDR's, and foreign exchange (June 1976) U.S. $213 million. Budget (1974–75 est.): revenue 5,594,000,000 taka; expenditure 4,702,000,000 taka (development budget 5,250,000,000 taka). Money supply (April 1976) 8,887,000,000 taka. Cost of living (Dacca; government employees; 1970 = 100; May 1976) 249.

Foreign Trade. (1975) Imports 15,627,000,000 taka; exports 3,688,000,000 taka. Import sources (1974): U.S. 24%; Australia 9%; Japan 7%; India 7%; West Germany 7%; Canada 6%. Export destinations (1974): U.S. 20%; U.K. 9%; India 8%; Australia 5%. Main exports: jute products 60%; jute 21%.

Transport and Communications. Roads (1973) c. 24,000 km (excluding c. 150,000 km dirt roads). Motor vehicles in use (1972): passenger 31,700; commercial (including buses) 24,800. Railways: (1974) 2,874 km; traffic (1973–74) 3,331,000,000 passenger-km, freight 639 million net ton-km. Navigable waterways (1974) c. 8,000 km. Shipping (1975): merchant vessels 100 gross tons and over 120; gross tonnage 133,016. Shipping traffic (1971–72): goods loaded 1,023,000 metric tons, unloaded 5,759,000 metric tons. Telephones (Dec. 1972) 48,000. Radio licenses (March 1969) 531,000.

Agriculture. Production (in 000; metric tons; 1975): rice c. 18,500; potatoes 880; sweet potatoes (1974) 637; onions c. 157; mangoes (1974) 301; bananas (1974) c. 622; tea 29; tobacco 41; jute c. 791; meat c. 250; timber (cu m; 1974) c. 16,821; fish catch (1974) 247. Livestock (in 000; 1975): cattle c. 27,418; buffalo (1974) c. 674; sheep c. 753; goats (1974) c. 11,938; chickens c. 30,477.

Industry. Production (in 000; metric tons; 1973–74): salt c. 170; crude steel 73; cement (1975) 102; petroleum products (1974) c. 454; nitrogenous fertilizers (nutrient content; 1974–75) 33; jute fabrics 508; cotton yarn 41; paper 52; electricity (kw-hr; 1975) 1,352,000.

Balance of Payments: *see* Economy, World

Ballet: *see* Dance

Ballooning: *see* Aerial Sports

Banking: *see* Economy, World

Baptist Churches: *see* Religion

WIDE WORLD

Maulana Bhashani leads Bangladesh's National Awami Party. Here he addresses marchers protesting an Indian dam on the Ganges River.

The most significant achievement was in the agricultural sector, which accounted for 55% of the gross domestic product and 80% of employment, as well as providing the basis for the country's one sizable industry, jute. Farm production rose by 16%, and the 1975 crop of paddy rice, which accounted for 75 to 80% of the cultivated area, was excellent. The government forecast total food production of 13.1 million tons in 1976, including both rice and wheat. On September 6 it was announced that 29 nationalized tea plantations would return to private ownership.

In industry, two major problems in the past had been overmanning of units as a result of trade-union pressure and scarcity of imported spare parts and equipment. The regime used its powers to cope with the unions and to deploy foreign exchange resources to meet the urgent needs of industry. Other hopeful economic signs included containment of inflation, a decline of 10% in the general price index, and satisfactory revenue collections.

On July 29 the government issued an ordinance allowing political parties to hold indoor activities, to enable them to prepare policy documents for government approval. The country's four major political groupings were the Awami League, once led by Sheikh Mujibur Rahman; the National Awami Party of the pro-Peking octogenarian leader Maulana Bhashani; the moribund United People's Front; and a new party being formed by former president Khandakar Mushtaque Ahmed. It was not clear to what extent they would be allowed to function in the open. The elections scheduled for early 1977 were postponed indefinitely, and Ahmed was among the approximately 100 advocates of early elections arrested in December.

Foreign policy was directed toward improving relations with China and Pakistan; diplomatic relations were established with Pakistan in December 1975 and with China a month later. In October Dacca and Islamabad were linked by satellite communication. The regime's anti-Indian posture, a residue of India's support for Sheikh Mujib's government, was linked with the controversy over the Indian barrage constructed on the Ganges at Farakka to save Calcutta port from silt. Dacca's view was that the barrage might deprive Bangladesh of the Ganges waters. Talks in New Delhi in early September ended in deadlock.

(GOVINDAN UNNY)

[976.A.3.b]

Barbados

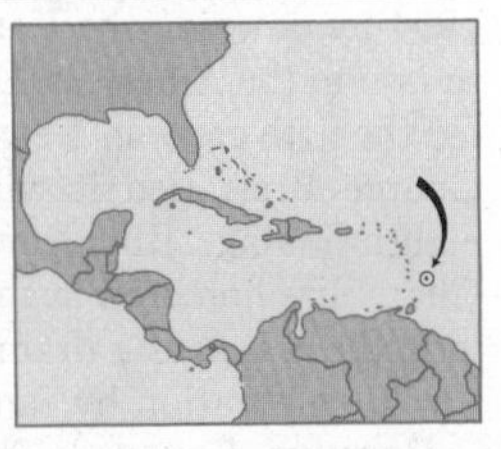

The parliamentary state of Barbados is a member of the Commonwealth of Nations and occupies the most easterly island in the southern Caribbean Sea. Area: 166 sq mi (430 sq km). Pop. (1975 est.): 251,200; 91% Negro, 4% white, 4% mixed. Cap. and largest city: Bridgetown (pop., 1970, 8,900). Language: English. Religion: Anglican 53%; Methodist 9%; Roman Catholic 4%; Moravian 2%; others 32%. Queen, Elizabeth II; governor-general in 1976, Sir Winston Scott until August 9; prime ministers, Errol Walton Barrow and, from September 3, J. M. G. Adams.

Barbados went to the polls on Sept. 2, 1976, and the Barbados Labour Party (BLP), led by 44-year-old J. M. G. (Tom) Adams, was returned to power for the first time since 1961 with 17 seats in the House of Assembly to 7 for the Democratic Labour Party of Errol Barrow. There was little ideological difference between the two parties, but the BLP was reportedly somewhat more to the right, less enthusiastic about links with Cuba, and less concerned about allegations of U.S. Central Intelligence Agency plots to "destabilize" Barbados and other governments in the region. Nevertheless, the uncovering of another such plot was announced on November 1. In late 1975 Cuban Airways flights had visited Barbados on their way to and from Angola, but after December 18 such flights were banned.

The sugar crop for 1976 was expected to yield between 110,000 and 115,000 metric tons, well in excess of the 1975 figure of 97,000 tons but with an estimated drop in price of about half. A new sugar levy introduced in November 1975 was expected to bring in Bar$30 million in 1976. Plans were announced in early 1976 to develop a small-hotel resort at Heywords, St. Peter, for lease to Barbadian nationals only.

The governor-general, Sir Winston Scott, died on August 9.

(SHEILA PATTERSON)

[974.B.2.d]

BARBADOS

Education. (1972–73) Primary, pupils 43,246, teachers 970; secondary, pupils 24,640, teachers 1,020; vocational, pupils 497, teachers 55; higher, students 1,089, teaching staff 75.

Finance and Trade. Monetary unit: Barbados dollar, with (Sept. 20, 1976) an official rate of Bar$2 to U.S. $1 (free rate of Bar$3.45 = £1 sterling). Budget (1975–76 est.): revenue Bar$171 million; expenditure Bar$187 million. Cost of living (1970 = 100; May 1976) 242. Foreign trade (1975): imports Bar$437,440,000; exports Bar$217,090,000. Import sources (1974): U.K. 21%; U.S. 19%; Trinidad and Tobago 12%; Venezuela 10%; Canada 9%. Export destinations (1974): U.K. 26%; U.S. 16%; Windward Islands 7%; Trinidad and Tobago 6%; Canada 6%. Main exports: sugar 42%; clothing (1973) 10%; petroleum and products (1973) 9%; chemicals (1973) 7%. Tourism (1974): visitors 231,000; gross receipts U.S. $76 million.

Agriculture. Production (in 000; metric tons; 1974): sweet potatoes *c.* 7; corn *c.* 2; sugar, raw value *c.* 112.

Baseball

In a season that featured almost as much activity off the field as on, there remained one constant—the Cincinnati Reds. The "Big Red Machine," considered one of the finest teams ever assembled, captured its fourth pennant in seven years and then became the first National League franchise to achieve consecutive World Series championships since the New York Giants in 1921–22. Three other teams wrested division titles from 1975 incumbents; there emerged a new folk hero in Detroit; and the national pastime made considerable strides in the tender area of labour relations.

World Series. The Reds, who until 1975 had not won a World Series in 35 years, claimed their second in as many seasons by sweeping the New York Yankees in four straight games during the annual best-of-seven October event. The Reds triumphed 5–1 in the Series opener at Cincinnati on October 16. Don Gullett, a hard throwing left-hander, allowed five hits and one run for the Reds before being lifted in the eighth inning because of an ankle injury. By that time, Tony Pérez, a clutch-hitting, 34-year-old first baseman, had batted in three runs for the Reds before 54,826 spectators.

The second game, a rare Sunday night encounter, also was won by the Reds 4–3 on October 17. After leading 3–0, Cincinnati was tied 3–3 when the Yankees scored twice in the top of the seventh inning. The score remained that way until the bottom of the ninth when, with two outs, Cincinnati's Ken Griffey reached second base on a throwing error by New York shortstop Fred Stanley. Joe Morgan was intentionally walked, but then the redoubtable Pérez lined the game-winning single to left field off losing pitcher Catfish Hunter. At the game's end, the crowd of 54,816 was enduring temperatures of 39° F.

Joe Morgan of the Cincinnati Reds makes it to third base as teammate Ken Griffey (right) is caught in a rundown in the eighth inning of the third game of the 1976 World Series at Yankee Stadium.

WIDE WORLD

The Series shifted to New York's remodeled Yankee Stadium for the third game on Tuesday night, October 19. The results were the same, however. Cincinnati assumed a 3–0 advantage in games with a 6–2 conquest behind Pat Zachry, a 24-year-old right-hander, and Will McEnaney, left-handed star of the Reds' impressive bullpen. The Reds reached Yankee starter Dock Ellis for three runs in the second inning when Dan Driessen singled, stole second, and scored on George Foster's double. Two other runs scored on Johnny Bench's single, a force-out, a stolen base, and a single by shortstop Dave Concepción.

The fourth game of the Series, scheduled for October 20, was postponed until the next evening because of rain. But the reprieve was all too short for the Yankees, who were eliminated before a quiet home throng of 56,700 by a score of 7–2. Bench, Cincinnati's outstanding catcher, stroked a two-run homer and a three-run homer to clinch the award as most valuable player for the Series. He batted .533 in the four games.

"I'm glad that I could contribute something to this club after the bad season I had," said Bench, who batted only .234 during the regular schedule and was beset by shoulder problems.

"We have the best ball club in the game, and I think we proved it," said Cincinnati manager Sparky Anderson (*see* BIOGRAPHY).

The World Series was bereft of the drama that had highlighted the classic 1975 struggle between victorious Cincinnati and the Boston Red Sox. Indeed, most of the conversation concerning the 1976 Series dealt with the decision to play night games under such cold conditions. Baseball Commissioner Bowie Kuhn was criticized for acquiescing to the wishes of the network televising the Series (NBC), which gladly paid increased prices to gain prime-time scheduling. Had the Series gone the limit, four of the seven games would have been played under lights.

"By holding the World Series at night during the week," said Kuhn, "we are supplying a service to loyal fans around the country who wouldn't be able to watch during the days because they are working. Our audiences for night games stand to be twice as large. Had the weather been inclement because of cool temperatures, the games would have been postponed just as they would have been postponed because of rain."

Cincinnati Reds president Bob Howsam disagreed vigorously. "What about loyalty to the fans who have paid all season to come to the ball park?" he asked. "Asking them to watch our showcase event in this weather is a disgrace."

Yankee Stadium, where the final two games of the 1976 World Series were played, was refurbished by the city of New York at costs variously reported as being from $57 million to $100 million.

UPI COMPIX

The Reds reached the World Series by achieving another sweep, this in the best-of-five National League championship play-offs against the Philadelphia Phillies. The scores were 6–3, 6–2, and 7–6. In the last game, the Reds trailed 6–4 entering the bottom of the ninth inning, but won on homers by George Foster and Bench and a bases-loaded infield single by Griffey.

The Yankees had captured their first pennant since 1964 by downing the Kansas City Royals three games to two in the American League play-offs. The Yankees led the fifth game in New York 6–3 until Kansas City's George Brett tied it with a three-run homer in the eighth inning. But New York first baseman Chris Chambliss homered in the bottom of the ninth to provide the Yankees a dramatic 7–6 triumph that ignited a wild celebration by fans.

Regular Season. The Reds qualified for postseason competition by winning the West Division with ease; the second place Los Angeles Dodgers finished ten games in arrears. The Philadelphia Phillies, who had not won a pennant since 1950, enjoyed an excellent season. They won 101 games, one fewer than Cincinnati, and fended off a September rush by Pittsburgh to capture the National League East Division by nine games.

The Yankees' return to glory was attributed in large part to their manager, Billy Martin, a fiery competitor who had been a valuable second baseman during the team's pennant-winning years. Martin, who insisted that "my players play the game my way —aggressively," piloted New York to a 10½-game romp over runner-up Baltimore in the American League East Division. The best race in baseball was in the American League West, where the Royals halted the string of five straight division titles by the Oakland A's. The margin of victory was close; after trailing badly most of the summer, the A's charged to finish only 2½ games back.

If the division races lacked suspense, the vying for batting titles did not. Both league champions were crowned on the last day of the regular season. Third baseman Bill Madlock of the Chicago Cubs went 4-for-4 to collect his second straight title with a .339 average. Griffey finished at .336. The American League title was won by Brett with a .333 mark. His Kansas City teammate, Hal McRae, finished at .332, and Minnesota's Rod Carew, winner of five American League batting crowns, wound up at .331. Brett won the championship in his last time at bat with an inside-the-park home run.

Graig Nettles, New York Yankee third baseman, won the American League home run title with 32, while third baseman Mike Schmidt of Philadelphia stroked 38 to capture the National League crown. Baltimore Oriole Jim Palmer won 22 games to top American League pitchers; Boston's Luis Tiant won 21, and Baltimore's Wayne Garland 20. Randy Jones of the San Diego Padres led the National League with 22 wins; Jerry Koosman of the New York Mets and Don Sutton of the Los Angeles Dodgers each copped 21, while Steve Carlton of the Phillies and James Rodney Richard of the Houston Astros garnered 20.

But by far the most discussed pitcher and perhaps the most discussed baseball personality of the 1976 season was Mark ("The Bird") Fidrych (*see* BIOG-

UPI COMPIX

No, not leapfrog—Yankee second baseman Willie Randolph forces out Cincinnati's César Gerónimo and relays the ball to first during the third game of the World Series.

RAPHY) of the Detroit Tigers. A veritable unknown in spring training, the colourful right-hander started brilliantly, won 19 games for a fifth-place team, and attracted attention with his uninhibited and unorthodox antics. Fidrych was not averse to talking to the ball before he delivered it, kneeling down on the mound to landscape it, or running over to shake hands with a fielder after a good defensive play.

For the second straight year Joe Morgan of the Reds was voted the most valuable player in the National League, while Thurman Munson of the Yankees won the award in the American League. Rookie of the year honours went to Fidrych in the American League and, for the first time in the 30-year history of the award, to two men in the National League, Pat Zachry of the Reds and Butch Metzger of the Padres. All three of the rookies were pitchers. The Cy Young award for outstanding pitcher was given to Randy Jones of the Padres in the National League and, for a record-tying third time, to Jim Palmer of the Orioles in the American. Named as managers of the year were Whitey Herzog of the Kansas City Royals in the American League and Danny Ozark of the Philadelphia Phillies in the National.

The A's, as always, made news through their peripatetic owner, Charles O. Finley. Just before the trading deadline June 15, he shocked the baseball world by selling three of his superstars for $3.5 million. Vida Blue was sent to the New York Yankees for $1.5 million; the Boston Red Sox purchased Rollie Fingers and Joe Rudi for $1 million each. Kuhn later negated the sales because "they are not in the best interests of baseball."

Finley attempted to get something for the players, none of whom had signed Oakland contracts, before they achieved free-agent status at the season's end. At that time, the still unsigned Fingers and Rudi and about two dozen other players became eligible for the novel "reentry draft," wherein free agents were to be wooed by as many as 12 other clubs.

The "reentry" procedure was one of several parts of a new agreement reached in mid-July between owners and the Players Association. A stalemate in negotiations had caused a two-week delay in spring training until Kuhn ordered the camps to open on March 18. Both sides acclaimed the pact as a step toward coexistence, if not lasting peace. In November, 24 players entered the free-agent draft.

Latin America. Starting in October, a winter league season featuring numerous players from the U.S. major leagues took place in Puerto Rico, Mexico, the Dominican Republic, and Venezuela. In 1975 Hermosillo, champions of the nine-team Mexican Winter League, captured the Caribbean title over Bayamón, winners of the six-team Puerto Rican League; Aragua, victors in Venezuela; and Águilas, Cibaeñas, which triumphed in the four-team Dominican circuit. Hermosillo was paced by Bump Wills, son of former major league star Maury Wills.

(ROBERT WILLIAM VERDI)

Japan. The Hankyu Braves of Nishinomiya won the Japan Series, four games to three, over the Yomiuri Giants of Tokyo. This was the second consecutive Series victory for the Braves. After the first three games, the Braves led 3–0, but the Giants rolled back to win the next three. The Braves captured the final contest by a narrow margin, 4–2. The success of the Braves was due mainly to overall team play, in both batting and fielding.

During the regular season the Yomiuri Giants, who finished in the cellar in 1975, captured the 1976 Central League pennant. This was the team's 29th title since it was founded in 1934.

Much credit for the Giants' success was given to manager Shigeo Nagashima. Those who helped him included left fielder Isao Harimoto and first baseman Sadaharu Oh (*see* BIOGRAPHY), who hit effective home runs in many of the important games in the latter half of the season. Also outstanding were pitcher Hajime

Final Major League Standings, 1976

American League
East Division

Club	W.	L.	Pct.	G.B.	N.Y.	Balt.	Bos.	Clev.	Det.	Mil.	Cal.	Chi.	K.C.	Minn.	Oak.	Tex.
New York	97	62	.610	—	—	5	11	12	8	13	7	11	5	10	6	9
Baltimore	88	74	.543	10½	13	—	7	7	12	11	8	8	6	4	4	8
Boston	83	79	.512	15½	7	11	—	9	14	12	7	6	3	7	4	3
Cleveland	81	78	.509	16	4	11	9	—	6	11	5	9	6	9	4	7
Detroit	74	87	.460	24	9	6	4	12	—	12	6	6	4	4	6	5
Milwaukee	66	95	.410	32	5	7	6	6	6	—	8	5	4	4	5	10

West Division

Club	W.	L.	Pct.	G.B.	K.C.	Oak.	Minn.	Cal.	Tex.	Chi.	Balt.	Bos.	Clev.	Det.	Mil.	N.Y.
Kansas City	90	72	.556	—	—	9	10	10	7	10	6	9	6	8	8	7
Oakland	87	74	.540	2½	9	—	7	12	7	9	8	8	8	6	7	6
Minnesota	85	77	.525	5	8	11	—	10	11	11	8	5	3	8	8	2
California	76	86	.469	14	8	6	8	—	12	11	4	5	7	6	4	5
Texas	76	86	.469	14	11	11	7	6	—	11	4	9	5	7	2	3
Chicago	64	97	.398	25½	8	8	7	7	7	—	4	6	3	6	7	1

National League
East Division

Club	W.	L.	Pct.	G.B.	Phil.	Pitt.	N.Y.	Chi.	St.L.	Mon.	Atl.	Cin.	Hou.	L.A.	S.D.	S.F.
Philadelphia	101	61	.623	—	—	8	13	10	12	15	7	7	8	7	8	6
Pittsburgh	92	70	.568	9	10	—	8	10	12	10	9	4	10	3	7	9
New York	86	76	.531	15	5	10	—	13	9	10	8	6	6	5	7	7
Chicago	75	87	.463	26	8	8	5	—	12	11	6	3	5	3	6	8
St. Louis	72	90	.444	29	6	6	9	6	—	11	8	6	3	2	8	7
Montreal	55	107	.340	46	3	8	8	7	7	—	4	3	2	2	4	7

West Division

Club	W.	L.	Pct.	G.B.	Cin.	L.A.	Hou.	S.F.	S.D.	Atl.	Chi.	Mon.	N.Y.	Phil.	Pitt.	St.L.
Cincinnati	102	60	.630	—	—	13	12	9	13	12	9	9	6	5	8	6
Los Angeles	92	70	.568	10	5	—	13	8	6	10	9	10	7	5	9	10
Houston	80	82	.494	22	6	5	—	10	10	11	7	10	6	4	2	9
San Francisco	74	88	.457	28	9	10	8	—	10	9	4	5	5	6	3	5
San Diego	73	89	.451	29	5	12	8	8	—	8	6	8	5	4	5	4
Atlanta	70	92	.432	32	6	8	7	9	10	—	6	8	4	5	3	4

Kato and Shigeru Takada, who was converted to an infielder from an outfielder.

In the Pacific League, the Hankyu Braves won the pennant for the second straight year. The combination of good pitching by Hisashi Yamada, Takashi Yamaguchi, and Mitsuhiro Adachi and good defense by both infielders and outfielders made it possible for the Braves to beat the closely following Lotte Orions of Sendai and Nankai Hawks of Osaka.

Oh, who won the home-run title with 49 and the runs-batted-in crown with 123, was given the Central League's most valuable player laurel. He broke the career record of 714 home runs set by Babe Ruth, and at the year's end was only surpassed by Hank Aaron with 755. Kenichi Yazawa of the Chunichi Dragons of Nagoya captured the Central League's batting title with an average of .3548 (the Giants' Harimoto, the runner-up, batted .3547).

The Pacific League's most valuable player title was captured by pitcher Hisashi Yamada of the Braves, who obtained 28 wins. Clarence Jones of the Kintetsu Buffaloes of Osaka won the home-run crown with 36. Satoru Yoshioka of the Taiheiyo Club Lions of Fukuoka was the leading hitter with .309, while Hideshi Kato of the Braves with 82 obtained the runs-batted-in crown for the second consecutive year.

(RYUSAKU HASEGAWA)

[452.B.4.h.iii]

Basketball

United States. PROFESSIONAL. Perhaps the greatest triumph of the year in U.S. professional basketball was the victory of the Boston Celtics over the upstart Phoenix Suns for the National Basketball Association championship. Or perhaps it was the one Julius Erving (*see* BIOGRAPHY), the game's most astounding performer, gave the New York Nets in their struggle with the Denver Nuggets for the American Basketball Association title. But in all probability it was that of the NBA over the ABA.

Certainly there was no triumph more absolute. The ABA ceased to exist after the owners of four franchises, the Nets, Denver, Indiana, and San Antonio, decided that joining the NBA, with its seniority and its television contract, was worth $3.2 million apiece to them. That was not the only expense, however. The NBA-bound teams also had to pay the two that refused to budge, Kentucky and Utah (formerly St. Louis), approximately $3 million each. And the Nets had to promise the New York Knicks, perhaps the richest team in the NBA, $4 million in the future as reparation for infringing on their territory. After all that had been agreed upon and the players' associations in both leagues had been appeased, the NBA team owners were still uncertain. Convincing them required an intense lobbying campaign by Larry O'Brien, NBA commissioner and former national chairman of the Democratic Party.

Guard Paul Westphal of the Phoenix Suns tries a jump shot over Steve Kuberski of the Boston Celtics during the National Basketball Association play-offs won by the Celtics in June.

WIDE WORLD

For all their apparent reluctance, the NBA franchise holders likely would profit from the merger. Their fans were eager to see Erving, the ABA's most valuable player and scoring leader, and Denver's springy-legged David Thompson, the league's rookie of the year. Moreover, some of the weaker NBA clubs strengthened themselves by drafting proven talent from a pool of the players on the disbanded ABA teams. The most expensive of the lot was 7-ft 2-in Artis Gilmore, the ABA rebounding champion from Kentucky. The Chicago management hoped Gilmore, who cost $1.1 million, would change the Bulls from the team with the NBA's worst record into a bona fide threat to Boston.

The Celtics found themselves facing threat enough when they played Phoenix in the 1976 championship series. The Suns were not expected to be nearly so obstinate. Although they had edged most valuable player Kareem Abdul-Jabbar and the Los Angeles Lakers out of a play-off berth, the Suns had finished 17 games out of first place in the Pacific Division. No one took them seriously until they defeated the Golden State Warriors, the defending NBA champions, for the chance to play the Celtics. Then the public began noticing Alvan Adams, the 6-ft 9-in centre who was the rookie of the year, and the splendid young backcourt of Ricky Sobers and former Celtic Paul Westphal.

They were trying to keep Boston from claiming its 13th championship, but the Celtics responded with the muscle of Dave Cowens and Paul Silas, the finesse of Jo Jo White, the raw talent of Charlie Scott, and, most of all, the spirit of John Havlicek, who was feeling both his 36 years and the pain of a bruised heel. The Celtics' attributes lasted them through the sixth and deciding game, a typically gritty 87–80 victory. The game that would be remembered longest, however, was number five. It featured three overtimes, a fight between a referee and a fan, and heroics by Sobers, Curtis Perry, and Garfield Heard for Phoenix and Havlicek, Scott, White, and reserve Glenn McDonald for Boston. McDonald's two baskets and two free throws in the final minutes gave the Celtics a 126–120 advantage, and they held to win, 128–126.

The ABA play-offs were cut from different cloth. The Nets brawled with San Antonio so violently in the semifinals that New York coach Kevin Loughery asked centre Rich Jones to sit out one game in San Antonio for fear that the fans might attack him. Regular-season champion Denver, loaded with Thompson, Dan Issel, and Bobby Jones, barely won its semifinal round from Kentucky, four games to three. Then Thompson and the Nets' Erving traded one acrobatic move after another through the finals. When guard John Williamson backed up Erving with 24 second-half points in the sixth game, the Nets won, 112–106, to become the last champions of the ABA.

COLLEGE. Spurred by the fear of failures past, Indiana University shot first, asked questions later, and marched to a 32–0 record and the National Collegiate Athletic Association championship. In 1975 virtually the same group of players had been undefeated until Kentucky upset them in the NCAA Mideast Regionals. This time they made no allowance for imperfection.

The Hoosiers established their sense of purpose in the first game of the season when they met UCLA, which possessed its usual wealth of talent. Indiana stunned the Bruins, 84–64, with the vengeful, hammer-handed style that brought it victory after victory by an average of 17.3 points.

The style reflected the personality of Bobby Knight, the Hoosiers' 35-year-old coach, whose brash ways and barbed tongue frequently took the spotlight away from his team. But without the talent Knight had assembled, few people would have noticed him. Scott May, a fluid, 6-ft 7-in senior forward, poured in 23.5 points a game. Kent Benson, a Bible-quoting, 6-ft 11-in, 245-lb junior centre, grabbed rebounds with a roughhouse style that seemed more professional than collegiate. In big games, guard Quinn Buckner, who was drafted by the Washington Redskins to play pro football, could be counted on to come up with a crucial play. Balancing the starting five were Bob Wilkerson, a 6-ft 7-in guard, and forward Tom Abernathy, whose best performances often came at critical times.

After roaring through their Big Ten schedule, the Hoosiers found the competition stiffer in the Mideast Regionals. But they kept Southeastern Conference champion Alabama from so much as taking a shot in the tense final moments of a 74–69 victory. Then they frustrated Marquette's frenetic style, 65–56, getting an unexpected boost when Warrior coach Al McGuire was hit with two technical fouls for bickering with the officials.

When the Hoosiers arrived at the semifinals in Philadelphia, they again faced UCLA, which had regrouped after that season-opening loss to win the Pacific Eight title. The other contest matched Michigan, the second-place team in the Big Ten and twice a victim of the Hoosiers, and Rutgers, with a 93.3-points-per-game average and a 31–0 record.

Once the playing started, the Big Ten proved to be the toughest conference. Michigan upset Rutgers with surprising ease, 86–70, and Indiana gave UCLA a 65–51 replay of its earlier thrashing. The only question left was whether the third time was going to be a charm for Michigan. Quick Rickey Green did what he could to make it so, leading the Wolverines to a 35–29 halftime lead. But after the Hoosiers tied the game at 51-all, May, who finished with 26 points, and Benson, who deposited 25, asserted themselves. The result was an 86–68 victory that gave Indiana the championship.

May received more honours after the season. *The Sporting News* named him player of the year, and he was selected for the weekly publication's All-American team along with forward Adrian Dantley of Notre Dame, centre Robert Parish of Centenary, and guards John Lucas of Maryland and Phil Ford of North Carolina.

(JOHN SCHULIAN)

World Amateur. In the Olympic Games at Montreal in July 1976 the men's basketball tournament was contested in two pools of six teams each. The U.S.S.R. and Canada finished first and second in pool A, and the U.S. and Yugoslavia first and second in pool B. The first of the semifinals, U.S.S.R. *v.* Yugoslavia, proved to be bitter, tense, and at times ill-tempered. At the half the score was tied 42-all, and in the second half the U.S.S.R., losing two of its starting five with five fouls each, was struggling. Meanwhile, brilliant individual performances clinched the game for the Yugoslavs, 89–84, and gave them a chance for the gold medal. The other semifinal, U.S. *v.* Canada, was something of an anticlimax, resulting in a comfortable win for the U.S., 95–77. The final between the U.S. and Yugoslavia was played on July 27 before a capacity crowd of 18,000 at the Montreal Forum. The U.S. team gave a scintillating display of aggressive basketball. The Yugoslavs had had a difficult passage to the final; the particularly hard match the previous day against the U.S.S.R. had left them fatigued and in poor form. They were no match for the U.S., which led 50–38 at the half and 95–74 at the final whistle. The U.S.S.R. took third place and Canada fourth.

UPI COMPIX

Kentucky's Bob Fowler reaches for a rebound during the National Invitation Tournament title game, played at Madison Square Garden against the University of North Carolina at Charlotte and won by Kentucky 71–67. Larry Johnson (12) and Don Pearce (31) stretch for it too.

The first women's Olympic basketball tournament took place at Montreal, with six teams competing. The U.S.S.R. proved to be invincible, winning the maximum of 10 points and the gold medal. The U.S. team was impressively organized and well coached, their wins against Bulgaria (95–79) and Czechoslovakia (83–67) assuring them of a silver medal, while Bulgaria edged into third place by narrowly defeating Czechoslovakia (fourth) 67–66. (*See* TRACK AND FIELD SPORTS: *Special Report.*)

Mobilgirgi (Italy), formerly Ignis Varèse, retained the men's European Champions' Cup by defeating Real Madrid (Spain) in the final at Geneva 81–74. In the men's European Cup-Winners' Cup final, Cinzano Milan (Italy) beat ASPO Tours (France) 88–83. In the third men's cup competition, the Korac Cup, Italy narrowly failed to make it a clean sweep when China Martini of Turin lost to the Yugoslav team Yugoplastika in Split, Yugos.

In the women's cups Soviet teams were not entered, preferring to concentrate on preparation for the Olympics, and so for the first time the cups went outside the U.S.S.R. In the European Champions' Cup, Sparta CKD Prague (Czech.) defeated Clermont-Ferrand in France 58–55 and made certain of the title in Prague with a convincing win, 77–57. In the Ronchetti Cup, the European Cup-Winners' Cup for women, Slavia Prague defeated Industramontaza from Zagreb (Yugos.). The European championships for women were played in Clermont-Ferrand during May. The U.S.S.R. retained its title, and Czechoslovakia finished second. (K. K. MITCHELL)

[452.B.4.h.iv]

Behavioural Sciences

The year 1976 seemed to be one of self-doubt for behavioural scientists in spite of, or perhaps because of, their advances in the understanding and control of behaviour. The theme of the annual convention of the American Psychological Association, for example, was "Prospects for Control, Implications for Freedom." Physiological psychologist Donald O. Hebb of McGill University, Montreal, reassured the conventioneers that they were among the good guys in science. Hebb rejected the view that "psychology is busy mechanizing the mind, depriving man of his humanity, developing new means of control to help all those who would rob us of freedom and turn us into puppets." But some behavioural scientists spent 1976 worrying about their science and their society.

Life and Death. Psychologist Paul Cameron of Fuller Theological Seminary in California worried about a general decline in society's regard for individual rights and for life itself. In one study, Cameron reviewed every article on suicide listed in the *Readers' Guide to Periodical Literature* over the past 50 years. He wanted to find out whether suicide had become more acceptable, so he had each article rated on the degree to which it expressed a negative attitude toward the act. He found that 50 years ago authors spoke out strongly against suicide, but each decade their views became less negative until some of the most recent articles spoke favourably of taking one's own life.

Cameron's concern about the devaluation of life seemed to be supported by the fact that in 1976 California passed the first law allowing a person to direct that, should he become hopelessly ill, life-sustaining machinery could be turned off. The sponsor of this right-to-death legislation argued that it would be a blessing to those individuals who have no hope of recovery and who "for psychological reasons, have been isolated." An opponent of the bill said, "The trend seems to be to get rid of the senile, insane and crippled people."

Learning. Some of the most promising developments in the behavioural sciences came in the area of brain chemistry. Nicholas Plotnikoff of Abbott Laboratories studied the hypothalamic peptide (protein) TRH and concluded that it may help schizophrenics. John Crabbe of the University of California at Santa Barbara gave injections of physostigmine to mice for five days to study its effects on learning. Forty-eight hours after the last injection, Crabbe trained his mice in a brightness discrimination problem and found that the injections had improved their ability to learn the task.

Efforts to improve learning chemically were not limited to mice. Abba J. Kastin, an endocrinologist at Tulane Medical Center in New Orleans, La., and his colleagues found that certain peptides can improve attention and memory in the mentally retarded. In one study, ten retarded patients were injected with either a saline solution (a placebo) or a peptide and then tested on a visual discrimination learning task.

COURTESY, DANCE THERAPY PROGRAM, HUNTER COLLEGE, CITY UNIVERSITY OF NEW YORK

"I hate you," these dancers seem to be saying in a dance therapy class at Hunter College in New York City. The object is to relieve emotional stress by giving vent to feelings.

Those who received the peptide attended better and mastered the task more quickly than those who got the saline.

Women. Feminist researchers began to find evidence that the women's liberation movement, actively supported by many behavioural scientists for several years, might have adverse effects. For example, sociologist Freda Adler of Rutgers University, New Brunswick, N.J., found evidence that the movement may mean an increase in crime. Adler analyzed the FBI's *Uniform Crime Reports* and found that crimes by women went up as women broke away from their traditional roles. Adler found that while arrests for burglary rose 169% for men between 1960 and 1972, the number of women arrested for burglary went up 277% in the same period. Arrests for larceny went up 303% for women over the 12-year span, compared with an 82% rise for men. Most other crimes showed similar trends, especially among young women who were most likely to have adopted the newer, liberated sex roles. Adler also found that increased female crime is as much a phenomenon of the suburbs as it is of the city.

Another blow to the feminists came from a study by Tsipora Peskin of the Institute for Human Development at the University of California at Berkeley. She compared the personalities of divorced women with those who were still married. Using the results of personality tests the women had taken in adolescence, Peskin found that the divorced women had scored lower on measures of conventionality and submissiveness than had those who were still married. Peskin's data could be interpreted to mean that women who adopt the less traditional, more assertive behaviours associated with feminism are more likely to have short-lived marriages.

Not all of the news from the behavioural sciences was bad for feminists, however. For example, Myra Ferree of the University of Connecticut at Storrs compared the attitudes of working-class housewives who worked full time with those who did not. She found that those who worked felt much more satisfied with their lives; only 25% of the unemployed housewives were happy, about half as many as in the employed group.

Help or Harm? The effectiveness of psychotherapy has long been a topic for argument among behavioural scientists, but in 1976 researchers began to speak of "psychonoxious therapy"—therapy that actually does the client more harm than good. About 40% of all disturbed people get better even without treatment. Of those who receive psychotherapy of some sort, 65% improve. But research by Allen E. Bergin of Brigham Young University, Provo, Utah, and others made it clear that psychotherapy can be hazardous as well as helpful. These studies show that while about 5% of those who go untreated get worse, about 10% of those who get therapy go downhill.

Perhaps it was partly the growing realization that psychotherapy can hurt as well as help that made 1976 a year for consumer guides to therapy. The most publicized was *Through the Mental Health Maze,* written by Sallie Adams and Michael Orgel and published by Ralph Nader's Health Research Group. This guide offers hints on how to select a therapist and explains the differences among the various kinds of therapies. Other guides included *What's Psychotherapy and Who Needs It* by Herbert L. Collier and *You Are Not Alone* by Clara Park and Leon Shapiro.

New Therapies. Neither doubts about the safety of psychotherapy nor the abundance of established cures kept psychologists from generating new treatment approaches. The development of movement therapy, feeling therapy, poetry therapy, and music therapy among others ensured that those seeking new paths to mental health would not be disappointed.

In Triad Therapy, developed by Alabama psychologists Charles and Eileen Slack through their work with juvenile offenders, the client meets with a therapist and with a layman who once had the client's problem but has overcome it. The lay therapist may be a reformed drug addict, prostitute, mugger, or thief, and is supposed to offer the insights and understanding that only a person who has "been there" can provide.

Skip Heck, an Arizona psychologist, reported his efforts to perfect wilderness workshops. Heck took people in search of fulfillment into the wilderness where they experienced therapeutic solitude. Name therapy was a method of self-discovery in which the client named and gave identity to various aspects of his personality. The idea is that by naming parts of himself the person gets to know his complete self better.

A group called Homebuilders in Tacoma, Wash., offered therapy to severely troubled families. What was new about Homebuilders was that they made house calls. Their therapists were on call 24 hours a day to client families, and all therapy was done in the home. Finally, 1976 was the year when psychotherapists discovered that fun is good for people. There was even a symposium at the APA meetings on "Fun as the Preferred Mode of Treatment."

One area of the behavioural sciences that showed considerable growth during the year was behavioural medicine. Specialists in this field applied the findings from research in learning, biofeedback, hypnosis, and other areas to medical problems. Epileptics were treated with behaviour modification techniques and learned to control their seizures; the neurologically impaired were helped with biofeedback to overcome their handicaps; and patients in pain learned to reduce their suffering with hypnosis and guided fantasy. Given the success so far, it seemed likely that this field would be among the fastest growing areas of the behavioural sciences for the next several years.

Getting Laymen Involved. One of the most encouraging developments in 1976 was the greatly increased emphasis on getting behavioural science information to the public. Therapists spent less time treating patients themselves and more time training parents, teachers, and paraprofessionals to work with disturbed people. A number of research studies concentrated on training parents to work with unruly, mentally retarded, or autistic children.

Laymen were also taught how to apply behavioural science skills to solving their own problems. Lynn Rehm of the University of Pittsburgh, for example, studied the self-control of depression. She and her colleagues taught self-control techniques to moderately depressed persons and found that they improved as much as patients who received more traditional therapies.

Researchers were finding that, in general, laymen can learn to apply behavioural science skills about as well as professionals. Susana Krivotsky and Thomas Magoon of the University of Maryland, for instance, compared college students who received traditional career counseling with students who used a self-directed career counseling program. The students who worked on their own seemed to get as much benefit from their efforts as those who had had help from a professional counselor.

In 1969 psychologist George Miller implored his colleagues to make the findings and skills that the behavioural sciences produce available to the general public. In 1976 behavioural scientists finally seemed to be responding to his call. It appeared likely that the trend toward turning the behavioural sciences over to the "unwashed" would continue.

(PAUL CHANCE)

See also Prisons and Penology.

[436.B.1; 522.C.3.a; 438.D.4.b]

ENCYCLOPÆDIA BRITANNICA FILMS. *The House of Man, Part II—Our Crowded Environment* (1969); *View from the People Wall: A Statement About Problem Solving and Abstract Methods* (1973).

Belgium

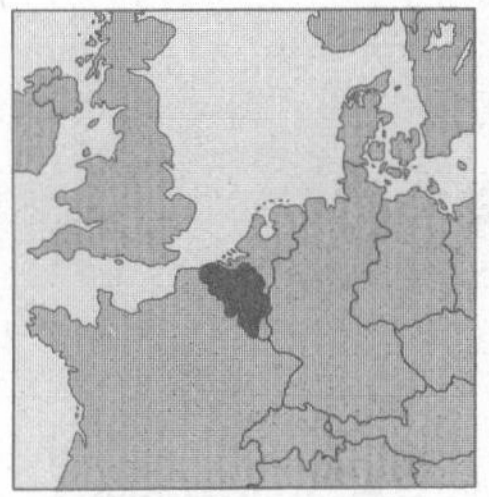

A constitutional monarchy on the North Sea coast of Europe, Belgium is bordered by The Netherlands, West Germany, Luxembourg, and France. Area: 11,782 sq mi (30,514 sq km). Pop. (1976 est.): 9,813,200. Cap. and largest urban area: Brussels (pop., 1976 est., commune 153,400, urban agglomeration 1,050,800). Language: Dutch, French, and German. Religion: predominantly Roman Catholic. King, Baudouin I; prime minister in 1976, Léo Tindemans.

Throughout 1976 the government of Prime Minister Tindemans (*see* BIOGRAPHY) tried hard to fight inflation and to bring down the high level of unemployment. An economic recovery program encountered strong Socialist and Social-Christian trade-union opposition because it included a kind of incomes policy. Plans to suspend the automatic indexation program tying wages to the cost of living were shelved, and the trade unions' suggestion that workers be pensioned off at age 62 provided their jobs went to workers under 30 was accepted. A freeze was ordered for dividends, rates, and rents as well as for monthly wages in excess of BFr 40,000. The legislation became effective on April 1, three months later than planned.

Another controversy with the trade unions developed when the minister of economic affairs temporarily removed fruit and vegetables from the newly revised consumer price index, a move intended to prevent a series of wage increases and a new inflationary spurt. Facing possible social unrest on the eve of the municipal elections, the government rescinded the measure as of September 1. Trade-union leaders also opposed a bill providing for the creation of a public holding company because it did not allow for the unconditional public industrial initiatives they believed were necessary to reduce unemployment.

Government proposals to curb public expenditures, including a virtual standstill for teachers' college enrollments and cutbacks in subsidies to the universities, led to a new round of protests and strikes in educational circles. A report warning that, unless drastic cuts were ordered, the health insurance system deficit would reach BFr 93 billion in the next four years got a cool reception.

Filibustering tactics by the Socialist opposition failed to stop a vote by Parliament on municipal reorganization which, from Jan. 1, 1977, would reduce the number of Belgian communes from 2,359 to 587. Elections for the new councils were held Oct. 10, 1976. The results showed strong gains by the Christelijke Volkspartij/Parti Social Chrétien (CVP/PSC; Christian Social Party) in Flanders and by the Belgische Socialistische Partij/Parti Socialiste Belge (BSP/PSB; Belgian Socialist Party) in Wallonia, and spectacular gains by the Front Démocratique des Francophones (FDF; French-speaking Democratic Front) in the officially bilingual area of Brussels.

The campaign was marked by fresh attempts to stir up tension between the Dutch- and French-speaking (Walloon) communities, culminating in a protracted debate in Parliament and outside it about the separated information desks—five for French speakers, two for foreigners, and one for Dutch—in the town hall of the Schaerbeek commune in the (bilingual) Brussels agglomeration. The government ordered a former attorney general to compel the mayor of the commune to comply with the law by ceasing to discriminate against Dutch-speaking citizens.

Dissatisfaction over slanted news and information put out by the official state-subsidized radio and television networks came to a head when Tindemans, speaking before the Radio-Télé-Luxembourg microphone, advocated the establishment of a private network in order to break their broadcasting monopoly. The difficulties of the press in the face of increased competition from radio and TV were brought to public attention by the spectacular bankruptcy of *De Standaard,* generally regarded as the mouthpiece of the Flemish intelligentsia. Though the newspapers of *De Standaard* group survived, some 1,500 people lost their jobs when new owners took over.

After a long winter marked by flooding along the Schelde River, where ill-maintained dikes collapsed, prolonged drought caused serious damage to agricultural production. Water also became a source of contention between the two communities when Walloon representatives demanded that they be given responsibility for the water supplies of the Ardennes reservoirs. King Baudouin's silver jubilee as chief of state was widely celebrated. (JAN R. ENGELS)

[972.A.7]

BELGIUM

Education. (1974–75) Primary, pupils 974,652, teachers (1967–68) 47,902; secondary, pupils 469,093, teachers (1967–68) 40,074; vocational, pupils 319,680, teachers (1966–67) 47,956; teacher training (third level), students 19,371, teachers (1967–68) 6,089; higher, students 132,758, teaching staff (universities only; 1973–74) *c.* 5,300.

Finance. Monetary unit: Belgian franc, with (Sept. 20, 1976) a free commercial rate of BFr 38.30 to U.S. $1 (BFr 66 = £1 sterling). Gold, SDR's, and foreign exchange (June 1976) U.S. $4,302,000,000. Budget (1975 est.): revenue BFr 595.6 billion; expenditure BFr 692.7 billion. Gross national product (1975) BFr 2,352,000,000,000. Money supply (March 1976) BFr 723.2 billion. Cost of living (1970 = 100; June 1976) 162.

Foreign Trade. (Belgium-Luxembourg economic union; 1975) Imports BFr 1,127,200,000,000; exports BFr 1,057,000,000,000. Import sources: EEC 67% (West Germany 22%, France 17%, The Netherlands 17%, U.K. 6%); U.S. 6%. Export destinations: EEC 70% (West Germany 22%, France 19%, The Netherlands 17%, U.K. 6%). Main exports: iron and steel 14%; machinery 13%; chemicals 12%; motor vehicles 10%; food 9%; textile yarns and fabrics 7%; petroleum products 5%. Tourism (1974): visitors 7,477,000; gross receipts (Belgium-Luxembourg) U.S. $695 million.

Transport and Communications. Roads (1974) 92,850 km (including 1,012 km expressways). Motor vehicles in use (1974): passenger 2,474,000; commercial 249,000. Railways: (1974) 4,004 km; traffic (1975) 8,257,000,000 passenger-km, freight 6,731,000,000 net ton-km. Air traffic (1975): 3,886,000,000 passenger-km; freight 289,109,000 net ton-km. Navigable inland waterways in regular use (1974) 1,534 km. Shipping (1975): merchant vessels 100 gross tons and over 252; gross tonnage 1,358,425. Shipping traffic (1975): goods loaded 34,842,000 metric tons, unloaded 49,292,000 metric tons. Telephones (Dec. 1974) 2,667,000. Radio licenses (Dec. 1973) 3,662,000. Television licenses (Dec. 1973) 2,376,000.

Agriculture. Production (in 000; metric tons; 1975): wheat 703; barley 635; oats *c.* 263; potatoes 1,272; tomatoes *c.* 131; apples (1974) 175; sugar, raw value 654; pork (1974) *c.* 692; beef and veal (1974) *c.* 275; milk *c.* 3,760; fish catch (1974) 46. Livestock (in 000; May 1975): cattle 2,889; pigs 4,666; sheep 80; horses (1974) 56; chickens 31,790.

Industry. Fuel and power (in 000; 1975): coal (metric tons) 7,478; manufactured gas (cu m) 2,514,000; electricity (kw-hr) 41,148,000. Production (in 000; metric tons; 1975): pig iron 9,068; crude steel 11,586; copper 359; lead 116; tin 5.4; zinc 229; sulfuric acid 1,841; fertilizers (nutrient content; 1974–75) nitrogenous 639, phosphate 603; cement 6,883; newsprint 77; cotton yarn 44; cotton fabrics 55; wool yarn 71; woolen fabrics 30; rayon and acetate yarn and fibres 13.

Belize:
see Dependent States

Benelux:
see Belgium; Luxembourg; Netherlands, The

Bermuda:
see Dependent States

Biathlon:
see Target Sports

Bicycling:
see Cycling

Benin

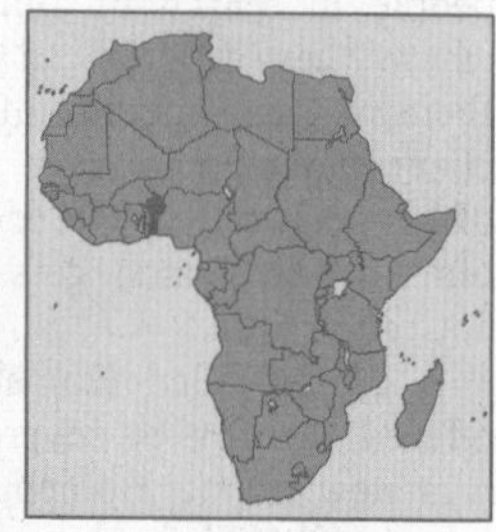

A republic of West Africa, Benin (called Dahomey until it was renamed the People's Republic of Benin on Nov. 30, 1975) is located north of the Gulf of Guinea and is bounded by Togo, Upper Volta, Niger, and Nigeria. Area: 43,475 sq mi (112,600 sq km). Pop. (1975 est.): 3,112,000, mainly Dahomean and allied tribes. Cap.: Porto-Novo (pop., 1972 est., 100,000). Largest city: Cotonou (pop., 1972 est., 175,000). Language: French and local dialects. Religion: mainly animist, with Christian and Muslim minorities. President in 1976, Lieut. Col. Mathieu Kerekou.

BENIN

Education. (1973–74) Primary, pupils 244,032, teachers 4,708; secondary, pupils 39,744, teachers 1,112; vocational, pupils 854, teachers (1968–69) 102; teacher training, students 170, teachers 5; higher, students 1,911, teaching staff 119.

Finance. Monetary unit: CFA franc, with (Sept. 20, 1976) a parity of CFA Fr 50 to the French franc and a free rate of CFA Fr 245.90 to U.S. $1 (CFA Fr 423.62 = £1 sterling). Budget (1974 est.): receipts CFA Fr 12,485,000,000; expenditure CFA Fr 13,572,000,000.

Foreign Trade. (1974) Imports CFA Fr 27.2 billion; exports CFA Fr 12,621,000,000. Import sources (1972): France 40%; U.S. 7%; West Germany 6%; The Netherlands 6%; U.K. 6%. Export destinations (1972): France 37%; West Germany 16%; The Netherlands 15%. Main exports (1971): palm products 31%; cocoa 24%; cotton 19%.

Agriculture. Production (in 000; metric tons; 1975): sorghum *c.* 65; corn (1974) 310; cassava (1974) *c.* 720; yams (1974) *c.* 600; dry beans *c.* 30; peanuts *c.* 55; palm kernels *c.* 70; palm oil *c.* 47; coffee (1974) *c.* 2.5; cotton, lint *c.* 16. Livestock (in 000; 1974): sheep *c.* 690; cattle *c.* 740; goats *c.* 700; pigs *c.* 430.

Although the military regime under Lieutenant Colonel Kerekou was Benin's longest-lasting (its fourth anniversary was celebrated on Oct. 26, 1976), it had clearly not succeeded in unifying the country. On February 3, after a political trial before the National Revolutionary Council at Cotonou, 11 persons were condemned to death for having taken part in a plot to overthrow the government in October 1975.

For several weeks after Jan. 28, 1976, a dispute between Benin and Togo caused their common frontier (opened only a month earlier) to be closed. Benin had accused Togo of granting asylum to Kerekou's political opponents. Successful mediation by Pres. Sékou Touré of Guinea resulted in the reopening of the border on March 27, and on October 6 Kerekou approved a draft convention under which Benin and Togo would assist each other in countering subversion.

In foreign affairs, the government strengthened its ties with the "progressive" camp in Africa, notably by its recognition of the Saharan Arab Democratic Republic (the former Spanish Sahara, declared an independent nation by a rebel group after the colony was divided between Morocco and Mauritania). On his return from an official visit to Peking, ended on July 20, Kerekou stopped off in Algeria. On November 4 Kerekou attended the 11-nation meeting at Lomé, Togo, to launch the Economic Community of West African States. (PHILIPPE DECRAENE)

Bhutan

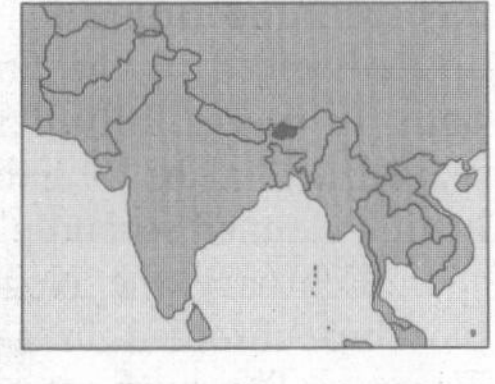

A monarchy situated in the eastern Himalayas, Bhutan is bounded by China and India. Area: 18,000 sq mi (47,000 sq km). Pop. (1976 est.): 1,202,000. Official cap.: Thimphu (pop., approximately 10,000). Administrative cap.: Paro (population unavailable). Language: Dzongkha (official). Religion: approximately 75% Buddhist, 25% Hindu. Druk gyalpo (king) in 1976, Jigme Singye Wangchuk.

Relations with India remained on a friendly level in 1976, and India continued to take a keen interest in Bhutan's economic development. The Indian government confirmed its grant-in-aid of Rs 702.9 million for the fourth five-year plan, starting with Rs 120 million for the first year, 1976–77. Nevertheless, Bhutan continued the efforts to reestablish the kingdom's separate identity that had begun with its admission to UN membership in 1971 and included the launching of a new currency unit, the ngultrum, at par with the Indian rupee; Bhutanese nationals were notified that they would lose their citizenship if they married foreigners.

India's army chief of staff, Gen. T. N. Raina, visited Bhutan in May at the invitation of King Jigme Singye Wangchuk. General Raina inspected the defense installations and noted there was calm on the strategic borders with China. The king visited India in August on his way to the fifth summit conference of nonaligned nations in Colombo, Sri Lanka, and was warmly received by Indian leaders. The king sought assistance from India for the exploitation of the vast mineral resources detected in various parts of the country by an Indian geological survey team.

(GOVINDAN UNNY)

BHUTAN

Education. (1972) Primary and secondary, pupils 11,420, teachers 492; vocational, pupils 285, teachers 19; teacher training, students 39, teachers 5.

Finance and Trade. Monetary unit: ngultrum, at par with the Indian rupee (which it replaced and which is also in use), with (Sept. 20, 1976) a free rate of 9.25 ngultrum to U.S. $1 (15.94 ngultrum = £1 sterling). Budget (1973–74): revenue 21 million ngultrum; expenditure 46 million ngultrum. Virtually all external trade is with India. Main exports: timber, coal, fruit and fruit products.

Billiard Games

Billiards. The 1976 world three-cushion championship was held during May in Ostend, Belgium. The 12 men who played a round robin of 22 sessions, consisting of three games each, included Nobuaki Koyabashi and Junichi Komori of Japan, Raymond Ceulemans and Ludo Dielis of Belgium, Roland Dufetelle of France, George Ashby of the U.S., Humberto Suguimizu of Peru, Avalino Rico of Spain, Mustapha Diab of Egypt, John Korte of Denmark, Wolfgang Anreiter of Austria, and Alfonso González of Colombia.

So intense was the interest in this international field

Fred Davis of England takes his shot as Canadian snooker champion Cliff Thorburn watches. The ten best snooker players in the world were matched in the Benson and Hedges Masters tournament in London.

SYNDICATION INTERNATIONAL/PHOTO TRENDS

COURTESY, BILLIARD CONGRESS OF AMERICA

Pocket billiards champ Jean Balukas ponders a shot in the course of winning her fifth consecutive U.S. women's open.

of champions that all sessions were completely sold out. Fans anxiously wondered whether 11-time world champion Ceulemans could regain his crown from Koyabashi. In the seventh round, Ceulemans' hopes dimmed when he was defeated by Komori 60–51 in 32 innings. As things turned out, however, it was Ceulemans' only loss.

When the final round began, Koyabashi and Ceulemans once again faced each other for the world championship. Early in the game the lead switched several times, but slowly Ceulemans took a commanding lead, finally winning 60–37 in 33 innings. In the process of regaining his title he set eight records, but did not better his one-game world play record of 2.5 (60 points in 24 innings), set in Peru in 1966.

In August a three-cushion U.S. open, sanctioned by the Billiard Congress of America (BCA), was held in Elizabeth, N.J. In the finals Larry ("Boston Shorty") Johnson held off Californian Allen Gilbert but saw his 19-point lead fade before he finally won 50–47. The winner received $2,000 for his first place finish. Other contestants in the open were Dick Reid, Bob Ameen, Murray Shapiro, Jimmy Cattrano, Bill Hawkins, Luis Campos, Abe Rosen, Vince Sbarbati, Bob Below, and George Ashby, who a month earlier had won the New England championship held in Connecticut.

Pocket Billiards. In August Chicago was host to the 11th U.S. open pocket billiards championship, sponsored by the Billiard Congress of America. There were 32 men and 12 women on hand vying for the most prized crowns in pocket billiards and for the $23,000 in cash prizes. The contestants were the most diverse ever seen at the open finals. Besides such seasoned veterans as defending champion Dallas West of Illinois and two-time open winner Joe Balsis of Pennsylvania, there were also national champions Lou Condo (Australia), Tetsuro Kakuto (Japan), and William Lake (West Germany). In addition there were the American College Union champions John Cianflone and Melissa Rice and two superb high school players, Mark Beilfuss and Jean Balukas.

No one quite expected what happened in the men's division. Tom Jennings, a quiet, unassuming mathematics teacher from Edison, N.J., methodically shot his way to victory through the four-day double-elimination tournament. To accomplish this he defeated West 150–52, Danny DiLiberto 150–122 and 150–91, Mark Beilfuss 150–62, and—in the "upset of the year"—Joe Balsis 200–52. On the final day, Jennings played five matches over a period of 14 hours and lost an early match to Balsis before picking up the winner's check for $4,500.

In the women's division, the action was more predictable. Jean Balukas, from Brooklyn, N.Y., garnered her fifth consecutive women's open championship in as many years, thereby equaling the record set by Dorothy Wise, who reigned from 1967 through 1971. Balukas triumphed in straight wins, defeating runner-up Gloria Walker of Pennsylvania in the finals 75–46. The $1,700 first place prize brought her total open winnings to $12,200.

During August the Professional Pool Players Association convened in Asbury Park, N.J., for what was billed as the first world open pocket billiard championship. The tournament, organized by professionals who were dissatisfied with prize money elsewhere available, attracted such well-known names as Pete Margo, Steve Mizerak, Ray Martin, Jim Rempe, Larry Lisciotti, Luther Lassiter, and Irving Crane. In the finals, Lisciotti earned the first place prize of $10,000 by defeating Mizerak 150–47 and 150–108.

Tournament play for women received a boost during 1976 with the advent of the Women's Professional Billiard Alliance. In its first year, the WPBA promoted four contests for its members and participation in the U.S. open.

Snooker. In the Western Hemisphere, the current season started with the Canadian snooker championship in October 1975 at Ottawa. All of the 20 Canadians who took part were previous contenders in provincial tournaments. Cliff Thorburn, Bill Werbeniuk, Robert Paquette, and Julien St. Denis were seeded and advanced to the finals with little opposition of note. In successfully defending his crown, Thorburn played a total of 29 games, winning all but 2. Werbeniuk claimed second place in the field of 20.

In February the North American snooker championship unfolded in a less predictable manner in Toronto. Thorburn was considered a heavy favourite to wrest the title from Werbeniuk. But early in the tournament Thorburn suffered his first loss at the hands of the defending champion, 11–2. On the last day they once again faced a showdown, with Werbeniuk needing only two games to retain his crown and claim the $3,200 prize money. Thorburn tied the series at 9–9, then 10–10, and needed only to clear the red in the 21st game to win the series and title. He missed, and Werbeniuk walked away from the table with the victory.

U.S. Open Pocket Billiards Championships, 1976

Men	bpi*	Women	bpi*
1. T. Jennings	6.86	1. J. Balukas	3.44
2. J. Balsis	10.49	2. G. Walker	2.37
3. D. West	10.60	3. G. Titcomb	2.26
4. D. DiLiberto	8.56	4. S. Adams	1.62
5. W. Weir	6.88	5. B. Billing	1.63
6. M. Beilfuss	6.35	6. V. Frechen	1.39
7. L. Hubbart	8.34	7. B. Gums	1.88
8. S. Cloyd	3.96	8. B. Marietta	1.37
9. N. Varner	7.98	9. M. Rice	1.88
10. J. Ervolino	6.76	10. L. Smith	1.49

*Average balls per inning.

The scene moved in April to Manchester, England, site of the world snooker championship. Ray Reardon of England, the 1975 world champion, was expected to survive stiff competition from the two champions of Canada; from Alex ("Hurricane") Higgins of Ireland; from John Spencer and Fred Davis of England; from Perri Mans of South Africa; and from Eddie Charlton of Australia. After a seesaw battle, it was the systematic Reardon who collected the £6,000 first prize. Although Higgins lost in the finals, his quick shooting style and flamboyant dress attracted a strong following among the spectators.

Snooker continued to be dominated by players from the Commonwealth nations. Though the U.S. received encouragement from the International Snooker Federation, it presented no serious challenge to England, Canada, and Australia.

(ROBERT E. GOODWIN)

[452.B.4.h.v]

Board Games

Chess. After being named world champion in April 1975, Soviet grandmaster Anatoly Karpov set out to justify his title in a series of important matches between July 1975 and August 1976. In July he played in the Spartakiad in Riga and scored $3\frac{1}{2}$ points out of 5 on top board for his native city, Leningrad; it was the best score achieved in the competition by a top-board player. The Association Internationale de la Presse d'Echecs in January 1976 awarded Karpov the chess Oscar as the best player of the year. In March Karpov finished first in a strong international tournament at Skopje, Yugos., and in May he was again victorious in a four-player tournament in Amsterdam. In July he was runner-up to Philippines grandmaster E. Torre in a Manila tournament, and he easily defeated his opponents at Montilla, Spain, in August.

In contrast to Karpov, former world champion Bobby Fischer (U.S.) did not play in any competition during this period, although the American tried to arrange a match with Karpov without official mediation. At the time of the Manila tournament, Fischer met Karpov in Tokyo to discuss terms for a match. Karpov indicated that he was willing to play a match, but that it would not be for the world title. A press rumour that $5 million had been proposed for the match was subsequently denied by Karpov. Another meeting between the two took place in Córdoba, Spain, in August. Karpov announced that if he played and lost the match to Fischer he would resign his title, but there were no further developments.

In the cycle of qualifying events for the world championship, zonals were played in 1975 and interzonals in 1976. The 1975 zonal in Barcelona (won by G. Sosonko, Neth.) was marred by the intrusion of politics when the Eastern European nations withdrew their players because the matches were played in a fascist country. The World Chess Federation (FIDE) arranged special small tournaments so that two of its members could play in the interzonals. The first was held in Manila during June–July and the other at Biel, Switz., during July–August 1976. The three Manila qualifiers for the Candidates Tournament were H. Mecking (Brazil), V. Hort (Czech.), and L. Polugayevsky (U.S.S.R.). Bent Larsen (Den.) qualified at Biel, but a triple tie for the remaining two places had to be settled. In a play-off T. Petrosian (U.S.S.R.) and L. Portisch (Hung.) qualified and M. Tal (U.S.S.R.) was eliminated. The lineup for the semifinals of the 1977 Candidates matches was: Fischer *v.* Hort; Korchnoi *v.* Petrosian; Mecking *v.* Polugayevsky; Larsen *v.* Portisch. If Fischer did not play, his place would be taken by the former world champion Boris Spassky; and if Spassky was not available he would be replaced by Robert Byrne. Spassky married a French woman on Sept. 30, 1975, and obtained Soviet permission to live in France for a year, but he was banned from playing in competitions during that period. Petrosian won the U.S.S.R. men's championship and L. Belavenetz the women's. In a women's world championship match at Tbilisi, U.S.S.R., N. Gaprindashvili defeated N. Alexandria. The Soviet Union lost one of its finest players when Victor Korchnoi sought and was granted asylum in The Netherlands during the July 1976 IBM tournament, in which he shared first place with Britain's Tony Miles.

Politics also affected the biennial FIDE Olympiad and FIDE Congress that took place at Haifa, Israel, during October and November 1976. Neither the Soviet Union nor the Arab bloc nations sent representatives, and Libya even organized a "Counter-Olympiad" in Tripoli at the same time as the FIDE Olympiad. Without competition from such countries as the U.S.S.R., Hungary, and Yugoslavia, the U.S. won the gold medal at Haifa, The Netherlands took the silver, and England the bronze. In the women's Olympiad the top team was Israel, with England second and Spain third. Perhaps the most controversial decision taken by the FIDE Congress was the readmission of the South African Chess Federation to full membership. Among those who received the title of international grandmaster were: Sosonko (Neth.); James Tarjan (U.S.); Boris Gulko, Oleg Romanishin, and Yuri Rasuvaev (U.S.S.R.); and Tony Miles and Ray Keene (England).

(HARRY GOLOMBEK)

Checkers. While Americans were celebrating two hundred years of independence from Great Britain, Derek Oldbury of Devon, Eng., invaded Sanford,

Ruy Lopez, Morphy Defense (played in the interzonal tournament at Biel, Switz., 1976)

White M. Tal	Black L. Portisch	White M. Tal	Black L. Portisch
1 P—K4	P—K4	20 B—B5	P—B5
2 Kt—KB3	Kt—QB3	21 Kt—Kt3	R—B3
3 B—Kt5	P—QR3	22 K—Kt2	R—K1 (f)
4 B—R4	Kt—B3	23 R—R1	P—B3
5 O—O	B—K2	24 P—KR4	P×KP
6 R—K1	P—QKt4	25 P×KP	B—B4
7 B—Kt3	P—Q3	26 R—K1	B—Kt5
8 P—B3	O—O	27 R—K3	P—Q5 (g)
9 P—Q4	B—Kt5	28 Q×P	B—B4
10 B—K3 (a)	P×P (b)	29 Q—K4	B×B
11 P×P	Kt—QR4	30 Kt×B (h)	B×R (i)
12 B—B2	Kt—B5	31 Q×R	B×B
13 B—B1	P—B4	32 P—K61	Kt—Kt1
14 P—QKt3	Kt—Kt3	33 Q—Kt7	B—Kt7
15 QKt—Q2	KKt—Q2 (c)	34 Q—B7 ch	K—R1
16 P—KR3	B—R4	35 R—Q1	Q—B1
17 P—KKt4 (d)	B—Kt3	36 Kt—Kt5 (j)	B—B3
18 Kt—B1	P—Q4 (e)	37 Kt—R6	resigns (k)
19 P—K5	R—B1		

(a) Black has a good game after 10 P—Q5, Kt—QR4; 11 B—B2, P—B3. (b) Not 10 . . ., Kt×KP; 11 B—Q5. Or if 10 . . ., P—Q4; 11 KP×P, P×P; 12 B—Kt5, P×P; 13 Kt×Kt, with advantage to White. (c) He cannot keep the pawn by 15 . . ., P×P on account of 16 P—KR3. (d) Tal plays most vigorously; safer, but not so forceful, is 17 B—Kt2, as Smejkal played against Portisch at Prague in 1970. (e) Portisch too likes to be forcetul; but safer was 18 . . ., R—B1. (f) White's dangerous KP must be kept under observation; at the same time he bears in mind the possibility of strengthening the king-side defenses by Kt—B1. (g) A critical position has been reached; if now 28 Kt×P, Kt×P and Black is winning. (h) If 30 Q×R, Black plays R—K3 before capturing the rook. (i) And now this capture is disastrous since he has not seen the force of White's 32nd move. (j) Threatening 37 Q—R5, P—R3; 38 Kt×RP, P×Kt; 39 Q×P ch, etc. (k) Since if 37 . . ., B×Kt; 38 Q—Kt8 ch, R×Q; 39 Kt—B7 mate. Or if 37 . . ., R—K2; 38 Q×R, B×Q; 39 Kt(Kt5)—B7 mate.

Biochemistry: *see* Life Sciences

Biographies: *see* People of the Year *beginning on page 24*

Biological Sciences: *see* Life Sciences

Biophysics: *see* Life Sciences

Birth Statistics: *see* Demography

FRANK C. DOUGHERTY—THE NEW YORK TIMES

A chess master at 13, Michael Wilder of Princeton, N.J., also plays football, basketball, tennis, and other games. He tied for first place in the Greater New York championships in February.

N.C., in July and departed with the American tournament championship, the master's trophy, and the first place prize of $1,000. (Hugh Henderson of Scotland and Walter Hellman of Sweden had previously won the American title, but both remained in the U.S. and became naturalized citizens.) Runner-up Karl Albrecht, who made his best showing yet in a national tournament, was followed in order by Ed Bruch, Elbert Lowder, Don Lafferty, Ed Scheidt, Everett Fuller, and Ed Markusic. World champion Marion Tinsley won the St. Petersburg tournament in Florida with a total of seven victories and one draw (against Fuller).

Because Tom Wiswell had earlier announced his intention to resign as freestyle world champion in 1976, the American Checkers Federation and the English Draughts Association decided that Leo Levitt, the U.S. master, and Derek Oldbury, Britain's top master, would play a 20-game match for the vacant title. The two met at Glasgow, Kentucky, in mid-March at the invitation of Col. J. Mitchell Ellis. The score at the end of 24 games was: Levitt 1, Oldbury 1, draws 22! In such circumstances the American Checkers Federation and the English Draughts Association both agreed that the deadlock could not be officially broken by declaring either one the new champion. It was suggested that a second freestyle match between the two contenders might take place in 1977 and that one or the other of them would emerge a decisive winner.

At the strong Lakeside (Ohio) Masters' Tournament in August Elbert Lowder of Sanford, N.C., carried off first honours with a total of 24 points; Louis Cowie of Painesville, Ohio, was runner-up with 20 points. Next in order of finish were Elzy Langdon, Karl Albrecht, Victor Monteiro, and Ed Bruch. The Southern Masters' Tournament that was held during August in Houston, Texas, was won by Lloyd Taylor of Birmingham, Ala.; Hugh Burton was second, E. T. Rolader third, and Elbert Lowder fourth.

(TOM WISWELL)

Boating:
see Rowing; Sailing; Water Sports

Bobsledding:
see Winter Sports

Boccie:
see Bowling

Backgammon. During the year the World Backgammon Club (WBC) continued an active program under the presidency of Prince Alexis Obolensky. The club organized tournaments in various parts of the world and continued to award master points to players on the basis of their performances in sanctioned tournaments. Heading the list were Arthur Dickman of Miami, Fla., Claude Beer of Palm Beach, Fla., and Paul Magriel of New York City. For those who wanted to keep abreast of recent developments, Joseph Pasternack of the WBC edited the *Backgammon News* six times a year. Some 100 affiliated clubs and societies held local tournaments that qualified for official master points. A certified teachers' program was also instituted with instructors licensed by the WBC. During the finals of the 1976 world championship, Baron Vernon Ball of the Virgin Islands defeated Lona Holland of New York City. It was only the second time that a woman became a finalist in this prestigious tournament. The European championship was won by Joseph Dwek of London, and the Grandmasters Tournament at the Las Hadas resort in Mexico was won by Tony Goble of Dallas, Texas, who bested Tobias Stone of New York City in a close 35–34 contest. Only 16 players were invited to participate. Paul Magriel won the American championship by defeating his former teacher Sidney Hecht. The WBC decided to change the pattern of the American championship by first holding tournaments in all major cities, then having the winners convene for a final showdown.

(PRINCE ALEXIS OBOLENSKY)

[452.C.3.c.i and ii]

Bolivia

A landlocked republic in central South America, Bolivia is bordered by Brazil, Paraguay, Argentina, Chile, and Peru. Area: 424,165 sq mi (1,098,581 sq km). Pop. (1975 est.): 5,634,000, of whom more than 50% were Indian. Language: Spanish (official). Religion (1975 est.): Roman Catholic 94.2%. Judicial cap.: Sucre (pop., 1973 est., 88,000). Administrative cap. and largest city: La Paz (pop., 1973 est., 697,500). President in 1976, Col. Hugo Banzer Suárez.

In August 1976 President Banzer's military regime completed five years in office, giving Bolivia an appearance of stability and implying some expertise on the part of the president in view of his country's turbulent history. During 1976 the government overcame or suppressed industrial and student unrest as well as disquiet generated by the murder of former president Juan José Torres Gonzales in Buenos Aires, Argentina, on June 2; on June 9 a three-month state of siege was imposed. The regime remained publicly committed to a return to a democratic system by 1980.

In foreign affairs the government's principal concern continued to be the attainment, once more, of sovereign access to the Pacific Ocean. Banzer accepted, as a basis for negotiation, the offer made by Chile at the end of 1975 of an exchange of territory, subject to the approval of Peru as required by treaty. The government's attitude to this offer hardened as negotiations continued and as opposition manifested itself both within the government and in the country at large. Though discussions among the three countries on a nonaggression pact continued, Bolivian

BOLIVIA

Education. (1973) Primary, pupils 769,968, teachers 33,084; secondary (1972), pupils 122,124, teachers 7,531; vocational (1971), pupils 10,452, teachers 549; teacher training, students 5,896, teachers 314; higher (at 9 universities only; 1974), students 34,030, teaching staff 2,270.

Finance. Monetary unit: peso boliviano, with (Sept. 20, 1976) an official rate of 20 pesos to U.S. $1 (free rate of 34.46 pesos = £1 sterling). Gold, SDR's, and foreign exchange (May 1976) U.S. $161.9 million. Budget (1974 est.) balanced at 5,034,000,000 pesos. Gross national product (1974) 36,553,000,000 pesos. Money supply (March 1976) 4,490,000,000 pesos. Cost of living (La Paz; 1970 = 100; April 1976) 260.

Foreign Trade. (1975) Imports U.S. $558 million; exports U.S. $443.2 million. Import sources (1974): U.S. *c.* 26%; Brazil *c.* 16%; Argentina *c.* 15%; Japan 14%; West Germany *c.* 8%. Export destinations (1974): U.S. *c.* 19%; Argentina 10%; Japan *c.* 6%; Brazil *c.* 5%. Main exports: tin 43%; crude oil 26%; zinc 9%; silver 6%; tungsten 5%.

Transport and Communications. Roads (1975) 37,075 km. Motor vehicles in use (1974): passenger 29,600; commercial (including buses) 33,000. Railways: (1975) 3,579 km; traffic (1973) 270 million passenger-km, freight 365 million net ton-km. Air traffic (1975): 331 million passenger-km; freight 2,770,000 net ton-km. Telephones (Jan. 1974) 49,000. Radio receivers (Dec. 1968) 1,350,000. Television receivers (Dec. 1972) 11,000.

Agriculture. Production (in 000; metric tons; 1975): barley *c.* 76; rice (1974) 75; corn (1974) 277; wheat (1974) *c.* 63; cassava (1974) *c.* 270; potatoes *c.* 775; bananas (1974) *c.* 263; sugar, raw value (1974) 204; coffee *c.* 15; cotton, lint *c.* 15; rubber *c.* 4. Livestock (in 000; Oct. 1973): cattle 2,326; sheep 7,508; goats 2,748; pigs 1,104; horses *c.* 328; asses *c.* 685.

Industry. Production (in 000; metric tons; 1974): cement 199; crude oil (1975) 1,855; electricity (kw-hr) 967,000 (77% hydroelectric); gold (troy oz) 42; tin 30; lead 18; antimony 11; tungsten (oxide content) 2.2; zinc 39; copper 7.8; silver 0.1.

leaders in September were expressing concern about a possible arms race between Peru and Chile. In November a Peruvian proposal for tripartite sovereignty over the access territory was rejected by Chile. After the March coup in Argentina, Bolivia improved relations with that country, completing a network of good relations with all its more powerful neighbours.

Bolivia continued to be popular among international lending agencies and foreign banks in spite of a balance of payments reversal in 1975. Provisional figures for 1975 showed a trade deficit of $49.5 million as against a surplus of $193.9 million in 1974, while the overall balance of payments showed a deficit of $49.9 million, as compared with a surplus of $112 million in 1974. The 1976–80 five-year plan required an investment of $3 billion, much of which had to be financed externally; although the foreign debt at the end of 1975 had reached $1,664,000,000, the government believed that future external finance requirements were within acceptable limits. The plan envisaged an annual growth rate of 7%, as compared with 6.8 and 6.7% in 1975 and 1974, respectively. Indications were that improved export prospects in 1976 and the planned high level of public investment would allow the target to be achieved.

While the prospects of achieving plan targets were good, Bolivia remained an underdeveloped country, with a small population largely engaged in semisubsistence agriculture. Average income per head in 1974 was $255, and the plan target for 1980 was $400. The important state mining sector required modernizing and needed to become more profitable. Improvement in national administration and planning indicated the possibility of progress. (JOHN HALE)

[974.D.3]

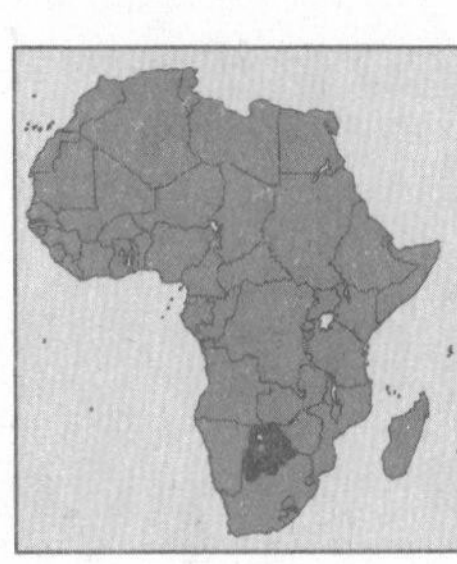

Botswana

A landlocked republic of southern Africa and a member of the Commonwealth of Nations, Botswana is bounded by South Africa, South West Africa, Zambia, and Rhodesia. Area: 222,000 sq mi (576,000 sq km). Pop. (1976 est.): 718,000, almost 99% African. Cap. and largest city: Gaborone (pop., 1976 est., 36,900). Language: English (official) and Tswana. Religion: Christian 60%; animist. President in 1976, Sir Seretse Khama.

The difficulty of reconciling political disapproval of South Africa with the fact of economic dependence on that country muted Botswana's cooperation with Tanzania and Zambia in 1976, and its attitude to refugees and terrorists on its soil was one of strict neutrality. It resisted pressure from other black African governments to close the section of the Rhodesian railways that passed across its territory, a step that would be economic suicide for Botswana. Seretse Khama was one of the five "front-line" southern African presidents whose September 26 Lusaka meeting called for a Rhodesia conference. He also visited India to ask for help in nationalizing the railway and China to explore the possibility of building a railway to link with the Tanzam railway.

BOTSWANA

Education. (1975) Primary, pupils 116,293, teachers 3,509; secondary, pupils 12,098, teachers 522; vocational, pupils 1,699, teachers 200; teacher training, students 489, teachers 48; higher (1973), students 289, teaching staff 30.

Finance and Trade. Monetary unit: pula, which replaced the South African rand at par from Aug. 23, 1976, with (Sept. 20, 1976) a free rate of 0.87 pula to U.S. $1 (1.50 pula = £1 sterling). Budget (1974–75 net est.): revenue 63.3 million pula; expenditure 62.6 million pula. Foreign trade (1974): imports 122 million pula (65% from South Africa in 1966); exports 76 million pula (18% to South Africa in 1966). Main exports: mineral products (mainly diamonds) 45%; meat and products 40%.

Agriculture. Production (in 000; metric tons; 1974): sorghum *c.* 40; corn *c.* 10; millet *c.* 4; peanuts *c.* 6. Livestock (in 000; 1974): cattle *c.* 2,200; sheep *c.* 415; goats *c.* 1,050; chickens *c.* 520.

Industry. Production (in 000; 1974): diamonds (metric carats) 2,718; electricity (kw-hr) 237,000.

The nation's 1976–77 budget, announced in May, drew attention to conditions of financial stringency and an annual inflation rate of 15%. Revenue was expected to fall by a quarter, and two-thirds of the expenditure for development would depend on foreign aid. Not least of the Botswana government's worries was the violence of opposition leader P. Matante, whose radical policies supporting the Selebe-Pikwe miners' strike cast doubt on the regime's stability, the basis of foreign investment. During the year the government decided to replace the South African rand at par with a new unit of currency, the pula.

(MOLLY MORTIMER)

[978.E.8.b.ii]

Bowling

Tenpin Bowling. WORLD. The last major event of 1975 was the international finals of the 11th Bowling World Cup, staged at Manila in November. The eliminations for the finals had been started over half a

Bonds:
see Stock Exchanges

Books:
see Art Sales; Literature; Publishing

Botanical Gardens:
see Zoos and Botanical Gardens

Botany:
see Life Sciences

year earlier, and in November the best men from 32 countries and best women from 28 countries were ready for the week-long international play-off. Progressively the best were separated out from the rest until on the final day there were only two players left in each of the two divisions. Among the men, Lorenzo Monti added Italy's name as the seventh country since 1965—when the tournament was started—to share the glory. In a three-game final match he beat Venezuela's Carlos Lovera, 561–544. In the ladies' final between Cathy Townsend from Canada and Hattieann Morrissette from Bermuda, Mrs. Townsend won 540–509.

The European youth championships for competitors under 18 were held in Brussels in April 1976. This was the third time that the European zone of the Fédération Internationale des Quilleurs (FIQ) had arranged such a tournament. Nine countries entered their junior champions in this two-day competition for three titles. Sweden and West Germany won all but one of the nine medals, the third place in the team-of-five event being taken by Ireland. The winners were: team of five, Sweden, 5,448, followed by West Germany, 5,427, and Ireland, 5,419; doubles, Sweden, 2,409, followed by West Germany, 2,400; individual (18 games), Michael Schäfer, West Germany, 3,576, followed by Anders Sandstrom, Sweden, 3,493, and Ove Jonasson, Sweden.

Records clattered like dishes in a china shop as the U.S. faced its stiffest competition ever at the 14th annual Tournament of the Americas in July at Miami, Fla., which had sponsored this competition from its inception. During the week-long event the U.S. won only one of eight events in a tournament it usually dominated. One hundred ten bowlers from 23 countries of North and South America and the Caribbean competed in this 36-game contest sponsored annually by the city of Miami. Mrs. Townsend from Canada added another victory to her achievements in winning the women's 36-game all-events. She was well supported by her countryman Glen Watson, who won the corresponding men's title. The winners were: mixed foursomes, Canada, 4,682; mixed doubles, Mexico, 2,446; women's doubles, U.S., 3,420; men's doubles, Canada, 3,733; women's singles, Regina Penaloza, Venezuela, 2,805; men's singles, Thomas Barria, Panama, 3,060; women's all-events, Cathy Townsend, Canada, 6,733; men's all-events, Glen Watson, Canada, 7,473.

Earl Anthony watches his pins fall. He was top money winner among U.S. professional bowlers for the third straight year.

COURTESY, NATIONAL BOWLER'S JOURNAL

During the season Iran, Malta, and Poland joined the FIQ to increase the membership to 55; the number of individual bowlers topped 10 million.

(YRJÖ SARAHETE)

UNITED STATES. Women's professional bowling has never approached the prominence attained by the male professionals, but a performance by Betty Morris in the opening round of the U.S. Women's Open in Tulsa, Okla., attracted nationwide attention. Mrs. Morris began her six-game qualifying round with a 300 game, followed it with scores of 254, 245, 227, 238, and then closed with another 300. The 1,564 total by the Stockton, Calif., resident was the highest six-game score in Women's International Bowling Congress records, and it was the first time that a woman had ever rolled two perfect games in sanctioned competition on the same day.

Mrs. Morris finished second in the U.S. Women's Open, losing to Patty Costello of Scranton, Pa., 235–233, in the final game. Miss Costello won $6,000. Mrs. Morris, however, had taken the $13,000 first prize in the Brunswick Women's World Invitational in April, and as the year neared a close she led in the earnings standings maintained by the Professional Women Bowlers Association with $23,310. Miss Costello's $17,035 ranked second.

Among the men, Earl Anthony outclassed his opposition for the third consecutive year. Anthony, a 38-year-old left-hander from Tacoma, Wash., won the Professional Bowlers Association (PBA) tournaments in Windsor Locks, Conn., Tamarac, Fla., Fresno, Calif., Los Angeles, Calif., and Waukegan, Ill. For the third straight year his tournament earnings approximated $100,000. Mark Roth, from New York City, was first in the PBA events in St. Louis, Mo., and Pittsburgh, Pa., and his earnings of $60,200 gained the 25-year-old right-hander second place among bowling's money winners.

The 73rd annual American Bowling Congress tournament was held on specially constructed lanes in Oklahoma City, Okla., in the spring, and the entries included 5,679 five-man teams. The champions were: Classic Division (for professionals)—team, Munsingwear No. 2, Minneapolis, Minn., 3,281; doubles, Don Johnson, Las Vegas, Nev., and Paul Colwell, Tucson, Ariz., 1,442; singles, Jim Schroeder, Buffalo, N.Y., 750; all-events, Gary Fust, Des Moines, Iowa, 2,050. Regular Division—team, Andy's Pro Shop, Tucson, 3,187; doubles, Gary Voss and Fred Willen, Sr., St. Louis, 1,356; singles, Mike Putzer, Oshkosh, Wis., 758; all-events, Jim Lindquist, Minneapolis, 2,071. In the Masters Tournament, held on the ABC tournament lanes, Nelson Burton, Jr., St. Louis, swept through seven matches undefeated and won the championship.

The Women's International Bowling Congress' 57th annual meet, held at Celebrity Sports Center in Denver, Colo., attracted 9,237 teams. The winners included: Open Division (combined average of 851 or over)—team, PWBA No. 1, Oklahoma City, 2,839; doubles, Eloise Vacco and Debby Rainone, Cleveland Heights, Ohio, and Georgene Cordes and Shirley Sjostrom, Bloomington, Minn., tied with 1,232; singles, Bev Shonk, Canton, Ohio, 686; all-events, Betty Morris, Stockton, Calif., 1,866. Division I (726 through 850)—team, Famous Brand Shoes, St. Louis, 2,753; doubles, Barbara Siemrzuch and Shirley Mansfield, Northglenn, Colo., 1,198; singles, Vanda Philson, Sidney, Neb., 666; all-events, Ethel Coverdell, Orlando, Fla., 1,748. Pam Rutherford of Oroville, Calif., won the WIBC Queens Tournament.

Duckpins. In the National Duckpin Championships the winners were: men—team, Connecticut Frozen Food, Hamden, Conn., 2,125; doubles, Tony Adams and Mike Piersanti, East Haven, Conn., 923; singles, Bob Atkins, Baltimore, Md., 501; all-events, Mike Piersanti, 1,426. Women—team, Overlea Exxon, Baltimore, Md., 1,926; doubles, Lorraine Watts and Kathy Cahoon, Willimantic, Conn., 810; singles, Doris Shortt, Baltimore, Md., 467. Mixed—team, Tin Can Cuties, Glastonbury, Conn., 1,914.

(JOHN J. ARCHIBALD)

Lawn Bowls. The year 1976 was dominated by the world championships held in February–March in South Africa at Zoo Lake Bowling Club, Johannesburg. The stands were conceived for a peak crowd of 7,000, but had to be enlarged on several days when 9,000 spectators viewed some of the finest bowls ever seen in the republic. Promotional costs soared above the R 560,000 raised, but the huge crowds spent a king's ransom at the gates. They were well rewarded, the home players taking the gold medals in all four events. Unquestionably, the outstanding player was Douglas Watson, winner of the singles. Presaging what was to follow with a devastating 21–9 win over the defending world champion, Maldwyn Evans of Wales, he won his first 14 matches with little or no danger of defeat and was already assured of the title when he met the first world champion, David Bryant, in his 15th and final encounter. Bryant, who took the bronze medal for finishing third, recaptured his 1966 form with a brilliant victory 21–10. Despite this, experts at Zoo Lake, recalling that Watson had only just taken the South African Masters championship for an unbelievable fourth year in succession, were rating him as the supplanter of Bryant as the best ever to play the game.

Before the singles, Watson had won the pairs event with Bill Mosely. His teammates, Kevin Lightfoot (skip), Nando Gatti, and Kevin Campbell, won the triples and, with Mosely, also took the fours event to give South Africa an unprecedented clean sweep of the world championships.

(C. M. JONES)

Boccie. Boccie is a form of bowls that developed in Europe, especially in France (as boules) and Italy, and is played also in Africa, the Americas, and Australia. The controlling body of the sport is the Fédération Internationale de Boules, formed by national associations, with headquarters at Turin, Italy. It is a game in which players throw a metal or synthetic composition ball weighing about two pounds at a small wooden ball called a jack in order to place it as near the jack as possible, or to knock the jack away. The game can be played in a court or on open, level, hard ground. The player runs about 20 ft with the ball before releasing it, and the throwing area beyond the foot-fault line measures about 60 ft by 12 ft. Individuals play each other with four balls each, whereas teams of two use three balls per player and teams of three and of four use two balls per player.

The Prince of Monaco World Cup and the world championships, which are held in alternate years, are the most important events. In 1975 the Prince of Monaco Cup was won by Italy, from France and Switzerland. The 1976 world championship, held in Turin in October, was won by Italy (beat France 15–11 in the final). These were followed, in order, by Morocco, Switzerland, Monaco, Yugoslavia, Tunisia, Belgium, Spain, Australia, West Germany, and Luxembourg.

(LUIGI SAMBUELLI)

[452.B.4.h.vi]

Brazil

A federal republic in eastern South America, Brazil is bounded by the Atlantic Ocean and all the countries of South America except Ecuador and Chile. Area: 3,286,500 sq mi (8,512,000 sq km). Pop. (1975 est.): 107,145,200. Principal cities (pop., 1975): Brasília (cap.; federal district) 763,300; Rio de Janeiro 4,857,700; São Paulo 7,198,600. Language: Portuguese. Religion: Roman Catholic 88%. President in 1976, Gen. Ernesto Geisel.

Domestic Affairs. At the beginning of 1976 there was an atmosphere of pessimism among political leaders of both the party supporting the government, the National Renewal Alliance (ARENA), and the opposition party, the Brazilian Democratic Movement (MDB). The ARENA leaders complained that they had little to say with regard to government decisions, while the opposition leaders claimed that there could not be real political freedom in the country so long as the emergency measures (the Institutional Act known as AI-5 and decree-law 477) were in force. These measures authorized the government to cancel the mandates of any elected or appointed official and to suspend that person's political rights for ten years. On January 5 a decree was signed by President Geisel canceling the mandates of a federal deputy and a member of a state legislature, both of whom belonged to the MDB. They were accused of having had some

WIDE WORLD

Flags of Brazil and Japan decorate Tokyo's main street, the Ginza, in honour of the visit of Brazil's President Geisel in September.

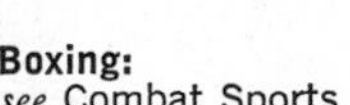
Boxing:
see Combat Sports

connection with the outlawed Communist Party and of refusing to appear for questioning before the Army's Intelligence Operations Detachment. In March and April three more members of the MDB suffered similar loss of mandates and political rights.

The government was accused of continuing to impose direct or indirect censorship on the press and other mass media. Many believed that President Geisel had abandoned his avowed intention of returning the country to a democratic regime by means of what he called "perfecting of the institutions." It was feared by many that new coercive measures would be taken by the government to prevent the opposition from gaining a significant victory in the November municipal elections. Both parties were prohibited from campaigning on radio or television, but the government's achievements were frequently praised in the media.

About 40 million persons voted in the municipal elections, which were held November 15. ARENA won approximately 70% of the mayoralties and city councils in the more than 3,700 municipalities. The MDB, which did not even present candidates in over 1,300 districts, gained control of the councils in several major cities, including Rio de Janeiro and São Paulo, but the mayors in these cases were appointed by the regime.

Furthermore, it was claimed that the torture of political prisoners had continued despite repeated denials. In October 1975 Vladimir Herzog, the news director of an educational television station in São Paulo, was found dead in an army prison. The authorities claimed that he had committed suicide. He had been called for questioning about possible inmander of the 3rd Army (with headquarters in São Paulo issued a declaration criticizing the arrest and torture of citizens on mere suspicion of subversive activities.

At the beginning of 1976 another man was found dead in an army prison. This time, President Geisel took immediate action to remove the general commander of the 3rd Army (with headquarters in São Paulo) as responsible for permitting such excesses. The president's action was hailed as a courageous condemnation of the arbitrariness of the military authorities in their investigation of supposed subversive actions.

In August the country mourned the death, in an automobile accident, of former president Juscelino Kubitschek de Oliveira (*see* OBITUARIES). Kubitschek promoted the industrialization of Brazil during his five-year term of office (1956–1961) and engineered the transfer of the capital from Rio de Janeiro to Brasília.

Foreign Affairs. During the year the government showed great interest in promoting friendly relations with the new African nations. Brazil had been one of the first to recognize the Soviet-backed Popular Movement for the Liberation of Angola, an action that had provoked a warning from the U.S. At the time there was an exchange of views between the U.S. and Brazil on a probable alteration of the strategic conditions in the South Atlantic if Soviet influence were to predominate in the new West African nations.

On February 19 U.S. Secretary of State Henry Kissinger (*see* BIOGRAPHY) arrived at Brasília as part of his visit to six Latin-American countries. Government officials expected to discuss with him the pending problems between the two countries, especially trade relations. It was pointed out that the deficit in trade unfavourable to Brazil amounted to $1.6 billion in 1975. The only significant result of the visit, however, was the signing at Brasília, on February 21, of a consultation agreement giving formal character to an informal system of bilateral relations that had existed for the last two years. It provided for meetings every six months between the foreign minister of Brazil and the U.S. secretary of state, along with other government officials, to discuss matters of common interest. Kissinger announced afterward that the first questions to be discussed would be those relating to energy and technical and scientific cooperation.

The consultation agreement was criticized by some in the United States as offensive to the other Latin-American nations, who saw in it an attempt to separate Brazil from the rest of the region by the promise of special treatment. Other observers saw the agreement as the result of the need felt in the United States to reformulate Brazil-U.S. policy in light of the Soviet Union's increasing influence in Africa. The first meeting under the agreement, scheduled to be held in Washington, D.C., in mid-1976, was postponed until after the U.S. presidential elections.

BRAZIL

Education. (1973) Primary, pupils 20,135,898, teachers 837,268; secondary (1971), pupils 3,464,088, teachers 228,143; vocational (1971), pupils 797,487, teachers 68,846; teacher training (1971), students 300,551, teachers 39,223; higher, students 772,800, teaching staff 59,760.

Finance. Monetary unit: cruzeiro, with (Sept. 20, 1976) a free rate of 11.29 cruzeiros to U.S. $1 (19.46 cruzeiros = £1 sterling). Gold, SDR's, and foreign exchange (Dec. 1975) U.S. $3,898,000,000. Budget (1975 actual): revenue 95,447,000,000 cruzeiros; expenditure 95,374,000,000 cruzeiros. Gross national product (1973) 473.2 billion cruzeiros. Money supply (March 1976) 178,860,000,000 cruzeiros. Cost of living (São Paulo; 1970 = 100; May 1976) 355.

Foreign Trade. (1975) Imports U.S. $13,558,000,000; exports U.S. $8,655,000,000. Import sources (1974): U.S. 24%; West Germany 12%; Saudi Arabia 10%; Japan 9%; Iraq 5%. Export destinations (1974): U.S. 22%; The Netherlands 8%; Japan 7%; West Germany 6%; U.K. 5%. Main exports: iron ore 11%; coffee 10%; sugar 9%.

Transport and Communications. Roads (1974) 1,312,675 km. Motor vehicles in use (1974): passenger 3,679,000; commercial (including buses) 1,002,000. Railways: (1974) 30,394 km; traffic (1973) 10,603,000,000 passenger-km, freight 42,698,000,000 net ton-km. Air traffic (1975): 9,600,000,000 passenger-km; freight 469,687,000 net ton-km. Shipping (1975): merchant vessels 100 gross tons and over 482; gross tonnage 2,691,408. Shipping traffic (1974): goods loaded 78,467,000 metric tons, unloaded 55,109,000 metric tons. Telephones (Jan. 1975) 2,652,000. Radio receivers (Dec. 1973) 6,250,000. Television receivers (Dec. 1972) 6.6 million.

Agriculture. Production (in 000; metric tons; 1975): wheat 1,500; corn 16,491; rice 7,674; cassava (1974) *c.* 30,000; potatoes 1,664; sweet potatoes (1974) *c.* 1,938; peanuts 441; sugar, raw value *c.* 5,950; dry beans 2,280; soybeans *c.* 10,200; coffee *c.* 1,300; cocoa *c.* 288; bananas (1974) *c.* 7,500; oranges (1974) *c.* 3,500; cotton, lint 515; sisal 324; tobacco 273; rubber *c.* 20; timber (cu m; 1974) *c.* 163,800; beef and veal (1974) *c.* 2,132; pork (1974) *c.* 723; fish catch (1974) *c.* 605. Livestock (in 000; Dec. 1974): cattle *c.* 92,480; pigs *c.* 35,000; sheep *c.* 26,500; goats (1973) *c.* 16,000; horses (1973) *c.* 9,500; chickens *c.* 272,000.

Industry. Fuel and power (in 000; metric tons; 1975): crude oil 8,434; coal (1974) 2,580; natural gas (cu m) 560,000; electricity (kw-hr; 1974) 70,480,000 (95% hydroelectric). Production (in 000; metric tons; 1975): pig iron 6,966; crude steel 8,323; iron ore (68% metal content; 1974) 59,420; bauxite (1974) *c.* 900; manganese ore (metal content; 1973) 1,141; gold (troy oz; 1974) 189; cement 16,297; asbestos (1973) 819; wood pulp (1974) 1,311; paper (1974) 1,855; passenger cars (including assembly; units) 553; commercial vehicles (including assembly; units) 370.

In April President Geisel, with a large number of technical assistants, visited France. Negotiations on economic and technical cooperation were carried on, and a joint declaration was issued that described priority questions to be considered by both countries. After returning to Brazil to attend the May 1 (Labour Day) ceremonies at Volta Redonda, the president went to London for a three-day official visit. Problems of economic cooperation and an exchange of views on Africa and the Middle East were on the program. (RAUL D'EÇA)

[974.G]

Bulgaria

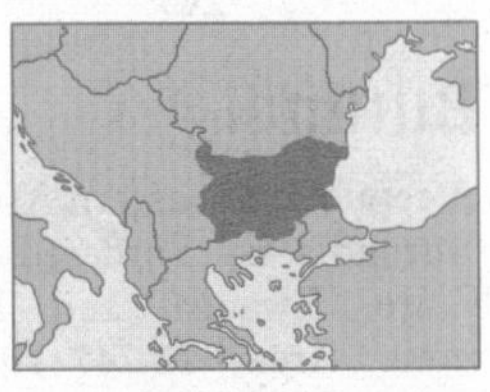

A people's republic of Europe, Bulgaria is situated on the eastern Balkan Peninsula along the Black Sea, bordered by Romania, Yugoslavia, Greece, and Turkey. Area: 42,823 sq mi (110,912 sq km). Pop. (1975) 8,729,700. Cap. and largest city: Sofia (pop., 1975, 965,700). Language: chiefly Bulgarian. First secretary of the Bulgarian Communist Party in 1976 and chairman of the State Council, Todor Zhivkov; chairman of the Council of Ministers (premier), Stanko Todorov.

The 11th congress of the Bulgarian Communist Party was held in Sofia from March 29 to April 2, 1976. It was attended by 1,575 delegates representing 789,796 party members (an increase of 90,320 since the tenth congress of 1971). In his five-year report on the Central Committee's activities, Zhivkov attacked Maoism and upheld Soviet leadership of the socialist camp. Reviewing the satisfactorily fulfilled sixth five-year plan (1971–75), Zhivkov announced that national income had risen by 46%.

For the seventh five-year plan (1976–80), a new approach to planning would emphasize the profit motive. Production of light industry was planned to rise by 45%, of the foodstuffs industry by 40%, and of agriculture by 20%. The average monthly salary (which rose from 65 to 146 leva in 1970–75) was expected to reach 170 leva by 1980.

The congress elected a Central Committee of 154 full and 121 associate members which, in turn, reelected Zhivkov as first secretary. Full membership of the Politburo was reduced from 12 to 9, the 6 associated members being reelected. On May 30, out of 6,379,348 citizens entitled to vote, 99.93% voted for the 400 official candidates for the National Assembly. On June 16 the Assembly elected the new State Council and the new Council of Ministers. Zhivkov was reelected chairman of the State Council and Stanko Todorov chairman of the Council of Ministers.

(K. M. SMOGORZEWSKI)

[972.B.3]

BULGARIA

Education. (1973–74) Primary, pupils 996,949, teachers 49,929; secondary, pupils 116,789, teachers 7,530; vocational, pupils 292,779, teachers 19,009; higher (including 3 universities), students 124,662, teaching staff 10,805.

Finance. Monetary unit: lev, with (Sept. 20, 1976) a free commercial exchange rate of 0.96 lev to U.S. $1 (1.70 lev = £1 sterling). Budget (1974 est.): revenue 8,060,000,000 leva; expenditure 8,045,000,000 leva.

Foreign Trade. (1975) Imports 5,236,000,000 leva; exports 4,541,000,000 leva. Main import sources (1974): U.S.S.R. 44%; East Germany 9%; West Germany 7%; Poland 5%. Main export destinations (1974): U.S.S.R. 50%; East Germany 8%; Poland 5%. Main exports (1974): machinery 31%; tobacco and cigarettes 11%; transport equipment 9%; fruits and vegetables 8%; iron and steel 6%; wines and spirits 5%. Tourism (1974): visitors 3,818,026; gross receipts U.S. $198 million.

Transport and Communications. Roads (1974) 31,157 km. Motor vehicles in use (1970): passenger *c.* 160,000; commercial (including buses) *c.* 38,000. Railways: (1974) 4,283 km; traffic (1975) 7,569,000,000 passenger-km, freight 17,286,000,000 net ton-km. Air traffic (1974): 385 million passenger-km; freight 7 million net ton-km. Navigable inland waterways (1973) 471 km. Shipping (1975): merchant vessels 100 gross tons and over 179; gross tonnage 937,458. Telephones (Dec. 1974) 718,000. Radio licenses (Dec. 1973) 2,266,000. Television licenses (Dec. 1973) 1,383,000.

Agriculture. Production (in 000; metric tons; 1975): wheat *c.* 3,100; corn *c.* 2,000; barley *c.* 1,500; sunflower seed *c.* 420; tomatoes *c.* 864; grapes (1974) *c.* 1,310; apples (1974) *c.* 358; tobacco *c.* 145; meat (1974) *c.* 472. Livestock (in 000; Jan. 1975): sheep 9,791; cattle 1,554; goats (1974) 286; pigs 3,422; horses (1974) 142; asses (1974) 312; chickens 32,694.

Industry. Fuel and power (in 000; metric tons; 1975): lignite 27,480; coal 320; crude oil 120; natural gas (cu m; 1974) 180,000; electricity (kw-hr) 25,233,000. Production (in 000; metric tons; 1975): iron ore (32% metal content) 2,340; manganese ore (metal content; 1974) *c.* 12; copper ore (metal content; 1974) 50; lead ore (metal content; 1974) 110; zinc ore (1974) 80; pig iron 1,510; crude steel 2,265; cement 4,361; sulfuric acid 853; soda ash (1974) 642; cotton yarn 79; cotton fabrics (m) 368,000; wool yarn 30; woolen fabrics (m) 33,000.

Brazilian Literature: *see* Literature

Bridge: *see* Contract Bridge

Bridges: *see* Engineering Projects

British Commonwealth: *see* Commonwealth of Nations; *articles on the various member states*

British Honduras: *see* Dependent States

Brunei: *see* Dependent States

Buddhism: *see* Religion

Building and Construction Industry: *see* Engineering Projects; Industrial Review

Bullfighting: *see* Arena Sports

EASTFOTO

Bulgaria's new atomic power station on the Danube at Kozloduy. It has two reactors with a total capacity of 880 megawatts.

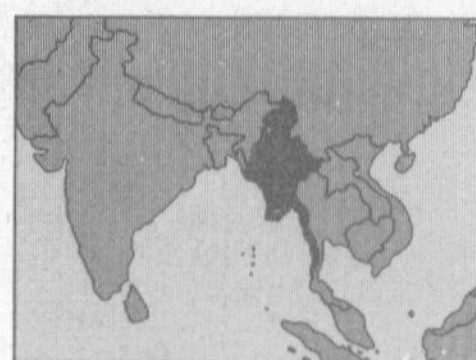

Burma

A republic of Southeast Asia, Burma is bordered by Bangladesh, India, China, Laos, Thailand, the Bay of Bengal, and the Andaman Sea. Area: 261,789 sq mi (678,030 sq km). Pop. (1976 est.): 31,992,000. Cap. and largest city: Rangoon (metro. pop., 1973, 3,186,900). Language: Burmese. Religion (1970): Buddhist 85%. Chairman of the State Council in 1976, U Ne Win; prime minister, U Sein Win.

Chairman U Ne Win's hopes for rapid progress in Burma through a socialistic program of development remained as much a dream in 1976 as in previous years. Despite an increase of 7.3% in agricultural output, the highest in 15 years, overall economic growth failed to catch up with the increase in population—a steady 2.2% a year. Mounting discontent arising from inflation and unemployment among the educated erupted in March into a further round of student demonstrations, leading to a long closure of the colleges. Martial law in Rangoon, imposed in December 1974, was lifted on September 1. A welcome rise in petroleum production to 7.8 million (U.S.) bbl made the nation almost self-sufficient in oil. In presenting the 1976–77 draft budget, Finance Minister U Lwin estimated a deficit of 803 million kyats.

U Ne Win's visit to Peking in November 1975 had resulted in the usual "friendly" communiqué, but there was no commitment from the Chinese to be discreet in their support of the Burmese Communist Party rebels. The following months saw a spurt in rebel activities, and there was evidence that the Chinese had in no way reduced their aid to the insurgents on the northern borders. Periodic skirmishes occurred between the security forces and insurgents of the Karen, Shan, and other ethnic minorities, some of whom regrouped in May 1976 to form a National Democratic Front. The arrest of several army officers accused of plotting to kill U Ne Win was announced in July. Foreign aid remained at a moderate level, with Japan assisting in oil exploration and West Germany and the Asian Development Bank in agricultural development. Burma signed a trade agreement with Vietnam in July. (GOVINDAN UNNY)

[976.B.1]

BURMA

Education. (1972–73) Primary, pupils 3,300,153, teachers 74,266; secondary, pupils 860,675, teachers 25,461; vocational, pupils 6,777, teachers 570; teacher training, students 4,428, teachers 301; higher, students 56,310, teaching staff 3,989.

Finance. Monetary unit: kyat, with (Sept. 20, 1976) a free rate of 6.91 kyats to U.S. $1 (11.90 kyats = £1 sterling). Gold, SDR's, and foreign exchange (June 1976) U.S. $143.2 million. Budget (1975–76 est.): revenue 14,472,000,000 kyats; expenditure 15,521,000,000 kyats.

Foreign Trade. (1975) Imports 806.1 million kyats; exports 1,015,200,000 kyats. Import sources (1973): Japan 28%; China 18%; West Germany 9%; U.K. 8%. Export destinations (1973): Japan 26%; Singapore 11%; U.K. 10%; West Germany 6%; Belgium-Luxembourg 6%; Pakistan 5%; Denmark 5%. Main exports (1974): rice 41%; teak 26%; oilcakes 5%.

Transport and Communications. Roads (1974) 21,745 km. Motor vehicles in use (1974): passenger 36,300; commercial (including buses) 39,300. Railways: (1973) 4,324 km; traffic (1974) 3,121,000,000 passenger-km, freight 395 million net ton-km. Air traffic (1974): 180 million passenger-km; freight 2.5 million net ton-km. Shipping (1975): merchant vessels 100 gross tons and over 39; gross tonnage 54,548. Telephones (Dec. 1974) 30,000. Radio licenses (Dec. 1973) 627,000.

Agriculture. Production (in 000; metric tons; 1975): rice *c.* 8,700; dry beans *c.* 160; onions *c.* 138; sugar, raw value *c.* 100; bananas (1974) *c.* 220; sesame seed *c.* 130; peanuts *c.* 500; cotton, lint *c.* 14; jute *c.* 112; tea (1974) *c.* 46; tobacco *c.* 75; rubber *c.* 15; timber (cu m; 1974) *c.* 21,170. Livestock (in 000; March 1974): cattle *c.* 7,875; buffalo *c.* 1,800; pigs *c.* 1,961; goats *c.* 790; sheep *c.* 214; chickens *c.* 18,000.

Industry. Production (in 000; metric tons; 1975): crude oil 956; electricity (excluding most industrial production; kw-hr) 630,000; cement (1974) 172; lead concentrates (metal content; 1974) 9.8; zinc concentrates (metal content; 1974) 4.3; tin concentrates (metal content; 1974) 0.6; tungsten concentrates (oxide content; 1974) 0.4.

Burundi

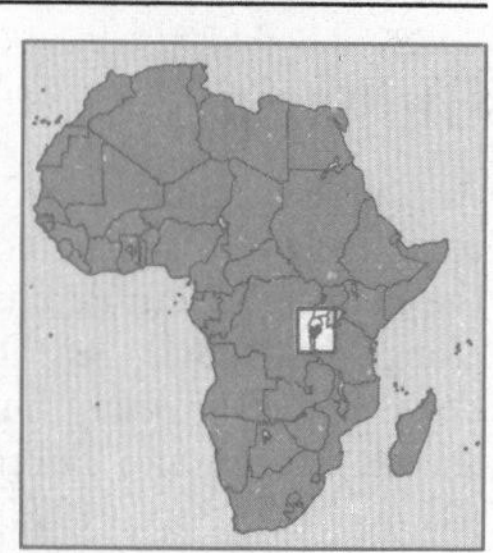

A republic of eastern Africa, Burundi is bordered by Zaire, Rwanda, and Tanzania. Area: 10,747 sq mi (27,834 sq km). Pop. (1976 est.): 3,863,000, mainly Hutu, Tutsi, and Twa. Cap. and largest city: Bujumbura (pop., 1970 est., 110,000). Language: Kirundi and French. Religion: Roman Catholic 60%; most of the remainder are animist; there is a small Protestant minority. Presidents in 1976, Michel Micombero and, from November 10, Lieut. Col. Jean-Baptiste Bagaza; prime minister from November 13, Lieut. Col. Edouard Nzambimana.

On Nov. 1, 1976, President Micombero was overthrown in a bloodless coup by army officers, who set up a Supreme Revolutionary Council. The head of the council, Lieut. Col. Jean-Baptiste Bagaza, was formally nominated as president of the republic on November 10. The new regime announced that Burundi would seek to maintain unchanged foreign relations.

Micombero visited Rwanda on June 17 in an attempt to improve relations between the two countries and to overcome tribal difficulties between the Tutsi and Hutu. An agreement was signed on joint agricultural and fishing projects and on strengthening social and economic ties. Agreements with Tanzania covered a joint shipping company for Lake Tanganyika and development in the Kagera River basin.

Burundi continued to rely on foreign and interna-

BURUNDI

Education. (1974–75) Primary, pupils 130,048, teachers (1971–72) 4,980; secondary, pupils 6,309, teachers (1971–72) 343; vocational, pupils 905, teachers (1971–72) 290; teacher training, students 5,078, teachers (1971–72) 243; higher, students 920, teaching staff (1971–72) 108.

Finance. Monetary unit: Burundi franc, with (Sept. 20, 1976) an official rate of BurFr 90 to U.S. $1 (free rate of BurFr 159.60 = £1 sterling). Gold, SDR's, and foreign exchange (June 1976) U.S. $26,880,000. Budget (1974 rev. est.): revenue BurFr 2,989,000,000; expenditure BurFr 2,629,000,000.

Foreign Trade. (1975) Imports BurFr 4,916,000,000; exports BurFr 2,148,000,000. Import sources (1974): Belgium-Luxembourg 25%; France 11%; West Germany 9%; Iran 6%; Japan 5%; China 5%. Export destinations (1974): U.S. 35%; West Germany 16%; France 10%; Belgium-Luxembourg 8%; Italy 7%; Spain 7%; U.K. 5%; Portugal 5%. Main export coffee 87%.

Agriculture. Production (in 000; metric tons; 1975): corn *c.* 350; cassava (1974) *c.* 4,000; sweet potatoes (1974) *c.* 1,200; millet *c.* 75; sorghum *c.* 100; dry beans *c.* 252; dry peas *c.* 30; bananas (1974) *c.* 1,540; coffee *c.* 18; cotton, lint (1974) *c.* 2.2. Livestock (in 000; Dec. 1973): cattle 761; sheep 203; goats 631; pigs 27.

tional aid, which in 1976 included $6 million from the African Development Bank for road and bridge links with Tanzania; a $6 million credit for fisheries from the International Development Association (IDA), supplemented by $1 million from Abu Dhabi; and another IDA credit of $5.2 million to increase production of coffee by small landholders in Ngozi Province. (MOLLY MORTIMER)

Cambodia

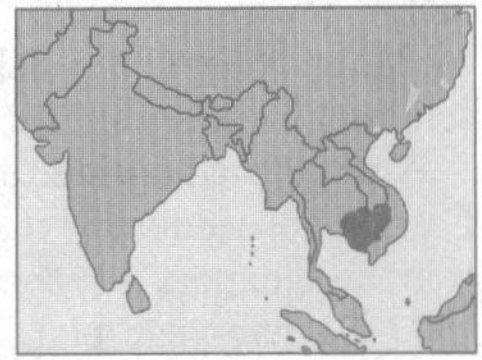

A republic of Southeast Asia, Cambodia (officially Democratic Kampuchea) is the southwest part of the Indochinese Peninsula, on the Gulf of Thailand, bordered by Vietnam, Laos, and Thailand. Area: 69,898 sq mi (181,035 sq km). Pop. (1976 est.): 7,735,300 according to official figures, although foreign observers estimated that figure to be overstated by as much as one million persons. It is estimated to comprise: Khmer 93%; Vietnamese 4%; Chinese 3%. Cap.: Phnom Penh (pop., 1976 est., between 40,000 and 100,000). Language: Khmer (official) and French. Religion: Buddhist. Heads of state in 1976, Prince Norodom Sihanouk and, from April 11, Khieu Samphan; premiers, Samdach Penn Nouth and, from April 11, Pol Pot.

The trickle of news that came out of Cambodia during 1976 helped confirm the postwar regime's reputation as a harshly different entity from its brother victors in neighbouring Vietnam and Laos. It started quietly enough. A new constitution, in force from January 5, gave the country a new name (Democratic Kampuchea), a new flag (the Angkor Wat emblem backed in yellow on a red field), and a new national anthem ("The Great Victorious April 17"). It called for state ownership of "important general means of production" but allowed private ownership of "property for everyday use," banned polygamy, guaranteed freedom of religion except when it was "detrimental," and provided for a legislature with farmers holding 150 seats, workers 50, and soldiers 50.

CAMBODIA

Education. (1973–74) Primary, pupils 429,110, teachers 18,794; secondary, pupils 98,888, teachers 2,226; vocational, pupils 4,856, teachers 202; teacher training, students 553, teachers 18; higher, students 11,570, teaching staff 276.

Finance. Monetary unit: riel, with (end February 1975) a free rate of 1,650 riels to U.S. $1 (4,000 riels = £1 sterling). Budget (1974 est.): revenue 22.8 billion riels; expenditure 71 billion riels.

Foreign Trade. (1973) Imports 14.2 billion riels; exports 2,732,000,000 riels. Import sources: U.S. *c.* 69%; Thailand *c.* 11%; Singapore *c.* 5%; Japan *c.* 5%. Export destinations: Hong Kong *c.* 23%; Japan *c.* 22%; Malaysia *c.* 18%; France *c.* 12%; Spain *c.* 10%. Main export rubber 93%.

Transport and Communications. Roads (1973) 15,029 km. Motor vehicles in use (1972): passenger 27,200; commercial (including buses) 11,100. Railways: (including sections not in operation; 1972) 649 km; traffic (1973) 54,070,000 passenger-km, freight 9,780,000 net ton-km. Air traffic (1974): 48 million passenger-km; freight 500,000 net ton-km. Inland waterways (including Mekong River; 1974) *c.* 1,400 km. Telephones (Dec. 1972) 9,000. Radio receivers (Dec. 1973) 1,110,000. Television receivers (Dec. 1973) 26,000.

Agriculture. Production (in 000; metric tons; 1975): rice *c.* 800; corn (1974) *c.* 70; bananas *c.* 90; oranges (1974) *c.* 33; dry beans *c.* 18; rubber *c.* 8; jute *c.* 3. Livestock (in 000; 1974): cattle *c.* 1,800; buffalo *c.* 840; pigs *c.* 950.

SARAH WEBB BARRELL—THE NEW YORK TIMES

Refugees from Cambodia line up for food at a camp in Thailand in January. They fled to escape forced migration from one part of Cambodia to another.

Other acts of consolidation followed swiftly. Information Minister Hu Nim announced on Radio Phnom Penh that elections had duly taken place on March 20. He said the right of franchise had been exercised by 98% of the registered voters (3,635,581 out of a total population of 7,735,300). Head of State Prince Norodom Sihanouk resigned on April 5, and on April 11 his Cabinet's resignation was accepted by the newly elected National Assembly. The assembly then named Khieu Samphan, who had been in the forefront of the guerrilla war, as head of state and Cambodian Communist Party Secretary-General Pol Pot as premier. Ieng Sary remained as deputy premier in charge of foreign affairs, Son Sen as deputy premier in charge of defense, and Hu Nim as minister of information. One name that figured nowhere was that of Sihanouk. After a tour including some of the third world countries, he had returned to Phnom Penh and presided over the Cabinet meeting that formally approved the constitution. With that his role apparently ended; in late October fears grew for the safety of the prince, reportedly under virtual house arrest.

Attempts that began in 1975 to set up a government in exile fizzled out, but sporadic resistance against the new regime persisted. Throughout the year refugees kept arriving in Thailand, most of them bringing horror stories about hardship and atrocities. U.S. sources went so far as to claim that some 500,000 Cambodians had either been killed or had died from starvation and disease after the Khmer Rouge victory.

In an unusual statement in August, Premier Pol Pot himself said that life was difficult. Admitting that "we have not yet achieved any noteworthy results except a revolutionary movement of the masses," he said postwar Cambodia was left with no formal schools, barely enough food, no means to build new factories, a serious medical problem, and no cultural activities. This was in sharp contrast to an earlier anniversary speech made by Khieu Samphan in which he claimed significant advances during the first year of the revolutionary government, including a record rice harvest.

While the true state of affairs inside the country remained a mystery to the outside world, the government by midyear had shown some interest in improving its image. It invited carefully selected foreigners to visit the country. It also sent out a steady stream of official delegations to conferences abroad. Foreign Minister Ieng Sary was a frequent caller in various world capitals, and Khieu Samphan traveled to Colombo in Sri Lanka to attend the fifth summit conference of nonaligned nations. Phnom Penh also established diplomatic relations with several countries and special trade arrangements with Thailand.

On April 30 Lieut. Pech Lim Kuon, a Cambodian Air Force pilot who had made headlines in 1973 by bombing Lon Nol's presidential palace and then defecting to the Khmer Rouge side, now defected from the Khmer Rouge and escaped to Thailand in a helicopter. He claimed that Khieu Samphan and Pol Pot, though important, were not among the top leaders. What he called "the organization" consisted of five: Communist Party boss Saloth Sar, a man known only as Nhun, Ieng Sary, Son Sen, and another man identified as Yan or Yang. (T. J. S. GEORGE)

[976.B.4.f]

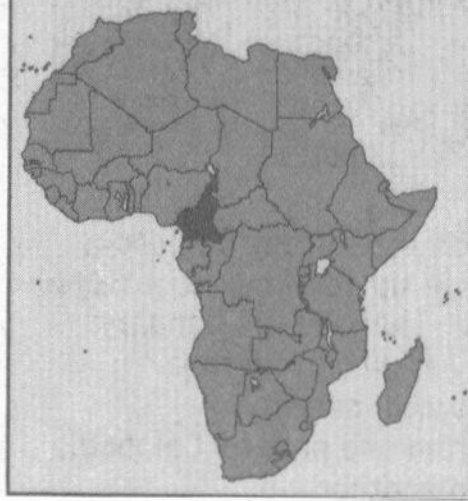

Cameroon

A republic of west Africa on the Gulf of Guinea, Cameroon borders on Nigeria, Chad, the Central African Empire, the Congo, Gabon, and Equatorial Guinea. Area: 179,600 sq mi (465,100 sq km). Pop. (1975 est.): 6,539,000. Cap.: Yaoundé (pop., 1975 est., 274,400). Largest city: Douala (pop., 1975 est., 485,800). Language: English and French (official), Bantu, Sudanic. Religion: mainly animist, with Roman Catholic (24%), Protestant, independent Christian, and Muslim minorities. President in 1976, Ahmadou Ahidjo; prime minister, Paul Biya.

Loyal to its traditional foreign policy of nonalignment with any form of political grouping, Cameroon did not participate in the Franco-African conference at Paris and Versailles, France, in May 1976. On July 19–22, however, President Ahidjo made an official visit to France, the second since he came to power in 1960. African affairs and bilateral relations were discussed and France pledged continuing aid to Cameroon's development projects, including modernization of the Douala-Yaoundé railway.

In February Cameroon announced its recognition of the People's Republic of Angola; but, no doubt because of the personal friendship between President Ahidjo and Pres. Moktar Ould Daddah of Mauritania, recognition was not given to the Algerian-supported Saharan Arab Democratic Republic (formerly Spanish Sahara), part of which was claimed by Mauritania. China delivered two coastal patrol vessels for the Navy in October.

A diversified agriculture continued to dominate the Cameroon economy, centred mainly on the production and export of cocoa, coffee, and timber. The 1977–81 five-year plan, totaling CFA Fr 725 billion, gave top priority to agricultural development, including rejuvenation of cocoa and coffee plantations.

The University of Yaoundé was to be divided into five regional campuses. The country's first national census was begun. (PHILIPPE DECRAENE)

CAMEROON

Education. (1974–75) Primary, pupils 1,074,021, teachers 20,803; secondary, pupils 93,934, teachers 3,699; vocational, pupils 27,524, teachers 1,240; teacher training, students 1,115, teachers 130; higher, students 6,171, teaching staff (1972–73) 328.

Finance. Monetary unit: CFA franc, with (Sept. 20, 1976) a parity of CFA Fr 50 to the French franc and a free rate of CFA Fr. 245.90 to U.S. $1 (CFA Fr. 423.62 = £1 sterling). Federal budget (1974–75 est.) balanced at CFA Fr 69.2 billion.

Foreign Trade. (1974): Imports CFA Fr 104,830,000,000; exports CFA Fr 114.9 billion. Import sources: France 47%; West Germany 9%; U.S. 6%; Italy 6%; Gabon 5%. Export destinations (1973): France 29%; The Netherlands 24%; West Germany 10%; U.S. 7%; Japan 5%. Main exports: cocoa 28%; coffee 25%; timber 14%; cocoa butter 5%.

Transport and Communications. Roads (1973) 43,508 km (including 2,913 km with improved surface). Motor vehicles in use (1972): passenger 39,100; commercial (including buses) 37,300. Railways (1974): 1,173 km; traffic 245 million passenger-km, freight 407 million net ton-km. Telephones (June 1973) 22,000. Radio receivers (Dec. 1973) 225,000.

Agriculture. Production (in 000; metric tons; 1975): corn *c.* 355; millet 386; sweet potatoes (1974) *c.* 550; cassava (1974) *c.* 1,000; bananas (1974) *c.* 90; peanuts *c.* 165; coffee *c.* 90; cocoa *c.* 112; palm kernels *c.* 60; palm oil *c.* 60; rubber *c.* 12; cotton, lint *c.* 15. Livestock (in 000; Dec. 1973): cattle *c.* 2,013; pigs *c.* 370; sheep *c.* 2,000; goats *c.* 1,500; chickens *c.* 8,600.

Industry. Production (in 000; 1974): aluminum (metric tons) 49; electricity (kw-hr) *c.* 1,123,000.

Canada

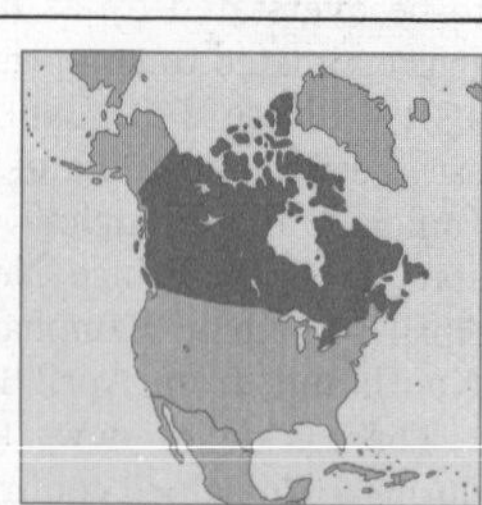

Canada is a federal parliamentary state and member of the Commonwealth of Nations covering North America north of conterminous United States and east of Alaska. Area: 3,851,810 sq mi (9,976,140 sq km). Pop. (1976 prelim. census): 22.6 million, including (1971) British 44.6%; French 28.7%; other European 23%; Indian and Eskimo 1.4%. Cap.: Ottawa (metro. pop., 1976 prelim. census, 668,000). Largest city: Montreal (metro. pop., 1976 prelim. census, 2,759,000). Language (mother tongue; 1971): English 61%; French 27%; others 13%. Religion (1971): Roman Catholic 46%; Protestant 42%. Queen, Elizabeth II; governor-general in 1976, Jules Léger; prime minister, Pierre Elliott Trudeau.

Domestic Affairs. The year 1976 was one of difficulty and uncertainty in Canada. Two issues dominated the news: the future course of the federal policy of bilingualism, and controversy over the system of wage and price controls introduced in October 1975. Both issues posed severe problems to the eight-year-old Liberal government of Pierre Trudeau. For most of the year public opinion polls ran strongly against the Liberals under Trudeau's leadership. Forced on the defensive by the unpopularity of its policies, the Cabinet was weakened by the resignation of some of its key ministers.

The issue of bilingualism came to the fore over a proposal to increase the use of French in ground-air communications at certain Canadian airports. For two years French had been allowed for noninstrument flights at five small Quebec airports. The federal government was anxious to extend its use to large international fields such as those at Montreal and Ottawa. The majority of air controllers and pilots in Canada opposed the extension on the ground that it would jeopardize air safety.

A settlement was negotiated by the federal minister of transport, Otto Lang. It involved the appointment of three judges to evaluate and report on procedures for bilingual air communications. They had the responsibility of reaching a unanimous judgment that, "beyond a reasonable doubt," bilingual air control would be safe. Their report would then be presented to Parliament. Here there would be a full debate in which members would vote according to their consciences and not by party solidarity.

Bilingualism in the air aroused intense feeling throughout Canada. To French-speaking Quebecois it symbolized their right to speak their own language in their own province. As one of their number put it, "All over the world, except in Quebec, the language of a country is the prime language in air communication. What we want is nothing more than this fundamental right." Quebec controllers and pilots denounced the Lang agreement, claiming that, in its insistence on unanimity among the commissioners, the inquiry was weighted against the position of the French language groups. They supported L'Association des Gens de l'Air in its stand that it would not take part in the commission of inquiry.

English-speaking Canadians appeared to have a genuine concern over flight safety in a system of bilingual communications. In addition, the issue touched on a widespread feeling in English Canada that the federal government was moving too quickly and too rigidly in imposing bilingualism in its activities. Prime Minister Trudeau warned of the danger that the quarrel over the issue could harden into a serious rift between French- and English-Canadians. "This country is in very serious danger of being divided on as basic an issue as has ever divided the country in the past 34 years. . . . The issue in this regard is indeed national unity."

The bilingual question threatened to split the Trudeau Cabinet. On June 30 one of the prime minister's closest colleagues, Jean Marchand, minister of the environment, resigned to express his indignation at the Lang settlement. He made it clear that in his view the settlement had undercut the principle of bilingualism and that he could not remain in a Cabinet that had approved it. He later resigned his seat in Parliament to run in the Quebec provincial election on November 15, but was defeated by a Separatist candidate. Just after Parliament opened for its new session, on October 13, another minister resigned, this time because of opposition to the possibility of bilingualism being entrenched in the constitution under a Quebec veto. James Richardson, minister of national defense, took this stand. He claimed that Trudeau's plan to transfer the legal power of amending the Canadian constitution from Great Britain to Canada would give both Quebec and Ontario a veto over constitutional change.

Wage and price controls proved another source of unpopularity for the federal government in 1976. Both business and organized labour opposed the government's intervention into the economy to restrain inflation. Announced to the Canadian people by Prime Minister Trudeau in October 1975, the program aimed to bring inflation down from a projected 8% in 1976 to 4% by the end of 1978. The plan required the cooperation of the provinces to be effective. Provincial adherence to the plan's guidelines was obtained during the first half of 1976, when most of the ten provinces signed agreements acknowledging the authority of the federal Anti-Inflation Board.

In March the 2.3 million-member Canadian Labour Congress, after vainly trying to persuade the Cabinet to drop the controls, proceeded to withdraw from government advisory bodies on which it was represented. At its convention in Quebec on May 17, it decided to

UPI COMPIX

Thousands of Quebec teachers march along Quebec City's Grand Allée in April to protest lagging contract talks.

mount a national day of protest against the controls on their first anniversary, October 14. The day of protest, called by some a general strike, was unique in Canada and perhaps in North America. For the first time a labour organization rallied its members from the Atlantic to the Pacific, not to press for better working conditions but to oppose a political decision. Demonstrations were held in Ottawa and in provincial capitals, and about 1,055,000 workers stayed off the job for the day.

As the year ended it was difficult to assess the results of the anti-inflation program. Inflation was clearly down from 1975, but some of the decrease was due to the fall in food prices, which were not under restraint. Hardships had been experienced by some groups of workers since it proved impossible to ensure equity in all decisions on wages and salaries. A positive accomplishment of controls was that they broke an attitude of inflationary expectations. The controversy over controls began to focus on the shape of the economy after controls would be removed—on Dec. 31, 1978.

Faced with dissension, the Trudeau government appeared indecisive and at times inept. The Cabinet suffered a number of losses. On March 16 André Ouellet, minister of consumer and corporate affairs, resigned after being convicted of contempt of court for criticizing a decision of a judge of the Quebec Superior Court. Another minister, C. M. Drury, offered his resignation when he was criticized for having made inquiries about a case before the courts. Trudeau refused to accept Drury's resignation, but in September, when he reconstructed his Cabinet, he allowed the veteran minister to leave. A new 31-member Cabinet was sworn in on September 15. There were seven new ministers drawn from the Liberal majority in the Commons. One, Leonard Marchand, named minister of state to the minister of industry, trade, and commerce, was an Indian from British Columbia, the first Indian to be appointed to a federal Cabinet. For the first time three women were given posts in the same Cabinet. The most important transfer among ministers was that of Allan MacEachen from external affairs to his old post as president of the privy council, with responsibility for steering legislation through Parliament. MacEachen was also named deputy prime minister. A former broadcaster from Newfoundland, Donald Jamieson, became secretary of state for external affairs. On November 3 Barnett Danson became minister of national defense, while Richardson's place as Manitoba's representative on the Cabinet was taken by Joseph-Philippe Guay, who was named minister of state. At the same time, Ouellet was recalled to succeed Danson as minister of state for urban affairs.

There were two by-elections in 1976, both lost by the Liberals. In St. John's West a seat held by a Conservative was retained by the party in an election on October 18. More serious was the loss of John Turner's riding on the outskirts of Ottawa on the same day. A Conservative, Mrs. Jean Pigott, won the riding by a larger margin than Turner had gained in the 1974 election.

The by-elections, resignations, and a death left the standings in the House of Commons as follows: Liberals 135; Progressive Conservatives 96; New Democratic Party 16; Social Credit 11; independent 1; vacancies 5.

The opposition Conservative Party gained a new national leader on February 21 when in a convention in Ottawa it chose 36-year-old Joseph Clark (*see* BIOGRAPHY), member for the Alberta riding of Rocky Mountain. Clark won over 11 other candidates on the fourth ballot. The new leader was bilingual, a former journalist and party organizer who once worked for the retiring leader, Robert L. Stanfield.

The longest parliamentary session in Canada's history, running from Sept. 30, 1974, ended on Oct. 12, 1976. The second session of the 30th Parliament began immediately. During the 1976 sittings a number of important bills were passed. One of the stormiest debates was provoked by a measure to remove the 100% tax deduction for advertisers in Canadian editions of foreign magazines. The chief examples of this type of publication were *Time* and *Reader's Digest*, but there were also about 20 U.S. border television stations affected by the legislation. In order to qualify for tax deductions for advertisers, it was proposed that a magazine must have 75% Canadian ownership, together with contents that were at least 80% different from material appearing in other editions. These regulations were interpreted during the course of the debate to allow *Reader's Digest* to count material as "Canadian content" if it was edited and condensed in Canada. *Time* could not meet the new stipulations and ceased publication of its Canadian edition after the legislation received final approval on February 25. The U.S. edition would still be available in Canada. The government argued that the measure was needed to give Canadian periodicals and television stations a fair chance to attract advertising.

Parliament also passed a law abolishing the death penalty. The last executions in Canada took place in 1962, after which time all death sentences had been commuted by order of the federal Cabinet. The legislation provided that for first-degree, premeditated murder there would be a 25-year sentence, with no eligibility for parole until at least 15 years had been served. In an effort to reduce mounting federal costs for health care, Parliament passed a bill on June 29 setting limits for the next two years on the federal contribution to provincial programs. Previously Ottawa had paid half the expenses regardless of the costs of the provincial plans. A new national lottery, Loto-Canada, was established to assist in reducing the deficit of the 1976 Olympic Games in Montreal, as well as to help amateur sport. (*See* Special Report.)

A controversial issue between Ottawa and the provinces was the patriation of the Canadian constitution. This was a favourite objective of the prime minister, who regarded it as anomalous that Canada's constitution, the British North America Act, could only be amended in another country, Britain. The problem lay in the inability of Canadians to agree on how their constitution should be changed in certain vital areas such as provincial rights. In April Trudeau suggested an amending formula by which both Ontario and Quebec would be given a permanent veto over changes. The smaller provinces would only have the power to block amendments through combining in groups. At a conference of provincial premiers at Banff, Alta., in August, British Columbia and Alberta criticized the plan for amendment and proposed that they also should have a veto over constitutional changes. Other provinces felt that this would impose too much rigidity upon the document.

CANADA

Education. (1975–76) Primary, pupils 2,821,500; secondary, vocational, and teacher training, pupils 2,673,400; preprimary, primary, and secondary, teachers 278,300; higher (including 45 main universities), students 592,000, teaching staff 48,000.

Finance. Monetary unit: Canadian dollar, with (Sept. 20, 1976) a free rate of Can$0.97 to U.S. $1 (Can$1.67 = £1 sterling). Gold, SDR's, and foreign exchange (June 1976) U.S. $5,261,000,000. Budget (1974–75 est.): revenue Can$24,909,000,000; expenditure Can$26,055,000,000. Gross national product (1975) Can$161,130,000,000. Money supply (April 1976) Can$23,180,000,000. Cost of living (1970 = 100; June 1976) 153.

Foreign Trade. (1975) Imports Can$36,926,000,000; exports Can$34,167,000,000. Import sources: U.S. 68%; EEC 9%. Export destinations: U.S. 66%; EEC 12% (U.K. 5%); Japan 6%. Main exports: motor vehicles 19%; crude oil 10%; wheat 6%; wood pulp 6%; nonferrous metals 5%; metal ores 5%; newsprint 5%. Tourism (1974): visitors 36,397,000; gross receipts U.S. $1,731,000,000.

Transport and Communications. Roads (1974) 3,032,985 km (2,765 km expressways in 1971). Motor vehicles in use (1974): passenger 8,472,000; commercial (including buses) 2,390,000. Railways: (1973) 70,131 km; traffic (1974) 3,023,000,000 passenger-km, freight 202,433,000,000 net ton-km. Air traffic (1975): 23,111,000,000 passenger-km; freight 580,675,000 net ton-km. Shipping (1975): merchant vessels 100 gross tons and over 1,257; gross tonnage 2,566,000. Shipping traffic (includes Great Lakes and St. Lawrence traffic; 1975): goods loaded 102,029,000 metric tons, unloaded 63,635,000 metric tons. Telephones (Jan. 1975) 12,454,000. Radio receivers (Dec. 1973) 19,133,000. Television receivers (Dec. 1973) 7,705,000.

Agriculture. Production (in 000; metric tons; 1975): wheat 17,100; barley *c.* 9,500; oats 4,440; rye 522; corn *c.* 3,600; potatoes 2,116; tomatoes *c.* 326; apples (1974) 407; rapeseed 1,635; linseed 445; soybeans 367; tobacco *c.* 102; beef and veal (1974) *c.* 920; pork *c.* 645; timber (cu m; 1974) 137,825; fish catch (1974) 1,027. Livestock (in 000; Dec. 1974): cattle 15,268; sheep 702; pigs 5,254; horses (1973) 345.

Industry. Labour force (Dec. 1975) 10,076,000. Unemployment (May 1976) 6.9%. Index of industrial production (1970 = 100; 1975) 120. Fuel and power (in 000; metric tons; 1975): coal 21,770; lignite 3,581; crude oil *c.* 70,000; natural gas (cu m; 1974) 73,370,000; electricity (kw-hr; 1974) 279,000,000 (75% hydroelectric and 5% nuclear). Metal and mineral production (in 000; metric tons; 1975): iron ore (shipments; 55% metal content) 31,135; crude steel 13,025; copper ore (metal content) 721; nickel ore (metal content) 240; zinc ore (metal content; 1974) 1,207; lead ore (metal content; 1974) 301; aluminum (1974) 1,007; uranium ore (metal content; 1974) 3.4; asbestos (shipments) 1,183; gold (troy oz) 1,624; silver (troy oz) 39,386. Other production (in 000; metric tons; 1975): cement 9,739; wood pulp (1974) 19,214; newsprint 7,056; other paper and paperboard (1974) 4,379; sulfuric acid 2,720; synthetic rubber 184; passenger cars (units) 1,045; commercial vehicles (units) 379. Dwelling units completed (1975) 217,000.

There were two provincial elections in the year ended in November. The first New Democratic Party (socialist) government in British Columbia's history was resoundingly defeated on Dec. 11, 1975, by the free-enterprise Social Credit Party under William H. Bennett, son of a former premier. There were 35 Social Credit members elected, 18 New Democratic Party, and one member each from the Liberal and Conservative parties. David Barrett, leader of the NDP and head of the defeated government, lost his seat but won another in a by-election in June.

Quebec held an election November 15, the results of which posed another challenge to Canadian unity. The separatist Parti Québécois won 71 of the 110 seats in the assembly to topple the six-year-old Liberal government of Robert Bourassa. The Liberals took 26 seats while a third party, the Union Nationale, gained 11. Under its founding leader, René Lévesque (*see* BIOGRAPHY), 55, the PQ did not stress separatism in the campaign but offered an efficient reform government. It promised to hold a referendum on the issue of independence before raising the matter with Ottawa. A few days later Bourassa resigned as head of the Quebec Liberal Party, effective Jan. 1, 1977.

Foreign Affairs. Canada's growing need for imported oil brought higher prices for domestic oil and gas in 1976 and cut into oil exports to the United States. Ottawa and the provinces held two meetings to try to reach agreement on a new national petroleum price. Alberta, the leading producing province, wanted an immediate increase in the wellhead price from $8 to the world price of $13.50 a barrel. This increase was strongly resisted by Ontario, the leading consuming province, and by the Maritime Provinces, which are dependent upon foreign oil for most of their energy needs. In late May it was announced that new prices would be effective after July 1, raising wellhead prices to $9.05 a barrel, with natural gas prices going up proportionally. Most provinces imposed a 60-day freeze on prices while old stocks were being consumed. The new levels were designed to encourage oil companies to carry out more exploration in Canada, to help in the conservation of energy, and to assist the federal government in meeting the higher price of imported oil, now amounting to about one-third of Canadian consumption.

The 515-mi, $200 million pipeline from Sarnia to Montreal was completed and put into operation by early summer. It brought Canadian prairie oil to the area east of the Ottawa River, which had previously obtained its supplies from foreign sources. As the pipeline came into use, oil exports to the United States were cut back by a formula that for every two additional barrels of domestic oil delivered to Montreal, exports would need to be reduced by one barrel.

There were several meetings between Canadian and United States leaders during the year. On June 16 Prime Minister Trudeau visited Washington to present President Ford with Canada's bicentennial present, *Between Friends—Entre Amis,* a book of scenes taken along both sides of the Canada-United States border. The two leaders discussed Canada's forthcoming purchase of the Lockheed Orion antisubmarine aircraft. On August 18 External Affairs Minister MacEachen met Secretary of State Henry Kissinger in Washington to discuss a number of border issues, including the Canadian plan to delete commercials from U.S. television signals carried by Canadian cable systems. The issue was referred to officials for further study. A new extradition treaty between Canada and the United States, in effect from March 22, provided that neither country would grant political asylum to terrorists or aircraft hijackers.

Canada was host to two large international gatherings in 1976. The first was Habitat, the UN Conference on Human Settlements, attended by 5,000 delegates from 140 countries, held in Vancouver from May 31 to June 11. The conference ended on a bitter political note as a resolution linking Zionism with racism was forced into the final declaration. (*See* ENVIRONMENT: *Special Report.*) The Games of the XXI Olympiad were held in Montreal from July 17 to August 1. At the last moment Canada announced it could not allow athletes from Taiwan to compete in the

continued on page 188

CANADIAN PRESS

Meeting in Ottawa's Civic Centre in February, Canada's Progressive Conservative Party chose a new leader, 36-year-old Joseph Clark.

MONTREAL—HOST TO THE WORLD

By Bruce Kidd

Unlike previous Olympic Games, which came about as a result of carefully integrated national economic and cultural planning, the 1976 Olympics represented the genius of one man, the 60-year-old mayor of Montreal, Jean Drapeau. Acting virtually alone, Drapeau in the late 1960s quietly lobbied the International Olympic Committee to bring the 1976 Games to his island city at the same time that Canadian sports officials and the federal government were preparing a bid to bring the 1976 Winter Games, considered more appropriate to Canada's climate, sporting traditions, and treasury, to Vancouver.

After gaining the Games for his city Drapeau personally selected the architect for the Olympic buildings, the controversial Frenchman Roger Taillibert, and then approved the plans and awarded the construction contracts. Men personally loyal to Drapeau largely controlled the Comité Organisateur des Jeux Olympiques (COJO), the corporation that administered the Games. A master of the political whipsaw, Drapeau waited until after he secured the Games and then persuaded the provincial government in Quebec to cover any deficit that might occur and the federal government to pay for television and security. Although control was wrested from his hands by Quebec Province seven months before the Games actually opened, neither friend nor foe doubted that the Games were principally his. Though he played a minor role in the opening ceremonies, his ovation was loudest and longest.

It was Drapeau's contention that a successful Games would proclaim to an audience even wider than that for the popular 1967 Montreal World's Fair the brilliance and bonhomie of the French Canadian community in North America, of which Montreal is the economic and intellectual capital. At the same time, he hoped that the Games would focus attention on Canadian amateur sports, which had suffered from a long period of neglect. He was successful on both counts.

Despite the gloomy predictions of many Olympic officials, including the late IOC president Avery Brundage, that the Montreal Games would never be held, they went off without a hitch. "Gold medal for Montreal," proclaimed the headline in a leading Oslo newspaper, *Verdens Gang,* the day after the closing ceremonies had taken place. It echoed the sentiments of the majority of Games visitors. Also, in the weeks preceding and during the competitions, the Canadian news media, traditionally oriented toward the commercial side of sports, gave overwhelming coverage to the Games.

City Improvements Postponed. But within Canadian society as a whole, the process left many bitter and confused. Although Drapeau repeatedly promised that "the Games won't cost the taxpayers a cent," costs were expected to exceed revenues by about $1 billion. This deficit was to be borne by the Quebec and Montreal governments and by an extended national lottery. Within Montreal itself, major parks acquisition, a subway extension, and a long overdue sewage treatment plant had to be postponed. Even municipal recreation services were cut back to help finance the Games.

About one-quarter of Montreal's 2.8 million people live on or below the poverty line, according to a major social agency, and many of these people are chronically ill, particularly from malnutrition. About 250,000 Montrealers earn the minimum wage of $2.87 an hour for an average annual salary of $5,740, compared with the $8,483 desired minimum for a family of four set by the Canadian Council on Social Development. About 91,000 persons, or 5.7% of the labour force, were unemployed at the time of the Olympics, and both business and labour leaders fear that the Games will be followed by a long slump. There is also a need for approximately 200,000 units of low-cost housing in the city. These problems have led many critics to argue that social services and public housing were more pressing priorities than the Games.

"There's no glamour in public housing," Drapeau has replied. "People know we cannot build 200,000 dwellings, one for everyone in need. They know that when we build a few thousand, none will be for them. It's impossible to get them behind you." Drapeau has the distinction of being the only mayor to be awarded the Games who remained in office during the period in which the Games were held, but he saw an opposition coalition win 19 of 55 seats in the city council during the 1974 elections. Until then, his handpicked Civic Party had held virtually every seat since 1960. Drapeau first served as mayor from 1954 to 1957, and he has held the office without a break since 1960. His present term expires in 1978.

Cause of the Deficit. The Olympic deficit resulted primarily from the large amount of money needed to build the spectacular facilities for the Games: a main stadium that contains a 70,000-seat track and field amphitheatre, now converted for use by the Montreal Expos baseball team and the Montreal Alouettes football team; a 9,200-seat swimming and diving pool, which when finally completed will also contain 20 floors of tennis and basketball courts; a 7,200-seat velodrome (cycling track); a 932-unit, four-block apartment complex built to house the athletes; and several lavish training centres. Almost all of the structures are located in the city's traditionally working-class east end. In 1970 Drapeau had told the IOC that Montreal would stage a "modest" Games to show the world that a nation need not be very rich to act as host to the competition. In 1976, however, the price tag for the facilities alone was estimated at $1.1 billion, not including $130 million needed to complete the stadium's tower and roof.

Inflation, overtime, and labour struggles all contributed to the high costs. So, possibly, did bribes and kickbacks, four major contractors having been arrested on charges of fraud and conspiracy. Throughout the construction, according to an auditor from Quebec Province, "there was always the feeling from the mayor's office that money was no object. There were many ways in which costs could have been trimmed, but no one was interested." Unlike Expo 67, when Drapeau had a strong lieutenant to veto unworkable ideas, there seemed to be no one at the Olympic site to check the rising expenses. The Quebec Chamber of Commerce has called for a full-scale public inquiry.

If Drapeau had managed to keep costs within his original $310 million budget, he would have made a profit on the Games, for his "self-financing" revenue schemes, necessitated by the initial refusal of both federal and provincial governments to share the expense, proved quite successful. The most spectacular of these was a national Olympic lottery, with individual tickets selling for $10 and a top prize of $1 million tax-free. Originally estimated to bring in $32 million, the lottery had netted $200 million by the opening of the Games. Considerable revenue was also earned by the specially minted sets of commemorative coins. There were 29 different designs in all, 28 in silver and 1 in gold. Despite a slow start when the federal government, which administered both lottery and coins, was caught by a rapidly rising silver market, the coins were expected to net $200 million.

Bruce Kidd, a championship runner who represented Canada in the 1964 Olympic Games, is assistant professor of physical education at the University of Toronto. His numerous writings on sports include The Death of Hockey *(1972) with John Macfarlane.*

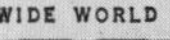

WIDE WORLD

Montreal's Olympic Stadium as it looked less than four months before the start of the 1976 Games. Beset by a myriad of problems, its construction left the taxpayers of Quebec with an Olympian debt.

Amateur sports have benefited significantly from both schemes, as 5% of each lottery ticket goes to the government sports agency in the province where it is sold and 3% of the coin revenue goes to the national Olympic committee in the country where the coins are sold. Drapeau consistently maintained that a worldwide lottery—what he likes to call a "voluntary tax"—and coin sales would make it possible to stage the Games on a break-even basis anywhere in the world. If expenditures had not risen so precipitously, the Montreal experience would have confirmed this.

No Shared Decisions. The other source of public irritation about the Games was what Drapeau believed to be his strongest suit—he kept the decisions to himself. "Nothing gets done if you involve lots of people in the plans," he once said. "They talk it to death." Throughout the six years of Olympic developments, the general public learned of his plans only after they had materialized. Very few were involved outside his city and the COJO executives. Even James Worrall, the IOC member for Canada who sat on COJO's executive board, would often say that he did not know what was going on. The secrecy touched off a constant flood of rumours, and alienated many people who under other circumstances might have been Drapeau's allies.

Resentment was particularly high in English-speaking Canada, where amateur sports had always involved hundreds of volunteers. When Vancouver staged the British Empire Games in 1954 and Winnipeg the Pan-American Games in 1967, thousands of people were involved in the preparations and the organizers attempted to make those events national efforts. Neither Drapeau nor COJO made a concerted effort to involve such volunteers in the Montreal Games. As a result, English Canada, both suspicious and jealous of Quebec, forgot about the sport and worried about the costs, remembering that during Expo 67 estimates of $137 million ballooned to a final cost of $414 million and a nationally shared deficit of $123 million.

In Quebec architects were angered by the announcement that there would be no public discussion of the Games facilities and that the commission had been awarded to the Frenchman Taillibert. A Montreal coalition of architects, environmentalists, and community groups collected 22,000 signatures on a petition opposing plans to build the Olympic village on public parkland. In neither case did Drapeau or COJO seem to consider alternatives to their plans. During the Games a $439,000 provincially sponsored public art project that was mildly critical of the city's role in the demolition of single-family housing in order to make room for high-rise and commercial development was hastily torn down by public works employees.

The Games did not greatly benefit Montreal's tourist industry, despite 3,250,000 paid admissions, second only to the 1972 Olympics at Munich. Few hotels were completely full, and during the Games taxi drivers staged a one-day tie-up of downtown traffic to protest the loss of business to COJO's 1,035-car fleet. Many Olympic visitors were athletes, coaches, and parents of competing athletes who came to watch the Games but not to spend money. They camped, brought their bicycles, and packed sandwich lunches.

Post-Games Assessment. The final balance sheet can only be drawn up after it becomes clear how well the costly facilities are used after the Games and whether the two weeks of breathtaking performances by the world's best athletes were sufficient to have convinced other politicians and civil servants in Canada to appropriate funds for amateur sports and physical recreation. Because of the new facilities in Montreal, the potential for accelerated sports development there is high. The problem facing provincial authorities, which took over control from the city in November 1975, is the cost of maintenance, estimated to be an exorbitant $50,000 a day for the stadium alone. The only facility opened to the public soon after the Games was the Olympic pool, where daily fees were set at $1 per person—likely to be too high for regular use by most east-end families. In these circumstances, the province might succumb to the well-rumoured alternative of turning the pool into a casino, with the velodrome becoming a convention centre.

The man who started it all, Jean Drapeau, is confident that the facilities will be kept for sport. "After all the money that has been spent," he says, "I don't see how they can close them." Throughout his administration, Drapeau has sought to inspire French-Canadians "not to be poor copies of others, but to make our own mark in this country and on this continent." First a major arts centre, then a subway, then Expo, now the Olympics. As one of his major critics once said privately, "He's like the devil in the morality play. No matter how much he ignores human suffering to pay for bread and circuses, he ends up smelling like roses." That was certainly the majority verdict during the 1976 Olympic Games.

". . and people were so impressed by this government initiative in cutbacks that inflation was soon overcome."

ULUSCHAK—EDMONTON JOURNAL, CANADA/ROTHCO

continued from page 185

games as representatives of the Republic of China. The Canadian position, based on the country's recognition of the People's Republic of China in 1970, was reluctantly accepted by the International Olympic Committee. Thirty-one countries, mainly black African and Arab, withdrew from the Games in protest against a tour of South Africa by a New Zealand rugby team. (*See* TRACK AND FIELD SPORTS: *Special Report.*)

The Economy. The economy showed a weak recovery in 1976. Real growth was expected to reach 5%, bringing the value of the gross national product to approximately $182 billion. The moderate growth helped to reduce the increase in the consumer price index to 6.5% for the year ended in September, the comparable figure for the previous year having been 10.6%. Unemployment stubbornly remained at just over 7% of the labour force, seasonally adjusted. The rate of growth of the labour force, one of the highest among industrialized countries, turned down slightly during 1976. The federal government's monetary policy was designed to reduce gradually the rate of expansion of the money supply in order to accommodate a reasonable improvement in the economy as well as to achieve progressively lower rates of inflation. During 1976 the central bank met its target of keeping the growth in currency and demand deposits to about 12%. Wage settlements began to move downward, and the outlook for costs and prices was brighter than it had been at the end of 1975. High rates of interest in Canada attracted an inflow of foreign capital which brought the Canadian dollar to a level of U.S. $1.025.

Finance Minister Donald Macdonald presented his first budget on May 25. Allowing for a moderate rate of growth in the economy, it held back government spending to a 16% increase. Total revenues were expected to increase to $34.4 billion, with expenditures running at $39.4 billion. Thus the budget deficit would amount to about $5 billion, slightly more than for 1975. (D. M. L. FARR)

[973.B]

ENCYCLOPÆDIA BRITANNICA FILMS. *The Legend of the Magic Knives* (1971); *The Canadians: Their Cities* (1974); *The Canadians: Their Land* (1974).

Canadian Literature: *see* Literature

Canoeing: *see* Water Sports

Catholic Church: *see* Religion

Cave Exploration: *see* Speleology

Census Data: *see* Populations and Areas; *see also the individual country articles*

Cape Verde Islands

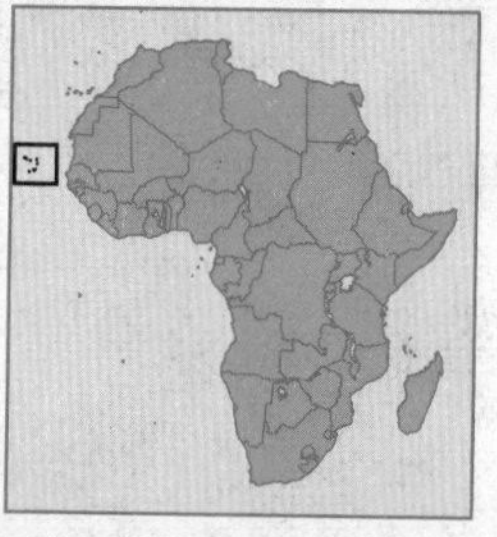

An independent African republic, Cape Verde is located in the Atlantic Ocean about 385 mi (620 km) off the west coast of Africa. Area: 1,557 sq mi (4,033 sq km). Pop. (1975 est.): 294,000. Cap.: Praia (pop., 1970, 21,500). Largest city: Mindelo (pop., 1970, 28,800). Language: Portuguese. Religion: mainly Roman Catholic. President in 1976, Aristide Pereira; premier, Maj. Pedro Pires.

The independence of the Cape Verde Islands was further recognized in November 1975 when they became one of four new members admitted to the Food and Agriculture Organization of the UN and on Jan. 5, 1976, when they joined the World Health Organization. Diplomatic relations had already been established with East Germany and Mongolia in the second half of 1975 and were established with China after meetings in Praia early in 1976 between China's ambassador in Guinea-Bissau and President Pereira and Premier Pires. Relations with Guinea-Bissau continued to be friendly; the possibility of a union between the two states remained likely, with the two presidents attending meetings of the councils of state of the two territories as joint general secretaries. But Cape Verde also shared with its sister republic the economic difficulties inherited from Portugal. Though the collectivist approach to economic reform adopted by the ruling African Party for the Independence of Guinea-Bissau and Cape Verde appeared to have the support of the bulk of the population in both countries, the main prospect for economic development rested on external aid. (KENNETH INGHAM)

CAPE VERDE ISLANDS

Education. (1973–74) Primary, pupils 63,734, teachers 1,078; secondary and vocational, pupils 3,712, teachers 186.

Finance and Trade. Monetary unit: Cape Verde escudo, at par with the Portuguese escudo and with (Sept. 20, 1976) a free rate of 31.10 escudos to U.S. $1 (53.60 escudos = £1 sterling). Budget (1973 est.): revenue 282 million escudos; expenditure 158 million escudos. Foreign trade (1973): imports 1,091,855,000 escudos; exports 306,605,000 escudos. Import sources: Portugal 53%; U.K. 13%; Angola 11%. Export destinations: Portugal 61%; U.S. 25%; ship's stores 6%. Main exports (excluding transit trade): fish 33% (shellfish 12%); fish products 20%; salt 8%; bananas 6%; metals 6%.

Transport. Ships entered (1972): vessels totaling 5,977,000 net registered tons; goods loaded 45,000 metric tons, unloaded 427,000 metric tons.

Central African Empire

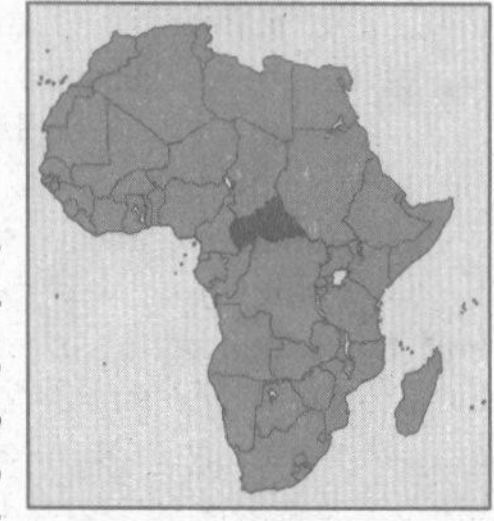

The landlocked Central African Empire (Central African Republic until Dec. 4, 1976) is bounded by Chad, the Sudan, Congo, Zaire, and Cameroon. Area: 241,305 sq mi (624,977 sq km). Pop. (1975 est.): 1,790,000 according to estimates by external analysts;

CENTRAL AFRICAN EMPIRE

Education. (1972–73) Primary, pupils 193,866, teachers 2,987; secondary, pupils 14,710, teachers 396; vocational, pupils 1,397, teachers 141; teacher training, students 451, teachers 48; higher (1973–74), students 380, teaching staff (1971–72) 6.

Finance. Monetary unit: CFA franc, with (Sept. 20, 1976) a parity of CFA Fr 50 to the French franc and a free rate of CFA Fr 245.90 to U.S. $1 (CFA Fr 423.62 = £1 sterling). Budget (1974 est.): revenue CFA Fr 15,706,000,000; expenditure CFA Fr 17.2 billion. Cost of living (1970 = 100; Feb. 1976) 166.

Foreign Trade. (1974) Imports CFA Fr 11,090,-000,000; exports CFA Fr 11,622,000,000. Import sources (1973): France 57%; U.S. 9%; West Germany 7%. Export destinations (1973): France 41%; U.S. 15%; Israel 11%; Italy 6%. Main exports (1973): diamonds 32%; cotton 31%; coffee 30%.

Agriculture. Production (in 000; metric tons; 1975): millet *c.* 50; cassava (1974) *c.* 1,100; corn (1974) *c.* 55; sweet potatoes (1974) *c.* 51; peanuts *c.* 85. Livestock (in 000; 1974): cattle *c.* 460; pigs *c.* 60; sheep *c.* 72; goats *c.* 550; chickens *c.* 1,200.

Industry. Production (in 000; 1974): diamonds (metric carats) 435; cotton fabrics (m) 6,000; electricity (kw-hr) 53,000.

recent official estimates range up to 750,000 persons higher. Cap. and largest city: Bangui (pop., 1968, 298,600). Language: French (official); local dialects. Religion: animist 60%; Christian 35%; Muslim 5%. President in 1976, Eddine Ahmed Bokassa (styled, from December 4, Emperor Bokassa I); premiers, Elisabeth Domitien until April 4 and, from September 5, Ange Patasse.

On Sept. 5, 1976, President Bokassa dissolved the government and replaced it by a 30-member Council of the Revolution. Already life-president of the republic, he relinquished all his ministerial offices and, as 31st member of the council, appointed himself the council's president. He also retained his posts of head of the armed forces and life-president of the country's sole political party. Ange Patasse, minister of state since 1969, was made premier. This post had been abolished when Elisabeth Domitien's Cabinet was dismantled on April 4. On December 4 Bokassa, who had converted to Islam and adopted the names Eddine Ahmed in place of Jean-Bédel, declared his country a parliamentary monarchy, with himself as emperor, and changed its name from Central African Republic to Central African Empire.

On February 3 Bokassa narrowly escaped an assassination attempt at Bangui airport organized by his son-in-law Fidel Odrou, commander of an air force squadron. Two of the perpetrators were reported killed on the spot, and eight others, including Odrou, were executed on February 14.

In August diplomatic relations with China were re-established. (PHILIPPE DECRAENE)

[978.E.7.a.ii]

Chad

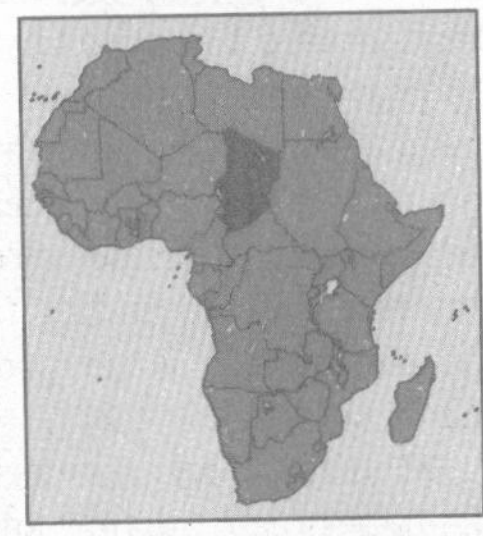

A landlocked republic of central Africa, Chad is bounded by Libya, the Sudan, the Central African Empire, Cameroon, Nigeria, and Niger. Area: 495,750 sq mi (1,284,000 sq km). Pop. (1975 est.): 4,030,000, including Saras, other Africans, and Arabs. Cap. and largest city: N'Djamena (pop., 1975 est., 224,000). Language: French (official). Religion: Muslim 52%; animist 43%; Roman Catholic 5%. President and premier in 1976, Brig. Gen. Félix Malloum.

CHAD

Education. (1973–74) Primary, pupils 198,030, teachers 2,540; secondary, pupils 11,418, teachers (1969–70) 313; vocational (1971–72), pupils 1,104; teacher training (1971–72), students 317, teachers (1969–70) 33; higher, students, 605, teaching staff 85.

Finance. Monetary unit: CFA franc, with (Sept. 20, 1976) a parity of CFA Fr 50 to the French franc and a free rate of CFA Fr 245.90 to U.S. $1 (CFA Fr 423.62 = £1 sterling). Budget (1976 est.) balanced at CFA Fr 15,785,000,000. Cost of living (N'Djamena; 1970 = 100; Dec. 1975) 154.

Foreign Trade. (1974) Imports CFA Fr 22,051,-000,000; exports CFA Fr 8,753,000.000. Import sources (1973): France 42%; Nigeria 12%. Export destinations: not separately distinguished 62%; Nigeria 6%; Congo 5%. Main exports (1973): cotton 63%; beef and veal 7%; cattle 5%.

Although President Malloum's government had abolished the arbitrary powers of the police and released political prisoners held under Pres. N'Garta Tombalbaye's regime, the president's call for national unity was not accepted by the Chad National Liberation Front (Frolinat), which in 1976 controlled most of the northern part of the country and kept up its demand for a socialist order for all Chad. On April 13 Malloum escaped injury when an attempt was made on his life during a parade to mark the first anniversary of the coup that brought him to power. Four persons were reported killed. Abba Siddick, the Algerian-based head of Frolinat, claimed responsibility for the attack.

A visit to N'Djamena by French Premier Jacques Chirac in March was marked by the signing of new civil and military agreements by which French aid to Chad would be greatly increased. The visit officially sealed the Franco-Chadian reconciliation after the crisis resulting from the detention of French ethnologist Françoise Claustre in April 1974 by splinter-group rebels under Hissen Habre. In November it was rumoured that she would be "tried or set free" by regular Frolinat forces. Financial and military aid was believed also to have been supplied by Chad's northern neighbour Libya in exchange for the cession of some 96,000 sq km of territory. Although foreign aid was essential, there was optimism over the cotton, millet, and sorghum harvests, hydrocarbon drilling in the east, and the possibility of a uranium discovery. (PHILIPPE DECRAENE)

Chemistry

Physical and Inorganic Chemistry. The year 1976 witnessed a sustained effort by scientists to develop new materials with unusual properties. Of particular interest to physical chemists were organic compounds that exhibited electrical conductivity and other metal-like characteristics. The unusual result reported in 1973 that the organic salt TTF-TCNQ (tetrathiofulvalene tetracyanoquinodimethan) exhibited signs of superconductivity at 58° K (−355° F) could not be substantiated. Nevertheless, the claim stimulated extensive research activity in synthesizing and studying analogous compounds. Some of these showed good room-temperature conductivity values, which increased upon cooling, but instead of becoming superconductors at low temperatures they were found to undergo an abrupt loss of conductivity in the temperature range of 40°–80° K, a phenomenon known as the

Central America: *see* Latin-American Affairs; *articles on the various countries*

Ceramics: *see* Materials Sciences

Ceylon: *see* Sri Lanka

Checkers: *see* Board Games

Chemical Industry: *see* Industrial Review

Peierls transition. However, a recently synthesized HMTSF-TCNQ (hexamethylene tetraselenafulvalinium TCNQ) demonstrated increased conductivity upon cooling to 45°–75° K, then decreased conductivity at still lower temperatures; it showed no Peierls transition, however, even at 0.008° K. Another related material, abbreviated $(DEPE)^{2+}(TCNQ)_4^{2-}$, was reported to be the first organic complex to show a monotonic increase in conductivity upon cooling from room temperature to 0.03° K.

Another intriguing class of new materials is that of shape-memory alloys, which upon change of temperature undergo a phase change in their crystalline structure that results in reversion to an earlier shape or recovery of previous mechanical properties. The alloys are made from precious and transition metals, the most notable example being Nitinol, which contains equal numbers of nickel and titanium atoms. During its fabrication the shape-memory alloy is given a desired configuration, such as that of a spiral wire, and then annealed at high temperature to fix the shape. Next it is lowered below its phase-transition temperature and given another shape; for instance, a straight wire. Subsequently on heating to a temperature above the phase-transition but below the annealing temperature, the alloy will return to its initial shape. Such alloys were finding uses as temperature sensors and weldless tubing connectors, in movements for electrical meters, in surgical and orthodontic devices, and in heat engines that can exploit small temperature differences.

Liquid membranes, neglected for several years after their discovery by Norman N. Li of Exxon Research & Engineering Co., became subjects of great interest during the year because of their ability to maintain a substance in isolation or to separate it from other substances. Liquid-membrane systems are formed when an oil, an aqueous solution, and a detergent are agitated together. Typically, small droplets of aqueous solution, about 0.1 mm in diameter, become encapsulated in a thin film, or membrane, of oil; these droplets in turn can be suspended in another aqueous solution where they coalesce into aggregates about 1 mm in diameter. Alternatively, droplets of oil may be encapsulated in a water membrane, which is then suspended in oil. Most applications of these membrane systems depended upon the selective permeability of the membrane to various chemicals. A substance soluble in the membrane and in both of the liquids that it separates will easily cross the membrane. If the substance is insoluble in the membrane, however, it will remain isolated in either the encapsulated liquid or the exterior one. Applications under development included water purification systems, the encapsulation of enzymes and drugs, and the scavenging of toxic substances from the human body.

(JOHN TURKEVICH)

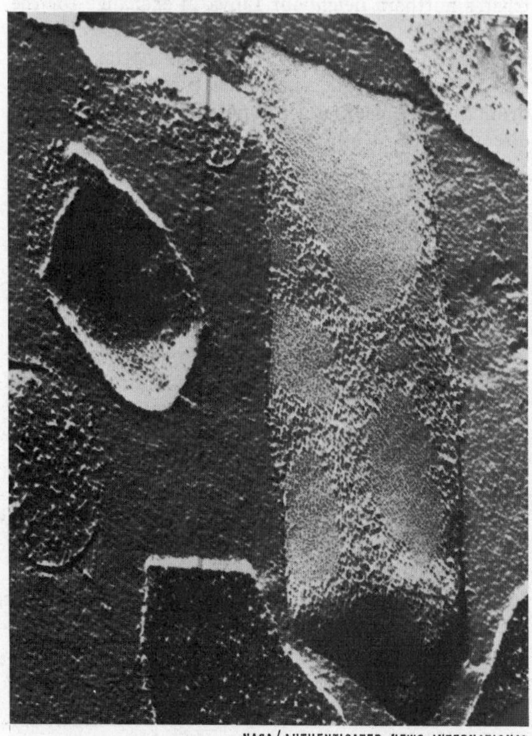

NASA/AUTHENTICATED NEWS INTERNATIONAL

Closeup of a frozen, fractured bacterium seen by electron microscope. A team of researchers in California is working on a bacterial system for converting sunlight into chemical energy and food.

Organic Chemistry. Among the more notable recent accomplishments and of considerable importance to the biological and health sciences were reports of the syntheses of the macrolide antibiotics methymycin and vermiculine, two members of a class of compounds that possess the unusual structural feature of many-membered rings. A major problem in the synthesis had been achievement of the desired cyclization.

Development of new methods for achieving selective changes in bonding continued. Noteworthy successes in this field included the selective conversion of a carbon-hydrogen bond by reaction with molecular fluorine; *e.g.*, steroids were converted directly into 9-α-fluorosteroids, compounds of medical importance. In another study, replacement of a preselected carbon-hydrogen bond in a steroid was achieved by a biomimetic reaction; that is, one designed to mimic nature. An activating group was attached to the steroid, activated (by light, for example) to produce the desired chemical modification in the steroid, and then removed.

The isolation and characterization of naturally occurring materials received powerful assistance from two new improvements in instrumentation. High-performance liquid chromatography,, a liquid-solid adsorption technique, facilitated the isolation and purification of substances, and high-resolution mass spectrometry, possessing greatly increased sensitivity in measurement of mass/charge values, made possible the assignment of composition and, to an increasing extent, of structure (based on computer analysis of fragmentation patterns) to substances that were available only in microgram quantities.

Search for selective methods of pest control focused on species-specific pesticides. The sex pheromone of the Japanese beetle was isolated, identified, and synthesized, thus providing a potentially efficient means of trapping insects or confusing their mating habits. The active pheromone is a delicate balance of cis, trans, and optical isomers of a gamma lactone of an unsaturated 14-carbon hydroxy acid. Other approaches to pest control involved studies on growth-regulating insect juvenile hormones and on antiallatotropic compounds, which were chemical substances capable of suppressing juvenile-hormone activity. Of particular interest was the finding that plants produce chemicals possessing this latter property. (*See* LIFE SCIENCES: *Entomology*.)

Studies of organic derivatives of metals, a borderland between organic and inorganic chemistry, were providing information on the nature of chemical bonding and a wide range of novel substances, some useful for synthesis and others for their special properties. One synthetic transformation, catalyzed by any of

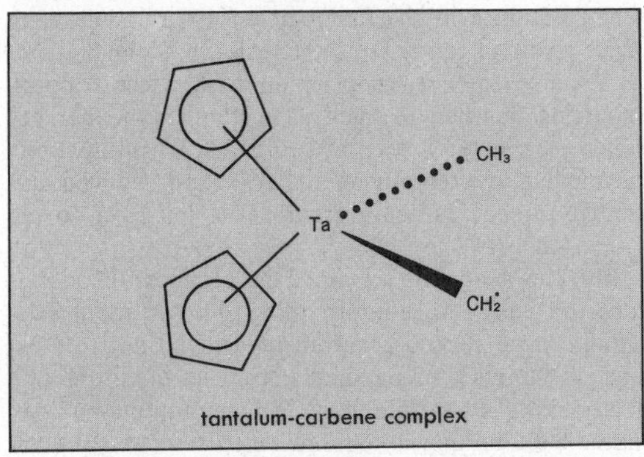

tantalum-carbene complex

several different organometallic complexes usually containing tungsten, molybdenum, or rhenium, is the olefin metathesis reaction $2R_1HC{=}CHR_2 \rightleftarrows R_1HC{=}CHR_1 + R_2HC{=}CHR_2$, in which R_1 and R_2 represent different generalized substituents. Contrary to most earlier suggestions, experiments reported during the year indicated that the reaction proceeds by a metal-carbene complex, formally a species in which a metal atom is associated with a divalent carbon atom. The nature and synthetic utility of metal-carbene species were under intense investigation in several laboratories, and one important advance was the isolation and characterization of a tantalum-carbene complex (*see* figure). Another active field of organometallic research involved the investigation of substances capable of duplicating the oxygen-transport capability of hemoglobin. Recently several organometallic substances were synthesized that possessed this ability to bind diatomic oxygen reversibly. One, a manganese-porphyrin complex, was of interest because its behaviour differed markedly from that of hemoglobin.

(FREDERICK D. GREENE)

[122.A.6.a and c; 122.B.5.b; 122.E.1.c; 321.B.3.b.ii]

Applied Chemistry. Major advances in applied chemistry included improvements in pest-control methods and in various materials and products. Organophosphate pesticides (substitutes for DDT) were being encapsulated by Pennwalt Corp., Philadelphia, into minute time-release beads less than 50 micrometres in diameter. Applied to crops, they release their contents gradually and in relatively small amounts, thereby reducing the need for costly repeated applications. By encapsulating natural and synthetic insect sex pheromones (sex-attractant substances) chemists were also able to extend the effectiveness of these relatively expensive materials; in some applications the encapsulated product contained both a pheromone and a pesticide so that insects would be lured to a site and then destroyed by the poison.

A plastic fibre-optic cable that can transmit visible light signals for military, marine, and control instrumentation applications as far as 50 m (over twice the distance previously attainable with plastic fibres) was developed by scientists at du Pont & Co., Wilmington, Del. The cable consists of a clear polymethyl methacrylate core reinforced with aramide fibres and coated with flame-retardant polyester. Unlike conventional glass-fibre strands, it can be cut easily with a razor for coupling to light source and detector. A novel structural material, the product of PPG Industries, Inc., Pittsburgh, Pa., was claimed to be four times stronger than steel but to weigh only half as much. Glass fibres are impregnated with liquid resin, crisscrossed on a revolving drum, unrolled, and cut into sheets that can be molded by compression into a desired shape. Called XMC, it was expected to find uses in home appliances and automobiles.

A water-insoluble carboxymethylcellulose fibre developed by Hercules, Inc., Hopewell, Va., can absorb 45 times its own weight of water. The biodegradable material is particularly suited for absorbent products such as medical dressings and diapers, but because the absorbed water is not releasable under pressure, such products can be used only once. Another superabsorbent material, developed by chemists of the U.S. Department of Agriculture, is even more thirsty; it can absorb 2,000 times its weight of water. Made of starch graft copolymers, it was being produced in powder, flake, film, and sheet form, and was considered a strong competitor of cellulose materials because of its greater absorbency and lower production cost.

(FREDERICK C. PRICE)

See also Nobel Prizes.

Chile

A republic extending along the southern Pacific coast of South America, Chile has an area of 292,135 sq mi (756,626 sq km), not including its Antarctic claim. It is bounded by Argentina, Bolivia, and Peru. Pop. (1975 est.): 10,253,000. Cap. and largest city: Santiago (metro. pop., 1975 est., 3,263,000). Language: Spanish. Religion: predominantly Roman Catholic. President in 1976, Gen. Augusto Pinochet Ugarte.

The military government that had seized power by a coup in September 1973 continued to rule as a dictatorship and by decree as an anti-Marxist, pro-Western regime. Three years after the overthrow of the constitutionally elected leftist president Salvador Allende, Chile continued to be a nation with a long democratic tradition in which all political parties were banned and the shape of the future had not yet emerged.

The curfew imposed on the day of the military coup remained in force, but the hours were reduced to the period from 1 AM to 5 AM. The regime continued to hold political prisoners, though under pressure from the U.S. and other democratic nations the number was reduced. There were estimated to be around 2,000 people held for political reasons at any given time. The government claimed that reports of prisoners being tortured were untrue. Nevertheless, U.S. Secretary of State Henry A. Kissinger was moved to criticize the Chilean regime when he addressed a meeting of American foreign ministers in the Chilean capital on June 8. He said that violations of human rights had "impaired [the U.S.] relationship with Chile," and called on all American countries to observe "fundamental standards of humane conduct."

The government's image suffered a serious setback in September when former ambassador to the United States Orlando Letelier, a Socialist who had been a minister in the Allende government at the time of its overthrow, was assassinated in Washington. He had been an active enemy of the current regime, denouncing its alleged use of torture and other rights violations. Shortly before his death the government had revoked Letelier's Chilean citizenship, and he had told friends and associates of threats against his life. Antijunta leaders charged that Letelier had been murdered by the DINA, Chile's secret police organization. He had been a prisoner of the junta for a year after the coup and reportedly had been in contact with other leaders of Chile's non-Marxist parties since then.

Chess:
see Board Games

Child Welfare:
see Education; Social and Welfare Services

ADN–ZB / EASTFOTO

Demonstrators in Washington, D.C., protest the slaying in September of Orlando Letelier, who had been prominent in the Chilean government of Salvador Allende before it was overthrown in 1973. Attributing his murder to the present government of Chile, the demonstrators wore masks so they could not be identified by photos.

The government denied any complicity in the murder.

Central to the question of Chile's political future was the refusal of the military leaders to deal with the non-Marxist, democratic politicians who had ruled Chile prior to the election of the Marxist front government in 1973. The traditional Christian Democratic, Radical, and National parties, which at first had seen the overthrow of Allende as offering them an opportunity to pursue their own programs, found no place in the plans of Pinochet and his military followers.

The junta formed a commission of jurists and lawyers to draw up a new constitution under which Chile would someday return to government by election. But the junta was obviously in no hurry, and there were predictions that a return to constitutional government might take five to ten years. Whatever form the constitution might assume, Chile seemed unlikely to return to its traditional party system in the foreseeable future. There would be no room for such elements as former president Eduardo Frei Montalva, the anticlerical Radicals, or the union of Conservative and Liberal parties.

Observers expected that Chile would eventually produce a new government party with a built-in majority and a controlled minority opposition party—a situation not unlike that imposed in Brazil or that which had evolved spontaneously in Mexico.

Chile under the junta remained four-square on the side of the U.S. in international relations and strongly antagonistic toward the Soviet Union and Cuba. In one diplomatic maneuver, the Pinochet government offered landlocked Bolivia an outlet to the Pacific—but through territory seized by Chile from Peru in the War of the Pacific a century ago. Peru's cooperation was obviously needed for such a transaction, and a joint commission was appointed to examine it. In exchange for the corridor, Chile was said to want concessions from Bolivia including not only territory but exclusive use of the waters of the Lauca River and demilitarization of the corridor. Opposition to the land exchange idea came from Bolivian mining interests. Negotiations among the countries involved were continuing at year's end.

As always, copper exports remained crucial for the economy. Copper accounts for about four-fifths of Chile's export earnings. The international price of the metal dropped sharply in 1975, going as low as 53 cents, but rose in the first part of 1976 and leveled off at about 64 cents. During the slump, Chile had cut its exports 15% in cooperation with other copper-exporting countries in an effort to stabilize the market. When prices rose it returned to full-scale production. Meanwhile, a program of austerity had reduced the annual rate of inflation from 340% in 1975 to an estimated 174% in 1976.

But the economy remained in perilous shape because of Chile's huge international debt of about $4.2 billion. Even so, the government decided not to seek any rescheduling of payments from its creditors and even paid off $800 million while accumulating an estimated $386 million in hard currency reserves. It continued its efforts to attract foreign investment, including a search for buyers for some of the nationalized enterprises inherited from the Allende regime. This brought Chile into conflict with its fellow members of the Andean Group—Colombia, Peru, Bolivia, Ecuador, and Venezuela—who had agreed with Chile to limit the amount of profits that foreign investors might take out of the area and were opposed to the liberal terms Chile was offering. The other members, at a meeting in late September, decided that Chile must drop out so that they could proceed with their plan to develop an integrated Andean economy. On October 6 Chile withdrew. (JEREMIAH A. O'LEARY, JR.)

[974.E]

CHILE

Education. (1975) Primary, pupils 2,314,411, teachers 75,400; secondary, pupils 285,806, teachers 17,799; vocational, pupils 163,105, teachers 11,768; higher (including 6 main universities), students 190,-535, teaching staff (1965) 8,835.

Finance. Monetary unit: peso, with (Sept. 20, 1976) a free rate of 14.22 pesos to U.S. $1 (24.50 pesos = £1 sterling). Gold, SDR's, and foreign exchange (June 1976) U.S. $380 million. Budget (1975 est.): revenue 7,703,500,000 pesos; expenditure 7,242,300,000 pesos. Gross national product (1973) 1,235,700,000 pesos. Money supply (Dec. 1975) 3,279,000,000 pesos. Cost of living (Santiago; 1970 = 100; May 1976) 75,537.

Foreign Trade. (1975) Imports U.S. $1,811,000,-000; exports U.S. $1,761,000,000. Import sources (1974): U.S. 22%; Argentina 17%; West Germany 8%; Australia 5%; Saudi Arabia 5%. Export destinations (1974): Japan 16%; West Germany 14%; U.S. 12%; U.K. 9%; Argentina 7%; Italy 6%; Brazil 6%; China 5%. Main exports (1974): copper 67%; nitrates 20%.

Transport and Communications. Roads (1974) 63,735 km. Motor vehicles in use (1974): passenger 197,800; commercial (including buses) 151,400. Railways: (1973) 8,995 km; traffic (principal only; 1975) 2,101,000,000 passenger-km, freight 1,926,000,000 net ton-km. Air traffic (1974): 1,159,000,000 passenger-km; freight 57 million net ton-km. Shipping (1975): merchant vessels 100 gross tons and over 138; gross tonnage 386,322. Telephones (Dec. 1974) 446,000. Radio receivers (Dec. 1973) 1.5 million. Television receivers (Dec. 1973) 525,000.

Agriculture. Production (in 000; metric tons; 1975): wheat 1,003; barley 121; oats 131; corn 329; potatoes 738; rapeseed 61; dry beans 74; tomatoes *c.* 210; sugar, raw value (1974) 127; apples (1974) *c.* 155; peaches (1974) *c.* 92; wine (1974) *c.* 600; beef and veal (1974) *c.* 136; wool *c.* 9; timber (cu m; 1974) 8,215; fish catch (1974) 1,127. Livestock (in 000; 1975): cattle 3,606; sheep 5,194; pigs *c.* 900; horses (1974) *c.* 470; poultry (1974) *c.* 19,500.

Industry. Production (in 000; metric tons; 1975): crude oil 1,167; natural gas (cu m) 3,645,000; coal (1974) 1,390; electricity (kw-hr) 8,855,000 (65% hydroelectric in 1974); iron ore (63% metal content) 11,028; pig iron 410; crude steel (ingots) 458; copper ore (metal content; 1974) 905; nitrate of soda (1974) 738; manganese ore (metal content; 1974) 11.5; sulfur (1974) *c.* 31; iodine (1973) 2.2; molybdenum concentrates (metal content; 1973) 4.8; gold (troy oz; 1974) 119; silver (troy oz; 1974) 6,655; woven cotton fabrics (m; 1973) 72,000; fish meal (1974) 194.

China

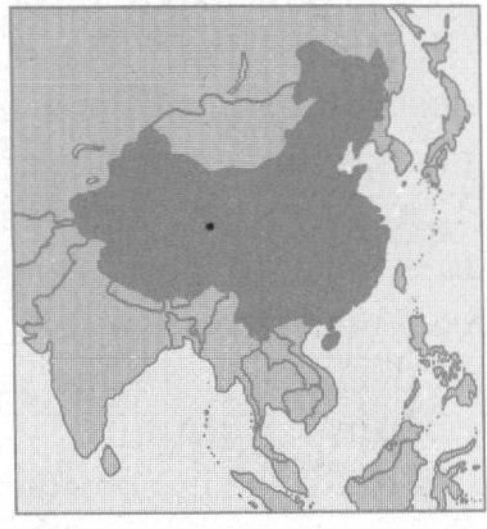

The most populous country in the world and the third largest in area, China is bounded by the U.S.S.R., Mongolia, North Korea, Vietnam, Laos, Burma, India, Bhutan, Nepal, Pakistan, and Afghanistan and also by the Sea of Japan, the Yellow Sea, and the East and South China seas. From 1949 the country has been divided into the People's Republic of China (Communist) on the mainland and on Hainan and other islands, and the Republic of China (Nationalist) on Taiwan. (*See* TAIWAN.) Area: 3,691,500 sq mi (9,561,000 sq km), including Tibet but excluding Taiwan. Pop. of the People's Republic: official figures total to 853 million; other, unofficial estimates ranged upward to 964 million in 1976. Cap.: Peking (metro. pop., 1975 est., 8,487,000). Largest city: Shanghai (metro pop., 1975 est., 10,888,000). Language: Chinese (varieties of the Mandarin [or Peking] dialect predominate). Chairmen of the Communist Party in 1976, Mao Tse-tung to September 9 and, from October 7, Hua Kuo-feng; chairman of the Permanent Standing Committee of the National People's Congress (nominal chief of state) to July 6, Marshal Chu Teh; premiers, Chou En-lai to January 8 and, from February 7, Hua Kuo-feng (acting premier until April 7).

The most important event of the year was the death of Chairman Mao Tse-tung, at the age of 82, on September 9, nine months after the passing of Premier Chou En-lai (*see* OBITUARIES). Mao had been head of the Chinese Communist Party and its Military Commission since 1935 and had proclaimed the establishment of the People's Republic at Peking's T'ien An Men (Gate of Heavenly Peace) Square on Oct. 1, 1949. For 27 years he had sought to create selfless "Maoist" individuals and to reshape traditional Chinese society, and he had often acted as the supreme leader over and above the party, state, and nation. Under his leadership and with the able assistance of Chou, China had become unified on the mainland and in recent years had played an effective role in world power politics.

Mao's death intensified the power struggle that had begun in late 1975 when Chou fell gravely ill. Observers had confidently expected that Chou would be succeeded as premier by the moderate first vice-premier, Teng Hsiao-p'ing. Instead, in an apparent victory for the leftists, Teng disappeared from sight, and the premiership devolved on the relatively young and obscure minister of public security, Hua Kuo-feng (*see* BIOGRAPHY). Within two months of Mao's death, however, Hua had succeeded to Mao's titles and the leading leftists, including Chiang Ch'ing (Mao's widow), were under arrest and the subjects of a campaign of vilification.

Domestic Affairs. In the late 1960s, Mao's Great Proletarian Cultural Revolution had proclaimed the supremacy of proletarian ideology, but it failed to resolve the fundamental contradiction between the urgent need for modernization and the continued demand for class struggle. The two opposing camps—the revolutionary-minded radicals and the pragmatic moderates—continued to fight for supremacy, although the ideological cleavage seemed to be less severe than the bitter personal rivalries dividing the top leadership.

SYGMA

Living on the street in Peking. After an earthquake occurred in northern China in July, destroying the city of T'ang-shan and causing severe damage elsewhere, the population of Peking evacuated their homes, fearing another quake, and camped out.

Conflicts over educational policy and economic development were at the forefront of the leadership struggle. While both camps agreed that the national economy must be developed and modernized, they differed on the methods of implementation and control. The pragmatic moderates favoured orderly social and economic development, with material incentives to encourage greater production. The doctrinaire radicals, fearful that a new elite class would emerge if this program were carried out, insisted on the class struggle and the primacy of politics over economics.

During the Cultural Revolution, Teng Hsiao-p'ing had been condemned as a "capitalist roader," but in 1973 he was rehabilitated and given the rank of a vice-premier with Chairman Mao's apparent approval if not by his design. In January 1975 the long-delayed fourth National People's Congress, presided over by Chou from his sickbed, established a new government leadership in which Teng was the leading figure. He was elected a vice-chairman of the party as well as a standing member of the Politburo, and was appointed as the most senior vice-premier and the chief of staff of the People's Liberation Army (PLA). He became de facto head of the government during Chou's illness.

Teng and his close associates maintained that China could not be modernized rapidly if the educational system was primarily concerned with ideological indoctrination, and they sought to reintroduce conventional education. This, together with Teng's enthusiasm for promoting economic development and his efforts to rehabilitate and promote capable officials who had been purged during the Cultural Revolution, alarmed the Maoist radicals. However, the critical debate on these matters did not begin until Chou En-lai became seriously ill, suggesting that the leftists were unable to mobilize while Chou remained in control.

On January 8 Chou, the first and only premier of the People's Republic, the architect of its foreign policy, and its chief stabilizing force in times of political crisis, died at the age of 78. Contrary to the general expectation that Teng would succeed to the premiership after Chou's death, that event precipitated a new power struggle initiated by the leftists with the evident support of Chairman Mao. In the antirightist campaign, Teng became the chief enemy of Chiang Ch'ing and the Cultural Revolution Group, who apparently tried to assert and consolidate their power while Mao was still alive—overturning, in the process, Chou's carefully laid plans for an orderly succession and collective leadership.

On February 8 the official Chinese news agency, Hsinhua, announced that Hua Kuo-feng, a long-time provincial administrator of Hunan Province and an agricultural specialist, had been named acting premier. The appointment bypassed the Maoist second vice-premier, Chang Ch'un-ch'iao, and in this regard was seen as a compromise. However, Hua's appointment did not augur well for Teng, and from this point the attacks on him became more direct. On February 17 the *People's Daily* published a long and vehement statement denouncing "capitalist roaders" who "unscrupulously split the Central Committee headed by Chairman Mao." The statement confirmed that Mao's decision against Teng did not have the support of a number of senior leaders, including Defense Minister Yeh Chien-ying and Marshal Chu Teh. In March the campaign to oust Teng took a definite turn with a personal attack on him by Chairman Mao, but Teng held his posts in the party until the T'ien An Men riots in early April.

Before the unprecedented incident at T'ien An Men, there were reports of factional disturbances in the country as workers and peasants, increasingly discontented with their low standard of living, looked to the moderate leaders to give them higher pay and more consumer goods. While the campaign against the moderates failed to generate widespread public enthusiasm, the movement in their support gathered momentum, culminating at T'ien An Men. The demonstration began on Saturday, April 3, with the placement of memorial wreaths in honour of the deceased premier. Subsequently, a ban was laid on further tributes, and the wreaths were removed during the night.

On April 5, the traditional Ch'ing-ming Festival or Tomb-sweeping Day, a huge crowd that had gathered at T'ien An Men Square to pay tribute to Chou became enraged at the removal of the wreaths. Demonstrators hoisted signs and shouted such slogans as "Down with Ch'in Shih Huang Ti," "Gone for good is Ch'in Shih Huang Ti's feudal society," and "Down with the Empress Dowager"—alluding to Chairman Mao and his wife and insultingly comparing them to the despotic 3rd-century BC emperor best known to history for his "burning of the books" and to Tz'u-hsi, who ruled China through a clique of corrupt officials in the last years of the Ch'ing (Manchu) dynasty.

In the late morning demonstrators attempting to enter the Great Hall of the People to present a petition clashed with the police and militia. In the fighting "more than 100 Peking worker-militia were injured, and a dozen of them were seriously wounded," according to the official press release. Not until evening, when "tens of thousands of worker-militiamen," mobilized by the Peking Revolutionary Committee "in coordination with the people's police and the PLA guards," began to arrest demonstrators did the crowd start to disperse. The official version of the T'ien An Men incident blamed a handful of class enemies for having "engineered and organized" the disorders, thus holding Teng personally responsible. Within 48 hours the Politburo was convened in special session and, on the proposal of Chairman Mao, agreed to dismiss Teng and to appoint Hua first vice-chairman of the party and premier.

As the party's first vice-chairman, Hua appeared to be the heir-designate, but fundamental internal policy differences and factional divisions remained. The devastating earthquakes of July and August, which virtually leveled the industrial city of T'angshan and caused severe damage in Peking and Tientsin (*see* DISASTERS), diverted the attention of the authorities from the anti-Teng campaign. Anticipating Mao's death, the editorial in *People's Daily* on August 23 played down the campaign against rightists and stressed the importance of unity.

Chou's death had weakened the position of the moderates, but with Mao's passing the radicals lost their protector and legitimist. On October 9, as the official month of mourning for Mao ended, wall posters appeared in Peking praising Hua's accession to the

CHINA

Education. Primary (1959–60), pupils 90 million, teachers (1964) *c.* 2.6 million; secondary (1958–59), pupils 8,520,000; vocational (1958–59), pupils 850,000; teacher training (1958–59), students 620,000; higher (1962–63), students 820,000.

Finance. Monetary unit: yuan, with (Sept. 20, 1976) a free exchange rate of 1.92 yuan to U.S. $1 (3.32 yuan = £1 sterling). Gold reserves (1973 est.) U.S. $2 billion. Budget (1960 est.; latest published) balanced at 70,020,000,000 yuan. Gross national product (1974 est.) U.S. $246 billion.

Foreign Trade. (1974) Imports *c.* U.S. $7.4 billion; exports *c.* U.S. $6.3 billion. Import sources: Japan *c.* 32%; U.S. *c.* 13%; Canada *c.* 7%; West Germany *c.* 7%; Australia *c.* 5%. Export destinations: Japan *c.* 21%; Hong Kong *c.* 19%; Singapore 5%. Main exports: foodstuffs (meat and products, cereals, fruit and vegetables) *c.* 40%; crude oil *c.* 20%; textiles and clothing *c.* 20%.

Transport and Communications. Roads (1974) *c.* 700,000 km (including *c.* 400,000 km all-weather). Motor vehicles in use (1973): passenger *c.* 30,000; commercial (including buses) *c.* 650,000. Railways: (1975) *c.* 48,000 km; traffic (1959) 45,670,000,000 passenger-km, freight (1971) 301,000,000,000 net ton-km. Air traffic (1960): 63,882,000 passenger-km; freight 1,967,000 net ton-km. Inland waterways (including Yangtze River; 1974) *c.* 160,000 km. Shipping (1975): merchant vessels 100 gross tons and over 466; gross tonnage 2,828,290. Telephones (1951) 255,000. Radio receivers (Dec. 1970) *c.* 12 million. Television receivers (Dec. 1973) 500,000.

Agriculture. Production (in 000; metric tons; 1975): rice *c.* 114,000; corn *c.* 33,000; wheat *c.* 41,000; barley *c.* 21,000; millet *c.* 24,000; potatoes *c.* 40,000; dry peas *c.* 4,900; soybeans *c.* 12,000; peanuts *c.* 2,700; rapeseed *c.* 1,250; sugar, raw value *c.* 3,300; pears *c.* 990; tobacco *c.* 950; tea *c.* 300; cotton, lint *c.* 2,150; jute *c.* 550; cow's milk *c.* 3,500; beef and buffalo meat (1974) *c.* 2,000; pork (1974) *c.* 9,200; timber (cu m; 1974) 182,000; fish catch (1974) *c.* 7,000. Livestock (in 000; 1975): horses *c.* 7,000; asses *c.* 11,600; cattle *c.* 63,200; buffalo *c.* 30,000; sheep *c.* 73,000; pigs *c.* 238,000; goats *c.* 60,000.

Industry. Fuel and power (in 000; metric tons; 1975): coal (including lignite) *c.* 500,000; coke (1974) *c.* 28,000; crude oil *c.* 79,000; electricity (kw-hr; 1974) *c.* 120,000,000. Production (in 000; metric tons; 1974): iron ore (metal content) *c.* 40,000; pig iron (1974) *c.* 35,000; crude steel *c.* 24,000; lead *c.* 100; copper *c.* 100; zinc *c.* 100; bauxite *c.* 600; aluminum *c.* 150; antimony ore (metal content) *c.* 12; magnesite *c.* 1,000; manganese ore *c.* 300; tungsten concentrates (oxide content) *c.* 11; cement *c.* 20,000; salt *c.* 18,000; sulfuric acid (1966) *c.* 2,500; fertilizers (nutrient content; 1974–75) nitrogenous *c.* 3,000, phosphate *c.* 1,300, potash *c.* 300; cotton yarn (1969) *c.* 1,450; cotton fabrics (1971) *c.* 9,000; man-made fibres *c.* 80; paper *c.* 4,700.

posts of party chairman and chairman of the Military Commission. At about the same time, wall posters attacked Chiang Ch'ing and three other prominent leftists, Chang Ch'un-ch'iao; Wang Hung-wen, a vice-chairman of the Communist Party; and Yao Wen-yuan, the second secretary of the Shanghai Communist Party. As the campaign against them increased in intensity, they were accused of a variety of crimes including plotting against the party, tampering with the words of Mao, and opposing the official plan to place Mao's body in a crystal sarcophagus and display it in Peking, in the manner of Lenin's body in Red Square.

Hua's appointments were officially confirmed by Hsinhua on October 22. Hsinhua also reported that an attempt by the four leftists to "usurp party and state power" had been "shattered" and the perpetrators "liquidated," although this was not taken to mean that they had been killed. There were reports that the "gang of four" had been under arrest since October 6 or 7 and that some sort of trial was being planned. Following the official announcement, demonstrations celebrating the leftists' downfall occurred in several major cities, and a huge rally acclaiming Hua was held in T'ien An Men Square on October 24.

Hua continued to hold the post of premier, although late in October it became apparent that many of the duties connected with that post were being performed by Li Hsien-nien, a vice-premier with experience in economics and foreign affairs. By late November there was still no official information on the convocation either of a plenum of the tenth party congress to ratify Hua's appointment as the party chairman or of the National People's Congress to restructure the government. Underlining the passing of the old order, Chu Teh (*see* OBITUARIES), the founder of the Red Army, died July 6 at 90. His position as chairman of the National People's Congress was not filled, although Wu Te, the mayor of Peking and vice-chairman of the Congress, was authorized to perform the functions of nominal chief of state.

The Economy. The 1976 New Year's Day editorials in the official press stated that the target for gross agricultural and industrial output set in the fourth five-year plan (1970–75) had been met successfully and that efforts were being made to fulfill the fifth plan (1976–80). Because Teng's interpretation of the plan as regards technology and the degree of China's dependence on foreign trade was under severe attack, alterations in the plan were made in the wake of his dismissal. However, following the purge of Chiang Ch'ing and her close allies, the program of economic development and modernization enunciated by Chou was reinstated. Late in October the minister of foreign trade, Li Ch'iang, told a group of Western diplomats and businessmen that implementation of the plan would not begin until early 1977.

Peking's Ministry of Agriculture gave total grain production in 1974 as 294.9 million tons, compared with 262 million tons for 1973. The projected grain output for 1975 was 288 million tons. It was expected that the factional struggle, labour unrest, and the aftermath of the earthquakes would inevitably impede the rate of economic growth. To raise morale and to show its resolve after Mao, Peking announced China's 19th nuclear test on September 26. On November 17 China set off its largest nuclear test device to date, estimated by U.S. authorities as having a force of four megatons, 20 times stronger than the September blast.

Foreign Affairs. The deaths of Chou and Mao and the leadership struggle had a negative effect on China's foreign relations. However, the policy guidelines of opposition to the hegemonism of the two superpowers, solidarity with the nonaligned nations of the third world, and friendship with the countries of the second world as a counterbalance to Soviet expansion and U.S. dominance remained. The withdrawal of the U.S. from Indochina, the emergence of a unified Vietnam with strong ties to the Soviet Union, and the latter's growing influence in the Pacific and Indian oceans and Africa prompted China to strengthen governmental relations with the Asian states, Australia, and New Zealand.

There was growing rivalry between China and the Soviet Union over Vietnam. Relations between Hanoi and Peking became cool, and territorial disputes over the control of the Spratly and the Paracel islands in the South China Sea became more acrimonious. While Hanoi labeled the Association of Southeast Asian Nations a cover for U.S. influence, Peking supported ASEAN's February decision to establish regional economic cooperation and moved to strengthen its relations with Thailand, Malaysia, and the Philippines. Diplomatic ties between China and Indonesia had not been restored, and Peking opposed Indonesia's annexation of former Portuguese Timor. Singapore's Prime Minister Lee Kuan Yew held talks with Chairman Mao and Premier Hua in May, but observers thought it unlikely that Singapore would establish diplomatic relations with Peking before Indonesia did. (*See* SOUTHEAST ASIAN AFFAIRS.) Friendly relations were maintained with Cambodia and Laos. On January 23 direct fortnightly air service between Peking and Phnom Penh resumed after a break of several years.

In the spring India and China decided to exchange ambassadors after an absence of 15 years. Peking invited Prime Minister Zulfikar Ali Bhutto of Pakistan and King Birendra of Nepal for state visits in May and June, respectively. Bhutto was the last head of state received by Chairman Mao. Both China and Pakistan supported the proposals of Sri Lanka and the king of Nepal for making the Indian Ocean and Nepal a zone of peace.

At the end of December 1975 Peking freed the Soviet helicopter crew captured inside Sinkiang in

For China the year 1976 was a year of deaths, beginning with that of Premier Chou En-lai in January. On T'ien An Men Square a group of mourners, wearing white paper flowers on their padded winter jackets, raise their clenched fists in salute to the departed Chou.

SYGMA

KEYSTONE

Wall posters constitute an important medium in China's political infighting. These posters were put up in spring 1976 in a campaign against rightists.

March 1974 with a statement that the Soviet airmen had not been spying. Apparently, the gesture was intended as an olive branch, but any response that Moscow might have made was quickly overtaken by the events following Chou's death. In his speech to the 25th congress of the Communist Party of the Soviet Union (CPSU) on February 24, party secretary Leonid I. Brezhnev sharply attacked Maoist ideology and policy as "incompatible with Marxist-Leninist teaching" and left the next efforts at reconciliation up to the Chinese. Instead, Peking denounced Soviet intervention in Angola and expressed delight over Egypt's abrogation of its friendship treaty with the Soviets. On April 29 an explosion at the gates of the Soviet embassy in Peking killed two Chinese guards, and Peking blamed "counterrevolutionary" saboteurs for the incident. The Communist Party of the Soviet Union and its allies dispatched a friendly condolence message upon the death of Mao, but it was rejected by Peking on the ground that the Chinese and Soviet ruling parties no longer had relations.

The status of Taiwan remained the stumbling block in the way of full relations with the U.S. In February the Chinese government invited former U.S. president Richard Nixon to visit China during February 21–29 and provided a special plane for both legs of the journey. The visit was apparently timed to coincide with the 25th congress of the CPSU and the anniversary of Nixon's first visit in 1972, and was intended to demonstrate Peking's determination to maintain good relations with Washington despite the slow pace of normalization.

In March, U.S. Pres. Gerald Ford dramatized the importance of U.S. relations with Peking by personally announcing the appointment of Thomas S. Gates, Jr., a former defense secretary, to replace George Bush as head of the U.S. liaison mission in Peking. U.S. visitors to China included a congressional delegation in April, Senate minority leader Hugh Scott in July, former secretary of defense James Schlesinger, who arrived just before Mao's death, and Senate majority leader Mike Mansfield, who visited just afterward. (HUNG-TI CHU)

[975.A]

ENCYCLOPÆDIA BRITANNICA FILMS. *China: Education for a New Society* (1976).

Chinese Literature: *see* Literature

Christian Church (Disciples of Christ): *see* Religion

Christianity: *see* Religion

Churches of Christ: *see* Religion

Church Membership: *see* Religion

Church of England: *see* Religion

Cinema: *see* Motion Pictures

Cities: *see* Environment

Civil Rights: *see* Race Relations

Clothing: *see* Fashion and Dress

Coal: *see* Energy

Coins: *see* Philately and Numismatics

Colleges: *see* Education

Colombia

A republic in northwestern South America, Colombia is bordered by Panama, Venezuela, Brazil, Peru, and Ecuador and has coasts on both the Caribbean Sea and the Pacific Ocean. Area: 439,700 sq mi (1,138,900 sq km). Pop. (1976 est.): 24,411,300. Cap. and largest city: Bogotá (pop., 1976 est., 3,153,000). Language: Spanish. Religion: Roman Catholic (96%). President in 1976, Alfonso López Michelsen.

President López Michelsen was unable to end the state of emergency (imposed in June 1975) by early 1976. He had hoped to do so in order that midterm local elections in April could take place under normal conditions. Elements in the Army wanted the state of emergency to continue to avoid the possibility of an investigation by a civil court of the trial of eight people accused of murdering Gen. Ramón Arturo Rincón Quiñones in September 1975; the military authorities had so mishandled the trial as to arouse suspicions that the murder was an internal army plot. A number of senior air force officers also wished to avoid a civilian inquiry into alleged dealings with the Lockheed Aircraft Corp. of the U.S. In January the Army clashed with striking sugar workers in the Cauca Valley and with rioting students at the Uni-

COLOMBIA

Education. (1974) Primary, pupils 3,791,543, teachers 115,310; secondary, pupils 1,003,492, teachers 49,931; vocational, pupils 199,987, teachers 11,314; teacher training, students 64,638, teachers 3,896; higher, students 141,718, teaching staff 16,199.

Finance. Monetary unit: peso, with (Sept. 20, 1976) an official rate of 34.70 pesos to U.S. $1 (free rate of 60.64 pesos = £1 sterling). Gold, SDR's, and foreign exchange (June 1976) U.S. $741 million. Budget (1975 actual): revenue 38,442,000,000 pesos; expenditure 39,579,000,000 pesos. Gross national product (1974) 322,560,000,000 pesos. Money supply (Dec. 1975) 58,915,000,000 pesos. Cost of living (Bogotá; 1970 = 100; May 1976) 271.

Foreign Trade. (1975) Imports U.S. $1,383,000,000; exports U.S. $1,453,000,000. Import sources (1974): U.S. 40%; West Germany 9%; Japan 9%. Export destinations (1974): U.S. 37%; West Germany 12%; Spain 5%. Main exports: coffee 44%; sugar 7%; textile yarns and fabric 6%; cotton 6%; fuel oil 6%. Tourism (1974): visitors 363,000; gross receipts U.S. $102 million.

Transport and Communications. Roads (1973) 48,761 km. Motor vehicles in use (1974): passenger 377,000; commercial 87,000. Railways (1974): 3,431 km; traffic 483 million passenger-km, freight 1,329,000,000 net ton-km. Air traffic (1974): 2,567,000,000 passenger-km; freight 121.5 million net ton-km. Shipping (1975): merchant vessels 100 gross tons and over 53; gross tonnage 208,507. Telephones (Dec. 1974) 1,090,000. Radio receivers (Dec. 1973) 2,793,000. Television receivers (Dec. 1972) *c.* 1.2 million.

Agriculture. Production (in 000; metric tons; 1975): corn *c.* 847; rice 1,614; barley *c.* 130; potatoes *c.* 950; cassava (1974) *c.* 1,320; sorghum *c.* 345; soybeans *c.* 130; coffee *c.* 540; bananas (1974) *c.* 954; cane sugar, raw value 970; palm oil *c.* 57; tobacco *c.* 54; cotton, lint *c.* 136; beef and veal *c.* 552. Livestock (in 000; Dec. 1974): cattle *c.* 23,222; sheep *c.* 2,071; pigs 1,877; goats (1973) *c.* 675; horses (1973) *c.* 860; chickens *c.* 39,000.

Industry. Production (in 000; metric tons; 1975): crude oil 8,102; natural gas (cu m; 1974) *c.* 1,700,000; coal (1974) *c.* 3,140; electricity (kw-hr; 1974) *c.* 11,950,000 (*c.* 69% hydroelectric); crude steel 265; gold (troy oz; 1974) 265; emeralds (carats; 1972) 1,750; salt (1974) 1,545; cement 3,091.

versity of Medellín. Strike action spread to other groups in other regions, and at the end of February the brief visit of Henry Kissinger, U.S. secretary of state, prompted a resumption of rioting, which intensified during March and resulted in several universities being occupied by troops or closed.

The April 18 election results were moderately encouraging for the ruling Liberal Party. While the percentage that did not go to the polls was very high (76%), reflecting public apathy at the internal squabbling of the Liberals and the ineffectiveness of the Conservatives, there was no swing by those who did vote toward either the Conservatives or the minority left-wing parties. Despite an upsurge of guerrilla activity during the spring, the state of emergency was lifted on June 22; it was reimposed, however, on October 7 after a strike of doctors and health service employees had disturbed public order, and on October 18 troops occupied the university in Bogotá. In July and August the president made several appointments that tended to strengthen his control and to shift the government slightly to the left.

The disturbances in Colombia had stemmed from economic, rather than political, discontent. By the end of 1976 the effects of the government's measures to enable the economy to function more efficiently and more equitably had yet to reach the bulk of the population. The economic recovery that began in mid-1975 was maintained during the year, but inflation was rekindled, the workers' cost-of-living index rising by 17.6% in the first eight months of 1976, as against 17.9% during all of 1975. This was attributable chiefly to the expansion of export earnings from coffee, which enriched the big coffee producers and exporters, a small group of heavy consumers. The government took measures to freeze part of the coffee income and channeled more of it into investment to absorb excess liquidity and, thereby, to curb price increases. The coffee boom benefited the economy, however. It was estimated that in 1976 the balance of payments current account would show a surplus of $600 million, as against $30 million in 1975, and the gross domestic product would grow by 8%, as against 4.8% in 1975. (JOAN PEARCE)

[974.C.2]

Combat Sports

Boxing. Notice of the end of an era was given by Muhammad Ali (U.S.) when the world heavyweight champion announced after outpointing Ken Norton (U.S.) over 15 rounds in New York in September 1976 that he intended retiring as undefeated champion. Ali continued to be listed as the world heavyweight champion until his status was officially clarified.

Before outpointing Norton, Ali had again dominated world boxing, defending his title against Jean-Pierre Coopman (Belgium) in 5 rounds, Jimmy Young (U.S.) over 15 rounds, and Richard Dunn (England) in 5 rounds. Ali also took part in a much-publicized contest against Japanese wrestler Antonio Inoki in Tokyo, but this bout, declared a draw, was regarded as a flop. Though the three U.S. judges unanimously awarded Ali the decision over Norton in Yankee Stadium, there was controversy over the verdict, the majority of U.S. boxing writers scoring in favour of Norton.

Even if Ali were to decide to defend his title in a proposed fight against George Foreman (U.S.) for $7 million or against some other contender, the Ali era might be said to be almost over. Ali would be 35 years old on Jan. 17, 1977, and had been a professional since October 1960, having won the Olympic light heavyweight championship in Rome that year when only 18. In 16 years as a professional he had taken part in 55 contests, winning 53. The only two opponents to gain decisions over him were Joe Frazier (U.S.) and Ken Norton, but he avenged those defeats, beating both men twice each in later contests.

SYNDICATION INTERNATIONAL/PHOTO TRENDS

Britain's Richard Dunn (right) became heavyweight champion of Europe in April when he knocked out West Germany's Bernd August in the third round. Dunn himself took a beating from Muhammad Ali (U.S.) in May.

In the light-heavyweight division Víctor Galíndez (Arg.) retained the World Boxing Association (WBA) title, while John Conteh (England) kept the World Boxing Council (WBC) championship. Conteh was inactive from August 1975 until September 1976 after breaking his right hand against Willie Taylor (U.S.) in the U.S. While training to defend the title against Alvaro Lopez (U.S.) in Uganda, he broke the same hand again and the fight was postponed. It eventually took place in Copenhagen, Denmark, and Conteh won on points.

A unanimous middleweight champion was accepted when Carlos Monzón (Arg.), the WBA champion, beat Rodrigo Valdes (Colombia), the WBC titleholder. Thus, out of 13 world divisions, Monzón and Ali were the only two world champions recognized by both the WBC and WBA in 1976. A surprise was that the junior middleweight division was taken over by two champions from Europe. Eckhard Dagge (West Germany) won the WBC title from Elisha Obed (Bahamas), while José Durán (Spain) captured the WBA crown from Koichi Wajima (Japan), who had taken it from Yuh Jae Do (South Korea). Durán, in turn, had to surrender the title to Miguel Angel Castellini (Arg.).

In the welterweight division, Carlos Palomino (U.S.) took the WBC title from John Stracey (England), stopping him in 12 rounds in London; in the WBA version José Cuevas (Mexico) stopped the defending champion, Ángel Espada (Puerto Rico), in the second round in Mexicali, Mexico. Saensak Muangsurin (Thailand), a kick-boxer who had caused a sensation by winning the WBC world junior welterweight title in only his third contest, lost the championship to Miguel Velasquez (Spain) in Madrid, being disqualified after knocking down Velasquez several times. In a return contest, in Segovia, Muangsurin regained the title with a two-round knockout.

Wilfredo Benítez (Puerto Rico) set a new record by outpointing Antonio Cervantes (Colombia) to win

Colonies: *see* Dependent States

KEYSTONE

Muhammad Ali reportedly made $6 million when he took on Japanese wrestler Antonio Inoki in Tokyo in June. Inoki made flying leaps at Ali's legs in the hope of getting him onto the mat. After boring the audience for 15 rounds, the match was declared a draw.

the WBA junior welterweight title; Benítez, only 17, became the youngest boxer in history to gain a world championship. Later, he successfully defended it.

The new WBC lightweight champion was Esteban de Jesús (Puerto Rico), who beat defender Gattu Ishimatsu (Japan) on points. The WBA junior lightweight champion, Ben Villaflor, was dethroned by Sam Serrano (Puerto Rico). Danny López (U.S.) won the WBC featherweight crown from David Kotey (Ghana). A new weight division, the junior featherweight (122 lb), which had been operating in the Orient for years, was introduced by the WBC but was not recognized by the WBA. Rigoberto Riasco (Panama) became the first champion, stopping Waringe Nakayama (Japan) in nine rounds in Panama City. Riasco was then involved in a controversial title fight against Yum Dong Kyun (South Korea) in Pusan. Initially Yum was declared the winner, but the WBC reversed the referee's verdict. Later Royal Kobayashi (Japan) won the title from Riasco.

Carlos Zárate (Mexico) took the WBC bantamweight title from Rodolfo Martínez (Mexico). Juan Guzmán (Dominican Rep.) gained the WBA junior flyweight title from Jaime Ríos (Panama), only to lose it to Yoko Gushiken (Japan).

Joe Bugner (England), who relinquished the European heavyweight championship and retired after losing to Ali in a world title contest in Kuala Lumpur, Malaysia, in 1975, returned to the ring and regained the European, Commonwealth, and British championships, knocking out Richard Dunn (England) in one round in London. Following Bugner's retirement 15 months earlier, Dunn had captured the British and Commonwealth titles from Bunny Johnson (England) and the vacant European championship by beating Bernd August (West Germany).

Britain, which held six European titles in 1974, finished 1976 with only three champions. Apart from Bugner, Maurice Hope (England) won the junior middleweight championship from Vito Antufermo (Italy) and Dave Green (England) the junior welterweight from Jean-Baptiste Piedvache (France). Italy dominated the European scene, claiming 5 champions out of the 11 European divisions. One surprise new champion was Mate Parlov (Yugos.), who took the light-heavyweight championship from Domenico Adinolfi (Italy).

The U.S. dominated the Olympic Games at Montreal. Five members of the team won gold medals, while Cuba was the next most successful country with three titles. (*See* TRACK AND FIELD SPORTS: *Special Report.*)

(FRANK BUTLER)

[452.B.4.h.vii]

Wrestling. The top event in wrestling in 1976 was the Olympic Games in Montreal. There, the U.S.S.R. was again victorious in both freestyle and Greco-Roman competition. The U.S. finished second in freestyle with Japan third and Bulgaria fourth. The U.S.S.R. achieved an almost perfect score in the Greco-Roman contests, winning seven gold medals, two silver medals, and one bronze medal. Romania and Bulgaria tied for second, and Poland finished fourth.

The U.S. National Collegiate Athletic Association championship was won by the University of Iowa. Iowa State University placed second, Oklahoma State University third, and University of Wisconsin fourth.

(MARVIN G. HESS)

See also Track and Field Sports: *Special Report.*

[452.B.4.h.xxix]

Judo. Japanese judoka suffered a series of shock upsets during the 1976 Olympics when Sergei Novikov (U.S.S.R.) won the heavyweight class, Hector Rodríguez (Cuba) the lightweight title, and Vladimir Nevzorov (U.S.S.R.) the gold medal for light middleweights. Haruki Uemura, however, solidified his claim to the world judo championship by adding the Olympic open-weights gold medal to his open-weights title won in the 1975 world championships. Japan had other Olympic gold medalists in light-heavyweight Kazuhiro Ninomiya and in middleweight Isamu Sonoda. In the world's only major judo tournament without weight classifications, Sumio Endo won the All-Japan Championships, defeating Takafumi Ueguchi in the finals with a sukuinage throw. Uemura, two-time Japan champion, and Chonosuke Takagi, former world heavyweight champion, lost in the semifinals. Endo also captured the heavyweight category by defeating Takagi in the All-Japan Weight Class Championships, which served to qualify athletes for the Olympic team. Ninomiya beat Ueguchi in the light-heavyweight contest; Sonoda upset three-time world champion Shozo Fujii for the middleweight title; Kuramoto won the light-middleweight class; and Minami was victorious in the lightweight category. (*See also* Track and Field Sports: *Special Report.*)

Karate. Karate activity in Japan in 1976 was largely confined to the national scene, with Japanese karateka participating in only one major international tournament. More than 20 countries competed in the Asian-Pacific Union of Karate-do Organizations Tournament held in late October in Jakarta; Japan defeated Indonesia 3–0 in the finals. In the most important tournament of the year in Japan, the sixth All-Japan All-Styles Championships held in Osaka in October, Junichi Hamaguchi took the title 1–0 with an upper punch in the two-minute final against Goju-kai stylist Kihei Sakamoto. Headed by Hamaguchi, Osaka won the team championship 2–0 against Tokyo. Hiroyuki Miyano of Shito-kai captured the men's competition in the prescribed forms (*kata*), while Wakako Yamaguchi, daughter of famed tenth-degree Gogen "Cat" Yamaguchi, won the women's *kata* title. The 6-ft, 170-lb Hamaguchi, runner-up for the individual title in the third world championships the previous year, also won the national Rengo-kai championships in Osaka, thus establishing himself as the year's premiere karate performer in Japan.

All of the major karate schools, the Self-Defense Forces, and the university clubs held national championships, but the industrial championships were postponed to March 1977. Hisao Murase won the Wado-kai title, Koji Matsuo the Shito-kai championships, and Yoichi Fukuda the All-Japan Rembu-kai title. The Japan Karate Association (JKA), which follows the Shotokan style, held its national championships in May; 28-year-old Yoshiharu Osaka emerged victorious. Toshikazu Sato outkicked and outpunched 22-year-old Joko Ninomiya in the finals of Mas Oyama's Kyokushinkai's All-Japan Open Championships. It was Japan's only major full-contact karate tournament of the year. Neither JKA nor Kyokushinkai are affiliated with the million-member Federation of All-Japan Karate-do Organizations. In the year's last

A.F.P./PICTORIAL PARADE

John Peterson of the U.S. won the middleweight gold medal in freestyle wrestling at the 1976 Olympic Games in Montreal. Here he is shown in action against the Soviet Union's Viktor Novojilov.

Table I. Boxing Champions

As of Dec. 31, 1976

Division	World	Europe	Commonwealth	Britain
Heavyweight	Muhammad Ali, U.S.	Joe Bugner, England	Joe Bugner, England	Joe Bugner, England
Light heavyweight	John Conteh, England* Víctor Galíndez, Arg.†	Mate Parlov, Yugos.	Tony Mundine, Australia	Tim Wood, England
Middleweight	Carlos Monzón, Arg.	Germano Valsecchi, Italy	Monty Beetham, N.Z.	Alan Minter, England
Junior middleweight	Eckhard Dagge, West Ger.* Miguel Angel Castellini, Arg.†	Maurice Hope, England	Maurice Hope, England	Maurice Hope, England
Welterweight	Carlos Palomino, U.S.* José Cuevas, Mexico†	Marco Scano, Italy	Clyde Gray, Canada	Henry Rhiney, England
Junior welterweight	Saensak Muangsurin, Thailand* Wilfredo Benítez, Puerto Rico†	Dave Green, England	Hector Thompson, Australia	Dave Green, England
Lightweight	Esteban de Jesús, Puerto Rico* Roberto Durán, Panama†	Perico Fernandez, Spain	Jonathan Dele, Nigeria	Jim Watt, Scotland
Junior lightweight	Alfredo Escalera, Puerto Rico* Sam Serrano, Puerto Rico†	Natale Vezzoli, Italy	Billy Moeler, Australia	...
Featherweight	Danny López, U.S.* Alexis Argüello, Nic.†	Pedro "Niño" Jiminez, Spain	vacant	Vernon Sollas, Scotland
Junior featherweight	Royal Kobayashi, Japan*	...	...	...
Bantamweight	Carlos Zárate, Mexico* Alfonso Zamora, Mexico†	Salvatore Fabrizio, Italy	Paul Ferreri, Australia	Paddy Maguire, Northern Ireland
Flyweight	Miguel Canto, Mexico* Guty Espadas, Mexico†	Franco Udella, Italy	Patrick Mambwee, Zambia	John McCluskey, Scotland
Junior flyweight	Luis Lumumba Estaba, Venez.* Yoko Gushiken, Japan†	...	...	...

*World Boxing Council champion.
†World Boxing Association champion.

Table II. U.S. Collegiate Wrestling Champions and Runners-up, 1976

Weight class	Champion	School	Runner-up	School
118 lb	Mark DiGirolamo	California Polytechnic State (San Luis Obispo)	John Jones	Iowa State
126 lb	Jack Reinwand	Wisconsin	Harold Wiley	California (Santa Barbara)
134 lb	Mike Frick	Lehigh	Pat Milkovich	Michigan State
142 lb	Brad Smith	Iowa	Gene Costello	Slippery Rock
150 lb	Chuck Yagla	Iowa	Pete Galea	Iowa State
158 lb	Lee Kemp	Wisconsin	Tom Brown	Washington
167 lb	Pat Christenson	Wisconsin	Dan Wagemann	Iowa
177 lb	Chris Campbell	Iowa	Mark Johnson	Michigan
190 lb	Evan Johnson	Minnesota	Frank Santana	Iowa State
Heavyweight	Jim Jackson	Oklahoma State	Greg Gibson	Oregon

major tournament, Akio Takahashi won the final match of the All-Japan Goju-kai Championships. [452.B.4.h.xxix]

Sumo. Wajima's spectacular comeback highlighted the year's sumo activities in Japan; the 28-year-old *yokozuna* (grand champion) was named wrestler of the year for compiling the most victories (77) in the 90 annual bouts. Though driven to the brink of forced retirement in 1975 by consistently poor performances, the former college sumo champion captured two of the six annual 15-day *basho* (tournaments) and finished as runner-up in the four others. Kitanoumi, the other *yokozuna,* actually captured one more *basho* than his arch rival Wajima, but was runner-up only once and finished with 72 wins in the year. Former champion Kaiketsu won the other *basho.*

Mienoumi gained, lost, and regained the second highest rank of *ozeki* (champion) during the year. He was promoted in January after winning the 1975 November tournament, but dropped out before the end of both the March and May *basho,* then managed to recapture his lost rank in July. Kaiketsu, who lost his *ozeki* rank in 1975, stood on the brink of regaining it after his 14–1 performance in September and a fine 11–4 record in November. Wakamisugi was also laying claim to an *ozeki* promotion with two successive 11–4 marks.

Hasegawa, who held sumo's third-highest rank of *sekiwake* for several *basho,* set a new all-time record of 1,024 consecutive appearances in the *makuuchi* division, the highest of the six major league sections, before announcing his retirement. Hawaiian-American Jesse Kuhualua then became the oldest wrestler in the top division at 32 and the record holder among active wrestlers for the most consecutive appearances in the *makuuchi* division with 810. Known in sumo as Takamiyama, the 6-ft $3\frac{1}{2}$-in, 407-lb *sumotori* completed his 12th year of competition in 1976.

The sumo world received a shock when six youthful wrestlers from Tonga were forced to quit the sport after just two years because of a prolonged dispute between their stable master and the widow of the former master. But two bright young prospects from Hawaii, Reid Asato and John Collins, joined Futagoyama Beya, one of 31 stables where some 650 sumo wrestlers live and train.

(ANDREW M. ADAMS)

[452.B.4.h.xxix]

A.F.P./PICTORIAL PARADE

An armlock by Tahashimi Uegushi (Japan) overcomes defending world champion Jean-Luc Rouge (France) at the 1976 Paris judo tournament.

SVEN SIMON/KATHERINE YOUNG

West Germany's Alexander Pusch defeats Hungary's Gyozo Kulcsar. Pusch went on to win a gold medal in the individual épée at the summer Olympic Games.

Fencing. The increasing strength of West Germany in world competition, the capture of the coveted Prince Rainier Cup by the Soviet Union, and a scandal at the Olympic Games provided the year's chief items of interest. After shifting its emphasis from national club-type programs to broader ones with international goals, West Germany made such an impressive showing that experts ranked the West Germans directly behind the powerful U.S.S.R. and Italy. France was moved into fourth place and Hungary, a perennial contender, was dropped from third to fifth.

During the Olympic Games in Canada the Soviet Union enjoyed moments of great glory and a moment of considerable embarrassment. Its greatest triumph came in the men's sabre events when Soviet fencers won all three individual medals as well as the team championship. When Viktor Krovopouskov, Vladimir Nazlimov, and Viktor Sidyak received the gold, silver, and bronze medals, it marked the first time in 24 years that athletes from a single nation had swept all three places in any Olympic fencing event.

West Germany made its finest showing in the épée, Alexander Pusch winning the gold medal and Jurgen Hehn the silver. In épée team competition, the West Germans took second place behind Sweden. Fabio Dal Zotto of Italy won the individual gold medal in foil, and the West Germans the team gold medal.

In women's competition, which is limited to the foil only, Ildiko Schwarczenberger of Hungary was the women's gold medalist and replaced fellow Hungarian Katalin Jencdik-Stahl as the international women's champion. In the Olympic women's team foil, once again Soviet athletes emerged victorious.

But the Soviet Union also had its moment of em-

LONDON DAILY EXPRESS/PICTORIAL PARADE

The 1976 world kendo championships were held in Britain. Kendo players wield bamboo swords and wear helmets, chest protectors, and quilted gloves.

barrassment. During an early round of the pentathlon event (which, besides fencing, also includes horseback riding, shooting, swimming, and cross-country), Boris Onischenko was accused of using an épée that was so wired as to light up and register a hit without any contact having been made with an opponent. Onischenko, who won the 1972 Olympic silver medal and was favoured to win first place at Montreal, was summarily dropped from the Soviet squad and ordered to fly home. The individual modern pentathlon gold medal was won by Janusz Pyciak-Peciak of Poland and the team title by the U.K.

U.S. fencers, who had not won any Olympic medals since 1960, came through with one of their strongest showings in years. They placed three men in the final round of 16 in each of the three different individual events, and in each of three team events they were among the eight finalists. Though no U.S. fencer returned home with a medal, it was an encouraging performance. An additional cause for optimism about the future was the considerable increase in the number of persons who were seriously attempting to improve their skills. The number of such athletes had increased from about 5,000 to some 20,000 during the last five years and did not include a large group that was interested in fencing only as a recreational pastime.

(MICHAEL STRAUSS)

See also Track and Field Sports: *Special Report.*
[452.B.4.h.xii]

Kendo. Japanese kendo activities in 1976 were highlighted by victories in both the team and individual events of the third World Kendo Championships in London, April 17–18. In the all-Japanese final, Eiji Yoko defeated Kuniyuki Ono 2–1 with a *men* strike against his opponent's face mask and another on the forearm protector (*kote*). Ono beat Y. Hosoda in one semifinal bout, and Yoko took the other with a 2–0 victory over T. Go of Taiwan. Japan's five-man team of Akashi, Yamada, Kawazoe, Ono, and Sato blanked the Canadians 5–0 in the finals to capture the team championship. In semifinal matches, Japan took the measure of the U.S., and Canada bested Taiwan. Besides various local and regional tournaments, there were the All-Japan Police Championships held on May 12 in Tokyo, with Yuji Ono of the Tokyo Metropolitan Police Department coming out on top. Setsuro Hirai of Daito Cultural University won the All-Japan Men Students Championships on June 27 in Tokyo, while Akemi Horibe of Tokyo Educational University took the All-Japan Women Students title. Oita Prefecture defeated Tokyo Metropolis in the All-Japan Team Championships on May 3 in Tokyo. Atsuko Kurosu of Tokyo defeated Y. Takei of Yamaguchi Prefecture 2–0 to capture the All-Japan Women's Championships. In a battle between two kendo instructors at the Budokan on December 5, 23-year-old Kojiro Migita won the title at the All-Japan Championships by defeating 28-year-old Haruo Saiyama 2–0, scoring *men* and *kote* strikes against his opponent's helmet and forearm guard. In martial arts activities closely related to kendo, the 17th All-Japan Iaido (Quick-Sword-Draw) Championships were held on October 31 in Fukushima Prefecture and the All-Japan Jodo (Short Stick) Championships were held July 25 in Tokyo.

(ANDREW M. ADAMS)

Commonwealth of Nations

On June 28, 1976, Seychelles became an independent republic and the 36th member of the Commonwealth. Tensions in Commonwealth Africa led to Britain's breaking off diplomatic relations with a fellow member for the first time, when relations with Uganda became untenable in July as a result of the conduct of Pres. Idi Amin and his government. Nigeria sought stability after an attempted coup had been put down, and members in southern Africa were involved in stress with Rhodesia and South Africa.

Canada and the Caribbean. World conflicts, albeit in a lower key, were evident when Canada acted as host to two purportedly nonpolitical international events: the UN Conference on Human Settlements (Habitat), held in Vancouver, B.C., May 31–June 11 (*see* ENVIRONMENT: *Special Report*) and the Olympic Games in Montreal in July (*see* CANADA: *Special Report*). Each provided a focus for Middle East and Communist conflicts. Canada, despite its own internal division between French and English communities, highlighted by the Parti Québécois's success in the November elections, maintained efficient security. Queen Elizabeth II and other members of the royal family attended the Games, and the queen, as head of the Commonwealth, officially declared the Games open.

Canada continued to work with the Caribbean Community and Common Market, though during the

Comecon:
see Economy, World
Commerce:
see Economy, World
Commodity Futures:
see Stock Exchanges
Common Market:
see Economy, World; European Unity

year fears were expressed concerning "externally inspired destabilization"—the suspected U.S. promotion of unrest in Caribbean countries under left-wing governments. Barbados, The Bahamas, and Trinidad and Tobago stressed the prosperity of their free mixed economies while Jamaica and Guyana moved toward increased socialization and closer relations with Cuba. The tenth anniversary of Guyana's independence in May saw some healing of the breach between Forbes Burnham's ruling People's National Party government and Cheddi Jagan's People's Progressive Party. Burnham's nationalization of the Booker-McConnell holdings, a British conglomerate that had controlled over 40% of the economy, was applauded by Jagan's powerful sugar union. The state of emergency declared by Jamaica's Prime Minister Michael Manley (*see* BIOGRAPHY) in June was the climax of months of violence and discontent arising from economic ills and unemployment. The prime ministers of Trinidad and Tobago, Guyana, and Barbados took concerted action, including a loan of $87 million, to avert a breakdown in Jamaica.

The Pacific and Southeast Asia. The new right-wing governments of Australia and New Zealand both sought to further their regional leadership. Malcolm Fraser's government in Australia, turning from Gough Whitlam's Labor policy of third world alignment to one of Western alliance, came out firmly against a Soviet buildup in the Indian Ocean, supported the construction of a U.S. base on Diego Garcia, and offered accommodation to U.S. ships. In light of the Communist insurgent threat to Malaysia, Australia increased its support of the Association of Southeast Asian Nations and the ANZUS treaty. At home, new land grants were offered to Aboriginals in the Northern Territories, and an Aboriginal was appointed governor of South Australia. As required by the World Bank, Australia guaranteed A$930 million over five years to Papua New Guinea, as well as providing technical assistance. Relations with Papua New Guinea were complicated by an unresolved dispute over the Torres Strait Islands. Though part of Queensland for nearly 100 years, the three islands of Boigu, Dauan, and Saibai, with their potential mineral wealth, were claimed by Papua New Guinea as lying within its territorial waters.

In New Zealand the government of Prime Minister Robert Muldoon (*see* BIOGRAPHY) showed the same concern over Soviet expansion in the Pacific as Fraser's government showed over that in the Indian Ocean. The development of diplomatic rights and fishing facilities with Fiji, Western Samoa, Papua New Guinea, and, especially, with Tonga was discussed at the Commonwealth South Pacific Forum meeting in Nauru in July. Though some satisfaction was expressed over economic progress in the Commonwealth Pacific, political strains were evident. Racial stress in Fiji, where the immigrant Indian population had reached 51% (Fijians 42%), found expression in an angry split between the two main parties and a demand by Fiji nationalists that the 283,000 Indians be deported.

The Mediterranean and Africa. Neither the Commonwealth Committee nor the UN succeeded in altering the separatist views of Greeks and Turks on Cyprus. Dom Mintoff retained power in the Maltese elections, despite the embarrassment caused when Col. Muammar al-Qaddafi of Libya declared, during a May visit, that the Maltese were 80% Arab and that he would support any anti-NATO party.

The 13th meeting of the 47-member Organization of African Unity (OAU) took place on the Commonwealth island of Mauritius in July, and the current and future chairmen were both Commonwealth citizens. Few heads of state attended, and the meeting, rent by dissension, was thrown into disarray by the Israeli rescue of the passengers of a hijacked plane at Entebbe, Uganda. The Israeli action was also a matter of Commonwealth concern, since it affected not only Kenya's deteriorating relations with Uganda—later somewhat repaired—but also the final breach between Britain and Uganda. In Nigeria, following the assassination of Gen. Murtala Ramat Mohammed in an abortive coup in February, Lieut. Gen. Olusegun Obasanjo was brought in to head the provisional military government. The fourth UN Conference on Trade and Development (UNCTAD 4) was held in May at Nairobi, Kenya.

Economic Affairs. Emphasis on economic questions reshaped Commonwealth priorities and relations between developed and less developed countries in 1976. The Commonwealth Group of Experts, set up by the Kingston, Jamaica, Commonwealth conference of 1975, met early in 1976 to work out concrete details of its report on a new international economic order; it recommended an empirical approach, based on commodity negotiation. Commonwealth delegates to UNCTAD 4 met before it opened to discuss their approach on commodities, debt, and industrialization and did much to soften the deadlocked acrimony of the Group of 77 (at the start of the conference comprising 111 third world countries). Final agreement on an integrated commodity program was accepted with reservations. Agreement was complicated by the Lomé Convention (of February 1975), which came into force on April 1, 1976. The convention, covering trade and aid between the European Economic Community and 46 less developed African, Caribbean, and Pacific countries, left many Asian and South American countries deprived of its economic benefits.

The Commonwealth was particularly concerned in UNCTAD 4 because primary commodities constituted the bulk of its less developed members' trade, which, in turn, was largely with its developed members. Of the 17 basic commodities in the UNCTAD integrated program, Commonwealth countries supplied more than 70% of the tea and jute, over 60% of the tin and rubber, two-thirds of the bauxite, half the vegetable oils, one-third of the meat and iron, and a large proportion of the sugar, coffee, cocoa, copper, and fibres that entered into world trade. Despite European Economic Community policies, Commonwealth trade improved. British aid to the less developed world continued to increase, from £352 million (gross) in 1974 to an estimated £432 million in 1975. A further 17% rise by 1980 was to be directed toward the poorer rural areas, with India and Kenya the chief beneficiaries.

The Colombo Plan, established by the Commonwealth in 1951, celebrated its 25th anniversary in London on July 1; since its founding its membership had grown from 6 to 27, and total aid disbursed amounted to £20,000 million. Substantial discoveries of on- and offshore oil in India suggested that it might become an exporter of both oil and aid, instead of a recipient, by the 1980s. Hopes for the Economic Community of West African States faded as a result of Nigerian unrest, Anglo-French differences, and the fact that West African trade with Europe increased so much that only about 3% was left for interstate

Communications: *see* Industrial Review; Television and Radio exchange. The Commonwealth Development Corporation agreed to launch its new projects (including 25 agricultural ventures) in the poorest areas. As 1976 opened, there were 230 projects in some 40 countries, with approved capital of £268 million.

(MOLLY MORTIMER)

See also articles on the various political units. [972.A.1.a]

Communist Movement

In the future 1976 might be seen as a major turning point in the history of the international Communist movement, but the extent and even the direction of the change were as yet unclear. It was possible that the death of Mao Tse-tung would open the way to reconciliation between China and the Soviet Union, and that the compromises that allowed the leaders of the European Communist parties to meet together in June would limit the growth of revisionism among them. On the other hand, the fact that the Chinese leadership did not respond favourably to Soviet suggestions for reconciliation after Mao's death could indicate that the schism transcended personality, while the fact that the European Communists recognized party autonomy but were unable to agree on a number of basic questions might mean that the old tradition of conformity and discipline within the movement was effectively dead.

Soviet and European Parties. For the Communist Party of the Soviet Union and for the movement as a whole, one of the major events of the year was the 25th congress of the CPSU in Moscow in February–March. All evidence indicated that General Secretary Leonid I. Brezhnev, who was awarded the rank of marshal in May, was continuing to consolidate his hold on the Soviet leadership, particularly in light of reports that Premier Aleksey N. Kosygin was seriously ill.

Although a record 103 foreign parties from 96 countries sent delegations to the congress, the absence of certain parties bore witness to continued disunity. Not only did the Chinese, Albanians, and other Maoist parties fail to attend, but the ruling Cambodian party was also missing. In addition, the Japanese, Dutch, Icelandic, and Australian Communists refused to send delegations, and the general secretaries of the French and Spanish parties decided not to head their respective delegations.

Even before the congress the previously loyal French party, at its 22nd congress in February, annoyed the Soviet leaders by emphasizing its commitment to a particularly French and democratic route to power and by altering Marxist-Leninist doctrine concerning the need for a post-revolutionary "dictatorship of the proletariat." The most prominent spokesman for this independent view at the Soviet congress was Italian Communist leader Enrico Berlinguer, whose policy of moderation and compromise brought his party close to winning a plurality in the Italian national elections in June.

It was in the hope of containing this trend that the Soviet Communists and their supporters sought an all-European Communist conference that would adopt something like a "general line." After 20 months of fruitless negotiation, the Soviets agreed to make concessions in order to restore the image of unity. A two-day summit conference of the leaders of 29 European parties was finally held in East Berlin in late June on the basis of a nonbinding statement that, in essence, endorsed the principle of party autonomy and rejected Soviet hegemony or even primacy within the movement. Coming as it did on the 28th anniversary of his party's expulsion from Stalin's Cominform, this statement represented a special victory for President Tito of Yugoslavia.

Several of the pro-Soviet Communist regimes had cause to resent the criticism leveled at them by the independent Western parties. The Polish leader Edward Gierek, who prided himself on his good relations with both Moscow and the independent Western parties, was clearly annoyed by Berlinguer's appeal for moderation and clemency in the handling of those arrested during riots protesting higher food prices in Poland. The Czechoslovak Communists found to their great irritation that their offer to readmit repentant liberals who had been removed from the party in the post-1968 purges by no means stanched criticism of their regime by Italian, Yugoslav, and other independent Communist newspapers. Similarly, the hard-line East German Communists came into conflict with the Italian Communists in August over the killing of an Italian Communist party member by border guards.

Communism in Asia. China was shaken in 1976, both by a series of devastating earthquakes and by the deaths of its outstanding leaders: Premier Chou

Communist election posters cover the wall in a working-class district of Rome. The elections in June brought the Communists closer to power in Italy.

KEYSTONE

HENRI BUREAU—SYGMA

There were no surprises at the 25th congress of the Soviet Communist Party in Moscow in February. Most of the 4,998 delegates who assembled in the Palace of Congresses were middle-aged or elderly men and women.

Membership of the Major Communist Parties of the World*

Countries with a membership of 2,500 or more persons

Country	Membership
Albania	100,000
Argentina	147,000
Australia	6,000
Austria	25,000
Bangladesh†	2,500
Belgium	15,150
Brazil†	7,000
Bulgaria	790,000
Burma†	6,500
Cambodia	10,000
Canada	2,500
Chile†	‡
China	28,000,000
Colombia	12,000
Cuba	200,000
Cyprus	12,000
Czechoslovakia	1,331,000
Denmark	10,000
Finland	49,000
France	500,000
Germany, East	1,950,000
Germany, West§	48,000
Greece	28,000
Guadeloupe	3,000
Hungary	800,000
Iceland	2,500
India	538,900
Indonesia†	800
Iraq	2,000
Israel	‡
Italy	1,716,000
Japan	370,000
Korea, North	2,000,000
Laos	5,000
Lebanon	2,500
Malaysia†	2,500
Mexico	5,000
Mongolia	66,900
Nepal†	5,000
Netherlands, The	11,500
Norway	2,500
Paraguay†	3,500
Peru	3,200
Philippines†	8,000
Poland	2,453,000
Portugal	50,000
Romania	2,500,000
Spain	22,000
Sri Lanka	3,000
Sudan†	3,500
Sweden	17,000
Switzerland	6,000
Syria	3,500
Turkey†	2,000
U.S.S.R.	15,000,000
United Kingdom	31,000
United States	15,000
Uruguay†	30,000
Venezuela	6,000
Vietnam	1,400,000
Yugoslavia	1,192,000

*Latest available figures.
†Communist Party illegal.
‡No estimate available.
§Including West Berlin.
Sources: U.S. Department of State, Bureau of Intelligence and Research, *World Strength of the Communist Party Organizations*, (1973); subsequent reports and communications, official or otherwise.

En-lai in January, Marshal Chu Teh in July, and Party Chairman Mao Tse-tung in September (*see* OBITUARIES). Chou's death was followed by the fall of the moderate Vice-Premier Teng Hsiao-p'ing amid riots and a strong antirightist campaign and by the rise of the relatively obscure Hua Kuo-feng (*see* BIOGRAPHY) to the posts of premier and vice-party chairman. Believed to be a middle-of-the-roader himself, Hua apparently aligned himself with the rightists in October to gain the party chairmanship and purge some of the most prominent members of the radical Maoist faction. (*See* CHINA.)

The ruling parties in Vietnam, Laos, and Cambodia each faced in its own way the difficult tasks of rebuilding its country and establishing relations abroad. In all three countries, major efforts were made to revive the rural economy and to "reeducate" former opponents, but the Cambodians were clearly the most draconian in their approach. The Cambodian Communists also contrasted with their neighbours in maintaining a self-imposed diplomatic isolation and a pro-Chinese orientation. North and South Vietnam were officially reunited in July as the Socialist Republic of Vietnam with Hanoi as its capital. The Vietnamese leaders sought to maintain their long-standing policy of neutrality in the Sino-Soviet dispute, but there were indications that the Soviet Union was becoming the more influential. Although the Laotians also emphasized their nonalignment, the Soviet mission was by far the largest in Vientiane.

The fact that the North Korean delegation to the Soviet Party congress was headed by Premier Pak Sung Chul, rather than by the reputedly ill party leader Kim Il Sung (*see* BIOGRAPHY), did not seem to indicate any worsening in North Korean-Soviet relations. On the contrary, while the North Koreans remained officially neutral in the Sino-Soviet dispute, they supported the Soviet-backed forces in Angola rather than their Chinese-backed rivals.

The two largest nonruling Asian Communist parties, those of India and Japan, presented a sharp contrast. The Indians remained firmly pro-Soviet. The Japanese Communists, already very nationalist and annoyed by Soviet support of a splinter group, rejected Soviet leadership, dropped the doctrine concerning the "dictatorship of the proletariat" from their program, and replaced the term "Marxism-Leninism" with "scientific socialism."

Africa and Latin America. Sino-Soviet competition for influence in the third world was nowhere more evident than in Africa. A growing number of African governments and movements had identified themselves as "Marxist-Leninist," but—with the exception of the small, illegal South African and Sudanese parties and the recently legalized Senegalese party—the Soviet Communists still preferred to treat them as "national democratic parties and organizations" rather than as "fraternal parties." A new element in the competition was the use of Cuban troops to assist the Soviet-backed Popular Movement for the Liberation of Angola (MPLA) to achieve power. Cuba's status as a nonaligned nation in spite of its ties with the Soviet Union was reflected in the decision to hold the next summit conference of nonaligned nations in Havana. This status was of great assistance to the Cubans in Africa, where they could claim to be third world revolutionaries rather than agents of a great power.

(DAVID L. WILLIAMS)

See also Economy, World.

[541.E.3.d.ii]

SPECIAL REPORT

HOW MANY COMMUNISMS?

By Neil McInnes

It was still possible to say in an earlier edition of *Encyclopædia Britannica* that "Communism in the late 1960s was a movement with many variations of thought held together by a common purpose to remake the world without the capitalist system, but divided sharply on how to do it." By 1976 this no longer seemed to be true. Communists still show a common antipathy to capitalism, in varying degrees, but all common purpose has vanished in disputes that are no longer about "how to do it" but about whether all Communists really want to abolish capitalism. The Chinese Communists assert that the Soviet leaders have "restored capitalism" in the U.S.S.R., while both the Chinese and the Soviet Communists doubt whether Western and Japanese Communists still seek to overthrow capitalism at all. Communists in the advanced countries as well as in the less developed world have split into pro-Soviet and pro-Chinese factions (of unequal importance from country to country), and often there is a third "autonomous" faction that declines to take sides. Even Communist parties of similar allegiance—parties belonging to Moscow's sphere of ideological influence, for example—were found in 1976 taking contrary positions on such issues as the fate of the Palestinian refugees, the future of Lebanon, and their countries' membership in Western military alliances.

Doctrinal Unity and National Interest. There is, then, no longer one Communist movement. The main reason for the fragmentation is that national realities, such as differences of character and interest between peoples, or ancient historical rivalries, have reasserted themselves at the expense of doctrinal unity. Disputes between Communist parties are carried on in ideological terms but often they are about national interests; the veritable cold war between the Soviet Union and China is the best example.

It is possible that, although the movement has split, Communism as an ideal or objective has retained its identity. The only tenet actually abandoned by the Communists might be the one embodied in a famous phrase of the Communist Manifesto, "Workers of the world, unite!"—that is, the claim that proletarians in different nations have common interests. Apart from that, all Communists might be practicing, or aiming at, an identical social system, adapted for local differences. They would thus be in the situation of protectionist capitalist states in the first half of the 20th century, all practicing comparable economic policies but all at loggerheads, if not at war, with one another.

This possibility, that the movement has split but Communism has not, is of more than theoretical interest. In the view of many Western politicians, what matters most is that, for all their differences, Communist societies show these common characteristics: abolition of the market in capital goods and hence of the freedom to start independent businesses; nationalization of most industries and many services; the collectivization of agriculture (with exceptions such as Poland); the dictatorship of a Communist Party that is rigidly and undemocratically organized; and the cultural monopoly of "Marxism-Leninism." Such politicians conclude that division within the Communist world does nothing to diminish the Communist threat to other social systems, although it does create opportunities for tactical maneuvers by Western diplomacy. Similarly, an orthodox Communist would argue that, since Communists agree on the points just listed, they could one day start to cooperate again, exactly as protectionist capitalist states have given up their hostilities and seek to collaborate in the Organization for Economic Cooperation and Development. The commonest form of this hope (or fear) is the thought that the Sino-Soviet split will be mended.

The reconciliation may occur one day, but if so it will probably be on the basis of a new estimate of national interests rather than any common conception of Communism. There are good reasons for thinking that it is not simply the Communist movement that has split, but the very doctrine of Communism. In other words, one can no longer say that all Communist parties are trying to install variants of one pattern of society, the classic form of which was fixed by Stalin in the 1930s. That was still true in 1948, when China came increasingly under Communist rule and Yugoslavia was in the Soviet camp. At that time, a dozen states covering much of the Earth had one official model of Communism. Today those same states and others that have joined them in using the Communist label, as well as the nonruling Communist parties, profess different views of the Communist society of tomorrow, and they already show different characteristics today. They have some common characteristics too, but many of these they share with other political models—classical tyrannies, fascism, Nazism, and the sundry one-party states of the contemporary non-Communist world.

Diversification of the Stalinist Model. For all the destalinization campaigns of the past 20 years, it is the Soviet system that has changed least from the Stalinist model, although the changes that have occurred have been warmly welcomed by Soviet citizens. In the Eastern European satellites, the pace of change has often been quicker, and Soviet intervention has sought to restrain it (by armed intervention in the case of Czechoslovakia in 1968). Within the narrow limits set by Moscow, it is possible that this process of diversification will continue, but it can scarcely go as far in the satellites as in Yugoslavia and Albania, which have simply gone their own way since they left the Soviet camp. The Yugoslav system has a particular claim to originality, because its market socialism, workers' control, decentralized planning, and relative openness to the non-Communist world diverge radically from the Soviet pattern. Politically, the differences are less marked because there are no autonomous political organizations in Yugoslavia, official doctrines are protected from criticism, and workers' control is itself controlled from above. Nevertheless, the style and objectives of Yugoslav Communism are so much at variance with the Soviet system that oppression is occasionally exercised by the Yugoslav authorities precisely to combat Soviet influence.

Chinese Communism had begun to diverge (for example, over the agricultural communes) at a time when Peking still recognized Moscow's hegemony over the world Communist movement. The differences continued to accumulate and, although they did not cause the break that occurred in the 1960s, they were exacerbated by it, until now each party denounces the other's conception of Communism as pernicious. The political disturbances of 1976 which preceded and, with greater violence, followed the death of Mao Tse-tung show that it is still too early to say just what the Chinese model of Communism is, because the Chinese Communist Party is deeply divided on fundamental economic and even political issues. Yet there is a common repudiation of the Soviet model. Quite apart from disagreements about Marxist philosophy and revolutionary theory, most Chinese Communists feel that the Soviet model could not be applied in their circumstances, just as India's present rulers feel that the U.S. system would not work in their country. The Sino-Soviet rivalry is complicated (as Indo-U.S. differences are not) by acute national security fears and, for both Moscow and Peking, leadership in the Communist movement can mean influence over neighbouring states and other

---

Neil McInnes, a specialist in Communist affairs and associate editor of Barron's, *is the author of* The Western Marxists *(1972) and* The Communist Parties of Western Europe *(1975).*

allies and hence greater security. Thus it is likely that whatever form it finally takes, Chinese Communism will set itself off sharply from Soviet practice.

The striking advances made by Communism in the Indochinese Peninsula after 1973 were the work of parties that are not committed to copying either the Soviet or the Chinese pattern. Capitalism had impinged on these nations merely as foreign colonialism, and therefore the transition to Communism was primarily a struggle against imperialism and foreign interference, rather than an effort to move from a market economy to a planned economy. Accordingly, the parties that now rule in Vietnam, Cambodia, and Laos are more intensely nationalist than the revolutionary internationalists who earlier won power in Russia and China. They have opted for one-party, centrally controlled regimes, but neither Moscow nor Peking is confident of its influence over these new practitioners of Communism.

Communism in the West. The varieties of Communism so far discussed prevail in nations that are seeking to "modernize" and industrialize without relying on free enterprise or capital imports or even extensive international trade. It has been suggested by Western socialists that this sort of Communism, far from being a "superior stage" of historical development coming after capitalism, is a prior, inferior stage that will end in a democratic revolution once society has been modernized and industrialized. Whatever the value of this neo-Marxist speculation about contemporary history (which assumes that Communism *can* successfully modernize a nation), it is clear that the modernizing, industrializing emphasis in Eastern European and Asian Communism is irrelevant in Western societies. Those latter are the very criterion the Communists have chosen to represent industrial modernity, and therefore Western Communists have little to learn from less developed, imitative countries. Besides, the advanced countries are part of a network of international trade and investment that Communists could break only at the cost of instant impoverishment. For those reasons, Western and Japanese Communists came to see (or rather, were forced by critics to admit) that all the established sorts of Communism were unsuitable and politically embarrassing models for the Communism they hoped to install in mature capitalist democracies.

These parties have spent the past 20 years gradually taking their distance from the Soviet archetype. (The Japanese party was tempted by sympathy with the Chinese experiment, but that was a brief interlude. By 1976 the Japanese had lined up with Western European Communists.) This process made rapid progress in 1976, but it is still far from complete. To visualize what "complete" would mean, one could imagine these parties not only declaring that their Communism would be "different" but describing it, specifically denouncing Soviet Communism whenever it diverged seriously from that description, and then, in order to avoid confusion, changing their party names and breaking off their links with Moscow. They are still far short of doing that, but the path they entered in 1976 could conceivably lead in that direction.

Soviet Primacy Rejected. In that year, the Italian, French, Spanish, Japanese, and British parties all explicitly rejected Soviet leadership, or even primacy, of the Communist movement. They insisted so firmly on their independence that the very notion of "the Communist movement" became vague. Indeed, after attending a meeting of European Communist parties, ruling and nonruling, in East Berlin in June, some Western party leaders declared they would never again attend such a rally, because even that compromised their independence. They, and the Japanese party, proclaimed their attachment to democratic principles and civil liberties to which Communist states have paid lip service while violating them. Going further, the dissident parties asserted their loyalty to parliamentary institutions, constitutional government, and durable alliances with non-Communist parties, all of which are entirely incompatible with Leninist doctrine.

Going further still, they abandoned essential tenets of Marxist doctrine, such as the dictatorship of the proletariat and proletarian internationalism (which had meant in practice, respectively, exclusive rule by a Communist party and solidarity between Communist parties under Soviet leadership). The hierarchical structure of the dissident Communist parties was carefully preserved, but at the base there was a relaxation of discipline and militancy. The cell, formerly the basic unit holding individual members together, was dropped in the Spanish party and had fallen into neglect in the Italian party. As a result, those parties became more like other, constituency-based political parties and less like conspiratorial Leninist organizations.

The Western Communist parties (at least the biggest of them, for the U.S., Danish, and West German parties remained unswervingly loyal to Moscow) felt that they had established their right to be different at the East Berlin meeting in June 1976. Yet, within a few weeks, the Soviet party was saying that this was not so. The official newspaper *Pravda* said in July, "Obviously, the considerable differences [between parties], which from time to time go beyond mere national peculiarities, are not permanent but only temporary, and they merely reflect, for the most part, different levels of development. As socialism becomes more mature, its common characteristics become more and more obvious." In other words, for Moscow there is still only one Communism, the Soviet sort, and the other parties will draw closer to it as they gain experience. By implication, the Soviet party, as the most experienced, would retain the privilege of guiding, and intervening in, the less mature parties. This is just what most of the latter, from the immense Chinese party down to the small British party, reject. Moscow was thus claiming a right it could not enforce except where it had the capacity for military intervention, as in Eastern Europe.

Can Communists Be Democrats? The Communist parties of the industrialized world changed their policies when they came nearer to exercising real political influence if not actual power. That fact presented their potential allies, and indeed all participants in Western parliamentary institutions, with an acute dilemma: could one acquiesce in the admission of Communists to "bourgeois" political systems and military alliances that, until quite recently, they were pledged to destroy, by violence or by guile? Answers to that question differed widely, even among people of comparable political experience and democratic conviction. In 1976 this was one of the subjects at a summit meeting of leaders of seven industrialized countries in Puerto Rico in June, one of the issues in the U.S. presidential election campaign, one of the concerns of the Socialist International, and one of the first problems of the restored Spanish monarchy. The political calendar in southern Europe suggests it will be a live issue for at least the next few years.

The common ground in such discussions was that, if the Communists were practicing subterfuge (which would be quite consistent with Leninism), advanced societies would risk disruption by admitting them to power or influence. So elaborate a subterfuge seemed unlikely to most observers, however, and the debate mainly centred about which of two possible sequences of events would be set off by the Communists' new role. On the one hand, their accession to high office might give rise to a leftward-moving dynamic, raising widespread expectations of sudden, radical change in industrialized democracies and inviting the Communists to anticipate what they would see as "the course of history"—until a revolutionary situation arose and the Communists turned to the Soviet Union for help against their opponents. On the other hand, their involvement in solidly based democratic institutions might soften and compromise them, obliging them to break with the Soviet Union and to return to the constitutional consensus they quit after the Bolshevik Revolution. Even that latter hypothesis, of course, would entail a notable leftward shift in the political balance of forces in Japan and in Mediterranean Europe, with extensive consequences for the economic policies of those countries and for their contribution to (or claim on) Western defense.

Comoro Islands

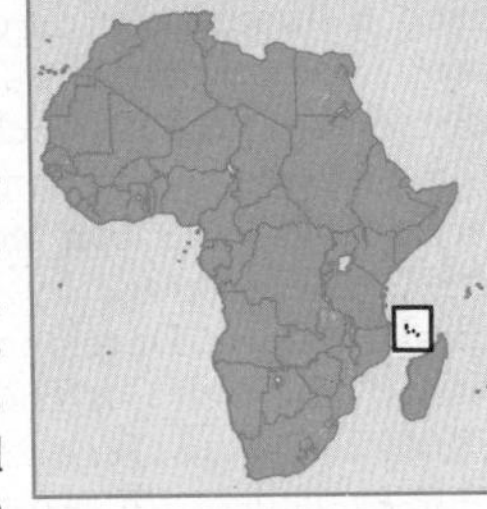

An African island state lying in the Indian Ocean off the east coast of Africa between Mozambique and Madagascar, the Comoros in 1976 administratively comprised three main islands, Grande Comore, Moheli, and Anjouan; the fourth island of the archipelago, Mayotte, continued to be a de facto dependency of France, although its final administrative status remained undetermined. Area: 719 sq mi (1,862 sq km). Pop. (1975 est.): 265,000. Cap. and largest city: Moroni (pop., 1973 est., 15,900), on Grande Comore. Mayotte: area 146 sq mi (378 sq km); pop. (mid-1970s) about 40,000. Language: French. Religion: mainly Muslim. President from Jan. 2, 1976, Ali Soilih; premier from January 6, Abdallah Mohammed.

On Jan. 2, 1976, Ali Soilih, leader of a successful coup the previous August, was elected head of state by a joint session of the National Revolutionary Council and the Executive Council, and on January 6 he appointed Abdallah Mohammed premier. Previously, on Dec. 13, 1975, France had enacted a law by which the islands of Grande Comore, Anjouan, and Moheli ceased to be part of the French republic and by which the future status of the island of Mayotte was to be decided by further referenda. These were held on February 8 and April 11 when, respectively, over 99% of votes cast were for continuance under French rule and over 97% for Mayotte to become a French département. However, France was subject to considerable pressure from within the UN by African and other countries who called for its withdrawal on the ground that a continued French presence in Mayotte constituted a threat to the national unity of the independent Comoro Islands, and on September 17 France announced that Mayotte would simply be granted a "special status."

The effects of the French withdrawal were alleviated by an $814,500 grant under the UN World Food Program and 2,500 tons of rice from Australia.

(PHILIPPE DECRAENE)

COMORO ISLANDS

Education. (Includes Mayotte; 1973–74) Primary, pupils 23,194, teachers 554; secondary, pupils 3,175, teachers 125; teacher training, students 22, teachers 3.

Finance and Trade. (Includes Mayotte) Monetary unit: CFA franc, with (Sept. 20, 1976) a parity of CFA Fr 50 to the French franc and a free rate of CFA Fr 245.90 to U.S. $1 (CFA Fr 423.62 = £1 sterling). Budget (1975 rev. est.) balanced at CFA Fr 2,949,000,000. Foreign trade (1973): imports CFA Fr 3,369,000,000; exports CFA Fr 1,106,000,000. Import sources: France c. 50%; Madagascar c. 15%; Kenya c. 5%. Export destinations: France c. 75%; Madagascar c. 19%; Italy c. 7%. Main exports (1971): essential oils c. 40%; vanilla c. 30%; spices c. 17%.

Computers

According to *EDP Industry Report* slightly more than 200,000 general-purpose computers existed in the United States in early 1976. Figures compiled by the International Data Corp. as of the beginning of the year showed that manufacturing, business, and miscellaneous business services held 55.1% of the installed computer base; banking, finance, and insurance, 13.4%; the education community, 5.7%; state and local government, 5.7%; and the federal government, 3.4%; the remaining 16.7% was spread among all other sectors of the economy. Most dramatic was the drop in the percentage of computers owned by the federal government since the early 1950s, when it had held more than 95% of the installed base.

WIDE WORLD

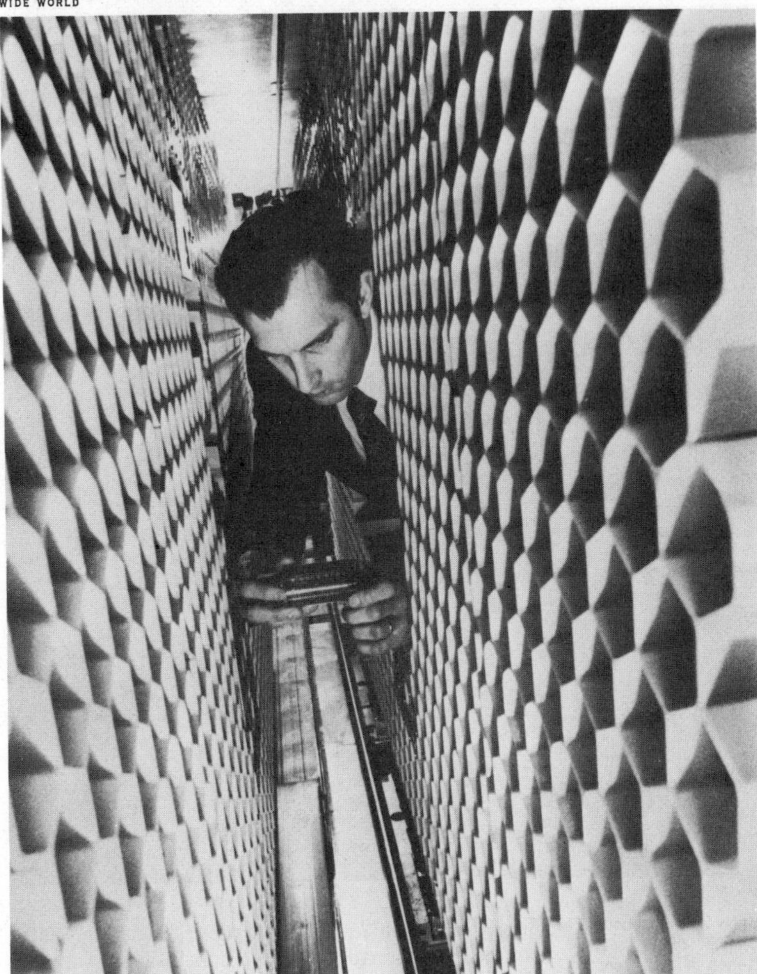

Systems engineer George Middleton holds a four-inch data cartridge, one of 3,382 that are kept in this new computer storage unit named TELOPS. The unit is designed to handle information transmitted by 25 U.S. scientific satellites now orbiting the Earth.

In addition to the shift in computer ownership another significant trend was evident in the increased use of minicomputers for tasks previously assigned to larger general-purpose computers. There is no good definition of minicomputers. The U.S. General Accounting Office used one of the more common definitions; namely, a simple computer system having a central processing unit that costs $50,000 or less. Under this definition more than 60% of the computers in use in the U.S. were minicomputers.

Digital Equipment Corp. remained the largest minicomputer vendor with 37% of the minicomputer market in early 1976. Hewlett-Packard Co. was second with 17.4% of the market. However, mainframe vendors were beginning to move seriously into the minicomputer market. In January, Honeywell Information Systems Inc. introduced a new minicomputer line, and in April Burroughs Corp. introduced a new series of minicomputers featuring the same architecture as its mainframes.

Applications. Microprocessors, the smallest of all electronic data-processing devices, continued to lead technological and application advances in 1976. Rang-

A new industrial computer terminal allows users to feed in data from the plant floor. It is designed to withstand hot and humid operating conditions.

ing from $10 to $500 in price, these single large integrated circuits made possible the inclusion of complex control, calculation, and processing capabilities in a wide variety of devices and instruments. General Motors included microprocessors as part of the control systems of its 1977 line of automobiles. Digital watchmakers found wristwatches to be a natural carrier for electronic calculators or logical devices and marketed several that matched in capability the simpler of the hand-held calculators.

Point-of-sale (POS) equipment emerged with unexpected strength as a giant in the retail industry. POS systems were basically real-time, data-collection computer terminal systems. They replaced traditional electromechanical cash registers and checkout devices. There were some 12 vendors of POS equipment as 1976 began. As the importance of POS equipment skyrocketed, the withdrawal of the Singer Co. from the POS sales market heralded more competition problems within the computer industry.

IBM took its first major step as a force to be considered in the U.S. communications market in late 1975 with its joint-venture application to the Federal Communications Commission for a domestic communications satellite network. Its partners were Comsat General Corp. and Aetna Life & Casualty and their goal was to develop the first all-digital communications system covering the 48 contiguous states by 1979. This venture was expected to make 1976 a hallmark year with respect to the convergence of computers and communications in practical applications.

Computer-aided manufacturing (CAM), which refers to any of a variety of applications of computers to manufacturing, received considerable attention in 1976. The most popular uses of the term referred to either industrial robots or computer control of production through control of the machine tools used to turn raw materials into finished parts. The year saw an industrial robot population of about 2,000 in the U.S. and roughly the same number in the rest of the world. The three high-technology robots available in the U.S. were made by Unimation, Inc., AMF Electrical Products Development Division, and the Cincinnati Milacron Co. They ranged in base price from $3,000 to $85,000 for a computer-controlled unit, and were available with two to six axes of motion. Memories of sophisticated robots were minicomputers and in some manufacturing applications entire banks of robots were under the control of a simple computer.

Office automation, best described as a wide-ranging systems approach to revolutionize office functions, emerged in full bloom in 1976. The equipment that epitomized office automation in 1976 included some combination of intelligent terminals, word processors, microform viewers, electronic displays, computer networks supplying information services, computer-controlled facsimile equipment, and copier devices under minicomputer control. In the context of office automation, word processing (WP) was the manipulation of words, sentences, and paragraphs by advanced hardware. There was wide consensus that WP was the springboard from which office automation would take off.

In 1976 Xerox Corp. and IBM were the two principal vendors of office automation hardware. After IBM, Redactron Corp., a small business, had the second-largest installed base of text-editing typewriters. There were also several other companies supplying sizable quantities of the differing equipment units that constitute office automation. It was estimated that about 12,000–15,000 cathode-ray-tube word-processing terminals would be installed in 1976.

Information Protection Systems. Public and congressional concerns with computer applications centred on computer abuse, computer crime, and invasion of privacy. The Privacy Act of 1974, which became effective in September 1975, imposed constraints on all computer systems within the federal government that processed information about individuals. Simulated attacks, or illicit attempts to extract information, showed that no operating system against which an attack was mounted was invulnerable. Both customers and vendors began redesigning system hardware and software to include lockout features, access controls, and audit procedures. *EDP Analyzer* reported on some 16 audit packages for sale in 1976, and about seven companies were found that sold computer terminals that required either keys or identification cards before they could be used.

Encryption as a means of providing security for data in transit within computer systems and networks or for selected data in residence in system files became popular for the first time. The National Bureau of Standards proposed a Data Encryption Standard for government use, and encryption algorithms attracted considerable attention from the academic and computer communities. The proposed standard claimed to be sufficiently secure from attack that it would take more than 2,000 years for the largest commercially available computer devoted to the attack to recover the encryption key and read the encrypted data. Several companies planned to announce data-encryption devices that used large-scale-integration (LSI) technology, sold in the $50–$100 range, and met the Data Encryption Standard.

Technology. The maximum feasible number of components on a single silicon integrated-circuit (IC) chip continued to increase, approaching 50,000 in 1976. This improvement in density was achieved without a rise in the price of maximum-complexity IC's, which remained roughly comparable to that of 1960–61. The three highest density circuit technologies for LSI applications (circuits having more than 100 gates) were complementary metal-oxide semiconductor (MOS)/silicon-on-sapphire, n-channel MOS, and integrated injection logic, with densities, expressed in gates per square millimetre, of 80–100, 80–100, and 100–200, respectively. A 20% yield in chip fabrication was the practical limit.

One severe limitation on high-speed LSI circuit complexity was the attainable density of connections from the chip to other components, a factor commonly connoted by LSI-package pin count. The state of the art in 1976 was about 64 pins with no breakthroughs in sight. This limitation affected LSI microprocessor capabilities to the extent that full parallelism in memory addressing and data paths desirable for high-speed, central-processing-unit operation were not feasible.

The principal successors to present storage devices being advanced in 1976 were charge-coupled-device memories and magnetic-domain (bubble) memories; the latter were touted as good replacements for cassettes and floppy-disk memories with wide microprocessor applications. One of the first companies to announce its plans for commercialization of bubble memories was Texas Instruments Inc. Bubble-memory systems were in some customers' hands in 1976 and were to be on the market in 1977, with 100-kilobit memories available in a single ceramic dual-inline package. IBM was working on bubbles four microns in diameter with a density of 64 kilobits per chip, and Bell Laboratories had two pilot-production lines in operation at a Western Electric plant.

Computer Networks. Computer networks were the principal modality of computer use in 1976, and some 100–200 commercial network data-processing services were available. The increased use of computer networks, some using packet-switching technology and satellite links, placed severe strains on software systems. Computer network operating systems, which were software designed to pull the network together and allow even the unsophisticated user to perform normal jobs, were still both novel and few in number.

By 1976 all general-purpose-computer manufacturers were offering software tools for networking, the most sophisticated being Burroughs' Network Definition Language (NDL) and Message Control Language (MCL). At the end of the year most computer manufacturers were offering comprehensive network architecture. Generally, these commercial data-processing network services were tailored to the more common 9.6–19.6 kilobit communications lines. Probably the most significant competitive happening in commercial networking was the announcement of bankruptcy by the Data Transmission Co. (Datran) in August 1976. As the single largest specialized common carrier competitor to AT&T, the exit of Datran from the market could signal higher communications costs for network users. (RUTH M. DAVIS)

See also Mathematics.

[735.D; 10/23.A.6–7]

ENCYCLOPÆDIA BRITANNICA FILMS. *What is a Computer?* (1970); *A Computer Glossary* (1973).

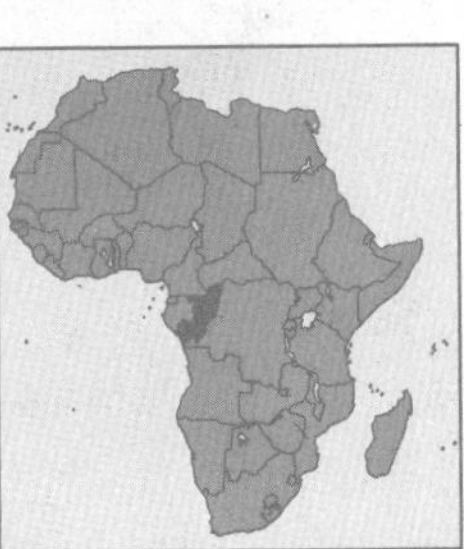

Congo

A people's republic of equatorial Africa, the Congo is bounded by Gabon, Cameroon, the Central African Empire, Zaire, Angola, and the Atlantic Ocean. Area: 132,000 sq mi (342,000 sq km). Pop. (1976 est.): 1,380,000, mainly Bantu. Cap. and largest city: Brazzaville (pop., 1974 prelim., 310,500). Language: French (official) and Bantu dialects. Religion: Roman Catholic 38%; most of the remainder are animist. President in 1976, Maj. Marien Ngouabi; premier, Maj. Louis Sylvain Goma.

A wholesale reorganization of government structures begun at the end of 1975 continued into 1976. On January 3 a new nine-member Council of State was created, with President Ngouabi as chairman and including Maj. Louis Sylvain Goma, who three weeks earlier had succeeded Henri Lopes as premier.

The authorities, capitalizing on the outbreak of an "illegal" strike, arrested several trade-union leaders on March 25, including Ekamba Elombé, but released them following a commission of inquiry.

The Congolese government decided at the last minute not to participate in the Franco-African conference held in Paris and Versailles, France, in May. Active support was given to the Algerian-backed Polisario independence movement in the "Saharan Arab Democratic Republic" (formerly Spanish Sahara). In June the Cuban defense minister, Raúl Castro, visited the Congo, but reports that Cuban troops were being transferred from Angola to the Congo were later denied. On May 27 it was announced that all property of foreigners who had left the country during the previous five years would be taken over by the state, with compensation. An African committee to promote information on environmental problems was established at a conference in Brazzaville in September. (PHILIPPE DECRAENE)

[978.E.7.a.iii]

CONGO

Education. (1973–74) Primary, pupils 293,138, teachers 4,650; secondary, pupils 66,710, teachers 1,289; vocational, pupils 5,002, teachers 342; teacher training, students 805, teachers 50; higher (1972–73), students 2,098, teaching staff 194.

Finance. Monetary unit: CFA franc, with (Sept. 20, 1976) a parity of CFA Fr 50 to the French franc and a free rate of CFA Fr 245.90 to U.S. $1 (CFA Fr 423.62 = £1 sterling). Budget (1975 est.) balanced at CFA Fr 56,352,000,000.

Foreign Trade. (1975) Imports *c.* CFA Fr 48,540,-000,000; exports *c.* CFA Fr 51,930,000,000. Import sources (1972): France 54%; West Germany 8%; U.S. 6%; China 5%. Export destinations (1972): France 16%; West Germany 14%; South Africa 8%; The Netherlands 5%. Main exports (1974): crude oil 62%; timber 19%.

Transport and Communications. Roads (1974) *c.* 11,000 km. Motor vehicles in use (1974): passenger 19,000; commercial (including buses) 10,500. Railways: (1974) 801 km; traffic (1975) 223 million passenger-km, freight 461 million net ton-km. Air traffic (including apportionment of Air Afrique; 1974): 111 million passenger-km; freight 11.6 million net ton-km. Telephones (Dec. 1974) 10,000. Radio receivers (Dec. 1973) 3,800.

Agriculture. Production (in 000; metric tons; 1974): cassava 607; sweet potatoes 91; peanuts 27; sugar, raw value *c.* 44; bananas 34; palm oil *c.* 4. Livestock (in 000; 1974): cattle 45; sheep *c.* 33; goats *c.* 45; pigs *c.* 15; chickens *c.* 700.

Industry. Production (in 000; metric tons): crude oil (1975) 1,789; potash (oxide content; 1974) 442; electricity (kw-hr; 1974) 97,000.

Congregational Churches: *see* Religion

Conservation: *see* Environment

Construction Industry: *see* Engineering Projects; Industrial Review

Consumerism

"Is Nader Fading?" ran the headline on a U.S. newsmagazine article in June 1976. After interviewing some of Ralph Nader's friends and associates, the authors concluded that the numerous groups Nader had sponsored in his ten years of consumer organizing were still going strong. His litigation group, for example, had just won two cases before the U.S. Supreme Court. In one, the court upheld the right of airline passengers to sue when they were "bumped" from flights because of overbooking. In the other, the court held that states could not forbid drugstores to advertise the prices of their prescription drugs.

Another Nader group released a study in June showing that when consumers took action they often got results. The study found that consumers experienced problems in one-fourth of their household purchases, but that only one problem in three was reported to the authorities. Whether a problem was reported or not seemed to depend on the consumer's economic level and the price of the product. However, those who did complain got satisfaction more than half of the time. The study estimated that the courts, Better Business Bureaus, and other third-party complaint-handling systems hear only about 1% of the problems encountered by consumers. Services drew more complaints than products, with repairs of homes, appliances, and cars high on the list. Among products, the categories drawing the most complaints were mail-order purchases, toys, cars, and clothing.

World Consumerism. Consumer organizations flourished all over the world. Many of them had joined together in federations, believing that the strength of the consumer movement lay in such cooperation: their combined membership made them powerful bodies exerting considerable influence, and their advice was often sought by national and international bodies. In 1976 the Bureau Européen des Unions de Consommateurs began a study of consumer education in schools and another on the transport requirements of consumers, on behalf of the European Economic Community (EEC). On the other side of the globe, the Australian Federation of Consumer Organizations marked its first anniversary with a doubling of its membership.

The International Organization of Consumers Unions (IOCU), with over 100 affiliated organizations in 50 countries, continued to work in consultation or liaison with several international and intergovernmental agencies. IOCU's proposal for a model code of consumer protection to be drawn up by the UN for the use of member nations was given further airing at the second session of the UN Commission on Transnational Corporations in Lima, Peru, in March. The statement submitted by the IOCU representative there suggested that it was time to place consumer protection within an international framework and under the scrutiny of the UN. It proposed that the code of conduct under study by the commission be extended to embrace a model code of ethics designed to protect consumers with respect to labeling, advertising, and promotion practices, rights and obligations of seller and buyer, opportunities for redress through judicial or administrative processes, and a model code of standards paralleling that of the Food and Agriculture Organization/World Health Organization code on food standards but applied to such necessities as housing, materials, textiles, and appliances.

The call for better standards was reiterated at the UN Conference on Human Settlements (Habitat) in Vancouver, B.C., in June. The statement submitted by

UPI COMPIX

One way of saving gasoline is to turn off half the motor whenever full power isn't needed. Ford Motor Co. is developing a Dual Displacement Engine equipped with "valve selectors" that cut out half the cylinders at speeds over 45 miles per hour.

the IOCU representative there asked that performance standards be established in the construction industry for safety, durability, availability, quality, accuracy, and completeness of information. The purpose should be to enable consumers to obtain housing of reasonable quality at a reasonable price and on reasonable terms. Later in the year the International Organization for Standardization issued a statement stressing the urgent need for international standardization in the construction industry.

Consumer Organizations. The activities of specific consumer organizations were various, depending on the problems facing consumers in different lands. In Switzerland, consumer organizations drew up guidelines for the introduction of standardized informative labeling on electric appliances. Japanese consumer groups joined in protest against the use of orthophenylphenol as a fungicide on imported citrus fruit, demanding that priority be given to the safety of food over the economies involved. The National Consumers' League in Jamaica urged its members to save money by growing their own vegetables. The high cost of living was also a target of the Consumers' Association of Canada, which demanded a reduction of 10–15% in the price of eggs, while in Switzerland the Schweizerischer Konsumentenbund supported the federal decision to enforce price control.

A survey of air pollution in the Delhi area, carried out by the Consumer Council of India, revealed that about half of Delhi's buses emitted a quantity of exhaust fumes above the danger level. In Singapore, consumer organizations joined with advertisers, advertising agencies, and media owners to produce a self-regulating code of advertising to be administered by an Advertising Standards Authority. The head of the legal department of The Netherlands' Consumentenbond reported that it had won 15 out of 17 cases taken on behalf of individual consumers.

A coalition of nine U.S. consumer organizations filed suit against the Department of Agriculture in August because it had allowed meat processors to redefine "meat" to include bits of crushed bone. The bits were introduced when meat containing soft bones was put through "deboning" machines. The consumer groups obtained an injunction from a federal court against the new regulations pending a showing by the department that no health hazard would be involved.

Eight national and local U.S. consumer organizations in September charged Pres. Gerald R. Ford with 82 "counts" of anticonsumer behaviour. They released their charges in the form of a criminal indictment. Among the "counts" were the following:

• President Ford had used his authority to increase the tariffs on imported oil.

• He had favoured the relaxation of automobile emission and safety standards.

• In 1975 he had vetoed legislation that would have provided milk and reduced the price of school lunches for some of the poorest children in the country.

• He had twice vetoed legislation that would have required strip miners to restore land to its original contours.

• His tight money policies had "made home ownership an impossible dream for millions of Americans."

• In 1975 he had opposed budget increases that would have enabled the Federal Trade Commission (FTC) and the Department of Justice to improve their abilities to investigate unfair competition and unfair restraint of trade by corporations.

• He had opposed a bill that would have enabled private citizens to sue government agencies for illegal actions.

WIDE WORLD

Joan Braden was appointed coordinator of consumer affairs for the U.S. Department of State. Her job was to make the department more responsive to consumers.

The groups represented labour unions, cooperatives, and local citizens' groups. Their broadside was seen as an effort to make the consumer movement felt as a political force in the November presidential election campaign. One of the spokesmen said that "the worst indictment of Mr. Ford is that during his two years in office he refused even to talk to consumer groups."

Government Participation. A growing concern for the problems of consumers in less developed countries could be seen in the staging of the IOCU Regional Seminar on Consumer Testing and Research, which took place in Penang, Malaysia, in October. The seminar was financed by a grant from The Netherlands government, the first instance in IOCU's history of substantial financial aid from a national government. Speaking at the opening of the seminar, the Dutch ambassador reminded participants that "to improve the standard of living in the world, protection of consumers and particularly of the poor, both in the developed and in the developing countries, and in cities as well as in rural areas, is of the utmost importance." One of the main objectives of the seminar was to provide executives of consumer organizations in the less developed countries with practical training in product testing.

In the U.S., President Ford ordered 17 executive departments and agencies of the federal government to develop consumer representation plans in an effort to make consumers "a part of the decision-making process." He said on September 27 that the new guidelines were designed to ensure "that the individual consumer with a complaint or a criticism must not only be heard, but that those complaints will be acted upon by the government." Each of the agencies would be required to name a person who would be responsible for carrying out the program, and for issuing an annual report detailing what had been done.

A congressional investigation of regulatory agencies of the U.S. government concluded with a report issued late in the year. The report said that the major weaknesses of the nine federal agencies studied were their lack of concern for the public and their ties to the industries being regulated. It rated the Interstate

COURTESY, PEPSI-COLA COMPANY

On the front line in the cola war: More people preferred brand "L," said the Pepsi ads. The "L" glass contained Pepsi while the "S" glass contained Coca-Cola. The Coke ads replied that of course people preferred "L." "L stands for liberty and lunch . . . all the things that really made our country great."

Commerce Commission and the Federal Power Commission lowest and put the Federal Trade Commission, the Securities and Exchange Commission, and the Environmental Protection Agency at the top.

In a move that aroused some controversy, the FTC in May issued a new rule to protect consumers from arrangements requiring them to pay for purchases that had proved to be unsatisfactory. It altered the "holder in due course" doctrine, under which a third party such as a bank or a collection agency could continue to collect money owed by a consumer even though the merchandise was not what the purchaser had anticipated. In a typical case, a consumer bought a sofa and agreed to pay for it in installments. The sofa fell apart, but when the purchaser complained he found that the seller had sold the installment contract to a finance house. He was legally compelled to keep on paying the finance house for the sums outstanding even though the seller of the sofa refused to repair or replace it. The new rule extended liability for the merchandise to the bank or finance company that purchased the installment contract.

In January the U.S. Food and Drug Administration (FDA) banned the dye known as Red No. 2, a widely used dye in foods, drugs, and cosmetics. Though there was no evidence of a public health hazard from any currently available product made with it, the agency decided to ban it because laboratory tests had shown that high dosages of the dye caused cancer in rats. In September the FDA banned the use in foods of Red No. 4 and carbon black.

The FDA also decided to pay fees to lawyers representing public-interest and consumer groups in proceedings before the agency.

Legislation. In the U.S., President Ford in May signed a bill that strengthened the charter of the Consumer Product Safety Commission and permitted consumers to sue the commission when it failed to exercise its powers to keep dangerous products off the market. Among the highlights of the revised charter were authority for the commission to override state product-safety laws, and power to set uniform standards for the packaging of poisonous substances and for the regulation of flammable fabrics. The provision affected, for example, bicycle manufacturers who were faced with a bewildering patchwork of state and local regulations on items such as reflectors and brakes. The legislation also gave the commission power to remove unsafe products from store shelves quickly by seeking court injunctions. Previously the commission had been required to hold hearings before banning the sale of a product.

A noteworthy development in the U.S. was legislation—adopted by 19 states and the District of Columbia, as of late 1976—encouraging or requiring physicians to prescribe generic equivalents for more costly brand-name drugs whenever feasible.

In India, Parliament passed an amendment to the Prevention of Food Adulteration Act (1954) under which offenders would face life imprisonment. Another law made it mandatory for manufacturers to print their names and addresses on packaged goods together with a description of the contents, the date of manufacture, the price, and the net weight. A Central Consumers' Council, with statutory powers, was set up in India to help implement the new legislation.

In Mexico, a new Consumer Protection Law established standards of quality, regulated installment purchase agreements, provided for the fixing of price ceilings, and set up a federal agency to enforce the law.

In Canada, new regulations dealing with open-date marking on the labels of prepackaged foods came into force. In Denmark, textile labeling rules were introduced, adopting in full the measures set out by the EEC.

Consumer Education. The Consumers' Association of Penang, Malaysia, organized a seminar in June on "the role of schools in promoting consumer education," the object being to familiarize students with the need for consumer education and with the methods and procedures for carrying out such a program.

The Consumer Guidance Society of India began a project for consumer education among low-income groups that sought to "improve the living conditions of those groups by creating awareness of consumer rights, . . . and to help them utilize their meagre resources."

(ISOLA VAN DEN HOVEN; EDWARD MARK MAZZE)

See also Economy, World; Industrial Review: *Advertising.*
[532.B.3; 534.H.5; 534.K]

Cosmetics:
see Fashion and Dress

Contract Bridge

To be runners-up in both the Bermuda Bowl (the official world championship) and the Olympiad would represent a great achievement for almost any bridge-playing country. For Italy, however, which surrendered both titles in Monaco in May 1976, this performance represented the end of a 20-year reign, 20 years in which teams that included Benito Garozzo, Pietro Forquet, and Giorgio Belladonna had come to be regarded as invincible.

Defending champions Italy and the five zonal representatives, Australia, Brazil, Hong Kong, Israel, and North America, contested the Bermuda Bowl for seven strenuous days. Italy began its defense of the title against the background of startling new allegations of misconduct, emanating this time from an unsuccessful competitor in its own selection trials. He was able to produce taped recordings of conversations in which a former member of successful Italian teams had apparently acknowledged that he and other members of the team had used improper methods. The validity of the tapes was questioned, and at the end of 1976 the findings and decision of the Italian Bridge Federation had yet to be promulgated.

The story of the "tapes" made world news on the eve of the Bermuda Bowl and placed a strain on the Italians that was clearly reflected in their play. Their place in the two-team final was in doubt until almost the last board of the five-day qualifying stage. In the final they took an early lead against North America, represented by a wholly U.S. team. After the opening session, however, they were unconvincing, and the winners owed more to Italian mistakes than to their own accuracy. The new champions, William Eisenberg, Fred Hamilton, Ira Rubin, Paul Soloway, Hugh Ross, and Eric Paulsen, with their nonplaying captain Dan Morse, won by 232–198. The U.S. made it a double victory when their women beat Great Britain, the European champions, 395–211. The winners were represented by Ruth MacConnell (nonplaying captain), Emma Jean Hawes, Betty Ann Kennedy, Dorothy Truscott, Carol Sanders, Gail Moss, and Jacqui Mitchell.

Forty-five countries competed in the open series of the fifth world team Olympiad, played over 14 days. It would be difficult to imagine a more dramatic climax. When play began for round 45, the final round, there were three possible winners, Italy 645, Brazil 634, and Great Britain 629. In the final match Great Britain was to meet Turkey, Brazil was opposed by Canada, and Italy by Greece. Italy had to do no more than divide the points with Greece 10–10 to retain the title. Great Britain was the first to finish, winning 17–3. Brazil, faced with the most difficult task, scored a maximum 20 points against Canada, and there was still time for most people to watch the closing stages of Italy versus Greece on the Vu-Graph screen. At the halfway stage the teams were almost even. Shortly afterward there came the hand which decided the Olympiad (*see* box).

Greece went on to win the match 17–3, and the final standings were Brazil 654, Italy 648, and Great Britain 646. The new Brazilian champions were Gabriel Chagas, Pedro-Paul Assumpcão, Christian Fonseca, Gabino Cintra, Sergio Barbosa, and Marcello Branco, with their nonplaying captain Adelstano Porte D'Ave.

Italy found a measure of consolation when Anna Valenti, Rina Jabes, Maria Robaudo, Lucianna Capodanno, Marisa D'Andrea, and Marisa Bianchi, with nonplaying captain G. Pelucchi, retained the women's title ahead of Great Britain and the U.S. And, to show the transitory nature of bridge glory, some four months later Brazil's nine-year reign as South American champion came to an end with a second-place finish to Argentina. The Olympiad champions would, therefore, be missing from the next Bermuda Bowl contest.

Julius Rosenblum, president of the World Bridge Federation (WBF) for six years, was scheduled to end his term of office at the end of the Olympiad. Unfortunately, he fell seriously ill during the first days of the Olympiad, and it became necessary to elect a new president. He was 47-year-old Jaime Ortiz-Patino of Switzerland, whose personal dynamism and considerable business experience were expected to help the WBF maintain the significant progress made during the previous six years. The International Bridge Press Association nominated Mrs. Rixi Markus of Great Britain as "bridge personality of the year."

(HAROLD FRANKLIN)

[452.C.3.a.1]

NORTH
♠ K Q 7 2
♥ 8 7
♦ A Q 6 4 2
♣ 6 4

WEST
♠ J 9 6 4
♥ Q 10 3
♦ 7 3
♣ K 10 9 7

EAST
♠ 10 8
♥ J 9 4 2
♦ 10 9 8
♣ Q J 3 2

SOUTH
♠ A 5 3
♥ A K 6 5
♦ K J 5
♣ A 8 5

Dealer, East. Game all.

When the hand came on the screen, the result in the closed room was already known: Greece had played in a contract of four spades and had made 11 tricks after a club lead. Benito Garozzo and Arturo Franco reached a superior contract of six diamonds with Franco declarer from the North hand. If he made his contract, Italy would be the certain winner.

East led the queen of clubs. Declarer played low from dummy, and West overtook with the king and returned a club. Franco drew the outstanding trumps, played two top hearts, ruffed a third heart, and then played his remaining trump, discarding a spade from dummy. His chances were excellent: he would win if the spades divided 3–3 or if either opponent had begun with four hearts and four spades. Unfortunately, both chances failed and he was down one.

Another line of play that offered about the same chance would have succeeded. After winning the second club, declarer ruffs a third club in hand. Two hearts and a heart ruff are followed by the ace of diamonds, a diamond to the jack, and a final heart, ruffed with the queen of diamonds. Declarer can now reenter dummy with the ace of spades, then draw the outstanding trump with the king and claim the remaining spade tricks in his hand. This line of play, a "dummy reversal," called for little more than a 3–2 trump break.

Costa Rica

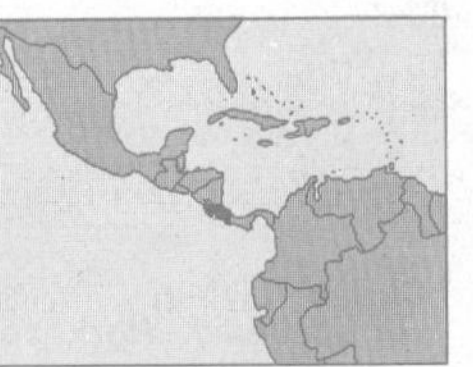

A Central American republic, Costa Rica lies between Nicaragua and Panama and has coastlines on the Caribbean Sea and the Pacific Ocean. Area: 19,652 sq mi (50,898 sq km). Pop. (1976 est.): 1,993,800, including white and mestizo 98%. Cap. and largest city: San José (metro. pop., 1976 est., 538,900). Lan-

COSTA RICA

Education. (1974) Primary, pupils 367,901, teachers 12,643; secondary, pupils (1972) 68,499, teachers 3,505; vocational, pupils (1972) 9,329, teachers (1970) 406; higher (1973), students 24,256, teaching staff 1,195.

Finance. Monetary unit: colón, with (Sept. 20, 1976) an official rate of 8.57 colones to U.S. $1 (free rate of 14.82 colones = £1 sterling). Gold, SDR's, and foreign exchange (June 1976) U.S. $75.1 million. Budget (1974 actual): revenue 1,936,000,000 colones; expenditure 2,113,000,000 colones. Gross national product (1975) 16,019,000,000 colones. Money supply (Feb. 1976) 2,895,000,000 colones. Cost of living (San José; 1970 = 100; Dec. 1975) 203.

Foreign Trade. (1975) Imports 6,023,700,000 colones; exports 4,179,600,000 colones. Import sources (1974): U.S. 34%; Japan 10%; Venezuela 7%; West Germany 6%; Guatemala 6%; Nicaragua 5%; El Salvador 5%. Export destinations (1974): U.S. 32%; West Germany 13%; Nicaragua 9%; Guatemala 7%; El Salvador 6%; The Netherlands 5%. Main exports: bananas 28%; coffee 20%; meat (1974) 8%; chemicals (1974) 8%; sugar (1974) 6%. Tourism: visitors (1973) 247,000; gross receipts (1974) U.S. $44 million.

Transport and Communications. Roads (1974) *c.* 18,000 km (including 650 km of Pan-American Highway). Motor vehicles in use (1973): passenger 52,100; commercial (including buses) 34,400. Railways: (1974) 650 km; traffic (1973) *c.* 97 million passenger-km, freight *c.* 20 million net ton-km. Air traffic (1975): 306 million passenger-km; freight 9,094,000 net ton-km. Telephones (Jan. 1975) 99,000. Radio receivers (Dec. 1973) 140,000. Television receivers (Dec. 1973) 122,000.

Agriculture. Production (in 000; metric tons; 1975): sorghum 18; corn (1974) *c.* 55; rice (1974) *c.* 107; potatoes (1974) *c.* 36; dry beans 20; bananas (1974) *c.* 1,100; oranges (1974) *c.* 65; sugar, raw value (1974) 176; cocoa *c.* 7; coffee *c.* 88; palm oil *c.* 23. Livestock (in 000; 1974): cattle *c.* 1,878; horses *c.* 116; pigs *c.* 288; chickens *c.* 4,600.

Industry. Electricity production (1974) 1,467,000,000 kw-hr (85% hydroelectric).

guage: Spanish. Religion: predominantly Roman Catholic. President in 1976, Daniel Oduber Quirós.

The main political issue of 1976 in Costa Rica was the nomination of presidential candidates for the 1978 election. A constitutional change that would have allowed successive reelection of presidents was rejected in mid-1976 by the Legislative Assembly, and José Figueres Ferrer, three times president in the past, resigned on September 12 as chairman of the governing party, the Partido de Liberación Nacional (PLN). Two ministers, Gonzálo J. Facio Segreda (foreign affairs) and Hernán Garrón Salazar (agriculture), left the government in September to campaign for the PLN nomination. In November the assembly voted to repeal the 1974 law that had sheltered fugitive millionaire Robert Vesco from extradition to the U.S.

The Costa Rican economy recovered in 1976 from two difficult years. An austere government program improved the growth rate (an estimated 6% in 1976, as compared with 3.4% in 1975), and the balance of trade showed satisfactory foreign reserves with an expected $116.6 million at the end of 1976, compared with $59.2 million at the end of 1975; the austerity also contributed to a slowdown in the rate of inflation from 20.5% in 1975 to about 10% in 1976. The San José stock exchange opened in August. Emphasis was put on tourism during the year, to increase exchange earnings and employment; the state allocated $1.2 million to various projects, and banks might grant loans up to $30 million. A new export market was created with the establishment of trade relations with Cuba, and Cuban orders were valued at $5 million by September 1976. (FRANÇOISE LOTERY)

[974.B.1.e]

Cost of Living: *see* Economy, World

Council for Mutual Economic Assistance: *see* Economy, World

Court Games

Handball. Fred Lewis of Miami, Fla., completely dominated the third season of the $50,000 Spalding Handball Tour by capturing six of eight scheduled tournaments. In the grand finale at Las Vegas, Nev., in June he repeated his 1975 triumph over Chicagoan Dennis Hofflander, winning 21–18, 21–4. Probably the most exciting action of the week-long play at Las Vegas was Lewis' victory over Nati Alvarado, a sensational 20-year-old pro newcomer and a native of Mexico. Alvarado broke into the pro ranks in brilliant fashion at the Tucson (Ariz.) Athletic Club in March. After qualifying, he successively eliminated the top-seeded Lewis, Gordy Pfeifer, Stuffy Singer, and Steve August. Lewis and Alvarado faced each other in the semifinals at Las Vegas. Alvarado lost the first game 21–8, but he took a 20–19 lead in the second game before missing a setup and finally losing 21–20.

In the finals of the United States Handball Association (USHA) open singles, Vern Roberts, Jr., the 1975 national intercollegiate titlist from Lake Forest College in Illinois, outclassed John Bart of Tucson. After Bart lost the first game 21–5, he was trailing 3–10 in the second when leg cramps forced him to default. In the open doubles, Dan O'Connor of St. Paul, Minn., also an all-American softball player, teamed with Gary Rohrer of Minneapolis, Minn., to defeat the San Francisco team of Bob Brady and Henry Chapparo, 21–14, 21–16. Jack Scrivens of Portland, Ore., repeated in the over-40 age masters singles, besting the highly touted Bob ("Buzz") Shumate of Dallas, Texas, 15–21, 21–19, 21–11. Arnold Aguilar and Gabe Enriquez of Los Angeles captured their second successive masters doubles victory by beating Tom Rohrback and Del Moro, another Los Angeles area team, 21–8, 18–21, 21–17. The first golden masters singles (plus-50 years) was won by Murray Marcus of Miami, who still retained fine court skills in beating John Sabo, Jr., of Orange, N.J.,

A glass-walled handball court at the Northwest Suburban YMCA in Des Plaines, Illinois, site of the seventh Spalding Handball Tour. The new court makes handball a spectator sport.

COURTESY, THE UNITED STATES HANDBALL ASSOCIATION

21–15, 21–15. Rudy Stadlberger and Tom Kelly of San Francisco took the golden masters doubles, overcoming Bill Badham of Los Angeles and Earl Russell of Long Beach, Calif., 21–14, 21–2. In the super masters doubles, open to veterans over 60, Ted Bystock of Miami and Jack Weitz of Larchmont, N.Y., defeated George Brotemarkle of Los Angeles and Marty Grossman of Lawrence, N.Y., 14–21, 21–17, 21–13.

Lake Forest College won its third straight USHA national intercollegiate team title by placing all three entries in the finals and winning the doubles with Jack Roberts and Mickey Guzman. Ken Ginty of Manhattan College, Bronx, N.Y., won the A singles and Pete Cristaudo of Memphis (Tenn.) State University the B singles.

(MORTON LEVE)

[452.B.4.h.xv]

Jai Alai. During the world amateur jai alai championships held in Mexico City in December 1975 the U.S. won its first international competition. The team of Víctor Gómez in the frontcourt and Linsey Bruce in the backcourt dominated the 40-point matches and was strongly supported by Larry Heffer and J. J. Castrello. All were from the Miami area. France, which won the title the previous year, finished second in the competition.

The Federación Internacional de Pelota Vasca, which has its headquarters in Spain, authorized the United States Amateur Jai-Alai Players Association to conduct the 1976 world amateur championships in Miami. The event coincided with the association's tenth anniversary. It was only the second time that such a tournament had been held in the U.S. and marked Italy's return to world competition after an absence of more than ten years.

The ninth annual U.S. amateur championships were held on July 18 in Miami and were decided by cumulative scores after four 25-point games. When Castrello in the frontcourt and Sergio Peiega in the backcourt emerged victorious, they became the youngest U.S. national champions ever; both were 16 years old. Each was named to represent the U.S. in the world championships, as were also Heffer and Alberto Pozo.

It was also an important year for professional jai alai in the U.S. New frontons were opened in Hartford and Bridgeport in Connecticut and in Newport, R.I. The Hartford fronton, built at a cost of $12 million and with a seating capacity of 10,000 persons, had 36 players on its roster. The average daily attendance exceeded 7,000 and the mutuel handle often hit $500,000 in an evening. The Bridgeport fronton, which cost $16 million and seated 12,000, had 40 professionals under contract. The success of the new frontons clearly indicated the rapidly growing popularity of jai alai in the U.S.

(ROBERT H. GROSSBERG)

[452.B.4.h.xix]

Volleyball. Though the Olympic Games in Montreal provided the most important international competition of the year, a notable tournament was inaugurated in Moscow in June. The first annual V. Savvin Memorial Tournament for men was held to honour the memory of a player and promoter, who at one time was both the captain of the Soviet national team and the president of the U.S.S.R. Volleyball Federation. The Soviet team won the event, followed in order by Poland, Czechoslovakia, Hungary, Cuba, Yugoslavia, and the U.S.

Of the men's teams that participated in the XXI Olympiad, Canada automatically qualified as the host country, Japan as the defending Olympic champion, and Poland as the current world champion. An additional five national teams, each representing a world zone, were chosen through prior eliminations: U.S.S.R. from Europe; Egypt (which withdrew for political reasons) from Africa; Brazil from South America; Cuba from North-Central and Caribbean America; and Korea from Asia. Italy and Czechoslovakia completed the list after qualifying as at-large teams in a pre-Olympic competition.

CANADIAN PRESS

Ryszard Bosek seems to float over the court as he makes a save during the final men's volleyball game between Poland and the Soviet Union at the Montreal Olympics. The Poles rallied from behind to win three games to two, taking their first Olympic medal in volleyball.

Among the eight women's teams that took part in the Olympics, Canada was included as host country, the U.S.S.R. as defending Olympic champion, and Japan as the current world champion. Four other teams represented world regions: Hungary from Europe; Peru from South America; Cuba from North-Central and Caribbean America; and Korea from Asia. The African zone was not represented. The only at-large women's team came from East Germany. For the Olympic results, *see* TRACK AND FIELD SPORTS: *Special Report*.

(ALBERT M. MONACO, JR.)

See also Racket Games; Tennis.

[452.B.4.h.xxviii]

Cricket

Four major test series were played in 1975–76: Australia *v.* West Indies, New Zealand *v.* India, West Indies *v.* India, and England *v.* West Indies. This meant a heavy program for the West Indians, who played the rubber match against India at home between full-length tours of Australia and England. Captained by C. H. Lloyd, they were overwhelmed 5–1 by Australia, severely challenged by India before winning 2–1, then finished in a blaze of glory with a 3–0 victory over England.

Australia v. West Indies. West Indies had problems in Australia similar to those faced by England the year before, namely, inability to cope with the fast bowling of D. K. Lillee and J. R. Thomson. Australia also had fast-medium bowler G. J. Gilmour. Though West Indies had fast bowlers in A. M. E. Roberts and M. A. Holding, Roberts became overworked and Holding needed more experience. The West Indies players made a fight of it during the first four tests, winning the second, but they lost their morale and Australia easily won the last two games.

The West Indians had talented batsmen in I. V. A. Richards, A. I. Kallicharran, R. C. Fredericks, and Lloyd, but the captain lost authority off and on the field and played only two big innings himself. During the tour, off-spinner L. R. Gibbs set a new world record of 308 test wickets. G. S. Chappell, who succeeded his brother I. M. as captain and won five tosses, had an outstanding season with the bat, and vice-captain I. R. Redpath invariably gave the innings a resolute start. Six Australians made centuries, G. S. Chappell and Redpath scoring three each.

Australia won the first test (Brisbane) by 8 wickets: West Indies made 214 and 370 (L. G. Rowe 107, Kallicharran 101); Australia 366 (G. S. Chappell 123) and 219 for 2 (G. S. Chappell 109 not out). West Indies won the second test (Perth) by an innings and 87 runs: Australia 329 (I. M. Chappell 156) and 169 (Roberts 7 for 54); West Indies 585 (Fredericks 169, Lloyd 149). Australia won the third test (Melbourne) by 8 wickets: West Indies 224 (Thomson 5 for 62) and 312 (Lloyd 102); Australia 485 (Redpath 102, G. J. Cosier 109) and 55 for 2. Australia won the fourth test (Sydney) by 7 wickets: West Indies 355 and 128 (Thomson 6 for 50); Australia 405 (G. S. Chappell 182 not out) and 82 for 3. Australia won the fifth test (Adelaide) by 190 runs: Australia 418 (Redpath 103, V. A. Holder 5 for 108) and 345 for 7 declared (A. Turner 136); West Indies 274 and 299 (Richards 101). Australia captured the sixth test (Melbourne) by 165 runs: Australia 351 (Redpath 101) and 300 for 3 declared (R. B. McCosker 109 not out); West Indies 160 (Lillee 5 for 63, Gilmour 5 for 34) and 326.

English and Australian women's cricket teams battle it out in August at Lord's Cricket Ground—the first women's game ever held on the famous London playing field.

KEYSTONE

West Indies v. India. At home West Indies had to face Indian spinners and no fast bowlers, and in an erratic performance won the first of four tests easily, drew the second, lost the third convincingly, and won the decisive fourth by ten wickets. This last victory, however, was a hollow triumph because the West Indian fast bowlers used a dangerous pitch so effectively that three Indian batsmen were seriously injured; moreover, B. S. Bedi, the Indian captain, ended his team's second innings with only five wickets down. Richards was the most outstanding West Indies batsman, continuing where he left off in Australia by making two more centuries. Kallicharran and Lloyd were his chief supporters in a patchy batting display. Holding's great speed was the most significant factor in the Indian defeat. India's leading batsmen, S. M. Gavaskar and G. R. Viswanath, made centuries in the remarkable victory at Port of Spain. After Lloyd had declared to set them 403 to win, they made the runs for only four wickets, a fourth innings total only once before achieved in test history. The Indian spin bowlers Bedi and B. S. Chandrasekhar took 39 of the 50 West Indies wickets that fell.

West Indies won the first test (Bridgetown) by an innings and 97 runs: India 177 (D. A. J. Holford 5 for 23) and 214; West Indies 488 for 9 declared (Richards 142, Lloyd 102). The second test (Port of Spain) was drawn: West Indies 241 (Richards 130, Bedi 5 for 82) and 215 for 8; India 402 for 5 declared (Gavaskar 156, B. P. Patel 115 not out). India won the third test (Port of Spain) by 6 wickets: West Indies 359 (Richards 177, Chandrasekhar 6 for 120) and 271 for 6 declared (Kallicharran 103 not out); India 228 (Holding 6 for 65) and 406 for 4 (Gavaskar 102, Viswanath 112). West Indies won the fourth test (Kingston) by 10 wickets: India 306 for 6 declared and 97; West Indies 391 (Chandrasekhar 5 for 153) and 13 for no wicket.

England v. West Indies. After a brief rest, the West Indian players undertook a full tour of England and had overwhelming success. Their victories were credited to the use of four fast bowlers to the exclusion of spin, and to the tremendous batting of Richards (two double centuries and one single) and C. G. Greenidge (three centuries, two in one match). There was also good support play all down the order. Roberts and Holding spearheaded the attack, sharing 56 wickets, and Holding had a memorable triumph in the fifth test at the Oval by taking 14 wickets. England was outclassed when its sparse bowling resources could not match the all-round strength of the West Indies batting. Only in the drawn second test at Lord's did England look as if it could hold its own, but the loss of a day through rain deprived the team of any slender chance it might have had for victory after England's two leading bowlers, J. A. Snow and D. L. Underwood, secured a first innings lead for the only time in the series. In the fourth test at Headingley, England came nearest to victory when their captain, A. W. Greig, made 116 and 76 not out, and A. P. E. Knott added another 116. In the fifth test D. L. Amiss made a triumphant comeback for England with a double century. Earlier in the summer, 45-year-old D. B. Close was recalled in an effort to bolster the batting and he played three staunch innings. England's only other centurion was D. S. Steele.

The first test (Trent Bridge, Nottingham) was drawn: West Indies 494 (Richards 232) and 176 for 5 declared; England 332 (Steele 106) and 156 for 2. The second test (Lord's, London) was also drawn:

England 250 (Roberts 5 for 60) and 254 (Roberts 5 for 63); West Indies 182 (Underwood 5 for 39) and 241 for 6 (Fredericks 138). West Indies won the third test (Old Trafford, Manchester) by 425 runs: West Indies 211 (Greenidge 134) and 411 for 5 declared (Richards 135, Greenidge 101); England 71 (Holding 5 for 17) and 126 (Roberts 6 for 37). West Indies won the fourth test (Headingley, Leeds) by 55 runs: West Indies 450 (Greenidge 115, Fredericks 109) and 196 (R. G. D. Willis 5 for 42); England 387 (Greig 116, Knott 116) and 204. West Indies won the fifth test (Oval, London) by 231 runs: West Indies 687 for 8 declared (Richards 291) and 182 for no wicket declared; England 435 (Amiss 203, Holding 8 for 92) and 203 (Holding 6 for 57).

West Indies further proved its superiority by winning all three one-day internationals for the Prudential Trophy by 6 wickets, 36 runs, and 50 runs, respectively.

New Zealand v. India. Early in the year New Zealand under G. M. Turner had a three-match series with India which ended with each team winning one game. In a wet, cheerless summer, New Zealand proved superior even though catches were too often dropped. Whereas New Zealand relied on the medium and fast bowling of R. O. Collinge, the brothers D. R. and R. J. Hadlee, and B. E. Congdon, India relied on the spin of Bedi, Chandrasekhar, and E. A. S. Prasanna. For New Zealand the best batting came from Turner and former captain Congdon. For India it was Gavaskar, Viswanath, and brothers S. and M. Amarnath who were outstanding.

India won the first test (Auckland) by 8 wickets: New Zealand 266 (Chandrasekhar 6 for 94) and 215 (Prasanna 8 for 76); India 414 (S. Amarnath 124, Gavaskar 116, Congdon 5 for 65) and 71 for 2. The second test (Christchurch) was drawn: India 270 (Collinge 6 for 63) and 255 for 6; New Zealand 403 (Turner 117, Madan Lal 5 for 134). New Zealand won the third test (Wellington) by an innings and 33 runs: India 220 and 81 (R. J. Hadlee 7 for 23); New Zealand 334. New Zealand proved its all-round superiority by winning both one-day internationals, the first at Christchurch by 9 wickets and the second at Auckland by 80 runs.

County Cricket. Middlesex won the championship for the first time since 1947. In a close finish it held off the challenge of Northamptonshire (second) and Gloucestershire (third). In a season of almost unbroken sunshine and drought conditions, the spin bowling of F. J. Titmus, P. H. Edmonds, and N. G. Featherstone proved decisive after the fast bowling of M. W. W. Selvey and A. A. Jones established a strong position early in the summer. The invaluable batting and leadership of captain J. M. Brearley was supported by M. J. Smith, C. T. Radley, and G. D. Barlow. Pakistan cricketers played a prominent part in the success of Northamptonshire and Gloucestershire. Zaheer Abbas (11 centuries) and Sadiq Mohammad (7 centuries) made most runs for Gloucestershire as Zaheer established a season's record aggregate of 2,554 runs. Mushtaq Mohammad, captain and leading batsman, and Sarfraz Nawaz, chief wicket-taker, excelled for Northamptonshire. The leading English batsmen were G. Boycott (Yorkshire) and Amiss (Warwickshire), and the most successful bowlers were Selvey and R. D. Jackman (Surrey).

The winners of one-day, limited-over competitions were Northamptonshire, which beat Lancashire by 4 wickets for the Gillette Cup, and Kent, which beat Worcestershire by 43 runs for the Benson and Hedges Cup. Kent also won the John Player League.

National Cricket. In Australia, South Australia won the Sheffield Shield; in South Africa, Natal retained the Currie Cup; in New Zealand, Canterbury won the Shell Shield; and in West Indies, Trinidad and Barbados shared the Shell Shield. Winners of the knockout, one-day competitions were Queensland in Australia, Eastern Province in South Africa, Canterbury in New Zealand, and Barbados in the West Indies. In India, Bombay won the Ranji Trophy, South Zone the Duleep, Bombay the Irani, and Sri Lanka the Topalan Trophy. In Pakistan, National Bank won the Patron's Trophy, the Qaid-i-Azam Trophy, and the A. S. Pirzada Memorial Tournament; Pakistan International Airlines won both the Pentangular Tournament and the S. A. Bhutto Memorial Tournament; and Lahore (A) won the Punjab championship. (REX ALSTON)

[452.B.4.h.ix]

Crime and Law Enforcement

Violent Crime. TERRORISM. Of countless terrorist incidents recorded in 1976, none attracted greater publicity than the hijacking in late June of an Air France jet en route from Tel Aviv, Israel, to Paris. Following the jet's diversion to Entebbe airport, Uganda, the pro-Palestinian hijackers issued demands for the release of imprisoned colleagues. Within a few hours of the hijackers' deadline, Israeli armed forces mounted a daring rescue mission, successfully freeing the hostages and killing or capturing the terrorists. (*See* DEFENSE.)

In the aftermath of the Entebbe raid, Israel re-

THE GUARDIAN, LONDON AND MANCHESTER

The bust of Karl Marx watches as youthful offenders clear the paths of Highgate Cemetery in London, part of a program intended to turn probationers into "lawful wage-earning local citizens."

A.F.P./PICTORIAL PARADE

Paris police watched the front entrance, but the thieves came underground. Bank robbers dug a tunnel from the sewers into the basement of the Société Générale Bank on the Île Saint Louis in August, escaping with a haul worth millions of dollars. A similar approach was used to rob the bank's branch in Nice in July.

newed its call for a coordinated international effort to strengthen airline security. Scarcely a month later, tight security measures at the Istanbul (Turkey) airport resulted in the foiling of an attempted hijacking by pro-Palestinian terrorists of a Tel Aviv-bound El Al flight. Turkish airport police spotted the terrorists among boarding passengers. A gun battle ensued, during which a number of the passengers were killed or wounded and the terrorists captured.

In September five Croatian nationalist terrorists penetrated the security screen of New York City's La Guardia Airport and hijacked a Chicago-bound TWA jet. This was the first successful hijacking of a U.S. domestic airliner in almost four years. Following a transatlantic flight, the jet and its 93 passengers and crew finally landed in Paris, where French authorities prevented further travel by shooting out the aircraft's tires. Meanwhile, a bomb left by the terrorists in New York City exploded while being disarmed by bomb squad experts, killing one policeman and injuring three others. Faced with a French ultimatum to surrender and be sent back to New York or face execution in France, the hijackers gave themselves up and were returned to the U.S. to be charged with murder and air piracy.

The flurry of hijackings prompted the West German foreign minister, Hans-Dietrich Genscher, to propose to the UN General Assembly that an international convention dealing with the issue be drafted. Genscher urged that the draft convention provide for "banning the taking of hostages and making sure that the perpetrators are either extradited or brought before court in the country in which they were seized." Observers felt that the chances for adoption of such a proposal were more promising than in previous years. Even the Arab countries, which in the past had been reluctant to take action against Palestinian groups, were taking tough measures against terrorist acts within their borders. In August Egyptian troops, in an Entebbe-style commando raid, rescued 75 passengers being held hostage on a hijacked Egyptair jet at Luxor airport, and the terrorists subsequently went on trial before a military court. In the same month, Syrian troops stormed a Damascus hotel where 90 hostages were being held, capturing three terrorists who were summarily hung in front of the hotel. Similarly, in November, Jordanian troops recaptured a hotel that had been taken over by terrorists in Amman.

Tough antiterrorist measures were also reported by other countries. Following the July slaying in Dublin of the British ambassador to Ireland and his secretary in a bomb explosion, the Irish government introduced stringent new laws making it easier to jail and hold Irish Republican Army (IRA) guerrillas. (*See* IRELAND.) In Spain and France police authorities cracked down on Basque extremists. In the U.S., Rex Davis, director of the Treasury Department's Bureau of Alcohol, Tobacco and Firearms, told the Senate Judiciary Internal Security Subcommittee that the number of bombings in the U.S. had risen from 893 in 1974 to 1,313 in 1975, with a correspondingly high injury and death rate—69 deaths and 326 injuries in 1975, compared with 24 deaths and 207 injuries in 1974. The subcommittee hearings were believed likely to result in stricter federal and state controls on explosives. Meanwhile, the former foreign minister in the Chilean government of the late president Salvador Allende, Orlando Letelier, was killed in Washington, D.C., during September by a bomb planted in his car. The identity of those responsible had not been determined by year's end, although it was suggested that the Chilean secret police might have arranged the killing.

ASSASSINATION AND KIDNAPPING. Fresh investigations of the assassinations of Pres. John F. Kennedy in 1963 and civil rights leader Martin Luther King, Jr., in 1968 were initiated by the newly created House Select Committee on Assassinations. Official findings that both slayings were the work of lone gunmen had failed to still public suspicions that others may have been involved. Conspiracy theories in the case of Kennedy's assassination were rekindled by allegations that the U.S. Central Intelligence Agency (CIA) had been behind efforts to kill Cuban Prime Minister Fidel Castro. In August the body of organized crime figure John Roselli, who had testified before a U.S. Senate committee regarding his role in recruiting underworld figures to assassinate Castro, was found floating in an oil drum off the Florida coast. Roselli's former boss, Momo Salvatore ("Sam") Giancana, who was also recruited for the assassination effort, had been murdered in 1975 days before he was to testify about the CIA-Castro plot.

Sara Jane Moore, one of two women who had made separate assassination attempts against U.S. Pres. Gerald Ford during 1975, was sentenced to life in prison in January. A few weeks earlier, Lynette Fromme, a former member of the Charles Manson "family" which had been implicated in a number of murders, had also received a life sentence.

Following a highly publicized trial in San Francisco, Patricia Hearst, a kidnap victim who allegedly joined forces with her revolutionary abductors, the Symbionese Liberation Army (SLA), was convicted in March of bank robbery charges and sentenced to seven years in prison. Pending appeal, the 22-year-old defendant was released on $1,250,000 bail in November after her father, millionaire publisher Randolph Hearst, posted bond and submitted a plan to guarantee her security. She also faced further criminal charges stemming from the period she was with the SLA. Two of her alleged abductors, William and Emily Harris, were found guilty in August on kidnap, robbery, and auto theft charges. Sentenced to serve 11 years to life, the Harrises were still to go on trial for the Hearst kidnapping itself.

The alleged kidnappers of Samuel Bronfman II, 21-year-old heir to the Seagram distillery fortune, went on trial in Westchester County, N.Y., in September. In a bizarre development, one of the kidnappers claimed that the whole affair was conducted in concert with Bronfman to extort money from his multimillionaire father, and the jury found the defendants guilty of extortion but not of kidnapping. In another dramatic kidnapping case a school bus with 26 children and a driver aboard was seized in the small town of Chowchilla, Calif., and taken to Livermore, Calif., where the kidnappers forced their captives into a truck body buried in a quarry. The victims eventually escaped unharmed and their alleged captors, three men in their early 20s, were arrested.

CAPITAL PUNISHMENT, GUN CONTROL, AND VIOLENT CRIME. With opinion polls indicating the highest levels of public support for capital punishment in 25 years, opponents of the death penalty in the U.S. suffered a severe setback in July when the Supreme Court upheld the constitutionality of death penalty statutes in Georgia, Florida, and Texas. (*See* LAW.) Spearheaded by the American Civil Liberties Union, opponents of capital punishment nevertheless vowed to fight, on a case-by-case basis, the executions of the more than 600 men and women on death rows around the U.S., including convicted murderer Gary Mark Gilmore, whose execution by firing squad was scheduled for November 15. The Gilmore case took a strange turn when the convicted man resisted efforts to help him, insisted that he be allowed to die, twice attempted suicide when the execution was postponed, and called the judge who finally fixed the date at Jan. 17, 1977, a "moral coward" for delaying it so long.

The first execution in France since 1973 took place in July. Refused a reprieve by Pres. Valéry Giscard d'Estaing, an acknowledged opponent of capital punishment, the kidnapper and murderer of an eight-year-old girl was guillotined in Marseilles. Opponents of capital punishment met with greater success in the U.K. and Canada. The U.K. Parliament refused to reintroduce the death penalty despite opinion surveys showing overwhelming public support for the hanging of convicted terrorists. In July the Canadian Parliament abolished the death penalty for all civilian crimes after a long and bitter struggle. At the same time, attempts were made to strengthen gun-control laws and provide stiffer sentences for violent criminals.

Crime—especially violent crime—was the subject of extensive debate during the U.S. presidential campaign. Both President Ford and his Democratic opponent, Jimmy Carter, promised improved law enforcement, and Carter also criticized the Law Enforcement Assistance Administration (LEAA) for spending $5.2 billion while making almost no contribution to reducing crime. On gun control, Carter supported and Ford opposed the registration of handguns. Although opinion polls showed 79% of the U.S. public favouring registration, a proposition to outlaw private ownership of guns with barrel lengths of less than 16 in in Massachusetts was defeated in a November referendum by three to one.

In Thailand the massive amount of weapons left behind by the departing U.S. forces contributed to a frightening increase in the incidence of violent crime. In 1975 more than 13,000 people were murdered in Thailand, an average of 37 per day. Indian authorities were alarmed by an apparent resurgence of activities by "dacoits" and "thugs." These organized bands of criminals, who in the 19th century waylaid travelers and, after robbing them, made a religious rite of strangling them, had been largely eliminated by the British. Bandit gangs again became active following independence in 1947, but many surrendered to the police in 1972. Recent robberies and murders by bandits stimulated fresh police drives against the dacoits in their thickly forested hideouts in central India.

UPI COMPIX

Five Croatian nationalists hijacked a New York–Chicago jet in September and forced it to fly to Europe, ordering propaganda leaflets to be dropped over Montreal, Chicago, New York, London, and Paris. They were taken prisoner in Paris.

China, long viewed as a country with a remarkably low crime rate, showed evidence of change in 1976. Foreigners traveling in China, and Chinese newspapers and radio broadcasts, gave accounts of breakdowns in law and order including bank robberies, looting, rape, and murder. The members of one gang, who held up a bank in Chengchow in Honan Province, were said to have become something like folk heroes, evading capture for several years. These reports preceded the death of Mao Tse-tung and may have been attributable to political unrest. In Portugal, another country experiencing major political upheaval, a substantial rise in violent crime was reported. Bank robberies and bombings increased, and in July a traffic policeman was shot and killed when questioning a motorist.

Italy continued to experience a crime wave of unprecedented proportions. In 1974 robberies in Italy increased 51% over the preceding year, while kidnappings in 1975 ran at the rate of five a week. Extremist violence escalated in 1976 prior to the June elections. In April suspected acts of arson caused damage estimated at $4 million at the giant Fiat automobile plant. In the same month the managing director of the Italian branch of the Chevron Oil Co. and president of the Italian Oil Companies Association was gunned down in the street; a leftist guerrilla group claimed responsibility. (*See* ITALY.)

Nonviolent Crime. WHITE-COLLAR CRIMINALS. No single scandal in 1976 penetrated as many political Cabinets and company boardrooms as that concerning the Lockheed Aircraft Corp. In Japan the government's investigation of bribery by the U.S. company resulted in the arrest in July of a number of leading Japanese businessmen, including former prime minister Kakuei Tanaka, on charges involving $12.6 million in alleged bribes spent by Lockheed to promote its aircraft sales. The scandal rocked the ruling party in Japan and threatened Prime Minister Takeo Miki's government. (*See* JAPAN.) A similar impact was felt in The Netherlands in August when Prime Minister Joop den Uyl told the Dutch Parliament that a commission of inquiry had found Prince Bernhard (*see* BIOGRAPHY), Queen Juliana's husband, to have been close enough to Lockheed bribery to have "harmed the interests of the State." (*See* NETHERLANDS, THE.) As a result of the Lockheed disclosures, the U.S. Congress considered a number of measures designed to prevent bribery by U.S. corporations doing business abroad, but no action was taken before adjournment.

The lenient treatment received by many convicted white-collar criminals was a topic of debate in a number of U.S. jurisdictions. For instance, over 1,000 persons convicted of cheating on their federal income taxes could have been sent to prison in 1975, but more than two-thirds of them were not, and most of the 367 who were imprisoned received sentences of less than a year. Bank robbers, on the other hand, went to prison in almost every case handled by federal courts, and most were sentenced to five years or longer. A case that provoked particularly angry comment was that of Bernard Bergman, a New York nursing home entrepreneur. A central figure in investigations of widespread nursing home fraud and abuse, Bergman was convicted on charges of federal Medicaid and tax fraud involving millions of dollars and given a four-month prison term.

Despite very stringent punishment for white-collar offenses, the Soviet Union continued to be plagued with a high rate of graft and embezzlement. In one case recorded in the Soviet press, truck drivers reported the removal of two million tons of snow in order to qualify for bonuses, although such a quantity could only have fallen over 20 years. In another case, five officials were sentenced to death by firing squad for their involvement in the sale of $12 million worth of nonexistent vegetables to the government.

THEFT. The theft of art treasures and antiquities continued to present a problem to many nations. According to the International Association of Art Securities, art thefts in the U.S. in 1975 rose 27% to almost 34,000, compared with slightly over 26,000 the year before. The theft in September of about $750,000 worth of Spanish coins and jewelry from the Museum of Sunken Treasure at Cape Canaveral, Fla., was only one of many major larcenies of art objects during the year. The Egyptian Parliament, in a somewhat belated attempt to curb the theft of statues, jewels, and other objects from sites in the Nile Valley, passed a law increasing the maximum punishment for such crimes from a $25 fine to imprisonment. In India, where public anger was mounting over the disappearance of many priceless art treasures from temples and palaces, experts accused the Indian government of gross negligence in failing to stop illicit dealings in art works.

The latest in crime fighting in Sweden is identifying fingerprints by computer. The man who developed the technique, Chief Supt. S. A. Eriksson of the police fingerprint section, sits at the computer terminal.

SVENSKT PRESSFOTO/PHOTO TRENDS

Also on the increase were crimes committed with the aid of computers. According to a study by the Stanford Research Institute, reported U.S. cases of "computer abuse" rose from 2 in 1966 to 66 in 1973. Losses running into millions of dollars were involved, though none approached the Equity Funding insurance fraud of 1973, in which 63,000 fake insurance policies were produced through company computers. Among recommended security measures were better methods of user identification; the development of more advanced built-in electronic computer safeguards; and more frequent checks by individuals of computer printouts to detect both machine errors and intentional crimes. Another form of modern technology presenting crime control problems was a recently marketed colour copying machine, said to be used increasingly to counterfeit U.S. currency and other documents. Several committees of printers, certificate issuers, and government agencies were formed to study the problem.

French police announced the apprehension of several persons suspected of being involved in what had come to be called *le fric-frac du siècle* ("the heist of the century"). It occurred on a July weekend when highly skilled thieves entered the sewer system of Nice, on the French Riviera, and dug a 30-ft tunnel leading into the vault of a bank. They brought along chairs, food, and wine and hung pornographic pictures on the walls before escaping with $10 million in cash and other valuables taken from safe-deposit boxes. During August thieves used a similar method to steal some $5 million in money and valuables from a bank in Paris.

VICTIMLESS CRIME. Following three years of extensive research, the U.S. National Gambling Commission released a controversial report to Congress in October. Major recommendations included eliminating federal income tax on legal wagering winnings so states could compete with illegal gambling and permitting each state to accept or reject legalized gambling without federal interference. The commission found that about two-thirds of the U.S. population spent more than $22 billion on gambling each year, most of it illegally. (*See* GAMBLING.)

In June the U.S. Supreme Court declared constitutional zoning regulations adopted by the city of Detroit to separate residential areas from a variety of "adult" entertainment activities such as X-rated bookstores and movie theatres. The establishment of such "quarantine zones" for pornography gave rise to new problems, however. Boston, for example, found that its zone became a kind of no-man's-land that attracted criminals of all types. In Copenhagen, the former pornography capital of the Western world, business reportedly slumped after a police crackdown on live sex shows. The police action was taken under pressure from the Danish Ministry of Justice, which said it had strong information that profits from such shows were going into narcotics traffic.

Law Enforcement. The police role in vice enforcement came under close scrutiny in the U.S. following the release of the Gambling Commission's report. The commission reported that of the 62,000 gambling arrests in the U.S. in 1974, 80% involved streetcorner "cards and dice" games and 75% of those arrested were black. Conceding that there was some organized crime control of gambling, the commission urged the federal government to concentrate its attack against top syndicate operators. One such operator, Carlo Gambino, died peacefully at his home in Long Island, N.Y., in October. Law enforcement officials alleged that Gambino commanded the largest, richest, and strongest organized crime "family" in the country.

Job actions on the part of many U.S. policemen continued, becoming ugliest in such cities as New York and Detroit where financial crises limited salaries and forced layoffs. A growing association between policemen and the powerful International Brotherhood of Teamsters, a union expelled from the AFL-CIO in 1957 for corruption and believed to have links with organized crime, raised serious questions of public concern. Promising substantial pay increases and fringe benefits, the union was attracting a growing membership of law officers, raising the possibility of police being forced to pursue investigations of the very officials who represented them in labour negotiations. Meanwhile, federal and state authorities studied allegations of mismanagement of the union's pension funds and continued their unsuccessful search for James R. Hoffa, former president of the Teamsters, missing since July 1975 and believed murdered.

The FBI, already battered in 1975 by revelations of misconduct, suffered further embarrassing disclosures. U.S. Justice Department investigations into the bureau's activities, including illegal break-ins of premises occupied by radical groups and the misuse of bureau funds, resulted in the firing of a number of top FBI officials. FBI Chief Clarence Kelley came under personal censure for accepting gifts of nominal value from subordinates, as well as permitting bureau carpenters to provide decorations for his Bethesda, Md., apartment. The chief of the exhibits section, a bureau veteran of 28 years, pleaded guilty in federal court to a criminal charge of converting government property to his own use.

The image of London's Scotland Yard was also tarnished. In February, following a two-and-one-half-year investigation, Scotland Yard detectives arrested 12 retired or suspended detectives, including three senior officers, in a dawn raid. The 12 were arraigned on charges of conspiring to receive bribes from London pornography shops and clip joints. It was alleged that "drinks money" had been paid regularly to the officers assigned to the Soho district of London, and obscene material confiscated by the police was regularly sold back to the owners.

Late in August a riot in the Notting Hill area of London resulted in a major clash between police and blacks in which 325 police and 131 civilians were injured. Admitting that relations between blacks and police were bad, London's commissioner of police, Sir Robert Mark, met with little success in recruiting nonwhites into the 22,000-strong metropolitan police force. Young blacks in particular were said to regard police with a hostility almost as intense as that of the IRA in the Roman Catholic ghettos of Belfast.

The general quality of the police-criminal investigation process came under fire in an important U.S. study, funded by the LEAA and conducted by the Rand Corporation. Limited to an analysis of serious crimes, the study concluded that differences in investigative training, staffing, workload, and procedures appeared to have no appreciable effect on crime, arrest, or clearance rates. Furthermore, substantially more than half of all serious reported crimes in the U.S. received no more than superficial attention from police investigators. Of the cases that were ultimately cleared in which the offender was not identifiable at the time of the initial police report, most were solved as a result of routine police work rather than by specialized investigations. The findings were criticized by some police chiefs as misleading and exaggerated.

One imaginative police method that proved highly effective in Washington, D.C., and several other cities was a storefront operation run by police to catch burglars and thieves. Posing as dealers in stolen goods, members of the Washington, D.C., force and the FBI established a business called PFF, Inc. (for Police-FBI Fencing, Incognito) and for five months bought a wide array of stolen property. Then, at a going-out-of-business party, the agents blew their cover and rounded up scores of thieves, recovering $2.4 million in stolen goods in the process.

(DUNCAN CHAPPELL)

International Criminal Police Organization. Interpol's affiliate membership rose to 125 countries in 1976. The 45th General Assembly was held in Accra, Ghana, October 14–20. Among the subjects covered in reports submitted were international illicit drug traffic and currency counterfeiting in 1975, international frauds and commercial crime, fraud involving arson, and crime in port and dock areas.

Activities by National Central Bureaus (NCB's) during 1975–76 involved the exchange of 176,444 items of information and led to 1,284 arrests. Between June 1975 and June 1976 the Interpol General Secretariat examined 27,584 cases resulting in 363 arrests; 11,084 items of information were supplied to NCB's, and 517 persons were the subjects of international notices.

Interpol's Paris headquarters was damaged by a bomb on October 28. The incident coincided with the visit to Paris of King Juan Carlos of Spain, and responsibility for it was claimed by a group protesting Interpol's role in rounding up Spanish exiles in France.

See also Drug Abuse; Prisons and Penology.

[522.C.6; 543.A.5; 552.C and F; 737.B; 10/36.C.5.a]

ENCYCLOPÆDIA BRITANNICA FILMS. *Our Community Services* (1969).

Cuba

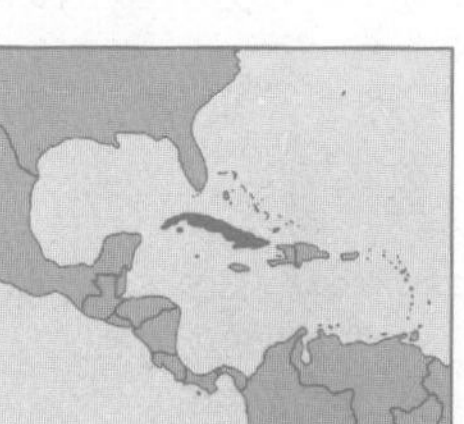

The socialist republic of Cuba occupies the largest island in the Greater Antilles of the West Indies. Area: 42,800 sq mi (110,900 sq km), including several thousand small islands and cays. Pop. (1975 est.): 9,265,900, including (1953) white 72.8%; mestizo 14.5%; Negro 12.4%. Cap. and largest city: Havana (pop., 1974 est., 1,838,000). Language: Spanish. Religion: Roman Catholic (52%). President to Dec. 2, 1976, Osvaldo Dorticós Torrado; prime minister, Fidel Castro; from December 3, president of the Council of State (combining the offices of president and prime minister), Fidel Castro.

Cuba experienced political stability and some economic progress during 1976. Headway continued to be made toward the formation of permanent government institutions, bringing the administrative system more in line with those of Eastern European countries. A new constitution, ratified by the first congress of the Cuban Communist Party, was promulgated in Febru-

Croatian Literature: *see* Literature

Crops: *see* Agriculture and Food Supplies

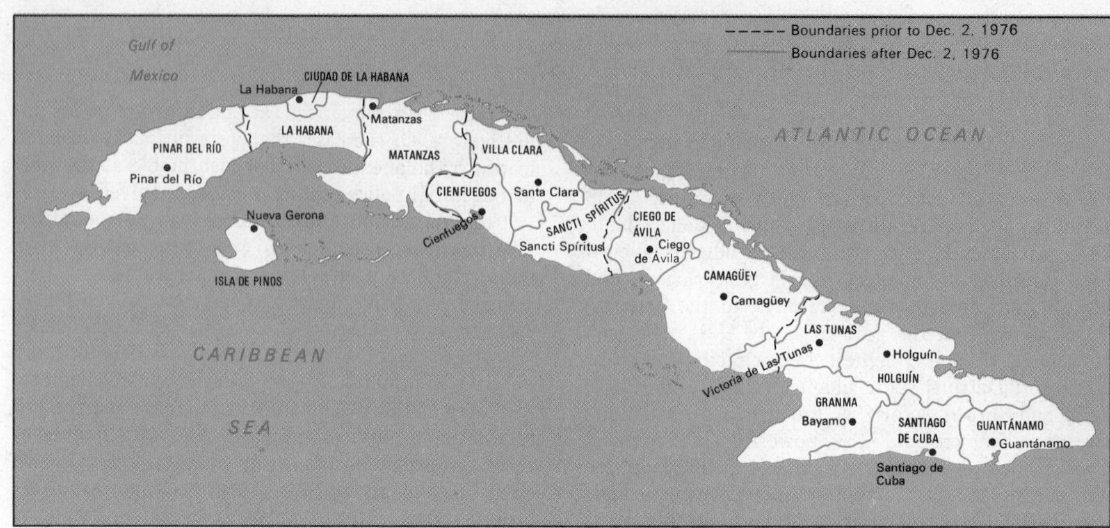

ary. The 6 existing provinces were raised to 14, and provisions were made for greater popular participation in government. Elections for local assemblies were held October 11. At the end of October, the 10,743 victorious candidates in the 169 assemblies, now given wide responsibilities for local affairs, elected 481 deputies to the National Assembly. They, in turn, convened December 2 and elected a 31-member Council of State, with Castro as president.

Much attention was focused during the year on the Cuban military intervention in the Angolan civil war on the side of the Soviet-backed Popular Movement for the Liberation of Angola (MPLA). It was estimated in January that 4,500–7,000 Cuban combat troops fought alongside the MPLA, and their presence was the key factor in its military victory over the two Western-supported factions. It was reported in April that the families of Cuban soldiers were arriving in Angola, indicating that a permanent garrison was being established there. Private U.S. sources announced in January that Cuba had military training missions in Malawi, Mozambique, South West Africa (Namibia), Guinea, Cameroon, Gabon, and Somalia, and in February it was reported that Cuban advisers were assisting the pro-Algerian guerrilla movement, Polisario, in the former Spanish Sahara. The growing Cuban involvement in Africa was further demonstrated by the visit of Fidel Castro to Conakry, Guinea, in March, following a visit to Moscow for the 25th congress of the Soviet Communist Party.

A five-year trade agreement, signed between Cuba and the U.S.S.R. in February, provided for trade of $3.4 billion in 1976 ($2.9 billion in 1975), rising to $8 billion by 1980. It was announced in April that the U.S.S.R. was to supply a nuclear plant to Cuba in 1978 for installation at Cienfuegos and a complex to produce one million tons of steel ingots a year; Soviet supplies of crude oil to Cuba were to be guaranteed until 1980.

Cuba continued to develop trade with Western countries in 1976. Cuban imports from these countries were estimated at about $1.5 billion in 1976 ($1.4 billion in 1975), with Japan, Canada, and the U.K. accounting for about half the 1976 total. These imports were largely being financed from credits of about $3 billion granted by the U.K., Canada, Japan, and other countries in recent years.

The Cuban authorities began the implementation of the country's first comprehensive five-year development plan, which called for capital investment of $14 billion to $18 billion by 1980. The main aim of the plan was to reduce dependence on sugar.

The intervention in Angola temporarily ended initiatives to normalize diplomatic and trade relations with the U.S. The deputy prime minister, Carlos Rafael Rodríguez, stated in June that Cuba was prepared for a rapprochement with Washington provided that the economic blockade against his country was withdrawn. In October Castro renounced the U.S.-Cuban antihijacking treaty in retaliation for alleged U.S. Central Intelligence Agency involvement (denied by the U.S.) in the loss of a Cuban airliner that crashed off Barbados October 6, with the loss of 73 lives, after a bomb explosion on board. A number of Cuban exiles were subsequently arrested in Trinidad and Tobago and Venezuela in connection with the incident. (ROBIN CHAPMAN)

[974.B.2.c]

CUBA

Education. (1973–74) Primary 1,899,266, teachers 75,921; secondary, pupils 265,589, teachers 21,475; vocational, pupils 56,959, teachers 5,454; teacher training, students 30,398, teachers 2,331; higher, students 55,435, teaching staff (1970–71) 4,129.

Finance. Monetary unit: peso, with (Sept. 20, 1976) a free rate of 0.83 peso to U.S. $1 (1.44 peso = £1 sterling). Budget (1966; latest published) balanced at 2,718,000,000 pesos.

Foreign Trade. (1974) Imports 2,210,000,000 pesos; exports 2,224,000,000 pesos. Import sources: U.S.S.R. 47%; Japan 8%; U.K. 5%. Export destinations: U.S.S.R. 36%; Japan 17%; Spain 7%; East Germany 5%. Main exports: sugar 86%; nickel and copper ores 6%.

Transport and Communications. Roads (1974) 18,900 km (including 1,220 km of the Central Highway). Motor vehicles in use (1973): passenger *c.* 70,000; commercial (including buses) *c.* 33,000. Railways: (1974) 14,872 km (including *c.* 11,000 km plantation); traffic (1972) 946 million passenger-km, freight 1,504,000,000 net ton-km. Air traffic (1974): 528 million passenger-km; freight 12.1 million net ton-km. Shipping (1975): merchant vessels 100 gross tons and over 272; gross tonnage 476,279. Telephones (Dec. 1973) 281,000. Radio receivers (Dec. 1973) 1,790,000. Television receivers (Dec. 1973) 525,000.

Agriculture. Production (in 000; metric tons; 1975): rice *c.* 420; corn (1974) *c.* 125; cassava (1974) *c.* 238; sweet potatoes (1974) *c.* 245; tomatoes *c.* 100; sugar, raw value *c.* 5,700; coffee *c.* 27; oranges (1974) *c.* 125; tobacco *c.* 50; jute *c.* 3. Livestock (in 000; 1975): cattle *c.* 5,450; pigs *c.* 1,450; sheep *c.* 330; goats (1974) *c.* 89; horses (1974) 799.

Industry. Production (in 000; metric tons; 1974): crude oil *c.* 140; petroleum products (1973) 5,293; electricity (kw-hr) 6,016,000; copper ore (metal content) 5.9; chrome ore (oxide content; 1973) 13; nickel ore (metal content) *c.* 32.

Curling:
see Winter Sports
Cybernetics:
see Computers

Cycling

Cycling events at the 1976 Olympic Games were not affected by the withdrawal of African nations, whose riders were still a minor force in international competition. Europeans took all the track titles at the Games, where the defeat of Daniel Morelon—on his 32nd birthday—robbed the French star of a third consecutive Olympic sprint victory. Morelon was fairly beaten by Anton Tkac (Czech.), who found the 287-m velodrome (cycle track) more to his liking than did the Frenchman, who needed a full-length "home straight" on which to show his speed. The size of the track had no influence on other Olympic track events, in which time, not tactics, was vital. The two Germanys were strongest, but the British quartet of Ian Hallam, Michael Bennett, Ian Banbury, and Robin Croker won bronze medals by beating the East Germans in the 4,000-m team pursuit event.

Later in the season two world amateur championship events not on the Olympic program, tandem sprint and 50-km motor-paced, were contested during the professional and women's championship week in Italy. Highlight of the week was the 288-km (178.9-mi) professional road race, in which, 12 mi from the finish, victory seemed probable for Italian star Francesco Moser. He was, however, caught and eventually outsprinted for the title by Freddy Maertens (Belgium), who had been the outstanding rider in earlier one-day and multistage races. After a few days Moser's defeat was forgotten by Italian enthusiasts who saw their idol take the world 5,000-m pursuit championship from the defending champion, Roy Schuiten (Neth.), a major surprise since Moser had little track racing experience.

A.F.P./PICTORIAL PARADE

Gerben Karstens of The Netherlands whizzes down the Champs Elysées in Paris in the final stage of the Tour de France. The overall winner of the race that covered 2,500 miles mostly in France and Belgium was Lucien Van Impe of Belgium.

European riders were almost out of the picture in the two sprint championships. John Nicholson (Australia) retained his professional title, and Japanese riders confirmed their emergence as top cycle racers by taking third and fourth places. The women's sprint final was an all-U.S. match between the titleholder, Sue Novarra, and the 1973 champion, Sheila Young. The verdict went to Young, an outstanding athlete who earlier in the year had won a gold medal for speed skating at the Winter Olympic Games.

Although Eddy Merckx won his seventh Milan–San Remo classic in March, he had a comparatively lean

1976 Cycling Champions

Event	Winner	Country
WORLD AMATEUR CHAMPIONS—TRACK		
Men		
Tandem sprint	B. Kocot and J. Kotlinski	Poland
50-km motor-paced	G. Minneboo	The Netherlands
Women		
Sprint	S. Young	U.S.
Pursuit	K. van Oosten Hage	The Netherlands
WORLD PROFESSIONAL CHAMPIONS—TRACK		
Sprint	J. Nicholson	Australia
Pursuit	F. Moser	Italy
One-hour motor-paced	W. Peffgen	West Germany
WORLD AMATEUR CHAMPIONS—ROAD		
Women		
Individual road race	K. van Oosten Hage	The Netherlands
WORLD PROFESSIONAL CHAMPIONS—ROAD		
Individual road race	F. Maertens	Belgium
WORLD CHAMPIONSHIPS—CYCLO CROSS		
Amateur	K.P. Thaler	West Germany
Professional	A. Zweifel	Switzerland
MAJOR PROFESSIONAL ROAD-RACE WINNERS		
Het Volk	W. Peeters	Belgium
Milan–San Remo	E. Merckx	Belgium
Tour of Flanders	W. Planckaert	Belgium
Paris–Roubaix	M. Demeyer	Belgium
Amstel Gold Race	F. Maertens	Belgium
Ghent–Wevelghem	F. Maertens	Belgium
Flèche Wallonne	J. Zoetemelk	The Netherlands
Liège–Bastogne–Liège	J. Bruyère	Belgium
Grand Prix of Frankfurt	F. Maertens	Belgium
Bordeaux–Paris	W. Godefroot	Belgium
Paris–Brussels	F. Gimondi	Italy
Tours–Versailles	R. de Witte	Belgium
Tour of Lombardy	R. de Vlaeminck	Belgium
Grand Prix des Nations time trial	F. Maertens	Belgium
Tour de France	L. Van Impe	Belgium
Tour of Italy	F. Gimondi	Italy
Tour of Spain	J. Pesarrodona	Spain
Tour of Belgium	M. Pollentier	Belgium
Semana Catalana	E. Merckx	Belgium
Four of Sardinia	R. de Vlaeminck	Belgium
Tour Days of Dunkirk	F. Maertens	Belgium
Dauphiné–Libéré	B. Thévenet	France
Paris–Nice	M. Laurent	France
Midi–Libre	A. Meslet	France

Czechoslovakia's Anton Tkac (right) won the gold medal in the sprint at the velodrome in Montreal, beating Daniel Morelon (left) of France.

A.F.P./PICTORIAL PARADE

season, partly due to an attack of the racing cyclist's occupational complaint of acute saddle soreness. This prevented him from starting in the Tour de France, but Lucien Van Impe won again for Belgium. Most of the other important races were also won by Belgians. The third finisher in the Tour de France was 40-year-old Raymond Poulidor, still the best all-round French road rider.

In amateur road racing the most important event was the Olympic individual road championship, won by the Swedish rider Bernt Johansson, who had won the 1975 Tour of Britain. The 1976 version of Britain's "Milk Race" went to Bill Nickson, the first British winner since 1967, and the Great Britain "A" selection took the team award. In the two other major amateur stage races, there were wins for Hans-Joachim Hartnick (East Germany) in the "Peace Race," and for Sven Åke Nilsson (Sweden) in the Tour de l'Avenir, the amateur edition of the Tour de France.

(J. B. WADLEY)

See also Track and Field: *Special Report.*
[452.B.4.h.x]

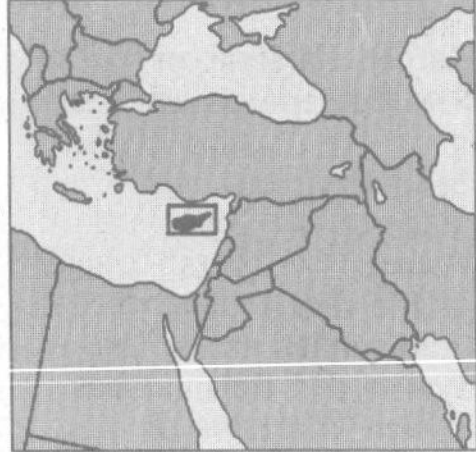

Cyprus

An island republic and a member of the Commonwealth of Nations, Cyprus is in the eastern Mediterranean. Area: 3,572 sq mi (9,251 sq km). Pop. (1975 est.): 638,900, including Greeks 82%; Turks 18%. Cap. and largest city: Nicosia (pop., 1974 est., 117,100). All these population figures should be considered unreliable, as they do not take into account the extensive internal migration or the recent and reportedly extensive Turkish immigration and Greek emigration, for which authoritative data are not available. Language: Greek and Turkish. Religion: Greek Orthodox 77%; Muslim 18%. President in 1976, Archbishop Makarios III.

On Nov. 20, 1975, the UN General Assembly passed a resolution calling for the speedy withdrawal of Turkish troops from Cyprus and the return of the island's refugees to their homes; the Turkish authorities in Cyprus were also urged to prohibit the settlement of mainland Turks in the northern zone. The resolution proved ineffectual. None of the 200,000 Greek Cypriots who had fled or had been driven from their homes in the north during the 1974 Turkish invasion were able to return there in 1976, and about 20,000 Turks were reported to have been established in the northern zone after June 1975. In the south, 18,000 Greek Cypriot refugees were still living in tents in the autumn of 1976; the rest—many of them unemployed—were living in crowded conditions in the towns. To prevent conflict between the communities the UN was obliged, in December 1975 and June 1976, to extend the mandate for its Cyprus peace-keeping force.

A meeting between the Greek and Turkish foreign ministers in December 1975 made it possible for UN Secretary-General Kurt Waldheim to arrange a resumption of the intercommunal talks broken off in September. The Greek and Turkish Cypriot interlocutors, Glafkos Clerides and Rauf Denktash, met in Vienna Feb. 17–21, 1976, and agreed to exchange proposals about the territorial and constitutional aspects of the Cyprus problem by April 3. Before and after this meeting Denktash sought to persuade the Cyprus government to sign a joint agreement that the island would not be partitioned and that there would be no union (*enosis*) between the Greeks in Cyprus and Greece. The Makarios government found the provisions of this agreement acceptable but would not sign before the "frontier" between the two communities had been negotiated. Denktash did not want to discuss the "frontier" until the Greek Cypriots took steps to allay the deeply rooted fears of his people about *enosis*. Furthermore, delay in reaching a settlement could only strengthen the eventual constitutional and territorial claims of the Turkish Cypriots, through the longer establishment of their self-proclaimed Turkish Federated State of Cyprus. Accordingly, Denktash, having obtained secretly from Clerides a draft of the Greek Cypriot proposals, declared on March 30 that this draft was unrealistic.

This revelation put an end to the negotiations and caused the resignation of Clerides, who, in his anxiety to speed progress toward a settlement, had deemed it necessary to keep his government in ignorance of his private arrangement with Denktash. Clerides lost his position as president (speaker) of the Cyprus House of Representatives (his successor, Tassos Papadopoulos, had also taken Clerides' place as Greek Cypriot interlocutor), and his party obtained no seats in the elections of September 5. All the seats were won by pro-Makarios candidates whose parties publicly expressed their determination that a Cyprus settlement should accord with the UN resolution of November 1975. On June 20, 1976, Denktash won almost 80% of the vote in the first "presidential" election in the Turkish Cypriot zone and now demonstrably had the strength to use the threat of a unilateral declaration of independence as a weapon in future negotiations. On November 12 the General Assembly again approved a resolution calling for Turkish withdrawal.

(L. J. D. COLLINS)

[978.A.4]

CYPRUS

Education. (Greek schools; 1974–75) Primary, pupils 56,649, teachers 2,074; secondary, pupils 41,037, teachers 1,829; vocational, pupils 5,763, teachers 357; higher, students 611, teaching staff 71. (Turkish schools; 1972–73) Primary, pupils 16,014; secondary, pupils 7,190; vocational, pupils 753; teacher training, students 13.

Finance. Monetary unit: Cyprus pound, with (Sept. 20, 1976) a free rate of C£0.41 to U.S. $1 (C£0.71 = £1 sterling). The Turkish lira is also in use in northern Cyprus (Turkish Federated State). Gold, SDR's, and foreign exchange (May 1976) U.S. $237.6 million. Budget (1975 est.): revenue C£46.6 million; expenditure C£64.5 million. Turkish Federated State budget balanced at 105 billion Turkish liras.

Foreign Trade. (1975) Imports C£113,650,000; exports C£56,090,000. Import sources: U.K. 20%; Greece 12%; France 7%; Iraq 7%; West Germany 7%; U.S.S.R. 7%; Italy 6%. Export destinations: U.K. 35%; Syria 8%; Libya 7%. Main exports: potatoes 14%; cement 11%; citrus fruit 9%; wine 6%; clothing 6%; copper ores 5%. Tourism (1974): visitors 151,000; gross receipts U.S. $38 million.

Transport and Communications. Roads (1974) 9,477 km. Motor vehicles in use (1974): passenger 67,018; commercial 15,414. Air traffic (1975): 115 million passenger-km; freight 1,392,000 net ton-km. Shipping (1975): merchant vessels 100 gross tons and over 735; gross tonnage 3,221,070. Telephones (Dec. 1974) 68,000. Radio licenses (Dec. 1973) 171,000. Television licenses (Dec. 1973) 66,000.

Agriculture. Production (in 000; metric tons; 1974): wheat 100; barley 120; grapes *c.* 170; potatoes *c.* 180; oranges *c.* 122; grapefruit *c.* 64; olives *c.* 8. Livestock (in 000; Dec. 1973): sheep 430; cattle 33; pigs 151; goats 340.

Industry. Production (in 000; metric tons: 1974): asbestos 37; iron pyrites (exports) 287; copper ore (exports; metal content) 13; chromium ore (oxide content) 17; cement (1975) 612; electricity (kw-hr; 1975) 717,000.

Czechoslovakia

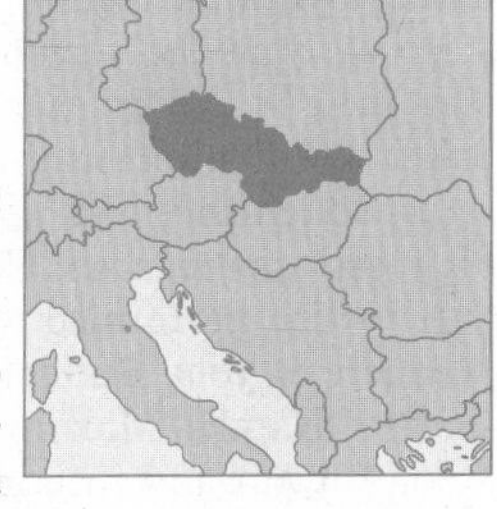

A federal socialist republic of central Europe, Czechoslovakia lies between Poland, the U.S.S.R., Hungary, Austria, and East and West Germany. Area: 49,374 sq mi (127,877 sq km). Pop. (1976 est.): 14,918,200, including (1975 est.) Czech 64%; Slovak 30%. Cap. and largest city: Prague (pop., 1976 est., 1,173,000). Language: Czech and Slovak (official). General secretary of the Communist Party of Czechoslovakia and president in 1976, Gustav Husak; federal premier, Lubomir Strougal.

During 1976 the inherent instability of the Czechoslovak political situation continued with its basic paradox of a divided Communist Party leadership ruling over an apathetic population and challenged by a small group of dissidents. At the top, neither the moderate conservatives led by President Husak nor the hard-liners were able to make any headway; each proved strong enough to show its hand when necessary. So, for example, while the discussions leading up to the 15th congress of the Czechoslovak Communist Party in April tended to be dominated by hard-liners like Vasil Bilak and Alois Indra, at the congress itself the conservative line prevailed, and neither of the two hard-line spokesmen addressed the congress. Husak himself brought up the question of the party members purged after 1969 for their support of the 1968 reforms associated with Alexander Dubcek, and announced that they could now seek readmission to the party. But readmission was to be assessed by local party branches, and it was generally expected that in practice these would sabotage Husak's conciliatory move.

Although the Czechoslovak economy had performed adequately since 1968, certainly well enough to provide a fair measure of prosperity for the people, the coming period of the late 1970s was regarded by Czechoslovak planners and economic policymakers with some concern. Labour productivity had remained unsatisfactory, and slower growth was expected in the future. A Central Committee plenum in September 1976 was highly critical of the state of the machinery sector, vital for a healthy export balance. The competitiveness of Czechoslovak industry had been declining steadily for many years. Economic difficulties were compounded by poor harvests in 1976, necessitating increased imports of grains and other farm products.

The small group of 1968 reformers who refused to accept the "normalization" policies of Husak continued to criticize the official program, despite regular police harassment. Western sources reported that several dozen books were circulating illegally in manuscript and that numerous underground newspapers were publishing information about developments among the dissidents. The aims of the opposition were to end the Soviet occupation and to return to the ideals of the 1968 reforms. A noteworthy development was the rise of political opposition among rock musicians. Members of two groups, the Plastic People of the Universe and DG 307, were tried in July and September for spreading antisocialist concepts in their songs, and seven of them received prison terms ranging from 8 to 30 months.

Although the Czechoslovak authorities made a concerted effort to break out of the international ghetto to which the country was still consigned—contacts at foreign minister or higher level were made with Britain, Austria, Turkey, Greece, Portugal, and others—Czechoslovakia's main role was played in international Communist forums. Bilak in effect became the leading spokesman for the hard line in the discussions leading up to the conference of European Communist parties in East Berlin. As a consequence, Czechoslovakia became embroiled in acrimonious polemics with the Yugoslav and Italian parties.

The dispute with Yugoslavia involved ideological matters—notably Czechoslovak support for the Soviet thesis of the future evolution of "a single socialist people" and the Soviet downgrading of the role of Yugoslav partisans during World War II—and also bilateral relations such as the treatment of Yugoslav workers employed in Czechoslovakia and the withdrawal of the Prague correspondent of the Belgrade newspaper *Politika* because the Czechoslovak authorities made it impossible for him to carry out his functions. The polemics with the Italian Communists concerned the attempted 1968 reforms during the "Prague Spring," a perennial subject of dispute. The Italian Communist newspaper continued to give support both to the ideals of 1968 and to dissident Communists in Czechoslovakia. Interestingly, relations between the two parties grew so poor that no Italian

CZECHOSLOVAKIA

Education. (1973–74) Primary, pupils 1,890,081, teachers 96,781; secondary, pupils 119,563, teachers 7,829; vocational, pupils 553,760, teachers 26,443; teacher training, students 6,812, teachers 457; higher (including 9 main universities), students 108,646, teaching staff 16,697.

Finance. Monetary unit: koruna, with (Sept. 20, 1976) an official exchange rate of 5.95 koruny to U.S. $1 (10.25 koruny = £1 sterling) and a tourist rate of 10.35 koruny to U.S. $1 (17.85 koruny = £1 sterling). Budget (1974 est.): revenue 263,750,000,000 koruny; expenditure 259,180,000,000 koruny.

Foreign Trade. (1975) Imports 50,716,000,000 koruny; exports 46,651,000,000 koruny. Import sources (1974): U.S.S.R. 27%; East Germany 12%; Poland 8%; West Germany 7%; Hungary 6%. Export destinations (1974): U.S.S.R. 30%; East Germany 11%; Poland 9%; West Germany 6%; Hungary 6%. Main exports (1974): machinery 35%; iron and steel 12%; motor vehicles 8%; chemicals 6%; food 5%.

Transport and Communications. Roads (1974) 145,455 km (including 79 km expressways). Motor vehicles in use (1974): passenger 1,234,437; commercial 265,000. Railways (1974): 13,241 km (including 2,685 km electrified); traffic 18,190,000,000 passenger-km, freight (1975) 69,271,000,000 net ton-km. Air traffic (1975): 1,366,100,000 passenger-km; freight 17,528,000 net ton-km. Navigable inland waterways (1974) 483 km. Shipping (1975): merchant vessels 100 gross tons and over 13; gross tonnage 116,148. Telephones (Jan. 1975) 2,481,000. Radio licenses (Dec. 1973) 3,793,000. Television licenses (Dec. 1973) 3,404,000.

Agriculture. Production (in 000; metric tons; 1975): wheat *c.* 4,500; barley *c.* 2,900; oats *c.* 650; rye *c.* 650; corn *c.* 600; potatoes 3,565; sugar, raw value *c.* 763; beef and veal (1974) 412; pork (1974) *c.* 676. Livestock (in 000; Jan. 1975): cattle 4,566; pigs 6,719; sheep 811; chickens 38,017.

Industry. Index of industrial production (1970 = 100; 1975) 138. Fuel and power (in 000; metric tons; 1975): coal 28,121; brown coal 85,635; crude oil 142; manufactured gas (cu m) 7,900,000; electricity (kw-hr) 59,790,000. Production (in 000; metric tons; 1975): iron ore (30% metal content) 1,800; pig iron 9,442; crude steel 14,322; cement 9,304; sulfuric acid 1,245; fertilizers (nutrient content; 1974–75) nitrogenous 483, phosphate 380; cotton yarn 128; cotton fabrics (m) 586,000; woolen fabrics (m) 69,000; rayon and acetate yarn and fibres 71; nylon, etc., yarn and fibres 69; passenger cars (units) 174; commercial vehicles (units) 65. Dwelling units completed (1975) 143,000.

delegate was sent to the Czechoslovak party congress, and even the delegate of the French party, with which relations were deteriorating, was not permitted to address the congress. Talks with the Vatican were resumed in December 1975 and July 1976, but no progress was officially reported. The antireligious campaign continued, especially in Slovakia.

(GEORGE SCHÖPFLIN)

[972.B.2.c]

Dance

Dance events constituted part of the 1976 bicentennial celebrations in the United States. During the year Martha Graham, a pioneer of modern dance and its most famous exponent, celebrated the 60th anniversary of her debut as a dancer (with Ruth St. Denis, Ted Shawn, and the Denishawn Dancers in 1916) and the 50th anniversary of the founding of her company (1926), the first major modern dance group in the U.S. The Martha Graham Dance Company also was honoured by being the first modern dance troupe ever to appear at the Royal Opera House in London. On the home scene, Graham was honoured by an award of the Medal of Freedom, the highest U.S. civilian honour, in a presentation by Pres. Gerald Ford at the White House. Graham reached her 82nd birthday on May 11, 1976.

Other bicentennial events included the U.S. debut of the Dutch National Ballet in a one-week Broadway engagement as a bicentennial gift from the government of The Netherlands; the Cincinnati Ballet's production of *Dear Friends and Gentle Hearts,* a new ballet by Donald Saddler to music of Stephen Foster arranged by Frank Proto; the New York City Ballet's production of George Balanchine's *Union Jack,* with a score by Hershy Kay based on English and Scottish themes and with scenery and costumes by Rouben Ter-Arutunian; the new production by the Joffrey Ballet (formerly the City Center Joffrey Ballet) of Agnes de Mille's historic American ballet *Rodeo* (1942), with the original costume designs of Kermit Love restored; a restoration, directed by Klarna Pinska, of an entire program of dances created by Ruth St. Denis, Ted Shawn, and the Denishawn dancers during the Denishawn era (1915–30), produced by Joyce Trisler's Danscompany; and a continuation (beginning in 1975 and throughout 1976) of an extensive series of large and small dance works utilizing music by Duke Ellington by the Alvin Ailey American Dance Theater (formerly the Alvin Ailey City Center Dance Theater).

The American Ballet Theatre's productions included ballets presented elsewhere previously but in new stagings and/or castings as they joined ABT repertory for the first time. Among these were Mikhail Baryshnikov's staging of *The Nutcracker;* a full-length *Sleeping Beauty* with the Oliver Messel original designs for the Sadler's Wells Ballet production and staged by Mary Skeaping; John Neumeier's *Hamlet Connotations,* set to music by Aaron Copland; Glen Tetley's *Sacre du Printemps* (music of Stravinsky); and the world premiere of Twyla Tharp's *Push Comes to Shove,* using for audio background a combination of ragtime music and Haydn themes and starring Baryshnikov. Yoko Morishita, Japanese ballerina and winner of a gold medal at the International Ballet Competition at Varna, Bulgaria, in 1974, made her debut with ABT. The company's principal U.S. ballerina, Cynthia Gregory, retired temporarily from the stage early in the year but returned in December to star in *The Nutcracker.* Alicia Alonso, the Cuban ballerina and director of the Ballet Nacional de Cuba, returned to dance with ABT, her alma mater, in a series of guest appearances. Carla Fracci of Italy, also a guest artist, performed with Baryshnikov in the U.S. premiere of John Butler's *Medea,* to music of Samuel Barber. Natalia Makarova doubled as a prima ballerina for ABT and Britain's Royal Ballet.

The New York City Ballet, in addition to its major bicentennial production, *Union Jack,* featured the U.S. premiere of Balanchine's *Chaconne* (to music of Gluck), first done for the Hamburg Opera Ballet. The troupe, returning to Paris after an absence of many years, enjoyed a critical and popular triumph in the French capital; it returned to New York late in the year to launch its 65th Manhattan season. The Joffrey Ballet, in addition to its major revival of *Rodeo,* featured the world premieres of Gerald Arpino's *Orpheus Times Light,* with a score by José Sérébrier and elaborate settings and costumes by Willa Kim; Twyla Tharp's *Happily Ever After* (using "country" music) in which Tharp's company joined the Joffrey dancers on stage; and Margo Sappington's *Face Dancers* (Michael Kamen). Two old ballets by Kurt Jooss, *Pavane on the Death of an Infanta* (Ravel) and *A Ball in Old Vienna* (Joseph Lanner), were added to the Jooss restagings of *The Green Table* and *The Big City* and were reunited in a single program, duplicating, on the occasion of the choreographer's 75th birthday, the U.S. debut program of the Jooss Ballet in 1933.

The Dance Theater of Harlem, the world's first permanent all-black classical ballet company, added Ruth Page's *Carmen and José* (quasi-Bizet; a Caribbean version of the Carmen tale) and William Dollar's *Mendelssohn's Concerto* to its swiftly growing repertory. The Eliot Feld Ballet played two repertory seasons at the Public Theater in New York, featuring Feld's new *Impromptu,* a solo created to music of Albert Roussel especially for the guest ballerina Birgit Keil of the Stuttgart Ballet.

The dozen-plus professional ballet troupes in the U.S. based outside of New York City and the more than 200 regional (nonprofessional) ballet and modern dance groups produced bicentennial dance works and many dealing with other themes. Among the leading troupes were the Pennsylvania Ballet, which included among its premieres Margo Sappington's *Under the Sun,* suggested by Alexander Calder mobiles and with music by Michael Kamen and costumes by Willa Kim; the Boston Ballet, with new productions of *The Sleeping Beauty* (traditional) and *Cinderella* (newly choreographed by Ron Cunningham); the Pittsburgh Ballet Theatre, with John Butler's new *Othello;* the Chicago Ballet, directed by Ruth Page and Frederic Franklin and with Robert Joffrey as artistic adviser, in Minsa Craig's *November Steps* and William Scott's *Love, How Many Colors;* and the Houston Ballet in James Clouser's *Caliban.* The Connecticut Ballet promoted such choreographic newcomers as Bruce Wells (*Renaissance Dances* and other new pieces), while the San Francisco Ballet staged a new full-length *Romeo and Juliet.*

Visiting ballet troupes from other countries included the Australian Ballet, with Dame Margot Fonteyn, in Sir Robert Helpmann's and Ronald Hynd's ballet version of the Franz Lehár operetta *The Merry Widow;* the National Ballet of Canada,

Czechoslovakian Literature: *see* Literature

Dahomey: *see* Benin

Dams: *see* Engineering Projects

with Rudolf Nureyev as guest artist; and the Royal Winnipeg Ballet, featuring new works by Oscar Araiz (*Mahler 4—Eternity Is Now*) and Stuart Sebastian (*The Seasons*). Britain's Royal Ballet toured with a repertory featuring Sir Frederick Ashton's *A Month in the Country* (new production) along with traditional works and ballets by Kenneth MacMillan. A visit by the Royal Danish Ballet featured the U.S. premiere of the avant-garde *The Triumph of Death* by Flemming Flindt (*see* BIOGRAPHY), with music by Thomas Koppel. The Dutch National Ballet staged works by its three major choreographers, Rudi van Dantzig, Hans van Manen, and Toer van Schayk.

In the modern dance field, active companies, dancers, and choreographers, in addition to Graham and Ailey, included the Paul Taylor Dance Company in a Broadway engagement featuring *Runes* (Gerald Busby); the José Limón Dance Company offering novelties and also a revival of Doris Humphrey's *Two Ecstatic Themes* ("Circular Descent" and "Pointed Ascent"); and the Phyllis Lamhut Dance Co. dancing Lamhut's *Hearts of Palm*. A new company, the American Dance Machine, was formed by Lee Theodore to retain, restore, and perform major dances from Broadway shows, with the first program featuring the musical comedy dances of Jack Cole. There was a major Broadway engagement by the Alwin Nikolais avant-garde troupe featuring Nikolais's new multimedia *Styx* and a new piece, *Glances*, choreographed by his disciple Murray Louis.

Dance on television included the launching of a Public Broadcasting Service series called "Dance in America"; a joint Soviet-U.S. production of the Bolshoi Ballet's *Romeo and Juliet;* and a "first," a live telecast of a Lincoln Center performance of the American Ballet Theatre in the full-length *Swan Lake*. A feature-length movie on a ballet theme, *The Turning Point*, went into production. The New York City Opera's new production of Offenbach's *La Belle Hélène* featured a major ballet by Thomas Andrew, and the Metropolitan Opera's *Faust* (Gounod) featured "Walpurgis Night," a new ballet by Stuart Sebastian. Norbert Vesak, newly appointed director of ballet at the Metropolitan, choreographed Massenet's *Esclarmonde*.

(WALTER TERRY)

An important 50th anniversary for British ballet was celebrated in 1976. On June 15, 1926, a short ballet, *A Tragedy of Fashion* (with music by Eugene Goossens), was first seen in the revue *Riverside Nights* at the Lyric Theatre in the inner London suburb of Hammersmith. It was the first creation by the then 20-year-old Frederick Ashton on the instigation of his teacher, Marie Rambert. *A Tragedy of Fashion*, in which they both danced, led to the formation of the Ballet Club and, later, Ballet Rambert; these organizations were entirely responsible for the first generation of British choreographers.

It was a coincidence that the 1975–76 season also marked the return from his retirement of Sir Frederick Ashton, now one of the foremost creators in the world, to choreography. His *A Month in the Country* (to music of Chopin), based on the Ivan Turgenev play, for the Royal Ballet at Covent Garden brought the company one of its biggest successes of recent years. The other creation for the company was *Rituals* (music by Bela Bartok) by Kenneth MacMillan, who also made some changes in his full-length *Romeo and Juliet* (Prokofiev).

The Royal Ballet's smaller company was rechristened the Sadler's Wells Royal Ballet in the autumn of 1976, when the Sadler's Wells Theatre became its permanent London base. Ashton's *La Fille Mal Gardée* (Louis-Joseph-Ferdinand Herold) was added to the repertory of full-length works; creations included David Morse's *Pandora* (Roberto Gerhard) and Jack Carter's *Lulu* (Darius Milhaud). The Royal Ballet's demonstration group, Ballet for All, added two works to the programs it took to Britain's small theatres and universities: *Romeo and Juliet—Ballet and Play* and *Tchaikovsky and His Ballets*.

MARTHA SWOPE

Jacques d'Amboise of the New York City Ballet dances the Highland fling in George Balanchine's new ballet "Union Jack" which opened at Lincoln Center in May.

After the popular success of Nureyev's *The Sleeping Beauty* in 1975, London Festival Ballet turned to strengthening its repertory of one-act works. Nicholas Beriosoff revived, for its first performance by a British company, Michel Fokine's shortened and danced version of the opera *Le Coq d'Or* (Rimsky-Korsakov) as well as his *Spectre de la Rose* (Carl Maria von Weber). Creations included Barry Moreland's *Dancing Space* (Mozart) and Ronald Hynd's *The Sanguine Fan* (Elgar), partly financed by Princess Grace of Monaco for the company's season in Monte Carlo.

As usual, it was the smaller companies that produced the greatest number of creations. Ballet Rambert preceded its 50th anniversary season at Sadler's Wells with *Collaboration Three* when artists in the company worked with design students from the Central School of Art and Design. Among the many creations were Blake Brown's *Steppes* (Tony Scott), Judith Marcuse's *Four Working Songs* (Carlos Miranda), Julia Blaikie's *there is a dream that is dreaming me* (Miranda), Leigh Warren's *Hot Air* (Paul Winter), Zoltan Imre's *Fixations* (Richard Crosby), Nicholas Carroll's *Widdershins* (John Eaton), Joseph Scoglio's *Small Hours* (Scarlatti), and Lenny Westerdijk's *5-4-3-2-1* (Nicholas Hooper). Creations for the anniversary season included Christopher Bruce's *Girl with Straw Hat* (Brahms) and *Black Angels* (George Crumb), Norman Morrice's *The Sea Whisper'd Me* (Miranda), and Robert North's *Reflections* (Howard Blake); also new to the repertory was Glen Tetley's *Moveable Garden* (Lukas Foss).

MARTHA SWOPE

Mikhail Baryshnikov performing in "Push Comes to Shove," a ballet by avant-garde choreographer Twyla Tharp presented by the American Ballet Theatre in January.

London Contemporary Dance Theatre, in addition to its London seasons and provincial touring, began residencies in regional colleges, a practice common in the U.S. but never before done in Britain. The company's artistic director, Robert Cohan, created *Class* (Jon Keliehor), a stage presentation of a Martha Graham modern dance class, and also *Stabat Mater* (Vivaldi); other creations included Richard Alston's *Headlong* (Anna Lockwood), Micha Bergese's *Da Capo al Fine* (Dominic Muldowney), Siobhan Davies' *Diary* (Gregory Rose), and Robert North's *David and Goliath* (Carl Davis).

Of Britain's regional companies, Scottish Ballet was firmly established in the Theatre Royal, Glasgow, converted into an opera house. Additions to its already extensive repertory included Murray Louis' *Moments* (Ravel), Peter Darrell's *The Scarlet Pastorale* (Frank Martin), and Norbert Vesak's pas de deux "Belong," from *What to Do Till the Messiah Comes* (Syrinx). Most important was Peter Darrell's three-act work to a commissioned score, *Mary Queen of Scots* (John McCabe).

The future of Britain's other principal regional company, Northern Dance Theatre in Manchester, which had seemed uncertain after a proposed merger with the Royal Ballet's smaller company fell through, looked brighter with the appointment of a new artistic director, Robert de Warren. The principal additions to the repertory were Walter Gore's *Street Games* (Jacques Ibert), *Peepshow* (Jean Françaix), and *Eaters of Darkness* (Benjamin Britten), Jack Carter's *Impromptu for Twelve* (Rossini), Ray Powell's *Just for Fun* (Shostakovich), Royston Maldoom's *Adagietto No. 5* (Mahler) and *The Four Seasons* (Vivaldi), and Jonathan Thorpe's *Spring Song* (Dvorak).

William Louther's Welsh Dance Theatre was disbanded after a London season at The Place in the spring of 1976. The Irish Ballet, in its third year, was becoming firmly established with seasons in its home theatre, the Cork Opera House, and also in Dublin and frequent provincial tours. The company's director, Joan Denise Moriarty, created two works with a local flavour, *They Come, They Come* (Ernest Mocran) and *The Devil to Pay* (Sean O'Riudu). Peter Darrell revived *The Prisoners* (Bartok) and *Grand Pas Gitane* (Saint-Saens). The important creation of 1976 was Domy Reiter-Soffer's *Yerma* (Crumb).

On the mainland of Europe the Paris Opéra, in addition to its second company, Troupe Favart, which gave seasons at the Théâtre de Champs-Elysées, also had an experimental group, GRTOP, which performed on the stage of the Opéra. The most important full-evening work of GRTOP was Carolyn Carlson's *Wind, Water, Sand* (John Surman/Barre Philips). The main Opéra company presented a Homage to Ravel program that included Balanchine's *Sonatine, Le Tombeau de Couperin, Tzigane,* and *La Valse;* also programs in homage to Nijinsky and his sister, Bronislava Nijinska, including Nijinska's *Les Noces* (Stravinsky), Serge Golovine's production of *Petrushka* (Stravinsky), and both Nijinsky's and Jerome Robbins' versions of *L'Après-midi d'un faune* (Debussy). Roland Petit, returning to the Opéra where he was formerly a student, created *Mouvances* (Verdi), *La Nuit Transfigurée* (Schoenberg), and *Nana* (Marius Constant).

West Germany continued to provide the greatest number of ballet companies in any one European country, with those of Stuttgart and Hamburg leading the way. The Stuttgart Ballet lost its artistic director, Glen Tetley, who was replaced by ballerina Marcia Haydée. Before Tetley left he created *Greening* (Arne Nordheim) and *Alegrías* (Carlos Chavez), and revived his *Pierrot Lunaire* (Schoenberg); his version of *Rite of Spring* (Stravinsky), created for the Munich Ballet, also went into the Stuttgart repertory. Jiri Kylian, a former Stuttgart dancer who had become artistic director of Netherlands Dance Theatre, returned to create *Return to an Unknown Land* (Janacek).

The most important works created for the Hamburg State Opera Ballet by its director, John Neumeier, were an entirely new conception of *Swan Lake* (Tchaikovsky) and *Le Sacre* (Stravinsky), part of a historic program dedicated to Nijinsky. The Frankfurt Ballet's main company gave Alfonso Catá's *Sweet Carmen* (Bizet) and Kent Stowell's *Variations on "I Lombardi"* (Verdi); the Frankfurt Chamber Ballet gave Stowell's *L'Heure bleue* (Ravel) and Catá's *The Golden Broom and the Green Apple* (Duke Ellington). In Cologne, Tanz-Forum staged Grey Veredon's full-length *Romeo and Juliet* (Berlioz), Glen Tetley's *Moveable Garden,* Norman Morrice's *That Is the Show* (Berio), and Jochen Ulrich's *The Rule Was Unalterable—Requiem in Five Movements* (Johannes Fritsch).

In The Netherlands the most notable addition to the repertory of the Dutch National Ballet was Rudi van Dantzig's *Blown in a Gentle Wind* (Richard Strauss). The oldest established Dutch company, Scapino Ballet, gave Roberto Trinchero's *Divertimento* (Poulenc), Kathy Gosschalk's *Interviews* (Bob Uschi), and Hans van Manen's *Ajakaboembie* (Chopin/Bob Scraggs).

For his Ballet of the Twentieth Century, Maurice Béjart created two productions, *Pli selon pli* (Pierre Boulez) and the full-length *Nôtre Faust* (Bach). Belgium's regional company, Ballet de Wallonie, offered Attilio Labis' new version of *Coppélia* (Delibes).

(PETER WILLIAMS)

See also Music; Theatre.

[625]

Danish Literature: *see* Literature

Darts: *see* Target Sports

Deaths: *see* Demography; *see also biographies of prominent persons who died in 1976, listed under People of the Year*

SPECIAL REPORT

THE BOLSHOI BICENTENNIAL

By Walter Terry

TASS / SOVFOTO

The Bolshoi Ballet, one of the world's premier dance troupes, celebrated its 200th birthday in 1976. Although critics believe that the Soviet company has not kept pace with modern developments in the dance, none can dispute the magnitude and influence of its past contributions.

Origins. Officially the Ballet Company of the State Academic Lenin Prize Bolshoi Theatre of the Union of Soviet Socialist Republics, the Bolshoi had its beginnings in 1773 when the trustees of the Moscow Orphanage instituted classes in ballet. Three years later, in 1776, an ensemble from the orphanage, trained by Filippo Beccari (a former dancer with the Imperial Ballet in St. Petersburg), gave its first performance and was considered sufficiently professional to form the core of Moscow's first ballet troupe.

Of the first ballet class of 62 orphans, 24 were chosen as soloists to dance outside the orphanage in performance. When the Petrovsky Theatre in Moscow was completed in 1780, all 62 became the official ballet company of the new house. The Petrovsky burned down in 1805 and was replaced at the same location, after some delays, by a new building called the Bolshoi Theatre. It too was destroyed by fire, in 1853, but from its ruins and with some of the original structure remaining the Bolshoi Theatre as it is today reopened in 1856.

Moscow-St. Petersburg Rivalry. Professional Russian ballet (as distinct from earlier European court ballets in which royalty and nobles were participants) had first been established in 1738 in St. Petersburg (now Leningrad), the capital of imperial Russia, with the founding of the Imperial School of Ballet under the direction of a Frenchman, Jean-Baptiste Landé. The academy was situated in the Winter Palace, and the pupils were children (both boys and girls) of the empress Anna's servants; the first graduating class performed in 1742. The present-day descendant of this troupe is Leningrad's Kirov Ballet (the Imperial Ballet of the Maryinsky Theatre).

The Kirov and the Bolshoi are the two major companies in the Soviet Union, and there is considerable rivalry between them. Until the overthrow of the monarchy in 1917 the St. Petersburg company was the more prestigious. It was, of course, in the nation's capital and literally in the presence of the tsars. In comparatively recent times it has produced such renowned dancers as Anna Pavlova, Vaslav Nijinsky, Tamara Karsavina, and Alexandra Danilova and such towering creative figures as the choreographers Michel Fokine and George Balanchine. The school of ballet that produced these artists also developed the ballet style and teaching methods that spread beyond Russian borders to strongly influence ballet style abroad, particularly in Great Britain and the U.S.

Moscow's Bolshoi (also an Imperial Ballet), though under the shadow of the St. Petersburg troupe until post-Revolution days, was by no means unknown or lacking in influence. Nadezhda Bogdanova, Moscow-born and trained, in the middle of the last century became the first Russian ballerina to win success in Western Europe. In this century the Bolshoi's Mikhail Mordkin made dance history as Anna Pavlova's partner when the two first performed in the U.S. in 1910, thereby instituting a renascence of ballet in the United States. Subsequently, Mordkin settled in the U.S., and it was his company of the 1930s, the Mordkin Ballet, that evolved into one of the world's major ballet troupes, the American Ballet Theatre. Also from Moscow came Léonide Massine, who joined Sergey Diaghilev's Ballets Russes as Diaghilev's special protégé, first as a dancer and then as a choreographer. Marius Petipa, the great choreographer whose reign in Russia spanned a half century, made his headquarters in St. Petersburg, but some of his ballets, including the masterpiece *Don Quixote,* were first created for the Bolshoi.

Long before the capital of Russia was transferred from St. Petersburg to Moscow, the Bolshoi Ballet had developed its own style. The differences between ballet style in Moscow and in St. Petersburg were instantly clear to the trained eye and instinctively recognized by even the untutored. It was not that different steps were used by dancers in each city but was instead the way that the steps, the *port de bras* (classical ballet positions of the arms) and whole *enchaînements* (combinations of classical steps), were done. St. Petersburg ballet was elegant, restrained in deportment, cool, perhaps "underplayed." Moscow's ballet style was broader, freer, more open, even flamboyant. Until recently, if one praised a Bolshoi performance to a dancer from Leningrad, the response would be, "Well, if you like circus dancing. . . ." And to the Muscovite, the dancers to the north were "boring," "classroom students." In 1964, however, Yuri Grigorovich, trained in Leningrad and a member of the Kirov Ballet as dancer and choreographer for almost 20 years, became artistic director and principal choreographer of the Bolshoi. His policy, in his own words, was to consolidate "the best of both schools" for ballet in the U.S.S.R.

Rise of the Bolshoi. With the overthrow of the monarchy and the transfer of the capital from Leningrad to Moscow, the national and international ascendancy of the Bolshoi Ballet began. The prelude to this could be symbolized by the rise in Moscow of a young St. Petersburg-born choreographer, Aleksandr Gorsky, a pupil of Petipa. When he was assigned to the Bolshoi, he began to evolve his own choreographic ideas. His new creations were said to have taken on the vigour of the city of Moscow. Today, in Soviet ballet repertory, especially at the Bolshoi, the fruits of his choreographic efforts remain in a dominant position.

With respect to performing, St. Petersburg and the Maryinsky certainly lent Pavlova to the world, but Moscow and the Bolshoi also produced a great ballerina, Yekaterina Geltzer, acclaimed in London and Paris as well as in Russia. Although Geltzer was described as having vivid and daring qualities in her dancing,

---

Walter Terry, Jr., is dance critic and dance editor of Saturday Review *magazine. His books include* The Dance in America *(1956; rev. 1973),* Ballet Guide *(1975), and* Frontiers of Dance: The Life of Martha Graham *(1975).*

SOVFOTO

The young, spectacular Maya Plisetskaya performed this leap in "Don Quixote," set to music by Léon Minkus, in February 1950. Largely unknown to Western audiences then, the Bolshoi made impressive debuts in its trips to London in 1956 and to the U.S. in 1959.

she herself at the start of her career in the 1890s had asked to go to St. Petersburg in order to acquire the polish and the exactitude of *pointe* work available there. Thus, she had anticipated Grigorovich's contemporary desire of combining the best of the two schools. Geltzer, unlike the expatriate Pavlova, was the most significant dancer to bridge the imperial and Soviet eras. She was the star of *The Red Poppy,* the first "revolutionary" ballet created (1927) in the Soviet Union, and was the first dancer to be named Peoples' Artist of the Republic.

During the 1920s choreographers such as Gorsky, Asaf Messerer, Mikhail Gabovich, and Igor Moiseyev (later the founder-director of the internationally famous folk dance-based Moiseyev Dance Company) brought new ideas to the Bolshoi. They tended to abjure the old classics in search of more modern dance expressions. But the government disapproved of modern art and the experiments faded away, leaving areas of modernity principally in matters of theme (ballets reflecting the viewpoints of the new regime) and in the restudying of the classics to remove old-fashioned mime and replace it with a broader style of semi-realistic acting.

Except for foreigners visiting the Soviet Union, the West's first glimpse of the Bolshoi Ballet came through motion pictures. The films included a dance performed by Olga Lepeshinskaya, who had made her Bolshoi debut in 1933 and who epitomized the vigorous and flamboyant Moscow style. The West also saw for the first time in these films Galina Ulanova, Kirov-trained but transferred to Moscow; the very young and blazing Maya Plisetskaya, who had some Kirov training; the elegant Marina Semeyonova, transferred from the Kirov to the Bolshoi; and the fantastically virtuosic Georgian Vachtang Chabukiani, who helped immeasurably in restoring the male dancer to prominence, through his Kirov performances, his choreography, and his reworking of male solos in the classics.

The Bolshoi troupe itself made its London debut in 1956 and its U.S. debut in 1959. The effect on both public and performers was spectacular. The West had never seen such virtuosity in ballet: one-arm lifts, with a strapping male holding a female dancer high above his head; hurtlings through space, as a female tossed herself bulletlike through the air only to be caught at the final split second by a sturdy male; multiple and dizzying floor turns and air turns by the men. Audiences gasped; dancers imitated. Choreographers were quick to use features of Bolshoi prowess in new ballets, and the dancers embellished their standard versions of the ballet classics with manifestations of Bolshoi bravura. The girls in British and U.S. ballet troupes emulated the arched backs of the Bolshoi ballerinas and the split (instead of the arc) leaps.

In turn, Soviet dancers were strongly influenced by Western ballet, especially by the faster tempos and by the abstract (rather than dramatic) themes found in the ballets of the most influential U.S. choreographer, George Balanchine. Bolshoi males, by the time of the troupe's second tour outside the U.S.S.R., were considerably slimmer than they had been, and even some aspects of the prudish male dress (long tunic or little pants over ballet tights) had been modified.

Contemporary Appraisal. By the time of the Bolshoi Ballet's bicentennial in 1976 the dance world of the West had had time to discover not only the strengths but also the weaknesses of the company. From the start it was clear that choreographically all Soviet ballet was at least 50 years behind the times. Isolation of the U.S.S.R. had kept the Bolshoi from experiencing the continuing innovations in Western ballet; indeed, Soviet dancers had to study outside their country to learn the work of their own innovator, Fokine, and his turn-of-the-century ballet developments. Also, there had been no exposure whatsoever to the powerful influences of modern dance.

In the 1950s Leonid Lavrovsky's ballet of Sergey Prokofiev's *Romeo and Juliet,* both as a movie (with Ulanova) and on stage (also with Ulanova), made a tremendous impression in the West. But by the time a new filming of the ballet with a Bolshoi cast headed by the foremost stars was released in 1976 it seemed sadly dated and was both a critical and popular failure. For in that 20-year period had come Frederick Ashton's choreography for the same ballet (for the Royal Danish Ballet), Kenneth MacMillan's for Britain's Royal Ballet, and John Cranko's for the Stuttgart Ballet. All of these represented a far larger vocabulary of dance movement and displayed considerably more subtleties of style and characterization than were present in the Lavrovsky version.

The case of *Romeo and Juliet* is symptomatic of the problems facing the Bolshoi Ballet. The troupe has remained static while other companies have advanced or, at the very least, explored in new directions. Since 1956 each succeeding Bolshoi tour to the West has had less effect on audiences and dancers. By 1975, on the eve of the company's bicentennial, the Bolshoi Ballet's chief claim to success lay in its massive productions, *Spartacus* and *Ivan the Terrible.*

"Bolshoi" in Russian means "big" or "great." Though certain Bolshoi artists who are "great" in any language, Plisetskaya, Natalya Bessmertnova, Vladimir Vasiliev, retained eminence for Soviet ballet along with aspects of the choreography of Grigorovich, the stature of Soviet ballet was swiftly receding in the eyes of the world. Despite some talented and brilliant junior dancers, the technical level of the dancers was inferior to that of their predecessors, particularly in matters of accuracy, neatness, and, especially, deportment. Several Soviet ballet expatriates explained defections by Soviet dancers to the West on a combination of unrewarding, standstill choreography and a "lack of good teachers." Both reasons seem valid as the Bolshoi Ballet, two centuries old, finds itself still "big" but no longer "great."

TOP LEFT) A. BATANOV—TASS/SOVFOTO; (TOP RIGHT) L. ZHDANOV—CAMERA PRESS/PHOTO TRENDS; (BOTTOM) CAMERA PRESS/PHOTO TRENDS

(Top left) Galina Ulanova and Yuri Zhdanov were the principals in Sergey Prokofiev's "Romeo and Juliet" at its hundredth performance by the Bolshoi on March 20, 1957. (Top right) Yekaterina Maximova in "The Mazurka," as staged by Kasian Goleizovsky. (Bottom) The Bolshoi making its long-awaited London debut in 1956, shown in a scene from "Swan Lake."

Defense

The strategic and political relationship between the superpowers, the U.S. and the U.S.S.R., reemerged as the dominant defense issue in 1976. The concept of détente promoted by U.S. Secretary of State Henry Kissinger and embodied in the 1972 strategic arms limitations talks agreement (SALT I) had collapsed. Instead of collaborating with the U.S. to limit the strategic arms race and avoiding interventions in local conflicts that might bring about superpower confrontations, the Soviet Union was acquiring a strategic and conventional military superiority that its leadership apparently believed could produce political gains. The U.S.S.R. was also using its new potential for global intervention wherever opportunities presented themselves, as in the Soviet use of Cuban soldiers and Soviet equipment to secure victory for the Moscow-backed Popular Movement for the Liberation of Angola (MPLA) in Angola. (See *Africa South of the Sahara,* below.)

Because Kissinger had made arms control agreements—notably SALT I, the 1974 Vladivostok accords, and the projected but still elusive SALT II agreement—the keystone in his structure of détente, the debate over those agreements assumed major importance. The individual issues were highly technical, but an overall pattern emerged in which Kissinger defended the agreements against charges that they were not being observed by the U.S.S.R. and were harmful to U.S. interests.

Kissinger and his supporters, including a lukewarm Pres. Gerald Ford, argued that SALT I had prevented Soviet (and U.S.) deployment of antiballistic missile (ABM) systems and the introduction of new Soviet intercontinental ballistic missiles (ICBM's) of sufficient throw weight (payload) and numbers to threaten a disabling first strike against the U.S. ICBM force. The resultant strategic stability had provided the foundation for détente, which in turn ensured that the U.S.S.R. would observe the *spirit* of these and any other arms control agreements. Kissinger's critics countered by arguing that the Soviets had observed only the *terms* of the SALT I agreement, and then only in the most legalistic sense.

SALT I actually consisted of several separate sets of agreements falling into two parts. The first part included the ABM treaty, of unlimited duration, and the Interim Agreement on strategic offensive arms, which would expire in October 1977; both had been signed by the U.S. and the U.S.S.R. The second part consisted of 12 "Agreed Interpretations," 6 "Common Understandings," and 7 U.S. "Unilateral Statements." These spelled out in detail the U.S. understanding of the key provisions of the ABM treaty and the Interim Agreement, but they were not legally binding on the Soviets and were not accepted by them. Instead, the Soviets had exploited the many ambiguities in a poorly drafted set of documents to render them meaningless.

According to critics of SALT I, the U.S.S.R. had developed a significant ability to deploy an effective, tested, ABM system, including an air-defense system that could be upgraded to give it ABM capabilities. In offensive forces, the Soviets had deployed a new generation of ICBM's, notably the SS-19 to replace the SS-11, that threatened the U.S. ICBM forces. Furthermore, the U.S.S.R. had interfered with the U.S. "national technical means of verification" of SALT I (chiefly satellites), despite a clear agreement not to do so. The U.S. administration countered these charges by saying that, though the SALT I package had its defects and was proving difficult to implement, such difficulties were to be expected in a major new venture. They were being worked out through negotiations, including those in the Standing Consultative Commission set up for this purpose in SALT I, and would be remedied in SALT II. The critics replied that nothing in the administration's arguments could alter the emergence of a Soviet advantage in throw weight of six to one.

Kissinger dismissed this as a phony argument, but he found it difficult to marshal support for SALT II. The projected agreement was to be based on the guidelines set up in the 1974 Vladivostok accords, which allowed each superpower 2,400 strategic delivery vehicles (SDV's) including 1,320 SDV's carrying multiple independently targetable reentry vehicles (MIRV's). Liberal critics charged that these limits would allow the superpowers to deploy far more SDV's than were necessary for defense and enough MIRVed SDV's to threaten stability. Conservative critics claimed that Kissinger's interpretation of these guidelines increased the Soviet threat to the U.S. strategic forces.

Since Vladivostok, two new issues had arisen to complicate the SALT II debate. The first was the Soviet deployment of the Backfire bomber. According to Kissinger it had only a medium range (3,500 mi), too low for a strategic weapon. His opponents, including the U.S. Department of Defense, insisted that with in-flight refueling it had an intercontinental range (6,000 mi) and so should be counted as an SDV, just as the U.S. B-1 supersonic bomber would be if it were deployed.

The second issue, that of the cruise missile, was more important. This new weapons system being developed by the U.S. crossed all the existing lines between conventional and nuclear, tactical and strategic weapons on which arms control agreements had been built. The cruise missile was unmanned, flew at subsonic speeds, and used an extremely accurate terrain contour matching (Tercom) guidance system, capable of putting it within 30 ft of its target after a flight of 1,500 mi. It utilized to the full the U.S. lead in miniaturized computer technology and could give the U.S. much-needed tactical and strategic capabilities against the U.S.S.R., especially in Europe.

"Did I have a nightmare last night! I dreamed they had a billion missiles and we had only a MILLION!"

ROSS—ROTHCO

UPI COMPIX

A Tomahawk cruise missile is launched from a U.S. Navy A-6 Intruder over the Pacific missile range. The missile flew more than 300 miles.

Two versions were under development, the Air Force's air-launched cruise missile (ALCM), with a range of about 600 mi, and the Navy's submarine-launched cruise missile (SLCM), which could be fired from the standard 21-in-diameter torpedo tube and had a range of 1,500 mi. Both the ALCM and the SLCM could carry conventional warheads or nuclear warheads with yields of up to 200 kilotons. To further complicate matters, the A/SLCM's accuracy meant it could take out fixed-based ICBM's using a conventional warhead. Because A/SLCM's were small, relatively cheap, and could have their range and warhead altered quickly, no verification of the numbers deployed or their capabilities (conventional or nuclear) would be possible.

The only way of restraining A/SLCM deployment would be for the U.S. to forgo the military advantages they represented and halt their deployment at very low levels. This was what Kissinger suggested during his January 1976 visit to Moscow, when he proposed that all bombers with long-range ALCM's (1,000–1,500 mi) be counted as MIRVed SDV's against the Vladivostok ceiling of 1,320. This would limit U.S. deployment to 34 bombers equipped with ten or more ALCM's unless other planned deployments of MIRVed SDV's were canceled. U.S. surface-launched cruise missiles would be limited to 25 surface vessels, each carrying ten short-range (360–372 mi) missiles, to be excluded from the Vladivostok SDV total. U.S. SLCM's would be limited to the same range, although the Soviets already had large numbers of cruise missiles deployed on surface vessels and submarines for strategic and tactical roles, notably the SSN-3 (450-mi range) which was to be replaced by the SSN(X)-12 (500-mi range).

In addition, Kissinger accepted Soviet deployment of the SS-19 as a replacement for the SS-11 without securing final agreement as to what constituted a "heavy" ICBM counting toward the SALT I subceiling of 313 for these missiles. This indicated probable acceptance of the Soviet proposal that any ICBM with a volume greater than that of an SS-19 (96 cu m) be considered "heavy." In exchange for these U.S. concessions, the Soviets would deploy, from 1977 to 1982, no more than 250 Backfire bombers, carrying cruise missiles of an unspecified range, which would not be counted as SDV's under the Vladivostok limits. After 1982 it could deploy as many Backfires as it wished, however, and restrictions on Backfire deployment and training and on the development of a tanker fleet to give them extra range, intended by Kissinger to limit the bomber's strategic capabilities, were meaningless, since they could easily be circumvented.

Despite criticisms that these proposals favoured the U.S.S.R. at the expense of the U.S. and that Kissinger had negotiated badly by making them without waiting for Soviet proposals, the secretary continued to seek a SALT II along these lines. What if any changes of policy would be initiated by President Ford's successor, Jimmy Carter, when he took office in January 1977 were unclear. Throughout the 1976 political campaign Carter had criticized Kissinger's negotiating style and accused the administration of weakening the U.S. defense posture, but he offered little in the way of substantive alternatives. That Ford himself had felt a political need to maintain some distance from Kissinger's policies was indicated by his decision, early in the campaign, to stop using the word détente.

To many observers, it appeared that the détente SALT II was supposed to support had indeed disappeared, and that the U.S. faced the task of reestablishing a strategic and political position of perceived equality with the U.S.S.R. that the Soviet leadership would recognize and respect. Otherwise, the Soviet government, in what one of Kissinger's chief aides, Helmut Sonnenfeldt, described as its imperial phase, would seek to expand its influence at the expense of the U.S. and its allies.

UNITED STATES

Manpower of the U.S. forces dropped again in 1976, by 43,000 to 2,086,700. So did the defense budget as a percentage of gross national product (GNP), to 5.9%, although in dollar terms it rose slightly, from the $102,691,000,000 actually spent in fiscal 1976 to a budget authority of nearly $112 billion for fiscal 1977. Significantly, President Ford's defense budget encountered far less opposition than any such budget since the U.S. involvement in Vietnam ended. The majority of representatives and senators apparently felt that U.S. defense spending had been trimmed back enough in light of the Soviet force buildup.

In the strategic forces the emphasis was on providing for survivability of the land-based ICBM force in case of a Soviet attack. This force remained constant at 550 Minuteman III's, each with three 170-kiloton MIRV's; 450 Minuteman II's, each carrying a single one–two-megaton warhead; and 54 Titan II's, each with a five–ten-megaton warhead. Development of a new 370-kiloton Mk 12A MIRV for the Minuteman III continued, and the Minuteman III production lines were kept open with the purchase of 60 new missiles, providing the option of replacing the Minuteman II with the Minuteman III.

In the short run, refinements in guidance, retargeting, and silo-hardening continued to improve ICBM survivability. In the longer run, the U.S. was considering land-mobile ICBM's and development of a new, advanced ICBM (designated the M-X) with a larger payload and a terminally guided warhead to replace the Minuteman. With these improvements, the U.S. ICBM force could provide the president with the options for selective nuclear strikes against military targets in the U.S.S.R., including missile silos, with minimum civilian casualties that had been recommended by former U.S. secretary of defense James Schlesinger.

The deployment of 496 Poseidon submarine-launched ballistic missiles (SLBM's), each with 10–14 50-kiloton MIRV's, in 31 Lafayette-class SSBN's (ballistic missile submarines, nuclear) was completed, leaving 10 older SSBN's carrying 16 Polaris A-3 missiles apiece. These were to be replaced by Trident SSBN's, each of which would carry 24 Trident I SLBM's equipped with 8 50-kiloton MIRV's and having a 4,600-mi range; deployment was to start in 1978. Also in 1978, the Trident I SLBM was to replace Poseidon in 10 SSBN's. Eventually the Trident SSBN would carry the Trident II SLBM, with 14 MIRV's and a 6,000-mi range.

The strategic bomber force was again reduced to 453 aircraft (66 FB-111A's, 151 B-52G's, 90 B-52H's, 75 B-52D's, and 71 B-52D/F's used for training) carrying 1,500 short-range attack missiles (SRAM's), each with a warhead in the kiloton range. The new Air Force supersonic bomber, the B-1, with an estimated cost of $71 million each, became the centre of a fierce congressional debate over its utility, given Soviet air defenses and the possibility of substituting large numbers of cheap ALCM's as strategic delivery vehicles. It was finally agreed to keep the production lines open, leaving the final decision on procurement of the 241 requested by the Air Force until after the new president had taken office. The Safeguard ABM site at Grand Forks, N.D., was deactivated, and ABM research and development were held to very low levels. Already minimal air defenses were reduced still further to 331 interceptors.

The 782,000-man Army continued its restructuring program, designed to raise the number of divisions (each with 16,000 men) from 13½ to 16. Two additional 4,000-man brigades were moved to Western Europe, bringing total U.S. forces there to virtually five divisions. The Army had four armoured, five mechanized, five infantry, one airmobile, and one airborne division, one armoured and one infantry brigade, and three armoured cavalry regiments. Tank strength rose: to about 10,000 medium tanks, including 5,900 M-60s (M-60A2s carried the Shillelagh antitank guided weapon) and 3,300 M-48s, plus 1,600 M-551 Sheridan light tanks with the Shillelagh; the number of armoured personnel carriers increased to 21,000. Other equipment included 3,000 self-propelled guns and howitzers, 2,500 towed guns and howitzers, Honest John, Pershing, and Lance surface-to-surface missiles (SSM's), 2,400 TOW and Dragon antitank guided weapons, 600 antiaircraft guns, and 20,000 Redeye and Chaparral/Vulcan gun/missile systems. The 900 older Nike Hercules and HAWK surface-to-air missiles (SAM's) were being supplemented by the Roland SAM. Helicopter strength rose to 8,600 and fixed-wing aircraft to 1,000. The primary mission of these forces was the defense of Western Europe and of vital U.S. interests elsewhere, chiefly in South Korea, Japan, Taiwan, and, in dire need, Israel.

In November, after a two-year competition, Chrysler was chosen over General Motors to build the new U.S. main battle tank, to be called the Abrams (after the late Gen. Creighton W. Abrams, former army chief of staff). The Army had recommended in July that the General Motors version be adopted, but the Department of Defense reversed the decision and ordered both manufacturers to modify their prototypes in order to incorporate some of the features of the West German Leopard 2. Under an agreement reached during the year by the U.S. and West Germany, the U.S. turret would be designed to accept the 120-mm gun used by West Germany as well as the 105-mm gun favoured by the U.S. Army. The West Germans, in turn, would adopt a turbine engine under development in the U.S. in place of a diesel engine, and it was also agreed to standardize tracks, transmission, fuel, and fire control and to use metric sizes in both tanks. In September a Leopard 2 was brought to the U.S. for

This U.S. Navy craft rides on a bubble of air at speeds of over 100 miles per hour. It is propelled by three gas turbine engines.

WIDE WORLD

Approximate Strengths of Regular Armed Forces of the World

Country	Military personnel in 000s Army	Navy	Air Force	Warships: Aircraft carriers/ cruisers*	Submarines†	Destroyers/ frigates	Total major surface combat vessels	Jet aircraft: Bombers‡	Fighters	Tanks§	Defense expenditure as % of GNP
I. NATO											
Belgium	64.0	4.3	19.9	—	—	—	—	90 FB	36	419	3.0
Canada	28.5	13.4	36.0	—	3	23	23	—	116	226	2.2
Denmark	21.8	5.8	7.1	—	6	2	2	60 FB	40	200	2.2
France‖	338.5	70.0	104.4	2 CV, 2 CA	23, 4 SSBN	48	52	273 FB, 36 SB	136	1,060	3.9
Germany, West	345.0	39.0	111.0	—	24	17	17	409 FB	78	4,000	4.4
Greece	160.0	17.5	22.0	—	8	13	13	109 FB	84	1,075	6.9
Italy	240.0	42.0	70.0	3 CA	8	18	21	162 FB	72	1,300	2.6
Luxembourg	0.6	—	—	—	—	—	—	—	—	—	1.1
Netherlands, The	75.0	18.2	19.0	—	6	18	18	106 FB	36	800	3.6
Norway	20.0	9.0	10.0	—	15	5	5	97 FB	16	116	3.1
Portugal	36.0	13.8¶	10.0	—	3	7	7	18 FB	20	115	6.0
Turkey	375.0	40.0	45.0	—	14	14	14	268 FB	54	2,500	9.0
United Kingdom	177.6	76.3¶	90.2	1 CV, 1 CVH, 2 CA	19, 9 N, 4 SSBN	70	76	88 FB, 106 B	135	910	4.9
United States	978.0¶	524.6	584.1	13 CV, 26 CA	10, 65 N, 41 SSBN	137	176	1,400 FB, 453 SB	1,240	10,000	5.9
II. WARSAW PACT											
Bulgaria	131.0	8.5	25.0	—	4	—	—	72 FB	144	2,000	2.7
Czechoslovakia	135.0	—	45.0	—	—	—	—	158 FB	240	3,400	3.8
Germany, East	105.0	16.0	36.0	—	—	3	3	36 FB	310	3,000	5.5
Hungary	80.0	—	20.0	—	—	—	—	—	140	1,300	2.4
Poland	204.0	25.0¶	61.0	—	6	2	2	230 FB, 23 B	452	3,400	3.1
Romania	145.0	11.0	25.0	—	—	—	—	75 FB	230	1,800	1.7
U.S.S.R.	1,825.0	450.0	1,000.0	1 CV, 2 CVH, 32 CA	122, 40 N, 51 SSBN, 7 N/BMSS, 20 BMSS, 44 N/CMS, 21 CMS	80	214	3,000 FB, 990 B	4,000	41,500	11–13
III. OTHER EUROPEAN											
Albania	36.0	3.0	8.0	—	4	—	—	—	48	100	...
Austria	33.0	—	4.3	—	—	—	—	30 FB	—	234	1.0
Finland	30.3	2.5	3.0	—	—	2	2	—	80	...	1.4
Ireland	12.8	0.5	0.7	—	—	—	—	6 FB	—	—	1.6
Spain	220.0	46.6¶	35.7	1 CVH	9	26	27	20 FB	80	545	1.8
Sweden	46.0	11.2	8.2	—	17	8	8	132 FB	360	650	3.4
Switzerland	37.5	—	9.0	—	—	—	—	290 FB	39	620	1.8
Yugoslavia	200.0	20.0	30.0	—	5	1	1	195 FB	110	2,150	5.6
IV. MIDDLE EAST AND MEDITERRANEAN; SUB-SAHARAN AFRICA; LATIN AMERICA♀											
Algeria	61.0	3.8	4.5	—	—	—	—	90 FB, 24 B	40	400	...
Egypt	295.0	17.5	30.0	—	12	5	5	238 FB, 50 B	490	1,945	...
Iran	200.0	18.5	81.5	—	—	7	7	285 FB	15	1,360	17.4
Iraq	140.0	3.0	15.0	—	—	—	—	170 FB, 19 B	110	1,290	...
Israelδ	135.0/375.0	4.5/6.0	19.0/25.0	—	5	—	—	537 FB	—	2,700	35.9
Jordan	61.0	—	6.6	—	—	—	—	48 FB	18	490	12.2
Lebanon□	17.0	—	1.0	—	—	—	—	16 FB	6	60	...
Libya	22.0	2.7	5.0	—	—	1	1	89 FB	30	715	1.7
Morocco	65.0	3.0	5.0	—	—	1	1	24 FB	23	150	2.8
Saudi Arabia	40.0	1.5	10.0	—	—	—	—	30 FB	37	325	...
Sudan	50.0	0.6	2.0	—	—	—	—	17 FB	20	130	...
Syria	200.0	2.0	25.0	—	—	—	—	190 FB	220	2,300	15.1
Ethiopia	47.0	1.5	2.3	—	—	—	—	27 FB, 4 B	—	24	2.9
Nigeria	221.0	3.5	5.5	—	—	1	1	24 FB	—	—	...
South Africa	38.0	5.0	8.5	—	3	7	7	45 FB, 18 B	43	161	5.3
Zaire	40.0	—	3.0	—	—	—	—	—	5	—	...
Argentina	83.5	32.3¶	17.0	1 CVH, 2 CA	4	9	12	80 FB, 11 B	14	120	...
Brazil	170.0	45.8¶	41.4	1 CVH, 1 CA	8	14	16	39 FB	14	150	1.3
Chile	45.0	23.8¶	10.8	3 CA	3	8	11	—	32	76	...
Colombia	40.0	8.0¶	6.3	—	2	8	8	—	16	...	...
Cuba	146.0	9.0	20.0	—	—	—	—	75 FB	120	600	...
Mexico	319.0	14.5¶	6.0	—	—	3	3	—	—	—	0.7
Peru	46.0	8.0¶	9.0	3 CL	8	6	9	32 B	44	260	3.1
Venezuela	28.0	8.0¶	6.0	—	3	11	11	29 B	55	—	1.7
V. FAR EAST AND OCEANIA♀											
Afghanistan	90.0	—	10.0	—	—	—	—	86 FB, 30 B	36	700	...
Australia	31.6	16.2	21.6	1 CV	4	12	13	80 FB	—	143	3.2
Bangladesh	59.0	1.0	3.0	—	—	—	—	—	9	30	...
Burma	153.0	9.0	7.5	—	—	2	2	—	—	—	2.9
Cambodia	80.0	—	—	—	—	—	—	—	—	—	...
China	3,000.0	275.0¶	250.0	—	55	18	18	500 FB, 520 B	3,650	8,000	...
India	913.0	42.5	100.0	1 CV, 2 CL	8	29	32	340 FB, 80 B	525	1,880	3.0
Indonesia	180.0	38.0¶	28.0	—	3	9	9	16 FB	—	—	3.8
Japan	153.0	39.0	43.0	—	16	47	47	150 FB	280	600	0.9
Korea, North	430.0	20.0	45.0	—	8	—	—	330 FB, 70 B	200	1,150	...
Korea, South	540.0¶	25.0	30.0	—	—	7	7	192 FB	—	840	5.1
Laos	40.0	—	2.0	—	—	—	—	—	—	—	...
Malaysia	52.5	4.8	5.0	—	—	2	2	14 FB	—	—	4.0
New Zealand	5.4	2.8	4.3	—	—	4	4	13 FB	—	—	1.8
Pakistan	400.0	11.0	17.0	—	3	8	8	196 FB, 15 B	—	1,000	7.2
Philippines	45.0	17.0¶	16.0	—	—	1	1	20 FB	20	—	2.6
Taiwan	365.0¶	35.0	70.0	—	2	18	18	250 FB	—	1,500	...
Thailand	141.0	27.0¶	42.0	—	—	7	7	26 FB	—	—	3.7
Vietnam◇	600.0	3.0	12.0	—	—	—	—	110 FB, 8 B	80	900	...

Note: Data exclude paramilitary, security, and irregular forces. Naval data exclude vessels of less than 100 tons standard displacement. Figures are for July 1976.
*Aircraft carriers (CV); helicopter carriers (CVH); heavy cruisers (CA); light cruisers (CL).
†Nuclear hunter-killers (N); ballistic missile submarines (SSBN); (nuclear/) ballistic missile submarines, short-range (BMSS, N/BMSS); (nuclear/) long-range cruise missile submarines (CMS, N/CMS).
‡Medium and heavy bombers (B), fighter-bombers (FB), and strategic bombers (SB).
§Medium and heavy tanks (31 tons and over).
‖French forces were withdrawn from NATO in 1966, but France remains a member of NATO.
¶Includes marines.
♀Sections IV and V list only those states with significant military forces.
δSecond figure is fully mobilized strength.
□Pre-civil war figures.
◇Equipment and manpower of former South Vietnamese forces not included.
Sources: International Institute for Strategic Studies, 18 Adam Street, London, *The Military Balance 1976–77*, *Strategic Survey 1975*.

"comparative evaluation." At one time it had been hoped that a single tank would be adopted for use throughout NATO, but it now appeared that the adoption of some common components was the best that could be expected.

In Europe the U.S. 7th Army totaled 189,000 men with 2,500 medium tanks, plus one brigade in West Berlin. These could be reinforced by one armoured and two mechanized divisions and one armoured cavalry regiment from the U.S.-based Strategic Reserve; except for one mechanized division, these forces had their heavy equipment stockpiled in West Germany. The remaining Strategic Reserve comprised one armoured, one mechanized, three infantry, one airmobile, and one airborne division. Remaining major overseas deployments were 30,000 men in South Korea (described as one division) and one infantry division less one brigade in Hawaii. Reserve strength fell to 212,400 in the Army Reserves and 380,000 in the Army National Guard. The Marine Corps decreased slightly to 196,000 men, manning three large divisions of 18,000 men each, with 430 M-48 tanks (being replaced by M-60s) and 950 armoured personnel carriers. The three air wings had 386 combat aircraft. Two divisions and two air wings were in the U.S. and one division and one air wing were in the Pacific.

The Navy had 176 major surface combat ships and 75 attack submarines (65 nuclear and 10 diesel), about the same as in the preceding year. The carrier force was reduced from 15 to 13 with the retirement of two Hancock-class vessels. A second nuclear-powered carrier, the "Nimitz" (96,000 tons), had joined the "Enterprise" (90,000 tons) in 1975, and a third, the "Eisenhower," was scheduled to enter service in 1978. There were also eight Forrestal/Kitty Hawk-class (78,000–87,000 tons) and three Midway-class (64,000 tons) carriers, one a training carrier; the larger vessels had 85–95 aircraft and the smaller, 75. The F-14 Tomcat interceptor entered service in significant numbers, together with the Aegis air-defense system. Five carriers and 68 surface combatants were deployed in the 2nd Fleet (Atlantic); 4 carriers and 59 surface combatants in the 3rd Fleet (Eastern Pacific); 2 carriers, 16 surface combatants, and one marine amphibious unit (seaborne battalion) in the 6th Fleet (Mediterranean); and 2 carriers, 18 surface combatants, and one marine amphibious unit in the 7th Fleet (Western Pacific). The Middle East Force in the Persian Gulf was a token force of two surface combatants.

Air Force personnel fell to 584,100 and the number of combat aircraft to about 4,500. These included 74 fighter/attack squadrons (52 with F-4 Phantoms; 12 with F-111 fighter-bombers; 2 with the new F-15 Eagle air superiority fighter; and 8 with the A-7D, which was being replaced by the A-10), 9 tactical reconnaissance squadrons with RF-4C Phantoms, and 6 electronic countermeasures squadrons with EB-57s and EF-111A's. Heavy transport was provided by 70 C-5A Galaxys and 234 C-141s, and tactical transport by 234 C-130 Hercules. A total of 82,000 men and 37 fighter squadrons were stationed in the U.S., together with 64,500 men in the Military Airlift Command; 73,000 men and 21 fighter, 3–6 tactical reconnaissance, and 2–8 tactical airlift squadrons were in U.S. Air Force, Europe; and 50,000 men and 9 fighter squadrons were in the Pacific Air Forces stationed in Japan, Okinawa, South Korea, the Philippines, and Taiwan.

The rapid growth of U.S. arms sales abroad came under attack during the year from some members of Congress and was used as an issue in the election campaign by Jimmy Carter. Such sales had been encouraged by the government in recent years as a means of improving the balance of payments and also to reduce U.S. military expenses. A study by the Congressional Budget Office staff, made at the request of the House Armed Services Committee, indicated that selling $8 billion in arms during 1975 had enabled the U.S. to cut its own military costs by $560 million, chiefly by spreading out the costs of research and development and of production overhead. The study also noted that the greater the sophistication of the weapons system being sold, the greater the savings.

U.S.S.R.

Official U.S. estimates of Soviet defense spending (made by the Central Intelligence Agency) indicated that it was substantially higher than had been previously thought, averaging 11–13% of GNP as against earlier estimates of 6–8%. Defense spending in 1975, the latest year for which revised estimates were available, was put at U.S. $114 billion, although alternative estimates went as high as $125 billion, equivalent to 10–14% of GNP. Total manpower rose again, by 75,000 men to 3,650,000.

The Strategic Rocket Forces buildup continued with the deployment of 100 SS-19s, each carrying six kiloton-range MIRV's; 36 SS-18s, each with eight megaton-range MIRV's or one 20–25-megaton war-

A Soviet destroyer passes through the Strait of Dover off the English coast. One of the newest Krivak-class vessels, it carries guided missiles.

WIDE WORLD

head; and 20 SS-17s, each with four kiloton-range MIRV's. These replaced the older SS-11s, of which 900 remained, and the large SS-9s, of which 252 remained. The 140 SS-7s and 19 SS-8s were being phased out in favour of new SLBM's. A land-mobile ICBM, the SSX-16, and a MIRVed derivative, the SSX-20, were under development; it was uncertain whether the SSX-20 was an ICBM or an intermediate-range ballistic missile (IRBM). There were also 100 SS-5 IRBM's and 500 SS-4 medium-range ballistic missiles (MRBM's), the majority near the western border covering Western Europe, the rest east of the Urals aimed at China.

Soviet SLBM deployment moved closer to the SALT I ceiling of 950 (allowed if SLBM's replaced existing ICBM's). There were 785 SLBM's in this category: 7 H-class SSBN's each had 3 SS-N-5 SLBM's, 34 Y-class SSBN's each had 16 SS-N-6 SLBM's (1,750-mi range, megaton warhead), 13 D-1-class SSBN's each had 12 SS-N-8 SLBM's (4,800-mi range, megaton warhead), and 4 new D-II-class SSBN's each had 16 SS-N-8 SLBM's. Four to six Delta-class boats were being constructed per year. The Long-Range Air Force had 30 new Backfire B supersonic bombers capable of inflight refueling. Other aircraft included 450 Tu-16 and 170 Tu-22 medium-range bombers, 70 tankers (20 Tu-16s and 50 Mya-4s), and 100 Tu-95 and 35 Mya-4 bombers dating from 1956.

The massive Air Defense Force was enlarged further to 550,000 men, and equipment was being improved, notably through large-scale deployment of the MiG-25 interceptor and upgrading of the SA-5 SAM to give it a limited ABM capability. Actual ABM deployment remained at 64 Galosh missiles around Moscow, with another Try Add engagement radar being added. SAM launchers totaled 10,000 at over 1,000 sites, and interceptors numbered about 2,650, including 1,550 Yak-28P's, Tu-28P's, Su-15s, and MiG-25s.

The Army of 1,825,000 men was organized into 50 tank, 111 motor rifle, and 7 airborne divisions. Equipment was being improved to equal that of the West; the BMP-1 armoured personnel carrier, effectively an armoured fighting vehicle, was being introduced, together with the T-72 tank (formerly designated T-64 or M-1970), 1,000 of which had been built in the last two years. Total equipment included 41,500 tanks, 37,500 armoured fighting vehicles, 17,500 field and self-propelled guns and howitzers, and 8,500 mortars. Nuclear-capable SSM's numbered 1,000. Deployment had altered little, with the main concentration of forces aimed against Western Europe (31 divisions in Central and Eastern Europe, including 16 tank divisions with 9,000 medium and heavy tanks, and 64 divisions, including 23 tank divisions, in the European U.S.S.R.) and against China (43 divisions, including 7 tank divisions, on the China-Soviet border). The 31 divisions in Eastern Europe and a third of those in the European U.S.S.R. and the Far East were in the category 1 state of readiness, three-quarters to full strength with complete equipment.

Air Force strength also increased, to 450,000 men with 5,350 combat aircraft. Geared to support the Army, the Air Force was increasingly equipped with deep-interdiction, ground-attack aircraft such as the MiG-21J, MiG-23D, and Su-19, and with MiG-25 reconnaissance planes. There were 1,550 aircraft in the Air Transport Force, including 50 of the An-22 giant transports whose effectiveness was demonstrated in the Soviet airlift of Cuban forces to Angola. The defection of a Soviet pilot who flew his MiG-25 interceptor to Japan gave Western experts their first detailed look at the most advanced Soviet aircraft in service. This was a major intelligence windfall for the West, since examination of the plane would presumably reveal much about the state of Soviet aviation and electronics technology. It was later indicated to the press that the aircraft was not as advanced as had been previously believed. (*See* JAPAN.)

Naval modernization continued with the introduction of improved antiship missiles and torpedoes. The force of 450,000 men with 214 major surface combat vessels and 231 attack and cruise missile submarines (84 nuclear, 147 diesel) was second only to that of the U.S. The first Kiev-class carrier was operational in the Mediterranean, and two more were under construction. In combination with the heavy antiship missile armament carried by their escorting cruisers and destroyers and with the Naval Air Force of 645 combat aircraft, the new carriers could threaten the air superiority so long enjoyed by Western forces. The Navy's qualitative improvements and quantitative expansion had done much to counter the weakness inherent in its separation into four fleets: the Northern (126 submarines, including 54 nuclear; 51 major surface combat ships), the Baltic (12 submarines; 46 ships), the Black Sea, including the Mediterranean squadron (19 submarines; 59 ships), and the Pacific (74 submarines, including 30 nuclear; 57 ships).

NATO

The Vienna negotiations on mutual and balanced force reductions (MBFR) between NATO and the Warsaw Treaty Organization remained deadlocked. On Dec. 16, 1975, NATO had offered a new proposal, known as Option III, which offered the withdrawal of 1,000 obsolete tactical nuclear weapons, 54 F-4 nuclear-capable aircraft, 36 Pershing SSM's, and 29,000 U.S. troops in exchange for the withdrawal of a Soviet force of 1,700 tanks and 68,000 men. This would be linked to NATO's aim of a common ceiling for manpower, now set at 900,000 for each alliance.

The Soviet/Warsaw Pact response in February 1976 was to call for equal percentage cuts and ceilings for each country, and in June they submitted their first figures for the NATO-Warsaw Pact military balance from which reductions would be made. These figures (965,000 men for the Warsaw Pact against 977,000 for NATO) were unrealistic, however, and grossly underestimated the Pact's numerical superiority. In the area covered by MBFR, the Pact outnumbered NATO (including French forces) in ground troops (899,000 to 792,000), main battle tanks (15,700 to 6,755), and tactical aircraft (3,000 to 1,320).

Contrary to earlier assumptions, increased Pact interdiction capabilities made it unlikely that NATO could receive substantial U.S. reinforcements once war broke out. NATO was therefore increasingly dependent on the early, widespread use of the new generation of smaller, cleaner tactical nuclear weapons (mininukes) being deployed by the U.S. to stop a Pact attack. This, in turn, was linked to the credibility of the U.S. threat to go to strategic nuclear war in defense of Western Europe, and thus to the debate on the superpowers' strategic nuclear balance.

UNITED KINGDOM

The U.K. budget was tightened still further, reducing defense spending to $10,353,000,000 (£5,632 million) for 1976–77. Service manpower was not substantially reduced, however. The total armed forces of 344,150 were designed to contribute to NATO's defense of the

Central Front and to provide an independent nuclear deterrent against the U.S.S.R. The 174,900-man Army was equipped with 910 Chieftain medium battle tanks, 270 FV-101 Scorpion light tanks, 270 armoured fighting vehicles (with the Striker entering service), 120 armoured and 1,720 scout cars, 2,120 armoured personnel carriers (with the Spartan entering service), Vigilant and Swingfire antitank guided weapons (with the Milan antitank guided weapon on order), and Lance SSM's. The British Army of the Rhine (BAOR; to become the 5th Field Force) had 55,000 men. The U.K. Mobile Force, consisting of one division plus one parachute brigade, was earmarked to reinforce the BAOR, while the ACE Mobile Force (land) would protect its flanks. The need to find some 16,000 troops to police Northern Ireland was a constant strain, and the political debate over whether they should be withdrawn continued. (*See* UNITED KINGDOM.)

Air Force personnel totaled 90,200, equipped with 450 combat aircraft. The RAF was geared to support of the BAOR, including nuclear strikes, for which 50 Vulcan B2s and 56 Buccaneers were available. Close-support aircraft included the Anglo-French Jaguar (40 deployed, with more on order) and 48 Harriers. Phantom FG1/FGR2s were replacing Lightnings as the main interceptor.

The 76,350-man Royal Navy had 76 major surface combat vessels, including one aircraft carrier, one antisubmarine warfare carrier, 2 assault ships, 2 cruisers, 10 destroyers, and 60 frigates, mostly armed with Seaslug or Seacat SAM's. The four SSBN's with 16 Polaris A-3 missiles each were protected by 9 nuclear and 19 diesel attack submarines.

FRANCE

The effective reorientation of France's defense effort around deterrence of a Soviet attack on West Germany, as well as on France, was confirmed by the chief of staff, Gen. Guy Méry, who described it as a policy of "wider sanctuarization." This meant that France's modernized conventional forces would participate in the forward defense of NATO, although they had not been under NATO command since 1966.

Defense spending at $10,661,000,000 (3.9% of GNP) provided for a significant independent nuclear deterrent consisting of two SSBN's with 16 M-1 missiles (500-kiloton warhead, 1,550-mi range) each; one SSBN with 16 M-2s (1,900-mi range); and one with 16 M-20s (3,000-mi range, 1-megaton warhead) entering service. A fifth SSBN was building, and plans for a sixth were being studied. Additional underground tests for improved nuclear and thermonuclear warheads were conducted in the Pacific. Older nuclear forces included 18 S-2 IRBM's (1,875-mi range, 150-kiloton warhead), 36 Mirage IV-A bombers, and 24 Pluton SSM's (75-mi range, 15–25-kiloton warhead).

The 338,500-man Army was to be reorganized in the next four years. The Forces de Manoeuvre (58,000 men in two mechanized divisions in West Germany, plus three mechanized divisions in support in France) would be combined with the Territorial Defense Forces (Défense Opérationnelle du Territoire or DOT; about 52,000 men) to form eight armoured, six infantry, one parachute, and one alpine division. The new divisions would be smaller: 8,200 men to an armoured division and 6,500 men to an infantry division. Armour included 1,060 AMX-30 medium tanks, 1,120 AMX-13 light tanks, and 950 armoured fighting vehicles. A total of 22,000 men from all services were deployed overseas.

The Air Force, with 104,400 men, included 8 interceptor squadrons armed with Mirage III-C's, Mirage F-1s, and Super Mystère B-2s and 18 fighter-bomber squadrons with Mirage III-E's, Mirage M5-F's, and Jaguars. The 70,000-man Navy had 52 major surface combat vessels, including 2 aircraft carriers with 40 aircraft each, and 23 submarines; 4 more submarines were under construction.

WEST GERMANY

In size ($12,605,000,000), West Germany's defense budget was the largest in Western Europe and ranked high as a percentage of GNP (4.4%). The Army, with 345,000 men, was being restructured to form 16 armoured, 17 armoured infantry/*Jäger*, and 3 airborne brigades. Equipment included 2,600 Leopard and 1,400 M-48A2 medium tanks; 660 HS-30, 2,100 Marder, 1,300 Hotchkiss PZ4-5, and 3,350 M-113 armoured personnel carriers (700 M-113s were on order); and 1,120 antitank armoured fighting vehicles, including 350 with the SS-11 antitank guided weapon. Cobra, Milan, TOW, and HOT antitank guided weapons

West Germany's Leopard 2 battle tank carries a 120-millimetre gun. It has essentially the same armament, track, and engine as the new U.S. Army Abrams tank.

SVEN SIMON—KATHERINE YOUNG

KEYSTONE

The new British-French tactical strike/trainer Jaguar is designed for low-level close support, interdiction, and reconnaissance. It is being built under international agreement by British and French firms.

were being deployed in large numbers. The Lance SSM was entering service.

The Air Force had 111,000 men and 462 combat aircraft, including 120 F-4F Phantoms (interceptors and fighter-bombers), 144 F-104G interceptors, and 120 G-91 fighter-bombers, the last to be replaced by Alpha Jets. Missiles included 72 Pershing SSM's, 216 Nike Hercules, and 216 HAWK SAM's.

The Navy of 39,000 men (including the Naval Air Arm) had 24 coastal submarines, 11 destroyers, and 21 fast patrol boats with Exocet SSM's; 200 more Exocet SSM's were on order. Naval aircraft included 85 F-104G fighter-bombers and 30 RF-104G reconnaissance planes.

THE MIDDLE EAST

The Israeli airborne commando raid on Entebbe airport in Uganda the night of July 3/4 reinforced the Israelis' reputation for military ingenuity and efficiency. Three Hercules C-130H planes flew 100–200 elite antiterrorist troops 2,500 mi from Israel to Entebbe to free 103 hostages (mostly Israelis) from an Air France jet that had been hijacked by Palestinian terrorists en route from Tel Aviv to Paris and flown to Uganda. Seven of the terrorists were killed and seven MiG-21s and four MiG-17s supplied to Uganda by the U.S.S.R. were destroyed. Refueling of the Israeli planes for the return journey in Kenya was possible because Ugandan Pres. Idi Amin's threats against Kenya had led to strained relations between the two countries.

Although the September 1975 Sinai disengagement agreement with Egypt and the cease-fire with Syria on the Golan Heights remained in effect, Israel still felt that in the long run its only security lay in deterrence through conventional superiority over its Arab opponents, maintained with the help of increased U.S. support, and a minimal nuclear deterrent for use if Israel faced destruction. Israeli defense spending rose to $4,214,000,000, one of the highest defense budgets in the world in terms of percentage of GNP (35.9). The Army of 135,000, including 120,000 conscripts, could be brought to its full strength of 375,000 within 72 hours of mobilization. Equipment included 2,700 medium tanks with additional M-48s and M-60s on order from the U.S.; about 3,600 armoured fighting vehicles with M-113 armoured personnel carriers on order; Lance and Ze'ev SSM's with more Lance on order; and Redeye SAM's, again with more on order from the U.S.

The number of Air Force combat aircraft had increased to 543, among them 204 F-4E Phantoms, 50 Mirage III, and 33 Israeli-built Kfir ground-attack/interceptor-fighters, and 250 A-4H/N Skyhawk ground-attack aircraft. Those on order included 25 F-15 Eagles and 35 F-4s; more HAWK SAM's were also on order to supplement the 90 already deployed. The Navy consisted of 12 Saar- and 6 Reshef-class fast patrol boats armed with the Gabriel SSM; 6 more Reshef-class boats with the longer-range U.S. Harpoon SSM were on order.

It had become tacitly accepted that Israel had a small (10–20) stockpile of nuclear weapons of at least 20-kilotons yield which could be delivered against Arab capitals by Phantoms and Kfirs. The nuclear-capable Jericho SSM, with a 280-mi range, still had not been deployed, but an improved version was under development. The U.S. had quietly dropped plans to supply Israel with the 450-mi-range Pershing SSM but remained committed to a guarantee of Israel's physical survival.

Of Israel's main opponents, Egypt had been virtually cut off from Soviet military aid. It was still spending $4,859,000,000 on defense, however, and maintained large standing forces. The 295,000-man Army included the Air Defense Command with 75,000 men and about 200 MiG-21MF interceptors; 635 SA-2, SA-3, and SA-6 SAM's; and 2,500 antiaircraft guns tied into a highly sophisticated radar network. Armour included 1,100 T-54/55 and 820 T-62 medium tanks and 2,500 armoured personnel carriers, with artillery support from 1,300 guns ranging in calibre from 76 to 180 mm, antitank guided weapons, and Soviet-supplied SSM's with conventional warheads. The 30,000-man Air Force maintained its strength of about 500 combat aircraft, but 44 Mirage F-1s were on order from France.

Syria under Pres. Hafez al-Assad continued to receive Soviet aid. Some $1,003,000,000 was spent on defense, representing 15.1% of GNP. The 200,000-man Army included the Air Defense Command, equipped with SAM batteries, antiaircraft artillery, interceptors, and radar. Armoured strength, which had increased slightly, included 800 of the new Soviet T-62 medium tanks and 1,400 T-54/55 tanks; Syria also had 1,200 armoured personnel carriers. FROG-7 and Scud SSM's were deployed in small numbers. The Air Force, with 25,000 men, had increased its combat aircraft to 440, including 80 MiG-17, 60 Su-7, and 50 MiG-23 fighter/ground-attack aircraft and 220 MiG-21 interceptors. Soviet pilots probably manned the 20 MiG-25 reconnaissance aircraft.

Ironically, Syria's main military involvement in 1976 was not against Israel but in the Lebanese civil war. The entrance into Lebanon of a small Syrian force in April was followed by a major incursion beginning May 31. Syria's aims appeared to be a de facto partition of Lebanon between the warring Muslim and Christian factions and control over the Palestinian groups, notably Yasir Arafat's Palestine Liberation Organization (PLO), which had joined forces with the Lebanese Muslims.

In the face of guerrilla resistance, the Syrian intervention became stalled during the summer, but by October Syria had some 20,000 troops deployed in Lebanon and these, acting in combination with the Lebanese Christians, appeared to be gaining the upper hand. In mid-October six Arab leaders meeting in Saudi Arabia signed a peace plan calling for a ceasefire and an enlarged Arab peacekeeping force. Meanwhile, Israel was reportedly assisting Christians in southern Lebanon with the aim of preventing the return of the Palestinians to the border areas. (*See* LEBANON.)

U.S. support for Iran came under increasing domestic criticism as it became known that some 24,000 American advisers and their dependents were in the country and that this number was scheduled to rise to 60,000 by 1980. The presence of the Americans in Iran made it impossible for the shah to go to war without Washington's approval, but it also provided potential hostages for U.S. agreement to Iranian policies. Iranian arms purchases from the U.S. were unprecedented in size, totaling some $10.4 billion from 1972 through 1976. They included F-14A Tomcat fighters (15 operational and 65 on order), F-4D/E Phantoms (173 operational and 36 on order), and F-5A/E's (112 operational and 41 on order). A new order was also placed for 160 F-15 fighters. The Army had increased to 200,000 men and had more Chieftain tanks than the BAOR. Some 3,000 troops were deployed in Oman.

INDIA AND PAKISTAN

The Indo-Pakistani military balance remained stable at the conventional level, while India continued its policy of developing a military nuclear option without openly declaring that it was producing weapons. India's military forces, second only to China's in the area, were still capable of deterring any Chinese attack but were insufficient to extend India's influence overseas. At $2,812,000,000, defense spending was only 3% of GNP, but it provided for increased armed forces totaling 1,055,500 personnel.

The 913,000-man Army was equipped with 1,880 medium tanks and 700 armoured personnel carriers, plus 2,850 guns and howitzers ranging from 75 mm to 5.5 in. The Air Force, with 100,000 men, had about 950 combat aircraft; major modern types included 130 Su-7B and 80 HF-24 Marut 1A fighter-bombers and 275 MiG-21PFMA/MF/FL and 250 Gnat Mk I interceptors; 110 MiG-21MF's and 100 Ajeets (Gnats) were on order. The 42,500-man Navy, primarily a coastal defense force, had 26 frigates and 8 Osa-class fast patrol boats armed with the Styx SSM, plus 8 more on order.

Pakistan, which spent proportionately more on defense (7.2% of GNP; $807 million), had also increased its armed forces, to 428,000 personnel. Of these, 400,000 were in the Army, which was equipped with about 1,000 medium tanks, 400 armoured personnel carriers, and 1,000 guns and howitzers, ranging from 25 pounders to 155 mm. The 17,000-man Air Force had 217 combat aircraft, including 28 Mirage III-EP/DP's and 28 Mirage 5-PA's; 10 Mirage III-RP's were on order. The Navy, with 11,000 personnel, included four destroyers, four frigates, and three Daphne-class submarines, with three more on order.

FAR EAST

After the initial shock of North Vietnam's defeat and occupation of South Vietnam in 1975, the strategic picture in the Far East altered less than had been ex-

JEAN-PIERRE COUDERC—CAMERA PRESS

French tanks line up for night maneuvers near Versailles. They are armed with Pluton missiles.

KEYSTONE

Britain, West Germany, and Italy shared in the development and production of the FH-70 155-millimetre field howitzer, shown in demonstration in September.

pected. The dominant problem was still the trilateral struggle for power between the U.S., the U.S.S.R., and China, with each supporting indigenous groups favourable to its side and with the U.S. and China in a tacit alliance to contain the U.S.S.R. Chairman Mao Tse-tung's death in September further complicated an already uncertain scene.

North Vietnam, victor in the 30-year Indochinese war, incorporated South Vietnam into the Democratic Republic of Vietnam which, with a population of about 45 million, constituted a formidable second-rank power in the area. The North Vietnamese armed forces were reduced only slightly, to 615,000 personnel. The Army of 600,000 included 18 infantry divisions equipped with 900 T-34, T-54, and T-59 medium tanks, and 20 SAM regiments with 18 SA-2 launchers each. The 12,000-man Air Force had 80 MiG-17 and 30 Su-7 fighter/ground-attack aircraft and 30 MiG-19 and 50 MiG-21 interceptors.

In addition, North Vietnam had captured great quantities of South Vietnamese equipment, including 500 M-48 medium and M-41 light tanks, 1,200 M-113 armoured personnel carriers, 1,300 105-mm and 155-mm guns and howitzers, and 1,100 aircraft of various types. Nominally, these were worth some $2 billion, but their actual military value was uncertain since they depended on captured stocks of U.S. spare parts for maintenance. Captured small arms could be of use to Communist guerrilla groups supported by Vietnam. In practice, however, the Vietnamese leaders seemed preoccupied with domestic reconstruction, consolidating their hold on the South, and securing the Communist position in Laos, where a contingent of 35,000 Vietnamese troops posed a potential threat to Thailand.

In Cambodia the Khmer Liberation Army remained at about 80,000 men, organized into four divisions and three independent regiments. Deployed in small detachments on internal security duties, they were ruthlessly carrying out the xenophobic policies of the government. The 40,000-man Lao People's Liberation Army, successor to the Royal Lao Army, inherited limited amounts of U.S. equipment from its predecessor. On paper, the Thai armed forces with 210,000 personnel offered a good defense capability, but their combat value was doubtful, especially as U.S. aid diminished. A right-wing coup in October emphasized the determination of the Thai military to resist Communist influence and guerrillas.

To the south, Malaysia maintained armed forces totaling 62,300 personnel, including an army of 52,500 and an air force and navy with about 5,000 each. Malaysia was facing a limited revival of Communist insurgency, but it was shifting from the countryside to the cities and was being contained. About one-third of Indonesia's 180,000-man Army was tied down with civil and administrative duties. The Air Force of 28,000 men had only 30 combat aircraft, not all of them operational; a number of Soviet-supplied aircraft were in storage. The 38,000-man Navy also had a number of nonoperational ex-Soviet ships. Nevertheless, Indonesia consolidated its hold on the former Portuguese colony of Timor, which it had occupied late in 1975, and was receiving increased U.S. military aid. The U.S. was also building up its Diego Garcia base in the Indian Ocean as a major naval support facility. The Philippine armed forces of 78,000 included an army of 45,000 infantry and a navy and air force of 17,000 and 16,000 men, respectively—relatively small forces to deal with the guerrilla problems posed by Maoist and Muslim insurgents.

In China the People's Liberation Army (PLA), totaling three million men, continued to play an important political role. In the struggle for power that followed the death of Chairman Mao Tse-tung, the PLA supported the moderate Hua Kuo-feng, who had become premier after the death of Chou En-lai in January, against the radical group led by Mao's widow, Chiang Ch'ing, and including the chief political commissar of the PLA, Chang Ch'un-ch'iao. In October the radicals were arrested, and Hua Kuo-feng succeeded to Mao's positions of chairman of the Communist Party and head of the Military Commission, effectively commander in chief. (*See* CHINA.)

The PLA's senior officers had already indicated their fears that Mao's policy of depending on the two extremes of minimal nuclear deterrence and "people's war" to deter the Soviet Union might no longer be adequate. North Vietnam's victory had shown that large-scale operations by mechanized forces could still bring rapid military and political gains, leading PLA commanders to wonder whether they could deter or contain a similar action by the U.S.S.R. against, for example, the industrial base of Manchuria. The PLA was poorly equipped to do this. It had only ten armoured divisions with 8,000 tanks, mostly obsolete. The bulk of the PLA strength was infantry (121 divisions) and artillery (40 divisions). Similarly, the 250,000-man Air Force, although large numerically, had only relatively elderly armament, including CSA-1 (SA-2) SAM's and, among its 4,250 combat aircraft, 1,500 MiG-17 and 2,000 MiG-19 interceptors.

Four nuclear tests were held during the year, bringing the total to 21 since testing began in 1964, but the nuclear deterrent force remained minimal. About 20–30 IRBM's with a range of 1,500–1,750 mi had been deployed, as well as 30–50 MRBM's with a range of 600–700 mi. There were also 65 Tu-16 medium bombers with a radius of action of up to 2,000 mi, and fighter aircraft, including the Chinese built F-9, could be used for tactical nuclear delivery. But the stockpile of both nuclear and thermonuclear weapons was small (200–300); yields, from 20 kilotons to 3 megatons, were relatively low; and the delivery systems could become vulnerable to a Soviet first strike by the end of the decade.

One possible way for the Chinese to upgrade their forces was through the importation of Western technology. An example of this was China's agreement with Rolls Royce of the U.K. to provide the technology for the manufacture of the Spey jet engines used in British and U.S. military aircraft. It was being argued in Washington that a selective transfer to China of certain defensive technologies would be to the West's advantage, given the shared Western and Chinese interest in containing the U.S.S.R.

Of China's neighbours, Japan maintained only minimal conventional forces. The $5,058,000,000 (0.9% of GNP) spent on defense provided an army of 153,000 with 600 medium tanks, an air force of 43,000 with 448 combat aircraft, including 80 F-4EJ Phantoms, and a navy of 39,000 with 30 destroyers. The deficiencies of the air defense system were demonstrated when a Soviet defector landed his MiG-25 interceptor at Hakodate Airport without being intercepted. (See *U.S.S.R.*, above.) Japan finally ratified the 1968 nuclear nonproliferation treaty, but its major nuclear energy industry would enable it to manufacture nuclear weapons on short notice if necessary.

The continuing tension in divided Korea was brought to public attention by the killing of two U.S. officers in the demilitarized zone in August. (*See* KOREA.) U.S. forces in South Korea, including tactical nuclear weapons, remained as evidence of the U.S. guarantee of the South's independence. The South had 595,000 men under arms, including 520,000 in an army equipped with 840 M-47/48 medium tanks and 30,000 in an air force with 204 combat aircraft, among them 72 F-4D/E's, and 78 on order from the U.S. This compared with the North's 495,000-man armed forces: an army of 430,000 men with 1,150 T-34, T-54/55, and T-59 medium tanks and an air force of 45,000 men with 600 combat aircraft, including 300 MiG-15/17s and 150 MiG-21s.

Taiwan remained able to deter a conventional Chinese attack. It spent $1 billion on its 470,000-man armed forces, which included an army of 330,000 men with 1,500 medium tanks and an air force of 70,000 men with 268 combat aircraft.

AFRICA SOUTH OF THE SAHARA

The victory of the MPLA in the postindependence fighting for control of the former Portuguese colony of Angola was part of a general Soviet drive for influence in Africa that seriously threatened Western interests in that continent and reinforced black pressures against the white-controlled governments of Rhodesia and South Africa. By the end of 1976 Rhodesia had apparently accepted the inevitability of black majority rule, and South Africa's once unassailable position seemed threatened by external guerrilla activity and domestic unrest.

In Angola, the MPLA's two indigenous opponents, the National Front for the Liberation of Angola (FNLA) and the National Union for the Total Independence of Angola (UNITA), had been supported by a South Africa anxious to lessen the threat to Namibia (South West Africa) from guerrillas of the South West African People's Organization (SWAPO). South Africa feared that the guerrillas, then operating out of Zambia, could also use Angola as a base if the MPLA won. By October 1975 South African forces were directly intervening in support of FNLA/UNITA forces, and by mid-November they threatened the MPLA-controlled capital of Luanda.

The Soviet Union, which had been aiding the MPLA with military supplies, responded by increasing this aid and sending regular Cuban troops into Angola. The number of Cubans rose from 2,500 in November to 11,400 in January 1976, and they played a decisive role in the defeat of the anti-MPLA forces, which was largely accomplished by February. Soviet military aid to the MPLA amounted to over $200 million. U.S. military aid to the FNLA and UNITA had been much lower and was terminated by Congress, assuring the MPLA of an easy victory.

Secretary Kissinger's protests against the Soviet intervention by Cuban proxy had no effect, since they had no military or political backing. Nor was it clear that he was correct in arguing that the Angolan conflict was a test of strength between the two superpowers. The U.S.S.R. had long been committed to the MPLA and was unlikely to let its ally go down to defeat when decisive action could secure a quick victory. But the precedent was ominous. As experience had shown, successful intervention in one local conflict encouraged further interventions elsewhere, and the U.S.S.R. seemed certain to step up support for African guerrillas operating against Rhodesia and Namibia.

The Rhodesian government of Prime Minister Ian Smith, which had unilaterally declared its independence from the U.K. in 1965, found itself, by mid-1976, unable to ensure the security of the ruling white minority. The government of neighbouring Mozambique was allowing the Chinese-backed Zimbabwe People's Army (Zipa) under Robert Magube to launch guerrilla attacks across the border, and Rhodesian guerrillas were also based in Zambia. Rhodesia had only 278,000 whites in a population of 6,420,000. Its army totaled 7,900 men, with a reserve of 10,000, and its paramilitary force, the British South African Police, had 8,000 men active and 35,000 reservists. By May 1, 1976, increased guerrilla activity had forced partial mobilization, so that all men 17 through 25 years old who had completed conscript service were liable to be retained in the forces indefinitely.

The key factor in Rhodesia's independence had always been South African support, including the provision of military aid, but South African Prime Minister B. J. Vorster had clearly decided that the Smith regime was a lost cause. He had withdrawn the paramilitary forces of the South African Police and put pressure on Smith to transfer power to an African government. This Smith agreed to do in September, and although difficult negotiations appeared to lie ahead, it seemed clear that the days of white minority rule in Rhodesia were numbered.

South Africa, where 4.3 million whites ruled a population of 26,230,000, also faced increasing pressures on white minority rule. To counter guerrilla raids on Namibia, large-scale military operations had been undertaken to clear a fire-free zone along the border with Angola. Whether this would diminish the guerrillas' activities seemed doubtful, however, since large-scale Soviet aid would be available to them. South African military forces were capable of repelling a conventional attack. Army personnel numbered 38,000 plus reserves of 138,000, and equipment included 161 medium tanks and 1,050 armoured cars. The 8,500-man Air Force had 133 combat aircraft. How effective these forces would be against guerrillas with sophisticated Soviet equipment remained open to question, however. Domestic rioting by nonwhites during the year posed further problems for the South African security services, and defense spending rose to $1,494,-000,000, or 5.3% of GNP. (ROBIN J. RANGER)

See also Space Exploration.

[535.B.5.c.ii; 544.B.5–6; 736]

Demography

Birthrate trends in most of the industrialized countries, including the U.S., Canada, Australia, New Zealand, and Western Europe, had been generally downward since the late 1950s, with the decline more rapid in the years 1970–73 and less rapid in 1974 and 1975. In the few other countries that had reliable annual statistics the rates apparently fell slowly or remained stationary. During the same period death rates fell slowly or rose somewhat in countries like Denmark, Sweden, and the U.K. with "older" populations. The most significant effect of these changes was a slowing of the rate of population growth in industrialized countries. Countries for which reliable annual vital statistics were not available tended to have higher vital rates and rapid population growth. During this period the marriage rate had risen in some industrialized countries and fallen in others, with decreases predominating in 1974 and 1975, while the divorce rate rose steadily.

Birth Statistics. The rapid fall of the U.S. birthrate between 1970 and 1973 slowed in 1974–76. According to provisional figures, both the number of births and the birthrate (births per 1,000 population) decreased less than 1% from 1974 to 1975. Decreases of about 3% occurred in the first seven months of 1976 compared with the same period in 1975. The fertility rate (births per 1,000 women aged 15–44 years) also decreased in 1975 and the first seven months of 1976.

The birthrate and the fertility rate were 14.8 and 66.7, respectively, in 1975, compared with 15 and 68.4 in 1974. For the first seven months of 1976 the birthrate was 14.3, compared with 14.7 for the corresponding period of 1975, and the respective fertility rates were 64.1 and 66.4. The rate of natural population increase (excess of births over deaths per 1,000 population) was 5.8 in 1975 and 5.7 in 1974.

The latest available U.S. birth data by colour, age of mother, birth order, and other characteristics were for 1974. The crude birthrate for the white population, 14, continued to be much lower than for all other groups, 21.4. The fertility rate for white women in 1974, 64.7, was only 71% of the rate for women of all other races, 91. Of all births to white women in 1974, 6.5% were reported to be illegitimate, whereas the corresponding figure for nonwhite women was 42.7%. The number of white illegitimate births rose 3% in 1974, and the number of nonwhite illegitimate births went up 2%. However, the rate (illegitimate births per 1,000 unmarried women) fell slightly for the fourth consecutive year.

Birthrates declined between 1970 and 1974 for women in all age groups except those under 15 years. The largest declines, over 30%, were in the age groups 35 years and above, and the smallest was in the 15–19 year group. Rates for all birth-order groups fell between 1970 and 1974, the decline ranging from about 11% for second births to over 50% for fifth- and higher-order births. The most recent (June 1975) survey by the U.S. Bureau of the Census indicated that this trend toward fewer births per mother was likely to continue. The number of lifetime births expected per married woman was 2.2 for women aged 18–24 years and 2.3, 2.7, and 3.1 for the next three five-year age groups. The expectation data, combined with the continuing rapid declines in the rates for third- and higher-order births and for women at the higher ages, provided strong evidence that the two-child family was now regarded as the preferred size by most women.

In other countries where birth registration was considered by the UN to be 90% or more complete, the birthrate fell in 22 countries from 1974 to 1975 and rose in 7. As in the U.S., the rates of most developed countries had fallen between 1970 and 1975. The most recent UN data indicated that birthrates around the world ranged from about 10 per 1,000 population to over 50.

In recent decades the birthrate had been the most dynamic factor influencing rates of population increase in all parts of the world. The annual rate of natural increase ranged from an actual decrease or increases

Table I. Birthrates and Death Rates per 1,000 Population and Infant Mortality per 1,000 Live Births in Selected Countries, 1975*

Country	Birth-rate	Death rate	Infant mortality
Africa			
Egypt†	35.5	12.4	100.4
Mauritius†	27.5	7.3	46.3
Nigeria‡	49.3	22.7	...
South Africa‡	42.9	15.5	...
Tunisia	33.9	6.9	62.6‡
Asia			
Cyprus	16.9	9.1	29.2
Hong Kong†	19.7	5.2	16.8
Israel	28.3	7.2	22.0
Japan	17.2	6.4	10.1
Kuwait	43.6	4.8	44.3†
Lebanon§	24.5	4.3	13.6‖
Malaysia	33.2	6.5	36.4
Philippines†	26.1	6.9	58.9
Singapore	17.8	5.1	13.9
Thailand§	29.3	6.0	21.8
Europe			
Austria	12.3	12.7	20.8
Belgium	12.2	12.2	16.2†
Bulgaria	16.6	10.3	22.9
Czechoslovakia	19.5	11.5	20.9
Dermark†	14.1	10.2	11.5§
Finland	14.2	9.4	10.2†
France	14.1	10.6	11.1
Germany, East	10.8	14.3	15.7
Germany, West	9.7	12.1	21.1†
Greece	15.6	8.9	24.1
Hungary	18.4	12.4	32.6
Iceland	20.6	6.9	11.1
Ireland†	22.3	11.2	17.1
Italy	14.8	9.9	20.7
Netherlands, The	13.0	8.3	10.6
Norway	14.0	9.9	10.5†
Poland |	19.0	8.7	24.8
Portuga†	19.6	11.0	37.9
Romania†	20.3	9.1	35.0
Spain	18.3	8.2	13.8†
Sweden	12..6	10.8	8.3
Switzerland	12 4	8.8	12.5†
United Kingdom	12·4	11.8	16.0
Yugoslavia	18.1	8.6	40.5
North America			
Antigua†	18.3	7.1	31.4
Bahamas, The	18.1	3.9	29.2
Barbados†	19.5	8.4	37.7§
Canada†	15.4	7.4	15.0
Costa Rica†	29.5	5.0	37.6
Cuba†	22.3	5.7§	28.9§
El Salvador	40.1	8.0	58.3
Guatemala§	43.1	12.5	79.6
Jamaica	29.8	7.2	26.3†
Mexico	41.9	7.2	48.2
Panama	31.7	5.2	32.9†
Puerto Rico§	23.3	6.5	24.2
United States	14.8	9.0	16.1
Oceania			
American Samoa	40.1	4.4	21.4
Australia†	18.4	8.7	16.5§
Fiji	28.8	6.9	20.6†
Guam	30.4	4.2	20.2
New Zealand	18.4	8.1	16.0
Pacific Islands, Trust Terr. of	31.8	4.5	31.8
Western Samoa	34.9	7.0	40.1
U.S.S.R.	18.2	9.3	27.7†

*Registered births and deaths only.
†1974.
‡1970–75 UN estimate.
§1973.
‖1960.
Sources: United Nations, *Population and Vital Statistics Report;* various national publications.

of less than 10 per 1,000 population in most developed nations to well over 30 in some countries of Africa, Latin America, and Asia. Recent rates for some of the largest countries were U.S. 6; U.S.S.R. 9; Japan 13; China 18; Egypt 22; Pakistan 24; Nigeria 25; India 27; Brazil 28; and Indonesia 29.

Death Statistics. The provisional crude death rate for the U.S. in 1975 was 9 per 1,000 population, slightly below the rate of 9.2 for 1974. The rate for the first seven months of 1976, at 9.2, was slightly below that recorded for the same period in 1975 (9.3). All the age-specific death rates were lower in 1975 than in 1974. Rates for the 45–54 and 55–64 age groups were the lowest ever recorded in the U.S. However, the largest percentage declines between 1974 and 1975 were 5 and 7.4% in the 5–14 and 85-plus age groups, respectively.

The most recent available age-adjusted U.S. death rates were for 1974. Substantial differences by sex and by colour continued to be observed: in 1974 the age-adjusted rate for the male population was 1.8 times the rate for females, and the rate for persons other than white was 1.4 times the rate for the white population. By major causes of death, all rates were much higher for males than for females, except for diabetes, and much lower for whites than for all other races combined except for arteriosclerosis, suicide, and bronchitis, emphysema, and asthma.

The ranking of the ten leading causes of death in the U.S. in 1975 is shown below. There were no

Cause of death	Estimated rate per 100,000 population
All causes	896.1
Diseases of the heart	339.0
Malignant neoplasms (cancer)	174.4
Cerebrovascular diseases	91.8
Accidents	47.6
Influenza and pneumonia	27.0
Diabetes mellitus	16.8
Cirrhosis of the liver	15.1
Arteriosclerosis	13.7
Certain diseases of early infancy	12.8
Suicide	12.6

changes from the 1974 rank order. Rates for all these causes were lower in 1975 than in 1974, except for malignant neoplasms, influenza and pneumonia, and suicide, which were higher. Over the longer period of 1950–74, the age-adjusted rates for 5 of the 15 leading causes of death rose: cancer, cirrhosis of the liver, suicide, homicide, and bronchitis, emphysema, and asthma. Rates for all other leading causes fell.

As for the U.S., the crude death rates for European countries, Canada, Australia, New Zealand, Japan, and a few others had fluctuated within narrow limits for a decade or longer with a slowly downward trend. The few countries in other parts of the world that had reasonably complete statistics had generally reported declining rates, reflecting improvements in standards of living and health services. In 1975, among countries with at least 90% complete registration, 15 reported higher crude death rates than in 1974, 11 showed lower rates, and 1 reported no change.

Infant and Maternal Mortality. The infant mortality rate for the U.S. continued its long downward trend, falling from 16.7 deaths under 1 year per 1,000 live births in 1974 to the provisional rate of 16.1 in 1975, the lowest annual rate ever recorded for the U.S. Rates for white and nonwhite infants were also the lowest ever recorded for those groups, 14.4 and 22.9, respectively. Both the neonatal rate (infants under 28 days) and the postneonatal rate (28 days to 11 months) fell, the former from 12.3 to 11.7, the

"Welcome?"

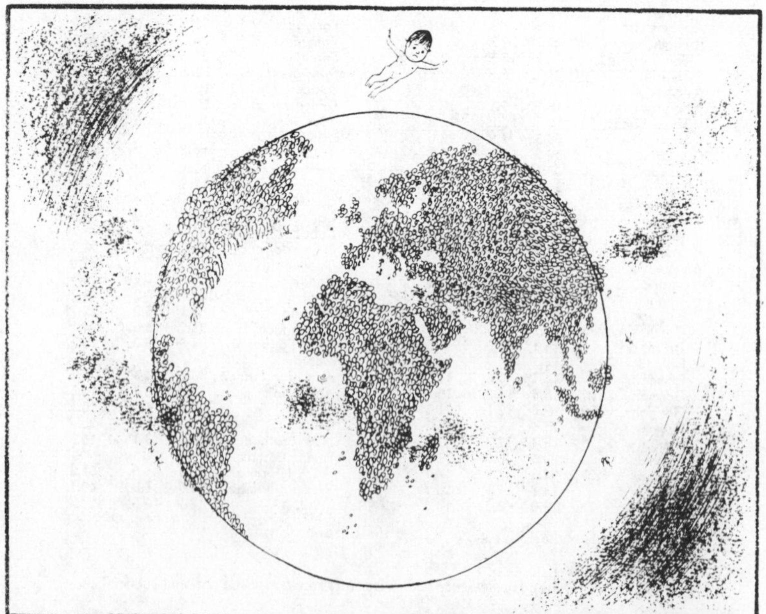

BEHRENDT—HET PAROOL, AMSTERDAM/ROTHCO

Table II. Life Expectancy at Birth, in Years, for Selected Countries

Country	Period	Male	Female
Africa			
Burundi	1975*	41.4	44.6
Egypt	1966	48.5	51.2
Liberia	1971	45.8	44.0
Madagascar	1966	37.5	38.3
Nigeria	1965–66	37.2	36.7
Upper Volta	1975*	37.5	40.6
Asia			
Hong Kong	1971	67.4	75.0
India	1966–70	48.2	46.0
Indonesia	1970–75	46.4	48.7
Israel	1973	70.2	73.2
Japan	1975	71.8	77.0
Korea, South	1970	63.0	67.0
Pakistan	1975*	52.4	52.1
Taiwan	1972	66.8	72.0
Thailand	1964–67	53.9	58.6
Europe			
Albania	1969–70	66.5	69.0
Austria	1974	67.4	74.7
Belgium	1968–72	67.8	74.2
Bulgaria	1969–71	68.6	73.9
Czechoslovakia	1973	66.8	73.6
Denmark	1972–73	70.8	76.3
Finland	1972	66.6	74.9
France	1972	68.6	74.4
Germany, East	1969–70	68.9	74.2
Germany, West	1972–74	67.9	74.4
Greece	1970	70.1	73.8
Hungary	1972	66.9	72.6
Iceland	1966–70	70.7	76.3
Ireland	1970–72	68.8	73.5
Italy	1970–72	69.0	74.9
Netherlands, The	1973	71.2	77.2
Norway	1972–73	71.3	77.6
Poland	1974	67.8	74.6
Portugal	1973	64.7	71.1
Romania	1972–74	66.8	71.3
Spain	1970	69.7	75.0
Sweden	1969–73	72.0	77.2
Switzerland	1969–72	70.2	76.2
United Kingdom	1972–74	69.2	75.6
Yugoslavia	1970–72	65.4	70.2
North America			
Barbados	1975*	68.0	73.0
Canada	1970–72	69.3	76.4
Costa Rica	1975*	68.5	72.1
Guatemala	1975*	54.9	56.6
Mexico	1965–70	61.0	63.7
Panama	1970	64.3	67.5
Puerto Rico	1971–73	68.9	76.1
United States	1974	68.2	75.9
Oceania			
Australia	1972	68.2	75.0
New Zealand	1970–72	69.1	75.2
South America			
Argentina	1970–75	65.2	71.4
Brazil	1975*	58.8	63.1
Chile	1969–70	60.5	66.0
Peru	1965–70	56.5	59.6
Surinam	1963	62.5	66.7
Uruguay	1963–64	65.5	71.6
Venezuela	1970–75*	62.9	66.7
U.S.S.R.	1970–71	65.0	74.0

*Projection.
Sources: United Nations, *Demographic Yearbook* (1974); *Statistical Yearbook 1975* (1976); official country sources.

latter from 4.4 to 4.3. Improvement continued in the first seven months of 1976, with a total infant mortality rate of 15.5, compared with 16.5 for the same period in 1975.

Among countries with 90% or more complete registration, the infant mortality rate ranged from about 12 for some Western European countries to over 30 for some other European countries. Rates for most countries in Africa and Asia were estimated by the UN to range from 75 to over 150, but reliable data were not available.

The provisional maternal mortality rate (deaths from complications of pregnancy per 100,000 live births) for the U.S. in 1975 was 10.8, below the record low reported final rate of 14.6 in 1974. Because of differences in definitions and classification procedures, maternal death rates are not comparable between the countries of the world.

Expectation of Life. The expectation of life at birth in the U.S. in 1975, based on provisional figures, was 72.4 years, appreciably higher than the 71.9 years for 1974. Expectation of life is the average number of years that an infant could be expected to live if the age-specific death rates observed during the year of birth were to continue unchanged throughout its lifetime. Obviously it is a hypothetical figure, but it is one that is very useful in measuring changes in the intrinsic rate of mortality.

According to 1974 final figures, the life expectancy for males was 68.2 years and for females, 75.9 years. For white persons it was 72.7 years and for all other persons, 67 years. It was significant that the expectation of life at birth in the U.S. was now 7.7 years longer for females than for males. This differential was also observed in the other technically advanced countries. In the less developed nations the female advantage was usually two or three years, and in a few countries of Africa and Asia estimated life expectancy for females was less than for males. (*See* Table II.)

Marriage and Divorce. In the U.S. both the number of marriages and the crude marriage rate per 1,000 population fell in 1975. The rate for 1975 was 10, compared with 10.5 in 1974. The decline began in 1973 when the number increased only slightly and the rate fell slightly. However, both the number and rate rose in the first seven months of 1976, the latter figure being 9.6, compared with 9.5 for the corresponding months of 1975.

Among countries where reporting was believed to be at least 90% complete, the marriage rate rose from 1974 to 1975 in 7 countries and fell in 12, with no change in 4 countries. Comparability of marriage rates between countries is limited by several factors in addition to completeness of reporting, most notably the frequency of unofficial or common law marriages in many countries of Africa, Asia, and Latin America.

Both the number and rate of divorces granted in the U.S. continued to increase in 1975. Provisional data indicated that the crude rate (divorces and annulments per 1,000 married persons) in 1975 was 4.8, compared with 4.6 in 1974. The number of divorces for the first seven months of 1976 was 9% above the same period in 1975.

The latest final U.S. statistics for 1974 showed that the median duration of marriage prior to divorce continued to fall and was 6.5 years in that year. However, it was only 8.3 years in 1900, indicating that, although more marriages now ended in divorce, the average time required for the marriage to fail had not changed greatly.

The average number of children affected was 1.1 per divorce in 1974, not significantly different from the previous four years. However, because more divorces were occurring, the number of minor children affected by divorce each year was now estimated to be about 1 million, compared with about 340,000, 20 years earlier.

Few or no divorces occur in Africa, Asia, and Latin America. In many countries divorce is forbidden or not recognized by law. Among the countries where divorce is permitted and reported with some reliability the U.S. consistently had the highest rate. Next highest in 1974 was Sweden, with 3.3 per 1,000 population. Other countries with high rates were East Germany, Denmark, Hungary, and the U.S.S.R. The trend of the divorce rate in most reporting countries had been upward for many years. (ROBERT D. GROVE)

See also Populations and Areas.
[338.F.5.b; 525.A; 10/36.C.5.d]

Denmark

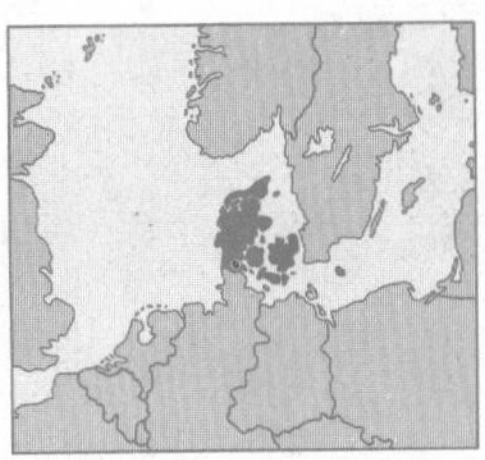

A constitutional monarchy of north central Europe lying between the North and Baltic seas, Denmark includes the Jutland Peninsula and 100 inhabited islands in the Kattegat and Skagerrak straits. Area (excluding Faeroe Islands and Greenland): 16,630 sq mi (43,074 sq km). Pop. (1975 est.): 5,059,000. Cap. and largest city: Copenhagen (pop., 1975 est., 729,400). Language: Danish. Religion: predominantly Lutheran. Queen, Margrethe II; prime minister in 1976, Anker Jørgensen.

The beginning of 1976 found the Danes on a buying spree as a result of the 1975 "September compromise," the reduction in value-added tax from 15 to 9¼% from the end of September 1975 to March 1, 1976, and also of the abandonment of a compulsory savings scheme. Imports increased and brought the balance of payments deficit to hitherto unseen heights. The tax reduction was intended to boost industry and create more jobs, but unemployment was only marginally influenced.

The April budget for 1976–77 was approved by the Folketing (Parliament). It forecast expenditures of 79 billion kroner and a deficit of about 15 billion kroner, with an estimated foreign debt of about 30 billion kroner. In parliamentary debate about the budget, the five parties behind the "September compromise"—the Social Democrat minority government with its allies—had difficulty keeping together. There were rumours of an early summer election which faded when it was seen that Mogens Glistrup's antitax Progress Party would be the only one to gain.

During the summer, the introduction of nuclear power in Denmark was vehemently debated, and popular opposition was strong enough for the government to decide to postpone the bill introducing nuclear power, pending further research into the question. A dispute between the government and the concession holder for the Danish North Sea sector about prospecting for natural gas there was settled; in 1977 Denmark would decide whether to exploit this natural gas.

Early in August the government negotiated the largest foreign loan in Denmark's history, borrowing $292.5 million from an international group of bankers. The loan was to cover the country's balance of payments deficit for the first half of 1976.

In an effort to stabilize the economy, the Social Democratic government tried to work out arrangements for an economic compromise that would be acceptable to other parties in Parliament and to employers and trade unions. It presented this as a package of 17 bills in August. Faced with strong opposition in Parliament, it was forced to ally itself with the Conservative Party in order to get the program passed. The program called for a cut in spending, controls on prices, profits, and dividends, and a limit of 6% a year on wage increases. It also raised taxes on consumer goods such as tobacco, alcoholic beverages, cars, gasoline, coffee, and sugar. The higher levies were expected to cost the average Danish family between $500 and $600 a year.

While the austerity plan was being debated, more than 15,000 workers gathered in front of the Parliament building to protest the wage clause. The left-wing parties vigorously opposed the "August compromise" for abolishing free negotiation in the labour market and as bearing oppressively upon the working class. They also opposed its tax provisions. Glistrup and his Progress Party attacked the compromise as destroying "the will to work" and advocated cuts in the public sector and in taxes.

Glistrup's party gained increasing popular support (20–25% of the electorate, according to autumn opinion polls), and the threat of his success was the one issue that promised to unite the other ten parties in Parliament which accused him of irresponsibility.

When Parliament reopened in October Prime Minister Jørgensen urged the legislators to unite in confronting Denmark's economic problems. The problems included 100,000 unemployed; a growing balance of payments deficit; and the desperate need to restrain rising prices and costs in order to keep Denmark's goods competitive in world markets. Indeed, inflation was slacking off: in 1974 prices had risen by 15%, in 1975 by 9%, and in the first six months of 1976 by an annual rate of 6%; but an export increase of 11% was overmatched by imports at 25%. Holding down wage increases would be the most important prerequisite for the success of the "August compromise," although there was some question as to whether the incomes policy would be able to survive the spring 1977 round of wage negotiations. (STENER AARSDAL)

See also Dependent States.

[972.A.6.a]

DENMARK

Education. Primary, pupils (1974–75) 559,745; secondary, pupils (1974–75) 283,318; primary and secondary, teachers (1974–75) 58,425; vocational and teacher training (1973–74), pupils 112,159, teachers (teacher training only) 1,119; higher (including 5 main universities), students (1973–74) 85,284, teaching staff (1974–75) 7,865.

Finance. Monetary unit: Danish krone, with (Sept. 20, 1976) a free rate of 5.95 kroner to U.S. $1 (10.26 kroner = £1 sterling). Gold, SDR's, and foreign exchange (June 1976) U.S. $931 million. Budget (1974–75 est.): revenue 65,123,000,000 kroner; expenditure 61,402,000,000 kroner. Gross national product (1974) 183,710,000,000 kroner. Money supply (March 1976) 49,960,000,000 kroner. Cost of living (1970 = 100; May 1976) 169.

Foreign Trade. (1975) Imports 59,708,000,000 kroner; exports 50,031,000,000 kroner. Import sources: EEC 46% (West Germany 20%, U.K. 10%, The Netherlands 6%); Sweden 14%; U.S. 6%; Norway 5%. Export destinations: EEC 47% (U.K. 19%, West Germany 13%, Italy 5%); Sweden 15%; Norway 7%; U.S. 5%. Main exports: machinery 21%; meat 15%; chemicals 7%; ships and boats 6%; dairy products 5%.

Transport and Communications. Roads (1974) 65,664 km (including 367 km expressways). Motor vehicles in use (1974): passenger 1,256,318; commercial 211,128. Railways: (1974) state 1,999 km; private 494 km; traffic (state only; 1974–75) 3,190,000,000 passenger-km, freight 2,040,000,000 net ton-km. Air traffic (including apportionment of international operations of Scandinavian Airlines System; 1975): 2,185,000,000 passenger-km; freight 97,767,000 net ton-km Shipping (1975): merchant vessels 100 gross tons and over 1,371; gross tonnage 4,478,112. Shipping traffic (1974): goods loaded 7,852,000 metric tons, unloaded 31,701,000 metric tons. Telephones (including Faeroe Islands and Greenland; Dec. 1974) 2,164,000. Radio receivers (Dec. 1974) 1,680,000. Television licenses (Dec. 1974) 1,527,000.

Agriculture. Production (in 000; metric tons; 1975): wheat 541; barley 5,194; oats 379; potatoes 661; sugar, raw value 423; apples (1974) *c.* 100; rapeseed *c.* 100; butter 138; cheese 152; pork (1974) *c.* 760; beef and veal (1974) *c.* 235; fish catch (1974) 1,835. Livestock (in 000; July 1975): cattle 3,048; pigs 7,748; sheep 59; horses (1974) *c.* 50; chickens *c.* 16,124.

Industry. Production (in 000; metric tons; 1975): crude steel 557; cement (1974) 2,493; fertilizers (nutrient content; 1974–75) nitrogenous 83, phosphate 102; manufactured gas (cu m) 319,000; electricity (net; excluding most industrial production; kw-hr) 17,151,000. Merchant vessels launched (100 gross tons and over; 1975) 983,000 gross tons.

Dependent States

One dependent state, Seychelles, achieved full independence with international recognition in 1976; the independence of Transkei, proclaimed on October 26, was recognized only by South Africa. (*See* SEYCHELLES; SOUTH AFRICA; TRANSKEI.) Other dependent territories, in the Caribbean and the Pacific, drew in their horns and opted for a year or two's postponement of the grant of independence; still others demanded self-government rather than full independence; and all were aware that in the prevailing state of world trade their insecure economies had need of external support, either through direct aid from the sovereign power or through association with partners. In North and East Africa belligerent politics cast a shadow over the former Spanish Sahara and the French Territory of the Afars and Issas. However small the dependent territories and wherever they were, most of them nursed vociferous and easily excited independence movements.

Europe and the Atlantic. In Gibraltar elections held on September 29 produced a clear victory for the Labour Party and its rejection of accommodation with Spain over the colony's future status.

In the French North Atlantic islands of Saint Pierre and Miquelon, the French government, with the agreement of the local population, proposed that the territory's status should advance toward that of an overseas département after a period of transition. The proposed plan of development was approved by the territory's General Council in June and was adopted by the French Senate in July.

Argentina's claims to the British Falkland Islands in the South Atlantic were sharpened by rumours of oil. The British Shackleton Mission sent out to the Falklands in January was obliged to proceed by Royal Navy survey ship, since air access, only possible via Argentina, was refused by the Argentine government. The 2,000 Falklanders, like the Gibraltarians, unanimously desired to stay British, and the Shackleton report recommended £5 million in aid for development and for the construction of an adequate airstrip.

Caribbean. It seemed likely in 1976 that each of the Commonwealth Caribbean associated states, despite the basic drawbacks of small size and limited resources, would seek and attain independence within

Dentistry:
see Health and Disease

two years. This had been advocated by the Caribbean Community and Common Market heads of government conference in December 1975. Whether or not this independence would be coupled with interdependence remained an open question.

St. Lucia, which had long advocated multi-island interdependence, was quick to announce that it would seek to go it alone by the end of 1976, but this date was subsequently postponed. The opposition St. Lucia Labour Party (SLP) wished Prime Minister John Compton to hold an election or a referendum first. At the beginning of 1976 St. Lucia suffered further outbreaks of violence, attributed to SLP fringe elements, including members of a Ras Tafarian (politico-religious) cult. Independence was seen as likely to remove British governmental constraints on the desired expansion of the island's tourist and agro-industrial investments. A banana workers' strike in June lasted six weeks and cost ECar$170,000.

In St. Kitts-Nevis, Prime Minister Robert Bradshaw's Labour Party, in power for 25 years, was returned again on Dec. 1, 1975; the main issues in the election were independence, public ownership of all sugar lands, and no secession for Nevis. However, both seats on Nevis were won by the separatist Nevis Reformation Party, which embarked on the type of separatist campaign waged by Anguilla in 1967. Anguilla officially became a self-governing British territory in February 1976. Issues in an election held in mid-March included possible leasing of Dog Island to the U.S. Department of Defense for artillery practice, a proposal that incensed local fishermen. Ronald Webster and his Progressive People's Party won 58% of the vote and six out of seven seats in the Legislative Assembly.

In Antigua the mechanics of granting independence rather than independence itself became a platform issue in the February elections. Prime Minister George Walter's Progressive Labour Movement (PLM), which favoured negotiation, was ousted, though by a minority vote, by Vere Bird's Labour Party, which was campaigning for a referendum. Bird won 10 out of 17 seats to Walter's 5. After his victory Bird, long a supporter of regional integration, tended to soft-pedal immediate independence and to emphasize plans for improving the economy and rebuilding overseas investors' confidence. Unemployment stood at 47%, the island had an ECar$90 million deficit, and sugar production on its dry and poorly cropped land had stopped in 1971. Bird's plans included a Bahamas-style abolition of the income tax, the development of tourism, the reintroduction of cane, and the expansion of agriculture.

Milton Cato's St. Vincent Labour Party was committed to independence but seemingly in no hurry to fix a date. A revival of the island's sugar industry for local consumption was planned, and moves were started to assist the dwindling tourist trade. In Dominica the idea of political independence caused little excitement. Prime Minister Patrick John took the view that it was of no value unless the state could be economically independent, and in December 1975 he stated his commitment to some sort of interdependence including a possible arrangement with the neighbouring French territories of Martinique and Guadeloupe. John visited France in January 1976 to discuss economic and cultural cooperation.

In the French Antilles the most publicized event was the evacuation of 70,000 people from Guadeloupe in August after the volcano La Soufrière became active. In Martinique Émile Maurice was reelected president in the cantonal elections. The economy was reported to be stagnating and tourism was suffering, while the population was expanding. Unemployment stood at 25%. In French Guiana the plan put forward by France's secretary of state for overseas departments and territories, Olivier Stirn, to recolonize the territory in order to exploit its resources found many thousands of French applicants and also galvanized into opposition the independence movement and extreme-left organizations. In May Stirn announced his "green plan" for development, including pulp plants and Fr 300 million to improve ports and roads.

CAMERA PRESS/PHOTO TRENDS

This wine-making establishment on the east coast of Corsica became a symbol of Corsican nationalism. Owned by a resettled French colonist from Algeria, it was seized by a group of Corsican nationalists in August 1975 in protest against French policies. One of the leaders, Edmond Simeoni, received a five-year prison sentence in June 1976.

The Netherlands Antilles—Curaçao, Aruba, Bonaire, St. Martin, Saba, and St. Eustatius—were reported to fear independence, except for Aruba, which was taking a go-it-alone line and seeking support from Venezuela. Antilles Prime Minister Juancho Evertsz won a promise from the Dutch government not to push independence until at least 1980 and to retain the Dutch garrison until that date.

Independence for Belize continued to be complicated by Guatemala's claim to the territory. The military threat from Guatemala abated after the earthquake of February 1976, which also forced the postponement of talks. These subsequently ended in failure. Meanwhile Belize had won overwhelming UN support for its right to self-determination, territorial integrity, and independence, marking a considerable shift in Latin-American attitudes. The issue was further complicated by the possibility of offshore oil.

In Bermuda the ruling United Bermuda Party retained a majority in the May general election (26 seats to 14) but lost 4 seats to the Progressive Labour Party led by Lois Browne Evans. A coroner's jury cited two men serving sentences for armed robbery as the killers of former Gov. Richard Sharples and his aide, Capt. Hugh Sayers, in March 1973. At the trial in June and July 1976 one of them was cleared; the other, Erskine Burrows, was sentenced to death.

The 1966–74 development explosion in the Cayman Islands had slowed to near stagnation by 1976. Tourism had risen from 8,054 visitors in 1966 to 54,145 in 1975, and the offshore financial sector remained healthy, despite a flurry of liquidations in 1974 and the continuing threat that the U.S. Internal Revenue

Service would investigate possible tax evasion. The construction sector was shrinking, however, and there were no alternative industries to offer employment. The government's notable improvements in education and other services were balanced against its land-development plans, reportedly resented by many of the electorate. In the elections of Nov. 10, 1976, for the 12-member Legislative Assembly, seven members lost their seats, including all four elected members of the Executive Council, but policy was expected to remain unchanged.

Despite the U.S. recession, the British Virgin Islands showed a modest rise in tourism, from 58,486 visitors in 1974 to 64,568 in 1975. Tourism had been largely limited to the luxury trade, however, and further development depended on attracting a broader socioeconomic cross-section of visitors. In the U.S. Virgin Islands fears that the runway at Charlotte Amalie's Harry S. Truman Airport on St. Thomas Island was dangerously short were reawakened when an airliner crashed there on April 27. (*See* DISASTERS.)

In October, at the end of a week of talks, the U.S. assured the Panamanian government that a solution would be found to the Canal Zone dispute. Panama, in its statement, said that it would press for a reasonable arrangement leading to a treaty extending no further than the year 2000. (*See* PANAMA.)

In Puerto Rico the severity of recession had been somewhat eased by U.S. financial aid and by the Food Stamp Program, under which the poor could buy cheap coupons that could be exchanged for food. Although Puerto Rico's per capita income of nearly $2,000 was higher than that of any Latin-American country except Venezuela, unemployment, chronic at about 10%, was running at 22% by January. Both right and left acknowledged the economy's critical state, and there was a revival of the movement for independence from the U.S., but the parties favouring independence received only about 6% of the vote in the November election. Carlos Romero Barceló of the pro-statehood New Progressive Party defeated incumbent governor Rafael Hernández Colón, candidate of the Popular Democratic Party which supports continued commonwealth status, and the New Progressives captured both houses of the legislature.

Africa. The situation in South West Africa (Namibia) was complicated by the Angolan war and the support given to the South West Africa People's Organization (SWAPO), which demanded complete and unified independence from South Africa, by the victorious Popular Movement for the Liberation of Angola (MPLA). The MPLA government harboured SWAPO guerrillas, who continued to operate despite the clearing of the border on the Namibian side by South African forces (in Operation Cobra) and the setting up of a checkpoint at Ruacana for workers on the Cunene Dam. The dam, of immense economic importance to both Angola and Namibia, was condemned by liberation movements because of its current political implications. The security of the dam was also vital to British interests in the Rossing uranium mine (expected to become the world's biggest), which feared that SWAPO had already come to terms with the U.S.S.R. regarding future control of the mine. South African plans to set up an interim government (protecting minorities) in Namibia and to grant independence in 1978, still under discussion at a constitutional conference at Windhoek, were opposed by SWAPO.

Two other areas continued to divide the Organization of African Unity (OAU), and no solution was in sight. Under the Madrid Agreement of November 1975, Spain had finally ceded Spanish Sahara to Morocco and Mauritania. The last Spanish troops left for the Canary Islands on Jan. 12, 1976, and there was a final handover on February 26. Partition of the territory between Morocco and Mauritania was unacceptable to Algeria, however, and after some border skirmishing Algeria broke off diplomatic relations in March with Morocco and Mauritania and declared its firm support for Polisario, a largely indigenous movement prepared to fight for independence. Arab and French attempts at mediation failed, and Morocco and Mauritania threatened to leave the OAU if it recognized Polisario's "Saharan Arab Democratic Republic." Polisario continued to mount raids, culminating with an attack on the Mauritanian capital of Nouakchott in June. The issue was complicated by economic and international questions. Algeria sought an outlet for its Tindouf iron ore, coveted by Morocco; Morocco for its part aimed to control the Bu Craa phosphate deposits and become the world's largest phosphate producer.

The second area over which OAU opinion was divided was the French Territory of the Afars and Issas, or Djibouti. On tribal and strategic grounds, the territory was the subject of rival claims by Somalia and Ethiopia, backed, respectively, by the U.S.S.R. and the U.S. In December 1975 France had agreed to Djibouti's independence, provided there was a constitutional referendum first, and its sizable contingent of soldiers remained to keep rival factions at bay. In an incident that cast a shadow over the negotiations concerning independence, a bus carrying some 30 French schoolchildren was hijacked near Djibouti on February 3 by members of an illegal Somalia-based independence group. French troops attacked the bus near the Somali border, killing six hijackers; one child was also killed and several were injured, and the troops exchanged fire with Somali soldiers across the border.

On July 17 the head of the Djibouti government, Ali Aref Bourhan, resigned under pressure, together with his ministers, and was succeeded by Abdallah Mohammed Kamil. The change of leadership came six months after the nomination of a new French high commissioner and was interpreted as a step to decrease local tension. In October it was announced that the referendum to decide the question of independence would be held in the spring of 1977. Somalia

Puerto Ricans seeking independence for their island from the U.S. gather outside the capitol in San Juan to hear their leader, Rubén Berríos Martínez. Neither of the two pro-independence parties made significant gains in the November election, which was won by a party favouring statehood.

UPI COMPIX

refused to agree to the referendum or to guarantee the territory's independence, since this would "limit the people's option."

Indian Ocean. In the Comoro Islands, which unilaterally declared their independence from France in July 1975 and were admitted to the UN in November of that year, one island, Mayotte, which had a considerable French base, twice overwhelmingly voted to remain French. In the February 1976 referendum the vote was 17,845 to 104. France itself was attacked in the UN and elsewhere for its acquiescent support of Mayotte's stand. In spite of financial aid from France, the economy of Réunion continued to stagnate.

Pacific. When the separation of Tuvalu (created on Oct. 1, 1975; formerly Ellice Islands) from the Gilbert Islands went into effect on Jan. 1, 1976, Funafuti, the capital of Tuvalu, was still recovering from the devastation of a hurricane in 1972. The U.K. pledged A$4 million as an establishment and development grant and Tuvalu was also aided to the extent of A$400,000 in its recurrent budget of A$1 million. Tuvalu might opt for independence in 1977 without a prior period of self-government, since in practice many of the reserved powers, such as foreign affairs, were already being exercised by a triumvirate of ministers elected from the House of Assembly. The Gilbert Islands were to receive self-government on Jan. 1, 1977, with independence to follow in 1978. By 1978 the phosphate resources of Ocean Island (Banaba), which provided considerable employment and revenue, would be exhausted. The people of Banaba claimed independence and association with Fiji, but their claim was not recognized by Britain despite the islanders' litigation in England's High Court of Justice. In one suit, for additional royalties as compensation for the sale of Banaban phosphates at prices that were too low, the judge ruled that the matter was not in the court's jurisdiction but called attention to "grave breaches of . . . obligations" by the British government.

France faced increasing unrest in its Pacific territories, caused not only by its proposed use of Wallis and Futuna as a nuclear experimental base but also by deepening divisions in the New Hebrides condominium, which it shared with Britain, and by greater demands for self-government in nickel-rich New Caledonia. In the New Hebrides the movement for autonomy, Nagriamel, demanded French and British withdrawal from the territory before August 1976. Elected in November 1975, the first representative assembly met on April 29, 1976, in a strained atmosphere; it was not until June 29 that it held its first session, in the course of which British and French representatives reaffirmed their countries' willingness to further independence.

In New Caledonia the year was marked by a mounting tide of opinion in favour of internal autonomy, which swung the territorial assembly in its favour in October. In July Olivier Stirn had to postpone a visit to Nouméa. There were demonstrations in January, after the killing of a Melanesian by a policeman the previous month. The adherents of self-determination in French Polynesia kept up their pressure. In June they forced suspension of the territorial assembly, and in September autonomist deputy Francis Sanford was reelected. Economic and social difficulties and the continuation of nuclear tests (two at Mururoa Atoll on July 10 and 22) by the French contributed to the support for autonomy.

NORMA/KATHERINE YOUNG

On guard in Afars and Issas. The French territory, soon to become independent, is located on the strategic Strait of Bab el-Mandeb, which connects the Red Sea with the Gulf of Aden and the Indian Ocean.

The Solomon Islands attained self-government on January 2, following the 1975 London constitutional talks with Chief Minister Solomon Mamaloni. Independence within two years was promised, but this was contested locally as coming too soon. In U.S. Micronesia, the last of the 11 trusteeship territories, the northern Mariana group took another step toward commonwealth status within the U.S. when Pres. Gerald Ford signed enabling legislation on March 24. The draft constitution for the independence of the Marshall Islands and the Caroline Islands remained in dispute, largely over the question of U.S. land use and control.

Portuguese Timor was taken over by Indonesia as a 27th province in July, following military intervention in December 1975 and a rubber-stamp acquiescence by the People's Assembly at Dili. The takeover was reluctantly accepted by Australia in the face of UN inaction. Rebel bands continued to operate on the borders of Irian Jaya (former West New Guinea), to the embarrassment of the Papua New Guinea government which feared further Indonesian interference. A West New Guinea government-in-exile established in Senegal in July 1975 continued to receive support from African states, which saw the Melanesian peoples as the eastern flank of the pan-black world.

The governor of the Portuguese possession of Macau was authorized by Lisbon on October 9 to conduct relations with foreign states and conclude international agreements. The sultan of Brunei, fearing Malaysian designs on the territory, endeavoured in 1976 to discourage the British from their proposed withdrawal of protection over the sultanate.

(PHILIPPE DECRAENE; BARRIE MACDONALD; MOLLY MORTIMER; SHEILA PATTERSON)

See also African Affairs; Commonwealth of Nations; United Nations.

Dependent States

ANTARCTIC

Claims on the continent of Antarctica and all islands south of 60° S remain in status quo according to the Antarctic Treaty, to which 19 nations are signatory. Formal claims within the treaty area include the following: Australian Antarctic Territory, the mainland portion of French Southern and Antarctic Lands (Terre Adélie), Ross Dependency claimed by New Zealand, Queen Maud Land and Peter I Island claimed by Norway, and British Antarctic Territory, of which some parts are claimed by Argentina and Chile. No claims have been recognized as final under international law.

AUSTRALIA

CHRISTMAS ISLAND

Christmas Island, an external territory, is situated in the Indian Ocean 875 mi NW of Australia. Area: 52 sq mi (135 sq km). Pop. (1976 est.): 3,300. Cap.: The Settlement (pop., 1971, 1,300).

COCOS (KEELING) ISLANDS

Cocos (Keeling) Islands is an external territory located in the Indian Ocean 2,290 mi W of Darwin, Australia. Area: 5.5 sq mi (14 sq km). Pop. (1976 est.): 540.

NORFOLK ISLAND

Norfolk Island, an external territory, is located in the Pacific Ocean 1,035 mi NE of Sydney, Australia. Area: 13 sq mi (35 sq km). Pop. (1976 est.): 1,600. Cap. (de facto): Kingston.

DENMARK

FAEROE ISLANDS

The Faeroes, an integral part of the Danish realm, are a self-governing group of islands in the North Atlantic about 360 mi W of Norway. Area: 540 sq mi (1,399 sq km). Pop. (1975 est.): 40,400. Cap.: Thorshavn (pop., 1975 est., 11,300).

Education. (1974–75) Primary, pupils 5,958; secondary, pupils 2,276; primary and secondary, teachers 421; vocational, pupils 1,301, teachers (1966–67) 88; teacher training, students 107, teachers (1966–67) 12; higher, students 24.

Finance and Trade. Monetary unit: Faeroese krone, at par with the Danish krone, with (Sept. 20, 1976) a free rate of 5.95 kroner to U.S. $1 (10.26 kroner = £1 sterling). Budget (1974–75 est.): revenue 196,314,000 kroner; expenditure 195,077,000 kroner. Foreign trade (1974): imports 607 million kroner; exports 487 million kroner. Import sources: Denmark 65%; Norway 19%; U.K. 5%. Export destinations: Denmark 22%; U.K. 12%; Italy 11%; Spain 11%; U.S. 8%; Norway 6%; West Germany 5%; France 5%. Main exports: fish and products 89% (including fish meal 15%).

Transport. Shipping (1975): merchant vessels 100 gross tons and over 151; gross tonnage 49,617.

Agriculture and Industry. Fish catch (metric tons; 1974) 247,000. Livestock (in 000; Dec. 1973): sheep *c.* 72; cattle *c.* 3. Electricity production (1974–75) *c.* 90 million kw-hr (*c.* 61% hydroelectric).

GREENLAND

An integral part of the Danish realm, Greenland, the largest island in the world, lies mostly within the Arctic Circle. Area: 840,000 sq mi (2,175,600 sq km), 84% of which is covered by ice cap. Pop. (1975 est.): 49,500. Cap.: Godthaab (pop., 1975 est., 8,300).

Education. (1974–75) Primary, pupils 10,385; secondary, pupils 2,190; vocational, pupils 722; primary, secondary, and vocational, teachers 1,044; teacher training, students (1970–71) 58, teachers (1967–68) 3.

Finance and Trade. Monetary unit: Danish krone. Budget (1973 est.) balanced at 58,282,000 kroner. Foreign trade (1974): imports 634 million kroner (89% from Denmark, 6% from U.K.); exports 551 million kroner (32% to Denmark, 26% to France, 23% to Finland, 11% to West Germany, 7% to U.S.). Main exports: zinc ores 49%; fish and products 34%; lead ores 12%.

Agriculture. Fish catch (metric tons; 1974) 51,000. Livestock (in 000; Nov. 1973): sheep 21; reindeer 0.8.

Industry. Production (in 000; metric tons; 1974): lead ore (metal content) *c.* 24; zinc ore (metal content) *c.* 88; electricity (kw-hr; 1973) 110,000.

FRANCE

AFARS AND ISSAS

The self-governing overseas territory of Afars and Issas is located on the Gulf of Aden between Ethiopia and Somalia. Area: 8,900 sq mi (23,000 sq km). Pop. (1976 est.): 226,000. Cap.: Djibouti (pop., 1976 est., 120,000).

Education. (1975–76) Primary, pupils 10,469, teachers 336; secondary, pupils 1,644, teachers 96; vocational, pupils 670, teachers 59; teacher training, students 11, teachers 4.

Finance. Monetary unit: Djibouti franc, with (Sept. 20, 1976) a free rate of DjFr 163 to U.S. $1 (DjFr 280 = £1 sterling). Budget (1973 est.) balanced at DjFr 2,955,000,000.

Foreign Trade. (1973) Imports DjFr 12,675,060,000; exports DjFr 3,498,540,000. Import sources: France 49%; Ethiopia 12%; Japan 6%; U.K. 6%. Export destinations: France 84%. Main exports: ships and boats 16%; leather and shoes 7%.

Transport. Ships entered (1971) vessels totaling 5,788,000 net registered tons; goods loaded (1973) 142,000 metric tons, unloaded 728,000 metric tons.

FRENCH GUIANA

French Guiana is an overseas département situated between Brazil and Surinam on the northeast coast of South America. Area: 34,750 sq mi (90,000 sq km). Pop. (1974 census): 55,100. Cap.: Cayenne (pop., 1974, 30,500).

Education. (1973–74) Primary, pupils 6,830, teachers (1971–72) 315; secondary (1972–73), pupils 4,227, teachers 229; vocational, pupils 1,240, teachers 79.

Finance and Trade. Monetary unit: French (metropolitan) franc, with (Sept. 20, 1976) a free rate of Fr 4.92 to U.S. $1 (Fr 8.47 = £1 sterling). Budget (1974 est.) balanced at Fr 117 million. Foreign trade (1974): imports Fr 271 million; exports Fr 7 million. Import sources: France 68%; Trinidad and Tobago 9%; U.S. 8%. Export destinations: U.S. 62%; France 19%; Surinam 6%; Guadeloupe 5%; Martinique 5%. Main exports: timber 39%; shrimps 39%; hides and skins 5%.

FRENCH POLYNESIA

An overseas territory, the islands of French Polynesia are scattered over a large area of the south central Pacific Ocean. Area of inhabited islands: 1,261 sq mi (3,265 sq km). Pop. (1976 est.): 129,800. Cap.: Papeete, Tahiti (pop., 1971, 25,600).

Education. (1975–76) Primary, pupils 28,658, teachers 1,510; secondary, pupils 7,280, teachers 424; vocational, pupils 1,719, teachers 142; higher, students 111, teachers 7.

Finance and Trade. Monetary unit: CFP franc, with (Sept. 20, 1976) a parity of CFP Fr 18.18 to the French franc and a free rate of CFP Fr 89.40 to U.S. $1 (CFP Fr 154.05 = £1 sterling). Budget (1975) balanced at CFP Fr 10,071,000,000. Foreign trade (1975): imports CFP Fr 22,317,000,000 (59% from France, 15% from U.S. in 1973); exports CFP Fr 1,969,000,000 (82% to France in 1973). Main exports: copra, vanilla, mother of pearl, coffee, citrus fruit. Tourism (1972) 111,300 visitors.

GUADELOUPE

The overseas département of Guadeloupe, together with its dependencies, is in the eastern Caribbean between Antigua to the north and Dominica to the south. Area: 658 sq mi (1,705 sq km). Pop. (1974 census): 324,500. Cap.: Basse-Terre (pop., 1974, 15,500).

Education. (1974–75) Primary, pupils 75,036, teachers 2,473; secondary, pupils 35,624, teachers 840; vocational, pupils 7,516, teachers 381; higher, students 1,614, teachers 33.

Finance and Trade. Monetary unit: French (metropolitan) franc. Budget (1972 est.) balanced at Fr 583 million. Cost of living (Basse-Terre; 1970 = 100; June 1976) 183. Foreign trade (1974): imports Fr 1,104,230,000 (73% from France, 5% from Martinique, 5% from U.S. and Puerto Rico); exports Fr 277,730,000 (85% to France, 8% to Martinique). Main exports: bananas 47%; sugar 30%; rum 9%; wheat meal and flour 5%.

MARTINIQUE

The Caribbean island of Martinique, an overseas département, lies 24 mi N of St. Lucia and about 30 mi SE of Dominica. Area: 417 sq mi (1,079 sq km). Pop. (1974 census): 324,800. Cap.: Fort-de-France (pop., 1974 census, 98,800).

Education. Primary, pupils (1973–74) 61,428, teachers (1971–72) 2,714; secondary (1972–73), pupils 35,866, teachers 1,978; vocational (1972–73), pupils 3,136, teachers 245; teacher training (1972–73), students 219, teachers 20.

Finance and Trade. Monetary unit: French (metropolitan) franc. Budget (1972 est.) balanced at Fr 392 million. Cost of living (Fort-de-France; 1970 = 100; Jan. 1976) 176. Foreign trade (1974): imports Fr 1,405,110,000 (63% from France, 6% from Venezuela, 5% from Saudi Arabia, 5% from U.S. and Puerto Rico); exports Fr 347,110,000 (66% to France, 26% to Guadeloupe). Main exports: bananas 44%; petroleum products 22%; rum 12%; fruit preserves 6%.

NEW CALEDONIA

The overseas territory of New Caledonia, together with its dependencies, is in the South Pacific 750 mi E of Australia. Area: 7,366 sq mi (19,079 sq km). Pop. (1974 census): 131,700. Cap.: Nouméa (pop., 1974 census, 59,100).

Education. (1975) Primary, pupils 31,138, teachers 1,353; secondary, pupils 5,604, teachers 235; vocational, pupils 2,221, teachers 218; teacher training, students 135, teachers 30; higher, students 337, teaching staff 26.

Finance and Trade. Monetary unit: CFP franc. Budget (1974 est.) balanced at CFP Fr 7,760,000,000 (including special French grants of CFP Fr 1,810,000,000. Foreign trade (1975): imports CFP Fr 27,049,000,000; exports CFP Fr 22,380,000,000. Import sources (1973): France 49%; Australia 12%. Export destinations (1973): France 46%; Japan 33%; U.S. 11%. Main exports (1973): ferronickel 45%; nickel 26%; nickel castings 24%.

Industry. Production (in 000; 1974): nickel ore (metal content; metric tons) 137; electricity (kw-hr) 1,790,000.

RÉUNION

The overseas département of Réunion is located in the Indian Ocean about 450 mi E of Madagascar and 110 mi SW of Mauritius. Area: 970 sq mi (2,512 sq km). Pop. (1974 census): 476,700. Cap.: Saint-Denis (pop., 1974 census, 104,600).

Education. (1973–74) Primary, pupils 124,120, teachers 3,942; secondary, pupils 44,450, teachers 2,123; vocational, pupils 4,013, teachers 275; teacher training, students 560, teachers 47; higher, students 1,295, teaching staff 56.

Finance and Trade. Monetary unit: French (metropolitan) franc. Budget (1974 est.) balanced at Fr 1,927,000,000. Cost of living (Saint-Denis; 1970 = 100; May 1976) 178. Foreign trade (1975): imports Fr 1,757,740,000 (61% from France, 8% from Italy, 7% from Madagascar in 1974); exports Fr 268,480,000 (76% to France, 19% to Italy in 1974). Main exports (1974): sugar 80%; essential oils 9%; rum 5%.

SAINT PIERRE AND MIQUELON

The self-governing overseas département of Saint Pierre and Miquelon is located about 15 mi off the south coast of Newfoundland. Area: 93 sq mi (242 sq km). Pop. (1974 census): 5,800. Cap.: Saint Pierre, Saint Pierre.

Education. (1974–75) Primary, pupils 1,287, teachers 53; secondary, pupils 377, teachers 32; vocational, pupils 107, teachers 12.

Finance and Trade. Monetary unit: French (metropolitan) franc. Budget (1973 est.) balanced at Fr 3,406,000. Foreign trade (1974): imports Fr 125,553,000; exports Fr 59,352,000. Import sources: Canada 54%; France 38%. Export destinations (excluding ship's stores): Canada 70%; U.S. 25%; France 5%. Main exports: petroleum products (as ship's stores) 53%; cattle 30%; fish 12%.

WALLIS AND FUTUNA

Wallis and Futuna, an overseas territory, lies in the South Pacific west of Western Samoa. Area: 98 sq mi (255 sq km). Pop. (1975 est.): 9,000. Cap.: Mata Utu, Uvea (pop., 1969, 600).

NETHERLANDS, THE

NETHERLANDS ANTILLES

The Netherlands Antilles, a self-governing integral part of the Netherlands realm, consists of an island group near the Venezuelan coast and another group to the north near St. Kitts-Nevis-Anguilla. Area: 383 sq mi (993 sq km). Pop. (1975 est.): 244,100. Cap.: Willemstad, Curaçao (pop., 1970 est., 50,000).

Education. (1972–73) Primary, pupils 39,192, teachers 1,344; secondary, pupils 11,820, teachers 536; vocational, pupils 6,879, teachers 367; higher, students 434, teaching staff 34.

Finance. Monetary unit: Netherlands Antilles guilder or florin, with (Sept. 20, 1976) a par value of 1.80 Netherlands Antilles guilder to U.S. $1 (free rate of 3.08 Netherlands Antilles guilders = £1 sterling). Budget (1972 rev. est.): revenue 116 million Netherlands Antilles guilders; expenditure 126 million Netherlands Antilles guilders. Cost of living (Curaçao; 1971 = 100; Dec. 1975) 160.

Foreign Trade. Imports (1975) 4,372,000,000 Netherlands Antilles guilders; exports (1974) 4,776,000,000 Netherlands Antilles guilders. Import sources (1973): Venezuela 57%; Nigeria 17%; U.S. 8%. Export destinations (1973): U.S. 69%. Main exports (1973): petroleum products 84%; petroleum 8%. Tourism: visitors (1972) 553,000; gross receipts (1973) U.S. $145 million.

Transport and Communications. Roads (1972) 1,150 km. Motor vehicles in use (1973): passenger c. 39,000; commercial (including buses) c. 8,000. Shipping traffic (1973): goods loaded 42,960,000 metric tons, unloaded c. 46,-878,000 metric tons. Telephones (Jan. 1975) 35,000. Radio receivers (Dec. 1973) 130,000. Television receivers (Dec. 1973) 34,000.

Industry. Production (in 000; metric tons; 1974): petroleum products c. 36,030; phosphate rock c. 107; electricity (kw-hr) c. 1,600,000.

NEW ZEALAND

COOK ISLANDS

The self-governing territory of the Cook Islands consists of several islands in the southern Pacific Ocean scattered over an area of about 850,000 sq mi. Area: 93 sq mi (241 sq km). Pop. (1974 est.): 19,500. Seat of government: Rarotonga Island (pop., 1971, 11,400).

Education. (1971) Primary, pupils 6,077, teachers 276; secondary, pupils 1,130, teachers 65; teacher training, students 75, teachers 10.

Finance and Trade. Monetary unit: New Zealand dollar, with (Sept. 20, 1976) a free rate of NZ$1 to U.S. $1 (NZ$1.73 = £1 sterling). Budget (1971 actual): revenue NZ$1,702,000 (excluding New Zealand subsidy of NZ$2,943,-000); expenditure NZ$4,695,000. Foreign trade (1973): imports NZ$4,947,000 (83% from New Zealand, 7% from Japan and Hong Kong); exports NZ$2,877,000 (98% to New Zealand in 1970). Main exports: citrus juices 41%; bananas 6%; canned fruit 6%; pineapple juice 5%.

NIUE ISLAND

The self-governing territory of Niue Island is situated in the Pacific Ocean about 1,500 mi NE of New Zealand. Area: 100 sq mi (259 sq km). Pop. (1974 est.): 4,000. Capital: Alofi (pop., 1971 census, 1,000).

Education. (1975) Primary, pupils 925, teachers 69; secondary, pupils 387, teachers 23.

Finance and Trade. Monetary unit: New Zealand dollar. Budget (1973–74 actual): revenue NZ$1,104,000 (excluding New Zealand subsidy of NZ$1,588,000); expenditure NZ$2,-407,000. Foreign trade (1973): imports NZ$721,-000 (79% from New Zealand in 1971); exports NZ$137,000 (90% to New Zealand in 1971). Main exports: passion fruit 23%; copra 15%; plaited ware 10%; honey 8%.

TOKELAU ISLANDS

The territory of Tokelau Islands lies in the South Pacific about 700 mi N of Niue Island and 2,100 mi NE of New Zealand. Area: 4 sq mi (10 sq km). Pop. (1975 census): 1,600.

NORWAY

JAN MAYEN

The island of Jan Mayen, a Norwegian dependency, lies within the Arctic Circle between Greenland and northern Norway. Area: 144 sq mi (373 sq km). Pop. (1973 est.): 37.

SVALBARD

A group of islands and a Norwegian dependency, Svalbard is located within the Arctic Circle to the north of Norway. Area: 23,957 sq mi (62,050 sq km). Pop. (1975 est.): 3,500.

PORTUGAL

MACAU

The overseas territory of Macau is situated on the mainland coast of China 40 mi W of Hong Kong. Area: 6 sq mi (16 sq km). Pop. (1975 est.): 260,200.

Education. (1974–75) Primary, pupils 22,025, teachers 677; secondary, pupils 7,006, teachers 466; vocational, pupils 1,258, teachers 130; teacher training, students 66, teachers 5; higher, students 55, teachers 3.

Finance and Trade. Monetary unit: patacá, with (Sept. 20, 1976) a free rate of 5.16 patacás to U.S. $1 (8.90 patacás = £1 sterling). Budget (1974 est.) balanced at 79,220,000 patacás. Foreign trade (1974): imports 714,492,000 patacás; exports 616,990,000 patacás. Import sources: Hong Kong 65%; China 25%. Export destinations: France 16%; West Germany 16%; U.S. 10%; Hong Kong 10%; Portugal 9%; Italy 6%; The Netherlands 5%. Main exports: clothing 51%; textile yarns and fabrics 28%.

Transport. Shipping traffic (1974): goods loaded 147,000 metric tons, unloaded 299,000 metric tons.

SOUTH WEST AFRICA (NAMIBIA)

South West Africa has been a UN territory since 1966, when the General Assembly terminated South Africa's mandate over the country, renamed Namibia by the UN. South Africa considers the UN resolution illegal. Area: 318,251 sq mi (824,-268 sq km). Pop. (1975 est.): 883,000. National cap.: Windhoek (pop., 1975 est., 77,400). Summer cap.: Swakopmund (pop., 1975 est., 13,700).

Education. (1973) Primary and secondary: Bantu, pupils 116,320, teachers 2,662; Coloured, pupils 15,941, teachers 797; white, pupils 22,775, teachers 1,232.

Finance and Trade. Monetary unit: South African rand, with (Sept. 20, 1976) an official rate of R 0.87 to U.S. $1 (free rate of R 1.49 = £1 sterling). Budget (1974–75): revenue R 85 million; expenditure R 91 million. Foreign trade (included in the South African customs union; 1972 est.): imports c. R 170 million (c. 80% from South Africa); exports c. R 240 million (c. 50% to South Africa). Main exports: diamonds c. 40%; fish and products 20%; livestock 15%; karakul pelts c. 14%.

Agriculture. Production (in 000; metric tons; 1974): corn c. 14; millet c. 14; beef and veal c. 127; mutton and goat meat c. 23; fish catch (excluding Walvis Bay) c. 30. Livestock (in 000; 1974): cattle c. 2,700; sheep c. 4,400; goats c. 1,900; horses c. 40; asses c. 61.

Industry. Production (in 000; metric tons; 1974): lead ore (metal content) 55; zinc ore (metal content) 81; copper ore (metal content) 26; tin concentrates (metal content) 1.1; vanadium ore (metal content; 1973) 0.7; silver (troy oz; 1972) 1,125; diamonds (metric carats) 1,569; salt (1973) 147; asbestos (1969) 90; electricity (kw-hr; 1963) 188,000.

UNITED KINGDOM

ANTIGUA

The associated state of Antigua, with its dependencies Barbuda and Redonda, lies in the eastern Caribbean approximately 40 mi N of Guadeloupe. Area: 171 sq mi (442 sq km). Pop. (1975 est.): 73,000. Cap.: Saint John's (pop., 1974 est., 23,500).

Education. (1973–74) Primary, pupils 12,138, teachers 440; secondary, pupils 6,300, teachers 290; vocational, pupils 153, teachers 23; teacher training, students 82, teachers 13.

Finance and Trade. Monetary unit: East Caribbean dollar, with (Sept. 20, 1976) an official rate of ECar$2.70 to U.S. $1 (free rate of ECar$4.65 = £1 sterling). Budget (1974 est.) revenue ECar$34 million; expenditure ECar$33 million. Foreign trade (1973): imports ECar$94,-504,000; exports ECar$59,445,000. Import sources: Venezuela 31%; U.K. 22%; U.S. 16%; Canada 6%. Export destinations: bunkers 37%; U.S. 21%; Switzerland 11%; Canada 9%; Bermuda 5%. Main exports: petroleum products 84%; aircraft and engines (reexports) 6%. Tourism (1974) 69,850 visitors.

BELIZE

Belize, a self-governing colony, is situated on the Caribbean coast of Central America, bounded on the north and northwest by Mexico and by Guatemala on the remainder of the west and south. Area: 8,867 sq mi (22,965 sq km). Pop. (1975 est.): 139,200. Cap.: Belmopan (pop., 1975 est., 320).

Education. (1973–74) Primary, pupils 33,396, teachers 1,170; secondary, pupils 4,987, teachers 411; vocational, pupils 117, teachers 10; higher, students 110, teaching staff 22.

Finance and Trade. Monetary unit: Belize dollar, with (Sept. 20, 1976) an official rate of Bel$2 = U.S. $1 (free rate of Bel$3.45 = £1 sterling). Budget (1975 est.) balanced at Bel$49.5 million. Foreign trade (1974): imports Bel$115 million; exports Bel$99.7 million. Import sources (1970): U.S. 34%; U.K. 25%; Jamaica 7%; The Netherlands 7%. Export destinations (1970): U.S. 30%; U.K. 24%; Mexico 22%; Canada 13%. Main exports (1970): sugar 48%; timber 8%; orange juice 7%; clothing c. 6%; grapefruit segments 5%; lobster 5%.

BERMUDA

The colony of Bermuda lies in the western Atlantic about 570 mi E of Cape Hatteras, North Carolina. Area: 18 sq mi (46 sq km). Pop. (1976 est.): 56,000. Cap.: Hamilton, Great Bermuda (pop., 1970 census, 2,100).

Education. (1974–75) Primary, pupils 6,919, teachers 397; secondary, pupils 4,700, teachers 325; vocational, pupils 510, teachers 49.

Finance and Trade. Monetary unit: Bermuda dollar, at par with the U.S. dollar (free rate, at Sept. 20, 1976, of Ber$1.72 = £1 sterling). Budget (1973–74 actual): revenue Ber$56,084,-000; expenditure Ber$54,096,000. Foreign trade (1974): imports Ber$154,620,000; exports Ber$33,828,000. Import sources: U.S. 44%; U.K. 15%; Netherlands Antilles 9%; Canada 9%. Export destinations (1973): U.S. 14%; The Netherlands 10%; New Zealand 7%; Italy 6%; South Africa 6%; Portugal 6%. Main exports: drugs and medicines 48%; liquor 5%. Tourism: visitors (1972) 340,000; gross receipts (1971) U.S. $97 million.

Transport and Communications. Roads (1973) 212 km. Motor vehicles in use (1974): passenger 12,200; commercial (including buses) 2,200. Shipping (1975): merchant vessels 100 gross tons and over 59; gross tonnage 1,450,387. Telephones (1975) 36,000. Radios (1973) 49,-000. Television receivers (1973) 20,000.

BRITISH INDIAN OCEAN TERRITORY

Located in the western Indian Ocean, this colony consists of the islands of the Chagos Archipelago. Area: 23 sq mi (60 sq km). No permanent civilian population remains. Administrative headquarters: Victoria, Seychelles.

BRITISH VIRGIN ISLANDS

The colony of the British Virgin Islands is located in the Caribbean to the east of the U.S. Virgin Islands. Area: 59 sq mi (153 sq km). Pop. (1975 est.): 11,000. Cap.: Road Town, Tortola (pop., 1973 est., 3,500).

Education. (1974–75) Primary, pupils 2,181, teachers 108; secondary and vocational, pupils 796, teachers 46.

Finance and Trade. Monetary unit: U.S. dollar (free rate, at Sept. 20, 1976, of U.S. $1.72 = £1 sterling). Budget (1975 est.): revenue U.S. $5,374,000; expenditure U.S. $6 million. Foreign trade (1973): imports U.S. $9,467,000; exports U.S. $441,400. Import sources: U.S. 24%; Puerto Rico 19%; U.K. 16%; U.S. Virgin Islands 15%; Trinidad and Tobago 8%. Export destinations: U.S. Virgin Islands 59%; Netherlands Antilles 12%; St. Martin 8%; U.K. 7%. Main exports: motor vehicles (reexports) 15%; nonelectric machines (reexports) 14%; gravel and sand 10%; fish 9%; timber (reexports) 6%; beverages (reexports) 5%.

BRUNEI

Brunei, a protected sultanate, is located on the north coast of the island of Borneo, surrounded on its landward side by the Malaysian state of Sarawak. Area: 2,226 sq mi (5,765 sq km). Pop. (1975 est.): 162,400. Cap.: Bandar Seri Begawan (pop., 1975 est., 44,000).

Education. (1974) Primary, pupils 32,120, teachers 1,625; secondary, pupils 12,906, teachers 884; vocational, pupils 197, teachers 33; teacher training, students 601, teachers 42.

Finance and Trade. Monetary unit: Brunei dollar, with (Sept. 20, 1976) a free rate of Br$2.50 to U.S. $1 (Br$4.30 = £1 sterling). Budget (1975 est.): revenue Br$1,173,000,000; expenditure Br$471 million. Foreign trade (1974): imports Br$450.9 million; exports Br$2,352,680,000. Import sources: Japan 27%; U.S. 20%; Singapore 15%; U.K. 11%. Export destinations: Japan 78%; Malaysia 8%; South Africa 5%. Main exports: crude oil 82%; natural gas 12%.

Agriculture. Production (in 000; metric tons; 1974): rice *c.* 6; cassava *c.* 3; rubber *c.* 0.5. Livestock (in 000; Dec. 1973): cattle *c.* 3; buffaloes *c.* 17; pigs *c.* 14; chickens *c.* 800.

Industry. Production: crude oil (1974) 9,284,000 metric tons; natural gas *c.* 5,000,000,000 cu m.

CAYMAN ISLANDS

The colony of the Cayman Islands lies in the Caribbean about 170 mi NW of Jamaica. Area: 102 sq mi (264 sq km). Pop. (1976 est.): 14,000. Cap.: George Town, Grand Cayman (pop., 1970 census, 3,800).

Education. (1975–76) Primary, pupils 1,964, teachers 72; secondary, pupils 1,355, teachers 93.

Finance and Trade. Monetary unit: Cayman Islands dollar, with (Sept. 20, 1976) a free rate of CayI$0.83 to U.S. $1 (CayI$1.44 = £1 sterling). Budget (1974 actual): revenue CayI$8,277,337; expenditure CayI$6,949,749. Foreign trade (1974): imports CayI$22 million; exports CayI$287,000. Most trade is with the United States and Jamaica. Main export turtle products 93%. Tourism (1974) 53,100 visitors.

Shipping. (1975) Merchant vessels 100 gross tons and over 56; gross tonnage 49,320.

DOMINICA

The associated state of Dominica lies in the Caribbean between Guadeloupe to the north and Martinique to the south. Area: 290 sq mi (751 sq km). Pop. (1975 est.): 75,000. Cap.: Roseau (pop., 1974 est., 10,200).

Education. (1973–74) Primary, pupils 16,989, teachers 448; secondary, pupils 5,535, teachers 217; vocational, pupils 972, teachers 45; teacher training, students 40, teachers 4.

Finance and Trade. Monetary unit: East Caribbean dollar. Budget (1973 est.) balanced at ECar$26.9 million. Foreign trade (1973): imports ECar$31,209,000; exports ECar$16,710,000. Import sources (1969): U.K. 33%; U.S. 15%; Trinidad and Tobago 11%; Canada 10%; The Netherlands and Antilles 6%; West Germany 5%. Export destination (1969) U.K. 84%. Main exports: bananas 46%; citrus fruit 7%; essential oils 6%.

FALKLAND ISLANDS

The colony of the Falkland Islands and Dependencies is situated in the South Atlantic about 500 mi NE of Cape Horn. Area: 6,280 sq mi (16,265 sq km). Pop. (1975 est.): 1,900. Cap.: Stanley (pop., 1976 est., 1,100).

Education. (1975–76) Primary, pupils 200, teachers 17; secondary, pupils 105, teachers 10.

Finance and Trade. Monetary unit: Falkland Island pound, at par with the pound sterling (U.S. $1.72 = £1 sterling). Budget: (1975–76 est.): revenue FI£1,184,000; expenditure FI£955,000 (excludes dependencies; revenue FI£30,000, expenditure FI£21,000). Foreign trade (1974): imports FI£805,000 (83% from U.K. in 1971); exports FI£4,916,000 (93% to U.K. in 1971). Main export wool.

GIBRALTAR

Gibraltar, a self-governing colony, is a small peninsula that juts into the Mediterranean from southwestern Spain. Area: 2.25 sq mi (5.80 sq km). Pop. (1974 est.): 29,400.

Education. (1974) Primary, pupils 3,923, teachers 185; secondary, pupils 1,549, teachers 120; vocational, pupils 52, teachers 22.

Finance and Trade. Monetary unit: Gibraltar pound, at par with the pound sterling. Budget (1974–75 est.): revenue Gib£11,850,000; expenditure Gib£12,190,000. Foreign trade (1974): imports Gib£25,089,000 (71% from U.K.); reexports Gib£10,484,000 (31% to EEC, 16% to U.K. in 1971). Main reexports: petroleum products 89%; tobacco 9%. Tourism (1974) 140,000 visitors.

Transport. Shipping (1975): merchant vessels 100 gross tons and over 11; gross tonnage 28,850. Ships entered (1974) vessels totaling 13,973,000 net registered tons; goods loaded 5,000 metric tons, unloaded 411,000 metric tons.

GILBERT ISLANDS

The Gilbert Islands comprise 16 main islands, together with associated islets and reefs, straddling the Equator just west of the International Date Line in the western Pacific Ocean. Area: 102 sq mi (264 sq km). Pop. (1976 est.): 53,300. Seat of government: Bairiki, on Tarawa Atoll (pop., 1974 est., 17,100).

Education. (1976–77) Primary, pupils 11,823, teachers 300; secondary, pupils 669, teachers 38; teacher training, students 53, teachers 11.

Finance and Trade. Monetary unit: Australian dollar, with (Sept. 20, 1976) a free rate of A$0.80 to U.S. $1 (A$1.38 = £1 sterling). Budget (including Tuvalu; 1973 est.): revenue A$5,497,000; expenditure A$5,509,000. Foreign trade (including Tuvalu; 1973): imports A$6,670,000 (54% from Australia, 14% from U.K., 5% from New Zealand); exports A$9,732,000 (62% to New Zealand, 30% to Australia, 5% to U.K. in 1972). Main exports: phosphates 89%; copra 11%.

Industry. Production (in 000; 1974): phosphate rock (metric tons) 562; electricity (kw-hr) *c.* 3,000.

GUERNSEY

Located 30 mi W of Normandy, France, Guernsey, together with its small island dependencies, is a crown dependency. Area: 30 sq mi (78 sq km). Pop. (1971): 53,700. Cap.: St. Peter Port (pop., 1971, 16,300).

Education. (1974–75) Primary, pupils 5,563, teachers 251; secondary, pupils 4,137, teachers 279; vocational, pupils 557, teachers 19.

Finance and Trade. Monetary unit: Guernsey pound, at par with the pound sterling. Budget (1974): revenue £14,793,000; expenditure £11,308,000. Foreign trade included with the United Kingdom. Main exports: tomatoes, flowers. Tourism (1974) *c.* 300,000 visitors.

HONG KONG

The colony of Hong Kong lies on the southeastern coast of China about 40 mi E of Macau and 80 mi SE of Canton. Area: 403 sq mi (1,045 sq km). Pop. (1976 prelim.): 4,407,000. Cap.: Victoria (pop., 1971, 520,900).

Education. (1975–76) Primary, pupils 642,611, teachers 20,089; secondary, pupils 347,146; vocational, pupils 21,509; secondary and vocational, teachers 12,254; higher, students 20,427, teaching staff 1,935.

Finance. Monetary unit: Hong Kong dollar, with (Sept. 20, 1977) a free rate of HK$4.88 to U.S. $1 (HK$8.40 = £1 sterling). Budget (1975–76 est.): revenue HK$6,184,000,000; expenditure HK$6,615,000,000.

Foreign Trade. (1975) Imports HK$34,020,000,000: exports HK$31,455,000,000. Import sources: Japan 21%; China 20%; U.S. 12%; Taiwan 6%; Singapore 6%; U.K. 5%. Export destinations: U.S. 25%; West Germany 9%; U.K. 9%; Japan 6%; Singapore 5%. Main exports: clothing 33%; electrical machinery 10%; textile yarns and fabrics 9%; toys and games 5%. Tourism (1974): visitors 1,295,000; gross receipts U.S. $476 million.

Transport and Communications. Roads (1974) 1,049 km. Motor vehicles in use (1974): passenger 127,000; commercial 42,000. Railways: (1974) 36 km; traffic (1975) 279.1 million passenger-km, freight 51.7 million net ton-km. Shipping (1975): merchant vessels 100 gross tons and over 104; gross tonnage 418,512. Ships entered (1974) vessels totaling 37,938,000 net registered tons; goods loaded (1975) 5,083,000 metric tons, unloaded 13,520,000 metric tons. Telephones (Jan. 1975) 989,000. Radio licenses (Dec. 1973) 1 million. Television licenses (Dec. 1973) 748,000.

ISLE OF MAN

The Isle of Man, a crown dependency, lies in the Irish Sea approximately 35 mi from both Northern Ireland and the coast of northwestern England. Area: 221 sq mi (572 sq km). Pop. (1975 est.): 55,600. Cap.: Douglas (pop., 1971, 20,400).

Education. (1974–75) Primary, pupils 5,641, teachers 214; secondary, pupils 4,329, teachers 251; vocational, pupils 133, teachers 32.

Finance and Trade. Monetary unit: Isle of Man pound, at par with the pound sterling. Budget (1975–76 est.): revenue £29 million; expenditure £29.2 million. Foreign trade included with the United Kingdom. Main exports: meat and livestock, fish. Tourism (1975) 529,913 visitors.

JERSEY

The island of Jersey, a crown dependency, is located about 20 mi W of Normandy, France. Area: 45 sq mi (117 sq km). Pop. (1971): 72,600. Cap.: St. Helier (pop., 1971, 28,100).

Education. (1974–75) Primary, pupils 5,017; secondary, pupils 4,051.

Finance and Trade. Monetary unit: Jersey pound, at par with the pound sterling. Budget (1974): revenue £33,647,000; expenditure £24,890,000. Foreign trade included with the United Kingdom. Main exports: manufactures, potatoes, tomatoes. Tourism (1974): visitors *c.* 1.1 million; gross expenditure U.S. $110 million.

MONTSERRAT

The colony of Montserrat is located in the Caribbean between Antigua, 27 mi NE, and Guadeloupe, 40 mi SE. Area: 40 sq mi (102 sq km). Pop. (1976 est.): 13,300. Cap.: Plymouth (pop., 1974 est., 3,000).

Education. (1975–76) Primary, pupils 2,623, teachers 107; secondary, pupils 486, teachers 34; vocational, pupils 60, teachers 8.

Finance and Trade. Monetary unit: East Caribbean dollar. Budget (1975 est.) balanced at ECar$8,064,000. Foreign trade (1974): imports ECar$15,298,000; exports ECar$260,570. Import sources (1973): U.K. 27%; U.S. 17%; Trinidad and Tobago 17%; Canada 8%. Export destinations (1973): Antigua 25%; Barbados 22%; St. Kitts-Nevis and Anguilla 14%; Dominica 9%; St. Maarten 7%; U.K. 5%; St. Lucia 5%. Main exports (1973): tomatoes 33%; recapped tires 30%; limes 11%.

PITCAIRN ISLAND

The colony of Pitcairn Island is in the central South Pacific, 3,200 mi NE of New Zealand and

1,350 mi SE of Tahiti. Area: 1.75 sq mi (4.53 sq km). Pop. (1976 census): 67, all of whom live in the de facto capital, Adamstown.

ST. HELENA

The colony of St. Helena, including its dependencies of Ascension Island and the Tristan da Cunha island group, is spread over a wide area of the Atlantic off the southwestern coast of Africa. Area: 159 sq mi (412 sq km). Pop. (1974 est.): 5,000. Cap.: Jamestown (pop., 1974 est., 1,600).

Education. (1974–75) Primary, pupils 729, teachers 37; secondary, pupils 509, teachers 29; vocational, pupils 10, teachers 2; teacher training, students 4, teachers 2.

Finance and Trade. Monetary unit: pound sterling. Budget (1974–75 est.): revenue £1,356,000; expenditure £1,520,000. Foreign trade (1974): imports £610,834 (61% from U.K., 28% from South Africa in 1968); exports nil.

ST. KITTS-NEVIS-ANGUILLA

This associated state consists of the islands of St. Kitts and Nevis; Anguilla received a separate constitution in 1976. Area: (excluding Anguilla) 100 sq mi (259 sq km). Pop. (excluding Anguilla; 1976 est.): 48,000 (Anguilla about 6,500). Cap.: Basseterre, St. Kitts (pop., 1976 est., 15,900).

Education. (1975–76) Primary, pupils 9,629, teachers 344; secondary, pupils 4,966, teachers 253; vocational, pupils 183, teachers 22.

Finance and Trade. Monetary unit: East Caribbean dollar. Budget (1974 est.) balanced at ECar$31,290,700. Foreign trade (1973): imports ECar$35.9 million; exports ECar$15.8 million. Import sources (1969): U.K. 28%; Canada 14%; U.S. 14%; Trinidad and Tobago 10%; Barbados 5%. Export destinations (1969): U.K. 76%; Canada 10%. Main exports (1969) sugar and molasses 88%.

ST. LUCIA

The Caribbean island of St. Lucia, an associated state, lies 24 mi S of Martinique and 21 mi NE of St. Vincent. Area: 241 sq mi (623 sq km). Pop. (1975 est.): 111,800. Cap.: Castries (pop., 1970, 3,600).

Education. (1975–76) Primary, pupils 30,577, teachers 930; secondary, pupils 4,105, teachers 232; vocational, pupils 237, teachers 32; teacher training, students 156, teachers 15.

Finance and Trade. Monetary unit: East Caribbean dollar. Budget (1974 est.): revenue ECar$29,390,000; expenditure ECar$49,504,000. Foreign trade (1974): imports ECar$91,115,000; exports ECar$32,909,000. Import sources (1973): U.K. 30%; U.S. 16%; Trinidad and Tobago 13%; Canada 5%. Export destinations (1973): U.K. 60%; Jamaica 10%; Barbados 8%; U.S. 6%; Leeward and Windward Islands 6%. Main exports: bananas 64%; cardboard boxes 10%; coconut oil 10%. Tourism (1974) 51,800 visitors.

ST. VINCENT

St. Vincent, including the northern Grenadines, is an associated state in the eastern Caribbean about 100 mi W of Barbados. Area: 150 sq mi (389 sq km). Pop. (1975 est.): 93,000. Cap.: Kingstown (pop., 1973 est., 22,000).

Education. (1971–72) Primary, pupils 34,521, teachers 1,765; secondary, pupils 3,647, teachers (1968–69) 92; teacher training, students 362, teachers 11.

Finance and Trade. Monetary unit: East Caribbean dollar. Budget (1975–76 est.) balanced at ECar$23.9 million. Foreign trade (1974): imports ECar$46,540,000; exports ECar$11,820,000. Import sources (1971): U.K. 36%; Trinidad and Tobago 14%; U.S. 8%. Export destinations (1971): U.K. 59%; Barbados 19%; Trinidad and Tobago 9%; U.S. 7%. Main exports (1971): bananas 51%; arrowroot 7%; coconut oil 6%.

SOLOMON ISLANDS

The Solomon Islands is a self-governing protectorate in the southwestern Pacific east of the island of New Guinea. Area: 10,983 sq mi (28,446 sq km). Pop. (1976 est.): 190,000. Cap.: Honiara, Guadalcanal (pop., 1973 est., 15,300).

Education. (1973) Primary, pupils 25,952, teachers 1,088; secondary, pupils 1,303, teachers 99; vocational, pupils 696, teachers 61; teacher training, students 88, teachers 18.

Finance and Trade. Monetary unit: Australian dollar. Budget (1975 est.) balanced at A$9,050,000 (excluding capital expenditure of A$6.5 million). Foreign trade (1974): imports A$15,696,000; exports A$17,013,000. Import sources (1973): Australia 45%; U.K. 13%; Japan 12%; Singapore 7%. Export destinations (1973): Japan 53%; American Samoa 13%; West Germany 7%; Australia 7%; Norway 5%. Main exports: copra 53%; timber 25%; fish 17%; canned fish 5%.

TURKS AND CAICOS ISLANDS

The colony of the Turks and Caicos Islands is situated in the Atlantic southeast of The Bahamas. Area: 193 sq mi (500 sq km). Pop. (1975 est.): 6,000. Seat of government: Grand Turk Island (pop., 1970, 2,300).

Education. (1972–73) Primary, pupils 1,791, teachers 90; secondary, pupils 354, teachers 17.

Finance and Trade. Monetary unit: U.S. dollar. Budget (1974 actual): revenue $2,630,897; expenditure $2,552,684. Foreign trade (1974): imports $6,597,000; exports $563,000. Main exports: crayfish 73%; conchs 25%.

TUVALU

The colony of Tuvalu comprises nine main islands, together with their associated islets and reefs, located just south of the Equator and just west of the International Date Line in the western Pacific Ocean. Area: 9½ sq mi (26 sq km). Pop. (1976 est.): 6,500. Seat of government: Funafuti (pop., 1976 est., 1,300).

Education. (1975–76) Primary, students 1,570, teachers 39; secondary, pupils 250, teachers 12.

For additional statistics *see* GILBERT ISLANDS.

UNITED KINGDOM and FRANCE

NEW HEBRIDES

The British-French condominium of the New Hebrides is located in the southwestern Pacific about 500 mi W of Fiji and 250 mi NE of New Caledonia. Area: 5,700 sq mi (14,800 sq km). Pop. (1976 est.): 97,500. Cap.: Vila (metropolitan area pop., 1976 est., 16,600).

Education. (1974) Primary, pupils 19,834, teachers 814; secondary, pupils 1,016, teachers 67; vocational, pupils 167, teachers 18; teacher training, students 112, teachers 11.

Finance. Monetary units: Australian dollar and New Hebrides franc, with (Sept. 20, 1976) a free rate of NHFr 79.47 = U.S. $1 (NHFr 136.93 = £1 sterling). Condominium budget (1975 est.) balanced at A$11,268,000; British budget (1974–75 est.) balanced at A$7,885,000; French budget (1973 est.) balanced at A$7,524,000.

Foreign Trade. (1974) Imports NHFr 3,858,000; exports NHFr 2,371,000. Import sources: Australia 33%; France 15%; Japan 15%; New Zealand 7%. Export destinations: France 59%; U.S. 22%; Japan 13%. Main exports: copra 64%; fish 27%.

Agriculture. Copra production (1975) *c.* 37,000 metric tons. Livestock (in 000; 1974): cattle *c.* 90; pigs *c.* 62.

Industry. Production (in 000; 1974): manganese ore (metal content; exports; metric tons) 18; electricity (kw-hr) *c.* 13,000.

UNITED STATES

AMERICAN SAMOA

Located to the east of Western Samoa in the South Pacific, the unincorporated territory of American Samoa is approximately 1,600 mi NE of the northern tip of New Zealand. Area: 76 sq mi (197 sq km). Pop. (1974): 29,200. Cap.: Pago Pago (pop., 1974, 4,700).

Education. (1974–75) Primary, pupils 7,213, teachers 333; secondary, pupils 2,367, teachers (1971–72) 142; vocational, students 800, teachers 38; higher, students (1972–73) 909, teaching staff (1971–72) 32.

Finance and Trade. Monetary unit: U.S. dollar. Budget (1973 est.) balanced at $33,921,000 (including U.S. grants of $30.4 million). Foreign trade (1973–74): imports $46.5 million (91% from U.S. in 1970); exports $83 million (95% to U.S. in 1970). Main exports (1970): canned tuna 90%; pet food 5%.

CANAL ZONE

The Canal Zone is administered by the U.S. under treaty with Panama and consists of a 10-mi-wide strip on the Isthmus of Panama through which the Panama Canal runs. Area: 558 sq mi (1,445 sq km). Pop. (1975 est.): 44,000. Administrative headquarters: Balboa Heights (pop., 1970, 200).

Education. (1972–73) Primary, pupils 9,435; secondary and vocational, pupils 3,581; primary and secondary, teachers 552; higher, students (1973–74) 1,632, teaching staff (1971–72) 120.

Finance. Monetary unit: U.S. dollar (Panamanian balboa is also used). Budgets (1975): Canal Zone government, revenue $69.4 million, expenditure $67.9 million; Panama Canal Company, revenue $253.7 million, expenditure $262.6 million.

Traffic. (1974–75) Total number of ocean-going vessels passing through the canal 13,609; total cargo tonnage 140,101,000; tolls collected U.S. $142 million. Nationality and number of commercial vessels using the canal: Liberian 1,950; British 1,368; Japanese 1,225; Greek 1,142; U.S. 1,097; Panamanian 1,050; Norwegian 832; West German 766; Dutch 420; Swedish 373.

GUAM

Guam, an organized unincorporated territory, is located in the Pacific Ocean about 6,000 mi SW of San Francisco and 1,500 mi E of Manila. Area: 209 sq mi (541 sq km). Pop. (1975 est.): 107,400. Cap.: Agana (pop., 1974 est., 2,500).

Education. (1976–77) Primary, pupils 18,525, teachers 718; secondary, pupils 12,253, teachers 440; vocational, pupils 878, teachers 49; higher, students 2,337, teaching staff (1971–72) 140.

Finance and Trade. Monetary unit: U.S. dollar. Budget (1974 est.): revenue $112.6 million (including U.S. grants of $11.5 million); expenditure $99.1 million. Foreign trade (1973): imports $211 million; exports $11 million. Tourism (1974) 234,000 visitors.

Agriculture and Industry. Production (in 000; metric tons; 1974): fruit and vegetables 1.6; fish catch 0.1; petroleum products *c.* 1,625; electricity (kw-hr) *c.* 1,250,000.

PUERTO RICO

Puerto Rico, a self-governing associated commonwealth, lies about 885 mi SE of the Florida coast. Area: 3,421 sq mi (8,860 sq km). Pop. (1975 est.): 3,120,900. Cap.: San Juan (pop., 1975 est., 1,087,000).

Education. (1975) Primary, pupils 478,335, teachers 17,181; secondary, pupils 330,454, teachers 12,455; vocational, pupils 26,699, teachers (public only) 490; higher, students 82,385, teaching staff (1971–72) 4,400.

Finance. Monetary unit: U.S. dollar. Budget (1973–74 actual): revenue $2,149,000,000; expenditure $2.1 billion. Gross domestic product (1974–75) $8,135,000,000. Cost of living (1970 = 100; April 1976) 154.

Foreign Trade. (1974–75) Imports $4,951,000,000 (62% from U.S., 10% from Venezuela); exports $3,139,000,000 (85% to U.S.). Main exports (1972–73): chemicals 20%; textiles 18%; machinery 9%; fish products 9%; petroleum products 9%. Tourism (1974–75): visitors 1,339,000; gross receipts U.S. $380 million.

Transport and Communications. Roads (1974) 16,827 km. Motor vehicles in use (1974): passenger 608,000; commercial (including buses) 124,500. Railways (1974) 96 km. Telephones (Jan. 1975) 466,000. Radio receivers (Dec. 1974) 1,752,000. Television receivers (Dec. 1974) 605,000.

Agriculture. Production (in 000; metric tons; 1974): sweet potatoes 8; yams *c.* 12; pumpkins 16; sugar, raw value (1975) *c.* 271; pineapples *c.* 40; bananas *c.* 112; oranges 31; grapefruit *c.*

Dependent States

8; coffee (1975) *c.* 12; tobacco 3. Livestock (in 000; Jan. 1974): cattle 541; pigs 233; poultry 4,635.

Industry. Production (in 000; metric tons; 1973): sand and gravel 6,786; stone 14,195; cement (1975) 1,427; electricity (kw-hr; 1974) 14,590,000.

TRUST TERRITORY OF THE PACIFIC ISLANDS

The Trust Territory islands, numbering more than 2,000, are scattered over 3 million sq mi in the Pacific Ocean from 450 mi E of the Philippines to just west of the International Date Line. Area: 728 sq mi (1,884 sq km). Pop. (1975 est.): 115,000. Seat of government: Saipan Island (pop., 1972 est., 10,700).

Education. (1973–74) Primary, pupils 30,-746, teachers 1,433; secondary, pupils 7,358, teachers 457; vocational, pupils 268, teachers 39; teacher training, pupils 122, teachers 17.

Finance and Trade. Monetary unit: U.S. dollar. Budget (1972–73 est.): revenue $79,605,000 (including U.S. grant of $59.4 million); expenditure $62,812,000. Foreign trade (1973): imports *c.* $30 million (*c.* 50% from U.S., *c.* 27% from Japan in 1972); exports $1.9 million (54% to Japan in 1972). Main exports: copra 50%; fish 28%; handicraft items 10%; vegetables 5%.

Agriculture. Production (in 000; metric tons; 1974): sweet potatoes *c.* 3; cassava *c.* 5; bananas *c.* 2; copra *c.* 10. Livestock (in 000; June 1974): cattle *c.* 16; pigs *c.* 29; goats *c.* 6; chickens *c.* 160.

VIRGIN ISLANDS

The Virgin Islands of the United States is an organized unincorporated territory located about 40 mi E of Puerto Rico. Area: 133 sq mi (345 sq km). Pop. (1975 est.): 92,000. Cap.: Charlotte Amalie, St. Thomas (pop., 1970, 12,200).

Education. (1972–73) Primary, pupils 19,-267, teachers (1971–72) 723; secondary and vocational, pupils 6,359, teachers (1971–72) 487; higher, students (1973–74) 1,698, teaching staff (1971–72) 50.

Finance and Trade. Monetary unit: U.S. dollar. Budget (1972 est.): revenue $90.7 million; expenditure $90,280,000. Foreign trade (1973): imports $850,336,000 (32% from U.S. in 1971); exports $636,093,000 (92% to U.S. in 1971). Main exports: petroleum products, sugar, rum, watches, woolen fabrics. Tourism (1972–73): 1,312,000 visitors; gross receipts U.S. $100,020,-000.

Disasters

The loss of life and property from disasters in 1976 included the following.

AVIATION

Jan. 1 Saudi Arabia. A Lebanese Middle East Airlines Boeing 707, on a flight from Beirut to Persian Gulf states, crashed in a desert area of Saudi Arabia; all 82 persons aboard lost their lives.

Jan. 21 Southern China. A Soviet-built An-24 airliner, with a capacity of 44 passengers, went down in southern China. In its first public announcement of a local air disaster, the Chinese government reported that one American and two Danish businessmen were among the undisclosed number of fatalities.

March 5 Near Yerevan, Armenian S.S.R. A four-engine Soviet Il-18 turboprop airliner crashed as it neared the end of a flight from Moscow to Yerevan; unofficial sources placed the death toll at about 120.

April 14 Neuquén Province, Argentina. A British-made Avro 748 belonging to Yacimientos Petrolíferos Fiscales, a government-owned oil company, crashed in west-central Argentina with the loss of 37 lives.

April 23 Gulf of Mexico. A Bell 205 helicopter, on a routine morning flight to an offshore drilling rig, went down in the Gulf of Mexico; the bodies of seven victims were recovered, and five other persons aboard were presumed dead.

April 27 Charlotte Amalie, Virgin Islands. An American Airlines Boeing 727 jetliner, on a flight from Rhode Island to St. Thomas island, overran the runway at the Harry S. Truman Airport, knocked down two fences, swept across an embankment, then burst into flames when it smashed into several buildings; 37 of the 88 persons aboard were killed, and many survivors were seriously injured.

Thirty-seven persons were killed in April when an American Airlines Boeing 727 landing at St. Thomas in the Virgin Islands overran the field and crashed into buildings beyond. The plane carried 88 persons.

WIDE WORLD

May 3 Monze, Zambia. A Twin Otter aircraft manufactured by de Havilland Aircraft of Canada crashed in south central Zambia while the Canadian pilot was demonstrating the aircraft to Zambian Air Force officers; of the 13 persons aboard, only 2 survived.

May 9 Near Huete, Spain. A Boeing 747 cargo plane belonging to the Iranian Air Force caught fire and crashed during a storm as it was heading for a stopover in Madrid; all 17 persons aboard the aircraft were killed.

June 1 Malabo Island, Equatorial Guinea. A Soviet Aeroflot Tu-154 crashed on a flight from Luanda, Angola, to Moscow; 46 bodies were recovered after the wreckage was located in mid-June.

June 4 Guam. An Air Manila Lockheed Electra, after taking off from Guam International Airport, crashed into a hill, bounced over a highway, struck a small truck, and burst into flames; the truck driver and all 45 persons aboard the aircraft were killed.

July 28 Near Bratislava, Czech. A Soviet-made Il-18 turboprop aircraft belonging to Czechoslovakia caught fire and crashed into Zlate Pisky Lake as it neared the end of a domestic flight from Prague; only 6 of the 76 persons aboard survived.

Aug. 28 Near Peterborough, England. A U.S. Air Force C-141 jet transport, en route from New Jersey to a military base at Mildenhall, England, crashed near Peterborough; all 18 persons aboard the StarLifter were killed in the accident.

Aug. 28 Søndre Strømfjord, Greenland. A U.S. Air Force C-141 StarLifter transport burst into flames after landing at Søndre Strømfjord; 21 of the 27 persons who had made the flight from Thule, Greenland, were killed.

Sept. 4 Terceira Island, Azores. A Lockheed Hercules C-130 belonging to the Venezuelan Air Force crashed on the outskirts of Lajes Airport during a hurricane; the dead included all 8 members of the crew and the 60 members of a choir which was to represent the Central University of Venezuela at a festival in Barcelona, Spain.

Sept. 4 Near Cochrane, Ont. A single-engine DHC-3 Otter aircraft, on an intraprovince flight from Moosonee to Timmins, hit three transmission lines before crashing into a hill and burning; ten persons, including two staff members of the Royal Commission on Electric Power Planning, were killed.

Sept. 6 Near Sochi, U.S.S.R. According to unofficial reports, two Soviet airliners collided in midair near the Black Sea resort town of Sochi; at least 90 persons were believed to have died.

Sept. 9 Managua, Nicaragua. A military helicopter, carrying 8 survivors of a plane crash to a hospital in the nation's capital, crashed on its way to Managua; all 13 persons aboard were killed.

Sept. 10 Near Zagreb, Yugos. In the world's worst midair collision to date, a British Airways Trident jet, flying from London to Istanbul, Turkey, collided at 33,000 ft with a Yugoslav Inex-Adria DC-9 heading for Cologne, West Germany; the 176 fatalities included all 63 persons aboard the British plane and all 113 on the chartered Yugoslav aircraft.

Sept. 19 Near Isparta, Turkey. A Turkish Airlines Boeing 727, on a flight from Italy to Antalya, Turkey, via Istanbul, crashed into the 7,220-ft Karakaya Mountain some 50 mi short of its destination; a pilot's miscalculation was blamed for the crash, which killed all 155 persons aboard.

Sept. 26 Near Alpena, Mich. A U.S. Air Force KC-135 Stratotanker crashed and burned in rugged terrain some 12 mi from Alpena; 5 persons survived the crash that took 15 lives.

Oct. 12 Bombay, India. An Indian Airlines Caravelle jet, scheduled to fly to Madras, crashed and burned shortly after taking off from Bombay's Santa Cruz Airport; none of the 95 persons aboard survived the crash.

Oct. 13 Santa Cruz, Bolivia. An American-owned Boeing 707 cargo plane crashed through the downtown area of Santa Cruz shortly after leaving El Trompillo Airport; of the estimated 100 persons who were killed, many were children attending classes in a primary school that was partly destroyed by one of the plane's wings.

Oct. 25 Villavicencio, Colombia. A DC-3 plane belonging to the El Venado airline company crashed in flames soon after taking off from Yopal Airport in Villavicencio; the 32 fatalities included one of Colombia's few female commercial pilots.

Sept. 26 Near Hot Springs, Va. A Grumman Gulfstream II jet aircraft owned by the Johnson & Johnson Corp. crashed about 500 ft short of the Blue Ridge Airport runway when the pilot attempted an instrument landing; the three-man crew together with four company executives and their wives were all killed.

Nov. 6 Northern Peru. A Peruvian Air Force helicopter crashed in the Andes; officials listed all 11 persons aboard as missing and presumed dead.

Nov. 23 Greece. An Olympic Airways YS-11A two-engine plane, on a domestic flight from Athens to Kozani, crashed and burned about 250 mi N of Athens; none of the 50 persons aboard the plane survived.

Nov. 28 Near Moscow. A Soviet Tu-104 crashed shortly after taking off from Sheremetyevo Airport on a flight to Leningrad; unconfirmed reports said there were no survivors among the 72 persons aboard the aircraft.

Dec. 25 Near Bangkok, Thailand. An Egyptian Boeing 707 crashed into a textile factory on the outskirts of Bangkok as it prepared to land some three hours after midnight; all 55 persons aboard the aircraft were killed and 18 night-shift factory workers were listed as dead or missing.

FIRES AND EXPLOSIONS

Jan. 1 La Louvière, Belgium. A fast-spreading fire that set off a gas explosion in a small ground-floor café gutted a three-story building and trapped many of the young patrons inside; 15 were burned to death and nearly 40 others were injured.

Jan. 9 Hamburg, West Germany. A boiler explosion aboard the 18,500-ton "Anders Maersk," under construction at the Bloehm und Voss shipyard, claimed 18 lives when the workmen were engulfed in searing steam; at least 20 other workers were seriously injured.

Jan. 10 Fremont, Neb. A gas leak in the basement of the six-story Pathfinder Hotel triggered an explosion and fire that killed 18 persons and injured about 50.

Jan. 30 Chicago, Ill. A fire that apparently started in a clothes closet on the fourth floor of the Wincrest Nursing and Rest Home took the lives of 23 elderly persons, most of whom succumbed from heavy smoke that poured into the chapel during morning services. Fire department officials suspected arson.

Feb. 4 New York, N.Y. An intense early morning fire that started in a back apartment on the ground floor spread quickly upward through a six-story building; 7 of the 10 persons who died were young children.

Feb. 16 Tiaret, Alg. A gas explosion that demolished two houses took the lives of 35 persons and injured 36 others.

April 13 Lapua, Fin. In the nation's worst industrial accident to date, a brick unit of an ammunition factory was totally destroyed by an explosion of gunpowder; the casualty toll included more than 40 dead and some 70 injured.

Aug. 12 Chalmette, La. An explosion in the fractionating tower of a refinery operated by the Tenneco Oil Co. killed 13 workers and seriously injured 6 others.

Aug. 29 Bangkok, Thailand. A chemical explosion and fire in a Bangkok factory killed 14 persons, 12 of whom were teenaged girls.

Dec. 24 Chicago, Ill. A three-story brick building was set ablaze when a can of lighter fluid, used to ignite an indoor charcoal grill, burst into flames; the burning fluid sloshed onto the hall floors and staircase when someone tried to carry it outdoors; among the 12 fatalities were 10 children attending a Christmas Eve birthday party on the upper floor.

Dec. 26 Numazu, Japan. A predawn explosion and fire, probably triggered by a gas leak in a bar, claimed the lives of at least 15 persons.

Dec. 26 Goulds, Newfoundland. Chafe's Rest Home, a two-story wooden structure, was totally destroyed by an early morning fire that apparently started with an electrical malfunction; 21 persons inside the building lost their lives.

MARINE

Jan. 3 Rangoon River, Burma. A double-deck ferryboat burned and sank after an explosion was set off by careless smoking near a leaking drum of gasoline; 12 persons were known to have died, 27 were severely burned, and some 150 were missing.

Jan. 9 Off Surat Thani Province, Thailand. Two ferryboats collided in predawn darkness off the southern coast of Thailand; though many passengers were rescued after one of the boats sank, 15 lost their lives and 50 others were reported missing.

Jan. 18 Off east coast of Mindanao, Phil. Two crewmen from the 224,000-ton Norwegian supertanker "Berge Istra" were rescued by a Japanese fishing boat after being adrift on a life raft for 20 days. They reported that three explosions on Dec. 30, 1975, ripped apart the hull of the "Berge Istra," which sank with the loss of 30 lives. The freighter was the largest ship ever lost at sea.

WIDE WORLD

A rescue worker covers a victim of aviation's worst midair collision. Two airliners, one British and the other Yugoslav, crashed head on near Zagreb, Yugoslavia, in September, killing all 176 persons aboard the two planes.

Jan. 19 Southern Bangladesh. A tidal wave that swept into the Ganges Delta from the Bay of Bengal took the lives of an estimated 800 fishermen in the vicinity of Barisal.

Jan. 20 Ichamati River, India. A launch carrying about 150 persons capsized in the Ganges Delta; early reports indicated that probably more than 40 persons drowned.

Late January Off southern Burma. About 160 of an estimated 200 passengers aboard a ferryboat reportedly lost their lives after a collision with a fishing trawler in the Andaman Sea.

March 25 Southern coastal waters, Haiti. About 100 persons died when fire broke out aboard the ferryboat "St. Sauveur" as it was making its way eastward from Dame Marie to Port-au-Prince.

Aug. 7 Gulf of Thailand. An overloaded three-deck ferryboat, operated by an unlicensed skipper, capsized several hundred miles south of Bangkok; nearly 30 persons were known to have died, but dozens of others were missing and presumably drowned.

Aug. 16 Gulf of St. Lawrence, Canada. A 14-ft motor launch capsized in stormy weather after setting out from Percé, Quebec; all of the nine French tourists and three Canadians were presumed drowned after the empty boat was recovered and one body retrieved from the water.

Aug. 29 Mindanao Province, Phil. Huge waves capsized a boat at the mouth of the Davao River; 19 of the 25 persons aboard were missing and presumed drowned.

Oct. 15 West of Bermuda. The 590-ft vessel "Sylvia L. Ossa," en route from Brazil to Pennsylvania with a cargo of iron ore, broke up in heavy seas and sank about 140 mi due west of Bermuda; rescue teams spotted pieces of wreckage but found no evidence that any of the 37 crewmen survived.

Oct. 20 Near Luling, La. The Norwegian tanker "Frosta" and the car ferry "George Prince" collided on the Mississippi River just before dawn; rescue divers recovered 71 bodies and more than 30 vehicles from the river, but an estimated 27 other persons were missing and presumed drowned; 18 persons survived.

Mid-October English Channel. Two small German ships, the tanker "Böhlen" and the freighter "Antje Oltmann," were lashed by gales in the English Channel; a total of 32 seamen were presumed to have lost their lives in the turbulent waters.

Rescuers look for survivors from the Mississippi ferry boat "George Prince" after it collided with a tanker at Luling, Louisiana, in October. Only 18 persons survived of about 120.

WIDE WORLD

Oct. 19 Off Newfoundland, Canada. The small Dutch freighter "Gabriella" was abandoned in heavy seas about 60 mi off the coast of Newfoundland; all but 2 of the 15 persons aboard lost their lives.

Nov. 11 Northwest of Honolulu, Hawaii. The 486-ft Japanese lumber ship "Carnelian 1" flooded and sank in stormy seas about 1,400 mi from Honolulu; 14 crewmen were rescued but 19 others were missing and presumed dead.

Dec. 25 Red Sea. An Egyptian passenger ship, the "Patria," caught fire and sank about 50 mi from Jidda, Saudi Arabia; most of the passengers were Muslim pilgrims returning to Egypt after visiting sacred shrines in Mecca and Medina; early estimates put the death toll at about 150.

MINING

March 9 and 11 Near Whitesburg, Ky. An explosion of methane gas in a mine operated by the Scotia Coal Co. claimed the lives of 15 workers; a second explosion some 36 hours later killed 11 more persons, including three federal safety inspectors, who attempted to investigate the mine and render it secure.

Aug. 5 Breza, Yugos. An explosion killed 17 miners who were working 600 ft underground; of the 100 workers who escaped, only a few were injured by the blast.

Sept. 7 Walbrzych, Poland. An explosion that shattered a coal mine shaft killed at least 17 workers and injured more than 30 others; some 70 other miners escaped unhurt.

Mid-September Near Tete, Mozambique. A gas explosion inside a coal mine claimed the lives of more than 100 workers.

October 4 Near Dhanbad, India. An explosion in a Sudamdih coal mine killed 39 workers and injured about 30 others.

Dec. 31 Chlebovice, Czech. A gas explosion at the Staric coal mine trapped 45 workers underground; despite frantic rescue efforts, none of the 45 was expected to survive.

MISCELLANEOUS

January Jamaica. A shipment of imported flour contaminated by the insecticide parathion was blamed for the deaths of 17 persons.

March 9 Cavalese, Italy. A cable car, carrying vacationing skiers back to their lodgings at the end of the day, swung precariously when a cable loosened, then plunged 200 ft to the frozen ground; most of the 42 persons who died were from West Germany.

April 16 Gulf of Mexico. A survival capsule, launched from a storm-battered oil-drilling rig that sank off the Texas coast, landed upside down in heavy seas; 13 workers who were trapped inside the capsule died.

June 5 Snake River Valley, Idaho. The 307-ft-high Teton Dam, criticized as potentially dangerous even before its construction began, collapsed from its own inadequacy as its reservoir was being filled for the first time; the vast quantity of water that roared into the upper Snake River Valley killed 14 persons, made some 30,000 homeless, and caused damage estimated at hundreds of millions of dollars.

Early July Madras, India. Bootleg liquor containing methyl alcohol and other toxic ingredients killed 84 persons and hospitalized about 100 others, some of whom faced possible death or blindness.

Late July. Philadelphia, Pa. A mysterious flu-like disease attacked members of the American Legion attending a convention in Philadelphia; despite intense monitoring of patients and extensive laboratory research, medical authorities were unable to identify the disease that claimed 29 lives and hospitalized 151.

Sept. 13 Karachi, Pakistan. A one-year-old six-story residential building collapsed because of inadequate foundations; of the 140 persons who were killed, 6 belonged to the family of the man who owned the building.

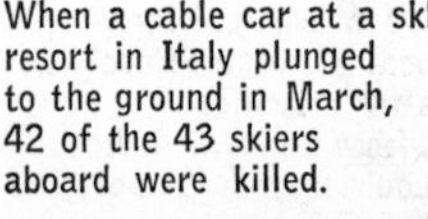

When a cable car at a ski resort in Italy plunged to the ground in March, 42 of the 43 skiers aboard were killed.

UPI COMPIX

NATURAL

Jan. 2–3 Northern Europe. A violent storm packing winds in excess of 100 mph struck England with devastating force before moving on to the Continent; there were 26 fatalities reported in Britain, 12 in West Germany, and a total of 17 others in Denmark, Belgium, The Netherlands, Sweden, Austria, France, and Switzerland.

Feb. 4 Guatemala. An earthquake that measured 7.5 on the Richter scale caused extensive damage in the heavily populated capital of Guatemala City and virtually destroyed several other towns and villages. As rescue operations proceeded, the estimate of casualties increased dramatically to an estimated 23,000 dead and some 75,000 injured.

Feb. 11 Esmeraldas, Ecuador. At least 60 persons were believed to have been killed when a landslide hit a section of Esmeraldas.

Mid-February Bitlis Province, Turkey. A series of avalanches in eastern Anatolia claimed the lives of 27 persons; intense snowstorms knocked out power lines, isolated towns, and trapped some 500 passenger buses on open roads.

April 9 Esmeraldas, Ecuador. An earthquake that struck the port city of Esmeraldas claimed at least ten lives and caused damage estimated at $4 million.

April 10 Faridpur, Bangladesh. A tornado that struck at least a dozen villages in Faridpur District in central Bangladesh killed 19 persons and injured more than 200 others.

May 2 Near Fresno, Colombia. Torrential rains triggered a landslide on an east-west road crossing the Andes Mountains of Colombia; 13 persons died and 16 others were injured.

May 6 Northeast Italy. A major earthquake that struck the northeastern area of Italy during the night caused extensive damage in several towns; late reports indicated that nearly 1,000 persons were killed.

Mid-May Luzon, Phil. Record-breaking rains unleashed on the island of Luzon by Typhoon Olga caused massive flooding that took 215 lives and left at least 600,000 persons homeless; property damage and crop losses were estimated at $150 million.

June 4 Pahire Phedi, Nepal. An early morning landslide took the lives of an estimated 150 villagers in central Nepal.

Mid-June Bangladesh. Persistent torrential monsoon rains were responsible for the deaths of at least 143 persons, some of whom were buried under landslides; the rains also caused major rivers to overflow their banks.

June 26 Irian Jaya, Indon. A major earthquake that struck the Indonesian province of Irian Jaya on the island of New Guinea claimed an estimated 500 to 1,000 lives.

Mid-July Mexico. After nearly two weeks of almost constant rain, an estimated 120 persons were dead and some 50 others missing as a result of floods in central and eastern Mexico; in addition, hundreds of thousands were homeless and millions of acres of fertile farmland were inundated.

July 14 Bali, Indon. An earthquake measuring 5.6 on the Richter scale killed more than 500 persons and injured about 3,400 others; fatalities included schoolchildren who were killed when their building in Seririt collapsed.

July 28 T'ang-shan, Hopeh Province, China. Two devastating earthquakes, measuring 8.2 and 7.9 on the Richter scale, struck northeast China 16 hours apart. Though no official report on damage or casualties was released at the time, it was learned that the industrial city of T'ang-shan had been virtually leveled and that extensive damage had also taken place in Tientsin and Peking. The death toll was later reliably estimated to be about 700,000, which made the T'ang-shan disaster the second worst in recorded history. In 1556 an earthquake in Shensi Province, China, claimed some 830,000 lives.

July 31 Big Thompson River Canyon, Colo. A 30-ft high wall of water raced through the narrow Big Thompson River Canyon after unusual meteorological conditions caused more than a foot of rain to fall in six hours; though rescuers recovered 130 bodies, fears remained that other vacationers were still buried beneath the mud and rubble.

Aug. 7 Chonju, South Korea. Torrential rains killed at least 25 persons, 15 of whom were buried by a landslide while attending religious services.

Aug. 10 Northern Pakistan. Heavy rains that caused the Ravi River to overflow its banks caused extensive damage in northern Pakistan; more than 150 persons died in the floodwaters that extended to some 5,000 villages.

Aug. 17 Philippines. A severe earthquake in the Moro Gulf created a 15–20-ft-high tidal wave that struck the island of Mindanao and the Sulu Archipelago with devastating force; Pres. Ferdinand Marcos estimated that the death toll would reach 8,000 and the damage to property would exceed $100 million.

Aug. 25 Hong Kong. The worst tropical storm to hit Hong Kong in nearly 50 years killed at least 11 persons, injured 62 others, and left about 3,000 persons homeless.

Sept. 5 Baluchistan Province, Pakistan. Floodwaters that eroded and then demolished the 442-ft-high earthen Bolan Dam washed away entire villages and inundated more than 5,000 sq mi of land; though no statistics were immediately available the death toll was expected to be high.

Sept. 8–13 Southern Japan. Typhoon Fran battered southern Japan with 100-mph winds and deposited 60 in of rain on the land; 104 persons were killed, 57 were missing, and an estimated 325,000 were made homeless.

Oct. 1 La Paz, Mexico. A 30-ft-high earthen dam burst under the impact of Hurricane Liza, which packed 130-mph winds and dumped 5½ in of rain on the city; a 5-ft wall of water swept across a shantytown in La Paz and killed at least 630 persons; tens of thousands of persons were rendered homeless by the disaster.

Oct. 6 Near Pereira, Colombia. Heavy rains caused a dike to burst shortly after midnight; at least 47 persons lost their lives and about 30 others were injured.

Oct. 29 Irian Jaya, Indon. A severe earthquake in the Bime, Eipomek, and Nalka areas of Irian Jaya on the island of New Guinea killed at least 133 persons.

Nov. 6 Trapani, Sicily, Italy. Heavy rains, which could not be carried off by Trapani's inadequate sewer system, generated floodwaters that took the lives of ten persons.

Nov. 7 Khorasan Province, Iran. A moderately severe earthquake that struck Vandik and several other villages in northeastern Iran killed at least 16 persons and inflicted injuries on about 30 others.

Nov. 20 Chameza, Colombia. A landslide that occurred about 190 mi from Bogotá smashed into a cluster of peasant huts in Chameza and claimed an estimated 20 lives.

Nov. 24 Van Province, Turkey. A major earthquake, measuring 7.9 on the Richter scale, struck eastern Turkey in the afternoon; heavy snows and rugged terrain impeded the work of rescue teams which expected the final death toll to reach about 4,000.

Late November Eastern Java, Indon. Heavy rains that inundated large areas of eastern Java caused extensive property and crop damage and claimed the lives of at least 136 persons.

Dec. 20 Aceh, Sumatra, Indon. Torrential rains caused severe flooding in villages within the administrative district of Aceh in Sumatra; at least 25 persons were killed.

RAILROADS

Feb. 17 Near Alexandria, Egypt. At least 11 persons died when a speeding train smashed into a train that was not in motion; about 50 other persons were seriously injured.

Feb. 20(?) Near Caborca, Mexico. A collision between a train and a bus killed 30 persons and injured 50 others.

April 21 Near Ta-ch'eng, Taiwan. An express train that crashed into a bus in central Taiwan killed 40 persons, about half of whom were students in their early teens.

April 27 Northeast Egypt. A collision between two trains about 90 mi from Cairo took the lives of 12 persons and caused injuries to more than 50 others.

May 4 Schiedam, Neth. The ten-coach Rhine Express, on a run from the Hook of Holland to West Germany and Austria, crashed head-on into a slowly moving local train during the morning rush hour. All 23 fatalities, some of them children, were aboard the badly damaged Dutch train.

May 23 Near Seoul, Korea. A truck loaded with 200 drums of fuel oil exploded in flames after striking a commuter train filled with families on their way to Sunday outings; flaming oil was mainly responsible for the 19 dead and 95 injured.

June 14 Jasen, Bulg. Ten persons were killed and three injured when a passenger train collided with a freight train about 100 mi from Sofia.

June 27 Neufvilles, Belgium. A crowded express train traveling from Amsterdam to Paris jumped the tracks in southern Belgium; 11 persons were killed and about 30 injured.

Sept. 6 Benoni, South Africa. A commuter train crashed into an express train that had halted for a red light at the Benoni station, 16 mi from Johannesburg; most of the 31 fatalities and 70 injured were aboard the express train, which was demolished.

Sept. 9 Cameroon. Two passenger trains collided in southern Cameroon; though initial reports were sketchy, more than 100 were feared killed and about 300 injured.

Sept. 20 Near Ljubljana, Yugos. An express train traveling to Trieste collided head-on with a local passenger train; at least 17 persons lost their lives and about 40 others were injured, some seriously.

Oct. 10 Northwestern Mexico. A glass-domed passenger train traveling through scenic Sierra Madre Occidental slammed into a freight train after the engineer failed to heed a stop signal; the Red Cross reported 24 fatalities.

Nov. 3 Near Czestochowa, Poland. A passenger train, making a scheduled stop at the small town of Julianka, was struck by an express train during a heavy fog; 25 persons were killed and 60 others injured.

Nov. 10 Near Zagreb, Yugos. An express train, speeding past a crossing that had not been closed off by the attendant, crashed into the back half of a crowded bus and killed 10 of the persons aboard.

Nov. 29 Near Kathekani, Kenya. An express train traveling from Mombasa to Nairobi plunged into the Ngaineithia River when the weight of the train caused a bridge, already weakened by swirling floodwaters, to give way; of the nearly 650 persons aboard the express, about 200 suffered injuries and at least 14 were killed.

TRAFFIC

Jan. 4 Natal State, South Africa. Nineteen persons were reported killed and 38 injured when a bus plunged into the Umtawalumi River.

Jan. 26 Near Nongoma, South Africa. A bus crash in a remote area of eastern South Africa killed 19 persons and injured 76 others.

KEYSTONE

Twenty-three persons on a commuter train were killed when it collided head-on with an express train at Schiedam, Neth., in May.

Feb. 7 Beckemeyer, Ill. A camper truck that was crossing an unguarded railroad track at night was hit by a fast-moving Baltimore & Ohio 67-car freight train; a grandfather and 11 young children were killed on their way to a roller-skating rink.

Feb. 7 Konya Province, Turkey. Ten persons were killed and eight injured when a driver lost control of his bus on an icy road in central Turkey.

Feb. 10 Near Kinshasa, Zaire. A truck transporting workmen to their jobs crashed when the driver lost control of the vehicle; 23 were killed and dozens were injured.

March 5 Shivalli, India. A bus, jam-packed with guests traveling to a wedding reception, went off the road, overturned, and plunged into a deep irrigation canal when the driver swerved to avoid a bullock cart; 79 persons were killed.

March 29 Near Hoshiarpur, India. A reported 20 persons were killed and 40 injured when a bus crashed into a tree in northwestern India.

Late March Near Poona, India. A tractor-drawn wagon transporting wedding guests between villages fell into a canal; 45 bodies were recovered, but the death toll was expected to increase as recovery operations progressed.

April 29 Luzon Province, Phil. A bus heading for the resort city of Baguio in northern Luzon crashed into a tree and burned; 22 persons were killed and 7 were injured.

April 30 Near Baguio, Phil. A bus carrying trade school employees and their families to Baguio slipped over the edge of a 250-ft cliff that bounds the zigzag MacArthur highway; casualties included 29 persons dead and 27 seriously injured.

May 21 Near Martinez, Calif. A bus carrying members of a Yuba City high school choir smashed through a guardrail and landed upside down 30 ft below a bridge ramp that was part of a freeway exit; 28 students and one adult were killed and many teenagers were seriously injured.

May 28 Near Rishikesh, India. Forty persons lost their lives in northern India when a bus skidded and plunged into the Ganges River.

Aug. 25 Northeast Iran. A passenger bus and a tank truck crashed into each other some 50 mi from Shahrud in northeastern Iran; the accident claimed 21 lives.

September Near Trinidad, Cuba. A bus exploded in flames after colliding with a truck near Trinidad; 27 persons were reported killed.

Sept. 2 Near Mexico City, Mexico. A passenger bus went over a 150-ft embankment about 25 mi W of the nation's capital; at least 15 persons died in the mishap and some 30 others were injured.

Sept. 19 Santiago, Chile. A runaway truck crashed into a crowd of people celebrating Chile's independence day; 23 persons died and 62 were injured.

Oct. 15 Eastern Cuba. Two freight cars that broke away from an ore train at the Nicaro nickel mines smashed into a crowded bus at a lower level crossing; 54 persons were reported killed.

Nov. 14 Near Manaus, Brazil. A bus loaded with voters failed to stop at an Urubu River ferry crossing and was swept downstream after plunging into the water; 38 persons were killed in the mishap.

Nov. 29 Near Van, Turkey. A bus and taxi fell over a precipice and into Lake Van after colliding on a road; 25 persons were killed and 15 seriously injured.

Dec. 12 Near São Paulo, Brazil. A bus traveling between São Paulo and Igautu plunged into the Pardo River when the driver swerved to avoid hitting a group of pedestrians; 20 persons were killed and 16 injured.

Dec. 21 Lyon, France. A school bus transporting handicapped children went off the road in heavy fog as the driver attempted to make a sharp turn; 17 persons died in the waters of the Rhône River and 2 others were reported missing.

Disciples of Christ: *see* Religion

Diseases: *see* Health and Disease

Divorce: *see* Demography

Docks: *see* Transportation

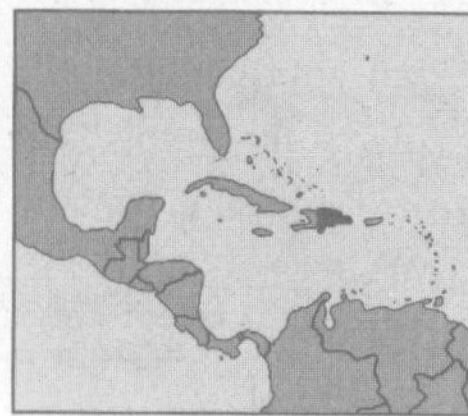

Dominican Republic

Covering the eastern two-thirds of the Caribbean island of Hispaniola, the Dominican Republic is separated from Haiti, which occupies the western third, by a rugged mountain range. Area: 18,658 sq mi (48,-323 sq km). Pop. (1975 est.): 4,696,800, including (1960) mulatto 73%; white 16%; Negro 11%. Cap. and largest city: Santo Domingo (pop., 1975 est., 922,500). Language: Spanish. Religion: mainly Roman Catholic (94%), with Protestant and Jewish minorities. President in 1976, Joaquín Balaguer.

In 1976 the country continued to be one of the most dynamic and stable nations in Latin America. However, agriculture, the basic sector of the economy, continued to suffer the consequences of the previous year's severe drought. Added to this, the fact that the agrarian reform programs were not pursued with the same vigour as in past years prompted continued land invasions by the peasants. The sugar industry suffered from both the sudden drop of prices on the world market and the increased duties placed by the U.S. on sugar imports.

In the mining sector the government strove for revision of agreements with foreign mining corporations. This was the case with the Aluminum Company of America's new contract, which provided greater returns to the nation. The tourist industry continued its economic boom sustained by U.S. investments. There was notable construction of new hotels. The Lowe's International Hotel was said to be the largest tourist facility in the Antilles. The high cost of oil imports and a shortage of electrical power forced a 20–30% cutback in industrial production.

The principal international events were the official visits in June of the king and queen of Spain and U.S. Secretary of State Henry Kissinger. There were also a number of discussions with Venezuelan leaders as part of the government's effort to broaden cultural and economic ties.

On the domestic scene the opposition parties were in the process of reorganization, attempting to improve their position for participation in the national elections of 1978. The Roman Catholic Church made public its concern about increasing corruption at all levels of Dominican life. On April 27 Msgr. Octavio Beras Rojas, archbishop of Santo Domingo, was named a cardinal by Pope Paul VI, the first Dominican to achieve that honour. (GUSTAVO ANTONINI)

[974.B.2.b]

DOMINICAN REPUBLIC

Education. (1972–73) Primary, pupils 833,439, teachers 15,216; secondary (1971–72), pupils 118,-190, teachers 5,381; vocational (1971–72), pupils 6,923, teachers 409; teacher training (1971–72), students 621, teachers 51; higher (1973–74), students 37,538, teaching staff 1,709.

Finance. Monetary unit: peso, at parity with the U.S. dollar, with (Sept. 20, 1976) a free rate of 1.72 pesos to £1 sterling. Gold, SDR's, and foreign exchange (June 1976) U.S. $60.9 million. Budget (1975 actual): revenue 652.4 million pesos; expenditure 639.9 million pesos. Gross national product (1973) 2,265,-700,000 pesos. Money supply (July 1976) 381 million pesos. Cost of living (Santo Domingo; 1970 = 100; March 1976) 170.

Foreign Trade. (1975) Imports 888.6 million pesos; exports 893.8 million pesos. Import sources: U.S. 71%; Japan 9%. Export destinations: U.S. 67%; The Netherlands 7%. Main exports: sugar 65%; coffee 5%.

Transport and Communications. Roads (1971) 10,467 km. Motor vehicles in use (1974): passenger *c.* 59,000; commercial (including buses) *c.* 29,000. Railways (1975) 475 km. Telephones (Jan. 1975) 95,-400. Radio receivers (Dec. 1973) 180,000. Television receivers (Dec. 1973) 155,000.

Agriculture. Production (in 000; metric tons; 1975): rice 231; corn (1974) *c.* 38; sweet potatoes *c.* 100; cassava (1974) *c.* 205; dry beans *c.* 29; tomatoes *c.* 86; peanuts *c.* 93; sugar, raw value *c.* 1,245; oranges (1974) *c.* 64; avocados (1974) *c.* 129; mangoes (1974) *c.* 143; bananas (1974) 315; cocoa *c.* 30; coffee *c.* 54; tobacco *c.* 17. Livestock (in 000; June 1974): cattle *c.* 1,560; sheep *c.* 49; pigs *c.* 800; goats *c.* 340; horses *c.* 170; chickens *c.* 7,200.

Industry. Production (in 000; metric tons; 1974): cement 643; bauxite 1,196; electricity (kw-hr) 1,512,-000.

Drama:
see Motion Pictures; Theatre

Dress:
see Fashion and Dress

Drug Abuse

Narcotics and Dangerous Drugs. Marijuana received a mild degree of official support at the beginning of the year when the National Institute on Drug Abuse in the U.S. issued its fifth annual *Marijuana and Health* report. While the main message of the report was that pot smoking poses significant hazards for drivers, pilots, factory workers, and others who cannot afford any diminution in mental alertness or physical coordination, new research showed that the drug is of value in reducing the internal pressure of the eye in glaucoma patients, that it may be useful in controlling vomiting in cancer patients undergoing chemotherapy, and that it can dilate the air tubes and ease breathing in asthmatics.

The report stressed that any eventual medical uses of cannabis were likely to involve synthetic compounds rather than the natural drug, and it added a warning that chronic users appeared to develop a tolerance, so that cannabis might not be the answer for the distressed asthmatic seeking a safe and pleasant means of permanent relief. Research conducted after publication of the previous report had failed to support earlier fears that chronic use of marijuana leads to genetic damage, lower fertility rates, or serious impotence problems. While not giving the drug a clean bill of health, which many had hoped for, the report did support the view that cannabis has only a low biological toxicity and stated that it is questionable whether any death can be attributed to an overdose.

The report stated that use of marijuana in the U.S. was increasing, and that more than half of all Americans between the ages of 18 and 25 had tried it at least once. "In the past seven years," said the report, "what was once statistically deviant behavior has become the norm for this age group." As a result of the increasing use and social acceptability of the drug, trade in cannabis had become a seller's market. The price in the U.S. had risen steeply, so that material which once cost between $10 and $20 an ounce now cost $150 an ounce or more.

An expert from Nepal, writing in the *British Journal of Psychiatry*, took a less rosy view of the drug's innocence. B. P. Sharma of Kathmandu, reporting a study of long-term cannabis users, found that, out of 166 married users, only 31 had a normal interest in the sexual side of marriage. He described their conversation as monotonous, full of unnecessary details, and tending to be restricted to a few topics—delicious food, kind angels who provided every sort of thing without any effort on their part, their own health, and how their families neglected them. However, Sharma pointed out that in Nepal cannabis users had always been thought of as people of "rather low calibre." Thus it might be that his findings reflected the fact that only persons who had inadequate personalities in the first place would normally become users.

Apart from the effects of cannabis on the mind, a report from Indiana University's department of chemistry suggested that marijuana cigarettes may contain higher concentrations of several cancer-causing agents than tobacco cigarettes. The study was based on a comparison of the chemical composition of the smoke obtained from 2,000 Mexican marijuana cigarettes and 2,000 tobacco cigarettes, using a smoking machine.

In the U.S. considerable publicity was focused on a $120,000, two-year study set up at the Southern Illinois University School of Medicine aimed at determining whether the sexual arousal produced in male volunteers in response to pornographic films was affected by the smoking of marijuana cigarettes. The sex hormones circulating in their blood were also to be measured before and after they had indulged in "joints." Critics in Congress branded the study as "tax-paid debauchery," and the National Institute on Drug Abuse withdrew its support.

After a fatal traffic accident in Britain, the blood plasma of the dead driver was found to contain very high levels of the active cannabinoids present in marijuana smoke, as measured by a new, highly accurate radioimmunoassay method. Reporting the case in the *Lancet,* the doctors concerned suggested that it should now be possible to accumulate evidence concerning the influence of cannabis on road safety. They suggested that, because of its widespread use, cannabis, just like alcohol, may be particularly dangerous, not only to those actually using it but to others as well. This danger was emphasized by the fact that the victim of the road accident, who had almost certainly died as a result of smoking pot before driving, was a railway signalman. Narcotic drugs do not pose the same problems because the majority of heroin users do not drive.

Newborn babies may suffer dangerous drug withdrawal symptoms if their mothers have been taken off opiates during pregnancy. This can happen when the drug to which the mother is addicted is withheld during labour or is withdrawn rapidly during the period immediately preceding birth. A team from London's University College Hospital reported that it is necessary to wean addicted mothers from their drugs slowly if danger to their unborn children is to be avoided.

During the year a number of papers were published on enkephalin, a substance produced naturally in the brain, which appears to act like morphine (although it is chemically dissimilar) and to have some specific pain-dampening function. It was suspected that morphine may work on the brain by taking part in reactions normally involving enkephalin, and it was hoped that further study of this newly discovered and newly synthesized brain chemical would throw light on the mechanisms of morphine addiction, thus leading to an effective treatment for addicts. Researchers in several countries, including Britain, the U.S., and Sweden, were working on the problem.

The barbiturates remained under a cloud in the eyes of most doctors. Barbiturate overdosage was responsible for some 10,000 hospital admissions each year in the U.K. and accounted for more than one-third of all drug overdose deaths. A survey carried out among 226 family physicians in two British towns revealed that 75% of those who returned questionnaires had stopped prescribing barbiturates entirely, and a further 20% said they seldom prescribed them. According to Eric Wilks of the Department of Community Medicine at the University of Sheffield, who conducted the survey, this meant that "a practice that was, until recently, no more than uncommon has now become an inexcusable eccentricity." It seemed likely that this local finding reflected a general trend.

Alcohol. Little progress appeared to have been made in tackling the worldwide problem of alcoholism. A World Health Organization report, prepared by WHO's European regional office in collaboration with Finnish and Canadian researchers, pointed out that in many countries cirrhosis of the liver had become a leading cause of death among middle-aged men. It was also clear that alcohol played a major role in deaths from accidents and in cancers of the upper digestive and respiratory tracts.

Governments, and those with an economic interest in alcohol supply, had accepted the desirability of educating people to refrain from harmful drinking and of the need to identify and treat "problem drinkers." However, general restrictions on the availability of alcohol were vigorously opposed. According to the WHO report, it is almost useless to attempt to tackle the problem by influencing those who have already acquired the drinking habit. The main aim should be to reduce the number of new alcoholics.

The Scottish Council on Alcoholism predicted that alcoholism would reach epidemic proportions in Scotland by the mid-1980s and would affect one-fifth of the population. There had been a sixfold increase in hospital admissions of alcoholics in Scotland since 1957, and drunkenness offenses and crimes of violence related to excessive drinking were steadily rising. The council estimated that each of Scotland's 60,000 alcoholic employees cost the economy approximately £600 a year through substandard work.

A report published in August showed that the quality of food eaten in Britain over the four years from 1972 to 1975 had undergone a steady decline, and that its energy value had fallen by 3%. By contrast, the consumption of spirits rose by 30% over the same period, from 3.4 proof pints per capita in 1972 to 4.5 proof pints in 1975. Wine and beer drinking also rose steadily.

There was more drinking among young people, and the onset of drinking was occurring at an earlier age.

Mexican agents took to helicopter in their war against the narcotics growers. Alejandro Gertz Manero (left) examines marijuana that had been sprayed with herbicide.

ALAN RIDING—THE NEW YORK TIMES

There was also evidence that those who start younger have a higher level of consumption. Most disturbing was the increase in the number of young persons under age 14 who were being diagnosed as having an alcohol problem. Many observers believed that young persons were turning to alcohol because, unlike marijuana and other illegal drugs, it was relatively cheap and easy to obtain and its use did not involve the risk of heavy penalties. At the same time, many adults tended to ignore drinking by their children or even to express relief that the children were not using illegal substances.

A long-smoldering argument on the treatment of alcoholism surfaced in June, when the Rand Corporation, a U.S. research institution, published a study suggesting that some alcoholics can safely return to social drinking. The report was vigorously attacked by many organizations concerned with the treatment of alcoholics, including the National Council on Alcoholism and Alcoholics Anonymous, which stressed total abstinence as the only way to prevent relapse. Although the Rand study had stated that there was no way to predict which persons could safely resume drinking in moderation, critics of the report feared that it might encourage many alcoholics to try, with potentially disastrous results. Further fuel was added to the controversy in August, when two studies published in the *Journal of Studies on Alcohol,* one conducted by the Addiction Research Foundation, Ontario, the other by the Center of Behavioral Medicine of the University of Pennsylvania, appeared to support the Rand findings.

As with opiates, a baby in the womb may be affected by the alcohol its mother drinks. During the year several studies confirmed the existence of a fetal alcohol syndrome, which includes a much higher risk of death immediately following birth, lower intelligence, stunted growth, a possible heart defect, and joint defects. Examination of the brains of affected babies who had died showed evidence of extensive developmental defects. An editorial in the *Lancet* suggested that serious consideration should be given to termination of pregnancy in mothers suffering from chronic severe alcoholism who have continued to drink throughout the first three months of pregnancy.

Tobacco. Despite vigorous efforts by some governments, the consumption of tobacco worldwide continued to increase. More cigarettes were smoked in the U.S. in 1975 than ever before. In particular, more American women and teenage girls were smoking than before, and they were starting at an earlier age. Cigarette sales rose to 602 billion in 1975 from 594 billion in 1974 and 547 billion in 1971, the year cigarette advertising on television was banned. However, the first year of a total ban on tobacco advertising in Norway produced encouraging results. Sales fell 15% in the first half of 1976 as compared with the latter half of 1975. New curbs on the advertising and promotion of cigarettes were introduced in Britain, where tobacco was said to cause at least 50,000 premature deaths annually.

Results of an American Cancer Society study released in September showed that the death rate from lung cancer and heart disease among smokers of low-tar and low-nicotine cigarettes was 16% lower than that among those using the high-tar, high-nicotine brands. Nevertheless, smokers of low-tar cigarettes still suffered an appreciably higher death rate than did nonsmokers.

A paper published in the *Lancet* revealed that the amount of carbon monoxide yielded by a number of filter-tipped cigarettes was, on average, 28% higher than that of untipped brands. The author said there was clear epidemiological evidence that the switch to filter tips since the mid-1950s had led to a reduction in lung cancer mortality among men aged less than 60 years, but his findings suggested that filter tips, because of their higher carbon monoxide yield, may carry a greater risk of heart disease.

(DONALD W. GOULD)

[522.C.9]

ENCYCLOPÆDIA BRITANNICA FILMS. *Scag (Heroin)* (1970); *Ups/Downs (Amphetamines and Barbiturates)* (1971); *Weed (Marijuana)* (1971); *Acid (LSD)* (1971); *The Drug Problem: What Do You Think?* (1972); *The Tobacco Problem: What Do You Think?* (1972); *The Alcohol Problem: What Do You Think?* (1973); *Alcohol: Pink Elephant* (1976).

Earth Sciences

GEOLOGY AND GEOCHEMISTRY

Many specific achievements in geology and geochemistry that merit review took place in 1976, but the year was especially significant for developments in the exploration and interpretation of planetary bodies and the oceanic crust. It was significant also because the Geodynamics Project began formulating a program for the 1980s that might be directed toward the continents and Earth resource systems.

Mars. The U.S. Viking mission, an unmanned field expedition to Mars, was the greatest geological achievement of 1976. Geologists sat in comfort before their television sets and watched with vicarious pleasure the survey of a really red Martian landscape through the eyes of a remote-controlled electro-optical camera. The titillating hope that evidence would be found for existing life forms, or fossil remains represented by organic compounds in the soil, was at first raised by the results of one test at both landing sites, but proof was not forthcoming from other tests.

The ingredients for life were found. The polar caps are composed dominantly of ice rather than of frozen carbon dioxide as previously believed. The photographic evidence from the Viking orbiters revealed beyond dispute that massive flows of water have at one time coursed across the Martian surface. Chemical reactions of the Martian soil in the biology laboratories of the two Vikings corresponded to those anticipated from the activity of microorganisms, but the gas/chromatograph mass spectrometer did not detect any organic compounds. One project scientist was quoted thus: "There is every sign of life except death. Where are the bodies?"

The magnificent new photographs from the Mars orbit and surface, together with the recent peek at the surface of Venus, would certainly be followed by significant developments in extraterrestrial geomorphology. The spectacular scenery raises many intriguing questions about tectonic and geomorphic processes. (*See* SPACE EXPLORATION.)

25th International Geological Congress. The Viking landings, on July 20 and September 3, straddled the sessions of the 25th International Geological Congress. Once every four years, geologists from throughout the world convene for approximately ten days of lectures, symposia, and international geopolitical meetings. The 1976 host was Sydney, Australia.

The U.S. Geodynamics Committee prepared a report to be available at the congress. This included

Dutch Literature: *see* Literature
Earthquakes: *see* Disasters; Earth Sciences

reference to the development of an approach to solid-earth studies in the 1980s, based on the findings of an ad hoc Working Group that convened in Washington, D.C., on June 3, 1976. A report of this meeting, "Crustal Dynamics," was also discussed at the congress. Whatever the outcome of these recent and future discussions, it was already evident that there was likely to be a shift of research emphasis from the ocean basins toward the origin and evolution of the continents.

The solution of many geological problems depends on an understanding of the structure of deep continental rocks. The petroleum industry developed a powerful seismic reflection profiling technique for depths of a few kilometres. This technique was successfully tested in 1975 to probe the continental crust to a depth of 50 km (30 mi). An extensive project to apply it was being planned by a consortium of scientists as part of the U.S. Geodynamics Program.

Earth Resource Systems. The U.S. Geodynamics Committee reports noted that the model of plate tectonics that had been developed during the past decade could now be applied to the evolution of the Earth's crust and the consequential formation of energy resource and ore deposits. The utility of plate tectonics as an exploration tool was a major topic of discussion in connection with oil and geothermal resources at the annual meeting of the American Association of Petroleum Geologists and Society of Economic Paleontologists and Mineralogists.

At a Penrose Conference (Geological Society of America) in March on "Function of the Geologist in Society" a group of representatives from government, academia, and industry informally initiated the proposal that the current Geodynamics Program should be followed by a global program aimed directly at better understanding of solid-Earth resource systems. They maintained that Earth resource systems must be considered on a global scale, in terms of both exploration and utilization. The United States, for example, had become increasingly dependent on foreign nations for petroleum and various mineral commodities, while at the same time foreign-assistance programs since 1945 permitted the U.S. Geological Survey and U.S. Bureau of Mines to provide geological assistance to less developed countries. Recent modifications eliminated most U.S. geological assistance, however, thereby terminating the cooperative relations that had been developed with reserve agencies and officials of other nations. This meant that U.S. information about known and potential mineral resources in less developed countries sharply decreased. The U.S. National Committee on Geology recommended a new program of technical cooperation aimed at improvement of the resource institutions and programs of the less developed countries.

During the year the Association of Geoscientists for International Development held its first general assembly, at the International Geological Congress. The association was committed to a more effective development of Earth resources, concern for their responsible management, and promotion of activities related to the needs of the less developed countries. A theme common to the association and to the participants of the Penrose Conference, reviewed above, was that geologists have in general failed to educate government and the public on the role of Earth sciences in the orderly development of natural resources.

The 1976 UN Conference on the Law of the Sea, the latest in a series begun almost 20 years earlier, involved 150 nations. These divided into two groups, the industrialized maritime nations and the less developed countries. The primary issue was the control of mining projects on the deep ocean floor, well away from national shorelines. This continuing debate was no longer an academic dispute because the geological exploration of the ocean floor had advanced sufficiently that the time for exploitation had arrived. (*See* LAW: *Special Report*.)

The Oceanic Crust. A December 1975 conference reviewing the results of the Deep Sea Drilling Project (see *Oceanography*, below) presented a complex picture of crustal magnetism, with an unexpected abundance of reversed polarity samples, shallow inclinations of remanent (residual) magnetism, and low intensities of magnetization. The relationships between observed basement rock magnetic complexities and the magnetic anomaly patterns observed at the ocean surface remained problematical.

Recent seismic studies have been interpreted in terms of the existence of shallow magma chambers, with 30% melt, beneath ocean ridges. Chemical studies of major and trace elements in oceanic basalts suggested that there are at least two mantle chemical systems beneath spreading ocean ridges, and that each basalt system has undergone extensive crystal fractionation. This is consistent with the evidence for magma chambers.

A major topic of discussion was the use of ophiolite complexes and data (an ophiolite complex is a group of igneous and sedimentary rocks including basalt, gabbro, and peridotite, and their metamorphic alteration products such as serpentine) from the ocean crust to develop models of vertical crustal structure. The ratio of intrusive to extrusive rocks in holes drilled in the deep-sea project appears to be higher than expected from comparison with ophiolites. According to ophiolite models, the basaltic crust should exhibit a steep metamorphic gradient caused by penetrative convection of seawater near the spreading axis. Unfortunately, the single deep hole available penetrated 600 m into virtually unmetamorphosed basalts. Is this to be considered a typical cross-section until proved otherwise, or is it to be considered atypical because it does not correspond with the ophiolite models?

The effect of penetration and convection of seawater into the rocks of the spreading ridge is significant in the geochemical budget of the igneous rock-marine sediment-seawater system. Studies of rare gases in submarine rocks and ocean water indicated that the formation of new crust in the region of the East Pacific Rise is associated with injection of primordial ^{3}He into the crust-seawater system.

There is a continuing strong trend in marine geochemistry to concentrate on the nature of the fluxes in the benthic (ocean bottom) boundary layer. An early version of a planned Bottom Ocean Measurement package designed to study fluxes in connection with the origin and formation of manganese nodules was being deployed in the Pacific Ocean.

Magnetostratigraphy. Although continued exploration of the magnetic properties of ocean floor rocks appeared to provide more questions than answers, there was a rapid growth in the applications of paleomagnetic methods to many problems in continental stratigraphy and paleontology. The Polarity Time Scale Subcommission of the International Union of Geological Sciences' Commission on Stratigraphy set up rules for evaluation of the magnetic data in magnetostratigraphic studies, and for correlation of stratigraphic zones and magnetic polarities. The ultimate aim is to correlate the magneto-chrono-biostratigraphy. An adjunct volume for this task is the Hedberg Guide, published in 1976 after 20 years of work by another arm of the Commission on Stratigraphy, the Subcommission on Stratigraphic Classification. The publication sets forth recommendations for procedures to be used by geologists on a worldwide basis.

Evolution of the Moon. At the seventh Lunar Science Conference in March, significant progress was reported toward understanding the first 500 million years of the Moon's history. Agreement was reached that the Moon's accretionary phase overlapped with melting and differentiation, and that the Moon melted to a considerable depth very early in its history. The mare basalts produced by remelting of mafic cumulates (minerals rich in iron and magnesium) between 3.9 billion and 3.1 billion years ago caused little disturbance of the closed chemical systems established 4.4 billion years ago. It is now possible to erect more elaborate models for specific whole-Moon compositions and to test these against the various geochemical constraints.

Comparative Planetology. The Apollo exploration of the Moon and the photographs and data returned from Mars, Mercury, Venus, and Jupiter greatly increased the understanding of planetary processes. During the year a new phase of extraterrestrial geology emerged. The term "comparative planetology" was applied to studies that examine a process or property on several planets.

An international organization was established at the September 1975 General Committee Meeting of the International Council of Scientific Unions. A Coordinating Committee for the Moon and Planets (CCMP) was established with the International Astronomical Union as parent, and with participation of five other unions. Its aims were to facilitate coordination of interdisciplinary research and exchange of information, to stimulate distribution of data, and to coordinate international meetings on planetary topics.

The Lunar Science Institute in Houston, Texas, organized and managed a project entitled "Basaltic Volcanism in the Terrestrial Planets: A Pilot Program in Comparative Planetology." This three-year program, which began in June, involved 50 to 90 scientists organized into ten study teams. One aim was to remove the boundaries that had developed between terrestrial, lunar, and planetary sciences, and to enhance communication among participants with expertise in various areas. For example, basaltic volcanism on the Earth should be more clearly understood when the process is seen in the perspective of its degree and stage on other planetary bodies. This program could initiate the same kind of stimulus for planetary sciences that the Geodynamics Project provided for the Earth sciences.

(PETER JOHN WYLLIE)

[133.A.3; 133.C.1.d; 133.E.5; 212.B.4; 212.F.1; 213.A; 214.C; 231.D]

How earthquakes are made: a highway cut through a California hill shows slippage scars above the San Andreas Fault, where two sections of the Earth's crust are sliding in opposite directions.

WIDE WORLD

GEOPHYSICS

Although the number of earthquakes, including large ones, occurring during the year was not exceptional, several major shocks centred in populous regions caused great loss of life and extreme damage. Two of these, including the largest to occur since the Alaska earthquake of 1964, occurred in a heavily industrialized area of northeastern China.

On July 28, 1976, at 3:40 AM and at 6:50 PM Peking time, earthquakes of magnitudes 8.2 and 7.9, respectively, struck the Peking-Tientsin-T'ang-shan area, which has a population of more than 15 million. The epicentres of the shocks were 145–160 km (90–100 mi) SE of Peking (pop. 7.5 million) and 65 km (40 mi) N of T'ang-shan (pop. 1 million). Hsinhua, the official news agency in China, reported: "A strong earthquake occurred in the T'ang-shan-Fengnan area on July 28, 1976, and affected the Tientsin and Peking municipalities causing great loss of life and property. T'ang-shan city, in particular, suffered extremely serious damage and losses." Unofficial sources estimated the dead, injured, and missing in the hundreds of thousands.

An earlier, smaller shock of magnitude 7.5 occurred on Feb. 4, 1976, in Guatemala and resulted in the deaths of 23,000 persons and injury of 75,000. Property damage was estimated at $1.1 billion. This earthquake was the subject of an intensive study by seismologists of the U.S. Geological Survey in cooperation with the government of Guatemala with support from the Organization of American States. Engineering studies were also made by the Portland Cement Association. The resulting reports gave a comprehensive picture of the seismicity, tectonic processes, and damage pertaining to the shock.

The earthquake occurred in a relatively inactive area on the Motagua Fault at a depth of 29 km (18 mi). This fault sharply defines the boundary between two large crustal plates, the North American and the Caribbean. The former is moving westward with respect to the latter at an average of 2.1 cm per year. The fault movement accompanying the earthquake represented a violent continuation of this long-term motion and was the largest surface displacement recorded in the Americas since the San Francisco earthquake of 1906. The area of damage was 33,000 sq km, and the communities and small towns where 100% damage was incurred covered 1,700 sq km. Many buildings of modern design were severely damaged, but most casualties resulted from the collapse of adobe structures and from massive landslides that completely covered two villages; destroyed highways, railways, and communication lines; and dammed a river. A partial count showed 88,404 homes destroyed and 435,000 left homeless.

On Aug. 17, 1976, another great earthquake occurred. This shock had a magnitude of 8.0 and took place off the south coast of Mindanao in the Philippine

Islands. In addition to major damage due to the earthquake directly, giant waves from 6 to 7.5 m high surged inland as far as 0.4 km (0.25 mi). Reports indicated over 8,000 dead and 175,000 left homeless. A quake of magnitude 7.9, centred on the northeast shore of Lake Van, devastated a mountainous area of eastern Turkey on November 24. The death toll was estimated at about 4,000 and help for the survivors was delayed by snow and frigid weather.

Earthquake prediction research received additional impetus as a result of these disasters. This augmented the increased interest generated by the successful prediction by Chinese seismologists of the Feb. 4, 1975, earthquake, magnitude 7.3, which destroyed the city of Haicheng and severely damaged several factories in the vicinity. There was little loss of life because authorities were able to evacuate thousands of persons in anticipation of the shock.

The Chinese were reported to have 10,000 trained earthquake observers operating in 17 centres, receiving data from 250 seismograph stations and 5,000 auxiliary observation points. Their predictions were based not only on recognized instrumentally recorded precursor phenomena such as dilatancy, increased radon content in groundwater, marked changes in the rate of Earth tilt, and changes in the geomagnetic conditions but also on such secondary phenomena as anomalous animal behaviour and disturbances in water wells and aquifers.

The research efforts in the U.S. on earthquake prediction were modest in comparison with those of China. Two events in the U.S. did, however, stimulate interest in the field. On Nov. 27, 1974, data gathered by seismologists of the U.S. Geological Survey from a highly instrumented section of the San Andreas Fault led them to believe that a moderate earthquake was imminent. They did not make a public prediction, but on the following day an earthquake of magnitude 5.3 occurred in the area where it was expected. Later, and possibly more important, the Palmdale uplift was discovered. Centring on Palmdale, Calif., this area, estimated at 12,000 sq km, has risen 0.25 m over the past 15 years. The most rapid rise occurred in 1962 and, on the basis of experience in other regions, should have resulted in an earthquake. Since no shock occurred, seismologists believe it is important to discover how this area differs from others exhibiting the same precursor characteristics and also to determine whether the bulge may still presage an earthquake.

Seismologists at the Weizmann Institute of Science, Rehovot, Israel, discovered that in 1943 an earthquake in the Jordan Rift Valley had produced a white material that discoloured the adjacent Dead Sea for about five months. A check of previous earthquakes revealed that another shock, occurring in 1834, had produced similar white material. This suggested a unique geophysical clock. By analyzing sedimentary profiles in samples taken from the Dead Sea floor, seismologists were able to correlate 65% of the layers of white deposits with known earthquakes. The relative depths corresponded to the time of occurrence, and the thickness of each layer was roughly proportional to the earthquake magnitude. The current profiles covered 2,000 years, and the investigators believed that deeper sampling would reveal evidence of earlier events, mentioned in the Bible and elsewhere, that have occurred during the last 4,000 years.

The models describing the migration of the Indian subcontinent across the ancient Tethys Sea and its collision with the Asian continent to form the Himalayas leave many factors unexplained. Tibet is less seismic than required and has no history of geologically recent volcanism that should be characteristic. Also, no previous hypothesis has explained the presence of the well-defined Precambrian crystal core of the Himalayas, and stratigraphic, paleontological, and paleomagnetic data are thought by some to argue against a wide oceanic separation between India and Tibet. To resolve some of these questions, an investigator at the Geological Survey of India in Calcutta suggested that a series of microcontinents lay between India and Tibet and that during the collision these continental structures were tilted and uplifted to form the Himalayas.

One of the fundamental constants that plays an important part in geophysics and geophysical theory is the gravitational constant (G). The usual method of measuring the Moon's orbital time, by determining the Ephemeris Time based on the Earth's orbit around the Sun, cannot demonstrate a change in G because the orbits of both the Sun and the Moon would be affected in the same degree by such a variation. Astronomers at the Astronomical Institute of the University of Utrecht in The Netherlands have, however, analyzed the Moon's orbit from 1955 through 1974 by using an atomic clock as a standard. They found the lengthening of the orbital time to be considerably greater than it was when determined by Ephemeris Time. The external deterrent force that contributes to this increase in period—tidal friction, solar wind, meteorite impacts, and drag exerted by the interplanetary medium—can account for only a portion of the change. It is postulated that the remainder of the effect is due to a decrease of G by 8 parts in 10^{11} per year. Among the experiments being undertaken to test this hypothesis were the lunar laser-ranging experiment, which allows a much more precise measurement of the Moon's orbit, and radar ranging measurements, which make more precise determinations of the orbits of Mercury and Venus.

LAJOS SOS—INTERFOTO MTI/EASTFOTO

Observer's deck of the photographic telescope at Hungary's new Cosmic Geodetic Observatory near Budapest. It will use data sent by Earth satellites to make geodetic measurements.

An experiment that produced negative results was an attempt to determine the various rotational and orbital parameters of the Sun and the Moon by studying fossil corals. An estimate of the lengths of the year and day was determined from the annual growth rings and intermediate ridges of corals for various periods extending as far back as 529 million years. These values were then used to calculate the changes in angular momentum and in the radius of the Earth. A decrease in G would indicate an increase in the radius of the Earth, but the analysis of the coral indicated that the radius has been essentially constant for the last 500 million years.

(RUTLAGE J. BRAZEE)

[131.B.5; 213.B; 241.D]

HYDROLOGY

In the United States most sources of cheap water by 1976 were either being used or had already been allocated, and most suggestions for conservation, treatment, and reuse carried what seemed to be unacceptably high price tags. One result was increasing attention to groundwater. During the past year, more than ever before, groundwater and the subsurface environment were studied, evaluated, and talked about in terms of water supply, waste disposal, storage and living space, and natural hazards.

Withdrawal of groundwater doubled in the U.S. in the past 20 years. By 1976 groundwater provided between one-quarter and one-third of all water used for all purposes, and about half the people in the U.S. depended on it for their domestic supplies.

The emphasis of investigations during the year was on the maintenance of groundwater quality. This is particularly a problem where wastes are being or are planned to be injected into the subsurface either directly through wells or indirectly by infiltration of polluted water from sanitary landfills and waste-spreading practices. New studies clearly showed that planning for groundwater use requires consideration of surface-water resources, actual and proposed land and water use, and actual and proposed waste disposal practices.

The occurrence of groundwater in the U.S. is known well enough for national, regional, and large-area purposes. In addition, many small areas have been studied intensively and the available information is adequate for foreseeable managerial purposes. However, the groundwater resources of many localities would have to be studied in greater detail to meet most of the needs of planners and managers in the immediate and more distant future. This is especially so in large urban areas, and several recent studies showed the adverse effect of urbanization on underlying groundwater resources. The increase of impermeable areas—buildings, streets, and parking lots—decreases local recharge to the underlying aquifers. More critically, particularly in highly industrialized zones, the water that is recharged is polluted with organic and inorganic wastes, some of which are toxic.

Widespread concern for the continuing supply of clean fresh water resurrected interest in the use of mineralized and saline waters for nonpotable domestic, industrial, and agricultural purposes. A joint study by the Colorado Water Institutes and U.S. Bureau of Reclamation indicated that the cost of using low-quality water for domestic purposes is about double previous estimates, which themselves were not favourable.

Advances in Applications of Research. The use of combinations of data from Landsat 1 and 2 and other satellites demonstrated the practicality of using remote sensing from satellites and high-flying aircraft for preliminary hydrological assessments of the water regimens of large areas. Satellite equipment used for hydrological studies was now able to sense, record, and transmit information from as many as 20 different sensors for areas as small as an acre. With the launching of Landsat 2 in 1975, three different proven systems of satellite data collection became available. These were Landsat 2, which receives bursts of data from collecting platforms and transmits them immediately to receiving stations; the three Geostationary Operational Environmental Satellites (GOES) launched in 1974 and 1975, which interrogate data-collection platforms on command of the receiving stations; and the commercial Telesat satellite, which demonstrated its capabilities of transmitting hydrological data.

Satellite sensors record several spectra of infrared, ultraviolet, and visible light reflections, and magnetic and microwave emissions. They are able, when related to data gathered on the ground, to monitor some aspects of water quality, detect sources of fresh water and the extent of streamflows, measure differences in water temperature, and locate point pollution sources. During the past year, using satellite imagery gathered for other purposes, a study gave the Yemen Arab Republic its first countrywide hydrological assessment; several new and enlarged existing areas for agricultural use were located, and other areas requiring ground-based investigation to determine their water-bearing potentials were identified. Elsewhere, thermal imagery was used both to detect freshwater discharges and losses to the sea and to assist with construction and highway planning, as in Florida where it was used to locate potential sinkholes.

During the year a dramatic shift took place, from regarding liquid wastes from effluents as substances to be treated and disposed of at considerable cost to considering them as sources of useful materials for many sectors of society. In St. Louis, Mo., the country's first waste exchange was organized. Its purpose was to capitalize on the concept that the waste from one process is the raw material for another. Several

THE NEW YORK TIMES

An iceberg calving from the Greenland ice cap (lower left) may appear in the North Atlantic shipping lanes in two or three years.

studies showed that a combination of waste treatment and reuse of salvaged materials lessens the requirements for additional supplies of water and the overall costs of water treatment and pollution control.

At the same time, there was no diminution in practical research applied to wastewater. In Puerto Rico scientists found that pollution from effluents from cane-sugar processing, a major contaminant of receiving streams, can be reduced nearly 90% by a combination of treatments with activated sludge, activated charcoal, aeration, trickling filtration, and anaerobic (absence of free oxygen) digestion. Work in the industrially polluted waters of Delaware was providing the basis for a new technology for the removal of high concentrations of organic substances in industrial wastewater. The catalytic oxidation process used was shown to be economically competitive with other physical-chemical treatment techniques and to be particularly useful where the pollution contained high concentrations of organic compounds.

International Developments. Reports of working groups of the U.S. National Committee for the International Hydrological Decade stressed the need in the United States for better coordination of research in snow-and-ice hydrology, increased application of already proven nuclear techniques in field studies and investigations, more realistically structured programs for drainage-basin research, and additional emphasis on basic hydrology in the university curricula of future water resources experts.

The UN called for a worldwide Water Conference to be held in Mar del Plata, Argentina, in March 1977. The conference was to focus on better management of the available supplies and the policy issues that must be resolved to avert water crises.

(L. A. HEINDL)

[222.A.2.b; 737.A.2]

METEOROLOGY

Far-ranging researches into changes in climate and weather and the close linkages between the sciences of the atmosphere and ocean were strikingly shown in a report on the abnormal behaviour of the El Niño Current, a usually minor part of the circulation in the Pacific off the coasts of Ecuador and Peru. In 1972–73, 1965–66, 1957–58, and at similar irregular intervals in the past El Niño brought to the region abnormally large quantities of warm water from the Equator. The usual areas of upwelling cold water were missing. Marine life was displaced and fish became scarce, reducing food supplies for humans and birds. The warmer water also heated the overlying air. The resulting convection produced cumulonimbus clouds, and the prevailing winds transported rainfall in torrents to the adjacent coastal regions.

The economic effects of El Niño on Peru and Ecuador have been disastrous, and it has become urgent to find methods for predicting these emergencies so that preparations for them can be made. The reported research expeditions indicated that prediction may depend on the broader overall system of ocean and atmosphere relations over the Pacific. Realizing the great importance of this global air-sea interface, hundreds of research scientists in Canada, China, Japan, the U.K., U.S., U.S.S.R., and several Western European countries reported progress in their studies during 1976, but no major new methods for predicting the changing patterns in the circulations of atmosphere and oceans were found.

At the opposite extreme of the Earth's atmosphere, the high stratosphere, the ozone layer was again studied with apprehension by some scientists. They determined that the immediate situation was not serious, but warned that over the long term man might inflict catastrophic damage on the layer.

WIDE WORLD

Scientists launch a stratosphere balloon to collect samples of gas in the upper atmosphere. They were trying to find out whether man-made chemicals have been adversely affecting the ozone layer.

In simplified summary, ozone in the high atmosphere intercepts most of the ultraviolet radiation from the Sun which would be lethal to life on Earth if it penetrated the atmosphere and reached the surface with full intensity. Ozone molecules are disintegrated by certain chemicals being discharged into the air from industrial effluents, commercial and domestic aerosols (such as spray can-propellant fluorocarbons), and other pollutants. How serious is the possibility that these chemicals might destroy the protective ozone? A panel of scientists chosen by the U.S. National Academy of Sciences reported in September that it had found no evidence of critical loss of ozone up to that date but that the possibility of such a loss occurring in the future is considerable. Further research was considered urgent, and within a period of two years definite conclusions should be drawn on placing restrictions on the use of chemicals destructive to the ozone layer.

The Viking spacecraft probes of Mars, the stepped-up investigations of core samples of layers of sedimentation on the ocean floor, and an impressive variety of research projects between these vertical extremes added greatly to knowledge and hypotheses about solar-atmosphere-ocean relationships and the probable causes of the changing climate of the Earth. For example, one authentic report showed how an extended period of very intense solar flares millions of years past may have decimated the ozone layer long enough for the lethal rays from the sun to destroy many forms of life on the Earth. This would explain why many species once plentiful became extinct eons ago.

Weather Forecasting. During 1976 the World Meteorological Organization (WMO) achieved a membership embracing 143 countries (131 sovereign states and 12 recognized territories). These ranged from among the largest (China, U.S., and U.S.S.R.) to a few small countries with very few reporting stations. But practically all were under constant urging from economic, social, and scientific bodies to improve the accuracy and extent into the future of their weather forecasts. Despite considerable effort over the years and great progress in technology, such as space satellites that provide "eyes" in the sky overlooking atmospheric conditions all over the globe, the accuracy of the regular daily weather forecasts has improved rather slowly. For most practical purposes and by most unbiased standards the 24-hour forecasts during 1976 were in error about 10–20% of the days. By contrast the predictions of certain weather events, in particular the warnings of tropical cyclones (hurricanes and typhoons), had improved greatly.

By 1976 the frequent duplication and contradictions in forecasts published by private or commercial sources independent of government meteorological centres reflected discredit on the science. Within government, however, duplication between civil and military branches in meteorological facilities was tolerated as a stimulus toward progress in research and optimum utilization of weather services.

There were improvements during the year in the worldwide communications facilities for gathering and exchanging weather data, a system that transmits many millions of items every day with noteworthy promptness and reliability through internationally coordinated scheduling set up by WMO committees. Such global coverage was vital to forecasting.

Technology. The acronym AFOS was given to the most advanced and comprehensive automation for field operations and services undertaken so far by a large national meteorological body. During 1976 the National Weather Service of the U.S. continued development and installation of AFOS, a complex of modern electronic equipment that was expected to require several years for ultimate completion. Technological progress in space satellites for atmospheric sensing and comparable improvements in other sectors (meteorology) also were impressive.

In regard to the year's weather itself, the number and severity of droughts, hurricanes, tornadoes, and other destructive weather events were near or perhaps slightly less than the yearly average. Nevertheless, many localities and several large regions suffered disasters and heavy losses of life from atmospheric disturbances of one kind or another.

(F. W. REICHELDERFER)

[221.A.1; 223.C; 224.C]

OCEANOGRAPHY

Since 1968 the specially designed and stabilized deep-sea drilling vessel "Glomar Challenger" had been investigating the sediments underlying most of the world's oceans. Approximately 400 holes had been drilled at sites in all parts of the world, excluding only the Arctic Ocean, in a reconnaissance that had confirmed the hypothesis of sea-floor spreading. According to this hypothesis, hot material upwells for unknown reasons at the crests of the great mid-ocean ridge systems that mark the centres of the major basins. The upwelled material moves laterally away from the ridge crests at speeds up to an inch or so per year, slowly subsiding as it cools and becoming covered with sediment as it spreads. The oldest sediments should thus be the deepest ones at the edges of ocean basins farthest from the ridges. The Deep Sea Drilling Project (DSDP) confirmed this hypothesis in detail and provided a detailed reconstruction of the evolution of ocean basins over the past 200 million years.

Late in 1975, the DSDP entered the International Phase of Ocean Drilling (IPOD). The main objectives of this program were detailed study of the boundaries of the oceans plus systematic drilling through the open ocean sediment layer into the underlying basaltic rock. The deep-sea part of this work would provide knowledge about the development of crustal material that may allow a global approach to local geology. On the continental shelves, exploration geologists may use the broad knowledge developed by this work to seek oil and gas reservoirs. IPOD was financed by an international consortium including the U.S., U.S.S.R., United Kingdom, France, West Germany, and Japan. It would require the development of new blowout protection technology in case oil or gas is encountered. To date, the DSDP had carefully avoided regions thought to contain oil or gas and, at the first sign of hydrocarbons, drill holes had been sealed with cement. Industrial practice is to provide blowout protection by installing a steel pipe between the driller and the sea floor. Such pipes have been used to depths of 1,000 ft. IPOD would require a similar capability in water 10,000 to 14,000 ft deep.

In January the "Glomar Challenger" sailed from San Juan, Puerto Rico, for drilling east of the Mid-Atlantic Ridge. It continued to the western edge of Africa, there finding evidence of powerful currents that once scoured the ocean floor free of sediments. Proceeding northward through the Bay of Biscay to Rockall Plateau, the voyage discovered that an ancient mountain range existed between Greenland and Europe about 60 million years ago and that western Europe was once bounded by a swampy marginal sea filled with coral reefs. Such previously unknown facts are typical of the results IPOD hoped to achieve in its study of ocean boundaries.

Just north of the place where the French-American Mid-Ocean Undersea Study (FAMOUS) project in 1975 took scientists to the ocean bottom for a firsthand look at sea-floor spreading, the "Glomar Challenger" found the youngest crustal material yet retrieved—about one million years old. On September 12 it departed from the Canary Islands with the aim of drilling over two miles into the bottom. This would top by 50% the ship's previous record depth of 5,709 ft. The goal was to obtain information about the Atlantic when it first began to open and to fill with seawater. This happened about 180 million years ago, and the depth of sediment accumulated since then made the record-breaking drill hole necessary.

Reconstructions of Climate. Among the dividends of coring the ocean floor are reconstructions of the climate that existed from thousands to millions of years ago. Such reconstructions allow scientists to study the response of climate to shifts in the distribution of land and water, sea surface temperature, ice cover, and surface reflectivity.

Results from deep-sea cores gathered by project CLIMAP were combined in 1976 into a model of global climate at the height of the last ice age, some 18,000 years ago. Sea-surface temperatures were then determined by measuring the relative abundance, in the upper sedimentary layers, of the remains of various temperature-sensitive, surface-dwelling planktonic organisms. From these data, ice-age sea surface temperatures could be estimated with an accuracy of about 1.6° C. Many areas of the equatorial oceans and high-latitude waters were found to be some 6° C cooler than at present, but the central regions of mid-ocean current systems were at about present-day temperatures. The Gulf Stream was displaced hundreds of miles south of its present course, and the cold waters north of it correspondingly filled much of the North Atlantic. Ice covered the ocean at very high latitudes in both hemispheres. Ice sheets almost two miles thick extended into North America and Europe, but little change in Southern Hemisphere land ice occurred. The global response on land was a spread of deserts, steppes, and grasslands with a corresponding reduction in forested areas. Computer experiments using this picture of ice cover and sea surface temperature also suggest that the ice-age climate was dry as well as cool compared with today.

The cores indicate that these conditions persisted from about 24,000 to 14,000 years ago. The selectivity in sediment age needed to identify samples within this range was obtained by measuring the oxygen isotope composition of the cores. This composition reflects the global amount of water locked up in continental ice at any time. It varies so uniformly throughout the globe that it can be used as a sedimentary clock with an accuracy of about 2,000 years.

Material gathered by the DSDP allows somewhat similar reconstruction of climate over the past 100 million years. The motion of continents disrupted the ancient equatorial current that once connected the world's oceans and replaced it with the present-day Antarctic Circumpolar Current. As the climate cooled, the present polar ice caps formed. This process took place as a chain of many climate fluctuations, the reconstruction of which had just begun.

Satellite Sensing of Ocean Surface Conditions. Oceanographers continued to be intrigued by the possibility of studying wide areas of the ocean's surface simultaneously from Earth-orbiting satellites. Work using presently orbiting sensors continued during the year, and plans were being made for a satellite dedicated to oceanographic research.

Satellite-borne infrared scanners yield images of the sea surface upon which temperature differences appear as different shades of gray. Because the scanner data are telemetered to the Earth, the images may be enhanced with a computer to bring out any desired range of temperatures. Thus, instead of one image of the sea surface there are many, each one displaying a different range of temperature variation. Work during the year concentrated upon the comparison of such images with actual measurements of sea surface temperature by ships at sea. Immediate practical application included tracking the Gulf Stream and locating coastal upwellings. In a related application, satellite images were enhanced to bring out oil slicks, a technique of potential utility in coastal zone management.

Satellite-borne radar was used to study ocean surface waves in a variety of ways. Differences in arrival time between reflections from wave crests and troughs broaden reflected radar pulses and thus provide an all-weather measure of local wave heights that could be useful in forecasting wave conditions for ocean shipping. Synthetic radar techniques employed computers to combine all the radar reflections the satellite receives over several miles of satellite track into a single high-resolution image. The result was that waves a few tens of metres long could be imaged directly under almost all weather conditions. Such images could help in seeing how wave energy shapes coastlines and transports sediments near shore.

Tracking Submerged Floats. Satellites are not the only way to monitor ocean conditions continuously. During the International Decade of Ocean Exploration (IDOE), a complementary technique of acoustically tracking submerged floats was developed as part of the Mid-Ocean Dynamics Experiment (MODE). It continued to be employed in 1976 in the North Atlantic. These SOFAR (Sound Fixing and Ranging) floats are fitted with acoustic transmitters that emit precisely timed sound pulses every minute. They are heavier than seawater at the surface, but the pressure at great depths compresses seawater more than it does the floats so that, at great depths, they are lighter than seawater. Thus they float at a depth of about 1,500 m and drift with the water there. This is the local depth of the oceanic sound channel. Because sound travels slowest there, sound pulses starting to leave this channel tend to return to it with the result that the floats can be heard for distances of hundreds of miles by microphones submerged in the sound channel. If the times of arrival of the signal at several widely spaced microphones are measured as accurately as present technology allows, the float can be located within about a quarter of a mile.

ADN-ZB/EASTFOTO

A harbour dredge outside the East German port of Rostock uses laser beams to guide it in deepening the shipping lane.

The bulk of the tracking was done continuously from coastal or island stations (Bermuda, Eleuthera, Puerto Rico, and Grand Turk Island). Float tracks analyzed during the year revealed a wide variety of motions. Many floats migrated in irregular paths, changing direction and speed appreciably over weeks to months in apparent response to the field of ocean eddies earlier documented in MODE. Several others began in this manner but then followed the rim of the Blake Plateau (the continental shelf of the east coast of the U.S.) southward for hundreds of miles, outlining deep currents with unprecedented clarity. Such float measurements reveal where water goes, and they are of particular relevance to the question of how rapidly the ocean can dispose of concentrated pollutants by diluting them. (MYRL C. HENDERSHOTT)

See also Disasters; Energy; Life Sciences; Mining and Quarrying; Physics; Space Exploration; Speleology.

[223.A–C; 224.D.1; 231.D; 231.G; 242.G]

ENCYCLOPÆDIA BRITANNICA FILMS. *Erosion—Leveling the Land* (1964); *Rocks that Form on the Earth's Surface* (1964); *Evidence for the Ice Age* (1965); *What Makes the Wind Blow?* (1965); *What Makes Clouds?* (1965); *Waves on Water* (1965); *The Beach—A River of Sand* (1965); *Why Do We Still Have Mountains?* (1966); *Rocks that Originate Underground* (1966); *How Solid Is Rock?* (1968); *Reflections on Time* (1969); *Heartbeat of a Volcano* (1970); *How Level Is Sea Level?* (1970); *The Ways of Water* (1971); *A Time for Rain* (1971); *A Time for Sun* (1971); *Earthquakes—Lesson of a Disaster* (1971); *Fog* (1971); *Geyser Valley* (1972); *Glacier on the Move* (1973); *The Atmosphere in Motion* (1973); *Volcanoes: Exploring the Restless Earth* (1973); *Monuments to Erosion* (1974); *Storms: The Restless Atmosphere* (1974); *The San Andreas Fault* (1974); *Energy for the Future* (1974); *Weather Forecasting* (1975); *What Makes Rain?* (1975); *Erosion and Weathering: Looking at the Land* (1976); *The Moon: A Giant Step in Geology* (1976); *Volcano: Birth of a Mountain* (1976).

Eastern Orthodox Churches: *see* Religion

Ecology: *see* Environment; Life Sciences

Economics

The year 1976 was the bicentennial of that famous work by Adam Smith, *An Inquiry into the Nature and Causes of the Wealth of Nations.* At the University of Glasgow, where the Scottish professor held the chair of moral philosophy from 1752 to 1763, a conference in his honour drew some 200 economists from Western countries. In four days of papers and discussions they seemed to agree that they were doing more than memorializing a distinguished ancestor. A common theme was that Smith's emphasis on the competitive price system was a contribution to social thought that could stand some reviving in an age of socialism and big government. This view was not restricted to conservative or "free enterprise" delegates, but was held by some who had worked for socialist or labour governments.

The Glasgow gathering was a quiet, academic affair, and the world took little notice. It had not always been thus. A hundred years earlier, the centenary of *The Wealth of Nations* had been celebrated in London at the Political Economy Club, with William Gladstone presiding (between stints as prime minister). At that moment the era of free trade seemed destined to last forever. Smith's book had been the bible of the free trade movement. He had argued powerfully against the old mercantilist philosophy which held that nations could increase their wealth by controlling the production and distribution of goods. Such efforts were self-defeating, he said, because government regulations only interfered with the natural working of the market.

Perhaps his most famous thesis was that of the invisible hand. He wrote that men in search of profits are often led as though "by an invisible hand" to advance the general welfare. The aspiring businessman not only enriches himself but improves the lot of his fellowmen. This comes about because, in a market economy, goods and services and the means of producing them move to the places where they are needed most, and competition brings prices down.

The Wealth of Nations was more than a tract for the times. It was also the first systematic appproach to economics as a science. Previous writers had dealt with economic subjects such as trade and foreign exchange, but Smith set forth a comprehensive picture of the whole economy as a dynamic system. In his book one found an explanation of how prices were determined, how labour was reimbursed, why capital and manpower moved from one industry to another, and why an economy grew. Economists ever since have looked upon Smith as the founder of their science.

Is he still relevant? Some say no. Smith wrote at a time when the Industrial Revolution was just getting under way, but there is no evidence in his book that he was even aware of it. His world was one of trade, agriculture, and small-scale industry—not of mechanized assembly lines and giant corporations. Even the famous pin factory he described in his account of the division of labour was hardly more than a group of artisans working together. If Smith were writing today he would have to rephrase his famous dictum, "It is not from the benevolence of the butcher, the brewer, or the baker that we expect our dinner, but from their regard to their own interest," to something like: "It isn't from the kindness of the supermarket or the airline or the food packer that we expect our dinner, but from their concern for their stockholders."

This is more than a problem of description. The modern economy does not work the way Smith's 18th-century one did, and much of the concern of 20th-century economists has been with adding to or revising the theoretical structure they inherited from him. The everyday behaviour of large sectors of the economy does not conform to Smith's competitive model. Nothing in his work is very helpful in understanding such present-day problems as inflation and unemployment, the setting of prices in heavy industry, or the fiscal and monetary policies of governments.

Smith remains the intellectual hero of the competitive school of economists who strongly oppose socialism and government regulation of business. His appeal for them lies in his moral emphasis on the individual and his hostility to the concentration of power, whether by government or by private monopoly. They point out that Smith began his career as a moral philosopher and that his economics was not separate from his concern with human conduct. According to his famous maxim, "People of the same trade seldom meet together, even for merriment and diversion, but the conversation ends in a conspiracy against the public, or in some contrivance to raise prices." About feudal barons and men of power he was even more trenchant: "All for ourselves, and nothing for other people, seems, in every age of the world, to have been the vile maxim of the masters of mankind." This jaundiced view of the human animal in its relation to power linked Smith the moral philosopher with Smith the economist. The market system was the best means of controlling "the mean rapacity, the monopolizing spirit of merchants and manufacturers, who neither are, nor ought to be, the rulers of mankind."

If Smith were writing today he would find little reason to change his view of men in power. He could doubtless fill a whole new book with the excesses of modern governments, both totalitarian and other, and with the malfeasances of industrial barons. He might point out how the number of government agencies has tended to grow more rapidly than the population in recent years, and how government programs set up to deal with social ills such as bad housing or lack of medical care often create new opportunities for exploiters and cheaters. He would probably be appalled at the way military expenditures have kept pace with increasing national wealth in the last two centuries. He would perhaps say that too much is spent on education, particularly in keeping the young out of the labour market for their first 25 or 30 years.

In these observations he would be supported by economists of various schools. But if he wanted to be taken as seriously as he was in the 18th century, Smith would have to add to his economic theory. He would have to find room in it for the behaviour of giant corporations that now employ so much of the labour force and for the torrents of purchasing power that flow in and out of government treasuries and from one country to another. If he did this, he might then be able to offer advice on how to achieve full employment without inflation—a task at which contemporary economists seem to have failed.

(FRANCIS S. PIERCE)

See also Nobel Prizes.

[531; 10/36.D]

Economy, World

General Overview. The year 1976 began as one of rapid recovery from the recession of 1975, which was by most measures the severest slump since World War II. Among the 24 countries of the Organization for Economic Cooperation and Development (OECD), industrial production fell 7.7% in 1975 and gross national product fell 1.2%. It was expected that the comparable figures for 1976 would show rises of about 8.5 and 5.5%, respectively, for the group as a whole. (The OECD countries are Australia, Austria, Belgium, Canada, Denmark, Finland, France, West Germany, Greece, Iceland, Ireland, Italy, Japan, Luxembourg, The Netherlands, New Zealand, Norway, Portugal, Spain, Sweden, Switzerland, Turkey, the U.K., and the U.S.) The larger industrial market countries entered 1976 with exceptionally rapid rates of growth, but these were not maintained in the second and third quarters.

The United States, which accounts for over 45% of the output of all OECD countries, started 1976 with an annual rate of growth in GNP of some 8%. This slowed to about 4% in the second and third quarters. But Great Britain's National Institute of Economic and Social Research (NIESR) estimated that U.S. GNP would increase by 6.4% for the year as a whole. Similarly, Japan (accounting for 11% of the OECD total) began the year with an 8% growth rate which slowed down in the second quarter but picked up somewhat during the second half. Japan would record a 7% rise in GNP for the year, the NIESR estimated. West Germany, while level in the second quarter, was estimated as having a GNP 6% higher for the year. France, Italy, and Canada also began the year strongly and then faltered. In Italy's case, the rapid expansion continued through midyear, when it encountered renewed difficulties in the form of an external payments crisis following deflationary fiscal and monetary policies. Yet Italy was expected to show an increase in GNP of 4.5% for the year.

The United Kingdom was among the OECD member countries having the lowest rates of growth in 1976, generally estimated at barely more than 1%, compared with the Treasury's forecast of about 2.5% at the beginning of the year. In the U.K., too, the year began with tangible growth but there was an absolute fall in the second quarter, and while consumption recovered in the third (aided by income tax concessions) the effect of this was partly offset by a rather surprising fall in the volume of exports. The case of the U.K. was also somewhat special in that the persistently adverse payments deficit, combined with the government's desire to support the exchange rate, provoked two bouts of measures to reduce the budget deficit: the first in July after the raising of a $5.3 billion central bank credit line; and the second, as the year ended, in the course of negotiations with the International Monetary Fund for a maximum drawing (145% of the U.K. quota in the Fund).

Canada's recovery proved a disappointment, in that the labour force expanded rapidly, making the expected 5% growth in GNP insufficient to prevent unemployment from rising above its mid-1975 peak.

The smaller OECD countries experienced much more sluggish recovery, in the majority of cases, than the large ones. Leaving aside the seven biggest OECD countries, GNP rose by a mere 2.5% for the others.

ROSS—ROTHCO

"Try as I may, I can't stop worrying about the cost of living."

Sweden was in a recession, due partly to the Swedish economy's typical time lag in the wake of the European economic cycle; Switzerland's recovery was apparently impeded by the rise of its exchange rate; Spain found it necessary to introduce anti-inflationary measures; while Australia was stagnating, partly as a consequence of slashes in public expenditure.

But the most singular feature of the behaviour of the industrial market economies in 1976 was the wide movements in exchange rates. In 1974 and through much of 1975 most industrial countries managed to finance their external deficits in a way that supported their exchange rates; and a few had surpluses. But toward the end of 1975, the cohesion of the pattern of exchange rates broke down. First the lira fell, then sterling and the French franc, and subsequently there were two more sharp declines in the weighted exchange rate of sterling. The Canadian dollar, which had been at a premium over the U.S. dollar through much of the year, fell to between 97 and 98 U.S. cents after the victory of the separatists in the Quebec provincial election. Among the depreciating currencies, sterling fell 21% in the 12 months to December 3 (as measured by the U.K. Treasury's weighted exchange rate index), the lira 22%, and the French franc 13%. The U.S. dollar remained almost stable, the Japanese yen rose a mere 2% (despite a slow domestic recovery and a current account external surplus of nearly $3 billion in the first half of 1976), while the mark appreciated by 11%. The Swiss franc and the guilder also rose—by 10 and 7%, respectively. The mark was easily the strongest currency in the second half, and was revalued within the European Economic Community (EEC) "snake"—the joint European float—in October.

The payments surplus of the oil-exporting countries recovered from its sharp dip in 1975, though estimates differed as to the extent of the recovery. Clearly the surplus would not be as large as in 1974. The Organization of Petroleum Exporting Countries (OPEC) surplus was in fact the result of varied national situations. Some oil-exporting countries, such as Iran and Indonesia, were taking steps in 1976 to reduce deficits that had appeared rather earlier than expected, while Saudi Arabia appeared to be having difficulty in implementing its plans for spending its revenues.

The economic situation of the other less developed countries was even more varied. Prices of third world commodities rose strongly in the first half of the year, leveling off somewhat in the second half. But in some cases—as with Brazil's coffee and Zambia's copper—supply problems that aggravated the price rises also prevented the countries in question from gaining any net benefit. The non-oil-producing third world, taken as a group, increased its external debt by a very large amount once again (over $20 billion for the second year in a row, by an OECD estimate).

The Soviet bloc also suffered from trade imbalances. Indeed, the reduction in industrial output targets in the annual plans of some of these countries was largely due to factors aggravating the balance of payments. This was the first time that member countries of the Council for Mutual Economic Assistance (CMEA, or Comecon) had deliberately reduced their rates of industrial growth because of difficulties with external payments. These difficulties, particularly in the form of rising prices of imported industrial materials, affected the Eastern European countries much more than the Soviet Union. The volume of Soviet imports in 1975 increased by a remarkable 18%. Much of this was grain, but imports of machinery rose steeply in both 1975 and early 1976. Soviet industrial production was said to have risen at an annual rate of 5% in the first half of 1976, compared with 7.5% in 1975.

NATIONAL ECONOMIC POLICIES

Developed Market Economies. In 1975 the Western world faced the deepest recession of the postwar period, resulting in a decline in real GNP of over 1%. However, as a result of the various reflationary measures taken from the spring of 1975, by the third quarter of that year most of the OECD countries were on a gentle recovery trend. This gathered strength in the early part of 1976, giving rise to a 6.5% real GNP gain for the OECD as a whole during the first half. Although the advance varied from country to country (from 4% in Italy to 9% in France), in general terms the recovery was less pronounced than in comparable phases of past recessions. By and large, this was regarded as a matter for satisfaction and confidence rather than concern, since it was felt that by keeping the upturn to moderate proportions it would be possible to avoid renewed inflationary pressures. By the first quarter of 1976, the annualized increase in OECD consumer prices was down to 9% from about 14% 12 months previously, and since this was still regarded as unduly high it was not surprising that governments everywhere were reluctant to take further reflationary measures. On the contrary, the Federal Reserve Board in the U.S. did not hesitate to apply the monetary brakes as soon as the recovery seemed to be established. Similarly, the Japanese authorities stopped inflating in November 1975 and it took some six months of relatively sluggish growth, as well as the imminence of critical parliamentary elections, to persuade them to provide an extra boost to the economy. At the same time, Great Britain—beset by a still unacceptably high rate of inflation and a very large external payments deficit—had little choice but to pursue a moderately deflationary policy. Neither West Germany nor France provided any significant boost to the economy in the first half, although—largely because of the ambitious expansionary programs introduced in late 1975—both countries started the year on a buoyant keynote.

Another reason for the general reluctance to pursue strongly reflationary policies was the rather difficult financial position of most governments. In their efforts to get the recovery going in 1975 most of them incurred very heavy deficits which put considerable strain on the money markets. As a result of the 1975 measures, many countries were still running large deficits in 1976. This, in turn, gave rise to a growing desire to reverse the trend which—in most cases—ruled out the injection of large additional funds into the economy.

Up to the middle of 1976, the broad indications were that the relatively cautious fiscal and monetary policies pursued would lead to a moderate but sustained recovery without any significant acceleration in inflation. The second half of the year, however, saw the emergence of some doubts about what had been previously regarded as a fundamentally satisfactory medium-term outlook. On the basis of the evidence available at the end of 1976, most major OECD members saw a deceleration in growth in the second half of the year. In Japan, for example, growth was thought to have come back from an annual rate of about 8% in January–June to 5–6% in the subsequent six months, while in West Germany the first half's annualized gain of 8% appeared to have been followed by an increase of only 3–4% in the second. The growth of the OECD group as a whole was provisionally estimated to have fallen back from 6.5 to 4.5%. This indicated that the strength of the expansionary forces present in the system might have been overestimated and that further stimuli would be desirable to ensure that the recovery did not peter out prematurely and that the still excessively high unemployment was brought down to acceptable levels. At the same time, however, the trend of inflation seemed to have taken a turn for the worse. Although this was partly explained by the growing strength of commodity prices, it seemed to argue for a careful, and even stricter, policy of demand management. Governments therefore faced a difficult dilemma and their response was not uniform. Japan stood firmly against any new boost to demand but finally gave in at the end of the year. The Ford administration in the U.S. stuck to its policy of no further reflation, but the indications were that President-elect Jimmy Carter would adopt a less restrictive approach. At the same time, France reacted with the introduction of strict price controls, while West Germany remained faithful to its original policy but took some steps to provide additional incentives to investment. Great Britain, on the other hand, had little choice but to follow a deflationary policy in spite of the prospect that the gain in real GNP might not even reach 2% in 1976. Furthermore, faced with a steady deterioration in the external value of sterling, the British government was forced to apply to the International Monetary Fund (IMF) for a standby facility of $3.9 billion and, just before the conclusion of the negotiations, it was widely assumed that the terms would require further curbs on private consumption and government expenditure in 1977.

So as the year drew to a close the major Western economies were characterized by a still high but faltering growth rate, a high level of unemployment, some tentative signs of renewed inflationary pressures, and a lack of clear-cut policies to deal with a difficult situation. The outlook for 1977 was regarded as uncertain, although it was generally expected that fears of a new inflationary spiral would ensure a cautious policy causing a further slowdown in economic growth. Thus an OECD forecast spoke of an increase of only 4–4.5% in real GNP during the initial six months of 1977, followed by a further cutback to 3.5% in the second half. However, since the world's productive

Table I. Real Gross National Products of OECD Countries

% change, seasonally adjusted annual rates

Country	Average 1960–73	From previous year 1975	1976*	From previous half year 1976 first half	second half*
Canada	5.1	0.6	5.0	6.0	4.5
France	5.9	−2.4	6.2	9.2	4.5
Germany, West	4.9	−3.4	5.2	8.0	3.7
Italy	5.6	−3.7	1.5	4.2	−2.2
Japan	10.9	2.2	6.5	7.7	5.7
United Kingdom	3.3	−1.6	2.2	4.7	1.2
United States	4.2	−2.0	7.0	7.0	6.0
Total major countries	5.5	−1.5	6.0	7.2	4.7
Australia	4.9	0.8	3.0	...	...
Austria	5.2	−2.0	2.7	...	...
Belgium	4.9	−1.4	3.7	...	...
Denmark	4.7	−0.8	5.0	...	...
Finland	5.4	0.2	−1.0	...	...
Greece	7.8	3.7	5.0	...	...
Ireland	4.1	−0.5	2.2	...	...
Netherlands, The	5.2	−1.0	4.0	...	...
New Zealand	3.5	−0.5	−3.5	...	...
Norway	4.9	3.3	5.5	...	...
Spain	7.3	0.8	2.2	...	...
Sweden	4.1	0.5	1.5	...	...
Switzerland	4.6	−7.0	1.0	...	...
Total OECD	5.5	−1.3	5.5	6.5	4.5

*Estimate.
Source: Adapted from OECD, *Economic Outlook*, July 1976. The countries belonging to OECD are: Australia, Austria, Belgium, Canada, Denmark, Finland, France, West Germany, Greece, Iceland, Ireland, Italy, Japan, Luxembourg, The Netherlands, New Zealand, Norway, Portugal, Spain, Sweden, Switzerland, Turkey, the United Kingdom, and the United States.

capacity was estimated to be growing at 4–5% per annum, this raised the prospect of no further fall, and perhaps even an increase, in the level of unemployment.

In broad terms, GNP growth for the OECD area during 1976 was estimated at around 5.5%, compared with a decline of 1.3% in the preceding year. However, because of the cautious monetary and fiscal policies pursued, the advance was fairly narrowly based. The leading element of the recovery had been private consumption expenditure. This was fairly buoyant in all countries except the U.K. (where there was a conscious policy to shift resources to investment and exports) and Italy; in fact—taking the OECD area as a whole—consumption was probably responsible for over half of the overall gain in GNP. To a large extent, this was the result of a gradual increase in disposable incomes—which benefited from the fiscal policies introduced in 1975 and the cutback in the rate of inflation. However, the reduction in the level of savings, which reflected an improvement in consumer confidence, also played a significant part. Another contributory factor appeared to have been a strong recovery in demand for consumer durables in reaction to the depressed levels seen in 1974 and most of 1975.

An even more buoyant area of demand was inventory-building. Following the furious destocking drive seen in 1975, the level of stocks saw a rapid rise in most OECD countries except Japan, where stocks fell in the first half of the year, and Great Britain, where the second half was thought to have seen some decline. The principal reason for the generally good performance in this sector was the recovery in output and the improvement in the financial situation of the corporate sector which made restocking desirable and possible. Most other areas of economic activity exhibited a comparatively sluggish trend. Despite the recovery in output, much of 1976 was characterized by considerable excess capacity in most countries and industries. This, together with the still widely held doubts about the strength and durability of the recovery, could not but have a strongly adverse effect on investment programs. The result of this was that during the first half of the year, when total GNP was on a strongly rising trend, expenditure on plant and equipment was falling in Great Britain, Canada, Italy, France, and Japan, and it was only because of the relatively strong performance of the U.S. and West Germany that the OECD group recorded a marginal increase. Over the whole OECD area the increase in fixed investment was estimated to have been responsible for less than 0.5 percentage point of the gain in GNP, compared with nearly 2 points attributed to inventory expansion. In contrast, however, private residential investment proved to be a source of some strength but, once again, performance varied strongly from country to country. Thus West Germany, France, Great Britain, and Italy saw little if any increase, but Japan (which benefited from the good availability of housing credit), the U.S., and Canada did rather well in this field. Public demand, on the other hand, was relatively weak, reflecting the efforts of most governments to contain their large deficits. In fact, growth in this area was generally sluggish, representing a deceleration from the advance registered in the preceding year in five of the seven most important OECD countries. The odd men out were the U.S., where government spending contributed 0.5 point to the gain in GNP, and France, where its contribution was nearer one percentage point.

In sharp contrast, export demand picked up strongly but, since a large part of OECD exports went to OECD countries, this was accompanied by a similar increase in imports. As a result the net foreign trade effect on the level of demand was largely negligible during 1976. The situation, however, varied from country to country. Japan, for example, saw a very rapid growth in overseas sales without an accompanying rise in purchases in the first half and, although the position was thought to have seen a sharp turnaround in the second, over 20% of the rise in GNP was attributable to this factor. In Italy and Great Britain, where the steady deterioration in the external value of the currency boosted exports and provided a disincentive for imports, there was also a strong positive effect (in Italy some two-thirds of the GNP gain came from foreign trade) but in the U.S., France, and Canada the overall performance of the economy was adversely affected by the excess of imports over exports.

During 1976 the external payments situation of most OECD countries saw a significant deterioration. In 1975 exports fell but this was more than compensated for by a reduction in imports, and the OECD countries as a whole had a positive trade balance of approximately $6 billion, with only Great Britain, Italy, Canada, and a number of smaller countries registering a deficit. However, under the impact of lively stockbuilding activities during the first half of 1976, imports—including those from third world countries—increased rapidly and the indications were that the second half saw a further, if somewhat slower, advance. At the same time, import prices rose faster than those of exports—the estimate was for gains of 8 and 6%—further inflating the bill for overseas purchases. However, the trend exhibited significant variations from country to country. On the one extreme was the U.S., where a trade surplus of around $9 billion in 1975 was estimated to have been turned into a deficit of $6 billion–$7 billion, but in Japan the 1975 surplus of $5 billion was thought to have risen to $10 billion in 1976. An improvement was also seen in Canada (where a deficit was turned into a small surplus) and The Netherlands (where the surplus of 1975 was enlarged in the following year). By contrast, France saw the emergence of a deficit after running a positive balance and Italy faced a widening of its adverse balance recorded in 1975. West Germany may have seen a reduction in the surplus achieved in 1975, but—at around $16 billion—this was still the largest of any OECD country. It was estimated toward the end of the year that the entire OECD area may have faced a deficit of $7 billion in 1976—quite a deterioration compared with the positive figure of $6 billion in 1975 but well below the deficit of $26.5 billion recorded in 1974 as a result of the explosion in oil prices.

By and large the trend of output reflected that of demand as outlined earlier in this section. In the first half of 1976 the index of industrial production was rising at a satisfactory, if somewhat erratic, rate in most countries and it is estimated that during this period the output of the OECD group recorded an annualized gain of about 12%. As already discussed, demand became weaker in the second half and the growth of production fell back to some 7%, giving an average of 9% for the whole year. The relatively strong growth recorded in the first half of 1976 had a visible effect on unemployment, cutting the number of jobless to about 14 million from the peak of just over 15 million in October 1975. However, in mid-1976 the unemployment rate (the number of jobless expressed as a percentage of the civilian labour force) was still a historically high 5.5% and even at the end of the year it was not thought to have fallen below 5%. As discussed earlier in this section, 1976 drew to a close amid growing uncertainty about the prospects for 1977, and there were widespread fears that, in the absence of further stimuli to demand which could have an adverse effect on inflation, economic growth might not be rapid enough to produce a further significant drop in unemployment rates.

UNITED STATES. The performance of the U.S. economy at the end of 1975 aroused doubts as to the quality and strength of the recovery. However, these fears were dispelled by the first quarter's national income statistics which showed that during January–March the economy grew at an annual rate of over 9% in real terms. Inventories fell and consumer confidence was strong, with sales of durable goods, in particular motorcars, setting the pace. As in previous recoveries, unemployment began to respond and the number of jobless fell below the 7 million mark by May (the 1975 peak had been 8.5 million). Industrial production raced ahead, unused capacity declined, and investment began to pick up.

At the same time, the first quarter's money supply figures registered what the chairman of the Federal Reserve Board, Arthur Burns, termed "explosive" growth rates. Taking heart from the highly satisfactory rate of economic expansion, but alarmed by the prospects of renewed inflation, the Fed decided to play safe and gave the monetary brakes a gentle touch. Accordingly, the long-range target for money supply was reduced and the Fed's open-market operations engineered a rise in short-term interest rates.

By tightening the reins on economic expansion at such an early stage of the recovery, the authorities served notice that inflation was still the number one enemy. However, subsequent developments demonstrated that the dangers of triggering a deceleration had been underrated and those of inflation exaggerated.

In formulating his budget strategy for July–September 1976 and the 1976–77 fiscal year, Pres. Gerald Ford and his advisers overestimated the amount of fiscal stimulus that was present in the system from the previous year's budget. Although the budget deficit for the first nine months of the 1975–76 fiscal year was a huge $67.8 billion (as against $31.6 billion the previous year), in the last three months of this period the shortfall ran below forecast and pointed to a falling trend. This was confirmed in the subsequent quarter, but the president and his advisers put forward proposals for 1976–77 which would have cut back the budget deficit to $44.6 billion. Although this was subsequently voted up by Congress to nearer $50 billion, the broad strategy of reduced fiscal stimulus was still the order of the day in late 1976.

The vigorous economic growth of the first quarter was not expected to continue unabated, but many economists were taken aback by the results of the second quarter, published in the summer. The growth rate was halved to 4.5% and most other economic indicators presented a sluggish picture. However, the administration and, to a lesser extent, the Congress were not perturbed by the magnitude of the slowdown. It was felt that this was largely a transitory phase attributable to the ending of stockbuilding and that a faster rate of expansion would be resumed in the next quarter. But the monthly economic statistics released through the summer, and the GNP figures for the third quarter, confirmed that there had been no improvement in the rate of growth.

The relaxed, steady-as-you-go approach of President Ford's economic advisers, together with Burns's concern for inflationary dangers, failed to produce measures that could have checked the slowdown. The political consequences of the policy were not clear, but some observers suggested that the failure to boost growth played into the hands of Jimmy Carter during the election campaign and contributed to the narrow defeat of President Ford.

The growth rates achieved in the second and third quarters (4.5 and 3.8%, respectively) were not high enough to prevent an increase in unemployment levels. From the low point of 7.5% reached in May, unemployment rose to 7.9% in August. This abnormally high level was held with minor fluctuations until November, when it rose to 8.1%. Given the weak keynote of the economy in the second and third quarters it is not surprising that consumer confidence was not very strong, leading to a seesaw in retail sales. Another reason for this was the fall in real disposable incomes; in August, for example, they were 0.6% lower than a year before and, more importantly, they were also lower than in July 1976.

Inflation, which since the spring had been repeatedly singled out as the most potent danger, remained largely unchanged at an annual rate of 4–5% in the six-month period to October, but now there were grounds for believing that this moderate trend might be jeopardized by the higher wholesale prices that were working their way through the economy.

So as the year drew to a close, the U.S. economic climate was not dissimilar to that of a year before. There were question marks over the strength of the expansion; unemployment was far too high; and inflation—though temporarily under control—had not been successfully tamed. However, with a new president taking over in January 1977, the chances of the deceleration gathering pace were practically nil. President-elect Carter was committed to a more expansionist policy—at least in the short run. Depending on the pace of expansion in the final months of 1976, an immediate tax cut for the medium-to-low income groups seemed in the cards. Barring unforeseen events, the U.S. during 1977 could be expected to continue to lead the world (except the U.K. and Italy) along a path of gradual economic expansion into the final stages of recovery.

GREAT BRITAIN. Unlike most developed countries, the U.K. had seen a weakening in economic activity during 1975, with real GNP falling by 2%. The recession, however, hit bottom around the end of the year, and the country entered 1976 on a note of cautious recovery. In the event, this turned out to be considerably more sluggish than expected and by early December the indications were that growth for the whole year would not exceed 1.5%. The main reason for this was the government's decision not to provide any significant boost to domestic demand. This represented a significant change from the policy pursued in previous recessions, but with a rapid rate of inflation, an unacceptably large balance of payments deficit, and steady pressure on the pound sterling, the option to reflate was simply not available to the authorities. At the end of 1975, Great Britain's inflation rate had been 25%, but as a result of the deflationary policies followed and the introduction of an even stricter incomes policy (providing for a maximum rise in wages of 4.5%) in August, this dropped to 14% by September. However, it was still considerably higher than the government's target and in excess of the rate seen in most other developed countries.

Furthermore, during the autumn there were some signs of an acceleration in the underlying trend of inflation, principally as a result of the continuing fall in the external value of sterling. Between January and December 1976, the dollar/sterling exchange rate dropped from $2.025 to $1.689, the rate of decrease being particularly sharp in the second half of the year. This was largely due to the deterioration in the external payments situation (after a fairly encouraging performance in the first quarter) as a result of which the current account deficit for 1976 was likely to reach some £1,900 million, compared with £1,573 million the preceding year. Other contributory factors were anxiety about the growing voice of the extreme left wing, fears of labour troubles, a large government deficit, and the failure of the Bank of England to support sterling on a number of critical occasions. Because of the persistent weakness of sterling, the chancellor of the Exchequer was forced to apply to the IMF for a loan of $3.9 billion in October; negotiations with Fund officials continued throughout the fourth quarter, and at the end of the year the indications were that this would be granted only if the government agreed to further curbs on expenditure leading to a reduction in the public sector borrowing requirement. Monetary policy during the year had not been particularly restrictive, mainly because the authorities were anxious to encourage investment. However, because of the attack on sterling, the Bank of England was forced to increase the minimum lending rate to 15% in October.

Not unexpectedly, the authorities' inability to provide any significant reflation had an adverse effect on most major components of domestic demand. Personal consumption was hit by income restraints, unemployment, uncertainty about the future, and a relatively rapid rise in prices. As a result—and despite a reduction in the level of savings—its volume during the first three quarters of the year was some 0.5% lower than in the corresponding period of 1975, and in December the signs were that 1976 as a whole would see a small decrease for the second successive year. The tempo of investment expenditure was also sluggish. Although 1976 saw a recovery in the corporate sector's financial situation, weak demand meant that most companies worked well below full capacity. This, and the lack of confidence in the future, provided a serious disincentive to spending on new plant and equipment, which was only partially offset by the relatively good supply of funds for investment purposes and the availability of official investment assistance in selected industries. With the benefit of three quarters' statistics, it was estimated that the volume of fixed investment would register a decrease of about 2% for the whole year compared with a fall of just over 1% in 1975. However, toward the end of 1976 there were some signs of a cautious recovery—particularly in the manufacturing sector—and it was widely felt that 1977 would see a modest increase.

Inventory movements also exerted a negative influence on demand largely because, notwithstanding the reduction in the previous year, most manufacturers took the view that the level of stocks was still too high in relation to the level of output. In contrast, government current expenditure was fairly strong despite attempts to economize; in the first half of the year its volume was nearly 4% higher than in the same period of 1975, and it was widely expected that the statistics for the second half would show a further increase. Exports—benefiting from the recovery in the world economy, the existence of much spare capacity in Britain, and the deterioration in sterling's external value—were also a positive influence on aggregate demand. In volume terms, exports of goods and services were up 3.5% in the first half and—despite some weakening in the second—the year as a whole was expected to see a gain of 4–5%. Imports of goods and services showed a broadly comparable increase, with the gain for the whole year estimated at around 4.5% in volume terms.

The trend of industrial output reflected the rather sluggish and erratic growth of demand. During the first two quarters of the year it was on a modestly rising curve, but in the third quarter it lost much of its earlier momentum. However, the underlying trend appeared to point upward at the end of the year and it was thought that the outcome for 1976 was a gain of just over 1%. This, however, was not large enough to cut back the level of unemployment. In fact, the

BAS—TACHYDROMOS, GREECE/ROTHCO

number of those out of work continued to increase; on a seasonally adjusted basis this accounted for 5.1% of the labour force in January 1976 and by October reached 5.5% (1,306,200).

On several occasions during the year, the official policy of maintaining a large margin of spare resources and cutting public expenditure came under severe attack from the left wing of the Cabinet and the trade union movement, which advocated high levels of public expenditure and severe import controls as a means of boosting domestic demand and reducing the trade deficit. The differences in approach came into particularly sharp focus at the end of the year in discussing the terms of the IMF loan of $3.9 billion asked for by the government. In December the discussions were still going on, although it was expected that agreement would be reached on an accelerated program of reducing public spending and the government's borrowing requirement. The outlook for the economy during 1977 could not be assessed accurately in the absence of a detailed evaluation of the IMF terms accepted by the government, although it seemed likely that even if these did not impose additional deflation on the economy, the gain in real GNP would not exceed 2.5%.

JAPAN. At the end of 1975, the Japanese economy had evidenced a sluggish tempo of growth, a gradual fall in the rate of inflation, and a rapidly strengthening external payments position. In spite of this, however, the authorities were reluctant to try significant demand-boosting measures since they felt that, as a result of the increases in public spending and relaxation in monetary policy up to November 1975, there was enough reflation in the pipeline to ensure a rapid recovery during 1976. The results for the first quarter of the year—showing a gain of 3.5% in real GNP over the previous quarter—provided some justification for this view, and many forecasters concluded that growth for fiscal 1976 (ending in March 1977) would exceed 7%. However, the euphoria did not last long. During the subsequent quarter, growth slowed down to 1.1% and key economic statistics for ensuing months provided further evidence that the recovery was losing momentum. To a large extent this was the result of a cutback in the growth of exports from an unsustainable and clearly abnormal 9% in the January–March period to a still highly satisfactory 4%. However, the tempo of economic activity was also adversely affected by the continuous political infighting within the ruling Liberal-Democrat Party, which—apart from damaging business confidence—delayed a substantial part of the public works program by holding up legislation.

By the second half of 1976, therefore, the government came under increasing pressure to provide a further boost to domestic demand. Facing crucial elections in December, the authorities obliged by announcing a $3.4 billion package in November aimed at higher public spending and investment. As a result, a GNP growth of 5–6% seemed likely during fiscal 1976, roughly in line with the government's original forecast and considerably better than the 4.1% achieved in fiscal 1975.

On the basis of the economic indicators available in December 1976, most major components of GNP were heading for a satisfactory increase. Exports were particularly buoyant. Thanks to the rapid growth in the world economy in early 1976, these started off on a strong underlying trend; and although there was a noticeable slowdown in the subsequent six or nine months, the outlook for fiscal 1976 pointed to a volume gain of about 8%, twice as large as during fiscal 1975. Private consumption, which makes up over half of GNP, saw a substantially slower rise. Like exports, it started off on a relatively buoyant keynote, but in the second quarter it grew at an annual rate of only 4.5%. This was largely the result of the relatively small wage increase (9%) negotiated during the spring wage offensive and a high propensity to save in the face of growing unemployment and general uncertainty about the future. Both of these conditions continued into the second half, and the outcome for 1976–77 was thought to be a real growth of only about 4%, compared with 5% in fiscal 1976.

Public investment and current spending started off well in the first few months of 1976, but during the following six months there was a loss of momentum—mainly because of the authorities' failure to get the bill authorizing the sale of government bonds enacted in time. Toward the end of 1976 the tempo of public works expenditure speeded up, but in spite of this it was felt that the gain for the fiscal year would not exceed 4%, compared with an increase of over 8% in 1975–76. The stock situation, however, saw a dramatic turnaround; under the impact of cash flow difficulties and weak demand the level of inventories had seen rapid decline in 1975–76, but the first two quarters of the subsequent fiscal year saw a steady increase. Private plant and equipment investments also did well. Despite the easy monetary policy, these were falling up to the end of 1975, but from then on the results pointed to a gradually strengthening recovery. In January–March 1976 the gain over the previous quarter was 0.4%, but in the April–June period there was an increase of 1.7%. All in all, it was anticipated that the 1976–77 fiscal year would see a gain of some 4.5%, compared with a fall of nearly 11% in 1975–76. Private housebuilding, stimulated by the good availability of housing credit, was also strong, but its anticipated growth—at 12%—was broadly the same as in the preceding year.

In line with the gentle upward trend of the economy, industrial output also saw an increase and most of the production limitation schemes, introduced as a defensive measure during the recession, were abandoned or relaxed. Inflation continued to moderate throughout most of the year—with the rate falling from 10% in January to 8% in September—although in the final quarter there were signs of an acceleration. Along with the rapid growth of exports, the year saw a fast rise in the trade surplus which was expected to total $10 billion for the whole fiscal year. This led to growing criticism from Japan's trading partners, forcing Tokyo to agree to restrictions on some of its exports and to improve access to its own markets.

Japan entered 1977 on a note of modestly growing aggregate demand (pointing to a 7–8% gain in real GNP in 1977–78), a continuing but probably unsustainable increase in the external payments surplus, and some tentative signs of an acceleration in inflation. The situation did not appear to call for any major initiative by the authorities. However, as a result of the poor showing of the ruling Liberal-Democrats in the December elections there was widespread uncertainty about the government's likely economic strategy. In the main, the doubts concerned the effects of Prime Minister Takeo Miki's replacement by Takeo Fukuda, widely recognized as a highly experienced but conservative economist, with the consequence that the Liberal-Democrats would have to seek the support of other conservative-oriented politicians to ensure a workable majority.

West Germany. The economic recovery confidently heralded for early 1975 did not get under way until late in the year. Consequently, 1975 witnessed a drop of 3.5% in real GNP instead of the small economic growth officially forecast. The year 1976 opened with high hopes of a strong economic performance, and national accounts statistics for the first quarter confirmed that such hopes were founded on strong ground. GNP rose by over 6% in real terms, while industrial production, after falling continually for over two years to mid-1975 and recovering only hesitantly after that, made up nearly half its lost ground. Industrial capacity utilization began to improve, and encouraging progress was made on the unemployment front. The outlook for industrial investment and exports appeared relatively sanguine.

In the early part of the year, the government's economic strategy was that—following successive doses of reflation administered during 1974 and 1975 (amounting to a total of DM 35 billion)—there was no need for further expansionary measures. The main aim was to encourage a steady and broadly based recovery underpinned by increased investment and export growth. Since the investment climate is largely conditioned by the level of company profits, the government took steps to improve them. One such measure, aimed at easing liquidity problems, was the introduction of new tax relief with a carryback provision—*i.e.,* companies that had made a loss in 1975 but a profit in 1974 were allowed to carry back that loss to 1974 and claim tax relief accordingly.

Another reason for planning no further general reflationary measures—apart from limited action such as the tax relief for companies—was the huge public-sector deficit built up during the recession. At a forecast level of DM 68 billion for 1976 this was nearly as high as the previous year's record shortfall. Although the long-term aim of a balanced budget remained, the government felt that, given high unemployment and the unexpectedly low levels from which the recovery was progressing, a sharp reduction in the public-sector deficit could damage economic recovery. At the same time, however, further stimulus could undo the progress made on the inflation front.

The Bundesbank's overall monetary policy was broadly in step with the government's fiscal stance. It favoured a steady-as-you-go approach with a slight accent on tighter control of the money supply lest it rekindle inflationary flames—a fear that subsequently proved to be unfounded. From spring onward, the monetary authorities periodically had to ward off flushes of speculative currency flows resulting from the continued weakness of the pound sterling and the franc. In March, and again in August, speculation aimed at breaking up the EEC snake and/or forcing a revaluation of the mark was successfully beaten back. In the course of this the money supply was managed too tightly and in consequence the first three quarters of the year saw a growth of less than the target rate of 8%. The discount rate stayed at the low level of 3.5% reached in August 1975. However, renewed currency crises in October 1976 precipitated by the sharp and seemingly uncontrollable fall in the value of sterling, mainly against the dollar, succeeded in forcing up the value of the mark by 2.5% within the snake.

As in the U.S. and the other major OECD countries, the rapid West German growth rate of the first quarter could not be maintained for the rest of the year. Statistics published in the summer showed that the growth rate slumped to a mere 2.7%. Inventory growth, which had been the engine of the recovery in its early stages, leveled out and private consumption became hesitant. Industrial investment, on which the hopes for a sustained recovery were pinned, had not responded sufficiently vigorously and although exports were well up on the previous year, imports—encouraged by the rise in the value of the mark—also grew at a fairly fast rate. A further set of figures published in the autumn did not relieve the gloom. The GNP was still rising by only 3% and personal incomes were barely ahead of inflation, which was growing at an annual rate of 4%. Furthermore, unemployment was far too high in relation to the recovery phase; although it fell below the critical one million mark in May, the rate of improvement during the summer and autumn was highly disappointing. Not surprisingly, resentment against foreign "guest workers" increased and the government came under greater pressure to do something about reducing their numbers.

ADN-ZB / EASTFOTO

A former part of Germany is now in the Soviet sphere. This plant in Frankfurt an der Oder in East Germany produces pig iron.

Even after narrowly winning the general election in October, the government refused to be panicked into stimulating the economy, firmly believing that the "summer pause" was coming to an end. All indications were that the final quarter would indeed show a slight acceleration in the growth rate. But in early December doubts still remained as to whether the underlying currents were strong enough to maintain a steady growth during the next year. In their autumn report Bonn's "wise men" (the Council of Economic Advisers) advocated reflationary measures totaling DM 3 billion to ensure that growth did not peter out in 1977. It was recommended that the bulk of the assistance be directed toward industry.

The outlook for 1977 was for a moderate growth of about 4%. However, the government's policy would depend on the outcome of the year as a whole, as well as such developments as the effect on currency markets of the IMF loan to Britain and the magnitude of the stimulus President-elect Carter might provide the U.S. economy in 1977. On balance, a guarded relaxation in West German fiscal and monetary policy seemed likely, which could push the growth rate to around 5%.

France. The French government entered 1976 riding the crest of a vigorous economic upswing fueled by the ambitious reflationary package introduced in September 1975. Having been criticized for doing too little too late to get the economy moving, the government appeared to have produced a hat trick. Economic indicators for the first quarter were encouraging and showed that industrial output had risen by an annual rate of 12% and was well on the way to recovering to prerecession levels. As in other OECD countries, consumer expenditure and stockbuilding led the way, but in France the demand for intermediate products, *e.g.*, steel, shared in the early stages of the upswing. Demand for capital goods, thanks to a large number of government contracts, was strong and there were increasing signs that external demand was picking up.

In spite of this buoyant economic scene, unemployment failed to respond accordingly. However, although the number of unemployed remained relatively stable, short-time working, which had been widespread during 1975, came down sharply (French employers, faced with high unemployment benefit costs, had reacted to the 1974–75 recession by introducing much more short-time working than anywhere else in Europe). The inflation rate was another source of disappointment to economic policymakers, for it stayed over the 10% mark during the first half of 1976, far above the government's target.

During the summer, as the effects of the September stimulus wore off and stocks were adjusted to the level of final sales, a slowdown set in. Industrial production leveled out and consumer demand became sluggish. The output of capital goods, highly sensitive to government incentives, suffered particularly and showed an actual fall from the corresponding quarter of 1975. In contrast to this general economic slowdown, real hourly wages marched on, adding to the inflationary pressures threatening the recovery. By the third quarter, increases in real wages were running almost at the same level as the 1975 average of 3.5%, while inflation appeared set to exceed the previous year's average of 10% by 1.5 points.

Given the delicate nature of the unemployment situation earlier in the year, these inflationary pressures weakened industrial confidence and worsened the problem. By the end of October, the crude unemployment figures exceeded the November 1975 peak of 1,020,000. Seasonally adjusted totals were less frightening, but the underlying trend was unmistakable.

The initial strategy of the government in the spring was to encourage a controlled but rapid economic recovery. So in March the bank lending ceilings imposed in the previous year were confirmed while, at the same time, the controls over retail margins were removed. Because of the authorities' desire not to do anything that might discourage private investment, the discount rate was not altered in this period in spite of a currency crisis that pushed the franc out of the EEC snake and forced a 5% depreciation within five days. But in the aftermath of the slowdown, with both inflation and the money supply rising faster than targeted and the franc under continual pressure, a more restrictive approach was taken. Once again, fighting inflation became the number one priority. The new premier, Raymond Barre, took decisive action. Private sector prices were frozen until the end of the year and public sector charges until the end of March. A new, lower inflation target of 6.5% by the end of 1977 was set (1976: 11% overall) accompanied by proposals to restrict increases in the money supply to 12.5% (as against 15% in the second quarter and 21% in the first). Bank liquidity was further reduced by Fr 3 billion and the discount rate raised again from 9.5 to 10.5%.

A stricter fiscal approach meant that the budget for 1977 would be balanced—that for 1976 was 2% in deficit—and state spending would be kept in line with the growth of gross domestic product. To bring about a balanced budget, taxes on motorcars, gasoline, and alcoholic drinks were raised. However, while squeezing private consumers, the authorities continued to find schemes to encourage investment so as to create a basis for a sustained rate of recovery in the future. Faster depreciation allowed for equipment delivered in 1977 and a state fund set up to encourage small and medium-sized companies were notable examples.

France ended 1976 on a distinctly less optimistic note than the one it started with, but the corrective medicine of Premier Barre seemed likely to have the desired effect of controlling inflation and giving the economy a chance to recover its strength.

Table II. Non-Oil Less Developed Countries: Financing of Current Account Deficits, 1972-75

In $000,000,000

	1972	1973	1974	1975
Current account deficit	9.2	9.9	28.4	37.0
Financing through transactions that do not affect net debt positions	5.1	7.8	9.1	10.0
Net borrowing and use of reserves	4.1	2.1	19.3	27.0
Reduction of reserves	−6.4	−8.1	−2.5	+0.8
Net external borrowing	10.5	10.2	21.8	26.2
Long-term official loans	3.6	5.1	7.6	12.6
Other long-term borrowing*	4.4	4.5	8.7	9.3

*Including from private banks abroad and suppliers' credit.
Source: Adapted from the International Monetary Fund, *Annual Report 1976*, Table 9.

Less Developed Countries. During the last few years the economic performance of the non-oil-producing less developed countries (LDC's) largely mirrored the cyclical fluctuations of the industrial world, albeit with a time lag. The effect of the 1974–75 international recession was not fully felt until 1975 when the demand for imports—other than oil—fell by nearly 10% in volume terms. Furthermore, with a few exceptions, prices of commodities on which the LDC's rely for their foreign exchange earnings fell sharply. But because of the cushioning effect of agriculture and additional heavy external borrowings, the fluctuations in the rate of economic growth were less violent than in the developed world. According to World Bank statistics, the annual economic growth of non-oil LDC's during the three-year period 1973–75 was 5.4%, compared with 6% in the previous five-year period. But these average figures tended to disguise the extremely low pace of economic activity in the poorest countries—especially in South Asia and Africa south of the Sahara.

But the most important effects of the world economic crises on the LDC's were seen in the sharply deteriorating trade accounts. These were already overburdened by the oil price increases of 1973–74, but as a result of the slowdown in export volumes and the deterioration in the terms of trade in 1975, the deficit saw a spectacular increase (*see* Table II). This put an enormous strain on the import-financing capacity of many of the weaker and poorer countries. Economic policymakers, therefore, had to take steps to restrain private consumption, encourage agricultural production and exports, reduce oil consumption, and adopt other monetary and fiscal measures to reduce inflation and improve social equity.

Thanks to favourable weather conditions during the latter part of 1975 and most of 1976, as well as the relative economic recovery in the developed world, the fortunes of the LDC's during 1976 improved noticeably. The early stages of the upswing, however, were rather slow because of the historically low levels some commodity prices were recovering from, *e.g.*, those of rubber and textile fibres. As the world economic recovery reached a more mature phase, commodity prices more than made up the ground lost during the recession. The Economist Commodity Index (measured in U.S. dollars) showed gains of over 30% in the 12-month period to December 1976, and the trend was still strongly upward. The net result of these developments seemed likely to be a 10–15% reduction in the current account deficits of the LDC's during 1976. In spite of this moderate improvement, the external financial position remained precarious, largely because of heavy borrowings undertaken in 1974 and 1975 to maintain the flow of essential imports and to safeguard living standards.

In some countries, the outstanding external debt and debt service payments were inevitably rising to a high level in relation to export earnings. This situation was exacerbated by short-term commercial bank loans secured in the last few years. These were often at less advantageous terms than the traditional development assistance provided by international agencies such as the IMF and the World Bank. But the scale of the current account deficits faced by the LDC's in the wake of the oil price crisis was such that these new types of borrowing were essential to avoid serious economic dislocation. Few countries found the problems of servicing their external debts unmanageable, partly because of the mitigating effects of inflation on previously incurred debts.

Fluctuations in the currencies of the major countries often tend to trigger undesirable ripples in the foreign earnings of the LDC's, causing anxiety and uncertainty, especially if their currency is tied to that of a major country. For this reason a number of countries severed their links with the pound sterling or the dollar during 1976 so as to avoid unnecessary fluctuations in their own currencies.

Not surprisingly, economic growth among the oil-exporting LDC's remained fairly buoyant at around 10–12% on average. This was made possible by increased domestic expenditures in the wake of an increase in oil revenues. (It will be remembered that the price of oil was increased by 10% in September 1975, and that a new revision of 5% for Saudi Arabia and 10% for most other oil producers was decided on in late 1976.) During 1975 and in the early part of 1976 most oil-producing LDC's pursued policies aimed at encouraging rapid development, combating inflation, and curtailing excess government expenditure. These policies had varying degrees of success; the year under review saw the appearance of severe bottlenecks, structural imbalances, and inflationary pressures in a number of countries.

Partly as a result of the massive development program based largely on imports and partly because of rapid inflation and reduced demand for oil in the developed countries, the huge current account balance of the oil exporters was cut by nearly 50% in 1975. Although the demand for oil remained relatively strong during 1976, imports of the oil exporters rose rapidly.

The total flow of resources, including export credits, to LDC's by members of the Development Assistance Committee (DAC) of the OECD rose by 40% during 1975 to reach $37.5 billion. According to DAC estimates that figure accounted for 0.99% of DAC members' combined GNP. If grants by private agencies

Table III. Production of Crude Oil in Selected Countries

Average output per month; in 000 metric tons

Country	1969	1970	1971	1972	1973	1974	1975
Abu Dhabi	2,398	2,774	3,733	4,205	5,227	5,637	5,614
Algeria	3,655	3,934	3,034	4,112	4,136	4,055	3,754
Argentina	1,514	1,669	1,798	1,844	1,790	1,762	1,681
Australia	167	707	1,227	1,340	1,595	1,580	1,680
Canada	4,597	5,239	5,500	6,282	7,334	6,878	5,825
Indonesia	3,064	3,525	3,675	4,480	5,518	5,665	5,343
Iran	14,041	15,948	18,902	20,994	24,403	25,071	22,301
Iraq	6,207	6,371	6,981	5,927	8,281	8,078	9,164
Kuwait	11,610	12,553	13,453	13,787	12,650	10,675	8,760
Libya	12,490	13,309	11,049	9,969	8,740	6,114	6,068
Mexico	1,755	1,792	1,784	1,847	1,938	2,463	3,037
Nigeria	2,250	4,517	6,365	7,577	8,480	9,305	7,361
Oman	1,348	1,382	1,211	1,176	1,218	1,207	1,420
Qatar	1,432	1,448	1,704	1,957	2,308	2,088	1,770
Romania	1,104	1,115	1,149	1,177	1,191	1,207	...
Saudi Arabia	13,296	15,701	19,890	24,989	31,459	35,116	29,347
U.S.S.R.	27,364	29,420	31,423	33,370	35,753	38,246	40,917
United States	37,967	39,607	38,892	38,913	37,849	36,066	34,371
Venezuela	15,660	16,192	15,440	14,028	14,648	12,984	10,228

Source: UN, *Monthly Bulletin of Statistics*.

Table IV. Production of Coal in Selected Countries

Average output per month; in 000 metric tons

Country	1969	1970	1971	1972	1973	1974	1975
Australia	3,318	3,768	3,662	4,548	4,624	4,831	5,591
France	3,396	3,111	2,825	2,548	2,196	2,003	1,868
Germany, West	9,478	9,695	9,702	8,980	8,583	8,408	7,699
Poland	11,251	11,675	12,124	12,558	13,052	13,500	14,302
U.S.S.R.	35,483	36,060	36,785	37,593	38,435	39,448	...
United Kingdom	12,929	12,260	12,453	10,152	11,003	9,190	10,722
United States	42,786	45,866	41,921	44,716	44,180	44,928	47,319

Note: Figures relate to all grades of anthracite and bituminous coal, but exclude lignite and brown coal except in the U.S.S.R.
Source: UN, *Monthly Bulletin of Statistics*.

Table V. Production of Bauxite in Selected Countries

Average monthly output; in 000 metric tons

Country	1969	1970	1971	1972	1973	1974	1975
Australia	526.0	691.0	920.0	1,144.0	1,225.0	1,545.0	1,846.0
Brazil	29.3	42.5	47.2	63.8	70.8	75.0	...
Dominican Republic	91.9	90.5	86.0	90.6	90.5	99.6	...
France	231.0	249.0	260.0	273.0	275.0	242.0	210.0
Ghana	20.5	28.5	27.4	28.3	29.1	29.8	...
Greece	158.0	190.0	236.0	203.0	228.0	234.0	237.0
Guinea	205.0	208.0	219.0	221.0	305.0	634.0	...
Guyana	359.0	342.0	353.0	309.0	302.0	254.0	...
Haiti	62.3	56.1	59.6	60.4	64.9	66.1	...
Hungary	161.0	168.0	174.0	196.0	215.0	228.0	241.0
India	90.0	115.0	126.0	140.0	108.0	93.0	105.0
Indonesia	64.0	102.0	103.0	106.0	102.0	108.0	83.0
Italy	18.0	18.8	15.9	7.0	4.2	2.7	2.7
Jamaica	885.0	1,009.0	1,045.0	1,082.0	1,124.0	1,269.0	942.0
Malaysia, West	89.4	94.9	81.4	89.7	95.3	79.0	58.6
Romania	52.7	64.7	74.9	74.5	75.0	68.0	...
Sierra Leone	38.0	37.0	49.0	58.0	55.0	54.0	...
Surinam	520.0	501.0	560.0	565.0	560.0	572.0	...
Turkey	0.2	4.3	12.8	39.3	29.3	55.4	52.6
United States	156.0	176.0	168.0	153.0	159.0	166.0	153.0
Yugoslavia	177.0	175.0	163.0	183.0	181.0	198.0	188.0

Source: UN, *Monthly Bulletin of Statistics*.

Table VI. Production of Copper Ore in Selected Countries

Average monthly output; in metric tons of Cu content

Country	1969	1970	1971	1972	1973	1974	1975
Australia	10,400	11,900	14,400	14,300	16,600	21,400	19,300
Austria	200	190	220	190	230	240	220
Bulgaria	3,280	3,360	3,580	4,000	4,000	4,170	...
Canada	43,300	50,900	54,500	60,000	68,700	68,900	60,100
Chile	58,300	59,200	59,800	60,500	61,900	75,400	...
Finland	2,740	2,810	2,220	2,720	3,000	3,060	3,230
Germany, West	120	110	120	110	120	140	160
India	860	850	1,000	1,220	1,430	2,340	3,250
Japan	10,090	9,960	10,090	9,340	7,600	6,850	7,050
Mexico	5,510	5,080	6,280	6,560	6,710	6,890	...
Morocco	200	270	270	320	360	450	400
Namibia	2,130	1,900	2,160	1,790	2,360	2,180	2,170
Norway	1,760	1,650	1,810	2,170	2,500	1,920	2,410
Peru	17,500	17,200	17,700	18,100	18,300	17,800	14,700
Philippines	11,000	13,400	16,500	17,800	18,400	18,800	18,900
Poland	4,000	6,900	10,200	11,200	12,900	16,500	...
Rhodesia	1,760	1,920	1,940	2,650	2,670	2,670	2,000
South Africa	11,500	12,400	12,700	13,000	14,600	14,900	...
Spain	880	790	2,840	3,010	2,410	3,160	1,780
Turkey	2,070	1,870	1,870	1,840	2,520	3,390	...
United States	117,000	130,000	115,000	126,000	130,000	120,000	107,000
Yugoslavia	6,810	7,570	7,870	8,590	9,320	9,340	9,580
Zaire	30,300	32,300	33,900	36,300	40,700	41,200	...
Zambia	71,800	69,700	65,400	73,400	73,600	73,700	67,200

Source: UN, *Monthly Bulletin of Statistics*.

Table VII. Production of Lead Ore in Selected Countries

Average monthly output; in metric tons of Pb content

Country	1969	1970	1971	1972	1973	1974	1975
Algeria	620	700	380	410	310	250	400
Australia	34,800	38,300	34,700	35,100	32,100	30,900	34,400
Austria	570	500	640	560	510	480	...
Bulgaria	7,960	8,210	8,330	8,500	8,750	9,170	...
Canada	25,000	29,800	30,700	27,900	29,200	24,700	26,200
Chile	70	70	70	40	40	30	20
France	2,520	2,400	2,480	2,220	2,080	1,920	1,820
Germany, West	3,280	3,380	3,430	3,200	2,870	2,540	2,700
India	190	210	250	310	610	880	1,020
Italy	3,110	2,900	2,530	2,710	2,070	1,770	2,860
Japan	5,290	5,370	5,880	5,290	4,410	3,690	4,170
Korea, South	800	890	880	780	790	670	670
Mexico	14,200	14,700	13,100	13,400	14,900	18,200	...
Morocco	6,700	7,000	6,400	7,900	8,600	7,000	5,500
Norway	290	250	260	290	260	260	260
Poland	5,400	5,600	5,800	5,700	5,800	5,800	...
Spain	5,980	6,060	5,850	5,790	5,380	5,060	4,820
Thailand	140	100	120	130	290	120	...
Tunisia	1,990	1,830	1,680	1,690	1,300	1,040	910
United Kingdom	330	340	400	380	550	550	...
United States	38,500	43,200	43,700	46,800	45,600	50,600	46,900
Yugoslavia	9,800	10,600	10,400	10,000	9,900	10,000	10,600

Source: UN, *Monthly Bulletin of Statistics*.

Table VIII. Production of Passenger Automobiles

Average output per month

Country	1969	1970	1971	1972	1973	1974	1975
Argentina*	13,000	14,100	16,300	16,800	18,300	17,800	...
Australia*	28,600	32,500	31,200	32,800	30,700	33,200	30,100
Austria	100	100	50	30	20	160	20
Brazil*	20,200	21,300	29,000	34,800	38,800	46,800	46,200
Canada	86,100	76,900	91,400	96,200	102,300	97,200	87,100
Czechoslovakia	11,000	11,900	12,400	12,900	13,700	14,100	14,500
France	181,000	205,000	224,000	249,000	267,000	254,000	246,000
Germany, East	10,100	10,600	11,200	11,600	12,300	12,900	13,300
Germany, West	286,000	294,000	308,000	293,000	304,000	237,000	242,000
India†	3,590	3,750	4,160	4,330	4,580	3,910	2,620
Italy†	123,000	143,000	142,000	144,000	152,000	136,000	112,000
Japan	218,000	265,000	310,000	335,000	373,000	328,000	381,000
Mexico*	9,500	11,400	13,300	14,200	17,300	21,600	22,000
Netherlands, The	5,050	5,600	6,500	6,580	7,050	4,660	4,190
Poland	4,000	5,400	7,200	7,600	9,600	11,100	13,700
Romania	540	610	750	870	1,080	1,150	...
Spain	31,700	37,900	38,300	51,000	59,900	60,200	59,100
Sweden‡	20,400	22,700	24,300	26,800	28,800	27,300	26,500
U.S.S.R.	24,500	28,700	44,100	60,800	76,400	93,200	...
United Kingdom	143,000	137,000	145,000	160,000	146,000	128,000	106,000
United States§	685,000	546,000	709,000	735,000	805,000	611,000	559,000
Yugoslavia	4,300	5,200	5,000	5,900	8,200	9,600	10,800

*Including assembly from imported parts.
†Production for the military or by ordnance factories not included.
‡Beginning 1974; deliveries only.
§Factory sales.
Source: UN, *Monthly Bulletin of Statistics*.

Table IX. Foreign Trade of the U.S.S.R. by Areas and Countries of Origin and Destination

In millions of rubles and percentages of total

Area		Imports				Exports			
		1960	1965	1970	1975	1960	1965	1970	1975
Total	Value	5,066	7,253	10,558	26,669	5,007	7,357	11,520	24,030
	%*	100	100	100	100	100	100	100	100
Developed market economies	Value	1,052	1,639	2,766	10,468	963	1,477	2,448	6,912
	%	20.8	22.6	26.2	39.3	19.2	20.1	21.3	28.8
Less developed market economies	Value	575	1,042	1,611	4,457	371	1,348	2,416	4,458
	%	11.4	14.4	15.3	16.7	7.4	18.3	21.0	18.6
Centrally planned economies	Value	3,439	4,571	6,182	11,744	3,674	4,532	6,657	12,660
	%	67.9	63.0	58.6	44.0	73.4	61.6	57.8	52.7
Selected Countries and Areas									
U.S. and Canada	Value	63	286	221	1,901	27	43	66	164
	%	1.2	3.9	2.1	7.1	0.5	0.6	0.6	0.7
Latin-American countries	Value	126	406	536	2,215	96	383	588	1,285
	%	2.5	5.6	5.1	8.3	1.9	5.2	5.1	5.3
Western Europe	Value	885	1,095	2,155	6,957	865	1,265	2,035	6,070
	%	17.5	15.1	20.4	26.1	17.3	17.2	17.7	25.3
Warsaw Pact countries	Value	2,538	4,205	5,970	11,312	2,806	4,097	6,083	11,866
	%	50.1	58.0	56.5	42.4	56.0	55.7	52.8	49.4
Africa	Value	158	224	483	864	90	296	522	572
	%	3.1	3.1	4.6	3.2	1.8	4.0	4.5	2.4
Japan	Value	55	160	311	1,254	69	167	341	669
	%	1.1	2.2	2.9	4.7	1.4	2.3	3.0	2 8
Middle East	Value	37	60	121	690	60	94	380	472
	%	0.7	0.8	1.1	2.6	1.2	1.3	3.3	2.0

*Percentages given may not add to 100 because of rounding.
Source: UN, *Monthly Bulletin of Statistics*.

are included, the total net flow exceeded 1%. This was an encouraging development in that it was the first time that the target of 1% for all flows had been reached. The oil-exporting countries were equally generous in their aid program to LDC's. Total commitments by OPEC reached $9 billion in 1975, an increase of nearly 7%. Net disbursements, however, rose more rapidly to $5.6 billion compared with $4.6 billion the year before.

(EIU)

Centrally Planned Economies. The 30th plenary session of the Council for Mutual Economic Assistance (CMEA), held in East Berlin July 7–9, found "with satisfaction" that the five-year plans for 1971–75 had been "successfully fulfilled." The premiers of the member states approved the new five-year plans for 1976–80, laboriously coordinated and dovetailed under the supervision of the CMEA general secretariat in Moscow, and also discussed the joint programs for cooperation in key sectors of production for a 10- to 15-year period. These programs, according to the official communiqué, would decide practical steps to meet the economic requirements of the CMEA member states: first, in the output of basic types of energy, fuel, and raw materials; second, in the joint development of machine building on the basis of specialization and cooperation in production; third, in the satisfaction of the requirements of staple foods and consumer goods; and finally in the modernization and development of transport links between members.

Aleksey Kosygin, the Soviet premier, said at the opening of the session that the main goal of the CMEA was "the creation and building of a new society free from exploitation of man by man and from wars and strife between nations." He reminded the session that in April 1969, at a special meeting of the leaders of the Communist and Workers' parties and heads of government of the member countries, a joint plan had been adopted for integrating their national economies. He pointed out that more had been accomplished in the sphere of economic cooperation since then than in many years before. "Attaching particular significance to the deepening and expansion of socialist economic integration," said Kosygin, "the Central Committee of the Communist Party of the Soviet Union and the Soviet government believe that the time has come to carry out a number of major measures in improving mutual long-term joint programs of cooperation."

Stanko Todorov, the Bulgarian premier, seconded this. He called for "a gradual drawing closer and unification of the mechanisms of management and planning of our national economies." But Gyorgy Lazar, the Hungarian premier, said comprehensive reforms were needed within the CMEA to make it more flexible and efficient. For instance, the CMEA was not moving fast enough toward its stated goal of making its unit of account, the "transferable" ruble, fully convertible into Western currencies. The CMEA nations continued to trade largely by barter. A country that had a surplus in trade with a neighbour could not use it to buy goods elsewhere. Manea Manescu, the Romanian premier, said that the less advanced members of the CMEA should be given help to catch up through a new 15-year program to wipe out gaps in development and living standards.

The proposal to undertake joint economic planning appeared to mark a new departure for the CMEA, which thus far had coordinated the national plans of member states but had not undertaken to set international economic targets. The final communiqué, however, avoided the sensitive term "joint planning."

The possibility of cooperation between the CMEA and the EEC was reopened late in the year. With a foreign trade deficit with the West estimated at $33.4

Table X. Rates of Industrial Growth in Eastern Europe*

Country	1956–60	1961–65	1966–70	1971–75	1976†
Bulgaria	15.9	11.7	11.2	9.0	9.1
Czechoslovakia	10.5	5.2	6.3	6.7	6.0
Germany, East	9.2	5.9	6.4	6.3	6.6
Hungary	7.5	8.1	6.1	6.3	4.4
Poland	9.9	8.6	8.3	10.5	13.0
Romania	10.9	13.0	11.8	13.1	12.4‡
U.S.S.R.	10.4	8.6	8.5	7.4	5.0

*Yearly average percentages.
†First six months.
‡1975.
Source: National statistics.

Table XI. Foreign Trade of Eastern Europe

In $000,000

Country	Exports 1973	Exports 1974	Exports 1975	Imports 1973	Imports 1974	Imports 1975
Bulgaria	3,297	3,833	4,601	3,267	4,322	5,309
Czechoslovakia	5,912	6,898	7,808	5,993	7,360	8,489
Germany, East	7,504	8,729	10,065	7,836	9,625	11,265
Hungary	4,316	4,817	5,355	3,767	5,148	6,221
Poland	6,432	8,321	10,289	7,862	10,489	12,545
Romania	3,729	4,863	5,329	3,497	5,132	5,330
U.S.S.R.	21,159	27,768	32,175	20,813	25,212	35,711

Source: National statistics.

Table XIII. Soviet Trade with Eastern European Countries

In 000,000 rubles, current prices*

Country	Exports 1974	Exports 1975	Exports 1976†	Imports 1974	Imports 1975	Imports 1976†
Bulgaria	1,478.5	2,059.6	1,663.5	1,425.6	1,931.2	1,605.0
Czechoslovakia	1,511.1	2,019.5	1,648.6	1,518.4	1,891.7	1,596.2
Germany, East	2,164.6	2,980.3	2,275.9	2,150.7	2,643.1	2,052.4
Hungary	1,134.5	1,657.7	1,297.9	1,147.8	1,616.0	1,217.7
Poland	1,838.2	2,447.2	1,984.9	1,745.4	2,406.1	1,778.3
Romania	578.5	702.1	529.8	612.3	823.7	618.9

*The average official exchange rate, used only in foreign trade, was in 1974, 1975, and 1976, respectively, 0.78, 0.75, and 0.755 ruble to U.S. $1.
†January-September.
Source: Ministry for Foreign Trade of the U.S.S.R.

Table XIV. Soviet Crude Petroleum and Products Supplied to Eastern Europe

In 000 metric tons

Country	1973	1974	1975
Bulgaria	9,322	10,855	11,553
Czechoslovakia	14,340	14,836	15,965
Germany, East	12,985	14,424	14,952
Hungary	6,294	6,729	7,535
Poland	12,336	11,855	13,271

Source: Ministry for Foreign Trade of the U.S.S.R.

Table XV. Percentage Changes in Consumer Prices

	Average 1962–72	1973	1974	1975	12 months to Nov. 1976
Total OECD	3.9	8.0	13.6	11.5	8.5
Australia	3.4	9.5	15.1	15.1	14.0*
Canada	3.3	7.6	10.9	10.8	5.5†
France	4.4	7.3	13.7	11.7	10.0
Germany, West	3.2	6.9	7.0	6.0	4.0
Italy	4.3	10.8	19.1	17.0	20.0
Japan	5.7	11.7	24.5	11.8	8.5
Netherlands, The	5.4	8.0	9.6	10.2	9.0
Sweden	4.7	6.7	9.9	9.8	9.5†
United Kingdom	4.9	9.2	16.0	24.2	14.5
United States	3.3	6.2	11.0	9.1	5.5

*To September.
†To October.
Sources: OECD, *Economic Outlook*, July 1976; OECD, *Main Economic Indicators*; The Economist, *Key Indicators*.

billion at the end of 1975, and a growing burden of debt repayments, the CMEA countries had expressed interest in preferential access to Western markets for their exports and also in export credits—both of which might be obtained from the EEC. On November 15 the foreign ministers of the nine countries of the EEC approved the general outlines of a cooperation agreement they would be willing to conclude with the seven members of the CMEA. They decided to exclude substantive trade questions from the proposed talks on cooperation.

The difficulties on the trade front stood in ironic contrast to some of the economic bragging that appeared in the Eastern European press. The Polish Statistical Office claimed that in 1974 the CMEA countries had produced 24.1% of the world's energy-generating raw materials, 20.3% of the world's electric power, 26.5% of its steel, 24.6% of its sulfuric acid, and 23.8% of its cement. But their share of world trade was less than 10%. According to a Barclays Bank estimate, between 1970 and 1975 total CMEA trade grew at an annual average rate of 17.2%. More than half of CMEA trade was among the member countries. The proportion of CMEA trade carried on with the industrial countries of the West grew from 23% in 1970 to 30% in 1975, but part of the increase reflected higher price levels in the West.

At the same time, there was a shift in the balance of trade between the Soviet Union and the other members of the CMEA, resulting mainly from higher prices for Soviet oil exports to those countries. Until 1975 Soviet exports to the Eastern European countries had been more or less equal to imports from them. But in 1975 and the first nine months of 1976 the U.S.S.R. ran surpluses with all except Romania (Table XIII).

(K. M. SMOGORZEWSKI)

ECONOMIC CONDITIONS

In this section the impact of economic developments on individuals and households is examined. The discussion focuses on wages and prices; employment and unemployment; taxation and social benefits; and housing, interest rates, and consumer credit availability.

Prices and Wages. A major feature of the 1974–75 recession, the longest and deepest since World War II, was the accompanying inflation. Major progress was made in 1976 in cutting it back from the peak levels of

Table XII. Output of Basic Industrial Products in Eastern Europe, 1975

In 000 metric tons except for natural gas and electric power

Country	Hard coal	Brown coal	Natural gas (000,000 cu m)	Crude petroleum	Electric power (000,000 kw-hr)	Steel	Sulfuric acid	Cement
Bulgaria	300	23,998*	100	100	25,200	2,300	854	4,400
Czechoslovakia	28,119	86,272	900	—	59,238	14,323	1,245	9,305
Germany, East	500	246,706	—	—	84,500	6,500	1,002	10,700
Hungary	3,000	21,887	5,175	2,006	20,457	3,671	647	3,759
Poland	171,625	39,865	5,963	600	97,169	15,004	3,413	18,543
Romania	7,300	19,789*	28,900*	14,600	53,700	9,500	1,448	11,500
U.S.S.R.	485,000	216,000	289,000	491,000	1,038,000	141,000	18,642	122,000
Total	695,844	654,517	330,038	508,306	1,378,264	192,298	27,251	180,207

*1974.
Source: National statistics.

Table XVI. Average Change in Real Earnings

Country	Average 1962–72	1973–74	1975–76	12 months average to latest month 1976
Australia	...	10.5	−0.1	2.2
Canada	2.7	2.3	1.2	8.1 June
France	4.4	4.3	5.8	4.5 1st quarter
Germany, West	4.2	3.4	2.0	1.1 April
Italy	5.6	2.5	3.0	10.0 August
Japan*	7.3	1.4	−2.7	−0.5
United Kingdom	3.1	0.9	−10.8	2.1 June
United States	1.0	0.6	−0.1	2.3 August

*Monthly earnings.
Source: OECD, *Economic Outlook*, July 1976; OECD, *Main Economic Indicators*.

1974, but it remained at a historically high level (Table XV). In the U.S., for example, the 1976 average increase in consumer prices was likely to be 5–5.5%, a significant improvement on the 1974 average of 11% but still 2 percentage points higher than the long-term trend (1962–72 average). A similar picture is seen in Japan where the rate of improvement was more impressive because of the dizzier heights reached by inflation in 1974.

Italy, and to a lesser extent the U.K. and Australia, had only limited success in bringing down the high inflation rates. Consequently, inflation in these countries was running at three to four times the historical average. By contrast, West Germany in 1976 enjoyed an enviable inflation rate of less than 5%, the lowest in Europe except for Switzerland.

CHART 1.

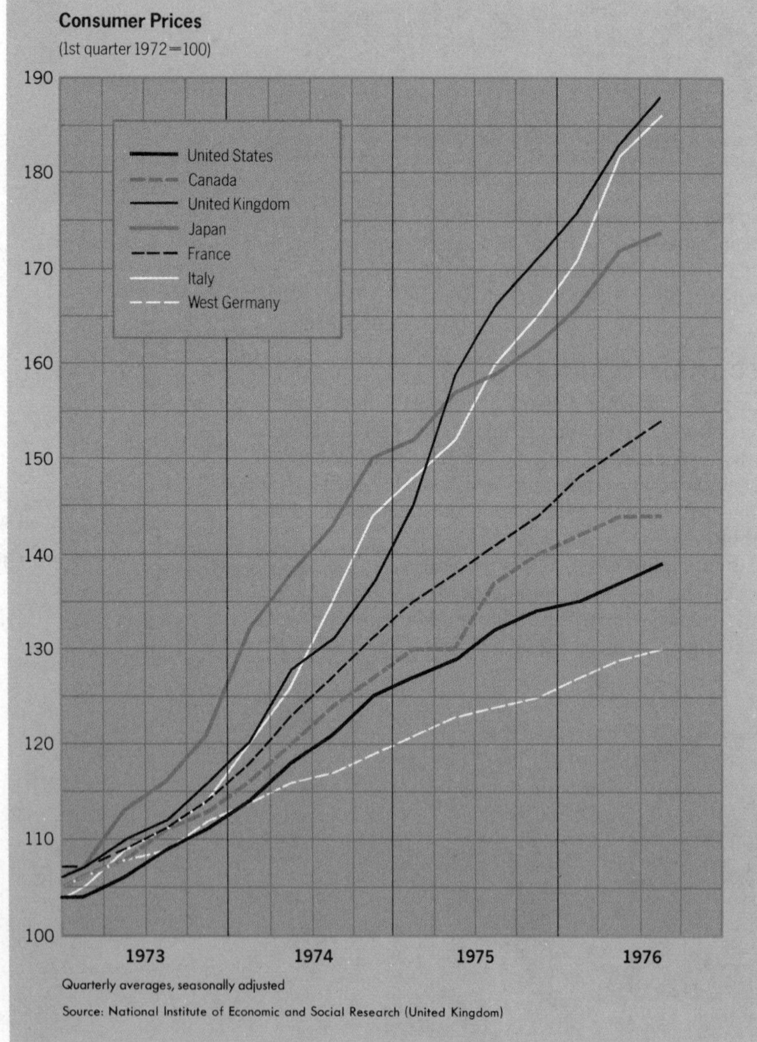

The most discouraging aspect of inflation during the year under review was that price levels showed signs of resuming their upward march at an early stage of the economic recovery. One factor in this was increases in commodity prices. Since November 1975 commodity prices had risen by over 30% and the trend was firmly upward (the latest monthly increase expressed as an annual rate was over 50%). Initially, the upswing was concentrated on fibres, forest products, rubber, and tropical beverages, but prices of other industrial materials had been rising rapidly since the spring.

A significant moderation in wage bargaining attitudes prevailed. In the U.S. 1976 was the first substantial bargaining year since the phasing out of price and wage controls, and did not produce settlement rates much above the average inflation rates. In the U.K. the extension of the "social contract" that limited pay increases to £6 per week eased the pressure on wage costs.

There were, however, signs of a gradual improvement in the real incomes of workers (*i.e.*, money earnings adjusted for changes in the cost of living). In Canada and in Italy the sharp increases during 1976 were likely to have inflationary effects unless matched by productivity gains, which seemed highly unlikely.

Employment and Unemployment. Politicians looking for a silver lining in the economic picture could point to the fact that more people were employed than ever before. In nearly all of the industrial countries, the second quarter of 1976 witnessed higher employment levels than in the preceding year (*see* Table XVII). The largest increases were in Canada, Australia, and the U.S.

Nevertheless, unemployment remained uncomfortably high in most of the countries. Throughout the recession the rates of unemployment had been much higher than those seen in previous postwar recessions, and they remained high even when output began to recover after the middle of 1975. In most countries unemployment peaked in the third or fourth quarter of 1975 and began to diminish, but as the recovery slowed down in the summer of 1976 the unemployment rates leveled off. In the U.S., France, and West Germany unemployment began to climb again. One plausible explanation for this is that the official unemployment figures had underestimated the weakness of the labour market, and when conditions began to improve employers were able to increase output by using workers who had been on reduced hours rather than by hiring from the ranks of the unemployed.

Published unemployment figures do not necessarily measure the full extent of unemployment because not

Table XVII. Total Employment in Selected Countries
(1970=100)

Country	1974	1975	1976 First quarter	1976 Second quarter
Australia	108	108	110	110
Canada	116	118	117	122
France	105	104	99	103
Germany, West	98	95	94	...
Italy	101	102	100	101
Japan	103	103	101	104
Sweden	103	105	105	106
United Kingdom	101	101	...	...
United States	109	108	108	111

Source: OECD, *Main Economic Indicators*.

everybody who becomes unemployed during a recession continues to look for work. Many simply drop out. Married women, in particular, "opt out" in this way. Others, particularly those nearing retirement age, may find it extremely difficult to find a job and, growing discouraged, cease to look for one.

The extent of unemployment also depends on the statistical methods and definitions adopted by government statisticians. Two main methods of counting are used: labour force surveys, as in the U.S., and official registration, as in the U.K. The former method employs interviewers to sample households to determine the numbers out of work and looking for a job. The other method counts those looking for jobs who have registered with the appropriate government department. Often the registration system provides a lower estimate than the sampling system. Caution is therefore needed in interpreting unemployment statistics and in making international comparisons. The figures given in Table XVIII are based on differing national definitions. The final two columns, however, show the unemployment rates for 1975 and the third quarter of 1976 adjusted to conform with U.S. definitions. In Japan and West Germany, the rates in past years were extremely low, reflecting the strong rates of economic growth. In West Germany, however, the 1974–75 recession brought a large shakeout, sending the number of unemployed over the million mark, in spite of the fact that a large number of immigrant workers from southern Europe were encouraged to return home. In Japan the tendency for employers to hold onto labour even during slack periods kept the unemployment rate well below those elsewhere.

Taxation and Social Benefits. One effect of inflation is to push up income taxes. This happens as rising incomes lift taxpayers into higher tax brackets. From the standpoint of economic policy this may be welcome because it siphons purchasing power out of the economy and thus helps to reduce inflationary pressures. At some point, however, it becomes necessary to make downward adjustments of the income tax system.

Inflation-prone countries such as Chile, Brazil, and Iceland have automatic adjustments for taxation. But even more stable economies have in recent years introduced similar arrangements. For instance, The Netherlands and Canada have provisions for automatic adjustment, and France has a partially auto-

A plumber in Mexico City waits for customers on a downtown street. His toolbox and a blowtorch advertise his trade. More than half of Mexico's workers have less than full-time employment.

WIDE WORLD

CHART 2.

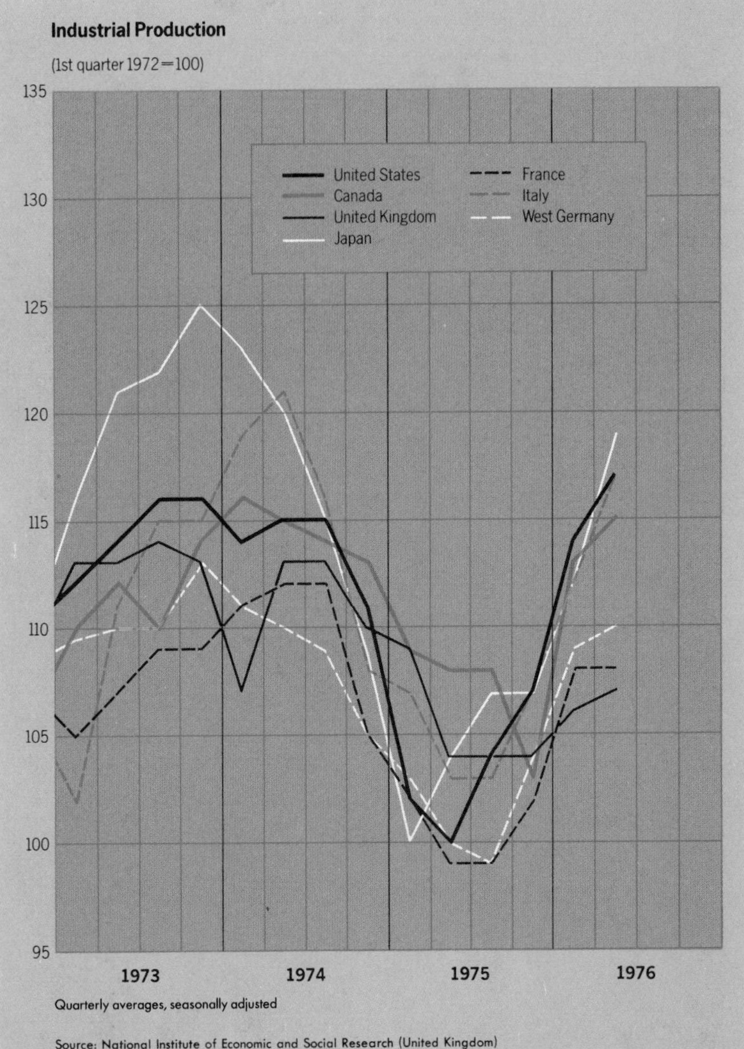

Quarterly averages, seasonally adjusted

Source: National Institute of Economic and Social Research (United Kingdom)

Table XVIII. Unemployment in the Developed Economies

Country	Unemployment rates (Percent of civilian labour force)* Average 1962–73	1974	1975	Latest month 1976	Number unemployed latest month 1976 (in 000)		Standardized annual unemployment rate (%) 1975	1976 third quarter
Australia	1.6	2.1	4.7	5.2	320	August	...	...
Canada	5.3	5.4	7.0	7.3	753	September	7.0	7.3
France	1.8	2.3	3.8	...	935	October	4.0	4.3
Germany, West	1.3	2.7	4.9	4.6	1,042	October	3.6	3.3
Italy	3.6	2.9	3.4	3.8	780	July	3.6	4.2
Japan	1.3	1.4	1.7	2.0	1,120	August	2.0	2.0
Netherlands, The	1.3	2.8	4.1	...	224	October	...	...
Spain	...	3.2	4.0	...	...		...	...
Sweden	2.1	2.0	1.6	1.7	70	September	...	...
United Kingdom	2.4	2.5	3.9	5.5	1,306	October	4.6	5.8
United States	4.9	5.6	8.5	7.9	7,569	October	8.3	7.7

*Seasonally adjusted.
Sources: OECD, *Economic Outlook*, July 1976; OECD, *Main Economic Indicators*; The Economist, *Key Indicators: Major Economies*; NIESR, *Economic Review*, November 1976.

Table XIX. Economically Active Population

Latest census or estimate

Country	% of economically active population in Agri-culture*	Indus-try†	Ser-vices‡
AFRICA			
Afars and Issas	50	—	50
Algeria	50.1	11.7	38.2
Angola	63	...	37§
Benin (Dahomey)	90	...	10§
Botswana	86	4	10§
Burundi	95	1	4
Cameroon	80	10	10
Cape Verde Islands	40.1	1.2	58.7
Central African Empire	87	...	13§
Chad	96	4	—
Comoro Islands	63.9	17.6	18.5
Congo	40	...	60§
Egypt	53.2	13.1	33.7
Equatorial Guinea	95	—	5
Ethiopia	85	...	15§
Gabon	84.1	7.0	8.9
Gambia, The	85	...	15§
Ghana	58.0	11.9	30.1
Guinea	83	...	17§
Guinea-Bissau	86	...	14§
Ivory Coast	86.4	1.9	11.7
Kenya	86.5	3.6	9.9
Lesotho	91	1	8
Liberia	80.9	8.5	10.6
Libya	32.5	24.3	43.2
Madagascar	80	2	18
Malawi	87	...	13§
Mali	91	...	9§
Mauritania	85	...	15§
Mauritius	32.8	23.1	44.1
Morocco	50.6	15.3	34.1
Mozambique	73.4	12.5	14.1
Niger	91	...	9§
Nigeria	55.9	12.1	32.0
Réunion	29.5	7.3	63.2
Rhodesia	63	...	27§
Rwanda	91	...	9§
São Tomé & Príncipe	...	...	...
Senegal	72.7	7.0	20.3
Seychelles	28.4	29.7	41.9
Sierra Leone	75.2	9.8	15.0
Somalia	82	...	18§
South Africa	28.0	21.3	50.7
South West Africa	58.5	10.2	31.3
Sudan	80	...	20§
Swaziland	19.4	6.9	73.7
Tanzania	91.0	1.7	7.3
Togo	75	...	25§
Transkei‖	68.2	6.6	25.2
Tunisia	41.0	9.5	49.5
Uganda	86	...	14§
Upper Volta	89	...	11§
Zaire	78	...	22§
Zambia	43.7	20.0	36.3
ASIA			
Afghanistan	77.0	8.2	14.8
Bahrain	6.6	14.0	79.4
Bangladesh	70.5	...	29.5§
Bhutan	...	...	...
Brunei	11.9	22.1	66.0
Burma	68	...	32§
Cambodia	80.3	2.8	16.9
China	66.5	...	33.5§
Cyprus	33.6	25.2	57.8
Hong Kong	4.0	53.3	42.7
India	68.6	...	31.4§
Indonesia□	61.8	7.5	30.7
Iran	54.6	21.4	24.0
Iraq	55.3	6.9	37.8
Israel	7.5	24.8	67.7
Japan¶	13.6	33.3	51.9
Jordan	35.3	10.8	53.9
Korea, North	53.2	...	46.8§
Korea, South	50.8	15.2	34.0
Kuwait	2.5	20.2	77.3
Laos	78	...	22§
Lebanon¶	18.3	23.5	56.3
Macau	0.4	0.4	99.2
Malaysia	46.0	11.8	42.2
Maldives	...	...	...
Mongolia	45.4	22.3	32.3
Nepal	94.4	1.2	4.4
Oman	82.7	4.0	13.3
Pakistan	56.2	13.0	30.8
Philippines	51.5	15.6	32.9
Qatar	...	...	...
Saudi Arabia	60	...	40§
Singapore	3.5	28.9	67.6
Sri Lanka	50.4	10.0	39.6
Syria	47.9	12.7	39.4
Taiwan	36.6	19.3	44.1
Thailand	82.1	4.4	13.5
Turkey	67.0	11.9	21.1
United Arab Emirates	...	...	...
Vietnam	...	...	...
Yemen (Aden)	62	...	38§
Yemen (San'a')	73.3	...	26.7§
EUROPE			
Albania	62	...	38§
Andorra	8.3	28.6	63.1
Austria	13.8	40.7	45.5
Belgium	4.5	34.3	61.2
Bulgaria	44.3	26.4	29.3
Channel Islands♀	8.3	22.5	69.2
Czechoslovakia	16.4	48.0	35.6
Denmark	9.5	32.7	57.8
Faeroe Islands	26.2	30.7	43.1
Finland	20.3	34.3	45.4
France	6.3	15.9	77.8
Germany, East	12.6	48.8	38.6
Germany, West	7.5	48.9	56.4
Gibraltar	—	21.8	78.2
Greece	40.5	24.8	34.7
Hungary	24.5	43.2	31.4
Iceland	16.8	36.8	46.4
Ireland	24.4	27.5	48.1
Isle of Man	9.1	31.1	59.8
Italy	16.7	42.0	41.3
Liechtenstein	6.2	56.6	37.2
Luxembourg	7.5	42.7	49.8
Malta	7.5	24.3	68.2
Monaco	0.1	21.5	78.4
Netherlands, The	6.1	35.3	58.6
Norway	11.9	35.0	53.1
Poland	38.6	34.4	27.0
Portugal	31.4	31.5	37.1
Romania	56.8	19.4	23.8
San Marino	8.5	54.1	37.4
Spain	24.8	36.6	38.6
Sweden	6.6	33.9	59.5
Switzerland	7.6	48.3	44.1
United Kingdom	1.7	45.3	53.0
Yugoslavia	43.9	17.7	38.4
NORTH AMERICA			
Antigua	10.6	20.0	69.4
Bahamas, The	6.9	17.7	75.4
Barbados	21.3	13.8	64.9
Belize	33.9	12.8	53.3
Bermuda	1.6	19.4	79.0
British Virgin Islands	7.8	9.9	82.3
Canada	6.2	28.3	65.5
Cayman Islands	10.9	27.6	61.5
Costa Rica	36.4	18.9	44.7
Cuba	30.0	26.2	43.8
Dominica	39.4	7.9	52.7
Dominican Republic	44.3	10.5	45.2
El Salvador	46.6	10.4	43.0
Greenland	18.6	28.2	53.2
Grenada	71.6	17.5	10.9
Guadeloupe	32.4	25.7	41.9
Guatemala	57.2	18.0	24.8
Haiti	77	...	23§
Honduras	58.8	14.4	26.8
Jamaica	32.8	19.4	47.8
Martinique	28.1	20.4	51.5
Mexico	39.4	22.5	38.1
Montserrat	20.4	5.8	73.8
Netherlands Antilles	0.9	32.9	66.2
Nicaragua	46.4	16.3	37.3
Panama	38.4	13.8	47.8
Puerto Rico	7.3	16.9	75.8
St. Lucia	10.5	5.3	84.2
St. Pierre & Miquelon	11.3	17.5	71.2
Trinidad and Tobago	15.4	18.7	65.9
United States	4.0	30.8	65.2
Virgin Islands (U.S.)	1.2	25.5	73.3
OCEANIA			
American Samoa	5.1	29.2	65.7
Australia	6.4	30.6	63.0
Christmas Island	—	80.3	19.7
Cook Islands	34.1	24.1	41.8
Fiji	55.2	7.0	37.8
French Polynesia	37.1	22.3	40.6
Gilbert Islandsδ	65.5	3.8	30.7
Guam	0.7	22.8	76.5
Nauru	0.1	31.4	68.5
New Caledonia	34.1	18.3	47.6
New Hebrides	82.5	2.5	15.0
New Zealand	11.5	34.0	54.5
Niue	11.4	—	88.6
Norfolk Island	6.1	15.9	78.0
Papua New Guinea	56.4	4.5	39.1
Solomon Islands	23.2	12.5	64.3
Tonga	34.0	1.5	64.5
Western Samoa	67.3	—	32.7
SOUTH AMERICA			
Argentina	14.8	20.6	64.6
Bolivia	48	16	36
Brazil	44.3	19.2	36.5
Chile	21.4	17.8	60.8
Colombia	32	19	49
Ecuador	32.5	11.5	56.0
French Guiana	18.4	28.5	53.1
Guyana	29.6	23.1	47.3
Paraguay	47.7	18.2	34.1
Peru	45.1	16.9	38.0
Surinam	34.9	14.9	50.2
Uruguay	18.5	27.8	53.7
Venezuela	20.3	14.6	65.1
U.S.S.R.	26.3	45.1	28.6

*Includes forestry and fishing.
†Includes mining and construction.
‡Includes all other economic activities, including government employment.
§Includes all nonagricultural activities.
‖Excludes Herschel and Glen Grey districts.
¶Detail does not add to 100% because of the omission of some categories.
♀Jersey only.
δIncludes Tuvalu (Ellice) Islands.
□Excludes East Timor.

matic system whereby the tax schedule is changed whenever the annual rate of inflation exceeds 5%. Premier Barre, however, suspended this arrangement for 1977 as part of his fight to bring inflation under control. In The Netherlands the allowances and tax brackets in the income tax tables are adjusted by a factor equal to the increase in consumer prices. But the effect of indirect taxes and subsidies on the prices of goods is excluded from the correction factor. Furthermore, the finance minister may adjust the correction factor downward by 20% at his discretion. The Canadian system is similar to the Dutch, though no prior adjustment is made for sales tax changes.

Many countries adjust pensions and other welfare payments to take account of inflation. Their methods of doing this are given in Table XX. Even in those countries, such as the U.K., which do not have automatic adjustment schemes, in recent years the adjustments have not been far short of increases in consumer prices.

Old-age pensions account for a larger proportion of government expenditure than welfare benefits (including unemployment benefits). The number of elderly people as a proportion of the population has increased considerably in recent years, as shown in Table XX. This trend is expected to continue until 1980, followed by a slight decline between 1980 and 1985.

Housing, Interest Rates, and Consumer Credit. Trends in housing conditions are summarized in Table XXI. Although there is some evidence of progress in recent years, care must be taken in interpretation and in making international comparisons. For example, a fall in the number of persons per household (as shown in the first column) may occur because more people are setting up homes—a sign of greater prosperity. But it may also reflect a trend toward having smaller families. Again, when a large proportion of households own their own homes this may reflect economic prosperity but not all the figures in the second column of Table XXI support this hypothesis. The comparatively low proportions in such rich countries as Sweden and West Germany show that preferences in home ownership differ from country to country.

Other measures of progress in housing conditions, such as the percentage of houses with running (piped) water, flush toilets, and electric lighting, are less ambiguous. But the urban-rural composition of a country's population affects these figures, since they tend to be lower in rural areas. The final column of Table XXI shows the rates of new housing construction in different countries. Again, factors such as urbanization, types of housing built (*e.g.*, high rise or low rise), and policies toward urban renewal all create difficulties in making international comparisons.

In the short term, housing is highly sensitive to changes in economic climate. This can be seen in figures for housing starts (Table XXII). Housing starts in 1974 were sharply down in most countries, reflecting the gathering forces of recession. As the economy turned upward in 1975, housing starts rose in several countries. In 1976 confidence returned to the housing sector. The upswing in the U.S. and Canada was particularly vigorous following one of the sharpest declines in their history. An important factor in housing construction is the availability of financing at reasonable rates. After reaching record levels in 1974, short-term interest rates fell in 1975 and—with the notable exception of Italy, the U.K., and to a lesser extent France—continued to decline or level out in 1976.

Currency crises in Italy, the U.K., and France reversed the tendency to falling interest rates, and in the former two raised them to new highs. Table XXIII shows the decline of consumer credit available for automobile purchases in the U.S. and U.K. during 1974, and the subsequent improvement in 1975 and in the first two quarters of 1976. In the U.K. most of the credit extended by the finance houses is for car purchases.

INTERNATIONAL TRADE

World trade increased sharply in volume during the first half of 1976 under the impulse of a rapid recovery in manufacturing production in the industrialized world. During the second half of the year there were some signs that increased export earnings might allow less developed countries to ease the restrictions on imports they had imposed at the end of 1975, and that a number of oil-exporting countries were increasing their purchases. But these developments were not strong enough to counter a marked slowdown in the pace of recovery in the West. International trade continued to grow in the second half of 1976, but at a slow rate. It was expected that when the final figures became available they would probably show that for the year as a whole trade grew by around 10% in volume and rather less than twice that in value.

Industrial countries increased their trade with each other sharply in the first half of 1976, with restocking providing most of the impetus. The greatest part of this expansion, which resulted in a growth rate of around 14% in volume for both imports and exports originating in the OECD countries, consisted of growth in trade between industrial nations. But there was also a continued rise in imports from non-oil-producing less developed countries, and oil imports also rose, though less sharply than in the last half of 1975. For 1976 as a whole, it seemed likely that oil imports by industrialized countries would return to the 1974 level.

For the oil-producing nations, the most important effect of this increase in oil prices was to increase their surplus on current account, which had fallen sharply during 1975. It was expected to increase by some $2 billion, to $35 billion, during 1976, a measure of the rapid increase in production in Saudi Arabia where physical constraints limit the growth of imports. Other oil-producing nations, which had limited imports because of payments constraints, tended not to be able to increase production as rapidly.

The CMEA countries, the Soviet Union and its allies, increased their trade with each other rapidly in value terms during the early part of 1976, a result of the sharp increase in prices in intra-area trade caused by the change in policy within the area. This reinforced the trend toward an increase in the CMEA's share of total world commerce during 1975, but there was no significant erosion of its concentration within the area; the Soviet Union increased its sales of raw materials to its partners more rapidly than they increased sales of manufactured goods to the Soviet Union. Good harvests in 1976 seemed likely to reduce grain imports from outside the area.

In 1975 the total value of world exports reached $880 billion. This was an increase of 5% over 1974, but it was more than accounted for by an increase in prices of 10%. Although higher than the average for the previous decade, this price increase was considerably less than the increases of 25% in 1973 and 40% in 1974. The increase was confined to the first quarter of the year, after which export unit values actually

Table XX. Number of Persons Aged 65 and Over as a Percent of Total Population and Methods of Adjustment of Old-Age Pensions

Country	1951	1965	1975	1985	Methods of adjustment of old-age pensions (as of 1973)
Belgium	11.1	12.5	14.2	13.4	An annual increment larger than the increase in the price index.
Canada	—	7.6	8.0	—	Based on increases in the price index. From 1976, will increase with changes in national average wages.
France	11.4	12.0	13.3	11.7	Semiannual adjustment (January and July); related to increase in salaries.
Germany, West	9.3	11.9	14.2	12.6	Adjusted annually, taking account of progress in economic efficiency and productivity, and changes in the national income per employed person.
Italy	8.1	9.7	11.7	12.0	Annual adjustment (by decree), when cost of living rises 2% or more.
Japan	—	6.3	7.9	9.5	
Netherlands, The	7.8	9.5	10.6	10.8	Pensions adjusted by decree, when wage index changes by more than 3%.
Sweden	10.2	12.6	14.7	15.9	Automatic adjustment based on changes in price level.
U.K.	10.9	12.0	13.5	13.5	Special legislation, once a year.
U.S.	—	9.3	9.8	10.2	Automatic cost of living adjustment.

Sources: "Old Age Pensions' Level, Adjustment and Coverage," in *The OECD Observer*, No. 77, September–October 1975; OECD, *Demographic Trends in Western Europe and the United States;* OECD, *Demographic Trends 1970–1985 in OECD Member Countries.*

Table XXI. Trends in Housing Conditions in Selected Countries

Country		Average number of persons per household	Percent of owner-occupants	Percent of dwellings with Piped water	Flush toilet	Electric lighting	Dwellings constructed*
Australia	1966	3.5	70.8	—	—	98.3	9.7
	1971	3.3	67.3	—	89.5	98.4	11.1
Belgium	1961	3.0	49.7	76.9	47.6	99.6	4.3
	1971	3.0	55.9	86.6	62.5	100.0	4.8
Canada	1967	3.7	65.4	95.2	92.5	—	7.4
	1971	—	60.0	96.1	94.3	—	9.4
France	1962	3.1	42.7	78.3	37.2	97.6	7.0
	1968	3.1	43.3	90.8	51.8	98.8	8.4
Germany, West	1968	2.9	34.3	99.7	87.4	99.9	8.6
	1972	2.7	33.5	99.2	94.2	99.7	10.7
Italy	1961	3.6	45.8	62.3	—	95.9	8.2
	1971	3.3	50.9	86.1	—	99.0	6.7
Japan	1968	3.9	59.5	94.9	17.1	—	12.7
	1973	3.6	58.8	98.3	31.4	—	18.7
Spain	1960	4.0	...	45.0	—	89.3	10.0
Sweden	1965	2.7	35.5	94.3	85.3	—	12.5
	1970	2.6	35.2	97.3	90.1	—	13.6
U.K. (England and Wales)	1966	2.9	47.8	—	97.9	...	7.4
	1971	2.9	50.1	—	98.9	...	—
U.S.	1960	3.3	61.9	92.9	89.7	—	8.7
	1971	3.2	62.9	97.5	96.0	—	7.2

*Per 1,000 population.
Source: UN, *Statistical Yearbook* (1974 and 1975).

Table XXII. Housing Starts in Selected Countries

(Average 1970=100)

Country	Total 1970 (000)	1973	1974	1975	1976 First quarter	1976 Second quarter	Percent change from a year earlier 1976 First quarter	Second quarter
Australia	138.8	120	91	86	92	97	12	1
Belgium	42.7	137	152	178	160	...	...	...
Canada	190.5	141	117	127	91	169	82	37
France	481.7	115	114	107	100	111	−7.5	4
Italy	71.5	102	77	80	81	...	...	...
Japan	1,484.6	128	89	91	90	105	27	16
Netherlands, The	127.3	111	88	88	89	86	6	−10
Sweden	106.7	75	76	48	40	58	29	45
U.K.	331.1	102	79	101	103	124	30	15
U.S.	1,469.0	140	92	80	77	120	45	35

Source: OECD, *Main Economic Indicators.*

declined. The physical volume of exports throughout the year declined by around 5%.

The trade recovery that began in the last quarter of 1975 continued forcefully into the new year, and at one time seemed likely to be as strong as the expansion of 1972. Although inflationary pressures seemed likely to assert themselves, they were expected to be felt less than in 1975.

Primary Producing Countries. Imports by the members of OPEC fell slightly in the first quarter of 1976 from the high point reached in 1975, but there appeared to be little change for the year as a whole compared with the previous year. Import constraints on OPEC members had now assumed two quite separate forms, financial and physical. For the four Arab states

Table XXIII. New Consumer Credit in the U.S. and U.K.

	1972	1973	1974	1975	1976 first quarter	1976 second quarter
U.S. ($000,000,000)						
Total new credit	11.67	13.35	13.33	13.62	13.49	15.95
New credit, automobiles	3.36	3.84	3.60	4.01	4.20	4.90
U.K. (£000,000)						
New credit, retail shops	106	118	123	149	165	163
New credit, finance houses	102	121	86	100	114	128

Source: OECD, *Main Economic Indicators.*

on the south of the Gulf, of which Saudi Arabia and Kuwait are the most important, the problems were largely physical and organizational. Port congestion remained very severe and had an important effect in both raising prices and reducing import volumes. Shortages of labour and administrative difficulties in carrying out ambitious development plans also made it difficult for these countries to increase imports even though they had very large surpluses from their sales of oil. But most of the other countries would probably have found some difficulty in ensuring sufficient revenue in the early part of the year, even if they had not experienced any practical problems in importing. The majority of OPEC countries were within a few hundred million dollars of balance in their payments, and many found it necessary to borrow.

The same pattern of differences showed itself in the exporting experience of the OPEC countries, the most remarkable variation being exhibited by Saudi Arabia whose output is to some extent a regulator of total OPEC output. Having experienced a fall of 20.3% in its rate of exports compared with the first quarter of 1975, far above the OPEC average of 13.8%, Saudi Arabia returned to its former level of earnings in the first half of 1976 and then surpassed them in the second half of the year as demand from industrial nations continued to hold up because of fears of a new round of price increases.

During the first six months of 1976, Saudi Arabian exports totaled $17,084,000,000, compared with imports of $5,027,000,000. Kuwait had earnings in the first half of the year of $3,995,000,000, compared with imports of less than one-third that rate.

The increase in exports of oil during the year was not restricted to these countries, however. Iran's exports of $11,022,000,000 in the first half of 1976 compared favourably with its earnings of $9,856,000,000 in 1975. Imports increased even more sharply, however, and by the middle of the year the Iranian government was having to take actions clearly designed to slow down the flow of goods into the country. In addition, it became clear during the autumn that the Iranians were considering tying future purchases from abroad to barter arrangements to purchase Iranian oil. The Iranian government had made it clear on a number of occasions throughout the year that it felt that the oil companies had not taken enough oil from Iran as compared with other countries.

The less developed countries that did not produce oil had a less testing time during 1976 than had at first seemed possible. Their exports of $94,290,000,000 in 1975 were insufficient by a wide margin to pay their import bill of $139,150,000,000, and at the beginning of 1976 there were fears both about the cuts in consumption that would need to be imposed and the possibility that their credit might cease to be good. But the problems proved somewhat more tractable than expected, in part because industrialized countries ran a much larger deficit than had seemed likely.

East Asian countries such as the Philippines and South Korea recovered the export markets they had lost during the recession of early 1974. Average increases of 20% in export value in the first half of 1976 were not matched by equivalent increases in imports, with a consequent dramatic reduction in payments deficits and an easing of the need to borrow in international capital markets. In the Western Hemisphere the improvement in exports was also considerable, with exports from Brazil rising some 25% in the first half of 1976 from the $8,760,000,000 annual rate in 1975. But there was still pressure on the trade balances of such countries since their long-term trade position was relatively less favourable than that of the East Asian countries, which traditionally have lower imports.

All of the less developed countries suffered, however, during the second half of the year when recovery in the West slowed down remarkably, and with it the imports of the industrialized world. Countries that relied on exports of commodities rather than manufactured products, such as Zaire, also suffered when the expected increase in commodity prices fell short.

Industrial Countries. The recession of 1974 and early 1975 originated in the industrialized Western world and was concentrated most sharply on imports. Manufacturing production declined more than the rest of the economy, and trade in manufactured goods between countries declined more sharply than in internal markets. The 24 OECD nations did not suffer a big drop in exports. The value of exports actually rose under the impact of increased purchases by CMEA countries and oil producers. Total exports in 1975 totaled $145.4 billion in each quarter, 4.9% higher in value terms than in 1974, though lower in volume.

There was, however, a very sharp drop in the total imports of the OECD area, some of it caused by a fall in oil purchases but mostly accounted for by a decline in imports from within the OECD area itself. In the first half of 1976, imports recovered to reach $317.4 billion, compared with $294.3 billion in the first half of 1975.

The increase in the first half of 1976 was, in effect, a continuation of a recovery that had begun at the end of 1975 but did not become apparent until the turn of the year. The turnaround showed itself in both the value and the volume of trade. Average values in dollar terms, which provide the best means of assessing changes in prices, actually declined by 10.5% for both imports and exports of OECD countries during the second half of 1975, after rises of 14 and 19%, respectively, in the first half. In 1976 this downward trend was reversed; the average unit value of exports rose by 2% in the first half of the year and the unit value of imports went up by 5% during the same period. The result was that the increase in volume was greater than the increase in value for the last half of 1975, but in the first half of 1976 value grew more than volume.

The total trade balance of the OECD countries was in deficit by around $7 billion during 1976 as a whole, compared with a surplus of $6 billion in 1975. This deficit, sharp in itself, concealed even sharper turnarounds in the positions of some countries.

It seemed likely that the United States, which had run a surplus of $9 billion in 1975, would show a deficit of $6,750,000,000 in 1976. About half of this deterioration was due to an increase in demand for petroleum, and the rest was explained by a sharp increase in other imports. During the first quarter of 1976, U.S. exports were $27,359,000,000 and in the second quarter they were $29,695,000,000. These figures were some 4% higher than in the equivalent period of 1975, when exports for the year as a whole totaled $107,652,000,000. Export unit values rose at an annual rate of 6% in the first half of 1976, in part reflecting an increase in costs caused by a 10% increase in the price of oil. U.S. imports rose very sharply in value during the first half of the year. In the first half of 1976 they totaled $60,989,000,000, compared with $50,897,000,000 in the first half of 1975. During 1975, total imports were $103,389,000,000. As 1976 proceeded, evidence began to mount that the pace of economic expansion was slackening, but not sufficiently to prevent the U.S. running a significant trade deficit during the year.

The deterioration in the U.S. position was counterbalanced by an improvement in that of Japan. During the year, Japan recovered the competitive advantage that it had had during 1972 and which had been eroded by the higher import cost structure imposed on it by the increase in oil prices. Japanese exports totaled $55,817,000,000 in 1975, but rose to $61,418,000,000 at an annual rate during the first half of 1976. The increase was largely accounted for by increases in volume, since Japanese unit export prices were some 5.5% below the average figure for 1975. This would imply a growth in volume of exports of some 23%. Imports, on the other hand, which stood at $30,593,000,000 in the first half of 1976, hardly increased at all in volume terms. Toward the end of the year there were signs that a number of countries in Europe and certain industries in the United States were concerned by the Japanese penetration of their markets.

West Germany's trade balance had remained firmly in surplus during 1975, though there was a slight reduction in its magnitude. Exports had risen sharply in the last quarter of 1975 to total $90,166,000,000 for the year as a whole, slightly higher in value terms than in the previous year. Imports in 1975 were $74,924,000,000. During the first half of 1976 imports were $41,718,000,000, up $3,942,000,000 over the equivalent period in 1975, an increase of 10.4% in value terms. The level of German imports, which remained strong throughout the year even though the German economy weakened, was a major factor in the rapid expansion in the first half of 1976 in the exports of other OECD countries. German exports also did well, increasing to $48,037,000,000 in the first half of the year, but their growth was not as rapid as that of imports. The revaluation of the mark in the autumn contributed to a further weakening of sales. It was expected that final figures would probably show a surplus on trade for the year as a whole of around $16 billion, compared with $15.2 billion in 1975.

France experienced a rapid domestic wage inflation during 1976, which forced the government to introduce austerity plans. During 1975 the country had run a small trade deficit, with exports of $52,951,000,000 and imports of $53,964,000,000. During the first half of 1976 imports totaled $31,715,000,000, considerably higher than the equivalent period in 1975, and pressure on the franc forced it to leave the snake of European currencies. Exports of $29,041,000,000 pointed the way to a trade deficit for 1976 considerably larger than that seen in 1975, possibly on the order of $3 billion or more.

KEYSTONE

The British pound fell precipitously in 1976, forcing the government to take emergency measures.

The U.K., on the other hand, may have marginally improved its payments position during 1976. For the first time, U.K. trade figures were significantly affected by the production of North Sea oil, which contributed some $2 billion to the balance of payments through reduced imports. During the year there was a rapid depreciation of the exchange rate of the pound. This led to higher prices for imports in the latter part of the year, but generally flat domestic demand held down their volume except in certain special sectors such as motorcars. Total imports in the first half of 1976 were $27,654,000,000, up from $27,642,000,000 in the first half of 1975. Their volume for the year as a whole probably increased by around 6%, less than the OECD average. The increase in export volumes was also limited, being probably around 8%, but their value increased much more. This was because exporters chose to use the depreciation of the pound to restore profit margins previously eroded. Exports in the first half of 1976 were $23,148,000,000, and it was expected that when final figures became available they would probably show an increase for the year as a whole of 30%, with the unit value of exports rising by over 20%.

Italy took a series of measures throughout the year in an effort to restrict imports, which continued to grow quickly. In 1975 imports totaled $38,365,000,000. In the first six months of 1976 they were $20,604,000,000. Three measures were taken. The first, deflation, seemed ineffective and failed to slow down a rapid decline in the parity of the lira. It was supplemented by a scheme requiring deposits to cover the cost of imports and by a tax on the purchase of foreign currency. Both these latter measures met strong international protest and were being phased out at the end of the year. In the cases of both Italy and the U.K., the trade results for 1976 had not yet had time to reflect fully the improvement which might result from the fall in their exchange rates.

Centrally Planned Economies. The countries of the CMEA made progress during 1976 toward the target of bringing their trade deficits with Western countries under control. Final figures for 1976 were not available at the end of the year, but it seemed likely that the Soviet Union would succeed in reducing its deficit below the $1,770,000,000 recorded during 1975. At the same time, higher prices charged for raw materials allowed the Soviet Union to record a trade surplus with its other CMEA partners.

Figures for 1975 show that the CMEA area as a whole recorded a deficit of $9.2 billion on its trade with the

West. During the first half of 1976 there was some success in reducing the growth of imports from Western countries, but the fact that many of these were tied to long-term contracts limited the scope for any real cuts. During the first half of 1976, the value of imports probably grew at around 7%, while exports grew at around 10% in value terms. A slight worsening in the terms of trade probably meant that the volume of exports grew less than 10%.

One new development in the policies of the CMEA countries was to seek arrangements with oil-producing states under which deliveries of oil were guaranteed in return for CMEA assistance in industrialization projects. One factor in this was concern on the part of borrowers and lenders alike over the rapid increase in CMEA debt. However, worries about this were to some extent countered by increased export earnings by CMEA countries from sales to the West, and the fact that the good harvest in the Soviet Union reduced the need for that country to import grain.

Commodity Trade. The prospect of a very rapid world recovery during the spring led to a sharp spurt in the price of all commodities. During April, May, and June the dollar price of all commodities rose at a monthly rate of between 6 and 7%, close to the rate it had achieved in 1974. The slackening in growth that became apparent later in the year, however, resulted in there being little overall increase in the second half of 1976. Commodities closed the year about 25% up in price over the level at the end of 1975.

This increase was not, however, uniform. During the early part of the year the increase in metals prices was particularly sharp, with an 18% rise in April alone. The cause of this increase was belief that 1976 could be similar in form to the boom of 1972, when metals performed very well. But later in the year there were losses which meant that by the end of the year metals prices stood only about 10% above the end-1975 level.

The movement of the price of copper on the London metal exchange is usually the key indicator for movements in metals prices generally. Although sometimes distorted by movements in the parity of sterling, it tends to set the trend of copper prices throughout the world. This rose to a peak of £895 a ton in the spring, significantly above the level of end-1975 but well below the nearly £1,400 a ton seen in the early 1970s. As the year proceeded, prices drifted downward. The realization that substantial levels of stocked copper existed (estimated at half a million tons at the beginning of the year) was one negative factor. So, too, was lack of consumer demand for final use, as opposed to speculative or precautionary purchases for stock. Other metals moved in sympathy, with the exception of tin which was unique in breaking through its previous peak and closing the year at around £5,000 a ton.

Agricultural products fared slightly better during the year, in part because their production was held down, in part because of the low prices obtained in 1975. As a group, fibre prices rose 38% over the year. Wool production appeared to be down significantly, possibly by as much as 8% for the year, while cotton output, at just over 60 million bales, was below demand, forcing a rundown in stocks. These shortages pushed prices up sharply in the summer, but prospects of higher production in the next year and the chance of a swing to synthetic fibres, where substantial overcapacity existed, stabilized values again by winter. Rubber production was below demand during the year, but the consequent rise in price was only gradual.

Grain production was in surplus for 1976 for the first time in five years. Even more important as far as world trade was concerned, there were good harvests in every major area, with record crops in the Soviet Union. The International Wheat Council forecast at the end of 1976 that total wheat production during the year would be 409.5 million tons, the highest ever recorded. The grain market weakened progressively throughout the year as forecasts of total production were repeatedly revised upward. Early uncertainties about Soviet production receded as it became clear that total production of grain in 1976 was going to reach 223.8 million tons, 1.3 million tons above the level reached in 1973, which was the highest in Soviet history. The Soviet crop was only 165 million tons in 1975, and heavy purchases from the U.S. were necessary to meet Soviet needs. Estimates by the U.S. Department of Agriculture and by outside experts suggested that Soviet grain purchases totaled roughly 26 million tons during 1976. At the beginning of the year there was some concern about the possibility of renewed pressure on demand if harvests were bad in the Soviet Union or the United States. Stocks at the beginning of the year stood at about 90 million tons, compared with the level of 150 million tons at which they had begun the 1970s.

None of these fears was realized. In addition to a record Soviet performance, which removed the largest buyer from the scene, the less developed countries also recorded good harvests. India announced that its grain production had been 116 million tons during 1975–76, allowing it, like other less developed countries, to cut down on imports. During 1976–77, the International Wheat Council estimated, only one-fifth of all wheat sales would be made to less developed countries, compared with two-thirds 25 years before.

The United States and Canada reasserted their dominance of world trade in wheat, accounting for 67% of the total sales. The United States also had around half of the 57 million tons of stocks with which exporting countries were expected to end the 1976–77 crop year. European production of cereals was reduced by a prolonged drought. According to preliminary estimates, production in the EEC countries was around 90 to 91 million tons, down 7% from the previous year.

The price of both coffee and cocoa rose sharply throughout the year, in large part because of continuing shortages. The frosts of the previous year in Brazil, combined with political difficulties in Angola, were the major factors.

Commercial and Trade Policy. The institutions of international trade marked time in 1976. There was little progress in any of the forums established to help liberalize trade between nations or to find new forms of relationship between industrialized and less developed nations. On the other hand, the year ended with no major recourse to protection to deal with the problems of high unemployment affecting most of the world.

The talks under the auspices of the General Agreement on Tariffs and Trade (GATT) that were aimed at producing a more liberalized framework for world trade, generally known as the Tokyo round, made no apparent progress on any major issue. Procedural difficulties over the extent to which agriculture should be brought into the talks, as the United States wanted and as a number of European countries did not want, made it difficult to do detailed studies of the problems in the talks. The major issues, apart from agriculture, were tariff reduction and measures to protect industries that were threatened with severe damage because of competition from abroad. There were also difficulties in deciding the relationship between industrialized and less developed nations in the talks.

The fear that measures designed to help domestic industries facing severe competition might lead on to generalized protection was shared by many at the beginning of the year. In the event, there were far fewer actions in defense of industries than had originally been expected. The U.S. government was required by law to investigate a number of complaints against alleged dumping by foreign industries. The two most important actions involved special steels, where import limitations were imposed, and motorcars. The imposition of import restraints on special steels provoked a strong reaction from the EEC, which accused the U.S. of resorting to protectionism. Partly in response to this feeling, however unjustified, the U.S. did not take similar action against European and Japanese motor manufacturers accused of dumping in a complaint brought by automobile workers in the U.S. Instead, the U.S. Treasury negotiated a voluntary agreement with the carmakers under which they pledged themselves to change their pricing policy. A demand for protection by the U.S. shoe industry was not conceded.

In Europe the two countries that were most active in this sphere were the U.K. and Italy. The Italians, as already mentioned, imposed an import deposit scheme under which it was necessary to deposit in advance with the central bank 50% of the price of imports. The U.K. imposed antidumping duties on imports from Taiwan and Japan in the electronics field and from a number of CMEA countries. These covered only a small proportion of the country's total imports.

Relations between the industrial world and less developed countries failed to improve during the year. The Conference on International Economic Cooperation (CIEC) had been set up in Paris to provide a forum for a dialogue between "North" (industrial) and "South" (less developed) countries. Twenty-six countries and the EEC, which participated as a unit, took part in talks throughout the year in four commissions designed to deal with energy, raw materials, finance, and development. The goal of these commissions was to prepare detailed proposals for action to be presented to a much larger ministerial meeting in December. During the spring the less developed countries expressed great dissatisfaction with the progress being made on ways to assist them. At a meeting of the United Nations Conference on Trade and Development (UNCTAD) in Nairobi, Kenya, they reasserted their belief in the need for agreements to maintain commodity prices and the importance of international action to relieve the burden of accumulated debt on the less developed countries. A compromise formula worked out at the UNCTAD talks averted a breakdown and stressed the role of the dialogue in improving relations between rich and poor nations.

However, the four commissions made no real progress during the summer, and plans for a ministerial meeting in December 1976 had to be abandoned. It was hoped that a ministerial session could be held at a later date, but strains were evident between the industrial countries and the less developed world and also within the industrial world itself over what attitude to adopt to the negotiations. (EIU)

INTERNATIONAL EXCHANGE AND PAYMENTS

The return to economic growth in the major industrial countries in 1976 brought with it a massive current account deficit with the oil-exporting countries. In addition, the rebuilding of stocks of primary commodities, and the price rises stimulated by this, probably worked to reduce the existing surplus with non-oil-producing less developed countries. The total deficit and the deficits of most individual countries were much lower than in 1974, but the problems arising from the deficits were at least as serious because the same countries had the largest deficits. Even more serious were the positions of the non-oil-producing less developed countries and the centrally planned economies, most of which had not had even a partial recovery in 1975. There was some reduction in their deficits in 1976, but the improvement ended after the first half. By the end of the year, it was clear that these countries and the industrial countries in deficit had based their strategy of borrowing heavily in 1974, 1975, and 1976 on a false assumption. They had relied on acceptance by all oil importers of deficits as counterparts to the oil exporters' surplus. They assumed an international consensus that "oil deficits" were not a normal imbalance requiring conventional domestic adjustment policies, but a medium-term problem justifying unusual financing arrangements. They had expected reflation by the major countries after the cyclical recession in 1974 which would return the international economy to the growth path of the late 1960s and early 1970s and permit them to increase exports and repay the borrowing. In 1976, when they needed more rapid growth of exports than in the past to finance interest and repayments as well as to pay for current imports, they faced instead the prospect of lower exports as the major countries began to fall below normal growth rates. As the oil producers' surplus remained high, all countries faced the same choice as in 1974 between accepting deficits or attempting to reduce them by slowing down their economies. Those that had made the first choice in 1974, however, had to carry the burden of three years' debts, while those that had taken the alternative path had fewer, or no, debts and had benefited from the continued expansion in the first group. The first group would not be likely to risk relying a second time on joint international reflation; more important, their financial position was now far worse, so that their ability to follow an independent nondeflationary policy was reduced.

Current Balances. A more than 10% growth in merchandise trade in 1976 encouraged a rapid rise in the services associated with it, particularly in shipping. Because of inefficient ports, the deficit of the oil exporters on services probably continued to grow more rapidly than the average. Tourism continued to recover from the fall caused by the rise in oil prices, despite higher fares and currency realignments.

The principal change in invisibles was the same as in 1975: interest payments increased for most of the countries that were in deficit. For the industrial countries as a group, there may have been little change from 1975 other than a further transfer of indebtedness from the smaller countries to the larger. The main change was in payments from the non-oil-producing less developed countries to the oil exporters, after a 1975 deficit as large as that in 1974 (Table XXIV). Their payments rose again by $2 billion or $3 billion to about $18 billion (including all returns on capital, but no repayments), 18% of export earnings. The ratio may have been near 30% for the most advanced in the group, whose ability to obtain medium-term finance at commercial rates as well as export credits was highest. The highest ratios of interest to income were therefore found among non-oil-producing Middle Eastern countries, particularly Egypt and Israel, and Latin-American countries, including Mexico, Brazil, Peru, and Uruguay. The rate of rise in these payments at the end of 1976 and in 1977 may have slacked off because of the growing share of official borrowing (generally at lower interest rates), a fall in interest rates in industrial countries, and smaller deficits. In spite of the growing burden of existing debt on some countries, there does not appear to have been any general increase in the relative interest rates charged to them; countries that might have been considered greater risks seem instead to have stopped borrowing entirely, although South Africa accepted an unusually high spread on one loan, and higher differentials for Eastern European countries, particularly the Soviet Union, were discussed.

OECD Countries. The largest part of the change in the industrial countries' current balance was accounted for by the United States (Table XXIV). An improvement in the invisibles balance offset only a small part of the massive deterioration in the merchandise balance. There was a small reduction in the deficit on travel and in military and other official grants, but the principal change was in net receipts of interest and profits (Table XXV). Lower interest rates reduced the cost of U.S. government interest payments, but the major change was in earnings from direct investment abroad; there may have been recovery of oil company profits because of higher oil production, as well as a return from lending abroad in 1974 and 1975. Although West Germany, with the United States, led the return to growth, there was little change in its current balance. The reduction in the trade surplus was balanced by a lower deficit on services. Although there was a small increase in the deficit on travel, receipts from interest payments doubled. Transfers were unchanged: private payments were lower as the employment of migrant workers continued to decline, but official contributions both to the EEC (subsidizing the agricultural policy) and to other international organizations were much higher. There was little change in the United Kingdom balance on invisibles; the current deficit probably fell slightly. Net receipts from travel rose because of the

Table XXIV. Current Balances of Payments
In $000,000

Country	1973	1974	1975	1976*
Canada	+14	−1,673	−4,885	−4,700
France	−691	−5,943	+330	−3,800
Germany, West	+4,341	+9,759	+3,907	+3,400
Italy	−2,510	−7,817	−514	−3,000
Japan	−133	−4,650	−680	+3,500
United Kingdom	−1,805	−7,829	−3,727	−3,200
United States	+22	−3,598	+11,650	−2,000
Other OECD countries	+4,142	−12,202	−10,802	−10,000
OECD total	+3,384	−33,953	−4,721	−19,800
Other advanced countries	+648	−2,461	−3,072	−2,500
Centrally planned economies*	—	−2,000	−5,000	−3,000
Oil-exporting countries*	+5,000	+60,000	+34,000	+40,000
Other less developed countries*	−9,000	−21,000	−21,000	−15,000

*Estimate.
Sources: International Monetary Fund, *International Financial Statistics;* national sources.

pound's devaluation, and the demand for construction and other services by oil-producing countries rose. The devaluation also helped to explain the improvement in the balance on property income, in spite of a further rise in interest on financing the deficit; there was also a rise in the earnings of British companies, especially oil companies, abroad. The Canadian deficit remained extremely serious as the deficit on invisibles rose sharply, offsetting most of the improvement in the trade balance. This was largely because of high interest payments to finance past deficits. The improvement in the Japanese balance and France's return to deficit were entirely because of trade changes. There was a deterioration in the Italian invisibles account because of lower receipts from workers abroad and higher interest payments, but this was minor compared with the trade balance change. Among the smaller OECD countries, changes in the trade and current balances were much smaller. Lower earnings from migrant workers further increased the deficits of the southern European countries, while higher interest payments hurt all but The Netherlands and Switzerland. Probably only these two countries remained in surplus. Belgium's surplus on current account may have been eliminated by the large increase in its trade deficit. Australia's trade balance deteriorated in the first half, but may have improved sufficiently in the second to leave its current deficit unchanged at about $500 million. Finland and Sweden may have reduced their deficits, but for the other countries worse trade balances probably brought larger current deficits.

Centrally Planned Economies. A reduction in the Soviet Union's trade deficit may have reduced the total deficit of the centrally planned economies. However, it probably remained higher than in any year except 1975.

Oil-Producing Countries. The surplus of the OPEC members rose in spite of still rapid import growth because of the relative rise in the price of oil and the revived demand for it in the developed countries, particularly the United States. Their invisibles deficit probably rose slightly in spite of an increase of perhaps $4 billion to $5 billion in interest receipts because of higher services imports. There was again a large gap between those with large surpluses and relatively slow import growth, especially in the Middle East, and those with small surpluses or even deficits because of large populations or ambitious development plans such as Algeria, Indonesia, and Nigeria, but the increase in exports saved Iran and possibly Iraq from the deficits that threatened them at the end of 1975.

Other Developed Countries. The deficits of South Africa and New Zealand were higher. South Africa was particularly badly hit by the fall in the price of gold in the first half of the year. But as for all primary producers, developed and less developed, their principal problem was the very brief recovery of primary prices, while those of oil and manufactures continued to rise.

Other Less Developed Countries. Among the non-oil-producing less developed countries, the worst deficits were probably suffered by the more advanced, which benefited less from the increase in commodity prices and continued to face low demand for their manufactures (and import restrictions on them) as well as high oil prices. Increased interest payments were the most important change in the invisibles accounts of Latin-American countries; Mexico also had a decline in tourism in 1975 and 1976 because of the overvaluation of the peso against the dollar (until its devaluation in September). Kenya, with an increase in tourism, and Jordan, which increased its earnings from workers employed abroad, were exceptional in improving their services balances.

Capital Movements. The demonstration in 1975 that some current balances could be improved even while oil prices and net saving by oil exporters remained high, combined with unwillingness on the part of both borrowers and lenders to continue increasing international debts when slow growth meant that the prospect of repayment was becoming more distant, brought by 1976 a move away from the acceptance of continuing deficits as the counterpart of a continuing oil surplus. The IMF and some of the major countries that had achieved temporary surpluses took the view that these deficits should be eliminated, although it was difficult to see how all countries could eliminate their deficits as long as there were oil producer surpluses to be accommodated. The IMF director in his annual report claimed that the more rapid growth of trade in 1976 offered the opportunity to reduce the deficits, apparently in spite of the higher OPEC surplus: "The time has come to lay more stress on the adjustment of external positions and less emphasis on the mere financing of deficits." As he recognized, for a change in attitudes to be effective commercial lenders would need to agree, since it had been almost entirely through their lending, rather than that by official agencies, that the 1974–76 deficits were financed. Even with stricter criteria, commercial lending would retain two of the advantages that gave it its central role: its volume, because OPEC members preferred to deposit their surpluses in the commercial banking institutions, and its ready availability as compared with the prolonged negotiations and variety of eligibility limits for official loans. Commercial lending stood to lose its third advantage for borrowers, that of being outside the traditional official bilateral or multilateral sources of aid, and thus offering greater independence from both the actions and the policies of the major countries. The poorer medium-term prospects and creditworthiness of the borrowing countries also encouraged commercial lenders to return to more cautious lending policies, although the continuing high surplus of the OPEC members required lenders to continue to search for possible borrowers.

INTERNATIONAL CAPITAL MARKETS. Commercially arranged finance, including export credits as well as medium-term loans and bond issues, remained the most important source of finance. In the first half of 1976 (Table XXVI) there were large rises in bond issues compared with the average for 1975, implying a rise of 40% for the year. Almost the whole of these were as usual from advanced countries. There was a sharp fall in the proportion issued in marks in the first half of the year, perhaps because of expectations of West German revaluation. Eurodollar issues, whose rise was smaller (perhaps 25%), continued to be mainly for the less developed countries. There was a fall in the share of the centrally planned economies and a rise, particularly in the second half of the year, in that of the oil exporters. Generally, long-term capital outflows from the major countries (Table XXV) were lower than in 1975, largely because of the inflows to West Germany that eliminated its large net outflow.

OFFICIAL AID. Bilateral aid to oil-importing less developed countries was about $9 billion in 1975. In the first three quarters of 1976, total IMF aid was almost 20% higher than the total for 1975, implying a growth of over 50% for the year as a whole. The share of OECD countries increased (to about 60%). The IMF was able to increase its lending because of the increased quotas and compensatory financing arrangements made at the end of 1975. In the year ended in June 1976, the World Bank increased its lending by only 12% compared with the preceding year, less than 10% in real terms, because of the slow growth in its income. The bank therefore hardened the terms of its loans, requiring more rapid amortization and raising its interest rate, relating it to the rate it pays on bond issues. By early 1976, however, it had begun its "third window" scheme that provided loans to the poorest countries at 4% below the normal interest rate and that would continue to have more generous amortization provisions; this lending was about $500 million. The World Bank attempted to increase its capital by 25% to $41 billion. This proposal was blocked, at least temporarily, by the United States which asked that any increase be tied to increased funds for natural resource development in association with private investors and greater control of borrowers' general economic policies. These proposals were opposed by most other lenders and borrowers.

OECD COUNTRIES. Commercial borrowing remained the major source of funds for deficit countries, although Australia, Portugal, and the United Kingdom began borrowing from the IMF as well. Direct investment both in and by the United States was reduced in 1976. There was an increase in purchases of foreign securities because of the higher issues by other countries and by the World Bank. There was a large shift in the balance on short-term capital into surplus because of increased private foreign inflows and large unidentified flows. The level of foreign official inflows in the first half was about twice the rate for 1975, financing an increase in official reserves as well as the large outflow on long-term capital. There was a slight fall in the United Kingdom surplus on private foreign investment in the first half of the year because of increased flows abroad. This was more than

Hungary extended economic assistance to Laos. Officials of the two countries sign the agreement in the Parliament building in Budapest.

GEZA SZEBELLEDY—INTERFOTO MTI/KEYSTONE

Table XXV. Foreign Investment by Major Countries
In $000,000

Country	Long-term capital flows 1973	1974	1975	1976*	Net interest, dividends, profits 1973	1974	1975	1976*
Germany, West	+4,846	−2,531	−6,727	+1,700	+582	−67	+415	+850
Japan	−9,750	−3,881	−272	−900	+490	−451	−273	−300
United Kingdom	−417	+5,139	+2,091	+3,500	+3,391	+3,256	+2,108	+2,200
United States*	−1,239	−7,256	−11,858	−12,000	+5,178	+10,227	+6,007	+8,400
Total	−6,560	−8,529	−16,766	−7,700	+9,641	+12,965	+8,257	+11,150
France	−2,239	−181	−1,239	...	+399	+497	+400*	...

*Estimate.
Source: National sources.

Table XXVI. Official Aid and International Capital Flows
In $000,000

	Official international aid			International capital markets			
		1976			1976 issues		
Areas and principal borrowers	1975, IMF and IBRD lending	IMF credit*	IBRD and IDA loans	Total 1975 issues	in Euro-dollars†	Foreign bonds‡	in foreign curren-cies‡
OECD	2,743	3,095	346	21,243	7,021	6,648	5,978
Austria	—	—	—	1,249	—	83	20
Canada	—	—	—	4,628	190	3,320	1,982
Finland	103	131	—	718	—	57	71
France	—	—	—	2,421	664	398	422
Japan	—	—	—	1,967	207	105	772
New Zealand	179	106	—	633	373	—	39
Norway	—	—	—	1,119	62	246	306
Spain	614	75	—	1,234	1,701	—	39
Sweden	—	—	—	1,279	88	196	111
United Kingdom	—	1,950	—	854	1,017	181	210
United States	—	—	—	932	327	28	185
Eastern Europe	277	172	170	2,043	1,000	—	47
Oil exporters	619	—	725	2,950	3,500	—	89
Algeria	48	—	150	535	768	—	59
Indonesia	332	—	517	1,570	460	—	—
Iran	52	—	—	245	740	—	30
Other countries	6,743	2,068	5,390	10,133	11,011	97	311
Brazil	426	—	498	2,342	3,137	—	77
India	1,050	−352	894	—	—	—	—
Israel	239	72	—	166	—	—	—
Mexico	360	—	315	2,492	1,981	77	140
Morocco	62	132	150	257	300	—	10
Philippines	318	210	268	213	777	—	—
South Africa	—	179	—	741	355	20	—
International agencies and companies	—	—	—	5,933	2,240	2,486	2,067
Total	10,382	5,335	6,632	42,367	24,925	9,230	8,494

*January–September. †January–November (partly estimated). ‡First half.
Sources: International Monetary Fund, *International Financial Statistics;* World Bank, *Annual Report 1975, 1976;* OECD, *Fianncial Statistics;* IMF, *Survey.*

Table XXVII. International Reserves of Market Economies
End of period

Countries and areas	1972	1973	1974	1975	1976*
Countries with major changes (in $000,000)					
Developed countries					
Australia	6,141	5,697	4,269	3,256	3,257
France	10,015	8,529	8,852	12,593	9,371
Germany, West	23,785	33,171	32,398	31,034	35,026
Italy	6,085	6,436	6,941	4,774	5,080
Japan	18,365	12,246	13,519	12,815	16,489
Netherlands, The	4,785	6,547	6,957	7,109	6,466
Portugal	2,312	2,839	2,354	1,534	1,291
South Africa	1,290	1,234	1,159	1,216	887
Spain	5,014	6,772	6,485	6,090	5,650
Sweden	1,575	2,529	1,736	3,077	2,904
Switzerland	7,557	8,520	9,011	10,428	10,959
United Kingdom	5,647	6,476	6,939	5,459	5,217
Oil exporters					
Indonesia	574	807	1,492	586	1,202
Other less developed countries					
Brazil	4,183	6,415	5,272	4,034	3,716
Chile	148	180	102	109	410
India	1,180	1,142	1,325	1,373	2,665
Mexico	1,164	1,355	1,395	1,533	1,501
South Korea	740	1,094	1,056	1,550	2,263
Distribution by (in $000,000)					
Developed countries	126,834	139,523	141,001	139,828	145,652
Oil-exporting countries	10,428	14,526	47,024	56,560	60,891
Other less developed countries	21,340	29,611	32,433	31,011	37,218
Total	159,077	183,660	220,456	227,398	243,760
Value in relation to imports (in percentages)					
Developed countries	40.1	32.0	22.7	22.4	21.3
Oil-exporting countries	79.2	73.0	138.7	104.0	95.0
Other less developed countries	36.7	37.0	24.8	22.3	28.2
Total	40.9	34.2	28.1	27.8	27.7

*Estimate.
Source: International Monetary Fund, *International Financial Statistics.*

balanced by increased medium-term borrowing by public sector industries, which was higher in the first three quarters than in any previous year ($2.5 billion); for the year, it probably approximately equaled the current deficit. Outflows of short-term capital from the U.K., both private and official, were extremely high because of fears of devaluation and the continued efforts by some traditional holders of sterling reserves to diversify their reserves. These were partly offset by the $2 billion borrowed from the IMF in the first half of the year; an application for a further loan of $3.9 billion was made in the fourth quarter. Canada's issues of bonds in the first half of the year exceeded total issues in all of 1975, and more than financed its expected current deficit. Interest rates were relatively high in Canada throughout the year. The inflow of long-term capital to Germany was the result of both a large increase in official inflows and a move into surplus on private flows; outflows on portfolio investment and lending were lower and inflows higher, probably reflecting expectations of a revaluation and faster economic growth. Direct investment abroad was higher; this account moved into deficit in 1975, possibly reflecting a long-term shift to investment in other countries because of past and expected revaluations. Italy received two loans from the EEC, financed by issues made in the name of the Community. Italy's application to increase its borrowing from the IMF was unsuccessful because it could not meet the policy conditions required. Japan continued to borrow on the international markets in spite of its current surplus; there was probably a small increase in its outflow of long-term capital, although this remained far below the levels of the early 1970s. Short-term inflows were high, probably because interest rates remained high.

Oil Exporters. Iran remained a heavy borrower on international markets in spite of the improvement in its balance, and Algeria increased its borrowing, but Indonesia raised slightly less, receiving higher aid from the World Bank. The OPEC members in surplus continued to reduce their reserve holdings in sterling, and private deposits from these countries in the United Kingdom also fell, giving a total fall of $1.4 billion in the first half. The share of their surplus kept in the United States continued to rise (to about 40%), although there was a fall in new direct investment there. Deposits in other countries rose more slowly.

Centrally Planned Economies. The Soviet Union reduced its borrowing on international markets in 1976. Its lower trade deficit explained some of the change, but there may also have been growing reluctance to lend to it and to other centrally planned economies as the level of their foreign debts increased, as well as greater hesitation on their part in borrowing. Some of these countries expected to have difficulty in increasing their exports to the Western industrial countries in the next few years.

Oil-Importing Less Developed Countries. The share of commercial sources in financing the deficits of the oil-importing less developed countries may have fallen slightly in 1976. Their deficits were smaller, IMF and World Bank loans were higher, and there was probably some increase in bilateral aid from OECD and OPEC. Their higher medium-term borrowing indicates that any reduction must have been from direct investment or bilateral credits. Export credits from advanced to less developed countries were estimated by OECD at $6 billion in 1975, an increase of

$3.5 billion over 1974. Estimates of the total external indebtedness of these countries vary widely, and high levels are not surprising after many years of borrowing to finance development projects and of accepting inflows of private investment. It is more useful to identify the additional deficits of recent years above the level which they and their creditors had come to regard as normal and tolerable. Their total deficit in 1974–76, using estimates at the low end of the possible range, was $57 billion. If a deficit of $7 billion a year is normal, the additional deficit equaled more than a third of their exports in 1976. Although they also received some additional aid from OPEC, the level of a tolerable deficit may have become lower because of the slower growth in the industrial countries.

Latin-American countries, particularly Brazil, remained among the heaviest borrowers on the international capital markets. Mexico's borrowing may have been slightly lower than in 1975; it had to obtain additional assistance from the IMF to cover capital outflows prompted by fears of devaluation because of its high inflation compared with the United States and its continued high current deficit. The poorer Asian countries used mainly official sources, although some, including India, had much-improved balances and therefore a reduced need for external finance. The Philippines and South Korea increased their commercial borrowing substantially in 1976, but both also received assistance from the IMF. Egypt was forced to look to support from the IMF because of pressure from the OPEC members, especially Saudi Arabia and Kuwait, which were unwilling to continue financing its deficit. It was no longer able to meet its interest payments and had to arrange renegotiation of its loans by agreement with its creditors. Zaire also had to make a formal rearrangement of its repayments; low and unstable export income made it unable to pay interest on existing loans or obtain new finance. South Africa found it increasingly difficult to expand borrowing during the year; its commercial borrowing was less than originally planned, and it obtained finance from the IMF.

Official Reserves and Exchange Rates. The change in total reserves was similar to that in 1975; the difference is exaggerated in Table XXVII because of the rise during 1975 in the value of the dollar in which they are measured. With the exception of South African gold sales, most use of reserves was not to finance deficits on current account. Changes were more closely tied to short-term capital movements, usually unexpected or unwanted, in response to interest rate differentials or expectations about changes in exchange rates; other finance was arranged for anticipated deficits. The principal differences from 1974 and 1975 were slower growth in oil exporters' reserves (a shift into more medium- and long-term assets probably balanced their new surplus) and the first large rise since 1973 for other less developed countries. Except for a temporary benefit from improved terms of trade, most of this went to India, Malaysia, and South Korea. For the other groups and for most less developed countries, the rises were less than the rise in imports (a rough measure of reserves' adequacy for financing temporary fluctuations in trade and capital movements). The composition of the increase in reserves was divided about equally between dollar liabilities and other foreign currencies, excluding sterling. Sterling liabilities fell 35% measured in dollars and over 25% even in sterling terms, from 3.5% of total reserves at the end of 1975 to about 2%.

The fluctuations of some major currencies, and of those linked to them, should not obscure the remarkable stability of the majority of rates. The timing of the successive bouts of speculation that developed against individual currencies is difficult to explain by economic arguments, but the results by the end of the year were as follows: massive devaluation for the two countries whose inflation rates greatly exceeded the OECD average, the United Kingdom, with about twice the average, and Italy, with lower inflation but greater political and economic uncertainty; a revaluation for the major country with the lowest inflation (West Germany); and little change among the other countries (by the third quarter, France, Iceland, Portugal, Spain, and Turkey had had small devaluations). The magnitude of the changes did not correspond precisely with the inflation differences among the respective countries. The steadiness of the yen and the Swiss franc was, however, probably less the result of market forces than of government intervention; both countries increased their foreign exchange reserves, and Switzerland tightened the already strict controls on the entry of foreign capital. The changes in other countries' effective rates were the result of these changes and changes in non-OECD countries' rates (Chart 4). Much of the speculation around the snake currencies was caused by expectations about an alteration in their relationships with each other, rather than about their rate relative to other currencies. Within the snake, the mark was at the upper end throughout the year, with pressure intensifying, as can be seen in the rise in German reserves, until it was finally revalued in October. Belgium and The Netherlands abandoned their narrower band within the snake in the spring, and Belgium devalued further relative to the mark in October. The French franc left the snake in March, and depreciated relative both to the snake currencies and to the dollar during the rest of the year, in spite of government use of reserves to retard the fall. Although the aggregate ratio of reserves to imports of the developed countries was probably adequate, under floating rates, for countries making only temporary interventions in the market, the need of some countries that persistently attempted to prevent or regulate devaluations to arrange standby finance with other central banks indicates that they found existing reserve ratios too low. In March selling of the pound probably began because it appeared that the continuing reduction in interest rates by the Bank of England was intended to bring about a fall in the exchange rate. The resulting devaluation may have encouraged a further reduction in sterling holdings and greater pressure on the rate in the second quarter, although interest rates were raised (Chart 3). In June, a $5.3 billion standby credit was arranged with the United States Federal Reserve and other central banks for six months. This was a change in the normal short-term swap arrangements among central banks that provide mutual support to prevent fluctuations. These are normally on a shorter-term basis and not announced at the time they are made. Although the declaration of apparent formal support for the pound's rate by other governments may have had a temporary effect, and the standby permitted the Bank of England to continue its intervention in the exchange markets at a time when the reserves were insufficient, the further devaluation of the pound while the standby was still

CHART 3.

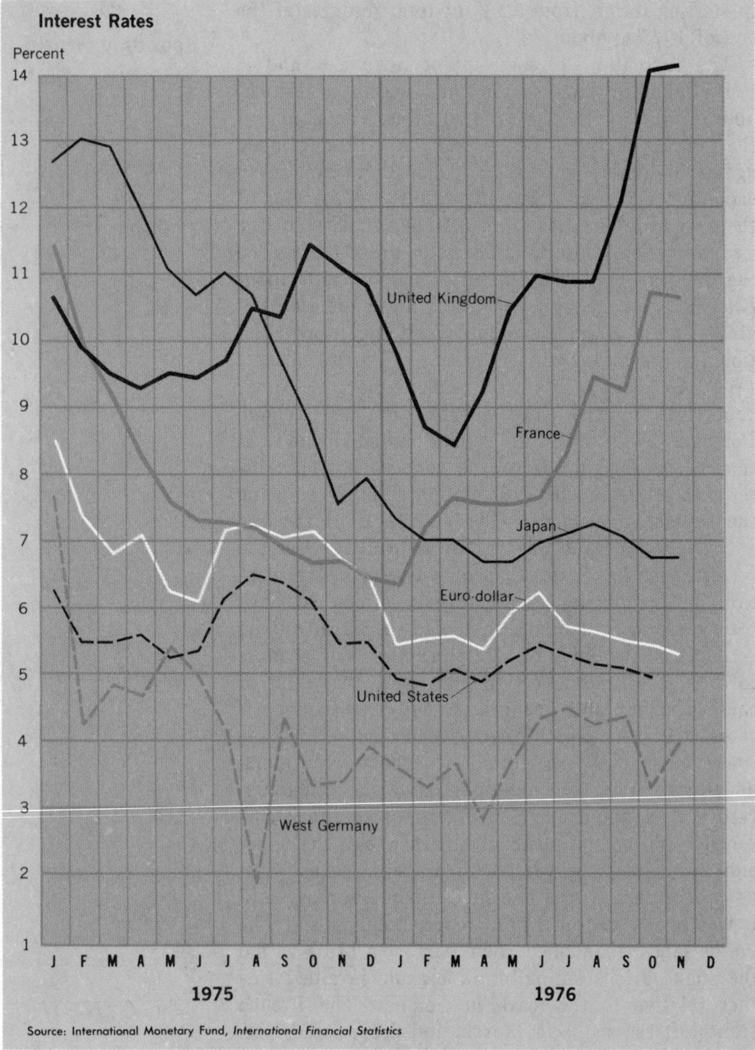

available made obvious the inadequacy of such temporary finance to permit a continuing exchange rate policy. A declaration of international support was not a substitute for intervention, and the standby could not be used against sustained pressure on the rate because of the need to repay it within six months. Excluding the amount used from the standby, the ratio of United Kingdom reserves to imports at the beginning of December was less than 7%.

The inter-central bank swap agreements were used more conventionally when the United States gave temporary support to Italy in March. Pressure on the lira began in January after it had been quite stable for several months. In attempting to maintain the rate, almost half of Italy's foreign currency reserves were sold. (As over $3.3 billion of Italian reserves are gold, which is not used for market intervention, the figures in Table XXVII exaggerate available reserves.) The government increased its resources with a total of $750 million in swaps from the United States, of which it drew $500 million; it also applied for further credit from the IMF. Renewed pressure in the second quarter, and the failure to obtain the IMF loan, weakened the lira further, but tighter foreign exchange controls and the usual summer improvement from tourism earnings strengthened it sufficiently to permit repayment of the swaps in summer; additional pressures in September and October were allowed to take the rate back to its second-quarter level.

The devaluation of the Australian dollar by 17% in November was not the result of an unfavourable trade balance. It appears to have been intended to stimulate the economy by restricting imports. Such a policy had not been used by any of the larger countries in this recession. (The avoidance of revaluation by Japan and Switzerland had probably been directed more at supporting exports.) Fears that the cumulative effect of competing devaluations on trade and output will wipe out any temporary advantage to an individual country are usually the only protection from such policies. This time, however, exceptionally high inflation had accompanied depressed output in most countries; there may also therefore have been fear of the effect of higher import prices after a devaluation.

After relatively little change in 1975, in spite of their deficits and high inflation, the oil-importing less developed countries turned increasingly to large devaluations in 1976. Because of the importance of world prices rather than domestic prices for most primary commodities, most major devaluations were by countries with relatively high dependence on exports of manufactures or of services such as tourism. (Controlling the growth of imports was usually done through direct controls or duties.) Mexico devalued by about 50% after high inflation had hurt its tourism and export earnings from the United States and after expectations of devaluation had led to large outflows of short-term capital. Argentina, Brazil, Chile, Peru, Uruguay, and Zaire were among other less developed countries with devaluations of over 20% against the dollar. In attempting to avoid devaluation, which had, at least temporarily, the effect of reducing the foreign currency value of exports and therefore further increasing the burden of external debt, Brazil, Mexico, Peru, Uruguay, and Zaire lost large parts of their reserves. Mexico also used its swap arrangement with the U.S., which could only be repaid out of its IMF loan. The ability of these countries to finance future deficits even temporarily, and therefore their economic independence, was thus greatly reduced.

In most major countries, interest rates were unusually stable during most of the year (Chart 3); this probably reflected the greater emphasis being given to domestic monetary policy in determining the levels except in the countries with an active exchange rate policy. At the middle of the year there were sharp divergences, with the largest rises in the United Kingdom and Italy whose rates had been above those of the other countries since the beginning of the year; there were also small rises among the smaller snake countries: Belgium, Denmark, The Netherlands, and Sweden. Swiss rates fell throughout the year.

International Monetary Reform. At the beginning of 1976, after four years of negotiations, the IMF introduced new provisions for borrowing and a few administrative changes, but there were no proposals

Table XXVIII. The Price of Gold
Averages for year

Measure	1970	1972	1973	1974	1975	1976*
Dollars per ounce	35.96	58.20	97.22	158.80	160.87	125.09
SDR's per ounce	35.96	53.61	81.55	132.06	132.46	108.39
Indices of gold's relative price, 1970=100						
To exports of manufactures	100	138	203	273	246	192
To all primary commodities	100	129	150	143	148	114
To other metals	100	151	208	252	225	166

*Estimate.
Sources: International Monetary Fund, *International Financial Statistics;* United Nations, *Monthly Bulletin of Statistics;* Samuel Montagu and Co. Ltd., *Annual Bullion Review* and *Monthly Review.*

for controls over international liquidity or exchange rates, although these had been the original reasons for attempting a reform. The normal provisions for borrowing, determined by countries' quotas in the Fund's capital and thus favouring the richer countries, were increased in total by a third and there was a redistribution increasing the oil producers' share by 10%. For the less developed countries, whose quotas are small, the Fund established an extended facility, offering credit for more than the usual five years; raised the limits on compensatory finance for falls in export income; and increased financing for approved buffer stock arrangements. These countries were also to receive the profits (receipts in excess of the official price) from the Fund's sales of one-sixth of its gold holdings. There was a temporary increase of 45% in all quotas until the ratification procedures could be completed on the proposed reforms (probably in 1977), which was most useful for the poorer developed countries; these gained little from the general increase but had the largest temporary need for credit. The currency created by the Fund, the SDR (Special Drawing Right; defined in terms of 16 major currencies), was to become the "principal reserve asset," but no provisions were made for new allocations; its share of total reserves could rise from its present 4.5% through exchange arrangements, or its importance could be increased through specification of a minimum ratio of SDR's to total reserves, but the only proposal made was for consultation. The new articles included greater emphasis on each member's responsibility to use domestic stabilization policies to control exchange rate fluctuations, but the only obligation was to inform the Fund how it determined its rates. This might be through floating, a par value system, or an intermediate system such as the snake; the only restriction was that a rate might not be tied to gold or to a single currency. The switching of less developed countries' currencies from a link to a single currency to the SDR or other groups of currencies continued in 1976.

The price of gold fell in the second and third quarters (the first IMF sale of gold was in June) with its lowest monthly average in August, $110 an ounce. This was followed by a partial recovery in the third quarter; demand at the IMF auctions remained high, with some purchases by central banks. Other supplies were probably lower than normal, however, at least in the middle of the year, when the Soviet Union, usually one of the major suppliers, stopped sales temporarily because of the low price. Probably partly because of the risk that the U.S.S.R. might resume selling to finance its deficit and that South Africa might need further sales, the recovery of the price stopped in November at about $130 an ounce, still below the average for 1975 or 1974 even if allowance is made for the relative rise in the dollar by measuring the price in SDR's (Table XXVIII). After floating currencies became widespread in 1973, the price of gold rose less than other prices in international trade. Although this could have been in part because of a relative fall in industrial demand owing to the high initial relative price of gold and the abnormal rise in supplies of it from Soviet, South African, and IMF sales, it also indicated that the efforts by the IMF and the major countries to reduce the role of gold in the international monetary system had begun to discourage its use as an asset in times of uncertainty, at least by private holders. (SHEILA A. B. PAGE)

[533; 534; 535; 536; 537]

CHART 4.

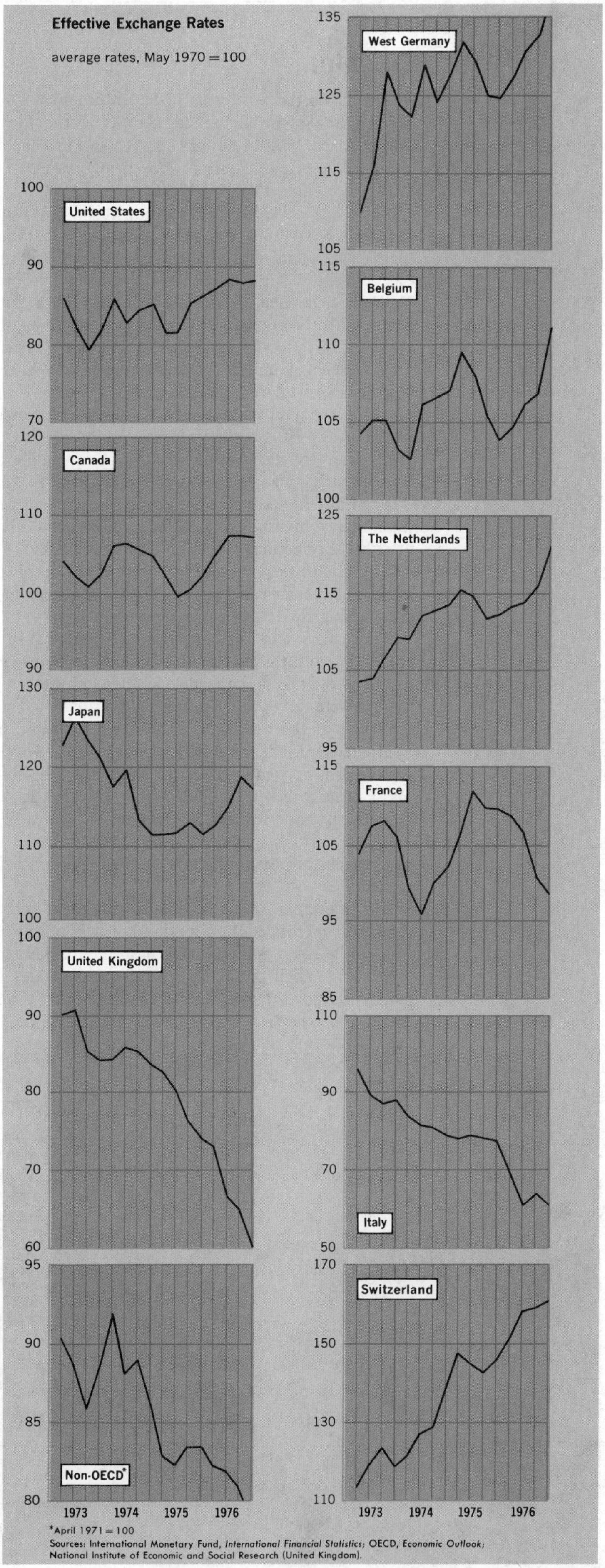

Effective Exchange Rates

average rates, May 1970 = 100

*April 1971 = 100

Sources: International Monetary Fund, *International Financial Statistics*; OECD, *Economic Outlook*; National Institute of Economic and Social Research (United Kingdom).

Ecuador

A republic on the west coast of South America, Ecuador is bounded by Colombia, Peru, and the Pacific Ocean. Area: 109,484 sq mi (283,561 sq km), including the Galápagos Islands (3,075 sq mi), which is an insular province. Pop. (1975 est.): 6,733,000. Cap.: Quito (pop., 1974, 597,100). Largest city: Guayaquil (pop., 1974, 814,100). Language: Spanish, but Indians speak Quechuan and Jivaroan. Religion: Roman Catholic about 93%, others 7%. President until Jan. 11, 1976, Brig. Gen. Guillermo Rodríguez Lara; from January 11, the country was ruled by a military junta formed by Vice-Adm. Alfredo Poveda Burbano (Navy), Gen. Guillermo Durán Arcentales (Army), and Gen. Luis Leoro Franco (Air Force).

A military junta headed by Vice-Admiral Poveda Burbano (*see* BIOGRAPHY) assumed power on Jan. 11, 1976, after the resignation of Brig. Gen. Guillermo Rodríguez Lara as president. Despite pressure from local parties for an immediate return to civilian rule, the military government said only that it would hold presidential elections sometime before January 1978.

The authorities succeeded in slowing down the growth of the inflation rate, with the consumer price index rising by 10.2% in the year ended July 1976, as compared with 15.6% for July 1975. Efforts to increase agricultural production through improvements in infrastructure and the development of the credit system were only partly successful because of uncertainty about the new Agrarian Reform Law and bad weather conditions, as well as damage caused by an earthquake early in October. In the industrial sector, major new projects included the Esmeraldas and Oriente oil refineries and the Esmeraldas-Quito pipeline, as well as petrochemical, gas, cement, and pharmaceutical developments and 14 electrification projects.

Oil production, still the major source of income for Ecuador, totaled 33.6 million bbl in the first half of 1976, a 32% increase over the total for January–June 1975. A dispute over petroleum revenues between the government and Gulf Oil of the U.S., a member of the Cepe (the state oil company)-Gulf-Texaco consortium, resulted in a recommendation by the Ministry of Natural Resources that Cepe should acquire Gulf's 37.5% share in the consortium to bring its total interests to 62.5%. On October 1, Gulf announced it would be closing down its operations in Ecuador; Texaco reaffirmed its intention to stay.

(BARBARA WIJNGAARD)

An oil pipeline in the Ecuadorian Andes.

MANUEL GUEVARA JR.—THE NEW YORK TIMES

ECUADOR

Education. (1972–73) Primary, pupils 1,101,586, teachers 28,380; secondary, vocational, and teacher training, pupils 268,388, teachers 17,659; higher (1971–72), students 43,743, teaching staff 2,867.

Finance. Monetary unit: sucre, with (Sept. 20, 1976) an official rate of 25 sucres to U.S. $1 (free rate of 47.14 sucres = £1 sterling). Gold, SDR's, and foreign exchange, central bank (June 1976) U.S. $320.1 million. Budget (1975 actual): revenue 12,617,000,000 sucres; expenditure 12,311,000,000 sucres. Gross national product (1974) 86,870,000,000 sucres. Money supply (Feb. 1976) 14,155,000,000 sucres. Cost of living (Quito; 1970 = 100; April 1976) 201.

Foreign Trade. (1975) Imports U.S. $943.2 million; exports U.S. $912.1 million. Import sources (1974): U.S. 37%; Japan 14%; West Germany 10%. Export destinations (1974): U.S. 41%; Trinidad and Tobago 11%; Panama 10%; Chile 8%; Peru 6%; West Germany 5%. Main exports: crude oil 57%; bananas 17%; coffee 7%; cocoa 5%.

Transport and Communications. Roads (1972) 18,345 km (including 1,392 km of Pan-American Highway). Motor vehicles in use (1972): passenger 33,000; commercial (including buses) 51,500. Railways (1972): 1,071 km; traffic 63 million passenger-km, freight 43 million net ton-km. Air traffic (1974): 189 million passenger-km; freight 8.4 million net ton-km. Telephones (Jan. 1975) 167,500. Radio receivers (Dec. 1971) 1.7 million. Television receivers (Dec. 1972) 178,000.

Agriculture. Production (in 000; metric tons; 1975): rice 330; barley 56; corn (1974) *c.* 255; potatoes 450; cassava (1974) 543; cabbages (1974) *c.* 74; dry beans 30; sugar, raw value *c.* 300; bananas (1974) *c.* 2,800; pineapples (1974) *c.* 60; oranges *c.* 173; coffee 80; cocoa 91. Livestock (in 000; 1974): cattle *c.* 2,690; sheep *c.* 2,060; pigs *c.* 1,440; horses *c.* 260; chickens *c.* 8,247.

Industry. Production (in 000; metric tons; 1974): petroleum products 1,687; crude oil 8,999; electricity (kw-hr) *c.* 1,270,000; cement (1973) 480; gold (troy oz) 7.7; silver (troy oz) *c.* 30.

[974.D.1]

Education

In most countries 1976 was at best a period of stability and at worst one of severe retrenchment for education. Economic difficulties were chiefly responsible for this, but partly it reflected the view, shared by all the advanced countries of the West, that educational expenditure could not go on expanding at the pace of the *explosion scolaire* of the 1960s. Along with most other kinds of public expenditure, it would have to be brought into line with the requirements of national economic viability. In Britain, for example, zero growth was decreed for education from 1977 through 1980. Indeed, it was expected that spending would actually be reduced in higher education—in the universities by as much as 4%. In France the seventh five-year plan (1977–81) foresaw a deceleration in spending, although in 1976–77 an increase of 18% in the cash budget was allowed; at least 9% of this, however, would be taken up by inflation.

One consequence was a sharp reduction in the demand for teachers. As many as 20,000 newly trained teachers in Britain were unable to get jobs in schools. In West Germany the figure was reported to be 7,000. Even in Sweden, the country with the most developed educational system in Western Europe, as few as 1 in 50 graduates entered teacher training in 1976, compared with 1 in 5 eight years previously. Likewise, in Belgium and in The Netherlands opportunities for teaching jobs were reduced, although in The Netherlands efforts were made to create an additional 800 vacancies for teachers and a scheme was proposed for encouraging head teachers to retire at the age of 63 on 80% of their salary instead of at 65. Early retirement schemes were also proposed in Britain.

At the same time, observers such as those at the Organization for Economic Cooperation and Development (OECD) believed that the long-term trend for educational expenditure was not wholly negative. A "guesstimate" published by the OECD (*Public Expenditure on Education*) in July 1976 suggested that there might well be a slight growth in spending between the early 1970s and 1985.

In the U.S. the eighth annual Gallup Poll on "The Public's Attitudes Toward the Public Schools" suggested that public criticism of the schools had crested. The public seemed to want the schools to assume some responsibility for supporting traditional values and learning. Discipline remained the top-rated problem. In second place, as before, was integration/segregation/busing, and in third place was school financing. Concerns about school curriculum moved from the previous year's seventh place to fourth. The other top ten concerns included drugs, getting "good" teachers, school and class size, lack of parent and student interest, and school board policies. Asked to rate schools, 42% assigned them "A" or "B" marks while only 6% gave failing grades.

Enrollments declined on the elementary, secondary, and collegiate levels in the U.S. for the first time since World War II. Federal officials estimated that the downward trend would continue. Costs, on the other hand, were rising. There was also a small increase in the number of education personnel.

Three out of every ten Americans were primarily students in 1976, and many more were enrolled in some formal part-time educational activity. Altogether, there were 60.1 million students, 3.2 million teachers, and 300,000 supervisory and supporting personnel. Public and private elementary students accounted for 34.2 million, secondary students for another 15.8 million, and college students for the remaining 10.1 million.

Pres. Gerald Ford stressed the need to move toward block grants in support of state education programs. He recommended $3.3 billion to consolidate 24 separate programs, an amount 2% more than that appropriated to the currently separate programs. States would develop comprehensive education plans which federal funds would partially finance. At least 75% of the funds would have to be spent for the educationally disadvantaged and the handicapped. Further, a major portion of the federal funds would have to be spent on vocational education.

The top U.S. education post changed hands again. U.S. Commissioner of Education Terrell H. Bell resigned to take a state job, and his chief deputy also resigned to take a higher paying job with a research group. President Ford nominated Edward Aguirre to the post, and the Senate rapidly concurred.

Nursery and Primary Education. Despite the austere outlook for education, France gave priority in 1976 to spending on nursery education, the aim being to get 45% of all children aged two into nursery classes and 90% of three-year-olds. The big gap in nursery provision in France was thought to be in the rural areas, and 1,275 more nursery school teachers were planned for in order to maintain class sizes of not more than 35. In The Netherlands a Green Paper was published proposing the merger of nursery and primary schools to form "basic schools" for the 4-to-12 age groups by 1983.

There were signs in the less developed countries of serious efforts to get universal primary education moving. In Nigeria an enactment came into force on September 7 providing for free universal primary education for six-year-olds, though regrettably it could not at that stage be made compulsory. South Korea undertook a reform of its elementary and middle schools along lines proposed in the Florida State University analysis of South Korea's education, completed in 1969. In South Africa there was a significant demand by industrialists, notably the Transvaal Chamber of Industries, for improved education facilities for blacks. The black population provided 70% of the economically active labour force, yet less than 7% of them were in the skilled category.

In Venezuela efforts were made to train local women to run day-care centres in villages and urban slums, the plan being to accommodate 750,000 children in this way by 1980. Experimental courses were begun in 1976 aimed at moving to nine-year schooling (six years primary and three years secondary). A very high dropout rate was reported, however—50% failing to complete the primary stage. In India a midterm appraisal of the 1974–79 education plan seemed to suggest that the situation would actually be worse at the end of the period than at the beginning. The intention of the plan was to get 90% of the children enrolled in schools for 6-to-11-year-olds, and 47% in schools for 11-to-14-year-olds. The long-term aim was to create a ten plus two plus three system—ten years of school, two years of junior college, and three years of university. Cuts in government spending seemed to have made this a very distant prospect. One report from India suggested that as many as six out of every ten entering class one of the primary school were dropping out by class five. In Algeria,

UPI COMPIX

Pres. Gerald Ford chats with Ruby S. Murchison of Fayetteville, North Carolina, after presenting her with the Teacher of the Year award at the White House in March. The Teacher of the Year awards are sponsored by the Encyclopædia Britannica Companies, the Council of Chief State School Officers, and the "Ladies' Home Journal," which presented a feature article on the winner in its April issue.

Ecumenical Movement: *see* Religion

where about 70% of children of primary age were at school, a gesture was made toward free schooling by abolishing all private schools—in practice, the Roman Catholic schools. The schools were compensated and the 40,000 children affected integrated into the state system.

In countries with more advanced educational systems, the standards achieved in primary schools continued to occupy much public attention. In England a parents' revolt at one London primary school led to the suspension of the entire teaching staff and a public inquiry into the so-called progressive methods that were being employed. A research inquiry conducted by Lancaster University threw doubts on the value of progressive methods compared with traditional methods of teaching, though the research was subjected to severe criticism by other educationists. The Lancaster inquiry showed, however, that the single most successful teacher in the inquiry was, in fact, using progressive methods. A research inquiry published in Sydney, Australia, in April 1976 suggested that one in every seven Australians was functionally illiterate. A large proportion of the illiterates were, however, new immigrants to Australia, and a significant proportion were native-born Australians over the age of 60.

Busing of students to overcome patterns of segregation was a familiar procedure in several U.S. cities, accepted with relative calm in most. The most publicized city was Boston, where the massive violence of the first two years was replaced by scattered incidents during the third year of federal court-ordered busing. Federal Judge W. Arthur Garrity returned most control of the schools to the Boston School Committee. But large numbers of students stayed out of the schools, while many parents eluded busing by moving to the suburbs or enrolling students in private schools. Several other cities were cited for their careful preparation for desegregation and their subsequent peaceful transitions.

Pasadena, Calif., one of the first cities in the nation to undergo court-ordered busing, found that residential shifts had led to resegregation. The U.S. Supreme Court decided that such a situation did not warrant an annual redistribution of pupils among schools.

The U.S. Commission on Civil Rights issued a report maintaining that school desegregation was working well. It noted that 82% of 1,300 districts had reported desegregation efforts as proceeding smoothly. While 50% of the nation's students were being bused, only 3.6% were bused for purposes of desegregation. The commission claimed that there had not been a lowering of academic standards in desegregated schools, or a white exodus from them.

KEYSTONE

Boy choristers of Regensburg in Bavaria celebrate the 1,000th anniversary of their choir, the famed Regensburger Domspatzen. The choir has 200 members.

P.A. INTERPRESS/AUTHENTICATED NEWS INTERNATIONAL

Children in a primary school in Warsaw. A 1973 reform provided for a comprehensive ten-year school curriculum in Poland.

The U.S. Supreme Court ruled that housing subsidized by the federal government could not be confined to low-income, nonwhite areas. The effect of the ruling could be to open more housing options to nonwhites outside central city areas.

After hearing much about declining student achievement, the U.S. public learned that reading scores for some students had increased in recent years. A testing organization noted a dramatic increase in reading scores for black children. Comparing test data for 1970–71 with those for 1974–75, it found that nine-year-old blacks had improved four times as much as whites of that age. Older students of both races showed little change.

Secondary Education. The most sensitive area continued to be secondary education. In some Western countries it even became a hot potato politically, notably in Britain where the Labour government introduced a bill into Parliament in 1976 to make comprehensive, or common, secondary schools obligatory. The bill was fought tooth and nail by the Conservative opposition, which, although not opposing comprehensive schools, was determined to allow freedom of selection at the age of 11 for those who wanted it. But the Labour government was insistent that selective education should end, and even withdrew grants from 170 state-supported private schools known as direct grant schools. Fifty of these schools decided to enter the local authority school system; the remainder decided to go entirely independent and charge full fees to their pupils.

World Education

Most recent official data

Country	1st level (primary)			General 2nd level (secondary)			Vocational 2nd level			3rd level (higher)			Literacy	
	Students (full-time)	Teachers (full-time)	Total schools	Students (full-time)	Teachers (full-time)	Total schools	Students (full-time)	Teachers (full-time)	Total schools	Students (full-time)	Teachers (full-time)	Total schools	% of population	Over age
Afghanistan	621,437	16,293	...	160,458	7,376	...	10,061	871	...	9,399	1,264	...	8.0	15
Albania	555,300	18,944	1,374	32,867	7,157	46	50,072	1,205	85	25,500	926	5	71.0	9
Algeria	2,435,365	60,179	7,794	406,565	15,340	524	23,454	1,316	46	35,887	4,041	15	26.4	15
Angola	536,599	13,230	5,585	59,209	3,060	177	15,845	1,154	99	2,942	274	1	30.0	...
Argentina	3,579,304	195,997	20,646	454,194	62,334	1,794	788,864	99,525	2,973	596,736	45,204	846	92.6	15
Australia	1,819,358	78,390	8,009	1,099,922	74,041	2,244	...	...	...	171,889	19,920	96	...	...
Austria	540,732	61,093	5,920	607,033	*	*	267,426	14,517	995	84,349	10,607†	35	98.0	15
Bangladesh	7,750,000‡	155,023‡	36,165†	1,955,200	80,500	8,083	7,373‡	616‡	53‡	27,940‡	1,532‡	12‡	22.7	15
Bolivia	769,968	33,084	...	122,124	7,531	...	8,114	1,060	80	37,692	3,026	16	39.8	15
Botswana	116,293	3,509	323	12,098	522	29	2,188	248	29	289	30	1	18.4	15
Brazil	20,135,898	837,268	186,563	3,464,088	228,143	9,323	788,662	...	...	772,800	77,951	...	79.8	15
Brunei	32,120	1,625	149	12,906	884	26	798	75	4	—	—	—	64.0	15
Bulgaria	1,000,442	50,738	3,544	116,586	7,637	328	265,900	19,408	561	92,582	12,230	52	91.4	8
Burma	3,300,153	74,266	...	860,675	25,461	...	11,205	871	...	56,310	3,989	...	68.3	8
Cambodia	429,110	18,794	1,021	98,888	2,266‡	79	5,409	220	73	11,570	276	35	36.1	...
Cameroon	1,074,021	20,803	4,349	93,934	3,699	226	28,639	1,370	...	6,171	...	8	12.0	...
Canada	2,821,500	278,300	16,500	2,673,400§	*	*	...	...	...	592,000	48,000	254	95.6	14
Chile	2,314,411	75,400	8,263	285,806	17,799	570	163,105†	11,768	282	190,535	...	40	88.2	15
China	90,000,000	...	...	8,520,000	...	...	1,470,000	...	...	820,000	...	...	40.0	...
Colombia	3,791,543	115,310	32,230	1,003,492	49,931	3,252	264,625	15,210	932	141,718	16,199	70	78.5	15
Congo	293,138	4,650	...	66,710	1,289	...	5,807	392	...	2,098	194	2	28.8	...
Costa Rica	367,901	12,643	...	68,499	3,505	...	9,329	...	...	17,366	1,275	5	84.7	15
Cuba	1,899,266	75,921	15,561	265,589	21,475	563	83,095	7,450	137	55,435	...	4	...	...
Czechoslovakia	1,890,081	96,781	10,247	119,563	7,829	339	560,572	26,900	1,548	108,646	16,697	44	98.5	15
Denmark	559,745	58,425	2,474	283,318	*	1,336	112,159	...	154	85,284	7,865	60	100	15
Dominican Republic	833,439	15,216	...	118,190	5,381	...	7,544	460	8	37,538	1,709	...	67.3	15
Ecuador	1,101,586	28,380	...	268,388	17,659	...	...	...	...	43,743	...	15	67.5	...
Egypt	4,096,863	100,119	...	1,383,335	45,403	...	326,830	18,680	...	351,522	18,143	...	26.3	14
El Salvador	759,725	15,665	3,103	29,559	1,546§	161	22,172	...	91	26,692	1,275	14	49.0	...
Fiji	135,092	4,229	...	26,202	1,103	...	2,221	224	...	1,348	...	...	72.7	15
Finland	393,242	21,248	4,449	405,203	17,536	1,049	111,776	11,212	748	67,881	4,940	27	100	15
France	6,367,523	255,919‖	59,967	2,945,192	173,934‡	6,282	981,058	69,501	4,478	763,980	38,000‡	278	100	7
Germany, East	2,649,886	158,543§	5,636	47,854	*	285	453,000	44,213	979	186,267	33,570	292	100	15
Germany, West	4,242,458	379,634	25,871	5,472,448	*	*	598,493†	20,633†	7,316†	729,207	68,286	288	99.0	15
Greece	925,495	29,921	9,738	504,031	16,595	1,137	133,361	...	...	97,131	5,068	137	86.0	15
Guatemala	585,015	16,451	5,902	86,215¶	5,934¶	493	15,810	1,380	...	21,715	1,314	5	36.7	15
Honduras	420,714	11,712	4,245	56,692	3,038	163	18,597	...	1,394	9,204	533	2	60.4	10
Hong Kong	642,611	20,089	1,013	347,146	12,254	326	21,509	¶	42	20,427	1,935	20	80.9	...
Hurgary	1,051,095	66,861	4,468	99,656	6,663	285	110,820	7,751	251	61,160	11,799	48	98.2	15
India	60,641,993	1,602,515	404,418	8,400,000	523,341	124,360	¶	¶	¶	2,540,000	119,000	3,721	33.3	15
Indonesia	13,314,246	443,015	66,994	1,651,439	105,169	6,744	860,030	74,960	3,912	117,587	11,763	965	56.6	15
Iran	4,119,157	135,021	35,796	1,818,323	62,936	5,592	82,803	3.452	365	115,311	4,128	156	22.8	15
Iraq‡	1,523,955	57,621	6,194	457,763	16,862	1,133	29,572	1,814	82	73,991	2,577	52	52.0	15
Ireland	542,849	17,908	3,839	252,994	14,618	843	3,658	215	65	30,989	2,682	61	100	15
Israel	561,858	30,488	1,901	76,667	5,654	355	73,847	6,980	370	84,399	...	...	91.9♀	14♀
Italy	4,835,449	252,637	35,080	3,322,014	283,043	8,868	1,517,705	119,388	6,639	886,894	50,662	77	93.9	...
Ivory Coast	606,263	13,158	...	83,456	2,804	...	2,342	136	...	6,034	368	...	20.0	...
Japan	10,364,855	415,039	24,652	9,095,163	457,565	15,697	1,252,605	47,696	8,017	2,087,866	105,104	933	99.9	...
Jordan	386,012	11,120	1,165	157,745	7,248	990	6,441	345	14‡	11,873	627	23	62.1	15
Kenya	2,881,155	86,109	8,161	226,835	9,230	1,160	3,525†	237†	11†	5,977	...	3	40.0	15
Korea, South	5,503,737	109,530	6,405	3,370,311	87,142	3,174	507,430	16,536	484	313,608	14,730	194	88.5	13
Kuwait	111,820	5,444‡	177	106,943	7,972‡	199	3,528	784	16	1,858	269	5	64.0	10
Laos	273,357	7,320	2,125	14,633	613	37	5,977	413	27	875	136	3	58.8	...
Lebanon	497,723	32,901*	2,319	167,578	*	1,241	7,836‡	...	159	50,803	2,313	13	88.0	...
Lesotho	221,932	4,228	1,081	15,611	605	60	...	66†	11†	847	130	9	56.5	15
Liberia	149,687	4,111	843	26,426	1,015	275	1,511	...	6	2,214	...	3	21.5	15
Libya	538,070	24,424	2,121	107,577	8,074	523	22,429	1,779	100	12,162	596	16	52.4	15
Luxembourg	35,589	1,691	472	8,214	739	12	9,631	874	44	341	11	2	100	15
Malawi	641,709	10,588	2,140	14,489	748	61	1,822	181	15	1,247	166	1	16.5	15
Malaysia	1,843,514	57,693	6,370	799,284	28,949	1,179	21,922	1,024	82	28,601	2,137	23	60.8	10
Mali	276,307	7,848	...	6,786	511	...	4,543	...	...	731	151	4	2.2	...
Mauritius	152,417	5,568	240	60,441	1,921	125	1,212	83	10	1,341	84	2	61.6	12
Mexico	11,885,509	275,558	...	2,477,999§	139,001§	...	76,550	5,131	...	451,947	27,855	...	76.2	9
Morocco	1,547,646	39,244	...	486,173	19,613	...	...	...	...	35,037	991	...	22.2	...
Mozambique	469,351	6,855	...	26,668	1,431	...	16,200	1,130	...	1,982	193	...	7.0	...
Nepal	392,229	15,500	...	217,524	7,749	...	17,051	...	...	...	...	...	12.5	15
Netherlands, The	1,529,529	59,544	9.358	740,280	45,790	1,503	469,905	40,500♂	2,024	209,920♂	26,000♂	364	100	15
New Zealand	525,323	21,187♂	2,544	219,754	11,107♂	396	2,387	1,136	21	35,078	4,502§	33	100	15
Nicaragua	350,519	8,817	2,297	76,763	...	251	6,945	429	44	11,618	694	6	57.6	15
Nigeria	4,368,778	129,399	13,183	476,507	18,441	1,270	68,013	3,307	198	23,707	2,361	6	25.0	15
Norway	386,559	29,605	3,745	262,889	*	*	65,921	...	665	64,469	...	...	100	15
Pakistan	4,813,134	115,698	50,574	1,514,904	87,171	7,328	40,356	2,582	314	256,340	13,198	443	16.3	5
Panama	342,043	11,185	2,171	81,928	3,472	70	43,563	2,170	138	26,289	1,022	2	81.3	15
Papua New Guinea	243,080	7,824	1,815	30,492	1,282	82	11,232	745	122	2,624	324	3	32.1	15
Paraguay	459,393	15,871	2,709	66,746	6,829	652	848	66	2	11,194	1,388□	4	79.7	15
Peru	2,970,708	76,445	20,055	758,320	30,051	1,560	250,788	10,320	446	320,038	16,095	629	71.6	15
Philippines	7,622,424	247,551	...	1,631,363	45,594	...	159,813	12,378	...	678,343	32,651	...	83.4	10
Poland	4,523,435	201,101	17,823	647,992	26,166	1,249	1,848,211†	74,067†	9,029†	521,899	45,014	89	97.8	15
Portugal	933,112	34,596	14,656	491,248	34,055	1,962	176,043	14,751	285	58,918	4,353	184	71.0	...
Puerto Rico	478,335	17,181	1,755	330,454	12,455	264	26,669†	...	83†	82,385	...	12	87.1	15
Rhodesia	885,547	22,898	3,786	75,951	3,849	198	5,290	461	38	2,666	346	6	28.6	16
Romania	2,882,109	137,405	14,722	344,585	14,818	434	580,125	29,579	...	162,767	14,147	...	100	8
Rwanda	386,719	7,854	1,824	8,663¶	707¶	64¶	2,564	...	...	1,023	206	4	23.0	15
Saudi Arabia	577,734	26,384	2,711	148,520	7,831	749	16,508	1,286	78	17,253	1,454	20	5.2	...
Senegal	283,276	6,294	...	59,039	2,198	...	7,408	920	124	7,773	...	...	45.6	6
Singapore	328,401	11,570	391	176,224	7,745	124	7,825	837	13	13,965	970	4	76.2	10
South Africa	4,683,401	149,651*	20,262*	979,755*	*	*	49,075	3,146	179	109,476	8,128	52	89.0	...
Soviet Union	39,040,000	2,415,000*	157,800*	15,400,000	*	*	4,477,800	208,600	...	4,751,100	302,000	...	99.7	10
Spain	6,215,093	206,948	187,187	792,179	49,100	2,405	308,704	25,313	1,277	380,196	24,523	147	90.1	15
Sri Lanka	2,117,706	...	6,970	480,264	98,925	1,673	12,936	895	39	19,286	2,453	...	78.1	10
Sudan	1,257,339	28,926	4,440	231,311	8,651	1,075	12,077	1,073	37	22,204	750	20	20.0	9
Sweden	713,149	43,000	4,934	533,214	54,000	...	18,324	...	63	108,000	...	40	100	15
Syria	1,184,122	34,247	6,676	423,922	20,082	1,010	25,989	2,479	73	...	...	6	46.6	10
Taiwan	2,364,961	62,803	2,376	1,221,538	50,281	800	282,415†	10,103†	177†	289,435	13,606	101	84.3	15
Tanzania	1,126,165	23,580	...	47,125	2,127	...	5,180	391	...	2,683	353	...	...	...
Thailand	6,609,239	239,128	42,179	958,889	41,445	2,391	232,900	13,451	288	80,675	10,206	31	81.8	10
Togo	329,443	5,627	1,199	44,306	1,111	112	4,695	393	23	1,619	243	2	10.5	...
Tunisia	910,532	22,225	...	158,643	...	...	38,004	...	...	9,246	884	...	32.2	10
Turkey	5,324,707	156,476	...	1,231,433	40,351	...	285,447	16,848	...	185,285	11,773	...	54.7	6
Uganda	940,920	27,597	3,417	75,582	2,812	268	11,192‡	524‡	43‡	5,635‡	604‡	4‡	31.0	15
United Kingdom	6,012,655	247,127	27,048	4,491,552	262,791	5,947	381,530†	67,692†	764†	397,621	52,947	286	100	15
United States	25,405,249	1,171,695	...	15,447,000§	1,083,000§	...	...	...	...	9,023,446	633,000	...	98.8	14
Uruguay	355,328	13,935	2,327	143,852	...	261	42,340‡	...	23‡	33,664	2,545	3	90.5	15
Venezuela	1,924,040	58,457	...	543,104	...	...	41,107	...	...	168,632	...	...	83.4	...
Western Samoa	32,642	968	152	15,093	773	159	621	40	3	249	9	1	98.3	10
Yugoslavia	2,869,344	126,327	13,661	203,296	10,164	450	519,957	10,540	1,475	328,536	19,197	273	83.5	10
Zaire	3,292,020	80,481	5,924	229,473	13,792	2,511	87,374	...	...	19,294	2,550	36	15.0	15
Zambia	810,234	16,916	2,654	61,354	2,880	110	7,197	...	23	2,324	...	2	47.7	...

*Data for primary include secondary. †Excludes teacher training. ‡Public schools only. §Includes vocational. ‖Includes preprimary education. ¶General includes vocational and teacher training. ♀Jewish population only. ♂Estimate. □Excludes private 3rd-level teacher training.

In West Germany comprehensive schooling continued to make very slow progress indeed. Some 180 pilot comprehensives were reported to be in operation, but half of them were run on "multilateral" lines—that is, the pupils were taught in separate streams. There was some evidence in West Germany, as in England, of a backlash against comprehensives, principally because of their large size. It was first thought that schools of 2,000 or even 3,000 pupils were necessary to span the 11-to-19 age group. It was apparent by 1976 that views had radically changed on school numbers, which were now thought to be optimal at the 750-to-900 level. Some major research was, however, produced in June 1976 by Helmut Fend of Konstanz University on behalf of the federal government, suggesting that comprehensive schools had decided virtues. Fend produced opinions from pupils, parents, and teachers to the effect that integrated comprehensives were more relaxed and humane than the traditional secondary schools. The Fend report had considerable effect, because school stress had become a source of anxiety. Suicides among teenagers in West Germany had been running at about 500 a year for the past ten years, and anxiety over the school-leaving examinations—especially the *Abitur*—had frequently been given as the cause.

The examination rat race preceding university entrance was also an issue in Japan, where a very much higher proportion of pupils remain in school after the end of compulsory school age than in Western Europe—more than double that of most European countries. The pressure to get children into university had led to the enormous growth of private cramming establishments (*jukus*). It was reported in April 1976 that 30% of Tokyo families were using them for their children.

In Sweden the replacement of the Social Democrats, who had been in office for 44 years, by a conservative coalition was thought unlikely to make a significant difference to the educational system. The major reform initiated by the Social Democrats—SIA (*Skolans inre Arbete*)—had general support. This reform incorporated the Swedish version of a community school involving pupils and parents as well as teachers. It consisted of organizing work units to resemble a school within a school, each composed of 90 pupils; *i.e.,* between two and four classes. The staff working with each of these units was to be known as the "work team" and would include teachers, special teachers, welfare personnel, and recreational leaders. All this was seen to mean developing a new style of teaching; much emphasis, therefore, was put on in-service training. The outcome of this experiment was awaited with great interest, though obviously it would take many years to prove itself.

Changes in the other Scandinavian countries were less dramatic, though in oil-prosperous Norway there was an expansion of numbers in the upper secondary schools to 37% by 1975–76. Evidently more girls stayed on in school than boys and, unlike Sweden, Norway saw no swing against science. In Denmark the emphasis was on changing the curriculum so as to allow more freedom of choice.

In The Netherlands the proposals of the minister of education, the *Contours Memorandum,* continued to be a centre of controversy. The memorandum proposed that by the year 2000 there should be three school types—6-to-12, 12-to-16, and 16-to-18. This attracted some criticism from the Dutch Educational Council, an advisory body, which thought that six was too early to begin formal schooling and did not consider that compulsory education should continue to 18.

Although there were strong religious differences of opinion in The Netherlands, the religious issue affected schooling most in the Republic of Ireland. Efforts by the Irish government to introduce community schools at the secondary level ran into conflict with the views of the Roman Catholic Church. In Northern Ireland a plan for encouraging comprehensive schooling was published in 1976, but the serious religious tension between Protestants and Roman Catholics made the prospect of an integrated system remote.

In Czechoslovakia an important school reform was launched in September in which an attempt was made to shift the emphasis in secondary schools to vocational subjects in the hope of steering more students to technical and vocational courses, notably engineering. More emphasis was also to be put on the learning of foreign languages.

Higher Education. By the time of Mao Tse-tung's death, China's Cultural Revolution had lost its impact. The effects it had had on the organization of higher education had been largely repaired. For example, the practice of taking unqualified older peasants and workers into universities had been abandoned in undergraduate courses, though short programs were still arranged for them. The universal practice of requiring two or more years of manual work from high school graduates before entry into higher education was, however, still maintained, just as it was still a standard practice for children to spend block-time in factories or in the countryside.

Much the same emphasis was to be found in Cuba, where the same cult of "new man" was prevalent. It was announced in Havana that the objective for 1980 was a total of 140,000 students in higher education. In 1976 the figure was 83,000, though a large proportion of them were part-time (57% in the University of Havana). Cuba was still suffering in 1976 from a grave shortage of qualified teachers, many of whom had emigrated to the United States after Castro's takeover. The emphasis in higher education was, not surprisingly, on science and technology. Of the 54,000 higher education students in Havana, only 600 were studying Spanish language and literature.

Much the same could be said of Mozambique's university, newly named the University of Maputo (previously Lourenço Marques). Of 1,300 full-time students in the university, only 113 were in the faculty of letters.

Manpower planning in the interests of a more productive society was not an obsession of Communist countries alone. In both Britain and France, for example, there were official expressions of anxiety about the need to attract more people into science and industry. In France the new minister for higher education, Mme Alice Saunier-Seïté, made herself very unpopular by introducing reforms of the courses leading to master's degrees, making them vocationally oriented. But having trained qualified graduates for particular occupations, it was not always easy to induce them to go where they were most needed. In certain elite French colleges it had long been the tradition to commit students to public service for a number of years, unless they were willing to buy themselves out. The same principle had also been applied in Eastern Europe where, in Romania for example, graduates were expected to commit themselves to a

FOX PHOTOS/PICTORIAL PARADE

In February, thousands of students marched in London to protest a government cutback in funds for education. Here they are entering High Holborn on their way from the Department of Education to Speakers Corner in Hyde Park.

particular three-year stint somewhere. Notwithstanding this, in Hungary it was reported that there were 10,000 physicians in the Budapest area while 4,000 positions for doctors in the countryside remained vacant.

France had an uproar over higher education, affecting not only master's degrees but also the new institutions established in 1966 known as Instituts Universitaires de Technologie (IUT). Fifty of the 66 directors of the IUT's actually walked out of a meeting with the minister for higher education over her insistence on cuts in the number of teaching posts. In fact, the IUT's had not attracted the number of students that had been anticipated—only 45,000 as against an expected total of 85,000 by 1976.

In most countries of the West efforts were made to reduce the pressure on higher education. In West Germany the University Framework Law (*Hochschulrahmengesetz*) was passed in January 1976. This was intended to bring about a rational partnership between the universities and the Länder or provinces. The Länder were required to agree on admission procedures to the universities by 1979, or the federal ministry would intervene directly. The *numerus clausus* (that is, the numerical limit on entry to particular faculties) became an election issue in the fall of 1976, Chancellor Helmut Schmidt calling for a relaxation of it for certain subjects—though interestingly this did not include oversubscribed subjects like medicine, pharmacology, psychology, dentistry, and veterinary surgery.

Not surprisingly, part of the criticism of the *numerus clausus* was that it would turn the universities into more elitist institutions than they already were. This criticism was heard in France in relation to the École Nationale d'Administration (National School of Administration), set up by Pres. Charles de Gaulle in 1945. The school's student body was held to be unrepresentative of French society, with a declining enrollment of children of farmers and of clerical and industrial workers. There was also alleged to be prejudice against students with socialist convictions.

Political differences even emerged in Switzerland over a White Paper issued by the Swiss federal government in April. About 70% of the Swiss are German-speaking, but there were only four universities for the 16 German cantons whereas the five French cantons also had four universities. The university authorities were predicting a shortage of 10,000 places by 1985.

In Denmark, where the expansion of higher education had been considerable—from 13% of the 19-year-olds in 1960 to 30% in 1975—the government determined to stabilize the system at 20,000 admissions. This meant a 25% cutback in admissions to the universities of Copenhagen and Aarhus and a 24% cutback in teacher training places. Similarly, in Greece it was announced that university entry would have to be cut by 25% to relieve congestion on the campuses.

There continued to be keen interest in the Open University system. This was seen in its most complete form in Britain where 5,000 Open University students graduated in 1976, all of them taught by TV, radio, and correspondence courses, but Open University systems of some kind existed in 14 other countries.

Ending a free-tuition tradition started in 1847, the City University of New York (CUNY) began charging students the same tuition as the State University of New York. After a 30% budget cut, the university actually closed for several days at the end of the 1975–76 academic year. CUNY's problems were part of the city's brush with bankruptcy. Those money problems destroyed the city's open admissions policy which had opened the city university to all comers, regardless of their readiness for college-level work.

On the national level, education appropriations were continued by Congress at about the same level as previously. Broad categories included $336,920,000 for student assistance programs, $14.5 million for institutional assistance programs in language training and area studies and for university community services, and $750,000 for personnel development. Substantial funds were also appropriated for the student loan insurance fund; for the higher education loan and insurance fund; for educational activities overseas; for the operation of the assistant secretary for education, Department of Health, Education, and Welfare (HEW); and for support for federally related Howard University, Gallaudet College, and the National Technical Institute for the Deaf. Appropriations for a number of higher education programs, plus some other HEW programs, were deferred since the authorizing legislation was not passed.

U.S. Census Bureau studies released at midyear showed that in the last 25 years the percentage of people graduating from high school and college had doubled. In 1975 two of every three adults completed high school. Four times as many black males graduated from college in 1975 as did in 1950.

An analysis of 1972–74 survey data suggested that about half of U.S. colleges were not in sound financial condition, and that more than 14% were edging toward insolvency. In the survey about half of some 3,200 institutions were in the "less than healthy" category, second from the bottom on a five-point scale of financial health. The picture was uneven, with best health reported by two-year colleges, public four-year colleges, predominantly white colleges, and institutions in the Far West and Southwest.

The cost of attending U.S. colleges continued to spiral. The increase for the 1976–77 academic year ranged from 5 to 9%, reflecting added costs of food, fuel, faculty salaries, and other operating expenses. The estimated cost to students at private colleges was $7,000 per year, since these could no longer depend on endowments and contributions to keep tuition down. Public institutions, on the other hand, are

YOUTH TELLS ITS VIEWS

Food for thought for parents and educators emerged from the second annual opinion poll of junior high school students, conducted in 1976 by the Encyclopædia Britannica Educational Corp. Despite the fears of many concerned citizens that violence on television is harmful to young people, fewer than 10% of the nearly 2,000 teenagers polled found TV violence objectionable. Students questioned in the 1975 poll, however, had rated television as the most important media influence in their lives.

No clear-cut preferences emerged when the students were asked to list their favourite TV programs. Among those mentioned most frequently were "Happy Days," "Charlie's Angels" (also first and second among the viewing audience at large, according to the A. C. Nielsen Co. ratings), "Starsky and Hutch," and "Saturday Night."

On another subject much discussed among adults, namely reading, the students displayed ambivalent views. Almost 85% of those polled said they liked to read, chiefly books and magazines, but when they were asked to rank nine specific activities in order of preference, reading was at the bottom, well below getting together with friends, participating in sports, and hobbies. Nevertheless, John H. Benton, chairman of Encyclopædia Britannica Educational Corp., found the results encouraging. "We were glad to find that teenagers overwhelmingly like to read," he said. "TV *is* an acknowledged influence, but obviously so are books, films, magazines, and newspapers."

Also somewhat ambivalent were the answers to a question on favourite school subjects. Math and social studies headed the list among both boys and girls (26%), but an almost equal number liked these least. There was much more agreement on the students' choice of audiovisual materials for classroom use; 80% preferred film.

Of the students aged 12 to 14, 67% had already decided what they wished to do after completing their formal schooling. Careers in teaching, medicine and related fields, and professional sports were high on the list, while less conventional choices included taking time off to travel and being the first to live on the Moon.

Despite their tolerance for television violence, 60% of the teenagers believed that achieving world peace should be the chief priority for President-elect Jimmy Carter after taking office. More predictable, perhaps, was the second choice—increasing the number of jobs for young people—but it was picked by only 22%. Twelve percent favoured safeguarding the country's natural resources as the number-one goal, and 5%, increasing funding for health research.

On one subject, the answers were almost unanimous. Ninety percent of those questioned believed, from personal observation, that alcohol, tobacco, and drugs are harmful, and also that their use among teenagers is increasing. Most of the students questioned reported that their schools had a sex education program which, by and large, they rated as average.

subsidized by tax moneys. Student expenses at four-year public institutions were approximately $2,790 per year, of which $621 was for tuition. The cost at public two-year colleges was about $2,454, with $387 for tuition.

Research. The International Association for the Evaluation of Educational Achievement (IEA) completed its massive series of nine reports comparing achievements in 21 countries over the period 1966–73 in science, literature, reading comprehension, English and French, and civic education. Some of the findings were not wholly palatable to educationists. Taken altogether, there was an association between pupil-teacher ratio and achievement, but when the developed countries were considered separately there was virtually no correlation between pupil-teacher ratios and achievement. "Student teacher ratios and class size alone are not adequate predictors of student achievement," the study concluded. "While planners will need to take class size into account for a variety of reasons, they may well question the conventional notion of smaller is better and insist on other measures to support such proposals."

It also turned out that countries with the longest period of compulsory schooling had by no means the highest achievement levels. For example, England and Scotland, with two additional early years of compulsory schooling, did not attain the average achievement levels of Finland and Sweden in either science or reading comprehension.

A study published in Britain entitled *Early Experience: Myth and Evidence,* by Ann and A. D. B. Clarke, challenged the widely held view that deprivation in early childhood is permanently damaging. The study was based largely on evidence drawn from some severely deprived Czechoslovak twins; it laid stress on the importance of a stable family background, however. Also published in Britain was the follow-up study conducted by the National Children's Bureau of all the children born in Britain between March 3 and 9, 1958. No evidence was found of any significant generation gap between the 16-year-olds and their parents, except in dress and physical appearance.

After years of study and debate, the U.S. Congress passed a new copyright law. The old law (1909) was written long before the existence of technology such as photocopying machines. The new law provided guidelines on how much material could be photocopied without payment of royalties.

In a move to implement the 1974 Education of the Handicapped Act, the U.S. Office of Education announced plans to spend approximately $4 billion to help severely handicapped students participate more fully in regular education programs and to reduce the number in institutionalized programs. Handicapped children and youth were to be grouped to the greatest extent possible with normal ones. The public schools would thus have to assume responsibility for many students previously served by institutions. Advocates claimed that all children and youth would benefit from learning together in school, in the same way that adults live and work together.

(TUDOR DAVID; JOEL L. BURDIN)

See also Libraries; Motion Pictures; Museums.

[562; 563]

ENCYCLOPÆDIA BRITANNICA FILMS. *Learning with Today's Media* (1974); *Expanding Math Skills with the MiniCalculator* (1976).

SPECIAL REPORT

FUNCTIONAL ILLITERACY IN THE UNITED STATES

By George Weber

A century ago it seemed useful for the decennial census to find out how many Americans were illiterate. The question was asked directly. In the census of 1870, 20% of Americans ten years of age or older were recorded as illiterate. They could not read and write a simple passage in any language. By 1969, when a Bureau of the Census survey asked those 14 years of age or older who had completed less than six years of formal schooling whether they could read and write, the roughly comparable figure had fallen to 1%.

Although the census keeps asking this question, it is no longer of practical interest. In a modern society, much more is required in the way of literacy than the mere ability to read and write a simple passage. This fact was recognized as early as 1930 by Finland, which in that year classified its population into three categories: illiterates, semiliterates, and literates. The term "functional illiterate" originated during World War II, when the U.S. Army used it to describe a person who was not necessarily illiterate by the census definition but who was unable to understand written instructions about basic military tasks. The distinction was important, because in that war the nation's armed services, for the first time, operated on the assumption that all personnel could read and write. With very large manpower requirements, the Army took in hundreds of thousands of these functional illiterates and taught them to read and write well enough to meet military needs. In later wars (Korea and Vietnam), most such men were simply rejected. In the Korean War 19% of those drafted were rejected for military service on the grounds of "educational deficiencies" (a euphemism that by then had replaced "functional illiteracy" in military usage).

The definition of functional illiteracy varies over time. A hundred years ago it would have been a meaningless concept, since an illiterate could cope with the minimal economic, social, cultural, and political demands of daily living. But, like the modern army, modern civilian society takes for granted a relatively high level of literacy in the routine conduct of business, politics, cultural activities, and communication. The result is a paradox: because of the achievement of ever higher levels of education, modern America has become so literate that it has far more "functional illiterates" than was the case a century ago. That is, there are far more Americans who, because of their low level of literacy, find it impossible or very difficult to function at even a minimal level in society. Exactly what that minimal functional level is now is open to debate, but it certainly includes the ability to read and write well enough to get and to perform satisfactorily the most routine jobs, to fill out common forms, to read an average daily newspaper, signs, instructions, and directions, and to write simple messages and letters.

Literacy and Grade Levels. Two approaches have been used to determine the number of people who cannot read at the minimal functional level. One is to decide what average grade-level performance is necessary and then to estimate how many fail to attain that level. This approach presents difficulties, the first of which involves determining the necessary average grade-level performance. In a 1976 study Ted K. Kilty of Western Michigan University at Kalamazoo found that the modern version of the 23rd Psalm is written at the 5th-grade level, the manual to obtain a Michigan driver's license and instructions to make a cup of coffee at the 6th-grade level, directions to prepare a frozen ham TV dinner at the 8th-grade level, some lead articles in *Time* magazine at the 11th-grade level, life insurance policies at the 12th-grade level, and apartment leases at the college level.

David Harman, an Israeli adult education expert, contended in 1970 that perhaps half the adults in the United States were functional illiterates because of those life insurance policies and apartment leases, but most people in the field would not agree with him. There are regulatory bodies to deal with the provisions of these documents, and individuals can turn to more literate friends, social workers, and lawyers for help. In the past, a fifth-grade level has been cited as the minimum needed if a person is to function successfully. More recently an eighth-grade level has been advocated, and that seems reasonable. On that basis, perhaps 10 to 20% of American adults are functional illiterates.

The main reason this approach has not led to better estimates, however, is that U.S. public schools today have no widely used

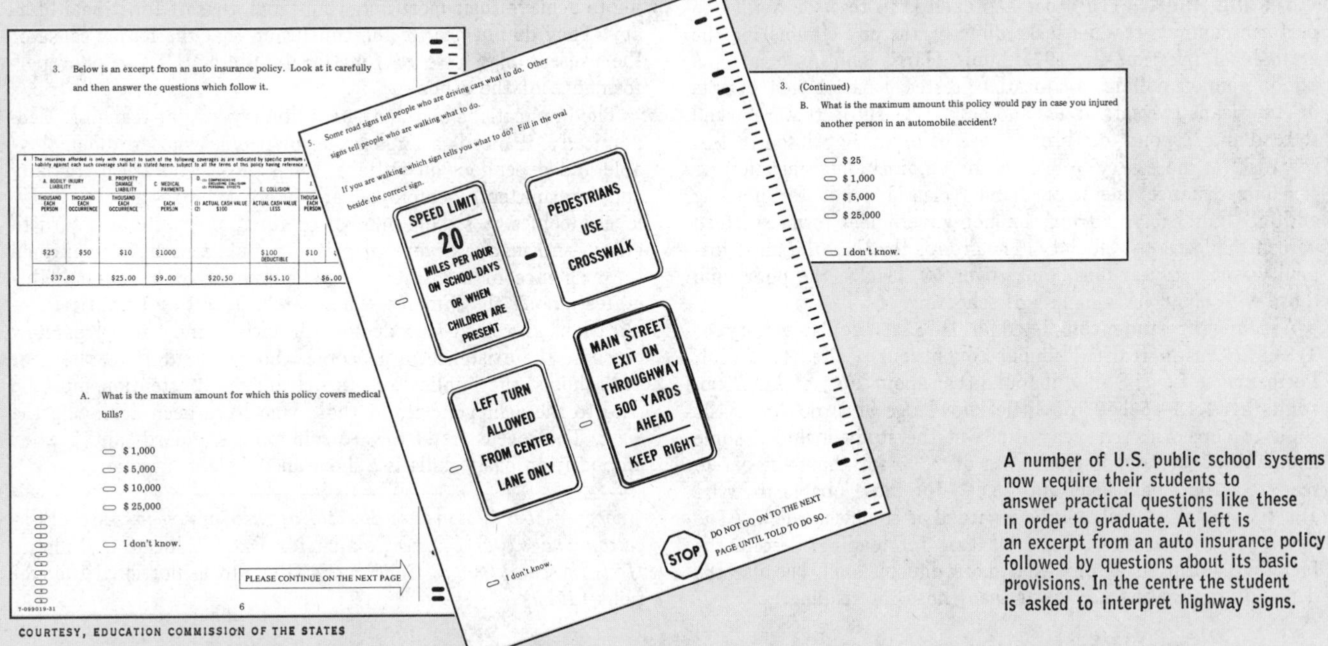

3. Below is an excerpt from an auto insurance policy. Look at it carefully and then answer the questions which follow it.

A. BODILY INJURY LIABILITY		B. PROPERTY DAMAGE LIABILITY	C. MEDICAL PAYMENTS	D.	E. COLLISION	
THOUSAND EACH PERSON	THOUSAND EACH OCCURRENCE	THOUSAND EACH OCCURRENCE	EACH PERSON	(1) ACTUAL CASH VALUE (2) $100	ACTUAL CASH VALUE LESS	THOUSA[ND] EACH PERSON
$25	$50	$10	$1000		$100 DEDUCTIBLE	$10
$37.80		$25.00	$9.00	$20.50	$45.10	$6.00

A. What is the maximum amount for which this policy covers medical bills?

- $ 1,000
- $ 5,000
- $ 10,000
- $ 25,000
- I don't know.

PLEASE CONTINUE ON THE NEXT PAGE

6

7-099019-31

5. Some road signs tell people who are driving cars what to do. Other signs tell people who are walking what to do.

If you are walking, which sign tells you what to do? Fill in the oval beside the correct sign.

I don't know.

STOP DO NOT GO ON TO THE NEXT PAGE UNTIL TOLD TO DO SO.

3. (Continued)

B. What is the maximum amount this policy would pay in case you injured another person in an automobile accident?

- $ 25
- $ 1,000
- $ 5,000
- $ 25,000
- I don't know.

COURTESY, EDUCATION COMMISSION OF THE STATES

A number of U.S. public school systems now require their students to answer practical questions like these in order to graduate. At left is an excerpt from an auto insurance policy followed by questions about its basic provisions. In the centre the student is asked to interpret highway signs.

MARION BERNSTEIN—COLLEGE NEWSPHOTO ALLIANCE

Experts say that 15% of American adults cannot read well enough to cope with the tasks of everyday life.

minimum standards of performance. Generally speaking, children are passed on from grade to grade because of their age. Many children read far below the average performance for their grade, and a few young people graduate from high school as functional illiterates. Thus, even if an average grade-level performance could be agreed upon as equivalent to minimum functional literacy, currently available data provide only rough approximations of how many people have not achieved that level.

Testing Ability. The other approach is to test the ability to perform common reading tasks directly, thereby eliminating the grade-level question. In 1971 Louis Harris and Associates, a public opinion polling organization, tested a nationwide sample of Americans 16 years of age and older. The subjects were asked to read and respond to a broad range of ordinary printed matter regarded as necessary for daily living, including instructions for long distance telephone dialing, classified ads for housing and jobs, and excerpts from common government forms. Fifteen percent had serious difficulty. The groups that had the most difficulty were 16-year-olds, those over 50, blacks, the poor, and those with eight years or less of schooling.

A four-year study completed in 1975 at the University of Texas at Austin reached similar conclusions. Called the Adult Performance Level Study, it found that about 20% of American adults aged 18–65 had too little knowledge and too few basic skills to cope with everyday life. But the study included some debatable tasks, and its estimates of 22% for those unable to read at a functional level and 16.6% for those unable to write at a functional level should be regarded as somewhat high. (The figure for writing was lower than that for reading, despite the fact that writing is a somewhat more difficult skill, because the demands for writing are lower than those for reading.)

A third nationwide study of functional literacy is the reading segment of the National Assessment of Educational Progress, a federally financed survey of educational achievement begun in 1969. In 1971 the National Assessment conducted a survey of 17-year-olds and young adults (ages 26–35). The project did not reach a formal conclusion per se, but an examination of the results of the survey indicates that these groups had a functional illiteracy rate of 15 to 20%.

From these three recent nationwide studies using the second (and superior) approach to determining the extent of functional illiteracy, it can be concluded that roughly 15% of American adults are now functional illiterates.

Have the Schools Failed? There are several causes for the presence of functional illiteracy in the United States today. One that has been mentioned is the high literacy level required by modern society. Another, which applies almost entirely to the middle-aged and elderly, is too little schooling. For several decades, almost all young people in the U.S. have completed at least eight years of schooling. If that alone were sufficient to produce functional literacy, the younger people would have it. But some of the middle-aged and elderly, particularly blacks and persons who only recently immigrated to the United States, received far less formal education.

The main cause of functional illiteracy, however, is a deficiency in the quality of schooling. As has been mentioned, in recent decades U.S. public schools have followed the practice of passing children on year after year without regard to their attainments. Thus a significant number of young people finish 8, 10, or 12 years of schooling without achieving functional literacy. Recently the embarrassment created by these young functional illiterates has led some states and local school districts to adopt proficiency standards for promotion from grade to grade and for high school diplomas. To the extent that this trend continues, the incidence of functional illiteracy among young people can be expected to decline.

It cannot be denied that certain nonschool factors make the school's job more difficult. A few children are so limited in intelligence that they cannot achieve functional literacy, but they probably account for only 2 or 3% of the population at most. Some children have home environments that give them relatively little motivation to learn to read and write well. They never see older members of the family reading or writing, and they are taught little or no reading and writing in the home. Finally, some children have little or no opportunity to practice reading and writing in the home; there are no reading materials available, and physical conditions are not conducive to reading and writing. But these nonschool factors cannot excuse the schools for failing to achieve their most important goal, that of functional literacy. They do not change the conclusion that the major cause of the present high rate of functional illiteracy is the poor performance of the schools.

The implications of functional illiteracy are far-reaching. Economically, it means a large group of people who are unemployable and dependent on welfare. Even those who are marginally and intermittently employed are likely to earn only poverty-level incomes. A sizable number of functional illiterates turn to crime, and many surveys of prison populations have confirmed the existence of a disproportionate number of functional illiterates among the inmates. There are cultural and political implications as well. A free, democratic society and a free press now presume the existence of a people who can read and write. For the schools, the implications are clear: more attention must be paid to the achievements of those who have been achieving the least. The recent trend toward minimum standards and greater emphasis on basic skills is a move in the right direction.

George Weber is associate director of the Council for Basic Education and editor of the Council for Basic Education Bulletin. *He is the co-author of* Consumer's Guide to Educational Innovations *(1972)*.

Egypt

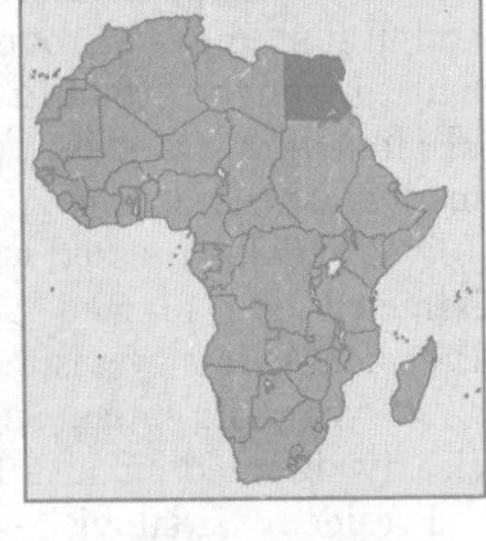

A republic of northeast Africa, Egypt is bounded by Israel, Sudan, Libya, the Mediterranean Sea, and the Red Sea. Area: 386,900 sq mi (1,002,000 sq km). Pop. (1976 est.): 38,067,000. Cap. and largest city: Cairo (pop., 1976 est., 6,133,000). Language: Arabic. Religion: Muslim 93%; Christian 7%. President in 1976, Anwar as-Sadat; prime minister, Mamdouh Salem.

Domestic Affairs. At home in 1976 the adaptation of the political system created by Pres. Gamal Abd-al-Nasser continued, although it remained strictly controlled and directed by the regime. On January 25 a committee of the Arab Socialist Union (ASU) was appointed to study applications for the formation of *manabir,* or platforms, within the ASU. This committee reported on March 14 its rejection of a multiparty political system and its acceptance of three "platforms": one for the right, known as the Socialist-Liberal Organization and headed by Mustafa Kamal Mourad; one for the centre, led by the prime minister, Mamdouh Salem; and one for the left, known as the Progressive Unionist Organization and led by Khaled Mohieddin. President Sadat expressed approval of this arrangement but said there was no reason why it should not develop into a multiparty system in the future. Certain groups, such as the Muslim Brotherhood and the Young Nasserists, declared that none of the three groups represented them.

In March President Sadat decreed major changes within the Egyptian press. The main trend was toward silencing leading left-wing journalists and intellectuals. They were not dismissed but were suspended from writing for the daily press, although a left-wing weekly, *Rose el-Youssef,* and the monthly *al-Talia* continued to appear. In January the left-wing writers tried to resist government attempts to control the writers' union, and in March there was a brief journalists' strike.

The main causes of public discontent were inflation, overcrowding, and some ostentatious spending by wealthy Egyptians and non-Egyptian Arabs. In March there were strikes by industrial workers near Cairo and in the Delta and in September by Cairo bus drivers. On September 8 there was some serious rioting in the poor quarters of Cairo. In Upper Egypt there were several signs of resistance to attempts by former big landowners to recover some of their lands. On August 8 there were two bomb explosions in Cairo and on August 14 one on a train in Alexandria, causing several casualties. The authorities blamed the bombs on Libyan subversion, but it seemed likely that Egyptian elements were involved—especially as on August 9 the government announced it had uncovered an organization of Muslim extremists.

On March 19 a Cabinet reshuffle led to the formation of a 32-man government which gave posts to four new men but retained most of the senior ministers. On June 3 Mustafa Khalil replaced Rifaat Mahgoub in the key post of first secretary of the ASU. President Sadat, having agreed to run for the presidency again at the end of his six-year term, was nominated as sole candidate by the People's Assembly, and his election was declared to have been approved by popular referendum on September 16 by 95.7% of the voters.

Preliminary results of the parliamentary elections on October 28 gave 280 out of 360 seats (18 still to be filled) to the centre group of the Arab Socialist Union. On November 11 Sadat announced that the groups would now be political parties in a move toward full democracy: the centre group would be Arab Socialists; the right, Free Socialists; and the left, National Progressive Unionists.

Foreign Relations. Egypt began 1976 somewhat on the defensive in the Arab world because of its second Sinai disengagement agreement with Israel in September 1975. To Syria, Iraq, and the Palestine Liberation Organization (PLO) this agreement indicated that Egypt had opted out of the Arab-Israeli struggle for its own interests. Israeli withdrawals in Sinai under the agreement were completed on February 22. Sadat continued to maintain that Egypt was championing the Palestinian cause and seeking international recognition for the PLO, and Egypt strongly criticized Jordan for reconvening its Parliament in February on the ground that this contravened Arab agreements recognizing the PLO as representing the Palestinian Arabs. When the PLO clashed with Syria over the latter's intervention in Lebanon, Egypt seized the opportunity for a rapprochement with the PLO. Sadat denounced Syrian aims in Lebanon and the Lebanese rightists, and called for joint Arab action although he refused to send Egyptian troops. The proposal by Khaled Mohieddin, leader of the leftist

JACQUES PAVLOVSKY—SYGMA

More than 12,000 vessels passed through the Suez Canal in the first year after it reopened in 1975. The canal was closed by the 1967 war with Israel, and badly damaged in the October 1973 war.

group in the ASU, that Egypt should send volunteers to fight on the Palestinian-leftist side in Lebanon was firmly rejected by the ASU first secretary, with government approval. On June 7 the PLO radio in Cairo was allowed to reopen. After attacks on the Egyptian Relations Office in Damascus by Syrian and other Arab students on June 5, Egypt withdrew its diplomats from Syria and closed the Syrian Relations Office in Cairo. Relations with Syria remained strained even after the June 23–24 meeting in Riyadh, Saudi Arabia, between the Egyptian and Syrian prime ministers, Mamdouh Salem and Mahmoud Ayoubi, arranged through Saudi-Kuwaiti mediation. At a meeting in Riyadh of six Arab leaders, including Sadat and Syrian Pres. Hafez al-Assad (*see* BIOGRAPHY), on October 18 a Lebanon cease-fire and the establishment of a peacekeeping force there were agreed upon, and this was confirmed at an Arab summit conference in Cairo attended by 14 Arab heads of state and the PLO leader, Yasir Arafat, on October 25. Relations with Syria improved thereafter, and on December 21 agreement to plan for Egyptian-Syrian political unity was announced.

Relations with Libya were exacerbated after Omar Muhaishi, a leading member of the Libyan Revolution Command Council, was granted asylum on February 8 and subsequently made anti-Libyan broadcasts from Cairo. As mentioned above, bomb incidents in Egypt in August were blamed on Libya, and Egypt moved troops to the frontier. President Sadat strongly attacked Libya's chief of state, Col. Muammar al-Qaddafi, referring to him as "Libya's madman." After the attempted coup in Sudan on July 2 Sadat expressed warm support for Pres. Gaafar Nimeiry and blamed the events on Libya. When President Nimeiry visited Alexandria on July 13–17, a 25-year Egyptian-Sudanese defense agreement, clearly directed against Libya, was signed.

President Sadat visited Saudi Arabia and the Persian Gulf states in February and again in June, following a state visit to Iran. His main purpose was to secure increased aid for Egypt from the oil states. He maintained that they had not provided enough for Egypt's needs and that they owed financial support to Egypt because it had borne the main cost of Arab wars with Israel. On March 29 Sadat began a tour of West Germany, France, Italy, Austria, and Yugoslavia in which he sought aid and also new sources of arms and spare parts to offset the lack of Soviet supplies. Egypt failed to obtain spare parts for its MiG-21s from Yugoslavia or India during 1976, but it purchased some helicopters and military hovercraft from Britain, took delivery of Mirages from France, and discussed with Italy the adaptation of Egypt's Soviet tanks to Western artillery. Egypt also obtained six C-130 military transport planes from the U.S. despite some congressional opposition.

Relations with the Soviet Union did not improve, and on March 14 Egypt abrogated the 1971 15-year Soviet-Egyptian friendship and cooperation treaty on the ground that the Soviet Union, by withholding arms spare parts, had not fulfilled its obligations. Egypt also stopped providing facilities for the Soviet Navy in Egyptian ports, which had existed since 1968. Economic relations were not affected, however, and a new Soviet-Egyptian trade protocol for $640 million was signed in April after a visit by the Egyptian trade and supply minister to Moscow. Vice-Pres. Husni Mubarak was warmly received during his visit to Peking in April, and the government reported that the Chinese had offered arms and aid.

The Economy. In 1976 Egypt continued the *infitah*, or "open-door" policy, initiated in 1974 to facilitate foreign investment, and gave new encouragement to the private sector. The results remained meagre, however, and early in the year it was revealed that of 244 projects approved under the "open-door" policy only 17 had been implemented. Two major new projects for a $50 million French-financed tire factory and for an Arab aluminum company with U.S. and Arab capital were approved. The balance of payments deficit was serious. In January President Sadat estimated the expected deficit for 1976 at $2.4 billion, but later in the year this estimate was increased to $4.5 billion. The country was said to need approximately $2.7 billion a year to service debts that included an estimated $4 billion to the Soviet Union for arms.

Despite Sadat's visits to the Arab oil states they remained reluctant to commit themselves to the extent Egypt wanted. After lengthy discussions, Saudi Arabia, Kuwait, Qatar, and the United Arab Emirates agreed in July to the establishment of a Gulf Authority for Egyptian Development with a capital of $2 billion. U.S. aid was promised for $1 billion in 1976, including the provision of 500,000 tons of wheat on easy payment terms.

On January 1 Port Said became a free zone. During

EGYPT

Education. (1972–73) Primary, pupils 4,096,863, teachers 100,119; secondary, pupils 1,383,335, teachers 45,403; vocational, pupils 299,057, teachers 16,402; teacher training, students 27,773, teachers 2,278; higher (including 8 universities; 1973–74), students 351,522, teaching staff 18,143.

Finance. Monetary unit: Egyptian pound, with (Sept. 20, 1976) an official rate of E£0.39 to U.S. $1 (free rate of E£0.70 = £1 sterling) and a tourist rate of E£0.72 to U.S. $1 (E£1.22 = £1 sterling). Gold, SDR's, and foreign exchange (May 1976) U.S. $334 million. Budget (1975 est.): revenue E£3,961 million; expenditure E£4,345 million. Gross national product (1974) E£3,949 million. Money supply (April 1976) E£1,991.5 million. Cost of living (1970 = 100; Feb. 1976) 140.

Foreign Trade. (1975) Imports E£1,467.6 million; exports E£548.6 million. Import sources (1974): U.S. 17%; France 15%; Australia 9%; U.S.S.R. 9%; West Germany 6%. Export destinations (1974): U.S.S.R. 33%; Japan 10%; Czechoslovakia 7%. Main exports (1974): cotton 47%; cotton yarn 11%; fruit and vegetables (1973) 9%; rice 7%.

Transport and Communication. Roads (1972) *c.* 26,000 km (including 12,100 km main highways). Motor vehicles in use (1974): passenger 184,500; commercial (including buses) 40,200. Railways: (1974) 4,510 km; traffic (1973) 7,258,000,000 passenger-km, freight 2,561,000,000 net ton-km. Air traffic (1974): 1,285,000,000 passenger-km; freight 17.7 million net ton-km. Shipping (1975): merchant vessels 100 gross tons and over 143; gross tonnage 301,383. Telephones (Jan. 1975) 503,200. Radio licenses (Dec. 1973) 5.1 million. Television licenses (Dec. 1973) 600,000.

Agriculture. Production (in 000; metric tons; 1975): wheat 2,033; barley 118; millet *c.* 900; corn *c.* 2,600; rice *c.* 2,450; potatoes *c.* 750; sugar, raw value *c.* 582; tomatoes *c.* 1,750; onions *c.* 700; dry broad beans (1974) 234; watermelons (1974) *c.* 150; dates (1974) *c.* 380; oranges (1974) *c.* 725; tangerines and mandarin oranges (1974) *c.* 96; lemons (1974) 80; grapes (1974) *c.* 167; cotton, lint *c.* 392; cheese (1974) *c.* 189; beef and buffalo meat (1974) *c.* 233. Livestock (in 000; 1975): cattle *c.* 2,312; buffalo (1974) *c.* 2,150; sheep *c.* 2,097; goats (1974) *c.* 1,278; asses (1974) *c.* 1,480; camels (1974) *c.* 110; chickens *c.* 26,070.

Industry. Production (in 000; metric tons; 1975): cement 3,605; iron ore (50% metal content) 1,120; crude oil 11,445; petroleum products (1974) *c.* 7,010; fertilizers (nutrient content; 1974–75) nitrogenous 100, phosphate *c.* 95; salt (1973) 454; sulfuric acid 232; cotton yarn 181; cotton fabrics (m) 561,000; electricity (kw-hr; 1974) 8,200,000.

the year moves were made toward making the Egyptian pound convertible, and in early October the official exchange rate was abolished for all except the import of a few essentials. This amounted to a heavy devaluation. Despite subsidies of food and essentials maintained at more than $1.5 billion a year, inflation was running at an annual rate of about 30% as shortages forced the public to revert to the black market. The most encouraging sectors of the economy were the Suez Canal and the oil industry. On February 4 work was started on the first stage of enlarging the Suez Canal to take ships up to 150,000 tons fully loaded by 1979. Canal revenues were expected to exceed $200 million in 1976. New oil discoveries offered the prospect that output would rise from about 370,000 bbl a day to 1 million bbl a day by 1980. (PETER MANSFIELD)

[978.B.3.e]

El Salvador

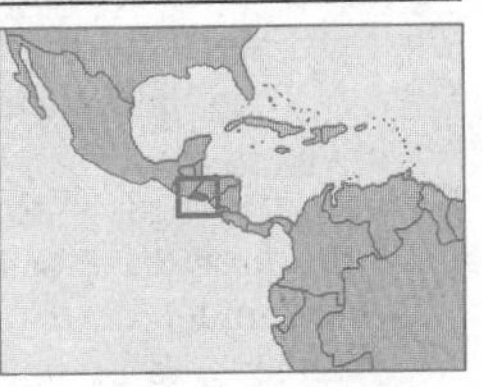

A republic on the Pacific coast of Central America and the smallest country on the isthmus, El Salvador is bounded on the west by Guatemala and on the north and east by Honduras. Area: 8,124 sq mi (21,041 sq km). Pop. (1976 est.): 4,240,000. Cap. and largest city: San Salvador (pop., 1974 est., 416,900). Language: Spanish. Religion: Roman Catholic. President in 1976, Col. Arturo Armando Molina.

The incumbent National Conciliation Party (PCN) won a clean sweep in the March municipal and congressional elections. One important result was the return of the capital city's government to the PCN after 12 years of Christian Democrat control. The PCN nominated War Minister Col. Carlos Humberto Romero and Public Health Minister Julio Astacio as its candidates for the nation's presidency and vice-presidency, respectively, in the 1977 elections.

The National Association of Private Enterprise softened its opposition to the government's year-old Agrarian Transformation Act when the government agreed in October to set up a committee, in which the private sector of the economy would have representation, to work out a plan for implementation of the act.

The signing on October 6 of an agreement between El Salvador and Honduras providing for mediation by a third-country jurist was hailed as a positive step toward restoration of peace between the two nations. The ceremony took place in the Washington, D.C., headquarters of the Organization of American States, which had contributed substantially to the negotiations that made the agreement possible.

(HENRY WEBB, JR.)

[974.B.1.c]

EL SALVADOR

Education. (1975) Primary, pupils 759,725, teachers 15,665; secondary, pupils 29,559; vocational, pupils 21,552; secondary and vocational, teachers 1,491; teacher training, students 620, teachers 55; higher, students 26,692, teaching staff 1,275.

Finance. Monetary unit: colón, with (Sept. 20, 1976) a par value of 2.50 colones to U.S. $1 (free rate of 4.29 colones = £1 sterling). Gold, SDR's, and foreign exchange (Sept. 1976) U.S. $206.8 million. Budget (1976 est.) balanced at 844 million colones. Gross national product (1974) 3,884,000,000 colones. Money supply (May 1976) 728.2 million colones. Cost of living (1970 = 100; May 1976) 161.

Foreign Trade. (1975) Imports 1,502,300,000 colones; exports 1,286,800,000 colones. Import sources (1974): U.S. 31%; Guatemala 12%; Venezuela 8%; Japan 8%; West Germany 7%; The Netherlands 5%. Export destinations (1974): U.S. 26%; Guatemala 17%; West Germany 14%; Nicaragua 8%; Costa Rica 7%; Japan 7%; The Netherlands 6%. Main exports: coffee 33%; cotton 15%; textiles (1973) 9%; sugar (1973) 7%.

Transport and Communications. Roads (1971) 10,733 km (including 625 km of Pan-American Highway). Motor vehicles in use (1973): passenger 38,500; commercial (including buses) 19,000. Railways (1974) 590 km. Telephones (Dec. 1974) 50,000. Radio receivers (Dec. 1971) 350,000. Television receivers (Dec. 1973) 110,000.

Agriculture. Production (in 000; metric tons; 1975): corn 381; sorghum 146; rice (1974) 30; dry beans 37; sugar, raw value 257; coffee 146; cotton, lint 78; jute 5. Livestock (in 000; 1974): cattle *c.* 1,200; pigs *c.* 421; horses *c.* 64; poultry 8,643.

Industry. Production (in 000; metric tons; 1974): cement 296; petroleum products 605; cotton yarn 6.2; electricity (kw-hr) 986,000.

Energy

No single event dominated developments in the field of energy during 1976, but in several countries public opposition to an increase in power production, especially nuclear power, continued. In the United States attention was drawn to the defeat of an antinuclear initiative in California's June primary election. The initiative called for the banning of new nuclear plant construction after one year unless utilities assumed full financial liability for nuclear accidents and for the phasing out of existing plants unless the legislature certified (by a two-thirds vote) that the reactors were safe and that adequate disposal of the nuclear wastes could be assured. The initiative was defeated by vote of two-to-one. In the general election in November voters faced similar initiatives or referenda in six other states (Arizona, Colorado, Montana, Ohio, Oregon, and Washington). These were all defeated, by a three-to-two margin in Montana and Oregon and at least two-to-one in the other states.

A piece of adverse news for nuclear power advocates was the announcement by Pres. Gerald Ford in October of a new government policy concerning plutonium. Until the worldwide problem of "nuclear proliferation" (the spread of nuclear weapons capability to more nations) has been adequately dealt with, it would be U.S. policy to regard the reprocessing of nuclear fuel to produce plutonium as not "a necessary and inevitable step in the nuclear fuel cycle." This raised the possibility of a future complete ban on the reprocessing of spent fuel.

In the courts, nuclear foes scored victories in July. In three separate decisions, the U.S. Court of Appeals for the District of Columbia agreed with the argument that licensing hearings for nuclear plants must consider the effects of the entire nuclear fuel cycle, including reprocessing and waste disposal, and must also consider the conservation of electricity as a means of forestalling the need for a nuclear plant. This led to some confusion as to the status of plants already licensed and those undergoing the licensing process. By October the Nuclear Regulatory Commission had decided to continue with the licensing process under an interim proceeding pending final resolution of the issues.

Environmental opposition forced the cancellation in April of a giant coal-fired power plant, to be located in the Kaiparowits region of southern Utah. In

Eire:
see Ireland

Electrical Industries:
see Energy; Industrial Review

Electronics:
see Computers

Employment:
see Economy, World

the planning stage for 13 years, the 3 million-kw plant would have been the largest in the country and would have supplied consumers in Arizona and southern California. On a smaller scale, in September voters in three counties in southern Idaho rejected a proposal to build a 500,000-kw coal-fired plant in that area.

Similar opposition to nuclear power appeared in Europe. The Social Democratic Party in Sweden was unexpectedly voted out of office in September after 44 years in power, a defeat attributed in part to the promise of one of the victorious parties to abandon plans for additional nuclear reactors and close down those already operating. (The new prime minister modified his position, however, after assuming office and agreed not to close down existing plants and to allow existing plans to proceed.) Elsewhere in Europe a British royal commission issued a report urging delay in further expansion of nuclear power in Great Britain in order to conduct a lengthy debate on its desirability. Plans to build nuclear plants were postponed in Denmark, Norway, and The Netherlands, and there were antinuclear sit-ins and bombings in France and West Germany.

The U.S. continued to adjust its policies, a process necessitated by the assumption of control over the world's exportable oil supplies by the Organization of Petroleum Exporting Countries (OPEC) in 1973. The U.S. Federal Energy Administration (FEA), as directed by the Energy Policy and Conservation Act of 1975, established a schedule for a gradual rise in the controlled price of domestically produced crude oil until the termination of controls in 1979. During 1976 the FEA decontrolled the prices of home heating oil, residual fuel oil, jet fuel, and other products. Gasoline price controls remained, however.

The changing circumstances of the U.S. with respect to oil were exemplified by statistics for the first week of March, which showed that for the first time in history the nation had imported more oil than it produced. By no coincidence a bill enacted in April authorized the use of the Naval Petroleum Reserves established some 50 years earlier to provide a strategic oil reserve for emergency use during wartime. These consisted of four developed fields with shut-in wells: at Elk Hills and Buena Vista, Calif.; at Teapot Dome, Wyo. (the subject of a major scandal during the Harding administration in the 1920s); and on the western part of the Alaskan north coast. The new act directed that the three fields in California and Wyoming be brought into full production and that the Alaskan reserve be transferred from the jurisdiction of the secretary of the navy to the secretary of the interior in 1977 for exploration and development. An unexpected result of this action was the announcement by the FEA in September that the new oil supply would make the West Coast self-sufficient in oil, with no need for the output from the Alaska pipeline. This began a vigorous debate over the merits of continued production from the reserves and the trading of the surplus Alaskan oil to Japan in return for Middle Eastern oil for delivery to the East Coast.

Scientists overhaul the Lawrence Livermore Laboratory's 2XII-B fusion fuel injection system. The machine injects superhot nuclear fuel into a powerful magnetic "trap." The aim is to develop controlled thermonuclear fusion, the energy source of the Sun and stars.

AUTHENTICATED NEWS INTERNATIONAL

In another move by the U.S. to improve its oil position, the first steps were taken to explore and develop the outer continental shelf of the Atlantic coast. Two test wells were drilled, one 80 mi E of Atlantic City, N.J., in the Baltimore Canyon area and the other about 75 mi off Cape Cod in the Georges Bank Trough. In August the Bureau of Land Management held the first lease sale of Atlantic tracts. The sale was held under dramatic circumstances. Last-minute legal maneuvers by opponents (including the state of New York) threatened its cancellation, but it was finally held late on the appointed day. The results were unexpected. High bids on 101 of the 154 tracts offered for lease totaled $1.1 billion, well above the maximum of $600 million expected by the U.S. Department of the Interior.

The winter of 1975–76, the third mild winter in a row, minimized the adverse effects of the curtailment of gas supplies in many parts of the U.S. In a major change of policy, the Energy Research and Development Administration (ERDA) announced in April that it would give "the highest priority" to work on energy conservation. This action came in response to sharp criticism of the agency's program, issued the previous year, which gave prime emphasis to the development of new sources of energy. In January the secretary of the interior lifted the moratorium on the leasing of federal coal lands that had been in effect four years. In August Congress overrode the presidential veto of a bill revising the conditions of such leasing. The new law discouraged speculation in coal leases by requiring production within ten years; encouraged small companies to seek leases; raised the minimum royalty from 5 cents per ton to 12.5% of the value; increased the state's share of royalties from 37.5 to 50%; and limited the maximum leaseholding by one company to 100,000 ac nationally.

In matters related to natural gas yet another unsuccessful attempt was made early in the year to pass legislation ending the authority of the U.S. Federal Power Commission (FPC) to regulate the wellhead price of gas in interstate commerce. The deregulation issue may well have been made moot, however, by the commission's establishment of new national price ceilings in July. The major provision of the new regulation was a ceiling of $1.42 per thousand cubic feet for new gas sales after Jan. 1, 1975. This new ceiling was nearly two and three-quarters times the previous level. The new price ceilings were immediately challenged in court, and the process of judicial review was begun.

In other gas developments a well in the Texas Panhandle established a record of 24,482 ft for the world's deepest production. ERDA announced that two gas wells that had produced gas from underground caverns formed by nuclear explosions were being sealed and abandoned. This marked the end of attempts to recover through nuclear explosions the very large gas resources of western Colorado that cannot be commercially produced by conventional means. Although the explosions did increase the flow of gas, the production was not great enough to justify the expense of the technique.

On the world scene, divisions began to appear in OPEC's hitherto united front. After holding the world oil price steady through most of the year, largely at the urging of Saudi Arabia, in December, 11 of the member countries announced that they would raise the price 15% in two steps during the next year. However, Saudi Arabia and the United Arab Emirates planned only a 5% raise, and the Saudis intimated that they might increase production. Meanwhile, OPEC's opposite number, the International Energy Agency (IEA), adopted detailed rules for sharing vital energy resources in the event of another OPEC embargo. The IEA, with a membership of 19 industrialized countries that are oil importers, was established in 1974 to meet the problem of the OPEC cartel power. Continuing the move by OPEC members toward direct control of oil activities within their borders, Venezuela nationalized all 19 of the foreign oil companies operating on its territory.

In the North Sea new discoveries continued to be made, and additional fields already discovered reached the production stage. A historic event was the occasion, in April, of the United Kingdom's first export of crude oil, from the Forties Field to West Germany. In June the first production from a well with the production control assembly located on the seafloor inaugurated a new generation of offshore production technology. The well was at a depth of 385 ft. In February the British government signed an agreement with a company operating in the North Sea whereby the government obtained the rights to 51% of the oil production. This constituted the beginning of the government's move to obtain the same degree of control over all North Sea oil operations within its territory.

Another development in the U.K. offered the possibility of an embarrassment of energy riches in that country in the 1980s. In October the development of a new coalfield at Selby, Yorkshire, was begun. The Selby reserves, discovered in the 1960s, were estimated to contain 600 million tons. Production was scheduled to begin in 1980.

New discoveries, some of major significance, others of potential importance, and still others the first indication of oil in the area, were made throughout the world. Saudi Arabia, which already led the world in oil reserves, announced that exploration the previous year had discovered three large new fields with reserves of 7,000,000,000 bbl (equivalent to the total reserves of Canada and more than one-fifth those of the United States). All of the fields are in the northern part of Saudi Arabian territory, two offshore and one onshore. Oil was discovered for the first time in the offshore waters of the Philippines, 90 mi SW of Manila, and good discoveries were made off both the east and west coasts of Spain. In March the discovery of a gas field off the mouth of the Amazon River constituted the first proof of the occurrence of petroleum hydrocarbons on the continental shelf in that area of South America. Production began from India's large Bombay High field 120 mi W of Bombay in the Arabian Sea.

AUTHENTICATED NEWS INTERNATIONAL

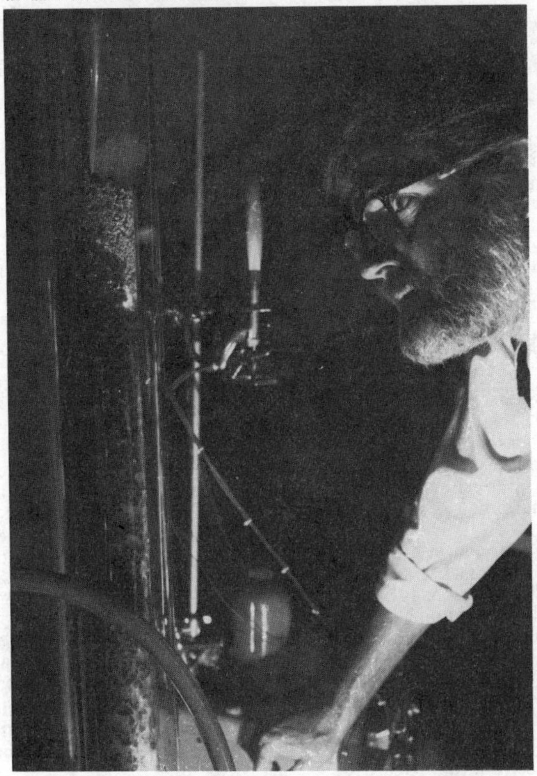

The extraction of energy from coal is investigated at the Lawrence Livermore Laboratory. The coal is burned to release energy in the form of methane and other gases.

The Kangan gas field in the Persian Gulf off southeastern Iran was found to be one of the largest, if not the largest, gas fields in the world. The field was discovered in 1965 but was not developed because of lack of demand. Drilling during 1976 indicated reserves of 180 trillion cu ft and possibly even more than the 210 trillion cu ft in the Urengoiskoye field of the U.S.S.R., currently the world's largest. The world's first offshore plant to separate natural gas liquids from natural gas went into operation in the Java Sea, 90 mi NE of Jakarta, Indon.

Several developments took place in the field of unconventional energy resources. ERDA and the National Aeronautics and Space Administration announced the joint funding of an experimental 1.5-Mw wind turbine of 200-ft diameter, the output to be fed into a local utility system. The U.S. Department of Housing and Urban Development announced a $1 million grant program for the installation of 143 solar heating units throughout the country. The program included space heating and cooling and water heating, in both new and existing housing, in a variety of different types of dwelling units. During the year work began on the world's first application of solar energy to provide hot water for an industrial process. The installation was at a uranium mill near Grants, N.M. The FPC in May authorized the commercial sale to a pipeline of synthetic methane produced from animal wastes at feedlots.

The first geothermal well ever drilled into a volcano yielded "clean" steam. A test well drilled into Kilauea Volcano on the island of Hawaii produced steam for four hours in an experimental run. In France the world's first solar-thermal power plant went into operation at Odeillo, in the French Pyrenees. The experimental plant was scheduled to feed between 70 and 100 kw into the French national grid for one year. (BRUCE C. NETSCHERT)

ENCYCLOPÆDIA BRITANNICA FILMS. *Energy: A Matter of Choices* (1973); *Energy for the Future* (1974).

COAL

A forecast in 1976 estimated that world coal production would almost double by the end of the century because of depletion of other fossil fuel reserves. The world's estimated economically recoverable reserves of coal in 1976 amounted to 478,000,000,000 metric tons, three times greater than the proven reserves of oil and natural gas and enough to last for many centuries at the present rate of consumption.

Many nations achieved record production levels in 1975 despite the economic recession, and nations with reserves announced plans to step up production. Research continued on a worldwide basis into the utilization of coal for the production of liquid and gaseous hydrocarbons as synthetic fuels and feedstuffs.

World hard coal production in 1975 was an estimated 2,397,630,000 metric tons, an increase of 107 million tons over 1974. Increases occurred in the U.S., the U.S.S.R., China, Poland, Canada, the U.K., Australia, and India. In Western Europe production reversed an established downward trend and increased by 9.9%, accounted for entirely by increased output in the U.K. Eastern European production (including the U.S.S.R.) showed a continued increase of just under 3%. (In the context of this article, hard coal refers to both bituminous and anthracite.)

China's output in 1975 was estimated at 470 million metric tons, an increase of 20 million tons over 1974. The earthquake centred on the northern Chinese coal-deposit area of Kailuan in July 1976 was certain to affect future coal production. In 1975 about 25.2 million tons were produced there, representing 6% of the total Chinese production.

U.S.S.R. A total of 701 million metric tons of raw coal and lignite was produced in the Soviet Union in 1975, an increase of 2.4% over 1974. Surface operations accounted for 32.2% of this total, and this method was being expanded during the current five-year plan because of its great productivity and the favourable location of reserves suitable for surface mining.

The U.S.S.R. produced 165 million tons of lignite in 1975, an increase of 5 million tons over 1974. Production of hard coal rose by 11 million tons to 535 million tons, and the coking coal component of this total rose by 5 million tons to 181 million tons.

United States. Coal production in the U.S. in 1976 was expected to exceed the record level set in 1975; during the first half of the year, production was 4.7% ahead of the similar period for 1975. For the same period, however, coal exports declined 14.8%, mainly attributable to lower shipments to Japan.

Total hard coal production in 1975 (about half from surface operations) amounted to a record 643.2 million short tons, despite a record number of wildcat miners' strikes. This production represented a healthy gain of 6% over 1974, due to the recovery after the low level of 1974 caused by a lengthy strike and the introduction of new mining capacity that outweighed the effects of the economic recession. Anthracite production continued to decline, by 6.3% from 1974 to 6.2 million tons.

Bituminous coal exports in 1975 totaled 65,667,000 short tons, a significant increase over the strike-reduced 1974 figure of 50,620,000 short tons. About 406 million tons of coal were used for electricity generation; 85 million tons were used for coke production; and 62 million tons for other industrial uses.

Due to price increases and environmental restrictions, the rate of growth of the industry was expected to be slightly lower than previously predicted. Production, however, was expected to reach 1,100,000,000 tons by the end of the century.

European Economic Community. Total hard coal production in 1975 for the EEC amounted to 257.8 million metric tons, an increase of 20.8 million tons over the 1974 level, thus halting the decline of past years. In 1976 it was expected that EEC coal production would increase slightly because of increases in the U.K. and France.

Belgium produced 7.5 million tons, a reduction of 8% from 1974. In France production was maintained at just below the 1974 level with 22.4 million tons of hard coal and 3 million tons of lignite.

Nuclear power plants may prove to be more costly than coal-fired plants. This New Mexico plant, fueled by inexpensive deposits of coal, supplies power for a large area of the West.

WIDE WORLD

Hard coal production in West Germany dropped 2.4 million metric tons to 92.4 million tons. Though lignite production fell by 2.6% to 123.4 million tons, West Germany retained its place as the world's third largest lignite producer. In 1975 sales of hard coal dropped a dramatic 25% to 80 million tons, and the government financed the formation of a 10 million-ton national reserve.

The National Coal Board of the U.K. finished the financial year 1975–76 with its second consecutive operating profit, which amounted to £52 million, despite reduced government grants. Output from deep mines was 112.5 million long tons, 2.2 million tons less than in the previous financial year. Opencut operations contributed 10,190,000 tons, an increase of 1,080,000 tons, and licensed mines provided an additional 1.1 million tons. Despite the overall reduction in energy demand, power station consumption increased by more than 3 million tons.

Poland. Hard coal production rose to a record level of 170.6 million metric tons, a significant increase of 5.9% over 1974. Lignite output climbed to 39.9 million tons. This combined production marked the largest single-year increase ever. The increased output in recent years had been achieved by the development of new mines and modernization, both below and above ground, of existing mines.

In 1975 development of the large Lublin coalfield started with the construction of the first pilot extraction mine. Piast Colliery, planned to be the largest Polish hard coal mine, began production in December 1975, with a production target of 24,000 metric tons per day by 1981. Coal exports in 1975 were 38.5 million tons of hard coal, slightly down from 1974.

India. In the fiscal year 1975–76 approximately 99,880,000 metric tons of coal were produced, 11,470,000 tons more than for the fiscal year 1974–75. By 1990–91 Indian production was expected to reach 340 million tons per year. This would, however, depend on improved rail links and port facilities and greater internal demand.

India made significant strides toward developing a coal export trade, and in late June the first shipments were made to EEC destinations. Exports during 1976 were expected to be 1.5 million tons, and it was hoped that by 1985 exports would have reached 12 million–15 million tons.

Japan. Japan's imports during 1975 declined for the first time in five years, to 62,110,000 metric tons, compared with 64,150,000 tons in 1974. Australia regained its position as principal supplier with 23 million tons. The U.S. provided 22,420,000 tons. During the first half of 1976 increased tonnages were reported from Australia and Canada and decreases from the U.S. and U.S.S.R.

Japan's indigenous production in 1975 amounted to 19,063,000 metric tons of coal and lignite, a decrease of 1,309,000 tons. Production thus was beginning to stabilize at about the planned 20 million tons per year.

South America. Coal production in 1975 amounted to 8,350,000 metric tons, recording a modest increase of 130,000 tons over 1974. Colombia was the largest producer, with 3.6 million tons, while Brazil produced 2.5 million tons and Chile 1.5 million tons. Colombia, with 60% of Latin America's coal reserves, was reported to be investigating the possibility of exporting coal to Venezuela to replace the coal that nation previously obtained from Brazil.

Africa. Of the estimated total of 74,921,000 metric tons of hard coal mined in Africa in 1975, some 69,921,000 tons were produced by South Africa, an increase of 7.5% over

1974. Rhodesia's production amounted to 2.6 million tons. Although Mozambique only produced 500,000 tons in 1975, output was expected to increase with the development of surface-mining operations.

With South Africa producing some of the world's cheapest coal, its exporters were hoping to increase shipments. This depended, however, on government export limits being raised, rail links being improved, and price increases to finance mine development. South African production was expected to rise to 150 million tons by 1985.

AUSTRALIA. Production of bituminous coal continued to rise in 1975 to a record 66.2 million metric tons, an increase of 2,570,000 tons over 1974. This was due mainly to increased surface operations in Queensland. About 45% of this total was exported, mainly to Japan. Lignite output from Victoria also reached record levels at 27 million tons and was expected to rise further when new power stations in the Latrobe Valley were commissioned. It was forecast in 1976 that by the year 1979 production of coal would have reached 88 million tons per year.

CANADA. Production in 1975 reached a record 27.8 million short tons, a 15% increase over 1974, and was expected to rise to about 29 million tons in 1976. The rise resulted from increases in sub-bituminous production for electricity generation in Alberta and increased production capacity in Nova Scotia.

Exports were again a record, increasing 1 million tons to 12.9 million tons. Exports to Japan represented 11.9 million tons of coking coal and were expected to rise to 13.5 million tons in 1976. Imports increased to approximately 15.3 million tons in 1975, from 13.6 million tons, and were expected to maintain that level in 1976.

(R. J. FOWELL)

ELECTRICITY

In 1973 world electricity consumption had continued to increase (by 7.6% over the previous year, a figure slightly above the established annual average), but the rate of increase fell in 1974 to approximately 2.7% and in 1975 to 2.5%. There was, however, a noticeable rise in consumption during the first months of 1976.

While there were vast reserves of coal worldwide, Europe (excluding the U.S.S.R.) had only about 2% of these, and a return to coal as a primary energy source to replace oil was out of the question. Geothermal and solar energy, wind power, and similar energy sources had the advantage of being virtually inexhaustible and might be of great value in a number of specific cases, but it was expected to be a long time before such methods could ensure production of electricity in the massive quantities required. Electricity producers were faced with a problem demanding short- and medium-term solutions, and a meeting of European electricity authorities at Vienna concluded that the answer for the present lay in nuclear power.

Nuclear power, which had become economically competitive against fuel oil, continued to carry a psychological handicap. Public opinion remained sensitive despite extensive and rigorous precautions taken by those responsible to ensure the safety of nuclear installations and to protect human lives. A referendum on the issue was organized in California on June 8, 1976, at the time of the U.S. presidential primaries. Opposition to nuclear power stations had been the subject of a particularly intense campaign in the U.S., yet although 33% of those taking part in the referendum declared their opposition to nuclear power, 66% accepted it as a means of meeting energy needs. In Sweden, on the other hand, public opposition to further expansion of nuclear power contributed significantly to the Social Democratic government's fall in the 1976 election.

NUCLEAR ELECTRICITY. Figures published by the U.S. Atomic Industrial Forum indicated 454 reactors in service, under construction, on order, or planned, worldwide, by March 31, 1976; the total capacity was 343,355 Mw. This compared with a figure of 426 reactors with a capacity of 294,278 Mw in 1975, a rise of 17%. The U.S., on March 31, 1976, had 228 reactors (50% of the world total), with a capacity of 226,189 Mw (66% of the world total). Progress, which had been rapid over the past few years, slowed down considerably in 1975. Five reactors went into service, three were authorized to start operation, 17 had their entry into service delayed by one year or longer, five were the subject of firm orders, and ten previously ordered were canceled. Sales in 1976 were not expected to exceed six reactors with a total capacity of 7,150 Mw, though there was a possibility that three additional reactors might be ordered toward the end of the year.

In West Germany, the Brünsbüttel (one boiling water reactor of 806 Mw), Neckarwestheim (one pressurized water reactor [PWR] of 855 Mw), and Biblis B (one PWR of 1,300 Mw) plants went into service. There was continued interest in the prototype high-temperature reactor reported working satisfactorily at the Jülich atomic research centre. The consortium with interests in the plant intended to set up a project on an industrial scale during 1977.

The ambitious French nuclear power program involved the start of construction work for 6,500 Mw annually. The target had been met in 1974 and 1975 but was revised downward to 6,000 Mw for 1976 and 1977 and to 5,000 Mw for 1978. Power stations at Fessenheim 1 (a PWR of 890 Mw) and Bugey 2 (a PWR of 925 Mw) went into service in 1976.

In the U.K., a study of power stations in 1975–76 showed that the cost of electricity produced by the nine Magnox-type power stations that had gone into service between 1962 and 1971 (total capacity 3,782 Mw) was lower than that of power stations using coal or fuel oil. The first reactor in the second British program, one of the two reactors at Hinkley Point B, began to produce electricity in February 1976, as did one of two reactors at Hunterston in southern Scotland. In 1974, the British government had chosen to use the steam-generating heavy water reactor. Six such reactors were projected, each having a capacity of 660 Mw, but plans remained at the preliminary stage. The coming into service in October 1975 of the Dounreay prototype breeder with a capacity of 250 Mw had faced the authorities with the difficult problem of deciding whether to follow the French example by moving forward to the industrial stage and building a breeder with a 1,300-Mw capacity. In September 1976 a royal commission published a 200-page report setting out reasons for delaying the project for as long as possible, but the U.K. Atomic Energy Authority stated that the dangers the report mentioned had been greatly exaggerated.

In July 1976 first contracts were signed for carrying out the June 1975 agreement between West Germany and Brazil to supply Brazil with a complete system for production of nuclear power. The contracts were for the building of two power stations out of five planned. They would be situated on the coast and would have a unit capacity of 1,325 Mw.

Iran planned a huge nuclear electricity program aiming for 20 power stations and a total capacity of 23,000 Mw by 1990. Two 1,300-Mw plants were ordered from West Germany and two of 900 Mw from France,

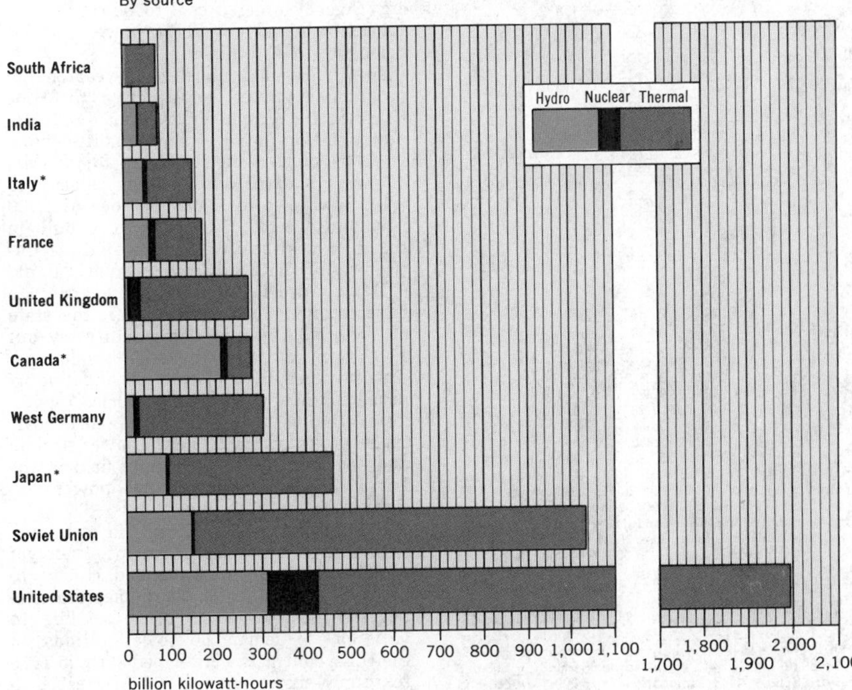

Installed Capacity and Production of Electric Power in Selected Countries, 1974-75

Country	Hydroelectric power: Operating plants: Installed capacity (000 kw)	Hydroelectric power: Operating plants: Production (000,000 kw-hr)	Total electric power: Installed capacity (000 kw)	Total electric power: Production (000,000 kw-hr)
World	...	...	...	6,245,400
Albania	...	1,200	...	1,700
Algeria	286*	484*	1,107	2,628*
Angola	368†	850	499†	1,050
Argentina‡‖	1,918	4,820	9,260	27,990
Australia	4,221¶	13,555	16,215¶	74,112§
Austria	6,008	22,662	9,240	35,208§
Bangladesh*	80	352	661	1,356§
Belgium‡‖	503	688	8,980	41,016§
Bolivia	236	747	345	967
Brazil	13,762	66,960	16,807	70,480
Bulgaria‡‖	1,558	2,080	6,169	25,236§
Burma	101	463	263	758
Cameroon	197	1,073	225	1,123
Canada‡‖	36,747	210,159	56,864	278,954
Chile	1,464	6,049	2,572	9,297
Colombia	2,287	8,200	3,663	11,950
Costa Rica	241	1,253	407	1,467
Cuba	44*	110	1,645	6,016
Cyprus	...	...	215	729
Czechoslovakia‡‖	1,592	4,042	12,806	59,232§
Denmark	9	24	6,284	17,646
Dominican Republic	96*	189*	443	1,512
Ecuador	104	440	407	1,270
Egypt	2,500*	5,200*	4,100	8,200
El Salvador	108*	515*	306	986
Finland	2,320	12,301	6,793	28,764§
France‡‖	16,600	56,830	49,302	180,402
Germany, East‡‖	725	1,337	15,808	84,564
Germany, West‡‖	4,878	17,877	69,792	301,800
Ghana	912	3,600	976	3,645
Greece	1,289*	2,340	3,969	14,628
Guatemala	106*	375*	246	1,050
Hong Kong	—	—	2,275*	6,420§
Hungary	20	80	3,738	20,460§
Iceland♀♁	376*	2,266*	493	2,292§
India‡‖	7,523	27,454	20,196	79,920§
Indonesia	404*	1,779	1,044*	3,246
Iran	850*	5,500	4,200	12,500
Iraq	—	—	...	2,600
Ireland	531*	1,011	2,041*	7,885
Israel	—	—	1,913*	9,720§
Italy‡‖♀♁	16,821	38,825	42,309	144,792§
Ivory Coast	224*	277	350*	855
Jamaica	21*	122*	677	2,328§
Japan‡‖♀♁	23,546	82,287	105,156	460,705
Kenya	80*	465	210*	900§
Korea, South	621*	1,906*	4,934	19,836§
Kuwait	—	—	...	4,000*
Lebanon	246	820	608	1,975
Liberia	73	317	298	860
Libya	—	—	300*	750*
Luxembourg	932*	...	1,157	1,476§
Malaysia	...	...	1,092	5,844
Mexico♀♁	3,679	16,708	9,647	40,766
Mongolia	—	—	251	741
Morocco	399*	1,337*	730	2,775
Netherlands, The‡‖	—	—	13,861	54,252§
New Caledonia	68	262	323	1,790
New Zealand♀♁	3,590*	14,214	4,449*	19,680§
Nigeria	320*	1,958§	860	2,828
Norway	16,000	76,570	16,158	77,580§
Pakistan‡‖	586*	2,750	1,920*	6,400
Panama	15*	95	315	1,195
Papua New Guinea	55	170	255	943
Peru	1,399	5,582	2,354	7,530
Philippines	890	2,988*	3,019	13,047
Poland	824	2,459	19,130	97,164§
Portugal	1,875	7,888	2,848	10,464§
Rhodesia	705	5,173	1,192	6,132§
Romania	2,384	8,476	10,576	49,062
Singapore*	—	—	1,109	4,176
South Africa	169*	1,132	13,435	74,916§
Spain‡‖	11,500	30,680	24,000	82,380§
Sri Lanka	195	800	281	1,050
Sweden‡‖	12,314	57,285	20,768	79,224§
Switzerland‡‖	9,800	28,922	11,400	41,796§
Syria	—	—	370	1,366
Thailand	910*	2,446*	2,432	7,789
Tunisia	29*	22*	382	1,275
Turkey	1,013	3,346	3,113	15,564§
U.S.S.R.‡‖	36,978	132,030	205,442	1,038,000§
U.K.‡‖	2,308	4,796	79,560	272,232§
U.S.‡‖♀♁	64,283	303,952	495,361	1,999,680§
Uruguay	252*	1,366*	671	2,458
Venezuela	1,348	7,299	4,305	18,396
Vietnam□	164	20	870	1,345
Yugoslavia	4,570	20,659	8,694	39,876§
Zaire	1,159	3,850	1,217	4,000
Zambia	759	5,736	1,031	6,264§

*Public sector only. †1973. ‡Includes nuclear (in 000 kw): Argentina 319; Belgium 22; Bulgaria 440; Canada 2,666; Czechoslovakia 100; France 2,942; East Germany 515; West Germany 3,504; India 640; Italy 670; Japan 3,906; The Netherlands 524; Pakistan 126; Spain 1,120; Sweden 1,062; Switzerland 1,006; U.S.S.R. 4,521; U.K. 5,814; U.S. 31,622. §1975. ‖Includes nuclear (in 000,000 kw-hr): Argentina 750; Belgium 152; Bulgaria 928; Canada 13,864; Czechoslovakia 486; France 13,932; East Germany 2,183; West Germany 12,136; India 2,160; Italy 3,410; Japan 19,699; The Netherlands 3,277; Pakistan 1,000; Spain 6,700; Sweden 2,054; Switzerland 6,635; U.S.S.R. 8,000; U.K. 33,617; U.S. 112,696. ¶1972. ♀Includes geothermal (in 000 kw): Iceland 2; Italy 406; Japan 48; Mexico 78; New Zealand 192; U.S. 441. ♁Includes geothermal (in 000,000 kw-hr): Iceland 8; Italy 2,503; Japan 312; Mexico 200; New Zealand ...; U.S. 2,453. □Figures for South Vietnam only.

Sources: United Nations, *Statistical Yearbook, 1975; Monthly Bulletin of Statistics.*

Y. KOPYT—TASS/SOVFOTO

Electricians at work on a high-voltage transmission line in the Soviet Ukraine. When finished it will carry electricity a distance of 1,110 kilometres (688 miles).

with options for the supply by France of six additional plants at a later date. Iran had large uranium deposits and was to receive 10% of the enriched uranium to be produced at the factory being built by Eurodif at Tricastin (France). Iran also had a 20% stake in the Coredif group, other members being France, Italy, Spain, and Belgium. Coredif decided to build an enrichment plant similar to that at Tricastin.

THERMOELECTRICITY. With the rise in oil prices, the use of coal in power stations excited renewed interest in most countries. In the U.S., in application of the Energy Supply Environment Coordination Act passed by Congress in 1974, the Federal Energy Agency ordered coal to be substituted for fuel oil and gas in 74 power stations belonging to 41 utilities.

In Canada the published 15-year energy program envisaged construction at Hatt Creek in the Fraser Valley of a 4,800-Mw power station fueled by high-quality lignite. In India plans were drawn up for a series of power stations with a total capacity of 6,200 Mw (two of 2,000 Mw, one of 1,200 Mw, and one of 1,000 Mw), to be built in the three coal-bearing regions of the country, possibly with aid from the World Bank.

Having decided for the present not to have recourse to nuclear power, the state of Victoria, Australia, decided to carry out a program of thermal power production. This involved the construction at Newport of a 1,000-Mw power station fueled by gas, installation of two additional 375-Mw coal-fueled groups at the Yallourn power station, and development of the lignite field in the Latrobe Valley to supply two power stations, each of 2,000 Mw.

HYDROELECTRICITY. Except in countries with a large hydroelectric potential not yet exploited, interest was directed chiefly to pumped storage plants. They offered a particularly flexible means of responding to variations in demand in power stations. In the U.K., contracts were signed early in 1976 to supply six groups, of 300 Mw each, to the Dinorwic (South Wales) pumped storage installation. They were scheduled to come into service in 1981.

Construction of the hydroelectric complex at Guri on the Caroní River in Venezuela neared completion with the coming into service of the tenth 290-Mw group. The existing dam would be raised by 52 m to supply a second station with ten groups of 720 Mw each. This would bring total capacity to 10,100 Mw and average annual productive capacity to 50,000,000,000 kw-hr. The agreement between Brazil and Uruguay for joint development of water resources along the section of the Uruguay River bordering the two countries included provision for building three power stations with a total capacity of 5,200 Mw and an annual productive capacity of 195,000,000,000 kw-hr.

(LUCIEN CHALMEY)

NATURAL GAS

Reserves of gas in the U.K. were higher in 1976 than in 1975 by an amount that was greater than that year's total consumption from the British sector of the North Sea. The North Sea continued to attract bids for oil and gas exploration licenses despite the fact that 51% of all production was taken by the government-created British National Oil Corporation. The British Gas Corporation was also successful with three out of four wells drilled off Blackpool on the northwest coast of England.

The American Gas Association (AGA) Committee on Natural Gas Reserves estimated that proved gas reserves in the U.S. totaled 228.2 Tcf (trillion cubic feet) in December 1975, down 3.8% from the previous year and the fifth straight year of decline. Net production in 1975 totaled 19.7 Tcf, down 7.5% from 1974. New reserves discovered in 1975 added 4.1 Tcf to the AGA's estimates, while revisions and extensions of previous estimates accounted for 6.4 Tcf. The Netherlands Ministry of Economic Affairs put Dutch natural gas reserves at 87.4 Tcf in January 1976, a 4.5% drop from the 1974 estimate. Proved reserves accounted for 65.2 Tcf, probable and possible reserves for 22.2 Tcf. About 75.4 Tcf of reserves were onshore and the remaining 12 Tcf were on the continental shelf. Canada's proved gas reserves were estimated at 56.97 Tcf in 1975, a 0.5% increase over 1974.

Worldwide, there appeared to be a shortage of reported gas well successes, but a Dutch North Sea well was tested by Eason Oil Co. A consortium of U.S. and European companies reported in March having tested up to 18 million cu ft a day of gas in the British North Sea sector, a few miles west of the Viking fields, and Phillips Petroleum Co. tested 12 million cu ft a day of gas from a well in the British North Sea in July. The Canadian Association of Oilwell Drilling Contractors reported a total of 2,401 oil and gas well completions in Canada in the first half of 1976, a 38% increase over the same period in 1975.

A well drilled in the Persian Gulf by Zapata Exploration Co. tested between 15 million and 26 million cu ft a day of gas. A flow of 26 million–30 million cu ft a day of gas was reported by the Phillips Petroleum Group and Pertamina in May from a well in the southern part of Salawati Island west of New Guinea. Continental Oil Co. reported a flow of 13.2 million cu ft a day of gas from an exploratory well south of Port Said and west of the Suez Canal in the first discovery ever made in the Nile Delta. The Japanese newspaper *Asahi* reported that Kangan Liquefied Natural Gas Co. had discovered what could be the world's largest single gas field in the Gulf of Iran. The deposit, off the Iranian coast and 11,600 ft below the sea bottom, was thought to hold over 180 Tcf of gas. Two wells were sunk in May, with two more in process.

An exploratory well off Ellef Ringnes Island in 200 ft of water showed the presence of an eighth gas field in the Canadian Arctic Islands. Tests indicated high productive levels. Shell Canada, Ltd., reported that five successful gas wells drilled in the Rosevean area of Alberta had boosted reserves from an originally estimated 100 Bcf (billion cubic feet) to 400 Bcf.

In the U.S.S.R. tests at the Berkutovskoe well near Orenburg indicated a flow of 35 million cu ft a day of gas at 13,000 ft, in a predominantly oil-producing region. The Soviet Union was reported as intensifying exploration efforts off the Crimean Peninsula. Tests from a well in the Golitsyna Uplift off the Crimea's Tarkhankut Peninsula in the Black Sea indicated a flow of 35.3 million cu ft a day of gas. Another well was drilled nearby to help delineate the size of the Golitsyna field.

Brazil's state-owned petroleum agency reported a flow of 25 million cu ft a day of gas from an exploratory well in the Atlantic Ocean. This was the first gas discovery ever made off the Amazon Delta.

Norway and the U.K. agreed to divide output from the Frigg gas field on the Norwegian-U.K. boundary in the North Sea. All gas from the field would be transported through a pipeline to a terminal under construction at St. Fergus, Scotland. Reserves in the field were estimated at 10 Tcf.

Abu Dhabi dissolved its partnership with British Petroleum Co., the Royal Dutch Shell Group, Compagnie Française des Pétroles, Exxon Corp., and Mobil Oil Corp. to build a $1.2 billion liquefied natural gas (LNG) plant, intending instead to construct the plant through the state-owned Abu Dhabi National Oil Co. Following a six-month study of LNG import policy in the U.S. by the LNG Import Task Force, the president's Energy Resources Council considered 2 Tcf a year of LNG imports an acceptable level. The council recommended that for national security reasons LNG imports from a single country be limited to 0.8 Tcf–1 Tcf a year. A floating LNG processing plant developed in Norway could liquefy 4 million cu ft a day of gas at the site of an offshore field, store it, and load it into LNG tankers.

LNG had become well established as a means of transporting gas, but a consortium of companies headed by Westinghouse Electric Corp.'s Oceanic Division sought federal funding to study the feasibility of converting Alaskan North Slope gas into methanol. Methanol produced in Alaska would be sent through the oil pipeline and shipped down the West Coast in conventional tankers. A more ambitious second phase would involve transporting the methanol by nuclear-powered submarine under the polar ice cap to the U.S. East Coast.

The Soviet Union awarded a $575 million contract to two West German firms to supply 17 gas turbine compressor stations for a 1,400-mi gas pipeline between Orenburg in the Urals and Chust in the western Ukraine. Later in the year a British compressor manufacturer obtained a similar Soviet order.

Interest remained high in all potential methods of gas production. In the first stage of a program to explore new underground coal gasification technology, coal was fractured at a depth of 150 ft in an attempt to produce a medium BTU (British thermal unit) gas that could be upgraded to pipeline quality from coal resources too deep for economic recovery by existing mining methods. In West Germany a $25 million prototype coal gasification plant, expected to be operational by 1977, was designed to use a new high-pressure process capable of converting 150 tons a day of coal into 300-BTU gas without forming by-products. Both New York State and the California State Energy Commission funded $100,000-plus projects to investigate gasification of solid refuse.

(DAVID RICHARD BUTLER)

PETROLEUM

Whereas 1973 and 1974 had been years of confrontation in oil affairs, 1975 and 1976 were years of discussion. After maintaining Saudi Arabia's imposed price freeze for most of the year, OPEC members split in December, with Saudi Arabia and the United Arab Emirates raising the oil price by 5% and the remaining 11 members by 10%, with a further 5% rise to come in mid-1977.

Nineteen less developed and eight industrialized countries met in Paris in October 1975, and again in December, as the Conference on International Economic Cooperation. They set up four commissions, including one on energy which met in April 1976. The International Energy Agency sponsored cooperation on conservation, a floor price for oil, emergency sharing schemes, and other measures to alleviate members' overdependence on oil. The EEC Commission, however, despite ministerial meetings, failed to formulate a satisfactory policy to reconcile different government policies on energy with the conflicting claims of different fuel priorities.

The international economic recession, mild weather, buyers' resistance to increased prices, and the reduction of stocks combined to bring about the first important reduction for decades in world petroleum production, down 5.4% in 1975. Consumption also declined by 1%, but with the upturn in the U.S. economy and signs of recovery in other countries, production revived in 1976. Production in non-Communist countries, at an average of 43 million bbl a day in the first six months of 1976, was nearly 7% above the level of the corresponding period in 1975. Saudi Arabia, producing over 8 million bbl a day, was 20% over 1975. Total U.S. oil demand rose 2.3% to nearly 17 million bbl a day, and imports were up 14.5%. Production increased 6.5% in the U.S.S.R. and 12%, some 1.6 million bbl a day, in China. The devastating effects of the earthquake in Tangshan may have cut China's production in the second half of the year.

There was growing interest in establishing national oil corporations. Early in 1976 the U.K., Canada, and Norway each established their own. In December 1975 Kuwait completed the takeover of the Kuwait Oil Co., and Saudi Arabia continued to discuss the takeover of Aramco without

A giant oil platform was built at Loch Kishorn in Scotland. Photo shows the concrete base being floated into the loch. Later it was to be floated out to sea.

PRESS ASSOCIATION

reaching a decision. Also in December 1975 the Egyptians repossessed the Sinai oil fields from Israel. Iraq nationalized the remaining foreign shareholdings and constructed an internal pipeline linking the producing northern oil fields with the new oil terminal at Fao, at the head of the Persian Gulf. This removed the need for transit arrangements with Syria and Lebanon.

Exploration continued worldwide. In the U.S. there were more well completions than in any year since 1965, and the total production figure was just maintained. In the North Sea five fields were in production. In Australia, by contrast, exploration activity declined. The importance of offshore drilling stimulated much scientific and engineering research into new methods and equipment, as technology was carried into deeper and more turbulent waters. The world's largest and heaviest platform jacket was completed in July 1976 for a field in the North Sea. Weighing 38,000 tons, it stood 606 ft high and had been designed to withstand 94-ft waves and 120-mph winds for operation in 530 ft of water. In Alaska there was tremendous effort to begin production on schedule in 1977.

There was an unprecedented world surplus of oceangoing tankers. At the end of 1975 surplus carrying capacity was reckoned at over 40% of available capacity, and it was estimated that about $35 billion of shipping debt was outstanding. The tanker fleet totaled 3,565 ships, an aggregate tonnage of 288.7 million tons deadweight (dw). Total carrying capacity increased by 35 million tons dw during the year, with new deliveries of 44.3 million tons dw and 8.8 million tons dw for scrap or losses. OPEC members owned only 5 million tons dw. Liberia continued to have the largest flag-registered tanker fleet, 30.7% of the world total, followed by the U.K. with 11.2%, Japan 10.9%, and Norway 8.9%.

RESERVES. At the beginning of 1976 total world "published proved" reserves had fallen to 666,100,000,000 bbl, compared with 720,400,000,000 bbl in the previous year. The Western Hemisphere share fell to 82,500,000,000 bbl, 12.3% of the total. Middle East reserves also fell, to 368,300,000,000 bbl, 55.5% of the total, while those of the U.S. were fractionally higher at 5.6%, compared with 5.4% in 1975. Western Europe, the U.S.S.R., Africa, and China figures were 25,600,000,000 and 3.8%, 80,400,000,000 and 12.1%, 65,100,000,000 and 9.6%, and 20,000,000,000 and 3%, respectively. Seismic and drilling activity continued in most parts of the world with considerable activity in the North Sea, Saudi Arabia, the U.S., and the U.S.S.R.

PRODUCTION. World oil production in 1975 decreased by 5.4%, or 8.5% if Eastern Europe, the U.S.S.R., and China are excluded, almost the same factor by which it had increased during 1969–74. For 1975, production was 55,095,000 bbl a day, compared with 58,170,000 bbl a day in 1974. The Western Hemisphere, with North America's production falling 6.2% and South America's 11.1%, registered an overall drop of 7.6%, 16,170,000 bbl a day and 28.9% of the world total against 17,465,000 bbl a day and 29.7% of the total in 1974. The Middle East easily retained its share of the world total at 35.9%, with 19,640,000 bbl a day, but registered a drop in production of 10.3%, compared with an annual average increase of 7.1% for 1970–75. The drop in production was not uniform. Dubai, Iraq,

AUTHENTICATED NEWS INTERNATIONAL

This self-propelled oil rig, built by two Japanese firms, travels at speeds of over six knots and can operate in rough seas. When drilling for undersea oil, it partly submerges.

Oman, and Sharjah recorded rises, while Abu Dhabi, Iran, Kuwait, Qatar, and Saudi Arabia had declines. Saudi Arabia retained the largest share of the world total for the Middle East, 12.7% and 6,970,000 bbl a day, compared with 14.3% and 8,350,000 bbl a day in 1974. Iran had 9.9% and 5,395,000 bbl a day in 1975, and 10.6% and 6,065,000 bbl a day in 1974. African production fell by 9.9% to 5,010,000 bbl a day in 1975, compared with 5,565,000 bbl a day in 1974, but its share of the total at 9.1% was little different from the previous year's 9.6%. In the U.S.S.R., Eastern Europe, and China, production increased in both volume and percentage terms. Figures were, respectively, 9,740,000 bbl a day and 17.9% of the world total, an increase of 7.3%; 400,000 bbl a day and 0.8%, an increase of 1.5%; and 1,305,000 bbl a day and 2.4%, an increase of 20.4%. In the North Sea oil production for Norway and the U.K. began, giving Western Europe a 1% share of production for the first time in years.

CONSUMPTION. World petroleum consumption registered a decline in 1975 similar to that of 1974, 1% compared with 1.2%. Western Europe registered the greatest fall, a drop of 5% to 13,540,000 bbl a day in 1975, or 24.6% of the world's total, compared with 14,180,000 bbl a day and 25.6% in 1974. Belgium and Luxembourg (3.4%), Denmark (3%), France (9.7%), Italy (5.1%), Switzerland (4.4%), the U.K. (13%), and West Germany (4.3%) all had consumption decreases, but consumption rose in Finland (3.3%), Greece (8.7%), Norway (4.3%), Portugal (5.1%), Spain (5.7%), and Turkey (9.1%). U.S. consumption of 15,845,000 bbl a day, 2.3% less than in 1974, remained the greatest single figure at 28.3% of the world total. The U.S.S.R. had the next largest share at 13.7%, 7,480,000 bbl a day, an increase of 8.3% over 1974. Japan was third with 8.9%, 4,905,000 bbl a day, a decline of 7.4% from 1974.

Imports into the U.S. fell 100,000 bbl a day in 1975. Reduced supplies from Canada and Latin America were balanced by increased supplies from the Middle East of 125,000 bbl a day. Middle East exports to Western Europe and Japan fell to 8,815,000 bbl a day and 3,675,000 bbl a day, respectively, but exports to Canada and Latin America increased.

PRODUCTS. In the U.S. gasoline dominated demand with 40%, followed by middle distillates with over 20%, fuel oil, and other products. In Western Europe, middle distillates and fuel oil predominated, taking more than two-thirds of the market with fuel oil having the greater share. In Japan fuel oil took over half of the market.

REFINING. The increasing surplus of refinery capacity throughout the world was perhaps most marked in Western Europe. About two-thirds of the total capacity of some 20,000 bbl a day was utilized in 1975. Nevertheless, refining capacity increased by 5.5% to 72,120,000 bbl a day, compared with 68,350,000 bbl a day in 1974. In the Western Hemisphere capacity was 25,190,000 bbl a day, 34.9% of the world total and an increase of 2.5% compared with 24,575,000 bbl a day and 35.6% of the total in 1974. In Western Europe, particularly Italy and Spain, capacity increased 8.7% to 20,920,000 bbl a day, in comparison with 19,250,000 bbl a day in 1974; this amounted to a world total share of 29% and an increase of 0.5% over the previous year. Japan retained its world share at 7.4% with 5,345,000 bbl a day, a 4.9% increase over 1974 but less than half the average annual increase of 10% for 1970–75. The U.S.S.R., Eastern Europe, and China slightly increased their total world share by 0.5% to 17%, a total of 12,250,000 bbl a day.

PETROCHEMICALS. Demand for products and construction of new plants dropped approximately 14.5% in 1975. The U.S. retained its position as leader in national construction projects. Fertilizer demand remained relatively high, and ammonia and urea plants represented a large proportion of new investment. In West Germany petrochemical output declined for the first time in 25 years. Western Europe, like Japan, experienced a substantial reduction in demand. The Middle East continued to build new plants, particularly in Iran, but technological and management problems tended to retard progress. With recovery from the economic recession of 1975 anticipated, demand for petrochemicals picked up in the first half of 1976. (R. W. FERRIER)

See also Engineering Projects; Industrial Review; Mining and Quarrying; Transportation.

[214.C.4; 721; 724.B.2; 724.C.1–2; 737.A.5]

Engineering Projects

Bridges. Following World War II there was a great surge in bridge building. Many bridges had to be rebuilt, and many planned before the war had never been built; also, the war itself had increased man's desire to move about. The need for transport within and between communities grew, and bridges became more necessary.

Appreciable changes in bridge design and construction took place during the postwar period. The quality of steels and concrete improved as did methods of construction. Rising labour costs and increased resistance to poor working conditions shifted bridge construction away from piece-by-piece erection at the site to prefabrication and assembly in shops. On larger projects, units weighing 100 tons or more were lifted into position. Riveting disappeared, to be replaced by welding and grip bolts. Steel plate replaced rolled sections, and prestressed concrete frequently replaced steel, at least for short-span bridges.

During the past few years many bridges planned at the height of the construction program were completed. By 1976 there was a lull in bridge construction while engineers rewrote codes of practice and specifications, taking account of changes in accepted practice and of lessons learned. The slackening-off in construction provided an opportunity to get complex analytical methods into perspective, paying due regard to the behaviour of structures.

Many new bridges would be required in the future. Rapid increases in transport costs and the need to transport more and more food and goods required route distances to be cut to the minimum. Bridges more than 40 years old would have to be replaced. Growth in bridge construction up to the end of the 20th century would be greatly aided by the recent significant increase in economic span length. Longer spans, making it possible to reduce the number of spans required, enabled construction to be transferred from the substructure—always liable to uncertainties due to unforeseen ground conditions or the difficulties of river flow—to the superstructure, where engineering problems could be resolved in advance of erection. The shift fitted in with the demand for better working conditions by transferring work away from the "dirty" job of foundation engineering to the cleaner tasks of off-site shop fabrication and assembly and the more spectacular work of superstructure erection. With the use of either steel or concrete box construction, spans of 300 m were expected to become standard rather than exceptional.

Moving day for a bridge. The new Oberkassel Rhine River bridge in West Germany slides into place after being moved 155 feet from approach at left where it was built.

WIDE WORLD

With general adoption of longer spans, ways of reducing the deadweight at mid-span would have to be found. The challenge of aerodynamics would have to be met if the tendency of such structures to oscillate in a steady wind or under a regular traffic load was to be avoided. Reduction in the deadweight of the structure would involve still greater use of orthotropic steel decks and of lightweight concretes, possibly with vented decks. Stayed girder bridges would become familiar structures. Wide acceptance of a thin epoxy resin coat in place of bitumen for the wearing surface on steel bridges would do much to eliminate wasteful deadload, but it would usually be cheaper to build more substantial structures.

Use of thin epoxy coatings forfeits the stress-distribution benefits of the thicker bitumen surface which in turn calls for better detail design of the structure to avoid local fatigue failures. The bitumen blanket offers a convenient opportunity to cover up variations in the steel surface and so provide a uniform running surface for the traffic.

With high-grade steel wire only slightly more costly than fabricated steelwork, designs making greater use of wire strands were expected to become more commonplace, both for stayed girder bridges and for suspension bridges. Recent studies in Britain aimed at improving the aerodynamic efficiency of decks and at reducing deadweight and making use of steel wire could form the basis for a completely new range of suspension bridges that would be economic at spans as low as 300 m. Designs had been prepared for spans of 3,000 m, more than twice the world's longest span of 1,410 m over the River Humber in England.

Despite the relative lull in bridge construction, a number of notable bridges were being built during 1976. In France, over the Seine River at Meules, a cable-stayed concrete bridge with a span of 300 m was under construction. In the U.S. a similar structure, the Pasco-Kennewick Intercity bridge, the first of its kind in North America, was being built over the Columbia River in Washington. In Britain the anchorages and concrete towers for the Humber Bridge were well advanced. About a quarter of the deck had been assembled in an adjacent yard. The bridge was planned for completion early in 1979.

Still nearer completion was the magnificent New River Gorge Bridge, near Fayetteville, W.Va. When finished, the steel arch bridge, with a span of 518.5 m, or 15 m more than that of the Kill Van Kull Bridge

KEYSTONE

Tomorrow's Paris? Multicoloured skyscrapers of unusual design are being built in the Paris outskirts. Their windows are round, square, and water-drop shaped.

between Bayonne, N.J., and Staten Island, N.Y., would be the biggest bridge of its type in the world. With its 23 approach spans it would carry the Appalachian Highway across the 915-m-wide gorge, 267 m above the New River.

In August 1976 one of Vienna's main road bridges, the 40-year-old Reichsbrücke, collapsed into the Danube, blocking one of Europe's main waterways. The 790-ft-span suspension bridge, one of the largest in Europe, had been the only bridge in Vienna to escape destruction during the German retreat at the end of World War II. Shipping on the Danube had to be held up for several weeks, and three temporary bridges were brought in to take road traffic.

(DAVID FISHER)

Buildings. The worldwide economic recession continued to affect the international construction market in 1976, and even the oil-rich Middle East nations were not immune. With what seemed almost limitless revenues anticipated from their oil, those countries had been envisaging unprecedentedly comprehensive and grandiose projects. During 1976, however, their expansion programs were pruned drastically. In Iran, for instance, cash flow difficulties placed an unexpected constraint upon development plans, which were re-evaluated in recognition of the need for controlled development.

A typical example of a project undergoing reevaluation was Shahestan Pahlavi, the planned new centre of Teheran, Iran. Approximately 5 million sq m of floor space were envisaged, including premises for ministries, government agencies, and banks as well as shopping and cultural centres, entertainment and recreational facilities, and residential accommodations for 50,000 inhabitants. An additional commuter population of 250,000 was foreseen, served by a subway system. The value of the transportation engineering studies, roads, and earthworks grading design alone was $32 million.

Several other large projects were under way despite cutbacks. In Qatar the Gulf University was planned to accommodate 3,000 students by the year 2000. Unlike many of the new buildings in the Middle East, where Western designs seemed to have been grafted unthinkingly and incongruously onto indigenous styles, this project made sensitive and sensible use of traditional Arab methods of cooling, ventilating, and indirect lighting. Two-story octagonal buildings, each topped by a "Tower of Winds" for ventilation, would be grouped around small courtyards, again a traditional feature of Islamic architecture, with shaded walkways connecting different parts of the campus. Despite the huge size and significance of the university, an intimate human-scaled environment was ensured for students and staff. Its traditional design notwithstanding, the project was to be realized by using the most up-to-date techniques of industrialized building through the setting up of a highly automated, precast-concrete factory.

In the West the pressures of growing ecological awareness and the need to conserve energy, coupled with the ever increasing costs of materials and skills, resulted in a low-key approach to changing needs. This often showed itself in the sensitive rehabilitation of old buildings rather than in the construction of sophisticated new ones. Rehabilitation of existing buildings depends on an engineering assessment of the viability of their structure. Given a sound structure, rehabilitation is a potential reality worthy of detailed study. The Theatre Royal, Glasgow, for Scottish Opera, was an example. While the neighbouring Edinburgh city council finally abandoned its long-planned and expensive scheme for a new opera house, this Victorian theatre in Glasgow was converted in a year into a versatile and efficient modern opera house, recreating the sumptuous warmth and plushness of the original. A similar problem of reuse was approached in a different way in Manchester, England. Within the empty Great Hall of the city's abandoned Cotton Exchange, a new theatre to seat 700 was constructed. A freestanding lightweight tubular steel and glass structure perched in the middle of the hall, accessible by steps from the existing floor, formed an entirely self-contained environment within the existing building.

Rehabilitation had its limitations in meeting new demands, even in ancient cities. On the outskirts of Vienna, Austria, the structure for a huge office complex was completed to be occupied jointly by the UN Industrial Development Organization and the International Atomic Energy Agency. Known as UN City, it was expected to cost the equivalent of $700 million when completed in 1979. The centre consisted of a cluster of buildings each Y-shaped in plan, ranging in height from 60 to 120 m, grouped irregularly around a circular central conference hall. The conference hall was supported from the roof. At the extremities of the "Y" of each office building stood a slip-formed

Putting a roof on "The Egg": The meeting centre at New York State Plaza in Albany nears completion. The state office building complex will cost nearly a billion dollars.

WIDE WORLD

load-bearing concrete tower. Three more stood at the hub enclosing a nonload-bearing core, so that the floors making up the arms of each "Y" were supported between the pairs of concrete towers.

A single but highly spectacular private commercial tower that employed a similar structural system to support its floors was the OCBC Centre in Singapore. Two vertical transportation and service towers 35 m apart were slip-formed to a height of nearly 200 m, and three huge transfer girders were constructed to link them at the 29th, 35th, and 49th floors. The lowest of the girders was of prestressed concrete, and the upper two of composite construction. This arrangement allowed a grandiose four-story-high, column-free banking hall to be built at ground level, while three stacks of 14 office floors above a plant room could each be constructed independently.

The largest cigarette factory in Europe, covering 13 ac near Bristol, England, and designed jointly by Skidmore, Owings & Merrill of Chicago and Yorke Rosenberg Mardall of London for W. D. & H. O. Wills, was completed. The most striking building in the complex was the production and packing area, a column-free space 180 by 90 m supported by nine Cor-ten steel lattice girders standing 10 m above the roof.

Off the California coast a $67 million oil platform was completed in 260 m of water. In effect a building about 290 m high, the platform was a relatively conventional earthquake-resistant welded steel structure. In contrast, the world's largest offshore concrete platform, weighing 400,000 tons and destined for the North Sea Ninian Field, was floated out from the construction yard.

Completion of the Arlanda Airport terminal in Stockholm, Sweden, and the Bush Lane office building in London demonstrated the structural versatility of stainless steel, but the most innovative design was the new, almost 200-m-high cooling tower for the Schmehausen nuclear power plant in West Germany. This consisted of a central pylon supporting an aluminum-covered steel web net weighing one-third of the equivalent conventional concrete design.

(PETER DUNICAN)

Dams. In 1976 increasing public awareness of their environmental consequences, galloping inflation worldwide, and a number of disastrous failures combined to make life difficult for those who had to plan, design, finance, construct, and manage large dam projects. Throughout the world projects were being increasingly opposed by factions representing particular interests, in many cases minority interests. In

Major World Dams Under Construction in 1976*

Name of dam	River	Country	Type†	Height (ft)	Length of crest (ft)	Volume content (000 cu yd)	Gross capacity of reservoir (000 ac-ft)
Agua Vermelha	Grande	Brazil	EG	295	13,090	25,689	8,900
Amaluza	Paute	Ecuador	A	558	1,345	1,513	97
Auburn	American (N. Fork)	U.S.	A	685	4,150	6,000	2,300
Balimela	Sileru	India	E	230	15,200	29,600	3,100
Bilandi Tank	Bilandi	India	EG	105	2,320	26,907	51
Chicoasen	Grijalva	Mexico	R	787	1,568	15,700	1,346
Fierze	Drin	Albania	R	518	1,312	916	2,124
Finstertal	Finstertalbach	Austria	R	518	2,034	5,742	49
Gura Apelor Retezat	Riul Mare	Romania	R	568	1,575	11,772	170
Hasan Ugurlu	Yesilirmak	Turkey	E	574	1,427	11,827	874
Inguri	Inguri	U.S.S.R.	A	892	2,513	4,967	801
Itaipu	Paraná	Brazil-Paraguay	ERG	591	25,918	35,316	23,510
Itumbiara	Paranaíba	Brazil	EG	328	21,981	47,088	13,806
Karakaya	Euphrates	Turkey	A	591	1,293	1,779	7,767
Kolnbrein	Malta	Austria	A	650	2,034	1,995	162
Kolyma	Kolyma	U.S.S.R.	R	427	2,461	16,415	12,000
La Grande No. 2	La Grande	Canada	ER	525	9,300	30,000	50,264
La Grande No. 3	La Grande	Canada	ER	320	12,800	30,000	49,615
La Grande No. 4	La Grande	Canada	ER	385	11,400	25,000	15,322
Las Portas	Camba	Spain	A	498	1,587	977	609
Miyagase	Nakatsu	Japan	G	505	1,348	2,551	167
Mornos	Mornos	Greece	E	414	2,677	22,235	632
Nader Shah	Maroon	Iran	E	574	722	9,418	1,313
Nurek	Vakhsh	U.S.S.R.	E	1,040	2,390	75,864	8,424
Olmapinar	Manavgat	Turkey	A	607	1,181	739	243
Oosterschelde	Vense Gat Oosterschelde	Netherlands, The	E	148	29,527	91,560	2,351
Patia	Patia	Colombia	R	787	1,804	30,869	15,322
Poechos	Chira	Peru	E	164	32,808	22,890	973
Raúl Leoni	Caroni	Venezuela	G	532	4,606	100,000	110,000
Rogunsky	Vakhsh	U.S.S.R.	E	1,066	2,506	91,560	9,485
São Simão	Paranaíba	Brazil	ERG	394	11,847	35,822	10,166
Sayano-Shushenskaya	Yenisei	U.S.S.R.	A	794	3,504	11,916	25,353
Sobradinho	São Francisco	Brazil	ERG	139	12,795	17,265	27,700
Sterkfontein	Nuwejaarspruit	South Africa	E	305	10,039	22,236	2,153
Takase	Takase	Japan	R	577	1,188	14,911	62
Tedorigawa	Tedori	Japan	R	502	1,355	12,613	187
Thomson	Thomson	Australia	R	530	1,800	12,600	892
Toktogol	Naryn	U.S.S.R.	G	699	1,476	3,787	15,800
Ukai	Tapi	India	EG	226	16,165	33,375	6,900
Ust-Ilim	Angara	U.S.S.R.	EG	344	11,695	11,382	48,100
Warm Springs	Dry Creek	U.S.	E	318	2,999	30,385	245
Yacyreta-Apipe	Paraná	Argentina-Paraguay	EG	125	164,000	91,560	14,079
MAJOR WORLD DAMS COMPLETED IN 1975 AND 1976*							
Beas	Beas-Indus	India	G	435	6,400	45,800	6,600
Chirkeyskaya	Sulak	U.S.S.R.	A	764	1,109	1,602	2,252
Chivor	Batá	Colombia	R	778	919	14,126	661
Cochiti	Rio Grande	U.S.	E	253	26,891	64,631	513
Dartmouth	Mitta-Mitta	Australia	R	591	2,264	20,012	5,232
Emosson	Barberine	Switzerland	A	591	1,818	1,439	182
Marimbondo	Grande	Brazil	EG	295	12,297	24,328	5,184
Mratinje	Piva	Yugoslavia	A	722	879	971	713
New Melones	Stanislaus	U.S.	R	625	1,600	15,970	2,400
Reza Shah Kabir	Karun	Iran	A	656	1,247	1,570	2,351
Tabka (Thawra)	Euphrates	Syria	E	197	14,764	60,168	11,350
Tarbela	Indus	Pakistan	ER	486	9,000	186,000	11,100

*Having a height exceeding 492 ft (150 m); or having a total volume content exceeding 20 million cu yd (15 million cu m); or forming a reservoir exceeding 12 million ac-ft capacity (14,800 x 10^6 cu m).
†Type of dam: E=earth; R=rockfill; A=arch; G=gravity; B=buttress.

ZENTRALFOTO/EASTFOTO

Bulgaria's new Antonyvanovtzi Dam will add 227 million kilowatt-hours annually to the country's energy capacity.

Canada, for example, the James Bay power project had been held up since November 1973 when the Supreme Court ruled that the works infringed on the rights of the Cree Indians and Eskimos. Compensation of more than $225 million was eventually awarded to the Crees and Eskimos for the ceding of territorial rights. Changes to the face of nature such as the creation of huge lakes at Kariba and Cabora Bassa in southern Africa brought with them other effects such as climatological changes and ecological problems, but on balance their benefit to the human race was undeniable.

The price of cement and labour costs resulted in a swing toward embankments and rock-fill dams to the extent that only 2% of the dams under construction in the U.S. were of concrete. The preponderance of embankment dams under construction lent point to the occurrence of a number of recent failures in this type of dam. In June 1976 the Teton Dam in eastern Idaho collapsed. Eleven persons were killed, and damage to property was such that 30,000 people had to be evacuated. The dam was an earth embankment with a crest length of 929 m and a height of 93 m. At the time of failure it was 97% complete and already impounded 308 million cu m. Leakage was noted two days before the collapse but did not increase to a level sufficient to cause alarm until the morning of the failure, giving only a few hours in which to warn the inhabitants of the valley. After the collapse of the dam, an avalanche of water surged toward Rexburg and Idaho Falls, spreading into a lake covering 25 sq mi.

Controversy had surrounded the Teton Dam from its inception, and the project was questioned on safety grounds by those opposed to its construction, who cited fears concerning the walls and floor of the canyon. These are formed of porous rocks with large fissures, and extensive grout curtains were to be provided to counter this situation. The U.S. had introduced the Dam Safety Act of 1972 to deal with safety aspects of dam construction, prompted by the Buffalo Creek Dam failure in West Virginia in February 1972, when 125 people were killed and some 4,000 made homeless by the collapse of a tailings dam. The Teton Dam, however, was not covered by this act as it was under the jurisdiction of the U.S. Bureau of Reclamation. Another embankment dam to fail in 1976 was that at Ropptjern, Norway, causing extensive damage but no loss of life.

Although the Tarbela Dam was completed in 1975, the fertile plains of Pakistan still awaited the huge volume of irrigation water promised by this project. The outlet works upon which the whole project depended had suffered an astonishing series of mishaps whose causes seemed far from clear to the many experts called upon to express an opinion. In August 1974 extensive damage occurred to tunnels 1 and 2, when concrete and debris were observed being discharged at the downstream end. This meant drawing down the reservoir and the loss of another year's impounding. More troubles were in store, however, for the outer chutes for tunnels 3 and 4 were badly damaged during the drawdown operation; damage was also suspected in the stilling basins of the reservoir, but this could not be observed because of the amount of debris deposited.

In the spring of 1975 tunnels 3 and 4 were again used to supply irrigation water, but this led to massive damage to the floors of the stilling basins and erosion and undercutting of the dividing walls to the extent that huge caverns were formed in the foundation rock. The situation was critical and the danger of a complete collapse was averted only by remarkable work involving divers and the placing of some 56,000 cu yd of concrete under water in less than a month. Although this work was successful in stabilizing the dividing walls, the floors of the stilling basins again suffered severe damage when the tunnels were operated in 1976. Huge blocks of concrete were taken out, but experts failed to agree as to the cause of the repeated failures in this area of the work. Some attributed it to cavitation and faulty design, and others to uplift, suggesting a possible connection with the troubles experienced immediately upstream of the dam where the location and plugging of sinkholes that had repeatedly formed in the area amounted to a major remedial operation on its own.

Recent legislation in a number of countries reflected the increasing awareness of the hazard that a large reservoir represents to life and property in the valley below. The French and British were among the first to establish regulations or pass legislation on the safety of dams, but the application and effect of these measures varied from country to country. The British Reservoirs Act of 1975 established the firm principle that the inspecting engineer must be truly independent and not in any way associated with the engineer responsible for the original certificates covering the construction of the work.

A major project completed in 1976 was the Emosson arch dam (height 180 m, crest length 555 m, storage 225 million cu m) on the Franco-Swiss border 20 mi N of Mont Blanc. Total cost of the dam and the associated pumped storage hydroelectric plant, to be shared by France and Switzerland, was SFr 700 million, 35% more than originally budgeted for. Turkey continued to harness the potential of the Lower Firat (Euphrates) for power and irrigation. Following the completion of the Keban Dam, the Karakaya project was begun; final design studies were also completed for the Golkoy and Karababa dams and power stations, which were to provide 1,300 Mw and the potential for an extensive irrigation project. Taiwan intended to develop further the famous Sun Moon Lake, a tourist attraction in the centre of the island already used for hydroelectric power, with a 1,600-Mw pumped storage project. In

Brazil many impressive dam projects were under construction, with a potential future capacity of approximately 20,000 Mw.

(J. C. A. ROSEVEARE)

Roads. Although no major single road project was completed during the year, there was no decline of activity in terms of starting new projects or road mileage actually completed. The reasons for the continued growth varied from one region of the world to the next.

In the less developed countries of Africa, for example, road construction increased as a result of the need to transport agricultural produce to ports for export and to open up new areas of country for agricultural development. In a number of such countries, there was also a change in the basic thinking that a road should be a subsidiary of the railway system.

In other parts of the world, such as the Middle East, the impetus given to road construction had other origins. Iran, Iraq, and Saudi Arabia embarked on ambitious road-building programs in the realization that their oil reserves were a finite asset. Their aim, therefore, was to establish the transport infrastructure that would serve an industrialized and commercial economy in the future. This involved not only the construction of roads spanning the country but also the construction of secondary roads linked to the major highways. These secondary roads, serving comparatively remote towns and villages, were regarded as essential to the agricultural development required for an enlarged industrial population in the future.

In the industrialized countries of the world, emphasis on road building varied as a result of the economic recession. In a number of cases, road-building programs were either reduced or delayed for budgetary reasons. Despite these cuts the vehicle population continued to increase, and the growth in the transport of goods by road continued in the face of campaigns to divert more of this traffic to other systems. The overall effect of the reduction in road construction was to aggravate environmental problems and to hinder recovery from the recession as trade improved during the year.

Development of the Middle Eastern countries greatly accelerated the growth of traffic originating from many European countries and converging on Turkey. The extent of this increase can be judged from the traffic using the Bosporus Bridge, which was opened in 1973. An average of 55,000 vehicles were using the bridge daily in 1976. In the planning stages of the bridge, it had been estimated that this rate would only be attained in 1989. In early 1976 the toll revenue had completely paid for the bridge construction costs, and a feasibility and engineering study of a second crossing was commissioned.

Urban road construction and traffic management was a major consideration of the year. The problem of commuter traffic to and from major cities was the subject of studies in many countries throughout the world. While the problem varied in detail according to the geographic characteristics of the city under consideration, it became evident that many solutions proposed in the past, based on mass transit systems, failed to meet the cities' needs. Evident from many of the studies, and in certain cases from practical experiments, was resistance to change on the part of the commuting public, with the result that even a massive increase in mass transport facilities produced a minimal reduction in private vehicle traffic.

(IRF)

FOTO-TANJUG/KEYSTONE

Bulldozers at work on a new trans-Yugoslav highway. The old two-lane road is in the background.

Tunnels. The construction of the world's longest railway tunnel was again held up in May 1976 when the 54-km (33-mi) Seikan Tunnel in Japan was flooded. Work on the pilot and main drives was resumed before the end of the year, and the expected completion date became spring 1983. A consortium of Japanese and Danish contractors developed three unique construction methods on the submerged tube under the Keihin Channel in Japan. A sand injection method prevented settling under the tubes as a result of earthquake. The use of alignment towers allowed easier placement of, and access to, submerged components, and a new form of jointing used water pressure panels and rubber gaskets rather than conventional concrete packing. In Hong Kong work began on the first section of the subway, which was to include an immersed tube under Victoria Harbour. The system was to have 15 stations and was expected to be operational in 1980. In Sydney, Australia, a cut-and-cover tunnel project costing A$10 million was completed. The tunnel, under Kings Cross in the centre of Sydney, had taken three years to complete.

In South Africa work began on driving 32 km (20 mi) of tunnel required to provide additional water supplies to Cape Province. Ground conditions were so variable that cut-and-cover, drilling and blasting, and conventional shield tunneling methods all had to be employed. In Egypt work commenced at Shallufah on the first road tunnel to be driven under the Suez Canal. One of the world's largest soft-ground tunneling machines, weighing nearly 800 tons, was to be used to drive the 10.4-m-diameter Ahmed Hamdi Tunnel. Completion was expected in 1980. In the United Arab Emirates traffic could now use the tunnel under the Dubai Creek, constructed by cut-and-cover methods. The contract had been completed in three years, exactly on schedule.

A historic breakthrough was achieved in March 1976 in Switzerland when the north and south sections of the safety tunnel in the St. Gotthard Tunnel were joined. The 16-km road tunnel, the world's longest, was expected to be in use by 1980. Work on the Furka Tunnel, the second longest rail tunnel in Switzerland, was delayed on account of bad ground conditions, and completion was expected at the end of 1978. The tunnel was one of the world's first civil engineering projects to use hydraulic rock drills exclusively. Austria and Yugoslavia agreed in 1976 to drive a 40-km-long road tunnel through the Karawanken range between the two countries.

In Vienna considerable ingenuity was employed in order to pre-grout the ground prior to tunneling for the new subway system. A 55-m length of tunnel was constructed in the Karlsplatz underground complex, beneath a large brick culvert carrying the subterranean Wien River. Spray concrete was then instantly applied to provide ground support in combination with steel arches and wire mesh.

In France an ingenious method of ground support was used during the construction of twin railway tunnels in Paris. An arch of horizontal bored tubes was installed to provide support to a sand stratum, prior to tunnel driving. The umbrella arch resembled a curved grid and later formed the crown of the excavated tunnel. At Marseilles work continued on the new Métro (subway), and it was expected to be functional in 1977.

In Frankfurt am Main, West Germany, the new Austrian tunneling method employing spray concrete was successfully used in conjunction with a large tracked heading machine for extending the subway. The 4.5-m-diameter tunnels were constructed using heading and bench methods through soft clay, and ground support was provided with gunite, steel arches, and mesh. In The Netherlands one of the widest submerged tube tunnels in the world was completed at Rotterdam under the Oude Maas River. The tunnel segments were 49 m wide and 115 m long. In Finland work continued on the project to provide water for Helsinki, and the longest continuous rock drive in the world at 120 km was expected to be complete in 1980. Fourteen headings were used.

In the U.K. the second annual meeting of the International Tunneling Association was held in February 1976. Work proceeded on the first immersed tube to be constructed in the U.K., a tunnel for the circulating water system for the new power station at Kilroot in Northern Ireland. Junctioning of the two main drives on the second Dartford Tunnel under the River Thames was scheduled to take place by the year's end.

Swiss workers excavating a ten-mile road tunnel deep in the Gotthard massif, due to be completed in 1980. It will speed north–south highway travel.

KEYSTONE

In the U.S. work on the Washington Metropolitan Area Transit scheme included all varieties of tunneling: hard rock, soft ground, cut-and-cover, and an immersed tube section. Construction started on the second bore of the Eisenhower Memorial Tunnel at Straight Creek in Colorado. In New York work resumed on the controversial water supply tunnel, the largest public works undertaking in the history of the city. The latest estimated cost was $500 million. In Canada part of the long-awaited massive extension to the Montreal subway system was completed in time for the 1976 Olympic Games. Work on this project was scheduled to continue until 1981.

(DAVID A. HARRIES)

[733; 734.A]

ENCYCLOPÆDIA BRITANNICA FILMS. *The Mississippi System: Waterways of Commerce* (1970).

Environment

In 1976 environmentalists found themselves concerned mainly with matters affecting land use and planning in urban areas. The principal controversy, arousing fierce debate in all the developed countries, was over nuclear power. The most dramatic and tragic incident of the year was the accidental release of large quantities of dioxin, a toxic by-product of the manufacture of a herbicide, at the village of Seveso in northern Italy.

INTERNATIONAL COOPERATION

UN Environment Program (UNEP). Maurice Strong retired from the executive directorship of UNEP at the end of 1975 and was succeeded by Mostafa K. Tolba of Egypt. UNEP experienced considerable financial difficulty during 1976 as subscribing governments reduced their contributions to its funds. It managed to continue its program, however, with a budget of $34 million for 1976 and $35.7 million for 1977. The program included organization of the UN Conference on Human Settlements (Habitat), held in Vancouver, B.C., May 31–June 11, 1976 (*see* Special Report), and preparation for the 1977 UN Conference on Desertification, to be held in Nairobi, Kenya. UNEP's information service was augmented in 1976 by the creation of Earthscan, an independent, but UNEP-funded, press agency based in London. Earthscan aimed to publicize environmental issues through articles commissioned from leading writers and published in newspapers and magazines, especially in less developed countries.

Marine Pollution. At a UNEP-sponsored conference held in Barcelona, Spain, February 2–16, 12 of the 16 nations attending signed a convention and protocols to "prevent, abate, and control pollution of the Mediterranean and to protect and enhance the marine environment in that area." The speed with which the signatories reached agreement suggested that a real determination existed to improve the quality of the Mediterranean. Building on the 1972 London Convention on the Prevention of Marine Pollution by dumping, the convention forbade the discharge of organosilicon compounds, all petroleum hydrocarbons, all radioactive wastes, and acids and alkalies from sources as yet unspecified, in addition to those substances listed in the earlier convention.

Following the Barcelona conference, UNEP or-

WIDE WORLD

The British-French Concorde supersonic transport aroused strong opposition among U.S. environmentalists when permission was sought for it to land at New York's Kennedy International Airport and Washington's Dulles International Airport.

ganized in Paris (June 16–18) a meeting of UN agencies to consider other regional seas, especially what it called "areas of concentration": the Persian Gulf, the Caribbean, the Malacca Strait and adjacent waters, and the Atlantic coast of West Africa. Guidelines were agreed on and principles established for comprehensive plans to protect regional seas through environmentally sound developmental strategies.

By August UN officials had visited the Persian Gulf and arranged an intergovernmental conference to be held in Kuwait in 1977; had consulted ten states bordering the Caribbean and planned a workshop to be held at the end of 1976 under the auspices of UNEP and the Inter-Governmental Oceanographic Commission; and had visited 14 of the West African coastal states for discussions. A workshop to examine the problems of the Malacca Strait was held earlier, in April. UNEP's efforts were augmented by the Arab League's Educational, Cultural, and Scientific Organization (ALECSO), which held two discussions, in December 1974 and in January 1976, to consider the pollution of the Red Sea and the Gulf of Aden. At the second meeting agreement was reached on a convention and protocols and a declaration of cooperation in a scientific research program.

The International Chamber of Shipping (ICS), representing the shipowners of 25 countries, announced on April 28 a new voluntary code of practice that would prevent the discharge of oil by ships at sea and would permit water used for washing tanks to be discharged only according to a strict standard of cleanliness and even then not less than 50 mi from the nearest coast. Similar provisions were contained in the 1973 Convention on the Prevention of Pollution from Ships, but because of technical difficulties this was not expected to become effective before 1980. In August 1976 the ICS described as "an extreme example of unilateralism" a U.S. proposal that would require all ships of 70,000 tons or more entering U.S. waters to have segregated ballast tanks. Such a move was considered inevitable, but its immediate introduction would confront tanker owners with conversion costs of up to $4 million per ship.

Ocean Resources. Hopes that the UN Conference on the Law of the Sea might offer guidance on marine pollution control and resource management were dashed when the latest session ended in New York City on September 17, still without having reached agreement. The next session would be held in New York from May 23 to July 9, 1977. (*See* LAW: *Special Report.*)

Progress was made in conserving whale stocks, however. The annual meeting of the International Whaling Commission, held in London on June 21–26, 1976, produced a confrontation between the conservationist nations, led by Mexico and the U.S., and the two leading whaling nations, Japan and the U.S.S.R. The whaling nations asked for sperm whale quotas roughly twice the size of those recommended by the IWC's Scientific Committee, but the IWC refused to compromise. Any member nation may lodge an objection to the IWC quota within 90 days, but on September 28, just after the 90-day period expired, Japan and the U.S.S.R. signed quota agreements.

European Economic Community. In May the EEC issued a directive designed to protect bathers in rivers, lakes, and coastal waters. The agreement on which the directive was based had been signed in December 1975, and it required all waters used for bathing to be brought up to the specified minimum standards of physical, chemical, and bacteriological quality within ten years. In Britain, where large quantities of sewage are discharged into the sea, there was consternation when it was realized that the directive would close many popular beaches.

NATIONAL DEVELOPMENTS AND POLICIES

There was concern over the condition of Laguna de Bay in the Philippines, one of the largest freshwater lakes in Southeast Asia, with a surface area of 900 sq km, and one of the shallowest, with an average depth of 2.8 m. The lake receives sewage from a population of six million living in its 4,500-sq-km catchment area, which includes Manila, Quezon, and three other cities, and industrial effluent from factories that doubled in number between 1974 and 1976. It also supports a thriving fishing industry, and fish farming, introduced in 1971, produced some 4,000 kg of fish per hectare annually by 1976. A major fish kill in 1975 aroused fears that the industries dependent on the lake would collapse. In September 1976 a semipublic body, the Laguna Lake Development Authority, announced that, with help from several UN agencies, the Asian Development Bank, the Colombo Plan, and the U.S. Agency for International Development, it had prepared a program to control pollution and develop the lake's resources.

England: *see* United Kingdom

English Literature: *see* Literature

Entertainment: *see* Dance; Motion Pictures; Music; Television and Radio; Theatre

Entomology: *see* Life Sciences

Lake Nakuru in Kenya was threatened by pollution from a factory making copper oxychloride fungicide. In January 1976 the Ministry of Finance and Planning accepted the recommendations of an official investigation into the operation of the factory, which would have required the withdrawal of its license. The Ministry of Commerce and Industry refused to act, however, and the pollution continued.

Stringent measures introduced by the Soviet government in 1975 produced signs of improvement in Lake Baikal, which had been seriously polluted by the effluent discharged by pulp and cellulose mills situated in its catchment area. In January 1976 it was announced that all sunken timber had been cleared from the beds of rivers that feed the lake, fish stocks had recovered, fishing was permitted once more, and two large fish farms had been opened.

The General Electric Co. was found guilty in February of having violated New York State's environmental protection laws by discharging polychlorinated biphenyls (PCB's) into the Hudson River. In September the company agreed to pay $3 million toward the cost of cleaning the river—probably by dredging out the bottom mud and incinerating it at a high temperature—and to spend some $5 million on modifying its own plant, so that all PCB discharges could end by July 1977. High levels of PCB's had also been discovered in some of the Great Lakes, and during the year they were found in the mother's milk of 30 women living in Michigan. A toxic substances control bill passed by Congress called for a complete ban on the manufacture and distribution of PCB's by early 1979.

In October a federal district judge in Richmond, Va., levied a fine of more than $13 million against the Allied Chemical Corp. for its part in contaminating the James River with the chemical Kepone, used in insecticides. The company had pleaded no contest to 940 counts of pollution relating to the period when it had operated a plant at Hopewell, Va., that manufactured the substance. Allied was cleared of charges that it had participated in the pollution of the James with the defunct Life Science Products Co., which had taken over the plant and supplied Allied with Kepone under contract. Allied and Life Science Products were among the defendants in civil suits for damages amounting to nearly $200 million, filed by former employees of the plant who had suffered neurological disturbances, including tremors and visual impairment, as a result of their exposure to Kepone, and by fishermen who had lost their livelihood when the lower James was closed to fishing. It was feared that the long-lasting chemical would eventually contaminate Chesapeake Bay. A possible similar incident came to light toward the end of the year, when it was discovered that some employees of a Velsicol Chemical Corp. plant in Bayport, Texas, where the pesticide Phosvel was manufactured, were exhibiting symptoms of severe nerve damage. The U.S. Environmental Protection Agency began a study of possible contamination of Galveston Bay, and the National Institute for Occupational Safety and Health planned to investigate other plants producing the chemical.

Damage from polybrominated biphenyls (PBB's) continued to plague residents of the state of Michigan. In 1973 PBB's, used chiefly in fire extinguishers, were inadvertently mixed with a livestock feed additive that was subsequently distributed to Michigan farmers. As a result, some 30,000 cattle, over a million chickens and other livestock, and thousands of tons of produce had to be destroyed. In November 1976 a large-scale testing program was begun to discover whether symptoms being reported by Michigan farmers and their families were traceable to the chemical and, if so, whether the health of these people was seriously threatened.

The Seas and Beaches. There were several incidents involving the confiscation of fish contaminated with mercury compounds. A quantity of tuna was seized by the authorities in Venice, Italy, and several consignments of dogfish ("rock salmon") were condemned by the Port of London Authority on their arrival from North American waters; ten tons were destroyed in this way in September 1976. In Japan the trial of two former executives of the Chisso Corp. on charges of involuntary manslaughter began on September 22. It was mercury waste discharged into Minamata Bay by the Chisso fertilizer factory that was blamed for causing Minamata disease.

Fears of substantial oil pollution grew as European offshore oil wells came into full production. The Norwegian State Oil Directorate published a report in April warning that in the event of a major accident, such as a blowout, 1.5 million tons of oil might be released before the situation could be brought under control. In May the Central Unit on Environmental Pollution of the British Department of the Environment also issued a report, giving its opinion that, by

Radioactive waste will be buried in these million-gallon tanks at Hanford, Washington, built by the Energy Research and Development Administration. The double-shelled concrete tanks are more than ten feet underground.

VICTOR K. MC ELHENY—THE NEW YORK TIMES

KEYSTONE

A West German group demonstrated against the building of a nuclear power plant near Brokdorf.

the time North Sea production reached its peak, 2,000 tons of oil would be released each year. A further report, published in September, stated that by 1981 there could be three or four large oil spills a year from tankers, one or two of them of more than 135 tons, and four or five spills of a similar magnitude from oil platforms.

Solid Wastes. On Jan. 12, 1976, the Waste Management Advisory Council, created a year earlier by the British government, published its first annual report, timed to coincide with the announcement that the government was to invest up to £1.1 million over four years in two plants that would sort wastes mechanically. The plants, at Newcastle upon Tyne and Sheffield, would be under the control of local authorities, and each plant would have a minimum capacity of ten tons an hour. One would extract ferrous metals and leave a residue rich in shredded paper and plastic that could be used as a fuel, while the other would test the mechanical separation of a wider range of materials.

The Control of Pollution Act, 1974, regulating the disposal of solid wastes, especially toxic ones, came into force in Britain in June 1976.

Land Use. In the U.S. the Federal Land Policy and Management Act, popularly known as the BLM (for the Bureau of Land Management in the Department of the Interior) Organic Act, was passed by Congress in October after several months of controversy. As originally passed by the Senate in February, the bill sought to consolidate the administration of almost all publicly owned land under the BLM and to increase the agency's authority, and it was strongly supported by environmental bodies, led by the Sierra Club. However, amendments proposed in the House favouring grazing and mining interests caused the club to mobilize its members in a campaign of opposition. In the bill's final form, the House provisions were substantially modified.

In Britain, the major land-use argument centred on expressways (motorways), and it brought environmentalists into bitter dispute with the Department of the Environment at a series of public inquiries. The environmentalists, led by the Conservation Society, argued that neither Parliament nor the public had debated and agreed on a comprehensive road policy and that the road-building program was being forced through by a powerful lobby. Their spokesman, John Tyme, appeared at several major inquiries, and those at Airedale, West Yorkshire, which began in December 1975, at Winchester in June 1976, at Hornchurch, Essex, in early July, and at Archway, in north London, in September were brought to a standstill and adjourned. By the end of the year it seemed likely that the procedure at the inquiries would be reformed. In September the Ministry of Transport was partly separated from the Department of the Environment. Environmentalists were not certain whether this would make the comprehensive examination of transport policy easier or more difficult.

Nuclear Power. In the world as a whole, the environmental argument of the year concerned nuclear power. The issues were not always simple. Generally they centred on reactor safety, the disposal of radioactive wastes, the transport and reprocessing of spent fuel, and the political implications of dependence on plutonium. In Britain there was also government indecision over the type of reactor that could best meet future needs, and some uncertainty over those needs themselves, since on March 10 the Electricity Council issued a forecast of future demand for electricity that was considerably lower than earlier estimates.

The U.K. prototype fast-breeder reactor at Dounreay, Caithness, Scotland, was brought up to its full power by late August. On September 22, however, the future of the fast breeder was placed in still deeper doubt by the publication of a report by the Royal Commission on Environmental Pollution, chaired by Sir Brian Flowers, which warned that the widespread use of plutonium fuel carried "grave potential implications for mankind," including the risk of nuclear blackmail by terrorists and environmental contamination from the accidental discharge of small amounts of radioactive material. The report advised against any expansion of the nuclear power program, or commitment to breeder reactors, until the major safety problems had been overcome.

The U.S. nuclear program fared no better. On Dec. 19, 1975, the Natural Resources Defense Council (NRDC), representing several environmental groups, filed a lawsuit to prevent the Nuclear Regulatory

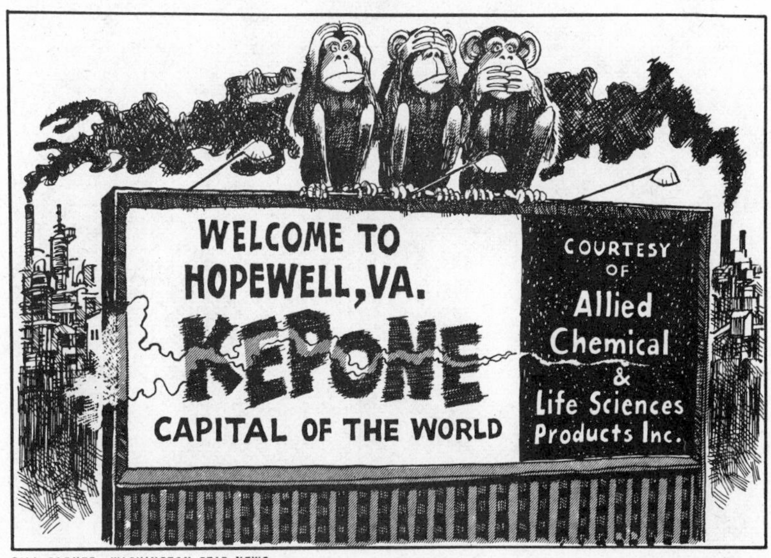

BILL GARNER—WASHINGTON STAR NEWS

AUTHENTICATED NEWS INTERNATIONAL

A Canadian pulp mill installed these 100-foot towers to cut down air pollution. Each tower contains a "scrubber" that removes corrosive sulfur compounds from the boiler gases.

Commission (NRC) from licensing facilities to recycle plutonium for fuel in U.S. reactors. In February the resignation of three nuclear engineers from the General Electric Co. was followed by the resignation of an NRC safety officer at the Indian Point reactor complex on the Hudson River. All four men joined antinuclear groups, and it appeared that morale within the industry was low.

In January the New York City Department of Health banned all movement of plutonium and spent fuel through the city, and on April 10 the American Civil Liberties Union joined the fray because it feared that security measures planned by the NRC would impinge on civil liberties. The Worldwatch Institute, in Washington, D.C., in its *Worldwatch Paper 6: The Fifth Horseman,* published on May 15, concluded that rising costs, uninsurable risks, and the necessity of a police state to supervise it meant that nuclear power might never contribute significantly to world energy supplies. The paper pointed out that in 1975, 25 nuclear power stations proposed in the U.S. were canceled or deferred for every one that was commissioned. The licensing activities of the NRC were further curtailed by a series of successful court suits filed against it by citizen groups during the summer. The debate became overtly political, and both major candidates in the presidential election campaign were drawn into it. However, propositions that would have limited nuclear energy development in several states were defeated in the November elections.

No such doubts were expressed in the U.S.S.R., where the fast-breeder program continued and the safety problems were considered to have been solved. France also continued to develop its nuclear power capacity, despite vigorous campaigns by the antinuclear environmental movement. In Switzerland, where work on a nuclear plant at Kaiseraugst, near Basel, was halted late in 1975 when protesters occupied the site, critics of the Swiss Federal Energy Department demanded a referendum on nuclear planning. The West German government encouraged public discussion of the issues, but there was little sign of any agreement between the two sides. In August 1976 the opponents of nuclear power were strengthened by the discovery, during a routine inspection, of a series of potentially serious faults at the world's largest nuclear power station, at Biblis near Frankfurt am Main.

In Australia a 24-hour strike brought all trains to a standstill on May 24 as rail workers protested against the dismissal of a supervisor who had refused to load chemical supplies destined for a uranium mine. It was in Sweden, however, that the issue produced its most dramatic political results. The defeat of the Social Democratic Party in the September general election was attributed by many observers, and by the outgoing prime minister, Olof Palme, to the unpopularity of the party's commitment to expansion of the nuclear industry.

If opposition to nuclear power was often emotional, it may have received firm scientific support in an article published in *Nature* in July. The article described a study of 13,000 people in Kerala, India, where natural background radiation levels are unusually high and where an apparent correlation was found between these radiation levels and mental retardation in children.

Pollution Hazards: Seveso. In the summer 29 members of the American Legion who had attended a state convention in Philadelphia died, and a number of others became seriously ill. It was later reported that their deaths may have been due to poisoning by nickel carbonyl, possibly released by the burning of refuse nearby, although the exact cause of the outbreak remained a mystery. (*See* HEALTH AND DISEASE.)

The British Health and Safety Commission urged much stricter control of potentially dangerous industrial plants and processes in its report published on September 13, and a Derbyshire factory making the herbicide 2,4,5-T (trichlorophenoxyacetic acid) closed voluntarily because it feared a major accident.

The type of accident the British firm feared occurred on July 10 at the Icmesa chemical plant at the village of Seveso, near Milan, Italy. This plant, a subsidiary of the Swiss multinational combine Hoffmann-La Roche, was also manufacturing the 2,4,5-T inter-

World's 25 Most Populous Urban Areas*

		City proper		Metropolitan area	
Rank	City and country	Most recent population	Year	Most recent population	Year
1	Tokyo, Japan	8,586,900	1976 estimate	27,037,300	1975 census
2	New York City, U.S.	7,567,800	1975 estimate	16,848,000	1975 estimate
3	Osaka, Japan	2,759,300	1976 estimate	16,772,900	1975 census
4	London, England	7,111,500	1975 estimate	12,606,700	1974 estimate
5	Mexico City, Mexico	8,628,000	1976 estimate	11,943,100	1976 estimate
6	Shanghai, China	5,700,000	1970 estimate	10,820,000†	1970 estimate
7	Los Angeles, U.S.	2,745,300	1974 estimate	10,316,600	1975 estimate
8	Ruhr, West Germany‡	—	—	10,278,000	1975 estimate
9	São Paulo, Brazil	7,198,600	1975 estimate	10,041,100	1975 estimate
10	Nagoya, Japan	2,071,400	1976 estimate	9,417,500	1975 census
11	Paris, France	2,289,800	1975 census	8,614,600	1975 census
12	Buenos Aires, Argentina	2,977,000	1975 estimate	8,498,000	1975 estimate
13	Moscow, U.S.S.R.	7,563,000	1976 estimate	7,734,000	1976 estimate
14	Chicago, U.S.	3,150,000	1975 estimate	7,623,300	1975 estimate
15	Peking, China	...	...	7,570,000†	1970 estimate
16	Rio de Janeiro, Brazil	4,857,700	1975 estimate	7,080,700	1975 estimate
17	Cairo, Egypt	6,133,000	1976 estimate	7,066,900	1976 estimate
18	Calcutta, India	3,148,700	1971 census	7,031,400	1971 census
19	Seoul, South Korea	...	...	6.964,860†	1976 estimate
20	Jakarta, Indonesia	...	...	6,178,500†	1977 estimate
21	Bombay, India	...	...	5,970,600†	1971 census
22	Philadelphia, U.S.	1,824,900	1975 estimate	5,764,500	1975 estimate
23	Manila, Philippines	1,450,000	1975 census	5,369,900†	1974 estimate
24	Teheran, Iran	...	...	4,716,000†	1975 estimate
25	San Francisco, U.S.	675,600	1974 estimate	4,579,800	1975 estimate

*Ranked by population of metropolitan area.
†Municipality or other civil division within which a city proper may not be distinguished.
‡A so-called industrial conurbation within which a single central city is not distinguished.

mediate compound trichlorophenol, an accidental by-product of which is a highly toxic dioxin, tetrachlorodibenzo-*p*-dioxin or TCDD. A pressure buildup in the process led to the release into the atmosphere of a vapour cloud variously estimated to contain from 2 to 130 kg of TCDD. Within three weeks, 700 people had to be evacuated from the danger area. No fewer than 500 of these showed symptoms of TCDD poisoning. Pregnant women who were affected were advised to have abortions, for the chemical was known to produce malformations in fetuses. Over 600 domestic animals were poisoned by the gas residues, and all those that survived were destroyed. All contaminated crops had to be destroyed by fire over a zone extending five miles south of the factory. A British expert on dioxin poisoning called in by the Italian government recommended that everyone in the area should undergo lifelong medical checks.

On September 26 another Italian pollution hazard occurred when a cloud containing heavy concentrations of arsenious oxide escaped from a fertilizer factory at Manfredonia on the Adriatic coast. People were forbidden to sell or eat local produce or to fish in the sea.

THE URBAN ENVIRONMENT

The centres of many older cities in the developed countries had been deteriorating for years, and by 1976 this had become a matter of urgent concern. As city centres became less pleasant places in which to live, the wealthier citizens moved out, eroding the tax base and leading to further deterioration and poverty. The most extreme example was that of New York City, where public expenditure had to be curtailed sharply, but other cities experienced similar difficulties. It was feared that Paris might find itself in a position similar to that of New York as the cost of providing its services was shifted from the state to the local government.

In Britain the secretary of state for the environment, Peter Shore, announced in September a major change in urban policy. No more new towns were to be planned. Housing densities in the suburbs would be allowed to increase, towns and villages would accommodate larger populations mainly by "in-filling," and housing would be provided in cities more by the renovation and modernization of old houses than by costly demolition and new building. It seemed likely that the opposition Conservative Party would adopt a similar approach. Peter Walker, a former Conservative secretary of state for the environment, told a Tory Reform Group seminar on September 9: "We have failed to learn from the appalling American experiences in which one inner city area after another has been destroyed because of lack of positive action when the trend of deterioration began."

Venice, too, had social problems. Michael Pacione, lecturer in geography at the University of Strathclyde, Scotland, told the annual meeting of the British Association for the Advancement of Science that the emigration of younger and abler citizens was leaving Venice populated by the old, the very poor, and tourists. He said the population of the city had fallen by one-third between 1951 and 1969. This was due

UPI COMPIX

The world's deserts are on the increase, often because of man-made damage to the soil. This wooded field in Kenya shows the marks of overgrazing by cattle and goats, which removed too much vegetation. The result has been erosion of topsoil and the formation of gullies.

in part to fears that the material fabric of the city could not survive much longer. In December 1975, however, Giuseppe Gambolati of IBM, who had made a computer model of the subsoil in the area, told journalists that subsidence was likely to stop and might have been arrested already.

On May 6, 1976, the Council of Europe adopted a five-year plan of intergovernmental cooperation covering regional planning, with special emphasis on urban development, the preservation of Europe's architectural heritage, improved town planning, and the protection of nature and the management of natural resources.

Shortly before the Habitat conference opened, the World Health Organization held its own 29th Assembly in Geneva, devoted to "Health Aspects of Human Settlements." The most essential urban improvement in many of the world's cities was the provision of reliable supplies of potable water and the hygienic disposal of sewage. In January the WHO had published *Community Wastewater Collection and Disposal,* suggesting ways of attacking sanitation problems, but it was criticized by some scientists for placing too much emphasis on waterborne sewerage systems, which are expensive in terms of capital and water, when alternatives were available.

(MICHAEL ALLABY)

THE NATURAL ENVIRONMENT

Land Conservation. A major forestry conference took place at Oslo, Norway, in June 1976, organized by the International Union of Forestry Research Organizations with support from the Food and Agriculture Organization of the UN. In a symposium entitled "Ways and Means of Reconciling Silvicultural and Operational Methods in Modern Forestry," a recurring theme was the conflict between the slow, natural growth of virgin forests and man's sudden, drastic interventions. These occur, for example, when timber is harvested by clear-cutting, followed by overall, artificial replanting on a large scale. Ulf Sundberg of Sweden's Royal College of Forestry declared that forestry had survived in Scandinavia only through the introduction of massive mechanization and large-scale clear-cutting, which offset soaring wages and shortages of skilled labour.

In the alpine forests of Switzerland, by contrast, mechanization was only permissible on a limited scale because the protective functions of the tree cover, as a shield against avalanche, flood damage, and associated soil erosion, were paramount. A Swiss expert commission reported that the cessation of timber harvesting, carried on over centuries by peasant farmer-foresters, was leading to a deteriorating forest with stands of aging trees, many of them dying slowly on their feet. The regular rejuvenation of growing stock, caused by seedlings filling in gaps left by fellings, had ceased. Artificial rejuvenation, through fellings carried out regardless of profit, appeared a possible, but costly, remedy.

A curious aspect of nature conservation was discussed in a paper by Madhav Gadgil of the Indian Institute of Science, Bangalore, and V. D. Vartak of the Maharashtra Association for the Cultivation of Science, Poona, entitled "The Sacred Groves of the Western Ghats in India." In these hillside groves, some as much as 50 ac in extent, all forms of vegetation are under the protection of the local reigning deity, represented by a shrine or statue. The removal of timber, or even dead wood, is taboo. As a result, many groves had survived for centuries as miniature nature reserves. Others had vanished, including a valuable timber stand at Ghol, where the timber merchant propitiated the resident god by sacrificing animals. As taboos weakened, more and more groves were being cut by villagers for firewood or charcoal. The authors recommended that temple trustees, forestry departments, or the Indian Board of Wild Life should undertake their protection.

Writing in the FAO's international journal of forestry, *Unasylva,* Joseph A. Tosi, director of the Tropical Science Centre, San José, Costa Rica, and R. F. Voertman of Grinnell College, Iowa, made a plea for the studied conservation of tropical forests, particularly in the Americas. Techniques of temperate zone plantation forestry and agriculture, they held, were out of place. Instead, the land-use system should maintain or imitate the natural vegetation of each site. Evidence was accumulating that in the humid and wetter tropical life zones, agriculture and animal husbandry can be integrated with sustained timber production to the benefit of both.

Studies by Margaret Bryan Davis of the Department of Biology, Yale University, at Frains Lake near Ann Arbor in southeastern Michigan, showed how rates of soil erosion may vary with changes in land use. By examining sediments that had accumulated in the lake from its closed watershed, she revealed a dramatic increase coinciding with the settlement of the region around 1830. The original, forested area lost only 9.5 metric tons of mineral matter per square kilometre each year. During the years of forest clearance and the first breaking of the litter layer by the settlers' plows, the amount of loss was 30 to 80 times greater. Later it became stabilized, but at a figure still ten times that under forest cover.

Paul D. Kilburn, a leading ecological consultant in the Rocky Mountain region, examined the environmental implications of oil-shale development, which was likely to begin in the foreseeable future in Wyoming, Utah, and Colorado. The extraction process involves heating the shale in retorts, leaving a residue of sterile, oil-free mineral ash that is difficult to revegetate. Commercial exploitation, on the scale of a million barrels (159 million litres) of oil produced daily, would pose enormous problems of soil and water conservation and of air pollution from extraction plants, as well as social problems arising from the influx of workers into thinly peopled regions. Combined

Environmental issues are sometimes difficult to settle. Court battles have raged for years over whether taconite tailings from an ore plant in Silver Bay, Minnesota, shown being discharged into Lake Superior (upper right), are a threat to public health.

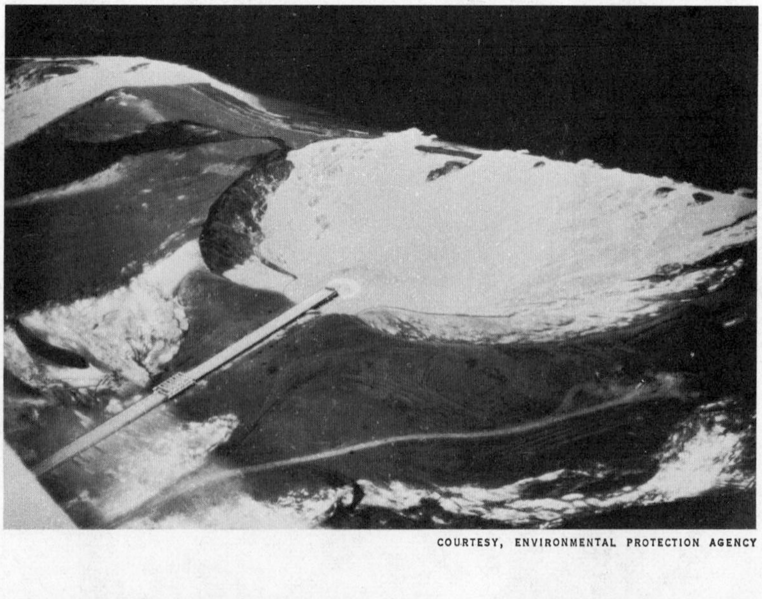

COURTESY, ENVIRONMENTAL PROTECTION AGENCY

resource planning, by developers and local government authorities, was essential to protect this unspoiled countryside, with its rich wildlife, from degradation into a man-made desert.

Water Conservation. Extremes of flood and drought, experienced in widely separated parts of the globe, showed that man's appreciation and control of his vital water resource were still inadequate. A major disaster was the collapse, on June 5, 1976, of the newly constructed Teton Dam on the Teton River in Idaho, which had been built despite the objections of experts. Eleven lost their lives as a result, and an estimated 30,000 were rendered homeless. (*See* ENGINEERING PROJECTS.) Two months later, on August 1, a freak flash flood in the Big Thompson Canyon in Colorado claimed more than 130 victims, many of them vacationers camping along the canyon. Downstream the river swelled to a lake 15 mi wide, strewn with the debris of automobiles and recreational vehicles, trees, homesteads, and farm machinery.

Maurice Arnold of the U.S. Department of the Interior advanced the view that most floods are man-made disasters, the outcome of faulty land management and unwise governmental programs. Planners placed too much reliance on artificial structures to control the immense energy of water flowing downhill and too little on overall control of the water regimes. A better plan would be to avoid close settlement and intensive agriculture on floodplains protected by levees and to use the areas at risk for conservation, recreation, and seasonal grazing. The levees themselves, however well sited, frequently lead to the silting up of channels, followed by bursts that start disastrous inundations. It might be better to let a great river, like the Mississippi, expend its energy over the bends of a wandering course.

England and Wales, together with the Channel Islands and the French region of Normandy across the English Channel, suffered a prolonged drought of unprecedented severity in 1976. Virtually no rain fell between April and September, resulting in parched grassland—a major resource for the pastoral farming communities—and low crop yields. In certain heavily populated areas, notably South Wales and Devon, which are dependent on surface runoff, local reservoirs sank to alarmingly low levels and for a time domestic users were restricted to standpipes in the streets, operated for only an hour or two each day.

Surprisingly, the Thames Valley water catchment, supplying London, was only lightly affected, since it relies on the previous winter's rainfall stored underground in an immense aquifer of porous chalk bedrock. By September, however, hydrologists calculated that the Thames had "sprung a leak," with more water flowing into this bedrock than emerged from it. The River Mole, a leading tributary, justified its name by disappearing underground, and at this point restrictions on consumption became inevitable.

Realizing, rather late in history, that Britain was an island with finite water resources, the government speedily passed a Drought Act, added water supply to the not too onerous duties of the minister for sport, and appointed a National Water Council. This body proposed a national water grid of pipelines to pool the resources of 11 catchment authorities, only recently established to succeed a multitude of local organizations having no overall responsibilities for supply and drainage. A start was made with the construction of the Kielder Dam, designed to divert water from the North Tyne River south toward the Tees.

AUTHENTICATED NEWS INTERNATIONAL

Three hundred green sea turtles launched themselves from a Florida beach. Classed as an endangered species, they were raised in tanks in an effort to repopulate the coastal waters.

In May an international dispute, smoldering since the completion of the Farakka Barrage across the Ganges River, flared up when thousands of Bangladesh protesters marched along the Indian border. India had built this dam, just within its frontier, to ensure that a quota of the Ganges water was diverted into the Hooghly River, which flows south to Calcutta. Bangladeshi farmers claimed a larger share for irrigation during the dry season and said navigation had also suffered. Indian road and river guards patrolled the barrage, which obviously checked the main flow of the Ganges eastward through Bangladesh.

In August Pakistan suffered disastrous floods involving 19 of the country's 21 districts, as well as the Pakistani-held portion of Kashmir. Over 150 people lost their lives, no fewer than 5,281 villages were reported to be entirely submerged, and a vast lake, with no land visible for miles, spread over the southern Punjab.

In the Sudan the Gezira Research Station faced new problems as farmers switched from cotton to food crops, particularly wheat. Agriculture over two million acres was dependent on the Sudan's share of the Nile waters, limited there to 32 million cu m a day. Peak demands occur in autumn, and the farmers preferred to flood their fields to soil capacity at that time, rather than promote trickles along furrows over longer periods. This made it exceptionally difficult for the Ministry of Irrigation to allocate fair shares.

Farther south, the Sudanese government pursued its ambitious scheme to drain 38,000 sq mi of swamps. By digging a 175-mi canal across a bend in the White Nile, from Jonglei in the south to the Sobat River above Malakal in the north, the authorities planned to prevent seepage and conserve supplies for agriculture downstream. Conservationists, who opposed the scheme, maintained that when water no longer evaporated from the swamp, rainfall would decrease over wide areas of semidesert. The nomadic way of life of the Dinka tribesmen who inhabit this marshy Sudd would inevitably be disrupted.

In Jamaica the Ministry of Health and Environmental Control admitted that an enormous lake of caustic red mud, a waste product of the aluminum industry, constituted a serious threat to the purity of the great underground water basin that supplies the southern part of the island. No action was taken, possibly because the bauxite and aluminum industries are a major source of national revenue.

(HERBERT L. EDLIN)

Wildlife. On Dec. 21, 1975, the Convention on Wetlands of International Importance, Especially as Waterfowl Habitat came into force—important because of the scientific, educational, and recreational value of wetlands which provide migrating and winter refuges for waterfowl and other birds. On Jan. 1, 1976, the U.K. introduced a licensing system to implement the Washington Convention on International Trade in Endangered Species of Wild Fauna and Flora. The Nature Conservancy Council became responsible for advice on policy; the Royal Botanic Gardens, Kew, for flora; and a committee appointed by the Department of the Environment, for fauna. This replaced and enlarged the scope of the organization that had administered the Animals (Restriction of Importation) Act, 1964. On Aug. 3, 1976, the U.K. became the 28th state to ratify the Washington Convention. In February the Royal Society for the Protection of Birds launched a new inquiry into the importation of captive birds through London Airport in conditions contravening the regulations of the International Air Transport Association.

In February the National Parks Service of the Galápagos Islands (Ecuador), in collaboration with the Charles Darwin Foundation, held a training course for guides covering the natural history of the archipelago. Special emphasis was given to tourism; the existence of the Galápagos park depended on the promotion of tourism which, at the same time, constituted a threat to the park's ecology. Elimination of the wild goats, which had devastated the vegetation and thus destroyed most of the habitat of the giant tortoises and other unique fauna, continued. On San Salvador (James) Island, where some plants were in imminent danger of extinction, quadrants of representative vegetation improved dramatically after being enclosed with goatproof fences.

On May 26 the Agreement on Conservation of Polar Bears came into force following ratification by the U.S.S.R. Norway and Canada had already ratified; Denmark and the U.S. had signed but not yet ratified. The agreement, drafted by the International Union for Conservation of Nature, prohibited the hunting, killing, or taking of polar bears, except for scientific or conservation purposes or by local (Eskimo) peoples who depended on polar bears and other Arctic animals for food. Parties to the agreement also undertook to protect the ecosystems of which polar bears form a part, with special attention to habitat requirements such as denning, feeding sites, and migration patterns.

In July the Fauna Preservation Society (FPS) drew attention in *Oryx* to the threat to two other Arctic animals: the narwhal, one of the toothed whales, whose long, spiral frontal tusk made it a much prized quarry; and the walrus. At the same time FPS reported the discovery in West Malaysia of a group of from 10 to 20 Sumatran rhinoceroses. This hairy rhinoceros is the smallest and most active of the five species of rhinoceros, three of which are Asiatic. Its ultimate survival might depend on the preservation of a small area of forest essential to this newly discovered group.

In June the International Council for Bird Preservation published its fifth report on Cousin Island, its 27-ha reserve in the Seychelles. This tiny island carried a breeding population of over one million birds, among which the brush warbler, which breeds not in pairs but in groups of three to five birds, and the fairy tern were few in number but especially important. Cousin also provided sanctuary for the endangered hawksbill and green turtles; the decline in the hawksbill was attributed mostly to the Japanese tortoiseshell trade. Conservation and scientific work on Cousin, including the tagging of breeding turtles, continued throughout the year. Another step to save the world's turtles had been taken in February when, on the advice of FAO adviser Robert Bustard, the exploitation of a newly discovered breeding ground in Orissa (northeast India) was stopped and the area was included in the Bhitar Kanika sanctuary, formed in 1975 to protect the salt-water crocodile, *Crocodylus porosus*.

Throughout 1976 the New Zealand Wildlife Service, supported by the Royal Forest and Bird Protection Society, intensified its efforts to save from extinction two of the world's rarest birds—the black or Chatham Islands robin and the kakapo, a large, flightless, browsing, nocturnal parrot. The black robin was believed extinct until it was "rediscovered" on Little Mangere Island in 1937. By the end of the 1976 breeding season the total robin population on this tiny island was 12, and the survival of the species depended on the success of reafforestation on the larger Mangere Island, being carried out in order to reintroduce the robin there.

The kakapo, of which only ten were known to exist, was threatened directly by stoats and rats while its habitat, in Fiordland (South Island, N.Z.), was endangered by deer, chamois, and opossums. Hope for the kakapo centred on the success of its introduction into a reserve on Maud Island in the Marlborough Sounds, which was free of man-introduced pests and within the historic range of the kakapo. Water points were built and fruit trees planted to provide an autumn berry supply similar to that in the birds' remaining wild habitat. Three introduced kakapo, two males and one of unknown sex, established territories on Maud Island, and in 1976 courtship booming was heard.

The 1975 J. Paul Getty $50,000 Wildlife Conservation Prize was awarded in February 1976 in Washington, D.C., to the veteran Indian ornithologist Salim A. Ali.

(C. L. BOYLE)

See also Agriculture and Food Supplies; Energy; Fisheries; Historic Preservation; Life Sciences; Transportation.

[355.D; 525.A.3.g and B.4.f.i; 534.C.2.a; 724.A; 737.C.1]

ENCYCLOPÆDIA BRITANNICA FILMS. *The House of Man, Part I—Our Changing Environment* (1965); *The Pond and the City* (1965); *Waterfowl: A Resource in Danger* (1966); *Problems of Conservation: Air* (1968); *The Everglades: Conserving a Balanced Community* (1968); *The House of Man, Part II—Our Crowded Environment* (1969); *Problems of Conservation: Forest and Range* (1969); *Problems of Conservation: Minerals* (1969); *Problems of Conservation: Soil* (1969); *Problems of Conservation: Water* (1969); *The South—Roots of the Urban Crisis* (1969); *The Industrial City* (1969); *The Rise of the American City* (1969); *The Garbage Explosion* (1970); *Problems of Conservation: Our Natural Resources* (1970); *Problems of Conservation: Wildlife* (1970); *A Field Becomes a Town* (1970); *What Is a Community?* (2nd ed., 1970); *The Aging of Lakes* (1971); *Turn Off Pollution* (1971); *The Ways of Water* (1971); *Noise—Polluting the Environment* (1971); *Poison Plants* (1972); *The Great Lakes: North America's Inland Seas* (2nd ed., 1972); *The Environment: Everything Around Us* (1972); *Buffalo: An Ecological Success Story* (1972); *Controversy over Industrial Pollution: A Case Study* (1972); *Our Changing Cities: Can They Be Saved?* (1972); *The Image of the City* (1973); *Energy: A Matter of Choices* (1973); *The Salt Marsh: A Question of Values* (1975).

Epidemics: *see* Health and Disease

Episcopal Church: *see* Religion

HABITAT AND THE HUMAN CONDITION

By Harford Thomas

Within four years the United Nations has staged five world conferences on special themes of global concern: the Conference on the Human Environment at Stockholm in 1972; the World Population Conference at Bucharest, Rom., and the World Food Conference at Rome, both in 1974; the World Conference of the International Women's Year at Mexico City in 1975; and the Conference on Human Settlements (Habitat) at Vancouver, B.C., in 1976. Together they constitute a searching reappraisal of the human condition, marking a reversal of many of the assumptions of the recent past.

The 1950s and 1960s were years of rapid economic growth in Western countries. They also saw the beginning of industrialization in the less developed world, where the expectation of life increased as health conditions improved. Food production seemed to be keeping pace with population. In this period most of the former colonial territories won their independence. The prevailing mood was thus one of confidence in the future.

Then doubts began to set in. Pollution became a threat to the whole environment. Food production declined in the poor harvest years of 1972 and 1973. How could the planet's resources of food, energy, and raw materials sustain both a hectic rate of growth in the developed world and the population explosion in the third world? This was the agenda for the world conferences of the 1970s.

Forums for New Thinking. Habitat, therefore, was part of an interconnected sequence, a complex of global unease and anxiety that represented a great awakening from the bland disregard of a decade ago and could come to be seen as a watershed in world thinking. These conferences have been criticized for generating little but mountains of paper and clouds of words. This criticism misses the point. They are not in the normal run of UN activities. Their function has been to assemble world opinion, information, and ideas on a single broad theme. They have been set up in great detail by preparatory committees that have brought together the knowledge and views of the world's leading experts. They have provided the focal point and the occasion for pooling and exchanging information and the best-informed opinion from all countries of the world. So even before the conference opens, a massive operation in global education has been set in motion.

Constitutionally, the conferences do not have the authority to make decisions. They draft declarations and recommendations for action that go forward to the UN General Assembly and other appropriate UN organizations such as the Food and Agriculture Organization or the Economic and Social Council. To answer the question, what have they done, one would have to trace the effect of their recommendations back through numberless channels of the UN structure and the administration of each of the UN's member governments. Some things have been done directly at the instigation of a conference, such as the setting up of the UN Environment Program (UNEP) with its Earthwatch monitoring system and the formation of the World Food Council. But the main achievement of the conferences has been to clarify, crystallize, and broadcast new ideas, new strategies, and new techniques for meeting the needs of mankind. They have acted as catalysts for changing ideas and attitudes.

It is in this sense that Habitat should be considered. Judged simply (oversimply, that is to say) as a 12-day conference (May 31–June 11) it was something of a disaster. The Palestine Liberation Organization (PLO) and its attendant lobby of like-minded countries chose to make the conference their platform. The conference was split wide open by an amendment associating the Vancouver Declaration on Human Settlements with the condemnation of Zionism as racism in the terms of the General Assembly resolution of November 1975. This was unacceptable to 25 countries, including most of the leading Western nations. To have any force, a declaration of principles must be carried by consensus. The Vancouver declaration lacks this authority.

All was not lost, however. A complementary document listing "Recommendations for National Action" (64 of them, filling 80 pages of text) was adopted by consensus except for two PLO amendments. The document embodies in some detail all the central features of the new thinking on human settlements and was described by Habitat's secretary-general, Enrique Peñalosa (Colombia), as "revolutionary in scope."

Exploding Cities. World population, doubling from 2,000,000,000 in 1930 to 4,000,000,000 in 1976 and likely to redouble to 8,000,000,000 in the next 35 years, sets the scale of the crisis of human settlements that Habitat had to consider. In 1900 there were 11 cities with populations of a million or more; in 1950 there were 75; in 1975, 191; and by 1985 there will probably be about 300. Projections suggest that by the year 2000 there will be a dozen or so cities with populations approaching 20 million or more, a few of them around 30 million. But while the big cities provide the most sensational statistics, about two-thirds of the world's people still live in rural areas. By the end of the century the urban-rural distribution is likely to be about half and half if present trends continue, for the population of the world's exploding cities, as they have been called, is being fed by migration from country to town.

This migration is on a scale far beyond anything known before. The city administrations cannot cope with the problem and the migrants therefore become shantytown squatters. In many cities of the third world one-third or more of the population is made up of squatters. Meanwhile, the poverty of the villages has been growing worse, often, paradoxically, as the result of the introduction of modern farming techniques that call for the use of machines and improved seed and fertilizers that only the relatively well-to-do farmers can afford. The poorer peasants cannot compete and are forced to sell out, slipping into the category of "marginal men" living at the rock-bottom level of subsistence. The enterprising ones leave for the big city where there is more hope, even in the squalor of the shantytowns.

It follows that one of the basic causes of the crisis of human settlements is sheer poverty, and one precondition for any early solution is the transfer of a proportion of the huge spending power of the developed world to the third world. This is mentioned in the Habitat Declaration, which confirms the UN call for a new international economic order to shift the balance of economic advantage in favour of the third world—a theme also at the 1976 meeting of the UN Conference on Trade and Development (UNCTAD) and that of the International Labour Organization (ILO) on world employment.

Urban Pioneers. But Habitat was more immediately concerned with determining what practical action could be taken to improve conditions of living in the world's towns and villages. Here the experts had already been at work and were coming up with answers that suggest the situation is not so hopeless as it may look. The message that came out of Habitat is that the one great untapped resource is human skill. The people who migrate to the cities are, as it were, urban pioneers, with resource, ingenuity, and fortitude. Perforce, they have to fend for themselves. The planners and sociologists who have studied "the

---

Harford Thomas, a regular contributor to the Britannica Book of the Year, *was formerly deputy editor of* The Guardian, *London.*

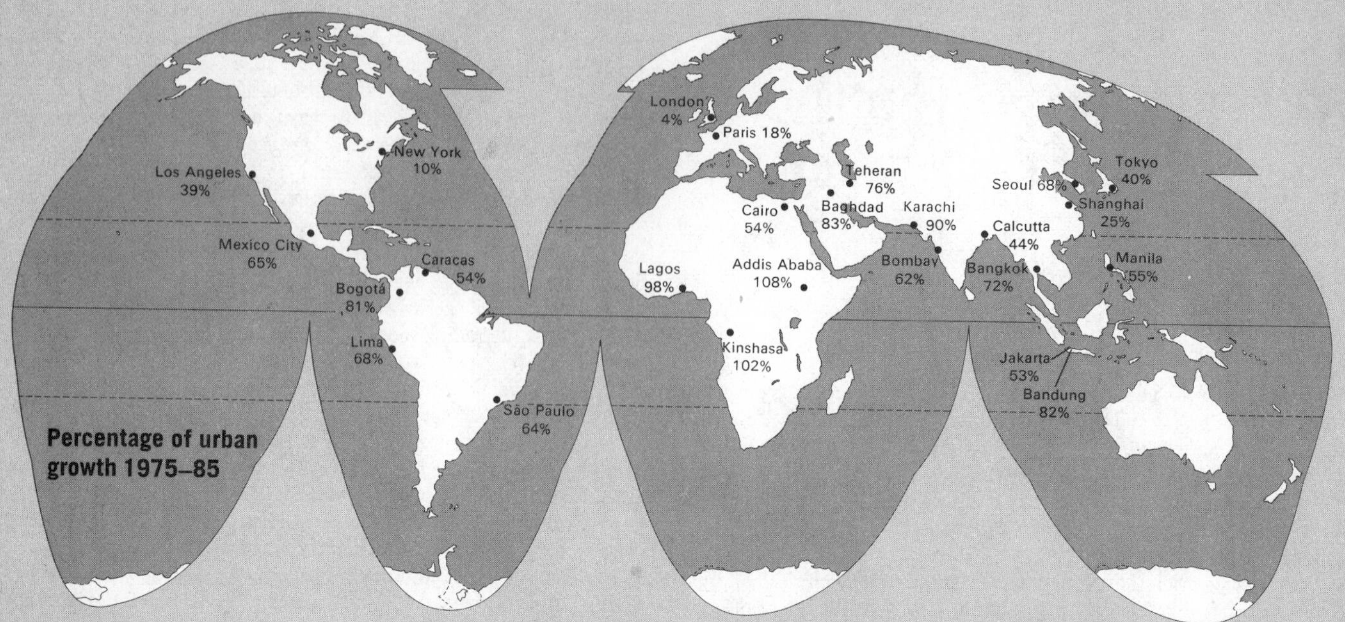

informal sector," as the shantytowns are euphemistically called, see it as a triumph of self-help. The migrant typically starts in the roughest shack and finds some sort of occasional work. Over the years he may establish himself as an independent craftsman or tradesman, and gradually he extends and improves his home, which as likely as not is built on a patch of ground with no legal right of tenure.

The theory now advanced is that urban authorities should encourage and support this potential for self-help. It is far beyond the capacity of the authorities to build dwellings for all the people who need them. Indeed, those who need them cannot afford to rent the kind of apartments an urban authority may provide. Hence, a more realistic approach is being developed: to provide site and services: a plot of land with basic services such as water and sewerage and road access, possibly some building materials, and cheap loans. The rest is up to the urban settler.

The philosophy of self-help also underlies the development of small-scale, labour-intensive technologies, which are now favoured as preferable alternatives to costly and inappropriate high technology imported from the West. This new approach expresses both the practicality and the personal satisfaction to be found in small-scale enterprise. It is the theme of E. F. Schumacher's book *Small Is Beautiful* and of the Intermediate Technology Development Group he founded. These ideas can be found in many sections of the Habitat Declaration and recommendations.

Human Scale in Housing. Rather unexpectedly, perhaps, much of the new philosophy of housing and town planning was found to fit the developed world as well as the third world. Each country had been asked to report to the conference on its own experience. From the developed world came evidence of a disenchantment with large-scale technology, a return to the attractions of human scale, and a greater reliance on personal initiative and participation in housing and town planning. In the U.S. the prizewinning Pruitt-Igoe public housing project in St. Louis, Mo., had been vandalized to such an extent that it had to be demolished. In Britain, London and Liverpool also had their vandalized tower blocks, and the faceless anonymity of the high-rise housing developments of the 1950s and 1960s was ferociously exposed in the U.K.'s official film made for Habitat. In the U.K. policy had shifted away from wholesale clearance and redevelopment to the rehabilitation of existing housing and the building of smaller, more intimate groups of low-rise housing in close-knit patterns of streets and squares.

The notion of self-help and participation also found favour. Housing cooperatives and tenant cooperatives were given official support in the U.K. Procedures were devised to help people manage their own housing improvement schemes. At the same time, local authorities were finding it more and more difficult to build the increasingly expensive old-style giant housing developments and to let dwellings at rents people in lower income groups could afford. Architects were beginning to turn their attention to designing cheaper and more simple buildings. Some of these new trends are examined in a book by the English architect John F. C. Turner, *Housing by People* (1976), which makes the point that centralized and bureaucratic institutions are incapable of providing *for* people the kind of housing they want. Although it strikes many responsive chords in recent British experience, Turner's views are derived largely from his studies in the shantytown areas of the cities of Peru and Mexico.

One obvious point that Habitat confirmed is that there is no single solution. The answers must spring from the local situation and employ local skills and local materials. Yet certain general ideas were found to have universal application. One was the need to consult and involve the individual in decisions about his own home. The Vancouver recommendations include a long section on participation, which is declared to be "a human right, a political duty, and an instrument essential for national development." Similarly, they give much attention to land ownership, which is an obstacle to good planning in many countries, and insist that the use of land must be subject to control in the public interest.

The Unofficial Forum. These world conferences of the 1970s have themselves applied the principle of participation by inviting nongovernmental organizations (NGO's; charities, amenity protection groups, conservationist societies, and the like) to take part in a parallel conference or forum. It has been a strikingly successful innovation, of great importance educationally, and a significant influence on official thinking. One of the leaders of this movement of the NGO's has been the economist Barbara Ward (Lady Jackson), joint author of *Only One Earth,* written for the Stockholm conference, and author of *The Home of Man,* written for Habitat. She and her colleagues were instrumental in securing the adoption of one of the most practical and perhaps the most urgent recommendation for action: a target objective for clean water for all by 1990.

It may appear starry-eyed at the moment, but in fact the clean water objective epitomizes one key conclusion about the human condition. The situation is not hopeless. The skills are available, in the intelligence and capacity of millions of underemployed people. The money could be made available. The World Bank has calculated the annual cost of a ten-year program to provide clean water for all human settlements at about U.S. $3 billion. That is a mere 1% of what the world spends each year on arms.

Equatorial Guinea

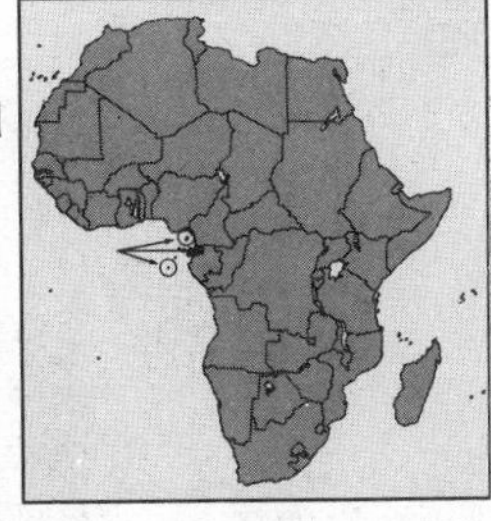

The African republic of Equatorial Guinea consists of Río Muni, which is bordered by Cameroon on the north, Gabon on the east and south, and the Atlantic Ocean on the west; and the offshore islands of Macías Nguema Biyogo (until 1973 called Fernando Po) and Pagalu (formerly Annobón). Area: 10,830 sq mi (28,050 sq km). Pop. (1976 est.): 316,000. Cap. and largest city: Malabo, on Macías Nguema Biyogo (pop., 1970 est., 19,300). Language: Spanish. President in 1976, Francisco Macías Nguema.

Ill treatment and nonpayment of wages of Nigerian nationals employed on Equatorial Guinea's cocoa plantations on Macías Nguema Biyogo led the Nigerian government to repatriate up to about half of the 45,000 Nigerians so employed by the beginning of 1976.

Alarm at the consequences to the country's agriculture led President Macías' government to attempt to block the continuing evacuation, and on January 7 troops fired on Nigerians at Malabo, killing 11. Nigeria demanded compensation and did not discourage clamour from its citizens for the annexation of Macías Nguema Biyogo. President Macías then ordered the pressing of more than 20,000 Equatorial Guinea mainlanders into work on the plantations under conditions of slave labour; the Anti-Slavery Society prepared a report on the subject for the UN Human Rights Commission in August.

The exiled opposition, the Alianza Nacional de Restoración Democrática (ANRD), based in Geneva, Switzerland, held a congress in April at which a 21-member central committee and a 7-member executive committee were appointed. The ANRD, which published an information journal, *La Voz del Pueblo*, claimed that the numbers of refugees abroad in 1976 amounted to approximately a quarter of the population—60,000 in Gabon, 30,000 in Cameroon, and others in Spain and Nigeria—and demanded help from Europe to end Macías' tyranny. Meanwhile, executions and assassinations of prominent people and the burning of villages on Macías' orders were reported.

(MOLLY MORTIMER)

[978.E.7.b]

EQUATORIAL GUINEA

Education. (1973–74) Primary, pupils 35,977, teachers 630; secondary (1972–73), pupils 4,713; vocational (1972–73), pupils 586; teacher training (1970–71), students 213; secondary, vocational, and teacher training (1970–71), teachers 175.

Finance and Trade. Monetary unit: ekpwele, at par with the Spanish peseta, with (Sept. 20, 1976) a free rate of 67.82 ekpwele to U.S. $1 (116.85 ekpwele = £1 sterling). Budget (1970): revenue 709.4 million ekpwele; expenditure 589.3 million ekpwele (excludes capital expenditure of 650.7 million ekpwele). Foreign trade (1970): imports 1,472,100,000 ekpwele (80% from Spain); exports 1,740,900,000 ekpwele (91% to Spain). Main exports: cocoa 66%; coffee 24%; timber 9%. Trade with Spain (1975): imports 453 million ekpwele; exports 822 million ekpwele.

Agriculture. Production (in 000; metric tons; 1975): sweet potatoes *c.* 30; bananas *c.* 12; cocoa 14; coffee *c.* 7; palm kernels *c.* 2; palm oil *c.* 4. Livestock (in 000; 1974): sheep *c.* 31; cattle *c.* 4; pigs *c.* 7; goats *c.* 7; chickens *c.* 80.

Equestrian Sports

Thoroughbred Racing and Steeplechasing.

UNITED STATES AND CANADA. Forego was almost unanimously acclaimed horse of the year, as well as outstanding older colt or gelding, for the third consecutive time in 1976. Although six, he had his finest season while successfully carrying the highest weights of his career. After launching the season with victory in a seven-furlong allowance race, Forego won five of seven stakes starts. He began with the 1-mi Metropolitan, carrying 130 lb, and the 1⅛-mi Nassau County under 132 lb. He then lost by a nose to Foolish Pleasure in the 1³⁄₁₆-mi Suburban (134 lb) and won the 1¼-mi Brooklyn (134 lb). Forego finished third to Hatchet Man and Intrepid Hero in the Haskell (136 lb), beaten by only a length, and then climaxed the season with brilliant triumphs in the 1⅛-mi Woodward (135 lb) and the 1¼-mi Marlboro (137 lb). Bill Shoemaker (*see* BIOGRAPHY), who rode Forego for the first time in the Woodward, said of the Marlboro, "That was the greatest race a horse ever gave me." Racing over a sloppy track in the Marlboro, Forego was forced wide on the final turn and was four lengths behind Honest Pleasure (119 lb) at the furlong pole. Victory seemed impossible, but Shoemaker and Forego combined their rare talents to win by a head.

Forego suffered an injury to the ankle of his right foreleg on the eve of the $300,000 Jockey Club Gold Cup, for which he would have been a prohibitive favourite. Under the season-long care of Frank Y. Whiteley, Jr., who had replaced ailing and retired trainer Sherrill Ward, Forego increased his career earnings to $1,655,217 to rank only behind Kelso ($1,977,896) and Round Table ($1,749,869).

Other Eclipse Award winners were Karen L. Taylor's Seattle Slew (Bold Reasoning-My Charmer, by Poker), in the two-year-old colt or gelding division; Mill House's Sensational (Hoist the Flag-Meritus, by Bold Ruler), two-year-old filly; Esteban Rodriguez Tizol's Bold Forbes (Irish Castle-Comely Nell, by Commodore M), three-year-old colt or gelding; Wil-

Bold Forbes held the lead all the way in the 102nd running of the Kentucky Derby in May. He was ridden by Angel Cordero. Honest Pleasure was second. Bold Forbes went on to win the Belmont Stakes in June.

UPI COMPIX

A 10-to-1 shot named Empery won the English Derby at Epsom in June. Lester Piggott rode the American-owned horse to victory.

CENTRAL PRESS/PICTORIAL PARADE

liam Haggin Perry's Revidere (Reviewer-Quillesian, by Princequillo), three-year-old filly; Montpelier's Proud Delta (Delta Judge-Loving Sister, by Olympia), older filly or mare; Nelson Bunker Hunt's Youth (Ack Ack-Gazala II, by Dark Star), turf; George Weasel's My Juliet (Gallant Romeo-My Bupers, by Bupers), sprinting; and Mrs. Ogden Phipps's Straight and True (Never Bend-Polly Girl, by Prince Bio), steeplechasing.

Seattle Slew made only three starts but won them all easily, a six-furlong maiden race by 5 lengths in 1 min 10.2 sec, a seven-furlong allowance race by $3\frac{1}{2}$ lengths in 1 min 22 sec, and the one-mile Champagne Stakes by $9\frac{3}{4}$ lengths in 1 min 34.4 sec. Sensational won 5 of her 11 starts including four stakes.

In the Triple Crown events Bold Forbes, a speed horse trained by Lazaro Barrera to race farther than anticipated, earned top honours in the Kentucky Derby and the Belmont Stakes. Bold Forbes finished third to Elocutionist in the Preakness Stakes after engaging in a suicidal duel with Honest Pleasure, running the first six furlongs in 1 min 9 sec. Bold Forbes also won the San Jacinto, the Bay Shore, and the Wood Memorial and earned $460,286 for the year.

Revidere, trained by Frank Whiteley's son, David, was dominant in her division. She garnered eight firsts, one second, and one third from ten starts and won five stakes. Optimistic Gal, which won five major stakes, was another prominent member of the division.

Proud Delta was first in six stakes, including the Beldame, in which she bested Revidere. Youth, a three-year-old colt, started only twice in North America but completely outclassed the opposition. He captured the Canadian International by four lengths and the Washington (D.C.) International by ten lengths, both under the guidance of jockey Sandy Hawley. Previously Maryland-bred Youth had won five stakes in France, including the Prix du Jockey Club, and had an overall record of seven victories in nine appearances and earnings of $669,286.

The four-year-old filly My Juliet clinched the sprint title by defeating male horses, including Bold Forbes, in the seven-furlong Vosburgh Handicap in her last race of the campaign. That marked her fifth consecutive victory, including four stakes.

Norcliffe, owned by Charles Baker and trained by Roger Attfield, dominated three-year-old racing in Canada. He won the first two events of the Canadian Triple Crown, the Queen's Plate and the Prince of Wales Stakes. Heavily favoured in the final race, the Breeders' Stakes, Norcliffe failed on the soft track and finished out of the money; the winner was Tiny Tinker. Norcliffe also won the Carling O'Keefe Invitational. In other major Canadian races the French horse Youth won the Canadian International Championship Stakes, and Bye Bye Paris took the Maple Leaf Stakes.

(JOSEPH C. AGRELLA)

EUROPE AND AUSTRALIA. The 1975–76 National Hunt racing season in Britain was brightened by the performances of the hurdler Night Nurse, owned by R. Spencer, trained by P. Easterby at Malton in Yorkshire, and ridden by P. Broderick. At five years old this young gelding won the Champion Hurdle at Cheltenham in March 1976 from Bird's Nest and Flash Imp, with the previous champion, Comedy of Errors, fourth. Night Nurse had already beaten Comedy of Errors twice, most recently in the Irish Sweeps Hurdle in December 1975. Night Nurse also took the Scottish and Welsh champion hurdles in his stride.

The Cheltenham Gold Cup Steeplechase was won by Sir E. Hanmer's Royal Frolic, trained by F. Rimell and ridden by J. Burke, from Brown Lad and Colebridge. Rag Trade, also trained by Rimell and ridden by Burke, won the Grand National Steeplechase from Red Rum and Eyecatcher; Red Rum had now won the race twice and been second twice in four successive years. The Irish Grand National went to Brown Lad. In November 1975 the Mackeson Gold Cup went to Clear Cut, and the Hennessy Cognac Gold Cup Steeplechase was won by April Seventh. In December Easby Abbey won the Massey-Ferguson Gold Cup Steeplechase and Captain Christy the King George VI Steeplechase from Bula. Irish Fashion won the Schweppes Gold Trophy, over hurdles, in February, and in April Otter Way took the Whitbread Gold Cup Steeplechase. J. Francome was National Hunt champion jockey. In June, at Auteuil, Paris, Plomares won the Grand Steeplechase de Paris.

The 1976 flat racing season in Britain and France reflected depressingly on the merits of the English-bred racing Thoroughbred. The long, hot, dry summer saw valuable prize after valuable prize swept away from England by French horses. Of the five English classics, only the Two Thousand Guineas was won by an English horse. Furthermore, a fair proportion of winners of European prestige races were U.S.-bred.

French stables contained a galaxy of brilliant colts and fillies of all ages. The strongest hands were held by the following owners, with their trainers and leading jockeys: Texas millionaire N. Bunker Hunt, with trainer M. Zilber and jockeys L. Piggott and F. Head, whose top colts were the three-year-olds Youth and Empery, and again Hunt, with trainer F. Mathet, for whom Exceller completed an exceptional three-year-old trio; D. Wildenstein, with trainer A. Penna and jockey Y. Saint-Martin, whose three-year-old filly Pawneese was a star successor to the same owner's Allez France and whose three-year-old colt Crow and filly Flying Water won English classics. F. Boutin trained the three-year-olds Malacate, Lagunette, and the luckless Trépan, while his five-year-old Sagaro could claim to be the best long-distance runner in Europe; Boutin's principal jockey, P. Paquet, enjoyed a brilliant season. A. Head trained Red Lord and Ivanjica for J. Wertheimer, with his son F. Head as jockey. Among two-year-olds the Aga Khan's Blushing Groom, trained by Mathet, was exceptional.

Of the English classics, the Two Thousand Guineas was won for England by C. d'Alessio's Wollow, trained by H. Cecil and ridden by G. Dettori, from the French Vitiges; Flying Water took the One Thousand Guineas; Empery a substandard Derby (in which his rider Piggott scored his seventh Derby victory and surpassed S. Donoghue's previous record), from Relkino and Oats. Pawneese won the Oaks, from Roses for the Star and African Dancer; and Crow won the St. Leger, from Secret Man and Scallywag.

One English horse withstood the foreign challenge consistently: C. and D. Spence's powerful sprinter, four-year-old Lochnager, trained in Yorkshire by M. W. Easterby and ridden by E. Hide, won Royal Ascot's King's Stand Stakes, Newmarket's July Cup, and York's William Hill Sprint Championship (formerly the Nunthorpe Stakes), becoming the first horse to win this triple crown since Abernant did so in 1949.

In the French classics, the equivalents of the One Thousand and Two Thousand Guineas were won respectively by Mrs. A. Head's Riverqueen, trained by C. Datessen and ridden by Head, and Red Lord; the Prix du Jockey Club (French Derby) by Youth from Twig Moss and Malacate; the Prix de Diane (French Oaks) by Pawneese, from Riverqueen and Lagunette; and the Prix Royal-Oak (French St. Leger) by Exceller. Before he went on to transatlantic successes, Youth also won the Prix Lupin. Exceller, ridden by Saint-Martin, won the Grand Prix de Paris. Pawneese added to her classic victories her triumph in Ascot's King George VI and Queen Elizabeth Diamond Stakes, in which she held off Bruni and Orange Bay. Riverqueen won the Prix Saint-Alary and the Grand Prix de Saint-Cloud. The four-year-old filly Ivanjica won the Prix de l'Arc de Triomphe at Longchamp, Paris, in which she beat Crow and Youth, with Norway's first runner in this race, Noble Dancer, a creditable fourth. Malacate beat Empery and Northern Treasure in the Irish Sweeps Derby. Sagaro won the Prix du Cadran and, for the second successive year, Ascot's Gold Cup. Wildenstein's successes in major races put him at the head of the winning owners in England, with £244,500.

In England, Wollow, although beaten in the Derby, won the Eclipse Stakes on the disqualification of Trépan, the Sussex Stakes at Goodwood, and the Benson and Hedges Gold Cup at York, but failed in the Champion Stakes at Newmarket. Rose Bowl came out after a long absence to win Ascot's Queen Elizabeth II Stakes, but in the Champion Stakes she was just caught by Vitiges, on that occasion only trained by P. Walwyn and ridden by P. Eddery. Epsom's Coronation Cup was won by Quiet Fling; Royal Ascot's St. James's Palace Stakes by Radetzky; and the Hardwicke Stakes by Orange Bay, which had also won the Jockey Club Stakes. Wildenstein's El Rastro took Newbury's Lockinge Stakes. Sarah Siddons won the Yorkshire Oaks, African Dancer the Park Hill Stakes, and Sea Anchor the Doncaster Cup.

Among the two-year-olds, Blushing Groom claimed preeminence by his victories in France's major two-year-old races: the Prix Robert Papin, the Prix Morny, the Prix de la Salamandre, and the Grand Critérium; in the last he crushed the English-trained (U.S.-bred) J. O. Tobin, winner of the Richmond Stakes and the Champagne Stakes. Both from Ireland, Nebbiolo won the Gimcrack Stakes and The Minstrel the Dewhurst Stakes. Eddery was champion jockey again and Cecil the leading trainer (£261,300), edging Walwyn (£260,110). After 41 years of training, Noel Murless retired at the end of the season. He had trained the winners of 19 classic races in England.

Boutin's Trépan won both Royal Ascot's Prince of Wales Stakes and the Eclipse Stakes, but a routine drug test on him was positive in each case and, after a lengthy Jockey Club inquiry, the horse was disqualified and Boutin fined £1,250. The affair underlined the need for a common international policy on the subject. Breeders in Britain supported proposals for a new, more representative body under the Home Office to administer racing.

In Ireland, the One Thousand Guineas was won by Sarah Siddons, trained by P. Prendergast; the Two Thousand Guineas by Northern Treasure, trained by K. Prendergast; and the Irish Oaks by Lagunette from Sarah Siddons. (Lagunette also won France's Prix Vermeille from Sarah Siddons.)

Steve Lobell collapsed of heat exhaustion after winning the Hambletonian trotting classic in September. Stablehands worked for two hours to revive the horse. The race was unusually arduous, requiring four heats to decide the winner.

WIDE WORLD

The Italian Derby was won by Red Arrow and the Gran Premio di Milano by Rouge Sang. In West Germany the Grosser Preis von Baden-Baden was won by Sharper; the Grosser Preis von Nordrhein-Westfalen by Windwurf; the Grosser Preis von Düsseldorf by Whip It Quick from Windwurf; and the Preis von Europa by Windwurf.

In Australia, the Melbourne Cup was taken by the five-year-old New Zealand horse Van der Hum, owned in partnership by W. Abel of Hamilton, New Zealand, and the Robinson brothers and ridden by New Zealand jockey R. J. Skelton, from Gold and Black and Kythera. The Caulfield Cup was won by How Now from Battle Heights and Van der Hum.

(R. M. GOODWIN)

Harness Racing. In major events in the U.S., the $100,000 Kentucky Futurity for trotters was won by Quick Pay, while two-year-old pacer Jade Prince took the International Stallion Stake in two straight heats. At Lexington, Ky., in October Jade Prince set a new world record for the mile in a race of 1 min 54.2 sec. The $153,799 Little Brown Jug for three-year-old pacers was won by Keystone Ore. In the Oliver Wendell Holmes $101,000 three-year-old pace, Oil Burner prevailed by a head in 1 min 55.2 sec over Armbro Ranger. The $263,524 Hambletonian trot at Du Quoin, Ill., went to Steve Lobell, with Zoot Suit and Armbro Regina the other heat winners. (Steve Lobell equaled a trotter's mile world record for three-year-olds of 1 min 56.4 sec.) The $105,721 Fox Stake for two-year-old pacers at Indianapolis went to Crash. The $200,000 Cane Pace at Yonkers Raceway was won in record time of 1 min 57.2 sec by Keystone Ore.

Tad Coffin of the U.S. won an Olympic gold medal in the three-day event for equestrians. Here he takes his horse Bally-Cor over a jump at Bromont, Quebec.

WIDE WORLD

At the Meadows the Adios Pace of $125,000 went to Armbro Ranger. The $202,000 Yonkers Trot was a triumph for the Billy Haughton stable, with Steve Lobell winning from stablemates Quick Pay and Zoot Suit. The "Off Track Betting" $300,000 Classic went to Oil Burner, the other two heat winners being Wolf Pack and Precious Fella. The Dexter Cup of $166,290 for three-year-old trotters at Roosevelt Raceway in New York was won by Soothsayer. At Sportsman's Park, Chicago, Time Breaker won the $119,000 Langley Memorial Pace. Tarport Hap won the $50,000 U.S. pace championship at Roosevelt Raceway, and Meadow Bright the $50,000 American trotting championship. French entry Equileo captured the $200,000 International Trot of $1\frac{1}{4}$ mi at Roosevelt with Bellino II, also of France, second and Meadow Bright third. Over $1\frac{1}{2}$ mi Equileo could only finish third to Dream of Glory and Cash Minbar in the Challenge Cup, run in world record time of 3 min 5.4 sec.

Paleface Adios broke all money-winning records in Australia. In the trotting division Cocky Adios took the $15,000 Australasian trotters' championship, and Bay Johnny won the Interdominion Trotters' final. South Australian Carclew won the Interdominion $60,500 pacing championship final in Adelaide from Pure Steel and Don't Retreat. The $53,300 Hunter Cup in Melbourne was won by Truant Armagh from Adios Victor and Alphalite. Among the juveniles Rip Van Winkle won 10 of his 14 starts, and Mister Karamea established a three-year-old record in the West Australian Triple Crown before leaving for California, where by winning in 1 min 56.6 sec he became the fastest pacer ever bred in Australia. Willie Rip won the $35,000 Australia Day Cup in Sydney and Paleface Adios took Sydney's Lord Mayor's Cup. High Advice won the Victorian and South Australian Derbies; Nixon Adios the West Australian Derby; Capri Glenfern the New South Wales Derby; Rodilo Bronze the Victorian Trotters' Derby; and Nicks Lad the Queensland Derby. The Miracle Mile was won by Paleface Adios from Don't Retreat and Hondo Grattan.

In New Zealand pacer Lunar Chance won the 1975 Miracle Mile in Christchurch from Noodlum and was later voted horse of the year. The 1975 New Zealand Derby was won by Main Adios from Direct Magic. The Auckland Cup of $35,000 went to Captain Harcourt, and the National Trot at Auckland was won by Topeka. New Zealand's leading two-year-old pace, the Sapling Stakes, was taken by Castle Derg and the juvenile championship at Auckland by Bronze Trail. After winning the Interisland Challenge Stakes at Auckland, Stanley Rio put up a fine performance for a four-year-old by winning the $60,000 New Zealand Cup at Christchurch.

In Europe, Wayne Eden won the trotters' Premio Mario Locatello at Milan. Colta won the Italian Derby, and three-year-old Atollo took the $41,000 Premio Elwood Medium and the $41,000 Premio Napoli. The Prix de Washington at Enghien, Paris, was won by Clarissa and the Prix d'Atlantique by the great French trotter Bellino II. Bellino II again won the $266,000 Prix d'Amérique and the Prix de France, but came in second to Equileo in the $200,000 Roosevelt International.

The Danish Derby was won by Tarok, which had also won the Grand Prix and the Derby Trial. The Jutland Grand Prix for three-year-olds went to Vetra from Umbra M. and Willi Hanover, and the Danish Criterium to U'Lejue from Uggla Nora and Wembley.

The $40,000 Jugend Preis of West Berlin for two-year-olds was won by Corner. Hegrina triumphed in the $32,000 Dreijährigen Trophy at Recklinghausen, West Germany, the $41,000 Breddenbrock Stake in West Berlin, and a $19,800 trot at Hamburg. At Solvalla in Sweden Wiretapper won the Princess Christina Trot. The Nordic championship was a dead heat between Frances Marie and Inside. The Swedish Derby of $49,600 was an easy win for Cal Min over Icky and Quick Label. Stockholm's Elite race went to Dimitria, from Duke Iran and Clissa. The Finnish Derby was won by Assessori, Veuve Clicquot taking the Grand Prix from Viking and Charme Asserdal. The top event of the season at Helsinki was won by the Danish-bred Silius. In The Netherlands Monty Buitenzong won the Merevold Mijerecord. The Austrian Derby was won by Damara S.

(NOEL SIMPSON)

Show Jumping. The 1976 show jumping season was entirely dominated by the Olympic Games. The individual grand prix, held in Bromont, near Montreal, was won for West Germany by Alwin Schockemöhle on Warwick Rex. Michel Vaillancourt, a French-Canadian 22-year-old from the Montreal area, finished second on seven-year-old Branch County, and François Mathy was third for Belgium on Gai Luron. The two other medallists, and Debbie Johnsey of Great Britain on Moxy—the only girl and the youngest rider in the field—had to jump-off for the places. Vaillancourt made only one mistake, and Mathy had two fences down, while Johnsey incurred 15¼ faults to finish fourth.

The team event, in the Olympic stadium, was won by France, which had taken the silver medals in Tokyo in 1964 and in Mexico City in 1968. The French team consisted of Hubert Parot on Rivage, Marc Roguet on Belle de Mars, Michel Roche on Un Espoir, and Marcel Rozier on Bayard de Maupas. They had 24 faults in their first round and 16 in the second, to win from the defending champions, the West Germans, who also had 24 faults in their first round but 20 in the second. The West German team comprised Alwin and Paul Schockemöhle on Warwick Rex and Agent, respectively, Sonke Sonksen with Kwept, and veteran Hans-Günter Winkler on Torphy. Belgium, represented by Edgar Cuepper on Le Champion, Stanny van Paeschen with Porsche, Eric Wauters on Gute Sitte, and Mathy on Gai Luron, won the bronze medals with 63 faults.

The U.S. team won the gold medals in the three-day event, from West Germany and Australia, the scores being 441, 584.6, and 599.54, respectively. Britain, the defending champion, was forced to retire when two horses went lame in the speed and endurance phase. The U.S. also won the individual gold and silver medals, with Edmund ("Tad") Coffin, aged 22, riding Bally-Cor and John ("Mike") Plumb on Better and Better. The individual bronze medal went to Karl Schultz of West Germany on Madrigal.

In dressage, West Germany provided the winning team, with Switzerland second and the U.S. third; the individual gold medal went to Christine Stückelberger of Switzerland on Granat, with Harry Boldt on Woycek and Reiner Klimke on Mehmed, both of West Germany, second and third, respectively.

(PAMELA MACGREGOR-MORRIS)

See also Track and Field Sports: *Special Report*.

Polo. In 1976 Argentina continued to lead the world in the production of polo ponies and polo players. Except in Australia and South Africa, the Argentine imported pony predominated. At Palermo, Arg., the Argentine Polo Association staged the "perfect" match, with all eight players handicapped at ten goals. Such an abundance of talent had never before been gathered together on the same ground. The older stars played together with H. Heguy as number one, Gaston Dorignac number two, J. C. Harriott number three, and Francisco Dorignac back. The slightly younger opposing team consisted of Alberto Heguy number one, Daniel Gonzalez number two, Gonzalez Tanoira number three, and Alfredo Harriott back. Thousands of spectators saw the young "tens" beat the old "tens" 10–8. Afterward a team from England defeated South Africa in two games.

KEYSTONE

Rag Trade (left) pulled ahead of Red Rum in the last few yards to win the Grand National Steeplechase at Aintree, England, in April.

Because of the extensive drought polo in England was played on fast grounds. Perhaps the most outstanding player was Sinclair Hill from Australia, who won two cups before he ran out of ponies. For the Cowdray Gold Cup the 1975 winner, Greenhill, was the favourite, but brilliant play by E. Moore (8) and H. Barrantes (7) gave Stowell an 8–6 victory. In the Wills international match between England—A. Kent (4), H. Hipwood (8), J. Hipwood (8), John Horswell (5)—and South America—G. Pierez (5), A. Herrera (8), E. Moore (8), A. García (5)—England lost 6–2.

The Spanish Gold Cup at Soto Grande was won by Villa Franca, defeating Casarajo 8–5. In the American National Open, Willowbent beat Tulsa 10–6. For the Australian Gold Cup, New South Wales beat Victoria 7–6.

(ANDREW HORSBRUGH-PORTER)

[452.B.4.h.xvii and xxi; 452.B.5.e]

Ethiopia

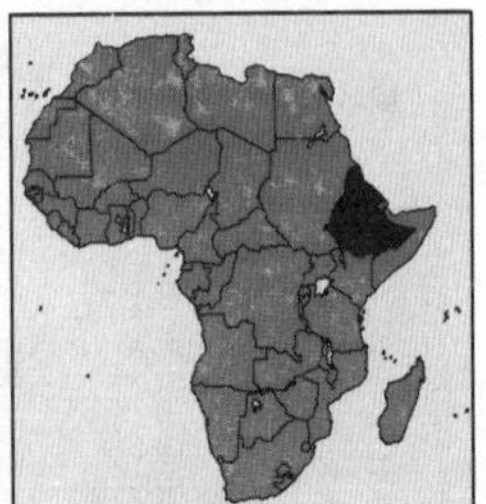

A socialist state in northeastern Africa, Ethiopia is bordered by Somalia, the French Territory of the Afars and Issas, Kenya, the Sudan, and the Red Sea. Area: 471,800 sq mi (1,221,900 sq km). Pop. (1975 est.): 27,030,400. Cap. and largest city: Addis Ababa (pop., 1975 est., 1,174,000). Language: Amharic (official) and other tongues. Religion: Ethiopian Orthodox (Coptic) and Muslim, with various animist minorities. Head of state and chairman of the Provisional Military Administrative Council in 1976, Brig. Gen. Teferi Benti.

In September 1976, the country celebrated the second anniversary of the Ethiopian revolution. The Provisional Military Administrative Council (PMAC) continued to govern, but steps were taken toward a more widely based participation by the population.

It was now claimed that over 22,000 rural peasant associations had been formed with a membership of more than five million families, on the basis of individual plots of 10 ha, with a maximum of 800 ha for an association. Teferi Benti announced in his anniversary address that the process of grouping the associations at district and regional levels was "now nearing completion." Teferi Benti also stated that about 1,800 urban *kebeles*, or community associations, had been formed in 600 towns, with the largest number (291) in Addis Ababa. These rural and urban associations had already been given considerable powers. Peasant associations were given legal status in a proclamation issued in February, which also detailed the powers and duties of the hierarchy of committees in the process of formation, including collection of the single, consolidated income tax proclaimed in January. Both rural and urban associations were given control of primary and secondary school programs, expenditure, and staff under the Education Proclamation issued in September. Popular control of the schools was seen as essential if education was to be effective and relevant to local needs.

The more difficult terms of reference of the authority granted to *kebeles* were announced in the Proclamation on the Consolidation and Organization of Urban Dwellers' Associations issued on Oct. 9, 1976. There were complex problems in management, rent collection, and security and social functions, involving distribution of consumer goods in short supply, such as grain and sugar. *Kebeles* in several urban districts launched consumer cooperatives.

The third mechanism for popular participation required the scrapping of the Confederation of Ethiopian Labour Unions (CELU). In line with the Labour Proclamation of December 1975, an All-Ethiopian Trade Union, with membership organized in nine trade groups, was to be formed instead. When organized, groups would send representatives to an All-Ethiopian Conference to decide the form of the National Union. The end of November was set as the target for completion of this process. Teferi announced a figure of 1,207 labour unions, with a membership of 274,000, in his anniversary speech of September 11.

These measures encountered opposition. The nationalization of rural land and the formation of associations succeeded most in the southern regions where the tenancy rates and the degree of absentee landlordism were highest. Even so, there was resistance everywhere from threatened groups. Teferi declared on September 11 that numerous reactionaries had been liquidated.

Reports of the surrender, capture, and killing of the regime's opponents increased after the formation of a people's militia and the arming of the peasants. The Political Bureau made it known in June that "arming the masses is our time's principal task." On June 20 the *Ethiopian Herald* declared that "a people's militia of close to half a million has already been organized by the initiative of the oppressed masses." Centres of feudal landowner resistance grew weaker, but pockets remained in such areas as eastern Gojam, Begemdir, and northern Wollo, and along the southeastern borders in Bale and Borana where Somali support was available.

In urban areas, resistance came from a more confused grouping of dissident trade-union leaders, students, and teachers, and from nascent but clandestine political organizations such as the Ethiopian People's Revolutionary Party (EPRP). The initial meeting of workers' representatives, held in the old Parliament building in June, was stopped after disturbances, and there were arrests of "saboteurs" and "anarchists."

September saw the attempted assassination of Maj. Mengistu Haile Mariam, first vice-chairman of the PMAC. On October 1 Fikre Merid, a prominent member of the political advisory group, the Provisional Office for Mass Organizational Affairs (POMOA), was shot in his car in Addis Ababa. The Dirgue (PMAC armed forces committee) weathered these storms, although, internally, it removed six members in January "in disgrace" and executed Maj. Sissay Habte, previously chairman of the PMAC Political Committee, and several of its other members in July. It was claimed that this group of plotters was linked with EPRP and with the Ethiopian Democratic Union (EDU) based in London. Also in July, the 26th Battalion, located in Asseb, executed its commanding officer and one other for "counterrevolutionary action." The execution of some 50 "dissidents" was reported in November.

A number of appointments within the Dirgue were clarified. Apart from the chairman and two vice-chairmen, there were heads of committees as follows: Capt. Moges Wolde-Mikael (economic); Lieut. Col. Asrat Desta (information and public relations); Maj. Berhanu Baye (legal); and Lieut. Alemayehu Haile (administration). A replacement for Maj. Sissay Habte (political) was awaited. The chairmanship of the influential POMOA was held by a civilian, Hailu Fida. POMOA probably prepared the "Program of the National Democratic Revolution of Ethiopia," the basic policy statement announced in April. It analyzed in Marxist terms the class structure and alliances of contemporary Ethiopia; announced such basic aims as the abolition of feudalism and capitalism, achievement of the transition to socialism, and establishment of the "people's democratic republic"; and outlined the revolutionary program and its tasks—arming the masses and forming a "true proletarian party" in an alliance with all progressive forces to eliminate the enemies of the masses. A final and significant section declared that after a popular revolutionary front had been formed,

KEYSTONE

Prisoners in a silent war: Ethiopian peasant soldiers after their capture by rebels in Eritrea Province in October.

an assembly that would assume state power would be established. The assembly would comprise representatives of parties and popular organizations that had participated in the front elected democratically and through secret ballot.

The civilian ministerial group was given a major overhaul in February, when seven Cabinet members were dismissed. The governor of the National Bank was arrested shortly after. In July the heads of most of the army units were replaced, and in August new administrators were appointed to the majority of the regions (formerly provinces). In February, Abuna Tewoflos (Theophilos), the head of the Ethiopian Orthodox Church, was dismissed and accused of a number of malpractices. A new patriarch, Aba Melaku Wolde-Mikael, a man of more humble origins, was elected in July, and efforts were clearly being made to bring the church, in its new disestablished role, into the mainstream of development activity rather than to suppress it. Official policy supported freedom of religion, and Islamic holidays were celebrated officially.

In the economic sector, the government continued with measures designed to place major concerns under public ownership and to control activities still under private ownership. The year began with the Proclamation on Commercial Activities (published Dec. 29, 1975), which limited private capital in industry to Eth$500,000; in wholesale trade to Eth$300,000, and in retail activities to Eth$200,000. The Ethiopian Insurance Corporation and the Addis Bank, both embracing previous private concerns, were established on January 1. Major government measures included the Monetary Proclamation in September, a multiobjective operation to wipe out the imperial image, bring currency back into circulation, and remove financial support from clandestine opposition groups. A new currency, designated the birr, replaced the Ethiopian dollar at par.

THE NEW YORK TIMES

A hot May sun blazes upon a government-organized rally in Addis Ababa. Leaders sought to drum up support for the war against rebels in Eritrea, once an Italian colony and now an Ethiopian region.

ETHIOPIA

Education. (1973–74) Primary, pupils 859,831, teachers 18,646; secondary, pupils 182,263, teachers 6,181; vocational, pupils 5,533, teachers 554; teacher training, students 3,126, teachers 194; higher, students 6,474, teaching staff 434.

Finance. Monetary unit: birr, which replaced the Ethiopian dollar at par from Oct. 14, 1976, with (Sept. 20, 1976) a par value of $2.07 birr to U.S. $1 (free rate of 3.57 birr = £1 sterling). Gold, SDR's, and foreign exchange (June 1976) U.S. $293.2 million. Budget (1975–76 est.): revenue 1,175,000,000 birr; expenditure 1,330,000,000 birr. Gross national product (1974) 5,586,000,000 birr. Money supply (May 1976) 1,082,300,000 birr. Cost of living (Addis Ababa; 1970 = 100; May 1976) 155.

Foreign Trade. (1975) Imports 644.9 million birr; exports 497.8 million birr. Import sources (1974): Italy 15%; Japan 14%; West Germany 12%; U.K. 8%; Iran 7%; U.S. 6%. Export destinations (1974): U.S. 21%; Afars and Issas, 8%; Japan 8%; West Germany 7%; Saudi Arabia 7%. Main exports: coffee 31%; oilseeds 17%; pulses 13%; hides and skins 7%.

Transport and Communications. Roads (1973) 23,000 km. Motor vehicles in use (1974): passenger 43,380; commercial (including buses) 12,000. Railways (1974): 988 km; traffic (including traffic of Afars and Issas portion of Djibouti-Addis Ababa line; excluding Eritrea) 95 million passenger-km, freight 244 million net ton-km. Air traffic (1974): 455 million passenger-km; freight 19.4 million net ton-km. Telephones (Dec. 1974) 66,000. Radio receivers (Dec. 1973) 175,000. Television receivers (Dec. 1973) 20,000.

Agriculture. Production (in 000; metric tons; 1975): barley *c.* 700; wheat *c.* 618; corn *c.* 1,077; millet *c.* 200; sorghum *c.* 855; sweet potatoes (1974) *c.* 265; potatoes *c.* 170; sugar, raw value *c.* 140; linseed *c.* 50; sesame *c.* 100; chick-peas *c.* 236; dry peas *c.* 75; dry broad beans (1974) *c.* 154; lentils (1974) *c.* 113; dry beans *c.* 95; coffee *c.* 186; cotton *c.* 24. Livestock (in 000; 1975): cattle *c.* 24,000; sheep *c.* 22,320; goats (1974) 17,322; horses (1974) *c.* 1,453; mules (1974) *c.* 1,451; asses (1974) *c.* 3,945; camels (1974) *c.* 1,001; poultry *c.* 53,833.

Industry. Production (in 000; metric tons; 1972–73): cement 203; petroleum products (1974) *c.* 600; cotton yarn 11.7; cotton fabrics (sq m) 82,000; electricity (kw-hr) *c.* 664,000.

A major economic problem was the malfunctioning of the national market mechanism, resulting in considerable increases in prices of consumer goods (particularly food) and widespread shortages. The PMAC took measures, and merchants were summarily executed or imprisoned for holding large stocks.

Ethiopian Shipping Lines made profits during 1975 and 1976 (Eth$1.5 million in the first six months of 1976); in 1975–76, 637 km of roads were built. Tea cultivation progressed in the Gumaro district of Illubabor region under an Eth$3.4 million agreement with the Commonwealth Development Corporation; the World Bank provided Eth$55 million for the Southern Rangelands Livestock Development Scheme in Borana, near the border with Kenya, and the UN Development Program was providing Eth$14 million in an Eth$23 million project for the development of 100 coffee-processing stations. It was from coffee production that Ethiopia would gain considerable financial strength in 1976. Reports indicated that earnings, as the result of high international prices and a reasonable crop, would be considerably in excess of Eth$200 million.

Measures were taken to keep unemployment in check in the modern sector. In 1975–76 Eth$50.3 million was earmarked for projects designed to provide employment for 44,250, and the 1977 budget was to cater for an additional 48,000. To these measures must be added projects in the rural sector. During 1975–76 21 settlements were established in nine regions for a total of more than 12,000 families. A "settlement authority" was established under the Ministry of Agriculture to implement the "land to the tiller" concept and to "ease the country's unemployment problem." The continuation of the drought in the lowland areas caused particularly severe conditions in Ogaden. In August it was announced that 65,000 people in Gardula district of Gamu-Gofa region were in a desperate condition. The World Food Program contributed Eth$46.8 million to the Relief and Rehabilitation Commission (RRC) for the settlement of pastoral nomads, and the Awash Valley Development Authority settled 4,231 Afars on 11,300 ha. The U.S. granted Eth$8.5 million to construct roads in drought-affected areas and to develop an early warning system to prevent future disasters.

The government adopted a more conciliatory attitude to the conflict in Eritrea in 1976. In May the PMAC issued a nine-point policy statement indicating willingness to consider a degree of political autonomy for the territory short of actual secession, but without result. A peasant army levied to march against the Eritrean secessionist guerrillas dissolved by the end of June after early reverses. In July a special commission was established to assist with the rehabilitation and resettlement of refugees, and Teferi Benti said in his anniversary speech on September 11 that over 2,500 had returned and accepted this offer. On July 16, Maj. Berhanu Baye of the PMAC Legal Committee was appointed to head a "dialogue team" on Eritrean problems, after his reportedly successful tour of Arab countries when eight Arab states were said to have affirmed their support for the nine-point governmental policy on Eritrea. An outstanding difficulty was the continued retention by the Eritrean Popular Liberation Front and the Tigrean People's Liberation Front of a number of foreign nationals, for whom ransom was demanded. Relations with Sudan were also strained after a complaint that the Ethiopian Air Force had violated air space and caused damage during March.

On the future of the French Territory of Afars and Issas, the PMAC issued a White Paper in April; this was followed by a three-point statement at the Organization of African Unity summit conference in July which insisted on the renunciation of all claims on the territory by contending parties and an end to all interference in Djibouti affairs, but no improvement in relations with Somalia followed.

[978.E.5.a]

KEYSTONE

Young people favouring European federalism lift their placards outside the Brussels meeting place of the European Council. The Council is composed of the heads of government of the nine European countries belonging to the Common Market.

European Unity

For the European Economic Community (EEC), 1976 began with the publication of the report on European union by Léo Tindemans (*see* BIOGRAPHY), the Belgian prime minister, on January 7. At its meeting in Luxembourg on April 1–2, the European Council (of the heads of government of the nine EEC countries), under the presidency of Gaston Thorn (*see* BIOGRAPHY) of Luxembourg, considered the report, which it had asked Tindemans to make, as a basis for discussion about the Community's future development. His report proposed such steps toward a federalist Community as he considered practical: moves toward a common external policy; resumption of progress toward economic and monetary union, with a two-tier system in which the second-tier countries would be excused from the rigours of monetary integration; a "citizen's Europe," including the right of appeal by Community citizens to the Court of Justice against violation of their rights by Community institutions; and strengthening of Community institutions, including greater powers for the European Parliament, majority voting as normal practice in the Council of Ministers, and an enhanced role for the Commission.

The broad sweep of the Tindemans report contrasted with the economic difficulties and political uncertainties of the member states. Unemployment in the member countries remained around 5% or more throughout the year. Inflation was well over 10% in Britain and Italy and started to rise again in France after a promising decline into single figures; only in West Germany was inflation reduced below 5%. In both Italy and Britain the economic crisis was reflected in severe political problems. The Italian elections in June were followed by the formation of a minority Christian Democrat government dependent on Communist support. In Britain the "social contract" between the Labour government and the trade unions was upheld, with pay rises limited to about 5%, and the transition from the Wilson to the Callaghan prime ministership was smooth; as in Italy, however, financial weakness remained a source of political weakness. In France, too, political uncertainty appeared along with economic deterioration, as Jacques Chirac resigned and was replaced as premier by Raymond Barre (a former vice-president of the EEC Commission). Only West Germany, among the big four, remained free from pressing economic difficulties, and the German elections in October brought little change in the government.

Given these troubled circumstances, and the reluctance of major member governments to relinquish any power to the European institutions, it was not surprising that little action was taken on the Tindemans report. More surprising, perhaps, was the fact that the Community did take some important steps toward unity in 1976. The most striking was the signature, on September 20, of the agreement to hold direct elections to the European Parliament, planned for May or June of 1978. The heads of government agreed, moreover, to appoint a major political figure, Roy Jenkins (*see* BIOGRAPHY), as president of the new Commission that would take office in January 1977, and to give him a consultative role in the nomination of commissioners. There was little progress on such crucial economic issues as monetary and energy pol-

European Economic Community:
see Economy, World; European Unity

icy, but significant advances were made in some sectoral policies, particularly the agreement on the Community's 200-mi fishing limit. External relations continued to be a field of active development, with the Greek application for membership, the full entry into force of the Lomé Convention associating African, Caribbean, and Pacific (ACP) countries with the Community, and the negotiation of trade and aid agreements with a number of Mediterranean countries.

Direct Elections. Drawn-out negotiations had taken place among the member governments about the size and composition of the directly elected Parliament. France and Britain sought representation more nearly proportionate to their populations, while the smaller countries endeavoured to maintain the existing weighting in their favour. The European Council finally reached agreement at its meeting in July on a Parliament of 410 members: 81 each from France, West Germany, Italy, and the U.K., 25 from The Netherlands, 24 from Belgium, 16 from Denmark, 15 from Ireland, and 6 from Luxembourg. The members were to be elected for five-year terms, and they might also be members of their national parliaments. Each member country was to choose its own electoral method for the first elections, and the Parliament itself would choose a method that would apply to the whole Community in subsequent elections.

The signing of the agreement was delayed by dispute over a matter of detail. The British government agreed that, if possible, the elections should be held in the same week in May or June of 1978 by all member countries, but it would not guarantee that the necessary legislation would be passed in time by the U.K. Parliament. The French would not accept an agreement in which different governments made differing commitments. It was not until September that the foreign ministers were able to sign the agreements, with the timing of the elections treated in a separate document.

Council and Commission. The European Council, formally constituted in 1975 as a triannual meeting of the heads of member governments, continued its uneven course. Some meetings disappointed by their meagre results, as in April 1976, and others, like that of July, moved the Community significant steps forward. In addition to agreeing on the basis of direct elections and on the appointment of Jenkins as president of the Commission, the Council decided in July to establish an antiterrorist convention under which the nine would prosecute or extradite kidnappers, hijackers, and terrorists.

Jenkins' appointment was greeted as a substantial boost for the Community. The Commission had been losing influence for some years, and by early 1976 it was rapidly becoming a lame-duck administration. Altiero Spinelli left to enter the Italian Parliament, and it was known that several other commissioners wanted to leave at the end of the year. The early agreement on the appointment, as president, of a major politician with a strongly pro-European record was expected to improve the standing and balance of the Commission as a whole.

External Relations. External relations continued to be an eventful area. Most important for the Community's future was the opening, on July 27, of formal negotiations for Greek accession. The Commission's opinion on the Greek application had been discouraging, especially as regards the threat to integration that would be posed by still wider divergences in economic development and political stability among the membership. Nevertheless, the Council of Ministers decided that negotiations should go ahead.

On the other hand, the negotiations with Greece prejudiced the Community's relations with Turkey. The Turks, like the Greeks, had an association with the Community, and they had been wanting to improve its terms. In particular, they had hoped to obtain free movement into the Community for their workers, better access for their agricultural products, and more financial aid. Nevertheless, they refused to start negotiations, on the ground that the Community's offers were inadequate.

The Community made more progress with other Mediterranean countries. Agreements signed in April with Algeria, Morocco, and Tunisia provided free access for those countries' manufactures and preferences for their agricultural products, financial aid, and nondiscriminatory conditions for their migrant workers; in return, the Community received only most-favoured-nation treatment. Preliminary negotiations with Egypt, Jordan, and Syria began early in 1976. Earlier agreements had been concluded with Israel (1975) and a number of other Mediterranean countries. Thus the prospects were for a network of similar agreements between the Community and most Mediterranean countries and the likelihood of at least one or two, and perhaps three or eventually four, additions to EEC membership. These included Portugal, which had concluded a further agreement, for financial aid, with the EEC in September, and Spain, with which, in the expectation of more democratic government,

A common summer traffic jam on the Yugoslav-Bulgarian border brings transport to a halt. A two-lane highway links Zagreb, Belgrade, Sofia, and Istanbul.

KEYSTONE

ALAIN NOGUES—SYGMA

Heads of state and government pose for photos at the July meeting of the European summit in Brussels. In centre, French Pres. Valéry Giscard d'Estaing shakes hands with Dutch Prime Minister Joop den Uyl. British Prime Minister James Callaghan stands between them.

the EEC had resumed the trade talks broken off in October 1975 after the execution of five Basque terrorists.

The Lomé Convention came fully into force in April, and the number of ACP signatories was enlarged to 51. There was an acrimonious negotiation about the current year's level of the preferential price paid by the Community for ACP sugar; the Community made its first payments to ACP countries under the Stabex commodity support scheme; and the first meeting of ministers of the ACP countries and the nine was held in July. Partly because of French reluctance, the Community made less progress in formulating trade and aid policies toward other less developed countries, although a large number of fairly liberal multifibre agreements providing for increased textile and yarn imports were concluded. On the other hand, the Community played a leading part in the Conference on International Economic Cooperation, which France promoted and which opened in Paris in February.

The Community's first trade negotiations with a state-trading country—in this case, China—were opened in February. Formal relations between the Community and the Eastern European countries were developing only slowly, however; the Community received Comecon's counterproposals for negotiations between the two groups in February and rejected them in November.

The Community's experience in its trading relations with the advanced industrial countries was checkered. There were disputes with the U.S. about Community treatment of soybean imports and U.S. policy toward some imports from Europe, including cars, but these were contained within a generally good relationship that kept protectionist pressures at bay during a time of acute economic difficulties. Relations with Canada were cemented by the conclusion of a cooperation agreement . Relations with Japan were severely strained, however, as a result of the swift inroads of a range of Japanese exports into the Community market. The multilateral trade negotiations in the General Agreement on Tariffs and Trade (GATT) were stalled pending the changeover in U.S. administrations.

Economic and Monetary Policies. It was another bad year for the Community's project for monetary union based on the "snake" of jointly floating currencies. After months of weakness reflecting intractable inflation and external deficit, the French franc was removed from the snake in March and subsequently floated downward. With the British, Irish, and Italian currencies already outside the snake, West Germany was left as the only large member of the Community adhering to it, together with Belgium, Denmark, Luxembourg, The Netherlands, and (outside the Community) Norway and Sweden. In October the currencies in the snake were realigned to reflect the continuing strength of the mark.

The disorder among the Community's currencies was the result of widely divergent rates of inflation and external deficits, which had persisted since the quintupling of oil prices in 1973 and prevented the tight linking of parities demanded by the snake. Accordingly, proposals were made for a Community system that would accommodate the weaker currencies. The French put forward an outline for a more flexible snake. The president of the Commission suggested strengthening the Community's own monetary instruments, in particular by increasing the reserve assets of the European Monetary Cooperation Fund and developing the European unit of account as a parallel currency. The Dutch used their presidency of the Council of Ministers in the second half of the year to promote their proposals for "target zones" for the Community's nonsnake currencies, with credits to help countries that followed policies compatible with those of the Community but that needed help to stay in their target zone. Meanwhile, the Community was using its financial resources to support the Italian and Irish balances of payments, and by November the finance ministers were discussing ways in which the Community might join in the funding of sterling balances.

Agriculture and Fisheries. The common agricultural policy (CAP) continued to take the lion's share of the Community's agriculture budget and to suffer from the backlash of the Community's monetary and economic crises. The greatest strain on the CAP resulted from the floating exchange rates. To avoid continual price adjustments, the common prices, fixed for agricultural products in European units of account, were converted into member countries' currencies at fixed exchange rates; thus there were divergent price levels inside different member countries when they were converted at the current, floating rates. For purposes of trade between member countries, the difference between the current (floating) exchange rate which traders used and the fixed ("green") rate was made up by monetary compensation amounts (MCA's). For example, imports of butter into Britain from France or The Netherlands attracted an MCA subsidy from the Community budget which insulated the sterling price of the butter from the fall in the sterling exchange rate.

Since sterling had been devalued by over 40% from its 1971 level, at which the green pound was fixed, imports into Britain from other Community countries attracted a huge subsidy—over £1 million a day by the autumn of 1976. Other importers, in particular Italy, also received MCA's, but the Italians agreed to a modest devaluation of the green lira. Further, Britain was by far the largest Community importer of foodstuffs. Although the expenditure on price supports for farmers under the CAP was still much larger than the consumer subsidies represented by the MCA's, the British came under heavy pressure from the Commission and other member governments to accept devaluation of the green pound. During 1976 Britain resisted this proposal, thus keeping food prices down, in line with the anti-inflation "social contract." This

Evangelical Churches:
see Religion

Exhibitions:
see Art and Art Exhibitions; Museums; Photography

Faeroe Islands:
see Dependent States

Falkland Islands:
see Dependent States

Farming:
see Agriculture and Food Supplies

also ensured a much more favourable balance between British payments to and receipts from the Community budget than had been envisaged in the debates on British entry.

Among more strictly agricultural problems, dairy products continued to cause concern. In March the Council of Ministers fixed a higher price for butter than the Commission, foreseeing a continued surplus, had proposed. The Commission's main proposal to reduce butter production, which included a tax on vegetable oils, encountered bitter opposition, not only from the U.S. with its soybean exports but also from the British, who were determined to keep down the price of margarine.

With the extension of fishing limits to 200 mi by Iceland, Norway, and many other countries, there was an urgent need for the Community to agree on a common fisheries policy. The British were particularly eager that the Community should negotiate with the Icelanders; British fishing ships would have to leave Icelandic waters before the end of the year if no new bargain were struck, and the Community, which imported substantial amounts of fish from Iceland, would have more bargaining power than Britain. The Council of Ministers did agree, on October 30, to extend the Community's limits to 200 mi and to negotiate with Iceland, Norway, and other non-EEC countries on that basis. There were still sharp differences among the member countries about policy within the Community's waters, however. The British and Irish sought national zones up to 50 mi and the French favoured minimal national waters. The Commission had proposed 12-mi national limits and, beyond that, quotas weighted in favour of fish-dependent regions, together with a program of aid for restructuring the fishing industry. The Council of Ministers agreed that special consideration be allowed to Greenland, Ireland, Scotland, and northern England. (*See* FISHERIES.)

Energy and Research. Three years after the start of the oil crisis, the Community still had no energy policy. Consumption of energy by member countries had begun to rise again, and a Commission paper forecast that by 1985, despite North Sea oil, the Community would be even more dependent on the Organization of Petroleum Exporting Countries. A floor price for Community oil was demanded by the British and supported by the Commission, but in the French view this was conditional on agreement on energy policy as a whole. The Community's Joint European Torus nuclear fusion research project was stymied by the governments' failure to agree on its location, though by autumn the Commission appeared to have secured Italy's agreement to relinquish its claim in return for a new four-year program for the joint research centre at Ispra, near Lake Maggiore.

Industrial Policy. Harmonization moved forward with Community agreement on 18 new directives setting forth common specifications for a variety of industrial products. Much of the Community's activity relating to industry, however, concerned sectors hard hit by the recession. The member countries' textile industries were pressing for more protection, particularly since the multifibre agreements negotiated by the Commission with a number of less developed countries allowed for a 6% annual increase in the volume of imports. But the most pressing problems came from Japan. To prevent Japan from taking an expected 80% of the stagnant world market for ships, the Commission in May proposed a program that would favour Community shipping and set limits to competition among shipbuilders. This scheme was not accepted by the Council of Ministers. By November, however, the Commission seemed to be near agreement with governments and steel industries on proposals to provide for production quotas in times of recession, and Japan appeared ready to accept more effective export restraint. (JOHN PINDER)

See also Defense; Economy, World.
[534.F.3.b.iv; 971.D.7]

Fashion and Dress

Just as jeans had become a basic for summer wear throughout the world, loden coats settled in as the ubiquitous fashion hit for town wear in the winter of 1975–76. Whether the real thing from Austria or a copy, the pea-soup-colour coat made its appearance with the first gray skies. Practical, warm, wrinkle- and rainproof, and also very inexpensive, it was teamed with pants, a turtleneck sweater and muffler or a shirt and knotted scarf, and a down-to-the-eyebrows knitted hat with a wide cuff.

Capes gave way to ponchos with high side indents, the newest having bold stripes in combinations of nutshell colour and earth brown. Many of the models, striving for an ethnic look, featured materials of the handwoven type and thick fringe trimming. The Peruvian influence showed in ponchos with strong designs.

The heavy-knit pullover, chunky or long, preferably handmade of extra-thick, off-white wool in the Aran Islands style, became the base for a display of imaginative and intricate stitches. The more chic models had fawn leather patches at the elbow. Narrow pants rolled into a heavy cuff at boot top completed the outfit. Boots for the young trendsetters were of the straight pull-on type, on the heavy side with thick crepe soles in natural colour. Others still preferred the high-heeled, crushed leather, riding-boot style.

Other utilitarian garments becoming high style were workmen's clothes, particularly overalls and the mechanic's jumpsuit. American women, always keenest for the pants look, were the first to adopt the jumpsuit for day wear, often choosing models in jersey.

LEFT, WIDE WORLD; RIGHT, SYNDICATION INTERNATIONAL/PHOTO TRENDS

Givenchy's winter collection included an evening dress in purple crepe georgette worn with a high-belted skirt (on left). Mary Quant brought out a one-piece cotton jumpsuit with drawstrings at waist and ankles.

A dress in Moroccan crepe with a cape of Russian sable (left) was featured in Christian Dior's fall-winter collection. Halston took a length of printed chiffon and let it flow, for the new "natural" look.

LEFT, AGIP/PICTORIAL PARADE; RIGHT, DON HOGAN CHARLES—THE NEW YORK TIMES

Parisians preferred a snappier version in lacquered nylon, dark red, midnight blue, or gunmetal brown, worn with a side-tilted beret. For evening, jumpsuits became more feminine, with a low neckline or strapless, and with accessories adding dash. With a glance toward the Orient, some of the satin versions were puffed just above the ankle.

Spring came early, and with it the tube line, slits, and a mania for blazers. The U.S. Bicentennial encouraged a wave of romanticism. In New York City the omnipresent blazer appeared in all sorts of shades, including poison green, but in Paris it was more often plain white, navy, or fire-engine red—for a time the Paris streets were a montage of red, white, and blue. Bright red, instead of white, trimmed the classic navy blazer, and gold braid appeared on many white models. The London blazer, in black velvet, navy gabardine, or flannel, was worn with easy pleated skirts and sensible shoes to produce the "dependable English look." The pure white blazer was often chosen as a companion to short silk party dresses or bare-shouldered black crepe ones. Pants suits, in classic gray flannel or sandy beige gabardine, were strictly tailored, but the look was softened by feminine silk blouses with loosely knotted collar bands.

The alternative to pants was the tube-line skirt, so narrow that a high slit, centre front, was indispensable for walking. High slits on unlined navy coats turned the skirts into circles of flying panels. High side slits were also featured on long, slim tunics worn over trousers or narrow, accordion-pleated skirts, and on caftans with elaborate jeweled trimming. Later in the season stripes appeared: pin stripes, hairline stripes, candy stripes—usually black, gray, or navy on a white background. Stripes were much more popular than florals in the spring.

Another tendency was to balance the tube-line skirt with a bulky top in the form of a long inflated blouson that brought the waistline down to hip level. This idea was carried over from sportswear to evening clothes, where plain gabardine, corduroy, and jersey gave way to florals in silk jersey or crepe de chine and to sheer chiffon. A successful London version of the blouson was in soft cashmere with kangaroo pockets and hood, worn with a pleated tartan skirt. In New York it appeared in thin, supersoft, rice-coloured wool and in tan twill, worn over pants. A French summer version was short sleeved and hooded, with horizontal red and white striping, rounded at the sides and reaching just below the waistline. Top bulk was also the effect of the T-line—wide, deep armholes, straight sleeves to the elbow, and rounded shoulders over a slim skirt. This silhouette was found frequently in plain cotton dresses with high waistlines and inserts of Liberty florals.

As soon as the hot weather set in, the cruise and beachwear look dominated the fashion scene in all large cities. There were fewer jeans and more dresses and skirts, though jeans were rejuvenated with matching tops in amusing shapes—judo jackets or tiny cropped waistcoats worn over Liberty print blouses. The strapped, sleeveless T-shirt also gave a new touch to the old jeans uniform.

But it was the cotton dress that won the fashion race in the summer. The milkmaid dress with ruffles and apron straight from England had a tremendous effect on the younger generation. Many were in Liberty prints in subtle tones, with parma, raspberry, and olive among the prevailing nuances as background for little black flower designs. Others were in cotton prints from the French provinces, always with small floral patterns. Most were cut with a square neckline and had a raised waistline with gathers just below the seaming, back and front. Shoulders were rounded and dropped and sleeves wide and square, Japanese style. As the temperature rose and the European drought set in, dresses became sleeveless. The sun dress with wide shoulder straps was soon followed by a strapless version, both styles having small fitted bodices with smocking across the rib cage The strapless look became epidemic in New York. It continued into the fall for evening wear, vying with the one-bare-shoulder style and the off-centre V-neck introduced by Halston.

Plain black cotton was a popular choice for the high-waisted sun dress styled with double shoestring shoulder straps and a dirndl skirt. It was frequently worn with a fringed shawl to complete the all-black look, very effective with a good suntan. Floral-printed upholstery material was another choice for the gathered skirt attached to a smocked brassiere top.

There was a hot weather version of overalls—in cotton, plain white or with red and white or navy and white stripes, cut with a square neckline and shoulder straps, and worn over a printed blouse. The Indian-squaw look descended on the beaches as white cotton fringing was attached to everything from skirts to bikinis, pants, handbags, and belts. The look was completed by an armload of Indian-style beaded bracelets. All were made in France and were a huge success in the U.S. The universally adopted accessory was the wedge-heeled espadrille or open-toe canvas sandal, laced up the leg and preferably black. This meant the end of the awkward clog. Head scarves twisted to hide all trace of hair or scarves with attached visors completed the summer fashion picture.

White or natural cheesecloth and hospital gauze were mandatory for the cocktail hour at Saint-Tropez. The dresses seemed to float around the body, an effect produced by a loose tabard over a full skirt. Alternatives were a free-flowing tunic over matching pants puffed at the ankle and a style inspired by the sari, draped and caught up at the centre. The link among all these models was transparency.

With the two-piece bathing suit reduced to a few strings held together by a patch or two, cover-ups were offered by designers who thought the beach towel unimaginative. Accordingly, tunics, hooded beach robes in the spirit of the Arab djellaba, wraparound skirts, shorts, and sarongs were displayed in shop windows and on the beaches. But the surprise was the success of the one-piece suit, admittedly styled with daring cutouts at the sides and no straps.

The first signs of winter confirmed the strength of the ethnic look as tabards, blousons, and ponchos emphasized the top-heavy silhouette. Blousons were the favourite, in blanket wool, quilted gabardine, jersey, and leather for day wear and in lace or taffeta for evening. Stoles and shawls were piled on. Skirts remained slim and pants narrow, the latter tucked into boots or puffed at the ankles. Bold blanket-type stripes in new strong colours updated the perennial duffle coat. Colours were striking: bright red, indigo blue, grass green, raspberry, fuchsia, black currant. Some of the ethnic paraphernalia was the real thing, imported directly from the source.

Then a turnabout occurred. The tube line seemed to be sidetracked and a far more feminine silhouette appeared. This really originated in the winter collection shown in April by Yves Saint Laurent (*see* BIOGRAPHY). This designer, apparently tired of neat masculine clothes, presented full dirndl skirts cinched at the waist and soft Russian-peasant blouses with billowy sleeves and colourful embroidery trimming. Some of the gathered skirts even had underskirts. Coats, also gathered from under a raised waistline, carried braid in contrasting colours up and down the seams. Evening clothes glittered with gold tinsel. Still ethnic, the inspiration ran from Mongolia to North Africa and Turkey. The full-skirted look led to a shift from chiffon to taffeta. Inclined to discard the long-standing shapeless look and limp chiffon dresses, women started moving toward this full dancing skirt, which could set off a trim waistline. In the fall, the spring and summer collections of some Paris houses, such as Kenzo and Dorothée Bis, set off shock waves by reintroducing the mini, and the look quickly appeared on Paris streets. U.S. designers, who had only just succeeded in coaxing American women into longer skirts, were less enthusiastic, although a few minis appeared in their collections, generally in the guise of sportswear.

Cosmetics and Hairstyles. In the spring cosmetics were tuned to match the lively fashion colour range. Playing with rose and brown, Helena Rubinstein suggested "Burnt Almond" for a base, combined with a matching burnt-pink lipstick called "Sheer Smoky Pink." Fifteen shades of pink were offered by Estée Lauder in her "Runaway Roses" line in an effort to wake up the all-white fashion look, and eyelid shadow played with flower shades of rose and lilac. Elizabeth Arden insisted on "Basic Beige" for a "Believable Color," with "Cherrywood" as a sponge-on cheek colour.

The autumn fashions with their vivid colours, bold designs, and strong ethnic influence called for makeup in deep rich shades. Inspiration often came from nature, as in the "Apple Country" line at Estée Lauder, with deep rich reds for lips, cheeks, and nails, or the red currant or "Groseille" at Lancôme. For a dramatic look, Helena Rubinstein contrasted a pale, clear face with bright red or "Follement Rouge" and plum "Cream Shadow" on the eyelids.

Hairstyles drifted toward more youthful and natural cuts, epitomized by the short brush and thick bangs popularized by Olympic skating champion Dorothy Hamill. The long and lanky Alice-in-Wonderland look, popular through the spring and summer, gave way in the autumn to shorter, neater, even boyish, and occasionally crew-cut styles.

(THELMA SWEETINBURGH)

The ethnic look was exemplified in this light tunic coat of cashmere from Emanuel Ungaro (left) and a Russian-inspired coat of blue monk's cloth by Yves Saint Laurent.

LEFT, J. P. METAYER; RIGHT, JEAN-LOUIS GUEGAN—WOOL

Men's Fashions. Comfort and elegance were characteristic of men's clothes in 1976. In most countries the single-breasted two-piece suit continued to be the most popular. Easier to wear because the jacket was looser fitting and the materials, including the interlining, were lighter in weight, these suits also appeared in much lighter colours: silver grays, light blue-grays, beige and biscuit shades, and some camel. The styling remained classic; there was less padding at the shoulders, the lapels were narrower and longer, and there was a slight accentuation at the waist.

These lounge suits in worsted and man-made fibre blends and the safari-style leisure suits and blouson jackets in cotton, denim, and drills, many in the lighter shades and not a few in white and off-white, dominated the major trade exhibitions in Europe, as well as in the U.S. and Canada. They were equally in evidence at the two new exhibitions held in Britain in the fall, the Menswear Association of Britain International Fashion Fair at Birmingham and the Menswear Fashion Fair International at Manchester.

Sales of lounge suits generally were helped by the International Wool Secretariat's "Man in Wool" suit promotion in 18 countries. The hot dry summer in Britain and some other European countries found many more men wearing tropical-weight suits. Blue denim jeans and jackets, which had become almost a universal uniform for the younger generation, were also worn by some older men during the midsummer hot spell.

There were a number of changes in shirt patterns,

(LEFT) RODEX OF LONDON; (OTHERS) AUTHENTICATED NEWS INTERNATIONAL

Lightweight white hats were worn with the brims turned down all around (above). Saint Laurent featured a blazer of soft chamois-like suede (centre) and a more sophisticated blazer suit with an elegant low-cut vest (right).

notably to handkerchief checks and border stripes. The fashion for white collars and cuffs with a patterned body cloth was short-lived. Because shirt collar points were shorter, ties tended to become narrower. Patterns were neater and colours stronger. Dress shirts were enlivened by frills, embroidery, and pleated fronts. The black or coloured velvet bow tie continued to be fashionable.

There was more variety in dinner jackets (tuxedos), with velvet and cotton needlecord and mohair/worsted and polyester/worsted blends providing more comfortable alternatives to the traditional black barathea. The earlier trend to the layered look in knitwear continued, and many new knitted jacket-type garments made their appearance in this context.

The emphasis on comfort also was seen in hats. White cotton summer hats were worn with the brim turned down all around, and tweed hats in a similar style were popular for the fall and winter. Comfort in footwear was provided by "earth" shoes or natural shoes finished without a built-up heel.

Sales of sports and leisure clothing continued to rise in most countries. Clothes worn by the active sportsman when playing influenced the styles worn by those who only watched. (STANLEY H. COSTIN)

See also Industrial Review: *Furs.*

[451.B.2.b; 451.B.2.d.i; 629.C.1]

ENCYCLOPÆDIA BRITANNICA FILMS. *Culture and Costumes: The Great Clothes Put-On* (1974).

Fencing: *see* Combat Sports

Field Hockey and Lacrosse

Field Hockey. Men's hockey was turned upside down in 1976 when the longtime dominance of Asian and European teams came to an end during the Olympic Games at Montreal in July. When the dust settled, New Zealand had won the gold medal and Australia the silver. Women's hockey, too, was in mild confusion after competition for the second Women's World Cup. The tournament was sponsored by the Fédération Internationale de Hockey (FIH) in Berlin in May. When West Germany defeated Argentina in the final, women's hockey had two world champions. The previous September in Edinburgh, England won a world championship organized by the International Federation of Women's Hockey Associations (IFWHA). The prospects for an accommodation, however, brightened with the establishment of a Supreme Council on which both groups were represented.

During the nine Olympiads held from 1928 through 1968 India won 7 gold medals and Pakistan 2. In 1972 at Munich, however, West Germany broke the sequence of Asian victories, though Pakistan and India were still very much in contention, finishing second and third, respectively.

The first stage of the Olympic Games competition, the pool matches, ran reasonably true to form, except for a disappointing display by West Germany. The Netherlands headed Pool A with a maximum 10 points, 4 points better than either Australia or India. Pakistan led Pool B with 7 points, besting both New Zealand and Spain, which garnered 4 points each. The play-off matches to break second-place ties were won by Australia and New Zealand, a hint of what was to happen next. Contrary to early expectations, The Netherlands was beaten in the semifinal round by New Zealand, and Pakistan fell victim to Australia. The victory put New Zealand in its first Olympic final and its team made the most of it, winning 1–0. For Australia it meant a second silver medal in Olympic field hockey; in 1968 Australia was runner-up to Pakistan in Mexico City. The Montreal tournament was the first international title decided on artificial turf. The final Olympic standings were: (1) New Zealand; (2) Australia; (3) Pakistan; (4) The Netherlands; (5) West Germany; (6) Spain; (7) India; (8) Malaysia; (9) Belgium; (10) Canada; (11) Argentina.

(R. L. HOLLANDS)

[452.B.4.h.xvi]

See also Track and Field Sports: *Special Report.*

Lacrosse. MEN. The exchange of international visits at both senior and junior levels continued during 1976, but everyone was looking forward to the quadrennial World Series of lacrosse scheduled for 1978.

In the U.S., Cornell University won the National Collegiate Athletic Association (NCAA) championship in a thrilling game against the University of Maryland, which was appearing in its fourth consecutive national final. Cornell, which like Maryland was undefeated when it took the field, was down 2–7 at halftime, but it built up a 12–10 lead with just three minutes remaining to be played. Then the incomparable four-time All-American Frank Urso scored for Maryland. In the final second of regular play Urso staved off defeat by setting up the tying goal with a pass. In a mandatory double overtime, Cornell clinched the title 16–13. The game was the first to be carried on nationwide U.S. television.

In Canada there was no professional 1976 National Lacrosse League champion because the League, beset with financial problems and other difficulties, was unable to continue operations. The Mann Cup was won four games to three by New Westminster of British Columbia against Brampton of Ontario. The President's Cup, symbol of the Senior B championship, was awarded to the Edmonton (Alta.) Fullers at the end of a round robin competition. The Canadian national Junior A championship was won by the Victoria (B.C.) MacDonalds, which captured the Minto Cup with four straight victories over Bramalea of Ontario.

The English club championship (Iroquois Cup) was won by Hampstead over Old Hulmeians 20–8. Sheffield University was again crowned British university champion.

While touring the U.S., Australia defeated Southern California All-Stars 18–6, West Florida All Stars 31–5, Mount Washington 20–19, Chesapeake Club 13–11, Rutgers University 18–7, and Cortland State University College 18–6; it lost to Washington and Lee University 10–15, University of Maryland 10–22, and Long Island 16–22. In Canada the Australians outscored the Canada All Stars 27–12. In England, Australia lost to Manchester 14–11, but easily defeated a Southern President's team in London.

(CHARLES DENNIS COPPOCK)

WOMEN. In the U.S. in 1976, during the national tournament in May, while the U.S. and reserve teams were being selected, the first division championship was won by the superb Philadelphia I team which beat its closest rival, Southern I. In fact, the rivalry between these two teams dominated U.S. club lacrosse throughout the season. The second division championship was won by the New England team. An Australian team was scheduled to tour the U.S. in 1977. Fierce competition for places on the U.S. squad and a new coach were expected to reinforce the high standard of women's lacrosse in the U.S.

In Great Britain the 1975–76 season was highlighted by the five-week visit of the U.S. team. Managed by Kathy Heinze, an Englishwoman, the U.S. squad won all 13 matches and scored an incredible total of 189 goals against the opponents' 27. The Americans returned home unbeaten, with the enviable distinction of being the first tourists ever to defeat the South (12–4), England (6–5), and Great Britain (8–6). Their success was attributed to supreme fitness, speed, stickwork skills, esprit de corps, and above all to determination.

In the home internationals, England was again victorious, defeating Scotland 16–1 and Wales 17–0. Scotland outscored Wales 11–4. The territorial championship was won by the Midlands, a powerful, well-coordinated team, which beat all four of the other territories, including the South, the 1975 champions. South pride was partially restored when the South Reserves repeated their success of last season with a victory in the Territorial Reserves Tournament. The All England Clubs and Colleges Tournament in April was again won by Bedford College of Physical Education. The first-ever British Universities Touring Team, which visited the U.S. East Coast for three weeks, played 17 matches and lost only one; against college teams it scored 242 goals and conceded 51. A British Redcoats team that visited the U.S. in May joined bicentennial celebrations to provide a fitting climax to a pleasurable international season.

(MARGARET-LOUISE FRAWLEY)

[452.B.4.h.xx]

CANADIAN PRESS

Canadian and Indian field hockey players race for the ball in their Olympic match in Montreal.

Fiji

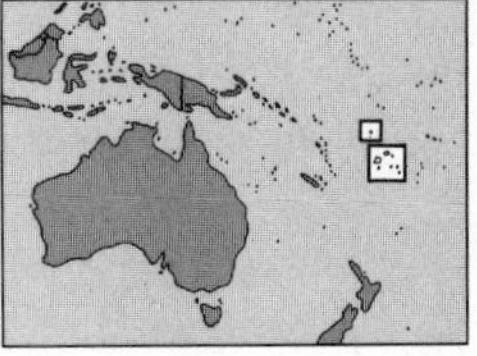

An independent parliamentary state and member of the Commonwealth of Nations, Fiji is an island group in the South Pacific Ocean, about 2,000 mi. E of Australia and 3,200 mi. S of Hawaii. Area: 7,055 sq mi (18,273 sq km), with two major islands, Viti Levu (4,011 sq mi) and Vanua Levu (2,137 sq mi), and several hundred smaller islands. Pop. (1975 est.): 569,000. Cap. and largest city: Suva (pop., 1974 est., 71,600). Language: English, Fijian, and Hindi. Religion: Christian and Hindu. Queen, Elizabeth II; governor-general in 1976, Ratu Sir George Cakobáu; prime minister, Ratu Sir Kamisese Mara.

In February 1976 the royal commission appointed to make recommendations on the most appropriate method of electing members to the House of Representatives presented its report. The existing constitution reflected the plural nature of Fiji's society, 27 seats being filled on a racially based vote on a communal roll and 25 by a cross-voting system in which all races vote together. The commission recommended abolition of the cross-voting seats and introduction of a system by which half of the seats would be ra-

FIJI

Education. (1974) Primary, pupils 135,092, teachers 4,229; secondary, pupils 26,202, teachers 1,103; vocational, pupils 1,715, teachers 174; teacher training, students 506, teachers 50; higher (University of the South Pacific; 1973), students 1,348, teaching staff 113.

Finance and Trade. Monetary unit: Fiji dollar, with (Sept. 20, 1976) a free rate of F$0.90 to U.S. $1 (F$1.54 = £1 sterling). Budget (1974): revenue F$88.8 million; expenditure F$83.3 million. Foreign trade (1975): imports F$221,750,000; exports F$141,760,000. Import sources (1974): Australia 30%; Japan 18.6%; New Zealand 11%; U.K. 10%; Singapore 8%. Export destinations: U.K. 30%; U.S. 26%; Australia 10%; New Zealand 7%. Main exports (1974): sugar 54%; petroleum products 12%; coconut products 9%; gold 7%. Tourism: visitors (1971) 152,000; gross receipts (1973) U.S. $49 million.

Transport and Communications. Roads (1973) 2,661 km. Motor vehicles in use (1974): passenger cars 19,800; commercial (including buses) 9,200. Railways (1973) *c.* 650 km (for sugar estates). Shipping (1975): merchant vessels 100 gross tons and over 28; gross tonnage 7,674. Ships entered (1974) vessels totaling 2,624,000 net registered tons; goods loaded 480,000 metric tons, unloaded 682,000 metric tons. Telephones (Dec. 1974) 25,556. Radio receivers (Dec. 1973) *c.* 150,000.

Agriculture. Production (in 000; metric tons; 1975): sugar, raw value *c.* 285; rice (1974) *c.* 18; sweet potatoes *c.* 16; cassava *c.* 90; copra *c.* 25; bananas (exports; 1974) *c.* 4. Livestock (in 000; Sept. 1974): cattle *c.* 165; pigs *c.* 30; goats *c.* 57; horses *c.* 33.

Industry. Production (in 000; 1974): cement (metric tons) 85; gold (troy oz) 69; electricity (kw-hr) 223,000.

cially based and half would be elected on a "common roll." Adoption of the recommendations was doubtful, as the ruling Alliance Party appeared not to support them.

The general mood of cooperation that had characterized post-independence politics was dispelled by the formation of splinter groups from both major parties. Late in 1975 a representative seeking "Fiji for the Fijians" called for the repatriation of Fiji's Indian population, and this was followed by heated exchanges among the party leaders. In August 1976 the government introduced legislation making it an offense to incite racial hatred.

Despite improved access to overseas markets, Fiji's sugar earnings fell because of lower world prices and a drop in production. In October Fiji was host to a special meeting of the South Pacific Forum at which it was agreed that, if the UN Conference on the Law of the Sea failed to reach agreement, members would consider unilateral declarations of a 200-mi economic zone. (BARRIE MACDONALD)

[977.A.3]

Finland

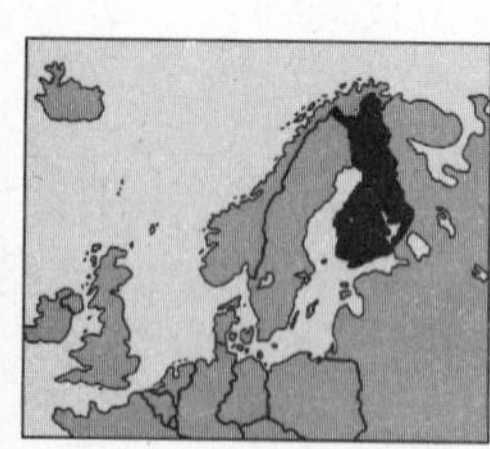

The republic of Finland is bordered on the north by Norway, on the west by Sweden and the Gulf of Bothnia, on the south by the Gulf of Finland, and on the east by the U.S.S.R. Area: 130,129 sq mi (337,032 sq km). Pop. (1976 est.): 4,736,000. Cap. and largest city: Helsinki (pop., 1976 est., 492,300). Language: Finnish, Swedish. Religion (1974): Lutheran 91.4%; Orthodox 1.2%. President in 1976, Urho Kaleva Kekkonen; prime minister, Martti J. Miettunen.

Political instability dominated the Finnish scene in 1976. A proposed increase in the sales tax led to interparty dissension in the left-centre coalition led by Miettunen—the only Western European government to contain Communists as part of the ruling coalition—and the prime minister attempted to resign on May 13. President Kekkonen, however, devised a formula by which the other four parties would allow the Communists to record their opposition to a higher tax within the Cabinet and urged him to continue in office. On September 17 the president accepted Miettunen's resignation after quarrels erupted inside the government over the 1977 budget: the Communists wanted higher housing and employment allocations than their partners would countenance, while the Social Democrats and the rural-based Centre Party clashed over financing the disposal of an unexpectedly large harvest. On September 29, at the president's insistence, Miettunen formed a three-party centrist minority coalition holding only 58 of the 200 seats in Parliament. In local elections on October 17–18 the four large parties consolidated their positions.

The one-year centralized wage agreement, hammered out in January, provided for all-round increases of 7%, but nine unions dissociated themselves from this settlement. A wave of strikes ensued, including, in February, the first postwar police stoppage in Europe. The most serious blows to a sluggish economy were strikes in March–April by food-processing workers and seamen. Unemployment peaked at 96,400 (4.2% of the work force), and the net emigration to Sweden was resumed. In June the quinquennial congress of the 900,000-strong Federation of Finnish Trade Unions (SAK) revealed widespread accord between Social Democrats and Communists. Neverthe-

FINLAND

Education. (1973–74) Primary, pupils 393,242, teachers 21,248; secondary, pupils 405,203, teachers 17,536; vocational, pupils 110,355, teachers 10,823; teacher training, students 1,421, teachers 389; higher (including 11 universities), students 67,881, teaching staff 4,940.

Finance. Monetary unit: markka, with (Sept. 20, 1976) a free rate of 3.86 markkaa to U.S. $1 (6.64 markkaa = £1 sterling). Gold, SDR's, and foreign exchange (June 1976) U.S. $519.6 million. Budget (1976 est.): revenue 28,519,000,000 markkaa; expenditure 27,970,000,000 markkaa. Gross national product (1975) 96,180,000,000 markkaa. Money supply (Feb. 1976) 8,770,000,000 markkaa. Cost of living (1970 = 100; June 1976) 198.

Foreign Trade. (1975) Imports 28,011,000,000 markkaa; exports 20,246,000,000 markkaa. Import sources: U.S.S.R. 17%; Sweden 16%; West Germany 14%; U.K. 9%; U.S. 6%. Export destinations: U.S.S.R. 21%; Sweden 18%; U.K. 14%; West Germany 8%; Norway 5%. Main exports: paper 28%; machinery 12%; ships 8%; wood pulp 7%; timber 7%; clothing 6%.

Transport and Communications. Roads (1974) 73,347 km (including 167 km expressways). Motor vehicles in use (1974): passenger 936,681; commercial 124,897. Railways: (1974) 5,948 km; traffic (1975) 3,132,000,000 passenger-km, freight 6,438,000,000 net ton-km. Air traffic (1975): 1,259,200,000 passenger-km; freight 31,551,000 net ton-km. Navigable inland waterways (1974) 6,675 km. Shipping (1975): merchant vessels 100 gross tons and over 361; gross tonnage 2,001,618. Telephones (Dec. 1974) 1,678,870. Radio licenses (Dec. 1974) 1,997,000. Television licenses (Dec. 1974) 1,261,000.

Agriculture. Production (in 000; metric tons; 1975): wheat 559; barley 1,155; oats 1,423; rye 69; potatoes 680; sugar, raw value (1974) 82; butter 78; eggs *c.* 76; timber (cu m; 1974) 40,780; fish catch (1974) *c.* 100. Livestock (in 000; June 1975): cattle 1,843; sheep 124; pigs 1,036; horses 38; poultry 9,391.

Industry. Production (in 000; metric tons; 1975): pig iron 1,355; crude steel 1,623; iron ore (metal content; 1974) 615; copper (1974) 38; cement 2,063; sulfuric acid 1,030; petroleum products (1974) 8,279; plywood (cu m; 1974) 530; cellulose (1974) 4,067; wood pulp (1974) mechanical 2,140, chemical 4,452; newsprint 1,253; other paper and board (1974) 4,296; electricity (kw-hr) 28,766,000; manufactured gas (cu m) 27,100.

Finnish Literature: *see* Literature
Fires: *see* Disasters

less, the Communist hard core, frequently blamed for wildcat strikes, castigated their revisionist comrades inside and outside the unions. Attempts to check inflation (35% in 1974–75) achieved only partial success. Despite a semiofficial target of 5% and a price freeze between February and June, an 11% rise in the cost of living for the year seemed likely. Restraint was practiced by the central bank which, as forecast by the president when he called for a "national emergency government" in November 1975, was at loggerheads with the politicians. The Bank of Finland's tough line on credit was instrumental in halving the record 7.7 billion markkaa trade deficit of 1975. On July 1 the bank, faced with a foreign debt of 22 billion markkaa, obtained a seven-year, $300 million standby credit facility from 14 North American banks. A midterm review of the one-year pay deal broke down on October 27, after employers had rejected union demands for a 4% increase. This, together with dismissals and layoffs, led to talk of a crisis of confidence in industrial relations and forecasts of strikes for the winter of 1976–77. Early in November, 670 station guards went on strike illegally for a reduction of retirement age from 63 to 58, but the intervention of the prime minister brought the strike to an end on November 11.

Foreign policy was pursued in light of the 1975 Helsinki Conference on Security and Cooperation in Europe. The Belgrade follow-up meeting, fixed for June 1977, was a special concern, as a visit by the Yugoslav foreign minister indicated. The friendship treaty of 1948 with the U.S.S.R., renewed until 1990, was widely debated after publication of a Soviet study. The foreign minister, Kalevi Sorsa, denied that the Finnish and Soviet governments put differing interpretations on the agreement.

On April 13 an explosion at the Lapua munitions works killed 40 people and injured 69 others. One of the century's greatest Finns, the architect Alvar Aalto (*see* OBITUARIES), died in Helsinki at the age of 78. On the brighter side was the unprecedented achievement of the Finnish runner Lasse Viren (*see* BIOGRAPHY), who repeated his 1972 Munich Olympics feat by winning both the 5,000 m and the 10,000 m at the Montreal Olympic Games. For the expulsion of North Korean diplomats from Finland on October 20, *see* KOREA. (DONALD FIELDS)

[972.A.6.d.i]

Finland's Pres. Urho Kekkonen met with Pres. Gerald Ford during a visit to the United States in July and August.

JACQUES TIZIOU—SYGMA

Fisheries

Although optimistic observers had predicted that an international 200-mi fisheries limit—or, more accurately, zone of control—would be agreed on by the end of 1975, it was apparent that legal and political problems had been underestimated. By the end of 1976 little progress had been made, other than a general increase in support for the new concept.

This was, in fact, the only visible result of the third UN Conference on the Law of the Sea (UNCLOS III), which met twice in New York in 1976. (*See* LAW: *Special Report.*) Eventually, the conference was expected to set the seal on a 200-mi regime, under which coastal nations would be responsible for fish stocks in their exclusive economic zone (EEZ). The coastal nation would also have first claim on fish stocks within the zone, subject to need (for domestic use or export) and the ability to catch the quantity claimed. Other nations—especially those with historic rights—would then bargain for the right to fish specific species in prescribed quantities.

It was not just the scientists who were sounding the note of alarm. It was painfully apparent to fishing enterprises of many nations that the average catch rate, or "catch per unit effort," was far below what it had been—so much so that some fisheries had become uneconomic for nations that had to steam long distances to the fishing grounds; in 1966–76, for example, a fivefold increase in fishing capacity in the northwest Atlantic saw total catch rise by only 15%.

Someone had to be blamed for allowing stocks to get so low, and the various international controlling bodies were the most convenient targets. Thus, in the area of the Newfoundland Grand Banks, it was the International Commission for the Northwest Atlantic

Table I. Whaling: 1974-75 Season (Antarctic); 1974 Season (Outside the Antarctic)
Number of whales caught

Area and country	Fin whale	Sei/ Bryde's whale	Hump-back whale	Minke whale	Sperm whale	Total	Percentage assigned under quota agree-ment*
Antarctic pelagic (open sea)							
Japan	598	2,251	—	3,500	307	6,656	54.1
Norway†							
U.S.S.R.	381	1,608	—	3,500	3,855	9,344‡	45.9
Total	979	3,859	—	7,000	4,162	16,000‡	100.0
Outside the Antarctic§							
Japan	240	1,947	—	—	4,164	6,351	
U.S.S.R.	173	696	—	—	3,963	5,015‖	
South Africa	21	13	—	—	1,783	1,817	
Peru	5	521	—	—	1,286	1,812	
Australia	—	—	—	—	1,080	1,080	
Iceland	285	9	—	—	71	365	
Others	63	452	9	—	196	741¶	
Total	787	3,638	9	—	12,543	17,181‖¶	

*Antarctic only.
†Norway had no expeditions in the Antarctic in the 1974–75 season.
‡Includes others (bottlenose, killer, gray, right, and blue whales).
§Excluding small whales.
‖Includes 183 gray whales.
¶Includes 21 other whales.
Source: The Committee for Whaling Statistics, *International Whaling Statistics*.

Fisheries (ICNAF) that came under fire for setting overoptimistic catch quotas for the nations engaged in that area. These quotas were based on the total allowable catch (TAC) for any species in any specific zone, and this TAC was agreed on by fisheries scientists of the signatory nations of ICNAF. However, the scientists were quick to point out that quotas had become international currency in political bargaining, and politicians were allocating quotas of fish which, when added together, exceeded the TAC, thus dipping heavily into reserves and preventing recovery of the stock. Scientist and politician alike also claimed that the quota system was almost impossible to enforce, and that nations with excessive catching capacity were taking more than their fair share.

It was conceded that nothing short of local control by the nation with the most to lose would reverse this downward trend. Canada, whose fleet-expansion program had been scrapped because of the state of the fish stocks, claimed that its fleet was landing only half its fishing capacity. Canada was one of the most dedicated of the 200-mi club. In May the Canadian fisheries minister, Roméo LeBlanc, announced that Jan. 1, 1977, would be the date on which Canada would unilaterally claim its right to control fish stocks 200 mi from its coastlines, closing lines of bays, and islands. The U.S. was to follow on March 1, 1977.

LeBlanc's policy was "Canada's needs and requirements first, then share the remainder," and since Canada had never developed its deep-sea fishery to the level of some Western European, Eastern European, and Far Eastern nations, its share would not be excessive. The big cutback for other nations would be the result of reduced fish stocks rather than of reduced access. By mid-1976 some half dozen major fishing nations, including the U.S.S.R., Poland, and Portugal, had responded to the Canadians' invitation to sign bilateral fishing agreements.

Meanwhile, Iceland's claims of a 200-mi EEZ around its coasts had sparked yet another "cod war" with Great Britain, whose heavy reliance on these waters for its favourite cod had already involved it in two such confrontations. The inability of either side to accept the other's proposals for a settlement, despite offers of drastic catch reductions by the U.K., produced a stalemate that brought British naval vessels into Icelandic waters outside the accepted 50-mi limit. Britain's case, as stated by its Foreign Office, was that the Icelandic claim to 200 mi had not been approved by the International Court of Justice at The Hague, and therefore the Royal Navy was protecting British vessels going about their lawful business on the high seas. As for Iceland, its government was politically committed to "Icelandic fish for the Icelanders."

It took months of costly and dangerous confrontation at sea to prove that the Icelandic harassment of trawlers by cutting trawl wires could not be totally prevented by a force of naval frigates. Collisions were frequent and frightening; tempers grew frayed and catches became uneconomic because of lost gear and the "box" system of fishing in groups. A temporary settlement, finally reached in June, limited the number of British trawlers allowed to fish at any one time in the 200-mi zone and was to expire December 1. Rumour had it that the U.K.'s need to negotiate a new European Economic Community common fisheries policy, together with Iceland's threats to pull out of NATO (with the loss to NATO of the Keflavik air base), forced the settlement. But no fresh agreement was negotiated by the end of the year, and British trawlers remained excluded from Icelandic waters.

Britain's insistence on a renegotiation of the EEC common fisheries policy was dictated by the changed circumstances that would be created by the 200-mi

Gulls hover hungrily as fishermen off New Bedford, Massachusetts, hose down their deck. Catches have been getting smaller because of competition from large foreign fishing fleets.

WIDE WORLD

Table II. World Fisheries, 1974*
In 000 metric tons

Country	Catch		Disposition of catch†	
	Total	Freshwater	Fresh marketed	Frozen, cured, canned, etc.
Japan	10,733.4	179.4	3,223.9‡	7,495.5
U.S.S.R.	9,235.6	772.9	...	...
China	...	...	...	...
Peru	4,149.9	5.4	143.1§	3,980.1§
United States	2,743.7	82.0	811.0	1,932.7
Norway	2,644.9	...	68.6	2,576.5
India	2,255.3	783.3	1,437.0	818.3
Korea, South	2,001.3	1.3	1,090.2	933.2
Denmark	1,835.4	13.3	112.1‖	1,723.3‖
Thailand	1,626.0	238.0	600.0	1,028.0
Spain	1,510.7	14.0	518.1	659.4
South Africa	1,414.6	0.1	...	...
Indonesia	1,341.9	449.0	...	...
Philippines	1,291.4	102.7	1,038.6	259.7
Chile	1,126.7	...	94.2	1,032.4
United Kingdom	1,102.5	...	622.3¶♀	532.8¶
Canada	1,027.3	47.6	210.4¶	907.1¶
Vietnam	1,013.5	176.3	...	...
Iceland	945.4	...	63.0	875.5
France	807.5	...	...	...
Korea, North	800.0	...	...	...
Nigeria	684.9	347.1	...	...
Poland	679.0	21.9	...	...
Brazil	604.7	77.7	...	...
Germany, West	525.7	15.0	80.0δ	508.0δ
Angola	469.7	...	13.2¶	454.0¶
Mexico	442.1	14.1	171.8	270.2
Malaysia	441.6	2.0	369.8§	153.9§
Burma	433.8	126.2	108.4	325.4
Portugal	428.0	0.2	220.9	169.1
Italy	425.4	17.5	347.9	78.2
Germany, East	363.3	13.5	...	...
Senegal	357.0	10.0	...	...
Netherlands, The	325.9	3.4	238.8‡	78.9
Argentina	301.3	10.1	99.8	166.9
Morocco	288.1	0.4	80.8	200.9
Turkey	259.4	14.4	...	...
Bangladesh	247.2	211.9	...	...
Faeroe Islands	247.0	...	44.7	202.5
Ghana	223.5	41.3	...	...
Sweden	210.7	10.6	64.0	132.0
Bermuda	199.9	...	...	...
Pakistan	191.8	28.5	49.8	121.5
Tanzania	167.7	144.7	62.6	93.8
Uganda	167.5	167.5	111.1	56.4
Cuba	165.0	2.2	24.5□	101.6□
Venezuela	162.4	17.9	120.4¶	41.9¶
Other	697.8	...	...	...
World total	69,844.6	9,803.8	21,000	27,800

*Excludes whaling.
†May include statistical discrepancy.
‡Includes freezing.
§Excludes freshwater fish.
‖Excludes aquaculture fisheries.
¶1973.
♀Includes cured fish other than herring.
δCatch includes imports but excludes exports. Data refer to period between July 1, 1972, and June 30, 1973.
□1971.
Source: United Nations Food and Agriculture Organization, *Yearbook of Fishery Statistics*, vol. 38 and 39.

zone—expected to result in an EEC zone of common waters. Iceland's action and similar restrictions by Norway (from Jan. 1, 1977) and Canada were throwing Britain's fleet more and more onto its own coastal resources. Under the original common fisheries policy, the U.K. would have to renegotiate its current 12-mi limit in 1982 and might, in fact, lose it. Now its fishermen, with one voice, were demanding a greater degree of control over North Sea and Irish Sea fish stocks and, as the principal fishing nation in the EEC, a larger share of the resource. The then British minister of agriculture, fisheries, and food, Fred Peart, took a demand for a 50-mi national limit to his fellow EEC ministers at Brussels, but confidence in this move was shaken when a Scottish newspaper allegedly "leaked" information suggesting that a general 12-mi limit with a few wider "special case" zones was already a fait accompli. On September 20 the U.K. foreign secretary, Anthony Crosland, announced at a meeting of EEC foreign ministers in Brussels that Britain intended to extend its EEZ to 200 mi, if necessary unilaterally, on Jan. 1, 1977. Agreement to declare a common EEC 200-mi zone as from that date was finally reached on October 30. Britain duly declared its 200-mi EEZ, Icelandic and other non-EEC vessels being excluded from it except that Norway, the Faroes, Finland, East Germany, Poland, Portugal, Spain, Sweden, and the U.S.S.R. (which on December 10 had announced its own 200-mi EEZ) would be permitted to negotiate reciprocal agreements with the EEC to fish there.

The Dutch instituted a plan for reducing and reshaping their fleet to match catching power with stock availability, and later an EEC plan was put forward to reduce the number of small, old, inefficient vessels while retraining and compensating fishermen forced to leave their profession. As for the big trawlers, an accelerated scrapping program still left all too many lying idle in port. The position was not improved by the appearance on the British and French markets of Polish frozen fillets at prices said to be below those Western countries' production costs.

The year also saw the development of an embarrassing situation between France and Great Britain, when large quantities of mackerel appeared off the Devon-Cornwall coasts. Some were caught by British fishermen and exported to France at prices that delighted the British but were construed by the French as constituting price cutting within the EEC. This illustrated the difficulties caused by varying species/value relationships in different countries. When big trawlers or purse seiners moved in to catch mackerel or herring for the fish-meal plant, blood pressures rose in countries where those species were delicacies.

For some years, fishery scientists had been drawing attention to unexploited stocks of fish and crustaceans, chiefly the deepwater (1,000 m and over) species such as grenadier, the North Atlantic blue whiting, and the Antarctic crustacean known as krill. Particularly tempting was the krill, a shrimp-like creature which was the main food of the baleen whale. It was estimated that over 50 million metric tons of krill could be caught each year without overfishing, and the U.S.S.R. had already caught krill and processed it into paste. In the spring of 1976, the West German fisheries research vessel "Walther Herwig," accompanied by the freezer stern trawler "Weser," headed for the Antarctic to explore this and other resources. The ships returned in June with 200 tons of krill which was officially sampled by politicians at the Düsseldorf marine fair. But whatever its appeal, the krill lived in waters a long way from Europe. Blue whiting, on the other hand, was found in relatively shallow water, had good colour and flavour, and could probably be filleted by adapting existing machinery. The blue whiting could be caught in large quantities by trawl, and it was hoped that development of this fishery would lessen the pressures of such overexploited species as cod and haddock.

WIDE WORLD

Conservationists chartered this boat to go "warring" on Russian whalers off the coast of California. Whalers are assigned quotas by the International Whaling Commission, but some authorities fear that whales are doomed to extinction.

Peruvian workmen shovel their way through tons of anchovies. Processed into fish meal, anchovies are one of Peru's largest exports.

KANDELL—THE NEW YORK TIMES

U.S. tuna fishermen faced a serious problem when the federal courts forbade them from killing porpoises. It was common practice to locate schools of yellowfin tuna by following porpoises, some of which then became trapped in the nets. Regulations outlawing the killing of certain species of dolphins were proposed by the National Marine Fisheries Service near the end of the year. New Zealand faced another kind of problem—the prospect that a 200-mi zone would enclose more fish than its fleet could possibly catch, leaving it with no justification for excluding the fleets of those nations both able and anxious to take their share, such as the Japanese and the Soviets. (H. S. NOEL)

See also Food Processing.
[731.D.2.a]

Food Processing

During 1976 environmental pollution, food additives, and the nutritional quality of foods occupied the attention of consumerist groups and legislative authorities throughout the world. A U.S. Central Intelligence Agency report predicted that catastrophic climatic changes attributable to the accumulation of carbon dioxide and man-made atmospheric pollutants could lead to a fall in temperature in the Northern Hemisphere and to severe droughts. A number of countries set up committees to investigate these potential hazards.

A U.S. publication claimed that many food additives caused behavioural problems (hyperkinesis or hyperactivity) in children. Although these claims were disputed, a committee representative of 13 specialist medical and scientific organizations reported that complete refutation was impracticable and proposed that controlled clinical trials be carried out. Governmental and food industry organizations were spending large sums of money in attempts to quantify the hazards of pollutants in the food chain, of food additives, and of food-processing techniques. Anxiety was expressed over the cost of this mushrooming administrative burden, which engaged 64,000 persons in the U.S. federal agencies at a cost of $2.2 billion annually, or about $30 per family. The indirect costs to U.S. business were estimated at $18 billion.

The U.S. Food and Drug Administration (FDA) proceeded with its proposals for nutritional labeling and the disclosure of nutrition information in food advertising, but a similar proposal in Britain did not gain support. The FDA warned against the indiscriminate use of high-protein foods in infant feeding and proposed that protein supplements carry a warning as to the hazards of improper use. The British authorities recommended modifications of a number of infant milk formulations and advocated breast feeding when practicable. Progress was made in the production of meat and dairy products rich in polyunsaturated fat and in the development of polyunsaturated margarines and low cholesterol food products, but there was much controversy in Britain concerning their dietary merit, and a government medical committee questioned the importance of diet in heart disease.

Xylitol was recommended as a noncarcinogenic sweetener on the basis of research carried out in Finland, West Germany, and Italy, but it faced legislative obstacles in many countries. Laws mandating date-marking focused attention on the importance of assessing shelf life, and a U.S. research institute launched a study of the deterioration of fatty foods. Canadian workers reported that exposure to fluorescent lights impaired the flavour and nutritional quality of dairy products and cooking oils.

SIDNEY HARRIS

"According to these latest tests, anything can cause anything."

According to an independent survey, the food additives market in Britain, Belgium, The Netherlands, West Germany, and France totaled almost $300 million. More food colourings were banned as unsafe, but a Danish company developed a natural red colour from beets which had good stability and colour fastness.

Fruit, Vegetable, and Bakery Products. Many Americans reacted to inflation by turning to gardening and the home preservation of fruit and vegetables. It was estimated that there were six million new gardeners, and approximately four billion containers for use in home preserving were sold. Inflation also stimulated the demand for vegetable protein meat extenders. The UN Food and Agriculture Organization (FAO) reviewed meat analogues and pointed out that they should be regarded as a challenge rather than a threat to the meat industry.

A new U.S. variety of seedless, squirt-free grapefruit being introduced in many countries was the culmination of some 15 years' research on mutants obtained by nuclear irradiation. A British research institute developed a new variety of the Cox's Orange Pippin apple, yielding 60% more fruit, which was said to be late maturing and to store well. A French agricultural institute succeeded in culturing truffles and claimed they could become as plentiful as potatoes. British agriculturalists developed new leafless and semileafless strains of the garden pea and a flat-podded bean free from string, especially suitable for mechanical harvesting. An inexpensive machine to obviate the laborious task of shelling peanuts (groundnuts) was invented in Malawi. A Dutch company developed a machine for removing peel from root crops without the use of water, thereby reducing waste and yielding a salable by-product.

A high-speed interleaving vacuum packer for frozen patties, pizzas, waffles, and fish cakes was developed in Britain. A Swedish company invented a sandwich-

Fishing:
see Hunting and Fishing

Floods:
see Disasters; Earth Sciences; Engineering Projects

Folk Music:
see Music

PHOTOS, DAVID A. O'NEIL—THE NEW YORK TIMES

Corn is processed into a sweet syrup at this Pennsylvania plant. Corn syrup has captured 25% of the sweetener market.

making machine that sliced and buttered the bread, interleaved it with meats or cheese, and added a garnish of pickles or salad. The Norwegian State Railways introduced a new line of vacuumized and gas-flushed hermetically-sealed Scandinavian open sandwiches with a shelf life of seven days. Czechoslovakia commissioned its largest bakery for the manufacture of dough products and frozen confectionery. A plant manufacturing dietetic cookies for infants, said to be the most modern cookie factory in Europe, was commissioned in Latina near Rome, Italy. Its two packaging lines had a capacity of 47,000 packs an hour. A British food research institute investigated a serious disinfectant-like taint detected in cookies and found it was caused by atmospheric contamination some miles away. The contaminant, chlorocresol, an impurity in the herbicide MCPA, was present in the atmosphere at a concentration of only one part in 10,000,000,000. Similar taints were encountered in several other countries.

Dairy Products. A Danish company developed a spray drier for the production of noncaking whey powders; these were especially suitable in products that are difficult to dry, such as those containing lecithin. A U.S. university established the feasibility of using cheese whey for the production of alcoholic beverages. A new creamery commissioned in Wales could process over one million litres of milk daily into butter and cheese, using highly mechanized equipment developed in New Zealand. The first fully automated plant for the manufacture of Gouda cheese was commissioned in The Netherlands. The production of UHT (ultraheat-treated) milk expanded throughout Europe.

Meat and Other Protein Foods. The European Economic Community (EEC) allocated £1.2 million toward improving meat-processing plants in Europe, and the British government provided £5 million to enable poultry-meat processors to comply with EEC hygiene requirements. A British company commissioned a new abattoir and meat factory at a cost of £5 million; a unique feature was the use of a computer to monitor some 700 environmental and mechanical functions. Syria commissioned a poultry facility that could produce 25 million eggs and one million broilers annually and a £2.5 million automated chicken-processing factory with a weekly capacity of 300,000 birds was opened in Northern Ireland. Scientists in Chile discovered a breed of Araucana fowl that lays eggs with an especially tough shell, which could save some 7,000 egg breakages daily in the larger poultry units. The shells were blue, however, and research was begun on cross-breeding to achieve a more acceptable shade.

The price of petroleum, coupled with legislative problems, led to the abandonment of several petroprotein projects in Europe, but expansion continued in the U.S.S.R. Saudi Arabia announced plans to construct a protein plant with a capacity of 100,000 tons. The development of edible protein from rapeseed made progress, and its feasibility as an alternative to soy protein was reviewed by Canadian and Swedish agronomists.

Seafoods. The FAO estimated that losses of edible fish due to poor handling, infestation, and damage amounted to some 2 million tons annually, and specialists from 46 countries met in London to discuss the problem. Improved handling and marketing techniques and the introduction of a wider range of attractive, deep-frozen, fish-based convenience foods resulted in a 12-million-ton expansion in U.K. consumption. A British company reported substantial improvements in the culture of Scotch salmon that reduced the mortality of fry to a few percent. By controlling the environment, an Indian research institute enabled catfish to spawn four times yearly instead of once. A Polish institute established a sperm bank for freshwater fish.

New Foods. Research at a crocodile farm in Cuba demonstrated that the meat is edible, nutritious, and tasty when boiled, roasted, or fried. An Australian scientist drew attention to the nutrient value of insects and the potential of insect farming; he noted that maggots, termites, beetles, pickled caterpillars, dried grasshoppers, locusts, and silkworm larvae are regarded as delicacies in some countries. A Nigerian institute demonstrated the value of snail culture on oil palm plantations; 1,000 mature snails will yield 70 kg of meat. A New Zealand company developed three new varieties of paté manufactured from oysters, rock lobsters, and smoked eels using a purification system to eliminate their "muddy" flavour.

The U.S. Department of Agriculture (USDA) developed a range of new products from secondary lamb cuts, including lamb patties, sausages, and reformed lamb steaks, which proved particularly popular. A French company invented a process for making sausages with flavoured centres by means of dual coaxial extrusion into casings. Several countries launched a novel "long egg" product manufactured with sophisticated equipment designed in Denmark. The egg roll had a completely uniform yolk/white cross-section, and a 16-oz roll was equivalent in weight and volume to 12 medium-sized eggs but yielded more centre-cut slices than 17 eggs. A U.S. company developed a line of flavoured whole-egg emulsion products suitable for home or institutional use. Several U.S. companies introduced low-cholesterol egg products in which part of the fat was replaced by vegetable oil, as well as liquid egg substitutes containing egg white and polyunsaturated fats.

The utilization of minced poultry meat separated from chicken bones became practicable through the development of a textured product consisting of 70% poultry meat and 30% vegetable protein. A number of snack foods in the form of dehydrated bars were made from skim milk, dried whey, soy protein, wheat flour, potato flakes, fats, and oils. A typical product produced by continuous extrusion contained 27% protein, 12% fat, and high levels of calcium, phosphorus, and riboflavin.

The USDA developed a soy yogurt by fermenting soy milk with a strain of *Lactobacillus acidophilus,* and a Swiss company prepared a similar product using a strain of *Rhizopus.* A line of yogurts prepared by blending with vegetable purées was introduced in the U.S. and Bulgaria, and frozen yogurt, with an ice-cream-like consistency, became popular in the U.S. The British market for continental and American-type cheesecake, once little known there, now exceeded £5 million. After two years' research, a British company introduced a line of canned textured vegetable protein products simulating stewed steak. Renewed interest in rice as a staple food led to the development of various new products in the U.S. and Japan, including a rice bread said to be suitable for people with digestive troubles and various precooked instant rice products. A U.S. product was based on a blend of rice with textured soy protein.

Soft-frozen yogurt was popular in the eastern U.S. This store in New York's financial district had 1,500 customers a day during the summer.

JACK MANNING—THE NEW YORK TIMES

According to a U.K. survey, one-third of all new foods disappear from the market within two years; the number of new foods introduced in the U.K. averaged 500–700 annually. (H. B. HAWLEY)

See also Agriculture and Food Supplies; Fisheries; Industrial Review: *Alcoholic Beverages.*

[451.B.1.c.ii; 731.E–H]

ENCYCLOPÆDIA BRITANNICA FILMS. *The Community Bakery* (1967); *Milk: From Farm to You* (3rd ed., 1972).

Football

Association Football (Soccer). The unsettled political situation in many parts of the world, particularly in Argentina, rubbed off on soccer during the 1975–76 season. Argentina was to be the site of the 1978 World Cup finals, a choice that was ratified after a visit by the International Federation of Association Football (FIFA) delegation during the year. The military government announced in the summer of 1976 a new committee to organize the event, describing the finals as "of national interest" and thereby qualifying for 5% of the national football pools revenue. The preliminaries of the tournament were under way during the year, and by September most of the groups had played some matches.

A spin-off from the world's warring factionalism was the recurring violence surrounding soccer. During a European championship match in Cardiff on May 22, when Wales was held to 1–1 by Yugoslavia, spectators hurled beer cans onto the field to show their anger at some decisions by the East German referee, Rudi Glöckner, who almost abandoned the game. Enver Maric, the visiting goalkeeper, was attacked by one man during the melee. As a result the Union of European Football Associations (UEFA) banned Wales from the next European championship. During Real Madrid's European Cup match with Bayern Munich Spanish fans attacked the referee, Erich Linemayr, and Bayern's Gerd Müller. After an appeal Real Madrid's one-year ban from European competitions was reduced to having to play its first three home legs at least 300 km (186 mi) away from its Bernabeu stadium. In Malta several brawling players were given jail sentences, and one referee in a South American game died after having been attacked by the players. During a dreary match in South America one frustrated fan pulled out a gun and shot the ball.

During the year several milestones were reached. They included Müller's 300th goal, and the completion of 470 league games and retirement at the age of 37 of the fine Italian player Tarcisio Burgnich of Napoli and Inter-Milan.

EUROPEAN CHAMPIONSHIP. Formerly called the Nations' Cup, this quadrennial tournament, played on similar lines to those of the World Cup, produced a double shock in the summer of 1976 when Czechoslovakia first beat the redoubtable Dutch side in a semifinal that had three players sent off and then went on to topple West Germany, the favourites, in the last round at Belgrade. It was the first international trophy for the Czechoslovakians.

Key player on the Czechoslovakian team was goalkeeper Ivo Viktor, who produced many splendid

ADN-ZB / EASTFOTO

East Germany's soccer team kicked its way to a gold medal at the Montreal Olympics. Here fullback Gerd Kische (right) tries to take the ball away from Poland's Grzegorz Lato.

saves to thwart the West German attack, which owed much to the skillful midfield men Herbert Wimmer and Rainer Bonhof. As it was, the championship had to be decided on penalties. The score in the final game on June 20 after 90 minutes of play was 2–2, and an extra half hour could not produce a goal. Czechoslovakia had raced into the lead through Jan Svehlik, after Sepp Maier had saved his first attempt, and Karol Dobias added a second goal when he fastened onto a headed clearance by Franz Beckenbauer to shoot home. The West Germans fought back, and Bonhof crossed for Dieter Müller to score. Czechoslovakia then went on the defensive and tried desperately to keep out the West Germans, with Viktor performing wonders. But in the closing seconds Bonhof curled the ball into a corner, and Bernd Holzenbein headed it into the goal to force the 30-minute overtime and the penalty-taking contest. After seven penalty attempts had scored, Uli Höness shot wide and then Antonin Panenka sent the trophy to Prague with a fine kick.

EUROPEAN CUP. On May 12 at Hampden Park, Glasgow, Bayern Munich (West Germany) retained the senior European club trophy by beating the French champions, Saint-Étienne, with a goal scored by Franz Roth. The West German club thus completed a hat trick of victories in the competition, but their performance, though efficient, lacked the sparkle of those triumphs of their immediate predecessors, Ajax, of Amsterdam, and Real Madrid, which dominated the early years of the tournament.

Most of the flair and inventiveness came, in the final, from Saint-Étienne, and the West Germans were content to contain them where they could. The French twice hit the Bayern crossbar in the opening half, though they too had a scare in the opening skirmishes; Gerd Müller jabbed Bernd Durnberger's pass into the net but was offside. Saint-Étienne then swept forward and rattled "Emperor Franz" Beckenbauer and his dour men, who were forced to call on their depth of experience and upon some superb goalkeeping by Maier to hold off the French. The vital goal came in the 57th minute when Müller was pulled down by Oswaldo Piazza as he broke from defense. Beckenbauer touched the free kick to Roth, who blasted the ball into the net past the outstretched fingers of goalkeeper Yvan Curkovic.

EUROPEAN CUP-WINNERS' CUP. As if to make sure the honours were passed around, Anderlecht became the first Belgian club to win a major European trophy and Belgium became the tenth country to collect the Cup-Winners' Cup. Anderlecht defeated the English entrants, West Ham, 4–2 in the final at Brussels on May 5 in a game decided largely by pre-match tactics. During the season West Ham had played most of its football from the back, and to combat this method the Belgian team concentrated mainly on defense and almost entirely did without a man playing an orthodox centre-forward role; Anderlecht used its midfielders to dart through the middle and spearhead mass raids on the Londoners' goal.

The Belgians were helped in their endeavours by a miscued pass from England full-back Frank Lampard; it let in Peter Ressel, who slipped the ball to Robbie Rensenbrink to tie the score before halftime. Pat Holland had previously scored for West Ham. Lampard strained a groin in attempting the pass back and did not return for the second half. Alan Taylor, a striker, substituted, and John McDowell moved into the back four. Another setback for the English came when Rensenbrink sent François Van der Elst clear of their defense to drive the ball home from inside the penalty area. Though West Ham trailed, they fought back and evened the score when Keith Robson headed a centre from Trevor Brooking in off a post. But the Londoners did not have a firm grip on the game, and the Dutch star Rensenbrink, brought down by Holland as he was bursting through, earned and converted the penalty after 74 minutes and laid on the fourth goal for Van der Elst to seal the victory.

UEFA CUP. Liverpool gained the UEFA Cup by defeating FC Bruges 4–3 on aggregate in the two-legged final. The Merseyside team's second success in three years came on May 19 when they held the Belgians to a 1–1 draw to add to a 3–2 victory in England three weeks previously. In between the two games they had become English champions. The experience of such campaigners as captain Emlyn Hughes, Ian Callaghan, Ray Clemence, and Tommy Smith allowed the natural flair of such as Kevin Keegan and Steve Heighway to have a firm launching pad. Yet in the second leg in Bruges both goals stemmed from free kicks, by Keegan and Raoul Lambert.

Table I. Association Football Major Tournaments

Event	Winner	Country
European Championship	Czechoslovakia	
European Super Cup	Anderlecht	Belgium
European Cup	Bayern Munich	West Germany
European Cup-Winners' Cup	Anderlecht	Belgium
UEFA Cup	Liverpool	England
South American Champions' Cup	Cruzeiro	Brazil
UEFA Youth Cup	U.S.S.R.	

Table II. Association Football National Champions

Nation	League winners	Cup winners
Austria	Austria WAC	Rapid Vienna
Belgium	FC Bruges	Anderlecht
Bulgaria	CSKA Sofia	Levski Spartak
Czechoslovakia	Banik Ostrava	Sparta Prague
Denmark	Koge BK	Esbjerg
England	Liverpool	Southampton
Finland	Turun Pallseura	Lahden Reipas
France	Saint-Étienne	Olymp. Marseilles
Germany, East	Dynamo Dresden	Loko Leipzig
Germany, West	Borussia Mönchengladbach	SV Hamburg
Greece	PAOK Salonika	Iraklis
Hungary	Ferencvaros	Ferencvaros
Iceland	IA Akranes	IBK Keflavik
Ireland	Dundalk	Bohemians
Italy	AC Torino	Napoli
Luxembourg	Jeunesse d'Esch	Jeunesse d'Esch
Netherlands, The	PSV Eindhoven	PSV Eindhoven
Northern Ireland	Crusaders	Carrick Rangers
Norway	Viking Stavanger	Bodo-Glimt
Poland	Stal Mielec	Slask Wroclaw
Portugal	Benfica	Boavista
Romania	Steaua Bucharest	Steaua Bucharest
Scotland	Rangers	Rangers
Spain	Real Madrid	Atletico Madrid
Sweden	Malmö	AIK Stockholm
Switzerland	FC Zürich	FC Zürich
Turkey	Trabzonspor	Galatasaray
U.S.S.R.	Dynamo Kiev	Dynamo Tbilisi
Wales		Cardiff
Yugoslavia	Partizan Belgrade	Hajduk Split

BRITISH ISLES CHAMPIONSHIP. Scotland deservedly won the British Isles championship tournament held in May, triumphing in all three of their matches for their first outright victory in nine years. In their last match, before nearly 86,000 spectators at Hampden Park, Glasgow, the Scots beat England 2–1, with goals by Ken Dalglish (Celtic) and Don Masson (Queen's Park Rangers) after Mick Channon (Southampton) had taken the lead for England. Previously, the Scots had beaten Wales 3–1, with goals by Willie Pettigrew (Motherwell), Bruce Rioch (Derby County), and Eddie Gray (Leeds United), and Northern Ireland 3–0, Archie Gemmill (Derby), Masson, and Dalglish scoring. Arfon Griffiths (Wrexham) scored the lone goal for Wales. England beat Wales 1–0, with a goal by Peter Taylor (Crystal Palace), and Northern Ireland 4–0, Gerry Francis (QPR), Stuart Pearson (Manchester United), and Channon (twice) scoring, to finish second. Wales beat Northern Ireland 1–0 on a goal by Leighton James (Derby).

(TREVOR WILLIAMSON)

See also Track and Field Sports: *Special Report.*
[452.B.4.h.ii]

Rugby. RUGBY UNION. The 1975–76 period was a time of much touring by national teams including major tours of the British Isles by the Wallabies of Australia from October 1975 to January 1976, and of South Africa by the All Blacks of New Zealand from June to September 1976. The latter led to the boycott of the Olympic Games by many African nations. (*See* TRACK AND FIELD SPORTS: *Special Report.*) There were a few interesting tours in which the travelers did not meet their hosts' full strength, such as Romania's visit to New Zealand and Japan's tour of Canada. The first tour during the period that involved international matches was Wales's visit to Japan in September 1975. Wales played one match in Hong Kong and four in Japan, winning all of them and scoring 261 points (45 tries) to 31. The tour was managed by Les Spence with John Dawes as coach and Mervyn Davies as captain. The results of the two international matches were crushing defeats for the Japanese, the scores being 56–12 at Osaka and 82–6 in Tokyo.

The Wallabies' record in the British Isles was played 25, won 18, drawn 1, lost 6, points for 472, points against 337. Their 472 points included 63 tries, and 154 of their points were scored by Paul McLean, a record for an Australian player on a tour of the British Isles. Three of the Wallabies' six defeats were suffered in international matches. They lost to Scotland 10–3 at Murrayfield, to Wales 28–3 at Cardiff, and to England 23–6 at Twickenham. In the last international match of their tour, however, the Wallabies beat Ireland 20–10 at Lansdowne Road, Dublin. John Hipwell, the scrum half and captain, had to have a knee cartilage operation before the end of the tour. The tour was managed by Ross Turnbull and coached by Dave Brockhoff. On their way home the Wallabies beat the U.S. 24–12, at Los Angeles, Calif., the first international match for the U.S. since the formation of the U.S. Rugby Union at Chicago

The ball comes out after a scrum-down of French and Irish forwards during the five-nations rugby tournament in Paris in February. France (light-coloured shirts) won this match.

A.F.P./PICTORIAL PARADE

in June 1975. The U.S. players took part in their second international competition in June 1976 when France, on a brief tour, beat them 33–14 in Chicago.

The home international championship tournament was again dominated by Wales. The Welshmen won all four of their matches, defeating England 21–9 at Twickenham, Scotland 28–6 at Cardiff, Ireland 34–9 in Dublin, and France 19–13 at Cardiff. Their game against France was the vital match of the season, for France had won its other three matches, defeating Scotland 13–6 at Murrayfield, Ireland 26–3 in Paris, and England 30–9 in Paris. Scotland finished in third place by beating England 22–12 at Murrayfield and Ireland 15–6 in Dublin. Ireland's only victory was by a point, 13–12, over England at Twickenham. England lost all four matches.

Ireland made a seven-match tour of New Zealand in May and June 1976, winning four games and losing three. Under the management of Kevin Quilligan, the coaching of Roly Meates, and the captaincy of Tom Grace, Ireland used the tour in part for rebuilding its team after the retirement or loss of form of several veterans. The All Blacks won the only international match of the tour 11–3 at Wellington.

The All Blacks, with Noel Stanley as manager, J. J. Stewart as coach, and Andy Leslie as captain, played 24 games on their tour of South Africa including a match against a multiracial team. In the crucial games, the four test matches, South Africa's Springboks came out clearly on top. They won the first match 16–7 at Durban, lost the second 9–15 at Bloemfontein, and won the third at Cape Town and the fourth at Johannesburg by scores of 15–10 and 15–14. The Springboks relied to a large extent on powerful scrummaging and skillful kicking.

Rugby League. The chief events of 1975–76 were the ten matches in the second stage of the experimental world championship involving England, Wales, France, Australia, and New Zealand. These took place during September–November 1975. Australia, which had finished first at the end of the first stage, held earlier the same year, maintained its lead and finished first in the final classification with 13 points from their total of eight games. In the second stage Australia beat New Zealand 24–8 at Auckland, Wales 18–6 at Swansea, and France 41–2 at Perpignan but lost to England 16–13 at Wigan. England, beating Wales 22–16 at Warrington, France 48–2 at Bordeaux, and New Zealand 27–12 at Bradford, finished second with 12 points. Wales and New Zealand each finished with 6 points, but third place went to Wales because it had a better points average than New Zealand. France finished last with three points.

(DAVID FROST)

[452.B.h.xxiv]

U.S. Football. The Oakland Raiders won their first National Football League championship by defeating the Minnesota Vikings 32–14 in the Super Bowl on Jan. 9, 1977. The game was held in the Rose Bowl in Pasadena, Calif. Pittsburgh was voted the best college team in the country.

College. None of the familiar college football powers was unbeaten in 1976, but three upstarts from the East had perfect records. There was considerable doubt, though, that Pittsburgh, Maryland, and Rutgers had very stern opponents in their 11–0 regular seasons. When those colleges claimed they were number one, fans outside the East were raising their eyebrows instead of their index fingers.

Post-season bowl games gave Pittsburgh and Maryland a chance to show how good they really were, and only Pittsburgh won. The 27–3 victory in the Sugar Bowl over Georgia clinched Pittsburgh's national championship in both major polls. Maryland lost 30–21 to Houston in the Cotton Bowl. Georgia had won the Southeast Conference title and Houston the Southwest Conference. Ranked behind Pittsburgh was Southern California, a 14–6 winner over Michigan in the Rose Bowl. After the season Pittsburgh coach Johnny Majors resigned to go to his alma mater, Tennessee.

Rutgers, with a schedule considered weaker than those of the other undefeated teams, was not invited to a major bowl game and turned down a bid to the new Independence Bowl. "I think we're ready for a big-time schedule," coach Frank Burns said, apparently agreeing with those critics who felt that his team lacked one in 1976.

Regardless of which team was the best, there was no argument about which running back gained the most yards in college history. Tony Dorsett of Pittsburgh broke Archie Griffin's year-old record and finished his four-year career with 6,082 yd. Dorsett, the Heisman Trophy winner, set 11 National Collegiate Athletic Association (NCAA) records, tied three others, and became the first player ever to gain more than 6,000 yd. He had 1,948 of them in 1976, leading the nation with 177.1 yd rushing per game, 134 points, and 2,021 yd all-purpose (which includes yards gained on kick returns and pass receptions). Pittsburgh, which does not play in a conference, also had another national leader, Bob Jury, with nine pass interceptions.

Rutgers, another independent, was the nation's top team in total defense, rushing defense, and scoring defense, allowing its opponents averages of 7.4 points, 83.9 yd rushing, and 179 yd total a game. Maryland

WIDE WORLD

Pittsburgh's Tony Dorsett charges over right guard during the football game with the University of West Virginia on November 13. Dorsett, the all-time college ground gainer, won the 1976 Heisman Trophy. His team was undefeated.

UPI COMPIX

Oakland's Fred Biletnikoff (25) is downed by Minnesota's Bobby Bryant after taking a pass from Ken Stabler in the Super Bowl XI game on Jan. 9, 1977. Oakland won 32–14 and Biletnikoff was named the game's most valuable player.

also stressed defense, allowing 7.7 points and 211 yd a game in winning the Atlantic Coast Conference.

Both Michigan and Southern California had to beat highly rated traditional rivals to reach the Rose Bowl, but they had surprisingly little trouble in disposing of Ohio State and UCLA, respectively. The victories gave both teams 10–1 records going into the Rose Bowl.

Led by running back Rob Lytle, Big Ten champion Michigan was the country's best team in total offense, rushing offense, and scoring offense and it tied Rutgers for the scoring defense lead. Michigan's offense averaged 448.1 yd and 38.7 points per game. Ricky Bell of Pacific Eight champion Southern California was fifth nationally in rushing with 1,417 yd and had the busiest and most productive single day when he ran 51 times for 347 yd in one game.

The passing and receiving leaders both were from schools that bowl watchers were not accustomed to seeing. Tommy Kramer of Rice was the national passing leader with 24.5 completions per game, and Billy Ryckman of Louisiana Tech led the country with 77 catches. Surprising Western Michigan had the leading pass defense, allowing 78.5 yd per game, and the second leading runner, Jerome Persell with 150.5 yd per game.

Several of the familiar New Year's Day bowl teams wound up in less prestigious post-season games. Notre Dame and Penn State played each other in the Gator Bowl after disappointing seasons with Notre Dame winning 20–9. Oklahoma settled for the Fiesta Bowl, where it beat Wyoming 41–7, and UCLA and Alabama had a Liberty Bowl match-up that was won by Alabama 36–6. After four straight Rose Bowl appearances, Ohio State changed New Year's Day locations and beat Colorado 27–10 in the Orange Bowl. Colorado had tied Oklahoma and Oklahoma State for the Big Eight title.

October 16 was a good day for place kicking. Tony Franklin of Texas A&M, the national leader with 17 field goals, had a 65-yarder in the Southwest that was the longest in NCAA football history. Vince Fusco of Duke tied a college record that day in the Southeast by kicking six field goals.

Yale beat Harvard and Navy beat Army in the East's most traditional battles. Yale's 21–7 victory gave it a share of the Ivy League championship with Brown. Navy won 38–10 and made its record against Army 35-36-6. Among the highlights of the game were Joe Gattuso's three touchdowns and the 128 yd he gained rushing.

PROFESSIONAL. The Oakland Raiders, long notorious for not being able "to win the big one," ended their years of frustration in 1977 with a decisive 32–14 Super Bowl victory over the Minnesota Vikings for the championship of the NFL. The game was even more one-sided than the score indicated, with the Raiders dominating Minnesota thoroughly on both offense and defense. Most valuable player in the game, attended by more than 100,000 in the Rose Bowl, was Oakland's veteran wide receiver Fred Biletnikoff, who caught four passes from quarterback Ken Stabler for 79 yd. Willie Brown of the Raiders set a new Super Bowl record by intercepting a pass from Fran Tarkenton and returning it 75 yd for a touchdown. Oakland's offensive line was outstanding, and their defensive line held the Vikings to 71 yd rushing.

In the first round of the NFL play-offs Minnesota defeated the Washington Redskins 35–20; the Los Angeles Rams beat the Dallas Cowboys 14–12; Oakland edged the New England Patriots 24–21; and the Pittsburgh Steelers trounced the Baltimore Colts 40–14. In the second round for the conference championships, Minnesota defeated Los Angeles 24–13, and Oakland triumphed over injury-riddled Pittsburgh 24–7.

During the regular season the Pittsburgh Steelers seemed to be taking the season off when they won only one of their first five games in 1976. Then they simply took off. They landed in the play-offs nine games later with a 10–4 record. The Steelers' nine-game winning streak was one of the most impressive stretches any professional team had had. Five of the

Oakland's Pete Banaszak (40) catches a touchdown pass against Pittsburgh in their AFC championship game on December 26.

UPI COMPIX

games were shutouts, tying a league record for shutouts in a season, and in eight of the nine games the Steelers did not allow a touchdown.

Cincinnati tied Pittsburgh for the American Conference Central Division lead, but Pittsburgh won the division's play-off berth because it beat Cincinnati twice, the second game a 7–3 decision played on a snow-covered field.

In a season with several surprising teams, New England was the most astonishing. The Patriots, led by quarterback Steve Grogan (*see* BIOGRAPHY), were trying to improve on their 3–11 record of 1975 when they won consecutive early games against heavily favoured Miami, Pittsburgh, and Oakland (the Raiders' only loss). Their eight-game improvement to 11–3 was the best in the league, but Cleveland was not far behind with a six-game improvement to 9–5. San Diego improved its record by four games with a 6–8 finish, and San Francisco and Chicago had three-game improvements to 8–6 and 7–7, respectively.

The most disappointing teams were Buffalo, Miami, and Houston, all of which had hoped to go to the play-offs but had losing records. Miami was decimated by injuries for the second straight season, and its record fell from 10–4 to 6–8. Houston, a surprising 10–4 in 1975, finished 5–9. Buffalo lost quarterback Joe Ferguson and blocking back Jim Braxton to injuries early in the season, and coach Lou Saban resigned early in the team's nosedive. Losing their last 10 games, the Bills finished 2–12 after a 1975 record of 8–6.

One thing Buffalo did not lose was star running back O. J. Simpson, although he asked to be traded to a team closer to his West Coast home and sat out the exhibition season waiting for a deal. The Bills could not trade him and signed Simpson to what was reported as a three-year $2.7 million contract. Simpson led the league in rushing with 1,503 yd, despite gaining fewer than 40 yd in his first three games and being thrown out of another game in the first quarter. He set league records with 273 yd rushing in one game and the fifth and sixth 200-yd games of his career.

Oakland had the league's best record, 13–1, and made the play-offs for the ninth time in ten years behind league-leading passer Stabler. Stabler's 66.7% passing record was the second best in league history, and his favourite receiver, Cliff Branch, had 1,111 yd on receptions, one behind league leader Roger Carr of Baltimore. The Raiders cut George Blanda before the season, ending his 26-year career with a record 2,002 points.

Pittsburgh not only had the league's best defense in total yards and rushing yards, but also led the league in rushing offense. Rocky Bleier and Franco Harris gained 1,036 and 1,128 yd, respectively, and Pittsburgh became the second team ever to have two 1,000-yd running backs. The Steelers also tied a league record by allowing only 14 touchdowns, and gave up 9.9 points a game, lowest in the league.

Minnesota had the best passing offense in the National Conference. Fran Tarkenton, the top full-time passer, set a league record for career passing yardage and had three receivers with at least 50 catches. The Vikings' pass defense also led the league. Fullback Chuck Foreman was second in the conference in receiving and fourth in rushing, and the Vikings also blocked 13 kicks, two of them in one-point victories.

Los Angeles' rushing yardage and its defense against the rush led the National Conference, as did Monte Jackson's ten interceptions, three of them for touchdowns. The Rams turned back a surprising challenge for their fourth straight Western Division title from San Francisco, which led the league with 61 quarterback sacks and had ten of them in a victory against Los Angeles.

The 49ers also had the conference's stingiest defense in terms of total yardage, and halfback Delvin Williams' 4.9-yd per carry average led the conference. Williams' 1,203 yd rushing made him second in the conference to Chicago's Walter Payton (*see* BIOGRAPHY), who had 1,390. With Roland Harper running for 625 yd, the Bears were the National Conference's only team to have two backs totaling over 2,000 yd.

Kansas City, with league-leading pass receiver MacArthur Lane, led the league in passing offense. Lane, 34 years old, had 66 catches. Rich Upchurch of Denver led in punt returns with a 13.7-yd average, and Duriel Harris of Miami led in kickoff returns with a 32.9-yd average. Leading punter John James of Atlanta had a net average of 36.2 yd for kicks minus returns. Cincinnati led the American Conference in pass defense, and its cornerback, Ken Riley, led in interceptions.

As the season ended, the courts had struck down the annual college draft, the method by which rookies had been assigned to teams. The draft was to have been modified in collective bargaining or eliminated so that players starting their careers would have some choice of employment.

Canadian Football. Tony Gabriel of Ottawa was the leading pass receiver in the Canadian Football League's regular season, but he saved his biggest catch for the last 13 seconds of the final play-off game. Gabriel's 24-yd touchdown catch gave Ottawa a 23–20 victory and the league championship over Saskatchewan in the Grey Cup game at Toronto.

Passing was the strength for both Saskatchewan, which led the Western Conference with an 11–5 record, and Ottawa, the Eastern Conference winner with a 9–6–1 record. They had the league's best quarterbacks, Ron Lancaster of Saskatchewan completing 60.1% of his passes and Tom Clements of Ottawa completing 59.9%.

The teams were league leaders in passing offense, total offense, and total points. Ottawa had the total offense edge, 5,873 yd to 5,800, but Saskatchewan had a 427–411 advantage in points and a 4,089–3,894 edge in passing yards and was the Grey Cup favourite.

After Ottawa took an early 10–0 lead on Gerry Organ's 31-yd field goal and Bill Hatanaka's 75-yd punt return, Saskatchewan led by 20–10 early in the third quarter. Lancaster threw touchdown passes to Steve Mazurak and Bob Richardson, and Bob Macoritti kicked field goals of 32 and 51 yd for Saskatchewan.

Organ's second and third field goals, 40 and 32 yd, cut Saskatchewan's lead to 20–16 midway through the fourth quarter, but Saskatchewan apparently clinched the game by stopping Ottawa at Saskatchewan's one-yard line with little more than a minute to play. Then Ottawa had another chance.

Gabriel had 72 catches for 1,320 yd during the regular season, and he had six in the final game when Ottawa got the ball back with 44 seconds remaining. Ottawa reached the end zone and won by throwing him two more. (KEVIN M. LAMB)

[452.B.4.h.xiii]

Table III. NFL Final Standings and Play-offs, 1976

	W	L	T
AMERICAN CONFERENCE			
Eastern Division			
*Baltimore	11	3	0
*New England	11	3	0
Miami	6	8	0
N.Y. Jets	3	11	0
Buffalo	2	12	0
Central Division			
*Pittsburgh	10	4	0
Cincinnati	10	4	0
Cleveland	9	5	0
Houston	5	9	0
Western Division			
*Oakland	13	1	0
Denver	9	5	0
San Diego	6	8	0
Kansas City	5	9	0
Tampa Bay	0	14	0
NATIONAL CONFERENCE			
Eastern Division			
*Dallas	11	3	0
*Washington	10	4	0
St. Louis	10	4	0
Philadelphia	4	10	0
N.Y. Giants	3	11	0
Central Division			
*Minnesota	11	2	1
Chicago	7	7	0
Detroit	6	8	0
Green Bay	5	9	0
Western Division			
*Los Angeles	10	3	1
San Francisco	8	6	0
Atlanta	4	10	0
New Orleans	4	10	0
Seattle	2	12	0

*Qualified for play-offs.

Play-offs

American semifinals
Oakland 24, New England 21
Pittsburgh 40, Baltimore 14

National semifinals
Minnesota 35, Washington 20
Los Angeles 14, Dallas 12

American finals
Oakland 24, Pittsburgh 7

National finals
Minnesota 24, Los Angeles 13

Super Bowl
Oakland 32, Minnesota 14

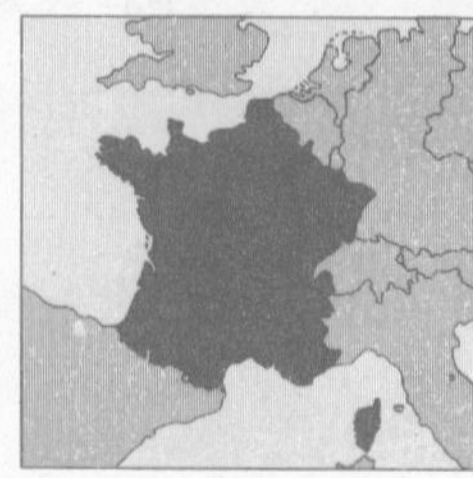

France

A republic of Western Europe, France is bounded by the English Channel, Belgium, Luxembourg, West Germany, Switzerland, Italy, the Mediterranean Sea, Monaco, Spain, Andorra, and the Atlantic Ocean. Area: 210,040 sq mi (544,000 sq km), including Corsica. Pop. (1976 est.): 52,904,000. Cap. and largest city: Paris (pop., 1975 census, 2,289,800). Language: French. Religion: predominantly Roman Catholic. President in 1976, Valéry Giscard d'Estaing; premiers, Jacques Chirac and, from August 25, Raymond Barre.

In 1976 there was an accentuation of the "presidentialist" character of the regime. The cantonal elections in March, in which the left gained a considerable victory over the majority parties, served as a warning to the government, and in August Premier Chirac, who was also leader of the Union des Démocrates pour la République (UDR), the Gaullist party, resigned. President Giscard d'Estaing replaced him with a man independent of party ties, Raymond Barre (*see* BIOGRAPHY), who took over the major task of fighting inflation.

Domestic Affairs. On January 12, Giscard d'Estaing (*see* BIOGRAPHY) undertook his sixth government reshuffle. It was a "technical rearrangement," no doubt, but one that brought some lowering in the average age of the Cabinet and a note of "feminization" in the government with the arrival of Alice Saunier-Seïté as secretary of state for universities and of Christiane Scrivener as secretary of state for consumer affairs at the Ministry of Economy and Finance; they joined the other women members of the Cabinet, Simone Veil, Françoise Giroud, and Hélène Dorlhac. The minister of justice, Jean Lecanuet, was granted the title of minister of state and raised to the same rank as Michel Poniatowski. But the main focus of attention was the entry into the government of two men who advocated strong ties with other European countries: Raymond Barre, former vice-president of the European Commission, and Jean François-Poncet, to assist Jean Sauvagnargues in the Ministry of Foreign Affairs.

At the beginning of February the congress of the Communist Party opened at Saint-Ouen under the presidency of its secretary-general, Georges Marchais, and confirmed the abandonment of the doctrine of "dictatorship of the proletariat." By following the lines of Italian Communism, Marchais endeavoured to give the French party a more acceptable face.

The cantonal elections for the general councils of the départements, held on March 7 and 14, resulted in gains by the left. These elections, affecting half the cantons of all the départements in metropolitan France (except Paris, which would not vote until the spring of 1977) and of the four nonmetropolitan départements overseas (French Guiana, Guadeloupe, Martinique, and Réunion), were a trial run for the 1977 municipal elections and the 1978 legislative elections. There were gains for the Communist Party, but it was the Socialist Party that benefited most. According to figures published by the Ministry of the Interior, the Socialist Party led all other electoral groups with 520 seats; the Communist Party took 249 seats, the moderate majority 208, the Independent Republicans (IR) 182, and the UDR 182. The Socialists and the Communists were the only parties to gain seats (194 and 75, respectively), while the "Giscardians" lost 36. Even allowing for the fact that the left-wing parties had put up more candidates than the "majority" group, the Socialist Party under François Mitterrand nonetheless confirmed its place as "the first party in France."

After the elections relations between the president and his staff at the Élysée Palace and Premier Chirac began to deteriorate. After a summer of increasing unease in the governing majority, the new secretary-general of the Élysée, François-Poncet (who had replaced Claude Pierre-Brossolette), announced on August 25 that Chirac had resigned from his post as premier. The choice of Barre to replace Chirac was a significant one. Aged 52, Barre belonged to no political party and merely adhered to the presidential majority (pres. maj.). For the first time in the history of the French Republic, the post of premier was occupied by a professor of political economy at a time when problems of inflation, unemployment, finance, and the trade balance were in the forefront.

Barre began at once to form his government. In addition to his responsibilities as premier, he took

A hundred thousand copies of the Paris newspaper "Parisien Libéré" were dumped on the Champs Élysées one day in February by demonstrators protesting against the publication of the paper by nonunion employees.

A.F.P. / PICTORIAL PARADE

Foreign Aid:
see Economy, World

Foreign Exchange:
see Economy, World

Forestry:
see Environment; Industrial Review

Formosa:
see Taiwan

on those of minister of economy and finance. He appointed to his Cabinet several nonparliamentarians who, like himself, were not attached to any specific political group; these were designated as members of the presidential majority. He had three ministers of state: Olivier Guichard (UDR), minister of justice; Poniatowski (IR), minister of the interior; and Lecanuet (president of the new Centre of the Social Democrats), minister for planning and regional development. Those three represented the three party groupings within the presidential majority in Parliament. Among other ministers were: Louis de Guiringaud (pres. maj.), foreign affairs; Michel Durafour (Radical), delegated to the premier; Yvon Bourges (UDR), defense; René Haby (pres. maj.), education; Robert Galley (UDR), cooperation; Jean-Pierre Fourcade (IR), supplies; Robert Boulin (UDR), relations with Parliament; Christian Bonnet (IR), agriculture; Christian Beullac (pres. maj.), labour and employment; Mme Veil (pres. maj.), health; Michel d'Ornano (IR), industry and research; Vincent Ansquer (UDR), quality of life (environment); Pierre Brousse (Radical), trade and crafts; André Rossi (Radical), foreign trade. Autonomous secretaries of state included: Norbert Ségard (pres. maj.) in posts and telecommunications; Mme Giroud (Radical), culture; and Mme Saunier-Seïté (pres. maj.), universities. The keynote was change with stability, but the real action was elsewhere. It came with the change in the premiership and the principal task that confronted Barre, the struggle against inflation. Barre realized that inflation in France, at 10%, was too high as compared with other countries, in particular with the 4% level in West Germany.

On September 22, Barre's counterinflation plan was adopted by the Council of Ministers. It envisaged a three-month freeze of all prices and a price freeze until April 1977 in the public sector. The so-called normal rate (20%) of value-added tax was to be lowered to 17.6% as of January 1 on a large number of items. The price of alcohol on the other hand was to be increased by 10%. Income taxes would be increased by 4% for those contributing between Fr 4,500 and Fr 20,000 in income taxes, and by 8% for those paying over Fr 20,000. Company taxes would be increased by 4%. Gasoline prices would be raised by 15%, and fees for car licenses increased between 43 and 127% according to the vehicle's horsepower. Farmers hit by the year's drought were to be compensated up to a total of Fr 6.2 billion. There were to be further restrictions on credit; the major banks could not grant more than 5% in supplementary credits in any one year and would have to set up reserves in the Banque de France, which would receive Fr 3 billion in liquid funds in this way and so be able to control the money supply and the short-term money market more closely.

CHRISTOPHER CLARITY—THE NEW YORK TIMES

The Maurice Ravel concert hall is part of the new civic centre in Lyon. Some critics say it resembles a horizontal potato.

The philosophy of the Barre plan was much in line with steps taken by Giscard d'Estaing in 1972 and 1973, when he was himself minister of economy and finance. They had included a temporary freeze on public sector charges and some prices, a credit squeeze with restrictions in the money supply, and a measure of restraint in public spending.

At this time a 175-page book, *Démocratie française*, reached the bookstores. It was by Giscard d'Estaing, and within a few days 650,000 copies had been sold. The event was unprecedented, for never before had a serving head of a modern Western state written and published a political work during his term of office. To coincide with the government changes, Giscard had tried to give a new impetus to presidential policy. In his view, the traditional ideologies of Marxism and classical liberalism did not provide a lasting solution

FRANCE

Education. (1973–74) Primary, pupils 6,367,523, teachers (including preprimary) 255,919; secondary, pupils 2,945,192, teachers 173,934; vocational, pupils 953,235, teachers 66,549; teacher training, students 27,823, teachers 2,952; higher, students 763,980, teaching staff 38,000.

Finance. Monetary unit: franc, with (Sept. 20, 1976) a free rate of Fr 4.92 to U.S. $1 (Fr 8.47 = £1 sterling). Gold, SDR's, and foreign exchange (June 1976) U.S. $8,733,000,000. Budget (1977 est.): revenue Fr 334.1 billion; expenditure Fr 333.3 billion. Gross national product (1974) Fr 1,324,800,000,000. Money supply (Feb. 1976) Fr 404,320,000,000. Cost of living (1970 = 100; June 1976) 166.

Foreign Trade. (1975) Imports Fr 231,180,000,000; exports Fr 221,530,000,000. Import sources: EEC 49% (West Germany 19%, Belgium-Luxembourg 9%, Italy 9%, The Netherlands 6%, U.K. 5%); U.S. 8%; Saudi Arabia 6%. Export destinations: EEC 49% (West Germany 17%, Belgium-Luxembourg 10%, Italy 10%, U.K. 7%, The Netherlands 5%); Switzerland 5%. Main exports: machinery 21%; motor vehicles 11%; chemicals 11%; iron and steel 9%. Tourism (1974): visitors (at classified hotels) 9,838,000; gross receipts U.S. $2,660,000,000.

Transport and Communications. Roads (1974) 794,130 km (including 2,830 km expressways). Motor vehicles in use (1974): passenger 15,180,000; commercial 2,075,000. Railways: (1974) 34,390 km; traffic (1975) 50,980,000,000 passenger-km, freight 64,033,000,000 net ton-km. Air traffic (1975): 23,272,000,000 passenger-km; freight 1,086,122,000 net ton-km. Navigable inland waterways in regular use (1974) 7,028 km; freight traffic 13,738,000,000 ton-km. Shipping (1975): merchant vessels 100 gross tons and over 1,393; gross tonnage 10,745,999. Telephones (Dec. 1974) 12,405,000. Radio licenses (Dec. 1972) 17,034,000. Television licenses (Dec. 1973) 12,332,000.

Agriculture. Production (in 000; metric tons; 1975): wheat 15,041; barley *c.* 9,727; oats *c.* 1,947; rye *c.* 307; corn *c.* 8,143; potatoes 7,219; rice *c.* 39; sorghum *c.* 334; sugar, raw value *c.* 3,232; rapeseed 532; sunflower seed 110; tomatoes 639; onions 132; carrots (1974) *c.* 544; apples (1974) 3,162; pears (1974) 424; peaches (1974) *c.* 500; wine (1974) *c.* 8,736; tobacco *c.* 50; milk 28,660; butter *c.* 553; cheese 935; fish catch (1974) 808. Livestock (in 000; Oct. 1974): cattle 24,700; sheep 10,429; pigs 12,000; horses (1974) 434; poultry *c.* 203,095.

Industry. Index of production (1970 = 100; 1975) 112. Fuel and power (in 000; 1975): coal (metric tons) *c.* 23,600; electricity (kw-hr) 177,440,000; natural gas (cu m) 7,357,000; manufactured gas (cu m; 1974) 7,098. Production (in 000; metric tons; 1975): bauxite 2,527; iron ore (32% metal content) 49,653; pig iron 17,920; crude steel 21,513; aluminum 493; lead 122; zinc 189; cement 29,370; cotton yarn 244; cotton fabrics 181; wool yarn 148; wool fabrics 70; rayon, etc., filament yarn 28; rayon, etc., staple fibre 59; nylon, etc., filament yarn 95; nylon, etc., staple fibre 124; sulfuric acid 3,757; petroleum products (1974) 117,631; fertilizers (nutrient content; 1974–75) nitrogenous 1,694, phosphate 1,720, potash 2,078; passenger cars (units) 2,952; commercial vehicles (units) 345. Merchant shipping launched (100 gross tons and over; 1975) 1,315,000 gross tons.

KEYSTONE

A guest curtsies to King Juan Carlos of Spain, who visited Paris in October. Others in the receiving line are France's President Giscard d'Estaing, Queen Sofía, and Mme Giscard d'Estaing.

to the problem of building a humanist society. He attacked collectivism, which, as he saw it, did not meet the basic aspirations of the French people; the society of the future required complete pluralism, that is to say, the possibility of expressing all tendencies and opinions.

Meanwhile, Chirac was not idle. In Égletons (Corrèze), he called on the UDR to establish a "vast popular movement." An extraordinary national convention of the Gaullist movement took place on December 5. There, the delegates founded the Rassemblement pour la République, which replaced the UDR and was to prepare itself—under Chirac's leadership—to offer a renewed and broadened Gaullism at the elections of 1978.

In Parliament the ordinary spring session (April–June) and the extraordinary session that ended on July 10 would be remembered as those associated with "surplus value." The proposal, inspired by Giscard, to tax "surplus values" was a test of the president's desire for reform and for justice. By taxing capital gains when they were speculative, it was an attempt to reduce fiscal inequalities among Frenchmen and to bring France into line with foreign practice. The bill was passed by the National Assembly on June 23 by 256 votes against 197 and in the Senate on July 10 by 141 in favour, 107 against. An additional 70 bills were passed, including a draft setting up and organizing the region of Île-de-France (to include Paris) and the draft law on nature conservation.

Another stage in reform was marked by the autumn parliamentary session. It was devoted chiefly to the 1977 budget, with its provisions for improving social security, and to drafts of bills on industrial reform.

Apart from the Barre plan, the main economic and financial event was the removal on March 15 of the French franc from the European "snake" (joint float of European currencies). Since the start of the year, the Banque de France had been obliged to commit some Fr 14 billion in foreign currency to support the franc. The French currency had rejoined the "snake" in July 1975. Its withdrawal was a blow to European economic and monetary union.

Strikes and student unrest took place in the spring. There were clashes between the police and students at the universities of Paris, Clermont-Ferrand, and Rennes. In March and April, more than 100,000 university students in Paris and the provinces participated in protests against reforms introduced by the minister of education. The two-month duration of the demonstrations, the number of institutions involved, and the extent of the strikes made them appear the most important protest movement since 1968. The students in general were demonstrating their concern with the economic crisis and the lack of job opportunities. The labour unions called for a day of national strikes against the Barre plan on October 7. The call was widely taken up, but the strikes did not paralyze the country.

Autonomist movements in Corsica in 1976 produced a series of violent episodes, and on November 9 they organized a "Dead Island Day" of general work stoppage. Early in the year wine growers throughout southern France protested actively against the importation of cheap Italian wine, under EEC terms; agreement on the issue was later reached between France and Italy. The mysterious affair of the Fr 8 million missing from the private account of Marcel Dassault, aircraft manufacturer, in connection with which his firm's former accountant Hervé de Vathaire was charged with embezzlement, led at the end of October to the government setting up an investigation into the financial affairs of the Dassault company and certain nationalized industries.

The position of the press continued to deteriorate. During the year, Robert Hersant (*see* BIOGRAPHY), whose group already controlled some ten daily newspapers, bought *Le Figaro* from Jean Prouvost. The latter accepted the breakup of his empire, *Paris-Match* coming under the control of Daniel Filipacchi (*see* BIOGRAPHY), and *Télé 7 Jours* reverting to Hachette. Finally, France-Editions et Publications (Hachette Group) handed over *France-Soir* to Paul Winkler of Opera-Mundi, and he in turn immediately sold half the shares to Hersant. The press empire that Hersant was carving out for himself highlighted the role played by banks in press matters. In other publishing developments discussions started between the Syndicat du Livre and the Syndicat de la Presse Parisienne, aimed at reaching an agreement that, while recognizing the need for modernization of equip-

French-Canadian Literature:
see Literature
French Guiana:
see Dependent States
French Literature:
see Literature
Friends, Religious Society of:
see Religion
Fuel and Power:
see Energy
Furniture Industry:
see Industrial Review
Furs:
see Industrial Review

ment in printing, would allow staff numbers to be adapted gradually to a reduction in the number of jobs. A strike by printers halted the publication of newspapers in Paris for five days in December before negotiations were resumed.

Foreign Policy. In the field of foreign affairs there was stress on the head of state's role as conciliator. France's European outlook was confirmed, with strong leanings toward a form of "internationalism" based on independence. In May the president and his wife went to the United States to celebrate the bicentenary of the two countries' friendship. France will "continue to contribute to the effectiveness of the Atlantic Alliance," Giscard declared in a speech in English to the U.S. Congress. The following month Giscard with his wife made a state visit to Great Britain. There, he talked with the British prime minister, James Callaghan, and received a warm welcome at the Houses of Parliament. The joint declaration issued on June 23 provided for annual meetings between the French president and the British prime minister, to be held alternately in France and Britain. The first took place at Rambouillet, France, on November 11–12.

First in Nice in February and then in Hamburg in July, the two regular Franco-West German summit conferences allowed Giscard and West German Chancellor Helmut Schmidt to confirm that the close cooperation between France, the U.K., and West Germany was to be beneficial to the whole of the European Economic Community (EEC). A visit to Iran in October and Giscard's talks with the shah developed economic cooperation between the two countries.

Giscard took the opportunity during the France-U.S.S.R. week in October to reaffirm in an interview televised in both France and the U.S.S.R. that "cooperation with the U.S.S.R. is a fundamental and permanent dimension of our policy." The official visit at the end of October of King Juan Carlos I of Spain and his queen, the first time in 50 years that a Spanish head of state had come to France, provided a "new departure" in relations between the two countries and led to speculation that Spain might join the EEC. Previously, Giscard had visited Réunion, Poland, and Gabon.

After the Comoro Islands became independent in 1975, the islands of Grande Comore, Anjouan, and Moheli ceased to belong to the French Republic. In the UN 46 African countries asked France to withdraw from the island of Mayotte, which had chosen by referendum to remain within the French state.

(JEAN KNECHT)

See also Dependent States.

[972.A.2]

Gabon

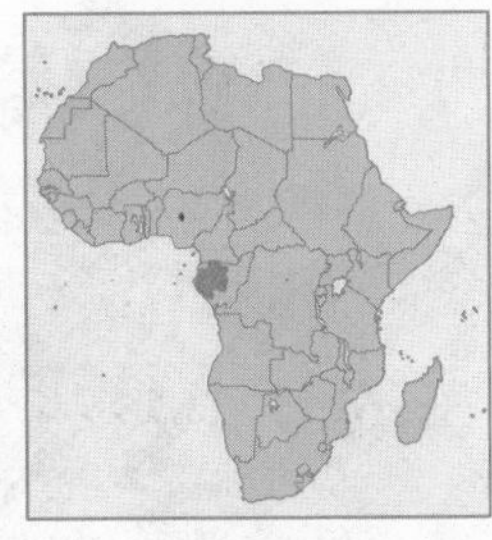

A republic of western equatorial Africa, Gabon is bounded by Equatorial Guinea, Cameroon, the Congo, and the Atlantic Ocean. Area: 103,347 sq mi (267,667 sq km). Pop. (1975 est.): 1,155,800. Cap. and largest city: Libreville (pop., 1975 est., 169,200). Language: French and Bantu dialects. Religion: traditional tribal beliefs; Christian minority. President in 1976, Omar Bongo; premier, Léon Mébiame.

GABON

Education. (1973–74) Primary, pupils 114,172, teachers 2,438; secondary, pupils 14,490, teachers 437; vocational, pupils 2,708, teachers 272; teacher training, students 346, teachers 34; higher, students 799.

Finance. Monetary unit: CFA franc, with (Sept. 20, 1976) a parity of CFA Fr 50 to the French franc (free rate of CFA Fr 245.90 = U.S. $1; CFA Fr 423.62 = £1 sterling). Budget (1975 est.) balanced at CFA Fr 151,448,000,000.

Foreign Trade. Imports (1975) CFA Fr 100,560,000,000; exports CFA Fr 201,920,000,000. Import sources (1974): France 57%; U.S. 10%; West Germany 9%; Sweden 8%. Export destinations (1974): France 31%; U.S. 18%; West Germany 10%; The Bahamas 9%; U.K. 6%; Italy 5%. Main export crude oil 77%.

Transport and Communications. Roads (1973) 6,848 km. Motor vehicles in use (1973): passenger 9,400; commercial (including buses) 7,500. Construction of a trans-Gabon railway (330 km) was begun in 1974, with completion planned for 1978. Telephones (Dec. 1973) 11,000. Radio receivers (Dec. 1971) *c.* 65,000. Television receivers (Dec. 1971) *c.* 1,300.

Agriculture. Production (in 000; metric tons; 1974): sweet potatoes *c.* 3; cassava *c.* 170; corn *c.* 2; peanuts *c.* 2; coffee *c.* 1; cocoa *c.* 5; bananas *c.* 10; palm oil *c.* 2.5; timber (cu m; 1974) 2,747. Livestock (in 000; 1974): cattle *c.* 5; pigs *c.* 5; sheep *c.* 57; goats *c.* 62.

Industry. Production (in 000; metric tons; 1974): manganese ore (metal content) 1,091; uranium 0.4; petroleum products 804; crude oil (1975) 11,320; electricity (kw-hr) 173,000.

Although he received an official visit from French Pres. Valéry Giscard d'Estaing in August 1976, President Bongo's relations with France became increasingly cool. As early as on his own visit to France in February, Bongo had been outspoken in his criticism of French policy over the Comoro Islands and the affair of Mme Françoise Claustre, in which he had attempted to mediate between France and Chad. (*See* CHAD.) In March, at the celebration of the eighth anniversary of the founding of the state's single party, the Parti Démocratique Gabonais, Bongo lashed out against "savage capitalism," referring in particular to the exploitation of the country's mineral wealth by foreign corporations. On September 7, a month after Giscard's visit to Libreville, he announced that Gabon would quit the Common African and Mauritian Organization (OCAM). In explaining this decision, Bongo declared that OCAM was "an anachronistic and sectarian organism, a carry-over of the old schemes of the former colonial powers in Africa."

Although the internal state of the country appeared to be calm, President Bongo carried out four ministerial reshuffles, in March, July, August, and October.

(PHILIPPE DECRAENE)

[978.E.7.a.iv]

Gambia, The

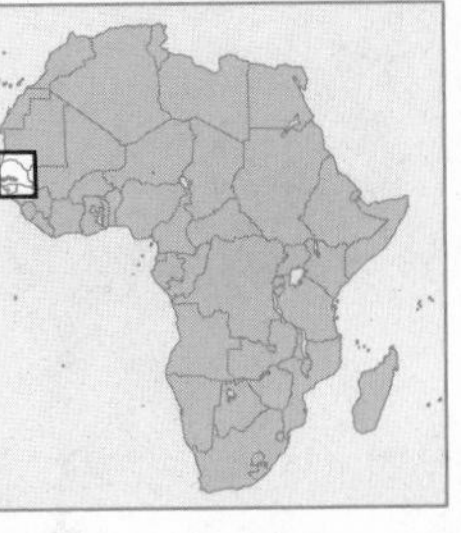

A small republic and member of the Commonwealth of Nations, The Gambia extends from the Atlantic Ocean along the lower Gambia River in West Africa and is surrounded by Senegal. Area: 4,467 sq mi (11,569 sq km). Pop. (1975 est.): 524,000, including (1973) Malinke 42.3%; Fulani 18.2%; Wolof 15.7%; Dyola 9.5%; Soninke 8.7%; others 5.6%. Cap. and largest city: Banjul (pop., 1975 est., 42,400). Language: English (official). Religion: predominantly Muslim. President in 1976, Sir Dawda Jawara.

President Jawara improved relations with Senegal in 1976 through an exchange of visits. Cooperation

GAMBIA, THE

Education. (1975–76) Primary, pupils 24,617, teachers 948; secondary, pupils 1,896, teachers 107; vocational, pupils 4,282, teachers 197; higher (including teacher training), students 440, teachers 43.

Finance and Trade. Monetary unit: dalasi, with (Sept. 20, 1976) a free rate of 2.31 dalasis to U.S. $1 (par value of 4 dalasis = £1 sterling). Budget (1975–76 est.): ordinary revenue 27,075,000 dalasis; expenditure 47,845,000 dalasis. Foreign trade (1975): imports 108,170,000 dalasis; exports 77 million dalasis. Import sources (1973–74): U.K. 24%; China 10%; The Netherlands 6%; France 5%; Poland 5%; U.S. 5%; Senegal 5%. Export destinations: U.K. 37%; France 23%; The Netherlands 17%; Portugal 8%; West Germany 7%; Italy 6%. Main exports: peanuts 51%; peanut oil 32%; peanut meal and cake 11%.

based on common elements in the countries' respective five-year plans included the promotion of a customs union to end smuggling. The Gambia's five-year plan (1975–80, released in February 1976) was to receive financial support from the Middle East, Britain, and France and $12 million in aid from the European Economic Community. Under the plan the nation's peanut (groundnut)-based economy would be diversified toward fishing and tourism. In 1976 The Gambia was host to 25,000 tourists. The 1975–76 peanut crop declined from the previous year, partly because some farmers switched to rice and millet.

The July budget revealed that inflation had raised the price index by 30% in 1974–76 though the gross domestic product had risen too, by 19%. Estimated total trade for 1976 stood at 200 million dalasis, but the trade gap was estimated at 71 million dalasis because of low commodity prices and increased imports. Estimated expenditure for 1976–77 at 44.3 million dalasis exceeded revenue by 1.3 million dalasis, the deficit to be covered by increased taxation and a levy on wages. (MOLLY MORTIMER)

[978.E.4.b.ii]

Gambling

Beginning in January 1977 anyone in the United States winning $1,000 or more on any lottery or by betting on or off any racetrack would have 20% of the payoff withheld against taxes. Proponents of legalized gambling criticized the new law on the ground that it would drive many bettors to illegal games, where the payoff was often in cash and could therefore be easily left off income tax returns. By contrast, the winnings were tax-free in most of the approximately 50 lotteries held in other nations.

Probably no country, certainly none in the West, made such varied provisions for legal gambling as Great Britain. The form of gambling that attracted the greatest sums in 1976 was betting on horse and greyhound races, but bookmakers offered betting facilities for many other contests, including tennis matches, the Miss World competition, and even the selection of archbishops. The total amount of bets placed in 1976 was about £2,300 million. Of this, approximately £160 million was taken by the government and £8 million was used to help sustain organized horse racing.

Horse Racing. Wagering on horse races became legal in Connecticut for the first time in April 1976 when offtrack betting parlours opened throughout the state. Other states allowing offtrack betting included Nevada and New York, where a witness at a congressional hearing testified that the parlours had created 90,000 new customers for illegal bookies in New York City alone.

The Irish Sweepstakes, a lottery based on the results of several major horse races in the U.K. and Ireland, was reported to be in financial trouble in 1976. The main reasons for this were that inflation had driven up costs and newly established lotteries in the United States and Canada were drawing away customers. In 1972 the Hospitals Trust, which administers the sweepstakes, sold about $8.5 million worth of tickets for the drawing based on the Cambridgeshire Stakes; in 1975 ticket sales for the same race were almost $3 million less.

Sporting Events. A survey in the U.S. for the National Gambling Commission revealed that approximately half of the illegal betting in the country was on nonracing sports events. The state of Delaware decided during the year to try to benefit legally from this huge cash flow by issuing computerized football cards on which bets could be placed on National Football League games. To discourage big-time gamblers the state offered bettors a return of only about 45% above the amount wagered. The scheme fell short of the state's expectations, however, with revenue averaging about $55,000 per week for the first six weeks, compared with an expected weekly sum of $400,000.

Betting on jai alai, long a fixture in Florida, moved north during the year into Connecticut and Rhode Island. Approximately $1 million per day passed through the betting windows in Hartford and Bridgeport, the two cities in Connecticut in which the sport was introduced.

In numbers of participants in gambling in Great Britain, betting on football (soccer) pools led the

This woman croupier on a cruise ship is one of a growing band who help passengers to part with their excess cash.

JAMES TUITE—THE NEW YORK TIMES

field, with about 15 million people taking part each week during the winter. The pools were based on the results of the English and Scottish Football League matches (Australian matches in the summer). They are a form of long-odds gambling to which people were attracted by the magnitude, often £500,000, of the largest individual prizes, of which there were, of course, very few. The total turnover of the football pools for the year was about £230 million. Taxes on the winnings were taken by the government at the rate of 40%, except for a small number of pools that contributed to charities and were taxed at a slightly lower level.

Casinos. In a statewide referendum in November the voters of New Jersey approved the introduction of casino gambling into the decaying ocean resort of Atlantic City. New Jersey thus joined Nevada as one of the two states in the U.S. allowing this form of betting. Property values in Atlantic City reportedly soared after the referendum, although the promoters of the casinos did not expect them to be ready for operation for at least a year.

Gambling continued to maintain its popularity in Nevada as the state's casinos grossed a record income of $1,190,000,000 in fiscal 1976, an increase of 11.5% over the previous year. The largest gains were in the Reno-North Lake Tahoe area.

Macau remained a flourishing centre of casino gambling in Asia, and the territorial government decided during the year to take a larger proportion of the profits of the syndicate that operated the casinos. Consequently, Stanley Ho, head of the syndicate, sold some of his Macau properties and expanded his operations to other countries. He invested $25 million to build two racetracks for horses and one for greyhounds in Teheran, Iran, and $3.5 million for a casino-nightclub complex in Karachi, Pak. He also owned a part of Australia's first casino, in Hobart.

Next to pool betting, the playing of games of chance for winnings in money or money's worth, which was legal only in licensed or registered clubs, was the most popular form of gambling in the U.K. An estimated six million people played bingo regularly and provided the nation's approximately 1,800 licensed bingo clubs with an annual turnover in the region of £290 million. Casino gambling attracted only about 400,000 fairly regular players, but the stakes were much higher; about £400 million was exchanged for casino chips during the year. About 108,000 gambling machines of various types were in use in the U.K. in 1976; some 33,000 of them were unlimited jackpot machines in clubs, and the balance, having more of an amusement element and offering small prizes, were in public houses, amusement arcades, and the like. About £400 million was fed into those machines during the year.

Lotteries. The cost of the summer Olympic Games, held in Montreal in 1976, exceeded revenues by about $1 billion. One of the ways in which Canada decided to make up this deficit was a national Olympic lottery. Individual tickets sold for $10, and the top prize was $1 million tax-free. Though first estimated to bring in $32 million, the lottery had netted approximately $200 million by the time the Olympics started. The lottery was extended to operate after the Games, and proceeds from it were committed to the Olympic fund through 1979. The Soviet Union in August began a national lottery to help develop Soviet sports and to finance construction of facilities for the 1980 summer Olympic Games, to be held in Moscow. In other Canadian developments, Ontario launched a new lottery in September.

In the U.S. it was reported in February that in the 12 years since the first state lottery began operating in New Hampshire the games had netted the 13 states operating them almost $1.5 billion; in fiscal 1975 alone the figure was $500 million. One major advantage of the lotteries was their relatively low overhead. In Pennsylvania in fiscal 1975 the lottery commission payroll was $3 million, while the profit from the games was more than $50 million.

So-called "instant lotteries," in which a ticket buyer can find out immediately if he is a winner, enjoyed considerable popularity in the U.S. during the year. The nation's Bicentennial was the theme in New Jersey, where the "1776 Instant Lottery Drawing" was introduced. The biggest winners of this game received $1,776 per week for life, the richest prize in any lottery in the nation's history. Maryland also achieved success with its instant lottery, introduced during the year; in a state with a population of approximately four million, some 20 million lottery tickets at $1 apiece were sold in five weeks.

New York had suspended its state lottery late in

A.F.P. / PICTORIAL PARADE

A croupiers' school holds classes in the cellar of a 17th-century building in Nice, on the French Riviera.

TONY KORODY—SYGMA

Adrian Doyle Brunson, alias Texas Dolly, won the world poker championship at Las Vegas in May, after playing for 32 hours straight.

1975 because of charges of irregularities in its operation, including misleading advertising, the printing of duplicate tickets, and failure to award prizes. The entire lottery commission was fired. In mid-1976 the state opened a new instant lottery. During the first week of the lottery's operation New York sold 18.9 million tickets for it, more than twice as many as any other state had ever sold in one week.

Australia also gained success with lotteries. In 11 days more than half of the 100,000 tickets in Western Australia's A$1 million lottery were sold. In the U.K. only small-scale lotteries were permitted. They were organized by charitable or other noncommercial organizations. Total annual ticket sales were estimated at about £45 million.

Although state lotteries in the U.S. were generally successful, they were not popular in areas where similar, often illegal games, such as numbers and bolita, were well established. This was particularly true among the poor in large cities, where the outlay for a numbers ticket was usually less than that for a lottery card. (DAVID R. CALHOUN)

See also Equestrian Sports.
[452.C.2]

Games and Toys

Although buyers at the major international toy fairs early in 1976 tended to be cautious and selective, favouring well-supported lines and established toys, the year promised to be a better one for toy manufacturers than 1975 had been.

A welcome boost to the West German industry, whose production and exports had been falling (by 8 and 5%, respectively, in 1975) and imports rising in recent years, came from the runaway success of two impressive lines of small plastic figures, Playmobil and Play-Big. Inspired by the play family figures of Fisher-Price, these West German newcomers were rapidly reaching the number one position in most of the countries in which they were sold. Indeed, 1976 was very much the year of the "little people."

The figures were stylized toy characters rather than lifelike miniature representations of people, but they had clothes and various sets of accessories to go with them. They came dressed as kings and queens, knights in shining armour, cowboys and Indians, doctors and nurses, builders and road construction workers, even divers and skiers. They could grip objects in their hands and move their arms up and down, bend at the waist and turn their heads, and had legs that could be moved separately and also ankle joints.

The versatility of the Playmobil and Play-Big figures was undoubtedly the key to their success. Manufacturers elsewhere were quick to follow the lead. In Britain Dunbee-Combex-Marx Ltd. (DCM) produced its 3-in-high semiarticulated Playpeople, reckoned suitable for 3-to-9-year-olds, and Playcraft (Mettoy Co.) their larger, fully articulated Busybodies, for 4-to-12-year-olds.

Other big crazes of the year involved outdoor toys. Skateboards returned to the top of the popularity list in the U.S. and Australia, with some U.S. schools even starting courses in skateboarding. The sport had still to catch on in Europe, however, and indeed there were moves to try to prevent this on the grounds that skateboards could be dangerous. In Britain, for example, the Royal Society for the Prevention of Accidents demanded they be banned, but other organizations, such as the British Safety Council, strongly opposed this, arguing that facilities for the sport should be provided by local authorities. One of the zaniest examples of skateboarding was its use as a form of transport by a Los Angeles, Calif., air freight company; Emery Air Freight had four messengers skating around its station.

In 1976 the popularity of kites soared to unprecedented heights in Britain following wide press and television coverage of three new types of stunt kite.

Anatomically correct dolls were produced by U.S. manufacturers for the first time. This is Baby Brother Tender Love by Mattel Toys.

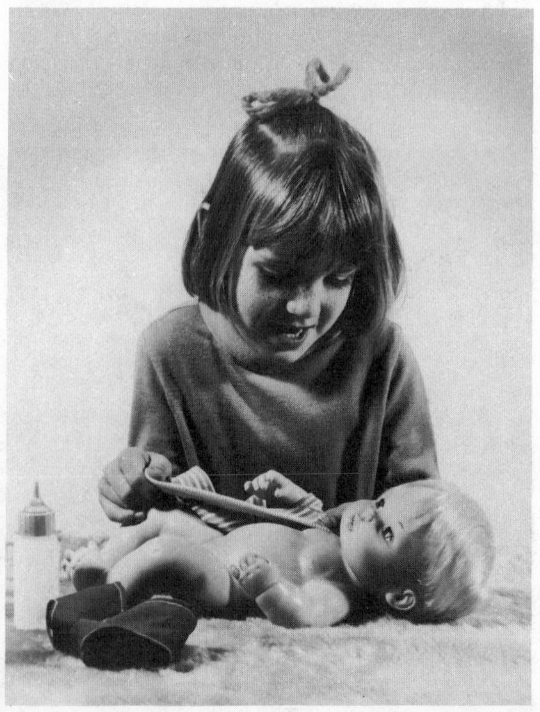

AUTHENTICATED NEWS INTERNATIONAL

During the summer every imaginable variety, from the simplest to the most exotic and colourful, could be seen flying above parks and beaches. The fever spread to Japan, where kite flying, although always a popular sport, had dwindled in interest in recent years.

Continuing to grow in popularity were electronic games such as Pong and Odyssey, in which two-dimensional hockey rinks, tennis courts, and other playing fields are simulated on a screen and moving dots of light on the screen represent the action. Coin-operated models became common in restaurants and entertainment arcades, and home versions of the games could be hooked up to television sets and displayed on the TV screen.

Noticeable at the Brighton Toy Fair in England was a return to favour of model train sets, with new versions launched by Airfix Products Ltd. and Palitoy (General Mills [U.K.] Ltd.) in competition with the market leader, Hornby (owned by DCM). Lego, the Danish interlocking plastic brick constructional system, with world sales totaling in excess of $150 million, won the National Association of Toy Retailers' "Toy of the Year" title and *Toys International*'s "Top Toy Trophy," the British toy industry's two major awards.

The overall economic climate for the world toy industry shifted somewhat during the year. One of the largest U.S. toy manufacturers, Louis Marx Inc., a subsidiary of Quaker Oats, was bought by the British DCM company for $15 million. DCM, which had owned Louis Marx's British subsidiary since 1967, also took control of the Louis Marx Hong Kong company. British toy manufacturers were beginning to challenge the Hong Kong supremacy simply because the prices of Hong Kong-made products were no longer as competitive. Indeed, toward the end of 1976 one Far Eastern manufacturer of boxed games found that it was cheaper to have his goods made in Britain and shipped back to the Far East than to have them made locally. The decline in the value of the pound sterling was the cause of this shift in balance. Hong Kong, nevertheless, was still the largest toy exporter, with exports totaling $325.4 million in 1975 and $234 million during January–July 1976, an increase of 33.2% over the corresponding period of 1975. The U.S. was Hong Kong's biggest market for toys, accounting for more than half its total exports, while the U.K. was second, followed by West Germany, Canada, Australia, and Japan. (GORDON A. WEBB)

The skateboard craze spread to Britain in 1976, despite opposition by accident prevention bodies.

SYNDICATION INTERNATIONAL/PHOTO TRENDS

See also Board Games.

[452.B.6; 452.C–D]

Gardening

Hope that the American chestnut tree could be saved from blight and restored to American forests was held out in 1976 by Richard A. Jaynes, associate geneticist at the Connecticut Agricultural Experiment Station, New Haven. The chestnut once covered most of the eastern U.S. from Maine to Minnesota and south to Florida and Mississippi. Around 1900 a fungus, *Endothia parasitica,* entered the U.S. on trees from northern China, and within less than 25 years it had killed most of the chestnuts on the eastern seaboard. The blight had not yet spread to the Midwest, and a few chestnut trees of timber size remained there, but they had no resistance to the disease.

In France, where European chestnut trees infected by the disease began to recover, research showed that a new and weaker strain of the fungus was inhibiting growth of the Asiatic strain. Jaynes imported this strain and found that it had the same effect on the American chestnut. In 1976 workers were attempting to determine whether the new fungus would spread itself or whether it would have to be spread by man. A determination was also being made as to whether the new strain would harm oak trees. The chestnut-blight fungus can live on oak trees but does not injure them. Meanwhile, extensive efforts were being made to breed a well-formed, blight-resistant hybrid chestnut. In addition, chestnut seeds were treated with radioactive cobalt in the hope of speeding the process of mutation.

A new systemic fungicide, Lignasan BLP, was approved by the U.S. Environmental Protection Agency for use against Dutch elm disease. Research at the Louisiana Agricultural Experiment Station indicated that Benlate, another systemic fungicide, could be used successfully to treat mimosa wilt, a supposedly fatal disease of mimosa trees. An intensive investigation was begun at the University of Florida to solve the mystery of the "lethal yellowing" that was killing the state's coconut palms. Meanwhile, Malayan Dwarf, a semidwarf coconut palm with high resistance to the disease, was introduced as a replacement.

In Europe losses resulting from the worst drought in two centuries were expected to be high, even among long-established trees and plants, and the effect on newly planted stock was catastrophic. This was particularly true in areas ravaged by Dutch elm disease. Also severely affected were those areas of the U.K. where mature stock and standard trees had been planted in an effort to counter the rise in vandalism against small, young plants. This type of vandalism was becoming a serious problem, and it was proposed that schools place greater emphasis on agricultural science in the hope of inculcating greater respect for

WIDE WORLD

The worlds most expensive rose, the hybrid Rosa persica, was sold in London in sets of five different hybrids at about $450 a set. It was developed from a wild Iranian variety.

gardens, the landscape, and the environment in general.

Worldwide interest was being shown in the nutrient film technique (NFT) of hydroponic crop culture devised at the U.K. Glasshouse Crops Research Institute. The NFT system consists of continuous lengths of self-supporting canal made from a chemically inert, nonrip plastic—black on one side and white on the other—with fastening studs at four-inch intervals to exclude light and allow stringing. Along the canal, plants, retained in cubes of rock wool, paper pots, or polyurethane foam, are placed at suitable intervals. A nutrient solution is constantly recirculated from a reservoir, partly by gravity and partly by pump, using capillary matting to ensure even distribution.

House plants grown by a technique called hydroculture or aquaculture were being sold in the U.K. with a six-month guarantee. The plants were grown in undrained containers filled with expanded clay granules. Water was added containing a slow-release fertilizer that needed renewing at intervals of 6 or 12 months. The containers were fitted with a simple float gauge to indicate the level of the water, which needed to be topped-up about once every three weeks.

Three new roses won 1977 All America awards: Double Delight, a hybrid tea with creamy white buds that open to carmine-red flowers; Prominent, a grandiflora with orange-red flowers; and First Edition, a floribunda with coral coloured blooms. Prominent, created by Reimer Kordes of West Germany, had already received awards in Europe and a gold medal in Portland, Ore., in 1975. All-America flower awards went to Showgirl, a hybrid geranium; Primrose Lady, a marigold hybrid; Yellow Galore, a marigold hybrid; and Blushing Maid, a petunia hybrid. A new variety of cabbage, Savoy Ace, was a 1977 winner of the rarely awarded gold medal of All-America Vegetable Selections. Melody, a spinach hybrid, won a silver medal, and Scallopini, a hybrid squash, and Spirit, a pumpkin hybrid, received bronze medals.

The first awards made by the British Association of Rose Breeders since its founding in 1973 went to Eye Paint and Dublin Bay from Sam McGredy Roses International, New Zealand, and Dame of Sark from R. Harkness & Co. Ltd. The selection was made from 41 new cultivars planted at 11 centres and grown for three seasons. Over 980 delegates from four continents attended the centenary conference of the Royal National Rose Society of Great Britain. Considerable interest was aroused by a line of hybrids introduced by Jack Harkness of the U.K. which have yellow flowers with a red "eye." A hybrid of this type with *Rosa persica* from Iran as a parent was raised in Paris in 1836, but had not been seen since. Three new apple varieties, Prima, Priscilla, and Sir Prize, were introduced in the U.S. Developed through cooperative research by the agricultural experiment stations of Illinois, Indiana, and New Jersey, all three have practical immunity to apple scab and considerable resistance to apple mildew and fire blight. In France a new large, yellow apple, Charden, was being given extended market trials.

The *Classified List and International Register of Tulip Names* was revised by the Royal General Bulbgrowers' Society, Hillegom, Neth.; 200 new cultivars were included and 600 regarded as extinct were deleted. The *Classified List and International Register of Hyacinths* was also revised and listed eight new genera. The appearance of the European Economic Community's *Common Catalogue of Varieties of Vegetable Species* and the U.K. *National List of Vegetable Varieties* made possible a significant cutback in synonyms and in the names by which a single variety is offered.

(J. G. SCOTT MARSHALL; TOM STEVENSON)

See also Agriculture and Food Supplies; Life Sciences.
[355.C.2–3; 731.B.1]

Garment Industry:
see Fashion and Dress

Gas Industry:
see Energy

Gemstones:
see Industrial Review

Genetics:
see Life Sciences

Geochemistry:
see Earth Sciences

Geography

Approximately 2,000 geographers attended the 23rd congress of the International Geographical Union in Moscow, July 27–Aug. 3, 1976. The president of the U.S.S.R. Academy of Sciences, A. Alexandrov, in his welcoming message, described the most important task facing geography today: dealing with the problem of consistently protecting and transforming the environment, which is an organic part of the broader problem of the relationship between nature and society. He noted that study of the interaction of man and his environment had created a body of sciences intermediate between the natural and the social, among which geography was of signal importance. The three major themes of the congress were: scientific forecasts of man-made changes in the environment; the lines of regional economic development; and geographic aspects of urbanization processes.

Most current geographic research problems can be subsumed under these three broad themes, and range from global systems studies of the natural and man-made environment to microanalytic studies of small settlements and ecosystems. The subjects of environmental management and settlement patterns were currently seeing much useful research. An ever expanding volume of work was being done in historical geography, physical geography, natural hazard assessment, medical geography, and humanistic geography. New journals of historical and medical geography now provided outlets for such research.

A myriad of environmental problems prompted a renewed interest in field studies. In his presidential address to the more than 1,700 geographers assembled at the 72nd annual meeting of the Association of American Geographers (AAG), James J. Parsons exhorted geographers to pay more attention to field study and to focus upon specific areas in order to learn and to appreciate the lessons their landscapes teach. He called upon them to rise above the mere marketing of techniques, to take stands on moral

KEYSTONE

The world is ever with us. This 28-foot globe was built at Babson College in Wellesley, Massachusetts. It weighs over 21 tons.

issues, to ask more critical questions about the devastation of resources and environment, and to challenge the suicidal materialistic philosophy of the day.

Applied geographic studies were enjoying a healthy resurgence. The *Geographical Review* instituted a new section on applied geography to bring before the profession and the general public examples of geographic problem-solving in real world situations. The American Geographical Society announced plans to move its world-renowned library, rare manuscript, map, and globe collection from New York City to the library of the University of Wisconsin-Milwaukee. The collection would remain as a discrete entity and would continue to serve research geographers and the general public from its new base.

The National Geographic Society celebrated the U.S. Bicentennial in the July issue of the *National Geographic Magazine* with a remarkable Landsat (formerly the Earth Resources Technology Satellite) colour photomosaic of the conterminous United States. Close-ups of this map reveal extensive modification of the natural environment. The society also supported innovative research projects on the Earth's changing climate, global plate tectonics, Ethiopian early man, analysis of the grizzly bear habitat using Landsat imagery, paleoenvironmental research in Alaska, culture and ecology of the New Guinean pig complex, western African settlement geography, ecology of sea turtles, solar energy, earthquake prediction, and India's program of wildlife conservation.

In May the National Science Foundation sponsored a workshop on trends in geographic research and the role of the NSF in assisting such research. Important discussion topics included the growing interest of geographers in man/land research, requiring new responses by the scientific community to such interdisciplinary research. Two focal points of such research deal with resource information systems that go beyond data acquisition and identification, and decision-making about energy use, management exploration of energy-related resources, federal and local land use policies, and environmental impact analysis.

The recently completed Metropolitan Analysis Project sponsored by the AAG with NSF funding produced an important atlas, a series of metropolitan vignettes, and urban policy studies. The products could provide significant guidance for future urban policies. A follow-up of this urban research pointed toward more research on overall settlement patterns and population redistribution and their implications for transportation policy, location-allocation problems for public facilities, and numerous governmental and private-sector decisions.

For geographers and public land use decision-makers, the appropriateness of land use policies was underscored tragically when more than 100 people lost their lives in the floodwaters rushing through the Big Thompson Canyon in Colorado on July 31/August 1. (*See* ENGINEERING PROJECTS.)

Geographic education research interests widened to include special attention to geographic components of environmental education and to assessing geographic learning in elementary education. The National Council for Geographic Education sponsored such projects during the year and would highlight them at its annual meeting. A number of other geographers had been exploring some of the significant processes that affect geographic learning in young children. (SALVATORE J. NATOLI)

See also Earth Sciences.
[10/33.B.1]

ENCYCLOPÆDIA BRITANNICA FILMS. *The Earth: Man's Home* (1970).

Geology:
see Earth Sciences
Geophysics:
see Earth Sciences

German Democratic Republic

A country of central Europe, Germany was partitioned after World War II into the Federal Republic of Germany (Bundesrepublik Deutschland; West Germany) and the German Democratic Republic (Deutsche Demokratische Republik; East Germany), with a special provisional regime for Berlin. East Germany is bordered by the Baltic Sea, Poland, Czechoslovakia, and West Germany. Area: 41,826 sq mi (108,328 sq km). Pop. (1976 est.): 16,820,200. Cap. and largest city: East Berlin (pop., 1976 est., 1,098,200). Language: German. Religion (1969 est.): Protestant 80%; Roman Catholic 10%. First secretary of the Socialist Unity (Communist) Party (SED) in 1976, Erich Honecker; chairmen of the Council of State, Willi Stoph and, from October 29, Erich Honecker; presidents of the Council of Ministers (premiers), Horst Sindermann and, from October 29, Willi Stoph.

A leadership reshuffle at the end of October 1976 was thought to be a consequence of the state's economic difficulties. The first secretary of the SED, Erich Honecker, was additionally elected to the chairmanship of the Council of State. In this role he replaced Willi Stoph, who became president of the Council of Ministers, or premier, succeeding Horst Sindermann. Sindermann was elected president of the Volkskammer, the East German Parliament, an office without great significance. Stoph had been premier from 1964 to 1973. He said of the new changes that "social developments" had made it advisable that the leader of the party should also be the head of state. As former party chief in Halle, Sindermann had shown a particularly sure hand in steering economic policy; as premier, however, he was less successful in this field. Nonetheless, his importance in the East German hierarchy was still recognized. There was speculation that he would encourage Parliament to become a forum for the "controlled" airing of the people's grievances.

In his government statement of policy, Stoph said that economic growth depended on ever increasing productivity. This appeal to work harder was not new. There were signs that the public was becoming more and more restive about increasing prices. Since the oil crisis of 1973 East Germany's deficit in its trade with the Western countries had grown by 50%. Economists doubted whether this development could be reversed by stepping up productivity. As it was, East German citizens were working longer hours than almost anybody else in Eastern Europe. The government was urged by economic experts to increase its exports to the West so as to reduce its deficit and build up its reserves of hard currency. But the Soviet government was reported to be demanding that East Germany send more of its high-technology products to the U.S.S.R.

At the election to the Volkskammer on October 17 99.86% of the electorate voted for candidates on the National Front's list, the only candidates on the ballot.

During the summer, relations between East and West Germany were strained by a number of incidents at the border. A man from Hamburg on a holiday trip was fired on and injured when he accidentally strolled across the border. An Italian truck driver, incidentally a member of the Italian Communist Party, was killed by shots from East German guards as he returned to their post to have his papers rechecked. Busloads of young West Germans traveling to West Berlin for a demonstration on the anniversary of the building of the Berlin Wall were refused transit across East Germany. Despite provocation from East Berlin and Moscow and shrill opposition cries for more action, the West German government resolutely turned the other cheek, protesting only when necessary, in the hope that the confrontation would simmer down. West German opposition reaction to the incidents was condemned by the East German Communist Party organ *Neues Deutschland* as an anti-East German campaign. The paper questioned whether East Germany could reasonably be expected to continue to grant West German citizens, who were being incited to hatred, the degree of free movement within East Germany that they now enjoyed. On August 11 the Soviet ambassador in East Berlin, Pjotr Abrassimov, called on Honecker for a talk about intra-German relations. On the following day Honecker received Günter Gaus, head of the West German mission in East Berlin, and from this conversation the West German government gained the impression that "the leadership of East Germany is not interested in escalating the recent tensions between the two German states."

In August the suicide of a Protestant pastor led to the first open confrontation between the East German government and the country's largest church. A letter from Protestant leaders, read in churches throughout the country, said that the suicide of 47-year-old Pastor Oskar Brüsewitz of Zeitz in Saxony, who set himself on fire in the town's market square in protest against the repression of religion, "demonstrated the tensions in our society and the tests which many have to undergo." The letter criticized the government for not giving the church's leaders a chance to discuss their demand for guarantees of equal treatment for young Christians in state schools. It hinted that the church in the past might have been too weak in its dealings with the government. The East German government had, in fact, treated its Christians relatively liberally. Unlike the churches in other Communist countries, those in East Germany ran their own hospitals, old people's homes, and institutions of higher learning.

East Berlin's Palace of the Republic was finished in May. The two-story lounge has murals by East German artists. Located on Marx-Engels Platz, the building houses the East German Parliament (People's Legislature).

KEYSTONE

GERMAN DEMOCRATIC REPUBLIC

Education. (1975–76) Primary, pupils 2,649,886; secondary, pupils 47,854; primary and secondary, teachers 158,543; vocational (1974–75), pupils 453,000; higher (1974–75), students 186,267, teaching staff 33,570.

Finance. Monetary unit: Mark of Deutsche Demokratische Republik, with (Sept. 20, 1976) a free exchange rate of M 2.48 to U.S. $1 (M 4.27 = £1 sterling). Budget (1974 est.): revenue M 99,563,000,000; expenditure M 99,518,000,000. Net material product (at 1967 prices; 1974) M 135 billion.

Foreign Trade. (1975) Imports M 39,290,000,000; exports M 35,105,000,000. Import sources (1974): U.S.S.R. 30%; West Germany 9%; Czechoslovakia 7%; Poland 7%; Hungary 5%. Export destinations (1974): U.S.S.R. 33%; Czechoslovakia 10%; West Germany 10%; Poland 9%; Hungary 6%. Main exports (1970): machinery 38%; transport equipment 11% (ships and boats 5%); chemicals; lignite; textiles; furniture.

Transport and Communications. Roads (1974) 126,900 km (including 47,603 km main roads and 1,531 km autobahns). Motor vehicles in use (1974): passenger 1,703,000; commercial 225,653. Railways: (1974) 14,252 km (including 1,406 km electrified); traffic (1975) 21,304,000,000 passenger-km, freight 49,681,000,000 net ton-km. Air traffic (1974): 1,315,000,000 passenger-km; freight 42,809,000 net ton-km. Navigable inland waterways in regular use (1974) 2,546 km; freight traffic 2,326,000,000 ton-km. Shipping (1975): merchant vessels 100 gross tons and over 437; gross tonnage 1,389,000. Telephones (Dec. 1974) 2,451,010. Radio licenses (Dec. 1973) 6,082,000. Television licenses (Dec. 1973) 4,966,000.

Agriculture. Production (in 000; metric tons; 1975): wheat *c.* 2,900; barley *c.* 3,000; rye *c.* 1,800; oats *c.* 900; potatoes 7,673; sugar, raw value *c.* 685; cabbages (1974) *c.* 345; rapeseed *c.* 270; apples (1974) *c.* 304; fish catch (1974) 363. Livestock (in 000; Dec. 1974): cattle 5,585; sheep 1,847; pigs 11,519; goats (1973) 78; horses used in agriculture (1973) 82; poultry 47,530.

Industry. Index of production (1970 = 100; 1975) 137. Production (in 000; metric tons; 1975): lignite 246,612; coal 539; electricity (kw-hr) 84,409,000; iron ore (25% metal content) 58; pig iron 2,457; crude steel 6,480; cement 10,652; potash (oxide content; 1974) 2,864; sulfuric acid 1,001; synthetic rubber 142; cotton yarn (1974) 58; rayon, etc., filaments and fibres 138; passenger cars (units) 159; commercial vehicles (units) 48.

The government could have done without criticisms of the tensions in society. In September it was revealed that approximately 55,000 people were said to have applied to emigrate to West Germany within recent months.

In October the Vatican acknowledged the existence of two Germanies. It announced that it was giving ecclesiastical independence to East Germany's 1.3 million Roman Catholics. Until then, East Germany, from the Vatican's point of view, had been part of the German bishops' conference whose seat was at Fulda in West Germany. East Germany's ten Catholic bishops had been unable to go to Fulda since the East German government built the Berlin Wall in 1961. But the Vatican did not give full recognition. For the moment there was to be no papal nuncio in East Germany.

Wolf Biermann, an East German protest singer who had frequently been extremely critical of the East German brand of socialism, was deprived of his East German citizenship in November, while on a professional tour of West Germany.

(NORMAN CROSSLAND)

[972.A.3.b.iii]

Germany, Federal Republic of

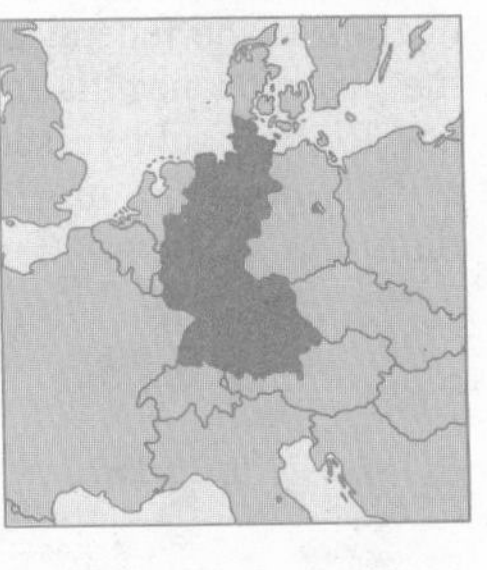

A country of central Europe, Germany was partitioned after World War II into the Federal Republic of Germany (Bundesrepublik Deutschland; West Germany) and the German Democratic Republic (Deutsche Demokratische Republik; East Germany), with a special provisional regime for Berlin. West Germany is bordered by Denmark, The Netherlands, Belgium, Luxembourg, France, Switzerland, Austria, Czechoslovakia, East Germany, and the North Sea. Area: 95,993 sq mi (248,620 sq km). Pop. (1976 est.): 61,644,600. Provisional cap.: Bonn (pop., 1976 est., 283,700). Largest city: Hamburg (pop., 1976 est., 1,717,400). (West Berlin, which is an enclave within East Germany, had a population of 1,984,800 in 1976.) Language: German. Religion (1970): Protestant 49%; Roman Catholic 44.6%; Jewish 0.05%. President in 1976, Walter Scheel; chancellor, Helmut Schmidt.

After the federal election on Oct. 3, 1976, the coalition of the Social Democratic Party (SPD) and the Free Democratic Party (FDP) remained in power but with a much reduced majority. During the year the government met with considerable success in maintaining economic stability. By October the rate of inflation had been cut to less than 4%, but unemployment was above 900,000.

Domestic Affairs. It was a surprise to many that the record of Helmut Schmidt since he became chancellor in May 1974 was so poorly rewarded in the federal election. The Christian Democratic Union (CDU) and its Bavarian sister party, the Christian Social Union (CSU), polled 48.6% of the total vote, as compared with 44.9% in 1972. The SPD's share of the poll was 42.6% (45.8%) and the FDP's 7.9% (8.4%). This meant that the coalition's majority in the Bundestag, or lower house, was cut from 46 to 8 seats. Clearly, many West Germans were not unduly impressed by the chancellor's argument that they had little to complain about in comparison with their neighbours.

Even so, the "Schmidt effect" undoubtedly played an important, perhaps decisive, role in keeping his party in power. He was to the right of the Social Democratic Party, a position that suited the country's conservative mood, and his qualities were likely to have persuaded many waverers to give him another chance. It looked like a last chance, for unmistakably the tide was running against Social Democracy in West Germany. The federal election of 1972, when Willy Brandt was returned to office

West German candidates for chancellor faced each other on TV in their hard-fought fall campaign. Shown from left are: Chancellor Helmut Schmidt of the governing Social Democratic Party; his ally Hans-Dietrich Genscher of the Free Democratic Party; Helmut Kohl, leader of the opposition Christian Democratic Union; and Franz-Josef Strauss of Bavaria's Christian Social Union.

REGIS BOSSU—SYGMA

WIDE WORLD

The drought in Western Europe took its toll in many harbours along the Rhine River such as this one at Duisburg, West Germany.

on a wave of personal sympathy, was exceptional. Since then the Social Democrats had lost ground in every Land (state) election but one. There was a great huddle around the political centre. Voters were not stampeded by the opposition's slogan, "freedom instead of socialism," but it stirred an emotional undercurrent.

The opposition's chancellor candidate, Helmut Kohl, who after the election resigned the premiership of the Rhineland-Palatinate to lead his party in the federal Parliament, caught the mood of the electorate with his constant assertion that the West German government was becoming too powerful and oppressive, stifling individual freedom. The electoral setback was expected to put the new government under some strain. But there was no parallel between the outcome of this election and that of 1969 when the first SPD/FDP coalition had a 12-seat majority that was gradually eroded by defections to the opposition. The Free Democrats went into the 1976 election with the unanimous backing of a party conference to continue the alliance. Kohl cordially invited them to join him in forming a government, but this was no more than a gesture, even though he had a point in saying that it was less than democratic for the strongest political force in Parliament to be excluded from office.

The opposition already had a majority of 26–15 in the Bundesrat, the upper house of the federal Parliament in which the Länder were represented. The result of the election did not affect this. Nor did it alter the composition of the important committee for the joint consideration of bills, in which each side had equal strength. Bundestag committees in the future would have fewer coalition members, but they would still be in the majority.

No sooner was the election over than Franz-Josef Strauss, chairman of the CSU, blew the dust off an old plan to extend the operations of his right-of-centre party beyond the borders of Bavaria. In the election the CSU polled 60% of the total Bavarian vote. Clearly, argued Strauss, what was needed was the Bavarian touch throughout the federal republic.

In Strauss's view the CDU had a sick left wing that must either be healed or discarded. If, for instance, the northerners had not been so halfhearted in raising the banner "freedom or socialism," victory would have been possible. Now, said Strauss, his party "must break loose." At the end of November, after 27 years of existence as the Bavarian sister of the CDU, the CSU broke its connection with the CDU and voted to form an entirely separate party.

After the election, the CDU invited the Free Democrats to form coalition governments in two states, Lower Saxony and the Saarland. In Lower Saxony, Ernst Albrecht, the Christian Democrat who was elected prime minister in February with the help of defectors from the former coalition benches, had been leading a minority government. In Saarbrücken Franz-Josef Röder of the CDU had presided since the state election in May 1975 over a government whose parliamentary strength equaled that of the Social Democrats and Free Democrats combined. The CDU had a major interest in lining up with the Free Democrats in both of those states, and not only for practical reasons. A renewal of cooperation between the two parties in the Länder would be an important step toward reforging an alliance of conservatives and liberals at the federal level. The main problem facing the coalition negotiations was that neither Albrecht nor Röder could reasonably expect the Free Democrats to join him unless they had the assurance that the votes of Lower Saxony and the Saarland in the

GERMANY, FEDERAL REPUBLIC OF

Education. (1973–74) Primary, pupils 4,242,458; secondary, pupils 5,472,448; primary and secondary, teachers 379,634; vocational, pupils 598,493, teachers 20,633; higher (including 54 universities), students 729,207, teaching staff 68,286.

Finance. Monetary unit: Deutsche Mark, with (Sept. 20, 1976) a free rate of DM 2.48 to U.S. $1 (DM 4.27 = £1 sterling). Gold, SDR's, and foreign exchange (June 1976) U.S. $30,877,000,000. Budget (federal; 1975 actual): revenue DM 130,120,000,000; expenditure DM 164,180,000,000. Gross national product (1975) DM 1,040,400,000,000. Money supply (May 1976) DM 167 billion. Cost of living (1970 = 100; June 1976) 141.

Foreign Trade. (1975) Imports DM 184,310,000,000; exports DM 221,590,000,000. Import sources: EEC 50% (The Netherlands 14%, France 12%, Italy 9%, Belgium-Luxembourg 9%); U.S. 8%. Export destinations: EEC 44% (France 12%, The Netherlands 10%, Belgium-Luxembourg 8%, Italy 7%, U.K. 5%); U.S. 6%. Main exports: machinery 29%; motor vehicles 13%; chemicals 13%; iron and steel 12%; textile yarns and fabrics 6%. Tourism (1974): visitors 6,951,000; gross receipts U.S. $2,338,000,000.

Transport and Communications. Roads (1974) 462,155 km (including 5,748 km autobahns). Motor vehicles in use (1974): passenger 17,356,000; commercial 1,244,000. Railways: (1974) 32,072 km (including 10,018 km electrified); traffic (1975) 37,759,000,000 passenger-km, freight 55,062,000,000 net ton-km. Air traffic (1975): 13,635,000,000 passenger-km; freight 993,414,000 net ton-km. Navigable inland waterways in regular use (1974) 4,393 km; freight traffic 50,972,000,000 ton-km. Shipping (1975): merchant vessels 100 gross tons and over 1,964; gross tonnage 8,516,567. Telephones (Dec. 1974) 18,767,033. Radio licenses (Dec. 1973) 20,586,000. Television licenses (Dec. 1973) 18,486,000.

Agriculture. Production (in 000; metric tons; 1975): wheat 7,013; barley 6,971; rye 2,125; oats 3,445; potatoes 10,853; sugar, raw value c. 2,510; apples (1974) 1,282; wine (1974) 626; cow's milk c. 21,604; butter 521; cheese 618; beef and veal (1974) 1,248; pork (1974) 2,275; fish catch (1974) 526. Livestock (in 000; Dec. 1974): cattle 14,420; pigs 20,213; sheep 1,040; horses used in agriculture (1974) 320; chickens 89,377.

Industry. Index of production (1970 = 100; 1975) 105. Unemployment (1975) 4.7%. Fuel and power (in 000; metric tons; 1975): coal c. 94,300; lignite 123,378; crude oil 5,742; coke (1974) 34,854; electricity (kw-hr) 301,803,000; natural gas (cu m) 18,813,000; manufactured gas (cu m) 17,118,000. Production (in 000; metric tons; 1975): iron ore (28% metal content) 3,288; pig iron 30,332; crude steel 40,413; aluminum 963; copper 422; lead 253; zinc 421; cement 33,053; sulfuric acid 4,179; cotton yarn 192; woven cotton fabrics 166; wool yarn 51; rayon, etc., filament yarn 52; rayon, etc., staple fibres 63; nylon, etc., filament yarn 302; nylon, etc., fibres 306; petroleum products (1974) 105,630; fertilizers (1974–75) nitrogenous 1,574, phosphate 900, potash 2,659; synthetic rubber 316; plastics and resins 4,994; passenger cars (units) 2,908; commercial vehicles (units) 284. Merchant vessels launched (100 gross tons and over; 1975) 2,545,000 gross tons. New dwelling units completed (1975) 436,000.

Bundesrat would not be used to block federal government legislation.

It was reported in September that since the ban on the import of foreign labour was imposed in November 1973 about 500,000 foreign workers had left the country. But some 2 million remained, with another 2 million dependents. The Ministry of Development Aid was promoting a scheme devised by Turkish workers to set up small factories at home with the money and skills they had acquired in West Germany. The signs were, however, that most foreign workers were content to stay in West Germany at any price.

West Germany's nuclear energy program ran into stiff opposition from citizens' initiative groups, which had strong misgivings about the safety aspects of atomic power stations. In October and November there were violent demonstrations at the site of a nuclear power station on the Lower Elbe at Brokdorf in Schleswig-Holstein. Work was still held up on constructing an atomic power station at Wyhl in Baden-Württemberg. West Germany had 11 nuclear power stations in operation, 12 being built, and 7 in the planning stage. It was still hoped that by 1980 about 9% of primary energy needs would be met by nuclear stations, but there were indications that this forecast would have to be revised.

On October 17 the mark was revalued upward with a range of 2 to 6% within the joint European floating bloc known as the "snake." It continued, however, to float freely against all other currencies, including the dollar and sterling.

Ulrike Meinhof (*see* OBITUARIES), political journalist turned urban guerrilla, committed suicide by hanging in her prison cell at Stammhein near Stuttgart on May 9. She was already serving an eight-year sentence for helping to free by force a fellow terrorist, Andreas Baader, when he was in prison for committing arson. Since May 1975 she, Baader, and two others had been on trial charged with involvement in 5 murders, 54 cases of attempted murder, and a series of bomb attacks and bank robberies. Lawyers representing Meinhof said she was pushed into committing suicide by the conditions of her confinement. Certainly the years since her arrest in 1972 had taken their psychological toll. In September 1975 doctors and psychiatrists pronounced all four accused to be capable of standing trial only to a limited extent and to be in need of treatment. Afterward the conditions of their imprisonment were improved.

Foreign Affairs. The Bundesrat in March voted unanimously in favour of the "money for people" agreements with Poland. A few hours before the vote took place the opposition representatives decided that their misgivings had been removed by new assurances from Warsaw. Under the agreements West Germany was to pay Poland DM 2.3 billion. Of this DM 1 billion was a loan, repayable in 25 years at $2\frac{1}{2}$% interest. The remainder was to cover Polish citizens' pension claims against West Germany and to provide compensation for Polish victims of Nazi concentration camps. In return the Polish government was allowing 125,000 Polish citizens of German origin to leave Poland for West Germany in the next four years. The deal was approved by an overwhelming majority of the Bundestag in February when 15 members of the opposition voted for it. But the official opposition line continued to be that no limit should be imposed on the number of ethnic Germans allowed out by the Poles. The agreements contained a clause, inserted at the West German government's request, that the question of approving further applications should be left open. This was not good enough for the opposition, although some of their leaders had been saying privately that the West German economy, faced with unemployment, could not cope even with an influx of 125,000. To make the agreements acceptable to the opposition, there was an exchange of letters between the two governments, making it clear that applications could be approved beyond the four-year period.

Pres. Anwar as-Sadat of Egypt paid a three-day visit to West Germany in March, and although West Germany agreed to increase its development aid to Egypt it rejected Sadat's suggestion that Bonn should be a guarantor of a Middle East settlement or that German troops should be part of a peacekeeping force. At a press conference Sadat said he had not even spoken about arms because he had known before he left Cairo that West Germany pursued a "restricted policy" in this sphere. But, he added, he had discussed with Chancellor Schmidt the possibility of West Germany's recognizing the Palestine Liberation Organization.

In June the leader of the French Socialist Party, François Mitterrand, set up a committee to "protect civic and professional rights" in West Germany. A Belgian television program decided that West Germany's approach to civil liberties had something in common with that of Spain, Chile, and Argentina. Alfred Grosser, the Frenchman who was awarded the German book trade's peace prize in 1975, considered that although the federal republic was the most democratic state Germany had ever had it was not as democratic as it was ten years ago. One thing all these people had in common was their criticism of West Germany's attempt to keep political extremists out of the civil service.

The comments abroad produced a reaction at home. There was talk of an international conspiracy against Germany. One German commentator said that the world was growing uneasy about West Germany's increasing economic and political power, and about the strictures of Schmidt against France and Italy. Schmidt did not like the idea of an alliance of Socialists and Communists in France or anywhere else and had not disguised his feelings. Earlier in the year, how-

Riot police used water cannon to disperse a crowd of demonstrators in Frankfurt am Main in May. It was the day after Ulrike Meinhof of the Baader-Meinhof urban guerrilla band committed suicide in her jail cell.

UPI COMPIX

ever, the chancellor told the federal Parliament that with a few exceptions members of the European Economic Community had withstood the temptation to engage in national eccentricities and the world economic crisis had not broken up the Community. The task was to safeguard what had already been achieved and to concentrate on those matters that were of immediate importance.

West Berlin. Four women prisoners, one a convicted terrorist, the others accused of acts of terrorism, escaped on July 7 from the jail in the Lehrter Strasse in West Berlin. The senator of justice in the city, Hermann Oxfort, took political responsibility for the escape and resigned. Some believed that, had it not been an election year, the mayor, Klaus Schütz, would have been persuaded to go as well. Security at the prison turned out to have been exceedingly lax. The local branch of the prison warders' association reported that the locks on the cell doors were so worn that they could be opened with a comb. A few days before the breakout a supervisor of a handicrafts class making models from wax and clay had temporarily mislaid her keys. To add to the difficulties West Berlin was disproportionately burdened with terrorist or alleged terrorist prisoners. Of the 29 politically motivated prisoners suspected of murder or attempted murder, 9 were in West Berlin. The city's prisons housed almost 25% of the West Germans awaiting trial for or convicted of terrorist crimes of all kinds.

The Berlin problem in the wake of Willy Brandt's era of *Ostpolitik,* when political relations had been established with East Germany, was the subject of an article in October in the journal of the West German Society for Foreign Affairs, written by the head of the political department of the West German Foreign Ministry, Günther van Well. He pointed out that the Soviet Union was still denying the right, anchored in the four-power agreement on Berlin of 1972, of the West German government to represent West Berlin's interests abroad. He recalled that when the Soviet leader, Leonid Brezhnev, visited Bonn in 1973 he and the then chancellor Brandt signed a declaration of intent to conclude a number of agreements, covering such matters as cultural exchanges and health and energy policy. The agreements were held up, however, because the U.S.S.R. refused to allow them to apply also to West Berlin.

Over the years, and with the consent of the three Western powers, a number of organizations and institutions of importance to international cooperation had been established in West Berlin, among them the German Archaeological Institute, the Federal Cartel Office, and the Federal Office for the Protection of the Environment. All were ignored by the U.S.S.R. even though the four-power agreement laid down that the ties between West Germany and West Berlin should be maintained and developed. Moreover, the Soviets inevitably protested when citizens of West Berlin were included in federal delegations at international conferences or when such conferences were held in West Berlin. Well said that this constant argument about the four-power agreement should not be underestimated. After all, it was that agreement which had put West Germany and its allies in a position to take the next major steps to reduce tension—to ratify the Moscow and Warsaw treaties, come to terms with East Germany, and prepare for the 1975 Conference on Security and Cooperation in Europe.

(NORMAN CROSSLAND)

[973.A.3.b.ii]

German Literature: *see* Literature

Ghana

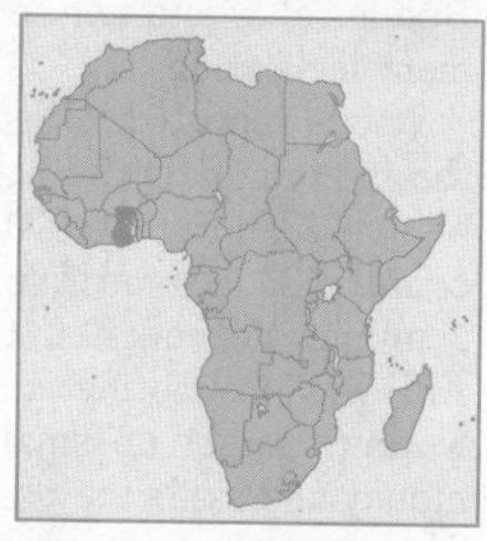

A republic of West Africa and member of the Commonwealth of Nations, Ghana is on the Gulf of Guinea and is bordered by Ivory Coast, Upper Volta, and Togo. Area: 92,100 sq mi (238,500 sq km). Pop. (1975 est.): 9,552,200. Cap. and largest city: Accra (pop., 1975 est., 716,600). Language: English (official); local Sudanic dialects. Religion (1960): Christian 43%; Muslim 12%; animist 38%. Chairman of the National Redemption Council and of the Supreme Military Council in 1976, Gen. Ignatius Kutu Acheampong.

After the establishment of the Supreme Military Council (SMC) in 1975, superseding the National Redemption Council as Ghana's highest legislative and administrative body, Colonel Acheampong (chairman of both) disclosed in his Jan. 13, 1976, address on the fourth anniversary of the revolution plans for a return to civilian rule in a near but undated future. Some observers saw this as no more than a sop to the cynical. The new SMC, consisting of Acheampong and six army chiefs, clamped military rule even more firmly on the country, providing, as the chairman said, "full participation of the military forces." This meant more power for army elements dissatisfied with four years of the "old guard," which had failed to root out corruption and tribalism or to solve economic problems.

GHANA

Education. (1973–74) Primary, pupils 1,014,964, teachers 33,752; secondary, pupils 508,554, teachers 20,351; vocational, pupils 15,671, teachers 788; teacher training, students 10,621, teachers 702; higher, students 7,466, teaching staff 952.

Finance. Monetary unit: new cedi, with (Sept. 20, 1976) an official rate of 1.15 cedi to U.S. $1 (free rate of 1.98 cedi = £1 sterling). Gold, SDR's, and foreign exchange (June 1976) U.S. $160.8 million. Budget (1974–75 est.): revenue 698.5 million cedis; expenditure 986.5 million cedis. Gross national product (1972) 2,787,000,000 cedis. Money supply (May 1976) 1,064,300,000 cedis. Cost of living (Accra; 1970 = 100; Jan. 1976) 279.

Foreign Trade. (1975) Imports 925.8 million cedis; exports 943.5 million cedis. Import sources (1974): U.K. 15%; West Germany 13%; U.S. 11%; Nigeria 7%; Japan 6%; France 5%. Export destinations (1974): U.K. 18%; U.S. 12%; Switzerland 11%; West Germany 11%; The Netherlands 10%; Japan 7%; U.S.S.R. 5%. Main exports (1974): cocoa 54%; timber 12%; veneers and plywood 9%.

Transport and Communications. Roads (1975) *c.* 31,000 km. Motor vehicles in use (1972): passenger 40,400; commercial (including buses) 31,000. Railways: (1974) 953 km; traffic (1971) 520 million passenger-km, freight 305 million net ton-km. Air traffic (1974): 149 million passenger-km; freight 4 million net ton-km. Shipping (1975): merchant vessels 100 gross tons and over 82; gross tonnage 180,351. Telephones (Dec. 1974) 55,000. Radio receivers (Dec. 1974) *c.* 1 million. Television receivers (Dec. 1974) *c.* 30,000.

Agriculture. Production (in 000; metric tons; 1975): corn *c.* 525; cassava (1974) *c.* 2,900; taro (1974) *c.* 1,200; yams (1974) *c.* 600; millet *c.* 141; sorghum *c.* 170; peanuts *c.* 95; oranges (1974) *c.* 90; cocoa *c.* 400; palm oil *c.* 24; timber (cu m; 1974) *c.* 9,760; fish catch (1974) 223. Livestock (in 000; 1974): cattle *c.* 1,100; sheep *c.* 1,600; pigs *c.* 340; goats *c.* 1,600.

Industry. Production (in 000; metric tons; 1974): bauxite 357; petroleum products *c.* 1,055; gold (troy oz) 614; diamonds (metric carats) 2,573; manganese ore (metal content: 1973) 313; electricity (kw-hr) *c.* 3,645,000.

A serious problem was the Ewe (Togo) secession movement, affecting the valuable Volta Region. Proscribed in March after several attempts at gentler measures, the movement was linked with an alleged attempted coup of November–December 1975. That attempt led to treason trials in May–July. Five alleged conspirators were sentenced to death, though the leaders (Brig. A. K. Kattah and Corp. K. Kwashiga) were said to have escaped abroad.

Ghana's economic problems were far from solved. Although Operation Feed Yourself had succeeded in producing basic foodstuffs, General Acheampong (promoted in rank on March 7) launched the fourth stage in May with an exhortation to produce oil-bearing crops. The 1976 development budget was estimated at 360 million cedis. The July budget showed that 117 million cedis of the 180 million cedis commercial debt inherited from the Busia regime had been paid off; expenditure for 1976 was estimated at some 1.2 billion cedis (a 15% increase) and revenue at 743 million cedis. Tax increases and a cocoa export duty were expected to fill the gap. The 1975 Foreign Investment Decree for the indigenization of business, which had its deadline extended to Dec. 31, 1976, led to the exodus of many Nigerian and Ivory Coast traders. But the World Bank and other foreign aid sources looked favourably on Ghana's plan to develop bauxite deposits and convert them into aluminum, thus greatly increasing the contribution already made by the Valco smelter to the balance of payments and employment. (MOLLY MORTIMER)

[978.E.4.b.ii]

Golf

With the notable exception of Jerry Pate, who won a spectacular success in the U.S. Open, established players continued to dominate the major championships, but the honours were more evenly divided than usual in 1976. Ray Floyd began the process with a victory in the Masters at Augusta, Ga., which was the start of his finest year as a professional. He was fourth to Johnny Miller in the British Open, at the Royal Birkdale, Southport, Merseyside, and finished only one stroke behind Dave Stockton, who won his second Professional Golfers' Association (PGA) championship at the Congressional Country Club near Washington, D.C. Though 1976 seemed a comparatively quiet year for Jack Nicklaus, he won the Tournament Players championship in March and the World Series of Golf in September. The first prize of $100,000 in the latter event took him to the head of the PGA money-winners' list, where he remained at the end of the season with $266,438. Nicklaus also tied for second in the British Open and finished third in the Masters and fourth in the PGA championship.

Floyd's Masters victory was the most commanding since Nicklaus won by nine strokes in 1965, and was one of the greatest front-running performances in modern championship golf. An opening round 65 gave him the lead, which he steadily increased and never for a moment seemed likely to surrender. His final total of 271 equaled Nicklaus' record for the event. Only Ben Crenshaw, 8 behind, finished within 11 strokes. The key to Floyd's supremacy was the ruthless fashion in which he mastered the par-five holes. Of the 12 played in the first three rounds, Floyd had 11 birdies and an eagle, a feat that must be without precedent in championship history. Many of these were achieved with a five wood, which Floyd preferred to a one iron because it gave him a softer landing shot.

KEYSTONE

Californian Johnny Miller won the British Open in July.

By winning the U.S. Open less than two years after being U.S. amateur champion, Pate joined Nicklaus and Bobby Jones in the elite group of those who had won both titles by the age of 22. That he should win at the Atlanta (Ga.) Athletic Club, where so much had been done to preserve the memory of Jones, was a felicitous coincidence. The tournament provided championship golf with one of its most dramatic finishes. With three holes to play only one stroke separated John Mahaffey, runner-up the previous year, Pate, Al Geiberger, and Tom Weiskopf. On the last hole, with its menacing carry over a lake, Geiberger and Weiskopf both drove into the rough but then made their pars with brave pitches and putts. Thus, Pate and Mahaffey, playing behind them, knew the extent of their tasks. After their first shots both were on the fringe of the rough. Mahaffey, whose cause had declined on the previous two holes, needed a birdie to tie. His desperate second shot went into the lake.

Pate then faced a fearsome prospect. His lie was fair. Should he go for the green, risking the lake, or lay up, making sure of a tie with Geiberger and Weiskopf, and hope for a single putt to win? No such doubts beset him. So "pumped up" he felt sure he could make the carry, he thought of a four iron, changed to a five, and hit a 190-yd stroke to within two feet of the hole. Even Ben Hogan and Nicklaus had never produced a greater finishing stroke.

Three weeks later, after two rounds at Birkdale, Pate was just in contention for the British Open. A day later he was out of the championship, having scored an unbelievable 87 in the third round, and so was Tom Watson, the defending champion. Pate's astonishing collapse was swiftly redeemed with victory in the Canadian Open, where Nicklaus found that a final round of 65 was not good enough. Pate moved further ahead of him with a closing 63. A tie for

Gibraltar: *see* Dependent States
Glass Manufacture: *see* Industrial Review
Gliding: *see* Aerial Sports

fourth place in the PGA established Pate, with his beautiful swing and superb rhythm, as the supreme young golfer of the year. Meanwhile, another young man, Severiano Ballesteros from Spain, was making a comparable impact on the European scene, and he was only 19. Although Miller, second in 1973 and only one stroke out of the play-off in 1975, deservedly won at Birkdale, the skill, courage, and enduring appeal of Ballesteros made a lasting memory for thousands. In torrid heat, the like of which Britain rarely experienced, Ballesteros opened with a pair of 69s and led Miller by two strokes. The next evening he was still two ahead, but his instinct to attack betrayed him on the final day. While Miller, who said later that he had never played a more conservative tournament, frequently used a one iron from the tees to keep the ball in play on the fast narrow fairways, Ballesteros hammered away with his driver. The deadly willow scrub and rough took its toll of these shots, but Ballesteros was not finished. Remarkable recoveries, two long putts, and a great chip at the last enabled him to tie with Nicklaus for second. Far from suffering any letdown, Ballesteros not only won the Dutch Open but was in contention week after week for the rest of the summer. In October he won the Lancôme Trophy in Paris, and he easily headed Europe's PGA Order of Merit, thereby winning the Vardon Trophy.

Continental European youth had its greatest season. Joining Ballesteros in the victor's circle was Baldovino Dassu, who at the age of 23 became the first Italian to win a major event in Britain by withstanding the challenge of Hubert Green in the Dunlop Masters. Three weeks later he left a strong field far behind in the Italian Open in Sardinia, winning by eight strokes.

The Piccadilly Match Play championship at Wentworth, Virginia Water, Surrey, later abandoned for economic reasons, produced a memorable climax in the last of its 13 years. Hale Irwin, winner the two previous years, endured an experience probably without parallel in losing the final to the deadly putting of David Graham. Never once in 38 holes was Irwin over par, and never was he down in the final match until Graham won with a birdie on the second extra hole. The previous day Graham had recovered from four down and beaten Floyd on the last green. This was a great climax to Graham's most successful season since he left Australia five years previously to compete regularly in the U.S. He won the Westchester and American Classics, and with victories in Australia, Japan, and Britain, was the leading world money winner. Although Hubert Green and Ben Crenshaw each won three tournaments and eight others won two apiece, the great depth of strong players on the U.S. tour became increasingly evident. The tour produced no fewer than 29 different winners, and more players than ever before won over $100,000.

In December at Palm Springs, Calif., Ballesteros and M. Pinero won the World Cup for Spain with a score of 574. The U.S. (Pate and Stockton) was second with 576, followed by Taiwan (581), Scotland (583), and Mexico (584). Ernesto Acosta (Mexico) was the individual champion with 282.

Money-winning records were also set by the women. By the end of the Ladies' Professional Golfers' Association season Judy Rankin, with $150,734, had become the first woman ever to pass the $100,000 mark during a single year. JoAnne Carner won the U.S. Open for the second time, and while she, Jane Blalock, Sandra Palmer, and Donna Young were the foremost winners after Mrs. Rankin, young players such as Pat Bradley, Jan Stephenson, and Amy Alcott were in close pursuit. In the Carlton Tournament in California the women played for over $200,000, and Donna Young won $35,000, the largest first prize in the history of women's golf. History was also made by Chako Higuchi of Japan, who became the first Asian golfer to win in Europe. In the Colgate European championship at Sunningdale, Berkshire, she finished six strokes ahead of Sandra Palmer and Kathy Whitworth and fascinated everyone by the consistency of an unusual swing and by her unshakable calm.

The biennial world amateur team championships were played in Portugal in October, and Great Britain and Ireland won the Eisenhower Trophy at Penina by two strokes from Japan. Australia finished third, the Republic of China (Taiwan) fourth, and the U.S. fifth, nine strokes behind the winning total. The British, whose previous victory was in 1964, had the best-balanced side for the occasion. They were the only team that did not have rounds in the 80s or worse, their highest being a pair of 78s. Had all four scores in each round counted instead of three, they would have won by a large margin. The Americans, with the exception of Dick Siderowf, were inexperienced in this form of competition. U.S. amateur champion Bill Sander, for all his fine style and great power, did not have the lasting control for the demanding course, where missing the fairways almost invariably cost a stroke. Fred Ridley's 70 was the lowest score the team could muster. The climax of the championship developed into an absorbing contest between Ian Hutcheon of Britain, Micho Mori of Japan, and Anthony Gresham of Australia, the last members of their teams to finish. With nine holes to play they were almost even; then Hutcheon played the last eight in four under par and resisted Mori's brave challenge.

Sally Little of South Africa won the Women's International Golf Tournament at Hilton Head, South Carolina, in May. Here she laments a putt that missed.

WIDE WORLD

No such glory had awaited the British the previous week in the women's world amateur golf championship at Vilamoura, where the U.S. won its sixth successive title by the commanding margin of 17 strokes over France. Nancy Lopez was the outstanding player of the championship with the lowest individual total, ten strokes ahead of Catherine Lacoste, still a great golfer, who won the U.S. Open and amateur titles in the late 1960s. Britain and Ireland finished 13th, 40 strokes behind the Americans. Relatively, they fared little better in the Curtis Cup match at Lytham St. Anne's, Lancashire, in June. The U.S. won by 11½–6½ without ever being seriously challenged, and retained the trophy they had held since 1960.

(P. A. WARD-THOMAS)

[452.B.4.h.xiv]

Greece

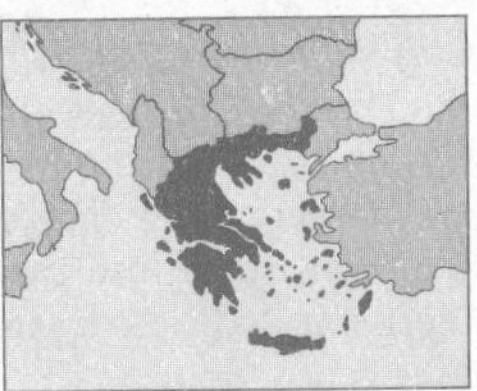

A republic of Europe, Greece occupies the southern part of the Balkan Peninsula. Area: 50,960 sq mi (131,986 sq km), of which the mainland accounts for 41,227 sq mi. Pop. (1975 est.): 9,046,000. Cap. and largest city: Athens (pop., 1971, 867,000). Language: Greek. Religion: Orthodox. President in 1976, Konstantinos Tsatsos; prime minister, Konstantinos Karamanlis.

The Greek-Turkish dispute over continental shelf rights in the Aegean dominated national life in Greece throughout 1976. The economy was burdened with the cost of massive arms orders, but the crisis united the Greeks and limited political and social friction. Karamanlis' proposal in April for a treaty to repudiate the use or the threat of force in bilateral disputes was eventually snubbed by Turkey, and emphasis shifted to the purchase of sophisticated weaponry, the establishment of war industries, creation of the new 4th Army Corps in Thrace, and, despite Turkish protests, military reinforcement of Greek islands near the Anatolian coast. At the same time the government pressed the European Economic Community to speed up Greece's admission as a full member. Talks were formally launched in July and negotiations began in November. If all went well Greece hoped to join in 1979.

The delicate equilibrium with Turkey that Athens was trying to establish was threatened in March when the U.S. and Turkish governments signed a new defense cooperation agreement, granting Turkey military aid worth more than $1 billion over four years in exchange for reopening the U.S. bases in that country. Greece demanded equal treatment. On April 15 the U.S. offered Greece military aid worth $700 million over four years, plus a quasi-guarantee that the U.S. would not tolerate any attempt to change the Aegean status quo by force. In addition, the Greeks would be given more control over the four main U.S. military installations in their country. The final signing was postponed until after the U.S. election. There were many anti-U.S. manifestations, but the government renewed its pledges of loyalty to the West.

Karamanlis' efforts toward a Balkan rapprochement culminated in January and February in an Athens meeting of delegates from five Balkan countries (Albania abstained) who agreed to pursue multilateral cooperation on technical and economic matters. Shortly afterward the heads of government of Romania, Bulgaria, and Yugoslavia came to Athens on state visits.

GREECE

Education. (1973–74) Primary, pupils 925,495, teachers 29,921; secondary, pupils 504,031, teachers 16,595; vocational, pupils 133,361; higher (including 6 universities), students 97,131, teaching staff 5,068.

Finance. Monetary unit: drachma, with (Sept. 20, 1976) a free rate of 36.95 drachmas to U.S. $1 (63.66 drachmas = £1 sterling). Gold, SDR's, and foreign exchange (June 1976) U.S. $869.8 million. Budget (1975 est.) balanced at 140 billion drachmas (excluding investment of 32 billion drachmas). Gross national product (1975) 696.8 billion drachmas. Money supply (March 1976) 117,390,000,000 drachmas. Cost of living (1970 = 100; June 1976) 204.

Foreign Trade. (1975) Imports 172,010,000,000 drachmas; exports 74,160,000,000 drachmas. Import sources: EEC 43% (West Germany 16%, Italy 8%, France 6%, U.K. 5%); Saudi Arabia 8%; Japan 8%; U.S. 7%. Export destinations: EEC 50% (West Germany 21%, Italy 8%, France 7%, The Netherlands 6%, U.K. 5%); Libya 6%; U.S. 5%. Main exports: fruits and vegetables 19%; petroleum products 11%; textile yarns and fabrics 8%; tobacco 7%; iron and steel 7%. Tourism (1974): visitors 1,956,000; gross receipts U.S. $437 million.

Transport and Communications. Roads (1974) 36,447 km (including 76 km expressways). Motor vehicles in use (1974): passenger 379,927; commercial 170,713. Railways (1974): 2,542 km; traffic 1,594,000,000 passenger-km, freight (1975) 931 million net ton-km. Air traffic (1975): 3,430,000,000 passenger-km; freight 36,521,000 net ton-km. Shipping (1975): merchant vessels 100 gross tons and over 2,743; gross tonnage 22,527,156. Telephones (Dec. 1974) 1,862,050. Radio receivers (Dec. 1972) c. 1.3 million. Television receivers (Dec. 1973) 950,000.

Agriculture. Production (in 000; metric tons; 1975): wheat 2,078; barley c. 924; oats c. 100; corn c. 537; rice c. 94; potatoes c. 801; sugar, raw value (1974) 187; tomatoes c. 1,826; onions c. 135; watermelons (1974) c. 650; apples (1974) 210; oranges (1974) c. 590; lemons (1974) c. 160; peaches (1974) c. 259; olives c. 1,020; olive oil c. 220; wine (1974) c. 453; raisins (1974) c. 144; figs (1974) c. 145; tobacco c. 109; cotton, lint c. 111. Livestock (in 000; Dec. 1974): sheep c. 8,400; cattle c. 1,206; goats (1973) c. 4,400; pigs c. 858; horses (1973) c. 180; asses (1973) c. 325; chickens c. 31,000.

Industry. Production (in 000; metric tons; 1975): lignite 17,907; electricity (kw-hr) 14,627,000; petroleum products (1974) c. 9,850; bauxite 2,849; magnesite (1974) 1,315; cement 7,870; sulfuric acid 920; fertilizers (1974–75) nitrogenous c. 265, phosphate c. 166; cotton yarn 67. Merchant vessels launched (100 gross tons and over; 1975) 76,000 gross tons.

The Greek-Turkish crisis reached its climax between July and September. Turkey dispatched the survey ship "MTA Sismik I" to prospect for oil in Aegean seabed areas claimed by Greece under the Geneva Convention of 1958, which provides that islands are entitled to a continental shelf. This right was not recognized by Turkey, which had not signed the convention. The Greek government appealed to the UN Security Council and the International Court of Justice. A Security Council resolution on August 25 urged bilateral negotiations, while the International Court denied the first Greek request to stop the Turkish research ship but reserved judgment on the second plea that the bench should demarcate the Aegean continental shelf boundary. The two countries agreed to open negotiations on the dispute on November 2 and during the month reached agreement on procedure amounting to a virtual truce.

The possibility that the confrontation over the Aegean might lead to war affected the political behaviour of the Greeks. Although the economy was overburdened with defense expenses and the rate of inflation was expected to rise by 12% in 1976, there was little labour unrest. Student agitation subsided, and relations between government and opposition parties became exceptionally civil. The exception was the riot-

Great Britain: *see* United Kingdom

STEVEN V. ROBERTS—THE NEW YORK TIMES

Time, tourism, and pollution are taking their toll on the Acropolis of Athens. In 1975 countermeasures were studied to preserve the sacred hill. Traffic is still being rerouted, and tourists can no longer walk inside the Parthenon.

ing, with one dead and about 100 wounded, in Athens on May 25 during a 48-hour strike in protest against legislation restricting the right to strike. When Alexandrov Panagoulis (*see* OBITUARIES), jailed under the dictatorship for his attempt to assassinate Georgios Papadopoulos, was killed in a car crash on May 1, the opposition claimed this was a political assassination.

Eager to eliminate social unrest at a time of external crisis, the government made economic concessions to workers and took strict action against delinquent bankers and industrialists. In reaction, right-wing political groupings were formed, some supporting a restored monarchy, others sheltering disgruntled conservatives and former collaborators of the dictatorship. (MARIO MODIANO)

[972.B.3]

Grenada

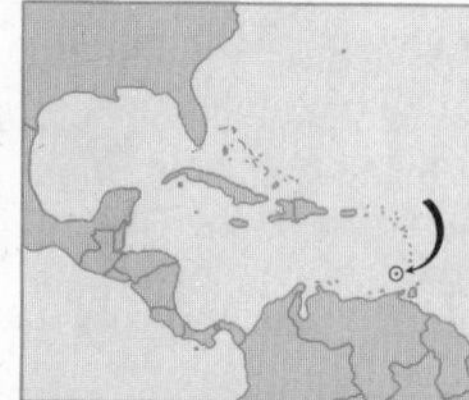

A parliamentary state within the Commonwealth of Nations, Grenada, with its dependency, the southern Grenadines, is the southernmost of the Windward Islands of the Caribbean Sea, 100 mi N of Trinidad. Area: 133 sq mi (344 sq km). Pop. (1974 est.): 106,200, including Negro 53%, mixed 42%, white 1%, and other 4%. Cap.: Saint George's (pop., 1974 est., 6,600). Language: English. Religion: Christian. Queen, Elizabeth II; governor-general in 1976, Leo de Gale; prime minister, Eric Gairy.

Despite 20–25% unemployment, reported corruption, and a decline in tourism, Prime Minister Gairy continued in 1976 to promote a carnival atmosphere and to ignore recommendations of the 1975 Duffus Commission of Enquiry into the Breakdown of Law and Order and Police Brutality in Grenada. No inquiry was held into the losses of businessmen during looting in 1973–74 by members of the police aides (or Mongoose Squad). The squad was ostensibly disbanded, but most members were absorbed into the defense force or the Grenada Volunteer Constabulary. Meanwhile the Guyanese-born attorney general, Desmond Christian, was sacked by Gairy and banned from returning to the island; he was reinstated after a tribunal cleared him of charges brought by the government but was reported hesitant to return. In the December 6 general election Gairy's United Labour Party was returned with a reduced majority.

The minister of finance, presenting the 1976 budget, confessed that public finance was in a critical state and would need to rely on external budgetary support from Britain and the Caribbean Community and Common Market (Caricom). The budget provided for a total expenditure of ECar$50 million (ECar$6.3 million more than in 1975). Commercial banks were to lodge 5% of their deposit liabilities with the accountant general and to surrender all accounts that had been dormant six years—with a consequent run on the banks.

In July, some weeks after Trinidad and Tobago set its dollar at TT$2.40 to U.S. $1, Grenada announced a parity of ECar$2.70 to $1, instead of the expected ECar$2.40 or ECar$2.50. This provoked strong reaction, since Grenada had considerable trading links with Trinidad, and the effect was to raise import costs and lower export earnings. (SHEILA PATTERSON)

[974.B.2.d]

GRENADA

Education. (1971–72) Primary, pupils 29,795, teachers 884; secondary, pupils 4,470, teachers 182; vocational, pupils 497, teachers 10; teacher training, students 101, teachers 6.

Finance and Trade. Monetary unit: East Caribbean dollar, with (Sept. 20, 1976) a par value of ECar$2.70 to U.S. $1 (free rate of ECar$4.65 = £1 sterling). Budget (1975 est.) balanced at ECar$44 million. Foreign trade (1974): imports ECar$38.1 million; exports ECar$17.8 million. Import sources (1972): U.K. 26%; U.S. 10%; Canada 9%. Export destinations: U.K. 36%; U.S. 7%. Main exports: cocoa 29%; nutmegs 28%; bananas 16%; mace 9%. Tourism (1972): visitors 38,000; gross receipts U.S. $12 million.

Greek Literature: *see* Literature

Greek Orthodox Church: *see* Religion

Greenland: *see* Dependent States

Gross National Product: *see* Economy, World

Guiana: *see* Dependent States; Guyana; Surinam

Guatemala

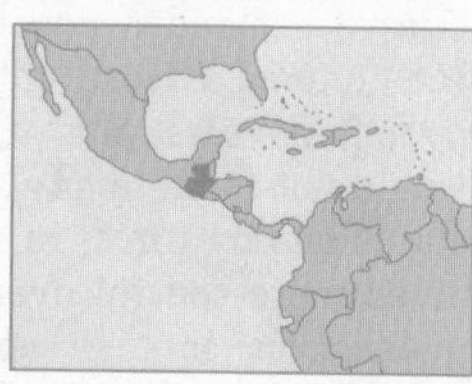

A republic of Central America, Guatemala is bounded by Mexico, Belize, Honduras, El Salvador, the Caribbean Sea, and the Pacific Ocean. Area: 42,042 sq mi (108,889 sq km). Pop. (1973): 5,175,400. Cap. and largest city: Guatemala City (pop., 1973, 700,500). Language: Spanish, with some Indian dialects. Religion: predominantly Roman Catholic. President in 1976, Kjell Eugenio Laugerud García.

The earthquakes of early February 1976, affecting primarily the central highland belt, had a devastating

GUATEMALA

Education. (1973) Primary, pupils 585,015, teachers 16,451; secondary, vocational, and teacher training, pupils 86,215, teachers 5,934; higher, students 21,715, teaching staff (university only) 1,314.

Finance. Monetary unit: quetzal, at par with the U.S. dollar (free rate, at Sept. 20, 1976, of 1.72 quetzales to £1 sterling). Gold, SDR's, and foreign exchange (June 1976) U.S. $446.6 million. Budget (1976 est.) balanced at 553.7 million quetzales. Gross domestic product (1974) 3,097,000,000 quetzales. Money supply (May 1976) 450.2 million quetzales. Cost of living (Guatemala City; 1970 = 100; May 1976) 160.

Foreign Trade. (1975) Imports 800 million quetzales; exports 646.8 million quetzales. Import sources (1974): U.S. 32%; Venezuela 12%; El Salvador 10%; Japan 9%; West Germany 8%. Export destinations (1974): U.S. 33%; El Salvador 11%; West Germany 11%; Nicaragua 7%; Costa Rica 6%; Japan 5%. Main exports: coffee 25%; sugar 18%; cotton 11%.

Transport and Communications. Roads (1973) 13,450 km (including 824 km of Pan-American Highway). Motor vehicles in use (1972): passenger 54,100; commercial (including buses) 36,900. Railways: (1974) *c.* 910 km; freight traffic (1970) 106 million net ton-km. Air traffic (1974): 100 million passenger-km; freight 4.8 million net ton-km. Telephones (Jan. 1974) 53,000. Radio licenses (Dec. 1973) 260,000. Television receivers (Dec. 1973) 105,000.

Agriculture. Production (in 000; metric tons; 1975): corn 934; sugar, raw value 386; tomatoes *c.* 74; dry beans 87; bananas (1974) *c.* 450; coffee *c.* 165; cotton, lint *c.* 105. Livestock (in 000; March 1974): cattle *c.* 1,839; sheep *c.* 650; pigs *c.* 1,022; chickens *c.* 11,000.

Industry. Production (in 000; metric tons; 1974): petroleum products 940; cement (1973) 316; zinc ore (metal content) *c.* 0.3; electricity (kw-hr) 1,050,000.

effect on the country. Nearly 23,000 lives were lost, a million persons were made homeless, and damage was estimated at $2 billion. The disturbed conditions of the post-earthquake period might also have been partly responsible for the renewed wave of political terrorism that hit the country.

Despite earthquake damage, it was expected that 1976 figures would show a continuation of the improving economic trends of 1975, with a growth rate as high as 10% and inflation reduced to 7–10%. A factor of considerable long-term importance was the discovery of additional oil reserves in the Rubelsanto area. Production potential was estimated at 30,000 bbl a day, and studies of a projected export pipeline were being undertaken. Further exploration was also being carried on near the Mexican border. Offshore oil exploration along the Caribbean coastline had proved unsuccessful so far. In June Guatemala claimed a 200-mi offshore zone for exploitation of fisheries and natural resources.

Talks with Britain over the disputed colony of Belize continued. No progress was reported from the negotiations, however, and there were occasional rumours that Guatemala was preparing for an invasion of the territory. (JOHN HALE)

[974.B.1.a]

Guinea

A republic on the west coast of Africa, Guinea is bounded by Guinea-Bissau, Senegal, Mali, Ivory Coast, Liberia, and Sierra Leone. Area: 94,926 sq mi (245,856 sq km). Pop. (1975 UN est.): 4,527,000; however, a census held on Dec. 30, 1972, reported 5,143,284 persons, of whom 1.5 million were living abroad. Cap. and largest city: Conakry (pop., 1974, 412,000). Language: French (official). Religion: mostly Muslim. President in 1976, Sékou Touré; premier, Louis Lansana Beavogui.

Relations between Guinea and France, which had been unsatisfactory since Guinea's unilateral declaration of independence in 1958 and had been broken off since late 1965, were at last normalized in February 1976 with an exchange of ambassadors. In August French Pres. Valéry Giscard d'Estaing sent a personal message to President Touré proposing that he pay an official visit to Conakry in 1977 and received Touré's assent. In October, to please Guinea's leaders, the French government seized a book published in France by an opponent of Touré's regime.

In June President Touré claimed that he had uncovered an assassination plot planned for May 13, and in July the authorities announced the arrest of (among others) Diallo Telli, minister of justice and a former secretary-general of the Organization of African Unity.

WIDE WORLD

The earthquake that devastated Guatemala in February shattered this highway bridge outside Guatemala City.

GUINEA

Education. (1971–72) Primary, pupils 169,132, teachers 4,698; secondary, pupils 68,410, teachers (1970–71) 2,360; vocational (1970–71), pupils 2,013, teachers 150; teacher training (1970–71), students 1,478, teachers 275; higher (1970–71), students 1,974, teachers (1965–66) 95.

Finance. Monetary unit: syli, with a free rate (Sept. 20, 1976) of 21.83 sylis to U.S. $1 (37.61 sylis = £1 sterling). Budget (1972–73 est.) balanced at 4.5 million sylis.

Foreign Trade. (1974) Imports *c.* 2.6 billion sylis; exports *c.* 2.8 billion sylis. Import sources: U.S.S.R. *c.* 22%; France *c.* 15%; U.S. *c.* 12%; Italy *c.* 7%; Belgium-Luxembourg *c.* 6%. Export destinations: Spain *c.* 11%; U.S. *c.* 10%; West Germany *c.* 10%; Cameroon *c.* 8%; Canada *c.* 8%; Norway *c.* 6%; U.S.S.R. 5%; France 5%; Yugoslavia 5%. Main exports (1971): alumina and bauxite 72%; pineapples 10%; coffee 6%; palm kernels 6%.

Alioune Drame, the minister of planning, was arrested in August. In their alleged confessions, those arrested sought to implicate the Ivory Coast and Senegal.

Touré scored a notable diplomatic success by arranging a meeting at Conakry on March 15–16 of Prime Minister Fidel Castro of Cuba, presidents Luis Cabral of Guinea-Bissau and Agostinho Neto of Angola, and himself. (PHILIPPE DECRAENE)

[978.E.4.b.ii]

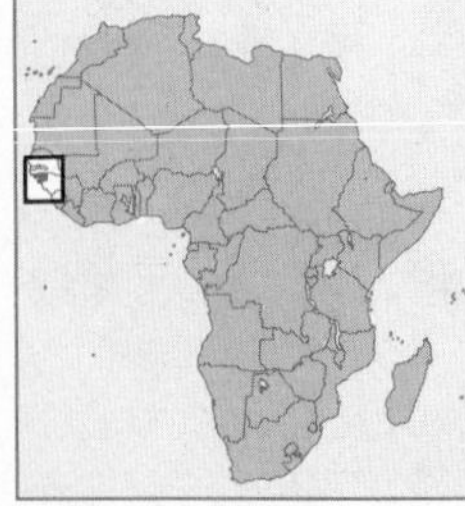

Guinea-Bissau

An independent African republic, Guinea-Bissau has an Atlantic coastline on the west and borders Senegal on the north and Guinea on the east and south. Area: 13,948 sq mi (36,125 sq km). Pop. (1976 est.): 534,000. Cap. and largest city: Bissau (metro. area pop., 1970, 71,200). President in 1976, Luis Cabral; premier, Francisco Mendès.

The country's main problems in 1976 were still those of rehabilitation after the war of independence of 1974 and financing development. The resettlement of refugees and the reversal of the movement from the rural areas to the capital was an urgent task, along with the revival of agriculture. Some rice still had to be imported in 1976 because of the drop in output before and during the war. The foundations of a primary educational system were laid, and attention was given to developing a commercial road system. All these undertakings depended upon foreign aid, and the government, anxious to maintain its position of nonalignment, accepted technical assistance and advice from the U.S.S.R. and Eastern Europe, while also cultivating friendly relations with the West. President Cabral, for example, visited France during the year and also traveled to Romania. Guinea-Bissau changed its currency from the colonial escudo to the peso in March. In an effort to support the peso, it froze the assets of the Portuguese Banco Nacional Ultramarino, which was issuing escudos, at the end of February. This was followed by an agreement by Portugal to support the peso on June 21. The plan for an eventual union with the Cape Verde Islands continued to be pursued. (KENNETH INGHAM)

[978.E.4.b.ii]

Guinea-Bissau's Pres. Luis Cabral is greeted by French Pres. Valéry Giscard d'Estaing on the former's visit to Paris in April.

A.F.P./PICTORIAL PARADE

GUINEA-BISSAU

Education. (1972–73) Primary, pupils 48,007, teachers 1,148; secondary and vocational, pupils 4,133, teachers 176.

Finance and Trade. Monetary unit: Guinea-Bissau peso (replaced the escudo at par in March), with (Sept. 20, 1976) a free rate of 31.02 escudos to U.S. $1 (53.45 escudos = £1 sterling). Budget (1972 est.): revenue 433 million escudos; expenditure 408 million escudos. Foreign trade (1973): imports 1,122,269,000 escudos (56% from Portugal, 7% from Spain, 5% from U.K., 5% from Japan); exports 121,698,000 escudos (90% to Portugal). Main exports: peanuts 46%; transport equipment (transit) 21%; petroleum and products (transit) 8%; palm kernels 7%; metals 6%; timber 5%.

Agriculture. Production (in 000; metric tons; 1974): peanuts *c.* 27; rice *c.* 30; cassava *c.* 40; palm kernels *c.* 9; palm oil *c.* 5. Livestock (in 000; 1974): cattle *c.* 253; pigs *c.* 165; sheep *c.* 68; goats *c.* 178.

Guyana

A republic and member of the Commonwealth of Nations, Guyana is situated between Venezuela, Brazil, and Surinam on the Atlantic Ocean. Area: 83,000 sq mi (215,000 sq km). Pop. (1975 est.): 789,100, including (1970) East Indian 51.8%; African 31.2%; mixed 10.3%; Amerindian 4.9%. Cap. and largest city: Georgetown (pop., 1970, 63,200). Language: English (official). Religion: Protestant, Hindu,

GUYANA

Education. (1973–74) Primary, pupils 132,023, teachers 4,077; secondary, pupils 64,314, teachers 2,830; vocational, pupils 3,539, teachers 159; higher, students 2,307; teaching staff 231.

Finance. Monetary unit: Guyanan dollar, with (Sept. 20, 1976) a par value of Guy$2.55 to U.S. $1 (free rate of Guy$4.39 = £1 sterling). Budget (1976 est.): revenue Guy$450 million; expenditure Guy$664 million.

Foreign Trade. (1975) Imports Guy$803.6 million; exports Guy$852.9 million. Import sources (1974): U.S. 26%; Trinidad and Tobago 23%; U.K. 20%; Canada 5%. Export destinations (1974): U.S. 25%; U.K. 21%; Trinidad and Tobago 7%; Morocco 5%; Jamaica 5%; Canada 5%. Main exports (1974): sugar 48%; bauxite 21%; rice 8%; alumina 8%.

Agriculture. Production (in 000; metric tons; 1975): rice *c.* 260; sugar, raw value 311; cassava *c.* 14; oranges *c.* 11; copra *c.* 4. Livestock (in 000; 1974): cattle *c.* 265; sheep *c.* 108; goats *c.* 52; pigs *c.* 106.

Industry. Production (in 000; 1974): bauxite (metric tons) 3,048; diamonds (metric carats; 1973) 53; electricity (kw-hr) *c.* 387,000.

Roman Catholic. President in 1976, Arthur Chung; prime minister, Forbes Burnham.

In 1976 the rapprochement between Prime Minister Burnham and Cheddi Jagan of the opposition Marxist-Leninist People's Progressive Party continued with the latter's agreeing to cooperate in "critical support" for Burnham, and in May Jagan returned to Parliament after a three-year boycott. This strengthened the governing People's National Congress and accelerated the drive toward socialism.

By summer Burnham's government controlled over 70% of the economy, following the takeover of a Canadian aluminum company and of Booker McConnell sugar holdings. The eventual takeover of banking resources was forecast in September. In 1976 the government also took charge of some 380 private nursery schools, 300 primary schools, and 16 secondary schools, some of them church-run, to control all the nation's education.

In April, along with Barbados and Jamaica, Guyana stressed the theme of U.S. attempts to "destabilize" leftist-oriented Caribbean states. In late October Burnham launched a strident anti-U.S. Central Intelligence Agency campaign through the government-controlled press and radio, in support of similar Cuban allegations in connection with the blowing up of a Cuban airliner by Cuban counterrevolutionaries.

(SHEILA PATTERSON)

[974.B.2.d]

Gymnastics and Weight Lifting

Gymnastics. During the 1976 Olympic Games in Canada gymnastics reached a new height of popularity. Capacity crowds of more than 16,000 attended all eight sessions of the men's and women's competitions and millions more watched on television. Before the advent of worldwide television, only relatively small groups had ever witnessed first-class gymnasts in action, but in 1972 the world was electrified by the breathtaking performances of ebullient Olga Korbut of the Soviet Union, who in the process of winning three gold medals and one silver also won the hearts of people all over the world. There was, as a consequence, intense anticipation when the 1976 Games opened in Montreal.

Nadia Comaneci (*see* BIOGRAPHY), a 14-year-old Romanian who became European champion in 1975, replaced Korbut as the undisputed queen of gymnastics. In winning her crown, however, Comaneci was closely pressed by Nelli Kim, a Korean-born teenager from the Soviet Union who also displayed dazzling skills. Although charges of favouritism had often been leveled at Olympic judging in the past, few voices were raised to challenge the unprecedented perfect 10 scores that both Comaneci and Kim were awarded. In the all-around competition, Comaneci scored 10 on the uneven parallel bars and on the balance beam; Kim received a perfect score on the horse vault. In the finals of the individual events, Comaneci repeated her previous scores and Kim was given a 10 in the floor exercise, the first time such an event was ever judged perfect at this level of competition. In the individual events, the floor exercise was so closely contested that only a perfect performance by Kim assured her of a gold medal. Ludmila Tourischeva, a former all-around champion from the Soviet Union, won the silver medal, and Comaneci the bronze. In the all-around event, Kim finished second behind Comaneci, who in turn was followed by Tourischeva, Teodora Ungureanu of Romania, and Korbut. The U.S. had only one gymnast with previous Olympic experience, Kim Chace, who finished 14th in the all-around—the best placing for an American girl since the event was introduced in 1948. For the first time, each nation was limited to its top three gymnasts in the individual all-around finals.

In the men's competition, Nikolay Andrianov of the Soviet Union had no rival. He won six individual Olympic medals (4 gold, 1 silver, 1 bronze), and as a member of the Soviet team that finished in second place received another silver medal. After executing a series of exceedingly difficult routines with near-perfect form, Andrianov was acclaimed by experts to be the greatest all-around champion in history and the finest gymnast on the Olympic program. Despite the presence of Andrianov, the men's team championship was not decided until the Japanese and Soviet athletes completed their final events. Amid great excitement, Japan won the team title by a scant 0.40 point (576.85 to 576.45) after Mitsuo Tsukahara completed his 30-second routine on the horizontal bar and was awarded a score of 9.9. Shun Fujimoto provided one of the great human interest stories of the Games. Despite a fractured knee, he completed his routine on the rings with a solid landing after executing a triple somersault and twist. The crowd cheered his display of courage and the incredible body control he demonstrated when he touched the floor. Though thrilled by their team victory, the Japanese probably realized they had little hope of maintaining their supremacy

CANADIAN PRESS

The Japanese men's gymnastic team won a gold medal at the Montreal Olympics. It was the fifth victory in a row for Japanese gymnasts.

CANADIAN PRESS

Little Nikolai Kolesnikov of the Soviet Union lifted 160 kilograms (over 352 pounds) to win the gold medal and set a new Olympic record in the featherweight clean and jerk competition.

at the world championships in 1978. Whereas the average age of their team was 26, the Soviets had four 19-year-olds and three in their early 20s, all of whom (including Andrianov) were expected to compete in the 1980 Olympics. Nonetheless, Japan could take well-founded pride in its Olympic champions: Sawao Kato, performing in his third Olympics, won his second successive gold medal on the parallel bars, and Tsukahara remained Olympic champion on the horizontal bar. The Soviet and Japanese men gymnasts took the gold medals in every event except the pommeled horse, won by Zoltan Magyar of Hungary. Peter Kormann of Massachusetts captured third place in the floor exercise and gave the U.S. its first Olympic medal in men's gymnastics in 44 years.

An important development in gymnastics during the past four years was the introduction of new safety equipment that permitted athletes to practice daring new maneuvers such as the double flyaway with a double full twist off the horizontal bar and other spectacular dismounts. Without special equipment to prevent serious injury during practice, it would have been impossible to master the movements that were executed so superbly at Montreal. As in certain other Olympic sports, the objectivity of the judging continued to be much discussed. Some felt that the criticism would not subside until the panel of judges had been sufficiently broadened to ensure that narrow national interests could play no significant part in the final results.

Weight Lifting. The 1976 Olympics provided convincing evidence that the Soviet and Bulgarian weight lifters were far superior to even their closest rivals. Four years earlier in Munich, West Germany, five nations shared the nine first-place medals. At Montreal the Soviet Union was awarded five gold medals and Bulgaria three. The only other country to produce a champion was Poland, and its gold medalist was later deprived of his award for using prohibited drugs. The seriousness of the drug problem became apparent during the competition. A Romanian, a Czechoslovak, and a U.S. athlete were disqualified for violating Olympic rules that forbade the use of stimulants and body-building anabolic steroids. Amid charges that others were equally guilty of the same infractions, a formal investigation was undertaken. A month after the conclusion of the Games, the International Weightlifting Federation (IWF) sent a report to the International Olympic Committee (IOC) stating that tests taken after the competition indicated that five other athletes were guilty of using anabolic steroids. On the basis of these findings, the IOC deprived Poland's lightweight champion of his medal and took similar action against two Bulgarians; both the heavyweight champion and the light-heavyweight silver medalist lost their Olympic awards. The decision was also made not to change the original position of any other medalist. All eight weight lifters who were found guilty of using banned substances were suspended from international competition by the IWF for one year (until July 31, 1977). In addition, the IOC warned the IWF that unless effective measures were taken to stop the use of steroids and stimulant drugs, the sport would be dropped from the Olympic program after the 1980 Games in Moscow. Responding to the challenge, the IWF decreed during its November meeting that no world record performance would be considered in the future unless the application was accompanied by certified documents showing negative test results for all banned drugs. It was also announced that all lifters would be subject to tests starting with the 1977 world championships.

Once the competition got under way, it was apparent that nothing vital had been lost by the elimination of the press. In both the snatch and the clean and jerk events, gamesmanship was a vital factor in the final outcome as athletes successively announced the weights they would attempt to lift. There were, however, no startling upsets. Four recognized world record holders won gold medals and two former Olympic champions retained their titles. In four weight classes the winner lifted 5 kg (11 lb) more than the second place finishers, but in the other five divisions the margin of victory was much greater. Superheavyweight Vasily Alekseyev (U.S.S.R.) gained some satisfaction in retaining his Olympic title even though he fell 2.5 kg (5.5 lb) short of the world record set in May by Christo Platchkov of Bulgaria who hoisted 442.5 kg (975.5 lb) at Sofia, Bulg. Though everyone was waiting to see the two in direct competition, it was not to be. The Bulgarians announced that Platchkov had injured himself training at the Olympic site and could not compete. During the European championships earlier in the year Gerd Bonk of East Germany took the world record from Alekseyev, who later regained it and then lost it to Platchkov. At Montreal Bonk's total combined lift assured him of a second place finish and the Olympic silver medal. Of the 24 medals that were officially awarded in weight lifting (the three that were recalled for drug violations after the Olympics were not reawarded), the Soviets won eight, the Bulgarians six, the East Germans three, and the Japanese two. Other medalists came from France, Hungary, Iran, Poland, and the U.S. (CHARLES ROBERT PAUL, JR.)

See also Track and Field Sports: *Special Report.*

[452.B.4.f]

PETER MARLOW—SYGMA

Collecting stones to build a new school for a Haitian village.

Haiti

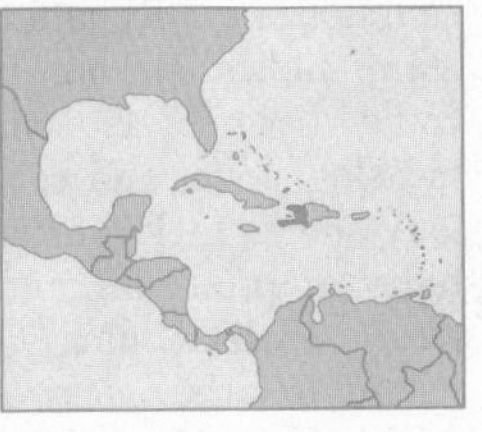

The Republic of Haiti occupies the western one-third of the Caribbean island of Hispaniola, which it shares with the Dominican Republic. Area: 10,714 sq mi (27,750 sq km). Pop. (1975 est.): 4,583,800, of whom 95% are Negro. Cap. and largest city: Port-au-Prince (pop., 1975 est., 625,000). Language: French (official) and Creole. Religion: Roman Catholic; Voodooism practiced in rural areas. President in 1976, Jean-Claude Duvalier.

During 1976 President Duvalier maintained his backing in the Cabinet and the armed forces. Though the old-guard supporters of the president's late father secured the dismissal of several liberal-inclined ministers in the spring, the president and the technocrats in the administration rallied enough support to secure the ouster of powerful old-guard Henri Siclait, head of the state tobacco company, in September. Minor manifestations of discontent in rural areas and in the Air Force early in the year were easily quelled.

Performance in the economy was unsatisfactory. The growth rate fell from over 4% in 1974 to less than 2% in 1975, mainly because of poor domestic food crops. Exports declined in value in 1975 and early 1976, while imports rose sharply over the period because of an expansion of credit, the need to make up for the shortage in domestic food supplies, and the speedier execution of some public-investment projects.

Revenue from tourism, usually $13 million a year, declined drastically during 1975–76. The International Monetary Fund and the World Bank provided, respectively, standby credit to purchase currencies up to 6,880,000 Special Drawing Rights and a credit of $5.5 million for an educational project. In October a Venezuelan concern won a contract to explore for petroleum in Haitian territorial waters.

(ROBIN CHAPMAN)

[974.B.2.a]

HAITI

Education. (1973–74) Primary, pupils 336,511, teachers 8,470; secondary and vocational, pupils 51,174, teachers 1,735; higher (University of Haiti), students 2,100, teaching staff 211.

Finance. Monetary unit: gourde, with (Sept. 20, 1976) a par value of 5 gourdes to U.S. $1 (free rate of 8.61 gourdes = £1 sterling). Gold, SDR's, and foreign exchange (Feb. 1976) U.S. $20.5 million. Budget (1975–76 est.) balanced at 216.6 million gourdes. Cost of living (Port-au-Prince; 1970 = 100; March 1976) 200.

Foreign Trade. (1974) Imports 545.6 million gourdes; exports 358.3 million gourdes. Import sources: U.S. 45%; Netherlands Antilles 7%; Canada 7%; Japan 6%; France 6%; West Germany 5%. Export destinations: U.S. 68%; France 8%; Belgium-Luxembourg 7%; Italy 5%. Main exports: coffee 33%; sugar 9%; bauxite 8%.

Transport and Communications. Roads (1974) c. 4,000 km. Motor vehicles in use (1973): passenger 11,700; commercial (including buses) 1,300. Telephones (Jan. 1974) 9,000. Radio receivers (Dec. 1973) 90,000. Television receivers (Dec. 1973) 13,000.

Agriculture. Production (in 000; metric tons; 1975): coffee c. 32; sweet potatoes (1974) c. 91; cassava (1974) c. 137; sugar, raw value (1974) c. 138; corn c. 250; millet c. 219; dry beans c. 44; bananas (1974) c. 183; mangoes (1974) c. 94; cocoa c. 4; sisal c. 19. Livestock (in 000; 1974): pigs c. 1,682; cattle c. 737; goats c. 1,316; sheep c. 77.

Industry. Production (in 000; metric tons; 1974): cement 138; bauxite (exports) 793; electricity (kw-hr) c. 145,000.

Health and Disease

General Overview. The year saw a sharply growing concern regarding the risks of a rapid spread across national frontiers of dangerous virus infections that had remained isolated before flying became the standard means of international travel. Several industrial nations were fearful of the possibility of outbreaks of deadly Lassa fever occurring within their boundaries as a result of its importation by travelers from West Africa. Several such travelers who had developed fever and malaise of unknown cause shortly after visiting a region in which Lassa is endemic were kept under observation in countries as far apart as Canada, Australia, and the U.K. Almost all alarms proved false. In August the disease was made notifiable in the U.K. as a matter of urgency following the refusal of a woman laboratory assistant to enter an isolation hospital for observation when she developed a fever and sore throat after handling material from a recovered victim of Lassa fever. Both the World Health Organization (WHO) and Great Britain's Department of Health warned laboratories not to import

Handball: *see* Court Games

Harbours: *see* Transportation

Harness Racing: *see* Equestrian Sports

the rat *Mastomys natalensis* for research purposes, because it was known to carry the Lassa virus without showing signs of disease.

Another killer-virus infection, Marburg disease, was shown to be responsible for many deaths in an epidemic that struck southern Sudan and northern Zaire in the autumn of 1976. This outbreak also caused alarm among authorities in other parts of the world who feared imported cases. Control measures were tightened at ports and airports throughout the world. Travelers arriving from the affected regions generally were warned to contact a doctor or local health authority if they developed any illness within the following week.

Although viral infections were more difficult to control and treat than bacterial infections, a number of bacteria continued to cause problems. The two major venereal diseases, syphilis and gonorrhea, appeared to be out of control, despite the fact that until recently both diseases were readily curable (at least in their early stages) by a brief course of penicillin. To the major difficulty of tracing and treating contacts was added the serious matter of the emergence of penicillin-resistant strains of gonococcus. Resistant strains had been appearing with increasing frequency within recent years, but victims usually could be treated effectively with larger doses of the antibiotic. In the autumn of 1976, however, it became clear that strains almost completely insensitive to penicillin had become established in several parts of the world, including the U.K., the U.S., and the Far East. These new strains produce an enzyme, penicillinase, that destroys the drug. They acquired this ability by contact with basically harmless organisms (coliform bacteria) that commonly inhabit the gut of man and other animals. The proliferation of resistant coliforms had been due largely to the indiscriminate use of penicillin by many doctors, veterinarians, and stock breeders. The effect of the new strains on venereology was certain to be great, particularly in less developed countries, because alternative antibiotics are much more expensive and often unavailable. A similar mechanism threatened to render gonococci resistant to some of the alternative drugs as well.

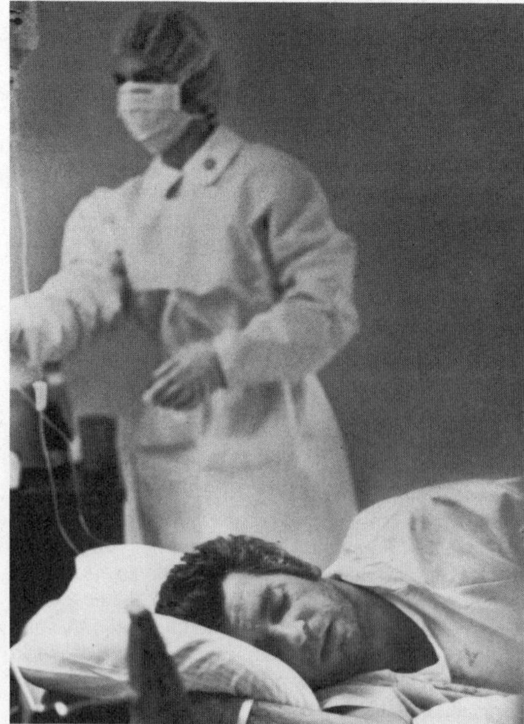
WIDE WORLD

Philadelphia's mystery "Legionnaire's disease" laid this truck driver low though he had only delivered a load of canned goods to the hotel in which the victims had been housed.

The increasing development of drug resistance among bacteria raised the fear that the enormous advantages gained from the major antibacterial drugs might be lost. Since resistant strains come to the fore by a process of natural selection after a particular antibacterial drug has been in widespread use for some time, WHO's Regional Office for Europe felt moved to recommend in a report published in June that new antibiotics be used only in particular hospitals for "specific well-defined conditions." In this way the possibility of such dangerous bacterial infections as typhoid fever once again becoming untreatable might be avoided.

In other news concerning syphilis, a team at the Florida Institute of Technology claimed success in culturing *Treponema pallidum,* the organism responsible for syphilis, thus opening the way to the production of a vaccine. Previously it had been possible to grow the spirochete only in living animals. Preliminary immunization experiments with rabbits were encouraging, and Ronald H. Jones, leader of the Florida team, indicated that immunization against syphilis could become as commonplace as those against measles, polio, and several other infectious diseases.

A similar achievement raised hopes of the possibility of producing an effective vaccine against malaria, of which some 96 million new cases were estimated to arise each year, with a million deaths in Africa alone. Late in the year a means for growing the malaria parasite outside the body was reported almost simultaneously by two separate teams of U.S. workers, one from the Rockefeller University, New York City, and the other from the Walter Reed Army Institute of Research in Washington, D.C. Both teams used a growth medium of red blood cells and serum exposed to a gas mixture low in oxygen and high in carbon dioxide. As with the spirochete of syphilis, once a good harvest of the infective organism was obtained, it should be possible to manufacture a vaccine.

Rabies continued to spread westward across the European continent at the rate of about 25 mi per year, largely due to the red fox, whose population had multiplied following elimination of its natural competitor, the wolf. Humans were put at greater risk because increased land cultivation was driving foxes from the countryside to seek food in areas surrounding towns and villages. Stringent new laws were introduced in the U.K. in an effort to prevent the spread of the disease across the English Channel, and during the first nine months of 1976 about 100 people were prosecuted for smuggling in pets or allowing dogs or cats ashore from visiting yachts and ships. But despite fines of up to £400 and the threat of jail sentences, breaches of the law continued. Many experts believed it was only a matter of time before Great Britain, which had been free of indigenous rabies for some 50 years, once again suffered the infection among its wildlife.

Efforts to control the spread of the disease among animals on the continent by slaughter, vaccination, and other means had little effect. However, an awareness of the dangers and the development of effective and safe new vaccines (particularly a vaccine made from rabies virus grown in a culture of human cells) meant that human deaths from rabies were likely to remain rare, even if the spread among animals could not be checked.

Two major public health events dominated the U.S. medical scene in 1976, one a sudden outbreak of a mysterious upper-respiratory disease, and the other a massive effort to prevent recurrence of the devastating "swine" influenza epidemic of 1918–19.

The mystery disease centred on a four-day Pennsylvania state convention of the American Legion in Philadelphia. Three days after the Legionnaires and their families returned to their homes, sudden illnesses developed among them. Symptoms included high fever, chills, headache, and malaise, followed by dry cough, muscle pain, pulmonary congestion, and shortness of breath. The more severe cases developed extensive pneumonia and succumbed to shock. Within a month 29 persons died and at least 179 others were stricken but recovered following medical treatment.

The outbreak set off the most intensive epidemiological investigation in modern medical history. Scientists of the U.S. Public Health Service's Center for Disease Control (CDC) in Atlanta, Ga., and of the Pennsylvania state and Philadelphia health departments promptly determined that the disease was not communicable and that the general population was not in peril. Nevertheless, efforts to find a cause of the outbreak, which became known variously as "American Legion fever," "Legionnaire's disease," and the "Philadelphia killer," were unavailing. Viruses, bacteria, and other infectious agents were ruled out by blood and tissue analyses. None of the potentially toxic substances found in tissue samples of some of the victims could be linked conclusively to the outbreak. Efforts to construct scenarios that would have exposed victims to a specific agent in a single place at a specific time were fruitless. Pennsylvania Secretary of Health Leonard Bachman concluded that the malady probably was new to medical science. David Sencer, director of the CDC, agreed that the disease was a sporadic, one-time phenomenon, the cause of which might never be found. However, the CDC announced its intention to pursue the investigation for several years if necessary.

The spectre of the World War I swine influenza pandemic that took 20 million lives, including over 500,000 in the U.S., prompted the federal government to push forward with the largest mass-immunization program in history. Following an outbreak of influenza among army recruits at Ft. Dix, N.J., in February near the end of the annual flu season, Pres. Gerald R. Ford signed a bill appropriating $135 million to immunize virtually all of the nation's population against the causative virus, which was found to be closely related to the agent responsible for the disaster 60 years earlier. The Canadian government also made plans to protect about half that nation's population against the infection, but most other countries, including the U.K., felt that the Ft. Dix outbreak was insufficient cause for taking such costly and extraordinary measures.

Many health authorities pointed out that the 1976–77 season could mark the end of the ten-year interval during which a major mutation in the flu virus occurs, leaving the population with no established immunity. Previous epidemics occurred in 1957 when the Asian flu virus evolved and in 1968 when the Hong Kong strain appeared. With identification of a major new virus early in its ecological cycle and prior to the beginning of its pandemic spread, U.S. health authorities for the first time had the necessary lead time to produce and distribute a protective virus.

Nevertheless, the program found itself beset by doubts, setbacks, and eventual suspension. Several prominent health authorities contended that mass immunization was unnecessary. These negative views, together with an unwillingness of drug manufacturers to deliver the vaccine without assurance of government protection against possible lawsuits, caused a month's delay of the program, which began on October 1. In mid-October the deaths of three elderly recipients hours after inoculation in the same clinic in Pennsylvania prompted 11 states to halt their programs until it was determined that the deaths were not due to the vaccine. Following a nationwide investigation of several dozen such deaths that occurred within two days of inoculation, the CDC concluded that most of the victims, whose mean age exceeded 71, had succumbed to some preexisting high-risk disease. In mid-December, after 40 million Americans had been inoculated, U.S. officials suspended the program when about half of over 100 reported cases of a little-understood paralytic syndrome showed possible links with receipt of the vaccine. By year's end many health experts conceded that inoculations would probably not be resumed, even if exonerated.

WIDE WORLD

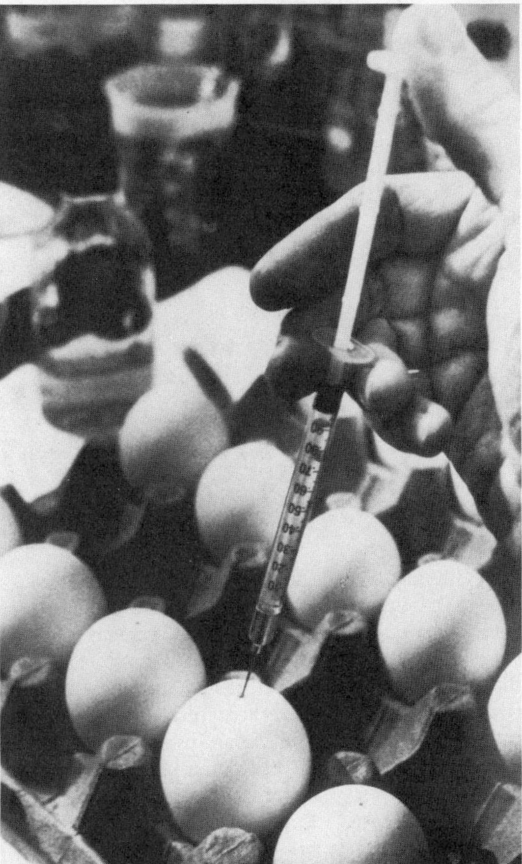

UPI COMPIX

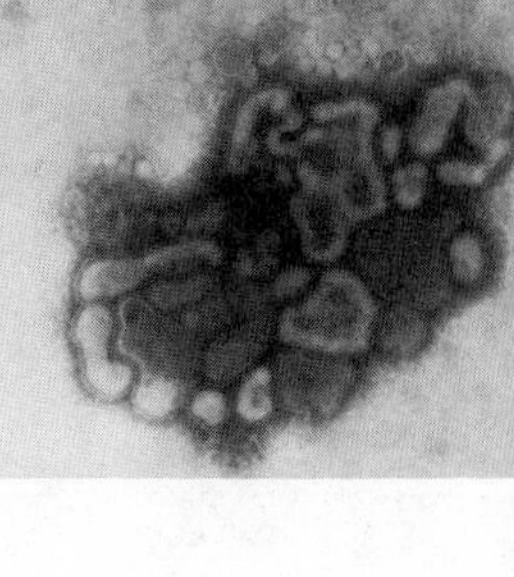

Swine flu virus (shown above magnified 132,300 times) was cultured in eggs to produce a vaccine for mass inoculation. Millions of Americans lined up for shots to avoid a possible epidemic.

In another domain of public health, a controversy ensued over a recommendation by the U.S. National Cancer Institute that mammography (the use of X-rays to detect breast cancer) not be used in asymptomatic women under age 50 unless there were specific grounds for doing so, such as a prior breast tumour or a family history of the disease. Previous guidelines had allowed mammographic examination in women over age 35. An advisory panel to the institute calculated that a single mammogram delivering a conventional radiation dose would increase the risk of developing cancer from about 7% in a normal lifetime to almost 7.1%. It recommended that women, who probably would be examined more frequently in

COURTESY, UNITED NATIONS. PHOTO BY RAY WITLIN

A blind man being led through his village in Upper Volta. The disease from which he suffers, known as river blindness, is endemic in the Volta basin countries of Benin, Ghana, Ivory Coast, Mali, Niger, Togo, and Upper Volta. UN agencies have begun a 20-year program to eradicate it.

their lifetimes, not be subjected to routine mammography. Dissenters, including the American College of Radiology, said the new guidelines were of dubious validity in determining carcinogenic risk because of the absence of objective scientific data. They stressed that the benefits of mammography outweighed any risk. In a group of about 260,000 women, more than 300 cancers were found in women under age 50 during the first four years of a national demonstration project; of these, 100 would not have been found without mammography.

In March the New Jersey State Supreme Court overturned a lower court's decision that had blocked efforts of the parents of Karen Ann Quinlan to remove respiratory support from their daughter, who had been in a coma since April 1975 and had been given no reasonable chance of regaining consciousness. The high court said that in such cases an individual's right to choose death takes precedence over the interest of the state in preserving life. The lower court had held that the nature, extent, and duration of medical care were the responsibility of physicians, who were vested by the morality and conscience of society. As guardian of his daughter, Joseph T. Quinlan had appealed to the state supreme court when the lower court upheld the refusal of the 22-year-old woman's physicians to turn off the respirator so that she could die "with grace and dignity." The court held that people have a right not to be forcibly treated by artificial life support and that the practical way to prevent violation of that right was to permit the family or guardian to render their best judgment.

In June Miss Quinlan was moved from a private hospital in New Jersey to a county nursing home after her respirator was permanently disconnected. Surprisingly she continued to breathe on her own and as 1977 began she was still alive, although comatose. Soon after the Quinlan decision, the Supreme Court of Massachusetts upheld the decision of a probate court judge who had ordered life-prolonging equipment withheld from a mentally retarded, 67-year-old victim of terminal leukemia.

California became the first state to legalize the right of the terminally ill to decree their own deaths. Effective Jan. 1, 1977, the new law recognized the validity of "living wills," which could be made out at any time in life and renewed every five years in the presence of two persons not related to the patient. The directive legally authorized an attending physician, in consultation with a colleague, to shut off life-sustaining equipment in the event the patient is terminally ill.

In the field of reproduction the greatest interest centred around contraception and abortion. Tests on an oral contraceptive for men containing the drug cyproterone acetate, which had been used to reduce the libido of sex offenders, were mounted in Great Britain, West Germany, India, and Hong Kong, with encouragement and financial aid from WHO. Indian proposals for the compulsory sterilization of one partner of couples who had exceeded their quota of three children met with such opposition and resentment that programs were shelved. However, voluntary sterilization remained a major item in the nation's efforts to reduce its present population growth rate of one million per month.

The likelihood of an early development of simple and safe "do-it-yourself" abortion techniques, in any case, was expected to make things more difficult for those who wished to impose stricter controls. At the John Radcliffe Infirmary in Oxford, England, trials began on a gel containing certain prostaglandins (naturally occurring, biologically active substances). Insertion of one dose of the gel into the vagina proved effective, and the gynecologist who developed the technique anticipated distribution of the gel by family planning clinics within two years.

The U.S. Food and Drug Administration (FDA) approved stronger warnings concerning the use of estrogen after medical reports had linked the female sex hormone to an increased incidence of uterine and breast cancer. The revised labeling recommended that estrogen be used for treating only moderate to severe symptoms of menopause. The FDA said there was no evidence that estrogens were effective in the treatment of nervous disorders or depressions that might occur during menopause and did not contribute to "maintaining youth." The FDA also ordered that major tranquilizers carry warnings on labels against use in the first trimester of pregnancy. Meprobamate, diazepam, and chlordiazepoxide, commercially marketed under a variety of popular names, were found to be associated with increased risk of congenital malformations.

Diethylstilbestrol (DES), a hormone given to pregnant women in the 1940s and 1950s to prevent miscarriages and found in recent years to produce a rare type of vaginal cancer in female offspring of those women, was discovered in 1976 to diminish the fertility of male offspring as well. One-third of such males tested at the University of Chicago showed sperm counts so low as to be considered sterile. Use of DES was halted except as a "morning-after" birth-control measure.

Poisons in the environment attracted a good deal of attention during the year. The most dramatic incident occurred in July when a chemical plant at Seveso near Milan, Italy, overheated and vented into the atmosphere a cloud of TCDD, a highly toxic dioxin by-product encountered in the manufacture of certain herbicides and disinfectants. At least 3,000 ac of land were contaminated by the poison, which is extremely stable and can linger indefinitely in untreated soil. Several hundred people were evacuated from the most seriously affected area, but many thousands more were exposed to the dangerous chemical. (*See* ENVIRONMENT.)

The first definitive evidence that smoking low-tar

continued on page 385

EPIDEMIC CONTROL: THE ERADICATION OF SMALLPOX

By Donald A. Henderson

The World Health Organization's ten-year campaign to eradicate smallpox throughout the world appeared to have reached its goal in October 1976, approximately two months ahead of the original target date. The last known case of smallpox occurred in Muqdisho, Somalia, on October 12. The case was one of 13 that occurred following the importation of smallpox from the final outbreaks in Ethiopia, the world's last endemic country. An intensive search for cases continued throughout Ethiopia and Somalia as well as in previously infected and neighbouring countries to be certain that no foci of infection remained. Final confirmation that eradication has been achieved will be possible only after two full years of intensive search following occurrence of the last case. Then an international commission of scientists specially convened by WHO will review activities in the field to satisfy themselves that the search was sufficiently thorough to detect cases of smallpox if they had been present. If they determine that smallpox has been eradicated, it will be the first time in history that mankind has succeeded in the global elimination of any disease.

Smallpox, a virus infection, was once prevalent throughout the world. Before Edward Jenner's discovery of a protective vaccine (1796) few escaped having smallpox at some time during their lives, and of those infected about 15–40% died; two-thirds of the survivors bore disfiguring facial scars, and blindness was sufficiently frequent that smallpox represented the principal cause of blindness in Europe as recently as the early 19th century. Because smallpox can spread in any geographic area and in any season and because there is no effective treatment, even those countries that have experienced no cases for many years have continued routine vaccination programs. Smallpox vaccination certificates have been required of all travelers in order to prevent importations from infected areas.

Although the eventual elimination of smallpox was foreseen by Jenner himself, effective smallpox control and, ultimately, eradication were not practicable in most parts of the world until potent, heat-stable vaccine could be produced in quantity. Not until after World War II were commercially feasible procedures developed for the production in quantity of freeze-dried vaccines that would remain potent for weeks even when they were exposed to tropical heat.

First Steps. The first impetus toward smallpox eradication was provided by the Pan-American Health Organization in 1950 when the countries of the Americas decided to undertake eradication in the Western Hemisphere. This was followed in 1959 by a declaration of the World Health Assembly that global smallpox eradication would be an objective of WHO and all its member states. Following passage of these resolutions, a number of countries instituted mass vaccination programs and became free of smallpox. The number of countries reporting cases of smallpox gradually decreased from 77 in 1950 to 50 in 1966. In the less developed countries, however, progress was discouragingly slow, and the few countries that did undertake intensive campaigns experienced frequent reintroductions of smallpox from infected neighbours. Only limited funds were available to support the program; vaccine supplies were insufficient and often of poor quality; and few resources were available in WHO for central planning, coordination, and support.

Recognizing these problems, WHO's director general proposed to the 1966 World Health Assembly that a special budget of $2.5 million per year be made available in support of an intensified campaign with the stated objective of eradicating the disease within a ten-year period. Although there was considerable doubt as to whether the eradication of smallpox or any other disease was feasible, the proposal was accepted. The intensified program began in January 1967.

In addition to the availability of a heat-stable vaccine that provides long-lasting protection, there are other aspects of smallpox that facilitate its eradication. The prevalence and extent of smallpox is more easily determined than for most diseases, thus permitting resources to be concentrated in those areas where problems are greatest. Diagnosis can almost always be decided without laboratory assistance, and the disease is recognized and known even to illiterate villagers. Since there are no insect or animal reservoirs of the disease and because its transmission almost always requires face-to-face contact, the continuous chain of infection from person to person can readily be identified. By determining the source of infection for each outbreak, unsuspected outbreaks can be detected and contained.

Of considerable importance is the fact that a recovered patient is immune to a second attack of smallpox. Thus, when the disease is introduced into remote areas, the chain of infection often is interrupted spontaneously as more and more people contract it and the number of susceptible persons thereby decreases. It is possible, therefore, to concentrate resources in the more densely populated and more accessible areas, knowing that in many of the more difficult areas the disease will die out spontaneously.

An initial step when the program began in 1967 was to define the extent of the problem. That year, 133,003 cases of smallpox were reported to WHO. Later surveys revealed that only about 1% of all cases that occurred were eventually reported. In 33 countries smallpox was considered to be endemic (that is, constantly present), while cases in 11 other countries were considered to have resulted from importations. The endemic countries could be divided into four geographic areas, each of which had sufficiently limited contact with the others that importation of cases from one area to another was considered unlikely. The four areas included South America, where Brazil was the only endemic country; Africa south of the Sahara, where almost all countries were endemic; South Asia, specifically, India, Pakistan, Afghanistan, Nepal, and Bangladesh (then East Pakistan); and the Indonesian archipelago. Campaign plans were developed with ministries of health in each of the endemic countries as well as adjacent nations where there was a risk of smallpox being imported. Emphasis was given initially to the two smallest areas, Brazil and Indonesia, with the hope of rapidly eliminating smallpox there in order to free limited resources for the other regions. By 1969 programs were under way in all the endemic countries except Ethiopia, which started its campaign in 1971.

Campaign Strategy. The strategy of the WHO campaign was twofold: first, to conduct systematic vaccination programs in each country over a two-to-three-year period with the objective of vaccinating 80% of the population; and second, to develop the case notification system so that when the vaccination program had been completed reporting would be sensitive enough to detect any remaining foci of infection. Within a year, however, it was discovered in eastern Nigeria that even in an area where as little as half the population had been vaccinated an intensive search for cases and containment of the outbreaks could successfully and rapidly eliminate smallpox. With subsequent confirmation of these findings in other areas, the strategy of the campaign

Donald Henderson, M.D., has been director of the World Health Organization's Smallpox Eradication Program since 1967.

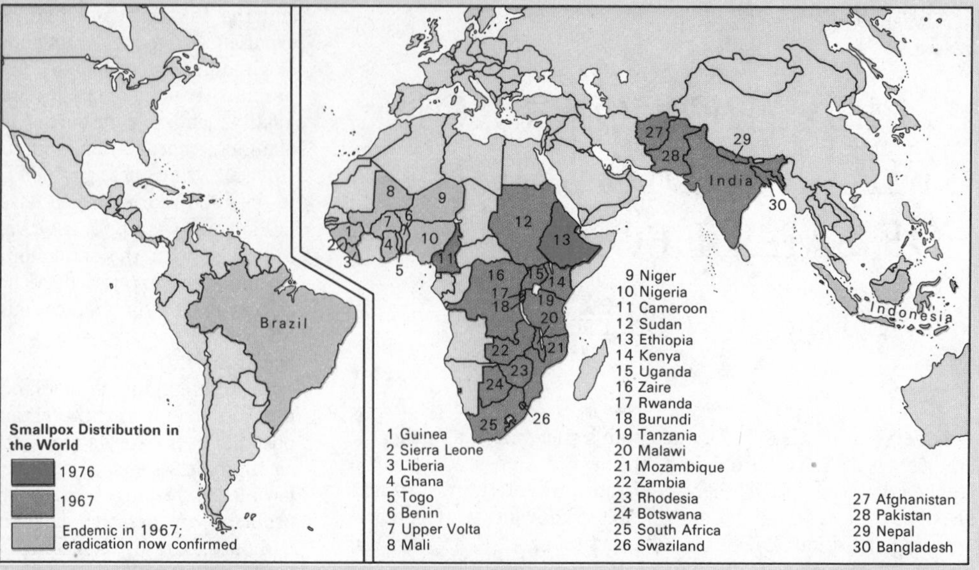

was altered to place the principal emphasis on surveillance (the reporting and detection of cases) and containment of outbreaks. Vaccination programs were continued in all countries, but they were modified to emphasize primary vaccination because it was found that very few cases were occurring among persons who had ever previously been inoculated.

A laboratory in The Netherlands and one in Canada agreed to monitor the quality of all vaccines used in the program. In 1966 virtually none of the vaccine in use in the endemic countries met WHO basic standards of potency and stability, but by 1970 all vaccine did so. Vaccine production in the originally endemic regions steadily increased so that by 1974 approximately 80% of all vaccine used in the program was produced in the less developed countries.

The technique for vaccination was improved and simplified. In 1967 jet-injector guns, which propel vaccine under high pressure through the skin, were first introduced for use in Brazil and western and central Africa. These had the advantages of permitting vaccination of 1,000 or more persons per hour and of requiring smaller quantities of vaccine virus. Vaccinations were more frequently successful than with the older scratch technique. The jet injectors were expensive, however, and required regular maintenance and repair. A more versatile instrument for vaccination was the bifurcated needle. This was developed by Wyeth Laboratories of the U.S. and tested in 1967–68 by WHO for use with a technique called multiple-puncture vaccination. The two-inch-long needle has a small fork at the end, which, when dipped into vaccine, holds just enough vaccine between the tines for one vaccination. It is held at right angles to the skin and is then used to make 15 rapid skin punctures. The technique could be quickly taught to vaccinators; less than one-fourth as much vaccine was required as with older techniques; and a high proportion of vaccinations were successful. The needles could be sterilized and reused hundreds of times.

By December 1972 the two primary target areas, Brazil and Indonesia, had detected their last cases, Brazil in April 1971 and Indonesia in January 1972. In the 20 countries of western and central Africa that had been assisted and supported by the U.S. Center for Disease Control and the U.S. Agency for International Development, the last case had been reported in April 1970, one year ahead of schedule. Elsewhere in Africa, smallpox was to be found only in Ethiopia, whose program had started in 1971, and in Botswana, which had become infected from South Africa just as smallpox was eliminated there. There remained, however, a heavily infected belt in Asia that stretched from Bangladesh across northern India and Nepal into Pakistan. Progress in most of those areas was discouraging, and health authorities despaired of success.

Final Drive. In the summer of 1973 a new plan was developed for the detection of smallpox cases in India. More than 100,000 health workers undertook a one-week search each month during which each village was examined for cases. Once an outbreak was found, intensive vaccination was performed in the village to stop further spread of the disease. Over the following year these techniques for search and containment steadily improved, and the system was extended to other countries in Asia.

With far better case detection, the number of reported cases rose sharply in 1974. Soon afterward, however, country after country became smallpox-free: Pakistan in October 1974; Nepal in April 1975; India in May 1975; and Bangladesh in October 1975. The last case of the severe form of smallpox (variola major), once prevalent throughout Asia, occurred on Bhola Island, Bangladesh, on Oct. 16, 1975.

In Africa, Botswana's last case had occurred in December 1973, leaving only one infected country, Ethiopia. The elimination of smallpox there, however, proved more difficult than had been anticipated. Political instability, a population that frequently resisted vaccination, and lack of communication facilities and supplies severely handicapped a program that until late 1974 consisted of fewer than 100 workers. In 1975 additional funds were made available for the program. Local staff was increased eventually to more than 1,000 and helicopters and additional cross-country vehicles were supplied. The numbers of cases and the extent of the infected areas began to decrease. The last known case in Ethiopia occurred on Aug. 9, 1976.

The premise of the WHO program is that when the last human case has been detected and the last chain of infection interrupted, smallpox as a human disease will have been eradicated. This assumes that there is no animal reservoir or potentially infective virus in old scabs or other material that might cause human infection. The best evidence that such is unlikely is the fact that for at least ten years all outbreaks in smallpox-free countries have been traced to travelers coming from areas known to be infected with the disease.

The likelihood that any other disease will be eradicated during this century is not great. For some, such as yellow fever, cholera, rabies, or plague, in which there is a large natural reservoir, the logistical problems are forbidding; for others, such as diphtheria or poliomyelitis, the diseases do not pose sufficiently major problems globally to warrant the effort and expenditure. The best candidates for eventual eradication programs are those diseases recognized in all countries as significant problems and for which natural reservoirs, if present, would not preclude the interruption of transmission. Such might include measles, leprosy, tuberculosis, yaws, syphilis, and certain of the parasitic diseases such as onchocerciasis and malaria.

continued from page 382
and low-nicotine cigarettes can lessen the harmful effects of tobacco was reported by the American Cancer Society. Death rates from lung cancer and heart disease were 26% and 14% lower among smokers of these varieties of cigarette, but were still 33% higher than death rates among nonsmokers.

A trial was launched to assess the effects of a single dose of aspirin taken immediately after a coronary attack. An earlier but statistically insignificant study in the U.K. had suggested that mortality rates might be reduced by 25% by the use of aspirin. Aspirin was thought to inhibit synthesis of a prostaglandin that would otherwise encourage blood platelets to clump together to form clots.

In October scientists at the Wellcome Institute in Great Britain announced discovery of an enzyme, produced by the walls of arteries, that appears to prevent clot formation. Once again prostaglandins were implicated. The researchers, led by John R. Vane, suggested that this enzyme transforms prostaglandins that encourage platelet clumping into ones that actively inhibit the process. This discovery could lead to the production of a drug capable of preventing heart attacks and strokes.

(ARTHUR J. SNIDER; DONALD W. GOULD)

[421; 423; 424; 10/35]

MEDICAL-SOCIAL POLICY

The escalating cost of health care in 1976, coupled with an increasing realization that prevention is both far more desirable and more economical than cure, led national governments to question the manner in which the money and resources available for dealing with the problems of illness were deployed. In the past the money and effort allocated to any particular health problem often depended upon the enthusiasm of the workers involved, upon fashion, or upon some other chance factor. This did not usually result in the best possible use of the necessarily finite means available to meet an always infinite demand.

The Crisis of Rising Costs. Early in the year Great Britain's Department of Health and Social Security released figures compiled during the course of a study aimed at relating the money spent upon various specific health problems and the importance of those problems to the economy and to the well-being of the community. Amazingly, no such study had been undertaken previously in the U.K., despite the fact that the government, through the National Health Service, had provided almost all funds devoted to health care within the U.K. since 1946. A typical instance of the kinds of anomalies that were revealed was the discovery that the money spent upon research into the causes of congenital defects each year was equivalent to about £23 per person so afflicted. On the other hand, skin diseases, which can be quite disabling and even fatal, attracted research funds at the yearly rate of only 3 pence per patient.

Health care expenditures continued to absorb an increasingly large share of U.S. resources during 1976 amid predictions that the public might be nearing a limit to the percentage of the gross national product it was willing to allocate. Several government programs were instituted in an effort to abate skyrocketing costs.

The February *Social Security Bulletin* reported that health expenditures in the U.S. had increased an average of 12% per year since 1965 and 14% between 1974 and 1975. During the decade ended in 1975, annual health dollar outlays more than tripled, to $118.5 billion, and health's share of the gross national product rose from 5.9 to 8.3%. In this period the gross national product itself doubled. The 10% of the U.S. population that was over age 65 in 1976 accounted for 30% of health care expenditures. A Bureau of the Census study estimated that 17% of the population would be 65 years or older by AD 2030, reflecting a growth twice as rapid as that of the total population.

The American Medical Association (AMA) calculated that out-of-pocket payments plus insurance premiums totaled $898 for the average American family during 1975, or about 6.2% of the family's income (after taxes) of $14,500. Health insurance paid about 82% of the family's hospital expenses and 53% of the doctor bills. Premium costs to U.S. industry, according to a survey by *Business Week* magazine, forced some companies to double and triple their employee health-insurance outlays.

The President's Council on Wage and Price Stability predicted that health care costs in the U.S. would continue to rise faster than the consumer price index. However, H. Robert Cathcart, chairman of the American Hospital Association's board of trustees, said the public might be willing to accept a 10–11% allocation of the gross national product but was not likely to permit the health industry to corner a much larger proportion of the national wealth.

The staggering costs of health care cooled enthusiasm for any national health insurance legislation in the U.S. Congress during 1976, but other government measures were implemented. Among these was the 1974 National Health Planning and Resources Development Act, geared toward reducing outlays and inefficiency by seeking to avoid overbuilding and duplication of medical facilities and by perceiving less expensive ways of taking care of the ill. In order for providers of medical services to purchase expensive

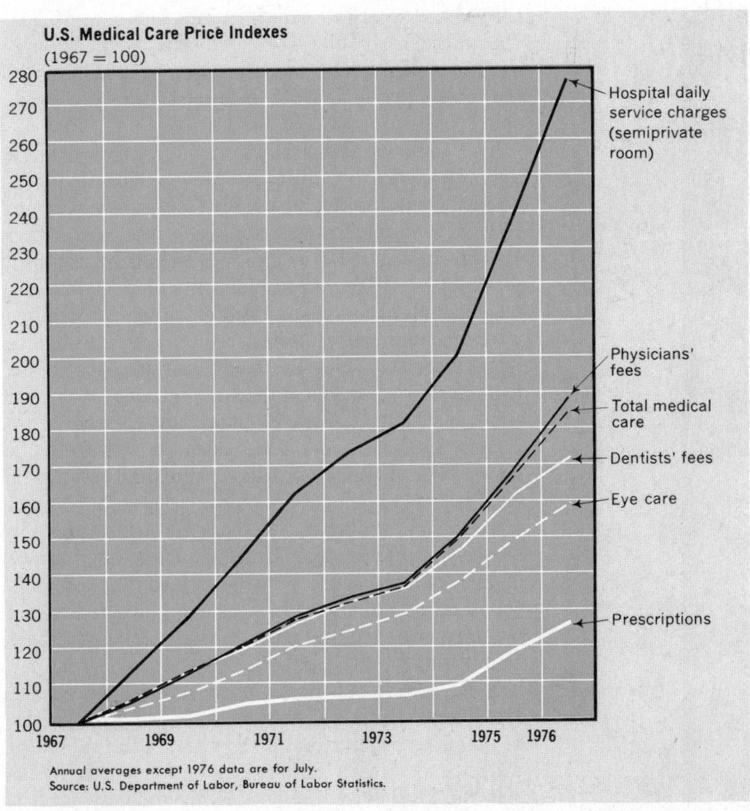

Annual averages except 1976 data are for July.
Source: U.S. Department of Labor, Bureau of Labor Statistics.

WILLIAM E. SAURO—THE NEW YORK TIMES

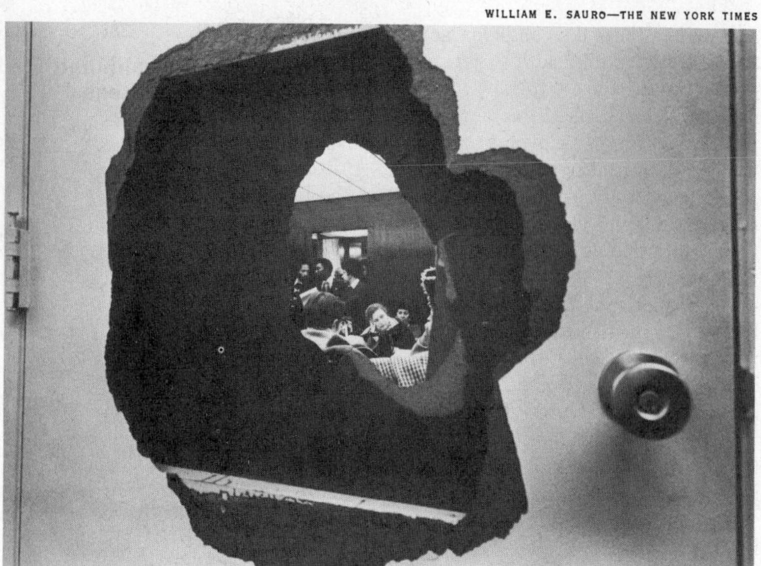

When the board of New York City's Health and Hospitals Corporation met in January to consider closing hospitals, angry demonstrators kicked a hole in the door.

new equipment or expand facilities, certificates of need were required from local health systems agencies (HSAS) designated by the Department of Health, Education, and Welfare (HEW). New York City's HSA announced that one of its first goals would be a reduction in the number of expensive open-heart-surgery units in hospitals.

The AMA joined in a suit filed by the State of North Carolina seeking to have the planning act declared unconstitutional. North Carolina contended that the certificate of need and other requirements interfered with the rights of individual states to determine their own policies. The AMA challenged the law on the more general constitutional grounds that it illegally delegated too much rule-making power to HEW.

In another cost-saving proposal, HEW instituted maximum-allowable-cost (MAC) regulations after weathering protests and court tests by organized medicine, pharmaceutical manufacturers, and pharmacists. Under the new laws, Medicare and Medicaid prescription bills would be reimbursed on the basis of the lowest price at which a drug is generally available.

The American Hospital Association announced that tighter controls by utilization review committees in hospitals cut the average length of patient stay to 7½ days, one full day less than five years earlier. At an average cost of $150 a day, 35 million hospitalized patients in 1975 saved $5.2 billion. Preadmission testing and one-day surgery for minor procedures were among the administrative tactics used to reduce the average stay. New mothers were being sent home from obstetrical wards in four or five days.

Of a sampling of 1,000 physicians by the AMA's Center for Health Services Research and Development, 35% of 419 respondents said that because of high premiums they were considering dropping all malpractice insurance; 13% reported they had already let their insurance lapse. Under an increasing barrage of medical malpractice suits, the medical profession counterattacked in 1976. A Skokie, Ill., radiologist became one of the first physicians in the U.S. to win a countersuit against a patient and her lawyer who had brought a $250,000 malpractice action against him. An Illinois Circuit Court awarded Leonard Berlin $8,000 in damages after he had accused the patient of willful and wanton misconduct in filing a frivolous suit and her lawyers of not having properly investigated the facts before instituting the suit. In the weeks immediately following the victory, medical liability lawsuits dropped 16% in Cook County.

Health Care Delivery. A major exercise in health care planning was launched in the U.K. when a Royal Commission on the National Health Service began work, its terms of reference being "to consider in the interests both of the patients and of those who work in the National Health Service the best use and management of the financial and manpower resources of the National Health Service."

This newly awakened realization of the need to deal with the basic causes of disease, and the social and environmental factors necessary for healthful living, was expressed at a fundamental level in Norway, where the government began consideration of a new food and nutrition policy. The plan under study involved the whole question of food supply, including domestic agricultural production and regulation of the amounts spent on food imports, but its most remarkable feature dealt with the strategy for persuading Norwegians to adopt better eating habits, and for reinforcing this persuasion with food pricing and production policies. The whole scheme was to be underpinned by an intensive program of nutrition education aimed at the entire population from infancy to old age. The planners particularly had in mind the influence of diet on such major causes of death and disability as coronary heart disease and probably some forms of cancer.

At the international level the World Health Assembly considered a report urging member nations to make extended use of auxiliary health workers. The report, which was adopted as official World Health Organization (WHO) policy, pointed out that many of the simpler medical tasks that traditionally were regarded as the preserve of fully qualified medical practitioners could be performed more economically, and sometimes with even greater competence and efficiency, by paramedical personnel with limited but intensive training. In this way (particularly in the less developed countries) a relatively small expenditure could achieve delivery of a valuable level of health care to whole populations who did not have direct access to fully trained physicians. This report marked a significant change in the standing policy, which regarded medical aides as second-best, to be employed in deprived regions until they could be replaced by the proper article.

The same report urged member nations to take steps to prevent or reduce the "medical brain drain," through which fully qualified physicians and nurses, trained at great expense in less developed countries, were leaving to pursue careers in such countries as the U.S., Canada, the U.K., and West Germany. Less developed nations, said the report, should adapt training programs to produce various grades of professional health workers fitted to their own particular needs, a process that incidentally would make the trainees less attractive to potential foreign employers. In 1976 more than 140,000 doctors were working outside their own countries, and about £700 million a year was being spent throughout the world on training medical students who eventually would emigrate.

The major donors of medical manpower included the Philippines, Syria, Iran, India, Pakistan, and the West Indies. Some of these, including Sri Lanka and Pakistan, introduced restrictions on the emigration of trained medical workers, and some of the recipient nations began to impose new conditions on would-be medical immigrants. Roughly two-thirds of foreign doctors undergoing the language and competence tests recently imposed by Great Britain's General Medical Council continued to fail their examinations.

The U.S. Congress passed new national genetic-disease legislation, replacing a former act dealing with only sickle-cell and Cooley's anemia. Deemphasizing the racial overtones of the previous program, it provided for research, testing, counseling, and education concerning such additional genetic diseases as Tay-Sachs, cystic fibrosis, hemophilia, retinitis pigmentosa, Huntington's chorea, and muscular dystrophy.
(ARTHUR J. SNIDER; DONALD W. GOULD)

[425.D.1–2; 425.G; 425.I–J]

HEART DISEASE AND HIGH BLOOD PRESSURE

It had been apparent for some years that there had been a changing pattern in mortalities due to heart disease and high blood pressure. Deaths due to heart disease from diphtheria essentially disappeared early in the 20th century with the introduction of immunization programs, and those from syphilis and rheumatic fever greatly diminished with the advent of penicillin. Total mortality from congenital heart disease (that form present at birth) also dropped by 30% from 1964 to 1974, perhaps due in part to a decreasing birthrate but also to improved treatment. In addition the death rate from high blood pressure over the past 30 years declined more than 50%.

In 1976 statistics were published to indicate that the mortality from coronary heart disease (heart trouble attributable to hardening of the small blood vessels nourishing the heart muscle) at last was beginning to drop in the United States. Depending upon age, sex, and race, this constituted a decline during 1968–74 of 13–37%. Although some experts attributed this last encouraging sign to a reduced number of severe respiratory infections precipitating the deaths of persons with heart conditions, it seemed very likely that a lesser amount of high blood pressure, dietary changes, and less cigarette smoking among adults were important factors.

High Blood Pressure. Despite the worldwide reduction in the prevalence of high blood pressure, or hypertension, over the past 30 years, this condition remained a major health problem and many issues remained to be clarified. In general, it seemed that a detailed and complex laboratory evaluation was not routinely required in the proper diagnosis and management of hypertension. However, it was not entirely clear what segments of the population should be considered for treatment. Thus, it was far from certain at precisely what levels of blood pressure drug treatment should begin, especially in children, in women, and in older individuals. There was no dispute, however, over the value of identifying and treating moderate to severe hypertension; *i.e.,* that indicated by upper (systolic) pressures of 160 or more and lower (diastolic) pressures of 100 or more in adults.

There was an increasing recognition that excess weight was an important contributing factor in high blood pressure; hypertension prevailed among the obese and those gaining excess weight, whereas blood pressure could be controlled more easily if excess weight were removed. There was also some increase in enthusiasm for a restriction of salt in the diet to improve the effects of drug management and possibly to lessen the incidence of hypertension, although evidence was far from convincing.

In the United States the basic medicines employed since the 1950s for the treatment of high blood pressure had been diuretics, which promoted the loss of salt, potassium, and water from the body, and such agents as rauwolfia, hydralazine, methyldopa, and guanethidine. Over the past several years, an additional group of agents called beta-adrenergic blockers have been employed in Europe and particularly in Great Britain. One member of this family, propranolol, was beginning to receive considerable attention in the U.S. in the management of high blood pressure following approval for this purpose by the Food and Drug Administration. It had the advantage of relatively few side effects and often lowered blood pressure best when taken in conjunction with one of the diuretics.

The Heart Valves. Abnormalities of one or more of the four heart valves had long been a matter of great interest and study. One of the great recent advances was the introduction and widespread use of artificial valves. For a time, human valves obtained from corpses at autopsy were transplanted into patients, but this practice was largely abandoned because of technical difficulties and signs that the valves would undergo deterioration. The mid-1970s saw increasing use of valves obtained from pigs. Porcine valves were expected to resist deterioration and be less inclined to induce clot formation than plastic and metal artificial valves. Further, they had the advantage of being noiseless, whereas artificial valves produced a very audible clicking sound with each heartbeat.

There was also a great deal of interest in a relatively newly recognized form of valve disease that involved the mitral valve on the left side of the heart. Called mitral valve prolapse, it consisted of an abnormality of one of the valve's free margins, resulting in a backward leakage of blood through the valve with each heartbeat. Such a process could often be detectable with the stethoscope as a particular kind of noise or murmur sometimes associated with a clicking sound. The condition was known to be more com-

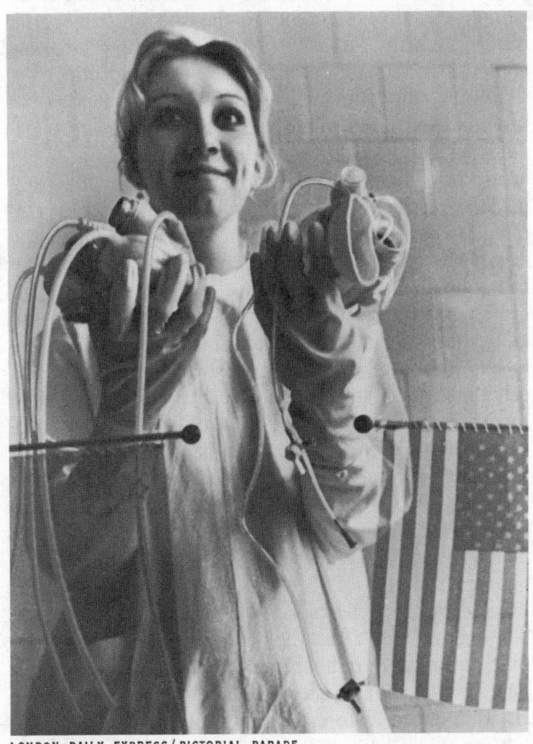

LONDON DAILY EXPRESS/PICTORIAL PARADE

U.S. and Soviet surgeons implanted these artificial hearts into calves in Moscow in March. It was the first step in a joint program to develop an artificial heart for human use.

UPI COMPIX

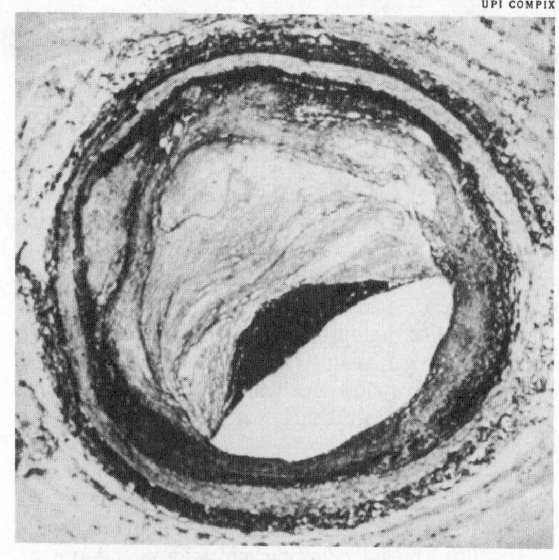

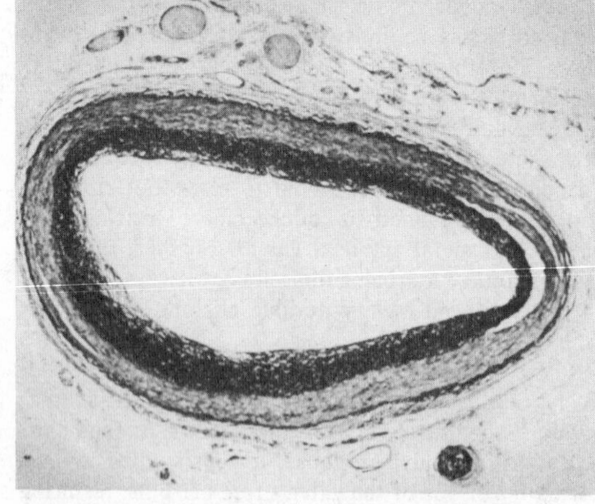

How cholesterol affects the arteries. (Top) A cross-section of a coronary artery partially occluded by deposits of cholesterol, cellular debris, and calcium. (Bottom) An artery from a 100-year-old woman who had no cardiac problem.

mon in females than in males, tended to occur in families, and was unrelated to rheumatic fever. Surveys indicated that this condition was indeed very common and was probably of little or no significance in most patients. In a few individuals, however, it might be complicated by infection of the mitral valve and, rarely, by serious and even life-threatening valve incompetence and irregularities of heart rhythm.

Echocardiography. The condition of mitral valve prolapse and other valve problems were being clarified by study with a new noninvasive technique called echocardiography. This important diagnostic tool utilized ultrasound, that is, sound waves of a frequency above the threshold of hearing, in much the same way that sonar is employed to explore the ocean depths. High-frequency sound waves were generated and transmitted into the chest, reflecting back as "echoes" when they encountered an interface between tissues of differing acoustical properties. The echoes were converted into electric signals that were recorded on paper for analysis or electronically processed to provide a moving image on a TV screen. Characteristic wave forms so obtained were proving of great value in identifying not only abnormal valve motion, as in mitral valve prolapse, but other heart conditions such as thickening of the walls of the heart, abnormal motion of these walls, and the presence of fluid in the sac (pericardium) surrounding the heart. The method had advantages of complete safety, mobility, economy, and ease of interpretation. Recently described modifications of the technique and of analysis were expected to extend its usefulness.

Diagnosis of Heart Attacks. The electrocardiogram was the basic laboratory tool for the diagnosis of the usual type of heart attack (myocardial infarction) due to hardening of the small blood vessels (coronary arteries) feeding the heart. Support for such a diagnosis had also been provided in recent years by measurement in the blood of levels of certain enzymes released from heart muscle cells damaged in a heart attack. Detection of these enzymes had been relatively easy, but one problem had been lack of specificity. None of the enzymes was found solely in the heart; thus, their presence in the blood might represent release from other tissues. Recent developments refined these tests by isolating certain enzyme types essentially unique for heart muscle damage. These "myocardial" fractions were especially valuable in improving the basis for heart-attack diagnosis.

An even newer approach was that of the use of radioactive substances. The earliest studies, undertaken about 1960, employed radioactive cesium in an attempt to visualize the heart muscle and chambers. In 1976 the two tracer substances found to be quite useful were radioactive thallium and technetium, one or both of which were injected intravenously, followed by a photographic record, using a scintillation camera, of their concentration and distribution throughout the heart. Thallium has an affinity for muscle tissue. A focal defect in the heart muscle appearing in a thallium scan was characteristic of a heart attack. The technique with thallium was also employed to estimate the presence of areas in the myocardium with reduced blood supply. The tracer technetium behaves differently; it binds to the protein albumin and remains within the blood compartment. It therefore was able to be used to evaluate the chambers of the heart and the nature of the contractile process of their walls. Although the images obtained using these radioactive materials still appeared quite crude, there was every evidence that the energetic and ingenious investigators employing them would make them increasingly applicable to the study of heart function and disease.

(OGLESBY PAUL)

[422.A; 424.C]

RHEUMATIC DISEASES

Rheumatic diseases is a collective term that connotes pain and disability of the musculoskeletal system. These disorders include about 100 diseases that in 1976 continued to be the leading causes of crippling in the United States. Over 22 million Americans, or at least 10% of the population, were afflicted with these conditions to some extent. Similar information concerning prevalence and other facts regarding the effect of these conditions on the nation were part of a comprehensive report transmitted in 1976 to the U.S. Congress. The report, "Arthritis: Out of the Maze," was developed by the National Commission on Arthritis and Related Musculoskeletal Diseases with the help of numerous expert consultants and other health professionals. In it the current status of research, education, community programs, data systems, epidemiology, and public policy in arthritis and the rheumatic diseases in general was appraised and comprehensive recommendations were made for long-range actions in each of these areas.

This landmark effort was in response to the National Arthritis Act of 1974 and was intended to be the beginning of a national arthritis initiative. Implementation and financing of the recommendations depended mainly upon the federal government, which invested an estimated $39.2 million in 1975 for arthritis research and education, or approximately $2 for each person having such disorders. Although the commission's recommendations were to triple national expenditures for new and expanded arthritis programs, only limited increases were expected to be approved. In spite of such funding restrictions, the detailed reports developed by the commission in response to the National Arthritis Act provided a most valuable planning resource for coping with these major health problems.

Autoimmune Theory. In the recent past emphasis had been given to human and animal studies of the immunological system under the assumption that a constitutional or acquired disorder in such functions played an important role in rheumatoid arthritis and the acquired connective-tissue diseases. Consequently by 1976 abundant evidence existed of quantitative differences in antibody and cell-mediated immune responses to some of the host's own tissues and gamma globulins, *i.e.,* antibody proteins, and such reactions were suspected to contribute to disease manifestations, the so-called autoimmune responses. It previously had been believed that the body was normally tolerant to its own natural tissue and plasma proteins and would not react to them immunologically. However, important exceptions to the theory of absolute immunological self-tolerance were becoming recognized in otherwise healthy individuals who seemed to react immunologically to their own tissue components and proteins, albeit at a lower average degree than patients with some of the rheumatic diseases. These observations suggested that some of the immunological phenomena were secondary. Increased or abnormal antigenic stimulation could explain immunologic differences found in some of the rheumatic diseases. Whether or not affected individuals acquired or were constitutionally predisposed to qualitative alterations in immunological responsiveness required further study.

Virus Theory. A popular hypothesis was that an occult virus infection could be contributing to the cause of some of the rheumatic diseases, especially systemic lupus erythematosus (SLE). This theory was stimulated by observations that viruses were involved in certain animal diseases that had immunological alterations or defects similar to those found in SLE. Virus expression was found in several animal models and the virus or its antigens were believed to produce disease by affecting the function of certain lymphocytes, rendering native tissue components antigenic, or providing a large amount of foreign antigen for continuing low-grade immunological reaction.

In humans, evidence of viral infections was still indirect and mainly implicated type C oncornaviruses. These viruses, found in birds, reptiles, and mammals, had a genetic component, or genome, of ribonucleic acid (RNA) as well as certain enzymes (RNA-directed deoxyribonucleic acid [DNA] polymerases) that were thought to allow viral information to become integrated into the host's cellular DNA. If DNA virogenes were present in all cells of an organism, the virus was called endogenous and its expression could be most difficult to demonstrate. As yet the experimental evidence for type C virus involvement in SLE was conflicting. Genetic factors were believed important in a possible host-viral disease relationship but specific mechanisms were still unknown.

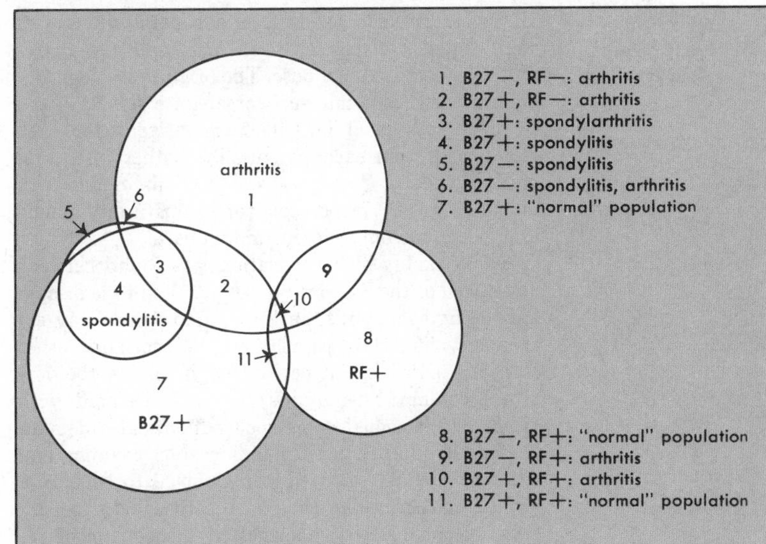

Correlation of the presence or absence of the human-leukocyte antigen B27 and an antibody protein called the rheumatoid factor (RF) with the incidence of various rheumatic diseases is illustrated in this Venn diagram of human populations. Recent investigations implicated both genetic predisposition and immunological mechanisms in several of these conditions.

Vascular Alterations. The original term for the acquired connective-tissue disorders, collagen-vascular diseases, indicated the early recognition of the role of the vascular system in their pathogenesis. Different disease mechanisms were known to cause vascular alterations. For example, certain circulating complexes of antigen (*e.g.,* chronic virus infection) and antibody were injurious to blood vessels by activating an inflammatory response or by occluding small blood vessels such as those in the kidney. Such mechanisms of damage were believed to occur in SLE, in various types of chronic viral infections (*e.g.,* hepatitis), and in serum sickness. However, in scleroderma the most impressive vascular alteration was a decrease in the number of nutritive capillaries in skin and muscle and a narrowing of small arteries in certain organs due to proliferation of the arterial lining. Such changes occurred for unknown reasons and resulted in decreased blood supply to tissues. Abnormality in the function of small blood vessels, *e.g.,* increased permeability, was also recognized in some of the rheumatic diseases. Causes of vascular changes included immunological or inflammatory reaction, hormonal or chemical alterations, and possibly direct virus infection, but less was known about this aspect of the rheumatic diseases than the previously mentioned areas of research.

Continued research in pathogenesis was important to improved therapy as well as to an understanding of primary causes. Although research progressed considerably faster in experimental areas of inflammation than in the discovery of new treatments or preventions, progress was being made in the latter areas as well.

HL-A Correlations. Recent progress was made in the categorization of certain rheumatic disorders by virtue of recognizing significant correlations with the human-leukocyte-antigen (HL-A) system, analogous to the ABO and Rh typing systems for circulating red blood cells, which normally do not have nuclei. Most nucleated cells of the body, including tissues, blood, and sperm, possess antigenic markers on their membrane surfaces that can be recognized immunologically by tissue-transplantation techniques or laboratory tests. Human somatic cells contain 46 chromosomes in 23 pairs, one set of maternal and one of paternal origin, and the HL-A system was known to be controlled by genes on each of the number six autosomal chromosomes. This system was found to be present in all species studied to date, and genetic similarities were found between that of man and the better studied system in the mouse. The original serologically defined antigens comprise two separate series, A and B. Each individual inherits two antigens for each series, one from each parent. Two other histocompatibility series, C and D, were later discovered with one of them (D) responsible for compatibility among lymphocytes from different individuals.

A remarkably high correlation was found between an antigen of the B series (HL-A B27) and the disease ankylosing spondylitis, an association which may exceed 90% in certain populations. Furthermore, other forms of arthritis, not necessarily involving the vertebral column (spondylitis), were correlated with HL-A B27, although most such patients also demonstrated sacroiliac changes on radiographic examination. Although the B27 antigen was believed to be only a genetic marker, rather than a causative factor per se, these recent discoveries suggested a spectrum of related, genetically conditioned arthritic disorders that affect the spinal, sacroiliac, or peripheral joints and other tissues, such as the skin. The term spondylarthritis was often used to refer to this spectrum of arthritis that did not overlap with classical rheumatoid arthritis, except by chance.

The benefit of these discoveries was that certain arthritis patients could be more accurately classified in early stages of disease. Interestingly, the spondylarthritic diseases predominate in males, whereas rheumatoid arthritis and related connective-tissue diseases predominate in females. Also B27-associated arthritis tends to manifest itself first about the time of puberty or in the early adult ages, whereas the risk of developing rheumatoid and related arthritis tends to increase with age. Immune responses, endocrine factors, and other biological control mechanisms seemed to be mediated by genes close to the HL-A system on the sixth chromosomes. Further study of the HL-A system in arthritis promised to reveal biological relationships of importance in the predisposition and course of disease.

(ALFONSE T. MASI)

[421.B.2; 422.I.3–5; 424.L.1–4]

NEUROLOGICAL DISEASES

Several refinements in computerized axial tomography (CAT) extended its influence on the diagnosis and management of patients with neurological diseases. A painless, noninvasive procedure that carried no risk to the patient, the CAT scan used computer analysis of a narrow X-ray beam passed sequentially through the skull to produce a two-dimensional image of a cross section of the brain and its environs. One of the principal problems faced by the clinical neurologist was determination of the cause of a patient's stroke, which could be due to hemorrhage (bleeding into the substance of the brain or its surrounding membranes), thrombosis of a cerebral blood vessel (blockage due to vascular clot), or cerebral embolism (blockage of a brain blood vessel by a clot formed elsewhere in the body). It was essential to differentiate accurately between these causes of stroke because treatment for one condition could be harmful if used in another. Before the advent of CAT scanning, the decision as to which of the three events was occurring was often made on clinical grounds alone. CAT scanning allowed rapid identification and localization of cerebral hemorrhage and, in the process, provided evidence that this event was a more frequent cause of stroke than had been previously suspected. Patients felt to have cerebral thrombosis on clinical grounds alone often were found to have unsuspected cerebral hemorrhage on CAT scanning. Prompter recognition of cerebral hemorrhage was expected to lead to more rational approaches to effective therapy.

As CAT scanning methods were becoming refined, resolution of relatively minor changes within brain substance was becoming possible. Abnormal changes were found by CAT scans in the brains of patients with demyelinating diseases, a group of disorders that included multiple sclerosis. Attempts were made to complement routine CAT scanning by supplementary techniques, including the intravenous injection of contrast substances to enhance the appearance of intracranial tumours and the instillation of nonionic, water-soluble myelographic contrast agents into the spinal canal to define more clearly the spaces and cisterns that surround the brain. These methods extended the sensitivity of the CAT scans and permitted better study of the brain in certain neurological disorders.

The year was marked by continued efforts to define

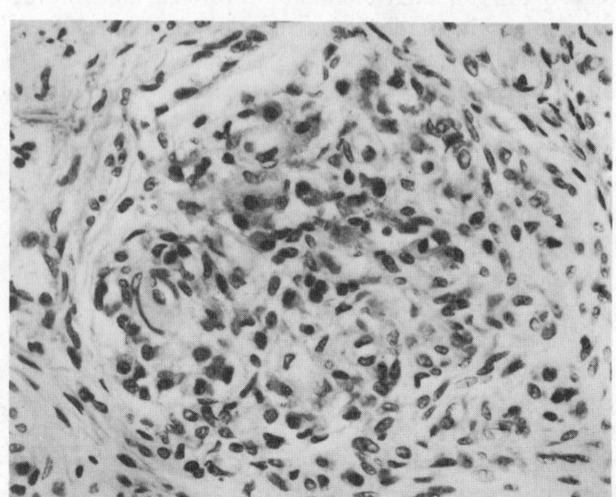

Researchers may have found a clue to crib deaths in abnormalities of the carotid body, which monitors oxygen and carbon dioxide levels in the blood and indirectly regulates respiration. (Far right) A cross-section of carotid body under the microscope. (Right) An infant sleeps under watch by a machine that signals breathing abnormalities.

COURTESY (RIGHT), DR. RICHARD L. NAEYE, DEPARTMENT OF PATHOLOGY, PENNSYLVANIA STATE UNIVERSITY, HERSHEY; (LEFT) THE WASHINGTON POST the cause of multiple sclerosis, one of the major unsolved neurological disorders. Results originally reported in 1972 were confirmed by Richard Carp and his co-workers at the New York State Institute for Mental Retardation. Carp reported that mice inoculated with extracts from brains of patients with multiple sclerosis developed a depression in the number of circulating polymorphonuclear neutrophils (PMN), a species of circulating white blood cell. Serums and spinal fluids from patients with the disease caused a similar PMN depression. By contrast normal human-brain extracts failed to elicit any change in the number of PMN cells. These results suggested that a transmissible agent, called multiple sclerosis associated agent (MSAA), was present in tissues of multiple sclerosis patients.

Recently Carp's work was confirmed and extended by Ursula Koldovsky, Gertrude Henle, and their associates at the Children's Hospital of Philadelphia. The PMN lowering effect was found not only in mice, but also in rats, hamsters, and guinea pigs. High titres of MSAA were detected in the brain and spinal fluid of multiple sclerosis victims. Nearly all serums and spinal fluids from sclerotic patients also contained antibodies antagonistic to the PMN-depression effect. In addition patients' relatives and nursing personnel had serum antibodies to MSAA. Further studies were required before a causal relationship between MSAA and the development of multiple sclerosis could be established, but the results suggested that a novel microorganism might be associated with the disease.

A more effective drug treatment for Parkinson's disease was introduced during the year. The symptoms of Parkinson's disease were known to be related to depletion of brain dopamine; replacement of dopamine by the oral administration of a precursor, levodopa (L-dopa), often dramatically reversed the signs of the disease. When levodopa was given alone, however, much of the drug was destroyed in the body before it could enter the brain. Combination of levodopa with carbidopa, a dopa decarboxylase inhibitor that prevented the peripheral breakdown of levodopa, resulted in a more satisfactory treatment. Some patients who were unable to tolerate large doses of levodopa because of undesirable side effects, such as gastrointestinal upset, could be given carbidopa-levodopa preparations. Although the benefits of levodopa replacement in Parkinson's disease often could not be sustained for long periods of time, control of many disabling features of Parkinsonism was being achieved in an increasing number of patients.

(DONALD H. HARTER)

[422.K.1–4; 424.M.1–6]

MENTAL HEALTH

Little emerged during the course of the year to indicate that medical science was approaching a true understanding of the causes of mental illness or improving its methods of treatment. What progress there was found itself hampered by skimpy research support and further constriction of mental health training programs. The lack of job opportunities for graduates in the field of mental health dissuaded many new applicants from entering related school programs, raising the alarming possibility that there would be fewer graduates to meet the increasing incidence and prevalence of mental illness.

Mental health continued to be an illusive goal to attain. Its definition clamoured for consensus, as leaders in the field continued to use concepts of exclusion, in which mental health became defined by the absence of specific psychopathologies. Techniques of coping and meeting "one's level of expectation" were being used increasingly as measures of adjustment to everyday life stress. And it was clear that many were not making such adjustments. At least 10% of the U.S. population suffered from some form of mental illness, and about one-seventh of these (over three million persons) had received or were receiving some form of professional care.

As advances in health care increased life expectancy to about 75 years in the developed countries, there appeared an increasing number of "worried well" among the clientele of most nonpsychiatric physicians. Surveys in the U.S. revealed that some 80% of patients in physicians' offices suffered from minor ailments and/or mild anxiety states. One of four adults was classified as "emotionally tense" with major complaints of anxiety, depression, boredom, and fatigue. Other studies revealed that about 48% of nonworking women in the U.S. were or had been on some form of mood-altering drugs obtained through legitimate prescriptions. Most of these were antianxiety agents to calm one down, but a substantial number were "uppers," or amphetamines. A 1976 study reported that the desire for paid employment among a sample of housewives was the one critical variable that differentiated women who were complaining, bored, and frustrated from those who were not. These unhappy women also overutilized medical personnel and mood-altering medication.

The overuse and overprescribing of minor tranquilizers, barbiturates, sedatives, stimulants, and pain killers gave rise to concerns that modern society was becoming drug dependent. The psychological dependence on a drug often occurred because the drug could relieve the symptom but did not uncover the cause. The illicit use of "hard" drugs (heroin, cocaine, etc.) remained as a major problem in mental health, although the increasing consumption of alcohol was thought to have surpassed hard drug usage. The effectiveness of detoxification techniques using replacement maintenance programs (*e.g.*, those using methadone in the treatment of heroin addiction) was being questioned. Recent research indicated that depression was prevalent among hard drug abusers, but whether such depression was a precursor to or a consequence of drug usage remained to be explored.

In Great Britain figures for admissions to mental hospitals published recently suggested that one in six U.K. women and one in nine men would enter a hospital as a result of mental illness at some time during their lives. Almost half the country's hospital beds were occupied by the mentally disordered, and mental illness caused the loss of 40 million working days each year. Yet well under one-tenth of the total budget of the National Health Service was spent on hospital psychiatric services, and a sum equivalent to only about one-fiftieth of this inadequate allocation was devoted to the provision of residential and day-care facilities for handling the mentally ill within the community. Consequently mental hospitals were grossly overcrowded with patients who did not need to be there at all. Large numbers of patients were detained for many years with virtually no active treatment save for sedatives to keep them quiet. Overworked nurses tended to become callous so that instances of cruelty and neglect were commonplace. Unfortunately this state of affairs was widespread throughout the developed nations.

During the year Britain's Department of Health and Social Security published a consultative document designed to promote discussion of desirable changes in the present Mental Health Act. This document dealt with certain matters of concern to people interested in the handling of the mentally ill everywhere, including safeguards aimed at preventing the unjustifiable compulsory detention of mental patients and the right of such patients to resist certain treatments (particularly electroconvulsive therapy) and procedures that produce an irreversible effect (such as brain surgery).

In general there was an increasing tendency to question the wisdom of allowing psychiatrists too much individual freedom in their handling of the mentally ill. It was feared that too many patients were too often and too casually labeled as mentally ill in a manner that could prejudice their career prospects and their status in society for the rest of their lives.

WHO launched a major multinational study into depressive illness, which affected about 100 million people in the world each year. The studies, to be based in Switzerland, Canada, Japan, and Iran, were to determine the social effects of depression on patients, their families, and the community within four different cultures and to establish some common factor or factors that might give a clue to its causation.

As anxieties and frustrations burdened individuals in the context of economic strain, high jobless rates, and increasing crime, depression in the U.S. rose to compete with anxiety as a major state of dysphoria, and self-destructive urges became increasingly viewed as a way out. The suicide rate continued to climb, most tragically among young people. In the adolescent age range (13–19) the suicide rate had almost doubled since 1966 (from 1.7 to 3.1 per 100,000), making suicide a leading cause of death even though most suicides were not recorded as such; usually they were tabulated under "accidents," the leading cause of death among young persons in this age group. Overall, the suicide rate remained at 11 per 100,000 in the U.S., or about 27,000 annually.

Clinical depression was also on the increase among adolescents. Several reasons were given, including the increasing number of persons in this age group who underwent stresses with which conventional social institutions could not cope, as well as the shrinking economy, which blocked economic gain and rising expectations of all young adults. The resulting replacement of self-esteem with self-doubt was seen to underlie the depressions that evolved. A serious question that emerged was whether these "reactive" depressions would continue into the future, developing a generation of chronic depressives and ushering in an age of melancholy to replace the age of anxiety.

Research yielded some promising techniques for quantifying some aspects of human behaviour. Electromyography measured subtle, typically covert facial expressions and provided a relatively objective index of various clinical mood states. The technique was claimed to differentiate depressed from nondepressed persons with methods more accurate than direct observation.

The major tranquilizers persisted in popularity in the "treatment" of schizophrenia, a serious mental disorder in which the victim's perception of reality is usually profoundly distorted. Some criticism arose that such drugs were being overused in many hospital settings, creating a "zombie" effect and raising ethical issues of what constituted proper treatment and whether the rights of the patient were being violated.

The search continued for some biochemical factor that was responsible for schizophrenic behaviour, and several papers appeared during the year examining the theory that at least some types of schizophrenia are associated with an abnormal activity of dopamine, a chemical involved in the transmission of nerve impulses among brain cells. An excess of this chemical, or a lack of some other substance that normally counteracts its effect, could lead to an overactivity of certain brain circuits, which in turn might induce the schizophrenic state. This work arose from a growing understanding of the pharmacology of the phenothiazines, a group of drugs effective in controlling the symptoms of schizophrenia in a significant proportion of patients, and from the observation that amphetamines produce a state resembling schizophrenia in some people.

Although it appeared increasingly likely that much, if not all, mental illness is associated with some organic or biochemical abnormality in the brain, it also appeared likely that psychological stress was often a precipitating factor, just as a faulty heart might function adequately until the demands put upon it became too great. Several British studies published during the year emphasized the possible role of stress in mental illness. One noted an increasing incidence of depression among Asian women immigrants who were isolated from the rest of the community by cultural and linguistic barriers. There was also a high incidence of paranoia among minority groups, a phenomenon that might be related to the prejudice and discrimination with which these groups must contend. Another study associated aircraft noise with an increased admission rate to psychiatric hospitals among people living near London's Heathrow Airport.

(ROBERT I. YUFIT; DONALD W. GOULD)

[438.D]

DENTISTRY

Although inflation continued to escalate the costs of health care in the U.S. during 1976, dental costs were held in check because of dramatic productivity increases by dentists. An analysis of health care costs by the American Dental Association (ADA) based on consumer price index figures revealed that dentists' fees had increased only 61.9% since 1967, compared with a 68.6% rise for all medical care and a 69.4% hike in physicians' fees. ADA president Robert B. Shira ascribed the containment to productivity increases and increased emphasis on preventive care, which allowed time for additional patients. The average number of patients per dentist in 1972 was 1,663, a 40% increase over 1962. Hence, holding the line on fees proved possible, despite a 132.5% increase in the costs of operating a dental office.

A University of Michigan dental scientist reported that the amount of tooth decay remaining in a community supplied with fluoridated water was reduced by two-thirds in children treated with a combination of five decay-preventive techniques. "The reduction in tooth decay is impressive," explained Robert A. Bagramian, "especially when you realize that fluoridating the community water supplies in Ypsilanti and Willow Run, Mich., already has reduced the incidence of tooth decay by about 60%." Preventive methods included cleaning of teeth, coating the chewing surfaces with a plastic sealant, twice-a-year application of a fluoride gel, supervised instruction in oral-hygiene practices, and filling of all decayed teeth.

Changing the immune response of white blood cells could aid in the treatment of patients with destructive gum disease, a scientist of the National Institute of Dental Research in Bethesda, Md., reported. William E. Wright observed in laboratory tests that lymphocytes, a type of white blood cell, reacted to foreign substances or antigens derived from bacterial plaque that forms on teeth. Normally lymphocytes multiply at a rather slow rate, but those that had been previously sensitized to plaque antigens and then reexposed were found to grow and divide at a much faster rate. Wright suggested that once a severely diseased individual's lymphocytes were sensitized to plaque antigens, "lymphocyte memory" allowed the cells to "remember" these antigens and respond to them even years later.

Dental scientists at the University of Alabama's Institute of Dental Research were experimenting with an oral vaccine that induced the production of antibodies against a principal causative agent of tooth decay, *Streptococcus mutans.* Still in the animal testing stage, the vaccine, which was composed of killed cells of *S. mutans,* proved effective when added to the drinking water of germ-free rats. Previous studies had produced a vaccine that could be injected into the oral tissues, salivary glands, or parotid duct to stimulate the production of IgA antibodies, which fight tooth decay. However, these inoculations were uncomfortable and were not expected to be suitable for use in humans.

Early detection of oral cancer, when chances of cure were greatest, was improved by biopsy of very small red or red-and-white speckled lesions in three high-risk regions of the mouth—the floor of the mouth, the sides or undersides of the tongue, and the soft-palate complex. These criteria, reported Arthur Mashberg of the East Orange, N.J., Veterans Administration Hospital and Lawrence Garfinkel of the American Cancer Society, were contrary to the established view that most precancerous or cancerous lesions in the mouth are white.

Three famed, largely educational children's television programs were found by a University of Connecticut dental scientist to lower a youngster's anxiety and heartbeat rate during dental office visits. Larry L. Venham explained that in his test, 51 preschool children were randomly divided into two groups. Whereas the control group saw no television during their visits, the remainder watched "Sesame Street," "Mr. Rogers' Neighborhood," or "The Electric Company" as they sat in the dental chair. Electrodes and a photoelectric sensor were attached to each youngster's hand to measure heart rate and electrical conductivity of the skin. Venham found that the children seemed most interested in the television programs during restorative work and least interested when injections were given.

An elaborate chewing machine, designed to help dentists precisely measure the action of a patient's jaw and teeth during chewing, was developed by University of Florida dental researchers. Co-inventor Charles H. Gibbs said the system could pave the way for designing simpler diagnostic instruments for use in dental offices. The instrument mechanically duplicated the motions of a patient's jaws and the mandibular joints that hinge the jaw to the skull. These movements were then recorded on magnetic tape and played back in slow motion so that the dentist could

COURTESY, DR. ROBERT G. SCHALLHORN, PROFESSOR AND CHAIRMAN, DIVISION OF PERIODONTICS, UNIVERSITY OF COLORADO SCHOOL OF DENTISTRY, DENVER

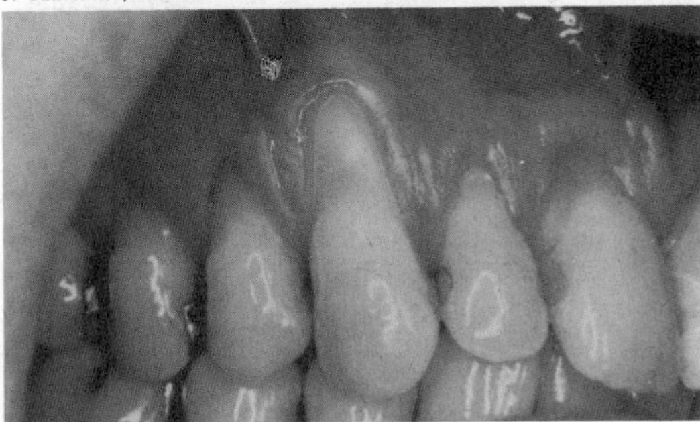

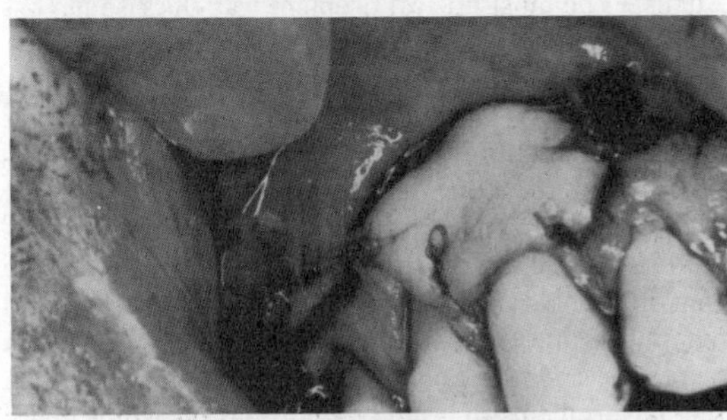

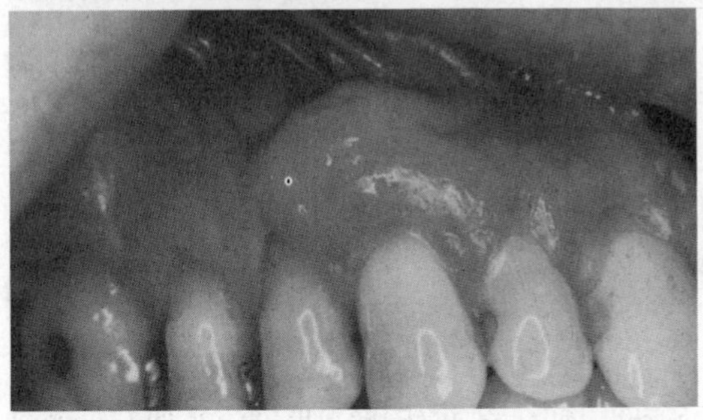

How a gingival graft is done. The gum has receded on an upper tooth (top). A thin layer of tissue is removed from the roof of the mouth and positioned over the exposed root (centre photos). Within a few weeks the transplanted tissue is firmly attached, and after three years the graft has completely healed (bottom).

closely observe action of the jaw joints normally hidden from view. "Such instrumentation could aid dentists in maintaining proper bite and proper mandibular joint function when fitting patients with such restorative devices as bridges and crowns," Gibbs explained. (LOU JOSEPH)

[422.E.1.a; 10/35.C.1]

See also Demography; Drug Abuse; Life Sciences; Nobel Prizes; Social and Welfare Services.

ENCYCLOPÆDIA BRITANNICA FILMS. *Work of the Heart* (1968); *The Ears and Hearing* (2nd ed., 1969); *Muscle: Chemistry of Contraction* (1969); *Muscle: Dynamics of Contraction* (1969); *Radioisotopes: Tools of Discovery* (1969); *Respiration in Man* (1969); *The Nerve Impulse* (1971); *Health: Eye-Care Fantasy* (1972); *Health: Toothache of the Clown* (1972); *The Drug Problem: What Do You Think?* (1972); *Work of the Kidneys* (2nd ed., 1972); *Regulating Body Temperature* (2nd ed., 1972); *The Tobacco Problem: What Do You Think?* (1972); *Intern: A Long Year* (1972); *Venereal Disease: The Hidden Epidemic* (1973); *The Alcohol Problem: What Do You Think?* (1973); *Exercise and Physical Fitness* (1973); *The Heart and Circulatory System* (1974); *The Living Cell: An Introduction* (1974); *The Lungs and Respiratory System* (1975); *Senses and Perception: Links to the Outside World* (1975); *Learning About Cells* (1976); *The Living Cell: DNA* (1976); *Alcohol: Pink Elephant* (1976).

Hebrew Literature: *see* Literature

Highways: *see* Engineering Projects; Transportation

Hinduism: *see* Religion

Historic Preservation

In February 1976 representatives of 43 member states of UNESCO met in Warsaw, Poland, to prepare a final draft of the "International Recommendation on the Preservation of Historic Quarters, Towns and Sites and their Integration into a Modern Environment." The draft recommendation underlined the problems resulting from indiscriminate urban renewal programs that lead to the destruction of established neighbourhoods and their replacement by stereotyped and depersonalized construction, as well as the value of maintaining the architectural heritage of urban societies. It was adopted at UNESCO's General Conference, held in Nairobi, Kenya, during October–November.

The UNESCO-sponsored project to save the temples on the island of Philae in Egypt, threatened by the waters of the Nile, progressed satisfactorily. Most of the temples had been dismantled and the stones stored nearby. The task of reassembling the temples on the neighbouring island of Agilkia was begun in August. The most critical problem was the rise in cost caused by inflation, now estimated at $18.5 million, compared with the 1971 estimate of $14 million.

In Indonesia the task of restoring the Buddhist monument at Borobudur made rapid progress. Dismantling of the north and south faces of the temple was well advanced, and the pouring of concrete foundations for the terraces began in March. Among the contributions received were technical services and computer time from International Business Machines Corp., steel reinforcing bars for the foundations from the government of India, and finance from many other foreign governments. Rising costs were again a problem, the original budget of $7,750,000 in 1972 having risen to $11.9 million.

In Venice the construction of aqueducts to permit the closure of artesian wells responsible for the city's sinking continued. Some of the deeper wells, particularly those serving industry, were closed, with a resultant rise in the water table of five to six metres. Sensitive measurements suggested that the sinking of the island due to compression had been arrested. The international consultative committee, at its 1975 session, had questioned the plan to close off the lagoon by constructing permanent barriers and narrowing the entrance of the ship canals in the belief that such measures might adversely affect the ecology of the lagoon. The tides were currently a major factor in reducing pollution, and it was feared by some that their flushing action would be lessened. As part of an overall program to introduce new cultural and educational activities to the city, the Italian government purchased the Abbey of the Misericordia and renovated it to serve as a centre for research in the preservation of stone and for training specialists in this field.

Restoration of the Hanuman Dhoka Palace in Kathmandu, Nepal, was continued under the supervision of a UNESCO/UN Development Program expert. Work was concentrated on the buildings surrounding the Lohan Chowk, or courtyard. The structure of the Lalitpur Tower had been shored, but careful examination revealed that it was not stable and some of the shoring timbers showed signs of strain. As a result it had to be demounted and rebuilt. Other projects, such as the master plan for the preservation and presentation of cultural and natural sites in Kathmandu Valley, were completed, and an inventory of historic buildings was published. In Pakistan work continued on the Bronze Age site of Mohenjo-daro. The Pakistan Water and Power Development Authority prepared tender documents for the construction of tube wells and a diversion barrage for the Indus River.

In June the World Bank announced an International Development Association loan of $6 million to Jordan for a tourism project for the preservation and presentation of the sites of Petra and Jerash and the improvement of tourist facilities. The total budget approved by the Jordanian government amounted to $12.1 million. This was the World Bank's first involvement in such a project; it was based on the consideration that important economic benefits could be realized, through tourism, from the sound development of historical sites.

International assistance was also given to a project to safeguard the Acropolis, Parthenon, and Erechtheum temples of Athens. A team of UNESCO experts was sent to examine the site. Several causes of deterioration were identified: atmospheric pollution, mainly sulfur dioxide from domestic fuels and nitric acids from automobile exhausts; former repairs, particularly rusting iron clamps installed during 1913–31; frost action; and increased wear on steps, footpaths, etc., caused by the large numbers of tourists. Little was in fact known about the condition of the Acropolis. Springs have occurred at the base from ancient times, and erosion may have taken place from within. The caryatids of the Erechtheum temple and the friezes of the Parthenon were now so weathered that it was recommended that they be dismounted and consolidated. As a temporary measure, replicas

The Battle of Hastings took place on this field in 1066. The abbey was built by William the Conqueror after his victory. The owners of the site sold it to the British government and an unnamed American academic institution in June.

SYNDICATION INTERNATIONAL/PHOTO TRENDS

would be made to replace them. An international campaign to raise the funds required was under consideration by the Greek government and UNESCO.

A UNESCO expert sent to Pagan, Burma, where damage to the ancient pagodas was caused by an earthquake in July 1975, reported that restoration using traditional methods was well under way. Damage was particularly serious in high, isolated superstructures, especially to the finial ornamentation of the *sikhara* peaks and the tops of stupas. Deep fissures and cracks had appeared in the walls and vaults of many temples, reflecting subsidence or inclination movements. Vaulted structures such as the temples of Manuha and Mimalaung Kyaung had proved to be particularly vulnerable. The expert, in collaboration with Burmese specialists, established priorities for restoration work. Contributions for equipment were being sought.

During 1976 major earthquakes occurred in Guatemala and Italy, causing extensive damage and loss of life. Historic monuments also suffered severely. In Guatemala the highland city of Antigua (capital of the old Spanish captaincy general) reported damage to many of its monuments, including churches and the palace. Some historic monuments, preserved as ruins since the 1773 earthquake, suffered further damage including collapsed arches and wide cracks in surviving walls. In northeastern Italy, in the province of Friuli, churches, ancient fortifications, and castles were seriously damaged in historic municipalities such as Gemona, Venzone, and Collaredo di Monte Albano. It was estimated that repairs and reconstruction of surviving monuments alone might amount to $375 million.

Preservation projects for church buildings were undertaken in several countries. One of the most striking projects was the transfer of the 16th-century Church of the Virgin Mary in Most, Czech. The village of Most was located over extensive lignite (brown coal) beds, and in order to get at the seams the people of the village were moved to a new location about a kilometre away from the original site, leaving the church behind. The final decision was to move the church as a unit, in the fear that taking it apart might cause unnecessary damage. At the request of the government, a team of UNESCO experts reviewed the plans prepared by Czechoslovak engineers. A reinforced-concrete cradle was built about the church (the bell tower was dismantled and transferred separately), and within the nave a system of steel braces was installed. It was then mounted onto four cars running upon four sets of steel rails, with motive power furnished by computer-controlled hydraulic jacks to inch the church toward the new site of the village.

In England a campaign was under way to raise £3.5 million to finance the restoration of Canterbury Cathedral. Humidity, atmospheric pollution, and damage suffered during World War II were underlying causes for the deterioration of the stone fabric and the famed 13th-century stained glass windows. The Bell Harry Tower had suffered erosion of the stone facing, and the roofs of the nave, choir, and transepts had to be repaired. After cleaning and treatment the stained glass was to be protected from dampness with a glass sheath and the humidity controlled by a steady flow of warm air.

In Moscow the Soviet government was restoring many church buildings no longer used for religious purposes. The Novospassky Monastery on the Moscow River was among them; it also served as the centre for all state-supported restoration work. A 15th-century cupola was restored and its crumbling walls shored.

KEYSTONE

Egyptian engineers set to work designing concrete foundations for the twin statues of the pharaoh Amenhotep III near Luxor. After 3,000 years the statues are threatened by a rising water table from the Aswan High Dam. Photo shows only one statue.

In The Netherlands, Amsterdam's Ronde Kerk in the 17th-century herring packers' quarter, which had been deconsecrated in 1935 but still served as a landmark, was restored. An adjacent block of houses had been converted into a modern hotel, and the church's restoration and conversion were undertaken by the hotel owners, with the aid of grants, to serve as a cultural and convention centre.

In the U.S. the bicentennial celebrations reinforced movements to preserve the historic ambiance of the central cores of cities throughout the country. Inevitably this was particularly noticeable among those cities that had played a leading role in the Revolution. In Philadelphia the National Park Service undertook the restoration of Franklin Court, a site including five buildings three of which were designed by Benjamin Franklin. Elsewhere, the Philadelphia Museum of Art undertook a major renovation program including refurbishing of more than 50 period rooms, while many homes of historic and architectural interest were opened to the public.

Changes in the ecology of cities because of modern construction practices continued to affect older centres. A recent example of this problem was to be found in Copenhagen, where much of the city had been built on land reclaimed from the sea into which timber piles were driven to support the foundations of buildings. As in Venice, the piles retained their ability to support the load while the water table was high. But excavations for new buildings, improved sewer and storm drain systems, and the replacement of cobblestone pavements by concrete and asphalt had resulted in lowering Copenhagen's water table and weakening the wooden piles. The Royal Theatre, home of the Royal Danish Ballet, had already required extensive repairs to its foundations, and Amalienborg Palace was among many other buildings threatened with foundation problems.

The tendency to restore was gradually increasing in importance. Among the most recent examples was the decision to restore the Café de la Paix (Place de l'Opéra), one of the most famous sidewalk restaurants of Paris, to its original appearance as built during the Belle Époque in 1872. The sidewalk part of the café was glassed in with curved glass and the furniture included bentwood and cane chairs. The interior of the Restaurant Opéra was redecorated in pale blue to match the painted ceiling, and Louis XVI chairs were installed. Many of the old fixtures, which were found stored in the basement, were restored and placed within the restaurant. (HIROSHI DAIFUKU)

See also Architecture; Environment; Museums.
[612.C.2.d]

Honduras

A republic of Central America, Honduras is bounded by Nicaragua, El Salvador, Guatemala, the Caribbean Sea, and the Pacific Ocean. Area: 43,277 sq mi (112,088 sq km). Pop. (1975 est.): 2,982,000, including 90% mestizo. Cap. and largest city: Tegucigalpa (pop., 1974, 270,600). Language: Spanish; some Indian dialects. Religion: Roman Catholic. President in 1976, Col. Juan Alberto Melgar Castro.

Prospects for a definitive peace settlement with El Salvador brightened with the signing on October 6 of an agreement providing for a mediated settlement of the long-standing differences between the two countries. The signing took place in the headquarters of the Organization of American States, which had sent observers to patrol the border following armed clashes in July and assisted with the negotiations.

HONDURAS

Education. (1974) Primary, pupils 442,668, teachers 12,302; secondary and vocational, pupils 59,451, teachers 3,093; teacher training, students 2,685, teachers 91; higher (university only), students 9,226, teaching staff 617.

Finance. Monetary unit: lempira, with (Sept. 20, 1976) a par value of 2 lempiras to U.S. $1 (free rate of 3.45 lempiras = £1 sterling). Gold, SDR's, and foreign exchange (June 1976) U.S. $130,010,000. Budget (1975 actual): revenue 271.9 million lempiras; expenditure 320.1 million lempiras. Gross national product (1975) 1,948,000,000 lempiras. Money supply (May 1976) 326.5 million lempiras. Cost of living (Tegucigalpa; 1970 = 100; August 1976) 143.8.

Foreign Trade. (1975) Imports 800.1 million lempiras; exports 566.6 million lempiras. Import sources (1974): U.S. 40%; Venezuela 13%; West Germany *c.* 11%; Japan 7%; Guatemala 6%. Export destinations (1974): U.S. 44%; West Germany 12%; Canada *c.* 5%. Main exports: coffee 20%; bananas 16%; timber 14%; lead and zinc (1974) 7%; meat (1974) 7%; petroleum products 6%; silver 5%.

Transport and Communications. Roads (1973) 5,943 km (including *c.* 150 km of Pan-American Highway). Motor vehicles in use (1974): passenger *c.* 14,700; commercial (including buses) 22,900. Railways (1974) *c.* 990 km. Air traffic (1974): 226 million passenger-km; freight 2.7 million net ton-km. Shipping (1975): merchant vessels 100 gross tons and over 60; gross tonnage 67,923. Telephones (Jan. 1975) 14,984. Radio receivers (Dec. 1973) 155,000. Television receivers (Dec. 1973) *c.* 60,000.

Agriculture. Production (in 000; metric tons; 1975): corn *c.* 220; cassava (1974) *c.* 40; coffee *c.* 51; sorghum *c.* 38; sugar, raw value (1974) *c.* 89; dry beans *c.* 48; bananas (1974) 1,360; oranges (1974) *c.* 45; cotton, lint (1974) *c.* 5; beef and veal (1974) *c.* 47; timber (cu m, 1974) *c.* 4,434. Livestock (in 000; 1974): cattle *c.* 1,657; pigs 511; horses *c.* 280; chickens *c.* 7,700.

Industry. Production (in 000; metric tons; 1974): petroleum products *c.* 630; silver 0.1; gold (troy oz) 2.1; lead ore (metal content) 20: zinc ore (metal content) 21; electricity (kw-hr) 460,000.

The military government created an advisory council, with representatives from all segments of society, to draft an electoral law that would govern a general election which President Melgar Castro said could not be anticipated until 1979. Labour unions and liberal forces supported the creation of the council and the election date. Conservative elements, including the two major political parties, opposed both.

Movement in the government's land-reform program included expropriation of a few parcels of land for distribution to the peasantry. This satisfied neither the latter, who pressed for accelerated action, nor the property owners, who were alarmed at the general trend.

Transfer of the properties of two United States-owned banana corporations, United Brands and Standard Fruit, to Honduran government ownership proceeded harmoniously. Active company participation in management operations continued.

The February 4 earthquake that caused extensive damage in Guatemala was also felt in Honduras, where the towns of Santa Bárbara and Santa Rosa de Copán near the Guatemalan border were destroyed and some damage occurred in San Pedro Sula, where 29 houses were reported to have collapsed, and in Puerto Cortés. (HENRY WEBB, JR.)

[974.B.1.b]

Hungary

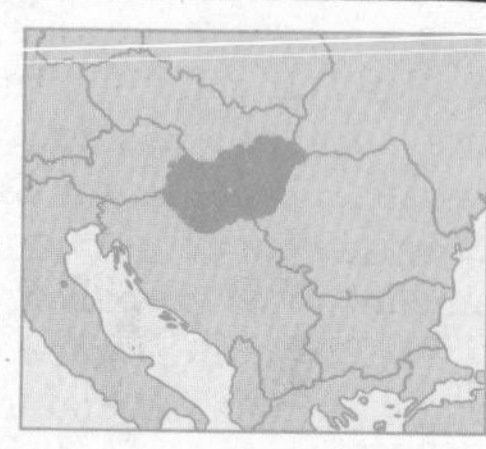

A people's republic of central Europe, Hungary is bordered by Czechoslovakia, the U.S.S.R., Romania, Yugoslavia, and Austria. Area: 35,920 sq mi (93,032 sq km). Pop. (1976 est.): 10,572,000, including (1970) Hungarian 95.8%; German 2.1%. Cap. and largest city: Budapest (pop., 1976 est., 2,071,000). Language (1970): Magyar 95.8%. Religion (1970): Roman Catholic about 60%, most of remainder Protestant or atheist. First secretary of the Hungarian Socialist Workers' (Communist) Party in 1976, Janos Kadar; chairman of the Presidential Council (chief of state), Pal Losonczi; president of the Council of Ministers (premier), Gyorgy Lazar.

Legislation governing the development of Hungary's economy during the years 1976–80 was passed by Parliament in December 1975, when proposals for the fifth five-year plan were presented by Deputy Premier Istvan Huszar. Reviewing the growth of the national economy during the 1971–75 period, Huszar stressed that all the main targets had been achieved despite the adverse effects on Hungary's trade of "the crisis in the capitalist world." In that period the national income had risen yearly by 6.3% instead of the planned 5.5%; the average annual rate of increase in industrial output was 6.6%, as against the expected 6%; and agricultural production had risen by 3.5% instead of the planned 2.8%. Foreign trade, calculated at constant prices, had risen by more than 60% instead of the planned 45%. Exports accounted for 50% of the national income in 1975, compared with 36% five years earlier.

Under the 1976–80 plan Hungary's national income was scheduled to rise by 30–32%, industrial production by 33–35%, and agricultural output by 16–18%. But Huszar warned that domestic spending was in excess of the available national income, that the defi-

Hockey:
see Field Hockey and Lacrosse; Ice Hockey

Holland:
see Netherlands, The

Honduras, British (Belize):
see Dependent States

Hong Kong:
see Dependent States

Horse Racing:
see Equestrian Sports; Gambling

Horticulture:
see Gardening

Hospitals:
see Health and Disease

Housing:
see Architecture; Industrial Review

Hungarian Literature:
see Literature

cit in the state budget was considerable, and that the Hungarian balance of payments was in deficit. One of the necessary conditions for improving the balance in the next five years was that the rate of increase in domestic spending should be lower than the planned increase in the national income.

Parliament adopted a new National Defense Bill on March 10, 1976. Presenting the bill, Col. Gen. Lajos Czinege, the minister of defense, defined the fundamental aims of Hungary's defense policy as safeguarding the peace and independence of the country and enabling it to fulfill its international commitments under the Warsaw Treaty alliance. Under the new legislation national service was cut to 24 months instead of 36, and the age limit for military service was raised from 50 to 55, except in the case of professional officers. Women were liable for military service in the fields of health and communications, but only in the event of war; the age limit was 45.

The government announced on July 4 that meat and fish prices would rise by 30% and poultry prices by 20%. The increases were necessary, it was explained, because between 1973 and 1975 food subsidies had climbed from a few billion forints to 30 billion forints ($1.4 billion at the official rate of exchange). The bitter but not unexpected news was accompanied by wage and pension increases: from July all employees were to receive a monthly supplement of 60 forints, and pensions went up by the same amount.

ANTAL MANEK—CAMERA PRESS / PHOTO TRENDS

A Hungarian photographer made this prizewinning study of an apartment development in Diosgyor in central Hungary. The architects had tried to avoid creating another urban jungle.

HUNGARY

Education. (1975–76) Primary, pupils 1,051,095, teachers 66,861; secondary, pupils 99,656, teachers 6,663; vocational, pupils 107,661; teacher training, students 3,159; vocational and teacher training, teachers 7,751; higher (including 18 universities), students 61,160, teaching staff 11,799.

Finance. Monetary unit: forint, with (Sept. 20, 1976) a commercial free rate of 44.78 forints to U.S. $1 (77.15 forints = £1 sterling) and a noncommercial (tourist) rate of 20.44 forints to U.S. $1 (38.57 forints = £1 sterling). Budget (1975 est.): revenue 318,488,-000,000 forints; expenditure 323,418,000,000 forints.

Foreign Trade. (1975) Imports 61,537,000,000 forints; exports 52,170,000,000 forints. Import sources: U.S.S.R. 35%; East Germany 10%; Czechoslovakia 7%; West Germany 7%; Poland 5%. Export destinations: U.S.S.R. 39%; East Germany 11%; Czechoslovakia 8%; West Germany 5%; Poland 5%. Main exports: machinery 24%; transport equipment 13%; chemicals 7%; fruits and vegetables 6%; meat and meat preparations 5%; iron and steel 5%.

Transport and Communications. Roads (1974) 100,577 km (including 158 km expressways). Motor vehicles in use (1974): passenger 490,760; commercial 107,163. Railways: (1974) 8,379 km; traffic (1975) 13,686,000,000 passenger-km, freight 22,961,-000,000 net ton-km. Air traffic (1974): 558 million passenger-km; freight 6.2 million net ton-km. Inland waterways in regular use (1975) 1,302 km. Telephones (Dec. 1974) 1,013,731. Radio licenses (Dec. 1975) 2,538,000. Television licenses (Dec. 1975) 2,390,000.

Agriculture. Production (in 000; metric tons; 1975): corn *c.* 7,100; wheat 4,084; rye *c.* 171; barley *c.* 735; potatoes *c.* 1,670; sugar, raw value *c.* 331; cabbages (1974) *c.* 200; tomatoes *c.* 401; onions *c.* 183; rapeseed *c.* 67; sunflower seed *c.* 149; green peas (1974) *c.* 197; dry peas *c.* 113; peaches (1974) *c.* 147; plums (1974) *c.* 200; apples (1974) *c.* 800; wine (1974) *c.* 430; tobacco *c.* 18; milk *c.* 2,111; beef and veal (1974) *c.* 199; pork (1974) *c.* 515. Livestock (in 000; March 1975): cattle 2,017; pigs 8,293; sheep 2,021; horses (1974) 172; chickens 54,329.

Industry. Index of production (1970 = 100; 1975) 136. Production (in 000; metric tons; 1975): coal 3,020; lignite 21,868; crude oil 2,005; natural gas (cu m) 5,175,000; electricity (kw-hr) 20,457,000; iron ore (25% metal content) 642; pig iron 2,220; crude steel 3,672; bauxite 2,890; aluminum 70; cement 3,760; petroleum products (1974) 8,410; sulfuric acid 630; fertilizers (1974–75) nitrogenous 416, phosphate 199; cotton yarn 6; wool yarn 10; commercial vehicles (units) 13.

According to an agreement announced on April 1 by Jozsef Biro, the Hungarian minister of foreign trade, the U.S.S.R. would provide Hungary with additional crude oil and other raw materials over the next five years in return for Hungarian beef and grain.

Premier Lazar paid a four-day official visit to France in June and another to Poland in August. Oskar Fischer, the new East German foreign minister, visited Budapest in June.

On February 12 it was announced from the Vatican that Pope Paul VI had appointed Bishop Laszlo Lekai as archbishop metropolitan of Esztergom, from 1452 the see of Hungarian primates. Msgr. Lekai was enthroned on February 24 at a ceremony attended by many Hungarian bishops, Franz Cardinal König, archbishop of Vienna, and Imre Miklos, head of the Hungarian State Committee for Church Affairs. This appointment put an end to a painful situation that had been created by the arrest of Jozsef Cardinal Mindszenty in December 1948. For 27 years the primatial see had had no resident archbishop, and only in February 1974 was the pope able to appoint Msgr. Lekai as apostolic administrator of the archdiocese of Esztergom. On May 24 Archbishop Lekai was made a cardinal.

The 20th anniversary of the Hungarian popular uprising of Oct. 23, 1956, saw the appearance in other countries of newspaper articles and books reflecting upon that outbreak and its swift suppression.

(K. M. SMOGORZEWSKI)

[972.B.2.b]

Hunting and Fishing

Game Shooting. Despite such factors as dwindling habitats, antihunting sentiment, and increasingly complex regulations, the sport of hunting appeared to be growing in North America and at least holding stable in much of the rest of the world. In the United States the number of hunting licenses, permits, tags, and stamps sold during 1976 was expected to surpass 26 million for the first time ever. In Britain 600,000 shotgun permits plus more than 300,000 authorized users of rifles indicated growth of the sport there.

Wheat sales to the U.S.S.R. by the U.S. and Canada could have a substantial effect on waterfowl populations. Enormous tonnages contracted for during 1976 would stimulate additional destruction of nesting habitats in Canada. Another waterfowl development was the implementation of a federal law requiring the use of steel shot for waterfowl hunting in parts of nine of the eastern United States. The restriction was aimed at reducing lead poisoning of ducks and geese.

Declines in the populations of two U.S. big-game species were particularly notable during 1976. The decline in mule deer in the western states was blamed variously on habitat deterioration, excessive predation, and overhunting. Several states initiated research projects to pinpoint the cause and reverse the situation. The other serious decline involved Alaska's northern caribou herd, which by 1976 had dwindled to about 50,000 from a high of several hundred thousand. The Alaska pipeline and subsistence hunting were thought to be major factors. On the other hand, the range of the wild turkey in the U.S. was spreading rapidly, thanks largely to stocking programs. More states than ever had huntable populations.

A landmark decision by the U.S. Supreme Court held that the U.S. Congress had the authority to regulate and protect the wildlife on federally administered public lands, state laws notwithstanding. The ruling was expected to cause widespread controversy, especially in western states.

In Europe big-game populations in general continued to increase. Efforts were being made to keep the numbers of animals down to a level the habitat could support. Goals were a relatively high harvest of younger animals, minimal take of mature animals, and an emphasis on taking animals past their reproductive prime. Among European game animals that made a notable comeback during 1976 were the ibex and the brant. Species declining in some areas included the black grouse and the capercaillie. The gray partridge made a surprising resurgence in the U.K. after being a rarity for two decades. Deerstalking, with the red stag the quarry, flourished in Scotland.

(WILLIAM R. ROONEY; WILSON STEPHENS)

Safaris. Africa continued to be the scene of many political developments that affected big-game hunting. Some of the newly independent countries banned hunting altogether, and many others enacted stringent regulations affecting the range and scope of game that could be hunted. Some of the most important reasons behind this new development included increasing worldwide antihunting sentiment, the growing pressure of human population on the traditional habitats of wild game, and the actual decrease of many species. These developments led to the formation of the Convention on International Trade in Endangered Species of Wild Fauna and Flora. No nation that is party to the convention can allow trade in specimens of species listed as being threatened with extinction.

The traditional hunting countries have been those of eastern, central, and southern Africa. Of those, only Zambia in 1976 allowed the taking of all five of the most coveted trophies, the elephant, lion, leopard, buffalo, and rhinoceros. Hunting on a somewhat limited scale was still possible in Sudan, Ethiopia, Kenya, Uganda, Central African Empire, Cameroon, Gabon, Botswana, Rhodesia, South Africa, and South West Africa (Namibia). Countries that imposed a complete ban on hunting were Somalia, Tanzania, Chad, Mozambique, Angola, and Zaire.

In India tigers increased to the extent that there were huntable populations. There was as yet no open season, however.

(ERNEST PAUL PROSSNITZ)

Fox Hunting. More accurately known as riding to hounds, fox hunting was under some pressure during the year in Britain. Though the readiness of farmers and landowners to allow others to ride over their land was undiminished, there were inevitable reservations about the numbers currently availing themselves of the opportunity. In 1976 there were 242 packs of hounds in Great Britain operating on an average of three days a week with an average of 70–80 mounted followers each, rising to hundreds on Saturdays. During a wet season the effect of riding to hounds on cultivated land was a cause for anxiety that increased as the numbers grew. In addition, there were 89 packs of beagles and basset hounds in the U.K. for hunting hares with followers on foot. Riding to hounds continued to be practiced in the U.S., with most hunt clubs located on the edges of large metropolitan areas.

Adverse pressure on ideological grounds had been directed against hunting in Britain uninterruptedly for two centuries. During 1975–76 it was again evident but not unusually strong. Hare coursing, in which two greyhounds at a time are judged against each other in pursuit of a hare that is given a long start, had long attracted considerable antipathy from non-participants, and four bills to prohibit it had been introduced into Parliament. The last went far enough before it failed for a Select Committee of the Upper House to be given the task of establishing what the sport in fact involved, as distinct from what its critics said it involved. Following the committee's report, the sport continued.

(WILSON STEPHENS)

Angling. Though maintaining a lower profile than such glamour sports as skiing or tennis, angling in the U.S. rivaled the former two activities combined in number of participants. Despite a softness in many areas of the economy, manufacturers of fishing tackle reported an excellent year and looked forward to continued gains in 1977.

In 1976 there was considerable interest in battling large fish on light lines. Tarpon of 79 lb 4 oz and 92 lb 13 oz set new men's and women's records, respectively, for 6-lb test lines. Records for various classes (tests) of line were beginning to be kept for freshwater species, and many entries were expected.

Aerospace programs plus continuing research were responsible for the increasing sophistication of fishing

The leader (left) of this band of desert bighorn sheep in the mountains of Arizona is believed to have the world's longest horns. An Arizona rancher stirred controversy when he offered $10,000 for the right to hunt the animal.

WIDE WORLD

tackle. Improved fibreglass, carbon filaments, and composites of the two found their way into rod construction. Electronics miniaturization and improvement nurtured an industry devoted to electronic aids for angling.

A continued upswing in popularity of inland warm water species, especially the largemouth bass, resulted in great pressure on some of those fish. Results, however, were not entirely negative. Increased fish studies were forthcoming, including a trend to telemetry. The latter involved the implanting of miniature transmitters into living fish, which were then tracked by researchers. New information, especially concerning bass, was gained as a result of this work.

The suspense novel and motion picture *Jaws* resulted in a sudden upsurge in sport fishing for sharks. Some anglers became interested in tagging sharks for science, which produced considerable data regarding shark movements and habits.

The worst drought in years occurred in Europe during 1976, and it affected angling, especially in the British Isles. Ireland's Atlantic salmon stocks were unable to swim upstream due to the low water. On the Hampshire Avon in England trucks were used to transport salmon downstream, there being insufficient water for them to swim.

Atlantic salmon restoration efforts continued in the Connecticut River despite setbacks involving the death of a 40-in fish that had survived a return to the river and was scheduled for breeding in autumn. Biologists were attempting to develop a strain of Atlantics that would show a preference for the Connecticut River. International action to control the netting of Atlantic salmon on the high seas continued.

On June 27 Robert Stahl caught a 52½-lb striped bass upriver from Lake Havasu, Arizona. It was believed the largest ever taken of striped bass that had spent their entire lifetimes in a completely landlocked body of water.

Chemical pollution continued to plague many of the world's waters, but in some areas there was a happy turnabout. The use of DDT around the shores of Maine's Lake Sebago had caused the collapse of the smelt population, which in turn resulted in a decline of landlocked salmon stocks. A ten-year cessation in the use of the pesticide resulted in the return to nearly normal levels of both species.

(JERRY GIBBS; WILSON STEPHENS)

[452/B.5.b–c; 731.D]

Ice Hockey

North American. While the brutality of some teams made headlines, fans also saw an elevation of style during the 1975–76 season in North American ice hockey. With devastating power the Montreal Canadiens swept the National Hockey League's Stanley Cup away from the two-time defending champions, the Philadelphia Flyers, by beating them in four straight games. In three play-off rounds the Canadiens lost just one game.

Scotty Bowman, the Canadiens' coach, had strengthened the defense of the "Flying Frenchmen" and produced a team that had the fewest goals scored against it in the NHL. In the regular 80-game season Montreal lost only 11 games.

In the World Hockey Association a similar team of swift-skating players, ten of them from Europe, won the Avco World Trophy. The Winnipeg Jets, rallying around the irrepressible 37-year-old Bobby Hull, defeated the defending champion Houston Aeros in four straight games.

WIDE WORLD

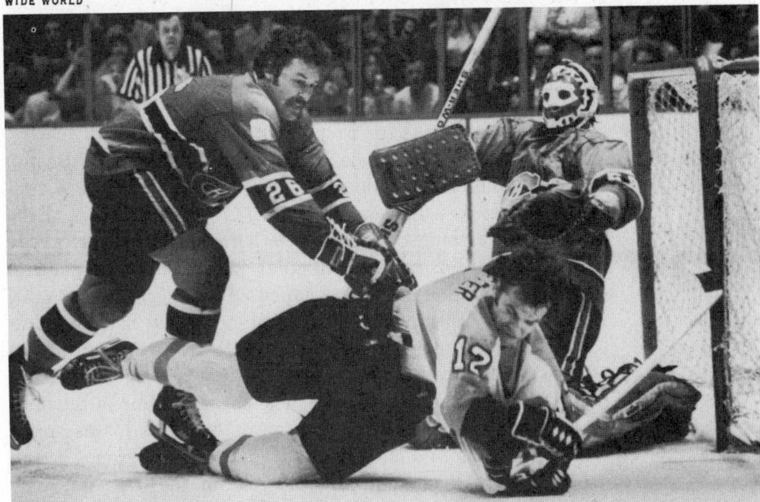

Gary Dornhoefer (12) of the Philadelphia Flyers hits the ice after trying for a goal and Pierre Bouchard (26) of the Montreal Canadiens plows into him during Stanley Cup play in May. Defending the goal is Ken Dryden. Montreal swept the final series of the ice hockey championship 4–0.

Both leagues' play-off series were marred by violent incidents that spurred legal action by civil authorities. In a game on April 11 Rick Jodzio of the Calgary Cowboys went after Marc Tardif of the Quebec Nordiques and felled the WHA's highest scorer and most valuable player of the season. Both team benches emptied for an all-out brawl. Tardif spent the summer recovering from brain contusions but was able to play in the new season. Jodzio was charged with assault with intent to injure, and along with his coach, Joe Crozier, was suspended indefinitely by the WHA.

In an explosive quarterfinal NHL play-off game with the Toronto Maple Leafs, the Philadelphia Flyers, incited by the crowd, attacked both players and spectators. Joe Watson, Mel Bridgman, and Don Saleski of the Flyers were charged with various degrees of assault. Earlier in the season, also in Maple Leaf Gardens, Dan Maloney of Detroit had knocked Brian Glennie's head against the ice but subsequently was acquitted of charges of assault.

The best hockey of the year, besides the artistry of the Winnipeg and Montreal teams, came in the Canada Cup, a six-team international tournament that for the first time brought together the world's best professionals and amateurs. The tournament, engineered by Alan Eagleson and located in six North American cities, opened the door for further international competition involving North American professionals.

The predictable winner of the Canada Cup was the all-star Team Canada, which with little exertion won the final from Czechoslovakia by taking the first two games of the three-game series. Other participants in the tournament were Finland, Sweden, the Soviet Union, and the United States. North American professional players were eligible to play for the country of either their birth or citizenship.

In January two Soviet club teams played an eight-game series with eight different NHL clubs. The Soviets lost only two games, to Buffalo and Philadelphia. After ten minutes in the Philadelphia Spectrum the Soviet Central Army team walked off the ice in protest against the Flyers' rough tactics, but returned eventually to lose 4–1.

In addition to the outstanding hockey of the tournament, Canada Cup fans were cheered to see Bobby Orr (*see* BIOGRAPHY) back in action after a fifth operation

Hurricanes: *see* Disasters; Earth Sciences

Hydroelectric Power: *see* Energy; Engineering Projects

Hydrology: *see* Earth Sciences

Ice Boating: *see* Winter Sports

on his left knee. The stellar defenseman had not played a game since November 1975. Over the summer, however, without testing his knee, Orr was able to negotiate a blockbuster contract with the Chicago Black Hawks for a reported $3 million over five years. As a free agent he had chosen to leave the Boston Bruins after a decade with them. The Chicago contract was remarkable in that Orr was guaranteed the full amount of money whether or not he ever played again. Boston had balked at such a guarantee, and so negotiations there had failed.

In other player movements virtually half the New York Rangers were traded followed by the firing of Emile Francis, who had been the team's general manager-coach for 12 years. The changes came in the midpoint of a disastrous season of spiritless losses, many of them by more than five goals.

The man with the best year in the NHL was Guy Lafleur of Montreal, the scoring champion, who had 56 goals and 69 assists. Bobby Clarke of Philadelphia was the league's most valuable player. The rookie-of-the-year award went to Bryan Trottier of the New York Islanders, while his teammate, Denis Potvin, was named the best defenseman. Ken Dryden of Montreal won the Vezina Trophy as the league's outstanding goalkeeper, and Jean Ratelle of Boston was awarded the Lady Byng Memorial Trophy for ability combined with sportsmanship. In the WHA Paul Shmyr of Cleveland was named the top defenseman, while Mark Napier of Toronto was rookie of the year.

The WHA was relatively stable in its fourth year of existence, losing its Minnesota and Denver franchises to economic troubles. At the season's end the Toronto Toros moved to Alabama and became the Birmingham Bulls. A Minnesota franchise was reestablished with the relocation of the Cleveland team. A basic realignment blending the Canadian division into the East and West divisions simplified the 12-team lineup for the 1976–77 season.

The NHL did not expand, but two franchises moved. The California Golden Seals relocated in Cleveland, and the Kansas City Scouts found new owners and became the Colorado Rockies of Denver.

In the minor leagues Nova Scotia won the American Hockey League championship, beating Hershey four games to one in the best-of-seven series. The Central Hockey League championship went to Tulsa, which completed the best-of-seven series in five games to defeat Dallas. Dayton beat Port Huron in four straight games to win in the International Hockey League, while Philadelphia beat Beauce four games to two for the North American Hockey League title. In the Southern Hockey League Charlotte defeated Hampton four games to one, while Milwaukee won a best-of-five series with Green Bay, 3–0, to capture the United States Hockey League championship.

(ROBIN CATHY HERMAN)

Table I. NHL Final Standings, 1975–76

	Won	Lost	Tied	Goals	Goals against	Pts.
Prince of Wales Conference						
JAMES NORRIS DIVISION						
Montreal	58	11	11	337	174	127
Los Angeles	38	33	9	263	265	85
Pittsburgh	35	33	12	339	303	82
Detroit	26	44	10	226	300	62
Washington	11	59	10	224	394	32
CHARLES F. ADAMS DIVISION						
Boston	48	15	17	313	237	113
Buffalo	46	21	13	339	240	105
Toronto	34	31	15	294	276	83
California	27	42	11	250	278	65
Clarence Campbell Conference						
LESTER PATRICK DIVISION						
Philadelphia	51	13	16	348	209	118
New York Islanders	42	21	17	297	190	101
Atlanta	35	33	12	262	237	82
New York Rangers	29	42	9	262	333	67
CONN SMYTHE DIVISION						
Chicago	32	30	18	254	261	82
Vancouver	33	32	15	271	272	81
St. Louis	29	37	14	249	290	72
Minnesota	20	53	7	195	303	47
Kansas City	12	56	12	190	351	36

CANADIAN PRESS

Bobby Clarke (16) routes a Bobby Hull rebound through the legs of Czechoslovak goalie Vladimir Dzurilla to tie the final game of the Canada Cup in September. Team Canada beat Czechoslovakia in overtime. Other players shown are Bill Barber (17) of Team Canada and Milan Kajki (17) of Czechoslovakia.

European and International. The continuing expansion of ice hockey during 1976 was particularly pronounced in the six nations that had the sport's biggest following. It was estimated that nearly one million Canadians took part in the game at some level. The U.S.S.R. had over 600,000 registered players; the U.S. 250,000; Sweden 200,000; Czechoslovakia 55,000; and Finland 53,000. Despite the limited ice time in Britain, owing to the heavy demands of skating and curling, the number of players exceeded 1,000 for the first time. Areas newly developing the sport included New Zealand, where the first national championships were held, and Singapore.

An important lessening of friction regarding amateur and professional status was widely accepted to be in the game's best long-term interests. Early-season challenge matches in North America between top Soviet clubs and U.S. and Canadian NHL teams suggested no great difference in ability between the world's top professionals and players who had been the cream of so-called amateur events. But a general agreement that maintenance of amateur status at the highest level of the sport was no longer desirable or workable did not bring about the long-projected European League for senior professional club teams, a seemingly inevitable development still hampered by unresolved financial problems.

The 43rd world championships, contested in three groups by 21 nations during March and April, were the first to be thrown open to professionals and the second in an Olympic year to be held separately from the Winter Games, for which some of the players would have been ineligible. Sweden, Finland, and the U.S. took most advantage of the new rules, which inspired an assurance from the still-absent Canada that it would reenter the tournament in 1977 after a break of seven years.

The eight title contenders competed in Group A at Katowice, Poland. Undefeated throughout, Czechoslovakia decisively recaptured the title it had last won in 1972, to become for the second time the only nation

Table II. WHA Final Standings, 1975–76

	Won	Lost	Tied	Goals	Goals against	Pts.
CANADIAN DIVISION						
Winnipeg	52	27	2	345	254	106
Quebec	50	27	4	371	316	104
Calgary	41	35	4	307	282	86
Edmonton	27	49	5	268	345	59
Toronto	24	52	5	335	398	53
EASTERN DIVISION						
Indianapolis	35	39	6	245	247	76
Cleveland	35	40	5	273	279	75
New England	33	40	7	255	290	73
Cincinnati	35	44	1	285	340	71
WESTERN DIVISION						
Houston	53	27	0	341	263	106
Phoenix	39	35	6	302	287	84
San Diego	36	38	6	303	290	78
Minnesota*	30	25	4	211	212	64
Denver-Ottawa*	14	26	1	134	172	29

*Withdrew from league.

to depose the U.S.S.R. in 14 years. It was the fourth Czechoslovakian victory since the event began in 1920. The competition was in two stages. After facing each other once, the top four and bottom four teams formed two sections and played three more games apiece. The Czechoslovakians took three points from their two encounters with the defending champion U.S.S.R. The Soviets also lost to Poland and Sweden and, despite finishing second, registered probably their least impressive performance since 1961. Third-place Sweden finished a point behind. The U.S. team, which finished fourth, included nine professionals. In the closely fought second section, Finland and West Germany only headed Poland by having better goal averages. Poland and East Germany were relegated to Group B for 1977, their places to be taken by Canada, in view of its obvious strength and past record, and Romania. The three top scorers in Group A, each with nine goals, were all Czechoslovakian forwards: Vladimir Martinec, Jiri Novak, and Milan Novy. The most points were obtained by Martinec, with 20 from his 9 goals and 11 assists. Jiri Holecek was outstanding in the Czechoslovakian goal. The best defenders were Frantisek Pospisil, the Czechoslovakian captain, and Mats Waltin of Sweden.

Romania topped the eight teams in Group B at Aarau and Biel, Switz., to qualify for its first entry into Class A. Norway, Switzerland, and Yugoslavia, third, fourth, and fifth, were split only by goal average

Table III. World Ice Hockey Championships, 1976

	Won	Lost	Tied	Goals	Goals against	Pts.
GROUP A SECTION 1						
Czechoslovakia	9	0	1	67	14	19
U.S.S.R.	6	3	1	50	23	13
Sweden	6	4	0	36	29	12
United States	3	6	1	24	42	7
GROUP A Section 2						
Finland	2	4	4	35	41	8
West Germany	3	5	2	26	41	8
Poland	3	5	2	32	47	8
East Germany	2	7	1	19	52	5
GROUP B						
Romania	5	1	1	40	33	11
Japan	5	2	0	34	17	10
Norway	4	3	0	29	21	8
Switzerland	4	3	0	25	28	8
Yugoslavia	4	3	0	37	26	8
Netherlands, The	3	4	0	22	30	6
Italy	2	4	1	23	41	5
Bulgaria	0	7	0	23	47	0
GROUP C						
Austria	4	0	0	38	9	8
Hungary	3	1	0	30	9	6
France	2	2	0	14	18	4
Denmark	1	3	0	16	24	2
Great Britain	0	4	0	6	44	0

(of scores in games between the three). The two bottom teams, Italy and Bulgaria, were relegated to Group C, to be replaced by Austria and Hungary, first and second in that division. Returning after an absence of two years, Britain failed to win a game but gained the Fair Play Cup as the nation least penalized for infringements.

The international club competition for the Ahearne Cup, at Stockholm in January, was won for the second time running by Dynamo Moscow of the U.S.S.R., with maximum points. Sparta Prague of Czechoslovakia was again runner-up. The Allan Cup, contested by U.S. and Canadian clubs, was won for a third time by the Spokane Flyers of the Western International Hockey League, who defeated the Ontario Senior Hockey League team, Barrie Flyers, 4–0 in the best-of-seven play-off. (HOWARD BASS)

See also Winter Sports: *Special Report.*
[452.B.4.h.xviii]

Iceland

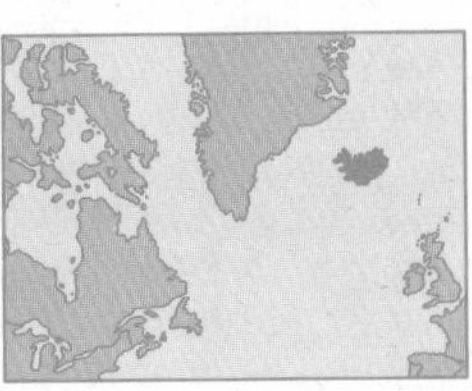

Iceland is an island republic in the North Atlantic Ocean, near the Arctic Circle. Area: 39,769 sq mi (103,000 sq km). Pop. (1976 est.): 219,000. Cap. and largest city: Reykjavik (pop., 1975 est., 84,900). Language: Icelandic. Religion: 97% Lutheran. President in 1976, Kristjan Eldjarn; prime minister, Geir Hallgrimsson.

In 1976 Iceland's efforts to conserve fishing resources took on a new and more serious form. The nation had extended its fishing limit to 200 mi on Oct. 15, 1975, but the extension was not recognized by the two principal nations affected, the United Kingdom and West Germany. An agreement on fishing concessions with the U.K. was in effect at the time of the extension and was not affected until it expired in November 1975, after which began the third and most serious "cod war" between the two countries. The conflict was marked by numerous collisions between British naval vessels and Icelandic coast-guard boats, some of them serious but without the loss of any lives.

A new interim agreement was concluded with the U.K. on June 1, 1976. It allowed an average of 24 British trawlers to fish within the 200-mi limit on each day and was to cover the period up to Dec. 1, 1976. As no further agreement was reached, British trawlers then withdrew from Icelandic waters. The fishing agreement with West Germany, which was made in November 1975, was to run for two years and would expire in December 1977. In conjunction with the fishing settlement with the U.K., a set of important tariff concessions from the European Economic Community (EEC) for fish products became effective for Iceland.

Iceland's apprehension over the state of its fish stock was heightened by a government research report published in late 1975. It concluded that the principal bottom-feeding species, including cod and haddock, were overexploited and that catches should be sharply reduced. This meant that not only would Iceland have to seek all means to divert foreign fishing fleets out of Icelandic waters, but also that it would have to reduce the catches of its own fleet. The government did not come to grips with this issue during the year, instituting only minor limitations on domestic fish catches. The EEC's adoption of a common 200-mi fishing limit, to become effective Jan. 1, 1977, imposed new problems, as it would exclude Icelandic vessels from rich waters to which they currently had access.

After two years of recession and high deficits on the current account of the balance of payments, the Icelandic economy began slowly to turn the corner toward expansion in early 1976. The terms of foreign trade improved by about 11% in 1976 after a deterioration of 24% during the previous two years.

Because Iceland exported about 40% of its gross national product, the sharp swings in foreign prices had a paramount importance for the development of domestic production. Real national income declined by 6.5% in 1975 and continued to decline into early 1976, after which it made a modest recovery. For 1976 as a whole, real national income improved by about 2.5%.

The balance of payments improved sharply in 1976, following record deficits of $155 million and $140 million, respectively, in 1974 and 1975. The current account deficit for 1976 was cut by at least one-half, probably declining to $60 million–$65 million for the year as a whole.

Construction work on the 150-Mw hydroelectric plant at Sigalda was continued in 1976, and the plant was brought close to completion by the end of the year. The construction of the Krafla geothermal electric plant ran into difficulties, as earthquakes disturbed the steam field in the course of 1976 and delayed the drilling of adequate holes to bring energy to the plant.

An agreement was concluded between Elkem Spigerverket A/S and the Icelandic government for the former to take over the participation of Union Carbide Corp. of the U.S. in a projected 52,000-ton-per-year ferrosilicon plant.

(BJÖRN MATTHÍASSON)

[972.A.6.d.ii]

ICELAND

Education. (1973–74) Primary, pupils 27,046, teachers (including preprimary) 1,466; secondary, pupils 19,921, teachers 1,459; vocational, pupils 4,685, teachers 624; teacher training, students 87, teachers 19; higher, students 2,429, teaching staff 410.

Finance. Monetary unit: króna, with (Sept. 20, 1976) a free rate of 189.64 krónur to U.S. $1 (326.75 krónur = £1 sterling). Gold, SDR's, and foreign exchange (June 1976) U.S. $82.8 million. Budget (1975 est.): revenue 47,626,000,000 krónur; expenditure 47,266,000,000 krónur. Gross national product (1975) 185,220,000,000 krónur. Money supply (May 1976) 20,269,000,000 krónur. Cost of living (Reykjavik; 1970 = 100; May 1976) 389.

Foreign Trade. (1975) Imports 71,697,000,000 krónur; exports 47,436,000,000 krónur. Import sources: U.K. 11%; West Germany 11%; Norway 10%; U.S.S.R. 10%; Denmark 10%; U.S. 9%; The Netherlands 7%; Sweden 6%; Australia 6%. Export destinations: U.S. 29%; Portugal 12%; U.S.S.R. 11%; U.K. 10%; West Germany 6%. Main exports: fish 70%; aluminum 11%; fish meal 8%. Tourism: visitors (1972) 68,000; gross receipts (1974) U.S. $16 million.

Transport and Communications. Roads (1974) 11,206 km. Motor vehicles in use (1973): passenger 56,396; commercial 6,070. There are no railways. Air traffic (1974): 1,930,700,000 passenger-km; freight 31,155,000 net ton-km. Shipping (1975): merchant vessels 100 gross tons and over 363; gross tonnage 154,381. Telephones (Dec. 1974) 87,288. Radio licenses (Dec. 1974) 64,000. Television licenses (Dec. 1974) 50,000.

Agriculture. Production (in 000; metric tons; 1974): potatoes *c.* 6; hay *c.* 320; milk *c.* 129; mutton and lamb *c.* 14; fish catch 945. Livestock (in 000; 1974): cattle 67; sheep 846; horses 42; chickens *c.* 220.

Industry. Production (in 000): electricity (public supply only; kw-hr; 1975) 2,296,000; aluminum (metric tons; 1974) 68.

Icelandic Literature: *see* Literature

Ice Skating *see* Winter Sports

India

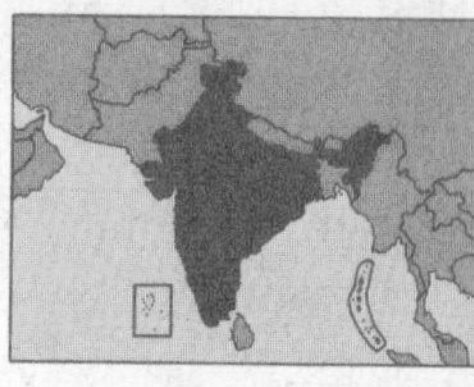

A federal republic of southern Asia and a member of the Commonwealth of Nations, India is situated on a peninsula extending into the Indian Ocean with the Arabian Sea to the west and the Bay of Bengal to the east. It is bounded (east to west) by Burma, Bangladesh, China, Bhutan, Nepal, and Pakistan; Sri Lanka lies just off its southern tip in the Indian Ocean. Area: 1,269,420 sq mi (3,287,782 sq km), including the Pakistani-controlled section of Jammu and Kashmir and Sikkim (annexed in 1975). Pop. (1976 est.): 610 million; Indo-Aryans and Dravidians are dominant, with Mongoloid, Negroid, and Australoid admixtures. Cap.: New Delhi (pop., 1971, 301,800). Largest cities: Calcutta (metro. pop., 1971, 7,031,400) and Greater Bombay (metro. pop., 1971, 5,970,600). Language: Hindi and English (official). Religion (1971): Hindu 83%; Muslim 11%; Christian 3%; Sikh 2%; Buddhist 0.7%. President in 1976, Fakhruddin Ali Ahmed; prime minister, Indira Gandhi.

The state of emergency continued throughout 1976. A comprehensive amendment of the constitution was undertaken to secure Parliament's power from judicial challenge and prevent misuse of fundamental rights. Parliament also extended its life by another year. The opposition charged that by these actions the nation's democratic institutions had been further dismantled.

The Constitution (44th Amendment) Act, intended "to spell out expressly the high ideals of socialism, secularism and the integrity of the nation, to make the directive principles more comprehensive and give them precedence over those fundamental rights which have been allowed to frustrate socio-economic reforms," broadly followed the recommendations of a committee appointed by the Congress Party, which rejected the suggestion for a changeover to the presidential form of government. A later proposal for a new constituent assembly was not followed up. The 59-clause bill, which was adopted by the Lok Sabha (lower house) on November 2 by 366 votes to 4 in a special session and later by the Rajya Sabha (upper house), amended 37 articles, inserted a new chapter and 13 new articles, and substituted 4 others. Besides placing Parliament's power to amend the constitution beyond the purview of the courts, the act stipulated that only the Supreme Court could determine the constitutional validity of central laws, provided for tribunals to hear administrative disputes, curtailed the high courts' powers to issue writs except in cases of substantial injury and failure of justice, permitted an emergency to be declared in any part of the country, fixed the normal term of the Lok Sabha and state assemblies at six years instead of five, prescribed ten fundamental duties for citizens, gave power to the union government to send troops into the states in times of disorder, and made special provisions to deal with antinational activities. The bill was supported by the Communist Party of India and the Muslim League, while the Communist Party of India (Marxist), the Jan Sangh, the Bharatiya Lok Dal, and the Opposition Congress (the old organization) boycotted the session.

Among other important legislative measures adopted by Parliament during the year were the

INDIA

Education. (1973–74) Primary, pupils 60,641,993, teachers (1970–71) 1,602,515; secondary and vocational, pupils (1971–72) 8.4 million; secondary (1970–71), teachers 523,341; higher (including 88 universities), students 2,540,000, teaching staff (1970–71) 119,000.

Finance. Monetary unit: rupee, with (Sept. 20, 1976) a free rate of Rs 9.25 to U.S. $1 (Rs 15.94 = £1 sterling). Gold, SDR's, and foreign exchange (May 1976) U.S. $2,258,000,000. Budget (central government; 1975–76 est.): revenue Rs 84,531,000,000; expenditure Rs 107,954,000,000. Gross domestic product (1973–74) Rs 525.3 billion. Money supply (March 1976) Rs 126,690,000,000. Cost of living (1970 = 100; April 1976) 157.

Foreign Trade. (1975) Imports Rs 51,343,000,000; exports Rs 36,003,000,000. Import sources (1974–75): U.S. 16%; Iran 11%; Japan 10%; U.S.S.R 9%; West Germany 7%; Saudi Arabia 7%; U.K. 5%. Export destinations (1974–75): U.S.S.R. 13%; U.S. 11%; U.K. 9%; Japan 9%; Iran 6%. Main exports (1974–75): sugar 10%; jute fabrics 9%; tea 7%; cotton fabrics 7%; iron ore 5%.

Transport and Communications. Roads (1974) 1,232,300 km (including 28,750 km main highways). Motor vehicles in use (1974): passenger 771,890; commercial 413,000. Railways: (1973) 60,149 km; traffic (1975) 134,747,000,000 passenger-km, freight 143,098,000,000 net ton-km. Air traffic (1974): 4,926,000,000 passenger-km; freight 182 million net ton-km. Shipping (1975): merchant vessels 100 gross tons and over 471; gross tonnage 3,869,187. Telephones (Dec. 1974) 1,689,530. Radio licenses (Dec. 1973) 14,034,000. Television licenses (Dec. 1973) 163,000.

Agriculture. Production (in 000; metric tons; 1975): wheat *c.* 25,800; rice *c.* 70,500; barley *c.* 2,900; corn *c.* 5,500; millet *c.* 9,600; sorghum *c.* 10,500; potatoes 6,171; cassava (1974) 6,358; sugar, raw value 5,300; sugar, noncentrifugal (1974) *c.* 8,110; chick-peas *c.* 4,055; mangoes (1974) *c.* 8,550; bananas (1974) *c.* 3,200; rapeseed *c.* 2,211; linseed *c.* 538; peanuts *c.* 6,600; tea *c.* 513; tobacco 395; cotton, lint 1,250; jute 803. Livestock (in 000; 1975): cattle *c.* 180,269; sheep *c.* 40,000; pigs *c.* 7,101; buffalo (1974) *c.* 60,000; goats (1974) *c.* 69,000; poultry *c.* 118,378.

Industry. Production (in 000; metric tons; 1975): coal 95,929; lignite 2,823; iron ore (61% metal content) 40,271; pig iron 8,543; crude steel 7,800; electricity (excluding most industrial production; kw-hr) 76,170,000; aluminum 167; cement 16,237; cotton yarn 991; woven cotton fabrics (m; 1974) 8,285,000; petroleum products (1974) *c.* 19,030; sulfuric acid 1,291; caustic soda 442; gold (troy oz; 1974) 55; manganese ore (metal content; 1974) 550.

Bonded Labour Abolition Bill and the Urban Land Ceiling and Regulation Bill (both in pursuance of the Twenty-Point Program), a bill to provide equal remuneration for men and women, another to make divorce easier, and a bill for registration of antiques and art treasures. The Code of Civil Procedure was amended. Restrictions against the press, introduced the previous year, continued. A new Prevention of Publication of Objectionable Matters Act was enacted, and the protection given to newspapers in reporting parliamentary proceedings was withdrawn. A single news agency, Samachar, was formed.

Some opposition leaders were released from detention, notably Asoka Mehta, Charan Singh, Biju Patnaik, Piloo Mody, and H. K. Mahtab. Jayaprakash Narayan, leader of the antigovernment agitation of 1974–75, continued his efforts to form a united opposition party. George Fernandes, chairman of the Socialist Party, who had evaded arrest in 1975, was apprehended in June and brought to trial in October on a charge of "hatching conspiracy to overawe government by means of criminal force." Two members of Anand Marg, a politico-religious organization, were sentenced to 17 years' imprisonment for an attempt on the life of the chief justice.

President's rule was promulgated in the state of Tamil Nadu on January 31, removing the government of the Dravida Munnetra Kazhagam. A commission was appointed to inquire into charges of corruption and misuse of power against the chief minister of the state, Muthuvel Karunanidhi. The Janata Front government in Gujarat resigned on March 12 after many of its supporters transferred their allegiance to Congress. President's rule was renewed in Nagaland and Pondicherry. The life of the Kerala assembly was extended. Syed Mir Qasim, former chief minister of Jammu and Kashmir, was inducted into the union Cabinet in June. (In December 1975 G. S. Dhillon, Bansi Lal, and P. C. Sethi had been appointed to the Cabinet on the resignation of Swaran Singh and Uma S. Dikshit.) Bansi Lal was given charge of defense and Bali R. Bhagat was elected speaker of the Lok Sabha. Shyam C. Shukla became chief minister in Madhya Pradesh, and Banarasi D. Gupta in Haryana. On January 22 president's rule was ended in Uttar Pradesh and a ministry under Narain D. Tewari installed. On December 16 president's rule was imposed in Orissa.

Two other notable developments of the year were the emergence of Sanjay Gandhi (*see* BIOGRAPHY), the prime minister's son, on the political scene, and the new impetus given to the family planning campaign. Between April and September, 3.7 million sterilizations were performed, bringing the total number of those sterilized to 22,380,000. The Maharashtra legislature adopted a bill requiring compulsory sterilization of persons with three children, but at the year's end the bill had not received presidential assent. On October 27 Prime Minister Gandhi told Parliament that there had been clashes in some places with the police on the question of sterilization but that it was not the government's intention to employ compulsion. Acharya Vinoba Bhave gave up a threat to fast from September 11 on assurances from government that it would gradually enforce a countrywide ban on slaughtering of cows.

T.S. SATYAN—CAMERA PRESS/PHOTO TRENDS

The statue of the Jain saint Gomateshwara, about 60 feet high, gets a ritual washing down every 12 years. The festival in the state of Mysore draws thousands of pilgrims.

The Economy. The economy showed confidence and thrust. Grain production (in the agricultural year July 1975 to June 1976) was a record 118 million metric tons, enabling a buffer stock of 17 million metric tons to be built up. The outlook for the coming year was hopeful, in spite of drought conditions in Kerala, Tamil Nadu, and Karnataka. Industrial production also demonstrated a marked advance, state undertakings doing especially well. The overall growth rate was a comfortable 6.5%. Exports were up by 18%, and with a generous inflow of invisibles (capital and service transactions not reflected in statistics of foreign trade), the foreign exchange reserves reached a new high of Rs 18,850,000,000, an increase of Rs 9,160,000,000 over the previous year. The rupee improved in relation to the pound (from £5.5 per 100 rupees in January to £6.8 in October).

Anti-inflationary policy was relaxed somewhat to stimulate consumer industries. Although wholesale prices rose steadily from March 1976, the level in October was lower than it had been two years earlier.

The upturn in the economy enabled revision of the fifth five-year plan, 1974–79. As approved by the National Development Council in September, the plan provided for a total public sector outlay of Rs 393,030,000,000 over the five-year period. Additional resources of Rs 146,930,000,000 were to be mobilized along with foreign assistance of Rs 58,340,000,000. The union budget for 1976–77, presented on March 15, increased the allocation for development by 31.6%. Revenue receipts in the coming year were computed at Rs 82,270,000,000, including Rs 480 million by new taxation. With revenue expenditure of Rs 76.9 billion and capital receipts and disbursements of Rs 44,230,000,000 and Rs 52.8 billion, respectively, a deficit of Rs 3.2 billion was left uncovered.

The Twenty-Point Program made tangible progress. The number of house sites distributed rose to 7.1 million; 2.6 million ac of land were identified as surplus and 1 million ac distributed to 505,000 families. Some 80,500 bonded labourers were freed. Hidden income and wealth of Rs 15 billion were disclosed under the Voluntary Disclosure Scheme, which had been announced in December 1975.

The Burmah Shell refinery in Bombay was taken over and renamed Bharat Refineries. With the purchase of 26% of shares from Esso, Hindustan Petroleum became fully state-owned. Among major projects commissioned during the year were the Idukki hydroelectric project in Kerala, the Jayakwadi Dam in Maharashtra, the Lower Sileru power station in Andhra Pradesh, and a hot strip mill at Bokaro. Preliminary work on the Kudremukh iron-ore project made progress. The award of the Krishna tribunal and an agreement among three southern states on the sharing of Cauvery River waters ended two long-standing disputes.

Large areas of Calcutta and its outskirts were flooded by rains in August. Volunteers carry food to the victims.

PANA-INDIA/AUTHENTICATED NEWS INTERNATIONAL

At the Chas Nala Colliery in Bihar, which was the scene of a major tragedy in December 1975, some 343 bodies were recovered after six weeks of search. On Oct. 4, 1976, an explosion killed 39 workers in a coal mine in Sudamdih. Also in October, 95 persons were killed in a crash of an Indian Airlines plane in Bombay. An Air India plane was hijacked to Lahore in Pakistan on September 10, but the passengers and crew were released the next day and the plane was returned.

Foreign Affairs. The effort to normalize relations with neighbours continued. Diplomatic links as well as air and rail traffic were resumed with Pakistan in July. There was an exchange of ambassadors with China. Events in that country consequent on the deaths of Chou En-lai and Mao Tse-tung evoked great interest. Prime Minister Gandhi visited the Soviet Union in June; East Germany and Afghanistan in July; and Mauritius, Tanzania, Zambia, and Seychelles in October. She also went to Colombo, Sri Lanka, in August for the fifth summit conference of nonaligned countries.

Relations with Bangladesh continued to be strained because of the demand of Bangladesh for a larger share of the waters of the Ganges, which, India said, would mean virtual abandonment of the Farakka Barrage. Canada's revocation of the agreement to supply nuclear fuel for the nation's power program evoked disappointment. Among notable visitors to India during the year were Pres. Julius Nyerere of Tanzania, Prime Minister Emir Abbas Hoveida of Iran, Conservative Party leader Margaret Thatcher and leader of the House of Commons Michael Foot from Britain, and Todor Zhivkov of Bulgaria.

(H. Y. SHARADA PRASAD)

[976.A.2]

Indonesia

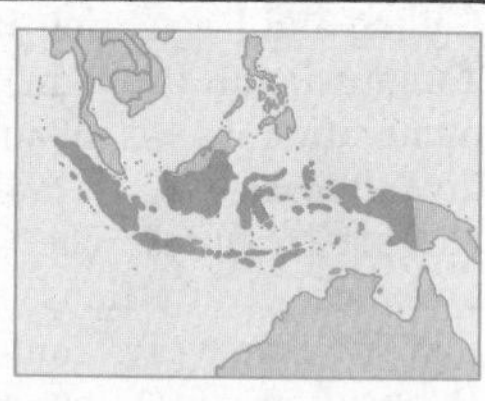

A republic of Southeast Asia, Indonesia consists of the major islands of Sumatra, Java, Kalimantan (Indonesian Borneo), Celebes, and Irian Jaya (West New Guinea) and approximately 3,000 smaller islands and islets. Area: 741,100 sq mi (1,919,400 sq km). Pop. (1977 est.): 138,133,500. Area and population figures include former Portuguese Timor. Cap. and largest city: Jakarta (pop., 1977 est., 6,178,500). Language: Bahasa Indonesian (official); Javanese; Sundanese; Madurese. Religion: mainly Muslim; some Christian, Buddhist, and Hindu. President and prime minister in 1976, General Suharto.

The Suharto administration was beset in 1976 by the worst loss of confidence at home and abroad in a decade. Indonesia was troubled by the deepening multibillion-dollar scandal involving Pertamina Oil Co., the state-owned oil enterprise; two coup attempts by religious zealots; and concern among officials and citizens over a ground swell of corruption inside and outside the government. In foreign affairs, Indonesia annexed Portuguese Timor, the last foreign foothold in the Indonesian archipelago. Relations with the newly installed Communist regime in Vietnam were strained.

Although Pertamina had in some years grossed more than $5 billion, the state oil agency was unable to meet its short-term borrowing obligations and verged on bankruptcy. The government had assumed the agency's financial problems in 1975 and restored confidence. However, a complete audit of Pertamina's books during 1976 stunned the government, and confidence again sagged. On May 20 the government disclosed that Pertamina's debt was $10.5 billion. By means of intensive renegotiations with creditors, the debt was reduced to $6.2 billion. By Indonesian standards, the scale of debt was staggering, 2.5 trillion rupiah as compared with the entire national budget of 3.5 trillion rupiah for fiscal 1976–77.

President Suharto dismissed the head of Pertamina, a controversial army general, and announced the sale of the agency's non-oil-producing enterprises, from golf courses to luxury hotels. Suharto's emergency bailout operation cut into Indonesia's foreign exchange, raised the country's debt service ratio uncomfortably, and slowed five-year-plan projects.

To earn more foreign exchange, Indonesia also renegotiated production-sharing agreements with foreign oil producers in Indonesia. The new accords, which strained relations between Indonesia and the investment community, provided for an 85–15 profit split in the government's favour, as compared with former ratios of largely 65–35. This development was expected to earn the government an additional $35 million annually.

NASA/PICTORIAL PARADE

Indonesia entered the space age in July with this communications satellite launched from Cape Canaveral in the U.S. The spacecraft, named Palapa, was placed in orbit over the 3,000-mile archipelago, linking stations in each of the country's 26 provinces through radio, TV, and telephone signals.

INDONESIA

Education. (1974) Primary, pupils 13,314,246, teachers 443,015; secondary, pupils 1,651,439, teachers 105,169; vocational, pupils 783,935, teachers 67,653; teacher training, students 76,095, teachers 7,607; higher (1971), students 251,870, teaching staff (1967) 21,309.

Finance. Monetary unit: rupiah, with (Sept. 20, 1976) an official rate of 415 rupiah to U.S. $1 (free rate of 715 rupiah = £1 sterling). Gold, SDR's, and foreign exchange (June 1976) U.S. $953 million. Budget (1975–76 est): revenue 2,496,000,000,000 rupiah; expenditure 2,735,000,000,000 rupiah. Gross national product (1974) 9,329,000,000,000 rupiah. Money supply (April 1976) 1,455,100,000,000 rupiah. Cost of living (Jakarta; 1970 = 100; May 1976) 286.

Foreign Trade. (1975) Imports U.S. $4,708,500,000; exports U.S. $7,103,200,000. Import sources (1974): Japan 30%; U.S. 16%; West Germany 8%; Singapore 7%. Export destinations (1974): Japan 53%; U.S. 20%; Singapore 7%. Main exports: crude oil 69%; timber 7%; rubber 5%; petroleum products 5%.

Transport and Communications. Roads (1972) 84,891 km. Motor vehicles in use (1973): passenger 307,622; commercial (including buses) 174,212. Railways: (1974) *c.* 7,800 km; traffic (1973) 2,726,000,000 passenger-km, freight 1,068,000,000 net ton-km. Air traffic (1974): 2,204,500,000 passenger-km; freight 44,890,000 net ton-km. Shipping (1975): merchant vessels 100 gross tons and over 724; gross tonnage 859,378. Telephones (Dec. 1974) 284,830. Radio licenses (Dec. 1972) 6 million. Television receivers (Dec. 1974) *c.* 330,000.

Agriculture. Production (in 000; metric tons; 1975): rice 23,100; corn *c.* 3,500; cassava (1974) *c.* 9,399; sweet potatoes (1974) *c.* 2,180; sugar, raw value *c.* 1,207; bananas (1974) *c.* 1,940; tea *c.* 65; copra 782; soybeans *c.* 557; palm oil *c.* 370; peanuts *c.* 541; coffee *c.* 192; tobacco (1974) *c.* 81; rubber *c.* 850; fish catch (1974) 1,342. Livestock (in 000; Dec. 1974): cattle *c.* 6,687; pigs *c.* 4,378; sheep *c.* 3,151; horses (1973) *c.* 690; buffalo (1973) *c.* 5,870; goats *c.* 7,468; chickens *c.* 115,000.

Industry. Production (in 000; metric tons; 1975): crude oil 63,800; petroleum products (1974) 14,632; coal 208; tin concentrates (metal content) 24; bauxite 993; electricity (excluding most industrial production; kw-hr; 1974) 3,246,000.

The Pertamina affair, coupled with an upsurge of corruption, created a debilitating moral atmosphere in Jakarta and generated two plots against the government. A Javanese mystic succeeded in persuading five of Indonesia's most respected elder statesmen and religious leaders to sign documents calling for Suharto's resignation and replacement by the mystic himself. The plot had comic overtones.

The signatories said that they had not read the documents thoroughly and signed them only to get rid of the mystic, who claimed he spoke directly to God. The other plot was serious. A student leader was arrested and charged with planning to kill Suharto and his family on the eve of the Islamic New Year and then launch a concerted attack against corruption, gambling, drug addiction, and prostitution. There was no connection between the two affairs, but they pointed up the growing uneasiness about moral corruption. In September Suharto issued stringent guidelines aimed at putting an end to what Radio Jakarta called "a misuse of public funds." The president urged the nation not to lose self-confidence.

Following a year-long civil war on Portuguese Timor between moderates who sought integration with Indonesia and leftist extremists who proclaimed unilateral independence, Indonesia tipped the balance in favour of the moderates by sending them military assistance. On July 17 Indonesia formally annexed the territory, and Portugal promptly recognized the action. However, tension between Indonesia and Vietnam sharpened over Timor when Vietnam, which had been supporting the leftists, declared, "We reaffirm our militant solidarity with the peoples of East Timor."

In August, at the fifth summit conference of nonaligned nations at Colombo, Sri Lanka, Vietnam announced its opposition to the creation of a "zone of peace, freedom, and neutrality in Southeast Asia" (ZOPFAN). Since 1971 the proposal had been pressed by the Association of Southeast Asian Nations (ASEAN), composed of Indonesia, the Philippines, Singapore, Thailand, and Malaysia. Vietnam's oppo-

sition surprised Indonesia and other ASEAN member states because a month earlier Phan Hien, the Vietnamese deputy foreign minister, toured the region on a goodwill mission and expressed Hanoi's desire to establish friendly relations with Indonesia and ASEAN. (ARNOLD C. BRACKMAN)
[976.C.1]

Industrial Relations

More than 200 years after the Industrial Revolution it might be expected that settled patterns of behaviour in industry would have been established, but such are the vagaries of human nature and the rate of change in the economic and social forces that shape industrial relations systems that each year presents at least some different aspects from the last. Not that 1976 was a year of great change, as industrial relations activities were somewhat overshadowed by the rather sombre overall economic situation. Under the circumstances changes in industrial relations were more notable in terms of reactions to external constraints and continuation of existing trends rather than intrinsic innovations.

Again it was the advanced industrial "market" economies where change was most noticeable, though among the Communist countries there were, for instance, strikes against higher food prices in Poland in June. Developments in the rest of the world included the national charter in Algeria, which incorporated the idea of a national occupational classification system, and a new and tough decree in Nigeria on settlement of disputes in essential services.

Wages, Job Security, and Inflation. In the advanced market economies the main focuses of attention in industrial relations were on how to regulate wages with business activity still fairly low and with inflationary tendencies continuing and how to protect workers from unemployment. These factors were reflected alike in steps by governments to achieve agreement with labour unions and employers on wage increases; in governmental measures to help the unemployed; and, in collective bargaining, by a generally sober attitude in negotiations as to what could be afforded, again accompanied by an increased emphasis on job security.

To illustrate, agreements providing relatively modest wage increases were made in the United States, where inflation was lower than in most countries. Examples included the trucking, rubber (after an 18-week strike), electrical equipment, and automobile industries. The key automobile settlement was made in October after a United Automobile Workers strike against the Ford Motor Co. Apart from the wage increases its main features were concerned, directly or indirectly, with job security. They included supplementary unemployment benefits, holidays, and working hours, and contained a provision that could prove a stepping-stone toward a four-day week. The United Steelworkers of America decided to claim in forthcoming negotiations a guarantee of paid lifetime employment.

Canada's wage and price control measure, launched in October 1975, met with heavy union opposition during the year. However, an attempt to get the federal act declared unconstitutional failed before the nation's Supreme Court.

In Western Europe a number of governmental measures sought to alleviate unemployment, particularly the high levels commonly experienced by young people. Wage negotiations were often difficult, but on the whole settlements were on a basis that took account of the economic background. In Denmark, though the usual national collective bargaining session was not due until the spring of 1977, the government set a general framework of 6% for wage increases for the next two years. West German wage increases were relatively modest. Ireland, with particularly high unemployment, experienced long-drawn-out negotiations to arrive at an interim and temporary 1976 national wage agreement.

Britain followed up its government-union agreement of 1975 with a new one-year agreement operative from August 1. It provided an upper limit of about 5% on annual earnings increases, with a maximum figure of £4 a week and a minimum of £2.50. Certain tax changes announced in the budget in April and made conditional on a satisfactory wage deal were thereupon implemented by the government. The inflationary pressures arising from the decline of the pound on the international markets appeared threatening, but at the end of the year the agreement was still in effect; a national seamen's strike that might have broken the agreement was narrowly averted in September.

In The Netherlands the government again found a need to intervene in collective bargaining, in July, with a new incomes policy. It included not only continued wage restraint but also reduction of national insurance contributions. This step followed publication of an outline of a bill proposing that a proportion of the capital growth of enterprises be placed in a national fund. In Japan, for the second straight year, the spring wage round produced a moderate outcome without undue disturbance.

The trend of 1976, then, seemed to be one of some moderation on the part of unions and, in a number of countries, an increasingly close involvement between wage negotiations and government economic policy.

Participation and Quality of Working Life. One might have expected that the anxieties in 1976 about unemployment and inflation would have deflected attention from issues of workers' participation on company policymaking boards and the improvement of work and working conditions. Changes in these areas did take place, however.

In West Germany the long-running conflict about codetermination was resolved, at least for the time being, by a compromise that was given legislative effect on July 1. There was to be equal representation of workers and stockholders on the supervisory boards of the approximately 600 enterprises employing more than 2,000 people. The workers' side, however, was to include managerial representation, and the chairman of each board (with a casting vote) was to be elected by the representatives of the stockholders.

Sweden in June also passed a bill about codetermination at work, bringing together and adding to three earlier laws. The new measure placed new duties to negotiate on the employer and added constraints on management's freedom to make decisions, including the right of interpretation of agreements. Constraints on freedom to strike were eased. Both Ireland and Israel proposed plans for worker representatives to be appointed to the boards of public sector enterprises.

The Netherlands initiated legislative changes to provide for the membership of works councils to be confined to workers, though the councils would continue to meet regularly with the employer. In the United Kingdom the Bullock Committee was due to report at the end of the year with proposals to strengthen workers' participation in formulating company policies.

One country took a decision against extending workers' rights to participate. Switzerland held a referendum in March that resulted in a substantial majority against proposals to give workers constitutional rights to participate in the management of enterprises. The debate about participation in Switzerland was by no means ended by this result, however.

Workers' participation in ownership of industry continued to be much discussed. In Sweden such legislation seemed likely after the trade union congresses of the summer, but the change of government in September put an end to that possibility for the time being. In both Sweden and West Germany, employers put forward their own proposals designed to enable workers to acquire a greater stake in the ownership of industry.

Working conditions continued to be the subject of attention in a number of countries. The Danish Working Environment Act, passed at the end of 1975, was followed by the final report of the Work Environment Commission in Sweden, proposing a new bill to strengthen the Workers' Protection Act. A similar measure was also initiated in Norway. In Sweden a central collective agreement on the working environment was signed in April. In Australia the report of the Jackson Committee on policies for manufacturing industry laid heavy stress on the need to improve the quality of working life. In July France established a substantial fund to help enterprises carry out projects for improving working conditions. Considerable government attention was given, in particular, to improvements in the status and conditions of manual workers. West Germany introduced new regulations on dangerous substances and on conditions to be observed in constructing and operating workplaces.

Despite all efforts to reduce them, occupational illnesses and accidents remained at a high level. During recent years some new and serious hazards had been produced in work associated with asbestos and with polyvinyl chloride. Several measures introduced during the year were aimed at reducing such hazards as well as improving general standards of working conditions.

National Developments. In several countries industrial relations developments occurred after significant political changes. Thus, in Australia and New Zealand the electoral defeats of Labour governments were followed by changed attitudes in industrial relations. In Australia a one-day general strike was called on July 12 in relation to a medical assistance plan. New Zealand, too, suffered a number of strikes, many in relation to a government wage freeze.

Political changes and a difficult economic situation in Argentina led to tough emergency labour legislation in March. Chile tightened up its legislation covering strikes in the public sector.

In May the Greek government enacted legislation concerning unions, banning politically motivated and wildcat strikes. A number of workers reacted by striking, and there were demonstrations and some rioting in Athens. The strike was opposed by the Greek Confederation of Labour.

In the uncertain social situation in Spain that followed the death of Gen. Francisco Franco the unofficial trade unions set out to wrest authority from the official *sindicatos,* long-established bodies incorporating both employers and workers. There were many strikes, and the three main unofficial organizations called a day of industrial action to protest against government economic measures, which included a limit on pay increases and more freedom for employers to dismiss workers.

KEYSTONE

Students picket trade union leaders in London in June. They were protesting the policy of going slow on pay increases, adopted by the unions as an anti-inflationary measure.

After the disturbances of 1975 a need for stability and a mood of reconstruction were felt in Portugal, and 1976 proved much more peaceful, despite the government's introduction of austerity measures. In April a new constitution was proclaimed, laying down economic and social rights and responsibilities for workers.

Political events in the southern part of the African continent led to a new militancy among black African workers in South Africa, and there were ugly scenes of disturbance in the industrial areas. In November the South African government banned nine labour activists from involving themselves in labour activities for five years.

The World Scene. In industrial relations, as in political and economic matters generally, there has been a tendency for international contacts to become more frequent and closer. This trend continued during the year, as was evidenced by the considerable number of international meetings to discuss industrial relations topics.

Employment was the subject of the International Labour Organization's World Employment Conference in June and the main topic at the meeting of ministers of labour held by the Organization for Economic Cooperation and Development in March. The latter meeting led to the adoption of a Recommendation on a General Employment and Manpower Policy. At the ILO conference the U.S. and Israel protested the inclusion of the Palestine Liberation Organization with a brief walkout. (R. O. CLARKE)

R. O. Clarke is a principal administrator in the Social Affairs and Industrial Relations Division of the Organization for Economic Cooperation and Development, Paris. The views expressed in this article are his own and should not be attributed to the OECD.

See also Economics; Economy, World; Industrial Review.

[521.B.3; 534.C.1.g; 552.D.3 and F.3.b.ii]

ENCYCLOPÆDIA BRITANNICA FILMS. *The Rise of Labor* (1968); *The Industrial Worker* (1969); *The Rise of Big Business* (1969); *The Progressive Era* (1971).

Industrial Review

The spectacular boom in 1972–73 and the stagnation in 1974 was followed in 1975 by the most severe recession since the end of World War II for the manufacturing industries in the developed industrial countries. Their aggregate output fell by 7%. This was only marginally offset by the rise of manufacturing production in the less developed countries, resulting in a decline of 6% in the total output of manufactures in the Western world. The centrally planned economies successfully isolated themselves, in this particular respect, from the world recession, and their industry continued to expand at a rapid rate (Table I).

Table I. Index Numbers of Production, Employment, and Productivity in Manufacturing Industries
1970=100

Area	Relative importance 1963	Relative importance 1970	Relative importance 1975	Production 1974	Production 1975	Employment 1974	Employment 1975	Productivity* 1974	Productivity* 1975
World†	1,000	1,000	1,000	121	114	...	...	...	...
Industrial countries	876	896	870	119	111	...	...	...	...
Less industrialized countries	124	104	130	137	146	...	...	...	...
North America‡	480	409	391	120	109	...	...	...	...
Canada	28	27	28	126	119	109	103	116	116
United States	452	381	364	122	109	104	95	118	115
Latin America§	49	59	76	141	146	...	...	...	...
Mexico	8	13	16	132	136	...	...	...	...
Asia‖	88	137	144	125	120	...	...	...	...
India	16	11	11	113	116	112	...	101	...
Iran	...	4	...	...	...	...	...	...	...
Japan	55	99	96	124	110	105	99	118	111
Pakistan¶	3	3	(3)	120	(115)♀	...	...	...	...
Europeδ	350	365	365	118	114	...	...	...	...
Austria	7	6	6	128	117	107	102	120	115
Belgium	11	11	11	123	111	...	...	...	...
Denmark	6	5	...	...	...	98	88	...	...
Finland	4	4	4	129	121	111	110	117	110
France	51	67	66	125	113	103	100	121	113
Germany, West	89	104	94	110	103	96	90	115	114
Greece	2	3	4	144	151	118	119	122	127
Ireland	1	1	1	124	116	103	95	120	122
Italy	36	37	35	119	107	107	107	111	100
Netherlands, The	12	13	12	115	107	92	89	125	120
Norway□	4	4	4	117	114	101	104	109	102
Portugal	2	3	3	140	132	...	...	...	...
Spain	12	12	15	155	144	115	115	135	125
Sweden	14	13	13	117	115	108	109	108	106
Switzerland	10	12	10	111	95	95	86	118	110
United Kingdom	73	54	48	108	102	95	91	114	113
Yugoslavia	13	13	17	140	149	121	124	116	120
Rest of the world◊	33	30	...	...	...	...	...	...	...
Australia¶	14	14	13	109	110	102	94	107	117
South Africa	5	6	7	122	124	113	116	108	107
Centrally planned economies▲	...	...	...	142	155	...	...	...	...

*This is 100 times the production index divided by the employment index, giving a rough indication of changes in output per person employed.
†Excluding Albania, Bulgaria, China, Czechoslovakia, East Germany, Hungary, Mongolia, North Korea, North Vietnam, Poland, Romania, and the U.S.S.R.
‡Canada and the United States.
§South and Central America (including Mexico) and the Caribbean islands.
‖Asian Middle East and East and Southeast Asia, including Japan.
♀Estimate.
¶Years beginning July 1.
δExcluding Albania, Bulgaria, Czechoslovakia, East Germany, Hungary, Poland, Romania and the U.S.S.R.
□Employment and productivity based on 1972=100.
◊Africa and Oceania.
▲These are not included in the above world total and consist of Albania, Bulgaria, Czechoslovakia, East Germany, Hungary, Poland, Romania, and the U.S.S.R.

Table II. Industrial Pattern of Boom and Recession, 1972–75
Percent change from previous year

	World*				Developed countries				Less developed countries				Centrally planned economies			
	1972	1973	1974	1975	1972	1973	1974	1975	1972	1973	1974	1975	1972	1973	1974	1975
All manufacturing	7	10	1	−6	7	9	0	−7	8	10	7	7	8	9	10	9
Heavy industries	8	12	2	−7	7	12	1	−8	11	12	10	7	10	10	11	11
Base metals	9	11	2	−13	8	12	1	−15	11	3	13	7	6	6	7	10
Metal products	7	13	1	−6	7	12	1	−7	14	19	13	11	11	11	12	11
Building materials, etc.	7	9	−1	−7	7	9	−2	−8	9	10	7	7	7	8	7	7
Chemicals	8	10	2	−5	8	10	2	−7	9	9	6	4	9	12	11	12
Light industries	6	5	0	−2	6	6	−1	−4	8	7	4	6	6	7	7	7
Food, drink, tobacco	4	6	4	0	4	5	2	0	7	7	7	4	5	5	8	6
Textiles	6	6	−3	−3	6	6	−4	−5	6	6	1	4	5	6	7	6
Clothing, footwear	7	4	−1	−1	7	2	−3	−5	6	13	6	15	5	5	7	8
Wood products	9	8	−2	−6	6	0	3	1	6	0	3	1	5	7	6	7
Paper, printing	6	7	−1	−7	6	7	−1	−8	15	13	1	1	7	7	6	7

*Excluding centrally planned economies.
Source: UN, *Monthly Bulletin of Statistics*.

The worst hit were the heavy industries in the industrial countries (−8%), base metals having suffered the greatest loss (−15%). The light industries were slightly better off (−4%), but the food industry was the only one to escape an actual decline (Table II).

Apart from the reaction to the preceding boom, several factors aggravated the recession. In most industrial countries restrictive monetary and fiscal measures were introduced in order to check the rapid rate of inflation and to counter balance of payments deficits caused chiefly by the higher oil prices. Stocks of basic materials and of intermediate and finished products had been severely reduced at all levels in the industrial countries. Rapidly rising prices and increasing unemployment depressed real purchasing power; consumer demand for certain industrial products, especially automobiles, fell dramatically. The gradually deepening crisis in confidence further reduced investment activity, especially in view of the low level of utilization of industrial capacities.

The trough of the recession was generally reached about the middle of 1975; in the second half there were signs of a recovery, which was well under way in the first half of 1976. In the first quarter of 1976 industrial output was already 7% above the low mark of 1975, and the expansion continued during the later months, though at a slower pace.

In the aggregate of the industrial countries, the main generators of the recovery were revived private consumption, fixed investment, and the rebuilding of stocks. There was also a modest revival in exports, but because of correspondingly increased imports it did not generate a balance for additional industrial demand and so, with the exception of a few countries, was a less important factor in influencing industrial activity.

Industrial activity in the United States rebounded in the summer of 1975. The dominant factor in this recovery was consumers' expenditure, boosted by tax rebates; it remained the main force in the following upswing. Much of its strength was attributable to sales of automobiles, which by the spring of 1976 were 50% higher than a year earlier and had regained most of the ground lost during the fuel crisis and the recession. Residential investment rose approximately 3% in the first months of 1976 and then continued to grow at a much reduced rate. Public expenditure and industrial

Table III. Manufacturing Production in the U.S.S.R. and Eastern Europe*
1970=100

Country	1973	1974	1975
Bulgaria†	131	142	156
Czechoslovakia	122	130	140
East Germany†	120	128	137
Hungary	120	131	137
Poland	135	151	168
U.S.S.R.	124	135	145

*Romania not available.
†All industries.
Source: UN, *Monthly Bulletin of Statistics*.

Table IV. Output per Hour Worked in Manufacturing
1970=100

Country	1971	1972	1973	1974	1975
France	105	114	122	126	120
Germany, West	105	111	118	122	126
Italy	103	111	124	126	120*
Japan	104	114	133	136	132
U.K.	105	112	118	118	117
U.S.	104	107	111	113	115

*Estimate.
Source: National Institute, *Economic Review*.

COURTESY, GENERAL ELECTRIC RESEARCH AND DEVELOPMENT CENTER

Scientists at General Electric found a way of creating pressures of more than eight million pounds per square inch. They used a pair of tungsten-carbide pistons like the one shown, tipped them with synthetic industrial diamonds, and installed them in a hydraulic press.

investment were retarding factors; the first faced financial difficulties and was expected to remain restrained, but orders for investment goods and other indicators in that sector seemed to herald faster growth in investment activity in the future. By the middle of 1976 output was running well over 10% higher than in the preceding year.

The recession in Canada was milder than in the U.S., and so was the recovery. By the middle of 1976 output had returned to prerecession levels. This was also the case in Japan, where, however, the turnaround of industrial activity started somewhat earlier, after a drop of 18%. The Japanese exporting industries were particularly successful; stockbuilding, public works, and private housing were other buoyant sectors of demand.

After a forceful increase in the second half of 1975, French industry's advance in 1976 was somewhat sluggish. Investment in productive equipment was particularly low, leading to promotional measures by the government. The rapid initial rise in private consumption slowed down, while export demand was fairly well maintained.

The West German manufacturing industry made a powerful recovery from its 10% decline and reached the previous peak as early as February 1976. The main agents of this recovery were private consumption and, to a lesser extent, exports, with stockbuilding as another contributory factor. West Germany remained the leading force behind the European revival, but the advance during the middle of the year was only moderate, although more evenly spread over most industrial sectors than in the early upswing phase.

Italian industrial production fell 15% from peak to trough; its recovery was partial and sluggish, largely owing to political and social obstacles to continued development. The decline in British industry was smaller (10%), but severe anti-inflationary measures restrained domestic demand and consequently the upswing was very slow.

Most of the smaller European countries (Belgium, Denmark, Ireland, The Netherlands, Portugal, Spain, Switzerland) shared the fate of their larger neighbours; in some of them the 1975 industrial recession was relatively mild (Austria, Finland, Norway), and a few were even able to escape a decline altogether (Greece, Yugoslavia). Output started to increase in 1976 in practically all of these countries. One notable exception was Sweden where the recession was delayed, reaching its deepest point in 1976.

The recession caused industrial productivity (output per employee) to fall in most countries, though in some the decline was marginal. Industrial unemployment rose to high levels. Productivity started to pick up in the revival, but the reduction of unemployment seemed likely to be a difficult and slow process. One of the reasons for the latter was that many were not working full time; by giving these workers full-time status it would be possible to raise output considerably with unchanged numbers employed.

Output per man-hour worked developed differently in the six largest Western industrial countries in 1975. It fell in France, Italy, and Japan, declined fractionally in Britain, and rose in West Germany and the U.S.

In contrast to the recession in the industrial world, manufacturing output in the less developed countries rose 7% in 1975. In the centrally planned economies the gains were even greater. Manufacturing in the Soviet Union advanced 7½%; the fastest growers in Eastern Europe were Bulgaria and Poland (10–12%) and the slowest Hungary (5%); East German and Czechoslovak output rose at a rate of 7–8%.

(G. F. RAY)

ADVERTISING

The economic climate for advertising improved in 1976. In the U.S. advertising expenditures reached a record $32 billion, largely as a result of increased activity by national advertisers, new product introductions, and large expenditures for the Winter Olympics, the bicentennial celebration, and the presidential election.

According to a *Standard & Poor's* survey, expenditures on television, both national and local, gained 11% in 1976, following an increase of 9% in 1975. Newspaper advertising revenues rose almost 10%, as compared with 4% in the preceding year. Magazine revenues increased 9% after a 1% drop in 1975. In late 1975 most magazines had announced rate increases, leading to an immediate decline of page volume. In the print media the single largest increase came from durable goods manufacturers who had cut back advertising schedules in the past two years. All this meant more activity, employment, and profits for advertising agencies, many of which had had to trim their staffs to a minimum in recent years.

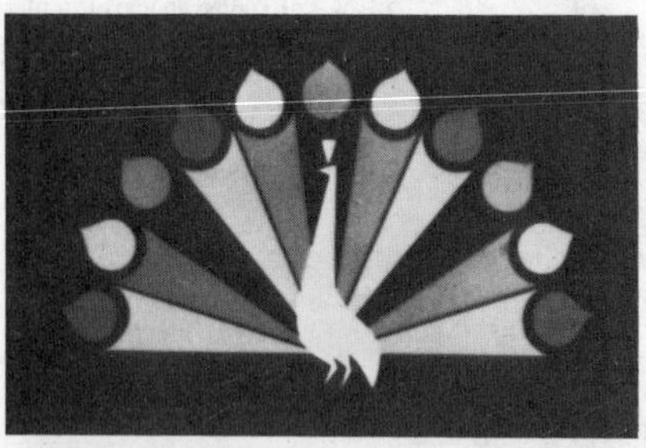

PHOTOS, WIDE WORLD

When NBC decided to replace its TV symbols (top and centre) it paid a six-figure sum for its new trapezoidal N (bottom). Then it found that the Nebraska Educational Television Network had already invented the same design. NBC finally agreed to pay NETV $55,000 to forgo using the N.

Despite the American Bar Association's decision to postpone action on major changes in its ethics code to allow advertising, some members of the legal profession moved ahead on their own and tested state laws that forbid advertising by attorneys. In Seattle, Wash., an attorney placed an ad in the *Post-Intelligencer,* and in North Carolina an attorney brought a legal suit to test the state law prohibiting lawyers from advertising, claiming that the current professional ethics code violates the rights of freedom of speech, due process, and equal protection under the law. It was estimated that, if it were permitted, lawyer advertising in the U.S. would amount to about $360 million a year.

In May a U.S. Supreme Court decision struck down Virginia's ban against advertising of prescription drug prices. The decision meant that similar restrictions in more than 30 other states would be unenforceable. It was also expected to result in a more thorough examination of advertising restrictions imposed on various professional groups, including lawyers and doctors, and on the advertising of cigarettes and liquor.

Violence on television was a major concern of national advertisers in 1976. As one measure of this concern, Best Foods and Samsonite luggage withdrew their advertising from excessively violent programs. Ted Bates and Co., a major advertising agency, reported that several of its clients had directed it not to buy time on shows with "gratuitous violence." There was a growing feeling among advertisers that violence actually had a negative effect on consumers. The National Citizens Committee for Broadcasting issued a "violence index" rating shows and sponsors, and none of the ten most popular programs was on the "ten most-violent" list prepared by the committee. A study showed that 1.4% of the consumers it surveyed had boycotted products advertised on violent shows.

The U.S. Federal Trade Commission, in a sweeping consent order with a vitamin marketer, said that advertising aimed at children was an "unfair" practice when the children were "unqualified by age or experience" to decide whether they needed the product. In particular, the FTC criticized the advertiser for using Spider-Man, a character in a children's TV series, to promote vitamins. The FTC held that such a "hero figure" might induce children to take excessive and possibly injurious amounts of vitamins, and it established restrictions on any future ads for these products. Action for Children's Television, a citizen's group, had complained about the Spider-Man ads and had petitioned the FTC to take action.

Statistics reported in August indicated that the 100 largest national advertisers, based on measured media expenditures, increased their advertising and promotion investment 6.7% to $6.4 billion in 1975. The largest of the increases was $35 million by Procter and Gamble, which maintained its number one position in national advertising by spending $360 million. Other advertisers in the top five included General Motors Corp., Sears, Roebuck and Co., General Foods Corp., and Bristol-Myers Co. In 1975 Procter and Gamble was the largest user of network and spot television time. The Warner-Lambert Co. was the largest buyer of network radio time, and the Chrysler Corp. purchased the most spot radio time.

In advertising, 1976 was the year of the cola war. Previously, Pepsi-Cola had run advertisements with the theme of "the Pepsi Generation," while Coca-Cola had emphasized that it was "the Real Thing." Then, Pepsi challenged Coca-Cola by running comparative ads, and these were followed by counter-ads and counter-counter-ads, all purporting to show that Coca-Cola drinkers prefer Pepsi or vice versa. Bottlers of both drinks were said to feel that this type of advertising was destroying the images of both companies, and the advertising community claimed that intense comparative advertising hurts the credibility of all advertising.

The Mexican government passed a "mexicanization" trademark bill requiring all brand names used in Mexico to be prefixed or suffixed by a Mexican name or symbol approved by the government. The move followed similar nationalistic legislation in France.

Dentsu Advertising of Japan remained the world's largest advertising agency. During the year it attempted to establish a new image by labeling itself as consultants on life-styles and society. The agency increased its special projects staff by 500.

Beginning Sept. 1, 1976, all cigarette and tobacco advertising on television was banned in Australia. Meanwhile, in Brazil, which had no restrictions on cigarette advertising or promotion, the world's three biggest tobacco companies saturated television with $50 million worth of advertising.

(EDWARD MARK MAZZE)

[534.I; 629.C.4.c]

AEROSPACE

The outstanding aeronautical event of 1976 was the introduction into airline service of the Anglo-French Concorde supersonic transport (SST), more than 13 years after the two-nation agreement was signed that launched the project and two decades after active planning had begun. British Airways and Air France flew their initial services on January 21, London–Bahrain and Paris–Rio de Janeiro, respectively. But most important were the first flights into the U.S.; Concordes of the two airlines touched down within minutes of each other at Dulles International Airport near Washington, D.C., on May 24. The U.S. secretary of transportation, after public hearings, allowed the Concorde into Dulles for a trial period of 16 months, and traffic rights into New York were to be negotiated. In November Britain and France agreed to build no more than 16 Concordes unless they gained new orders for the aircraft. Concorde's Soviet rival, the Tupolev Tu-144 SST, had begun mail and freight operations in December 1975 between Moscow and Alma Ata.

For the airlines the year was a slow trek back to profitability. TWA slimmed down by selling nine Boeing 747s and two Lockheed L-1011 transports, while United, with the largest fleet of any Western airline, announced its intention of buying 28 Boeing 727s. With 1,400 delivered or on order, the 727 remained the world's top-selling jet transport, and production continued at the rate of 5 a month. The world's largest airliner, the Boeing 747, also remained popular, even at $50 million per plane, and few reached the secondhand market. A 747 powered by a more powerful version of the Rolls-Royce RB.211 engine made its first flight. It was scheduled to join British Airways' fleet.

At the biennial Farnborough (England) International Air Show in September, Boeing announced three versions of a short-haul twin-engined airliner designated the 7N7 and development of the projected three-engined

WIDE WORLD

Boeing is testing a short-takeoff jet for the U.S. Air Force designed to lift large cargoes from short, rough airfields. The YC-14 prototype is shown taking off from Boeing Field in Seattle.

7X7 transport. Other manufacturers, notably McDonnell Douglas, continued to refine schemes for new transports. No airline was likely to choose a completely new design without waiting to see what Boeing would do, but the Seattle company was cautious and stated that much more market research would be necessary before irrevocable commitments were made. Meanwhile, Europe courted the U.S. manufacturers: Dassault and Aérospatiale pressed McDonnell Douglas to join them in a derivative of Dassault's Mercure, and Britain's aerospace minister, Gerald Kaufman, visited U.S. companies in October to sound out possibilities for Anglo-U.S. cooperation. British Airways' decision to buy six long-range Lockheed TriStars emphasized the lack of a cohesive European aircraft industry in the face of continuing U.S. domination.

Lockheed was in the news during the summer when agreement was reached on its refinancing with a consortium of 24 U.S. banks. The company had been in severe financial trouble owing to slow sales of its TriStar, on which it had not yet broken even. Investigation of various financial deals with Lockheed led to the resignation of a number of officials from the Japanese airline All Nippon, and in The Netherlands the implication of Prince Bernhard's involvement rocked the government.

The defection of a Soviet pilot to Japan, along with his MiG-25 fighter, was an event of considerable interest for U.S. military aerospace technologists. The MiG-25 ("Foxbat") had long been the bête noire of Western defense planners, and its unchecked intrusions into the airspace of Iran and Israel led those countries to purchase the latest U.S. fighters, the F-14 and F-15, both designed with the Foxbat as principal target. U.S. technical experts were quickly on the scene to examine the aircraft, which landed at Hakodate airport, Japan, on September 6, despite vigorous and repeated demands for its return by the U.S.S.R. It was finally returned in mid-November. The three-year-old plane seemed representative of the most modern Soviet engineering.

In July the Soviet aircraft carrier "Kiev," first of its type, sailed from its yard in the Black Sea through the Bosporus and Mediterranean into the Atlantic and up to Murmansk. It carried a vertical-takeoff-and-landing (VTOL) fighter, the Yak-36, seen by Western experts for the first time. Photos taken by ships and aircraft showed the Yak-36 to be about the same size as Britain's Harrier VTOL fighter.

Also in July, the U.S. Department of Defense approved development of the McDonnell Douglas AV-8B, an improved version of the Harrier, for service with the U.S. Marine Corps in about 1984. Two test aircraft were to be built, and if full production was eventually sanctioned, a total of 336 AV-8B's would be built for the U.S. forces. British companies would share in the program, and Rolls-Royce would build all the Pegasus engines.

Two competing prototypes in the U.S. Air Force's Advanced Medium STOL (short-takeoff-and-landing) Transport (AMST) program to replace the ubiquitous C-130 Hercules made their initial flights. First to take the air was the four-engined McDonnell Douglas YC-15, which later flew to Britain and demonstrated its short-takeoff-and-landing abilities convincingly at the Farnborough International Air Show. It was followed into the air a few months later by the equally advanced twin-engined Boeing YC-14. Whichever company won the competition stood to supply the West with more than 1,000 tactical transports over the next two decades. These advanced aircraft and many more like them in the U.S. emphasized the increasing disparity between that country and Europe.

For Britain the most important topic was the nationalization of the aerospace industry, put forward by the Labour government in its Aircraft and Shipbuilding Industries Bill. The resulting single company would be called British Aerospace Corporation. Because of the uncertainties arising from the proposed nationalization, the British aerospace industry took fewer initiatives in 1976 than it might have done otherwise.

(MICHAEL WILSON)

[732.B.1]

ALCOHOLIC BEVERAGES

Beer. World beer consumption rose by 3.3% in 1975, reaching about 776 million hectolitres (hl), compared with about 751 million hl in the previous year (1 hl = about 26.5 U.S. gal). In terms of per capita consumption, West Germany ranked first, followed by Czechoslovakia and Australia. The U.S., with per capita consumption of 81.7 litres in 1975, stood 13th on the list, maintaining the same position as in 1974, although total consumption showed a healthy rise of 7.4%. (*See* Table V.)

The excitement of crop estimates showing record world wheat harvests in country after country of America and Europe in 1976 concealed the problem of brewers for the coming year. Sales during the summer of 1976 were brisk because of the sustained drought in Europe, notably in the countries of the European Economic Community (EEC), but beer drinkers in these and many other countries had to pay more for their beer. There were many reasons for this, but two were of outstanding importance. First was the towering price of oil for transport—all brewers are big users of transport for their distribution networks. Of equal significance in many countries, notably those of the EEC, was the enormous increase in the price of barley. The 1976 crop, affected by the long drought, was high-nitrogen barley. For the brewer this meant a lower yield of extract from a given tonnage of grain; in other words, more barley would be required to produce a given quantity of beer. In addition, the price increase for grain itself caused an upward leap in raw materials costs.

The British figures were typical of what had happened elsewhere in the EEC. In August 1971 the price of malting barley in the U.K. was £24.80 per metric ton. By August 1975 this price had increased to £82.70 per ton. Incidentally, with British beer probably the most highly taxed of all except that of Ireland (where duty was increased by 5 pence per pint in 1975 in a desperate attempt to balance the country's books), the British government expected the beer duty to raise £1,000 million a year.

West Germany had in recent years insisted that home production of beer should be confined to all-malt grist. In view of the shortages and high prices of malting barley, the dangers of such a policy, loudly voiced by brewers in other countries, could clearly be seen. For seven centuries or more, other countries such as the U.K., Denmark, and The Netherlands had used admixtures of other grains, such as unmalted barley, wheat flour, corn, and rice. The last-named was also widely used in brewing in the U.S. The European Commission hoped to secure the adoption of common EEC standards for the brewing industry that would permit the use of a wide range of ingredients, as opposed to West Germany's "purity" norm, which in effect protected its brewers from outside competition.

(ARTHUR T. E. BINSTED)

Spirits. In the U.K. consumption of spirits was again affected adversely by an increased excise duty. The April 1976 budget added 32 pence to a standard bottle of spirits. This followed a rise of 64 pence imposed the previous year, so that 79% of the retail price (about £4) of a bottle of Scotch whisky was for duty and value-added tax (VAT). A further increase in duty was expected in the near future.

V. CERNIK—CZECHOSLOVAK NEWS AGENCY/EASTFOTO

Two of the new brewing tanks at the pilsner beer breweries in Plzen, western Bohemia, Czechoslovakia. The plant has been undergoing renovation in recent years. Its output is expected to reach 2.7 million hectolitres by 1980.

In the first eight months of the year the total U.K. spirits market declined by 2.7%, although in real terms consumers were spending a larger proportion of their incomes on spirits. Vodka continued to increase its market share, by 8%, to 10.3%, and seemed likely to take third place after whiskey and gin by the year's end. Gin's market share fell by 4.1%, to 16.37%. Scotch whisky's share fell by 3.3%. Whiskey production fell by 23% in the first half of 1976.

Scotch suffered from an apparent worldwide trend toward lighter spirits, particularly vodka. The U.S., Scotch's most important export market, took 9 million proof gallons of bulk blends of Scotch in the January–September period of 1976, one-fifth less than in the corresponding period of 1975. Exports to the U.S. of bottled-in-Scotland blends, however, rose by 11% to 13.9 million proof gallons.

Discrimination against Scotch whisky continued in Italy, the second biggest market for bottled malt whiskey, where VAT on grain-based spirits was raised from 30 to 35%. VAT on grape-based spirits rose only from 12 to 18%. The EEC Commission considered this move contrary to the provisions of the Treaty of Rome. Italy, a large wine producer, counterclaimed that Britain's high duties on wine discriminated in favour of beer.

In the U.S. there had been a marked slowdown in the growth of spirits consumption, from 5–6% a year before 1970 to 2–3% in 1970–74, and only 1.5% in 1975. More than in the U.K., wine competed directly with spirits in the U.S. as a pre-dinner cocktail and party drink.

(COLIN PARNELL)

Wine. World production of wine in 1976 was estimated at 327 million hl, an increase of about 3% over the previous year. Of the 1976 total, 77% originated in Europe and 16% in the Americas. The year's increase was mainly accounted for by France, whose output was 7 million hl higher than in 1975, and Argentina, with output up by 5 million hl. In Spain production dropped by 5 million hl, and there were lesser declines in Portugal and West Germany.

The French harvest, at 73 million hl some 11% greater than that of 1975, was gen-

Table V. Estimated Consumption of Beer in Selected Countries
In litres* per capita

Country	1973	1974	1975
Germany, West	146.7	146.9	147.8
Czechoslovakia	145.5	142.7	142.2
Australia†	130.5	141.3	141.1
Belgium‡	150	140	140
New Zealand	125.2	126.1	133.2
Luxembourg	144.2	135	129
Germany, East	112	114.9	117.6
United Kingdom	112	114.3	117.6
Denmark	113.52	111.96	117.19
Austria	110.1	105.4	103.8
Canada§	81.6	85.0	85.9
Ireland	80.82	85.97	84.37
United States	76.5	80.1	81.7
Netherlands, The	73.46	75.72	78.92
Switzerland	75.7	75.4	71.8
Hungary	61.6	66.8	62.9
Sweden	56.6	58.3	60.2
Finland	54.3	56.2	54.7
Bulgaria	43.62	52	...
Venezuela	40.8	40.4	50
Spain	42.6	44.3	47
Norway	42.02	43.85	45.44
France	44.47	44.19	45.22
Yugoslavia	37.2	44.3	...
Poland	37.8	36.1	36.8

*One litre=1.0567 U.S. quart=0.8799 imperial quart.
†Years ending June 30.
‡Including so-called "household beer."
§Years ending March 31.

Table VI. Estimated Consumption of Potable Distilled Spirits in Selected Countries
In litres* of 100% pure spirit per capita

Country	1973	1974	1975
Poland	4.2	4	4.6
Japan	...	3.74	3.95
Canada†	2.96	3.38	3.61
Luxembourg	3.3	3.1	3.5
Germany, East	3.2	3.4	3.4
Netherlands, The	2.55	2.75	3.39
U.S.S.R.	3.3	3.3	3.3
United States	3.03	3.12	3.13
Germany, West	3.02	2.64	3.04
Yugoslavia	3	3	...
Hungary	2.91	3.11	3
Czechoslovakia	2.64	2.78	2.98
Sweden	2.66	2.94	2.97
Finland	2.45	2.9	2.8
France‡	2.4	2.7	2.6
Spain	2.3	2.5	2.6
Surinam	2.5§	...	...
Iceland	2.53	2.65	2.4
Ireland	1.81	1.91	2.03
Italy	2.2	2	2
Bulgaria	2	2	...
Belgium	1.75	1.9	1.99
Switzerland	2.32	2.15	1.94
Norway	1.66	1.82	1.84
Cyprus	1.8	1.4	1.8

†Years ending March 31.
‡Including aperitifs.
§1972.

Table VII. Estimated Consumption of Wine in Selected Countries
In litres* per capita

Country	1973	1974	1975
Portugal	80.4	133.4	120
Italy	109.3	109.2	107.5
France†	105.49	104.1	103.7
Argentina	73.1	77.2	85.7
Spain	85.2	77	76
Switzerland‡	46.5	46	43.9
Luxembourg	40.9	49.6	41.3
Chile	38.2	40	40
Greece	37	36.5	38
Hungary	38.5	34.6	37
Austria	36.8	35.4	35.1
Romania	35.6	30	33
Yugoslavia	29.2	28.6	...
Uruguay	25.4	25.1	...
Germany, West	21.5	20.3	23.2
Bulgaria	20	19.98	...
Belgium	15.3	15.8	17.2
U.S.S.R.	16	16	16
Czechoslovakia	14.5	15.2	15
New Zealand	8.7	9.2	11.8
Denmark	10.74	9.66	11.48
Australia§	9.9	11.1	11.2
South Africa	10.72	11.34	10.41
Netherlands, The	8.89	10.37	10.25
Finland	6.42	9.2	8.86
United States	6.39	6.29	6.55

†Excluding cider (c. 20 litres per capita annually).
‡Excluding cider (c. 6 litres per capita 1975–76).
§Years ending June 30.

Sources: Produktschap voor Gedistilleerde Dranken, *Hoeveel alcoholhoudende dranken worden er in de wereld gedronken?*; U.S. Department of Commerce.

KEYSTONE

Britain's long hot summer proved ideal for wine grower Sir Guy Salisbury-Jones. He and his wife watch as a picker empties her basket at the five-acre Hambledon vineyard. He calls his wine "le vin Hambledon."

erally of very good quality and in some regions exceptional. In the Bordeaux region quantity and quality compared well with 1975, which had been an extremely good year in all respects. In Burgundy, where climatic conditions were particularly favourable, wines were of an exceptionally high quality and 1976 promised to be a great year. In the Beaujolais region, too, with production of 1 million hl, quality was excellent.

Italian production totaled about 70 million hl in 1976. In Piedmont the wine was of excellent quality, and it was even better in Lombardy, although there the harvest was smaller than in 1975. In Puglia, Italy's most important wine-producing region, conditions were disastrous, with heavy rains causing much damage and affecting the quantity and quality of the wines.

In the U.S. production of wine in 1975 reached 11.5 million hl, a 40% increase over average production during 1964–68. The French wine and spirits combine Moët-Hennessy (controlling the Moët et Chandon champagne house), with vineyards in Napa Valley, Calif., planned to expand its U.S. operation by marketing a U.S.-grown "champagne," Domaine Chandon.

The glut of ordinary table wines within the EEC continued to be a matter of contention, particularly between France and Italy. Clashes between police and French growers protesting cheap Italian imports resulted in the deaths of a policeman and one of the protesters near Narbonne, southern France, in March.

(PAUL MAURON)

[731.E.8.a–c]

AUTOMOBILES

The year 1976 was filled with events that seemed likely to mold the automobile industry for years to come. Volkswagen bought an unfinished Chrysler Corp. plant in New Stanton, Pa., and mapped plans to build 200,000 cars a year in the U.S. by 1980; U.S. domestic car sales in 37 consecutive ten-day periods were higher than in the corresponding periods of the previous year; and General Motors Corp. brought out a lighter and shorter standard-size car that signified the shape of future motor vehicles. Just when things looked their best, the U.S. Congress failed to act on more lenient emission-control regulations, and the U.S. industry threatened to close down after the 1977 model assembly run since it could not meet the regulations established for 1978 models.

If one word could sum up 1976, it might be "unpredictable." Automakers in 1975 geared their plants to manufacture more small cars, the gas-saving models that flourished following the Arab oil embargo of 1974. In 1976, however, consumers turned to big cars, and by late summer there was such a shortage of these that automakers could not keep up with demand even into several weeks of the 1977 model run.

The small cars gathered dust and remained near or over 100 days' supply of unsold inventory for almost the entire year. The big cars hovered between 20 and 30 days' supply, 60 days being considered normal. Analysts and industry observers were of the opinion that consumers turned back to bigger cars because small-car buying was a knee-jerk reaction to gas shortages and because people found out that small cars were not suitable for all families. Also, and perhaps most important, General Motors made it clear that its 1977 models would be nearly a foot shorter and from 600 to 1,000 lb lighter than the 1976 models. Expecting GM's move to signal the beginning of an industry-wide movement toward smaller cars, consumers rushed to get their hands on the last of the "big" 1976 GM cars early in the year.

Small cars became such a burden on the market that AMC and GM decided to offer cash rebates on some models. AMC in November reduced the price of its subcompact Gremlin by $253 to $2,995. It followed with an offer of discount allowances of from $25 to $225 on any of its 1977 cars and Jeeps purchased by members of certain retiree associations. Finally, it offered a $253 rebate on the purchase of any new 1977 Pacer sedan or any unsold 1976 sedan still in stock. GM's Chevrolet and Pontiac divisions attempted to generate sales of the subcompacts Vega and Astre and the mini Chevette by offering $200 cash rebates on any of the 1976 or 1977 models.

Ironically, while big cars sold strongly early in the year, they went even better early in the fall when the 1977 models came out. This presented another problem for GM. The company found that while consumers accepted its lighter cars, they had been accustomed to buying large engines for full-size cars. GM brought out several lighter-weight power plants to work in tandem with the lighter-weight cars, but consumers continued to choose the large engines and supplies of them ran short.

In the 1976 calendar year the four major U.S. manufacturers sold 8,632,080 cars, a 21.5% increase over the 7,099,173 sold in 1975. GM captured 55.6% of the market, up from 52.7% in 1975; Chrysler rose to 15% from 14%; Ford Motor Co. slipped to 26.4% from 28.6%; and AMC plunged to 2.8% from 4.5%. AMC, which had capitalized on the popularity of small cars a year earlier, felt the effects of the switch back to big cars as it offered no car larger than an intermediate.

U.S. import sales declined, partly the result of the decline in small-car popularity. The Japanese manufacturers Toyota, Datsun, and Honda did well, however. Toyota held onto the title as the best-selling import for the second consecutive year. Revaluations of European currencies kept those import car prices relatively high compared with the Japanese models. For the 1976 calendar year import sales totaled 1,490,000 units, compared with 1,580,000 a year earlier. They accounted for 14.8% of industry sales, versus the record 18.3% in 1975.

Volkswagen hoped to recover from its decline to third place in import sales by signing a multimillion-dollar deal to build subcompact Rabbits in Pennsylvania. Pilot production was scheduled for late 1977, and actual output in February or March 1978. The plant was a move by VW to help sta-

The Continental Mark V for 1977 is more angular and rakish than its predecessor. It has new front-fender louvres, and is nearly 400 pounds lighter. An engine with a 400-cubic-inch displacement is standard.

WIDE WORLD

bilize prices by making them less susceptible to changes in the value of the West German mark. Volvo also planned to begin producing cars at its new $150 million plant in Chesapeake, Va., early in 1977.

As had become standard in the last several years, the automakers once again raised prices when the 1977 models appeared. GM prices rose 5.9% or $339; Ford 5.1% or $310; Chrysler 5.9% or $326; and AMC 4.8% or $167. During the last three years prices had risen an average of $1,000.

But, unlike the situation in 1975, the price increases did not keep consumers out of the market. Rather, many industry analysts said that consumers had come to accept the increases as a side effect of inflation. As long as consumer incomes were going up, there was no resistance.

The pricing policies meant there was only one U.S. car offered under $3,000, and that was the single-seat, two-passenger Chevette from Chevrolet which missed $3,000 by 70 cents at $2,999.30. Later, however, AMC reduced the Gremlin to below $3,000, and GM followed suit by offering a $200 rebate on the Chevette.

As a further indication of the rise in prices, when the '77 models came out in the fall there were 70 models in the $3,000–$4,000 category against 91 a year earlier; 95 at $4,000–$5,000 versus 99 a year earlier; and 71 at $5,000–$6,000 versus 41 the previous year. The average selling price of the 1977 cars was $6,050.

Although prices were higher, the number of model offerings decreased to 252 from 295 the previous year. This was the lowest total since 1960 when only 244 were offered. The reduction was planned by the manufacturers in an effort to reduce their own costs and to conserve on materials.

Import prices also increased, by an average of 2.5–2.8%, or only slightly more than $100 per car. The increase was partly the result of government charges of "dumping" against many imports; importers agreed to raise prices to avoid charges that they were selling the cars more cheaply in the U.S. than in their home countries.

While prices went up, so did fuel economy. A few years earlier, consumers thought that 40 miles per gallon (mpg) in fuel economy was unattainable. In 1975 a host of models obtained that level. They did it again in the 1976 model year, and then late in the summer, when the Environmental Protection Agency listed 1977 figures, the diesel-engine Volkswagen Rabbit recorded 52 mpg in highway fuel economy and a combined city/highway figure of 44 mpg. Overall fuel economy on an industry-wide basis rose 6% to 18.6 mpg. Among the top ten, imports accounted for nine. The Chevette was the only U.S. car ranked among the leaders.

The U.S. Congress had been expected to relax emission standards for the 1978 models but failed to act before it adjourned on October 2. Therefore, strict laws postponed since 1975 were scheduled to go into effect in the fall of 1977. The automakers countered by saying that they could not meet those standards and therefore could not build cars. The standards that had been in effect called for emissions of 1.5 g per mi of hydrocarbons; 15 g of carbon monoxide; and 2 g of oxides of nitrogen. The stricter laws called for 0.41 g of hydrocarbons; 3.4 g of carbon monoxide; and 0.4 g of oxides of nitrogen. The automakers said that the biggest drawback was the oxides of nitrogen, claiming that the best they could achieve was 1.5 g. The automakers pleaded for a reconsideration by Congress, but no decision would be made until after it reconvened in January 1977.

AUTHENTICATED NEWS INTERNATIONAL

The new Lancia Scorpion from Italy is for sports-car enthusiasts who want four-wheel disc brakes and leather interiors. The engine is mounted crosswise forward of the rear axle. Curb weight is 2,370 pounds.

While uncertain what the future would bring, the present seemed rather rosy for both Chrysler and GM on the ledger sheets. In the second quarter of the year GM reported profits of $909 million, not only a record for the automaker but also the most ever for a quarter by any industrial manufacturer. It fell short only of the $940 million earned by American Telephone & Telegraph Co.

Chrysler Corp., which went into the year with six consecutive quarters of losses, reversed the trend in the third quarter by reporting record three-month earnings. For the first nine months of the year profits totaled $303 million, surpassing the previous full-year earnings high of $302.9 million in 1968.

When not making money, the automakers were making new cars, and the big news came out of GM, where its standard-size cars underwent a dramatic size and weight reduction of from 6 to 12 in in length and 600 to 1,000 lb in weight depending on the model. The end result was that the full-size cars were built on 116-in wheelbases and were about 212 in in length, some 2 in longer than the mid-size cars. The cars were also narrower but taller than in 1975. GM announced that it would decrease the size of its intermediates in the 1978 model year and its compacts in 1979.

Both Ford and Chrysler said that they would eventually follow GM's lead in resizing their cars, but on a different timetable. Both were expected to reshape their standard-size cars in 1979. Ford also announced that it would completely revamp its compact lines in 1978, eliminating the Maverick/Comet in favour of an expanded line of coupes, sedans, and wagons.

While the U.S. industry made news throughout the year, things were comparatively quiet in other countries. Ford invested $800 million into bringing out the mini Fiesta in Spain, a car that eventually would be shipped to the U.S. Volkswagen unveiled its diesel Golf model in October, with the engine that would be put in the Rabbit in the U.S.

Automakers in West Germany, Italy, France, and Brazil experienced healthy years, while those in the U.K., Mexico, Portugal, and Argentina did not fare as well. The Venezuelan industry expected to lose $50 million in 1976, primarily because of strict government price regulations. Overall, sales in 1976 were about 6% higher than in 1975.

Europeans were having good years in their home markets, but did poorly in the U.S. Currency revaluations made their cars expensive when imported to the U.S., and the trend away from small cars hurt many manufacturers. The Japanese, by contrast, did not have a very good year in their home market but accounted for three of the top four imports in the U.S., Toyota, Datsun, and Honda. All three firms introduced new models into the U.S. Toyo Kogyo, maker of the Mazda, recovered from its deficit of 1975.

The West German market was very strong. Like the U.S., it was shaking off the effects of recession. Volkswagen's profit of DM 500 million in the first half of 1976 compared with a loss of DM 350 million during the same period of 1975. The British manufacturers faced a serious problem, however. Imports into the U.K. reached 43% of the market, with no letup in sight. In an effort to help counter this, British Leyland introduced its first new Rover sedan in 13 years.

Japan's problem was that its employment practices, though they encouraged exports, also flooded its own market with cars. In Japan traditional lifelong employment with the same company necessitated continuous running of production lines even though the cars had nowhere to go.

Perhaps the biggest event outside the U.S. was the salvation of the U.K. operations of the Chrysler Corp. After Chrysler threatened to abandon the country, the British government agreed to bail the company out in order to preserve jobs. The agreement called for the government to provide more than $325 million under a complex plan in which Chrysler would be reimbursed for its losses over a four-year period and share a small portion of its profits with the British government if it went in the black during the same time span.

(JAMES L. MATEJA)

[732.B.2]

BUILDING AND CONSTRUCTION

During the first half of 1976 the total expenditures for new construction in the United States were at an annual rate of $140.5 billion. This level of activity was expected to continue throughout the year, which would constitute a new high level of dollar outlays for construction put in place in the United States on a current dollar basis. The previous highest levels of total outlays occurred in 1973 and 1974, when the respective figures were $137.9 billion and $138.5 billion. When adjustment was made for inflation, however, the picture changed considerably. On a constant dollar basis (1967 dollars) the mid-year 1976 value of construction put into place was at an annual rate of $72.5 billion. On a comparable basis the level of outlays was higher than the expenditure of $69.7 billion in 1975 but below the outlays in each of the preceding four years. The highest level was attained in 1973 when outlays on this basis amounted to $93.3 billion.

While the upturn in construction activity in 1976, which brought it above the low level experienced in 1975, was welcomed, it was still clear that construction would not attain the desired levels of 1972 and 1973. It was encouraging, however, that on both a current and a constant dollar basis residential construction during the first half of 1976 showed sizable gains over 1975. The doldrums in residential construction, which started in 1973 and continued through 1975, had been a major contributing factor to the depressed conditions in the construction industry. On a current dollar basis outlays for residential construction in 1976 were up 28%, while on a constant dollar basis they were up 20%.

In Canada in 1976 the recovery from the recession was slower than in the United States and unemployment remained high. The demand for housing was weak, but housing investment during the last half of 1975 was stimulated by countercyclical policies of the government. During the first quarter of 1976 housing outlays rose about 5%.

In Western Europe there was some modest recovery in building and construction in 1976, but the conditions of inflation and depression had a continuing adverse effect. In the U.K. in 1975 the starts of both public and private dwellings increased over 1974 and moved up again in the first quarter of 1976. Housing starts showed improvement over the comparable period in 1975, and it was expected that private investment would improve in 1976. The pace of recovery in 1976 exceeded expectations in West Germany and France. In 1976 in West Germany, private building demands had begun to improve, and a government subsidy was stimulating investment in plant and equipment. In France recovery accelerated in 1976 because of the upturn in private consumption. In Belgium, Denmark, and Switzerland the recovery in 1976 was less pronounced than in other continental countries, and construction fared poorly. Investment in Sweden in 1975 had declined about 3% because of an 8½% decline in the housing sector.

In Australia the outlook for the gross national product in 1976 was for an increase of about 2%, but construction continued to lag. In New Zealand the recession was still deepening, and construction continued to be down. Construction also continued to lag in South Africa. In Japan, however, an increase in government expenditures was expected to have a favourable effect on the economy in 1976 and stimulate growth in construction and production.

(CARTER C. OSTERBIND)

[733.A]

CHEMICALS

The pickup in U.S. chemical activity continued through the third quarter of 1975 and the first half of 1976. The increase was not, however, sufficient to offset the sharp drop in the first half of 1975. And although chemical industry shipments were higher in 1976 than they were in 1975, the change was due to higher prices rather than to higher production.

According to the U.S. Department of Commerce, chemical shipments in 1975 totaled $85,967,000,000, 5.3% above the $81,377,000,000 registered in 1974. In the first half of 1976, they climbed to $50,071,000,000, 16.3% higher than the $41,886,000,000 worth of chemicals shipped in the corresponding period of 1975. Indications were that the growth had reached a temporary plateau by the end of the first half of the year. By the start of the fourth quarter of the year, it was expected that shipments for the full year 1976 would be 10–15% higher than they were in 1975.

The Federal Reserve Board's index of chemical production averaged 147.3 (1967 = 100) for 1975, 7.6% below the 159.4 average for 1974. But the figures were considerably higher for the second half of the year. And the upward trend continued through the first half of 1976, reaching 170.6 (seasonally adjusted) in March.

The sharp upturn in long-depressed chemical prices that occurred in 1974 continued through 1975. The U.S. Department of Labor's wholesale price index for chemicals increased 23.5% in 1975 to 181.3 (1967 = 100). The rate of increase slowed in 1976, and by the start of the fourth quarter it appeared that the average price for the year would be 5–6% above that for 1975.

Chemicals continued to play a key role in U.S. trade. The U.S. Department of Commerce reported that U.S. chemical exports dropped slightly in 1975, to $8,691,200,000 from $8,819,200,000 in 1974. Imports fell more, however, from $4,017,700,000 in 1974 to $3,696,400,000 in 1975. As a result, the country's favourable trade balance in chemicals rose 4%. Net chemical exports for the U.S. in the first six months of 1976 amounted to $2,674,100,000, on exports of $4,924,100,000 and imports of $2,250,000,000.

While net exports were growing, sales of foreign affiliates of U.S. chemical companies increased handsomely too. The Bureau of Economic Analysis (BEA) of the U.S. Department of Commerce completed a study in 1976 of sales of majority-owned affiliates of U.S. companies. Based on a sample survey, it estimated that sales of chemical affiliates rose 42% in 1974 to $36.2 billion. Among developed countries, the increase was particularly strong in The Netherlands (where sales doubled to $3.6 billion) and in the U.K. (where they went up 57% to $5 billion). Among the less developed nations, the increase in sales by U.S. affiliates was concentrated in South Korea, Brazil, and Mexico.

Confidence in the continued growth of chemical demand was reflected in a U.S. Department of Commerce study on capital spending plans. The survey, completed in late November and early December 1975, showed that chemical companies boosted their capital outlays from $5,690,000,000 in 1974 to $6.3 billion in 1975 (preliminary figure) and planned another increase in 1976 to $6,840,000,000. The percentage increases were 10.7% in 1975 and 8.6% in 1976, higher than the 5% increase in each period for all manufacturing industries.

In the U.S.S.R., ambitious plans for chemical expansion were being made as part of the country's new five-year plan. Chemical production was to be increased 60–65% by 1980, while the target for overall industrial growth for the period was 35–39%. Special emphasis was being given to agricultural fertilizers. Soviet chemical production increased substantially during the first three quarters of 1976, but was having trouble meeting targeted levels.

In other major chemical industries, recovery lagged behind that of the U.S. but appeared to be well under way by the first half of 1976. One trouble area continued to be man-made fibres. Worldwide man-made fibre production fell 8% in 1975 to 10.4 million metric tons, placing it at the 1972 level. In Western Europe production dropped 19% to 2,570,000 tons; in Japan, 12% to 1.4 million tons; and in the U.S., 11% to 2.9 million tons. In June 1976, the president of a Dutch firm estimated that Western European fibre makers lost a combined total of at least $1 billion in 1975.

Despite fibre problems and others, Japan increased its chemical sales 10% in 1975 to $34.6 billion, thereby moving into second place among non-Communist chemical industries. Most of the increase was due to higher prices. The Bank of Japan reported the average chemical price index for the first three quarters of 1975 was 166.4 (1970 = 100), compared with 157.3 in 1974. The chemical production index, according to the

"Here's a nice bungalow in your price range . . . actual size."

ULUSCHAK—EDMONTON JOURNAL/ROTHCO

Ministry of International Trade and Industry (MITI), fell to 115.8 (1970 = 100) for the first three quarters of 1975, from 1974's average of 124.9. In the first half of 1976, MITI reported that chemical expansion plans for fiscal 1976 (which started in April) were $2.1 billion, 20.9% below fiscal 1975.

In West Germany chemical sales dropped 11% in 1975 to $30 billion, according to the German Chemical Industry Association. Chemical exports, which customarily account for 40% of industry sales, were a major factor in the decline. In 1975 they went down 21% to $11.8 billion. A turnaround appeared to have taken place in December 1975, when exports shot up 23%. And for the first half of 1976, sales moved up nicely. The association was looking for a 10% sales increase for the full year. It was expecting, moreover, that most of that would be accounted for by increased output rather than higher prices.

The U.K. chemical industry managed a sales increase of 11% in 1975 to over $18 billion. The government in 1976 was projecting a growth rate of 8% per year for the next four years. The nation's Chemical Industries Association, however, believed that the estimate was too optimistic. A weak economy, steady devaluation of the pound, and escalating plant costs in 1976 were making it difficult to meet targeted growth projections. The association had projected a capital expenditure for chemicals in 1976 of $1,297,000,000 but a Department of Industry survey in the second half of the year indicated that spending would be only $950 million. (DONALD P. BURKE)
[732.D.1]

ELECTRICAL

In 1976 the effects of a continuing low growth in the demand for electricity in most industrialized countries compelled serious consideration of cutbacks in the building of new heavy electrical power plants. A survey conducted in the U.S. for the National Electrical Manufacturers Association reported that utilities that had prepared for high growth now had excess capacity in service and on order. Manufacturers experienced only moderate demand for electrical equipment and reacted by canceling plans for expansion and permanently removing facilities from operation.

In Britain the Central Electricity Generating Board (CEGB), with 40% overcapacity, told manufacturers that no additional generating plants would be required for at least ten years. British plant manufacturers pressed the government to step in and order the construction of new power stations, thereby enabling manufacturers to stay in business in expectation of the reestablishment of a large home market in the 1990s. The government, however, while conscious of the effect of plant closings on unemployment, was not convinced that the optimistic energy demand forecasts for the 1990s would be achieved.

A warning that the world would shortly face another energy crisis, similar to the one that had ended the cheap energy era in 1973, came in October 1976 from the chairman of the International Energy Agency (IEA). He claimed that the industrialized countries, even with only a low 3% annual growth rate in gross national product, would, by 1985, want to consume more oil than the producer countries would be willing to make available.

In spite of such pessimism and forecasts of further increases in energy costs, the West German, Italian, and Japanese heavy electrical plant industries continued to plan for large increases in domestic orders for power plants. Even more optimistically, Sweden's Allmänna Svenska Elektriska Aktiebolaget (ASEA) decided to construct a new factory at Västerås to build power station generators with unit capacities up to 2,000 Mw.

With home markets in the industrialized countries generally unpredictable, the world's heavy electrical manufacturers turned their attention to the Middle East, South America, Southeast Asia, and parts of Africa. The Japanese were particularly successful in the Persian Gulf nations. In September the Mitsubishi Electric Corp. decided to set up a 100% self-financed local corporation at Dubai in the United Arab Emirates. In competition with eight international consortia, Mitsubishi had already won the first of an expected series of contracts for a large power development in Dubai. Mitsubishi also was to fill large power-plant orders in Iraq, Saudi Arabia, and Malaysia. In South Africa, British and West German companies had notable successes.

In other sectors of the electrical industry, a distinct upturn in trade took place in the early months of 1976, but this was short-lived, particularly in Europe. In September the chairman of AEC-Telefunken Konsumgüter admitted that the boom in the home market for household equipment was over although exports continued relatively buoyant. The Dutch Philips group began cutting back on operations in West Germany, where 33,000 workers were employed in 18 wholly owned subsidiaries, and there were signs that the company would shift more resources to the U.S.

Research resources in most industrialized countries were concentrated on alternative

Tiny Schottky diodes developed at General Electric (left) are about the size of a match. In the foreground is the silicon wafer that when sectioned will form the heart of the device. The sodium-sulfur battery (right) is intended for bulk storage of electrical energy for use during peak periods.

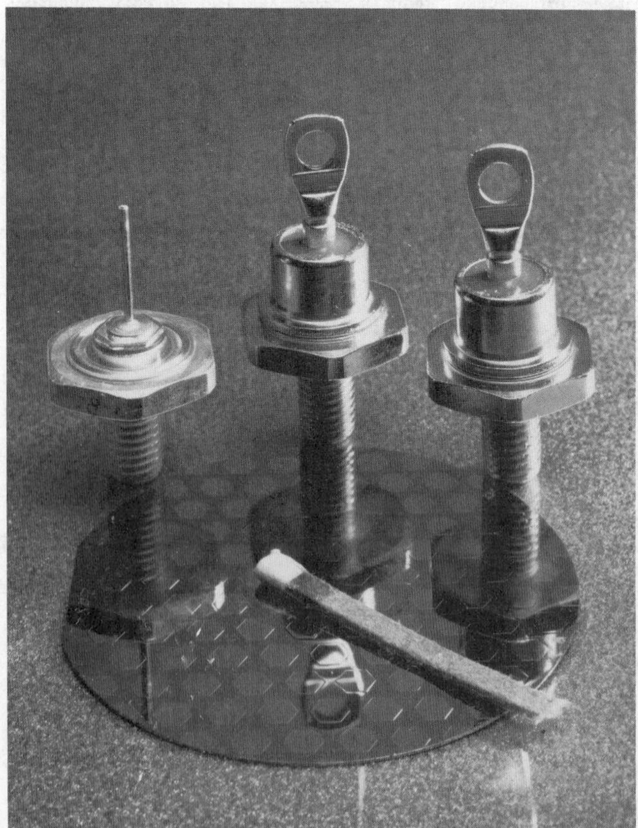

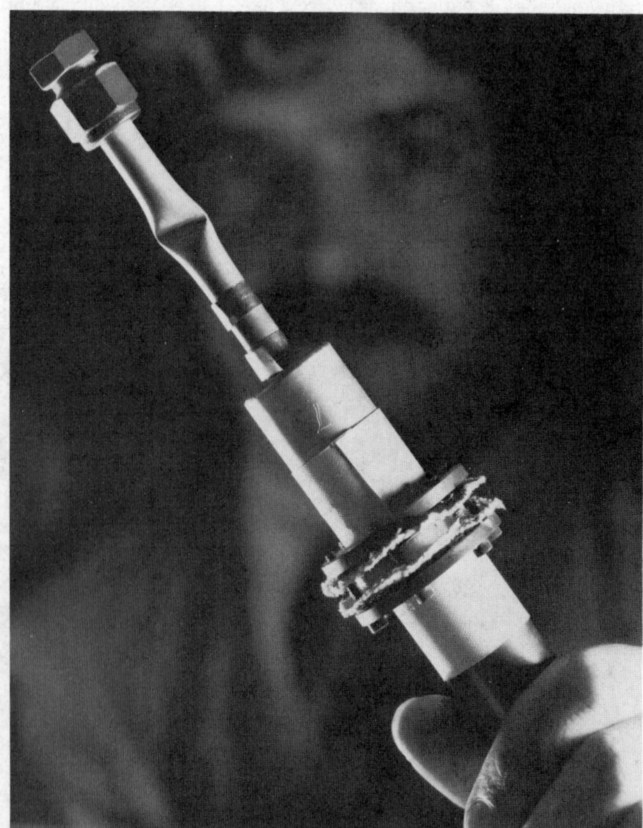

PHOTOS, COURTESY, GENERAL ELECTRIC RESEARCH AND DEVELOPMENT CENTER

methods of generating electricity from renewable energy sources, particularly wind, wave, and solar power; on the development of new types of batteries for vehicles; and on conservation devices such as heat pumps. In the U.S. the price of photovoltaic cells dropped by more than 25% in six months, to $15.50 per watt output. But it remained a long way from the 1986 goal of 50 cents per watt that would enable such cells to compete with conventional sources of electric power in an important number of uses.

(T. C. J. COGLE)

[732.C.6; 10/37.B.5.d]

FURNITURE

Worldwide, the furniture industry showed improvement in 1976, but growth was slower than expected. Both sales and production rose gradually. The total furniture production in Europe was estimated at £8,000 million for 1975. The estimated figure for the U.S. was £5,000 million.

The world's largest furniture exporter in 1975 was West Germany (£385 million) followed by Italy (£217 million) and Belgium (£178 million). Belgium lost second place in 1975 to Italy, whose exports that year increased by 40%. During the first six months of 1976, West Germany increased its exports by 30% over the comparable period of 1975.

Concerning the use of material, wood remained the uncontested king. Production and sales of plastic furniture dropped because of the increased price of this petrochemical material.

In regard to styles, the two major trends in Europe were the Italian, which emphasized rounded corners, and the Scandinavian, featuring straight lines. To these must be added traditional furniture, reproduction or antique, the market for which flourished during the year. Many buyers considered the purchase of this type of furniture as an investment that would act as an effective hedge against inflation. Rustic-style furniture also maintained its popularity, and contemporary furniture slowly gained ground.

Furniture was mostly sold by the manufacturers at fairs and trade marts. The largest furniture fair in the world continued to be the Cologne International Furniture Fair, held every second year in January. In the U.S. the twice-yearly fair at High Point, N.C., the Southern Market Center, was the largest furniture event.

(HENRY MAURICE VALCKE)

The economic downturn of 1974 caused a pent-up demand for household furniture, and in the second half of 1975 sales in the U.S. began a strong comeback. In the spring of 1976, new orders slowed and the year ended about 7% ahead of 1975, with half the dollar increase due to inflation. The slowdown was due principally to sluggishness in housing starts and to inflation-wary consumers putting more of their disposable income into appliances and automobiles. Retail furniture sales rose to $15 billion.

Early American and Colonial furniture had been expected to enjoy increased consumer orders in the U.S. in 1976 because of the Bicentennial. But the boom in those styles failed to materialize. Reclining chairs enjoyed the greatest single product growth in the U.S. in 1976, with sales up 40% compared with 1975. Consumers continued to adopt leisure living as a way of life and helped the summer and casual furniture manufacturers to remain the healthiest industry segment with a shipment increase of almost 30% in 1976.

The use of natural wood finishes increased in the U.S. during the year, and the "country look" continued as a strong style trend. An increase in glass and chromium in contemporary styles reflected the popularity of those materials with consumers. The newest trend was the introduction of a "nostalgia" group by a number of manufacturers. These were reproductions of furniture designs from the early 1900s, including such pieces as fainting couches, sideboards with stained glass doors, and hat racks.

(ROBERT A. SPELMAN)

[732.B.4]

FURS

Furriers continued to do well in 1976, despite economic problems in many countries. Good consumer demand was sparked not only by the importance of furs in the fashion picture but also by the appeal of a luxury investment in a time of inflation. Significantly, fur sales were best in the most expensive categories.

In the U.S. the industry experienced its fifth consecutive good year, and retail sales appeared to have reached a new high of approximately $550 million. Mindful of their inability to meet demand in the previous year, manufacturers introduced their new collections a month earlier. Buying by stores slackened somewhat around midyear, reflecting a general sluggishness in all retail sales, but picked up again when cool weather set in.

The industry's attrition, which had its roots in the difficult years of the 1950s and 1960s, continued in the U.S. and most of Western Europe. New manufacturing industries were springing up in some of the less developed nations, particularly in the Far East, but as yet most of these efforts were little more than training programs.

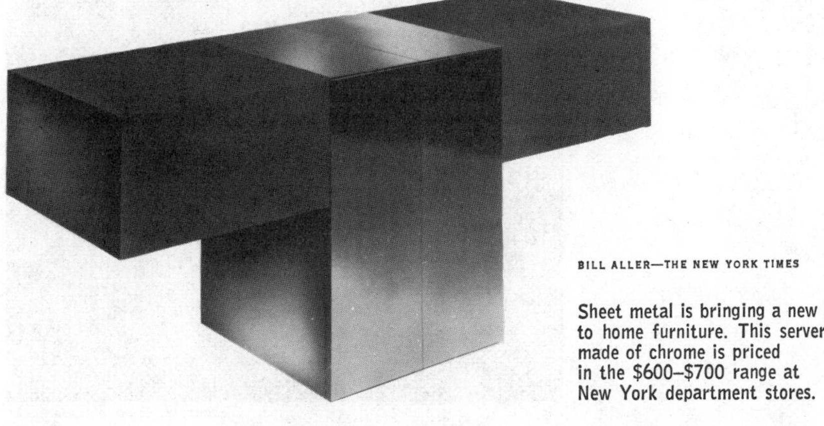

BILL ALLER—THE NEW YORK TIMES

Sheet metal is bringing a new look to home furniture. This server made of chrome is priced in the $600–$700 range at New York department stores.

To help alleviate the shortage of skilled labour in the U.S., the government, through the Human Resources Administration of the Department of Health, Education, and Welfare, authorized a $500,000 training program designed to bring nearly 200 new workers into New York fur factories.

After several years of quiescence, humane societies and some conservationist groups attempted to revive antifur sentiment among consumers. Much of their activity was directed against the trapping of wild animals, particularly the use of traps that caused the animals to suffer. An effort to ban such traps through a state constitutional amendment in Ohio was defeated.

The number of fur ranchers continued to decline, reflecting the retirement of many ranchers and their failure to bring their children into the business during the lean years. There were fewer than 1,100 ranches producing mink in the U.S. in 1976, 11% less than in the previous year. The number of mink produced—3.1 million pelts—was virtually unchanged, however, indicating a trend to larger ranches. In Wisconsin, the chief mink-producing state, production actually rose 3% to 915,000 pelts.

Worldwide, the 1976 mink crop (to be marketed in 1977) was unchanged from the previous year, about 18 million pelts. Production of ranched fox, which also enjoyed good demand, rose about one-third to 1.3 million pelts.

(SANDY PARKER)

[724.C.8.e; 732.C.4]

GEMSTONES

As had been expected in the gem and jewelry industry, the favourable markets of 1975 extended into 1976, reflecting not so much recovery from recession as the continuation of a rapid expansion.

Diamonds still comprised the bulk of the market, with U.S. imports of cut and uncut stones rising by an estimated $25 million and exports by $50 million over 1975. The Central Selling Organization in London, source of most of the world's diamonds, had reported sales of $1,070,000,000 during 1975, down from $1,254,000,000 in 1974, but demand rose briskly in 1976, particularly for larger diamonds and those of less than top quality. As a result, a price rise of almost 3% faced wholesale buyers at the beginning of the year. This worked out to retail price increases of almost 20% for finished smaller diamonds in the U.S. Nevertheless, retail sales expanded, and jewelers frequently had difficulty finding enough larger, better-quality diamonds to fill their orders.

A number of news stories involving diamonds helped to fuel the demand. During 1976, India's Geological Survey announced the discovery of six new diamond-bearing pipes. It was also reported that diamond mining had resumed in Angola as military operations tapered off. The year ended with news of two superb, large diamonds. Cartier held a gala unveiling of the new 107.07-carat Cartier Diamond at its New York salon, and Harry Winston, Inc., presented its newly cut 76-carat diamond, Star of Independence, at the Smithsonian Institution in Washington, D.C.

The rapidly expanding demand for coloured gems, so evident in 1975, also continued into 1976. Supply could not keep pace with demand. Disturbances throughout Asia interfered with mining and drastically reduced gem production. Rubies became scarce and larger stones, such as 10-carat

WIDE WORLD

This 107.07-carat diamond from South Africa was offered for sale by Cartier's at $5 million.

cat's-eyes and 15-carat peridots, practically disappeared from the market. Colombian emeralds were still available, but they tended to be of lesser size and quality.

As a result of the shortage, the price of rubies rose a drastic $1,300 per carat for small stones, and the price of large, top-quality emeralds went as high as $25,000 per carat. Similar price pressures were in evidence for all coloured gems, although emeralds, rubies, and chrysoberyl cat's-eyes, in all sizes, led the parade. Aquamarine appeared to have stabilized, perhaps because of competition from new supplies of topaz turned aquamarine-blue by irradiation.

Public interest in coloured gems was not discouraged by the price rises, however, and there was increased enthusiasm for finding new sources. Sri Lanka encouraged gem exports through tax incentives and the distribution of new mining lands near Ratnapura, and they rose by an estimated $5.6 million in 1976. Drought in southern Sri Lanka, in the Hinidumpatti area, exposed rich gem gravels in dry rice paddies and on banks of streams, causing a local gem rush. Increased demand also encouraged the flow of synthetic, altered, and other substitute stones into the market, creating increased work for such authentication agencies as the Gemological Institute of America.

(PAUL ERNEST DESAUTELS)

[724.C.4]

GLASS

For glassmakers 1976 was a depressing year. Tonnage of glass produced in the EEC countries in 1975 had been 10% below that of 1974. The Belgian-based Glaverbel-Mécaniver group went through a particularly difficult period, with five of its sheet-glass plants shut down and the remaining three running below capacity. Hoya Glass Works of Japan, specialists in optical glass, reported a sharp decline in profits. The French company of Saint-Gobain-Pont-à-Mousson weathered the recession and forecast a 10% growth in turnover in 1976. In Sweden contraction among the hand-made glass companies was expected as competition from imported machine-made glassware intensified.

The U.S. giant Corning Glass signed a scientific and technical cooperation agreement with the Soviet Union. The U.K. firm Pilkington Brothers Ltd. began operations at its float-glass plant at Halmstad in Sweden, and this led to a merger among the remaining flat-glass interests. The Halmstad plant, set up on the presupposition that the float process would eventually supersede all other flat-glass-manufacturing methods, would be capable of supplying 60% of the current Scandinavian demand for float glass. Pilkington Brothers extended their interests by acquiring the largest producer of safety glass in Finland, Lamino Oy, and licensed their float process to the Polish enterprise Pilimex-Cekop.

Environmental matters continued to be a subject of concern, and the emission of toxic fumes, use of energy, and disposal of containers after use were major areas of discussion and activity. The first created a need for capital investment, the second for investigation into methods of improving melting techniques, and the third for active reuse of cullet (waste glass). Most countries with developed glass container industries became actively concerned with reclaiming glass from household waste. The problem was to acquire the cullet in a satisfactory condition, so that it would neither damage the furnace nor impair the quality of the finished product, and at a price lower than that for basic raw materials. Pressures for greater use of returnable bottles increased, but the U.S. Bureau of Domestic Commerce claimed that a complete change to a returnable bottle system for soft drinks and beer would not reduce fuel usage or litter.

Glass fibre became a product area of increasing interest. Pilkington Brothers began large-scale exploitation of glass-fibre-reinforced cement following development of a commercial method of manufacturing a nonreactive fibre. The U.S. Energy Research and Development Administration supported the development of a small car powered by a flywheel made of composite glass fibre material. Philips Research Laboratories in The Netherlands produced experimental fluorescent lamps incorporating a small amount of glass fibre and claimed that they used only one-third of the energy consumed by the equivalent incandescent lamp. The large, self-lubricating universal joints used in the Concorde supersonic aircraft, made of impregnated glass fibre fabrics, were rustproof and were said to have ten times the life of conventional joints.

(CYRIL WEEDEN)

[724.C.5.a; 733.A.4.a.vii]

INSURANCE

Insurance sales growth continued at record levels in 1976. During the preceding decade global insurance premiums of private insurers had more than tripled, but expansion was uneven. Average annual rates of increase were approximately 20% in Asia, 15% in Europe, and 9% in the U.S.

Life Insurance. With annual purchases at the $300 billion level in the U.S. by the end of 1976, more than 150 million people were insured for total life insurance in force of approximately $2.3 trillion. This averaged more than $33,000 for each insured family. Life insurance companies had assets of close to $300 billion at midyear.

Review of life insurance programs and estate plans to reflect changes in estate and gift tax laws incorporated in the U.S. Tax Reform Act of 1976 became a major sales and service task for life insurance agents, attorneys, and tax accountants. Other sales opportunities resulted from increased public knowledge of the 1974 Employee Retirement Income Security Act, which permitted life insurers to compete with banks and

Chunks of a cellular ceramic developed by Corning Glass for use in catalytic converters in automobile exhaust systems. The ceramic is coated with platinum that converts hydrocarbons and carbon monoxide into harmless carbon dioxide and water. The same ceramic, coated with a different catalyst, can be used to reduce nitrogen oxides in the exhaust.

COURTESY, CORNING GLASS WORKS

other investment institutions for individual retirement accounts.

Two major U.S. life insurer associations merged in 1976 to form the American Council of Life Insurance. As a result of consumer protection activities, almost all life insurance companies in the U.K. agreed to limit first-year commissions and to structure them on premiums rather than on sums insured. Four associations were joining to form the British Insurance Brokers' Council and were seeking a registration plan that would obviate the need for government regulation.

Property and Liability Insurance. Statutory underwriting losses continued to plague U.S. insurers, but midyear reports indicated they were slowing to $500 million after first-quarter losses of $1.4 billion. Investment gains were a more than offsetting $2.3 billion for the first six months.

Trouble spots were concentrated in the liability insurance area, but were not limited to it. Medical malpractice and products liability costs escalated rapidly, with many insurers reducing their writings. The swine flu inoculation program (*see* HEALTH AND DISEASE) required a combined industry and government effort to provide liability protection for manufacturers of the vaccine. New medical malpractice "joint underwriting associations" were required in many states, and some medical groups formed new insurers. Automobile insurance rates rose approximately 20%, but claims also increased rapidly. Inflation added to repair costs, and citizens band radio thefts reached epidemic proportions.

Serious financial difficulties were encountered by the Government Employees Insurance Co., a major U.S. auto insurer. A combined issue of convertible preferred shares and an industry reinsurance pool were in process to raise additional capital of more than $50 million. In the U.K. similar problems were being partially met under the new Policyholders Protection Act, providing compensation of 90% of sums due in insurance company insolvencies. Early 1976 was poor for U.K. insurers, with worldwide underwriting losses at the £175 million level. Throughout the world, earthquakes were unusually severe, and a spectacular fire in Sakata, Japan, in November caused more than $138 million in damages.

(DAVID L. BICKELHAUPT)

[534.J]

IRON AND STEEL

While 1976 began with modest hopes for the recovery of the steel industry from acute depression, it ended in disappointment and renewed uncertainty. The economies of most industrial countries had been gradually adjusting to the rise in oil prices and to the other unbalancing developments of 1973–74, and inflation had abated in some measure. A slow but soundly based growth in real steel consumption was expected to result from these circumstances. In the first part of 1976 there were indications that this was taking place; many countries experienced a rise in demand for consumer durables, especially automobiles, and the depletion of industrial stocks came to an end. This favourable trend in turn induced some rebuilding of steel stocks held by merchants and consumers. Steel production began to rise in many countries, and the general tone of the steel market strengthened.

At this point in the cycle the steel industry looked for an increase in demand from the industrial investment sector to reinforce and extend the strengthening market. This failed to emerge on any substantial scale, so that growth in real steel consumption tended to level out and confidence generally faltered. By late summer prices were weakening again and international trade pressures growing, with complaints by the U.S. and EEC steel producers about the export activities of the Japanese steel industry in particular.

By the fall it was clear that although world steel output might reach 690 million–700 million metric tons (against 650 million in 1975 and 710 million in 1974), any wide-ranging recovery would be deferred until well into 1977. Toward the year's end many of the major producing areas, and especially much of the EEC, were facing market prospects only slightly less forbidding than those of 1975. Meanwhile, the steel industries of the countries with centrally planned economies continued to develop at about their accustomed pace, and a number of the less developed countries were achieving significant increases in output.

The general market situation was reflected in the finances of Western steel companies. The improvement in utilization rates, as compared with the disastrous 1975 position, and such price rises as the market was able to bear (significant at least in some areas and for certain products) together brought some relief. But in many regions it was only the companies with substantial diversified interests in nonsteel fields or in sectors of the steel market that had remained fairly buoyant (such as oil pipes) that avoided losses. Moreover, in the current recession, the prices of the industry's most important raw materials generally showed themselves more resistant to the downward pressures of the low cycle than did the prices of steel products. This development tended to increase concern about the industry's overall profitability in relation to the finance required for investment in new and replacement capacity to meet anticipated future demand and in the anti-pollution equipment necessitated by legal and social considerations.

The U.S. economy was the first to show signs of a real recovery, which broadened during the first part of 1976. But investment in industrial plant and in nonresidential construction did not respond similarly, and this provoked a hesitation in late summer. For the steel industry this resulted in a first half year better than the second. Price increases were made earlier in the year and capacity utilization was high, but in late summer further proposed price increases on certain products were withdrawn. During the fall estimates of deliveries of finished products and of earnings for the year were revised downward, while some temporary plant closings and layoffs occurred. For all of 1976 the U.S. industry was expected to produce about 119 million metric tons (against 106 million in 1975 and 132 million in 1974). The prospects for renewed expansion in 1977 looked reasonably good.

Table VIII. World Production of Crude Steel
In 000 metric tons

Country	1971	1972	1973	1974	1975	1976 Year to date	1976 No. of months	Percent change 1976/75
World	582,500	630,100	697,300	709,900	650,500	—	—	—
U.S.S.R.	120,640	125,590	131,480	136,200	141,000	84,800	7	+ 4.0
U.S.	109,060	120,750	136,460	131,990	105,940	89,970	9	+10.2
Japan	88,560	96,900	119,320	117,130	102,310	78,760	9	+ 0.7
Germany, West	40,310	43,700	49,520	53,230	40,410	32,860	9	+ 5.3
United Kingdom	24,240	25,390	26,720	22,400	19,840	16,690	9	+11.4
France	22,840	24,050	25,270	27,020	21,530	17,190	9	+ 5.9
China*	21,000	23,000	25,000	27,000	30,000	—	—	—
Italy	17,450	19,810	21,000	23,800	21,870	17,320	9	+ 4.5
Poland	12,690	13,420	14,060	14,560	15,100	9,027	7	+ 4.7
Belgium	12,440	14,530	15,520	16,230	11,580	9,240	9	+ 4.9
Czechoslovakia	12,070	12,730	13,160	13,640	14,320	7,310	6	+ 1.3
Canada	11,040	11,860	13,390	13,610	13,030	9,870	9	− 0.1
Spain	8,020	9,530	10,800	11,500	11,100	8,190	9	− 1.6
Romania	6,800	7,400	8,160	8,840	9,550	†		
Australia	6,750	6,750	7,700	7,810	7,870	5,980	9	+ 0.4
India	6,100	6,860	6,890	7,070	7,990	6,820	9	+18.0
Brazil	6,000	6,520	7,150	7,520	8,390	6,860	9	+10.9
Germany, East	5,750	6,070	5,860	6,170	6,480	3,350	6	+ 4.4
Sweden	5,270	5,260	5,660	5,990	5,610	3,800	9	− 9.9
Luxembourg	5,240	5,460	5,920	6,450	4,620	3,500	9	− 0.4
Netherlands, The	5,080	5,580	5,620	5,840	4,820	3,760	9	+ 2.4
South Africa	4,880	5,340	5,720	5,840	6,830	5,290	9	+ 2.1
Austria	3,960	4,070	4,240	4,700	4,070	3,430	9	+11.0
Mexico	3,820	4,430	4,760	5,120	5,280	4,000	9	+ 1.5
Hungary	3,110	3,270	3,330	3,470	3,670	1,840	6	+ 0.8
Yugoslavia	2,450	2,590	2,680	2,840	2,920	2,010	6	− 4.8
Bulgaria	1,950	2,120	2,250	2,190	2,260	1,440	7	+11.7
Argentina	1,910	2,150	2,210	2,350	2,210	1,920	9	+14.3
South Korea	470	590	1,160	1,950	1,995	2,440	9	+63.4

*Estimated.
†1976 figures not yet available.
Sources: International Iron and Steel Institute; British Steel Corporation.

Table IX. World Production of Pig Iron and Blast Furnace Ferroalloys
In 000 metric tons

Country	1971	1972	1973	1974	1975
World	422,550	446,940	495,430	508,090	472,900
U.S.S.R.	89,250	92,300	94,900	99,870	102,960
U.S.	74,110	81,110	91,610	87,010	72,510
Japan*	72,740	74,060	90,000	90,440	86,880
Germany, West	29,990	32,000	36,830	40,220	30,070
China†	19,000	21,000	23,000	26,000	27,000
France	18,340	19,000	20,290	22,520	17,890
United Kingdom	15,420	15,320	16,850	13,900	12,130
Belgium	10,530	11,900	12,660	13,150	9,070
Italy	8,550	9,440	10,030	11,690	11,350
Czechoslovakia	7,960	8,360	8,530	8,910	9,420
Canada*	7,830	8,490	9,540	9,420	9,420
Poland	7,190	7,420	8,140	7,790	8,200
India	6,940	7,020	7,340	7,260	8,290
Australia*	6,240	6,000	7,660	7,250	7,570
Spain*	4,850	5,930	6,290	6,890	6,830
Brazil*	4,690	5,290	5,470	5,980	7,220
Luxembourg	4,580	4,670	5,130	5,470	3,890
Romania	4,380	4,890	5,710	6,080	6,600
South Africa	4,040	4,430	4,330	4,620	5,180
Netherlands, The	3,760	4,290	4,710	4,800	3,970
Austria*	2,850	2,850	3,000	3,440	3,060
Sweden	2,580	2,360	2,570	2,980	3,310
Germany, East	2,030	2,150	2,200	2,280	2,460
Hungary	1,980	2,060	2,110	2,290	2,230
Mexico*	1,680	1,890	2,800	3,210	2,960
Yugoslavia*	1,510	1,820	1,960	2,130	2,000
Bulgaria	1,340	1,510	1,610	1,480	1,580

*Pig iron only.
†Estimated.
Source: British Steel Corporation.

COURTESY, U.S. STEEL

The U.S. Steel Corporation's Gary, Indiana, plant made its 300 millionth ton of steel in April. The photo shows a basic oxygen process furnace. The plant has produced more steel than any other plant in the world.

The Japanese steel industry was badly affected by the general recession conditions in 1975, compounded in the early months of 1976 by an accentuation of the movement to deplete stocks. Trading profits suffered correspondingly, especially in the case of companies with relatively small nonsteel activities. The position improved significantly during the summer; domestic steel prices were raised and production rates improved. For the year as a whole an output of 107 million metric tons was expected (against 102 million in 1975 and 117 million in 1974), with further expansion in prospect for 1977. But the increase in Japanese output in 1976 was very largely due to export sales (up more than 20% over 1975), which provoked complaints by other major producers during the fall.

The EEC steel industry benefited from some increase in real demand early in the year and from a technical adjustment of steel stocks. During this period prices were raised in relation to the exceptionally depressed levels to which they had fallen in 1975. But during the summer the order position began to fall away again and confidence faltered badly, especially in West Germany, France, and the Benelux countries. Output appeared likely to reach 135 million metric tons in 1976 (against 125 million in 1975 and 156 million in 1974). In this situation, many of the Community steel companies that had incurred losses in the past year were having great difficulty in returning to profitability.

The steel industries of the Communist countries were relatively little affected by the recession, and all increased their output. These countries generally account for about 30% of crude steel production, but in a world recession the proportion rises (to 35% in 1975). The Soviet Union, which was likely to produce 145 million metric tons of steel in 1976, remained the world's largest producer, a position it first took from the U.S. during the 1971 recession, while Poland and Czechoslovakia, with annual production of over 15 million metric tons and over 14 million metric tons, respectively, were now by any standards highly important steel producers. But in relation to its size the steel industry of the Communist bloc played a relatively small role in international steel trade.

Many less developed countries had ambitious plans to expand steel output if financing and technical problems could be resolved. The UN Industrial Development Organization (UNIDO) was increasingly active in the steel field and sponsored a global study and international meetings on the prospects for expansion of steel and of ferrous raw materials production in the less developed countries.

Despite the relapse of late 1976, the outlook for the world steel industry in 1977 seemed to be an improving one. Expansion of output to a level significantly above that of 1974 was almost certain, though boom conditions of the kind associated with that year appeared improbable.

(TREVOR J. MACDONALD)

[724.C.3.g; 732.C.2]

MACHINERY AND MACHINE TOOLS

The sales picture for machine tools was much brighter in 1976 than in 1975. Following a precipitous decline in orders from an all-time high in the first quarter of 1974, sales bottomed out in the first quarter of 1975 and then began an upward trend that continued into the fourth quarter of 1976. Total sales for machine tools were 75% greater for the first three quarters of 1976 than for the same period in 1975. Metal-cutting tools increased 67% and metal-forming tools registered a 118% gain over 1975.

Depending on the type and complexity of a machine tool, the manufacture and shipment of the equipment usually lags far behind the sales of the equipment. This is because of the long lead time needed to obtain such parts as the castings, bearings, motors, and controls, as well as the long time needed to manufacture the many complex, and sometimes large, component parts. For these reasons the manufacturing picture for 1976 was quite different from the sales picture. Reflecting the drop in orders in 1974 and early 1975, the production of machine tools declined steadily from the second quarter of 1975 through the third quarter of 1976. Actual shipments in the first three quarters of 1976 declined 19% compared with the same period in 1975. The production of metal-cutting machines was down 23% and of metal-forming machines down 4% from the comparable period. Because of the countertrends in sales and shipments, the industry backlog of unfilled orders declined continuously through 1975 and came to a low point in June 1976. After that time there was a steady and substantial increase in the backlog.

Fortuitously coinciding with the upturn in sales, numerous machine tool shows were held during the year. Sponsored by the National Machine Tool Builders' Association, the International Machine Tool Show was held in Chicago's McCormick Place and International Amphitheatre from September 6 to September 17. This show, among the largest manufacturing expositions in the U.S., attracted more than 78,000 visitors from all parts of the world. Truly international in nature, it included exhibitors from

Turbine department of the Bucharest Heavy Machine Enterprise in Romania. Besides turbines, the enterprise produces cement mills and other equipment for heavy industry.

AGERPRES BUCHAREST/EASTFOTO

26 countries other than the U.S. Displayed were the latest machine tool developments, with an increased emphasis on the numerically controlled types. The use of numerical control units was spreading beyond the turning, boring, and milling types of machines to equipment such as grinding machines. For the first time a tape-controlled band saw was shown.

During 1976 other large machine tool shows were held in Birmingham, England; Milan, Italy; and Tokyo. Early in the year West Germany exhibited a large number of its machines in Moscow.

Machine tool builders in the U.S. would be among the first to be affected by the changeover to the metric system, authorized by legislation in 1975. Since the industry had long supplied metric-sensitive measurement elements on the machine tools for export, machines purchased in the U.S. could be readily equipped with the necessary devices. The conversion of the basic machine to the metric system would, however, depend upon the availability of component parts built to metric units and on the expected life of the current designs.

(EDWARD J. LOEFFLER)

[722.B–C; 732.C.7]

NUCLEAR INDUSTRY

Orders for new nuclear power plants remained low in 1976. Only three nuclear units were ordered in the U.S., though operation of nuclear plants had greatly improved and had allowed savings in oil purchases estimated at $1 billion for the year.

West German utilities did not order until the end of the year, but Spain continued strong, ordering three plants. France ordered several units, including a first at 1,300 Mw. France reorganized its industry, removing most of the holdings of the Westinghouse Electric Corp. in the single French nuclear supplier, Framatome, and altering the functioning of the Commissariat of Atomic Energy to make it more commercially responsive.

South Africa and the Philippines placed new orders, and contracts were signed for projects already announced. Brazil ordered two units from West Germany, and Iran ordered from France and West Germany. Israel, Egypt, and Turkey firmly committed themselves to order, and India and Pakistan announced large programs. Finland ordered a third Soviet unit, larger than the others. The U.S.S.R. announced a large-scale ten-year building program. Both pressurized water and graphite-moderated, water-cooled 1,000-Mw units were already in operation within the U.S.S.R.

Britain had expected to order the first steam-generating heavy-water reactors in 1976, but, due to low growth predictions and needed cuts in public spending, did not do so. The government's technical advisers reassessed the new system and concluded that it would never be commercially successful; they suggested that another proven system such as the British advanced gas-cooled reactor (AGR) or the U.S. light water reactor be reconsidered. The first AGR stations finally started operation, several years late, and the prototype fast breeder reactor (FBR) reached full power.

A referendum on nuclear power held in California produced a 2–1 vote in favour. In the year's elections in the U.S., Sweden, and West Germany, nuclear power was a major issue. Pro-nuclear forces seemed to lose ground, though the influence of nuclear policy in the results could be questioned.

The nuclear debate in Britain focused on reprocessing of Japanese fuels; British industry wanted to place a large order from Japan. The government organized a formal public debate resulting in acceptance of the deal, but by then France had taken half of the order. A public report critical of the FBR's resulted in a government decision to delay plans to build a full-sized unit.

WIDE WORLD

The white dome houses a nuclear reactor at the Idaho National Engineering Laboratory near Idaho Falls, where safety tests were conducted on equipment for nuclear power plants.

Japan's political situation following the Lockheed scandals stopped consideration of such nuclear power issues as siting of advanced reactors and funding of reprocessing and enriching projects. West Germany too suffered due to election uncertainties. France, despite an active campaign against the FBR, began contracting for the first full-sized 1,200-Mw FBR, the SuperPhénix. The U.S. Congress passed virtually no nuclear legislation.

Also on the political front was the issue of nuclear weapons proliferation. This had intensified following India's explosion of a nuclear device in 1974 and the sale of reactors and plutonium reprocessing and uranium enrichment technology by West Germany to Brazil in 1975. Some consensus and agreement as to control was reached, but actual success was limited. France sold a reprocessing plant to Pakistan and was only stopped from selling one to South Korea by strong U.S. intervention. France also won the South African nuclear order, perhaps because the U.S. and West German governments may not have allowed their suppliers to take it. (In November the French government announced that it would make no more sales of nuclear reactors to South Africa after the two presently on order were delivered.) These sales and Brazil's contract with West Germany were to be under the control of the UN International Atomic Energy Agency. In the U.S., a court decision halted licensing of new plants for several months. The decision questioned the completeness of the Nuclear Regulatory Commission's assessment of the environmental impact of reprocessing and the disposal of nuclear contaminated wastes, and a reassessment was ordered.

Other significant developments included the beginning of operation of two demonstration enrichment plants by Urenco, a tripartite company set up by Britain, West Germany, and The Netherlands. The international enriching company, Eurodif, led by France, was well advanced in construction of a large plant, and its sister company, Coredif, announced the building of another.

With the development of advanced reactor systems, the high-temperature reactor was brought to a complete standstill when General Atomic (U.S.) lost its last order and the Dragon HTR facility, an OECD project built in the U.K., was ended. In the U.S. a project to build a test reactor for fusion power was begun, but the Joint European Torus (JET) was halted by political indecision. The nonpower segments of the industry continued to grow, with the radioisotope market for industrial detection and measuring systems, medical and pharmaceutical research, and environmental analysis expanding by some 30% annually. There were further developments in food preservation by irradiation.

(RICHARD W. KOVAN)

[721.B.9]

PAINTS AND VARNISHES

As it fought for sales in the aftermath of the recession, the paint industry in 1976 continued to be beset by environmental and consumer pressures. In the U.S. the trade association made strenuous efforts to ward off a reduction in the permitted lead content of household paints from 0.5 to 0.06%. Such a reduction would have had a drastic effect on formulations and, the industry argued, was not justified by current medical evidence. Although a stay of execution was secured, it seemed likely that the lower level would be enforced in 1977.

Another heavy metal under attack was mercury. In the U.K. an official report identified the marine paint industry as a major nonagricultural source of mercurial pesticides entering the seas. Although the industry challenged the figures, restrictions and prenotification would probably be demanded in the near future. Alleged new carcinogens continued to be found among the paint industry's raw materials, and the important class of yellow, orange, and red pigments based on chromates came under suspicion. The absence from coating systems of more exotic carcinogens, such as vinyl chloride monomer and bischloromethyl ether, had to be demonstrated.

Expected agreement within the EEC on a directive for the labeling of paints and allied products failed to materialize. The Netherlands entered a late objection to the requirement that a number of risk and safety phrases be shown in appropriate languages, arguing that a system of pictograms would be preferable. The suggestion seemed unlikely to win early approval.

In most countries economic recovery reached the paint industry too late to affect results for 1975. In Europe reported contractions in volume ranged from 1.8% in France to 15% in Switzerland, with West Germany (the largest manufacturer) showing a 2.9% fall, Scandinavia 4%, and the U.K. 5.9%. The U.S. paint industry experienced a 6% decline in output, selling about 890 million gal for $4 billion. However, manufacturers in most countries were able to raise prices in step with costs. In the U.S. sales value grew by some 8%, and in Scandinavia by 6%, while U.K. companies increased their income by 15.7%. Only in Austria, Portugal, and Switzerland were paintmakers unable to cover the effects of inflation.

Competition in export markets intensified, and many countries were unable to hold the gains of previous years. The world's largest exporter, West Germany, sold 12.5% less by volume overseas, but The Netherlands (third in the world) just managed to hold its own with a late surge. The South African paint industry achieved a small increase in sales, to some 108 million litres worth about R 120 million. Japanese output, however, barely exceeded 80% of the 1973 record level of 1,450,000 tons. The Australian industry saw a 6% decline in 1974–75, with production amounting to 160.6 million litres; this contrasted with a steady growth of some 5% a year since 1970, mainly in water-thinned emulsion (latex) paints.

(LIONEL BILEFIELD)

[732.D.7]

PHARMACEUTICALS

Despite occasional complaints from drug industry executives about the "staggering" cost of research and development (estimated by more than one company president at 12% of industry sales) and about how much of this went into "nonproductive" research to prove and re-prove efficacy and safety, the pharmaceutical industry continued to set new sales and production records.

After a "dry" period of four or five years, there was evidence that the research and development effort was beginning to pay off again in new products. For example, the Pharmaceutical Manufacturers Association (PMA) compiled a "bright new developments" list that included several new broad-spectrum antibiotics for the treatment of urinary tract infections; a new drug to correct potassium depletion in hypertension; a new antibiotic effective against gram-negative bacteria; a drug useful as an adjunct in the management of minimal brain dysfunction in children; and a new drug for use against schistosomiasis, which debilitates millions in Africa, the Middle East, and Latin America.

Domestic volume of ethical (prescription) pharmaceuticals in 1976 was expected to reach $8.1 billion in the U.S. and $14.3 billion worldwide, according to the PMA. In 1975 the respective figures were $6.9 billion domestically (13.3% above 1974) and $12.2 billion worldwide (up 13.6%). These high percentage gains were somewhat misleading, however, since to a large degree they reflected inflationary pressures on industry costs and prices rather than actual business gains. The two largest single categories of ethical drugs were tranquilizers and antibiotics, each of which accounted for slightly more than $500 million in U.S. sales.

For the over-the-counter (OTC) or proprietary drug market, U.S. Bureau of the Census figures for 1974 (the latest available) indicated sales of $1,690,000,000, 6.7% above the previous year. Analgesics ($431.8 million) were the leading product, followed by respiratory or cough and cold preparations ($300.4 million), skin preparations ($259.8 million), and vitamins and nutrients ($247.9 million).

Two regulatory developments had great significance for the proprietary drug industry: the issuance of "monographs" or efficacy-safety-ingredient guidelines by special U.S. Food and Drug Administration panels, and the issuance by the FDA of Good Manufacturing Practices Regulations for OTC drugs. The first would force the reformulation of many such drugs, mostly to eliminate less-than-effective ingredients. The second would improve the quality of manufacturing techniques.

The OTC monograph program was expected to affect the industry more profoundly than any governmental action since passage of the Food, Drug and Cosmetic Act in 1938. Possibly as many as 40% of the 196,000 OTC drugs on the market would have to be reformulated, relabeled, repackaged, or otherwise changed. Further, the U.S. Federal Trade Commission indicated that it would use these monograph label-claim restrictions as the basis for a trade regulation rule sharply limiting advertising claims.

(DONALD A. DAVIS)

[732.D.4]

PLASTICS

In most of the world the plastics industry improved steadily in 1976 following the 1975 recession. Japan was something of an exception because, although increased exports of cars and electrical goods helped certain component sectors, they did not compensate for continuing flatness in domestic demand for end products. The welcome revival that began in the U.S. in mid-1975 was fueled early in 1976 by restocking as confidence returned. With many schemes for new plastics materials capacity delayed or canceled during the downturn, spasmodic shortages of certain polymers reemerged and new investment recommenced, although cautiously and selectively. These factors combined with continuing inflation to edge up plastics prices still further.

There was some feeling early in the year that the sudden turnaround in inventory

This isn't a radar dish or a giant mushroom. It's the bottom of a distillation tower for the production of styrene, in process of construction for a Canadian manufacturer of plastics and synthetic rubber.

AUTHENTICATED NEWS INTERNATIONAL

policies had created an artificial impression of boom. However, activity continued to build up, even extending to the manufacturers of plastics-processing machinery. Toward the end of the year notes of caution were heard from the U.S., where there was some lessening of expansion during the presidential election campaign, and from those European countries, notably the U.K., with specific industrial problems. Nevertheless, 1977 was expected to be another year of improvement, if at a slower pace.

Statistical patterns had been completely disrupted by the violent swings in the supply/demand pattern since the energy crisis of 1973–74, but, overall, the output of plastics in 1976, in Western Europe at least, was expected to return to the 1974 level of 17 million metric tons. The U.S. did considerably better, and its output was expected to equal that of Europe, nearly 20% more than in 1975. Including some 7 million metric tons from Japan, total world plastics production in 1976 was estimated at around 43 million metric tons, compared with 41 million tons in 1974 and rather less in 1975.

The industry everywhere had to contend with the increasingly complex problems of dealing with a multitude of official and other regulatory agencies concerned with various environmental, health, and safety aspects of the production, processing, and use of plastics. On the manufacturing side, following the discovery of carcinogenic properties in vinyl chloride monomer (the feedstock for polyvinyl chloride [PVC]) in 1974, no other potential health hazard of comparable dimensions had been identified in the production of plastics or of their intermediates. After exhaustive reviews of permissible levels of monomer concentrations in plant locations, and with practical compromises mostly established, PVC, one of the largest-tonnage materials, was again on a growth curve, even in food packaging.

Requirements concerning flame retardance and toxicity in end use proliferated. The situation was at its most complicated in the U.S., and the most exacting demands probably came from Sweden, while the rest of the plastics world tended to draw on U.S. practice in setting the standard in these matters. The industry recognized its responsibilities and attempted to make compliance more realistic by seeking to work more closely with the government departments and other bodies involved. The year saw even greater concentration on plastics with improved flame-retardation characteristics for all sorts of uses in construction and in consumer appliances.

One plastics material with enormous potential became more generally recognized in 1976. Polypropylene could be used as a general purpose molding and extrusion material, as well as in the form of sheet, film, and fibre. It was easily processed and converted into end products, and it had economic advantages partly resulting from a relatively favourable feedstock-supply position. Polypropylene had been discovered in Italy in 1954. Although its level of production was still well below the "big three," PVC, polyethylene, and polystyrene, it was expected to become the volume leader by the year 2000.

Developments in 1976 confirmed the direction in which the industry had been moving since the energy crisis forced new attitudes. Greater efficiency in conversion, through improved machinery and techniques, and utilization of material-saving foam structures and extended use of fillers were constantly to the fore. The recession had taught individual firms not to become overdependent on business associated with consumer purchasing of luxury items or of durable goods, such as cars, furniture, and appliances, whose replacement could be postponed. The less sensitive sectors involved essential purchasing of a kind that could provide continuing, noncyclic opportunities; for example, agricultural and other specialized vehicles and machinery; equipment and components for social and institutional building; and educational and hospital requisites.

(ROBIN C. PENFOLD)

[732.D.5]

PRINTING

The year brought improvement and perhaps consolidation, but few revolutionary innovations. Ink-jet printing for extra-speed printout of information became more widespread. A. B. Dick Co. started selling ink-jet printers in Europe, mainly to newspaper and magazine publishers. Mead Dijit in the U.S. introduced attachments to permit in-line personalization of printed products. IBM brought improved quality to ink-jet printing of type.

A number of newspapers changed to Di-Litho direct lithographic printing, using offset printing plates and water or alcohol dampening. Tokyo Kikai Seisakusho, Ltd., of Japan became the first manufacturer to supply a web press especially built for direct lithographic printing.

The length of printing runs went down as magazine circulations shrank and the high cost of paper encouraged publishers and print buyers to print shorter initial runs and to reprint later. Printers searched for smaller presses, designed to cater to short-run demands and provide for rapid changeover to new work. In web offset, the first miniwebs capable of producing book-quality printing became operational. The Timson Major book web press system was a compact, low-level machine design with wheel-on folders to permit rapid change of work. *The Times* of London became the first newspaper to print on new extra-light thermomechanical newsprint from Finland; developed by UPM United Paper Mills, it provided wood base savings of 25% against conventional newsprint production.

In Sweden a newspaper pressroom in which the presses were entirely separated from the operators and supervised via closed-circuit television was intended to reduce noise damage to hearing. Lower noise on folders was sought by most manufacturers, but mechanical noise reduction was difficult to achieve, and architectural solutions to the problem gained ground. Japan became the world's largest user of electronic colour scanners. A laser system for gravure cylinder production was proposed in Britain, and in Finland a large publisher-printer used a U.S.-designed laser system to work directly from phototypesetting machines.

In wallpaper printing, the world's biggest reel-fed rotary screen-printing machine was announced. In textile printing, heat transfer printing by ink sublimation became worldwide big business. Sheet-fed offset remained the favourite for commercially merchandised designs in short runs.

Phototypesetting and electronic editing continued to gain adherents as low-cost, versatile, compact machines with keyboards, visual display editing and correction screens, and medium-fast photosetting units became available. Many publishers felt that the time had come to investigate the possibility of handling their own typesetting and origination, leaving the printer to print and bind.

(W. PINCUS JASPERT)

[735.E.3–4]

RUBBER

The U.S. rubber industry suffered a severe setback in 1976 as a result of the four-month strike by the United Rubber Workers, which

In the pressroom of Madrid's daily "El Pais." The newspaper uses a Harris N-1650 web offset press.

started in April. The business climate for the rubber industry had been favourable early in the year, reflecting the general business upturn. However, the strike affected all segments of the industry and its suppliers adversely. The settlement called for an increase in wages of approximately 36% spread over three years, plus some fringe benefits. These wage raises, combined with increasing materials costs, were resulting in higher prices for rubber products. Also because of the strike, tires were in short supply at year's end.

The raw materials situation had stabilized somewhat with regard to supply and demand, but not price. The Association of Natural Rubber Producing Countries took steps to stabilize the price of natural rubber at a value equitable to both producer and consumer. This followed the temporary stockpile plan implemented in 1975 by the Malaysian government. Product and market trends indicated that natural rubber would gain a greater share of the market. Some forecasts suggested an increase in use of natural rubber from 33% of total rubber as of 1976 to 42% by 1980. On Oct. 1, 1975, natural rubber sold for 30 cents per pound for smoked sheets and on Oct. 1, 1976, for 40⅝ cents per pound; throughout the year it fluctuated between 30 and 42 cents. The price of non-oil-extended, 1500-type styrene butadiene rubber (SBR), the most widely used synthetic, rose from 31 to 34 cents per pound during the same period.

World production of natural rubber in 1975 was estimated at 3,292,000 metric tons, a decrease of 156,000 tons from 1974. Production for 1976 was expected to rise to 3.5 million tons. The Management Committee of the International Rubber Study Group (IRSG) also estimated world natural rubber supplies in 1976 at 3.5 million tons and synthetic rubber supplies at 7,850,000 tons. It was estimated that the world would consume 3.6 million tons of natural rubber and 7.7 million tons of synthetic rubber during the year. (Estimates for synthetic rubber production include rubber produced in the U.S.S.R., nonmember countries of the IRSG in Eastern Europe, and China, and could be in error from 2 to 3%. Estimated production and consumption of natural rubber may also be in error by the same amount.)

The U.S. continued to be the largest single buyer of natural rubber: 669,966 tons in 1975. World consumption of natural rubber latex (dry basis) was estimated at 254,250 tons. Statistics on world consumption of synthetic latexes were not complete, but U.S. consumption was 92,000 tons (dry basis) of the SBR type. Total consumption of both natural and synthetic rubbers worldwide was estimated at 10,387,500 tons in 1975. Production of reclaimed rubber continued to decline, from 262,955 tons in 1974 to 184,417 tons in 1975.

Oil has traditionally been the starting material for synthetic rubber, but Melvin Calvin of the University of California proposed that oil might be made from rubber produced by the *Euphorbia tirucalli* plant. This plant flourishes in such regions as the semiarid southwestern U.S., and there are 44 varieties of the plant family that secrete rubber latex. Preliminary estimates of the cost were $3 to $10 per barrel of oil, compared with $11.50 a barrel for imported oil. Additional experimental work was planned. A team headed by Arnold Peterson of Goodyear developed a method that reportedly controlled South American leaf blight, which had been responsible for the abandonment of natural rubber culture in South America. It involved systematic aerial spraying with standard fungicides. The recovery of isoprene from new ethylene plants using petroleum fractions rather than gas fractions gave promise of reducing the cost of isoprene markedly by late 1977. It was predicted that by 1980, 550 million lb of isoprene per year would be available as a by-product of ethylene production.

Table X. Natural Rubber Production
In 000 metric tons

Country	1973	1974	1975
Malaysia	1,542	1,549	1,478
Indonesia	886	855	825*
Thailand	382	379	349
Sri Lanka	155	132	149
India	123	128	136
Liberia	84†	88	83
Nigeria	49	60*	45*
Zaire	40*	27	25*
Brazil	23	19	19
Others	228	211	183
Total	3,512	3,448	3,292

*Estimate, or includes estimate.
†Preliminary.

Table XI. Synthetic Rubber Production
In 000 metric tons

Country	1973	1974	1975
United States	2,607	2,498	1,941
Japan	967	858	789
France	458	463	350
United Kingdom	353	327	253
Germany, West	349	324	278
Netherlands, The	263	245	216
Italy*	230	240	200
Canada	230	209	173
Germany, East	133	139	144*
Brazil	125	155	129
Poland	94	100	108
Romania	83	92	100
Spain	68	67	...
Mexico	54	65	66*
Belgium*	65	65	60
Czechoslovakia*	50	51	53
Argentina*	47	50	53
Australia	43	45	37
South Africa	28	32	32
Others*†	1,258	1,365	1,526
Total	7,505	7,390	6,508

*Estimate, or includes estimate. †Includes estimated production for the Soviet Union (about 1,355,000 tons in 1975) and China (about 70,000 tons in 1975).
Source: The Secretariat of the International Rubber Study Group, *Rubber Statistical Bulletin.*

A new tire-wheel combination was ready for production by Michelin of France. The TRX steel-belted, tubeless radial tire had a height-to-width ratio of 0.5 to 0.6, depending on size, and the new wheel rim profile distributed the tire bead stresses more uniformly, resulting in a safer, longer-lasting wheel. The open blocky tread pattern of the tire was said to function well on dry, wet, or snowy roads. Pirelli of Italy developed the first steel-belted radial tires recommended for all types of automobile racing. Seventeen sizes with three types of tread pattern and tread compound were available. Heretofore steel-belted radial tires had not been considered suitable for extremely high speeds. It was expected that 75% of 1977 model cars in the U.S. would be on radial tires, compared with 4.8% in 1972.

(J. R. BEATTY)

[732.D.6]

SHIPBUILDING

Shipbuilding activity reached a new low in 1976. While world capacity still totaled 35 million gross registered tons (grt), 17 million grt of it in Japanese yards, new orders were estimated at a maximum of 12 million grt. Of this, half, 6 million grt, went to Japan, leaving the rest to be shared among yards in the rest of the world, excluding the U.S. and the Council for Mutual Economic Assistance (Comecon) countries.

Prospects remained poor. Tanker tonnage ran at a surplus of some 50 million tons deadweight (dw), and the surplus in bulk carriers continued to grow, reaching 10 million tons dw at midyear. Almost all new orders were for dry cargo ships. Japanese shipyards were quick to produce attractive designs for multipurpose vessels that could be fitted with non-Japanese equipment.

Orders for new tankers—428 ships, amounting to 56 million tons dw—were the lowest since 1968. A year earlier 804 tankers (123 million tons dw) had been on order. Orders for 70 tankers (12 million tons dw) were canceled during the year, and by mid-1976 the world order book had fallen to 3,651 vessels (128,795,891 tons dw), compared with 4,798 ships (180 million tons dw) a year earlier.

Dry cargo ships on order, not including containerships, totaled 1,467 vessels (14,-

Bulgaria's port of Varna on the Black Sea is a shipbuilding centre. A new tanker nears completion at the Georgi Dimitrov shipyards. The 100,000-ton vessel was to carry a crew of 50.

CAMERA PRESS/PHOTO TRENDS

412,442 tons dw); there were 53 ore/oil and ore/bulk/oil carriers on order (6,195,-230 tons dw); 171 tankers of more than 150,000 tons dw (46,456,726 tons dw); and 546 tankers of less than 150,000 tons dw (26,105,363 tons dw). Bulk carriers on order totaled 764 ships (30 million tons dw), and there were 231 new containerships on order and under construction (3.5 million tons dw). Japanese shipyards led with 42,537,-674 grt of new orders; Sweden was second, with 7,180,452 grt, and West Germany third with 6,099,466 grt. British yards still had a reasonable order book, 5,390,870 grt, putting them in fourth place.

The growth in overcapacity of world shipbuilding was taken up at government level. Efforts were made through the Association of West European Shipbuilders and builders in Scandinavia and Japan to agree on cutbacks, but the size of Japan's shipbuilding industry was the real problem. In Sweden capacity was to be reduced by nearly 40%, and the Swedish government encouraged the yards to build for stock. The situation in the U.K. was overshadowed by the impending nationalization of shipbuilding and ship repairing. Worldwide, yards engaged in restructuring, changed building docks into drydocks, offered repair facilities, and began to offer specialized shipbreaking facilities.

Overcapacity seriously affected the new yards with the latest equipment and production techniques. Two new docks in South Korea had great difficulty in obtaining orders, despite the offer of financial inducements. Several plans for new yards were postponed, including a 330,000-ton-capacity building facility for liquefied natural gas (LNG) tankers at Saldanha Bay in South Africa, and a new yard at Curaçao, Netherlands Antilles. A giant Polish-built floating dock to lift 200,000-ton-dw tankers was placed in position at a repair yard in Göteborg, Sweden. In the Persian Gulf work continued on the large 400,000-ton repair dock at Bahrain and on a three-dock complex to handle vessels of up to 500,000 tons dw at Dubai. One of the world's largest covered-in shipbuilding complexes was opened at Sunderland in the U.K. This yard was to concentrate on smaller tonnage.

By the fall of 1976 prices in Japan were 30 to 40% below those in Western Europe. At a meeting in Rome in September it was made clear that the Japanese did not intend to soften their sharp price policy. With the Western European shipbuilding industry threatened by Japanese competition and the jobs of 450,000 men in jeopardy, the president of the large Dutch Rhine-Schelde-Verolme group of yards said that governments and shipyards must ensure that at least 60% of the West's shipbuilding capacity was preserved.

(W. D. EWART)

[734.E.7]

TELECOMMUNICATIONS

Major developments in telecommunications in 1976 involved more than just a further application of technology. The telephone, which celebrated its 100th birthday, might be finally getting a new look thanks to technological advances, while the American Telephone and Telegraph Co. (AT&T), after years of fighting to establish itself as a monopoly, took some bold steps to maintain that position and eliminate competition. It was a year in which optical fibre cables that can carry much more information than conventional copper cables were given field trials, and a more conventional undersea cable of 3,402 nautical miles across the Atlantic Ocean from the U.S. to France was completed.

Telephones. During the year an all-electronic telephone developed by Bell Northern Research, the research arm of Bell Canada, was tested by approximately 200 subscribers in the Canadian telephone system. The electromagnetic bell ringer, dial-pad assembly, and other components of the conventional telephone were replaced by tiny solid-state integrated circuits. Because these all-electronic components take much less room than their electromechanical counterparts, new shapes became possible and there was plenty of space for adding convenience features. Such features would allow a user to redial the last number dialed by simply pushing a button, dial any one of several most used numbers in a similar fashion, and, by using the pushbuttons on the telephone, perform such functions as turning on the lights when away from home with a simple telephone call.

Without a doubt the U.S. enjoyed the finest telephone system in the world. AT&T controlled more than 80% of the nation's telephone system and, as such, was a controlled monopoly regulated by government agencies. Over the past several years, the Federal Communications Commission (FCC) had promoted competition with AT&T. In an attempt to retain the biggest share of existing U.S. telephone service, AT&T in 1976 lobbied for a bill in Congress that would not only effectively wipe out the new forms of competition authorized by the FCC to offer communications services to business but also would guarantee AT&T the biggest share of future markets.

In looking for congressional support for the bill, officially called the Consumer Communications Reform Act, AT&T insisted that residential phone rates would jump by as much as 80% unless competition was reduced. AT&T officials claimed that home telephone service loses money and must be subsidized by the more lucrative revenues from long-distance tolls, special private lines, and commercial telephone equipment.

Those opposing the bill claimed that home phones were subsidizing other services. Opponents of the bill were also quick to point out that AT&T earned more than $1 billion in the third quarter of 1976, the largest amount ever reported by a U.S. company in a single quarter and an increase of 25% over the same period in 1975.

Cables. Bell Telephone Laboratories demonstrated during the year the much greater information-carrying capacity of optical fibre communications links using light transmitted over hair-thin solid-glass fibres instead of radio waves. They installed an experimental telephone link near Atlanta, Ga., using a cable only one-half inch in diameter containing 144 individual glass fibres. This cable could carry almost 50,000 simultaneous two-way telephone conversations. In contrast, it would take one and one-half coaxial cables, each with a 3-in diameter, to carry that many messages.

Bell was not alone in looking to optical fibre cables to meet the increasing needs of communications of the future. General Telephone and Electronics Corp. (GTE), the second largest telephone company in the U.S., put the final touches on a similar fibre optic telephone link that was to carry actual voice messages between telephone exchanges. And in July TelePrompter Manhattan Cable Television tested a system that carried television signals over optical fibres from an antenna on the roof of a tall New York City building to the main equipment some 800 ft below. But the most ambitious undertaking was started by the Japanese. Their fibre optic interactive computer-controlled network was designed to carry two-way video information to and from households in Japan, and eventually to provide services ranging from request entertainment through computer-aided instruction, cashless shopping, police and fire protection, medical assistance, and remote telemetering.

Satellites. Satellites played an increasing role in international and domestic voice and data communications. During the year, for the first time, full pages of the *Wall Street Journal* were sent via satellite between printing plants located several thousand miles apart; the transmission took about three minutes. Several U.S. domestic communications satellites were launched, including all three maritime satellites (Marisats). These linked ships at sea and offshore facilities in remote ocean areas with world-

Looking upward through the struts of a digital microwave radio tower undergoing tests in Ontario. It was to become part of Bell Canada's new computer-age communications network.

COURTESY, CARL BYOIR & ASSOCIATES, INC.

Engineers checking out the second Comstar communications satellite before launching. It handles long-distance phone calls for AT&T and GTE. About 20 million long-distance phone calls are made in the U.S. every workday.

wide telecommunications networks. Also, the second of RCA's Satcoms went up in 1976, as did two of the three planned Comstar satellites shared by AT&T and GTE.

Planned for 1977 was a different kind of satellite network. Operated by Satellite Business Systems, a joint venture of IBM, Aetna Life and Casualty Co., and Comsat General Corp., it would, unlike existing systems, carry voice, facsimile, and data directly to the end user, thus completely bypassing common carrier telephone lines.

The Communications Technology Satellite (CTS), a joint U.S. and Canadian effort that could influence future satellite communications systems throughout the world, was launched during the year. CTS was designed to test the technology involved, the applications, and the social effect of satellites that offer expanded service by using low-cost Earth stations with antennas small enough to fit on rooftops.

(RICHARD GERARD GUNDLACH)

[735.I.2–3 and 6]

Table XII. Countries Having More Than 100,000 Telephones

Telephones in service, 1975

Country	Number of telephones	Percentage increase over 1965	Telephones per 100 population	Country	Number of telephones	Percentage increase over 1965	Telephones per 100 population
Algeria	229,673	64.5	1.38	Luxembourg	141,686	77.7	39.69
Argentina	2,373,665	61.2	9.41	Malaysia	259,405	97.0	2.21
Australia*	4,999,982	87.3	37.49	Mexico	2,546,186	251.2	4.37
Austria	1,986,733	112.2	26.37	Morocco	189,000	33.2	1.13
Belgium	2,666,701	81.6	27.32	Netherlands, The	4,678,945	114.6	34.41
Brazil	2,651,728	107.6	2.50	New Zealand	1,494,587	55.3	48.12
Bulgaria	718,325	188.6	8.18	Nigeria	111,478	62.2	0.16
Canada	12,454,331	77.4	54.96	Norway	1,355,142	56.0	33.90
Chile	447,014	69.8	4.26	Pakistan*	195,325	42.2	0.29
Colombia	1,186,205	189.6	4.74	Panama	139,241	194.9	8.61
Cuba†	274,949	19.1	3.16	Peru	333,346	143.5	2.14
Czechoslovakia	2,480,801	77.4	16.83	Philippines	446,262	170.7	1.09
Denmark	2,183,847	88.2	42.48	Poland	2,399,249	101.0	7.09
Ecuador	167,505	285.1	2.58	Portugal	1,011,177	93.7	11.67
Egypt	503,200	67.0	1.37	Puerto Rico	466,465	129.7	15.25
Finland	1,678,873	115.8	35.78	Rhodesia	171,881	69.8	2.77
France	12,405,000	117.5	23.52	Romania	1,076,566	152.4	5.10
Germany, East	2,451,011	54.5	15.04	Singapore	280,280	222.6	12.53
Germany, West	18,767,033	129.8	30.25	South Africa	1,935,831	70.8	7.77
Greece	1,862,050	331.7	20.71	Spain	7,042,968	178.7	19.96
Hong Kong	988,545	350.0	22.75	Sweden	5,178,082	116.9	63.32
Hungary	1,013,731	88.2	9.65	Switzerland	3,790,351	77.8	59.46
India	1,689,528	122.3	0.29	Syria*	143,320	83.7	2.08
Indonesia	284,831	65.5	0.23	Taiwan	900,605	509.2	5.68
Iran	805,560	344.7	2.40	Thailand*	270,840	248.4	0.66
Iraq	152,932	135.3	1.42	Tunisia	114,250	126.8	2.03
Ireland	393,879	81.4	12.78	Turkey	899,923	192.1	2.30
Israel	735,156	241.9	21.57	U.S.S.R.	15,782,000	122.3	6.23
Italy	13,695,006	147.7	24.62	United Kingdom	20,342,457	104.2	36.26
Japan	41,904,960	242.1	37.88	United States	143,971,718	62.1	66.02
Kenya	113,688	112.1	0.88	Uruguay	247,923	33.8	8.97
Korea, South*	1,014,016	269.6	3.09	Venezuela	554,197	113.0	4.65
Kuwait	108,587	317.0	11.00	Yugoslavia	1,142,883	209.0	5.38
Lebanon‡	227,000	116.2	7.67				

*1974. †1972. ‡1973.

Sources: American Telephone and Telegraph Company, *The World's Telephones, 1975;* Statistical Office of the United Nations, *Statistical Yearbook 1967.*

TEXTILES

Research and technological developments offered the most encouragement to the textile industry in 1976, although signs of recovery from the recession were observable in some sectors. Britain's Shirley Institute set up a unit to research the use of fibres, yarns, and fabrics in medicine and hospital practice. Low-cost production of polyolefin continued to give the producers a growing share of the market in yarns and fabrics for such products as carpets and bags.

High rates of heating and cooling and savings in water consumption were claimed for a U.K. advance in jet-dyeing technology. Swiss, West German, Belgian, and Spanish loom engineers announced improved performances in conventional, shuttleless, and jet-type models. A Belgian firm developed a semisynthetic lubricant for lubrication of industrial sewing machines. A French company announced a laboratory tensile strength tester for studying the mechanical behaviour of fibre aggregates.

An unprecedented rate of inflation in 1976, an enormous balance of payments deficit, major industrial strikes in many sectors, and rising unemployment all had adverse effects on the U.K. textile industry. Rising imports of textiles resulted in more mill closures, more short-time working, and rapidly mounting unsold stocks. Desperate appeals for tougher import quota arrangements met with litttle response.

(ALFRED DAWBER)

Natural Fibres. COTTON. World output of raw cotton was substantially reduced in 1975–76, but the effect on supplies was largely offset by extensive stocks held at the beginning of the period. Consumption reached record levels, and carry-over stocks at the start of the 1976–77 season in August were down to 21.7 million bales, four months' consumption at current levels.

Steep reductions in acreage planted and in average yields led to a dramatic drop in output, and total crops fell to 55.6 million bales. The decline was attributed to lower prices at planting time, advancing costs of production, and government policies to stimulate food crops. The U.S. crop fell by more than 3 million bales and that in Mexico by over 1.3 million bales.

The Liverpool index of average values began the 1975–76 season at nearly 55 cents a pound, advancing to 62.5 cents at the end of 1975. During 1976 the average price continued to rise, and in July a new record of 92.65 cents was posted. The index then fell below 83 cents but recovered to 86.5 cents by mid-October. The largest rises in consumption, totaling a record 63.7 million bales, were in the U.S. and the Far East.

(ARTHUR TATTERSALL)

WOOL. By January 1976 it was clear that the wool textile industry was emerging from the severe recession of 1974–75. During most of 1975 wool prices held firm only because of governmental floor price support in Australia, New Zealand, and South Africa, but as commercial demand grew the proportion bought by grower organizations tended to decline. Eventually, the rising trend was sufficient to enable grower organizations to raise floor prices for the start of the 1976–77 selling season without any significant new support purchases.

Consumption rose considerably from the extremely depressed levels of 1975. The Commonwealth Secretariat estimated that consumption of virgin wool in nine representative Western countries was 28% higher in the first quarter of 1976 than in the corresponding quarter of 1975, and the rising trend was maintained. The increase was partly due to a swing back from man-made

EDWARD HAUSNER—THE NEW YORK TIMES

The international fabric exhibit at the New York Coliseum in May had displays by more than 150 mills, converters, and yarn companies. Fifty European companies were represented.

fibres, which had benefited from the sharp rise in wool prices during 1973.

(H. M. F. MALLETT)

SILK. In 1976 the madness that had seized the Chinese silk market four years before subsided. In August 1972 the price of 3A 20/22 denier stood at 43.65 yuan per kilo; by April 1973 it had been pushed up to 92.25 and by February 1975 it was down again to 37.40. Following the 3% advance set by the Chinese corporation in September 1975 in an attempt to reverse the downward movement that had persisted for two years, buyers began to regain confidence. Four additional modest advances followed at regular intervals, amounting in all to 17½%, until by October 1976 the price stood very much at the level from which it was launched in August 1972. Meanwhile, world demand for silk goods had not only revived, but was experiencing steady growth.

Other problems, however, persisted. The bonanza in domestic silk consumption in Japan, which began to fade at the time of the 1973 oil crisis, had ended, and Japan, still in some measure insulated by its ban on raw silk imports, was faced with the problem of finding a market for its own cocoon farmers at prices commensurate with those to which they had grown accustomed in the good years. Meanwhile, South Korea, Brazil, and other producers were demanding entry for their own silk, production of which had been growing steadily with the Japanese market in view.

(PETER W. GADDUM)

Man-Made Fibres. A revival in textiles was expected for the first quarter of 1976, but the upturn, when it came, was marginal. Plants continued to run at half capacity, and fibre producers were unable to raise prices high enough to regain profitability. Plants operating at 85% capacity were the exception.

The collapse of the textured polyester double jersey trade had left fibre producers with excess capacity. In 1975–76 new U.S. very fine filament yarns generated impressive new business and enabled knitters to make fabrics with a more "natural" handle, resembling silk but with the easy care of the synthetics. Finer yarns were brought to Britain in 1976 and attempts were made to spin them. The yarns, spun in Japan, mostly reached Europe as high quality fabric.

ICI Fibres extended the use of heterofil spunbonded nonwovens. Fabrics could be made from these specialty fibres that had a strong affinity for water and a lack of affinity for oil. When oil-polluted water in which the oil was emulsified was filtered through such fabrics, the minute droplets of oil were caused to agglomerate and to float up to the surface. There they could be continuously extracted, and the water could be passed through the fabric to emerge as a potable effluent.

(PETER LENNOX-KERR)

[732.C.1; 732.D.9]

A.F.P./PICTORIAL PARADE

A Belgian firm makes cigars 32 centimetres (about a foot) long, and names them for French presidents. From left to right: Presidents de Gaulle, Pompidou, and Giscard d'Estaing.

TOBACCO

World production of leaf tobacco rose by 2½% during 1975, but with early forecasts for the 1976 harvest suggesting a decline of perhaps 2% to 11,500,000,000 lb, supply of leaf would become considerably tighter as the developed countries pulled out of their industrial recession and consumption increased. North American farmers were dissatisfied over prices after the bumper harvest of 1975 and were reluctant to maintain acreage. Adverse weather conditions were reported from Asia, and the only area to record significant increases in 1976 would probably be Africa.

Demand for tobacco products in the industrialized countries rose by 1½% during 1975. Utilization of tobacco leaf—most accurately assessed by the output of tobacco manufacturers—in the less developed countries increased by a significantly higher proportion, about 2½%. In the centrally planned economies consumption appeared to have risen by 2%. Prospects for 1976 were for a somewhat higher rate of leaf utilization, perhaps a 2½% increase against a total increase of slightly less than 2% in 1975. Production of tobacco goods was expected to rise significantly in North America, and an increase in aggregate EEC output seemed likely, particularly in West Germany and The Netherlands. However, steep price increases could temper expansion in Japan and Italy.

The anticipated decline in the world's supply of tobacco leaf in 1976, coupled with a projected increase in global demand for tobacco products, was expected to push prices for leaf upward, but large stocks of 1975 crops reportedly held by the U.S., Canada, India, Brazil, and Italy could restrain the increases. Although production costs (fuel, fertilizers, insecticides, farm machinery, and labour) continued to rise, producers in many countries received guaranteed support or minimum prices. Prices for U.S. flue-cured tobacco, on average $1 per pound in 1975, were expected to rise by at least 12% in 1976. The price of American Burley rose by 19% in 1975, and the 1976 support price was 14% more than that. Prices of oriental tobaccos continued to rise more steeply. Greek oriental tobacco reached such a high level in 1975 that only 36% of the entire 1975 crop had been sold by the following April.

World exports of tobacco leaf in 1975 proved slightly heavier than previously estimated, but they were still 9% below 1974, reflecting a weakening of import demand by tobacco manufacturers faced with recessionary conditions. The drop was accounted for chiefly by reduced shipments of flue-cured tobacco from the U.S., Canada, and India, oriental leaf from Greece, Turkey, and Italy, Burley from Greece and Mexico, and dark leaf from Indonesia and the Dominican Republic. Only Brazil (+7%), South Korea (+5%), the Philippines (+11%), Argentina (+71%), and Malawi (+13%) recorded notable increases in exports. World imports of unmanufactured tobacco, at 2,740,000,000 lb in 1975, were 3% above 1974. The bulk of the increase was accounted for by West Germany, Japan, France, and the U.S.

Total 1975 output of tobacco goods in the U.S. increased by 1.8% (manufactured weight), an improvement over the static performance of 1974. After another punishing tax increase, the U.K. experienced a drop in tobacco goods output for the second consecutive year. The original six EEC members showed a slight increase in output, much more modest than the 4% of 1974.

EEC harmonization continued. In 1976 the U.K. introduced an ad valorem excise duty on cigarettes in a move toward the ad valorem/specific EEC system. Aggressive pricing policies by British manufacturers kept prices lower than anticipated, and consumption was expected to improve during the year. The French government abolished the exclusive rights of its monopoly, as required by the Treaty of Rome. Italy also drafted laws to disband its tobacco monopoly. The Benelux countries planned to introduce identical excise duties in 1977.

The only two major synthetic tobacco supplement developers (one British, one U.S.) left by mid-1976 were awaiting U.K. government clearance.

(MARINA THAINE)

[731.B.4.e]

TOURISM

Tourism had a mixed year in 1976. The progress of international tourism, in particular, was uneven. Some destinations continued the recovery begun in 1975; others failed to progress beyond 1973 levels. There was increased movement to and from the U.S., a result of Bicentennial promotional efforts on the one hand and of a more stable dollar on the other. But travel from West Germany, the world's biggest international travel spender, grew only slightly in 1976. Mediterranean destinations had an uneventful year, and political uncertainties clouded Spain's international tourist season. The U.K., however, continued to enjoy spectacular growth in the number of visitors, from both the Continent and North America, in line with the fall in value of sterling. Altogether, 10 million visitors, including 1.6 million from the U.S., were welcomed by the U.K. in 1976.

Domestic tourism (the travel of residents of a country within its own frontiers) did better than international tourism. An unusual contributory factor was climate. The dry, hot summer enjoyed by northern Europe favoured stay-at-home tourism, while the absence of gasoline rationing made automobile tourism a convenient possibility. At the same time, European and U.S. railroads continued to attract travelers through modernization efforts and new, higher-speed services.

On the key North Atlantic air route, passenger traffic experienced the long-awaited upturn in 1976. Numbers of available seats and numbers of passengers filling them both rose substantially in the first half of the year; passengers increased by 11.1%; load factors by 3.4%; charter passengers by 30%; and the number of charter flights by 28.3%. However, the North Atlantic was probably among the more favoured sectors, and in the view of at least one European government intra-European air fares were too high to permit proper recovery of mass European tourism.

In 1975 international tourism had recovered from the 1974 fall resulting from the energy crisis. Total international arrivals numbered 213 million (up 2%). Receipts from international tourism grew from $29 billion in 1974 to between $34 billion and $35 billion in 1975, although this 17–20% increase reflected price rises and fluctuations in exchange rates more than increases in actual numbers of spending tourists or their length of stay. Countries earning more than $2 billion from international tourism in 1975 were the U.S., $4,827,000,000; Spain, $3,404,000,000; West Germany, $2.9 billion; Austria, $2,781,000,000; France, $2,663,000,000; Italy, $2,579,000,000; and the U.K., $2,442,000,000.

The major spenders were West Germany ($8,457,000,000) and the U.S. ($6,345,000,000). Most spending by residents of West Germany was in neighbouring countries, while roughly half of U.S. travel was intercontinental. Despite a 10% increase in U.S. expenditures abroad in 1975, there was a slight fall in the number of U.S. travelers, especially in the first six months of the year. U.S. travel to Europe and the Mediterranean dropped 4% in 1975 to 3.2 million travelers (compared with a 15% decline in 1974). Trip duration of U.S. travelers was 24 days and average daily expenditure was $25. Among countries experiencing growth in U.S. tourist arrivals in 1975 were Austria, Switzerland, Belgium, The Netherlands, and Ireland.

Viewing tourism by region in 1975, South Asia showed the highest rate of growth in arrivals—30%—probably as a result of promotional efforts within the framework of the 1975 "South Asia Tourism Year." For Africa the rate was 16–17% and for the Pacific area, 11%, while for the Americas and Europe it did not exceed the world average of 2%. Incoming tourism dropped 25% in the Middle East, but outgoing tourism from newly rich oil states was reported strong.

Government policies toward tourism remained broadly neutral in 1976. There was, however, a new awareness of the importance of the social role played by tourism in providing individuals with a desirable change of routine and with mental and physical refreshment. Thus, in the EEC, paid vacations moved toward the four-week minimum set by the European Commission, ahead of the three weeks enjoyed by most

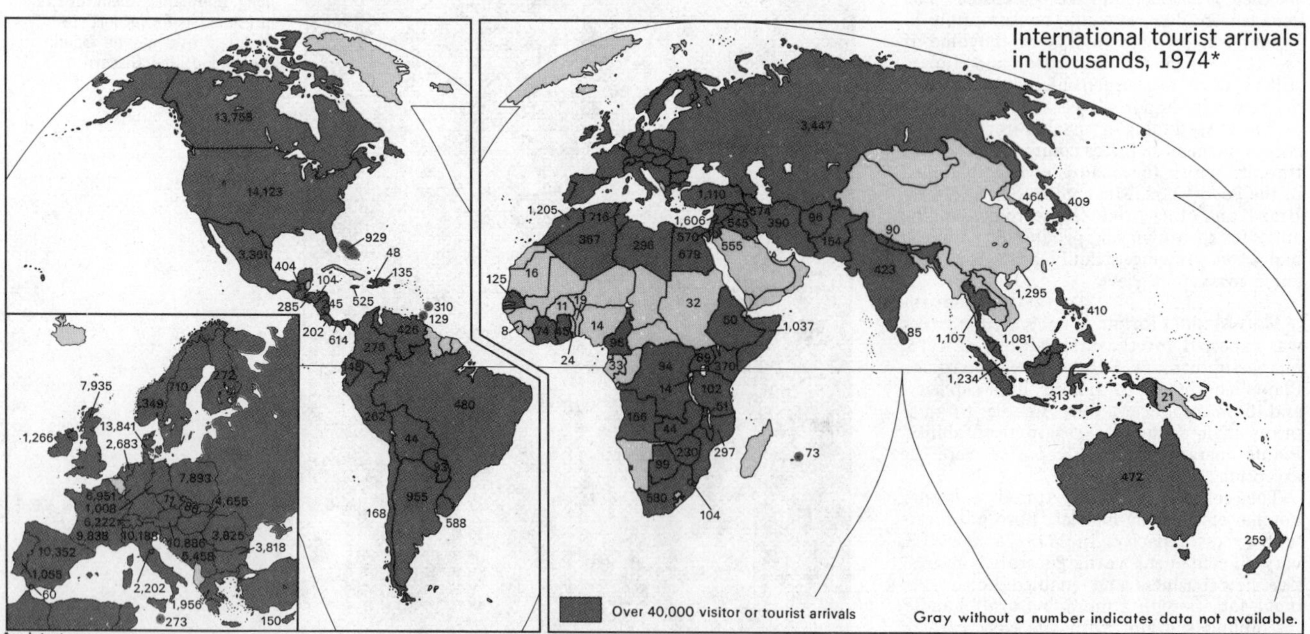

*or latest year.
Source: International Union of Official Travel Organizations, *International Travel Statistics*.

Americans. Problems of health and environmental protection in the context of travel received attention from the World Health Organization in the form of guidelines for health protection of tourist establishments. There were signs that the painstaking efforts of European governments to stagger vacations would at last bear fruit. French automobile manufacturers agreed to stagger the start of the notorious August vacations and, in Austria, schools and colleges in different Länder (states) agreed to break up for vacations at different times.

On the commercial side, the merger process that had characterized the early 1970s was virtually complete by 1976, and those tour operators that remained generally held strong market positions. However, floating currencies made planning difficult, and uncertainties remained about the effect of oil price rises on charter costs. The travel agent, still responsible for over 80% of tour sales in most major countries, reasserted his role as a friendly counselor, ready to unravel the complexities of airline fares or to wrestle with the timetable problems created by Europe's failure to agree on a standard year-round clock time.

The hotel industry spent a nervous year watching costs spiral. Some hotels responded by hiking prices (rises up to 20% were authorized in Spain, and an independent survey showed London hotel prices up by one-quarter in sterling terms); others, notably the Swiss, made stern efforts to peg increases. In the face of rising labour costs and difficulties in filling vacancies, the International Hotel Association (Paris) called upon governments to be more flexible in issuing work permits to foreign hotel staff.

While beach tourism retained its classic popularity in 1975–76, two other forms of leisure enjoyment were growing rapidly. One was history and historic houses; the British Tourist Authority reported 47.6 million visits made to historic homes in 1975, and there were indications that 1976 would also be a record year. The other was water-borne tourism, with canal cruising becoming a fast-growing attraction in France and elsewhere.

(PETER SHACKLEFORD)

[732.F.1]

WOOD PRODUCTS

The market for forest products strengthened in 1976. The United States led the way back from the severe worldwide recession that had started in 1974 and extended through part of 1975. Both forest industry giants of North America, the U.S. and Canada, showed improved performance in 1976. But Canada's labour disputes in 1975 and early 1976 and its greater dependence on exports kept its forest products industry lagging behind that of the U.S. Together, the U.S. and Canada supplied one-third of the world harvest of industry roundwood (logs). The Soviet Union alone accounted for one-fourth of the harvest.

Because home construction is the major market for wood products, the industry was particularly cheered in the fall of the year when new housing starts in the U.S. reached their highest level in nearly three years. It appeared that 1976 would be one of the best years on record for single-family housing starts, and more than 80% of all single-family homes are framed with wood.

Lumber production in the U.S. in 1976 was expected to reach 36,000,000,000 bd-ft, 14% above 1975 production, according to the National Forest Products Association. Paper and paperboard production in the U.S. rose briskly in the first half of 1976 and then slumped a bit in the third quarter. But the rate of production for the first nine months of the year averaged about 61 million tons per year according to the American Paper Institute. This was about 20% above the recession level of 1975.

WIDE WORLD

Chinese arborists at work pruning a stand of birch trees in Shensi Province.

Plywood production was targeted at about 18,000,000,000 sq ft in 1976, with the value of shipments at an all-time high, 55% above that of 1975. Wood pulp output reached a new high of 48.4 million tons in 1976, some 19% above 1975. Demand for hardwoods, used mainly in the furniture industry, also showed gains.

A crisis for the timber industry in the U.S. was resolved late in the year with the passage of a landmark law, the National Forest Management Act of 1976. The new law preserved the concept of multiple use of the forests for timber, recreation, wildlife, and other uses, and also outlined policies for land management planning in the federally owned National Forest System, which contains half of the nation's inventory of softwood sawtimber. Sawtimber is raw material for building products, in contrast to trees of smaller size that are used primarily for the manufacture of pulp and paper.

Most important, the new law resolved a threat to the supply of timber for wood and paper products from the national forests, which include 187 million ac of land available for growing, sale, and harvesting of timber. The supply was threatened by a court interpretation of an 1897 law governing the harvesting of timber from the national forests, an interpretation that severely restricted modern forestry practices. Without the new law, the timber supply from all 155 federal forests could have been sharply curtailed.

Internationally, one significant development was the long-term agreement between a consortium of Swedish pulp and paper producers and 100 southern U.S. sawmills for the purchase of wood chips. The five-year contract was valued at $130 million. Under the agreement, some 300,000 tons per year of chips would be shipped to Sweden.

The Soviet Union in 1976 started its tenth five-year development plan for the nation's economy. Output in the forest industry sector was scheduled to increase by 22–25%, with relatively low growth in logging. But in the area of particle board production (an engineered product of wood chips bonded together), the plan called for an increase of from 60 to 85% by 1980. Paper and paperboard production also were to increase at a faster rate than logging.

The United Nations Development Program in 1976 projected that worldwide supply and demand of wood for the next ten years would be approximately in balance, but that there could be serious local and regional shortages, particularly in Western Europe and Japan. (TAIT TRUSSELL)

[732.D.3]

See also Agriculture and Food Supplies; Computers; Consumerism; Economy, World; Energy; Food Processing; Games and Toys; Industrial Relations; Materials Sciences; Mining and Quarrying; Photography; Television and Radio; Transportation.

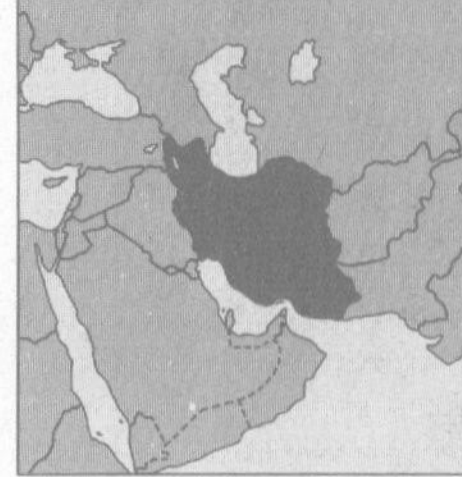

Iran

A constitutional monarchy of western Asia, Iran is bounded by the U.S.S.R., Afghanistan, Pakistan, Iraq, and Turkey and the Caspian Sea, the Arabian Sea, and the Persian Gulf. Area: 636,000 sq mi (1,648,000 sq km). Pop. (1976 est.): 33,957,000. Cap. and largest city: Teheran (pop., 1974 est., 3,931,000). Language: Farsi Persian. Religion (1972 est.): Muslim 98%; Christian, Jewish, and Zoroastrian minorities. Shah-in-shah, Mohammad Reza Pahlavi Aryamehr; prime minister in 1976, Emir Abbas Hoveida.

During 1976 Iran continued to exert a stabilizing influence throughout the West Asian and South Asian regions. The agreements reached with Iraq over border security and demarcation in June 1975 were ratified in June 1976. Earlier in the year the shah used his influence with Afghanistan and Pakistan to ease the dangerously strained relations between the two countries. Iran also concluded a series of commercial and industrial agreements with India; Teheran's friendly contacts with New Delhi and its understanding with Islamabad assisted in the implementation of the Simla agreement of 1972 between the prime ministers of India and Pakistan. But the shah's tentative suggestion that India and Afghanistan might join the Regional Cooperation for Development (RCD) group was coolly received.

A conference of RCD ministers held in Lahore, Pak., early in the year reported good progress in the fields of cultural exchanges, currency facilities, internal communications, and tourism, but the economic potentialities of the group, it said, were not being properly exploited. A summit conference attended by the shah, Prime Minister Zulfikar Ali Bhutto of Pakistan, and Pres. Fahri Koruturk of Turkey met in Izmir, Turkey, in April, and an accord was signed on April 22. The agreement pledged all three countries to a gradual reduction of tariff and nontariff barriers to interregional trade in accordance with a new protocol aiming at establishing an RCD free-trade area within ten years. Meanwhile, improved credit facilities were to help exporters to member countries; an industrial and development bank was to be set up to encourage collaboration in viable projects; and an RCD shipping company was made responsible for encouraging sea trade by establishing more frequent services and by pooling cargo. Three new RCD institutions were to be set up immediately: an institute of science and technology in Iran, a school of economics in Pakistan, and a school of tourism and hotel management in Turkey. A new RCD science foundation in Islamabad was to provide a reservoir of highly skilled manpower for all three countries. Economically the strongest, Iran was able to help its two partners effectively.

The breakup of the great landed estates in Iran and the distribution of land to the farmers, begun in 1962, was accelerated. The establishment of heavy and light industry, more dependent upon Western technology, was proving a slower process. On October 6 in Teheran the shah and Pres. Valéry Giscard d'Estaing of France clinched deals worth Fr 40 billion, which included the building in Iran of eight nuclear power plants. The defense forces continued to rely upon Europe and the U.S. for their equipment, and inflation in Europe in 1976 made such equipment cost more. For that reason, Iran's influence in the meetings of the Organization of Petroleum Exporting Countries was generally cast on the side of fixing higher prices for crude oil, although in February, faced with a declining market, Iran had

IRAN

Education. (1974–75) Primary, pupils 4,119,157, teachers 135,021; secondary, pupils 1,818,323, teachers 62,936; vocational (1972–73), pupils 56,745, teachers 2,817; teacher training (1972–73), students 26,058, teachers 635; higher (including 8 universities; 1972–73), students 115,311, teaching staff 4,128.

Finance. Monetary unit: rial, with (Sept. 20, 1976) a free rate of 70.52 rials to U.S. $1 (121.50 rials = £1 sterling). Gold, SDR's, and foreign exchange (June 1976) U.S. $7,408,000,000. Budget (1974–75 est.): revenue 1,347,000,000,000 rials; expenditure 1,368,000,000,000 rials. Gross domestic product (1973–74) 2,033,200,000,000 rials. Money supply (April 1976) 502,250,000,000 rials. Cost of living (1970 = 100; March 1976) 167.

Foreign Trade. (1975) Imports 700.3 billion rials; exports 1,351,200,000,000 rials. Import sources: U.S. 20%; West Germany 18%; Japan 16%; U.K. 8%. Export destinations: Japan 29%; The Netherlands 9%; U.K. 9%; U.S. 9%; West Germany 8%; France 7%; Italy 7%; Canada 5%. Main exports: crude oil 92%; petroleum products 5%. Tourism (1974): visitors 390,000; gross receipts U.S. $158 million.

Transport and Communications. Roads (1972) 43,442 km. Motor vehicles in use (1972): passenger 393,900; commercial (including buses) 87,600. Railways: (1974) 4,560 km; traffic (1973) 2,144,000,000 passenger-km, freight 4,432,000,000 net ton-km. Air traffic (1974): 1,390,000,000 passenger-km; freight 20.6 million net ton-km. Shipping (1975): merchant vessels 100 gross tons and over 135; gross tonnage 479,718. Telephones (Jan. 1975) 805,560. Radio receivers (Dec. 1973) c. 8 million. Television receivers (Dec. 1974) c. 2 million.

Agriculture. Production (in 000; metric tons; 1975): wheat 5,483; barley 1,438; rice 1,386; potatoes c. 570; sugar, raw value c. 660; onions c. 328; tomatoes c. 220; watermelons (1974) c. 850; melons (1974) c. 400; dates (1974) c. 350; grapes (1974) c. 680; soybeans c. 70; sunflower seed c. 76; tea c. 25; tobacco c. 11; cotton, lint 165. Livestock (in 000; Oct. 1974): cattle c. 5,680; sheep c. 38,000; goats (1973) c. 14,600; horses c. 380; asses (1973) c. 2,000; chickens c. 55,000.

Industry. Production (in 000; metric tons; 1974): petroleum products c. 29,876; crude oil (1975) 267,293; natural gas (cu m) 22,126,000; cement (1973) 3,489; coal c. 1,100; lead concentrates (metal content) c. 60; chromite (oxide content; 1974–75) c. 12,500; electricity (kw-hr; 1974) 12,504,000.

A steel mill near Isfahan. Steel is seen as the key to Iran's industrialization, still in its early stages.

THE NEW YORK TIMES

Information Science and Technology: *see* Computers

Insurance: *see* Industrial Review

International Bank for Reconstruction and Development: *see* Economy, World

International Law: *see* Law

International Monetary Fund: *see* Economy, World

Investment: *see* Economy, World; Stock Exchanges

had to reduce its price for heavy crude oil. At the December OPEC meeting in Qatar, Iran was among the majority of members who agreed to a two-stage, 15% oil price rise in 1977.

In government, departmental efficiency increased; there was a successful drive against corruption launched by the shah in January. The one-party rule of the Rastakhiz (National Resurgence) Party, though firmly supported in the Majles (Parliament), was criticized by Iranians resident abroad. In Iran there were occasional assassinations of security police and, more rarely, of visiting foreign experts, by underground subversive elements. The Iranian press accused Libya of supplying the subversives with arms, and diplomatic relations with Cuba were broken off because of contacts between its leader, Fidel Castro, and the leader of the banned Tudeh Party, Iraj Eskandari. The activities of the security services and the stern punishment of convicted offenders were criticized in the report of a group of legal experts appointed by the International Commission of Jurists, but the government did not change its attitude, though the shah often exercised clemency.

(L. F. RUSHBROOK WILLIAMS)

[978.C.1]

Iraq

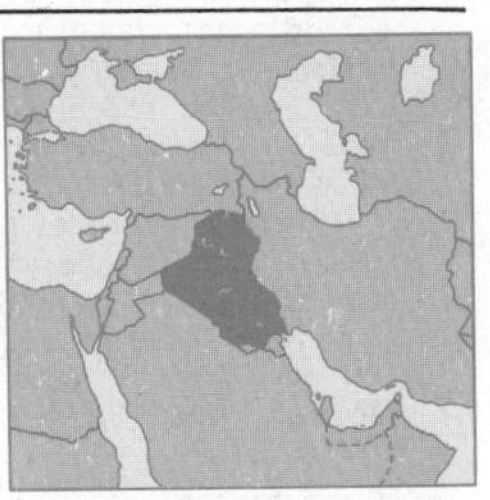

A republic of southwestern Asia, Iraq is bounded by Turkey, Iran, Kuwait, Saudi Arabia, Jordan, Syria, and the Persian Gulf. Area: 168,928 sq mi (437,522 sq km). Pop. (1975 est.): 11,124,300, including Arabs, Kurds, Turks, Assyrians, Iranians, and others. Cap. and largest city: Baghdad (pop., 1974 est., 2.8 million). Language: Arabic. Religion: mainly Muslim, some Christian. President in 1976, Gen. Ahmad Hassan al-Bakr.

In 1976 Iraq continued to pursue its militant radical role as a leading member of the Arab "rejection front," refusing all political settlements of the Middle East problem. It stopped short of any military intervention, however. Although it remained critical of Egypt for having accepted the second Sinai disengagement agreement with Israel, Iraq directed its strongest enmity against the rival Baathist regime in Syria, and throughout the year it maintained a barrage of criticism of Syria's actions and motives in intervening in the civil war in Lebanon. On June 8 Iraq warned of sending troops to the Syrian border, although it officially maintained that it wanted them to march through to confront Israel. Iraq continued to claim that it wished to form a united front against Israel consisting of Syria, Iraq, Libya, Algeria, and the Palestine Liberation Organization, but only if Syria repudiated UN Security Council resolutions calling for a Middle East political settlement.

Iraq's other means of pressure on Syria was through the oil that it conveyed over Syrian territory. Talks began on February 12 for the revision of the financial terms of the 15-year oil transit agreement signed in 1973 under which Syria had been receiving Iraqi oil at about one-quarter of the world price as well as substantial transit revenues. Iraq's hand was strengthened by its project for a new pipeline via Turkey that would bypass Syrian territory and also by increasing the export of oil from Iraq's northern fields via Basrah. The talks were resumed on April 6 but remained deadlocked, and by the summer Iraq was reported to have cut the flow of oil to Syria entirely. In the summer and autumn Iraq sent "volunteers" to fight in the Lebanese civil war on the Palestinian-leftist side against the rightist and Syrian forces.

In contrast, relations with Egypt were friendly, and Iraq supplied Egypt with some aid and cheap oil and promised to build a town in the Suez area. Government sources said that about 30,000 Egyptians, including several thousand farmers, were working in Iraq as part of a new experiment. Relations with Iran were much improved as a result of the March 1975 agreement in Algiers between the two countries, and the demarcation and security border agreement of June 1975 stemming from this was ratified in June 1976. Some problems still arose over Iran's insistence on referring to the "Persian Gulf" rather than "Arabian Gulf" and over Iraq's strict limitations on the number of Iranian pilgrims allowed to visit the Shi'ite holy places in Iraq. The Iraqi-Iranian accord inhibited Iraq from pursuing its former militantly nationalist policies in Arabia and the Gulf. In February Iraq signed an agreement with Saudi Arabia to demarcate their common border, and in April the Iraqi strong man Saddam Hussein Takriti paid his first visit to Saudi Arabia.

Internally, the Baathist regime benefited from the collapse in 1975 of the Kurdish rebellion, which was the most important result of the Iraqi-Iranian agreement, and reconstruction of the Kurdish autonomous region in northern Iraq continued. However, there were reports during the spring of 1976 from Kurdish

IRAQ

Education. (1974–75) Primary, pupils 1,523,955, teachers 57,621; secondary, pupils 457,763, teachers 16,862; vocational, pupils 21,033, teachers 1,508; higher, students 73,991, teaching staff 2,577.

Finance. Monetary unit: Iraqi dinar, with (Sept. 20, 1976) an official rate of 0.296 dinar to U.S. $1 (free rate of 0.517 dinar = £1 sterling). Gold, SDR's, and foreign exchange (June 1976) U.S. $2,852,200,000. Budget (1973–74 est.): revenue 592.6 million dinars; expenditure 820,190,000 dinars (including development expenditure of 310 million dinars). Gross national product (1973) 1,582,100,000 dinars. Money supply (April 1976) 626.6 million dinars. Cost of living (Baghdad; 1970 = 100; May 1976) 152.

Foreign Trade. Imports (1974) 700.1 million dinars; exports (1975) 2,592,100,000 dinars. Import sources: Japan 11%; West Germany 8%; U.S. 8%; France 7%; Brazil 5%; U.K. 5%. Export destinations: France *c.* 15%; Italy *c.* 14%; Brazil *c.* 8%. Main export crude oil 95%. Tourism (1974): visitors 545,000; gross receipts U.S. $81 million.

Transport and Communications. Roads (1974) 11,096 km. Motor vehicles in use (1974): passenger 83,400; commercial (including buses) 59,000. Railways: (1974) 1,955 km; traffic: (1973–74) 633 million passenger-km, freight 1,707,000,000 net ton-km. Air traffic (1975): 532.7 million passenger-km; freight 7,504,000 net ton-km. Shipping (1975): merchant vessels 100 gross tons and over 56; gross tonnage 310,594. Telephones (Jan. 1975) 152,930. Radio receivers (Dec. 1973) 1,250,000. Television receivers (Dec. 1973) 520,000.

Agriculture. Production (in 000; metric tons; 1975): wheat *c.* 860; barley *c.* 400; rice *c.* 200; aubergines (1974) *c.* 120; cucumbers (1974) *c.* 170; watermelons (1974) *c.* 530; melons (1974) *c.* 170; tomatoes *c.* 410; dates (1974) *c.* 350; tobacco *c.* 10; cotton, lint (1974) *c.* 15. Livestock (in 000; 1975): sheep *c.* 15,829; goats (1974) *c.* 2,450; cattle *c.* 2,116; buffalo (1974) *c.* 309; camels (1974) *c.* 322; horses (1974) *c.* 128; asses (1974) *c.* 590.

Industry. Production (in 000; metric tons): cement (1971) 1,856; crude oil (1975) 109,860; petroleum products (1974) *c.* 5,780; electricity (kw-hr; 1974) *c.* 2,600,000.

sources outside Iraq that the rebellion would be resumed and that fighting had actually started in border areas in protest against the government's policy of transferring thousands of Kurds to the south. On August 26 the government announced a new amnesty for Kurds in the Iraqi armed forces.

In 1976 Iraq's crude oil reserves were estimated at 34,300,000,000 bbl, and oil revenues in 1975 were given as $7.6 billion, compared with $5.7 billion in 1974. The 1976 budget was estimated at about $17 billion, a 3.9% increase over the previous year. Some 30% of expenditure was allocated to investment. There were signs that the government was anxious about overheating the economy, and the start of the five-year plan was delayed until early 1977. In February it was announced that the $1 billion Japanese loan to Iraq in return for Iraqi oil, agreed to in 1974, would be doubled.

On February 7 the name of Kirkuk Province was officially changed to Tamim. Also, two new provinces were created, Salaheddin and Najaf.

(PETER MANSFIELD)

[978.B.3.c]

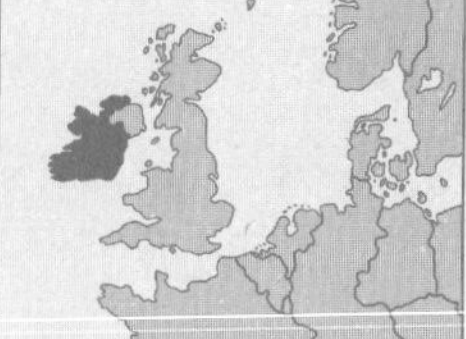

Ireland

Separated from Great Britain by the North Channel, the Irish Sea, and St. George's Channel, the Republic of Ireland shares its island with Northern Ireland to the northeast. Area: 27,136 sq mi (70,283 sq km), or 83% of the island. Pop. (1976 est.): 3,163,000. Cap. and largest city: Dublin (pop., 1971, 567,900). Language (1971): mostly English; 28% speak English and Irish or Irish only. Religion: 95% Roman Catholic. Presidents in 1976, Carroll O'Daly until October 22 and, from December 3, Patrick J. Hillery; prime minister, Liam Cosgrave.

The assassination of the British ambassador; the passing of major new emergency laws; and the continued bombings, bank raids, mail train holdups, and the escapes of prisoners placed a heavy emphasis on security throughout 1976. In the autumn this led directly to the constitutional crisis that resulted in the resignation of the head of state, President O'Daly.

The first major piece of legislation to tighten up security was the Criminal Law (Jurisdiction) Bill, introduced in 1975 and passed by both houses of Parliament on March 3, 1976. The bill received a stormy passage, with strong public opposition to its main provision, the setting up of legal means for the trial in the republic of offenders suspected of crimes in Northern Ireland. On March 10 the president referred the bill to the Supreme Court for a test of its constitutionality. The court found it constitutional, and it became law on May 6. In spite of the urgency with which the government pushed the measure through, it was not used in 1976.

Ireland's new president, Patrick J. Hillery.

WIDE WORLD

During the first half of the year there were a number of violent episodes, and challenges to the government's authority by the Provisional Irish Republican Army (IRA). Several bank and post-office raids at the end of January were followed on February 13 by the bombing of the Shelbourne Hotel in Dublin and the burning of a number of city department stores. On February 19 the body of a Republican prisoner, Frank Stagg, who had died after a hunger strike in Wakefield Gaol in Britain, was brought back for burial in Ireland. The body was taken over by the police and sent on to Shannon, and from there to the Stagg family's burial place in Robeen, County Mayo, for interment, under police control, on February 21. At commemoration ceremonies in the graveyard the following day there was violence. During the same weekend the U.K. secretary of state for Northern Ireland, Merlyn Rees, visited Dublin for security talks with the justice minister, Patrick Cooney, and the foreign minister, Garret FitzGerald. On March 31 the biggest mail train robbery in the history of Ireland took place in County Kildare, when an estimated £209,000 was stolen.

In a major display of strength, the Provisional IRA held a rally in Dublin on April 25. Although it was banned by the government, 10,000 attended, including an elected Labour Party deputy in the Dail (lower house), David Thornley. He was subsequently expelled by the party and charged in court.

On July 3 there were more bombings of hotels in Dublin and provincial centres, this time by a Northern Ireland, Protestant extremist organization, the Ulster Freedom Fighters (UFF). On July 15 a bomb was exploded in Dublin under the Special Criminal Court, the court dealing with extremist offenses. Four prisoners escaped, though three were immediately recaptured. Then, on July 21, less than 200 yd from his residence in the Dublin Mountains, the new British ambassador to Ireland, Christopher Ewart-Biggs (*see* OBITUARIES), was killed by a terrorist bomb explosion. Judith Cook, a British civil servant, was also killed, and two others in the car were seriously injured. A week later the government ordered the drafting of stiffer emergency legislation on subversive activities. The two Houses of Parliament were called

IRELAND

Education. (1974–75) Primary, pupils 542,849, teachers 17,908; secondary, pupils 252,994, teachers 14,618; vocational, pupils 3,658, teachers 215; higher, students 30,987, teaching staff 2,682.

Finance. Monetary unit: Irish pound, at par with the pound sterling, with a free rate (Sept. 20, 1976) of U.S. $1.72 = £1. Gold, SDR's, and foreign exchange (June 1976) U.S. $1,479,000,000. Budget (1975 actual): revenue £1,295 million; expenditure £1,795 million. Gross national product (1974) £2,915 million. Money supply (May 1976) £730.3 million. Cost of living (1970 = 100; May 1976) 219.

Foreign Trade. (1975) Imports £1,699.6 million; exports £1,441.4 million. Import sources: EEC 69% (U.K. 49%, West Germany 7%, France 5%); U.S. 7%. Export destinations: EEC 79% (U.K. 54%, West Germany 8%, The Netherlands 6%); U.S. 6%. Main exports: beef and veal 14%; dairy products 11%; machinery 9%; cattle 8%; chemicals 8%; textile yarns and fabrics 5%. Tourism: visitors (1974) 1,266,000; gross receipts U.S. $254 million.

Transport and Communications. Roads (1973) 87,182 km. Motor vehicles in use (1974): passenger 487,483; commercial 52,910. Railways: (1974) 2,189 km: traffic (1975) 824.3 million passenger-km, freight 475.3 million net ton-km. Air traffic (1975): 1,487,100,000 passenger-km; freight 70,965,000 net ton-km. Shipping (1975): merchant vessels 100 gross tons and over 93; gross tonnage 210,389. Telephones (Dec. 1974) 393,879. Radio licenses (Dec. 1974) *c.* 600,000. Television licenses (Dec. 1974) 527,000.

Agriculture. Production (in 000; metric tons; 1975): barley 886; wheat 212; oats 159; potatoes *c.* 1,000; sugar, raw value *c.* 199; cow's milk *c.* 4,200; butter 84; cheese *c.* 57; beef and veal *c.* 345; pork *c.* 136; fish catch (1974) 90. Livestock (in 000; June 1975): cattle *c.* 7,000; sheep *c.* 4,000; pigs *c.* 947; horses (1974) 94; chickens *c.* 10,232.

Industry. Index of production (1970 = 100; 1975) 116. Production (in 000; metric tons; 1974): coal 68; cement 1,536; petroleum products *c.* 2,590; electricity (kw-hr; 1974–75) 7,885,000; manufactured gas (cu m) 254,000; beer (hl; 1973–74) *c.* 5,050; wool fabrics (sq m; 1973) 5,000; rayon, etc., fabrics (sq m; 1972) 7,300.

back into emergency session at the end of August, and a state of emergency was declared on September 1.

By mid-September both the Emergency Powers Bill, raising the period of detention by the police before charge from 48 hours to seven days, and the Criminal Law Bill, imposing a wide range of stiffer penalties, were passed. But the president decided to refer the Emergency Powers Bill to the Supreme Court. On October 15 the Supreme Court found the bill to be constitutional, and on October 16 President O'Daly signed it.

Then, on October 18, the most senior of the prime minister's Cabinet colleagues, Patrick S. Donegan, minister for defense, described the president as "a thundering disgrace." He did so before an audience of army officers and in the presence of the minister for justice. The president, who is supreme commander of the defense forces, refused to accept the limited apology offered. Donegan offered to resign, but was told not to by the prime minister. In a vote in the lower house the action by the minister for defense was endorsed, and President O'Daly resigned on October 22. A subsequent confidence debate was also won by the government.

The crisis coincided with the coalition government's decision not to reappoint as its commissioner in Europe Patrick J. Hillery, who had originally been appointed to the job by the Fianna Fail Party, when it had been in power. The party then nominated Hillery as its candidate for the presidency, and his election was not opposed. In two by-elections in midsummer the national coalition won one seat, and the other went to an independent.

The security situation, though it produced violence and political confrontation, was in reality much less serious than appeared on the surface, and was referred to as a "technical emergency" by Cabinet ministers. The real emergency was the economic one. Continued high unemployment, the highest rate of inflation in Europe, balance of payment problems caused by the decline of the pound sterling, and the incapacity of the government to control wages caused grave problems for the economy. A shutdown of all banks from the end of June to September because of a bank clerks' strike further complicated industry's difficulties.

The former prime minister, John A. Costello (*see* OBITUARIES), who was responsible for establishing Ireland as a republic, outside the British Commonwealth, in 1948, died in January. It was the driest summer in 30 years, with widespread shortages of water. This was rectified in the autumn, with the wettest October in living memory. (BRUCE ARNOLD)

See also United Kingdom.

[972.A.1.b.i]

Israel

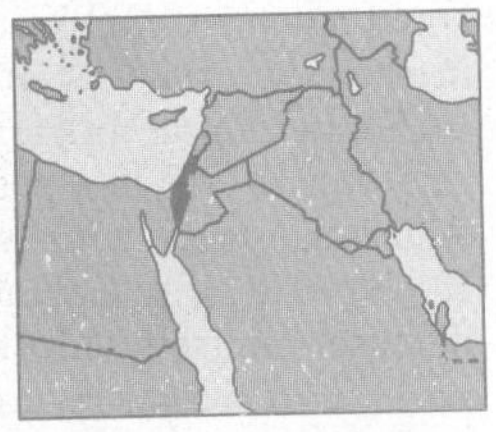

A republic of the Middle East, Israel is bounded by Lebanon, Syria, Jordan, Egypt, and the Mediterranean Sea. Area (not including territory occupied in the June 1967 war): 7,992 sq mi (20,700 sq km). Pop. (1976 est.): 3,530,800. Cap.: Jerusalem (pop., 1974 est., 344,200). Largest city: Tel Aviv-Yafo (pop., 1976 est., 353,800). Language: Hebrew and Arabic. Religion: predominantly Jewish (1975 est., 84.6%) with Muslim, Christian, and other minorities. President in 1976, Ephraim Katzir; prime minister, Yitzhak Rabin.

For Israel, 1976 was an almost uncanny carbon copy of 1975; on the surface everything was the same but, if anything, a little blacker and somewhat sharper. The achievements, especially in the reconstruction and reorientation of the defense potential, were even more impressive, with Israel reasserting itself as the ranking military power in the Middle East. But so were the problems of the economy and of international relations; they, too, had grown in size and complexity, as had the failures in labour relations, in civic conduct, and, particularly, in the social architecture of the nation. There were strikes, financial scandals, disunity in the dominant Labour Party, Cabinet differences, uncertainties about relations with the U.S., deficits in the balance of payments, and the problem of coexistence with none-too-friendly neighbours.

But there was also something else, a new perspective, far more significant in its way even than the dramatic raid and rescue of the hostages at Entebbe. It was given its most articulate expression in a lecture and subsequent television interview by the archaeologist and former chief of staff, Yigael Yadin, on October 24. He called on the Israelis, in their preparation for the general elections of 1977, to give priority to the internal conditions of the country rather than to questions of war and peace. Yadin expressed a halting preparedness to return to the political arena in support of a program of what was in effect a call

ISRAEL

Education. (1975–76) Primary, pupils 561,858, teachers 30,488; secondary, pupils 76,667, teachers 5,654; vocational, pupils 73,847, teachers 6,980; higher (1972–73), students 70,431, teaching staff 9,127.

Finance. Monetary unit: Israeli pound, with (Sept. 20, 1976) a free rate of I£8.19 to U.S. $1 (free rate of I£14.11 = £1 sterling). Gold, SDR's, and foreign exchange (June 1976) U.S. $1,211,900,000. Budget (1975–76 est.): revenue I£44,520 million; expenditure I£65,726 million. Gross national product (1975) I£74,864 million. Money supply (May 1976) I£11,201 million. Cost of living (1970 = 100; May 1976) 375.

Foreign Trade. (1975) Imports I£38,323 million (including I£11,716 million military goods); exports I£12,404 million. Import sources: U.S. 23%; U.K. 16%; West Germany 14%. Export destinations: U.S. 16%; U.K. 9%; West Germany 8%; The Netherlands 7%; Iran 6%; Hong Kong 6%; France 6%; Japan 6%. Main exports: diamonds 33%; chemicals 12%; machinery 7%; oranges 7%; clothing 5%. Tourism (1974): visitors 570,000; gross receipts U.S. $200 million.

Transport and Communications. Roads (1976) 10,657 km. Motor vehicles in use (1974): passenger 267,400; commercial 94,758. Railways: (1975) 902 km; traffic (1974) 323 million passenger-km, freight 464 million net ton-km. Air traffic (1975): 3,106,700,000 passenger-km; freight 135,139,000 net ton-km. Shipping (1975): merchant vessels 100 gross tons and over 65; gross tonnage 451,323. Telephones (Dec. 1974) 735,156. Radio receivers (Dec. 1972) 680,000. Television licenses (Dec. 1973) 385,000.

Agriculture. Production (in 000; metric tons; 1975): wheat 220; barley (1974) 38; sorghum *c.* 25; potatoes *c.* 158; watermelons (1974) *c.* 109; tomatoes *c.* 205; oranges (1974) *c.* 1,180; grapefruit (1974) *c.* 400; grapes (1974) *c.* 82; apples (1974) 84; olives *c.* 30; bananas (1974) *c.* 55; cotton, lint *c.* 51; fish catch (1974) 24. Livestock (in 000; 1974): cattle 280; sheep *c.* 185; goats 138; pigs *c.* 74; chickens 11,136.

Industry. Index of production (1970 = 100; 1975) 138. Production (in 000; metric tons; 1975): cement 2,189; petroleum products (1974) *c.* 6,760; sulfuric acid 194; electricity (kw-hr) 9,720,000; salt (1973) 61; potash (oxide content; 1974–75) *c.* 600. New dwelling units completed (1975) 53,800.

Ireland, Northern: *see* United Kingdom

Iron and Steel Industry: *see* Industrial Review

Islam: *see* Religion

RACHEMANI—SYGMA

Joy bordering on hysteria swept Israel's Ben Gurion Airport on July 4 when Hercules transports brought back 103 hostages from Entebbe, Uganda. Man in centre is the pilot of the Air France plane that was hijacked en route to Paris and forced to fly to Uganda.

for "Israel First" as more important than international diplomacy or seeking accommodation with Israel's Arab neighbours. Although the reception of Yadin's viewpoint seemed barely lukewarm, there was evidence that he had struck a responsive chord in the mood of the country and had significantly addressed the needs of Israeli society. For one of the principal consequences of Yadin's address was that it gave perspective to the domestic and economic achievements of the Israelis. For example, in the field of taxation and development, the nation's record was no less heroic than it was in military affairs.

In a remarkable address delivered on June 10, Moshe Sanbar, retiring governor of the Bank of Israel, gave the country the necessary facts and figures to assess its economic and social achievements. It was a timely intervention, for the Israeli public was inclined to minimize its own economic record much as it had minimized the achievements of its armed forces during the October 1973, or Yom Kippur, war. In 1976 Israel was devoting "a full one-third of its national product to defense." This was a tremendous burden. Even so, it did not reflect the entire picture. More than 20% of Israel's labour force was tied to the security effort. Sanbar estimated that if this defense burden were reduced to the same proportion as that carried by the U.S. at the height of the Vietnam war, 8–9% of the national product, Israel would have been able to shift each year the equivalent of $2,250,000,000 to productive purposes. Sanbar noted that on the eve of the Egyptian revolution in 1951, Israel's national product was only 40% of that of Egypt. Now, 25 years later, "it is about the same as Egypt's," although Egypt had roughly ten times the population of Israel. Similarly, Israel's exports, though still lagging behind Israel's needs, had grown fivefold since 1966, from $800 million to $4 billion in 1976. Even more noteworthy were the nation's agricultural exports of $330 million in 1976 after meeting virtually all requirements of the home market.

Another unusual factor in the economic development of the country was the marked increase in defense cost after the war in 1973. In most cases, countries drastically reduce the cost of defense after a war. Not so Israel. And, though U.S. aid substantially assisted Israel in making good the losses of the Yom Kippur war, much of the basic burden of defense was carried by the Israeli taxpayer. The Bank of Israel calculated that income tax and compulsory loans paid by Israelis increased from I£4,500 million in 1972 to I£13,500 million in 1975, and preliminary estimates put the total for 1976 at I£17,000 million. Direct taxes increased from I£6,000 million in 1972 to I£17,600 million in 1975; and indirect taxes for the same period increased from I£5,000 million to I£15,500 million and were estimated at I£18,000 million for 1976. In this setting, Israel's economy had managed to maintain a degree of full employment that was unique in a world beset by unemployment. In 1975 the number of job offers was roughly double that of job seekers, and unemployment rarely exceeded 3%. Some 27% of Israel's labour force, about 300,000, was Arab, and about 60,000 Arabs from the occupied administered territories traveled daily into Israel to work.

The combination of manifest confidence in the security of the country, provided by the defense forces and by Arab disunity, and the condition of virtual full employment was the setting for massive labour unrest, especially in the public sector. On November 8, the authorities noted that one in four employees in the public sector was either on strike or in open dispute with the authorities.

There were outcries concerning publicized but not always proven cases of official malfeasance, over high living by a minority of officials and businessmen, over the report that approximately 250,000 Israelis managed to evade paying taxes altogether, and against the rampaging inflation (40% in 1975 and estimated at 30–35% in 1976). Also, the cutting of food subsidies and the high cost of living fueled labour discontent on all levels. There was also a marked increase in inequality among the Israelis. According to the report of the government statistician made public on November 4, in 1967 the three lowest income groups comprised 11% of the population; in 1975 that number had risen to 14%, and the proportion for 1976 was expected to be higher. At the same time, the Jewish population of Israel had reached 3 million in September out of a total population of 3,549,000, giving a non-Jewish proportion of 15%. For the first time, women outnumbered men. At the end of 1975 there were 1,000 women for every 998 men. The life expectancy of the women was longer than that of the men: 74¼ years against 71. In 1975 immigration declined to 19,756, as compared with 32,000 in 1974 and 55,000 in 1973. Emigration figures, insofar as they could be established, roughly equaled the immigration totals for 1975 and the estimated number for 1976. The number of Soviet Jews who left for Israel in 1975 was 11,000 and for 1976 somewhat smaller. But only about half of those actually went to Israel. The remainder sought other destinations once they had reached Vienna.

Yadin recognized that the overburdened nation could not successfully undergo the throes of what was in effect an economic and social revolution while tied to Western precepts. He was not alone in thinking this. But he was in a position and he had an authority which the prime minister did not have, hamstrung as the latter was by Cabinet and party ties. The former defense minister, Moshe Dayan, also restated his position in similar terms with a remarkable book that was as much a political statement as a memoir.

These then were the factors that mattered most, more than the endless reports of differences between the prime minister and the minister of defense over future policy, or reports about the erosion of U.S. support for Israel—another hardy annual of which

Italian Literature: *see* Literature

the Israeli media never tired. Lebanon was also a factor but curiously muted in 1976 apart from the "understanding" reached through U.S. mediation that none of the combatants would establish themselves too close to the Israeli border. But it was no more than an "understanding" and could be breached at any time without Israel's policy having been clearly stated as to the consequences. The South African prime minister, B. J. Vorster, visited Israel in April and signed a wide-ranging economic cooperation agreement.

The rescue on July 3–4 of the Jewish hostages on the Air France jetliner taken by Palestinian hijackers to Entebbe in Uganda, by a raiding party under Brig. Dan Shomron (*see* BIOGRAPHY), fired the imagination of the country and raised the stock of the prime minister and the government for a time. (*See* DEFENSE.) But it was no substitute for an attack on the domestic economic and social problems. It was they that required an "Entebbe."

The internal political conflict intensified as the year drew to a close. Late in the afternoon of Friday, December 10, Prime Minister Rabin held a welcoming ceremony for three F-15 fighter aircraft being delivered from the U.S. Rabin later insisted that the ceremony had ended 17 minutes before the start of the Sabbath, but the United Torah Front claimed that the Sabbath had been desecrated and brought a motion of no confidence in the Knesset. Although the National Religious Party was part of the government coalition, its members abstained from the voting, costing the government its majority. Rabin then expelled the party from the government, and on December 20 he resigned and called for elections in May or June, rather than November as originally scheduled. Until then, Rabin would remain at the head of a caretaker government.

Israel bade farewell, at least temporarily, to the man who for three years had dominated Israeli politics more than any Israeli politician, U.S. Secretary of State Henry Kissinger. There was not much gratitude or even understanding evident in the country for what Kissinger had done for Israel during and after the October war. Only Prime Minister Rabin warned his countrymen that they might yet be looking back to the Kissinger years "with nostalgia." Meanwhile, many of the familiar issues of past years would have to lie fallow, and these included the future of the Palestinians and of a peace settlement with Israel's neighbours. The new Israelis were prepared to wait for the new generation of Arab leaders, who might be more inclined to consider peace as preferable to more war. (JON KIMCHE)

[978.B.3.d.i]

ENCYCLOPÆDIA BRITANNICA FILMS. *Israeli Boy: Life on a Kibbutz* (1973); *Kibbutz Kfar Menachem: Crossroads* (1974).

Italy

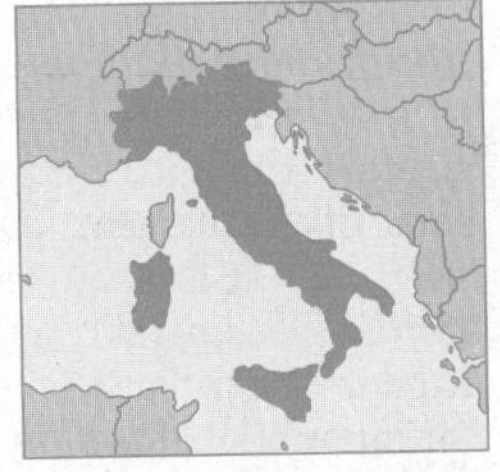

A republic of southern Europe, Italy occupies the Apennine Peninsula, Sicily, Sardinia, and a number of smaller islands. On the north it borders France, Switzerland, Austria, and Yugoslavia. Area: 116,311 sq mi (301,245 sq km). Pop. (1976 est.): 56,014,200. Cap. and largest city: Rome (pop., 1976 est., 2,874,900). Language: Italian. Religion: predominantly Roman Catholic. President in 1976, Giovanni Leone; premiers, Aldo Moro and, from July 30, Giulio Andreotti.

General elections in which the Communist Party scored gains, a tragic earthquake in the northeastern region of Friuli, a strained economic situation, and the local ramification of the Lockheed scandal were the highlights of a year that confirmed the country's difficulty in recovering from the political and economic troubles of the previous two years.

Domestic Affairs. On the political scene 1976 started with yet another government crisis. Premier Moro's coalition with Ugo La Malfa's Republican Party, formed on Nov. 23, 1974, became the 37th Cabinet to fall in the 30 years of the republic. Moro was again asked by President Leone to lead a new government, and he tried to do so in several ways. These included a coalition with the Socialist Party, another one with Socialists and Republicans, and a third one with Social Democrats and Republicans. None of them, however, could guarantee sufficient support to survive the quicksands of Italian politics. In the end Moro was forced to choose the only alternative left: a minority government, formed by Christian Democrats alone with the support of parties from the former centre-left coalition.

Moro's Cabinet, his 5th and Italy's 38th, was voted in by the Chamber of Deputies on February 21 and by the Senate on February 24. The new government proved to be unmanageable, and the lack of agreement by parties to form a more durable setup induced Moro, on April 30, to call for elections. Held on June 20 and 21, they resulted in a clear advance by the left and a strong showing by the Christian Democrats, who appeared to be gaining by defections from right-wing parties and from former allies in past centre-left coalitions. Voting for the Chamber of Deputies was as follows (1972 election figures in parentheses): Christian Democrats 38.7% and 262 seats (38.7 and 267), Communists 34.4% and 228 (27.1 and 179), Socialists 9.6% and 57 (9.6 and 61), Social Democrats 3.4% and 15 (5.1% and 29), Republicans 3.1% and 14 (2.9 and 15), Liberals 1.3% and 5 (3.9 and 20), Neofascist MSI-DN Party 6.1% and 35 (8.7 and 56). Voting for the Senate followed the same pattern. Christian Democrats collected 38.8% of the votes and 135 seats, Communists 33.8% and 116, Socialists 10.2% and 29, Social Democrats

During the Italian political crisis in the spring, a crowd gathered in a Roman square to hear a leader of the far right, neofascist Giorgio Almirante.

ALAIN NOGUES—SYGMA

ITALY

Education. (1975–76) Primary, pupils 4,835,-449, teachers 252,637; secondary, pupils 3,322,-014, teachers (1972–73) 283,043; vocational, pupils 1,321,209, teachers (1972–73) 100,579; teacher training, students 196,496, teachers (1972–73) 18,809; higher (including 73 universities), students (1974–75) 886,894, teaching staff (1973–74) 50,662.

Finance. Monetary unit: lira, with (Sept. 20, 1976) a free rate of 843 lire to U.S. $1 (1,453 lire = £1 sterling). Gold, SDR's, and foreign exchange (June 1976) U.S. $5,235,000,000. Budget (1975 actual): revenue 24,364,000,000,000 lire; expenditure 38,101,000,000,000 lire. Gross national product (1974) 97,182,000,000,000 lire. Money supply (Dec. 1975) 67,193,000,000,000 lire. Cost of living (1970 = 100; May 1976) 198.

Foreign Trade. (1975) Imports 25,090,000,-000,000 lire; exports 22,750,000,000,000 lire. Import sources: EEC 43% (West Germany 17%, France 13%, The Netherlands 5%); U.S. 9%; Saudi Arabia 6%. Export destinations: EEC 45% (West Germany 19%, France 13%, U.K. 5%); U.S. 7%. Main exports (1974): machinery 22%; chemicals 10%; motor vehicles 8%; petroleum products 8%; food 6%; iron and steel 6%; textile yarns and fabrics 6%; clothing 5%. Tourism (1974): visitors 12,442,000; gross receipts U.S. $2,668,000,000.

Transport and Communication. Roads (1973) 288,400 km (including 5,090 km expressways). Motor vehicles in use (1974): passenger 14,295,000; commercial 1,080,930. Railways: state (1974) 16,072 km, other (1972) 3,974 km; traffic (1975) 11,377,000,000 passenger-km; freight 461 million net ton-km. Air traffic (1975): 11,491,000,000 passenger-km; freight 1,460,000,000 ton-km. Shipping (1975): merchant vessels 100 gross tons and over 1,732; gross tonnage 10,136,989. Telephones (Jan. 1975) 13,695,000. Radio licenses (Dec. 1974) 12,641,000. Television licenses (Dec. 1974) 11,-816,000.

Agriculture. Production (in 000; metric tons; 1975): wheat 9,620; corn *c.* 5,290; barley 610; oats 506; rice 931; potatoes *c.* 3,035, cabbages (1974) 653; dry broad beans (1974) 268; onions 477; sugar, raw value *c.* 1,450; tomatoes 3,545; grapes (1974) 11,823; wine (1974) *c.* 7,100; olives 2,950; oranges (1974) 1,700; tangerines and mandarin oranges (1974) 357; lemons (1974) *c.* 830; apples (1974) 1,886; pears (1974) 1,507; peaches (1974) 1,252; figs (1974) 145; tobacco *c.* 96; cheese *c.* 480; beef and veal (1974) *c.* 710; pork (1974) *c.* 672. Livestock (in 000; Jan. 1975): cattle *c.* 8,140; sheep *c.* 7,831; pigs *c.* 8,960; goats *c.* 950; poultry *c.* 110,000.

Industry. Index of production (1970 = 100; 1975) 108. Unemployment (1975) 3.3%. Fuel and power (in 000; metric tons; 1975): lignite 1,233; crude oil 1,017; natural gas (cu m) 14,-560,000; manufactured gas (cu m) 3,408,000; electricity (kw-hr) *c.* 149,900,000. Production (in 000; metric tons; 1975): iron ore (50% metal content) 631; pig iron 11,644; crude steel 21,808; aluminum 194; lead 38; zinc 182; cement 34,221; cotton yarn (1974) 150; rayon, etc., filament yarn 41; rayon, etc., fibres 48; nylon, etc., filament yarn 113; nylon, etc., fibres 193; fertilizers (nutrient content; 1974–75) nitrogenous 1,132, phosphate 410, potash 166; sulfuric acid 3,005; petroleum products (1974) 119,421; passenger cars (units) 1,348; commercial vehicles (units) 109. Merchant vessels launched (100 gross tons and over; 1975) 843,-000 gross tons. New dwelling units completed (1975) 214,700.

3.1% and 6, Republicans 2.7% and 6, Liberals 1.4% and 2, and the MSI-DN 6.6% and 15.

After the leaders of the Chamber, Communist Pietro Ingrao (*see* BIOGRAPHY), and of the Senate, Christian Democrat Amintore Fanfani, were chosen, the formation of a government proved to be a formidable task. The Christian Democrats' main allies of the past, the Socialists, refused to participate in a coalition unless the Communist Party was present as well. The Christian Democrats rejected this solution, but Giulio Andreotti (*see* BIOGRAPHY), who formed in July his third Cabinet (Italy's 39th), won a vote of confidence by both houses only because the Communist Party members abstained. Andreotti's government was regarded as the first main concession to the Communists, and with their consent it managed to introduce a series of unpopular but necessary financial and economic measures.

Social unrest during the year originated from both extremes of the nation's political spectrum. After "Red Brigades" leader Renato Curcio was captured on January 18, Rome witnessed battles between police and left-wing extremists. Later both left- and right-wing movements were at the centre of a series of attacks in Milan and in Rome on party offices, army barracks, and supermarkets. In May Neofascist Representative Sandro Saccucci was involved in a shooting at a political rally at Sezze, near Rome, where one man was killed. He was later arrested in London, but extradition proceedings were interrupted upon his reelection to Parliament.

On June 8 Red Brigades in Genoa ambushed and killed General Prosecutor Francesco Coco and both his escorts. A few weeks later another ambush caused the death of Rome Judge Vittorio Occorsio. Later inquiries indicated right-wing connections to his murder. In December ambushes by NAP's (proletarian armed groups) in Rome and Red Brigades near Milan caused the deaths of police as well as two of the agitators.

Kidnappings continued throughout the year; increasingly they were tied to political extremist action, although most were still considered to be of a purely criminal nature. A ruling by a Milan judge had the effect of "freezing" all funds of families trying to pay ransom for one of their relatives. In some cases family members were even prosecuted as "accomplices" for paying ransom rather than helping police with their investigations.

The greatest national calamity in many years was recorded on the evening of May 6, when a severe earthquake hit towns in the northeastern region of Friuli. Almost 1,000 people died, over 2,000 were injured, and 75,000 were left homeless. Subsequent tremors hampered rescue and reconstruction work. As winter came, most of the homeless had to be transferred to other cities because building programs were severely delayed. Another major disaster occurred at Seveso (near Milan), when a cloud of poisonous gas, commonly called dioxin, burst out of a chemical factory. A large area had to be evacuated after physical damage was suffered by the inhabitants. (*See* ENVIRONMENT.) Drought during the summer months, the most severe in decades, seriously damaged crops. When rain finally fell in the autumn, it was with unexpected violence; a sudden flood killed 12 people in the Sicilian town of Trapani.

Foreign Affairs. Apart from Egyptian Pres. Anwar as-Sadat's trip to Rome in April, when he met President Leone and Premier Moro, diplomatic activity mainly consisted of trips by Foreign Minister Arnoldo Forlani to the UN and, later in the year, to London. In December Premier Andreotti paid a visit to outgoing U.S. Pres. Gerald Ford.

Italy was involved during the year in two international scandals. In January the U.S. Central Intelligence Agency was accused of paying large amounts of money to Italian politicians belonging to government parties. Soon afterward, the Lockheed Aircraft Corp. bribery scandal exploded, with heavy repercussions in Italy. The sale of Hercules C-130 planes to Italy was investigated, and as a result the parliamentary committee charged with investigating members of Parliament put former defense ministers Luigi Gui (Christian Democrat) and Mario Tanassi (Social Democrat) and former Premier Mariano Rumor (Christian Democrat) on trial. Another cause for international malaise was a series of statements by U.S. Secretary of State Henry Kissinger and West German Chancellor Helmut Schmidt denouncing economic aid to Italy in case members of the Communist Party gained government positions.

The Economy. All figures related to Italy were in the red in 1976. The balance of trade showed a 3,304,000,000,000 lire deficit in the first eight months of the year (compared with 962 billion lire in the same period of 1975), while the balance of payments showed a loss of 1,069,000,000,000 lire (against 370 billion lire). The national budget had a deficit of more than 11.5 trillion lire.

The Italian economy was sustained by a series of loans by the International Monetary Fund and the European Economic Community and by direct deals with other countries (mainly West Germany and the U.S.). The lira had to be supported in January and February by closing the foreign exchange markets, and again in autumn, when it started falling against the dollar. A special tax was introduced on all currency dealings, with a deposit payable on all foreign currency purchases, and unlawful exportation of capital was made subject to severe penalties. Other government measures were a special "once only" tax on cars (although this was officially destined for rebuilding expenditures after the Friuli earthquake), the freezing of "cost-of-living" pay for salaries above a certain level, and an increase in the gasoline tax.

Inflation was still galloping; by September the cost of living was 17.4% above a year earlier, and the tendency was toward an even higher rate late in the year. The automobile industry, often taken as an indication of general trends, increased production by 9.8% in the first nine months of the year, but housing was at a standstill, while unemployment rose from 693,000 in July 1975 to 776,000 in July 1976. Industry seemed to lack investment incentives, but an unexpected boost took place at the beginning of December when the Libyan Arab Foreign Bank acquired about 10% of the shares of the automaker Fiat. (FABIO GALVANO)

[972.A.4]

Ivory Coast

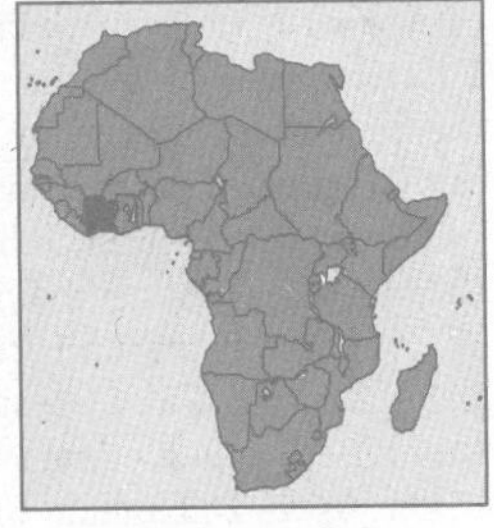

A republic on the Gulf of Guinea, the Ivory Coast is bounded by Liberia, Guinea, Mali, Upper Volta, and Ghana. Area: 123,484 sq mi (319,822 sq km). Pop. (1975 prelim.): 6,673,000. Cap. and largest city: Abidjan (pop., early 1970s est., 650,000). Language: French and local dialects. Religion: animist 65%; Muslim 23%; Christian 12%. President and premier in 1976, Félix Houphouët-Boigny.

On March 4, 1976, President Houphouët-Boigny reorganized his government, enlarging it from 29 to 36 members and appointing Jean-Baptiste Mockey as minister of state for public health and population. Mockey had been a leading politician when the Ivory Coast became an independent republic within the former French Community in 1960. In 1963 he was arrested for plotting against the security of the state, was sentenced to death in January 1965, and then pardoned in May 1967 and released. This appointment was seen as being in line with the president's policy of promoting national unity.

In May Houphouët-Boigny paid his second state visit to France in 16 years and afterward took part in the Franco-African conference at Paris. Despite almost unanimous disapproval from fellow black African leaders, the president remained faithful to his policy of dialogue with South Africa, while declaring himself totally opposed to apartheid (South Africa's policy of racial separation) in all its forms. In March Connie Mulder, the South African minister of information and the interior, visited Abidjan, and in July William Schaufele, U.S. assistant secretary of state for African affairs, made an exploratory visit prior to U.S. Secretary of State Henry Kissinger's Rhodesian mission, which Houphouët-Boigny actively supported. (*See* RHODESIA.) Economic expansion continued, and on April 2 black Africa's only stock exchange opened in Abidjan.

(PHILIPPE DECRAENE)

IVORY COAST

Education. (1973–74) Primary, pupils 606,263, teachers 13,158; secondary, pupils 86,563, teachers 2,693; vocational, pupils (1971–72) 5,242, teachers (1970–71) 613; teacher training, students 2,342, teachers 136; higher, students 6,034, teaching staff 368.

Finance. Monetary unit: CFA franc, with (Sept. 20, 1976) a parity of CFA Fr 50 to the French franc (free rate of CFA Fr 245.90 = U.S. $1; CFA Fr 423.62 = £1 sterling). Gold, SDR's, and foreign exchange (June 1976) U.S. $99.8 million. Budget (1975 actual): revenue CFA Fr 165 billion; expenditure CFA Fr 140 billion. Money supply (April 1976) CFA Fr 196,570,000,000. Cost of living (Abidjan; 1970 = 100; March 1976) 157.

Foreign Trade. (1975) Imports CFA Fr 241,390,000,000; exports CFA Fr 254,570,000,000. Import sources (1974): France 39%; U.S. 7%; West Germany 6%; Iraq 6%; Nigeria 5%. Export destinations: France 27%; The Netherlands 10%; U.S. 10%; West Germany 9%; Italy 7%. Main exports: coffee 24%; cocoa 19%; timber 14%; petroleum products 6%.

Agriculture. Production (in 000; metric tons; 1975): rice *c.* 470; corn (1974) *c.* 130; yams (1974) *c.* 1,600; cassava (1974) *c.* 625; millet *c.* 50; peanuts *c.* 45; bananas (1974) *c.* 230; palm kernels *c.* 36; palm oil *c.* 140; coffee *c.* 280; cocoa *c.* 225; cotton, lint *c.* 24; rubber *c.* 18; timber (cu m; 1974) *c.* 10,895. Livestock (in 000; 1974): cattle *c.* 480; pigs *c.* 195; sheep *c.* 950; goats *c.* 960; poultry *c.* 6,400.

Jamaica

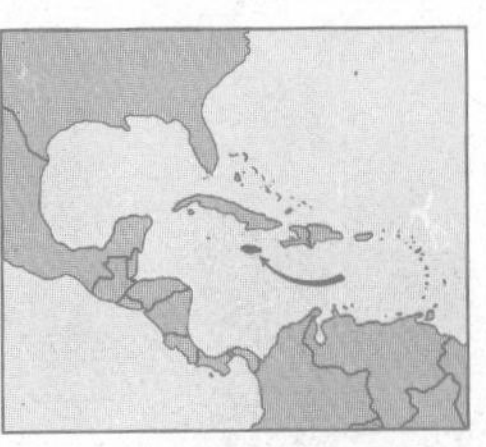

A parliamentary state within the Commonwealth of Nations, Jamaica is an island in the Caribbean Sea about 90 mi S of Cuba. Area: 4,244 sq mi (10,991 sq km). Pop. (1976 est.): 2,060,400, predominantly Negro, but including Europeans, Chinese, Indians, and persons of mixed race. Cap. and largest city: Kingston (pop., 1974 est., 169,800). Language: English. Religion: Christian, with Anglicans and Baptists in the majority. Queen, Elizabeth II; governor-general in 1976, Florizel Glasspole; prime minister, Michael Manley.

In 1976 the Jamaican economy moved into deeper crisis, with low domestic production, unemployment, strikes in the vital aluminum and sugarcane industries and on the waterfront and railways, a further decline in tourism, poor export performance, and a continuing flight of capital despite currency controls. In June the country's foreign exchange reserves stood at minus $61.7 million, and a loan of $87 million to help Jamaica out was rapidly put together by Trinidad and Tobago, Barbados, and Guyana, Jamaica's regional partners in the Caribbean Community and Common Market.

The private sector and overseas investors lacked confidence in the government, which was strengthening ties with Cuba despite the declared allegiance of Prime Minister Manley (*see* BIOGRAPHY) to "dem-

Jai Alai: *see* Court Games

JAMAICA

Education. (1974–75) Primary, pupils 440,235, teachers (1972–73) 9,888; secondary, pupils 103,680; vocational, pupils 5,169; secondary and vocational, teachers (1972–73) 3,549; teacher training, students 2,104, teachers (1972–73) 142; higher, students 2,451, teaching staff (1972–73) 638.

Finance. Monetary unit: Jamaican dollar, with (Sept. 20, 1976) a par value of Jam$0.91 to U.S. $1 (free rate of Jam$1.57 = £1 sterling). Gold, SDR's, and foreign exchange (June 1976) U.S. $123 million. Budget (1975–76 est.): revenue Jam$475,065,000; expenditure Jam$864,884,000.

Foreign Trade. (1975) Imports Jam$1,021,400,000; exports Jam$712.7 million. Import sources: U.S. 37%; Venezuela 14%; U.K. 13%; Canada 5%; Trinidad and Tobago 5%. Export destinations: U.S. 38%; U.K. 23%; Norway 11%; Iran 5%. Main exports: alumina 41%; sugar 20%; bauxite 13%. Tourism (1974): visitors 433,000; gross receipts U.S. $133 million.

Agriculture. Production (in 000; metric tons; 1974): sweet potatoes *c.* 16; yams *c.* 127; cassava *c.* 15; corn *c.* 12; sugar, raw value 372; bananas *c.* 190; oranges *c.* 46; grapefruit *c.* 32; copra *c.* 8. Livestock (in 000; 1974): cattle *c.* 274; goats *c.* 378; pigs *c.* 222; poultry *c.* 3,600.

Industry. Production (in 000; metric tons; 1975): bauxite 11,304; cement 405; petroleum products (1974) 1,614; electricity (kw-hr; 1974) 2,218,000.

ocratic socialism." North American tourists were deterred by the violent crime and endemic political warfare between the governing People's National Party (PNP) and Jamaica Labour Party (JLP) extremists that had escalated in Kingston until the introduction of a state of emergency in mid-June.

The campaign for the December 15 elections was marked by charges by the governing PLP that the JLP, the U.S. Central Intelligence Agency, and U.S. bauxite interests were attempting to "destabilize" Jamaican society, while the JLP claimed harassment and countercharged the government with attempting to create a "red axis" in alliance with Cuba. Despite the economic crisis and endemic politico-criminal violence, the PLP won an overwhelming 48 seats to the JLP's 12.

(SHEILA PATTERSON)

[974.B.2.d]

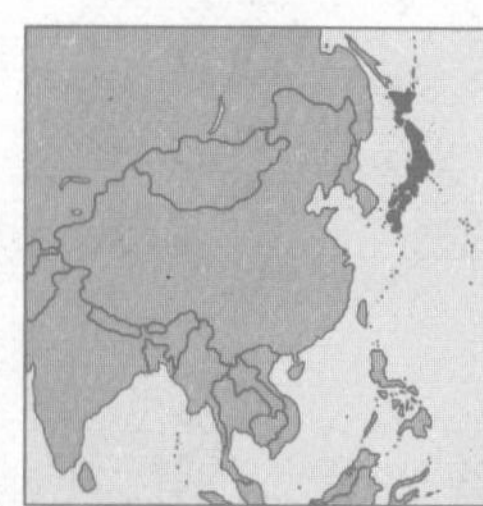

Japan

A constitutional monarchy in the northwestern Pacific Ocean, Japan is an archipelago composed of four major islands (Hokkaido, Honshu, Kyushu, and Shikoku), the Ryukyus (including Okinawa), and minor adjacent islands. Area: 145,767 sq mi (377,535 sq km). Pop. (1976 est.): 112,550,000. Cap. and largest city: Tokyo (pop., 1976 est., 8,586,900). Language: Japanese. Religion: primarily Shinto and Buddhist; Christian 0.5%. Emperor, Hirohito; prime ministers in 1976, Takeo Miki and, from December 24, Takeo Fukuda.

Domestic Affairs. During 1976 Japan was completely absorbed in the unfolding "Lockheed affair," the nation's equivalent to the U.S. Watergate scandal, which cost the ruling Liberal-Democrats their absolute majority in the lower house of the Diet and brought down the government of Prime Minister Miki. In the testimony and in evidence subsequently presented to a closed hearing held by the U.S. Securities and Exchange Commission, former vice-chairman A. Carl Kotchian of Lockheed Aircraft Corp. testified that his company had been advised to send bribes to Japanese government officials to gain their help in the sale of airplanes to Japan.

Both the U.S. and Japanese governments immediately clamped a lid of secrecy on the case, so that Japanese newspapers found it difficult to engage in investigative reporting. On February 9 government and majority Liberal-Democratic Party (LDP) leaders did, however, comply with the opposition parties' demand that the Diet subpoena certain persons, including Yoshio Kodama (*see* BIOGRAPHY), a wealthy ultrarightist suspected of involvement in the Lockheed payoff case.

In September 1972, two years before he resigned amid another political scandal, Prime Minister Kakuei Tanaka (*see* BIOGRAPHY) met then U.S. Pres. Richard Nixon in a summit conference at Honolulu. An agreement that supplemented the Tanaka-Nixon communiqué provided that Japanese commercial airlines were to purchase civil aircraft, including wide-bodied airbuses, valued at about $320 million in order to help correct the U.S.-Japanese trade imbalance of more than $1 billion. On Aug. 23, 1972, and again on Oct 14, 1972, Pres. Hiroshi Hiyama of Marubeni Corp., Lockheed's sales agent in Japan, called on Prime Minister Tanaka in his home, and on Oct. 24, 1972, Pres. Tokuji Wakasa of All Nippon Airways (ANA) similarly visited the prime minister. On July 27, 1973, Lockheed concluded a consultant contract with Kodama. These were the only facts on the case available to the Japanese press.

On March 12, 1976, at the request of Prime Minister Miki, U.S. Pres. Gerald Ford stated in a letter that information on the Lockheed case could be supplied to the Japanese government but only on a conditional basis. On March 24 Japan's Justice Ministry and the U.S. Department of Justice signed a mutual assistance agreement providing for the supply of information, which was to remain confidential except in connection with open court proceedings in Japan. The first batch of data arrived in Tokyo on the evening of April 10, and a week later two officials of the Tokyo District public prosecutor's office returned home from the U.S. carrying the remaining Lockheed documents but Miki claimed that even he could not see them.

Meanwhile, on March 23 the case took a bizarre turn when a young movie actor, dressed in a World War II kamikaze uniform, crashed a light plane into the suburban Tokyo residence of Kodama. The pilot was killed, but Kodama remained unhurt.

On April 2 Tanaka broke a long silence with his first public statement on the Lockheed affair. In addressing a meeting of his powerful LDP faction, he denied complicity in the case.

Nonetheless, the net drew tighter as Kodama was indicted on May 10 for violating the foreign exchange control law by receiving payments of 440 million yen in cash from Lockheed in 1973. By June two arrested ANA officials had admitted that during 1974 more than 50 million yen in Lockheed payments had been distributed through President Wakasa. The latter flatly denied this charge on June 27. Two more persons were arrested on July 2, a former director of Marubeni and an aide of Kodama, for having received a total of 500 million yen in the period 1973–74. On July 9 Vice-Pres. Naoji Watanabe became the sixth ANA official and the tenth person arrested in the case. On July 22 the seriously ill Kodama, in a bedside interrogation by a Diet member, denied allegations that he had received bribes of more than one billion yen from Lockheed. Kodama claimed that he had received no funds except for 50 million yen in annual consultant fees.

JAPAN

Education. (1974–75) Primary, pupils 10,364,855, teachers 415,039; secondary, pupils 9,095,163, teachers, 457,565; vocational, pupils 1,252,605, teachers 47,696; higher (including 41 main state universities), students 2,087,866, teaching staff 105,104.

Finance. Monetary unit: yen, with (Sept. 20, 1976) a free rate of 287 yen to U.S. $1 (495 yen = £1 sterling). Gold, SDR's, and foreign exchange (June 1976) U.S. $14,215,000,000. Budget (1975–76 est.): revenue 25,977,000,000,000 yen; expenditure 27,323,000,000,000 yen. Gross national product (1975) 144,865,000,000,000 yen. Money supply (June 1976) 51,787,000,000,000 yen. Cost of living (1970 = 100; June 1976) 188.

Foreign Trade. (1975) Imports 17,174,000,000,000 yen; exports 16,572,000,000,000 yen. Import sources: U.S. 20%; Saudi Arabia 11%; Iran 9%; Australia 7%; Indonesia 6%. Export destinations: U.S. 20%; Liberia 5%. Main exports: machinery 23% (telecommunications apparatus 6%); iron and steel 18%; motor vehicles 15%; ships 11%; chemicals 7%; textile yarns and fabrics 5%.

Transport and Communications. Roads (1974) 1,058,912 km (including 1,454 km expressways). Motor vehicles in use (1974): passenger 15,854,000; commercial 10,825,000. Railways: (1973) 27,517 km; traffic (1975) 323,192,000,000 passenger-km, freight 47,911,000,000 net ton-km. Air traffic (1975): 17,544,000,000 passenger-km; freight 841,952,000 net ton-km. Shipping (1975): merchant vessels 100 gross tons and over 9,932; gross tonnage 39,739,598. Telephones (Dec. 1974) 41,905,000. Radio receivers (Dec. 1972) 70,794,000. Television licenses (Dec. 1974) 25,564,000.

Agriculture. Production (in 000; metric tons; 1975): rice 17,101; wheat *c.* 241; barley 221; sweet potatoes (1974) *c.* 1,024; potatoes *c.* 3,000; sugar, raw value 464; onions *c.* 1,000; tomatoes *c.* 880; cabbages (1974) *c.* 1,400; cucumbers *c.* 1,150; watermelons (1974) *c.* 1,220; apples (1974) *c.* 924; pears (1974) *c.* 514; mandarin oranges and tangerines (1974) 3,568; grapes (1974) 265; tea *c.* 103; tobacco *c.* 157; milk *c.* 4,970; eggs 1,786; pork (1974) *c.* 1,100; timber (cu m; 1974) *c.* 43,060; fish catch (1974) 10,773; whale and sperm oil (1974–75) 18. Livestock (in 000; Feb. 1975): cattle *c.* 3,676; sheep *c.* 13; pigs *c.* 8,243; goats (1974) 127; chickens *c.* 280,391.

Industry. Index of production (1970 = 100; 1975) 110. Fuel and power (in 000; metric tons; 1975): coal 19,000; crude oil 607; natural gas (cu m) 2,764,000; manufactured gas (cu m) 5,481,000; electricity (kw-hr; 1974) 460,705,000. Production (in 000; metric tons; 1975): iron ore (55% metal content) 897; pig iron 89,016; crude steel 102,314; petroleum products (1974) 217,514; cement 65,522; cotton yarn 460; woven cotton fabrics (sq m) 2,124,000; rayon, etc., filament yarn 103; rayon, etc., fibres 288; nylon, etc., filament yarn 491; nylon, etc., fibres 570; sulfuric acid 6,002; fertilizers (nutrient content; 1974–75) nitrogenous *c.* 2,341, phosphate 769; cameras (35-mm still; units) 4,466; wrist watches (units) 30,239; radio receivers (units) 14,188; television receivers (units) 10,625; passenger cars (units) 4,569; commercial vehicles (units) 2,373; motorcycles (units) 3,801. Merchant vessels launched (100 gross tons and over; 1975) 17,740,000 gross tons. New dwelling units started (1975) 1,540,000.

A climax in the case came on July 27 when Tanaka was arrested on a charge of accepting 500 million yen in secret payments from Lockheed's agent, the Marubeni Corp. Later in the day, Tanaka's private secretary was also detained. The charge held that there were three channels for the payments: Marubeni Corp., consultant Kodama, and ANA, which had purchased the aircraft.

On August 16 Tanaka became the first Japanese prime minister ever to be indicted on a charge of bribery stemming from his official duties. The charge filed by the Tokyo prosecutor alleged that on Aug. 23, 1972, Marubeni President Hiyama urged Tanaka "to endeavour to persuade ANA to purchase Lockheed Aircraft's L-1011 TriStars." Tanaka was promised a reward of 500 million yen on completion of the deal. ANA announced its decision to purchase the aircraft on Oct. 30, 1972, and signed the contract with Lockheed on Jan. 12, 1973. Tanaka faced one count for violation of the exchange law (maximum sentence, three years) and one for the bribe "in response to an entreaty" (maximum, five years).

The Lockheed affair, of course, affected all political maneuvers during the year. In March and April opposition parties boycotted Diet business in an attempt to force the government into complete disclosure of the U.S.-supplied data. In a poll conducted in April, voters were asked if they supported the manner in which the Miki Cabinet operated; only 29.9% replied in the affirmative, while 49.1% answered no. On May 25 the 77th regular Diet adjourned its 150-day session, barely passing the 24,296,000,000,000 yen budget for fiscal year 1976–77.

Six dissident members of the Diet, led by Yohei Kono, on June 25 submitted letters of secession from the LDP, which they described as "a gerontocracy bent on chamber room power struggles." They announced formation of a Shin Jiyu (New Liberal) club. At the time, the party standings in the Diet were as follows: (lower) House of Representatives: LDP 269, Japan Socialists (JSP) 114, Japan Communists (JCP) 39, Komeito 30, Democratic Socialists (DSP) 19, New Liberals 5, independent 1, vacancies 14 (total 491); (upper) House of Councillors: LDP 128, JSP 62, Komeito 24, JCP 20, DSP 10, Niin Club 5, independents 3 (total 252).

Late in July Prime Minister Miki expressed his determination to stay in power and to hold a general election after dissolving the lower house. He listed three priority tasks: (1) to unravel the Lockheed scandal; (2) to carry out a drastic reform of the LDP; and (3) to pass key bills carried over from the last session of the Diet. On August 23, however, Deputy Prime Minister Takeo Fukuda and Finance Minister Masayoshi Ohira called for the resignation of Miki. There was no alternative, Fukuda said, but to plunge into the general election under a "fresh, powerful leadership." On August 30 party executives proposed a compromise: the LDP Cabinet would be reshuffled and would then call an extraordinary session of the Diet to pass key pending measures, and the LDP would prepare for the general election, which, under law, had to be held by December 9. The anti-Miki party elders flatly rejected the mediation and in turn called

KEYSTONE

The Nippon Press Centre in Tokyo opened in July. Financed by newspaper and business groups, it provides office space for the press plus a conference hall on top.

WIDE WORLD

WIDE WORLD

Japan's Watergate. A political scandal rocked Japan when high government officials were accused of accepting multimillion-dollar bribes from the Lockheed Aircraft Corp. (Left) Trade union members parade in Tokyo in February, demanding a thorough investigation. (Right) Kenji Osano, director of All Nippon Airways, tells a parliamentary committee that he was not involved.

a meeting of LDP members of both houses on August 31.

Party members, who had once thought Miki too weak to pursue the Lockheed investigation, now began to realize that public opinion was on the side of the prime minister, who insisted on strict law enforcement. On September 11 a compromise was reached within the LDP: the Cabinet was to call an extraordinary session of the Diet to process economic bills; Miki would remain temporarily in power; and an extraordinary party convention would be held in October to choose the LDP leadership for the forthcoming elections. The convention was postponed, however, when it appeared that factional disputes might injure the party at the polls.

On September 15 Miki reorganized his Cabinet, retaining powerful faction leaders Fukuda and Ohira. The new foreign minister, Zentaro Kosaka, had held the post in a previous administration.

The extraordinary Diet session opened on September 16 on an ominous note. The LDP alone determined the 50-day duration of the session, proposing passage of the overdue bill for deficit-finance bonds and two acts designed to raise national railway fares and telephone rates. Opposition parties were adamant, maintaining that the Lockheed probe should be given first priority. In a speech to the Diet on September 24, Miki pledged his determination to aid the Diet in uncovering the rest of the Lockheed case.

In the December 5 elections the LDP suffered its worst setback in more than 20 years and, although Tanaka retained his seat, the Lockheed affair was held to be a major factor. In an expanded lower house of 511 seats, the LDP won only 249, but an alliance with several independents gave it a slim majority. The standings of the other parties were: JSP 123, Komeito 55, DSP 29, JCP 17, New Liberals 17, and independents and minor parties 21. The LDP's percentage of the popular vote fell from 46.9 in 1972 to 41.8. In a letter to the LDP executive on December 17, Miki accepted responsibility for the election results and announced his intention to resign. Takeo Fukuda was chosen as LDP leader, and on December 24 was elected prime minister by a margin of two votes in the House of Representatives and one vote in the House of Councillors. In a Cabinet that stressed expertise in economic affairs, Iichiro Hatoyama became foreign minister and Hideo Bo, finance minister.

Foreign Affairs. Had it not been for the Lockheed affair, the U.S.-Japan trade balance would have been the most serious issue between the two nations. Early in September in Washington, D.C., Japan's ambassador to the U.S., Fumihiko Togo, denied an allegation made by U.S. Rep. Henry Reuss (Dem., Wis.) that Japan was artificially holding down the value of the yen to boost its exports. Togo stated that Japan's current account in the first seven months of 1976 posted a surplus of $1.1 billion. At an annual rate, this sum was much smaller than the $11.7 billion chalked up by the U.S. in 1975 and the $9.7 billion by West Germany in 1974.

Friendly ties between Japan and the Soviet Union, according to a *Pravda* dispatch on September 1, had helped reinforce the tendency toward relaxation of tension in the world. The Soviet Union's volume of trade with Japan increased by 160% during the period covered by the U.S.S.R.'s ninth five-year plan (1971–75).

Movement toward the settlement of differences between Japan and the U.S.S.R. became stalled on September 6 when a Soviet high-performance MiG-25 jet fighter made an emergency landing at Hakodate civil airport. The pilot, Lieut. Viktor Ivanovich Belenko, promptly announced his intention to seek political asylum in the U.S., and a few days later was granted his wish by the Japanese government. In a meeting with Foreign Minister Kosaka at the UN in New York City on September 28, Soviet Foreign Minister Andrey Gromyko denounced Japan's handling of the MiG-25 incident as "unfriendly." Gromyko expressed strong dissatisfaction with the fact that the aircraft was jointly dismantled by Japanese and U.S. military personnel. He also showed an unbending attitude on various pending issues, such as the "northern territories" (islands off Hokkaido held by the U.S.S.R. since World War II), fishing operations in the northern Pacific, and requests by Japanese to visit graves of relatives in the Soviet Union. In Tokyo the Foreign Ministry delivered a four-page letter to the Soviet embassy, branding as "slanderous perversion" the claim that the Soviet lieutenant had been sent to the U.S. against his will.

Relations between Japan and China dipped to the lowest point since the two nations normalized relations (in 1972) when, on July 19, China formally protested the Japanese foreign minister's statement urging the U.S. to move slowly in improving its ties with Peking. The *People's Daily* of China charged a violation of the joint Japan-China statement of 1972, in which Japan stated that it understood and respected the principle that Taiwan is an integral part of China.

Relations with South Korea continued to be troubled by a long-standing case, in which Japan had interested itself since 1973. In that year Kim Dae Jung, a leader of the opposition to South Korean Pres. Park Chung Hee, had been abducted from a Tokyo hotel to South Korea under unusual circumstances that suggested the involvement of a staff member of South Korea's embassy in Tokyo. A diplomatic agreement was reached in 1975 whereby the Korean staff member was removed from official status and Japan in turn agreed to exercise surveillance over anti-Park movements. On August 28 the Foreign Ministry in Tokyo objected to the sentencing of Kim in Seoul, recalling previous assurances to Japan that the political prisoner would be freed. The same day more than 100 protesters demonstrated before the Korean embassy in Tokyo, calling attention to the sentencing of Kim and former Pres. Yun Po Sun to eight years' imprisonment.

Japan's "hostile policy" toward North Korea was denounced by North Korean Foreign Minister Ho Dam, attending a conference of nonaligned nations held in Colombo, Sri Lanka, in August. At the end of September the official North Korean Central News Agency accused Japan of committing a "grave provocation" by sending naval ships and fighter planes to obstruct the peaceful passage of a North Korean ship on the high seas. The incident, according to the news agency, was part of an "American campaign" to increase tension and to encourage South Korea.

(ARDATH W. BURKS)

[975.B]

Jordan

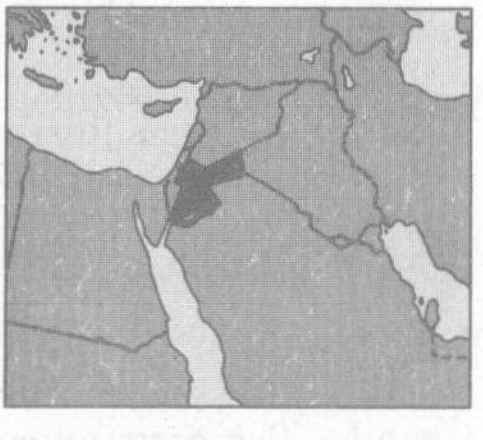

A constitutional monarchy in southwest Asia, Jordan is bounded by Syria, Iraq, Saudi Arabia, and Israel. Area (including territory occupied by Israel in the June 1967 war): 36,832 sq mi (95,394 sq km). Pop. (1975 est.): 2,702,000. Cap. and largest city: Amman (pop., 1975 est., 615,000). Language: Arabic. Religion (1961): Muslim 94%; Christian 6%. King, Hussein I; prime ministers in 1976, Zaid ar-Rifai and, from July 13, Mudar Badran.

In 1976 Jordan reaffirmed its new close relationship with Syria and was the only Arab state to give unequivocal support to Syrian intervention in Lebanon. Apart from King Hussein's visits to Damascus in March, August, and September and Pres. Hafez al-Assad's visit to Amman in December there were frequent meetings between top Syrian and Jordanian officials, and of the countries' Joint Supreme Committee. Accepting that the Syrian ties would involve Jordan directly in any future Arab-Israeli conflict, Jordan was concerned with military needs. The new national service law passed at the end of 1975 was designed to draft 8,000 men a year and raise the Army's strength to 85,000. It also aimed to add skilled urban workers to the armed forces to handle sophisticated equipment. It was announced in January that the Army would be fully mechanized in 18 months.

Jordan's chief military weakness lay in air defense; as negotiations to buy U.S. antiaircraft missiles and artillery continued to be prolonged, owing to U.S. congressional opposition, the king and the prime minister spoke of the possibility of buying Soviet SAM's instead, even if this meant an important change in Jordan's normally pro-Western foreign policy. After a visit to Jordan in May by the Soviet deputy defense minister, Marshal Pavel S. Kutakhov, King Hussein paid an 11-day visit to the Soviet Union in June and on his return said Moscow had offered to sell Jordan an air defense system that would be 40% cheaper than the American. However, no deal went through, and in August it was reported that Jordan would after all buy Hawk and Redeye missiles and Vulcan antiaircraft guns from the U.S. for about $540 million, to be provided by Saudi Arabia (which was thought to have refused to finance any purchase of Soviet arms).

Apart from his Moscow visit, King Hussein made several diplomatic missions during the year, visiting Australia, Japan, Singapore, and Iran in March and the U.S., Canada, and Britain in April. He constantly emphasized the need for the U.S. to help toward a final solution of the Middle East problem.

On February 4 the government announced that general elections would be postponed indefinitely beyond the period prescribed by the constitution because of the unsettled circumstances prevailing in the region. The old Chamber of Deputies and Senate that had been dissolved in 1974 were reconvened on February 5 by royal decree and then dissolved on February 7 after much criticism by Palestinians and some Arab states. They charged that the recall of the old Parliament, with its representation of the West Bank, contravened the decision of the 1974 Rabat Arab summit conference that the Palestine Liberation Organization (PLO) was the sole legitimate representative of the Palestinian people. King Hussein maintained he still stood by the Rabat resolutions, but he was critical of the PLO role in Lebanon and condemned Egypt's support of the PLO against Syria. The Arab National Union, the country's single political organization since 1971, was also dissolved on February 18.

JORDAN

Education. (1975–76) Primary, pupils 386,012, teachers 11,120; secondary, pupils 157,745, teachers 7,248; vocational, pupils 6,441, teachers 345; higher, students 11,873, teaching staff 627.

Finance. Monetary unit: Jordanian dinar, with (Sept. 20, 1976) a free rate of 0.32 dinar to U.S. $1 (0.55 dinar = £1 sterling). Gold, SDR's, and foreign exchange (June 1976) U.S. $485.2 million. Budget (1975 est.): revenue 206 million dinars; expenditure 218 million dinars. Gross national product (1974) 374 million dinars. Money supply (May 1976) 259,330,000 dinars. Cost of living (Amman; 1970 = 100; May 1976) 192.

Foreign Trade. (1975) Imports 234,030,000 dinars; exports 48,870,000 dinars. Import sources: West Germany 12%; U.S. 11%; Saudi Arabia 11%; U.K. 10%; Japan 8%; Italy 5%. Export destinations: Saudi Arabia 10%; Iran 9%; Syria 8%; Romania 7%; Turkey 6%; Iraq 5%; Kuwait 5%; Lebanon 5%. Main exports: phosphates 39%; vegetables 10%; cement 8%; oranges 7%. Tourism (1974): visitors 554,900; gross receipts U.S. $54 million.

Transport and Communications. Roads (1974) 5,972 km (including 28 km expressways). Motor vehicles in use (1974): passenger 24,922; commercial 7,574. Railways (1974) 480 km. Air traffic (1975): 711.3 million passenger-km; freight 13,460,000 net ton-km. Telephones (Dec. 1973) 40,000. Radio receivers (Dec. 1973) 521,000. Television receivers (Dec. 1973) 80,000.

Agriculture. Production (in 000; metric tons; 1975): wheat *c.* 60; barley (1974) *c.* 35; lentils (1974) *c.* 25; tomatoes 145; watermelons (1974) *c.* 45; olives *c.* 5; oranges (1974) *c.* 12; grapes (1974) *c.* 25; tobacco *c.* 1.5. Livestock (in 000; 1974): cattle *c.* 40; goats *c.* 360; sheep *c.* 670; camels *c.* 9; asses *c.* 44; chickens *c.* 2,700.

Industry. Production (in 000; metric tons; 1974): phosphate rock 1,676; petroleum products 701; cement 596; electricity (kw-hr) 310,000.

Japanese Literature: *see* Literature

Jazz: *see* Music

Jehovah's Witnesses: *see* Religion

Jewish Literature: *see* Literature

On July 13 Prime Minister Zaid ar-Rifai resigned and was replaced immediately by Mudar Badran, a former intelligence chief and the king's special adviser on the occupied territories, who also took over the portfolios of defense and foreign affairs. The new 18-member Cabinet included ten members of the outgoing government. The new prime minister promised to tackle inflation and make the country more reliant on its own resources. Many economic sectors were enjoying boom conditions, partly caused by the Lebanese crisis and the transfer of foreign and Arab business from Beirut to Amman, but the rapid increase in prices was causing serious social strain. The balance of payments was greatly helped by aid from the Arab oil states and the U.S. and other Western sources, but the visible trade deficit continued to increase. The near doubling of the volume of imports and of the number of ships using Aqaba port in 1975 over 1974 required extensive plans for expanding the port. May 31 marked the official launching of the 1976–80 development plan which forecast a total investment of over $2.3 billion and a 12% annual economic growth rate. (PETER MANSFIELD)

See also Middle Eastern Affairs.

[978.B.3.d.ii]

Kenya

An African republic and a member of the Commonwealth of Nations, Kenya is bordered on the north by Sudan and Ethiopia, east by Somalia, south by Tanzania, and west by Uganda. Area: 224,961 sq mi (582,646 sq km), including 5,172 sq mi of inland water. Pop. (1975 est.): 13,399,000, including (1969) African 98.1%; Asian 1.5%. Cap. and largest city: Nairobi (pop., 1975 est., 700,000). Language: Swahili (official) and English. Religion: Protestant 36%; Roman Catholic 22%; Muslim 6%; others, mostly indigenous 36%. President in 1976, Jomo Kenyatta.

Kenya's continuing balance of payments deficit led to restrictions on imports in 1976; this in turn inhibited economic development, and the country remained heavily dependent upon external aid. Two years of drought brought fears of famine, particularly in the Machakos district and in Masailand to the southeast and southwest of Nairobi. The links that had bound the East African Community together were growing weaker, and an exchange of missions with Zambia led to hopes of an increase in trade with that country that would offset the loss in trade with Uganda. The government was worried also about the growing military strength of Somalia, being armed by the U.S.S.R.

Relations with Uganda posed the most serious problems. Claims by Uganda's Pres. Idi Amin to a portion of western Kenya aroused fierce resentment in February. Mombasa dockworkers voted to boycott exports to and from Uganda, and Kenya's western frontier was closed for two days. The government refused to allow gasoline supplies to enter Uganda unless payment was made in advance because of Uganda's heavy indebtedness, and in March the government also demanded an inquiry into the shooting of a Kenyan student at Makerere University and the disappearance of another.

Late in April the U.S. secretary of state, Henry Kissinger, visited Kenya. Questions of defense occupied the main position in his discussions with government ministers. This was followed in June by a visit from the U.S. secretary of defense, Donald Rumsfeld, that led to an agreement in principle to supply Kenya with 12 F-5 jet fighter aircraft as a counterbalance to the growing supplies of arms from the Soviet Union to Somalia and Uganda. Relations with Uganda became still worse early in July when Uganda accused the Kenya government of complicity in the Israeli raid on Entebbe airport, Uganda. (Israeli planes had landed in Nairobi on their way back to Israel; *see* DEFENSE.) Each country accused the other of massing troops along the common border. Kenyan workers fleeing

Kenya's Pres. Jomo Kenyatta (dark suit) received Tanzania's Pres. Julius Nyerere (holding baton) in August to discuss their common difficulties with Uganda.

PASCAL VILLIERS LE MOY—SYGMA

KENYA

Education. (1975) Primary, pupils 2,881,155, teachers 86,109; secondary, pupils 226,835, teachers 9,230; vocational, pupils (1973) 3,525, teachers (1973) 237; teacher training, students 8,666, teachers 541; higher, students 5,977.

Finance. Monetary unit: Kenyan shilling, with (Sept. 20, 1976) a free rate of KShs 8.40 to U.S. $1 (KShs 14.48 = £1 sterling). Gold, SDR's, and foreign exchange (June 1976) U.S. $222.3 million. Budget (1974–75 est.): revenue KShs 4,240,000,000; expenditure KShs 3,720,000,000. Gross national product (1974) KShs 18,184,000,000. Cost of living (Nairobi; 1970 = 100; June 1976) 164.

Foreign Trade. (1975) Imports KShs 6,948,000,000; exports KShs 4,464,000,000. Import sources: U.K. 20%; Iran 15%; Japan 9%; West Germany 8%; Saudi Arabia 8%; U.S. 7%. Export destinations: Uganda 12%; U.K. 10%; Tanzania 9%; West Germany 9%. Main exports: petroleum products 26%; coffee 16%; tea 10%; chemicals 6%; fruit and vegetables 5%. Tourism (1974): visitors 377,000; gross receipts U.S. $76 million.

Transport and Communications. Roads (1974) 49,699 km. Motor vehicles in use (1974): passenger 122,357; commercial 18,226. Railways: (1973) 2,073 km (operated under East African Railways Corporation, serving Kenya, mainland Tanzania, and Uganda with a total of 5,893 km); traffic (total East African; 1966) 4,529,000,000 passenger-km, freight (1974) 3,998,000,000 net ton-km. Air traffic (apportionment of traffic of East African Airways Corporation; 1974): 715 million passenger-km; freight 21.4 million ton-km. Telephones (Dec. 1974) 114,000. Radio receivers (Dec. 1973) 508,000. Television receivers (Dec. 1973) 36,000.

Agriculture. Production (in 000; metric tons; 1975): corn *c.* 1,600; wheat *c.* 160; millet and sorghum *c.* 360; sweet potatoes (1974) *c.* 540; cassava (1974) *c.* 640; sugar, raw value *c.* 133; coffee *c.* 70; tea *c.* 56; sisal *c.* 43; cotton, lint *c.* 5; fish catch (1974) 29. Livestock (in 000; May 1975): cattle *c.* 7,610; sheep *c.* 3,200; pigs *c.* 68; goats (1974) *c.* 3,600; camels (1974) *c.* 330; chickens (1974) *c.* 14,600.

Industry. Production (in 000; metric tons; 1974): soda ash 152; salt (1973) 35; cement (1975) 897; petroleum products *c.* 2,733; electricity (kw-hr; 1975) 904,000.

Uganda reported harassment and actual cruelty, and in response to an appeal from President Kenyatta Britain offered to send supplies of arms to Kenya immediately. President Amin accused Kenya of operating an economic blockade that was paralyzing his country by cutting off supplies of gasoline. Early in August, after considerable argument, a meeting in Nairobi between representatives of the two countries ended in an agreement to put an end to the bellicosity and to reopen trade; Uganda offered to pay the £27 million owing to Kenya. In September Kissinger again visited Kenya in order to brief President Kenyatta on the results of his Rhodesian mission.

Troubles with Uganda tended to overshadow criticism of the government by some of Kenya's own members of Parliament. In March one member, Mrs. Chelagat Mutai, was sentenced to 30 months' imprisonment for inciting people to damage a sisal estate in September 1975. Paul Ngei, a long-term Cabinet minister and close associate of the president, who had been expelled from office and from Parliament in November 1975 after being found responsible for irregularities in the 1974 elections, was reelected to Parliament in January with a large majority and became a minister once more in March. Parliament, which was prorogued early in the year after criticizing the government's handling of relations with Uganda, reassembled in June. In his address at the reopening the president called for a movement toward greater national unity. In August the minister for local government, Robert Matano, had to postpone the election for Nairobi's mayor because the municipal council split its support between the then mayor, Margaret Kenyatta, and the deputy mayor, Andrew Ngumba, who had put himself forward for election in defiance of the Kenya African National Union. The minister also dissolved the Mombasa municipal council after receiving reports of inefficiency and corruption and appointed a seven-man commission to run the town's affairs. (KENNETH INGHAM)

[978.E.6.b.v]

Korea

A country of eastern Asia, Korea is bounded by China, the Sea of Japan, the Korea Strait, and the Yellow Sea. It is divided into two parts at the 38th parallel.

For a tense moment, on Aug. 18, 1976, it looked as though the bitter antagonists of the Korean War were about to pick up where they had left off in 1953. In the border truce village of Panmunjom, where long-winded negotiations had helped maintain a facade of peace for a quarter century, a work party under the UN Command's flag went out on a tree-pruning mission. Suddenly about 30 North Korean guards wielding axes and clubs pounced upon them. A brutal fight followed and two U.S. officers were killed—the first to die in Panmunjom in nine years.

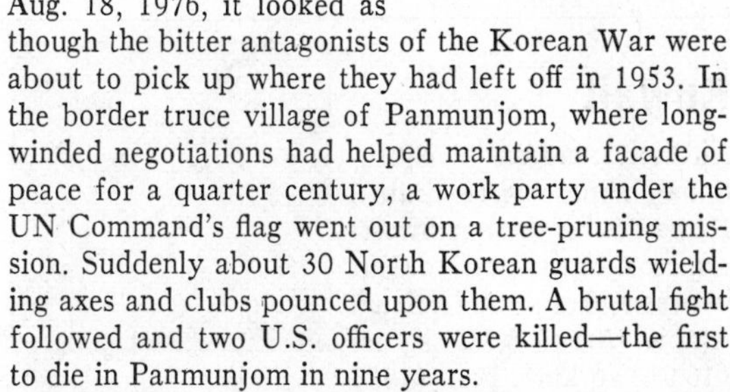

All parties immediately ordered a military alert. The U.S. rushed F-4 Phantoms and F-111 fighters to Seoul and ordered the carrier "Midway" to the Korean coast. Pyongyang ordered its own massive (more than 2 million) Army and militia into full combat readiness. U.S. officers at Panmunjom accused North Korea of "an open and flagrant act of belligerency," while North Korean officers charged the UN Command with "vicious and provocative acts" against their border guards. Within two days, however, it became clear that cool heads in Washington, Seoul, and even Pyongyang were determined to avoid armed conflict. In Washington the White House announced that North Korea had expressed regrets for the killing of the two army officers. North Korean Pres. Kim Il Sung (*see* BIOGRAPHY) had chosen the unusual method of a personal message to the U.S. commander of UN forces to convey the regrets. Both the U.S. and South Korea rejected the expression of regrets, hinting that it was no more than a Communist maneuver to distract attention.

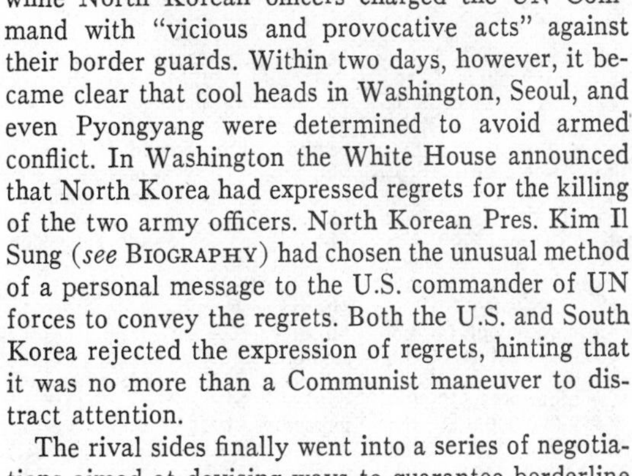

The rival sides finally went into a series of negotiations aimed at devising ways to guarantee borderline peace in the future. New proposals on such matters as the number of security guards and the extent of the Joint Security Area were discussed and agreed upon. With that the threat of another Korean war seemed to recede. But the possible motivations for the border killings remained the subject of continuing speculation and a source of worry. The prevailing view among U.S. officials seemed to be that Kim, beset by economic crisis and political isolation, was trying to gain attention. The South Koreans promoted the view that the assault indicated a growing fear in the North that it soon would be no match militarily or economically for South Korea.

Republic of Korea (South Korea). Area: 38,130 sq mi (98,758 sq km). Pop. (1975 prelim.): 34,708,500. Cap. and largest city: Seoul (pop., 1975 prelim., 6,889,500). Language: Korean. Religion: Buddhist; Confucian; Tonghak (Chondokyo). President in 1976, Gen. Park Chung Hee; prime minister, Choi Kyu Hah.

Internally 1976 was a relatively easy year for President Park. He had put into motion in December 1975 another round of ministerial "musical chairs." Kim Chong Pil had been replaced as prime minister by Choi Kyu Hah while Park Thong Chin was named foreign minister. The reshuffle was seen as a move to toughen the South's position in anticipated wranglings with the North.

Apparently for the same reason, there was no letup in Park's strict rule. Dissidents detained by the powerful police establishment continued to receive severe treatment. The most celebrated of them, one-time presidential candidate Kim Dae Jung and former president Yun Po Sun, were both sentenced to eight years in prison in August 1976, and 16 others received jail terms ranging from two to eight years, but the sentences were later reduced. All had been arrested for violating Park's 15-month-old Emergency Decree No. 9, which banned all political dissension in the country. Park's view, expressed to a Swedish interviewer in January, was that liberal democracy was unrealistic in South Korea where the first concern was "maximum national survival."

South Korea's economic planners continued to pin much of their hopes on striking oil in the East China Sea. These hopes were brightened by reports in January that an anticline believed to contain a large oil pool was discovered in the section of the sea known as Block 7. The total deposits in the area were estimated at between 5,000,000,000 and 10,000,000,000 metric tons. A joint agreement had been signed in 1974 between South Korea and Japan to exploit the oil resources. Following the discovery of the anticline in January, Japan said it would proceed with plans to ratify the agreement on oil exploration and develop-

Journalism: *see* Publishing
Judaism: *see* Israel; Religion
Judo: *see* Combat Sports
Karate: *see* Combat Sports
Kashmir: *see* India; Pakistan
Kendo: *see* Combat Sports
Khmer Republic: *see* Cambodia

KOREA: Republic

Education. (1975–76) Primary, pupils 5,503,737, teachers 109,530; secondary, pupils 3,370,311, teachers 87,142; vocational, students 507,430; teachers 16,536; higher, students 313,608, teaching staff 14,730.

Finance. Monetary unit: won, with (Sept. 20, 1976) an official rate of 485 won to U.S. $1 (free rate of 848 won = £1 sterling). Gold, SDR's, and foreign exchange (June 1976) U.S. $2,044,000,000. Budget (1975 est.): revenue 1,306,000,000,000 won; expenditure 1,430,000,000,000 won. Gross national product (1975) 9,051,800,000,000 won. Money supply (June 1976) 1,258,200,000,000 won. Cost of living (1970 = 100; May 1976) 232.

Foreign Trade. (1975) Imports 3,520,800,000,000 won; exports 2,459,200,000,000 won. Import sources: Japan 33%; U.S. 26%; Saudi Arabia 8%; Kuwait 8%. Export destinations: U.S. 30%; Japan 25%; West Germany 6%. Main exports: clothing 23%; textile yarns and fabrics 13%; electrical machinery and equipment 9%; fish 7%; iron and steel 5%. Tourism (1974): visitors 518,000; gross receipts U.S. $159 million.

Transport and Communications. Roads (1974) 44,177 km (including 1,013 km expressways). Motor vehicles in use (1974): passenger 76,500; commercial (including buses) 96,900. Railways: (1973) 5,541 km; traffic (1975) 12,703,000,000 passenger-km, freight 9,107,000,000 net ton-km. Air traffic (1974): 2,753,000,000 passenger-km; freight 204.7 million net ton-km. Shipping (1975): merchant vessels 100 gross tons and over 828; gross tonnage 1,623,532. Telephones (Dec. 1974) 1,158,000. Radio receivers (Dec. 1972) 4,115,000. Television receivers (Dec. 1973) 1,182,000.

Agriculture. Production (in 000; metric tons; 1975): rice 6,485; wheat 150; barley 2,225; potatoes c. 469; sweet potatoes (1974) c. 1,670; soybeans c. 320; cabbages (1974) c. 850; watermelons (1974) c. 145; tomatoes c. 55; onions (1974) c. 72; apples (1974) c. 300; tobacco 105; fish catch (1974) 2,000. Livestock (in 000; Dec. 1974): cattle c. 1,260; pigs c. 1,452; goats 194; chickens 23,071.

Industry. Production (in 000; metric tons; 1975): coal 17,584; iron ore (60% metal content) 524; steel 2,009; cement 10,129; tungsten concentrates (oxide content; 1974) 3.2; zinc (1974) 11; gold (troy oz; 1974) 23; silver (troy oz; 1974) 1,307; sulfuric acid 462; petroleum products (1974) 14,617; electricity (excluding most industrial production; kw-hr) 19,837,000.

KOREA: Democratic People's Republic

Education. (1973–74 est.) Primary, pupils c. 1.5 million; secondary and vocational, pupils c. 1.2 million; primary, secondary, and vocational, teachers c. 100,000; higher, students c. 300,000.

Finance and Trade. Monetary unit: won, with (Sept. 20, 1976) a nominal exchange rate of 1.03 won to U.S. $1 (1.77 won = £1 sterling). Budget (1975 est.) balanced at 11,517,000,000 won. Foreign trade (approximate; 1974): imports c. 1.2 billion won (c. 50% from China, 20% from U.S.S.R., 20% from Japan); exports c. 1.1 billion won (c. 65% to China, 18% to U.S.S.R., 10% to Japan). Main exports (1965): metals 50%; minerals 12%; farm produce 11%.

Agriculture. Production (in 000; metric tons; 1975): rice c. 3,700; corn c. 2,058; barley c. 366; millet c. 410; potatoes c. 1,110; sweet potatoes (1974) c. 320; soybeans c. 263; apples c. 130; tobacco c. 40; fish catch (1974) c. 800. Livestock (in 000; Dec. 1974): cattle c. 767; pigs c. 1,491; sheep c. 205; chickens c. 22,000.

Industry. Production (in 000; metric tons; 1974): coal c. 33,900; iron ore (metal content) c. 3,760; pig iron c. 3,000; steel c. 2,900; lead c. 100; zinc c. 132; magnesite c. 1,700; silver (troy oz) c. 700; cement (1973) c. 5,800; tungsten concentrates (oxide content) c. 2.7; electricity (kw-hr; 1965) 13,300,000.

ment. Development experts conceded that, even if no setbacks occurred, it would be some time before oil became a significant factor in the economy. In the short term they were buoyed by growing trade and investment links with Arab countries, where Korean labour became a favoured import.

South Korea's gross national product growth rate reached 17.4% during the first half of the year, making economists predict a 14% rate in real terms for the whole year. The unexpected spurt (originally the government had envisaged a growth rate of 7 to 8%, later revised to 12%) was forcing an upward revision of targets in price control and money supply.

A major scandal erupted in Washington, D.C., in the fall involving charges that officials of the Korean Central Intelligence Agency (KCIA) and other South Koreans had attempted to influence U.S. policy toward Korea by bribing congressmen. The KCIA denied the allegations. (*See* UNITED STATES.)

Democratic People's Republic of Korea (North Korea). Area: 46,800 sq mi (121,200 sq km). Pop. (1975 est.): 15,852,000. Cap.: Pyongyang (metro. pop., 1975 est., 1,157,000). Language: Korean. Religion: Buddhist; Confucian; Tonghak (Chondokyo). General secretary of the Central Committee of the Workers' (Communist) Party of Korea, president, and chairman of the Council of Ministers (premier) in 1976, Marshal Kim Il Sung.

Kim Il Sung's customary exhortations for peace and unity in the Korean Peninsula carried little conviction during the year because of the violent incident in Panmunjom on the one hand and persistent reports of a power struggle in Pyongyang on the other. In the wake of reports that Kim's cancerous tumour of the neck was causing concern, his brother Kim Yong Ju and son Kim Chong Il were mentioned as possible contenders for power. By October there were reports that Yong Ju also was seriously ill. Tokyo's *Mainichi* newspaper reported in October that former vice-president Nam Il had suddenly died and that Park Sung Chol had been appointed prime minister while the army chief of staff, Gen. Oh Jin Wu, had been promoted to defense minister. These moves were interpreted as reflecting the intensity of the internal power struggle. Significantly, Pyongyang's official media failed to list the leaders attending the mass meeting on October 10 to mark the 31st anniversary of the founding of the party.

It was a bad year for North Korea's economy. Its confidence boosted by the profitable market enjoyed by its coal, tungsten, and iron ore, Pyongyang had ordered, from 1970 onward, large quantities of industrial machinery on credit. The collapse of the raw materials market following the oil crisis plunged the country into indebtedness; concerned Japanese sources estimated this now to be in the region of $10 billion, $1.4 billion of which was owed to Japan alone. Early in 1976 North Korea defaulted on interest payments on its debt and asked its Western and Japanese creditors for a moratorium. Not only Japan and West Germany but even the Soviet Union were refusing to enter into fresh deals with Pyongyang—a stance that could cripple essential purchases for North Korea's new economic plan scheduled to start in 1977 and generally slow down its economic growth rate. In October there were reports, again out of Tokyo, that Kim Il Sung was planning to visit the Soviet Union to plead for economic assistance. Also in October, North Korean diplomats in Denmark, Norway, Sweden, and Finland were found to be smuggling cigarettes and drugs and were expelled from the countries concerned, except that those from Sweden departed of their own accord. (T. J. S. GEORGE)

[975.C]

Kuwait

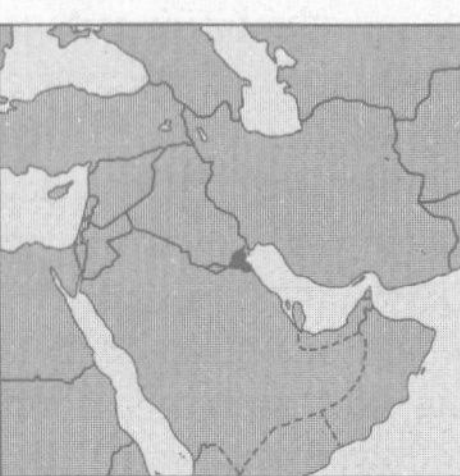

An independent constitutional monarchy (emirate), Kuwait is on the northwestern coast of the Persian Gulf between Iraq and Saudi Arabia. Area: 6,532 sq mi (16,918 sq km). Pop. (1975 census): 994,800. Cap.: Kuwait (pop., 1975 census, 78,000). Largest city: Hawalli (pop., 1975 prelim., 130,300). Language: Arabic. Religion (1975): Muslim 94.9%; Christian 4.5%. Emir in 1976, Sheikh Sabah as-Salim as-Sabah; prime minister, Crown Prince Sheikh Jabir al-Ahmad al-Jabir as-Sabah.

Kuwait's 13-year-old system of parliamentary

democracy was suspended in 1976. The government resigned on August 29, charging the National Assembly with having made its task impossible by irresponsibly obstructing vital legislation. At the same time the ruler dissolved the assembly and suspended certain key articles in the constitution requiring fresh elections. The ruler then asked the prime minister to form the new government. A committee of experts was appointed to revise the constitution and report in six months, and the function of parliamentary committees was taken over by new ministerial committees. New curbs were imposed on Kuwait's relatively free press, and several newspapers were suspended for fomenting disorder. The country was affected internally by repercussions of the Lebanese civil war, especially among the non-Kuwaiti half of the population, which included an estimated 270,000 Palestinians, and there were bombing and sabotage incidents. The Kuwait government maintained its neutral stance in inter-Arab affairs and joined with Saudi Arabia in trying to mediate between Egypt and Syria.

Kuwait's oil production had fallen by 18% in 1975, and both revenues and exports had declined. However, the 1976–77 budget forecast a 25% increase in revenues to $7,156,000,000. Estimated expenditure was also increased by 25%, but the budget forecast a comfortable surplus. During the year Kuwait committed itself to a variety of loans to Arab and third world countries through the Kuwait Fund for Arab Economic Development and other agencies. In January the finance minister announced that Kuwait had ordered an undisclosed amount of Soviet weapons; it also bought 150 British Chieftain tanks and some French arms. (PETER MANSFIELD)

[978.B.4.b]

Laos

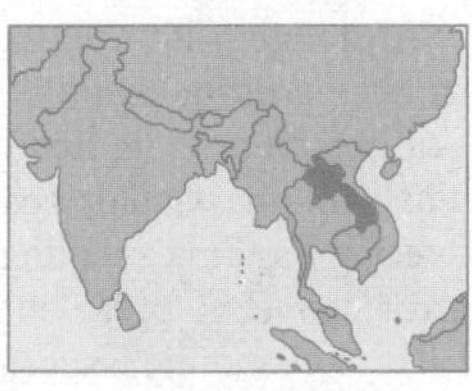

Nominally a constitutional monarchy until Dec. 3, 1975, when the People's Democratic Republic of Laos was proclaimed, Laos is a landlocked country of Southeast Asia, bounded by China, Vietnam, Cambodia, Thailand, and Burma. Area: 91,400 sq mi (236,800 sq km). Pop. (1976 est.): 3,381,000. Cap. and largest city: Vientiane (pop., 1973, 176,600). Language: Lao (official); French and English. Religion: Buddhist; tribal. President in 1976, Prince Souphanouvong; premier, Kaysone Phomvihan.

The new Communist government of Laos appeared to be consolidating its position during 1976, although there were reports of resistance groups fighting government forces, of refugees constantly escaping into neighbouring Thailand, and of riots and repression. Premier Kaysone Phomvihan stayed in the limelight with official visits to the Soviet Union and China, as well as to Vietnam and Cambodia.

That unrest marked the early stages of the Communist consolidation was clear from such news as trickled out of the country. In a June speech to the Supreme People's Assembly, Kaysone Phomvihan noted the suppression of "reactionary forces" that had organized subversive activities against the new regime during its first three months. The activities, he admitted, had led to insecurity and serious economic difficulties in several regions of the country.

The situation was apparently brought under control by strong-arm measures against suspected dissenters and by the appointment of a large network of neighbourhood and village supervisors. Those supervisors who failed to keep their areas quiet were arrested. By the end of March the antigovernment Lao People's Front resistance movement conceded that it was collapsing for lack of outside assistance and agreement on a leader around whom scattered groups could rally. With that the problem of resistance seemed solved, although the government kept up the pressure. The official newspaper *Sieng Prasason* reported in October that the Laotian militia was to undergo a major overhaul to make it a force "of the people and for the people." Declaring that reactionary forces existed in the militia, the paper called for a thorough purge in accordance with the constitution.

With the first signs that its opponents were being effectively neutralized the government turned its attention to establishing working relations with neighbouring countries, especially Thailand, whose hostility could block the Mekong River and choke the economy. For several months the river frontier remained tense, with shooting incidents and refugee crossings punctuating on-and-off negotiations. In August Thailand's foreign minister, Pichai Rattakul, visited Vientiane and Hanoi, and the Mekong became a "river of peace" across which trade began to move. But the military takeover of Thailand in October was expected to cause strained relations again. In a reverse flow of refugees, several hundred students and leftists from Thailand escaped into Laos following the coup.

Premier Kaysone Phomvihan told the Assembly in June that Laos would welcome good relations with all nations, whatever their political system. He specifically mentioned the U.S. but added that Washington should stop its "imperialist maneuvers against the new Laotian regime." At the same time the official news media vigorously denied reports that foreign (Chinese, Soviet, Vietnamese, or Cuban) troops were on Laotian soil or that radar systems had been installed by Chinese and Soviet allies.

LAOS

Education. (1972–73) Primary, pupils 273,357, teachers 7,320; secondary, pupils 14,633, teachers 613; vocational, pupils 1,946, teachers 186; teacher training, students 4,031, teachers 227; higher (1973–74), students 875, teaching staff 136.

Finance. Monetary unit: new kip (which replaced the old kip in June 1976 at 1 new kip = 20 old kip), with (Sept. 20, 1976) an official exchange rate of 60 new kip to U.S. $1 (free rate of 103.38 new kip = £1 sterling). Budget (1973–74 rev. est.): revenue (excluding foreign aid) 13,485,000,000 old kip; expenditure 28,437,000,000 old kip (including defense expenditure of 14,142,000,000 old kip).

Foreign Trade. (1973) Imports 34,298,000,000 old kip; exports 3,045,000,000 old kip. Import sources: Thailand 47%; Japan 13%; France 10%; U.S. 7%; Switzerland 5%; Singapore 5%. Export destinations: Thailand 65%; Malaysia 29%. Main exports: timber 62%; tin 29%.

Transport. Roads (1973) 7,291 km. Motor vehicles in use (1974): passenger 14,100; commercial (including buses) 2,500. Air traffic (1974): 22 million passenger-km; freight 500,000 net ton-km. Inland waterways (Mekong River) 715 km. Telephones (Dec. 1973) 5,000. Radio licenses (Dec. 1973) 102,000.

Agriculture. Production (in 000; metric tons; 1974): rice 905; corn *c.* 30; onions *c.* 29; melons *c.* 20; oranges *c.* 17; pineapples *c.* 27; coffee *c.* 2; tobacco *c.* 4; cotton, lint *c.* 3. Livestock (in 000; 1974): cattle *c.* 464; buffalo *c.* 1,040; pigs *c.* 1,292; chickens *c.* 14,000.

Industry. Production (1974): tin concentrates (metal content) 612 metric tons; electricity (excluding most industrial production) *c.* 255 million kw-hr.

Labour Unions: *see* Industrial Relations
Lacrosse: *see* Field Hockey and Lacrosse

As part of the Communist consolidation process, the national economy was completely revamped during the year. In June the government announced that the Laotian kip was being replaced by a new currency following a decision of the Supreme Assembly. The new kip or "kip pot poy" (sometimes called Sam Neua kip in relation to the jungle hideout that had for long been the base of the Pathet Lao) was pegged at one to 20 old kip, or 60 to U.S. $1. A week before the announcement the rate of the old kip had slipped to 14,000 to $1 on the black market. Cadres and workers were allowed to exchange up to 100,000 old kip, each family a maximum of 200,000, traders 500,000, and certain private companies one million. The rest of the wealth was required to be deposited in the national bank and could be withdrawn at some future date.

In May Laos signed a series of agreements with the Soviet Union. The U.S.S.R. declared that it would give Vientiane "assistance in reviving and developing its national economy." (T. J. S. GEORGE)

[976.B.4.e]

Latin-American Affairs

On March 27, 1976, the foreign ministers of Venezuela, Colombia, Costa Rica, and Peru agreed with Gen. Omar Torrijos of Panama to cancel the congress planned for June 1976 to celebrate the 150th anniversary of the Bolivarian congress, organized by Simón Bolívar in 1826. The only president who had publicly refused to come was Juan María Bordaberry of Uruguay, who stated that he would not attend because Fidel Castro of Cuba had also been invited. This view was shared by a number of other countries, showing that the Cuban involvement in Angola had already had an effect on Latin America. When the congress was first proposed early in 1974, it represented a wave of Latin-American nationalism manifested in a determination to confront the U.S. on trade, political, and defense issues. The idea of holding the conference, however, was progressively undermined as a result of political changes in many countries of the region and Cuba's involvement on the African continent.

Cuba's Fidel Castro (left) talks with Panamanian strong man Omar Torrijos in January.

WIDE WORLD

On October 6 El Salvador and Honduras signed an agreement providing for a mediated settlement of the conflicts between the two countries. The signing took place in the headquarters of the Organization of American States (OAS), which had assisted in the negotiations.

U.S. Policy. Henry Kissinger, the U.S. secretary of state, undertook a tour of six Latin-American countries during Feb. 16–24, 1976. He visited Venezuela, Peru, Brazil, Colombia, Costa Rica, and Guatemala. The journey yielded no dramatic proposals for new U.S. policy initiatives, but it did confirm the trend toward more realism in the relations between the U.S. and Latin America. The tour had been pending since the Tlatelolco, Mexico, meeting in February 1974, at which a declaration providing for a "new dialogue" had been adopted, but it had been postponed, largely as a result of conflicts within the OAS.

During his visit to Venezuela Kissinger delivered a major speech outlining six ways in which U.S. policy toward Latin America would be implemented: (1) by supporting the more industrialized nations in Latin America in their efforts to participate in the world economy; (2) by continuing foreign aid to the poorer countries in the region; (3) by supporting subregional organizations such as the Andean Group, the Central American Common Market, and the Caribbean Community and Common Market; (4) by negotiating all disputes on a basis of equality and dignity; (5) by accepting commitment to the mutual security of the hemisphere; and (6) by modernizing the OAS. The low-key expectations that characterized the mood in Latin America were underscored by the fact that no matter what good intentions Kissinger had, his ability to carry them through was limited by the U.S. Congress' growing role in foreign policy making.

Although Kissinger said that his trip was not meant to be a crusade against Cuba's role in Angola, the issue came up sporadically, particularly in Costa Rica. The Panama Canal treaty was barely mentioned, reflecting Panama's willingness to let the issue lie quietly until the U.S. presidential election was over. In regard to economic issues, Kissinger stated that the U.S. would cooperate with the new Latin-American Economic System (SELA), established in October 1975, and suggested that useful negotiations could take place between the U.S. and SELA on defining a "code of conduct" for the behaviour of transnational concerns.

SELA and the OAS. The first high-level meeting of SELA was held in January 1976 and was related mainly to organizational matters, but the members were also able to work out a joint Latin-American position to be presented at the May 1976 meeting in Nairobi, Kenya, of the UN Conference on Trade and Development. Although SELA was bound to find plenty of areas of conflict with the U.S., it continued to make clear that it did not want to initiate an adversary relationship. The main administrative and technical body of the organization was the secretariat, headed by Jaime Moncayo García, former finance minister of Ecuador. All his actions had to be reviewed and approved by the Latin-American Council, SELA's highest authority, in which each member country had one vote and most decisions were adopted on a two-thirds majority basis. The council established the general policies, approved the working program and the budget, established members' quotas, and determined the common positions for international meetings.

The sixth annual assembly of the OAS was held in

PARTNERS OF THE AMERICAS

Fifteen years after Pres. John F. Kennedy, amid considerable fanfare, launched the Alliance for Progress, that program of U.S. assistance to Latin America appeared to have sunk with scarcely a trace. But if the governmental component of the Alliance had fallen victim to changing economic conditions and political attitudes, the private-citizen component was still quietly but effectively going about its business. Partners of the Americas, founded in 1964, was the largest private, nonprofit organization linking the peoples of the Western Hemisphere in projects to promote economic, social, and human development.

Under the Partners program, each of the 43 participating U.S. states was paired with one of 20 Latin-American or Caribbean countries or (in the case of the larger nations) with a section of a country. Thus Delaware was the partner of Panama, Kansas the partner of Paraguay, Illinois the partner of the state of São Paulo in Brazil. In each U.S. Partner state, a committee of volunteer professionals worked with its counterpart in Latin America to develop projects and exchanges. In the U.S. these activities were coordinated by the National Association of the Partners of the Alliance, Inc.

Over the 12 years of its existence, Partners had generated more than $56 million in projects in such diverse fields as health, education, culture, agriculture, sports, and rehabilitation. Every project was operated as a two-way street. Thus, in the area of sports, Latin-American soccer coaches were sharing their skills with youth and coaches in the U.S., while U.S. basketball coaches traveled to Latin America to conduct clinics.

Health programs made up more than a third of all Partner activities. For nine years, the Wisconsin-Nicaragua Partners had maintained a program of continuing health care on the east coast of Nicaragua. The Florida-Northern Colombia and Connecticut-Paraíba, Brazil, Partners were exchanging techniques in advanced medical training. Partners was one of the few international programs addressing the hemisphere's needs in rehabilitation, special education, and mental health. Through exchanges with Panama's Special Education Institute, the Delaware Partners developed model programs on nursing care for the mentally retarded.

Another important component of the program was agriculture. In addition to working at the local level, Partners agriculture programs linked governments and research institutions interested in increasing food production and combating malnutrition. The University System of Georgia, for example, was developing such a project with the Federal and Rural University in its partner state of Pernambuco, Brazil. The national association organized several special projects, including an agriculture workshop in Honduras.

Financial support for the Partners of the Americas came from tax-deductible contributions, corporate, foundation, and government grants, membership dues, and donated gifts-in-kind, including technical services, equipment, and scholarships.

Santiago, Chile, on June 4–18, 1976, and was attended by 23 American foreign ministers. The matters discussed were related to reform of the organization; cooperation for the development of the region; the role of multinational concerns; and the U.S. Trade Reform Act of 1974. For Kissinger's personal standing in Latin America, the conference was something of a triumph. He spoke against the abuse of human rights but did not antagonize Chile; he assured Ecuador and Venezuela, affected by the 1974 Trade Reform Act, that he had nothing to do with it; and produced a joint document of agreement with Panama to continue negotiations on the canal.

Namucar, the Caribbean shipping company established in 1975, began operations in March 1976 with a 5,200-ton chartered cargo vessel, the "City of Bochum." Namucar was jointly owned by Costa Rica, Cuba, Jamaica, Mexico, Nicaragua, and Venezuela. Its aim was to open new markets to regional importers and exporters by providing a low-cost and full Caribbean shipping service.

LAFTA, the Andean Group, and CACM. Collective negotiations under the Latin American Free Trade Association (LAFTA) continued during 1976, but no meetings were held to discuss changes in the organization and the tariff-cutting mechanism. In September 1976 the central banks of the LAFTA countries began to issue Latin-American negotiable bills, known as *aceptaciones Bancarias Latinoamericanas* (Ablas), in U.S. financial markets. The bills were expected to produce a total of $600 million in new short-term export finance.

Progress in the Andean Group was delayed in 1976 as a result of discrepancies among the member countries in relation to the regulations affecting foreign investment in the subregion. The Commission of the Cartagena Agreement issued an additional protocol on April 10, 1976, together with a number of other decisions, aimed at postponing deadlines for the industrial, tariff reduction, and external tariff programs and changing some of the negotiation procedures. However, when the representatives of the six member countries met in Lima, Peru, early in August, to ratify the protocol amending the agreement, the Chilean representative refused to sign the document, stating that this would only be done after the group had modified Decision 24, governing foreign investment. Representatives of Bolivia, Colombia, Ecuador, Peru, and Venezuela met in Sochagota, Colombia, in mid-August, to discuss the Chilean position regarding Decision 24 and agreed to propose a number of changes, such as that the limit on profit remittances be raised from 14 to 20% and the limit on the reinvestment of profits from 5 to 7%. But the mid-September meeting of the Commission of the Cartagena Agreement failed to agree on the proposed changes, and at the beginning of October a protocol was signed outlining the terms on which Chile would withdraw from the Andean Pact at the end of that month unless an arrangement providing for partial membership for Chile in the pact could be found. On October 6 Chile dropped out.

The proposed changes reflected the extension of the concept that unequal conditions should compensate for unequal development in the four most developed countries, Chile, Colombia, Peru, and Venezuela. The Andean Pact had always allowed preferential treatment for Bolivia and Ecuador, as the two least-developed members of the group, but the proposed idea was that the other four countries would be allowed to vary, within specified limits, the conditions under which they complied with any particular program. Before leaving office, on March 31, 1976, the members of the governing council of the Andean Group released two new industrial programs dealing with the electronics and steel industries, along with an extension of the light manufacturing program to include Venezuela.

The Central American Common Market (CACM) continued its progress toward integration. On March 23, 1976, a high-level committee completed a final draft treaty for the restructuring of the CACM within a new integrated organization to be known as the Central American Social and Economic Community (CASEC). Like an earlier version, the final draft proposed eliminating all obstacles to free movement of people, goods, and capital as well as coordinating policies in such fields as agriculture, taxation, energy, and finance. At the same time, and unlike other schemes in Latin America, it encouraged foreign investment in the five Central American republics.

Inter-American Development Bank. The IDB annual survey on economic and social progress in Latin America showed that the combined gross domestic product of the Latin-American and Caribbean countries increased by only 3% in 1975, as compared with 7.2% in 1974. The report noted that the external position of Latin America during the first half of the 1970s reflected, on the one hand, the favourable developments in 1972 and 1973 and, in contrast, the adverse effects of the soaring oil prices in 1974 and the weakening of prices for primary commodity exports during 1975. For the region as a whole, the merchandise account registered a rapidly growing surplus from $256 million in 1972 to $4,230,000,000 in 1974, but the combined current account deficit, which was reduced from $4,321,000,000 in 1972 to $3,044,000,000 in 1973, soared to $6,302,000,000 in 1974. Capital movements more than compensated for this deficit, and the overall balance was a surplus of $3,383,000,000 in 1972 and one of $4,157,000,000 in 1974.

The Board of Governors of the IDB unanimously elected Antonio Ortíz Ména of Mexico as president of the bank for a second five-year term beginning on March 1, 1976. The 17th annual meeting of the board was held in Cancún, Mexico, May 17–19, 1976. The IDB's president reported that the bank had granted 70 loans totaling $1,375,000,000 to Latin-American countries in 1975. This amount represented a $200 million increase over the amount approved in 1974 and was distributed as follows: agriculture, 24%; electric power, 22%; transport and communications, 22%; industry and mining, 13%; sanitation, 8%; education, 5%; urban development, 3%; and preinvestment, export financing, and tourism, 3%.

In June 1976 the IDB member countries resolved to increase the authorized resources of the institution by about $7 billion and approved an amendment to the agreement establishing the bank so as to facilitate the admission of 13 nonregional countries, 9 of which (Belgium, Denmark, West Germany, Israel, Japan, Spain, Switzerland, the U.K., and Yugoslavia) joined on July 9. (JAIME R. DUHART)

See also articles on the various political units.

[971.D.8; 974]

ENCYCLOPÆDIA BRITANNICA FILMS. *Venezuela: Oil Builds a Nation* (1972); *Central America: Finding New Ways* (2nd ed., 1974); *Costa Rica: My Country* (2nd ed., 1974).

Latin-American Literature: *see* Literature

Latter-day Saints: *see* Religion

Law

Court Decisions. Two death penalty decisions handed down by the U.S. Supreme Court were generally considered the most important of the year by the world's legal scholars, but other significant decisions from West Germany, India, Rhodesia, and the U.S. on freedom of speech also occupied their close attention. In addition, notable cases were decided in Argentina and West Germany on the question of the rights of Communist Party members, and two cases from Britain had important consequences for international traders.

DEATH PENALTY. In 1976 the Supreme Court of the United States set new standards to determine when and if the death penalty could be imposed on individuals convicted of certain crimes. In the opinion of some scholars, these decisions seemed to overturn the celebrated *Furman* case, in which the Supreme Court in 1972 apparently had ruled that the death penalty always violated the U.S. Constitution, either because of its "cruel and unusual" penal nature or because its imposition is arbitrary and capricious.

In *Gregg* v. *Georgia,* the Supreme Court upheld by a 7–2 majority the constitutionality of a death penalty statute enacted by the state of Georgia. In the decision, announced by Justice Potter Stewart, the majority of the court held that (1) the death penalty is not necessarily a cruel and unusual punishment proscribed by the Eighth Amendment to the Constitution; and (2) it is not necessarily imposed in an arbitrary and capricious manner forbidden by the Fourteenth Amendment to the Constitution where the decision-making process involved in its imposition is carefully controlled by clear and objective standards aimed at evenhanded treatment. Each statute under which a death penalty is imposed and the procedures employed in its imposition, however, must be separately reviewed to determine whether they meet constitutional standards.

Furman and other cases had made it clear that the constitutional prohibition against cruel and unusual punishment "must draw its meaning from the evolving standards of decency that mark the progress of a maturing society," so that a penalty appropriate in the 19th century might be found to be cruel and unusual in the 20th. Even if a penalty meets the standards of decency of present society, it must accord with the "dignity of man." This means that the punishment must not involve the unnecessary and wanton infliction of pain and must not be grossly out of proportion to the severity of the crime.

While all the judges seemed to agree as to these standards under the Eighth Amendment, they disagreed sharply as to their application. In the *Furman* case, Justices William J. Brennan, Jr., and Thurgood Marshall stated that the death penalty always violates the Eighth Amendment because it subjects the individual to a fate forbidden by the principle of civilized treatment and is morally unacceptable to most well-informed Americans. In *Gregg* v. *Georgia,* Justice Brennan continued to maintain this position, but Justice Marshall seemed to abandon it in part, pointing out that, "[S]ince the decision in *Furman,* the legislatures of 35 states have enacted new statutes authorizing the imposition of the death sentence for certain crimes, and Congress has enacted a law providing the death penalty for air piracy resulting in

UPI COMPIX

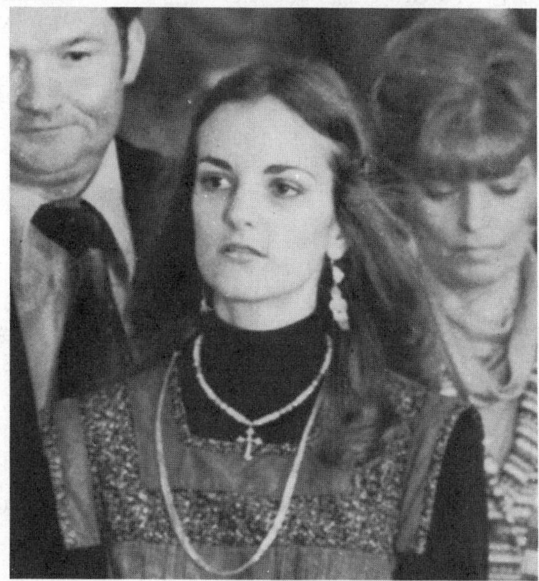

Newspaper heiress Patricia Hearst failed to convince a jury that she had not willingly taken part in a San Francisco bank robbery after being kidnapped by the Symbionese Liberation Army in 1974.

death. I would be less than candid if I did not acknowledge that these developments have a significant bearing on a realistic assessment of the moral acceptability of the death penalty to the American people." Nevertheless, these death penalty statutes are still unconstitutional under the Eighth Amendment, according to Justice Marshall, because they are excessive forms of punishment.

In the past Chief Justice Warren E. Burger and Justices Byron R. White, Harry A. Blackmun, and William H. Rehnquist had indicated for a variety of reasons that statutes imposing death penalties were constitutional, and they maintained those positions in the case at hand. The balance of power thus consisted of Justices Stewart, Lewis F. Powell, Jr., and the newly appointed John Paul Stevens (*see* BIOGRAPHY). They held, in *Gregg* v. *Georgia,* that the American people had accepted the morality of the death penalty, and that it is not an excessive penalty for a limited range of extremely serious crimes in that it serves the social purposes of retribution and deterrence of capital crimes by prospective offenders. With regard to retribution, they said, "In part, capital punishment is an expression of society's moral outrage at particularly offensive conduct. This function may be unappealing to many, but it is essential in an ordered society that asks its citizens to rely on legal processes rather than self-help to vindicate their wrongs."

Regarding the contention that a death penalty statute is unconstitutional under the Fourteenth Amendment because the procedures used to employ it result in arbitrarily and capriciously imposing the penalty on some but not others, the majority found that the statute under consideration had been carefully drafted to avoid such uneven treatment. The Georgia statute provides for two trials, one to determine the guilt of the accused and a second to determine his or her sentence. At the sentencing stage the jury is told that it cannot consider imposing the death sentence unless it first finds, beyond a reasonable doubt, some carefully defined "aggravating circumstance." In addition, the jury's attention is focused on the characteristics of the person who committed the crime, including any record of prior convictions for capital offenses, and any mitigating circumstances, such as youth or cooperation with the police. As a result, while some jury discretion exists, the procedure is designed to control the exercise of that discretion by clear and objective standards. Moreover, the Supreme Court of Georgia is required to review each case and to compare each death sentence with sentences imposed on similarly situated defendants.

Unlike Georgia, North Carolina, Louisiana, and a number of other states had responded to *Furman* by replacing discretionary sentencing in capital cases with mandatory death penalties. These statutes were designed to overcome the charge that the death penalty is imposed wantonly and freakishly where discretion exists. In *Woodson* v. *North Carolina,* the court held that such statutes violate the Eighth Amendment. In this case, Justices Stewart, Powell, and Stevens joined with Brennan and Marshall.

Possibly stimulated by the consideration of the death penalty cases in the U.S., the Canadian government reviewed its position on the question. After a long and somewhat acrimonious debate in which many of the concerns reflected by the U.S. justices were voiced by members of Parliament, Canada enacted legislation outlawing the death penalty.

FREEDOM OF SPEECH. In India a high court ruled that the detention of a newspaper editor, Kuldip Nayar, under the Internal Security Laws was unlawful. The court held that it had the right to review detention cases, even under the "emergency situation" in India, and pointed out that personal liberty is a common law right which cannot be taken from a person arbitrarily. This right cannot be abridged by an arbitrary arrest or without a showing by the authorities that a genuine need to detain a person can be supported by factual grounds.

The Appellate Division of the High Court of Rhodesia held that an individual's right to privacy may be greater than the right of a newspaper to publish a true story of local interest about that individual. The case involved two divorced people whose

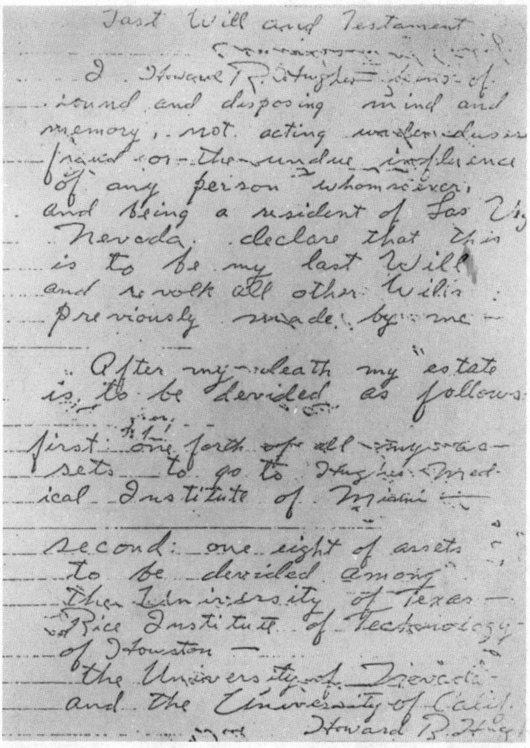

Last Will and Testament

I Howard R. Hughes being of sound and disposing mind and memory, not acting under duress fraud or the undue influence of any person whomsoever, and being a resident of Las Vegas Nevada. declare that this is to be my last Will and revolk all other Wills previously made by me —

After my death my estate is to be devided as follows:

first: one forth of all my assets to go to Hughes Medical Institute of Miami —

second: one eight of assets to be devided among the University of Texas — Rice Institute of Technology of Houston — the University of Nevada — and the University of Calif.

Howard R. Hughes

WIDE WORLD

Billionaire Howard Hughes apparently left no will. This is one of the many forgeries that turned up.

children were in the custody of their ex-spouses. The two individuals married, moved to Rhodesia, and then abducted their children and brought them to Rhodesia. The story created local interest, and a newspaper planned to print an accurate account of it. It was restrained from doing so by a trial court, and this decision was affirmed on appeal. U.S. legal scholars found the case interesting and important because the Rhodesian appellate court announced that it was basing its decision on principles found in the U.S. law, specifically those articulated in the American Restatement of Tort Law, sec. 867.

On the other hand, the public's "right to know" was held to be greater than an individual's right of privacy by the Federal Administrative Court of West Germany in a limited-fact situation in which a person tried in vain to prevent his name from being listed in a phone directory. The court sustained the listing, pointing out that names are normally excluded only in cases of security risks and where there have been repeated nuisance calls.

In the U.S. a consumer group successfully attacked the constitutionality of a Virginia statute that made it illegal for pharmacists to advertise the prices of prescription drugs. The U.S. Supreme Court found the law to be a restriction on free speech in violation of the First and Fourteenth Amendments to the Constitution. (*See* INDUSTRIAL REVIEW: *Advertising*.)

POLITICAL RIGHTS. In Argentina the National Criminal Court, the highest criminal appeals court, held that the emergency decree of 1974 was unconstitutional and invalid with respect to granting the government the power to make arrests on political grounds. The case involved the arrest and detention of a Communist professor.

In West Germany the Federal Supreme Court held that government employees owe special duties of good faith toward the state constitution, especially to art. 33 which mandates a "free democratic basic order." As a result, the court held it was proper to reject an application of a Communist to join the judiciary service. Viewed narrowly, the case only involved a lawyer who had belonged to a "red cell" at a university, but the court took the occasion to consider generally the duty of public employees to support the constitution.

The electric chair in Florida's Raiford Prison, unused since 1964. The U.S. Supreme Court decided that the death penalty did not violate the Eighth Amendment ban on cruel and unusual punishment.

UPI COMPIX

RACE RELATIONS. The U.S. Supreme Court held that the Civil Rights Act prohibits private schools from excluding children solely because of their race. In so doing, the court confronted two issues on which scholarly opinion had been divided. First, the court held that the Civil Rights Act was not limited to public situations but was meant to prohibit racial discrimination in the making and enforcing of virtually all private contracts as well. Second, the court determined that it was within the power of Congress to enact such legislation. The court did not resolve the question of whether a religious school might discriminate on the basis of race where such discrimination is mandated by the tenets of its religion.

COMMERCIAL LAW. Great Britain's standing as the leading arbitrator of commercial disputes had been attained because international traders routinely inserted in their contracts "choice of law" and "choice of forum" terms directing that English courts try all disputes arising under the contract pursuant to English procedural and substantive law. This preeminence had been declining in recent years because some international merchants felt that British substantive law had fallen behind the times and that its procedural law, particularly its rule that all judgments must be awarded in pounds sterling, was too locally oriented. Two 1976 decisions from high courts in England might help to reverse this trend. In the first case, the House of Lords reversed the rule that money judgments must be in sterling only. The facts showed that Switzerland had the closest contacts of any country to the dispute, and the House of Lords held that the judgment could be awarded in Swiss francs.

In the second case, the Privy Council reversed the previous rule that all state-owned ships were entitled to sovereign immunity. Under this rule, no action could be brought against a state-owned ship for its debts or actions (*e.g.*, collisions) unless the owner-state consented to the lawsuit. The Privy Council held that state-owned ships operated entirely for commercial purposes are no longer entitled to sovereign immunity, although publicly operated ships (*e.g.*, naval vessels) would continue to enjoy it.

(WILLIAM D. HAWKLAND)

International Law. MARITIME AFFAIRS. The third UN Conference on the Law of the Sea (UNCLOS III; *see* Special Report) held its fourth and fifth sessions in 1976, both in New York City, but no final outcome was in sight. The sense of urgency sharpened, however, as plans for serious exploitation of ocean-floor nodules advanced and, more seriously still, as the North Atlantic states prepared to claim 200-mi exclusive economic zones (EEZ's) in 1977. At the end of October the member states of the European Economic Community agreed that the EEC would declare a 200-mi EEZ for all EEC waters on Jan. 1, 1977, and also agreed on a "framework mandate" for EEC negotiations with nonmember countries such as Norway and Iceland. EEZ's were also being prepared in other regions (South Africa, India, Sri Lanka, Seychelles, Mexico).

The reason for the increasing pressure to extend

economic zones was fish, and considerable diplomatic activity on that subject was seen during the year. Thus the U.S. entered into fishery agreements with Poland (relating to the forthcoming U.S. EEZ) and the U.S.S.R. (relating to mid-Atlantic fishing). Canada reached agreement about fishing in its projected EEZ with the U.S.S.R., Poland, Spain, and Portugal; and the Canada-Norway Fisheries Agreement of December 1975 came into force the following May. India and Norway signed an agreement to cooperate in the development of fisheries in Indian waters. Iceland entered into agreements covering foreign fishing in its new EEZ with Belgium and Norway (both indefinite, terminable on six months' notice), West Germany (to run for two years from November 1975), and the U.K. (for six months ended on Dec. 1, 1976). The U.S. and Canada gave notice to withdraw from the International Commission for the Northwest Atlantic Fisheries as of the end of 1976.

Perhaps of even greater significance was the situation in the Barents Sea. In October Norway and the U.S.S.R. entered into a fisheries agreement that did not recognize the former's right to claim an EEZ unilaterally but nevertheless regulated the mutual rights of the two states on the introduction of EEZ's. A number of unresolved related problems remained, however; *e.g.,* the right of Norway to claim a continental shelf and EEZ around Svalbard (Spitsbergen) and the disputed area of some 60,000 sq mi (155,000 sq km) between the Norwegian Soviet equidistance line and the line claimed by the U.S.S.R. on the "polar sector" principle. (*See* FISHERIES.)

The signature in February of the Barcelona Convention for Protection of the Mediterranean Sea Against Pollution was a major achievement of the UN Environment Program. (*See* ENVIRONMENT.) The convention was also significant in that it was specifically open to signature "by the European Economic Community and by similar regional economic groupings at least one member of which is a coastal state of the Mediterranean Sea Area and which exercises competence in fields covered by the Convention." Two months later Italy passed a statute controlling the discharge of waste into the sea. In the eastern Mediterranean, however, the dispute between Greece and Turkey over the continental shelf under the Aegean Sea made little progress; Greece brought an action against Turkey before the International Court of Justice in August, but the court refused a Greek request for interim measures of protection arising out of Turkish exploration of the Aegean seabed.

Of particular importance for the future was the adoption in November 1975 of far-reaching amendments to the constitution of the Intergovernmental Maritime Consultative Organization (IMCO), which would widen its area of activity and change its name to the International Maritime Organization. Its 1972 Convention on the International Regulations for Preventing Collisions at Sea would come into force in July 1977.

A Danish regulation prohibited foreign warships from entering the inner three-mile belt of Danish territorial waters (thus forcing Warsaw Pact naval vessels to use the Great Belt to get in and out of the Baltic). A treaty between Guatemala and Mexico defined the territorial water limits between the two countries, both of which claimed 200 mi. In the North Sea the apparent phenomenon that nearly all the oil strikes were in the middle near the continental shelf

HENRI BUREAU—SYGMA

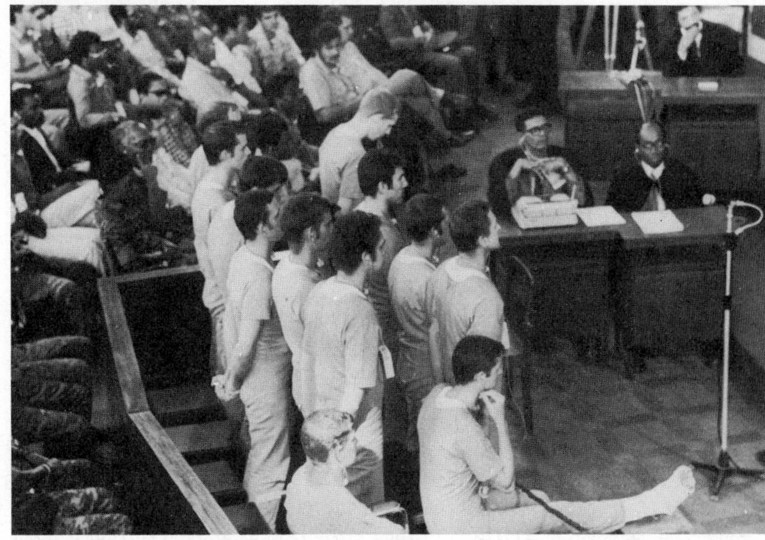

Angola charged these white mercenaries with "war crimes." One American and three Britons were executed. Nine others were given prison terms.

boundary lines at last found recognition in the signature, on May 10, 1976, of an Anglo-Norwegian agreement regulating the exploitation of the Frigg gas field which straddles the boundary.

INTERNATIONAL ORGANIZATIONS. The review of the UN Charter and strengthening of the role of the UN were the subjects of a General Assembly resolution in December 1975, which reconvened a 1974 committee to examine in detail the observations received from governments concerning suggestions and proposals already made on the subject. The World Health Organization amended articles 24 and 25 of its constitution. Extensive changes were also made in April 1976 to the rules of procedure of the International Court of Justice.

Two new international organizations were created: the International Fund for Agricultural Development, in June, to mobilize and provide finance for less developed countries, primarily for projects to introduce, expand, or improve food production systems; and the International Maritime Satellite Organization, in February and September, under the auspices of IMCO, to coordinate land-satellite-ship communications throughout the world (except the Arctic).

The tempo of nuclear energy agreements, both bilateral and multilateral, increased. Members of the International Energy Agency signed two agreements in May relating to cooperation on nuclear reactor safety and to the development of thermonuclear fusion power. Euratom and the International Atomic Energy Agency (IAEA) signed a cooperation agreement in Vienna in December 1975, and this was followed in September 1976 by an agreement between those organizations and the U.K. providing that the peaceful nuclear activities of the U.K. would be subject to IAEA control in collaboration with Euratom; this was the first time a nuclear-weapons state had subjected itself to such controls in the context of the nuclear nonproliferation treaty of 1968. The EEC published draft legislation to empower IAEA inspectors to inspect nuclear plants within the Community. However, the draft regulation to implement the guarantee agreement of April 1973 between the nonnuclear-weapons member states of Euratom and the IAEA relating to nonproliferation encountered difficulties in the European Parliament on the ground that it would involve double-checking of installations by both Euratom and IAEA inspectors. Also in the context of nonproliferation, seven states (Canada, the

U.S., France, West Germany, the U.K., Japan, and the U.S.S.R.) signed an agreement in January 1976 to restrict the sale of nuclear reactors and other nuclear installations so as to prevent the purchasers' using them to make atomic weapons. They were later joined by Belgium, Italy, The Netherlands, Sweden, Poland, Czechoslovakia, and East Germany.

TERRITORY AND SOVEREIGNTY. A boundary treaty between The Gambia and Senegal was initialed in June. In the same month, Iran and Iraq ratified a treaty covering the crossing of their common frontier by terrorists. In September Czechoslovakia and East Germany signed a treaty on cooperation concerning their joint frontier.

Seychelles became independent in June and was admitted to the UN in September. However, the new state of Transkei, formed in October, was studiously ignored by UN members. (*See* TRANSKEI.) In the Pacific, the Mariana Islands, part of the Trust Territory of the Pacific Islands, moved further toward commonwealth status within the U.S. when Pres. Gerald Ford signed enabling legislation in March.

Mauritania and Morocco signed an agreement in April dividing the Western Sahara (previously the Spanish Sahara) between them and providing for joint exploitation of its phosphate deposits. In October 1975 the International Court of Justice had delivered an advisory opinion to the effect that: (1) Western Sahara at the time of colonization by Spain (1884) was sufficiently organized tribally not to be characterized as *terra nullius*; (2) there were at that time no "legal ties" of sovereignty between Morocco and the territory, although a legal tie of allegiance did exist between the sultan of Morocco and some of the nomadic peoples of the territory; and (3) the "Mauritanian entity" at that time did not have corporate personality, but some of the nomadic peoples possessed some rights in relation to the lands through which they migrated and this constituted legal ties between Western Sahara and the Mauritanian entity.

HUMAN RIGHTS. The UN International Covenant on Civil and Political Rights came into force in March 1976 after 35 ratifications had been deposited. However, the diplomatic conference considering revision of the 1949 Geneva Conventions on the laws of war ended its third session in June with only 103 of the proposed 140 articles in the two draft protocols having been approved.

The European Court of Human Rights gave judgment in three cases involving trade-union rights, two in Sweden (the *Swedish Engine Drivers' Union Case* and *Schmidt & Dahlström* v. *Sweden*) and one in Belgium (the *National Union of Belgian Police Case*). In a further judgment relating to military discipline in The Netherlands, it held that measures of provisional military arrest and hearings in camera before the Supreme Military Court constituted a violation of the 1950 European Convention for the Protection of Human Rights and Fundamental Freedoms (*Engel & Ors.* v. *The Netherlands*).

The European Commission on Human Rights adopted the court's reports in two cases involving art. 10 of the European Convention (freedom of expression): *Handyside* v. *U.K.* (the "Little Red School Book" case), in which the operation of the British laws on obscenity was held not to violate the convention, and *De Geillustreerde Pers NV* v. *The Netherlands*, which involved a copyright monopoly for the publication of radio and television program details. It also adopted the court's reports in two cases brought by member states—*Cyprus* v. *Turkey* and *Ireland* v. *U.K.*—both of which were transmitted to the Committee of Ministers for action.

DIPLOMACY. An almost unprecedented occurrence in the field of diplomatic practice was the expulsion by Denmark, Norway, and Finland of the North Korean embassies in those countries (the embassy in Sweden left that country voluntarily) following the discovery by the Danish police that the embassy staff had been systematically involved in drug and cigarette smuggling. This was thought to have originated as a means of financing a long series of full-page advertisements in leading Western newspapers promoting the political views of North Korean Pres. Kim Il Sung, but a link with some terrorist activities was also revealed. (NEVILLE MARCH HUNNINGS)

See also Crime and Law Enforcement; Prisons and Penology; United Nations.
[552; 553]

ENCYCLOPÆDIA BRITANNICA FILMS. *Justice Under Law—The Gideon Case* (1967); *Freedom to Speak—People of New York vs. Irving Feiner* (1967); *Equality Under Law—The Lost Generation of Prince Edward County* (1967); *Free Press vs. Fair Trial by Jury—The Sheppard Case* (1967); *Equality Under Law—The California Fair Housing Cases* (1969); *The Schempp Case—Bible Reading in Public Schools* (1969); *The United States Supreme Court: Guardian of the Constitution* (2nd ed., 1973).

Spain turned over its Sahara colony in northwest Africa to Morocco and Mauritania. The signing ceremony (right) took place in the capital, El Aaiún.

UPI COMPIX

SPECIAL REPORT

LAW OF THE SEA III

By Tony Loftas

In 1976 the world still awaited a comprehensive legal regime for the oceans and seabed. The first and second UN Conferences on the Law of the Sea had met in Geneva in 1958 and 1960, respectively. The third UN Conference on the Law of the Sea (UNCLOS III) continued to progress slowly after its first, preparatory meeting in New York in December 1973 and its second meeting at Caracas, Venezuela, in June–August 1974, when the family of nations began in earnest the task of drafting an international convention on the subject. Following this second session—the first working one—a third was held at Geneva in March–May 1975, and it was there that a picture of what the convention might entail began to emerge. In 1976 UN headquarters in New York City was host to two further sessions: the fourth, from March 15 to May 7, and the fifth, from August 2 to September 17. At the fifth session, for the first time since the marathon debate began, complete deadlock arose over a major issue, deep-ocean mining. Its solution would test as never before the commitment of the negotiating nations to creating a new international law of the sea.

If 1976 was a crucial year for the conference, it was even more crucial for some of the subjects under discussion. Trials of strength occurred between nations over marine resources, both living and nonliving. The "cod war" between Iceland and the United Kingdom started again in the autumn of 1975 and carried through into the first half of 1976. Later a confrontation occurred between Greece and Turkey over the latter's right to search for oil and gas in the Aegean. Above all, many major coastal states, among them Canada and the U.S., prepared to extend their fishing limits to 200 mi in light of a consensus at UNCLOS on the rights of coastal states to a 200-mi-wide exclusive economic zone (EEZ).

By the end of the year every country bordering on the North Atlantic had decided to extend its fishing limits. Thus the U.K., having resisted Iceland's unilateral extension of its limits from 50 to 200 mi with both Royal Navy warships and civilian tugs, found itself, within months of the end of the conflict, pressing for the same kind of action by the European Economic Community. In Western Europe, North America, and elsewhere, customary international law began to overtake the UNCLOS negotiations. A hoped-for "package deal" involving trade-offs among the various interested groups lost ground when confronted by the common interest of many coastal states, both rich and poor, in owning the resources lying off their shores. Meanwhile, another UNCLOS session, the sixth, was set for New York City between May 23 and July 9, 1977, in the hope that the deadlock would be broken, allowing speedy progress to an international convention.

The Negotiating Texts. In common with its precursor, the Sea-Bed Committee, UNCLOS III had established, in Caracas in 1974, three negotiating committees, each with different areas of responsibility. The First Committee dealt with the international regime and machinery for overseeing the seabed and ocean floor beyond national jurisdiction. The Second Committee was responsible for a wide number of issues, including the breadth of territorial seas and economic zones, definition of the continental shelf, passage through straits, the needs of geographically disadvantaged states, and the many other aspects involved in defining the limits of national jurisdiction. Finally, the Third Committee was concerned with the problems of scientific research, pollution, and the transfer of technology.

The Caracas session had been used by nations to outline their views on the many issues confronting the negotiators. Its main achievement was the conclusion of a working document containing the different alternatives for every item before the conference. With the problem defined, the hope was that the third, Geneva, session, which followed six months later in March 1975, would produce hard negotiation. The decision was made not to indulge in formal debate or statements of national positions but instead to devote most of the time to informal consultations. Unfortunately, these discussions tended to become divisive. Toward the end of the session the conference decided that a single informal negotiating text was needed covering all the subjects entrusted to the three committees.

The chairman of each committee prepared a text that in his view reflected the informal discussion. The texts were a clever device to restore the flagging spirit of the conference. Even though they were not binding on any delegation, they gave the first real indication of what a final convention might look like. Shortly after their circulation on the last day of the Geneva session, the president of the conference, Hamilton Shirley Amerasinghe of Sri Lanka, independently submitted a fourth document, covering the settlement of disputes, in order to provide a more complete text. The stage was set for the fourth session in New York, March–May 1976.

The Fourth and Fifth Sessions. In contrast to previous sessions, the gathering in New York for the fourth session recognized from the start that at least one more meeting, apart from a formal treaty-signing ceremony, would be needed. Nevertheless, the delegations set out with a will to review the informal texts. The results of their endeavour were summed up in a four-part revised single negotiating text consisting of 397 articles and 11 annexes, issued on the closing day of the session. Like the original Geneva version, the revised draft remained informal, a procedural device to provide a basis for negotiation. After much debate the fifth session was set to take place from August 2 to September 17, again in New York.

Toward the end of the first New York gathering, it became clear that trouble lay in store for the fifth session. Many less developed countries felt they were being pushed into decisions by cliques of nations, particularly the industrial powers. They disliked the idea of meeting again so soon. They disliked even more the revised texts, which seemed far less favourable to them than the original versions. The landlocked and other geographically disadvantaged states, a group of 49 nations both rich and poor, were disgruntled at the willingness of resource-rich coastal states to trade among themselves. Some delegations were even in favour of abandoning the long-standing "gentleman's agreement" to negotiate by consensus; they wanted to force a vote to demonstrate the depth of their dissatisfaction.

Voting on major issues before a conference is anathema to most delegates experienced in multinational negotiation. They realize that international agreement cannot be created or imposed in this way. Certainly voting could easily have proved fatal to the UNCLOS negotiations because the various interest groups did not form along traditional political lines. Their composition could vary from committee to committee according to the issues. For example, the U.S. and Canada agreed in the Second Committee to a 200-mi-wide EEZ, but they were at odds in the Third Committee over allowing freedom of scientific research for other nations in it. As many as nine different interest groups could be identified. Not one had the same overall membership.

Once the fifth session was under way, the threatened disputes,

---

Tony Loftas, who reported on earlier sessions of UNCLOS III in the 1975 Britannica Book of the Year, *is editor of* Marine Policy, *marine consultant to* New Scientist, *and has been consultant to the FAO and special adviser to the UN. His publications include* Wealth from the Oceans *(1967) and* The Last Resource: Man's Exploitation of the Oceans *(1970; revised 1973).*

LONDON DAILY EXPRESS/PICTORIAL PARADE

An Icelandic gunboat rams a British frigate during the "cod war" off the coast of Iceland. The British naval vessel was protecting British trawlers in the quarrel over fishing limits.

at least in the Second Committee, began to recede. Efforts were made to dispel some fears of the landlocked and geographically disadvantaged countries. Provisions were made for access to the oceans, and greater agreement than before proved possible on the rights of these states to share in the living resources of neighbouring or better-endowed coastal states. Progress was even made on the vexed question of sharing of resources lying in or over the continental margins beyond the 200-mi EEZ. Coastal states regarded the seabed there as an extension of their land territory and therefore not a negotiable item, but they now seemed prepared to share at least the income derived from its material resources, principally oil and natural gas.

The Second Committee, which had by far the greatest number of topics to discuss, still had several major issues outstanding. Perhaps the two most important questions were how to fix the boundaries between adjacent and opposite coastal states, and what balance to strike between the needs of the international community and the rights of the coastal state in the waters of the EEZ. The Third Committee faced equally important and potentially divisive issues. For example, what controls should the coastal state exercise over scientific research in its EEZ and what regulations could it impose to prevent pollution from ships operating in this area? But in both committees negotiation and compromise continued. For the first time, for example, the Soviet Union withdrew its opposition to the need for the consent of coastal states for any marine research in the EEZ. Proposals were also in hand to meet the objections of the few industrial states, such as the U.S., West Germany, and The Netherlands, that still rejected this principle.

Deep Ocean Mining. Only in the First Committee did this process of negotiation become exhausted, leading to a deadlock that effectively halted any progress more than a week before the formal close of the session. Instead of examining the structure of the proposed International Sea-Bed Authority and its ancillary bodies, the committee found itself debating once again the system for exploiting seabed resources in the international area. Should the system provide a guaranteed permanent role in exploitation for states, other parties, and private industry? Should such a role be determined in the future by the proposed international authority? Or should it be considered only a temporary arrangement for a period perhaps set by the conference itself? According to the committee's chairman, Paul Bamela Engo of Cameroon, a positive show of political will was needed to enable one or the other of these options to be adopted.

Negotiating positions on deep-sea mining had changed since UNCLOS began, but the underlying issue remained basically the same. The majority of less developed countries wanted a powerful international authority, effectively controlled by them and with its own exclusive mining enterprise. The industrialized countries, particularly the U.S., would have preferred to limit the authority to the licensing of national or multinational mining groups, but they would settle for a "parallel system" comprising both the international enterprise and outside groups. In fact, U.S. Secretary of State Henry Kissinger, speaking outside the conference in April, had proposed that the U.S. government should finance the enterprise and arrange a transfer of the technology needed to make it operational. In the absence of specific details, however, many delegations believed that this was simply a ruse designed to sell the parallel system, and that the enterprise would remain little more than a paper entity.

In the eyes of all the negotiators a great deal was at stake. Deep-ocean minerals, mainly the potato-sized manganese nodules, promised to guarantee supplies of nickel, copper, cobalt, and manganese for hundreds if not thousands of years. To those countries with the mining and processing technology—and here the U.S. apparently led—these resources represented a secure base for future industrial life. To major producers of such minerals, particularly less developed countries, deep-ocean mining threatened both their future livelihood and any influence they enjoyed as suppliers of vital metals. And finally, to those countries that could benefit little from more conventional marine resources, the minerals of the deep were practically their only hope of deriving any substantial reward from the oceans.

Resolution of the deadlock was not furthered by pressure for unilateral action from mining companies within the U.S., where bills to permit deep-ocean mining had already been drafted. One company, Deepsea Ventures, a subsidiary of Tenneco Inc., actually attempted to file a claim to deposits of nodules lying over an area of approximately 60,000 sq km, or 23,000 sq mi, in the Pacific Ocean. The industry was pressing for legislation primarily because it offered insurance for the substantial investments required to establish a commercial ocean-mining system. The total costs, including exploration and research and development, for a system yielding 3 million tons of nodule ore annually were estimated variously at between $460 million and $700 million. Another important factor was a determination to maintain the country's technological lead in order that its industry might benefit from any future ocean mining, whether corporately, nationally, or internationally inspired.

The Future of UNCLOS III. The sixth session in 1977 would decide whether the political will existed to establish a new order of international law in the oceans. The fact that nearly 150 nations had progressed so far without breaking up in disarray held some hope for success. The first three weeks would be devoted to breaking the impasse on seabed mining. Once the crucial decisions were made on the system of exploitation, many delegates believed that other provisions on seabed mining could be agreed on without delay. Agreement in the First Committee was also likely to help negotiations in the other committees, which had fallen under its shadow of dissent toward the end of the fifth session. It might even be possible to produce a draft convention at the sixth or a subsequent session in 1977. If, on the other hand, the conference finally failed, the world would not fall into chaos, but ocean development would be less ordered, heightening the possibility of serious conflicts between nations in years to come.

XAVIER BARON—A.F.P./PICTORIAL PARADE

Lebanon

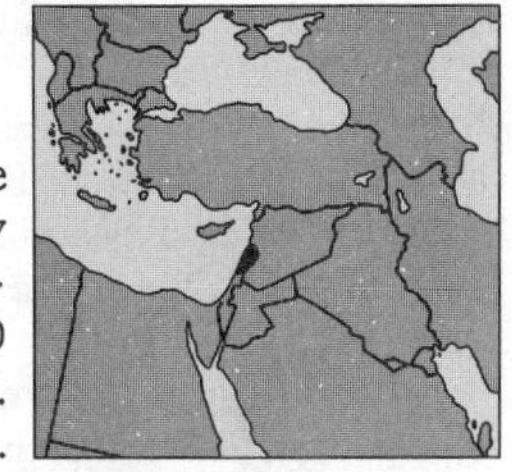

A republic of the Middle East, Lebanon is bounded by Syria, Israel, and the Mediterranean Sea. Area: 3,950 sq mi (10,230 sq km). Pop. (1975 est.): 2,869,000. Cap. and largest city: Beirut (metro. pop., 1975 est., 1,172,000). Language: Arabic. Religion: Christian and Muslim. Presidents in 1976, Suleiman Franjieh and, from September 23, Elias Sarkis; prime ministers, Rashid Karami and, from December 9, Selim al-Hoss.

In 1976 Lebanon passed from the relative calm of a temporary cease-fire in the civil war to a violent renewal of the fighting and massive Syrian intervention. Finally, a joint Arab decision on united action to end the war brought some hope of peace at the end of the year. The war had killed some 45,000 people, injured 100,000, and caused some 500,000 to emigrate.

The sources of the Lebanese conflict did not lie only in the Palestine problem and the presence of some 400,000 stateless Palestinian Arabs in the country, although this was one of the principal factors. Severe social and political tensions had long existed. First, the laissez-faire system on which the country's commercial prosperity was based left much of the population poor and deprived—especially in the largely Shi'ite Muslim areas in the south of the country. Second, the Muslims, aware that they were almost certainly a majority, increasingly resented the Christians' domination of the country. Third, the post-1967-war period witnessed the rise of the Palestinian guerrilla movements and their combination in the Palestine Liberation Organization (PLO). All the ingredients for the explosion existed in the spring of 1975. The incident that may be said to have sparked off the war was the massacre of the Palestinian occupants of a bus by Christian militia, but the conflict was almost certainly inevitable.

LEBANON

Education. (1972–73) Primary, pupils 497,723; secondary, pupils 167,578; primary and secondary, teachers 32,901; vocational, pupils 4,603, teachers (1970–71) 508; teacher training, students 3,233, teachers (1970–71) 466; higher, students 50,803, teaching staff 2,313.

Finance. Monetary unit: Lebanese pound, with (Sept. 20, 1976) a free rate of L£3.28 to U.S. $1 (L£5.65 = £1 sterling). Budget (1976 est.) balanced at L£1,716 million. Gross national product (1972) L£6,358 million. Cost of living (Beirut; 1970 = 100; July 1975) 129.

Foreign Trade. (1973) Imports L£3,465 million; exports L£1,522 million; transit trade L£1,345 million. Import sources: U.S. 12%; West Germany 11%; France 10%; Italy 10%; U.K. 8%. Export destinations: Saudi Arabia 15%; France 9%; U.K. 8%; Libya 7%; Kuwait 6%; Syria 5%. Main exports: machinery 14%; fruit and vegetables 12%; chemicals 8%; aircraft 6%; clothing 6%; textile yarns and fabrics 5%; motor vehicles 5%. Tourism (1974): visitors 2,262,000; gross receipts U.S. $415 million.

Transport and Communications. Roads (1971) 7,400 km. Motor vehicles in use (1974): passenger 214,400; commercial (including buses) 24,100. Railways: (1973) 417 km; traffic (1974) 1,890,000 passenger-km, freight 42 million net ton-km. Air traffic (1974): 1,773,800,000 passenger-km; freight 423.6 million net ton-km. Shipping (1975): vessels 100 gross tons and over 123; gross tonnage 167,490. Telephones (Jan. 1973) 227,000. Radio receivers (Dec. 1971) 605,000. Television receivers (Dec. 1973) 321,000.

Agriculture. Production (in 000; metric tons; 1975): potatoes *c.* 80; wheat (1974) *c.* 60; sugar, raw value (1974) *c.* 24; tomatoes *c.* 60; grapes (1974) *c.* 115; olives *c.* 32; bananas (1974) *c.* 40; oranges (1974) *c.* 230; lemons (1974) *c.* 85; apples (1974) *c.* 200; tobacco *c.* 10. Livestock (in 000; 1974): cattle *c.* 84; goats *c.* 330; sheep *c.* 227; chickens *c.* 6,555.

Industry. Production (in 000; metric tons; 1974): cement 1,744; petroleum products 2,200; electricity (kw-hr) 1,975,000.

Parts of Beirut were completely destroyed in the civil war. This photo was taken in May.

During the first half of January 1976 there was fighting throughout the country as the Phalangist right-wing Christian forces blockaded the Palestinian refugee camps and the leftist Palestinian forces responded by attacking Christian villages on the coast. Syria, which had sworn to prevent Lebanon's partition by force if necessary, intervened by allowing Palestine Liberation Army forces (belonging to the PLO) under its control to enter the country, and this led to a Syrian-sponsored cease-fire on January 22 and the formation of a Syrian-Lebanese-Palestinian Higher Military Committee to supervise it. Prime Minister Karami withdrew his resignation announced on January 18, and the country returned to relative peace as schools and offices reopened. Cabinet discussions of a reform program led to the issue of a proposed new national pact on February 14 under which the president would still be a Maronite Christian but the Sunni Muslim prime minister would be elected by a simple majority of Parliament whose members would be equally divided between Christians and Muslims instead of in a 6–5 ratio. Lebanese leftists led by Kamal Jumblatt (*see* BIOGRAPHY) declared these reforms inadequate and demanded partial secularization of the state. An uneasy calm prevailed, but it was broken by political kidnappings, and a group of army deserters broke away to form a Lebanese Arab Army under Lieut. Ahmed al-Khatib.

On March 11 the military commander of Beirut, Brig. Gen. Abdul Aziz al-Ahdab, declared a state of emergency and called on President Franjieh to resign. Franjieh refused and barricaded himself in the presidential palace at Baabda. Syrian troops then halted the leftist advance on Baabda, first revealing the split between Syrians and the leftist Palestinian forces that was eventually to develop into an open alliance between Syria and the Lebanese right. Fighting re-

Law Enforcement: *see* Crime and Law Enforcement

Lawn Bowls: *see* Bowling

Lawn Tennis: *see* Tennis

sumed in Beirut on March 13 and 14 and became general during the second half of the month. The leftists made gains in the Beirut hotel district; on March 25 President Franjieh left his bombarded palace for the Christian coastal base town of Juniyah.

Parliament met, and 90 deputies voted on April 10 to amend the constitution to enable a new president to be elected six months before the expiration of the incumbent's term. On April 24 Franjieh reluctantly signed the amendment, and on May 8 Elias Sarkis (*see* BIOGRAPHY) was elected president by Parliament. Sarkis was supported by Syria and the Christian right; his election was criticized by the leftists. Fighting was general throughout the country in the second half of April and May, and the leftists made significant gains. On June 1 Syrian troops, which had already crossed the border in some strength, made their first large-scale intervention, advancing to occupy the Beqaa Valley and over Mount Lebanon where they met fierce resistance from the Palestinian leftist forces.

Mediation by the Libyan prime minister and the decision of the Arab foreign ministers in Cairo to send an Arab League peace force failed to stop the fighting, although the peace force succeeded in July in establishing itself between the two sides in Beirut. President Franjieh refused to make way for President-elect Sarkis and appointed the hard-line interior minister, Camille Chamoun, as foreign minister on June 16. On the same day the U.S. ambassador to Lebanon was assassinated in leftist-held Beirut, and most remaining foreigners began to leave the country. Christian forces besieged Palestinian refugee camps in their territory, and one of them, Tel az-Zaatar in eastern Beirut, became a symbol of Palestinian resistance. This fell on August 12–13 after seven weeks of siege and heavy loss of life.

Areas of control in Lebanon and Beirut at the time of the cease-fire on October 21.

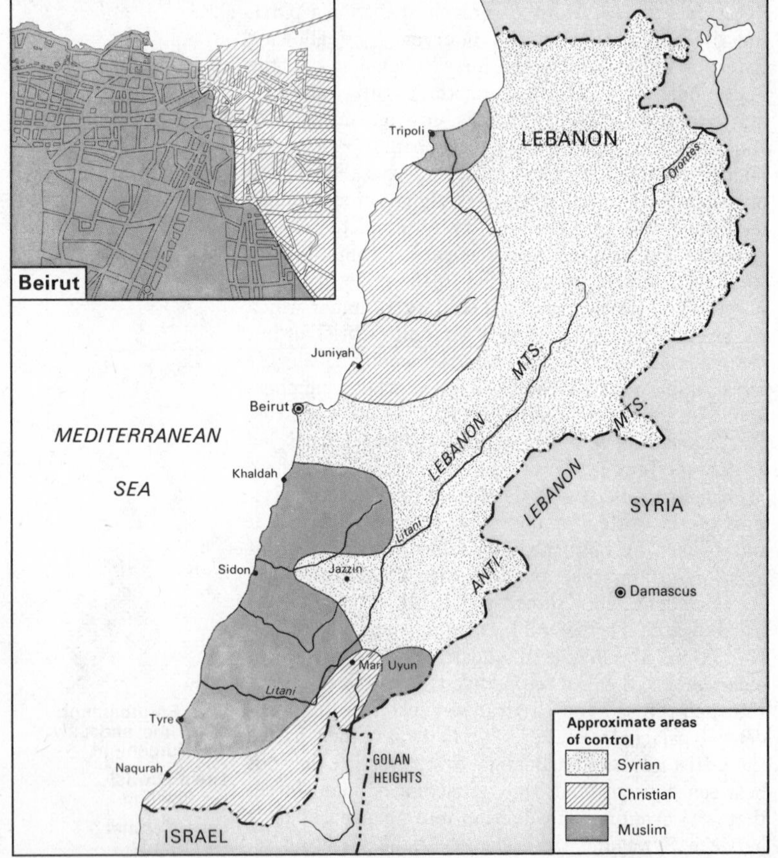

On September 23 President Sarkis was sworn in at Syrian-held Shtawrah and asked Karami to stay as prime minister until a new government was formed. On September 28 the Syrians launched an offensive in the mountains east of Beirut and forced the stubbornly resisting Palestinians to retreat. The Syrians began another offensive on October 12 against leftist-held Marjayoun in the south. Several meetings of Palestinian, Syrian, Lebanese, and Arab League representatives in September and October still failed to find a solution; but a limited summit meeting of Syria, Egypt, Lebanon, Kuwait, and the PLO in Riyadh, Saudi Arabia, on October 17–18 agreed on a cease-fire, which generally came into force on October 21, and on the increase of the Arab League peace force to 30,000. These decisions were endorsed by the general Arab summit in Cairo on October 25–26. There, it was agreed that the "deterrent force" should be under the authority of President Sarkis, who on November 4 appointed Lieut. Col. Ahmed al-Haj to head it. Initial doubts of Lebanese rightist leaders about allowing the force into their territory were overcome, and during the second week of November Syrian troops, which formed the bulk of the force, advanced gradually into Beirut to separate the combatants and reopen key roads. On December 9 Sarkis appointed a new interim Cabinet. Composed of four Christians and four Muslims, all of whom were described as technocrats rather than politicians, it was headed by Prime Minister Selim al-Hoss, a Muslim banker.

(PETER MANSFIELD)

[978.B.3.a]

Lesotho

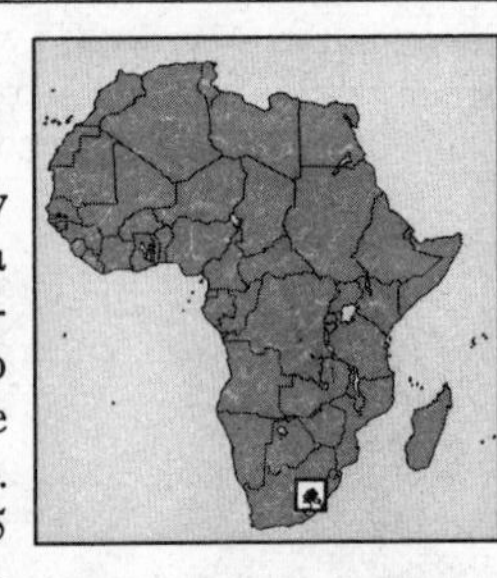

A constitutional monarchy of southern Africa and a member of the Commonwealth of Nations, Lesotho forms an enclave within the republic of South Africa. Area: 11,720 sq mi (30,355 sq km). Pop. (1976 prelim.): 1,214,000. Cap. and largest city: Maseru (pop., 1976 prelim., 14,700). Language: English and Sesotho (official). Religion: Roman Catholic 38.7%; Lesotho Evangelical Church 24.3%; Anglican 10.4%; other Christian 8.4%; non-Christian 18.2%. Chief of state in 1976, King Moshoeshoe II; prime minister, Chief Leabua Jonathan.

Lesotho established formal diplomatic relations with Swaziland in February 1976 for the first time. Relations with Botswana and Swaziland had deteriorated, however, after Chief Jonathan nationalized the jointly administered University of Botswana, Lesotho, and Swaziland in October 1975. After fruitless negotiation, Botswana and Swaziland threatened to take their claim for compensation to the International Court of Justice. Jonathan had reacted against the left-wing policies of Joel Moitse, a former vice-chancellor and ex-minister of trade and industry, who was expelled, and in fear of a coup by the opposition Basutoland Congress Party. In other moves to the right, Foreign Minister J. R. L. Kotsokoane was replaced by Charles Molapo. In December the UN Security Council discussed Lesotho's charge that its Transkei border had been closed by South Africa, which said the matter concerned Transkei.

In his May budget speech, Finance Minister E. R.

LESOTHO

Education. (1975) Primary, pupils 221,932, teachers 4,228; secondary, pupils 15,611, teachers 605; vocational (1972), pupils 623, teachers 170; teacher training, students 345, teachers 57; higher, students 502, teaching staff 73.

Finance and Trade. Monetary unit: South African rand, with (Sept. 20, 1976) an official rate of R 0.87 to U.S. $1 (free rate of R 1.49 = £1 sterling). Budget (1974–75 est): revenue R 17,251,000; expenditure R 16,008,000. Foreign trade (1973): imports R 60.5 million; exports R 8.8 million. Main exports: wool 36%; cattle 18%; mohair 17%; sheep and goats 5%. Most trade is with South Africa.

Agriculture. Production (in 000; metric tons; 1974): corn *c.* 100; wheat *c.* 50; sorghum *c.* 60; wool *c.* 1.5. Livestock (in 000; 1974): cattle *c.* 490; goats *c.* 970; sheep *c.* 1,600.

Sekhonyana announced that recurrent expenditure would be locally financed. A European Economic Community mission visited Lesotho to discuss an R 32 million aid program. In July a second five-year plan, involving expenditure of R 111.6 million by the end of 1980, was announced. Extensive floods damaged crops and washed away roads, isolating the Maloti Mountain people. (MOLLY MORTIMER)

[978.E.8.b.ii]

Liberia

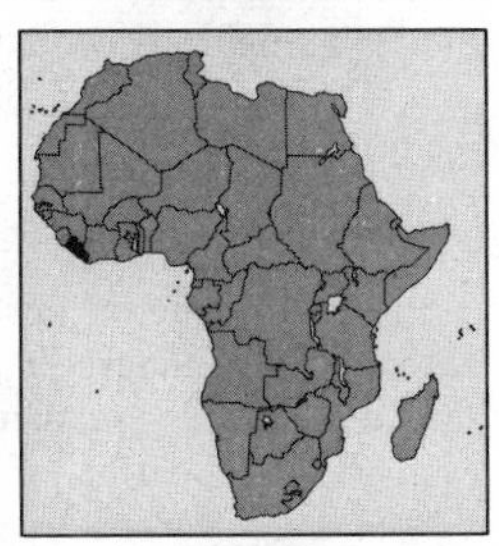

A republic on the west coast of Africa, Liberia is bordered by Sierra Leone, Guinea, and Ivory Coast. Area: 43,000 sq mi (111,400 sq km). Pop. (1976 est.): 1,750,000. Cap. and largest city: Monrovia (pop., 1974, 180,000). Language: English (official) and tribal dialects. Religion: mainly animist. President in 1976, William R. Tolbert, Jr.

LIBERIA

Education. (1974) Primary, pupils 149,687, teachers 4,111; secondary, pupils 26,426, teachers 1,015; vocational, pupils 1,087, teachers (1970) 66; teacher training, students 424, teachers 41; higher, students 2,061, teaching staff 141.

Finance. Monetary unit: Liberian dollar, at par with the U.S. dollar, with (Sept. 20, 1976) a free rate of L$1.72 to £1 sterling. Budget (1974 actual): revenue L$124.2 million; expenditure L$124.5 million.

Foreign Trade. (1975) Imports L$331,230,000; exports L$394.4 million. Import sources (1974): U.S. 28%; Saudi Arabia 18%; U.K. 9%; West Germany 9%; Japan 5%. Export destinations (1974): U.S. 24%; West Germany 19%; The Netherlands 13%; Italy 12%; Belgium-Luxembourg 11%; France 8%. Main exports: iron ore 74%; rubber 12%; diamonds 5%.

Transport and Communications. Roads (main: 1973) 10,260 km. Motor vehicles in use (1974): passenger 12,100; commercial (including buses) 10,000. Railways (1973) 496 km. Shipping (1975): merchant vessels 100 gross tons and over 2,520 (mostly owned by U.S. and other foreign interests); gross tonnage 65,820,414. Telephones (Jan. 1974) 3,000. Radio receivers (Dec. 1973) *c.* 260,000. Television receivers (Dec. 1973) 8,500.

Agriculture. Production (in 000; metric tons; 1974): rice *c.* 146; cassava *c.* 260; bananas *c.* 62; palm kernels *c.* 18; rubber (1975) *c.* 90; palm oil *c.* 21; cocoa *c.* 3; coffee *c.* 3. Livestock (in 000; 1974): cattle *c.* 33; sheep *c.* 168; goats *c.* 165; pigs *c.* 88.

Industry. Production (in 000; metric tons; 1974); iron ore (metal content) 24,461; petroleum products 541; diamonds (exports; metric carats) 636; electricity (kw-hr) 860,000.

GLYN GENIN—CAMERA PRESS/PHOTO TRENDS

Aerial view of Monrovia shows the president's office and residence on the left and, behind it, the Parliament building.

On Jan. 5, 1976, President Tolbert was inaugurated to an eight-year term. Tolbert, who had succeeded the late Pres. William V. S. Tubman in 1971, had been returned to office unopposed in October 1975. At the same election, a constitutional amendment limiting the tenure of a president to a single eight-year term had been approved by the voters. At his inauguration, Tolbert laid down his general policy, including a four-year, $413 million National Development Plan (1977–80) emphasizing agricultural self-sufficiency. Citizens were to be encouraged to buy government lands, and tribal chiefs were to be elected and paid. In a Cabinet reshuffle, Mrs. Abeodu Jones was named minister for posts and telecommunications, the first Liberian woman to hold such an office.

Liberia's budget showed gross domestic product at $635 million in 1975 (20% above 1974, due mainly to the high price of iron ore). Though the Firestone Tire and Rubber Co.'s 50-year-old tax exemption was canceled, foreign investment was encouraged. A $1 billion iron-ore development project was arranged with West Germany and Japan and, after Tolbert's May visit to the Ivory Coast, a $1.5 million project was set up to help Liberia develop palm oil, coconuts, cocoa, and coffee. (MOLLY MORTIMER)

[978.E.4.a]

Libraries

Two important centenaries were celebrated by librarians in 1976. The conference of the American Library Association (ALA) in Chicago in July, with keynote addresses on "Libraries and the Life of the Mind in America," commemorated the foundation of the ALA in 1876 under the aegis of such famous librarians as Justin Winsor of the Boston Public Library and the first ALA president; Charles A. Cutter, well known for his *Expansive Classification;* R. R. Bowker, founder of the publishing firm; and Melvil Dewey. Simultaneously, the ALA published the first, centennial edition of *The ALA Yearbook.*

The second centenary was that of the publication in 1876 of the first edition of the Dewey Decimal Classification, now used in nearly all public libraries in the Anglo-Saxon world as well as in many libraries in France, Italy, and elsewhere. A European Centenary Seminar also was organized by the British Library Association (BLA) at Banbury, England, in September, attended by representatives of the Dewey Decimal Classification from Forest Press and from the Library of Congress and some 40 European delegates and guests. Methods of cooperative compilation were discussed, including the revision of class 780 Music just completed by the Department of Librarianship of Leeds Polytechnic, England, and the new area tables -41 and -42 for Great Britain compiled by Ross R. Trotter following the reorganization of local government boundaries, both contributions to be included in the coming 19th edition of the Dewey classification. A history of the Dewey system, *The Eighteen Editions* by John P. Comaromi, was published by Forest Press.

In the international field emphasis was on better cooperation between libraries in the face of the still rising prices of books, the sheer quantity of publications, and the decrease of available funds. At the International Federation of Library Associations (IFLA) General Council in August at Lausanne, Switz., the advantages of centralized lending were described by Maurice B. Line, director of the British Library Lending Division, which in 1976 received over 2.5 million requests and published its *Brief Guide to Centres of International Lending and Photocopying.* Other speakers also explained that the much-mooted universal bibliographical control would not solve library problems unless universal availability of publications could also be achieved. Meanwhile, in West Germany the Deutsche Forschungsgesellschaft recommended the rational cooperation of leading libraries to supply research literature to the nation, rather than centralized lending. In August the IFLA agreed on its new statutes, in which the most important change was the creation of a Division of Regional Activities, divided into Asia, Africa, Latin America, and the Caribbean, with regional chairmen. IFLA held a worldwide seminar at Seoul, Korea, May 31–June 5, attended by delegates from 28 countries, with a special meeting of Asian librarians convened by the chairman of the IFLA Regional Section for Asia; there it was emphasized that less developed countries needed to create public library networks, in addition to their existing academic and special libraries, in order to promote literacy and economic development.

UNESCO further implemented its plan for promoting national information systems (NATIS) by sending consultants to 17 countries; in Venezuela the government drew up a program to develop the National Library, with a new building, and to link it with a system of libraries; in Argentina a project was formed for a national system for agricultural information in cooperation with the Central Library of the Faculty of Agronomy of the University of Buenos Aires; in Somalia the government recognized the need for a national library; and a meeting of librarians from ten African countries in September 1975 at Accra, Ghana, initiated plans for an integrated library policy for African countries. An enlarged edition of UNESCO's *National Information Systems* was published, and an important report on "Planning and Organizing Public Libraries in Ethiopia . . . 1975–2000" appeared in the *Unesco Bulletin for Libraries* in March–April.

Other national developments included Bolivia's new plan for public and school libraries; Bulgaria's new International Centre of Sources of Balkan History (CIBAL), in Sofia; France's creation of the Centre Bibliographique National at the Bibliothèque Nationale, Paris, to serve all French libraries; Great Britain's *Atkinson Report on Self-renewing Libraries,* produced by the University Grants Committee; and Switzerland's automation of procedures at the university libraries in Lausanne and Zürich.

In the field of techniques and standardization, a general International Standard Bibliographical Description, ISBD(G), was established by the IFLA Committee on Cataloguing as the basis for cataloging books, periodicals, music, maps, and all other data carriers, with the purpose of facilitating compatibility with ISBD (Monographs), ISBD (Serials), ISBD (Music), etc. Another milestone in cataloging was reached with the publication of the Yugoslav librarian Eva Verona's *Corporate Headings: Their Use in Library Catalogues and National Bibliographies.* Two new standards on documentation were published by the International Organization for Standardization (ISO): ISO 690, *Documentation—Bibliographical References—Essential and Supplementary Elements;* and ISO 1086, *Title-Leaves of a Book.* The new version of the Bibliographic Classification of Henry E. Bliss was completed under the editorship of Jack A. Mills and explained by him to librarians in Denmark, Norway, and Sweden. Mills's and Ruth Daniel's *Classification*

Vast oil revenues have transformed the face of Libya. Below are two views of the new library at the University of Benghazi. The university had 8,815 students in 1975–76.

PHOTOS, COURTESY, JAMES CUBITT & PARTNERS

of Library and Information Science was published by the BLA. An international survey of cataloging-in-publication was completed by L. R. Swindley for UNESCO, while in Canada the cataloging-in-publication program was operational from January. The use of microforms in libraries was analyzed at the first annual Microform Conference held in New York in late 1975, and a Computer/Microfilm Interfaces Seminar critically examined computer-output-microfilm (COM) techniques in October 1976. The Library of Congress published its computer-produced *Main Reading Room Reference Collection Subject Catalog* of some 11,000 books and 3,000 serials.

In North America and Western Europe the trend toward full-time graduate training for library personnel continued; in Scandinavia efforts were made to standardize the curricula, and an all-Scandinavian journal of library education was started. In the U.S.S.R. some two-thirds of professional librarians qualified by part-time study, while in West Germany from October 1976 a full-time course for documentalists began at the Lehrinstitut für Dokumentation, Frankfurt am Main, and in France in-service training for documentalists continued to be given by the Association Française des Documentalistes et des Bibliothécaires Spécialisés. The ALA published a statement on security of employment to support its Library Bill of Rights of 1948 (amended 1961 and 1967). Three important initiatives taken by the BLA were publication of *New Readers Start Here,* a handbook for new literates, financed by a grant from the Adult Literacy Resource Agency; appointment of a journalist as editor of the *Library Association Record,* who gave it a new style for 1976; and computerized production of *Library and Information Science Abstracts,* the leading English-language abstracting journal in Europe for the literature of libraries and librarianship.

(ANTHONY THOMPSON)

[441.C.2.d; 613.D.1.a; 735.H]

ENCYCLOPÆDIA BRITANNICA FILMS. *Library Story* (1952); *The Library—A Place for Discovery* (1966); *Library of Congress* (1969); *Look in the Answer Book* (1972); *Smithsonian Institution* (1973).

Libya

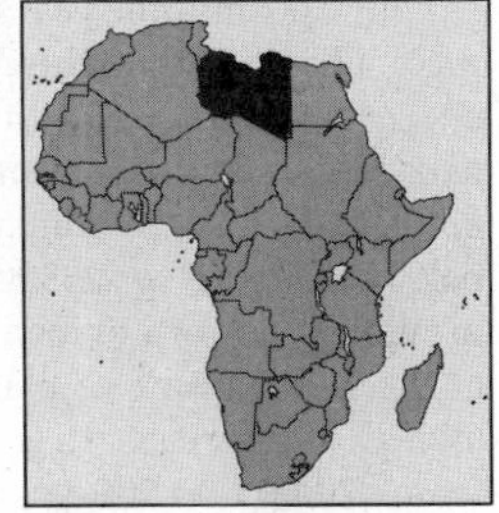

A socialist republic on the north coast of Africa, Libya is bounded by the Mediterranean Sea, Egypt, the Sudan, Tunisia, Algeria, Niger, and Chad. Area: 675,000 sq mi (1,749,000 sq km). Pop. (1975 est.): 2,444,000. Cap. and largest city: Tripoli (pop., 1973 census, municipality, 551,000). Language: Arabic. Religion: predominantly Muslim. Leader of the Revolutionary Command Council in 1976, Col. Muammar al-Qaddafi; prime minister, Maj. Abdul Salam Jalloud.

After the uneasy decline in oil production and revenues in 1975, Libya's economy took a steadier course in 1976 with demand firm at about 1.9 million bbl a day, almost twice the lowest level of the previous year. Demand for the desirable light Libyan crude was sufficient to justify a price rise (10–20 cents a barrel) in July when other producers such as Kuwait were reducing prices. In December Libya was one of the 11 oil producers that raised prices by 10%.

Relations with neighbouring Sudan were severely strained in July when Libyan involvement in an attempted coup in Khartoum was loudly claimed by Sudanese Pres. Gaafar Nimeiry. These accusations were equally loudly denied. Relations with Egypt followed a similar pattern. Cairo sources asserted the involvement of Libyan agencies in bombings in Egyptian cities, attempted kidnappings of fugitive Libyan politicians, and other incidents. Such propaganda only abated in September when a story that Libyan agents had hijacked an Egyptian internal flight was revealed as spurious. Libya countered by expelling thousands of Egyptian nationals from Libya. Libyan involvement in the Lebanese hostilities, long suspected in the form of clandestine payments to left-wing forces, became explicit in the spring with Prime Minister Jalloud's frequent visits to Lebanon. His attempts at mediation were abandoned in July.

At home the role of the "popular committees" in government was confirmed in a number of areas, especially in municipal affairs and education. A further extension of this version of democracy was outlined in the first part of the *Green Book* of President Qaddafi, published in August. Violence broke out at the universities and serious incidents occurred in April in Benghazi, resulting in changes in university administration. The government attempted to woo the potentially important but easily alienated Libyan students studying abroad. They were called to a meeting in Tripoli (there had been a similar gathering in 1975) where they were indulgently treated and encouraged to participate in the celebration of the seventh anniversary of the revolution.

In January the government's expectation of a continuously expanding economic future was given substance in the five-year development plan, 1976–80. It

LIBYA

Education. (1974–75) Primary, pupils 538,070, teachers 24,424; secondary, pupils 107,577, teachers 8,074; vocational, pupils 2,883, teachers 265; teacher training, students 19,546, teachers 1,514; higher, students 12,162, teaching staff 596.

Finance. Monetary unit: Libyan dinar, with (Sept. 20, 1976) a par value of 0.296 dinar to U.S. $1 (free rate of 0.510 dinar = £1 sterling). Gold and foreign exchange (June 1976) U.S. $2,449,000,000. Budget (1973 actual): revenue 966,109,000 dinars (including petroleum revenue of 614,480,000 dinars); expenditure 1,301,833,000 dinars. Gross national product (1973) 1,875,000,000 dinars. Money supply (March 1976) 903.8 million dinars. Cost of living (Tripoli; 1970 = 100; Sept. 1975) 124.

Foreign Trade. (1975) Imports (fob) *c.* 1,184,000,000 dinars; exports 1,812,300,000 dinars. Import sources (1974): Italy 25%; West Germany 11%; France 10%; Japan 7%; U.K. 5%. Export destinations: Italy 33%; West Germany 22%; U.K. 12%; France 6%; Japan 5%. Main export crude oil 100%.

Transport and Communications. Roads (with improved surface; 1972) *c.* 5,200 km (including 1,822 km coast road). Motor vehicles in use (1974): passenger 227,500; commercial (including buses) 104,900. Air traffic (1974): 414 million passenger-km.; freight 3.8 million net ton-km. Shipping (1975): vessels 100 gross tons and over 27; gross tonnage 241,725. Ships entered (1974): vessels totaling 5,166,000 net registered tons; goods loaded 70,524,000 metric tons, unloaded 6,413,000 metric tons. Telephones (Dec. 1971) 42,000. Radio licenses (Dec. 1973) 100,000. Television licenses (Dec. 1973) *c.* 15,000.

Agriculture. Production (in 000; metric tons; 1975): barley *c.* 200; wheat *c.* 70; potatoes (1974) *c.* 80; watermelons (1974) *c.* 100; tomatoes (1974) *c.* 194; olives *c.* 100; dates (1974) *c.* 62. Livestock (in 000; 1974): goats *c.* 1,109; sheep *c.* 3,200; cattle *c.* 121; camels *c.* 120; asses *c.* 73.

Industry. Production (in 000; metric tons; 1974): petroleum products *c.* 400; crude oil (1975) 72,900; electricity (Tripolitania; excluding most industrial production; kw-hr) *c.* 750,000.

involved about $20 billion, with more than $4 billion allocated for 1976. Agriculture continued to receive the major share (17%), but the commitment to extend the industrial base beyond the already productive petrochemicals sector into heavy industry, especially iron and steel, remained firm. In December it was announced that Libya had purchased a 10% interest in Fiat, the giant Italian automobile-manufacturing firm, for $415 million. (J. A. ALLAN)

[978.D.2.a]

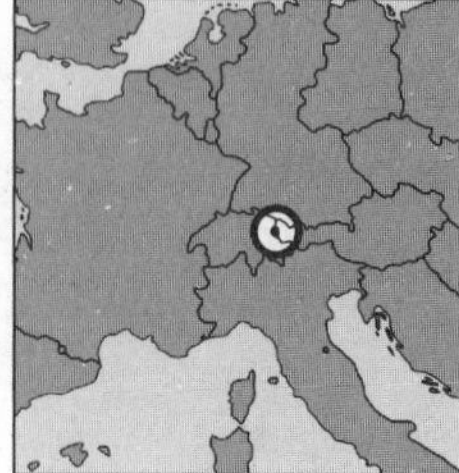

Liechtenstein

A constitutional monarchy between Switzerland and Austria, Liechtenstein is united with Switzerland by a customs and monetary union. Area: 62 sq mi (160 sq km). Pop. (1976 est.): 23,900. Cap. and largest city: Vaduz (pop., 1975 est., 3,900). Language: German. Religion (1970): Roman Catholic 90%. Sovereign prince, Francis Joseph II; chief of government in 1976, Walter Kieber.

On Aug. 16, 1976, with the unanimous approval of Parliament, Prince Francis Joseph signed a law granting women the vote in communal elections, subject to popular consultation and approval.

According to the West German weekly *Der Spiegel,* the number of "letter box" foreign enterprises, trusts, and foundations registered in Liechtenstein rose in 1976 to about 30,000. As each company paid 2% of its declared capital on registering and 1% per year afterward, the increment from this source represented about 40% of the principality's yearly internal revenue. Walter Walser, owner of the "Bürotel" at Schaan, near Vaduz, who was also honorary consul of Chad, boasted that his office alone was "the turntable of many thousands of businesses" in this tax-free sanctuary, although he did not deny that from time to time some fraudulent dealings were discovered. However, the value of these activities, together with the sale of postage stamps and tourism, was being overtaken by that of industrial production, the real source of the country's prosperity.

For the first time, citizens of Liechtenstein won Olympic medals when Willy Frommelt and Hanny Wenzel came in third in the men's and women's slaloms, respectively, at the 1976 Winter Games at Innsbruck, Austria. (K. M. SMOGORZEWSKI)

LIECHTENSTEIN

Education. Primary (1976), pupils 2,114, teachers 89; secondary, pupils 1,582, teachers 76.

Finance and Trade. Monetary unit: Swiss franc, with (Sept. 20, 1976) a free rate of SFr 2.48 to U.S. $1 (SFr 4.26 = £1 sterling). Budget (1976 est.): revenue SFr 183,075,000; expenditure SFr 182.8 million. Exports (1975) SFr 522.3 million. Export destinations: Switzerland 41%; EEC 27%. Main exports: metal manufactures, furniture, pottery. Tourism: visitors (1975) 78,550; gross receipts (1971) *c.* SFr 18 million.

Life Sciences

Excitement over the search for manifestations of biological activity on the planet Mars was paced by important progress in 1976 in understanding the extraordinary complexity of life on Earth. For example, since the classic work of François Jacob and Jacques Monod (*see* OBITUARIES) in the late 1950s, it was known that in bacteria a genetic operon (gene complex) only becomes active when the action of a repressor gene is itself repressed. Recently scientists at Stanford University found an additional control gene, the "attenuator," that stops synthesis by the operon at a particular intermediate stage, thus constituting another link in the delicate mechanism by which the nature and amount of the products of gene action are adjusted to the needs of the organism. In eucaryotes (nucleated cells) the corresponding controls are almost unknown, but work on nitrogen metabolism in the fungus *Aspergillus* (Fungi Imperfecti) showed them to be extremely complex. In multicellular organisms the on-and-off switching of gene activity is influenced by neighbouring cells, either by direct contact or through chemical messengers.

The essential agent by which cells recognize and react to such external influences is the cell membrane, and the properties of this structure continued to be a major field of research. The nature, distribution, and mechanism of action of specific chemical receptors on the cell membrane were related to a very wide range of scientific and medical investigations, including those of the movements and differentiations of embryonic cells, regeneration and repair of tissues, transmission across the nerve synapse, immunity, and reactions to drugs. Of particular note were studies of the ways by which correct neuronal connections develop between retina and brain and of the actions of drugs and their natural analogues on specific cell groups in the brain (*e.g.,* opium and its analogue enkephalin).

Some outstanding advances were made in knowledge of prehistoric organisms and of the conditions under which they lived. Finds in several countries, while not yet revealing the direct ancestry of modern man, gave greater precision to the time scale involved and furthered understanding of the evolutionary radiation of the hominids in relation to the climatic changes of Plio-Pleistocene times (as much as seven million years ago). The age of the vertebrates was extended by some 20 million years through the discovery of fishlike skeletal plates in a Lower Ordovician deposit (about 500 million years old) on Spitsbergen in Norway. The fact that this was a marine deposit cleared up the anomaly that the earliest known vertebrates had been freshwater animals. Burrows, presumably made by metazoan animals, found in Zambian copperbelt rocks were some 300 million years older than any previously known evidences of metazoan life. The isolation and staining of filaments showing close morphological similarities to modern *Sphaerotilus* bacteria from 2,000,000,000-year-old Australian rocks supported belief in the role of bacteria in the formation of iron deposits during Precambrian time (between 4,600,000,000 and 570 million years ago).

With the general (but not universal) acceptance of safety guidelines for work on recombinant DNA in bacteria, the way was opened for genetic engineering to become a major tool of science. The first completely chemical synthesis of a fully functional bacterial gene was reported by a team of scientists from the Massachusetts Institute of Technology. (See *Genetics,* below.) Eucaryotic genes (from yeast) were incorporated into a bacterium, a procaryote (a cell lacking a distinct nucleus). Several successful fusions of plant and animal cells were made. Though composite plant-animal multicellular organisms could not be developed, the technique opened up new possibilities for research in cell biology. (See *Botany,* below.)

Life Insurance:
see Industrial Review

Among the practical results that could be expected in the near future from these lines of investigation were: (1) the use of cultures of viruses carrying human genes for the manufacture of therapeutically important human proteins; (2) a great extension of the use of bacteria in other industrial processes; and (3) an increase in the number of plant species with the ability to fix atmospheric nitrogen and improved efficiency of the biological nitrogen-fixation process.

The year 1976 saw the complete worldwide extermination (subject to future confirmation) of one of the most deadly of parasitic organisms, the smallpox virus. (*See* HEALTH AND DISEASE: *Special Report.*) Concerning this accomplishment, two points deserve special note. First, conservationists had argued for years that any unique combination of genes was a potential asset that merited conservation. This position was strongly questioned, however, when it was suggested that the smallpox virus be preserved in laboratory cultures to ensure its future availability. Second, the eradication of smallpox did not depend upon "big science" at prestigious institutes. Although organized by the UN World Health Organization (WHO), it depended essentially on the accumulated experience and devotion of doctors and hospital staffs.

This kind of reliance was typical of many aspects of the life sciences. Whereas some of these sciences, notably molecular biology, resembled the physical sciences in their concern with the universal characteristics of the materials of life and with the application of these characteristics to particular cases, others sought to apply experiences with particular cases to the unique, unpredictable phenomena of whole organisms and communities. It was this synthesis of the universal and the particular, of the orderly and the disorderly aspects of nature, that offered the life sciences a central place in any philosophy of nature.

(HAROLD SANDON)

[339.C.3.c]

ZOOLOGY

Some of the most interesting findings about animals reported in 1976 concerned sex and reproduction. For example, P. M. Narins and R. R. Capranica of Cornell University, Ithaca, N.Y., reported a sexual difference in the response of female tree frogs of the species *Eleutherodactylus coqui* to the call of the male. This frog is found in Puerto Rico, Florida, and the U.S. Virgin Islands. The male call consists of two notes, "co-qui," emitted in the evening from sunset until midnight or shortly thereafter. In a series of acoustic playback experiments carried out in the natural habitat, both natural and synthetic sounds were played on a tape recorder and the responses of frogs recorded. Three recorded calls were presented in random order: a natural two-note "co-qui" call, a synthetic "qui," and a synthetic "co." In general, males responded to all three types of call with one of two types of their own, either a two-note "co-qui" or a one-note "co." On the other hand, females responded only to "co-qui" or to "qui" (not to "co" alone) by hopping toward the source of the call. This behaviour was taken as a measure of the degree of attractiveness of the call. It was concluded that the first note, "co," must play a role in male-male interactions, but it does not attract the female. The experimenters suggested that the first note may serve to maintain spacing between adjacent males. This frog is apparently the first known example of a vertebrate in which the peripheral auditory sensitivity shows a sexual difference.

A related study involved the effect of the male song on the reproductive development of inbred Belgian "Wasserschlager" canaries (*Serinus canarius*). D. E. Kroodsma of Rockefeller University, New York City, subjected virgin female canaries to recorded long or short segments of the male song and assessed their reproductive activity by counting the number of eggs laid and measuring the birds' inclination to gather strings for nest building from a standard ball of string lengths. After several weeks the birds sub-

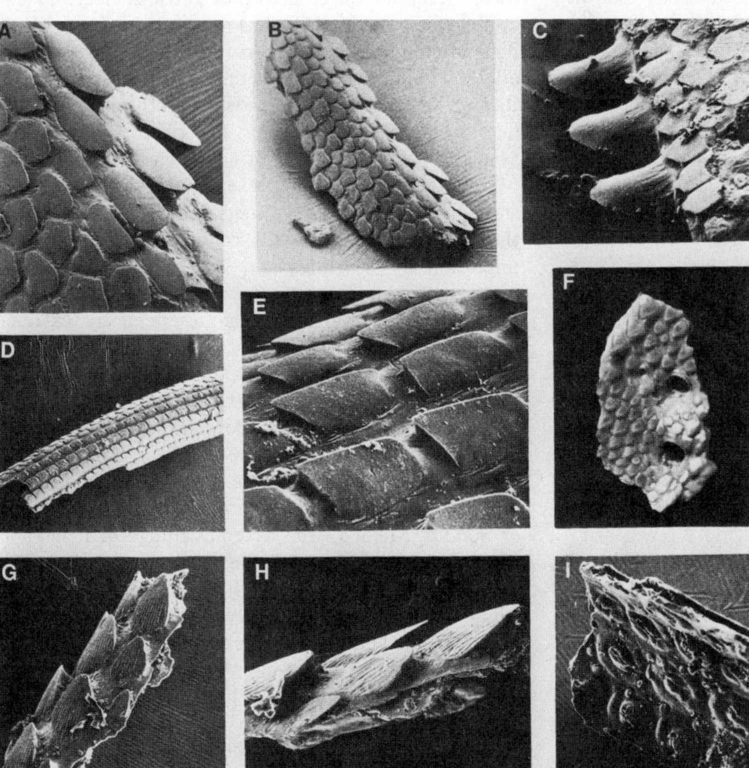

Fossil vertebrate remains have been found that date back 500 million years. These fragments of Heterostracan fishes were discovered in Norway's arctic region of Spitsbergen. Photos A, B, D, E, G, and H show scales. Photo C shows part of a spinelike fragment. Photo F shows a fragment with circular perforations that apparently represent original openings in the animal's exoskeleton. Photo I shows the inner surface of a fragment.

jected to the longer male song segments had pulled out much more string and laid more eggs than those subjected to the short song segments. The exact mechanism remained unknown, but it may be that the longer songs contained more of the specific components required to trigger a reproductive response.

A third study involved a test of the hypothesis of R. L. Trivers of Harvard University that, in those species in which the male contributes extensively to parental care, it is vital to the male to fertilize the eggs by his own sperm; otherwise his extensive parental investment would be wasted. C. J. Erickson and P. G. Zenone of Duke University, Durham, N.C., studied this question in the ring dove, *Streptopelia risoria,* a species in which the male makes a large parental investment. One group of males was observed first with females that had been "preexposed" to other males and then with "unexposed" females; another group of males was presented with females in the reverse order. Males of both groups engaged in much more nest-soliciting activity with unexposed than with preexposed females, supporting Trivers' hypothesis. In addition, males were more aggressive toward preexposed females, indulging in more chasing and pecking. There was no difference in the amount of male bowing and cooing, but these were regarded as being important only for sexual identification. It was considered likely that the male can determine if a female has been preexposed to another male and possibly inseminated. He thus avoids her and thereby maximizes his reproductive efforts.

The deleterious effect of acidic precipitation on embryonic development was studied recently by F. H. Pough of Cornell University, who observed the effect of pH on the development of the spotted salamander *Ambystoma maculatum.* Numerically "pH" is the negative logarithm of the hydrogen ion concentration; low pH values indicate high acidity and high values low acidity. Many amphibians breed in temporary ponds, which are especially susceptible to the effects of acidic precipitation. Laboratory studies have shown a hatching success of 90% or more for Jefferson salamanders (*A. jeffersonianum*) only at pH 5–6, and for spotted salamanders at pH 7–9; pH values other than these have been associated with heightened mortality and the presence of specific embryonic malformations. In order to determine if a similar situation exists in nature, the development of spotted salamanders was studied in five ponds in Tompkins County, New York. The ponds varied in pH from 4.5 to 7.0 when the eggs were laid and had increased by 0.25 to 0.5 pH units by time of hatching. Below pH 6, embryonic mortality increased markedly. Furthermore, sensitivity to acidity was confined to the same embryonic stages as those observed in the laboratory. Although the possibility exists that various stresses were working together to produce the mortalities and abnormalities, it was deemed likely that pH was the critical variable. The general problem of the deleterious effects of acidic precipitation on forests and fisheries had been studied for two decades in Scandinavia and more recently in North America. Although there was some evidence that amphibians may be in the process of evolving some tolerance of acidity, it seemed unlikely that this is occurring at a rate sufficient to counteract the long-term negative effect on their reproduction.

Other interesting behavioural findings also were reported. Experimental proof was obtained for the odour hypothesis of salmon homing, which states that a juvenile salmon imprints to the unique chemical odours of its natal stream during the spawning migration. In 1973 and 1974 A. D. Hasler and co-workers of the University of Wisconsin at Madison exposed hatchery-raised and tagged juvenile coho salmon to morpholine or phenethyl alcohol (p-alcohol) for 1½ months and then released them in Lake Michigan. Eighteen months later morpholine and p-alcohol were added to separate Wisconsin streams that fed into the lake and the number of exposed fish returning to each stream was determined. Monitoring was also carried out at 17 other locations. In 1974, 94.1% of morpholine-treated fish were found in the morpholine-treated stream and 90.5% of all p-alcohol-treated fish were captured in an area scented with p-alcohol. Similar results were obtained in 1975. By contrast, large numbers of unexposed control fish were captured at other locations.

Another interesting and unusual behavioural phenomenon, reverse migration, was observed by D. G. Raveling of the Canadian Wildlife Service in Winnipeg during a three-year study of geese (*Branta canadensis*). Geese were captured at a breeding marsh on the southeastern shore of Lake Manitoba, marked with individually identifiable neck tags, and released. Marked geese were observed at the marsh for an average of two days per week between September 20 and November 20 (1968–70), a period encompassing all normal and reverse autumn migrations of this flock. The main normal wintering site of the flock is located at Rochester, Minn., 855 km SE of the breeding site. However, 2.1% of all adults (geese more than 2½ years old) practiced reverse migration; *i.e.*, they migrated to the wintering grounds in Rochester in the spring and returned to the nesting area in Manitoba in autumn. In addition, 5.5% of all yearlings (1½ years old) and 0.6% of the immatures (observed in summer and autumn of the year of hatching) practiced reverse migration. This process usually was attributed to untoward weather conditions and was most prevalent among individuals that were not associated with families, the dominant structure of goose society. Of 252 adults who were identified as members of normal families, none practiced reverse migration. Those few adults who did were (1) members of gang-brood families (families including goslings other than those hatched by the adult pair); (2) paired, but without young; (3) single; or (4) of unknown status. The high percentage of yearling reverse migrants included three sibling birds that always migrated as a group. From these observations it was concluded that irregular migration by yearlings and singles could provide a major mechanism of gene flow between populations of Canada geese, which are characterized by extreme isolationism and morphological variation.

Finally, a behavioural characteristic was reported that actually may threaten the survival of a species. The condition of winter dormancy in sea turtles (*Chelonia mydas*) from the Gulf of California makes them exceedingly vulnerable to overfishing. Winter dormancy had been discovered by the Seri Indians of Sonora, Mexico, who take advantage of it in their winter turtle-fishing operations, and recently was verified by R. S. Felger, K. Cliffton, and P. J. Regal. In winter, turtles bury themselves three to five metres apart along the muddy or sandy edges of undersea troughs, which often occur at the perimeters of eelgrass beds. Indian fishermen hunt with harpoons from boats during low tide, when the turtles lie at water depths of about four to eight metres and can be located by observing small portions of their shells exposed above the sand. In this condition harpooned turtles are very torpid and easily boated. In 1976 *C. mydas* was very scarce and, although not all populations of this species exhibit dormancy, it was felt that governments and others interested in conservation should be alerted to this phenomenon.

(RONALD R. NOVALES)

[342.A.5.b and c; 342.A.6]

Entomology. By the mid-1970s pest-control research had spawned three generations of insecticides: the first were inorganic stomach poisons; the second, the primarily neurotoxic contact insecticides; and the third, compounds that mimicked insect hormones. In 1976 William S. Bowers and colleagues at the State Agricultural Experiment Station, Geneva, N.Y., claimed discovery of a new, fourth generation. Noting that plants produce compounds representative of most of the known categories of insecticide, Bowers and his group searched for further examples and found two, called precocene I and II, in the common bedding plant *Ageratum houstonianum*. These chemicals were shown to prevent production of insect juvenile hormone, a master hormone that, among other functions, controls metamorphosis. The precocenes cause development of precocious, nonreproductive adults of plant bugs, prevent egg maturation in flies and beetles, cause premature winter diapause (a period of reduced metabolic activity) in the Colorado potato beetle, and kill eggs of other insects including the Mexican bean beetle. It had been known for many years that plants produce compounds that mimic the effects of juvenile hormone, preventing susceptible insects from developing into reproductive adults; but synthetic hormone mimetics had had limited success mainly because insects have effective systems that regulate hormone concentrations by destroying excesses.

The second generation insecticides continued to fall foul of environmentalists. The U.S. Bureau of Land Management predicted that the Arctic race of peregrine falcon might soon disappear from Alaska, and blamed DDT runoff into the Pacific Ocean and accumulation in the anchovies on which the birds feed. The bureau reported that the falcons displayed a well-recognized side effect of DDT—thin eggshells that collapsed when the birds sat on them. Meanwhile, the U.S. Food and Drug Administration found evidence of another insecticide, Kepone, contaminating fish marketed along the U.S. East Coast. (*See* ENVIRONMENT.)

Screwworm had been very effectively controlled in the southern U.S. for over a decade by regular release of large numbers of sterilized male flies; these mated with wild females, causing them to lay sterile eggs. A scare began in 1972 when the screwworm population built up again, seemingly because wild females were rejecting their laboratory-bred beaux. The U.S. Department of Agriculture (USDA) restocked with new insects from the wild, and by 1974 control had been restored.

Guy L. Bush of the University of Texas and his co-workers finally determined what had happened. Rearing the insects in the laboratory at high, constant temperatures for several generations had favoured the survival of individuals with a normally rare, congenital form of α-glycerol dehydrogenase, an enzyme involved in respiratory metabolism. The enzyme worked particularly well under conditions of mass rearing, but when the flies were released they found themselves literally out in the cold, where their hothouse metabolism put them at a disadvantage.

Experimenters continued to try ways of trapping or confusing insects with chemical attractants, including their intraspecies chemical signals, called pheromones, while other workers concentrated on another form of insect communication, acoustic signaling. Working with bark beetles, Lee C. Ryder and J. A. Rudinsky of Oregon State University at Corvallis reported that the male makes a variety of chirping sounds by rubbing its wing cases together: a stress signal (*e.g.*, when handled); an "attractant" chirp when entering the gallery of a virgin female; and an intermittent "rivalry" chirp that threatens other males. The female too has a stress signal; she chirps in reply to the attractant signal of the male, and when he has finally found her, she gives a distinctive "greetings" chirp before courtship begins.

Fruit flies also have a vocabulary, according to J. C. Webb and co-workers of the USDA, Florida. The male Caribbean fruit fly makes four distinct sounds, one in normal flight, the others by "buzzing" its wings. Of these, one is attractive to females, one is a premating sound made after mounting the female but before copulating, and one is an aggressive sound that challenges other signaling males for their territory. Water boatmen, aquatic bugs of the family Corixidae, signal each other under water by rubbing together a ridge and comb on their abdominal sclerites; I. M. King of Monash University, Victoria, Australia, described a variety of chirps, clicks, and chatterings that were also clearly audible above the surface.

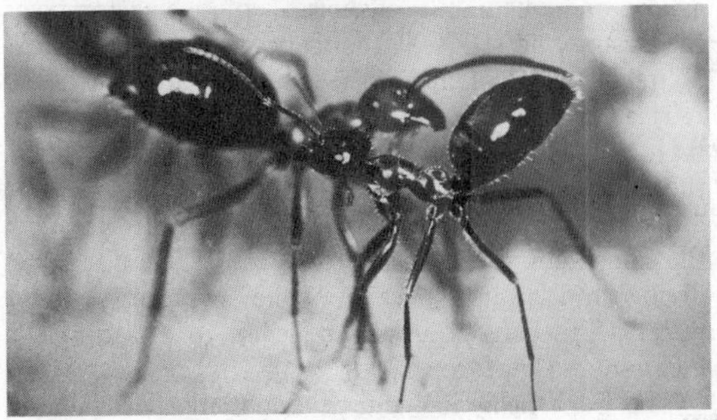

COURTESY, DR. BERT HÖLLDOBLER, DEPARTMENT OF BIOLOGY, HARVARD UNIVERSITY; PHOTOS BY TURID HÖLLDOBLER

Warriors of opposing colonies of the honeypot ant conduct highly ritualized tournaments. Vulnerable to physical violence, they confine themselves to head-on confrontation (top), lateral display (centre), and drumming with their antennae on each other's abdomens (bottom). Once a colony has been cowed into submission, its workers allow themselves to be carried off as the "slaves" of the victors.

Death knell for the house fly? A tiny parasitic wasp lays its eggs in the pupa of a housefly. The developing eggs will feed on the fly, destroying it. Researchers in Florida have found this effective in controlling fly populations in poultry houses and cattle barns.

Outbreaks of the forest-defoliating gypsy moth may well be precipitated by litterbugs, according to Robert W. Campbell of the Northeastern Forest Experiment Station, Syracuse, N.Y. He found that man-made objects left at the edges of forests provide the larvae of *Porthetria dispar* with resting and pupation sites, thus improving their chances of survival and triggering outbreaks from otherwise numerically innocuous levels of population.

In subzero weather, some insects survive temperatures below −15° C (5° F) because of an antifreeze (glycerol) in their tissues. Other insects, however, have adopted a different strategy: they freeze, but not quite solid. Karl Erik Zachariassen of the University of Oslo, Norway, and Harold T. Hammel of the Scripps Institution of Oceanography, La Jolla, Calif., found that some ground beetles (Tenebrionidae) have a nucleating agent that ensures formation of ice in the blood above −10° C. As a result, their blood becomes more concentrated and progressively draws water from tissue cells, thereby lowering the cellular freezing point and preventing the formation of lethal intracellular ice crystals.

(PETER W. MILES)

[321.B.9.c.i; 321.E.2.a; 342.A.6.d.ii]

Ornithology. The main conclusion of a summary of recent work on dinosaurs was that they are not extinct, but survive in the form of birds! Taxonomically, it argued, birds should no longer merit an order of their own but should be placed among the Dinosauria. The best known fossil bird, *Archaeopteryx,* is thought to be descended from a carnivorous dinosaur, not a more primitive thecodont as previously supposed. Prior to the advent of *Archaeopteryx,* the dinosaurs may have developed warm-bloodedness and a featherlike insulating layer.

Penguins have been studied almost exclusively when ashore or immediately offshore. A pioneer attempt at the systematic study of the Cape or jackass penguin in its principal element, the open sea off southwest Africa, was made by W. R. Siegfried and others. The majority of the seagoing population lives in groups, the average size of which is 8, though flocks of over 50 were recorded. All members of a group perform the same actions in unison; for example, simultaneous diving and group cohesion while swimming under water. This behaviour was believed to assist in the location and capture of prey.

The Cape penguin—and no doubt most, if not all, penguin species—is highly adapted to withstand the cold waters in which it hunts. When ashore, however, it finds itself in a hot climate and is overinsulated. To cope, it has evolved a number of behavioural adaptations, as shown in another study by Siegfried and his colleagues. At its island breeding stations the bird is mainly crepuscular and nocturnal; it reduces the effects of daytime sun by burrowing, by evaporative cooling, and most interestingly by orientating its body with its back to the Sun. Thus the lightly feathered areas of the body are shaded, and heat loss by convection and reradiation from these shaded surfaces is facilitated. Heat gain is restricted by the efficient insulation of its heavily feathered back. Predictably, on overcast days body orientation is nondirectional.

A review of the relationship between birds and human welfare prepared by W. R. P. Bourne showed that birds present the greatest hazard to their most devoted admirers, the birders, who in the course of their pursuits expose themselves to a variety of incidental risks, notably falling from cliffs and drowning. The study also pointed out that, although birds have been incriminated as carriers of such diseases as ornithosis and of arboviruses and *Salmonellae,* these cases occurred less often than might have been expected.

T. C. Grubb's work on Leach's storm petrel showed that birds returning under cover of darkness to their burrows on offshore islands navigate by smell, a sense that very few avian species even possess. The burrow entrance becomes impregnated with a musky smell given off by the bird's feathers as it passes in and out, and the petrel homes in on this source.

Turnstones, arctic wading birds that nest on either side of the Bering Strait, were proved by banding studies to conduct a circular migration to and from their breeding grounds. Southward movement in autumn takes them through the central Pacific Ocean, especially to the Marshall Islands. In spring they fly north through the western Pacific and Japan. The southward migration can be very rapid, one bird averaging 650 mi a day.

Various myths and suggestions that attempted to explain why the male baya weaver of India often lines its nest chamber with mud were discarded by T. A. Davis. The mud is not to hold fireflies for lighting the nest but serves as a binder for the nest fibre. The mud provides general structural strength and helps the nest resist rather vigorous testing by house-hunting females.

The production of a television film, *The Private Life of the Cuckoo*, by Maurice Tibbles stimulated research into this unconventional family. In the region featured in the film cuckoos were laying eggs in the nests of reed warblers. Of 136 warbler nests found by Ian Wyllie, 25 were parasitized. At least 25% of the unparasitized warbler nests had been visited by adult cuckoos that removed warbler eggs and, in one case, a brood of young warblers. It was thought that the main reason for this predation of nests of the host species was to maintain a continuity of suitable nests in which the female cuckoos could lay their eggs, because the warblers that lose their eggs or young then rebuild, providing cuckoos with new opportunities to parasitize nests at the appropriate stage of the host's breeding cycle.

H. E. McClure and Puntia Kwanyuen reported on the effects on other animals of the annual occupancy of a colony in Thailand by 5,000 pairs of open-billed storks. The yearly presence of these birds was found to affect the annual cycle of ticks and mites that depend upon them. Several species of myna bird rely upon dropped food from under the nests, and monitor lizards, snakes, crows, and dogs subsist on stork eggs and on the dead and dying young that fall from trees.

In the Estonian Soviet Socialist Republic the nesting population of white storks increased from one pair in 1841 to 1,060 pairs in 1974. In some other parts of its European range this species was decreasing. At Pune, India, a flock of 200 tawny eagles displaced vultures as the scavengers at a poultry processing plant.

Among the year's publications were *British Birds of Prey* by Leslie H. Brown, the world's leading expert on raptors, and Edward S. Gruson's *A Checklist of the Birds of the World*, which provided a complete record of the world's birds. *Avian Biology*, edited by Donald S. Farner and James R. King, probably the most important ornithological textbook currently available, was completed with the issue of its fourth and fifth volumes.

(JEFFERY BOSWALL)

[313.J.6]

MARINE BIOLOGY

Conditions governing planktonic growth were studied as part of a West German interdisciplinary research program. A 32-metric-ton steel tower set up in Kiel Bay in the western Baltic Sea carried up to four large cylinders of nylon fabric extending to the seabed. In addition to the study of conditions in the water column itself, this "plankton tower" permitted for the first time in the sea an assessment of interactions between the water and the bottom sediment.

A rare opportunity to study the effects of isolation from the sea on marine organisms was expected to occur in Russell Fiord, located at the head of Yakutat Bay, Alaska. The Hubbard Glacier had advanced across the mouth of the fjord and was projected to isolate it from marine influence within the next few years. In anticipation of closure, the existing water circulation was studied as a basis for comparison.

Studies of contemporary coral reefs in the tropical eastern Pacific had generally noted the scattered and relatively poor state of development of those reefs, with the notable exception of those on Clipperton Island, 1,072 km SW of Acapulco, Mexico. A new overview of the prevailing oceanographic conditions by Thomas F. Dana suggested that the region is marginal for coral-reef development (1) owing to the persistence of a strong, shallow thermocline with relatively cold water very close below the warm surface layer and (2) because of the annual north–south migration of the intertropical convergence zone, an equatorial belt of converging trade winds and rising air that results in very pronounced wet and dry seasons, the heavy annual rains inducing low salinity and high turbidity in the inshore environments.

The life cycles of many marine animals differ from their freshwater counterparts in their dependence upon a pelagic larval stage disseminated by water currents. Some larvae feed during their pelagic life; others do not feed but are provided with energy stores derived from the large yolky egg. The latter forms can only remain active as long as the energy supplies last, which is usually no longer than 12 hours. In these forms the urge to settle and metamorphose to the adult increases steadily with age, suggesting that the breakdown of instinctive patterns of settlement behaviour is related to energy exhaustion.

In other behavioural work, diving studies by H. W. Fricke and others in the Red Sea and elsewhere led to the accumulation of much observational data on the role of behaviour in mutualistic associations between marine animals. Fascinating problems arise relating to the evolution and ecological significance of such behaviour as that of the shrimp *Alpheus djiboutensis*, which emerges from its burrow only when its partner, the fish *Cryptocentrus cryptocentrus*, is in position at the mouth of their shared burrow. When moving outside the burrow the shrimp keeps the tip of its long antenna in constant physical contact with the fish.

In the past the age of elasmobranch fishes such as sharks and rays could not be judged by scale or otolith readings as could that of certain bony fishes. Consequently little had been known about the longevity and growth rates, particularly of the larger sharks. A new technique using silver nitrate staining of shark vertebrae clearly revealed annual growth rings, which indicated, for example, that blue sharks grow from 45 cm in length at birth to 300 cm in ten years.

New work on the growth of the queen conch (*Strombus gigas*) suggested that its mariculture was feasible but not yet economically practicable. At best,

WIDE WORLD

Tired of living? In what looked like suicide, 25 long-snouted spinner dolphins beached themselves on a Florida key near Sarasota in July. Marine biologists had no explanation for their behaviour.

seeding subtidal algae flats with hatchery-reared individuals seemed the most likely method of reestablishing local fisheries in the Caribbean Sea where this economically important species had been overfished. Overfishing off Nova Scotia, Canada, of the lobster *Homarus americanus* had resulted in decreased abundance of nearly 50% in 14 years. In the same region there also had occurred during the past six years a 70% reduction in the size of the beds of the large brown alga *Laminaria,* a phenomenon that appeared to be causally related to the lobster decline. The sea urchin *Strongylocentrotus droebachiensis,* which grazes on the alga, appeared to have done so increasingly following reduced predation by the lobster, a major predator of sea urchins.

Because the male and female gametes of many marine invertebrates are shed directly into the water, it is important that spawning should occur when conditions are favourable for both fertilization and the development of pelagic larvae. The impressive regularity and abruptness of spawning in *S. droebachiensis* and two chitons, *Tonicella lineata* and *T. insignis,* was thought to be cued by the spring outburst of phytoplanktonic abundance. Though previously known to be a cue for the release of phytoplankton-feeding larvae, this phenomenon had never before been considered a signal for the release of gametes.

(ERNEST NAYLOR)

[354.B.2 and 4]

BOTANY

The importance of plants to civilization has long been recognized, and increasing concern had been expressed in preceding years over the dangers of neglecting or misusing this vital natural resource. A recently published report of the U.S. National Academy of Sciences stressed the importance of exploring the potential of underexploited tropical crop plants and identified several that might become staples in the future. The 1976 Cabot Symposium, held at Harvard Forest, Petersham, Mass., also dealt with the tropics; while pointing out that many aspects of the biology of tropical trees are still poorly understood, it served as a focus for the principles emerging from research in this field.

Scientists have found a new source of hydrogen and nitrogen. Growing in the leaves of this water fern, a microscopic alga releases hydrogen from water and fixes nitrogen from the air.

AGRICULTURAL RESEARCH MAGAZINE

AGRICULTURAL RESEARCH MAGAZINE

Profile of a grim eater: a Hessian fly sucks the sap from a wheat seedling. Researchers are working to control the fly.

Another symposium, held at Kew, England, reiterated the importance of conserving endangered species, particularly wild relatives of economically important plants. Continued survival of several crop plants may depend on preservation and utilization of related gene pools. This point was well illustrated by experiments in which genetic resistance to mildew attack was bred into the cultivated oat *Avena sativa* from a wild relative, *A. barbata.*

Despite the economic importance of the susceptibility of plants to pathogenic diseases, until recently little had been known of those plant-pathogen interactions responsible for either resistance or sensitivity. One basis of resistance to fungal attack is the accumulation at the site of infection of compounds toxic to the potential pathogen. The production of these "phytoalexins" by the host is triggered by chemical "elicitors" of pathogenic origin. In a series of experiments reported in 1976, an elicitor from the fungus *Phytophthora* was isolated and identified as a substituted glucan, a normal polysaccharide component of *Phytophthora* cell walls. When applied to soybean cells, the potent compound triggered the production of large amounts of a phytoalexin and was observed to increase the activity of one of the enzymes involved in phytoalexin synthesis. However, because phytoalexin production was induced experimentally by elicitors from races of *Phytophthora* to which soybean is sensitive as well as from races to which it is resistant, it was stressed that race-specific resistance could not be accounted for solely by the elicitor-phytoalexin system. One hypothesis held that race-specific resistance might be determined by host response to a fungal-wall glycoprotein, an additional discriminating factor superimposed on the general resistance provided by phytoalexins. The similarities between such host-pathogen interactions and recognition phenomena in animal cells were quite apparent.

The central role of the pigment phytochrome in mediating developmental responses of higher plants to light continued to attract the efforts of plant physiologists toward elucidation of its mechanism of action. That phytochrome can be associated with the membranes of cells appeared to be clearly established, and in 1976 additional evidence was provided that the activity of phytochrome depends in some way on this association. Earlier work had confirmed the presence of phytochrome in etioplasts (incompletely developed chloroplasts) of leaves of barley plants grown in darkness. Illumination of the etioplasts with red light, which converts the pigment to its biologically active form, resulted in release of growth regulators known as gibberellins from the etioplasts. Recently phytochrome was shown to be associated with the membranous envelope of the etioplast; this evidence could be taken as support for the hypothesis that phytochrome influences functions associated with specific membranes within the cell, perhaps by regulating membrane permeability.

Among the most notable strides in recent months was the achievement reported from Brookhaven (N.Y.) National Laboratory of the successful fusion of animal and plant cells. Tobacco-cell protoplasts prepared by enzymatic removal of the cell walls were mixed in culture medium with human HeLa cells, derived from human tumour tissue. Within a few hours of mixing under appropriate conditions, membrane fusion occurred and HeLa cell nuclei could be recognized inside the tobacco cells. The interkingdom fusion of cells was confirmed by the detection of radioactively labeled HeLa cell nuclei within the tobacco protoplast after mixing. A recorded instance of the observed reproduction of an HeLa nucleus within a tobacco cell several days after fusion indicated that such heterokaryons might be maintained in a viable state. If this could be achieved with reproducible consistency, many new avenues of research would be opened, including the possibility of using plant cells in the study of human genetics. (*See also* GARDENING.)

(PETER L. WEBSTER)

[321.B.6.b.ii; 338.B.1.c; 341.A.3.a]

MOLECULAR BIOLOGY

Biochemistry. Avoiding danger and seeking nutrition are universal necessities among motile organisms, be they as complex as man or extremely primitive. Consider the fascinating behaviour of a suspension of the common aerobic colon bacillus, *Escherichia coli,* on a microscope slide and under a glass coverslip. Bacterial metabolism soon exhausts the dissolved oxygen; the only way more can enter between the slide and the coverslip is by diffusion from the edges, where the liquid is exposed to air. Eventually the bacteria congregate along the edges, where the concentration of dissolved oxygen is highest. Just as these organisms can sense and move toward oxygen, so can they respond to certain sugars and amino acids. In contrast, high concentrations of such substances as alcohols, acids, or indoles repel them. These responses are called chemotaxis—positive when the movement is toward an attractant and negative when it is away from a repellant.

How can an organism as apparently unsophisticated as *E. coli* sense attractants or repellants and having done so give the response appropriate to each? Given its minuscule dimensions, how can it detect a gradient of concentration? Moreover, how can the bacterium control the movement of its flagella, the threadlike appendages arising on its cell surface, to propel itself correctly up or down this gradient? Although complete answers were not available in 1976, some of the fundamental aspects of bacterial chemotaxis were clarified.

Observation of a single bacterium as it swims in the absence of any gradient revealed that its movement alternates between runs and tumbles. It swims in a straight line for a few seconds and then gyrates briefly before gliding off again in some random direction. It was discovered that when this cell swims up a gradient of attractant it tumbles less frequently, thereby lessening the likelihood of a change in direction. Conversely, moving down an attractant gradient elicits more frequent tumbling, inhibiting progress in that direction. In the case of a gradient of repellant the opposite responses are given. Thus, this behaviour has the net effect of favouring movement in the appropriate direction, whether it be toward food or away from danger.

How does the bacterium know which direction is up the gradient and which is down? Simultaneous comparison of the concentrations at its anterior and posterior ends would not be feasible because over such a small distance the difference in concentration would be undetectable. It must be that the bacterium somehow remembers a concentration it experiences at least until it has moved to a point sufficiently distant for a difference in concentration to be apparent. In cleverly conceived experiments D. E. Koshland, Jr., and co-workers at the University of California, Berkeley, demonstrated that the bacterium indeed can remember a concentration experienced in the past, an ability called sensing of temporal gradients. To understand how such a memory is possible, suppose the existence of a substance, called TI, that inhibits tumbling. Further suppose that TI is produced in a reaction that is rapidly accelerated by an attractant and that TI is eliminated by a second reaction that is only slowly accelerated by the attractant. During movement up a gradient, the TI production reaction would speed up quickly in response to the rising concentration of the attractant, but the rate of the reaction that eliminates TI would increase more slowly. This lag in the response of the TI elimination reaction is the memory factor; it allows the concentration of the tumble inhibitor to rise, thereby favouring linear swimming. For a bacterium moving down an attractant gradient, the ratio of TI production to TI elimination would diminish and tumbling would be favoured. It was shown that the memory of attractant concentration lasts as long as five minutes. For gradients of repellants, one can presume inhibition, rather than acceleration, of the reactions that make and destroy the tumble inhibitor.

What is the nature of the sensory mechanism by which the bacterium can detect substances? Julius Adler at the University of Wisconsin discovered the existence of proteins between the cell wall and the cell membrane that can bind specific attractants and repellants. He showed that when a mutant bacterium was produced that had a defect in one of these binding proteins, it lost sensitivity to the relevant compound. At least 20 proteins, each serving as a chemosensor for a particular compound, were found in *E. coli.* Many of these were isolated and studied, but the manner in which they signal the flagellum that they have bound their relevant compound remained unknown.

(IRWIN FRIDOVICH)

[333.B.1.b.iii; 341.A.2.b]

Biophysics. By 1976 most cancers were believed to be induced by environmental agents. This conclusion was based essentially on three different kinds of evidence. First, some chemicals encountered in particular occupations were known to produce specific neoplasms. Second, according to recent surveys, frequencies of occurrence for many different kinds of cancer were found to vary significantly with location of human populations, and higher rates of incidence of certain cancers were correlated with particular geographical regions or with proximity to manufacturing centres. Third, many industrial chemicals were known to damage DNA, and further evidence indicated that such damage might be potentially carcinogenic.

Until the mid-1970s progress in identification of carcinogens had been slow, due mainly to the difficulties in screening chemicals for potential carcinogenicity. Ideally, for many environmental chemicals the most direct method would be to base identification upon human population studies. Most cancer frequencies, however, were too low for practical epidemiological analysis. In addition, cancer frequencies did not necessarily relate to the patient's present location but might depend upon a location during exposure many years earlier. Furthermore, most carcinogens were known to induce not one but a variety of common cancers, so population studies alone would not identify particular carcinogenic agents. The alternative approach of testing in laboratory animals, while feasible, was both laborious and expensive, usually requiring several years and about $100,000 per compound. These difficulties led Bruce Ames and his colleagues at the University of California, Berkeley, to develop a rapid, sensitive, and inexpensive bacterial testing system, which subsequently was adopted by most major carcinogenic research laboratories. Selected strains of the bacterium *Salmonella typhimurium* were grown in the presence of the suspected compound under conditions that allow only mutated bacteria to survive. The frequency of mutated cells was believed to reflect the carcinogenicity of the compound. The range of this test was greatly increased recently by addition of enzyme-producing granular bodies, called microsomes, obtained from liver cells. These structures provided mixed-function oxidases that convert many precarcinogens into their active carcinogenic forms, duplicating a metabolic process that occurs within the body.

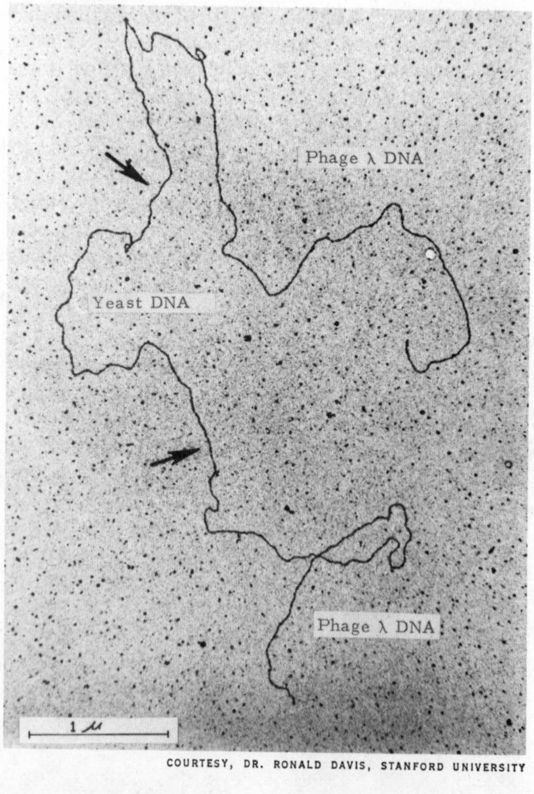

Several bacterial strains were selected for the test to demonstrate the different kinds of DNA damage produced by different classes of carcinogens. Using these strains, Ames's team examined the mutagenicity of a large number of chemical compounds, including 179 known carcinogens and 157 compounds believed to be noncarcinogens. The tester system correctly identified both the carcinogens and the noncarcinogens approximately 90% of the time. This striking correlation between carcinogenicity and mutagenicity supported an older proposal that carcinogens cause cancer by somatic mutation, and therefore that all carcinogens are mutagens.

Another promising assay for carcinogens, developed by H. F. Stich and his colleagues at the University of British Columbia, depended upon estimating the amount of DNA repair that was initiated in repair-proficient cells from destructive action of the carcinogen. Repair was measured by the incorporation of radioactive thymidine into the DNA of cultured human skin fibroblasts that had been prevented from carrying out normal DNA replication. By late 1976 Stich and R. H. C. Han found that each of 50 directly acting carcinogens elicits DNA repair whereas none of 16 noncarcinogens does so.

Although relatively reliable, these simple tests for mutagenicity and for DNA repair were not yet adequate to establish carcinogenicity or its absence for any chemical. Some types of DNA damage might conceivably give rise to mutagenicity but fail to be carcinogenic; alternatively, some carcinogens might test falsely negative. Reliability still requires that each suspected substance be tested for carcinogenesis in mammalian systems. Significant positive results then would indicate a potential hazard for man, although again negative results unfortunately would not rule out possible hazard. Furofuramide is a telling example. This food additive was used extensively in Japan, where it had tested negative in two carcinogenicity trials with mammals. Later, when found to be mutagenic in bacteria, it was retested and shown to produce cancerous tumours in fetal and young mice, and was banned. The problem of false negatives was, of course, most serious at the level of mammalian tests, and usually arose from the time and expense required to establish reliable results in mammals. Clearly neither mammalian tests nor rapid tester systems alone were adequate. The commonly suggested solution was to use rapid tests to detect potential carcinogens, and then to examine the suspected agents in mammals.

(H. E. KUBITSCHEK)

[424.B.1.a]

Phage λ DNA

Yeast DNA

Phage λ DNA

1 μ

COURTESY, DR. RONALD DAVIS, STANFORD UNIVERSITY

Can genes transferred from a higher organism into a lower one still function? Yes, say some scientists. They introduced genetic DNA from bakers' yeast into the chromosome of the bacterium Escherichia coli. As a carrier they used a bacterial virus called phage lambda. Photo shows the hybrid molecule that did the carrying. Arrows indicate joints.

Genetics. Among the most notable events in genetics in recent years has been the development of techniques to overcome the natural barriers to genetic exchange. The potentially dangerous aspects of this new technology, the result of recombinant DNA research, was recognized early and in July 1973 led a group of prominent scientists to issue an unprecedented warning against uncontrolled experiments. A report from a committee of the U.S. National Academy of Sciences, released in mid-1974, called for a moratorium on further recombinant DNA research until guidelines for its conduct could be formed, and prompted the National Institutes of Health (NIH) to organize a Recombinant Advisory Committee. Following open discussion and considerable input from the scientific community, the committee set to work to develop detailed and complete guidelines, which were published in final form on June 23, 1976.

The potential uses of recombinant DNA research can be assigned to two broad categories. First, it allows scientists to produce working amounts of one small DNA segment of an organism's total genetic makeup in purified form by attaching the DNA segment to the DNA of a vector (*i.e.*, a plasmid or virus that is capable of infection and self-replication in a host cell) and then isolating that segment in quantity from a cloned population of the host cell. Gene purification can lead to further understanding of the structure and function for that gene. Second, together with the knowledge and tools from microbial and molecular genetics, the ability to transplant genes—especially from complex organisms to simpler microorganisms—makes possible the manipulation and development of rapidly reproducing biological "factories" from which such important chemicals as antibiotics, hormones, and enzymes might be extracted abundantly and economically. Concern over this kind of experimentation arose when it grew apparent that microbes with certain transplanted genes could prove hazardous to man or to other forms of life. For example, given genetic capabilities it would not naturally possess, a normally innocuous bacterium might be transformed into a highly infectious and antibiotic-resistant pathogen. Hence, it became necessary to formulate precautionary guidelines that would chart a safe course for future research.

The NIH guidelines subdivided experiments into two categories, permissible and nonpermissible. Experiments not permitted were those in which the risk was considered too great and the level of available containment insufficient. Listed among experiments of this type was the transfer of drug resistance from one organism to another, if that drug was used therapeutically to control the recipient organism. Cloning of DNA from pathogenic organisms or oncogenic viruses or from cells infected with these agents was also prohibited, as was cloning of DNA from organisms that produce toxins or venoms. The deliberate release into the environment of any organism containing recombinant DNA likewise was prohibited although this ban could be lifted in the future for particular organisms shown to be both harmless and beneficial.

Experiments that were permitted were to be conducted under conditions that matched containment with potential risk. Containment methods are of two kinds, physical and biological. Physical containment involves the use of techniques, laboratory practice and design, and special equipment to keep the microbe carrying recombinant DNA within defined and controlled territories. The object of biological containment is to develop and employ a host organism that is incapable of survival outside controlled laboratory conditions. A major effort to construct such a host was made by Roy Curtiss III and his colleagues of the University of Alabama Medical Center at Birmingham who combined a number of mutations into the intestinal bacterium *Escherichia coli* K12 that made it unable to survive in the outside environment.

Adherence to the guidelines, though basically voluntary, was more than a moral or ethical compunction for those scientists whose research was supported by

BROOKHAVEN NATIONAL LABORATORY

Animal or vegetable? Researchers have combined animal cells with plant cells to form the first interkingdom protoplasts. Photo shows large cell nuclei from a tumour together with small cell nuclei from tobacco.

NIH; anyone in that category who did not adhere to the guidelines would not receive financial support for research. Ready acceptance of these guidelines by all federal agencies was expected to widen the scope of coverage to the national laboratories and other federally supported researchers including those working in universities and nationally sponsored laboratories. In June a meeting was held between NIH officials and the Pharmaceutical Manufacturers Association to discuss the applicability of the proposed guidelines to industrial research. Willingness of the editors of scientific journals to require submitted papers to include a full description of the containment used to accomplish the work was making guideline acceptance a necessity for publication in the open literature.

Pursuing a line of investigation that shared some of the goals of DNA recombinant research, Nobel laureate Har Gobind Khorana (*see* BIOGRAPHY) and his associates at the Massachusetts Institute of Technology announced achievement of the first completely chemical synthesis of a fully functional bacterial gene. In an effort that spanned nearly ten years and enlisted the cooperation of 24 postdoctoral fellows, Khorana's team approached their monumental problem by first chemically synthesizing several dozen short double-stranded chains of nucleotides from commercially available starting materials; these were then joined with appropriate enzymes to complete the molecule, which measured 207 nucleotides in overall length and coded for tyrosine transfer RNA in *E. coli.* Proof that the gene worked was obtained by inserting it into a genetically defective strain of bacterial virus that depended for its survival on the functionality of the gene. The significance of Khorana's method of synthesis was that it would allow deliberate changes in genes to be made at will and observed in vivo, thus revealing how the genetic structure of an organism affects its form. Using this knowledge it might be possible to ascertain the genetic causes of such diseases as cancer and to tailor synthetic genes to code for desired biological products. (JAMES C. COPELAND)

See also Earth Sciences; Environment.

[321.B.5; 339.C.2.b]

ENCYCLOPÆDIA BRITANNICA FILMS. *The Ears and Hearing* (2nd ed., 1969); *Muscle: Dynamics of Contraction* (1969); *The Origin of Life: Chemical Evolution* (1969); *Radioisotopes: Tools of Discovery* (1969); *Theories on the Origin of Life* (1969); *The Nerve Impulse* (1971); *Seed Dispersal* (3rd ed., 1971); *The World of Up Close* (1971); *How Do They Move?* (1971); *Some Friendly Insects* (1971); *Investigating Hibernation* (1972); *A Bird of Prey—The Red-Tailed Hawk* (1972); *The Cactus: Profile of a Plant* (1973); *Nematode* (1973); *The Mayfly: Ecology of an Aquatic Insect* (1973); *Insect Life Cycle (The Periodical Cicada)* (2nd ed., 1975); *Migration: Flight for Survival* (1976).

Liquors, Alcoholic: *see* Drug Abuse; Industrial Review

Literature

The 1976 Nobel Prize for Literature was awarded to Saul Bellow, a novelist whose passionate fluency had been so widely admired for a decade or more that the result came almost as a surprise in this contest in which victory often seems to go to darker horses. Certainly no novelist since Dos Passos had wrestled with language more mightily to register the complexity of modern consciousness, and none represented more centrally that toughly intelligent urban Jewish sensibility that had dominated American cultural life in the postwar decades. (*See* NOBEL PRIZES.)

Bellow produced no fiction in 1976, but some of his reflections in *To Jerusalem and Back,* a one-man commission of inquiry into the clouded future of the state of Israel, gave clear form to anxieties that seemed widely shared during the year among writers, many of whom, like Bellow, could not avoid preoccupation with "the merciless problems—the butcher problems—of politics." Foremost was a dawning realization that they had been guilty of a childlike faith in the power of rationality in the conduct of affairs. Having reported sensible-sounding prognostications in Jerusalem from a group of writers, diplomats, and scholars, Bellow remarks: "Such intelligent discussion hasn't always been wrong. What is wrong with it is that the discussants invariably impart their own intelligence to what they are discussing. Later, historical studies show that what actually happened was devoid of anything like such intelligence. . . . History and politics are not at all like the notions developed by intelligent, well-informed people." The other, related concern was with what seemed to be a general attenuation of the sense of history, which in turn led to what Bertrand Russell once called the problem of not being able "to take an interest in anything after one's own death"—and this at a time when Aleksandr Solzhenitsyn was pointing to the brink of "an upheaval similar to that which marked the transition from the Middle Ages to the Renaissance."

The result of these dwindling perspectives, discussed in many articles and reviews in Britain and the United States particularly, was a retreat into solipsism and narcissism which showed up in poetry as a low-spirited minimalism, in fiction as a growing preoccupation with fantasy, in the "raiding" of history to produce collages of personal myth, and in still grosser forms of brutality and eroticism in the more commercial kinds of science fiction and Western ("two genres," as Gore Vidal remarked, "that appear to reflect the night mind of the race").

Novelist Saul Bellow, who won the Nobel Prize for Literature in 1976, wrote from an urban Jewish sensibility central in American cultural life.

NANCY CRAMPTON

None of these evidences of what was being described commonly and complacently as "the New Decadence" would have come as a surprise to Solzhenitsyn who, before he moved from Switzerland to the U.S. in 1976, excoriated the spiritual weakness of Western civilization in terms almost harsher than those he had customarily used in dealing with the Soviet society from which he was expelled in 1974. These criticisms, leveled first at Britain, were made in two broadcasts for the BBC in March, but their echoes rumbled on ominously throughout the year. Octavio Paz, the Mexican poet and philosopher (who was obliged by political pressure to resign from the editorship of *Plural,* the most influential intellectual review in Latin America), suggested that "Solzhenitsyn's is not so much a style as a conscience." But *Lenin in Zurich,* published in 1976, contained some of his most striking pages since *The First Circle* and was admired for more than its moral tone. (See *Expatriate Russian Literature,* below.)

There were significant developments in the posthumous reputation of another famous exile of Zürich. The long-awaited second German translation of James Joyce's *Ulysses* appeared and was generally reckoned to be an improvement. A contract was also signed for its publication in East Germany, where Joyce had long been deplored as one of the more pernicious of bourgeois formalists. The Soviet Union did not go so far, but the appearance there of the first translation of *A Portrait of the Artist as a Young Man* was felt to be an advance. Visitors noted a new reading boom in the Soviet Union, where considerably more foreign literature in translation was made available during the year (including, from English, four novels of Iris Murdoch, two of Evelyn Waugh). It was also observed, however, that many of the translations included elements of political and sexual censorship. (Students of comparative censorship thought Soviet censors marginally more prudish than their South African counterparts.) Two studies were made of such suppressions in the Soviet edition of Heinrich Böll's *Gruppenbild mit Dame.* Konstantin Bogatyrev, the Russian translator of Rainer Maria Rilke and part author of one of these analyses, was brutally beaten up outside his Moscow apartment on April 26, shortly after his study appeared in a U.S. academic review; he died in hospital some weeks later without regaining consciousness.

ENGLISH

United Kingdom. An extravagant amount of attention was devoted to nostalgia for yesterday's chic. In 1975 the completion of Anthony Powell's novel sequence *A Dance to the Music of Time* was rightly celebrated. But in 1976 too much time and space, surely, was allotted to gossipy review of *Infants of the Spring,* the bumbling first volume of Powell's autobiography, to the prolix alcoholic fugues of Evelyn Waugh's diaries, and to other dandified, elderly memoirs such as Christopher Hollis' *Oxford in the Twenties* and Peter Quennell's *The Marble Foot.*

At times the whole scene took on the aspect of parody, as when the *Times Literary Supplement* (TLS) gave the longest review of the year to a biography of Noel Coward by his valet; or when the same reviewer (Alastair Forbes) was rebuked for a particularly juicy account of Cyril Connolly's death bed levees by

Evelyn Waugh's novelist son Auberon, appearing in the lists as Connolly's biographer (and later, in *The Spectator,* as reviewer of his father's diaries—Waugh on Waugh). So late in the day another kind of attention to this milieu and its writers might have been more appropriate, and more interesting. For example, Alastair Forbes in another of his TLS reviews remarked that "Like most of his Oxford contemporaries, Waugh was almost exclusively homosexual while at the university." But even by 1976 no coherent study had been published of the effect on the English sensibility of this powerful homosexual strain from Froude through Strachey, Forster, and the Oxbridge-Bloomsbury line to the English writers of the 1930s and beyond.

FICTION. In the novel what seemed most lacking was not seriousness but new sources of imaginative vitality. The point was made in a review by Anthony Burgess of Robert Nye's fictional autobiography of *Falstaff,* one of the few new works that showed something of the verbal energy and inventiveness of the best American contemporaries and which secured for Nye *The Guardian*'s 1976 fiction prize. "In choosing Falstaff as hero," wrote Burgess from his tax exile in Monaco, "Nye is registering a protest not only against the bland nullity of the contemporary British novel but against the dull society that begets it."

When the smoke from these critical barrages had cleared, it could be observed, of course, that much good writing had gone on as before; that established and gifted novelists like Patrick White, Iris Murdoch, Muriel Spark, and, from a later generation, William Trevor and Beryl Bainbridge, had all published highly accomplished work. But there was not much new and wonderful to report, and it was hardly surprising that at the end of a gloomy year the books that were still being read and talked about with most pleasure and gratitude were those that came from more vigorous phases of English history and sensibility—the two volumes of Byron's vivid and bloody-minded *Letters,* for example, and the ninth and final volume of the marvelous unexpurgated modern edition of *The Diary of Samuel Pepys,* that "happy extrovert, happy egoist," wrote Geoffrey Grigson in a parting salute, "whose troubles blow away like petals from a cherry tree."

Some of the most vigorously imaged fiction came once more from writers of the Commonwealth countries, perhaps less cramped psychologically than their British cousins during the last decade or so. *A Fringe of Leaves* by Patrick White, the 1973 Nobel Prize winner, set on the wilder shores of early 19th-century Australia, records the liberation of a repressed and passionate woman into her own nature after shipwreck in the storm that kills her English husband. As in almost all his work, the writing sometimes thickened and curdled with the heat of his vision, but this novel ranked not far below *Voss* and *The Solid Mandala.*

Season in Purgatory, by Patrick White's younger compatriot Thomas Keneally (*see* BIOGRAPHY), was another of his versions of episodes from more recent history, a wartime partisan hospital off the Adriatic coast this time, formidably present, but a shade enthusiastic with the gore and gallantry. The scenes from Indian family life in the stories *How I Became a Holy Mother* by Ruth Prawer Jhabvala (*see* BIOGRAPHY) were no less present, but her art was far removed from Keneally's in its cool intimacy and tact.

Two of the stranger fictions of the year came from Kingsley Amis and Muriel Spark, though strangeness from Miss Spark was no great surprise. In fact, *The Takeover,* though rum enough, was longer and slightly less enigmatic than the novellas of recent years. Set in a Spark-lit Italy, it brought a group of rich cosmopolitans to the realization that, as Solzhenitsyn might have said, they were on the brink of "the Dark Ages II"; or rather (as the Communist successes in the 1975 elections indicated) about to experience "a change in the meaning of money and property"—this daylight meaning being cunningly complicated with variations on the Diana myth. Its message, thought one reviewer, was that the takers-over can always be taken over. In *The Alteration* Kingsley Amis imagines an England in our time under Roman rule yet, a comprehensive fantasy, with darkly comic roles for A. J. Ayer, Sartre, and sundry British politicos, and a plain blunt Yorkshire pope whose new basilica is adorned with an Ecce Homo by David Hockney. It turned, hilariously at first, savagely in the end, on the proposed castration of a silver-throated choirboy, and it divided the reviewers more sharply than most of the things they looked at during the autumn.

KENNETH SAUNDERS—CAMERA PRESS

Ruth Prawer Jhabvala, a Polish-born author living in India and writing in English, whose collection of stories, "How I Became a Holy Mother," appeared in 1976.

Grisly conclusions were also reached in *Henry and Cato,* another of those elaborately decorated metaphysical melodramas of Iris Murdoch's which left most critics drunk with the joys of explication and no doubt wondering furiously, in the hangover of publication day, just what her dazzling fluency would amount to in the literary history books. The question hardly arose with Jean Rhys, whose *Sleep It Off Lady* was a matched set of very short stories marking out the stations of a woman's life from the bright days of a Caribbean childhood to loneliness and death under gray English skies a world and most of a century later. As usual, she sounded, this woman, uncomfortably like Jean Rhys, a writer who disarms criticism to the point of embarrassment, and is loved, not graded, for her candour, her courage, and a talent that seems as unwilled and vulnerable as beauty in a child. Beryl Bainbridge, for all their differences in generation and milieux, had something of the same disturbing personality, the omnivorous eye of a too-experienced child. In *A Quiet Life* she turned it once more on the world whose detail she had so lovingly collected, exploring the darker emotional corners of cramped lower middle-class family life in the flatlands of East Lancashire in the years just after World War II.

The dourness and violence of some of David Storey's novels had made reviewers reach for their Lawrence more than once, but the ambitious scale and descriptive power (not merely the pit-village setting, the miner father, and the alienated clever son) made *Saville*—for which Storey was awarded the year's Booker Prize—a novel that one could sensibly look at in the light of *Sons and Lovers. The Survivors,* the last book of Simon Raven's multinovel *Alms for Oblivion,* left its upper-crust cast stranded in Venice (the "Titanic" of our times, perhaps), and left even fans of Raven's clever caddishness feeling a little let down.

Fantasy was not quoted so highly on the London market as in New York, but there were three interesting new enterprises. Martin Bax's *The Hospital Ship,* which tours the world picking up casualties from a psychic epidemic at every port, was built largely as a collage of catastrophic items from improbably diverse printed sources. There was more craft and imagination in Brian Aldiss' *The Malacia Tapestry,* which pictures a whole quasi-Venetian city-state, doomed to eternal stasis and a rather too heavily detailed decor. But the real rushing thing came from the twin fancies of Peter Redgrove and Penelope Shuttle, tapping once more the deep old stream of native English surrealism, which bubbled up brilliantly in *The Glass Cottage,* subtitled "a nautical romance," a Lear-like logging of preoccupations and perceptions on a trip to the U.S.

In *The Children of Dynmouth,* William Trevor, master of the matter-of-fact bizarre, created an alarmingly autonomous adolescent monster, terrorizing younger children in a Dorset seaside town; and *The Doctor's Wife* was another of Brian Moore's remarkable empathizing portraits of a woman caught up from the detailed mess of life by the whoosh of middle-aged love, with a grim backdrop of Belfast's smoking despair. Two older Irish writers, Sean O'Faolain (*Foreign Affairs*) and Liam O'Flaherty (*The Pedlar's Revenge*), published collections of characteristic short stories, as did one of the best English practitioners, Francis King (*Hard Feelings*), and the novelist and critic Malcolm Bradbury (*Who Do You Think You Are?*).

Paul Theroux's *The Family Arsenal* was an excellent, coolly observed entertainment from the London of art thefts and bomb factories in seedy flats, almost in the Graham Greene class. The fashionable entertainment of the autumn, however, was *The Death of the King's Canary,* a spoof detective story about the murder of the poet laureate, jointly authored in 1940 by Dylan Thomas and John Davenport (writing alternate chapters stuffed with the characters of such poets of the time as Auden, Day Lewis, and George Barker). A quaint corpse, unlikely to stay revived for long. The most likely debut was Caroline Blackwood's claustrophobic little novel *The Stepdaughter,* penned, in every way, in a posh New York apartment where the narrator, abandoned by her husband, writes letters in her head all day long, refracting her resentment and self-hatred onto her ugly, equally rejected stepdaughter and the pretty, baffled French au pair girl who are cooped up with her deadly inertia.

LETTERS, LIVES. Three daunting collections of writers' letters spanned the year, the most daunting, without doubt, being Sylvia Plath's *Letters Home*—more than 600 of them written weekly over 13 years, mostly to her mother. What was disturbing was the apparently unbridgeable distance between the persona revealed here—the chattery bright all-American Smith girl, wife and mother—and the fierce author of the poems.

Richard Ellmann's *Selected Letters of James Joyce,* which appeared in the same week in April, would have disturbed some readers more, including as they did the 60-odd previously unpublished and violently erotic letters to his wife Norah written when they were apart for a period in 1909. "Less love letters than highly effective masturbatory devices," Anthony Burgess suggested, in which Joyce outblooms Bloom in his masochism, fetishism, and infantilism. The second volume of Virginia Woolf's letters, *The Question of Things Happening,* covered her 30s (the years in which she wrote her first three novels, was twice mad, and helped her husband to found the Hogarth Press), and underlined once more her total devotion to literature and to the circle of her friends; a devotion which, in the latter case, did not exclude many pages of fine feline malice. Another Bloomsbury relic was *Ottoline,* a biography of Lady Ottoline Morell by Sandra Jobson Darroch, which showed her sympathetically, as the victim of the talented people she admired or loved, and included memorable pictures of her affair with Bertrand Russell.

The richest lives to appear were surely *The Autobiography of Arthur Ransome* and Hugh Trevor-Roper's biography of that most cunning of all Old China hands, Sir Edmund Backhouse (*A Hidden Life*). Ransome, the author of *Swallows and Amazons* and other beloved children's books of the 1930s, appeared in his autobiography in quite other roles as a Bohemian friend of the Georgian poets who helped Strindberg's daughter to run away from home, reported the Russian Revolution for the *Manchester Guardian,* and married Trotsky's secretary. If that seemed rich, Sir Edmund Backhouse's career was strange beyond belief. Known previously only as a scholar of Chinese history who left a valuable collection to the Bodleian Library, he emerged through study of a manuscript "autobiography" not so much a new Corvo as a liar who outbid Baron Munchhausen himself.

There was a good study of *The Auden Generation* by Samuel Hynes. Other useful critical work appeared in John Bayley's *The Uses of Division;* in *Keywords,* in which Raymond Williams greatly expanded the set of definitions out of which his *Culture and Society* grew; and in F. R. Leavis' *Thought, Words and Creativity.* George D. Painter, the foremost English Proust scholar, wrote what would clearly remain the definitive account of the life and work of Britain's founding master printer, *William Caxton.*

Among writers who died during the year were Richard Hughes (*A High Wind in Jamaica*), Elizabeth Taylor (whose last novel, *Blaming,* was published posthumously), William Sansom, underestimated in the last decade or so, and Colin MacInnes, whose novels and essays said more (and sooner) than any other writer's about the social changes that were pushing their way like fireweed through the shabbiness of postwar Britain in the 1950s and early 1960s. (*See* OBITUARIES.)

(W. L. WEBB)

POETRY. If 1976 failed to produce any work of major significance either by a well-known poet or by one of the numerous young poets hoping to take the literary world by storm, it was by no means an unexciting year for those interested in poetry. It was marked early on by the award to Philip Larkin (*see* BIOGRAPHY) by the FVS Foundation of Hamburg, West Germany, of its Shakespeare Prize for 1976, for outstanding Anglo-Saxon contributions to European culture.

Throughout the period, controversies of one kind or another, of varying intensity depending upon the personal involvement of the participants, engaged the attention of the poetry-reading (and poetry-writing) sections of the public—controversies about the relative merits of volumes such as Ted Hughes's *Season Songs* or Thom Gunn's *Jack Straw's Castle,* about the function and operation of the Arts Council, or arising from the widely publicized struggle for power within the Poetry Society between opposing groups of "activists" and "centrists," both of whom held support meetings and issued manifestos. There was plenty of diversity in style, technique, and use of language in the work placed before readers, a few interesting experiments, and, despite the increasing gravity of the economic situation, an extraordinary number of books and booklets published.

Among the best of an impressive array of first collections were *Catacomb Suburb* by Alastair Fowler, *Separations* by Tony Flynn, *Black and Sepia* by Eleanor Murray, *The Noise of the Fields* by Hugh Maxton, *Bridging Loans* by Rodney Pybus, the stark *Sky Made of Stone* by Paul Yates, dealing with the realities of the conflict in Northern Ireland, and *Owl Shadows* and *Whispering Stone,* parallel booklets by the 14-year-old Zoë Brooks. In *Brass Rubbings* by David Day most of the poems were centred upon the author's reflections and activities while engaged upon the absorbing task of hunting down brasses and taking rubbings in ancient churches situated in some of the most inaccessible parts of the country. For *The Horwich Hennets,* Edmond Leo Wright invented an entirely new form—the "hennet," a 12-line hendecasyllabic verse, rhyming *abacbcde deff*—to delineate his childhood experiences.

Season Songs by Ted Hughes, if originally intended for children, made a powerful impact upon adults, and not always a favourable one. Divided into four sections corresponding to the cyclical phases of the year, and therefore emphasizing the natural rotation of birth, animation, and death, against a rural background, this volume was reminiscent of Hughes's earliest poetry in its sharpness of image and clarity of observation. His split chestnut "opens an African eye," his spring buds "burst in tatters—like firework stubs"—exhilarating after the macabre antics of *Crow!* In *Jack Straw's Castle,* on the other hand, the tough and assured Thom Gunn of former times seemed suddenly to have developed a surprising vulnerability, and assumed a more questioning, if uncertain, approach to his themes while exploring the darkest dungeons of his castle.

Some unusual collected editions appeared during the year. In addition to the *Complete Poems of Hugh MacDiarmid* and the *Collected Poems of W. H. Auden* (edited by Edward Mendelson), readers had the choice of *The Best of Adrian Henri, Last Poems* by Luke Parsons, *Selected Poems* by Glyn Jones, and the *Collected Poems* of Kenneth Allott, Elizabeth Daryush, Humphrey John Moore, and Peter Levi. Anthologies that contributed to the general liveliness of the scene were *Here and Human* edited by F. E. S. Finn, *Scottish Love Poems* edited by Antonia Fraser, *Poetry Dimension Annual 4* edited by Dannie Abse,

WILSON S. GROAT

English poet Alastair Fowler published an impressive book of verse in 1976, "Catacomb Suburb."

and the PEN anthology *New Poems 1976/77* edited by Howard Sergeant.

Other volumes deserving mention were *The Bearing Beast* by Patric Dickinson, *Another Full Moon* by Ruth Fainlight, *Sea Grapes* by the West Indian Derek Walcott, *Vanishing Trick* by Brian Patten, *Winterfold* by George Mackay Brown, *The Little Timekeeper* by Jon Silkin, *A View of the North* by David Wright, and, published posthumously, *The First Known* by Frances Bellerby.

(HOWARD SERGEANT)

United States. FICTION. American fiction in 1976 continued to move from an embattled existential ethos toward a cool, mock-structuralist outlook. It tended still further away from recognizable literary forms to elusive and intricate patterns vanishing in their own intricacies. Yet fiction also acknowledged the enormous diversity of American culture, its stubborn facts and fluid fantasies, its outer conformity and violence within. With a radical innocence, the fictional hero(ine) still sought the sources of love and of freedom, the sources of being and meaning. The search for love sometimes brought him (her) to the edge of metaphysical experience; the search for freedom sometimes immersed the hero in the destructive element—crime, anarchy, self-annihilation, the alienated's way of death.

The two quests, starting from different points, often met in the figure of the rebel-victim, the holy schlemiel, eternally the outsider, who incarnated in American literature the ancient dialectic of the primary "Yes" and the everlasting "No." Now and then, the character of the hero and the nature of his quest appeared to change, though perhaps only superficially. Still the scapegoat redeemer, still the misfit hero, he became more knowing, campy, vaudevillian, a player king in the lands of unreality. Yet despite the unreality of his world, despite the chaos of his own motives, his perduring hope remained classic: the renewal of life through supreme fictions of the mind.

Slapstick: Or Lonesome No More, by magus of fantasy Kurt Vonnegut, was Vonnegut as you knew him or loved him, or didn't, with the reductivist simplicities and more than faintly identifiable referrals and the one-pea-in-a-peapod story.

Richard Brautigan's *Sombrero Fallout,* subtitled "A Japanese Novel," is a word play about an American humorist, "dashing tears forth" after his pretty Japanese lover of two years, a psychiatrist, leaves him and he sits alone—tearing up pieces of paper and dropping them in a wastebasket where they look like Japanese origami turning into hamburgers and tuna sandwiches—plotting sentimental hara-kiri. In *Doctor Rat* William Kotzwinkle is the imaginative impresario of the might-almost-be-true, spinning a new fable on cyclometered wheels in the laboratory of Doctor Rat, friend to man and foe to all other species—and filled with happy distractions such as the whale, useful for perfume and the occasional girdle, or the poor leader of the elephants whose tusks never descended.

Two long-standing avant-garde cult figures proffered fugal works: In *Travesty* by experimentalist John Hawkes, we are moving toward and through horror with a madman-narrator, locked up with the sealed-off acceleration of his mania, incapable of interrupting or deflecting the suave nihilism of his resolve to crash his car containing his daughter and his wife's lover into a particularly thick wall. A disturbing novel testifying to those faint and sinister qualities of the artistic mind that no writer knows better how to exploit than Hawkes; and Edward Dahlberg scored with *The Olive of Minerva or The Comedy of a Cuckold,* the theme being that "grievous are all earth-born men with puissant testicles."

In the canon of Women's Movement fiction, seashells of pink kink and pearls of transsexual wisdom pervaded Lois Gould's *Sea-Change,* the story of Jessie Waterman (a "seasick Emily Brontë") who starts to fantasize about a Black Gunman she calls B. G. and then goes off to a remote island. After storms, death games, and lesbian interludes, Jessie's role reversal is complete when she assumes the identity of B. G. and disappears with her children. *Kinflicks,* a novel by Lisa Alther, is recalled by Ginny Hull Babcock between her vigils at the hospital for her spine-stiffening mother who is now dying; she remembers all those kinflicks or home movies which were her mother's record of all the family firsts—the first tooth, the first smile. Ginny's tone-deafening equivalents: her time at Hullsport High as a flag swinger, her first romance, failed sex and sex redivivus, marriage, motherhood, and divorce. On the comic side, Gail Parent offered *David Meyer Is a Mother,* about male submission to women's liberation as one David Meyer from Long Island, reared as a superior boychik with paternal send-offs on *schtupping,* becomes a victim of the sexual revolution at 32. His personhood and puissance destroyed, he falls for a girl who renews him, only to learn her name months later when she writes a *Playboy* article.

More traditionally, the John Updike constants continued to scratch up the personable surfaces in *Marry Me*—namely, sexuality versus that Higher Vision, "the idea of God lending a roundness of significance." The lack of a vaulting significance materially and immaterially dooms the love affair between Jerry, a dimly successful cartoonist afraid of death, and Sally, a shiny and seductive Unitarian. And blue blood ran colder than ever in *The Winthrop Covenant* by Louis Auchincloss, following a pride of Winthrops from early Puritan times to the present-day "world falling apart," but not theirs—granted a natural immunity through genealogical and social distinction.

Fantasist Kurt Vonnegut published "Slapstick: Or Lonesome No More" in 1976. For one reader it was "Vonnegut as you knew him."

Another family opus was Helen Yglesias' *Family Feeling,* a work of authentic imagination and ubiquitous vitality. Moving backward and forward through the years, when the Goddards (from Poland to Miami) grew up in relative accord—seven children under a proverbial Jewish mother—they all come together at her death, and later Papa's, in the knowledge that "we're all finished as a family. We'll meet at funerals."

Two brilliant first novels made their appearance: *Speedboat* by Renata Adler, essentially a New York collage of bits and pieces—many of them the verbal equivalent of found objects—shaped for us by the sensibility of a highly intelligent, vulnerable woman in her mid-30s—whose name we barely know. A work of strong emotional impact, but one that derives more from a painfully exact transcription of the life many of us lead than from the creation of a powerfully imagined fictional world; and Judith Guest's extraordinary *Ordinary People,* the story of a real family, or what's left of it. Responsible and guilty for the death of a brother in a boating accident, Conrad returns home (after hospitalization and a suicide attempt) to an indifferent mother and protective father, attempting to deal with everyone's unease, particularly his own—until someone he knew in the hospital kills herself, shattering his (and the reader's) precarious stability.

Large in length and ambition, Vance Bourjaily's *Now Playing at Canterbury* used Chaucerian multiple tales to bring to life a group of people staging a new American opera at a Midwest university; preparations for the production are repeatedly interrupted as one by one they tell their stories out of their own pasts—tales ranging from realism to folk comedy to Gothic horror. *The Auctioneer,* Joan Samson's almost-might-be-true horror story, is grounded in the rural life of a small New Hampshire village where things are just like they used to be until the arrival of Perly Dunsmore, the auctioneer, who pesters the natives for wheels in the woodshed or quilts in the attic.

After the sale of a new kind of livestock, the town's children, and much sustained suspense, the final town meeting waits for the gavel of justice. Magnolia-scented Gothicisms abounded in Southern novelist James Purdy's *In a Shallow Grave,* a four-person vehicle moving swiftly from disabled war vet Garnet Montrose's "romance" with a widow, and the development of a languid boy-boy-girl triangle, to the table-turning conquest of the lady.

In 1976 the novel also came into its own as a medium for highly topical, political, and behavioural communication. Once again as in *Burr* (1973), Gore Vidal centred on politics as the manifestation and shaper of American identity. In *1876: A Novel,* a toy for the Bicentennial set in the Centennial year, Vidal illuminates one of the nation's dark moments, the disputed Tilden-Hayes election along with the centralizing drift of money, power, and sectional interests toward the Capital. Charlie Schuyler is again the journalist-narrator, returned to New York after 37 years in France with his beautiful daughter Emma and some Rip Van Winkle obsessions. In this rich, talky achievement—rarefied *escritoire* to bock-beer blunt—Vidal revolutionizes the genre with a seriousness and a muscle both firm and new. *The Company* was John Ehrlichman's unabashed roman à clef, dealing with pre-Final Days from Monckton/Nixon's election to the bugging of Democratic headquarters; William F. Buckley's *Saving the Queen* offered an entertaining suede-gloved intrigue under not-so-deep CIA cover in the 1950s; and John V. Lindsay's *The Edge* treated a story of a fledgling congressman's experiments with government at the Top, adultery, and other miscellaneous self-fulfillments.

Finally, popular successes were scored by Ira Levin's *The Boys from Brazil,* a post-Nazi nightmare concerning the fate of 94 babies cloned from Hitler's cells; Robert Littell's *The October Circle,* a Realpolitikal thriller about counterrevolution in Bulgaria and Czechoslovakia; *The Gemini Contenders* by Robert Ludlum, another cliff-hanging search for hidden documents bound to overthrow countries, churches, and the faith of faiths; and Leon Uris' *Trinity,* devoted with partisan magnanimity to another popular/unpopular lost cause, the Fenian struggle. Also notable: *The Deep* by Peter Benchley, a treasure hunt without the maxillary crunch of his *Jaws;* and Barbara Howar's sentimentally chic *Making Ends Meet,* which does not laugh all the way through.

Several important short-story collections appeared in 1976. Most remarkable was *Bloodshed* by Cynthia Ozick, where irony and ambiguity often hedged its statements, and its heroes were characters of mixed innocence and sophistication caught between memories of holocausts abroad and anxieties of assimilation at home. Wright Morris' *Real Losses, Imaginary Gains* contained moving pieces exploring the dreads and joys of youth: a bereaved youngster's terrible empathy with the swinging corpse of an animal or young boys' roughhousing in an earthly paradise of brotherhood and peace. *Dream Children* by Gail Godwin presented stories sometimes skimming the frangible surfaces of her *Glass People,* sometimes drifting into the bizarre dimensions of her *Perfectionists;* most interesting were her lives or loves in transit—movable partners, changing patterns, quick dissolves.

The young man whose stance is one of avoidance was symptomatic of many of the stories in Sue Kaufman's *The Master,* though others evoked memories of her most successful books of not-quite-mad housewives and headshrinkers and precarious falling bodies. And finally, take a household name, toss it up against the wall that barricades reality from fantasy—and *voilà:* a Max Apple story. In *The Oranging of America,* with guest stars such as Nixon, Castro, and G. R. Ford, Apple is free not only to develop his themes under adequate cover but also to create, in each of the tales, a man or woman Friday who is realer, richer, and more important than any myth-man.

© THOMAS VICTOR

Alex Haley's "Roots" told of his search into his ancestors' African past. It was a sobering birthday present for America in its bicentennial year.

History, Biography, and Belles Lettres. "The true history of the human race," wrote E. M. Forster, "is the story of human affections. In comparison with it all other histories—even economic history—are false." This maxim took on special meaning in 1976 in two major works of historical reconstruction. An extraordinary wave of critical acclaim greeted Alex Haley's *Roots: The Saga of an American Family,* a feast of research and powerful imagination regarded by many as the Book of the Year and a sobering birthday present for America in its bicentennial year. Haley took the essence of a family story told on summer nights and traced his roots back to Kunta Kinte, an African captured while gathering wood and brought to America in 1767. Haley sensitively reconstructs everyday life in Juffure (Gambia). He verified the genealogy and bare facts using government records, but the search in Africa was more unconventional, taking him to his family's *groit* (oral historian), who recited the complete Kinte history; and the listening villagers shared the significance of the discovery: they had Haley embrace their children—the laying on of hands.

An indelible story handled with strenuous determination was *The World of Our Fathers* by famed critic Irving Howe. "The central promise of Jewish survival," writes Howe, "is a defiance of history; the cost, beyond measure." Perhaps no survival was more moving than that of the Yiddish-speaking Ashkenazim who came to New York City between 1880 and World War I. This long and loving act of homage is examined: the painful journeys from pogrom-racked Eastern Europe to Hamburg or Rotterdam; the dreadful passage to Ellis Island and the dank warrens of the Lower East Side; the transmutation of European socialist ferment into pioneering

GETSUG / ANDERSON

Judith Guest's first novel, "Ordinary People," was an extraordinary success in 1976.

triumphs of unionization. The American opportunity for assimilation called forth a contradictory wealth of responses; but paradoxically, it was these very contradictions that gave American Yiddish culture its outrageous, precarious vitality.

Journalism's most famous partnership produced *The Final Days,* a spectacular piece of reporting by Bob Woodward and Carl Bernstein, whose explosive unveiling maximized its exposure almost at the expense of the drama. Anyone who had been awake knew the worst: Kissinger's contempt for "our meatball President" and his siege with a kneeling, sobbing Nixon the night before resignation; the wire-pulling of Leon Jaworski by Alexander Haig; the bullishness of Ronald Ziegler. In the final two weeks, Nixon is nudged toward resignation through balks, wavers, liquor, and tears.

A more subdued postmortem was *Nightmare: The Underside of the Nixon Years,* J. Anthony Lukas' enormous narrative of the dirty tricks, financial misconduct, subversive efforts, and cover-up attempts conducted by the Nixon forces; but Jonathan Schell's *The Time of Illusion* was an elaborate tour de force on the submerged ideological context of Watergate, centring on that tendentious cliché "credibility." Schell makes clear the kinship of major national policies, over more than a decade, with the thought processes of psychosis.

In the domain of academic history, Lawrence Goodwyn's *Democratic Promise* offered an exhaustive scholarly study of the Populist movement in America, treating it as an inspiring resurgence of the democratic ideal in the midst of Gilded Age centralization; it will doubtless provoke high-decibel debate and remain a basic reference on a period whose contemporary parallel Goodwyn does not fail to underline. Another major work of historical inquiry was Eric Foner's *Tom Paine and Revolutionary America,* wherein one of the purist "ideologues" of the Revolution is shown to be speaking consistently on behalf of an *economic* interest. Paine emerges as the elite stylist and radical cutting edge of American democracy giving voice to a proletariat of men who were rising indeed, but remained in economic competition with the merchant class.

Underscoring the trenchancy of economics in contemporary American life, two important books on capitalism appeared: Michael Harrington's *The Twilight of Capitalism* and Daniel Bell's *The Cultural Contradictions of Capitalism.* Harrington sought to identify "the authentic Marx," thereby rescuing him from misinterpretation, and to demonstrate his relevance to present-day conditions—thus implicitly disproving the contention that capitalism's persistence beyond its allotted span gives the lie to Marx's expectations; while Bell argued a return to "tradition" and a commonsense division of social spheres into economic, political, and cultural. Having gained prominence by announcing "the end of ideology" in the '50s, Bell here defends humane liberalism and traditional capitalism. Barry Commoner was less optimistic in *The Poverty of Power,* revealing that the coming ecological crisis would be the harbinger of a full-blown economic crisis rooted in the fundamental flaws of our institutions. Another challenging approach to an important aspect of capitalism was Stuart Ewen's *Captains of Consciousness,* which argued that mass advertising was both the greatest clouder of class distinctions and the greatest tool of class manipulation—the matrices of a world "commodified" beyond the wildest dreams of 19th-century corporate greed.

Two seminal legal studies were *The Role of the Supreme Court in American Government* by former Watergate prosecutor Archibald Cox, offering the theme that the judiciary power is approaching the limits of its utility for major strategic innovation; and John Noonan's *Persons and Masks of the Law,* arguing the thesis that law will not shed its "masks" until lawyers rethink the relationship of past to present realities so as to focus not on that vague abstraction "the spirit of the law" but on the human persons who have tried to embody worthy and abiding purposes in law. And finally, *The Uses of Enchantment* by famed psychologist Bruno Bettelheim imaginatively explored the essential need of children for fairy tales, because they acknowledge that good and evil are attractive, that struggle is a crucial part of human existence, and that there are advantages to moral behaviour.

The calls upon the imagination and intuition of the year's biographers were as challenging as ever. All the ingredients were there in *Lyndon Johnson and the American Dream,* Doris Kearns's brilliant and sweeping examination of the ebullient, secretive, visionary, cynical, vulgar, princely practitioner of Realpolitik who became America's 36th president—the major biography of the year. In her opinion, Johnson's lifelong inability to deal openly with conflict, his equation of love with performance rewarded, and his intense need to be needed stemmed from a childhood of intense parental competition. A compulsive conciliator, he was paralyzed by true differences of belief. "The biggest danger to American stability," said Johnson, "is the politics of principle." What is unique is Kearns's access to Johnson's own words and thoughts, by turns pointed, rambling, holier-than-thou, Rabelaisian—the voiceprint of a man whose appetite for the human animal in all its sweaty diversity might almost have served him in place of principle.

The Rockefellers by Peter Collier and David Horowitz was another eminent biography taking voyeurism and gossip to a grand scale to clarify an era of American industrial growth. The basic motifs: the nature of Rockefeller philanthropy and power; and the rise and decline of the Rockefeller family as an institution, from malefactors to benefactors to merely factors. Also noteworthy: John Martin's *Adlai Ste-*

venson in Illinois, where the pieces come together to make by far the best portrait of the compulsive role-playing politician who presented himself to the world and equally to his friends as he liked to believe he was; *Norman Thomas* by W. A. Swanberg, a large, engrossing biography of the man who came to embody anti-Bolshevik socialism in the U.S., viewed not as a quixotic diehard for sticking to the shell of the Socialist Party but as a seminal and flexible political symbol; and *Ezra Pound,* a "political" biography by David Heymann, focusing on the ugly, degenerative time when the great poet, always querulous, vituperative, and strident in the name of his beliefs, redirected his energy to a hyper-naive, paranoid theory of utopian economics.

In the genre of self-revelation, famed dramatist Lillian Hellman ventured *Scoundrel Time,* a disturbing partial memoir of her defiant testimony before the House Committee on Un-American Activities in 1952, those "cheap baddies." She agreed to answer questions about herself but refused to discuss others. Memorable: the years of blacklisting by Hollywood, the sale of the much-beloved farm she owned with Dashiell Hammett, her lover, the anxious poverty—all with an eloquence the more so for what remains unsaid. Other important memoirs included: *The Right and the Power* by Leon Jaworski, the story of how the former Watergate prosecutor came to the rescue; the fourth volume of Anne Morrow Lindbergh's diaries and letters, *The Flower and the Nettle;* and renowned behaviourist B. F. Skinner's *Particulars of My Life.*

Hailed as a major contribution to 20th-century literary criticism was *Poetry and Repression,* the concluding volume of the tetralogy that Yale professor Harold Bloom initiated in *The Anxiety of Influence,* his 1973 manifesto for "antithetical criticism." His concept of repression is neo-Freudian, referring to a tutelary primal scene of instruction: "It is only by repressing creative 'freedom' through the initial fixation of influence, that a person can be reborn as a poet." Also notable belles lettres: Steven Marcus' *Representations,* essays remarkable for their treatment of sociology as literary text; and two major and controversial offerings by theatrical watchdog John Simon, *Uneasy Stages* and *Singularities.* He awards high marks to Ibsen and Brecht while his bêtes noires include just about everything written recently by Albee, Miller, Osborne, and Williams.

The American Bible Society completed its translation of the Old Testament in the "natural, modern English of everyday conversation" and published it, together with an earlier colloquial version of the New Testament, as the Good News Bible. It was intended for readers who find the vocabulary of standard versions difficult to understand, particularly when read aloud.

Finally, the James Russell Lowell Prize was awarded by the Modern Language Association to Jonathan Culler for his *Structuralist Poetics: Structuralism, Linguistics, and the Study of Literature.*

Poetry. The poetic event of the year was the publication of Robert Lowell's *Selected Poems.* This most honoured of living poets is a maker and chronicler of contemporary consciousness whose poetry has the broadest historical sense of any in the past quarter century. The underlying theme of the early poems was that of temporality, of "Time and the grindstone of the knife of God." Set against a number of opposing forces—innocence and corruption, liberation and constriction—Lowell's aggressive metrics and prophetic religiosity wrought finely balanced, if dissonant, landscapes of a puritan past and a heathen present. Later, with *Life Studies,* Lowell depressurized his style and gave us the famous confessional poems of the 1950s, suffused with humour as much as with scandal. Since then, however, while still preserving his characteristic elegiac and ironic strains, Lowell's world has grown increasingly notational; still, at every stage of his development, his imaginative powers reveal a master.

Dead by her own hand, poet Anne Sexton spoke from beyond the grave in her 1976 volume "45 Mercy Street."

A contribution of extraordinary accomplishment was James Merrill's seventh collection, *Divine Comedies,* featuring a superlative long narrative poem, "The Book of Ephraim." It was, as Merrill quipped, something of a low-budget remake of the Paradiso. His Virgil is Ephraim, a familiar who, operating via Ouija board and teacup pointer, reveals to Merrill the secrets of Time and the lives beyond Death. Within these heavenly circles reside the uninhibited, hedonistic dramatis personae of Merrill's previous incarnations as well as his (current) life in Stonington, Conn. In James Dickey's *The Zodiac,* an equilibrium between stability of form and violence of subject was tipped toward power rather than finish. The persona was a Dutchman, at home in Amsterdam after years of travel, struggling to relate himself by means of poetry and aqua vitae to the sea, the land, and to the "beastly stars."

A well-received first volume also on "celestial" themes was *The Planets* by Diane Ackerman, devoted to the choreography of planets, the cumulative effect of which is a small, beautifully arranged museum of solar artifacts. Anne Sexton's heroic and appalling voice persisted posthumously from beyond the grave in *45 Mercy Street,* the culmination of a career of suicide notes that seemed to say I told you so. The "Leaves That Talk" to her that last spring invited her to die. Insanity frightened her, and religion did not assuage her; and their threats, now realized, became bolder.

More stolid and down-to-earth was Irving Feldman's *Leaping Clear,* recreating the reality of contemporary cities through the resurrected rhythms and simplisms of his New York City boyhood, the lamentations of tormented Jews and other oppressed and hounded, the "dull" and "unperceiving" consciousness of those at "the bottom of every heap."

Also particularly notable was Robert Creeley's *Selected Poems,* showing Creeley as the most skillful practitioner of Charles Olson's polemical efforts—called "projective verse"—to recreate sensibility by breaking up received assumptions.

Social sympathies linked to an imperfect search for the proper form characterized Muriel Rukeyser's *The Gates,* where the act of will everywhere predominates: "Pay attention to what they tell you to forget." The voice of James Tate's *Viper Jazz* was that of a Trickster persistently turning everything upside down, pyrotechnically unraveling all the usual connections and showing us that the spirit is fragile and there are no nets beneath our feet: "A sign said YIELD/ and a woman ran through the streets/ actually crying."

(FREDERICK S. PLOTKIN)

Canada. English Canadian fiction in 1976 produced an unusually large group of novels concerned with personal liberation and exotic experience. Margaret Atwood's *Lady Oracle* provides the image of a fat girl teetering on a tightrope and symbolizes the precarious life-style of a secretive wife, eager mistress, Gothic writer, and spiritualist whose faked suicide ends in nightmare. Resisting such mental anguish, Bill Farthing, at 95, boasts of his follies in Richard B. Wright's picaresque *Farthing's Fortunes,* the ribald adventures of a mortician's apprentice turned Klondike racketeer, front-line soldier, railroading hobo, and chorus girl's lover. The themes of moral ethics and women's liberation were treated in both Marian Engel's *Bear,* a symbolic search for historical roots and primitive experience in which a lonely woman achieves spiritual and sexual rebirth through a bear's companionship; and Brian Moore's *The Doctor's Wife,* an erotic love affair between a young man and an older married woman. Carol Shields detailed the disguises imposed by mannered behaviour in *Small Ceremonies,* incidents surrounding a biographer's attempt to grasp the inner personalities of her family, her friends, and her subject, early Canadian writer Susannah Moodie. *The Viking Process* by Norman Hartley was a superior example of the adventure story as an international terrorist group tries to destroy a multinational corporation.

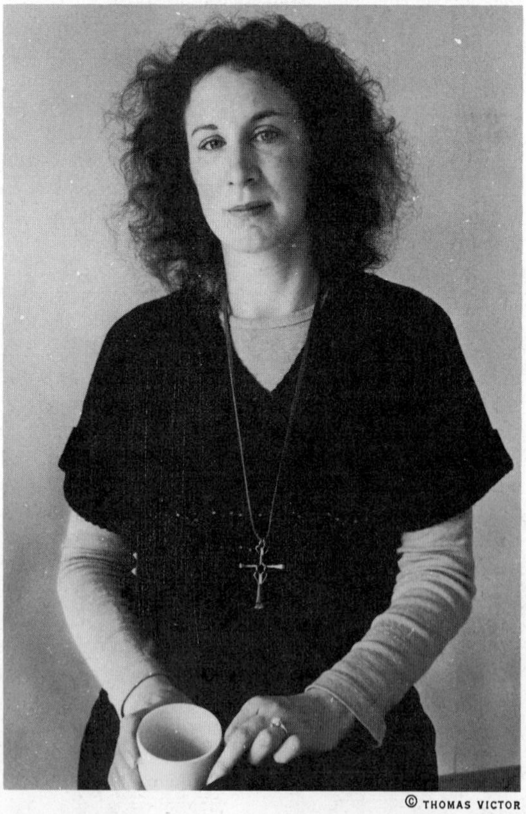

Canadian novelist Margaret Atwood published "Lady Oracle" in 1976.

In the field of short stories, there was more concern with actuality. Maritime fishing and mining communities provided the realistic settings for Alistair McLeod's stories of personal relationships and domestic conflicts in *The Lost Salt Gift of Blood.* In *Dark Glasses* Hugh Hood exposed the restless cares of ordinary people protected by the shades of dark glasses, phony identities, and self-righteous arrogance.

Many Canadian writers provided works dealing with Canada's past. In *The Forked Road, Canada 1939–1957,* Donald Creighton gave his assessment of Canada's evolution during World War II and after. Barry Broadfoot recorded the experiences of 200 Prairie citizens to produce a tribute to the homesteader in *The Pioneer Years 1895–1914: Memories of Settlers Who Opened the West.* Peter Stursberg utilized political recollections in *Diefenbaker: Leadership Lost, 1962–67.* William Stevenson's *A Man Called Intrepid: The Secret War* detailed the career of industrialist Sir William Stephenson, who became director of the British Intelligence Services during World War II.

Dramatists' subjects ranged from ordinary daily routines to figures of literature and history. In *The Farm Show,* director Paul Thompson's improvised vignettes of a farming community promoted the grass roots genre that celebrates regional culture and lifestyles. In their attempt to remain faithful to the spirit of Victorian melodrama, Alden Nowlan and Walter Learning added universal mythology and Wildean paradox to their adaptation of *Frankenstein.* George Hulme's *The Life and Death of Adolf Hitler* portrayed man as a monster seeking an outlet for his demonic hatred.

More than 200 works of poetry appeared, including many translations from the French-Canadian. Al Purdy's *Sundance at Dusk* confirmed the poet's defiant attitude, with a wandering anecdotal style which befitted a mind that reaches for comradeship with prehistoric and cosmic frontiers. Irving Layton strove hard to break new ground, but the polemics of *For My Brother Jesus* overshadowed the poems. He adopted the perspective of a Judaic prophet blaming Christian ideology for Auschwitz and Gulag. Gary Geddes' *War & Other Measures* was a sequence of poems probing the mind of a Canadian activist who destroys himself as an agent of the apocalypse in a lavatory of the Ottawa House of Commons. *Miron* by Roland Giguere was a first English translation of two long poems by one of Quebec's best poets.

Canadian biography again dealt largely with political figures. With his usual wit and energy, John Diefenbaker related his often turbulent term as prime minister in *One Canada: The Years of Achievement, 1956–1962,* the second volume of his memoirs. *Edward Blake, Leader and Exile, 1881–1912* by Joseph Schull completes the account of Blake's years as leader of the Canadian Liberal Party, relates his eventual rift with the party, and continues with his later career in the British House of Commons as an Irish nationalist. Blair Neatby, in *William Lyon Mackenzie King: The Prism of Unity,* thoroughly covers the years 1932–39 in King's life by concentrating on the political legislation, debates, decisions, and conferences of the period. King's private life is almost ignored, but emerges as the major focus of C. P. Stacey's *A Very Double Life: The Private World of Mackenzie King.*

Much of the most creative writing in present-day Canada is focused on the country's role in international, social, and economic development. This writing is a powerful stimulus to national thinking. Peter Newman in volume 1 of *The Canadian Establishment* provided a much-sought-after insight into the manners and habits of those Canadian leaders who dominate business life and manage much of the affairs of the country. Gwen Matheson's collection of essays, *Women in the Canadian Mosaic,* reflects the frank and personal reactions of 18 women, engaged in a variety of occupations, to the issues of feminism as it exists in Canada. Poet-writer Andreas Schroeder in *Shaking It Rough: A Prison Memoir* describes his life in maximum security and less strict correctional camps, while in prison on a drug charge, and provides his own insights into present-day Canadian moral standards.

(H. C. CAMPBELL)

FRENCH

France. FICTION. The French Academy, awarding its Grand Prix du roman, said that it had grown tired of the "new novel" and had consequently appreciated, in Pierre Schoenderfer's book, the modern feeling and the existence of a plot in which the reader could find his bearings: so the prize was awarded to *Le Crabe-Tambour* which recalled Joseph Conrad in its nautical spirit. The Prix Goncourt went to Patrick Grainville's *Les Flamboyants;* set in a baroque Africa dominated by a character who calls to mind Uganda's Pres. Idi Amin, the novel is a succession of orgiastic scenes, written in sumptuous style. *L'Amour les yeux fermés* by Michel Henry, winner of the Prix Renaudot, resolutely opposed leftist intellectual tendencies and was an elegant and sophisticated satire of a student revolt in a wonderfully realized imaginary town. The sexual activities of some rather perverted couples were the subject of Marc Cholodenko's *Les États du désert,* which won the Prix Médicis.

These awards confirmed the supremacy of well-made novels, as did the runners-up for the year's prizes: Guy Croussy's *Le Loup-cervier,* Jean Blot's *Les Cosmopolites,* Guy Rohou's *La Prairie dans la ville,* Jacques Lanzmann's *Le Têtard,* Didier Martin's *Il serait une fois,* and Michel Bernard's *Le Coeur du paysage.* In *Un Crime de notre temps,* Pierre Moustiers used a concise and captivating style to protest against contemporary indifference toward the victims and the lenient attitude taken toward those guilty of crimes. *La Constellation des lévriers,* in which the characters are attractive puppets of the "dolce vita," was perhaps Camille Bourniquel's best novel. Bernard Clavel, in *La Saison des loups,* evoked the province of Franche-Comté ravaged by the plague during the 17th century. The same historical period was chosen by Raymond Jean in *La Fontaine obscure,* a remarkable story of love and sorcery. Marcel Brion continued in a vein of fantasy with *Algues,* drawing on Germanic myth. Paul Vialar, in *Le Triangle de fer,* studied a group of Europeans stranded in the mountains of Asia. Great and deserved success went to Gaston Bonheur's *La Croix de ma mère,* the adventures of a modern Quixote, and to Max Gallo's *La Promenade des Anglais,* the final episode in the story of an Italian family. A number of leading writers published collections of short stories: *Salido* and *O.K. Joe* by Louis Guilloux, *Sous la lame* by André Pieyre de Mandiargues, *L'Étage noble* by Louis Curtis, *Quat'saisons* by Antoine Blondin, and *Des Yeux de soie* by Françoise Sagan.

WIDE WORLD

Michel Henry won the 1976 Prix Renaudot for "L'Amour les yeux fermés" ("Love with Closed Eyes"), satirizing a student revolt.

Françoise Mallet-Joris' *Allegra,* a considerable best-seller, was very much a novel about women. Others in the same vein included *Un mari, c'est un mari* by Frédérique Hébrard, *Va voir Maman, Papa travaille* by Inès Cagnati, *Jérémie la nuit* by Claire Gallois, and *Un Crime si juste* by Lucie Faure. *Le Trajet,* describing the monotonous daily life of a woman divided between her office and her suburban home, gained for Marie-Louise Haumont the Prix Fémina. The Prix Interallié went to Raphaële Billetdoux for *Prends garde à la douceur des choses,* a feminine version of the Narcissus myth.

Youth and maturity, respectively, inspired Jean Frustié in *L'Aventure familiale* and *Proche de la mer.* Also partly autobiographical were *Une Journée dans la vie d'Henri* by Henry Bonnier, *Un jour* by Maurice Génevoix, *La Fantaisie du voyageur* by François-Régis Bastide, *La Mort du connétable* by Michel Droit, and *Le mauvais temps* by Paul Guimard. Set in Italy, Michel Déon's *Je ne veux jamais l'oublier* was reminiscent of Henry James. A successful first novel was *La Rencontre de Santa-Cruz,* set in South America, by the well-known critic Max-Pol Fouchet.

POETRY. The French Academy awarded its Grand Prix de poésie to Eugène Guillevic, a militant Marxist with a talent described as "sharp and brilliant." In *Morale élémentaire,* Raymond Queneau (*see* OBITUARIES) indulged in astounding wordplay accompanied by typographical fantasies. Hervé Bazin, in *Traits,* showed the black humour and aggressivity characteristic of his work elsewhere; there was humour also in Roland Bacri whose poems, in free verse, had as their title the author's name. *Grand Bal du printemps,* Jacques Prévert's "armful of popular flowers," appeared in a new edition. Jean Berthet attained the full flowering of his talent in *L'éternel instant.* Robert Houdelot's *Les Treize,* a passionately lyrical ode to love, was inspired by sunlight and warm countries; intensity and clarity were to be found also in Philippe Chabaneix's *Dix nouvelles romances,* while Christian Dedeyan's *Chant du Houlme* was full of love expressed with confident craftsmanship. *Verger des rêves,* written in nostalgic seven-syllable lines, was the best work of Jacques Marlet. The Belgian Marcel Thiry's collected works appeared in France under the title *Toi qui pâlis au nom de Vancouver,* in which mastery of the traditional Alexandrine vied with a liking for free verse. John Jackson published a timely and pertinent study of Yves Bonnefoy whose work is largely written in free verse. Finally, J. P. Seguin's *L'Année poétique 1975* contained extracts of works of Jean Orizet and others.

NONFICTION. Autobiography was the dominant genre in 1976. With *Frêle Bruit* Michel Leiris completed the fourth and last volume of an autobiography in which he delved into his own thoughts with masochism and biting humour. *Ce n'est pas une vie* by a leading critic, Robert Poulet, had as its central theme his sentencing to death by a Belgian court in the purges following the World War II Liberation: he was freed after six years in prison which he underwent at the time with serenity but which he now looked back on with resentment. Several writers examined their philosophy of life or their faith. *Somme toute,* perhaps Claude Roy's best book, gave a picture of the writer and his work and striking impressions of other writers including Aragon and Sartre. Both the title and the contents of Maurice Clavel's *Dieu est Dieu, nom de Dieu!* were memorable: here was a Christian attacking the church and a progressive attacking the politicians of the left. José Cabanis, awarded the French Academy's Grand Prix de littérature for the whole of his work, published an intimate journal of the World War II years, *Les profondes années,* which was full of tender feeling and religious concern. *Le Cadavre de Dieu bouge encore* by Georges Suffert was a profession of faith, not without humour and amplified by interviews with contemporary personalities. André Frossard proclaimed his faith in an essentially spiritual autobiography, *Il y a un autre monde.* Gilbert Cesbron's *Mourir étonné* was a collection of sometimes horrifying stories expressing anguish and seeking consolation in love for one's fellow men. Paul Guth's *Lettre à votre fils qui en a ras le bol* was a little masterpiece of savage and irresistible humour which attacked the present educational system but left room to hope for a return to lasting values. Jacques Laurent wrote his memoirs in *Histoire égoiste* as an intellectual aristocrat; as Cecil St. Laurent he also published three erotic tales under the title *Les Voyeurs jaloux.*

Politicians continued to write, some showing literary merit in the expression of their ideas, but not surprisingly it was Pres. Valéry Giscard d'Estaing who had by far the greatest success, with his *Démocratie française,* the first political work published by a French head of state during his term of office.

In *La Fontaine ou La Vie est un conte,* a comprehensive and fascinating biography, Jean Orieux discussed La Fontaine's work in the context of his time and gave a brilliantly successful picture of a libertine who was also a thinker and a man of genius. The centenary of George Sand's death was the occasion for a study by Francine Mallet which illuminated every aspect of its subject. *La beauté et la gloire,* a monumental biography of Nelson and Emma Hamilton by Georges Blond, joined rigorous historical research to exceptional storytelling ability. Although revealing no new facts, Jacques Levron's *Choiseul* attracted renewed interest in the career of Louis XV's great and unjustly neglected foreign minister.

The death of André Malraux (*see* OBITUARIES) removed a giant figure from the French literary, cultural, and political scene of the 20th century. Prior to his death *La Corde et les souris,* the second volume of his *Miroir des Limbes* (of which *Antimémoires* was the first volume), appeared; art occupied the forefront of the stage in this latest volume. In *Malraux, être et dire,* Martine de Courcel brought together articles by writers from many countries, but the principal interest of this sizable work lay in the postscript or "néo-critique" by Malraux himself. In *Le coeur battant,* Suzanne Chantal revealed a passionate and tragic episode in Malraux's private life at the time of his liaison with Josette Clantis.

Besides Malraux and Queneau, other well-known writers who died during the year were the poet Pierre-Jean Jouve and the novelists Henri Bosco and Paul Morand (whose *L'Allure de Chanel* appeared shortly before his death). (*See also* OBITUARIES.)

(ANNIE BRIERRE)

Canada. In reviewing French-Canadian literature produced in 1976, one notes somewhat disappointedly that the output of fiction diminished in comparison with other genres. With several exceptions, the year produced few novels of real distinction. Among those works that merit mention were *Eugélionne* by Louki Bessianik, a three-part novel about a woman who, in her search for the true man, lives in a fictional world drawn from biblical and surrealistic sources; *L'Ile au dragon* by Jacques Godbout, about a bottle with a message inside that is one day thrown out to sea; *Les Pins parasols* by Gilles Archambault; *Une Liaison parisienne* by Marie-Claire Blais, which was judged rather harshly by the critics; and *Le Déroulement* by Wilfrid Lemoyne, the sequel to the story of the tightrope artist Sébastien.

In poetry Paul-Marie Lapointe received the International Poetry Forum prize for the entire body of his work, translated excerpts of which were to be published under the title *The Terror of the Snows.* The year was also marked by the return of Georges Cartier, author of *Le Poisson pêché* (1964), with his new *Chanteaux* in which the meaning sometimes overshadows all the spontaneity and fantasy of which the author is quite capable. Also of note was the publication of an interesting collection *Poèmes de la mère pays* by Paul Chanel Malenfant.

In theatre the year was a very active one. *La Nef des sorcières,* which might also have been called "Women Have Their Say," was the work of a Quebec feminine collective. Elsewhere, the magic of Michel Garneau's fiction was brought to the stage in the provinces, in Montreal, and in Paris. Experimental theatre at the University of Montreal boldly dealt with the problem of incest in *Les Mûres de Pierre,* a play written in 1967 by Pierre Sauvageau. *Septième ciel* by François Beaulieu was the story of a young professor's love for one of his students, a story in which all the serious problems of current society are reflected. With *Ma corriveau* Victor Lévy-Beaulieu took Canadians back to the heart of their traditions and history. Finally of interest was the revival of *Médium saignant,* written in 1970 by Françoise Loranger.

With respect to essays, several works stood out: *Le Théâtre québécois, instrument de contestation sociale et politique* by Jacques Cotman; *L'Étrangeté du texte* by Claude Lévesque, composed of four essays on Nietzsche, Freud, Blanchot, and Derrida; *Un Génocide en douce* by Pierre Vadeboncoeur, a study of the dramatic situation of the Quebecois; and an index prepared by Pierre Pagé on *Le Comique et l'humour à la radio québécoise.*

Among the year's most important reissues were *Andante* by Félix Leclerc; *La Pension Leblanc* by Robert Choquette; and *Pour la patrie* by Jules Tardivel, a sort of grand historic fresco on the end of the 19th century and the beginning of the 20th century.

(ROBERT SAINT-AMOUR)

DUTCH

Two of the foremost Dutch writers, Harry Mulisch and Gerard Reve, each published a new novel in 1976. Mulisch departed from the complex and cryptic mode he had adopted in *De Verteller,* and in *Twee Vrouwen* he gave a sensitive account, written in a crystal-clear style, of a lesbian relationship that foundered on the desire of one of the partners to have a child. Gerard Reve remained true to his subject of male homosexual love in *Een Circusjongen,* but even his incomparable stylistic qualities and his celebrated black humour could not obscure the fact that he was more and more repeating himself.

Anton Koolhaas, who seemed to have forsaken the animal stories that made him famous, analyzed a precarious marriage in *Tot Waar Zal Ik Je Brengen?* In the midst of a destructive hurricane and spring tide, a man and a woman realize that their seemingly ideal marriage has been disintegrating for a long time. Though the relationship was handled with intelligent insight, the most important aspect of the book was the powerful evocation of nature run wild, which Koolhaas achieved with a minimum of words.

A still greater master of understatement than Koolhaas was Albert Alberts. Recognition of his ability had been slow in coming, but he now seemed well established as one of The Netherlands' best storytellers. A new collection of short stories, *Haast Hebben in September,* and a welcome reprint of an older collection under the new title of *In en Uit het Paradijs Getild* helped to underscore this.

Dutch novelist Harry Mulisch wrote of lesbian love in his 1976 novel "Twee Vrouwen."

Understatement was also the main characteristic of the young writer Mensje van Keulen. In her choice of subject she confined herself to the most ordinary events in the lives of the most ordinary people. In her new novel, *Van Lieverlede* ("By Degrees," but the wordplay on *lief en leed,* "sweet and bitter," is untranslatable), she portrayed a sick mother and her daughter who live together in a love-hate relationship. In her clinical and yet compassionate description of this claustrophobic situation she added a new flavour to realist writing in The Netherlands.

Hella Haasse's intricate and highly original novel *Een Gevaarlijke Verhouding of Daal-en-Bergse Brieven,* though at first glance seemingly far removed from reality and realism, dealt with the topical subject of a woman's place in society. The book consisted of letters exchanged between Madame de Merteuil, a character from Choderlos de Laclos' *Les Liaisons Dangereuses,* and a 20th-century woman.

Jos Vandeloo, one of the most prolific storywriters in Flanders, published a new collection, *Mannen,* depicting in his usual laconic style several men in a variety of bewildering predicaments. The underlying theme of all these stories was the harshness and cruelty of modern society.

For poetry it was another lean year. It was significant that the poets of the 1950s were now bringing out their collected editions. After Lucebert and Remco Campert, Gerrit Kouwenaar, the most cerebral poet of the period, followed suit with his *Verzamelde Gedichten.*

(REINDER PIETER MEIJER)

GERMAN

West Germany, Austria, Switzerland. The main political issue that exercised writers in West Germany was the legislation designed to prevent "radicals" from entering public service. A poem by Alfred Andersch, *Artikel 3 (3),* which equated the new measures with those taken by the Nazis, created a storm of controversy when a television recital of it was banned. Earlier, Peter Schneider found success with *. . . schon bist du ein Verfassungsfeind,* the story of a liberal but not very politically minded teacher who is dismissed for security reasons. Were the prosperity and stability that impressed those who viewed West Germany from the outside only superficial?

The number of major works devoted to psychiatric cases might be regarded as symptomatic. Ernst Augustin's *Raumlicht* described a psychiatrist's attempt to cure Evelyne B. by devoting himself wholly to her, taking her seriously almost to the extent of reversing their roles. Heinar Kipphardt's *März* had a similar theme, with the patient in this case a poet; schizophrenia was viewed as a superfluity of the inner life, and there was a more specific attempt to relate mental illness to the social pressures to conform. Günter Steffen's autobiographical *Annäherung an das Glück* described in compelling manner his wife's death from cancer and his own subsequent mental and physical disintegration. Against this background it seemed no coincidence that Peter Härtling's bestselling novel *Hölderlin* related the life of the poet whose last 35 years were spent in madness.

© LUTFI ÖZKÖK

Alfred Andersch's poem "Artikel 3(3)" aroused controversy in West Germany in 1976 for its attack on a new civil service law designed to exclude radicals from public service.

Suicide too was a prominent motif. Rolf Hochhuth's monodrama of Ernest Hemingway's last hours, *Tod eines Jägers,* was just one example. In Thomas Bernhard's *Korrektur,* the "correction" was, among other things, self-destruction—life itself is an error. Bernhard's novel was abstract, his hero's life based on that of Wittgenstein; his pessimism was intellectual. Equally pessimistic, but in political terms, was Martin Walser's much more readable *Jenseits der Liebe,* although critics were divided on its merits. It treated Walser's familiar themes, the misery of the uncommitted liberal intellectual, alienation in capitalist society, the law of the weakest to the wall. Michael Scharang told a similar story but at proletarian level in his *Der Sohn eines Landarbeiters.*

Other novels gave a wider, historical picture, but here too the introspective, autobiographical element was strong. August Kühn's "family chronicle" *Zeit zum Aufstehen* covered exuberantly and realistically the life of a working-class family over the past 100 years, while Georg Lentz's *Muckefuck* was a further contribution to the list of books describing the lives of young people in the Third Reich. Max Fürst's *Talisman Scheherezade* continued his autobiography into the 1920s. With *Dichterleben* Heinz Piontek, who received the 1976 Büchner Prize, provided a more poetic and disguised account of his progress through life. But the most important and ultimately disappointing work of this kind was Peter Weiss's *Die Ästhetik des Widerstands,* the first volume of an autobiography "as he would like it to have been."

The Hoffmannesque tradition with its mixture of fantasy and accurately observed reality received further support. Arno Schmidt's *Abend mit Goldrand* owed more to Jean Paul but delighted its author's coterie by its linguistic virtuosity and whimsical inventiveness. Closer to Hoffmann were Herbert Rosendorfer's entertaining *Grosses Solo für Anton,* whose hero awakens one morning to find himself alone in the world, and especially Urs Widmer's *Die gelben Männer,* whose narrator finds the exotic, the simple life, and above all the threat from the Andromeda nebula within walking distance of Basel railway station.

Among shorter fiction, Peter Handke's story *Die linkshändige Frau* was a counterpiece to his previous novel. This time it is a woman who "breaks out," sending her husband away. Erich Fried's *Fast alles Mögliche,* subtitled "true stories and valid lies," mingled general observations on human life with more directly polemical statements about present-day Germany. Both H. C. Buch (*Aus der Neuen Welt*) and Klaus Stiller (*Die Fascisten*) treated historical manifestations of fascism—but in other countries, the U.S. and Italy, respectively. Ilse Aichinger impressed with *Schlechte Wörter,* a collection of prose poems and a play for radio on the tyranny of language.

Lyric poetry included collections by Horst Bienek (*Gleiwitzer Kindheit*) and Michael Kruger (*Reginapoly*), the former nostalgic, the latter pervaded with melancholy over the collapse of the hopes of yesteryear. Ernst Meister's *Im Zeitspalt* contained miniatures of great precision on more universal themes of life and death, time and eternity. The most successful collection was H. M. Enzensberger's *Mausoleum,* subtitled ironically "37 ballads from the history of progress," and consisting of brief biographies of historical personalities, some obscure, others less so, Babbage and Bakunin, Leibniz and Molotov, with political glosses on each.

East Germany. The relation between individual and socialist collective continued to be a prominent theme. From the old guard, Bruno Apitz' novel *Der Regenbogen* described the fortunes of a proletarian family from 1900 to the Spartacus uprising of 1919 and its development from individualism to acceptance of Communism. Younger writers were less optimistic. Jurek Becker's *Der Boxer* related the story of Arno Blank, who lives his life in complete self-reliance to the detriment of all personal and social relationships—individualism leads to failure. However, by making his hero a Jew who survived the extermination camps, Becker created a fruitful tension between sympathy and antipathy. Rolf Schneider's broken-backed *Das Glück* covered the same period, 1945 to the present, with another outsider as central figure, this time a girl from a "problem family." If Hanna did not find "happiness," Schneider made it clear that she was

East German novelist Klaus Schlesinger's "Alte Filme" (Old Films), published in 1976, features a former film actress.

ROGER MELIS—CARL HINSTORFF VERLAG

not solely to blame and the leitmotivs from the Book of Job suggested that it was not as easily attainable as official ideology implied. More satisfying as a novel was Klaus Schlesinger's *Alte Filme,* whose hero is jolted out of a routine existence by the discovery that the old lady who shares his cramped accommodation was once a film actress. His search for a more vital life leads only to the police station and the novel's "happy ending" is ironic.

One form of escapism was watching "old films," others were dreams and fantasy. The heroes of Manfred Pieske's *Luftschlösser* and Joachim Nowotny's *Ein Gewisser Robel* seek refuge in the imagination and if both are brought back to their responsibilities in the end, it was nevertheless the fictional realm that remained memorable. Nowotny's work was particularly impressive. The fantastic was the domain of Irmtraud Morgner's picaresque *Leben und Abenteuer der Trobadora Beatriz.* But the most interesting work was Gerhard Dahne's *Die ganz merkwürdigen Sichten und Gesichte des Hans Greifer* with its mixture of historical anecdotes, Utopian visions, contemporary love story, and byplay between "author" and hero. A self-reflecting novel, it combined political orthodoxy with an appeal for artistic freedom.

Dahne's novel was poorly received in the East. Rainer Kunze's collection of short prose pieces, *Die wunderbaren Jahre,* appeared only in the West, where it was highly praised. In the domain of lyric poetry Erich Arendt produced an important cycle, *Memento und Bild,* poems inspired mainly by landscapes and artists, with the theme of death most prominent. Here too a turning away from social to inner realities was apparent.

A much-discussed collection of literary essays was Franz Fühmann's *Erfahrungen und Widersprüche.*

(J. H. REID)

NORDIC

Danish. A year rich in memoirs saw the publication of Knud Thestrup's *Mit livs gågade.* Other political memoirs, the unfortunate A. C. Normann's *Erindringsbilleder* (1975), were partly self-defense. Life and opinions rather than politics were at the centre of Elsa Gress's *Campania,* largely concerned with the 1950s. Nobel Prize winner Johannes V. Jensen was the subject of Villum Jensen's *Min fars hus,* while Jacob Paludan (1896–1975) wrote of himself in his final, posthumous, autobiographical volume, *Låsens klik.* Ole Wivel's *Tranedans* also had literary overtones, telling of the author's work with the Gyldendal publishing house. The publication of Karen Blixen's *Efterladte fortællinger* (1975) was another echo from the past, but it contained material the author herself hesitated to publish and met with a mixed reception.

It was a year of poetry, too. Jørgen Nash published his collected poems *Her er jeg,* while Klaus Rifbjerg produced a volume called *Stranden.* Jørgen Gustava Brandt, awarded the Aarestrup Medal, wrote in two genres: a poetic recreation of Copenhagen, *Mit hjerte i København,* and two volumes of poetry in his religious, mystical vein, *Jathåram* and *Regnansigt.* Outstanding among poetry published late in 1975 were Thorkild Bjørnvig's *Delfinen* and *Stoffets krystalhav,* both protests against the despoilment of the environment, for which he received the Danish Critics' Prize. One writer of poetry, Inger Christensen, turned to prose in an experimental historical novel, *Det malede værelse,* exhibiting the same preoccupation with structure as her earlier "meta-poetical" work *Det* (1969).

© LUTFI ÖZKÖK

Danish poet Jørgen Gustava Brandt, who was awarded the 1976 Aarestrup Medal, published three volumes of poetry.

In fiction "worker novels," some written by quite unsophisticated authors, emerged as a new genre. A more accomplished version was Villy Karlsson's autobiographical novel *Firkanten* revealing conditions in Copenhagen in the 1930s. One result of this new trend was a fresh interest in Martin Andersen Nexø (1869–1954), about whom various works appeared; his biographer and bibliographer Børge Houmann was awarded the Brandes Prize.

Established novelists were in evidence: Willy-August Linnemann moved on to society and politics in Copenhagen in *Himlens genskær i byens ruder,* while in *Andre måder* (1975) Christian Kampmann, completing his study of a Copenhagen family, examined the question of a family as a unit and came down in favour of the collective. Anders Bodelsen's *Penge og livet,* a successful sequel to *Tænk på et tal* (1968), was again a thriller, but with serious overtones. Another comedy thriller was Rifbjerg's *Kiks,* inventive and chaotic, while exciting if not a thriller was Leif Panduro's *Høfeber,* revealing the goings-on behind a bland middle-aged facade.

Frank Jaeger's *Udsigt til Kronborg* was a mixture of short stories and essays, some centred on Helsingør and some on figures such as the poet and novelist Tom Kristensen (1893–1974). Rifbjerg's *De beskedne* was a four-volume edition of 20 radio plays making up a family "saga," based on reality and less superficial than many such sagas.

The Danish Academy's prize went to Jørgen Sonne, and the Otto Gelsted Prize to Sten Kaalø.

(W. GLYN JONES)

Finnish. As the 60th year of Finland's independence approached, Finnish writers, especially novelists, looked back over the major events of recent history and took stock. Eeva Joenpelto evoked the atmosphere of the early years of Finnish prohibition in *Kuin kekäle kädessä,* contrasting the commercialism and mass religious hysteria of the 1920s and at the same time chronicling the revival of the Social Democratic movement after the trauma following the 1918 Civil War. The same period and the years leading up to World War II were illuminated by the

© LUTFI ÖZKÖK

Finnish novelist Paavo Rintala wrote of the 1939 Russo-Finnish War in his 1976 novel "Nahkapeitturien linjalla."

posthumous publication of Pentti Haanpää's diary, *Muistiinmerkintöjä vuosilta 1925–1939,* and his collected works.

Paavo Rintala's novel *Nahkapeitturien linjalla* examined the attitudes of officers and men during the Winter War of 1939–40, when the Soviet threat united the Finns. The war years also provided the pivot for two novels by Pirkko Saisio. In *Elämänmeno,* awarded the Erkko Prize, she portrayed the life of a Karelian refugee in a Helsinki slum, while her second novel, *Sisarukset,* was set in the years before and after the war. Together, her books provided a social study of first-generation city dwellers from the 1930s to the late 1950s. Questions of social identity occupied Hannu Salama. In *Kosti Herhiläisen perunkirjoitus* he examined the despair experienced by left-wing intellectuals of working-class origin when they lose their roots.

Changing attitudes characterized contemporary poetry, although it remained uncertain whether they marked a pause to take stock or pointed to new directions. Little trace of Paavo Haavikko's usual obsession with economic and political power could be detected in his bacchanal *Viiniä, kirjoitusta.* Anxious introspection permeated Hannu Mäkelä's *Synkkyys pohjaton, ninn myös iloni, onneni* and Jarkko Laine's *Viidenpennin Hamlet.* Matti Rossi employed the rhythms and themes of Finnish folk poetry to depict love and death as forces of social change in his *Laulu tummana tulevi.* The revival of interest in folk poetry, with its inward-looking national associations, was typified by Matti Kuusi's *Kansanruno Kalevala,* a reconstruction of the folk poems that formed the basis of Elias Lönnrot's *Kalevala* (1849), a work long regarded as Finland's national epic.

(MICHAEL ARTHUR BRANCH)

Icelandic. Fiction was the most popular genre in Iceland, but poetry came close behind. If few or no works appearing since late 1975 could be termed great, most of the best-known authors contributed—and typically in styles that had come to be associated with them.

Nobel laureate Halldór Laxness received predictable applause for an account of his youth as seen from a distant vantage point, and Ólafur Jóhann Sigurdsson, though chiefly a novelist, got a Nordic award for poetry. Both authors were largely within the mainstream of epic-narrative fiction—a style ultimately deriving from saga tradition and still preferred by much of the general readership. Among the prime representatives of the active avant-garde are those mentioned below.

Thor Vilhjálmsson added a novel to the corpus in which he dispensed with all conventional techniques, substituting a plethora of imagery, allusions, and associations that bring forth a vision of humanity ill at ease in the modern world. Gudbergur Bergsson published a sequel to his existing slice-of-life fiction and showed further mastery of the stream-of-consciousness mode.

A play by Svava Jakobsdóttir had a premiere run; it was in part an elaboration on the theme of her 1969 allegorical protest novel (on Iceland-U.S. relations), though also containing a strong feminist element; noted for her short-story successes, she was fast gaining a reputation for skilled rendering of Kafkaesque scenes. Jökull Jakobsson, her brother and the foremost living Icelandic playwright, published a novel for a change—and Björn Th. Björnsson aroused attention with a creative documentary work on the fate of Icelandic convicts sent into exile in the mid-18th century.

A breakthrough for free verse occurred in the late 1940s, and many held that Icelandic fiction in the 1970s was in a transitional phase; if so, the experimenters—still overshadowed by Laxness—would seem to be destined for a larger future role. A recurrent theme was the culture shock of urbanization, often taking on colouring from resentment at the U.S. military presence—a polarizing issue since World War II.

(HAUKUR B. BÖDVARSSON)

Norwegian. Penetrating psychological analysis, mastery of language, and exciting storytelling combined to make Tor Edvin Dahl's *Romanen om Eva* an outstanding event. Gradually, the main character, Ragnar Hermansen, was unmasked as a sadistic, destructive self-deceiver, and religious overtones added

The 70th birthday of Norwegian author Torborg Nedreaas in 1976 was marked by the publication of five radio plays and a TV play.

ASCHEHOUGS FORLAG

an extra dimension to this exceptionally moving and disturbing novel. Outstanding also was the concluding volume of Knut Faldbakken's apocalyptic vision of the collapse of our technological civilization, *Uår. Sweetwater*. The main message in Gunnar Lunde's novel *Kanskje fins det fine dager* was that one must take budding neofascist tendencies very seriously, but this message was combined with a witty survey of most of the problems facing the average apartment-house dweller in contemporary Norway. Neo-Nazism and teenage unemployment leading to delinquency were main themes in Kjell Askildsen's short novel *Hverdag*. In a mixture of prose and poetry Finn Carling took a critical view of tourism in underdeveloped Africa in *Hvite skygger på svart bunn*. He also gave intimate glimpses of his own experiences as a spastic child in *I et rom i et hus i en hage*. Reminiscences of a countryside childhood in the 1930s provided the material for Simen Skjønsberg's nostalgic novel *Gitter i lyset*, valuable both as sensitive fiction and as cultural history.

Boomerang effects of attempts to solve the mystery of wartime informing 30 years later were excitingly dealt with in Bernt Vestre's psychological thriller *Understrømmer*. Tor Obrestad's *Stå på!* was a documentary novel based on a recent Norwegian industrial labour conflict. Ragnhild Magerøy's *Baglerbispen*, concluding a cycle of five historical novels, was an attempt to restore the reputation of the 13th-century Bishop Nikolas, much maligned in Ibsen's play *Kongsemnerne* (*The Pretenders*). Among several other historical novels Asbjørn Øksendal's *Dronning Astrid av Viken* told of a 10th-century widowed queen trying to save her son from being killed by rivals fighting for supremacy in Norway. Ebba Haslund's short stories, *Hver i sin verden*, centred round the theme of expectations going sour and covered a wide spectrum of female experiences. A number of topical themes were taken up in a collection of short stories by Vigdis Stokkelien, *Vi*. The 70th birthday of Torborg Nedreaas was marked by a *Festschrift* in her honour, as well as by the publication of five radio plays and a television play, *Det dumme hjertet*. Stein Mehren's *Den store søndagsfrokosten* was a play operating on many levels with its mixture of realism, surrealism, and poetry and putting up for discussion a variety of attitudes to life and human relationships. Pessimistic attitudes were foremost in two outstanding collections of poems, Rolf Jacobsen's *Pusteøvelser* and Ragnvald Skrede's *Brenning*, whereas a welcome sense of humour coloured much of Peter R. Holm's *Portrettalbum*.

Unforgettable and almost unbearable in its low-key account of the inhuman treatment of prisoners in the Auschwitz concentration camp were the memoirs of one of the few surviving Norwegian Jews, Herman Sachnowitz, *Det angår også deg*, impeccably penned by Arnold Jacoby and appropriately appearing in the year that saw the untimely death of the indefatigable defender of human values, Jens Bjørneboe, whose articles on education appeared posthumously under the title *Under en mykere himmel*.

(TORBJØRN STØVERUD)

Swedish. After the austere political commitment of the 1960s, imaginative literature flourished once more. A striking feature was the number of multi-volume novels. Sven Delblanc's *Stadsporten* concluded his quartet on the inhabitants of Hedeby (actually Södertälje), now turned town dwellers. His richly mannered language distanced his human tragedies, whereas young Per Holmer's *Allmänheten*, the first part of a trilogy, described life and class tensions in and around the fire station in the same town (Södertälje) with artless realism. His contemporary Ann-Charlotte Alverfors published *Hjärteblodet*, the second part of her autobiographical suite, with a vivid portrait of the rural community in which her alter ego Gertrud grows up. Göran Tunström's *Prästungen* provided the autobiographical key to his earlier bizarre and colourful novels from Värmland. This account of a vicar's son whose father's death traumatically affects his subsequent development was straight narration. On the other hand, Lars Gustafsson's *Sigismund*, fourth volume of a pentalogy, was a sophisticated literary presentation of an intellectual Western liberal's subconscious dreams and conflicts. Gustafsson almost succeeds in switching places with Sigismund III in his magnificent Cracow sarcophagus, while a German lady painter descends into a temperate hell, ciceroned by three urbane devils. These books all ultimately derived from personal experience and made no attempt to simulate objectivity and documentary. Lars Forsell's *De rika* probably also derived from the personal sphere, but its bitter, stylized scenes from upper-class family life were in effect a cautionary tale about haves and have-nots, both individual and national. Hans Granlid's *Noll* mirrored the author's undisguised descent into personal and sexual chaos and his attempts to find a way out via Buddhism.

Per Holmer's "Allmänheten" (1976) described life in and around a fire station in a town near Stockholm.

Straight political documentaries may have been out, but Jan Myrdal's *Karriär* was a wicked satire in the form of letters exchanged by members of the Establishment in connection with the so-called "IB affair" (1973–74), when two journalists were jailed for leaking official secrets. Genuine documents in the shape of diaries, letters, and the testimony of Strindberg's late plays underlay the fiction in Ole Söderström's novel *Röda huset* about August Strindberg and his third wife, Harriet Bosse. C.-G. Ekerwald's *Citron-*

pressen was a delightful collection of stories about the fictive municipality Kumminåkern, a Swedish microcosmos, irresistibly absurd yet true. Anna Wahlgren's *Kärleksberättelser,* short stories about human relationships, were written with mastery reminiscent of Maupassant or Turgenev, yet absolutely modern. Nothing if not modern in approach was Elvira B. Holm's *Ensam* (with the author's address on the title page inviting young readers' responses), sympathetically dealing with adolescent hetero- and homosexual love. Ingrid Arvidsson's *Ensamheten* was a simple account of the inevitable loneliness of aging. And Sven Olsson's *Vigmannen* was a straight, old-fashioned, and zestful story about Viking times.

Göran Sonnevi's *Det omöjliga* confirmed his status of outstanding poet, intellectually and linguistically. Sten Hagliden's *Kvällsordat* was muted poetry from the evening of life, and Barbro Lindgren's *Rapporter från marken* were engagingly simple messages from the living countryside.

The novelist Eyvind Johnson, co-winner of the 1974 Nobel Prize for Literature, died on August 25 (*see* OBITUARIES).

(KARIN PETHERICK)

ITALIAN

Italy's economic difficulties and social and political instability found significant reflection in the literature of 1975–76. An interesting novel inspired by the contemporary political situation was Ferdinando Camon's *Occidente,* an attempt to investigate the psychological and ideological roots of the neofascist movements. Although couched in a somewhat surrealistic style, it was based on actual events and made use of public documents as well as secret pamphlets and psychoanalytic studies. *Tanto la rivoluzione non scoppierà* by the well-established author Carlo Bernari also had surrealistic effects; it too was made up by merging multiple source material and different languages, and it also became concerned with the activities of revolutionary groups. But it was a "revolution-which-anyway-would-not-happen," financed as such precisely by those who retained power and whom it was to have overthrown. The author's object was to illustrate the critical impasse of the Italian situation, where revolution and stagnation, like truth and falsity, seemed to be continually exchanging roles in a state of anguishing circularity.

Italian novelist Alberto Bevilacqua published a volume of poetry in 1976, "La crudeltà."

Aspiring to a fierce denunciation of contemporary society was Pier Paolo Pasolini's posthumously published *La divina mimesis,* written as an imitation of Dante's *The Divine Comedy* and meant to portray the sinful and sterile hell in which all Italians, regardless of political faith or social class, were struggling: another step forward in what had lately become for Pasolini an increasingly personal and isolated crusade.

A notable, if posthumous, success was achieved by Guido Morselli, a formerly unknown writer who committed suicide in 1973, with his novels *Roma senza papa, Contropassato prossimo, Divertimento 1889,* and *Il comunista.* The last named, taking place in 1958–59, was the story of a Communist deputy of working-class origins who finds himself in a crushing conflict with the party because, on the one hand, he sees in the official process of destalinization the danger of a bourgeois involution, and on the other, convinced of the intrinsically accursed nature of labour, he does not believe in the all-redeeming possibilities of Communism.

Interesting among feminist productions were *Un matrimonio perfetto* by Giovanna Cerati and *Un quarto di donna* by Giuliana Ferri, but the most considerable achievement in this genre was attained by Dacia Maraini, an already successful writer, with her *Donna in guerra.* This was the story, written in diary form and in a personal and uninhibited language, of a short summer holiday in which the narrator achieves her own maturity and liberation through a series of discoveries, ranging from the obsessive superstitions of the South to the political activities of an extraparliamentary group.

Directly related to recent Italian history also were the two most widely acclaimed memory novels of the year, *Il busto di gesso* by Gaetano Tumiati and *Le quattro regazze Wieselberger* by Fausta Cialente. The latter told the story of the author's family from the 1890s to the present. Its main setting is Trieste, but the narrative shifts widely throughout Italy and into Egypt where the writer was involved with British Intelligence in anti-Fascist broadcasting. A memory novel of a special kind was *Ernesto* by the poet Umberto Saba (1883–1957), who wrote it in 1953 but never published it. With a marvelous candour, underlined by the frequent use of Triestine dialect, it tells the story of a short-lived homosexual love that came to life and died in the Trieste of 1898. Despite the awkwardness of the subject matter, the book was a small literary masterpiece.

Vincent Consolo's documentary novel *Il sorriso dell'ignoto marinaio,* possibly the best work of the year, was the story of a series of disquieting discoveries related to Sicilian history of the 1850s. Falling between history and fantasy, learned and popular tradition, language and dialect, the novel treats of problems still much alive in contemporary Italy: the political commitment of intellectuals, the writer's attitude to history, the "neutrality" of science, the mystification of literature.

The year's poetry included *Morte segreta* by Dario

Bellezza, *La crudeltà* by Alberto Bevilacqua, better known as a novelist, *Documento 1966–73* by Amelia Rosselli, and *Lo splendido violino verde* by Angelo M. Ripellino. Although each of these concentrated on a personal predicament, they all seemed to reflect aspects of the contemporary malaise, thereby attaining some degree of social resonance.

(LINO PERTILE)

SPANISH

Spain. Much ferment followed the restoration of the Spanish monarchy, but little noteworthy literature appeared. Spanish presses were a couple of years behind Portugal in turning out a dazzling variety of formerly controlled matter: feverish esoterica, dubious erotica, lurid religiomagical tracts full of mumbo-jumbo, and dated Spanish novels first printed outside the country. The censorship did not operate, except to quell the more exhortatory Communist propaganda and to regulate the number of nudes and their layout per metre. Communist authors were published and even won prizes. Writers as a community gave themselves over to instant politics and left literature to foreigners, mainly Hispanic-Americans: the Argentine Jorge Luis Borges, for example, was probably the most widely read in the numerous editions of and about his work. In a reversal of the censorship role, a monographic issue of *Cuadernos hispano-americanos* devoted to Borges was canceled by the left-wing editors when Borges accepted a decoration from right-wing Chile. The left was also much incensed by Aleksandr Solzhenitsyn's visit to Spain. New magazines sprang up like mushrooms, and it was mainly into these that writers put their energy.

Literary prizes reflected the upheaval. The Premio de la Nueva Crítica, intended for experimental novels by young Spaniards, went unaccountably to the same Borges—neither "experimental," young, nor even Spanish. The Premio de la Crítica, a prestigious noncommercial prize designed for established writers, went to an unknown 33-year-old, Eduardo Mendoza; his *La verdad sobre el caso Savolta* was a well-constructed, old-fashioned novel of bombs and violence (anarchists versus entrepreneurs) in the radical Barcelona of 1917–19. The Premio Planeta, a thoroughly commercial prize given by a Francoist businessman, usually to regime supporters, went to a youth out of jail on provisional liberty, Jesús Torbado, for *En el día de hoy,* an upside-down political fiction of the detective novel class, in which the Nationalist forces lose the Spanish Civil War, Franco is exiled to Cuba, whence he writes for *Life* magazine, and in which the narrator is Ernest Hemingway.

Eduardo Mendoza won Spain's 1976 Premio de la Crítica for his novel "La verdad sobre el caso Savolta."

COLITA FOTOGRAFIA

Poetry fared far better, with an excellent book of verse by Antonio Colinas, *Sepulcro en Tarquinia,* a highly competent collection running a classical gamut of form, which won the Premio de la Crítica in its category. Another excellent collection, *El vuelo de la celebración* by Claudio Rodríguez, contained some fine and delicate erotic celebrations characterized by truth and innocence.

A solid book of criticism was José Luis Cano's *Heterodoxos y prerománticos,* concerned with the cruel dilemma of the Frenchified classical "liberals" who formed the background in literature and thought for Goya's work and art. Worthy of note were Manuel Andújar's *El destino de Lázaro* and Gonzalo R. LaFora's *Don Juan, Los milagros y otros ensayos.*

Many Argentines were flocking to the new, more liberal Spain, and one at least, Mario Satz, published a noteworthy novel, *Sol.*

(ANTHONY KERRIGAN)

Latin America. Two important writers died during 1976—the Cuban poet and novelist José Lezama Lima, and the Mexican novelist José Revueltas. Lezama Lima, who wrote some of the most hermetic poetry of modern times, was best known for his novel *Paradiso,* a baroque, eccentric account of the childhood and adolescence of a poet. One or two chapters of a sequel, *Purgatorio,* had appeared in Cuba, though it was not clear how much of it had been completed before he died. José Revueltas was grossly underrated by critics. A political militant, he was several times in prison—an experience that provided the basis for many of his novels and stories. When he died, he was at work on a novel, *Hegel y yo,* the germ of which had appeared as a short story.

It was a year of repression and censorship throughout the continent. Among the literary publications forced to shut down was the Argentine journal *Crisis,* some of whose editorial staff were arrested. The Buenos Aires branch of the publishing house Siglo xxi also closed. A galaxy of writers, including David Viñas, Noé Jitrik, and the poet Juan Gelman were living abroad in 1976. Even in Mexico, considered one of the more liberal countries of Latin America, the government forced changes in the editorial staff of *Excelsior,* the country's leading daily. The resignations included the editorial staff of *Plural,* the paper's literary monthly edited by the poet Octavio Paz. Paz said he would start a new magazine, *Vuelta.*

Under the circumstances, it was not surprising that the writing of Latin Americans in exile assumed major importance. The French literary review *L'Europe* announced its decision to dedicate an issue to Chilean literature in exile, and the Cuban journal *Casa de las Américas* devoted one of its 1976 issues to Uruguayan writing that included poems by Mario Benedetti, Juan Carlos Onetti, Hugo Achúgar Ferrari, Ibero Gutiérrez, and Juan Carlos Somma.

Outside Latin America the prestige of its leading writers had seldom been higher. During the year translations appeared of two important works, Carlos

SOPHIE BAKER—CAMERA PRESS/PHOTO TRENDS

Colombian novelist Gabriel García Marquez' "The Autumn of the Patriarch" appeared in English translation in 1976.

Fuentes' historical novel *Terra Nostra* and Gabriel García Marquez' *The Autumn of the Patriarch*, both of which received favourable reviews.

Despite this international attention, 1976 was a fairly quiet year for literature within Spanish America. Several of the *Casa de las Américas* prizes went to writers of the English-speaking Caribbean. A novel prize was awarded for the first time to a Chicano writer, Rolando Hinojosa, for *Klael City y sus alrededores*. The prizes for poetry went to Jorge Alejandro Boccanera of Argentina for *Contraseña* and Hernán Miranda of Chile for his collection *La Moneda y otros poemas*. Short-story prizes were awarded to the Argentine writers Pedro Orgambide for *Historias con tango y corridos* and Eduardo Mignogna for the collection *Cuatrocasas*. Theatre prizes went to Colombians: to Esteban Navajas Cortés for *La agonía del difunto* and to the La Candalaria theatre group for their collective work *Guadalupe años sin cuenta*.

Poetry. One of the few substantial new collections of poetry by an established writer to appear was *Islas a la deriva* by José Emilio Pacheco of Mexico. A sensitive, talented writer, he attempted in this poem to make the text speak for itself, without the obtrusive mediation of an authorial voice. After ten years' silence, Guadalupe Amor published a new collection, *El zoológico de Pita Amor*, and Jomi García Ascot brought out a nostalgic collection, *Un modo de decir*. Symptomatic of a new trend was the collective volume *Doce modos* published by a workshop of "synthetic poetry" in Mexico.

Fiction. Literary criticism increasingly focused on the practice of *escritura*, the kind of text that cannot easily be incorporated into the ideological structures of society. An example of the self-consciously avant-garde text was the Mexican José Martin Artajo's *Fiesta a oscuras*. Most writers preferred a more judicious blend of innovation and irony. The Argentine writer Ricardo Piglia produced a collection of stories, *Nombre falso*, which seemed to owe something to both Roberto Arlt and Jorge Luis Borges in their use of Buenos Aires as a location while at the same time conveying a sense of estrangement. The talented Argentine writer Eduardo Gudiño Kieffer published *Será por eso que la quiero tanto*, a novel that can be described as a melodrama of the tango. It is the story of a peasant and his family in Buenos Aires, a soap opera theme treated with a fine sense of parody. It was a productive period for Poli Délano, the Chilean writer living in exile in Mexico. His short-story collection *Sin morir del todo* had won a literary prize in San Luis Potosí in 1974 and was now published in Mexico City. One critic compared his stories, in mood at least, to those of F. Scott Fitzgerald.

In a more traditional vein, the Mexican anthropologist and short-story writer Eraclio Zepeda published a collection, *Asalto nocturno*, and in Cuba Manuel Cofiño's novel *Cuando la sangre se parece al fuego* explored the ideological changes of a mulatto with deep roots in Afro-Cuban culture during and after the revolution. Finally, no year would be complete without its novel of dictatorship—in 1976 it was *General, general*, a satire by the Paraguayan writer Lincoln Silva.

(JEAN FRANCO)

PORTUGUESE

Portugal. After 18 months of ceaseless bombardment by political tracts, ranging from anarchically proliferating rival editions of the same Marxist classics to the mushroom growth of smudged pamphlets and manifestos apparently translated in some haste from the Albanian, the satiation and disenchantment of a long-suffering reading public coincided with a measure of precarious political stability to encourage the gradual return of literature to its normal (and, thanks to the revolution, incomparably airier and more spacious) place in the national life.

Poets in particular used the enforced moratorium for retrospection and stocktaking, subsequently publishing revised versions of previously censored (or self-censored) works, often supplemented by a modest amount of new writing; and if the hints of unpublishable masterpieces hidden away against the day of liberation predictably proved exaggerated, enough good work emerged from locked drawers to silence the more extreme skeptics. The two volumes of Carlos de Oliveira's *Trabalho Poético* (1941–71) should at last earn this poet's verse the esteem his more conventional novels had long enjoyed. Another graduate of neorealism, Egito Gonçalves, continued his emancipation from its apron strings with *Luz Vegetal*. The latest volume of Eugénio de Andrade's complete poems to date, *Limiar dos Pássaros*, while faintly self-conscious in its exploiting of the new freedom for explicit celebration of deviant eroticism, maintained his deserved prestige. António Ramos Rosa's stature was further enhanced by his long Freudian dream-poem in 72 quasi-sonnets, *Ciclo do Cavalo*, perhaps the most important new work of the year in verse. Pedro Tamen moved firmly into the front rank of somewhat younger poets with the contained intensity of *Agora, Estar*. It was not clear what extrapoetic point was being made (conceivably about the "marketing" of literature) by the four poets—A.-F. Alexandre, H. Moura Pereira, J. M. Fernandes Jorge, and J. M. Magalhães—who collaborated in publishing a limited edition of untitled paper bags stuffed at random with texts of their most recent poems on crumpled slips of paper; the last-named collaborator's earlier book of poems, *Consequência do Lugar*, had implied that poetry, as a process of successive encoding by the poet and decoding by the reader, cannot constitute true communication between them.

In fiction, Agustina Bessa Luís's reputation for subtly allusive novels of great complexity was heightened by the appearance of *As Pessoas Felizes* and *Crónica do Cruzado Osb,* while Jorge de Sena's collection of short stories dating from 1961–62 (and clearly unprintable on both political and "moral" grounds at the time), *Os Grão-Capitães,* was the major single revelation of buried treasure so far.

(STEPHEN RECKERT)

Brazil. The year 1976 was a productive one for Brazilian literature. Fiction showed a continued predominance of regionalism. Josué Montello's *Os Tambores de São Luís,* an absorbing historical novel that vividly recounted a century of slavery and religious cult life in northeastern Maranhão, received wide critical attention and acclaim. Djalcídio Jurandir, who was awarded the Machado de Assis Prize for his overall literary production, published *Chão dos Lobos,* another volume in his series of novels portraying life in the northern state of Pará; the work was notable for its presentation of local customs and linguistic varieties. Paulo Jacob dealt poetically with Amazon River life in *Vila Rica das Queimadas,* a first-person narrative about an immigrant Syrian family.

Speculation about the future was another principal trend in fiction. Herberto Sales's *O Fruto de Vosso Ventre* was a science-fiction satire about a technocratic government's attempts to prevent further overpopulation of its robotlike society through repressive contraceptive measures. J. J. Veiga once again returned to his futuristic world of fantastic, inexplicable events in *Os Pecados da Tribo.* Maria Alice Barroso's *Um Dia Vamos Rir Disso Tudo* viewed Cariocan pseudo-intellectual life of the 1960s from the 1990s.

Collections of short fiction brought attention to two novices. Jair Vitória's *Cuma-João* presented poignant episodes in the life of the poor of southeastern Minas Gerais state. A regionalistic orientation also characterized *O Azul da Montanha* by Enéas Athanazio. Notable works of established writers included Hernani Donato's *Babel,* brief stories replete with contemporary slang; Juarez Barroso's *Joaquinho Gato,* short "documentaries" of the perilous existence in Ceará state; and *As Curtições do Pitu,* Elias José's first volume of juvenile fiction.

None of Brazil's outstanding poets published a new collection of poetry, but one poem by Drummond de Andrade aroused great critical interest. Marcus Accioly's epic of man entitled *Sísifo* contained all forms of poetry, from the classical sonnet to concrete and popular Brazilian forms. Yolanda Jordão's latest volume was *Biografia do Edifício e Anexos.* A newcomer of note was Adélia Prado; her *Bagagem* celebrated the (pro)creative role of women.

Drama continued to be heavily censored. By midyear over 80 plays had been held up by censorship, with a crippling effect on Brazilian theatre. Dramatists turned to other endeavours; Ariano Suassuna published another volume of his folk-chivalric novel, and Jorge Andrade continued to write for television.

The fourth volume of Assis Brasil's important study of contemporary literature discussed Brazilian literary criticism in a world perspective. The growing influence of "new criticism" in Brazil was evident in critical studies of the works of poet Drummond de Andrade by Silviano Santiago and J. Guilherme Merquior. Ana Maria Machado evaluated the psycho-symbolic meaning of proper names in the works of Guimarães Rosa in *Recado do Nome.*

(IRWIN STERN)

RUSSIAN

Soviet Literature. A noteworthy feature of recent Soviet literature has been a growing interest on the part of writers, above all novel and short-story writers, in presenting a study of life in depth and on many planes simultaneously. Examples of this in works published during 1975–76 were Yuri Bondarev's novel *The Shore,* Yuri Trifonov's short stories *Another Life* (1975) and his novel *The House on the Embankment,* and V. Beekman's novel *Night Fliers* (translated from Estonian), which portrayed events during World War II and the postwar years and dealt with a great many ethical, philosophical, and other problems.

The theme of links between different times and generations was of special significance. It ran through Vasily Zakrutkin's novel *The Creation,* dealing with the establishment of the young Soviet state, Oles Gonchar's *Shore of Love* (in Ukrainian), and Mirmukhsin's *The Smelter's Son* (translated from Uzbek), and was to be seen in the works of the contributors to *Great Roads: Stories of Our Contemporaries.*

As before, many works were historical in character: I. Yesenberlin's trilogy *Nomads* (in Kazakh), the story of the Kazakh people's struggle for their independence; I. Kalachnikov's novel *A Grim Age,* about the terrible days of Genghis Khan; and B. Tumasov's novel *Savage Dawns,* dealing with the formation of a centralized Russian state.

The time of the Revolution of October 1917 and the Civil War found reflection in Sergey Zalygin's novel *The Commission* and S. Drozdov's semidocumentary *No More Waiting,* based on historical documents, personal recollections of old Bolsheviks, and so on. World War II and the heroic feats of Soviet people at the front and in the rear were featured in I. Akulov's *The Baptism,* F. Niyazi's novel *Don't Say That the Forest Is Empty . . .* (translated from Tadzhik), Y. Ebanatsky's documentary stories *We're Not from a Legend* (translated from Ukrainian), and I. Novikov's *Not Long Till Dawn* (translated from Belorussian), about partisans.

NOVOSTI

Soviet writer Yuri Bondarev published "The Shore" in 1976.

There was increasing interest in works about contemporary life and above all those dealing with controversial social and moral problems. Among these was G. Radov's collection of essays *The Chairman's Block* and M. Kolesnikov's novel *Altunin Takes a Decision,* which raised questions concerning the improvement of quality and efficiency in production; others were V. Astafyev's "narrative in folk tales" *The Tsar-Fish,* which called for rational use of the gifts of nature; V. Kondrashov's novel *Ginger Is Not Ginger* about the upbringing of the rising generation; a novel by V. Bubnis, *The Flowering of the Unsown Rye* (in Lithuanian), and another by V. Lama, *The Result of a Lifetime* (translated from Latvian); S. Veliev's book *Links: Novel and Stories* (translated from Azerbaijani); and R. Solntsev's *A Day in the Defense of a Good Man Story,* presenting a serious discussion on true and false moral values.

Many dramatic works provided evidence of a heightened interest in moral problems involving people whose lives follow a complex course: Vasily Shukshin's posthumous *Call Me into the Bright Distance,* Aleksey Arbuzov's *Old Fashioned Comedy,* and E. Damian's *Idol* (translated from Moldavian) were three examples. There was lively public interest in A. Gelman's play *Minutes of a Meeting,* which posed the question of individual responsibility in the Soviet Union.

Continuity of generations was what one might call the theme of many works by Soviet poets. These included Mikhail Dudin's *Boundaries: Poems,* Sergey Vikulov's *The Bonfire That Warmed You: Verses,* and the anthology *Those Years: Verses,* which included some of the finest works by modern Soviet poets. Poems that were in effect meditations on things lived through and suffered, and on moral values, were T. Sunnanen's *Red Bridge* (in Finnish), Yulia Drunina's *Star of the Trenches,* L. Martynov's *Earthly Burden,* Yevgeny Yevtushenko's *A Father's Ear,* Mikola Bazhan's *Night Reflections of an Old Worker* (in Ukrainian), Rasul Gamzatov's *Cherish Our Mothers* (translated from Avarish), and M. Jangaziev's *My House in the Golden Valley* (translated from Kirgiz).

(NOVOSTI)

Expatriate Russian Literature. The growing influence of the new Russian literature in exile brought to mind more and more in 1976 that minor 19th-century prophet, quoted by Nadezhda Mandelstam in her memoirs, who said that "Russia exists only for the purpose of teaching the world a lesson." The thought grew not only out of Aleksandr Solzhenitsyn's always didactic and increasingly minatory speeches and interviews but from the spreading awareness of literature's extraordinary role in Russian history, before and after the Revolution. Solzhenitsyn's strictures struck home to Western audiences preoccupied with economic crisis and the shifting balance of power in the world, but a more significant response was that described by the British playwright Dennis Potter in a review of *A Voice from the Chorus,* letters from prison by the critic Andrey Sinyavsky published under his "subversive" pseudonym of Abram Tertz. "The camps of the East are turning into the monasteries of the West," wrote Potter, and we were learning to read their literature "not just to confirm a prejudice or damn a hope about the nature of Soviet Communism but more and more to look for insights into our own condition." In fact, it was possible to see more clearly during the year that not merely the literature of the camps but the whole of modern Russian literature, with the lessons to be learned from the harsh circumstances of its production and precarious preservation, was becoming a dominant influence, widely and deeply pondered.

Sinyavsky, teaching at the Sorbonne in 1976, demonstrated how remarkably productive the new "monastic" discipline could be by publishing two major critical works on Pushkin and Gogol (*Progulki s Pushkinym* and *V teni Gogolya*) that had also been written during his six years in the Dubrovlag forced labour camp. Sinyavsky's Pushkin essay, wrote Max Hayward in the *Times Literary Supplement,* went far to explain "the uncanny power that poets have exercised not only over the minds of the Russian nation but also over the minds of even its most oppressive rulers," for, thanks to Pushkin, "the poet is high priest, wielding a spiritual power equal to the Tsar's in the temporal domain." The example of Gogol supplies a complementing, darker version of this role—the poet as a being gifted with terrifying insight into the more mysterious energies at work in nature: Sinyavsky presents him as one afflicted with the ancient shaman's vision.

Solzhenitsyn's fascinating portrait of *Lenin in Zürich* was a strange, scarcely classifiable work which he presented as a bringing together of elements dealing with Lenin from his huge historical novel in progress.

A significant new voice from the chorus of exile was that of David Markish, whose talented novel *The Beginning* recounted a quest for a lost father and the eventual discovery of his Jewishness. It was dedicated to the author's murdered father, the Yiddish poet Peretz Markish, who was one of Stalin's later victims, and it closely reflected his own experience, which included banishment to a remote area of Kazakhstan as a "member of the family of an Enemy of the People."

(W. L. WEBB)

GREEK

The democratic climate created after the fall of the dictatorship (1967–74) continued to influence Greek intellectual life. The suppression in the new constitution of the article that had imposed *katharevusa* as the official language of the state and education was followed by a government decision (1976) to introduce demotic in the schools, two steps that can justifiably be called historic.

The most significant poetry collections in 1976 were older works, previously unpublished or now appearing in collected editions. The *Apanta-Piitika* of the critic Markos Avgeris revealed him as one of the most noteworthy poets of his generation (1910). George Seferis' *Tetradio Gymnasmaton B* included many unpublished satirical and political poems written between 1934 and 1971. *Piimata 1938–1971 Vol. 4* and *Epikairika 1945–1969* by Yannis Ritsos expressed the struggles and sufferings of the Greeks during this troubled period. These dramatic events also inspired postwar poets such as Takis Sinopoulos in his *Syllogi 1, 1951–1964,* Titos Patrikios in his *Poiimata 1, 1948–1954,* and Dimitris Christodoulou in his *Aikhmes (1965–1975).* Sinopoulos, who views the postwar world torn apart and in ruins, produces many unusual images, sometimes terrifying but full of truth. Patrikios turns nostalgically to the heroic years of the Resistance but principally expresses the anger and bitterness that many Greeks felt after the defeat of the leftist movement and the frustration of its hopes.

A collection of poems by Greek poet Nikiforos Vrettakos, "Apogevmatino Iliotropio," appeared in 1976.

These sentiments are also expressed by Christodoulou, as they evolved before, during, and after the dictatorship. Perhaps the most significant poetry collection of 1976 was Nikiforos Vrettakos' *Apogevmatino Iliotropio*—thoughtful poems, almost classical in their simplicity, having as their theme the quest for beauty, light, and life.

The most important novel of 1976 was Kosmas Politis' unfinished *Terma,* set in the first decade of the century, with a plot skillfully woven from real, autobiographical, and fictitious elements. Also significant as a piece of political prose was *Kapetan Aris* by Kostis Papakongos—an exciting account of the guerrilla war in Greece from 1940 to 1945, with Aris, the principal guerrilla leader, as its central figure. In *Goupato* Christodoulou described the experiences of the generation that grew up during the dictatorship of 1936–40, the occupation, and the Resistance. Vasilis Vasilikos drew his inspiration from the immediate present in two novels: *To kalokairi toy Erotokritou* and *O Iatrodikastis,* the latter a documentary based on a crime as fantastic as that which he related in *Z.* Special mention must be made of *Selides Aftoviografias,* vol. 4, by the poet Giorgos Vafopoulos, which gives a composite picture of the intellectual life of Thessaloniki from between the wars to the present day.

Notable works of criticism were: Eratosthenis Kapsomenos' structuralist study *I syntaktiki domi tis piitikis glossas tou Seferi;* Kostas Profyris' literary historical study *O Andreas Kalvos karbonaros;* Andreas Karandonis' *I piisi mas meta ton Seferi;* and Giorgos Vrisimitzakis' *To ergo tou K. P. Kavafi.* Kitsos Makris' *Laiki tekhni tou Piliou* was the work of a lifetime and one of the most significant of its kind. Also based on many years' research was Giorgos Petris' art-study *Makryannis kai Panagiotis Zografos.* Sociohistorical and political studies dominated the year, among them *Istorika Dokimia A. Pos eftasama stin 2li Apriliou 1967 B. 1940—Ethniki antistasi* by former premier Panagiotis Kanellopoulos.

(CHRISTOS ALEXIOU)

EASTERN EUROPEAN LITERATURE

Polish. The death of Stanislaw Grochowiak stunned literary circles in Poland. Grochowiak was acknowledged as the finest poet-dramatist among those who had made their literary debut after 1956. Coming only a few months after the tragic death of the brilliant director Konrad Swinarski, Grochowiak's death left Poland's theatre bereft of two major talents.

More and more Polish directors were turning to Witkacy, Mrozek, and Gombrowicz to fill out their repertories. Unfortunately, Tadeusz Rozewicz' latest play had difficulties with the censors. Mrozek's latest efforts appeared in the third volume of his *Collected Works* containing *The Emigrés* (his best play since *Tango*), *The Slaughterhouse,* and the screenplay *The Island of Roses.* With the staging of Gombrowicz' third and final play, *Operetta,* by Kazimierz Dejmek in Lodz, Gombrowicz like Witkacy became an integral part of Polish theatre history.

Any year in which Tadeusz Konwicki publishes a novel becomes a banner year. His latest work, *The Calendar and the Hourglass,* although not as sensational as his *A Polish Dreambook,* was still worthy of his immense talent. Intimate and personal, sometimes self-deprecating, the work was Konwicki's *Apologia pro Vita Sua.* Stanislaw Lem, perhaps Poland's most famous novelist, continued his endless journey into private and scientific fantasy with *The Mask.* Wojciech Zukrowski's *The Beach on the River Styx* was proclaimed a best-seller by its publisher (Czytelnik) even before it appeared. It was in one way a modernized *Fathers and Sons;* in another, a polonized version of the American rat race—from the point of view of a woman. Bohdan Czeszko's *The Flood* was a sensitive account of a man's search for personal meaning among the inhabitants of an isolated fishing village. Andrzej Kusniewicz' *The Third Kingdom* was also derivative of Turgenev's novel: the fathers in this instance, former victims of Nazi concentration camps, seem more heroic and less pathetic than the old Bazarovs; the sons continue to protest in the usual ways and seem highly contrived and two-dimensional.

Noteworthy was Ewa Lipska's *Living Death,* a novel in the form of a schizophrenic's notebook. It marked an outstanding literary debut for a fine poet. Also important was Jerzy Andrzejewski's *The Time Has Come for Your Annihilation,* loosely based on the biblical myth of Cain and Abel, depicting a Cain who kills his brother out of "compassionate love."

The death occurred in July of Antoni Slonimski (*see* OBITUARIES), the finest of the older generation of poets. Despite the loss of Grochowiak and Slonimski, Polish poets continued to dominate the literary scene. Tadeusz Rozewicz' new volume of poetry, *Poems,* showed an urgency and a conflict between the poet and fame that were absent from his former works. Czytelnik published selections of poems by Wieslawa Szymborska and Urszula Kozioł, two of Poland's finest poets. Grochowiak's *Billiards,* published before his death, seemed in retrospect to be poetic arguments with the spirits he was soon to join: his love spats with the Polish Romantics, his caustic dialogues with the poets of the "Age of Reason," his ambivalent view of tradition—all these were gossamer excuses for his love of humanity and his race against the Hound of Heaven. He was not vanquished. Zbigniew Herbert added lustre to his reputation as a poet, critic, and essayist with his volume of sketches, *Elements.*

(EDWARD J. CZERWINSKI)

Czechoslovak. The publication in the U.S. and Canada of three major works by Czechoslovakia's two leading contemporary novelists, Ludvik Vaculik and Milan Kundera, constituted the major literary event of 1976. These works deal with the question of individual responsibility for political immorality. The narrator of Vaculik's *The Guinea Pigs* is a common bank clerk, homespun and stubbornly frank (like the author himself). He enjoys observing the habits of his docile pets, but his curiosity and latent sadism lead him to experiments that soon verge on torture. The kindly benefactor and later murderer of guinea pigs simultaneously falls prey to powers for whom he is but an annoying and insignificant nuisance. The complex narrative employs fantasy and grotesquerie in a manner recalling Kafka and Gogol. The novel is a chilling allegory about the banality of evil.

The subject of Kundera's *Life Is Elsewhere* is the mediocre lyrical poet who, driven by an immature and narcissistic vision, becomes the handmaiden of a totalitarian regime. The psychological motivation which Kundera places at the root of the process is the need to emerge from under the suffocating cloud of excessive maternal possessiveness and prove oneself a man. The young poet turns to violent and virile revolution, cruel and implacable, as a sublimation of unfulfilled sexual desire. Every poet needs a revolution, Kundera implies, alternating episodes from the life of his fictional hero Jaromil with vignettes from the lives of other "romantic" poets. Although Jaromil is a ridiculous parody of the rebel poet, and his socialist realist poetry readings and newspaper contributions are treated with biting satire, the novel is not without pathos. Many members of Kundera's generation began their careers as writers in service of the revolution.

Kundera's *The Farewell Party* first strikes the reader as an ironic view of the labyrinth of sexual psychology (in the vein of the author's earlier stories, *Laughable Loves*). However, the lovers in this satirical farce are also clearly representative of types in Czech society, from the petite bourgeoise who would willingly sacrifice others for her own advantage to the former political prisoner who prides himself on his own lack of vindictiveness, only to discover that he too, given anonymity, would murder his ideological enemies. The only hope in the novel is provided by a character who seems capable of loving and finding value in all humanity, the exploiter as well as the exploited.

The recent novels of Vaculik and Kundera clearly attempt to transcend the questions of immediate political blame and concentrate instead on the psychological constants of human nature which render difficult the achievement of a truly humane society. By exhibiting in their works an insight into the inevitable fallibility and culpability of all men, these two authors opened a way toward a reconciliation between the humanists of the Prague Spring of 1968 and the political leaders of the "normalized" Czechoslovakia of 1976. But how much time would elapse before these novels could be published in Czech in their native land was yet unknown.

(HERBERT J. EAGLE)

Hungarian. Nonfiction of literary distinction has always been held in high esteem in Hungary. In 1976 a work that revealed more about present-day Hungarian mores than many a novel was Gyorgy Moldova's *Akit a mozdony füstje megcsapott* ("A Whiff of Engine Smoke"), a series of reports about the

Sandor Weores, Hungary's most gifted living poet, published "Athallasok" ("Overheard Voices") in 1976.

Hungarian state railroad. The poet Istvan Vas continued publishing, in installments, his voluminous reminiscences entitled *Mert vijjog a saskeselyu?* ("Why Does the Vulture Screech?"). Vas's work shed light not only on his own intellectual and artistic development but on the crises of conscience faced by Hungarian writers in the last several decades. Pal Granasztoi's new book of essays, *Varosok, kepek, zene* ("Cities, Pictures, Music"), likewise contained reflections on art and society, in addition to interesting biographical material. An architect and city planner by profession, Granasztoi has also been called one of the outstanding figures of contemporary Hungarian literature. An émigré writer, Elemer Illyes, treated a highly emotional subject with exemplary restraint; his *Erdely valtozasa* ("Change in Transylvania") was a penetrating appraisal of Hungarian life in modern Romania.

Miklos Meszoly's *Film*, by far the most interesting new Hungarian novel, focused on a moment in the life of an ancient couple and superimposed on it a description of a murder that took place some 60 years earlier and possibly involved the couple. This multifaceted, curiously enigmatic, cinematically impersonal evocation of reality contained unmistakable allusions to crucial events in recent Hungarian history. Past and present often merged in another novel, Agnes Gergely's elliptical and self-consciously trendy *A chicagoi valtozat* ("The Chicago Variant"), which was about a Hungarian actress's experiences in the United States. A juxtaposition of past and present was also a provocative feature of Tibor Cseres' *Parazna szobrok* ("Lascivious Statues"), a novel tracing the fate of an army officer who led his troops into the formerly Hungarian provinces of Slovakia during World War II. Even Ferenc Karinthy's short novel, *Hazszentelo* ("Housewarming"), otherwise a perfect example of critical realism, made use of the sort of chronological backtracking favoured by avant-garde novelists. *Hazszentelo* recounts the circumstances surrounding a murder committed by a successful executive. Like other recent Karinthy tales, all of them ironic success stories, the novel questions the values of those who had made it to the top in modern Hungary.

A new volume of poetry, *Athallasok* ("Overheard Voices") by Sandor Weores, Hungary's most gifted and versatile living poet, proved to be disappointing since it was little more than a mildly amusing collection of improvisations and pastiches. Dramatist Istvan Orkeny showed his penchant for grotesque situations again in his new play, *Kulcskeresok* ("Looking for the Key"), in which a pilot casually lands his plane in a cemetery. Gyula Hernadi's *A tolmacs* ("The Interpreter"), a play about the 16th-century Peasants' War, and Andras Suto's *Csillag a maglyan* ("Star on a Burning Stake"), a historical drama concentrating on the clash between John Calvin and his rival Michael Servetus, were interesting mainly because of their modern overtones.

(IVAN SANDERS)

Romanian. The most generally applauded novel published in 1976 was Constantin Toiu's *Galeria cu vita salbatica.* Among the many fictional works to deal with the 1950s, it seemed so far the most forthright: in an almost Orwellian manner, it traces the destiny of a young man who is first excluded from the Communist Party, then arrested, and finally commits suicide. The harsh outlines of the plot are softened by the luxuriant variety of secondary characters, from law enforcers and sycophants to eccentric or serenely wise survivors. D. R. Popescu, a leading novelist of the middle generation, continued in *Ploile de dincolo de vreme* his allegorical saga of contemporary provincial Romania, in which the obsession of a confused guilt leads again and again to labyrinthine investigations and futile gestures of redemption. Fanus Neagu's much-awaited *Frumosii nebuni ai marilor orase* seemed to many just a succession of spectacular and improbable episodes, without significant characters or structure.

Romanian novelist Fanus Neagu, whose "Frumosii nebuni ai marilor orase" was published in 1976.

© LUTFI ÖZKÖK

Among the year's books of poetry, *Anotimpul discret* by Stefan A. Doinas stood out; it was a sophisticated and melancholy attempt to set up poetry as a solution to the conflicting claims of reality and nonreality in the world—even an imaginary world can act as moral judge against its creator, man's conscience. Remarkable also was Ion Gheorghe's *Noimele,* the work of a muscular and tortured psyche apprehensive about the fate of peasant values and dignity in an industrial environment.

As a mere curiosity, a new hybrid genre should be noted: lyrical rhapsodizing about figures of literary history, the equivalent perhaps of romanced biographies. Dan Verona's *Cartea runelor* and S. Banulescu's *Scrisori provinciale* were examples. Related to such endeavours, but on a higher level, was the venture of Eugen Barbu, a noted novelist, into critical writing: he launched a projected 15-volume history of Romanian literature by publishing volume 14, a survey of contemporary poetry that was often unjust, always fiercely arbitrary, but also full of startling insights and felicitous comments. I. Negoitescu's *Analize si sinteze* was part of his history of Romanian literature—its plan had been announced in 1968, but so far only fragments had appeared. Two other works of criticism deserve mention: N. Manolescu's monograph about Sadoveanu offered a surprisingly fresh exegesis of Sadoveanu's historical novels in terms of vast imaginary societal structures; Cornel Regman's *Colocvial* was a collection of current criticism, vigorous, fair, and witty, a most reliable assessment of present-day literary trends.

(VIRGIL P. NEMOIANU)

Yugoslavian. SERBIAN. The last unpublished works by Ivo Andric were published posthumously in 1976: poems, *Sta sanjam i sta mi se dogadja,* short stories, *Kuca na osami,* and an unfinished novel, *Omer-pasa Latas.* Although weaker than his earlier works, they enhanced Andric's overall reputation.

It was a bountiful year in Serbian literature. Among the poets, Desanka Maksimovic published *Letopis Perunovih potomaka,* in which she deals lyrically with the mythology of ancient Slavs. Another established poet, Miodrag Pavlovic, mixed his visits to the distant past with contemporary motifs in *Zavetine.* Bosko Bogetic evoked the translucent beauty of his native Mediterranean in *Vrt u Budvi.* And in *Subota* Ljubomir Simovic offered a psychological and sociological portrait of present society through a dialogue among the visitors to a night café.

In fiction Mihailo Lalic continued to trace the recent origins of the Montenegrins in his saga *Zatocnici.* Mirko Kovac's best book—and perhaps the best novel of the season—*Ruganje s dusom,* was a Faulknerian atmosphere piece of diabolic probings into the disintegrating soul of modern man. Danilo Kis dealt boldly with the monstrosity of Stalinist purges by following several victims on their way to perdition (*Grobnica za Borisa Davidovica*). Other important novels were *Upotreba coveka* by Aleksandar Tisma, *Srebrna ruka* by Borislav Pekic, and *Kolijevka* by Zarko Komanin.

The first five anthologies of Serbian criticism promised an excellent series. Predrag Palavestra brought to life a neglected genius who was very influential in the first decades of the 20th century in England (*Dogma i utopija Dimitrija Mitrinovica*). Leading critics Velibor Gligoric, Petar Dzadzic, and Zoran Gavrilovic also published books of criticism.

CROATIAN. Although the harvest in Croatian literature was not as bountiful, several outstanding works were published. Miroslav Krleza continued his saga of the Croatian people in the twilight of the Austro-Hungarian empire with another volume of *Zastave*. Another novel, *Gastarbajterce* by Ivan Slamnig, involved the problem of Yugoslav guest workers in a foreign country.

Well-known poets Vesna Parun (*Olovni golub*), Antun Soljan (*Izabrane pjesme*), and Jure Franicevic Plocar (*Bastina*) trod established paths yet managed to bring refreshing new spirit into their poetry, especially Parun with her highly emotional, confessional style.

In an interesting book of essays, *Izmisljotine,* the witty and erudite poet Danijel Dragojevic talked about art, religion, philosophy, and other cultural matters, attempting to bridge the chasm between classical values and modern civilization.

Of great importance were also several volumes of the history of Croatian literature, especially *Srednjovekovna knjizevnost* by Eduard Hercigonja and *Ilirizam i realizam* by M. Zivancevic and I. Franges. The last of the monumental 97-volume *Rjecnik hrvatskoga ili srpskoga jezika* was issued, bringing to a close a work of a hundred years.

SLOVENIAN. Slovenian literature celebrated the 100th anniversary of the birth of Ivan Cankar. His works were reissued, several critical studies were published, and there was even a biographical novel about him, *Tujec* by Anton Slodnjak.

In poetry several established poets published new books. Gregor Strnisa had two books, *Jajce* and *Rebernik,* in which he coupled the medieval morality with surrealistic metaphor, while imitating the balladic style of folk poetry. Kajetan Kovic wrestled in *Labrador* with problems of alienation of modern man in the technological age but found a way back to basic human values. In *Kras* Ciril Zlobec continued, with some novel approaches, to search for his childhood. Tone Pavcek was searching for his own self at the present time (*Poganske hvalnice*). Tomaz Salamun, one of the younger and most active poets, published three books, *Praznik, Druidi,* and *Turbine,* which pretty much confirmed his poetic idiom.

Among the fiction writers, Andrej Hieng attempted in *Cernodej* to scrutinize social and psychological foundations of the Slovenian man at the turn of the century and today. A tireless novelist, Pavle Zidar published several more short novels, of which *Dolenjski Hamlet hamletuje* and *Zivim* combined social criticism with moral concerns. Peter Bozic's *Zemlja* was a grotesque novel about the lower strata of society, mixing the real with the fantastic.

MACEDONIAN. The youngest of Yugoslav literatures, Macedonian literature showed a constant and healthy need to assert itself. One manifestation of this self-assertion was the publication of collected works of several writers (Kuzman A. Sapkarov, Vojdran Cernodrimski, Aco Sopov, Blaze Koneski, Mateja Matevski, etc.). Another manifestation was a flood of critical works; obviously, the critics felt that enough literature had been written to allow wide-ranging analyses and syntheses.

Several poets published new collections. Among the best, Aco Sopov drew on his experiences as an envoy to write *Pesni na crnata zena,* devoted to women of Africa. Mateja Matevski stressed in *Perunika* the native landscape and the abandonment of the native soil, displaying economy of expression and harmony between the language and the poet's ideas and emotions. Mihail Rendzov's poems in *Strav* were characterized by contemplation and refined emotions.

A leading playwright, Vasil Iljoski, dealt in *Svadba* with one of the oldest motifs in literature, a wedding, but with a new twist.

(VASA D. MIHAILOVICH)

ARABIC

Palestinian poet Mahmoud Darwish published two poems, *Tall Al-Za'tar* ("The Hill of Thims," named for a Palestinian camp in Lebanon), inspired by the revolutionary situation in the Middle East. Darwish succeeded in enriching his verse with dramatic characteristics and yet retaining a lyrical sweetness and warmth. The hero of the first poem is the revolutionary Ahmad; that of the second is the people. Iraqi poet Muthaffar an-Nawab, in his *Wattarryyat Layliyyah* ("String Tunes of the Night"), sought to write poetry for the people.

Syrian novelist Hanna Minah was still in the limelight with his book of short stories, *Al-Abanossa Al Baida* ("The White Abanossa Tree"). Egyptian Najib Mahfouz brought out two main works: *Qualb Al Layl* ("The Heart of the Night") and *Hadrat Al Muhtarram* ("The Respectable Esquire"). Iraqi Abdul Rahman Rabi'i put forth *Al-Quamar Wal Asswar* ("The Moon and Walls"), a sequel to his *Thikriat Al Madina* ("The Memory of the City"), published the previous year.

Among Egyptian novelists Jamal al-Ghitani was seen as the inheritor of the mantle of Najib Mahfouz. Among Palestinians, Yahya Yakhlaf was the heir apparent of the late Ghassan Kanafani, who was assassinated in Beirut. Yakhlaf's novel *Najran Tahta Al-Sifr* ("Najran Below Zero") was a sort of epic drama in modern experimental clothing. Two other leading Palestinians were Emil Habibi, whose *Al-Mutashael* ("The Optimistic-Pessimistic") appeared in 1975, and the late Ghassan Kanafani for his unfinished trilogy, *Al-Ashek* ("The Lover"), *Al 'Ama Wal Akhrass* ("The Blind and the Dumb"), and *Barkuk Nissan* ("The Prunes of April").

There was a revival of interest in the works of the Algerian novelists Katib Yassin, Mohammad Deeb, Mawlud Faraoun, Mawlud Muammari, Malek Haddad, and Asia Jabbar. Two interesting novels by Taher Wattar were published in 1976: *Al-Laz* and *Al-Zilzal* ("The Earthquake"). Wattar represents the realistic socialistic trend of thought in Algeria and in this sense can be considered in the same continuum of thought as Yassin, Haddad, and certain novelists in Algeria who wrote in French.

Also noteworthy was a novel by Nawal Sadawi of Egypt; her earlier book on sex, *Al-Mara' Wal Jins* ("Woman and Sex"), may have been the reason why her 1976 novel *Immrata'tan Fi Imra'* ("Two Women in One") was a best-seller.

The Algerian Khatib Yassin brought out a play, *Al Jutha Al Mutawaka* ("The Surrounded Corps"), and promised another on Vietnam. Egyptian Mahmud Diab's play *Rassoulon Min Karyat Tamira Lillistifham A'n Masa'lat Al-Harb Wal-Silm* ("A Messenger from Tamira to Inquire About War and Peace") was expected to be produced later in Syria. But the two main events in the drama were the one-act play by Naji George, *I'nni A'tarid* ("I Protest"), portraying social stratification and conflict; and the granting of permission to Palestinian Samih al-Kassim to have his play *Al-Maghtasseba* ("The Raped") published in the Orient Press.

(ABDUL RAHMAN YAGHI)

JEWISH

Hebrew. Hebrew literature had demonstrated steady growth as well as gaining a measure of prestige abroad, largely in translation. Recently, however, there had been what might be called a retrenchment, caused no doubt by insecure economic conditions in Israel.

The posthumous fiction of well-known authors such as S. Y. Agnon and H. Hazaz continued to appear. The prolific A. Oz offered volumes of stories, *Har ha-Etza ha-raa* and *Arzot ha-Tan.* Y. Kanuick's *Afar u-Teshuka* struck a familiar note, and Y. Orpaz' *ha-Yoman Shehelif et ha-Bedaya* proved technically adroit. M. Shamir's *Pirkai Saba Liova* was evocative of the past. The third volume of D. Shahar's *ha-Rozenet* was published.

Perceptive critical studies were Sh. Kramer's *Panim ve-Ofan* and A. B. Yoffe's *ha-Sifrut: Chadash Mul Yashan.* Complementing this was B. Kurzweill's provocative disquisition *Lenochach ha-Mevuch Ha-ruchanit shel Dorainu,* which appeared after his death. *Halifat Iggerot Bain Sh. Abramovich ve-Ch. N. Bialik* represented the correspondence between two classic Hebrew authors. R. Sivan's linguistic evaluation of contemporary Hebrew, *Ovnai Lashon Yomanu,* drew attention, as did Sh. Albeck's scholarly essay *Dinai ha-Memonot ba-Talmud.*

Many volumes by poets of various "schools" were published, among them Sh. Shalom's *Or Ganuz,* S. Tanai's *Raglai ha-Mevaser,* Y. Hurwitz' *Shirim 1960–1973,* and A. Yeshurun's *ha-Mashber ha-Suri-Afrikani.* The previously uncollected writings of an earlier modern Hebrew poet, Y. Shteinberg, appeared. A scholarly contribution was D. Pagis' work on Hebrew poetry of centuries past, *Shirat Hachol ha-Ivrit.*

The few Hebrew authors still residing in the U.S. had their books published in Israel, the natural centre for both critical reaction and readership. Nevertheless, a selection of essays on Y. D. Berkovich appeared, edited by A. Holtz. In addition three volumes of poetry made their appearance: E. Silberschlag's *Yesh Raishit Lechol Acharit;* G. Preil's *Shirim Mishnai ha-Kezavot,* and the transplanted American R. Ben-Yosef's slim volume *Kolot ba-Rama.*

(GABRIEL PREIL)

Yiddish. The Holocaust and Jewish life in Eastern Europe in the interwar period still dominated Yiddish literature.

In *The Silent Quorum* Chaim Grade re-created Jewish life in Poland on the eve of World War II in seminal prose and traditional form. Isaac Bashevis Singer's *The Mirror* contained esoteric stories told in realistic style which, though thematically similar, turned on nuances and images. Abraham Sutzkever's *Green Aquarium* was his first collection of prose poems. Experimental and symbolic, they created an apocalyptic mood.

Some Yiddish writers in the Soviet Union managed to free themselves in part from the limitations of the official socialist realism. In *The Story of a Love* Note Lurie wrote in an old-fashioned, sentimental style about the love of a young couple. The author invoked the traditional *shtetl* and the Holocaust. Irme Druker wrote in *Musicians* with nostalgia about their struggles and accomplishments. Elya Schechtman, an immigrant to Israel, continued his epic novel *Erev,* focusing on the fate of the Jewish community in Russia, the Revolution, the Ukrainian struggle for independence, and Zionism.

For Isaiah Spiegel's 70th birthday a two-volume collection of his stories was published, *The Stars Light in the Abyss.* In them Spiegel transformed the tragedy of the Holocaust into great literature. J. Finer's *Two Families* was a dramatic description of Jewish life in France under the Nazis—the suffering, deportations, mass murders, and the Resistance. *The Living Corpses* by Wolf Tambur (Bucharest) was a fantastic symbolic novella rich with allusions. Sholem Shtern dealt in verse in *The Family in Canada* with the life and struggles of a Canadian Jewish family.

A number of excellent collections of poetry were published. *The Jester and the Knight* by Shloyme Roitman, now in Israel, contained poems written in the Soviet Union between 1933 and 1970. Remarkably free of propaganda, they excelled in melody and images. Chaim Maltinsky's *The Earth Understands* was topical, idiomatic, and emotional. In *Wounds and Wonder* Selwyn Schwartz expressed his personal response through imagery and striking metaphors. I. Paner's *Traits in the Personality of Itsik Manger* contained recollections of this major lyric poet. Rochelle Weprinsky's *Night Fires* included exquisite poems and some excellent translations of Emily Dickinson. In *On Grass and Clay* Shifra Werber produced a number of delicate, sensitive poems. Melekh Ravitch's *The Story of My Life* described his life and activities in various Yiddish literary centres and his encounters with Yiddish writers.

(ELIAS SCHULMAN)

CHINESE

The quality of the short stories written in Taiwan in 1976 was not what one might expect from such a heavy concentration of authors in a single genre. There were some unimpressive experiments in time-shift and stream-of-consciousness in Chang Hsi-kuo's *Banana Boat* and Ch'i Teng-sheng's *I Love Black Iris* and *Cul-de-Sac.* The works of new young writers were represented in such collections as *Best Stories of the Year* edited by Hung Hsin-fu, *Annual Anthology of Modern Chinese Literature: The Short Story,* and *An Anthology of Serialized Short Stories.* These stories, invariably following a naturalistic, almost reportorial, narrative line and involving ordinary characters in ordinary situations, attempted to strike a note of anguish in the lower depths of Taiwan.

Work generally richer and artistically superior was apparent in the collections by Wang To, Cheng Ch'ing-wen, and Ch'en Ying-chen. Set in his native fishing village, the stories in Wang's *Chin Shiu Shen* probe, with realistic depth and symbolic force, the psychology of its inhabitants, exposing the ambivalence and angst of modern youth in a changing, declining environment. In his *Modern Hero,* in contrast, Cheng's style is almost bare, the better to depict the inarticulateness of his lowly, uneducated, "underdog" characters, yet is infused with a concrete vividness that suggests a hidden reservoir of feeling and thought. Ch'en's *The Tribe of Generals* is not free from melodrama, but at their best, his portrayals reveal a forceful grasp of the pathetic dilemma his bourgeois protagonists flounder in, between creative inclinations and the patterns of life they cannot break away from. Ch'en Jo-hsi's *District Magistrate Yin* is set in China and has an explicitly anti-Communist theme, but his personages are not distinctively characterized and the society that he attacks does not take on any complex, differentiated appearance.

The undisturbing novels produced in China in 1976 ironically smacked of the same kind of "bourgeois" self-righteousness that was displayed in Ch'en Jo-hsi's stories. Chin Ke and Ch'en Ch'iu's *The Story of Tung Ts'un-shui,* Li Hui-hsin's *By the Banks of Lan Ts'eng Chiang,* Li Yu-ch'ing's *All the Mountains Are Red,* and the collectively written *The River Beckons* are all formulistic in style and content, involving depersonalized heroes who wage an unceasing war of hatred against class enemies and elements that threaten national reconstruction. Hao Jan was almost alone among post-Cultural Revolution writers in being able to integrate lively description and believable characters with the ideological demands of his time. His stories in *The Wings of the Land* are informed with an almost Platonic vision of reality—one that sees the everyday consciousness of peasants and workers as forming a phenomenal backdrop at most to reveal the "reality" of the objective laws of social development or that of class consciousness, a reality given symbolic force by its association with the natural landscape.

(JOHN KWAN-TERRY)

JAPANESE

There were several literary issues during 1976, but they remained only marginal. One was the controversy between Tatsuzo Ishikawa, president of Japan's PEN Club, and Akiyuki Nosaka, author of *The Pornographers,* over obscenity and censorship. Another was concerned with the Akutagawa Award given to young promising novelists. The recipient in 1976 was Ryu Murakami, a 24-year-old art student whose novelette *Blue Almost Transparent* was labeled "shocking" and "dirty" by some of the literary critics and immediately got onto a best-seller list. It was a "scandalous" novel all right, because it was exclusively concerned with the behaviour of a group of young drug addicts—quite a new theme in contemporary Japanese fiction. There were straightforward descriptions of drug intoxication and even group sex between American soldiers and Japanese girls. But since there had been a number of American literary precedents in this genre, it was not a new theme at all in the literary sense.

ASAHI SHIMBUN

"Pleasures of a Country Gentleman" by Shizuo Fujieda was one of the most-discussed Japanese novels of 1976.

The forte of the Japanese imagination still seemed to lie in short, concise literary forms. One could be sure of finding a number of fine stories in the literary magazines each month. Particularly impressive was the combination of boldness in approach and spontaneity in style in the stories by female authors such as Taeko Tomioka, Takako Takahashi, and Chiyo Uno. There were several outstanding collections of short stories by male authors. In Tetsuro Miura's *Pistol and Other Stories* each story was worked out carefully, each in its own way. But the collection had an implicit theme: the contrast between Tokyo and the rural areas of northern Japan, the recent changes coming over the latter, and the vicissitudes of various members of one family—all suggested and implied rather than stated and described. Kazuo Ozaki's *Honeybee Falling* was autobiographical and ecological at the same time. His deceptively simple, lucid style was amazingly effective in conveying the delicate tremors of his uncannily acute sensitivity to the ecological omens. Hideo Takubo's *Ringlets of Hair* belonged to a different category; it was a sensitive evocation of lingering erotic atmosphere in a variety of situations, though some of the stories suffered from a touch of artificiality.

Kenzaburo Oe's *Documents on Pinchrunners,* Shizuo Fujieda's *Pleasures of a Country Gentleman,* and Takako Takahashi's *Temptress* were three remarkable novels of the year. Oe's Pinchrunners turn out to be two messengers sent from some other planet to save the Earth. It was an ambitious tour-de-force in the form of science fiction, though the whole tone was too serious and the author's implied message too obvious. *Pleasures of a Country Gentleman* was a fantastic novel too, though in very different vein—a wild fantasia on old curios, describing grotesque loveplay among the curios and alluding even to Buddhistic incarnations. Takahashi's *Temptress* was a delicate and sharp evocation and analysis of a death wish on the part of several female characters.

Ryuichi Tamura's *Dead Words* and Minoru Nakamura's *Landscape of Flying Insects* were two notable collections of poems, and Taeko Kono's *Affirmative Desires in Junichiro Tanizaki* and Nobuo Kasahara's *Kyoka Izumi* were two impressive books of literary criticism. (SHOICHI SAEKI)

See also Art Sales; Libraries; Nobel Prizes; Philosophy; Publishing; Theatre.
[621]

ENCYCLOPÆDIA BRITANNICA FILMS. *Bartleby by Herman Melville* (1969); *Dr. Heidegger's Experiment by Nathaniel Hawthorne* (1969); *The Lady, or the Tiger? by Frank Stockton* (1969); *The Lottery by Shirley Jackson* (1969); *Magic Prison* (1969); *My Old Man by Ernest Hemingway* (1969); *James Dickey: Poet* (1970); *Shaw vs. Shakespeare—Part I: The Character of Caesar, Part II: The Tragedy of Julius Caesar, Part III: Caesar and Cleopatra* (1970); *The Deserted Village* (1971); *The Lady of Shalott* (1971); *The Prisoner of Chillon* (1971); *Greek Myths—Part I: Myth as Fiction, History, and Ritual* (1971); *Greek Myths—Part II: Myth as Science, Religion, and Drama* (1971); *Walt Whitman: Poet for a New Age* (1972); *The Crocodile by Fyodor Dostoyevsky* (1973); *The Secret Sharer by Joseph Conrad* (1973); *John Keats: His Life and Death* (1973); *John Keats: Poet* (1973); *The Bible as Literature—Part I: Saga and Story in the Old Testament* (1973); *The Bible as Literature—Part II: History, Poetry and Drama in the Old Testament* (1973); *Talking with Thoreau* (1975); *The Hunt* (1975); *Fall of the House of Usher* (1975); *Voltaire Presents Candide: An Introduction to the Age of Enlightenment* (1976).

SPECIAL REPORT

FEMINISM AND LITERATURE

By Ellen Moers

Feminism, narrowly defined, is the ideology of woman's right to social justice, and literature, narrowly defined, is language used best. If we conceive of these definitions as two narrow lines traveling through modern history, we find they rarely intersect. Feminists write polemics, studies, and reports in order to effect change—to win voting or property rights, to enlarge educational and employment opportunities for women—and they must write logically and powerfully to do so. That feminist writings retain interest and readability is attested by the selections from Margaret Fuller, Frances Wright, Margaret Sanger, Emma Goldman, Simone de Beauvoir, Elizabeth Cady Stanton, and many more that have been edited by Alice S. Rossi. Rossi, a sociologist, calls her anthology *The Feminist Papers,* not Women's Literature, and she does not include selections by Jane Austen, Emily Dickinson, George Eliot, Mme de Staël, Willa Cather, Emily Brontë, or others of the great women writers whose place in literary history is secure. For, with few exceptions, they were not feminists in the narrow sense of the term. They were not joiners, not activists in any cause; they were writers.

Writers and Polemicists. Virginia Woolf may be counted one of the exceptions. Her fiction and criticism are, by any standard, works of literature, and she also participated to a degree in the women's movement of the early 20th century, when winning the vote was its principal issue. In her 20s, before publishing her first novel, she joined a suffrage group, addressed envelopes, taught classes of working women. Later, established as a novelist, Woolf lectured on the social inequities afflicting her sex. Two of these lectures, originally delivered to women students at Cambridge and published together in 1929 as *A Room of One's Own,* make a work that is both literature and feminism. There, however, Woolf also presents a strong and still controversial case against the carry-over of feminist polemics into the work of a woman whose principal intention is to make literature.

That special breed of woman, the writer, was always the central concern of Virginia Woolf's literary criticism, a genre to which (rather than feminist polemics) *A Room of One's Own* actually belongs, for it deals mainly with the Victorian women novelists, such as Charlotte Brontë, who were Woolf's predecessors. "It is fatal," Woolf concludes, "for a woman to lay the least stress on any grievance; to plead even with justice any cause; in any way to speak consciously as a woman. . . . The whole of the mind must lie wide open if we are to get the sense that the writer is communicating his experience with perfect fullness. There must be freedom and there must be peace."

The wide-open, well-educated mind, the freedom from daylong chores, the peace of solitude in "a room of one's own" have taken a heap of winning for women, and the main burden of the fight has been borne by the feminists, not by the literary women. For creative artists are by definition sensitive and self-absorbed, while social activists must be tough-skinned and self-denying in single-minded devotion to a cause. "I plead for my sex, not for myself," wrote Mary Wollstonecraft at the outset of her

Ellen Moers is university professor in the department of English, University of Connecticut. Her published works include Literary Women *(1976).*

COURTESY, NATIONAL ARCHAEOLOGICAL MUSEUM, ATHENS

The seated figure on this ancient Greek water jug is thought to be a likeness of Sappho, the celebrated lyric poet of Lesbos (*c.* 610–580 BC).

Vindication of the Rights of Woman, which began the feminist movement in the last decade of the 18th century. But at the start of her first novel, Wollstonecraft expressed her commitment to literature (rather than social action) by aligning herself with the "chosen few" who "wish to speak for themselves. . . . The paradise they ramble in, must be of their own creating. . . ." (Because of her original, sometimes exquisite prose style, Wollstonecraft like Woolf can be counted among the exceptional writers who belong to the history of literature as well as that of feminism.)

To define literature as feminist whenever the author is a woman is thus a distortion of history, but it would be equally distorting to make an absolute separation between the history of women's literature and the history of feminism. The two have run together, not in tandem, but in erratic, swerving parallels since the 18th century. Literature, indeed writing of any kind for publication, has a special place in women's history, including contemporary history. The current feminist movement owes its start in the 1960s and its continuance primarily to journalists such as Betty Friedan, Gloria Steinem, and Françoise Giroud, and secondarily to academics able and willing to address a general public on feminist issues in the press, such as Kate Millett, Germaine Greer, and Michele Murray. The relatively recent conquest of professional careers for women in journalism and the university was the result of generations of feminist agitation. Those careers in turn provide a public forum for feminist views.

But long before there were women professors and women reporters, literature opened to women as a profession—the first and for centuries virtually the only profession for women. Only as novelists, poets, essayists, and playwrights could women address a wide public, influence society, express their genius, and also—the sense in which literature is a profession—earn a respectable and comfortable living. Men could do all these things as clergymen, politicians, lawyers, professors, administrators in government and business, but through the 18th, the 19th, and the early 20th centuries, and to a degree today, women have been barred from these professions. Their pulpit, forum, platform has been literature, and literature alone. Simply to speak in public was unheard of for women until very recent times.

Literature and the Condition of Women. Throughout the Victorian age the Condition of Woman question absorbed men's minds (and not only in England) with an urgency surpassed only by the Condition of England question, dealing with the widening gulf between the rich and the industrial poor. Hardly a literary work of the age, whether *The Scarlet Letter* or *Idylls of the King* or *Madame Bovary,* was untouched by the century's debate over women's minds and education and work, over marriage and divorce. Because women too could speak through fiction and poetry, women's issues took on a multidimensional solidity in Victorian literature, and literature itself took on a new dimension from the anguish and the rage in women's voices.

The case in point, as Virginia Woolf made clear, is Charlotte Brontë, one of the most brilliant, perhaps the deepest of Victorian women writers. And it was on the deepest level of the creative imagination that Charlotte Brontë pondered the Woman Question, pondered those "evils—deep-rooted in the foundation of the social system," as she once put it, and produced not clear, sharp, feminist answers but the characters of Jane Eyre and Lucy Snowe. The exploitation of the governess and the schoolteacher are women's issues in Brontë's *Jane Eyre* and *Villette;* the denial of meaningful work and women's craving for travel and wide social experience are issues in *Shirley* and *The Professor.* But none of these novels is in any sense a polemic. Women's issues become, in Brontë's fiction, human issues, Christian ordeals, regional dramas, fantasies of fulfillment and passion.

The remarkable childhood chapters at the start of *Jane Eyre* and the Rochester-Jane romance later in the novel gain extra power if read with some grasp of the Woman Question in Victorian times. They were inspired in part by Brontë's acute and anguished sense that to grow up as a girl, to love as a woman were experiences in which women differed from men. However, the immediate consequence of the novelist's female self-consciousness was to transform the novel—to contribute the rebellious pain of childhood and the bold passion of adulthood to English fiction—not to alter legislation. Only indirectly, and on a scale possible to imagine but not to measure, did women's creative accomplishment in literature effect change in the position of women in society.

Feminists everywhere hailed the accomplishment of George Sand, for in the middle decades of the 19th century she was probably the most widely respected and influential novelist in the world. The eloquence of her prose stirred both Dostoyevsky and Whitman, and "the immense vibration of George Sand's voice upon the ear of Europe," Matthew Arnold predicted, "will not soon die away."

On women's issues, George Sand was actually rather conservative and refused to let herself be drawn into the lively feminist movement of her day in France. "Women cry out against slavery," she wrote; "let them wait until man is free, for slavery cannot give birth to liberty." Spokesman for the aspirations of *le peuple,* lifelong critic of religious and political tyranny, Sand was a progressive, sometimes a revolutionary in a general, not a feminist, context. And, in spite of her influential role in social and nationalist causes, she insisted that she was not an ideologue but an artist first of all. According to the American feminist Margaret Fuller, George Sand made her principal contribution to the cause of women through her artistry in prose: because of Sand's *style,* Fuller wrote, men would be "led to review their opinions, and perhaps to elevate and enlarge their hopes as to 'woman's sphere' and 'woman's mission.' " Because of Sand's *intelligence,* wrote the Italian feminist Anna Maria Mozzoni, she reflected glory on all women.

"To Speak . . . as a Woman." That women were absolutely, eternally, and by divine creation the inferior, the stupid sex was in the 19th century the established opinion against which all feminists did battle. They cited George Sand, who brought history, religion, music, nature, and philosophy into fiction; feminists cited George Eliot, first true intellectual among major Victorian novelists of either sex, though George Eliot expressed herself with even more cautious conservatism than George Sand on the Woman Question. As they expanded the terrain of fiction into the realm of ideas, both novelists wrote with a consciousness that, as women, they were members of the sex condemned as incapable of serious or consecutive thought.

All women writers, feminists or not, have been affected by the negatives imposed on women for centuries by family and society: you are not allowed to, therefore you do not, and this proves you cannot think, study, aspire, rebel, lead. . . . Greek philosophers and fathers of the church, scientists and lawmakers have told women they lack souls and independent moral natures; that they do not crave change or adventure; that they feel nothing deeply; that they have no bodies worth attending to; that they are timorous, passive, imitative, and narrow; that they never leave home, never look outside their "inner space." Thus the moral seriousness of Jane Austen, the Gothic fantasies of Mrs. Radcliffe and Mary Shelley, the raw passion in the Brontës and Emily Dickinson, the theme of slave or proletarian revolt in George Sand, Elizabeth Gaskell, and Harriet Beecher Stowe, the sensuality of Colette, the wide open spaces in Emily Brontë, Willa Cather, and Isak Dinesen—all owe either a little something or a very great deal to the literary woman's conscious intention to refute the denial to women of their full humanity.

From the snarling, battling little girls in the Brontës' fiction to the aggressive, foulmouthed wives in the poetry of Erica Jong and Adrienne Rich today, women writers have overturned narrowing, conventional ideas of womanhood and in so doing have widened the human base of literature. To break through conventions, expand human consciousness is the task of all serious writers, whether they be male or female. With all deference due to the authority of Virginia Woolf, "to speak consciously as a woman" has proved no more "fatal" to literature than to speak consciously as a man.

Women poets in America, to take only one species of current women writers, testify to the vitality that female self-consciousness contributes to literature. A whole fresh range of metaphor —the sensations of pregnancy and miscarriage, the squalor of housekeeping, the bitchery of neighbours—was opened for poets by Sylvia Plath, who brought the urgent, screeching sound of rage to poetry remarkable for precision, elegance, and control. Plath was no feminist (she died at age 30 before Women's Liberation began) but she taught a whole generation—Anne Sexton, Adrienne Rich, Diane Wakoski, Robin Morgan, Judith Johnson Sherwin, Cynthia Macdonald, Erica Jong, and many more—that late-20th century women had something new to say about the human condition, something that belonged to and invigorated poetry.

Post-Liberation Ironies. With heavier polemical emphasis, the novels and plays that women are writing everywhere today revolve around the new feminist matter, issues perhaps best summarized as the *post*-Liberation ironies of the modern woman's life. All that their ancestors fought for—contraception, higher education, political representation, easy divorce, easy money, easy travel, easy clothes, easy religion—now liberate the modern heroine to misbehave as heroes do. But the inexorable laws of female aging still hold; rape, drugs, alcoholism, abortion, and madness are distasteful consequences of free female living; and modern motherhood, with its guilts, its superhuman patience, its impossible standards and responsibilities, must now be carried out, for the first time in the recorded history of the gently reared, highly educated classes, without servants.

Humour, a bitter humour just short of lunatic laughter, turns out to be the best, perhaps the only possible response to such ironies in the novels of the '60s and '70s by Lois Gould, Penelope Mortimer, Margaret Drabble, Anne Roiphe, Sue Kaufman, Natalia Ginzburg, Margaret Laurence, Jean Rhys, Janet Frame, Monique Wittig, and many, many more. But no woman novelist of the Western world has as yet approached so closely to feminist tragedy as did Aleksandr Solzhenitsyn in his chapter on the domestic life of the chief surgeon, a woman, in *Cancer Ward.*

Luxembourg

A constitutional monarchy, the Benelux country of Luxembourg is bounded on the east by West Germany, on the south by France, and on the west and north by Belgium. Area: 999 sq mi (2,586 sq km). Pop. (1975 est.): 357,400. Cap. and largest city: Luxembourg (pop., 1975 est., 78,300). Language: French, German, Luxembourgian. Religion: Roman Catholic 97%. Grand duke, Jean; prime minister in 1976, Gaston Thorn.

On Nov. 8–10, 1976, Queen Elizabeth II and Prince Philip paid a state visit to Luxembourg, returning the visit that Grand Duke Jean and Grand Duchess Joséphine-Charlotte paid to the United Kingdom in June 1972. It was the first official call ever made to the grand duchy by a British monarch.

Albert Borschette, a prominent Luxembourger who had served from 1970 as a member of the European Commission (composed of the permanent representatives of the nine member states of the European Economic Community), was released from this post in July for reasons of health. Raymond Vouel, hitherto deputy prime minister and finance minister of the grand duchy, succeeded him on the Commission. Prime Minister Thorn (*see* BIOGRAPHY) appointed Benny Berg deputy prime minister and entrusted Vouel's portfolio of finance to Jacques Poos. Until that time Poos had been the editor in chief on the *Tagesblatt*, a Liberal daily newspaper.

(K. M. SMOGORZEWSKI)

[972.A.7]

Luxembourg ("Little Fortress") has long been a crossroads of Europe. Today it is the headquarters of many financial concerns. Photo shows the spires of the cathedral in Luxembourg city.

MARCEL SCHROEDER

LUXEMBOURG

Education. (1973–74) Primary, pupils 35,589, teachers 1,857; secondary, pupils 8,213, teachers 739; vocational, pupils 12,126, teachers 742; higher, students 458, teaching staff 169.

Finance. Monetary unit: Luxembourg franc, at par with the Belgian franc, with (Sept. 20, 1976) a free commercial rate of LFr 38.31 to U.S. $1 (LFr 66 = £1 sterling). Budget (1976 est.): revenue LFr 28,441,000,000; expenditure LFr 30,687,000,000. Gross national product (1974) LFr 82,770,000,000. Cost of living (1970 = 100; June 1976) 155.

Foreign Trade. *See* BELGIUM.

Transport and Communications. Roads (1974) 4,465 km (including 25 km expressways). Motor vehicles in use (1974): passenger 127,860; commercial 10,540. Railways: (1974) 271 km; traffic (1975) 292.4 million passenger-km, freight 660 million net ton-km. Air traffic (1974): 135 million passenger-km; freight 200,000 net ton-km. Telephones (Dec. 1974) 141,700. Radio licenses (Dec. 1973) 176,000. Television licenses (Dec. 1973) 85,000.

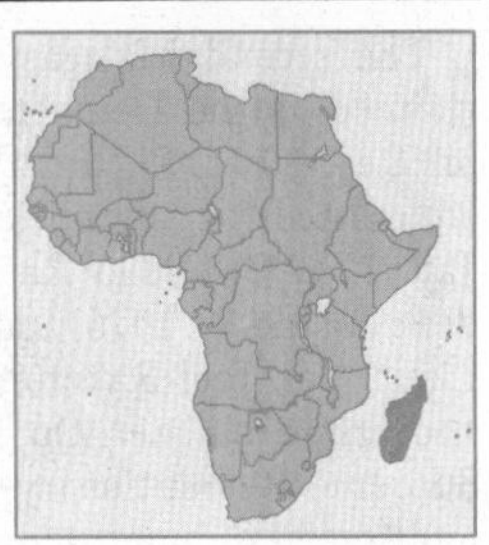

Madagascar

Madagascar occupies the island of the same name and minor adjacent islands in the Indian Ocean off the southeast coast of Africa. Area: 226,658 sq mi (587,041 sq km). Pop. (1975 est.): 8,044,000. Cap. and largest city: Antananarivu (the former name, Tananarive, was a corruption of the Malagasy and was replaced in 1976; pop., 1975 est., 438,800). Language: French and Malagasy. Religion: Christian (approximately 50%) and traditional tribal beliefs. President in 1976, Didier Ratsiraka; prime ministers, Joël Rakotomalala until July 30 and, from August 12, Justin Rakotoniaina.

MADAGASCAR

Education. (1972) Primary, pupils 1,030,342, teachers 15,600; secondary, pupils *c.* 175,000, teachers (1971) 5,181; vocational, pupils 10,200, teachers 684; teacher training (1971), students 2,019, teachers 215; higher (1971), students 6,683, teaching staff 260.

Finance. Monetary unit: Malagasy franc, at par with the CFA franc, with (Sept. 20, 1976) a parity of MalFr 50 to the French franc (free rates of MalFr 245.90 = U.S. $1 and MalFr 423.62 = £1 sterling). Gold, SDR's, and foreign exchange (June 1976) U.S. $66.8 million. Budget (1974 est.): revenue MalFr 71 billion; expenditure MalFr 93.4 billion.

Foreign Trade. (1974) Imports MalFr 67,260,000,000; exports MalFr 58.5 billion. Import sources: France 36%; West Germany 9%; U.S. 7%; Japan 5%. Export destinations: France 34%; U.S. 21%; Réunion 8%; Japan 6%; West Germany 5%. Main exports: coffee 27%; meat (1973) 10%; vanilla 8%; cloves 7%; petroleum products 6%.

Transport and Communications. Roads (1974) 26,992 km. Motor vehicles in use (1974): passenger 56,700; commercial (including buses) 43,700. Railways: (1973) 884 km; traffic (1975) 228 million passenger-km, freight 199.6 million net ton-km. Air traffic (1974): 271.8 million passenger-km; freight 10,475,000 net ton-km. Shipping (1975): merchant vessels 100 gross tons and over 50; gross tonnage 44,273. Telephones (Dec. 1974) 30,000. Radio receivers (Dec. 1973) 700,000. Television receivers (Dec. 1973) 6,300.

Agriculture. Production (in 000; metric tons; 1975): rice *c.* 2,000; corn (1974) 118; cassava (1974) 1,378; sweet potatoes *c.* 350; potatoes *c.* 125; dry beans *c.* 60; bananas (1974) *c.* 280; oranges (1974) *c.* 70; fish catch (1974) 64. Livestock (in 000; Dec. 1974): cattle *c.* 9,734; sheep *c.* 768; pigs *c.* 713; goats *c.* 850; chickens *c.* 13,000.

Livestock: *see* Agriculture and Food Supplies

Lumber: *see* Industrial Review

Lutheran Churches: *see* Religion

Macau: *see* Dependent States

Macedonian Literature: *see* Literature

Machinery and Machine Tools: *see* Industrial Review

Madagascar's most important crop is rice, grown in irrigated fields.

The second Malagasy republic was officially proclaimed as the Democratic Republic of Madagascar on Dec. 30, 1975, and the next day an amnesty was announced for all political offenses committed before Jan. 1, 1975. Didier Ratsiraka was sworn in as president on Jan. 4, 1976, and on January 11 he appointed Lieut. Col. Joël Rakotomalala as head of government and prime minister. On January 13 a new 12-member Supreme Revolutionary Council and an 18-member, multiracial Cabinet were announced. The composition of the Cabinet clearly reflected the president's call for national unity. In May an 18-member Executive Bureau of the Revolutionary Advance Guard was set up as the supreme ruling body under President Ratsiraka's chairmanship.

Following Rakotomalala's death in a helicopter accident on July 30, Justin Rakotoniaina was appointed as the new prime minister on August 12; on August 20 he announced his Cabinet. In September, faced with serious student strikes, the government dissolved the extreme left-wing party Power to the Underlings, which had played a significant role in the downfall of former president Philibert Tsiranana and which the government accused of inciting the strikes. Violence involving Comoro Islands nationals resident in Madagascar broke out in December, with many deaths reported. (PHILIPPE DECRAENE)

[978.E.6.c]

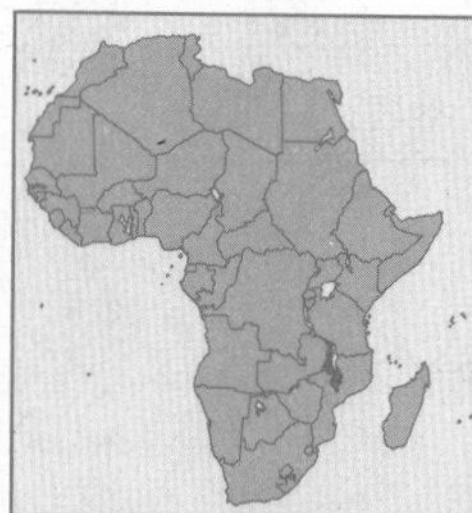

Malawi

A republic and member of the Commonwealth of Nations in east central Africa, Malawi is bounded by Tanzania, Mozambique, and Zambia. Area: 45,747 sq mi (118,484 sq km). Pop. (1975 est.): 5,044,000. Cap.: Lilongwe (pop., 1974 est., 86,900). Largest city: Blantyre (pop., 1972, 160,100). Language: English (official) and Nyanja (Chichewa). Religion: predominantly traditional beliefs. President in 1976, Hastings Kamuzu Banda.

The year 1976 opened with a buoyant economy, mainly because the country relied less upon imported fuel than did many of its neighbours and because of foreign investment in development projects. Nevertheless, the growing cost of imports was felt, and it seemed likely that for the first time in several years Malawi would have an unfavourable balance of payments. The economy also suffered as a result of Mozambique's decision in March to close its border with Rhodesia, thereby reducing Malawi's export trade by 20% (one of its main road links with Rhodesia ran through Mozambique).

The European Economic Community offered grant assistance to countries affected by the political conflict in southern Africa, but after President Banda had unexpectedly ordered the expulsion of several members of the Goan community (originating in Goa, India) in May and about 100 Goans, holders of British passports, had arrived in London, the British government warned that if other British passport holders were expelled British aid to Malawi—estimated at £9 million for 1976—would be cut. Banda gave assurances that no further action was contemplated, but the removal of Asians from rural areas to towns and official policy toward them suggested that about 7,000 would have to leave the country by the end of March 1978. Also disturbing to world humanitarian opinion was the continuing persecution of the Jehovah's Witnesses sect. (*See* RELIGION.)

(KENNETH INGHAM)

[978.E.8.b.iii]

MALAWI

Education. (1974–75) Primary, pupils 611,678, teachers 10,524; secondary, pupils 13,900, teachers 694; vocational, pupils 529, teachers 46; teacher training, students 1,283, teachers 95; higher, students 1,146, teaching staff 101.

Finance. Monetary unit: kwacha, with (Sept. 20, 1976) a free rate of 0.92 kwacha to U.S. $1 (1.59 kwacha = £1 sterling). Gold, SDR's, and foreign exchange (June 1976) U.S. $30,180,000. Budget (1975 actual): revenue 76.7 million kwacha; expenditure 117,130,000 kwacha.

Foreign Trade. (1975) Imports 216,630,000 kwacha; exports 119,670,000 kwacha. Import sources: South Africa 24%; U.K. 24%; Rhodesia 12%; Japan 8%. Export destinations: U.K. 35%; U.S. 7%; The Netherlands 6%; Rhodesia 6%; South Africa 5%. Main exports: tobacco 42%; tea 17%; peanuts 5%.

Transport and Communications. Roads (1974) 12,074 km. Motor vehicles in use (1974): passenger 10,600; commercial 9,500. Railways: (1974) 566 km; traffic (1975) 88.9 million passenger-km, freight 275 million net ton-km. Air traffic (1974): 79.9 million passenger-km; freight 1.1 million net ton-km. Telephones (Dec. 1974) 19,000. Radio receivers (Dec. 1973) 112,000.

Agriculture. Production (in 000; metric tons; 1975): corn *c.* 1,000; cassava (1974) *c.* 150; sweet potatoes (1974) *c.* 49; sorghum *c.* 45; sugar, raw value *c.* 53; peanuts *c.* 165; tea *c.* 26; tobacco *c.* 34; cotton, lint *c.* 7. Livestock (in 000; 1974): cattle *c.* 596; sheep *c.* 120; goats *c.* 620; pigs *c.* 180; poultry *c.* 7,500.

Industry. Production (in 000; 1975): electricity (public supply; kw-hr) 263,000; cement (metric tons) 109.

Malaysia

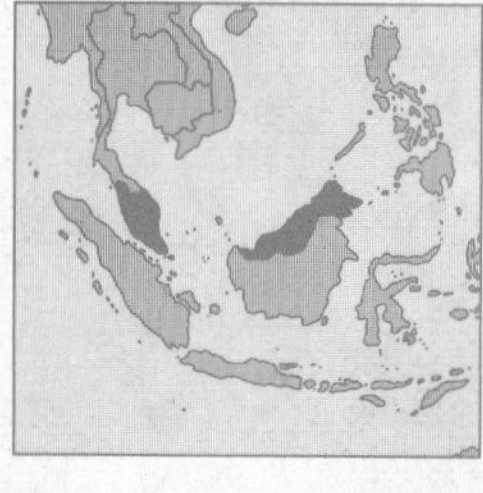

A federation within the Commonwealth of Nations comprising the 11 states of the former Federation of Malaya, Sabah, Sarawak, and the federal territory of Kuala Lumpur, Malaysia is a federal constitutional monarchy situated in Southeast Asia at the southern end of the Malay Peninsula (excluding Singapore) and on the northern part of the island of Borneo. Area: 127,316 sq mi (329,747 sq km). Pop. (1975 est.): 11.9 million. Cap. and largest city: Kuala Lumpur (pop., 1975 UN est., 557,000). Official language: Malay. Religion: Malays are Muslim; Indians mainly Hindu; Chinese mainly

Magazines: *see* Publishing

Malagasy Republic: *see* Madagascar

MALAYSIA

Education. *Peninsular Malaysia.* (1975) Primary, pupils 1,593,804, teachers 49,225; secondary, pupils 789,031, teachers 28,255; vocational, pupils 21,134, teachers 930; higher (1974–75), students 32,295, teaching staff 2,986. *Sabah.* (1974) Primary, pupils 123,419, teachers 4,764; secondary, pupils 43,257, teachers 1,702; vocational, pupils 285, teachers 30; teacher training, students 599, teachers 56. *Sarawak.* (1974) Primary, pupils 165,484, teachers 4,753; secondary, pupils 50,202, teachers 1,886; vocational, pupils 293, teachers 25; teacher training, students 695, teachers 68.

Finance. Monetary unit: ringgit (Malaysian dollar), with (Sept. 20, 1976) a free rate of 2.51 ringgits to U.S. $1 (4.32 ringgits = £1 sterling). Gold, SDR's, and foreign exchange (May 1976) U.S. $1,744,000,000. Budget (1975 est.): revenue 4,869,000,000 ringgits; expenditure 6,902,000,000 ringgits. Gross national product (1974) 19,562,000,000 ringgits. Money supply (May 1976) 4,647,000,000 ringgits. Cost of living (peninsular Malaysia; 1970 = 100; April 1976) 144.

Foreign Trade. (1975) Imports 8,618,000,000 ringgits; exports 9,218,000,000 ringgits. Import sources: Japan 20%; U.S. 11%; U.K. 10%; Singapore 9%; Australia 8%; West Germany 5%. Export destinations: Singapore 20%; U.S. 16%; Japan 14%; The Netherlands 8%; U.K. 6%. Main exports: rubber 22%; palm oil 14%; tin 13%; timber 12%; crude oil 9%.

Transport and Communications. Roads (1973) 23,862 km. Motor vehicles in use (1974): passenger 430,400; commercial (including buses) 140,300. Railways (1974): 1,814 km; traffic (including Singapore) 986 million passenger-km, freight 989 million net ton-km. Air traffic (1975): 1,633,000,000 passenger-km; freight 29,874,000 net ton-km. Shipping (1975): merchant vessels 100 gross tons and over 129; gross tonnage 358,795. Shipping traffic (1974): goods loaded 15,227,000 metric tons, unloaded 11,641,000 metric tons. Telephones (Jan. 1975) 259,000. Radio licenses (Dec. 1973) 462,000. Television licenses (Dec. 1974) 372,000.

Agriculture. Production (in 000; metric tons; 1975): rice *c.* 1,900; rubber *c.* 1,400; copra *c.* 164; palm oil *c.* 1,265; tea *c.* 3; bananas (1974) *c.* 460; pineapples (1974) *c.* 300; pepper (Sarawak only; 1974) 29; timber (cu m; 1974) *c.* 30,370; fish catch *c.* 526. Livestock (in 000; Dec. 1973): cattle *c.* 359; pigs *c.* 1,095; goats *c.* 348; sheep (peninsular Malaysia only) *c.* 41; buffalo *c.* 293; chickens *c.* 37,000.

Industry. Production (in 000; metric tons; 1975): tin concentrates (metal content) 64; bauxite 703; cement (peninsular Malaysia only) *c.* 1,430; iron ore (56% metal content) 349; crude oil (Sarawak only) 4,218; petroleum products (Sarawak only; 1974) *c.* 1,455; gold (troy oz; 1974) 4.5; electricity (kw-hr) 5,845,000.

Buddhist, Confucian, and Taoist. Supreme head of state in 1976, with the title of *yang di-pertuan agong,* Tuanku Yahya Putra ibni al-Marhum Sultan Ibrahim; prime ministers, Tun Abdul Razak and, from January 14, Datuk Hussein bin Onn.

Prime Minister Tun Abdul Razak died in London on Jan. 14, 1976 (*see* OBITUARIES). He was succeeded by his deputy and brother-in-law Datuk Hussein bin Onn (*see* BIOGRAPHY). Datuk Hussein announced a new Cabinet on March 5; the post of deputy prime minister was given to Mahathir bin Mohamed.

On March 18 the Supreme Council of the United Malays National Organization (UMNO) announced the expulsion of Datuk Harun bin Idris, the chief minister of the state of Selangor, who was due to face trial on charges of corruption and breach of trust. On March 25 the Selangor state assembly voted to censure him, and the following day Datuk Harun resigned his office. On May 18 he was found guilty by the Malaysian High Court and sentenced to two years' imprisonment; at the end of the month, further charges of forgery were brought against him arising out of the financing of the boxing match between Muhammad Ali and Joe Bugner held in Kuala Lumpur in 1975. On October 23 UMNO decided to accept Datuk Harun's application for readmission. Further signs of difficulties within UMNO and within the ruling National Front coalition generally came in November with the arrest of six prominent politicians, including two UMNO deputy ministers, Datuk Abdullah Ahmad and Abdullah Majid, and the executive secretary of the Malaysian Chinese Organization, Tan Ken Sin (the other three were from opposition parties). No immediate explanation was given, although the arrests were believed to be linked to rumours of Communist infiltration in high places and to an internal power struggle.

Escalation of insurgent activity was marked in late April by the downing of a helicopter, killing 11 servicemen, and the sabotage in Perak of a stretch of Malaysia's main northern railway line. In May Communist-inspired demonstrations in the Thai town of Betong on the Malaysian border followed a Malaysian hot-pursuit raid across the border after retreating insurgents. Malaysian forces stationed in Betong were withdrawn on June 6 at the Thai government's request, and it was not until November 10 that the two countries reached accord and announced joint operations against Communist guerrillas.

Elections in the state of Sabah in April were won by the Sabah People's Union (Berjaya). Tun Mohamed Fuad Stephens was sworn in as chief minister, but on June 6 he was killed in a plane crash. His deputy, Datuk Harris Salleh, succeeded him. For the arrest of newspaper editors Abdul Samad Ismail and Hussein Jahidin in June, *see* SINGAPORE. Also arrested was *Berita Harian*'s news editor, Samani Mohamed Amin. (MICHAEL LEIFER)

[976.B.2]

GEORG FISCHER—CAMERA PRESS/PHOTO TRENDS

The coffin of Tun Abdul Razak is carried through the streets of Kuala Lumpur on its way to Parliament House. Prime minister of Malaysia since 1970, Razak died in London in January, of leukemia.

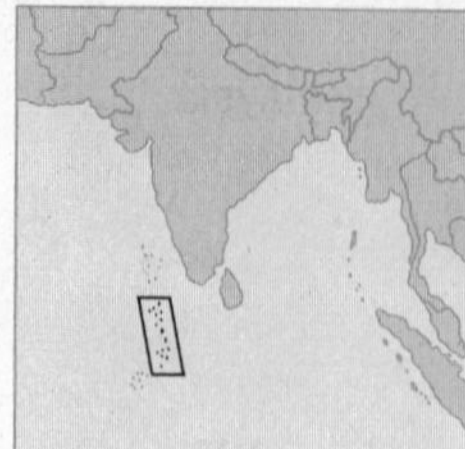

Maldives

Maldives, a republic in the Indian Ocean consisting of about two thousand small islands, lies southwest of the southern tip of India. Area: 115 sq mi (298 sq km). Pop. (1974): 128,700. Cap.: Male (pop., 1974, 16,250). Language: Divehi. Religion: Muslim. Sultan, Emir Muhammad Farid Didi; president in 1976, Ibrahim Nasir.

On Dec. 31, 1975, an era ended when the British pulled out of Gan Island in Addu Atoll, where for 34 years the Royal Air Force had maintained a staging post. The property handed over in April included a runway the whole length of Gan Island, with buildings and equipment, a modern medical centre, tennis and golf grounds, and a meteorological station. The British departure also meant the loss of an annual grant and over £300,000 earned by about 1,000 Maldivians employed on Gan. The Addu Atoll people, who had nearly doubled in number (to 17,000) and had improved in health during the RAF tenure, faced an uncertain future, though their skills and languages could be of value in the new tourist industry.

MALDIVES

Education. (1976) Primary, pupils 3,362, teachers 94; secondary, pupils 513, teachers 40; vocational, pupils 19, teachers 4.

Finance and Trade. Monetary unit: Maldivian rupee, with (Sept. 20, 1976) a free rate of MRs 8.57 to U.S. $1 (MRs 14.77 = £1 sterling). Budget (1974) expenditure MRs 22,130,000. Foreign trade: imports (1974) MRs 26,670,000; exports (1973) MRs 22 million. Trade is mainly with Sri Lanka and Japan. Main exports (metric tons; 1973): fish 7,760; shells 65; copra 20.

The government had undertaken a campaign for economic development on both inhabited and desert islands. This was accompanied by the creation of Air Maldivia and improvement of transport to the Maldives from Sri Lanka, as well as free port facilities. Tourism provided a stimulus to local crafts and market-garden crops. Rice, the staple food, was imported.

Most of the population fished, and fishing accounted for 90% of Maldivian exports in 1976, mainly to Sri Lanka, which took about £1 million of dried tuna. A fishing agreement with Japan, which processed fish on the spot, increased trade in that direction. When the 1975–76 season proved lean, the UN Food and Agriculture Organization approved £330,000 in emergency food aid and the World Food Program allotted rations for one-third of the population. (MOLLY MORTIMER)

Most people in the Maldives are fishermen, like those shown below in the capital city, Male.

SVEN SIMON—KATHERINE YOUNG

Mali

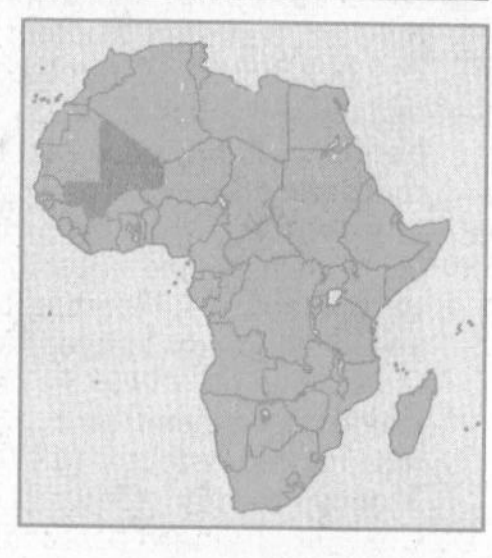

A republic of West Africa, Mali is bordered by Algeria, Niger, Upper Volta, Ivory Coast, Guinea, Senegal, and Mauritania. Area: 478,822 sq mi (1,240,142 sq km). Pop. (1976 est.): 5,842,000. Cap. and largest city: Bamako (pop., 1975 est., 243,000). Language: French (official); Hamito-Semitic and various tribal dialects. Religion: Muslim 65%; animist 30%. Head of military government in 1976, Col. Moussa Traoré.

The chief political event of 1976 was the creation of a new party, the Malian People's Democratic Union (UDPM). Announcing this on September 21, Colonel Traoré stated that conditions in the country were right for a return to normal political life. The UDPM would be the sole legal party and would replace all previous political formations, which had been dissolved after the military coup of Nov. 19, 1968, that overthrew the former president, Modibo Keita. Under the constitution adopted on June 2, 1974, all those who had held political posts between March 1, 1966, and the 1968 coup would be automatically barred from holding membership in the new party, the National Assembly, and the government for a period of ten years from the date of the proclamation of the constitution.

Mali's economy, seriously affected until 1974 by the Sahel drought, continued to improve, and growth in national production exceeded the 7% forecast for the 1974–78 five-year plan. Dependence on foreign aid increased, however, the principal donors being the U.S., China, the U.S.S.R., France, and the Arab countries. (PHILIPPE DECRAENE)

[978.E.4.b.ii]

MALI

Education. (1974–75) Primary, pupils 276,307, teachers 7,848; secondary, pupils 6,786, teachers 511; vocational, pupils 2,704, teachers (1970–71) 332; teacher training, students 1,839, teachers 126; higher (1970–71), students 731, teaching staff 151.

Finance. Monetary unit: Mali franc, with (Sept. 20, 1976) a parity of MFr 100 to the French franc and a free rate of MFr 500 to U.S. $1 (MFr 862 = £1 sterling). Gold, SDR's, and foreign exchange (May 1976) U.S. $5.3 million. Budget (1974 actual): revenue MFr 29.2 billion; expenditure MFr 33.1 billion.

Foreign Trade. (1974) Imports MFr 86,080,000,000; exports MFr 30,810,000,000. Import sources (1973): France *c.* 57%; Ivory Coast *c.* 15%; U.S. *c.* 7%; West Germany *c.* 6%; Belgium-Luxembourg *c.* 5%. Export destinations (1973): France *c.* 34%; Ivory Coast *c.* 28%; Upper Volta *c.* 8%; Japan *c.* 6%; West Germany *c.* 5%; U.K. *c.* 5%. Main exports (1971–72): cotton 38%; livestock 27%; peanuts 12%; fish 6%; peanut oil 6%.

Agriculture. Production (in 000; metric tons; 1975): millet and sorghum *c.* 700; rice (1974) *c.* 200; corn (1974) *c.* 87; peanuts *c.* 120; sweet potatoes *c.* 60; cassava (1974) *c.* 120; cotton, lint *c.* 21; beef and veal (1974) *c.* 35; mutton and lamb (1974) *c.* 23. Livestock (in 000; 1974): cattle *c.* 4,500; sheep *c.* 4,700; goats *c.* 4,000; camels *c.* 158; horses *c.* 125; asses *c.* 340.

Malta

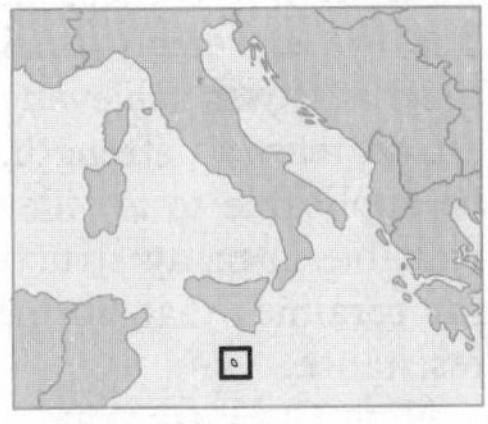

The Republic of Malta, a member of the Commonwealth of Nations, comprises the islands of Malta, Gozo, and Comino in the Mediterranean Sea between Sicily and Tunisia. Area: 122 sq mi (316 sq km), including Malta, Gozo, and Comino. Pop. (1976 est.): 300,900. Cap.: Valletta (pop., 1975 est., 14,000). Largest city: Sliema (pop., 1975 est., 20,000). Language: Maltese and English. Religion: mainly Roman Catholic. Presidents in 1976, Sir Anthony Mamo and, from December 27, Anton Buttigieg; prime minister, Dom Mintoff.

In September 1976 the Malta Labour Party, led by Dom Mintoff, was returned to power for a second five-year term. The Maltese islands were divided into 13 divisions, instead of 10 as previously, from which 65 instead of 55 members of Parliament were elected. Labour won 34 seats in the House of Representatives, against 31 for the Nationalist Party led by G. Borg Olivier. The voting age was lowered to 18 from 21, and 95% of the registered voters went to the polls.

For 1976–77 the government budgeted for a total expenditure of M£96 million, including M£32.5 million on capital account. In April the principle of equal pay for equal work for men and women came into force, and the minimum weekly wage was raised to M£13.25.

In May, at the end of an official visit by Libyan Pres. Muammar al-Qaddafi, the Maltese and Libyan leaders reaffirmed their belief in the establishment of a new international economic order that would take into consideration the interests of the third world. Malta's television service started test transmissions on a second channel, and a new television station, with Italian participation, was inaugurated. A direct-dialing automatic telephone service with Italy and the U.K. came into operation. (ALBERT GANADO)

This Nationalist Party clubhouse was burned out during the September election campaign in the Maltese capital.

KEYSTONE

MALTA

Education. (1973–74) Primary, pupils 32,569, teachers 1,718; secondary, pupils 25,509, teachers 1,954; vocational, pupils 4,161, teachers 331; higher, students 1,420, teaching staff 305.

Finance. Monetary unit: Maltese pound, with (Sept. 20, 1976) a free rate of M£0.43 to U.S. $1 (M£0.75 = £1 sterling). Gold, SDR's, and foreign exchange (June 1976) U.S. $527.1 million. Budget (1975–76 est.): revenue M£70,459,000; expenditure M£80,357,000.

Foreign Trade. (1975) Imports M£144,430,000; exports M£63,090,000. Import sources (1974): U.K. 25%; Italy 17%; West Germany 8%; The Netherlands 6%; U.S. 6%; France 5%. Export destinations (1974): U.K. 28%; West Germany 10%; Belgium-Luxembourg 9%; Italy 7%; Sweden 6%; Libya 5%. Main exports (1974): clothing 38%; petroleum products 11%; textile yarns and fabrics 10%; machinery 7%; rubber products 6%; food 6%. Tourism (1974): visitors 273,500; gross receipts U.S. $58 million.

Transport and Communications. Roads (1973) 1,248 km. Motor vehicles in use (1974): passenger 51,646; commercial 11,464. There are no railways. Air traffic (1974): 219.2 million passenger-km; freight 2,874,000 net ton-km. Shipping (1975): merchant vessels 100 gross tons and over 31; gross tonnage 45,950. Ships entered (1974): vessels totaling 1,522,000 net registered tons; goods loaded 91,000 metric tons, unloaded 914,000 metric tons. Telephones (Dec. 1974) 48,984. Radio licenses (Dec. 1973) 129,000. Television licenses (Dec. 1973) 61,000.

Materials Sciences

Ceramics. Activity in ceramics during 1976 derived its impetus from a broad range of energy-related concepts. Progress was made in new materials, in new processing techniques with the potential for lower fabrication costs, in research directed toward improved mechanical properties, and in new applications for ceramics.

New Materials. Silicon carbide filaments had been studied for many years as attractive reinforcements for high-temperature metals. Unfortunately they could be made only by chemical vapour deposition on tungsten or carbon substrates, and their expense (about $800/lb in research quantities) had limited their use in metal-matrix composites. Thus one of the most significant events of the year was the announcement by Seishi Yajima and co-workers at Tohoku Gakuen University in Sendai, Japan, of their success in preparing silicon carbide filaments with very good mechanical properties by pyrolyzing a polycarbosilane polymer precursor. This process offered tremendous potential for the production of low-cost filaments and showed promise of increasing the attractiveness of ceramic-fibre-reinforced metal-matrix composites. There was even speculation that the ability to prepare ceramics from organometallic polymer precursors might lead to new ways of making a range of mixed nitrides and carbonitrides in both filament and bulk form.

Another major development was the announcement by the Carborundum Co. at Niagara Falls, N.Y., of a sinterable alpha-phase silicon carbide powder amenable to fabrication into complex shapes, including turbine-engine parts, with good-quality surfaces

Manufacturing: *see* Economy, World; Industrial Review

Marine Biology: *see* Life Sciences

AUTHENTICATED NEWS INTERNATIONAL

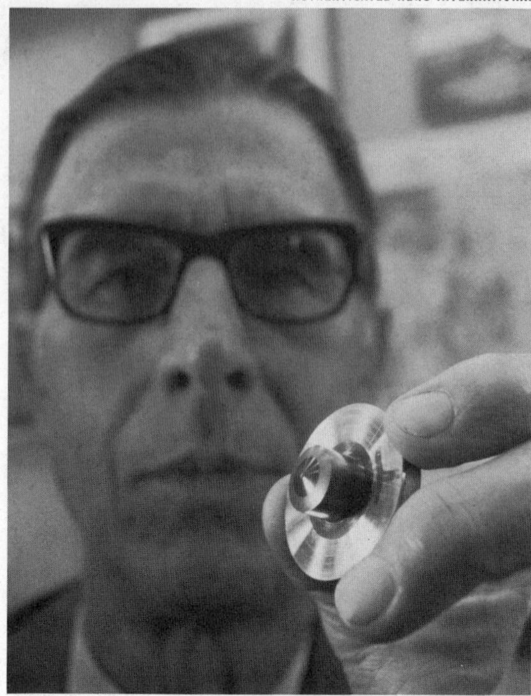

General Electric developed a tungsten carbide piston tipped with diamonds for generating pressures above eight million pounds per square inch—equivalent to placing four 50-ton locomotives on a tack.

that required little or no expensive finish grinding. This material thus joined a growing number of silicon nitride and silicon carbide powders with great potential for use in new ceramic structural applications.

PROCESSING. Hot isostatic pressing (HIP), a relatively new process employing high-temperature, inert-gas autoclaves for the densification of ceramic powders, was proving of great benefit in improving existing sintering methods. A. Traff and P. Skotte of ASEA in Sweden recently reported success in using the HIP process to close remaining porosity in traditionally sintered alumina tool tips used to machine metals. They found that the postdensification HIP treatment increased tool-tip lifetime by at least 25%. Similarly, they were able to more than double the rupture strength of boron carbide by HIP treating presintered parts. There also were indications in the U.S. and elsewhere that silicon nitride, which did not sinter or even hot press without the aid of generally harmful additives, might densify to a ceramic of high strength under the simultaneous high pressures and temperatures achievable in the HIP process. In view of the expense involved in grinding and finishing dense, fired ceramics, such processes as hot isostatic pressing and the newly emerging injection-molding process for ceramics, with their potential for producing shapes close to final configuration, were expected to have a tremendous effect on cost reduction.

MECHANICAL PROPERTIES. Many modern ceramics can be processed to high levels of strength, but they are inherently brittle, failing with little or no local plastic deformation. They also generally lack toughness, and though brittleness continued to pose a difficult challenge, some progress was made in toughness improvement. Several researchers demonstrated that partially stabilized zirconia, when properly processed, could have surprisingly high toughness values. Nils Claussen of the Max-Planck-Institut in West Berlin showed that the addition of unstabilized zirconia as a very finely divided second-phase dispersion could double the fracture toughness of alumina. The toughening mechanism in this case appeared to be associated with the formation of a very fine network of microcracks at the second-phase particles. Because extremely small cracks form, the increased toughness was achieved at the expense of only a modest decrease in strength. The technique, which might be applicable to a wide range of ceramics, should be valuable in many structural applications, particularly for ceramics that normally have poor thermal-shock resistance.

NEW CERAMIC APPLICATIONS. During the year the U.S. Energy Research and Development Administration (ERDA) and the National Aeronautics and Space Administration (NASA) proposed a large government-industry program aimed at developing ceramic-component automotive turbine engines that operated at 2,500°–3,000° F (1,370°–1,650° C). NASA studies indicated such engines would be cleaner and much more efficient than those currently available.

There was also a rise in demand for improved glasses for fibre-optic communications. Accelerating growth in communication requirements and the great information-carrying capacity of coherent light traveling along fibre waveguides made it increasingly probable that light waves would someday supplant current radio and cable systems. Central to the problem, however, was the need for improved low-loss optical fibres. For example, recent studies indicated that waveguide cable losses must not exceed ten decibels per kilometre if transmitter-receiver separations of five kilometres were to be achieved. In view of the small size, light weight, freedom from electrical interference, and low cost potential of fibre-optic systems, the development of ceramic waveguides with improved optical and mechanical properties seemed a certainty.

A third area of concentrated activity last year centred around the possibility of using ceramics as a means of safely storing radioactive wastes. Several groups, including the Pacific Northwest Laboratories in Richland, Wash., were studying the incorporation of wastes from nuclear reactors into solid, glassy ceramics that offered stability and ease of handling.

(NORMAN M. TALLAN)

Metallurgy. Metallurgical development continued rather slowly under the influences of worldwide economic and political problems and uncertainties. Economical, environmentally acceptable methods of extracting metal from ores, especially those of low grade, continued to be a pressing need. No repressive mineral cartels developed but many nontechnical problems affected mineral supplies.

EXTRACTIVE METALLURGY. With practically no bauxite deposits of its own, the Soviet Union was very active in developing processes to obtain aluminum from clay and other aluminum silicate minerals. One interesting method used bacteria to change a fraction of the silica to a soluble form, greatly simplifying later aluminum recovery. Among the most successful processes was a high-pressure nitric acid leach operating at temperatures near 180° C (355° F). A U.S. company obtained a license to use a Soviet process to obtain aluminum from alunite and began construction of a large pilot plant.

The relative cost in energy to extract metals by different processes had been a subject of debate for several years but appeared to be approaching agreement as energy-use audit procedures became more uniform. Recent studies of energy requirements made hydrometallurgical copper production methods appear competitive with pyrometallurgical approaches. The first flash smelter for copper in the U.S. went into production with apparently satisfactory control of its sulfur dioxide emission, which was one of the main attractions of the process. A nearly completed aluminum smelter was expected to consume about four kilowatt-hours of electricity per pound of extracted metal, about one-third less than the best existing plants. The enclosed smelting chamber made the process much cleaner than the Hall process and prevented the emission of fluorides. Reports from Japan, where the energy problem was very serious, told of a record low blast-furnace fuel consumption of 431 kilograms per metric ton of iron produced; industry-wide, however, the average was probably still in the 500-kg range.

Recently released figures for the U.S. showed nearly one-quarter of the aluminum cans produced in 1975 were returned for remelting, a procedure that consumed only about one-twentieth the power needed to extract aluminum. Although the high tin content of steel in municipal waste made it undesirable for recycling, tests indicated that it could safely be used in such items as reinforcing bars for concrete. Porcelain-enameled steel appliances had not been recycled for fear of damage to furnace linings by reaction with the enamel, but experiments showed that with care they could be included in remelt charges with little danger.

ALLOYS. Among the rapidly growing ranks of high-strength low-alloy steels, one new alloy combined good formability with very high strength in the cold-rolled condition without heat treatment. Such materials were of importance to automobile manufacturers, which sought car weight reductions to meet fuel-economy standards without expensive changes in production methods, and to the steel industry, which needed to meet competition from low-weight aluminum and plastics. Another new automotive steel used vanadium and nitrogen as alloying elements. Heat treatment of the steel produces a soft, highly formable two-phase structure that increases in strength by two-thirds during normal forming operations.

The superplastic alloys became firmly established for the production of complicated shapes with low forming force. For example, one very complex aircraft part nearly 12 ft long was being blow-molded like plastic or glass from a simple welded tube of a superplastic titanium alloy at only 950° F (510° C). The first commercial superplastic aluminum alloy was under production in England.

METAL FORMING. Because of its energy and labour efficiency and its vigorous development, powder metallurgy was probably the most active aspect of metal forming. The availability of split-die presses made practical the production of increasingly complex shapes. A line of heavy-duty bearings probably imposes the most stringent requirements for dimensional stability and mechanical properties of any product of powder metallurgy. A forging step after sintering brings the parts to full density; their critical dimensions are machined, and finally they are heated, treated, and ground to final size and finish. Aluminum powder-metallurgy bearings containing 10% of a proprietary antifriction alloy had properties comparable to bronze bearings, and had less weight and lower material cost.

Vacuum deposition of nickel found use in forming thin parts and as a corrosion-resistant coating. The use of vacuum-deposited aluminum continued to increase, and ionplating was being used in civilian products. Ionplating made possible the coating of complex shapes by using an electric field to attract charged aluminum ions to all areas of the part.

AUTHENTICATED NEWS INTERNATIONAL

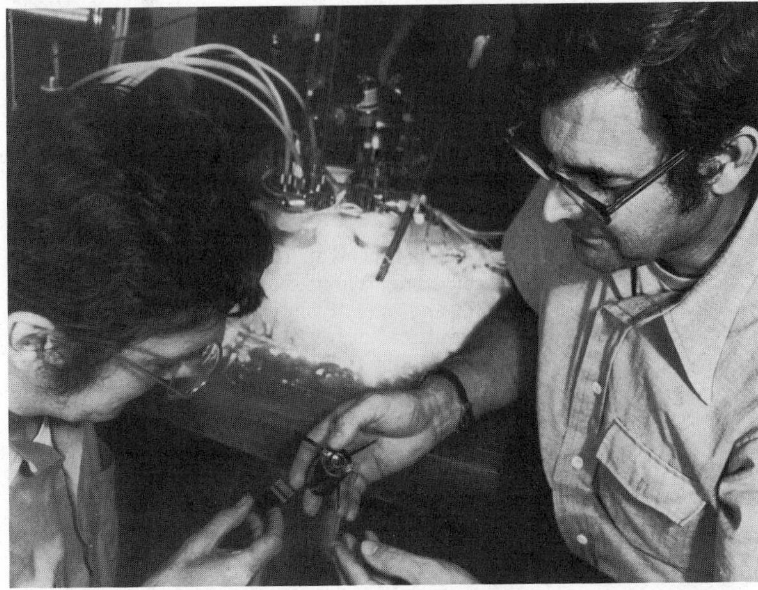

Two IBM scientists built a supervacuum chamber large enough to hold several experiments. It is used for studying superthin layers of material at temperatures close to absolute zero.

Because the relatively thick oxide film produced on aluminum by anodizing is porous, it can be impregnated with dye for colour or with other materials. A ten-year worldwide outdoor exposure test showed certain organic dyes to be stable over this length of time. Impregnation with Teflon or molybdenum disulfide was being used to improve wear-resistance. Cobalt-based alloys were being given a hard, potentially corrosion-resistant outer finish using a laser beam to melt a thin surface layer of metal. As the intense beam passes, the cold metal beneath causes the liquefied layer to cool at a rate of more than a million degrees per second to a glasslike, noncrystalline structure. (DONALD F. CLIFTON)

See also Industrial Review: *Glass; Iron and Steel; Machinery and Machine Tools;* Mining and Quarrying.
[725.B]

Mathematics

The normally restrained world of higher mathematics was jolted in the summer of 1976 when news from the University of Illinois indicated that a team of mathematicians had resolved the century-old four-colour conjecture. This simple problem, perhaps the most famous and widely known of the many unsolved puzzles of modern mathematics, asked the question: Can every map on a plane be coloured with four colours so that adjacent regions receive different colours? The affirmative answer, provided after a four-year research effort by Kenneth Appel and Wolfgang Haken, required an unprecedented and controversial synthesis of computer search and theoretical reasoning.

The four-colour conjecture was first posed in the early 1850s by Francis Guthrie, a mathematics student at University College, London. Simple examples (*e.g.*, a circular region surrounded by three adjacent regions) show that no fewer than four colours will suffice to properly colour a map. But despite the intense study of increasingly complex cases involving thousands of regions, no one had ever discovered a map that required more than four colours or, until now, showed that none could exist.

Appel and Haken adopted a very simple strategy for their proof. They created an immense catalog of nearly 2,000 "unavoidable" configurations that must be present in any graph, no matter how large. Then they showed how each of these configurations could be reduced to a smaller one so that, if the smaller one could be coloured with four colours, so could the original catalog configuration. Thus, if there were a map that could not be coloured with four colours, they could use their catalog to find a smaller map that also could not be four-coloured, and then a smaller one still, and so on. Eventually this reduction process would lead to a map with only three or four regions that, supposedly, could not be coloured with four colours. This absurd result, derived from the hypothesis that a map requiring more than four colours might exist, leads to the conclusion that no such map can exist. All maps are four-colourable.

The strategy involved in this proof is not particularly revolutionary. It dates back to 1879 when British mathematician A. B. Kempe published the first "proof" of the conjecture. Kempe produced a short list of unavoidable configurations, and then showed how to reduce each to a smaller case. In 1890, however, P. J. Heawood, also a Briton, discovered an example with 25 regions that could not be reduced in the manner outlined in Kempe's analysis. Of course, Heawood's map could be coloured with only four colours, but this fact could not be proved by Kempe's method.

To correct Kempe's oversight Appel and Haken replaced his brief list with their catalog of 1,936 cases. Treating all of these cases—verifying that every map contained at least one of them, and that each was reducible—required extensive computer analysis because each involved up to 500,000 logical options for full analysis. Their complete proof, itself several hundred pages long, required over 1,000 hours of computer calculations.

This reliance on computer analysis led to some unusual controversy. Many mathematicians were initially skeptical of the accuracy and logical validity of the proof because they could not actually carry out the necessary verification. But those experts who examined the work seemed quickly convinced that the argument was airtight, if not exactly elegant. For many mathematicians, however, there remained a deeply rooted suspicion that if one proof existed, no matter how grotesque, someone would eventually find

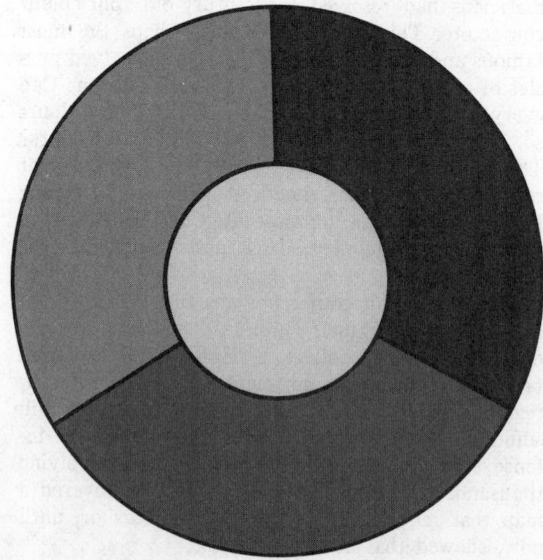

Can every map on a plane be coloured with no more than four colours? Yes, say the mathematicians, and at last they've proved it.

an elegant argument more in keeping with mathematical tradition.

Indeed, traditional mathematical arguments were of critical importance to the first part of the Appel-Haken proof. In this stage they had to reduce a potentially infinite number of cases to a finite but large number of cases. This proved possible because of the intricate geometric links that relate regions of a map. But once the problem had been made finite, there remained a major question: how many different cases are involved? As it turned out, the number of required cases was just barely within the processing capability of modern computers; had the problem been a few orders of magnitude larger, its solution would have had to wait upon future advances in the computer sciences.

The fact that the four-colour conjecture is true came as little surprise to the mathematical community, for almost everyone who had worked on the problem believed that it was true. Moreover, no crucial statements in other branches of mathematics rested on the four-colour conjecture, so the direct effect of the proof on the body of mathematical knowledge was slight.

But the effect of the method of solution on the progress of mathematical research could be profound. Appel and Haken demonstrated by this vivid example that certain mathematical truths may be so complex that no brief, elegant proof in the traditional form exists. Such truths, of which the four-colour conjecture is but one example, could be proved only by a new synthesis of theoretical and computational methods. Investigations of this type, involving the cooperation of mathematician and machine, may well become a new frontier of mathematical research.

(LYNN ARTHUR STEEN)

[10/22.E.1.c.iv]

Mauritania

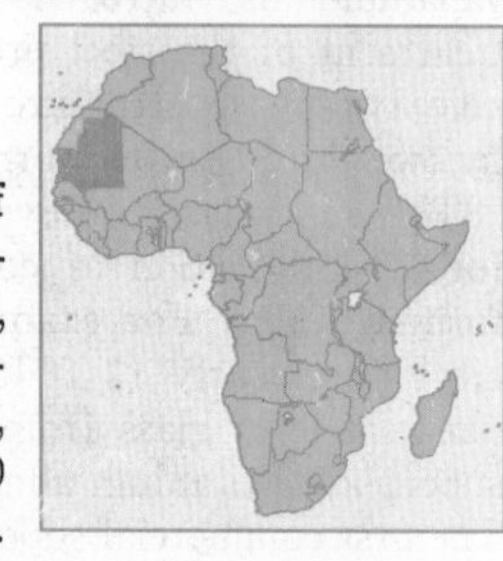

The Islamic Republic of Mauritania is on the Atlantic coast of West Africa, adjoining Western (Spanish) Sahara, Algeria, Mali, and Senegal. Area: 398,000 sq mi (1,030,700 sq km). Pop. (1975 est.): 1,318,000. Cap.: Nouakchott (pop., 1975 est., 103,500). (Data above refer to Mauritania as constituted prior to the purported division of Spanish Sahara between Mauritania and Morocco.) Language: Arabic, French. Religion: Muslim. President in 1976, Moktar Ould Daddah.

Following Spain's departure from Western Sahara on Feb. 26, 1976, and the proclamation of a Saharan Arab Democratic Republic at midnight on February 27–28 by the Saharan nationalist front, Polisario, fighting began between Mauritania and Morocco on the one hand and Polisario guerrillas on the other. This, in turn, led to the breaking off of diplomatic relations with Algeria when the latter recognized the new republic.

On April 14 Mauritania and Morocco signed a convention on the delimitation of their borders within Western Sahara and on the sharing of the area's mineral deposits and territorial waters. Mediation efforts by the Arab League and the Organization of African Unity proved fruitless, and Mauritania, with

MAURITANIA

Education. (1972–73) Primary, pupils 38,900, teachers (1971–72) 1,585; secondary, pupils 4,073, teachers (1971–72) 156; vocational, pupils 247; teacher training (1971–72), students 145.

Finance. Monetary unit: ouguiya, with (Sept. 20, 1976) a parity of 1 ouguiya to 5 CFA francs (free rate of 49 ouguiya = U.S. $1; 84.41 ouguiya = £1 sterling). Gold, SDR's, and foreign exchange (June 1976) U.S. $110.4 million. Budget (1974 est.) balanced at 3,125,000,000 ouguiya.

Foreign Trade. (1974) Imports 5,345,000,000 ouguiya; exports 8,175,000,000 ouguiya. Import sources: France *c.* 30%; Senegal *c.* 16%; Ghana *c.* 12%; U.S. *c.* 6%; U.K. *c.* 6%; West Germany 5%. Export destinations: Japan *c.* 16%; France *c.* 16%; Spain *c.* 13%; U.K. 13%; West Germany *c.* 12%; Belgium-Luxembourg *c.* 8%; Italy *c.* 8%. Main exports: iron ore 72%; fish (1972) 11%; copper concentrates (1972) 10%.

25% of its development budget diverted into military spending, suffered crippling economic consequences. On June 8 Nouakchott itself was attacked.

In a Cabinet reshuffle on June 17, Col. Vahi Ould Mayouf became the first military member of the government since Mauritania's independence in 1960. On August 8 Ould Daddah was confirmed president for a fourth consecutive five-year term. At the same time, seven candidates of the ruling Mauritanian People's Party were elected to the National Assembly to represent the new Saharan region of Tiris el Gharbia and Güera. (PHILIPPE DECRAENE)

Mauritius

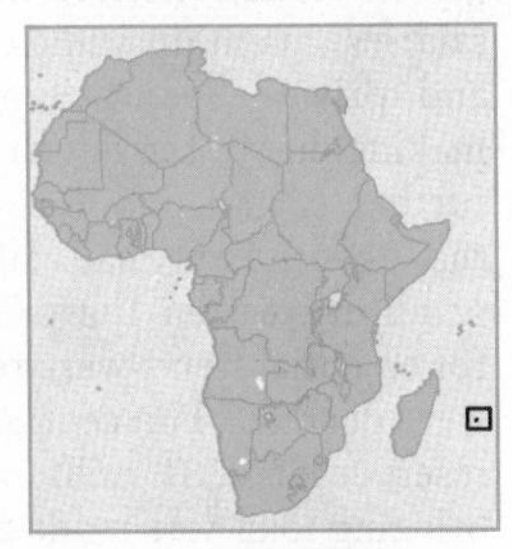

The parliamentary state of Mauritius, a member of the Commonwealth of Nations, lies about 500 mi E of Madagascar in the Indian Ocean; it includes the island dependencies of Rodrigues, Agalega, and Cargados Carajos. Area: 787.5 sq mi (2,040 sq km). Pop. (1975 est.): 882,300, including (1972) Indian 50%; Pakistani 16%; Creole (mixed French and African) 31%; others 3%. Cap. and largest city: Port Louis (pop., 1974 est., 138,400). Language: English (official). Religion (1974 est.): Hindu 51%; Christian 30%; Muslim 16%; Buddhist 3%. Queen, Elizabeth II; governor-general in 1976, Sir Abdul Rahman Muhammad Osman; prime minister, Sir Seewoosagur Ramgoolam.

For Mauritius the outstanding event of 1976 was the 13th meeting of the Organization of African Unity (OAU), held at Port Louis during July. The choice of Mauritius, 1,200 mi from Africa and with a predominantly Asian population, seemed odd and could have embarrassed the outgoing chairman, Pres. Idi Amin of Uganda. This did not happen, however, and Amin was succeeded by the first Asian chairman of the OAU, Sir Seewoosagur Ramgoolam (*see* BIOGRAPHY). Ramgoolam relinquished his foreign affairs portfolio to Sir Harold Walter in a Cabinet reshuffle in June. The right-wing Social Democratic Party, led by Gaëtan Duval, objected to membership in the OAU, because of the Asian majority in Mauritius and because the party favoured better relations with South Africa. In the December elections Paul Berenger's Marxist party, the Mauritius Militant Movement, won 34 seats out of 70 in Parliament, but Ramgoolam's Independence Party (28) formed a coalition government with the Social Democrats (8).

A project to harness energy from ocean waves was undertaken. The first phase was a pilot plant on the south coast to convert energy for hydroelectric development and also provide a wave-free area for commercial fish farming. (MOLLY MORTIMER)

MAURITIUS

Education. (1974) Primary, pupils 152,417, teachers 5,568; secondary, pupils 60,440, teachers 1,921; vocational, pupils 1,212, teachers 83; teacher training, students 645, teachers 19; higher, students 696, teaching staff 65.

Finance and Trade. Monetary unit: Mauritian rupee, with (Sept. 20, 1976) a free rate of MauRs 6.97 to U.S. $1 (MauRs 12.01 = £1 sterling). Gold, SDR's, and foreign exchange (June 1976) U.S. $103.2 million. Budget (1974–75 est.): revenue MauRs 744 million; expenditure MauRs 733 million. Foreign trade (1975): imports MauRs 1,995,300,000; exports MauRs 1,838,900,000. Import sources (1974): U.K. 14%; South Africa 9%; Taiwan 8%; Iran 8%; France 8%; West Germany 6%; Japan 6%; U.S. 5%; Australia 5%. Export destinations (1974): Canada 36%; U.K. 35%; U.S. 8%; Iran 7%. Main export (1974) sugar 86%. Tourism: visitors (1973) 68,000; gross receipts (1974) U.S. $20 million.

Agriculture. Production (in 000; metric tons; 1975): sugar 468; bananas (1974) *c.* 11; tea *c.* 4; tobacco *c.* 0.6; milk *c.* 22. Livestock (in 000; April 1974): cattle *c.* 51; pigs *c.* 4; sheep *c.* 3; goats *c.* 66; chickens *c.* 430.

Mexico

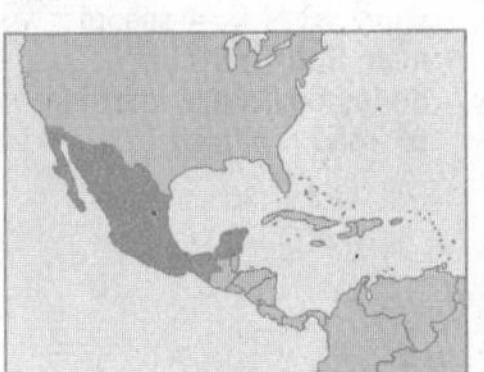

A federal republic of Middle America, Mexico is bounded by the Pacific Ocean, the Gulf of Mexico, the U.S., Belize, and Guatemala. Area: 761,600 sq mi (1,972,550 sq km). Pop. (1976 est.): 62,329,200, including about 55% mestizo and 29% Indian. Cap. and largest city: Mexico City (pop., 1976 est., federal district 8,628,000, metro. area 11,943,000). Language: Spanish. Religion: predominantly Roman Catholic. Presidents in 1976, Luis Echeverría Álvarez and, from December 1, José López Portillo.

In March President Echeverría granted amnesty to some 250 persons arrested during the student riots that preceded the 1968 Olympic Games. Apart from some university and peasant unrest, there were several major disturbances in 1976, mostly ascribed to the Liga Comunista 23 de Septiembre, a left-wing guerrilla group. They included assaults on banks and restaurants in which 22 Mexico City policemen were reported to have been killed. The most spectacular events were the kidnapping on May 25 of Nadine Chaval, the Belgian ambassador's daughter, who was later released after payment of a $400,000 ransom, and the attempt to abduct the sister of President-elect José López Portillo (*see* BIOGRAPHY) on August 11, during which the alleged leader of the 23 de Septiembre group, David Jiménez Sarmiento, was killed. In the presidential elections held on July 4, López Portillo, the candidate of the ruling Partido Revolucionario Institucional (PRI), won with 94.4% of the 18.5 million votes cast.

In two major unions, the electrical workers and the telephone workers, rebel factions disputed the official leadership; there was some violence and one death, but eventually the opposition subsided. After the devaluation of the peso, workers demanded wage increases of up to 65% and threatened a general strike on September 28. After discussions, however, the government was able to limit wage rises to 16–23%.

Medicine: *see* Health and Disease

Mental Health: *see* Health and Disease

Merchant Marine: *see* Transportation

Metallurgy: *see* Materials Sciences

Metals: *see* Industrial Review; Materials Sciences; Mining and Quarrying

Meteorology: *see* Earth Sciences

Methodist Churches: *see* Religion

WIDE WORLD

Mexico's Indians speak dozens of different languages. These youngsters in a school near San Cristóbal de las Casas are learning to read Spanish.

Julio Scherer García, editor of Mexico's influential daily newspaper *Excélsior*, was voted out of his job by an employees' cooperative in July. Scherer described the move as an attempt by the government to end independent criticism of its policies. The paper was taken over by the Mexican Editorial Organization, which had been formed by President Echeverría and already owned two leading newspaper chains.

In July torrential rains and floods affected 11 of Mexico's 31 states, and in October Hurricane Liza ravaged parts of Baja California, especially La Paz. About 215,000 people were left homeless.

Mexico's economic growth in 1975 was estimated at 4% in real terms, as compared with 6% in 1974. The most dynamic sectors were petroleum and petrochemicals, while mining declined because of a fall in external demand. Total industrial output grew by 4.2% and construction and manufacturing by 3.5 and 4%, respectively. Agricultural production improved, reflecting better irrigation and more adequate technical and credit facilities. The government succeeded in lowering the inflation rate to 11.6% in the year ended July 1976 (as compared with an annual rate of 15.9% at the end of July 1975). New import controls implemented in July 1975 helped to reduce the trade deficit for January–June 1976 to $1,460,000,000, 12.4% below the first half of 1975.

Despite these seemingly favourable trends—and regardless of frequent official denials—the government announced on Aug. 31, 1976, that the peso would be allowed to float freely against the U.S. dollar. For 22 years it had been fixed at 12.50 pesos to U.S. $1, which in 1976 amounted to an overvaluation of between 30 and 50%. No restrictions were imposed on the exchange market. The aims of the devaluation were to improve the terms of trade, particularly with the U.S., which took 60% of Mexico's exports, and to encourage foreign tourists. Persistent rumours of a devaluation had encouraged a flight of capital, resulting in an additional burden on the foreign debt (estimated at 18.8 billion at the end of March).

Early dealings moved the rate down to $1 = 20.50 pesos, representing an effective devaluation of 39%. On September 12 a new parity was established of $1 = 19.70/19.90 pesos, to be maintained as long as it was viable. On October 27, however, the central bank decided to refloat the peso until further notice so as to halt currency speculation. In the meantime measures had been taken to control prices, adjust salaries, maintain sufficient credit for both the public and private sectors, and prevent excessive profit-making due to the devaluation. A decree was issued to further curtail public spending, despite the fact that the government had succeeded in maintaining expenditure within the projected levels. Import duties for essential items were reduced, and new export levies were decreed. The central bank was said to have gross reserves of $381 million to support the float, and a bridging loan was made available by the U.S. Federal Reserve System until further assistance totaling $1.2 billion was granted by the International Monetary Fund in November. A loan of some $800 million (Eurodollars) was to be arranged by a group of international banks.

The inauguration of López Portillo on December 1 was clouded by disturbances involving the expropriation of land that, together with the uncertainties surrounding devaluation of the peso, led to rumours of

MEXICO

Education. (1974–75) Primary, pupils 11,885,509, teachers 275,558; secondary and vocational, pupils 2,477,999, teachers 139,001; teacher training, students (1973–74) 76,550, teachers (1970–71) 5,131; higher (including 44 universities), students 451,947, teaching staff 27,855.

Finance. Monetary unit: peso, with (Sept. 20, 1976) a free rate of 19.76 pesos to U.S. $1 (free rate of 34.04 pesos = £1 sterling). Gold, SDR's, and foreign exchange (March 1976) U.S. $1,388,000,000. Budget (1975 est.) balanced at 346,660,000,000 pesos. Gross domestic product (1974) 812.9 billion pesos. Money supply (Jan. 1976) 112,860,000,000 pesos. Cost of living (Mexico City; 1970 = 100; June 1976) 200.

Foreign Trade. (1975) Imports 82,252,000,000 pesos; exports 36,358,000,000 pesos. Import sources (1974): U.S. 62%; West Germany 8%. Export destinations (1974): U.S. 58%; Japan 5%. Main exports (1974): chemicals 9%; sugar 8%; fruit and vegetables 8%; textile yarns and fabrics 7%; cotton 6%; transport equipment 6%; machinery 5%; fish 5%; zinc 5%. Tourism (1974): visitors 3,361,000; gross receipts U.S. $2,056,000,000.

Transport and Communications. Roads (1974) 172,097 km (including 957 km expressways). Motor vehicles in use (1974): passenger 1,943,155; commercial 709,855. Railways (1972): 24,607 km; traffic (principal only) 4,614,000,000 passenger-km, freight 31,094,000,000 net ton-km. Air traffic (1974): 5,957,000,000 passenger-km; freight 76.4 million net ton-km. Shipping (1975): merchant vessels 100 gross tons and over 274; gross tonnage 574,857. Telephones (Dec. 1974) 2,546,000. Radio receivers (Dec. 1973) 16,870,000. Television receivers (Dec. 1973) 4,339,000.

Agriculture. Production (in 000; metric tons; 1975): corn c. 9,300; wheat c. 3,000; barley c. 260; sorghum c. 2,700; rice 414; potatoes c. 650; dry beans 1,202; soybeans c. 545; tomatoes c. 1,250; bananas (1974) c. 1,155; oranges (1974) c. 2,013; lemons (1974) 236; coffee c. 240; sugar, raw value c. 2,763; tobacco c. 52; agaves (1974) 149; cotton, lint c. 189; fish catch (1974) 442. Livestock (in 000; Dec. 1974): cattle c. 28,071; sheep c. 5,280; pigs c. 11,779; horses (1973) c. 4,459; mules (1973) c. 2,937; asses (1973) c. 2,945; chickens c. 153,000.

Industry. Production (in 000; metric tons; 1975): cement 11,569; crude oil 36,445; coal (1974) 5,166; natural gas (cu m) 22,357; electricity (kw-hr) 43,224,000; iron ore (metal content; 1974) 3,338; pig iron (1974) 3,307; steel 5,108; sulfur (1974) 2,322; petroleum products (1974) c. 29,445; sulfuric acid 1,872; nitrogenous fertilizers (nutrient content; 1974–75) c. 409; aluminum 40; phosphate c. 197; copper (1974) 68; lead (1974) 183; zinc (1974) 137; antimony ore (metal content; 1974) 2.4; manganese ore (metal content; 1974) 145; phosphate rock (1974) 194; gold (troy oz; 1974) 134; silver (troy oz; 1974) 37,550; cotton yarn (1974) 179; woven cotton fabrics (1974) 150; wool yarn (1974) 38; rayon, etc., filaments and fibres (1974) 34; nylon, etc., filaments and fibres (1974) 156.

unrest and a possible coup. Stringent security measures were taken at the ceremony, but it proceeded without incident. Twelve days before leaving office, President Echeverría had decreed that over 200,000 ac of rich farmland in Sonora and Sinaloa states be expropriated with compensation and distributed to landless peasants. Under Mexico's Agrarian Reform Law, individual ownership of irrigated land was limited to 100 ha (250 ac). The landowners, however, had claimed that although the land in question was owned by a few wealthy families, the holdings of individual family members were within the legal minimum. Within hours of Echeverría's proclamation, the land was occupied by peasants, while the landowners began a strike and business and industrial interests issued strong protests. In December a federal judge reversed the order on procedural grounds, but no final ruling was expected before Jan. 7, 1977. The peasant unions announced that they would appeal.

Mexico continued to improve its relations with other states in 1976. In January Prime Minister Pierre Trudeau of Canada came to discuss investments in livestock development, mining, tourism, and the manufacture of railroad cars. In March President Tito of Yugoslavia paid a state visit, and in April a memorandum of understanding on economic and industrial cooperation was signed with the U.K. Trade and economic assistance were again discussed when the president of the European Commission, François-Xavier Ortoli, visited the country in April.

In June Mexico declared a 200-mi territorial-waters limit and signed an agreement with Guatemala to establish the respective water limits between them; a document on mutual aid in oil exploration, development, refining, and transport was also initialed. Although the Mexican authorities had intimated that the country might soon join the Organization of Petroleum Exporting Countries, these intentions were denied after the U.S. warned that preferential treatment for Mexican goods and services would be at stake. Mexico refused to attend the Organization of American States meeting in June because it was to be held in Santiago and Mexico had severed relations with Chile.

(BARBARA WIJNGAARD)

[974.A]

Middle Eastern Affairs

There were no important developments in the Arab-Israeli conflict in 1976. The Arab states were concerned throughout the year with the Lebanese crisis. No new initiative toward a Middle East settlement came from the great powers in the period preceding the U.S. presidential election, and when it was over U.S. Secretary of State Henry Kissinger indicated he would take no actions that would commit the incoming government of President-elect Jimmy Carter. The likelihood of early peace moves was further diminished by the Israeli political crisis in December. The Palestinian Arabs—especially the Palestine Liberation Organization (PLO) leadership—were also much involved in Lebanese affairs, and this to some extent distracted their attention from the marked nationalist stirrings in the Israeli-occupied West Bank of the Jordan and the separate, though related, protest movement among Israeli Arabs in Galilee.

Arab-Israeli and Palestine Problems. In January 1976 the U.S. tried unsuccessfully to prevent the PLO from taking part in a UN Security Council debate on the Middle East on the ground, which the U.S. shared with Israel, that there could be no dialogue with the PLO. On January 26 the U.S. vetoed a resolution that would have affirmed the Palestinian people's right to self-determination, including the right to establish an independent state; France and the Soviet Union voted in favour while Britain abstained. The veto sparked serious rioting in the Israeli-occupied West Bank, and the situation was exacerbated by the decision of an Israeli court to allow Jews to pray on the Temple Mount near the Al-Aqsa Mosque and the Dome of the Rock in Jerusalem. The Israeli government's decision on February 4 to maintain its ban on Jewish prayer there failed to end the disturbances.

UPI COMPIX

Egyptian troops raise their flag at an outpost in the Sinai desert during the last stage of Israel's withdrawal from its former buffer zone in February.

On February 22 the Israeli government announced that it had authorized the U.S. to investigate, with the leaders of Egypt, Syria, and Jordan, the possibilities of ending the state of war with Israel, but the idea had little support even inside Israel. Similarly, an Israeli offer to start direct negotiations with Jordan was rejected by Jordan. Both Egypt and the Soviet Union continued to press for the resumption of the Geneva Middle East peace talks (which in September 1975 had produced the second Sinai disengagement agreement between Egypt and Israel after the October 1973 Arab-Israeli war but had led to nothing further), but this had no result as Israel and the U.S. continued to reject PLO participation.

After improving briefly in early March, the West Bank situation deteriorated again, and the mayors and municipal councils of four towns, including Nablus, resigned. The worst incident occurred on March 10 when Israeli troops broke into the Arab Bir Zeit University College to stop a student demonstration and many were injured. Rioting continued throughout the month, and curfews were imposed.

A UN Security Council debate was called on March 19 to discuss Israel's policies in East Jerusalem and the West Bank. Israel decided to attend, breaking its earlier decision never to take part in any proceeding when the PLO was present. The debate ended on March 25 with the U.S. vetoing a resolution criticizing Israel; this caused some surprise, since the U.S. ambassador to the UN, William Scranton, had strongly criticized Israel's policy of establishing Jewish settlements in the West Bank in a speech on March 23. Inside Israel the Arab population of Galilee organized a general

Microbiology: *see* Life Sciences

strike on March 30, which they called the Day of the Land, in protest against the Israeli government's expropriation of Arab land. In incidents that were given wide publicity in the world press, at least 6 Arabs were killed and 70 persons were injured, including 38 Israeli soldiers and police.

Municipal elections held in the West Bank on April 12 resulted in sweeping victories for Palestinian nationalist and left-wing candidates. In most of the major towns traditionalist mayors and councillors were replaced by younger and more radical representatives. On May 9 the Israeli Cabinet decided that the unauthorized Kadum settlement, established in Samaria by ultranationalist Gush Emunim settlers, should be moved to another site, although the decision had not been implemented by the end of the year. Clashes also occurred during the year between Arabs and members of another Gush Emunim settlement at Kiryat Arba outside Hebron, and in early October there were serious incidents when a mosque and a synagogue were both desecrated in the Tomb of the Patriarchs in Hebron.

By the midyear it was clear to all sides that no new Middle East peace initiative could take place until after the U.S. presidential election, and a planned visit to the Middle East by Pres. Gerald Ford was postponed indefinitely. At the end of May and again in November Syria agreed to a six-month extension of the mandate of the UN Disengagement Observer Force (UNDOF) in the Golan Heights, without any conditions (in November 1975 Syria had insisted that renewal should depend on the UN debating the Palestine question). On October 22 the UN Security Council similarly renewed the mandate of the UN Emergency Force (UNEF) in Sinai for one year.

On June 9 the Security Council began to debate a report prepared by the Committee on Palestinian Rights set up by the General Assembly in December 1975. Israel boycotted the session, and on June 29 the U.S. vetoed a Security Council resolution affirming the "inalienable rights" of the Palestinian people and the creation of a "Palestinian entity" in the West Bank and Gaza. On June 16 the U.S. ambassador to Lebanon was murdered in the Palestinian leftist-held area of Beirut, an act that was denounced by the PLO as "odious and immoral." Contacts between the U.S. State Department and the PLO over this and the evacuation of U.S. nationals from Lebanon drew protests from Israel, but on July 1 the Israeli government said it had been reassured by Washington that there had been no change in policy toward the PLO.

While civil war raged in Lebanon, many villagers in border areas looked to Israel for help in their daily lives. This Lebanese woman is waiting for treatment at an Israeli Army medical centre.

UPI COMPIX

On July 1 President Ford signed the foreign aid appropriation bill and the foreign aid authorization bill, which included $2.2 billion in aid for Israel for the fiscal year ended June 30, 1976, and $275 million for the period between July 1 and October 1, when the new U.S. fiscal year would begin. In what was seen as a compromise between President Ford and pro-Israeli members of Congress, the $5.6 billion aid bill also included $695 million for Egypt. In October, Rabin said President Ford had agreed to provide Israel with a number of the advanced weapons it had been seeking. The general opinion of military experts was that Israel was maintaining a strong military lead over its Arab neighbours.

On the night of July 3–4 Israeli commandos landed at Entebbe airport, Uganda, and rescued hostages from an Air France airbus hijacked by guerrillas after it left Athens on June 27. (*See* DEFENSE.) The exploit aroused great enthusiasm in Israel and strengthened the Rabin government. In another incident, at Istanbul on August 11, Arab guerrillas fired on passengers about to board an El Al plane, causing five deaths including that of one guerrilla. In general, however, Palestinian guerrilla activity against Israel in 1976 was muted because of the involvement in Lebanon.

Lebanon and Inter-Arab Relations. The split in the Arab states that resulted from Egypt's second Sinai agreement with Israel became even more acute as a result of the Lebanese crisis. The division was apparent in the UN Security Council debate in January, when Egypt and Saudi Arabia took a moderate approach based on UN Resolution 242 of 1967 and Syria called for immediate Israeli withdrawal from all occupied territory and recovery of the Palestinians' "inalienable rights." Libya and Iraq criticized Syria from an even more extreme position, claiming that it had accepted, through UN resolutions, the principle of a negotiated settlement with Israel.

In January it seemed that the Lebanon cease-fire mediated by Syria with PLO cooperation might bring a lasting settlement. A call on January 19 for an Arab summit conference on Lebanon from Arab League Secretary-General Mahmoud Riad was rejected by Lebanon on these grounds. The secretary-general then invited Arab heads of state to meet in April.

Jordan's action in summoning West Bank representatives to a reconvened Jordanian Parliament on February 5–7 was criticized in most of the Arab world, with the notable exception of Syria. The relationship between Syria and Jordan developed strongly throughout the year. The incident also revealed signs of a split within the PLO: al-Fatah and other groups, including the Palestinian Rejection Front, strongly attacked Jordan's action while the Syrian-backed as-Saiqa supported it. The Syrian-Jordanian axis also drew criticism from Egypt.

The breakdown of the Lebanese cease-fire in March, followed by some of the worst fighting of the civil war, caused a revival of Arab concern. On March 28 Egyptian Pres. Anwar as-Sadat said a joint Arab peacekeeping force to separate the warring factions was needed, and the proposal was submitted to the other Arab states. The Lebanese leftists then began to denounce Syria, and the split in the PLO deepened as the Rejection Front called for the expulsion of as-Saiqa. Syrian troops began entering Lebanon in early April. Syria's developing quarrel with the PLO and its de facto alliance with Lebanese rightists caused a remarkable realignment in the Arab world.

Riad proposed a limited Arab summit to end the Lebanese crisis, and the PLO called for a general Arab summit in June, but nothing came of either proposal. The Arab states were all concerned about a possible Israeli occupation of southern Lebanon if Syrian troops advanced near the area. The U.S. State Department announced on March 29 that it would oppose any foreign military intervention in Lebanon, especially by Syria or Israel, but that it regarded the Syrian-backed cease-fire as a reasonable basis for a solution.

On March 31 Dean Brown, president of the Middle East Institute in Washington, D.C., and an ex-diplomat, arrived in Lebanon as a special envoy and mediator between the warring factions. Although he succeeded in contacting the various sides in the war, his mediation was unsuccessful, and his presence aroused the strong hostility of the PLO. On April 20 President Ford praised both Israel and Syria for the "great restraint" they had shown over Lebanon, and a White House spokesman said that the U.S. was no longer implacably opposed to Syrian intervention.

Meanwhile, the PLO continued its efforts at mediation. PLO Chairman Yasir Arafat visited Damascus in mid-April with new proposals for a settlement, but PLO-Syrian relations deteriorated rapidly despite his efforts. Pro-Syrian and anti-Syrian Palestinian and leftist forces clashed in Beirut and other towns on May 11 and 12, while the Palestinian leadership issued a statement condemning Syrian action in Lebanon. At the same time, this led to a marked improvement in Egyptian-PLO relations, which had been cool since Egypt's acceptance of the second Sinai agreement. In his May Day speech President Sadat said that, whatever its differences with the PLO may have been, Egypt categorically opposed any attempt to weaken the body of the Palestinian revolution. Some Palestinian groups remained suspicious of Egypt, however. The Rejection Front said that Egypt was trying to buy the PLO's silence.

In May the Libyan government intervened in Lebanon in the belief that it could mediate because it had the confidence of both the Syrians and the Palestinians. The Libyan prime minister, Abdul Salam Jalloud, arrived in Damascus on May 15 for talks with Pres. Hafez al-Assad (*see* BIOGRAPHY), visited Beirut before returning to Damascus, then proceeded to Baghdad before returning to Damascus again. On June 2 the PLO called for an urgent meeting of the Arab League foreign ministers to discuss the Lebanese crisis and Syrian intervention. The meeting, held in Cairo on June 8, was attended by representatives of all 20 Arab League countries, including the Syrians, whose participation had been much in doubt. On June 9 the meeting adopted a seven-point resolution calling for the dispatch to Lebanon of "a symbolic Arab security force to preserve the security and stability of Lebanon and to replace the Syrian forces." The force was to be composed of several thousand men to be divided "more or less equally" between Algeria, Libya, Saudi Arabia, Sudan, Syria, and the PLO.

A committee including Riad and the Algerian, Bahraini, and Libyan representatives at the conference then went to Damascus to discuss implementation. At the same time, the Libyan prime minister organized a Syrian-Libyan-Palestinian committee to supervise the joint force. Jalloud continued his mediation efforts, shuttling between Damascus and Beirut during the first half of June, and he claimed that Syria had agreed that Syrian troops in Lebanon should be replaced by a joint Libyan-Algerian force. However, Jalloud's mediating role was overtaken by Riad who, after receiving Lebanese Pres. Suleiman Franjieh's consent to the Arab peacekeeping force (although he insisted on a continuing Syrian presence), became engaged in efforts in several Arab capitals to get the force established.

The arrival of the first Syrian, Libyan, and Saudi peacekeeping contingents—scheduled for June 18—was delayed because of Saudi insistence on extra security measures and on the appointment of a commander in chief. On June 22 Riad announced the appointment of the permanent Egyptian representative on the League secretariat's military command, Maj. Gen. Muhammad Hassan Ghunaim, and the first units began to arrive in late June. The buildup was slow, however, and the total force of less than 2,500 was quite incapable of separating the warring factions in different parts of the country. Effective joint action was still delayed, mainly because of the rift between Egypt and Syria. This was thought to have been healed by a meeting of the Syrian and Egyptian prime ministers in Riyadh, Saudi Arabia, arranged through Saudi and Kuwaiti mediation, which had been postponed twice but was finally held on June 23–24. However, the reconciliation did not last, and the two countries continued to abuse each other.

The lack of progress in Lebanon led the Arab foreign ministers to hold another meeting on June 30, at which they adopted a new six-point resolution calling for a cease-fire and established a three-man Arab League committee headed by Saudi Arabia to go to Beirut and persuade all parties to abide by the League's resolutions. The committee reported at a

A.F.P. / PICTORIAL PARADE

A Lebanese Army tank moves through the battlefront north of Beirut during the civil warfare in March.

further meeting on July 12 in Cairo, at which it called for the convening of an Arab summit. The proposal received little support, however, and instead Iraq and Libya proposed that an Arab "combat force" be sent to Lebanon to impose a cease-fire. Eventually, a third meeting on July 13 adopted an Algerian proposal that Syrian-Palestinian talks should start immediately.

During the second half of July the Arab League force managed to establish a small buffer zone along the "green line" dividing east and west Beirut, but its success was marred by opposition from Lebanese rightists, and several members of the force were killed or injured. An appeal for reinforcements from the special Arab League envoy, Hassan Sabry al-Kholi, went largely unanswered except for a small Libyan contingent. On the other hand, Iraqi volunteers were arriving in increasing numbers to support the Palestinian leftist side under the general leadership of Kamal Jumblatt (*see* BIOGRAPHY); by October estimates of their numbers varied between 3,000 and 8,000. Kholi pursued his efforts to hold a meeting of the tripartite Syrian-Lebanese-Palestinian committee, but the meeting was called off after Lebanese rightists alleged that Iraqi troops were in the country. On August 8 the Arab League force abandoned its efforts to establish buffer zones until the tripartite committee had worked out a timetable for a cease-fire.

In the second half of August new attempts were made to hold an Arab summit in answer to the now desperate appeals from the PLO to the Arabs to stop the fighting. However, Egypt's view was that a general Arab summit would be useless until fighting had ceased, and it called instead for a meeting of the heads of state of Egypt, Syria, Saudi Arabia, Kuwait, and Lebanon and the PLO. Although this plan was supported by Saudi Arabia, it failed because of Syria's insistence that Jordan should attend (unacceptable to Egypt and the PLO) and that the meeting should discuss the Sinai agreement (unacceptable to Egypt). Further diplomatic efforts were delayed because of the fifth summit conference of nonaligned nations held in Colombo, Sri Lanka, on August 16–20, which was attended by some of the key leaders. Finally, the Arab League foreign ministers' meeting in Cairo decided that the general summit should be held in Cairo on October 18. It was also decided to admit the PLO as the 21st full member of the Arab League.

Diplomatic efforts did not await the summit. The Arab League envoy attempted to arrange a tripartite meeting at Shtaurah in Syrian-controlled Lebanese territory as Elias Sarkis (*see* BIOGRAPHY) took office as Lebanese president on September 23. With its forces hard-pressed in Lebanon, the PLO was more prepared to negotiate with Syria. However, meetings held at Shtaurah on September 17 and 19 and again on October 9 came to nothing. Similarly, discussions held in Paris in the first week of October by the Egyptian foreign minister achieved no results because the Lebanese rightists refused to negotiate until the problem of the Palestinians in Lebanon had been settled. When Syria launched its offensive in the mountains east of Beirut, the PLO announced its intention of resisting to the end.

The Arab summit due for October 18 now seemed in jeopardy. President Assad had decided not to attend, and President Sadat had strongly intimated that he would not be present either. However, in a surprise move a heads-of-state meeting was arranged in Riyadh on October 17–18 with both Assad and Sadat attending, as well as Sarkis and Arafat. Assad announced he had ordered his troops in Lebanon—which now numbered some 20,000—to stop fighting, and Egypt and Syria agreed to settle their differences. A nine-point resolution was adopted calling for a cease-fire at 0400 hours on October 21, the return of all parties to positions held before the civil war began, and an increase of the Arab peacekeeping force to 30,000 men. Sadat withdrew his objections to the presence of Syrian troops in Lebanon on the ground that Sarkis had invited them. The Riyadh resolution was confirmed at an Arab summit in Cairo on October 25.

The main credit for the Riyadh agreement went to Saudi Arabia. To heal the Syrian-Egyptian breach that had so weakened the Arab world for a year, Saudi Arabia was prepared to exert strong pressure on Syria to abandon its insistence on Jordanian participation and on discussion of the Sinai agreement, and Syrian dependence on Saudi financial support made this pressure effective. The PLO declared itself satisfied with the agreement and willing to implement fully the Lebanese-Palestinian accords of 1969 limiting Palestinian action in Lebanon. The most skeptical elements were the Lebanese rightists, and reports in mid-October that they were receiving effective support from Israel in the south of Lebanon caused concern throughout the Arab world. The reconciliation of Egypt and Syria was further strengthened in December when, after four days of talks between Sadat and Hafez in Cairo, it was announced that the two countries would form a "united political leadership" and a joint military command. Joint committees were appointed to study the possibilities of even closer union, perhaps even extending to a revival of the old United Arab Republic of 1958–61.

There was a further deterioration in Libyan-Egyptian relations, although a complete break was avoided. An attempted coup in Sudan on July 2 was blamed on Libya by the Sudanese government, and the subsequent Egyptian-Sudanese defense agreement was clearly directed against Libya, as was a meeting in Saudi Arabia of the heads of state of Egypt, Sudan, and Saudi Arabia at which they agreed to coordinate their policies against subversion.

Oil and Economics. All the main Middle East oil-producing states increased their output in 1976, although it did not reach the record levels of 1974. Revenues rose substantially, but so did the prices of imported goods, and some members of the Organization of Petroleum Exporting Countries (OPEC) pressed for an increase in oil prices on these grounds. Iraq and Iran in particular demanded increases at the OPEC meeting in Bali, Indon., on May 27–28, but the meeting was deadlocked because of Saudi opposition, and it was decided to freeze oil prices until December. At the December OPEC meeting in Qatar, Saudi Arabia and the United Arab Emirates split with the remaining members, deciding to hold their price increases to 5% for 1977 while the others agreed to raise prices by 15% in two stages.

The Lebanese civil war deprived Beirut of its key role in the Middle East economy. The gap was filled to some extent by other Middle Eastern capitals, including Amman, Damascus, Nicosia, Cairo, and even Bahrain. With the reopening of the Suez Canal, some east-west trade was diverted through Egypt, but Egypt's economy remained precarious, and it was forced to pursue its search for increased aid from the Arab oil states. (PETER MANSFIELD)

See also Energy; articles on the various political units.
[978.B]

Migration, International

The number of third world migrants working in industrialized market-economy countries and in high-income, oil-producing Arab countries was estimated in 1976 at around 12 million, exclusive of dependents. Most migrants were unskilled or semiskilled, but the number of trained and professional persons among them was increasing.

Of the up to ten million undetected illegal immigrants in the U.S., over 60% were from Mexico, others from the Caribbean and Central and South America. A Cabinet committee was appointed to look into the problem, and an illegal alien bill was proposed. The large number of illegal immigrants contrasted with the 400,000 admitted annually for permanent residence and the 1.5 million people from less developed countries living as permanent resident aliens. A new immigration act was introduced in the Canadian Parliament. Based on the findings of a special joint committee, presented to Parliament on Nov. 6, 1975, it would require the minister of immigration, after consultation with the provinces, to set a "level of immigration" that would prevail for a specified period. The committee report had stated that Canada should continue to be a country of immigration, particularly in view of the spectacular decline in the Canadian birthrate since 1960. Immigration to Canada in 1975 decreased by 14% from 1974, to 187,881, only 43% of whom were destined for the labour force. Some 80,000–90,000 persons entered Canada annually under temporary employment visas, designed to admit nonimmigrant workers for up to 12 months.

In Western Europe recession and the tightening of migration controls led to stabilization of the existing migrant labour force, not to an exodus as in 1967–68. Migrant workers felt they were better off staying, even on unemployment allowances, and indigenous workers still fought shy of "migrant" jobs; moreover, receiving countries were moving toward policies of fuller integration rather than temporary migration, sometimes with an eye to declining birthrates. In 1975 the European Economic Community (EEC) had about 6,587,000 migrant workers (including 742,000 Italians, 672,000 Turks, and about 500,000 each from Yugoslavia, Portugal, and Algeria), and Switzerland, Austria, and Sweden had an additional million. Including dependents, these 12 countries together had a grand total of over 13.5 million.

Morocco, Tunisia, Algeria, and Egypt exported migrant workers; other Arab countries with smaller populations and greater oil resources attracted professional skilled expatriate labour, Western or Asian (mostly Arabs or non-Arab Muslims). Libya granted 225,000 work permits in 1974 and over 170,000 in 1975. Saudi Arabia's $142 billion five-year development plan (1975–80) called for one million foreign workers. Half a million foreign Arabs, Egyptians, Africans, and Pakistanis (representing one-third of the labour force) were in the country by the summer of 1976, evoking some conservative local criticism. In August the government announced the immigration of one million workers from Malaysia to fill skilled and semiskilled jobs over the following few years. One-third of Bahrain's labour force and three-fourths of Kuwait's consisted of migrant workers. There were reports of illegal immigration into the United Arab Emirates (U.A.E.). Some 50,000 Pakistanis, mostly professionals and skilled workers, were living in the U.A.E. and a further 30,000 in Kuwait.

Immigration and Naturalization in the United States

Year ended June 30, 1975

Country or region	Total immigrants admitted	Quota immigrants	Nonquota immigrants: Total	Nonquota immigrants: Family—U.S. citizens	Aliens naturalized
Africa	6,729	5,163	1,566	1,411	2,757
Asia*	132,469	94,032	38,437	33,539	44,915
China†	18,536	14,881	3,655	3,318	9,683
Hong Kong	4,891	4,179	712	632	...
India	15,773	14,827	946	746	2,720
Iran	2,337	1,534	803	791	601
Iraq	2,796	2,594	202	190	526
Israel	2,125	1,510	615	506	1,844
Japan	4,274	2,017	2,257	1,930	1,548
Jordan	2,578	2,124	454	422	1,364
Korea, South	28,362	19,782	8,580	6,391	6,007
Lebanon	2,075	1,701	374	350	796
Philippines	31,751	18,984	12,767	11,936	15,330
Thailand	4,217	1,348	2,869	2,603	411
Vietnam, South	3,039	411	2,628	2,267	1,369
Europe‡	73,996	54,499	19,497	17,445	50,268
Germany, West	5,154	1,556	3,598	3,209	5,187
Greece	9,984	8,023	1,961	1,822	6,647
Italy	11,552	9,213	2,339	2,143	8,798
Poland	3,941	3,042	899	830	3,069
Portugal	11,845	10,732	1,113	1,037	3,728
Spain	2,549	1,628	921	801	922
U.S.S.R.	5,118	4,908	210	167	550
United Kingdom	10,807	6,336	4,471	3,944	8,532
Yugoslavia	3,524	3,020	504	452	3,273
North America	146,668	109,714	36,954	31,564	34,794
Canada	7,308	3,342	3,966	3,300	3,548
Cuba	25,955	24,794	1,161	309	15,546
Dominican Republic	14,066	11,550	2,516	2,261	1,518
El Salvador	2,416	1,676	740	706	342
Haiti	5,145	4,498	647	594	1,966
Jamaica	11,076	9,357	1,719	1,600	2,152
Mexico	62,205	41,977	20,228	17,146	5,781
Trinidad and Tobago	5,982	5,060	922	889	987
Oceania	3,347	2,208	1,139	1,037	595
South America	22,984	15,944	7,040	6,508	6,722
Argentina	2,227	1,675	552	485	1,378
Colombia	6,434	4,032	2,402	2,241	1,699
Ecuador	4,727	3,758	969	915	807
Guyana	3,169	2,692	477	436	524
Peru	2,256	1,276	980	955	710
Total, including others	386,194	281,561	104,633	91,504	141,537

Note: Immigrants listed by country of birth; aliens naturalized by country of former allegiance.
*Includes Turkey. †Taiwan and People's Republic. ‡Includes U.S.S.R.
Source: U.S. Department of Justice, Immigration and Naturalization Service, *1975 Annual Report*.

For the first time some figures became available on labour movements in Eastern European countries (other than Yugoslavia, which exported labour to Western Europe). In 1975 East Germany employed some 50,000 Poles on the construction of roads and pipelines, as well as about 8,000 Hungarians and 5,000 Algerians. As in pre-1939 days, Poles supplied the largest migrant groups, with over 20,000 in Czechoslovakia and 20,000 in the Soviet Union.

In West Africa the traditional movement from Upper Volta, Mali, and Niger to the Ivory Coast and Ghana continued. South Africa employed over 400,000 foreign-born Africans in 1975, the majority in mines. Five out of every six Lesotho citizens were working in South Africa, which also received 25,387 immigrants from the U.K. and 8,825 from Europe in 1975. One of the largest emigration movements in Asia was from the Philippines to North America and Europe. In Australia the number of settlers dropped in the year ended June 1976 to 52,451, compared with 89,147 a year earlier. (SHEILA PATTERSON)

See also Refugees.
[525.A.1.c]

Mining and Quarrying

Recovering from the slump of the previous year, the U.S. mining industry in 1976 showed improvement in company earnings. In general, the iron ore, coal, and uranium sectors were buoyant, while nonferrous met-

Military Affairs: *see* Defense

Minerals: *see* Mining and Quarrying

als were improved though not yet healthy. Development of new nonferrous mines and expansions of existing ones were generally postponed, or else the work was slowed down. Capital expenditures were mostly related to modifications for the improvement of environmental quality.

The less developed nations with mineral resources continued to take more control and revenue from foreign developers. There were definite signs that national aspirations were gaining greater acceptance by investors in return for improved treatment, thereby lessening tensions. Southern Africa, because of racial tensions in Rhodesia, South Africa, and South West Africa, was an area in which investors were cautious. It appeared that uncertainties would slow mine development throughout that region for several years.

Industry Developments. U.S. mining companies planned to increase capital spending overseas in 1977, according to an annual survey. In 1977 approximately $1.4 billion, up from $968 million in 1976, would be divided as follows: Australia-Oceania, $538 million; Canada, $337 million; Latin America, $241 million; and the remainder in Europe.

The merger of General Electric Co. and the mining firm of Utah International Inc. was approved by the Federal Trade Commission (FTC) with the proviso that Utah sell its uranium mines. If stockholders approved it, this $1.9 billion merger would be the largest ever consummated in the U.S.

Kennecott Copper Corp. had been under orders from the FTC to divest itself of Peabody Coal Co., the largest coal company in the U.S., since 1971, on the ground that the 1968 acquisition diminished competition in coal. In October, Kennecott accepted an offer by a U.S. group of companies led by Newmont Mining Corp. for $1.2 billion for the purchase of Peabody. This also required approval by the FTC. Besides Newmont, the group consisted of the Williams Companies, Bechtel Corp., Fluor Corp., and the Equitable Life Assurance Society of the U.S. Peabody's Australian coal property was to be purchased by Broken Hill Pty.

A worldwide boom in prospecting for uranium was under way, with most finds being made in the western U.S. and Australia. The boom was a natural consequence of the fact that the price of a pound of uranium climbed from $9.50 in 1973 to $40 in 1976. The price was responding to estimates of shortages in the 1980s in meeting nuclear power industry requirements. The upward pressure on price was increased by the Westinghouse Electric Corp. situation. Westinghouse had sold reactors to utilities with a guarantee to supply uranium at an average price of $9.50 per pound. At the time there was ample uranium available at lower prices than quoted to its customers, and so Westinghouse maintained only a nominal stockpile. The company agreed to deliver uranium over a period of 20 years. In late 1975, when the market price had more than tripled, Westinghouse was confronted with a long-term commitment of 65 million lb of uranium in excess of its supply. Westinghouse said that it was "legally excused" from 80% of its commitments, with the result that the firm was being sued by many utilities. It was reported that the commitment at the present market price increased the company's indebtedness by an amount equal to the entire shareholders' equity.

The big caterpillar-tread vehicle below was developed by the Krupp firm of West Germany for pulling machinery like the conveyor belt-driving stations in the background, used for mining operations. The vehicle has tracks 2.5 metres wide.

KEYSTONE

In the U.S., a presidential veto of the coal-leasing law was overridden by Congress. This legislation, which provided ground rules for coal leasing on federal land, was claimed by its proponents to encourage mine development. A provision of the law, however, gave the U.S. Geological Survey the large task of analyzing coal reserves by drilling all unleased federal land, some 70 million ac, before any new leases could be granted. The law also set a 12% royalty on the sales price, half of which would be paid to the individual states. The *Coal Observer* claimed that the drilling would create delays of from two to eight years in new mine development. The federal lands in question are in the West. They have large reserves of low-sulfur coal that could be used economically in the Middle West and south-central U.S.

Four coal mines in the Powder River Basin of eastern Wyoming got a go-ahead from the U.S. Department of the Interior. The projects had been blocked for over a year by a temporary court injunction requested by the Sierra Club which was lifted in January by the U.S. Supreme Court. The mines were being developed by Atlantic Richfield, Carter Oil, Kerr-McGee, and Wyodak Resources. Secretary of the Interior Thomas Kleppe said that Wyoming's reclamation laws would apply to the four operations. Construction of Sun Oil Co.'s new Cordero mine near Gillette, Wyo., was completed in December. This mine was expected ultimately to reach a producing capacity of 15 million tons per year. When achieved, this would be 60% larger than the top U.S. producer in 1975.

Asarco, Inc., inaugurated the world's most modern copper refinery at Amarillo, Texas, in July. The new facility, which cost $190 million, could produce 420,000 tons per year of electrolytic copper. Construction took three years. The new plant made Texas the top-ranking copper refinery state in the U.S.

Canada's first producing mine north of the Arctic Circle began production in October. It is the Nanisivik lead-zinc mine on Baffin Island, discovered in the late 1950s by Texasgulf, Inc. The operation, designed to process 15,000 tons per day of ore yielding 125,000 tons per year of zinc concentrates and 20,000 tons of lead concentrates, was expected to employ about 300 men, including more than 50 Eskimos.

After protracted negotiations Alcoa and the Jamaican government announced that they had agreed on the terms of a joint venture company, Jamalco, to operate the former's bauxite mining and refining facilities on the island. The Jamaican government had a 6% interest in the new company, equivalent to 51% of the mine assets only, which was the government's objective. The agreement, when ratified by the legislature, would be in force for 40 years. Either party had the right, separately or jointly, to expand the operation.

Peru compensated Marcona Mining Co. of the U.S. in the amount of $61 million plus other deferred payments for the 1975 expropriation of the firm's iron-ore mines. The settlement, termed equitable by the involved parties, cleared the way for $200 million in loans to Peru from private U.S. banks, thus indicating that a nation can achieve control of its basic industry without economic retaliation if it pays fair compensation for expropriated property.

Technological Developments. Since the early 1920s, the process of flotation has been growing in importance as the principal method for separating minerals from their ores. The process, applicable to a large variety of minerals and capable of handling large tonnages, is applied to the ores at the mine site. The concentration step for most ores involves dry crushing and wet grinding to liberate the valuable minerals from the gangue or waste material. The output of the grinding mills is a slurry of water and ore that is almost as fine as powder. The slurry is treated with chemicals and then directed through batteries of tanks in which the flotation process takes place. In the tanks, the slurry is agitated by impellers and/or compressed air bubbles. The mineral particles become coated with a chemical that causes them to attach to the bubbles and rise to the surface, where they are swept off in a froth. To appreciate the degree of concentration, it should be observed that an ore containing 0.7% copper can be concentrated to 28%; zinc ore of 3% to a concentrate of 64%.

As the mining industry turned to extracting ores of diminishing grade, the tonnages were increased to compensate for the lesser mineral content. Machinery in all unit processes therefore tended to become larger. In the case of flotation, the numbers of small cells, less than 100 cu ft, were multiplied to process the larger tonnages. In the last decade, however, development of much larger flotation cells became the trend. Cells of 500–600 cu ft became common, and some installations contained a few gigantic cells such as those at Falconbridge's Opemiska concentrator in Canada, where twelve 1,900-cu ft flotation cells were employed. Advantages claimed in using large cells include reduced floor space, lower capital and operating cost, simplified instrumentation and controls, and better metallurgical results.

Dredging had been considered from time to time as a means of mining phosphate, but was never used. However, Texasgulf at Lee Creek, N.C., added a dredge to remove the top 40 ft of overburden from an 80-ft-thick section of overburden on the phosphate deposits. The cutter-head dredge removes overburden and pumps it to a mined-out area. Once the stripped area is drained, the remaining overburden is stripped and the phosphate extracted by dragline. Previously, the whole section had been stripped by dragline, but this resulted in high, unstable spoil banks that slipped back onto the phosphate bed and caused dilution.

Occidental Petroleum Corp. had been preparing for some time to recover oil from oil shale by in situ retorting. During 1976 the company ignited an in situ retort that was scheduled to have a capacity of 5,000 bbl of oil per day. Most oil shale experimental work has consisted of mining the shale and retorting it in plants constructed on the surface. In the Occidental procedure, an underground retort is constructed in two steps. First, 15–20% of the retort volume is mined by conventional methods. Then the remainder of the volume is drilled and blasted into the void. This rubbleized oil shale is then ignited with gas, but combustion is self-sustaining thereafter. The products are petroleum, drawn off the bottom through prepared channels, and gas, off the top. The technique eliminates building a retorting plant on the surface, use of large volumes of water, and the problem of disposing of the spent shale. Occidental invested five years and $30 million of its own money in the development. At the end of 1976 this was the only oil shale project performing significantly, as the others had been curtailed because of economics, environmental problems, and lack of interest by the government.

(JOHN V. BEALL)

CAMERA PRESS/PHOTO TRENDS

This surface mine in New South Wales, Australia, produces coking coal used in making iron and steel.

Production. During 1975 and 1976 the mining industries of the world continued to lose ground to other sectors of the global economy. For example, as the table illustrates, although world mining output in the first quarter of 1976 (the latest for which world data were available) was 17% higher than the 1970 base year adopted by the UN, manufacturing output for the same period was more than 30% higher.

Among the developed market economies, this loss of position was not only relative (to other sectors) but in the case of certain commodities, like coal, absolute as well. Coal production worldwide in 1976, despite the incentives offered by the energy crisis, was only about five-sixths that of 1970. For metals, both ferrous and nonferrous, virtually no growth had taken place over the previous seven years. Only in the case of petroleum and natural gas were there sufficient price incentives to raise production above 1970 levels, and even there growth was far below levels attained by the centrally planned economies of the third world.

Eastern Europe (the centrally planned economies) showed the only strong and sustained growth in mining and production as a region since the first quarter of 1975. Although those countries were insulated from the worst effects of the energy crisis by their own domestic and Soviet supplies, the U.S.S.R. announced in late 1976 that its export prices for those commodities would rise substantially in the near future. In

KEYSTONE

Mining sulfur in Poland's Rzeszow Province. A power shovel loads ore onto a conveyor belt. Poland is a leading exporter of sulfur.

the less developed countries increased energy costs were imposing severe limits on many development programs.

Generally, the mineral commodities most essential to national development tended to show high production levels in 1975 and 1976, in both the developed and less developed countries. Cement, for example, had attained by the second quarter of 1976 production levels that seemed certain to eclipse the best previous year's production. Iron and steel also remained at high levels because their health was critical to other sectors of national economies where steel was utilized, especially the automotive and construction industries. Nonferrous metals for which substitution or scrap utilization was possible lost ground generally. Only metals that continued to command world prices, such as copper, aluminum, nickel, or silver, retained high levels of production. A number of those materials (diamonds, copper, iron ore, and tin among others) were marketed with the help of more or less formal industry or intergovernmental organizations that limited or expanded production and exports.

Indexes of Production, Mining, and Mineral Commodities

(1970=100)

	1971	1972	1973	1974	1975	1976 I	1976 II
Mining (total)							
World	103	107	114	116	114	117	...
Centrally planned economies*	106	112	118	124	131	137	140
Developed market economies†	100	101	105	104	100	101	100
Less developed market economies‡	105	110	123	125	115	119	...
Coal							
World	100	97	96	96	98	101	...
Centrally planned economies*	103	105	107	109	113	114	115
Developed market economies†	97	89	86	83	85	87	84
Less developed market economies‡	103	104	104	112	121	134	...
Petroleum							
World	106	112	121	123	119	123	...
Centrally planned economies*	107	113	122	130	140	152	148
Developed market economies†	104	110	113	112	108	110	103
Less developed market economies‡	106	112	127	127	116	119	...
Metals							
World	101	102	107	109	105	106	...
Centrally planned economies*	106	112	118	120	121	122	124
Developed market economies†	98	96	101	101	97	95	103
Less developed market economies‡	101	104	109	113	107	112	...
Manufacturing (total)	104	112	123	127	125	131	...

*Bulgaria, Czechoslovakia, East Germany, Poland, Romania, U.S.S.R.

†North America, Europe (except centrally planned), Australia, Israel, Japan, New Zealand, South Africa.

‡Caribbean, Central and South America, Africa (except South Africa), Asian Middle East, East and South East Asia (except Israel and Japan).

Source: UN, *Monthly Bulletin of Statistics* (November 1976).

Aluminum. World production of bauxite, the primary ore of aluminum, was estimated to have fallen by about 4% during 1975, to about 79,442,000 metric tons; this was attributable mainly to decreased demand in the primary consuming countries, where, for example, the United States imported 25% less dried bauxite than during the preceding year. Major producers were Australia with 21,003,000 metric tons, Jamaica 11,571,000 tons, Guinea 10,641,000 tons, the Soviet Union an estimated 6 million tons, and Surinam 4,928,000 tons. Radical changes in production levels occurred in a number of those countries, with Guinea up some 40%, Jamaica down 24.5%, and Surinam down 26.5%. Production of aluminum metal during 1975 declined by 8.6%, from 13,128,000 tons in 1974 to 11,992,000 in 1975; the major producer was the U.S. with 3,519,000 tons, followed by the Soviet Union with an estimated 1.5 million tons and Japan with 1,013,000 tons.

Antimony. Total world production of antimony in 1975 was estimated to have risen by about 3.5%, from 70,700 metric tons in 1974 to 73,200 tons in 1975. Major producers were South Africa with some 16,200 tons, China about 12,000 tons, and Bolivia 11,915 tons. U.S. domestic production was some 860 tons, the highest annual production since 1971. In the U.S., which was the primary user of antimony, imports, smelter production, and consumption all declined during 1975, the two former by 13% and the latter by over 20%. The increasing use of antimony trioxide for flame-retardant materials led to major increases in its production capacity in the U.S., South Africa, and Bolivia. It was estimated that Bolivian production of concentrates would decline to about half of its 1975 level by 1977 and stabilize at about 6,500 tons annually.

Arsenic. Total world production of arsenic (in terms of its trioxide) declined slightly in 1975, from 49,700 metric tons the previous year to a preliminary estimate of 49,350 tons. The leading producer was Sweden with about 15,400 tons, down slightly from 1974's 16,000 tons. There were only four other major producers: Mexico at 9,400 tons, France 9,100, the Soviet Union 6,600, and South West Africa about 6,350. Recent research indicating the applicability of arsenic metal in strengthening cast ferrous alloys led to speculation about a major new application of the metal.

Cadmium. Total world production of cadmium metal in 1975 was 15,566 metric tons, a decline of about 10.6% from 1974. The major producers were the Soviet Union with an estimated 2,950 metric tons, gaining first place from Japan, which fell by more than 11% to 2,688 tons. The next three major producers were all North American—the U.S. 1,989 tons, Mexico 1,596 tons, and Canada 1,142 tons; the only other producers of more than 1,000 tons were Australia and West Germany. World consumption of the metal declined more drastically than supply, as estimated use fell from over 17,000 tons in 1974 to fewer than 12,300 in 1975 (almost a 28% decline). Although current projections of demand through 1980 showed only a 2% per annum increase, applications of cadmium in solar batteries might raise actual consumption to a higher rate.

Cement. Cement production rose by an estimated 5.5% worldwide during 1975, from 666 million metric tons in 1974 to some 703 million tons in 1975. The major producer was the Soviet Union at 121.9 million metric tons, followed by Japan 65,520,000 tons, and the U.S. 58.3 million tons. Both of the latter represented steep declines against 1974 production, 12 and 20%, respectively, although a change in U.S. reporting methods exaggerated somewhat the extent of the decline there. The decline in U.S. production was attributable to a decline in consumption by the construction industry, the extent of which was greater than anticipated (apparent consumption in 1975 was down some 15.1%, to the lowest level since 1964). The slowdown in activity and lower inventories provided many companies with the opportunity to initiate plant maintenance and modernization.

Chromium. Total world production of chromium ores fell during 1975 by 7.3%, from about 7.2 million metric tons in 1974 to about 6.7 million tons in 1975. Major producers of chromite ore were the Soviet Union and South Africa, each producing about 1.8 million tons, followed by a group of four countries in the range 450,000 to 700,000 tons—Albania, Rhodesia, the Philippines, and Turkey. U.S. imports reached their highest level since 1970, some 1.2 million tons, in a world market that was generally weaker than in 1974.

Cobalt. As with most other metals, mine production of cobalt in 1975 showed a decline—about 7.8%, from 30,500 tons (of contained cobalt) in 1974 to about 28,100 tons in 1975. Almost half of the production originated in a single country, Zaire, where about 13,600 tons were produced in 1975 (a decline of over 22% from 1974's 17,500 tons); other major (over 1,000 tons) producers were Zambia with 3,200 tons and five ranging between 1,000 and 2,000 tons—the Soviet Union, Canada, Cuba, Finland, and Morocco. Despite unsettled political prospects in Rhodesia, the Rio Tinto operation commissioned a new cobalt plant to be operational by the end of 1976. Increased capacity became available in late 1975 at the renovated Port Nickel, La., facility, which was expected to reach 75% of its ultimate capacity during 1976. Consumption in the U.S., the major market, declined steeply, by nearly 42% in 1975, reflecting declines in every category of end use except welding and hard facing rods.

Copper. World mine production of copper ores fell from 7,653,000 metric tons in 1974 to 7,296,000 tons in 1975, a decline of about 4.7%; the major producers were North American, the U.S. and Canada together accounting for 27% of the world total. In order, the main producers were the United States 1,280,000 tons, the U.S.S.R. an estimated 1.1 million tons, Chile 828,000 tons, Canada 724,000 tons, Zambia 677,000 tons, and Zaire 495,000 tons. Most producers were at or above levels of recent years, the main exception being the U.S., where a decline beginning in 1973 continued, with a drop of 11.7% from 1974. The exceptionally high copper prices of 1973 and 1974 returned to more normal levels in 1975 and 1976, although by mid-1976 London prices had regained almost 75% of the price as of the second quarter of 1974. Smelter production of copper metal also declined in 1975, from 7,537,000 metric tons in 1974 to 7,276,000 tons in 1975, a reduction of some 3.5%. There was no change in the relative ranks of the first five major producers in 1975; they were the U.S. with 1,312,800 metric tons, followed by the Soviet Union with an estimated 1.1 million tons, Japan 742,000 tons, Chile 724,400 tons, and Zambia 659,000 tons. Consumption of copper was drastically reduced worldwide during 1975, from 6,916,500 tons the preceding year to 6,295,000 tons in 1975. The U.S. continued as the leading consumer, with about a 16% share of the total.

Gold. World mine output of gold fell slightly during 1975, dropping from 39,780,000 troy ounces in 1974 to an estimated 38,710,000 oz in 1975. South Africa produced more than 58% of the world total, although the 1975 production of 22,765,000 oz represented a 14-year low and was some 7% below the 1974 level of 24,386,000 oz. The second leading producer, estimated at some 7.5 million oz, was thought to be the U.S.S.R., followed by Canada at 1,674,000 oz and the U.S. at 1,052,000 oz. The newly developed Pueblo Viejo mine in the Dominican Republic reached about 90% of its designed capacity (320,000 oz annually) by late 1975. The International Monetary Fund conducted five gold auctions during 1976 as part of a four-year program to disperse one-sixth of the Fund's holdings for the benefit of the less developed countries; five lots of 780,000 oz each were dispersed.

Iron and Steel. Total world output of iron ore during 1975 was estimated to have declined by only about 1.9% during the year, faring in this respect much better than the nonferrous industries. Of the world total of 879.5 million metric tons, more than a quarter was produced by the Soviet Union, which mined some 232.8 million tons during the year, registering an increase of about 3.5% over 1974. Australia finished in second place with 97,674,000 tons (a slight increase of 1%), followed by the United States, down 5.3% to 81,351,000 tons. Production of pig iron showed a more marked decline than ore production; the total for 1975 was estimated to be about 469.2 million tons, compared with 504 million tons the previous year, a drop of about 6.9%. The U.S.S.R. and Eastern Europe generally showed increases and the non-Communist countries mostly registered declines, the major exceptions being Australia, Spain, Sweden, South Korea, India, and South Africa.

Lead. World production of lead declined by about 1% based on preliminary data, from a total of 3,476,000 metric tons in 1974 to about 3,438,000 tons in 1975. Major producers were relatively unchanged from the preceding year. The world leader was the U.S. at 577,000 tons, followed by the Soviet Union at about 480,000 tons, Australia 407,000 tons, and Canada 338,000 tons. Of the major producers only the U.S. reported a decline in 1975; all of the others showed slight gains. Smelter production of lead declined by about 3.7% during 1975 to a total of about 3,364,000 tons. Of the major producers only the Soviet Union was thought to have increased its output during the year.

Manganese. World mine production of manganese in 1975 showed a slight increase (in terms of contained metal), rising from about 21.9 million metric tons to some 22.5 million tons in 1975. Major producers were unchanged from 1974; the U.S.S.R. was estimated to be the world leader with over 8.2 million tons, followed by South Africa at 4 million tons (down 11.1% from 1974), Gabon with 2.2 million tons, Brazil with an estimated 1.8 million tons, Australia 1.6 million tons, and India about 1,350,000 tons. The U.S. continued to be the major consumer of the metal on the world market, importing about 1,430,000 tons, up about 250,000 tons from 1974; U.S. domestic production of ferromanganese, the major end use of manganese, also rose during 1975.

Mercury. World production of mercury (in terms of flasks of 34.5 kg, or 76 lb) was estimated to be about 253,850 in 1975, a slight decline (some 3.2%) from 1974's 262,300 flasks. Leading producers were Spain with an estimated 60,000 flasks, almost 24% of world production, followed by the U.S.S.R at an estimated 54,000 flasks, China with about 26,000 flasks, Italy about 24,000, and Mexico about 20,000. Domestic U.S. production rose sharply in 1975, to 6,750 flasks, up from 2,190 in 1974, mainly as the result of the June 1975 opening of the Placer Amex Inc. mine near McDermitt, Nev.

Molybdenum. Mine production of molybdenum in 1975 showed a moderate decline compared with 1974, down by 5.9% from 86,356 metric tons in 1974 to an estimated 81,274 tons in 1975. The major producer was the United States with 48,264 tons in 1975, followed by Canada with 12,435 tons, down more than 10% from the preceding year. The only other major producers were Chile with 9,091 tons and the Soviet Union with an estimated 9,090 tons, the four countries together accounting for over 95% of world production. The U.S. General Services Administration dispersed virtually the last of the molybdenum in government strategic stockpiles, over 2,600 tons in 1975.

Nickel. World mine production of nickel declined slightly during 1975, off less than 0.5% from 1974's 749,000 metric tons to 745,000 in 1975. Three countries supplied about two-thirds of world production—Canada with 245,000 tons, New Caledonia with 127,000 tons, and the Soviet Union with an estimated 120,000 tons. Smelter production showed a much more severe decline during 1975, falling from about 703,000 metric tons in 1974 to about 653,000 tons in 1975, a loss of about 7%. The leading countries were Canada, which processed approximately 148,800 tons in 1975, followed by the Soviet Union at an estimated 134,000 tons, Japan at 78,700 tons, and New Caledonia 52,800 tons. U.S. domestic consumption of nickel was estimated to have declined by over 30% from 1974.

Phosphate. World mine production of phosphate rock was estimated to have declined by about 4%, from 110.8 million tons in 1974 to an estimated 107,650,000 tons in 1975. The major producer was the U.S. at 44,285,000 metric tons, comprising almost 42% of total world production; it was followed by the Soviet Union with about 24 million tons and Morocco at about 13,550,000 tons. Despite Morocco's newly obtained administration of the Bu Craa phosphate mines of the Western (Spanish) Sahara no phosphate was exported by Morocco from these mines during 1976, partially as a result of guerrilla activities and also because of the depressed world market in 1975 and 1976. Ocean Island, from which about 560,000 tons were produced in 1975, was the focus of a lawsuit, which alleged that the native Banabans were illegally displaced and disadvantaged by the British government with respect to the royalties earned and paid from phosphate mining on their island. Settlement of the claim by the United Kingdom might make the Banabans as rich as the beneficiaries of the Nauruan Trust Fund (also based on phosphates).

Platinum-Group Metals. Platinum-group metals were among the few nonferrous metals to show an increase in production levels for 1975 compared with 1974. Production of 5,748,000 troy ounces in 1974 rose to an estimated 5,801,000 oz the following year; virtually all of this production originated in South Africa, the leader at 2.7 million oz, and the Soviet Union at about 2.6 million oz (estimated). Canada was the only other important supplier, at 430,000 oz. Consumption of these metals in the U.S. market stabilized in 1975 at about 1,250,000 oz, comprising about 55% platinum and about 41% palladium.

Potash. World mine production of potash declined by about 6% overall in 1975, falling from 23,756,000 metric tons in 1974 to 22,364,000 tons. Major producers were the U.S.S.R., estimated at 6,050,000 metric tons, followed by Canada at 4,850,000 tons, East Germany 2.9 million tons, West Germany 2,372,000 tons, and the U.S. 2,269,000 tons. Of Western producers, only the Congo and Spain raised their total production during 1975, with Canada showing the largest drop of any of the major producers, a 16% loss from 1974.

Silver. Silver production fell slightly during 1975 (294,935,000 troy ounces in 1974 to 293,452,000 oz in 1975). The U.S.S.R. led all producers with 43 million oz; Canada was second with 39,101,000 oz, but third place was occupied by Mexico with 38,029,000 oz, displacing Peru with 37,783,000 oz. Handy & Harman reported that U.S. domestic consumption in 1975 changed radically from the previous year, declining overall by about 12.4% and falling by 55% in the commemorative objects category while jewelry use more than doubled. Worldwide, consumption for industrial uses and coinage fell about 15% from 1974.

Sulfur. World production of all forms of elemental sulfur rose slightly in 1975, from about 51.7 million metric tons in 1974 to an estimated 52.8 million tons in 1975. The results for the major producers for which authoritative 1975 data were available showed that the U.S. continued to lead with about 11,440,000 tons, followed by Canada, which fell substantially during 1975 (over 42%) to a level of 4,060,000 tons. Production in the Soviet Union was estimated to exceed 4 million tons. Although the U.S. domestic supply of sulfur exceeded demand for the eighth consecutive year, exports fell by nearly a half (49%) and domestic stocks rose by over a quarter.

Tin. World mine production of tin fell by approximately 6.4% during 1975, from 219,600 metric tons in 1974 to an estimated 205,500 tons in 1975. The major producer was Malaysia, with total production of 64,364 tons, off 5.5% from the 1974 level of 68,122 tons. No other country produced as much as 30 thousand tons; the leaders in this second rank of producers were Bolivia with 28,324 tons, Indonesia at 25,346 tons, and China estimated at 23,000 tons. Smelter production of tin metal remained virtually unchanged during 1975 at 222,300 tons (1974, 222,800 tons). Malaysia was also the largest smelter of tin, producing some 83,100 tons in 1975. No other producer except China was thought to have produced as much as 20 thousand tons. Consumption patterns in the U.S., the largest consumer, were approximately as follows during 1975: containers 43%, electrical 14%, transportation 12%, construction 11%, and machinery 9%.

Titanium. World production of titanium ilmenite concentrates amounted to some 3,180,000 metric tons in 1975, representing a 5.2% decline from production of 3.4 million tons in 1974. The leading producing countries were Australia about 810,000 tons, Canada about 725,000 tons, Norway 660,000 tons, and the U.S. 580,000 tons. World production of titanium rutile concentrates during 1975 declined by an estimated 8.4% from 1974, to 307,000 tons. Virtually all of this production was Australian, some 94.6% in 1975.

Tungsten. World output of tungsten (wolfram) ore and concentrates was estimated to have increased slightly in 1975, totaling 37,900 metric tons as against 37,350 tons in 1974. The leading producers were thought to be China and the Soviet Union, producing about 8,500 tons and 7,850 tons, respectively. Following these two were the United States at about 3,175 tons, South Korea 2,400 tons, and Bolivia 2,000 tons. Major increased mining and processing capacity were added to the U.S. during 1976 with the opening of the Union Carbide Tempiute, Nev., property.

Uranium. The strategic significance of uranium resulted in a dearth of statistics about annual production. Of the countries for which data were available, total output in 1975 amounted to approximately 22,400 metric tons, a 3.8% increase over 1974. The U.S. was the leading producer with 10,500 tons, followed by Canada with 5,557 tons and South Africa and France with about 3,300 tons each. The continuing rise in uranium prices over recent years reached the point that for some countries, Israel for example, it had become economically feasible to extract uranium from phosphate deposits for electrical power.

Zinc. World mine production of zinc fell slightly in 1975, down 2.4% from 1974 according to preliminary data. The total production for 1975 was estimated to be 5,563,000 metric tons, of which the main producing countries were Canada with 1,083,000 tons, the Soviet Union at about 690,000 tons (other estimates varied upward to 1 million tons), Australia 492,000 tons, the United States 425,000 tons, and Peru 360,000 tons. Smelter production of zinc fell steeply, dropping about 7.7% during 1975 to a total for the year of about 5,042,000 tons, compared with the previous year's 5,463,000 tons. Most of this decline was borne by the smelters of four countries: the U.S., Australia, West Germany, and Japan, the outputs of which fell by 10.7, 31.8, 25.6, and 17.4%, respectively. (WILLIAM A. CLEVELAND)

See also Earth Sciences; Energy; Industrial Review: *Gemstones; Iron and Steel;* Materials Sciences.
[724.B.1; 724.C.3]

ENCYCLOPÆDIA BRITANNICA FILMS. *Problems of Conservation: Minerals* (1969).

Monaco

A sovereign principality on the northern Mediterranean coast, Monaco is bounded on land by the French département of Alpes-Maritimes. Area: 0.73 sq mi (1.89 sq km). Pop. (1975 est.): 25,000. Language: French. Religion: predominantly Roman Catholic. Prince, Rainier III; minister of state in 1976, André Saint-Mleux.

By 1976 there were more than 2,000 foreign registered businesses in Monaco, including 20 banks and 42 other firms that had opened there during 1975. With the increase in commercial interests and in population, Monaco was experiencing an acute land shortage, though it was being overcome by the massive Fontvieille reclamation area—some 220,000 sq m with a new marina of 60,000 sq m.

On February 16, in Barcelona, Spain, Monaco was one of 12 countries whose delegates signed a convention against pollution of the Mediterranean Sea, under the auspices of the UN Environment Program. On May 10 France, Italy, and Monaco signed an agreement on the protection of Mediterranean coastal waters from Hyères to Genoa, which included the setting up of a 21-member commission with a laboratory vessel. Since 1970 Prince Rainier had been pressing for his Project Ramoge, the creation of a pilot zone of action against marine pollution extending from Saint-Raphaël to Genoa.

In August Princess Grace of Monaco spoke at a symposium on family life at the 41st International Eucharistic Congress of the Roman Catholic Church in Philadelphia. In September she appeared in poetry readings at the Edinburgh, Scotland, festival. (K. M. SMOGORZEWSKI)

WIDE WORLD

Monaco's Prince Rainier and Princess Grace celebrated their 20th wedding anniversary in April. (Left to right) Princess Caroline, Prince Albert, Princess Stephanie, Grace, and Rainier.

MONACO

Education. (1971–72) Primary, pupils 1,486, teachers 71; secondary, pupils 2,089, teachers 165; vocational, pupils 458, teachers 61.

Finance and Trade. Monetary unit: French franc, with (Sept. 20, 1976) a free rate of Fr 4.92 to U.S. $1 (Fr 8.47 = £1 sterling). Budget (1975 est.): revenue Fr 330,249,000; expenditure Fr 387.4 million. Foreign trade included with France. Tourism (1973) 137,100 visitors.

Missiles: *see* Defense

Molecular Biology: *see* Life Sciences

Monetary Policy: *see* Economy, World

Money and Banking: *see* Economy, World

Mongolia

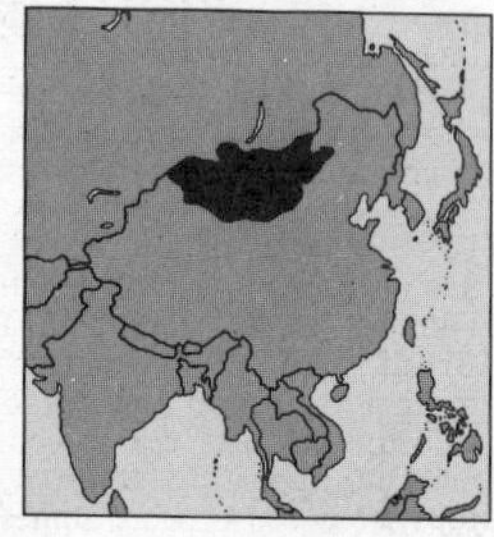

A people's republic of Asia lying between the U.S.S.R. and China, Mongolia occupies the geographic area known as Outer Mongolia. Area: 604,000 sq mi (1,565,000 sq km). Pop. (1976 est.): 1,489,000. Cap. and largest city: Ulan Bator (pop., 1974 est., 312,000). Language: Khalkha Mongolian. Religion: Lamaistic Buddhism. First secretary of the Mongolian People's Revolutionary (Communist) Party in 1976 and chairman of the Presidium of the Great People's Hural, Yumzhagiyen Tsedenbal; chairman of the Council of Ministers (premier), Zhambyn Batmunkh.

The 17th congress of the Mongolian People's Revolutionary Party was held in Ulan Bator on June 14–18, 1976. There were 813 party delegates and 57 fraternal delegations from Communist parties of the

V. MASTYUKOV—TASS/SOVFOTO

A new residential district in Ulan Bator. Round structure in the background is the circus building. Plans call for rebuilding the city by 1986.

world. First Secretary Tsedenbal said in his report that friendship with the U.S.S.R. was the main guarantee that the building of a socialist society in Mongolia would succeed. His country also desired to establish neighbourly relations with China, but he rejected the "Maoist clique."

Tsedenbal said that during the fifth development plan of 1971–75 Mongolia's industrial production rose by 55%, agricultural output by 26%, and national income by 38%. It was expected that with the fulfillment of the sixth five-year plan industrial production would rise by 60–65% and agricultural production by 26–30%. Educational achievements had been remarkable: 23,000 students had graduated from the institutions of higher education and technical colleges.

Party membership had risen since 1971 by 15.3% to 66,933; 31.3% of members were workers, 19% belonged to agricultural associations, and 49.7% were members of the "intelligentsia." The congress elected a new Central Committee which named eight full and two candidate members of the Politburo, the only changes being the election of a new candidate member, Damdiny Gombojav, and the dropping of one full member (Sonomyn Luvsan), who was succeeded by Tumenbayaryn Ragchaa, former candidate member. Tsedenbal was reelected first secretary for the fifth time. On September 17, on the occasion of his 60th birthday, he received many congratulatory telegrams from other Communist leaders.

(K. M. SMOGORZEWSKI)

MONGOLIA

Education. (1974–75) Primary, pupils 127,986, teachers 4,144; secondary, pupils 161,309, teachers 6,511; vocational, pupils 12,718, teachers 755; teacher training, students 1,461, teachers 157; higher, students 8,900, teaching staff (1971–72) 710.

Finance. Monetary unit: tugrik, with (Sept. 20, 1976) a nominal exchange rate of 3.38 tugriks to U.S. $1 (5.82 tugriks = £1 sterling). Budget (1976 est.): revenue 2,987,000,000 tugriks; expenditure 2,972,000,000 tugriks.

Foreign Trade. (1973) Imports *c.* 1,250,000,000 tugriks; exports *c.* 520 million tugriks. Import sources: U.S.S.R. *c.* 90%. Export destinations: U.S.S.R. *c.* 76%; Czechoslovakia *c.* 7%; East Germany *c.* 5%. Main exports: livestock *c.* 28%; wool *c.* 21%; meat *c.* 10%; fluorspar *c.* 5%.

Transport and Communications. Roads (1970) *c.* 75,000 km (including *c.* 9,000 km main roads). Railways (1973) 1,425 km. Telephones (Jan. 1974) 27,000. Radio receivers (Dec. 1973) 148,000. Television receivers (Dec. 1973) *c.* 34,000.

Agriculture. Production (in 000; metric tons; 1974): wheat *c.* 270; oats *c.* 64; barley *c.* 25; potatoes *c.* 27; milk *c.* 246; beef and veal *c.* 65; mutton and goat meat *c.* 120. Livestock (in 000; Dec. 1973): cattle *c.* 2,206; sheep *c.* 14,077; goats *c.* 4,442; horses *c.* 2,100; camels *c.* 670.

Industry. Production (in 000; metric tons; 1974): coal 137; lignite 2,337; salt 11; cement 171; electricity (kw-hr) 741,000.

Morocco

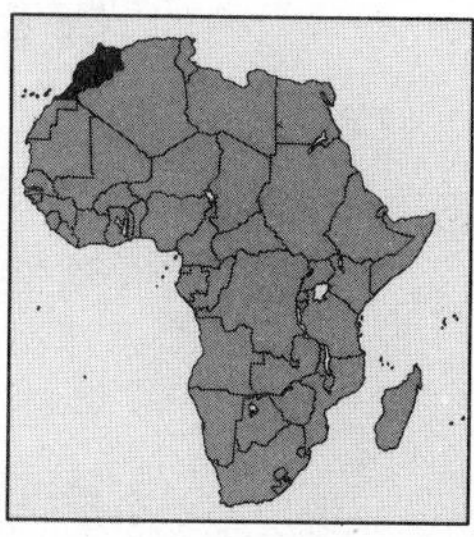

A constitutional monarchy of northwestern Africa, on the Atlantic Ocean and the Mediterranean Sea, Morocco is bordered by Algeria and Western (Spanish) Sahara. Area: 177,117 sq mi (458,730 sq km). Pop. (1975 est.): 17,305,000. Cap.: Rabat (pop., 1975 UN est., 654,000). Largest city: Casablanca (pop., 1975 UN est., 1,856,000). Data above refer to Morocco as constituted prior to the purported division of Spanish Sahara between Morocco and Mauritania. Language: Arabic; Berber. Religion: Muslim. King, Hassan II; prime minister in 1976, Ahmed Osman.

King Hassan, after his remarkable success in winning back by diplomacy the "lost territory" of the Spanish Sahara, was much preoccupied in 1976 in consolidating this achievement, both militarily and politically. The last Spanish troops left the Sahara on February 26; the division of the territory between Morocco and Mauritania was formalized in April; and by September the Moroccan Army claimed total control of its sector. The formation of a Saharan Arab Democratic Republic and a government-in-exile (in Algeria) was disregarded, and neither the UN nor the Organization of African Unity pressed their contention that the Saharans should exercise self-determination.

The consolidation of Morocco's position in the Sahara was not, however, won without effort. Militarily, the Moroccan Army had to fight off Algerian intervention—the Algerians captured but later lost the strategic town of Amgala—and the constant harassment of guerrillas from the Popular Front for the Liberation of Saguia el Hamra and Río de Oro (Polisario Front), actively supported by Algeria. On June 8 the Polisario guerrillas made a bold attack on Nouakchott, the Mauritanian capital, and thereafter Morocco pledged itself to the defense of Mauritanian as well as its own territory. Despite the heavy costs of the military op-

Mormons: *see* Religion

erations and the loss in men, King Hassan had the full support of all political parties and, on the diplomatic front, was able to send "opposition" leaders as royal emissaries to explain Morocco's case abroad. The king arrived in Paris on November 22 on a four-day state visit to France and was accorded exceptional marks of respect and expressions of cordiality by the French president and the government.

With the party leaders united behind his successful Sahara policy, the king felt strong enough to take the first steps along the road of return to democracy. On July 8 he promised that there would be a Parliament elected within nine months. The first step in a three-stage electoral process, as laid down in the dormant 1972 constitution, took place in November with municipal and rural community elections.

The disappointing trend in phosphates exports, severely cut from 20 million tons to 14 million tons in 1975, continued in 1976 and, coupled with a decline in the production of vegetables, the country's second biggest export category, caused a severe balance of payments deficit. After four years of the current five-year plan economic growth was lagging 20% below expectations, and it was unlikely that the gap would be filled in 1977, the last year of the plan. Foreign financial help, of which one-third came from the Arab states and the rest from the International Bank for Reconstruction and Development, the United States, and Western Europe, did much to ensure that development projects in agriculture, industry, and tourism were not curtailed. (PETER KILNER)

[978.D.2.c]

MOROCCO

Education. (1975–76) Primary, pupils 1,547,646, teachers 39,244; secondary, pupils 486,173, teachers 19,613; higher, students 35,037, teaching staff 991.

Finance. Monetary unit: dirham, with (Sept. 20, 1976) a free rate of 4.27 dirhams to U.S. $1 (7.36 dirhams = £1 sterling). Gold, SDR's, and foreign exchange (June 1976) U.S. $372 million. Budget (1974 est.): revenue 7,273,000,000 dirhams; expenditure 8,759,000,000 dirhams. Gross domestic product (1974) 26,710,000,000 dirhams. Money supply (March 1976) 12,975,000,000 dirhams. Cost of living (1970 = 100; April 1976) 141.

Foreign Trade. (1975) Imports 10,397,000,000 dirhams; exports 6,236,000,000 dirhams. Main import sources: France 30%; U.S. 8%; West Germany 8%; Iraq 5%. Main export destinations: France 21%; Italy 8%; Poland 7%; West Germany 7%; U.K. 7%; Belgium-Luxembourg 6%; Spain 6%. Main exports: phosphates 55%; citrus fruit 7%. Tourism (1974): visitors 1,204,700; gross receipts U.S. $349 million.

Transport and Communications. Roads (1973) 25,414 km (including 14 km expressways). Motor vehicles in use (1973): passenger 258,246; commercial 91,439. Railways: (1974) 2,071 km; traffic (1975) 792.1 million passenger-km, freight 2,843,000,000 net ton-km. Air traffic (1974): 693 million passenger-km; freight 7.8 million net ton-km. Shipping (1975): merchant vessels 100 gross tons and over 53; gross tonnage 79,863. Telephones (Jan. 1975) 189,000. Radio licenses (Dec. 1973) 1.2 million. Television licenses (Dec. 1973) 331,000.

Agriculture. Production (in 000; metric tons; 1975): wheat *c.* 1,267; barley *c.* 1,187; corn 420; potatoes *c.* 200; sugar, raw value 262; dry broad beans (1974) *c.* 200; tomatoes *c.* 315; grapes (1974) *c.* 290; oranges (1974) *c.* 765; mandarin oranges and tangerines (1974) *c.* 163; olives *c.* 303; figs *c.* 67; dates *c.* 92; fish catch (1974) 288. Livestock (in 000; 1974): cattle *c.* 3,820; sheep *c.* 19,000; goats *c.* 8,500; horses *c.* 400; mules *c.* 400; asses *c.* 1,140; camels *c.* 180; poultry *c.* 23,000.

Industry. Production (in 000; metric tons; 1975): coal 651; crude oil 20; cement 2,028; iron ore (55–60% metal content) 554; phosphate rock (1974) 19,749; manganese ore (metal content; 1974) 141; lead concentrates (metal content) 66; zinc concentrates (metal content) 17; petroleum products (1974) *c.* 2,260; electricity (kw-hr; 1974) 2,775,000.

Motion Pictures

In general 1976 seemed a year in which motion pictures were in the doldrums, no doubt reflecting widespread economic insecurity and political uncertainty. Everywhere in the Western world the commercial cinema struggled to maintain its diminishing audience with very much the same dispiriting appeals. Pornography, whether "soft" or "hard," was in plentiful supply, representative titles being Britain's *Keep It Up Downstairs* and *Secrets of a Superstud,* West Germany's *Wenn Mädchen mündig werden,* and Italy's *Professoressa di lingua.* Even Switzerland competed with, for instance, *Mädchen die sich selbst bedienen,* shown abroad under the balder title of *Bed Hostesses.* At a different level, the legacy of *Rosemary's Baby* and *The Exorcist,* in the form of a new fascination with satanism and the occult, brought a spate of ever more disagreeable films, such as the English-language Italian productions *The Antichrist* and *The Devil Within Her* and the Anglo-West German co-production *To the Devil a Daughter.*

In the Eastern socialist countries, too, film activity seemed at a low ebb. In Latin America political repression had dispersed the energetic growth of motion pictures that had appeared in the 1960s, and little that was outstanding emerged from the rest of the third world cinemas. Practically the only motion-picture industries that were thriving, barely touched by the competition of television, were those of India and the Far East.

The cinema's obituary list for the year included, among many others, directors Fritz Lang, Carol Reed, and Luchino Visconti; actors Richard Arlen, Jean Gabin, and Lee J. Cobb; screenwriter Dalton Trumbo; cameraman James Wong Howe; choreographer Busby Berkeley, creator of the greatest 1930s musicals: and producer Adolph Zukor, last and most illustrious survivor of the Nickelodeon years, creator of Famous Players Co. and Paramount Pictures Corp.

English-Speaking Cinema. UNITED STATES. Predictably, much of Hollywood's production was geared to repeating or imitating recent box-office successes. *That's Entertainment* was followed by another compilation of extracts from old MGM movies, *That's Entertainment, Part 2.* The futurist fantasy of *Westworld* was followed up with *Futureworld,* and *Walking Tall* by *Part 2 Walking Tall,* the further adventures of Sheriff Buford Pusser of McNairy County, Tennessee (the real-life Sheriff Pusser died in an automobile crash shortly after having agreed to play his own role in the new film).

The unprecedented box-office success of *Jaws* set off a spate of sequels and imitators, sending producers in frantic search of other perils from the animal kingdom. Among the resulting films were *The Swarm* (killer bees); *Bug* (giant cockroaches); *Squirm* (carnivorous worms); and *Grizzly* (a rampaging bear).

Richard Donner's *The Omen* brought a little more class to the satanism genre, with a cast headed by Gregory Peck and Lee Remick, some good special-effects work, and a novel twist to the story: the victim of the satanists is the U.S. ambassador to Great Britain, and the infant inhabited by the devil ends up adopted into the White House. This was, perhaps, a distant echo of Watergate, which in other respects, too, left its mark on Hollywood productions. One of the year's outstanding films was Alan J. Pakula's *All the President's Men,* a meticulous re-creation of the Carl Bernstein/Bob Woodward feat of investigative journalism on the Watergate affair. Thrillers unequivocally drew their villains from the CIA (Sam Peckinpah's *The Killer Elite*).

Apart from occasional flights into the future (Michael Anderson's cautionary tale of the year 2274, *Logan's Run,* as well as *Futureworld*), U.S. films were concerned with the past. Jack Smight's *Midway* diminished the historic World War II battle to a conventional war melodrama. Walter Hill's attractive *Hard Times* (*The Streetfighter,* in Britain) set its story of an invulnerable boxer, played by Charles Bronson, in the lean depression days of 1936.

Hollywood continued to evince a special nostalgia for its own past. Howard Zieff's charmingly oddball comedy *Hearts of the West* related the adventures of an ingenuous young man who accidentally falls into the role of star in 1930s B-picture Westerns. In *Nickelodeon* Peter Bogdanovich went back still further to 1912 and the period of the bitter war over patents that split the motion-picture industry in its pioneer days. F. Scott Fitzgerald's *The Last Tycoon,* based on the career of producer Irving Thalberg, was adapted to the screen by writer Harold Pinter and director Elia Kazan. Woody Allen starred in *The Front,* about Hollywood's blacklisted writers in the 1950s.

Nostalgic melancholy marked two Westerns that starred the aged giant of the Hollywood West, John Wayne. In Stuart Millar's *Rooster Cogburn* he resumed his role of the one-eyed old reprobate marshal from *True Grit,* this time finding his match in a formidable missionary maiden played by Katharine Hepburn. In Don Siegel's *The Shootist* Wayne was a superannuated gunfighter in the last few weeks of terminal cancer. Robert Altman's bicentennial offering was an equivocal compliment: *Buffalo Bill and the Indians* provided a portrait part satirical, part cruelly realistic of one of the great heroes of the West in his later years when, vain, boozy, and half convinced by his own legend, he was reenacting his exploits twice nightly for rustic audiences at his Wild West circus show.

Comedy was in the ascendant. With *Airport 1977* already on the way and a race to get the first film about Israel's Entebbe exploit onto the screen, the "disaster" cycle proved fair game for parody in James Frawley's *The Big Bus,* a sometimes surreal farce about the disaster-prone maiden voyage of the world's first nuclear-powered motor coach. Michael Ritchie's *The Bad News Bears* was a more genial satire on the American success syndrome than his earlier *Smile,* with Walter Matthau as the local drunk engaged by the town council to train a baseball team of misfit children—including Tatum O'Neal, since *Paper Moon* the highest paid child star in film history.

Major and continuing influences upon Hollywood comedy were still Altman's *M*A*S*H* (*Mother, Jugs and Speed* used the same formula in its comedy about a highly inefficient private ambulance service) and the zany genius of Mel Brooks. Brooks's influence was identifiable in *The Big Bus,* as well as in Melvin Frank's *The Duchess and the Dirtwater Fox* which insolently parodied each style and cliché of costume romance. Brooks himself made *Silent Movie,* a deliberate exercise in reviving a purely visual style of comedy. *Network,* written by Paddy Chayefsky and directed by Sidney Lumet, was a sharp satire of the U.S. television industry.

The black cinema was making notable strides forward from its early preoccupation with violent crime thrillers. Berry Gordy's *Mahogany,* a novelette story exploiting all the white cinema's gaudiest success dreams, was one of the less notable representatives. Gordon Parks's otherwise rather wooden biography of Huddie Ledbetter, *Leadbelly,* was distinguished by the title performance of Roger E. Mosley. Sidney Poitier's *Let's Do It Again* and John Badham's *The Bingo Long Traveling All-Stars and Motor Kings,* with similar themes (the first the attempt to exploit a boxer; the second a baseball team), managed their comedy with charm and dexterity.

Outstanding among the individual and individualist successes of the year was the adaptation of Ken Kesey's novel *One Flew over the Cuckoo's Nest* directed by the émigré Czechoslovak director Milos Forman. The story tells of the misadventures of a manic young petty criminal who sees a spell in a mental hospital as a soft option, but, in losing a battle of wits with an inhuman disciplinarian ward supervisor, finds himself instead in a Kafkaesque trap. Extraordinary performances by the principals confirmed Jack Nicholson's career, reestablished that of Louise Fletcher, and made the giant Indian Will Sampson (*see* BIOGRAPHY) a character actor greatly in demand.

Alfred Hitchcock's 53rd film, *Family Plot,* was an easy entertainment which showed that at 77 the veteran English-born director had lost none of his genius as a teller of tales, creating suspense and suspending disbelief even with the most patently implausible plot. Another veteran, John Huston, employed a comparable talent as narrator in filming *The Man Who Would Be King,* Rudyard Kipling's eerie story of a common soldier who becomes briefly the god-king of a northwest frontier state in British India. A third veteran, the 77-year-old George Cukor, had less good fortune with his adaptation of Maurice Maeterlinck's moral fairy tale *The Blue Bird,* which was remarkable only as being the first U.S.-Soviet co-production.

Martin Scorsese's earlier films had generally been autobiographical recollections of the gregarious society of New York's Little Italy. In *Taxi Driver* the hero is a loner who takes up nocturnal driving because of its solitary nature and becomes obsessed with the notion of making some gesture in the face of the City, which he sees as a kind of inferno. Robert De Niro gave an impressive performance as a man in whom

Dustin Hoffman (left) and Robert Redford played the roles of the Watergate reporters Carl Bernstein and Bob Woodward in "All the President's Men," directed by Alan J. Pakula.

COLUMBIA-WARNER DISTRIBUTORS LTD.

Scott Baio, 14, played Bugsy, a straightforward, honest guy with brains, in "Bugsy Malone," a movie about 1930s gangsters played by child actors. Baio said afterward that it was "just like any other job I might have done."

stunted intelligence and dreadful determination are dangerously combined.

The year's documentaries included Emile de Antonio's *Underground*, a startling series of interviews with members of the revolutionary Weathermen organization; a new film investigation by Frederic Wiseman, this time on the processes that result in the citizen's daily *Meat;* and David and Albert Maysles' *Grey Gardens*, a *cinéma vérité* portrait of the two Edith Bouvier Beales, mother and daughter, the idiosyncratic if not positively eccentric aunt and cousin of Jacqueline Onassis.

In the annual awards of the U.S. Academy of Motion Picture Arts and Sciences, *One Flew over the Cuckoo's Nest* ran away with the top prizes, receiving Oscars for best film, best actor (Jack Nicholson), best actress (Louise Fletcher), best director (Milos Forman), and best adapted screenplay (Lawrence Hauben and Bo Goldman). Stanley Kubrick's *Barry Lyndon* earned four awards, for best cinematography (John Alcott), best art direction (Ken Adams, Roy Walker, and Vernon Dixon), best costume design (Ulla-Britt Söderlund and Milena Canonero), and best scoring adaptation (Leonard Rosenman). Steven Spielberg's *Jaws* took Oscars for best editing (Verna Fields), best original music score (John Williams), and best sound (Robert L. Hoyt, Roger Heman, Earl Madery, and John Carter).

The best supporting actor was the octogenarian comedian George Burns, for *The Sunshine Boys;* the best supporting actress, Lee Grant, for *Shampoo*. The award for best original screenplay went to Frank Pierson for *Dog Day Afternoon*. The best foreign-language film was Akira Kurosawa's *Dersu Uzala;* best documentary feature, *The Man Who Skied Down Everest;* best documentary short, *The End of the Game;* and best animation short, Bob Godfrey's comic portrait of Isambard Brunel, *Great*.

BRITAIN. Early in 1976 the working party set up to consider the future of the British film industry published its report. Major proposals were to increase investment in production from £25 million (in 1975) to £40 million a year during a four-year period, and to set up a British Film Authority to assume responsibility for film functions currently fulfilled in the main by two government departments.

There was a tendency toward polarization in British film production. At one extreme were films in the large budget class. Sir Lew Grade followed up the massive box-office successes of *The Return of the Pink Panther* and a remake of *Farewell, My Lovely* by announcing other multimillion dollar productions, including an epic life of Christ to be directed by Franco Zeffirelli. Stanley Kubrick's monumental *Barry Lyndon*, adapted from a minor Thackeray novel about an incorrigible Irish cad moving in the best society of the 18th century, somehow managed to miss the point of the narrative, just as its exquisite images and decorations finally failed to evoke the Janus-faced world of the 18th-century aristocracy. A British production shot in the U.S., Nicolas Roeg's *The Man Who Fell to Earth*, endeavoured unsuccessfully to make a mystical experience out of an essentially rationalist science-fiction novel (by Walter Tevis). The pop star David Bowie made an impressive debut in the title role.

At the opposite end of the scale from such ambitiously budgeted films, the British commercial cinema seemed largely occupied with cheaply made films of the softest of soft-core pornography (*The Ups and Downs of a Handyman, Confessions of a Driving Instructor, Sextet*) or substandard horror films (Robert Fuest's *The Devil's Rain*). Again in 1976, however, the most encouraging signs of vitality were to be found in areas of independently financed low-budget film production. Derek Jarman (designer of such Ken Russell films as *The Devils*) and Paul Humfress made an idiosyncratic interpretation of the life of St. Sebastian, *Sebastiane*. A movie of stunning visual elegance, it was the first feature film ever made using classical Latin dialogue. Made for a mere fraction even of *Sebastiane*'s tiny budget, Giles Foster's *Devices and Desires* was a quiet and accurately observed portrait of a lonely obsessive recluse, based on the diaries of a misanthropic clergyman.

Lying somewhere in the area between the big-budget commercial productions and the shoestring independents, one of the most surprising British successes of the year was *Bugsy Malone*, directed by Alan Parker (*see* BIOGRAPHY). Eccentricity paid bonuses in this musical pastiche of a 1930s gangster film, played entirely by children, with bombs and tommy guns replaced by custard pies and "splurge guns." The joke sometimes seemed stretched a little thin, but this did not impair the enthusiastic box-office response in both Britain and the U.S.

AUSTRALIA. Peter Weir, whose skill in evoking atmosphere was already evident in his first feature film, *The Cars that Ate Paris*, made a movie of supernatural mystery, *Picnic at Hanging Rock*, involving the strange disappearance of some schoolgirls from a picnic in the early 1900s. Other noteworthy Australian films of the year were *The Devil's Playground*, a first film by Fred Schepisi which treated artlessly but with real feeling the frustrations and hypocrisies of life in a boys' seminary in the 1950s; and Philippe Mora's *Mad Dog*, an ironic saga of a 19th-century outlaw eventually run down by authorities who are perhaps more culpable in their violence than the criminal himself.

CANADA. New features by two Quebec directors were in markedly contrasting styles. Jean-Pierre Lefebvre's *L'Amour blessé* was practically a solo performance, the observation of a woman undergoing the pain and emptiness of marital breakup. André Forcier's *L'Eau chaude, l'eau frette* followed his earlier *Bar Salon* in presenting, through the vaguest of narrative structures, a comic gallery of eccentrics and ne'er-do-wells from Montreal's East End. Eccentricity was also the keynote of Peter Bryant's notable debut film, *The Supreme Kid*, the tragicomic adventures of a couple of drifters. It effectively combined a contemporary theme with tributes to old slapstick-comedy traditions.

Western Europe. FRANCE. By and large crime and comedy remained the staples of the French commercial cinema, with the two styles combining on occasion, as in Jacques Deray's *Le Gang.* François Truffaut's *L'Histoire d'Adèle H.* was based on the recently discovered diaries of Victor Hugo's younger daughter, who fell in love with a young English officer during her father's exile and followed him to Canada. Truffaut found a fine new actress for the taxing central role in Isabelle Adjani. *L'Argent de Poche* (*Small Change*), another Truffaut film, was a series of loosely linked episodes about the lives of schoolchildren that proved too slight to be sustained even by the director's evident affection for his characters.

In a Franco-West German co-production, Eric Rohmer adapted Heinrich von Kleist's story *La Marquise d'O . . . ,* evolving a dry, elegant, witty style to match Kleist's own irony in this tale of romantic notions of innocence and honour, tested severely when an aristocratic young lady becomes pregnant apparently without having known a man. Rohmer used German stage actors, notably the exquisite Edith Clever, with fine effect.

France's distinguished group of women directors, including Agnes Varda, Nelly Kaplan, Nadine Trintignant, Yannick Bellon, and Anna Karina, was joined by Jeanne Moreau, who completed *Lumière,* and novelist Françoise Sagan, who in the summer of 1976 was at work on a feature, *Les Fougères bleues* (*Blue Ferns*). Marguérite Duras, another novelist turned filmmaker, essayed the eccentric but stimulating experiment of using the whole sound track of her 1975 film *India Song* and substituting different images.

Several new directors of talent emerged in France during the year. The writer Eduardo de Gregorio in *Sérail* (*Surreal Estate*) gave new (and erotic) vitality to the favourite theme of a novelist haunted by his creations. Jean-Louis Commoli, a critic, made his debut with *La Cecilia,* which used a historical incident about a group of Italian anarchists endeavouring to set up a commune in 19th-century Brazil to illuminate contemporary social themes. Claude Miller's *La Meilleure Façon de Marcher* (*The Best Way to Make It*) was a perceptive portrayal of a competitive relationship, with erotic undertones, between two men working in a boys' summer camp.

Two foreign directors made films in which obsessive themes of the exchange of personality provided unexpected parallels. Joseph Losey's *Mr. Klein* related a fable about an opportunistic French art dealer who makes a fortune during the World War II German occupation by buying works of art from fleeing Jews. An irritating muddle when he is momentarily confused with another Mr. Klein, of Jewish origin, leads him into a dark Kafkaesque maze, in which identities become wholly confused until the original Mr. Klein finds himself taking the other's place on the way to the concentration camps. Roman Polanski's *Le Locataire* (*The Tenant*) was lighter in tone, with the director himself playing the leading role of a mild little man who rents a room in a Parisian lodging house. There is nightmare again, as the young man gradually finds himself taking over the personality of his predecessor in the room, a girl whom the other tenants' malice had driven to throw herself suicidally out of the window.

Roman Polanski as Paris clerk Trelkovsky on his balcony in "The Tenant," a psychological suspense thriller directed by Polanski.

ITALY. Within a year Italy lost two of its greatest film personalities, Pier Paolo Pasolini (murdered in November 1975) and Luchino Visconti. During the last months of his activity, though confined to a wheelchair, Visconti had succeeded in completing an elegant and detailed adaptation of Gabriele D'Annunzio's novel *L'Innocente* (*The Intruder*), the story of a wife who responds to her husband's insistence on keeping a mistress by herself taking a lover. When this liaison results in a child, the husband embarks on a path of self-destruction. Pasolini's last film, *Salo, o le Centoventi Giornate di Sodoma,* first shown a few weeks after the director's death, proved an awesome testament. De Sade's *120 Days of Sodom* is transposed to 1943 and Mussolini's short-lived republic of Salo; the four degenerates are now sadomasochistic officials who abuse and torment a group of adolescent boys and girls; and the whole becomes a parable on political power. More firmly structured than any previous Pasolini film, it was organized in three Dantesque "circles" of escalating horror.

Marie-Christine Barrault and Victor Lanoux starred in Jean-Charles Tacchella's "Cousin, Cousine," a slice-of-life film about two cousins who have a clandestine affair.

Apart from these, the two major films of the year were highly political in content. Bernardo Bertolucci's *1900* was an uncompromisingly biased view of the struggle between Communism and capitalism in Italy during the first three quarters of the 20th century. Pictorially magnificent, with a notable cast led by Burt Lancaster, Gérard Depardieu, and Robert De Niro, it disappointed even Bertolucci's most enthusiastic Communist supporters in its failure to work out its political message beyond the most superficial level. Francesco Rosi's enigmatic thriller *Cadaveri Eccellenti* (*Illustrious Corpses*) adapted Leonardo Sciascia's novel *Il Contesto* but made its political allusions—to a series of real-life political murders that happened in 1970 and to the much discussed "historical compromise" between Italian Communism and Roman Catholicism—more specific and critical. Lina Wertmüller (*see* BIOGRAPHY) continued her productive and controversial career with *Swept Away* and *Seven Beauties,* two films that reflected the director's fondness for paradox.

WEST GERMANY. The young West German cinema continued to flourish, and all its major directors were active during the year. The indefatigable Rainer Werner Fassbinder made an absurdist comedy, *Satansbraten.* Alexander Kluge's *Der Starke Ferdinand* (*Strongman Ferdinand*) had an unexpected thematic similarity to *Taxi Driver* in its story of the obsessive zeal of a factory security officer, whose enthusiasm finally breaks out into madness when he assassinates a politician. Wim Wenders' *Kings of the Road* followed the director's earlier films in chronicling a contemporary odyssey, this time the adventures of two acquaintances who traverse Germany servicing projectors in superannuated movie theatres.

Hans-Jürgen Syberberg's exploration of the wellsprings of Hitler's Third Reich took a new turn in *The Confessions of Winifred Wagner,* an extraordinary five-hour interview with the daughter-in-law of Richard Wagner, who cheerfully recalled her 24-year friendship with and admiration for Hitler. Werner Herzog's *Heart of Glass* pursued a characteristic theme of obsession, in this case the determination of the son and heir of the owner of a Bavarian glass factory of the early 19th century to rediscover the lost secret of a particular kind of ruby glass. Always unorthodox in his choice and use of actors, for this film Herzog hypnotized the players before each day's

French director François Truffaut's "Small Change" showed the world of children.

Liv Ullmann starred as a psychiatrist haunted by hallucinations in Ingmar Bergman's "Face to Face."

shooting, achieving a strange, hallucinatory style in his performers to suit the film's bizarre atmosphere.

SWITZERLAND. The late developing German-speaking sector of the new Swiss cinema was by 1976 firmly in its stride. Thomas Körfer adapted Robert Walser's part-autobiographical, part-fantastic *Der Gehülfe.* Set in the early years of the 20th century, it relates the bizarre adventures of an unemployed clerk who is taken on as assistant secretary to an inventor but finds himself drawn into a much more central position in the man's strange home and family. Daniel Schmid, director of *La Paloma,* adapted Fassbinder's play *The Judge, the City and Death,* allegedly written in the course of a transatlantic flight, as *Schatten der Engel.* Both play and film attracted notoriety in Germany and abroad for alleged anti-Semitism.

SWEDEN. Following *The Magic Flute* and an extraordinary self-revelation in a series of television interviews made by Jorn Donner, *Three Scenes with Ingmar Bergman,* Bergman (*see* BIOGRAPHY) returned to a more characteristic subject in *Face to Face.* This was the portrait of a woman psychiatrist (played by Liv Ullmann), living in a seemingly ideal social situation, who nevertheless becomes prey to acute and suicidal nervous depression. Through the portrait Bergman offers a brutal critique of a dehumanized technological society, a society which he and his collaborators had incidentally come hard against during 1975–76 in a series of much publicized tax investigations.

SPAIN. After Franco, and 40 years after the event, the cinema inevitably revisited the Spanish Civil War (the revised film section of the Venice Biennale in August was mainly dedicated to the theme). Jaime Camino's *Las Largas Vacaciones del 36* reexamined the war from the viewpoint of a well-to-do Catalan family, sitting it out in extended holidays near Barcelona. Carlos Saura's *Cría Cuervos* obliquely examined the war's legacies, through a girl's memories of a long-ago summer and a vanished Madrid.

Eastern Europe. U.S.S.R. The Soviet Union's minimal participation in international film events during 1976 seemed to reflect a continuing creative crisis. At the Cannes Film Festival the Soviet Union angrily withheld participation after the officially submitted entry was refused by the festival authorities on the grounds of its inadequate quality. The newly founded Cairo Film Festival, however, gave a prize to a modest and attractive little comedy about a country mouse in town—specifically, an old Armenian peasant (Armen Jigarkhanian) who visits Moscow, where his sophisticated, urbanized daughter and her circle find the old man can still teach them a thing or two about living. The director was Edmond Keosayan.

POLAND. Strikingly, Polish filmmakers seemed exclusively to seek subjects in the past. Bohdan Poreba's *Jaroslav Dabrowski* dealt with a Polish insurgent of the 1863 uprising who later became a general of the Paris Commune. Andrzej Konic's *These Early Spring Days,* Kazimierz Kutz's *From Nowhere to Nowhere,* and Stanislaw Rozevicz's *Fallen Leaves* all treated World War II subjects; while Pawel Kororowski's *Red and White* followed its hero through 50 years and two world wars. Wlodzimierz Haupe's *Doctor Judym* was based on a 50-year-old novel about social struggles in turn-of-the-century Poland; while Janusz Majewski's *Hotel Pacific* was based on a 1930s bestseller, portraying in meticulous detail the backstage dramas of a prewar Grand Hotel.

HUNGARY. The Hungarian cinema continued to suffer from a sense of crisis. The growing hold of television—allied perhaps to shortcomings in distribution and publicity techniques—had by 1976 begun to make appreciable inroads into the motion-picture audience. At the same time, there had been signs of a new spirit among Hungarian filmmakers. The influence of *cinéma vérité,* given a great impetus by Judit Elek's *A Hungarian Village,* had begun to indicate a reaction against the long-standing, essentially literary traditions that had dominated Hungarian films. For instance, Istvan Darday's *Holiday in Britain* treated a newspaper item about a young boy whose parents would not let him take the proffered opportunity of a visit to Britain. The film used an amateur cast and improvised dialogue, new departures for Hungarian cinema. When the film was criticized as "untypical," Darday's wife went to the village where the real-life family lived and made an interview film on *The Natural History of an Untypical Case.*

Among the best Hungarian films of the year was Zsolt Kezdi-Kovacs' *When Joseph Returns,* an uncompromisingly realistic portrait of an incurably feckless girl who drifts perilously when her sailor husband goes to sea, leaving her alone with her mother-in-law. It was particularly notable for the playing of two fine actresses, Lili Monori, a newcomer, and Eva Ruttkai, a well-loved star of the Hungarian stage and screen, as the two waiting women.

YUGOSLAVIA. Movies about World War II partisans remained staple fare. Two big-budget films, however, were clearly aimed (not very accurately perhaps) at an international market. Veljko Bulajic's *Assassination at Sarajevo,* with a multinational cast headed by Christopher Plummer, studiously avoided dealing with any real political issues. Vatroslav Mimica's *Anno Domini 1573* was a handsome and spectacular historical epic.

Asia. JAPAN. In a cinema fighting for its existence (in 1975 Japanese companies produced 134 films; a decade earlier the number would have been almost four times as great), production was oriented strictly to commercial demand, with a regular output of sex films, "yakuza" (gangster) films, and popular comedies. One Japanese film, however, made an intense impression at the international festivals where it was shown. This was Nagisa Oshima's *Empire of the Senses,* based on a true incident of 1936. It chronicles the love affair of a geisha and a pimp, which achieves its ultimate and inevitable culmination in the man's death and subsequent emasculation at the hands of his lover.

HONG KONG. The prolific Hong Kong cinema demonstrated its capacity to deal with other subjects than the martial arts. Li Han-hsiang, rated one of Hong Kong's best directors, completed a two-part epic of astonishing historical accuracy on the last days of the Ch'ing dynasty in the late 1890s. The year's most successful film, however, was directed by a disciple of Li Han-hsiang and former actor in his films, Michael Hui. His *The Last Message* was a black comedy about the attempt of an attendant in a mental hospital to secure information from an inmate who is obsessed with the notion of a hidden Ming treasure.

INDIA. The Indian cinema appeared to be making positive efforts—in several opposing directions—to break out of the pattern of low-budget, star-dominated melodramas punctuated with songs that had predominated for years. A major Indian producer, G. P. Sippy, enjoyed a huge success with a big-budget spectacle, modeled directly on European "Westerns" of the Sergio Leone type, directed (by the producer's son, Ramesh Sippy) and written with some panache. Concurrently, the independent movement for an Indian cinema of artistic and intellectual integrity was gaining ground. Like his earlier *Ankur* (*The Seedling*), Shyam Benegal's *Nishant* (*Night's End*) successfully bridged the gap between "art" and "commerce" with a melodrama containing an underlying sociopolitical message.

IRAN. Parviz Kimiavi's *The Stone Garden* was an imperfect but likable film in which the leading player re-created his own real-life role; Darvich Khan, a deaf-mute shepherd, was inspired to realize a mystical vision that came to him in the desert and spent ten years creating his bizarre garden of stones, dead trees, telegraph wire, and other detritus. The film showed how Darvich's own enthusiasm for his creation had given his garden a local reputation as a holy place.

LEBANON. Moustapha Akkad's massive life of Muhammad (the English title *Mohammad Messenger of God* was changed to *The Message* out of deference to Muslim sensibilities) met with religious objections both in the making and in its eventual exhibition, even though there was no attempt at any representation of the Prophet himself. This delicacy in any case presented the filmmakers with insuperable artistic problems, and in the end the film's worst enemy was its own banal and turgid conception, on the traditional lines of Hollywood costume epics.

Latin America. Chile remained a major theme for Latin-American filmmakers. In Cuba Patricio Guzman completed the second part of an intended trilogy, *The Battle of Chile: The Coup d'État.* One historical incident, a strike in the British-owned nitrate mines in 1907 when 3,600 workers were killed by Chilean troops, provided the inspiration for two strongly contrasted feature films. The Cuban director Humbert Solas made *Cantata de Chile,* a rather pretentiously conceived and self-conscious assembly of music and slogan, reconstructed documentary, and legend. In Mexico the exiled Chilean director Miguel Littin made *Actas de Marusia,* a more literal and eventually more impressive effort to evoke the attempt to create a labour movement in early 20th-century Chile.

(DAVID ROBINSON)

Annual Cinema Attendance*

Country	Total in 000	Per capita
Afghanistan	19,200	1.1
Albania	8,400	4
Algeria	89,300	6
Angola	3,700	0.6
Argentina	63,000	2.6
Australia	32,000	3
Austria	26,700	3.6
Bahrain	2,000	8.8
Barbados	1,800	7.4
Belgium	32,800	3.4
Benin	1,200	0.4
Bolivia	3,200	0.9
Brazil	234,700	3
Brunei	2,900	20.4
Bulgaria	114,000	13.2
Burma	222,500	8.1
Cambodia	20,000	3
Cameroon	6,200	1
Canada	92,300	4.3
Chad	1,300	0.4
Chile	44,600	5
Colombia	92,800	5
Cuba	124,300	14.2
Cyprus	6,100	9.5
Czechoslovakia	89,300	6.1
Denmark	19,300	3.8
Dominican Republic	5,200	1.2
Ecuador	16,000	2.5
Egypt	65,400	2
El Salvador	10,400	3
Finland	11,000	2.4
France	184,700	3.6
Germany, East	84,500	5
Germany, West	144,300	2.3
Ghana	18,700	2
Guatemala	8,300	1.5
Guyana	9,200	12.1
Haiti	1,500	0.3
Hong Kong	63,000	15.1
Hungary	73,500	7.1
Iceland	1,600	7.6
India	3,490,000	6.2
Iran	22,600	0.7
Iraq	8,300	1.3
Ireland	38,000	13
Israel	32,100	10.1
Italy	546,500	10
Ivory Coast	11,500	2.5
Japan	185,000	1.7
Jordan	3,200	1.8
Korea, South	125,200	3.9
Kuwait	3,600	4.1
Laos	1,000	0.3
Lebanon	49,700	18
Liberia	1,000	0.6
Luxembourg	1,100	3.2
Macau	21,200	8.1
Malaysia	136,000	11.7
Mali	2,500	0.5
Malta	3,000	9.5
Martinique	2,100	6
Mauritius	8,300	9.7
Mexico	220,000	4.1
Morocco	23,700	1.5
Mozambique	3,200	0.4
Netherlands, The	26,500	2
New Zealand	14,300	5
Nicaragua	7,500	5
Norway	17,400	4.4
Pakistan	194,800	3
Panama	7,100	4.8
Poland	140,700	4.2
Portugal	26,500	3.1
Puerto Rico	8,700	3
Réunion	1,200	3
Romania	177,400	8.5
Senegal	5,200	1.5
Singapore	37,400	17.1
Somalia	4,700	1.7
Spain	293,100	8.5
Sri Lanka	98,100	7.7
Sudan	24,000	1.4
Surinam	1,700	5
Sweden	22,100	2.7
Switzerland	27,000	4.2
Thailand	15,000	0.4
Trinidad and Tobago	8,400	8
Tunisia	12,500	2.3
Turkey	246,700	6.7
U.S.S.R.	4,583,300	18.4
United Kingdom	134,200	2.4
United States	920,600	5
Upper Volta	1,000	0.2
Venezuela	37,000	3.4
Yemen (San'a')	3,500	2.4
Yugoslavia	86,300	4.1
Zaire	1,100	0.1

*Countries having over one million annual attendance.
Source: United Nations, *Statistical Yearbook 1975.*

TOHO INTERNATIONAL (USA) INC.

Yoko Takaashi played a girl sold by her family into prostitution in the eloquent Japanese film "Brothel No. 8." The film also had first-rate performances by Kinuyo Tanaka and Komaki Kurihara.

Nontheatrical Motion Pictures. Film production in 1976 in the U.S. and Canada, as in recent years, was no longer done by sizable companies with large staffs and total production capability. Rising costs did not allow producers the luxury of large staffs. Most production companies were reduced to a bare minimum of nonproduction personnel and used free-lance talent for actual production work.

The quality of production, however, did not suffer. For example, again nearly 290 films were selected for Golden Eagle (260 professional) and Cine Eagle (28 amateur) recognition in 1976. These motion pictures were chosen by CINE, the Council on International (film) Events, to represent the U.S. in film competition around the world. Three U.S. motion pictures that took high honours abroad were *Twenty-Three/Twenty-Eight* by John J. Hennessy for Firestone Tire and Rubber Co.; *Trains,* produced by Mary Jo and Caleb Deschanel for the Corporation for Public Broadcasting and the American Film Institute; and *End of the Game* by Robin Lehman's Opus Films Ltd.

In the U.S., New York's American Film Festival, sponsored by the Educational Film Library Association, gave its top Emily Award to *The Gentleman Tramp,* produced by Bert Schneider and directed by Richard Patterson. *Angel and Big Joe,* produced by Bert Salzman, won an Oscar from the Academy of Motion Picture Arts and Sciences, the first such award for an educational film.

One of the most ambitious motion-picture programs ever attempted was staged in Vancouver, B.C., in June. For its Conference on Human Settlements, Habitat, the UN used 230 visual programs (approximately 195 motion pictures and 35 slide shows). In a unique experiment each of the 131 participating nations was invited to produce a film or slide show as a substitute for the traditional printed report.

During 1975 sales of educational films to schools fell below the 1974 level. In 1976 sales continued to be soft because of the reduction by many schools of the amount budgeted for instructional materials. The tight budgets resulted from inflation, higher teacher salaries, and other costs. Smaller student enrollment was also a contributing factor. Production of educational films, however, increased slightly in 1975 to about 1,900 after a dip in recent years.

Business and government purchases of motion pictures increased. Videotape production was being used primarily in producing television commercials and by business firms for training purposes. Most sponsored work continued to be made on film.

(THOMAS W. HOPE)

See also Photography; Television and Radio.
[623; 735.G.2]

ENCYCLOPÆDIA BRITANNICA FILMS. *Growing* (1969)—a computer-animated film; *Practical Film Making* (1972); *Acting for Film* (1976); *Directing a Film* (1976); *Editing a Film* (1976).

Motorboating: *see* Water Sports

Motor Industry: *see* Industrial Review

Motor Sports

Grand Prix Racing. Three new races were added to the grand prix calendar in 1976: the U.S. West, the Canadian (canceled in 1975), and the Japanese. Formula One racing was again run to the 3-litre formula, with engines required to use commercial gasoline. Again most of the front-runners were powered by Cosworth-Ford engines driving through Hewland gearboxes, such cars challenging the flat-12-cylinder Ferraris from Italy. Unfortunately, the season was characterized by disputes over race rules, which often left results in doubt for some time, and by the temporary withdrawal of the Ferrari team as Enzo Ferrari's comment on the situation. Highlight of the year was the world drivers' championship, which remained open to either Britain's James Hunt or Austria's Niki Lauda (*see* BIOGRAPHY) until the final battle in Japan in October.

The season began in January in Brazil, where Lauda won in a 312T Ferrari from Patrick Depailler of France in a four-wheeled Tyrrell 007. Tom Pryce was third in a Shadow DN5, and another Shadow driven by Jean-Pierre Jarier of France made the fastest lap. By March the grand prix tour had moved to South Africa's Kyalami circuit, and there the Hunt-Lauda conflict began. Lauda won for Ferrari on a slowly deflating rear tire, which allowed Hunt in the McLaren M23 to finish within 1.3 sec of him, followed by West German Jochen Mass's McLaren M23. Already the bickering had commenced, over the dimensions of the McLarens, which were corrected before the race.

At the end of March the U.S. Grand Prix West, run over 260 km of a street circuit at Long Beach, Calif., was won by Lauda's Swiss teammate Clay Regazzoni, who also had the fastest lap. Lauda finished second, and third place went to Depailler's Tyrrell. By the time of the Spanish race at Jarama, Hunt was in winning form, but the result was marred by a protest that Hunt's car was 1.8 cm too wide. He was eventually awarded the race, with Lauda relegated to second place. Sweden's Gunnar Nilsson's Lotus 77 was a good third. The next two races were a demonstration of Ferrari supremacy, with Lauda winning the Belgian Grand Prix, followed by his teammate Regazzoni and Jacques Lafitte of France in a Matra. Lauda then won the difficult Monaco Grand Prix. In the latter race, however, it was the unconventional six-wheeled Elf-Tyrrell P34s of South African Jody Scheckter and Depailler that came in second and third. This writing-on-the-wall was confirmed in the Swedish Grand Prix, which Scheckter won in the P34, with Depailler behind him; Lauda had to be content with third place. Hunt then triumphed in the French Grand Prix at the Paul Ricard Autodrome, but it was the Tyrrell P34 of Depailler that chased him home. Third place was given to Britain's John Watson driving a Penske PC4, but he was later disqualified for a reason

WIDE WORLD

Johnny Rutherford (right) overtaking A. J. Foyt in the Indianapolis 500 on May 30. The race was called because of rain after 102 laps, and Rutherford was declared the winner.

associated with the height of an airfoil. This let Carlos Pace's Brabham BT45 into that place.

Protests again flared up at Brands Hatch, when the Ferraris collided on the first lap of the British Grand Prix and the race was stopped, although no one had been seriously hurt. Hunt's car had been damaged while trying to avoid the Ferraris, but he was able to get it repaired while the race was stopped. Because he had not completed one lap, protests were entered that Hunt should not be allowed to compete when the race was restarted. But he did enter and drove a great race, finishing 52.05 sec ahead of Lauda's Ferrari. Scheckter was third, and Hunt made fastest lap, at 189.71 kph. But Hunt was eventually disqualified from the race under protest, and Watson was given third place.

In the German Grand Prix over 14 laps of the Nürburgring, Hunt proved his worth by winning at 168.586 kph, and Scheckter proved the technical merit of the Tyrrell by taking second place, ahead of Mass in a McLaren. The world championship took a dramatic turn in this race when Lauda crashed from an unstated cause and was taken to the hospital suffering from severe facial burns and other injuries. For a time his life appeared to be in danger, but he fought a courageous battle and was racing again at Monza. Meanwhile, Watson scored an unexpected but well-deserved victory in the Austrian Grand Prix in the well-prepared Penske, from Lafitte's Ligier JS5 and Nilsson's Lotus 77. Hunt finished in fourth place. In the Dutch Grand Prix at Zandvoort, Hunt saw his chance of the world championship sharpening. This 75-lap race was exciting, Hunt finally winning by 0.92 sec from Regazzoni. Hunt was still using the M23 McLaren in preference to the newer M26, and he had won a hard struggle, averaging 181.351 kph. Mario Andretti of the U.S. gave a little fresh hope to Lotus by taking third place, and Watson made fastest lap in the Penske to show that his Austrian performance was no fluke.

All eyes were on Lauda when he bravely returned for the Italian Grand Prix at Monza, but he was not quite up to his old form and finished fourth, with Ronnie Peterson of Sweden a happy victor for March in a 761, Regazzoni second for Ferrari, and third place filled by Lafitte for Ligier. A protest, this time over fuel octane ratings, put Hunt's McLaren at the back of the starting grid, and he was forced to retire from the race.

With the teams crossing the Atlantic for the Canadian and U.S. Grand Prix, Hunt had 47 championship points to Lauda's 64. At Mosport, Ont., Hunt drove another superlative race, getting his McLaren home first, ahead of Depailler's Tyrrell and Andretti's Lotus. Lauda was a lap behind, in eighth place. At Watkins Glen, N.Y., Hunt won again, pursued by a Tyrrell, this time in Scheckter's hands, and Lauda. That put Hunt within three points of Lauda, with the Japanese Grand Prix to decide the issue.

The Japanese Grand Prix, the first to be held in that country, started in heavy rain. Hunt led almost all the way until he was obliged, as the weather improved, to stop for a tire change. He reentered in fifth position and worked up to third, which was sufficient to give him the world drivers' championship by one point from Lauda, who retired early in the race because he thought the conditions too dangerous for him to continue. The winner was Mario Andretti, who pulled off the first Lotus win in a grand prix in two years; Depailler was second. Hunt and his Marlboro-McLaren-Ford with its 460 bhp Cosworth-DFV engine, Lucas fuel-injection system, Goodyear tires, and Lockheed brakes, thoroughly deserved their success because earlier in the year Hunt had won the Race of Champions at Brands Hatch and the International Trophy race at Silverstone, both in England. Ferrari won the constructors' championship. Jacky Ickx of Belgium and Gijs Van Lennep of The Netherlands won the 24 Hours of Le Mans in a Porsche 936.

International Rallying. The European rally championship, based on 39 events of varying importance,

James Hunt's Marlboro-McLaren-Ford careens on two wheels in a multicar crash at the British Grand Prix in July. Hunt went on to win but was disqualified.

LONDON DAILY EXPRESS/PICTORIAL PARADE

was won by Bernard Darniche of France, driving a privately entered Lancia Stratos. Lancia Stratos were first, second, and third in the Monte Carlo Rally. The Saab 96 V4s beat an Opel Ascona in the snowy Swedish event, and in Portugal Lancia scored over Toyota and Opel. In the tough East African Safari Rally Japan triumphed, Mitsubishi Lancers taking the first three places from two Peugeot 504s. Japan again won in the Acropolis, a Datsun Violet beating an Alpine Renault 110 in an event with only 34 finishing out of 136. In Morocco two Peugeot 504s vanquished the Munari/Maiga Lancia Stratos combination. Fiat, with a 131, took the Finnish Rally of a Thousand Lakes from a Ford Escort RS1800 and a Toyota Celica. At San Remo, Italy, the Lancia Stratos were back in form, filling the first four places. The Lombard-Royal Automobile Club Rally in Britain was won by a Ford Escort from a Saab 99.

(WILLIAM C. BODDY)

U.S. Racing. Familiar names dominated the complex world of U.S. automobile racing in 1976. Yet there was change, some controversy, and a great deal of extremely close competition.

The Indianapolis 500-mi classic, the world's richest race, went only 255 mi as rain made it the shortest in the Indy's 65-year history. Johnny Rutherford, the winner in a Team McLaren Offenhauser, earned $256,121 from the record $1,037,775 purse, or more than $10,000 a mile. It was Rutherford's second victory at Indianapolis in three years. Runner-up A. J. Foyt, a three-time Indianapolis winner, finished 15 seconds behind in the official standings after United States Auto Club (USAC) officials waited almost 2½ hours before halting the contest. He received $103,296 driving a Coyote of his own design with the Foyt-modified version of the V-8 Ford racing engine. Gordon Johncock placed third.

The Unser brothers, Al and Bobby, split the two lesser jewels of USAC's Triple Crown of 500-mi races. At the three-cornered Pocono International Raceway in Pennsylvania, Al won the Schaefer 500 in the Vel Miletich-Parnelli Jones racing team car powered by the team's own version of the racing Ford V-8. Averaging 143.622 mph, he earned $84,340 in edging Mike Mosely, Wally Dallenbach, and Johnny Rutherford. The race was so close that all finished in the same lap and Unser nipped Mosely by only 3.5 sec.

In the seventh annual California 500 at Ontario, Calif., Bobby Unser became the first two-time winner of that event. He swept from tenth place to nip Rutherford by 2.6 sec, thereby winning $82,986. Third was Johncock.

The season-long USAC national championship was contested to the final race of the season. Al Unser won the Bobby Ball 150 at Phoenix, Ariz., but Johncock by virtue of a second place in the race won the championship over Rutherford, who placed 16th. Meanwhile, Duane (Pancho) Carter, Jr., won his second USAC sprint crown, and Butch Hartman won USAC's stock car title. Sleepy Tripp was the midget car champion, and Billy Cassella the dirt car king.

USAC activity was enlivened by the entry of two women drivers. Arlene Hiss, wife of a driver, competed in a race in Phoenix but thereafter decided to gain experience by campaigning in a stock car. More serious was Janet Guthrie (*see* BIOGRAPHY), who became the first woman to qualify as a driver at Indianapolis. She did not make the starting field after her car was deemed noncompetitive by its owner, but she competed in two USAC races at Trenton, N.J.

KEYSTONE

Britain's Barry Sheene rides his 500-cc Suzuki to victory in the Grand Prix de France in April. He averaged 147 kilometres (88 miles) per hour.

The Winston Cup remained the dominant U.S. season series if total attendance and number of races are the measure. As usual its classic event was the Daytona 500, worth $46,800 to winner David Pearson from Spartanburg, S.C. In a race noted for its close finishes this was one of the closest and most bizarre. Pearson and Richard Petty touched and spun wildly into the infield grass 300 yd from the end of the race. Pearson then restarted his Purolator Mercury and crept across the finish line as Petty watched helplessly.

It was an exceptionally competitive season on the National Association for Stock Car Auto Racing (NASCAR) circuit. Pearson amassed ten victories but was not in contention for the Winston Cup because he skipped contests on smaller tracks. Petty won only three times yet contested the season title with Cale Yarborough, who returned to the limelight with nine victories in his Holley Farms Chevelle. The winner was decided at the Times 500 at Ontario, Calif. It was Yarborough, who earned enough points for the championship even though a burned clutch forced him out of the race after 420 mi.

Pearson, however, won the triple crown of stock car racing. Besides Daytona, he finally won the Southern 500 at Darlington, S.C., and also the longest race, the World 600-mi at Charlotte, N.C. It remained, however, for Buddy Baker to set a world record for a 500-mi race. At Talladega, Ala., he averaged 169.887 mph in his Norris Ford.

(ROBERT J. FENDELL)

Motorcycles. A new major-class world champion appeared in 1976. In the 500-cc class Barry Sheene of the U.K. on a Suzuki was a clear-cut winner from Teuvo Lansivuori of Finland (Suzuki), with Pat Hennen of the U.S. (Suzuki) third. Walter Villa of Italy (Harley-Davidson) finished first in the 350-cc class, with Johnny Cecotto of Venezuela (Yamaha) second and Charles Mortimer of the U.K. (Yamaha) third. Villa also won the 250-cc title for the third successive year, with Takazumi Katayama of Japan (Yamaha) second and G. Bonera of Italy (Harley-Davidson) third.

In the 125-cc class Pirpaolo Bianchi of Italy, riding a Morbidelli, won from Spanish rider Angel Nieto (Bultaco), with Paolo Pileri of Italy (Morbidelli) third. Nieto, who had won five titles in eight years, claimed the 50-cc crown, with H. Rittberger of West Germany (Kreidler) second and U. Graf of Switzerland (Kreidler) third. Rolf Steinhausen of West Germany drove his König-powered motorcycle to victory in the sidecar class.

In the Formula 750 class, for 1976 granted limited status by the Fédération Internationale Motocycliste but to be accorded world championship rating in 1977, the winner was Victor Palomo of Spain riding a Yamaha. In British national road racing, the senior (500-cc) class winners in the Isle of Man Tourist Trophy (TT) and the Manx Grand Prix were Tom Herron of the U.K. and Les Trotter of the U.K., respectively. Steve Baker of the U.S., riding a Yamaha, won the main event at the John Player-sponsored Grand Prix at Silverstone and the Race of the Year at Mallory Park.

In motocross, in the 500-cc class Roger de Coster of Belgium won the title for the fifth time for Suzuki; Heikki Mikkola of Finland (Husqvarna) was the 250-cc winner; and Gastin Rahier of Belgium took the 125-cc title. The European 1,000-cc sidecar class was won by the Swiss team driving a Norton Wasp. In the major team contest, the Moto Cross des Nations, the standings were Belgium first, The Netherlands second, and West Germany third.

(CYRIL J. AYTON)

See also Water Sports.
[452.B.4.c]

Mountaineering

In the Alps during the summer of 1975 new difficult routes included a direct route on the north face of the Pic Sans Nom, a line left of the Davaille route on the north face of Les Droites, a route by the south pillar of the Pointe Sud on the south face of the Aiguille d'Argentière, and a route left of the Dülfer route on the east face of the Fleischbank. Particularly difficult ascents were made left of the Gervasutti-Devies route on the northwest face of the Ailefroide, left of the Laurendau-Kemp route on the north face of the Aiguille de Bionnassay, and up the Lagarde-Segogne couloir on the north face of the Aiguille de Plan. In 1976 no less than four new routes were made on the north face of the Grandes Jorasses: left of the Shroud, on the right flank of the Walker Spur, direct up the Croz Spur, and direct to Punta Margherita. New routes in Norway made by Norwegian and British parties were on Store Vengetind in Romsdal, Vesle Galdhøpiggen in Jotunheimen, and Skalnut in Hemsedal.

In Africa in 1975 new ascents were made on the northeast face of Nyabubuya on Ruwenzori, the south face of Batian on Mt. Kenya, and on the Breach wall of Kibo and the Kersten Glacier on Kilimanjaro. In 1976 another new route was made on the Kersten Glacier, and others took place on the Ollier Couloir, the northeast buttress of Batian, the Diamond Buttress and southeast face of Nelion on Mt. Kenya, and the west ridge of Alexandra on Ruwenzori.

Pre-monsoon new ascents in the Himalayas in 1975 included Churen Himal west ridge by Japanese climbers. Post-monsoon ascents were: Makalu south face by Yugoslavians; Dunagiri north face by British; Sickle Moon by Indians after a disastrous Japanese attempt; Trisul by a U.S. team, one member of which was killed; Kwangde by Nepalese; and three peaks around Uttari Rishi Glacier, namely Garhwal (Japanese), Devistan (Japanese), and Brammah 2 (Japanese). Ascents before the monsoon in 1976 included: Jannu north face (Japanese); Makalu south spur (Czechoslovakians); Everest by South Col (British Army party, one member killed); Annapurna 4 south face (West Germans); Lamjung Himal east ridge (Japanese); and Changabang southwest ridge (Japanese). After the monsoon Nanda Devi was ascended from the north (U.S.). The 1975 pre-monsoon ascents in Karakoram included Chogolisa south face (Japanese), Chorta Kangri (British), Pyramid Peak (British), Malubiting Central (Japanese), Teram Kangri (Japanese), Grand Cathedral (Italians), Liara (Japanese), and Purian Sar (Japanese). No new ascents were reported in the post-monsoon period. In the pre-monsoon season of 1976 new ascents included Trango Tower (British), Paiju (Pakistanis), and Singri Kangri (Japanese). In the Hindu Kush in 1975 the Italians climbed the west spur of Tirich Mir.

The new ascents in New Zealand during the winter of 1975 included the Tasman face of Balfour, Whiplash Gully on Mt. Jagged east face (Arrowsmith Range), and Alarm south face (Kaikoura Range). In the summer of 1975–76 there were climbs on Hicks north rib, Teichelmann southwest face, Malaspina, Aspiring south face, and Karetai east face.

Ascents in Greenland in 1975 were: Ingolsfjeld south face (British); Apostelens Tommelsfinger south pillar (French); Ketil west face and south face (both French); Nalumassurtok south face and east arête (both French); Staunings Alps traverse from Kap Petersen to Syd Kap (British); Trillingerne Towers group, various ascents (Anglo-Danish); mountains east of Quinquedalen, various ascents (Irish); and Søndre Sermilikfjord area, various ascents (British, Royal Air Force). In the same year Mt. Asgard northwest face and other good routes, and in 1976 Overlord northwest face right-hand pillar, were climbed by British parties.

The Himalayas loom above the fog, viewed by members of the American Bicentennial Everest Expedition in August, from their camp at 13,900 feet.

WIDE WORLD

In Alaska and the Yukon 1976 climbs included McKinley by new direct south face route (British), Huntington west ridge (Japanese), North Hess northwest face, and Middle Triple Peak west face in the Kichatna Spires. In Canada in 1976 new routes were established on the north faces of Temple and Fay.

In the U.S. several new winter ascents in the Cascades were made in 1975–76. During the summer of 1976 new routes were established in the Sierra Nevada.

In the Andes in 1975 Japanese and U.S. parties made new climbs in Alpamayo. Other new routes were on Jancarurish, Uruashraju, Raurapalca, Cerro Catedral, Hualcán, and Cerro Potosí. Torre Egger, Cerro Fitzroy east pillar, and Aguja Pollone in Patagonia were climbed in 1975–76. (JOHN NEILL)

[452.B.5.d]

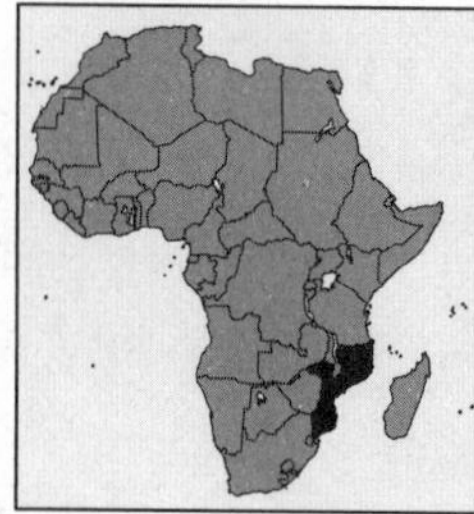

Mozambique

An independent African state, the People's Republic of Mozambique is located on the southeast coast of Africa, bounded by the Indian Ocean, Tanzania, Malawi, Zambia, Rhodesia, South Africa, and Swaziland. Area: 308,642 sq mi (799,380 sq km). Pop. (1976 est.): 9,454,000. Cap. and largest city: Maputo (Lourenço Marques; pop., 1970, 354,700). Language: Bantu languages predominate; Portuguese is also spoken. Religion: traditional beliefs 70%, Christian about 15%, Muslim 13%, with Hindu, Buddhist, and Jewish minorities. President in 1976, Samora Machel.

An attempted coup in December 1975 was thwarted by the government, and during the early months of 1976 those responsible were rounded up. Members of the Jehovah's Witnesses sect were also imprisoned because they refused to accept Marxist doctrines, which the government was attempting to introduce. Resistance to the government continued sporadically through the year, mainly because the peasant society, which comprised the greater portion of the population, found it difficult to respond to the collectivist methods by which the government sought to revive the country's economy, particularly in agriculture. The departure of more than three-quarters of the former Portuguese residents had deprived the country of needed skills and technology, a lack that was notably apparent in the delay in completing the Cabora Bassa Dam. This latter project was held up mainly through lack of supplies because the transport system had depended heavily upon the Portuguese for its operation. An additional problem arose from the destruction of a vital bridge on one of the main supply routes by Rhodesian troops raiding over the border.

Aid was forthcoming from a number of countries, notably China, which supplied doctors and medical stores. In May, however, President Machel visited the U.S.S.R. and entered into a cultural and technical agreement, as a result of which Soviet participation in Mozambique's affairs increased. Soviet geologists arrived to assist in surveying the mineral resources of the Zambezi Valley, and doctors came to strengthen the medical services. The Soviet government also agreed to send teachers and equipment for 16 schools, and Soviet technicians began construction of a runway for heavy aircraft at Bazaruto, a strategically important location near the coast between Beira and Maputo (Lourenço Marques until February 3). Visits to Mozambique by Presidents Julius Nyerere and Kenneth Kaunda resulted in agreements to create economic development commissions with Tanzania and Zambia, respectively, which, it was hoped, would improve communications between Mozambique and its neighbours. Earlier, Zambia had sent doctors and other medical personnel; Tanzania was training Mozambican troops. Meanwhile, crash courses were introduced to train Mozambican students to fill the gaps in the various technical services left by the Portuguese.

Relations with Rhodesia took a turn for the worse in March. Hitherto the Mozambican government had avoided becoming deeply involved in the sanctions campaign against Rhodesia because of the adverse economic effects any such action might have upon Mozambique itself. On March 3, however, in response to an attack upon a border village by Rhodesian air and ground troops, President Machel ordered the closing of the border with Rhodesia and the imposition of sanctions, coupled with the confiscation of Rhodesian property in Mozambique. A month earlier he had urged his people to be prepared to join the guerrillas operating against Rhodesian Prime Minister Ian Smith's regime if this became necessary, but his decision on sanctions was likely to have a much more immediate effect on Mozambique. At the Commonwealth conference in May 1975, however, the countries of the Commonwealth had agreed to give assistance to Mozambique if this were required, and immediately upon receiving news of the sanctions, Britain offered to give financial support and other Commonwealth countries also discussed means of honouring their pledge. In June Mozambique itself launched raids over the Rhodesian border which were said to be in response to Rhodesian incursions in the opposite direction.

MOZAMBIQUE

Education. (1971–72) Primary, pupils 469,351, teachers (1970–71) 6,855; secondary (1970–71), pupils 26,668, teachers 1,431; vocational (1970–71), pupils 15,031, teachers 1,016; teacher training (1970–71), students 1,169, teachers 114; higher (1970–71), students 1,982, teaching staff 193.

Finance and Trade. Monetary unit: Mozambique escudo, at par with the Portuguese escudo, with (Sept. 20, 1976) a free rate of 31.10 escudos to U.S. $1 (53.60 escudos = £1 sterling). Budget (1973 actual): revenue 11,789,000,000 escudos; expenditure 11,682,000,000 escudos. Foreign trade (1974): imports 11,741,000,000 escudos; exports 7,559,000,000 escudos. Import sources: South Africa 20%; Portugal 17%; West Germany 14%; Japan 7%; U.K. 6%; U.S. 6%; France 5%; Saudi Arabia 5%. Export destinations: Portugal 33%; U.S. 11%; South Africa 9%; India 6%; The Netherlands 5%. Main exports: cashew nuts (1973) 22%; cotton 20%; sugar 10%; minerals 6%; vegetable oils 5%.

Transport and Communications. Roads (1974) 39,173 km. Motor vehicles in use (1972): passenger 89,300; commercial (including buses) 21,500. Railways: (1974) 4,161 km; traffic (1973) 396 million passenger-km, freight 3,400,000,000 net ton-km. Ships entered (1974) vessels totaling 11,509,000 net registered tons; goods loaded 10,038,000 metric tons, unloaded 3,989,000 metric tons. Telephones (Dec. 1974) 56,000. Radio licenses (Dec. 1973) 176,000. Television receivers (Dec. 1974) 1,000.

Agriculture. Production (in 000; metric tons; 1975): corn *c.* 250; sorghum *c.* 180; cassava (1974) *c.* 2,160; peanuts *c.* 120; sugar, raw value 210; copra *c.* 65; bananas (1974) *c.* 68; cashew nuts (1974) *c.* 204; tea *c.* 17; cotton, lint *c.* 25; sisal *c.* 23. Livestock (in 000; 1974): cattle *c.* 2,250; sheep *c.* 250; goats *c.* 910; pigs *c.* 280.

Industry. Production (in 000; metric tons; 1974): petroleum products 485; cement 465; bauxite 2; electricity (kw-hr) 747,000.

President Machel joined with Presidents Nyerere, Kaunda, and Sir Seretse Khama of Botswana in attempting to bring diplomatic pressure upon the Smith regime and in trying to induce African party leaders in Rhodesia to agree to a uniform policy for the achievement of majority rule there. Machel's influence in these discussions was particularly important because the main Rhodesian guerrilla bases were in Mozambique, because he was believed by the black African Rhodesian leaders to be uncompromising in his attitude toward the Smith regime, and because of the sacrifice his country made in bearing the burden imposed by its acceptance of the policy of sanctions against Rhodesia. (KENNETH INGHAM)

[978.E.8.b.iv]

Museums

Financial problems continued to plague museums in the Western world in 1976, as the combined effects of inflation and recession pushed prices up and incomes down. In Britain, where cuts in government expenditure were particularly severe, publicly maintained museums faced reductions in staff and resources. The Victoria and Albert Museum and the Science Museum in London were to lose a fair proportion of their staff, and as a result the Victoria and Albert was obliged to abandon its existing regional extension services. A number of important projects in Scotland were also abandoned, although it was hoped that a new gallery to house the Burrell Collection in Glasgow would still be fitted into the curtailed building program. Financial problems were also a major source of concern in the U.S., where museums both large and small were curtailing services and instituting mandatory entrance fees. The Minneapolis (Minn.) Institute of Arts and the Worcester (Mass.) Art Museum began charging fees, and at the Art Institute of Chicago, where a fee was already in effect, a curtailment of hours was averted only through municipal and private grants. In Philadelphia the newly renovated Museum of Art made major service cuts in an effort to balance its budget.

The Museum of Modern Art, New York City, had been forced to take about $1 million from its endowment annually since 1969 to cover its operating expenses, partially as a result of the Rockefeller family's gradual withdrawal from its almost traditional role as the museum's benefactor. To ensure an adequate source of income in the future, the museum announced an intricate plan to construct a 40-story condominium complex on a portion of its air rights and adjacent properties in central Manhattan. The planned structure was approved by the city of New York late in the year.

Further examples of nontraditional attempts to deal with current conditions were seen in two U.S. exhibitions. The Guggenheim Museum, New York City, presented "Acquisition Priorities: Postwar Painting in America," where works already in the permanent collections were placed alongside works being considered for purchase. At the Everson Museum of Art in Syracuse, N.Y., viewers of "Panorama of American Art" could contribute a dollar and vote for the painting or sculpture in the exhibition that they felt the museum should purchase. These gestures were especially significant because the funding basis for many U.S. museums had been shifting to the public sector.

Several U.S. museums did receive substantial grants during the year. The Brown Foundation of Houston, Texas, pledged $11.8 million to the Houston Museum of Fine Arts over the next ten years with the stipulation that the museum raise an additional $9.8 million. The Detroit Institute of Arts received $3.5 million from the city of Detroit and the state of Michigan and planned to open five days a week without a fee. The Art Museum at Princeton University received a $2.5 million bequest, specifically for acquisition, from the Fowler McCormick estate, and in St. Louis, Mo., the Art Museum was given a $1 million matching fund gift for construction by a local manufacturer. Two large federally funded grants were awarded by the Arts Museum Restoration Program of the National Endowment for the Arts: $2 million to the Boston Museum of Fine Arts for a climate control system, provided an additional $8 million was raised; and $500,000 to the Baltimore (Md.) Museum of Art as part of its fund-raising campaign.

Despite financial difficulties, there was a steadily increasing interest in and expenditure on audiovisual presentation in museums, especially in North America. Although slide tape presentations were expensive to install and maintain, it was felt that their usefulness as interpretative tools often justified their cost. The trend toward increased specialization also continued, as did the growth in popularity of technology

KATHERINE YOUNG

The plane in which Charles A. Lindbergh flew the Atlantic in 1927 is displayed in the Smithsonian Institution's mammoth National Air and Space Museum which opened in July in Washington, D.C. The exhibits range from the first Wright Brothers plane to an atomic bomb and a moon rock.

and local history as basic themes. In Britain, a new gas gallery was opened in London's Science Museum. Financed in part by the British Gas Corporation, it presented a picture of the modern gas industry, tracing its growth from the early 19th century. The display included a full-scale representation of the drilling floor of a typical North Sea gas rig. A national collection on the history of medicine was established and loaned to the Science Museum, where it was to be housed in a gallery already under construction.

The Gladstone Pottery Museum, which opened in 1974 at Longton, Stoke-on-Trent, Staffordshire, was chosen as Britain's Museum of the Year, 1976. It was particularly impressive in that much of the actual building formed part of the exhibit. Devoted to the history of the ceramics industry, especially that of Staffordshire pottery, it comprised a restored central block of early Victorian factory buildings, including four distinctively shaped brick bottle-ovens, the engine house, sliphouse, and the throwing and casting departments. Live demonstrations formed part of the daily activities and, when feasible, visitors were allowed to handle exhibits. The museum was founded and administered by a charitable trust.

The Gladstone Museum, of course, also celebrated local history, a theme that recurred in the reorganized museum at Quimper in Brittany, France. A separate section was reserved for Breton art, and there was a particularly fine group of paintings by the artists of the Pont-Aven school. Quimper had become one of the most important French provincial museums, with a fine selection of paintings from the 17th century to the present. In June 1976 the buildings of the Joan-Miró Foundation were opened at Barcelona, Spain. The octogenarian artist Miró had created the foundation in 1971, and its translation into a physical entity was an important and internationally celebrated achievement. Partly a museum of Catalan art, the foundation also served as a centre for contemporary local art and as such was unique in Spain.

The Gladstone Pottery Museum at Stoke-on-Trent, Staffordshire, England. Photo shows an early Victorian potbank, with four brick bottle-ovens. The museum won a national prize as Museum of the Year.

ILLUSTRATED LONDON NEWS

Other developments in Europe included the reorganization of the Museum of Antiquities at Saint-Germain-en-Laye, France. The museum covered a large period of prehistory. At the other end of the time spectrum, Concorde 002, the British-built prototype of the Anglo-French supersonic airliner, was put on display at the Fleet Air Arm Museum in Yeovilton, Somerset. The aircraft had been presented to the Science Museum.

The Art Institute of Chicago completed its new East Wing expansion, part of its $46 million funding drive of the past few years. In addition to housing the new facilities of the School of the Art Institute and providing a new auditorium and additional gallery space, the wing would include Louis Sullivan Hall, with a reconstruction of the trading room from the architect's now-demolished Chicago Stock Exchange.

The Metropolitan Museum of Art in New York City reopened 16 galleries in its Egyptian wing, closed for the past 17 years. Also in New York, one of the world's major collections of the decorative arts, the Cooper-Hewitt Museum of Design, moved into its new quarters in a renovated 64-room mansion formerly owned by Andrew Carnegie. The museum had moved from its long-time home in the Cooper Union in 1963 because that institution could no longer afford upkeep of the collection. In 1967 Cooper-Hewitt became a part of the federal museum system within the Smithsonian Institution. At Yale University the four-story Center for British Art and Studies opened. Both the building, a $10 million structure designed by Louis Kahn, and the large collection of British art were the gift of Paul Mellon.

Two important university galleries in the Midwest expanded their facilities. The University of Kansas Museum of Art was constructing a new five-story building—the Helen F. Spencer Museum of Art—to replace the present structure dating from 1894, and the Allen Memorial Art Museum at Oberlin (Ohio) College reopened after construction. One of the major manuscript resources in the world, the Huntington Library in San Marino, Calif., announced a $6 million development program that would include renovation of its main exhibition halls. The San Francisco Museum of Art, the better to define its position among the three large museums in the city, changed its name to the San Francisco Museum of Modern Art.

One of the most satisfactory museum stories of 1976 was the full acceptance, by the local population as well as by foreign visitors, of the magnificent newly opened National Museum of Qatar, which owed its existence to the inspiration and drive of the emir, Sheikh Khalifah ibn Hamad ath-Thani. The core of the museum was the former Amiri Palace in Qatar's capital, Doha, and a new concrete building running along the north wall of the palace grounds was in keeping with the main architectural style. Although much money had been spent in funding foreign archaeological expeditions, and the region was known to be rich in sites, the supply of actual exhibits and artifacts was thin. As a result, there was considerable reliance on replicas and on audiovisual presentations. Work continued throughout the year on the addition of a maritime section to the museum; six newly built but traditionally styled Gulf vessels were anchored in an artificially constructed lagoon.

Museums continued to face problems resulting from the newly coined definitions of legality in the international traffic in antiquities. The Norton Simon Museum of Art, Pasadena, Calif., concluded its dispute with the government of India over an important sculpture of the god Nataraja. While the Indian government would receive title to the work, the Simon Museum could hold it for ten years and would thus be able to display it in the new Asian Art wing. In exchange, India agreed not to contest the Simon Foundation's ownership of art that had been obtained outside India.

Thailand asked the Metropolitan Museum of Art in New York City to return an important bronze statue, ostensibly obtained illegally. Harvard's Peabody Museum returned to the Mexican government a "priceless" treasure of 240 pieces of Mayan jade (*c.* 500–1300 AD). The hoard had been found in a sacrificial well in the late 1800s by a U.S. archaeologist who lived in Mexico. Harvard gave back the treasure, which had been extensively studied and cataloged, even though no laws existed at that time to prevent the export of such works. It was thought that about $1 billion worth of stolen and smuggled art works were currently in circulation. The six-year-old International Foundation for Art Research, a nonprofit organization offering impartial opinions in questions of authenticity, was awarded a grant of $100,000 by the Jerome Foundation in St. Paul, Minn., to study the ramifications of the situation.

Acquisitions. The Fitzwilliam Museum, Cambridge, England, was able to raise sufficient money to prevent the Van Dyck "Virgin and Child" from being exported to the U.S. The painting, which had been on loan to the Fitzwilliam for 16 years, was sold at Christie's in London in July to a U.S. museum for £220,000. An export license was temporarily withheld to allow the Fitzwilliam time to raise a matching sum by public appeal. Earlier in the year the National Gallery in London acquired, as a payment for estate tax, Rembrandt's fine portrait of his mistress, Hendrickje Stoffels. It was suggested that the painting's real value on the open market might have amounted to around £1 million.

The British Museum purchased an important collection of North American Indian Art formed over the last 40 years by Robert Bruce Inverarity of Philadelphia. The collection was especially strong in material from the cultures of the Northwest Coast, and it made the British Museum's collection one of the best of its type in the world. The Rijksmuseum, Amsterdam, acquired "The Musical Party" (1626), an early Rembrandt oil, with help from the Rembrandt Society, the Prince Bernhard Fund, and the Foundation for the Promotion of the Interests of the Rijksmuseum. This was the earliest of Rembrandt's paintings to find its way back to Amsterdam, where the painter did his major work.

The Kimbell Art Museum, Fort Worth, Texas, acquired a major work by Rubens entitled "The Duke of Buckingham." The equestrian portrait was painted in 1625 on a panel measuring $17\frac{1}{2}$ by $19\frac{1}{2}$ in and was considered lost for nearly 300 years. Another work once thought to have been lost, Caravaggio's "The Martyrdom of St. Andrew the Apostle," was acquired by the Cleveland (Ohio) Museum of Art. The dramatic 5-by-7-ft oil, painted about 1607, had dropped from sight for 300 years until it reappeared in Spain

AUTHENTICATED NEWS INTERNATIONAL

A gold mask of Tutankhamen was part of an exhibition of treasures from the tomb of the boy pharaoh that began a tour of the U.S. in November.

in 1973. It was now one of five by the artist in U.S. collections.

The most important contemporary work acquired by a U.S. museum was "Lavender Mist" (1950), a 7-by-10-ft painting by Jackson Pollock, the pioneer American nonrepresentational artist. One of the last major works of Pollock in private hands, it was purchased by the National Gallery of Art, Washington, D.C., for a rumoured $2 million. The Brooklyn Museum exchanged 11 paintings and $200,000 for an important work by the mid-19th-century American landscapist Albert Bierstadt, "Storm in the Rocky Mountains—Mt. Rosalie." The Los Angeles County Museum of Art displayed a portion of the Daumier collection of Armand Hammer, reputedly the world's largest private collection of that artist's works, and then announced that the entire collection had been promised to the museum.

A major graphic art collection, the drawings assembled by the New York dealer Eugene Thaw, was given to the Pierpont Morgan Library there. Also in New York, the Museum of Modern Art acquired the 54-ft-long cutout "The Swimming Pool" by Matisse. Several important works were sold to facilitate the purchase, including Jackson Pollock's "Number 5, 1950." It was thought that this important late work by Matisse would help take the place of Picasso's "Guernica," which, under the terms of the artist's will, would return to Spain should that nation become a democracy. In Canada the Art Gallery of Ontario in Toronto was given a vast collection of the satirical works of Walter Trier, as well as $500,000 for the administration of the gallery in the new wing of the museum where they were to be displayed. In Montreal the Museum of Fine Arts presented a new acquisition, an important painting by Rubens, "The Leopards."

Conservation. Conservation remained an important part of museum administration and a subject of much public interest. The publication *Museum* devoted an issue to conservation in South and Southeast Asia.

At the Rijksmuseum, Amsterdam, the restoration

of Rembrandt's "Night Watch," which had been slashed with a knife in 1975, was successfully completed. The oil was completely relined and cleaned, bringing to light some original colour and new details of costume never before seen in contemporary times. Visitors to the museum were able to watch the progress of the restoration at regular hours each day.

In Athens it was decided to move the remaining three figures on the west pediment of the Parthenon into the Acropolis Museum in order to protect them from further decay caused by weathering and air pollution. They were to be replaced by replicas. Other original features to be removed for conservation were the caryatids—the pillars sculpted as draped female forms. Plans were made for the removal of the museum from the Acropolis itself and for the restoration of the 4th-century BC theatre of Dionysos at the base of the Acropolis, which could then be used for the staging of classical drama.

(JOSHUA B. KIND; SANDRA MILLIKIN)

See also Art and Art Exhibitions; Art Sales.
[613.D.1.b]

Music

The event that caused the greatest stir in the musical world during 1976 was undoubtedly the production of Wagner's *Der Ring des Nibelungen* to mark the centenary of the Bayreuth Festival, created by the composer in 1876 for the presentation in ideal circumstances of this great tetralogy and his other major works. "Ideal" seemed hardly the adjective to describe the performances that took place. Wolfgang Wagner, the composer's grandson, had decided to ask a French team to present a new view of the work. The young producer, Patrice Chéreau (*see* BIOGRAPHY), obviously took him at his word, and placed the four operas firmly in the 19th century—indeed, about the time when Bayreuth was being built, rather than in their usual timeless setting. Wotan appeared in a frock coat; the Rhine maidens were dressed as Victorian tarts; Siegfried appeared at one time in a dinner jacket. The German audience was outraged by what had been done to their sacred works. One commentator jokingly said that this was the final revenge for the French defeat in the Franco-Prussian War. Boos and catcalls were heard at the end of each performance, but Wolfgang remained unperturbed, commenting that his brother Wieland's treatment of the operas in the 1950s had also been considered sacrilegious when first encountered but had later become the norm of Wagnerian productions for more than a decade. Conductor Pierre Boulez, who had been responsible for choosing Chéreau and reportedly made his appearance in the pit conditional on the young man's engagement, conducted a subdued account of the scores that was also received with a good deal of skepticism. Be that as it might, the Chéreau-Boulez *Ring* would be seen and heard again in 1977.

"I've been coming here for 70 years," said Artur Rubinstein, who made his American debut in Carnegie Hall, New York City, in 1906. In March the 89-year-old pianist celebrated his 70th anniversary by giving a recital and unveiling a bust of himself.

WIDE WORLD

A symposium (August 18–20), attended by many musicologists, discussed every aspect of the *Ring* as myth and music. The Bayreuth centenary was also marked by several important books about Wagner and Bayreuth. The most significant were undoubtedly Cosima Wagner's diary and *Wagner: A Documentary Study,* both emanating from Bayreuth. In addition, there was an album of family photographs, containing much previously unavailable material, the reissue of Ernest Newman's *The Life of Richard Wagner* in four paperback volumes, *The Forging of the "Ring"* by Curt von Westernhagen, a revised version of Geoffrey Skelton's book on Wagner at Bayreuth, and the first publication of Andrew Porter's English translation of the *Ring,* finely illustrated by Eric Fraser.

Various other opera houses contributed to the celebrations with new productions of the work. The most interesting of these were at Leipzig and Covent Garden. In Leipzig Joachim Herz fashioned a modern interpretation of the cycle that was reportedly free from the inexperience and eccentricities of Chéreau's reading. In London Götz Friedrich, like Herz a disciple of the late Walter Felsenstein, contributed a demythologizing view more interesting in its detail than in its total effect, as the producer chose to present each of the operas as a separate entity. Colin Davis, who conducted, showed signs of developing into a vital Wagnerian conductor.

The year closed with the sad news of the death on December 4 of Benjamin, recently Lord, Britten, which robbed the world of music of one whom many considered to be the greatest English musician since Henry Purcell and who was probably the best-known outside his own country of British 20th-century composers. Among conductors who died during 1976 were Rudolf Kempe, one of the leading Richard Strauss and Wagner interpreters of his day; Dean Dixon; and Jean Martinon. Among instrumentalists, the cellists Enrico Mainardi and Gregor Piatigorsky and the pianists Alexander Brailowsky and Geza Anda died. The operatic world mourned the loss of Lotte Lehmann, Elisabeth Rethberg, and Lily Pons. The composer Bernard Herrmann, noted for his film scores, died. So did Carrie Tubb, veteran English singer, just after celebrating her 100th birthday. (*See also* OBITUARIES.)

Opera. In the operatic field the most important events besides those at Bayreuth concerned the La Scala Opera Company, Milan. That company enjoyed a successful exchange visit with the Royal Opera, Covent Garden, London, during March. Giorgio

Strehler's production of *Simon Boccanegra* was much admired in London, while Jean-Pierre Ponnelle's *La cenerentola* of Rossini was praised to a slightly lesser extent. Milan praised *Peter Grimes, Benvenuto Cellini,* and *La clemenza di Tito,* none of them precisely a popular favourite but each admired for its sense of an ensemble performance. Then in September La Scala visited Washington, D.C., with Strehler's *Macbeth* and, once more, *La cenerentola.* The company's reception in the U.S. was mixed. The visit was planned as part of the bicentennial celebrations, which also encompassed a season at the Metropolitan Opera in New York by the Paris Opéra, which opened with Sir Georg Solti conducting *Le nozze di Figaro.* On December 7 the opening of the 1976–77 season with *Otello,* conducted by Carlos Kleiber, was marked by demonstrations against the fashionable audience attending the first night.

During the normal seasons at the Metropolitan new productions included Günther Rennert's disappointing *Le nozze di Figaro* (in November 1975), *Aida, Fidelio* (from which Leonard Bernstein withdrew), and Richard Strauss's *Ariadne auf Naxos.* The first new productions of the 1976–77 season were *Lohengrin* and Massenet's *Esclarmonde,* with Joan Sutherland, in November. James Levine, music director, was in charge of the *Lohengrin,* which was produced by August Everding. The New York City Opera suffered from a strike at the beginning of its autumn season, which included a new production of *La Belle Hélène* and Gian-Carlo Menotti's *The Saint of Bleecker Street.*

A significant development over the last few years had been the growing importance of opera companies outside the main centres. The Houston (Texas) Opera presented the premiere of Carlisle Floyd's *Bilby's Doll,* based on a novel about witchcraft trials in late 17th-century Massachusetts, with the composer writing his own libretto. In spite of Catherine Malfitano's fine portrait of Doll Bilby, the opera was not well received. Christopher Keene was the conductor. Sarah Caldwell's Boston Opera did much valiant work of resuscitation and in presenting novelties; for the Bicentennial, the company presented Roger Sessions' *Montezuma.* It seemed hampered by G. Antonio Borgese's limp libretto, and the music was considered rather dense in texture. The Baltimore Opera celebrated its 25th anniversary by giving the premiere of Thomas Pasatieri's *Ines de Castro,* especially commissioned for the occasion. Although only 30, the composer had already written 12 works for the stage. This work, conventional in musical style, was not considered a dramatic success. The central figure of Dom Pedro was sung by Richard Stilwell, a leading U.S. baritone (heard as Count Almaviva at the Metropolitan and as Ford at Glyndebourne, among other appearances). Keene was again the conductor.

Dallas, a company that once tempted Maria Callas to perform with it, stayed with more conventional fare and usually included leading personalities in one or another of their most sympathetic roles. Such, in December 1975, was Jon Vickers as Tristan, and later in the season Renata Scotto as the most compelling Anna Bolena in Donizetti's opera of that name since Callas herself, worthily supported by Tatiana Troyanos as Jane Seymour. The first performance of Alfredo Kraus in the title role of *Les Contes d'Hoffmann* completed Dallas' tally of eloquent portrayals.

In Britain, at Covent Garden, apart from the *Ring,* there were the premiere in July 1976 of Hans Werner Henze's (*see* BIOGRAPHY) controversial *We Come to the River,* with libretto by Edward Bond; the first performance of the revised version of Sir William Walton's *Troilus and Cressida,* with Dame Janet Baker as Cressida; and a new production of *Ariadne auf Naxos.* The English National Opera at the Coliseum presented at the end of 1975 a realistic production of *Salome,* staged by Herz, with Josephine Barstow in the title role. During the 1976–77 season there was a new production of *Don Giovanni* and then a production, the work of the New Opera Company, of Alberto Ginastera's *Bomarzo,* that lurid work's first performance in Europe. The Welsh National Opera in Cardiff presented a memorable production of Michael Tippett's *The Midsummer Marriage* in September, and the Scottish Opera a controversial staging of Verdi's *Macbeth* for the Edinburgh Festival.

Glyndebourne featured a new production of *Falstaff,* designed and staged by Ponnelle, and a disastrous *Pelléas et Mélisande.* The English Music Theatre Company got off the ground with the premiere of Stephen Oliver's *Tom Jones* at the Brighton Festival in May and the first performance since 1941 of the

BERNARD GOTFRYD—NEWSWEEK

Milan's La Scala opera company played in Washington in September. Photo shows a scene from "La cenerentola," Rossini's version of the Cinderella story. Paolo Montarsolo is the blustering stepfather, flanked by the stepsisters.

JACK MANNING—THE NEW YORK TIMES

The New York Philharmonic played its first concert in the reconstructed Avery Fisher Hall in October. Formerly Philharmonic Hall, it had proved an acoustical disaster when it first opened in 1962. The new hall received high praise.

Britten-Auden operetta *Paul Bunyan*, given at the Aldeburgh Festival. The company also presented more-or-less successful stagings of *The Threepenny Opera;* Mozart's rarely heard *La finta giardiniera*, here called *Sandrina's Secret;* Rossini's *Cinderella* (*La cenerentola*); and Britten's *The Turn of the Screw*. The same Britten work was one of the successes of the Wexford Festival along with rare revivals of Otto Nicolai's *The Merry Wives of Windsor* and Verdi's *Giovanna d'Arco*. Kent Opera, one of Britain's burgeoning young companies, gave an evocative new production, by Jonathan Miller, of Monteverdi's *Orfeo* at the Bath Festival. Roger Norrington, the company's musical director, presented a new and authentic edition of the score, which used the soloists as chorus too, as happened in early performances of the work at the Mantuan court.

At the Vienna State Opera, Otto Schenk produced *Boris Godunov* with Nicolai Ghiaurov in the title role. Ulrich Baumgartner produced *La clemenza di Tito* at the Theater-an-der-Wien in May. The new regime (with Egon Seefehlner as administrator) and the 1976–77 season began on September 1 with a gala performance of *Don Carlos*. Montserrat Caballé was Queen Elisabeth, Ghiaurov King Philip, Josephine Veasey the Eboli, and Piero Cappuccilli the Posa. The same opera, again with Ghiaurov and Cappuccilli, was revived at the Salzburg Festival with Herbert von Karajan as conductor and producer. The festival's new production was *La clemenza di Tito*, very much the year's leading Mozart opera, now wholly restored to favour. It was produced by Ponnelle and conducted by Levine. The 1973 production of *Idomeneo* by Gustav Sellner was revived with veteran Karl Böhm as conductor. At the Salzburg Easter Festival, Herbert von Karajan produced and conducted *Lohengrin*.

At the Deutsche Oper in West Berlin, Zubin Mehta (*see* BIOGRAPHY) conducted a new production of Puccini's *La fanciulla del West*, Dietrich Fischer-Dieskau sang his long-awaited first Hans Sachs in *Die Meistersinger von Nürnberg*, conducted by Eugen Jochum, and the first German performance of *We Come to the River* was given. At the Munich Festival, Josef Tal's *Die Versuchung* had its first performance, and Leos Janacek's *From the House of the Dead*, conducted by Rafael Kubelik, was revived. The 25th Handel Festival took place at Halle in East Germany, and the composer's rarely seen operas *Faramondo, Imeneo*, and *Deidamia* were performed. To celebrate the 150th anniversary of Weber's death, his opera *Euryanthe* was given in concert form at his birthplace, Eutin, in Schleswig-Holstein, and his *Abu Hassan* and *Der Freischütz* were staged. Large-scale commemorations of Weber took place at Dresden during June in a series of *Weber-Tage*, which included several concerts. At the Staatsoper, Horst Seeger produced *Der Freischütz;* then the same work was given in the open air at Rathen, produced by Joachim Schech with literal fidelity to Weber's score. At the Kleines Haus in Dresden, *Peter Schmoll und seine Nachbarn* and *Abu Hassan* were given.

At Amsterdam, as part of the Holland Festival, The Netherlands Opera gave the first European performance of Floyd's *Of Mice and Men*. A day later Martti Talvela sang the title role in a new production of *Boris Godunov* at Strasbourg. At the Paris Opéra the season's major production was *Otello* produced by Terry Hands and conducted by Solti. This production was later taken to Washington, D.C., and New York. Placido Domingo sang the title role in Paris, and Carlo Cossutta in the U.S. In December a new *Ring* cycle began, controversially produced by Peter Stein, conducted by Solti. At the Festival of Lyric Art and Music at Aix-en-Provence, Sylvia Sass, a rising star from Hungary, sang Violetta in a new production of *La Traviata*, and Richard Stilwell the title role in *Don Giovanni*. At the Roman Theatre at Arles as part of the same festival Leonie Rysanek sang her famous Medea in Luigi Cherubini's *Médée*.

The Maggio Musicale at Florence gave Henze's *König Hirsch* (in Italian as *Il re cervo*) and Paul Dessau's *Einstein* their first Italian performances, but most praise was reserved for Gluck's *Orfeo ed Euridice* in the original Viennese version, produced by Luca Ronconi and conducted by Riccardo Muti. Julia Hamari and Ileana Cotrubas sang the title roles. At the Spoleto Festival, Filippo Sanjust designed and produced Tchaikovsky's *Queen of Spades* (given in Italian), and Viktor Ullmann's 30-year-old *Der Kaiser von Atlantis*, given its premiere the previous December at Amsterdam, was also heard. Montserrat Caballé revived Donizetti's *Gemma di Vergy* for the first time this century at Naples. She sang it also in various other centres during the season. Naples gave the premiere of Nino Rota's *Torquemada*, and at Rome the Teatro dell'Opera gave the premiere of the same composer's *Aladino e la lampada magica* and presented Leos Janacek's *Jenufa*. At Milan Carlos Kleiber conducted a new production of *Der Rosenkavalier* at La Scala. At Venice, the Teatro la Fenice, Manno Wolf-Ferrari conducted a new production of his uncle's opera *La vedova scaltra* to mark the centenary of the composer's birth. Verona Arena began its season with a new production of *Boris Godunov*.

Symphonic Music. Chiefly in celebration of the Bicentennial, a number of new works were given their first performance in the U.S. Among these were Mario Davidovsky's *Synchronism 7* for electronics and instruments, given by the New York Philharmonic under Boulez; Lukas Foss's *Folksong* for full orchestra by the Baltimore Symphony; Roy Harris' 14th Symphony by the Washington National Symphony under Antal Dorati; Roger Sessions' *When Lilacs Last in the Dooryard Bloom'd* and Alan Stout's 2½-hour *Pas-*

PHOTOS, AUTHENTICATED NEWS INTERNATIONAL

Pianist Paul Shenly, harpist Heidi Lehwalder, and violinist Ani Kavafian were recipients of the first Avery Fisher Prizes in February. Another recipient was pianist Ursula Oppens. The awards are noncompetitive, given by recommendation, and include $1,000 each, an appearance with the New York Philharmonic, and six appearances with other U.S. orchestras.

sion at Chicago; Peter Mennin's *Voices* by Frederica von Stade and the Chamber Music Society of Lincoln Center; John Cage's *Renga* played with *Apartment House 1776* for four voices and orchestra by the Boston Symphony under Seiji Ozawa; and new pieces by Miklos Rosza, Gunther Schuller, and Ulysses Kay by the Washington National.

In his laudable crusade on behalf of modern music, Lorin Maazel with the Cleveland Orchestra gave at various times a program of Boris Blacher's music, one of Luciano Berio's, and the premiere of British composer Raymond Premru's specially commissioned *Concerto for Orchestra.* In New York City a nine-day festival of 20th-century music began on March 5. At the Kennedy Center in Washington, D.C., there was a year-long Bicentennial Parade of American Music. Riccardo Muti was appointed principal guest conductor of the Philadelphia Orchestra, and gave Menotti's first symphony its premiere at Saratoga Springs, N.Y. Other events of importance were the visit of the legendary Soviet pianist Lazar Berman for his first tour of the U.S., and a "Concert Celebration" on the 85th birthday of Carnegie Hall to promote a national endowment fund for the hall. At the latter, Isaac Stern (moving force in the affair), Yehudi Menuhin, Mstislav Rostropovich, Dietrich Fischer-Dieskau, Vladimir Horowitz, Leonard Bernstein, and Carnegie executive director Julius Bloom joined together to sing the Hallelujah Chorus from Handel's *Messiah.* On October 19 the Avery Fisher Hall was reopened in Lincoln Center after being completely gutted and rebuilt to improve its acoustics. If the Mahler month that its reopening inaugurated was a guide, the effort and expense had been worthwhile.

In London, after the considerable stir caused the previous year when John Boyden, then general manager of the London Symphony Orchestra (LSO), allegedly attacked the orchestra's habits while on tour and its musical director, André Previn, for being overpaid, Boyden was replaced by the more diplomatic Michael Kaye. Previn remained, but he was now supported by veteran Eugen Jochum, whose title was "conductor laureate"; Colin Davis carried on as principal guest conductor along with Claudio Abbado. The orchestra, on its better days, maintained its high reputation. Meanwhile, the London Philharmonic Orchestra (LPO) continued to stay at the peak of its form under its principal conductor, Bernard Haitink, and its chief guests, Solti, Daniel Barenboim, and Carlo Maria Giulini. In October at the start of the 1976–77 season it also gave a memorable series, including all the Tchaikovsky symphonies under Rostropovich, who had been appointed chief of the Washington National during the course of the year and intended to conduct as much as he played his cello. The New Philharmonia Orchestra (NPO), under new and youthful management, was the capital's most improved orchestra with dynamic Muti as its principal conductor. The Royal Philharmonic, under Dorati (who had moved from the Washington National), was in a state of change. The LSO and NPO visited Mexico, and the LPO went to the U.S. The British Broadcasting Company (BBC) Symphony Orchestra mourned the loss of its recently appointed principal conductor, Rudolf Kempe (*see* OBITUARIES), and replaced him with Charles Mackerras, who was to relinquish his post as musical director of the English National Opera.

During the year London was visited by the Berlin and Vienna Philharmonics and the Orchestre de Paris, which also appeared at the Edinburgh Festival along with the Vienna Philharmonic and the much-praised Leipzig Gewandhaus Orchestra. The Promenade Concerts continued to be a festival of concerts all on its own, while the contemporaneous South Bank Summer Music, under Neville Marriner's astute direction, provided a varied and well-liked series of chamber concerts at the Queen Elizabeth Hall. In Glasgow a

WIDE WORLD

Old Dixleland jazz holds a rapt audience in New Orleans' Preservation Hall. Homer Eugene (left) plays trombone with banjoist Emmanuel Sayles.

Musica Nova series was held during September. The Festival Hall in London celebrated its 25th anniversary in May with a dozen concerts given by many old friends and some distinguished guests. The festivities were launched by BBC Television, which provided from its archives of tapes a compendium of performances by great artists such as Otto Klemperer, Igor Stravinsky, David Oistrakh, and Maria Callas. In the hall itself there was an interesting but not very imaginatively presented exhibition of the hall's beginnings and history. Of the celebratory programs themselves, outstanding were the recitals by Clifford Curzon and Janet Baker and the concert by the Berlin Philharmonic, at least as far as Karajan's conducting of Richard Strauss's *Ein Heldenleben* was concerned. Another event of note on London's South Bank during the year was the World of Islam Festival, including programs by groups from the Indian subcontinent, from Morocco, and from Iraq.

For various reasons musical life in Australia was a burgeoning industry. The main one was the existence of the Sydney Opera House with its 2,700-seat concert hall and 1,550-seat opera theatre, but also important were the Musica Viva Society and the Arts Theatre in Adelaide. Under Richard Bonynge, its new musical director, the Australian Opera completed a successful summer season with four new productions during January and February: *Così fan tutte, Albert Herring, Salome,* and a double bill of Stravinsky's *Les Noces* and Orazio Vecchi's *L'Amfiparnaso*. The company's season in Melbourne during March–May included *Simon Boccanegra* and Janacek's *The Cunning Little Vixen* in its repertory, while at the Adelaide Festival of Arts in March the company gave the first Australian performances of Alban Berg's *Wozzeck*. The New Opera Company's presentations at Adelaide between July and November included *La Bohème* and *Il matrimonio segreto*.

Between them the Musica Viva Society and the Australian Broadcasting Commission (ABC) arranged most of the concerts, with Musica Viva bringing over groups such as the Amadeus Quartet and the Academy of St.-Martin-in-the-Fields. A privately run organization, Musica Viva received a government subsidy. ABC arranged as many as 800 concerts a year throughout the country.

The record industry continued to flourish, with growing emphasis on comprehensive boxes of a composer's output in a particular field. Meanwhile, the exploration of neglected works continued apace. In Philips/Phonogram's series of early Verdi operas, *Il corsaro,* based on Byron's *The Corsair,* was included. The same company began a series of Haydn operas, in collaboration with the European Broadcasting Commission, with *La fedeltà premiata,* conducted by Dorati, who had been responsible for the successful complete Haydn symphonies for Decca. John McCabe continued his marathon task of recording all the Haydn piano sonatas, and the Aeolian Quartet was close to completing its version of all the Haydn quartets. The Bayreuth celebrations brought forth a plethora of Wagner issues, among them rival versions of *Die Meistersinger von Nürnberg* conducted by Solti and Jochum with Norman Bailey and Fischer-Dieskau, respectively, as Hans Sachs. Deutsche Grammophon and Electrola (EMI's German label) brought out several volumes of historical reissues of performances by famous Wagnerian singers and conductors of the past. Janet Baker recorded her long-awaited version of *Das Lied von der Erde,* with James King as the tenor soloist and Bernard Haitink conducting the Amsterdam Concertgebouw. Fischer-Dieskau continued his recording of all the Hugo Wolf lieder. Verdi's *Macbeth* appeared in two rival versions, one conducted by Abbado, a souvenir of the Scala performances, and another conducted by Muti. The companies were also beginning to explore the huge field of French opera. Decca issued Joan Sutherland in *Esclarmonde,* a remembrance of her San Francisco and Metropolitan performances in the opera, and CBS

(Columbia Records in the U.S.) revived Gustave Charpentier's *Louise,* with Cotrubas in the title role and Domingo as her lover Julien.

(ALAN BLYTH)

Jazz. The extent to which gloom continued to pervade the jazz scene might be conveyed by the fact that not even the most rampant progressive would care to deny that all the events of any great significance during 1976 were of a posthumous nature. While the embarrassing absence of new younger players of unquestioned talent continued as it had done throughout the decade, the older masters became a little older, a few of them died, and the population of jazz's tiny principality therefore shrank still further. The blight had lasted for so long that several theorists applied themselves to the task of asking why, and doing what they could to provide an answer.

What seemed to have happened to the music was that it was caught between the twin pincers of technical complexity and social expediency. Ever since the great modernist movements of the 1940s jazz had been in danger of isolating itself from appreciation by laymen. But what was much more serious from the aesthetic viewpoint was the fact that since the innovations of such members of that generation as Charlie Parker and Dizzy Gillespie the harmonic load to be borne by the soloist had become a very nearly intolerable encumbrance. The music lost much of its old buoyancy and carefree effect, and this decline, in conjunction with the rise of a new consumer group too young and undiscerning to be able to follow the subtleties of a Duke Ellington score or a Parker solo, left a strong impression that jazz might after all prove to be a finite art.

This predicament was eloquently expressed in the marketplace, where the music remained commercially viable but only by leaning strongly on the posthumous elements of its appeal. During the year there were several major events in the recording industry, and one in particular would be seen in the future as among the most valuable of the last 20 years. Ever since his death in 1956, the pianist Art Tatum, arguably the greatest solo virtuoso that jazz had ever produced, had been conspicuous in most record catalogs by his absence. The deletion many years ago of his masterpieces had remained a grievance among connoisseurs ever since, and a particular bone of contention had been the series he concluded shortly before his death for the concert and recording impresario Norman Granz. During the year Granz, continuing his comeback in the recording business, reacquired the historic series of 21 long-playing albums that Tatum had made for him in the 1950s. The 13 solo piano albums, without question the most sustained burst of virtuosity ever preserved on record, were issued as a boxed set on the Pablo label, and these were followed later in the year by another set of the remaining eight albums showing Tatum working with a variety of small groups. From the moment the 21 Pablo albums became available, Tatum's art, in all its complexity, was there to be analyzed and evaluated. He would no doubt prove to have been one of the most extraordinary musicians of any kind who surfaced in the 20th century, with his baroque embellishments never quite obscuring the earthy foundations of his style.

Nothing appeared during the year, either in concert or on record, to challenge the might of Tatum, but it was during 1976 that the last albums ever made by two other dead giants, Ellington and Coleman Hawkins, were released. Of the Hawkins album, one could repeat what George Bernard Shaw once said of Dickens' *The Mystery of Edwin Drood,* that it was "a gesture by a man already three-quarters dead," but the Ellington farewell, a quartet recording entitled "Duke's Big Four," was an astonishing gesture by a man in his 70s and within months of death. The only comparable gesture in the year was that achieved by another veteran pianist, Count Basie, who, in his 70s and victim of a heart attack during the summer (from which he later recovered fully), turned up several times on small group recordings, playing the blues with a wit and sly cunning undiminished by the years.

As in recent years many jazz musicians died in 1976, although the most famous name in the year's obituary columns, that of Connee Boswell, was, strictly speaking, not a jazz name at all. Boswell (*see* OBITUARIES) was one of those singers whose commercial affiliations did not prevent her from being influenced benignly by jazz music in her emergent years. As part of the vocal trio the Boswell Sisters, she recorded with such jazzmen as Benny Goodman and Don Redman, and would also be remembered as being the prime influence on Ella Fitzgerald. Another singer who died during the year was blues specialist Victoria Spivey. Among the instrumentalists who passed away were trombonist Quentin Jackson, who had played for McKinney's

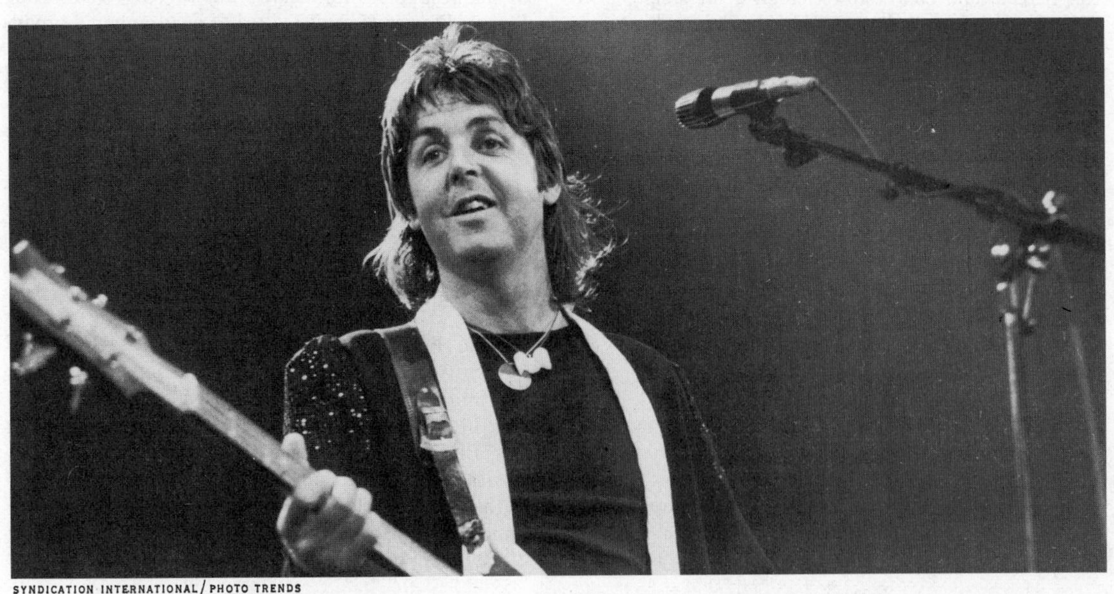
SYNDICATION INTERNATIONAL/PHOTO TRENDS

Paul McCartney toured the U.S. and Canada with his group, Wings, returning to the American stage after ten years. In Detroit he played to an audience of 17,000.

Cotton Pickers and Cab Calloway before joining the postwar Duke Ellington orchestra (1948–59), and saxophonist Rudy Powell, who had worked in the Don Redman and Calloway bands.

(BENNY GREEN)

Popular. For popular music 1976 was a depressing year. Many musicians died, including singer Phil Ochs, guitarist Paul Kossoff, bluesman Jimmy Reed, bandleader Percy Faith, and songwriter Johnny Mercer (*see* OBITUARIES).

In Britain nostalgia reached unhealthy proportions; old songs newly recorded (Art Garfunkel's "I Only Have Eyes for You") and rereleased hits (David Bowie's "Space Oddity" from 1969) were among the year's best-sellers. A craze for 1940s swing, begun in a Canvey Island discotheque, spread nationwide. Following a fans' demonstration, a weekly radio show was allocated to 1950s rock 'n' roll. A new generation lapped up repackaged Beatles records; in August a Beatles Convention was held in Norwich. Despite many offers, the Beatles refused to re-form, being occupied with their individual affairs. Paul McCartney's group Wings had its most successful year, touring and recording, and its "Band on the Run" was issued in the U.S.S.R. John Lennon won his pass from the U.S. immigration authorities. Less happily, George Harrison was found guilty of plagiarism in his hit song "My Sweet Lord," and he and Ringo Starr tried unsuccessfully to prevent the release of a record of Beatles interviews.

At the other extreme, the search for new talent became increasingly desperate. "Punk rock" was the journalistic term for the music of many new bands, denoting an untutored, aggressive style. Among its exponents were poet Patti Smith and the bands centred on CBGB's club in New York City; Stinky Toys and Bijoux in France, where the style was particularly popular; and the Sex Pistols in Britain. At best the punk bands were energetic, at worst downright bad.

There was, however, no shortage of fine contemporary music. Some artists, such as Canada's McGarrigle sisters, Welsh entertainer Max Boyce, and Irish band The Chieftains, "crossed over" from the folk field. Country-rock singer Emmylou Harris won international acclaim. Vocal duos such as Daryl Hall and John Oates were popular. The English group Genesis survived its lead singer's departure and progressed to new successes. Mike Oldfield's "Ommadawn" topped the U.K. album charts and yielded a hit single, "On Horseback." Jon Anderson, Yes's singer, achieved a remarkable tour de force in learning and playing himself every instrumental part for his album "Olias of Sunhillow." Reggae became increasingly serious in the hands of such artists as Bob Marley and Toots Hibbert. Record prices rose again, and although discount stores became commonplace, sales suffered and charts were sluggish. There was a revival of the EP (extended play) record, better value with four numbers than a single at the same price with two.

Live music continued active, with top artists such as Elton John and the Rolling Stones touring. A notable event was the "Rolling Thunder Revue," in which Bob Dylan and Joan Baez, together for the first time since the 1960s, toured the U.S. with a band including Roger McGuinn, Arlo Guthrie, and ex-Bowie guitarist Mick Ronson. West German trio Tangerine Dream performed their electronic music in English cathedrals. Increasingly unfavourable exchange rates diminished British promoters' profits from foreign artists; ticket prices increased, and several tours were canceled. The problem of where to hold concerts remained, large halls often having ruinous acoustics; some concerts were given at football stadia. The once-important British college circuit declined, students being unable to afford musicians' fees. Violence and drunkenness at concerts were increasing, but the Greater London Council's security proposals in March were denounced as unrealistic. Despite the exceptionally dry English summer, few festivals took place; a government inquiry was held with a view to finding a permanent festival site. The Walman Rink in Central Park, New York City, was temporarily reprieved from redevelopment. In San Francisco Bill Graham presented more successful "Days on the Green."

The Anglo-American domination of rock was being challenged by Europe, spearheaded by the catchy songs of the Swedish quartet Abba. Greek singer Demis Roussos, a longtime Continental favourite, finally broke through in Britain. Some Soviet bloc countries admitted Western pop; Cliff Richard toured the U.S.S.R., and the group Mud toured Poland. But in Czechoslovakia members of two indigenous groups went to prison for spreading "anti-socialism."

Outstanding among the year's many novelty records was C. W. McCall's "Convoy," a tale of U.S. long-distance truck (lorry) drivers; it became a hit not only in the U.S. but also in Britain, where it inspired a successful parody. Discos prospered, but despite a new dance, "The Hustle," generated by Van McCoy's instrumental hit, their music was becoming formularized and dull.

On the soul scene, Nat "King" Cole's daughter, Natalie, was a promising newcomer. In January Stax Records of Memphis, Tenn., once a leading producer of soul music, went bankrupt. In country music progress continued, with artists such as Waylon Jennings and Jerry Jeff Walker both extending the style and returning to the music's roots in western swing and folk. Black artists such as Dobie Gray entered the field. Favourite women included Dolly Parton and Tanya Tucker.

David Bowie, as well as returning to England for concerts, made his movie debut as Newton in *The Man Who Fell to Earth.* Andrew Lloyd Webber and Tim Rice produced a new work, *Evita,* based on the life of Eva Perón. The Thames Television series "Rock Follies," about a girl group, was a notable success. One of the best rock radio shows was the U.S. FM "King Biscuit Flower Hour," featuring quadraphonic broadcasts of top artists in concert.

Styles in popular music were becoming specialized and categories defined. There was more room for experiment in the U.S. than in Britain, where new artists battled against the nostalgia threatening to overwhelm the business. Some hope for the future lay in the punk bands which, despite their lack of technique, were bringing in new blood. Many observers believed that if they could abandon their nihilism, they might mature into the leading musicians of the 1980s.

(HAZEL MORGAN)

Folk. Probably the biggest show of folklore and folk music in 1976 took place in Washington, D.C., at the Smithsonian Institution and National Park Service's Festival of American Folklife. In honour of the U.S. Bicentennial, it ran from June 16 to September 6, with five simultaneous main sections: (1) Old Ways in the New World; (2) African Diaspora; (3) Regional Americans; (4) Native Americans; and (5) Working Americans. In all but the last section music and dance occupied the centre of attention, with demonstrations by each of the various regional and ethnic groups. In the section called Old Ways in the New World, representatives of at least 27 different nationalities came from abroad to meet with corresponding ethnic groups settled in the U.S. and to perform, above all, their music and dances. Each week two foreign countries appeared at the festival with their U.S. counterparts.

The Duquesne University Tamburitzans in Pittsburgh, directed by Walter Kolar, had long been known in the U.S. for their concerts of South Slavic and Balkan folk songs, music, and dances. In 1975–76 they produced a special U.S. bicentennial program in which folk music and dances of nearly all Eastern European nationalities were represented, including the Eastern Slavs, and also American traditional music. The Tamburitzans Institute of Folk Arts arranged with the governments of Yugoslavia and Bulgaria to bring leading specialists in folklore, folk music, and folk arts to Pittsburgh for two symposia, held in March and October.

A good example of the hundreds of relatively local European folk music festivals was the fifth Folklore Festival of the Republic of Serbia (Yugoslavia), held in Leskovac, southeastern Serbia, on June 25–27. The only amateur presentation of original folklore in Serbia, it included dances, songs, and instrumental music. Most of the instrumentalists were bagpipe players, but there were also players of the frula, the duduk, and the dvojnice (single and double vertical flutes).

(BARBARA KRADER)

See also Dance; Motion Pictures; Television and Radio; Theatre.

[624.D–J]

Nauru

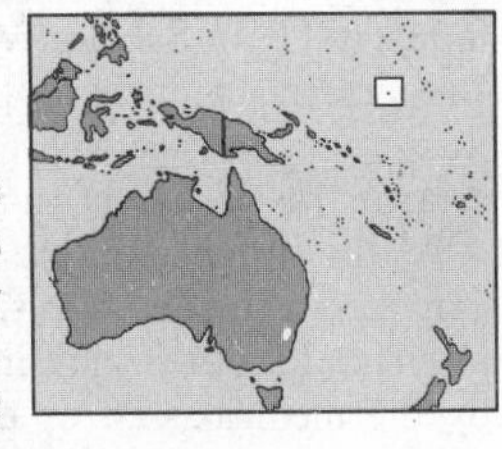

An island republic in the Pacific Ocean, Nauru lies about 1,200 mi E of New Guinea. Area: 8 sq mi (21 sq km). Pop. (1975 est.): 8,000. Capital: Yaren. Language: English and Nauruan. Religion: Christian. Presidents in 1976, Hammer DeRoburt and, from December 21, Bernard Dowiyogo.

The Nauruan economy continued to grow under the stimulus of reinvestment of its phosphate royalties. Much of the country's wealth was spent on improving transport and communications—high priorities in 1976. A satellite communications system, provided under contract by Cable and Wireless Systems (Hong Kong) at a project cost of U.S. $1.3 million, was operating at the beginning of the year. The Nauru Pacific Line chartered the "Weser Carrier," a semi-container ship, from West German owners to serve Fiji, New Zealand, and ports on the east coast of Australia. The "Weser Carrier" made two trips a month to Australia and Fiji with up to 5,000 tons of cargo.

Air Nauru expanded its services in 1976. An agreement was concluded with the French flag carrier Union de Transports Aériens (UTA) to serve Wallis Island, Nouméa, and Vila and to fly a new route to Hong Kong via Manila. The agreement with UTA was for two years initially, and Air Nauru flights were programmed to coincide with international schedules. Tourism was a growing component of the Pacific economy, and the New Hebrides in particular expected a sizable increase in tourism as a result of the new Air Nauru services.

(A. R. G. GRIFFITHS)

[977.A.3]

NAURU

Education. (1974) Primary, pupils 1,506, teachers 87; secondary, pupils 463, teachers 34; vocational, pupils 51, teachers 3.

Finance and Trade. Monetary unit: Australian dollar, with (Sept. 20, 1976) a free rate of A$0.80 to U.S. $1 (A$1.38 = £1 sterling). Budget (1973–74): revenue A$15,903,000; expenditure A$30,010,000. Foreign trade (1974 est.): imports A$10 million (*c.* 58% from Australia, *c.* 30% from The Netherlands); exports A$35 million (*c.* 57% to Australia, *c.* 23% to Japan, *c.* 18% to New Zealand). Main export phosphate.

Industry. Production (in 000): phospate rock (exports; metric tons; 1973–74) 2,288; electricity (kw-hr; 1974) *c.* 22,000.

Nepal

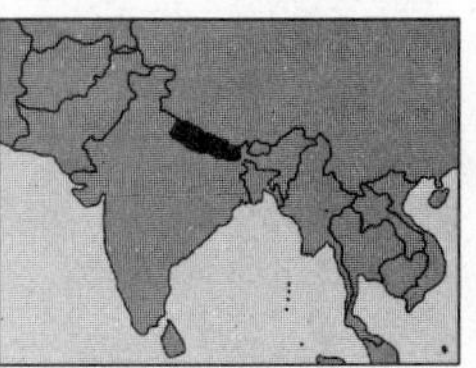

A constitutional monarchy of Asia, Nepal is in the Himalayas between India and the Tibetan Autonomous Region of China. Area: 54,362 sq mi (140,797 sq km). Pop. (1976 est.): 12,857,000. Cap. and largest city: Kathmandu (pop., 1971, 150,400). Language: Nepali (official); also Newari and Bhutia. Religion (1971): Hindu 89.4%; Buddhist 7.5%. King, Birendra Bir Bikram Shah Deva; prime minister in 1976, Tulsi Giri.

The replacement of Prime Minister Nagendra Prasad Rijal by Tulsi Giri in December 1975 provided an opportunity for Nepal to improve its relations with India, which had deteriorated following India's annexation of Sikkim in 1974. A visit by Giri to New Delhi in April 1976 cleared up some "misunderstandings," but Indian Prime Minister Indira Gandhi firmly reminded him that Nepal could not take India's friendship for granted. Two attempts to renew the five-year trade and transit treaty signed in August 1971 failed, and the treaty had to be temporarily extended until November 1976, when discussions were renewed. Despite differences, India continued to be Nepal's leading trade partner and major source of aid after the U.S.

King Birendra's visit to Tibet and Szechwan Province in China in June improved friendly ties with Peking, and Chinese Premier Hua Kuo-feng gave open support to the king's proposal (rejected by

NEPAL

Education. (1973) Primary, pupils 392,229, teachers 15,500; secondary, pupils 217,524; teachers 7,749; vocational, pupils 13,254; secondary and vocational, teachers 7,749; teacher training, students 3,797.

Finance. Monetary unit: Nepalese rupee, with (Sept. 20, 1976) a par value of NRs 12.50 to U.S. $1 (free rate of NRs 24.40 = £1 sterling). Gold, SDR's, and foreign exchange (May 1976) U.S. $119.8 million. Budget (1974–75): revenue NRs 960 million; expenditure NRs 1,741,000,000.

Foreign Trade. (1975) Imports NRs 1,885,000,000 (*c.* 80% from India, *c.* 10% from Japan in 1973–74); exports NRs 1,097,000,000 (*c.* 83% to India in 1973–74). Main exports: rice, jute products, jute.

Agriculture. Production (in 000; metric tons; 1975): rice *c.* 2,582; corn *c.* 784; wheat *c.* 357; potatoes *c.* 308; millet *c.* 143; mustard seed (1974) *c.* 60; jute *c.* 60; buffalo milk *c.* 450; cow's milk (1974) *c.* 210. Livestock (in 000; 1974): cattle *c.* 6,535; buffalo *c.* 3,831; pigs *c.* 324; sheep *c.* 2,266; goats *c.* 2,348; poultry *c.* 20,078.

Namibia: *see* Dependent States; South Africa

Narcotics: *see* Drug Abuse

NATO: *see* Defense

Navies: *see* Defense

India) to make Nepal a "zone of peace." Earlier, the 1966 trade pact with China was extended for another ten-year period. Mounting inflation continued to be the major economic difficulty, although rice production in fiscal 1974–75 was good. The Nepalese rupee was devalued to a new rate of NRs 12.50 to the U.S. dollar. (GOVINDAN UNNY)

[976.A.6]

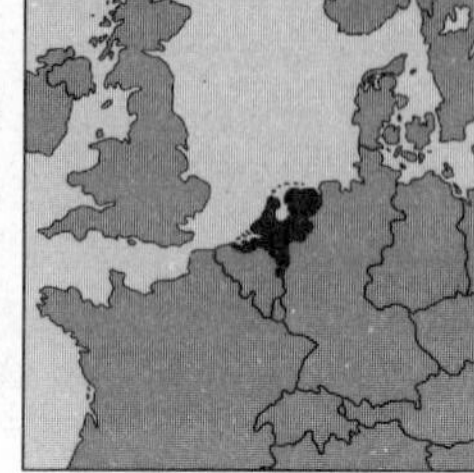

Netherlands, The

A kingdom of northwest Europe on the North Sea, The Netherlands, a Benelux country, is bounded by Belgium on the south and West Germany on the east. Area: 15,892 sq mi (41,160 sq km). Pop. (1975 est.): 13,745,000. Cap. and largest city: Amsterdam (pop., 1975 est., 758,000). Seat of government: The Hague (pop., 1975 est., 482,900). Language: Dutch. Religion (1971): Roman Catholic 39.6%; Dutch Reformed 23%; no religion 22.4%; Reformed Churches 7%. Queen, Juliana; prime minister in 1976, Joop den Uyl.

On Feb. 8, 1976, Prime Minister den Uyl, in a broadcast to the Dutch people, said that all were shocked by the disclosure made in evidence before a U.S. Senate subcommittee by the Lockheed Aircraft Corp., through a former president, A. Carl Kotchian, that in the past years large sums of money had been paid to a high government official of The Netherlands. The government, having acquired further information, inferred that the "high government official" was Prince Bernhard (*see* BIOGRAPHY).

A three-member committee, headed by Andreas M. Donner, a member of the Court of Justice of the European Economic Community, was instructed to investigate the Lockheed evidence to determine whether it was true. On August 26 the findings of the committee were made public. The report concluded that "his royal highness . . . originally entered much too lightly into transactions that were bound to create the impression that he was susceptible to favours. Later he showed himself open to dishonourable requests and offers. Finally, he allowed himself to be tempted to take initiatives that were completely unacceptable." The publication of the report was followed by a government statement, the conclusion of which was that the prince's activities had damaged the interest of the state and that he would have to

HENRI BUREAU—SYGMA

Wearing civilian clothes, Prince Bernhard waves to crowd from balcony of the Parliament building in September. At right, Queen Juliana; between the royal couple, son-in-law Prince Claus.

resign from official positions, among others that of inspector general of the Dutch Armed Forces. The report's findings dealt a severe blow to the Dutch people, for whom the integrity of the royal family had been above suspicion. Nevertheless, a nationwide opinion survey a few days later showed an increase in the percentage supporting the monarchy.

In the course of the year, the five-party, centre-left coalition Cabinet had to overcome three major internal conflicts. In May the Cabinet almost split in a conflict over the supply of essential parts for an atomic power station in South Africa. The minister of economic affairs, Ruud F. M. Lubbers, supported by his Christian Democratic colleagues, threatened to resign if the government should refuse to give an export guarantee to the consortium in which Dutch industry (Rijn-Schelde-Verolme, Verenigde Bedrijven Bredero en Comprimo) participated. A Cabinet crisis was averted when the government of South Africa awarded the contract to a French consortium.

At the same time, the minister of justice, Andreas van Agt, considered resigning after the police were prevented from seizing instruments used for abortion by the medical staff of the Bloemenhove Clinic. The public prosecutor, after consultation with the minister of justice, decided to act upon a complaint made by a West German married couple, but women's action groups and other demonstrators were able to prevent the police from closing part of the clinic on

NETHERLANDS, THE

Education. (1974–75) Primary, pupils 1,529,529, teachers 59,544; secondary, pupils 740,280, teachers 45,790; vocational, pupils 459,056, teachers *c.* 39,600; teacher training, students 10,849, teachers *c.* 900; higher (including 10 main universities), students *c.* 209,920, teaching staff *c.* 26,000.

Finance. Monetary unit: guilder, with (Sept. 20, 1976) a free rate of 2.60 guilders to U.S. $1 (4.48 guilders = £1 sterling). Gold, SDR's, and foreign exchange (June 1976) U.S. $5,145,000,000. Budget (1976 est.): revenue 62,228,000,000 guilders; expenditure 75,945,000,000 guilders. Gross national product (1975) 203,350,000,000 guilders. Money supply (April 1976) 51,370,000,000 guilders. Cost of living (1970 = 100; June 1976) 164.

Foreign Trade. (1975) Imports 89,851,000,000 guilders; exports 88,526,000,000 guilders. Import sources: EEC 57% (West Germany 25%, Belgium-Luxembourg 14%, France 8%, U.K. 6%); U.S. 10%; Iran 5%. Export destinations: EEC 70% (West Germany 31%, Belgium-Luxembourg 12%, France 10%, U.K. 9%, Italy 5%). Main exports: food 21%; chemicals 15%; petroleum products 13%; electrical machinery and equipment 7%; nonelectrical machinery 7%. Tourism (1974): visitors 2,683,400; gross receipts U.S. $1,039,000,000.

Transport and Communications. Roads (1974) 82,877 km (including 1,420 km expressways). Motor vehicles in use (1974): passenger 3,440,000; commercial 320,000. Railways: (1974) 2,832 km (including 1,712 km electrified); traffic (1975) 8,502,000,000 passenger-km, freight 2,722,000,000 net ton-km. Air traffic (1975): 10,132,000,000 passenger-km; freight 615,083,000 net ton-km. Navigable inland waterways (1974): 4,787 km (including 1,614 km for craft of 1,500 tons and over); freight traffic 33,196,000,000 ton-km. Shipping (1975): merchant vessels 100 gross tons and over 1,348; gross tonnage 5,679,413. Ships entered (1974) vessels totaling 154.9 million net registered tons; goods loaded (1975) 80,801,000 metric tons, unloaded 242,592,000 metric tons. Telephones (Dec. 1974) 4,678,945. Radio licenses (Dec. 1974) 3,845,000. Television licenses (Dec. 1974) 3,545,000.

Agriculture. Production (in 000; metric tons; 1975): wheat 528; barley 336; oats 158; rye 63; potatoes 5,003; tomatoes 355; onions 405; apples (1974) 370; pears (1974) 105; sugar, raw value 914; cabbages (1974) *c.* 229; cucumbers (1974) 325; carrots (1974) *c.* 140; rapeseed 37; fresh milk *c.* 10,000; condensed milk 473; butter 205; cheese 375; hen's eggs *c.* 281; beef and veal (1974) 356; pork (1974) 947; fish catch (1974) 326. Livestock (in 000; May 1975): cattle 4,953; pigs 7,272; sheep 760; chickens *c.* 64,457.

Industry. Index of production (1970 = 100; 1975) 115. Production (in 000; metric tons; 1975): crude oil 1,421; natural gas (cu m) 90,849,000; manufactured gas (cu m) 1,089,000; electricity (kw-hr) 54,249,000; pig iron 3,969; crude steel 4,823; cement 3,626; petroleum products (1974) 59,007; sulfuric acid 1,291; fertilizers (nutrient content; 1974–75) nitrogenous *c.* 1,289, phosphate *c.* 296; cotton yarn 29; wool yarn 9; rayon, etc., filament yarn and fibres 30; nylon, etc., filament yarn and fibres (1972) 113. Merchant vessels launched (100 gross tons and over; 1975) 944,000 gross tons.

May 18. After long deliberations in the Cabinet, the minister decided to call off the police, but very unwillingly. On December 15 a bill to legalize abortion was rejected by 41 votes to 34 in the Senate after it had been adopted by 83 votes to 58 in the lower house in September.

The third crisis occurred in October. The boards of the Socialist Party (PvdA) and the Radical Political Party (PPR) drew up a resolution making their participation in the next government conditional upon their winning a greater number of seats in the Second Chamber of Parliament in the 1977 election than they held in the current Parliament. The Cabinet members from the Christian Democratic parties, the Catholic People's Party and the Antirevolutionary party (KVP and ARP), felt themselves betrayed and insisted on a clear statement from their Socialist and Radical fellow ministers. The prime minister succeeded in postponing the conflict by getting the resolution toned down.

In the autumn the three confessional parties, KVP, ARP, and the Christian Historical Union (CHU), decided to cooperate in the Christian Democratic Appeal (launched the previous year) and appointed van Agt as their principal candidate. Some weeks before, the progressive parties, PvdA and PPR, had appointed den Uyl as their principal candidate. Thus the lines were drawn for the election campaign.

(DICK BOONSTRA)

See also Dependent States.
[972.A.7]

New Zealand

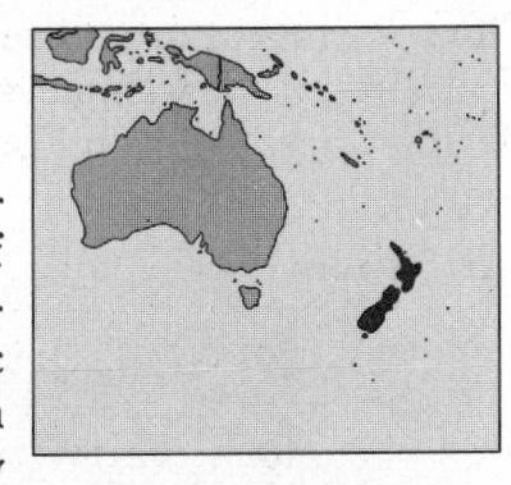

New Zealand, a parliamentary state and member of the Commonwealth of Nations, is in the South Pacific Ocean, separated from southeastern Australia by the Tasman Sea. The country consists of North and South islands and Stewart, Chatham, and other minor islands. Area: 103,747 sq mi (268,704 sq km). Pop. (1976 prelim.): 3,130,100. Cap.: Wellington (pop., 1976 prelim., 139,300). Largest city: Christchurch (pop., 1976 prelim., 171,800). Largest urban area: Auckland (pop., 1976 prelim., 743,600). Language: English (official), Maori. Religion (1971): Church of England 31%; Presbyterian 20%; Roman Catholic 16%. Queen, Elizabeth II; governor-general in 1976, Sir Denis Blundell; prime minister, Robert David Muldoon.

The belief of a majority of New Zealanders that South Africa could best be influenced to progressively abandon apartheid by contact rather than by isolation, and that governments should not interfere with the movement of individuals or sports teams, received a testing at the Olympic Games in July. The governments of 31 third world countries forced their athletes to withdraw from the Montreal events because a New Zealand rugby team was touring South Africa. After that, without going back on its policy of noninterference, the New Zealand government began to emphasize to sports organizations that they had to consider the national image abroad in arranging future tours.

The National Party did not convene the new Parliament until June 23, but then quickly used its 53–34 majority to revise some of the legislation of the Labour government it had defeated in November 1975. It returned broadcasting (two TV networks, one radio organization) to single corporation control under a ministerial portfolio with restrictions on government involvement; repealed the automatic suppression of the names of defendants before the courts until they had been convicted; and moved to amend ineffective legislation limiting therapeutic abortions to cases where the mother's life was in danger—on which it was defeated because a Labour-appointed commission had yet to report on a number of social issues including abortion.

UPI COMPIX

Antinuclear demonstrators in Wellington, New Zealand, sailed out in this little boat to protest the visit of the U.S. nuclear-powered warship "Truxton." Dock workers also went on strike in protest.

The Muldoon government had been returned mainly to retrieve a drifting economy in which extensive borrowing had averted unemployment in the face of reduced returns for exports and inflated prices for imported raw materials and consumer items. It declared that the country must take a 10% cut in its standard of living and did not wait for the convening of Parliament to make a start. Within weeks the government had clamped down on bank credit, lifted gasoline prices to $1.20 a gallon, approved bulk power and postal rate rises, and removed subsidies on milk and bread. In its incomes policy it tried to prevent inflationary wage increases. In May it approved a 7% general wage order and froze all special increases, the second part of the package provoking criticism from the unions, which sought to demonstrate "exceptional circumstances" that would enable them to return to direct bargaining. The budget, at the end of July, tried to stimulate farm production in small ways. It increased taxes on overseas travel, on liquor, cigarettes, television and sound equipment, and machinery not used in primary industry, but the new administration was still some way from arresting high inflation.

To no one's surprise, Prime Minister Muldoon (*see* BIOGRAPHY) dominated public affairs. The assertive former finance minister was determined that his administration would govern—he continued to charge the rejected Labour administration with not having done so—and his style of having a ready response for every press question indicated a detailed control of all the major portfolios that at times was the despair of ministers. While opponents clamoured for

Netherlands Overseas Territories:
see Dependent States

New Guinea:
see Indonesia; Papua New Guinea

New Hebrides:
see Dependent States

Newspapers:
see Publishing

the convening of Parliament, he visited Britain and Europe in April and continued on to Korea, Japan, and then Peking, where his stand against the development of Soviet naval strength in the Indian and Pacific oceans ensured a welcome for even a conservative New Zealander. Muldoon seemed to reflect a greater awareness of Pacific island responsibilities after attending a meeting of island leaders in Nauru, and he was obviously hurt by political opponents' charges that his administration, in paring immigration as an economic measure, was discriminating against islanders. In September he attended International Monetary Fund and World Bank meetings at Manila and went on to a Commonwealth finance ministers' conference at Hong Kong. On November 29, following the Australian devaluation, he announced a 7% devaluation of the New Zealand dollar.

A by-election came too early (February 28) in the government's term to measure its performance; the Labour opposition retained the electorate of its deceased speaker, Sir Stanley Whitehead, with an increased majority of 300-odd. Muldoon's warnings on Soviet naval emergence did not prevent trade unions from bringing the key port of Wellington to a standstill during the week-long visit at the end of August of a nuclear-powered U.S. cruiser with nuclear weapons capability, though nuclear ships had visited more than a decade earlier. (JOHN A. KELLEHER)

See also **Dependent States.**
[977.C]

NEW ZEALAND

Education. (1975) Primary, pupils 525,323, teachers 21,187; secondary, pupils 219,754, teachers 11,107; vocational, students 2,387, teachers 1,136; higher, students 35,078, teaching staff (universities and teacher training only) 4,502.

Finance. Monetary unit: New Zealand dollar, with (Sept. 20, 1976) a free rate of NZ$1 to U.S. $1 (NZ$1.73 = £1 sterling). Gold, SDR's, and foreign exchange (June 1976) U.S. $455 million. Budget (1974–75 actual): revenue NZ$2,962,000,000; expenditure NZ$2,602,000,000. Gross national product (1974–75) NZ$9,421,000,000. Cost of living (1970 = 100; 1st quarter 1976) 180.

Foreign Trade. (1975) Imports NZ$2,613,500,000; exports NZ$1,796,400,000. Import sources (1974–75): Australia 20%; U.K. 19%; Japan 14%; U.S. 13%. Export destinations (1974–75): U.K. 22%; Australia 12%; Japan 12%; U.S. 12%. Main exports (1974–75): meat and meat preparations 28%; wool 17%; butter 9%; wood pulp and paper 5%. Tourism (1974): visitors 259,300; gross receipts U.S. $131 million.

Transport and Communications. Roads (1973) 92,005 km (including 115 km expressways). Motor vehicles in use (1975): passenger 1,167,300; commercial 212,620. Railways: (1974) 4,797 km; traffic (1975) 537 million passenger-km, freight 3,272,000,000 net ton-km. Air traffic (1974): 3,779,000,000 passenger-km; freight 116.8 million net ton-km. Shipping (1975): merchant vessels 100 gross tons and over 109; gross tonnage 162,520. Telephones (Dec. 1974) 1,495,000. Radio receivers (Dec. 1973) 2.7 million. Television licenses (Dec. 1975) 817,000.

Agriculture. Production (in 000; metric tons; 1975): wheat 203; barley 334; oats 65; corn (1974) 132; potatoes (1974) 238; dry peas *c.* 75; tomatoes 66; apples (1974) *c.* 170; milk 6,086; butter 240; cheese 89; mutton and lamb (1974) *c.* 580; beef and veal (1974) 406; wool *c.* 210; sheepskins (1974) *c.* 120; timber (cu m; 1974) 7,468; fish catch (1974) 59. Livestock (in 000; Jan. 1975): cattle 9,653; sheep 55,320; pigs 500; chickens (1974) *c.* 5,704.

Industry. Fuel and power (in 000; metric tons; 1975): coal 458; lignite 1,931; crude oil (1974) 163; natural gas (cu m) 322,000; manufactured gas (cu m) 77,000; electricity (excluding most industrial production; kw-hr) 19,687,000. Production (in 000; metric tons; 1975): cement 1,074; petroleum products (1974) *c.* 3,480; phosphate fertilizers (1974–75) 301; wood pulp (1974–75) 816; newsprint (1974–75) 218; other paper (1974–75) 316.

Nicaragua

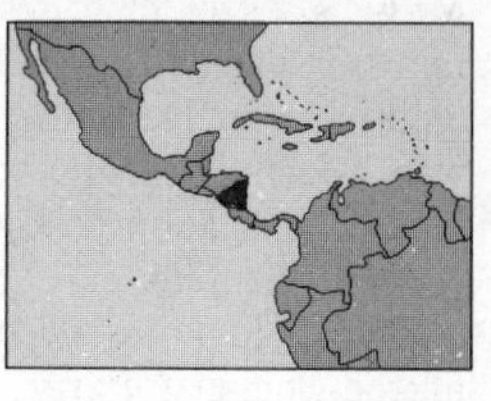

The largest country of Central America, Nicaragua is a republic bounded by Honduras, Costa Rica, the Caribbean Sea, and the Pacific Ocean. Area: 50,000 sq mi (130,000 sq km). Pop. (1975 est.): 2,155,000. Cap. and largest city: Managua (pop., 1974 est., 313,400). Language: Spanish. Religion: Roman Catholic. President in 1976, Anastasio Somoza Debayle.

A Jesuit priest from Nicaragua, Fernando Cardenal, appeared in June before a foreign affairs subcommittee of the U.S. House of Representatives that was investigating possible violation of human rights in Central American countries and accused the U.S. of supplying troops and planes for the Nicaraguan government's use against guerrillas. Both governments denied the charges.

Small-scale guerrilla warfare between Nicaraguan security forces and members of the Sandinist National Liberation Front continued. Captured Sandinists, according to government sources, confirmed President Somoza's claim that their campaign was being directed by Cuba's Fidel Castro.

July floods in the northeastern Caribbean area and the Pacific zone near Chinandega caused an undetermined number of deaths, left thousands homeless, and did considerable agricultural damage. A prolonged drought caused additional losses. The national economy fared well, nevertheless, due largely to high world prices for export crops, notably cotton and coffee. (HENRY WEBB, JR.)

[974.B.1.d]

NICARAGUA

Education. (1974–75) Primary, pupils 350,519, teachers 8,817; secondary, pupils 76,763; vocational (1972–73), pupils 5,613, teachers 336; teacher training (1972–73), students 1,332, teachers 93; higher (1972–73), students 11,618, teaching staff 694.

Finance. Monetary unit: córdoba, with (Sept. 20, 1976) a par value of 7 córdobas to U.S. $1 (free rate of 12.06 córdobas = £1 sterling). Gold, SDR's, and foreign exchange (May 1976) U.S. $178,460,000. Budget (1975 actual): revenue 1,327,000,000 córdobas: expenditure 1,968,000,000 córdobas. Gross national product (1975) 10,372,000,000 córdobas. Money supply (May 1976) 1,589,200,000 córdobas.

Foreign Trade. (1975) Imports 3,631,600,000 córdobas; exports 2,636,000,000 córdobas. Import sources (1974): U.S. 32%; Venezuela 9%; Guatemala 7%; Japan 7%; Costa Rica 7%; West Germany 7%; El Salvador 7%. Export destinations (1974): U.S. 19%; West Germany 11%; Japan 9%; Costa Rica 9%; El Salvador 6%; China 6%; Guatemala 6%; The Netherlands 5%. Main exports: cotton 25%; coffee 13%; sugar 11%; meat 7%.

Transport and Communications. Roads (1971) 13,147 km (including 485 km of Pan-American Highway). Motor vehicles in use (1973): passenger *c.* 32,000; commercial (including buses) *c.* 20,000. Railways: (1974) 373 km; traffic (1972) 28 million passenger-km, freight 14 million net ton-km. Air traffic (1974): 78 million passenger-km; freight 2 million net ton-km. Telephones (Dec. 1974) 29,000. Radio receivers (Dec. 1973) 125,000. Television receivers (Dec. 1973) 63,000.

Agriculture. Production (in 000; metric tons; 1975): corn 241; rice *c.* 82; sorghum 90; dry beans 51; sugar, raw value (1974) *c.* 160; bananas (1974) *c.* 250; oranges (1974) *c.* 54; coffee *c.* 41; cotton, lint *c.* 121. Livestock (in 000; 1974): cattle *c.* 2,858; pigs *c.* 660; horses *c.* 175; chickens *c.* 3,400.

Industry. Production (in 000; metric tons; 1974): petroleum products 577; cement (1971) 99; gold (exports; troy oz) 72; electricity (kw-hr) *c.* 845,000.

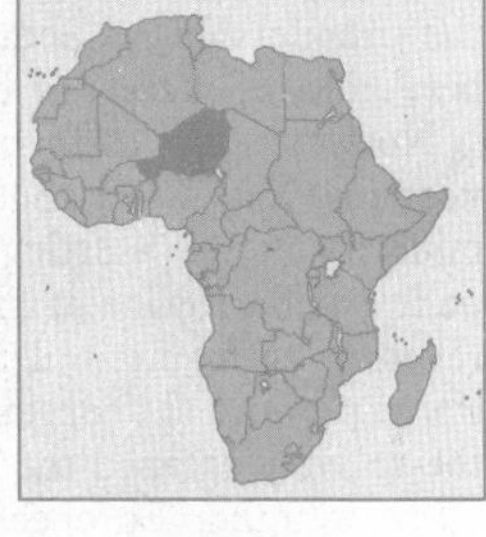

Niger

A republic of north central Africa, Niger is bounded by Algeria, Libya, Chad, Nigeria, Benin, Upper Volta, and Mali. Area: 458,075 sq mi (1,186,408 sq km). Pop. (1975 est.): 4,600,600, including (1970 est.) Hausa 53.7%; Zerma and Songhai 23.6%; Fulani 10.6%; Beriberi-Manga 9.1%. Cap. and largest city: Niamey (pop., 1975 est., 130,000). Language: French and Sudanic dialects. Religion: Muslim, animist, Christian. President in 1976, Lieut. Col. Seyni Kountche.

Dismissing four of the leading military members of his Cabinet on Feb. 21, 1976, President Kountche formed a predominantly civilian government for the first time since the coup that brought him to power in April 1974.

On March 15 Kountche disclosed that troops had foiled an attempted coup in Niamey earlier that day. Among the coup leaders was Maj. Bayere Moussa, formerly minister of rural economy, who had been replaced in the government reshuffle. Nine people were condemned to death for their part in the attempt, and on April 21 seven, including Major Moussa, were executed.

The attempt was not, however, the work of associates of former president Hamani Diori, who had been imprisoned since the 1974 coup, and on April 15, the second anniversary of Kountche's seizure of power, nine of these associates who had been detained as political prisoners since the coup were released.

Niger celebrated the 16th anniversary of its independence with a call from President Kountche for priority to be given to the country's economic and social development. He outlined a three-year development plan in which public works, agriculture, social facilities, and industry would be of first importance.

(PHILIPPE DECRAENE)

NIGER

Education. (1973–74) Primary, pupils 110,437, teachers 2,736; secondary, pupils 10,494, teachers 474; vocational, pupils 237, teachers 25; teacher training, students 377, teachers 40; higher, students 280, teaching staff 40.

Finance. Monetary unit: CFA franc, with (Sept. 20, 1976) a parity of CFA Fr 50 to the French franc (free rate of CFA Fr 245.90 = U.S. $1; CFA Fr 423.62 = £1 sterling). Gold, SDR's, and foreign exchange (June 1976) U.S. $55.9 million. Budget (1974–75 est.) balanced at CFA Fr 15.3 billion (including investment expenditures).

Foreign Trade. (1974) Imports CFA Fr 23,144,000,000; exports CFA Fr 12,621,000,000. Import sources: France 37%; U.S. 13%; Nigeria 9%; West Germany 8%. Export destinations: France 54%; Nigeria 27%; West Germany 7%. Main exports (1973): uranium 39%; peanuts 14%; cattle *c.* 7%.

Transport and Communications. Roads (1974) 6,944 km. Motor vehicles in use (1974): passenger 14,377; commercial 2,672. There are no railways. Inland waterway (Niger River) *c.* 300 km. Telephones (Dec. 1974) 5,000. Radio receivers (Dec. 1971) 150,000.

Agriculture. Production (in 000; metric tons; 1975): millet *c.* 800; sorghum *c.* 250; rice (1974) 43; cassava (1974) *c.* 160; dry beans *c.* 170; peanuts *c.* 100; goat's milk *c.* 102. Livestock (in 000; 1974): cattle *c.* 3,000; sheep *c.* 1,800; goats *c.* 4,800; camels *c.* 340.

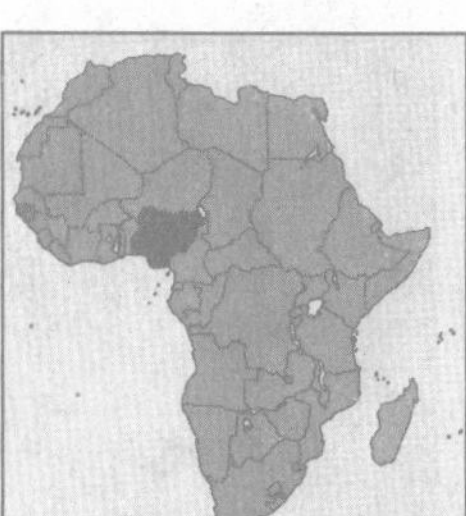

Nigeria

A republic and a member of the Commonwealth of Nations, Nigeria is located in Africa north of the Gulf of Guinea, bounded by Benin, Niger, Chad, and Cameroon. Area: 356,700 sq mi (923,800 sq km). Pop. (1974 est.): 72,833,000, including Hausa 21%; Ibo 18%; Yoruba 18%; Fulani 10%. Cap. and largest city: Lagos (pop., 1973 est., 970,300). Language: English (official). Religion (1963): Muslim 47%; Christian 34%. Heads of provisional military government in 1976, Brig. Murtala Ramat Mohammed to February 13 and, from February 14, Lieut. Gen. Olusegun Obasanjo.

Brig. Murtala Mohammed (*see* OBITUARIES) was assassinated by dissident troops on Feb. 13, 1976, but the coup, led by Lieut. Col. Bukar S. Dimka, failed, and the new head of state, Lieut. Gen. Olusegun Obasanjo (*see* BIOGRAPHY), announced the continuation of Mohammed's policies, including an eventual return to civilian rule (though political parties were still banned) and the encouragement of chiefs' participation in local government. On March 11, 30 plotters, including Mohammed's defense minister, were executed, and on May 15 seven others, including Dimka. The complicity of Gen. Yakubu Gowon (head of state deposed in July 1975 by Mohammed) was alleged and his extradition from Britain demanded. When the British refused, relations between Nigeria and Britain cooled, and Nigeria detained two British pilots who had strayed into its territory.

In February it was announced that a new capital centrally situated near Abuja was being planned to replace Lagos. Seven new states, bringing the total to 19, were to be created to reflect ethnic groupings and to split the larger, densely populated areas into more manageable units. Preparations for the World Black and African Festival of Arts and Culture, to open in January 1977 as a great celebration of black culture, were soured by a quarrel with Senegal over the inclusion of Muslims that led to Senegal's withdrawal; meanwhile costs accelerated, with allegations

NIGERIA

Education. (1973–74) Primary, pupils 4,368,778, teachers 129,399; secondary, pupils 476,507, teachers 18,441; vocational, pupils 20,423, teachers 1,057; teacher training, students 47,590, teachers 2,250; higher, students 23,707, teaching staff 2,361.

Finance. Monetary unit: naira, with (Sept. 20, 1976) a free rate of 0.66 naira to U.S. $1 (1.14 naira = £1 sterling). Gold, SDR's, and foreign exchange (June 1976) U.S. $5,516,000,000. Federal budget (1975–76): revenue 5,252,000,000 naira; expenditure 6,635,000,000 naira (including 4,914,000,000 naira capital expenditure). Gross domestic product (1973–74) 8.9 billion naira. Money supply (Feb. 1976) 2,681,100,000 naira. Cost of living (Lagos; 1970 = 100; March 1976) 220.

Foreign Trade. (1975) Imports 3,717,400,000 naira; exports 4,988,400,000 naira. Import sources: U.K. 23%; West Germany 15%; U.S. 11%; Japan 10%; France 8%; Italy 6%. Export destinations: U.S. 29%; U.K. 14%; The Netherlands 11%; France 11%; Netherlands Antilles 7%; West Germany 7%. Main export crude oil 93%.

Transport and Communications. Roads (1971) 89,000 km. Motor vehicles in use (1973): passenger *c.* 150,000; commercial (including buses) *c.* 82,000. Railways: (1973) 3,505 km; traffic (1973–74) 890 million passenger-km, freight 1,343,000,000 net ton-km. Air traffic (1974): 355 million passenger-km; freight 8.3 million net ton-km. Shipping (1975): merchant vessels 100 gross tons and over 84; gross tonnage 142,050. Telephones (Dec. 1974) 111,000. Radio licenses (Dec. 1973) 3.5 million. Television licenses (Dec. 1973) 85,000.

Agriculture. Production (in 000; metric tons; 1975): millet *c.* 3,200; sorghum *c.* 3,500; corn *c.* 1,000; rice *c.* 368; sweet potatoes (1974) *c.* 210; yams (1974) *c.* 15,000; taro (1974) *c.* 1,780; cassava (1974) *c.* 10,000; cowpeas (1974) *c.* 830; tomatoes *c.* 230; peanuts *c.* 280; palm oil *c.* 470; cocoa *c.* 230; cotton, lint *c.* 46; rubber *c.* 95; fish catch (1974) 685. Livestock (in 000; 1975): cattle *c.* 10,918; sheep *c.* 7,653; goats *c.* 22,400; pigs *c.* 891; poultry *c.* 85,000.

Industry. Production (in 000; metric tons; 1974): cement 1,206; crude oil (1975) 88,419; natural gas (cu m) 574,000; tin 5.6; petroleum products 2,703; electricity (kw-hr) 2,828,000.

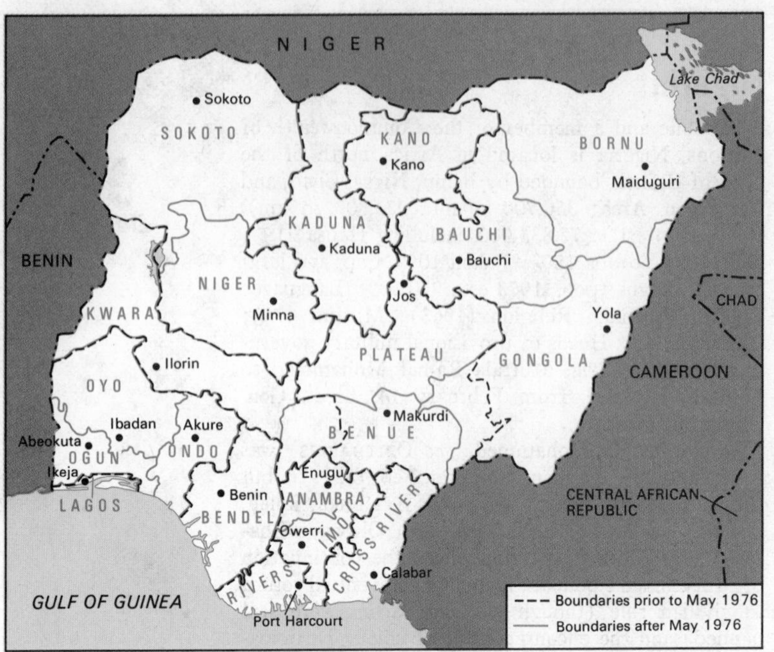

The Nigerian government redrew the country's political map, making 19 states instead of the previous 12.

of corruption. A massive repatriation of Nigerian workers from Equatorial Guinea's cocoa plantations on Macías Nguema Biyogo (Fernando Po) was made. (*See* EQUATORIAL GUINEA.)

Inflation at nearly 40%, congestion at Lagos port, corruption, and swollen army budgets did not create confidence, in spite of oil wealth. Though total oil output in 1975 moved down, oil accounted for 90% of export earnings and was expected to support the third national development plan, 1975–80 (ten times the level of the second plan). The ambitious program included the development of heavy industry and transportation. Investment in agriculture aimed at raising the output of cash crops and also at reversing the decline in food production. The government gave heavy publicity to Operation Feed the Nation in the hope of achieving self-sufficiency in food production within a year. Free education was opened to all six-year-olds under a plan that, by 1980, would provide free, compulsory primary education for all. The federal budget for 1976–77 was designed to reduce the balance of payments deficit by pegging government spending and restricting imports. An indigenization program (effective in 1977) required 100% Nigerian ownership of small retail businesses and Nigerian participation in banking (60%) and in major foreign businesses (40%). Nigeria continued to attract foreign investment: the United Kingdom exported £465 million to it in 1975. (MOLLY MORTIMER)

[978.E.4.b.ii]

Norway

A constitutional monarchy of northern Europe, Norway is bordered by Sweden, Finland, and the U.S.S.R.; its coastlines are on the Skagerrak, the North Sea, the Norwegian Sea, and the Arctic Ocean. Area: 125,053 sq mi (323,886 sq km), excluding the Svalbard Archipelago, 23,957 sq mi, and Jan Mayen Island, 144 sq mi. Pop. (1976 est.): 4,017,200. Cap. and largest city: Oslo (pop., 1976 est., 463,000). Language: Norwegian. Religion: Lutheran (94%). King, Olav V; prime ministers in 1976, Trygve Bratteli and, from January 9, Odvar Nordli.

On Jan. 9, 1976, Trygve Bratteli formally resigned the premiership, as announced the previous September, and was succeeded by Odvar Nordli.

Norway enjoyed another moderately prosperous year in 1976. The Labour government, ruling with a minority in the Storting (Parliament), continued its policy of borrowing against future offshore petroleum revenues to maintain demand at home. The gross national product (at constant prices) grew by 5.9%, and the country escaped the mass unemployment suffered by many other European nations. At year's end, the balance of payments deficit seemed likely to reach a record 18.3 billion kroner, but much of this reflected heavy investment in new ships for the merchant fleet and equipment for the offshore oil industry. The year brought a gradual revival in demand for important Norwegian export commodities such as aluminum, ferroalloys, and wood products, and unsold stocks began falling. During the slump, the government had provided credit to allow companies to produce for stock, in order to avoid production cutbacks and resultant layoffs. In October more than one-fifth of the

NORWAY

Education. (1974–75) Primary, pupils 386,559, teachers (including some secondary) 29,605; secondary, pupils 262,889, teachers (1971–72) 21,888; vocational, pupils 65,921, teachers (1971–72) 10,616; higher, students 64,469, teaching staff (1971–72) 5,291.

Finance. Monetary unit: Norwegian krone, with (Sept. 20, 1976) a free rate of 5.40 kroner to U.S. $1 (9.30 kroner = £1 sterling). Gold, SDR's, and foreign exchange (June 1976) U.S. $2,026,700,000. Budget (1976 est.): revenue 40,439,000,000 kroner; expenditure 48,544,000,000 kroner. Gross domestic product (1975) 147,930,000,000 kroner. Money supply (May 1976) 30,290,000,000 kroner. Cost of living (1970 = 100; June 1976) 164.

Foreign Trade. (1975) Imports 50,609,000,000 kroner; exports 37,778,000,000 kroner. Import sources: Sweden 19%; West Germany 16%; U.K. 10%; U.S. 7%; Japan 6%; Denmark 6%; The Netherlands 5%. Export destinations: U.K. 24%; Sweden 16%; West Germany 10%; Denmark 7%; U.S. 6%. Main exports: ships 14%; petroleum and products 12%; machinery 11%; chemicals 7%; aluminum 6%; fish 5%; paper 5%.

Transport and Communications. Roads (1974) 76,085 km (including 156 km expressways). Motor vehicles in use (1974): passenger 890,361; commercial 144,995. Railways (1974): 4,241 km (including 2,440 km electrified); traffic 1,884,000,000 passenger-km, freight 2,886,000,000 net ton-km. Air traffic (including Norwegian apportionment of international operations of Scandinavian Airlines System; 1975): 2,964,300,000 passenger-km; freight 105,795,000 net ton-km. Shipping (1975): merchant vessels 100 gross tons and over 2,706; gross tonnage 26,153,682. Shipping traffic (1974): goods loaded 40,425,000 metric tons, unloaded 22,644,000 metric tons. Telephones (Dec. 1974) 1,355,140. Radio licenses (July 1975) 1,272,000. Television licenses (July 1975) 1,031,000.

Agriculture. Production (in 000; metric tons; 1975): barley 445; oats 259; potatoes 435; apples (1974) 45; milk *c.* 1,798; cheese 61; beef and veal (1974) *c.* 64; pork (1974) *c.* 77; timber (cu m; 1974) 9,532; fish catch (1974) 2,645. Livestock (in 000; June 1974): cattle *c.* 963; sheep *c.* 1,632; pigs *c.* 785; goats 70; chickens *c.* 6,404.

Industry. Fuel and power (in 000; metric tons; 1975): crude oil 9,277; coal (Svalbard mines; Norwegian operated only) 389; manufactured gas (cu m) 25,000; electricity (kw-hr) 77,581,000. Production (in 000; metric tons; 1975): iron ore (65% metal content) 4,064; pig iron 1,509; crude steel 919; aluminum 591; copper 20; zinc 61; cement 2,791; petroleum products (1974) *c.* 5,890; sulfuric acid 333; fertilizers (nutrient content; 1974–75) nitrogenous 390, phosphate 127; fish meal (1974) 320; wood pulp (1974) mechanical 1,171, chemical 1,055; newsprint 434; other paper (1974) 910. Merchant vessels launched (100 gross tons and over; 1975) 1,035,000 gross tons. New dwelling units completed (1975) 43,600.

WALTER SULLIVAN—THE NEW YORK TIMES

Norway leads the race to exploit the oil deposits of the North Sea. The photo shows drilling and production rigs that will soon make Norway one of the richest countries of the Western world.

merchant fleet was still laid up, including one-third of the tanker fleet.

In the spring long-term wage contracts for large groups of industrial workers were renegotiated, and the government became a party to the settlement by promising tax relief, higher food subsidies, and increased social security benefits in exchange for agreement by the workers to accept relatively moderate pay increases. The declared aims were to raise wage-earners' real disposable incomes by 3% in 1976 and to keep price rises over the year down to 9.2%.

In September, when price rises showed signs of exceeding the agreed limit, the government increased credit curbs, raised the bank rate from 5 to 6%, introduced additional food subsidies, and imposed a profits margin and price freeze on a wide range of goods and services. The budget for 1977, introduced in October, channeled modest direct tax reliefs mainly to lower income groups and families with children, while increasing indirect taxes. However, Finance Minister Per Kleppe promised additional tax concessions later on if workers again showed restraint in the spring wage bargaining.

Delays, accidents, and escalating costs plagued the companies developing Norway's undersea oil and gas deposits. The Ekofisk field—the only one so far in production—yielded several million tons less than expected in 1976. In November 1975 an explosion and fire on an Ekofisk production platform caused the deaths of three workers. More lives were lost in March 1976, when a mobile platform being towed to Bergen for repairs was wrecked in a blizzard, killing six. During the year it became clear that the Frigg gas field would not become operative until 1978, and the giant Statfjord oil and gas field would not begin production until late 1978 or early 1979. In June the Storting approved a 20 billion kroner development program for Statfjord, and only two months later the government admitted the project would probably cost at least 30 billion kroner. The revelation caused a minor political storm, but the government insisted that the project was still well worthwhile.

A major foreign policy issue in 1976 was the government's much-heralded plan to establish a 200-mi exclusive economic zone around the mainland coast, in order to protect fish stocks. After a series of negotiations with countries affected by the move, Prime Minister Nordli announced on October 5 that the zones would be established from Jan. 1, 1977. (*See* LAW: *Special Report.*) The question of regulating fisheries around the Svalbard Archipelago, where Norway had special treaty obligations, was "still being studied."

(FAY GJESTER)

[972.A.6.c]

Oman

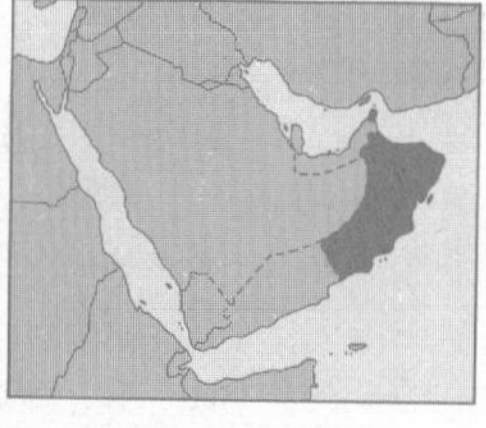

An independent sultanate, Oman occupies the southeastern part of the Arabian Peninsula and is bounded by the United Arab Emirates, Saudi Arabia, the Gulf of Oman, and the Arabian Sea. A small part of the country lies to the north and is separated from the rest of Oman by the United Arab Emirates. Area: 82,000 sq mi (212,400 sq km). Pop. (1975 UN est.): 776,000; for planning purposes the government of Oman uses an estimate of 1.5 million. No census has ever been taken. Cap.: Muscat (pop., 1973 est., 15,000). Largest city: Matrah (pop., 1973 est., 18,000). Language: Arabic. Religion: Muslim. Sultan in 1976, Qabus ibn Sa'id.

In December 1975 the Oman government declared that the rebellion conducted in the southwestern Dhofar Province by the Popular Front for the Liberation of Oman (PFLO) was over and only remnants of it remained; in January 1976, a $20 million development program for the province was launched. Several factors favoured the government in the conflict. On January 31 diplomatic relations were established with Iraq, a former supporter of the PFLO. Having settled its problems with Iran, Iraq was ready to play down its objections to the presence of some 3,000 Iranian

OMAN

Education. (1974–75) Primary, pupils 48,691, teachers 2,010; secondary, pupils 571, teachers 95; vocational, pupils 82, teachers 21.

Finance and Trade. Monetary unit: rial Omani, with (Sept. 20, 1976) an official rate of 0.345 rial to U.S. $1 (free rate of 0.582 rial = £1 sterling). Budget (1975 est.) balanced at 506 million rials. Foreign trade (1974): imports 135,580,000 rials; exports 298,430,000 rials. Import sources: United Arab Emirates 20%; U.K. 17%; Japan 8%; The Netherlands 8%; U.S. 8%; West Germany 7%. Export destinations: Japan *c.* 27%; Spain *c.* 15%; France *c.* 10%; Italy *c.* 6%; U.K. *c.* 5%; Norway *c.* 5%. Main export crude oil 99.9%.

Industry. Production (in 000): crude oil (metric tons; 1975) 17,043; electricity (kw-hr; 1974) *c.* 200,000.

Nobel Prizes: *see* People of the Year

Nordic Literature: *see* Literature

Norwegian Literature: *see* Literature

Nuclear Energy: *see* Defense; Energy; Industrial Review

Numismatics: *see* Philately and Numismatics

Obituaries: *see* People of the Year

Oceanography: *see* Earth Sciences

Oil: *see* Energy

Olympic Games: *see* Track and Field Sports; Winter Sports troops in Oman helping to fight the rebels. Also in March, when Saudi Arabia established diplomatic relations with the People's Democratic Republic of Yemen (South Yemen), the rebels' main source of aid, Saudi mediation achieved a cease-fire between Oman and South Yemen, and Oman offered an amnesty, valid for a fortnight, to Omanis involved in the rebellion. Later in the year, however, there were more shelling incidents across the Oman-South Yemen border. On August 23 an Oman government spokesman said that the Iranian troops would stay until South Yemen expressed good intentions.

In January the Oman oil minister claimed that new oil discoveries by international oil companies offered the prospect of increasing production from 380,000 bbl a day to 1 million bbl by 1979. Budget details announced in August showed a 20% increase over 1975 and a planned deficit of about $400 million. Defense spending was about 45% of the total and showed a 9% increase over 1975. (PETER MANSFIELD)

[978.B.4.b]

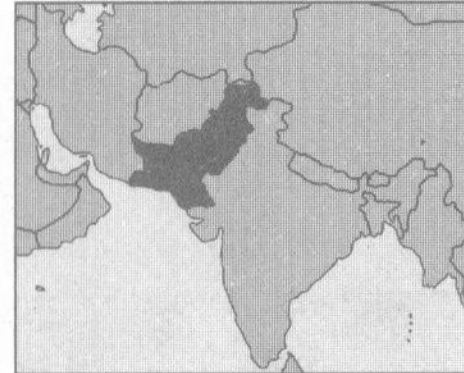

Pakistan

A federal republic, Pakistan is bordered on the south by the Arabian Sea, on the west by Afghanistan and Iran, on the north by China, and on the east by India. Area: 307,374 sq mi (796,095 sq km), excluding the Pakistani-controlled section of Jammu and Kashmir. Pop. (1975 est.): 70,260,000. Cap.: Islamabad (pop., 1972, 77,000). Largest city: Karachi (metro. area pop., 1975 est., 4,465,000). Language: Urdu and English. Religion: Muslim 90%, Hindu and Christian minorities. President in 1976, Chaudhri Fazal Elahi; prime minister, Zulfikar Ali Bhutto.

The centenary of the birth of Mohammed Ali Jinnah fell in 1976, which was declared memorial year by the government. Celebrations culminated in an international conference of historians and writers held in Islamabad in December to honour the memory of Pakistan's founder. Appropriately enough, the year brought a notable relaxation of tension between Pakistan and two countries with which Jinnah had always hoped to have neighbourly relations—India and Afghanistan.

A passenger train leaves Amritsar, India, for Lahore, Pakistan, 30 miles away. After a break of 11 years, service was resumed in July.

RAGHU RAI—THE NEW YORK TIMES

During 1975 there had been little progress in implementing the agreement concluded at Simla between Indira Gandhi, prime minister of India, and Prime Minister Bhutto in 1972. Pakistan resented India's policy in Kashmir; India accused Pakistan of spreading rumours that Indian forces were about to attack Pakistan or Bangladesh. This souring of the atmosphere was all the more unfortunate because Iran, Pakistan's firm ally, was concluding important industrial and commercial trading arrangements with India and deprecated the delay in normalizing Indo-Pakistani relations. In March 1976, Bhutto successfully broke the deadlock with a letter to Mrs. Gandhi, as a consequence of which meetings took place in May at Islamabad between delegations from each country. Both sides agreed to withdraw their complaints to the International Civil Aviation Organization and to resume air links and overflights. Freight and passenger traffic by rail through the frontier at Wagah-Attari was reopened; diplomatic relations (broken off in December 1971) were restored; and the participation of the private sector in Indo-Pakistani trade was sanctioned. By the end of the year a marked improvement had taken place in the relations between Islamabad and New Delhi.

At the close of 1975 tension between Kabul and Islamabad had almost reached a breaking point. Pakistan accused Afghanistan of encouraging secessionists working for the breakaway of the North-West Frontier Province (N.W.F.P.) and Baluchistan; Af-

PAKISTAN

Education. (1973–74) Primary, pupils 4,657,000, teachers 117,000; secondary, pupils 1,704,358, teachers 88,700; vocational, pupils 25,798, teachers 1,810; teacher training, students 37,201, teachers 1,398; higher, students 256,340, teaching staff 13,198.

Finance. Monetary unit: Pakistan rupee, with (Sept. 20, 1976) a par value of PakRs 9.90 to U.S. $1 (free rate of PakRs 16.75 = £1 sterling). Gold, SDR's, and foreign exchange (June 1976) U.S. $636 million. Budget (1975–76 est.): revenue PakRs 17,687,000,000; expenditure PakRs 30,819,000,000. Gross national product (1974–75) PakRs 107,730,000,000. Money supply (June 1976) PakRs 28,260,000,000. Cost of living (1970 = 100; April 1976) 228.

Foreign Trade. (1975) Imports PakRs 21,361,000,000; exports PakRs 10,416,000,000. Import sources: Japan 13%; U.S. 13%; Saudi Arabia 8%; U.K. 6%; Australia 6%; West Germany 6%. Export destinations: Hong Kong 11%; Japan 7%; Saudi Arabia 6%; U.K. 6%; West Germany 5%. Main exports (1974–75): rice 22%; cotton 15%; cotton fabrics 13%; cotton yarn 9%.

Transport and Communications. Roads (1972) 62,834 km. Motor vehicles in use (1973): passenger 177,300; commercial (including buses) 79,100. Railways: (1974) 9,808 km; traffic (1973–74) c. 11,600,000,000 passenger-km, freight c. 7,344,000,000 net ton-km. Air traffic (1975): 2,622,700,000 passenger-km; freight 129,990,000 net ton-km. Shipping (1975): merchant vessels 100 gross tons and over 84; gross tonnage 479,358. Telephones (Dec. 1974) 210,000. Radio receivers (Dec. 1972) c. 1.5 million. Television receivers (Dec. 1972) c. 195,000.

Agriculture. Production (in 000; metric tons; 1975): wheat 7,299; barley 137; corn 904; rice 3,657; millet c. 312; sorghum c. 371; sugar, raw value 547; sugar, noncentrifugal (1974) 1,422; chick-peas 535; onions c. 249; peanuts c. 71; rapeseed 248; oranges (1974) c. 330; mangoes (1974) c. 670; tobacco c. 74; cotton, lint c. 635. Livestock (in 000; 1975): cattle c. 13,389; buffalo (1974) c. 10,200; sheep c. 18,693; goats (1974) c. 12,749; camels (1974) c. 827.

Industry. Production (in 000; metric tons; 1975): cement 3,225; crude oil 387; coal and lignite (1973–74) c. 1,500; natural gas (cu m; 1974) c. 4,600,000; electricity (excluding most industrial production; kw-hr; 1974) c. 6,400,000; sulfuric acid 41; caustic soda 38; soda ash (1973–74) 91; nitrogenous fertilizers (nutrient content; 1974–75) 311; cotton yarn 357; woven cotton fabrics (m; 1973–74) 648,000.

ghanistan bitterly criticized the prosecution of National Awami Party (NAP) leaders by the Pakistan government. Both Iran and the Soviet Union used their influence in favour of moderation, and in April, when earthquakes and floods struck three provinces of Afghanistan, Bhutto sent a message of sympathy and offers of practical help to Pres. S. M. Daud Khan, following this up with a personal visit to Kabul in June. In return, Daud Khan not only visited Islamabad but gave a donation to the relief work necessitated by the devastating autumn floods in the Punjab and Sind. It was noted in the Pakistan press that certain professional advocates of Pakhtunistan and of an independent Baluchistan had left Kabul for Europe, while support for the NAP leaders was no longer featured in the Kabul press.

In February Bhutto shifted some of the portfolios in his Cabinet. No one was dropped; some new blood was added, including Gen. Tikka Khan, army chief of staff, who became special assistant to the president for national security, with Cabinet rank. Important appointments included new governors for Sind and the N.W.F.P.

During 1976 there was an improvement in internal security in the N.W.F.P. and Baluchistan, due partly to economic progress based on generous grants from the central government and partly to the abolition in April of the *sardari* system; the sardars, local chieftains who had exercised semifeudal powers, were forbidden to maintain private armies and private prisons, administer justice, or exact feudal dues or forced labour. Some shootings and bombings continued, but the hands of the executive were strengthened by constitutional amendments curtailing the scope of the judiciary, and the prosecution of certain NAP leaders for sedition was upheld by the Supreme Court.

In an effort to ensure fair prices for both consumers and producers, paddy husking, cotton ginning, and large-scale flour milling were nationalized. Smallholders were exempted from land tax, and the distribution of land to the cultivators and the conferring of proprietary rights on tenants made progress. The federal budget indicated a resilient economy but hopes of a record agricultural production were dashed by severe flooding in the Indus Valley regions.

(L. F. RUSHBROOK WILLIAMS)

[976.A.3]

Panama

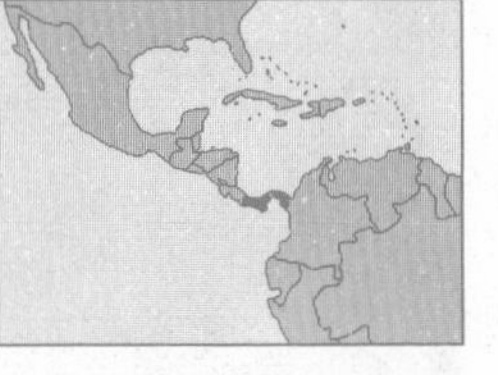

A republic of Central America, bisected by the Canal Zone, Panama is bounded by the Caribbean Sea, Colombia, the Pacific Ocean, and Costa Rica. Area: 29,209 sq mi (75,650 sq km). Pop. (1976 est.): 1,718,700. Cap. and largest city: Panama City (pop., 1976 est., 415,790). Language: Spanish. Religion (1971 est.): Roman Catholic 90%. President in 1976, Demetrio Lakas Bahas.

The proposal for the United States to transfer the Panama Canal and Canal Zone to Panama aroused the attention of more people in 1976 than ever before. Ambassador-at-large Ellsworth Bunker, the U.S. negotiator, disclosed in October 1975 that "conceptual" agreement had been reached on Panamanian participation in operating and protecting the canal and on the transfer of certain jurisdictional functions. No meeting of minds occurred on other problems, however, and little progress was expected before 1977.

CAMERA PRESS/PHOTO TRENDS

The Bayano Dam in Panama was built by a Yugoslav enterprise.

In April, after having strongly advocated Panamanian control over the canal, Brig. Gen. Omar Torrijos, Panama's strong man, silenced the Panamanian press and warned students to suspend agitation on the subject. In the U.S., however, Ronald Reagan, a formidable rival to U.S. Pres. Gerald Ford for the Republican nomination for president, raised the issue by charging the administration with approving a secret pact with Panama to yield sovereignty over the Canal Zone. Reagan declared that the United States had bought and paid for the Zone and had built the canal and should, therefore, keep them. The Department of State denied the allegation of a secret pact.

President Ford responded that the U.S. would never give up its defense and operational rights in the canal. A report of the hearings before a subcommittee of the U.S. House of Representatives on April 6–8 indicated, however, that Ambassador Bunker had been instructed to do just that after a period of years. Reagan capitalized on the issue and lost the nomination to Ford in August by a close margin. In a debate between candidates Ford and Jimmy Carter the former declared that the U.S. must maintain complete access to the canal and a defense capability over it. Carter insisted that he would never give up practical control, while sharing responsibilities. Torrijos reminded Carter that "never" had disappeared from the political dictionary and scolded Ford for talking "peace" while stationing 20,000 soldiers in the Zone.

The intensity of feeling generated by Reagan's campaign was due, in part, to Torrijos' posture of friendship with Castro. In October 1975 the Cuban armed forces entertained and instructed a Panamanian military mission, and in January Torrijos and an entourage of some 200 military, student, business, labour, and farm representatives made a five-day visit to Cuba. Castro piloted them to sugar mills, schools, construction camps, and museums. The substance of the advice which the Cuban offered Torrijos was to observe patience and depend upon Cuban aid. The revelation that such aid, in the form of an expeditionary force, had been dispatched to Angola chilled the pro-Castro sympathies of many Latin Americans. Torrijos went on planning a June conference of Latin leaders at which he anticipated that his demands upon the U.S. would be supported. The

Opera: *see* Music

Organization for Economic Cooperation and Development: *see* Economy, World

Organization of African Unity: *see* African Affairs

Organization of American States: *see* Latin-American Affairs

Ornithology: *see* Life Sciences

Orthodox Churches: *see* Religion

Painting: *see* Art and Art Exhibitions; Art Sales; Museums

Paints and Varnishes: *see* Industrial Review

Palestine: *see* Israel; Jordan

PANAMA

Education. (1975) Primary, pupils 342,043, teachers 11,185; secondary, pupils 81,928, teachers 3,472; vocational, pupils 37,713, teachers 1,926; teacher training, students 5,850, teachers 244; higher, students 26,289, teaching staff 1,022.

Finance. Monetary unit: balboa, at par with the U.S. dollar, with (Sept. 20, 1976) a free rate of 1.72 balboas to £1 sterling. Gold, SDR's, and foreign exchange (Dec. 1974) U.S. $39.4 million. Budget (1975 est.) balanced at 337 million balboas. Gross national product (1974) 1,688,400,000 balboas. Cost of living (Panama City; 1970 = 100; June 1976) 144.

Foreign Trade. (1975) Imports 869,780,000 balboas; exports 282,490,000 balboas. Net service receipts etc. from Canal Zone (1974) 227 million balboas. Import sources (1974): U.S. 27%; Ecuador 17%; Venezuela 11%; Saudi Arabia 8%; Japan 6%. Export destinations (1974): U.S. 52%; Canal Zone 17%; West Germany 6%; Italy 6%; The Netherlands 5%. Main exports: petroleum products 45%; bananas 21%; shrimps 7%.

Transport and Communications. Roads (1974) 7,128 km. Motor vehicles in use (1974): passenger 69,780; commercial 16,080. Railways (1975) 347 km. Shipping (1975): merchant vessels 100 gross tons and over 2,418 (mostly owned by U.S. and other foreign interests); gross tonnage 13,667,123. Telephones (Dec. 1973) *c.* 105,000. Radio receivers (Dec. 1973) 255,000. Television receivers (Dec. 1972) 200,000.

Agriculture. Production (in 000; metric tons; 1974): rice 178; sugar, raw value 104; bananas *c.* 970; oranges *c.* 59; coffee *c.* 5; cocoa *c.* 0.6. Livestock (in 000; 1974): cattle *c.* 1,361; pigs *c.* 188; horses *c.* 164; chickens *c.* 3,790.

Industry. Production (in 000; metric tons; 1974): petroleum products 3,587; cement (1971) 192; manufactured gas (cu m) 14,000; electricity (kw-hr) *c.* 1,195,000.

southern Latin-American states, however, prompted the cancellation of the meeting.

The close relations with Cuba and the warning words against the U.S. were intended, in part, as a distraction from the worries of a downtrend in the Panamanian economy. Unemployment and inflation continued to afflict the country. To provide more jobs required more money, but investors' confidence was such that no economic growth was registered; the foreign debt was 503.3 million balboas in August. The banking industry, object of special concessions from the Panamanian government and consisting of some 72 different banks, restricted its activities. New capital was sought in new ways. Thus, Texas Gulf Co. was induced to enter a contract to exploit the copper of the Cerro Colorado, while the government was to hold 80% of the capital stock in the new company. United Brands Co. agreed to turn over thousands of acres of banana plantations at a nominal price and to lease these back at a high figure.

Unhappy with the government's economic and political policies, business leaders took the unusual step of meeting in mid-January at David, Chiriqui Province, to proclaim their discontent. Torrijos swiftly moved against them with arrests and deportations. In protest the business organization called a general strike, which idled banks, factories, and offices for about three days. Again the government responded, this time by smashing the headquarters of the Association of Panamanian Business Executives. Beginning on Sept. 10, 1976, student riots and demonstrations took place, marked by stoning, looting, arson, tear gas, and arrests. Torrijos unsuccessfully tried to place the blame on the U.S. Student placards attacked the price of food and the cost of living, but the slogan "Yankee Go Home" was absent.

U.S. civilian employees in the Canal Zone, fearful that the ultimate policy of their own government was "Yankee Go Home" and angered by the Panama Canal Company's wage policy, struck back. Their absence from duty on "sick leave" in March caused a backup of 175 ships. (ALMON R. WRIGHT)

[974.B.1.f]

Panama Canal Zone: *see* Dependent States; Panama

Paper and Pulp: *see* Industrial Review

Papua New Guinea

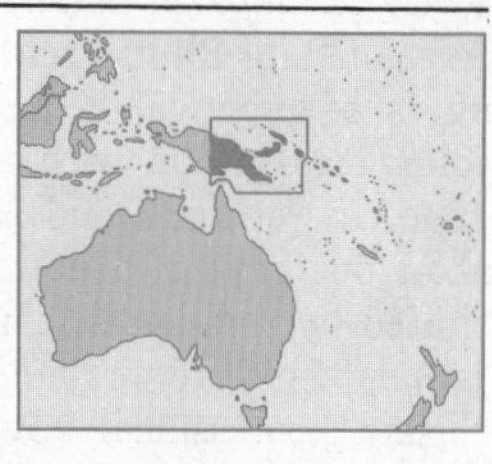

Papua New Guinea is an independent parliamentary state and a member of the Commonwealth of Nations. It is situated in the southwest Pacific and comprises the eastern part of the island of New Guinea, the islands of the Bismarck, Trobriand, Woodlark, Louisiade, and D'Entrecasteaux groups, and parts of the Solomon Islands, including Bougainville. It is separated from Australia by the Torres Strait. Area: 178,260 sq mi (461,690 sq km). Pop. (1975 est.): 2,756,500. Cap. and largest city: Port Moresby (pop., 1975 est., 104,500). Language: English, Police Motu (a Melanesian pidgin), and Pidgin English (or Neo-Melanesian) are official, although the latter is the most widely spoken. Religion (1966): Roman Catholic 31.2%; Lutheran 27.3%; indigenous 7%. Queen, Elizabeth II; governor-general in 1976, Sir John Guise; prime minister, Michael T. Somare.

In 1976, in an attempt to establish a sense of national identity, Papua New Guineans were encouraged by the prime minister to wear national dress to work every Friday. The plan was not successful, as it was difficult to be sure what constituted national dress. The major political event was the dismissal of the minister of culture, recreation, and youth development, Moses Sasakila, after a tribunal discovered that he had failed to provide the required accounting of his income, gifts, and business dealings.

In April the finance minister, Julius Chan, announced a tax on the boom earnings from coffee growing. Chan also introduced in the national Parlia-

Wearing national dress is Sir Maori Kiki (right), Papua New Guinea's minister for defense, foreign relations, and trade.

KEYSTONE

PAPUA NEW GUINEA

Education. (1975) Primary, pupils 243,080, teachers 7,824; secondary, pupils 30,492, teachers 1,282; vocational, pupils 9,031, teachers 569; teacher training, students 2,201, teachers 176; higher, students 2,624, teaching staff 324.

Finance. Monetary unit: kina, at par with the Australian dollar, with (Sept. 20, 1976) a free rate of 0.80 kina to U.S. $1 (1.38 kina = £1 sterling). Budget (1975–76) balanced at 400.1 million kinas (including Australian grants of 127 million kinas).

Foreign Trade. (1974–75) Imports 367,040,000 kinas; exports 426,250,000 kinas. Import sources (1974): Australia 50%; Japan 17%; Singapore 8%; U.S. 6%. Export destinations (1974): Japan 40%; West Germany 21%; Australia 12%; U.K. 7%; U.S. 6%. Main exports: copper ores 56%; cocoa 9%; coffee 8%; copra 7%.

Transport. Roads (1973) *c.* 16,000 km. Shipping (1975): merchant vessels 100 gross tons and over 54; gross tonnage 14,500.

Agriculture. Production (in 000; metric tons; 1975): cocoa *c.* 34; coffee *c.* 41; copra *c.* 140; cassava (1974) *c.* 82; taro (1974) *c.* 215; yams (1974) *c.* 165; rubber *c.* 6; timber (cu m; 1974) *c.* 5,291. Livestock (in 000; March 1974): cattle *c.* 83; pigs *c.* 1,150; goats *c.* 15; chickens *c.* 1,040.

Industry. Production (in 000; troy oz; 1974): gold 678; silver 1,286; copper ore (metal content; metric tons) 184.

ment in Port Moresby a statement of the World Bank's survey of the state's economy. The bank gave Papua New Guinea a high credit-worthiness rating and endorsed the government's financial policies. However, it referred to the country's economic reliance on Bougainville copper and underlined the point that, if Bougainville seceded, the picture could change. Bougainville had threatened to secede several times, and serious riots occurred there in January. However, an accommodation with the Bougainville leaders was announced later in the year. (For the dispute with Australia over the Torres Strait Islands of Boigu, Dauan, and Saibai, *see* COMMONWEALTH OF NATIONS.)

(A. R. G. GRIFFITHS)

[977.A.3]

Paraguay

A landlocked republic of South America, Paraguay is bounded by Brazil, Argentina, and Bolivia. Area: 157,048 sq mi (406,752 sq km). Pop. (1976 UN est.): 2,724,000. Cap. and largest city: Asunción (pop., 1975 UN est., 574,000). Language: Spanish (official), though Guaraní is the language of the majority of the people. Religion: Roman Catholic (official). President in 1976, Gen. Alfredo Stroessner.

General Stroessner's government faced more open opposition in 1976 in spite of a substantial victory (86% of votes cast) obtained by the governing Partido Colorado in the October 1975 municipal elections. The church experienced increased repression, and the Partido Liberal Radical and the Partido Liberal, which decided in September 1976 to iron out their differences and create a "true" liberal coalition, repeatedly expressed disapproval of the government. In July the Congress approved in principle a constitutional amendment that would allow Stroessner, president since 1954, to run in 1978 for another five-year term.

The Itaipú hydroelectric complex, under construction in collaboration with Brazil, attracted many foreign industrial projects such as cement production, steel manufacturing, and paper and cellulose mills; industrial investment in the first six months of 1976 reached $13.7 million, an increase of 120% over the corresponding January–June 1975 figure, as a result of a new investment law passed in December 1975 offering bigger and also new incentives. In 1976 various trade agreements were signed with neighbouring countries, and special efforts were made to increase trade with the European Economic Community. Inflation, a recurring major problem, reached 25.2% in 1974 but was brought down to 6.7% in 1975.

(FRANÇOISE LOTERY)

[974.F.3]

PARAGUAY

Education. (1975) Primary, pupils 452,249, teachers 15,398; secondary, pupils 75,424, teachers 10,406; vocational, pupils 1,361, teachers 67; higher (1973), students 12,212, teaching staff 1,529.

Finance. Monetary unit: guaraní, with (Sept. 20, 1975) an official rate of 126 guaranies to U.S. $1 (free rate of 214 guaranies = £1 sterling). Gold, SDR's, and foreign exchange (June 1976) U.S. $132,260,000. Budget (1975 est.) balanced at 18,329,000,000 guaranies. Gross national product (1974) 165,990,-000,000 guaranies. Money supply (March 1976) 17,-670,000,000 guaranies. Cost of living (Asunción; 1970 = 100; May 1976) 180.

Foreign Trade. (1975) Imports 26,786,000,000 guaranies; exports 21,804,000,000 guaranies. Import sources: Brazil 20%; Argentina 18%; U.S. 12%; U.K. 9%; West Germany 8%; Japan 5%. Export destinations: Argentina 28%; West Germany 13%; U.K. 10%; U.S. 9%; The Netherlands 9%; Switzerland 8%; France 5%. Main exports: meat 18%; timber 16%; cotton 11%; tobacco 7%; vegetable oils 6%.

Transport and Communications. Roads (1973) 15,956 km. Motor vehicles in use (1973): passenger 10,000; commercial (including buses) 19,000. Railways (1973): 498 km; traffic 26 million passenger-km, freight 30 million net ton-km. Navigable inland waterways (including Paraguay-Paraná River system; 1973) *c.* 3,000 km. Telephones (Dec. 1974) 34,500. Radio receivers (Dec. 1973) 175,000. Television receivers (Dec. 1973) 53,000.

Agriculture. Production (in 000; metric tons; 1975): corn *c.* 342; cassava (1974) 1,108; sweet potatoes (1974) 88; soybeans 216; peanuts *c.* 15; dry beans 30; sugar, raw value (1974) *c.* 80; tomatoes *c.* 52; oranges (1974) *c.* 119; mandarin oranges and tangerines (1974) *c.* 31; bananas (1974) *c.* 264; tobacco *c.* 33; palm kernels *c.* 15; cotton lint *c.* 33; beef and veal (1974) 111. Livestock (in 000; 1974): cattle *c.* 6,016; sheep *c.* 347; pigs *c.* 659; horses *c.* 731; chickens *c.* 6,724.

Industry. Production (in 000; metric tons; 1974): petroleum products *c.* 230; cement (1973) 74; cotton yarn 24; electricity (kw-hr) 504,000.

Peru

A republic on the west coast of South America, Peru is bounded by Ecuador, Colombia, Brazil, Bolivia, Chile, and the Pacific Ocean. Area: 496,224 sq mi (1,285,215 sq km). Pop. (1975 est.): 15,869,000, including approximately 52% whites and mestizos and 46% Indians. Cap. and largest city: Lima (metro. area pop., 1975 UN est., 3,901,000). Language: Spanish and Quechua are official; Indians also speak Aymara. Religion: Roman Catholic. President of the military government in 1976, Francisco Morales Bermúdez.

In the traditional rotation of positions in the military government, Gen. Jorge Fernández Maldonado became prime minister, minister of war, and commander in chief of the Army on Jan. 31, 1976. He had been minister of mines and energy under former pres-

Parachuting: *see* Aerial Sports

Penology: *see* Prisons and Penology

Pentecostal Churches: *see* Religion

WIDE WORLD

A crowd of his followers welcomes former Peruvian president Fernando Belaúnde Terry as he returns to Lima after five years in exile.

ident Juan Velasco Alvarado and had supervised the nationalization of the Cerro de Pasco and Marcona mining operations. He was commonly listed among the "radicals" of the military hierarchy.

The General Confederation of Workers of Peru (CGTP), which had spearheaded a wave of strikes in vital economic sectors in January, retreated in February when faced with a tough government crackdown on illegal strikes and a possible break between the government and the Communist Party. The campaign for a general strike had gained momentum when government conciliatory measures failed to quell labour unrest. A potentially devastating strike in the state-owned Pescaperú fishing fleet was broken rapidly, however, when the anchovy fishermen were threatened with immediate and noncompensated dismissal.

In a controversial speech on March 31, President Morales did not present the promised "Tupac Amaru" plan, which was to provide general guidelines for the "second phase of the Revolution" through 1981. There was a change of policy—after unrest had led to the declaration of a state of national emergency on July 1—and President Morales introduced changes in his Cabinet, including the dismissal of Fernández on July 16 and his replacement by Gen. Guillermo Arbulú Galliani. On July 21 the government announced that the Pescaperú fishing fleet would be largely denationalized.

In a related but more significant move, on March 15 directors of six "socialized" national newspapers were dismissed and replaced by more moderate editors, and by the end of July further dismissals severely constrained press freedom. The national daily press, "socialized" in 1974, had generally maintained an obsequious line of support for official policies, but the economic austerity measures announced in January 1976 had been increasingly criticized.

The reorientation of official policy became apparent in February when the small business law was passed, giving private enterprise a greater role in the Peruvian economy. Although some of Peru's problems had been caused by uncontrollable external factors, such as the 1975 fall in copper prices, productivity was severely affected by labour unrest, particularly in mining. In May and June 1976 the government announced a series of new measures designed to reduce Peru's balance of payments deficit and to stimulate the economy. The corrective measures included a curtailment of the investment expenditures of both the central government and public concerns, a freeze on current account budgetary outlay, a heavy tax on gasoline which more than doubled the retail price, a 15% tax on traditional exports, an additional 15% sales tax on imported products, and a ceiling on corporate dividend payments of 10% of a firm's net worth.

The country's economic problems had their effect on the sol, which was devalued from 45 to 65 soles per U.S. dollar in June; the government adopted a policy of periodic devaluations toward the end of the year. Foreign confidence in Peru remained quite high, however, with international loans to all sectors of the economy. External funds were essential to finance the ambitious $3.5 billion development plan. The government expected that the Peruvian economy would benefit by the middle of 1977 from a reduction in petroleum imports and the start of a period as an oil exporter. The petroleum would be available as a result of the coming into operation of Petroperú's pipeline linking the jungle area with the coast, at a cost of $700 million.

Some commentators believed that the Peruvian revolution was entering into a third stage, marked by a progressive demilitarization of the government and movement toward the political centre. The Communist Party, after strongly supporting the military in its quest for the military road to socialism, moved into opposition. (JAIME R. DUHART)

[974.D.2]

PERU

Education. (1975) Primary, pupils 2,970,708, teachers 76,445; secondary, pupils 758,320, teachers 30,051; vocational, pupils 250,788, teachers 10,320; higher, students 320,038, teaching staff 16,095.

Finance. Monetary unit: sol, with (Sept. 20, 1976) a par value of 65 soles to U.S. $1 (free rate of 112 soles = £1 sterling). Gold, SDR's, and foreign exchange (Nov. 1975) U.S. $507.6 million. Budget (1975 actual): revenue 86,762,000,000 soles; expenditure 106,975,000,000 soles. Gross domestic product (1974) 448.6 billion soles. Money supply (Nov. 1975) 113,210,000,000 soles. Cost of living (Lima; 1970 = 100; April 1976) 217.

Foreign Trade. (1974) Imports 59,232,000,000 soles; exports 58,021,000,000 soles. Import sources: U.S. 31%; Japan 12%; West Germany 10%; Ecuador 5%. Export destinations: U.S. 36%; Japan 13%; West Germany 8%; China 5%. Main exports: copper 23%; fish meal 13%; silver 11%; zinc 11%; sugar 10%; cotton 6%.

Transport and Communications. Roads (1974) 50,670 km. Motor vehicles in use (1972): passenger 256,400; commercial 136,100. Railways: (1972) 3,218 km; traffic (1973) 270 million passenger-km, freight 735 million net ton-km. Shipping (1975): merchant vessels 100 gross tons and over 677; gross tonnage 518,361. Telephones (Dec. 1974) 333,000. Radio receivers (Dec. 1973) 2,001,000. Television receivers (Dec. 1973) 411,000.

Agriculture. Production (in 000; metric tons; 1975): rice 500; corn c. 625; wheat 150; barley c. 170; potatoes 1,870; sweet potatoes (1974) 120; onions c. 178; cassava (1974) 266; dry beans c. 42; sugar, raw value c. 1,005; apples (1974) 73; grapes c. 63; oranges (1974) 214; lemons (1974) c. 75; coffee c. 65; cotton, lint c. 73; fish catch (1974) 4,150. Livestock (in 000; 1975): cattle c. 4,200; sheep c. 17,800; pigs c. 1,900; goats (1974) c. 1,950; horses (1974) c. 731; poultry c. 25,000.

Industry. Production (in 000; metric tons; 1974): coal c. 85; crude oil (1975) 3,657; natural gas (cu m) c. 530,000; cement 1,731; iron ore (metal content) c. 6,198; pig iron 305; crude steel 482; lead 81; zinc 69; copper 39; tungsten concentrates (oxide content) 1.1; gold (troy oz) 75; silver (troy oz) c. 41,000; fish meal 902; petroleum products c. 5,310; electricity (kw-hr) c. 7,530,000.

Petroleum: *see* Energy

Pharmaceutical Industry: *see* Industrial Review

COURTESY, THE POST OFFICE, LONDON

Philately and Numismatics

Stamps. The year was dominated by the U.S. bicentennial celebrations, which culminated for stamp collectors with Interphil 76 in Philadelphia from May 29 to June 6. This was the year's major international philatelic exhibition under the patronage of the International Philatelic Federation (FIP). The leading awards were: Grand Prix d'Honneur, Wallace W. Knox (U.S.), for early British stamps and postal history; Grand Prix National, Louis Grunin (U.S.), for U.S. stamps of 1847–57; Grand Prix International, Horst G. Dietrich (West Germany), for Afghanistan 1839–1881. Commemorative stamps for the Bicentennial were issued by many nations, providing material for a new theme for topical (thematic) collectors. In August an international exhibition, Hafnia 76, was held in Copenhagen to mark the 125th anniversary of Denmark's first stamps. There, the FIP Grand Prix d'Honneur was won by a Swedish collector (entering as "Per Fossum") with a collection of Norwegian stamps of 1855–71; the Grand Prix National went to H. Mott (Sweden) for specialized Denmark 1851–63; and the Grand Prix International to Tewfik Kuyas (Turkey) for specialized Brazil 1843–51.

Two other exhibitions were Themabelga 75 (December 1975) at Brussels, the first exclusively topical international exhibition, at which the Grand Prix went to H. Paikert (West Germany) for his history of the Universal Postal Union collection; and Juvarouen (at Rouen, France, in April 1976), a junior international confined to those under 21. At the latter, Robert Newton (U.K.) won the Grand Prix for "British Treaty Ports in China and Japan."

The new signatories to the Roll of Distinguished Philatelists were Sybil Morgan (U.K.), only the fourth woman to sign since the roll was inaugurated in 1921; John Gartner (Australia); Max Guggenheim (Switzerland); and Karl K. Wolter (West Germany). The Philatelic Congress Medal was awarded to Kathleen F. Goodman (U.K.). The Lichtenstein Medal of the Collectors Club of New York was awarded to Ernest A. Kehr (U.S.).

Auction prices everywhere continued to show steep rises for rare stamps and covers. In January Robert A. Seigel (New York) realized $57,500 for an unused imperforate U.S. 1851 one-cent stamp, Die I, the most ever paid for a single U.S. stamp. Princeton University sold a mint block of four U.S. 1918 24-cent airmail stamps with inverted centre at Harmer's in New York for $170,000, a record for any U.S. item at auction.

Britain issued a set of stamps marking the 500th anniversary of William Caxton's printing press. The stamps show the knight in "The Canterbury Tales," an extract from "The Tretyse of Love," a woodcut from "The Game and Playe of Chesse," and an early printing press.

Illustrative of the growing trend toward large, specialized auctions devoted to stamps and postal history of a single country were Stanley Gibbons Auctions' two-day sale of Malta, which realized £81,924; Harmer's (New York) three-day sale of U.S. Postmasters' Provisionals, Confederate issues, Carrier stamps, and telegraph and revenue stamps ($411,852); Harmer's (London) two-day sale of Victorian Great Britain (£158,515); and P. J. Downie's (Melbourne) record sale of Australian stamps (A$127,338).

The major auction houses all reported record turnovers for the season ended in July: Stanley Gibbons Auctions, £1,633,604 (including a Frankfurt, West Germany, sale totaling £380,952); Robson Lowe International, £4,284,000 (including first-time sales in

AUTHENTICATED NEWS INTERNATIONAL

A strip of four U.S. bicentennial stamps reproduced John Trumbull's famous painting "The Declaration of Independence 4 July 1776."

Bermuda and Melbourne); H. R. Harmer (London, New York, and Sydney, Australia), £4,776,028. In September Stanley Gibbons held its first sale in Hong Kong, which realized £154,375.

The decision of Thomas De La Rue and Co. Ltd to auction artwork, essays, and proofs from its reference collection of work carried out for former British colonial possessions caused considerable controversy. On one side were those who thought that the material should have remained on loan to the National Postal Museum in London, while others believed that it should be made available by purchase to private specialist collectors.

Stamp robberies remained worrisome, but more disturbing were the murders of two U.S. stamp dealers who were to be called as witnesses for the prosecution of suspected stamp thieves. For the first time in U.S. postal history, arrests were made of alleged forgers of current U.S. stamps, following the discovery of just over 1,000 forged 13-cent Liberty Bell "regular" stamps at Dayton and Columbus (both Ohio), produced for sale to mail users at 5 cents each. (KENNETH F. CHAPMAN)

Coins. In addition to the three coins with special bicentennial designs, which had actually been put into circulation in 1975, collectors of U.S. currency had one new item to acquire in the bicentennial year, a $2 Federal Reserve green-seal note with a new back design. This denomination, formerly a United States red-seal note, was last printed in May 1965 and officially discontinued by the U.S. Department of the Treasury on Aug. 10, 1966. The new note depicts John Trumbull's painting of the signing of the Declaration of Independence on its reverse and the series date 1976 on its face side. First released on April 13, 1976, it was expected to be produced indefinitely as part of the U.S. circulating currency. There were some objections because the signers from six states had been cut from the Trumbull picture. The bicentennial designs on the reverses of the quarter, half dollar, and dollar were discontinued at the end of 1976.

An experimental U.S. dollar coin (top); side on left shows a Liberty head and a cap on a pole (long a symbol of freedom). At bottom are Martha Washington/Mt. Vernon galvanos, used in testing coinage metals.

WIDE WORLD

Worldwide interest in the U.S. bicentennial celebration was evidenced by at least 15 other governments or their banks, as they ordered U.S. bicentennial design coins for release to their citizens. Furthermore, several countries observed the event on coinages of their own. A number of countries noted International Women's Year on their 1975 coinages.

Token and medal collectors could choose from numerous bicentennial pieces, issued by various organizations, cities, states, and the U.S. Department of the Treasury. Only one of these was the official national bicentennial medal, depicting the upper portion of the Statue of Liberty and the Great Seal of the United States. It was produced and distributed by the U.S. Bureau of the Mint in seven combinations of sizes and metals, ranging from $1\frac{1}{2}$-in-diameter bronze at $5 to a 3-in coin-gold at $4,000.

The issuance of more FAO (Food and Agriculture Organization) coins by many nations throughout the world helped to stimulate interest in collecting coins of other countries. Nearly $4 billion, in U.S. value, of such coins in more than 200 types had been issued by mid-1976, and others were planned to help stimulate production of food for the world's growing population.

Of the many new coins issued by countries of the world, the following were notable: The Bahamas, 1976, sterling silver $10 and gold $100 in celebration of its third anniversary of independence; Belgium, 1976, silver 250 francs (two types, Flemish and French legends) commemorating the 25th anniversary of King Baudouin's reign; Bolivia, 1975, 0.933 fine silver 100, 250, and 500 pesos in observance of the 150th anniversary of its independence from Spain; Canada, 1975, silver dollar for the centennial of the founding of Calgary; Netherlands Antilles, 1976, 0.900 fine gold octagonal 200 guilders observing the U.S. Bicentennial; Soviet Union, 1975, chervonetz (10 rubles), the first gold (0.900 fine) coin of the Soviets since 1923 and identical to that issue except for the date and mint master's initials; Turks and Caicos Islands, 1975, 0.500 fine gold 25, 50, and 100 crowns; and West Germany, 1975, 0.625 fine silver 5 marks in observance of the centennial of the birth of Albert Schweitzer.

Numerous medals were produced to honour persons and commemorate events, and a few were for purely artistic purposes. Among them were ones commemorating the birth of Michelangelo in 1475; honouring Jerusalem's mayor, Teddy Kollek, and Harriet Beecher Stowe, author of *Uncle Tom's Cabin;* and the "Happy Birthday U.S.A." quasi-official observance of the 200th anniversary of the Declaration of Independence.

The American Numismatic Association, with headquarters in Colorado Springs, Colo., held its 1976 convention in New York City with a recorded attendance far greater than in any previous year. General economic conditions and, to some extent, the decline in the market price of gold and silver had, however, checked the growth of coin collecting. One good omen for its future could be seen in the increasing demand for authoritative numismatic literature, many out-of-print works bringing ever higher prices when offered for sale. (GLENN B. SMEDLEY)

[452.D.2.b; 725.B.4.g]

Philippines

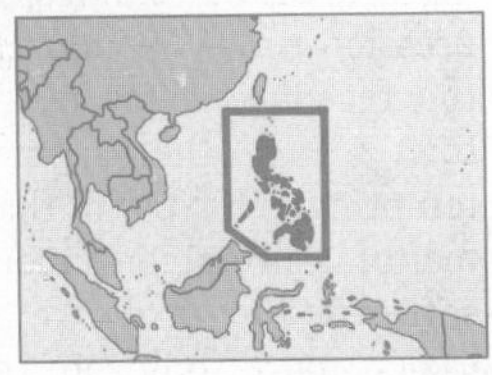

Situated in the western Pacific Ocean off the southeast coast of Asia, the Republic of the Philippines consists of an archipelago of about 7,100 islands. Area: 115,800 sq mi (300,000 sq km). Pop. (1975 census): 41,831,000. Cap. and largest city: Manila (pop., 1975 est., 1,454,400). Language: Pilipino (based on Tagalog), English, Spanish, and many dialects. Religion (1970): Roman Catholic 87%; Muslim 4.4%; Aglipayan 4%; Protestant 3.1%; others 1.5%. President in 1976, Ferdinand E. Marcos.

Approaching the fourth anniversary of his declaration of martial law, Pres. Ferdinand E. Marcos on Sept. 21, 1976, convened a new Legislative Advisory Council as a step toward a new form of government. The council was composed of 28 Cabinet members, 91 community assembly leaders, and 13 regional delegates, including Marcos' wife, Imelda, the governor of metropolitan Manila. Earlier Marcos said that he intended to call elections in 1977 for a parliament of about 120 members and that, under a future parliamentary system, the reforms of the martial law period must be protected.

Critics of Marcos were active but ineffectual. Diosdado Macapagal, president of the Philippines from 1961 to 1965 and head of the constitutional convention that drafted the 1973 constitution, accused Marcos of "blatant dictatorship." Roman Catholic Church groups were also critical. One, composed of 12,000 priests and nuns, charged on April 23 that the government was torturing prisoners, despite Marcos' denials. On June 26 the organization Amnesty International charged that political prisoners were tortured "freely and with extreme cruelty, often over long periods." The government announced an investigation of prisoner handling.

For most of the year, two rebellions continued, of Muslim separatists in the southern islands, chiefly Mindanao, and of Maoist revolutionaries scattered throughout the archipelago. On December 23, in Tripoli, Libya, a cease-fire agreement was reached by the government and the Moro National Liberation Front. Libya, which with other Muslim nations had assisted in the negotiations, announced that the agreement included autonomy for the Muslim regions.

Some leaders of the Maoist New People's Army were captured in August, but during 1976 the NPA became more active. Two NPA leaders were added to the sporadic trial for murder and subversion of former senator Benigno S. Aquino, Jr., who had been Marcos' main political challenger before martial law.

Moving slowly up Luzon Island in late May, Typhoon Olga caused extensive flooding, killing 215 persons and leaving at least 600,000 homeless. A severe earthquake under the Celebes Sea August 17 caused damage on Mindanao and the Sulu Archipelago, following which seismic waves some 15 to 20 ft high swamped coastal areas. The government estimated the death toll at over 8,000. A $160 million rehabilitation program was announced.

On a visit to Moscow, Marcos signed an agreement June 2 to establish diplomatic relations with the Soviet Union. Relations with Vietnam were agreed to in Manila on July 12, completing the Philippines' move to full diplomatic contacts with Communist countries. Under a tentative agreement reached in December, the U.S. would provide $1 billion in aid over five years in return for continued use of Philippine military bases.

On May 31 Marcos signed a decree formally changing the national capital from Quezon City to Manila. No physical transfer was involved.

Low prices for two main exports, sugar and copper, caused economic difficulties and forced the government to hold imports down. The country's first oil strikes, offshore northwest of Palawan Island, offered the prospect of reducing the main import bill, but offshore drilling led to disputes with China and Vietnam. Official figures indicated about 6% economic growth in 1976. (HENRY S. BRADSHER)

[976.C.2]

PHILIPPINES

Education. (1972–73) Primary, pupils 7,622,424, teachers 247,551; secondary, pupils 1,631,363, teachers 45,594; vocational, pupils 159,813, teachers 12,378; higher (including 40 universities), students 678,343, teaching staff 32,651.

Finance. Monetary unit: peso, with (Sept. 20, 1976) a free rate of 7.55 pesos to U.S. $1 (13.01 pesos = £1 sterling). Gold, SDR's, and foreign exchange (June 1976) U.S. $1,679,000,000. Budget (1975–76 est.): revenue 17,327,000,000 pesos; expenditure 22,399,000,000 pesos. Gross national product (1975) 113,410,000,000 pesos. Money supply (May 1976) 10,785,000,000 pesos. Cost of living (Manila; 1970 = 100; Feb. 1976) 247.

Foreign Trade. (1975) Imports 27,883,000,000 pesos; exports 16,434,000,000 pesos. Import sources: Japan 28%; U.S. 22%; Saudi Arabia 11%. Export destinations: Japan 38%; U.S. 29%; The Netherlands 8%. Main exports: sugar 25%; coconut oil 10%; copper 9%; timber 9%; copra 8%.

Transport and Communications. Roads (1974) 92,775 km. Motor vehicles in use (1974): passenger 362,500; commercial (including buses) 247,300. Railways: (1973) 1,150 km; traffic (1974) 899 million passenger-km, freight 70 million net ton-km. Air traffic (1974): 2,050,000,000 passenger-km; freight 51.3 million net ton-km. Shipping (1975): merchant vessels 100 gross tons and over 413; gross tonnage 879,043. Telephones (Jan. 1975) 446,260. Radio receivers (Dec. 1973) 1.8 million. Television receivers (Dec. 1973) 450,000.

Agriculture. Production (in 000; metric tons; 1975): rice 6,258; corn *c.* 2,650; sweet potatoes (1974) *c.* 640; sugar, raw value 2,471; coffee *c.* 57; bananas (1974) *c.* 1,100; tobacco *c.* 60; rubber *c.* 30; manila hemp (1974) *c.* 87; pork (1974) *c.* 390; timber (cu m; 1974) *c.* 32,380; fish catch (1974) 1,291. Livestock (in 000; March 1975): cattle *c.* 2,250; buffalo (1974) *c.* 5,000; pigs *c.* 9,700; goats (1974) *c.* 1,300; horses (1974) 310; chickens *c.* 51,000.

Industry. Production (in 000; metric tons; 1975): coal 101; iron ore (55–60% metal content) 1,352; chrome ore (oxide content; 1974) 192; copper ore (metal content) 226; gold (troy oz; 1974) 536; silver (troy oz; 1974) 1,700; cement 3,617; petroleum products (1974) *c.* 7,800; sulfuric acid (1974) 342; electricity (excluding most industrial production; kw-hr) 9,761,000.

Philosophy

In 1976 the philosophical profession moved actively to resolve a pair of persistent problems. While its traditional academic support had remained static in recent years, its research activities and the numbers of those seeking entry into the profession had burgeoned. Publishing and employment opportunities accordingly were at a premium. To cope with the first of these problems new journals were organized. The American and Canadian Philosophical associations cooperated with the Philosophy Documentation Center to print the first volume of *Philosophy Research Archives,* a microfiche journal in French and English. The University of Kansas began sponsorship of *Auslegung,* a journal that would offer publishing opportunities to graduate students and recent recipients of the Ph.D. In Europe *Grazer Philosophische Studien* ended its first season's efforts to strengthen communication between American and European analytical philosophers.

To improve the prospects for employment of those trained in philosophy, professional associations worked to find untraditional jobs for interested members. Suitable business and government positions were sought, for example—often with success. Philosophers also began joining the staffs of secondary schools and teacher-training programs. The year's major effort, however, went into placing qualified candidates on medical and law school faculties. The American Philosophical Association formed two committees whose joint charges included the task of designing model courses in ethics that might be incorporated permanently into medical- and law-school curricula.

Most facets of philosophy were represented by the publications and awards that appeared or were announced during the year. C. J. F. Williams' provocative book *What Is Truth?* challenged standard presumptions in epistemology. Lawrence Sklar won the third biennial Matchette Prize for his recent work in the philosophy of science, *Space, Time, and Spacetime.* A topical interest in the ethical problems of biological research was fed by several books, particularly *Animal Rights and Human Obligations,* edited by Tom Regan and Peter Singer. The history of philosophy, however, was the most widely treated subject. New editions of works by William James, Comte, Seneca, Kierkegaard, and Schopenhauer were published. Scholarly studies of historical figures were also prominent, ranging from Isaiah Berlin's *Vico and Herder* to separate analyses by Tracy Strong, Judith Shklar, Duncan Forbes, and John Cooper of Nietzsche, Hegel, Hume, and Aristotle.

An interest in the history of philosophy was quickened by other events during the year. The Charles S. Peirce Foundation was established to honour the memory and to promote the study of the founder of pragmatism and America's most distinguished philosopher. With the help of the U.S. National Park Service, the foundation's centre would be located at Arisbe, the Peirce homestead in Pennsylvania. The late English philosopher and historian R. G. Collingwood was honoured by the decision of Pembroke College, Oxford, to offer an annual essay prize named after him. Similar honours undoubtedly would be accorded to Martin Heidegger, for several decades the leading exponent of existentialism, who died in May at the age of 86 (*see* OBITUARIES). (JERRY S. CLEGG)

[10/51; 10/52; 10/53]

ENCYCLOPÆDIA BRITANNICA FILMS. *The Medieval Mind* (1969); *The Spirit of the Renaissance* (1971); *An Essay on War* (1971); *The Reformation: Age of Revolt* (1973).

Photography

Continuing a trend that was clearly evident during the past decade, photography in 1976 maintained strong growth in many areas—as a popular hobby, a tool of research and communications, a form of artistic expression, and a technology that was drawing more and more upon electronics. Historically a relatively "depression-proof" industry, photography weathered the recent stresses of recession and inflation better than many other segments of the economy. In attempting to expand the mass market, photographic manufacturers continued to search for innovations in software and hardware that would make photography easier, more foolproof, and closer to the goal of providing instant gratification to camera users. The adaptation of sophisticated electronic technology to photographic equipment continued to increase, as did the trend toward miniaturization. Photographic education remained a vigorous activity on the college and university level and through numerous workshops, seminars, and conferences, and an increasing number of high school and elementary school teachers included photography courses in the curriculum. Strong enthusiasm for collecting photographic works was reflected in the unprecedented prices being commanded by some photographic prints, in the opening of several new photographic galleries, and in the addition of photography to the stock of established art dealers and galleries.

Cameras. The most influential 35-mm single-lens-reflex (SLR) camera of the year was the Canon AE-1, introduced in Japan early in 1976 and subsequently placed on sale throughout the world. Although no single operating feature of the AE-1 was extraordinary, its combination of modular design, electronic chip circuitry adapted from the pocket-calculator industry, effective use of plastic and metal-reinforced plastic, and extensive automation in the manufacture and assembly of parts offered high sophistication at a very competitive price. A shutter-preferred, fully automatic exposure camera, the AE-1 had an electronically controlled focal-plane shutter with speeds from 2 to 1/1000 sec, a 50-mm Canon S.C. *f*/1.8 prime lens, and a hot shoe synchronized with a companion Speedlite 155A electronic flash unit that automatically set correct flash exposure. An optional auto winder attached to the base provided single-frame or sequential exposures at about two frames per second.

The Olympus OM-2, a fully automatic (aperture-preferred) version of the compact, trend-setting OM-1, reached the market in 1976. Having the same dimensions and weighing only ten grams more, the OM-2 offered an unusual dual-metering exposure system involving both cadmium sulfide (CdS) and silicon cells, which in automatic mode monitored the light and regulated the exposure as it was taking place. The OM-2 had an electronically controlled shutter with automatically set speeds from 1 min to 1/1000 sec (1 to 1/1000 sec manual) and a 50-mm Zuiko *f*/1.8 basic lens.

A number of other manufacturers introduced compact 35-mm SLR's during the year. Among the most interesting was the Asahi Pentax ME, first shown at the September Photokina exhibition in Cologne, West Germany. With body dimensions of 50 x 83 x 131 mm (about 2 x 3¼ x 5¼ in) and a weight of 460 grams (1 lb), it was smaller and lighter than the OM-2, setting a new standard for miniaturizing a complex fully automated SLR. Also it and its sister model, the Pentax MX, were the first cameras to utilize a gallium-arsenic-phosphorus photocell in the exposure system.

E. Leitz, Inc., added a new model to its line of SLR's, the Leica R-3. A truly multinational camera, with components from West Germany, Japan, and

WIDE WORLD

Only slight injuries resulted when three speedboats flipped over on Miami's Biscayne Bay in 1975. The picture won the 1976 World Press Photo Competition.

Canada and assembled in the Leitz Portugal plant, the R-3 offered full exposure automation with an interesting dual-range meter system. By flipping a switch, the user could select a narrow-range spot reading or a centre-weighted averaging reading.

Shown only in prototype form at Photokina was the Rollei SL-2000, a radical departure in 35-mm SLR design with its dual viewfinders (eye-level and waist-level), full-exposure automation in either the shutter-preferred or aperture-preferred mode, interchangeable backs and viewing screens, and built-in motor drive. When and if production models would reach the market was uncertain, but its innovative design stimulated much interest and discussion.

Numerous new 110 pocket cameras were introduced in 1976, including dual-range (normal and moderate-telephoto) models. Considerable interest was generated by the first 110 SLR to reach the market, the Minolta 110 Zoom SLR, with a 25–50-mm Zoom Macro Rokkor *f*/4.5 lens that focused to less than a foot, full-exposure automation, and a top shutter speed of 1/1000 sec. Fuji offered the Fujica Pocket 350 zoom, a non-SLR 110 with a 25–42-mm *f*/5.6 Fujinon zoom lens.

One of the major developments in photographic technology was the long-awaited introduction by Kodak of its instant-colour system. To utilize the Kodak product were two new cameras of unconventional design, the Kodak EK4 and EK6. Rather than incorporating a battery in the film pack itself, as with Polaroid SX-70 film, Kodak chose to place the power function in the cameras, the less expensive EK4 being crank-operated, and the EK6 ejecting the film automatically by means of a motor. The two relatively large cameras utilized a folded light path, ejected the film from the bottom of the body, and included a zooming circle distance finder, a 137-mm *f*/11 lens, and shutter speeds ranging from 1/20 to 1/300 sec. In what was becoming one of the legal and marketing battles of the decade in the photographic industry, Polaroid introduced the Pronto!, a new, relatively low-cost, plastic-body nonfolding camera for its SX-70 film. It featured a 116-mm *f*/9.4 lens that focused from three feet to infinity and a range of shutter speeds from 1 to 1/125 sec. A second model of the Pronto!, which included a rangefinder, also was marketed, as was the SX-70 Alpha 1 camera, a modified version of the original SX-70.

Lenses. Again 1976 saw a proliferation of lenses, mostly for 35-mm SLR cameras, but no remarkable technical breakthroughs. In general, lens manufacturers were achieving smaller, lighter lenses of high performance at realistic cost through the use of computers in lens design, new optical glasses with special characteristics, floating elements and groups of elements, aspheric surfaces, improved plastics, and metal alloys of low weight. Sometimes the result was speed, exemplified by the Nikon 58-mm Noct-Nikkor *f*/1.2 and the Asahi 20-mm *f*/1.4. Sometimes it was compactness, as with the Leitz 180-mm Elmar-R *f*/4, or ultracompactness as with the Olympus Zuiko Auto-S 50-mm *f*/2 and the Asahi 40-mm SMC *f*/2.8. An unusually compact Minolta 500-mm *f*/8–16 mirror lens attracted considerable attention. New PC (perspective-control) lenses included a 35-mm Shift CA Rokkor *f*/2.8 from Minolta and a 35-mm PC Distagon *f*/2.8 from Carl Zeiss (both for 35-mm use) and the first 75-mm *f*/4.5 perspective-correcting lens for the 6 x 7-cm format from Pentax. A large number of new zoom lenses were brought forth including a Schneider 180–240-mm *f*/5.6 zoom Variagon for various Hasselblad models, and several new wide-angle-to-telephoto models. Schneider's wide-angle enlarging lens, a 40-mm *f*/4, was designed to allow large enlargements to be made from 35-mm negatives without excessive lens-to-paper distance.

Films and Papers. Software made considerable strides in 1976. Kodak introduced its instant-colour print film in direct competition with the established Polaroid SX-70 product. Utilizing different, and controversial, chemical technology, the Kodak product was exposed through the back of the emulsion pack, eliminating the optical image reversal required with SX-70 film, which was exposed through the front. The new film also featured the release of pure dyes rather than dye couplers, plus the application of high-speed direct-positive emulsions. In terms of performance the two instant-print films rated something of a standoff; the Kodak material delivered a natural, realistic range of colours biased toward the cool, blue side while improved versions of SX-70 film tended toward a warmer, more contrasty rendition. Although both films were approximately equal in basic film speed (ASA 150) and in time of development (about eight minutes), SX-70 appeared to have the edge in terms of permanence. Both the chemical and mechanical technology of Kodak's instant-colour system were the subject of suits and countersuits involving patent infringements that seemed far from being resolved by the end of 1976.

Kodak also introduced a series of new E-6 processed Ektachrome professional emulsions, including an ASA 50 and 160 Type B (tungsten) and 64 and 200 daylight films. In a surprise move at Photokina, Fuji introduced a high-speed ASA 400 colour negative film available in 20- and 36-exposure rolls, while Agfa-Gevaert demonstrated both an Agfa version of a similar high-speed colour negative material and a sample of its instant-colour material, which approached both Kodak's and Polaroid's product in film speed, processing time, and no-peel concept. Ilford introduced a new high-speed black-and-white emulsion, HP-5, with a basic rating of ASA 400 but with a claimed flexibility in processing to exposure indexes of 800, 1600, and 3200.

WIDE WORLD

Kodak entered the instant-photography market with cameras that make prints in seconds.

Automatic Focusing. A new species of camera automation made significant strides in 1976, although it did not reach the point of effectiveness expected by some of its exponents. Stimulated by Honeywell Photographic's recently developed Visitronic device, an amalgam of optics and electronic-chip technology that might form the heart of a future self-focusing camera system, a number of camera manufacturers experimented with the concept. In the most advanced public demonstration of the state of the art, five firms at Photokina showed variations of possible techniques. The Leitz Correfot (which did not employ the Visitronic) was essentially a focusing indicator, an experimental approach designed to evoke discussion rather than to serve as a prototype of any prospective model. The Asahi Pentax 45–70-mm *f*/3.5 autofocusing Visitronic lens was an interesting, if unconvincing, demonstration of Visitronic technology applied to a lens for a 35-mm SLR. More impressive was a prototype Super-8 movie camera by Elmo, which incorporated the Honeywell device in a relatively compact and swiftly responding electronic "rangefinder" mounted above the camera lens. Similar approaches to Super-8 focusing automation were shown by Eumig and Sankyo.

Cultural Trends. In the U.S. bicentennial year the role of photography in documenting that birthday celebration was paradoxical. On the one hand, a large-scale, federally funded program called Project Documerica withered away and Photo-200, a second program in the mold of the Farm Security Administration's photographic efforts of the 1930s and 1940s, died stillborn. Yet, a large number of individual photographers, working on their own or with the aid of grant money from industry, federal, state, civic, or private sources, successfully created a penetrating photographic portrait of the United States at the start of its third century.

Among the notable achievements were Neal Slavin's colour portraits of various American groups, ranging from Electrolux salesmen at their national convention to the Lloyd Rod & Gun Club, Highland, N.Y. These were collected in a book and shown at the opening of Light Gallery's new quarters in uptown Manhattan, N.Y. A survey of rural Kansas, funded as a pilot project in 1974 by the National Endowment for the Arts (which until recently had concentrated on "art" photography rather than the documentary/photojournalistic mode), resulted in the initiation of five other projects throughout the country and in plans for an ambitious documentary program. An extraordinary photographic documentation of senility and death was *Gramp,* by Mark and Dan Jury, who recorded the decline and demise of their grandfather in a touching but unflinching visual story.

Karl Struss's "Gloria Swanson with Ball—III. 1919" was shown in a New York exhibition by the 90-year-old photographer and Hollywood cameraman.

THE NEW YORK TIMES

Colour photography as an art form, which in terms of prestige and collectability had tended to remain in the background, made considerable progress in 1976. In what was perhaps the most controversial photographic exhibition of the year, New York City's Museum of Modern Art presented its first large-scale colour exhibition in more than a decade with a showing of the prints of William Eggleston. Extolled by the museum's director of photography, John Szarkowski, as "near perfect" photographs and damned by many viewers as banal snapshots, the Eggleston prints typified a coolly objective yet highly personal approach in marked contrast to the romantic pictorialism and commercial slickness of much of the colour photography of the past. Images, the first photographic gallery in the U.S. devoted entirely to colour, opened in uptown Manhattan, and the prestigious George Eastman House in Rochester, N.Y., indicated that it would add colour photographs to its permanent acquisitions. However, the problem of permanence of colour prints and transparencies remained troublesome, and further research was required both in the manufacturing of colour materials and in techniques of archival storage.

The enthusiasm for photographic education at all levels continued at a high pace, with particular emphasis on workshops and conferences. The Visual Studies Workshop of Rochester, the Maine Photographic Workshops, the Apeiron Workshops in Millerton, N.Y., and, extending a typically American institution to Europe, the Arles workshop attracted large numbers of participants. In New York City the International Center of Photography, a unique nonprofit institution dedicated to socially meaningful photography, successfully entered its second year with a combination of exhibitions, lecture series, and workshops. High enrollment contributed to the continued proliferation of photography courses, which ranged from basic techniques to graduate-level programs in photography as art and communication. Although still far from a widely accepted part of the elementary school curriculum, photography was being introduced to increasing numbers of young students, not so much as a technique but as a form of "visual literacy" and personal expression.

Perhaps the most widely viewed photographs of 1976 were the panoramic scenes of the Martian desert taken by two U.S. space probes after their touchdown on the planet's surface. A marvel of sophisticated space-age technology, these colour pictures evidenced a basic appeal of the photographic image since its inception—to preserve in exact detail the image of things as they are in the domain of human vision. (ARTHUR GOLDSMITH)

See also Motion Pictures.
[628.D; 735.G.1]

Physics

Applied Magnetics. The past few years in physics have been notable for developments in superconducting materials and in particular for the discovery of materials with higher critical magnitudes of magnetic field and temperature. Within recent months one of these materials, vanadium-gallium, made possible the introduction of a second generation of superconducting magnets.

Using niobium-titanium cooled to 4.2° K (−269° C), superconducting magnets with fields approaching ten Tesla (T) had been commercially available for some time. More recently the use of stabilized niobium-tin (Nb_3Sn) superconducting tape enabled a magnet to be constructed for the Mullard Cryogenic Laboratory of the University of Oxford with a field of 15.8 T. The latest technological advance, that of a magnet enclosed concentrically within another magnet, raised the limits of the attainable field to 17.5 T at 4.2° K. The outer magnet is wound with niobium-tin tape and produces 13.5 T; inside is a vanadium-gallium magnet producing an additional 4 T. Vanadium-gallium was preferred for the inner magnet because it has a higher current-carrying capacity than niobium-tin at high fields. Because both materials remain superconducting to at least 22.5 T, the possibility of a 20 T magnet was well within reach.

In 1976 physicists stood on the threshold of a new application for conventional coil and superconducting magnets that could have far-reaching effects on society. It had been known for years that magnetic fields could be used to separate magnetic from nonmagnetic material, but the technique had been limited to those materials that are ferromagnetic at room temperature—iron, nickel, cobalt, and a few of their alloys and compounds. Paramagnetic materials, which are much more numerous, are also influenced by magnetic fields but much less strongly than the ferromagnetics. The force on a magnetic particle is proportional to the volume of the particle, to the intensity of magnetization induced in the particle by the applied magnetic field, and to the gradient of the field; that is, the difference between the strength of the magnetic field at one end of the particle and the strength at the other. Thus, efficient magnetic separation of paramagnetic material and of small particles of ferromagnetic material requires very intense magnetic fields with large field gradients. In addition, a large flow of material through the magnet dictates that its shape be short and fat and possess a large air gap.

These initially conflicting demands were overcome by workers at the Francis Bitter National Magnet Laboratory of the Massachusetts Institute of Technology using their research experience in very high magnetic fields and very careful design of the solenoid and its flux return paths. The air gap of the magnet is filled with a matrix of steel wool, which becomes magnetically saturated by the magnetic field and produces large field gradients at its many edges. The mixture to be filtered is pumped through the matrix and the magnetic particles attach themselves to the steel wool. These can be removed and collected after separation by switching off the magnet to demagnetize the steel and then backflushing with water.

One of the most far-reaching applications of magnetic separation is the purification of water from rivers, lakes, sewage, industrial processes, and the like. The contaminated water is "seeded" with small amounts of iron oxide that trap the impurities and carry them to the magnetized steel-wool matrix. Successful trials were carried out at a rate of 150 gal/min/sq ft of magnet surface; contaminants removed included bacteria, solid particles, phosphates, and even viruses. It was estimated that one large superconducting magnet could process 100 million gal of water per day economically because once in the superconducting state the magnet draws no further current.

The application of a superconducting magnetic separator was demonstrated for kaolin, a type of white clay. Very pure kaolin is used in the manufacture of glossy magazines, and natural resources of the required material were fast becoming exhausted. Impure kaolin contains mainly iron and potassium impurities, which were shown by J. H. P. Watson and D. Hocking of English China Clays Lovering & Pochin Co. Ltd., Cornwall, England, to be removable by magnetic separation in a matrix of stainless-steel wool. Other possible uses for the technique included the extraction of tungsten and molybdenum, the purification of low-grade iron ores, and the desulfurization of coal.

A totally different application of magnetic separation was reported by D. Melville and colleagues of the University of Southampton, England, who demonstrated that red blood cells could be separated from other blood components without serious damage using a high-gradient magnetic separator. About 28% of the volume of each red blood cell is taken up by hemoglobin, and each hemoglobin molecule contains only four iron atoms (of a total of 10,000 atoms per molecule). Nevertheless, these were sufficient to allow the paramagnetic red blood cells to be separated with a conventional electromagnet and stainless-steel wire matrix. Blood devoid of red cells was of considerable interest in immunological and cytological research.

Glassy-State Theory. A theoretical understanding of the glassy state has always eluded physicists. Of two standard approaches, neither is able to explain all features of the glassy state. The microcrystalline model explains the short-range order in glasses that has been observed by X-ray diffraction, Raman scattering, and infrared phonon work. The network model allows one to understand, at least qualitatively, how the addition of only a small percentage of certain constituents has a marked effect on the physical properties of the glass, extending the temperature range over which the glass has a workable viscosity.

A novel approach, suggested by C. H. L. Goodman of the Standard Telecommunication Laboratories Ltd., Essex, England, might best be described as a strained mixed-cluster model. Goodman pointed out that a very large number of the systems that form glasses have as a major constituent a material which exists simultaneously in two or more polymorphic crystalline forms that differ but little in free energy. He then suggested that this polymorphism could be a necessary condition for a material to form a glass. With this concept in mind the glass-forming process would take place as follows. Above its solidification temperature the glass has a large though finite viscosity; in this state it consists of clusters of all of its possible polymorphs. These clusters are prevented from reaching a size suitable for crystal growth, however, because the different polymorphs impede each other and because two clusters of the same polymorph do not necessarily have the correct relative orientation. As the glass solidifies, the clusters bond across parts of their surfaces, leaving liquidlike material in

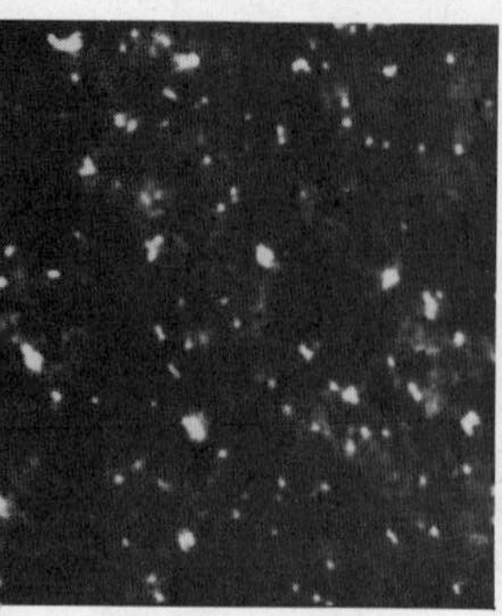

The first motion pictures of single atoms were produced at the University of Chicago using a scanning electron microscope (right). Shown above are uranium atoms magnified 5.5 million times.

PHOTOS, COURTESY, THE UNIVERSITY OF CHICAGO

the interstices. An attractive part of the argument is that glass additives of high effectiveness, although used in only small concentrations, may well concentrate in the interstices where they reduce the strain resulting from the differential thermal contraction of the clusters of different polymorphs. In 1976 the hypothesis was the subject of careful study, and various experiments were proposed or in progress to test its applicability to other properties of the glassy state.

Nuclear Physics. Working with a tandem Van de Graaff accelerator at Florida State University at Tallahassee, a team of U.S. physicists claimed evidence for the discovery of a range of superheavy elements in samples of ancient Madagascan mica. The existence of halos surrounding mineral inclusions in mica was well known, and their production had been traced to the radioactive decay of uranium and thorium at their centres. Some exceptional halos, however, have diameters approaching 200 micrometres, or twice the size of those expected from known radioactive nuclei. Theoretical work of the 1960s had predicted relative nuclear stability for certain groups of elements with atomic numbers higher than that of uranium (atomic number 92), the heaviest known naturally occurring element, and had derived values for their X-ray energy spectra. Subjecting several inclusions with giant halos to low-energy proton bombardment, the experimenters obtained X-ray spectra values that correlated with those predicted for elements 116, 124, and 126 and that gave weaker evidence for elements 114, 125, and 127. They cautioned against complete acceptance of the conclusions, however, until stronger evidence could be amassed. The observed X-ray spectra were weak and incomplete and varied from sample to sample; in addition, the elements for which the evidence seemed strongest were not among the most stable predicted by theory. (S. B. PALMER)

See also Nobel Prizes.

[121.A.5; 125.F; 127.C.5.c; 721.B.5]

Pipelines: *see* Energy; Transportation

Plastics Industry: *see* Industrial Review

Poetry: *see* Literature

ENCYCLOPÆDIA BRITANNICA FILMS. *Introduction to Holography* (1972); *Introduction to Lasers* (1973); *Time: Measurement and Meaning* (1974); *Learning About Electric Current* (2nd ed., 1974); *Learning About Heat* (2nd ed., 1974); *Learning About Magnetism* (2nd ed., 1975); *Learning About Nuclear Energy* (2nd ed., 1975); *Learning About Sound* (2nd ed., 1975); *Learning About Light* (1976).

Poland

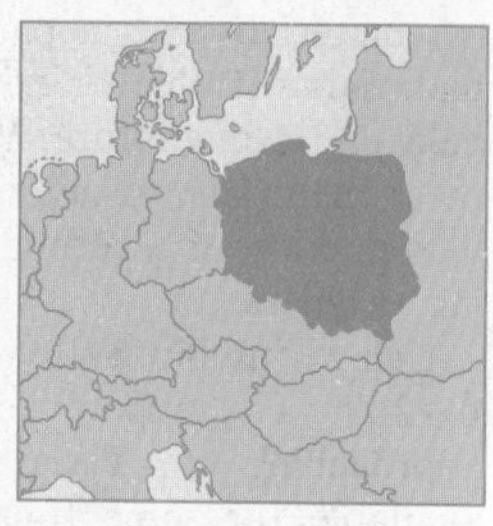

A people's republic of eastern Europe, Poland is bordered by the Baltic Sea, the U.S.S.R., Czechoslovakia, and East Germany. Area: 120,725 sq mi (312,677 sq km). Pop. (1976 est.): 34,362,000. Cap. and largest city: Warsaw (pop., 1975 est., 1,436,100). Language: Polish. Religion: predominantly Roman Catholic. First secretary of the Polish United Workers' (Communist) Party in 1976, Edward Gierek; chairman of the Council of State, Henryk Jablonski; chairman of the Council of Ministers (premier), Piotr Jaroszewicz.

Poland's leaders entered the year 1976 in a rather optimistic mood, though in a speech on Dec. 12, 1975, at the Polish United Workers' Party (PUWP) congress, First Secretary Gierek had spoken of the need to overcome both an unfavourable trend in foreign trade and a decline in agricultural production. A political hue and cry arose when the Politburo proposed to revise the constitution promulgated on July 22, 1952, and bring it into line with those of other states of the socialist camp, by describing the PUWP as "the leading political force in the country," the Polish-Soviet alliance as "inseparable and unbreakable," and all citizens' rights as "integrally linked with honest fulfillment of their duties to the socialist motherland." These amendments gave rise to protests by hundreds of intellectuals, among them Edward Lipinski, econo-

Polish workers get Italian technology: these Fiats are being assembled in a plant built by the Italian company in Tychy, Poland.

P.A. INTERPRESS/AUTHENTICATED NEWS INTERNATIONAL

POLAND

Education. (1974–75) Primary, pupils 4,523,-435, teachers 201,101; secondary, pupils 647,992, teachers 26,166; vocational, pupils 1,848,211, teachers 74,067; teacher training, pupils 17,851, teachers (1971–72) 2,251; higher (including 10 main universities), students 521,899, teaching staff 45,014.

Finance. Monetary unit: zloty, with (Sept. 20, 1976) a basic rate of 3.32 zlotys to U.S. $1 (5.90 zlotys = £1 sterling) and a tourist rate of 33.20 zlotys to U.S. $1 (59 zlotys = £1 sterling). Budget (1975 est.): revenue 684 billion zlotys; expenditure 680 billion zlotys. Net material product (1974) 1,209,300,000,000 zlotys.

Foreign Trade. (1975) Imports 41,424,000,-000 zlotys; exports 34,063,000,000 zlotys. Import sources: U.S.S.R. 25%; West Germany 8%; East Germany 7%; U.K. 5%; Czechoslovakia 5%; France 5%; U.S. 5%. Export destinations: U.S.S.R. 32%; East Germany 9%; Czechoslovakia 8%; West Germany 5%. Main exports: machinery 31%; coal 16%; chemicals 9%; textiles and clothing 9%; food 7%; metals 7%; ships and boats 7%.

Transport and Communications. Roads (1974) 299,600 km (including 139 km expressways). Motor vehicles in use (1974): passenger 920,310; commercial 386,030. Railways: (1974) 23,773 km (including 5,118 km electrified); traffic (1975) 42,918,000,000 passenger-km, freight 129,230,000,000 net ton-km. Air traffic (1975): 1,309,000,000 passenger-km; freight 13,856,000 net ton-km. Shipping (1975): merchant vessels 100 gross tons and over 696; gross tonnage 2,817,129. Telephones (Dec. 1974) 2,399,200. Radio licenses (Dec. 1974) 7,988,000. Television licenses (Dec. 1974) 6.1 million.

Agriculture. Production (in 000; metric tons; 1975): wheat *c.* 5,530; rye *c.* 6,810; barley *c.* 3,940; oats *c.* 3,230; potatoes 46,429; sugar, raw value *c.* 1,699; rapeseed *c.* 700; linseed *c.* 52; cabbages (1974) *c.* 1,600; onions *c.* 350; tomatoes *c.* 330; carrots (1974) *c.* 490; cucumbers (1974) *c.* 460; tobacco *c.* 80; flax fibre (1974) *c.* 52; butter *c.* 255; cheese 353; hen's eggs *c.* 447; beef and veal (1974) *c.* 685; pork (1974) *c.* 1,860; timber (cu m; 1974) *c.* 21,543; fish catch (1974) 679. Livestock (in 000; June 1975): cattle 13,254; pigs 21,311; sheep 3,175; horses (1974) 2,312; chickens *c.* 137,212.

Industry. Index of industrial production (1970 = 100; 1975) 165. Fuel and power (in 000; metric tons; 1975): coal 171,505; brown coal 39,865; coke (1974) 16,929; crude oil (1974) 550; natural gas (cu m) 5,964,000; manufactured gas (cu m; 1974) 7,280,000; electricity (kw-hr) 97,165,000. Production (in 000; metric tons; 1975): cement 19,546; iron ore (metal content; 1974) 398; pig iron 8,204; crude steel 14,907; aluminum (1974) 102; copper (1974) 194; lead (1974) 72; zinc (1974) 233; petroleum products (1974) 10,593; sulfuric acid 3,411; fertilizers (nutrient content; 1974) nitrogenous 1,457, phosphate 823; cotton yarn 212; wool yarn 102; rayon, etc., filament yarn and fibres 96; nylon, etc., filament yarn and fibres 117; cotton fabrics (m) 928,000; woolen fabrics (m) 125,000; rayon and synthetic fabrics (m; 1974) 110,000; passenger cars (units) 165; commercial vehicles (units) 79. Merchant vessels launched (100 gross tons and over; 1975) 617,-000 gross tons.

mist, Antoni Slonimski, poet and playwright (*see* OBITUARIES), and Stefan Cardinal Wyszynski, primate of Poland, who delivered outspoken sermons. The party leadership modified the amendments to read that the Polish People's Republic was a socialist state, that the PUWP was the leading political force in the construction of socialism, and that the republic would strengthen friendship and cooperation with the U.S.S.R. and other socialist countries. The Sejm approved the constitution Feb. 10, 1976. After a general election on March 21 the political composition of the seventh Sejm was identical to that of its two predecessors. (*See* POLITICAL PARTIES.) There were a few changes in the new Council of Ministers.

On an official visit on June 8–11 to West Germany, Gierek met Chancellor Helmut Schmidt, who described the encounter as the most important effort at reconciliation that West Germany had undertaken since Konrad Adenauer achieved the Franco-German rapprochement in 1963. Schmidt spoke of the barbaric behaviour of the German Nazis in Poland during World War II. Gierek replied that the Poles had never identified Hitler and his henchmen with the German nation and affirmed the importance of détente. Fourteen agreements between the Polish state and West German banks and industrial concerns were signed in Bonn on June 11. It was hoped that their cumulative effect would correct the imbalance in Polish-West German trade, in which, for the period 1972–75, Poland's deficit was more than DM 5 billion.

Two weeks later Gierek's regime was shaken by large-scale workers' demonstrations resembling those that had caused the downfall of his predecessor, Wladyslaw Gomulka, in December 1970. They occurred when the government raised the prices of foodstuffs, which had been frozen for five years. The cost of food subsidies had risen from 22 billion to 100 billion zlotys, nearly 8% of the national income, over the preceding five years.

Higher prices had become an economic necessity, but when, on June 24, Premier Jaroszewicz announced in the Sejm increases averaging 60% on many staples, industrial workers went on strike. Workers in Radom clashed violently with police. Near Warsaw the Ursus tractor factory workers cut the main railway line. As the protest movement spread, the government yielded: on June 25 Jaroszewicz announced on television that the bill was being withdrawn for further study. Except for two civilians accidentally crushed to death by a tractor, there was no bloodbath similar to that of December 1970. Hundreds of protesters accused of rioting, looting, and arson were summarily tried and many were sentenced to prison. A group of Polish intellectuals appealed to the Sejm for a free flow of information to avert further such disasters, and by the end of July had set up a committee to defend workers from repression (in September some sentences were reduced and trials postponed).

On November 9–15 Gierek visited the U.S.S.R. At a dinner in the Kremlin, Soviet Communist Party leader Leonid I. Brezhnev described the visit as a "milestone on the way toward further expansion of Soviet-Polish relations." It was believed that the U.S.S.R. promised extra deliveries of raw materials, capital goods, and consumer goods worth 1 billion rubles ($1.4 billion) over the next five years.

(K. M. SMOGORZEWSKI)

[972.B.2.d]

Political Parties

The following table is a general world guide to political parties. All countries that were independent on Dec. 31, 1976, are included; there are a number for which no analysis of political activities can be given. Parties are included in most instances only if represented in parliaments (in the lower house in bicameral legislatures); the figures in the last column indicate the number of seats obtained in the last general election (figures in parentheses are those of the penultimate one). The date of the most recent election follows the name of the country.

The code letters in the affiliation column show the relative political position of the parties within each country; there is, therefore, no entry in this column for single-party states. There are obvious difficulties involved in labeling parties within the political spectrum of a given country. The key chosen is as follows: F—fascist; ER—extreme right; R—right; CR—centre right; C—centre; L—non-Marxist left; SD—social-democratic; S—socialist; EL—extreme left; and K—Communist.

The percentages in the column "Voting strength" indicate proportions of the valid votes cast for the respective parties, or the number of registered voters who went to the polls in single-party states.

[541.D.2]

Police:
see Crime and Law Enforcement

Polish Literature:
see Literature

COUNTRY AND NAME OF PARTY	Affiliation	Voting strength (%)	Parliamentary representation
Afghanistan			
Presidential rule since July 17, 1973	—	—	—
Albania (October 1974)			
Albanian Labour (Communist)	—	99.9	250 (214)
Algeria			
Presidential regime since June 19, 1965	—	—	—
Angola, People's Republic of			
Movimento Popular de Libertaçao de Angola (MPLA)	—	—	—
Argentina			
Military junta since March 24, 1976	—	—	—
Australia (November 1975)			
Liberal-Country	CR	...	92 (61)
Democratic Labor	C	...	0 (0)
Australian Labor	L	...	35 (66)
Austria (October 1975)			
Freiheitliche Partei Österreichs	R	5.4	10 (10)
Österreichische Volkspartei	C	42.9	80 (80)
Sozialistische Partei Österreichs	SD	50.4	93 (93)
Kommunistische Partei Österreichs	K	1.2	0 (0)
Bahamas, The (September 1972)			
Progressive Liberal Party	C	60.0	30
Free National Movement	L	...	8
Bahrain			
Emirate, no parties	—	—	—
Bangladesh			
Military government since Nov. 6, 1975	—	—	—
Barbados (September 1976)			
Democratic Labour	C	...	7 (18)
Barbados Labour	L	...	17 (6)
Belgium (March 1974)			
Front Démocratique Francophone / Rassemblement Wallon	R	11.0	25 (27)
Volksunie (Flemish)	R	10.2	22 (21)
Parti de la Liberté et du Progrès	CR	15.2	30 (31)
Parti Social Chrétien	C	32.3	72 (67)
Parti Socialiste Belge	SD	26.7	59 (61)
Parti Communiste Belge	K	3.2	4 (5)
Benin (Dahomey)			
Marxist-Leninist military government since Oct. 26, 1972	—	—	—
Bhutan			
A monarchy without parties	—	—	—
Bolivia			
Military junta since Nov. 9, 1974	—	—	—
Botswana (October 1974)			
Botswana Democratic Party	C	...	27 (24)
Botswana People's Party	L	...	2 (3)
Botswana National Front	EL	...	2 (3)
Brazil (November 1974)			
Aliança Renovadora Nacional (ARENA)	CR	...	199 (223)
Movimento Democrático Brasileiro (MDB)	L	...	165 (87)
Bulgaria (May 1976)			
Bulgarian Communist Party	Fatherland Front	99.9	272 (266)
People's Agrarian Union			100 (100)
Nonparty			28 (34)
Burma (February 1974)			
Burma Socialist Program Party	—	99.0	...
Burundi (October 1974)			
Tutsi ethnic minority government	—	—	—
Cambodia, People's Republic of (March 1976)			
People's Kampuchea Revolutionary Party	—	—	—
Cameroon (May 1973)			
Cameroonian National Union	—	...	120
Canada (July 1974)			
Social Credit	R	5.0	11 (15)
Progressive Conservative	CR	35.6	95 (107)
Liberal	C	42.9	141 (109)
New Democratic	L	15.6	16 (31)
Independents	—	...	1 (2)
Cape Verde Islands (June 1975)			
African Party for the Independence of Guinea-Bissau and Cape Verde (PAIGC)	—	84.0	56
Central African Empire			
Military government since Jan. 1, 1966	—	—	—
Chad			
Military government since April 13, 1975	—	—	—
Chile			
Military junta since Sept. 11, 1973	—	—	—
China, People's Republic of			
Communist (Kungchantang)	—	—	—
Colombia (April 1974)			
Partido Conservador	R	...	66 } (90)
Partido Liberal	C	...	113 }
Others	—	...	20 (72)
Comoro Islands (December 1974)			
Single party rule from Aug. 3, 1975	—	—	—
Congo			
Military government since Sept. 1968	—	—	—
Costa Rica (February 1974)			
Partido de Liberación Nacional	R	...	27 (32)
Partido de Unificación Nacional	C	...	16 (22)
Others (six parties)	—	...	8 (3)
Cuba (November 1976)			
Partido Comunista Cubano	—	...	481
Cyprus			
De facto partition in two parts	—	—	—
Czechoslovakia (October 1976)			
Communist Party of Czechoslovakia / Czechoslovak People's Party / Czechoslovak Socialist Party / Communist Party of Slovakia / Slovak Freedom Party / Party of Slovak Revival	— National Front	...	...
Denmark (January 1975)			
Conservative	R	5.5	10 (16)
Liberal Democratic (Venstre)	CR	23.3	42 (22)
Christian People's	CR	5.3	9 (7)
Progress (M. Glistrup)	C	13.6	24 (28)
Radical Liberal (Radikale Venstre)	C	7.1	13 (20)
Single-Tax (Retsforbund)	C	1.8	0 (5)
Centre Democrats (E. Jakobsen)	L	2.2	4 (14)
Social Democrats	SD	30.0	53 (46)
Socialist People's	EL	4.9	9 (11)
Left Socialists	EL	2.1	4 (0)
Communists	K	4.2	7 (6)
Dominican Republic (May 1974)			
Partido Quisqueyano Demócrata	ER	...	...
Partido Reformista (J. Balaguer)	R	...	...
Partido Revolucionario Social-Cristiano	C	...	...
Partido Revolucionario Dominicano	L	...	...
Partido Demócrata Popular	L	...	...
Ecuador			
Military junta since Feb. 15, 1972	—	—	—
Egypt (October 1976)			
Arab Socialist Union	—	...	347
El Salvador (March 1976)			
Partido de Conciliación Nacional	R	...	52 (32)
Union Nacional de Oposición	C	...	0 (14)
Partido Popular Salvadoreño	L	...	0 (6)
Frente Unido Democrático Independiente	—	...	0
Equatorial Guinea			
Partido Único Nacional de los Trabajadores	—	—	—
Ethiopia			
Military government since Sept. 12, 1974	—	—	—
Fiji (April 1972)			
Alliance Party (mainly Fijian)	—	...	33
National Federation Party (mainly Indian)	—	...	19
Finland (September 1975)			
Conservative Party	R	18.4	34 (33)
Swedish People's Party	R	4.7	10 (11)
Centre Party (ex-Agrarian)	C	17.7	39 (35)
Liberal Party	C	4.4	9 (6)
Christian League	C	3.3	9 (4)
Rural Party	L	3.6	2 (5)
Social Democratic Party	SD	25.0	54 (55)
People's Democratic League	K	19.0	41 (37)
Others	—	4.0	2 (14)
France (March 1973)			
Union des Démocrates pour la République	R	31.3	185 (292)
Independent Republicans	CR	7.7	54 (61)
Centre Démocratie et Progrès	C	3.9	21 (33)
Other majority coalition	C	3.2	15 (0)
Radicals	L	3.8	12 (0)
Socialists	SD	21.9	89 (57)
Parti Socialiste Unifié	EL	0.3	3 (10)
Communists	K	20.6	73 (34)
Others	—	...	38 (3)
Gabon (February 1973)			
Parti Démocratique Gabonais	—	...	70
Gambia, The (March 1972)			
People's Progressive Party	C	...	28 (24)
United Party	L	...	4 (8)
German Democratic Republic (October 1976)			
Sozialistische Einheitspartei / Christlich-Demokratische Union / National-Demokratische Partei / Liberal-Demokratische Partei / Demokratische Bauerpartei	National Front —	99.9	500 (434)
Germany, Federal Republic of (October 1976)			
Christlich-Demokratische Union	R	38.0	190 (177)
Christlich-Soziale Union	R	10.6	53 (48)
Freie Demokratische Partei	C	7.9	39 (41)
Sozialdemokratische Partei Deutschlands	SD	42.6	214 (230)
Deutsche Kommunistische Partei	K	0.3	0 (0)
Ghana			
Military government since 1972	—	—	—
Greece (November 1974)			
New Democracy Party	CR	54.4	220
Centre Union—New Forces	C	20.4	60
Pan-Hellenic Socialist Movement	S	13.6	12
United Left	K	9.5	8
Grenada (December 1976)			
United Labour Party	L	...	9 (13)
People's Alliance (coalition of three parties)	—	...	6 (2)
Guatemala (March 1974)			
Partido Institucional Democrático / Movimiento de Liberación Nacional	CR	41.2	...
Frente Nacional de Oposición / Partido Demócrata Cristiano	C	35.7	...
Partido Revolucionario / Frente Democrático Guatemalteco	L	23.1	...
Guinea (December 1974)			
Parti Démocratique de Guinée	—	100.0	150
Guinea-Bissau (1975)			
African Party for the Independence of Guinea-Bissau and Cape Verde (PAIGC)	—	...	92

COUNTRY AND NAME OF PARTY	Affiliation	Voting strength (%)	Parliamentary representation
Guyana (July 1973)			
People's National Congress	C	...	37
People's Progressive Party	EL	...	14
Others	—	...	2
Haiti			
Presidential dictatorship since 1957	—	—	—
Honduras			
Military junta since Dec. 4, 1972	—	—	—
Hungary (June 1975)			
Hungarian Socialist Workers' Party	Patriotic People's Front	97.6	352
Young Communist League			
National Council of Women			
Hungarian Federation of Partisans			
Federation of National Minorities	—		
Iceland (June 1974)			
Independence (Conservative)	R	42.7	25 (22)
Progressive (Farmers' Party)	C	24.9	17 (17)
Union of Liberals and Leftists	L	4.6	2 (5)
Social Democratic	SD	9.1	5 (6)
People's Alliance	K	18.3	11 (10)
India (March 1971)			
Jan Sangh (Hindu Nationalists)	ER	...	22 (33)
Dravida Munnetra Kazhagam	R	...	23 (25)
Telengana Praja Samiti	R	...	10 (0)
Swatantra (Freedom)	R	...	7 (35)
Ruling Congress Party	C	...	349 (223)
Opposition Congress Party	L	...	16 (63)
Praja Socialist	SD	...	2 (15)
Samyukta Socialist	S	...	3 (17)
Communist-Marxist (pro-Chinese)	K	...	25 (19)
Communist (pro-Soviet)	K	...	24 (24)
Independents and others	—	...	33 (53)
Indonesia (July 1971)			
Sekber Golkar (Functional Groups)	—	65.5	261
Nahdatul Ulama (Muslim Teachers)	R	...	58
Partai Nasional	R	...	20
Parmusi (Liberal Muslims)	C	...	24
Sarikat Islam (United Muslims)	C	...	10
Partai Keristen Indonesia (Protestants)	C	...	7
Partai Katholik Indonesia	C	...	3
Perti (Islamic Party)	C	...	2
Partai Murba (Party of the Masses)	EL	...	0
West Irian	—	...	9
Iran (June 1975)			
Rastakhiz (National Resurgence) Party	—	52.0	268
Iraq			
Military and Baath Party governments since 1958	—	...	...
Ireland (February 1973)			
Fianna Fail (Sons of Destiny)	C	46.2	69 (75)
Fine Gael (United Ireland)	C	35.1	54 (50)
Irish Labour Party	L	13.7	19 (18)
Sinn Fein (We Ourselves)	—	1.1	0
Others	—	3.9	2
Israel (December 1973)			
Likud (Herut, Liberal Alignment, Free Centre, and State List)	R	...	39 (32)
Torah Front (Agudat Israel and Poalei Agudat Israel)	CR	...	5 (6)
National Religious	C	...	10 (12)
Independent Liberal	C	...	4 (4)
Civil Rights List (Mrs. S. Aloni)	L	...	3 —
Maarakh (Mapam, Mapai, Rafi, and Ahdut Avoda)	SD	...	51 (56)
Moked (pro-Israel Communists)	K	...	1 (1)
Rakah (pro-Soviet Communists)	K	...	4 (3)
Pro-government Arabs	—	...	3 (4)
Italy (June 1976)			
Movimento Sociale Italiano	F}	6.1	35 (56)
Partito di Unità Monarchica	R}		
Partito Liberale Italiano	CR	1.3	5 (20)
Democrazia Cristiana	C	38.7	262 (267)
Partito Repubblicano Italiano	C	3.1	14 (15)
Partito Social-Democratico Italiano	L	3.4	15 (29)
Partito Socialista Italiano	SD	9.6	57 (61)
Democrazia Proletaria	EL	1.5	6 (0)
Partito Comunista Italiano	K	34.4	228 (179)
Südtiroler Volkspartei	—	0.5	3 (3)
Others	—	1.4	5 —
Ivory Coast (November 1970)			
Parti Démocratique de la Côte d'Ivoire	—	99.9	100
Jamaica (December 1976)			
People's National Party	L	...	48 (35)
Jamaica Labour Party	S	...	12 (18)
Japan (December 1976)			
Liberal-Democratic	R	41.8	249 (271)
Komeito (Clean Government)	CR	10.9	55 (29)
New Liberals	CR	4.2	17 —
Democratic Socialist	SD	6.3	29 (19)
Socialist	S	20.7	123 (118)
Communist	K	10.4	17 (38)
Independents and others	—	5.7	21 (16)
Jordan			
Royal government, no parties	—	—	60
Kenya (October 1974)			
Kenya African National Union	—	...	158 (171)
Korea, North			
Korean Workers' (Communist) Party	—	...	...
Korea, South (February 1973)			
Democratic Republican	CR	38.7	73
New Democratic	L	32.6	52
Democratic Unification	S	10.1	2
Independents	—	18.6	19
Kuwait			
Princely government, no parties	—	—	30
Laos, People's Democratic Republic of			
Lao People's Revolutionary Party	—	...	...
Lebanon (April 1972)			
Maronites (Roman Catholics)	—	...	30
Sunni Muslims	—	...	20
Shi'ite Muslims	—	...	19
Greek Orthodox	—	...	11
Druzes (Muslim sect)	—	...	6
Melchites (Greek Catholics)	—	...	6
Armenian Orthodox	—	...	4
Other Christian	—	...	2
Armenian Catholics	—	...	1
Lesotho			
Constitution suspended Jan. 30, 1970	—	—	—
Liberia (October 1975)			
True Whig Party	—	...	41
Libya			
Military government since Sept. 1, 1969	—	—	—
Liechtenstein (February 1974)			
Vaterländische Union	CR	...	7 (8)
Fortschrittliche Bürgerpartei	C	...	8 (7)
Christlich-Soziale Partei	C	...	0
Luxembourg (May 1974)			
Parti Chrétien Social	CR	28.0	18 (21)
Parti Libéral	C	22.1	14 (11)
Parti Ouvrier Socialiste	SD	29.0	17 (15)
Parti Social Démocratique	S	9.1	5 (6)
Parti Communiste	K	10.4	5 (6)
Madagascar			
Military government since Oct. 13, 1972	—	—	—
Malawi			
Malawi Congress Party	—	...	58
Malaysia (August 1974)			
Barisan Nasional (National Front, 12 mainly Malay parties)	—	61.6	120 (125)
Democratic Action Party (mainly Chinese	L	...	9} (19)
Pekemas (Social Justice Party)	K	...	1}
Maldives			
Government by the Didi family	—	—	—
Mali			
Military government since Nov. 19, 1968	—	—	—
Malta (September 1976)			
Nationalist Party	R	48.7	31 (27)
Labour Party	SD	51.3	34 (28)
Mauritania (August 1971)			
Parti du Peuple Mauritanien	—	95.1	50
Mauritius (December 1976)			
Independence Party (Indian-dominated)	C	...	28 (39)
Parti Mauricien Social-Démocrate	L	...	8 (23)
Mauritius Militant Movement	K	...	34
Mexico (July 1976)			
Partido Revolucionario Institucional	CR	94.4	...
Partido Acción Nacional	C	...	...
Partido Auténtico de la Revolución Mexicana	L	...	...
Partido Popular Socialista	S	...	...
Partido Comunista Mexicano	K	...	...
Monaco (August 1970)			
Union Nationale et Démocratique	—	...	18
Mongolia (1973)			
Mongolian People's Revolutionary Party	—	99.0	295
Morocco (August 1970)			
Independents (pro-government)	CR	...	159
Popular Movement (rural)	CR	...	60
Istiqlal (Independence)	C	...	8
National Union of Popular Forces	L	...	1
Others	—	...	12
Mozambique, People's Republic of (1975)			
Frente da Libertação do Moçambique (Frelimo)	—	...	...
Nauru			
No political parties	—	—	—
Nepal			
Royal government since December 1960	—	—	—
Netherlands, The (November 1972)			
Boerenpartij (Farmers' Party)	R	1.9	3 (1)
Anti-Revolutionaire Partij (Calvinist)	CR	8.8	14 (13)
Christelijk Historische Unie (Lutheran)	CR	4.8	7 (10)
Katholieke Volkspartij	C	17.7	27 (35)
Volkspartij voor Vreiheid en Democratie	C	14.4	22 (16)
Democraten '66	C	4.2	6 (11)
Democraten-Socialisten '70	L	4.1	6 (8)
Partij van de Arbeid	SD	27.4	23 (39)
Communistische Partij	K	4.5	7 (6)
Five other parties	—	12.2	15 ...
New Zealand (November 1975)			
National (Conservative)	CR	...	53 (31)
Labour Party	L	...	34 (56)
Nicaragua (September 1974)			
Partido Liberal Nacionalista (A. Somoza)	R	60.0	42 (35)
Partido Conservador de Nicaragua	R	...	11 (17)
Others	—	...	0 (1)
Niger			
Military government since April 17, 1974	—	—	—

COUNTRY AND NAME OF PARTY	Affiliation	Voting strength (%)	Parliamentary representation	
Nigeria				
Military government since Jan. 15, 1966	—	—	—	
Norway (September 1973)				
Høyre (Conservative)	R	17.3	29	(29)
Kristelig Folkeparti	CR	11.8	20	(14)
Senterpartiet (Agrarian)	C	6.8	21	(20)
Venstre (Liberal)	C	3.4	1	(13)
Anti-EEC Venstre	C	2.3	2	—
Arbeiderpartiet (Labour)	SD	35.5	62	(74)
Socialistisk Folkeparti	S}	11.2	16	(0)
Kommunistiske Parti	K}			
Oman				
Independent sultanate, no parties	—	—	—	
Pakistan				
Presidential government since Dec. 20, 1971	—	—	—	
Panama				
No-party assembly of "corregidores"	—	—	—	
Papua New Guinea (1972)				
United Party	...	...	40	
Pangu Party (M. T. Somare) } National coalition	...	...	24	
People's Progress Party } National coalition	...	...	12	
National Party	...	...	12	
Paraguay (February 1973)				
Partido Colorado (A. Stroessner)	R	84.0	40	(80)
Partido Liberal Radical	C	12.0	16	(29)
Partido Liberal	C	3.0	4	(8)
Partido Revolucionario (Febrerista)	L	...	0	(3)
Peru				
Military junta since Oct. 3, 1968	—	—	—	
Philippines				
Martial law since Sept. 23, 1972	—	—	—	
Poland (March 1976)				
Polish United Workers' Party } Front of National Unity	—	99.4	255	(255)
United Peasants' Party } Front of National Unity			117	(117)
Democratic Party } Front of National Unity			39	(39)
Nonparty } Front of National Unity			49	(49)
Portugal (April 1976)				
Centro Democrático-Social	CR	15.9	41	(16)
Partido Popular-Democrático	C	20.0	71	(80)
Partido Socialista	SD	35.0	106	(116)
União Democrática Popular	EL	1.7	1	(5)
Partido Comunista Português	K	14.6	40	(30)
Eight other parties	—	...	0	(0)
Qatar				
Independent emirate, no parties	—	—	—	
Rhodesia (July 1974)				
Rhodesian Front (European)	R	72.0	50	(50)
Centre Party (mainly African)	C	...	6	(7)
Independents	—	...	2	—
African National Council (boycotted the elections)				
Romania (March 1975)				
Communist-controlled Socialist Unity Front	—	99.9	349	
Rwanda (July 1975)				
National Revolutionary Movement for Development	—	—	—	
San Marino (September 1974)				
Partito Democratico-Cristiano	CR	...	25	(27)
Partito Social-Democratico	SD	...	9	(11)
Partito Socialista	S	...	8	(7)
Partito Comunista	K	...	15	(14)
Others	—	...	3	(1)
São Tomé and Príncipe (1975)				
Movimento de Libertação de São Tomé e Príncipe	—	—	—	
Saudi Arabia				
Royal government, no parties	—	—	—	
Senegal (January 1973)				
Union Progressiste Sénégalaise	CR	99.9	100	
Parti Démocratique Sénégalais	L	...	0	
Seychelles (April 1974)				
Seychelles Democratic Party	C	...	13	
Seychelles People's United Party	L	...	2	
Sierra Leone (May 1973)				
All People's Congress	CR	...	84	
Others	—	...	13	
Singapore (December 1976)				
People's Action Party	CR	...	69	(65)
Six opposition parties	—	...	0	(0)
Somalia				
Somalian Revolutionary Socialist Party	—	—	—	
South Africa (April 1974)				
National Party	R	57.1	123	(118)
United Party	C	32.7	41	(47)
Progressive Reform Party	L	5.3	7	(1)
Others	—	4.9	1	(5)
Spain				
Provisional royal government from Nov. 20, 1975	—	—	—	
Sri Lanka (May 1970)				
United National (D. Senanayake)	R	...	17	(72)
Sri Lanka Freedom (S. Bandaranaike)	C	...	91	(41)
Federal (Tamil)	C	...	13	(14)
Lanka Sama Samaja (pro-Chinese)	K	...	19	(10)
Communist (pro-Soviet)	K	...	6	(4)
Others	—	...	5	(10)
Sudan				
Military government since May 25, 1969	—	—	—	
Surinam (1975)				
National Unity coalition (H. Arron)	—	...	22	
Vatan Hitkarie Party (J. Lachmon)	...	...	17	
Swaziland				
Royal government, no parties	—	—	—	
Sweden (September 1976)				
Moderata Samlingspartiet (ex-Höger)	R	15.6	55	(51)
Centerpartiet (ex-Agrarian)	CR	24.1	86	(90)
Folkpartiet (Liberal)	C	11.0	39	(34)
Socialdemokratiska Arbetarepartiet	SD	42.9	152	(156)
Vänsterpartiet Kommunisterna	K	4.7	17	(19)
Others	—	1.7	0	—
Switzerland (October 1975)				
Christian Democrats (Conservative)	R	20.6	46	(44)
Republican Movement	R	3.0	4	(7)
Evangelical People's	R	2.0	3	(3)
National Action (V. Oehen)	R	2.5	2	(4)
Swiss People's (ex-Middle Class)	CR	10.1	21	(23)
Radical Democrats (Freisinnig)	C	22.2	47	(49)
League of Independents	C	6.2	11	(13)
Liberal Democrats	L	2.3	6	(6)
Social Democrats	SD	25.4	55	(46)
Socialist Autonomous	EL	1.3	1	(0)
Communist (Partei der Arbeit)	K	2.2	4	(5)
Others	—	2.2	0	—
Syria				
Baath and military government	—	—	—	
Taiwan (Republic of China)				
Nationalist (Kuomintang)	—	...	773	
Tanzania (October 1975)				
Tanganyika African National Union	C	93.2	218	
Zanzibar Afro-Shirazi (nominated)	L	...	52	
Thailand				
Military dictatorship since Oct. 6, 1976	—	—	—	
Togo				
Military government since 1967	—	—	—	
Tonga (June 1972)				
Legislative Assembly (partially elected)	—	—	21	
Trinidad and Tobago (September 1976)				
People's National Movement (E. Williams)	C	...	24	(36)
Democratic Action Congress	—	...	2	
United Labour Front	L	...	10	
Tunisia (November 1974)				
Parti Socialist Destourien	—	99.0	112	(101)
Turkey (October 1973)				
Nationalist Action	ER	3.4	3	(1)
National Salvation (N. Erbakan)	R	11.8	49	(6)
Turkish Justice (S. Demirel)	CR	29.8	149	(257)
Democratic	C	11.9	44	—
Republican Reliance (T. Feyzioglu)	C	5.3	13	(15)
Republican People's (B. Ecevit)	L	33.3	185	(144)
Turkish Unity	EL	1.1	1	(8)
Others	—	...	6	(8)
Uganda				
Military dictatorship since Jan. 25, 1971	—	—	—	
Union of Soviet Socialist Republics (1974)				
Communist Party of the Soviet Union	—	99.8	767	
United Arab Emirates				
Federal government of seven emirates				
United Kingdom (October 1974)				
Conservative	R	35.8	276	(296)
Liberal	C	18.3	13	(14)
Labour	L	39.3	319	(301)
Communist	K	...	0	(0)
Scottish National Party	—	...	11	(7)
United Ulster Unionists	—	...	10	(11)
Plaid Cymru (Welsh Nationalists)	—	...	3	(2)
Others	—	...	3	(4)
United States (November 1976)				
Republican	CR	...	143	(144)
Democratic	C	...	292	(291)
Upper Volta				
Military government since Feb. 8, 1974	—	—	—	
Uruguay				
Rule by Council of State as of June 1973	—	—	—	
Venezuela (December 1973)				
Cruzada Cívica Nacional	ER	4.3	7	(21)
Unión Republicana Democrática	R	3.2	5	(17)
COPEI (Social Christians)	C	30.2	64	(57)
Acción Democrática	L	44.3	102	(68)
Movimiento al Socialismo	SD	5.3	9	(10)
Fuerza Democrática Popular	S	1.2	2	(5)
Movimiento Electoral del Pueblo	EL	5.0	8	(27)
Partito Comunista Venezuelano	K	1.2	2	(5)
Others (four parties)	—	...	4	—
Vietnam, Socialist Republic of (April 1976)				
North: Lao Dong (Communist Party)	K	...	249	
South: National Liberation Front	—	...	243	
Western Samoa				
No political parties	—	—	—	
Yemen, People's Democratic Republic of				
National Liberation Front	—	—	—	
Yemen Arab Republic				
Military government since June 13, 1974	—	—	—	
Yugoslavia (May 1974)				
Communist-controlled Federal Chamber	—	...	220	
Zaire (November 1975)				
Mouvement Populaire de la Révolution	—	98.0	420	
Zambia (December 1973)				
United National Independence Party	—	80.0	125	

(K. M. SMOGORZEWSKI)

Populations and Areas

World population had hovered somewhere around the 4,000,000,000 mark for several years. Estimates ranged from a moderate 4,029,000,000 to 4,300,000,000. However, there was no way to make an exact determination. Some countries had not held a census for more than 20 years, and China, which accounted for almost one-fourth of the world's people, held its last census in 1953. Differences in figures were related to varying estimates of growth.

The Environmental Fund, which believed the growth rate was increasing, estimated that world population was rising at a rate of 2 to 2.2% each year. This meant that another 4,000,000,000 people would be added in about 33 years. On the other hand, the U.S. Agency for International Development believed world growth might have slowed, from 2% annually to 1.6%. At that rate it would take 43 years to double the current population. A more widely accepted estimate for world growth was 1.8% a year, the figure used by the U.S. Bureau of the Census.

Most of the dramatic growth that had occurred since World War II had taken place in the less developed countries of Latin America, Asia, and Africa. In the two and a half decades since 1950, world population had risen from 2,500,000,000 to 4,000,000,000, an increase of 60%. However, the population of the industrialized countries of North America and Europe (including the Soviet Union) rose only 31% during that period, from 739 million to 965 million, while that of Latin America practically doubled (from 164 million to 323 million), Africa grew by 82% (219 million to 399 million), and Asia, the largest continent, increased by 65% (1.4 billion to 2.3 billion).

In the developed world people tended to have smaller families and birthrates were low, not too much above death rates. In the U.S. in 1975 there were 14.8 births and 9 deaths per 1,000 population, for a natural growth rate of 0.6% per year. Immigration raised the figure to 0.8%, but even so it would take 87 years for the U.S. population to double. By contrast, the Yemen Arab Republic, with 50 births and 21 deaths per 1,000 for a growth rate of 2.9%, would double its population in 24 years. In Mexico, which had a high birthrate of 41.9 and a low death rate of 7.2 per 1,000, the growth rate was about 3.5% and the population would double in about 20 years.

Other conditions also affected population estimates. War brought increased deaths and mass migrations. Poor economic conditions sent millions from their homelands in search of a better life. Conversely, countries with booming economies contained large concentrations of immigrants. In recent years many migrants from southern Europe and North Africa had gone to the more prosperous countries of northern Europe where they found jobs as semiskilled or un-

continued on page 568

Polo:
see Equestrian Sports; Water Sports

World Population and Areas*

Country	AREA AND POPULATION: MIDYEAR 1975			POPULATION AT MOST RECENT CENSUS					Age distribution (%)†					
	Area in sq mi	Total population	Persons per sq mi	Date of census	Total population	% Male	% Female	% Urban	0-14	15-29	30-44	45-59	60-74	75+
AFRICA														
Afars and Issas	8,900	234,000	26.3	1960-61	81,200	...	...	57.4	...	...	...	...	...	...
Algeria	896,592	16,776,000	18.7	1966	11,833,126	50.2	49.8	38.8	47.1	22.4	14.9	8.7	5.0	1.8
Angola	481,350	6,678,000	13.9	1970	5,646,166	52.1	47.9	14.2	...	...	...	...	...	...
Benin	43,475	3,112,000	71.6	1961	2,082,511	49.0	51.0	9.3	46.0	22.7	16.4	9.3	—5.6—	
Botswana	220,000	691,000	3.1	1971	574,094	45.7	54.3	8.4	46.1	21.7	12.8	9.0	5.0	5.4
British Indian Ocean Territory	23	—	—	1971	110	...	...	...	...	...	...	...	...	...
Burundi	10,747	3,763,000	350.1	1970-71	3,350,000	...	...	3.5	...	...	...	...	...	...
Cameroon	179,558	6,539,000	36.4	1960-65	5,017,000	...	...	...	...	...	...	...	...	...
Cape Verde Islands	385	294,000	763.6	1970	272,071	48.2	51.8	19.7	...	...	...	...	...	...
Central African Empire	241,305	1,790,000	7.4	1959-60	1,177,000	47.8	52.2	6.8	40.0	21.9	25.7	10.4	—2.0—	
Chad	495,750	4,030,000	8.1	1964	3,254,000	48.2	51.8	7.8	45.6	22.2	19.3	9.3	—3.6—	
Comoro Islands‡	719	265,000	368.6	1966	244,905	49.2	50.8	13.5	44.1	23.6	15.7	8.7	4.2	3.8
Congo	132,047	1,345,000	10.2	1974	1,300,120	48.7	51.3	39.8	...	...	...	...	...	...
Egypt	386,900	37,233,000	96.2	1966	30,075,858	50.5	49.5	41.2	...	...	...	...	...	...
Equatorial Guinea	10,830	310,000	28.6	1965	277,240	52.8	47.2	...	35.1	—48.5—		—16.4—		
Ethiopia	471,800	27,030,000	57.3	1970	24,068,800	50.7	49.3	9.7	43.5	27.0	16.3	8.8	3.7	0.7
French Southern and Antarctic Lands	2,844	—	—	—	—	—	—	—	—	—	—	—	—	—
Gabon	103,347	1,156,000	11.2	1970	950,009	47.9	52.1	26.9	35.4	19.2	22.2	16.3	6.3	0.6
Gambia, The	4,467	524,000	117.3	1973	494,279	50.9	49.1	13.1	41.3	26.5	17.6	8.3	4.3	1.7
Ghana	92,100	9,552,000	103.7	1970	8,559,313	49.6	50.4	28.9	46.9	24.4	15.8	7.5	3.8	1.6
Guinea	94,926	4,416,000	46.5	1972	5,143,284	...	...	...	...	...	...	...	...	...
Guinea-Bissau	13,948	525,000	37.6	1970	487,448	48.7	51.3	11.1	...	...	...	...	...	...
Ivory Coast	123,484	6,673,000	54.0	1975	6,673,013	...	...	...	...	...	...	...	...	...
Kenya	224,961	13,399,000	59.6	1969	10,942,705	50.1	49.9	9.9	48.4	25.1	13.6	7.5	3.9	1.5
Lesotho	11,720	1,143,000	97.5	1966	852,361	43.2	56.8	4.4	43.5	22.1	13.9	11.5	6.8	2.0
Liberia	43,000	1,533,000	35.7	1974	1,496,000	...	...	...	...	...	...	...	...	...
Libya	675,000	2,444,000	3.6	1973	2,257,037	53.2	46.8	...	...	...	...	...	...	...
Madagascar	226,658	8,044,000	35.5	1966	6,200,000	49.2	50.8	...	46.5	22.3	15.2	10.1	—5.9—	
Malawi	45,747	5,044,000	110.3	1966	4,039,583	47.4	52.6	5.0	43.9	25.2	15.5	9.7	—5.7—	
Mali	478,822	5,697,000	11.9	1960-61	3,484,500	49.7	50.3	...	...	...	...	...	...	...
Mauritania	398,000	1,318,000	3.3	1964-65	1,030,000	50.1	49.9	...	43.9	24.5	16.3	10.0	—5.3—	
Mauritius	788	882,000	1,119.3	1972	851,334	50.0	50.0	42.9	40.3	28.6	14.5	11.0	4.9	0.7
Mayotte	146	40,000	274.0	1966	32,494	50.3	49.7	...	48.9	—51.1—				
Morocco	177,117	17,305,000	97.7	1971	15,379,259	50.1	49.9	35.4	46.2	22.4	16.0	8.3	5.3	1.8
Mozambique	308,642	9,239,000	29.9	1970	8,168,933	49.4	50.6	...	45.3	22.5	19.1	9.1	3.8	0.3
Niger	458,075	4,601,000	10.0	1959-60	2,611,473	49.7	50.3	...	...	...	...	...	...	...
Nigeria	356,669	62,925,000	176.4	1973	79,760,000	...	...	...	...	...	...	...	...	...
Réunion	970	489,000	504.1	1974	476,675	...	...	...	...	...	...	...	...	...
Rhodesia	150,674	6,310,000	41.9	1969	5,099,340	50.3	49.7	16.8	47.2	25.4	15.7	8.4	—3.3—	
Rwanda	10,169	4,160,000	409.1	1970	3,735,585	47.8	52.2	3.2	43.8	24.2	15.2	11.6	—5.2—	
St. Helena	159	6,000	37.7	1966	4,649	48.0	52.0	0	39.0	21.2	13.9	13.2	10.0	2.7
São Tomé and Príncipe	372	80,000	215.1	1970	73,811	50.8	49.2	...	...	...	...	...	...	...
Senegal	75,955	4,961,000	65.3	1976	5,085,388	49.2	50.8	...	...	...	...	...	...	...
Seychelles	171	58,000	339.2	1971	52,650	49.8	50.2	26.1	43.4	21.0	15.1	11.2	7.0	2.3
Sierra Leone	27,925	2,798,000	100.2	1974	2,729,479	...	...	...	...	...	...	...	...	...
Somalia	246,300	3,170,000	12.9	—	—	—	—	—	—	—	—	—	—	—
South Africa	457,269	25,471,000	55.7	1970	21,448,169	49.2	50.8	47.9	40.8	26.1	16.7	10.0	5.0	1.3
South West Africa (Namibia)	318,251	883,000	2.8	1970	746,328	50.8	49.2	24.9	...	...	...	...	...	...
Sudan	967,500	18,268,000	18.9	1973	14,171,732§	...	...	...	...	...	...	...	...	...

World Population and Areas* *(Continued)*

Country	AREA AND POPULATION: MIDYEAR 1975 Area in sq mi	Total population	Persons per sq mi	POPULATION AT MOST RECENT CENSUS Date of census	Total population	% Male	% Female	% Urban	Age distribution (%)† 0–14	15–29	30–44	45–59	60–74	75+
AFRICA (cont.)														
Swaziland	6,704	494,000	73.7	1966	374,571	47.7	52.3	7.1	46.7	24.6	14.4	8.5	4.5	1.3
Tanzania	364,943	15,155,000	41.5	1967	12,313,469	48.8	51.2	5.5	43.9	24.7	15.4	8.6	4.1	3.3
Togo	21,925	2,198,000	100.3	1970	1,953,778	48.1	51.9	...	...	...	...	...	...	...
Transkei	14,176	1,900,000	134.0	1970	1,751,317	41.0	59.0	...	...	...	...	...	...	...
Tunisia	63,379	5,588,000	88.2	1975	5,588,209	50.8	49.2	...	...	...	...	...	...	...
Uganda	93,104	11,549,000	124.0	1969	9,548,847	50.5	49.5	7.7	46.2	24.0	15.7	8.3	4.2	1.6
Upper Volta	105,869	6,032,000	57.0	1975	6,144,013	...	...	...	...	...	...	...	...	...
Western (Span.) Sahara	103,000	117,000	1.1	1970	76,425	57.5	42.5	45.3	42.9	27.2	16.3	7.4	4.4	1.8
Zaire	905,365	24,902,000	27.5	—	—	—	—	—	—	—	—	—	—	—
Zambia	290,586	4,896,000	16.8	1969	4,056,995	49.0	51.0	29.6	46.3	24.0	16.6	9.4	3.0	0.7
Total AFRICA	11,926,600	402,035,000	33.7											
ANTARCTICA total	5,500,000	‖	—	—	—	—	—	—	—	—	—	—	—	—
ASIA														
Afghanistan	252,000	19,280,000	76.5	—	—	—	—	—	—	—	—	—	—	—
Bahrain	256	256,000	1,000.0	1971	216,078	53.8	46.2	78.1	44.3	25.3	16.9	9.0	3.7	0.8
Bangladesh	55,126	73,100,000	1,326.1	1974	71,316,517	...	...	...	...	...	...	...	...	...
Bhutan	18,000	1,173,000	65.2	1969	1,034,774	...	...	...	...	...	...	...	...	...
Brunei	2,226	162,000	72.8	1971	136,256	53.4	46.6	63.6	43.4	28.0	15.7	8.1	3.9	0.9
Burma	261,789	31,240,000	119.3	1973	28,885,867	...	...	...	...	...	...	...	...	...
Cambodia	69,898	8,110,000	116.0	1962	5,728,771	50.0	50.0	10.3	43.8	24.9	16.8	9.8	4.1	0.6
China	3,691,500	853,000,000	231.1	1953	574,205,940	51.8	48.2	13.3	35.9	25.1	18.8	12.9	6.3	1.0
Cyprus	3,572	639,000	178.9	1973	631,778	49.5	50.5	42.2	28.8	27.3	17.0	13.3	10.4	3.2
Hong Kong	403	4,367,000	10,836.2	1976	4,407,000	...	...	...	...	...	...	...	...	...
India	1,269,420	600,000,000	472.7	1971	547,949,809	51.8	48.2	19.9	41.9	24.1	17.8	10.2	4.9	1.1
Indonesia	741,100	131,255,000	177.1	1971	118,459,845	49.2	50.8	17.5	44.1	24.0	18.6	9.0	3.7	0.6
Iran	636,000	32,923,000	51.8	1966	25,788,722	51.8	48.2	38.0	46.1	21.7	17.6	8.0	5.4	1.2
Iraq	168,928	11,124,000	65.9	1965	8.047,415	51.0	49.0	44.1	47.9	21.0	15.3	8.7	4.9	2.2
Israel	7,992	3,450,000	431.7	1972	3,147,683	50.3	49.7	85.3	32.6	26.9	15.6	13.6	9.2	2.0
Japan	145,767	110,953,000	761.2	1975	111,933,818	49.2	50.8	75.9	24.3	24.9	23.1	15.9	9.2	2.5
Jordan	36,832	2,702,000	73.4	1961	1,706,226	50.9	49.1	43.9	45.4	26.1	13.7	7.5	5.1	1.8
Korea, North	46,800	15,852,000	338.7	—	—	—	—	—	—	—	—	—	—	—
Korea, South	38,130	34,709,000	910.3	1975	34,708,542	...	...	...	...	...	...	...	...	...
Kuwait	6,562	995,000	151.6	1975	994,837	54.7	45.3	...	44.3	26.7	19.3	7.0	2.1	0.5
Laos	91,400	3,303,000	36.1	—	—	—	—	—	—	—	—	—	—	—
Lebanon	3,950	2,869,000	726.3	1970	2,126,325	50.8	49.2	60.1	42.6	23.8	16.7	9.1	—7.7—	
Macau	6	260,000	43,333.3	1970	248,636	51.4	48.6	100.0	37.6	28.9	15.0	11.3	5.9	1.1
Malaysia	127,316	11,900,000	93.5	1970	10,434,034¶	50.4	49.6	26.1	44.9	25.5	15.2	9.2	—5.2—	
Maldives	115	132,000	1,147.8	1974	128,697	53.1	46.9	—	44.9	22.8	19.0	9.4	3.4	0.4
Mongolia	604,000	1,446,000	2.4	1969	1,197,600	49.9	50.1	44.0	...	...	...	...	...	...
Nepal	54,362	12,572,000	231.3	1971	11,555,983	49.7	50.3	13.8	40.5	25.5	18.7	9.7	—5.6—	
Oman	82,000	766,000	9.3	—	—	—	—	—	—	—	—	—	—	—
Pakistan	307,374	70,260,000	228.6	1972	64,892,000	53.0	47.0	...	...	...	...	...	...	...
Philippines	115,800	41,831,000	361.2	1975	41,831,045	...	...	...	...	...	...	...	...	...
Qatar	4,400	180,000	40.9	—	—	—	—	—	—	—	—	—	—	—
Saudi Arabia	865,000	7,188,000	8.3	1974	7,012,642	...	...	...	...	...	...	...	...	...
Singapore	230	2,250,000	9,782.6	1970	2,074,507	51.2	48.8	100.0	38.8	28.1	16.9	10.5	4.9	0.8
Sri Lanka	25,332	13,986,000	552.1	1971	12,771,143	51.3	48.7	22.4	39.3	27.8	15.9	10.5	5.2	1.3
Syria	71,498	7,346,000	102.7	1970	6,304,685	51.3	48.7	43.5	49.3	22.4	14.3	7.5	4.8	1.7
Taiwan	13,815	16,049,000	1,161.7	1975	16,190,808	...	...	...	...	...	...	...	...	...
Thailand	209,411	41,334,000	197.4	1970	34,397,374	49.6	50.4	13.4	45.5	24.9	16.1	8.6	—4.9—	
Turkey	300,948	40,198,000	133.6	1975	40.197,669	...	...	...	...	...	...	...	...	...
United Arab Emirates	32,300	656,000	20.3	1975	655,973	...	...	...	...	...	...	...	...	...
Vietnam	130,654	45,211,000	346.0	—	—	—	—	—	—	—	—	—	—	—
Yemen (Aden)	111,074	1,690,000	15.2	1973	1,590,275	49.5	50.5	33.3	47.3	20.8	15.8	8.6	—6.6—	
Yemen (San'a')	77,200	5,238,000	67.8	1975	5,237,893	47.6	52.4	8.2	...	...	...	...	...	...
Total ASIA§δ	17,186,000	2,325,792,000	135.3											
EUROPE														
Albania	11,100	2,482,000	223.6	1960	1,626,315	51.4	48.6	30.9	42.7	57.3				
Andorra	179	27,000	150.8	1975	26,558	...	...	...	...	...	...	...	...	...
Austria	32,376	7,523,000	232.4	1971	7,456,403	47.0	53.0	51.9	24.4	20.5	18.3	16.5	15.5	4.8
Belgium	11,782	9,796,000	831.4	1970	9,650,944	48.9	51.1	...	23.5	21.0	19.4	17.1	14.4	4.6
Bulgaria	42,823	8,722,000	203.7	1965	8,227,866	50.0	50.0	46.5	17.8	22.6	23.8	16.5	10.3	9.0
Channel Islands	75	126,000	1,680.0	1971	126,363	48.5	51.5	...	21.8	21.4	18.4	18.1	14.9	5.3
Czechoslovakia	49,374	14,802,000	299.8	1970	14,344,787	48.7	51.3	55.5	23.1	24.8	18.4	16.7	13.6	3.4
Denmark	16,630	5,059,000	304.2	1970	4,937,784	49.6	50.4	79.9	23.2	23.8	17.7	17.8	13.4	4.1
Faeroe Islands	540	41,000	75.9	1970	38,612	52.2	47.8	...	31.8	23.0	16.5	16.0	9.4	3.3
Finland	130,129	4,707,000	36.2	1970	4,598,336	48.3	51.7	50.9	24.3	26.0	18.6	16.6	11.6	2.9
France	210,039	52,913,000	251.9	1975	52,544,400	48.7	51.3	70.0	...	...	...	...	...	...
Germany, East	41,826	16,850,000	402.9	1971	17,068,318	46.1	53.9	73.8	23.3	19.9	20.1	14.7	16.9	5.1
Germany, West	95,993	61,832,000	644.1	1970	60,650,599	47.6	52.4	...	23.2	21.3	19.7	16.6	15.0	4.2
Gibraltar	2.25	29,000	12,888.9	1970	26,833	48.1	51.9	91.9	22.9	22.7	21.1	18.7	11.2	3.4
Greece	50,960	9,046,000	177.5	1971	8,768,640	49.8	50.2	53.2	24.9	20.4	21.9	16.5	12.5	3.8
Hungary	35,920	10,540,000	293.4	1970	10,322,099	48.5	51.5	45.2	21.1	23.6	20.5	17.7	13.6	3.5
Iceland	39,776	218,000	5.5	1970	204,930	50.6	49.4	...	32.3	25.1	16.4	13.7	9.0	3.5
Ireland	27,136	3,127,000	115.2	1971	2,978,248	50.2	49.8	52.2	31.3	22.0	15.2	15.9	11.6	4.0
Isle of Man	221	59,000	267.0	1971	56,289	47.0	53.0	55.7	19.9	18.3	14.9	19.0	20.9	7.0
Italy	116,313	55,810,000	479.8	1971	54,136,547	48.9	51.1	...	24.4	21.2	20.7	17.0	12.8	3.9
Jan Mayen	144	—	—	1973	37	...	...	—	...	...	...	...	...	...
Liechtenstein	62	24,000	387.1	1970	21,350	49.7	50.3	...	27.9	27.1	18.6	14.5	9.3	2.6
Luxembourg	999	357,000	357.4	1970	339,812	49.0	51.0	68.4	22.1	20.5	21.4	17.5	14.6	3.9
Malta	122	300,000	2,459.0	1967	314,216	47.9	52.1	94.3	29.8	25.9	17.6	13.8	10.2	2.7
Monaco	0.73	25,000	34,246.6	1968	23,035	45.2	54.8	100.0	12.9	17.5	18.4	20.9	21.2	9.1
Netherlands, The	15,892	13,653,000	859.1	1971	13,045,785	50.0	50.0	...	...	...	...	...	...	...
Norway	125,053	4,007,000	32.0	1970	3,888,305	49.7	50.3	42.6	24.4	22.5	16.0	18.8	13.5	4.8
Poland	120,725	34,020,000	281.8	1970	32,642,270	48.6	51.4	52.3	26.4	25.5	20.4	14.6	10.6	2.5
Portugal	35,383	8,762,000	247.6	1970	8,545,120	47.4	52.6	...	28.4	21.9	19.0	16.2	11.2	3.3
Romania	91,700	21,245,000	231.7	1966	19,103,163	48.9	51.1	38.2	26.3	23.1	23.3	15.3	9.9	2.1
San Marino	24	20,000	833.3	1947	12,100	49.3	50.7	...	...	...	...	...	...	...
Spain	194,885	35,472,000	182.0	1970	33,956,047	48.9	51.1	54.7	27.8	22.0	19.9	16.1	10.8	3.4
Svalbard	23,958	—	—	1974	3,472	...	...	...	...	...	...	...	...	...
Sweden	173,732	8,195,000	47.2	1970	8,076,903	49.9	50.1	81.4	20.6	22.8	17.4	19.3	14.8	5.1
Switzerland	15,943	6,403,000	401.6	1970	6,269,783	49.3	50.7	52.0	23.4	23.7	20.2	16.3	12.5	3.9
United Kingdom	94,222	56,042,300	594.8	1971	55,515,602	48.5	51.5	...	24.1	21.0	17.6	18.3	14.3	4.7
Vatican City	0.17	1,000	5,882.4	—	—	—	—	—	—	—	—	—	—	—
Yugoslavia	98,766	21,352,000	216.2	1971	20,522,972	49.1	50.9	38.6	27.2	24.6	22.7	13.5	9.8	2.2
Total EUROPEδ	4,055,800	664,052,000	163.7											

World Population and Areas* *(Continued)*

Country	AREA AND POPULATION: MIDYEAR 1975 Area in sq mi	Total population	Persons per sq mi	POPULATION AT MOST RECENT CENSUS Date of census	Total population	% Male	% Female	% Urban	Age distribution (%)† 0–14	15–29	30–44	45–59	60–74	75+
NORTH AMERICA														
Anguilla	35	7,000	200.0	1960	5,810	44.5	55.5	...	45.7	18.8	11.8	12.9	7.3	3.5
Antigua	171	70,000	409.4	1970	64,794	47.2	52.8	33.7	44.0	24.2	12.0	11.7	—8.0—	
Bahamas, The	5,382	204,000	37.9	1970	168,812	50.0	50.0	71.4	43.6	24.3	16.8	9.8	4.4	1.1
Barbados	166	245,000	1,475.9	1970	235,229	48.0	52.0	3.7	35.9	27.2	12.9	12.8	8.7	2.5
Belize	8,867	140,000	15.8	1970	119,934	50.6	49.4	54.4	49.3	22.5	13.0	8.7	5.0	1.5
Bermuda	18	56,000	3,111.1	1970	52,976	50.2	49.8	6.9	30.0	25.8	20.5	14.4	7.7	2.0
British Virgin Islands	59	11,000	186.4	1970	10,298	53.0	47.0	21.9	39.2	29.1	14.7	10.0	5.1	1.9
Canada	3,851,809	22,831,000	5.9	1976	22,598,016	...	...	...	...	...	...	...	...	...
Canal Zone	558	44,000	78.8	1970	44,198	53.9	46.1	5.8	31.8	31.3	19.8	14.1	2.2	0.8
Cayman Islands	111	11,000	99.1	1970	10,249	46.8	53.2	61.1	...	...	...	...	...	...
Costa Rica	19,652	1,968,000	100.1	1973	1,871,780	50.1	49.9	40.6	43.3	27.0	14.2	8.4	4.4	2.7
Cuba	42,827	9,266,000	216.4	1970	8,569,121	51.3	48.7	60.3	27.0	25.0	16.9	12.1	6.8	2.2
Dominica	290	75,000	258.6	1970	70,302	47.4	52.6	46.2	49.1	21.2	11.2	10.0	6.3	2.2
Dominican Republic	18,658	4,697,000	251.7	1970	4,006,405	50.4	49.6	40.0	47.2	24.8	15.2	7.8	3.8	1.2
El Salvador	8,124	4,007,000	493.2	1971	3,541,010	49.6	50.4	39.4	46.2	25.1	15.2	8.2	4.3	1.0
Greenland	840,000	54,000	0.06	1970	46,531	52.5	47.5	...	43.4	24.8	18.8	8.5	3.9	0.6
Grenada	133	106,000	797.0	1970	96,542	46.2	53.8	...	47.1	23.0	11.6	9.4	6.6	2.2
Guadeloupe	658	354,000	538.0	1974	324,500	...	...	41.9	41.2	22.8	14.3	10.4	5.3	1.7
Guatemala	42,042	5,175,000	123.1	1973	5,211,929	50.0	50.0	33.6	45.1	26.7	15.1	8.3	—4.8—	
Haiti	10,714	4,584,000	427.8	1971	4,314,628	48.2	51.8	20.4	41.5	25.8	16.5	9.5	5.0	1.7
Honduras	43,277	3,037,000	70.2	1974	2,653,857	49.5	50.5	37.5	...	...	...	...	...	...
Jamaica	4,244	2,029,000	478.1	1970	1,813,594	49.8	50.2	41.4	37.5	25.1	15.2	12.4	7.5	2.3
Martinique	417	363,000	870.5	1974	324,800	...	...	...	39.5	25.0	14.2	11.8	7.3	2.2
Mexico	761,604	60,145,000	79.0	1970	48,225,238	49.9	50.1	58.7	46.2	25.6	14.6	8.0	4.4	1.2
Montserrat	40	13,000	325.0	1970	11,458	46.9	53.1	31.7	37.9	20.6	9.8	12.1	10.7	8.9
Netherlands Antilles	383	242,000	631.8	1972	223,196	48.8	51.2	...	38.0	26.7	16.7	10.3	6.4	1.9
Nicaragua	50,000	2,155,000	43.1	1971	1,877,972	48.3	51.7	48.0	48.1	—51.9—				
Panama	29,209	1,668,000	57.1	1970	1,428,082	50.7	49.3	47.6	43.4	26.1	15.2	9.6	4.3	1.4
Puerto Rico	3,421	3,087,000	902.4	1970	2,712,033	49.0	51.0	58.1	36.5	26.1	15.9	11.9	7.1	2.5
St. Christopher-Nevis (-Anguilla)□	104	47,000	451.9	1970	44,884	46.9	53.1	31.7	48.4	18.9	9.5	12.1	8.7	2.4
St. Lucia	241	112,000	464.7	1970	101,064	47.5	52.5	54.2	49.6	21.3	11.6	9.8	5.5	2.2
St. Pierre and Miquelon	93	6,000	64.5	1974	5,762	...	...	...	...	...	...	...	...	...
St. Vincent	150	93,000	620.0	1970	89,129	47.4	52.6	...	...	...	...	...	...	...
Trinidad and Tobago	1,980	1,074,000	542.4	1970	931,071	49.4	50.6	...	42.1	—40.4—		—17.5—		
Turks and Caicos Islands	193	6,000	31.1	1970	5,588	47.4	52.6	—	47.1	20.4	12.0	11.1	7.0	2.5
United States	3,615,122	213,611,000	59.1	1970	203,211,926	48.7	51.3	73.5	28.6	24.0	17.0	16.3	10.4	3.7
Virgin Islands of the U.S.	133	92,000	691.7	1970	62,468	49.9	50.1	24.4	35.7	28.3	19.4	10.8	4.4	1.4
Total NORTH AMERICA	9,360,900	341,685,000	36.5											
OCEANIA														
American Samoa	76	29,000	381.6	1974	29,200	...	...	...	...	...	...	...	...	...
Australia	2,967,900	13,502,000	4.5	1971	12,755,638	50.3	49.7	...	28.8	24.6	19.9	15.4	8.6	2.2
Canton and Enderbury Islands	27	—	—	1970	0	—	—	—	—	—	—	—	—	—
Christmas Island	52	3,000	57.7	1971	2,691	64.4	35.6	0	30.8	34.6	22.0	10.8	1.4	0.4
Cocos (Keeling) Islands	6	1,000	166.7	1971	618	50.5	49.5	0	...	...	...	...	...	...
Cook Islands	93	25,000	268.8	1971	21,317	51.2	48.8	0	51.6	22.5	12.5	—14.4—		
Fiji	7,055	573,000	81.2	1966	476,727	50.9	49.1	33.4	46.7	26.6	14.6	8.2	2.9	1.0
French Polynesia	1,261	128,000	101.5	1971	117,664	53.1	46.9	19.0	45.5	23.7	16.6	9.0	3.7	1.5
Gilbert Islands	102	53,000	519.6	1973	51,932	...	...	...	45.0	23.8	14.3	9.9	5.2	1.3
Guam	209	104,000	497.6	1970	84,996	55.7	44.3	25.5	39.7	29.1	19.3	8.9	2.5	0.5
Johnston Island	1	1,000	1,000.0	1970	1,007	...	...	0	...	...	...	...	...	...
Midway Islands	2	2,000	1,000.0	1970	2,220	...	...	0	...	...	...	...	...	...
Nauru	8	8,000	1,000.0	1966	6,055	53.3	46.7	0	40.0	24.7	23.9	9.2	2.1	0.1
New Caledonia	7,366	136,000	18.5	1974	131,665	...	...	...	...	...	...	...	...	...
New Hebrides	5,700	95,000	16.7	1967	77,988	52.1	47.9	12.0	45.6	26.0	15.5	8.5	—4.4—	
New Zealand	103,747	3,087,000	29.8	1976	3,130,083	...	...	...	...	...	...	...	...	...
Niue	100	5,000	50.0	1971	4,990	50.2	49.8	0	50.7	21.0	13.3	7.8	5.2	2.0
Norfolk Island	13	2,000	153.8	1971	1,683	49.0	51.0	0	25.2	20.7	19.7	18.9	12.5	2.9
Pacific Islands, Trust Territory of the	728	120,000	164.8	1973	114,782	51.5	48.5	...	...	...	...	...	...	...
Papua New Guinea	178,260	2,756,000	15.5	1971	2,489,937	52.0	48.0	11.1	45.2	24.5	17.4	9.9	1.4	1.6
Pitcairn Island	2	67	33.5	1975	67	...	...	0	...	...	...	...	...	...
Solomon Islands	10,983	190,000	17.3	1970	160,998	52.9	47.1	7.0	44.6	25.3	15.9	8.9	4.0	1.3
Tokelau	4	2,000	500.0	1972	1,599	46.1	53.9	0	48.2	18.3	14.3	9.4	6.9	2.7
Tonga	270	102,000	377.8	1966	77,429	51.5	48.5	...	46.3	25.2	15.6	8.1	3.8	1.0
Tuvalu	10	6,000	600.0	1973	5,887	44.8	55.2	...	...	...	...	...	...	...
Wake Island	3	2,000	666.7	1970	1,647	...	...	...	...	...	...	...	...	...
Wallis and Futuna Islands	98	9,000	91.8	1969	8,546	48.9	51.1	...	—95.7—				—4.2—	
Western Samoa	1,075	152,000	141.4	1971	146,627	51.8	48.2	20.6	50.6	24.3	13.1	7.9	3.3	0.8
Total OCEANIA	3,285,200	21,093,000	6.4											
SOUTH AMERICA														
Argentina	1,072,163	25,383,000	23.7	1970	23,364,431	49.7	50.3	80.4	29.3	24.6	19.9	15.4	8.6	2.2
Bolivia	424,165	5,634,000	13.3	1950	2,704,165	49.0	51.0	34.9	39.6	27.2	16.6	9.4	5.5	1.7
Brazil	3,286,488	107,145,000	32.6	1970	93,139,037	49.7	50.3	55.9	42.2	26.7	16.3	9.4	—5.1—	
Chile	292,135	10,253,000	35.1	1970	8,884,768	48.8	51.2	75.1	39.0	25.5	16.6	10.4	5.6	2.9
Colombia	439,737	23,542,000	53.5	1973	12,962,204	...	...	...	...	...	...	...	...	...
Ecuador	109,484	6,733,000	61.5	1974	6,552,095	50.1	49.9	41.3	44.6	26.5	14.7	8.4	4.6	1.3
Falkland Islands	6,150	2,000	0.3	1972	1,957	55.2	44.8	44.7	26.7	22.4	—51.9—			
French Guiana	34,750	55,000	1.6	1974	55,125	...	...	...	...	...	...	...	...	...
Guyana	83,000	791,000	9.5	1970	699,848	49.7	50.3	33.3	47.1	25.1	13.4	9.0	4.4	1.0
Paraguay	157,048	2,647,000	16.8	1972	2,357,955	49.6	50.4	37.4	44.9	25.4	14.5	9.2	4.5	1.5
Peru	496,224	15,615,000	31.5	1972	13,567,939	50.0	50.0	59.6	43.9	25.8	15.6	8.7	—5.9—	
Surinam	70,060	350,000	5.0	1971	384,903	50.0	50.0	...	48.0	—52.0—				
Uruguay	68,536	3,064,000	44.7	1975	2,763,964	49.1	50.9	...	...	...	...	...	...	...
Venezuela	352,144	11,993,000	34.1	1971	10,721,522	50.0	50.0	75.0	35.1	31.7	17.5	10.0	4.4	1.3
Total SOUTH AMERICA	6,892,100	213,207,000	30.9											
U.S.S.R.δ	8,649,500	254,382,000	29.4	1970	241,720,134	46.0	54.0	56.3	30.9	19.9	23.5	13.8	—11.8—	
in Asiaδ	6,498,500	63,837,000	9.8											
in Europeδ	2,151,000	190,545,000	88.6											
WORLD TOTAL◊	58,206,600	3,967,864,000	75.3											

*Any presentation of population data must include data of varying reliability. This table provides published and unpublished data about the latest census (or comparable demographic survey) and the most recent or reliable midyear 1975 population estimates for the countries of the world. Census figures are only a body of estimates and samples of varying reliability whose quality depends on the completeness of the enumeration. Some countries tabulate only persons actually present, while others include those legally resident, but actually outside the country, on census day. Population estimates are subject to continual correction and revision; their reliability depends on: number of years elapsed since a census control was established, completeness of birth and death registration, international migration data, etc.

†Data for persons of unknown age excluded, so percentages may not add to 100.0.
‡Excludes Mayotte, shown separately.
§Sudan census excludes three southern autonomous provinces.
‖May reach a total of 2,000 persons of all nationalities during the summer.
¶West Malaysia only.
♀Includes 7,000 sq mi of Iraq-Saudi Arabia neutral zone.
δAsia and Europe continent totals include corresponding portions of U.S.S.R.
□Excludes Anguilla, shown separately.
◊Area of Antarctica excluded in calculating world density.

continued from page 565

skilled workers, but there were signs that the recent downturn in the world economy had reversed this trend. (*See* Migration, International.)

In the U.S. vast changes had occurred since the "baby boom" of the 1950s. With increased income and education, attitudes about family size had changed. Americans were having fewer children and were starting their families at a later age. As the children of the "baby boom" matured and the birthrate fell, there was a noticeable change in school statistics. From 1965 to 1975 the number of college students rose sharply, from 5.7 million to 9.7 million, while the number of children in elementary schools fell from 32.5 million to 30.4 million.

The U.S. population was growing older. Since 1900 the number of persons 65 years of age or older had increased at twice the rate of the total population. In 1976, 22 million people, or 10% of the population, were over 65, and it was expected that the percentage would rise drastically as the "baby boom" group aged. Projections suggested that the number of elderly might reach 51.6 million in 2030.

Other changes were also taking place in the U.S. population. According to the Bureau of the Census, there has been a drastic slowdown of growth in the densely populated Northeast and a continuing increase in the so-called Sun Belt states—Florida, Texas, and Arizona. There were also some signs of a reversal of the migration to large metropolitan areas and a return to smaller cities and towns. However, the rural population continued the decline of the last 50 years. Fewer than 9 million Americans lived on farms in mid-1975. (WARREN W. EISENBERG)

See also Demography.

[525.A]

ALAIN DEJEAN—SYGMA

Socialist Mário Soares, whose party got the most votes, formed Portugal's first democratic government in 50 years.

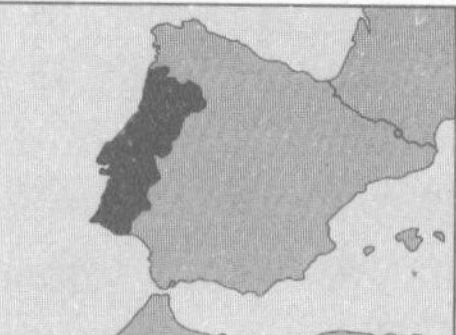

Portugal

A democratic republic of southwestern Europe, Portugal shares the Iberian Peninsula with Spain. Area: 35,383 sq mi (91,641 sq km), including the Azores (905 sq mi) and Madeira (308 sq mi). Pop. (1976 est.): 9,448,800, excluding about 550,000 refugees (mostly from Africa). Cap. and largest city: Lisbon (pop., 1976 est., 829,900). Language: Portuguese. Religion: Roman Catholic. Presidents in 1976, Gen. Francisco da Costa Gomes and, from July 23, Gen. António dos Santos Ramalho Eanes; premiers, Adm. José Baptista Pinheiro de Azevedo and, from July 23, Mário Soares.

On Feb. 26, 1976, the president, General Costa Gomes, and the leading political parties signed an agreement, to be incorporated into the draft constitution, guaranteeing full democratic elections and relegating the Supreme Revolutionary Council to the status of a presidential advisory council. On April 2, the constituent assembly approved Portugal's third constitution since the proclamation of the Portuguese Republic in 1910. It saw the country as a pluralistic society engaged in a task of transformation with the aim of attaining a classless society; this was to be attained through the development of social property via nationalizations, democratic planning, control of management, and democratic power for workers. Any future change in the constitution was to respect "the rights of workers, workers' committees, and trade unions"; the text of the constitution was to stand for at least four years and any further revisions had to be approved by a two-thirds majority in the People's National Assembly. The promulgation of the constitution on April 2 allowed the electoral campaign to commence on April 4 as foreseen. In the elections to the 263-member assembly held on April 25, the Socialist Party, which had polled the highest number of votes in the constituent assembly elections a year earlier, remained the largest single party but again failed to secure an absolute majority. The Popular Democratic Party was again second in strength, while the Communist Party was replaced by the Centre Democratic Social Party as the third strongest party in the assembly. The leader of the Socialist Party, Mário Soares, rejected a coalition on the ground that it would split his own party's support and announced that he would form a minority government to serve until it was defeated in the assembly or in elections.

Against this background of electoral impasse, the next elections, those for president, which duly took place on June 27, assumed major significance. Gen. António dos Santos Ramalho Eanes (*see* Biography) was elected, with 61.5% of valid votes, over two other military candidates and one civilian: Adm. José Pinheiro de Azevedo (the former premier), Gen. Otelo Saraiva de Carvalho (for the extreme left wing), and Octávio Pato (the Communist Party candidate). After a heart attack suffered by the admiral, the election was a foregone conclusion, although at the same time it represented a major defeat for Pato who polled only half the votes cast for the Communist Party in the legislative elections of April. The majority of the left-wing votes went to Carvalho, who finished in second place with 16.5% of valid votes cast. The result of the June 1976 presidential elections was a clear response to General Eanes' appeal for a mandate to introduce civil discipline within the new democratic constitution; it implied the choice of a Socialist and/or Christian Democratic government oriented toward integration with the European Economic Community (EEC) and loyalty to traditional alliances.

PORTUGAL

Education. (1974–75) Primary, pupils 933,112, teachers 34,596; secondary, pupils 491,248, teachers 34,055; vocational, pupils 167,255, teachers 14,130; teacher training, students 8,788, teachers 621; higher, students 58,918, teaching staff 4,353.

Finance. Monetary unit: escudo, with (Sept. 20, 1976) a free rate of 31.10 escudos to U.S. $1 (53.60 escudos = £1 sterling). Gold, SDR's, and foreign exchange (June 1976) U.S. $1,297,000,000. Budget (ordinary; 1975 est.): revenue 56,282,000,000 escudos; expenditure 45,185,000,000 escudos. Gross national product (1974) 341.6 billion escudos. Money supply (Dec. 1975) 227,280,000,000 escudos. Cost of living (Lisbon; 1970 = 100; May 1976) 214.

Foreign Trade. (1975) Imports 97,590,000,000 escudos; exports 49,340,000,000 escudos. Import sources: U.S. 12%; West Germany 11%; U.K. 9%; France 9%; Iraq 6%; Italy 5%. Export destinations: U.K. 21%; West Germany 10%; U.S. 7%; Sweden 7%; France 7%; Angola 6%. Main exports (1974): textile yarns and fabrics 17%; clothing 11%; machinery 11%; chemicals 8%; wine 7%; electrical equipment 7%; cork and manufactures 6%; fruits and vegetables 5%. Tourism (1974): visitors 2,622,000; gross receipts U.S. $513 million.

Transport and Communications. Roads (1974) 46,024 km (including 75 km expressways). Motor vehicles in use (1974): passenger 989,700; commercial (including buses) 48,001. Railways (1974): 3,563 km; traffic 4,552,000,000 passenger-km, freight 867 million net ton-km. Air traffic (1975): 3,135,400,000 passenger-km; freight 70,737,000 net ton-km. Shipping (1975): merchant vessels 100 gross tons and over 440; gross tonnage 1,209,701. Telephones (Dec. 1974) 1,011,177. Radio licenses (Dec. 1974) 1,516,000. Television licenses (Dec. 1974) 675,000.

Agriculture. Production (in 000; metric tons; 1975): wheat 646; oats 122; rye 155; corn 509; rice 141; potatoes 927; onions *c.* 65; tomatoes *c.* 839; figs (1974) *c.* 195; oranges (1974) *c.* 149; wine (1974) 1,405; olives *c.* 240; olive oil *c.* 33; cow's milk *c.* 531; meat *c.* 313; timber (cu m; 1974) 7,190; fish catch (1974) 428. Livestock (in 000; 1975): sheep *c.* 925; cattle *c.* 1,160; goats (1974) *c.* 739; pigs *c.* 2,220; chickens *c.* 14,872.

Industry. Fuel and power (in 000; 1975): coal (metric tons) 222; manufactured gas (Lisbon; cu m) 128,000; electricity (kw-hr) 10,459,000. Production (in 000; metric tons; 1975): iron ore (50% metal content) 23; crude steel 395; sulfuric acid (1974) 396; fertilizers (nutrient content; 1974–75) nitrogenous *c.* 129, phosphate *c.* 60; cement 3,326; tin (1974) 0.5; tungsten concentrates (oxide content; 1974) 1.9; gold (troy oz; 1974) 11; kaolin 61; preserved sardines (1973) 27; wood pulp (1974) 540; cork products (1973) 365; cotton yarn 77; woven cotton fabrics 47.

Once elected, General Eanes named Mário Soares his premier and on July 23 the Cabinet, composed largely of Socialist Party members and three military men, took office. Under the new constitution the Cabinet had three weeks to have its program passed in Parliament. The program approved on August 11 incorporated the first stage of the Socialists' political, economic, and social plans for the future in the face of rising unemployment (15 to 20%), budget deficits, inflation, and a balance of payments crisis. To restore local and international investors' confidence, the authorities stated that the government would indemnify in the case of further nationalizations and would clarify policy in those industrial sectors in which it intended to participate, allowing for "competitive coexistence" between itself and the private sector; incentives would be granted to firms that complied with government economic objectives and helped promote regional development, increase exports, or reduce unemployment. Labour policies included the definition of clearer prices and regulations, and legislation regarding worker discipline, participation, and incentive payments; the Ministry of Labour was to be restructured, labour courts set up, and the single union confederation disestablished and a freer system of unions instituted. Imports, especially of luxury goods, were further curtailed with the imposition of 30% surcharges on superfluous goods and 60% on luxury items; other measures included legislation to limit wage increases to 15% a year, cut "fringe benefits" and overtime working, raise prices, and severely discourage strikes. A public works program valued at $850 million was launched to help control unemployment.

The balance of payments current account deficit was forecast at $1,650,000,000 in 1976, as against $1,350,000,000 in 1975. As a result of the unfavourable payments position, total international reserves had fallen from $1,534,000,000 at end-1975 to $1,397,000,000 at end-March 1976. Falls in reserves were slowed from the beginning of 1976 by international loans of about $1.5 billion from the U.S., the EEC, the European Free Trade Association (EFTA), the International Monetary Fund, and the World Bank.

Agriculture and fishing were given high priority support. Prospects for the wheat harvest were good but other crops were only managing to maintain past average yields. The crisis in the fishing and wine industry continued although official credits were being made available. Agrarian reform was proceeding in the south, although illegally seized land in the north was being returned to its former owners.

International assistance was forthcoming from the EEC and the EFTA through tariff concessions and loans to help to develop the local industrial base; and the U.S. and many European countries made loans and technical aid and political support available. The municipal elections in December gave the Socialist Party about 33% of the vote, followed at a distance by the Social Democrats with about 24% of the vote. This seemed to guarantee the continuation of the Socialist Party in office. (MICHAEL WOOLLER)

See also Dependent States.

[972.A.5.b]

Prisons and Penology

Correctional policies continued to be contradictory, penology controversial, and the administration of prisons difficult throughout 1976. Different countries took quite opposite measures. Thus the Canadian House of Commons voted for abolition of the death penalty for civil offenses while, almost simultaneously, the U.S. Supreme Court moved in the opposite direction, effectively restoring the possibility of executions. Through a series of new rulings, intended to prevent arbitrary differences in different states and to define the law more closely, it enabled the death penalty to be imposed again, though in a limited way. New capital punishment laws in Georgia, Florida, and Texas were upheld, but the court ruled against mandatory death penalty laws in North Carolina, Louisiana, and Oklahoma. No death sentence had been carried out by year's end, however. Meanwhile, in France, 22-year-old Christian Ranucci was guillotined on July 28 for the abduction and murder of an eight-year-old girl—the first execution to have been held there since 1973.

Parole. It was a similar story with parole. In the U.K. it was extended so that almost 50% of those eligible were beginning to get parole. France, on the other hand, made it more difficult to be released on license, especially for those serving life sentences. But the very possibility of getting, or not getting,

Portuguese Literature: *see* Literature

Power: *see* Energy; Engineering Projects; Industrial Review

Presbyterian Churches: *see* Religion

Prices: *see* Economy, World

Printing: *see* Industrial Review

parole and the uncertainty about their eventual release date tended to create tensions and frustrations in the minds of prisoners. The 37th and latest of the U.S. federal prisons, which opened at Butner in North Carolina during the year, was set up on quite different lines, influenced by the thinking of the criminologist and criminal law expert Norval Morris. There, all prisoners knew their exact release date. Moreover, instead of having a rehabilitation program imposed on them, they were free to choose what work or educational training to follow. But Norman A. Carlson, director of the Federal Bureau of Prisons, made it clear that "we make no claims that this is the answer. We want to see if it works or if it is going to prove a failure like so many once highly touted ideas."

Prison Populations. The prison population in the U.S. reached a record level of around 250,000 inmates (excluding those kept in the small county jails). In terms of percentage of total population, this was higher than the highest in Europe: in West Germany and in England and Wales. U.K. Home Secretary Roy Jenkins (*see* BIOGRAPHY) emphasized in midsummer that a prison population of 42,000 would constitute a crisis point; that point was in fact reached during the autumn. The problem for penal administrators in many countries was that reductions in public spending meant the cancellation of new prison buildings, a halt in the recruitment of extra staff, and a reduction in overtime worked by existing staff. This, in turn, led to restrictions on prisoners' work and leisure activities, as well as to considerable overcrowding.

The further development of such alternatives for less serious offenders as the weekend community service programs in the U.K. and in New Zealand would also have meant more spending, however. More intensive community-based programs cost even more money, though still less than custodial treatment. Insufficient resources meant that society itself could become a sort of dustbin for less serious but perhaps

Scene outside Madrid's Caramanchel prison after King Juan Carlos granted amnesty to hundreds of political prisoners.

PABLOS—SYGMA

persistent offenders, alcoholics, and many of the mentally handicapped.

Although there were some jail demonstrations, including one at Tidaholm in Sweden and a much more serious disturbance at Hull maximum security prison in England which greatly damaged the building, it was remarkable that—despite the monetary pressures on penal institutions—fewer serious riots occurred than in previous years. A potentially explosive situation at the Lisieux high security prison in Normandy, France, when four guards were held hostage, ended quickly. So did an inmates' strike at the Attica state prison in New York, which was publicized largely because the facility had been the scene of a major riot, involving 43 deaths, in 1971. The most newsworthy escapes were those of four notorious women inmates of Moabit prison, West Berlin, where security was subsequently found to be rather lax.

Relaxed Regimes. The relative calm was partly a result of a gradual relaxation of prison rules, for example about communications with the outside world, and of experiments designed to reduce tensions and make life inside more normal. In one of these experiments, men and women were housed together in two of the six 16-cell blocks at Ringe prison in Denmark. Inmates were able to have sexual relations. Erik Anderson, the man in charge, found that the presence of women among the prisoners had improved the general atmosphere. At Ulriksfors prison in Sweden, prisoners could receive their wives on weekends, and in some Scandinavian penal institutions even visits by prostitutes were allowed. Public opinion was divided about such ideas, however, and they would not necessarily be acceptable in other parts of the world. Many countries did employ women staff in prisons for men and male staff in prisons for women. Experience showed that the selection of such staff had to be undertaken with the greatest care.

Coincident with these moves to make life more normal, there was also a move away from the use of tranquilizers for violent prisoners. It had been found that their use could lessen not only anxiety but also inhibitions. Well-considered programs of physical training did, however, provide acceptable outlets for aggression, not least among young women, as was shown at Bullwood Borstal in England.

More significant still were the lessons learned about the management of difficult and dangerous prisoners. Perhaps the best summary was written by Patrick Pope in the British *Prison Service Journal* (May 1976). He divided prisoners into various groups: the subversives; those with personality problems; prisoners needing protection; and the escapers. Prisoners in these groups were moved among a number of high security prisons and placed in different situations until the optimum conditions were found. Those with personality disorders were sent to the most appropriate psychiatric units. The mere possibility of rapid transfer of especially difficult prisoners reduced the pressure on staff, who were trained to be particularly patient and understanding. Transfers at the right moment were often a welcome change for the prisoners concerned as well.

Before long, staff had become very experienced at finding the best place for prisoners in the different categories and the regime most suited to each individual. Transfers were made not only between various prisons but from one unit to another within the same prison. Some institutions contained specialized units with different regimes, including psychiatric facilities

WEBB—MAGNUM

The new maximum security federal prison at Butner, North Carolina, received its first inmates in May. It has no gun towers, no cell blocks, and no bars on the windows.

and segregation units that could be used for punishment or simply to protect one inmate against violence from others.

Politics and Penology. Although such methods, when applied with skill and humanity, worked reasonably well and benefited all concerned, they were nevertheless attacked by opponents of imprisonment who saw custodial treatment principally as a form of political control designed to keep the ruling class in power. Some sociologists saw crime as being related to the class struggle and law enforcement as upholding the existing social structure. Offenses against property, they held, could be regarded as legitimate in Western societies. The way to reduce crime was to change the social structure. But property crimes were also committed in countries with different social structures. Where property was largely publicly owned, most thefts were considered to be crimes against the state and were regarded seriously. Whatever the structure of society, the majority of crimes occurred in large cities.

Arguments about the nature of crime, social control, and social support continued among those concerned with the treatment of lawbreakers. Established social work techniques used in probation, such as casework or group work, were increasingly questioned by some probation officers, especially in The Netherlands and in the U.K. A minority among them began to question their role as officers of the courts. They doubted whether they really ought to be concerned with maintaining or attempting to strengthen social cohesion. In many cases, they rejected some social work training and the concept of professionalism, since this might stop them from ranging themselves with their clients in the fight against social wrongs. Social work management was also viewed with suspicion because it was concerned with guidance, supervision, and the maintenance of professional standards. Attempts at considering the problems of offenders objectively and helping them to stay within the law were seen as propping up the system. Professional social work associations, in this view, ought to become trade unions.

Behaviour Modification. The majority of probation officers did not accept these views. Most of them continued to want to help offenders cope with their difficulties and improve their life situation by their own efforts. There were, however, uncertainties about training and about methods and techniques. Some advocated behaviour modification, but others criticized it as possibly constituting an unethical degree of pressure, even amounting to brainwashing. At the new prison at Butner, for example, behaviour modification has been ruled out. However, the use of action planning—in essence, a form of behaviour modification—achieved fairly good results with quite severely damaged people; this involved the joint setting, with the offender, of sometimes quite modest targets in the acquisition of new skills, together with the liberal use of praise if the target was achieved and judicious criticism if it was not. Transactional analysis (TA) was also found to be helpful with both prisoners and probationers in the U.S. and Europe, possibly because it is easily grasped. First developed by Eric Berne, TA sought to teach the subject to distinguish between the mature and less mature parts of his personality.

Self-Help. Outside the official field of corrections, the most important developments were in the area of voluntary offender self-help. Self-help day and community centres or clubs succeeded fairly well; partly staffed by ex-offenders turned social workers, they were used by those who realized they might get into trouble again but chose to make the effort to help themselves first. Self-help groups were also found useful for prisoners' wives. They would meet before or after visiting their husbands to share common problems while one of them supervised a play group for the children. This could assist them in coping with the absence of husband and father, with economic and social problems, and with the eventual reintegration of a man for whom the world had stood still with his family outside.

But such schemes, found chiefly in the U.S., Scandinavia, and the U.K., involved relatively small numbers. International and national research showed that different penal methods did not produce markedly different results. In any case, as Michael Hogan, England's chief probation inspector, put it in introducing PRISM—the initials stood for Probation Research Implication for Staff and Management—expectations about research were often unrealistic. No instant answers to complex problems could be expected, although the problems themselves could be clarified. It was shown, for example, that even the best social work inside penal institutions, undertaken in order to prepare prisoners for ultimate release, was ineffective if communications with the probation or parole officer outside were not improved. Effective plans beyond release and proper follow-up required that all who were involved be kept informed: families and future employers, hostels for the homeless, and the relevant persons who would provide support or supervision. (HUGH J. KLARE)

See also Crime and Law Enforcement; Law.
[521.C.3.a; 543.A.5.a; 10/36.C.5.b]

Publishing

Despite continuing economic problems the publishing industry in general had grounds for guarded optimism in 1976. Book publishers were encouraged by ever increasing sales, especially of paperbacks, with the reading public seemingly undeterred by the higher prices that followed still-mounting costs. For newspapers the picture was more varied. In Paris, London, and New York old-established mastheads changed hands, and in France at least there was disquiet at journalists' professional conscience being "included in the deals and delivered with the chattels," as Pierre Viansson-Ponté of *Le Monde* put it. Official, as distinct from economic, control and censorship remained rife in many countries, particularly in Africa, India, and Latin America. In Spain, however, there was a relaxation of censorship following the restoration of the monarchy. Third world countries expressed concern at the exclusive role of Western news agencies operating within their territories, but at the UNESCO general conference in Nairobi, Kenya, a Soviet-inspired draft declaration to impose governmental control over international news media operations within member countries was shelved.

At its 25th general assembly, held in Philadelphia, Pa., in May, the International Press Institute voted to move its headquarters from Zürich, Switz., to London, as an economy measure.

Newspapers. Britain's beleaguered national press got a chance to catch its breath in 1976 after the economic gloom and downward-spiraling circulations of 1975. Final circulation figures for that year, published in February 1976, showed an average 8% drop in sales, with some papers faring much worse; even the *Sun*'s soaring rise was checked to a tiny gain, with the *Daily Mail* the only other national daily to hold its own. But the spring of 1976 seemed to carry hints of a general improvement in the economy. Advertisers started to return and so did some of the lost readers, although the mass-circulation Sunday papers continued to face a downward trend. Of the dailies, the *Daily Express* clearly had competitive problems to overcome.

The respite was short-lived. By the autumn it became clear that the country's underlying economic problems were not being solved, nor was inflation fully checked. The implications of this for the newspaper industry were bad enough, but the October slump in the value of the pound sterling dealt a sharp and specific blow: the price of newsprint, mostly imported, rose as the pound fell. Since newsprint already absorbed 28% of the quality newspapers' total costs and no less than 36% of those of the big-circulation dailies, this was a real new burden. Percy Roberts, chief executive of Mirror Group Newspapers Ltd., told his staff in November that devaluation alone had added 14% to newsprint costs since August and that a New Year price increase by the manufacturers was likely to add an additional 15%. The outcome for MGN was that its expected improvement in profits for 1977–78 (£3 million was reported for 1975–76) would be wiped out. Yet another round of price increases, putting more pressure on sales, was therefore inevitable, as was made clear by Beaverbrook Newspapers Ltd., owners of the *Daily Express, Sunday Express,* and the London *Evening Standard.*

Following its 1975 financial crisis, in January 1976 the Sunday *Observer* acquired a new editor. Donald Trelford, who had previously been deputy to owner-editor David Astor, wrote in his first editorial: "Fleet Street has just survived its most dangerous year. In standing alone, with no outside sources of support, *The Observer* has achieved a unique independence." But by the autumn that too was threatened, through the need for £1 million capital—not, the management insisted, to underwrite losses, but for necessary expansion. A number of bidders, ranging from Far East interests to the heiress Olga Deterding, entered the ring, with two established newspaper empires, Rupert Murdoch's News International Ltd. (*Sun, News of the World*) and Associated Newspapers Ltd. (*Daily Mail,* London *Evening News*) seemingly the most likely contenders. The prospect of yet another newspaper shifting from a radical stance toward the political centre caused alarm. There was a surprise outcome, however, when it was announced on November 24 that the U.S. oil company Atlantic Richfield Co. (chairman Robert O. Anderson, also chairman of the Aspen Institute for Humanistic Studies) had taken a controlling interest in *The Observer* under conditions that seemed to ensure the 185-year-old paper's continued editorial independence. (Murdoch was able to console himself with his acquisition, some days previously, of the *New York Post.*)

Britain was not the only European country with problems, although the third-quarter circulation figures from West Germany showed all but one of the nationally distributed newspapers gaining circulation and the *Frankfurter Allgemeine Zeitung* rising to the best figures in its history. In France there was much concern over changes of ownership as 91-year-old Jean Prouvost, having sold *Le Figaro* to Robert Hersant (*see* BIOGRAPHY) in 1975, broke up the remainder of his empire. (See *Magazines*, below.) With *France-Soir* sold to Paul Winkler, a former staff man, concern focused on what interests might be providing the necessary finance. Strongly critical of the deals and of the lack of consultation with journalists was *Le Monde,* which itself did not escape unscathed during the year. In *Le Monde tel qu'il est* ("*Le Monde* as it really is"), published in March, Michel Legris,

Profits:
see Economy, World
Protestant Churches:
see Religion
Psychiatry:
see Health and Disease
Psychology:
see Behavioural Sciences; Health and Disease

a former staff journalist, accused the paper of spreading left-wing, even Marxist, views under the cloak of the reputation for objectivity built up by its retired founder Hubert Beuve-Méry. This did not inhibit *Atlas World Press Review* from naming *Le Monde*'s editor in chief, André Fontaine, "international editor of the year." Another award, the "golden pen of freedom" of the International Federation of Newspaper Publishers, went to Raul Rego, editor of the Lisbon socialist evening paper *A Luta*. Rego founded *A Luta* following the seizure in 1975 by Communist-dominated printing workers of *República,* of which he was previously editor.

In Italy the rising cost of newsprint was met with joint protective action by publishers in the form of a self-imposed limit on the number of pages, first to 16, with a threat of going down to 8 if there was no new agreement on government subsidies. Italy was also the scene of an unusual legal case when three journalists claimed damages after a leftward shift in the policies of the Milan paper *Corriere della Sera.* This, they said, had forced them to leave the newspaper (for the rival *Il Giornale*). The court came out in favour of the newspaper's editor, Piero Ottone; he had changed the policies, it found, but only if he had censored or changed copy would there have been a case to answer. In December there was concern that Turin's *La Stampa,* owned by Fiat, in which the Libyan government had just bought a share, might suffer Libyan interference.

One event of the year brought a reminder, albeit a melancholy one, of what was still possible in the newspaper industry. The death occurred of Lord Thomson of Fleet (*see* OBITUARIES), the Canadian-born owner of *The Times, The Sunday Times,* and a huge collection of newspaper, periodical, and other interests across the world. The many tributes to him, in newspapers other than his own, acknowledged Roy Thomson's capacity for running profitable businesses with great acumen, while still leaving editors free to run serious newspapers according to their own beliefs and judgment. His son, Kenneth Thomson, reaffirmed the family's intention of continuing to back *The Times* with a family trust.

(PETER FIDDICK)

For newspapers in the United States, 1976 was a year of intense judicial and legislative activity. Perhaps the most notable event was a unanimous U.S. Supreme Court ruling against the use of "gag" orders, judicial restrictions on press coverage of criminal trials. In recent years judges had been imposing such orders on the press with increasing frequency in order to help protect the right of a defendant to a fair trial. Before 1966 "gag" orders were virtually unknown; in that year, however, the Supreme Court overturned the murder conviction of Sam Sheppard because of adverse pretrial publicity. Consequently, during the next decade some 200 "gag" orders were imposed. Early in 1976 a judge in Nebraska ordered journalists not to report news about the case of Edward Simants, an out-of-work farmhand accused of murdering six members of a Sutherland, Neb., farm family. The judge was concerned that inevitable widespread publicity about the grisly killings would make it impossible to select an impartial jury for the trial. Newspapers and broadcasters in the state challenged the ruling, and the Supreme Court found that "gag" orders violate constitutional guarantees of a free press.

That decision was a decisive victory for newspapers,

World Daily Newspapers and Circulations, 1975–76*

Location	Daily newspapers	Circulation per 1,000 population
AFRICA		
Algeria	4	17
Angola	4	15
Benin	2	0.7
Botswana	2	21
Cameroon	2	3
Central African Empire	1	0.3
Chad	4	0.5
Congo	3	1
Egypt	14	22
Equatorial Guinea	1	4
Ethiopia	7	2
Gabon	1	1
Ghana	6	41
Guinea	1	1
Guinea-Bissau	1	12
Ivory Coast	3	10
Kenya	3	8
Lesotho	1	...
Liberia	2	4
Libya	6	...
Madagascar	13	15
Malawi	1	...
Mali	3	0.6
Mauritius	16	115
Morocco	11	15
Mozambique	5	5
Niger	2	0.5
Nigeria	17	...
Réunion	2	60
Rhodesia	3	15
Senegal	2	...
Seychelles	2	71
Sierra Leone	5	17
Somalia	2	1
South Africa	26	...
Sudan	22	8
Tanzania	3	...
Togo	3	6
Tunisia	4	22
Uganda	7	9
Upper Volta	1	0.4
Zaire	13	9
Zambia	2	23
Total	233	
NORTH AMERICA		
Antigua	1	4
Bahamas, The	2	155
Barbados	1	99
Belize	1	30
Bermuda	1	218
Canada	121	235
Costa Rica	8	112
Cuba	14	...
Dominican Republic	7	...
El Salvador	13	...
Guadeloupe	2	70
Guatemala	10	...
Haiti	7	16
Honduras	8	...
Jamaica	3	91
Martinique	3	79
Mexico	227	...
Netherlands Antilles	5	188
Nicaragua	6	...
Panama	9	92
Puerto Rico	4	120
Trinidad and Tobago	3	139
United States	1,756	352
Virgin Islands (U.S.)	3	343
Total	2,215	
SOUTH AMERICA		
Argentina	179	...
Bolivia	17	38
Brazil	274	40
Chile	128	94
Colombia	52	...
Ecuador	22	46
French Guiana	1	38
Guyana	3	88
Paraguay	11	...
Peru	70	...
Surinam	6	...
Uruguay	59	...
Venezuela	47	...
Total	869	

Location	Daily newspapers	Circulation per 1,000 population
ASIA		
Afghanistan	18	5
Bangladesh	30	...
Burma	10	...
Cambodia	16	10
China	392	...
Cyprus	12	123
Hong Kong	72	...
India	830	...
Indonesia	154	...
Iran	39	24
Iraq	7	...
Israel	23	...
Japan	188	537
Jordan	4	19
Korea, North	11	...
Korea, South	33	...
Kuwait	7	85
Laos	8	...
Lebanon	32	...
Macau	7	...
Malaysia	41	...
Mongolia	2	103
Nepal	29	...
Pakistan	88	...
Philippines	19	17
Saudi Arabia	11	11
Singapore	10	193
Sri Lanka	15	...
Syria	5	9
Taiwan	31	...
Thailand	35	24
Turkey	450	...
Vietnam	32	...
Yemen (Aden)	3	1
Yemen (San'a')	6	10
Total	2,670	
EUROPE		
Albania	2	49
Austria	32	305
Belgium	46	268
Bulgaria	13	215
Czechoslovakia	28	269
Denmark	52	364
Finland	61	...
France	106	233
Germany, East	40	443
Germany, West	1,211	301
Gibraltar	2	207
Greece	103	101
Hungary	27	226
Iceland	5	439
Ireland	7	234
Italy	78	120
Liechtenstein	1	263
Luxembourg	7	...
Malta	7	...
Netherlands, The	93	311
Norway	77	391
Poland	44	234
Portugal	29	86
Romania	58	179
Spain	115	97
Sweden	108	515
Switzerland	97	385
U.S.S.R.	658	373
United Kingdom	109	438
Vatican City	1	...
Yugoslavia	25	87
Total	3,242	
OCEANIA		
American Samoa	1	156
Australia	58	386
Cook Islands	1	48
Fiji	1	36
French Polynesia	3	87
Guam	2	234
New Caledonia	3	143
New Zealand	40	...
Niue	1	60
Papua New Guinea	1	6
Total	111	
Grand total	9,340	

*Only newspapers issued four or more times weekly are included.
Sources: UN, *Statistical Yearbook 1975* (1976); *1976 Editor & Publisher International Year Book* (1976); *Europa Year Book 1976, A World Survey.*

CENTRAL PRESS

British financier Sir James Goldsmith and his companion Lady Annabel Birley arrive for the start of his libel proceedings against the magazine "Private Eye."

but other Supreme Court actions were setbacks. The court ruled that some persons considered "public figures" can no longer be prevented from suing for libel by virtue of their notoriety; that ruling narrowed publishers' defenses against libel actions. The court also refused to dismiss an invasion of privacy suit in which the defendant admitted that injurious statements published about him were true; this could eliminate a journalist's long-standing ability to rely on truth as a defense against privacy-invasion suits.

Congress in 1976 passed the nation's first federal "sunshine law," a measure that would open the proceedings of some 50 government boards and agencies to the press. The legislators also deleted in committee some of the antipress provisions of Senate Bill No. 1, the proposed revision of the Federal Criminal Code.

While Congress was taking those generally favourable steps toward greater press freedom, it also was attempting to persecute a newsman for publishing a secret congressional report. Early in the year CBS reporter Daniel Schorr (*see* BIOGRAPHY) obtained a copy of a Senate committee's report on its investigation into alleged Central Intelligence Agency abuses. Schorr passed the document to *The Village Voice,* a Manhattan weekly newspaper, which published it in its entirety. Schorr was subpoenaed by the House Select Committee on Standards and Practices, which demanded that he name the person who furnished him with the report. Schorr refused, insisting that he had done nothing illegal, and that the First Amendment protects reporters from having to reveal the identity of confidential sources. Schorr could have been cited for contempt for his defiance, but the committee eventually voted not to punish him.

Newspaper circulation in the U.S. continued its downward slide, according to the *1976 Editor & Publisher International Year Book.* Total circulation declined nearly 2% from the previous year to 60,655,431, the lowest level in a decade. Evening circulation fell by 1.6% to 35,165,245, and morning circulation fell by 2.5%. Though morning papers lost more readers, evening readers lost more papers. The number of evening newspapers in the U.S. declined by 13 to 1,436; the number of morning papers fell by only one to 339. There were 19 "all day" newspapers, which publish editions at various times throughout the day, two fewer than the previous year. The disproportionately steeper mortality rate for evening newspapers was nothing new; according to one 1976 study, some 60% of all newspapers that had failed in the past decade were evening papers. One of the most important papers to close during 1976, the 159-year-old *Hartford* (Conn.) *Times,* was an evening daily; circulation had dwindled from 132,000 in 1972 to a final 69,000. One important factor in the demise of evening papers was television; more and more readers were taking their evening news from that medium.

Pulitzer Prize awards for the year reflected a renewed appreciation for "investigative reporting," the aggressive pursuit by hard-digging reporters of official misdeeds and other abuses of power. The 1976 Pulitzer Gold Medal for Public Service, probably the nation's single most prestigious newspaper award, went to the *Anchorage* (Alaska) *Daily News* for its 15-article investigation of the state's powerful Teamsters Union local 959. Among other investigative reporting feats to win Pulitzer Prizes: Gene Miller's stories in the *Miami* (Fla.) *Herald* exonerating two men sentenced to death for murder; *Chicago Tribune* exposés of public-housing abuses and misuse of public hospital funds; and James Risser's investigation for the *Des Moines* (Iowa) *Register* of large-scale corruption in the U.S. grain-exporting business. In addition, *New York Times* reporter Sydney Schanberg received a Pulitzer for his coverage of the Communist victory in Cambodia, and a *Times* colleague, Walter (Red) Smith, was cited for his commentaries on sports.

One investigative reporter became the first martyr to his profession since the 1930s. Don Bolles of the *Arizona Republic* was looking into organized crime and political corruption in the state when a bomb exploded under his car, killing him. Shortly after Bolles' death, 18 investigative reporters from 14 newspapers across the U.S. arrived in Arizona to continue his investigations.

(DONALD M. MORRISON)

Magazines. The Periodical Publishers' Association, in evidence to the Royal Commission on the Press, put the failure rate of new consumer magazines in Britain at 80%. There seemed reason to suspect that such a figure might indicate the liveliness of the magazine market, rather than its decline. There was certainly a marked inclination for new publications to be aimed at filling relatively narrow or short-term gaps in the market.

Some of the year's more orthodox new titles helped give the impression of an industry eager and ready for any sign of improvement in the economy. *Prima,* launched in October, was a monthly apparently aimed at the middle-road heart of the potential audience of young women, less aggressive than *Cosmopolitan* or *She,* and offering a wide range of traditional interests, from romantic fiction to homemaking. Sex might be obligatory in the mid-1970s, but there was at least one surprise move in the opposite direction: Penthouse Publications, a leading sex publisher, announced that *Viva,* its female-oriented magazine, would become less sexy and henceforth be distributed by eminently respectable Condé Nast. Another new aspirant was *Hi-Fi Weekly,* pushing boldly into a high-spending consumer market, but one already well-stocked with a range of highly competitive monthlies, each with its own distinctive approach.

While other, more established titles struggled against rising costs, prices edged up. The *New Statesman* rose to 25 pence, *Listener* to 20 pence, *The Tatler and Bystander* to 75 pence. Imported publications had the same problem of pricing; *Newsweek* and *Time* magazines were retailing in Britain at 40 pence. But in spite of the higher prices the increasingly colourful magazine racks abounded with frivolous newcomers, such as *National Rock Star* and *Oh Boy!* (for girls).

In a case that rumbled on through the year in a series of injunctions and counterclaims, Sir James Goldsmith (*see* BIOGRAPHY), the head of a Paris-based commercial empire, attempted to use the law of criminal libel against the satirical magazine *Private Eye*. This rarely used law carried harsher penalties than the civil version, including imprisonment, and the severity of the action was increased by Sir James's intention to involve all distributors rather than just the main publishers.

In the breakup of Jean Prouvost's French publishing empire (see *Newspapers,* above), *Paris-Match* was sold, in a package, to the Librairie Hachette subsidiary France-Éditions et Publications. The buyer kept the profitable television guide *Télé 7 Jours* but three weeks later sold *Paris-Match* to photographer-turned-publisher Daniel Filipacchi (*see* BIOGRAPHY). *Black-Hebdo*, a weekly tabloid aimed at French-speaking Africa and black communities in France, made its first appearance in April.

In India, under the continuing state of emergency, two magazines, the weekly *Opinion* (Bombay) and the monthly *Seminar* (Delhi), were forced to close down after having criticized the government in defiance of the current censorship rules.

(PETER FIDDICK)

Romping happily up the economic comeback trail, general magazine publishers in the U.S. in 1976 reported average increases of 20 to 30% in advertising revenues over 1975. Profits were assisted by continuing boosts in cover prices for the magazines. In fact, for the first time in memory several of the popular mass circulation magazines reported that circulation revenues exceeded those from advertising. The result was a continuing trend that seemed to prove the assumption that publishers can issue a magazine basically supported by revenue from subscriptions and newsstand sales rather than solely by advertising. For example, *Good Housekeeping* raised its newsstand price from 75 to 95 cents and claimed more money from sales than from advertising. A similar report came from *Ms* magazine.

The March *Reader's Digest* topped its own record in the *Guinness Book of Records* with an issue that included the most expensive single print ad ever to run anywhere. The Bicentennial Commission of Pennsylvania paid $1,280,000 for a 48-page insert, topping previous records (also claimed by the *Digest*) of $950,000 and $877,000.

Another relatively new phenomenon was the increasing number of supermarkets with magazine racks. High postal costs discouraged many mass magazine publishers from seeking mail subscribers, and they turned instead to racks placed near supermarket checkout counters or wherever one might be tempted to make an impulsive purchase. Supermarkets sold $455 million of magazines in 1975 out of a total of $2 billion.

TONY ROLLO—NEWSWEEK

Publisher Clay Felker holds a sample copy of his West Coast monthly "New West," which made its debut in February.

Among financial success stories of the year was the city magazine. Four of the five U.S. monthlies with the fastest growing volume of advertising in 1976 were what one commentator called the "urban survival manuals," *Chicago, Los Angeles, The Washingtonian,* and *Cleveland*. (The fifth impressive gainer was *The Smithsonian*.) Most of the better city magazines borrowed the format of *New York*, the pacesetting weekly by Clay Felker, which began a western version, *New West*, in 1976. And to prove that a mountain of money can still be made from failing to overestimate the U.S. male reader's taste, the comparatively hard-core sex magazine *Hustler* claimed a net income of about $16 million in 1976, moving from zero to third place among men's magazines in less than two years.

Business sponsorship of magazine articles along the same lines as commercials on television ended before it really began. Xerox Corp. paid Harrison Salisbury $55,000 for an article in *Esquire*'s bicentennial issue in return for mention of its sponsorship at the beginning and end of the article. Two more projects were planned, but were canceled after a heated debate over the propriety of such articles.

Among the new 1976 titles of promise were *Working Woman,* with a predicted circulation of over 400,000 by the end of 1977; *Firehouse,* edited by the author of *Report from Engine Co. 82* and directed to both firefighters and fire buffs; and *Weed,* a New York tabloid begun by John Wilcock, who helped to found *The Village Voice*. Among children's magazines the newest was *Children's Express,* distinctive in that all of the writers were children and the editor was only 17 years old.

The most controversial magazine of the year was *Counter-Spy,* a Washington, D.C., quarterly along the editorial lines of the old *Ramparts*. Its mission was to expose the secrets of government organizations such as the CIA and the FBI. Since 1974 it had named over 200 clandestine government agents. When CIA station chief Richard Welch was gunned down in

Athens, *Counter-Spy* was the target of criticism for identifying the agent. Although admitting discomfort, but not blame, the editors countered with a new list of names in a subsequent issue.

In a move to protect domestic periodicals, Canada's House of Commons voted in February to deny Canadian advertisers in U.S.-controlled magazines the same tax exemptions they received in Canadian-owned periodicals. The result was that after 30 years Time, Inc. closed its Canadian edition. At the same time, McGraw-Hill, the largest publisher of trade publications in the U.S., began distribution in China of the Chinese-language *American Industrial Report.*

(WILLIAM A. KATZ)

Books. INTERNATIONAL DEVELOPMENTS. Judging by attendance at the 1976 Frankfurt Book Fair, bigger than ever with more exhibitors (4,139) and more visitors, book publishers seemed to have survived the 1974–75 recession almost unharmed in most countries. In 1976 the number of novelties, new editions, and reprints reached new peaks. The North American market was attracting more and more companies from Europe, Australia, and Japan, with some securing footholds in the U.S. either by opening branches or by buying local imprints. A special exhibit was devoted to Latin America. Brazilian publishers were among the busiest at the fair. The Soviet Union released information about Moscow's first international book fair, to be held in September 1977.

The International Publishers Association's 20th congress, held in Kyoto, Japan, May 25–June 1, 1976, drew more than 1,000 publishers from more than 35 countries. Major themes of the congress included copyright and photocopying relations between publishers in developed and less developed countries, marketing and distribution of publications, and freedom to publish. Publishers from developed countries were asked to give priority to the private sector of the publishing trade in the less developed countries, to offer translation rights of their books to publishers in less developed countries at extremely low rates, and to transfer reprint rights to less developed countries instead of sending finished books. Congress participants expressed concern at the ever increasing postal rates and extra postage required for book parcels sent to some countries.

(JOSEPH A. KOUTCHOUMOW)

UNITED STATES. For U.S. publishers, the most significant events in 1976 were the passing of a new copyright act and the settlement of the 1974 antitrust suit by the U.S. Department of Justice against 21 publishers. On the economic front the book business, which began to pick up during the summer of 1975, maintained its upward trend in 1976. All book categories gained in sales and revenues for the first nine months of the year.

After more than 20 years of legislative effort, the first complete revision of the 1909 U.S. Federal Copyright Law was passed at the end of September. The new law, with an effective date of Jan. 1, 1978, does not change the fundamental relationship between authors and publishers except to include an extension of copyright protection from the current maximum of 56 years to the life of the author plus 50 years. At the same time, copyright protection begins from the time an author finishes a manuscript or renders his work in a tangible form, thus bringing unpublished as well as published works under statutory copyright. The new bill also extended copyright protection to two previously uncovered areas, jukeboxes and cable television, and went a long way toward resolving the question of "fair use" of copyright works by spelling out guidelines for classroom and library photocopying.

The Justice Department's antitrust suit against 21 U.S. publishers, charging them with carving up sales territories in other nations for the sale of English-language books, was settled at the end of July. All the publishers involved signed a consent agreement stating that they would not illegally divide foreign sales territories for their books. The antitrust proceedings came to an end only after the Justice Department was able to convince British publishers to revoke the traditional market agreement in effect since the end of World War II which stipulated that members of the British Publishers Association (named as a co-conspirator in the antitrust suit) would not accept a copyright license from a foreign publisher or author unless the license included the exclusive right for publishing and distributing in 70 English-speaking countries.

The Association of American Publishers (AAP) reported that sales for the first nine months of 1976 were ahead of the corresponding period of 1975 in most categories. Adult trade hardcover books rose 5.6%; juvenile hardcovers declined 1.1%; book clubs increased 15.7%; and mail-order publications were up 53%. In educational publishing, elementary and high school textbook sales declined 1.1% in the first nine months of 1976, but college textbook sales were up 3.4%.

The U.S. Department of Commerce estimated that sales of U.S. book publishers in 1976 would pass $4.1 billion, a 10% increase over 1975. The department estimated that by 1985 publishers' receipts should reach $8.4 billion.

Breaking down the total 1975 sales into different book categories, the greatest percentage increase in dollar sales for 1975 over 1974 occurred in general religious books, college texts, medical books, mass market paperbacks, and adult trade paperbacks. Sales in adult trade hardcover books increased only 1.7%. In view of the sizable average rises in book prices, this small total increase indicated that substantially fewer adult hardcover books were sold in 1975 than in 1974. Mass market paperbacks, on the other hand, brought in $339.6 million to their publishers, over 8% more than the adult hardcover sales total of $313.4 million. Adult trade paperback books continued to show healthy increases, including a rise of 14.3% in 1975 over 1974. Religious books showed a 13.5% sales rise in bibles, hymnals, and related works and a surprising 23.6% jump in general religious book sales.

The overall title output for U.S. publishers declined slightly in 1975, a drop of 2% in new books and 8.7% in new editions. The 1975 total output was 39,372, of which 30,004 were new books and 9,368 were new editions. This compared with a total of 40,846 published in 1974, of which 30,575 were new books and 10,271 were new editions. The book title output from U.S. publishers changed only slightly in the first three months of 1976 from the first three months of 1975. Listings of new books were almost the same, 6,543 in 1976 compared with 6,536 in 1975. New edition totals were down somewhat, 1,950 in 1976 compared with 2,122 in 1975.

Doubleday and Co., the largest hardcover trade publisher (with more than 700 titles published annually and estimated sales of more than $300 million through its printing, book club, and bookstore operations), was a principal party in one of the biggest publishing mergers in years. The other was the Dell Publishing Co., one of the five top mass market paperback firms. The merger was significant because it continued the trend of hardcover-paperback mergers.

Each year record-breaking sales of paperback rights are set, and in 1976 there were two. *The Final Days* by Robert Woodward and Carl Bernstein, the *Washington Post* reporters who broke the Watergate story, was sold by Simon and Schuster to Avon Books for $1,550,000, the highest reprint figure ever paid for a nonfiction book. The previous high for a nonfiction book was established when *The Joy of Cooking* was sold by Bobbs-Merrill to New American Library in 1974 for $1.5 million.

Setting a record for the prepublication sale of paperback rights in a work of fiction, Dodd, Mead auctioned the late Agatha Christie's last novel, *Sleeping Murder,* to Bantam Books for $1.1 million. Bantam paid the highest price ever for paperback rights in 1975 when it purchased from Random House E. L. Doctorow's novel *Ragtime* for $1,850,000, but that purchase was made after the book was published.

The Final Days was also one of the best-selling hardcover books during the year. It climbed to the top of best-seller lists within days of its publication date and maintained that position for four months. Sales for that period of time exceeded 600,000 copies.

(DAISY G. MARYLES)

UNITED KINGDOM. Prophets had forecast that 1976 would be a year of retrenchment for British book publishing. It was known that some larger publishing houses had cut back on their programs for the year. Figures for the first nine months of 1976, however, indicated that the reduction was less than might have been expected: new books were down by 1,422 and new editions by 819, representing a reduction of 8.35% compared with the corresponding period of 1975. Only the medical sciences showed an increase, and the most dramatic cut came in school textbooks, where the number of titles produced was reduced by almost one-third. This reflected the continued erosion of school budgets, which led teachers to be cautious about buying all but the most essential books. At the post-school level there were significant cuts in the output of titles in chemistry and physics, history, literature, and political science. Despite pessimism about the future of hardcover fiction, the number of novels published fell by only 1%.

Following several years of alarming inflation there was increasing concern that British books would become less competitive in world markets. (In 1975 list prices had risen 25% over the previous year.) The sharp decline in the value of the pound sterling, however, made British books much more attractive once again, even though, by raising paper and other input costs, it kept list prices rising faster than had originally been expected. In 1975 book exports fell slightly to just under 41% of a total turnover of £351 million. For 1976 the picture appeared to be uneven. The introduction of universal primary education in Nigeria provided an excellent opportunity for those firms established in that market. There were indications, however, that exports to some other important markets had fallen.

(MARTIN BALLARD)

WEST GERMANY. Book production in 1975, with 43,649 titles, was 12.3% lower than in 1974. The proportion of new editions was higher, and 11.4% of all titles published were in paperback. Book prices again rose. Competition among publishers grew in 1976, and was reflected in changes in book distribution. Direct sales of many publishing houses were impressive, while book offers by chain stores, especially coffee dealers, became a menace to the bookseller. Book clubs became more international. The Bertelsmann group (2.5 million members in West Germany) cooperated with foreign firms in France, Italy, Spain, and Austria. The French experiment resulted in a membership of 1.3 million in 1976 after a modest start in 1971 with 21,000 members. Bertelsmann also planned to enter the British market.

(SIGFRED TAUBERT)

CANADIAN PRESS

Browsers at the Montreal International Book Fair, the largest international book fair in North America.

SWITZERLAND. Swiss publishers issued 7,711 titles in 1975, up by 5.7% from the 1974 total of 7,294. However, fiction titles, the largest category, dropped from 1,229 to 1,157 titles. The slight trend of expansion in book production was reflected in two of the four national languages, German and Italian, while publication in the other two, French and Romansh, fell considerably. Books published in English rose by 54%—531 titles compared with 344 titles in 1974—to constitute 7% of book production.

Due to the worldwide economic recession and the strength of the Swiss franc, book exports to France, the U.S., and the U.K. fell by 20, 53, and 16.5%, respectively. Exports to West Germany, however, rose by 12%.

(KURT ERICH WETTSTEIN)

AUSTRALIA. For Australian book publishers 1976 was a difficult year. The change of government at the end of 1975 created both confusion and dearth in educational and institutional library spending, on which the prosperity of most Australian publishers depended. The total number of new titles increased from 1,212 to 1,422. The increase was due almost exclusively to the Australia Council's Literature Board, which in 1975–76 subsidized 183 titles at a cost of A$377,446. The total of volumes printed in Australia was 8,465,023, but the number of Australian published books printed in Southeast Asia, mainly Hong Kong and Singapore, rose to 33,066,756 volumes. The printing industry was therefore engaged in heavy lobbying to stem the flow of book imports.

(ANDREW FABINYI)

See also Literature.

[441.D; 543.A.4.e]

ENCYCLOPÆDIA BRITANNICA FILMS. *Newspaper Story* (2nd ed., 1973).

Puerto Rico: *see* Dependent States

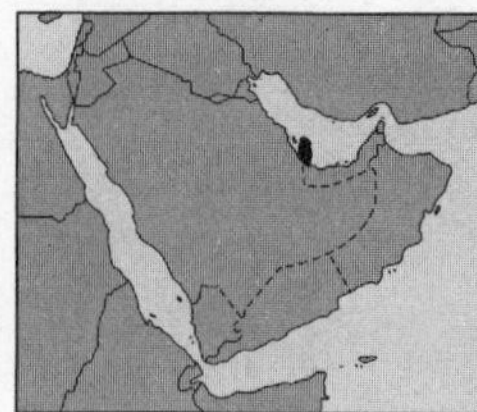

Qatar

An independent emirate on the west coast of the Persian Gulf, Qatar occupies a desert peninsula east of Bahrain, with Saudi Arabia and the United Arab Emirates bordering it on the south. Area: 4,400 sq mi (11,400 sq km). Pop. (1975 est.): 180,000. Capital: Doha (pop., 1975 est., 130,000). Language: Arabic. Religion: Muslim. Emir in 1976, Sheikh Khalifah ibn Hamad ath-Thani.

In 1976 Qatar launched plans to use its oil wealth to reduce its almost total dependence on oil exports. The 1976 budget announced in January was about $1 billion, more than double that of 1975, and the $376 million allocation to heavy industry marked a nearly fivefold increase over 1975. Industrial projects included iron and steel, petrochemicals, natural gas, fertilizers, and cement. In February the new Bunduq oil field owned jointly by Qatar and the United Arab Emirates started production. In May the oil minister said that Qatar planned to hold output at about 465,000 bbl a day, which would bring in revenues of about $2 billion a year.

Qatar started negotiations in June for a takeover of the remaining 40% interest held by foreign participants in the Qatar Petroleum Co. (QPC) and Shell Co. of Qatar, which jointly produced Qatari oil. Negotiations were complicated by Qatari claims that the takeover would be retroactive to December 1974, when the demand was first made. However, an agreement was reached with QPC in late September providing for a Qatari payment to the companies of about $20 million compensation. The companies would also receive 15 U.S. cents a barrel in return for continuing to provide managerial and operational services. A parallel agreement with Shell Co. of Qatar was expected to follow. In March Qatar's first earth satellite communications station, installed by Nippon Electric Co., Ltd., of Japan, came into operation and a new automatic telex exchange was inaugurated on August 1.

(PETER MANSFIELD)

[978.B.4.b]

QATAR

Education. (1974–75) Primary, pupils 20,152, teachers 1,068; secondary, pupils 6,985, teachers 620; vocational, pupils 190, teachers 46; teacher training, students 307, teachers 47.

Finance. Monetary unit: Qatar riyal, with (Sept. 20, 1976) a free rate of 3.93 riyals to U.S. $1 (6.78 riyals = £1 sterling). Gold and foreign exchange (March 1976) U.S. $101.5 million. Budget (1975 actual): revenue 7,315,000,000 riyals; expenditure 5,302,000,000 riyals.

Foreign Trade. (1975) Imports 1,621,600,000 riyals; exports 7,024,900,000 riyals. Import sources (1974): Japan 18%; U.K. *c.* 15%; U.S. 10%; Lebanon 6%; West Germany 6%. Export destinations (1974): U.K. *c.* 15%; France 10%; United Arab Emirates *c.* 10%; Italy *c.* 8%; Thailand *c.* 8%. Main export crude oil 98%.

Industry. Production (in 000; metric tons): crude oil (1975) 21,194; petroleum products (1974) 20.

Race Relations

World Review. By 1976 the dissolution of the great European empires was virtually accomplished. But the world remained divided between affluent, developed countries, mostly white, and impoverished, overpopulated new nations, mostly coloured. Many of these new nations had retreated into a narrow, oppressive nationalism, tyrannizing over neighbours or ethnic minorities within their boundaries. Such activities frequently went unnoticed in the uproar of the international campaign against racism, Zionism, and the remaining white-dominated states of southern Africa.

The active intervention and rivalry of the Soviet Union and China encouraged these tendencies. The most notable instance occurred in 1975–76 in the power vacuum of Angola. Here the Soviet Union intervened successfully in a struggle between competing forces. It used Cuban troops to defeat the mainly Bakongo National Front for the Liberation of Angola (FNLA), backed by Zaire and aided first by China and then by the U.S., and the moderate, Ovimbundu-centred National Union for the Total Independence of Angola (UNITA), the Ovimbundu being the largest ethnolinguistic and regional grouping in Angola (about 40% of the population).

The South West Africa People's Organization (SWAPO), a militant Marxist black nationalist liberation movement in Namibia (South West Africa), was operating southward from bases in Angola. SWAPO claimed to have a national, rather than an ethnic, base and perspective, as against the South West African National Union (SWANU; mainly Herero) and other black movements in Namibia. Ethnic differences of a Bantustan type were meanwhile being encouraged by the South African government, which proposed independence on a multiethnic basis, with 11 legislative assemblies, including whites and Coloureds.

In Rhodesia, Ian Smith's government appeared finally to have accepted the principle of black majority rule within two years. At the Geneva conference which met late in 1976 to discuss dates and terms, African political, socioeconomic, and ethnotribal differences emerged again, notably in Robert Mugabe's delegation and among the guerrilla factions, divided between the Zezuru and Karanga tribes of the Shona people. The whites seemed to be favouring more moderate representatives such as Bishop Abel Muzorewa, a Shona who commanded support among black Rhodesians at home and might not be eager to see a peaceful transition jeopardized by militant Marxist guerrillas from outside.

The civil war in Lebanon stimulated Lebanese emigration. One haven was Sierra Leone, where Lebanese had traditionally been shopkeepers and businessmen. This increased inflow elicited official words of concern in late 1976. The Sierra Leone Citizenship Amendment Act particularly affected the Lebanese community: it provided among other things that non-Negro Africans applying for citizenship must have resided in Sierra Leone for not less than 20 years and must be able to speak one indigenous language. Elsewhere in West Africa there was evidence of nationalist fervour, with traditional African ethnic minorities being winnowed out and forced to return to their countries of origin. Some moves were also reported in East Africa against the remaining Asian minority communities, notably in Malawi, where several hundred U.K. passport holders were expelled to Britain.

In the Middle East, late in 1976, a relative peace came to war-torn Lebanon. The Syrians hoped to reunite the country on the basis of a Feb. 14, 1976, reform program giving the Muslims greater representation than previously. Some extremist Maronite military groups took to the hills in protest, but the main losers in the conflict which they had done so

Quakers: *see* Religion

Quarrying: *see* Mining and Quarrying

MAQUBAWE—SYGMA

Houses burn in Soweto, a black township near Johannesburg, South Africa, during three days of rioting in June.

much to fan were the Palestinian refugees, whose camps were mostly destroyed. The Israeli-Arab conflict remained dormant.

In a number of ethnically plural Western societies, political moves toward devolution or fuller independence continued. In Canada, Quebec separatism was again on the march, and René Lévesque's Parti Québécois won a sweeping victory over Robert Bourassa's Liberals in November. Lévesque was committed to a referendum and ultimate independence for Quebec. Three-fifths of the voters, however, opted for pro-confederation parties and could probably be convinced of the confederation's value if the English-speaking majority were to implement bicultural policies more wholeheartedly. In Britain the 1976–77 parliamentary session was to consider legislation on devolution for Scotland and Wales but not for strife-torn Ulster despite the resurrection among some Protestants and Catholics in late 1976 of the idea of independence. Independent-minded Shetland, whose oil would provide much of the financial basis for the Scottish nationalists' dream of an independent Scotland, sought to promote a private bill in Westminster to exempt the island from the Scottish devolution proposals.

As Spain moved cautiously toward democracy, criticisms were heard of the constitutional reforms being proposed by Adolfo Suárez González. The equal senatorial representation of each mainland province would favour the more thinly populated, conservative rural areas as against the more progressive, industrialized peripheral regions, notably the Basque country and Catalonia. The Catalans remained largely withdrawn and focused on developing their own economy and culture, while violent protest and repression still continued in the Basque country. The Franco decree declaring Vizcaya and Guipúzcoa "traitor provinces" was revoked only in November 1976.

Home rule by 1980 was planned for Greenland, an integral province of Denmark since 1953, but a Danish commission found that the 50,000 Eskimo-Caucasian Greenlanders did not constitute a people, and thus did not own the oil or mineral resources that might be found under their feet. In The Netherlands, after years of tension and protest, sometimes violent, the 35,000 South Moluccans, who rejected absorption and sought an eventual return to the East Indies, were granted increased rights as from Jan. 1, 1977.

The biennial conference of UNESCO held in Nairobi, Kenya, in November 1976 showed more enlightenment than did the heavily politicized 1974 conference (which had supported the Arab-third world racist onslaught on Israel and caused several Western countries to reduce or suspend financial contributions). In 1976 conciliatory efforts by UNESCO's director general Amadou Mahtar M'Bow of Senegal secured agreement that every member be entitled to join a regional group, and Israel was thereupon accepted by the European group. The conference did, however, once again condemn Israel for continuing archaeological excavations in Jerusalem that were said to threaten Muslim shrines, and for allegedly depriving Arabs in the occupied territories of cultural opportunities.

The 1975–76 report of Amnesty International afforded a worldwide picture of human rights denied to various minorities, although information was often less readily available from areas in which institutionalized violation of human rights was most grave; *e.g.,* Iran, Iraq, Cambodia, the Soviet Union, Burma, Uganda, Mozambique, and the Central African Empire. Other reports, notably from the third world, concerned not only prisoners but long-standing repression, confrontation, or flight of racial and ethnic groups, particularly in Asia and Africa.

United Kingdom. In 1976 immigration numbers again became an issue, with the leaking in May of a confidential Foreign and Commonwealth Office report on the self-perpetuating pool of dependents said to be waiting in India and Pakistan, alarmist reports of an "Asian flood" from East Africa and the Indian subcontinent, and also reports of widespread illegal immigration. The National Front organized provocative marches and other activities. Black-police relations gave concern, with muggings of older white people by young blacks in some London districts and also arrests by police of young blacks on "sus" (suspicion of loitering with intent to commit a felony). Particular confrontations included: a demonstration in June in Southall by over 200 Asians, following the stabbing to death of a Sikh student by white youths, and a later peaceful multiracial protest march by 7,000 in Southall; and a day of racial tension and protest marches in the East End of London in which one white boy was stabbed to death and three Asian youths were wounded. In August, on the last day of the annual street carnival in Notting Hill, London, groups of young black pickpockets became particularly active and fighting broke out between West Indians and the police; 325 policemen out of a force of about 1,600 on duty at the carnival were injured, as well as at least 131 members of the public. Replying to accusations of excessive police pressure, the metropolitan police commissioner, Sir Robert Mark, said: "There is no question of our abdicating responsibility for law and order on the streets of London."

Revised official estimates of the coloured population of Great Britain for the years 1971–74 gave a total of 1,744,000, or 3.2% of the population. The number of persons from the New Commonwealth, mostly dependents, accepted for settlement in the first nine months of 1975 was 23,189, plus 5,482 citizens of Pakistan and 10,588 U.K. passport holders. In 1969–74 the births to mothers born in the New Commonwealth and Pakistan increased slightly, from 5.9% of all British births in 1969 to 6.3% in 1974.

At the autumn political party conferences the Liberals demanded less immigration control (including a repeal of the Immigration Act 1971) and more urban aid; the Labour Party called for the repeal of the Commonwealth Immigrants Act 1968 and the 1971 act, and for a campaign against racialism; and the Conservative Party endorsed stricter immigration controls but rejected renewed calls of the former Conservative MP Enoch Powell for massive repatriation and accepted a resolution that "all efforts must be made to ensure that the immigrants now in Britain are equal and welcome members of our society." The new Race Relations Act was due to come into force at the end of 1976. It was designed to strengthen the law against racial discrimination and to bring it into line with the Sex Discrimination Act (which had been in operation for one year).

During 1975, 1,138 complaints were made to the Race Relations Board (the highest total since 1969), and 1,083 cases were disposed of. Opinions of unlawful discrimination were formed in 233 cases, written assurances against further discrimination were secured in 191 cases, and settlements in addition in 77 cases. In the first six months of 1976, the high rate continued, with 559 complaints and 604 disposals, in 112 of which opinions of unlawful discrimination were formed.

A Political and Economic Planning (PEP) survey, *The Facts of Racial Disadvantage* (February 1976), indicated that overt discrimination in employment decreased considerably between 1966 and 1974, probably because of the effect of the Race Relations Act 1968. Registered unemployment figures for minority group workers increased by 302%, from 14,678 to 59,070, between August 1973 and August 1976 (as compared with 135% for the general population). An earlier (September 1975) PEP study found that the allocation of public housing tended to work to the disadvantage of coloured minority groups. The Greater London Council (GLC) decided in 1976 to carry out its own investigation, and an interim report published in May concluded that coloured tenants fared less well than whites.

Carnival turned to riot at London's annual Notting Hill Calypso Carnival, intended as a celebration of "love and peace." Tensions among the West Indian population run high.

SYKES—SYGMA

South Africa. In 1976 a Parliamentary Internal Security Commission was set up with wide powers to investigate individuals and organizations. The Internal Security Act gave the minister of justice practically uncurbed powers to intern, for repeated periods of one year with no access to the courts, anyone considered to be doing, or who might do, anything to endanger state security. The blacks also had increasingly stringent restrictions placed on them by the Squatters' Act and the Status of the Transkei Act, which withdrew South African citizenship from nearly 2 million Africans living outside the Transkei.

Rioting by young blacks began in the township of Soweto near Johannesburg on June 16 and later spread to other black townships. It was still continuing in December (*see* SOUTH AFRICA). The riots reflected the deep-seated black resentment against white domination. Prime Minister B. J. Vorster reacted with an uncompromising policy of tough action against violence, though in December there were signs of a more conciliatory approach. By December at least 433 persons, mostly black, were being held in detention under the Terrorism Act and Internal Security Act. About 80 had been released and about 100 detainees (most of them leaders of the "black consciousness" movement) held under sect. 10 of the Internal Security Act were to be released if there was no more unrest in the black townships. The Soweto Students' Representative Council promised a quiet return to classes in January provided detained students were released; but it also asked residents to cooperate with its Christmas call for a boycott on white-owned shops in Johannesburg. In December the schools boycott continued in Johannesburg and Cape Town, where 30,000 pupils in the three African townships were affected.

It was estimated that 8% of Africans were unemployed. The Environment and Planning Act bore hard on African workers by pegging the employers' African labour force at the January 1968 total. Some 6,000 more than the 1968 quota were employed in the clothing industry in 1976, but the government was initiating prosecutions against many employers. African advancement into operative and skilled work was still hampered by legislation preventing mainstream unionization or negotiation and denying Africans apprenticeship training, although the Bantu In-Service Training Act made concessions about training centres for African labour.

The Theron Commission recommended in 1976 that the political future of the Coloured people, who had no homeland of their own, be linked to the country's "white" Parliament and other decision-making bodies, that the Group Areas Act be drastically amended and many other disparities and inequalities removed, and that the laws prohibiting mixed marriages and miscegenation between Coloured and white be repealed. The government rejected the more radical proposals.

For Pretoria the granting of independence to the Transkei marked a first step in its grand design of separate development, whereby every African person in South Africa would eventually become perforce a citizen of one or another homeland, even though he or his ancestors had never lived there, and those nine or ten million who had to remain working in the republic would be "guest workers" who were citizens of foreign states and so not entitled to full political, economic, or social rights. Whites would thus eventually constitute the largest ethnic group in South Africa proper. The significance of this grand design was widely recognized, and international recognition of the Transkei did not accompany the independence celebrations in October 1976. It was also noted that the Transkei was retaining the basic South African apartheid laws and the repressive security laws.

Despite years of government threats, the press in South Africa continued to show considerable independence. In July Percy Qoboza, editor of South Africa's only black daily, *The World,* picked up Vorster's 1974 "give me six months" speech with "we give *you* six months, Mr. Vorster." *The World*'s circulation shot from 100,000 a day before Soweto to 185,000 afterward. Later, official harassment led to the detention of some 30 journalists, the trial of Donald Woods, white editor of the *Daily Dispatch,* and the interrogation of Qoboza in December. Some Nationalist Party intellectuals condemned current apartheid policy. Piet Cillié, editor of Cape Town's *Die Burger,* even called in November for full citizenship and freedom for all—white and black—living in the republic. In the same month Chief Gatsha Buthelezi, chief minister of the KwaZulu homeland, launched a new political party aimed at grouping middle-class blacks and church leaders from urban and rural cultural groups in a moderate, antiapartheid Black Unity Front, to resist the homelands policy and all apartheid legislation. Though ridiculed by the "black consciousness" Black People's Convention and the Soweto Students' Representative Council, Buthelezi proposed a loose black-white alliance with consultations between the Front and white opposition parties. The plan was welcomed by the Progressive Reform Party and seemed to offer a last hope of cooperation.

(SHEILA PATTERSON)

United States. Black American political gains over the past generation came to fruition in the presidential elections of 1976. About 70% of all black registrants went to the polls, and over 90% of them voted for the Democratic Party nominee. This effort more than made the difference in Jimmy Carter's victory. Thus the first U.S. president from the Deep South in over a century owed his narrow win to newly enfranchised black citizens.

Blacks had long been an important part of the Democratic Party coalition in such key northern urban areas as New York, Philadelphia, Pittsburgh, Cleveland, Detroit, and Chicago. But 1976 witnessed a new phenomenon: a Democratic sweep of the entire South (save for Virginia) even though white Southerners favoured the Republican candidate by about 55% to 45%. This startling new pattern reflected the broad racial changes in the South over the past generation in general, and the effectiveness of the Voting Rights Act of 1965 in particular.

This increment in black American political participation was also reflected at local levels of government. In 1970 there had been 1,469 black elected officials, according to the Joint Center for Political Studies. By 1976 there were over 3,600, though this figure still represented less than 1% of the nation's elected officials. And in July Kenneth Gibson, the mayor of Newark, N.J., became the first black president of the United States Conference of Mayors.

Language minorities also participated more fully in the 1976 presidential election, thanks largely to a 1975 amendment to the Voting Rights Act. In April the U.S. Department of Justice ruled that 513 political entities in 30 states would have to hold elections in more than one language. Heavy Mexican-American turnouts, aided by ballots in Spanish, were important for Carter—particularly in Texas.

Racial issues surfaced throughout the election but did not become dominant. The Rev. Andrew Young, once a chief assistant to the late Martin Luther King, Jr., and now a member of the U.S. House of Representatives from Atlanta, seconded Carter's nomination for president at the Democratic Party convention. Young was expected to become the closest black adviser any president had ever had. And Agriculture Secretary Earl Butz resigned on October 4 after acknowledging that he had been guilty of "gross indiscretion" in making a racist remark about blacks.

But the most explosive racial issue, that of the "busing" of public school children to achieve racial desegregation in education, failed to become a major campaign issue. The Democratic Party platform described busing as a "judicial tool of last resort"; Pres. Gerald Ford in May and June repeatedly championed strict curbs on the practice; and the Republican Party platform called for "consideration" of a constitutional amendment to prohibit the "assignment of children

SYNDICATION INTERNATIONAL/PHOTO TRENDS

Robert Relf sacrificed 42 pounds to his belief that England needs to be made safe for white people. After he put up a sign in his yard offering his home for sale "to an English family," a court ordered him to take it down. Jailed for refusing, Relf went on a hunger strike that lasted 45 days until a judge decided to free him. Coming home to his wife, Sadie, he called his release "a great victory for the white man."

WIDE WORLD

Police charge demonstrators near South Boston High School. White youths, protesting the busing of students to overcome racial segregation, hurl missiles at the police.

to school on the basis of race." Nonetheless, even Alabama Gov. George Wallace, an early presidential candidate in Democratic primaries, played down the issue.

Meanwhile, court orders for more extensive school desegregation continued to be handed down in 1976, including orders affecting the public schools of Dallas, Texas; Cleveland, Ohio; Los Angeles; Milwaukee, Wis.; and Wilmington, Del. Moreover, the Supreme Court of the United States on June 25 ruled against the denial of enrollment to black children by private, commercially operated, nonsectarian schools. And though sporadic protest confrontations over school desegregation continued throughout the year in Boston, racial busing programs in Detroit, Omaha, Neb., and many smaller communities began peacefully.

Economic issues were paramount in the presidential campaign, and these vitally concerned racial minorities. Throughout 1976, for example, adult unemployment among blacks in the labour force remained at about 13% or higher, compared with about 7% for whites. Understandably, the Caucus of Black Democrats, meeting in Charlotte, N.C., in early May, listed full employment legislation as having the highest priority for black communities. The Caucus also supported proposals for the postcard registration of voters, a domestic "Marshall Plan" for the nation's metropolitan areas, more revenue sharing funds for the poorest areas, and national health insurance based "on ability to pay." The Caucus, joined by the Congressional Black Caucus in Washington, made the passage of the Humphrey-Hawkins jobs bill their primary goal. This bill, which set a target of lowering unemployment to 3% in four years, was also endorsed by organized labour and seemed likely to be a focus for minority political efforts during 1977.

In March the Supreme Court aided minority employment efforts with a key decision. By 5 to 3, the court ruled that retroactive seniority applied to black employees who had been refused jobs after passage of the 1964 Civil Rights Act and since hired.

In April the Supreme Court rendered an important decision dealing with the issues of racial access and integration as opposed to the autonomy of local governments and neighbourhoods. In *Hills* v. *Gautreaux*, the court held that federal courts could order lower-income public housing to be located in white suburbs. In deciding against the Chicago Housing Authority and the U.S. Department of Housing and Urban Development, the court did say that nonviolating governments could not be interfered with and that local governments could still enforce zoning and other restrictions. Since racial progress in urban America depended ultimately on remedies of metropolitan scope, this case appeared to represent an opening round in a continued legal testing of suburban boundaries.

Mexican-Americans were primarily affected by another Supreme Court decision in July. By 7 to 2, the court allowed law officers trying to detect illegal aliens to stop automobiles at permanent checkpoints without a warrant or a specific reason. Further questioning at a backup inspection point was also allowed "even if . . . made largely on the basis of apparent Mexican ancestry."

The Northern Cheyenne Indian tribe fared better in a May ruling of the Supreme Court. In rare unanimity, the justices held that individuals "allotted" portions of tribal land did not have a vested right to mineral deposits beneath the land. Thus the tribe itself would benefit from the estimated $2 billion of coal underlying its Montana reservations. The militant American Indian Movement (AIM) also made news in 1976. Russell Means, AIM's leader, was acquitted in Rapid City, S.D., of a murder charge in August. Three months earlier on a reservation near Wagner, S.D., Means and another AIM member had been shot and wounded. In July Robert Robideau and Darelle Butler were acquitted of killing two FBI agents a year before on the Oglala Sioux reservation in South Dakota.

The National Association for the Advancement of Colored People (NAACP) had more difficulty in court. In Hinds County (Mississippi) Chancery Court in August, 12 white merchants of Port Gibson, Miss., were awarded a $1,250,000 judgment against the NAACP for conducting a boycott ten years earlier. In order to appeal the decision, the organization had to post a bond of more than $1.5 million. The need for such a vast sum threatened the existence of the 67-year-old group; and an organized effort to raise the money began nationally, accompanied by wide publicity. In October a federal judge in Mississippi reduced the bond to $110,000.

The year witnessed the deaths of three prominent black Americans. In January Paul Robeson (*see* OBITUARIES) died in Philadelphia at the age of 77. A famed singer and actor as well as a controversial political activist, Robeson had lived in near seclusion since 1963. Vivian Henderson, president of Clark College and a highly regarded labour economist, died in January at the age of 52 in Atlanta. And Mordecai Johnson, who served for 34 years as the first black president of Howard University, died in September at the age of 86 in Washington, D.C.

(THOMAS FRASER PETTIGREW)

[522.B]

ENCYCLOPÆDIA BRITANNICA FILMS. *Heritage in Black* (1969); *The Mexican-American Speaks: Heritage in Bronze* (1972); *The American Indian Speaks* (1973).

Racket Games

Badminton. The 66th All-England badminton championships held at Wembley in March 1976 produced two record performances that were likely to stand for a long time. Rudy Hartono of Indonesia, the world's greatest badminton player, won the title for a record-breaking eighth time, defeating his countryman Liem Swie King, 15–7, 15–7. Hartono's greatest competition came in a drama-packed semifinal match against Flemming Delfs of Denmark when Hartono had to come from behind to win 15–10, 7–15, 18–15. Gillian Gilks of England also entered the record book when she became the first player since 1952 to win all the titles open to her. In the finals of the women's singles she overwhelmed Margaret Lockwood 11–0, 11–3. Then, playing with Sue Whetnall, she won the women's doubles with a 15–10, 15–10 victory over Lockwood and Nora Gardner. Gilks next teamed up with Derek Talbot to take the mixed doubles title (15–9, 15–12) in an all-English final against Mike Tredgett and Gardner. The men's doubles championship went to the Swedish team of Bengt Froman and Thomas Kihlstrom, who beat Svend Pri and Steen Skovgaard of Denmark 15–12, 17–15. The U.S. Open championships held during April in Philadelphia produced some exciting come-from-behind triumphs for a galaxy of stars from overseas. Paul Whetnall, the English champion, earned a hard-fought 17–14, 15–10 win over Kihlstrom to take the men's singles title. All-England triple-crown winner Gilks played brilliantly in capturing the women's singles title 8–11, 11–5, 11–6 over Denmark's Lene Koppen. Gilks then won her second U.S. open women's doubles title when she and Sue Whetnall (wife of the men's champion) defeated Pam Bristol (the newly crowned U.S. amateur singles champion) and her partner Rosine Lemon 15–4, 15–10. Bristol also finished second in the mixed doubles; in the finals she and Kihlstrom were beaten by David Eddy of England and Whetnall 15–4, 7–15, 15–13. The West German team of Roland Maywald and Willie Braun upset Kihlstrom and Froman 18–15, 15–12 to take the men's doubles title. Indonesia's men's team successfully defended the Thomas Cup with a very convincing 9–0 record over Malaysia. The final round took place at Bangkok, Thailand, in June. The Uber Cup also resided in Indonesia by virtue of the women's team victory over Japan in 1975.

(JACK H. VAN PRAAG)

Squash Rackets. In 1975–76 squash not only made its first appearance in such countries as the U.S.S.R. but continued to grow in popularity as new courts were built in West Germany and elsewhere. In the U.S., where there were nearly 500,000 players, the first commercial courts were built in several cities and championships were sponsored for the first time. Because Canada showed more interest in the "soft ball" or British game, courts of British dimensions were built for the 1977 international amateur championships, which were to be played under British rules. National soft-ball championships were also held, in addition to the older hard-ball championships. The International Squash Rackets Federation authorized new rules and established new criteria for membership. No decision was taken about South Africa's participation in future international amateur championships. The standard of amateur play declined after top-notch amateurs joined the professional ranks.

The only 1976 world open championship recognized as such was the British Open. The title was won by Geoff Hunt of Australia who beat Mohibullah Khan of Pakistan in the final. The first Hashim Khan Gold Cup for teams was won by the Pakistan Professionals, who easily beat the Pakistan Amateurs. An individual event was won by Gogi Alauddin, who defeated fellow Pakistani Mohibullah Khan. At the fifth international amateur championships, held in England in May, Great Britain finally captured the team event after being runner-up to Australia on the four previous occasions. Pakistan was second and Australia third. In the individual event, in which some nonwhite players scratched against South African opponents, Kevin Shawcross of Australia beat Dave Scott of South Africa and then turned professional. In the European championships, held in Brussels, England again finished first, followed by Scotland and Sweden. Shawcross also won the British amateur championship against Aly Aziz, a little-known Stockholm-residing Egyptian. Hunt won the Australian Open championship with a victory over Mohibullah Khan.

In the U.S. Sharif Khan reversed his 1975 defeat in the North American Open championship by conquering Victor Niederhoffer and won the title for the seventh time. Peter Briggs won the U.S. amateur championship with a 3–0 triumph over John Reese.

Heather McKay continued to dominate women's squash with two important victories. She defeated Sue Newman 9–2, 9–4, 9–2, to take the British Women's Open championship and at Brisbane, Australia, overpowered Marion Jackman to capture the first women's world championship 9–2, 9–2, 9–0. In both tournaments all the finalists were Australians.

(JOHN H. HORRY)

CENTRAL PRESS/PICTORIAL PARADE

The world's greatest badminton player: Rudy Hartono of Indonesia won the All-England championship for the eighth time.

COURTESY, UNITED STATES RACQUETBALL ASSOCIATION

Marty Hogan unlimbers his backhand playing against Steve Strandemo, on the professional racketball circuit in Sacramento.

Rackets. William Boone, a 25-year-old left-hander, won the British amateur singles championship for the first time at Queen's Club, London. After saving one match point at 10–14 and three more at 13–14 in the final game of a thrilling five-set match, Boone defeated John Prenn 15–9, 11–15, 8–15, 15–5, 16–14. Howard Angus, titleholder for four previous years, lost to Prenn in a semifinal. Another great match was the semifinal of the Louis Roederer British Open championship at Queen's Club in March. Angus battled Boone for 100 minutes before winning 10–15, 15–10, 15–5, 12–15, 6–15, 15–12, 15–11. Boone had one remarkable service run of 19, but Angus outmaneuvered him and retained the championship by defeating Prenn in the final.

Boone and Tom Pugh retained the British amateur doubles championship with a 4–3 victory over Charles Hue Williams and Prenn in a tense seesaw encounter. In December 1975 Hue Williams and Prenn won the Noel-Bruce Cup for Harrow School. Runners-up were Richard Gracey and Martin Smith of Tonbridge School, champions the previous six years. Marlborough College (D. K. Watson and M. N. P. Mockridge) dethroned Malvern College (P. C. Nicholls and M. A. Tang) 4–3 in the public schools doubles championship in April. A. C. S. Pigott (Harrow) won the public schools singles championship when Nicholls lost 3–2 in the final in December 1975.

Real Tennis. Howard Angus became the first British amateur to win the world championship by twice defeating Eugene Scott, the U.S. champion. Angus won 7–3 in New York and 4–1 in London.

Angus also won the amateur singles championship, retaining the title he had held for 11 straight years. He outclassed John Ward 3–0 in the final in May, and he retained the British Open championship by again beating the professional champion, Frank Willis, 7–2. Angus and David Warburg regained the amateur doubles championship at Lord's in May, and Angus won the Gold Racket in the MCC Prizes competition for the 11th year running.

Willis and David Cull (Lord's) won the Cutty Sark British Open doubles championship for the first time together. They defeated two other professionals, Christopher Ennis (Leamington) and Michael Dean (Oxford University), 3–1 in a splendid final. Ennis emerged as a surprise winner of the Cutty Sark Open singles; in the final in November 1975 he beat Norwood Cripps 3–2. (CHRISTINA MARGARET WOOD)

[452.B.5.h.xxii and xxvii]

Radio:
see Television and Radio

Railroads:
see Transportation

Real Tennis:
see Racket Games

Recordings:
see Music

Reformed Churches:
see Religion

Refugees

In 1976 the task of providing international protection for refugees, the cornerstone of the activities of the Office of the United Nations High Commissioner for Refugees (UNHCR), became increasingly synonymous with physical protection as disregard of the rights of refugees persisted in many parts of the world. Latin America was the scene of the most flagrant violations that came to UNHCR's attention. Organized intimidation by uncontrolled elements in Argentina took the form of torture, abduction, and even assassination of refugees from Chile and Uruguay. UNHCR's ability to prevent such abuses was limited to urging the Argentine authorities to strengthen security measures. The only real solution lay in finding other countries that would admit the refugees, and in June, following new outrages, the high commissioner, Sadruddin Aga Khan, appealed for resettlement opportunities for 1,000 refugees. By mid-November 14 countries had responded, and refugees were leaving for new destinations at the rate of 200 to 300 a month.

In other areas there were equally tragic cases of refugees being forcibly returned to their country of origin—expressly forbidden by the 1951 Convention relating to the Status of Refugees. There was also a tendency in some regions to subordinate the humanitarian duty of granting asylum to efforts to maintain friendly relations with neighbouring states. UNHCR was charged with responsibility not only for promoting accessions to the 1951 Convention and its 1967 Protocol (to which by mid-November there were 68 and 63 parties, respectively) but also for supervising the application of these instruments.

UNHCR met the $14.8 million financial target for its 1976 annual program thanks primarily to contributions of exceptional size from the Nordic countries and The Netherlands. The Netherlands' donation of

$3,850,000 was in fact by far the largest amount ever contributed by a single government to a UNHCR annual program. The heaviest expenditures were in Latin America, where approximately 6,000 refugees in Argentina depended almost entirely on UNHCR funds for their subsistence, and in Africa. Efforts in Africa were centred on consolidating projects begun in previous years, although there was a substantial influx of new refugees from Rhodesia into Mozambique. In August UNHCR protested when an attack on a refugee camp at Nyazonia 40 km (25 mi) inside the Mozambique frontier killed and wounded hundreds.

In 1976 special operations entrusted to UNHCR called for $80 million in contributions; by mid-November approximately $60 million had been raised toward this target. The shortfall in funds notwithstanding, considerable progress was made in carrying out projects to promote the resettlement of displaced persons in Vietnam and Laos. In 1977 UNHCR's financial requirements in Indochina were expected to be sharply reduced, as multilateral assistance would be provided increasingly by other agencies of the UN system geared to long-term programs. In Thailand the influx from neighbouring countries continued, and by November UNHCR aid was supporting some 75,000 displaced persons, mostly Laotians of hill-tribe origin, who were still living in camps. In 1976 about 25,000 refugees left Thailand for other countries, mainly France and the U.S.

During the year the presence was reported in various parts of Southeast Asia of several thousand "boat people," who had left Indochina in small vessels in quest of a haven in neighbouring areas. By mid-November, of some 3,200 "boat people" brought to UNHCR's attention, 1,500 had found permanent homes.

As coordinator of UN humanitarian assistance in Cyprus, UNHCR in 1976 channeled approximately $33 million in aid for displaced persons throughout the island. In August, UNHCR was named by the UN secretary-general to undertake a similar task for the benefit of an estimated one million persons who had left Angola during the struggle for independence or who had been displaced within the country. A special operation begun in 1975 in Guinea-Bissau to return refugees and displaced persons to the country was concluded, while in Mozambique the organized repatriation of refugees was completed by mid-November 1976.

CARIBPRESS/SYGMA

Will it erupt or won't it? Without waiting for an answer, Guadeloupe authorities evacuated people from the island of Basse Terre when scientists predicted an eruption of La Soufrière volcano.

A dramatic new problem in North Africa was posed by the presence of tens of thousands of Sahrawis, people from the Western (formerly Spanish) Sahara, in the Tindouf region of southwest Algeria. After channeling some $1 million to the Algerian Red Crescent for emergency relief to the Sahrawis, whose number was estimated at 50,000 by Algeria in October, the high commissioner in that same month launched an appeal for 10,000 tons of food and $5,725,000 in cash to cover needs until October 1977. (UNHCR)

See also Migration, International.

[525.A.1.c.iii]

CLAUDE SALHANI—SYGMA

American citizens were among this group being evacuated from Beirut by sea during the Lebanese civil war. The U.S. Navy took them to Athens.

Religion

To the surprise of most citizens, the personal faith of the leading U.S. presidential candidates became a campaign issue in 1976. Most voters thought the day had long passed when candidates need parade their piety or see it examined in the months before an election. Yet the religious outlook of Gerald R. Ford and Jimmy Carter, two evangelical Protestants, was a public concern throughout the nation's bicentennial year.

Religion as such and the presidency have often been paired in the public mind, but almost always voter interest has centred on ceremony or policy. What will a president say about God in his inaugural speech? Will Alfred E. Smith or John F. Kennedy, as Roman Catholics, "take orders from Rome" and favour their church if elected? What religious resources does a candidate draw upon in forming attitudes toward war, peace, race, poverty, justice? Aside from a controversy over abortion, a practice that both candidates religiously opposed, ethics and policy issues rarely surfaced in 1976. An attempt to get aspirants to discuss such issues in Washington in January attracted few prime candidates or religious leaders, and RAP '76, "Religion and the Presidency," quietly left the scene.

Jimmy Carter addresses a black audience at Chicago's Tabernacle Baptist Church during his presidential campaign.

WIDE WORLD

Piety, not policy, remained an issue, and this focus mirrored perfectly the drastic change in Americans' spiritual mood in the 1970s. Gone were the headlines about clergy trying to change the world through pronouncements or demonstrations. In their place were obsessions with "being right with God," having personal experiences of the sacred, and the like. The two leading candidates invited scrutiny on precisely these lines.

The subject began to take shape on Aug. 8, 1974, when Ford took office after Richard M. Nixon resigned. After the Watergate scandal that had forced Nixon from office, people were curious about the character of the new president, the hidden forces that produced him. Most of them, conservative and fervent evangelicals in particular, were bitterly disappointed in Nixon. For a time they had numbered him among their own. A man of Quaker heritage, he gave visibility to worship in the White House East Room and made a point of his friendship with Billy Graham, the nation's best-known evangelist. Graham, in turn, often praised Nixon for his "deep religious past" and his "great sense of moral integrity." Feeling betrayed after Watergate, Graham promised to be more cautious in the future.

Religion was not a public "East Room" affair for Ford. He was a certified conservative churchgoing Protestant, the 11th Episcopalian president in a line that stretched from George Washington to Franklin D. Roosevelt. He took his turn as a church usher and his wife, Betty, on occasion taught Sunday School. Ford had long been a member of Capitol Hill's most consistent prayer cell, along with fellow congressmen John Rhodes and Albert Quie, and was a familiar figure on the "prayer breakfast" circuit.

Ford's staid piety was also subjected to more expressive influences. His son Michael was a student at the conservative Gordon-Conwell Seminary near Boston. When Mrs. Ford faced cancer surgery in September 1974, it became known that a flamboyant Grand Rapids, Mich., revivalist, Billy Zeoli, brought solace to the family. Zeoli, a producer of Gospel Films and an informal chaplain to professional football teams, was a man of colourful garb and worldly style who insisted that people be "born again" in Jesus Christ. But Ford and Zeoli agreed to be discreet about their ties, and evangelicals remained cautious. One unnamed Protestant congressman was quoted as having said, "Let's not make the same mistake" as they had with Nixon, "presenting him as a born-again Christian without really knowing his true commitment." Nonpartisan observers came to agree with *New York Times* columnist James Reston: "For him religion is not a role but a reality."

Before Catholics, Jews, other kinds of Protestants, and secularists learned to translate the language of evangelicalism, they began to hear a much more outspoken version of it from former Georgia governor Jimmy Carter. As he progressively eliminated opponents during the Democratic presidential primaries, he increasingly voiced the South's "old-time religion." While Ford had said, "I've never been one to be ostentatious about my religious views," Carter welcomed opportunities to spread his own.

In the course of time a critical public seemed to regard Carter's piety, as it did Ford's, as a natural expression of a faith held long before presidential candidacy came into view. But there were vast cultural differences between Washington Episcopalianism and Georgia Southern Baptist faith. Where Carter came from, people spoke of their experience of Jesus as naturally as others might say "Good morning." People around him believed that, just as one was once born physically, he or she must be "born again" spiritually with a vivid experience in which Jesus Christ is accepted in the heart. Such a language was inspiring and vote-getting in the ears of part of the electorate, but abrasive in others.

When Carter became the Democratic candidate, "Evangelicals for Carter" began to take out advertisements in his support. He found it necessary to court Catholics, particularly after some bishops were "disappointed" over his unwillingness to support a constitutional amendment banning abortion. In the process, he was able to reassure many Catholics that his piety was not at war or even at odds with their own. No Jew, of course, could accept his view of Jesus, but many found his support of Israel to be deeply grounded in his religion.

Carter claimed to have had his personal experience at age 11 and found it reinforced in a spiritual crisis attended by his faith-healing sister, Ruth Carter Stapleton. He was a deacon and a Sunday school teacher in Plains, Ga., and was thoroughly familiar with both black and white "gospel" styles of song and worship. Historians reached back to William Jennings Bryan's populist faith for comparison, though Carter, an admirer of more liberal thinkers like Reinhold Niebuhr, did not share Bryan's fundamentalism. Or they remembered the idealism born of puritan zeal in the instance of Woodrow Wilson. Carter's roots were deeper, reaching back to the Great Awakening of the 1730s and 1740s. In that event the nation's major Protestant style was born. After that, people did not merely inherit religion the way they did in Europe. They "got religion" through the conversion experience and showed it in holy lives and in forming voluntary groups with people who shared the faith. Since conversion was usually stimulated by revivalists, this faith was often emotional in tone. Since converts were often judgmental about the sinners around them, they were often ill-mannered, and in the fundamentalist disputes of the 1920s they acquired a bad name. Carter was a product of a gentler, revised conservative style.

Those with historical curiosity that reached back before Bryan and Wilson could note that the public regularly examined the piety of George Washington. They knew that he connected religion with morality, but they wanted more and swallowed fictions about him kneeling in prayer at Valley Forge. Thomas Jefferson, who envisioned a style of separating church and state to which both Ford and Carter adhered, was dismissed as an infidel by the pious. Abraham Lincoln, spiritually the most profound of the presidents but never a church member, had to take out handbills during an Illinois congressional race, defending himself against charges that he had "spoken intentional disrespect of religion in general." As recently as the 1950s, during the era of what William Lee Miller called "piety along the Potomac," the public was convinced that its beloved Pres. Dwight Eisenhower was, in Miller's words, "the most religious person I know," though Eisenhower's was a mildly stated faith in faith itself.

When presidential religion affects policy, it inevitably stirs controversy. So, it turned out, does candidates' piety because it affects character. For that reason voters inevitably took it into consideration when appraising candidates. During 1976 both Gerald Ford and Jimmy Carter learned what the nation's history could have told them: in matters of religion, the best advice seemed to be "handle with care."

After the election, the victorious Carter faced one more religious test. A maverick black minister from Albany, Ga., tested the ten-year-old decision of Carter's home church to exclude blacks from membership. Under the glare of international publicity, the members of the First Baptist Church in Plains changed the policy, thus relieving Carter of possible embarrassment even as the incident called attention to the still-segregated character of worship in countless locales in the U.S.

Analysts of voting patterns also determined that the antiabortion or "Pro-Life" forces had not played much of a part in the campaign's outcome and that Carter had retained much of the traditionally Democratic Catholic vote.

(MARTIN E. MARTY)

PROTESTANT CHURCHES

Anglican Communion. All over the world in 1976, Anglican churches continued to be preoccupied with the question of whether or not women may be priests. Opposition was loud and sustained, but even so further breaches were made in the bastion of the once all-male priesthood. The church in Canada ordained its first women in November, despite pleas from bishops of some other Anglican churches that action be deferred until more general agreement emerged. In New Zealand the General Synod amended the constitution of the church there to allow women to become priests and, astonishingly, the Church of Ireland's General Synod recorded a massive vote in favour of accepting the ordination of women in principle. Formal statements by the pope and by Orthodox leaders deploring the prospect of women priests and viewing

WIDE WORLD

The Rev. Jeannette Piccard, irregularly ordained in 1974, hears the long-awaited announcement that the Episcopal Church has approved admission of women to the priesthood.

The Church of England holds a synod three times a year to discuss the affairs of the Anglican Communion. Among the topics of concern in 1976 were attitudes toward political developments in Chile and euthanasia.

COLIN DAVEY—CAMERA PRESS/PHOTO TRENDS

their introduction by Anglicans as a serious obstacle to Christian unity were predictable, but they provided ammunition for opponents and caused dismay among those Anglicans who wanted both Christian unity *and* women priests. One of the most influential churches in the Communion, the Episcopal Church (U.S.), gave approval to the ordination of women at its triennial General Convention in Minneapolis, Minn., in mid-September; the vote was 95–61 in the House of Bishops and 64–49 for laymen and 60–54 for clergy in the House of Deputies. An initial proposal that would have required reordination of several women irregularly ordained since the last General Convention in 1973 was later eased.

Anglican reactions at the official level again gave rise to doubts over whether Anglicans really meant what they said about wanting Christian unity. In New Zealand, although the bishops and laity favoured the scheme, a plan for union with four Protestant churches was rejected because of a tie in the clergy voting; a majority in each of the three "houses" was required for approval. In Sri Lanka a group of Anglicans helped to bring the legal action that at the last moment caused postponement of the inauguration of a united church there. The Church of England gave only a cautious welcome to the Ten Propositions issued in January by the Churches' Unity Commission in an attempt to test the seriousness of the churches' ecumenical intentions.

Yet there were signs of growing interest by Anglicans in unity maneuvers on an international scale, particularly with the Roman Catholic and Orthodox churches. The Anglican-Roman Catholic joint commission began tackling its hardest issue—authority in the church, including the question of papal primacy and infallibility. A similar commission with the Orthodox Church met in Moscow in August, and it was there that the Anglican theologians made the historic declaration that they were prepared to see the *filioque* clause dropped from the Nicene Creed since, whatever its doctrinal merits or demerits, it had no place there. The Orthodox delegates expressed satisfaction—as well they might, for the clause, which asserts that the Holy Spirit proceeds both from the Father and from the Son, had been a cause of dissension between the church in East and West for a thousand years.

There were indications that liturgical experimentation was coming to an end in various parts of the world. In the U.S. a draft proposed Book of Common Prayer was endorsed by the General Convention, although final acceptance would require a further favourable vote at the next General Convention in 1979. In February the Church of England decided to go ahead with publication of a book of modern alternative services, and the Australian General Synod would have copies of a new Australian Prayer Book before it when it met in 1977.

The Anglican Consultative Council, meeting in Trinidad in May 1976, recommended the holding of a full-scale Lambeth-type conference of bishops in 1978 (at Canterbury, Kent), to the embarrassment of the Church of England delegates, who foresaw their church's having to meet most of the estimated £1.5 million cost and accordingly abstained from the vote. During the summer a fund drive was begun in the U.S. to save Canterbury Cathedral, deteriorating as the result of neglect and air pollution.

(SUSAN YOUNG)

Baptist Churches. A record registration of 18,672 messengers (delegates) attended the annual meeting of the Southern Baptist Convention in Norfolk, Va., in June. Apart from tension regarding inadequate facilities for the large group, the meetings went smoothly, with President Ford as the keynote speaker. The fact that a prominent SBC layman, Jimmy Carter, was seeking the presidency lent a note of excitement to the political atmosphere, though Carter did not make a personal appearance. The resolutions on social

WIDE WORLD

James L. Sullivan was elected president of the Southern Baptist Convention in June. Sullivan is a prominent Baptist minister and author of religious books for laymen.

issues were conservative, but many concluded that the SBC was moving toward a "centrist" position in American church life.

The only noticeable hostility in the three-day convention concerned a report on a controversial social studies curriculum called MACOS (Man: A Course of Study). Designed for use in elementary schools, MACOS described practices common in some non-Western cultures, most notably among the Netsilik Eskimo, that were deemed immoral by traditional Western standards. The SBC committee recommended that the Convention neither endorse nor condemn the material, a position unsatisfactory to some.

In September 1976 the 6.3 million-member National Baptist Convention, U.S.A., Inc., held its annual meeting in Dallas, Texas. Joseph H. Jackson was reelected to an unprecedented 24th term as president of the Convention, the largest of the black Baptist groups. "The Million Dollar Miracle" celebrated at this convention marked the culmination of a fund, first established by Jackson in 1962, which reached its $1 million goal in 1975; the fund was recognized as tax exempt by the U.S. Internal Revenue Service. In another action, the Convention's board of directors asked 2,000 persons to make an immediate gift or loan, interest free for one year, to the National Association for the Advancement of Colored People, which faced bankruptcy when it was ordered to post bond of more than $1.5 million with a Mississippi court pending appeal of a judgment awarding $1.2 million to Port Gibson, Miss., merchants for damages suffered in an NAACP-led boycott.

The Board of National Ministries of the American Baptist Churches in the U.S.A., an integrated but largely white denomination, suspended trading stock with Merrill Lynch, Pierce, Fenner and Smith Inc. after the U.S. Equal Employment Opportunities Commission charged the brokerage firm with bias in job practices. The current value of the ABC/USA stock was about $36 million. Merrill Lynch responded by pledging to hire fixed percentages of women and minorities at all staff levels through 1980.

The first checks were issued by the Fund for Renewal, a $7.5 million capital fund-raising program for minority education sponsored by the American Baptists and the Progressive National Baptist Convention. Fifteen Baptist minority institutions received checks totaling nearly $250,000. The director of the Fund announced that $4 million had been raised to date.

In Europe an ABC/USA missionary, William Thomas, pastor of a French-speaking congregation in Brussels, became the first black to hold evangelistic meetings in a German church. Thomas baptized two South African whites in his church in a service witnessed by others visiting from Cape Town. Also in Europe, General Secretary Aleksey Bichkov of the main Soviet Baptist body was elected president of the European Baptist Federation.

(NORMAN R. DE PUY)

Christian Church (Disciples of Christ). The government of Paraguay raided the Friendship Mission of the Christian Church (Disciples of Christ) in Asunción April 10, jailing several Paraguayan workers as "subversives" and ordering two missionaries out of the country. The raid was part of a drive that included Roman Catholics as well. The mission had been involved in community organization among the poor and the Indians. The incident was particularly significant since the Disciples of Christ were the National Council of Churches group working in Paraguay by agreement. The church's general board subsequently affirmed the work being done among the poor and said that it would continue.

Nineteen Disciples leaders, including Moderator James A. Moak and Kenneth L. Teegarden, the general minister and president, visited Kenya, South Africa, Zaire, and Liberia in a demonstration of support for African efforts to deal with Americans on a church-to-church rather than a missionary basis. The Disciples had conducted a similar "fraternal visit" to Asia in 1972.

The 1.3 million-member Disciples of Christ and the 1.8 million-member United Church of Christ took steps to reopen union talks, suspended in 1966 in the interest of concentrating on larger union possibilities through the nine-denomination Consultation on Church Union. Both churches reiterated their commitment to COCU.

(ROBERT L. FRIEDLY)

Churches of Christ. Ministries to prisoners, youth, and the family, as well as benevolence and evangelism received special emphasis in 1976. Since Churches of Christ have no centralized organization, these ministries were carried on by autonomous congregations.

Numerous "Let Freedom Ring" campaigns, with strong emphasis on personal evangelism, were held in conjunction with the U.S. Bicentennial. The number of youth ministers rose to more than 200; as an example of activities among college students, the Mid-America Mobilization Seminar, held in Springfield, Mo., attracted students from 61 universities and colleges in 33 states. The third annual Workshop for Jail and Prison Workers registered 120 workers from 14 states. Among efforts to strengthen the Christian home, Family Enrichment Seminars and Marriage Encounter sessions increased in popularity. The University Church in Austin, Texas, sponsored a seminar for divorced Christians. More than 3,000 persons attended the 40th annual Yosemite Family Bible Encampment in California.

Worldwide evangelism resumed its growth after a decline caused by the economic inflation. Some 1,400 missionaries in 200 countries were supported by Churches of Christ. American Military Evangelizing Nations (AMEN), a program to locate and enlist the efforts of Christian military personnel, was begun by White's Ferry Road Church in West Monroe, La.

(M. NORVEL YOUNG)

Church of Christ, Scientist. In 1976 members were urged to deepen their commitment to Christianity, including Christian healing. "Not just the Christianity that acknowledges Jesus as the Savior," said Lenore D. Hanks, chairman of the Christian Science Board of Directors, ". . . But the Christianity that follows the Christ so closely it adds spiritual dimension to everything we do." Mrs. Hanks spoke at the annual June meeting of members of the Mother Church, the First Church of Christ, Scientist, in Boston, where numerous accounts of healing solely through prayer were recounted.

Throughout the year, Christian Scientists gathered at meetings in the U.S., Australia, New Zealand, and Great Britain to discuss the denomination's healing ministry. At these meetings, and at a special session during the Boston gathering of members, question-and-answer discussions focused on church commitments most in need of membership support. These discussions included a review of the denomination's financial condition. According to the church treasurer, Marc Engeler, economies at the Church Center in Boston plus increased contributions had combined to keep church finances in sound condition.

Naomi Price, an associate editor of the church's religious periodicals, was named president of the Mother Church for 1976–77, succeeding Jules Cern.

(J. BUROUGHS STOKES)

Church of Jesus Christ of Latter-day Saints. The church continued to experience vigorous growth in 1976, with a total membership of approximately 3.8 million at the year's close. The most pronounced increase was in Mexico, where in the first six months of 1976 nearly 17,000 converts were baptized. Reflecting the expansion of missionary efforts, the church's presiding hierarchy had been expanded in October 1975 by the reestablishment of the First Quorum of Seventy. The First Quorum was organized by Joseph Smith in 1835 but had gradually become dysfunctional after the 1840s.

The restructuring process begun in mid-1975 was completed. Members of the Council of Twelve were assigned as area advisers over all geographic divisions of the church. Under their direction were area supervisors, who also were General Authorities and who had jurisdiction over local stakes (dioceses) and missions. A Correlation Department was organized at church headquarters to deal with long-range planning and to review church programs and publications.

Two revelations claimed by early church leaders were approved by the membership of the church in April 1976 for inclusion in the *Pearl of Great Price,* one of the four works considered by Latter-day Saints to be scriptures. These were Joseph Smith's "Vision of the Celestial Kingdom" (1836) and Joseph F. Smith's "Vision of the Redemption of the Dead" (1918).

(LEONARD JAMES ARRINGTON)

Jehovah's Witnesses. During 1976 the body of Christian evangelizers known as Jehovah's Witnesses experienced restrictions, total proscription, and violent opposition in over 40 lands. The most severe persecutions occurred in Benin, Mozambique, and, especially, Malawi, where eyewitness reports told of Witnesses being beaten, gang raped, robbed, driven from their homes, prevented from working, buying food, or drawing water from wells, and in some cases being detained in prison camps. The issue arose when the Witnesses, in keeping with the neutral, nonpolitical position prompted by their religious beliefs, declined to comply with the government requirement that they join the Malawi Congress Party.

Witnesses preached in 210 countries and territories in 1976. A total of 2,248,390 individuals spent 359,-258,019 hours going from door to door and conducting 1,339,466 weekly Bible studies in the homes of interested persons; 196,656 individuals were baptized following such a course of Bible study. Jehovah's Witnesses had 97 branch offices around the world, and during 1976 new branch office buildings were constructed in Greece and Venezuela. A series of 112 four-day "Sacred Service" assemblies, held throughout the summer in the United States and Canada, were attended by 1,076,990 persons. Six assemblies in the British Isles brought together 110,298 persons, and 109 assemblies on the European continent were attended by more than 570,000.

(N. H. KNORR)

Lutheran Churches. A new church body was formed at the close of 1976 by moderates in the Lutheran Church—Missouri Synod who disagreed with the theological conservatism espoused by Jacob A. O. Preus, president of the doctrinally divided 2.8 million-member denomination. The Association of Evangelical Lutheran Churches (AELC), activated in December, incorporated about 150 congregations with more than 70,000 members. William Kohn of Milwaukee was elected president.

Preus told the LCA's eighth biennial convention in July that "Missouri has overwhelmingly, at the synodical, the district, and the congregational level, decided . . . to remain Missouri." He predicted that only a handful of the Synod's 6,200 congregations would defect to the AELC, some of whose leaders claimed that as many as 40% would leave the Synod eventually.

A spokesman said the AELC would give "high priority" to putting itself out of business, but that a separate association rather than integration into existing church bodies was necessary because "we need each other at least for now and possibly for some brief time to come." Meanwhile, Evangelical Lutherans in Mission (ELIM) would continue as a "confessional voice of protest" within the LCMS to support those members who felt they could not as yet leave the 129-year-old Synod.

Four of eight district presidents censured for ordaining unapproved graduates of Concordia Seminary in Exile (Seminex) were removed from office. All were upheld by their districts, but several resigned during the year. The case of John H. Tietjen, who was absolved of the charges of false doctrine that had led to his dismissal as president of the official Concordia Seminary in St. Louis, was placed under review by Theodore F. Nickel, third vice-president of the LCMS. Tietjen was currently president of Seminex.

Lutheran leaders throughout the world led a wave of protests over death sentences imposed on a Lutheran and a Roman Catholic in South West Africa (Namibia). Two Lutheran nurses received seven and five years in prison, while charges against two defendants were dismissed. Said to be members of the

South West Africa People's Organization (SWAPO), all were accused of assisting those who assassinated Ovamboland Chief Minister Filemon Elifas in August 1975. The case was being appealed.

The Lutheran World Federation reported that 70.6 million persons belonged to the Lutheran confessional family, including 53.1 million in the 95 church bodies affiliated with the federation. Three new members were received by the LWF, the newly autonomous Evangelical Lutheran Church of Papua New Guinea, the Kinki Evangelical Lutheran Church in Japan, and the Evangelical Lutheran Church of Southern Africa, formed by recent merger of four black churches. Membership in Lutheran bodies in North America decreased for the seventh successive year, but the drop was the smallest in any of the last five years. A loss of 33,853 members, less than half of 1%, brought the total down to 8,930,581.

Lutheran and Roman Catholic theologians expressed guarded optimism over the prospects of formulating a common statement on papal infallibility acceptable to both communions. Six sessions had been held on the divisive dogma, and findings were not expected until 1977. Meanwhile, leaders of the two traditions urged their churches to respond to a recommendation of their theologians that they recognize the validity of each other's ministry and Eucharist. A volume on the ministry and Eucharist issued by the scholars in 1971 had met with a mixed and even cool reception in both Lutheran and Catholic circles.

Publication of a new hymnal and service book for most of Lutheranism in the U.S. and Canada might be delayed beyond the target date of late 1978 as the result of action taken by the Lutheran Church in America. Delegates to the LCA's eighth biennial convention approved the hymnal but called for "thorough review of the theology and whatever testing is deemed necessary" for the liturgical portion of the book. The Evangelical Lutheran Church of Canada had approved the new volume, which was being prepared by the Inter-Lutheran Commission on Worship; the American Lutheran Church gave its approval at its eighth biennial convention in October, and the Lutheran Church—Missouri Synod was to act in 1977.

(ERIK W. MODEAN)

Methodist Churches. In addition to the annual conferences that administer Methodist churches around the world, 1976 also saw the quadrennial General Conference of the United Methodist Church in the U.S. and the quinquennial World Methodist Council and Conference. Common to all these meetings was an increasing awareness of the church's role in its identification with the poor and oppressed.

At its General Conference in Portland, Ore., the United Methodist Church voted to assist its ethnic minorities, fight world hunger, and seek lost souls through evangelization. These priorities were set out under the theme "Committed to Christ—Called to Change." Hunger relief would include emergency food aid for the starving and supplies, technical help, and medical education for the hungry. Evangelism would be carried out through programs of the Board of Discipleship. An approved report on the "United Methodist Church and World Peace" called for world disarmament and an effective system of international peacemaking, help for the millions of people under oppressive rule, and support for the UN.

The British Methodist Conference heard that, for the first time since 1962, the number of new members joining during the past year had increased (by 13%). The conference expressed its continued concern for a speedy, just, and peaceful end to the struggle for equal human rights for all the people of Rhodesia and affirmed that African majority rule within two years should be a condition of independence.

The World Methodist Council and Conference in Dublin, August 25–31, brought together nearly 3,000 Methodists from 87 countries, representing 61 autonomous conferences. Under the general theme "The Day of the Lord," members gave a day each to the consideration of such subjects as mission, understanding, brotherhood, judgment, and God's power. A strong resolution on South Africa condemned the wanton slaughter of unarmed black men, women, and children; urged all nations, church groups, and multinational corporations to support UN economic sanctions; and insisted that all negotiations concerning South Africa must involve indigenous black African leaders.

The role of women in the church was emphasized by

WIDE WORLD

Congratulating a new bishop: the Rev. C. Dale White (left), newly elected bishop of the Northeast Jurisdiction of the United Methodist Church, being greeted by Bishop Edward G. Carroll of Boston.

a resolution brought from the World Federation of Methodist Women to "recognize and support the changing role of women throughout the world in all endeavours and to implement the full participation of women at all levels of the World Methodist Council in planning, policy, and leadership participation." It was decided that at least 20% of places on committees should be allocated to women. Perhaps the most significant sign of women's leadership was the "Dublin Peace March" on August 28, when over 30,000 women, including many Methodists, walked in silent procession to demonstrate their desire for peace in Ireland.

The process of africanization of church structures was demonstrated by the presence in Dublin of the "patriarch" of the Nigerian Methodist Church. Methodist churches historically linked with Britain had retained the single level of ministry, while those associated with the U.S. had had the threefold order of deacon, minister, and bishop. The Nigerian Conference created a new order of ministry: his preeminence Bolaji was patriarch of the church, which had four regional archbishops and area bishops.

(PETER H. BOLT)

Pentecostal Churches. The major event of 1976 for the Pentecostal churches was the triennial Pentecostal World Conference in London in September. Over 10,000 delegates heard reports of phenomenal growth.

In the U.S. Ray E. Smith resigned as general superintendent of the Open Bible Standard Churches at their 44th convention in Des Moines, Iowa, and was succeeded by Frank W. Smith. The Assemblies of God reported that in one year membership in the U.S. had increased 8.3% to a new high of 850,362. In observance of the U.S. Bicentennial, a giant rally was held in July on the steps of the Capitol in Washington. The well-known preacher and faith healer Kathryn Kuhlman died in February (*see* OBITUARIES). The *National Courier,* a tabloid produced in Plainfield, N.J., by Logos International, began publication of exclusively religious material during the year.

Among the traditional churches, the quadrennial General Conference of the United Methodist Church adopted guidelines that cautiously approved the charismatic movement in that church. Southern Baptist charismatics met for the first time, in Dallas, Texas, in a conference headed by the controversial pastor Howard Conatser. At the close of a five-year dialogue between the Vatican and Pentecostal leaders, Vatican radio pronounced the charismatic renewal to be "the springtime of the church." Plans for a new five-year dialogue were announced in September. (See *Roman Catholic Church,* below.)

(VINSON SYNAN)

UPI COMPIX

Holding a rattlesnake in his hands, a minister of the Holiness Church of God in Jesus' Name preaches at Newport, Tennessee, in April 1973. The Supreme Court of Tennessee has barred the handling of snakes and swallowing of poison by revivalists. Citing the Constitution's guarantee of freedom of religion, attorneys appealed the case to the U.S. Supreme Court, which declined to review the decision in March 1976.

Presbyterian and Reformed Churches. In the worldwide ecumenical debate on the theological basis of human rights, the World Alliance of Reformed Churches (Presbyterian and Congregational) put forward a two-part document giving theological guidelines and identifying a number of practical statements. The document was drafted at a consultation held in London on February 18–21 attended by church representatives from 16 countries. A study paper presented at the consultation by Jürgen Moltmann of the University of Tübingen, West Germany, included a summary and analysis of findings on human rights issues sent in by WARC member churches since the study was launched by the last WARC assembly, at Nairobi, Kenya, in 1970.

The consultation preceded the 1976 executive committee meeting, at which discussions on finance, administrative structures, and future program figured prominently. Preparations continued for the 1977 Centennial Consultation (augmented executive committee), which would replace the General Council (world assembly) scheduled for 1977 but canceled by the executive committee in 1975. A total of 65 persons would be invited by name to attend the Consultation, the theme of which was "The Glory of God and the Future of Man," and there would be room for an additional 135 participants, visitors, and staff. Cancellation of the General Council necessitated an alternative method of appointing a new WARC executive committee, normally elected at an assembly. Plans were devised for nominations by the member churches, the preparation by a nominations committee of a slate of 42 names for 21 vacancies, and submission of the list to the churches for a postal vote.

Two more churches were received into WARC membership: the 28,000-strong Evangelical Congregational Church of Brazil and the Reformed Church in Africa, formerly known as the Indian Reformed Church in South Africa, with just over 1,000 members. The Evangelical Church-Bethel in Ethiopia became a synod within the Evangelical Lutheran church Mekane Yesus, thereby technically severing its relation with the Alliance. WARC membership now stood at 143.

Alliance member churches continued to be involved in the search for church union. According to an ecumenical survey, 38 WARC churches were currently actively engaged in union negotiations. Theological conversations between the WARC and the Baptist World Alliance continued, while Reformed-Lutheran-Roman Catholic talks on the theology of marriage and the problems of mixed marriages were concluded after five years. The North American and Caribbean Area Council of the WARC agreed to continue Reformed-Roman Catholic conversations by "engaging in a three-year dialogue on mutual theological issues."

The United Presbyterian Church in the U.S.A. (UPCUSA) elected a black laywoman, Thelma Davidson Adair, as moderator of its general assembly. William P. Thompson was reelected stated clerk (general secretary) for a third term of five years. Voting that could lead to a merger between UPCUSA and the Presbyterian Church in the U.S. now seemed likely to occur at the 1977 assemblies of the two churches, with enactment of reunion, after 118 years of separation, taking place the following year.

(FREDERIK H. KAAN)

Religious Society of Friends. Early in the year a conference in Maryland on mission and service brought together Friends of two very different persuasions: those who emphasize evangelical mission and those whose main concern is for social action. As an example of the latter group, the American Friends Service Committee vigorously supported the United Farm Workers campaign to boycott California grapes and other produce and protested a U.S. Supreme Court decision opening the way for restoration of the death penalty in the U.S.

In recognition of the importance of Africa in international affairs and the large group of Friends in East Africa, Nairobi, Kenya, was added to the Quaker network of international representation. An office there would be directed jointly by an Indian and a Kenyan Friend.

British Friends devoted attention to more effective organization of their small society (membership had long been stable at around 20,000) and, in the difficult state of the British economy, to fund raising; in the event, it appeared that Friends were responding generously to the increasing needs. They also joined peace organizations in the Campaign Against the Arms Trade and helped to stage the International Forum for World Disarmament at York in March. An important gathering of world Friends, the triennial meeting of the Friends World Committee for Consultation, was held in Hamilton, Ont., in July.

(DAVID FIRTH)

Salvation Army. Under the slogan "Share Your Faith," the Salvation Army's worldwide evangelistic and social forces in 82 countries endeavoured to spread the Christian gospel through caring and sharing. Leading the Army's activities in this program was Gen. Clarence Wiseman, who in 1976 campaigned in India, Bangladesh, Sri Lanka, the Philippines, Japan, South Korea, North and South America, and many European centres.

The Salvation Army continued to provide accommodation for the homeless in more than 600 hostels throughout the world, in addition to occupational and alcoholic clinics and centres and 187 homes and residential centres for the aged. A U.K. government survey, the Peter Wingfield Digby report, revealed that the Salvation Army provided one-quarter of all sleeping accommodations for single, homeless people in Great Britain. The Army's inquiry department for missing persons, another worldwide service, showed a 60% success record.

COURTESY, THE SALVATION ARMY

The Salvation Army's Gen. Clarence Wiseman and Mrs. Wiseman shown with the Canadian consul general in Chicago. General Wiseman is the leader of worldwide Salvation Army operations in 82 countries.

Salvationists were much involved in disaster relief work in 1976. Within hours of the earthquakes that devastated many areas of Guatemala in February, Salvation Army rescue and relief teams were arriving on the scene to bring assistance and general supplies received from many parts of the world. Emergency services and relief teams were also set up following the earthquakes in the Philippines and in Italy, where for many weeks Italian and Canadian Salvationists, who had flown into the Friuli, Italy, area with a mobile canteen, continued to render essential services.

(JOHN M. BATE)

Seventh-day Adventist Church. Two new services for the world church were inaugurated at the denomination's Washington, D.C., headquarters: Home and Family Service, created to study and counteract influences challenging the stability of the home, and Christian Leadership Seminars, a program designed to improve church administration. On its seventh overseas mission, a medical team from Loma Linda (California) University spent two six-week terms in Saudi Arabia performing open-heart surgery. At the same time, two of the church's 421 health-care institutions, in Ethiopia and Nigeria, were lost through government nationalization.

The church had never ordained women to the gospel ministry, but the theology of this position was being subjected to further scrutiny. In the matter of minority groups, some black leaders advocated that the local conferences of all-black churches in North America be brought together into one or more union conferences in order to give black leaders more influence and to increase the effectiveness of the church's evangelistic thrust toward blacks.

Two major research centres for the study of the writings of Ellen G. White, a church founder whom Adventists consider inspired, were opened, at Loma Linda University and at Avondale College in Australia. This brought the total of such centres to four. Evangelistic work was carried on in 559 languages and dialects during the year. In 1975, 1,062 workers were sent as missionaries, world church membership reached a new high of 2,666,484, and literature with a value of more than $80 million was sold.

(KENNETH H. WOOD)

Unitarian Churches. Signs of the times were apparent in the widespread discussions of violence and militarism in Unitarian churches throughout the world. The 250th anniversary festivities of the Antrim Presbytery of the Non-Subscribing Presbyterian Church of Ireland (Unitarian), held in Dunmurry, Belfast, Northern Ireland, were guarded by a three-ring security cordon. Since the start of the troubles in Northern Ireland, explosions had seriously damaged churches and killed many members.

The 15th annual General Assembly of the Unitarian Universalist Association, covering North America, attracted 686 delegates and 400 observers from 48 states. Held June 21–27, it was the first assembly to meet on a college campus—at the Claremont Colleges, Claremont, Calif. For the first time in nine years contributions to the Annual Program Fund surpassed the goal. Resolutions were passed opposing the private ownership of handguns, government harassment, uncontrolled nuclear plant proliferation, and discrimination by sex or age. Other issues debated included disarmament, social justice, racial bigotry, support of farm workers, and busing of children to promote school desegregation.

Vandalism and violence were among the major problems considered at the British General Assembly of Unitarian and Free Christian Churches, held in Edinburgh, Scotland, in the spring. Resolutions were passed supporting amendments to the Scottish law on marriage that would recognize non-Christian religious leaders on an equal basis with Christians and opposing "closed shops" as undermining the fundamental right of conscientious objection in all issues of human association and community.

The Liberal Religious Peace Fellowship terminated its affiliation with the Unitarian Universalist Association through inactivity, reflecting the fact that the U.S. was not at war. Nearly 400 volunteers were working in the service corps of the Unitarian Universalist Service Committee; programs tailored to meet specific local problems were under way in Tanzania, Guatemala, Haiti, El Salvador, and Peru. In 1975, 50 Unitarian Universalist scholars had established Collegium, An Association for Liberal Religious Studies. Theology and philosophy, history, and ethics were the subjects of the first meeting, at the Meadville/Lombard Theological School in Chicago.

(JOHN NICHOLLS BOOTH)

When Pope Paul announced the names of 19 new cardinals in April, he kept two others secret. One of them turned out to be Joseph Marie Trinnhu-Khue, archbishop of Hanoi. In May Trin arrived in Rome to become the first Vietnamese prince of the church.

WIDE WORLD

United Church of Canada. The United Church of Canada, it has been said, "is as Canadian as the maple leaf and the beaver." It fought secularism, had close liaison with the Canadian government in matters of national and international affairs, abhorred lotteries, barely tolerated abortion, and had little enthusiasm for mass evangelism. Within the church, there were 42 ethnic congregations using their own languages.

Above all, the United Church regarded mission as the essence of the faith. Its largest mission field was suburbia, where thousands had no real association with the Christian church and missionaries, rather than organizers, were needed. Increasingly, churches of various denominations were finding that joint effort in this area was better than rivalry. Overseas, missionaries were still needed, but they had to be well qualified for their work; they were sent only when an overseas church requested them and were invited only to provide a definite form of leadership, usually as ministers. In 1976 five countries—Argentina, Haiti, Jamaica, Sierra Leone, and Japan—requested help from the United Church. Some other countries, including Angola, South Korea, Nepal, Malawi, and Madagascar, were receiving special assistance from doctors, nurses, teachers, a dentist, and an agronomist.

Together with the Anglican and Roman Catholic churches in Canada, the United Church was concerned about the morality of lending money to the South African government. Three Canadian banks that had good relations with the churches expressed abhorrence of the South African policy of apartheid but declined to stop lending money to the government that practiced it.

The first ordination of a woman candidate in the United Church took place in 1936. As of 1976 there were 115 ordained women, and in recent years the proportion of women among intended candidates had risen dramatically. During the year 90 young persons were sent to six overseas countries for 23 days in order to gain some understanding of how people in other cultures live. The Youth Exchange was designed to enable young Canadians to become sensitive to the feelings and values of other cultures.

(ARTHUR GUY REYNOLDS)

United Church of Christ. At the beginning of 1976 the membership of the United Church of Christ stood at 1,818,762. Total giving by church members rose from $214,328,960 in 1974 to $225,211,074 in 1975, despite a decline of 22,550 in membership and negative economic trends. The denomination surpassed $13 million in its campaign to raise $17 million for six predominantly black colleges and several overseas educational institutions by 1976.

Throughout 1976 major priorities within the United Church were determined by the pronouncements of the tenth biennial General Synod, which met in June 1975. Three pronouncements had been adopted by the General Synod. One, on "Civil Liberties Without Discrimination Related to Affectional or Sexual Preference," called for federal, state, and local legislation that would guarantee the civil liberties of homosexual persons as well as others. The General Synod also called for a major study of the biblical and theological foundations of the church's teachings about human sexuality. A second pronouncement, on the world food crisis, called upon members and agencies of the denomination to become aware of the critical nature of the crisis, to make changes in their life-style in order to release resources for the meeting of human hunger, and to engage in citizen action that would contribute to the resolution of the problem of hunger at home and abroad. A third pronouncement, on "The Role of Transnational Business in Mass Economic Development," affirmed that the church is called by its faith to ask those engaged in transnational business to accept as an integral and primary part of their responsibility a concern to improve the welfare and to enlarge the dignity of the people of the countries where they operate.

The General Synod had also directed that national programs be developed relating to priorities it approved, including the role and status of women in church and society, revitalizing the local church, evangelism, Christian education, stewardship, the search for faith, racial and economic justice, and criminal justice and penal reform.

(ROBERT V. MOSS)

[827.D; 827.G.3; 827.H; 827.J.3]

ROMAN CATHOLIC CHURCH

Throughout 1976 Pope Paul VI repeatedly appealed for unity within the church and criticized both the traditionalists who resisted all change and the progressives who questioned everything. In a typical statement on July 7, he said that the unity inherited from the past could not be taken for granted but that it had to be rebuilt anew in each succeeding generation. The dimensions and the difficulty of this task were illustrated by the year's events.

A 6,000-word *Declaration on Certain Questions Concerning Sexual Ethics* was published in January. It reaffirmed the traditional Catholic teaching which condemned premarital sex, homosexuality, and masturbation. It recommended compassion but no yielding on principle. Coolly received, it was said to ignore the findings of modern psychology and to be unhelpful to those struggling with tragic moral problems. In the heat of controversy, and to the chagrin of the Vatican, another document, on evangelization (*Evangelii nuntiandi*), passed almost unnoticed.

A bitter rearguard action was being fought to preserve the form of Mass laid down in the 16th century by the Council of Trent. Archbishop Marcel Lefebvre (*see* BIOGRAPHY), head of the traditionalist seminary at Ecône in Switzerland, became the champion of an international anti-Vatican movement which regarded developments after the second Vatican Council (1962–65) as a feeble capitulation to the modern world or to Protestantism. In July Lefebvre was "suspended *a divinis*," which meant that he could no longer celebrate Mass licitly. Undeterred, he continued to say Mass amid a blaze of publicity, particularly in France where the political right wing found his views sympathetic.

In the following month a blow was also delivered to the left when Giovanni Franzoni, formerly abbot of St. Paul's Outside the Walls, in Rome, was laicized. He had been suspended in 1974, but he incurred this final sanction because he had given public support to the Italian Communist Party in the months preceding the June elections. The Vatican was deeply committed in the election campaign, especially when six Catholic

UPI COMPIX

Ascension Day at St. Peter's in Rome, where Pope Paul VI (centre, at altar) is seen speaking to 20 new Roman Catholic cardinals standing in a semicircle before him.

SAL DI MARCO—SYGMA

Philadelphia's John Cardinal Krol opens the 41st Eucharistic Congress in August, attended by nearly one million Catholics. The eight-day faith festival, with marching bands and impassioned speeches, emphasized "Hungers of the Human Family."

laymen announced their intention of standing for election alongside the Communists. Antonio Cardinal Poma, president of the Italian Episcopal Conference, reasserted the incompatibility of Christianity and Marxism and uttered veiled threats about excommunication. They were not carried out, however, and Rome settled down under a Communist mayor for the first time in its history without immediate disaster. Although Italy was in the foreground of these moves, the Vatican became increasingly alarmed by developments in Latin America, where the "theologians of liberation" preached the need for a "strategic alliance" with Marxists.

Some comfort came to the beleaguered Vatican from the continued growth of the charismatic movement. Its congress at South Bend, Ind., toward the end of May gathered 35,000 Catholics who had been touched by modified Pentecostalism. Archbishop Joseph L. Bernardin, president of the National Conference of Catholic Bishops, gave the charismatics his blessing, though he confessed that not all his episcopal colleagues were equally enthusiastic. The congress was summed up as follows: "Vatican II turned the altars round; now it is time to turn the people round."

American Catholics received a letter from Pope Paul on the occasion of the nation's bicentennial celebrations. It listed a number of areas in which they were urged to show concern, including drugs, migrants, and abortion, and spoke of "those sound moral principles formulated by your Founding Fathers and enshrined forever in your history." Fidelity to these ideals, added the pope, would make the nation "a beacon for the world." The world's attention did in fact turn to the U.S. in August when a Eucharistic Congress was held in Philadelphia. Every effort was made to broaden its scope, and the speakers included Archbishop Helder Câmara from Brazil and Mother Teresa of Calcutta. Later, in the fall, Catholics were prominent among supporters of the Right to Life movement, which attempted to make abortion an issue in the U.S. presidential campaign.

The names of 19 new cardinals were announced in April, and there were two more *in petto* (in secret). One of the anonymous cardinals was discovered to be the archbishop of Hanoi, given this office as a gesture of friendship to the new Vietnam. Pope Paul's new appointments were widely interpreted as the final arrangements for the conclave that would elect his successor. They also revealed a concern for geographic representation in the College of Cardinals, with the balance tilting away from Europe and toward the third world. Among them were Basil Cardinal Hume (*see* BIOGRAPHY), formerly abbot of Ampleforth, the first Benedictine monk to be archbishop of Westminster, and Laszlo Cardinal Lekai of Esztergom, Hungary, whose appointment was intended to draw the veil over the controversies that had raged around his predecessor, Jozsef Cardinal Mindszenty.

The Vatican's *Ostpolitik,* however, continued to be attacked for its alleged naiveté and weakness. Disquieting reports of renewed persecution came from inside Czechoslovakia. In Poland the Znak group of Catholic intellectuals was dealt a severe blow after it had protested against constitutional changes; the rules of censorship were tightened to an alarming degree. The first congress of the Cuban Communist Party guaranteed "freedom of religion," but this was conditional on religion not being used "against the goals of the Cuban Revolution." Despite these and other setbacks, the Vatican continued to pursue its step by step policy of trying to secure basic rights for Catholics living under Communism.

These policies were regarded as illusory by many members of the Ukrainian Catholic Church. The head of this Uniate church, Josyf Cardinal Slipyj, had all the prestige of one who had spent 18 years in Soviet prisons and survived. A massive campaign was launched to establish a patriarchate for his church and to make Cardinal Slipyj the first patriarch. The Vatican had steadily refused this proposal, on juridical grounds. But the mood of defiance had grown, and it was even thought necessary to refuse Cardinal Slipyj permission to travel to Philadelphia for the Eucharistic Congress. The Ukrainians attributed the Vatican's coolness toward them to its desire to be on good terms with the Russian Orthodox Church.

Ecumenical relations marked time. While theologians continued to find common ground and inch forward together, church leaders lamented the distance that still separated them. An exchange of correspondence between the pope and the archbishop of Canterbury, Donald Coggan, was made public in July. While the tone was friendly enough, Pope Paul made it clear that the Anglican proposal to ordain women to the priesthood would prove an additional obstacle to the union of the two churches. Anglicans were divided on the appropriate response; some held that they should "do what was right" come what might, while others did not wish to upset their larger sister church. The fact that many Catholic women, especially in the U.S., were campaigning for the ordination of women was not mentioned in the correspondence.

One of the oddest events of the year was a conference on Christian-Muslim relations held in February at Tripoli, Libya, at the invitation of Col. Muammar al-Qaddafi, leader of Libya's Revolutionary Command Council. The head of the Vatican's Secretariat for Non-Christian Religions, Sergio Cardinal Pignedoli, led a strong delegation which went expecting a religious discussion on what Christians and Muslims have in common. They soon found themselves embroiled in political controversy, marked by speeches and telegrams denouncing the iniquities of Israel and the evils of "Zionism." In the end, the Vatican was obliged to disavow the anti-Israel resolutions of the conference, which had been pushed through in haste and in a confusion of languages at the last minute.

Yet the Vatican was not unsympathetic to the Pal-

LONDON DAILY EXPRESS/PICTORIAL PARADE

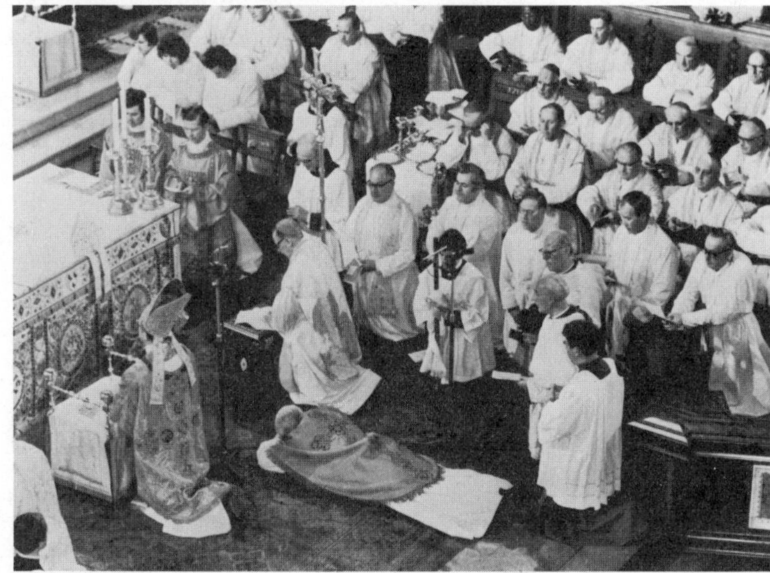

The new spiritual leader of four million Roman Catholics in England and Wales is Basil Hume, the first monk to become archbishop of Westminster. Here he prostrates himself before the altar in Westminster Cathedral.

estinian cause. In December 1975 Pope Paul had spoken of "the legitimate aspirations of the Palestinian people"—and the word *gente* was used in an endeavour to exclude political considerations. This did not mean that the Vatican was condemning Israel, or that it believed that dialogue with Islam excluded dialogue with Jews. To prove the point, the International Council of Christians and Jews met in Jerusalem during June 20–30 to examine the religious and political dimensions of the idea of "Israel." The silence of the Vatican on the military campaign of the Christian Maronites of the Lebanon was striking. The pope confined himself to deploring the tragic events of that war-torn country.

In Lent, Pope Paul spoke of his death as "an event that cannot be far distant." On Sept. 26, 1977, he would reach 80, the age when cardinals must retire. There was a sense of moving toward the end of a pontificate in which there had been an almost desperate attempt to hold the church together.

(PETER HEBBLETHWAITE)

See also Vatican City State.

[827.C; 827.G.2; 827.J.2]

EASTERN CHURCHES

The Orthodox Church. During April and May 1976, the ecumenical patriarchate of Constantinople (Istanbul), which enjoys honorary primacy in the Orthodox Church, sent a delegation headed by Metropolitan Meliton of Chalcedon to various centres of the Orthodox world to discuss the agenda of a future pan-Orthodox "Great Council." In contrast to previous consultations, when vast programs of doctrinal and disciplinary reform had been envisioned, the delegation suggested consideration of "a limited number of issues that are vital to the life of the Church." Among them were relations of the various Orthodox autocephalous (independent) churches among themselves and with the ecumenical patriarchate; the procedure for establishing new autocephalous churches; and the existence of parallel ethnic jurisdictions in America and Western Europe.

Clearly, the agenda implied a desire on the part of Constantinople to find a joint solution for the conflict that occurred when, in 1970, a new autocephalous church was established in America by an act of the church in Russia. The patriarch of Constantinople refused to grant official recognition to the new church, although maintaining full communion with it. Orthodox canon law prohibits parallel jurisdictions in the same area, a situation which, however, has existed de facto in America since 1921.

Some observers doubted that a full pan-Orthodox council would actually meet in the near future. The political situation and the antireligious attitude of the socialist governments of Eastern Europe, where 90% of Orthodox Christians live, were likely to be insurmountable obstacles. However, some concrete problems could also be resolved at a series of consultations, such as that held in the fall of 1976 at Chambésy, Switz.

At the meeting of the central committee of the World Council of Churches at Geneva in July, the general secretary presented a report on the persecution of Christians in the Soviet Union, and a special advisory group was created to deal with the matter. The report had been mandated by the fifth WCC General Assembly, held in 1975 in Nairobi, Kenya, despite the objections of delegates from the Soviet Union, including Metropolitan Nikodim of Leningrad, who was elected one of the council's presidents.

The new Greek constitution, adopted in 1975, significantly modified the legal status of the Orthodox Church in Greece. While still considered the "dominant" religion, it enjoyed less preferential treatment but also greater administrative freedom from the government. Some observers believed this was a prelude to further separation between church and state in Greece.

Eastern Non-Chalcedonian Churches. During the last months of 1975, the Ethiopian government proclaimed the separation of the church from the state. It confiscated church properties and appointed a committee of handpicked ecclesiastics to run church affairs. The reigning patriarch, Abuna Tewoflos (Theophilos), opposed these measures, and on Feb. 18, 1976, he was accused of corruption, deposed, and arrested. The monk Aba Melaku Wolde-Mikael was elected patriarch on July 7, and on August 9 an Ethiopian ecclesiastic delegation visited Cairo requesting the Coptic patriarch's participation in his consecration, according to custom. The Coptic Holy Synod refused, however, on the ground that it had no knowledge that the deposition of Tewoflos had been accomplished properly.

(JOHN MEYENDORFF)

[827.B; 827.G.1; 827.J.1]

JUDAISM

The Judaic tradition, with its emphasis on the centrality of morality in the religious life, found fresh expression within South African Jewry in 1976. At its meeting in Johannesburg on May 29, the national congress of the South African Jewish Board of Deputies, representing all institutions and organizations among the 120,000 Jews of that country, unanimously condemned the policy of apartheid. The congress called for equal rights for all citizens of the republic, without regard to race. In context, that resolution expressed concretely what Judaism has always maintained is the most important aspect of the faith.

In the U.S. another perennial issue, the nature and meaning of Israel, the Jewish people, came to the fore. The contemporary formulation of the classical category of peoplehood—structurally equivalent to ecclesiology in Christian theology—is in terms of the state of Israel and the relationship of the Diaspora communities to the state. While framed in practical and even chiefly political terms, the underlying question has to do with "who is Israel" and "who is authentic Israel."

Faced by the claim that the state of Israel is central and predominant among all Jewish concerns and for Judaism as well, some American Jews, few in number but considerable in communal standing and intellectual achievement, took exception. Organized as Breira, meaning "alternative," these Jews engaged in free discussion of Israeli and U.S. Jewish policies and programs, not hesitating to differ on important ethical and moral grounds from both.

In his paper "The Jewish Situation: 1976" (*New Outlook,* June 1976), Arthur I. Waskow, a leader of Breira, pointed out that for ten years endless war in the Middle East had exhausted the energies and emotions of the Jews so that "their sense of a Jewish content for their Jewish identity is emptied out." He called instead for a "focus on both creating a healthy Jewish identity and stopping the military drain on our money and energy, especially by ending the obsession with military means of protecting Israel and by substituting for it the political process and the achievement of peace as the crucial defense of Israel and of the whole Jewish people." Waskow argued further that a new definition of the meaning of Jewish peoplehood is called for, specifically, "a transnational movement for a renewed Jewish peoplehood." In the context of Judaism, Waskow's statement bears important theological meaning.

Arab youths attacked a Jewish shrine in Hebron, south of Jerusalem, ripping and defiling Torah scrolls. Here the chief rabbi inspects the scrolls before their burial.

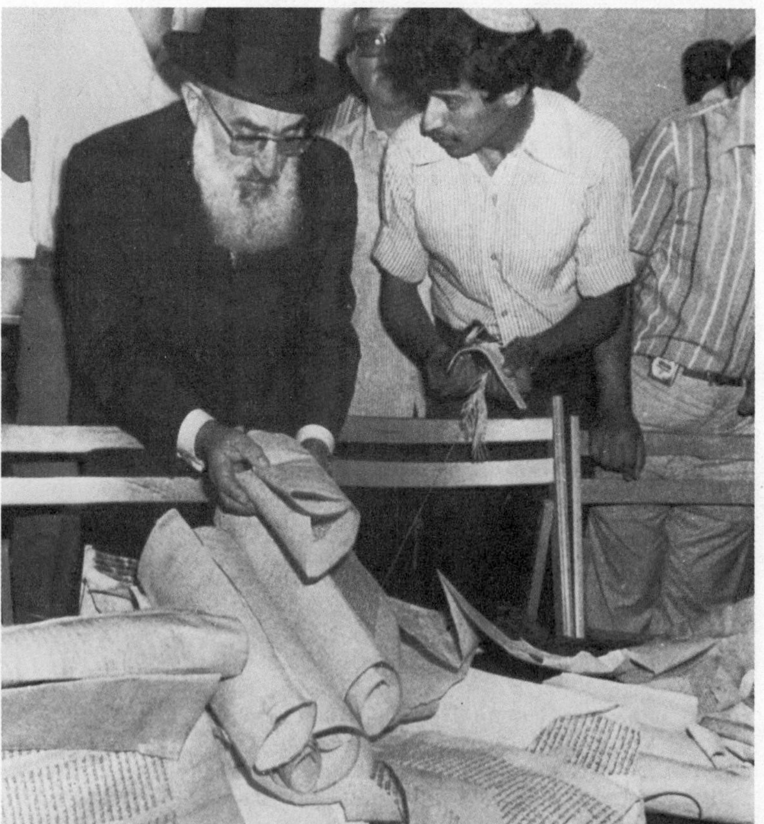

UPI COMPIX

The critics of Breira, for their part, maintained that public discussion of Israeli policy and other matters of Jewish concern outside the Jewish press and magazines is to be deplored. Forty-seven rabbis in Los Angeles signed a public statement condemning a rabbi in that community who condemned Israeli settlement on the West Bank. Rabbi Arthur Lelyveld told the Central Conference of American Rabbis, the Reform rabbinical organization, "It goes beyond criticism and becomes irresponsibility when we join the jackals who are tearing Israel's body. . . . It is totally inadmissible for a Jew to give aid and comfort through ill-calculated formulations to those who would cut aid to Israel and leave her defenseless before murderers and terrorists."

For his part, Lelyveld exercised the right of criticism to point out that the central activity of the American Jewish community, raising funds for the state of Israel and for local Jewish institutions, lacks all spiritual content. "Most of our people understand [raising funds for a Jewish] Federation. . . . The rest of Judaism is for many of them a vague context about which they feel sentimental but within which they rarely have perceptions of value and purpose." Lelyveld called upon synagogues and fund-raising agencies to form a partnership.

Certainly, during 1976, free discussion of Judaic issues took place within the Jewish communities of the U.S., Western Europe, and the state of Israel. Yet Irving Howe, writing in *Interchange* (June 1976), pointed out that while Israelis are free to advocate diverse positions on their religious and political life, "Things are not quite so ordered among American Jews. . . . It would be self-deceiving to say that the atmosphere of the American Jewish community is one that entirely encourages free exchange of opinion regarding such critical issues as Israeli settlement on the West Bank or Israeli relations with South Africa or Israeli treatment of Arabs. There are . . . no external forces of repression. But there is a good measure of self-repression, anxiety lest differences of opinion be used by enemies, and at times a certain mindless chauvinism." Observing that a good many American Jews "feel a strong reluctance to get involved in any debate concerning Israeli policies," Howe argued that without free discussion "American Jewish community life would be lifeless: a mere ritual of parades, resolutions, and generous checks." Clearly, under such circumstances, Judaism too becomes a religion of sheer ritualism rather than a commitment to the godly life defined for thousands of years in the Hebrew Bible and Talmud.

In these ways the issues of Judaism were phrased in acutely contemporary terms during 1976, yet turned out to be defined by the enduring and classical categories of the Judaic religious life.

(JACOB NEUSNER)

[826]

THE TIMES, LONDON

Ordination of a novice monk at the Buddhist Centre in Farmoor, England. The ceremony includes shaving the novice's head and a bath of purification.

BUDDHISM

During 1976 Buddhists celebrated the 26-hundredth anniversary of the birth of Prince Siddhārtha (Buddha Gautama) with pride in their past and cautious optimism for the present and future. That pride was enhanced by several archaeological finds, including the discovery of an ancient cave meditation centre near Trincomalee, Sri Lanka, and a 6th- or 7th-century Buddhist temple in the southern Tadzhik Soviet Socialist Republic, U.S.S.R. Of special historical significance was the discovery of an inscription on a fragmentary granite pillar at Sanchi, India, which mentions an envoy of Bindusara, father of the famous Buddhist king Asoka. This might change the traditional opinion that the Mauryan dynasty adopted Buddhism only after Asoka's Kalinga war.

Princess Poon Pismai Diskul was reelected as president of the General Conference of the World Fellowship of Buddhists, which met in Bangkok early in the year. The conference also passed a resolution asking for an international Buddhist women's conference for the purpose of "examining, defining and proclaiming the role of Buddhist women according to Buddhism and Buddhist culture."

In India, Buddhist activities centred around the Tibetan refugees headed by the Dalai Lama and the "new Buddhists," who were formerly outcastes. According to the director of the International Buddha Sravaka Society, the number of Buddhists in India now exceeded the entire population of Sri Lanka, but there were only 60 monks, excluding the Tibetan priests. A lack of adequate Buddhist leadership was also reported in Nepal. The government of Sri Lanka was actively promoting Buddhism; the Vidyalankara Institute of Post-Graduate Buddhist Studies was established at the University of Sri Lanka, and parents were encouraged to send their children to Dhamma schools. Nevertheless, the general secretary of the Buddhist Sangha Congress lamented the deterioration of Buddhist culture in that country.

The abdication of King Savang Vatthana in 1975 ended the traditional Buddhist monarchy in Laos. South Korea designated the Buddha's birthday (Vesak) as a national holiday, and Dongguk University in Seoul held its second world conference on Buddhism and the Modern World. It was reported that the second-ranking Tibetan prelate, the Panchen Lama, was well and studying politics in Peking.

Europe, the Americas, and the Southern Hemisphere reported a wide range of Buddhist activities. Of special interest were the establishment of the first Vietnamese Buddhist Temple in America (Los Angeles) and the formation of the Buddhist Union of Europe with representatives from West Germany, France, The Netherlands, Austria, Switzerland, and Great Britain.

(JOSEPH M. KITAGAWA)

[824]

HINDUISM

A marked feature of Hinduism in recent years has been the increase in the number of highly educated Indians and diverse Hindu groups placing more and more emphasis on Yoga as a resource for physical health as well as a technique for the individual seeker after spiritual strength and psychological serenity. Claims have been made that physical and meditational exercises associated with traditional Hindu religious yogic practices are especially well suited for dealing with diseases caused by the stresses of modern industrial and urban life.

In 1976 Indian research teams working at such scientific centres as the Institute of Medical Sciences of Benares Hindu University and the All-India Institute of Medical Sciences in New Delhi were receiving encouragement in their studies from the Ministry of Health. While these studies were deliberately dissociated from religious belief and cultic practice, for the general Hindu population the serious practice of Yoga continued to be limited to those individuals who were ready to devote full time to the arduous physical and mental discipline demanded by Yoga within Hinduism's traditional religious context. At the same time, in Europe and America, various movements exhibiting at least quasi-Hindu religious characteristics continued to present their own interpretations of Yoga, meditation, and Indian-Hindu life-style as the answer to the stresses of modern life and the key to human spiritual realization.

Because of the nonpolitical nature of Hinduism, the suspension of civil liberties in India by Prime Minister Indira Gandhi's government appeared to have had little effect on Hindu religious thought or activities. However, a political party with a strong Hindu religious orientation, the Bharatiya Jan Sangh (Indian People's Party), continued to be outlawed because of its alleged involvement in nondemocratic conspiracies and incitement to discord among the people. (*See* INDIA.)

Festivals and holidays remained at the centre of Hindu religious and social life. Varying throughout India in name, mythological content, and nature of observance, they served, along with pilgrimages to temples and shrines, to remind the devout of the gods and goddesses that are central to the multiformed religious traditions that combine to constitute all-India Hinduism. Reliable reports of increasing attendance attested to the continuing vitality of Hinduism in the religious and social life of India. In some instances hundreds of thousands of persons attended a single festival.

(PHILIP H. ASHBY)

[823]

ISLAM

The effects of the civil war in Lebanon extended to the wider Muslim world and once again underscored the inextricability of political and religious developments. (*See* LEBANON.) During the year the separation of Lebanon into Christian and Muslim areas became more distinct. The situation underscored the nagging question of how Muslims and non-Muslims might develop common goals and cooperative interests within a single national state.

The Lebanese civil war overshadowed news of other trouble spots: Jammu-Kashmir, still in dispute between India and Pakistan; parts of Africa; and in the Middle East itself. Rioting broke out among the Arab inhabitants of Jerusalem in February after an Israeli magistrate decided that Jews could not be prevented from praying in the raised site of the Temple area near al-Aqsa Mosque, even though this was forbidden by Israeli law. In March the Israeli Supreme Court upheld the law, and Israel restated to the UN its determination to prevent violence-provoking religious demonstrations by Jews. Outbreaks among the Arabs under Israeli rule appeared to have been increasing in recent years, and they might well continue as Jerusalem and the West Bank area became more closely integrated with the rest of Israel. (*See* ISRAEL.) A riot occurred in the Muslim quarter of the old city of New Delhi, India, late in April, apparently because of the municipality's attempt to clear away shanties of the poor; however, spokesmen claimed that Muslims were objecting to India's stringent measures favouring birth control, a subject about which Muslims in various areas have differing attitudes. After four years of fighting, a cease-fire agreement between the Philippine government and the Muslim inhabitants of Mindanao was reached in December through the efforts of several Islamic nations.

Two Islamic conferences held during the year were principally concerned with political events. A 44-nation conference in March denounced what it called Israel's systematic effort at obliterating Jerusalem's Christian and Muslim heritage. The seventh annual Islamic Foreign Ministers Conference, meeting in Istanbul in May, similarly reflected the difficulty of separating "religious" from "secular" concerns. Turkey, though emphasizing its stance as a secular state, announced plans to seek full membership. West African nations attending the meeting were unable to agree on the role of Islam in black Africa or to reconcile the seemingly incompatible concept of "Négritude" advanced by Pres. Léopold Senghor of Senegal and Islamic interests in such areas as Nigeria.

The 50th anniversary of the World Muslim Congress was celebrated at the beginning of the year. The Congress was formed in 1926, two years after the Turkish republic formally abolished the caliphate. After a long period of inactivity, it had held meetings and published a weekly journal in recent years. It attempted to deemphasize political events while pursuing Muslim unity and serving as a clearinghouse for Islamic information.

In early summer the long-suppressed Muslim Brotherhood in Egypt attempted to publish a new journal. Though the journal was stopped by the Egyptian censor, the Brotherhood seemed to be showing signs of renewed vigour, encouraged by the conservative religious attitude of Libya as well as by concerns over the allegedly lax moral standards evident in Egyptian cities.

Muslim activity in non-Muslim areas continued. In early March, the establishment of the Voice of Islam radio station in West Germany was announced; partly, this was an effort to respond to Christian broadcasts in Africa. Work on the $10 million mosque and Islamic cultural centre to be constructed in Rome was expected to begin early in 1977; $2 million in pledges had already been received by mid-1976. In the United States, where Wallace D. Muhammad had succeeded to the leadership of the Nation of Islam (often referred to as the Black Muslims) following the death of his father, Elijah Muhammad, in 1975, changes continued to be instituted in that organization. The name was changed to the World Community of Islam in the West, membership was opened to nonblacks, and activities were cosponsored with non-Muslim religious groups. These changes seemed to be increasing and broadening the organization's appeal.

An Islamic arts festival held in London in the late spring brought together art objects from all over the world. It was probably the most extensive display of Islamic art ever shown and reminded the world once again of the genius displayed by Muslim artists and craftsmen over the centuries. (*See* ART AND ART EXHIBITIONS.)

(R. W. SMITH)

[828]

WORLD CHURCH MEMBERSHIP

The study of religious statistics is still in its infancy. Some churches keep very exact information on their members but will not release the data to outsiders. Baha'i, a new and rapidly growing community of faith, has approximately 60,000 groups throughout the world but does not release membership statistics. Reports on the ethnic religions and even some branches of Christianity with centuries-old ethnic foundations tend to be based on percentages of population figures. Finally, no census of any kind has as yet been taken in some nations.

Some religions have "adherents," others designate "constituents," and others count "communicants"; in the latter case, normally only adults are counted. Only on the mission fields of Christianity, Buddhism, Islam, and Hinduism are fairly precise figures available in the more numerous religions. For Judaism, quite accurate published figures are available for communities outside the control of the Communist governments, but the figure for the third-largest concentration (in the U.S.S.R.) must remain an estimate.

A second major problem for the statistician is the uncertainty of reports from areas of persecution. Many millions of the world's refugees are religious as

Estimated Membership of the Principal Religions of the World*

Religions	North America†	South America	Europe‡	Asia	Africa	Oceania§	World
Total Christian	228,479,000	161,872,500	358,732,600	86,358,000	98,326,000	17,290,000	951,058,100
Roman Catholic	130,789,000	151,017,000	182,087,000	44,239,500	31,168,500	3,230,000	542,531,000
Eastern Orthodox	4,121,000	55,000	62,145,600	1,786,000	16,335,000‖	360,000	84,803,200
Protestant¶	93,569,000	10,800,500	114,500,000	40,332,500	50,822,500♀	13,700,000	323,724,500
Jewish	6,356,675	675,000	3,960,000	3,186,460	274,760	80,000	14,532,895
Muslim♂	248,100	197,800	8,277,000	427,035,000	101,889,500	66,000	537,713,400
Zoroastrian□	250	—	3,000	224,700	530	—	228,480
Shinto°	60,000	92,000	—	61,004,000	—	—	61,156,000
Taoist△	16,000	12,000	—	29,256,100	—	—	29,284,100
Confucian△	96,100	85,000	25,000	175,440,250	500	42,000	175,688,850
Buddhist+	155,000	195,300	220,000	244,212,000	2,000	16,000	244,800,300
Hindu⊕	80,000	547,000	330,000	516,713,500	473,650	650,000	518,794,150
Totals	235,491,125	163,676,600	371,547,600	1,543,430,010	200,966,940	18,144,000	2,533,256,275
Population**	347,934,000	224,154,000	733,454,000	2,304,929,000	412,183,000	21,729,000	4,044,433,000

*Religious statistics are directly affected by war and persecution; for example, recent events in Uganda, Vietnam, Cyprus, and Lebanon alter the estimates of religious affiliation substantially. There are c.18 million refugees throughout the world who are not as yet integrated into the population statistics and religious estimates of their lands of temporary (?) residence.

†Includes Central America and the West Indies.

‡Includes the U.S.S.R., in which the effect of a half century of official Marxist ideology upon religious adherence is evident, although the extent of religious disaffiliation and disaffection is disputed. The same difficulty in estimating religious adherence obtains in other nations with officially Marxist governments, although the degree of persecution varies from country to country and from time to time.

§Includes Australia and New Zealand as well as the islands of the South Pacific.

‖Includes Coptic Christians, numerous in Egypt and Ethiopia.

¶Protestant statistics outside Europe usually include "full members" only, rather than all baptized persons, and are not comparable to the statistics of state churches, ethnic religions, or of churches counting all adherents.

♀Including many sects and cults of recent appearance and rapid growth.

♂The chief base of Islam is still ethnic, although missionary work has recently begun in Europe and America. In countries where Islam is the official state religion, minority religions are frequently persecuted and reliable statistics are scarce.

□Zoroastrians (Parsees) were until recently found chiefly in Iran and India, but a number of refugees of that persuasion are now living in England.

°A Japanese ethnic religion, Shinto has declined markedly since the Japanese emperor gave up the claim to divinity (1947); neither (in contrast to Buddhism) does it transplant readily with Japanese moving out from the homeland. Japanese religious statistics are problematical because, as traditionally also in China, adherents are frequently related to several different religions simultaneously.

△General population figures for China are highly speculative, although minimal population growth has apparently been achieved. The effect of the Maoist-Marxist revolution has not yet been measured definitively. Although Buddhist intellectual leadership was slaughtered, there are reliable reports of continuing Buddhist observances and pilgrimages.

+Buddhism has several modern renewal movements, with energetic and successful missions outside the traditional ethnic-Buddhist areas.

⊕Hinduism's strength in India has been enhanced by nationalism but eroded by modern industrialization and contemporary secular ideologies. Modern Hinduism has also developed several renewal movements with growing communities of converts in America and Europe. Here the statistics include Jainism as well as other religions of India (except for Buddhism) which have emerged from Hinduism.

**Source: United Nations, Department of Economic and Social Affairs; data refer to midyear 1976.

(FRANKLIN H. LITTELL)

well as cultural, political, and/or economic victims. In some places genocide is still practiced by governments against countercultures. The effect upon traditional affiliations of religious/ideological revolutions in large populations such as those of China and the Soviet Union can only be estimated. Even before 1948, many millions in China had so blended their religious and ritual devotions from Taoist, Confucian, and Buddhist teachings that any separation of discrete numbers of adherents was problematical.

The data for free churches, where membership is based on a clear and uninhibited choice, are generally far more reliable than those from areas in which governments have intervened either to sponsor or to persecute. The accompanying table is revised regularly to reflect the latest surveys and estimates, but the reader is advised to use it with awareness that mixed styles of reckoning are necessarily involved.

(FRANKLIN H. LITTELL)

Rhodesia

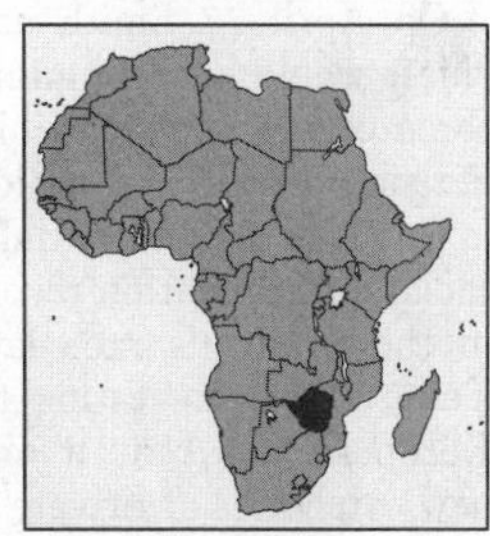

Though Rhodesia declared itself a republic on March 2, 1970, it remained a British colony in the eyes of many other nations. It is bounded by Zambia, Mozambique, South Africa, and Botswana. Area: 150,674 sq mi (390,245 sq km). Pop. (1976 est.): 6.4 million, of whom 95% are African and 5% white. Cap. and largest city: Salisbury (urban area pop., 1976 est., 569,000). Language: English (official) and Bantu. Religion: predominantly traditional tribal beliefs; Christian minority. Presidents in 1976, Clifford W. Dupont and, from January 14, John Wrathall; prime minister, Ian D. Smith.

Affairs in Rhodesia in 1976 were carried on against a background of guerrilla raids, mainly from Mozambique. The government claimed to have killed more than 1,000 guerrillas and to have lost about 70 members of the Rhodesian armed forces. Apart from the

ARGUS AFRICA NEWS SERVICE/PHOTO TRENDS

A Rhodesian soldier cleans his gun at a border post. Guerrilla forces were encamped a short distance away in neighbouring Mozambique.

KEYSTONE

The Geneva conference on Rhodesia opened in the Palais des Nations on October 28. Chairman Ivor Richard of Great Britain is in the foreground. On the left and right are the black delegations led by Joshua Nkomo, Robert Mugabe, Ndabaningi Sithole, and Bishop Abel Muzorewa. Rhodesian Prime Minister Ian Smith is in the background.

strain upon both Africans and whites living on the eastern border, the main concern arose from guerrilla attacks on road and rail communications with South Africa. From time to time these were cut by the raiders. On May 1 it was announced that officers and men of the Territorial Force who had completed a year of service would be required to remain in uniform for as long as might be necessary, and on May 5 the period of national service was extended from 12 to 18 months. The government announced that it would exercise its right of "hot pursuit" across national borders if Mozambique and Zambia continued to allow raiders to use bases there. Air strikes and ground operations were launched in August in a retaliatory attack upon what the government claimed to be a guerrilla camp in Mozambique. There were more than 300 casualties and the authorities in Mozambique maintained that the victims were defenseless refugees. The Rhodesian government strongly denied this.

On April 26 regulations were published aimed at censoring the dissemination of information held prejudicial to the security of the state. Although morale among the white population in general remained high, considerable numbers of whites, particularly in the age group liable for military service, continued to leave the country, and in spite of the arrival of Portuguese refugees from Mozambique and Angola the numbers of those leaving greatly exceeded the number of those arriving. At the beginning of March a blow was dealt to Rhodesia's economy when Mozambique closed the border between the two countries, thus severing the rail links with the Indian Ocean at Maputo (formerly Lourenço Marques) and Beira as well as cutting off Rhodesia's export trade with Malawi. In July the finance minister, David Smith, introduced a budget which forecast an increase of 40% in allocations for the military and 23% for the police. The cost was to be met by internal borrowing and by keeping down other expenditures.

In February talks began between Ian Smith (*see* BIOGRAPHY) and African leader Joshua Nkomo. The British government made it clear that it would play a part in negotiations only if Smith conceded the principle of majority (African) rule, and Lord Greenhill, formerly permanent undersecretary at the British Foreign Office, was sent to Rhodesia to clarify Smith's position. Greenhill returned with a disappointing report, and Smith's talks with Nkomo continued fruitlessly until March 19. Again Smith appealed to Britain, and on March 22 James Callaghan, then British foreign secretary, outlined Britain's settlement proposals. They included the acceptance of the principle of majority rule, elections for majority rule within 18 months or two years, no independence until majority rule had been achieved, and no long-drawn-out negotiations. Nkomo's reaction to this plan was unenthusiastic, and he called upon Britain to be more forthright in its dealings with Smith. Toward the end of March the presidents of Tanzania, Zambia, Mozambique, and Botswana—Julius Nyerere, Kenneth Kaunda, Samora Machel, and Sir Seretse Khama, respectively—met in Lusaka, Zambia, to discuss Rhodesia but issued no communiqué. Clearly there was no reconciliation between the two leaders of the African National Council (ANC), Nkomo and Bishop Abel Muzorewa, who were present in Lusaka. In May a third force began to make its presence felt when Robert Mugabe, former secretary-general of the Zimbabwe African National Union (ZANU), said that the Zimbabwe People's Army, operating from Mozambique, rejected the leadership of both ANC factions.

On April 27 Smith announced that four African chiefs would become ministers within the Cabinet and three others deputy ministers, but this only aroused derision among the nationalists. A report submitted in June by a presidential commission of inquiry into racial discrimination recommended important reforms in the country's race laws and criticized the Land Tenure Act, suggesting that the distinction between European and African land should be replaced by two new categories of private and state land.

In April a new factor appeared on the scene with the arrival in Africa of Henry Kissinger, U.S. secretary of state, to discuss with African leaders various issues affecting southern Africa. Kissinger announced U.S. commitment to majority rule in Rhodesia and set out ten points for the achievement of a just and durable solution. Early in August Smith demanded direct talks with the U.S. in an attempt to reach a settlement, and in mid-September Kissinger again

RHODESIA

Education. (1976) Primary, pupils 885,547, teachers 22,898; secondary, pupils 75,951, teachers 3,849; vocational, students 3,430, teachers 338; teacher training, students 1,860, teachers 123; higher (including University of Rhodesia), students 2,666, teaching staff 346.

Finance. Monetary unit: Rhodesian dollar, with (Sept. 20, 1976) a free rate of R$0.63 to U.S. $1 (R$1.09 = £1 sterling). Budget (1974 actual): revenue R$401 million; expenditure R$448 million. Gross domestic product (1974) R$1,845,000,000.

Foreign Trade. (1973) Imports *c.* R$316 million; exports R$380 million. Import sources (1965): U.K. 30%; South Africa 23%; U.S. 7%; Japan 6%. Export destinations (1965): Zambia 25%; U.K. 22%; South Africa 10%; West Germany 9%; Malawi 5%; Japan 5%. Main exports (1965): tobacco 33%; food 10%; asbestos 8%.

Transport and Communications. Roads (1974) 78,930 km. Motor vehicles in use (1974): passenger *c.* 180,000; commercial (including buses) *c.* 70,000. Railways: (1974) 3,394 km; freight traffic (including Botswana; 1975) 6,436,000,000 net ton-km. Telephones (Jan. 1975) 171,880. Radio receivers (Dec. 1973) 225,000. Television receivers (Dec. 1972) 57,000.

Agriculture. Production (in 000; metric tons; 1975): corn *c.* 1,400; millet *c.* 220; wheat (1974) *c.* 93; sugar, raw value *c.* 260; peanuts *c.* 120; tobacco *c.* 90; cotton, lint *c.* 43; beef and veal *c.* 65; cow's milk 253. Livestock (in 000; 1974): cattle *c.* 4,150; sheep *c.* 490; goats *c.* 740; pigs *c.* 150.

Industry. Production (in 000; metric tons; 1974): coal *c.* 3,500; cement (1975) 675; asbestos *c.* 80; chrome ore (oxide content) *c.* 292; iron ore (metal content) *c.* 305; gold (troy oz) *c.* 500; electricity (kw-hr) 5,823,000.

visited Africa. After consultations between Kissinger and some presidents of African states, the prime minister of South Africa, and Smith himself, Britain was invited to convene a Rhodesian constitutional conference. Smith, it appeared, had accepted a set of proposals formulated by the secretary of state as a basis for a settlement. Britain at once agreed to a conference, although leaders of some African states rejected parts of the plan when it was announced by Smith. Trouble arose, too, over who was to represent the African nationalists at the conference, and eventually Nkomo, Muzorewa, Mugabe, and Ndabaningi Sithole were all invited. When the conference opened in Geneva on October 28 under the chairmanship of a British civil servant, Ivor Richard, Nkomo and Mugabe were seen to be cooperating with each other while the supporters of Muzorewa and Sithole retained their distinctive approach. All agreed that two years was too long to wait for majority rule, but Smith claimed he had accepted a package deal with Kissinger and would discuss no modifications. The conference adjourned in December with no settlement in sight. (KENNETH INGHAM)

See also African Affairs.

[978.E.8.b.iii]

Romania

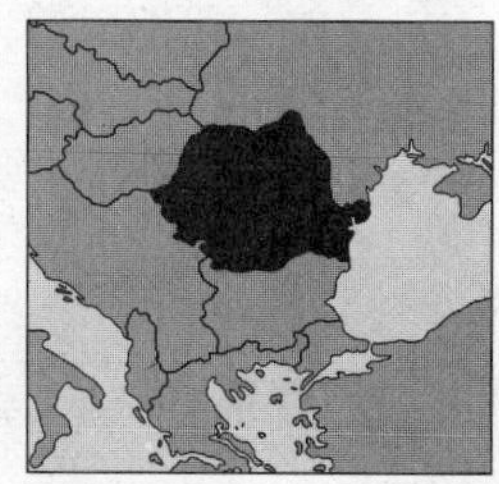

A socialist republic on the Balkan Peninsula in southeastern Europe, Romania is bordered by the U.S.S.R., the Black Sea, Bulgaria, Yugoslavia, and Hungary. Area: 91,700 sq mi (237,500 sq km). Pop. (1975 est.): 21,245,000, including (1966) Romanian 87.7%; Hungarian 8.5%. Cap. and largest city: Bucharest (pop., 1974 est., 1,681,600). Religion: Romanian Orthodox 70%; Greek Orthodox 10%. General secretary of the Romanian Communist Party, president of the republic, and president of the State Council in 1976, Nicolae Ceausescu; chairman of the Council of Ministers (premier), Manea Manescu.

Speaking at the Congress of Political Education in Bucharest on June 2, 1976, Ceausescu presented his own definition of the concept of "proletarian internationalism"; according to him, it simply meant "full equality and comradely mutual assistance among all socialist countries." He also denied the existence of a "Moldavian" nationality and language, affirming that the Romanian nation is composed of Moldavians, Walachians, and Transylvanians. (Shortly before this, two young Romanian historians, Ion Ardeleanu and Mircea Musat, had published a book entitled *Political Life in Romania from 1918 to 1921* in which they described Bessarabia, presently part of the U.S.S.R., as an ethnically Romanian land. Similarly, the periodical *Romania: Pages of History* [no. 2, 1976] had published the text of a treaty of alliance of April 13, 1711, signed at Lutsk [now in the Ukrainian S.S.R.] between Peter I of Russia and Dimitrie Cantemir, prince of Moldavia, stating that the Dniester River constituted the eastern frontier of the principality and thereby including Bessarabia in Romanian Moldavia.) Ceausescu declared that knowledge of national history was an important factor in the development of the people's self-awareness, but he added that problems inherited from the past should not cast a shadow on

ROMANIA

Education. (1974–75) Primary, pupils 2,882,109, teachers 137,405; secondary, pupils 344,585, teachers 14,818; vocational and teacher training, pupils 580,125, teachers 29,579; higher (including 12 universities), students 162,767, teaching staff 14,147.

Finance. Monetary unit: leu, with (Sept. 20, 1976) a commercial rate of 4.97 lei to U.S. $1 (8.61 lei = £1 sterling) and a tourist rate of 12 lei = U.S. $1 (20.79 lei = £1 sterling). Budget (1975 est.) balanced at 242.8 billion lei.

Foreign Trade. (1974) Imports 25,563,000,000 lei; exports 24,226,000,000 lei. Import sources: West Germany 15%; U.S.S.R. 15%; U.K. 6%; East Germany 5%; U.S. 5%. Export destinations: U.S.S.R. 17%; West Germany 10%; East Germany 6%; Italy 5%; U.K. 5%; Czechoslovakia 5%. Main exports: machinery and transport equipment 21%; food 20%; chemicals 11%; petroleum products 11%; industrial raw materials 7%.

Transport and Communications. Roads (1974) 95,216 km (including 96 km expressways). Motor vehicles in use: passenger (1972) *c.* 125,000; commercial *c.* 50,000. Railways (1974): 11,086 km; traffic 22,406,000,000 passenger-km, freight 61,618,000,000 net ton-km. Air traffic (1975): 574 million passenger-km; freight 8,240,000 net ton-km. Inland waterways in regular use (1974) 1,691 km. Shipping (1975): merchant vessels 100 gross tons and over 122; gross tonnage 777,309. Telephones (Dec. 1974) 1,076,566. Radio licenses (Dec. 1974) 3,066,000. Television licenses (Dec. 1974) 2,405,000.

Agriculture. Production (in 000; metric tons; 1975): wheat *c.* 2,900; barley *c.* 800; corn *c.* 7,000; potatoes *c.* 2,900; cabbages (1974) *c.* 630; onions *c.* 280; tomatoes *c.* 1,243; sugar, raw value *c.* 587; sunflower seed *c.* 724; dry beans *c.* 130; soybeans *c.* 330; plums (1974) *c.* 700; apples (1974) *c.* 300; grapes (1974) 1,700; linseed *c.* 40; tobacco *c.* 38. Livestock (in 000; Jan. 1975): cattle 5,983; sheep 14,212; pigs *c.* 8,652; horses (1974) *c.* 610; poultry 67,672.

Industry. Fuel and power (in 000; metric tons; 1974): coal 7,107; lignite 19,789; coke 1,525; crude oil 14,486; natural gas (cu m) 24,217,000; manufactured gas (cu m) 947,000; electricity (kw-hr) 49,062,000. Production (in 000; metric tons; 1974): cement 11,196; iron ore (metal content) 837; pig iron 6,081; crude steel 8,840; petroleum products *c.* 17,150; sulfuric acid 1,358; fertilizers (nutrient content) nitrogenous 980, phosphate 404; cotton yarn 157; cotton fabrics (sq m) 612,000; wool yarn 49; woolen fabrics (sq m) 94,000; rayon, etc., filament yarns and fibres 66; nylon, etc., filament yarns and fibres 77; newsprint 53; other paper 531. New dwelling units completed (1974) 164,000.

Roads:
see Engineering Projects; Transportation

Rockets:
see Defense; Space Exploration

Rodeo:
see Arena Sports

Roman Catholic Church:
see Religion

the solidarity of the respective Communist parties and states. Romania, he said, had no territorial or other disputes with the U.S.S.R. or with other neighbouring socialist states.

A few days before, on May 28–30, Konstantin Katushev, secretary of the Central Committee of the Communist Party of the Soviet Union (CPSU), paid a visit to Bucharest, and Ceausescu accepted his invitation to attend the conference of European Communist parties in East Berlin. Addressing the conference on June 29, Ceausescu repeated what he had said in Moscow on February 26 at the 25th congress of the CPSU, namely, that the Romanian Communist Party regarded the defense of vital national interests and the protection of independence and national freedom not as "national narrow-mindedness" but as its supreme duty.

From August 2 to 12 Ceausescu and his wife paid a visit to the U.S.S.R. At a dinner in Kishinyov in the Moldavian S.S.R. (which was formed out of a large part of historic Bessarabia), Ion Bodyul, first secretary of the Moldavian Communist Party, and his Romanian guests exchanged toasts in Romanian. On August 3 Ceausescu was received by the CPSU general secretary, Leonid I. Brezhnev, at the latter's Crimean villa. Afterward the Romanian couple visited the republics of Georgia and Armenia.

Ceausescu visited Greece in March, the Philippines in April, Turkey in June, and Yugoslavia in September. After a cordial meeting with Pres. Tito of Yugoslavia, agreements were signed on extended collaboration in exploiting the hydroelectric power potential of the Danube and on further development of Romanian-Yugoslav economic relations.

On July 2 the Grand National Assembly adopted the 1976–80 development plan, under which Romania's industrial output was to rise at an annual rate of 10.2 to 11.2%. By 1980 steel production would reach about 17 million tons and generation of electric power, 76,500,000,000 kw-hr. On September 16, at Calarasi on the Danube, the construction of the fifth Romanian iron and steel complex began; by 1980 it was expected to produce about two million tons of steel annually. In Bucharest on November 21, U.S. Secretary of Commerce Elliot Richardson signed a ten-year economic agreement between the U.S. and Romania.

On November 22–24 Brezhnev paid his first visit to Romania since 1966. Replying to Ceausescu's reference to "some differences of opinion on nonessential questions," Brezhnev urged wider cooperation within the framework of Comecon and the Warsaw Pact military alliance. Previously, addressing an army command in Bucharest in October, Ceausescu had stressed that the strategic objective of Romania's armed forces was the defense of the country's frontiers. (K. M. SMOGORZEWSKI)

[972.B.3]

Romanian Literature: *see* Literature

Rubber: *see* Industrial Review

Rugby Football: *see* Football

Russia: *see* Union of Soviet Socialist Republics

Russian Literature: *see* Literature

Rowing

East Germany dominated the 1976 rowing season, winning nine Olympic titles and three silver and two bronze medals in the five other events at Montreal. The U.S.S.R. collected nine Olympic rowing medals; other nations to earn distinction were Bulgaria, Czechoslovakia, West Germany, Great Britain, Norway, and the United States. Women's events were included in the Olympic rowing program for the first time. For the third consecutive year East Germany won five of the eight men's events in the world championships (the Olympic results in Olympic years).

Oxford's crew left Cambridge far behind in their annual boat race from Putney to Mortlake.

KEYSTONE

Eighteen nations reached the men's finals, and nine of them shared the 24 medals. The Hansen brothers, Frank and Alf, won Norway's first Olympic title in double sculls after Great Britain had squeezed East Germany out of second place. The biggest surprise of the regatta, however, was the defeat in the single sculls of the 1975 world champion, Peter Michael Kolbe of West Germany, who had the gold medal plucked from his grasp in the last few strokes. Newcomer Pertti Karppinen of Finland won the event to add his country to the Olympic roll of gold medal winners in rowing for the first time.

The U.S.S.R. lost narrowly in quadruple sculls to East Germany by 1.24 sec, but then avenged this defeat by twice the time difference to take the gold medal in coxed fours. Norway edged the U.S.S.R. out of a silver medal in the coxless fours, which East Germany won by 3.80 sec. The Landvoigt twins, Bernd and Jorg, defeated the United States by nearly as much for another East German victory in coxless pairs, but the remaining finals were more closely contested. East Germany beat the U.S.S.R. by 2.83 sec in coxed pairs, but had to produce its very best to overcome New Zealand—the defending champions—and Great Britain in the eights. After New Zealand made an explosive start, the British crew attacked at 750 m, took the lead, and stayed in front even when the East Germans challenged at 1,200 m. In the last 200 m East Germany increased the pressure again and finally broke through to win by 2.53 sec with New Zealand in third place.

Twelve nations reached the women's finals, but only the Bulgarians succeeded in preventing East Germany from making a clean sweep of the six events. They narrowly foiled East Germany by 0.42 sec in coxless pairs and won by a wider margin in the double sculls. East Germany avenged these losses by defeating Bulgaria in the coxed fours and then triumphed over the U.S.S.R. in the quadruple sculls and the eights. An unexpected threat to the East German world champion Christine Scheiblich in single sculls came from the U.S. competitor Joan Lind, who narrowly missed the gold medal by 0.65 sec. Six nations shared the medals. East Germany finished with four golds and two silvers; Bulgaria took two golds and a silver; and the U.S.S.R. reached every final to finish with two silver and three bronze medals. The U.S. collected a silver and a bronze, and the two remaining bronze medals went to West Germany and Romania.

The men's lightweight and junior world championships were held at Villach, Austria, where the East German junior team failed by a fraction of a second to make a clean sweep of all eight titles. The U.S.S.R. foiled them by 0.65 sec in a thrilling eights final. The U.S.S.R. gained a silver medal in another tight finish when East Germany won the coxless fours. Only six nations were among the medal winners. In addition to East Germany and the U.S.S.R., which had a gold, three silvers, and a bronze, there were West Germany with three silvers and two bronzes, the U.S. with a silver and two bronzes, and Spain and Yugoslavia with a bronze medal each. In the lightweight events France successfully defended the coxless fours, and Raimond Haberl won the single sculls for Austria. In eights West Germany also defended its title successfully. They led all the way with the U.S. team second until caught by Great Britain in the last 500 m.

At the Henley Royal Regatta in England the course record was broken in five events and six trophies went abroad. Three U.S. eights triumphed: in the Ladies' Plate (Trinity College, Hartford, Conn.), Thames Cup (Harvard University), and the Princess Elizabeth Cup (Holy Spirit High School, Atlantic City, N.J.). The University of British Columbia scored a victory for Canada in the Stewards' Cup (coxless fours), and there was a double triumph for the Australians. They won the Silver Goblets (coxless pairs), and E. O. Hale captured the Diamond Sculls.

Oxford, with the heaviest crew yet to row in the 147-year-old University Boat Race, broke 15 records in scoring its 53rd victory over Cambridge (68 wins). Aided by exceptionally favourable weather, Oxford clocked an astonishing 16 min 58 sec to lower the $4\frac{1}{4}$-mi course record by 37 sec. (KEITH OSBORNE)

See also **Track and Field Sports:** *Special Report.*
[452.B.4.a.ii]

Rwanda

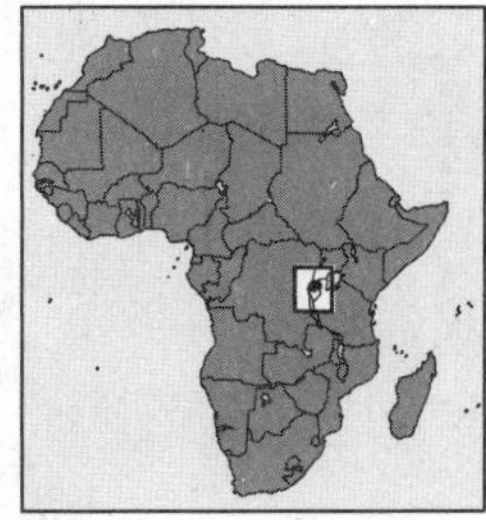

A republic in eastern Africa, and former traditional kingdom whose origins may be traced back to the 15th century, Rwanda is bordered by Zaire, Uganda, Tanzania, and Burundi. Area: 10,169 sq mi (26,338 sq km). Pop. (1976 est.): 4,321,000, including (1970) Hutu 90%; Tutsi 9%; and Twa 1%. Cap. and largest city: Kigali (pop., 1971 est., 60,000). Language (official): French and Kinyarwanda. Religion: Roman Catholic 39%; most of the remainder are animist; there are small Protestant and Muslim minorities. President in 1976, Gen. Juvénal Habyalimana.

Rwanda suffered considerably during 1976 from Uganda's quarrel with Kenya. Its industry and transport were brought to a virtual standstill when Pres. Idi Amin of Uganda refused to allow oil trucks through his country from Kenya on the only feasible route to landlocked Rwanda. An acute fuel shortage in Uganda led to the seizure in mid-July of more than 30 vehicles bound for Rwanda. President Habyalimana had flown to Kampala on April 7 to see Amin, but failed to get the blockade lifted. He was followed on July 29 by two of his senior ministers, who were likewise unsuccessful, but by early August the restrictions ended.

Rwanda's economy remained dependent on foreign

Drivers of tank trucks headed for Rwanda stand by the roadside near Mombasa in Kenya, refusing to drive through Uganda after previous oil trucks had been seized by Idi Amin's government.

CAMERAPIX/KEYSTONE

RWANDA

Education. (1974–75) Primary, pupils 386,719, teachers 7,854; secondary, pupils 8,663; vocational, pupils 1,722; teacher training, students 842; secondary, vocational, and teacher training, teachers 707; higher, students 1,023, teaching staff 206.

Finance. Monetary unit: Rwanda franc, with (Sept. 20, 1976) a par value of RwFr 92.84 to U.S. $1 (free rate of RwFr 164 = £1 sterling). Gold, SDR's, and foreign exchange (June 1976) U.S. $29,840,000. Budget (1974 actual): revenue RwFr 3,255,000,000; expenditure RwFr 3,765,000,000.

Foreign Trade. Imports (1974) RwFr 5,394,000,000; exports (1975) RwFr 3,888,000,000. Import sources: Belgium-Luxembourg 16%; Kenya 10%; Japan 9%; West Germany 9%; France 7%; Italy 7%; Iran 7%; U.S. 5%. Export destinations (1974): Kenya 65%; Belgium-Luxembourg *c.* 15%; West Germany *c.* 5%. Main exports: coffee 63%; tin 13%.

Agriculture. Production (in 000; metric tons; 1975): sorghum 135; corn (1974) *c.* 40; potatoes *c.* 110; sweet potatoes (1974) *c.* 400; cassava (1974) *c.* 370; dry beans *c.* 121; dry peas *c.* 60; pumpkins (1974) *c.* 45; bananas (1972) 1,681; coffee *c.* 20; tea *c.* 4. Livestock (in 000; July 1974): cattle *c.* 812; sheep *c.* 245; goats *c.* 630; pigs *c.* 55.

aid, though coffee production had expanded rapidly, reaching 367,000 bags in 1975. The Arab Bank sponsored a $5 million loan for rural development, and West German aid was provided for the development of unique methane gas deposits in Lake Kivu between Rwanda and Zaire. Rwanda sent representatives to the third French-sponsored African meeting in Paris and Versailles on May 10–11 to discuss joint economic problems. (MOLLY MORTIMER)

Sailing

The main sailing event of 1976 was at the Olympic Games in Canada. Many of the world's top yachtsmen concentrated their efforts on one of the six Olympic-class boats, Finn, 470, Flying Dutchman, Tempest, Soling, and Tornado catamaran.

The Finn class competitors sailed boats supplied by the host nation, but many top competitors brought their own rigs, as permitted for the first time. After a surprise first race win by Canadian outsider Sanford Riley, the contest lay between John Bertrand of Australia, Jochen Shumann of East Germany, and Andrey Balashov of the U.S.S.R. Shumann, with a strong first, second, and third in the last three races, made certain of the gold medal from Balashov with Bertrand finishing third.

Sabah:
see Malaysia

The 470 class, racing for the first time, produced more problems for the measurers than all the rest of the classes put together. Then, once racing started, there were many protests, often against the committee. The racing was, however, hard and closely contested. Frank Hübner of West Germany put together a convincing series, winning three of the races, with Antonio Gorostegui of Spain taking the silver medal and Ian Brown of Australia gaining the bronze.

The Flying Dutchman class started with Rodney Pattisson looking ready to take his third gold medal in succession, but the Diesch brothers from West Germany were not lagging far behind. Then, in the last two races, the Diesches added two steady fifth places, while Pattisson could only manage 12th and 11th and only just held off Reinaldo Conrad from Brazil, who took the bronze medal.

In the Tempest class John Albrechtson and Ingvar Hansson from Sweden won one of the clearest gold medals, with three firsts, two seconds, and a fourth. They beat the defending champion, Valentin Mankin of the U.S.S.R., by 16 points, with U.S. 12-m helmsman Dennis Conner taking the bronze medal.

The Soling class had attracted many gold medal winners from earlier Olympics. None of them, however, was able to win medals. The battle for supremacy was between Boris Budnikov from the U.S.S.R., who had to settle for fourth place; Dieter Below, the European champion from East Germany, who won the bronze medal; John Kolius of the U.S., who took the silver; and Danish sailmaker Poul Jensen, who won first place by less than a point.

The Tornado catamaran class, racing for the first time in an Olympics, had an entry of only 14 countries but an outstanding winner. The British entry, Reg White and his brother-in-law crew John Osborn, crossed the finish line first in four of the seven races and did not even need to start in the last race. Meanwhile, David McFaull from the U.S. and Jorg Spengler of West Germany fought a close series for

Spinnaker flying, the winner, "Great Britain II," of the Round-the-World Clipper Race passes under London's Tower Bridge in March.

FINANCIAL TIMES, LONDON

Eric Tabarly's Pen Duick VI (left) took first place in the singlehanded transatlantic race from Plymouth, England, to Newport, R.I., in June. The 73-foot ketch made the crossing in 23 days 20 hours after losing its electrical system in a storm.

the silver and bronze medals, respectively. (*See also* TRACK AND FIELD SPORTS: *Special Report.*)

In the Ton Cup events, an eighth-ton 16.3 and mini-ton 16 series were included. Only nine boats turned out for the eighth-ton series, won by the Dutch entry "Ocean II," a conventional-looking craft. The mini-ton series, however, was won by a real rule-cheater of almost quarter-ton proportions but sporting an enormous "cat"-rig mainsail; in the light-wind series, "L'Effraie" swept to victory, but if it had been windy things could have been very different. For the second year in succession, the Quarter-Ton Cup, sailed in the U.S., went to New Zealand, to "Magic Bus," a new design from Paul Whiting. In the half-ton event sailed off Trieste in the Adriatic Sea, Harold Cudmore from Ireland, who had earlier swept the opposition aside at Cowes, Isle of Wight, in his new Ron Holland-designed "Silver Shamrock," won a good series from "Perception" (E. Griener, Italy) and "Ziggurat" (P. Ferri, Italy). The three-quarter tonners had a close series, racing from Plymouth, England, with the amateur, owner-built, and owner-designed "Finn Fire," sailed by British sailmaker and champion yachtsman Bruce Banks, winning by one-eighth of a point from Richard Bagnall's "Golden Delight," a modified Nicholson 33. The one-ton event reestablished Britton Chance, a leading U.S. designer. His "Resolute Salmon" was a pure centreboarder with all the ballast inside the hull. The two-ton series went to the U.S. yacht "Williwaw," sailed by sailmaker Eckart Wagner from West Germany.

The major interest in the 1976 transatlantic race was the battle of the French giants "Pen Duick VI" and "Club Mediterranée," sailed by two of France's most experienced oceangoing yachtsmen, Eric Tabarly (*see* BIOGRAPHY) and Alain Colas. The early violent Atlantic storms soon took their toll among the competitors, mostly in masts and sails. "Club Mediterranée" lost most of its sails and had to limp into Halifax, Nova Scotia, costing it any chance of victory. The storms were followed by light winds and thick fog off the east coast of America, which masked the yachts over the last part of the course. After anxious days of waiting, Tabarly in "Pen Duick VI" appeared out of the gloom, winning the race again, although in a different boat. (ADRIAN JARDINE)

[452.B.4.a.ii]

World Class Boat Champions

Class	Winner	Country
Finn	C. Law	U.K.
Hornet	J. Stavenhuiter	The Netherlands
Optimist	H. Wallen	Sweden
Tornado	R. White	U.K.
505	F. Tolhurst	Australia
Star	J. Allsopp	U.S.
Enterprise	S. Robertson	U.K.
International Moths	T. Cansey	U.S.
Laser	J. Bertrand	Australia
Mirror Dinghy	J. Partridge	U.K.
420	C. Tanner	U.S.
O. K.	P. Kirketerp	Denmark

San Marino

A small republic, San Marino is an enclave in northeastern Italy, 5 mi SW of Rimini. Area: 24 sq mi (61 sq km). Pop. (1976 est.): 19,900. Cap. and largest city: San Marino (metro. pop., 1976 est., 4,600). Language: Italian. Religion: Roman Catholic. The country is governed by two *capitani reggenti,* or co-regents, appointed every six months by a Grand and General Council. Executive power rests with two secretaries of state: foreign and political affairs and internal affairs. In 1976 the positions were filled, respectively, by Gian Luigi Berti and Giuseppe Lonfernini until March 11 and, from that time, by Giancarlo Ghironzi and Clara Boscaglia.

Sanmarinese politics in 1976 resembled that of Italy, which surrounds the "serene republic." As in Italy, Christian Democrats were the strongest and the Communists the second strongest party. From 1957 the Christian Democrats had ruled San Marino in coalition with Social Democrats. In January 1973, 11 Social Democrats left the coalition over a question of economic policy and were replaced by seven Socialists and the only member of the tiny but resoundingly named Movimento per la Difesa della Libertà Costituzionale (Movement for the Defense of Constitutional Liberty). As the Christian Democrats then had 27 seats in the 60-member Grand and General Council, the coalition was assured until the next general election.

Salvador, El:
see El Salvador

Salvation Army:
see Religion

Samoa:
see Dependent States; Western Samoa

SAN MARINO
Education. (1974–75) Primary, pupils 1,698, teachers 167; secondary, pupils 1,140, teachers 96.
Finance. Monetary unit: Italian lira, with (Sept. 20, 1976) a free rate of 843 lire to U.S. $1 (1,453 lire = £1 sterling); local coins are issued. Budget (1975 est.) balanced at 23,918,000,000 lire. Tourism (1974) 2,202,000 visitors.

Though the Christian Democrats lost two seats in September 1974, the coalition was maintained, but in November 1975 the Socialists withdrew from it. In March 1976 Primo Bugli and Virgillio Cardelli succeeded Giovannito Marcucci and Giuseppe Della Balda as co-regents. The Christian Democratic-Socialist coalition was restored; Giancarlo Ghironzi (Christian Democrat) succeeded Gian Luigi Berti as secretary of state for foreign and political affairs, while Clara Boscaglia (also Christian Democrat) took over internal affairs from Giuseppe Lonfernini. Rémy Giacomini (Socialist) retained the portfolio for budget and finance. (K. M. SMOGORZEWSKI)

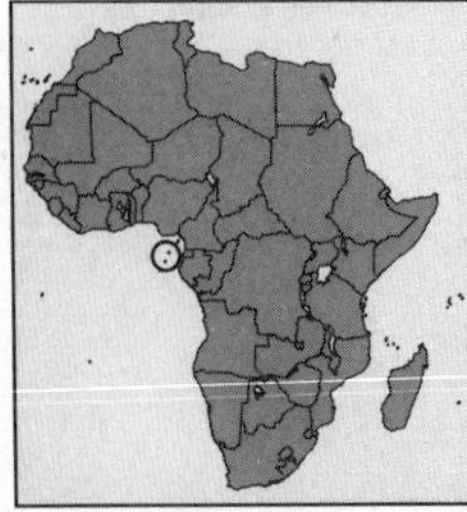

São Tomé and Príncipe

An independent African state, the Democratic Republic of São Tomé and Príncipe comprises two main islands and several smaller islets that straddle the Equator in the Gulf of Guinea, off the west coast of Africa. Area: 372 sq mi (964 sq km), of which São Tomé, the larger island, comprises 330 sq mi (854 sq km). Pop. (1975 est.): 80,000. Cap. and largest city: São Tomé (pop., 1970, 17,400). Language: Portuguese. Religion: mainly Roman Catholic. President in 1976, Manuel Pinto da Costa; premier, Miguel Trovoada.

On Dec. 11, 1975, President da Costa appointed a new Cabinet, but he retained a number of portfolios in his own hands. Miguel Trovoada remained premier but surrendered the ministries of foreign affairs (to L. M. d'Alva) and defense (to the president) to do so. In the same month the president visited China, where he signed an agreement establishing trade and economic and technical cooperation between the two countries. Moving on to North Korea, he signed a further agreement, which promised North Korean aid for São Tomé. Earlier, in October 1975, diplomatic relations had been established with another Far Eastern country, Mongolia, while by contrast it had been reported in August 1975 that São Tomé had forbidden South African Airways to use the country's airspace. In March 1976 São Tomé joined the World Health Organization. (KENNETH INGHAM)

SÃO TOMÉ AND PRÍNCIPE
Education. (1972–73) Primary, pupils 10,015, teachers 303; secondary, pupils 2,114, teachers 86; vocational, pupils 256, teachers 30.
Finance and Trade. Monetary unit: Portuguese escudo, with (Sept. 20, 1976) a free rate of 31.10 escudos to U.S. $1 (53.60 escudos = £1 sterling). Budget (1972 actual): revenue 171,138,000 escudos; expenditure 170,820,000 escudos. Foreign trade (1973): imports 247,259,000 escudos; exports 322,-591,000 escudos. Import sources: Portugal 47%; Angola 23%; The Netherlands 6%; France 5%. Export destinations: Portugal 36%; The Netherlands 32%; West Germany 12%; U.S. 8%. Main exports: cocoa 87%; copra 8%.
Agriculture. Production (in 000; metric tons; 1975): cocoa *c.* 10; copra *c.* 6; bananas *c.* 2; palm kernels *c.* 2; palm oil *c.* 1. Livestock (in 000; 1974): cattle *c.* 4; pigs *c.* 3; sheep *c.* 2; goats *c.* 1.

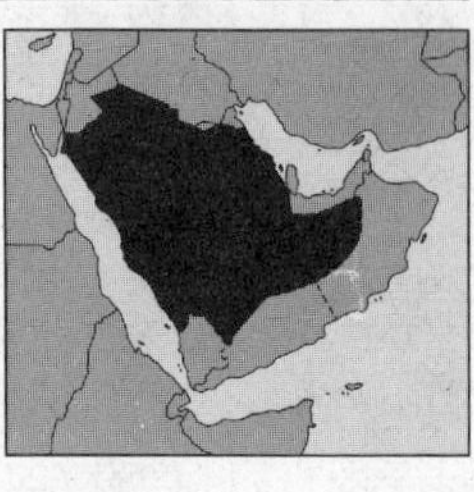

Saudi Arabia

A monarchy occupying four-fifths of the Arabian Peninsula, Saudi Arabia has an area of 865,000 sq mi (2,240,000 sq km). Pop. (1974 census): 7,012,600. Cap. and largest city: Riyadh (pop., 1974 census, 660,800). Language: Arabic. Religion: Muslim. King and prime minister in 1976, Khalid.

In 1976 Saudi Arabia enhanced its position as one of the leading Arab states and as a major international financial power.

Foreign Affairs. Saudi Arabia attempted with some success to mediate in inter-Arab disputes, especially that between Egypt and Syria arising out of Egypt's second Sinai agreement with Israel of 1975 and Syria's role in the Lebanese civil war. Egyptian and Syrian leaders paid several visits to Saudi Arabia during the year. In the spring the Saudi government tried to convene a "reconciliation summit" in Riyadh to include the heads of state of Egypt, Syria, and Jordan and the chairman of the Palestine Liberation Organization, Yasir Arafat. When this failed, Saudi Arabia pursued its efforts in cooperation with Kuwait, and on June 23 and 24 a meeting was finally held in Riyadh between the Egyptian and Syrian prime ministers in the presence of the Saudi first deputy prime minister, Crown Prince Fahd, and the Kuwaiti foreign minister. Egypt and Syria were declared to have settled their differences, but the two governments continued to

SAUDI ARABIA
Education. (1973–74) Primary, pupils 577,734, teachers 26,384; secondary, pupils 148,520, teachers 7,831; vocational, pupils 2,576, teachers 333; teacher training, students 13,932, teachers 953; higher, students 17,253, teaching staff 1,454.
Finance. Monetary unit: riyal, with (Sept. 20, 1976) a free rate of 3.52 riyals to U.S. $1 (6.07 riyals = £1 sterling). Gold, SDR's, and foreign exchange (June 1976) U.S. $22,020,000,000. Budget (1974–75 est.): revenue 98,247,000,000 riyals; expenditure 45,743,000,000 riyals (excluding amounts allocated under the second development plan, 1975–80). Gross national product (1973–74) 82,551,000,000 riyals. Money supply (Dec. 1975) 13,756,000,000 riyals. Cost of living (1970 = 100; 1st quarter 1976) 249.
Foreign Trade. (1975) Imports (fob) 23,020,000,-000 riyals; exports 97,380,000,000 riyals. Import sources (1973): U.S. 19%; Japan 15%; Lebanon 12%; U.K. 7%; West Germany 5%. Export destinations (1973): Japan 15%; Italy 10%; The Netherlands 9%; France 9%; U.K. 8%. Main exports: crude oil 93%; petroleum products 7%.
Transport and Communications. Roads (1974) 34,396 km (including 70 km expressways). Motor vehicles in use (1974): passenger 134,160; commercial 114,930. Railways: (1974) 612 km; traffic (1973) 61 million passenger-km, freight 62 million net ton-km. Air traffic (1974): 1,268,000,000 passenger-km; freight 37.4 million net ton-km. Shipping (1975): merchant vessels 100 gross tons and over 55; gross tonnage 180,246. Telephones (Jan. 1974) 85,000. Radio receivers (Dec. 1971) 87,000. Television receivers (Dec. 1974) 120,000.
Agriculture. Production (in 000; metric tons; 1975): millet *c.* 150; sorghum *c.* 200; wheat (1974) *c.* 175; barley (1974) *c.* 22; tomatoes *c.* 120; onions (1974) *c.* 37; grapes (1974) *c.* 26; dates (1974) *c.* 260. Livestock (in 000; 1974): cattle *c.* 310; sheep *c.* 3,030; goats *c.* 1,700; camels *c.* 590; asses *c.* 146; poultry *c.* 8,800.
Industry. Production (in 000; metric tons; 1974): petroleum products 28,161; crude oil (1975) 351,761; natural gas (cu m) 3,100,000; electricity (excluding most industrial production; kw-hr) 1,474,000; cement (1973) 964.

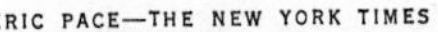
ERIC PACE—THE NEW YORK TIMES

The modern and the traditional vie with each other in Saudi Arabia, where the construction industry is booming. Photo shows a building site in Jidda.

criticize each other, and it was not until December, when the presidents of Egypt and Syria, at a meeting in Cairo, agreed to coordinate their political and military policies and examine the possibility of future union, that the reconciliation appeared to have been completed. Pres. Anwar as-Sadat of Egypt visited Saudi Arabia in February and again in June and August for talks with King Khalid. Saudi-Egyptian relations remained close, although there were some indications that President Sadat was disappointed with the $300 million in immediate aid promised by Saudi Arabia, less than it had provided before the 1975 Sinai agreement.

In Arabia and the Persian Gulf area, Saudi Arabia acted as a major power. In March King Khalid toured five of the Arab states of the Gulf and declared close identity of views with all their rulers; he promised $350 million in aid to Bahrain. The king also paid a friendly visit to Iran on May 24–27. Very close cooperation continued with the government of the Yemen Arab Republic (Yemen [San'a']), and the possibility of a merger of the two countries was even raised. Throughout the year there were frequent exchanges of visits of senior ministers and army officers between the two countries.

A shift in policy culminated in Saudi Arabia's recognition of the left-wing regime in the People's Democratic Republic of Yemen (South Yemen), with which it had been in constant dispute and on occasion at war since 1967. Diplomatic relations were established on March 9 "on a basis of good neighbourliness and noninterference in the internal affairs of each other" with the declared aim of "guaranteeing the security and stability of the Arabian peninsula and the interests of the Arab nation." One Saudi objective was to effect a reconciliation between Sultan Qabus of Oman and South Yemen, which had been supplying the Omani rebels in Dhofar; an Omani-South Yemen ceasefire was declared on March 11. Saudi Arabia was probably concerned with the continuing presence of Iranian troops in Oman and hoped this would enable them to be withdrawn. A senior South Yemen delegation visited Riyadh in early May, after the Saudis agreed to provide the hard-pressed South Yemen government with $100 million in aid.

In February Saudi Arabia and the government of Iraq agreed to have the borders between the two countries demarcated by an international company. Saudi Arabia contributed to the Arab League peacekeeping force in Lebanon; its contingent arrived there on July 1. Saudi efforts were concentrated on bringing the fighting to an end, and it voiced no public criticism of the various participants in the Lebanese civil war or of the Syrian intervention. On July 17–19 King Khalid held a meeting in Riyadh with President Sadat and Pres. Gaafar Nimeiry of Sudan to discuss the Lebanese civil war and the aftermath of the attempted coup in Sudan, led by the Sudanese ex-premier Sadik al-Mahdi with Libyan support. Saudi Arabia had formerly had close ties with the Mahdists, and the purpose of the meeting was to reconcile President Nimeiry with Saudi Arabia and form a common front against Col. Muammar al-Qaddafi's Libya; however, Saudi Arabia later strongly denied that a tripartite anti-Libyan military alliance had been formed.

In the oil sector, Saudi policy continued to be forcefully in favour of holding down price increases. The Saudi oil minister, Sheikh Ahmad Zaki Yamani, declared himself delighted with the result of the Organization of Petroleum Exporting Countries (OPEC) meeting in Bali, Indon., in May, where he successfully held the line against price rises, and at the December OPEC meeting in Qatar the Saudis broke the organization's united front by opting (together with the United Arab Emirates) for a 5% price rise in 1977 while the remaining members decided on a 15% rise in two stages. Sheikh Yamani warned, however, that any decision on increasing oil production was dependent on Western "appreciation" of the Saudis' restraint. Saudi oil production, with a potential capacity of 12 million bbl a day, had been held to an average of some 6 million bbl a day in the autumn of 1975. It rose to 7.1 million bbl a day in February 1976, however, and to 8,750,000 bbl a day in July, only slightly below the record of October 1974. Although average output in 1975 was 16.8% below 1974, revenues of nearly $25.7 billion represented a 13.7% increase. It was revealed during the year that in 1975 Aramco had discovered three huge new oil fields with estimated reserves of 7,000,000,000 bbl.

Negotiations took place during the year for a Saudi takeover of the remaining 40% share in Aramco owned by four U.S. companies. Saudi terms were reported to be compensation of the companies for the net book value of their assets (estimated by the companies at $3 billion) and a 12 U.S. cents a barrel

CENTRAL PRESS/PICTORIAL PARADE

To get around congestion in Saudi Arabian ports, the Cunard shipping company is using vessels that permit cargo containers to be rolled on and off by truck.

discount on oil bought by the companies from their former concession area. Prince Fahd said in a press interview in July that the companies would be allowed to buy 75% of production in the first five years of the agreement and 60% in the next five years, and that Saudi Arabia would consider expanding into oil marketing, refining, and distribution outside its own borders when the 100% takeover had been completed.

Domestic Affairs and the Economy. In the 1976–77 provisional budget announced in June, expenditure, at $31.4 billion, was about the same as for 1975–76; oil income accounted for 88% of revenues. About 67% was earmarked for development and 29% for defense—an increase of more than 30% over the previous year's allocation. Saudi reserves continued to increase, rising by $1.7 billion to $24.6 billion between the end of 1975 and March. In 1976 Saudi Arabia made substantial loans or grants to a number of Arab, Islamic, and third world countries, and to various international aid funds. However, the planning minister said in August that foreign aid, which had been running at $4 billion a year, had reached its peak.

There were also signs that the $142 billion five-year development plan launched in 1975 was encountering difficulties. The program was plagued by shortages of labour and housing, together with inflation estimated at 50% a year caused by rapidly increasing money incomes. The government tried to grapple with these problems in various ways, including crash programs to build houses and the allocation of about $2 billion in contracts for the desalination of seawater for urban dwellings and the electrification of all houses in the country. A campaign against profiteers was launched, a state consumer company was set up, and plans were made for the importation of workers from Morocco, Pakistan, and elsewhere. The most serious hindrance to development was port congestion. Dutch, West German, and Greek firms won a $1 billion contract to double Dammam port's capacity by 1980, and a similar contract went to Swedish, French, and Greek firms for the expansion of Jidda.

In March King Khalid inaugurated work on a new Riyadh University campus. The government publicly declared that it hoped to be host to the 1984 Olympics and announced plans to spend $440 million on building sports stadia in Riyadh, Jidda, Dammam, and Mecca. The expenditure of about $50 million on improving Saudi football (soccer) was also announced, and a former professional British football star, Jimmy Hill, was engaged to assist in the program.

A major aim of Saudi policy in 1976 was to purchase arms to strengthen its 40,000-man Army and 10,000-man Air Force with modern equipment. In April it was announced that Saudi Arabia planned to spend $16 billion to reequip its forces over ten years. Its main source was the U.S., but opposition in the U.S. Congress to massive arms sales to Saudi Arabia raised constant difficulties. The Saudis were dissuaded by the U.S. Department of Defense from buying F-16 fighters and other large aircraft in favour of building up its force of less sophisticated F-5s. Saudi Arabia placed a $1,140,000,000 order with a U.S. company, the Raytheon Corp., for Hawk antiaircraft missiles and construction and training. However, an order for 1,900 Sidewinder air-to-air missiles was opposed by some U.S. senators on the ground that it was excessive.

A further move by Congress to halt the sale of 650 air-to-ground Maverick missiles in late September provoked a crisis in U.S.-Saudi relations, which was only averted by vigorous U.S. administration lobbying. In a related development, the U.S. administration acted to block a move to forbid U.S. companies to give information to the Arab states relative to the boycott of Israel. The Saudi government had said that such a provision ran counter to Saudi laws and might make it impossible for U.S. firms to buy Saudi crude oil. The entire question of the boycott became an issue in the U.S. presidential campaign. (PETER MANSFIELD)

[978.B.4.a]

Scandinavian Literature: *see* Literature

Schools: *see* Education

Scotland: *see* United Kingdom

Scuba Diving: *see* Water Sports

Sculpture: *see* Art and Art Exhibitions; Art Sales; Museums

Securities: *see* Stock Exchanges

Seismology: *see* Earth Sciences

Serbian Literature: *see* Literature

Seventh-day Adventist Church: *see* Religion

Senegal

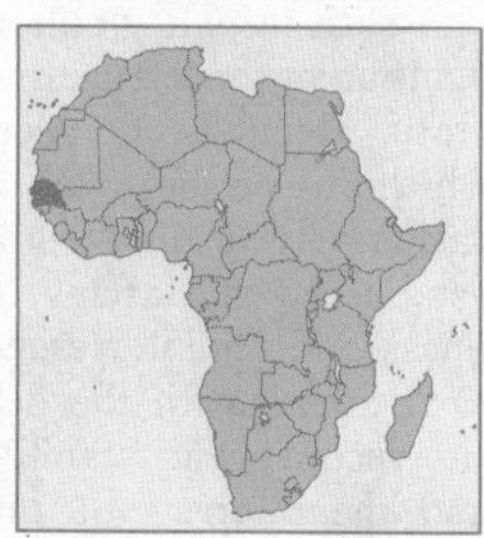

A republic of northwestern Africa, Senegal is bounded by Mauritania, Mali, Guinea, and Guinea-Bissau, and by the Atlantic Ocean. The independent nation of The Gambia forms an enclave within the country. Area: 75,955 sq mi (196,722 sq km). Pop. (1976 prelim.): 5,085,400. Cap. and largest city: Dakar (pop., 1976 prelim., 798,800). Language: French (official); Wolof; Serer; other tribal dialects. Religion: Muslim 90%; Christian 6%. President in 1976, Léopold Sédar Senghor; premier, Abdou Diouf.

On March 17, 1976, Senegal's National Assembly passed a constitutional amendment providing for a three-party system, and in August the African Independence Party, which had been dissolved in 1960, was reorganized as the third legal party, alongside the governing Senegalese Progressive Union (renamed

ALAIN NOGUES—SYGMA

The Empress Farah of Iran, on a tour of Senegal in February, visited a joint Senegalese-Iranian industrial project and dined with Pres. Léopold Senghor.

the Socialist Party in December) and the Senegalese Democratic Party. Another amendment, passed April 1, enabled the president to seek election for an indefinite number of terms (formerly limited to two) and set up a procedure by which the premier would succeed to the presidency, in case the office became vacant, and serve until the end of the current term. On April 3 President Senghor signed an amnesty law that allowed all remaining political prisoners to be released. At celebrations of Senghor's 70th birthday in October the World Health Organization announced the establishment at Dakar of an African Health Fund, to be named after him.

Relations with Guinea were again strained when, in July, Pres. Sékou Touré accused Senegal of conspiring against his regime. But tension between Senegal and Nigeria, because of the latter's decision to open the 1977 World Black and African Festival of Arts and Culture to the Arab countries, was finally eased. Expanding Senegal's circle of friends across the world, Senghor visited the Caribbean in February and Iran in April; he also maintained good relations with France. (PHILIPPE DECRAENE)

[978.E.4.b.ii]

SENEGAL

Education. (1972–73) Primary, pupils 283,276, teachers 6,294; secondary, pupils 59,039, teachers 2,198; vocational and teacher training, pupils 7,408, teachers 920; higher, students (1973–74) 7,773, teaching staff (university only; 1970–71) 237.

Finance and Trade. Monetary unit: CFA franc, with (Sept. 20, 1976) a parity of CFA Fr 50 to the French franc (free rate of CFA Fr 245.90 = U.S. $1; CFA Fr 423.62 = £1 sterling). Budget (1976 est.) balanced at CFA Fr 96 billion. Foreign trade (1975): imports CFA Fr 119,620,000,000; exports CFA Fr 96,660,000,000. Import sources (1974): France 41%; West Germany 6%; U.S. 6%; Nigeria 6%. Export destinations (1974): France 50%; The Netherlands 7%; U.K. 6%; Ivory Coast 6%; Mauritania 5%. Main exports (1974): phosphates 28%; peanut oil 22%; fish and products 7%; peanut oil cake 7%.

Seychelles

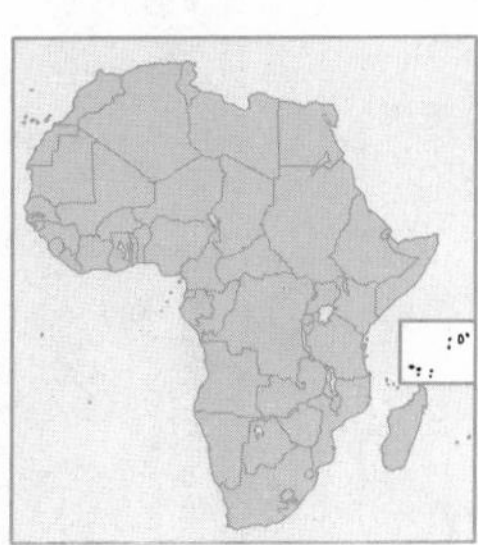

A republic in the Indian Ocean consisting of 89 islands, Seychelles lies 900 mi (1,450 km) from the coast of East Africa. Area: 171 sq mi (443 sq km), of which 64 sq mi (166 sq km) includes the islands of Farquhar, Desroches, and Aldabra. Pop. (1976 est.): 60,000, including Creole 94%, French 5%, English 1%. Cap. Victoria, on Mahé (pop., 1972 est., 14,500). Language: English and French are official, creole patois is also spoken. Religion: Roman Catholic 91%, Anglican 8%. President in 1976, James R. Mancham; prime minister, Albert René.

At midnight on June 28–29 Seychelles became an independent republic and the 36th member of the Commonwealth of Nations. Farquhar, Desroches, and Aldabra islands were returned to Seychelles on independence day, with U.S. and U.K. agreement. The government was a temporary coalition of divergent parties, with Prime Minister René of the Seychelles People's United Party looking to left-wing and African support and President Mancham and his Seychelles Democratic Party to Britain, France (with which a cultural, scientific, and technical agreement was signed in Paris on July 15), and the local Chinese and Indian merchants. Good relations with moderate Kenya were the cornerstone of Mancham's policy, which, though officially nonaligned, looked to U.S. support. Though officially anti-apartheid, Seychelles depended upon South African tourism and imports. Kenya became its chief trading partner, but Britain supported the faltering economy. Inflation and poor market prospects for Seychelles products had produced a soaring trade deficit, with exports less than a quarter of imports in value. British aid of over £15 million in the five previous years was increased by £10 million over a period of two years from independence, with additional budgetary help of £1.7 million spread over four years. The July summit conference of the Organization of African Unity in Mauritius admitted Seychelles as the organization's 48th member. (MOLLY MORTIMER)

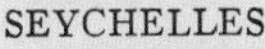

SEYCHELLES

Education. (1976) Primary, pupils 10,206, teachers 435; secondary, pupils 3,794, teachers 172; vocational, pupils 242, teachers 29; higher, students 142, teaching staff 13.

Finance and Trade. Monetary unit: Seychelles rupee, with (Sept. 20, 1976) a free rate of SRs 7.74 to U.S. $1 (official rate of SRs 13.33 = £1 sterling). Budget (1975 est.): revenue SRs 74.6 million; expenditure SRs 74.2 million. Foreign trade (1974): imports SRs 160,490,000; exports SRs 39,131,000. Import sources: U.K. 29%; Kenya 20%; South Africa 10%; Singapore 5%; Australia 5%. Export destinations: ship and aircraft bunkers 31%; Pakistan 13%; U.S. 10%; France 9%. Main exports: fuels 31%; copra 25%; cinnamon bark 18%. Tourism (1973) 19,500 visitors.

Ships and Shipping: *see* Industrial Review; Transportation

Shipwrecks: *see* Disasters

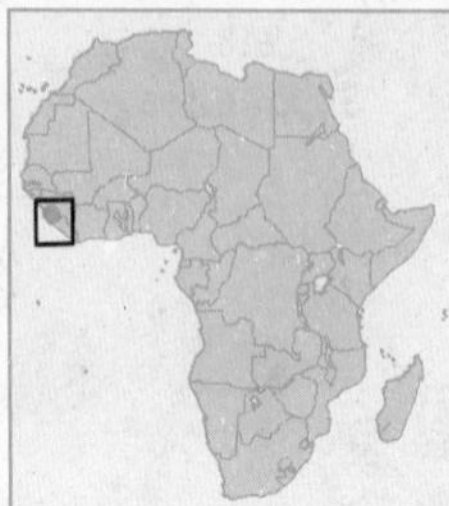

Sierra Leone

A republic within the Commonwealth of Nations, Sierra Leone is a West African state on the Atlantic coast between Guinea and Liberia. Area: 27,925 sq mi (72,325 sq km). Pop. (1974): 3,002,400, including (1963) Mende and Temne tribes 60.7%; other tribes 38.9%; non-African 0.4%. Cap. and largest city: Freetown (pop., 1974, 274,000). Language: English (official); tribal dialects. Religion: animist 66%; Muslim 28%; Christian 6%. President in 1976, Siaka Stevens; prime minister, Christian A. Kamara-Taylor.

Siaka Stevens was reelected as president in March 1976. Speaking at the July opening of Parliament, he emphasized the serious state of the economy, particularly the difficulties caused by the collapse of the Delco iron ore mines in October 1975. Diversity and self-sufficiency in agriculture must be increased, he said; on the credit side, European Economic Community aid under the Lomé Convention would assist agricultural projects over the next four years, and the opening of the Mano River bridge with Liberia had stimulated communication. Illicit diamond buying—made easier by the Mano bridge—remained a serious problem. Smuggling likewise accounted for nearly 80% of cigarette imports. The Fullah were the main smugglers, followed by Lebanese immigrants, who also handled most of the licit trade. The increase of Lebanese in Sierra Leone led to tightening of regulations and some danger of racial feeling as economic difficulties grew.

Finance Minister Sorie I. Koroma's July budget put the country at a "low ebb," with inflation soaring, debt servicing eating up over 18% of export earnings, and a trade deficit of 33 million leones. For 1976–77 estimated recurrent expenditure stood at 157 million leones and revenue at 104 million leones. Koroma cast a severe eye at public corporations, which after 12 years did not yet pay their way. The abrasive and honest budget speech was welcomed at home as a demand for discipline and productivity and abroad as a reasonable call for help in a situation not entirely the country's fault. (MOLLY MORTIMER)

[978.E.4.b.ii]

SIERRA LEONE

Education. (1971–72) Primary, pupils 176,658, teachers 5,599; secondary, pupils 35,507, teachers 1,706; vocational, pupils 1,156, teachers 68; teacher training, students 887, teachers 97; higher (1973–74), students 1,476, teaching staff 268.

Finance and Trade. Monetary unit: leone, with (Sept. 20, 1976) a free value of 1.16 leones to U.S. $1 (par value of 2 leones = £1 sterling). Budget (1975–76 est.): revenue 98.4 million leones; expenditure 105.8 million leones. Foreign trade (1975): imports 167,880,000 leones; exports 116,470,000 leones. Import sources (1974): U.K. 21%; Japan 10%; Nigeria 8%; West Germany 7%; Pakistan 5%; France 5%; China 5%. Export destinations (1974): U.K. 61%; The Netherlands 15%; U.S. 6%; Japan 5%. Main exports: diamonds 54%; iron ore 11%.

Agriculture. Production (in 000; metric tons; 1975): rice *c.* 500; cassava (1974) *c.* 83; palm kernels *c.* 52; palm oil *c.* 55; coffee *c.* 3; cocoa *c.* 7; fish catch (1974) 51. Livestock (in 000; 1974): cattle *c.* 280; sheep *c.* 64; goats *c.* 168; pigs *c.* 34; chickens *c.* 3,150.

Industry. Production (in 000; metric tons; 1974): iron ore (metal content) 1,502; bauxite 650; petroleum products *c.* 350; diamonds (metric carats) *c.* 1,670; electricity (kw-hr) 219,000.

Singapore

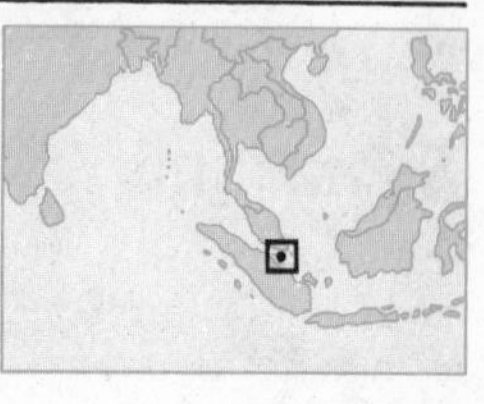

Singapore, a republic within the Commonwealth of Nations, occupies a group of islands, the largest of which is Singapore, at the southern extremity of the Malay Peninsula. Area: 230 sq mi (597 sq km). Pop. (1976 est.): 2,278,200, including 76% Chinese, 15% Malays, and 7% Indians. Language: official languages are English, Malay, Mandarin Chinese, and Tamil. Religion: Malays are Muslim; Chinese, mainly Buddhist; Indians, mainly Hindu. President in 1976, Benjamin Henry Sheares; prime minister, Lee Kuan Yew.

In February 1976 Amnesty International's imputations of violations of human rights in Singapore provoked an attempt to expel the ruling People's Action Party (PAP) from the (democratic) Socialist International. The PAP preempted expulsion by resigning from the International. Arrests in January were alleged to have broken up a network of Communist cells with links in Malaysia, Thailand, and Australia. Hussein Jahidin, editor of the Malay language newspaper *Berita Harian,* was arrested in June together with the former assistant editor, Azmi Mahmud. Hussein admitted in a televised confession that he had tried to break the religious faith of local Malays so as to turn them toward Communism under the instigation of Abdul Samad Ismail, managing editor of the *New Straits Times,* who was also detained.

The government of Singapore applied in June for the extradition from the U.K. of the financier Jim Slater (*see* BIOGRAPHY) and four former Slater Walker Securities executives in order that they could stand trial on charges relating to their involvement in the affairs of the Singapore company Haw Par Brothers International. (MICHAEL LEIFER)

[976.B.2]

SINGAPORE

Education. (1975) Primary, pupils 328,401, teachers 11,570; secondary, pupils 176,224, teachers 7,745; vocational, pupils 7,140, teachers 737; teacher training, students 685, teachers 100; higher, students 13,965; teaching staff 970.

Finance. Monetary unit: Singapore dollar, with (Sept. 20, 1976) a free rate of Sing$2.45 to U.S. $1 (Sing$4.23 = £1 sterling). Gold, SDR's, and foreign exchange (April 1976) U.S. $3,167,000,000. Budget (1975–76 est.): revenue Sing$2,647,000,000; expenditure Sing$2,646,000,000. Gross national product (1975) Sing$13,430,000,000. Money supply (April 1976) Sing$3,667,000,000. Cost of living (1970 = 100; June 1976) 161.

Foreign Trade. (1975) Imports Sing$19,269,000,000; exports Sing$12,758,000,000. Import sources: Japan 17%; U.S. 16%; Malaysia 12%; Saudi Arabia 9%; Iran 5%; U.K. 5%. Export destinations: Malaysia 17%; U.S. 14%; Japan 9%; Hong Kong 7%; Australia 5%. Main exports: petroleum products 27%; machinery 19%; rubber 10%; food 7%. Tourism (1974): visitors 1,234,000; gross receipts U.S. $310 million.

Transport and Communications. Roads (1973) 2,139 km. Motor vehicles in use (1974): passenger 149,000; commercial (including buses) 41,200. Railways (1973) 39 km (for traffic: *see* MALAYSIA). Air traffic (1975): 5,104,000,000 passenger-km; freight 156,280,000 net ton-km. Shipping (1975): merchant vessels 100 gross tons and over 610; gross tonnage 3,891,902. Shipping traffic (1975): goods loaded 19,374,000 metric tons, unloaded 33,563,000 metric tons. Telephones (Dec. 1974) 280,280. Radio licenses (Dec. 1973) 303,000. Television licenses (Dec. 1973) 231,000.

Social and Welfare Services

In many countries 1976 was a difficult year for social and welfare services. The immediate cause for concern was the impending or existing financial imbalance of many national social security programs.

European Developments. Social security spending continued to rise faster than national income in many countries, and was consuming an increasing share of the national product. For example, expenditure on social security as a percentage of gross national product (GNP) was 13.8% in The Netherlands in 1962 but had nearly doubled to 26.3% in 1975; for Italy, corresponding figures were 14.3 and 23%.

Deficits emerged or were imminent in several social security funds. In France, for example, the overall deficit of the social security system had reached Fr 4 billion by 1976, and in West Germany a deficit appeared at the end of 1976, which, it was predicted, would rise to DM 25 billion by December 1977.

The explanation for these deficits is complex. Over a number of years increases in earnings considerably exceeded the increases in living costs. As earnings rose, income from contributions increased. The result was the accumulation of substantial surpluses in the accounts of several social security systems.

This trend was further accelerated by high rates of inflation, which caused social security receipts to go up quickly along with increases in wages and salaries. In the early 1970s the U.S. Social Security Advisory Council issued a warning that the U.S. program was overfinanced and would produce accumulations of reserves the council deemed both "unnecessary and undesirable." As in several other countries, this assessment led to important liberalizations in the pension schemes, including the extension and improvement of automatic adjustment procedures, early retirement provisions, and raising of minimum pensions.

Assumptions about the overfinancing of social security programs proved to be short-lived, however, and by 1976 it was clear that any existing surpluses would soon disappear. The economic recession of the 1970s had radically altered the situation. High rates of unemployment led to increased expenditure on unemployment benefits and to declining social insurance contributions. In addition, the effect of the program liberalizations that had been made was soon felt in terms of rising costs.

The emerging volume of social security expenditures would have to be matched by a corresponding increase in income. This was complicated by two main factors, the indexation of benefits and demographic trends.

Increasingly, social security benefits, particularly pensions, were automatically adjusted to changes in price or wage levels. This was, of course, a device to ensure that pensions maintained their real value insofar as they were tied to prices and that they were kept in line with improvements in wages if they were linked with the wage index. With these methods of adjustment, pensioners were spared declining standards of living in times of inflation, but at the same time the pension bill rose considerably.

The other important factor was demographic change. Not only did the number of people over retirement age increase but, particularly in the European countries, the aging coefficient (the ratio of the population of pensionable age to the population of active age) would deteriorate significantly at least until the early 1980s.

Another demographic factor that bears directly on pension costs is the number of years the average person may expect to live after the age of retirement. At age 65, for example, in industrialized countries of Western Europe, men had a life expectancy of 12 to 13 years and women of 16 to 17 years. The figures for Sweden were 14 for men and 16.9 for women.

The social security systems reacted to this abnormal and unfamiliar situation of concurrent inflation and recession with a variety of short-term measures. At the same time, there were signs that some fundamental rethinking of the systems was under way. Measures to economize on increasingly limited resources and to deal with the deficits included limitations placed on existing programs and benefits in payment; the postponement of the implementation of new social security programs; and changes in financing.

The most common method of increasing social security revenue was to raise the contribution rate as well as the ceiling for the payment of insurance con-

Skating:
see Ice Hockey; Winter Sports

Skeet Shooting:
see Target Sports

Skiing:
see Water Sports; Winter Sports

Skin Diving:
see Water Sports

Slovenian Literature:
see Literature

Soccer:
see Football

KEYSTONE

Senior citizens of London march in protest at Trafalgar Square in October, demanding pension increases to meet higher living costs.

WIDE WORLD

Wearing shabby clothes and scuffed shoes, U.S. Sen. Frank E. Moss (Dem., Utah) pretended to be on welfare and got firsthand evidence of Medicaid frauds in New York City. His Senate subcommittee issued a report saying that fraudulent practices by doctors and clinics had bilked the government of millions of dollars. In the background are pictures of Moss as a Medicaid patient.

tributions. But, increasingly, both employers and insured persons were resisting the ever greater burden. In Switzerland, for example, because it was believed that a higher contribution rate would be excessive, consideration was being given to introducing a value-added tax to help pay pension costs.

Future trends in social security thinking were difficult to ascertain. The most discernible pattern appeared to be one of increased selectivity, in which increases in statutory payments would be restricted and new benefits granted only to certain categories of people and families. This seemed likely to ensure more effective use of available resources and also might serve to contain costs.

This move toward some selectivity in benefits raised a fundamental problem. Traditionally, social insurance programs were earnings-related, with benefits reflecting past earnings. They sought in this way to maintain a proportion of the former standard of living of the individual worker. The benefits were paid independently of income or other resources.

Under this definition of social insurance disadvantaged groups did not have the kind of preferential treatment that a selective system would accord. Increasingly, however, minimum pensions were being guaranteed. These took the form of minimum pensions under social insurance or income-tested social assistance grants.

IMPROVED UNEMPLOYMENT PROTECTION. Unemployment and partial unemployment remained major problems. In mid-1976, for example, nearly six million workers in the European Economic Community countries were unemployed, with another 2½ million on either short-time work or temporarily withdrawn from the labour market. Faced with an overall average rate of unemployment and underemployment of about 8%, the social security institutions continued to strengthen the protection offered by their unemployment insurance programs. In most systems, the amount of the unemployment benefit was increased as wages rose or in line with price changes; in many, the duration of benefits was extended to take into account the difficulties of finding new employment. In addition, new social security measures were evolving to deal with certain problem areas. These included protection of other social security rights during periods of extended unemployment, the extension of benefits for the long-term unemployed older worker whose opportunities for reemployment are minimal, and special benefits for the partially unemployed.

The importance of preserving other social security rights, such as medical care, during periods of full or partial unemployment as well as during approved courses of training was increasingly recognized. Although most social security systems either guaranteed or credited contributions, or permitted voluntary contributions for health insurance during periods of unemployment, the accumulation of pension rights during such times might be interrupted; if a worker is partially employed, his recorded earnings may be unusually low for a time and may thereby affect the amount of his pension.

Some new techniques to deal with such problems were developed during the year. In Finland employees could be unemployed for 200 days a year without losing any pension rights. In addition, if they were on a shortened workweek because of the economic recession, their pension was not calculated on the basis of these lower wages but rather on the basis of higher earnings in earlier years. In the U.K. the unemployed who undertook vocational training courses were credited with national insurance contributions for the period of their course.

"Unemployment pensions," as opposed to unemployment benefits, were becoming more commonplace and provided an income bridge for older unemployed workers. Payable for a period of up to five years before the normal retirement age, an unemployment pension is an extension of the unemployment benefit beyond its normal duration until the time when the beneficiary becomes eligible for a retirement pension. In Belgium, for example, a "prepension" became payable in 1976 to workers aged 60 who were dismissed, as well as to those who resigned. The pension was payable until retirement at age 65. As was the case for eligibility for an unemployment benefit, a worker must have worked 600 days during the preceding 36 months; moreover, he could not continue in paid employment nor could he receive any other unemployment benefit. The prepension was calculated in two parts. The first was equal to the unemployment benefit, and the second was a supplementary allowance equal to half the difference between the unemployment benefit and the previous net wage of the worker up to a maximum of BFr 40,250 a month. Vacancies arising from the retirement of workers on prepensions could be filled only by unemployed workers under 30.

Part-time work assumed increased importance as a measure to enable workers to avoid total unemployment during periods of economic recession. Reduced hours of employment and consequently lower earnings led to a variety of new compensation measures for workers so affected. In West Germany short-time allowances were paid by the National Employment Institute to an estimated 288,000 employed persons in 1975, significantly reducing the numbers who might have become unemployed. In Italy workers who were on reduced hours or who had been laid off for reasons beyond their control received a guaranteed payment of 80% of their former wages. In the U.K., under the Employment Protection Act of 1975, a worker received a "guaranteed payment" of £6 per day during short-time working or temporary layoff. In Belgium and in France recent collective bargaining agreements ensured that income lost from hours or days not worked due to the economic recession would be compensated.

As a complement to the measures to protect the unemployed worker, national authorities moved toward the payment of various kinds of allowances to help maintain employment. These took the form of subsidies to firms, either to retain otherwise unnecessary workers or to recruit the unemployed, and of increased benefits during periods of retraining.

Flexible Retirement Provisions. New legislation permitting and encouraging earlier retirement was enacted or implemented during the year. Although partially in response to the growing demand for an earlier retirement age, the legislation also reflected the desire to open up more jobs for the young and the unemployed. Although there were doubts as to whether early retirement provisions actually reduced the number of unemployed, Belgium, France, Sweden, and the U.K. made changes in 1976.

Early retirement was permitted for those with long years of service and/or arduous work in Belgium and in France. In Belgium a worker could retire at age 64 (instead of 65) with a full pension, provided that he had 45 years of employment. In addition, under another measure, early retirement with a full regular old-age pension became possible at age 64 for a worker who had been employed in arduous or unhealthy occupations during 5 of the 15 years preceding his 64th birthday, or during any 12 years of his career.

Similarly, in France, a retirement pension was payable at the maximum rate when a worker reached the age of 60 (instead of 65) if he had been insured for at least 42 years and if he had been in arduous work for at least 5 of the 15 years preceding the request for a pension. Women were eligible for the same pension after 30 years of insured work if they had raised three or more children.

Sweden also introduced greater flexibility in the retirement provisions for old-age pensions effective as of July 1976. New legislation, the Partial Pension Insurance Act of 1975, encouraged a reduction in work activity by paying a partial pension which, when combined with the lower wage from part-time work, provided between 85 and 90% of the worker's former net income.

A new retirement measure in the U.K. was clearly intended to open up job opportunities for the young unemployed. Men aged 64 and women aged 59 (the normal retirement age was 65 for men and 60 for women), who lived in specified areas with high rates of unemployment, would receive a flat-rate weekly £23 tax-free allowance if they left full-time employment. This would be operative during the six-month period starting Jan. 1, 1977. The allowance was payable only if the employer signed a declaration that the early retirement of the worker had resulted in the hiring of a registered unemployed person either for the job vacated or elsewhere in his firm.

(ISSA)

U.S. Developments. Social welfare programs encountered some difficulties in the U.S. in 1976. Two of the largest programs were shaken by revelations of fraud and abuse, and virtually all were caught in an election-year battle between Congress and Pres. Gerald Ford over spending levels. The struggle ended in a standoff, with no large cutbacks in government services but few significant new programs.

The most serious charges of fraud and waste were leveled against the Medicaid program, which helped provide health care for the needy. After a four-month study of Medicaid operations in eight cities, investigators for the Senate Subcommittee on Long-Term Care concluded that "rampant fraud and abuse" existed among both providers and recipients of Medicaid, matched by "an equivalent degree of error and maladministration by government agencies." Their report estimated that one-fourth of the $15 billion per year spent on Medicaid was wasted through fraud, care of poor quality, and the provision of services to ineligible persons.

Subcommittee chairman Sen. Frank Moss (Dem., Utah) and six staff members posed as Medicaid patients and visited clinics in five states. They told of unnecessary tests and treatments; filling of fictitious prescriptions; fraudulent billing by physicians and laboratories; and kickbacks to laboratories, landlords, and "Medicaid mill" owners. Senator Moss also charged that more than $300 million a year was fraudulently obtained by doctors under Medicare, which helps pay the health care costs of the elderly. He said that investigators estimated that 4–6% of the 250,000 physicians taking part in Medicare engaged in such fraud.

New abuses also were found in the food stamp program, which had been jarred by charges of mismanagement and errors in 1975. An audit by the U.S. Department of Agriculture revealed that food stamp vendors, the organizations authorized to sell food stamp coupons to program participants, had misused more than $34 million of the money they received from selling the coupons. They had been slow in depositing the money, had not made deposits at all, or had used the funds for private investment.

Congress took some action in response to the reports of mismanagement and fraud. It passed a measure that tightened the accountability of food stamp vendors, and it created an Office of Inspector General in the Department of Health, Education, and Welfare to investigate and audit all HEW programs.

Attempts were made by both the Ford Administration and Congress to revamp the food stamp program. The Department of Agriculture announced regulations designed to cut $1.2 billion from the $5.8 billion spent on it annually and to drop 5 million of the 19

In France it's called "the third age." This Yoga group meets at one of the new clubs established for senior citizens.

JEAN-LUCE HURE—THE NEW YORK TIMES

million recipients. However, legal action prevented those regulations from going into effect. Meanwhile, President Ford requested Congress to make large cuts in the program. The Senate instead passed a moderate bill that would have removed about 1.4 million persons from food stamp rolls while maintaining or increasing benefits for most others. The legislation died when the House of Representatives failed to vote on it.

Medicaid and Medicare revision did not even get as far as food stamp reform. Committees in both the House and Senate considered changes aimed at checking the rapid increase in the cost of the two programs, but took no final action. A related matter, national health insurance, was virtually ignored by Congress in 1976.

Welfare reform, another controversial and prominent issue, also received relatively little attention in 1976. The Ford administration made no major proposals, and Congress did not even hold committee hearings on the subject. Meanwhile, the nation's welfare rolls declined, reaching the lowest level in 18 months in June 1976, when 11,247,679 persons received Aid to Families with Dependent Children. Officials said that the decline was due to smaller families, a stronger economy, the drive to weed out ineligible recipients, and a year-old campaign to collect payments from absent parents.

Three important bills were enacted: a public works jobs program, an extension of emergency public service jobs, and an expansion of unemployment compensation. But the potentially most far-reaching measure, the Humphrey-Hawkins full-employment bill, was not passed. The public works bill, aimed primarily at chronic high unemployment in the construction trades, was one of the few new federal programs started in 1976, and it had to overcome two presidential vetoes. It authorized $2 billion in fiscal 1977 for state and local public works projects such as buildings, parks, and waterways, and $1,250,000,000 to help hard-pressed state and local governments maintain public services.

The Emergency Public Service Jobs Program, begun in 1974 to combat the recession, provided grants to states and municipalities to create jobs for unemployed persons in state and local governments. A significant portion of the new jobs was supposed to go to welfare recipients and the long-term unemployed.

A revision of the unemployment compensation laws brought more than 8.5 million additional workers, mostly nonelected state and local government employees, under the regular unemployment benefit coverage and raised taxes on employers who pay for the system. The new law also tried to close loopholes in unemployment compensation by restricting the eligibility of some groups.

The Humphrey-Hawkins bill would have set up coordinated long-range economic planning by the federal government to reduce unemployment to 3% for persons over 19, with the government serving as employer of last resort if monetary and fiscal policies failed to achieve that goal. It did not reach the floor of either house for a vote.

Another sharp confrontation between Congress and President Ford involved day-care centres for children of welfare recipients and other needy families. Early in 1976 Congress passed a measure that would have given states an extra $125 million to help them meet federal health, safety, and staffing standards for the centres. Ford vetoed the legislation, primarily, he said, because it imposed staff-to-child ratios that unduly restricted the states.

A second, compromise day-care bill was passed in August and, faced with a likely override if he vetoed it again, the president signed that measure. It provided $240 million through Oct. 1, 1977, to help states make general improvements in day-care programs. But it postponed the controversial staffing standards until Oct. 1, 1977, pending completion of a government study. An estimated 550,000 children from low- and moderate-income families were enrolled in day-care centres that received federal assistance.

Social programs became entangled in the controversy over abortion when Congress partially banned the use of Medicaid funds for abortions for low-income women. HEW estimated that Medicaid spent $45 million to $55 million a year for 250,000 to 300,000 abortions. The new restrictions stipulated that no money appropriated for HEW could be used "to perform abortions except where the life of the mother would be endangered if the fetus were carried to term." A report accompanying the bill explained that the provision meant that federal funds could be used for an abortion only when a physician deemed it "of medical necessity" and could not be used if the abortion was "a method of family planning or for emotional or social convenience."

But the constitutionality of the ban was left in doubt when U.S. District Judge John Dooling of Brooklyn, N.Y., ruled on October 22 that Medicaid patients are entitled to abortions at public expense. He said that a woman has a constitutional right to have an abortion and that she may not be barred from exercising that right simply because she lacks money.

Concern about the future financing of the Social Security system continued in 1976. President Ford proposed that payroll taxes, paid by both employers and employees, be raised from the current 5.85 to 6.15% on covered wages, but Congress did not go along with this. The maximum tax was to go up in 1977 anyway, because it was to be computed on the first $16,500 of each person's salary, as opposed to the first $15,300 in 1976. This caused an increase in payroll taxes of $70.20 to a total of $965.25 for workers who earned $16,500 or more a year.

An automatic 6.4% cost-of-living increase in Social Security benefits went into effect in June 1976 for the 32.6 million Social Security recipients. The maximum benefits for a worker retiring at age 65 rose from $364 a month to $387.30 and the minimum from $101.40 to $107.90. The average benefit for a retired worker went from $204 a month to $218 and for a retired couple from $348 to $372.

Although no major new programs were enacted in 1976, social welfare expenditures continued to climb. Preliminary estimates indicated that total social welfare spending by federal, state, and local governments would be about $330 billion for fiscal 1976, a one-year increase of approximately 15%.

The federal government financed about 60% of this social welfare spending, which included Social Security, unemployment insurance, Medicaid and Medicare, veterans' programs, public assistance, and Supplemental Security Income. In 1950 about 26% of the federal budget went into social welfare. The proportion rose to 33% in 1965 and was likely to reach 56% in 1976. (DAVID M. MAZIE)

See also Education; Health and Disease; Industrial Review: *Insurance.*
[522.D; 535.B.3.c; 552.D.1]

Sociology: *see* Behavioural Sciences

Soil Conservation: *see* Environment

Somalia

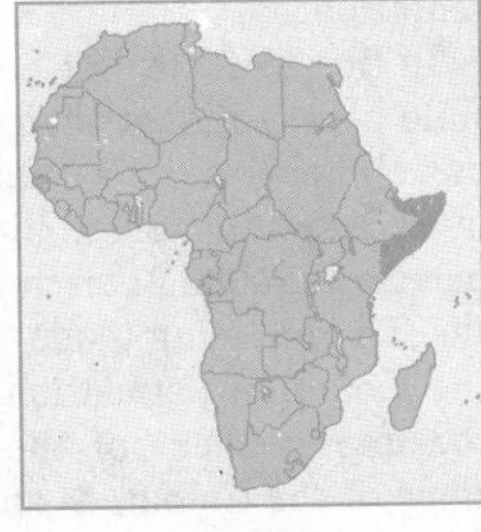

A republic of northeast Africa, the Somali Democratic Republic, or Somalia, is bounded by the Gulf of Aden, the Indian Ocean, Kenya, Ethiopia, and Afars and Issas. Area: 246,300 sq mi (638,000 sq km). Pop. (1976 est.): 3,258,000, predominantly Hamitic, with Arabic and other admixtures. Cap. and largest city: Muqdisho (pop., 1976 UN est., 285,000). Language: Somali. Religion: predominantly Muslim. President of the Supreme Revolutionary Council in 1976, Maj. Gen. Muhammad Siyad Barrah.

In 1976 Somalia was still suffering from the aftereffects of the 1974–75 drought and famine, which, together with world financial inflation, had left the country with an estimated balance of payments deficit of about 500 million Somali shillings. Major development projects connected with the farming and fishing cooperatives set up for destitute former herdsmen and farmers caused foreign aid and credit to increase to 1,220,000,000 Somali shillings, as against 423 million Somali shillings in 1975.

Bitter territorial disputes continued with neighbouring Ethiopia and with the French government in the Territory of the Afars and Issas, which was on the verge of independence. Somalia continued to press for self-determination for the latter, on the assumption that this would lead to amalgamation with Somalia.

On February 3 a group of guerrillas belonging to the Front for the Liberation of the Somali Coast (FLCS), which was based in Somalia, hijacked a school bus in the Afars and Issas containing about 30 children, mostly of French military personnel. In a rescue attempt French troops opened fire and one of the children as well as Somali civilians and policemen were killed at the border village of Loyada. The FLCS men escaped with one of the children, a seven-year-old boy, who was later handed over to the French ambassador by the Somali secretary of state for foreign affairs. The latter accused the French of invading Somali territory and massacring innocent villagers.

SOMALIA

Education. (1973–74) Primary, pupils 69,493, teachers 1,789; secondary, pupils 37,910, teachers 1,693; vocational, pupils 1,798, teachers 133; teacher training, students 954, teachers 44; higher (1971–72), students 958, teaching staff 51.

Finance. Monetary unit: Somali shilling, with (Sept. 20, 1976) an official rate of 6.23 Somali shillings to U.S. $1 (free rate of 10.74 Somali shillings = £1 sterling). Gold, SDR's, and foreign exchange (June 1976) U.S. $85.5 million. Budget (1975 est.): revenue 667 million Somali shillings; expenditure 583 million Somali shillings. Cost of living (Muqdisho; 1970 = 100; Feb. 1976) 153.

Foreign Trade. (1974) Imports 814.6 million Somali shillings; exports 390.6 million Somali shillings. Import sources (1972): Italy 29%; U.S.S.R. 10%; U.S. 6%; U.K. 6%; China 6%; Japan 6%; Kenya 5%; West Germany 5%. Export destinations (1972): Saudi Arabia 53%; Italy 18%; U.S.S.R. 6%; Kuwait 6%; Yemen (Aden) 5%. Main exports: livestock 57%; bananas 21%.

Transport and Communications. Roads (1971) 17,223 km. Motor vehicles in use (1972): passenger 8,000; commercial (including buses) 8,000. There are no railways. Air traffic (1974): 19 million passenger-km; freight 200,000 net ton-km. Shipping (1975): merchant vessels 100 gross tons and over 273; gross tonnage 1,813,313. Telephones (Jan. 1971) c. 5,000. Radio receivers (Dec. 1973) 65,000.

Agriculture. Production (in 000; metric tons; 1974): corn c. 165; millet c. 15; cassava c. 27; sesame seed c. 8; sugar, raw value c. 50; bananas c. 140. Livestock (in 000; 1974): cattle c. 2,972; sheep c. 3,906; goats c. 5,022; camels c. 3,022.

Nomads from drought-stricken regions of Somalia have been resettled in the south. After learning to master the waves of the Indian Ocean, they catch shark, tuna, and other fish for a processing plant nearby.

Later in February an amnesty was granted to 438 students who had "failed in their responsibilities in the Rural Development Campaign." The previous October amnesty had been granted to nearly all nonpolitical prisoners, as well as to many political ones. The latter group included the former prime minister, Haji Ibrahim Egal, who was made ambassador to India in October.

On July 1 the long-promised national political party was established. Somalia thus became a one-party socialist state, the responsibility for administering the country having been transferred from the Supreme Revolutionary Council to the Revolutionary Socialist Party. The party established 17 departments, each headed by a member of the party's Central Committee. President Barrah became secretary-general of the party and chairman of the Council of Ministers. In September, President Barrah published a book entitled *The Philosophy of the Somali Revolution.*

The foreign minister, Omar Arteh Ghalib, was removed from his post in April and given an obscure job in internal affairs. He had had a notable career in the international field, his outstanding achievement being the settlement by arbitration of the Uganda-Tanzania dispute of 1972. (VIRGINIA R. LULING)

[978.E.6.b.i]

South Africa

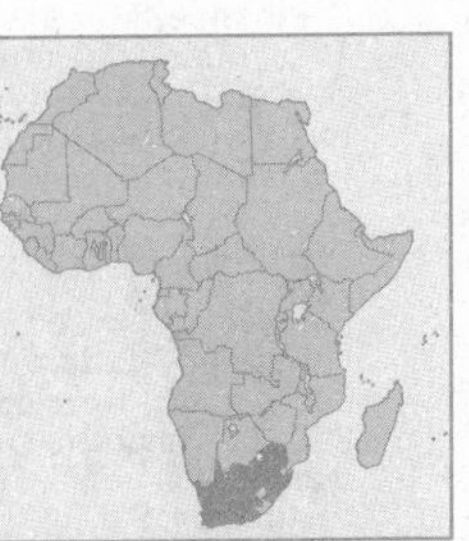

A republic occupying the southern tip of Africa, South Africa is bounded by South West Africa (Namibia), Botswana, Rhodesia, Mozambique, and Swaziland and by the Atlantic and Indian oceans on the west and east. Lesotho and, since independence on Oct. 26, 1976, the republic of Transkei are enclaves within South African territory. Area: 457,269 sq mi (1,184,321 sq km), excluding Walvis Bay, 372 sq mi. Pop. (1975

UPI COMPIX

U.S. Secretary of State Henry Kissinger met with South Africa's Prime Minister B. J. Vorster (left) and Foreign Minister Hilgard Muller (right) in Pretoria in September to discuss the problems of Rhodesia and South West Africa.

est.): 25,471,000, including Bantu 71.3%; white 16.9%; Coloured 9%; Asian 2.8%. After Transkei's independence, excluding its de facto population of 1,900,000, South Africa's population comprised Bantu 68.9%, white 18%, Coloured 10%, and Asian 3.1%. Executive capital: Pretoria (pop., 1975 est., 614,-400); judicial capital: Bloemfontein (pop., 1975 est., 234,000); legislative capital: Cape Town (pop., 1975 est., 818,100). Largest city: Johannesburg (pop., 1975 est., 1,498,700). Language: Afrikaans and English. Religion: mainly Christian. State president in 1976, Nicolaas J. Diederichs; prime minister, B. J. Vorster.

Domestic Affairs. A major constitutional development in South Africa in 1976 was the proclamation of the independent republic of the Transkei, the first Bantu homeland to acquire sovereign status under the policy of separate development formulated by H. F. Verwoerd in 1958. (*See* TRANSKEI.) Another self-governing homeland that declared its intention to seek full independence was Bophuthatswana, whose chief minister, Lucas Mangope, envisaged the establishment of a republic, with headquarters in Mafeking, by 1978, subject to the adequate land consolidation of the territory. The other seven homelands, generally speaking, did not favour independence in the foreseeable future, particularly because of consolidation problems and on economic grounds. The emphasis, notably in KwaZulu (Zululand), was rather on political and economic integration in an undivided South Africa emphasizing local self-government and representation.

In line with current South African thinking on possible constitutional changes to accommodate the various ethnic groups, a Cabinet committee was set up to investigate the possibility of reforming the parliamentary system. This followed a recommendation by the Theron commission of inquiry into the future of the Coloured population. It contained proposals for the improvement of the social and economic conditions of the Coloureds and for their political advancement. While the government accepted in principle most of the recommendations, it rejected a proposal by the majority of the commission for direct Coloured representation in the country's lawmaking machinery. Instead, both the Coloured and Indian groups were given representation on the newly formed Cabinet Council presided over by the prime minister, with the specific purpose of enabling these groups, jointly with the white representatives, to have a voice, at a high level, in decisions of common interest. Participation in the Cabinet Council, which first met in September, was refused by the majority Labour Party in the Coloured Persons' Representative Council, which also, for the second successive year, rejected the Representative Council's annual budget. In response to the request by leaders of the Coloured community for direct representation in Parliament, the government held out the prospect of more powers and responsibility for the Coloured Representative Council.

Racial unrest on a large scale erupted in the middle of June in the African township of Soweto, near Johannesburg. The disturbances started when approximately 10,000 schoolchildren, protesting against an order by the Department of Bantu Education enforcing the use of Afrikaans as well as English as dual media of instruction in Bantu schools, clashed with the police. The order was later rescinded, but meanwhile the unrest took a more serious turn. With a population approaching one million, Soweto became the scene of almost daily rioting, arson, destruction of property (mainly public buildings and schools), and a mounting toll of dead and injured. Hundreds were arrested. Buses were burned and trains attacked, and thousands of workers employed in Johannesburg were prevented from going there.

Disturbances continued in Soweto, and the unrest also spread into some of the Bantu homelands, to several universities, and subsequently to Coloured residential areas in the Cape Peninsula and nearby

SOUTH AFRICA

Education. (1976) Primary, pupils 4,683,401; secondary, pupils 979,755; primary and secondary, teachers 149,651; vocational and teacher training, students 49,075, teachers 3,146; higher, students 109,476, teaching staff 8,128.

Finance. Monetary unit: rand, with (Sept. 20, 1976) an official rate of R 0.87 to U.S. $1 (free rate of R 1.49 = £1 sterling). Gold, SDR's, and foreign exchange (June 1976) U.S. $1,171,000,-000. Budget (1975–76 est.): revenue R 5,909,-000,000; expenditure R 5,311,000,000. Gross national product (1975) R 24,631,000,000. Money supply (June 1976) R 4,408,000,000. Cost of living (1970 = 100; June 1976) 173.

Foreign Trade. (1975) Imports R 6,083,500,-000; exports (excluding gold bullion) R 3,955,-800,000. Import sources: U.K. 20%; West Germany 19%; U.S. 18%; Japan 11%. Export destinations: U.K. 23%; Japan 12%; U.S. 11%; West Germany 11%. Main exports: gold coins 15%; diamonds 11%; cereals 8%; sugar 7%.

Transport and Communications. Roads (1973) *c.* 320,000 km (including 185,846 km main roads). Motor vehicles in use (1974): passenger 1,950,347; commercial 719,148. Railways: (excluding Namibia; 1974) 19,910 km; freight traffic (including Namibia; 1975) 63,850,000,000 net ton-km. Air traffic (1975): 5,946,000,000 passenger-km; freight 155,107,000 net ton-km. Shipping (1975): merchant vessels 100 gross tons and over 286; gross tonnage 565,575. Telephones (Dec. 1974) 1,936,000. Radio receivers (Dec. 1972) 2,350,000. Television receivers (Jan. 1976) *c.* 250,000.

Agriculture. Production (in 000; metric tons; 1975): corn 9,516; wheat 1,815; oats 110; sorghum 526; potatoes 719; tomatoes *c.* 250; sugar, raw value 1,920; peanuts 288; sunflower seed *c.* 221; oranges (1974) *c.* 600; grapefruit (1974) *c.* 120; apples (1974) *c.* 260; grapes (1974) 1,085; tobacco *c.* 30; cotton, lint *c.* 47; wool *c.* 54; meat *c.* 791; milk *c.* 3,300; fish catch (1974) 1,415. Livestock (in 000; June 1975): cattle *c.* 10,600; sheep *c.* 31,000; pigs *c.* 1,050; goats (1974) *c.* 4,100; horses (1974) *c.* 230; chickens (1974) *c.* 12,650.

Industry. Index of manufacturing production (1970 = 100; 1975) 124. Fuel and power (in 000; 1975): coal (metric tons) 69,487; manufactured gas (cu m; 1974) *c.* 1,856,000; electricity (kw-hr) 75,606,000. Production (in 000; metric tons; 1975): cement 7,176; iron ore (60–65% metal content) 12,136; pig iron 5,924; crude steel 6,557; antimony concentrates (metal content; 1974) 15; copper ore (metal content; 1974) 179; chrome ore (oxide content; 1974) 826; manganese ore (metal content; 1974) 1,895; uranium (1974) 2.7; gold (troy oz) 22,800; diamonds (metric carats; 1974) 7,502; asbestos (1974) 335; petroleum products (1974) *c.* 11,200; fish meal (including Namibia; 1974) 259.

localities. Arson, destruction of property, and disruption of transportation were features common to most of the incidents, and students and schoolchildren were usually in the forefront of the trouble. From the early evidence at an inquiry into the causes of the unrest it appeared that, while there was a certain amount of organized agitation behind the riots, serious dissatisfaction with the socioeconomic and political conditions of the population groups concerned played a significant part. Another factor which emerged was that in complexes such as Soweto normal administrative machinery for the maintenance of law and order was inadequate, and the inhabitants themselves had insufficient responsibility for the administration of their own affairs. Various changes in those respects were announced or foreshadowed by the minister of Bantu administration and development, M. C. Botha, in the wake of the disturbances. Residents in Soweto and other townships were given the right, of which they had long been deprived, to acquire or build their own houses on a long-term leasehold basis; some restrictions on African traders in the townships were removed; and free compulsory education for African children within a few years was promised.

Additional security legislation was passed by Parliament during the year. The measures provided for the setting up of a parliamentary internal security commission of ten members to review security legislation and to investigate the activities of organizations and individuals deemed to be a threat to security; they also gave greater powers to the minister of justice to detain persons whose activities were considered to be an actual or potential threat to the state. A number of persons were held under this measure, the Internal Security Act, as well as under earlier legislation such as the Terrorism Act. Some were brought to trial, while others were released after a period or remained in detention without being charged.

Against the background of government pledges at the UN and elsewhere to move away from discrimination based on colour and with growing demands both inside and outside the country for radical changes in race policy, there were moves for the formation of a new and unified opposition party. Leaders of the three main opposition groups—the United Party, the Progressive Reform Party, and the Democratic Party—agreed at a meeting in Durban to set up a steering committee, under the chairmanship of a retired Supreme Court judge, J. F. Marais, to consider the feasibility of establishing a united opposition that would provide a political home for people of all parties who favoured liberal racial policies. Changes in official sports policies aimed at opening the door to racially mixed competition were announced during the year. At the same time, South Africa continued to be barred from many international sports events.

Foreign Affairs. South Africa, acting as a mediator, played a key role in international diplomatic moves concerning Rhodesia. After the failure of the 1975 Victoria Falls talks on Rhodesia and of the subsequent negotiations between the government of Rhodesian Prime Minister Ian Smith and the African nationalists, Prime Minister Vorster and U.S. Secretary of State Henry Kissinger met in June 1976 at Grafenau, West Germany, to discuss the Rhodesian issue, the future of South West Africa, and other matters concerning southern Africa. The talks were followed by another meeting in Zürich on September 4–6 and by a four-day meeting on September 17–20 at Pretoria. There, negotiations by Kissinger and Smith, with Vorster as intermediary, resulted in an agreement in which Smith accepted the principle of majority rule within two years and a multiracial interim government. The Geneva conference, opening in October, to negotiate a settlement with the African Rhodesian leaders was the sequel. (*See* AFRICAN AFFAIRS.)

In South West Africa the constitutional conference in the Turnhalle, Windhoek, initiated with South African approval in 1975 and attended by delegations from all the 12 (including white) ethnic groups in the territory, agreed on the principle of independence by the end of 1978. It was further agreed that steps should be taken to establish an interim government representing all groups on a unitary basis, with local self-government and guarantees for the rights of minorities. Proposals for a constitution providing for a three-tier form of government—central, regional, and local—were considered by a constitution committee. In the meantime, a number of measures aimed at the abolition of discriminatory practices in the territory were introduced on the initiative of the constitutional conference. In the background of the Turnhalle proceedings was the UN Security Council resolution adopted in January 1976, which set August 31 as the date for the withdrawal of South Africa from the territory and the threat of mandatory sanctions if South Africa failed to comply. A resolution in the Security Council in September, calling for such sanctions in view of South Africa's failure to withdraw, was vetoed by Britain, France, and the U.S., on the grounds that the Turnhalle conference showed evidence of progress and should be left to continue with its work.

The South West Africa People's Organization (SWAPO), recognized by the UN as the representative of the people of the territory (known to the UN as Namibia), was not represented at the Turnhalle conference. There were moves to have it included, provided it abandon violence. Its external wing, based in Angola, engaged in sporadic guerrilla operations across the border, where an unpopulated buffer zone one kilometre wide was established as a protection for the Ovambo territory. The South African forces that had been sent into Angola to guard the Cunene River irrigation and power installations constructed jointly with Angola were withdrawn on March 27 after operating for a time deep in Angolan territory. South

JAN KOPEC—CAMERA PRESS

South African troops arriving on the outskirts of Soweto during the riots that took place in June in the black township near Johannesburg.

Africa received assurances from Angola that work on the installations would not be disrupted.

South Africa continued to be the object of repeated criticism at the UN. Its active participation in the Angolan war, defended by South Africa as a necessary demonstration of concern over Soviet and Cuban intervention in southern Africa, was labeled by the UN as an act of aggression. On October 26, the day Transkei became independent, the General Assembly unanimously, with the U.S. abstaining, denounced it as merely an outcome of apartheid. An economic and cultural pact with Israel, concluded by Vorster during an official visit there in April, was attacked in a wide-ranging General Assembly debate on South African policies in October.

The Economy. Steadily mounting inflation, a declining growth rate, and rising unemployment, especially among the Africans, imposed a strain on the economy and were reflected in a slowing down of business activity, a drop in savings, and some lowering of living standards. The key building and motor industries were markedly affected by the prevailing climate of recession. While the national budget for 1976 was aimed, among other things, at stimulating exports and curbing imports, the deficit in the balance of trade remained large. This was partly because of the increased cost of essential imports, particularly of oil. The sharp fall in the price of gold was an important contributory factor in the decline of the foreign exchange reserves and the balance of payments, which also felt the impact of an appreciable reduction in the inflow of foreign capital. Cuts in state expenditure were offset by higher costs of defense and administration. Direct fiscal and monetary measures included an increase in bank rates, further restrictions on bank credit and liquidity, and a system of import deposits designed to break the influx of imports.

Long-term capital and development schemes completed during the year included the railway line from the Transvaal coalfields to the new port of Richards Bay, the line from the iron-ore deposits at Sishen to Saldanha Bay, and additional installations of the vast Orange River irrigation project. Work was pushed ahead on the Sasol II oil-from-coal plant in the Transvaal, estimated (by February 1976) to cost R 1.9 billion, and final plans were made for the construction of the nuclear power plant by a French consortium at Koeberg in the western Cape, at an estimated cost of R 1 billion. (LOUIS HOTZ)

See also Dependent States.
[978.E.8.b.i]

Southeast Asian Affairs

A wide range of security and diplomatic problems kept Southeast Asia on edge during much of 1976. The fears that countries in the region felt following the establishment of peace in Indochina seemed to materialize as insurgency movements stepped up their activities in Malaysia and Thailand, while Vietnam berated neighbouring countries for being imperialist camp followers. At the same time, there was something of an agonizing reappraisal of diplomatic options as Southeast Asian countries hovered between nonalignment and continuing dependence on some form of military protection from big powers.

Most of these developments centred on the Association of Southeast Asian Nations (ASEAN). Responding to the need to adjust to the changed post-war climate, ASEAN countries held the first summit meeting in the association's history early in the year. Two presidents (Indonesia, Philippines) and three prime ministers (Malaysia, Singapore, Thailand) met on February 23–24 on the Indonesian island of Bali. It was not an easy gathering of identical minds: there were contradictory pulls among the member countries. These, however, were resolved in the course of closed-door bargaining sessions by the leaders. The summit finally formalized two major documents, the Declaration of Concord and the Treaty of Amity and Cooperation. The declaration noted the members' determination "to expand and consolidate economic cooperation and move toward establishment of preferential trading agreements as a long-term objective." It also approved plans for the establishment of large regional industrial projects that would use resources in each member country. Subsequently, finance ministers of ASEAN countries met to work out the details of these projects and decide on their allocation.

The Treaty of Amity envisaged a High Council of ministers to settle disputes among members. It spoke of measures to facilitate closer contacts among peoples of the region, mutual assistance in technical and cultural fields, and improvement of the economic infrastructure for the common benefit of the contracting countries. The Declaration of Concord attached special importance to the accords on the sharing of food and energy in times of need.

The Bali summit, despite the wrangles and rhetoric that inevitably became a part of it, succeeded in infusing a new spirit of solidarity among the member countries. Officials attending the meeting indicated that the most important topic of discussion did not figure in the public documents. This pertained to the security situation in general and the intentions of Vietnam in particular.

There was some apprehension among the ASEAN countries that the massive quantity of weapons left behind by the retreating U.S. forces in Indochina would find its way to the insurgent groups in the rest of Southeast Asia. Persistent sabre rattling by Hanoi in the weeks preceding the Bali summit did nothing to assuage these fears. Vietnam regarded the summit as a case of Southeast Asian ganging-up against it under U.S. auspices and kept up a barrage of violent invectives against the regional grouping. The virulence of the attack intensified during and immediately after the Bali meeting. The Vietnam Army paper *Quan Doi Nhan Dan* charged that ASEAN was being used by U.S. imperialism "to rally all pro-American reactionary forces to oppose the revolutionary movement in Southeast Asia." Later, the official party paper *Nhan Dan* said that a new confrontation had emerged in Southeast Asia between revolutionary and reactionary forces.

ASEAN countries were undoubtedly disturbed by this belligerent note. At first they sent peace feelers to Vietnam, Laos, and Cambodia with assurances of their good intentions. Later, ministerial spokesmen began adopting a tougher stand. Typical was Singapore Foreign Minister Sinnathamby Rajaratnam's remark that "no amount of confrontation can destroy ASEAN countries." He added: "Indochina can choose to be Communist, but we have the right to be non-Communist. Don't interfere with us."

Behind the scenes, however, a different kind of game was going on, as became apparent later. An Indonesian diplomatic source claimed that the broadsides coming from Hanoi merely reflected the per-

UPI COMPIX

Five leaders of Southeast Asian nations met in Indonesia in February. From left: Prime Minister Lee Kuan Yew of Singapore; Prime Minister Datuk Hussein bin Onn of Malaysia; President Suharto of Indonesia; Pres. Ferdinand E. Marcos of the Philippines; and Prime Minister Kukrit Pramoj of Thailand.

sonal opinion of newspaper writers and that the Vietnamese government was far from hostile to the idea of ASEAN. This view was strengthened when Hanoi sent Vice-Minister of Foreign Affairs Phan Hien on a tour of Southeast Asian countries. He faintly hinted that Vietnam might someday join ASEAN, whose members, he said, obviously wanted peace and were not being used as tools by other countries.

Although the diplomatic problem posed by Hanoi seemed resolved with the Phan Hien visit, ASEAN still faced the challenge of growing insurgency. Thailand's preoccupation with party politics gave insurgents in its border districts time to strengthen themselves, and its arguments with Malaysia over the separatist Muslim movement in the south gave Communist forces in Malaysia a unique opportunity to assert themselves. The extent of Communist growth as a result of these developments was not known. But the arrest of, and subsequent public confessions by, leading journalists in Singapore and Malaysia gave the impression that ideological infiltration had succeeded to a considerable degree in those countries. The governments seemed to regain confidence and strength from the silent purges as well as from military campaigns against underground groups they launched during the year.

Against this background, few were surprised that an element of uncertainty crept into Southeast Asian countries' calculations about their association with the big powers. In general the tendency to steer clear of big power entanglements continued, but there was a new "pragmatic" mood in favour of ensuring "fall-back" positions to take care of contingencies. In June Singapore's Rajaratnam told a press conference in Manila that Southeast Asia could become a cold-war battleground for a long time because it would take a "miracle" for the great powers to renounce their rivalries in the region. That statement was with specific reference to the cold-shouldering given by the big powers to ASEAN's favourite idea, that of having Southeast Asia declared a zone of peace and neutrality. (The idea received a further setback in August when the conference of nonaligned nations, in Colombo, Sri Lanka, declined to endorse it following objections raised by the Indochina countries.) However, Rajaratnam did not seem to mind the big-power interest in the region. After attending the ninth ministerial conference of ASEAN, he indicated that there might be a need for U.S. bases in Southeast Asia for the time being if their aim was to ensure "our security."

On the other hand, Japan's *Mainichi* newspaper published what it said was a secret document obtained from ASEAN sources, according to which member countries had agreed to conclude nonaggression treaties with nonmember countries. This was envisaged as part of the plan to "secure recognition of and respect for Southeast Asia as a Zone of Peace, Freedom and Neutrality, free from any form or manner of interference by outside powers." The document also suggested that "under present circumstances, however, security and cooperation should not be formalized or institutionalized on an ASEAN basis."

Southeast Asia's perception of the Sino-Soviet split as the dominant rivalry in the region strengthened during the year. For one thing, although U.S. spokesmen continued to assert their interest and involvement in the region, it was clear to all concerned that the retreat of U.S. power was going to be a feature of Asian life for the foreseeable future. For another, there was no letup in the feuding between the Communist superpowers, with the Soviet Union remaining highly visible in its efforts to fill the vacuum left by the U.S. Making no reference whatsoever to the Asian collective security plan it had proposed many years earlier, Moscow quietly carried on a campaign to win Southeast Asian confidence. It did not go along with Vietnam's early attacks on ASEAN and refrained from assisting insurgents in the region. One Soviet official was quoted by U.S. sources as saying that the insurgents were "barely Communist" and that such ideological content as they had was China-oriented.

Peking for its part continued to present its best face in Southeast Asia, while continuously hammering at the U.S.S.R. The turmoil following the death of Mao Tse-tung in China caused some concern in Southeast Asian capitals, but did not disturb the general impression that China's strategic interests would continue to coincide with those of the U.S. and the non-Communist states of the region.

In July a U.S. environmental group, the Alternate Energy Coalition, which had studied the energy problems in Thailand, Malaysia, Indonesia, Singapore, and Japan over a period of ten months, reported that the pursuit of nuclear power by Southeast Asian countries would result in heavy financial burdens, overdependence on Western or Soviet technology, and proliferation of nuclear weaponry. It argued that the region's growing interest in nuclear energy reflected the needs of the nuclear industry to sell rather than the real energy needs of Southeast Asian societies. It also said that nuclear power plants could pose serious problems regarding the storage and disposal of nuclear wastes in countries that lacked the proper technology and facilities.

A somewhat reassuring economic picture for the region was painted by the Private Development Corporation of the Philippines. In a newsletter published in April, it said that inflation rates in Southeast Asia had gone down markedly during 1975 to less than 4% annually, compared with between 17 and 40% in 1974. Only Indonesia had recorded a rate of 18.8%. It also found that all Southeast Asian countries had experienced either declining trade surpluses or increasing deficits because of falling export revenues. But their international reserves had remained stable. The main source of optimism for economists and planners was the growing size of the Southeast Asian market. R. C. Cooper, financial adviser to a private firm in Singapore, estimated in January that the total market in the region by the end of the decade would be six to ten times greater than that of any single ASEAN country, affording major economies of scale to producers in the region. The projection was based on the combined ASEAN population reaching 300 million by 1980 and 360 million by 1990.

At a different level, the Stanford Research Institute reported in March that ASEAN as a group provided a better investment climate than the Latin-American, Middle Eastern, and African regions. Noting that "the foreign investor now realizes that in the developing world he must be content to be in the minority when it comes to holdings or joint-ventures involving natural resources and public utilities," the institute said ASEAN countries "have been more consistent in the application of their policies" in relation to foreign investment than their counterparts elsewhere. The report was presented to a three-day conference of private businessmen in Manila.

Any initiative that promised to accelerate economic growth was warmly welcomed by Southeast Asian governments during 1976. At the Bali summit, the heads of government unanimously agreed that the only effective solution to the problems of insurgency and subversion was the improvement of the people's economic lot. Looked at in that light, economic progress became no mere slogan with governments but a condition of their survival. (T. J. S. GEORGE)

See also articles on the various countries.
[976.B]

Southern Rhodesia: *see* Rhodesia

South West Africa: *see* Dependent States; South Africa

Soviet Literature: *see* Literature

Soviet Union: *see* Union of Soviet Socialist Republics

Space Exploration

With the exception of Vikings 1 and 2, the Bicentennial of the United States found space activities playing a minor role in national affairs. May 5, 1976, marked the 15th anniversary of the country's first manned spaceflight. On that day in 1961 Alan Shepard was boosted to a point 116.5 mi above the Earth in a voyage that lasted 15 minutes and 22 seconds, during which period he was weightless for a period of five minutes. On July 1, 1976, a signal from the Viking 1 space probe orbiting Mars was used to activate the ribbon-cutting device for the official opening of the National Air and Space Museum, in Washington, D.C. In a similar ceremony, photons of light that left the star Gamma Boötis on midnight July 3, 1776, were used to signal the lighting of a giant birthday cake atop the Superdome in New Orleans on July 4.

In commenting on the progress of the Soviets in space, Malcolm Currie, director of defense research and engineering at the U.S. Department of Defense, said, "The Soviets are investing increasing resources in space technology for military purposes. Their level of activity reached an all-time high in 1975, and the systems they put into orbit are significantly more sophisticated than those deployed in the past. The Soviets are innovating and taking greater technological risks in their space systems."

Manned Flight. Soviet manned spaceflight took a step forward late in 1975 with a mission that did not involve men at all. Soyuz 20, with no crew but a payload of biological experiments, was launched from Tyuratam on November 17. It automatically docked with the Salyut 4 space station, which had been placed into orbit on Dec. 26, 1974. For 91 days the two craft circled the Earth as engineers in the Soviet Union checked their performance. The purpose of the mission was to perfect techniques for supplying manned space stations by unmanned spacecraft.

On June 22, 1976, the U.S.S.R. launched the Salyut 5 space station from Tyuratam. The orbital parameters and telemetry from it soon indicated that it was primarily a military reconnaissance mission. It had a rather low, circular orbit of 144 mi by 139 mi that was characteristic of such missions.

On July 6 Col. Boris Volynov and Lieut. Col. Vitaly Zholobov, backup crewman on the military Salyut 3, lifted off from Tyuratam in Soyuz 21. A day later the two men docked with the Salyut 5. Aboard the space station were scientific experiments, several similar to those flown on the U.S. Skylab. The cosmonauts manipulated equipment that grew crystals, studied diffusion processes in molten substances, permitted the welding of steel rods, formed almost perfect spheres, and utilized surface tension effects for the movement of fluids.

During the fifth week of their life aboard the Salyut 5, the two cosmonauts concentrated on biological studies. They continued earlier experiments on the adaptation of the human organism to the weightlessness of orbital flight. On August 24 the two cosmonauts suddenly returned to Earth, landing in a wheat field in Kazakhstan. After 48 days the two men had become unable to cope with a very strong, acrid odour that had filled their space station. Later physical examinations of the men showed that, whatever their cause, the fumes had not harmed them.

On September 15 Col. Valery F. Bykovsky, making his second trip into space after 13 years on the ground, and Vladimir Aksenov, making his first voyage, were launched from Tyuratam in Soyuz 22. Their relatively brief eight-day mission was largely a scientific one, utilizing a special camera provided by East German scientists to photograph selected portions of their country in multispectral wavelengths.

On October 14 Lieut. Col. Vyacheslav Zudov and Lieut. Col. Valery Rozhdestvensky were launched in Soyuz 23 for a rendezvous with Salyut 5. Again, however, hard luck manifested itself in the Soviet manned spaceflight program. The attempt to make an automatic rendezvous and docking with the Salyut 5 went

UPI COMPIX

Space vehicle of the 1980s: The U.S. space shuttle orbiter "Enterprise" will be borne into orbit on a rocket and then glide back to Earth with its crew. The craft will make up to 100 flights. Initial tests begin in 1977.

wrong, and the two cosmonauts were forced to return to the Earth within 48 hours.

Manned spaceflight in the U.S. was, of course, nonexistent as, indeed, it would be until early 1980. However, results from the Apollo missions were still being received. Laser-ranging experiments resulted in measurements of the distance from the Earth to the Moon to an accuracy of six inches. They were made by means of telescopes in Hawaii flashing laser beams to Apollo reflectors on the Moon.

The first space shuttle orbiter in the U.S. was rolled out on September 17. It was named "Enterprise" after the spaceship in the television show "Star Trek."

Unmanned Satellites. A new communications satellite service was inaugurated on February 19 when Marisat 1 was launched as the initial satellite in a network designed to give the U.S. Navy greater communications capability. The system was also designed to furnish service for commercial shipping industry and shore facilities. Additional satellites in the series were orbited on June 9 and October 14. One satellite each was placed over the Pacific and Atlantic oceans, with a third over the Equator at longitude 73° E.

An experiment to obtain information on movements of the Earth's crust as well as its polar motions and to permit lasers to obtain accurate locations on the Earth was launched on May 4. The Lageos satellite was a sphere weighing 903 lb and only 24 in in diameter. Its surface was covered with small laser light reflectors.

Early in 1976 the Soviets resumed tests involving a maneuvering, "killer" satellite and a passive orbiting one. Cosmos 803 was placed into an almost circular orbit of 388 mi by 344 mi at an angle of inclination of 65°. On February 16 an SS-9 rocket from Tyuratam launched Cosmos 804 into an orbit of 436 mi by 92 mi at an angle of 65.1°. An intercept occurred, but no destruction took place. The mission could have failed or perhaps it could have been so designed.

Interplanetary Probes. Clearly the most important events in interplanetary probes during 1976 were the successful landings of Vikings 1 and 2 on Mars. Viking 1 had been launched from Cape Canaveral, Fla., on Aug. 20, 1975, and it was followed by Viking 2 on September 9. The former touched down on Mars on July 20, 1976, seven years to the day after the landing of the first men on the Moon. The originally scheduled landing on July 4, at an area 365 mi farther to the southeast, had to be canceled because the surface at the original site was too rough.

Once the Viking 1 lander had detached from its orbiter, its descent to the surface of the planet was entirely automatic. The first picture transmitted from the surface showed the lander's No. 3 leg and the soil immediately around it. From the photograph scientists determined that the leg had penetrated no more than 1.4 in into the Martian soil. Panoramic views of the landing site followed, showing a rocky, sandy scene that looked like deserts of the western U.S. Colour pictures showed a distinctly reddish soil and a pink sky.

On July 28 the soil-sampler scoop gathered in five loads to be analyzed by the Viking's automated laboratory to look for signs of earthlike microorganisms. Almost from the beginning of the operation minor problems plagued the attempt. The scoop appeared to be jammed, but it was later freed and worked satisfactorily. The seismometer refused to unlock and remained permanently nonfunctional. Communications between lander and mission control faltered but were later restored.

Meteorological instruments indicated that while winds gust up to 40 mph, they generally average only 19 mph. The temperatures at Viking 1's location

Soviet cosmonauts V. F. Bykovsky and V. V. Aksenov of Soyuz 22 in preflight training at the Gagarin cosmonaut training centre.

TASS / SOVFOTO

Major Satellites and Space Probes Launched Oct. 1, 1975–Sept. 30, 1976

Name/country/ launch vehicle/ scientific designation	Launch date, lifetime*	Physical characteristics: Weight in kg†	Shape	Diameter in m†	Length or height in m†	Experiments	Orbital elements: Perigee in km†	Apogee in km†	Period (min)	Inclination to Equator (degrees)
Tip 2/U.S./Scout/ 1975-099A	10/12/75	‡	‡	‡	‡	Communications satellite	578 (359)	830 (516)	98.8	90.3
GOES 1/U.S./Delta/ 1975-100A	10/16/75	295 (650)	cylinder	1.91 (6.25)	2.69 (8.83)	Meteorological satellite	35,759 (22,220)	35,808 (22,250)	1,435.9	0.3
Molniya 3/U.S.S.R./A IIe/ 1975-105A	11/14/75	1,500 (3,307)	‡	‡	‡	Communications satellite	518 (322)	39,831 (24,750)	717.6	62.8
Soyuz 20/U.S.S.R./A II/ 1975-106A	11/17/75 2/16/76	6,570 (14,484)	sphere and cylinder	2.72 (8.92)	7.48 (24.54)	Biological tests	339 (211)	345 (214)	91.3	51.5
Explorer 55/U.S./Delta/ 1975-107A	11/20/75	721 (1,590)	16-sided polyhedron	1.35 (4.43)	1.14 (3.75)	Atmosphere exploration	144 (89)	2,757 (1,713)	114.9	19.6
China 4/China/China B/ 1975-111A	11/26/75 12/29/75	3,500 (7,716)	‡	‡	‡	Military	‡	‡	‡	‡
Interkosmos 14/U.S.S.R./C I/ 1975-115A	12/11/75	700 (1,543)	octagon	1.1 (3.61)	2.5 (8.2)	Scientific satellite	334 (208)	1,682 (1,045)	105.2	73.9
Satcom 1/U.S./Delta/ 1975-117A	12/13/75	464 (1,023)	box	1.25 (4.1)	1.62 (5.3)	Communications satellite	35,779 (22,232)	35,793 (22,241)	1,436	0.1
Prognoz 4/U.S.S.R./A IIe/ 1975-122A	12/22/75	905 (1,995)	‡	‡	‡	Scientific tests	634 (394)	199,000 (123,653)	5,740	65
Raduga/U.S.S.R./D Ie/ 1975-123A	12/22/75	5,000 (11,023)	cylinder	‡	‡	Communications satellite	35,800 (22,245)	35,800 (22,245)	1,434	0.3
Meteor 23/U.S.S.R./A I/ 1975-124A	12/25/75	2,200 (4,850)	cylinder	1.5 (4.92)	5 (16.4)	Meteorological satellite	841 (523)	902 (560)	102.3	81.2
Molniya 3/U.S.S.R./A Ie/ 1975-125A	12/27/75	1,500 (3,307)	‡	‡	‡	Communications satellite	640 (398)	40,375 (25,088)	731.2	62.9
Helios 2/West Germany/Titan IIIe/1976-003A	1/15/76	350 (772)	16-sided polyhedron	2.74 (8.99)	2.13 (6.99)	Solar observatory	Orbit around Sun			
CTS/Canada/Delta/ 1976-004A	1/17/76	674 (1,485)	cylinder with two panels	1.91 (6.25)	3.54 (11.6)	Communications satellite	35,737 (22,206)	35,841 (22,271)	1,436.2	0.2
Molniya 1/U.S.S.R./A IIe/ 1976-005A	1/22/76	998 (2,200)	cylinder	‡	‡	Communications satellite	678 (421)	39,671 (24,650)	717.6	63.1
Intelsat 4A/U.S./Atlas Centaur/ 1976-010A	1/29/76	726 (1,600)	cylinder	2.38 (7.81)	2.82 (9.25)	Communications satellite	35,784 (22,235)	35,793 (22,241)	1,436.2	0.1
Marisat 1/U.S./Delta/ 1976-017A	2/19/76	655 (1,444)	cylinder	‡	‡	Communications satellite	35,765 (22,223)	35,813 (22,253)	1,436.3	1.9
UME/Japan/N/ 1976-019A	2/29/76	85 (187)	‡	‡	‡	Scientific tests	994 (618)	1,012 (629)	105.1	69.6
Molniya 1/U.S.S.R./A IIe/ 1976-021A	3/11/76	998 (2,200)	cylinder	‡	‡	Communications satellite	431 (268)	39,915 (24,802)	717.6	63
Molniya 1/U.S.S.R./A IIe/ 1976-026A	3/19/76	998 (2,200)	cylinder	‡	‡	Communications satellite	604 (375)	39,747 (24,698)	717.7	63.1
Satcom 2/U.S./Delta/ 1976-029A	3/26/76	464 (1,023)	box	1.25 (4.1)	1.62 (5.3)	Communications satellite	35,780 (22,233)	35,795 (22,242)	1,436.1	0.0
Meteor 24/U.S.S.R./A I/ 1976-032A	4/7/76	‡	cylinder	1.5 (4.92)	5 (16.4)	Meteorological satellite	841 (523)	893 (555)	102.2	81.2
NATO 3-A/U.S./Delta/ 1976-035A	4/22/76	310 (683)	cylinder	2.2 (7.22)	2.23 (7.32)	Communications satellite	35,782 (22,234)	35,794 (22,241)	1,436.2	2.7
NOSS 1/U.S./Atlas Centaur/ 1976-038A	4/30/76	‡	cylinder	‡	‡	Ocean surveillance (launched three subsatellites after achieving orbit)	1,086 (675)	1,126 (700)	107.3	63.4
Lageos 1/U.S./Scout/ 1976-039A	5/4/76	410 (903)	sphere	0.61 (2)	‡	Laser beam reflector experiment	5,836 (3,626)	5,950 (3,697)	225.4	109.8
Molniya 3/U.S.S.R./A IIe/ 1976-041A	5/12/76	1,500 (3,307)	‡	‡	‡	Communications satellite	585 (364)	39,768 (24,711)	717.4	63
Comstar 1/U.S./Atlas Centaur/ 1976-042A	5/13/76	‡	cylinder	‡	‡	Communications satellite	35,782 (22,234)	35,789 (22,238)	1,436.1	0.1
Meteor 25/U.S.S.R./A I/ 1976-043A	5/15/76	‡	cylinder	1.5 (4.92)	5 (16.4)	Meteorological satellite	843 (524)	897 (557)	102.3	81.2
Marisat 2/U.S./Delta/ 1976-053A	6/9/76	655 (1,444)	cylinder	‡	‡	Communications satellite	35,769 (22,226)	35,804 (22,248)	1,436.1	2.4
Interkosmos 15/U.S.S.R./B I/ 1976-056A	6/19/76	1,100 (2,425)	octagon	1.1 (3.61)	2.5 (8.2)	Scientific tests	484 (301)	517 (321)	94.6	74
Salyut 5/U.S.S.R./D I/ 1976-057A	6/22/76	19,000 (41,888)	cylinder with solar panels	4 (13.12)	10 (32.81)	Manned space station	257 (160)	268 (167)	89.7	51.5
Soyuz 21/U.S.S.R./A II/ 1976-064A	7/6/76 8/24/76	6,000 (13,228)	sphere and cylinder	3.1 (10.17)	10.7 (35.11)	Manned spacecraft	114 (71)	409 (254)	89.7	65
Palapa 1/Indonesia/Delta/ 1976-066A	7/8/76	‡	cylinder	‡	‡	Communications satellite	35,764 (22,223)	35,809 (22,251)	1,436.1	0.0
Comstar 2/U.S./Delta/ 1976-073A	7/22/76	‡	cylinder	‡	‡	Communications satellite	35,778 (22,231)	35,792 (22,240)	1,436	0.0
Molniya 1/U.S.S.R./A IIe/ 1976-074A	7/23/76	998 (2,200)	cylinder	‡	‡	Communications satellite	515 (320)	39,836 (24,753)	717.7	62.9
Interkosmos 16/U.S.S.R./B I/ 1976-076A	7/27/76	1,100 (2,425)	octagon	1.1 (3.61)	2.5 (8.2)	Scientific tests	463 (288)	518 (322)	94.4	50.5
NOAA 5/U.S./‡/ 1976-077A	7/29/76	409 (902)	cube with three rectangular panels	1 (3.28)	1.2 (3.94)	Meteorological satellite	1,507 (936)	1,522 (946)	116.2	102.0
Luna 24/U.S.S.R./D Ie/ 1976-081A	8/9/76 8/22/76	‡	sphere	‡	‡	Lunar soil sample vehicle	‡	‡	‡	‡
Soyuz 22/U.S.S.R./A II/ 1976-096A	9/15/76 9/23/76	6,000 (13,228)	sphere and cylinder	3.1 (10.17)	10.7 (35.11)	Scientific experiments in Earth resources—manned spacecraft	251 (156)	257 (160)	85.6	64.75

*All dates are in universal time (UT).
†English units in parentheses; weight in pounds, dimensions in feet, apogee and perigee in statute miles.
‡Not available.

(MITCHELL R. SHARPE)

ranged between a low of −122° F and a high of −24° F.

On August 7 Viking 2 entered orbit around Mars. Its lander detached itself and touched down on the planet on September 3. The first pictures from the lander indicated that it had set down in an extremely rocky region. They showed a great number of rocks with deeply pitted surfaces, features that puzzled geologists. In addition, they clearly showed that very fine soil had been blown among the rocks.

Temperatures at Viking 2 ranged from −114° F in the early morning to −23° F in mid-afternoon. A barometer measured the atmospheric pressure at 7.72 millibars, as compared with the 7.12 millibars at the Viking 1 site. (The pressure on the Earth's surface at mean sea level is about 1,000 millibars.)

From chemical analyses of the atmosphere, the two Vikings indicated that the air on Mars consists of 95% carbon dioxide, 2.7% nitrogen, 1.6% argon, and 0.15% oxygen. Results from experiments on both landers to determine whether some form of life exists on Mars were ambiguous and inconclusive.

Measurements from the Viking 2 orbiter revealed that the temperature over the north pole of Mars was −90° F. This is too high to permit the formation of frozen carbon dioxide ("dry ice"), and scientists concluded that the polar caps consist largely of frozen water.

More was learned about the planet Venus during the year from the Soviet probes Venera 9 and 10. From the planet's surface the landers transmitted information that Venusian rocks have a density and composition of natural radioactive elements similar to the basalts on Earth. Though both landers only survived an average of 60 minutes, the orbiters continued to function much longer. They telemetered data indicating that the top of the thick Venusian cloud cover is about 40 mi above the planet's surface. Instruments also showed that the mass of the planet is 0.81485 that of Earth.

Deimos is the smaller of the two moons of Mars. This photo was taken by Viking Orbiter 1 from a distance of 3,300 km (2,050 mi). It reveals numerous craters on a surface of substantial age.

COURTESY, NASA

COURTESY, NASA

The surface of Mars consists mainly of reddish, fine-grained material according to photos taken on the planet by the Viking 1 lander. The horizon is about 3 km (1.8 mi) from the camera.

On Feb. 10, 1976, Pioneer 10, launched on March 2, 1972, continued on its way out of the solar system by crossing the orbit of Saturn. The probe would become the first man-made object to leave the solar system in 1987, when it crossed the orbit of Pluto. Pioneer 11, launched on April 5, 1973, was well over half the way to its rendezvous with Saturn in September 1979. In March it was revealed that Pioneer 10 had discovered that Jupiter's magnetic tail, almost half a billion miles long, completely spanned the distance between the orbits of Jupiter and Saturn.

(MITCHELL R. SHARPE)

See also Astronomy; Defense; Earth Sciences; Industrial Review: *Aerospace; Telecommunications;* Television and Radio.
[738.C]

ENCYCLOPÆDIA BRITANNICA FILMS. *Man Looks at the Moon* (1971); *Controversy over the Moon* (1971); *Space Exploration: A Team Effort* (1972); *The Moon: A Giant Step in Geology* (1976).

Spain

A monarchy of southwest Europe, Spain is bounded by Portugal, with which it shares the Iberian Peninsula, and by France. Area: 194,885 sq mi (504,750 sq km), including the Balearic and Canary islands. Pop. (1976 est.): 35,848,900, including the Balearics and Canaries. Cap. and largest city: Madrid (pop., 1976 est., 3,750,900). Language: Spanish. Religion: Roman Catholic. King, Juan Carlos I; premiers in 1976, Carlos Arias Navarro to July 1 and, from July 3, Adolfo Suárez González.

New regulations for public meetings were approved on May 25, and as of July 14 political associations other than Communist, separatist, and anarchist parties might be formed under specific rules. Arias resigned on July 1, and Adolfo Suárez González (*see* BIOGRAPHY), secretary-general of the National Movement, was appointed to replace him on July 3. Five of the Cabinet's most liberal members, including Manuel Fraga Iribarne and José María de Areilza, would not serve under Suárez. On July 7 the king appointed a new Cabinet, which included many younger technocrats committed to instituting democracy. At the end of July political prisoners were amnestied,

NICOLE HERZOG-VERREY—CAMERA PRESS/PHOTO TRENDS

An unusual photograph of the Spanish police in action during a demonstration by assistant professors of the University of Madrid in April.

and by the end of September nearly half of the officially estimated 650 such prisoners had been released. In December Santiago Carrillo, general secretary of the Communist Party, who was in the country illegally, was arrested, provoking widespread demonstrations. He was released a week later.

From mid-January a 21-member, Cortes-National Council of the Movement commission worked out details of a political reform outlined by the Cabinet in December 1975. On April 28 Premier Arias announced the plans for a bicameral parliament, the creation of a Court of Constitutional Guarantees, and changes in the Law of Succession. Final details, modified in the direction of democracy by the new government, were published on September 12 and approved by the Cortes on November 18: the Lower House (Congress) was to comprise 350 deputies, all freely elected; the Senate would comprise 207 elected senators, plus up to an additional fifth (*i.e.,* up to 41) nominated by the king. Elections for the new parliament would take place before June 1977. The reform was overwhelmingly approved by the voters in a referendum held on December 15.

The first three months of 1976 were characterized by industrial action and political disturbances. Employees from the Madrid subway, the railway network, the telephone service, banks, mines, and other areas were involved in lengthy strikes. The workers demanded wage increases over the government's limit set in November 1975 (a 3% maximum above the cost-of-living index) and better working conditions; the government generally responded by drafting them into the armed forces and threatening them with court-martial when they refused to work. Industrial conflict affected 1.3 million workers, and 49 million hours were lost, compared with 10 million and 18 million hours in all of 1975 and 1974, respectively. At the same time, widespread demonstrations were held demanding wider amnesty for political offenders, speedier moves toward political freedom, and, in Catalonia and the Basque provinces, separatism. The police reacted harshly; many participants were arrested and some were injured. Strikes and demonstrations continued all year long, albeit at a slower rate.

In January Spain and the U.S. signed a new five-year treaty, providing for economic cooperation and joint action in the technological, cultural, defense, and scientific fields. The U.S. also agreed to support Spain's entry into the European Economic Community; negotiations toward this end resumed in March after a six-month suspension by EEC members following the execution on Sept. 27, 1975, of five Basque terrorists. A new trade agreement between Spain and the EEC was being drafted to replace the seven-year agreement that expired at the end of June. The king and queen visited the U.S. and the Dominican Republic in June and Colombia and France in October.

The peseta came under pressure on international currency markets early in the year and was supported by the Bank of Spain, but on February 9 it was allowed to float and fell to the equivalent of a 10% devaluation. The hoped-for increase in exports and tourism had not materialized by the autumn, and temporary import surcharges were imposed. Inflation was increasing (about 20%, as against 14.8% in 1975) and the rise in gross domestic product was smaller than expected (2%, as against a forecast of 5–6%, although this was better than the 0.5% registered in 1975). In August Spain received a $1 billion loan from foreign and Spanish banks. (FRANÇOISE LOTERY)

See also Dependent States.

[972.A.5.a]

SPAIN

Education. (1974–75) Primary, pupils 6,215,-093, teachers 206,948; secondary, pupils 792,179, teachers 49,100; vocational, pupils 262,633, teachers 23,147; teacher training, students 46,-071, teachers 2,166; higher (including 31 universities), students 380,196, teaching staff 24,-523.

Finance. Monetary unit: peseta, with (Sept. 20, 1976) a free rate of 67.82 pesetas to U.S. $1 (116.85 pesetas = £1 sterling). Gold, SDR's, and convertible currencies (June 1976) U.S. $5,298,000,000. Budget (1975 actual): revenue 704 billion pesetas; expenditure 722 billion pesetas. Gross national product (1974) 4,943,-000,000,000 pesetas. Money supply (May 1976) 1,786,000,000,000 pesetas. Cost of living (1970 = 100; May 1976) 209.

Foreign Trade. (1975) Imports 932.2 billion pesetas; exports 441.5 billion pesetas. Import sources: EEC 35% (West Germany 10%, France 8%, U.K. 5%, Italy 5%); U.S. 16%; Saudi Arabia 11%. Export destinations: EEC 45% (France 14%, West Germany 11%, U.K. 8%, The Netherlands 5%); U.S. 10%. Main exports: machinery 12%; iron and steel 9%; fruit 7%; motor vehicles 7%; footwear 6%; ships and boats 5%; textile yarns and fabrics 5%. Tourism (1974): visitors 30,343,000; receipts U.S. $3,209,000,000.

Transport and Communications. Roads (1974) 142,585 km (including 1,079 km expressways). Motor vehicles in use (1974): passenger 4,309,510; commercial 950,510. Railways: (1973) 15,967 km (including 4,105 km electrified); traffic (1974) 16,079,000,000 passenger-km, freight 11,887,000,000 net ton-km. Air traffic (1975): 10,694,000,000 passenger-km; freight 237,908,000 net ton-km. Shipping (1975): merchant vessels 100 gross tons and over 2,667; gross tonnage 5,433,354. Telephones (Dec. 1974) 7,042,968. Radio receivers (Dec. 1973) *c.* 8 million. Television receivers (Dec. 1973) 5,719,-000.

Agriculture. Production (in 000; metric tons; 1975): wheat 4,354; barley 6,877; oats 619; rye 247; corn 1,848; rice *c.* 384; sorghum 148; potatoes 5,162; dry broad beans (1974) 131; other dry beans 117; chick-peas 60; tomatoes 2,309; onions 859; cabbages (1974) 558; melons (1974) 683; apples (1974) 992; pears (1974) 452; peaches (1974) 390; oranges (1974) 1,830; mandarin oranges and tangerines (1974) 579; lemons (1974) 222; sugar, raw value *c.* 915; sunflower seed 338; bananas (1974) 380; olives *c.* 2,222; olive oil *c.* 480; wine (1974) 3,637; tobacco 23; cotton, lint *c.* 45; cow's milk *c.* 5,100; hen's eggs *c.* 600; meat *c.* 1,850; fish catch (1974) 1,511. Livestock (in 000; 1975): cattle 4,417; pigs 7,865; sheep 16,257; goats (1974) 2,403; horses (1974) 266; mules (1974) 377; asses (1974) 310; chickens *c.* 45,708.

Industry. Index of industrial production (1970 = 100; 1975) 143. Fuel and power (in 000; metric tons; 1975): coal 10,571; lignite 3,381; crude oil 1,745; manufactured gas (cu m) 2,733,000; electricity (kw-hr) 82,385,000. Production (in 000; metric tons; 1975): cement 23,970; iron ore (50% metal content) 8,217; pig iron 7,131; crude steel 11,115; aluminum 208; copper 139; lead 73; zinc 133; petroleum products (1974) *c.* 42,740; sulfuric acid 2,348; fertilizers (nutrient content; 1974–75) nitrogenous 819, phosphate 655, potash 381; cotton yarn 73; cotton fabrics 68; wool yarn 30; rayon, etc., yarn and fibres 50; nylon, etc., yarn and fibres 120; passenger cars (units) 710; commercial vehicles (units) 109. Merchant vessels launched (100 gross tons and over; 1975) 1,633,-000 gross tons.

SPAIN: THE POST-FRANCO ERA

By David Rudnick

When Generalissimo Francisco Franco died in November 1975, the world waited to see what sort of changes were in the offing. Would Spain begin a transition from Francoism to some sort of democracy? That was likely to be a difficult operation in a land where a bloody civil war had been followed by 36 years of political repression. There were, however, some hopeful signs.

The Chances for Democracy. For one thing, Franco's death did not leave as much of a political vacuum as the personal nature of his rule might have suggested. Although he had maintained his position by playing one group off against another, arbitrating between the National Movement (as the Falange was later reconstituted), the monarchists, and the Catholic Opus Dei technocrats, ultimately one broadly defined group did emerge ascendant. This was the business elite, the "civilized right" of new capitalists that had grown up through the boom years of Spain's rapid economic growth. Franco's heirs were hardheaded men who had been enriched by mass consumerism; they were conservative reformers who appreciated the connection between consumer sovereignty and popular sovereignty, between economic freedom and political freedom. The reactionary right, the "Bunker," was admittedly still a force to be reckoned with, but many of its members were also shareholders and beneficiaries of *desarrollo* (economic development).

Second, Spain's dependence on foreign investment for the maintenance of economic advance and its need for export markets combined to increase the influence of other countries over internal Spanish politics. When five alleged terrorists were executed in defiance of European protests in September 1975, the European Economic Community reacted by suspending trade talks then in progress until "freedom and democracy are established in Spain." Since the EEC takes some 47% of all Spanish exports, and since Spain's Mediterranean competitors have been increasing their trade with the EEC market, it was clear that in future Spain would have to observe certain democratic norms if it was not to suffer serious economic damage.

In the third place, rapid economic growth had transformed Spanish society, replacing the old division between landlord and peasant by a new, more complex and modern structure. A prosperous urban proletariat and sub-bourgeoisie had emerged, endowed for the first time with the rewards and the psychology of Western consumer society. Spaniards had joined their European neighbours and become less ideological and more materialistic. Their gains—however modest—gave them a stake in order and stability which, in the eyes of their rulers, qualified them for a say in the government of the country.

Vestiges of the Old Regime. Despite these favourable and probably decisive social and economic factors, democratic progress faces powerful obstacles, some institutional, some historic in nature. Institutionally, the Francoist machinery of government still has to be radically reformed, if not completely dismantled, before genuine representative forms can develop. The Cortes (Parliament), the Council of the Realm (Privy Council), the National Syndicate (state-run trade-union organization), and the extensive police and security apparatus are the four pillars of the old regime.

The unreformed Cortes, a rubber-stamp body of Franco followers, is to be replaced by a bicameral body comprising an entirely elected lower house (Congress) and a largely elective upper chamber (Senate). But since the Senate would be empowered to veto legislation by Congress, critics fear that constitutional deadlock would be inevitable. Spanish reformers sometimes point to Britain as their model, but the shape of such legislative reform suggests British democracy of the 19th rather than the 20th century. The precise method by which the new legislature will be elected and its relationship with the government defined have still to be clarified. Hitherto the Cortes has acted as a brake on reform. In June 1976 it employed procedural tactics to delay changes in the penal code legalizing political parties, and when in July it finally did approve the necessary changes it excluded organizations that, "subjected to international discipline, seek to implant a totalitarian system"—that is, the Communist Party.

The Communists, Trade-Union Reform, and the Democratic Game. The vexed question of the legality of the Spanish Communist Party (PCE) is linked to the problem of trade-union reform through Communist domination of the Workers Commissions, the most influential of the clandestine, class-based trade-union structures. In contrast, the Francoist National Syndicate is a vertically organized body that unites employers and workers with the government along corporatist rather than class lines, and the unofficial unions are determined to see it abolished. Although still illegal a year after Franco's death, these unions—besides the Workers Commissions there are the Socialist UGT and the smaller USO—are preferred as bargaining partners by employers because they are more representative (if also more militant) than the National Syndicate. Realistic Syndicate officials are ready to abandon the organization's corporatist character by ejecting the employers and declaring it independent from the government, but the clandestine unions will not cooperate in such plans. The Workers Commissions are particularly hostile; having emerged spontaneously around 1960 in the new industrial suburbs of Madrid, the Commissions rejected attempts seven years later to assimilate them to the Syndicate structure. This, however, has not stopped them from infiltrating the Syndicate, whose totalitarian associations make it a potentially easy (if paradoxical) target for Communist subversion.

For any new form of trade-union organization to be approved, the Cortes would first have to revoke a labour statute promulgated by Franco in 1938 (his first law), establishing the Syndicate as the instrument of state economic policy. However, since Syndicate representatives hold one-third of all seats in the unreformed Cortes, such a radical move could only happen after the Cortes has itself been reformed.

The Communist Party issue has further ramifications. A legalized PCE would mean that strikes called by the Workers Commissions, the party's industrial arm, would also be legalized and could no longer be broken by using troops as manpower, a tactic the government resorted to frequently in the first part of 1976. Labour militancy was already sharply on the increase during Franco's final years; in 1976 it positively exploded, and although the government usually responded with grossly inflationary wage settlements, it sometimes imposed militarization orders on the strikers. If strikers should ever ignore their call-up orders on any scale, the government would either have to use the Army in a possibly bloody act of repression or climb down and risk a furious backlash by Bunker forces in the police and among the higher army echelons.

Strikes have basically been motivated by demands for higher wages and better conditions—worker militancy being partly based on the belief that high growth rates in the past (averaging nearly 8%) were achieved at their expense. But strikers have also frequently demanded amnesty for political prisoners and

David Rudnick is a research fellow at the Royal Institute of International Affairs, London, and has written a number of articles on contemporary Spain.

R. ROYAL—SYGMA

Spain's new premier, Adolfo Suárez González, with King Juan Carlos (foreground) and Queen Sofía. Suárez, 43, became the century's youngest head of a Spanish government when he was sworn in on July 5.

liberty for all opponents of the regime, particularly clandestine union leaders like the Communist Marcelino Camacho.

Yet a further aspect of the Communist issue that could throw the government's reform plans off course is the unwillingness of other political parties to play "the democratic game" without Communist opponents. Early in 1976 the two opposition groups, the largely socialist-led Democratic Platform and the Communist-led Democratic Junta, came together in a popular front called the Democratic Coordination, demonstrating that the government's attempts to isolate the Communists had failed. Here again the government faces a potentially dangerous situation, unable to legalize the PCE for fear of the Bunker, yet apparently unable to gain the cooperation of other parties in excluding the Communists. Many observers, however, dismissed the Democratic Coordination as a mere paper creation, arguing that the other parties would soon desert the Communists.

Economic Problems. Economic problems have not made the government's task of achieving change with stability any easier. Spain was hit by the recent international recession somewhat later than other countries, and its recovery has been correspondingly delayed. After several years in surplus, the balance of payments fell to a deficit of nearly $3.5 billion in 1975 and was not expected to show much improvement in 1976. Inflation, officially 14.8% in 1975, was running at around 20% by mid-1976, and by the same period unemployment had increased to over 5% of the work force. Recession in Europe meant that fewer jobs were available for Spanish migrant workers and reduced the flow of foreign exchange remittances into Spain, thus hitting both unemployment and the payments gap at one blow. There was also a sizable outflow of private capital from Spain, partly impelled by the political uncertainty that also played a marginal role in the slight decline in tourism. Devaluation added to inflationary pressures and stimulated wage demands which (politically hard to resist) gave a further twist to inflation.

The Suárez Gonzalez government which took over from Arias Navarro's administration in July 1976 attacked the country's economic problems on a piecemeal basis. Fiscal reform, although long overdue, was a nettle the government was in no hurry to grasp. Similarly, austerity measures that would have made economic sense were delayed because of their political implications. Although wage increases on the scale of 1976 were certainly not justified by Spain's markedly lower growth rate, the government bought domestic peace by running down its sizable reserves and borrowing heavily abroad.

International Relations. Internationally, the first year of the post-Franco era was one of fence-mending with Europe, consolidation with the U.S., and exploration with the Soviet bloc. Priority was given in the first half of 1976 to unfreezing relations with the EEC, which Spain aspired to join as soon as practicable. Madrid was heartened by Greece's success in opening membership negotiations, which it saw as a test case. But little thought was given to the economic problems—particularly in agriculture—likely to flow from Community membership. Membership was seen both in Madrid and in the EEC capitals largely in political terms, as a prize to be awarded for democracy. Unquestionably, however, the aim of ultimate EEC membership was a powerful incentive driving the government along its reformist road.

Relations with the U.S. had always been easier, since the Americans were much less ideological than most Europeans in their approach to the Franco regime. Washington had seen Franco as a bulwark against Communism and disorder. Impressed by Spain's strategic importance at the gateway to the Mediterranean and the Atlantic, the U.S. began as early as 1953, with the cold war at its most glacial, a long and lone relationship with Franco's pariah regime. Spain gained much-needed international respectability, and the U.S. acquired valuable air and naval bases. Furthermore, U.S. investment contributed more significantly than any other to Spain's spectacular growth.

With Franco out of the way, however, and Juan Carlos on the throne, Washington made plain that it favoured speedy constitutional change, partly in the hope of overcoming European opposition to Spain's membership in NATO. Mounting uncertainty elsewhere on NATO's southern flank highlighted the importance of satisfactorily integrating Spain into the West's defense system. For his part, Juan Carlos needed sophisticated U.S. weaponry to keep his armed forces content. During the Spanish royal couple's state visit to the U.S. in June 1976, the king spoke out most openly and unequivocally in favour of democracy in Spain. Shortly afterward, the Cortes ratified the Spanish-U.S. Treaty of Friendship and Cooperation (worth $1.2 billion to Spain), upgraded by the U.S. since Franco's death from a mere executive agreement.

The end of the Franco regime also gave Spanish foreign policy more flexibility in its dealings with the Soviet bloc (although diplomatic relations already existed with East Germany). Determined opposition to Communism at home did not prevent Madrid from embarking on a diplomatic offensive to deepen commercial relations with the Communist countries.

Speleology

The known depth of the world's deepest cave system increased again in the fall of 1975. Two members of the Bristol Exploration Club discovered the entrance of a new cave in the French Pyrenees, the Gouffre Soum Couye 3, and explored it. At the bottom they found themselves in the Tête Sauvage cave, itself part of the overall Pierre Saint-Martin system. As the new entrance was 528 ft higher than that of the Tête Sauvage, the total depth of the system became 4,370 ft. The Jean Bernard cave, in the French Alps, became the second deepest; discovery of a connection between it and the B19 pothole resulted in a combined depth of 3,963 ft, and on Jan. 1, 1976, further exploration reached a terminal sump at 4,258 ft. Soviet speleologists attained a depth of 2,625 ft in the Kirk Tav plateau in the Pamirs, where exploration continued. In Austria, French cavers descended a 1,148-ft shaft in the lower part of the Hochlecken-höhle and reached a depth of 2,330 ft.

In Mexico the terminal sump of the Joya de las Conchas was reached at a depth of 1,693 ft, making that cave the third deepest in Mexico and the fourth in the Americas. A Polish-Venezuelan expedition descended a new cave in the Sarisariñama Plateau of Venezuela—the Sima de la Lluvia (663 ft). They also measured the exact depth of the two deeper holes in that area, the Sima Grande de Sarisariñama (1,030 ft) and Sima Pequeña de Sarisariñama (813 ft). In Guatemala Canadian cavers reached the bottom of an enormous open pit, El Grande, which at about 800 ft became the country's deepest.

The British expedition to the caves of New Guinea spent several months in the field. The biggest cave they found, called Selminum Tem, was at least 8.5 mi long and hence the longest in the Southern Hemisphere. At 1,200 ft it was also the second deepest in New Guinea and third or fourth deepest in the Southern Hemisphere. The Cave Exploration Group of East Africa explored Leviathan Cave in the lava of the Chyulu Hills, Kenya. At 6.8 mi long and with a vertical depth range of 1,542 ft it was the longest and deepest lava cave in the world. Ethiopian and British explorers made several original discoveries in Ethiopia and explored the country's deepest cave, Enkoftu Mohu, to 630 ft.

Cave diving had a fruitful year. In France the 3,000-ft-long sump in the Grotte de la Balme (Isère) —the second longest explored sump in the world—was passed by Bernard Léger, taking 2¾ hours. In North Yorkshire, England, the mile-long submerged passage between Kingsdale Master Cave and the karst spring at Keld Head slowly succumbed to British cave divers. Geoffrey Yeadon dived 2,350 ft downstream from the cave and Oliver Statham penetrated 2,750 ft upstream from the rising. Only some 500 ft in the middle remained unexplored. Also in North Yorkshire, a successful dive through a 730-ft-long sump linked Notts Pot and Ireby Cavern, giving a combined system over 3.5 mi long. The diving of sump 6 in Prod's Pot (Ireland) revealed a mile of spectacular stream passage. Oliver Statham and others penetrated even deeper into Wookey Hole (Mendip Hills, Somerset) in February when they dived a succession of new sumps in the cave. The new sections, Wookey 23 and 24, include a large chamber, a lake, and canyon passages containing the river.

In May three cavers from Newcastle University died while attempting to dive the sumps between Langstroth Cave and Langstroth Pot (North Yorkshire) without diving apparatus. They were not drowned but were asphyxiated by carbon dioxide that had rapidly accumulated in the intermediate air bell chamber.

In Japan a party of seven cavers was rescued after being trapped underground for three days by flooding from a heavy rain. They were 990 ft into Byakurendo Cave, the deepest in Japan.

The International Speleological Union was accepted as a member of UNESCO. (T. R. SHAW)

[232.A.5.a]

Sporting Record

Every four years the Olympic Games provide a magnificent forum for individual athletes and national teams to come together to test their speed, their strength, their endurance, their grace, their accuracy, and their courage against one another. The drama provided by the Games of the XXI Olympiad passed all expectations. One world record after another was broken, and television audiences throughout the world witnessed a series of individual accomplishments never before attained in Olympic competition. Indeed, the 1976 spectacular was sure to be remembered for many years to come. Even the intrusion of politics into the Games at Montreal was part of the drama and was certain to affect the Olympics in the years ahead.

This issue of the *Book of the Year* carries two Special Reports on the recent Olympics. A summary of the winter events in Austria, together with a complete list of results, will be found under WINTER SPORTS. Parallel coverage of the summer events will be found under TRACK AND FIELD SPORTS. In addition, the BIOGRAPHY section of the *Book of the Year* includes a three-page pictorial array of some of the most outstanding Olympians of 1976.

Readers are also reminded that text articles on a wide variety of sports can also be found in the *Book of the Year*. Because related sports are often grouped under a single heading (COMBAT SPORTS, for example, includes boxing, wrestling, judo, karate, sumo, fencing, and kendo), the simplest method for locating a specific sport is through the Index at the back of the book.

[452.B]

Sri Lanka

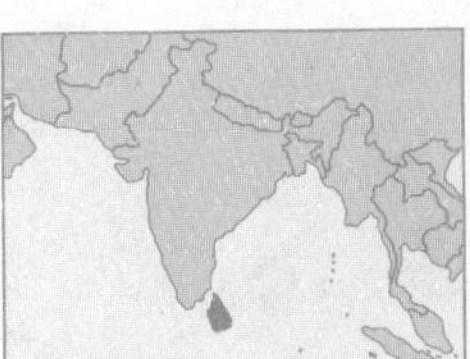

An Asian republic and member of the Commonwealth of Nations, Sri Lanka (Ceylon) occupies an island in the Indian Ocean off the southeast coast of peninsular India. Area: 25,332 sq mi (65,610 sq km). Pop. (1975 est.): 13,603,000, including Sinhalese about 72%; Tamil 21%; Moors 7%. Cap. and largest city: Colombo (pop., 1974 est., 592,000). Language: Sinhalese (official), Tamil, English. Religion (1971): Buddhist 67%; Hindu 18%; Christian 7%; Muslim 7%. President in 1976, William Gopallawa; prime minister, Mrs. Sirimavo Bandaranaike.

The fifth summit conference of nonaligned nations, held in Colombo in August 1976, provided the government only a brief respite from nagging economic difficulties and political tension. In May the government

Squash Rackets: *see* Racket Games

SRI LANKA

Education. (1973) Primary, pupils 2,117,706; secondary, pupils 480,264; primary and secondary, teachers 98,925; vocational, pupils 3,648, teachers 302; teacher training, students 9,288, teachers 593; higher, students 19,286, teaching staff 2,453.

Finance. Monetary unit: Sri Lanka rupee, with (Sept. 20, 1976) a free rate of SLRs 8.85 to U.S. $1 (SLRs 15.21 = £1 sterling) and an effective tourist rate of SLRs 14.57 to U.S. $1 (SLRs 25.10 = £1 sterling). Gold, SDR's, and foreign exchange (June 1976) U.S. $68 million. Budget (1975 actual): revenue SLRs 4,494,000,000; expenditure SLRs 6,562,000,000. Gross national product (1974) SLRs 21,318,000,000. Money supply (March 1976) SLRs 3,365,000,000. Cost of living (Colombo; 1970 = 100; June 1976) 146.

Foreign Trade. (1975) Imports SLRs 4,975,000,000; exports SLRs 3,934,000,000. Import sources (1974): China 8%; Japan 8%; France 8%; Pakistan 6%; Australia 6%; India 5%. Export destinations (1974): U.K. 10%; China 8%; Pakistan 8%; U.S. 7%; West Germany 6%. Main exports: tea 49%; rubber 17%; coconut products 10%.

Transport and Communications. Roads (1974) 26,218 km. Motor vehicles in use (1974): passenger 90,730; commercial 34,850. Railways: (1974) 1,535 km; traffic (1973–74) 2,778,000,000 passenger-km, freight 323 million net ton-km. Air traffic (1974): 258 million passenger-km; freight 3,020,000 net ton-km. Telephones (Dec. 1973) 68,000. Radio licenses (Dec. 1973) 515,000.

Agriculture. Production (in 000; metric tons; 1975): rice *c.* 1,105; cassava (1974) *c.* 600; sweet potatoes (1974) *c.* 95; onions *c.* 53; pineapples (1974) *c.* 40; copra *c.* 170; tea *c.* 214; coffee *c.* 9; rubber *c.* 150. Livestock (in 000; June 1974): cattle *c.* 1,650; buffalo *c.* 716; sheep *c.* 27; goats *c.* 549; pigs *c.* 112; chickens *c.* 8,000.

Industry. Production (in 000; metric tons; 1974): salt 120; cement (1975) 393; graphite (1973) 7.2; petroleum products *c.* 1,700; cotton yarn (1973) 7; electricity (kw-hr) *c.* 1,050,000.

declared a state of emergency after receiving reports that antigovernment forces were planning subversive action. Mrs. Bandaranaike referred particularly to the Tamil Federal Party's campaign for a separate state. Communal riots between Muslims and Sinhalese in Puttalam district of North Western Province triggered a demand for autonomy in the eastern districts where Muslims were in a majority.

Parliament's seven-year term would expire in May 1977, but the ruling Sri Lanka Freedom Party spurned the opposition's demand that a date for the election be set. There was a strongly voiced desire within the ruling party to postpone the election indefinitely.

Per capita national income in 1975 remained level at SLRs 716. The nationalization of tea, rubber, and coconut estates and the takeover of their management from the private agency houses had not improved production. In agriculture, only rice production increased, by 22% in 1974–75. In April the Aid Group for Sri Lanka pledged U.S. $180 million for the fiscal year 1976–77. (GOVINDAN UNNY)

[976.A.4]

Stamp Collecting: *see* Philately and Numismatics

Steeplechasing: *see* Equestrian Sports

Stock Exchanges

The year 1976 was one of declining stock prices and rising commodity prices. Stock prices generally increased early in the year in expectation that the business recovery would gather speed. The rise in stock prices came to a halt, however, when investors realized that recovery was slowing down while inflation was continuing at relatively high rates. Thus for the year as a whole, 11 of the 16 major stock market indexes in Europe, Asia, and Africa showed declines.

In contrast, commodity prices, as measured by selected indicators in London and Tokyo, rose during the year. The strength in commodity prices, particularly in the prices of industrial materials, reflected two major factors. One was premature buying by businessmen and speculators who feared renewed shortages or overestimated the revival of demand for materials by industry. The other factor was the International Monetary Fund's decision to start selling 25 million ounces of gold bullion; investors who normally bought gold as a hedge against declines in currency values were led to switch to commodities other than gold as a protection from currency depreciation.

In Europe stock markets were uniformly weak during 1976. Among the 11 European countries included in Table I, only Switzerland experienced higher equity prices. Elsewhere the trend in stock prices was mixed. In Japan, Hong Kong, and Singapore the markets put on relatively strong performances. Lower equity values prevailed in Australia and South Africa.

Worldwide economic recovery continued, though at a slower rate. The slowdown was due to a combination of factors: inflation and the expectation of further inflation; political instability in some countries; abnormally high unemployment; tight monetary pol-

Activity on the New York Stock Exchange hit an all-time high on February 20. Employees celebrated by tossing paper in the air when it was announced that 44,510,000 shares had been traded that day.

WIDE WORLD

icies; governmental controls; and the threat of rising oil prices. Uncertainty in foreign exchange markets led to devaluations of some currencies and created doubts about others. This tended to enhance the relative position of countries with strong economies and exacerbate the problems of those with weak economies. Some of the latter were forced to adopt deflationary policies in order to maintain their balance of payments.

As 1976 came to a close, the outlook for the world economy was highly uncertain. Many large and small nations faced the need to reverse the trend toward falling exports and rising imports, increase their production, and reduce levels of unemployment. Their success in adjusting to a slower but potentially more consistent growth pattern, without erecting barriers to international trade, would likely determine the overall direction of equity markets in 1977.

(ROBERT H. TRIGG)

United States. Stock markets in the U.S. began 1976 with a burst of bullish activity, only to follow this with many months of uncertain trading within a narrow range before resuming a forward momentum at year-end. The Dow Jones industrial average, having closed 1975 at 852.41, gained 14.5% during January of 1976, which saw many new records set for trading volume on the New York Stock Exchange. The high for the year was achieved on September 21 at 1014.79 but the Dow crossed the 1000 mark 12 times during the year, closing at 1004.65 for a year-to-year gain of 18%. Many U.S. investors found the year a frustrating one because of the absence of a clear trend. Widespread dissatisfaction with the performance of the economy, continued skepticism over the future, an economic slowdown in the second half of the year, and continuing high unemployment created investor uncertainty. The volume of trading on the New York Stock Exchange reached new levels for the second consecutive year. February 20 was the most active day in the 184-year history of the exchange, when 44,510,000 shares were traded (a record 13 million shares in the first hour). The 634,854,655 shares traded in January, and the 1,760,000,000 shares traded in the first quarter, were both new highs. There were 27 days in which 30 million or more shares changed hands, as compared with only 7 in 1975. The value of all New York Stock Exchange stocks rose by an estimated $150 billion in 1976.

Average prices on the New York Stock Exchange fluctuated within a narrow range throughout most of 1976 (Table II). The 500 stocks in Standard and Poor's composite index jumped from 96.86 to 100.64 in January and February, then settled within a narrow range until July when the index rose to an average of 104.20 before dipping in August, achieving a high of 105.45 in September, falling off in October and November, and rising abruptly in December. The 425 industrial stocks in the average rose from the 99.31 level of the previous year-end to 108.45 in January and 112.96 in February. The advance was slowed in May but later resumed to achieve a high of 118.15 in September.

Public utility stock prices fluctuated between a low of 45.67 attained in March and a high of 50.63 in September. These prices were substantially above the corresponding 1975 averages throughout 1976.

The railroad index paralleled the utilities, rising from 37.07 in December 1975 to 41.42 in January 1976 and climbing slowly but consistently through July, the peak month for this index. On a year-to-year basis, July represented a 26% gain over the corresponding month of 1975.

Yields on common stocks in 1976 were well below the corresponding values for 1975. In January the return was 3.80%, a drop of 27% from the preceding year. Yields declined irregularly throughout most of 1976, but in October the January level was surpassed temporarily. The reverse spread between stocks and bonds continued in 1976 with an average yield on Barron's ten highest grade bonds at 7.95% in November and the dividend yields on the 30 stocks in the Dow Jones industrial averages at 4.18%. This spread decreased in the latter half of the year. In January 1976 bond yields had been 8.5% and stock yields 4.5%.

Long-term government bond prices rose from an average of 55.75 in January 1976 to 59.33 by April, and, after a modest decline, recorded a high of 59.99 for the first ten months of the year (Table III). Bond yields, which began a downtrend in October 1975 from an average of 7.29, declined to 6.94 in January and, except for a brief interruption in May, drifted to a low of 6.70 in September. The municipal bond market registered the lowest yields in four years as prices surged to the highest levels since 1974 by December 1976. As measured by the Dow Jones municipal bond index, municipal bond yields moved down to 5.70% in December, the lowest level since 5.63% in the week

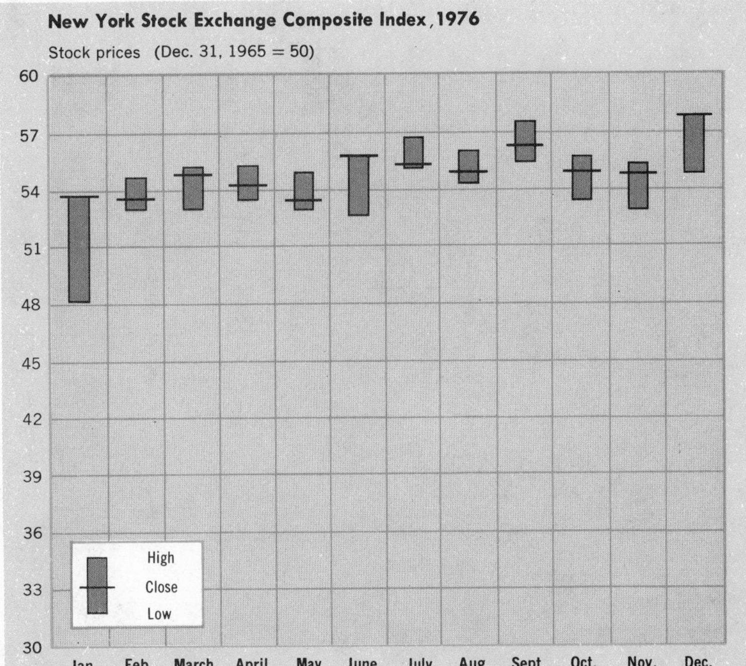

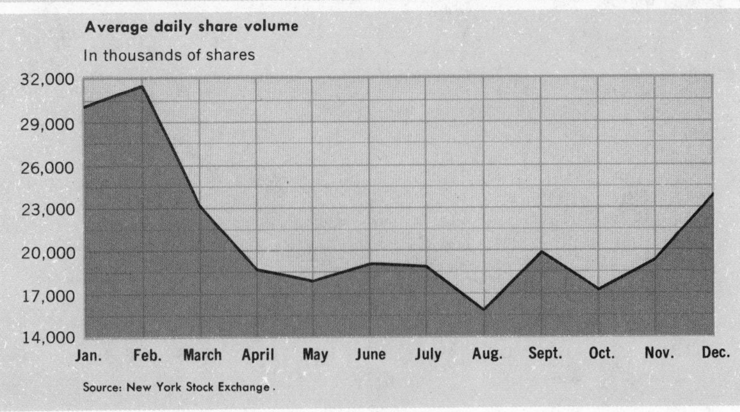

ended April 19, 1974. Even New York issues rose sharply in 1976 despite the default risk that worried the municipal bond markets earlier in the year.

Corporate bond prices increased very slightly over their 1975 levels, with a range between 56.5 and 59.3 during the first ten months of the year. The bond market staged a major rally in the final months as interest rates dropped to their lowest levels in four years and the Federal Reserve Board pursued a more accommodative monetary policy. The net volume of new corporate and foreign bond offerings in 1976 was about $34 billion, down from about $36 billion in 1975. The potential for refinancing the high-interest debt issues of 1969 and 1970 as interest rates declined was considered a bullish factor in the bond market. Yields on long-term securities declined within a very narrow range in 1976 from a level of 8.60 in January to a low of 8.38 in September (Table IV).

Investor expectations were mixed as a result of conflicting developments in the economy and in the stock markets. The slowdown in the economy, political uncertainties, continuing redemptions of mutual funds, changes in the demand and supply situation for common stocks, and the greater attractiveness of fixed-income investments because of high interest rates were depressants. The drop in interest rates was a bullish factor, particularly in the last quarter of 1976.

Volume for the year on the New York Stock Exchange was 5,360,116,438, a gain of 14.2% over the 4,693,426,508 record set in 1975. Bond sales, at $5,262,106,900, increased only slightly above the 1975 level of $5,178,337,500. On the American Stock Exchange (Amex), the volume of shares traded in 1976 was 648,330,290, a 19.7% gain over the prior year's 541,139,281. Bond trading increased to $301,095,000, as compared with $259,623,000 in 1975.

The booming market in options continued to capture the headlines as volume surged from 18.1 million contracts in 1975 to 32.3 million in 1976, representing 3,200,000,000 shares of stock. The number of securities on which listed options were available went from 137 to 202 and the number of exchanges from three to five. The American Stock Exchange, the Chicago Board Options Exchange, and the Philadelphia Stock Exchange were joined by the Pacific Stock Exchange and the Midwest Stock Exchange. At year-end the New York Stock Exchange went on record as favouring trading in options on that exchange as well. Several scandals were investigated involving the reporting of fictitious trades and "wash sales" in the options markets, but the impact of such misconduct was not very serious in 1976. The Chicago Board Options Exchange accounted for about 65% of options trading, with the American Stock Exchange representing about 30% of total volume. The significance of the shift in trading interest was reflected in the price of a seat on the exchange. A seat on the Big Board that sold for $515,000 in 1969 could be purchased for as little as $40,000 in 1976 and was priced at $75,000 bid and $100,000 asked at year-end. A seat on the Chicago Board Options Exchange sold for as much as $149,000, in recognition of the growing trading activity in options as compared with stocks.

The Securities and Exchange Commission (SEC) intervened actively in the stock market during 1976 pursuant to federal legislation mandating a national market with greater freedom of entry. Stock exchanges were obliged to remove all obstacles to membership by any financially qualified applicant. This required amendments to the Big Board constitution limiting to 45% the interest in a member firm's capital or profit that could be owned by a foreign non-Canadian entity, and the rule that an individual exchange member must be a U.S. citizen. There was much resistance to this set of amendments because of brokers' fear of competition from commercial banks that might seek membership on the exchange. The SEC also proposed a computerized national market system called CLOB (Composite Limit Order Book) whereby brokers would send all buy and sell orders into the computer in addition to buy and sell price limits for given quantities of stock. Such a system would enable potential buyers to look to a single market-making centre for price information and result in greater market efficiency. Perhaps more newsworthy in 1976 was the SEC's role in requiring public disclosures by more than 175 publicly traded corporations of more than $300 million paid in bribes and other questionable overseas payments during the previous five or six years. Among the disclosures were those by Lockheed, Gulf, and R. J. Reynolds.

New York Stock Exchange Common Stock Index Closing Prices

Stock prices (Dec. 31, 1965 = 50)

High
Close
Low

70
65
60
55
50
45
40
35
30
25
20
15
10
5
0
1954 1956 1958 1960 1962 1964 1966 1968 1970 1972 1974 1976

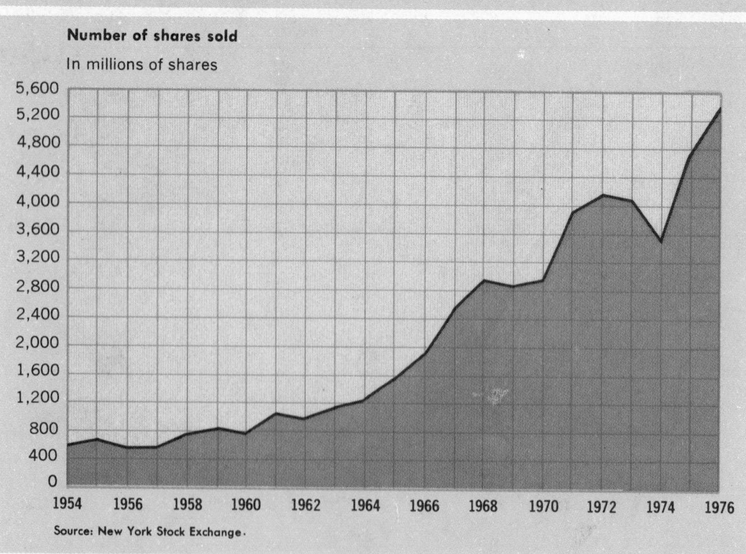

Source: New York Stock Exchange.

Canada. Canadian stock prices did not reflect the scale of gains achieved by their U.S. counterparts. The Toronto Stock Exchange composite index of 300 shares, corresponding to Standard and Poor's 500-share index, had a sharp rise in January and February from 950 to 1100 and then fluctuated narrowly between 1050 and 1100 from March through September before dipping to a low of 975 in October and regaining lost ground by the end of 1976. Industrials rose in the first and last quarters of the year and lagged during the middle half. Gold stocks were more volatile, with sharper movements over a wider range. The low for the year was 220.94 and the high 333.48, a 50.6% spread. Base metals and oils traded within a narrower price band. The Montreal Stock Exchange was relatively inactive during most of 1976 with the average index, which stood at 172.88 at the end of 1975, ending the following year at 168. The victory of the separatist party in Quebec on November 15 caused a sharp market setback that was short-lived. Market analysts reported that the continuation of controls over wages, prices, and dividends created resistance to foreign investment in Canada. They also blamed economic and political uncertainties.

Yields on 91-day Treasury bills, which paid 8.5% in January 1976, rose to 9.1% in March and remained at 9% or slightly above until November when they fell by stages to 8% in December. Because of the wide gap between Canadian and U.S. interest rates, the 30-day rate for Canadian commercial paper was 9.25% as compared with 4.75% for an equivalent security in the United States. At year-end, the prime rate in Canada was at 10% whereas the U.S. prime was split between 6 and 6.25%. The Canadian dollar was very strong most of the year, selling at a premium of as much as 3% above the U.S. dollar, but fell sharply in November to a discount before ending the year slightly below the U.S. dollar.

Long-term bonds gained in price during the year as investors anticipated a favourable outcome in the war on inflation. The government of Canada successfully floated several major bond issues on increasingly favourable terms with interest rates declining from 9.5% for long-term maturities in May to 8.5% by November and December of 1976.

(IRVING PFEFFER)

Western Europe. Of the four largest European economies, France had relatively the worst stock market performance, followed by Italy, Great Britain, and West Germany. Among the smaller countries, stocks declined most in Spain, The Netherlands, and Belgium; modest declines were experienced in Austria, Sweden, and Denmark; and Switzerland managed a 1% gain.

Economic and political crises were disruptive to the French stock market in 1976. Stock prices had been strong in January, but the upswing topped out in March. From April through December, the Paris Bourse was able to show higher prices only in May. Inflation in the first quarter was nearly twice as rapid as in West Germany, while the trade deficit amounted to $1.8 billion. During the same period, French factories were producing at only 80% of their capacity, compared with 84% a year earlier and 96% in 1974. The resulting weakness in the franc prompted the government to set controls on profits and freeze prices on selected consumer goods as a means of slowing inflation. The prolonged drought in Europe affected France more than any other country, since farm production accounts for 20% of the nation's export earnings. The economic program of Premier Raymond Barre, announced in September, included a three-month price freeze, a partial wage freeze, higher corporate taxes, and an increase in tax rates on individuals in high income brackets. The Parliament also enacted the nation's first tax on capital gains and endorsed a government study of a wealth tax. Equally disturbing to investors was the belief prevalent in the business community that a socialist-Communist victory was likely in the next general election in March 1978. Toward the end of 1976 there was a wave of labour unrest. Even the Paris Bourse was forced to close because of a strike by employees pro-

Table I. Selected Major World Stock Price Indexes*

Country	1976 range High	1976 range Low	Year-end close 1975	Year-end close 1976	Percent change
Australia	523	405	443	431	− 3%
Austria	2,674	2,492	2,547	2,497†	− 2
Belgium	113	87	105	96	− 9
Denmark	118	96	100	99	− 1
France	74	52	69	56	−19
Germany, West	822	688	776	727	− 6
Hong Kong	465	355	350	446	+27
Italy	91	65	83	75	−10
Japan	4,991	4,452	4,359	4,991	+14
Netherlands, The	1,065	78	97	83	−14
Singapore	286	236	237	255	+ 8
South Africa	215	174	212	184	−13
Spain	101	72	100	71	−29
Sweden	477	366	396	394	− 1
Switzerland	299	261	282	285	+ 1
United Kingdom	421	265	376	355	− 6

*Index numbers are rounded, and limited to countries for which at least 12 months' data were available on a weekly basis.
†As of Dec. 24, 1976.
Sources: *Barron's*, *The Economist*, *Financial Times*, and *The New York Times*.

Table II. U.S. Stock Market Prices and Yields

	Railroads (15 stocks)		Industrials (425 stocks)		Public utilities (55 stocks)		Composite (500 stocks)		Yield (200 stocks; %)	
Month	1976	1975	1976	1975	1976	1975	1976	1975	1976	1975
January	41.42	37.31	108.45	80.50	46.99	38.19	96.86	72.56	3.80	5.19
February	43.40	37.80	112.96	89.29	47.22	40.37	100.64	80.10	3.67	4.78
March	44.54	38.35	113.73	93.90	45.67	39.55	101.08	83.78	3.65	4.69
April	44.91	38.55	114.67	95.27	46.07	38.19	101.93	84.72	3.66	4.47
May	46.09	38.90	113.76	101.56	45.69	39.69	101.16	90.10	3.76	4.26
June	46.56	38.94	114.50	103.68	46.51	43.67	101.77	92.40	3.75	4.18
July	47.75	38.04	116.90	103.84	47.49	43.67	104.20	92.49	3.64	4.47
August	46.90	35.13	115.63	96.21	48.81	40.61	103.29	85.71	3.74	4.47
September	46.59	34.93	118.15	94.96	50.63	40.53	105.45	84.67	3.71	4.31
October	44.89	36.92	114.08	99.29	50.19	42.59	101.89	88.57	3.85	4.22
November	...	37.81	...	100.86	...	43.77	...	90.07	...	4.07
December	...	37.07	...	99.31	...	43.25	...	88.70	...	4.14

Sources: U.S. Department of Commerce, *Survey of Current Business*; Board of Governors of the Federal Reserve System, *Federal Reserve Bulletin*. Prices are Standard and Poor's monthly averages of daily closing prices, with 1941–43=10. Yield figures are Moody's composite index.

Table III. U.S. Government Long-Term Bond Prices and Yields
Average price in dollars per $100 bond

Month	Average 1976	Average 1975	Yield (%) 1976	Yield (%) 1975	Month	Average 1976	Average 1975	Yield (%) 1976	Yield (%) 1975
January	55.75	59.70	6.94	6.68	July	58.38	58.09	6.85	6.89
February	57.86	60.27	6.92	6.61	August	58.88	56.84	6.79	7.06
March	58.23	59.33	6.87	6.73	September	59.54	55.23	6.70	7.29
April	59.33	57.05	6.73	7.03	October	59.99	55.23	6.80	7.29
May	57.38	57.40	6.99	6.99	November	...	55.77	...	7.21
June	57.86	58.33	6.92	6.86	December	...	56.03	...	7.17

Source: U.S. Department of Commerce, *Survey of Current Business*. Average prices are derived from average yields on the basis of an assumed 3% 20-year taxable U.S. Treasury bond. Yields are for U.S. Treasury bonds that are taxable and due or callable in ten years or more.

Table IV. U.S. Corporate Bond Prices and Yields
Average price in dollars per $100 bond

Month	Average 1976	Average 1975	Yield (%) 1976	Yield (%) 1975	Month	Average 1976	Average 1975	Yield (%) 1976	Yield (%) 1975
January	57.0	56.4	8.60	8.83	July	57.1	56.6	8.56	8.84
February	57.1	56.6	8.55	8.62	August	57.9	56.6	8.45	8.95
March	57.3	56.2	8.52	8.67	September	58.8	55.8	8.38	8.95
April	58.2	55.8	8.40	8.95	October	59.3	56.0	8.39	8.86
May	56.5	56.6	8.58	8.90	November	...	56.3	...	8.78
June	56.8	56.7	8.62	8.77	December	...	56.1	...	8.79

Source: U.S. Department of Commerce, *Survey of Current Business*. Average prices are based on Standard and Poor's composite index of A1+ issues. Yields are based on Moody's Aaa domestic corporate bond index.

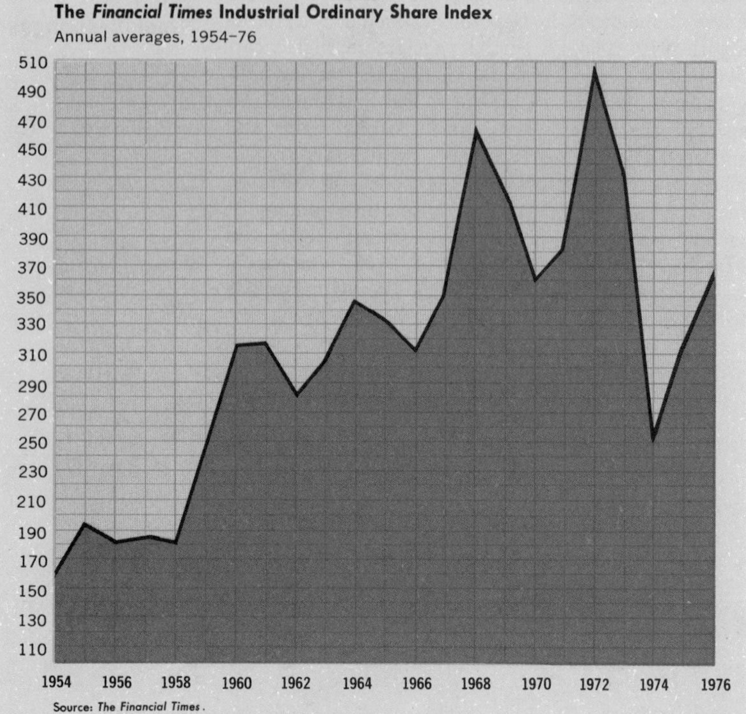

testing planned layoffs. News in October that unemployment had reached a record high was also discouraging to investors. At the close of December, stock prices were near their lowest level for the year. The overall decline in 1976 amounted to 19%.

In Italy the stock market slipped another 10% in 1976. The flight from equities was caused mainly by an unstable political environment and a dramatic fall in the value of the lira. The political crisis following Premier Aldo Moro's resignation of January 7 set off a sharp decline in the value of the lira, forcing the Bank of Italy to close the foreign exchange market. The depreciation of the lira raised the cost of imports, aggravating Italy's inflation which was already one of the highest in Europe. Prices on the Milan Stock Exchange dropped 3% in the first three months of 1976, the only equities market in Europe to experience a decline during that period.

In May, after President Giovanni Leone dissolved Parliament and announced national elections for June, the lira closed at 916 to the dollar compared with 680 in early January, representing a 26% depreciation in its value. The government imposed limitations on imports and restricted foreign exchange dealings. The narrow victory of the Christian Democrats in the June elections calmed investor fears. At the end of June, stock prices were 3% higher than on May 21. But by September inflation was proceeding at an annual rate of 22%, and the foreign trade deficit for the first nine months of 1976 had reached nearly $5 billion. On October 1 Premier Giulio Andreotti announced his plan to restore economic stability. This included a boost in the central bank's discount rate to 15 from 12%, partial wage controls for two years, a temporary 10% tax on all foreign exchange operations, the elimination of five paid holidays, and increases in the price of gasoline, train fares, and post office rates. The combined drop in stock values during September and October averaged 17%. About one-third of that loss was regained in November and December. Stock prices at the end of 1976, however, were 69% below the record high set in the early 1960s.

In Great Britain *The Financial Times* index of 30 industrial stocks traded on the London Stock Exchange declined 6% in 1976. It reached its 1976 high on May 4, and its low on October 27.

Following a 136% advance in 1975, stock prices had begun 1976 on a strong uptrend. January's rise amounted to 11%, but the index dropped nearly 4% in February and was relatively steady in March. In April it rose 2% and remained relatively strong in early May. The rally was propelled by sharply falling interest rates. The Bank of England's minimum discount rate to commercial banks dropped to 9.5% in early February. But unemployment stood at 6.1% of the labour force, the highest since World War II. In March, Prime Minister Harold Wilson submitted his resignation, having failed to end the "slumpflation" that had plagued the British economy since the Arab oil embargo in 1973. The subsequent lack of confidence in Britain's ability to discipline itself economically drove the pound to $1.72 in early June, down from the $2.35 level of a year earlier. This steep drop in the value of sterling precipitated a series of interest rate increases by the Bank of England, designed to make the pound more desirable to holders.

After hitting a recovery high of 421 at the beginning of May, *The Financial Times* index entered a steep downtrend which saw both the 400 and 300 levels broken. From July through October average equity prices declined each month. Britain's problems were compounded by a record trade deficit and the worst summer drought in history. The settlement of labour disputes with wage increases widely viewed as inflationary caused a new attack on the pound. These factors, combined with rising food and material prices and record interest rates, caused sterling to skid to a new low of $1.57. In response, the Bank of England raised its discount rate to a record 15%. In December stock prices rebounded strongly following the government's announcement that it would cut the budget in order to qualify for a $3.9 billion loan from the International Monetary Fund. The subsequent rise in the value of the pound to $1.70 allowed the Bank of England to lower its discount rate. From November 26 to the year's close, equity values rose 17%.

West Germany's stock markets experienced a decline in share prices averaging 6% in 1976. This occurred despite a relatively good economic performance and one of the lowest inflation rates in Europe (4½%). However, unemployment stood at about 4% of the labour force. In addition, West Germany's political stability and the strength of its economy relative to those of neighbouring countries, particularly France, exerted upward pressure on the mark. Persistent increases in the international value of the mark made it more difficult for German exporters to compete in world markets, and this put a lid on domestic economic expansion.

The economic, political, and social environment in Spain during 1976 could only be described as chaotic. Spain's inflation rate exceeded 20%, and unemployment was at 7% of the labour force. Economic activity was disrupted throughout the year by strikes and demonstrations against government policies. In July, Adolfo Suárez succeeded Carlos Navarro as premier. Promising to speed the pace of democratic reforms, he began in October with a bill authorizing free trade unions in Spain for the first time in 40 years. At the same time, he offered an emergency economic program that included a two-month price freeze and wage controls. Most investors apparently believed that a successful political transition was a necessary prerequisite if the country was to overcome inflation and rebuild its foreign reserves. The prices of equity securities traded on the Madrid Stock Exchange declined 29% in 1976.

Stock prices in The Netherlands followed a bearish pattern for the fourth consecutive year. Prices on the Amsterdam Stock Exchange dropped 14%, bringing the cumulative loss in the value of Dutch equities since the end of 1972 to 47%. The involvement of Prince Bernhard in the Lockheed bribery scandals unleashed a series of government investigations into business practices. The resulting wave of resentment against businessmen generated legislative proposals to restrict the growth of foreign-owned firms. The Dutch investment climate was further chilled with the imposition of temporary price controls in December that allowed industry to adjust prices for the higher costs of raw materials and semifinished parts, but not of wages. While the stock market staged a mild rally after mid-October, considerable doubt existed as to whether the long bear market had actually come to an end.

The trend of stock prices in Belgium was likewise bearish. Prices on the Brussels Bourse reached their highest point on February 5, nearly 8% above the 1975 close, but declined steadily over the next four months. At the end of June, prices were 12% below the February high. They remained relatively stable during July but resumed their decline in August. In mid-November unemployment reached a record 9.2%, surpassing the previous high of 8.8% registered 11 months earlier. Belgium's central bank raised its discount rate to 9%, the highest level since 1974. Stock prices staged a strong rally following the October bottom, but finished the year 9% lower than at the end of 1975.

Stock markets in Austria and Denmark also followed a bearish pattern. The Vienna Stock Exchange recorded its 1976 high in April, and Copenhagen's was reached on August 19. Stock prices in both countries fell sharply beginning in mid-October. For the year as a whole, the average decline in Austria was 2% and in Denmark 1%.

In Sweden the seesaw movement of stock prices resulted in a small net decline in the leading averages. After rising 29% in 1975, the stock market added an additional 17% in the first seven months of 1976. But within a period of just 13 weeks the 1976 advance was wiped out. The election defeat of Prime Minister Olof Palme's Social Democrats, after ruling for 44 years, suggested that the country faced a period of confusion until the economic philosophy of the new administration was clarified. In October reports regarding substantial deterioration in Sweden's balance of payments, and rumours about the krona's possible devaluation, caused an increase in the central bank's discount rate from 6 to 8%, the biggest change since World War II. Despite these bearish factors, stock prices managed to finish 1976 only 1% off.

Stocks in Switzerland began 1976 in a bullish atmosphere. The gains in equity values on the Zürich Stock Exchange during the January–March period (+3%) were an extension of the upward trend established in November 1975. But the rally softened and those gains were erased before the end of May. However, stock prices in June experienced a broad upswing that left equity values 5% higher for the first half of 1976.

During the final six months of 1976, Swiss stock prices reversed direction twice. From the end of June to mid-November, average share prices fell 12%. By the end of the year, however, this loss was trimmed by 9%. The net result for 1976 as a whole was a gain of 1%. Continued turmoil in foreign exchange markets, which greatly increased the value of the Swiss franc relative to other currencies, threatened the ability of the export and tourist industries to compete in world markets. To reduce the attraction of Swiss francs for foreign holders, the central bank cut its discount rate to 2%, a ten-year low, and imposed various restrictions to keep its currency from rising in foreign exchange markets. The relative attractiveness of Swiss equities reflected not only the strength of the Swiss franc but the country's relatively moderate monetary policies, low inflation rate, and social stability.

Other Countries. In 1976 stock prices in Hong Kong enjoyed the largest increase of any stock market. Prices rose sharply and virtually without pause until March 17, a gain of 27%. The market softened considerably during April and May, as investors took profits and potential buyers awaited new signs that the world economy would regain its upward momentum. From the end of March to the end of May, equity values dropped 12%. Following a technical rally in June, the market entered into a relatively narrow trading range until October when prices sank nearly 5%.

Singapore's stock market, which usually reflects equity price trends in Hong Kong, was up 8% in 1976. Both the Hong Kong and Singapore economies had not only recovered from the 1974–75 recession but surpassed the levels recorded during the 1973 boom. The resurgence of both countries could be traced to improving trade and relations with the People's Republic of China.

The stock exchange in Buenos Aires, Argentina, is in a cavernous old building. After the fall of Pres. Isabel Perón in March, the market shot upward. Some speculators made fortunes.

JUAN DE ONIS—THE NEW YORK TIMES

The stock market in Japan was also a star performer in 1976. The index of 225 common stocks traded on the Tokyo Exchange rose 14%, after jumping 14% in 1975. Prices ended the year at their highest level, the low having been set on January 5.

Throughout 1976 the Japanese government was pressured by other industrial countries to refrain from supporting the value of its currency in foreign exchange markets. Active intervention tended to keep the Japanese yen from appreciating against the U.S. dollar, thereby holding down the price of Japanese goods in world trade. Reflecting the pause in global economic activity, Japanese industrial production fell in both August and September. As a result, the government moved in October to lower interest rates and make borrowing easier in the hopes of encouraging spending on business capital equipment and private home construction. Two other encouraging developments as 1976 came to a close were the failure of the Organization of Petroleum Exporting Countries to agree on a uniform increase in the price of crude oil and the choice of Takeo Fukuda as the new prime minister.

In Australia, prices on the Sydney Stock Exchange ended 1976 3% lower than at the end of 1975. Equity values reached a peak on August 19 at 25% above the 1975 close. The subsequent decline reduced equity values by one-third before the end of November. Australia's deteriorating foreign trade position forced a 17½% devaluation of the Australian dollar on November 28, the largest in the nation's history.

The stock market in South Africa also took a beating in 1976, reflecting civil violence in the southern part of the country. For the year as a whole, industrial share prices on the Johannesburg Stock Exchange dropped 13%. Reflecting the upsurge in the price of gold bullion from $103 in September to $135 per ounce at year-end, gold shares traded on the Johannesburg Exchange rebounded. For 1976 as a whole the average decline was 23%, compared with 45% from January through August.

Commodity Markets. Bull markets were prevalent in international commodity markets during 1976. *The Economist*'s dollar index of 28 commodities traded predominantly in Great Britain jumped from 209 at the end of 1975 to 260 in early December a year later. The 24% increase was the third largest for this indicator since World War II, exceeded only by 48% in 1950 and 63% in 1973. The index established its 1976 high on July 6—a new record since this series was first compiled in 1860; the low was set in January.

The Economist's commodity index, which is heavily influenced by copper, coffee, sugar, beef, and grains, entered a strong upswing beginning in the first week of January. The index rose virtually without a significant correction until its peak in July. The subsequent retreat, however, lasted only until mid-September, and was relatively mild (−8%).

Reuter's United Kingdom commodity index also reached record highs in 1976. That index, which measures spot or futures quotations in sterling terms for 17 primary commodities weighted by their relative importance in international trade, experienced a 34% increase from the end of 1975 to the end of 1976. The index recorded its year's high on the final trading day of 1976, some 6% above the previous record.

The Nikkei Index of Commodity Prices, covering 17 of the most sensitive commodities traded in Tokyo, rose 12% from the end of 1975 to near the end of December 1976.

In sum, international commodity markets experienced strong demand in 1976. Farm commodity price movements reflected uncertainty over the size of the crop outlook because of drought conditions. Industrial commodities seesawed as buyers thought they saw signs of a strong global economic upturn. However, the major force underlying the trend in commodity prices in 1976 appeared to come from hedging and speculative considerations associated with the erosion of confidence in paper currencies.

(ROBERT H. TRIGG)

See also Economy, World.
[534.D.2.g.i]

Strikes:
see Industrial Relations

Sudan

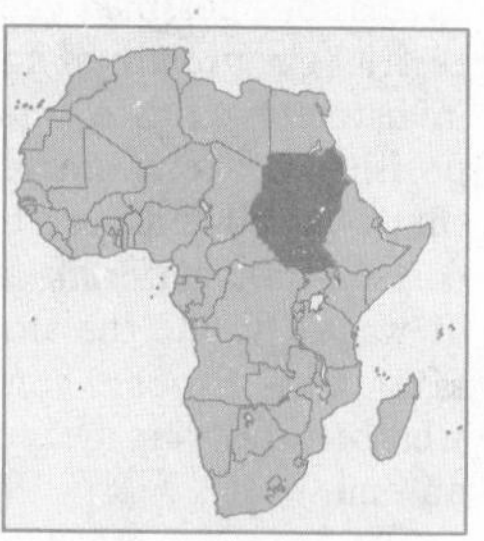

A republic of northeast Africa, the Sudan is bounded by Egypt, the Red Sea, Ethiopia, Kenya, Uganda, Zaire, the Central African Empire, Chad, and Libya. Area: 967,500 sq mi (2,505,813 sq km). Pop. (1974 est.): 17,324,000, including Arabs in the north and Negroes in the south. Cap. and largest city: Khartoum (pop., 1972 est., 300,000). Language: Arabic; various tribal languages in the south. Religion: Muslim in the north; predominantly animist in the south. President in 1976, Maj. Gen. Gaafar Nimeiry; prime ministers, Maj. Gen. Gaafar Nimeiry and, from August 9, Rashid Bakr.

President Nimeiry in July survived the most serious threat so far to his eight-year-old regime. A coup

SUDAN

Education. (1974–75) Primary, pupils 1,257,339, teachers 28,926; secondary, pupils 231,311, teachers 8,651; vocational, pupils 6,397, teachers 445; teacher training, students 5,680, teachers 628; higher, students 22,204, teaching staff 750.

Finance. Monetary unit: Sudanese pound, with (Sept. 20, 1976) a par value of Sud£0.348 to U.S. $1 (free rate of Sud£0.61 = £1 sterling). Gold, SDR's, and foreign exchange (June 1976) U.S. $32,800. Budget (1975–76 est.): revenue Sud£337 million; expenditure Sud£304 million. Money supply (June 1976) Sud£258,940,000. Cost of living (1970 = 100; Jan. 1976) 197.

Foreign Trade. (1975) Imports Sud£308,910,000; exports Sud£152,470,000. Import sources (1974): U.K. *c.* 15%; U.S. *c.* 12%; Japan *c.* 10%; West Germany *c.* 9%; Italy *c.* 7%; U.S.S.R. *c.* 6%; China *c.* 6%. Export destinations (1974): China *c.* 20%; France *c.* 11%; Italy *c.* 9%; West Germany *c.* 8%; U.S. *c.* 6%; Japan *c.* 5%. Main exports: cotton 46%; peanuts 23%; gum arabic 5%.

Transport and Communications. Roads (1974) *c.* 50,000 km (mainly tracks, including 450 km asphalted). Motor vehicles in use (1972): passenger 29,200; commercial (including buses) 21,200. Railways: (1973) 4,757 km; freight traffic (1971) 2,636,000,000 net ton-km. Air traffic (1974): 244 million passenger-km; freight 4.6 million net ton-km. Navigable inland waterways (1974) 4,068 km. Telephones (Jan. 1975) 56,150. Radio receivers (Dec. 1972) 1,310,000. Television receivers (Dec. 1973) 100,000.

Agriculture. Production (in 000; metric tons; 1975): millet 741; sorghum 2,333; wheat 246; sweet potatoes (1974) *c.* 495; sesame *c.* 271; peanuts *c.* 1,100; sugar, raw value (1975) *c.* 118; watermelons (1974) *c.* 312; dates (1974) *c.* 100; cotton, lint *c.* 229; cow's milk *c.* 1,364; beef and veal (1974) *c.* 198; mutton and goat meat (1974) *c.* 84. Livestock (in 000; 1975): cattle *c.* 15,012; sheep *c.* 12,800; goats (1974) *c.* 8,600; camels (1974) *c.* 2,620; asses (1974) *c.* 664.

Industry. Production (in 000; metric tons; 1974): salt 50; cement (1973) 208; petroleum products *c.* 730; electricity (kw-hr) *c.* 325,000.

attempt, masterminded by former prime minister Sadik al-Mahdi and former finance minister Hussein al-Hindi, both in exile, and heavily backed by Libya's Col. Muammar al-Qaddafi with arms and money, involved the infiltration of some 2,000 heavily armed civilians into Khartoum and Omdurman. The rebels caused much destruction, including the immobilizing of Sudan's Air Force on the ground, but their plans went wrong on two counts: they found themselves unable to operate the transmitters of Radio Omdurman and so could make no explanation to the people of their aims, and Nimeiry, returning from visits to the U.S. and France, arrived at Khartoum Airport earlier than expected and thereby thwarted the rebels' intention to kill him on touchdown. After a day-long shoot-out between the rebels and the Army, which remained loyal to Nimeiry, the president emerged in full control. In the fighting 700 rebels and 82 soldiers were killed.

Retribution was quick and severe; 98 were executed for their part in the plot, several hundred were imprisoned and, after an elaborate show trial, Mahdi and Hindi were sentenced to death in absentia and their property was confiscated. Nimeiry was also quick to heed some of the lessons of the July coup attempt. In an effort to diversify decision-making, he gave up the posts of prime minister (to a civilian, Rashid Bakr), defense minister, and secretary-general of the Sudan Socialist Union, the only authorized political organization. To strengthen his regime, he promised to expand the Army, form a people's guard, and introduce an identity card system to prevent infiltration.

The July coup attempt brought Sudan closer to its two most powerful neighbours. A mutual defense pact was signed with Egypt immediately after the attempt, and this was followed by tripartite talks with Egypt and Saudi Arabia that appeared aimed at isolating Libya politically and economically. Nimeiry repeatedly condemned Libya's Qaddafi for attempting to sow subversion in the Middle East and Africa and reiterated his belief that the Soviet Union was behind this subversion. Sudan's links, political and economic, with Saudi Arabia were consolidated during the October visit of King Khalid to Khartoum.

The Southern Region was isolated for two months until a mystery virus, later identified as the green monkey disease, was brought under control in mid-October. It killed 63 persons. (PETER KILNER)

[978.E.5.b]

Surinam

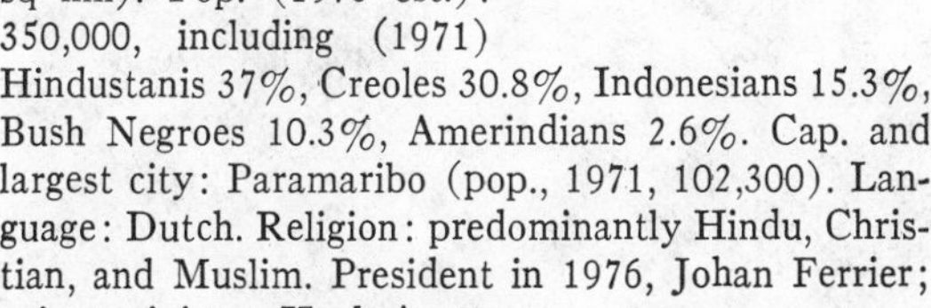

An independent republic of northern South America, Surinam is bounded by Guyana, Brazil, French Guiana, and the Atlantic Ocean. Area: 70,060 sq mi (181,455 sq km). Pop. (1975 est.): 350,000, including (1971) Hindustanis 37%, Creoles 30.8%, Indonesians 15.3%, Bush Negroes 10.3%, Amerindians 2.6%. Cap. and largest city: Paramaribo (pop., 1971, 102,300). Language: Dutch. Religion: predominantly Hindu, Christian, and Muslim. President in 1976, Johan Ferrier; prime minister, Henk Arron.

In May 1976 negotiations between the Surinam government, represented by the minister of reconstruction, Michael Cambridge, and the Suralco and Billiton companies were completed, with disappointing results for the government. The companies would pay the government 6% of the world market price for a pound of unalloyed aluminum per ton of bauxite, the same percentage as in 1975.

Emigration to The Netherlands in recent years had done much to create economic stagnation and uncertainty in Surinam. The government campaigned to woo back the emigrants—the country's most skilled, educated, and wealthy people. The decades-long migration from the countryside to the capital was another problem; the exodus had become so heavy that the country faced the prospect of importing sugar, vegetables, oils, and peanuts—products it formerly exported. To encourage farm work, Prime Minister Arron and other ministers personally took part in a sugarcane harvest. (DICK BOONSTRA)

[974.B.2.e]

JONATHAN KANDELL—THE NEW YORK TIMES

Street market in Paramaribo. The former Dutch colony lost a third of its population after becoming independent in late 1975.

SURINAM

Education. (1974–75) Primary, pupils 136,363, teachers 5,271; secondary, pupils 2,158, teachers 327; vocational, pupils 2,522, teachers 148; higher, students 2,138.

Finance. Monetary unit: Surinam guilder or florin, with (Sept. 20, 1976) a free rate of 1.80 Surinam guilder to U.S. $1 (3.08 Surinam guilders = £1 sterling). Budget (1976 est.): revenue 355 million Surinam guilders; expenditure 405 million Surinam guilders.

Foreign Trade. (1974) Imports 691,370,000 Surinam guilders; exports 606,370,000 Surinam guilders. Import sources (1973): U.S. 34%; The Netherlands 24%; Trinidad and Tobago 11%; Japan 6%; West Germany 5%; U.K. 5%. Export destinations (1973): U.S. 35%; West Germany 14%; The Netherlands 12%; Norway 10%; Spain 5%. Main exports (1973): alumina 46%; bauxite 27%; aluminum 14%; rice 7%.

Transport and Communications. Roads (1973) *c.* 2,500 km. Motor vehicles in use (1973): passenger 21,500; commercial (including buses) 5,600. Railways (1973) *c.* 50 km. Shipping traffic (1971): goods loaded *c.* 4.9 million metric tons, unloaded *c.* 1,145,000 metric tons. Telephones (Dec. 1973) 13,000. Radio receivers (Dec. 1973) 108,000. Television receivers (Dec. 1973) 31,000.

Agriculture. Production (in 000; metric tons; 1974): rice *c.* 130; oranges *c.* 10; grapefruit *c.* 5; bananas *c.* 35; sugar, raw value *c.* 11; coffee *c.* 0.4. Livestock (in 000; Jan. 1974): cattle *c.* 43; goats *c.* 6; sheep *c.* 3; pigs *c.* 13; chickens *c.* 850.

Industry. Production (in 000; metric tons; 1974): aluminum 57; bauxite 6,863; gold (troy oz) 0.4; electricity (kw-hr) 1,588,000 (63% hydroelectric).

Sumo: *see* Combat Sports

Surfing: *see* Water Sports

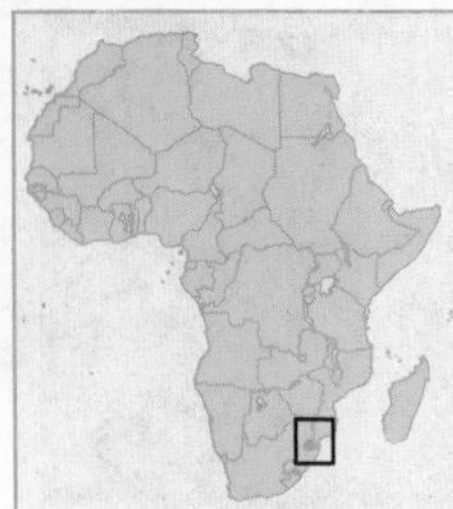

Swaziland

A landlocked constitutional monarchy of southern Africa, Swaziland is bounded by South Africa and Mozambique. Area: 6,704 sq mi (17,364 sq km). Pop. (1976 est.): 482,000. Cap. and largest city: Mbabane (pop., 1973 est., 20,800). Language: English and siSwati (official). Religion: Christian 60%; animist 40%. King, Sobhuza II; prime ministers in 1976, Prince Makhosini Dlamini and, from March 17, Col. Maphevu Dlamini.

Swaziland in 1976 walked a tightrope between Marxist Mozambique and South Africa, and not only because of the latter's pursuits of African National Congress guerrillas into Swaziland. On the one hand, Swaziland benefited from South African tourists (the Swazi government held a 30–60% interest in tourist hotels, besides levying a 40% company tax and a 15% casino tax); on the other, 85% of Swazi exports of sugar, iron, coal, and citrus fruits were sent out through Mozambique. In April King Sobhuza met Pres. Samora Machel of Mozambique to discuss border problems, trade, aid, and shipping. But Swaziland also took an interest in developing a rail outlet to Richard's Bay in South Africa, while South Africa planned to build and help finance a thermal power station at Mpaka in Swaziland.

Prince Makhosini Dlamini, 72 years old and prime minister since Swaziland became self-governing in 1967, was succeeded by Col. Maphevu Dlamini. The 1976–77 budget increased the company tax rate from 33.33 to 37.5%; customs revenue was to fall by about one-third (because of policy changes in South Africa); foreign aid funds would be used to develop the basic economic structure, a third sugar mill, and new coal reserves. The Umbuluzi dam scheme, which would irrigate 8,000 ha, was allotted a further 3 million emalangeni. A major sugar promotion scheme was backed by the government and Tate and Lyle of Great Britain, with 50 million emalangeni loan capital. (MOLLY MORTIMER)

See also Lesotho.

[978.E.8.b.ii]

Swedish Literature: *see* Literature

SWAZILAND

Education. (1974) Primary, pupils 86,110, teachers 2,220; secondary, pupils 14,301, teachers 611; vocational, pupils (1973) 615, teachers (1969) 10; teacher training, students 381, teachers (1969) 31; higher, students (1973) 369, teaching staff (1969) 15.

Finance and Trade. Monetary unit: lilangeni (plural emalangeni), at par with the South African rand, with (Sept. 20, 1976) a par value of 0.87 lilangeni to U.S. $1 (free rate of 1.49 lilangeni = £1 sterling). Budget (1973–74 est.): revenue R 28.1 million; expenditure R 23.9 million. Foreign trade (1974): imports 79.6 million emalangeni; exports 121,024,000 emalangeni. Export destinations (1970): U.K. 25%; Japan 24%; South Africa 21%. Main exports: sugar 36%; wood pulp 26%; iron ore 10%; asbestos 5%.

Agriculture. Production (in 000; metric tons; 1974): corn 95; rice *c.* 5; potatoes *c.* 7; sugar, raw value (1975) *c.* 214; oranges *c.* 70; pineapples *c.* 14; cotton, lint *c.* 5; beef and veal 13. Livestock (in 000; 1974): cattle *c.* 610; sheep *c.* 40; pigs *c.* 16; goats *c.* 275.

Industry. Production (in 000; metric tons; 1974): coal 117; iron ore (metal content) 1,314; asbestos 38; electricity (kw-hr) 121,000.

Sweden

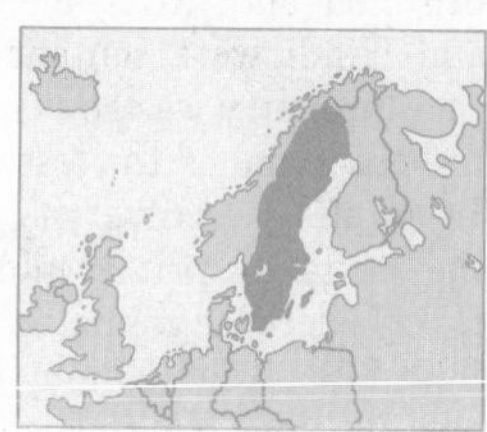

A constitutional monarchy of northern Europe lying on the eastern side of the Scandinavian Peninsula, Sweden has common borders with Finland and Norway. Area: 173,732 sq mi (449,964 sq km). Pop. (1976 est.): 8,208,400. Cap. and largest city: Stockholm (pop., 1976 est., 665,200). Language: Swedish, with some Finnish and Lapp in the north. Religion: predominantly Lutheran. King, Carl XVI Gustaf; prime ministers in 1976, Olof Palme until September 20 and, from October 4, Thorbjörn Fälldin.

An epoch ended in Sweden when the general elections on Sept. 19, 1976, resulted in the defeat of the Social Democratic Party after 44 years in power. The outgoing government of Olof Palme, prime minister since 1969, ascribed its defeat to the nuclear power issue in environment-minded Sweden. Thorbjörn Fälldin (*see* BIOGRAPHY), the new prime minister and

NORDFOTO/PICTORIAL PARADE

From commoner to queen. King Carl XVI Gustaf of Sweden and Queen Silvia leave the church after their wedding in June. Daughter of a West German businessman, Silvia met the king while acting as a hostess at the 1972 Olympic Games in Munich.

SWEDEN

Education. (1975–76) Primary, pupils 713,-149, teachers 43,000; secondary, pupils 533,214, teachers 54,000; vocational and teacher training, students 18,324; higher, students 108,000.

Finance. Monetary unit: krona, with (Sept. 20, 1976) a free rate of 4.33 kronor to U.S. $1 (7.45 kronor = £1 sterling). Gold, SDR's, and foreign exchange (June 1976) U.S. $3,085,000,-000. Budget (1975–76 est.): revenue 85,855,000,-000 kronor; expenditure 95,581,000,000 kronor. Gross national product (1975) 287,510,000,000 kronor. Money supply (April 1976) 30,820,000,-000 kronor. Cost of living (1970 = 100; June 1976) 162.

Foreign Trade. (1975) Imports 74,851,000,-000 kronor; exports 72,227,000,000 kronor. Import sources: West Germany 19%; U.K. 11%; Denmark 7%; Norway 7%; Finland 6%; The Netherlands 5%. Export destinations: Norway 11%; U.K. 11%; West Germany 10%; Denmark 9%; Finland 7%; U.S. 5%; France 5%. Main exports: machinery 27%; motor vehicles 11%; paper 8%; iron and steel 8%; wood pulp 8%; ships and boats 5%; chemicals 5%.

Transport and Communications. Roads (1974) 112,847 km (including 866 km expressways). Motor vehicles in use (1974): passenger 2,638,900; commercial 153,800. Railways (1974): 12,114 km (including 7,520 km electrified); traffic 5,332,000,000 passenger-km, freight 19,598,000,000 net ton-km. Air traffic (including Swedish apportionment of international operations of Scandinavian Airlines System; 1975): 3,629,-000,000 passenger-km; freight 152,446,000 net ton-km. Shipping (1975): merchant vessels 100 gross tons and over 775; gross tonnage 7,486,196. Telephones (Dec. 1974) 5,178,100. Radio receivers (Dec. 1974) *c.* 3,080,000. Television licenses (Dec. 1974) 2,841,000.

Agriculture. Production (in 000; metric tons; 1975): wheat 1,476; barley 1,956; oats 1,360; rye 324; potatoes 951; sugar, raw value 277; rapeseed 332; apples (1974) 135; cow's milk 3,130; butter 43; cheese 90; beef and veal (1974) *c.* 145; pork (1974) *c.* 278; timber (cu m; 1974) 56,813; fish catch (1974) 211. Livestock (in 000; June 1975): cattle *c.* 1,910; sheep *c.* 402; pigs *c.* 2,419; horses (1974) *c.* 52; chickens (1974) *c.* 11,954.

Industry. Index of industrial production (1970 = 100; 1975) 115. Production (in 000; metric tons; 1975): cement 3,121; electricity (kw-hr; 1974) 75,130,000 (76% hydroelectric); iron ore (60–65% metal content) 32,636; pig iron (1974) 3,181; crude steel 5,630; silver (troy oz; 1974) 4,530; petroleum products (1974) *c.* 9,585; sulfuric acid (1973) 938; rayon, etc., yarn and fibres (1974) 35; wood pulp (1974) mechanical 1,930, chemical 7,841; newsprint 1,183; other paper (1974) 4,300. Merchant vessels launched (100 gross tons and over; 1975) 2,470,000 gross tons. New dwelling units completed (1975) 74,500.

Centre Party leader, had vigorously campaigned to halt the development of nuclear power. He argued that safety risks could never be mastered.

In the elections the nonsocialist bloc, consisting of the Centre, Conservative, and Liberal parties, won 180 seats in the single-chamber Riksdag (Parliament). The Social Democrats and the small Communist Party, unofficial parliamentary allies, together captured 169 seats. In the old Parliament both blocs had held 175 seats and lots had been cast to break tie votes. So that such a situation would never again arise, a constitutional change was promulgated whereby the new Parliament was to consist of 349 seats. A record turnout of 90.4% of the electorate went to the polls. They included 18-year-olds, enfranchised for the first time. (*See* POLITICAL PARTIES.)

In October Fälldin announced the formation of his coalition government, a delicate balance of Conservative, Liberal, and Centre party members of Parliament. As foreign minister he chose Karin Söder, Europe's first woman to hold such a post since 1952. The new government made it clear that no major alterations in internal or external policies would occur, with the possible exception of the slowing down of the ambitious nuclear power program adopted by Parliament in 1975. That program proposed to increase the number of reactors from the existing 5 to 13 by 1985. Under the leadership of Fälldin the Centre Party, starting in 1971, became Sweden's second largest by focusing concern upon environmental questions and against nuclear power. Fälldin hoped eventually to eliminate dependence upon nuclear power.

Though the nuclear issue appeared to have tipped the balance in the elections, there were other issues. Nonsocialist parties received a boost in the spring with the bizarre case of Astrid Lindgren, a children's writer who for years had enjoyed one of Sweden's highest incomes. She told a newspaper that she had been informed that she would have to pay a 102% tax on her annual earnings of more than 2 million kronor. It turned out that she had been misinformed, but by then the damage had been done. Lindgren wrote a biting satire about the tax system which made a deep impression upon the public. Her attack coincided with the self-proclaimed exile of film director Ingmar Bergman (*see* BIOGRAPHY), who claimed he had been harassed about his taxes. The furor resulted in a sharp drop of support for the Social Democrats. They were accused of building a rigidly conformist society administered by heavy-handed tax collectors.

Throughout the year Sweden remained out of step with world business activity. For the first six months of 1976 production volume was about 3% less than during the same period in 1975. The reason was that the Swedes practiced countercyclical measures during the international recession of 1974–75, which meant that full production was maintained to achieve the central economic goal of full employment. Sweden thus weathered the international recession with negligible unemployment and rising industrial investment. In April the Organization for Economic Cooperation and Development (OECD) praised Sweden for its exemplary economic behaviour.

King Carl XVI Gustaf, aged 30, was married on June 19 to West German commoner Silvia Sommerlath amid a grass-roots outburst of royalist sentiment unusual in egalitarian-minded Sweden. In December his uncle, Prince Bertil, married British commoner Lilian Craig, a former Welsh actress.

(ROGER NYE CHOATE)

[972.A.6.b]

Swimming

The 1976 Olympic Games, July 17–August 1, in Montreal provided a showcase for the greatest competitive swimming the world had ever seen. Athletes from 53 nations competed in the swimming and diving events, but it was the male swimmers from the United States and the East German women who completely dominated all rivals. Over 9,200 spectators each day and millions more watching on worldwide television saw the swimmers set 22 world and 25 Olympic records.

The U.S. men swimmers, who justly could claim to be the greatest team ever assembled, set 11 of the world standards. Of a possible total of 13 gold medals and 11 additional silver medals, they won 12 and 10, respectively. They swept all three places in the 100-m and 200-m butterfly, the 200-m freestyle, and the 200-m backstroke. The individual star was John Naber, 20, who won four gold medals and one silver and set two individual world records.

Almost equaling the U.S. men's medal output was the women's team from East Germany, led by Kornelia Ender, 17, who won four gold medals and one silver and set two individual world records and equaled another (her own) in the process. In the 13 events the East Germans won 11 gold medals, 6 silvers, and 1 bronze, and set 8 world records.

The U.S. 400-m freestyle relay team of Kim Pey-

Jubilant U.S. women swimmers celebrate after winning the 400-m relay at the 1976 Olympic Games.

JEAN PIERRE LAFFONT—SYGMA

ton, Wendy Boglioli, Jill Sterkel, and Shirley Babashoff, in the last swimming event and trailing for half the race, rallied to win their only gold medal with a world record 3 min 44.82 sec. In the 1972 Olympics the U.S. women had been dominant, winning eight gold, five silver, and four bronze medals. At Montreal, they slipped to one gold, four silver, and two bronze even though they set nine U.S. records.

The 1980 Olympics were to be held in Moscow, and both the Soviet men and women swimmers showed that they had improved sufficiently to rank second to the U.S. in men's and third to East Germany and the U.S. in women's swimming. By 1980 the Soviets would have climaxed a four-year training plan and were expected to field a strong team.

During the year, world records were broken on 58 occasions, 27 by men and 31 by women. U.S. men gained all of the world standards except the 100-m freestyle and the 200-m breaststroke. The East German women possessed all but the 200-m breaststroke, the 400-m freestyle relay, and the 1,500-m freestyle.

Diving. A series of three international diving meets were held during April and May in Canada, the U.S., and Mexico. Winners in the men's 3-m springboard were Klaus Di Biasi, Italy; Phil Boggs, U.S.; and Franco Cagnotto, Italy. In the 10-m platform the winners were Sergey Nemtsanov, U.S.S.R.; Di Biasi; and Carlos Giron, Mexico. In the women's events the 1972 Olympic platform gold-medal winner, Ulrike Knape of Sweden, won all three platform competitions as well as the 3-m springboard in Canada. Irina Kalinina, U.S.S.R., was the winner in the springboard competition in the U.S., and Cindy Shatto of Canada won the event in Mexico.

In the Olympic Games the men's gold medals went to the older, more experienced competitors, Boggs in the springboard and defending champion Di Biasi in the platform. Boggs, 26, dominated the springboard event over an even older diver, 29-year-old Cagnotto. But Di Biasi, 28, had his hands full with runner-up Greg Louganis, a 16-year-old Samoan-American.

The women's events featured two young divers. Jennifer Chandler, a 17-year-old Alabaman, upset the field in the springboard with a surprising consistency. Then Elena Vaytsekhovskaia, from the Soviet Union, won the platform over defending titleholder Knape. Christa Kohler of East Germany placed second in the springboard.

(ALBERT SCHOENFIELD)

See also Track and Field Sports: *Special Report.*
[452.B.4.a.i]

CANADIAN PRESS

Elena Vaytsekhovskaia of the Soviet Union won the women's platform diving competition in Montreal.

World Records Set in 1976

Event	Name	Country	Time
MEN			
100-m freestyle	Jim Montgomery	U.S.	50.39 sec
100-m freestyle	Jim Montgomery	U.S.	49.99 sec
100-m freestyle	Jonty Skinner	S. Africa	49.44 sec
200-m freestyle	Bruce Furniss	U.S.	1 min 50.29 sec
400-m freestyle	Brian Goodell	U.S.	3 min 53.08 sec
400-m freestyle	Brian Goodell	U.S.	3 min 51.93 sec
800-m freestyle	Steve Holland	Australia	8 min 06.27 sec
800-m freestyle	Steve Holland	Australia	8 min 02.91 sec
800-m freestyle	Bobby Hackett	U.S.	8 min 01.54 sec
1,500-m freestyle	Steve Holland	Australia	15 min 10.89 sec
1,500-m freestyle	Brian Goodell	U.S.	15 min 06.66 sec
1,500-m freestyle	Brian Goodell	U.S.	15 min 02.40 sec
100-m backstroke	John Naber	U.S.	56.19 sec
100-m backstroke	John Naber	U.S.	55.49 sec
200-m backstroke	John Naber	U.S.	2 min 00.64 sec
200-m backstroke	John Naber	U.S.	1 min 59.19 sec
100-m breaststroke	John Hencken	U.S.	1 min 03.62 sec
100-m breaststroke	John Hencken	U.S.	1 min 03.11 sec
200-m breaststroke	David Wilkie	U.K.	2 min 15.11 sec
200-m butterfly	Roger Pyttel	E.Ger.	1 min 59.63 sec
200-m butterfly	Mike Bruner	U.S.	1 min 59.23 sec
400-m individual medley	Zoltan Verraszto	Hungary	4 min 26.00 sec
400-m individual medley	Rod Strachan	U.S.	4 min 23.68 sec
400-m medley relay	U.S. national team (Peter Rocca, Chris Woo, Joe Bottom, Jack Babashoff)		3 min 47.28 sec
400-m medley relay	U.S. national team (John Naber, John Hencken, Matt Vogel, Jim Montgomery)		3 min 42.22 sec
800-m freestyle relay	U..S national team (Doug Northway, Tim Shaw, Mike Bruner, Bruce Furniss)		7 min 30.33 sec
800-m freestyle relay	U.S. national team (Mike Bruner, Bruce Furniss, John Naber, Jim Montgomery)		7 min 23.22 sec
WOMEN			
100-m freestyle	Kornelia Ender	E.Ger.	55.73 sec
100-m freestyle	Kornelia Ender	E.Ger.	55.65 sec
200-m freestyle	Kornelia Ender	E.Ger.	1 min 59.78 sec
200-m freestyle	Kornelia Ender	E.Ger.	1 min 59.26 sec
400-m freestyle	Barbara Krause	E.Ger.	4 min 11.69 sec
400-m freestyle	Petra Thumer	E.Ger.	4 min 09.89 sec
800-m freestyle	Petra Thumer	E.Ger.	8 min 40.68 sec
800-m freestyle	Shirley Babashoff	U.S.	8 min 39.63 sec
800-m freestyle	Petra Thumer	E.Ger.	8 min 37.14 sec
100-m backstroke	Ulrike Richter	E.Ger.	1 min 02.60 sec
100-m backstroke	Kornelia Ender	E.Ger.	1 min 01.62 sec
100-m backstroke	Ulrike Richter	E.Ger.	1 min 01.51 sec
200-m backstroke	Antje Stille	E.Ger.	2 min 14.41 sec
200-m backstroke	Antje Stille	E.Ger.	2 min 13.50 sec
200-m backstroke	Birgit Treiber	E.Ger.	2 min 12.47 sec
100-m breaststroke	Carola Nitschke	E.Ger.	1 min 11.93 sec
100-m breaststroke	Hannelore Anke	E.Ger.	1 min 11.11 sec
100-m breaststroke	Hannelore Anke	E.Ger.	1 min 10.86 sec
200-m breaststroke	Marina Koshevaia	U.S.S.R.	2 min 33.35 sec
100-m butterfly	Kornelia Ender	E.Ger.	1 min 00.13 sec
200-m butterfly	Rosemarie Kother-Gabriel	E.Ger.	2 min 13.60 sec
200-m butterfly	Rosemarie Kother-Gabriel	E.Ger.	2 min 12.84 sec
200-m butterfly	Rosemarie Kother-Gabriel	E.Ger.	2 min 11.22 sec
200-m individual medley	Ulrike Tauber	E.Ger.	2 min 18.30 sec
200-m individual medley	Kornelia Ender	E.Ger.	2 min 17.14 sec
400-m individual medley	Birgit Treiber	E.Ger.	4 min 48.79 sec
400-m individual medley	Ulrike Tauber	E.Ger.	4 min 42.77 sec
400-m freestyle relay	Berlin Dynamo, E.Ger. (Barbara Krause, Monika Seltmann, Rosemarie Kother-Gabriel, Andrea Pollack)		3 min 48.80 sec
400-m freestyle relay	U.S. national team (Kim Peyton, Wendy Boglioli, Jill Sterkel, Shirley Babashoff)		3 min 44.82 sec
400-m medley relay	Berlin Dynamo, E.Ger. (Monika Seltmann, Carola Nitschke, Andrea Pollack, Barbara Krause)		4 min 13.41 sec
400-m medley relay	E.German national team (Ulrike Richter, Hannelore Anke, Andrea Pollack, Kornelia Ender)		4 min 07.95 sec

Switzerland

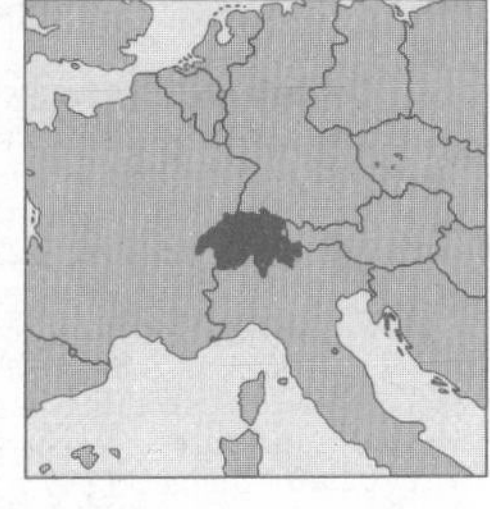

A federal republic in west central Europe consisting of a confederation of 25 cantons, Switzerland is bounded by West Germany, Austria, Liechtenstein, Italy, and France. Area: 15,943 sq mi (41,293 sq km). Pop. (1975 est.): 6,405,000. Cap.: Bern (pop., 1975 est., 152,200). Largest city: Zürich (pop., 1975 est., 395,200). Language (1970): German 65%; French 18%; Italian 12%; Romansh 1%. Religion (1970): Roman Catholic 49.4%; Protestant 47.7%. President in 1976, Rudolf Gnägni.

In its legislative and financial program of 1975–79, published in 1976, the government proposed a comprehensive reform of public finance, with a shift from the turnover tax to a 10% value-added pattern and better coordination of cantonal and federal taxes. In October the federal deficit was announced to be a record SFr 1,940,000.

The program stated that neutrality would continue to be followed in foreign affairs, with possible eventual full membership in the UN, an increase in aid to less developed countries, and ratification of the European Social Charter. Technological modernization was expected to increase defense expenditures from SFr 2,906,000,000 in 1976 to SFr 3,645,000,000 in 1979. An amendment of the military penal law would substitute civil for military service for conscientious objectors. A compulsory retirement benefit scheme would be introduced, and old-age and health insurance provisions would be revised.

The program also stated that increased government authority was required to control cyclical economic fluctuations, and that maintenance of full employment was to be a primary aim. Unemployment insurance was to be obligatory, and legislation concerning the status of foreign workers (and incidentally the right of asylum) were to be revised. Other proposals concerned urban and rural planning, exploitation of natural resources, energy supply, a revision of laws governing marriage and the family, protection of private spheres and persons, and better distribution of functions between the federal and cantonal authorities.

A constituent assembly for the new canton of Jura (formerly part of the canton of Bern) was elected on March 28 and installed on April 12, with the task of planning the canton's political and economic structure. Three dissenting communes resented the prospect of eventual inclusion in Jura and had support from the Bernese and federal governments.

The economy continued to be in recession, with the building industries still hardest hit, and the federal government announced a SFr 2 billion plan to create employment. The Swiss franc remained excessively strong, even while government policy limited the influx of foreign funds. In October the inflationary rate for the preceding 12 months was reported at 0.9%—the lowest among industrialized countries. Some strikes occurred, breaking the "labour peace" in effect since the celebrated industrial relations agreement of 1937. The presence of foreign workers, despite large-scale departures due to the recession, was still an unresolved issue. After a federal draft law on urban and rural planning was defeated by popular vote on June 13, the Federal Council fell back on existing emergency powers to cope with major problems until a new draft law could be submitted to the people. There was popular opposition to the construction of seven new nuclear power plants.

A proposed 50-year, interest-free loan of SFr 200 million to the International Development Association was defeated by popular vote, and less controversial methods of providing aid to third world countries were attempted. The federal expert commission studying the question of membership in the UN favoured Switzerland's full participation, but polls showed public opinion to be at least cool. The powerful Nestlé concern brought a successful libel suit against members of a group working on behalf of third world countries who had accused it of "killing babies" by promoting the sale of its powdered milk infant formula among backward populations. However, the court admonished the firm to "carry out a fundamental reconsideration of its promotion methods" in less developed areas. The Swiss chemical concern Hoffmann-La Roche accepted responsibility for the pollution of the region around Seveso, Italy, caused by an accident at a plant operated by its subsidiary Givaudan. (*See* ENVIRONMENT.) It was discovered that pro-Soviet military espionage activity had been carried on for 15 years by Jean-Louis Jeanmaire, a high-ranking Swiss Army officer. (MELANIE STAERK)

[972.A.8]

SWITZERLAND

Education. (1974–75) Primary, pupils 529,000, teachers (excluding craft teachers; 1961–62) 23,761; secondary, pupils 322,000, teachers (full-time; 1961–62) 6,583; vocational, pupils 155,172; teacher training, students 10,017; higher (including 10 universities), students 55,990, teaching staff 2,650.

Finance. Monetary unit: Swiss franc, with (Sept. 20, 1976) a free rate of SFr 2.48 to U.S. $1 (SFr 4.26 = £1 sterling). Gold and foreign exchange (June 1976) U.S. $10,726,000,000. Budget (1975 actual): revenue SFr 11,599,000,000; expenditure SFr 12,662,-000,000. Gross national product (1975) SFr 144.6 billion. Money supply (May 1976) SFr 57,890,000,-000. Cost of living (1970 = 100; June 1976) 147.

Foreign Trade. (1975) Imports SFr 34,271,000,-000; exports SFr 33,418,000,000. Import sources: EEC 66% (West Germany 28%, France 14%, Italy 10%, U.K. 6%); U.S. 8%. Export destinations: EEC 43% (West Germany 15%, France 9%, Italy 7%, U.K. 6%); U.S. 6%; Austria 6%. Main exports: machinery 33%; chemicals 21%; watches and clocks 9%; textile yarns and fabrics 5%. Tourism (1974): visitors 6,222,000; gross receipts U.S. $1,793,000,000.

Transport and Communications. Roads (1974) 61,274 km (including 628 km expressways). Motor vehicles in use (1974): passenger 1,728,100; commercial 165,400. Railways: (1973) 4,971 km (including 4,805 km electrified); traffic (1975) 7,984,000,000 passenger-km, freight 5,141,000,000 net ton-km. Air traffic (1975): 7,564,000,000 passenger-km; freight 308,487,000 net ton-km. Shipping (1975): merchant vessels 100 gross tons and over 29; gross tonnage 193,657. Telephones (Dec. 1974) 3,790,351. Radio licenses (Dec. 1974) 2,036,000. Television licenses (Dec. 1974) 1,714,000.

Agriculture. Production (in 000; metric tons; 1975): wheat 320; barley *c.* 180; oats *c.* 63; rye *c.* 32; corn (1974) 119; potatoes 960; rapeseed *c.* 25; apples (1974) *c.* 320; pears (1974) *c.* 120; sugar, raw value (1974) 72; wine (1974) 70; milk *c.* 3,361; butter *c.* 34; cheese 102; beef and veal (1974) *c.* 148; pork (1974) *c.* 239. Livestock (in 000; April 1975): cattle 1,975; sheep *c.* 360; pigs *c.* 2,170; chickens (1974) 6,536.

Industry. Index of industrial production (1970 = 100; 1975) 97. Production (in 000; metric tons; 1975): aluminum 79; cement 5,256; petroleum products (1974) 5,708; rayon, etc., yarn and fibre (1974) 4; nylon, etc., yarn and fibre (1974) 72; cigarettes (units; 1974) 27,995,000; watches (units; 1974) 59,-020; manufactured gas (cu m; 1974) 286,000; electricity (kw-hr) 41,796,000.

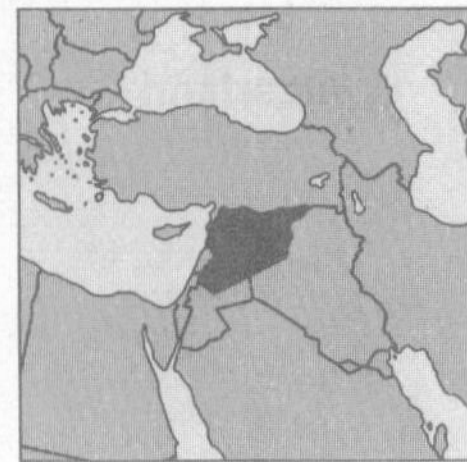

Syria

A republic in southwestern Asia on the Mediterranean Sea, Syria is bordered by Turkey, Iraq, Jordan, Israel, and Lebanon. Area: 71,498 sq mi (185,180 sq km). Pop. (1975 est.): 7,355,000. Cap. and largest city: Damascus (pop., 1975 est., 1,049,500). Language: Arabic (official); also Kurdish, Armenian, Turkish, and Circassian. Religion: predominantly Muslim. President in 1976, Gen. Hafez al-Assad; premiers, Mahmoud Ayoubi and, from August 1, Abdul Rahman Khleifawi.

The year 1976 was one of fateful decisions for Syria and the regime of President Assad (*see* BIOGRAPHY), as the country became increasingly involved in Lebanon's civil war and attracted criticism from most Arab states, the Palestine Liberation Organization (PLO), and the Soviet Union. Only Jordan steadily supported Syria, and the two countries grew closer together.

The year began hopefully when Syrian mediation led to a Lebanese cease-fire on January 22 and the Constitutional Declaration of February 14 which seemed to provide the basis for a permanent settlement. Lebanese Pres. Suleiman Franjieh visited Damascus on February 7 and Lebanon returned to relative peace. However, the situation began to deteriorate again in mid-March, when the Syrian-controlled guerrilla force as-Saiqa prevented the Palestinian-leftist forces from developing their advantage and driving President Franjieh from office. President Assad was forced to postpone a visit to Paris.

Syria's former Lebanese leftist allies turned against Syria and refused its mediation, and by the end of March Syria had cut off aid and arms to their side. On April 9 some 3,500–4,000 Syrian forces crossed the Lebanese border to back up the 7,000-man as-Saiqa. On April 16 a Syrian-Palestinian agreement was patched up, but this did not hold and, although the Syrian-supported candidate Elias Sarkis (*see* BIOGRAPHY) was elected president of Lebanon on May 8, the civil war, and with it destruction in Beirut, escalated. On May 31 Syria intervened on a more massive scale, occupying the Beqaa Valley and advancing along the road to Beirut against Palestinian-leftist opposition. As-Saiqa forces were badly beaten in Beirut, and the advance Syrian forces suffered losses, but President Assad stopped short of attempting an advance to the Lebanese capital at that time.

A Soviet-made T-62 tank of the Syrian Army rolls toward Beirut in November. The Syrian intervention in Lebanon surprised many nations, including the Soviet Union.

WIDE WORLD

SYRIA

Education. (1974–75) Primary, pupils 1,184,122, teachers 34,247; secondary, pupils 423,922, teachers 20,082; vocational, pupils 20,076, teachers 1,973; teacher training, students 5,913, teachers 506; higher (1972–73), students 51,797, teaching staff (1971–72) 1,200.

Finance. Monetary unit: Syrian pound, with (Sept. 20, 1976) an official exchange rate of S£3.925 to U.S. $1 (free rate of S£6.78 = £1 sterling). Gold, SDR's, and foreign exchange (May 1975) U.S. $1,147,000,000. Budget (1975 est.): revenue S£10,445 million; expenditure S£4,600 million (excluding development expenditure). Gross domestic product (1974) S£14,478 million. Money supply (Dec. 1975) S£6,965 million. Cost of living (Damascus; 1970 = 100; March 1976) 197.

Foreign Trade. (1975) Imports S£6,236 million; exports S£3,441 million. Import sources: West Germany 13%; Italy 9%; France 7%; U.S. 6%; Japan 5%; Brazil 5%. Export destinations: Italy 18%; Belgium-Luxembourg 11%; West Germany 10%; U.K. 8%; U.S.S.R. 7%; Yugoslavia 6%; Greece 6%. Main exports: crude oil 70%; cotton 15%.

Transport and Communications. Roads (1971) 16,710 km (including 63 km expressways). Motor vehicles in use (1974): passenger 37,300; commercial (including buses) 23,100. Railways: (1973) 902 km; traffic (1975) 145 million passenger-km, freight 152 million net ton-km. Air traffic (1974): 322 million passenger-km; freight 2.2 million net ton-km. Telephones (Dec. 1974) 152,000. Radio receivers (Dec. 1972) 2.5 million. Television receivers (Dec. 1974) 224,000.

Agriculture. Production (in 000; metric tons; 1975): wheat *c.* 1,500; barley 597; potatoes (1974) 111; lentils (1974) 98; tomatoes 508; onions 110; watermelons (1974) *c.* 400; melons (1974) *c.* 130; grapes (1974) 215; olives 146; cotton, lint *c.* 150. Livestock (in 000; 1974): cattle *c.* 510; sheep 5,738; goats 716; horses *c.* 63; asses *c.* 262; chickens 4,431.

Industry. Production (in 000; metric tons; 1975): crude oil 9,637; petroleum products (1974) *c.* 1,840; cement 860; cotton yarn (1974) 30; electricity (kw-hr; 1974) 1,366,000.

Syria attended the hastily convened Arab foreign ministers' meeting in Cairo on June 9 but insisted that its troops would only withdraw if replaced by an adequate Arab League force capable of restoring peace. Iraq and Egypt were both highly critical of Syria's action; Saudi-Kuwaiti mediation succeeded in arranging a meeting of the Syrian and Egyptian premiers in Riyadh, Saudi Arabia, on June 23–24, when differences were declared to have been removed, but relations showed little improvement until December when, during a visit by Assad to Cairo, agreement was reached on close political and military cooperation between the two countries.

Soviet Premier Aleksey Kosygin visited Damascus on June 1–4—at the very moment when large Syrian forces were entering Lebanon. Although he expressed no public criticism of Syria's role in Lebanon, the Soviet news agency Tass and other official Soviet sources began to comment unfavourably. A message from the Soviet leader Leonid Brezhnev to President Assad on July 11 urging Syrian withdrawal was widely reported. However, there was no break in Soviet-Syrian relations, and new quantities of Soviet arms arrived in Syria in June.

By the summer Syria was in the position of ally to the Lebanese-rightist forces against the Palestinian leftists. A new Syrian-PLO agreement of July 29, providing for a cease-fire under the supervision of a Syrian-Palestinian-Lebanese committee, also failed to hold. In late September Syrian forces joined Lebanese rightists in their offensive in the mountains east of Beirut. Egyptian and Iraqi reports of widespread disaffection among Syrians were not borne out, although there were some sabotage incidents. When four Arab guerrillas attacked a Damascus hotel and took 90 hostages on September 26, the three surviving guerrillas were publicly hanged the next day. Reports of massacres of Lebanese Druze villagers by rightist militia in early October caused some unrest among Syrian Druzes. Syrian forces launched fresh attacks toward Marjayoun, Sidon, and Beirut from October 10. In mid-October a summit meeting of Syria, Egypt, Lebanon, Kuwait, and the PLO in Riyadh agreed on a cease-fire and an increase in the Arab peacekeeping force to 30,000, decisions that were endorsed by a general Arab summit a week later. The cease-fire came into force on October 21, and by mid-November the Arab force, composed largely of Syrian troops already on the spot, had entered Beirut.

Syria agreed to renew the mandate of the UN Disengagement Observer Force on the Golan Heights at the end of May and again in November for a further six months. On August 1 Premier Mahmoud Ayoubi resigned and was replaced by Abdul Rahman Khleifawi, who had been premier in 1971–72. His new government was notable for having the first woman member in Syrian history as minister of culture and national guidance.

Intervention in Lebanon was estimated to be costing the equivalent of $1 million daily and the 1976–77 budget, which at about $4.5 billion represented a 60% increase over the previous year, had to be cut back to the 1975–76 level. The economy was helped by an excellent year in agriculture and a 1975–76 cotton harvest of 414,500 metric tons, as compared with the previous year's 386,500 tons.

(PETER MANSFIELD)

[978.B.3.b]

Table Tennis

The tenth European table tennis championships were decided in Prague, Czech., where representatives of 26 national associations vied during March and April for individual and team honours. For the first time sample drug tests were taken, all of which proved to be negative. The men's team title was won by Yugoslavia, the women's title by the Soviet Union. In singles competition Jacques Secretin of France and Jill Hammersley of England were both victorious. Stellan Bengtsson and Kjell Johansson of Sweden captured the men's doubles, and Linda Howard of England teamed with Hammersley to win the women's doubles. The mixed doubles was taken by Anton Stipancic and Erzebet Palatinus of Yugoslavia.

In the Premier Division of the 1975–76 European League, Yugoslavia emerged victorious over 18 rival entries. In a contest for the Europe Club Cup, Gstk Vjesnik of Zagreb, Yugos., won the men's competition by defeating defending champion Sparta of Prague; Statisztika of Budapest, Hung., captured the women's cup. The Division 2A and 2B titles were taken, respectively, by England and West Germany.

1976 World Rankings

MEN	WOMEN
1. Liang Ko-liang (China)	1. Pak Yung Sun (N. Korea)
2. J. Secretin (France)	2. Chang Li (China)
3. D. Surbec (Yugos.)	3. Ke Hsin-ai (China)
4. K. Johansson (Swed.)	4. Chung Hyan Sook (S. Korea)
5. S. Bengtsson (Swed.)	5. Chang Te-ying (China)
6. M. Orlowski (Czech.)	6. J. Hammersley (Eng.)
7. A. Stipancic (Yugos.)	7. A.-C. Hellman (Swed.)
8. Kua Yueh-hua (China)	8. M. Alexandru (Rom.)
9. Li Chen-shih (China)	I. Uhlikova (Czech.)
10. N. Takashima (Japan)	10. A. Lee (S. Korea)

The third annual Asian championships were held in Pyongyang, North Korea, during the spring. China won the men's team title, the men's singles (Liang Ko-liang), and the women's singles (Chang Li). North Korea captured the women's team title and the women's doubles (Pak Yung Sun and Kim Chang Ae). Among the 25 participating groups, Japan was the only other country to win any titles. Tetsuo Inoue teamed up with Mitsuru Kono to take the men's doubles, and he helped give Japan the mixed doubles title in partnership with Mitsuko Shimamoto.

Cotonou, Benin, was the venue for the fifth African championships that concluded in early October. Nigeria dominated the tournament by winning both team titles, both singles, the women's doubles, and the mixed doubles. Egypt prevented a Nigerian sweep by defeating Ghana in the finals of the men's doubles.

The third Asian, African, Latin-American Invitational Tournament, which took place during October in Mexico City, ended with China and Japan sharing the honours. China won both team titles and the singles for men (Kuo Yueh-hua) and women (Chang Li). But in the doubles the Japanese were invincible. Katsuyuki Aba and Kono took the men's title, and Yukie Ohzeki and Sachiko Yokota the women's. Kinji Koyama and Teruko Kuroko captured the mixed doubles in four sets.

December marked the 50th anniversary of the founding of the International Table Tennis Federation (ITTF), which now included 125 national associations and some eight million players. To meet the ever growing demands placed on the organization, a

Yugoslavia's Dragutin Surbec (right), ranked third in the world, defeats Desmond Douglas of England in the men's semifinals at the U.S. Open in Philadelphia. Surbec went on to take the title.

NEAL FOX

three-story building was purchased in January at St. Leonards-on-Sea, Sussex, Eng. A full-time professional secretary-general took up his duties in March.

During the year the Arab Federation, which was founded in 1956, moved its headquarters from Cairo to Riyadh, Saudi Arabia. An African seminar and training course took place in August in Alexandria, Egypt, during which a staff from England and West Germany instructed 51 African coaches and umpires. A general pattern for such seminars was established by the Asian Table Tennis Union the previous November when 100 coaches from 19 Asian countries attended an assembly in Otsu City, Japan.

(ARTHUR KINGSLEY VINT)

[425.B.4.h.xxvi]

Taiwan

Taiwan, which consists of the islands of Formosa and Quemoy and other surrounding islands, is the seat of the Republic of China (Nationalist China). It is north of the Philippines, southwest of Japan, and east of Hong Kong. The island of Formosa has an area of 13,815 sq mi; including its 77 outlying islands (14 in the Taiwan group and 63 in the Pescadores group), the area of Taiwan totals 13,893 sq mi (35,981 sq km). Pop. (1976 est.): 16,323,700. Cap. and largest city: Taipei (pop., 1976 est., 2,063,400). President in 1976, Yen Chia-kan; president of the Executive Yuan (premier), Chiang Ching-kuo.

By Oct. 10, 1976, when the Nationalist government celebrated the 65th anniversary of the revolution that created the Republic of China, it had spent 27 years in exile on Taiwan. Although the government made no overt change in its dedication to the recovery of the mainland, its policy theme had shifted to "self-strengthening," with emphasis on the importance of internal political solidarity, economic construction, and improvement of the standard of living as the best means of maintaining an independent existence. Under Premier Chiang's leadership the political base had been broadened. Taiwanese held most positions in the county and local governments, and their participation in the ruling Kuomintang party and the national government continued to expand. Since 1972, 6 of the 19 Cabinet posts had been held by local inhabitants, and in June, in the first Cabinet reshuffle since 1972, two more Taiwanese were named as ministers without portfolio.

Taiwan's Olympic team returned home after Canada refused to permit its members to participate in the summer Olympic Games at Montreal under the banner of "The Republic of China."

WIDE WORLD

TAIWAN

Education. (1975–76) Primary, pupils 2,364,961, teachers 62,803; secondary, pupils 1,221,538, teachers 50,281; vocational, pupils 282,415, teachers 10,103; higher, students 289,435, teaching staff 13,606.

Finance. Monetary unit: new Taiwan dollar, with (Sept. 20, 1976) a par value of NT$38 to U.S. $1 (free rate of NT$65.47 = £1 sterling). Gold and foreign exchange (June 1976) U.S. $1,394,000,000. Budget (1973–74 rev. est.): revenue NT$109 billion; expenditure NT$86.2 billion. Gross national product (1975) NT$547,250,000,000. Money supply (June 1976) NT$116,910,000,000. Cost of living (1970 = 100; June 1976) 181.

Foreign Trade. (1975) Imports NT$226,460,000,000; exports NT$201,470,000,000. Import sources: Japan 30%; U.S. 28%; Kuwait 7%; West Germany 6%. Export destinations: U.S. 34%; Japan 13%; Hong Kong 7%; West Germany 6%. Main exports: clothing 17%; electrical machinery and equipment 13%; textile yarns and fabrics 12%; footwear 6%; fruits and vegetables 5%; sugar 5%.

Transport and Communications. Roads (1974) 16,197 km. Motor vehicles in use (1974): passenger 126,000; commercial (including buses) 101,000. Railways (1974): 4,300 km; traffic 8,345,000,000 passenger-km, freight 2,853,000,000 net ton-km. Air traffic (1970): 954 million passenger-km; freight 25,175,000 net ton-km. Shipping (1975): merchant vessels 100 gross tons and over 428; gross tonnage 1,449,957. Telephones (Dec. 1974) 900,605. Radio licenses (Dec. 1975) 1,484,000. Television licenses (Dec. 1975) 912,000.

Agriculture. Production (in 000; metric tons; 1975): rice *c.* 2,537; sweet potatoes (1974) 3,100; corn *c.* 85; cassava (1974) *c.* 330; peanuts *c.* 91; sugar, raw value *c.* 987; citrus fruit (1973) 332; bananas (1973) 422; pineapples (1973) 328; tea (1973) 29; pork (1973) 523. Livestock (in 000; 1975): cattle *c.* 266; pigs *c.* 4,337; goats *c.* 267; chickens *c.* 14,053.

Industry. Production (in 000; metric tons; 1974): coal 2,898; crude oil 210; natural gas (cu m) 1,587,000; electricity (kw-hr) 20,534,000; cement 6,171; crude steel 1,029; salt 363; sulfuric acid (1973) 609; petroleum products *c.* 4,000; cotton yarn 111; man-made fibres 273; paper 463.

Taiwan's position as a major industrial area in Asia was pointed up by the fact that agriculture accounted for only about 38% of the gross national product. Per capita income for 1975 exceeded U.S. $700, the highest among the large countries of South and East Asia after Japan. Foreign trade, the backbone of the economy, totaled $11,254,000,000 in 1975 (about 79% of GNP) and $7,142,000,000 for the first six months of 1976; Japan and the U.S. were Taiwan's major trading partners. The policy of building Taiwan into an economic bastion was evident in the plan to complete, before 1979, the "Ten Projects" program for highway construction, railroad electrification, and the building of an integrated steel mill, nuclear power plants, and a shipyard. On July 1 a new six-year development program to improve the economic structure and speed the growth of heavy and chemical industries was launched.

Although Taiwan maintained trade relations with over 100 countries, only 26 of them (13 in Central and South America) recognized it as the legal government of all China. Next to the U.S., Saudi Arabia was the most influential of these countries, and the ties between Saudi Arabia and Taiwan were further strengthened with the conclusion of an economic agreement in March. The pact provided for new Saudi loans of $80 million to finance Taiwan's economic development and the assistance of Taiwanese technicians in modernizing the Saudi economy.

Peking's efforts to isolate Taiwan extended to foreign trade and sports. Under pressure from Peking, the Canadian government banned the athletic team of the Republic of China from participation in the Olympic Games in Montreal under its own name. U.S. companies that had joined the U.S.-Republic of China Economic Council for promoting understanding and trade were not invited to the Canton Trade Fair. However, the Republic of China retained its membership in the International Monetary Fund and the World Bank and its affiliated organizations.

Washington continued its dual policy toward China, recognizing Taiwan but pursuing closer relations with Peking. Taiwan's political, economic, and strategic importance in the Pacific and U.S. treaty commitments with the Republic of China, as well as Peking's strong opposition to recognition of "two Chinas," appeared to bar any easy solution to the Taiwan dilemma. In March the U.S. State Department decided on a sharp cutback in U.S. credit sales of military equipment to Taiwan, and it was reported that Pres. Gerald Ford had pledged to reduce by half the remaining 2,300 U.S. troops on the island. In June the White House announced the withdrawal of a small team of U.S. military advisers from the Nationalist-held islands of Quemoy and Matsu. Because of State Department objections, the Massachusetts Institute of Technology terminated a training program for engineers from Taiwan. (HUNG-TI CHU)

See also China.

[975.A.6]

Tanzania

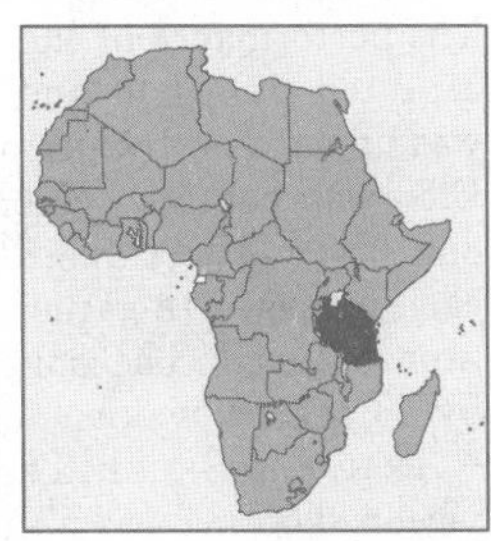

This republic, an East African member of the Commonwealth of Nations, consists of two parts: Tanganyika, on the Indian Ocean, bordered by Kenya, Uganda, Rwanda, Burundi, Zaire, Zambia, Malawi, and Mozambique; and Zanzibar, just off the coast, including Zanzibar Island, Pemba Island, and small islets. Total area of the united republic: 364,943 sq mi (945,198 sq km). Total pop. (1975 est.): 15,155,000, including (1966 est.) 98.9% Africans and 0.7% Indo-Pakistani. Cap. and largest city: Dar es Salaam (pop., 1972 est., 396,700) in Tanganyika. Language: English and Swahili. Religion (1967): traditional beliefs 34.6%; Christian 30.6%; Muslim 30.5%. President in 1976, Julius Nyerere.

Tanzania's lack of natural resources and its consequent poverty were the overriding factors in its affairs in 1976. In March the civil service was cut by 20%, an economy that seemed justified when shortly afterward auditing revealed mismanagement of funds and overspending by officers of both central and local governments. The closing of privately owned shops, to avoid duplication and facilitate price control, was slowed down when government-financed cooperatives could not fill the gap and shortages of goods were accompanied by higher prices. There was also a shortage of sugar because of the export of much of Tanzania's crop to Kenya. Although trade with Kenya remained steady, worsening relations within the East African Community encouraged Tanzania to look toward Zambia and Mozambique. Visits to India in January and to the Scandinavian countries and West Germany in April–May by Pres. Julius Nyerere (*see* BIOGRAPHY) resulted in offers of aid from several quarters, including The Netherlands. Completion of the Zambian portion of the Tanzam railway resulted in congestion at the port of Dar es Salaam, but this was largely cleared up by midyear.

By contrast with the poverty of the mainland, Zanzibar was in a sound economic position, though attempts were being made to reduce the island's re-

AUTHENTICATED NEWS INTERNATIONAL

Women in a Tanzanian village carry building materials for the construction of a primary school. The government declared it would provide primary schooling for all children by 1977.

TANZANIA

Education. (1973–74) Primary, pupils 1,126,165, teachers 23,580; secondary, pupils 47,125, teachers 2,127; vocational and teacher training, pupils 5,180, teachers 391; higher (1972–73), students 2,683, teaching staff (universities only) 353.

Finance. Monetary unit: Tanzanian shilling, with (Sept. 20, 1976) a free rate of TShs 8.40 to U.S. $1 (TShs 14.48 = £1 sterling). Gold, SDR's, and foreign exchange (June 1976) U.S. $91.8 million. Budget (1974–75 est.): revenue TShs 3,631,000,000; expenditure TShs 5,723,000,000. Gross national product (1974) TShs 15,607,000,000. Money supply (April 1976) TShs 4,483,000,000. Cost of living (1970 = 100; 4th quarter 1975) 191.

Foreign Trade. (1975) Imports TShs 5,694,000,000; exports TShs 2,764,000,000. Import sources: U.K. 13%; U.S. 12%; Saudi Arabia 10%; China 9%; West Germany 7%; Kenya 6%; Iran 6%; Japan 6%. Export destinations: U.K. 12%; West Germany 8%; Singapore 8%; Kenya 6%; U.S. 6%; Zambia 6%; India 5%. Main exports: coffee 17%; spices 12%; cotton 11%; sisal 10%; diamonds 6%; cashew nuts 6%; petroleum products 5%.

Transport and Communications. Roads (1974) *c.* 18,000 km. Motor vehicles in use (1974): passenger *c.* 39,100; commercial (including buses) *c.* 42,300. Railways (1975): 3,536 km (including *c.* 970 km of the 1,870-km Tanzam railway linking Dar es Salaam with Kapiri Mposhi in Zambia, completed in 1975; for traffic *see* KENYA). Air traffic (apportionment of traffic of East African Airways Corporation; 1974): 154 million passenger-km; freight 3.6 million net ton-km. Shipping traffic (mainland only; 1974): goods loaded 1,130,000 metric tons, unloaded 3,226,000 metric tons. Telephones (Dec. 1974) 58,000. Radio receivers (Dec. 1973) *c.* 230,000. Television receivers (Dec. 1969) 4,000.

Agriculture. Production (in 000; metric tons; 1975): corn *c.* 600; millet *c.* 120; sorghum *c.* 180; rice *c.* 170; sweet potatoes (1974) *c.* 306; cassava (1974) *c.* 3,500; sugar, raw value (1974) *c.* 124; dry beans *c.* 133; mangoes (1974) *c.* 150; bananas (1974) *c.* 720; cashew nuts (1974) *c.* 150; coffee *c.* 55; cotton, lint *c.* 41; sisal *c.* 125; timber (cu m; 1974) *c.* 32,672; fish catch (1974) *c.* 168. Livestock (in 000; 1974): cattle *c.* 12,098; sheep *c.* 2,850; pigs *c.* 23; goats *c.* 4,500; asses *c.* 161; chickens *c.* 19,800.

Industry. Production (in 000; metric tons; 1974): cement 445; salt 34; magnesite 0.1; diamonds (metric carats) *c.* 550; petroleum products *c.* 780; electricity (kw-hr) 533,000.

liance upon cloves as its main source of income. The more relaxed political atmosphere under the leadership of Aboud Jumbe was also encouraging non-Communist countries to show an interest in Zanzibar. Throughout the year President Nyerere played a prominent role in support of majority rule in Rhodesia and of the African cause in southern Africa in general.

(KENNETH INGHAM)

[978.E.6.b.iii]

Target Sports

Archery. During the 1976 Olympics 39 men and 28 women represented a total of 25 nations in the archery events. Though there were 28 fewer archers at Montreal than there were at Munich in 1972, the decrease resulted from a ruling by the International Olympic Committee and was not attributable to any lack of enthusiasm on the part of the potential Olympians. An indication of the calibre of the competition could be seen in the final results: every record established in the 1972 Olympics was broken in 1976. Darrell Pace (U.S.) once again displayed his amazing skills during the double International Archery Federation (FITA) round by piling up 2,571 points in the process of establishing new Olympic records at 90 m, 70 m, 50 m, and 30 m. Hiroshi Michinaga of Japan trailed Pace by 69 points, but outscored G. Carlo Ferrari of Italy to earn the Olympic silver medal. In the women's competition, Luann Ryon (U.S.) set a world record of 1,282 points during her second FITA round and established a new Olympic record for the double FITA with a total of 2,499 points. The next two best women archers were from the Soviet Union and in the final tally trailed Ryon by 39 and 92 points, respectively. Ryon finished first in the 50-m event, second at 30 and 60 m, and fifth at 70 m. Valentina Kovpan, the silver medalist, set Olympic records in three of the four events, but lost the gold medal by finishing tenth at 50 m.

The world field archery championship was another highlight of the year. The 68 men and 33 women who gathered in Sweden represented 18 different nations. T. Persson of Sweden captured the men's freestyle championship and A. Lehmann of West Germany won the women's title. In individual barebow competition, J. Virtanen of Finland took the men's title and S. Sandiford of Great Britain the women's.

Luann Ryon of Riverside, California, drew a mean bow at the summer Olympic Games. She set a world record and an Olympic record in target archery at Montreal.

WIDE WORLD

The third annual Championship of the Americas, held in Pennsylvania's beautiful Valley Forge National Park, proved to be another step forward for archery in the Western Hemisphere. U.S. archers established new records at all distances, outshining competitors from eight other countries.

During the year another world record went into the books when Bruce Odle (U.S.) shot an arrow a distance of 3,231 ft 3 in, bettering the old mark by 463 ft 9 in. Archers consistently demonstrated during 1976 that records are made to be broken and they were already looking forward to establishing even higher standards of accuracy during the 1977 world championships to be held in Australia.

(CLAYTON B. SHENK)

See also Track and Field Sports: *Special Report.*
[452.B.4.h.i]

Shooting. Two major international shooting competitions took place during the year, one at L'Acadia (near Montreal, Canada) as part of the 1976 Olympic Games, and the other at Camp Perry in Ohio, site of the Palma international long-range rifle matches. The Olympic competition comprises seven events, three using rifles, two using pistols, and two using shotguns. The performance of the East German marksmen, who captured two gold and two silver Olympic medals, was unmatched by any other national contingent. The U.S. was not far behind with two gold medals and one silver. The U.S.S.R. and West German shooters each managed to garner one gold, one silver, and one bronze medal. The only other gold medal was taken by a Czechoslovakian skeet shooter.

TRAP AND SKEET. The gold medal in Olympic clay pigeon shooting was won by Donald Haldeman (U.S.) with a score of 190. The silver medal was awarded to Armando Silva Narques (Port.), who won the shoot-off against Ubaldesc Baldi (Italy); each finished the regular competition with a score of 189. The Olympic gold medal for skeet went to Josef Panacek (Czech.), but not before he defeated Eric Swinkels (Neth.) in a shoot-off. Swinkels edged into a one-point lead in the fourth round and maintained his advantage with flawless shooting until the eighth and final round when he missed one of the 25 birds. That brief moment of inaccuracy evened the score and forced a shoot-off. The bronze medal was also decided in a shoot-off, which was won by Wieslaw Gawlikowski (Poland). A regulation adopted in June 1976 changed the sequence of skeet shooting in future international contests. Beginning in 1977, doubles would be shot at all stations except numbers four and eight, and the optional shot would be eliminated. In U.S. trapshooting, Frank Crevatin of Canada won the 1976 Grand American Handicap at Vandalia, Ohio, with a 99 x 100 from 21½ yd. The title, however, was not finally decided until Crevatin won a shoot-off against two other competitors who also scored 99 x 100 in the regulation rounds. Judith Whittenberger of Indiana won the women's title with a score of 97 from 18½ yd.

RIFLE. All rifle events during the 1976 Olympic Games were held at 50 m and only the small-bore weapon was fired in competition. In the prone shooting event, Karlheinz Smieszek (West Germany) captured the gold medal with a world-record-tying score of 599; fellow countryman Ulrich Lind won the silver medal with a score of 597. The bronze medalist was Gennady Lushchikov (U.S.S.R.) who finished with 595. Anton Mueller (Switz.) also finished with a score of 595 but lost the bronze medal when his performance was judged fourth best according to Olympic rules that are invoked to break ties. In the three-positions competition, Lanny Bassham (U.S.) and Margaret Murdock (U.S.) each finished with scores of 1,162. Though Bassham was officially declared the winner of the gold medal under the ruling that decided the winner on the basis of the final ten shots, he graciously shared the awards podium with his female teammate. The third place bronze medal went to Werner Seibold (West Germany), who scored 1,160. In the running target event, Aleksandr Gazov (U.S.S.R.) scored 579 to become the only 1976 Olympic marksman to set a new world and Olympic record in the rifle events. The second place silver medal went to Aleksandr Kedyarov (U.S.S.R.), who finished with a score of 576, five points better than third place finisher Jerzy Greszkiewicz (Poland).

The U.S. was host to the 1976 Palma long-range rifle matches at Camp Perry in conjunction with the U.S. national matches. During the international Palma team competition, which was first held in 1876, rifles were fired at 800, 900, and 1,000 yd. Observing an old tradition, the U.S. as host country supplied specially produced weapons and ammunition in cal. 7.62-mm. Maximum possible score for each 20-man team was 9,000 on the new decimal target. The U.S. team finished in first place (8,658—271X), followed in order by South Africa (8,497—227X), U.K. (8,465—220X), New Zealand (8,435—201X), Australia (8,432—201X), and Canada (8,425—184X). The U.S. national high-power championship was won by Gary Anderson, who scored 1,990—111X out of a possible 2,000. David Weaver captured the small-bore rifle prone title with a score of 6,396—538X. The national small-bore three-position championship went to nine-time winner Lones Wigger who scored 3,175—208X. Wigger also finished second in the prone small-bore competition and at Tucson, Ariz., won the national metallic silhouette championship.

World Archery Records

Event	Winner	Year	Record	Old record	Maximum possible
	Single FITA Round				
MEN					
FITA	D. Pace (U.S.)	1975	1,316	1,291	1,440
90 m	D. Pace (U.S.)	1975	309	303	360
70 m	D. Pace (U.S.)	1975	333	325	360
50 m	S. Spigarelli (Italy)	1976	340	331	360
30 m	D. Pace (U.S.)	1975	354	350	360
Team	United States	1976	3,812	3,775	4,320
WOMEN					
FITA	L. Ryon (U.S.)	1976	1,282	1,266	1,440
70 m	L. Myers (U.S.)	1974	310	307	360
60 m	V. Kovpan (U.S.S.R.)	1976	327	324	360
50 m	L. Sjoholm (Sweden)	1975	319	311	360
30 m	V. Kovpan (U.S.S.R.)	1976	346	344	360
Team	U.S.S.R.	1972	3,670	—	4,320
	World Distance Record				
	Bruce Odle (U.S.)	1976	3,231¼ ft		

Olympic Archery Records

Event	Winner	Year	Record	Old record	Maximum possible
	Double FITA Round				
MEN					
FITA	D. Pace (U.S.)	1976	2,571	2,528	2,880
90 m	D. Pace (U.S.)	1976	592	580	720
70 m	D. Pace (U.S.)	1976	634	630	720
50 m	D. Pace (U.S.)	1976	644	630	720
30 m	D. Pace (U.S.)	1976	701	688	720
WOMEN					
FITA	L. Ryon (U.S.)	1976	2,499	2,424	2,880
70 m	V. Kovpan (U.S.S.R.)	1976	589	580	720
60 m	V. Kovpan (U.S.S.R.)	1976	626	624	720
50 m	L. Ryon (U.S.)	1976	618	576	720
30 m	V. Kovpan (U.S.S.R.)	1976	686	670	720

The Americas Archery Records

Event	Winner	Year	Record	Old record	Maximum possible
	Single FITA Round				
MEN					
FITA	D. Pace (U.S.)	1976	1,278	1,235	1,440
90 m	D. Pace (U.S.)	1976	292	285	360
70 m	R. McKinney (U.S.)	1976	323	306	360
50 m	R. Bednar (U.S.)	1976	324	322	360
30 m	R. McKinney (U.S.)	1976	348	342	360
	D. Pace (U.S.)	1976	348	342	360
Team	United States	1976	3,812	3,656	4,320
WOMEN					
FITA	L. Ryon (U.S.)	1976	1,215	1,180	1,440
70 m	M. Silcocks (U.S.)	1976	303	288	360
60 m	I. Daubenspeck (U.S.)	1976	318	297	360
50 m	L. Ryon (U.S.)	1976	298	285	360
Team	United States	1976	3,636	3,466	4,320

SVEN SIMON—KATHERINE YOUNG

A biathlon competitor pauses to shoot at the Winter Olympics in February. The biathlon combines cross-country skiing with rifle marksmanship over a course of 20 kilometres (about 12.5 miles). The 1976 winner was Nikolay Kruglov of the U.S.S.R.

HANDGUNS. In the Olympic pistol events, East German shooters clearly demonstrated their superiority by finishing first and second in each of the two competitions. Uwe Potteck led his team with a sparkling score of 573 that established a new world and Olympic record for free pistol. In capturing the silver medal, Harald Vollmar scored 567 to give him a comfortable lead over Rudolf Dollinger (Austria), who scored 562. In the rapid fire event the East Germans again outclassed their competitors. Norbert Klaar set a new Olympic record and won the gold medal with a score of 597 and Jurgen Wiefel captured the silver medal with 596. Though three marksmen tied for third place with scores of 595, the bronze medal was awarded to Roberto Ferraris (Italy) on the basis of Olympic rules that govern such contingencies.

Bonnie Harmon successfully defended his 1975 title by capturing the U.S. pistol championship at Camp Perry with an aggregate score of 2,647—137X. Hershel Anderson, the U.S. champion in 1973 and 1974, was runner-up in that event and won the U.S. .22 rimfire pistol crown with a score of 889—52X.

BIATHLON. In the 1976 Winter Olympics in Innsbruck, Austria, 51 athletes participated in the individual 20-km biathlon and teams from 15 nations took part in the four-man 30-km biathlon relay. In the individual event, Aleksandr Tihonov (U.S.S.R.) set the pace through the first three stages, but could not keep his lead and finished in fifth place. First over the finish line was Nikolay Kruglov (U.S.S.R.), who traversed the 20-km course in 1 hr 14 min 12.26 sec, nearly 2 minutes faster than silver medalist Heikki Ikola (Fin.). The bronze medal went to Aleksandr Elizarov (U.S.S.R.), who could not quite overtake Ikola and finished some ten seconds behind the Finn. In the four-man team relay competition, Soviet and Finnish athletes once again battled for the gold and silver medals. The Soviet team of Aleksandr Elizarov, Ivan Biakov, Nikolay Kruglov, and Aleksandr Tihonov posted a combined time of 1 hr 57 min 55.64 sec over the 30-km course to best the Finnish team by nearly 4 minutes. The East German team finished a scant 3 seconds ahead of the West Germans to take the third place bronze medal.

(ROBERT N. SEARS)

[452.B.4.e]

Darts. The first of two major dart tournaments held in Great Britain during the year took place at Alexandra Palace in London, where representatives of 12 nations gathered for the finals of the News of the World championships. U.S. Open champion Tony Money, an Englishman by birth but currently residing in Ohio, represented the U.S. After a series of elimination victories, Bill Lennard reached the finals and won the title by defeating Leighton Rees. Despite this loss, Rees had reason to feel proud. While playing against Denny Gower at the Spotted Cow in Bristol, he set a new world record by finishing a game of 3,001 in just 81 darts. In the U.K. Unicorn world championships, dartists from 16 nations competed for top honours. In the finals Kevin White and George Foster of Australia defeated Willy Dalaere and Omer Bauwens of Belgium. The U.S. Unicorn championship was won by Jack Curry and Russ Zanardi of San Mateo, Calif. (EDMUND CARL HADY)

Television and Radio

Approximately 1,117,200,000 television and radio sets were in use throughout the world in 1976. With the introduction of tests in South Africa in 1975 and regular programming in 1976, all major countries had some form of television service. For years, none had lacked radio service. Radio sets in use numbered approximately 774 million, of which 413.1 million, or more than half, were in the U.S. An estimated 343.2 million television receivers were in use throughout the world, with 125 million of those in the U.S.

The Soviet Union, with approximately 45 million television sets, ranked next to the U.S., according to estimates published in the 1975 *Broadcasting Yearbook*. Japan was third with 26 million, followed by the United Kingdom with 22.9 million. Other *Broadcasting* estimates included West Germany, 17.4 million; France, 14.3 million; Italy, 11 million; Brazil, 8.8 million; Canada, 8 million; Spain, 6.8 million; Poland, 5.2 million; East Germany and Mexico, 5 million each; and Argentina, Australia, and The Netherlands, 4 million each.

There were about 6,675 television stations on the air throughout the world, distributed approximately as follows: 2,200 in the Far East, 2,100 in Western Europe, 1,031 in the U.S., 920 in Eastern Europe, 180 in South America, 105 in Mexico, 96 in Canada, and 43 in Africa. Radio stations, mostly of the amplitude modulation (AM) type but with an increasing number of frequency modulation (FM) stations, numbered about 14,790. The U.S. had 8,421, of which 3,892 were FM.

Organization of Services. Inflation and government reluctance to sanction increases in license fees for sets hit television hard in 1976, as broadcasting organizations in Britain, West Germany, and Japan sank into debt. Program budgets were, as always, the first victims of the inevitable financial cuts; other responses included scheduling more reruns and coproductions. The only exceptions to this trend were organizations in countries where advertising revenue continued to rise (such as the U.S. and South America) or where broadcasting was state-controlled (U.S.S.R. and China).

No significant progress was made in 1976 in efforts to reach an agreement on the future international distribution of television programs by satellite. In the United Nations the deadlock continued over the question of control of the airwaves at the time that broadcasting from one country directly into home television sets in other countries becomes feasible, perhaps by 1985. The U.S. advocated a free flow of information among countries; the U.S.S.R. and its supporters insisted that each country must have the right to forbid such broadcasts into the homes of its people.

While this disagreement continued, private and government-owned broadcasting organizations continued the cooperative arrangements through which international exchange of major news coverage via satellite had become commonplace. Portions of the Winter Olympic Games in Innsbruck, Austria, and the Summer Games in Montreal, Canada; the gala July 4 celebration of the U.S. Bicentennial; and coverage of the U.S. presidential election returns in November were among the broadcasts most widely distributed throughout the world. In another kind of international venture, the government of India completed in August a one-year experiment in which health, educational, and agricultural material was transmitted by television to 2,400 remote Indian villages by means of a U.S. satellite.

UNITED STATES. Approximately 54.9 million or 77% of all U.S. television-equipped homes had colour television sets in mid-1976, according to *Broadcasting* magazine. That total represented a gain of 3.6 million sets in 12 months. Virtually all programs were broadcast in colour, the main exceptions being old movies originally made in black-and-white. More than 90% of all television homes were equipped to receive programs from ultrahigh-frequency (UHF) stations; 45% had more than one TV set; and more than 15% were connected to cable television (CATV). Among the CATV subscribers, according to estimates published by *Broadcasting* early in 1976, about 600,000 also subscribed to pay-TV services on their CATV channels.

One of many disputes between cable operators and broadcasters was at least partially resolved in October when the U.S. Congress passed and Pres. Gerald Ford signed a new copyright law requiring, for the first time, that CATV systems pay broadcasters whose programs they picked up and delivered to their own subscribers. But it was an uneasy settlement, for most broadcasters contended that the payment rates prescribed in the law were too small.

In November NBC signed a conditional consent decree to settle its part of a four-year-old antitrust suit brought by the U.S. Department of Justice against all three commercial TV networks, designed to reduce their control over programming. Many of the restrictions that NBC accepted, however, would not go into effect until the same restrictions were imposed against ABC and CBS. In addition, many of the restrictions would give NBC greater leeway than it currently exercised. For instance, NBC would not be allowed to produce or hold financial interests in more than 2½ hours of programming a week, whereas in 1976 it owned or produced only one hour a week. Nevertheless, ABC and CBS criticized the agreement and indicated that they would continue to resist.

Tariffs:
see Economy, World
Taxation:
see Economy, World
Telecommunications:
see Industrial Review

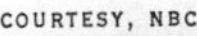
COURTESY, NBC

The presidential year brought a TV mini-series about a political family in NBC's "Captains and the Kings," based on Taylor Caldwell's novel. Presidential candidate Rory Daniel Armagh (Perry King) rides with his family in a 1912 parade. Also shown are wife Claudia (Cynthia Sikes) and brother Brian (Cliff DeYoung).

A plan for three-year federal funding of public broadcasting, replacing the year-to-year approach whose uncertainties had dismayed the noncommercial stations in the past, went into effect after being passed by Congress and then upheld over a veto by President Ford. The law specified that the Corporation for Public Broadcasting (CPB) should receive, under a system of matching grants requiring it to raise $2.50 for each federal dollar, $103 million in 1977, $107,150,000 in 1978, and $120.2 million in 1979. In fiscal 1975, according to a preliminary report by the CPB, gross income of public television stations (of which there were 157) totaled $277 million from all sources, an increase of 25.5% over 1974; the income of public radio stations, numbering 165, was $31 million, up 20.1%.

EUROPE. In July the European Broadcasting Union (EBU), the Communist-bloc International Radio and Television Organization (OIRT), and the Organización de la Televisión Iberoamericana (OTI) signed an agreement with the International Federation of Association Football (FIFA) for exclusive world rights to televise the 1978 World Cup finals in Argentina. Another example of EBU cooperation was the special operation to cover the U.S. political party conventions and presidential election.

A workshop for those concerned with the production of programs for children reflected a growing concern among EBU members that young people spent more time watching late-night adult material than watching programs specially prepared for them. Education and drama were other areas in which EBU discussions took place. The need for investment in drama productions was emphasized for two reasons: drama programs were among those most favoured for sales and exchanges, and although old films had been a staple diet of television programmers for years, their supply was becoming exhausted.

At the EBU Assembly in Helsinki, Fin., in July, Sir Charles Curran was reelected to a third term as president. Two new vice-presidents were Jean Autin, president of Télédiffusion de France, and Otto Oberhammer, director general of Österreichischer Rundfunk (ÖRF).

In Britain the continuing investigations of the Committee on the Future of Broadcasting, chaired by Lord Annan, effectively prevented the government from making any major policy decision and tended to discourage the broadcasters' energies. The BBC led independent (commercial) television (ITV) in the ratings battle but was accused of becoming dull and overbureaucratic. The director general of the BBC, Sir Charles Curran, announced his resignation as of the spring of 1977. He would be succeeded by Ian Trethowan, currently managing director of BBC television.

In Switzerland a proposal to set up a new independent organization to compete with the state monopoly was defeated in a referendum.

The growth of democracy in Spain was reflected in the setting up of a General Council of television and radio, which could criticize RTVE, the state broadcasting organization. In Greece the new, more independent broadcasting organization, ERT, took over responsibility for the first channel and was expected to take over the second channel in 1978. Television in Greece was marked by a more liberal and professional approach.

CANADA. The "border war" between the Canadian Broadcasting Corporation (CBC) and the cable companies intensified. Cable companies that bought time on U.S. channels and imported U.S. television signals were pressured to cease by the federal government.

The second symposium on "Radio in the 1980s" was held in Ottawa by the CBC. It reflected the awareness of radio's new importance, particularly in education, news, and audience-participation programs.

AFRICA AND AUSTRALASIA. After much internal debate, South Africa began regular television transmissions in January. The South African Broadcasting Corporation transmitted about 5½ hours daily, half in English and half in Afrikaans. The service was technically excellent and fairly popular, but was proving more expensive than estimated; it was thought advertising might have to be introduced.

In Australia and New Zealand new governments quickly overturned the reforms of their predecessors. The Australian Liberal government abolished the innovative minister for the media and set up an inquiry into broadcasting; this recommended that the Australian Broadcasting Commission (ABC) and the commercial companies be regulated by a single body. In New Zealand the government restored the monolithic New Zealand Broadcasting Corporation and made it responsible for all broadcasting.

In Japan Kichiro Ono, the president of Nippon Hoso Kyokai (NHK), resigned amid allegations that he was involved with former prime minister Kakuei

Tanaka in the Lockheed bribery affair. Vice-Pres. Tomkazu Sakamoto succeeded Ono. After an eight-year standstill, NHK raised its license fee in an effort to counter an alarming deficit ($63 million in 1975). In India a separate organization, Door Darshan, was set up to run television; its top priority was to extend television coverage beyond the current 0.1% of the population. Indonesia launched Asia's first national satellite system (outside the U.S.S.R.); it could provide 12 television channels. From China it was announced that Peking TV, which broadcast three nights a week, could reach every part of the country except Tibet. Radio still dominated Chinese broadcasting, however.

Programming. As in the past, coverage of major news events provided one of the principal program exports among countries in 1976. Besides the Olympic Games in Innsbruck and Montreal, the debates between Pres. Gerald Ford and Jimmy Carter, the U.S. election returns, and portions of the U.S. celebration of its Bicentennial on July 4 were distributed widely throughout the world.

In entertainment programming, mysteries, Westerns, and comedies produced in the U.S. were major television attractions in many countries. *Broadcasting* magazine estimated that foreign sales of U.S. TV programs and movies totaled about $160 million in 1975, an all-time high and about 25% higher than the 1974 total of $128 million. All indications suggested further gains in 1976. "The Six Million Dollar Man," "The Bionic Woman," "Rich Man, Poor Man," "Starsky and Hutch," "All in the Family," "Ironside," "The Odd Couple," and "The Mary Tyler Moore Show" were among the most popular U.S. exports.

UNITED STATES. The 1976–77 network television season, which opened in September, got off to an unaccustomed start. CBS, which had dominated prime-time audience ratings of the three networks for two decades, was running third, and ABC, which had run third for most of those years, was clearly in first place. In the sixth week of the season, going into November, ABC not only had won six weeks in a row but had the top three programs and six of the top seven. ABC's "Happy Days," a situation comedy featuring Henry Winkler (*see* BIOGRAPHY), was attracting almost half of the television viewing audience in its time period and had displaced the longtime favourite, CBS's "All in the Family," as the top-rated show; and ABC's "Charlie's Angels" and "The Bionic Woman" were in second and third positions. By mid-November, the season-to-date averages were: ABC 20.9, NBC 20.1, and CBS 18.4. (Each rating point represented 1% of the approximately 71.2 million U.S. television homes.)

Young John Adams, played by George Grizzard, arriving in Boston in 1758 in "The Adams Chronicles," a series that became a hit on U.S. public television.

WIDE WORLD

In preparing for the 1976–77 season the networks had thoroughly overhauled their evening schedules, canceling a total of 23 programs, introducing 24 new ones, and moving 9 others to new time periods. No night's lineup was exactly the same as it had been in 1975–76. The new series were predominantly situation comedies and, to a somewhat lesser extent, straight dramas or melodramas. Westerns, once a dominant part of the prime-time schedules, were represented by only one new entry, "The Quest" on NBC, and heavy-action programs, much criticized by opponents of violence on TV, were more evident by their absence than by their presence. In recognition of what it considered an audience trend toward the spectacularly unusual in programming, NBC introduced "The Big Event," to consist of rare occasions such as World Series baseball, "blockbuster" motion pictures, and a 4½-hour program, broadcast in November, commemorating the network's 50th anniversary.

Many well-established shows were canceled to make room for the 1976–77 entries. Among them were "Marcus Welby, M.D.," a seven-year veteran that for many years was a top-rated series on ABC; "The Rookies" and "Harry O," also on ABC; "Medical Center," which won high ratings for CBS for seven years; and "Bronk," a four-year-old CBS police show.

The 1976–77 prime-time schedules, according to estimates by *Broadcasting,* would cost the networks more than $500 million for regular series alone, or some $90 million more than the comparable cost in 1975–76. In addition, *Broadcasting* estimated that special programs would add $100 million to $120 million in production costs. The cost of regularly scheduled entertainment series was estimated to average about $10.9 million a week, or about 20% more than in 1975–76.

For all the expense, early returns in the ratings showed that the 1976–77 season would probably be no exception to the rule that six out of every ten series never get beyond their first season. The cancellations started early. Within a month after the season opened, CBS announced it was dropping "Ball Four" and "Doc," two situation comedies, and was suspending "The Blue Knight," an action drama, indefinitely. Within two weeks ABC announced that it would replace two new comedies, "Cos" and "Mr. T and Tina," and NBC disclosed plans to abandon "Gemini Man" and subsequently replaced a weekly movie with three new situation comedies. Replacements were to include a new movie night on CBS; "What's Happening," a situation comedy centring on three black urban high-school students, and a series of specials on ABC; and "Gibbsville," a drama series based on short stories by John O'Hara, on NBC.

The largest audience of the year was won by NBC's two-part showing of the motion-picture classic *Gone with the Wind,* on November 7–8. Its Nielsen rating averaged 47.5, almost two-thirds of all homes watching television during those hours. NBC estimated that 110 million persons had watched some or all of the movie, exceeding the former movie record of 85,820,000 set by *Ben Hur* on Feb. 14, 1971.

A decision that could have far-reaching future effects on programming was handed down by a federal court in Los Angeles in November, holding that the so-called family-viewing concept was unconstitutional in origin. The concept had evolved in 1975 in conversations between the chairman of the Federal Communications Commission (FCC), Richard Wiley, and leaders of the three networks and had subsequently been incorporated into the National Association of Broadcasters' standards of good practices. In essence, it provided that between 7 and 9 PM Eastern and Pacific Time (6–8 PM Central and Mountain Time), programming should be designed for all-family viewing, avoiding "sex and violence." But U.S. District Judge Warren Ferguson, ruling in a suit brought by a group of West Coast producers and talent unions, held that the FCC chairman's involvement represented a violation of the First Amendment's guarantees of freedom of speech.

Judge Ferguson said the evidence showed there had been "a successful attempt by the FCC to pressure the networks and the NAB into adopting a programming policy that they did not want to adopt." He also said, however, that broadcasters were free to continue the family-viewing policy if they wished, provided they did not do so out of fear of government reprisal. CBS and ABC said they would appeal the decision and would continue to observe the family-viewing principle. NBC said it did not plan to appeal on the main issue but would continue to honour the concept.

Local programming had not been materially affected by the family-viewing rule because stations had historically chosen to present nonviolent material, primarily games and nature shows, in the nonnetwork period covered by the plan (7–8 PM Eastern and Pacific Time, 6–7 PM Central and Mountain).

One of the most talked-about hits in syndication to individual stations was "Mary Hartman, Mary Hartman," an irreverent, plain-speaking takeoff on television's daytime serials that was produced by Norman Lear, creator of such network hits as "All in the Family." Because of its frank approach to adult themes, the networks would not buy "Mary Hartman, Mary Hartman" and many of the 100-plus stations that did buy it scheduled it late in the evening. Even there, however, it received high ratings and made a star of lead actress Louise Lasser (*see* BIOGRAPHY).

Syndication was also being considered for another purpose that could have a bearing on future programming: the formation of a "fourth network," though not necessarily one with the same kind of structure as ABC, CBS, and NBC. Those conventional networks and most stations were enjoying an economic boom of unprecedented proportions in 1976, so much so that the networks, in particular, had little advertising time left to sell. Advertisers who could not buy as much network time as they thought they needed, or who objected to the prices the networks were charging, began to explore the possibilities of organizing a nationwide group of independent stations on which, through syndication, they could place their own programs (and advertising) for broadcast during a limited but specified number of daytime or evening hours. Some of the leaders of this venture hoped to reach a decision on its feasibility early in 1977 and, if it was favourable, to have the new "network" in operation for the start of the 1977–78 season.

PHOTOS, WIDE WORLD

One hundred dollars a minute was Barbara Walters' new salary for co-anchoring the ABC "Evening News" with Harry Reasoner (top). The star of NBC's "Today" got a five-year $1 million-a-year contract. Her replacement on "Today" was Jane Pauley, shown (bottom) with host Tom Brokaw.

Programming for children was a matter of continuing concern for both networks and stations. Among the latter, cooperative program production increased, as more and more stations found it worthwhile to form groups in which they would pool their resources and produce programs at once more elaborate and more fitting than they could afford individually. The programs dealt with subjects ranging from books, music, and fantasy to current affairs and even the latest news reported in terms suitable for the young. The idea of the mini-series, which had proved so successful in prime-time programming, was adapted for the young audience in "Little Vic," a six-part series developed by ABC-owned stations, based on a novel by Doris Gates.

The networks introduced 16 new series in their Saturday-morning and Sunday-morning schedules for young viewers. They consisted of both live-action and animated features, but the trend away from heavy action-adventure continued in response to complaints of too much violence. The new entries included

"Animals, Animals, Animals" and "Short Story Specials" on ABC; "Tarzan: Lord of the Jungle" and "Ark II" on CBS; and "McDuff" and "Big John, Little John" on NBC. The networks also reduced to 9½ minutes per hour the amount of advertising permitted in their children's shows, completing a 40% reduction in two years.

Game shows and serials were the dominant formats in daytime programming, as in the past, with 60-minute dramas gaining widespread acceptance after "Another World," "Days of Our Lives," and "As the World Turns" were expanded from 30-minute to one-hour versions. One long-running game show, "Let's Make a Deal," a daytime staple for 12½ years, was dropped from the network schedule in mid-1976 but was widely sold in syndication for showing by local stations, usually in early-evening hours.

In the 28th annual Emmy awards, the National Academy of Television Arts and Sciences again voted "The Mary Tyler Moore Show" the outstanding comedy series of 1975–76 and named "Police Story" the outstanding drama series. "Eleanor and Franklin," a drama special about Pres. and Mrs Franklin D. Roosevelt, set an Emmy record by winning 11 awards; among them were those for outstanding drama or comedy special, outstanding directing in a special, and outstanding writing in a special. The choices for best lead actors and actresses in regular series were Peter Falk of "Colombo" and Michael Learned of "The Waltons" in drama and Jack Albertson of "Chico and the Man" and Mary Tyler Moore of "The Mary Tyler Moore Show" in comedy. "Upstairs, Downstairs" was named the outstanding limited series. Other program winners included "Gypsy in My Soul" as best comedy-variety or musical special; "Bernstein and the New York Philharmonic," outstanding classical music program; "You're a Good Sport, Charlie Brown" and "Huckleberry Finn," best children's specials; "NFL Monday Night Football," outstanding live sports series; and "XII Winter Olympic Games" and "Triumph and Tragedy . . . the Olympic Experience," best edited sports specials. Among daytime programs, top Emmy winners included "The $20,000 Pyramid" as the leading game or audience-participation show and "Another World" as the outstanding dramatic series.

Sports continued to command large audiences—and high prices. *Broadcasting* estimated that television and radio networks and stations were paying $81.6 million for rights to broadcast professional and college football games in 1976 and $50.8 million for similar rights to major-league baseball games. Those sums represented a gain of only about 1% over the 1975 costs of football rights but almost 15% for baseball. In general, the audiences for these sports, though large, seemed to have leveled off, but the championship events still attracted record or near-record viewing audiences. The Super Bowl football game between the Pittsburgh Steelers and Dallas Cowboys in January, for instance, took first place in Nielsen's list of the 25 highest-rated TV shows up to that date; it was seen, Nielsen estimated, in an average of 29,440,000 homes per average minute. In early October, two of the five highest rated shows of the week were World Series baseball games, each of which was seen in more than 21 million homes. Earlier in the year, coverage of the Olympic Games had scored even higher; in one July week the seven highest-rated shows were the seven nights of coverage of the Summer Olympics in Montreal, and in February the Winter Olympic Games had usually ranked among the weekly top-20 programs. ABC obtained TV rights to the 1980 Winter Games, and all three networks were negotiating for rights to the Summer Games in Moscow, though the Soviet Union was reported to be demanding up to four or more times the $25 million that ABC had paid for U.S. rights to the 1976 competition.

Basketball, tennis, and golf continued to attract consistent although relatively small audiences, but soccer seemed unable to generate genuine appeal and CBS dropped its option to carry the sport in 1977 and 1978. Ice hockey had been dropped earlier by NBC, for similar reasons, but late in 1976 the National Hockey League, encouraged by the acceptance of special coverage of its Stanley Cup play-off games, was attempting to put together a special lineup of independent TV stations to carry a series of 13 Monday-night NHL games, starting in January 1977.

News and public affairs remained basic television fare, and the most publicized attraction of 1976 was the series of three debates between President Ford and Jimmy Carter, the first such joint appearances since John Kennedy and Richard Nixon set the precedent in 1960. Televising the Ford-Carter debates was made possible by an FCC ruling that such appearances could be covered as news events, not subject to legal requirements of equal time for all other presidential candidates, if they were presented entirely under nonbroadcast auspices. The League of Women Voters then arranged the debates, which were held in Philadelphia on September 23, San Francisco on October 6, and Williamsburg, Va., on October 22, and were covered by ABC, CBS, NBC, the Public Broadcasting Service, and a number of independent stations. (*See* UNITED STATES: *Special Report: How the Debates Came to Be.*)

Despite the closeness of the balloting, coverage of the election returns on November 2 drew fewer viewers than normally watch television at night. For election coverage during the prime hours of 7–11 PM Eastern Time, the three-network average rating was 52.4%, as compared with about 57% for conventional programming one week earlier. *Broadcasting* estimated the audience at 120 million persons, about equal to that for Richard Nixon's quick win over George McGovern in 1972 but 15% short of the 142 million who watched when Nixon edged out Hubert Humphrey in 1968. Independent stations, which for the most part were carrying entertainment programs, found their audiences much larger than usual—24% of the total, compared with the usual 10–15%.

Television news made news when ABC hired Barbara Walters away from NBC's "Today" show, at $1 million a year for five years, to join Harry Reasoner on ABC's "Evening News" and thus become network television's first female "co-anchorperson." At the same time ABC suggested that it might lengthen the 30-minute evening newscast to 45 minutes or an hour. CBS and NBC took up the idea, but all three networks dropped it several months later in the face of almost solid opposition from their affiliates, who protested that the expansion would cut into their own program time, forcing many of them to curtail their own local newscasts and costing them, in total, millions of dollars in advertising revenues. Instead, both CBS and ABC were planning to replace a weekly hour of entertainment programming with "magazine type" news reports early in 1977.

One of the most colourful "programs" of the year was provided by network and local coverage of the nation's bicentennial celebration on July 4. It ranged

PHOTO TRENDS

Italian TV starred Renato Rascel in a series about a night watchman who works while others sleep. In this scene sleepy-eyed Rascel (right) breakfasts while his wife (Giuditta Santarini) and father-in-law (Mario Maranzana) are eating their dinner.

from Operation Sail in New York and fireworks displays in Washington, D.C., New York City, and Boston to ceremonies at the Liberty Bell in Philadelphia and local observances in scores of small- and middle-sized towns across the country. CBS devoted 16 hours to this coverage, NBC 15 hours, and ABC 3 hours of edited highlights; in addition, hundreds of individual TV and radio stations added their own special programs and coverage of local celebrations. *Broadcasting* estimated the three commercial networks alone spent $3.5 million on the day's events. The audiences were not up to normal in size, however, peaking at about 27,283,000 homes, or 39.2% of all TV homes. This was 10 percentage points below the usual level at 10:30–11 PM Eastern time.

Among television and radio stations as well as network news organizations the practice of employing specialists to report on and interpret the news in their fields continued to gain ground. Stations paid more attention to news of everyday importance to their viewers and listeners: ways to minimize the effects of inflation, conserve energy, attack housing and environmental problems, and the like. They also attempted to show how major national and international developments might affect their local communities. With lightweight electronic cameras coming into more widespread use, TV news crews were able to and did range farther from home in covering news of local interest, and many stations also expanded their main daily newscasts from 30 minutes to an hour. Surveys continued to show that television was the main source of news for most people.

In radio there was a surge in the number of all-news stations, thanks in part to NBC's formation of its round-the-clock News and Information Service (NIS) in mid-1975. NIS itself, however, was not successful; NBC announced late in 1976 that it had failed to attract enough revenues to offer any prospect of ever becoming profitable and would be shut down at the end of May 1977. But many of the 62 stations then subscribing to NIS, especially those in large markets, were expected to retain their all-news formats, using other sources for national and world news.

Radio news lost one of its oldest and best-known voices in 1976. Lowell Thomas (*see* BIOGRAPHY), a network newscaster for 46 years, retired from his nightly series on CBS Radio on May 14.

With the start of its 1976–77 season in September, the Public Broadcasting Service introduced a new concept, "Theme Night," under which PBS programming on most nights each week would be devoted to a specific variety or theme. Sunday nights concentrated on the performing arts, with programs including "Evening at Symphony" with the Boston Symphony Orchestra, "Masterpiece Theatre" (dramas), and "Great Performances" (music, theatre, and dance). Monday nights were set aside for variety, with repeat showings of the widely acclaimed "The Adams Chronicles," a third season of "In Performance at Wolftrap," and contemporary music on "Soundstage." Tuesday evenings featured outstanding specials, among them dramas from the "Hall of Fame" series and "National Geographic Specials." Wednesday nights were devoted to the sciences and arts, including "Nova" and "Book Beat"; Thursdays were set aside for drama; Fridays for such public affairs programs as "Washington Week in Review"; and Saturdays for all-family programming that included "Zoom," "Rebop," and "Once Upon a Classic."

PBS daytime programming included "The Infinity Factory," "World Press," and "Consumer Survival Kit"; repeats of some of the nighttime programs; and the much-praised "Sesame Street," "The Electric Company," "Mr. Rogers' Neighborhood," "Villa Alegre," and "Carrascolendas." Special surveys by Nielsen found that Americans spent 60.8% more time watching PBS programs in March 1976 than they had in October 1975, and that, in March, 50.4% of all TV households had tuned in to PBS programs. It was the first known time that more than half of all TV homes had watched PBS programming at least once during a month.

In radio, most stations presented a combination of music and news, with the emphasis on music. All-news stations, though increasing, were still few in number compared with those devoted primarily to music. A survey by *Broadcasting,* based on ratings compiled by the American Research Bureau, found that in the 50 largest U.S. cities the most popular program formats were, in order, contemporary music, "beautiful" music, middle-of-the-road music, country music, and all-news or news-and-talk programming. Radio dramas, both new works and replays of early radio favourites such as "The Green Hornet," "The

Filming the crucifixion scene from the TV epic "The Life of Christ." The British-Italian production stars Robert Powell as Christ. Also in the cast are Rod Steiger, Sir Laurence Olivier, Peter O'Toole, Sir Ralph Richardson, Michael York, James Mason, Anne Bancroft, Olivia Hussey, and Ernest Borgnine.

Shadow," and "Fibber McGee and Molly," continued to attract sizable and growing audiences.

EUROPE. In Britain interest grew in the extension of the "social use" of television, already exemplified by the BBC's adult literacy program and series such as Granada's "Reports Action" and London Weekend's "London Programme." Nevertheless, the familiar ratings battle continued, with the BBC claiming almost 60% of the national viewing audience thanks to its program planners' combination of imported U.S. successes, such as "Starsky and Hutch," with comedy, sports, and superior quizzes such as "Mastermind." The BBC's success against the independent channels caused considerable dismay among advertisers.

Repeats, reruns, and action replays were much in evidence. The BBC celebrated 40 years of television broadcasting with "Festival 40," and screened again some favourites from the past, as did the independent channels to commemorate the 21st birthday of commercial television in Britain.

One of ITV's longest-running successes was its nightly "News at Ten," and in an effort to counter its popularity the BBC restyled its "Nine O'Clock News," using a female newscaster regularly for the first time. The BBC's television and radio news services were supported by a worldwide team of reporters; altogether, the BBC had 20 foreign correspondents, ten times the foreign staff of International Television News (ITN). Some journalists criticized the BBC for separating "news" from "analysis" and called for greater coverage of major issues.

In spite of financial stringencies, British television continued to profit from exports, particularly in the documentary field. The BBC had sales in more than 80 countries, including China. In September Thames Television transmitted a week of British television on New York's Channel 9. Presented in conjunction with WOR-TV, New York, the "takeover" was aimed at boosting program sales. Reaction was mixed. Many U.S. viewers, however, praised the drama and documentary quality. Thames showed the Prix Italia winner for drama, "The Naked Civil Servant," which later won an Emmy award. Actor John Hurt's portrayal of Quentin Crisp, a homosexual on whose life the drama was based, won him the British Academy of Film and Television Arts' best actor award. Also featured was the documentary "Beauty, Bonny, Daisy, Violet, Grace and Geoffrey Morton," a film by Frank Cvitanovich about a Yorkshire farmer and his working horses, which took the Prix Italia documentary award—the second year in succession that British programs had taken the two top Prix Italia awards.

The U.S. Bicentennial inspired several series, of varying quality, including Thames' "Destination America" and BBC-2's "Goodbye America." "The World at War" team continued to extract fresh program material from the World War II film archives, while Granada's "Three Days in Szczecin" was a reconstruction of a Polish shipyard strike in 1971, based on taped records and the recollection of the strike leader, now an exile in Britain.

In drama series, the content was mixed. Associated Television Network, Ltd.'s (ATV) "Clayhanger" proved considerably less successful than had been hoped. Yorkshire Television offered "Dickens of London," with script by Wolf Mankowitz, and the BBC gained good audiences for "When the Boat Comes In," Julian Mitchell's series set in the depressed 1920s; "The Brothers," a remorseless saga of family intrigue and big business; and "The Duchess of Duke Street," which traced the fortunes of a Cockney girl making good as a cook and hotelier in Edwardian London. Television's oldest policeman, George Dixon of the fictitious "Dock Green," finally retired from duty after many years of service as portrayed by veteran actor Jack Warner. Dixon's less cozy successors, such as "The Sweeney," were regarded by some policemen as a possible threat to crime prevention because of their unflinching (and often violent) realism. "I, Claudius" was a BBC-2 adaptation of the novels of Robert Graves, and Thames' "Bill Brand" examined national politics in the person of a radical Labour Party MP.

Three British actors won Emmy awards in the U.S.; they were Anthony Hopkins for his portrayal of Bruno Hauptmann in "The Lindbergh Kidnapping Case"; Rosemary Harris for her part as George Sand in the BBC series about the French novelist; and Gordon Jackson for his performance as Hudson, the butler, in "Upstairs, Downstairs." Sir Laurence Olivier made what amounted to his television debut in Granada's series "The Best Play of the Year 19—." Olivier co-produced, starred in, and directed several of the plays shown.

The BBC's money problems affected its External Services, which broadcast more than 700 radio hours each week in 39 languages to a regular audience in excess of 69 million. Failure to reequip itself with new transmitters resulted in the BBC being "drowned" in some areas, particularly in the Middle East. At home, radio continued to cater to a widespread and loyal audience, its strengths being listener phone-ins, current affairs discussions, and music programs. Radio 3's coverage of the annual Proms concerts in London was marked by the use of stereo combined with simultaneous television broadcasting. London Weekend linked with Capital Radio, a London commercial channel, to broadcast a rock concert in the same way.

Throughout Europe money problems, tight budgets, and a general air of dissatisfaction prevailed. In France, program quality remained low. Pres. Valéry

Giscard d'Estaing criticized the monopoly of a few producers, which excluded new talent. The nation's new three-channel setup was also criticized for excessive screening of old films and foreign serials. The government threatened to interfere directly unless more original material was forthcoming.

In Eastern Europe, Czechoslovakia introduced its first colour studio equipped with home-produced technology. Poland opened a new radio channel, its fourth; it was to concentrate on music and on scientific and educational broadcasts. East German television played host to several teams of documentary filmmakers from abroad; among its 1976 programs were investigations into parapsychology and a showing of the classic films of Robert Flaherty, pioneer of documentaries. Competitions remained a popular feature of radio, with the audience being invited to write songs and critiques of radio plays. In the U.S.S.R. a highlight was the performance of Sergey Prokofiev's ballet *Romeo and Juliet* by the Bolshoi Ballet; a television recording was made by Soviet Television and the West German Telecom company, with the technical assistance of the BBC and CBS. The film of the ballet was shown in 114 countries to mark the 200th anniversary of the Bolshoi Ballet. (*See* DANCE: *Special Report*.) In Moscow preparations were under way for coverage of the 1980 Olympics. A new radio and television centre, with 70 radio studios and 18 television studios, was to be built. "Down the Mine," a program of folk songs from the British series "Something to Sing About" (ATV), won the folk art prize at the new Rainbow Festival in Moscow. The main award went to a Cuban documentary.

The Prix Italia, in its 28th year, attracted the usual assortment of entries. Switzerland's "Music Fermé" won the music award, and Japan took the RAI prize for "The Whistling of the Wind." Telefis Eireann made a film about Northern Ireland; the U.S.S.R. documented the success of the head of a hydroelectric project; the Spanish danced (to castanets), and so did the Australians (to the Beatles); the Swedes gazed thoughtfully at a runic stone; and in the U.S. entry, Danny Kaye and Beverly Sills became entangled with the Metropolitan Opera and *La Traviata*.

JAPAN. The Japanese broadcasting corporation NHK undertook a broad program revision of its five networks. Local news services were extended; the use of colour on the education channel was doubled; and a new cultural theme was introduced with such programs as "Japanese History in Everyday Life" and "History and Civilization." More interchange of programs between the educational and general television channels was planned, and there was also to be an expansion of programs aimed at teenage and preschool children. In the evenings, NHK undertook major new documentary and drama series.

(RUFUS W. CRATER; JOHN ANTHONY HOWKINS; SOL J. TAISHOFF; ICHIRO TSUJIMOTO; MICHAEL TYPE; BRIAN WILLIAMS)

Amateur Radio. The number of amateur radio operators increased dramatically in 1976. Figures compiled from the FCC by the American Radio Relay League (ARRL), the leading organization of amateur, or "ham," radio operators, put the number of amateur licenses outstanding in the U.S. at 268,192 as of April 30, a 4.36% gain in 12 months. By October 1, the total was put at 282,952, a rise of 5.5% in five months and almost 10% in 12. Much of the increase was attributed to the even bigger boom in the Citizens Radio Service (citizens band or CB), whose license total within a few years had reached 8 million or more. Many who went into CB were becoming interested in the greater sophistication of amateur radio, in which operators may use internationally allocated frequencies throughout the radio spectrum. In late 1976 the ARRL reported that some 35,000 prospective ham operators were enrolled in classes preparing for their amateur radio license examinations. Throughout the world the number of amateur operators was estimated at about 800,000. For CB radio operators the FCC increased the number of available channels from 23 to 40 as of Jan. 1, 1977.

WIDE WORLD

"This is First Mama, and I've got a lot of smokies on my front door." Mrs. Betty Ford, wife of the U.S. president, talks to citizens band listeners from a monitoring station in Texas during the Republican primary campaign in April.

In addition to the enjoyment they got in talking with other amateurs, ham radio operators in times of disaster had historically served as vital links when normal communications were down. When a disastrous earthquake struck Guatemala in February, for instance, ham radio was the only contact left with the outside; amateurs in the U.S. worked in teams around the clock for days relaying vital information. When a typhoon devastated Guam in May, hams again served as key emergency links.

There were also some major technological achievements in 1976. In one, Allen Katz (K2UYH) of West Windsor, N.J., became, according to the ARRL, the first ham operator to complete two-way communication with all six continents via radio signals reflected off the Moon.

(RUFUS W. CRATER; SOL J. TAISHOFF)

See also Industrial Review: *Advertising; Telecommunications;* Motion Pictures; Music.
[613.D.4.b; 735.I.4–5]

ENCYCLOPÆDIA BRITANNICA FILMS. *TV News; Behind the Scenes* (1973).

Tennis

During 1976 large amounts of prize money continued to be awarded to the successful tennis players in major events. The Women's Tennis Association (WTA), under the presidency of Chris Evert and later under Betty Stove of The Netherlands, took a step forward in its avowed aim of establishing parity of prize money between women and men, already achieved in the U.S. championships, by asking the management committee of the Wimbledon championships for equality in 1977. Previous agreement had established the proportion at Wimbledon as 80%, the first prize in the men's singles for 1976 being £12,500 and in the women's singles £10,000. When the Wimbledon authorities refused the WTA request, WTA announced that a rival tournament would be established in 1977 in which its members, which included the world's leading players, would take part.

There was some discord in the management of the Davis Cup competition because of the reluctance of several nations to compete against South Africa or Chile. The U.S. put forward a motion at the annual meeting of the Davis Cup nations in London on July 1 to impose a three-year suspension on nations withdrawing from the Cup for political reasons. The motion failed to pass and the U.S. announced its resignation from the organization and from the 1977 competition. Both France and Great Britain announced their withdrawal from the competition, but did not withdraw as members of the organization. The next week, at the annual meeting of the International Lawn Tennis Federation (ILTF) in Monte Carlo, the three nations agreed to participate after all following a Spanish proposal that 1977 should be a year of neutrality.

World Team Tennis (WTT) operated for the third year in the U.S., ten cities again taking part on a league basis from May to the end of August. The competition caused many leading players to be unavailable for European tournaments, with the exception of the Wimbledon championships. The quality of the women's entries for the Italian and French championships markedly declined.

A new issue for tennis was raised by the entry into women's competition of Renee Richards. Until she underwent a sex-change operation in 1975, the 42-year-old Richards had been Richard Raskind and had been ranked sixth in the U.S. in the men's 35-and-over division in 1972. Opinion was divided on the right of Richards to compete against women, and the U.S. Tennis Association announced that all women entrants in the U.S. Open must take a sex chromosome test to qualify for the tournament. Richards refused to take the test, claiming that it was "inconclusive at best."

WIDE WORLD

Jimmy Connors of the U.S. uses his two-handed backhand to beat Australian John Newcombe in the World Cup competition in March. The American team defeated the Australians in a four-of-seven match.

Men's Competition. The Grand Prix for 1975 concluded at the end of the year with Guillermo Vilas of Argentina winning for the second year. With his top bonus prize of $100,000, he earned from Grand Prix tournaments $237,392, bringing his total earnings up to $247,372. The Grand Prix Masters' tournament was staged indoors in Stockholm and was won for the fourth time in five years by Ilie Nastase of Romania. He defeated Björn Borg (*see* BIOGRAPHY) of Sweden in the final match 6–2, 6–2, 6–1.

The Australian championships, held in Melbourne at the turn of the year, had an entirely unexpected winner in Mark Edmondson from the Australian state of New South Wales. In the semifinal match he beat Ken Rosewall and in the final, played in hot, windy conditions, he defeated John Newcombe 6–7, 6–3, 7–6, 6–1.

The most successful player on the World Championship Tennis (WCT) circuit, held from January to May, was Arthur Ashe of the U.S. He won tournaments in Columbus, Ohio; Indianapolis, Ind.; Richmond, Va.; Rome; and Rotterdam, Neth. In the final tournament at Dallas, Texas, for which the eight leading players qualified, his fellow American Harold Solomon beat Ashe three sets to one in the first round. The tournament was won by Borg, who defeated Vilas in the final 1–6, 6–1, 7–5, 6–1.

Adriano Panatta of Italy took the Italian title in Rome. In the semifinals he beat Newcombe, and in the final Vilas 2–6, 7–6, 6–2, 7–6. Panatta won his first-round match against Kim Warwick of Australia after being within one point of losing 11 times.

In the French championships in Paris, Panatta again triumphed, winning in the quarterfinals against Borg, in the semifinals against Eddie Dibbs of the U.S., and in the final against Solomon 6–1, 6–4, 4–6, 7–6. The German championship was taken by Dibbs for the third time in four years. In the final he beat Manuel Orantes 6–4, 4–6, 6–1, 2–6, 6–1.

The Wimbledon meeting was played in the hottest weather within living memory. The singles winner was Borg. In the last three rounds he beat Vilas, Roscoe Tanner of the U.S., and, in a disappointingly one-sided final, Nastase 6–4, 6–2, 9–7. Borg lost no set in the tournament and was the most one-sided champion since Chuck McKinley of the U.S. won the singles title in 1963. Ashe, the defending champion, lost in the fourth round to Vitas Gerulaitis, also of the U.S. Jimmy Connors of the U.S. was widely expected to repeat his 1974 triumph but was beaten in the quarterfinal round by Tanner.

The U.S. Open championships, which attracted a record total attendance of 250,880, brought success to Connors. Reaching the final without losing a set (including a semifinal win against Vilas), he won a hard-hitting match against Borg 6–4, 3–6, 7–6, 6–4. Borg beat the 1975 champion Orantes in the quarterfinals and Nastase in the semifinals. Nastase was fined $1,000 for his behaviour in a second-round match against Hans Jürgen Pohmann of West Germany.

DOUBLES. The Grand Prix of 1975 included doubles, and the four leading pairs competed in the Masters' tournament in Stockholm at the end of the year. Orantes and Juan Gisbert of Spain, Jürgen Fassbender and Pohmann of West Germany, and Fred McNair and Sherwood Stewart of the U.S. all had two wins, while Brian Gottfried (U.S.) and Raúl Ramírez (Mexico) had none in a round-robin series.

Newcombe and Tony Roche won the Australian championship. The WCT event, played in Kansas City, Mo., had surprise winners in Wojtek Fibak of Poland and Karl Meiler of West Germany. McNair and Stewart won both the German and French titles. Gottfried and Ramírez shared the Italian title with Newcombe and Geoff Masters, another Australian,

SYNDICATION INTERNATIONAL/PHOTO TRENDS

Chris Evert of the U.S. won her second women's singles title at Wimbledon in July. She had previously won in 1974.

when failing light stopped play at two sets all. At Wimbledon, Gottfried and Ramírez beat Newcombe and Roche in the first round and then went on to win the final against two other Australians, Masters and Ross Case.

The U.S. tournament brought an early loss to Gottfried and Ramírez, and McNair and Stewart got no further than the quarterfinals. Marty Riessen (U.S.) and Tom Okker (Neth.) revived their prestige by winning.

DAVIS CUP. For the second successive year the U.S. failed early in the competition. In late 1975 in Mexico City, Mexico (Marcelo Lara and Raúl Ramírez) beat the U.S. (Connors, Gottfried, Dick Stockton, and Tanner) by 3–2, with Ramírez beating Connors in the decisive fifth match 2–6, 6–3, 6–3, 6–4. Mexico scratched to South Africa in the next round, and Chile then beat South Africa 3–2 in Santiago to win the American Zone.

The Eastern Zone was won by Australia. The final, against New Zealand, was uniquely staged in different continents. In Brisbane, Australia built a 2–1 lead, but bad weather and the professional commitments of the players caused the contest to be postponed from the beginning of March to the middle of June. Then, at Nottingham, England, Newcombe beat Brian Fairlie to establish a decisive 3–1 lead for Australia.

The U.S.S.R. and Italy were winners of the two European Zones. The Soviets, led by the experienced Alex Metreveli, beat Monaco, West Germany, Spain, and Hungary to qualify as winners of Section A of the Zone. Italy, led by Panatta, beat Poland and Yugoslavia to qualify for the section semifinal against the champion nation, Sweden, which had not been required to play up to that stage. Borg, Sweden's star player, who had just become Wimbledon champion, was unable to compete because of a pulled stomach muscle. Italy beat Sweden and won the section final by 4–1 against Great Britain at Wimbledon.

The interzone semifinals brought the U.S.S.R. against Chile. The U.S.S.R. withdrew in political protest against the Chilean regime; Italy met Australia in Rome and won 3–2. In the final in Santiago, Chile, in December, Italy beat Chile 4–1; Panatta played in two singles matches and one doubles, all of which were won.

Women's Competition. Two players were outstanding, Chris Evert and Evonne Goolagong Cawley; Martina Navratilova and Virginia Wade were notable rivals to their supremacy. Billie Jean King usually played in doubles only, and Margaret Court was semi-retired.

Cawley was unbeaten in both singles and doubles in the Australian championships. The losing finalist in the singles was Renata Tomanova of Czechoslovakia. Cawley was also the dominant performer in the Virginia Slims indoor circuit, in the U.S. from January to April. Out of the ten tournaments making up the qualifying series she won five, Evert won four, and Navratilova won one.

The Wimbledon title was won by the 1974 champion, Evert, who beat Cawley 6–3, 4–6, 8–6 in the final. In the semifinals Evert beat Navratilova 6–3, 4–6, 6–4, and Cawley beat Wade 6–1, 6–2.

The U.S. championship was dominated overwhelmingly by Evert, and the general level of competition was disappointing. Navratilova lost in the first round to Janet Newberry of the U.S., and Wade lost in the second round to Mima Jausovec of Yugoslavia. In the final Evert won over Cawley 6–3, 6–0.

In doubles Evert won at Wimbledon with Navratilova, defeating Billie Jean King and Betty Stove in the final 6–1, 3–6, 7–5. The most consistently successful partnership was that of Linky Boshoff and Ilana Kloss of South Africa. They won the German, Italian, and U.S. championships.

Commercially sponsored for the first time, the Federation Cup tournament was staged in August indoors at the Spectrum Stadium, Philadelphia. The presence of South Africa and Rhodesia brought objection from the U.S.S.R., which withdrew from the tournament. Czechoslovakia and Hungary also scratched, and the Philippines refused to play Rhodesia in the consolation event.

The tournament was disappointing in the intensity of the competition except for the final round between the U.S. and Australia. In this the U.S. beat Australia 2–1 to win the cup for the fifth time.

The U.S. broke Britain's two-year hold on the Wightman Cup by winning the tournament, held indoors in London in November, 5–2. Evert led the U.S. team by winning all three of her matches.

(LANCE TINGAY)

[452.B.4.h.xxvii]

Thailand

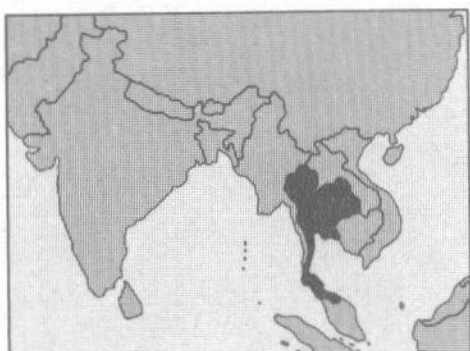

A constitutional monarchy of Southeast Asia, Thailand is bordered by Burma, Laos, Cambodia, Malaysia, the Andaman Sea, and the Gulf of Thailand. Area: 209,400 sq mi (542,400 sq km). Pop. (1976 est.): 42,391,500. Cap. and largest city: Bangkok (pop., 1976 est., 4,349,500). Language: Thai. Religion (1970): Buddhist 95.3%; Muslim 3.8%. King, Bhumibol Adulyadej; prime ministers in 1976, Kukrit Pramoj until April 16, Seni Pramoj from April 20 until October 6, and Thanin Kraivichien from October 8.

Even by Thai political standards two government

Textiles: *see* Industrial Review

CHRISTIAN SIMONPIETRI—SYGMA

Dennis A. Roland of Queens, New York, carrying two U.S. flags, crosses a railroad bridge over the Kwai River in Thailand that he helped build as a prisoner of the Japanese during World War II. With him are 42 one-time Japanese guards, 7 Australians, and 1 Briton. Thousands of men died building the railroad.

changes in one year, 1976, seemed rather much. The second, which turned out to be unusually bloody, put the country back in the hands of the military. And there, said the newly installed civilian prime minister, Thanin Kraivichien, it would remain for at least 12 years.

The holdover prime minister from 1975, Kukrit Pramoj, had lost his seat in the April 4 general election. His elder brother, 70-year-old Seni Pramoj, put together a four-way coalition of his own Democratic Party, the Thai Nation Party, the Social Justice Party, and the Social Nationalist Party, together holding 207 seats in a house of 279. Despite the numerical strength enjoyed by the coalition, the government was under constant pressure from left-wing students, right-wing military factions, and ruling politicians jockeying for power and portfolios. The final phase of violent crisis began in August with the dramatic return to Bangkok of former strong man Field Marshal Prapas Charusathiara. Along with Prime Minister Thanom Kittikachorn, he had been driven out of office and the country by popular uprising in 1973. His return, though clandestine, was evidently facilitated by well-placed army officers who received him at the airport and provided shelter.

As news of Prapas' homecoming spread, students led a public outcry for his arrest and trial. The government seemed undecided as to what to do; indeed, there was evidence that different leaders were pulling in different directions. Soon riots broke out between leftist and rightist students of Bangkok's Thammasat University, with government soldiers trying to restore order. In the face of the bloodletting, Prapas was finally persuaded to return to his exile in Taiwan. But hopes of any restoration of normality were shattered by public statements by Thanom that he, too, planned to return home from his exile in Singapore. Despite persistent government instructions against it, Thanom landed in Bangkok on September 19 and entered the Buddhist monkhood, purportedly to "earn merit" for his dying 91-year-old father.

Thanom's return was the signal for a fresh mobilization of student protesters. But this time the ultraright group among the students, the Red Gaur ("red bull"), was ready for battle. Bangkok exploded into savage campus war during the first week of October. Some students were lynched and many were injured. The right-wing group, displaying unexpected power that surprised even the government, massed in public parks for more action. Convinced that the Seni administration was in no position to control events, Defense Minister Adm. Sa-ngad Chaloryu took power in the name of an Administration Reform Council. Thailand's democratic interlude had lasted three years.

The new martial-law government, which installed former Supreme Court judge Thanin as prime minister and former foreign minister Thanat Khoman as adviser on foreign affairs, quickly introduced policies that indicated an intention to stay in power for a long time. The thrust of the policies was strident anti-Communism. Not only were some 4,000 suspected leftists arrested in the first fortnight but the press was also put under severe restrictions and school curricula were revised to eliminate courses in political theory. A new constitution was promulgated.

There was speculation as to whether the new toughness would suppress or nourish the leftist insurgency, already believed to have grown significantly in the north, northeast, and south. Many borderline leftists were said to have joined the underground fol-

THAILAND

Education. (1974–75) Primary, pupils 6,609,239, teachers 239,128; secondary, pupils 958,889, teachers 41,445; vocational, pupils 165,585, teachers 8,992; teacher training, students 67,315, teachers 4,459; higher, students 80,675, teaching staff 10,206.

Finance. Monetary unit: baht, with (Sept. 20, 1976) a par value of 20 baht to U.S. $1 (free rate of 35.29 baht = £1 sterling). Gold, SDR's, and foreign exchange (June 1976) U.S. $1,853,000,000. Budget (1975–76 est.): revenue 48,068,000,000 baht; expenditure 59,385,000,000 baht. Gross national product (1975) 295,670,000,000 baht. Money supply (March 1976) 37,380,000,000 baht. Cost of living (Bangkok; 1970 = 100; June 1976) 158.

Foreign Trade. (1975) Imports 62,660,000,000 baht; exports 48,378,000,000 baht. Import sources (1974): Japan 31%; U.S. 13%; West Germany 7%; Qatar 6%; Kuwait 5%; Saudi Arabia 5%; U.K. 5%. Export destinations (1974): Japan 26%; The Netherlands 9%; Singapore 8%; U.S. 8%; Hong Kong 7%; Taiwan 7%; Malaysia 5%. Main exports: rice 12%; corn 12%; tapioca 9%; rubber 7%. Tourism (1974): visitors 1,107,000; gross receipts U.S. $210 million.

Transport and Communications. Roads (1973) 27,506 km. Motor vehicles in use (1974): passenger 316,900; commercial 188,700. Railways (1974): 3,765 km; traffic 5,484,000,000 passenger-km, freight 2,296,000,000 net ton-km. Air traffic (1974): 2,845,-000,000 passenger-km; freight 63.3 million net ton-km. Shipping (1975): merchant vessels 100 gross tons and over 84; gross tonnage 182,554. Telephones (Dec. 1974) 270,840. Radio receivers (Dec. 1973) 3,009,000. Television receivers (Dec. 1973) *c.* 700,000.

Agriculture. Production (in 000; metric tons; 1975): rice *c.* 15,000; corn *c.* 3,000; sweet potatoes (1974) *c.* 320; sorghum *c.* 240; cassava (1974) *c.* 3,800; dry beans 326; soybeans *c.* 190; peanuts *c.* 260; sugar, raw value 1,021; pineapples (1974) *c.* 500; bananas (1974) *c.* 1,300; tobacco *c.* 69; rubber *c.* 375; cotton, lint *c.* 11; jute *c.* 9; kenaf *c.* 300; timber (cu m; 1974) *c.* 21,830; fish catch (1974) 1,626. Livestock (in 000; 1975): cattle *c.* 4,939; buffalo (1974) *c.* 5,700; pigs *c.* 4,962; chickens *c.* 66,000; ducks *c.* 7,500.

Industry. Production (in 000; metric tons; 1974): tin concentrates (metal content) 20; tungsten concentrates (oxide content) 1.8; lead concentrates (metal content) 1.5; manganese ore (metal content) 11; cement 3,923; petroleum products *c.* 7,160; electricity (kw-hr) 7,789,000.

lowing the crackdown by the new government. But there were indications that the armed forces were planning an anti-insurgency offensive "on a scale not seen before." It was reported that U.S. military personnel in civilian dress had begun rebuilding an air base near Bangkok; earlier in the year Thailand had closed down all U.S. military facilities in the country. U.S. sources reported in May that Thailand was rapidly becoming one of Asia's largest purchasers of arms. Among new acquisitions listed were a squadron of F-5E Freedom fighter jets, Sea Wolf patrol boats, and tanks. Of the $3.4 billion budget for fiscal 1977, presented before the military takeover, 19% was earmarked for defense, more than double the appropriation in 1973 when the country was last under a military government. (T. J. S. GEORGE)

[976.B.3]

Theatre

The theatre in most countries suffered a year of crisis in 1976, when inflation increased costs and at the same time reduced the purchasing power of governmental and municipal grants. In Great Britain the Arts Council Building Fund, set up in 1965 and having distributed £8 million on nearly 300 projects since that time, was reduced by half to £500,000 a year; plans for expansion were thereby halted. A notable victim of state parsimony was London's Old Vic Theatre, which had been vacated by the National Theatre ensemble on February 28 when the latter moved to its new premises on the south bank of the Thames. An Arts Council report revealed that the sums of £80,000 for restoration and £131,000 for upkeep in the first year were not available. A plan to offer the theatre to a consortium of dramatic, operatic, and dance troupes, headed by the successful touring company Prospect Theatre, had to be abandoned, leaving the governors no choice but to lease it to speculative managers. This move, as it turned out, brought unexpected financial rewards to the investors.

The annual report of Britain's National Theatre Board, under its new chairman, Lord Rayne, revealed that in the year ended March 1976, shortly before the company vacated the Old Vic, the costs (£2,670,000) had been covered by £823,000 in box-office receipts and a grant of £1,850,000. Approximately £450,000 had been swallowed up by the delays in completing the new complex and could not be recouped. The board argued that, because 50% of its grant (£3 million would be required for the new theatre's first full operating year) was related exclusively to the cost of keeping the building in working order, it should be funded by the state as were museums, galleries, and libraries.

The 100th annual report of the Royal Shakespeare Company (RSC) disclosed that the anticipated losses had been avoided by economy measures taken and by the unexpected financial success of its foreign tours, in the U.S., Canada, Europe, Asia, and Australia. Box-office receipts exceeded £1.5 million, a world record for any theatre, it was claimed, and the number of spectators at home and abroad also exceeded the record figure of 1.5 million. A partial return to the repertory system had been possible at its London home, the Aldwych Theatre, and the £118,000 raised by a special appeal enabled indispensable renovations to be carried out at its Stratford quarters.

The campaign for saving theatre buildings in the U.K. resulted in parliamentary legislation restricting the arbitrary powers of individual proprietors and local authorities. Former Prime Minister Sir Harold Wilson gave a special prize at the first annual awards organized by the Society of West End Theatre (formally the Society of West End Theatre Managers)—on the lines of the Tony awards in New York—to the campaign as such. Despite this, several theatres were still being threatened, if not by demolition or conversion at least by closing. The Greenwood, for example, had had to close after less than 12 months, notwithstanding an interesting season of French plays presented by companies from Paris. The Cambridge Theatre was converted into the first ice arena mounted inside a regular playhouse, for the British Olympic champion John Curry and a new-style show advertised as "Theatre of Skating."

In Ireland, on the other hand, the government created an Arts Council to fund theatres directly. And the highlight of 1976 in France was the reopening after two years of renovation of the radically modernized Salle Richelieu, the home of the Comédie Française, in the Place Colette. In Switzerland, the Zürich Schauspielhaus, gutted for rebuilding purposes, was temporarily vacated by Harry Buckwitz' players, who had to make do with the Corso, a converted movie theatre. In Rome Luigi Squarzina took over the new Teatro di Roma.

West German theatre attendances were declining in Frankfurt, Hamburg, and elsewhere, and adventurous directors came under managerial criticism. The Czechoslovakian premiere of Vaclav Havel's parody on John Gay, *The Thieves' Opera*, was raided by the police at an amateur performance in Prague. Sadly, film director and theatre producer Ingmar Bergman (*see* BIOGRAPHY) went into self-imposed exile from Sweden after harassment by tax authorities, and in Turku, Finland, Kalle Holmberg and Ralf Långbacka resigned after five years at the head of the City Theatre.

Great Britain and Ireland. The year's theatrical headlines were stolen by the National Theatre, which finally opened its doors to the public on March 15

NOBBY CLARK

Albert Finney was "Tamburlaine the Great" in an open-stage production of Marlowe's play at London's Olivier Theatre, part of the new National Theatre complex.

DONALD COOPER

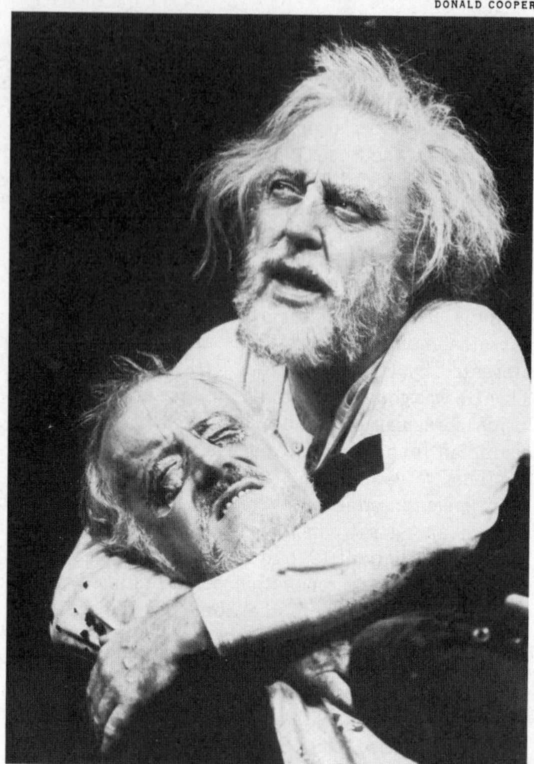

Donald Sinden as Lear (right) and Tony Church as Gloucester in the Royal Shakespeare Company's production of "King Lear" at Stratford.

with a gala charity performance of the 90-year-old Ben Travers' *Plunder,* a farcical thriller already seen at the Old Vic. It was one of six plays transferred to the proscenium stage of the Lyttelton Theatre. The final performance at the Old Vic, which the National players had occupied since Oct. 23, 1963, was *Tribute to the Lady,* staged on February 28 to commemorate Lilian Baylis, creator and promoter of the Old Vic company. On October 25 a specially invited audience attended the official unveiling of the entire complex by Queen Elizabeth II, who also watched the first performance, in the open-stage Olivier Theatre, of Carlo Goldoni's *Il Campiello,* while Princess Margaret was present at Tom Stoppard's *Jumpers* in the adjoining Lyttelton.

The opening of the National's third theatre, the flexible Cottesloe, had to be delayed until the spring of 1977. Partly to compensate for its absence as a home of theatrical experiment, the company ran a short season at the temporarily vacated Young Vic Theatre. Among their presentations were the British premieres of Peter Handke's *They Are Dying Out* and Slawomir Mrozek's *The Emigrés.* Other short tryout work could be seen in the foyers or on the forestages in the rest of the complex, which was conceived, both by its architect, Sir Denys Lasdun, and by Peter Hall, the National Theatre's director, as available for every sort of "happening" throughout the working day and not merely during the matinee or evenings.

The productions brought from the Old Vic to the Lyttelton, besides Michael Blakemore's exciting *Plunder,* were Hall's of Ibsen's *John Gabriel Borkman,* Harold Pinter's *No Man's Land,* Samuel Beckett's *Happy Days,* and *Hamlet,* and Bill Bryden's of John Osborne's latest black comedy, *Watch It Come Down.* Two other revivals at the Lyttelton, destined for eventual transfer to the open stage, were Pinter's studied production of Noel Coward's *Blithe Spirit* and Bryden's of John Millington Synge's *The Playboy of the Western World; Hamlet* also ended up there, much improved in appearance. *Weapons of Happiness,* by Howard Brenton, was a political fable that not only exploited the boundless technical facilities of the new stage in David Hare's production but was also notable for a realistic portrayal of Stalin in one scene. The first British production of a parabolic comedy by Thomas Bernhard of Austria, *The Force of Habit,* at the Lyttelton, marked the promising directing debut of the Australian-born Elijah Moshinsky, formerly of the Royal Opera House, Covent Garden.

The fan-shaped Olivier Theatre gave an indication of its remarkable potential to excite an audience and hold its attention in Peter Hall's sumptuously dressed open-stage production of the two parts of Marlowe's *Tamburlaine the Great,* performed in a single 4½-hour-long sitting, with Albert Finney in the arduous title role and with John Bury's imaginative decor. After a colourful, though disappointing version (directed by Bryden), of Goldoni's Venetian comedy *Il Campiello,* Bryden directed, on a far smaller scale, the world premiere of Edward Albee's two-handed self-styled "vaudeville" about married love, *Counting the Ways,* with Michael Gough and Beryl Reid. The continued West End run of John Dexter's production of Peter Shaffer's *Equus* was helping to improve the finances of the National. One innovation was the first visit (at the Lyttelton) of a foreign troupe since the demise of the World Theatre Season in 1975, that of the Lyon-based Théâtre National Populaire in Roger Planchon's production of *Tartuffe* and Patrice Chéreau's (*see* BIOGRAPHY) of *La Dispute.*

The RSC at the Aldwych carried off three top awards of the Society of West End Theatre: the best actor in a revival award going to Alan Howard in Terry Hands's production of the three Henry plays by Shakespeare; the best designer award to Abdel Farrah for the same plays; and the best actress in a new play award to Peggy Ashcroft in Aleksey Arbuzov's comedy *Old World.* By contrast the best director award was won by Jonathan Miller (with Michael Blakemore, one of two directors resigned from the National) for a privately presented *Three Sisters,* featuring Janet Suzman, on loan from the RSC, as Masha. Other attractions at the Aldwych were *The Merry Wives of Windsor, Much Ado About Nothing,* and *The Winter's Tale,* all earlier seen at Stratford-upon-Avon; Maxim Gorky's *The Zykovs;* Eugene O'Neill's marathon *The Iceman Cometh,* with Alan Tilvern replacing an indisposed Ian Holm; Shaw's *The Devil's Disciple,* featuring Tom Conti as Dick Dudgeon, and with Jack Gold making his directing debut; Chekhov's *Ivanov,* with John Wood and Mia Farrow; and the 18th-century actor-dramatist John O'Keeffe's boisterous comedy *Wild Oats,* starring Alan Howard. At the Round House the RSC also presented Peter Brook's Paris-based players in Colin Turnbull and Denis Cannan's *The Ik,* performed in English, and, from their Stratford-based The Other Place, a modern-dress *Hamlet* (with Ben Kingsley) and Bertolt Brecht's *Man Is Man.*

The Young Vic returned from a profitable transatlantic tour to appear in *Antony and Cleopatra,* with Delphine Seyrig speaking impeccable English as the queen of Egypt. The year's highlights at the Royal Court were the plays in a 70th-birthday Samuel Beckett season that included his own productions of *Waiting for Godot,* played in German by the actors of the Berlin-based Schiller Theatre, and of his latest playlets, *That Time* (with Patrick Magee) and *Footfalls* (written specially for and with Billie Whitelaw). Other events at the Royal Court, including the reopening of its Theatre Upstairs, were Christopher Hampton's comedy of sexual disparity *Treats;* two new comedies of immigrant life by West Indian playwrights; and Peter Gill's first original, autobiographical Welsh working-class family-drama *Small Change.*

The Actors Company returned once more to the Wimbledon Theatre, which toward the end of the year announced that it would soon close. Other subsidized theatres kept going, partly as a result of successful West End transfers. Examples were Mike Stott's sex-comedy *Funny Peculiar* (from the Mermaid Theatre) and Johnny Speight's *The Thoughts of Chairman Alf,* starring Warren Mitchell (from Stratford East). Hampstead also had two stimulating dramas on view, Michael Frayn's *Clouds,* a satire on Cuba, and Mike Stott's *Lenz,* about the 18th-century German writer of that name. Frayn's commercially staged comedy of university high jinks, *Donkey's Years,* carried off the best comedy award. Another hilarious comedy—or pair of comedies—to transfer emanated from the bicentennial celebratory season at Ed Berman's Ambiance Lunchtime Theatre, Tom Stoppard's doubleton of *Dirty Linen* and *New-Found-Land;* at the same theatre Edward Bond's two playlets condemning the racism and violence of U.S. society, *Grandma Faust* and *The Swing,* were also first seen.

Highlights of the purely commercial season were *Mardi Gras,* a musical set in New Orleans, by Melvyn Bragg; Alan Ayckbourn's (*see* BIOGRAPHY) bitter comedy (in five allied sketches) *Confusions;* the Brian Rix sex-comedy *Fringe Benefits;* Alec Guinness in his own dramatic homage to Swift, *Yahoo;* the prize-winning black comedy by Denis Cannan *Dear Daddy;* Somerset Maugham's *The Circle,* from the Chichester Festival; and a promising first play, *Family Dance,* by Felicity Browne, about a large middle-class family viciously at odds with itself. A successful private venture was the visit to the Round House of the Paris-based transvestite show *La Grande Eugène.* Other musical entertainments included *Spokesong* (from 1975's Dublin Festival), *Leave Him to Heaven,* a rock review of the 1950s by Ken Lee, *Betjemania,* about the poet laureate, at the Shaw Theatre, which celebrated the National Youth Theatre's coming-of-age, and an erotic show sponsored, among others, by Kenneth Tynan, *Carte Blanche.* Foreign visitors included Tadeusz Kantor's *The Dead Class* from Poland and participants in an international fringe festival at the Institute of Contemporary Arts, whose theatre became the first victim of the Arts Council axe.

In Ireland, highlights at the Abbey Theatre, Dublin, were the silver jubilee revival, directed by Tomás Mac Anna, of Sean O'Casey's *The Plough and the Stars,* starring Siobhan McKenna, Cyril Cusack, and his daughter Sorcha Cusack; the Dublin Festival production, directed by Max Stafford-Clark, of Tom Kilroy's *Tea and Sex and Shakespeare,* about a writer's fantasies, starring Donal McCann; and John Lynch's *All You Need Is Love,* about life in London and Dublin in the 1960s and 1970s, at the smaller Peacock. Among the 28 attractions at the festival were O'Neill's *More Stately Mansions* and Henry Montherlant's *The City Whose Lord Is a Child,* each an Irish premiere; Patrick Galvin's play about a Cork slum, *The Devil's Own People* (with Ray McAnally); Donal Donnelly's Shavian one-man-show; Kevin O'Connor's *Friends,* about James Joyce; and Jonas Arnason's wartime drama *Operation: Shield Rock,* acted by Icelandic players in English.

France. The Comédie Française staged Franco Zeffirelli's sumptuous production of Alfred de Musset's *Lorenzaccio,* with the splendid Claude Rich in the title role. Other noteworthy events at the Comédie Française were the English guest-director Hands's sensual production of *Twelfth Night,* with the company's manager Pierre Dux as Malvolio and Hands's wife, Ludmila Mikael, as Viola; Jorge Lavelli's brilliant debut there directing Eugène Ionesco's *Exit the King;* and the return of the veteran Raymond Rouleau to stage Eugène Scribe's *The Glass of Water.* At the subsidiary stages of the Odéon, the Young National Theatre players staged Frank Wedekind's *Spring Awakening,* Pinter's *The Dumb-Waiter,* and a first play by the novelist Yves Heurté.

At the Théâtre de l'Est Parisien the main events were *As You Like It,* staged by the Swiss-born guest from East Berlin, Benno Besson (transferred from the Avignon Festival), Max Frisch's *Biedermann and the Firebugs,* and Brecht's *Refugee Dialogues;* at the Théâtre de la Ville, there were revivals of Vercors' *Zoo,* Paul Claudel's *L'Echange* (with Geneviève Page), and Friedrich Dürrenmatt's *The Visit of the Old Woman* (with Edwige Feuillère); and Théâtre d'Orsay featured Restif de la Bretonne's *Paris Nights,* John Dexter's production of *Equus* (with François Périer and Stéphane Jobert), and the Freudian dramatic portrait *Portrait de Dora,* by Hélène Cixous, which contrasted interestingly with Pierre Bourgeade's *Dora* on a similar theme in a boulevard theatre.

The new plays included Jean Anouilh's backstage drama *Le Scénario* (with Daniel Gélin) and an extreme black comedy, *Chers Zoiseaux* (with Guy Tréjean), followed by Robert Bresson's *The Trial of Joan of Arc,* staged by Robert Hossein (with Anne Doat); *Jocaste,* by René Ehni, a modern view of an old story; and two remarkable first plays, *Dames* by the actress Loleh Bellon and *The Human Race* by Jean Edern Hallier.

Switzerland, Germany, Austria, The Netherlands. An outrageous production in Basel, by Hans Hollmann, of *Othello,* culminating in the rape of a topless Desdemona (Susanne Tremper), inflamed local tempers; they were, however, assuaged by his brilliant adaptation of Thomas Mann's novel *Buddenbrooks.* In Zürich Harry Buckwitz' players in an impressive one-night version of Schiller's trilogy of *Wallenstein*

The Comédie Française celebrated the opening of its renovated quarters with a production of Alfred de Musset's "Lorenzaccio," with Claude Rich in the title role.

KEYSTONE

KEYSTONE

Prague's "Drawn Theatre" presents drawings enlivened by people. The popular Czechoslovak ensemble toured West Germany in March.

(with Hans Dieter Zeidler) vied in popularity with a touring version of *The Cherry Orchard,* with the masterly Maria Becker as Ranevskaya.

In West Berlin Samuel Beckett celebrated his 70th birthday by staging the German premieres of his *That Time* and *Footfalls* at the Schiller's Workshop, while Hans Lietzau's amusing production of Ayckbourn's trilogy of *The Norman Conquests* packed the Schiller's substage, the Schlosspark. Novelties were Elias Canetti's *The Wedding,* the Austrian playwright Franz Buchrieser's drama of a former jailbird, *The Product,* and the first visit of an East German troupe to West Berlin, when Rostock brought Hanns Anselm Perten's productions of Rolf Hochhuth's *Lysistrata or NATO* and Peter Weiss's *Hölderlin* to the autumn Arts Festival. The highlight of the Schaubühne season was Else Lasker-Schüler's *The Wupper,* effectively staged by Luc Bondy. In East Berlin Fritz Marquandt staged Heiner Müller's revolutionary *The Peasants,* a world premiere, about postwar collectivization, at the People's Theatre; Peter Kupke presented a new version of Brecht's *The Caucasian Chalk Circle,* with Ekkehard Schall as Azdak, at the Berliner Ensemble; and Friedo Solter staged a new *King Lear,* with Fred Düren, at the Deutsches.

Peter Palitzsch came under fire in Frankfurt, where attendances were falling, despite his striking production of Chekhov's *The Seagull* and the selection of Peter Löscher's engrossing production of David Rudkin's *Afore Night Come* to represent the city at the West Berlin Theatre Review. Stuttgart, too, resisted official calls for cutbacks, and countered with a memorable world premiere, by Austria's Thomas Bernhard, of the biographical drama of an actor, *Minetti,* written especially for Bernhard Minetti to play himself. Düsseldorf welcomed the exiled Czechoslovakian director Otomar Krejca, who began his engagement as a full-time staff member with a much-debated adaptation of *The Cherry Orchard.* Peter Zadek's two provocative versions (some called them perversions) of *Othello,* in Hamburg, and *Spring Awakening,* in Bochum, created fiercely partisan arguments in both cities.

Before retiring to hand over the reins to Achim Benning, Vienna Burgtheater manager Gerhard Klingenberg supervised his theatre's 200th anniversary celebrations. Main events there were Krejca's guest production of *Faust* in 19th-century garb and the world premieres, at the Akademie substage, of Wolfgang Bauer's drama of a psychotic, *Magnet Kisses,* and Vaclav Havel's autobiographical Kafkaesque one-acters *Audience* and *Vernissage,* prohibited in his native Prague. The Vienna Festival premiere was Bernhard's skit on prominent festival personalities called *Famous People.* A new version of Tennessee Williams' failed *The Red Devil Battery Sign* was the key offering at Vienna's English Theatre.

The Brussels experimental Pocket Theatre celebrated its 25th birthday with a festival attended by Belgian, French, Italian, and U.S. troupes, the Belgian Mobile Theatre's *A Doll's House* proving to be outstanding. Pierre Laroche's stage adaptation of the French philosopher's writings as *Blaise Pascal,* directed by himself at the Rideau, and the French-language premiere of Trevor Griffiths' *Comedians* at the National were other attractions in Brussels, along with the premiere of Hugo Claus's adaptation of *Orestes* at the Royal Flemish Theatre. In The Netherlands, the new Rotterdam-based international group "Kiss" scored a success with a touring show of classical drama in Greek, Latin, and English by turns.

Italy and Spain. The Milan Piccolo celebrated its 30th birthday with Strehler's production of Jean Genet's *The Balcony* (with Anna Proclemer) and Lamberto Pugelli's of *Widowers' Houses;* Giorgio Albertazzi returned to his old theatre in his own adaptation of a monodrama based on the writings of Dostoyevsky and Nikolay Chernyshevsky. Giorgio De Lullo joined forces with Romolo Valli once more in Pinter's *No Man's Land,* played in a suitably drear decor by Pier Luigi Pizzi. In Trieste, Massimo De Francovich appeared in his own stage version of Italo Svevo's short story *The Cousins.* After producing his own version of the life of Rosa Luxemburg in Genoa, Squarzina opened in Rome in the new Teatro di Roma with a new production of Pasolini's *The Braggart.*

Two important events in Madrid marked a turn toward democracy in the Spanish theatre. The first was Víctor García's imaginatively symbolical rendering of Ramón María del Valle-Inclán's *Divines Paroles* with Nuria Espert at the head of her own troupe (which later toured several world festivals), and the second was the first stage appearance in Madrid since her exile in 1936 of María Casares, daughter of the former republican premier, in the European premiere of *Defiance,* written by the exiled Spanish playwright Rafael Alberti.

Eastern Europe. Moscow's Yuri Liubimov was given permission to leave the U.S.S.R. for the first time with his Na Taganke Theatre company to attend a foreign festival. He presented *Hamlet, Ten Days that Shook the World,* and *Here the Dawns Are Quiet* at the second itinerant Theatre of the Nations Festival in Belgrade. Back home he put on Yuri Trifonov's adaptation of his own novel *The Exchange,* the study of a failed marriage, with Anna Demidova and Leonid Flatov as the estranged couple. A visually beautiful, though slow-paced, *The Cherry Orchard* was Galina Volchyok's latest production at the Sovremennik (Contemporary), while Olga Yakovleva gave a fine rendering of the bride in Anatoli Efros' uproarious version of Nikolay Gogol's *The Wedding* at the Malaya Bronnaya.

For his outstanding performance in Andrzej Wajda's production of Buero Vallejo's Goya drama with which Warsaw's newest theatre, the Na Woli, was inaugurated, Tadeusz Lomnicki won the best actor award of the journal *Theatre.* Two separate productions of Slawomir Mrozek's *The Emigrés* were directed by Jerzy Kreczmar in Warsaw and Andrzej Wajda in

Krakow, and also of his absurdist allegory, *The Hunchback*, by Kazimierz Dejmek in Lodz and Jerzy Jarocki in Krakow. An important novelty was Tadeusz Kantor's terrifying re-creation of Poland's past called *The Dead Class*, which his Cricot 2 company also took to Edinburgh and London. National Theatre actress Zofia Kucówna had a great success in Ireneusz Iredynski's monodrama *Maria*.

In Czechoslovakia Krejca finally emigrated to West Germany; Jan Grossman carried on, in the City Theatre in Cheb, where his production of Molière's *School for Wives* attracted favourable criticism. At the Cinoherni Klub, Ladislav Smocek staged *The Wolf*, a Soviet drama about hyprocrisy by Leonid Leonov. Osvald Zahradnik's second play, *A Sonatina for a Peacock*, about the loneliness of a gregarious miner, was world-premiered in Bratislava. New plays in Hungary included the late Laszlo Nemeth's posthumous Huguenot drama *Colbert*, with Ferenc Bessenyi; Istvan Csurka's *Taken on Location*, about an incompetent film director, with Maria Sulyok; and Endre Illés's *Isabella of Spain*.

Scandinavia. At the Royal Dramatic, Stockholm, the highlights included Kent Andersson's *The Hole*, adapted from the production in Göteborg; the world premiere of Arnold Wesker's *The Merchant*, splendidly staged by Staffan Roos (with Ingvar Kjellson as Shylock); and Per Olov Enquist's second drama, about crime in modern Sweden, *Chez Nous*. The City Theatre, Stockholm, staged Weiss's *The Trial* (premiered in Göteborg), based on the novel by Franz Kafka, and Staffan Westerberg's imaginative production with a musical score by Lars Johan Werle of *The Growing Castle*. Sven Wollter took over the People's Theatre, where Étienne Glaser made his directing debut with an exciting production of Gerhart Hauptmann's *The Weavers*.

In Oslo Liv Ullmann gave a touching performance opposite Toralv Maurstad at the latter's New Theatre in O'Neill's *A Moon for the Misbegotten*, directed by José Quintero from New York. Other highlights included Per Aabel as a male Arcati in Coward's *Blithe Spirit* and a new production of Ibsen's juvenile drama *Catiline*, both at the National. At the New Norwegian, there was a revival of *The Insect Play* staged by a Czechoslovakian team. Wesker's *The Merchant* in Danish was staged at Århus. In Copenhagen, Ernst Bruun Olsen's biographical drama about Baron Holberg, called *Poetic Ecstasy*, with Erik Mörk, was the season's success at the Royal Theatre in Preben Neergård's colourful production. At Helsinki's City Theatre Paavo Liski's anachronistic production of *Paradise Lost*, adapted from Milton by the Hungarian Karoly Kazimir, with Pertti Palo as a benign Satan, had a rock band to provide the stage music.

(OSSIA TRILLING)

U.S. and Canada. A number of large-scale, ambitious ventures that looked promising on paper turned out to be disappointing onstage in 1976, and such excitement as the year afforded came largely from unexpected sources and odd configurations of talent. In honour of the Bicentennial, the annals of U.S. drama were ransacked in search of scripts to revive. The American Bicentennial Theatre, sponsored by the Kennedy Center and financed by the Xerox Corp., mounted a series of such revivals, lavishly produced, for performances at the Kennedy Center (Washington, D.C.) and on tour during the 1975–76 season. The most successful of these was *The Royal Family* by George S. Kaufman and Edna Ferber, which opened late in 1975 and moved to Broadway just before the new year for a substantial run followed by a tour. Other noncommercial theatres also went in heavily for U.S. revivals. And on Broadway, under commercial auspices, there was an impressive revival of *Who's Afraid of Virginia Woolf?* by Edward Albee, starring Colleen Dewhurst and Ben Gazzara, directed by the author.

Few of these revivals proved particularly popular; revivals of U.S. musicals did distinctly better at the box office. *My Fair Lady* (with Ian Richardson as Professor Higgins) and *Fiddler on the Roof* (with Zero Mostel in his original role) returned to Broadway, as did *Pal Joey* (in an unhappy revival at the Circle in the Square) and *Guys and Dolls* (with an all-black cast). *Porgy and Bess*, George Gershwin's masterpiece, is arguably not a musical at all but a full-fledged opera, and it seemed particularly so in its splendid Broadway revival, which came from the Houston Grand Opera with recitatives intact. It was certainly one of the sensations of 1976, and Clamma Dale as Bess made a personal sensation of her own.

Porgy and Bess, though written by whites, is set in a black community, and black modes of song and speech and living are the elements it is made of; it is played, of course, by a nearly all-black cast. It, and the all-black *Guys and Dolls*—along with *Bubbling Brown Sugar*, a revue that evoked the great period of Harlem nightlife, and *Your Arms Too Short to Box with God*, a gospel musical that came from Ford's Theatre in Washington, D.C.—testified to the black presence in the Broadway musical theatre. There was, moreover, a significant black Broadway audience to support plays about the black experience.

In general, however, it was not a happy year for new Broadway musicals. The most impressive, and controversial, of the 1976 crop was *Pacific Overtures*, produced and directed by Harold Prince, with music and lyrics by Stephen Sondheim. An audacious attempt to use the techniques of the Japanese theatre to tell the story of the "opening" of Japan to Western commerce by Commodore Matthew Perry in 1853, it won the New York Drama Critics Circle Award, ran

MARTHA SWOPE

Haruki Fujimoto, playing the role of Commodore Matthew Perry, does a Kabuki-style Lion Dance to celebrate his success in opening Japan to the West in 1853, in the musical "Pacific Overtures" produced and directed by Harold Prince.

MARTHA SWOPE

Andrew Smith as Crown and Clamma Dale as Bess sang in the first uncut version of George Gershwin's black opera "Porgy and Bess," which opened on Broadway in September.

from January to June, and closed at an estimated loss of $1.3 million. The new Richard Rodgers musical, *Rex,* starring Nicol Williamson as Henry VIII, was a failure; *1600 Pennsylvania Avenue,* with book and lyrics by Alan Jay Lerner and music by Leonard Bernstein, was an exceptionally dire failure.

In spite of these setbacks, "The Broadway legit season of 1975–76 was by far the biggest in history, at least on a financial basis," according to *Variety,* the theatrical trade paper. Though the biggest hits were mainly musicals from the previous season, there were high hopes that financial success would continue into the new year and stimulate artistic success as well. In fact, business held up well, but in terms of new creativity the fall Broadway season of 1976 was of a piece with the rest of the year: undistinguished.

Traditionally a source of theatrical creativity, Broadway had become more a destination for creative work from elsewhere. As usual, there were new plays from abroad, especially Great Britain. *A Matter of Gravity,* a rather feeble work about an indomitable grande dame by the author of *The Chalk Garden,* Enid Bagnold, had a short but profitable Broadway run as a vehicle for Katharine Hepburn. The original British production of Harold Pinter's *No Man's Land,* starring Sir John Gielgud and Sir Ralph Richardson, was brought over intact for a successful limited engagement. *Comedians* by Trevor Griffiths used a class of apprentice comedians on a rainy night in Manchester as a context for discussing the responsibility of the artist to society and to himself. Mike Nichols directed it for Broadway, and Jonathan Pryce, the only member of the original cast to repeat his role in the U.S., made a deep impression as the most talented, and most hostile, of the comedians.

As for new U.S. plays on Broadway, they were neither numerous nor distinguished, and few of them began as Broadway productions. *California Suite* by Neil Simon began its career at the Ahmanson Theatre in Los Angeles, but was at least clearly intended for Broadway from the beginning; composed of four playlets set in the same suite at the Beverly Hills Hotel, it was a hit on the strength of its resemblance to Simon's previous comedies. *Zalmen, or The Madness of God* by Elie Wiesel, about the plight of Soviet Jewry, came to Broadway from the Arena Stage in Washington, D.C. *The Runner Stumbles* by Milan Stitt, a sombre, scrupulous account of a doomed love affair between a Roman Catholic priest and a nun, came to Broadway from the Hartman Theatre Company in Stamford, Conn., and, before that, the Manhattan Theatre Club. *Knock Knock* by Jules Feiffer, a reflective yet zany comedy in which Joan of Arc appears to two elderly Jewish men, opened in a much-admired production at the Circle Repertory Theatre in Greenwich Village. The production was transferred to Broadway, and when business there proved disappointing it was restaged by a new director with a new cast; the new production got unenthusiastic notices and quickly closed.

Unquestionably the big disappointment of the fall Broadway season was *A Texas Trilogy,* three full-length, interrelated plays by Preston Jones about life in a West Texas town. The trilogy was originally mounted by the Dallas Theatre Center; one play of the three, *The Last Meeting of the Knights of the White Magnolia,* was produced at regional theatres throughout the country. Then the entire trilogy, directed by Alan Schneider, was produced by the Kennedy Center in Washington, D.C., with tremendous critical and popular success. This production, the three plays in repertory, was transferred to Broadway with high hopes. But the New York response was merely polite. Few thought they were bad plays, but few thought they were more than skilled but uninspired exercises in conventional American realism. They closed after a short run, at a considerable loss of money.

The balance of power in the U.S. theatre having shifted decisively to the noncommercial theatre, one of the major theatrical entrepreneurs in the U.S. was Joseph Papp of the New York Shakespeare Festival. In 1976 Papp had four major successes running simultaneously. *A Chorus Line* continued its successful Broadway career, and two touring companies were sent out. A thoroughly unlikely success was *For Colored Girls Who Have Considered Suicide/When the Rainbow Is Enuf,* a suite of poems by Ntozake Shange about being black and female in America, spoken and sometimes sung and danced by a cast of seven black women, including the author. First produced at a bar in Manhattan, it was moved to Papp's Public Theatre as a co-production by Papp and Woodie King, Jr., of the New Federal Theatre; from the Public Theatre it moved to Broadway. Its highlight, a story-poem about a crazy Vietnam veteran who kills his own children, was powerfully performed by Trazana Beverley.

Meanwhile, at the Vivian Beaumont Theatre in Lincoln Center, Papp presented the first New York revival in many years of *The Threepenny Opera* by Brecht and Kurt Weill. To direct, he engaged Richard Foreman, much admired among the avant-garde as the author-director-designer of such surrealist creations as *Rhoda in Potatoland.* Foreman's rigorously controlled, forbidding, coldly lavish *Threepenny* was controversial, and popular. To fill his smaller Lincoln Center auditorium, Papp imported from the Long Wharf Theatre in New Haven, Conn., Mike Nichols' staging of *Streamers,* David Rabe's new play about sexual, racial, and other tensions at an army camp in Virginia during the war in Vietnam. *Streamers* won the New York Drama Critics Circle Award as the best American play of 1975–76.

Other new U.S. plays were presented off-Broadway, off-off-Broadway, and in the regional theatres. The Folger Theatre Group in Washington, D.C., sent its production of *Medal of Honor Rag* by Tom Cole, about a Vietnam veteran with psychic scars, to New York for an off-Broadway engagement. The Virginia Museum Theatre presented *Children,* a sensitive play by A. R. Gurney, Jr., about a wealthy New England family, in February; in October, the Manhattan Theatre Club mounted its own production of *Children. Every Night When the Sun Goes Down,* an ominous, doom-ridden play by the black dramatist Philip Hayes Dean, appeared at the American Place Theatre in New York in February; *Vanities* by Jack Heifner, about the growing older of three former cheerleaders, opened off-Broadway in March; *Serenading Louie* by Lanford Wilson, about two prosperous but emotionally fraught couples, was produced by the Circle Repertory Company, Greenwich Village, in April; *Suicide in B-Flat* by Sam Shepard had its premiere at the Yale Repertory Theatre, New Haven, Conn., in October.

The most promising new U.S. dramatist to emerge was David Mamet, who had three plays produced in New York for brief engagements off-off-Broadway in the fall of 1975, after previous productions in Chicago. A double bill of his *Sexual Perversity in Chicago* and *Duck Variations* opened off-Broadway in June 1976 for a long run. *Sexual Perversity* was a sharply brilliant comic account of how modern young American men and women try to deal with their fear of each other.

The experimental-theatre event of the year, beyond question, was *Einstein on the Beach,* an "opera" devised and staged by Robert Wilson, with music by Philip Glass. A 4½-hour surrealistic extravaganza, a sort of huge-scale, meticulously organized happening, *Einstein,* though created by Americans, was first presented in Europe. After gaining favourable reviews at the Avignon Festival in Paris and elsewhere, it was presented for two much-discussed performances at the Metropolitan Opera House in New York.

In Canada theatre felt the effect of the Olympic Games at Montreal. The Arts and Culture Program of the Olympics brought performers and companies from all over Canada to Montreal for a festival of Canadian theatre, music, and dance; the organizers were later severely criticized because audiences for many events were disappointingly small. Two notable French-Canadian plays, both produced by Montreal companies, formed part of the festivities. *Évangéline Deusse* by Antonine Maillet, produced by the Théâtre du Rideau Vert, was a gentle little play about an old woman from Acadia, the French-speaking community in New Brunswick, who feels like an exile in busy metropolitan Montreal. *Sainte Carmen de la Main* by Jean Tremblay, produced by the Compagnie Jean Duceppe, was a harsh, jolting play about a nightclub singer who gets into trouble when her songs take on radical political implications; written in the form of a Greek tragedy, *Sainte Carmen* had a chorus of prostitutes, male and female, who work "the Main," Montreal's nightclub strip.

Meanwhile, the Lennonville Festival (located in Quebec, but English-speaking) had a success with *Sqrieux-de-Deux* by Betty Lambert, a cheerful sex-comedy imported from Vancouver. The Stratford (Ont.) Festival had a successful year with ten productions, including Congreve's *The Way of the World,* Shakespeare's *Antony and Cleopatra,* and Chekhov's *The Three Sisters,* all starring Maggie Smith, and two successful productions carried over from the previous year, Shakespeare's *Measure for Measure* and Oscar

SY FRIEDMAN

Katharine Hepburn played a grande dame in Enid Bagnold's "A Matter of Gravity" on Broadway.

Wilde's *The Importance of Being Earnest,* the latter starring William Hutt in a transvestite performance as Lady Bracknell. In Toronto it was not an exciting theatrical year; there was a new play by James Reaney entitled *Baldoon,* but no new work reached the Toronto stage from most of the other established English-speaking Canadian playwrights.

One event in the Canadian theatre had a symbolic importance. On April 1, 1976, the Canadian branch of Actors Equity, the stage performers' union, separated itself from the U.S. Actors Equity and became an independent organization. (JULIUS NOVICK)

See also Dance; Literature; Music.
[622]

ENCYCLOPÆDIA BRITANNICA FILMS. *Shaw vs. Shakespeare—Part I: The Character of Caesar, Part II: The Tragedy of Julius Caesar, Part III: Caesar and Cleopatra* (1970); *Medieval Theater: The Play of Abraham and Isaac* (1974); *Art of Silence* (1975); *The New Tenant* (1975); *The Well of the Saints* (1975); *The Long Christmas Dinner* (1976); *Tennessee Williams: Theater in Progress* (1976).

Togo

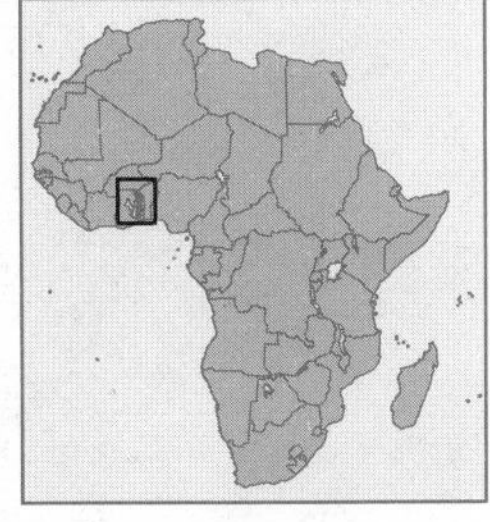

A West African republic on the Bight of Benin, Togo is bordered by Ghana, Upper Volta, and Benin. Area: 21,925 sq mi (56,785 sq km). Pop. (1975 est.): 2,197,-900. Cap. and largest city: Lomé (pop., 1975 est., 214,200). Language: French (official). Religion: animist; Muslim and Christian minorities. President in 1976, Gen. Gnassingbe Eyadema.

After months of bickering, Togo and Benin (formerly Dahomey) normalized their relations in March 1976, thanks to the mediation of Pres. Sékou Touré of Guinea.

In September, after a major ministerial reorganization, Ayi Houenou Hunlede, who had headed Togo's foreign ministry since General Eyadema seized power in 1967, surrendered the foreign affairs portfolio to Edem Kodjo, previously minister of finance and the economy.

The only shadow over an otherwise seemingly satisfactory domestic situation was a certain tension in relations between church and state, notably revealed in the disturbances at Lomé on May 2 at a bishop's

Theology: *see* Religion

Timber: *see* Industrial Review

Tobacco: *see* Drug Abuse; Industrial Review

Tobogganing: *see* Winter Sports

consecration. However, General Eyadema personally saw to it that conflicts of this nature did not lead to crisis, and the steps he took were effective. A return to civilian rule in the near future was forecast by the general in a speech at Piya in northern Togo in November, but he did not mention a specific date.

In October representatives of Togo, Zaire, Gabon, and the Ivory Coast met in Lomé in order to coordinate policies. (PHILIPPE DECRAENE)

[978.E.4.b.ii]

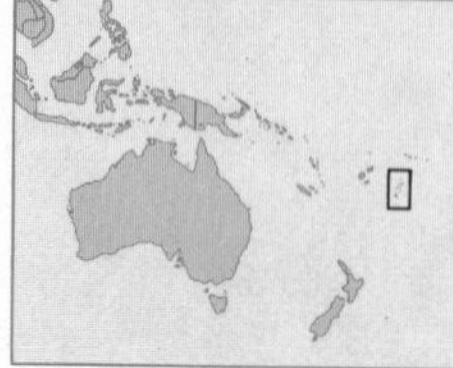

Tonga

An independent monarchy and member of the Commonwealth of Nations, Tonga is an island group in the Pacific Ocean east of Fiji. Area: 270 sq mi (700 sq km). Pop. (1975 est.): 102,000. Cap.: Nukualofa (pop., 1974 est., 25,000). Language: English and Tongan. Religion: Christian. King, Taufa'ahau Tupou IV; prime minister in 1976, Prince Tu'ipelehake.

On Nov. 4, 1975, Tonga celebrated its centenary as a constitutional monarchy. Among the events of 1976 it was understood that the U.S.S.R. had offered to upgrade Tonga's international airport and dockyard in return for the right to establish a fisheries base there. The terms and tone of the New Zealand government's comments on these developments caused a deterioration in relations with Tonga, in part because they coincided with an attempt by New Zealand to reduce immigration (especially of temporary workers from the Pacific islands) and to locate and, in some cases, deport illegal immigrants, many of whom were Tongans. Remittances from migrant workers were important for cash income in the villages of Tonga and as a means of reducing the nation's chronic balance of payments deficit.

There was a revival of Japanese interest in Tonga with offers of aircraft for regional services, hotel development, and a fisheries agreement. With other Pacific island nations, Tonga on March 9 accepted Australian and New Zealand proposals for a weakened version of the stand on a nuclear-free zone in the Pacific taken at the 1975 meeting of the South Pacific Forum and also agreed not to formalize any fisheries agreements until the Law of the Sea Conference (*see* LAW: *Special Report*) had completed its deliberations on the concept of a 200-mi exclusive economic zone. (BARRIE MACDONALD)

[977.A.3]

Track and Field Sports

An important (and long overdue) decision emerging from the International Amateur Athletic Federation (IAAF) congress meeting at Montreal in July 1976 concerned timing. Only approved fully automatic electronic timing for sprint events (up to and including 400 m) would be accepted in the future for world record consideration, and hand timings for all events would be released in tenths of a second. Thus, many records would be jettisoned from the world sprint lists, and athletes would know the marks at which to aim.

International Competition: Men. Predictably, most of the record breaking took place at the Olympic Games. (See *Special Report.*) But world records tumbled even as early as February, when Terry Albritton (U.S.) surprised the world with a shot put of 21.85 m (71 ft 8½ in) in Hawaii. The discus record was soon to follow, thanks to a very much in-form Mac Wilkins (U.S.). He reached 69.16 m (226 ft 11 in) at Walnut, Calif., in April and on May 1 capped a remarkable series of throws with a heave of 70.86 m (232 ft 6 in). Steve Williams, Harvey Glance (both U.S.), and Don Quarrie (Jamaica) all ran hand-timed 9.9 sec for 100 m during the early part of the season; none of these made the final world record lists because of the IAAF's new ruling. Albritton's shot put mark was destined to have a short life, for Aleksandr Baryshnikov (U.S.S.R.), using the dramatic "discus whirl" technique, reached an even 22 m (72 ft 2¼ in) in Paris on July 10 just before the Olympic Games opened in Canada.

High jumper Dwight Stones (U.S.) achieved a world record on each side of the Games. In winning the National Collegiate Athletic Association (NCAA) title in Philadelphia in June, he scaled 2.31 m (7 ft 7 in) and, four days after finishing a bitterly disappointed bronze medalist in Montreal, went over a bar set at 2.32 m (7 ft 7¼ in), again in Philadelphia. Two U.S. pole vaulters helped push the world mark closer to 5.80 m (19 ft). Earl Bell vaulted 5.67 m (18 ft 7¼ in) at Wichita, Kan., on May 29, and Dave Roberts won the U.S. Olympic Trials with a magnificent vault of 5.70 m (18 ft 8¼ in) on June 22 at Eugene, Ore. (Roberts was vaulting on Bell's pole after his own shattered on his first attempt at the new world record.)

On the track, New Zealander John Walker, in Oslo on June 30, turned in one of the most sensational middle distance exploits of all time, covering the rarely run 2,000 m in 4 min 51.4 sec. Michel Jazy's previous record (4 min 56.2 sec) had stood for ten years. In The Netherlands, Jos Hermens churned out his annual long distance chores on the track at the Papendal National Sports Centre, near Arnhem. On May 1 he became the first man ever to run more than 13 mi in an hour after passing 20 km (50 laps) in 57 min 24.2 sec. Decathlon competitor Bruce Jenner (U.S.) previewed his Montreal world record by amassing 8,444 points in Eugene in June. Due to faulty electrical timing and some events being wind-assisted, his score checked out five different ways, the most popular being 8,448 (electrical) and 8,542 (hand timing).

Table I. World 1976 Outdoor Records—Men

Event	Competitor, country, date	Performance
800 m	Alberto Juantorena, Cuba, July 25	1 min 43.5 sec
400-m hurdles	Edwin Moses, U.S., July 25	47.64 sec
3,000-m steeplechase	Anders Garderud, Sweden, July 28	8 min 08.02 sec
High jump	Dwight Stones, U.S., June 5	2.31 m (7 ft 7 in)
	Dwight Stones, U.S., August 4	2.32 m (7 ft 7¼ in)
Pole vault	Earl Bell, U.S., May 29	5.67 m (18 ft 7¼ in)
	Dave Roberts, U.S., June 22	5.70 m (18 ft 8¼ in)
Shot put	Terry Albritton, U.S., February 21	21.85 m (71 ft 8½ in)
	Aleksandr Baryshnikov, U.S.S.R., July 10	22.00 m (72 ft 2¼ in)
Discus	Mac Wilkins, U.S., April 24	69.16 m (226 ft 11 in)
	Mac Wilkins, U.S., May 1	70.86 m (232 ft 6 in)
Javelin	Miklos Nemeth, Hungary, July 26	94.58 m (310 ft 4 in)
Decathlon	Bruce Jenner, U.S., June 25–26	8,444 pt 8,448 pt* 8,542 pt†
	Bruce Jenner, U.S., July 29–30	8,618 pt
Nonstandard events		
2,000 m	John Walker, New Zealand, June 30	4 min 51.4 sec
One-hour run	Jos Hermens, The Netherlands, May 1	20,944 m (13 mi 10 yd)
20,000 m	Jos Hermens, The Netherlands, May 1	57 min 24.2 sec

*Wind-assisted.
†Hand timing.

Tornadoes:
see Disasters; Earth Sciences

Tourism:
see Industrial Review

Toys:
see Games and Toys

Men showing good early season 100-m sprint form included Americans Harvey Glance (10.11 sec) and Steve Riddick (10.18 sec), while over 200 m Millard Hampton led the world with 20.10 sec and Olympic gold medal winner Don Quarrie ranked sixth with a hand-timed 20.30 sec. Alberto Juantorena of Cuba gave a clear indication of his intentions by pacing the world 400-m rankings with 44.70 sec prior to his 44.26 sec victory in the Olympics, and his 1 min 44.9 sec ranked second in the 800-m lists going into the Games. After the Games, Mike Boit of Kenya, sadly missing from Montreal's action because of the African boycott, began to turn in some stirring marks. He ran 800 m in 1 min 43.6 sec in West Berlin in August to miss Juantorena's world mark by just 0.07 sec (he clocked 1 min 43.57 sec on the electronic timing) and beat bronze medalist Rick Wohlhuter (U.S.) and silver medalist Ivo Van Damme (Belgium) in Helsinki, Nice, and Zürich after the Games.

New Zealanders John Walker, Dick Quax, and Rod Dixon were prominent in Europe both before and after the Games. Quax missed Emile Puttemans' 5,000-m world record by a tenth of a second with a brilliant 13 min 13.1 sec victory in Stockholm in June, leading home Klaus-Peter Hildebrand (West Germany) in 13 min 13.8 sec and Dixon in 13 min 17.2 sec in their best-ever times. Walker ran 22 races after Montreal, winning most of them, including a mile in 3 min 53.1 sec from Thomas Wessinghage (West Germany), who cut the European record to 3 min 53.2 sec behind him. Lasse Viren (Finland) prefaced his triumphs in Montreal by churning out a fast 27 min 42.9 sec for 10,000 m in June, and after the Games little Carlos Sousa-Lopes of Portugal was within world record pace for 9 km in a race he won narrowly from Quax. Over the hurdles, Guy Drut ran a hand-timed 13.1 sec just before his Olympic win. In the 400-m hurdles, Edwin Moses ran a U.S. (electrical) record of 48.30 sec at Eugene before his world record at the Games. John Akii-Bua (Uganda) ran 48.58 sec in shaping up to defend his title, but suffered an injury while in Europe and did not race at the Games because of the African boycott.

Olympic high-jump champion Jacek Wszola of Poland beat the redoubtable Dwight Stones three times after Montreal, setting a European record of 2.29 m (7 ft 6 in) at Koblenz, West Germany, in difficult, dark conditions, to prove that he was no fluke Olympic winner. Pole vaulter Tadeusz Slusarski (Poland) cleared 5.62 m (18 ft 5¼ in) to share a European record with countryman Wladyslaw Kozakiewicz prior to his surprise win at Montreal. Hammer-throw champion Yury Sedykh led a Soviet clean sweep at Montreal, and his June 78.86-m (258 ft 9 in) throw with the ball-and-chain topped the world rankings. Prior to the Games, Seppo Hovinen of Finland showed consistency with several javelin throws of more than 90 m, led by one at 93.54 m (306 ft 11 in). The world record, however, was set by Miklos Nemeth (Hungary) in the opening round at Montreal with a throw of 94.58 m (310 ft 4 in).

International Competition: Women. Germans dominated the sprint events during the early part of the season. Inge Helten of West Germany cut 0.03 sec off the world 100-m best with 11.04 sec at Fürth in June, and Olympic champion-to-be Annegret Richter dashed the distance in a hand-timed 10.8 sec at Gelsenkirchen to equal Renate Stecher's controversial world record. Afterward, as mentioned above, all hand times were rejected for world record consideration. Christina Brehmer, an 18-year-old from East Germany, burned around 400 m in 49.77 sec at Dresden in May, but Irena Szewinska of Poland chopped this to 49.75 sec at Warsaw on June 22 prior to her stunning Olympic triumph in 49.29 sec.

ADN-ZB / EASTFOTO

Waldemar Cierpinski of East Germany was the surprise winner of the Olympic marathon in July. The favourite, Frank Shorter of the U.S., was second in the 26-mile race.

Soviet middle distance runners hit top form in 1976. Valentina Gerasimova broke the world 800-m record with 1 min 56.0 sec in Kiev but surprisingly was eliminated in the semifinals at the Olympics. Tatyana Kazankina ran an eye-boggling 3 min 56.0 sec for 1,500 m in Moscow on June 28 to break the

Table II. World 1976 Outdoor Records—Women

Event	Competitor, country, date	Performance
100 m	Inge Helten, West Germany, June 13	11.04 sec
	Annegret Richter, West Germany, July 25	11.01 sec
400 m	Christina Brehmer, East Germany, May 9	49.77 sec
	Irena Szewinska, Poland, June 22	49.75 sec
	Irena Szewinska, Poland, July 29	49.29 sec
800 m	Valentina Gerasimova, U.S.S.R., June 12	1 min 56 0 sec
	Tatyana Kazankina, U.S.S.R., July 26	1 min 54.94 sec
1,500 m	Tatyana Kazankina, U.S.S.R., June 28	3 min 56.0 sec
High jump	Rosemarie Ackermann, East Germany, May 8	1.96 m (6 ft 5 in)
Long jump	Angela Voigt, East Germany, May 9	6.92 m (22 ft 8½ in)
	Siegrun Siegl, East Germany, May 19	6.99 m (22 ft 11¼ in)
Shot put	Marianne Adam, East Germany, May 30	21.67 m (71 ft 1¼ in)
	Ivanka Khristova, Bulgaria, July 3	21.87 m (71 ft 9 in)
	Ivanka Khristova, Bulgaria, July 4	21.89 m (71 ft 9¾ in)
	Helena Fibingerova, Czechoslovakia, Sept. 25	21.99 m (72 ft 1¾ in)
Discus	Faina Melnik, U.S.S.R., April 24	70.50 m (231 ft 3 in)
Javelin	Ruth Fuchs, East Germany, July 10	69.12 m (226 ft 9½ in)
4 x 100 m	East German team, May 29	42.50 sec
4 x 400 m	East German team, July 31	3 min 19.23 sec
Nonstandard events		
1,000 m	A. Sorokina, U.S.S.R., July 3(?)	2 min 32.8 sec
2,000 m	Natalia Marescu, Romania, April 17	5 min 44.0 sec
3,000 m	Grete Waitz, Norway, June 21	8 min 45.4 sec
	Ludmila Bragina, U.S.S.R., August 7	8 min 27.1 sec
3 mi	Peg Neppel, U.S., May 14	15 min 41.8 sec
4 x 440 yd	U.S.S.R. team, August 8	3 min 29.1 sec
4 x 800 m	East German team, August 8	7 min 54.2 sec
	U.S.S.R. team, August 17	7 min 52.3 sec
4 x 200 m	East German team, August 13	1 min 32.4 sec

JEAN-PIERRE LAFFONT—SYGMA

Tadeusz Slusarski of Poland won the pole vault at the summer Olympic Games.

world record by 5.4 sec and become the first woman to run the distance in under 4 min; she later collected both 800-m (world record 1 min 54.94 sec) and 1,500-m titles at the Games. Only 1.62 m (5 ft 3¾ in) tall and weighing 47 kg (104 lb), she proved herself to possess the driving force of a racing car.

The formidable East German female athletes were responsible for several world records prior to the Games. Rosemarie Ackermann high-jumped 1.96 m (6 ft 5 in) with her immaculate straddle technique at Dresden in May, while at the same meeting Angela Voigt long-jumped 6.92 m (22 ft 8½ in). Two weeks later Siegrun Siegl bounded 6.99 m (22 ft 11¼ in). Javelin queen Ruth Fuchs then threw her spear 69.12 m (226 ft 9½ in) in East Berlin on July 10. The shot put record traded hands through the efforts of three young women; Marianne Adam (East Germany) reached 21.67 m (71 ft 1¼ in) at the end of May only to see Ivanka Khristova of Bulgaria reach 21.87 m (71 ft 9 in) and 21.89 m (71 ft 9¾ in) on successive days at Belmetten, Bulg. Khristova went on to win the Olympic title, but then in September Helena Fibingerova (Czechoslovakia) put the shot 21.99 m (72 ft 1¾ in). Though she lost her discus crown at the Games and had a bad time with Canadian officials, Faina Melnik (U.S.S.R.) achieved a mark of 70.50 m (231 ft 3 in) at Sochi in April. Of the nonstandard records, Ludmila Bragina's 3,000-m time of 8 min 27.1 sec stood out. She ran it in the U.S. versus U.S.S.R. match in Maryland after the Games, and it averaged out at 67.6 sec per lap.

(DAVID COCKSEDGE)

United States Competition. A discus thrower, a hurdler, and a decathlon performer highlighted the U.S. season as each won track and field's two most coveted prizes, the world record and the Olympic championship. Four other Americans achieved new world bests, three more global marks were equaled, and three additional Olympic gold medals were won by U.S. athletes.

Edwin Moses won his two prizes in the 47.64 sec it took him to run the 400-m intermediate hurdle race at the Olympic Games at Montreal. The Morehouse College (Atlanta, Ga.) student, who won his Olympic medal on July 25, had established a new U.S. record by running 48.30 sec in the Olympic Trials at Eugene, Ore., on June 21.

Bruce Jenner also won an Olympic gold medal and a world record in the same competition. But it took the San Jose Stars athlete two full days of competition (July 29–30) to score 8,618 points in his event, the decathlon. It was his second world record of the season; he totaled 8,542 in the Olympic Trials June 25–26.

Mac Wilkins won the Olympic discus throw with a mark of 221 ft 5 in (1 m = 3⅓ in) on July 25. But the Pacific Coast Club thrower achieved his two world records elsewhere. He threw 226 ft 11 in at Walnut, Calif., on April 24 and 232 ft 6 in at San Jose, Calif., on May 1.

Another athlete twice broke the world record. Dwight Stones of Long Beach State University set marks before and after the Olympic Games, where he placed third. He leaped 7 ft 7 in in the NCAA championships in Philadelphia on June 5, breaking his own record. A few days after the Olympics, on August 4, he cleared 7 ft 7¼ in, again at Philadelphia.

The world record also fell twice in the pole vault. First to break it was Earl Bell of Arkansas State University. He vaulted 18 ft 7¼ in at Wichita, Kan., on May 29. The former champion, Dave Roberts of the Florida Track Club, wasted no time in regaining the record. He made 18 ft 8¼ in in the Olympic Trials on June 22. Terry Albritton set a short-lived shot put mark of 71 ft 8½ in during February in Hawaii. The 100-m dash also saw two new entries in the international record book. Harvey Glance of Auburn (Alabama) University tied the mark of 9.9 sec at Baton Rouge, La., on May 1, and Don Quarrie repeated the performance at Modesto, Calif., on May 22. The University of Tennessee completed the rewriting of the world record book by breaking the 880-yd relay mark with a time of 1 min 21.7 sec at

Miklos Nemeth of Hungary won the javelin throw at the summer Olympic Games, with a distance of 94.58 metres (310 feet 4 inches).

WIDE WORLD

Knoxville, Tenn., on April 10, and by equaling the 800-m relay standard of 1 min 21.5 sec at Philadelphia on April 24.

Long jumper Arnie Robinson was the only other American to win an individual Olympic track and field event. The Maccabi Track Club member leaped 27 ft 4¾ in on July 29. Both relays were won by U.S. quartets on July 31. Winning the 400-m test in 38.33 sec were Glance; Johnny Jones, a recent graduate of Lampasas, Texas, High School; Millard Hampton of San Jose City College; and Steve Riddick of the Philadelphia Pioneer Club. The 1,600-m winners, in 2 min 58.65 sec, were Herman Frazier of Arizona State University, Fred Newhouse of the Baton Rouge Track Club, and Benny Brown and Maxie Parks of the Maccabi club.

National records were achieved by Duncan Macdonald, who ran 5,000 m in 13 min 19.4 sec on August 10 in Stockholm, and the University of Pennsylvania 6,000-m relay team, which was timed in 15 min 9.8 sec at Philadelphia on April 24. A world junior record of 3 min 4.8 sec was made by the United States national 1,600-m relay team at Ludenscheid, West Germany, on July 8.

In team competition, the U.S. defeated the Soviet Union 115 to 107, at College Park, Md., on August 7, but the U.S. junior team was beaten by the Soviets 123½–109½, at Tallinn, U.S.S.R., on July 3. The juniors beat West Germany 136–86.

The NCAA title was won by the University of Southern California with 64 points to 44 for the University of Texas, El Paso, at Philadelphia on June 5. The University of California at Irvine won the NCAA Division II meet, and Southern University of New Orleans captured the Division III competition. The National Association of Intercollegiate Athletics tournament was won by Eastern New Mexico University, and the Pacific Coast Club won the U.S. Track and Field Federation (USTFF) championships.

Indoors, Stones and pole vaulter Dan Ripley of the Pacific Coast Club were the leading performers. Stones bettered the world mark twice, clearing 7 ft 6¼ in at New York on February 20 and 7 ft 6½ in at San Diego the next night. Ripley set three records. His 18 ft 1¼ in at College Park, Md., on January 9, 18 ft 2¼ in at Inglewood, Calif., on February 6, and 18 ft 3¾ in at New York on February 20 were amateur bests although short of the professional standard.

Three indoor relay marks were achieved. Villanova (Pa.) University ran the four-mile relay in 16 min 19.0 sec at Hanover, N.H., on January 16; the University of Michigan performed the sprint medley in 3 min 23.6 sec at East Lansing, Mich., on February 7; and Villanova ran the distance medley in 9 min 38.4 sec at Louisville, Ky., also on February 7. A final U.S. indoor record to fall was in the triple jump, when Tommy Haynes of the U.S. Army leaped 55 ft 5½ in at New York on February 27.

The NCAA indoor title went to Texas, El Paso, and the Amateur Athletic Union (AAU) meet was won by the New York Athletic Club. The Soviet Union defeated the U.S. at Leningrad on March 7, by a 96–64 score.

U.S. women were not as successful as their male counterparts. They scored one world record in a seldom-contested event and earned three Olympic medals, none of them gold.

Peg Neppel of Iowa State University claimed the lone world mark by running three miles in 15 min 41.8 sec at Manhattan, Kan., on May 14. She also achieved U.S. records at 5,000 m (16 min 28.6 sec) and 10,000 m (34 min 19 sec). Placing second in the Olympics were Kathy McMillan in the long jump and the 1,600-m relay team, while Kate Schmidt won a bronze medal in the javelin.

WIDE WORLD

Long jumper Angela Voigt of East Germany grimaces as she lands in the sand. She won the women's long jump at Montreal with a leap of 6.72 metres (22 feet ½ inch).

National records were comparatively commonplace among the women. McMillan improved the long-jump standard three times with a best effort of 22 ft 3 in, and Schmidt moved the javelin mark up to 218 ft 3 in. Three members of the 1,600-m relay team took turns breaking the 400-m figure; Rosalyn Bryant ran 51.5 sec, followed by Sheila Ingram at 51.31 sec, Debra Sapenter at 51.23 sec, and Ingram at 50.90 sec before Bryant had the last word with 50.62 sec. The last four marks all were made in Olympic competition.

The U.S. 1,500-m record was reduced to 4 min 7.3 sec by Cyndy Poor of the San Jose Cindergals, to 4 min 7.2 sec by Francie Larrieu of the Pacific Coast Club, and then to 4 min 2.6 sec by Jan Merrill (Age Group Athletic Association). Larrieu also claimed the 3,000-m mark of 8 min 54.9 sec, while Merrill set a 5,000-m best of 16 min 16.2 sec. Madeline Jackson of the Cleveland Track Club twice lowered the 800-m record. She ran 1 min 59.8 sec and 1 min 57.9 sec. A 400-m hurdle record of 57.24 sec was set by Arthurine Gainer of Prairie View A & M University, Texas, while the Los Angeles Track Club A ran the two-mile relay in 8 min 34.4 sec.

Indoors, Deby LaPlante of Eastern Michigan University equaled the world mark for the 70-yd hurdles, timed in 8.8 sec, and Lorna Forde of the Atoms Track Club had the fastest time ever for 500 yd, 1 min 3.4 sec. Martha Watson of Lakewood International tied the national standard of 21 ft 4¾ in in the long jump, and Bryant claimed a U.S. best in the 200-m dash with 23.5 sec.

The national team lost to the Soviet Union twice, 104–42 outdoors and 75–53 indoors. The junior team lost to the U.S.S.R. 90–54 but edged West Germany 71–64. Prairie View A & M won the outdoor USTFF tournament, while the Atoms won the indoor AAU meet. (BERT D. NELSON)

[452.B.3.b]

SPECIAL REPORT

MONTREAL: THE XXI OLYMPIAD

By Chris Brasher

On behalf of the International Olympic Committee I appeal to every single sportsman and woman not to come to the Olympic Games if they wish to make use of sport for political purposes. . . . We all have our own beliefs; we all have our friends and enemies; but the aim of the Olympic Movement is to subjugate these in the fellowship which is enshrined in the intertwining Olympic rings representing the five continents of the world, wedded together in sport, peace, and friendship. If this is not accomplished then the Olympic Movement and all sport, whether amateur or professional, is doomed. Instead of progressing toward the common ideals, we shall retreat into barbarism.

Such was the appeal made by Lord Killanin, president of the International Olympic Committee (IOC), in 1974. On Aug. 1, 1976, when the XXI Olympiad of the modern era was brought to a close in the city of Montreal, many of those present believed that the progress toward common ideals had stopped and that the retreat into barbarism had begun. Never in the history of the Olympic Games had there been such conspicuous waste of money and resources; never had the Games been so callously exploited for political purposes; never had the lives of the athletes and coaches been so affected by the authorities' fear of terrorism; never had so many great athletes been missing from the greatest sporting occasion in the world; and never had those who cherished a belief in the Olympic ideal felt so helpless and disillusioned.

Finance and Politics. When the IOC accepted Montreal's bid for the Games, it was on the basis that they would be "modest and self-financing." Modesty was stripped away by the grandiose ambitions of Montreal's mayor, Jean Drapeau, who determined to use the Olympics as a means of acquiring a stadium designed not for the Olympic Games but for future use for professional baseball and football. The full cost of the stadium would not be known until it was finally completed in 1977, but the deficit on the entire Games was expected to exceed U.S. $1 billion—over three times the original budget for the whole "self-financing" operation. The citizens of Montreal and of the province of Quebec might well be reminded of this extravagance as they paid their taxes over the next 20 years. (*See* CANADA: *Special Report.*)

Throughout the years of argument that preceded the Games, Canada's Prime Minister Pierre Trudeau refused to be drawn into the political and financial infighting. Just eight days before the Games opened, however, he strode onto centre stage when he and his government refused to allow the Olympic team of the Republic of China (Taiwan) to enter Canada, an action Canada had warned of in May. This was a direct infringement of one of the most precious of all the Olympic ideals: free access to the Olympic city for all athletes, officials, and media personnel affiliated to their national Olympic committees. The problem arose because the Canadian government recognizes only one Chinese nation, the People's Republic of China. Eventually, only 48 hours before the Games opened, a compromise appeared to have been reached: the Taiwanese could enter Canada and would be allowed to fly their flag and play their anthem provided that they did not use the name "The Republic of China." However, on the day before the opening the Taiwanese decided this condition was unacceptable and withdrew.

Meanwhile, the Games were the target of another political threat. The representatives of 16 African nations signed a letter to the IOC in which they threatened to withdraw from the Games unless the New Zealanders were banned. The Africans objected to the fact that the New Zealand "All Blacks" rugby team (so-called because the players wear black shirts and shorts) was currently touring South Africa. The Africans referred to a UN resolution condemning all sporting associations with South Africa and said that their athletes could not compete in the Olympic Games against the New Zealanders. The IOC rejected the letter, saying that as rugby was not an Olympic sport they had no jurisdiction in the matter and that because the New Zealand Olympic Committee was properly affiliated, their athletes were entitled to take part in the Games.

Chaos ensued as the African delegations sought orders from their governments (national Olympic committees are supposed, under Olympic rules, to be independent of governmental control). Not until the teams marched into the stadium for the opening ceremony on July 17 was the extent of the defections known. All the major black and North African nations had withdrawn; so, too, had Iraq and Guyana.

Highlights of the Games. When at last the Games got under way, the rancour and turmoil of international politics were soon forgotten in the perfection of the performance by Romania's girl gymnast Nadia Comaneci (*see* BIOGRAPHY). On the first day of competition this beguiling 14-year-old, less than 5 ft tall and weighing only 86 lb, put the elaborate results computer into turmoil by doing something that nobody had ever done, scoring a maximum possible ten points, on the uneven parallel bars. She did it again on the balance beam and yet again on the bars. In all, Comaneci scored seven perfect "tens" during the first week of competition and emerged from the Games with three gold medals, the balance beam, the uneven bars, and the supreme title, for combined exercises.

In the women's gymnastics team event the U.S.S.R., led by the stately Ludmila Tourischeva, preserved the superiority that it had held since the 1952 Games in Helsinki. The team included the sensation of 1972, Olga Korbut; the smallest competitor of all, Maria Filatova, just 4 ft 3¼ in tall and only 66 lb in weight; and Nelli Kim, who won the individual gold medals in the horse vault and the floor exercises. But it was Tourischeva who won the sympathy of the experts. This striking woman had won the combined exercises in the 1972 Games, but then her sporting skill had been overshadowed by the 17-year-old Korbut. Now in Montreal she was upstaged again by children: Comaneci and her Romanian teammate Teodora Ungureanu, and the impish Filatova. Afterward Tourischeva announced her retirement, but those who had watched her at two Olympic Games would remember her as a true artist.

Meantime at the swimming pool, records were being overturned. If the men's results were spectacular, those of the women's events verged on the unbelievable. Until the Montreal Games no East German woman had ever won a gold medal for swimming, but there they were to win 10 of the 11 individual titles, breaking, indeed smashing, eight world records. Perhaps the advance in women's swimming standards is best represented by one fact. At the Tokyo Olympics in 1964 U.S. Swimmer Don Schollander broke the world and Olympic record in the 400-m freestyle with a time of 4 min 12.2 sec. In Montreal that time would have achieved only third place in the *women's* 400 m, and Schollander would have had to give way to Petra Thümer of East Germany and his countrywoman Shirley Babashoff.

The 17-year-old Kornelia Ender of East Germany was the heroine of the swimming pool. She won four gold medals and one silver and on one evening gained two of her titles in the space of half an hour, equaling her own world record in the 100-m butterfly and then winning the 200-m freestyle in a new

---

A gold medalist (3,000-m steeplechase) in the 1956 Olympics, Christopher Brasher is sports correspondent to The Observer *and a reporter and producer for BBC Television, London. He is author of* Tokyo 1964, Mexico 1968, *and* Munich 72.

SYGMA

New Zealand's team marches around the track at the opening of the Summer Games. International politics led to the withdrawal of most of the black and North African delegations when their governments opposed the New Zealanders' participation.

world record time. Such dominance by the sportswomen of one nation caused speculation as to how it was achieved. The explanation was simple. The East German sports medicine authorities decided that women can work just as hard in training as men. Indeed, they set work loads for their women that exceeded those of many male swimmers, totaling two hours of weight training and three hours in the water every day. This schedule was later adjusted to one hour of weights to every four in the water. Whatever the balance between weights and water, there was no doubt that five hours of hard training every day amounted to a full-time occupation.

East German domination of the women's events was equaled, if not surpassed, by the U.S. swimmers in the men's events. They won all the Olympic titles (11 of them with new world records) except for the 200-m breaststroke, which went to the British swimmer David Wilkie. Wilkie confessed, however, that he would never have won this gold medal (plus a silver medal in the 100-m breaststroke) if he had stayed in his native Scotland. He was only able to get the facilities he needed for training by attending the University of Miami (Florida).

At the end of the first week, the excitement produced by such outstanding performances was transferred to the Olympic Stadium itself, where a huge Cuban, Alberto Juantorena, was proving to be the sensation of the track and field events. In the heats of the 800 m he looked untutored in tactics and ungainly in stride, but his massive strength and quick brain soon overcame any lack of experience and by the third day he had won his first gold medal with a new world and Olympic 800-m record of 1 min 43.5 sec. Juantorena's tactics were simple: an electrifying first lap of 50.85 sec followed by a display of massive power around the second lap. He went on to win the 400 m as well in the fastest time ever achieved at sea level. (The world record of 43.81 sec by Lee Evans of the U.S. was set in the rarefied air of Mexico City in 1968.)

Equally unexpected was the dual victory of Finland's Lasse Viren in the 5,000 m and 10,000 m, unexpected because of the improbability that a man who had won those two punishing distance events in one Olympic meeting would be able to repeat such an achievement four years later in the next Games; it was something that had never been done before in Olympic history. But Viren, who had won the 10,000 m in 1972 in world record time even after falling in the race, dominated both the 5,000- and 10,000-m fields in Montreal. Undoubtedly, his task was made easier by the absence of the great African runners whose exuberance had made these events so exciting to watch on other occasions, but few people doubted that Viren would have won the two finals even if the Africans had been competing.

Unquestionably, the absence of the Africans affected the atmosphere, for it is the high excitement of knowing that all the best athletes in the world are assembled on the track that not only makes Olympic titles so satisfying for the few who win but which also produces world records. Only Juantorena in the 800 m, Edwin Moses (U.S.) in the 400-m hurdles, and Anders Garderud (Sweden) in the 3,000-m steeplechase were able to break world records on the track. The U.S. trackmen had an uncharacteristically bad Olympics, winning only four individual titles—the 400-m hurdles (Moses), the long jump (Arnie Robinson), the discus (Mac Wilkins), and the decathlon (Bruce Jenner).

What was expected to be the most keenly contested track event of the Games, the men's 1,500 m, proved a great disappointment. The world record holder, Filbert Bayi, stayed at home in Tanzania because of the African boycott, and in his absence John Walker of New Zealand seemed to terrify his opponents by the simple fact of being the only man in the world to have run the mile in less than 3 min 50 sec. And so the 1,500-m final, on the last day of track racing, was a pitiful dawdle with Walker winning in 3 min 39.17 sec, nearly 7 sec (or some 50 yd) slower than Bayi's world record.

Perhaps the disappointment of that race symbolized the Montreal Games: born in a time of comparative political peace (1970), they became dominated by the fear of a repetition of the terrorist attack on the 1972 Munich Games and were then disrupted by the African boycott. Certainly there were many problems, most of them political, which the IOC must try to resolve before the next Olympic Games in Moscow in 1980. (For additional commentaries on events in the Montreal Olympics *see also* BASKETBALL; COMBAT SPORTS; COURT GAMES; CYCLING; EQUESTRIAN SPORTS; FIELD HOCKEY AND LACROSSE; FOOTBALL; GYMNASTICS AND WEIGHT LIFTING; ROWING; SAILING; TARGET SPORTS; WATER SPORTS. Several of the leading athletes are profiled in a special illustrated section of the BIOGRAPHY article.)

OLYMPIC CHAMPIONS, 1976 SUMMER GAMES, MONTREAL

Archery

Men's round D. Pace (U.S.) 2,571 pt* Women's round L. Ryon (U.S.) 2,499 pt*

Basketball

Winning men's team United States (beat Yugoslavia 95–74 in final)	Winning women's team U.S.S.R. (won all five final matches)

Boxing

Light flyweight	J. Hernandez (Cuba)	Welterweight	J. Bachfeld (E. Ger.)
Flyweight	L. Randolph (U.S.)	Light middleweight	J. Rybicki (Pol.)
Bantamweight	Yong Jo Gu (N. Kor.)	Middleweight	M. Spinks (U.S.)
Featherweight	A. Herrera (Cuba)	Light heavyweight	L. Spinks (U.S.)
Lightweight	H. Davis (U.S.)	Heavyweight	T. Stevenson (Cuba)
Light welterweight	R. Leonard (U.S.)		

Canoeing

Men		
500-m Canadian singles	A. Rogov (U.S.S.R.)	1 min 59.23 sec
500-m Canadian pairs	U.S.S.R.	1 min 45.81 sec
500-m kayak singles	V. Diba (Romania)	1 min 46.41 sec
500-m kayak pairs	East Germany	1 min 35.87 sec
1,000-m Canadian singles	M. Ljubek (Yugoslavia)	4 min 09.51 sec
1,000-m Canadian pairs	U.S.S.R.	3 min 52.76 sec
1,000-m kayak singles	R. Helm (East Germany)	3 min 48.20 sec
1,000-m kayak pairs	U.S.S.R.	3 min 29.01 sec
1,000-m kayak fours	U.S.S.R.	3 min 08.69 sec
Women		
500-m kayak singles	C. Zirzow (East Germany)	2 min 01.05 sec
500-m kayak pairs	U.S.S.R.	1 min 51.15 sec

Cycling

Sprint	A. Tkac (Czechoslovakia)	10.78 sec (best 200 m)
1,000-m time trial	K.-J. Grünke (E. Ger.)	1 min 05.927 sec
4,000-m individual pursuit	G. Braun (West Germany)	4 min 47.61 sec
4,000-m team pursuit	West Germany	4 min 21.06 sec
100-km team time trial	U.S.S.R.	2 hr 08 min 53.0 sec
Road race	B. Johansson (Sweden)	4 hr 46 min 52.0 sec

Equestrian Sports

	Individual	*Team*
Dressage	C. Stückelberger (Switz.) on Granat	West Germany
3-day event	E. Coffin (U.S.) on Bally-Cor	United States
Show jumping	A. Schockemohle (W. Ger.) on Warwick Rex	France

Fencing

	Individual	*Team*
Foil	F. Dal Zotto (Italy)	West Germany
Epée	A. Pusch (West Germany)	Sweden
Sabre	V. Krovopouskov (U.S.S.R.)	U.S.S.R.
Women's foil	I. Schwarczenberger (Hungary)	U.S.S.R.

Football (Soccer)

Winning team East Germany (beat Poland 3–1 in final)

Gymnastics

	Men	*Women*
Combined exercises		
individual	N. Andrianov (U.S.S.R.)	N. Comaneci (Romania)
team	Japan	U.S.S.R.
Parallel bars	S. Kato (Japan)	—
Uneven parallel bars	—	N. Comaneci (Romania)
Horizontal bar	M. Tsukahara (Japan)	—
Horse vaults	N. Andrianov (U.S.S.R.)	N. Kim (U.S.S.R.)
Pommeled horse	Z. Magyar (Hungary)	—
Rings	N. Andrianov (U.S.S.R.)	—
Balance beam	—	N. Comaneci (Romania)
Floor exercises	N. Andrianov (U.S.S.R.)	N. Kim (U.S.S.R.)

Handball

Winning men's team U.S.S.R. (beat Romania 19–15 in final)	Winning women's team U.S.S.R. (beat East Germany 14–11 in final)

Hockey (Field)

Winning team New Zealand (beat Australia 1–0 in final)

Judo

Lightweight	H. Rodriguez (Cuba)	Light heavywt.	K. Ninomiya (Japan)
Light middlewt.	V. Nevzorov (U.S.S.R.)	Heavyweight	S. Novikov (U.S.S.R.)
Middleweight	I. Sonoda (Japan)	Open class	H. Uemura (Japan)

Modern Pentathlon

Individual	J. Pyciak-Peciak (Poland)	5,520 pt*
Team	United Kingdom	15,559 pt

Rowing

Men (2,000-m course)		
Single sculls	P. Karppinen (Finland)	7 min 29.03 sec
Double sculls	Norway	7 min 13.20 sec
Quadruple sculls	East Germany	6 min 18.65 sec
Pairs with coxswain	East Germany	7 min 58.99 sec
Pairs without coxswain	East Germany	7 min 23.31 sec
Fours with coxswain	U.S.S.R.	6 min 40.22 sec
Fours without coxswain	East Germany	6 min 37.42 sec
Eights with coxswain	East Germany	5 min 58.29 sec
Women (1,000-m course)		
Single sculls	C. Scheiblich (E. Ger.)	4 min 05.56 sec
Double sculls	Bulgaria	3 min 44.36 sec
Quadruple sculls	East Germany	3 min 29.99 sec
Pairs without coxswain	Bulgaria	4 min 01.22 sec
Fours with coxswain	East Germany	3 min 45.08 sec
Eights with coxswain	East Germany	3 min 33.32 sec

Shooting

Free pistol	U. Potteck (East Germany)	573 pt†
Small-bore rifle (prone)	K. Smieszek (West Germany)	599 pt§
Small-bore rifle (3-position)	L. Bassham (U.S.)	1,162 pt
Rapid-fire pistol	N. Klaar (East Germany)	597 pt*
Trapshooting	D. Haldeman (U.S.)	190 pt
Skeet shooting	J. Panacek (Czechoslovakia)	198 pt‡
Moving target	A. Gazov (U.S.S.R.)	579 pt†

*Olympic record. †World record. ‡Equals Olympic record. §Equals World record. ‖Best Olympic performance.

Swimming and Diving

Men		
100-m freestyle	J. Montgomery (U.S.)	49.99 sec†
200-m freestyle	B. Furniss (U.S.)	1 min 50.29 sec†
400-m freestyle	B. Goodell (U.S.)	3 min 51.93 sec†
1,500-m freestyle	B. Goodell (U.S.)	15 min 02.40 sec†
100-m backstroke	J. Naber (U.S.)	55.49 sec†
200-m backstroke	J. Naber (U.S.)	1 min 59.19 sec†
100-m breaststroke	J. Hencken (U.S.)	1 min 03.11 sec†
200-m breaststroke	D. Wilkie (U.K.)	2 min 15.11 sec†
100-m butterfly	M. Vogel (U.S.)	54.35 sec
200-m butterfly	M. Bruner (U.S.)	1 min 59.23 sec†
400-m individual medley	R. Strachan (U.S.)	4 min 23.68 sec†
800-m freestyle relay	United States	7 min 23.22 sec†
400-m medley relay	United States	3 min 42.22 sec†
Springboard diving	P. Boggs (U.S.)	619.05 pt
Platform diving	K. Di Biasi (Italy)	600.51 pt
Women		
100-m freestyle	K. Ender (East Germany)	55.65 sec†
200-m freestyle	K. Ender (East Germany)	1 min 59.26 sec†
400-m freestyle	P. Thümer (East Germany)	4 min 09.89 sec†
800-m freestyle	P. Thümer (East Germany)	8 min 37.14 sec†
100-m backstroke	U. Richter (East Germany)	1 min 01.83 sec*
200-m backstroke	U. Richter (East Germany)	2 min 13.43 sec*
100-m breaststroke	H. Anke (East Germany)	1 min 11.16 sec
200-m breaststroke	M. Koshevaia (U.S.S.R.)	2 min 33.35 sec†
100-m butterfly	K. Ender (East Germany)	1 min 00.13 sec§
200-m butterfly	A. Pollack (East Germany)	2 min 11.41 sec*
400-m individual medley	U. Tauber (East Germany)	4 min 42.77 sec†
400-m freestyle relay	United States	3 min 44.82 sec†
400-m medley relay	East Germany	4 min 07.95 sec†
Springboard diving	J. Chandler (U.S.)	506.19 pt
Platform diving	E. Vaytsekhovskaia (U.S.S.R.)	406.59 pt

Track and Field

Men		
100-m dash	H. Crawford (Trinidad and Tobago)	10.06 sec
200-m dash	D. Quarrie (Jamaica)	20.23 sec
400-m dash	A. Juantorena (Cuba)	44.26 sec
800-m run	A. Juantorena (Cuba)	1 min 43.50 sec†
1,500-m run	J. Walker (New Zealand)	3 min 39.17 sec
5,000-m run	L. Viren (Finland)	13 min 24.76 sec
10,000-m run	L. Viren (Finland)	27 min 40.38 sec
Marathon	W. Cierpinski (E. Ger.)	2 hr 09 min 55.0 sec‖
110-m hurdles	G. Drut (France)	13.30 sec
400-m hurdles	E. Moses (U.S.)	47.64 sec†
3,000-m steeplechase	A. Garderud (Sweden)	8 min 08.02 sec†
400-m relay	United States	38.33 sec
1,600-m relay	United States	2 min 58.65 sec
20-km walk	D. Bautista (Mexico)	1 hr 24 min 40.6 sec‖
High jump	J. Wszola (Poland)	2.25 m*
Long jump	A. Robinson (U.S.)	8.35 m
Pole vault	T. Slusarski (Poland)	5.50 m‡
Triple jump	V. Saneyev (U.S.S.R.)	17.29 m
Shot put	U. Beyer (East Germany)	21.05 m
Discus	M. Wilkins (U.S.)	67.50 m
Hammer throw	Y. Sedykh (U.S.S.R.)	77.52 m*
Javelin	M. Nemeth (Hungary)	94.58 m†
Decathlon	B. Jenner (U.S.)	8,618 pt†
Women		
100-m dash	A. Richter (West Germany)	11.08 sec
200-m dash	B. Eckert (East Germany)	22.37 sec*
400-m dash	I. Szewinska (Poland)	49.29 sec†
800-m run	T. Kazankina (U.S.S.R.)	1 min 54.94 sec†
1,500-m run	T. Kazankina (U.S.S.R.)	4 min 05.48 sec
100-m hurdles	J. Schaller (East Germany)	12.77 sec
400-m relay	East Germany	42.55 sec*
1,600-m relay	East Germany	3 min 19.23 sec†
High jump	R. Ackermann (East Germany)	1.93 m*
Long jump	A. Voigt (East Germany)	6.72 m
Shot put	I. Christova (Bulgaria)	21.16 m*
Discus	E. Schlaak (East Germany)	69.00 m*
Javelin	R. Fuchs (East Germany)	65.94 m*
Pentathlon	S. Siegl (East Germany)	4,745 pt

Volleyball

Winning men's team Poland (beat U.S.S.R. 3–2 in final)	Winning women's team Japan (beat U.S.S.R. 3–0 in final)

Water Polo

Winning team Hungary (won 4 and tied 1 of the final matches)

Weight Lifting

Flyweight	A. Voronin (U.S.S.R.)	242.5 kg§
Bantamweight	N. Nourikian (Bulgaria)	262.5 kg†
Featherweight	N. Kolesnikov (U.S.S.R.)	285.0 kg*
Lightweight	disqualification	—
Middleweight	Y. Mitkov (Bulgaria)	335.0 kg*
Light heavyweight	V. Shary (U.S.S.R.)	365.0 kg*
Middle heavyweight	D. Rigert (U.S.S.R.)	382.5 kg*
Heavyweight	disqualification	—
Superheavyweight	V. Alekseyev (U.S.S.R.)	440.0 kg*

Wrestling

	Freestyle	*Greco-Roman*
Paperweight	K. Issaev (Bulgaria)	A. Shumakov (U.S.S.R.)
Flyweight	Y. Takada (Japan)	V. Konstantinov (U.S.S.R.)
Bantamweight	V. Umin (U.S.S.R.)	P. Ukkola (Finland)
Featherweight	Jung-Mo Yang (S. Kor.)	K. Lipien (Poland)
Lightweight	P. Pinigin (U.S.S.R.)	S. Nalbandyan (U.S.S.R.)
Welterweight	J. Date (Japan)	A. Bykov (U.S.S.R.)
Middleweight	J. Peterson (U.S.)	M. Petkovic (Yugoslavia)
Light heavyweight	L. Tediashvili (U.S.S.R.)	V. Rezantsev (U.S.S.R.)
Heavyweight	I. Yarygin (U.S.S.R.)	N. Bolboshin (U.S.S.R.)
Superheavyweight	S. Andiev (U.S.S.R.)	A. Kolchinski (U.S.S.R.)

Yachting

Finn class	J. Shumann (East Germany)
Flying Dutchman class	J. Diesch (West Germany)
Tempest class	J. Albrechtson (Sweden)
Soling class	P. Jensen (Denmark)
Tornado class	R. White (U.K.)
470 class	F. Hübner (West Germany)

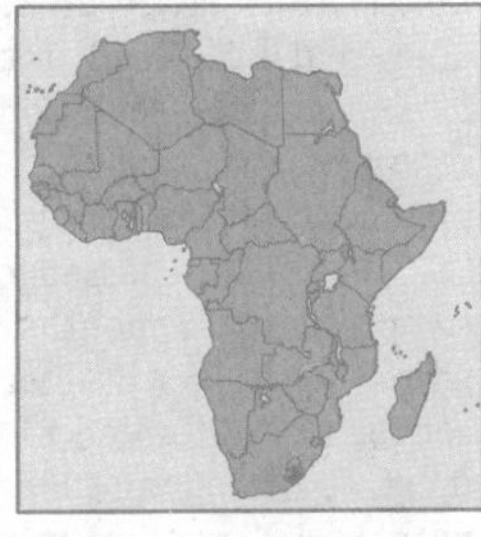

Transkei

A republic in southern Africa and a Bantu homeland, Transkei borders the Indian Ocean and is surrounded on land by South Africa. Area: 14,176 sq mi (36,716 sq km). Pop. (1976 est.): 1.9 million permanent, with 1,050,000 resident permanently outside Transkei (in South Africa) and 350,000 migrant workers temporarily outside; whites (1970 census) 9,556; Coloureds 7,645. Cap.: Umtata (pop., 1975 est., 29,100). Language: Xhosa, Sesotho, and English. Religion: largely Christian. President in 1976, Paramount Chief Botha Sigcau; prime minister, Paramount Chief Kaiser Daliwonga Matanzima.

Established as an independent republic on Oct. 26, 1976, by South Africa under the Status of the Transkei Act, Transkei has a single-chamber Parliament of 150 members, with a president and a Cabinet headed by the prime minister. At independence, the Transkei National Independence Party held 145 seats and was led by Kaiser Daliwonga Matanzima (*see* BIOGRAPHY), as prime minister.

Transkei established diplomatic relations with South Africa at the ambassadorial level. On October 26 the UN General Assembly decided unanimously, with one abstention (the U.S.), not to recognize Transkeian independence. An agricultural and pastoral region, Transkei continued to depend on financial aid from South Africa and on the earnings of Transkeians outside the territory. Under the Transkeian Development Corporation, sponsored by South Africa, secondary industries were encouraged, mainly at Umtata and Butterworth. Among the first acts of the new republic were acceptance of the principle of multiracial schools and the planning of a university.

Transkei joined the South African customs union in October. It had rail and air communications with South Africa and a small natural harbour, Port St. Johns. Transkei possessed a South African trained and officered defense force. (LOUIS HOTZ)

[978.E.8.b.i]

TRANSKEI

Education. (1972) Primary, secondary, and vocational, pupils 453,581, teachers 8,024; teacher training, students 1,624.

Finance and Trade. Monetary unit: South African rand, with (Sept. 20, 1976) an official rate of R 0.87 to U.S. $1 (free rate of R 1.49 = £1 sterling). Most trade is with South Africa.

Agriculture. Production (in 000; metric tons; 1974): wool 2; mohair 0.03. Livestock (in 000; 1974): cattle 1,306; sheep 2,200; goats 1,014; pigs 515; horses 76.

Transportation

Two major themes ran through 1976. The first, a continued demand by governments for economies in transport budgets, led to proposals in several countries to cut the railways' losses, even at the expense of eliminating routes, and to a critical approach toward large investments in mass transit. The second theme, a major debate in Britain, was set off by the publication in April of a consultation document on transport policy written by Anthony Crosland, then secretary of state for the environment. The document's tough attitude toward railways and its moderate approach to road transport excited much angry comment.

VICTOR DE LA PORTE—GAMMA/LIAISON

Farmers in the Transkei following their oxen home from the fields. About a third of the "citizens" of the new state live elsewhere.

Railway finances came under discussion in the U.S., Britain, West Germany, Japan, and Canada. In West Germany the Deutsche Bundesbahn published a plan to halve both the 18,000-mi rail system and the number of stations. The truncated network would still carry 90% of the freight and 95% of the passengers moved by the larger system. The plan also proposed that the work force be reduced from 360,000 employees to 250,000.

In Japan the railways promised greater efficiency and a tougher line with the unions, who would be sued for damages suffered during strike action. The Japan Economic Research Council opposed higher fares, arguing that increased prosperity had not resulted in more rail travel. Nonetheless, the Japanese government approved fare increases of 50%.

In Canada it was proposed that some services be cut and subsidies increased on the remainder. Duplication of services between Canadian National and Canadian Pacific on 2,000 mi of line was discussed. The prestigious transcontinental services attracted a large share of subsidy but a small share of passengers.

ConRail, a federally aided U.S. company established in 1975, embarked on the task of rejuvenating the seven bankrupt northeast railway companies that it had taken over. The Department of Transportation issued a study showing that 30% of the country's rail system (60,000 mi) moved only 1% of the rail freight.

The British government's annual review of public expenditure forecast that rail freight subsidies would be phased out gradually, that there would be no increase in the passenger subsidy, and that investment was to be 30% less than British Rail's original plan.

In his document, Crosland argued that car ownership would continue to grow despite the oil crisis; that road users, including trucks, paid far more than the direct cost of providing the roads, although the heaviest trucks were an exception to this; that, although railways received higher subsidies than buses, they were used largely by the rich while buses were more heavily used by the less affluent; and that even if British Rail could increase its freight by 50%, road traffic would only be cut by 2% and truck traffic by 8%. These conclusions raised a storm of protest, and Crosland's calculations, notably the road traffic fore-

Trade, International: *see* Economy, World

Trade Unions: *see* Industrial Relations

Traffic Accidents: *see* Disasters

DAVID POTTS NEWS (MIDLANDS) LTD.

Ancient Welshmen paddled around in coracles like this one, made by covering a hoop with tarpaulin. Eustace Rogers of Ironbridge, England, commutes to work in it across the River Severn.

casts, were questioned. Later in the year a more left-wing politician, Peter Shore, took over Crosland's job, and it appeared that the strategy might be scrapped. However, transport was then removed from the Department of the Environment altogether and given to a new secretary of state, William Rodgers, with Rodgers and Shore having joint responsibility for big road-building projects.

British action groups took the controversy into their own hands and shouted down several of the public inquiries that had to be held on the construction of major roads. Eventually, they won their point that such inquiries should consider the government's national transport forecasts and not merely the local proposal in isolation. (*See* ENVIRONMENT.)

Figures were released showing that road traffic in the U.S. had increased by nearly 2% in 1975, half the pre-oil-crisis growth rate. Pilot schemes for traffic restraint in some of the large cities were considered. In Britain the Greater London Council planned to tax office parking lots, while in Asia, Kuala Lumpur proposed to follow Singapore's successful use of road tolls to discourage commuters from using their cars. A British survey showed that two-thirds of car owners used their cars to get to work. Special lanes for cyclists were provided in a number of European cities.

(RICHARD CASEMENT)

AVIATION

The airline industry experienced somewhat improved conditions in 1976; traffic growth was more encouraging than in 1975, and financial results were better. Nonetheless, considerable doubt was expressed about the airlines' ability to finance new fleets. The International Air Transport Association (IATA) estimated that more than $45 billion would be needed for acquiring new aircraft within the next decade. Traffic growth in the first half of 1976 was described as "encouraging" by IATA's director general, Knut Hammarskjöld, in his annual report in November. IATA forecast an average growth rate of 8% per year in international scheduled passenger traffic for 1975–81.

In the first nine months of 1976, the 11 U.S. trunk airlines, which carried more than one-third of world traffic (U.S.S.R. included), reported a 14.6% increase in passenger traffic over the corresponding period of 1975, a total of 211,027,700,000 revenue passenger-km. With capacity up 8.7%, to 369,714,200,000 available seat-km, load factor improved from 54.2 to 57.1%. The Association of European Airlines (AEA) reported that for the 12 months to June 1976 its members' intra-European passenger traffic totaled 36,004,800,000 passenger-km, an 11% increase over the previous 12 months. Load factor was 56.2%, compared with 53.4%. On intercontinental flights passenger traffic totaled 81,727,000,000 passenger-km, an increase of 7%, and load factor was 56.8%, compared with 56.1%. AEA members' freight traffic for the period rose 7% to 619,227,000 metric ton-km on intra-European flights and 4,524,315,000 metric ton-km on intercontinental flights.

On the North Atlantic routes there were signs of renewed traffic growth. In the first half of 1976 the number of passengers carried by IATA airlines on scheduled and charter flights rose by 13% compared with the first half of 1975, representing a distinct improvement. In 1975 there had been a 4.2% decline in passengers compared with 1974; increases in scheduled traffic in 1975 had been the lowest recorded for ten years, and growth in freight was only 0.2%.

Data on scheduled airline traffic in 1975 released by the International Civil Aviation Organization (ICAO) put the U.S. in first place with 38% of traffic and the U.S.S.R. in second with 16%. The U.K., France, and Japan were third, fourth, and fifth with around 4% each.

International nonscheduled traffic in 1975 was down 0.8% from 1974 following a significant decrease in that year. The 1975 figures showed that 25.9% of the world's passenger traffic had been on nonscheduled flights, compared with 27% in 1974. Nonscheduled carriers had increased their share of nonscheduled traffic from 62% in 1974 to 65%. The financial situation remained poor. For IATA scheduled services, excess of revenue over costs in the 1975–76 fiscal year, at $110 million, amounted to less than 1% of operating revenue—a marginal improvement over 1974–75, when there was a slight operating loss. IATA quoted a $1,650,000,000 shortfall on its target of a 12.4% return on investment. The North Atlantic, the largest of IATA's main route areas, showed the greatest shortfall in 1975–76, more than $600 million.

Results for the 1976–77 fiscal year looked more encouraging. An operating result of $430 million, or 3.4% of revenue, was predicted toward the close of 1976. Nonetheless, IATA reported that the industry still faced "a massive shortfall from required earnings." Unit operating costs per available metric ton-kilometre for IATA scheduled international operations rose by more than 7% in 1975–76. In the current financial year a cost increase of less than 2% was anticipated, thanks to comparatively small rises in fuel costs and tighter control of other cost items.

World Total International and Domestic Air Traffic

	Passengers		Passenger-km		Freight (metric ton-km)		Total (metric ton-km)	
Year	In 000,000	Annual increase (%)	In 000,000	Annual increase (%)	In 000,000	Annual increase (%)	In 000,000	Annual increase (%)
1971	411	7.5	494,000	7.4	13,220	9.6	60,470	6.7
1972	450	9.6	560,000	13.4	15,020	13.6	68,160	12.7
1973	489	8.7	619,000	10.4	17,540	16.8	75,810	11.2
1974	514	5.1	654,000	5.8	19,010	8.4	80,550	6.3
1975	536	4.2	691,000	5.6	19,110	0.5	83,930	4.2

Note: Includes U.S.S.R.; excludes China and some small states not affiliated with the ICAO.
Source: International Civil Aviation Organization.

For the U.S. airlines, a spokesman for the Air Transport Association of America (ATA) predicted in September that net profit for 1976 would amount to between $250 million and $350 million. In the first half of the year, U.S. trunk carriers reported a net profit of almost $140 million, a considerable improvement over 1975 when, according to the U.S. Civil Aeronautics Board (CAB), the trunks suffered a net loss of $104,026,000. The eight local-service airlines had a loss of $1,772,000, but the supplemental or nonscheduled airlines showed a net income of $17.7 million in 1975.

Perhaps the most newsworthy event of 1976 was the inauguration of Concorde supersonic services by Air France and British Airways to Rio de Janeiro and Bahrain, respectively, on January 21. In the U.S., where environmentalists had voiced considerable concern over possible noise pollution, the authorities allowed both airlines to fly to Washington's Dulles International Airport for a 16-month trial period. Equally significant but attracting less public attention was the notice given by the U.K. in June that it would renounce the 1946 Bermuda Agreement—the bilateral agreement governing air services between Britain and the U.S.—12 months later unless a new agreement could be negotiated. The U.K. was concerned to redress a large alleged imbalance of earnings in favour of U.S. carriers on routes governed by the agreement. Observers believed that the British move might herald attempts by other countries to renegotiate bilateral agreements with the U.S.

In the U.S., 1976 closed with many important aviation issues clouded by doubts that would not be resolved until President-elect Jimmy Carter took office early in 1977. These included the international situation, particularly with regard to the British action. Control of aircraft noise and financing of noise reduction measures were also left pending, as was "deregulation"—liberalization of the system of economic regulation of the U.S. airline industry.

(DAVID WOOLLEY)

SHIPPING AND PORTS

World movement of nonliquid cargoes rose in 1976, but the increase was not significant, and experts feared a return to the traditional boom and bust cycle that had characterized shipping since the late 1960s. Seaborne trade for 1976 was below the 1975 level, which in turn had been 6.5% below 1974. The greatest drop was in the movement of oil, down nearly 10%, while iron ore, coal, and grain were down by nearly 8%. Although cargo movements fell, tonnage rose to a total of 560 million tons deadweight (dw).

There was little improvement in tankers and only a slight rise in freight rates. With tanker tonnage in surplus and a further 428 vessels on order, special efforts were made to reduce the excess. Several orders were canceled or converted to other vessel types, and the rate of scrapping was increased. Some 45 million tons dw of tankers were laid up, along with approximately 6 million tons dw of combined carriers. The Soviet tanker fleet, consisting almost entirely of vessels below 80,000 tons dw, continued to grow, however, reaching 481 vessels, an aggregate of 3.7 million gross tons, with a further 45 tankers on order.

As overage vessels were withdrawn from service and as oil-producing states took steps to develop their own home-based refining facilities and marketing structures, interest in product carriers increased. By 1976, 403 combined carriers (oil/ore) totaling 44.7 million tons dw were in service, and these provided nearly 44% of the capacity in the oil trade. This section was threatened, however, by the large number of new vessels—54—under construction.

Caution was the watchword in the dry cargo market, but several orders were placed for multipurpose, high-class cargo liners. More roll-on/roll-off vessels were needed to overcome port congestion, particularly in the Middle East. The use of very large seagoing barges pushed or pulled by high-powered tugs also increased. Worldwide grain movements fell by more than 15% compared with 1975, but general cargo business began to expand. It was estimated that by the end of 1976 all the 1975 losses would have been made good.

Port development was concentrated in the Middle East, particularly in the Red Sea area. A large harbour complex was being built at Port Rashid near Dubai. At Dammam $1 billion was committed to the doubling of the port's capacity by 1980, and at Jubail $944 million was to be spent on a new harbour with an annual capacity for 10 million tons of cargo. It was hoped to raise the capacity of Jizan from 100,000 tons per year to 500,000 tons at a cost of $118 million. In Europe container facilities were increased at Bremerhaven and Hamburg, West Germany. The giant new port at Marseilles-Fossé in France neared completion.

In the first full year after the Suez Canal was reopened in June 1975, average daily net tonnage through the canal was about 180,000. In July nearly 1,500 vessels had used the canal in both directions. The canal was to be deepened to increase the permissible draft from 38 to 53 ft, and maximum loaded deadweight of ships using it would eventually rise from 60,000 to 130,000 tons. A 250,000-ton-dw tanker could use the canal in ballast, but there would be no rush back to the canal until tanker freight rates rose and the current slow-steaming policy ended.

(W. D. EWART)

FREIGHT MOVEMENTS

Freight movements picked up in response to the slow economic recovery, though there was still plenty of spare capacity. The Swiss railways were among the beneficiaries. The West German railways revived a piggyback service (trucks on trains) because of shortages of road permits on routes to the prosperous Middle East. European road and rail freight was also helped by the European drought, since low river levels meant that much traffic normally carried by barges

The passengers on this ship sailing from Australia in April were 51,000 sheep bound for Iran. The former oil tanker was refitted with pens and a conveyor system for feeding the sheep twice a day. Iran does not import killed sheep because of religious laws.

UPI COMPIX

World Transportation

Country	Railways: Route length in 000 km	Railways Traffic: Passenger in 000,000 pass.-km	Railways Traffic: Freight in 000,000 net ton-km	Motor transport: Road length in 000 km	Motor transport: Vehicles in use: Passenger in 000	Motor transport: Vehicles in use: Commercial in 000	Merchant shipping (Ships of 100 tons and over): Number of vessels	Merchant shipping: Gross reg. tons in 000	Air traffic: Total km flown in 000,000	Air traffic: Passenger in 000,000 pass.-km	Air traffic: Freight in 000,000 net ton-km
EUROPE											
Austria	6.5	6,790	11,237	102.7	1,636.0	152.0	55	75	13.7	677	8.2
Belgium	4.0	8,257	6,731	92.8	2,474.0	249.0	252	1,358	48.4	3,886	289.1
Bulgaria	4.3	7,569	17,286	31.2	c.160.0*	c.38.0*	179	937	9.3	385	7.0
Cyprus	—	—	—	9.5	67.0	15.4	735	3,221	2.9	115	1.4
Czechoslovakia	13.2	18,190	69,271	145.5	1,234.4	265.0	13	116	24.6	1,366	17.5
Denmark	2.0†	3,190†	2,040†	65.7	1,256.3	211.1	1,371	4,478	31.0‡	2,185‡	97.8‡
Finland	5.9	3,132	6,438	73.3	936.7	124.9	361	2,002	29.2	1,259	31.6
France	34.4	50,980	64,033	794.1	15,180.0	2,075.0	1,393	10,746	239.6	23,272	1,086.1
Germany, East	14.3	21,304	49,681	126.9	1,703.0	225.7	437	1,389	24.3	1,315	42.8
Germany, West	32.1	37,759	55,062	462.2	17,356.0	1,244.0	1,964	8,517	170.4	13,635	993.4
Greece	2.5	1,594	931	36.4	379.9	170.7	2,743	22,527	32.3	3,430	36.5
Hungary	8.4	13,686	22,961	100.6	490.8	107.2	16	48	11.4	558	6.2
Ireland	2.2	824	475	87.2*	487.5	52.9	93	210	19.6	1,487	71.0
Italy	16.1†	36,387	14,962	288.4*	14,295.0	1,080.9	1,732	10,137	146.3	11,377	461.0
Netherlands, The	2.8	8,502	2,722	82.9	3,440.0	320.0	1,348	5,679	94.2	10,132	615.1
Norway	4.2	1,884	2,886	76.1	890.4	145.0	2,706	26,154	48.4‡	2,964‡	105.8‡
Poland	23.8	42,918	129,230	299.6	920.3	386.0	696	2,817	21.2	1,309	13.9
Portugal	3.6	4,552	867	46.0	989.7	48.0	440	1,210	55.4	3,135	70.7
Romania	11.1	22,406	61,618	95.2	c.125.0*	c.50.0*	122	777	13.7	574	8.2
Spain	16.0*	16,079	11,887	142.6	4,309.5	950.5	2,667	5,433	129.4	10,694	237.9
Sweden	12.1	5,332	19,598	112.8	2,638.9	153.8	775	7,486	60.1‡	3,629‡	152.4‡
Switzerland	5.0*	7,984	5,141	61.3	1,728.1	165.4	29	194	80.0	7,564	308.5
U.S.S.R.	263.8*	306,298	3,233,000	1,421.6	c.3,000.0	c.4,000.0	7,652	19,236	...	108,577	2,475.3
United Kingdom	18.2§	36,130§	24,168§	c.366.0	c.13,980.0	c.1,811.0	3,622	33,157	340.0	27,766	852.5
Yugoslavia	10.3	10,243	21,606	110.3	1,333.0	136.1	414	1,873	24.9	1,967	14.6
ASIA											
Bangladesh	2.9	3,331	639	c.24.0*	31.7*	24.8*	120	133	...	...	...
Burma	4.3*	3,121	395	21.7	36.3	39.3	39	55	6.8	180	2.5
Cambodia	0.6*	54*	10*	15.0*	27.2*	11.1*	3*	2*	1.0	48	0.5
China	c.48.0	45,670*	301,000*	c.700.0	c.30.0*	c.650.0*	466	2,828	...	64*	2.0*
India	60.1*	134,747	143,098	1,232.3	771.9	413.0	471	3,869	57.6	4,926	182.0
Indonesia	c.7.8	2,726*	1,068*	84.9*	307.6*	174.2*	724	859	47.2	2,204	44.9
Iran	4.6	2,144*	4,432*	43.4*	393.9*	87.6*	135	480	18.7	1,390	20.6
Iraq	2.0	633	1,707	11.1	83.4	59.0	56	311	6.6	533	7.5
Israel	0.9	323	464	10.7	267.4	94.8	65	451	29.8	3,107	135.1
Japan	27.5*	323,192	47,911	1,058.9	15,854.0	10,825.0	9,932	39,740	263.2	17,544	842.0
Korea, South	5.5*	12,703	9,107	44.2	76.5	96.9	828	1,624	32.4	2,753	204.7
Malaysia	1.8	986‖	989‖	23.9*	430.4	140.3	129	359	24.8	1,633	29.9
Pakistan	8.8	c.11,600	c.7,344	62.8*	177.3*	79.1*	84	479	25.1	2,623	130.0
Philippines	1.1*	899	70	92.8	362.5	247.3	413	879	38.5	2,050	51.3
Saudi Arabia	0.6	61*	62*	34.4	134.2	114.9	55	180	21.8	1,268	37.4
Syria	0.9*	145	152	16.7*	37.3	23.1	14	8	6.4	322	2.2
Taiwan	4.3	8,345	2,853	16.2	126.0	101.0	428	1,450	18.0*	954*	25.2*
Thailand	3.8	5,484	2,296	27.5*	316.9	188.7	84	183	27.4	2,845	63.3
Turkey	8.1	5,753	6,418	59.5	c.303.8	c.230.8	387	995	19.2	1,471	11.4
AFRICA											
Algeria	4.0	1,058	1,901	78.4	180.0	95.0	78	246	19.2	997	6.4
Benin	0.6	101	129	6.9	14.0	8.6	5	1	1.5¶	101¶	11.3¶
Central African Empire	—	—	—	21.5	c.9.1	c.3.9	—	—	2.0¶	106¶	11.3¶
Chad	—	—	—	30.7	5.8*	6.3*	—	—	2.6¶	119¶	12.2¶
Congo	0.8	223	461	c.11.0	19.0	10.5	8	2	2.4¶	111¶	11.6¶
Egypt	4.5	7,258*	2,561*	c.26.0*	184.5	40.2	143	301	19.3	1,285	17.7
Gabon	—	—	—	6.8*	9.4*	7.5*	15	107	3.1¶	128¶	11.4¶
Ghana	1.0	520*	305*	c.31.0*	40.4*	31.0*	82	180	3.6	149	4.0
Ivory Coast	0.7*	918	529	36.1*	c.90.5*	c.57.4*	49	119	2.0¶	109¶	11.4¶
Kenya	2.1*	4,529*♀	3,998♀	49.7	122.4	18.2	19	17	10.1♂	715♂	21.4♂
Malawi	0.6	89	275	12.1	10.6	9.5	—	—	2.6	80	1.1
Mali	0.6*	95*	152*	14.7	4.5*	5.7*	—	—	1.8	77	1.9
Morocco	2.1	792	2,843	25.4*	258.2*	91.4*	53	80	10.9	693	7.8
Nigeria	3.5*	890	1,343	89.0*	c.150.0*	c.82.0*	84	142	9.4	355	8.3
Rhodesia	3.4	...	6,436□	78.9	c.180.0	c.70.0	...	...	5.8	259	2.2
Senegal	1.0*	220	392	13.3*	44.8	25.0	56	23	2.2¶	112¶	11.3¶
South Africa	19.9	...	63,850◇	c.320.0*	1,950.3	719.1	286	566	55.0	5,946	155.1
Tanzania	3.5	4,529*♀	3,998♀	c.18.0	c.39.1	c.42.3	17	33	4.2♂	154♂	3.6♂
Tunisia	1.9*	588	1,283	18.8*	115.1	76.2	28	41	8.1	898	6.5
Uganda	1.2	4,529*♀	3,998♀	27.5	27.0	8.9	1	6	2.3♂	150♂	5.7♂
Zaire	5.3	447*	3,017*	c.140.0*	84.8	76.4	28	85	14.4	655	35.4
Zambia	c.2.2	320*	897*	35.0*	86.0	62.0	1	6	7.1	362	20.8
NORTH AND CENTRAL AMERICA											
Canada	70.1*	3,023	202,433	3,033.0	8,472.0	2,390.0	1,257	2,566	291.7	23,111	580.7
Costa Rica	0.6	c.97*	c.20*	c18.0*	52.1*	34.4*	14	6	6.3	306	9.1
Cuba	14.9	946*	1,504*	18.9	c.70.0*	c.33.0*	272	476	7.8	528	12.1
El Salvador	0.6	...	...	10.7*	38.5*	19.0*	2	2	...	...	...
Guatemala	c.0.9	...	106*	13.4*	54.1*	36.9*	7	10	2.8	100	4.8
Honduras	c.1.0	174*	3*	5.9*	c.14.7	22.9	60	68	5.7	226	2.7
Mexico	24.6*	4,614▲	31,094▲	172.1	1,943.2	709.9	274	575	87.8	5,957	76.4
Nicaragua	0.4	28*	14*	13.1*	c.32.0*	c.20.0*	26	33	2.2	78	2.0
Panama	0.3	...	...	7.1	69.8	16.1	2,418	13,667	...	...	...
United States	332.7	16,629▲	1,246,652▲	6,126.6*	104,269.7	23,699.2	4,346	14,587	3,633.9	262,137	8,555.9
SOUTH AMERICA											
Argentina	40.2*	13,177	12,324	309.1	2,160.0	966.0	374	1,447	57.5	4,080	106.5
Bolivia	3.6	270*	365*	37.1	29.6	33.0	...	...	4.7	331	2.8
Brazil	30.4	10,603*	42,698*	1,312.7	3,679.0	1,002.0	482	2,691	163.1	9,600	469.7
Chile	9.0*	2,101	1,926	63.7	197.8	151.4	138	386	21.9	1,159	57.0
Colombia	3.4	483	1,329	48.8*	377.0	87.0	53	209	48.4	2,567	121.5
Ecuador	1.1*	63*	43*	18.3*	33.0*	51.5*	44	142	9.7	189	8.4
Paraguay	0.5*	26*	30*	16.0*	10.0*	19.0*	26	22	...	...	...
Peru	3.2*	270*	735*	50.7	256.4*	136.1*	677	518	12.9	700	20.4
Uruguay	3.0	353	239	49.6*	c.151.6	c.85.7	38	131	2.7	80	0.1
Venezuela	0.2	42*	15*	65.7	820.0*	295.0*	152	516	36.5	2,269	73.1
OCEANIA											
Australia	40.4†	...	29,000†	863.9*	4,769.2	1,130.8	419	1,205	207.3	17,770	362.6
New Zealand	4.8	537	3,272	92.0*	1,167.3	212.6	109	163	48.3	3,779	116.8

Note: Data are for 1974 or 1975 unless otherwise indicated.
(—) Indicates nil or negligible; (...) indicates not known; (c) indicates provisional or estimated.
*Data given are the most recent available.
†State system only.
‡Including apportionment of traffic of Scandinavian Airlines System.
§Excluding Northern Ireland.
‖Including Singapore.
¶Including apportionment of traffic of Air Afrique.
♀Total for Kenya, Tanzania, and Uganda (East African Railways Corp.).
♂Including apportionment of traffic of East African Airways Corp. and Caspair Ltd.
□Including traffic in Botswana.
◇Including Namibia (South West Africa).
▲Principal railways.

Sources: UN, *Statistical Yearbook 1975, Monthly Bulletin of Statistics, Annual Bulletin of Transport Statistics for Europe 1974;* Lloyd's Register of Shipping, *Statistical Tables 1975;* International Road Federation, *World Road Statistics 1975.*

(M. C. MacDONALD)

had to switch to other modes. Piggyback was generally a strong sector, and Britain had growing success with a concept called SCIDS (small container intermodal distribution system), which suited many road freight customers and required less investment in heavy container cranes. In France a rail freight service carrying produce from farms in the south to Paris averaged 87 mph and was said to be the world's fastest.

The British government announced a 3,100-mi network for heavy trucks. However, much of it could not be implemented because the roads had yet to be built, and they were unlikely to be built for many years to come. Britain was in trouble with the European Economic Community (EEC) for failing to introduce tachographs—devices for monitoring the hours worked by truck drivers. The drivers vehemently opposed what they considered to be "spies in the cab."

In the U.S. the long-distance truck driver became something of a folk hero, and pop songs were even composed about him. The mystique was part of the fad for citizens band radios, long used by truckers to communicate among themselves. The government insisted that for safety the wheels of big trucks should be monitored by a microcomputer that would prevent skidding. Unfortunately, the computers were liable to interference from radios, and they sometimes put on the brakes at the wrong time.

The 1,857-km Tanzam railway, built by the Chinese to link Zambia's copper belt with the Indian Ocean, was completed in July. Afghanistan planned to build a 1,100-mi railway system.

PIPELINES

The 800-mi trans-Alaska oil pipeline burst on July 9 when the operator of a pressure gauge allowed the water pressure to build up too much during a test. The incident highlighted controversy over faulty welds on the pipeline. Both a government report and an audit by the pipeline's builders suggested that there were perhaps 4,000 problem welds, and the 1977 opening date for the $7.7 billion pipeline seemed threatened. After much argument it was decided to repair all the dubious welds.

Eastern European countries were active in the building of gas pipelines. Those under construction included one from the western tip of the U.S.S.R. to Orenburg, via Kharkov, and another from Czechoslovakia to Italy, via Austria. Negotiations were conducted on exploiting Siberian natural gas and carrying it by pipeline for transshipment to the U.S.

In the Middle East the Sumed pipeline from the Gulf of Suez to the Mediterranean was completed. However, Tipline, the trans-Israel pipeline, lost business to the newly reopened Suez Canal. In Kenya a 300-mi pipeline from Mombasa to Nairobi was under construction. Canada was studying a 2,200-mi gas pipeline from Alaska and the Mackenzie Delta to southern Canada and the U.S., while Britain was considering a £2,000 million pipeline to take gas from the North Sea oil fields to the Scottish coast.

INTERCITY RAILWAYS

In West Germany an experimental train suspended just above the rails by magnetic repulsion and propelled by magnets achieved a speed of 401 kph. British Rail's 125-mph High Speed Train, which used conventional technology, was introduced on the Western Region, but the chances of the more sophisticated Advanced Passenger Train reaching its design speed of 155 mph were reduced by the failure to develop a suitable gas-turbine engine. The U.S.S.R., however, decided to opt for gas turbines on its new trans-Siberian railway. The gas turbines were said to be lighter and to work better at cold temperatures.

COURTESY, CONRAIL

Six major U.S. railroads were combined in the federally financed Consolidated Rail Corporation (ConRail), serving 16 states.

Italy began a £1.3 million investment program, including a high-speed line from Rome to Florence. Lightly used lines continued to be a problem; 30% of the network carried only 2% of the traffic. The EEC suggested there should be more coordination of international investment for both roads and rail, notably at bottlenecks like the Alps. The West German railways planned to invest £1,600 million a year, and the government approved a new line from Stuttgart to Mannheim to relieve congestion. It was announced that the almost legendary Paris–Istanbul Orient Express would be discontinued in May 1977.

In Britain a book called *The Rail Problem,* written by two academics, attracted considerable attention, since it showed how, in the authors' opinion, British Rail could break even. However, neither British Rail's then chairman, Sir Richard Marsh, nor his successor, Peter Parker, agreed.

URBAN MASS TRANSIT

The continuing problems of the two showpieces of U.S. mass transit—the Bay Area Rapid Transit (BART) in San Francisco and the Washington, D.C., subway—encouraged proposals for light rail systems as a cheaper alternative. Buffalo, N.Y., was the first U.S. city to gain approval for such a system, with the government undertaking to contribute $269 million, 80% of the cost of a 6.4-mi route. Miami, Fla., also obtained federal approval for rail transit, but in Denver, Colo., the government refused to finance a $733 million light rail system and offered $31 million for bus improvements instead.

The first 4.6 mi of the Washington, D.C., subway opened in March. One estimate put running costs at $80,000 a day and receipts at $10,000. The rolling stock was air-conditioned and carpeted and the seats were padded. The cost of the full 98-mi system had been estimated earlier at $2.5 billion, but it was now expected to be nearly twice that figure.

In San Francisco BART's financial problems reached a crisis as the expiration date for the sales tax that subsidized it approached. A study by Melvin Webber of the University of California (Berkeley) suggested that the real cost of a trip on BART was 62% higher than an equivalent trip by private car. Fare revenue was about what had been estimated in 1962, whereas costs were nearly five times higher. The system, meant to carry 28,000 passengers across the bay in an hour, carried barely that number in a day. Rather than placing stations close together, and therefore near people's homes, BART had given priority to high operating speed on the trains themselves. This was proving to be a poor decision. Half of those who should have been using BART but did not stated that it was too far from their homes or offices and required time-consuming walks, waits, and transfers.

Rome was 12 years behind schedule on building its subway; most of the delays were caused by unexpected discoveries of archaeological sites. Brussels opened a new subway. London Transport reported a 4.2% fall in ridership in 1975; fares had risen 30% in March and another 26% in November, and costs had increased 47% during the year. The British government put the brake on mass transit subsidies, but the Greater London Council decided to defy it. Also in Britain, the light rail system under construction on Tyneside was threatened by a clash over British Rail's insistence on running the new trains. The estimated cost of construction had risen from £65 million to £160 million.

West Germany proposed a dual-mode bus that would be automated. Initially, only steering would be automatic, but eventually the bus would be entirely controlled by means of a cable under the road, and the "driver" would merely collect fares.

Interest in new demand-responsive forms of public transport continued to grow. The number of dial-a-ride services in the the U.S. increased to over 100. In Turkey an analysis conducted in cities that encouraged shared taxi services showed that the taxis attracted three times as many passengers as buses in Ankara and twice as many as buses in Istanbul.

(RICHARD CASEMENT)

See also Energy; Engineering Projects; Environment; Industrial Review: *Aerospace; Automobiles.*

[725.C.3; 734; 737.A.3]

ENCYCLOPÆDIA BRITANNICA FILMS. *The Mississippi System: Waterways of Commerce* (1970); *Rotterdam-Europort: Gateway to Europe* (1971); *The Great Lakes: North America's Inland Seas* (2nd ed., 1972); *Airplane Trip* (4th ed., 1973); *All the Wonderful Things that Fly* (1974).

Trinidad and Tobago

A republic and a member of the Commonwealth of Nations, Trinidad and Tobago consists of two islands off the coast of Venezuela, north of the Orinoco River delta. Area: 1,980 sq mi (5,128 sq km). Pop. (1973 est.): 1,061,900, including (1970) Negro 43%; East Indian 40%; mixed 14%. Cap. and largest city: Port-of-Spain (pop., 1973 est., 60,400). Language: English (official); Hindi, French, Spanish. Religion (1960): Christian 66%; Hindu 23%; Muslim 6%. Queen to Aug. 1, 1976, Elizabeth II; governor-general to August 1 and, from that date, transitional president (sworn in as president on December 30), Sir Ellis Clarke; prime minister, Eric Williams.

On Aug. 1, 1976, Trinidad and Tobago declared itself a republic within the Commonwealth. The new constitution was a moderate document, enshrining existing basic rights and adding certain safeguards. Other features included: reduction of the voting age to 18; abolition of voting machines; the retention of a bicameral Parliament (the House of Representatives with its current membership of 36 and a Senate enlarged from 24 to 31 members); and retention of judicial links with Britain, with appeals to the Privy Council.

In the September 13 elections Eric Williams' People's National Movement was returned for a fifth term, with 24 seats to 12. Two seats were won by A. N. R. Robinson's Democratic Action Congress and ten by the left-wing United Labour Front, an interracial coalition of trade-union interests.

Trinidad continued to enjoy the benefits of the oil boom, with reserves of TT$1,728,000,000 at the end of 1975, some months before the government revalued the TT dollar by 12% and tied it to the U.S. dollar in the ratio of TT$2.40 to $1. Inflation eased somewhat to an anticipated 11% for 1976, but problems of declining production, retrenchment, and unemployment (officially 16%) continued.

(SHEILA PATTERSON)

[974.B.2.d]

TRINIDAD AND TOBAGO

Education. (1972–73) Primary, pupils 222,928, teachers 6,704; secondary, pupils 49,225, teachers 2,151; vocational, pupils 2,909, teachers 112; higher, students 2,159, teaching staff 278.

Finance and Trade. Monetary unit: Trinidad and Tobago dollar, with (Sept. 20, 1976) a par value of TT$2.40 to U.S. $1 (free rate of TT$4.14 = £1 sterling). Budget (1975 est.): revenue TT$1,212,000,000; expenditure TT$1,294,000,000. Foreign trade (1975): imports TT$3,243,900,000; exports TT$3,878,500,000. Import sources: Saudi Arabia 26%; U.S. 22%; Indonesia 17%; U.K. 9%; Iran 5%. Export destinations: U.S. 68%; ship and aircraft bunkers 5%. Main exports: petroleum products 50%; crude oil 37%.

Transport and Communications. Roads (1972) 4,230 km. Motor vehicles in use (1974): passenger 88,800; commercial (including buses) 22,900. There are no railways in operation. Air traffic (1975): 992 million passenger-km; freight 20,402,000 net ton-km. Ships entered (1972) vessels totaling 24,244,000 net registered tons; goods loaded 20,624,000 metric tons, unloaded 14,808,000 metric tons. Telephones (Dec. 1974) 66,400. Radio receivers (Dec. 1971) 296,000. Television receivers (Dec. 1973) 93,000.

Agriculture. Production (in 000; metric tons; 1974): sugar, raw value 186; rice *c.* 12; tomatoes *c.* 9; oranges *c.* 13; grapefruit *c.* 19; copra 7; coffee 2. Livestock (in 000; 1974): cattle *c.* 71; pigs *c.* 54; goats *c.* 40; poultry *c.* 6,000.

Industry. Production (in 000; metric tons; 1975): crude oil 11,124; natural gas (cu m; 1974) 1,418,000; petroleum products (1974) 17,792; cement 259; nitrogenous fertilizers (nutrient content; 1974–75) *c.* 91; electricity (kw-hr) 1,124,000.

Tunisia

A republic of North Africa lying on the Mediterranean Sea, Tunisia is bounded by Algeria and Libya. Area: 63,379 sq mi (164,150 sq km). Pop. (1975 census): 5,588,200. Cap. and largest city: Tunis (pop., governorate, 1975 census, 944,100). Language: Arabic (official). Religion: Muslim; Jewish and Christian minorities. President in 1976, Habib Bourguiba; prime minister, Hedi Nouira.

In November 1976 the state of President Bourguiba's health gave rise to renewed anxiety, and he went to Switzerland again for medical treatment. At home, student opposition to the government continued throughout the year. In January dozens of students

Trapshooting: *see* Target Sports

TUNISIA

Education. (1974–75) Primary, pupils 910,532, teachers 22,225; secondary, pupils 158,643; vocational, pupils 34,977; secondary and vocational, teachers 9,231; teacher training, students 3,027, teachers 133; higher (1972–73), students 9,246, teaching staff 884.

Finance. Monetary unit: Tunisian dinar, with (Sept. 20, 1976) a free rate of 0.42 dinar to U.S. $1 (0.72 dinar = £1 sterling). Gold, SDR's, and foreign exchange (June 1976) U.S. $343 million. Budget (1976 est.) balanced at 641 million dinars. Gross domestic product (1975) 1,773,700,000 dinars. Money supply (May 1976) 462.2 million dinars. Cost of living (Tunis; 1970 = 100; May 1976) 134.

Foreign Trade. (1975) Imports 572,820,000 dinars; exports 345,580,000 dinars. Import sources: France 35%; Italy 9%; West Germany 8%; U.S. 7%; U.K. 5%. Export destinations: France 19%; Italy 17%; Greece 14%; U.S. 10%; West Germany 8%; Libya 6%. Main exports: crude oil 42%; phosphates 20%; olive oil *c.* 9%. Tourism (1974): visitors 716,000; gross receipts U.S. $201 million.

Transport and Communications. Roads (1973) 18,774 km. Motor vehicles in use (1974): passenger 115,100; commercial (including buses) 76,200. Railways: (1973) 1,928 km; traffic (1975) 588 million passenger-km, freight 1,283,000,000 net ton-km. Air traffic (1975): 898 million passenger-km; freight 6,491,000 net ton-km. Telephones (Dec. 1974) 114,000. Radio licenses (Dec. 1973) 277,000. Television licenses (Dec. 1973) 147,000.

Agriculture. Production (in 000; metric tons; 1975): wheat *c.* 890; barley 210; potatoes (1974) *c.* 80; tomatoes *c.* 267; watermelons (1974) *c.* 175; wine (1974) *c.* 95; dates (1974) *c.* 53; figs (1974) *c.* 21; olives *c.* 850; oranges (1974) *c.* 72. Livestock (in 000; 1974): sheep *c.* 3,300; cattle *c.* 690; goats *c.* 660; camels *c.* 180; poultry *c.* 13,000.

Industry. Production (in 000; metric tons; 1975): crude oil 4,611; natural gas (cu m) 210,000; cement 615; iron ore (55% metal content) 650; phosphate rock (1974) 3,826; lead 24; petroleum products (1974) 1,080; sulfuric acid (1974) 731; electricity (excluding most industrial production; kw-hr) 1,204,000.

were arrested; in May during disturbances at the University of Tunis some 30 people were wounded, and in the same month the challenge was taken up by other sections of society, even magistrates going on strike. Cabinet changes took place after the death of Hedi Khefacha, minister of defense, in Paris on May 25, and after the dismissal of Driss Guiga, minister of education who was held responsible for the persistence of student unrest, on May 31.

Relations with Libya deteriorated sharply in March; Tunisia recalled its ambassador at Tripoli after the Tunisian government had announced the arrest of a Libyan commando unit allegedly sent to kill Bourguiba. After a public trial on April 19–23 the three members of the unit were convicted and one was executed. In connection with the affair and in circumstances that were not made clear, Mohammed Masmoudi, former Tunisian minister of foreign affairs and former ambassador in Paris, was questioned in Cairo in March and briefly held by the Egyptian police. Some 15,000 Tunisian workers were said to have been expelled from Libya since the beginning of the year.

Relations with France remained excellent. On March 20, the 20th anniversary of the proclamation of Tunisia's independence, Michel Poniatowski, French minister of the interior, himself headed the French delegation to Tunis. A few days earlier Jean Sauvagnargues, French minister of foreign affairs, had been received in the Tunisian capital.

Their earlier conflict notwithstanding, Tunisia and Libya announced in a joint communiqué in August their decision to ask the International Court of Justice to demarcate their respective zones of the oil-bearing African continental shelf in the Mediterranean. In the meantime they would work out a temporary understanding for jointly exploiting the disputed area. The surprising move to end this long-standing dispute was understood to have come from the Libyan leader, Col. Muammar al-Qaddafi. It benefited Tunisia, which was especially anxious to work the offshore petroleum deposits.

(PHILIPPE DECRAENE)

[978.D.2.b]

Turkey

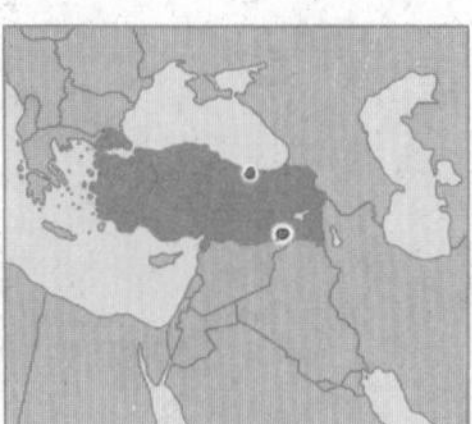

A republic of southeastern Europe and Asia Minor, Turkey is bounded by the Aegean Sea, the Black Sea, the U.S.S.R., Iran, Iraq, Syria, the Mediterranean Sea, Greece, and Bulgaria. Area: 300,948 sq mi (779,452 sq km), including 9,150 sq mi in Europe. Pop. (1975 prelim.): 40,197,700. Cap.: Ankara (pop., 1974 est., 1,522,400). Largest city: Istanbul (pop., 1974 est., 2,487,100). Language: Turkish, Kurdish, Arabic. Religion: predominantly Muslim. President in 1976, Fahri Koruturk; prime minister, Suleyman Demirel.

Although the four-party rightist coalition government headed by Suleyman Demirel, leader of the Justice Party, secured parliamentary approval for its first budget on February 29 by 231 votes to 205, the year 1976 was one of tension. The feud between rightist and leftist student radicals disrupted the universities and claimed more than 40 dead by the end of the academic year in June. When universities reopened in November, the violence and killings resumed. Security forces were involved in bloody clashes with leftist guerrillas in eastern Turkey, at Malatya in January and at Gaziantep in June, while in September there were riots in another eastern town, Elazig. Also in September, the smaller of the two labour confederations, the Confederation of Revolutionary Trade Unions (DISK), organized strikes against a government bill that provided for the continued existence of the state security courts, originally set up when martial law was lifted in 1973. Several union leaders were arrested; a radical association of teachers was closed down; and the mayor of Ankara was removed from office for having supported a strike. However, all these actions were disallowed by the courts, which also canceled the appointment of a new Air Force commander. The government bill lost, as a result of tactics by the opposition Republican People's Party, and the state security courts ceased to exist in October.

Foreign relations were dominated by the dispute with Greece over rights in the Aegean seabed and the control of air traffic over the Aegean. In July the seabed dispute came to a head, when Turkey sent the seismic research ship "MTA Sismik I" to prospect in disputed waters, and it was not until November that the two countries agreed to negotiate (*see* GREECE). A proposal made on October 29 by Turkish Foreign Minister Ihsan Sabri Caglayangil that a "temporary government" be established in Cyprus was unfavourably received both in Cyprus and in Greece. Apart from this and from supporting the continuation of talks between the two Cypriot communities, Turkey made no move on the Cyprus problem.

On March 26 Turkey and the U.S. signed a defense cooperation agreement providing for the disbursement of $1 billion of U.S. military aid to Turkey over four years (plus other aid put at more than $200 million).

Trucking Industry: *see* Transportation

Trust Territories: *see* Dependent States

Tunnels: *see* Engineering Projects

In return, 25 U.S. defense installations in Turkey were to be reopened, but under Turkish control instead of dual control as in the past. The agreement awaited U.S. congressional approval at year's end.

Friendly relations with the U.S.S.R. continued to develop, and two agreements were signed, in April on the construction of a large dam on the border river of Arpa Cayi and in November on the provision of electric energy by the U.S.S.R. On July 18, Turkey allowed the Soviet aircraft carrier "Kiev" to negotiate the Dardanelles Straits on its way from the Black Sea to the Aegean, thus interpreting in the Soviets' favour the relevant provision of the Montreux Convention.

Turkey was host to the annual conference of Islamic foreign ministers in Istanbul in May. The conference communiqué supported Turkish policy on Cyprus, and Turkey announced that the Palestine Liberation Organization would be allowed to open an office in Ankara.

The Demirel government pursued economic growth, in spite of inflation (21% in 1975 and 19% in most of 1976) and a trade deficit ($3.3 billion in 1975 and $1.2 billion in the first half of 1976). But growth in production was estimated at 7 and 8% in 1974 and 1975, respectively—during a period of world recession. Relations with the European Economic Community (EEC), with which Turkey had an association agreement, were difficult. Meetings of the Council of Association were postponed twice (in July and in October), the European Commission having failed to satisfy Turkey on issues of trade, aid, and migrant workers. An agreement was eventually signed on December 20, though with Turkish reservations on the concessions offered.

A violent earthquake shook eastern Anatolia east of Lake Van on November 24 and killed approximately 4,000 people. To support the rescue operation, other countries contributed medical supplies and equipment.

(ANDREW MANGO)

See also Cyprus.
[978.A.1–3]

TURKEY

Education. (1973–74) Primary, pupils 5,324,707, teachers 156,476; secondary, pupils 1,231,433, teachers 40,351; vocational, pupils 221,627, teachers 13,913; teacher training, students 63,820, teachers 2,935; higher (including 11 universities), students 185,285, teaching staff 11,773.

Finance. Monetary unit: Turkish lira, with (Sept. 20, 1976) a free rate of 16 liras to U.S. $1 (27.60 liras = £1 sterling). Gold, SDR's, and foreign exchange (June 1976) U.S. $913 million. Budget (1976–77 est.) balanced at 153.1 billion liras. Gross domestic product (1974) 403 billion liras. Money supply (Feb. 1976) 120,310,000,000 liras. Cost of living (Ankara; 1970 = 100; March 1976) 244.

Foreign Trade. (1975) Imports 66,309,000,000 liras; exports 20,075,000,000 liras. Import sources: West Germany 22%; Iraq 11%; U.S. 9%; Italy 8%; U.K. 7%; Switzerland 6%; France 6%; Japan 5%. Export destinations: West Germany 22%; U.S. 11%; Switzerland 7%; Italy 6%; U.S.S.R. 5%; U.K. 5%; Lebanon 5%. Main exports: cotton 17%; tobacco 13%; hazelnuts 11%. Tourism (1974): visitors 1,110,000; gross receipts U.S. $194 million.

Transport and Communications. Roads (1974) 59,532 km. Motor vehicles in use (1974): passenger *c.* 303,800; commercial *c.* 230,800. Railways (1974): 8,141 km; traffic 5,753,000,000 passenger-km, freight 6,418,000,000 net ton-km. Air traffic (1975): 1,471,000,000 passenger-km; freight 11,427,000 net ton-km. Shipping (1975): merchant vessels 100 gross tons and over 387; gross tonnage 994,668. Telephones (Dec. 1974) 900,000. Radio licenses (Dec. 1974) 4,091,000. Television receivers (Dec. 1974) 456,000.

Agriculture. Production (in 000; metric tons; 1975): wheat *c.* 14,750; barley 4,300; corn *c.* 1,100; rye 700; oats 400; potatoes 2,400; tomatoes *c.* 2,250; onions *c.* 666; sugar, raw value *c.* 986; sunflower seed *c.* 380; chick-peas 165; dry beans 130; cabbages (1974) 545; pumpkins (1974) 314; cucumbers (1974) 360; oranges (1974) 578; lemons (1974) 125; apples (1974) 860; pears (1974) 200; peaches (1974) 125; plums (1974) *c.* 125; grapes (1974) 3,120; raisins (1974) *c.* 330; figs (1974) 200; olives 625; tea *c.* 47; tobacco *c.* 120; cotton, lint *c.* 450. Livestock (in 000; Dec. 1974): cattle *c.* 13,387; sheep 40,539; buffalo (1973) 1,023; goats (1973) 18,007; horses (1973) 936; asses (1973) 1,616; chickens (1973) 38,329.

Industry. Fuel and power (in 000; metric tons; 1975): crude oil 3,094; coal 4,760; lignite (1974) *c.* 5,240; electricity (kw-hr) 15,561,000. Production (in 000; metric tons; 1975): cement 10,748; iron ore (55–60% metal content) 1,907; pig iron 1,197; crude steel 1,464; sulfur (1974) 10; petroleum products (1974) *c.* 12,520; sulfuric acid 20; fertilizers (nutrient content; 1974–75) nitrogenous 108, phosphate 161; chrome ore (oxide content; 1974) 270; manganese ore (metal content; 1974) 1.2; cotton yarn (factory only; 1970) 189; wool yarn (1971) 26; man-made fibres (1974) 50.

Unemployment: *see* Economy, World; Social and Welfare Services

Uganda

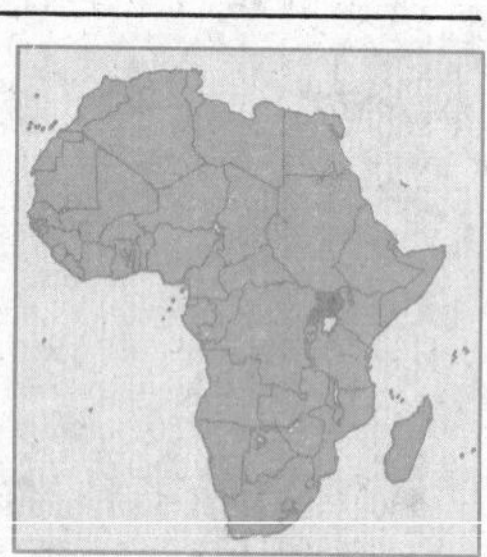

A republic and a member of the Commonwealth of Nations, Uganda is bounded by Sudan, Zaire, Rwanda, Tanzania, and Kenya. Area: 93,104 sq mi (241,139 sq km), including 15,235 sq mi of inland water. Pop. (1976 est.): 11,942,700, virtually all of whom are African. Cap. and largest city: Kampala (pop., 1975 UN est., 542,000). Language: English (official), Bantu, Nilotic, Nilo-Hamitic, and Sudanic. Religion: Christian, Muslim, traditional beliefs. President in 1976, Gen. Idi Amin.

On Dec. 18, 1975, Ugandan relations with the U.K. were restored to normal when James Hennessey was

UGANDA

Education. (1974–75) Primary, pupils 940,920, teachers 27,597; secondary, pupils 75,582, teachers 2,812; vocational, pupils 2,862, teachers 236; teacher training, students 8,330, teachers 288; higher, students 5,635, teaching staff 604.

Finance and Trade. Monetary unit: Uganda shilling, with (Sept. 20, 1976) a free rate of UShs 8.40 to U.S. $1 (UShs 14.48 = £1 sterling). Budget (1975–76 est.): revenue UShs 2,050,000,000; expenditure UShs 2,018,000,000. Foreign trade (1975): imports UShs 1,470,000,000; exports UShs 1,912,000,000. Import sources: Kenya 34%; U.K. 17%; Japan 8%; West Germany 6%; Italy 6%. Export destinations: U.S. 24%; U.K. 20%; Japan 8%; West Germany 5%. Main exports: coffee 75%; cotton 10%; tea 6%.

Transport and Communications. Roads (1974) 27,536 km. Motor vehicles in use (1974): passenger 27,000; commercial 8,900. Railways (1974) 1,240 km (for traffic *see* KENYA). Air traffic (apportionment of traffic of East African Airways Corporation; 1974): 150 million passenger-km; freight 5.7 million net ton-km. Telephones (Dec. 1974) 43,000. Radio receivers (Dec. 1973) *c.* 250,000. Television licenses (Dec. 1972) 15,000.

Agriculture. Production (in 000; metric tons; 1975): millet 720; sorghum 490; corn (1974) *c.* 350; sweet potatoes (1974) *c.* 720; cassava (1974) *c.* 1,100; peanuts *c.* 215; dry beans *c.* 170; coffee *c.* 180; tea 18; sugar, raw value (1974) *c.* 62; cotton, lint *c.* 31; timber (cu m; 1974) 14,675; fish catch (1974) 167. Livestock (in 000; Dec. 1973): cattle *c.* 3,840; sheep *c.* 750; goats *c.* 1,700; pigs *c.* 75; chickens *c.* 11,010.

Industry. Production (in 000; metric tons; 1974): cement 153; copper, smelter (1975) 9; tungsten concentrates (oxide content) 0.12; phosphate rock 19; electricity (kw-hr) *c.* 836,000.

appointed high commissioner, and on Jan. 24, 1976, President Amin paid over $1.6 million as compensation for Indian citizens expelled from Uganda in 1972, thus improving relations with India.

When, in February, Amin declared part of western Kenya to have been, historically, Ugandan territory, port workers in Mombasa, Kenya, boycotted goods traveling to and from Uganda, and Pres. Jomo Kenyatta affirmed Kenya's intention to safeguard its boundaries. President Amin then announced that Uganda had no desire to take any land belonging to Kenya. However, after the Israeli commando raid to rescue 103 hostages being held at Entebbe airport (*see* DEFENSE: *Middle East*), Amin learned that the Israeli planes had landed in Nairobi after the raid to refuel and became convinced of Kenya's complicity. Troops were massed on both sides of the Kenya-Uganda border. On July 8 Kenya called upon Uganda to pay for all goods and passengers in transit through Kenya in Kenyan currency because of Uganda's indebtedness, a request that Amin regarded as a threat of an economic blockade; further, by July 16 Kenyan truck and train drivers were refusing to enter Uganda. Faced with a cut of its petroleum supply, Uganda became more conciliatory, and on August 6 delegates from Uganda and Kenya, meeting in Nairobi, reached an agreement. But relations with Britain deteriorated after charges that one of the Entebbe hostages, Mrs. Dora Bloch, a British subject, had been murdered by agents of the Uganda government, and on July 28 Britain severed diplomatic relations with Uganda. On June 10 there had been an attempt to assassinate Amin, but on June 25 he was appointed president for life. Behind these political issues concern for the economy remained. (KENNETH INGHAM)

[978.E.6.b.iv]

Union of Soviet Socialist Republics

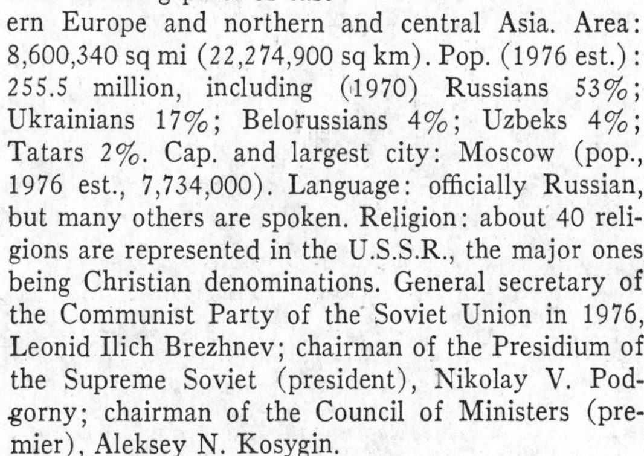

The Union of Soviet Socialist Republics is a federal state covering parts of eastern Europe and northern and central Asia. Area: 8,600,340 sq mi (22,274,900 sq km). Pop. (1976 est.): 255.5 million, including (1970) Russians 53%; Ukrainians 17%; Belorussians 4%; Uzbeks 4%; Tatars 2%. Cap. and largest city: Moscow (pop., 1976 est., 7,734,000). Language: officially Russian, but many others are spoken. Religion: about 40 religions are represented in the U.S.S.R., the major ones being Christian denominations. General secretary of the Communist Party of the Soviet Union in 1976, Leonid Ilich Brezhnev; chairman of the Presidium of the Supreme Soviet (president), Nikolay V. Podgorny; chairman of the Council of Ministers (premier), Aleksey N. Kosygin.

The year 1976 was Leonid Brezhnev's year. The personal position of the general secretary of the Communist Party of the Soviet Union reflected the relative stability of the regime he led, and the celebration of his 70th birthday at the end of the year (on December 19) served to underline his primacy.

Although Brezhnev could not dominate the Soviet scene as absolutely as Stalin did—and doubtless had never desired to—the praise and tributes he received on his birthday recalled the "personality cult" of the late 1940s and early 1950s. All the Eastern European allies of the U.S.S.R., along with Finland, bestowed their highest decorations on the aging general secretary. He was not only made a Hero of the Soviet Union for the second time and given his fifth Order of Lenin, but received a completely new honour—a sword bearing the hammer and sickle emblem embossed in gold. This new distinction bore some resemblance to the swords of honour the tsars used to bestow on their victorious generals and to the revolutionary arms of honour awarded to Bolshevik heroes of the civil war up to 1930. In May the traditional celebrations of the anniversary of the victory in World War II included the unveiling of a bronze bust of Brezhnev in Dneprodzerzhinsk, his birthplace. At the same time he was given the rank of marshal in recognition of his achievements as a strategist and organizer of his country's military power. His sword of honour later in the year was perhaps intended to emphasize his new "military" role and to underline the party's supremacy over the military. The promotion of two very senior policemen—Yury Andropov, the head of the KGB (the political police), and Nikolay Shchelokov, the minister in charge of the civilian police—to the rank of general of the army seemed to be part of the same process. The most significant development in this context was the appointment of Dmitry F. Ustinov (*see* BIOGRAPHY) to succeed Marshal Andrey Grechko (*see* OBITUARIES) as minister of defense. Ustinov, though immediately promoted to general of the army, was essentially a civilian of Brezhnev's generation who, since he became minister of defense industry in 1953, had been prominently associated with the Soviet military-industrial complex.

Grechko, who died in April, was one of the great field commanders of World War II; nine years earlier he had succeeded Marshal Rodion Y. Malinovsky, an old comrade-in-arms, and it is more than likely that the generals would have preferred to see another professional soldier, such as Gen. Viktor Kulikov, the chief of staff, in the ministry of defense.

Gymnasts and children march past the Lenin Mausoleum in Moscow on May Day 1976. Beyond the wall are buildings of the Kremlin.

LONDON DAILY EXPRESS/PICTORIAL PARADE

Brezhnev's birthday coincided with a decision to release Vladimir Bukovsky, a leading dissident who had spent many years in various penal institutions, and to exchange him for Luis Corvalan, the Communist leader imprisoned by the military junta in Chile. The arrival of Corvalan in Moscow, widely publicized in the Soviet press, was in no way linked to the departure of Bukovsky as far as the ordinary Soviet citizen was able to find out. But the international effect of this de facto exchange was considerable. As Bukovsky pointed out on his arrival in Switzerland, it was the first time that the Soviet government had admitted publicly that it still kept political prisoners. His statement that conditions in Soviet prisons had improved before the negotiations in Helsinki in 1975 but worsened after the Helsinki declaration had been signed did not come as a surprise in view of the Soviet government's attitude toward détente. Indeed, the authorities in Moscow had always insisted that the issue of human rights in the Soviet Union was a purely internal matter. Thus, for example, in May 1976 the police cracked down on a dissidents' committee calling itself the Public Group to Promote the Fulfillment of the Helsinki Accord, and TASS, the official news agency, issued a warning that similar activities would be regarded as anti-Soviet acts. When some European Communist parties were critical of the Soviet performance in human rights, their views were firmly rejected. In June the writer Andrey Amalrik (*see* BIOGRAPHY) was expelled from the Soviet Union.

At the end of the year the authorities broke up attempts to organize a conference on Jewish culture in the Soviet Union; several of the organizers were subjected to harassment and arrest. On the other hand, some 13,750 Jews were allowed to emigrate—an increase of 500 compared with 1975 but well below the 1974 total of 16,900.

Jews were not the only religious group to suffer from the attentions of the political police. According to information received by the World Council of Churches, young people in the U.S.S.R. were being subjected to "cures" in mental hospitals to rid them of the Christian faith. Thus there had been no change in the treatment of believing Christians since the Helsinki conference, except perhaps for the worse.

Another discontented minority that tried to attract world attention in 1976 were the Soviet Germans, of whom there were two million (compared with three million Jews) in the U.S.S.R. Most of them were the descendants of peasant farmers invited to Russia by Catherine the Great after 1764, and who settled on the Central Volga. During World War II they were deported to Siberia and thousands perished. After the war they were not repatriated to their former homes, since they provided much-needed labour in the east. Some 25,000 of these Germans had emigrated since 1971, and more wanted to go; early in 1976 there were demonstrations outside the West German embassy in Moscow by groups of people wanting to be allowed to leave for West Germany.

The Crimean Tatars, another national minority that was moved from its homeland to Siberia during World War II, had been trying to obtain permission to return to the Crimea. In April a Crimean Tatar named Mustafa Djemilev was put on trial in the Siberian city of Omsk, accused of "slandering the Soviet Union." The case received attention in the world press because Andrey Sakharov, the Soviet physicist and a prominent figure in the human rights movement, was refused entry to the courtroom by police. Sakharov described Djemilev's trial as "an unbearable mockery." The Tatar leader was sentenced to 2½ years in a strict-regime labour camp.

Yet the record was not entirely negative. The release of Bukovsky and a few other prominent dissidents such as Leonid I. Plyushch and Amalrik showed perhaps that the Soviet government was not as insensitive to world public opinion as it pretended to be. At the beginning of the year the government simplified procedures for those seeking to emigrate.

In February *Pravda* published an article setting out the official view on human rights in reply to critics in the West: that "the system of Soviet democracy far surpasses any bourgeois-democratic system," and that slander of Soviet society, based on "deliberately false fabrications," was punishable in law. The party newspaper denied that dissidents were imprisoned in psychiatric hospitals, and also emphasized that penalties for anti-Soviet slander had been made lighter, but concluded that "the Soviet people are categorically against granting freedom of action to those who damage socialist society and national security."

U.S.S.R.

Education. (1974–75) Primary, pupils 39,040,000; secondary, pupils 15.4 million; primary and secondary, teachers 2,415,000; vocational, pupils 4,477,000, teachers (1973–74) 208,600; teacher training (1973–74), students 363,600, teachers 209,000; higher (including 121 universities), students 4,751,000, teaching staff (1973–74) 302,000.

Finance. Monetary unit: ruble, with (Sept. 20, 1976) a free rate of 0.77 ruble to U.S. $1 (1.33 ruble = £1 sterling). Budget (1976 est.): revenue 223.7 billion rubles; expenditure 223.5 billion rubles.

Foreign Trade. (1975) Imports 26,699,000,000 rubles; exports 24,030,000,000 rubles. Import sources: East Germany 10%; Poland 9%; Bulgaria 7%; Czechoslovakia 7%; West Germany 7%; Hungary 6%; U.S. 5%; Cuba 5%; Japan 5%. Export destinations: East Germany 12%; Poland 10%; Bulgaria 9%; Czechoslovakia 8%; Hungary 7%; Cuba 5%. Main exports: machinery and transport equipment 19%; crude oil 16%; petroleum products 9%; iron and steel 8%; timber 6%.

Transport and Communications. Roads (1974) 1,421,600 km (including 628,300 km surfaced). Motor vehicles in use (1974): passenger *c.* 3 million; commercial *c.* 4 million. Railways: (1973) 263,800 km (including 136,800 km public and 127,000 km industrial); traffic (1974) 306,298,000,000 passenger-km, freight (1975) 3,233,000,000,000 net ton-km. Air traffic (1974): 108,577,000,000 passenger-km; freight 2,475,300,000 net ton-km. Navigable inland waterways (1974) 146,300 km; traffic 212,300,000,000 ton-km. Shipping (1975): merchant vessels 100 gross tons and over 7,652; gross tonnage 19,235,973. Telephones (Dec. 1974) 15,782,000. Radio licenses (Dec. 1973) 110.3 million. Television licenses (Dec. 1973) 49.2 million.

Agriculture. Production (in 000; metric tons; 1975): wheat *c.* 65,000; barley *c.* 35,000; oats *c.* 11,000; rye *c.* 9,000; corn *c.* 8,000; rice *c.* 2,000; millet *c.* 3,000; potatoes 88,480; sugar, raw value *c.* 7,532; tomatoes *c.* 3,590; watermelons (1974) *c.* 3,500; sunflower seed *c.* 5,000; linseed *c.* 350; dry peas *c.* 3,700; soybeans *c.* 600; wine (1974) 2,710; tea *c.* 83; tobacco *c.* 315; cotton, lint *c.* 2,500; flax fibres (1974) *c.* 450; wool 278; hen's eggs *c.* 3,175; milk *c.* 90,300; butter 1,320; cheese 1,362; meat *c.* 15,200; timber (cu m; 1974) *c.* 383,000; fish catch (1974) 9,236. Livestock (in 000; Jan. 1975): cattle 109,122; pigs 72,272; sheep 145,305; goats (1974) 5,900; horses (1974) 6,848; chickens 754,000.

Industry. Index of production (1970 = 100; 1975) 143. Fuel and power (in 000; metric tons; 1975): coal and lignite 696,100; crude oil 490,614; natural gas (cu m; 1974) 260,553,000; manufactured gas (cu m; 1974) 35,963,000; electricity (kw-hr) 1,015,000,000. Production (in 000; metric tons; 1975): cement 121,887; iron ore (60% metal content) 232,800; pig iron (1974) 99,868; steel 141,161; aluminum (1974) *c.* 1,430; copper (1974) *c.* 1,350; lead (1974) *c.* 475; zinc (1974) *c.* 680; magnesite (1974) *c.* 1,570; manganese ore (metal content; 1974) 2,847; tungsten concentrates (oxide content; 1974) 9.6; gold (troy oz) *c.* 7,500; silver (troy oz) *c.* 42,000; sulfuric acid 18,643; caustic soda (1974) 2,200; plastics and resins 2,840; fertilizers (nutrient content; 1974) nitrogenous 7,856, phosphate 3,868, potash 6,586; newsprint (1974) 1,334; other paper (1974) 6,862; cotton fabrics (sq m) 6,567,000; woolen fabrics (sq m) 738,000; rayon and acetate fabrics (sq m; 1974) 980,000; passenger cars (units; 1974) 1,119; commercial vehicles (units; 1974) 729. New dwelling units completed (1974) 2,231,000.

Foreign Policy. The problems confronting the Soviet Union reminded some observers of those that the tsar had to face a century ago: an outwardly monolithic regime, rejected by a small stratum of ill-organized dissident intellectuals and unable to cope with the nationalistic aspirations of various minority groups. Yet the analogy must not be pressed too far: the external power of Russia in the 19th century was more apparent than real, and the tsarist autocracy was ultimately brought down by the failure of its foreign policies and by military defeat. The Soviet Union, on the other hand, had become firmly established as one of the two most powerful states in the world, and its government was able to rely on a highly integrated military and industrial structure. There was no doubt that the power gap between the U.S.S.R. and the U.S. had continued to narrow more rapidly than had been expected. The U.S.S.R. had more intercontinental missiles than the U.S., although fewer warheads. The Soviet naval buildup had been dramatic, and although the Soviets could not match the Americans in the air, they continued to be superior in conventional ground forces which had been undergoing extensive modernization.

The Soviet attitude to détente was to be viewed in the context of this continually increasing military capability, and also in relation to the refusal of the Soviet government to make any major concessions on human rights. To many observers, Moscow seemed to be trying to maintain its advantages while relying on the spirit of détente to improve its economic position and to erode the military power of the NATO countries, particularly in Western Europe where disarmament by inflation was proceeding apace. In his policy statement to the 25th congress of the Soviet Communist Party in February, Brezhnev felt able to propose a reduction of American and Soviet forces in Central Europe while the level of forces of the other nations involved would be frozen, thus preserving the numerical advantage of the Warsaw Pact armies. Brezhnev had no qualms about calling for a worldwide agreement against resorting to force at a time when he could claim that the global revolutionary process was developing on the lines foretold by Marx and Lenin—as evidence for which he cited the "deep economic crisis" of capitalism, the Portuguese revolution, the fall of the military dictatorship in Greece, the changes in Spain, and the progress of decolonization in Africa. The Soviet success in establishing a Marxist regime in Angola by using Cuban troops was particularly significant in view of the deteriorating situation in southern Africa. This was marked by the signing of a 20-year Treaty of Friendship with Angola when Pres. Agostinho Neto visited Moscow in October. In August Sam Nujomo, the leader of SWAPO (the South West Africa People's Organization), which was trying to win independence for Namibia, was welcomed in Moscow.

Relations with China did not improve, and the succession crisis in Peking following Mao Tse-tung's death only added to the uncertainty. In his speech to the 25th party congress Brezhnev compared the rulers of China to the Western enemies of détente, and argued that China's policies were openly directed against the socialist camp. In April *Pravda* carried an important article describing Mao Tse-tung as "the mastermind of his country's anti-Soviet policy." The new Chinese leadership under Hua Kuo-feng told the Soviet Union in November in a message on the occasion of the 59th anniversary of the Bolshevik Revolution that quarrels on "questions of principle" should not affect relations at the intergovernmental level, but a few days later the Chinese representative in the United Nations denounced the U.S.S.R. as "the most dangerous source of war" in the world and the Chinese News Agency dismissed Moscow's claim that the Eastern European bloc was a voluntary association of sovereign states as "another piece of humbug mouthed by the new Tsars."

UPI COMPIX

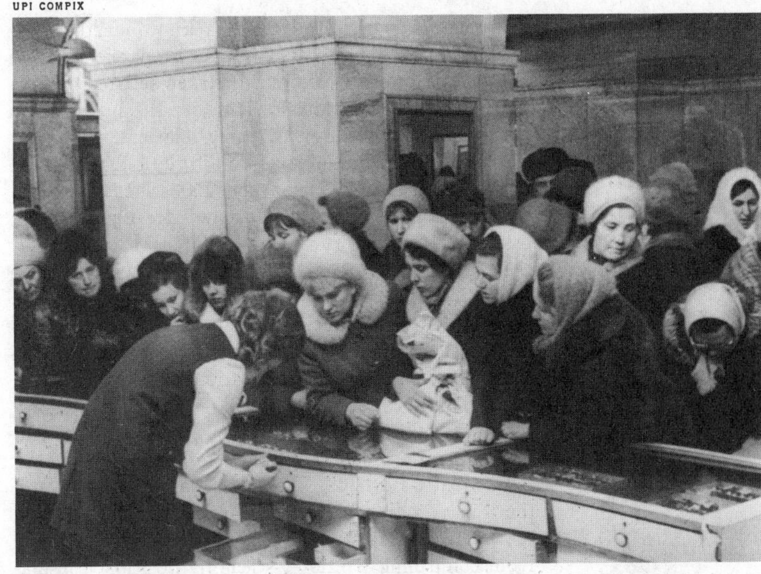

Shoppers crowded the counters of Moscow's GUM department store when more consumer goods became available during the Communist Party congress held in February–March.

The Soviet Union certainly did not neglect its Eastern European relations in 1976. The usual rounds of official visits included a journey to Moscow by Polish party leader Edward Gierek in November and, more important, an extended visit by Brezhnev to Romania later that month. The Romanian leaders had for some years pursued a relatively independent foreign policy; in a joint declaration issued after Brezhnev's talks with Pres. Nicolae Ceausescu, they obtained an endorsement of the "principles of equality and independence," but had to agree to consult regularly with the U.S.S.R. on international questions. *Pravda* commented that the declaration would "give serious food for thought to those who seize any pretext for their dirty purpose of sowing mistrust between the two countries." Before going to Romania, Brezhnev stopped off in Yugoslavia to reassure President Tito of the Soviet Union's peaceful intentions toward his country.

In the Middle East, Soviet diplomacy did not succeed in mending its fences. In March the Egyptians broke off the Soviet-Egyptian friendship treaty, and soon afterward signed a military cooperation agreement with China. Pres. Anwar as-Sadat had been exasperated by the Soviets' refusal to supply spares for his MiG-21 aircraft; the U.S.S.R. reacted by accusing him of anti-Soviet policies. One of the consequences of the abrogation of the treaty was the loss of major Soviet port facilities in Alexandria. However, trade negotiations between the Soviet Union and Egypt continued, and in November the Egyptian foreign minister met with his Soviet counterpart, Andrey Gromyko, in Bulgaria in an effort to normalize relations between their countries.

In summary, Soviet foreign policy in 1976 continued to enjoy the fruits of détente while waiting for the outcome of the presidential election in the United States. In Europe perhaps the major problem was the increasing independence of the Western European

Communists, which had to be acknowledged at the meeting of the European Communist parties held in East Berlin in June. The most marked setback was experienced in the Middle East, where the breach with Egypt was followed by worsening relations with Syria as a result of Syrian intervention in the Lebanese civil war against the Soviet-backed Palestine Liberation Organization. By contrast, Moscow's prestige in Africa rose after the victory of the Popular Movement for the Liberation of Angola (MPLA) in Angola, and there was some evidence of expanding Soviet influence in Mozambique and Tanzania at the expense of the Chinese position there. Moscow's most serious problem continued to be its poor relationship with Peking. Apart from economic and ideological considerations, the garrisoning of the vast Sino-Soviet frontier imposed a strain on the U.S.S.R.'s military capabilities.

Domestic Politics. The year's main political event, the 25th congress of the Soviet Communist Party, took place in Moscow at the end of February. Aside from confirming Brezhnev's leading position, the major speeches merely restated established policies. The most interesting change in the composition of the party leadership was the removal of Dmitry Polyansky from the Politburo, the relative failure of Soviet farming over the last five years having made his position untenable. He was later replaced as minister of agriculture by Valentin Mesyats, a party official from Kazakhstan. Two candidate members were advanced to full membership in the Politburo: Dmitry Ustinov, who was soon to succeed Marshal Grechko as minister of defense; and Grigory Romanov, the head of the party organization in Leningrad. Geidar Aliyev, party secretary in Azerbaijan, became a candidate member. Two additional secretaries to the Central Committee were also appointed: Mikhail Zemyanin, chief editor of *Pravda,* and Konstantin Chernenko, the head of the Central Committee's administration. In October the Central Committee appointed another member of the Secretariat: Yakov Ryabov, party secretary of the Sverdlovsk region, chosen to take over responsibility for defense industries from Marshal Ustinov.

The 25th party congress produced little change, thus underlining the static character of the Soviet system. Obedience, stability, and orthodoxy seemed to be the qualities needed for success and survival in Soviet politics. The leadership probably saw no need for change. Apart from the perennial difficulties of agriculture, the Soviet economy was doing reasonably well, and the foreign policy record was not unsatisfactory. Whether this continued investment in conformity would serve as well for the future remained to be seen. Possible problems to come were foreshadowed in the address to the party congress by Enrico Berlinguer, the Italian Communist leader, who advocated heretical views on sharing power with parties of different ideological persuasion and made an eloquent defense of civil liberty and the principles of parliamentary democracy.

The Economy. The party congress received the customary report on the state of the Soviet economy from Premier Kosygin, who reported that national income had risen by 34%, real wages by 20%, and retail trade by 36% in the last five years. Although targets were not fulfilled in agriculture and consumer goods, overall economic growth was declared to be satisfactory. Kosygin attacked "the excessive time taken to draw up plans, which undermines control over economic organs," and also criticized the uneven rhythm of technical progress. The congress approved the five-year plan for 1976–80, which had already been published in December 1975.

Soyuz 22 blasts off from its launching pad at Tyuratam in Soviet Central Asia in September. The spaceship carried two cosmonauts on an eight-day trip into orbit. The mission was a joint venture of the U.S.S.R. and East Germany.

A. PUSHKAREV—TASS / SOVFOTO

LONDON DAILY EXPRESS / PICTORIAL PARADE

A tall bronze statue of Lenin's wife, Nadezhda Krupskaya was unveiled in Moscow in June. The sculptors were A. M. Belashov and F. Belashova.

The chief problem was the massive failure of Soviet agriculture in 1975. The grain harvest of 140 million tons had been 75 million tons below target and the poorest in ten years. The effect on livestock production was disastrous. In consequence, the planned growth in the food industry for 1976–80 had to be cut back. The final plan also indicated that an effort would be made to increase the consumption of fish as a major source of protein. This was closely linked to the international issue of fishing limits and offshore zones. Toward the end of 1976 the U.S.S.R. imposed a 200-mi limit in the Pacific, a move much resented by the Japanese fishing industry. Recent changes in the international law of the sea compelled the U.S.S.R. to negotiate fishery agreements with Canada and Norway in 1976, and a treaty would have to be discussed with the European Economic Community, which had extended its members' limits to 200 mi in some traditional Soviet fishing areas in the North Atlantic and the North Sea. The problem was important for the U.S.S.R., which had the world's largest fishing fleet and earned significant foreign exchange from fish.

A possible reason for the failure of agriculture might be found in the relatively low standard of living in the Soviet countryside, which continued to drive young people from the villages to the towns. In June the party issued directives emphasizing the need to raise productivity and make good the shortage of labour by introducing factory farm methods. The creation of agrotowns—a project begun and abandoned by Nikita Khrushchev many years earlier—was to be resumed in an effort to make rural life more attractive to young people and to lay a foundation for the new farm policy. The program called for closing down 114,000 small villages in the central and northern parts of the country and moving the inhabitants into 29,000 population centres by 1990. Some 170,000 families were to be moved by 1980.

In the short term the Soviet leaders could take comfort from the successful 1976 harvest. The grain yield at the end of the year was reported to have been the largest in Soviet history. The disaster of the previous year was reflected in the trade statistics. Heavy purchases of grain, meat, and agricultural machinery in the West, coupled with a slackening demand for Soviet exports, brought about a foreign trade deficit of $3.6 billion in 1975, which had to be covered by borrowing from Western banks and by selling gold. (*See* AGRICULTURE AND FOOD SUPPLIES: *Special Report.*) (OTTO PICK)

[972.B.1]

ENCYCLOPÆDIA BRITANNICA FILMS. *The Soviet Union: Epic Land* (1972); *The Soviet Union: A Student's Life* (1972); *The Soviet Union: Faces of Today* (1972).

United Arab Emirates

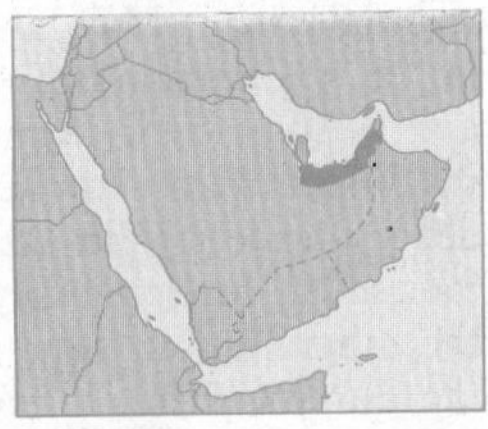

Consisting of Abu Dhabi, Ajman, Dubai, Fujairah, Ras al-Khaimah, Sharjah, and Umm al-Qaiwain, the United Arab Emirates is located on the eastern Arabian Peninsula. Area: 32,300 sq mi (83,600 sq km). Pop. (1975): 656,000, of whom (1968) 68% were Arab, 15% Iranian, and 15% Indian and Pakistani. Cap.: Abu Dhabi town (pop., 1975, 95,000). Language: Arabic. Religion: Muslim. President in 1976, Sheikh Zaid ibn Sultan an-Nahayan; prime minister, Sheikh Maktum ibn Rashid al-Maktum.

The United Arab Emirates (U.A.E.) in 1976 continued its economic development though there were some internal political disagreements. At a meeting in July the rulers of the emirates decided to extend the interim constitution for another five years from Dec. 2, 1976. In August President Sheikh Zaid intimated his unwillingness to run for a second term because of unsettled border disputes and lack of cooperation between member states. On October 12, however, an extraordinary session of the National Federal Council (Parliament) urged him to stay. Dubai caused a dispute by refusing to contribute to the federal budget, 50% of the revenues of which Abu Dhabi had undertaken in November 1975 to provide. In May the seven emirates agreed to merge their armed forces and a parade of arms marked the U.A.E.'s fifth anniversary on December 12; later in the month, 1,500 U.A.E. troops were reportedly moved to Lebanon's frontier with Israel.

Egypt looked to the U.A.E. for aid, and Egyptian Pres. Anwar as-Sadat visited the U.A.E. in February and June. Among development projects launched in the emirates during 1976 were the exploitation of onshore natural gas in Abu Dhabi; the building of an oil refinery to add to Abu Dhabi's first refinery, which opened during the year; an extension to Port Rashid and the dry dock in Dubai; and an aluminum smelter, also in Dubai. The U.A.E. followed Saudi Arabia in deciding to limit its oil price increase for 1977 to 5%. (PETER MANSFIELD)

[978.B.4.b]

SVEN SIMON—KATHERINE YOUNG

At the oasis of Al Ain in Abu Dhabi, the visitor can choose between a tent and the Hilton Hotel.

UNITED ARAB EMIRATES

Education. (1975–76) Primary, pupils 53,066, teachers 3,191; secondary, pupils 12,289, teachers 1,389; vocational, pupils 296, teachers 90; teacher training, students 118, teachers 8.

Finance. Monetary unit: dirham, with (Sept. 20, 1976) a par value of 3.95 dirhams to U.S. $1 (free rate of 6.80 dirhams = £1 sterling). Budget (federal; 1975–76 est.) balanced at 2,778,000,000 dirhams.

Foreign Trade. (1975) Imports *c.* 10,540,000,000 dirhams; exports *c.* 26,930,000,000 dirhams. Import sources (1974): Japan *c.* 18%; Qatar *c.* 14%; U.S. *c.* 14%; U.K. *c.* 14%; West Germany *c.* 5%; Kuwait *c.* 5%. Export destinations (1974): Japan *c.* 14%; West Germany *c.* 11%; U.K. *c.* 7%; U.S. *c.* 6%. Main export (1974) crude oil 98%.

Industry. Crude oil production (1975) 81,825,000 metric tons.

United Kingdom

A constitutional monarchy in northwestern Europe and member of the Commonwealth of Nations, the United Kingdom comprises the island of Great Britain (England, Scotland, and Wales) and Northern Ireland, together with many small islands. Area: 94,222 sq mi (244,035 sq km), including 1,174 sq mi of inland water but excluding the crown dependencies of the Channel Islands and Isle of Man. Pop. (1975 est.): 56,042,300. Cap. and largest city: London (Greater London pop., 1975 est., 7,111,500). Language: English; some Welsh and Gaelic also are used. Religion: mainly Protestant with Catholic, Muslim, and Jewish minorities, in that order. Queen, Elizabeth II; prime ministers in 1976, Harold Wilson and, from April 5, James Callaghan.

Politics. Halfway through the prospective life of the Labour government elected in 1974 there was a change of prime minister when Harold Wilson (*see* BIOGRAPHY) decided to retire after reaching the age of 60 and was succeeded by James Callaghan (*see* BIOGRAPHY). The statement Wilson made to the Cabinet on March 16 set out his reasons for retiring, emphasizing that he had been prime minister for nearly eight years, that the burden of office was heavy, that there was a risk of going stale, and that it was right to make a change in good time.

The Labour Party constitution provided for the election of a new leader in the House of Commons by the votes of Labour MP's and by the elimination of minority candidates in a succession of votes until one had a clear majority. Six candidates for the leadership lined up for the first round with the following result: Michael Foot (left) 90, James Callaghan (centre) 84, Roy Jenkins (right) 56, Anthony Benn (left) 37, Denis Healey (centre) 30, Anthony Crosland (right)

Unions: *see* Industrial Relations

Unitarian Churches: *see* Religion

United Church of Canada: *see* Religion

United Church of Christ: *see* Religion

17. Healey (*see* BIOGRAPHY) chose to run again in the second round, which put Callaghan ahead with 141, leading Foot 133 and Healey 38 but without a clear majority. In a final third round, on April 5, Callaghan was elected leader by 176 votes to 137.

In his reconstruction of the government Callaghan dropped some of the older stalwarts from the Cabinet, including Barbara Castle, Edward Short, William Ross, and Bob Mellish (at his own request). In the new Cabinet Michael Foot became leader of the House of Commons, Anthony Crosland (*see* BIOGRAPHY) foreign secretary, Peter Shore secretary of state for environment, and Shirley Williams (*see* BIOGRAPHY) paymaster general (in addition to secretary for prices and consumer protection). An additional small Cabinet reshuffle followed the announcement in September that Roy Jenkins, home secretary (*see* BIOGRAPHY), was to become president of the Commission of the European Economic Community (EEC). Merlyn Rees became home secretary, and Roy Mason, formerly defense secretary, took over from Rees as secretary of state for Northern Ireland; Shirley Williams became secretary for education and science, taking over from Fred Mulley, who became defense secretary; Fred Peart went to the House of Lords as its leader and was replaced by John Silkin as minister of agriculture, fisheries, and food. Reg Prentice, minister for overseas development, resigned on December 21 and was replaced by Frank Judd.

Callaghan quickly imposed his own style on affairs. Whereas Wilson had been rather reticent and even self-effacing in later years, Callaghan was readier to initiate a change of policy line, either by a major speech or on television. For example, he took the lead in opening up a wide-ranging debate on the quality of education, arguing at Oxford on October 18 that it had to be more purposefully directed toward the training of basic skills. He startled many in the government by detaching transport from the giant Department of the Environment and restoring it as an independent ministry.

Monty's last parade. The funeral cortege of Field Marshal Viscount Montgomery of Alamein, hero of North Africa in World War II, heads toward Windsor Castle for his state funeral in April.

FOX PHOTOS/PICTORIAL PARADE

The Conservative opposition led by Margaret Thatcher continued to move further to the right of the political spectrum, incorporating monetarist doctrines into its financial and economic policy and adopting a hawkish stance on foreign affairs and defense. A reconstruction of the so-called shadow cabinet in November confirmed this move to the right. Reginald Maudling, a former Cabinet minister in the governments of Edward Heath, was dropped, and a number of aggressive younger men brought in. William Whitelaw, known as a moderate, remained deputy leader. John Davies, a strong pro-European, took over foreign affairs from Maudling. Some of the other leading figures included Sir Keith Joseph, the party's theorist and a monetarist (policy and research); Sir Geoffrey Howe (Treasury affairs); James Prior (employment); Francis Pym (devolution); Michael Heseltine (environment); and John Biffen (industry).

The Liberal Party elected David Steel (*see* BIOGRAPHY) as its leader after the resignation on May 10 of Jeremy Thorpe, who had been leader since 1967. Thorpe had been at the centre of a controversy that had grown after allegations had been made in January during a court case (in which Thorpe was not involved) that he had had homosexual relations with a former male model named Norman Scott. Thorpe denied these allegations, and the Liberal parliamentary party reaffirmed its support for him. However, a number of newspapers continued to investigate the allegations. Also in January, the report of an official inquiry into the collapse of the investment bank London and County Securities, of which Thorpe was a nonexecutive director, was severely critical of the directors. While continuing to deny the Scott allegations, Thorpe decided he must resign for the sake of his party.

Jo Grimond, Thorpe's predecessor as Liberal leader, was called back as a caretaker leader while arrangements were made to elect a successor, but refused to stay for more than a minimum interim period. The Liberals introduced a novel system of election by constituencies, with each constituency vote of Liberal Party members weighted to take account of the number of Liberal votes cast in that constituency at the general election. There were two candidates, John Pardoe and David Steel. The result announced on July 7 showed Steel elected by 12,541 votes to 7,032 for Pardoe.

Parliament. Labour found its majority in the House of Commons increasingly insecure after losing two seats in by-elections on November 4. Earlier, in by-elections in March and June, Labour had held safe seats but with greatly reduced majorities. In November it lost two safe seats in the industrial areas of Workington and Walsall North with massive swings of votes to the Conservatives of 13 and 22%. (The Walsall North seat had been vacated in August by John Stonehouse—the MP who disappeared in 1974 and was later arrested in Australia—after he was sentenced to seven years in prison on charges of theft, forgery, and fraud.) In a Parliament of 635 members, and discounting the speaker and his three deputies who do not vote, this left Labour with 312 against 278 Conservative MP's, and the government could not always be sure which way the 41 members of smaller parties would vote. It could generally rely on the support of two Scottish Nationalists and two from Northern Ireland, while ten Ulster Unionists were likely to vote with the Conservatives. This left 13 Liberals, 11 Scottish Nationalists, and 3 Welsh Nationalists sometimes holding the balance.

On issues of confidence the government could expect to survive (except, perhaps, on issues of devolution, which might concentrate the nationalists against it), but it could not guarantee to win every vote, particularly when it was liable to occasional defections. Though the so-called "Tribune group" on the left was the most numerous and therefore seemed to be the most threatening, it was the abstention of two right-wingers that wrecked a bill to give the dockers' union (Transport and General Workers) a monopoly of all freight handling within five miles of the dockside. This was one episode during November in a flurry of amendments made to government bills by the Conservative opposition in the House of Lords (where there was a permanent majority of Conservative peers). Labour in the Commons retaliated by rejecting the Lords' amendments and returning the bills to the Lords. This raised the endemic constitutional issue of conflict between the two houses in sharper terms than for many years.

Constitution. In November 1975 the government postponed for another 12 months a decision on devolution of political power to Scotland and Wales in order to provide further time for discussion. Legislation was promised for the 1976–77 session opening in November, and the devolution bill was introduced on November 30. It proposed elected assemblies and an executive for Scotland and Wales, but would not give them revenue-raising powers. Meanwhile, as the devolution debate continued, doubts began to deepen on the one hand among those who were skeptical about the concept and its likely consequences for the future of the United Kingdom, while at the other extreme some of the nationalists were talking in terms of separatism.

The Economy. At the opening of 1976 the U.K. seemed to be climbing out of the nightmarish economic troubles of 1975. The pay ceilings that took effect from Aug. 1, 1975, together with price controls, had reduced the annual rate of inflation by more than half, from a peak figure of 36% in June 1975 to 13.6% in December. In January 1976 the Price Commission issued its most optimistic report in 2½ years, and the prices minister, Shirley Williams, said that inflation should be down to single figures by the end of the year. For the first time in six months Britain's gold and currency reserves increased in January. Consumer spending was depressed, but personal savings were high. The minimum lending rate, at 9½% was at its lowest in more than two years. The stock market responded cheerfully, and on one day in January the *Financial Times* industrial index registered the largest one-day and one-week increases in its history, rising to over 400 early in January (as compared with 146 at the bottom of the stock market collapse a year earlier). The trade deficit had been improving steadily over the previous six months. The question early in the year seemed to be how the government could stimulate economic activity while inflation was still high, for the world trade recession plus stagnant demand at home had pushed up unemployment, to 1,372,000 in January.

At that stage little was being said about two factors which, as it turned out, were about to go out of control. The Price Commission in its January report had noted that the main threat to a continuing reduction of the inflation rate would be a further decline in the value of sterling. Through November 1975 to February the sterling exchange rate remained steady at about $2.02 to the pound. Then early in March sterling began to slide, and was in a state of continuing crisis for the remainder of the year. It was not clear what set off the flight from sterling in March, though a fortnight earlier a routine document, the White Paper "Public Expenditure to 1979–'80," had been published. This showed that public expenditure (by the central government, local government, and public enterprise) had grown by 20% in volume in the previous three years, at a time when output had increased by only 2%, and was now accounting for 60% of the gross domestic product (GDP), as compared with 50% in 1972 and 42% in 1961. Government expenditure targets were then revised downward by £2,900 million but these cuts were to take effect only by 1978–79. At this point a group of Cambridge

continued on page 690

UNITED KINGDOM

Education. (1974–75) Primary, pupils 6,012,655, teachers 247,127; secondary, pupils 4,491,552, teachers 262,791; vocational, pupils 381,530, teachers 67,692; higher, students 397,621, teaching staff 52,947.

Finance. Monetary unit: pound sterling, with (Sept. 20, 1976) a free rate of £0.58 to U.S. $1 (U.S. $1.72 = £1 sterling). Gold, SDR's, and foreign exchange (June 1976) U.S. $5,302,000,000. Budget (1976–77 est.): revenue £33,197 million; expenditure £39,915 million. Gross national product (1975) £103,190 million. Money supply (June 1976) £17,405 million. Cost of living (1970 = 100; June 1976) 213.

Foreign Trade. (1975) Imports £24,163 million; exports £19,929 million. Import sources: EEC 37% (West Germany 8%, The Netherlands 8%, France 7%); U.S. 10%. Export destinations: EEC 32% (West Germany 6%, France 6%, The Netherlands 6%, Belgium-Luxembourg 5%, Ireland 5%); U.S. 9%. Main exports: nonelectric machinery 22%; chemicals 11%; motor vehicles 9%; electrical machinery and equipment 8%. Tourism (1974): visitors 7,935,000.

Transport and Communications. Roads (1974) *c.* 366,000 km (including 1,879 km expressways). Motor vehicles in use (1974): passenger *c.* 13,980,000; commercial *c.* 1,811,000. Railways (excluding Northern Ireland; 1974): 18,168 km; traffic 36,130,000,000 passenger-km, freight 24,168,000,000 net ton-km. Air traffic (1975): 27,766,000,000 passenger-km; freight 852,514,000 net ton-km. Shipping (1975): merchant vessels 100 gross tons and over 3,622; gross tonnage 33,157,422. Ships entered (1970) vessels totaling 137,888,000 net registered tons; goods loaded (1973) 56,157,000 metric tons, unloaded 221,043,000 metric tons. Telephones (March 1975) 20,342,500. Radio receivers (Dec. 1974) *c.* 38 million. Television licenses (Dec. 1975) 17,675,000.

Agriculture. Production (in 000; metric tons; 1975): wheat 4,435; barley 8,436; oats 802; potatoes 4,515; sugar, raw value *c.* 627; cabbages (1974) *c.* 772; cauliflowers (1974) *c.* 346; green peas (1974) *c.* 706; carrots (1974) 506; apples (1974) 365; dry peas 88; dry broad beans (1974) *c.* 215; tomatoes 114; onions *c.* 243; hen's eggs 799; cow's milk *c.* 14,000; butter 40; cheese 228; beef and veal 1,216; mutton and lamb 260; pork 816; wool 32; fish catch 802. Livestock (in 000; June 1975): cattle 14,641; sheep 28,125; pigs 7,471; poultry 136,249.

Industry. Index of production (1970 = 100; 1975) 101. Fuel and power (in 000; metric tons; 1975): coal 128,660; crude oil 1,600; natural gas (cu m) 34,216,000; manufactured gas (cu m; 1974) 7,806,000; electricity (kw-hr) 272,229,000. Production (in 000; metric tons; 1975): cement 16,891; iron ore (28% metal content) 4,490; pig iron 12,134; crude steel 20,157; petroleum products 86,640; sulfuric acid 3,166; fertilizers (nutrient content; 1974–75) nitrogenous 885, phosphate 429, potash 12; cotton fabrics (m) 405,000; woolen fabrics (sq m) 151,000; rayon and acetate fabrics (m) 503,000; passenger cars (units) 1,268; commercial vehicles (units) 378. Merchant vessels launched (100 gross tons and over; 1975) 1,294,000 gross tons. New dwelling units completed (1975) 310,000.

SPECIAL REPORT

THE IRISH QUESTION

by Bruce Arnold

The Northern Ireland Constitutional Convention came to an end on March 3, 1976. It had been elected ten months earlier, in May 1975, with "Loyalists" of the United Ulster Unionist Coalition gaining 46 of the 78 seats. Predictably, the report it made to the British government was a demand for a return to majority rule. The report was not supported by minority representatives in Northern Ireland, and was therefore unacceptable to Britain. The last and weakest of Northern Ireland political assemblies was disbanded, and the six Ulster counties, with a total population of just over 1.5 million, were left with a representation of 12 MP's in the British Parliament. Direct rule from Westminster was once again the only rule for the North.

This return to direct rule came about in an atmosphere of substantial change in political attitudes in Britain, in the Republic of Ireland, and among Northern Ireland politicians of all opinions. There was now no expectation of an early return to political independence of any type in Northern Ireland, little or no pressure for it within Britain, and only limited and uncertain pressure within the Republic of Ireland. What was most alarming for the Northern Ireland politicians, however, was the fact that within the province itself there was growing acceptance of direct rule from Britain as the most satisfactory option in the face of continuing violence. Since this was also the basis of the Republic's Northern Ireland policy, and since it was supported by the majority of people in Britain now that violence in British cities had ceased to be part of the Irish Republican Army's terrorist program, there was little or no prospect for the rekindling of Northern Ireland political initiatives.

Yet violence continued. The Protestant and Roman Catholic communities remained bitterly divided. The terrorist organizations showed no sign of abating their control over the communities and continued to use them as bases for launching further terrorist attacks.

British Policy. In the wake of the convention's failure to produce a report offering any realistic prospect for workable political devolution in the North, British policy hardened against any new initiatives. The British government was increasingly influenced by pressures for devolution coming from Scotland and Wales and by the knowledge that a Northern Ireland solution, in terms of a devolved parliament, would establish precedents that could be embarrassing. But this was only one of many factors affecting the overall Northern Ireland policy.

Militarily, the situation in the North had improved. Violence had been concentrated in the area of sectarian killings, which, to put it bluntly, had a local rather than a United Kingdom impact. The deaths of British Army personnel were at a militarily acceptable level. Numerically, they compared quite favourably with the general accident rate of the British Army in training either in Britain or in West Germany, and Northern Ireland offered valuable training experience in combating urban terrorism and civil disturbances.

The military aspects of the Northern Ireland problem should not be underestimated. In addition to the theory that an acceptable level of violence, in military terms, had been achieved, there was a growing conviction that British policy was now substantially influenced by the belief in a military solution to terrorism. This view was reinforced by the replacement, in September, of Merlyn Rees as secretary of state for Northern Ireland by the former U.K. defense minister, Roy Mason. The strong reaction to this appointment from the Social Democratic and Labour Party leader, Gerard Fitt, indicated that he felt it offered no possibility for new political solutions—a view shared by many others. There was a third strand in the military argument, namely, that overall defense policies for Britain and Europe would be gravely threatened by political instability in Northern Ireland resulting from initiatives such as a British undertaking to withdraw, which might have disastrous results. Military containment, combined with the British Army's hope for an eventual victory over terrorism, thus became a major element in the British government's thinking after the failure of the Northern Ireland convention to produce a power-sharing solution.

The strong military content of British policy called for political dovetailing by the Northern Ireland secretary. This led to charges that there was, in effect, no policy at all. But this was an unjust view of what was attempted in Northern Ireland during the period of political vacuum that followed the convention. Disappointing as it might be to politicians of widely differing views in both parts of Ireland, the main direction of Merlyn Rees's policy was to reestablish the Britishness of Northern Ireland. The ending of internment, the restoration of law and order, the effort to obtain convictions in courts, the treatment of terrorists as criminals, the phasing out of special category status for political prisoners were all aspects of a normalizing process that went hand in hand with the essential political reality of direct rule. In theory, the process also went hand in hand with a British government commitment to devolved government for Northern Ireland, but the onus now was on the Northern politicians to come up with an acceptable formula. And if there was little prospect of Merlyn Rees helping in this, there was even less chance that his successor, Roy Mason, would play a positive role or that the U.K. prime minister, James Callaghan, would propose wider British initiatives.

Irish Policy. The national coalition government in the Republic of Ireland played a significant part in making this low-key British policy possible. Foreign Minister Garret FitzGerald, who was primarily responsible for Northern Ireland policy, worked on the assumption that Northern Ireland Loyalist intransigence, while basically an attitude that had been necessary if the Loyalists were to retain power within the six Ulster counties, had fed on the fears of ordinary people at the threatening Republican noises coming from all the political parties in the South over the past half century. If the grounds for such fears could be reduced, in his opinion, the unity of Loyalist political feeling would begin to break up. New alignments would emerge, leading to the possibility of a form of political partnership that would make devolved government in Northern Ireland once again acceptable.

The Republic's policy, then, went no further than offering concern, understanding, and cooperation to people in the North, both Protestant and Catholic, combined with increased vigilance against terrorists and terrorist organizations south of the border. It was an approach fraught with difficulties, the most obvious being that it laid the coalition government open to the charge of doing nothing at all. The first major political action taken by the coalition after it came to power in March 1973 had been the Sunningdale initiative that led to the only Northern Ireland power-sharing administration. After so positive a start, to revert to a low-key and necessarily negative role in British-Irish relations was to invite criticism. The foreign minister and the minister for posts and telegraphs, Conor Cruise O'Brien, worked genuinely for a new approach and new attitudes toward Northern Ireland, but they were relatively isolated within the Cabinet. The coalition government as a whole, partly through lack of confidence in what it was doing, partly because of old political

---

Bruce Arnold is parliamentary correspondent of the Irish Independent, *Dublin.*

bitterness, failed to establish the first and by far the most important prerequisite for a workable Northern Ireland policy: true bipartisanship between itself and the previous government party, Fianna Fail, now in opposition. This would have been difficult but possible in 1973 and into 1974; by the fall of 1976 the possibility was no longer there.

Without the general endorsement of Fianna Fail on all major issues affecting the relationship between the Republic and Northern Ireland, the coalition government was in no position to give practical expression to its concern, to extend the framework of understanding by consultation at political or official levels, or to engage in joint cooperative activities across the border. Worse still, the sequence of security moves undertaken by the coalition, with the object of strengthening its hand against subversives, led to bitter political encounters. They were seen as a replacement for more positive policy measures; as a form of connivance with the military approach dominant in British policy; and as an attempt to discredit Fianna Fail on law-and-order grounds. While privately dismayed at the direction policy was taking and aware of the damage it was doing both in the North and in Britain, Foreign Minister FitzGerald was powerless to prevent the growing rift between government and opposition. The making of it was too firmly in the hands of Prime Minister Liam Cosgrave and Defense Minister Patrick Donegan, both of them strong law-and-order men and both opposed to any sharing of policy or responsibility with the opposition. Inevitably, the death of the British ambassador at the hands of terrorists in July was used as an excuse to bring in a state of emergency, special emergency powers of detention, and greatly increased sentences for terrorist offenses. And the rift became still wider.

This introduction of an emergency package had the further effect of driving the Republic of Ireland toward much more draconian and selective pressures on terrorists just when the whole trend of British policy in the North was toward the normal use of the police and the courts and the elimination of political status for extremists. It suggested less than adequate liaison between the Republic and Britain. It also suggested an overreaction, for political reasons, to a situation in the Republic that, in spite of certain specific events, could not be said to justify a state of emergency and seven-day detention.

Conclusions. The main emphasis in this article has been on British policy and policy in the Republic of Ireland. It might appear that this is because, over the past six years, undue emphasis has been placed on the Northern Ireland politicians. But the reality was that in 1976, for the first time since the period of troubles began, the politicians of the North—with the exception of the 12 who still had their seats at Westminster—were reduced to the status of public representatives whose mandate belonged to the past and who had no place to exercise it. Although some people expressed relief at this, particularly in British political circles, it was an extremely dangerous development. It threw back on the terrorist organizations the onus of action and the assertion of power and control.

A military campaign fought out within a virtual political vacuum still leaves that vacuum if and when the campaign ends. Even the most sanguine of militarists can find few examples of military campaigns against terrorism that succeeded without political concessions. In the Irish context, even if there should be further success in containing extremism, the political initiatives would still have to be taken, and the belief that this could or would be done in the unlikely event that terrorism ended grew ever more faint. The simple restoration of the belief in a better political future in Northern Ireland—in all of Ireland—was the basic priority for those who still retained power: the British government and the government of the Republic.

ALAIN DEJEAN—SYGMA

A British soldier crouches in a Belfast doorway. There were growing doubts whether British policy in Northern Ireland had anything more to offer than a military solution. Politically, the British seemed to have run out of ideas, and the Irish themselves had nothing new to propose.

PETER MARLOW—SYGMA

Irish women march for peace in Northern Ireland. Thirty thousand Catholics and Protestants took part in this Belfast demonstration in August calling for an end to the slaughter.

continued from page 687

University economists calculated that public expenditure was likely to be £3,250 million more in 1976–77 than had been planned. This set the stage for the rest of the year: an intermittent public debate about the actual level of public expenditure, runaway government borrowing to cover the gap, and a consequent collapse in confidence in sterling, interacting in a financial chain reaction.

It was difficult to follow the course of events exactly, partly because the figures themselves were distorted by inflation. The general drift, however, became reasonably clear. The fall in the sterling exchange rate increased the cost of imports and widened the balance of payments deficit. To shore up sterling, interest rates were increased, which in turn increased the cost of government debt and the size of the government's borrowing requirement. Higher interest rates and curbs on government spending held back economic recovery, which caused high levels of unemployment and thereby increased the cost of social security and the budget deficit. Higher import costs and interest rates added to domestic inflation, which led to a further decline in the exchange rate.

Some of the key stages in this process could be noted. Sterling declined from \$2.02 to \$1.85 in the six weeks before the April budget. Healey introduced one novel feature in his budget; some small reductions in the income tax were made conditional on the labour unions agreeing to a 4½% limit up to a £4 per week ceiling on any pay increases. At the same time, Healey increased the consumer taxes on gasoline, alcoholic beverages, and tobacco. His budget was designed to hold back inflation and also to provide for 4% annual growth that would rise to 5½% in following years. The Trades Union Congress agreed to pay limits of £4 a week up to a ceiling of 5% early in May. Yet sterling continued to fall, to \$1.71 by the beginning of June. At that time six months of standby credit from the Group of Ten (leading industrialized nations) was negotiated, and the level of sterling settled between \$1.80 and \$1.75 until mid-September.

Meanwhile, on June 17 a White Paper, "The Attack on Inflation—the Second Year," claimed that the halving of the inflation rate since July 1975 "has set Britain on the road to recovery," but acknowledged that single-figure inflation could not be reached, as intended, by the end of the year. A month later Healey submitted the July mini-budget, making additional expenditure cuts of about £1,000 million for 1977–78 and adding another £910 million to the national insurance payments made by employers from April 1977.

The run on sterling was renewed in mid-September. This time the Bank of England decided to let the rate slide without support, but the minimum lending rate was raised to 13%. With Healey and others saying that the pound was undervalued it slipped back to \$1.70 and below. Then on September 28, the day when Healey was setting out for the Commonwealth finance ministers' conference in Hong Kong and the annual meeting of the International Monetary Fund (IMF) in Manila, the pound fell by 4.40 cents, at that time the biggest one-day decline ever recorded. Healey broke off his journey at London airport to return to the Treasury. The following day Britain applied for an IMF loan of £2,300 million to stabilize sterling.

Yet worse was to come. By that time reports of rising money supply, liable to refuel inflation, had still further weakened confidence. The market had become so unstable that on October 25, on the strength of a newspaper report, sterling dropped 7 cents in a few hours to touch \$1.57. Later that week it drifted down to \$1.56. This for the time being proved the low point. With the minimum lending rate raised to an unprecedented 15% on October 7 and with an IMF team in London negotiating terms for the loan, confidence began to recover, for it was plain that sterling was now undervalued. Sterling's role as a reserve currency, with £6,000 million of sterling balances overhanging reserves that in October had fallen to a five-year low of around £3,000 million (at a \$1.60 exchange rate), was now a manifest embarrassment, and the prime minister said so. Discussions began for an international arrangement to fund the sterling balances.

On December 15 Healey introduced an interim budget to meet the terms of the IMF loan, with cuts of £2,500 million over the next two years in public spending, affecting defense, foreign aid, housing, food, and education, as well as increases in the price of tobacco, beer, spirits, and gas. The budget was attacked by the Labour left for its cuts in the area of social service.

On October 7 it was announced that Wilson would head a committee to inquire into "the role and functioning, at home and abroad, of financial institutions in the United Kingdom and their value to the economy." This reflected widespread disquiet with the recent financial performance of the City of London. Severely critical reports appeared. In July the Department of Trade attacked Lonrho, the overseas trading conglomerate, criticizing the chief executive Roland ("Tiny") Rowland, former chairman Lord Duncan-Sandys (an ex-Cabinet minister), and directors including Angus Ogilvy (married to Princess Alexandra, a cousin of the queen). In September a team of accountants reported on the collapses of Slater Walker Securities, whose chairman, Jim Slater (*see* BIOGRAPHY), had been replaced in October 1975 by the multimillionaire financier James Goldsmith (*see* BIOGRAPHY), and in November there was a Stock Exchange inquiry into stock dealings by Sir Hugh Fraser, chairman of the House of Fraser (the department store chain that owned Harrods) and of Scottish and Universal Investments (SUITS). From the latter probe it emerged that Fraser had sold 1.5 million shares to pay gambling debts.

Industry and Trade. The sterling crisis became such an obsession that it diverted attention from more hopeful developments. Callaghan told the House of Commons in October, "the pessimism is overdone."

He was able to point to the fact that pay agreements were working in the second year of the social contract, and in 1976 the number of work stoppages in industry was the lowest since the 1950s. Exports were rising. At the lord mayor of London's banquet on November 15, a traditional occasion for a prime minister's keynote speech, Callaghan said that the industrial strategy (worked out during the year between government, trade unions, and industry on a new tripartite basis) was aimed at giving absolute priority to industrial needs even ahead of social objectives. He drew attention to the solid ground for confidence in the near future: North Sea oil, which would make Britain self-sufficient in energy by the early 1980s.

Britain's biggest North Sea oil find, the Brent field, started production in November. Five other fields were already in production, yielding about 400,000 bbl a day, equivalent to a quarter of Britain's oil consumption. Exploration suggested that North Sea resources would be greater than earlier thought, putting Britain among the top ten oil producers in the world in the 1980s. North Sea gas was also being brought ashore in increasing quantities and earlier than expected.

Climate. Parts of Britain in 1976 suffered the worst drought since weather records began in 1727, and in some areas in the later part of the summer water supplies were severely restricted to both industrial and domestic users. Moreover, the parched, brown landscape was made desolate in the south and many other parts of Britain by leafless elms succumbing to the progress of Dutch elm disease. There was rationing of water in southwest England, south Wales, and parts of Yorkshire, and there were extensive heath and forest fires in August and September. The drought, which extended over Western Europe from the Scottish border to northern Italy, came as the climax to the driest five years in Britain since 1850. When it finally broke in September, nine weeks of exceptionally heavy rainfall followed, with October in some places in Britain the wettest on record.

Foreign Affairs and Defense. Foreign policy and defense policy were increasingly centred on Europe. The withdrawal of British defense forces from bases east of Suez continued. Almost the whole of the British defense effort (costing £5,632 million in 1976–77, 5.5% of gross national product) was devoted to the North Atlantic Treaty Organization (NATO). The U.K. found that its membership in the EEC was attracting greater benefits (especially in the cost of food) than the cost of its contributions. The government agreed to direct elections to a European Parliament to be held in 1978, Britain having 81 seats out of 410. The former U.K. Cabinet minister Roy Jenkins was appointed president of the European Commission as of Jan. 1, 1977, and it was the turn of the British foreign secretary (Anthony Crosland) to be chairman of the Community Council of Ministers for the first half of 1977.

The dispute with Iceland over fishing limits led to the breaking off of diplomatic relations. The Royal Navy put in escorts for British trawlers, and there were a number of incidents with Icelandic patrol boats involving 45 cases of collision. After Iceland had threatened to withdraw from NATO, an agreement was reached on June 1 which restricted the number of British trawlers fishing in the Icelandic 200-mi limit to an average of 24 a day. Diplomatic relations were resumed, but a final settlement remained to be adjusted to the EEC's own declaration of a 200-mi limit.

Britain was reluctantly involved in the gathering conflict between Rhodesia and its African neighbours. On March 22 Callaghan (then foreign secretary) called on Rhodesian Prime Minister Ian Smith to accept the principle of majority rule, with elections to take place within two years. Smith rejected the British initiative, and U.S. Secretary of State Henry Kissinger (*see* BIOGRAPHY) then took on the role of intermediary. This led to the opening in Geneva on October 28 of a conference to agree on a settlement, with Britain's permanent representative at the UN, Ivor Richard, as chairman. (*See* AFRICAN AFFAIRS.)

Northern Ireland. The so-called cease-fire of 1975 broke down in an escalation of sectarian violence, and the 1976 death toll of 296 was the highest since 1972. Among many violent incidents, two stood out: the assassination of Britain's newly appointed ambassador to Dublin, Christopher Ewart-Biggs (*see* OBITUARIES), when a land mine blew up his car near his Dublin residence on July 21; and the killing of Mrs. Maire Drumm (*see* OBITUARIES), a well-known leader of the Provisional Irish Republican Army, who was shot dead by Protestant gunmen in the Belfast hospital where she was being treated. The death of three small children who were run down by a gunman's car in Belfast prompted a wave of public protest, with a series of mass demonstrations by a women's peace movement set up in August by two Belfast women, Mrs. Betty Williams (a Protestant) and Miss Mairead Corrigan (a Roman Catholic). Prime Minister Callaghan, visiting Belfast in July, said that Northern Ireland would not cease to be part of the U.K. unless it was the clear wish of a majority, and he promised that the Army would remain as long as needed.

UPI COMPIX

A newspaper placard outside the Bank of England proclaims the bad news about Britain's pound. In October, after months of decline, it seemed to be heading toward $1.50.

The Royal Family. Arrangements were under way for silver jubilee celebrations on June 7, 1977, to mark the 25th anniversary of the accession of Queen Elizabeth II. The queen and Prince Philip visited the U.S. on the occasion of the 200th anniversary of the Declaration of Independence. On March 19 it was announced that Princess Margaret and the earl of Snowdon had "mutually agreed to live apart." There were no plans for divorce proceedings.

(HARFORD THOMAS)

See also Commonwealth of Nations; Dependent States; Ireland.

[972.A.1.a]

United Nations

Reporting in September to the General Assembly on United Nations activities during the previous year, Secretary-General Kurt Waldheim (whom the General Assembly on December 8 reelected by acclamation for a second five-year term) said that he was more than ever convinced that the UN was necessary, but also more worried than ever before at states' reluctance or halfheartedness in using or developing the organization. The UN, he said, should not be just "a last resort in critical situations" or "a repository for insoluble problems." Rather, the world needed an instrument of cooperation "with sufficient international solidarity and prestige not to be ignored in dangerous times or thrown off balance by sudden controversies and confrontations."

Southern Africa. Waldheim issued several warnings in 1976 of escalating crises and possible bloodshed in southern Africa because South Africa had refused to give independence to Namibia (South West

Africa) and white Rhodesians had refused to grant majority rule to indigenous blacks, who outnumbered them by a ratio of 20 to 1. The secretary-general's point was illustrated in January, when Zaire complained that "Soviet-Cuban forces . . . fighting in Angola" threatened its sovereignty, territorial integrity, and security, and again, on March 31, when the Security Council voted 9–0, with five abstentions (France, Italy, Japan, the United Kingdom, and the United States) and China not participating, to condemn South Africa for aggression against Angola and demanded that the republic desist from using the "international Territory of Namibia to mount provocative or aggressive acts" against Angola or any other African state. The abstaining council members characterized the resolution as unbalanced in not calling for all states to refrain from interfering in Angola, especially since, at the time, no South African troops were on Angolan territory—they had all been withdrawn by March 27—but Cuban soldiers were. Indeed, on June 23 the U.S. vetoed Angola's application for UN membership, arguing that Angola did not yet meet UN Charter requirements because of the continuing "massive" presence and "apparent influence" of Cuban troops in the country. In deference to African desires to see Angola in the UN, however, the U.S. abstained when the Security Council reconsidered Angolan membership on November 22, and Angola became the 146th member of the UN when the assembly admitted it on December 1.

Year-long protests by many UN organs and affiliated agencies against South African policies of apartheid came to a climax on November 9, when the 31st annual assembly, by large majorities, adopted various resolutions directed against South Africa: reaffirming the right of the people of South Africa to struggle by all means for "the seizure of power" and the exercise of their right to self-determination; condemning any collaboration with the republic as "a hostile act against the oppressed people of South Africa" and as "contemptuous defiance" of the UN and especially singling out France, West Germany, Israel, the U.K., and the U.S. as offenders; scoring Israel for "continuing and increasing collaboration with the South African racist regime"; urging the Security Council to impose a mandatory arms embargo against South Africa and specifically requesting France, the U.K., and the U.S. to reconsider their opposition to such action; requesting the council to consider ways of bringing to an end further foreign investments in South Africa; authorizing its special committee against apartheid to organize a world conference in Africa in 1977 on the problem and suggesting interim measures that governments, specialized agencies, churches, trade unions, and other organizations might take against South Africa; establishing a drafting committee to prepare an international convention against apartheid in sports; excoriating South Africa for "ruthless repression . . . of the oppressed people of South Africa and other opponents of apartheid"; reaffirming solidarity with South African political prisoners and demanding their immediate and unconditional release; and asking states to contribute more generously to the UN trust fund for Africa, which provides humanitarian assistance to victims of discriminatory legislation.

Votes opposing or abstaining on these resolutions were cast mainly by Western states, but also by some Latin-American and African countries. These UN members generally condemned apartheid, but argued that ending all contacts with South Africa was not an effective way to oppose racial separation, that apartheid could not properly be treated as a colonial situation, that encouraging violence was wrong, and that condemning particular countries was unwarranted.

During 1976 related Security Council actions directed against South Africa were sometimes frustrated by permanent council members with the right of veto. Thus, on October 19, the council did not adopt a resolution calling for a mandatory arms embargo against South Africa for having rejected council initiatives to transfer power to the people of Namibia. Ten members of the 15-member body wished to adopt the resolution, but France, the U.K., and the U.S. did not and Japan and Italy abstained. The three states voting no told the council that although they were in fact denying arms to South Africa, they regarded the resolution as inappropriate when U.S. Secretary of State Henry A. Kissinger had, in private talks with South African officials, opened up diplomatic prospects for achieving UN goals for Namibia. Supporters of the draft resolution generally argued that, far from meeting UN demands, South Africa was actually intensifying its "illegal and repressive grip" on Namibia and had used the territory as a springboard for aggression against neighbours; they insisted that stronger pressure on South Africa was needed.

Early in the year border incidents were reported between Mozambique and Rhodesia, but on the weekend of August 7–8 Rhodesian forces attacked deep inside Mozambique, an action Waldheim condemned as a "clear and admitted violation by force of the sovereign territory of a member state." The secretary-general also deplored the fate of hundreds of persons killed or wounded.

Middle East. Like the problems of Africa, problems of the Middle East commanded the attention of many UN groups during the year and culminated in council and assembly debates. On July 14 the council concluded a four-day debate on Israel's raid of July 3–4 on Entebbe airport, Uganda, where Israeli troops rescued 103 passengers and crew of a hijacked French airbus whom Palestinian terrorists were holding hostage. The council turned aside without vote an African draft resolution which would have condemned the Israeli action as a flagrant violation of Ugandan sovereignty and territorial integrity and would have de-

WIDE WORLD

Austrians call it UN City. These new buildings on the north bank of the Danube in Vienna will house agencies of the United Nations, including the International Atomic Energy Agency and the UN Industrial Development Organization.

manded compensation for damage and destruction. A U.K.-U.S. draft condemning aerial hijacking and calling for measures to prevent and punish all such terrorist acts, while reaffirming the need to respect territorial integrity and sovereignty of all states, received only six of the nine votes required for approval.

On November 29 the assembly endorsed recommendations of its committee on Palestinian rights that Israel withdraw completely by June 1, 1977, from areas it had occupied in 1967. Under the resolution, the UN would take over evacuated territories and, in cooperation with the Arab League, hand them over to the Palestine Liberation Organization (PLO) as the representative of the Palestinian people. As soon as an independent Palestinian entity had been established, the UN would arrange to give effect to the rights of the Palestinian people. The assembly urged the council to consider these recommendations and to put them into effect as soon as possible. In the assembly voting, the permanent council members took divergent positions: China and the U.S.S.R. voted in favour, the U.K. and U.S. against, and France abstained. Chaim Herzog of Israel denounced the resolutions as reflecting the PLO position and as conflicting with council decisions. Israel, he said, would not be dictated to and insisted on direct negotiations among the parties concerned. The assembly also adopted resolutions on Palestinian refugees that emphasized the serious financial problems of the UN Relief and Works Agency, called on all governments to contribute generously to the agency, and also urged continuing assistance to the refugees. The assembly, in addition, reaffirmed the right of the displaced inhabitants to return to their homes or to camps in occupied territory and called on Israel to facilitate the return. Israel responded by saying that the existing security situation did not permit large-scale returns of displaced persons, and, in the case of the Gaza Strip, charged that the assembly was asking it to return refugees from decent housing provided by Israel to the "wretched" conditions of Gaza Strip camps.

In a statement adopted by consensus on November 11, the Security Council "strongly deplored" measures Israel had taken altering the demographic composition or geographic nature of the Israeli-occupied territories, particularly by establishing settlements. Such measures, the council stated, had "no legal validity" and constituted "an obstacle to peace." The council once again asked Israel to ensure the safety, welfare, and security of the inhabitants of the territories and to help those who had fled since the outbreak of hostilities to return. It also asked Israel to comply with the Geneva Convention on the Protection of Civilians in Wartime and to rescind all measures tending to change the legal status of Jerusalem. The statement followed public debate and private consultations on Egypt's complaint earlier in the month that Israel was creating an explosive situation in the occupied territories. Ambassador Herzog cited the consensus statement as an example of the "biased selectivity, one-sidedness, and political expediency" that, he said, characterized the council's approach to the issues. It was unacceptable, he continued, because it ignored the root of the problem—the unwillingness of the Arab states to negotiate peace with Israel.

Economic Affairs. Among major economic and social actions in 1976, UN observers noted that the World Food Program, meeting in Rome in April, committed $600 million to support projects of economic and social development and $40 million to help meet emergency food needs of people affected by calamities; the UN Conference on Trade and Development ended its fourth session in Nairobi, Kenya, on May 31, after approving an integrated commodity program seeking both to stabilize and increase the earnings of less developed countries and also to promote their exports of manufactured products to industrial ones; the two-week-long UN Conference on Human Settlements (Habitat) in Vancouver, B.C., approved on June 11 a blueprint for national and international action to improve the living places of peoples (*see* ENVIRONMENT: *Special Report*); a working group on corrupt practices began work in November in an effort to elaborate a treaty to prevent and eliminate all illicit payments in international commercial transactions; and the UN Special Fund continued to solicit and distribute funds for projects designed to assist states most seriously affected by economic crises.

Other Matters. Two international covenants on human rights, adopted in 1966, came into force during 1976, the economic and social covenant on January 3 and the political and civil on March 23.

UN membership rose to 147 during the year with the admission of the Seychelles (September 21), Angola (December 1), and Western Samoa (December 17). The U.S. vetoed the admission of Vietnam on November 15. (RICHARD N. SWIFT)

[522.B.2]

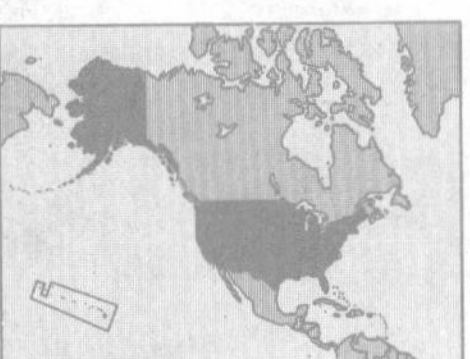

United States

The United States of America is a federal republic composed of 50 states, 49 of which are in North America and one of which consists of the Hawaiian Islands. Area: 3,615,122 sq mi (9,363,123 sq km), including 78,267 sq mi of inland water but excluding the 60,306 sq mi of the Great Lakes that lie within U.S. boundaries. Pop. (1976 est.): 215,135,000, including 87% white and 11.5% Negro. Language: English. Religion (1974 est.): Protestant 72.5 million; Roman Catholic 48.7 million; Jewish 6 million; Orthodox 3.7 million. Cap.: Washington, D.C. (pop., 1975 est., 716,000). Largest city: New York (pop., 1975 est., 7,567,900). President in 1976, Gerald Rudolph Ford.

Domestic Affairs. After an absence of eight years, the Democratic Party won control of the White House as Jimmy Carter (*see* BIOGRAPHY) defeated Republican incumbent Gerald Ford (*see* BIOGRAPHY) in the November 2 presidential election. The Democrats, in addition, retained their grip on Congress with sizable majorities of seats in both the House of Representatives and the Senate. Republicans suffered a net loss of one governorship to the Democrats, reducing their total to 12. But the GOP did come up with some promising new faces, led by James Thompson, a runaway winner in the Illinois gubernatorial election.

Carter's margin of victory over Ford was relatively narrow in terms of both popular and electoral votes. The Democratic nominee polled 40.8 million votes nationwide, while Ford received 39.1 million. Carter carried 23 states and the District of Columbia, with a combined total of 297 electoral votes, while Ford took 27 states with 241 electoral votes. (Ford's total in the Electoral College fell to 240 when one elector from Washington State voted for former California governor Ronald Reagan.) As expected, Carter scored an almost complete sweep of his native South, and he also won the populous states of New York, Ohio, and

OWEN FRANKEN—SYGMA

Two weeks after his defeat in the November election, Pres. Ford received Jimmy Carter at the White House. While the men talked, Mrs. Carter looked over the living quarters upstairs.

Pennsylvania. Ford's strength was concentrated in the Far West. Political analysts generally credited Carter's close victory to traditionally heavy pro-Democratic margins among blacks and members of organized labour. (*See* Special Report: *The 1976 Presidential Election.*)

While Ford's defeat was deeply disappointing to Republicans, the GOP failure to make significant gains in the House stunned party strategists who had expected a substantial comeback from the Democratic landslide in the Watergate year of 1974. Instead, the GOP carried only 143 districts, two fewer than in 1974. The Republicans fared better in the Senate races, but only by virtue of holding their own. The composition of the Senate was unchanged, with 62 Democrats and 38 Republicans, but 18 were freshmen, the largest number of newcomers in any Congress in the past 18 years. Nine of the new senators defeated incumbents, and eight took the seats of senators who declined to run for reelection. Gov. Wendell Anderson (Dem., Minn.) was appointed to replace Sen. Walter Mondale (*see* BIOGRAPHY), who was elected vice-president.

A number of issues on state ballots attracted nationwide attention. One of the most publicized votes was New Jersey's approval of a constitutional amendment to establish and regulate gambling casinos in Atlantic City. The state's share of casino revenues was to be used to help disabled and elderly persons. Massachusetts received considerable publicity for its rejection of a proposed statewide ban on handguns. California's Proposition 14, another nationally publicized ballot initiative, lost by 62 to 38%. The proposition, favoured by César Chávez and the United Farm Workers, would have established an independent state farm labour relations board.

FEDERAL LEGISLATION. Taxes, jobs, and congressional spending goals emerged as the key election-year issues. Congress approved the most sweeping tax-revision bill in seven years, an important feature of which extended personal and business income-tax cuts passed in 1975. Congress also left its mark on federal spending plans. In a surprisingly smooth exercise of its new budget powers, it set a spending limit of $413.1 billion in the fiscal year that began October 1, about $19 billion more than Ford had proposed in January. A $10 billion reduction in the president's $28 billion package of tax cuts offset part of the budget increase.

While leaving proposed defense spending virtually intact, Congress decided to spend more than the president wanted on domestic programs and new job-creation efforts. Despite two presidential vetoes, it successfully insisted on a new public-works job program. A state and local public-service jobs program won a one-year extension.

Ford continued his free use of the veto power. He issued 15 vetoes during the 1976 session, and only 4 were overridden. The president claimed that his vetoes since taking office in August 1974 had saved taxpayers $9 billion. The Ford-Congress deadlock had practical effects on legislative proposals. Given Ford's opposition, Congress decided not to consider national health insurance proposals. A veto threat stalled legislation creating a federal consumer protection agency even though the bill had passed both houses.

The president's proposals to trim federal costs and red tape fared no better. Congress ignored Ford's proposals to set up state "block grant" programs in the fields of health, education, child nutrition, and social services. His proposed increases in Social Security payroll taxes and payments by elderly patients under Medicare proved immediately unpopular in Congress. Several administration-backed energy bills never made it to the president's desk.

As always, though, there were some compromises. After a first veto, for instance, congressional sponsors cut more than $2 billion from the public works jobs bill. The more traditional pressures of time, lobbying, fear of campaign repercussions, and internal disputes laid other proposals to rest for the year. They included an ambitious plan to overhaul the nation's banking industry, strip-mining legislation, and a reworking of the food stamp program. Highly controversial oil company divestiture, gun control, and criminal code revision bills never made it to the floor.

Congress did complete work on a number of long-pending measures in such fields as health and moved to strengthen legislative oversight of foreign arms sales and U.S. intelligence operations. Other legislation winning final approval included a "government in the sunshine" bill requiring federal agencies to open their proceedings to the public. The federal revenue-sharing program got a last-minute lease on life, but amendments to the 1970 Clean Air Act were killed.

CONGRESSIONAL SCANDALS. A number of scandals concerning ethics, several involving sex, proved embarrassing to Congress in 1976. The most sensational disclosures led to the downfall of Rep. Wayne L. Hays

(Dem., Ohio), chairman of the powerful House Administration Committee. In a speech on the House floor on May 25, Hays admitted that he had had a "personal relationship" with Elizabeth Ray (*see* BIOGRAPHY), a member of the committee's staff. Hays denied, however, that he had hired Ray for the $14,000-a-year job solely so that she could be his mistress.

The *Washington Post* had carried the first report of Hays's affair with Ray in its editions of May 23. Ray was quoted as saying that Hays had hired her to be his mistress. She denied having the secretarial skills required for the job, saying, "I can't type, I can't file, I can't even answer the phone." When the story first broke, Hays denied having any intimate relationship with Ray, but in his House speech, he said he had "committed a grievous error in not presenting all the facts" of the matter. The relationship, he said, occurred after he had been separated from his first wife and before he married his second wife. Ray had not been hired, Hays said, on condition that she sleep with him; the sexual relationship, he insisted, had been "voluntary on her part and on mine."

By admitting to his affair with Ray, Hays apparently hoped to deflect any move by other House members to censure or take disciplinary action against him. But the stratagem failed. Under pressure from senior House Democrats, Hays resigned his chairmanships of the Administration Committee and the Democratic Congressional Campaign Committee. On August 13 he announced that he would not seek reelection. Finally, on September 1, two days after the House Select Committee on Standards of Official Conduct voted unanimously to hold public hearings on the allegations against him, he resigned from the House "effective immediately."

The Hays scandal directed attention to a number of other sex-related accusations against House members. Former House aide Colleen Gardner charged that her employer, Rep. John Young (Dem., Texas), had kept her on the House payroll primarily to have sex with him, and the *New York Post* reported that Rep. Joe D. Waggonner, Jr. (Dem., La.), had been arrested in Washington, D.C., on a charge of soliciting a police decoy for purposes of prostitution.

MICHAEL A. NORCIA—KEYSTONE

Queen Elizabeth II was made an honorary citizen of New York by Mayor Abe Beame during her bicentennial tour of the U.S. in July. Photo shows them in front of the statue of George Washington at Federal Hall. Prince Philip stands to the left of the queen.

Waggonner was released without formal charges because of a District of Columbia police practice, since revised, that prohibited the arrest of members of Congress on misdemeanour charges while Congress was in session. No official House action was taken against Waggonner or Young or against Rep. Allan Howe (Dem., Utah), who was convicted on July 23 of soliciting sex for hire from two undercover Salt Lake City policewomen. A Department of Justice spokesman announced on August 16 that an investigation had uncovered no evidence to support Gardner's allegations regarding Young. Howe was defeated in his reelection campaign, while Waggonner and Young were reelected.

The most pervasive congressional scandal of the year centred on money rather than sex. It began in December 1975, when a special committee of the Gulf

UNITED STATES

Education. Primary (1975–76), pupils 25,405,249, teachers 1,171,695; secondary and vocational (1974–75), pupils 15,447,000, teachers *c.* 1,083,000; higher (including teacher training colleges; 1974–75), students 9,023,446, teaching staff *c.* 633,000.

Finance. Monetary unit: U.S. dollar, with (Sept. 20, 1976) a free rate of U.S. $1.72 to £1 sterling. Gold, SDR's, and foreign exchange (June 1976) $14.7 billion. Federal budget (1976–77 est.): revenue $351 billion; expenditure $394 billion. Gross national product (1975) $1,516,300,000,000. Money supply (June 1976) $295.4 billion. Cost of living: (1970 = 100; June 1976) 146.

Foreign Trade. (1975) Imports $103,414,000,000; exports (excluding military aid exports of $461 million) $107,191,000,000. Import sources: Canada 23%; Japan 12%; West Germany 6%. Export destinations: Canada 20%; Japan 9%; West Germany 5%; Mexico 5%. Main exports: nonelectrical machinery 20%; cereals 11% (wheat 5%); motor vehicles 9%; chemicals 8%; electrical machinery and equipment 7%; aircraft 6%. Tourism (1974): visitors 14,123,000; gross receipts $4,034,000,000.

Transport and Communications. Roads (1973) 6,126,564 km (including 61,936 km expressways). Motor vehicles in use (1974): passenger 104,269,700; commercial (including buses) 23,699,200. Railways (1974): 332,746 km; traffic (class I only; 1974) 16,629,000 passenger-km, freight 1,246,652,000,000 net ton-km. Air traffic (1975): 262,137,000,000 passenger-km (including domestic services 218,835,000,000 passenger-km); freight 8,555,942,000 net ton-km (including domestic services 5,670,396,000 net ton-km). Inland waterways freight traffic (1974) 523,000,000,000 ton-km (including 184,000,000,000 ton-km on Great Lakes system). Shipping (1975): merchant vessels 100 gross tons and over 4,346; gross tonnage 14,586,616. Ships entered (including Great Lakes international service; 1973) vessels totaling 253,931,000 net registered tons; goods loaded (1975) 245,735,000 metric tons, unloaded 399,253,000 metric tons. Telephones (Jan. 1975) 143,430,000. Radio receivers (Dec. 1973) 368.6 million. Television receivers (Dec. 1973) 110 million.

Agriculture. Production (in 000; metric tons; 1975): corn 146,487; wheat 58,074; oats 9,535; barley 8,340; rye 454; rice 5,789; sorghum 19,265; soybeans 41,406; dry beans 780; dry peas *c.* 166; peanuts 1,750; potatoes 14,323; sweet potatoes (1974) 606; onions 1,425; tomatoes 8,620; sugar, raw value 6,058; apples (1974) 2,900; pears (1974) 645; oranges (1974) 8,740; grapefruit (1974) 2,428; lemons (1974) 641; peaches (1974) 1,415; grapes (1974) 3,805; sunflower seed *c.* 400; linseed 370; tobacco 990; cotton, lint 1,813; butter 443; cheese 1,588; hen's eggs *c.* 3,769; beef and veal (1974) 10,601; pork (1974) 6,203; timber (cu m; 1974) *c.* 336,866; fish catch (1974) 2,744. Livestock (in 000; Jan. 1975): cattle 131,826; sheep 14,538; pigs 55,062; horses (1974) 8,984; chickens 383,579.

Industry. Index of production (1970 = 100; 1975) 107; mining 97; manufacturing 107; electricity, gas, and water 120; construction 87. Unemployment (1975) 8.5%. Fuel and power (in 000; metric tons; 1975): coal 568,158; lignite 18,174; crude oil 412,019; natural gas (cu m) 567,415,000; manufactured gas (cu m) 25,460,000; electricity (kw-hr) 1,999,676,000. Production (in 000; metric tons; 1975): iron ore (55–60% metal content) 81,351; pig iron (1974) 89,281; crude steel 105,911; cement (shipments) 58,348; newsprint 3,110; other paper (1974) 49,215; petroleum products (1974) 591,561; sulfuric acid 27,750; caustic soda 8,422; plastics and resins *c.* 8,160; synthetic rubber 1,941; fertilizers (including Puerto Rico; nutrient content; 1974–75) nitrogenous 8,621, phosphate 6,049, potash 2,090; passenger cars (units) 6,713; commercial vehicles (units) 2,272. Merchant vessels launched (100 gross tons and over; 1975) 1,006,000 gross tons. New dwelling units started (1975) 1,166,000.

Oil Corp. reported to the Securities and Exchange Commission that Gulf over the previous decade had illegally contributed more than $5 million in corporate funds to the campaign efforts of members of Congress. Those named included some of the most influential legislators, among them Senate Minority Leader Hugh Scott (Rep., Pa.). At least two House members, James Jones (Dem., Okla.) and H. John Heinz III (Rep., Pa.), publicly admitted having received illegal Gulf contributions, although both denied knowing the nature of the money at the time it was received. Congress took no action against those three or any other members implicated in the case.

The House did, however, vote on July 29 to reprimand Rep. Robert L. F. Sikes (Dem., Fla.) for financial misconduct. Sikes was accused of failing to disclose ownership of 1,000 shares of stock in Fairchild Industries, a major defense contractor, and of using his position for personal gain in a matter of more than $2,500 worth of stock in the First Navy Bank in Florida. It was further alleged that Sikes, chairman of the House Military Construction Appropriations Subcommittee, had used his office on three occasions to advance the interest of companies in which he held stock. Sikes was reelected to office.

A federal grand jury began hearing testimony during the year concerning the operations of the South Korean Central Intelligence Agency (KCIA) in the U.S. Allegations had been made that officers of the KCIA and affiliated South Koreans had offered bribes and favours to congressmen in exchange for continued U.S. support of the regime of South Korean Pres. Park Chung Hee. A major subject of the investigation was Park Tong Sun, also known as Tongsun Park, a wealthy businessman who lived in Washington, D.C., and became known for entertaining government officials at lavish parties. Other figures in the investigation were Pak Bo Hi, head of the Korean Cultural and Freedom Foundation, and Suzy Park Thomson, Korean-born aide to House speaker Carl Albert; Thomson was granted immunity by the grand jury.

The KCIA denied that it had attempted to influence U.S. policy illegally. In November the agency ordered Park Tong Sun to stay out of the U.S. indefinitely and later asked a number of its U.S. officers to return to Seoul. Maj. Gen. Kim Yung Hwan, the Washington, D.C., station chief, agreed to return, but another official, Kim Sang Keun, refused the order and announced his defection to the U.S. Meanwhile, several leaders of the 70,000-member Korean community in Los Angeles charged that the KCIA was "systematically intimidating" those in the community who were critical of President Park.

A flotilla of sailing ships from many countries gathered in New York Harbor to help the U.S. celebrate its Bicentennial. Here one of them is greeted by a salvo from a fireboat.

JEAN-PIERRE LAFFONT—SYGMA

One line of the investigation was concerned with the U.S. Department of Agriculture. USDA officials were questioned about alleged attempts by two U.S. representatives, Otto Passman (Dem., La.) and Robert Leggett (Dem., Calif.), to influence departmental decisions involving rice and other export programs. Both Passman and Leggett denied the allegations.

LOCKHEED BRIBES. U.S. government officials were by no means the only recipients of illegal or improper donations. Exxon, Northrop, and Gulf Oil corporations and the United Brands Co. were among those that admitted funneling large amounts of cash to officials of foreign governments and then hiding the transactions from their shareholders and directors. But the clandestine overseas payments of Lockheed Aircraft Corp. attracted the most attention, because of the amount of money and the prominence of the persons involved.

The Lockheed scandal began to unfold in August 1975 when the company admitted, after months of denials, that it had paid at least $22 million to politicians and officials of foreign governments since 1970 to win lucrative aerospace contracts. Even then, Lockheed fought hard to protect the identities of those who got the money, saying that disclosure could have a serious adverse effect on the company's present backlog and "could result in a material adverse impact with respect to the company's future operations."

Lockheed's apprehensions were well founded. Subpoenaed company documents, made public in February 1976 by the Senate Subcommittee on Multinational Corporations, showed that Lockheed had secretly paid $7.1 million in cash to Yoshio Kodama (*see* BIOGRAPHY), a Japanese businessman who had served three years in prison following World War II. The ostensible purpose of the payoff was to promote the sale of Lockheed's L-1011 commercial jetliner to Japan.

Sensational as the Kodama disclosures were, greater shocks were yet to come. Former Japanese prime minister Kakuei Tanaka (*see* BIOGRAPHY) was arrested on July 27 and charged with having accepted Lockheed money that had been brought illegally into Japan during his term of office. Other Japanese who were indicted on charges of having accepted Lockheed bribes included a former transportation minister, a former vice-minister of transportation, and 13 businessmen. Justice Minister Osamu Inaba said on October 15 that 14 members of the Diet also had received cash payments from Lockheed in amounts ranging from $3,300 to $50,000, but he declined to name them. As the months passed, the Lockheed payoff scandal came to be known as "Japan's Watergate." It was the central issue in the national elections on December 5, in which the ruling Liberal-Democratic Party suffered a net loss of 16 seats.

Testimony before the Senate Subcommittee on Multinational Corporations also indicated that a "high government official" in The Netherlands was the recipient of a $1.1 million gift to aid Lockheed Aircraft sales. The Dutch Cabinet soon afterward confirmed that Prince Bernhard (*see* BIOGRAPHY), Queen Juliana's husband, was the person suspected of having taken the money. Prime Minister Joop den Uyl, in a television appearance soon after the government announcement was released, said that the Cabinet would set up an independent commission to investigate the allegations. The commission's report, issued August 26, sharply chastised Bernhard for being "extremely imprudent and unwise" in his dealings with Lockheed. Although it found no firm evidence that the prince had taken the money, the commission stated that he had "allowed himself to be tempted to take initiatives which were completely unacceptable." Bernhard resigned virtually all of his many military and business posts the day the report was released.

In all, Lockheed was accused of having paid bribes in at least 15 countries, including Italy, Sweden, Turkey, West Germany, and Australia. Not all of the allegations withstood scrutiny, and in some countries the bribe reports stirred only moderate interest. But the whole tangled episode raised disturbing questions about the manner in which U.S.-based multinational companies do business abroad. Because the distinction between a sales commission and a bribe is not always easy to draw, attempts to outlaw payoffs by legislation probably would have only limited effectiveness. Discouraging corporate bribery of foreign officials nonetheless was clearly in the national interest, for the improper activity by a powerful U.S. firm could imperil U.S. relations with friendly governments.

DEATH PENALTY REVIVAL. For more than a decade, the death penalty had been under attack in state and federal courts as being in violation of the Constitution's ban on "cruel and unusual" punishment. Largely as a result of the litigation, no one had been executed in the U.S. since 1967. In a group of decisions handed down on July 2, the Supreme Court upheld the death penalty as a legitimate punishment for murder. The court stated that capital punishment is permissable so long as the jury or judge who gives out the sentence receives enough guidance and information to be able to make a sound, nonarbitrary decision. (*See* LAW.) The court's opinion was seen as opening the way for execution of at least some of the prisoners on the nation's death rows. By far the most publicized such prisoner was Gary Gilmore, convicted of murder in Utah, who became a celebrity of sorts by insisting that his execution be carried out as scheduled. (*See* CRIME AND LAW ENFORCEMENT.)

SPACE ACHIEVEMENTS. Although the glamorous days of manned landings on the Moon were over, the National Aeronautics and Space Administration (NASA) again scored a triumph in 1976 by successfully placing two unmanned spacecraft on Mars. The first craft, Viking 1, touched down July 20 and the second, Viking 2, touched down on September 3. Both sent back spectacular colour photographs. NASA also provided a glimpse of space feats to come when it unveiled the first space shuttle orbiter at Palmdale, Calif., on September 17. The shuttle was designed to ferry men and equipment between the Earth and space. Suborbital test flights were to begin in 1977. (*See* SPACE EXPLORATION.)

BICENTENNIAL CELEBRATION. The year 1976 marked the 200th anniversary of the U.S. Declaration of Independence, and the nation celebrated the occasion with a year-long series of parades, concerts, fireworks displays, art exhibitions, and other commemorative events. The most spectacular was Operation Sail, during which 53 warships from 22 countries and 16 tall ships—square-rigged sailing vessels more than 100 ft in length from all parts of the world—passed in review July 4 in New York Harbor and the Hudson River. A crowd estimated at six million persons watched from the shore or from pleasure boats. Many who observed Operation Sail and other bicentennial celebrations on July 4 were struck by the spontaneous singing, flag-waving, and patriotic comments of the onlookers. This was interpreted as evidence that the U.S. was experiencing a "resurgence of spirit" after more than a decade of war and political turmoil.

HENRI BUREAU—SYGMA

A parade of covered wagons assembles at Valley Forge, Pa., on July 4.

In honour of the Bicentennial, a number of foreign heads of state and of government visited the U.S. in 1976. The most eagerly awaited was Britain's Queen Elizabeth II, who arrived in Philadelphia on July 6. She presented a bell, cast in the same foundry as the Liberty Bell, as a bicentennial gift from the British to the American people. She said in a speech that the Fourth of July had "taught Britain a very valuable lesson: 'To know the right time, and the manner of yielding what is impossible to keep.' "

Foreign Affairs. Keeping the peace in the Middle East was, as usual, a major concern of U.S. foreign policy officials in 1976. The country's principal aim in that troubled area was to bring an end to the bitter civil war in Lebanon and to discourage outside intervention in the conflict. After a meeting at the White House on March 30, President Ford and King Hussein of Jordan issued a joint appeal for a truce in Lebanon and stressed the need for "a basic political solution."

U.S. ambassador to Lebanon Francis E. Meloy, Jr. (*see* OBITUARIES), and his economic counselor, Robert O. Waring, were shot to death in Beirut on June 16. Two days later, the U.S. embassy in Beirut "strongly urged" all remaining U.S. citizens in Lebanon to leave the country. The U.S. Navy evacuated 110 Americans and 166 persons of 25 other nationalities from Beirut on June 20. Al-Fatah, the Palestinian guerrilla group, provided escorts for the civilians assembling on the Beirut beach. The U.S. sent a message through a third party thanking the Palestinian leadership, the State Department confirmed on June 21.

U.S. diplomats also were active in southern Africa. President Ford castigated members of Congress on February 10 for having "lost their guts" in voting to ban further aid to the forces in the Angolan civil war that were opposing the faction supported by the Soviet Union and Cuba.

In a major policy statement delivered in Lusaka, Zambia, on April 27, Secretary of State Henry Kissinger (*see* BIOGRAPHY) pledged concrete steps "to usher in a new era in American policy" toward southern Africa and declared U.S. support for black majority rule in Rhodesia, an independent Namibia (South West Africa), and the termination of apartheid (racial separation) in South Africa. Throughout his speech,

UPI COMPIX

Squaring off for their first TV debate in September, Pres. Gerald Ford and challenger Jimmy Carter faced an audience estimated at around 75 million Americans.

Kissinger stressed the urgency of these goals. He reiterated U.S. warnings against foreign intervention in southern Africa and proposed broad economic development programs in the region.

Later, Kissinger offered the good offices of the U.S. in negotiations for a peaceful transfer of power. Endorsing British proposals for a two-year transition to majority rule in Rhodesia, Kissinger pledged U.S. assistance to the people of Rhodesia and vowed continued aid to "a newly independent Zimbabwe" (the nationalists' name for Rhodesia) under black rule.

Kissinger met with South African Prime Minister B. J. Vorster (*see* BIOGRAPHY) in West Germany June 23–24, soon after several days of rioting had occurred in black South African townships. Their discussions were described as "worthwhile" and "sensitive," but they produced no agreement. "The problem," Kissinger said at a news conference in Munich on June 24, "is whether it is possible to start an evolution in southern Africa in which sufficient guarantees are given to the minority so a system can evolve that the majority of the people want and [that] is bearable for the minority."

U.S. diplomatic efforts in southern Africa bore fruit on September 24, when Rhodesian Prime Minister Ian Smith (*see* BIOGRAPHY) accepted Kissinger's proposal for the transfer of power to Rhodesia's black majority. The proposal provided for the establishment of majority rule within two years, immediate formation of an interim government, cessation of economic sanctions and guerrilla attacks against Rhodesia, and a program of foreign economic support to ensure continued Rhodesian economic growth. Representatives of the British and Rhodesian governments and of Rhodesian black nationalist groups met in Geneva on October 28 to consider ways of implementing the Kissinger plan, but no agreement had been reached by year's end.

President Ford and Soviet Communist Party General Secretary Leonid I. Brezhnev signed on May 28 a joint treaty placing limits on the size of underground nuclear explosions for peaceful purposes and providing for U.S. on-site inspection of Soviet tests. The pact was expected to pave the way for U.S. and Soviet ratification of a companion treaty limiting the size of underground nuclear weapons tests. The weapons treaty, which had been signed by Pres. Richard Nixon and Brezhnev in 1974, was to have gone into effect March 31, 1976. Its formal implementation was delayed to await the accord limiting peaceful tests.

President Ford joined the heads of government of six other industrialized nations for economic summit talks in Puerto Rico June 27–28. In a declaration issued at the conclusion of the meeting, the participants said: "Our objective now is to manage effectively a transition to [economic] expansion which will be sustainable, which will reduce the high level of unemployment which persists in many countries and won't jeopardize our common aim of avoiding a new wave of inflation." In agreeing to adopt a go-slow policy, the participants declared "this will involve acceptance, in accordance with our individual needs and circumstances, of a restoration of better balance in public finance as well as of disciplined measures in the fiscal areas and in the field of monetary policy, and in some cases, supplementary policies, including incomes policy." (RICHARD L. WORSNOP)

See also **Dependent States.**

[973.A]

ENCYCLOPÆDIA BRITANNICA FILMS. *The Rise of Labor* (1968); *Heritage in Black* (1969); *The Pacific West* (1969); *The South—Roots of the Urban Crisis* (1969); *The Industrial Worker* (1969); *The Presidency: Search for a Candidate* (1969); *The Rise of Big Business* (1969); *The Rise of the American City* (1969); *Chicano from the Southwest* (1970); *Linda and Billy Ray from Appalachia* (1970); *The Mississippi System: Waterways of Commerce* (1970); *Jesse from Mississippi* (1971); *Johnny from Fort Apache* (1971); *The Progressive Era* (1971); *An Essay on War* (1971); *The Great Lakes: North America's Inland Seas* (2nd ed., 1972); *Valley Forge* (1972); *The Shot Heard Round the World* (1972); *The Boston Tea Party* (1972); *The United States Congress: Of, By and For the People* (2nd ed., 1972); *President of the United States: Too Much Power?* (1972); *The United States Supreme Court: Guardian of the Constitution* (2nd ed., 1973); *The Amish: A People of Preservation* (1975); *Prelude to Revolution* (1975); *Thomas Paine* (1975); *City Government: Closest to the People* (1976); *Political Parties in the United States: Getting the People Together* (1976); *State Government: Resurgence of Power* (1976).

THE 1976 PRESIDENTIAL ELECTION

By Stanley W. Cloud

When a former governor of Georgia named James Earl Carter, Jr. (*see* Biography), was elected the 39th president of the United States in November 1976, his victory climaxed one of the most dramatic political success stories in U.S. history. Jimmy Carter—as he preferred to be called—had risen in only two years from a position of relative obscurity to one of immense power. In so doing, he had defied the odds and the predictions of many political experts. If his margin of victory over his Republican opponent, Gerald R. Ford (*see* Biography), was narrower than he and and his fellow Democrats might have wished, it was nonetheless considerably wider than those achieved by either John F. Kennedy in 1960 or Richard M. Nixon in 1968—the only other nonincumbents elected to the presidency since Dwight D. Eisenhower's landslide in 1952. Noting that fact, Carter said during his first formal press conference after the election: "I don't feel timid or cautious or reticent about moving aggressively to carry out my campaign commitments."

The Outsider. One of the many things the public learned about Carter in the course of his remarkable 22-month campaign was not to underestimate the effects of his self-confidence. With a political career that included only four years as an unheralded state senator and a single term as Georgia's governor (he was prohibited by state law from seeking a second term), Carter did not impress many people when, on Dec. 12, 1974, in Washington, D.C., he added his name to the list of Democrats—soon to grow to more than a dozen—who were seeking their party's nomination. Political observers pointed out that he would be stepping down as governor in January 1975, that he had no apparent political base in the nation, no organization, no standing in the polls, and little or no money with which to finance his campaign. Ambition, they said in effect, should be made of sterner stuff.

But Carter had been planning his campaign carefully for two years prior to his announcement. His executive secretary, Hamilton Jordan (who would become his campaign manager), had drafted the first installment of the Carter campaign plan before the presidential election of 1972. In it and subsequent installments, Carter's manifest political weaknesses were duly noted, but he and his aides preferred to dwell on his strengths. His background as a naval officer, peanut farmer, agribusinessman, and late-blooming state politician, as well as his extraordinary ability to campaign on such "fuzzy" issues as "love" and "trust," were ideally suited to the mood of a public that, thanks to Watergate and Vietnam, had grown weary and cynical toward officials in Washington and politics in general. Moreover, recent presidential elections had indicated that it is difficult, perhaps impossible, for a Democrat to win the presidency without the support of the old "Solid South" that had played such an important role in the Roosevelt coalition of the 1930s and 1940s. Carter, a nonracist "New Southerner" who could appeal to both whites and blacks, North and South, might well bring the South back into the Democratic fold. He would have to overcome the bias of many Northern liberals against Southerners, of course, and he would have to assuage fears about his fundamentalist, born-again Christian, Southern Baptist faith. (*See* Religion.) But these did not appear to be insurmountable obstacles.

Stanley W. Cloud is political correspondent for Time *magazine.*

Carter's plan called for him to enter all of the 31 presidential primaries that were held in 1976 (actually, he entered 30, having failed to qualify a slate of delegates in West Virginia). He correctly assumed that the record number of primaries—plus the limitations on campaign spending and fund raising imposed by the federal campaign finance law of 1974—would lead his better-known Democratic opponents to pick and choose among the state primaries in order to husband their resources. Carter's decision to "run everywhere" reflected his knowledge that, as a relative unknown, he needed as much exposure as possible and that the Democratic Party's new rules would give him a proportionate share of delegates even in states where he did not finish first.

Fighting for the Nominations. The plan served Carter well. Early victories in January's Iowa caucuses and February's New Hampshire primary, the results of his effective one-to-one campaigning techniques and his penchant for meticulous organization, put him on the covers of *Time* and *Newsweek* and established him as an early front runner. He went on to defeat Alabama Gov. George Wallace, an "Old Southerner" making what many felt was his last try for national office, in Florida and North Carolina (and in every other Southern primary, except in Wallace's home state). Carter scored an unexpectedly strong victory in Illinois and narrowly defeated his main liberal opponent, Rep. Morris K. Udall of Arizona, in Wisconsin. By the time of the Pennsylvania primary, April 27, only two other serious candidates remained in the race, Udall and Sen. Henry M. Jackson of Washington. Carter decisively whipped both of them in Pennsylvania, forcing Jackson out of the race and causing Sen. Hubert H. Humphrey of Minnesota, who had been waiting in the wings in the hope that the active candidates would eliminate each other, to decide against an active candidacy for himself.

Carter's drive for the nomination was certainly not without setbacks. He lost badly to Jackson in Massachusetts and New York and was embarrassed several times in May by two quixotic latecomers to the race, Gov. Edmund G. Brown, Jr., of California and Sen. Frank Church of Idaho. Still, Carter continued to pile up delegates in state after state even when he did not finish first. By the final day of the primaries, June 8, his nomination had become a foregone conclusion.

Meanwhile, Ford, the "accidental president" who had been appointed vice-president in 1973 after Spiro Agnew's resignation and succeeded to the presidency the next year when Richard Nixon resigned because of the Watergate scandal, was having a much harder time of it in the Republican primaries. Despite victories in New Hampshire, Massachusetts, and Florida, Ford was unable to force his right-wing challenger, former California governor Ronald Reagan (*see* Biography), out of the race. Reagan went on to beat Ford in North Carolina and to trounce him in Texas, Indiana, and California, as well as in Georgia and several other Southern states. Ford countered with victories in Illinois, New York, Pennsylvania, Wisconsin, and Michigan. Suddenly the Republican Party, which prides itself on its decorum, had a civil war on its hands, while the normally fractious Democrats were headed for their most peaceful convention in at least 12 years.

Convening in New York City in July, the Democratic delegates to the convention managed to suppress any nervousness they felt about Carter's "outsider" status and nominated him on the first ballot. They approved a platform in keeping with his generally moderate-to-liberal views and cheered his choice of a bona fide liberal, Sen. Walter Mondale of Minnesota (*see* Biography), as his vice-presidential running mate. Most delegates appeared to be impressed with Carter's basically liberal acceptance speech, which he would later describe as "populist" in tone. The harmony that prevailed in Madison Square Garden evidently had its effect on popular opinion; by the time the convention adjourned, Carter had a massive lead of more than 30 percentage points over Ford in the Gallup and Harris polls.

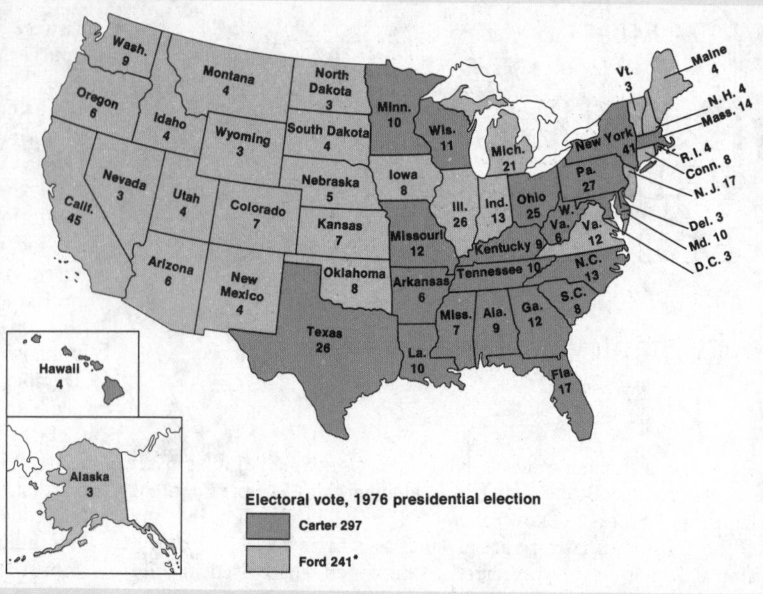

The election of 1976 split the states on roughly an east-west basis. Carter's victory was based on a sweep of the South and the border states, plus some industrial states in the northeast. In the West, Carter won only Hawaii. Altogether, Ford won 27 states while Carter won 23 states and the District of Columbia. But Carter's states were more populous, giving him a total of 297 electoral votes to Ford's 240. The total number of votes cast was 81,518,720, of which Carter got 40,827,292 or 50% and Ford 39,146,157 or 48%. About 55.8% of the eligible voters participated.

*WHEN THE ELECTORAL COLLEGE MET ON DECEMBER 13, ONE ELECTOR, FROM THE STATE OF WASHINGTON, CAST HIS VOTE FOR RONALD REAGAN, MAKING THE TOTAL NUMBER OF ELECTORAL VOTES FOR FORD 240

The Democratic nominee himself predicted that the lead would not hold, and he was correct. Despite the Ford-Reagan fight during the primaries and immediately afterward, the GOP gave Ford a first-ballot nomination at its convention in August. In an effort to strengthen his shaky base in the Midwest and the farm belt, the president surprised many delegates by choosing Sen. Robert Dole of Kansas (*see* BIOGRAPHY), known as a tough, hard-hitting campaigner, to be his running mate. Ford's acceptance speech, in which he challenged Carter to a series of televised debates, was probably the best of his career.

The Campaign. Ford's strategy would be to remain in the White House as much as possible during the first month of the fall campaign, projecting a "presidential image" by signing bills in the Rose Garden and holding televised press conferences. Dole would do most of the active campaigning at first, and Ford would blitz the country in person and on TV during the final weeks. There was reason for Ford strategists to think the plan might work; Carter's peripatetic campaigning was causing him to make mistakes and, by early September, his lead in the polls had dropped to ten points. It would continue to decline until, by election eve, pollsters would pronounce the race too close to call.

The economy, the character of the two candidates, and the desirability of change emerged as the basic issues of the campaign, although the antiabortion crusade of the Right to Life movement (which neither candidate fully satisfied) and the gaffes to which both men seemed prone usurped much of the headline space. Both committed serious errors. Having run in the primaries as an unorthodox politician who stressed personal integrity above all else ("I'll never tell you a lie"), Carter came out after the convention as a more traditional Democrat, calling for new federal initiatives to increase employment and for other measures to revive the lagging economy. He wavered, however, when the pitch did not seem to be going over well. While Ford castigated him as "the biggest flip-flopper I know," Carter proclaimed that inflation posed as great a problem as unemployment and reverted to his preconvention stance favouring a balanced federal budget. He renewed his pledge to reorganize the federal government and to seek tax and welfare reform. His desire to touch as many political bases as possible, and his occasionally harsh attacks on Ford, tended to confuse the voters—as did a remarkably revealing interview he granted to *Playboy* magazine, in which, among other things, he admitted to having "committed adultery in my heart many times."

Ford had even greater problems, not all of them of his own making. He had inherited an administration plagued by the Watergate scandal, the inglorious end to the war in Vietnam, the worst recession since the Great Depression of the '30s and the worst inflation in U.S. history. He was the nominee of a party that could claim the loyalty of only about 20% of the electorate, and he had no regional base of support. He was an uninspiring leader whose constant battles with the Democratic Congress suggested to many voters that he had an essentially negative approach to the presidency. In his efforts to deal with inflation, unemployment, and the energy crisis, he had switched policies several times. Republican liberals thought he was too conservative, while the GOP's conservatives thought he was too liberal. Though he was still haunted by his hasty pardon of Nixon, Ford had, as he claimed, restored a measure of "trust and confidence in the White House." That did not seem sufficient to impress the Democrats and independents whose votes he needed, however. Verified reports that, as a congressman, he had accepted free golfing trips from corporate lobbyists and apparently unfounded charges that he had illegally diverted Maritime Union campaign donations to his personal use further weakened his position.

Debates and Ballots. During the three Ford-Carter debates (a fourth featured the vice-presidential nominees), the president did little to dispel the doubts about him. Nor was he able to avoid the malapropisms that had led some critics to question his intellectual capacity. During the second debate, for example, he insisted, inexplicably, that Eastern Europe was free of domination by the Soviet Union. By the end of the third debate, Carter had shown himself to be at least as "presidential" as the president, in the opinion of most observers.

When the returns were in, it was clear that Carter's "Southern strategy" had won the election for him. The Solid South (except Virginia) had returned to the Democratic column for the first time since 1960, along with the border states (except Oklahoma) and most of the northeastern half of the country. Although higher than had been predicted, the relatively low turnout of 55.8% of eligible voters probably worked against Carter. Any disadvantage he might have suffered as a result, however, was offset by impressive support from blacks and labour union members. Except for Hawaii, the western half of the U.S. went for Ford, but he still fell short. The final tally showed Carter with about a two million-vote edge (50% to 48%) and an electoral vote victory of 297 to 240. (One elector from the state of Washington voted for Reagan.) In essence, most pollsters agreed, the voters had resolved any doubts they had about Carter in favour of their desire to see a change in Washington.

Returning to his home in the tiny southwest Georgia hamlet of Plains the morning after the election, Carter told the several hundred people who had gathered to greet him that "the only reason it was so close was that the candidate wasn't good enough as a campaigner." He paused, then added: "But I'll make up for that as president."

SPECIAL REPORT

HOW THE DEBATES CAME TO BE

By Charles Benton

The first television debates between major-party candidates in U.S. political history occurred during the 1960 presidential campaign, when John F. Kennedy and Richard M. Nixon met in four highly publicized confrontations that, it was later felt, probably helped Kennedy to win the election. Those debates were made possible by a suspension by Congress of the so-called equal time provision, sec. 315 of the Federal Communications Act.

A new ruling by the Federal Communications Commission in the fall of 1975 once again opened the way to presidential debates on television. The ruling broadened the interpretation of "bona fide news events," which were not subject to the equal time provision, by excluding from coverage under sec. 315 all events that were sponsored by organizations independent of the broadcasting media.

Six months earlier three citizen activists, Marjorie and Charles Benton and Gene Pokorny, had developed a proposal for a series of "presidential forums" to be held during the presidential primaries in the winter and spring of 1976. The idea was to hold a number of televised "town meetings" during the U.S. Bicentennial to which the presidential candidates of both parties would be invited to speak concerning the major issues confronting the nation. In July 1975 the William Benton Foundation made a grant of $50,000 to develop the idea. Jim Karayn, former head of National Public Affairs Center for Television, was named staff director, and discussions began with several major organizations involved in public television.

Immediately following the FCC ruling contact was made with the League of Women Voters, a leading voter education organization that had just announced its theme for the 1976 election as "Issues Not Images." When the League agreed to adopt the project, the Benton Foundation increased its grant to $200,000, and a further $100,000 was obtained by the Public Broadcasting System from the Ford Foundation to help fund public television coverage of the forums.

Four forums took place, although five were planned. The first occurred in Boston on Feb. 23, 1976, just before the Massachusetts primary. Seven Democratic hopefuls participated: Jimmy Carter, Morris Udall, Henry Jackson, Fred Harris, Sargent Shriver, Birch Bayh, and Milton Shapp. Participation fell off in later forums—in Miami, Fla., on March 1, in New York on March 29, and in Chicago on May 3—as the list of Democratic candidates contracted. No Republican joined any of the forums, although all were repeatedly invited by the nonpartisan steering committee. The last forum, scheduled to be held before the California primary, was canceled owing to a lack of candidate participation, but the earlier ones had attracted a solid audience on public television—between 1.5 million and 2 million viewers.

With the experience, staff, and credentials of the forums behind it, the League of Women Voters, at its annual spring convention, announced through its president, Ruth Clusen, that the League would invite the major party nominees to engage in television debates during the fall campaign. Along with this announcement the League launched a petition drive for four million signatures and an editorial and press campaign to mobilize public opinion in favour of such debates.

Early in August the League formed a steering committee for the debates comprised of distinguished Americans and headed by three co-chairpersons: Rita Hauser, Newton Minow, and Charles Walker. In late August in his acceptance speech at the Republican convention, Pres. Gerald Ford issued a challenge to his Democratic rival Jimmy Carter to engage in debates during the campaign. Ford had learned that Carter was going to issue a similar challenge the next day and, at the last minute, decided to seize the initiative. Carter immediately accepted.

Heated discussions ensued among representatives of the League, the U.S. television networks, and other interested parties as to who would sponsor the debates, and about their framework and format. The League was finally chosen and proposed four debates, three between the presidential candidates, with the first on domestic affairs and the second on foreign affairs, and one between the vice-presidential candidates. The Ford entourage wanted to begin with foreign affairs and to have longer debates; both Carter and Ford wanted less informality than the League did, preferring a more structured exchange with representatives of the print and electronic media acting as intermediaries.

The first presidential debate was held at the Walnut Street Theatre in Philadelphia, the second in San Francisco, and the third at William and Mary College in Virginia; the vice-presidential debate was held in Houston, Texas. Unlike 1960, when the viewing audience fell sharply as the debates followed one another, the television audience in 1976 stayed fairly constant, at least for the three Carter-Ford debates: the average audience was over 70 million people, or roughly one in every three Americans. While much ground was covered, certain specifics stand out, such as Ford's assertion that the Eastern European countries were essentially in control of their own destiny and free of Soviet domination. The debate between the vice-presidential candidates also seemed to accentuate the differences in the style and character of Senators Walter Mondale and Robert Dole.

Though commentators were uncertain of the overall impact on voter attitudes, there seemed to be a consensus that the debates helped to shape the 1976 presidential campaign. In a country of continental size, with its vast regional differences, the images of national candidates become blurred as they tailor their speeches to the special interests of different audiences and surroundings. In nationally televised debates, the candidates have to speak to all Americans.

There is also general agreement that the debates have raised some important questions for the future. Among them are these:

1. The year 1976 was the first in which the public directly, through the Campaign Reform Act of 1976, funded the primary and general election campaigns. Assuming that will continue, do candidates have a special obligation to be accountable to the public on the major issues through televised debates?

2. Television has become the most pervasive news medium. Assuming that, too, will continue, what is the proper balance between commercial time (bought by the candidates), news reporting (provided by the networks), and debates or forums organized independently of both candidates and networks?

3. In 1977 Congress will begin hearings on the revision of the Communications Act of 1934. How should sec. 315 and other provisions of this old law be changed to accommodate the needs of U.S. society now and in the future?

4. Finally, how can the issue of minor party participation in media debates be resolved, in fairness to such candidates but also keeping in mind the size of the constituencies—often relatively tiny—that they represent?

In American society today, how can mass communications technology play a role that supports, rather than erodes, the basic foundations of political democracy—public education, public understanding, and enlightened public choice? Since the technology itself is neutral, what is done with and through it remains the central issue.

Charles Benton is president of Films Incorporated and a member of the board of Encyclopædia Britannica Educational Corp.

United States Statistical Supplement

Developments in the states in 1976

Dissatisfaction with governmental bureaucracy, as typified by the federal government, plus cooperation between the states toward common goals made 1976 a significant year in the evolution of U.S. state governments. With a national economic upturn pumping increased revenues into state treasuries, most legislatures again avoided major new tax increases. To polish further the public image of state governments there was a marked reduction in corruption charges as compared with recent years.

The new mood, which seemed to favour smaller government, also resulted in a sharp decline in the quantity of new legislation. New laws concerning equal rights for women, no-fault insurance, environmental protection, and open public meetings were enacted at the lowest rate in five years. Led by Colorado, states began decreeing "sunset laws" requiring periodic review for state agencies and death for those whose usefulness was deemed to be ended.

The cooperation between states, especially in combating encroachment by the federal government, led to some notable victories, especially in modifying federal assistance programs for state and local governments. Serious cooperation between states was not universal, however. After the Iowa legislature declared the wild sunflower, official Kansas state flower, to be "a noxious weed" that "harms crops and should be eradicated," a Kansas legislative leader introduced a resolution labeling the official Iowa state bird, the eastern goldfinch, as "an unattractive, bothersome, obscene and raucously noisy creature which ... serves no useful purpose on God's green earth." But before a vote could be taken on the anti-goldfinch measure, the legislature adjourned. Thirty-seven states held regular legislative sessions, and 12 staged special sessions during the year.

Party Strengths. Democrats added slightly to their already decisive advantage in governorships during 1976. In November elections, Republicans wrested control of Delaware, Illinois, and Vermont, previously held by Democrats. But Democrats ousted Republican gubernatorial control in Washington, West Virginia, North Carolina, and Missouri, leaving the prospective lineup for 1977 at 37 Democrats, 12 Republicans, and 1 independent.

In state legislative balloting Democrats also retained their marked dominance, though Republicans scored minor gains. The prospective partisan breakdown for 1977 remained virtually identical to that of 1976, when Republicans controlled both houses of only five legislatures. For 1977, Democrats had a majority in both houses of 36 legislatures. They dominated the lawmaking process in every state except Colorado, Idaho, South Dakota, and Wyoming (where Republicans controlled both houses); Arizona, Indiana, Kansas, Maine, North Dakota, New York, Utah, and Vermont (where each party controlled one chamber); New Hampshire (where the upper chamber was tied while the Republicans controlled the House); and Nebraska (which had a nonpartisan, unicameral legislature).

Women continued to make progress in gaining top state offices, as former Atomic Energy Commission chairman Dixy Lee Ray, a Democrat, won the governorship in Washington. She joined Connecticut's incumbent, Ella Grasso, as the only female governors in U.S. history who had not been preceded by their husbands.

Finances and Taxes. With a nationwide economic recovery boosting revenue collections, legislative action on state taxes in 1976 was relatively light. A survey by the Tax Foundation revealed that 15 states moved to increase major tax levies during the year to yield an additional $975 million. More than half of that increase was to come in New Jersey, which became the first state since 1971 to enact a new personal income tax.

The New Jersey action came as the state supreme court pressured lawmakers to enact a new school finance plan to equalize spending among school districts throughout the state. It left only nine U.S. states without a comprehensive personal income tax. During the year, Maine and Nebraska increased their income tax rates; Utah lowered them slightly; and both Kentucky and Hawaii provided some tax relief by raising allowable credits.

Nebraska increased corporate income tax rates, and Washington imposed a surtax on its business-occupation tax. Incentives to business were extended by a dozen legislatures (often in the form of investment incentives), including Connecticut, Kansas, Hawaii, Indiana, Louisiana, Pennsylvania, and Tennessee.

Sales and use taxes were raised in Massachusetts, Nebraska, Rhode Island, Tennessee, and Washington; Vermont and Wisconsin expanded the list of items subject to sales tax. But new exemptions to sales tax levies were enacted in South Carolina, Tennessee, Utah, Kentucky, and New York.

Connecticut, Idaho, Kansas, and Wyoming increased motor fuel taxes, as special excises continued to be considered a relatively painless method of increasing revenue. Hawaii and South Dakota failed to allow the scheduled expiration of special gasoline taxes during the year. Levies on various alcoholic beverages were raised in Colorado, Virginia, South Carolina, and Vermont.

As inflation continued to erode the value of the dollar, Delaware, Idaho, Illinois, Iowa, Kentucky, South Dakota, West Virginia, and Vermont took steps to reduce their inheritance or estate taxes, and Ohio voters authorized the legislature to do so. Most new laws raised the amount that is exempted from inheritance taxes.

State tax collections in the 1975 fiscal year totaled $80.2 billion, up 8% from the 1974 figure. Of the new total, general sales and gross receipts taxes accounted for $24.8 billion; $18.6 billion came from selective sales taxes, $18.8 billion from individual income taxes, $6.6 billion from corporate income taxes, and $6.3 billion from motor vehicle and miscellaneous licenses.

Figures accumulated in 1976 showed that state revenue from all sources totaled $154.6 billion during the 1975 fiscal year, an increase of 9.8% from the preceding 12 months. General revenue (excluding state liquor and state insurance trust revenue) was $134.6 billion, up 10%. Total state expenditures rose 18.2% to $156.2 billion, creating a deficit of $1.6 billion for the year. General expenditures, not including outlays of the liquor stores and insurance trust systems, amounted to $138.3 billion, up 15.4% for the year. Of general revenue, some 59.5% came from state taxes and licenses; 12.4% from charges and miscellaneous revenue, including educational tuition; and 28.1% from intergovernmental revenue (most from the federal government).

The largest state outlay was $54 billion for education, of which $17.7 billion went to state colleges and universities and $36.3 billion to other schools. Other major outlays were $25.6 billion for public welfare, $17.5 billion for highways, and $10.2 billion for health and hospitals.

Federal-State Relations. By banding together, state governments achieved major breakthroughs during 1976 toward protecting themselves against federal government encroachment. As a result, states ended the year with a promising vitality, retaining many advantages of federal aid funding while loosening strings and controls traditionally imposed by Washington.

State and local governments scored a landmark victory on June 24 when the U.S.

Supreme Court ruled 5 to 4 that principles of federalism forbade extension of mandatory federal wage and hour laws to other governmental layers. Political conservatives, who feared that a distant federal government was moving toward control of virtually all proprietary and service functions, hailed the verdict as a badly needed reaffirmation of federalism.

Two important federal programs to aid states, the Law Enforcement Assistance Administration (LEAA) and federal revenue sharing, were renewed during the year but only after the aided governments obtained a louder voice in fund disbursement. LEAA, which had failed to stop a nationwide crime rate increase despite expenditures of $3 billion in five years, was extended for three more years; state courts and legislatures were given new consulting roles in the expenditure process. Revenue sharing was also renewed at the approximate level of recent years, but with tighter state auditing, increased citizen participation, and a strengthened antidiscrimination clause.

Typifying new state activism, 30 states joined Pennsylvania in a court test seeking the right to sue the federal government for money damages. A survey at midyear showed that 21 states had 137 "dispute conflict situations" with the federal government over a range of problems. Signs of disenchantment with the strings attached to federal funding were revealed when Texas began refusing LEAA prison grants during the year, and both Pennsylvania and Oklahoma required a special review procedure before state officials could apply for federal funds.

Two nationwide public opinion polls showed apparently conflicting results. A Harris survey indicated that a majority of citizens had more confidence in their state government than in the federal government, but a poll a month later showed a plurality favouring the federal government as the most effective spender of a tax dollar.

Other examples of state cooperation during the year included Maryland's court battle, supported by 34 other states, against a Health, Education, and Welfare education fund cutoff attempt. New York, Massachusetts, Ohio, Illinois, Wisconsin, Washington, California, Georgia, and New Jersey enlisted in joint efforts to combat federal Medicaid fraud, estimated at $750 million annually. Nebraska joined seven other state legislatures in seeking a U.S. constitutional amendment that would require a balanced federal budget every year.

Structures and Powers. Citizen dissatisfaction with the size of government was reflected by a variety of events during 1976. California and Nebraska created paperwork commissions in an effort to cut down on bureaucracy and red tape. New Mexico, Louisiana, and Oklahoma attempted government organizational streamlining, and Georgia, Kansas, and Missouri reorganized state court systems. A proposal to require citizen approval of any new taxes received widespread backing in Colorado, though voters turned it down in November.

The most important innovation was a "sunset law" approved by Colorado legislators in May. It provided that each of the state's 43 agencies be reviewed every six years and that they automatically expire unless the legislature specifically votes to renew them. By the year's end, Louisiana and Florida had approved separate sunset laws; an Ohio commission to detect obsolete state agencies had been formed; and the Iowa governor had vetoed a sunset law as unconstitutional.

Arkansas, Hawaii, and Texas scheduled new constitutional conventions for 1977. And Alaska voters chose Willow, a site more than 100 mi from Anchorage and other major population areas, to replace Juneau (reachable only by sea and air) as the state capital.

Ethics. After four consecutive years of high incidence of corruption, state governments managed to avoid major ethics scandals during 1976. No statewide elected official was indicted on new charges, although legislators impeached and convicted Texas judge O. P. Carillo for malfeasance and censured Georgia state senator Roscoe Dean for falsifying travel vouchers. West Virginia Gov. Arch Moore was acquitted by a federal jury of corruption charges.

New York Gov. Hugh Carey ordered state officials earning more than $30,000 to file complete financial and income statements, and Gov. Dan Walker of Illinois fired 19 top state officials who failed to comply with a similar 1973 order. Florida voters in November approved an initiative that would require complete financial disclosure by candidates and holders of state and county offices.

Reform of utility rate commissions, criticized by Common Cause in 31 states for secrecy and ethical conflicts, was a major item of concern. Voters in Colorado, Massachusetts, and Ohio rejected utility reform initiatives. But Missouri voters approved a similar measure, and the New Hampshire legislature pushed through utility rate reform over a gubernatorial veto.

Education. Many states moved to increase state funding for public schools in an effort to equalize tax receipt potentialities among rich and poor school districts. After considerable resistance, New Jersey complied with a state supreme court order to increase educational funding by approving a new state personal income tax.

The U.S. Supreme Court on June 21 approved Maryland's plan of providing aid for nonsectarian purposes to private colleges, including religious ones. Previous plans in several states had been rejected as an unconstitutional link between church and state, and the Maryland formula promised to provide a model for state assistance to hard-pressed private schools.

Many legislatures continued to look for ways around court decisions banning organized prayer in public schools. Arkansas, New Hampshire, Connecticut, Delaware, Kentucky, and Maine provided for either silent meditation or recital of the Lord's Prayer in classrooms, though the New Hampshire effort was voided by a federal judge.

Governors of Pennsylvania (for the third consecutive year) and New York vetoed antibusing bills during 1976. And Wisconsin joined Minnesota and Iowa in requiring periodic continuing legal education for practicing attorneys.

Health and Welfare. A hot debate over the "right to die" dominated medical news during the year, highlighted by court action over the future of an injured New Jersey woman, Karen Quinlan. The New Jersey Supreme Court ruled that Quinlan's parents and physicians could legally terminate artificial life-sustaining efforts in her case, even though medical experts testified the action would mean almost certain death. But after the equipment was removed in late May, Quinlan continued to live and, in fact, showed improvement through the end of the year. A Massachusetts court similarly decreed a right to die, and California became the first state to enact the right into law, providing for removal of vital equipment with the written consent of the patient.

The 1974–75 furor over medical malpractice insurance rate increases abated during the year, with another 18 states enacting new laws to ease financial burdens on physicians and, occasionally, to limit the amount of possible awards for "pain and suffering."

Ohio, Michigan, and Hawaii joined Minnesota in banning smoking from certain public places. Ten states filed a petition with the U.S. Consumer Product Safety Commission seeking a ban on aerosol products using fluorocarbons; one of the ten, Oregon, had previously prohibited their sale in that state.

U.S. Supreme Court decisions inspired several states to modify their health and public welfare practices. Connecticut and New Jersey moved to prohibit municipalities from using zoning regulations to exclude low-income housing. Hawaii and Wisconsin allowed involuntary commitment to mental hospitals only for dangerous patients, and a New Jersey court declared that a mental patient has a right to beneficial treatment and must not merely be held in custody.

Law and Justice. A historic U.S. Supreme Court decision on July 2 declared capital punishment to be a constitutional sentence for convicted murderers. Modifying a 1972 decision that labeled death as "cruel and unusual punishment" as it had historically been imposed in the U.S., the court stated that laws specifying capital punishment for specific crimes, with opportunity for examination of special circumstances, met constitutional requirements. The last imposition of capital punishment in the U.S. had occurred in 1967.

The decision voided mandatory death penalty laws in Louisiana and North Carolina but upheld different versions in Florida, Georgia, and Texas. By the end of 1976, approximately 450 prisoners in 19 states with apparently valid death laws were awaiting individual review and clemency proceedings. The execution of one convict, Gary Gilmore of Utah, by firing squad was set for January 1977 after he rejected efforts by various groups to assist him.

Thirty-five states had enacted new death penalty laws designed to meet objections raised by the high court's 1972 ruling. In its new opinion, the court cited the widespread legislative action as proof that the death penalty did not violate contemporary standards of decency. (*See* LAW.)

A trend toward mandatory minimum prison sentences for certain crimes continued, with Michigan, Hawaii, Mississippi, Kansas, and Missouri requiring prison time upon conviction for specified offenses. Studies released during 1976 showed that similar laws in Massachusetts and New York had been ineffective and had led to reduction of charges and imposition of fewer jail terms than under previous, more lenient laws.

Virginia, Michigan, Ohio, Colorado, and Pennsylvania enacted laws providing compensation for victims of crime, joining 18 other states with similar plans. Eight states funded their plans by fining offenders.

Massachusetts voters turned down an initiative that would have banned private possession of handguns. Following the death of a Phoenix investigative reporter looking into land fraud allegations, attorneys general in New Mexico and Arizona filed major lawsuits charging deception in land sales. And although the state attorney general insisted that organized crime had not infiltrated the state, Alaska was awarded a special $400,000 federal grant to combat it.

A federal court ruled that New Hampshire's attempts to prevent citizens from taping over the "Live Free or Die" state motto on automobile license plates were an unconstitutional interference with free expression. The U.S. Supreme Court stated in June that Massachusetts and other states could legally force uniformed state patrolmen to retire at age 50 if public policy demanded it.

Drugs. A nationwide trend toward drastic reduction in penalties for possession of marijuana continued during 1976. Minnesota and South Dakota decriminalized possession of small amounts, bringing to eight the number of states making possession subject only to a civil penalty, usually a small fine. Georgia also enacted a sharp reduction in criminal penalties for marijuana possession.

Gambling. Forces backing state-controlled wagering enjoyed a run of good luck during the year. Vermont and Colorado voters approved new sweepstakes-lottery proposals in November elections, joining 13 other states in holding revenue-raising games of chance.

In a major breakthrough, New Jersey voters authorized introduction of casino gambling, previously legal only in Nevada, for the decaying resort of Atlantic City. Bingo games under limited circumstances were approved by legislatures in Georgia and Ohio, but a bill authorizing pari-mutuel horse-race betting was vetoed by the Indiana governor. Voters also turned down proposals for legalization of slot machines in Delaware and of dog-race betting in California.

At the end of the year, 31 states had sanctioned some form of state-supervised gambling; betting on horse races was legal in 30 states, on dog races in 9, lotteries in 15, jai alai in 4, offtrack betting in 3, and numbers games in 4.

Environment. Protection against pollution, a preoccupation of state legislatures during the early 1970s, slowed markedly during 1976, with only a half-dozen states enacting new measures to counter threats to air, water, and the landscape. Environmentalists were able to make progress in combating individual threats to water resources, however.

The California legislature enacted a comprehensive protection bill for its 1,072-mi coastline, a measure that preserved seaside open space, established a coastal commission, and regulated local governmental use of land next to the water. Florida voters approved a special tax to be used for water resource management, and Minnesota joined New York and Indiana in banning phosphates in detergents. A major environmental disaster involving the chemical Kepone occurred in Virginia. (*See* ENVIRONMENT.) Use of polychlorinated biphenyls (PCB's) was severely restricted in Indiana, Michigan, and Wisconsin. Voters in Michigan and Maine approved a statewide ban on nonreturnable beverage containers, but similar measures in Colorado and Massachusetts were turned down in hotly contested elections. Environmentalists charged that a similar nonreturnable ban in South Dakota was rendered ineffective by overly generous exemptions for recyclable containers. Legislatures in California, Minnesota, and Virginia outlawed pull-tab cans.

New Jersey became the first state to enable farmland open space to be preserved through state subsidy. Under a pilot project to begin in 1977, the state was to buy development rights (easements) to an expected 5,000–10,000 ac of farmland and prohibit construction on that land. Maine voters decided to prevent a ski-condominium development on Mt. Bigelow, second highest in the state, by authorizing state purchase of 40,000 ac there.

Washington state officials, fearing an oil spill, continued to enforce a ban on supertankers in Puget Sound despite a federal court decision labeling the law illegal. New Jersey and New York officials, on noise and pollution grounds, succeeded, at least temporarily, in keeping the Anglo-French supersonic transport plane, the Concorde, from landing at state airports, but Virginia officials were unsuccessful in a similar attempt involving Dulles International Airport near Washington, D.C.

Energy. A drive by environmentalists to limit the growth of nuclear plants was resoundingly defeated in seven states during the year as voters apparently decided that the need for development of alternative energy sources outweighed possible health and safety risks. By a 2–1 margin, California voters June 8 defeated an initiative that would have placed stringent limits on development and operation of nuclear power plants. Similar initiatives, some authorizing a ban on nuclear construction until safety measures were foolproof, were decisively turned down by voters in Arizona, Colorado, Montana, Ohio, Oregon, and Washington in November 2 balloting.

Three bills that became law only a week before the California referendum accomplished most of that initiative's goals: they prohibited nuclear construction until safe procedures for fuel-rod reprocessing and waste disposal were developed, and they required studies of underground or shielded construction techniques.

California, Georgia, Kansas, Maryland, Massachusetts, Michigan, and Minnesota granted tax breaks to persons installing solar energy units. Pennsylvania and Wisconsin authorities, following deaths by freezing of elderly citizens, forbade disconnection procedures by utility companies for unpaid bills whenever human life was endangered by the process.

Equal Rights. No state ratified the Equal Rights Amendment to the U.S. Constitution, throwing the future of the proposed anti-sex discrimination clause into grave doubt. Only 34 of 38 states needed to ratify the amendment had done so, and proponents were not able to mount a serious effort in the eight states where it was introduced during 1976.

Advocates of equal rights for women were not without successes, however. Massachusetts voters approved a state equal rights constitutional amendment; Colorado turned down an initiative to rescind its state amendment; and Idaho and Kentucky legislatures refused efforts to retract their national ERA ratification.

Prisons. Overcrowding increased markedly in state correctional institutions during the year. A nationwide survey released in June revealed that a record 225,000 prisoners were housed in state prisons on a typical day, a population increase in 49 states over the previous year. State prisons were occupied at an average 125% of listed capacity, the survey showed.

Colorado, Florida, North Carolina, and Wyoming authorized major expenditures for building new prison facilities. Arkansas and Virginia began housing inmates in house trailers. Several states turned to furlough or early release programs to relieve crowding, but violent incidents involving those released caused temporary suspension of the furlough experiment in New Jersey, Massachusetts, and Maryland during the year. The year's worst state prison riots occurred in Carson City, Nev., where 2 inmates were killed and more than 60 wounded in fighting on September 28 and October 11, and in Reedsville, Ga., where 3 prisoners died and 17 were wounded on November 18.

Consumer Protection. For the first time in recent years, no state enacted new no-fault automobile insurance laws. Nonetheless, a survey by the National Conference of State Legislatures of 16 states with such laws revealed that all expressed satisfaction with the measure. Massachusetts, in 1971 the first state to enact a no-fault law, substantially modified its program; changes included eliminating property damage remuneration for the at-fault driver's own car.

Consumer groups scored a major victory when the U.S. Supreme Court, acting on a test case from Virginia, declared state laws banning drug price advertising to be illegal. The Federal Trade Commission, which had previously outlawed so-called fair trade measures in about half of the states, threatened to overturn state bans against advertising in the eyeglass, pharmacy, and mortuary businesses.

New York, California, and Michigan enacted measures to require disclosures of bank lending practices, a move designed to discourage "redlining," or blockage of mortgage funds for marginal neighbourhoods. No state joined Illinois, which in 1975 became the first to outlaw the practice, however.

Washington and Indiana enacted utility regulations to protect consumers against arbitrary billing and deposit practices. Iowa approved a "plain language" law requiring usually intricate insurance policies to be written on the seventh-grade-English level.

(DAVID C. BECKWITH)

Area and Population

Area and population of the states

State	AREA in sq.mi. Total	Inland water*	POPULATION (000) July 1, 1970	July 1, 1975†	Percent change 1970–75
Alabama	51,609	549	3,451	3,614	4.9
Alaska	586,400	15,335	305	352	16.3
Arizona	113,909	334	1,792	2,224	25.3
Arkansas	53,104	605	1,926	2,116	10.0
California	158,693	2,120	19,994	21,185	6.1
Colorado	104,247	363	2,225	2,534	14.7
Connecticut	5,009	110	3,039	3,095	2.1
Delaware	2,057	79	550	579	5.7
Dist. of Columbia	69	8	753	716	−5.4
Florida	58,560	4,308	6,845	8,357	23.0
Georgia	58,876	602	4,602	4,926	7.4
Hawaii	6,424	9	774	865	12.3
Idaho	83,557	849	717	820	14.9
Illinois	56,400	470	11,137	11,145	0.3
Indiana	36,291	106	5,208	5,311	2.2
Iowa	56,290	258	2,830	2,870	1.6
Kansas	82,264	216	2,248	2,267	0.8
Kentucky	40,395	532	3,224	3,396	5.4
Louisiana	48,523	3,417	3,644	3,791	4.1
Maine	33,215	2,203	995	1,059	6.6
Maryland	10,577	703	3,937	4,098	4.4
Massachusetts	8,257	390	5,699	5,828	2.4
Michigan	58,216	1,197	8,901	9,157	3.1
Minnesota	84,068	4,059	3,822	3,926	3.1
Mississippi	47,716	493	2,216	2,346	5.8
Missouri	69,686	548	4,693	4,763	1.8
Montana	147,138	1,402	697	748	7.7
Nebraska	77,227	615	1,490	1,546	4.1
Nevada	110,540	752	493	592	21.1
New Hampshire	9,304	290	742	818	10.9
New Jersey	7,836	315	7,195	7,316	2.0
New Mexico	121,666	156	1,018	1,147	12.7
New York	49,576	1,637	18,260	18,120	−0.7
North Carolina	52,712	3,645	5,091	5,451	7.2
North Dakota	70,665	1,208	618	635	2.7
Ohio	41,222	250	10,688	10,759	1.0
Oklahoma	69,919	1,032	2,572	2,712	6.0
Oregon	96,981	733	2,102	2,288	9.4
Pennsylvania	45,333	326	11,817	11,827	0.2
Rhode Island	1,214	156	951	927	−2.4
South Carolina	31,055	783	2,596	2,818	8.8
South Dakota	77,047	669	666	683	2.6
Tennessee	42,244	482	3,932	4,188	6.7
Texas	267,338	4,499	11,254	12,237	9.3
Utah	84,916	2,577	1,069	1,206	13.8
Vermont	9,609	333	447	471	5.9
Virginia	40,815	977	4,653	4,967	6.8
Washington	68,192	1,483	3,414	3,544	3.8
West Virginia	24,181	102	1,746	1,803	3.4
Wisconsin	56,154	1,449	4,433	4,607	4.3
Wyoming	97,914	503	334	374	12.5
TOTAL U.S.	3,615,210	66,237	203,805	213,121‡	4.8

*Excludes the Great Lakes and coastal waters.
†Preliminary.
‡State figures do not add to total given because of rounding.
Source: U.S. Department of Commerce, Bureau of the Census, *Current Population Reports.*

Largest metropolitan areas*

Name	Population 1970 census	1975 estimate	Percent change 1970–75	Land area in sq mi	Density per sq mi 1975
New York-Newark-Jersey City SCSA	17,033,367	16,848,000	−1.1	5,072	3,322
New York City	9,973,716	9,567,000	−4.1	1,384	6,913
Nassau-Suffolk	2,555,868	2,750,800	7.6	1,218	2,258
Newark	2,057,468	2,061,300	0.2	1,008	2,045
Bridgeport†	792,814	793,900	0.1	627	1,266
Jersey City	607,839	601,400	−1.1	47	12,796
New Brunswick-Perth Amboy	583,813	600,600	2.9	312	1,925
Long Branch-Asbury Park	461,849	473,000	2.4	476	994
Los Angeles-Long Beach-Anaheim SCSA	9,983,017	10,316,600	3.3	34,007	303
Los Angeles-Long Beach	7,041,980	6,944,900	−1.4	4,069	1,708
Anaheim-Santa Ana-Garden Grove	1,421,233	1,710,200	20.3	782	2,187
Riverside-San Bernardino-Ontario	1,141,307	1,223,400	7.2	27,293	45
Oxnard-Simi Valley-Ventura	378,497	438,100	15.7	1,863	235
Chicago-Gary SCSA	7,610,978	7,623,300	0.2	4,657	1,637
Chicago	6,977,611	6,982,900	0.1	3,719	1,878
Gary-Hammond-East Chicago	633,367	640,400	1.1	938	683
Philadelphia-Wilmington-Trenton SCSA	5,627,719	5,764,500	2.4	4,946	1,166
Philadelphia	4,824,110	4,933,400	2.3	3,553	1,388
Wilmington	499,493	515,300	3.2	1,165	442
Trenton	304,116	315,800	3.8	228	1,385
Detroit-Ann Arbor SCSA	4,669,154	4,701,100	0.7	4,627	1,016
Detroit	4,435,051	4,444,700	0.2	3,916	1,135
Ann Arbor	234,103	256,400	9.5	711	361
San Francisco-Oakland-San Jose SCSA	4,423,797	4,579,800	3.5	5,390	850
San Francisco-Oakland	3,107,355	3,128,800	0.7	2,480	1,262
San Jose	1,065,313	1,173,400	10.1	1,300	903
Vallejo-Fairfield-Napa	251,129	277,600	10.5	1,610	172
Boston-Lawrence-Lowell SCSA†	3,848,593	3,914,600	1.7	3,114	1,257
Washington, D.C.	2,909,355	3,029,600	4.1	2,812	1,077
Cleveland-Akron-Lorain SCSA	2,999,811	2,912,300	−2.9	2,917	998
Cleveland	2,063,729	1,975,400	−4.3	1,519	1,300
Akron	679,239	668,200	−1.6	903	740
Lorain-Elyria	256,843	268,700	4.6	495	543
Dallas-Fort Worth	2,378,353	2,535,500	0.7	8,360	303
Houston-Galveston SCSA	2,169,128	2,438,100	12.4	7,193	339
Houston	1,999,316	2,256,300	12.8	6,794	332
Galveston-Texas City	169,812	181,800	7.1	399	456
St. Louis	2,410,492	2,392,500	−0.7	4,935	485
Pittsburgh	2,401,362	2,315,900	−3.6	3,049	760
Miami-Fort Lauderdale SCSA	1,887,892	2,301,100	21.9	3,261	706
Miami	1,267,792	1,438,600	13.5	2,042	705
Fort Lauderdale-Hollywood	620,100	862,500	39.1	1,219	708
Baltimore	2,071,016	2,136,900	3.2	2,259	946
Minneapolis-St. Paul	1,965,391	2,027,500	3.2	4,647	436
Seattle-Tacoma SCSA	1,836,949	1,821,500	−0.8	5,902	307
Seattle-Everett	1,424,605	1,411,700	−0.9	4,226	334
Tacoma	412,344	409,800	−0.6	1,676	245
Atlanta	1,595,517	1,793,800	12.4	4,326	415
Cincinnati-Hamilton SCSA	1,613,414	1,628,600	0.9	2,620	622
Cincinnati	1,387,207	1,384,500	−0.2	2,149	644
Hamilton-Middletown	226,207	244,100	7.9	471	518
Milwaukee-Racine SCSA	1,574,722	1,602,300	1.8	1,793	894
Milwaukee	1,403,884	1,426,400	1.6	1,456	980
Racine	170,838	175,900	2.9	337	522
San Diego	1,357,854	1,587,500	16.9	4,261	373
Denver-Boulder	1,239,477	1,404,300	13.3	4,651	302
Tampa-St. Petersburg	1,088,549	1,365,400	25.4	2,045	668
Buffalo	1,349,211	1,327,200	−1.6	1,590	835
Kansas City	1,273,926	1,295,000	1.6	3,341	388
Indianapolis	1,111,352	1,147,400	3.2	3,072	374

*Standard Metropolitan Statistical Area, SMSA, unless otherwise indicated; SCSA is a Standard Consolidated Statistical Area, which may be comprised of SMSAs. †New England County Metropolitan Area. Sources: U.S. Dept. of Commerce, Bureau of the Census, *Current Population Reports;* U.S. Dept. of Justice, FBI, *Uniform Crime Reports for the United States, 1975.*

Population change

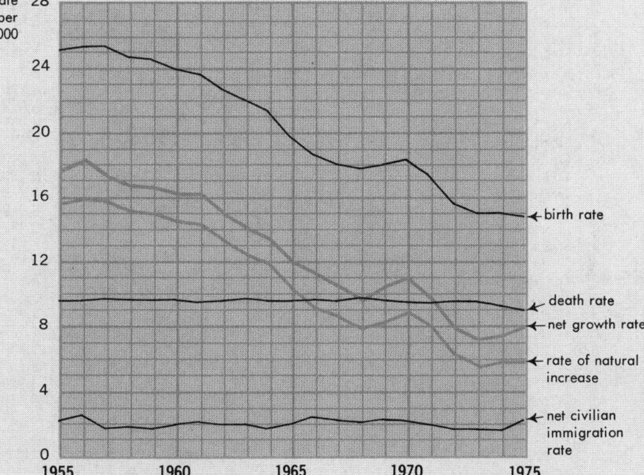

Source: U.S. Department of Commerce, Bureau of the Census, *Current Population Reports.*

Marriage and divorce rates

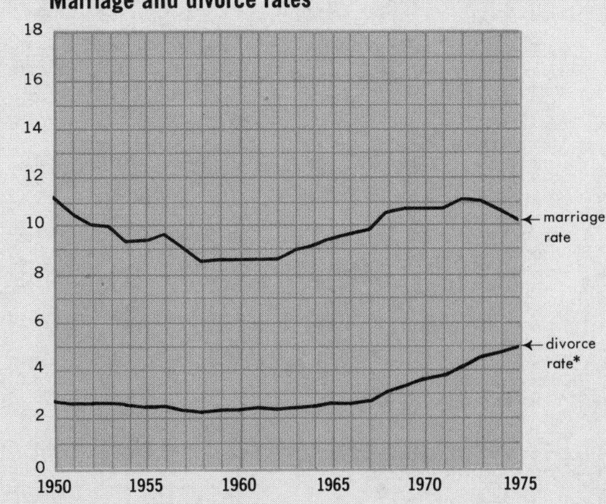

*Includes annulments.

Source: U.S. Department of Health, Education, and Welfare, Public Health Service, *Monthly Vital Statistics Report.*

Church membership

Religious body	Total clergy	Inclusive membership
Adventist, Seventh-day	3,606	479,799
Baptist bodies		
American Baptist Association	4,070	1,071,000
American Baptist Churches in the U.S.A.	8,564	1,579,029
Baptist General Conference	1,055	111,093
Baptist Missionary Association of America	2,650	211,000
Conservative Baptist Association of America	...	300,000
Free Will Baptists	3,700	215,000
General Baptists (General Association of)	1,125	70,000
National Baptist Convention of America	28,754	2,668,799
National Baptist Convention, U.S.A., Inc.	27,500	5,500,000
Natl. Bap. Evang. Life and Soul Saving Assembly	137	57,674
National Primitive Baptist Convention	601	1,645,000
Primitive Baptists	...	72,000
Progressive National Baptist Convention, Inc.	863	521,692
Regular Baptist Churches, General Assn. of	...	250,000
Southern Baptist Convention	54,150	12,513,378
United Free Will Baptist Church	784	100,000
Brethren (German Baptists): Church of the Brethren	1,948	179,387
Buddhist Churches of America	101	100,000
Christian and Missionary Alliance	1,196	144,245
Christian Church (Disciples of Christ)	6,567	1,312,326
Christian Churches and Churches of Christ	6,272	1,034,047
Christian Congregation	506	59,600
Church of God (Anderson, Ind.)	2,905	161,401
Church of the Nazarene	7,130	430,128
Churches of Christ	6,200	2,400,000
Congregational Christian Churches, Natl. Assn. of	475	90,000
Eastern churches		
American Carpatho-Russian Orth. Greek Catholic Ch.	68	100,000
Antiochian Orthodox Christian Archdiocese of N. Am.	124	130,000
Armenian Apostolic Church of America	34	125,000
Armenian Church of America, Diocese of the (Including Diocese of California)	67	372,000
Bulgarian Eastern Orthodox Church	11	86,000
Greek Orthodox Archdiocese of N. and S. America	675	1,950,000
Orthodox Church in America	558	1,000,000
Romanian Orthodox Episcopate of America	52	40,000
Russian Orth. Ch. in the U.S.A., Patriarchal Parishes of	60	51,500
Russian Orthodox Church Outside Russia	168	55,000
Serbian Eastern Orth. Ch. for the U.S.A. and Canada	64	65,000
Syrian Orthodox Church of Antioch	14	50,000
Ukrainian Orthodox Church in the U.S.A.	131	87,745
Episcopal Church	11,573	2,907,293
Evangelical Covenant Church of America	683	69,960
Evangelical Free Church of America	...	70,490
Friends United Meeting	611	67,431
Independent Fundamental Churches of America	1,252	87,582
Jehovah's Witnesses	None	539,262
Jewish congregations	6,400	6,115,000
Latter Day Saints		
Church of Jesus Christ of Latter-day Saints	18,096	2,683,573
Reorganized Church of Jesus Christ of L.D.S.	15,179	156,687
Lutherans		
American Lutheran Church	6,483	2,437,862
Lutheran Church in America	7,579	2,986,970
Lutheran Church—Missouri Synod	7,331	2,769,594
Wisconsin Evangelical Lutheran Synod	1,041	388,865
Mennonite Church	2,370	92,390
Methodists		
African Methodist Episcopal Church	7,089	1,166,301
African Methodist Episcopal Zion Church	6,873	1,024,974
Christian Methodist Episcopal Church	2,259	466,718
Free Methodist Church of North America	1,760	65,210
United Methodist Church	35,106	10,063,046
Moravian Church in America	203	54,892
North American Old Roman Catholic Church	109	60,098
Pentecostals		
Apostolic Overcoming Holy Church of God	350	75,000
Assemblies of God	12,810	1,239,197
Church of God	2,737	75,890
Church of God (Cleveland, Tenn.)	8,650	328,892
Church of God in Christ	6,000	425,000
Church of God in Christ, International	1,502	501,000
Church of God of Prophecy	5,475	62,743
International Church of the Foursquare Gospel	2,690	89,215
Pentecostal Church of God of America, Inc.	1,900	135,000
Pentecostal Holiness Church, Inc.	1,878	74,108
United Pentecostal Church, International	5,555	270,000
Polish National Catholic Church of America	144	282,411
Presbyterians		
Cumberland Presbyterian Church	713	93,948
Presbyterian Church in the U.S.	5,092	896,203
United Presbyterian Church in the U.S.A.	13,736	2,723,565
Reformed bodies		
Christian Reformed Church	1,065	206,000
Reformed Church in America	2,742	354,004
Roman Catholic Church	59,287	48,701,835
Salvation Army	5,178	366,471
Spiritualists, International General Assembly of	...	164,072
Triumph the Church and Kingdom of God in Christ	1,375	54,307
Unitarian Universalist Association	864	192,510
United Church of Christ	9,526	1,841,312
Wesleyan Church	2,489	94,215

Table includes churches reporting a membership of 50,000 or more and represents the latest information available.
Source: National Council of Churches, *Yearbook of American and Canadian Churches*, 1976.

(CONSTANT H. JACQUET)

The Economy

Gross national product and national income

in billions of dollars

Item	1965*	1970*	1975	1976†
GROSS NATIONAL PRODUCT	688.1	982.4	1,516.3	1,675.2
By type of expenditure				
Personal consumption expenditures	430.2	618.8	973.2	1,064.7
Durable goods	62.8	84.9	131.7	155.0
Nondurable goods	188.6	264.7	409.1	434.8
Services	178.7	269.1	432.4	474.9
Gross private domestic investment	112.0	140.8	183.7	239.2
Fixed investment	102.5	137.0	198.3	223.2
Changes in business inventories	9.5	3.8	−14.6	16.0
Net exports of goods and services	7.6	3.9	20.5	9.3
Exports	39.5	62.5	148.1	160.3
Imports	32.0	58.5	127.6	151.0
Government purchases of goods and services	138.4	218.9	339.0	362.0
Federal	67.3	95.6	124.4	131.2
State and local	71.1	123.2	214.5	230.9
By major type of product				
Goods output	336.6	456.2	681.7	758.4
Durable goods	133.6	170.8	254.4	301.2
Nondurable goods	203.1	285.4	427.3	457.1
Services	272.7	424.6	692.5	759.6
Structures	78.8	101.6	142.1	157.3
NATIONAL INCOME	566.0	798.4	1,207.6	1,337.4
By type of income				
Compensation of employees	396.5	609.2	928.8	1,017.2
Proprietors' income	56.7	65.1	90.2	100.3
Rental income of persons	17.1	18.6	22.4	23.1
Corporate profits	77.1	67.9	91.6	116.4
Net interest	18.5	37.5	74.6	80.3
By industry division‡				
Agriculture, forestry, and fisheries	20.4	24.5	44.4	48.6
Mining and construction	35.9	51.6	79.2	83.8
Manufacturing	170.4	215.4	309.9	360.0
Nondurable goods	65.4	88.1	126.7	146.8
Durable goods	105.0	127.3	183.2	213.2
Transportation	23.1	30.3	44.8	51.0
Communications and public utilities	22.9	32.5	49.3	53.2
Wholesale and retail trade	84.7	122.2	195.6	216.5
Finance, insurance, and real estate	64.0	92.6	137.6	148.6
Services	64.1	103.3	165.1	183.0
Government and government enterprises	75.4	127.4	199.7	215.4
Other	4.7	4.6	10.6	12.4

*Revised. †Second quarter, seasonally adjusted at annual rates.
‡Without capital consumption adjustment.
Source: U.S. Department of Commerce, Bureau of Economic Analysis, *Survey of Current Business.*

Personal income per capita

State	1950	1960*	1970*	1975
Alabama	$ 880	$1,519	$2,948	$4,643
Alaska	2,384	2,809	4,644	9,448
Arizona	1,330	2,012	3,665	5,355
Arkansas	825	1,390	2,878	4,620
California	1,852	2,706	4,493	6,593
Colorado	1,487	2,252	3,855	5,985
Connecticut	1,875	2,838	4,917	6,973
Delaware	2,132	2,785	4,524	6,748
District of Columbia	2,221	2,983	5,079	7,742
Florida	1,281	1,947	3,738	5,638
Georgia	1,034	1,651	3,354	5,086
Hawaii	1,386	2,368	4,623	6,658
Idaho	1,295	1,850	3,290	5,159
Illinois	1,825	2,646	4,507	6,789
Indiana	1,512	2,178	3,772	5,653
Iowa	1,485	1,983	3,751	6,077
Kansas	1,443	2,160	3,853	6,023
Kentucky	981	1,586	3,112	4,871
Louisiana	1,120	1,668	3,090	4,904
Maine	1,186	1,862	3,302	4,786
Maryland	1,602	2,341	4,309	6,474
Massachusetts	1,633	2,461	4,340	6,114
Michigan	1,701	2,357	4,180	6,173
Minnesota	1,410	2,075	3,859	5,807
Mississippi	755	1,222	2,626	4,052
Missouri	1,431	2,112	3,781	5,510
Montana	1,622	2,035	3,500	5,422
Nebraska	1,490	2,110	3,789	6,087
Nevada	2,018	2,799	4,563	6,647
New Hampshire	1,323	2,135	3,737	5,315
New Jersey	1,834	2,727	4,701	6,722
New Mexico	1,177	1,843	3,077	4,775
New York	1,873	2,740	4,712	6,564
North Carolina	1,037	1,590	3,252	4,952
North Dakota	1,263	1,704	3,086	5,737
Ohio	1,620	2,345	4,020	5,810
Oklahoma	1,143	1,876	3,387	5,250
Oregon	1,620	2,220	3,719	5,769
Pennsylvania	1,541	2,269	3,971	5,943
Rhode Island	1,605	2,217	3,959	5,841
South Carolina	893	1,397	2,990	4,618
South Dakota	1,242	1,784	3,123	4,924
Tennessee	994	1,576	3,119	4,895
Texas	1,349	1,936	3,606	5,631
Utah	1,309	1,979	3,227	4,923
Vermont	1,121	1,847	3,468	4,960
Virginia	1,228	1,864	3,712	5,785
Washington	1,674	2,360	4,053	6,247
West Virginia	1,065	1,621	3,061	4,918
Wisconsin	1,477	2,188	3,812	5,669
Wyoming	1,668	2,247	3,815	6,131
United States	1,496	2,222	3,966	5,902

*Revised.
Source: U.S. Department of Commerce, Bureau of Economic Analysis, *Survey of Current Business.*

Income by industrial source, 1975

State and region	SOURCES OF PERSONAL INCOME: Total personal income	Farm income	Govt. income disbursements: Federal	Govt. income disbursements: State, local	Private nonfarm income	SOURCES OF LABOUR AND PROPRIETORS' INCOME % OF TOTAL: Total	Farms	Mining	Construction	Mfg.	Wholesale, retail trade	Finance, insurance, real estate	Transportation, communications, public util.	Service	Govt.	Other
United States	$1,257,354	$33,878	$62,648	$110,676	$743,635	$950,837	%3.6	%1.4	%5.7	%25.5	%16.8	%5.3	%7.2	%16.0	%18.2	%0.4
New England	74,319	360	2,387	5,960	44,594	53,301	0.7	0.1	5.2	30.6	16.4	6.3	5.8	18.8	15.7	0.4
Maine	5,071	114	323	412	2,791	3,641	3.1	0.1	6.6	25.7	17.0	4.2	6.5	15.7	20.2	0.8
New Hampshire	4,346	22	167	328	2,421	2,939	0.7	0.2	6.1	30.5	17.3	5.0	5.6	17.2	16.9	0.4
Vermont	2,336	70	78	220	1,330	1,697	4.1	0.6	5.4	26.7	16.0	4.4	6.5	18.4	17.6	0.3
Massachusetts	35,568	66	1,100	3,040	21,886	26,092	0.2	0.1	4.9	27.8	17.0	6.4	6.4	20.9	15.9	0.4
Rhode Island	5,413	9	226	470	3,000	3,703	0.2	0.1	4.6	31.4	16.4	5.5	4.9	17.5	18.8	0.5
Connecticut	21,584	80	494	1,490	13,165	15,229	0.5	0.1	5.3	36.7	14.9	7.2	5.0	16.8	13.0	0.3
Mideast	274,420	1,460	13,799	25,716	165,604	206,579	0.7	0.6	4.7	25.7	16.2	6.7	7.6	18.4	19.1	0.3
New York	118,958	405	3,056	13,080	73,180	89,720	0.4	0.2	3.8	22.5	16.7	9.2	8.3	20.6	18.0	0.3
New Jersey	49,181	94	1,480	3,987	28,480	34,041	0.3	0.1	5.0	30.9	17.5	4.9	7.9	16.8	16.1	0.3
Pennsylvania	70,296	622	2,291	5,254	44,635	52,801	1.2	1.8	5.5	33.7	15.7	4.6	7.2	15.8	14.3	0.2
Delaware	3,908	104	148	308	2,501	3,062	3.4	0.2	6.3	38.5	13.9	4.2	5.2	13.1	14.9	0.3
Maryland	26,533	235	2,716	2,328	12,928	18,208	1.3	0.2	6.9	17.3	17.5	4.9	5.9	17.8	27.7	0.4
District of Columbia	5,544	*	4,108	758	3,880	8,746	†	†	3.4	2.8	7.2	4.2	5.9	20.2	55.6	0.6
Great Lakes	250,838	6,113	6,204	20,605	161,424	194,345	3.1	0.7	5.0	36.3	16.0	4.4	6.5	13.9	13.8	0.2
Michigan	56,526	585	1,054	5,378	36,716	43,733	1.3	0.5	4.3	41.3	14.9	3.6	5.2	13.8	14.7	0.2
Ohio	62,514	1,011	1,826	4,603	41,623	49,063	2.1	1.0	5.1	38.0	15.9	4.0	6.6	14.0	13.1	0.2
Indiana	30,023	1,265	777	2,115	19,558	23,715	5.3	0.6	5.4	39.5	14.9	4.1	6.3	11.5	12.2	0.2
Illinois	75,666	2,376	2,087	6,125	47,762	58,349	4.1	0.8	5.4	29.9	17.3	5.5	7.6	15.0	14.1	0.2
Wisconsin	26,109	876	459	2,384	15,765	19,485	4.5	0.2	5.1	35.6	16.0	4.2	5.8	13.5	14.6	0.3
Plains	96,533	8,452	3,754	7,993	53,397	73,596	11.5	1.0	‡	21.6	17.9	4.7	7.8	‡	16.0	‡
Minnesota	22,793	1,476	536	2,193	13,450	17,655	8.4	1.3	5.7	23.5	18.4	4.9	7.5	14.5	15.5	0.3
Iowa	17,440	2,397	323	1,374	8,860	12,954	18.5	0.4	5.4	23.7	16.7	4.2	6.1	11.5	13.1	0.5
Missouri	26,244	781	1,314	2,006	16,532	20,633	3.8	0.6	5.4	25.5	18.3	5.1	9.3	15.6	16.1	0.3
North Dakota	3,652	850	272	275	1,498	2,894	29.4	1.3	‡	6.3	17.3	3.2	6.1	‡	18.9	‡
South Dakota	3,365	552	226	289	1,422	2,489	22.2	1.3	5.4	8.1	18.7	3.9	6.3	12.7	20.6	0.7
Nebraska	9,384	1,421	401	801	4,585	7,207	19.7	0.4	5.7	13.9	17.6	5.2	8.1	12.5	16.7	0.2
Kansas	13,655	975	682	1,056	7,050	9,764	10.0	2.1	5.7	20.7	17.6	4.4	8.2	13.0	17.8	0.4
Southeast	241,406	7,648	16,004	20,044	135,826	179,522	4.3	2.3	6.4	22.7	16.9	4.9	7.2	14.8	20.1	0.3
Virginia	28,732	367	3,829	2,338	14,299	20,833	1.8	1.8	6.2	19.1	15.2	4.5	6.8	14.7	29.6	0.3
West Virginia	8,867	27	241	700	5,750	6,719	0.4	16.9	6.4	24.3	14.4	2.9	8.3	12.2	14.0	0.1
Kentucky	16,541	660	979	1,213	9,636	12,488	5.3	7.2	5.7	25.1	15.5	3.6	6.9	12.8	17.5	0.3
Tennessee	20,501	340	1,049	1,685	12,922	15,996	2.1	0.9	5.8	29.9	17.9	4.8	6.2	15.0	17.1	0.3
North Carolina	26,995	1,228	1,679	2,200	16,130	21,237	5.8	0.2	5.3	30.5	15.9	4.3	6.1	13.3	18.3	0.3
South Carolina	13,014	326	1,158	1,113	7,434	10,031	3.2	0.2	6.3	31.8	14.2	4.0	5.1	12.1	22.6	0.3
Georgia	25,052	833	1,700	2,180	14,874	19,586	4.2	0.4	5.3	22.3	19.3	5.6	8.6	14.0	19.8	0.2
Florida	47,055	1,287	2,250	4,115	23,843	31,493	4.1	0.4	7.7	12.2	19.5	7.0	8.2	19.9	20.2	0.6
Alabama	16,779	495	1,287	1,383	9,510	12,674	3.9	1.7	6.6	26.8	15.7	4.2	6.5	13.3	21.1	0.2
Mississippi	9,504	469	608	830	5,171	7,078	6.6	1.3	5.7	26.5	15.6	4.1	6.1	13.1	20.3	0.5
Louisiana	18,591	526	812	1,607	11,252	14,198	3.7	6.7	8.8	17.0	17.5	4.6	9.5	14.7	17.0	0.3
Arkansas	9,775	1,090	413	681	5,006	7,190	15.2	1.0	5.5	23.3	16.0	4.0	6.9	12.3	15.2	0.5
Southwest	100,523	2,848	6,646	8,268	58,517	76,280	3.7	5.0	7.1	18.0	18.4	5.2	7.5	15.0	19.5	0.4
Oklahoma	14,237	482	1,067	1,082	7,823	10,453	4.6	7.0	5.7	16.9	18.1	4.8	7.9	14.1	20.5	0.4
Texas	68,903	1,815	4,187	5,282	41,575	52,859	3.4	4.6	7.2	19.7	18.9	5.3	7.6	14.9	17.9	0.4
New Mexico	5,476	244	580	651	2,688	4,164	5.9	7.2	7.4	6.5	15.8	4.0	7.3	15.9	29.6	0.3
Arizona	11,908	307	812	1,253	6,432	8,804	3.5	4.2	8.1	14.9	16.9	5.6	6.3	16.5	23.4	0.5
Rocky Mountain	31,686	1,681	2,427	2,969	17,530	24,607	6.8	4.1	7.4	14.5	17.5	4.8	7.9	14.7	21.9	0.4
Montana	4,054	507	257	396	1,915	3,074	16.5	3.6	6.4	9.4	16.7	3.6	8.7	13.5	21.2	0.4
Idaho	4,234	470	226	369	2,226	3,291	14.3	1.5	7.9	16.5	17.3	3.8	6.6	13.4	18.1	0.6
Wyoming	2,294	58	144	219	1,364	1,785	3.2	16.9	14.3	6.3	14.1	2.9	10.2	11.1	20.3	0.6
Colorado	15,168	550	1,216	1,432	8,639	11,837	4.6	2.9	6.6	15.5	18.0	5.8	7.6	16.3	22.4	0.4
Utah	5,937	95	585	553	3,387	4,620	2.1	4.5	7.1	16.9	17.9	4.4	8.4	13.9	24.6	0.3
Far West	178,632	5,158	9,898	18,197	101,221	134,474	3.8	0.5	‡	21.4	17.2	5.2	7.1	‡	20.9	‡
Washington	22,158	979	1,482	2,131	11,919	16,511	5.9	0.2	6.0	21.9	17.3	4.6	6.9	14.6	21.9	0.7
Oregon	13,201	413	468	1,329	7,779	9,989	4.1	0.2	6.0	24.5	19.3	4.6	7.6	14.9	18.0	0.6
Nevada	3,935	41	238	373	2,483	3,136	1.3	1.9	‡	4.9	14.9	4.0	7.9	‡	19.5	‡
California	139,337	3,725	7,710	14,363	79,039	104,838	3.5	0.6	6.2	21.5	17.0	5.4	7.1	18.2	21.0	0.5
Alaska	3,324	3	556	417	2,680	3,656	0.1	3.0	29.8	4.3	10.2	2.5	11.1	11.1	26.6	1.3
Hawaii	5,674	155	973	507	2,843	4,477	3.5	‡	9.7	6.0	15.3	6.0	8.4	17.5	33.1	0.6

Dollar figures in millions. Percentages may not add to 100.0 because of rounding.
*Less than $500,000. †Less than 0.05%. ‡Figures not shown to avoid disclosure of confidential information. Data are included in totals.
Source: U.S. Department of Commerce, Bureau of Economic Analysis, *Survey of Current Business*.

Farms and farm income

State	Number of farms 1976*	Land in farms 1976 in 000 acres*	CASH RECEIPTS, 1975, IN $000* — Farm marketings: Total	Crops	Livestock and products
Alabama	77,000	14,700	1,384,731	545,223	839,508
Alaska	300	1,710†	7,802	4,079	3,723
Arizona	5,700	37,500	1,052,384	564,110	488,274
Arkansas	69,000	17,400	2,218,033	1,226,305	991,728
California	63,000	36,000	8,485,095	5,696,870	2,788,225
Colorado	29,500	39,900	1,947,868	608,202	1,339,666
Connecticut	4,400	540	214,676	96,455	118,221
Delaware	3,500	696	269,337	101,550	167,787
Florida	32,000	14,000	2,433,269	1,809,078	624,191
Georgia	73,000	17,000	2,218,929	1,102,527	1,116,402
Hawaii	4,300	2,300	372,271	314,565	57,706
Idaho	26,500	15,600	1,314,757	819,327	495,430
Illinois	122,000	29,100	5,404,907	3,513,362	1,891,545
Indiana	105,000	17,500	2,996,251	1,774,250	1,222,001
Iowa	135,000	34,200	6,614,245	2,711,698	3,902,547
Kansas	79,000	49,900	3,365,306	1,857,063	1,508,243
Kentucky	124,000	16,000	1,467,636	798,220	669,416
Louisiana	47,000	11,900	1,083,592	769,784	313,808
Maine	7,600	1,710	370,492	124,402	246,090
Maryland	17,600	2,925	666,343	260,853	405,490
Massachusetts	5,800	710	202,232	95,497	106,735
Michigan	80,000	12,400	1,656,218	943,417	712,801
Minnesota	118,000	30,600	3,855,294	1,812,357	2,042,937
Mississippi	84,000	17,100	1,374,702	707,749	666,953
Missouri	139,000	32,700	2,657,463	1,070,797	1,586,666
Montana	22,500	62,400	1,078,329	657,649	420,680
Nebraska	68,000	48,000	3,875,931	1,717,717	2,158,214
Nevada	2,000	9,000	132,070	37,102	94,968
New Hampshire	2,600	560	74,051	19,921	54,130
New Jersey	7,900	1,025	318,733	216,899	101,834
New Mexico	11,700	47,100	729,154	184,201	544,953
New York	58,000	11,400	1,546,147	494,259	1,051,888
North Carolina	125,000	13,200	2,673,305	1,676,989	996,316
North Dakota	40,000	41,600	1,983,705	1,530,897	452,808
Ohio	116,000	17,300	2,758,613	1,632,648	1,125,965
Oklahoma	86,000	36,800	1,900,458	825,562	1,074,896
Oregon	32,500	19,500	1,031,263	705,805	325,458
Pennsylvania	73,000	10,220	1,622,172	475,866	1,146,306
Rhode Island	680	65	27,345	15,559	11,786
South Carolina	47,000	7,800	829,031	558,451	270,580
South Dakota	43,000	45,500	1,815,769	559,461	1,256,308
Tennessee	124,000	15,300	1,095,202	514,093	581,109
Texas	205,000	141,800	5,846,591	2,785,683	3,060,908
Utah	12,600	13,000	328,818	95,877	232,941
Vermont	6,600	1,860	219,861	16,953	202,908
Virginia	72,000	11,000	1,008,206	483,481	524,725
Washington	40,000	16,500	1,891,915	1,449,733	442,182
West Virginia	26,500	4,750	144,571	43,868	100,703
Wisconsin	103,000	19,400	2,651,655	538,860	2,112,795
Wyoming	8,000	35,500	346,463	96,206	250,257
TOTAL U.S.	2,785,780	1,084,671	89,563,191	46,661,480	42,901,711

*Preliminary. †Exclusive of grazing land leased from the U.S. Government, Alaska farmland totals about 70,000 acres.
Source: U.S. Department of Agriculture, Statistical Reporting Service and Economic Research Service.

Principal minerals produced

State	Principal minerals, in order of value, 1973	Value in $000		% of U.S. total	
		1972	1973	1972	1973
Alabama	Coal, cement, petroleum, stone	$371,241	$413,056	1.15	1.12
Alaska	Petroleum, sand and gravel, natural gas, stone	286,138	328,789	0.89	0.89
Arizona	Copper, molybdenum, sand and gravel, cement	1,091,004	1,304,988	3.39	3.55
Arkansas	Petroleum, bromine, natural gas, cement	241,179	273,705	0.75	0.75
California	Petroleum, cement, sand and gravel, natural gas	1,851,365	2,041,686	5.75	5.55
Colorado	Petroleum, molybdenum, coal, sand and gravel	425,841	532,776	1.32	1.45
Connecticut	Stone, sand and gravel, feldspar, lime	33,123	36,804	0.10	0.10
Delaware	Sand and gravel, magnesium compounds, clays	2,871	3,869	0.01	0.01
Florida	Phosphate rock, petroleum, stone, cement	424,287	601,100	1.32	1.63
Georgia	Clays, stone, cement, sand and gravel	258,041	305,479	0.80	0.83
Hawaii	Stone, cement, sand and gravel, pumice	28,074	35,147	0.09	0.10
Idaho	Silver, phosphate rock, lead, zinc	106,206	136,081	0.33	0.37
Illinois	Coal, petroleum, stone, sand and gravel	769,737	825,608	2.39	2.24
Indiana	Coal, cement, stone, sand and gravel	322,608	351,405	1.00	0.96
Iowa	Cement, stone, sand and gravel, gypsum	134,496	158,800	0.42	0.43
Kansas	Petroleum, natural gas, natural gas liquids, cement	584,537	646,299	1.81	1.76
Kentucky	Coal, stone, petroleum, natural gas	976,910	1,164,762	3.03	3.17
Louisiana	Petroleum, natural gas, natural gas liquids, sulfur	5,411,543	5,819,610	16.80	15.82
Maine	Sand and gravel, cement, zinc, stone	22,922	33,493	0.07	0.09
Maryland	Stone, cement, sand and gravel, coal	115,501	131,907	0.36	0.36
Massachusetts	Stone, sand and gravel, lime, clays	52,428	59,682	0.16	0.16
Michigan	Iron ore, cement, copper, sand and gravel	694,767	789,022	2.16	2.14
Minnesota	Iron ore, sand and gravel, stone, cement	659,669	852,785	2.05	2.32
Mississippi	Petroleum, natural gas, sand and gravel, cement	260,681	281,738	0.81	0.77
Missouri	Lead, cement, stone, iron ore	451,817	512,634	1.40	1.39
Montana	Copper, petroleum, coal, sand and gravel	307,676	385,285	0.96	1.05
Nebraska	Petroleum, cement, sand and gravel, stone	73,675	80,821	0.23	0.22
Nevada	Copper, gold, sand and gravel, diatomite	181,702	201,813	0.56	0.55
New Hampshire	Sand and gravel, stone, clays, gem stones	10,111	14,119	0.03	0.04
New Jersey	Stone, sand and gravel, zinc, titanium concentrate	113,760	114,016	0.35	0.31
New Mexico	Petroleum, natural gas, copper, natural gas liquids	1,097,292	1,305,644	3.41	3.55
New York	Cement, stone, salt, sand and gravel	320,453	375,866	0.99	1.02
North Carolina	Stone, sand and gravel, cement, feldspar	116,323	146,930	0.36	0.40
North Dakota	Petroleum, coal, sand and gravel, natural gas	98,086	111,853	0.30	0.30
Ohio	Coal, stone, cement, lime	724,748	806,979	2.25	2.19
Oklahoma	Petroleum, natural gas, natural gas liquids, stone	1,210,728	1,323,626	3.76	3.60
Oregon	Sand and gravel, stone, cement, nickel	76,516	81,466	0.24	0.22
Pennsylvania	Coal, cement, stone, sand and gravel	1,231,485	1,401,900	3.82	3.81
Rhode Island	Sand and gravel, stone, gem stones	4,291	4,340	0.01	0.01
South Carolina	Cement, stone, clays, sand and gravel	82,313	88,361	0.26	0.24
South Dakota	Gold, sand and gravel, cement, stone	65,200	81,139	0.20	0.22
Tennessee	Stone, coal, cement, zinc	269,814	275,690	0.84	0.75
Texas	Petroleum, natural gas, natural gas liquids, cement	7,211,551	8,442,494	22.38	22.95
Utah	Copper, petroleum, coal, gold	542,809	674,210	1.68	1.83
Vermont	Stone, asbestos, sand and gravel, talc	34,868	29,366	0.11	0.08
Virginia	Coal, stone, sand and gravel, cement	489,791	540,595	1.52	1.47
Washington	Sand and gravel, cement, coal, stone	109,806	114,329	0.34	0.31
West Virginia	Coal, natural gas, stone, cement	1,430,632	1,503,045	4.44	4.09
Wisconsin	Sand and gravel, stone, iron ore, cement	89,353	114,339	0.28	0.31
Wyoming	Petroleum, sodium compounds, uranium, natural gas	746,743	928,105	2.32	2.52
TOTAL U.S.		$32,217,000	$36,788,000	100.00	100.00

Source: U.S. Department of the Interior, Bureau of Mines, *Minerals Yearbook.*

Principal crops, 1975, production and value*

State	Corn, grain (bu)		Hay (tons)		Soybeans (bu)		Wheat (bu)		Tobacco (lb)		Cotton† lint (bales)		Sorghum (bu)		Potatoes (cwt)	
	Production	Value	Production	Value	Production	Value	Production	Value	Production	Value	Production	Value	Production	Value	Production	Value
Ala.	34,980	$96,195	1,134	$47,061	31,440	$146,196	3,240	$9,558	1,260	$1,153	315	$78,019	1,360	$3,509	2,728	$22,888
Alaska	...	...	...	...	...	...	...	...	...	...	...	...	...	...	...	...
Ariz.	396	1,267	1,593	91,598	...	...	22,720	71,568	...	...	560	138,432	11,220	33,323	1,519	9,114
Ark.	1,900	5,035	1,452	67,518	112,800	513,240	15,600	44,460	...	...	700	169,680	9,800	21,364	...	...
Calif.	27,686	87,211	7,642	458,520	...	...	62,227	202,740	...	...	1,940	480,499	14,904	41,731	20,740	127,344
Colo.	49,290	133,083	2,793	150,822	...	...	50,950	165,588	...	...	...	...	7,540	17,945	10,485	41,625
Conn.	...	...	195	14,625	...	...	...	...	6,430	28,616	...	...	...	...	552	3,312
Del.	17,290	44,954	47	2,350	5,100	24,225	1,156	3,295	...	...	...	...	...	...	941	5,458
Fla.	17,730	47,871	404	22,220	7,080	31,152	520	1,612	29,865	33,853	2.5	660	...	...	5,344	24,796
Ga.	103,400	274,010	1,175	49,938	31,500	143,325	3,645	10,571	150,978	153,193	140	34,675	1,692	4,078	...	...
Hawaii	...	...	...	...	...	...	...	...	...	...	...	...	...	...	...	...
Idaho	2,075	5,810	4,441	202,066	...	...	60,050	202,972	...	...	...	...	...	...	75,090	311,624
Ill.	1,242,360	3,105,900	3,555	161,753	291,810	1,371,507	67,470	209,157	...	...	0	0	4,080	8,568	380	1,558
Ind.	551,740	1,351,763	2,258	124,190	119,790	563,013	64,500	206,400	16,500	17,160	...	...	1,152	2,615	1,644	11,870
Iowa	1,091,700	2,620,080	6,897	348,299	236,980	1,090,108	2,550	8,798	...	...	...	...	1,612	3,563	620	3,038
Kan.	137,760	351,288	4,743	227,664	22,140	99,630	350,900	1,175,515	...	...	...	...	144,060	327,016	...	...
Ky.	87,780	223,839	2,890	112,710	31,800	149,460	11,968	35,306	465,706	492,386	0.4	97	1,365	2,976	...	...
La.	3,120	9,360	777	36,131	43,680	205,296	400	1,180	60	87	350	85,008	924	2,486	182	819
Maine	...	...	354	25,134	...	...	...	...	...	...	...	...	...	...	26,840	163,724
Md.	50,050	130,130	617	30,542	8,904	41,849	5,304	15,116	24,150	23,087	...	...	...	...	306	1,805
Mass.	...	...	245	19,600	...	...	...	...	2,048	10,786	...	...	...	...	718	4,308
Mich.	152,800	359,080	3,290	143,115	15,555	69,998	38,760	120,156	...	...	...	...	...	...	8,076	48,698
Minn.	407,400	998,130	8,005	412,258	92,820	436,254	87,839	340,833	...	...	...	...	...	...	11,796	51,077
Miss.	5,945	16,943	1,172	51,568	68,640	319,176	4,440	12,210	...	...	1,050	252,504	1,330	3,059	171	1,454
Mo.	170,100	433,755	5,683	261,418	113,985	524,331	48,510	145,530	6,210	6,086	195	46,800	26,460	59,270	...	...
Mont.	730	2,044	4,409	187,383	...	...	155,925	541,695	...	...	...	...	...	...	1,748	11,362
Neb.	503,200	1,258,000	6,643	305,578	33,210	151,106	98,240	324,192	...	...	...	...	103,400	237,820	1,527	6,749
Nev.	...	...	885	50,888	...	...	1,175	3,995	...	...	1.4	370	...	...	4,125	12,788
N.H.	...	...	177	13,983	...	...	...	...	...	...	...	...	...	...	92	552
N.J.	6,723	16,808	305	18,148	2,054	9,243	1,944	5,638	...	...	...	...	...	...	1,365	8,149
N.M.	7,000	17,150	963	52,484	...	...	10,062	35,217	...	...	70	17,002	15,500	38,130	700	1,995
N.Y.	39,610	99,025	5,114	265,928	240	1,020	7,410	21,489	...	...	...	...	...	...	11,818	71,972
N.C.	103,180	278,586	533	28,249	32,660	151,869	9,300	26,040	953,125	950,817	46	10,908	4,080	9,710	2,400	20,784
N.D.	6,732	16,830	5,025	183,413	2,906	13,077	264,392	1,118,446	...	...	...	...	...	...	17,600	75,680
Ohio	321,080	786,646	3,620	195,480	100,750	468,488	74,340	241,605	25,000	25,051	...	...	...	...	2,393	14,358
Okla.	6,800	18,360	3,730	169,715	5,451	23,439	160,800	530,640	...	...	185	43,867	25,080	59,690	...	...
Ore.	935	2,852	2,398	141,482	...	...	56,370	211,388	...	...	...	...	...	...	22,779	92,711
Pa.	88,560	221,400	4,399	233,147	1,204	5,358	11,385	33,017	21,875	12,688	...	...	...	...	6,815	41,572
R.I.	...	...	17	1,326	...	...	...	...	...	...	...	...	...	...	987	4,293
S.C.	34,650	91,823	495	25,245	30,360	138,138	4,185	11,509	189,000	188,055	95	22,572	595	1,434	...	...
S.D.	83,250	203,963	5,719	251,636	8,425	37,913	63,294	250,591	...	...	...	...	6,162	14,173	598	1,854
Tenn.	36,900	97,785	1,822	78,346	45,325	206,229	9,610	27,389	124,678	125,687	220	53,434	1,248	2,870	425	3,188
Texas	113,300	305,910	5,245	241,270	9,065	38,526	131,100	432,630	...	...	2,400	495,360	374,400	891,072	2,975	21,837
Utah	1,650	5,115	1,670	87,675	...	...	7,164	24,358	...	...	...	...	...	...	1,508	5,580
Vt.	...	...	782	60,996	...	...	...	...	...	...	...	...	...	...	212	1,272
Va.	48,590	128,764	1,771	84,123	10,825	48,713	9,052	26,251	143,030	142,065	0.5	132	490	931	2,400	14,880
Wash.	3,264	9,629	2,391	136,287	...	...	145,140	551,532	...	...	...	...	...	...	48,300	178,710
W.Va.	5,525	14,918	1,002	45,090	...	...	544	1,686	2,970	3,044	...	...	...	...	266	1,875
Wis.	198,370	505,844	10,602	498,294	4,871	21,920	2,820	9,136	21,190	15,921	...	...	...	...	14,850	87,615
Wyo.	1,440	4,536	1,838	95,576	...	...	6,802	24,203	...	...	...	...	...	...	1,632	5,549
TOTAL	5,766,991	$14,381,692	132,917	$6,512,842	1,521,370	$7,043,799	2,133,803	$7,435,212	2,184,075	$2,229,735	8,271	$1,930,019	758,454	$1,787,333	315,647	$1,519,837

*In thousands. †Excludes pima cotton (55,800 bales). Source: U.S. Department of Agriculture, Statistical Reporting Service, Crop Reporting Board, *Crop Production* and *Crop Values.*

Livestock and products, with fisheries, 1975

State	Cattle and calves (lb)		Hogs and pigs (lb)		Sheep and lambs (lb)		Milk (lb)		Eggs (no)*		Chicken (lb)*		Fisheries, 1974 (lb)	
	Amount produced in 000	Value in $000	Amount produced in 000	Value in $000	Amount produced in 000	Value in $000	Amount produced in 000,000	Farm value of milk produced in $000	Amount produced in 000,000	Gross income in $000	Amount sold +farm consumption in 000	Gross income in $000	Commercial landings in 000	Value in $000
Alabama	744,395	164,571	258,164	115,141	123	45	686	72,990	2,951	132,303	57,800	5,144	36,962‡	17,087‡
Alaska	811	283	141	59	†	†	17	2,817	5	417	136	26	456,864	141,120
Arizona	567,775	207,759	36,550	18,019	22,245	6,816	840	78,876	159	6,148	1,785	96	...	...
Arkansas	665,770	169,492	89,873	40,083	252	59	707	62,570	3,594	182,096	96,132	8,748	13,067§	2,872§
California	1,853,800	664,838	40,357	18,080	59,816	24,455	10,853	1,006,073	8,467	351,381	70,228	3,511	745,047	130,381
Colorado	1,838,830	732,548	102,612	48,022	73,876	31,976	870	80,040	473	19,668	5,799	522	...	...
Connecticut	21,235	4,785	2,062	928	339	175	613	61,300	798	46,883	13,501	1,350	6,530	1,897
Delaware	9,835	2,736	18,455	8,655	107	34	133	12,648	115	6,584	2,773	300	8,576	1,618
Florida	709,520	174,421	57,834	25,852	167	37	1,958	223,408	2,779	102,128	38,119	2,211	171,394	66,367
Georgia	505,570	117,241	407,586	178,930	104	29	1,194	117,370	5,284	261,998	82,250	9,130	18,157	7,094
Hawaii	50,610	17,579	11,183	6,520	...	...	146	20,878	209	11,234	1,391	160	10,463	5,458
Idaho	661,275	230,747	18,542	8,288	47,365	19,439	1,535	125,563	184	7,743	2,230	112	1,310	47
Illinois	979,925	374,822	2,297,222	1,052,128	12,444	4,321	2,560	212,480	1,483	63,399	19,663	1,317	5,317‡	955‡
Indiana	656,075	232,041	1,337,938	627,493	10,441	3,576	2,210	192,712	2,609	107,404	38,309	2,298	334‡	121‡
Iowa	2,652,480	973,223	3,931,873	1,816,525	24,691	10,359	3,916	309,364	2,006	66,031	34,245	1,610	5,774	856
Kansas	2,384,015	711,906	527,907	237,558	12,063	4,726	1,403	122,622	599	19,667	13,359	668	49	14
Kentucky	848,100	231,653	329,820	155,675	3,111	1,193	2,319	192,941	518	21,195	11,820	1,088	2,728§	659§
Louisiana	484,970	113,672	50,094	21,490	371	129	1,054	109,616	658	29,390	12,075	1,075	1,228,906‡	86,694‡
Maine	29,420	6,664	2,481	1,116	785	375	619	60,848	1,650	87,587	42,040	4,288	147,822	41,410
Maryland	118,065	33,406	54,315	25,474	1,147	396	1,555	147,570	331	18,950	6,685	728	63,004	20,439
Massachusetts	27,430	6,251	18,957	8,531	412	225	601	59,980	541	29,845	9,623	991	268,659	61,784
Michigan	455,860	152,396	214,704	103,058	9,225	3,940	4,434	379,550	1,303	49,188	24,746	3,588	15,454	3,926
Minnesota	1,469,865	455,978	1,079,944	502,174	21,524	9,056	8,946	687,053	2,209	73,081	31,551	946	10,399‡	1,065‡
Mississippi	715,400	162,340	101,891	46,666	240	58	876	83,570	1,707	85,066	43,192	5,485	304,794‡	16,355‡
Missouri	2,079,535	640,416	1,134,709	528,774	10,429	4,165	3,021	242,586	1,241	49,123	36,353	4,071	929	152
Montana	963,050	287,421	60,773	27,044	23,955	8,366	284	24,538	197	9,095	3,480	192	793	117
Nebraska	2,696,990	960,911	998,325	470,211	14,184	6,274	1,431	113,335	782	24,307	7,344	309	158	16
Nevada	190,220	57,993	2,922	1,394	10,666	4,322	167	14,846	4	164	49	3	...	...
New Hampshire	18,050	3,999	3,024	1,361	341	174	343	32,859	283	15,848	7,390	754	2,488	1,057
New Jersey	31,240	7,856	19,472	7,516	395	131	527	49,380	620	29,966	9,714	641	166,962	16,607
New Mexico	562,460	213,274	30,055	14,366	20,014	7,978	368	38,860	234	11,329	3,338	250	...	...
New York	379,780	86,867	31,185	14,033	3,247	1,141	9,904	870,562	1,984	84,485	37,795	1,777	35,189	25,379
North Carolina	257,020	61,248	572,743	265,753	530	163	1,602	167,249	2,802	145,470	85,000	17,766	206,683	17,544
North Dakota	904,680	272,304	96,896	42,344	16,290	6,168	924	65,604	132	3,938	3,056	306	212	23
Ohio	708,430	250,485	624,815	291,789	27,953	10,769	4,254	381,584	1,999	75,795	29,815	1,729	8,573	1,746
Oklahoma	2,085,120	621,314	99,249	46,151	4,360	1,694	1,060	96,778	430	19,243	7,440	684	740§	169§
Oregon	471,715	144,765	36,486	16,419	23,690	9,218	990	91,872	519	22,187	5,496	275	95,542	34,450
Pennsylvania	423,730	134,579	178,669	82,366	5,598	2,302	7,140	672,588	3,299	140,757	46,998	9,682	442	155
Rhode Island	2,353	532	2,423	1,090	72	22	63	6,073	70	3,898	1,255	125	96,066	15,695
South Carolina	263,340	58,444	170,944	76,925	37	12	510	54,927	1,385	59,671	19,228	2,576	18,402	6,861
South Dakota	1,248,710	428,217	531,467	247,132	55,857	22,347	1,370	103,846	702	20,124	12,395	619	3,151	276
Tennessee	968,035	230,395	280,495	128,747	784	293	1,875	165,188	949	43,654	9,825	1,356	6,054§	1,187§
Texas	5,076,150	1,527,162	275,827	120,536	148,645	50,972	3,221	307,283	2,360	117,214	45,700	3,930	97,203‡	72,455‡
Utah	267,720	72,597	14,655	6,346	33,201	14,161	919	79,861	321	11,422	3,194	128	...	...
Vermont	71,030	15,513	2,205	992	383	180	2,009	184,426	105	6,536	1,624	165	...	...
Virginia	455,630	118,614	176,982	80,527	11,386	4,577	1,752	166,615	765	40,354	20,018	2,362	507,293	33,836
Washington	416,780	131,585	23,152	10,557	3,772	1,767	2,322	212,695	1,068	41,207	16,170	841	115,973	59,031
West Virginia	140,150	32,407	20,634	9,368	8,148	3,021	347	32,375	256	12,096	4,318	565	2	1
Wisconsin	1,032,050	266,954	436,139	200,624	5,914	2,221	18,900	1,540,350	1,194	44,775	17,504	2,188	55,135‡	3,524‡
Wyoming	515,070	160,917	9,002	3,907	41,053	15,430	110	9,636	30	1,368	332	19	—	—
TOTAL U.S.	40,680,069	12,728,121	16,823,753	7,762,737	771,752	299,287	115,458	10,148,755	64,362	2,813,412	1,094,253	108,705	4,939,600	898,500

*Dec. 1, 1974–Nov. 30, 1975. †Decrease in inventory and death loss of sheep resulted in deficit in number of pounds produced. ‡Catch in interior waters estimated. §Estimate.
Sources: U.S. Department of Agriculture, Statistical Reporting Service, Crop Reporting Board, *Chickens, Eggs, & Broilers, Meat Animals, Milk;* U.S. Department of Commerce, National Oceanic and Atmospheric Administration, National Marine Fisheries Service, *Fisheries of the United States.*

Value of construction contracts

in millions of dollars

State	1972	1973	1974 Total	1974 Non-residential	1974 Residential	1974 Non-building
Alabama	1,351	1,639	1,262	476	565	221
Alaska	373	421	773	222	126	425
Arizona	1,671	1,697	1,362	460	617	285
Arkansas	829	1,016	840	270	358	212
California	8,943	9,378	8,455	3,206	3,474	1,775
Colorado	1,708	1,989	1,515	703	496	316
Connecticut	1,217	1,022	1,175	438	436	301
Delaware	280	241	220	79	100	41
Dist. of Columbia	640	550	620	253	89	278
Florida	6,482	7,710	5,585	1,599	3,090	896
Georgia	2,533	2,694	2,133	784	959	390
Hawaii	655	820	999	247	583	169
Idaho	299	355	371	135	113	123
Illinois	4,772	4,938	4,544	1,920	1,493	1,131
Indiana	2,154	2,456	2,253	802	1,066	385
Iowa	829	1,099	1,068	323	381	364
Kansas	779	812	865	326	319	220
Kentucky	1,508	1,481	1,522	470	570	482
Louisiana	2,026	1,926	2,040	616	676	748
Maine	306	355	357	146	146	65
Maryland	1,752	2,078	2,058	705	599	754
Massachusetts	2,178	2,170	1,913	679	710	524
Michigan	3,388	4,275	3,461	1,355	1,314	792
Minnesota	1,339	1,745	2,058	684	633	741
Mississippi	885	1,002	2,066	252	319	1,495
Missouri	1,437	2,006	1,782	605	560	617
Montana	273	516	322	86	124	112
Nebraska	611	683	711	301	184	226
Nevada	627	624	442	144	184	114
New Hampshire	301	324	293	112	120	61
New Jersey	2,949	2,513	2,361	1,063	720	578
New Mexico	478	677	615	210	270	135
New York	6,016	5,755	4,805	2,032	1,527	1,246
North Carolina	2,646	2,463	2,220	803	1,047	370
North Dakota	331	297	283	78	108	97
Ohio	3,898	4,167	4,418	1,870	1,583	965
Oklahoma	1,328	1,377	1,409	488	498	423
Oregon	968	977	1,015	391	370	254
Pennsylvania	3,360	4,274	3,960	1,332	982	1,646
Rhode Island	207	257	235	108	84	43
South Carolina	1,307	1,776	1,418	461	600	357
South Dakota	210	244	239	67	92	80
Tennessee	1,843	2,232	2,089	769	753	567
Texas	5,819	6,217	6,596	3,164	2,205	1,227
Utah	509	596	810	234	296	280
Vermont	170	164	170	54	79	37
Virginia	2,735	3,023	2,672	733	1,068	871
Washington	1,557	1,633	2,188	626	680	882
West Virginia	586	609	565	325	81	159
Wisconsin	1,552	1,760	1,584	578	676	330
Wyoming	361	271	359	76	48	235
TOTAL U.S.	90,977	99,304	93,076	33,860	34,171	25,045

Source: U.S. Department of Commerce, Bureau of the Census, *Statistical Abstract of the United States 1975;* data compiled by F. W. Dodge Division, McGraw-Hill Information Systems Company.

Principal manufactures, 1974

monetary figures in millions of dollars

Industry	Employees (000)	Cost of labour*	Cost of materials	Value of shipments	Value added by manufacture
Food and kindred products	1,553	$14,788	$118,331	$162,104	$44,948
Meat products	312	2,943	33,688	40,035	5,987
Dairy products	181	1,709	16,211	20,880	4,824
Preserved fruits and vegetables	231	1,814	10,134	15,486	5,417
Grain mill products	114	1,216	15,362	20,225	4,942
Beverages	205	2,254	10,497	17,776	7,584
Tobacco products	67	604	3,966	7,140	3,179
Textile mill products	933	6,684	20,052	32,892	13,199
Apparel and other textile products	1,317	7,642	15,774	30,551	14,926
Lumber and wood products	675	5,490	15,600	26,853	11,561
Furniture and fixtures	459	3,570	6,360	13,197	6,983
Paper and allied products	646	6,995	23,162	41,665	18,957
Printing and publishing	1,076	11,139	12,527	35,822	23,610
Chemicals and allied products	866	10,547	41,467	83,801	44,488
Industrial chemicals	242	3,257	14,818	28,205	14,121
Plastics materials and synthetics	171	2,044	8,587	15,108	7,086
Drugs	146	1,843	2,879	9,897	7,269
Soap, cleaners, and toilet goods	111	1,221	5,281	12,147	7,073
Paints, allied products	65	742	2,890	5,007	2,228
Agricultural chemicals	50	550	3,787	7,422	3,813
Petroleum and coal products	146	1,920	50,140	58,876	9,951
Rubber, misc. plastics products	661	6,203	13,628	27,902	14,826
Leather and leather products	256	1,604	3,099	6,176	3,120
Stone, clay, and glass products	637	6,414	12,041	26,260	14,566
Primary metal industries	1,248	15,900	58,720	95,618	37,297
Blast furnace, basic steel products	611	8,641	29,199	49,649	20,061
Iron, steel foundries	239	2,750	3,913	8,535	4,724
Primary nonferrous metals	63	815	6,728	9,383	2,965
Nonferrous drawing and rolling	200	2,311	13,846	19,758	6,292
Nonferrous foundries	90	875	1,618	3,176	1,598
Fabricated metal products	1,575	16,570	33,858	67,570	35,221
Ordnance and accessories	97	1,033	1,280	2,891	1,695
Machinery, except electrical	2,126	$24,713	$43,549	$92,487	$52,495
Engines, turbines	131	1,710	4,065	7,439	3,666
Farm machinery	158	1,790	4,845	8,641	4,214
Construction and related mach.	327	3,973	8,725	16,696	8,887
Metalworking machinery	320	3,910	3,965	11,010	7,396
Special industry machinery	219	2,486	3,835	8,562	5,072
General industrial machinery	301	3,435	5,300	11,857	7,147
Service industry machines	202	2,092	5,256	9,806	4,715
Office, computing machines	247	3,002	5,414	12,179	7,141
Electric and electronic equipment	1,776	18,093	30,106	65,804	36,902
Electric distributing equip.	123	1,244	2,112	4,643	2,636
Electrical industrial apparatus	217	2,185	3,529	7,861	4,532
Household appliances	168	1,578	4,255	7,957	3,754
Electric lighting, wiring equip.	180	1,627	3,003	6,834	3,947
Radio, TV receiving equipment	107	886	3,372	5,452	2,171
Communication equipment	463	5,492	6,668	16,455	9,979
Electronic components, access.	382	3,686	4,635	11,301	6,963
Transportation equipment	1,738	22,609	64,875	108,245	44,973
Motor vehicles and equipment	798	10,468	46,797	68,633	22,301
Aircraft, parts	462	6,289	8,828	20,439	12,460
Ship, boat building, repair	200	2,044	2,824	5,925	3,061
Railroad equipment	60	735	2,165	3,539	1,603
Guided missiles, space vehicles	154	2,500	2,470	6,763	4,315
Instruments and related products	524	5,560	7,698	20,865	13,627
Measuring, controlling devices	180	1,873	1,957	5,457	3,646
Medical instruments and supplies	105	978	1,528	3,711	2,270
Photographic equipment and supplies	109	1,429	2,566	7,493	5,075
Miscellaneous manufacturing industries	435	3,477	6,625	14,044	7,666
All establishments, including administrative and auxiliary	19,844	208,312	581,580	1,017,873	452,497

*Payroll only. Source: U.S. Department of Commerce, *Annual Survey of Manufactures 1974.*

Services

Kind of service	Number of services 1972	Number of services 1973	Number of employees* 1972	Number of employees* 1973
Hotels and other lodging places	51,302	52,327	828,532	898,638
Hotels, tourist courts, and motels	34,156	34,225	675,358	732,591
Rooming and boarding houses	6,905	6,963	106,984	113,241
Personal services	166,095	163,479	917,065	909,415
Laundries and dry-cleaning plants	42,224	39,758	416,706	388,180
Photographic studios	6,608	6,598	36,626	39,136
Beauty shops	70,309	70,475	278,061	281,634
Barber shops	18,203	15,476	38,283	33,500
Funeral service and crematories	12,922	13,009	67,876	69,558
Miscellaneous business services	97,255	105,426	1,670,653	1,856,903
Advertising	8,120	8,308	107,083	109,958
Credit reporting and collection	5,509	5,375	66,338	66,094
Duplicating, mailing, stenographic	5,284	5,482	60,206	62,990
Building services	16,735	17,716	317,650	351,520
Private employment agencies	5,300	5,613	51,380	63,970
Research and development laboratories	1,966	1,982	74,133	77,650
Business consulting services	21,179	22,781	301,982	326,111
Detective and protective services	3,822	4,182	182,665	202,561
Equipment rental and leasing	7,801	8,140	73,452	81,281
Photofinishing laboratories	1,609	1,663	40,878	45,799
Temporary help supply services	2,149	2,304	167,455	203,706
Auto repair, services, and garages	73,275	76,841	405,871	435,549
Automobile rentals, without drivers	5,405	5,611	66,538	73,600
Automobile parking	3,428	3,293	37,136	35,976
Automobile repair shops	56,852	58,638	235,901	251,247
Automobile laundries	5,038	5,060	50,693	52,561
Miscellaneous repair services	38,586	40,798	212,509	222,642
Radio and television repair	8,281	8,315	38,248	38,361
Motion pictures	11,076	11,506	186,501	190,137
Motion picture filming and distribution	2,973	3,195	53,726	58,045
Motion picture theatres	7,627	7,495	120,658	118,948
Other amusement and recreation services	37,143	38,492	467,716	494,019
Producers, orchestras, entertainers	5,695	5,646	57,041	58,927
Bowling and billiard establishments	8,424	8,163	95,461	97,512
Golf clubs and country clubs	4,763	4,890	93,586	98,909
Race tracks and stables	1,420	1,489	37,018	40,338
Medical and other health services	223,732	231,495	3,240,295	3,425,013
Physicians' and surgeons' offices	108,484	110,872	438,478	470,349
Dentists' and dental surgeons' offices	66,406	67,973	190,945	208,818
Hospitals	5,135	5,098	1,868,469	1,922,794
Medical and dental laboratories	7,389	7,654	60,330	65,298
Sanatoria, convalescent and rest homes	11,097	11,081	517,271	563,645
Legal services	70,456	73,885	269,904	298,218
Educational services	37,074	39,577	959,860	1,012,312
Elementary and secondary schools	26,496	28,244	364,964	401,225
Colleges and universities	1,930	1,947	462,286	470,934
Correspondence and vocational schools	3,474	3,589	53,006	53,305
Museums, botanical, zoological gardens	869	912	20,447	21,266
Nonprofit membership organizations	128,515	132,719	1,248,140	1,312,704
Business associations	11,999	12,101	75,129	76,356
Labour organizations	20,829	20,690	147,234	148,679
Civic and social associations	28,872	29,230	260,255	267,806
Religious organizations	46,096	47,169	326,427	358,423
Charitable organizations	6,768	6,887	160,074	170,057
Miscellaneous services	63,066	68,918	620,896	698,946
Engineering and architectural services	23,343	25,019	268,478	303,647
Nonprofit research agencies	3,640	3,709	110,818	116,712
Accounting, auditing, bookkeeping	30,958	31,799	213,826	234,298
TOTAL†	1,000,729	1,038,505	11,102,077	11,830,536

*Mid-March pay period. †Includes administrative and auxiliary businesses not shown separately.
Source: U.S. Department of Commerce, Bureau of the Census, *County Business Patterns 1972* and *1973.*

Business activity

Category of activity	Wholesaling 1960	Wholesaling 1965	Wholesaling 1970	Wholesaling 1973	Retailing 1960	Retailing 1965	Retailing 1970	Retailing 1973	Services 1960	Services 1965	Services 1970	Services 1973
Number of businesses (in 000)												
Sole proprietorships	306	265	274	316	1,548	1,554	1,689	1,782	1,966	2,208	2,507	2,820
Active partnerships	41	32	30	30	238	202	170	168	159	169	176	178
Active corporations	117	147	166	201	217	288	351	378	121	188	281	365
Business receipts (in $000,000)												
Sole proprietorships	17,061	17,934	21,556	30,816	65,439	77,760	89,315	100,739	23,256	29,789	40,869	48,806
Active partnerships	12,712	10,879	11,325	13,688	24,787	23,244	23,546	26,540	9,281	12,442	18,791	23,564
Active corporations	130,637	171,414	234,885	379,758	125,787	183,925	274,808	376,347	22,106	36,547	66,460	95,988
Net profit (less loss; in $000,000)												
Sole proprietorships	1,305	1,483	1,806	2,537	3,869	5,019	5,767	6,768	8,060	11,008	15,063	16,968
Active partnerships	587	548	557	725	1,612	1,654	1,603	1,820	3,056	4,402	6,189	6,876
Active corporations	2,130	3,288	4,441	11,787	2,225	4,052	5,217	7,461	849	1,505	1,199	2,749

Data refer to accounting periods ending between July 1 of year shown and June 30 of following year.
Source: U.S. Department of the Treasury, Internal Revenue Service, *Statistics of Income: Business Income Tax Returns* and *Corporation Income Tax Returns.*

Retail sales

in millions of dollars

Kind of business	1960	1965	1970	1975
Durable goods stores*	70,560	94,186	114,288	180,725
Automotive group	39,579	56,884	64,966	102,105
Passenger car, other automotive dealers	37,038	53,484	59,388	93,046
Tire, battery, accessory dealers	2,541	3,400	5,578	9,059
Furniture and appliance group	10,591	13,352	17,778	26,123
Furniture, home furnishings stores	...	...	10,483	15,283
Household appliance, TV, radio stores	...	...	6,073	8,420
Building materials, hardware, farm equipment group	11,222	12,388	20,494	34,204
Lumberyards, building materials dealers	8,567	9,731	11,995	18,202
Hardware stores	2,655	2,657	3,351	5,772
Nondurable goods stores*	148,969	189,942	261,239	403,698
Apparel group	13,631	15,765	19,810	26,749
Men's, boys' wear stores	2,644	...	4,630	6,085
Women's apparel, accessory stores	5,295	...	7,582	10,396
Family clothing stores	...	...	3,360	4,726
Shoe stores	2,437	...	3,501	4,123
Drug and proprietary stores	7,538	9,186	13,352	18,098
Eating and drinking places	16,146	20,201	29,689	47,514
Food group	54,023	64,016	86,114	131,723
Grocery stores	48,610	...	79,756	122,666
Meat and fish markets	...	...	2,244	3,087
Bakeries	...	...	1,303	1,455
Gasoline service stations	17,588	20,611	27,994	43,895
General merchandise group	...	42,299	61,320	95,402
Department stores and dry goods general merchandise stores	...	...	45,000	73,429
Variety stores	...	...	6,959	9,120
Mail-order houses (department store merchandise)	...	...	3,853	5,995
Liquor stores	4,893	5,674	7,980	10,974
TOTAL	219,529	284,128	375,527	584,423

*Includes some kinds of business not shown separately.
Source: U.S. Department of Commerce, Bureau of the Census, *Monthly Retail Trade*, Bureau of Economic Analysis, *1975 Business Statistics*.

Unemployment trends

quarterly averages, seasonally adjusted

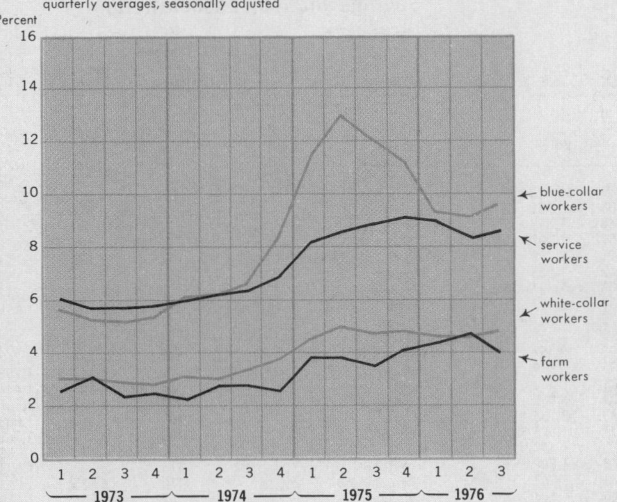

Source: U.S. Department of Labor, Bureau of Labor Statistics, *Monthly Labor Review*.

Sales of merchant wholesalers

in millions of dollars

Kind of business	1960	1965	1970	1975
Durable goods*	56,803	82,861	111,970	185,806
Motor vehicles, automotive equipment	7,883	12,140	19,482	33,526
Electrical goods	8,660	12,681	16,667	24,240
Furniture, home furnishings	2,910	3,777	5,199	6,682
Hardware, plumbing, heating equipment	6,422	8,413	10,858	17,177
Lumber, construction supplies	6,680	9,765	10,863	15,949
Machinery, equipment, supplies	14,287	20,561	27,638	51,802
Metals, metalwork (except scrap)	5,708	9,162	13,647	25,066
Scrap, waste materials	3,296	4,789	6,040	8,537
Nondurable goods*	80,477	104,470	135,029	253,061
Groceries and related products	27,661	38,068	53,411	89,682
Beer, wine, distilled alcoholic beverages	7,424	9,464	13,332	20,112
Drugs, chemicals, allied products	5,370	7,180	9,135	15,114
Tobacco, tobacco products	4,164	5,014	6,232	8,471
Dry goods, apparel	6,675	8,804	10,577	15,467
Paper, paper products	4,153	5,612	7,679	11,556
Farm products	11,683	13,711	13,987	44,416
Other nondurable goods	13,346	16,966	22,632	49,100
TOTAL	137,281	187,331	246,999	438,867

*Includes some kinds of business not shown separately.
Source: U.S. Dept. of Commerce, Bureau of the Census, *Monthly Wholesale Trade*.

Average employee earnings

September figures	AVERAGE HOURLY EARNINGS		AVERAGE WEEKLY EARNINGS	
Industry	1975	1976*	1975	1976*
MANUFACTURING				
Durable goods	$5.24	$5.66	$212.22	$229.80
Ordnance and accessories	5.39	5.86	224.76	237.33
Lumber and wood products	4.43	4.87	177.20	195.77
Furniture and fixtures	3.79	4.05	149.33	156.33
Stone, clay, and glass products	5.01	5.42	206.41	224.39
Primary metal industries	6.39	6.95	257.52	284.26
Fabricated metal products	5.17	5.54	209.39	226.59
Nonelectrical machinery	5.47	5.86	223.72	240.26
Electrical equipment and supplies	4.66	5.02	185.93	201.30
Transportation equipment	6.14	6.67	253.58	276.81
Instruments and related products	4.60	4.93	184.00	198.19
Nondurable goods	4.41	4.80	175.52	189.12
Food and kindred products	4.62	5.01	192.19	204.91
Tobacco manufactures	4.29	4.65	166.45	175.77
Textile mill products	3.48	3.78	143.03	148.93
Apparel and related products	3.22	3.49	116.56	122.85
Paper and allied products	5.11	5.57	217.18	236.73
Printing and publishing	5.49	5.79	204.78	218.86
Chemicals and allied products	5.48	6.03	226.32	253.26
Petroleum and coal products	6.61	7.23	278.94	309.44
Rubber and plastics products	4.41	4.84	178.61	196.99
Leather and leather products	3.26	3.48	124.53	127.02
NONMANUFACTURING				
Metal mining	6.36	6.98	258.85	296.65
Coal mining	7.30	8.00	290.54	324.00
Oil and gas extraction	5.45	5.86	240.35	266.63
Contract construction	7.42	7.81	278.99	287.41
Local and suburban transportation	4.97	5.52	198.80	220.25
Electric, gas, and sanitary services	6.12	6.66	252.14	276.39
Wholesale trade	4.94	5.24	190.68	203.84
Retail trade	3.39	3.59	109.50	115.24
Hotels, tourist courts, and motels†	2.83	3.06	88.86	96.08

*Preliminary. †Excludes tips. Source: U.S. Dept. of Labor, Bureau of Labor Statistics, *Employment and Earnings*.

Income levels of families and unrelated individuals

	Families, all races			Families, white			Families, black			Unrelated individuals		
Year and income level	Total*	Husband-wife	Female head	Total*	Husband-wife	Female head	Total*	Husband-wife	Female head	All races*	White	Black
March 1974												
Number of income earners (000)	55,712	46,971	7,242	49,451	42,969	5,212	5,498	3,346	1,940	18,872	16,252	2,347
Percent under $3,000	5.3	3.3	19.1	4.3	2.9	15.4	14.4	6.4	28.8	34.9	32.9	49.2
$3,000 to $4,999	7.8	5.9	19.8	6.8	5.5	16.7	17.1	10.9	27.7	19.6	20.3	15.8
$5,000 to $6,999	8.9	7.8	15.8	8.4	7.5	15.4	13.5	11.5	16.9	13.7	13.7	12.3
$7,000 to $9,999	13.8	13.3	16.9	13.5	12.9	18.5	16.5	18.3	12.5	13.9	14.3	12.1
$10,000 to $11,999	10.2	10.5	8.3	10.5	10.5	9.7	8.4	10.4	4.8	6.3	6.6	4.5
$12,000 to $14,999	14.1	15.2	7.8	14.6	15.2	9.3	10.7	14.9	3.7	5.5	5.9	2.9
$15,000 to $24,999	28.3	31.2	10.2	29.7	31.9	12.1	16.2	22.5	5.0	4.9	5.2	3.1
$25,000 and over	11.5	13.0	2.1	12.4	13.5	2.8	3.2	4.9	0.4	1.1	1.3	0.1
Median income, dollars	$12,836	$13,847	$6,413	$13,356	$14,099	$7,363	$7,808	$10,530	$4,465	$4,439	$4,636	$3,059
March 1970												
Number of income earners (000)	52,227	44,964	6,001	46,535	41,092	4,386	4,928	3,235	1,506	15,357	13,413	1,746
Percent under $3,000	8.9	6.4	27.4	7.5	5.8	22.7	21.1	11.8	41.3	48.6	46.9	60.3
$3,000 to $4,999	10.4	8.7	21.8	9.5	8.4	20.4	17.4	13.5	25.9	17.7	17.7	17.6
$5,000 to $6,999	11.8	11.0	17.4	11.3	10.5	18.1	17.0	17.8	15.5	12.2	12.4	10.8
$7,000 to $9,999	19.9	20.5	16.2	20.1	20.3	18.3	18.1	21.7	9.7	12.3	12.7	9.0
$10,000 to $11,999	12.7	13.5	6.5	13.1	13.7	7.6	8.8	11.0	3.8	3.7	4.0	1.3
$12,000 to $14,999	14.1	15.4	5.4	14.8	15.7	6.6	8.1	11.0	2.1	2.6	2.9	0.4
$15,000 to $24,999	17.7	19.5	4.7	18.7	20.1	5.7	8.5	12.0	1.3	2.3	2.6	0.4
$25,000 and over	4.6	5.1	0.7	5.0	5.4	0.7	1.0	1.1	0.4	0.5	0.7	0.2
Median income, dollars (current)	$9,867	$10,516	$5,093	$10,236	$10,723	$5,754	$6,279	$7,816	$3,576	$3,137	$3,283	$2,117

*Includes other male headed families. Percentages may not add to 100.0 because of rounding. Source: U.S. Department of Commerce, Bureau of the Census, *Current Population Reports*.

Commercial banks*

December 31, 1975

State	Number of banks	Total assets or liabilities $000,000	SELECTED ASSETS ($000,000) Loans†	Investments	Reserves, cash, and bank balances	SELECTED LIABILITIES ($000,000) Deposits Total	Demand	Time	Capital accounts
Ala.	299	10,859	9,166	3,126	1,294	9,164	3,796	5,368	837
Alaska	11	1,437	1,106	354	262	1,250	648	602	94
Ariz.	15	7,597	6,329	1,593	848	6,226	2,258	3,968	450
Ark.	258	6,944	5,772	1,994	943	6,018	2,570	3,448	521
Calif.	200	104,277	79,348	20,072	15,612	85,317	30,682	54,635	5,744
Colo.	277	8,765	7,148	1,921	1,248	7,393	3,425	3,967	659
Conn.	71	8,705	6,776	1,786	1,480	7,393	3,735	3,658	637
Del.	17	2,453	2,150	906	192	1,956	777	1,178	169
D.C.	16	4,427	3,512	1,018	748	3,673	2,110	1,563	376
Fla.	743	28,773	23,718	9,271	3,815	24,885	10,496	14,390	2,318
Ga.	440	15,783	12,410	2,681	2,257	12,357	6,014	6,343	1,284
Hawaii	8	2,954	2,450	695	333	2,599	1,017	1,582	209
Idaho	24	3,028	2,532	684	398	2,626	1,009	1,616	191
Ill.	1,206	74,493	63,863	20,281	7,272	59,446	21,134	38,312	5,088
Ind.	405	21,311	18,151	6,393	2,129	17,910	6,445	11,465	1,477
Iowa	654	13,370	11,565	4,121	1,495	11,799	4,212	7,588	977
Kan.	615	10,200	8,693	3,188	1,186	8,791	3,729	5,062	835
Ky.	341	11,464	9,630	3,149	1,415	9,798	4,494	5,305	833
La.	254	14,225	11,881	3,980	1,828	11,939	5,058	6,880	1,005
Maine	45	2,283	1,971	546	227	1,979	772	1,207	174
Md.	115	10,323	8,636	2,443	1,223	8,735	3,641	5,094	775
Mass.	145	18,524	14,305	3,858	2,712	14,935	7,388	7,547	1,399
Mich.	350	34,585	29,179	8,945	4,051	29,448	9,072	20,376	2,531
Minn.	745	17,777	15,196	4,681	2,032	14,738	5,276	9,462	1,315
Miss.	185	6,501	5,441	1,807	829	5,654	2,459	3,195	500
Mo.	700	21,191	17,644	6,105	2,963	17,260	7,887	9,372	1,608
Mont.	154	3,347	2,875	928	379	2,910	1,038	1,873	230
Neb.	448	7,257	6,074	1,945	940	6,251	2,799	3,452	548
Nev.	8	2,136	1,756	561	284	1,885	760	1,124	160
N.H.	77	1,902	1,632	406	207	1,639	540	1,099	158
N.J.	209	25,333	21,364	7,531	2,902	21,784	8,189	13,595	1,893
N.M.	80	3,408	2,765	836	505	2,987	1,215	1,772	245
N.Y.	267	164,253	120,792	24,942	28,945	126,412	64,834	61,577	12,823
N.C.	93	15,282	12,461	4,001	1,970	12,699	5,521	7,178	1,166
N.D.	169	2,950	2,611	971	271	2,612	996	1,615	216
Ohio	495	37,775	31,496	10,861	4,484	31,135	11,537	19,597	3,037
Okla.	462	11,801	9,635	3,370	1,759	10,202	4,421	5,781	932
Ore.	45	7,748	6,163	1,676	1,190	6,015	2,367	3,648	541
Pa.	392	55,542	46,369	12,557	6,312	44,486	15,451	29,035	4,235
R.I.	14	3,852	3,267	647	376	3,223	957	2,266	270
S.C.	90	4,873	3,971	1,310	707	4,124	2,323	1,801	399
S.D.	158	3,271	2,870	1,043	318	2,914	954	1,960	236
Tenn.	342	15,434	12,633	3,663	1,952	13,098	4,974	8,124	1,116
Texas	1,336	56,879	45,317	14,476	9,036	47,282	22,635	24,647	4,058
Utah	63	3,918	3,179	896	601	3,373	1,355	2,018	260
Vt.	31	1,521	1,339	329	141	1,353	372	981	110
Va.	290	16,083	13,626	3,804	1,751	13,721	5,015	8,706	1,199
Wash.	91	11,884	9,318	1,934	1,715	9,674	3,929	5,745	700
W.Va.	219	6,552	5,696	2,247	645	5,506	1,875	3,631	531
Wis.	623	17,532	15,030	4,796	1,848	15,008	4,961	10,046	1,263
Wyo.	77	1,870	1,588	570	225	1,634	629	1,004	139
TOTAL	14,372	944,654	762,400	221,898	128,256	775,209	319,751	455,458	68,474

*Detail may not add to total given due to rounding; excludes noninsured banks.
†Includes investment securities, trading account securities, federal funds sold, and securities purchased under agreements to resell.
Source: Federal Deposit Insurance Corporation, *Assets and Liabilities—Commercial and Mutual Savings Banks—December 31, 1975, 1975 Report of Income.*

Life insurance, 1975

Number of policies in 000s; value in $000,000

State	Total: Number of policies	Value	Ordinary: Number of policies	Value	Group: Number of certificates	Value	Industrial: Number of policies	Value	Credit*: Number of policies	Value
Ala.	11,789	$34,212	1,661	$15,965	1,515	$13,188	6,892	$2,546	1,721	$2,513
Alaska	466	3,305	105	1,571	241	1,550	12	3	108	181
Ariz.	4,303	22,621	1,512	13,338	1,235	7,276	193	114	1,363	1,893
Ark.	2,462	13,624	801	7,137	574	5,097	528	283	559	1,107
Calif.	29,440	205,406	9,996	103,120	10,581	92,128	2,237	1,448	6,626	8,710
Colo.	4,088	27,612	1,603	15,341	1,236	10,607	237	138	1,012	1,526
Conn.	5,476	39,463	2,333	18,835	1,752	19,065	353	236	1,038	1,327
Del.	1,419	8,446	467	3,509	366	4,306	248	154	338	477
D.C.	2,595	13,344	438	3,531	1,085	8,868	557	301	515	644
Fla.	14,702	73,166	4,653	41,432	2,877	24,755	3,937	2,522	3,235	4,457
Ga.	12,153	51,079	2,793	25,516	2,072	19,261	4,583	2,845	2,705	3,457
Hawaii	1,420	11,743	532	6,509	575	4,712	7	3	306	519
Idaho	1,225	7,021	508	3,965	403	2,532	29	14	285	510
Ill.	22,315	131,468	8,861	66,981	6,082	57,207	3,438	2,018	3,934	5,262
Ind.	10,145	53,868	3,815	27,781	2,364	21,878	1,793	1,053	2,173	3,156
Iowa	4,625	29,023	2,388	16,875	1,174	10,438	272	135	791	1,575
Kan.	4,109	23,244	1,830	14,296	1,033	7,313	375	198	871	1,437
Ky.	6,101	26,522	1,928	13,368	1,071	10,374	1,724	891	1,378	1,889
La.	8,955	34,030	1,750	16,977	1,478	12,598	4,049	2,192	1,678	2,263
Maine	1,760	8,683	679	4,686	527	3,325	98	58	456	614
Md.	7,930	42,562	2,644	21,893	1,646	17,458	1,932	1,053	1,708	2,158
Mass.	9,260	57,559	3,945	29,015	2,371	25,765	952	559	1,992	2,220
Mich.	16,269	102,036	5,345	40,093	5,210	55,184	2,151	1,265	3,563	5,494
Minn.	5,773	39,290	2,346	19,589	2,001	17,755	287	149	1,139	1,797
Miss.	3,399	15,496	792	7,876	730	5,709	769	458	1,108	1,453
Mo.	8,625	48,440	3,425	24,228	2,219	21,144	1,399	787	1,582	2,281
Mont.	1,006	6,066	400	3,583	311	2,009	27	11	268	463
Neb.	2,707	16,511	1,318	10,155	643	5,327	142	73	604	956
Nev.	1,040	6,706	225	2,540	360	3,282	17	8	438	876
N.H.	1,286	7,467	598	4,444	292	2,543	102	62	294	418
N.J.	11,916	86,942	5,475	44,766	2,919	38,521	1,522	1,091	2,000	2,564
N.M.	1,618	9,253	514	4,541	490	3,958	118	72	496	682
N.Y.	27,526	191,024	11,480	92,458	7,625	88,862	2,251	1,428	6,170	8,276
N.C.	11,595	47,500	3,264	24,343	2,157	17,953	3,765	2,104	2,409	3,100
N.D.	924	5,705	409	3,351	267	1,866	5	3	243	485
Ohio	20,090	114,578	7,800	59,269	4,748	47,141	3,644	2,228	3,898	5,940
Okla.	4,067	24,442	1,527	12,915	1,013	9,552	452	265	1,075	1,710
Ore.	3,103	19,922	1,108	10,053	1,137	8,806	103	48	755	1,015
Pa.	24,032	120,287	9,667	62,626	5,008	48,657	5,133	2,882	4,224	6,122
R.I.	1,856	9,443	775	5,267	539	3,633	213	122	329	421
S.C.	7,193	24,330	2,053	12,219	1,239	8,956	2,631	1,517	1,270	1,638
S.D.	904	5,745	488	3,748	208	1,585	5	3	203	409
Tenn.	8,918	39,334	2,218	18,679	1,985	16,172	2,803	1,628	1,912	2,855
Texas	21,488	120,018	7,203	63,753	5,566	46,913	3,395	2,048	5,324	7,304
Utah	1,903	10,416	648	5,599	710	3,997	108	46	437	774
Vt.	762	4,222	353	2,454	180	1,497	60	35	169	236
Va.	10,070	52,812	3,024	24,681	2,163	24,074	2,819	1,571	2,064	2,486
Wash.	4,714	32,769	1,788	16,466	1,787	14,939	198	89	941	1,275
W.Va.	3,053	13,830	902	6,168	657	6,110	632	377	862	1,175
Wis.	6,919	43,651	3,290	24,052	2,119	17,601	511	285	999	1,713
Wyo.	516	3,335	217	1,864	152	1,248	7	4	140	219
TOTAL U.S.	380,010	$2,139,571	133,894	$1,083,421	96,693	$904,695	69,715	$39,423	79,708	$112,032

*Life insurance on loans of ten years' or less duration.
Source: Institute of Life Insurance, *Life Insurance Fact Book 1976.*

Savings and loan associations

Dec. 31, 1975*

State	Number of assns.	Total assets ($000,000)	Per capita assets
Alabama	61	$2,733	$756
Alaska	4	213	606
Arizona	16	3,561	1,601
Arkansas	69	2,298	1,086
California	169	58,008	2,738
Colorado	47	4,850	1,914
Connecticut	36	2,901	937
Delaware	22	196	338
District of Columbia	16	3,598	5,026
Florida	124	24,654	2,950
Georgia	100	6,492	1,318
Guam	2	22	198
Hawaii	11	1,787	2,066
Idaho	11	600	732
Illinois	441	25,244	2,265
Indiana	170	6,418	1,208
Iowa	84	4,151	1,446
Kansas	87	4,233	1,867
Kentucky	109	3,423	1,008
Louisiana	108	4,402	1,161
Maine	21	405	383
Maryland	216	6,303	1,538
Massachusetts	170	6,135	1,053
Michigan	67	9,734	1,063
Minnesota	68	6,387	1,627
Mississippi	80	1,820	776
Missouri	119	9,066	1,904
Montana	15	577	772
Nebraska	43	2,924	1,891
Nevada	7	958	1,618
New Hampshire	18	666	815
New Jersey	242	13,547	1,852
New Mexico	36	1,157	1,009
New York	139	19,105	1,054
North Carolina	180	6,426	1,179
North Dakota	11	1,231	1,938
Ohio	423	23,616	2,195
Oklahoma	55	3,094	1,141
Oregon	29	3,613	1,579
Pennsylvania	450	14,848	1,255
Puerto Rico	12	984	317
Rhode Island	6	566	610
South Carolina	72	3,531	1,253
South Dakota	18	568	832
Tennessee	93	4,081	975
Texas	306	16,624	1,358
Utah	13	1,829	1,516
Vermont	7	160	339
Virginia	77	4,626	931
Washington	51	5,315	1,500
West Virginia	36	854	474
Wisconsin	122	7,284	1,581
Wyoming	14	501	1,340
TOTAL U.S.	4,964	$338,395	$1,581

*Preliminary. Components do not add to totals because of differences in reporting dates and accounting systems.
Source: U.S. League of Savings Associations, *1976 Savings and Loan Fact Book.*

Government and Politics

The national executive

December 20, 1976

Department, bureau, or office	Executive official and official title
PRESIDENT OF THE UNITED STATES*	Gerald R. Ford
Vice-President	Nelson A. Rockefeller
EXECUTIVE OFFICE OF THE PRESIDENT	
Assistant to the President	Richard B. Cheney
	Brent Scowcroft
Press Secretary to the President	Ronald H. Nessen
Counsel to the President	Philip W. Buchen
Counselor to the President	Robert T. Hartmann
	John O. Marsh, Jr.
Special Assistant to the President for Women	Jeanne M. Holm
Special Consultant to the President	Robert A. Goldwin
Office of Management and Budget	James T. Lynn, director
Council of Economic Advisers	Alan Greenspan, chairman
National Security Council	†
Central Intelligence Agency	George Bush, director
Domestic Council	James M. Cannon, executive director
Office of the Special Representative for Trade Negotiations	Frederick B. Dent, special representative
Council on Environmental Quality	Russell W. Peterson, chairman
Office of Telecommunications Policy	John M. Eger, director (acting)
Council on International Economic Policy	J. M. Dunn, executive director (acting)
Federal Property Council	vacancy (chairman)
Council on Wage and Price Stability	Michael H. Moskow, director
Energy Resources Council	Frank G. Zarb, executive director
DEPARTMENT OF STATE	Henry A. Kissinger, secretary (Cyrus R. Vance‡)
	Charles W. Robinson, deputy secretary
Political Affairs	Philip C. Habib, undersecretary
Economic Affairs	William D. Rogers, undersecretary
Security Assistance	Amos A. Jordan, undersecretary
Management	Lawrence S. Eagleburger, deputy undersecretary
Ambassador at Large	U. Alexis Johnson
Counselor of the Department	Helmut Sonnenfeldt
Agency for International Development	Daniel Parker, administrator
Permanent Mission to the Organization of American States	William S. Mailliard, permanent representative
Mission to the United Nations	William W. Scranton, permanent representative
African Affairs	William E. Schaufele, Jr., asst. secretary
European Affairs	Arthur A. Hartman, asst. secretary
East Asian and Pacific Affairs	Arthur W. Hummel, Jr., asst. secretary
Inter-American Affairs	Harry W. Shlaudeman, asst. secretary
Near Eastern and South Asian Affairs	Alfred L. Atherton, Jr., asst. secretary
DEPARTMENT OF THE TREASURY	William E. Simon, secretary (W. Michael Blumenthal‡)
	George H. Dixon, deputy secretary
Monetary Affairs	Edwin H. Yeo III, undersecretary
Comptroller of the Currency	Robert Bloom, comptroller
Bur. of Government Financial Operations	Dario A. Pagliai, commissioner
U.S. Customs Service	Vernon D. Acree, commissioner
Bureau of Engraving and Printing	James A. Conlon, director
Bureau of the Mint	Mary T. Brooks, director
Bureau of the Public Debt	H. J. Hintgen, commissioner
Internal Revenue Service	Donald C. Alexander, commissioner
Office of the Treasurer	Francine I. Neff, treasurer
Savings Bond Division	Francine I. Neff, national director
U.S. Secret Service	H. Stuart Knight, director
Bureau of Alcohol, Tobacco and Firearms	Rex D. Davis, director
Federal Law Enforcement Training Center	Arthur F. Brandstatter, director
DEPARTMENT OF DEFENSE	Donald H. Rumsfeld, secretary (Harold Brown‡)
	William P. Clements, Jr., deputy secretary
	Robert Ellsworth, deputy secretary
Joint Chiefs of Staff	Gen. George S. Brown, USAF, chairman
Chief of Staff, Army	Gen. Bernard W. Rogers, USA
Chief of Naval Operations	Adm. James L. Holloway III, USN
Chief of Staff, Air Force	Gen. David C. Jones, USAF
Commandant of the Marine Corps	Gen. Louis Wilson, USMC
Department of the Army	Martin R. Hoffmann, secretary
Department of the Navy	J. Wm. Middendorf II, secretary
Department of the Air Force	Thomas C. Reed, secretary
DEPARTMENT OF JUSTICE	
Attorney General	Edward H. Levi (Griffin B. Bell‡)
Solicitor General	Robert H. Bork
Community Relations Service	Benjamin F. Holman, director
Law Enforcement Assistance Admin.	Richard W. Velde, administrator
Antitrust Division	Donald I. Baker, asst. attorney general
Civil Division	Rex E. Lee, asst. attorney general
Civil Rights Division	J. Stanley Pottinger, asst. attorney general
Criminal Division	Richard L. Thornburgh, asst. attorney general
Land and Natural Resources Division	Peter R. Taft, asst. attorney general
Tax Division	Scott P. Crampton, asst. attorney general
Office of Management and Finance	Glen E. Pommerening, asst. attorney general
Federal Bureau of Investigation	Clarence M. Kelley, director
Bureau of Prisons	Norman A. Carlson, director
Immigration and Naturalization Service	Leonard F. Chapman, Jr., commissioner
Drug Enforcement Administration	Peter B. Bensinger, administrator
U.S. Marshals Service	William E. Hall, director

Department, bureau, or office	Executive official and official title
DEPARTMENT OF THE INTERIOR	Thomas S. Kleppe, secretary (Cecil D. Andrus‡)
	D. Kent Frizzell, undersecretary
Fish and Wildlife and Parks	Nathaniel P. Reed, asst. secretary
National Park Service	Gary E. Everhardt, director
Fish and Wildlife Service	Lynn A. Greenwalt, director
Bureau of Outdoor Recreation	John Crutcher, director
Energy and Minerals	William L. Fisher, asst. secretary
Office of Minerals Policy Development	Hermann Enzer, director
Geological Survey	Vincent E. McKelvey, director
Bureau of Mines	Thomas V. Falkie, director
Land and Water Resources	Jack O. Horton, asst. secretary
Bureau of Land Management	Curtis J. Berklund, director
Bureau of Reclamation	Gilbert G. Stamm, commissioner
Commissioner of Indian Affairs	Benjamin Reifel, commissioner
DEPARTMENT OF AGRICULTURE	John A. Knebel, secretary (acting) (Bob S. Bergland‡)
	John A. Knebel, deputy secretary
Rural Development	William H. Walker III, asst. secretary
Rural Electrification Administration	David A. Hamil, administrator
Farmers Home Administration	Frank B. Elliott, administrator
Marketing and Consumer Services	Richard L. Feltner, asst. secretary
Agricultural Marketing Service	Donald E. Wilkinson, administrator
International Affairs and Commodity Programs	Richard E. Bell, asst. secretary
Commodity Credit Corporation	Richard E. Bell, president
Conservation, Research, and Education	Robert W. Long, asst. secretary
Forest Service	John R. McGuire, chief
Soil Conservation Service	Ronello M. Davis, administrator
Agricultural Economics	Don A. Paarlberg, director
Statistical Reporting Service	William E. Kibler, administrator
DEPARTMENT OF COMMERCE	Elliot L. Richardson, secretary (Juanita M. Kreps‡)
	Edward O. Vetter, undersecretary
Domestic and International Business	Leonard S. Matthews, asst. secretary
Chief Economist	John Kendrick
Bureau of the Census	Robert L. Hagan, director (acting)
Bureau of Economic Analysis	George Jaszi, director
Science and Technology	Betsy Ancker-Johnson, asst. secretary
Office of Environmental Affairs	Sidney R. Galler, director
National Bureau of Standards	Ernest Ambler, director (acting)
Patent and Trademark Office	C. Marshall Dann, commissioner
Maritime Affairs	Robert J. Blackwell, asst. secretary
Tourism	Creighton D. Holden, asst. secretary
National Oceanic and Atmospheric Administration	Robert M. White, administrator
DEPARTMENT OF LABOR	W. J. Usery, Jr., secretary (F. Ray Marshall‡)
	Michael H. Moskow, undersecretary
Administration and Management	Albert J. Angebranndt, asst. secretary
Employment and Training	William H. Kolberg, asst. secretary
Labor-Management Relations	Bernard E. DeLury, asst. secretary
Employment Standards	Robert C. Chase, asst. secretary (acting)
Occupational Safety and Health	Morton Corn, asst. secretary
Labor Statistics	Julius Shiskin, commissioner
DEPARTMENT OF HEALTH, EDUCATION, AND WELFARE	F. David Mathews, secretary (Joseph A. Califano, Jr.‡)
	Marjorie Ward Lynch, undersecretary
Education Division	Virginia Y. Trotter, asst. secretary
Office of Education	Terrel H. Bell, commissioner
National Institute of Education	Harold L. Hodgkinson, director
Public Health Service	Theodore Cooper, M.D., asst. secretary
Food and Drug Administration	Alexander M. Schmidt, M.D., commissioner
National Institutes of Health	Donald S. Fredrickson, director
Health Resources Administration	Kenneth M. Endicott, administrator
Health Services Administration	Louis M. Hellman, administrator
Center for Disease Control	David J. Sencer, M.D., director
Social and Rehabilitation Service	Don I. Wortman, administrator (acting)
Social Security Administration	James B. Cardwell, commissioner
DEPARTMENT OF HOUSING AND URBAN DEVELOPMENT	Carla A. Hills, secretary (Patricia R. Harris‡)
	John B. Rhinelander, undersecretary
Community Planning and Development	Warren H. Butler, asst. secretary (acting)
Federal Housing Commissioner	John T. Howley
Fair Housing and Equal Opportunity	James H. Blair, asst. secretary
Policy Development and Research	Charles J. Orlebeke, asst. secretary
DEPARTMENT OF TRANSPORTATION	William T. Coleman, Jr., secretary (Brock Adams‡)
	John W. Barnum, deputy secretary
United States Coast Guard	Adm. Owen W. Siler, USCG, commandant
Federal Aviation Administration	John L. McLucas, administrator
Federal Highway Administration	Norbert T. Tiemann, administrator
National Highway Traffic Safety Administration	John W. Snow, administrator
Federal Railroad Administration	Asaph H. Hall, administrator
Urban Mass Transportation	Robert E. Patricelli, administrator
St. Lawrence Seaway Development Corp.	David W. Oberlin, administrator

*Jimmy Carter elected President and Walter F. Mondale elected Vice-President Nov. 2, 1976.
†Council comprised of the President of the United States and certain other members.
‡Nominated by Jimmy Carter after November elections.

Senate January 1977

State, name, and party	Term expires
Ala.—Allen, James B. (D)	1981
Sparkman, John J. (D)	1979
Alaska—Stevens, Ted (R)	1979
Gravel, Mike (D)	1981
Ariz.—DeConcini, Dennis (D)	1983
Goldwater, Barry M. (R)	1981
Ark.—Bumpers, Dale (D)	1981
McClellan, John L. (D)	1979
Calif.—Cranston, Alan (D)	1981
Hayakawa, S. I. (R)	1983
Colo.—Hart, Gary W. (D)	1981
Haskell, Floyd K. (D)	1979
Conn.—Ribicoff, Abraham (D)	1981
Weicker, Lowell P., Jr. (R)	1983
Del.—Biden, Joseph R., Jr. (D)	1979
Roth, William V., Jr. (R)	1983
Fla.—Stone, Richard (D)	1981
Chiles, Lawton M. (D)	1983
Ga.—Nunn, Sam (D)	1979
Talmadge, Herman E. (D)	1981
Hawaii—Inouye, Daniel K. (D)	1981
Matsunaga, Spark M. (D)	1983
Idaho—Church, Frank (D)	1981
McClure, James A. (R)	1979
Ill.—Percy, Charles H. (R)	1979
Stevenson, Adlai E., III (D)	1981
Ind.—Bayh, Birch (D)	1981
Lugar, Richard G. (R)	1983
Iowa—Clark, Richard (D)	1979
Culver, John C. (D)	1981
Kan.—Dole, Robert J. (R)	1981
Pearson, James B. (R)	1979
Ky.—Ford, Wendell H. (D)	1981
Huddleston, Walter (D)	1979
La.—Long, Russell B. (D)	1981
Johnston, J. Bennett, Jr. (D)	1979
Maine—Muskie, Edmund S. (D)	1983
Hathaway, William D. (D)	1979
Md.—Sarbanes, Paul S. (D)	1983
Mathias, Charles McC., Jr. (R)	1981
Mass.—Brooke, Edward W. (R)	1979
Kennedy, Edward M. (D)	1983
Mich.—Griffin, Robert P. (R)	1979
Riegle, Donald W., Jr. (D)	1983
Minn.—Humphrey, Hubert (D)	1983
Anderson, Wendell R. (D)	1979
Miss.—Stennis, John C. (D)	1983
Eastland, James O. (D)	1979
Mo.—Danforth, John C. (R)	1983
Eagleton, Thomas F. (D)	1981
Mont.—Metcalf, Lee (D)	1979
Melcher, John (D)	1983
Neb.—Curtis, Carl T. (R)	1979
Zorinsky, Edward (D)	1983
Nev.—Laxalt, Paul (R)	1981
Cannon, Howard W. (D)	1983
N.H.—Durkin, John A. (D)	1981
McIntyre, Thomas J. (D)	1979
N.J.—Case, Clifford P. (R)	1979
Williams, Harrison A., Jr. (D)	1983
N.M.—Domenici, Pete V. (R)	1979
Schmitt, Harrison H. (R)	1983
N.Y.—Javits, Jacob K. (R)	1981
Moynihan, Daniel P. (D)	1983
N.C.—Helms, Jesse (R)	1979
Morgan, Robert B. (D)	1981
N.D.—Young, Milton R. (R)	1981
Burdick, Quentin N. (D)	1983
Ohio—Glenn, John H., Jr. (D)	1981
Metzenbaum, Howard M. (D)	1983
Okla.—Bellmon, Henry L. (R)	1981
Bartlett, Dewey F. (R)	1979
Ore.—Hatfield, Mark O. (R)	1979
Packwood, Robert W. (R)	1981
Pa.—Heinz, H. John, III (R)	1983
Schweiker, Richard S. (R)	1981
R.I.—Pell, Claiborne (D)	1979
Chafee, John H. (R)	1983
S.C.—Thurmond, Strom (R)	1979
Hollings, Ernest F. (D)	1981
S.D.—McGovern, George (D)	1981
Abourezk, James G. (D)	1979
Tenn.—Sasser, James R. (D)	1983
Baker, Howard H., Jr. (R)	1979
Texas—Tower, John G. (R)	1979
Bentsen, Lloyd M. (D)	1983
Utah—Garn, Jake (R)	1981
Hatch, Orrin G. (R)	1983
Vt.—Leahy, Patrick J. (D)	1981
Stafford, Robert T. (R)	1983
Va.—Scott, William L. (R)	1979
Byrd, Harry F., Jr. (I)	1983
Wash.—Jackson, Henry M. (D)	1983
Magnuson, Warren G. (D)	1981
W.Va.—Byrd, Robert C. (D)	1983
Randolph, Jennings (D)	1979
Wis.—Nelson, Gaylord (D)	1981
Proxmire, William (D)	1983
Wyo.—Wallop, Malcolm (R)	1983
Hansen, Clifford P. (R)	1979

Supreme Court

Chief Justice Warren Earl Burger (appointed 1969)

Associate Justices (year appointed)

William J. Brennan, Jr.	(1956)	Harry A. Blackmun	(1970)
Potter Stewart	(1958)	Lewis F. Powell, Jr.	(1972)
Byron R. White	(1962)	William H. Rehnquist	(1972)
Thurgood Marshall	(1967)	John Paul Stevens	(1975)

House of Representatives membership at the opening of the first session of the 95th Congress in January 1977

State, district, name, party

Ala.—1. Edwards, Jack (R)
2. Dickinson, W. L. (R)
3. Nichols, William (D)
4. Bevill, Tom (D)
5. Flippo, Ronnie G. (D)
6. Buchanan, John H., Jr. (R)
7. Flowers, W. W. (D)
Alaska—Young, Don (R)
Ariz.—1. Rhodes, John J. (R)
2. Udall, Morris K. (D)
3. Stump, Bob (D)
4. Rudd, Eldon D. (R)
Ark.—1. Alexander, Bill (D)
2. Tucker, Jim Guy (D)
3. Hammerschmidt, J. P. (R)
4. Thornton, Ray (D)
Calif.—1. Johnson, Harold T. (D)
2. Clausen, Don H. (R)
3. Moss, John E. (D)
4. Leggett, Robert L. (D)
5. Burton, John L. (D)
6. Burton, Phillip (D)
7. Miller, George, III (D)
8. Dellums, Ronald V. (D)
9. Stark, Fortney H. (D)
10. Edwards, Don (D)
11. Ryan, Leo J. (D)
12. McCloskey, Paul N., Jr. (R)
13. Mineta, Norman Y. (D)
14. McFall, John J. (D)
15. Sisk, B. F. (D)
16. Panetta, Leon E. (D)
17. Krebs, John (D)
18. Ketchum, William M. (R)
19. Lagomarsino, Robert J. (R)
20. Goldwater, Barry M., Jr. (R)
21. Corman, James C. (D)
22. Moorhead, Carlos J. (R)
23. Beilenson, Anthony C. (D)
24. Waxman, Henry A. (D)
25. Roybal, Edward R. (D)
26. Rousselot, John H. (R)
27. Dornan, Robert K. (R)
28. Burke, Yvonne B. (D)
29. Hawkins, Augustus F. (D)
30. Danielson, George E. (D)
31. Wilson, Charles H. (D)
32. Anderson, Glenn M. (D)
33. Clawson, Del (R)
34. Hannaford, Mark W. (D)
35. Lloyd, Jim (D)
36. Brown, George E., Jr. (D)
37. Pettis, Shirley N. (R)
38. Patterson, Jerry M. (D)
39. Wiggins, Charles E. (R)
40. Badham, Robert E. (R)
41. Wilson, Bob (R)
42. Van Deerlin, Lionel (D)
43. Burgener, Clair W. (R)
Colo.—1. Schroeder, Patricia (D)
2. Wirth, Timothy E. (D)
3. Evans, Frank (D)
4. Johnson, J. P. (R)
5. Armstrong, W. L. (R)
Conn.—1. Cotter, William R. (D)
2. Dodd, Christopher J. (D)
3. Giaimo, Robert N. (D)
4. McKinney, Stewart B. (R)
5. Sarasin, Ronald A. (R)
6. Moffett, Anthony J. (D)
Del.—Evans, Thomas, Jr. (R)
Fla.—1. Sikes, Robert L. F. (D)
2. Fuqua, Don (D)
3. Bennett, Charles E. (D)
4. Chappell, William, Jr. (D)
5. Kelly, Richard (R)
6. Young, C. William (R)
7. Gibbons, Sam (D)
8. Ireland, Andrew P. (D)
9. Frey, Louis, Jr. (R)
10. Bafalis, L. A. (R)
11. Rogers, Paul G. (D)
12. Burke, J. Herbert (R)
13. Lehman, William (D)
14. Pepper, Claude (D)
15. Fascell, Dante B. (D)
Ga.—1. Ginn, R. B. (D)
2. Mathis, Dawson (D)
3. Brinkley, Jack (D)
4. Levitas, Elliott H. (D)
5. Young, Andrew (D)
6. Flynt, J. J., Jr. (D)
7. McDonald, Lawrence P. (D)
8. Evans, Billy Lee (D)
9. Jenkins, Edgar L. (D)
10. Barnard, Doug (D)
Hawaii—1. Heftel, Cecil (D)
2. Akaka, Daniel (D)
Idaho—1. Symms, S. D. (R)
2. Hansen, George V. (R)

State, district, name, party

Ill.—1. Metcalfe, Ralph (D)
2. Murphy, Morgan (D)
3. Russo, Martin A. (D)
4. Derwinski, Edward J. (R)
5. Fary, John G. (D)
6. Hyde, Henry J. (R)
7. Collins, Cardiss (D)
8. Rostenkowski, Dan (D)
9. Yates, Sidney R. (D)
10. Mikva, Abner J. (D)
11. Annunzio, Frank (D)
12. Crane, Philip M. (R)
13. McClory, Robert (R)
14. Erlenborn, J. N. (R)
15. Corcoran, Tom (R)
16. Anderson, John B. (R)
17. O'Brien, G. M. (R)
18. Michel, Robert H. (R)
19. Railsback, Thomas F. (R)
20. Findley, Paul (R)
21. Madigan, E. R. (R)
22. Shipley, George E. (D)
23. Price, Melvin (D)
24. Simon, Paul (D)
Ind.—1. Benjamin, Adam (D)
2. Fithian, Floyd J. (D)
3. Brademas, John (D)
4. Quayle, J. Danforth (R)
5. Hillis, Elwood H. (R)
6. Evans, David W. (D)
7. Myers, John (R)
8. Cornwell, David L. (D)
9. Hamilton, L. H. (D)
10. Sharp, Philip R. (D)
11. Jacobs, Andrew, Jr. (D)
Iowa—1. Leach, James (R)
2. Blouin, Michael T. (D)
3. Grassley, Charles E. (R)
4. Smith, Neal (D)
5. Harkin, Tom (D)
6. Bedell, Berkley (D)
Kan.—1. Sebelius, Keith G. (R)
2. Keys, Martha E. (D)
3. Winn, Larry, Jr. (R)
4. Glickman, Dan (D)
5. Skubitz, Joseph (R)
Ky.—1. Hubbard, Carroll, Jr. (D)
2. Natcher, William H. (D)
3. Mazzoli, Romano L. (D)
4. Snyder, Gene (R)
5. Carter, Tim L. (R)
6. Breckinridge, J. B. (D)
7. Perkins, Carl D. (D)
La.—1. Tonry, Richard E. (D)
2. Boggs, Lindy (D)
3. Treen, David C. (R)
4. Waggonner, Joe D., Jr. (D)
5. Huckaby, Jerry (D)
6. Moore, W. Henson, III (R)
7. Breaux, John B. (D)
8. Long, Gillis W. (D)
Maine—1. Emery, David F. (R)
2. Cohen, W. S. (R)
Md.—1. Bauman, Robert E. (R)
2. Long, Clarence D. (D)
3. Mikulski, Barbara A. (D)
4. Holt, Marjorie S. (R)
5. Spellman, Gladys N. (D)
6. Byron, Goodloe E. (D)
7. Mitchell, Parren J. (D)
8. Steers, Newton I. (R)
Mass.—1. Conte, Silvio O. (R)
2. Boland, Edward P. (D)
3. Early, Joseph D. (D)
4. Drinan, Robert F. (D)
5. Tsongas, Paul E. (D)
6. Harrington, M. J. (D)
7. Markey, Edward J. (D)
8. O'Neill, Thomas P., Jr. (D)
9. Moakley, John J. (D)
10. Heckler, Margaret (R)
11. Burke, James A. (D)
12. Studds, Gerry E. (D)
Mich.—1. Conyers, John, Jr. (D)
2. Pursell, Carl D. (R)
3. Brown, Garry E. (R)
4. Stockman, David A. (R)
5. Sawyer, Harold S. (R)
6. Carr, Bob (D)
7. Kildee, Dale E. (D)
8. Traxler, Bob (D)
9. Vander Jagt, Guy (R)
10. Cederberg, Elford A. (R)
11. Ruppe, Philip (R)
12. Bonior, David E. (D)
13. Diggs, Charles C., Jr. (D)
14. Nedzi, Lucien N. (D)
15. Ford, W. D. (D)
16. Dingell, John D. (D)
17. Brodhead, William M. (D)
18. Blanchard, James J. (D)
19. Broomfield, William S. (R)
Minn.—1. Quie, Albert H. (R)
2. Hagedorn, Tom (R)
3. Frenzel, William (R)
4. Vento, Bruce F. (D)
5. Fraser, Donald M. (D)
6. Nolan, Richard (D)
7. Bergland, Bob S. (D)
8. Oberstar, James L. (D)
Miss.—1. Whitten, Jamie L. (D)
2. Bowen, D. R. (D)

State, district, name, party

3. Montgomery, G. V. (D)
4. Cochran, Thad (R)
5. Lott, Trent (R)
Mo.—1. Clay, William (D)
2. Young, Robert A. (D)
3. Gephardt, Richard A. (D)
4. Skelton, Ike (D)
5. Bolling, Richard (D)
6. Coleman, E. Thomas (R)
7. Taylor, Gene (R)
8. Ichord, Richard H. (D)
9. Volkmer, Harold L. (D)
10. Burlison, Bill D. (D)
Mont.—1. Baucus, Max S. (D)
2. Marlenee, Ron (R)
Neb.—1. Thone, Charles (R)
2. Cavanaugh, John J. (D)
3. Smith, Virginia (R)
Nev.—Santini, James (D)
N.H.—1. D'Amours, Norman (D)
2. Cleveland, James C. (R)
N.J.—1. Florio, James J. (D)
2. Hughes, William J. (D)
3. Howard, J. J. (D)
4. Thompson, Frank, Jr. (D)
5. Fenwick, Millicent (R)
6. Forsythe, Edwin B. (R)
7. Maguire, Andrew (D)
8. Roe, Robert A. (D)
9. Hollenbeck, Harold C. (R)
10. Rodino, Peter W., Jr. (D)
11. Minish, Joseph G. (D)
12. Rinaldo, M. J. (R)
13. Meyner, Helen S. (D)
14. LeFante, Joseph A. (D)
15. Patten, Edward J. (D)
N.M.—1. Lujan, Manuel, Jr. (R)
2. Runnels, Harold L. (D)
N.Y.—1. Pike, Otis G. (D)
2. Downey, Thomas J. (D)
3. Ambro, Jerome A., Jr. (D)
4. Lent, Norman F. (R)
5. Wydler, John W. (R)
6. Wolff, L. L. (D)
7. Addabbo, Joseph P. (D)
8. Rosenthal, Benjamin S. (D)
9. Delaney, James J. (D)
10. Biaggi, Mario (D)
11. Scheuer, James H. (D)
12. Chisholm, Shirley (D)
13. Solarz, Stephen J. (D)
14. Richmond, Frederick W. (D)
15. Zeferetti, Leo C. (D)
16. Holtzman, Elizabeth (D)
17. Murphy, John M. (D)
18. Koch, Edward I. (D)
19. Rangel, Charles B. (D)
20. Weiss, Theodore S. (D)
21. Badillo, Herman (D)
22. Bingham, J. B. (D)
23. Caputo, Bruce F. (R)
24. Ottinger, Richard L. (D)
25. Fish, Hamilton, Jr. (R)
26. Gilman, B. A. (R)
27. McHugh, Matthew F. (D)
28. Stratton, Samuel S. (D)
29. Pattison, Edward W. (D)
30. McEwen, Robert (R)
31. Mitchell, D. J. (R)
32. Hanley, James M. (D)
33. Walsh, W. F. (R)
34. Horton, Frank J. (R)
35. Conable, B., Jr. (R)
36. LaFalce, John J. (D)
37. Nowak, Henry J. (D)
38. Kemp, Jack F. (R)
39. Lundine, Stanley N. (D)
N.C.—1. Jones, Walter B. (D)
2. Fountain, L. H. (D)
3. Whitley, Charles (D)
4. Andrews, Ike F. (D)
5. Neal, Stephen L. (D)
6. Preyer, L. R. (D)
7. Rose, C. G., III (D)
8. Hefner, Bill (D)
9. Martin, J. G. (R)
10. Broyhill, James T. (R)
11. Gudger, Lamar (D)
N.D.—Andrews, Mark (R)
Ohio—1. Gradison, Willis D. (R)
2. Luken, Thomas A. (D)
3. Whalen, Charles W., Jr. (R)
4. Guyer, Tennyson (R)
5. Latta, Delbert L. (R)
6. Harsha, William H. (R)
7. Brown, Clarence J. (R)
8. Kindness, Thomas N. (R)
9. Ashley, Thomas L. (D)
10. Miller, Clarence E. (R)
11. Stanton, J. William (R)
12. Devine, Samuel L. (R)
13. Pease, Donald J. (D)
14. Seiberling, John F., Jr. (D)
15. Wylie, Chalmers P. (R)
16. Regula, R. S. (R)
17. Ashbrook, John M. (R)
18. Applegate, Douglas (D)
19. Carney, Charles J. (D)
20. Oakar, Mary Rose (D)
21. Stokes, Louis (D)
22. Vanik, Charles A. (D)
23. Mottl, Ronald M. (D)

State, district, name, party

Okla.—1. Jones, James R. (D)
2. Risenhoover, Ted (D)
3. Watkins, Wes (D)
4. Steed, Tom (D)
5. Edwards, Mickey (R)
6. English, Glenn (D)
Ore.—1. AuCoin, Les (D)
2. Ullman, Al (D)
3. Duncan, Robert (D)
4. Weaver, James (D)
Pa.—1. Myers, Michael (D)
2. Nix, Robert N. C. (D)
3. Lederer, Raymond F. (D)
4. Eilberg, Joshua (D)
5. Schulze, Richard T. (R)
6. Yatron, Gus (D)
7. Edgar, Robert W. (D)
8. Kostmayer, Peter H. (D)
9. Shuster, E. G. (R)
10. McDade, Joseph M. (R)
11. Flood, Daniel J. (D)
12. Murtha, John P. (D)
13. Coughlin, R. L. (R)
14. Moorhead, William S. (D)
15. Rooney, Fred B. (D)
16. Walker, Robert S. (R)
17. Ertel, Allen E. (D)
18. Walgren, Doug (D)
19. Goodling, William F. (R)
20. Gaydos, Joseph (D)
21. Dent, John H. (D)
22. Murphy, Austin J. (D)
23. Ammerman, Joseph S. (D)
24. Marks, Marc L. (R)
25. Myers, Gary A. (R)
R.I.—1. St. Germain, Fernand (D)
2. Beard, Edward P. (D)
S.C.—1. Davis, Mendel (D)
2. Spence, Floyd D. (R)
3. Derrick, Butler C., Jr. (D)
4. Mann, James R. (D)
5. Holland, Kenneth L. (D)
6. Jenrette, John W., Jr. (D)
S.D.—1. Pressler, Larry L. (R)
2. Abdnor, James (R)
Tenn.—1. Quillen, James H. (R)
2. Duncan, John J. (R)
3. Lloyd, Marilyn (D)
4. Gore, Albert, Jr. (D)
5. Allen, Clifford (D)
6. Beard, Robin L., Jr. (R)
7. Jones, Edward (D)
8. Ford, Harold E. (D)
Texas—1. Hall, Sam B. (D)
2. Wilson, Charles (D)
3. Collins, James M. (R)
4. Roberts, Ray (D)
5. Mattox, Jim (D)
6. Teague, Olin E. (D)
7. Archer, William R. (R)
8. Eckhardt, Robert C. (D)
9. Brooks, Jack (D)
10. Pickle, J. J. (D)
11. Poage, W. R. (D)
12. Wright, James C., Jr. (D)
13. Hightower, Jack (D)
14. Young, John (D)
15. de la Garza, E. (D)
16. White, Richard C. (D)
17. Burleson, Omar (D)
18. Jordan, Barbara C. (D)
19. Mahon, George (D)
20. Gonzalez, Henry B. (D)
21. Krueger, Robert (D)
22. Gammage, Bob (D)
23. Kazen, Abraham, Jr. (D)
24. Milford, Dale (D)
Utah—1. McKay, K. Gunn (D)
2. Marriott, Dan (R)
Vt.—Jeffords, James M. (R)
Va.—1. Trible, Paul S. (R)
2. Whitehurst, G. W. (R)
3. Satterfield, D. E., III (D)
4. Daniel, R. W. (R)
5. Daniel, W. C. (D)
6. Butler, M. C. (R)
7. Robinson, J. Kenneth (R)
8. Harris, Herbert E. (D)
9. Wampler, William C. (R)
10. Fisher, Joseph L. (D)
Wash.—1. Pritchard, Joel (R)
2. Meeds, Lloyd (D)
3. Bonker, Don (D)
4. McCormack, Mike (D)
5. Foley, Thomas S. (D)
6. Dicks, Norman D. (D)
7. Adams, Brock (D)
W.Va.—1. Mollohan, R. H. (D)
2. Staggers, Harley O. (D)
3. Slack, John M., Jr. (D)
4. Rahall, Nick Joe (D)
Wis.—1. Aspin, Leslie (D)
2. Kastenmeier, Robert W. (D)
3. Baldus, Alvin J. (D)
4. Zablocki, Clement J. (D)
5. Reuss, Henry S. (D)
6. Steiger, William A. (R)
7. Obey, David R. (D)
8. Cornell, Robert J. (D)
9. Kasten, Robert W. (R)
Wyo.—Roncalio, Teno (D)

The federal administrative budget

in millions of dollars; fiscal years ending June 30 (1977, Sept. 30)

Source and function	1975	1976 estimate	1977 estimate
BUDGET RECEIPTS	$281,000	$297,500	$351,300
Individual income taxes	122,400	130,800	153,600
Corporation income taxes	40,600	40,100	49,500
Excise taxes	16,600	16,900	17,800
Social insurance taxes and contributions	86,400	92,600	113,100
Estate and gift taxes	4,600	5,100	5,800
Customs duties	3,700	3,800	4,300
Miscellaneous receipts	6,700	8,300	7,200
BUDGET EXPENDITURES	324,600	373,500	394,200
National defense	86,600	92,800	101,100
Department of Defense military functions	85,000	89,800	99,600
Military assistance	1,000	1,400	500
Atomic energy defense activities	1,500	1,600	1,800
Defense-related activities	−900	−100	−800
International affairs	4,400	5,700	6,800
Conduct of foreign affairs	700	800	900
Foreign economic and financial assistance	3,700	5,000	4,700
Foreign information and exchange activities	300	400	400
International financial programs	—*	—*	1,300
General science, space, and technology	4,000	4,300	4,500
Agriculture	1,700	2,900	1,700
Farm income stabilization	800	1,900	700
Agricultural research and services	900	1,000	1,000
Natural resources, environment, and energy	9,500	11,800	13,800
Water resources and power	3,300	3,800	3,900
Conservation and land management	1,300	1,300	1,000
Recreational resources	800	900	1,000
Pollution control and abatement	2,500	3,100	4,400
Energy	1,600	2,600	3,400
Other natural resources	800	900	900
Commerce and transportation	16,000	17,800	16,500
Mortgage credit and thrift insurance	2,800	1,300	−600
Payment to the Postal Service	1,900	1,700	1,500
Other advancement and regulation	900	900	900
Air transportation	2,400	2,700	2,800
Water transportation	1,500	1,700	1,900
Ground transportation	6,500	9,500	10,100
Other transportation	100	100	100
Community and regional development	4,400	5,800	5,500
Community development	3,100	3,900	3,700
Area and regional development	900	1,400	1,300
Disaster relief and insurance	400	600	600
Education, training, employment, and social services	$15,200	$18,900	$16,600
Elementary, secondary, and vocational education	4,600	4,600	4,400
Higher education	2,100	2,700	2,300
Research and general education aids	900	800	800
Training and employment	4,100	6,900	5,000
Social services	3,300	3,600	3,700
Health	27,600	32,100	34,400
Health care services	23,400	27,600	21,300
Health research and education	2,700	3,000	2,800
Prevention and control of health problems	900	1,000	900
Health planning and construction	700	600	400
General health financing assistance	—	—	9,000
Income security	108,600	128,500	137,100
General retirement and disability insurance	69,400	77,200	87,400
Federal employee retirement and disability	7,000	8,300	10,000
Unemployment insurance	13,500	19,400	16,900
Public assistance and other income supplements	18,800	23,600	22,900
Veterans benefits and services	16,600	19,000	17,200
Income security for veterans	7,900	8,400	8,300
Veterans education, training, and rehabilitation	4,600	6,000	4,200
Hospital and medical care for veterans	3,700	4,100	4,500
Other veterans benefits and services	500	600	600
Law enforcement and justice	2,900	3,400	3,400
Federal law enforcement and prosecution	1,600	1,900	1,900
Federal judicial activities	300	300	400
Federal correctional and rehabilitative activities	200	300	300
Law enforcement assistance	900	900	800
General government	3,100	3,500	3,400
Legislative functions	600	800	800
Central fiscal operations	1,800	1,900	1,900
General property and records management	400	300	300
Other general government	500	600	500
Revenue sharing and general purpose fiscal assistance	7,000	7,200	7,400
Interest	31,000	34,800	41,300
Allowances for contingencies, civilian agency pay raises	—	200	2,300
Undistributed offsetting receipts	−14,100	−15,200	−18,800
Employer share, employee retirement	−4,000	−4,200	−4,500
Interest received by trust funds	−7,700	−8,000	−8,400
Rents and royalties on the Outer Continental Shelf	−2,400	−3,000	−6,000

*Less than $50,000,000. Source: Executive Office of the President, Office of Management and Budget, *The United States Budget in Brief: Fiscal Year 1977.*

State government revenue, expenditure, and debt

1975 in thousands of dollars

	GENERAL REVENUE						GENERAL EXPENDITURE					DEBT		
		State taxes												
State	Total	Total	General sales	Individual income	Intergovernmental	Charges & misc.	Total	Education	Highways	Public welfare	Hospitals	Total	Issued 1975*	Retired 1975*
Alabama	2,089,570	1,111,317	354,751	189,964	687,309	290,944	2,049,795	997,798	298,959	291,705	110,858	895,835	79,523	60,290
Alaska	622,301	202,848	—	86,975	246,151	173,302	797,754	264,193	128,949	44,907	7,761	709,821	170,270	18,853
Arizona	1,419,017	938,399	397,374	157,537	309,395	171,223	1,459,718	736,869	217,707	83,687	56,461	87,359	5,300	2,020
Arkansas	1,138,889	652,646	211,274	126,192	383,514	102,729	1,135,590	457,190	233,161	169,347	56,683	122,922	6,564	4,510
California	15,562,855	9,564,630	3,380,652	2,456,573	4,564,061	1,434,164	15,271,687	5,866,345	1,216,912	3,786,452	448,264	6,470,355	543,830	320,418
Colorado	1,650,599	866,425	274,971	280,498	476,401	307,773	1,616,188	806,361	193,592	265,696	80,897	122,859	825	4,616
Connecticut	1,747,292	1,058,848	425,882	13,578	465,433	223,011	1,930,237	598,659	237,023	347,506	145,131	2,922,230	318,860	169,974
Delaware	522,360	336,393	—	137,598	92,508	93,459	514,979	242,727	50,532	60,658	26,299	592,920	60,300	36,967
Florida	4,253,460	2,791,223	1,200,061	—	1,023,773	438,464	4,528,405	1,942,131	725,917	422,829	171,463	1,597,560	148,650	55,794
Georgia	2,706,370	1,547,774	563,660	373,916	898,777	259,819	2,764,481	1,146,408	423,769	492,151	155,329	1,148,785	134,750	59,757
Hawaii	982,344	575,549	287,219	168,670	249,355	157,440	1,082,473	382,349	84,173	133,615	57,328	1,164,873	95,000	44,074
Idaho	527,557	298,069	79,110	91,244	163,440	66,048	536,390	201,188	109,467	59,019	9,805	39,583	4,361	2,184
Illinois	6,788,895	4,409,545	1,497,126	1,136,918	1,716,744	662,606	7,119,197	2,776,331	947,262	1,801,471	306,129	2,798,172	471,088	86,562
Indiana	2,901,780	1,853,950	849,144	400,793	579,334	468,496	2,706,998	1,204,103	427,064	291,714	129,877	615,210	15,818	20,976
Iowa	1,765,907	1,061,960	283,758	358,899	469,417	234,530	1,770,611	774,658	362,170	236,125	96,352	127,209	2,500	4,512
Kansas	1,278,662	769,035	263,732	170,044	335,011	174,616	1,228,422	518,783	216,860	188,352	80,137	306,294	6,000	11,962
Kentucky	2,184,711	1,283,705	371,819	249,449	630,275	270,731	2,032,510	836,529	375,757	324,455	65,037	1,965,352	104,835	50,249
Louisiana	2,609,465	1,528,692	364,972	108,870	688,883	391,890	2,585,136	960,038	489,912	323,578	187,824	1,224,700	51,235	46,664
Maine	701,636	369,015	137,369	44,603	240,662	91,959	736,675	257,165	94,513	153,040	30,153	460,035	105,586	23,277
Maryland	2,778,211	1,730,723	396,006	665,997	656,165	391,323	3,136,475	1,162,501	444,658	443,937	173,188	2,095,020	442,765	107,042
Massachusetts	3,724,025	2,218,537	252,946	985,616	1,117,672	387,816	4,360,815	1,301,924	312,592	1,336,541	236,658	3,940,953	584,175	157,441
Michigan	5,973,800	3,485,965	1,177,360	846,427	1,705,915	781,920	6,499,624	2,496,790	708,646	1,618,687	299,195	1,663,997	306,088	80,835
Minnesota	3,214,365	2,022,228	384,391	807,108	804,693	387,444	2,922,116	1,345,400	338,904	466,842	141,240	875,590	99,765	48,671
Mississippi	1,435,692	797,390	387,445	92,687	477,364	160,938	1,433,630	598,131	259,184	179,262	69,517	613,341	15,074	26,628
Missouri	2,158,568	1,302,972	481,807	311,334	645,017	210,579	2,219,820	894,145	441,476	356,491	140,978	277,455	91,900	27,322
Montana	505,749	232,712	—	88,599	188,913	84,124	476,517	190,104	94,964	52,957	20,085	81,399	—	5,190
Nebraska	790,594	424,805	142,021	78,436	245,889	119,900	818,798	302,321	153,530	121,423	49,741	68,673	—	4,562
Nevada	434,321	266,819	89,732	—	109,888	57,614	411,571	156,820	68,355	38,560	11,747	51,804	—	3,396
New Hampshire	368,869	172,410	—	8,562	131,713	64,746	433,954	124,512	89,423	68,647	21,141	248,790	34,485	12,535
New Jersey	3,854,833	2,100,903	770,381	45,942	1,196,657	557,273	4,325,766	1,417,357	405,302	983,266	210,060	3,886,307	400,070	218,881
New Mexico	1,004,947	519,551	218,291	56,575	276,127	209,269	857,584	400,260	131,175	88,690	38,802	152,723	23,730	29,363
New York	14,857,537	8,939,223	2,000,854	3,588,584	4,161,645	1,756,669	15,704,675	4,991,803	838,318	3,528,478	1,148,535	14,635,017	1,681,305	359,523
North Carolina	3,247,883	1,900,440	424,018	549,927	996,907	350,536	3,226,479	1,678,945	426,990	314,101	179,319	616,529	80,345	38,231
North Dakota	551,255	263,638	94,458	64,580	143,045	144,572	464,387	178,507	82,772	42,690	18,027	63,308	—	2,187
Ohio	5,111,134	3,039,163	929,725	481,785	1,376,886	695,085	5,449,408	2,050,174	763,018	904,180	268,994	2,661,620	322,794	146,484
Oklahoma	1,657,683	883,735	163,455	162,741	514,228	259,720	1,536,607	609,894	253,649	296,484	103,841	945,800	65,200	52,790
Oregon	1,534,872	793,010	—	427,002	483,104	258,758	1,499,491	516,076	251,418	238,543	61,168	1,676,559	454,645	46,122
Pennsylvania	7,236,912	4,733,435	1,271,015	995,409	1,865,592	637,885	7,933,758	2,909,866	1,104,708	1,674,825	492,086	5,359,575	428,470	169,893
Rhode Island	644,446	349,759	103,431	79,682	192,168	102,519	656,013	224,470	35,584	174,264	52,969	459,545	72,835	21,507
South Carolina	1,704,761	956,581	337,711	210,895	471,383	276,797	1,854,946	774,820	231,180	165,448	112,516	931,844	102,480	35,479
South Dakota	398,414	171,127	84,863	—	149,843	77,444	406,779	129,350	89,823	57,178	19,302	67,619	12,000	1,714
Tennessee	2,037,298	1,152,054	477,012	18,436	652,842	232,402	2,187,759	944,528	402,252	289,923	134,138	775,156	100,000	30,130
Texas	6,250,160	3,637,162	1,272,418	—	1,713,320	899,678	5,754,523	2,866,003	840,981	866,084	359,193	1,943,212	187,220	63,560
Utah	786,663	398,801	174,401	104,919	265,781	122,081	809,336	448,151	98,567	81,758	30,673	88,924	6,850	6,706
Vermont	397,929	186,995	26,523	55,140	143,371	67,563	411,128	138,340	58,103	74,015	13,949	461,606	71,460	25,613
Virginia	2,917,520	1,662,677	361,125	547,125	779,623	475,220	3,040,962	1,238,333	618,265	406,427	203,640	691,367	75,870	37,153
Washington	2,631,677	1,554,074	871,418	—	770,639	306,964	2,665,762	1,205,602	349,687	417,343	74,287	1,272,036	159,918	48,157
West Virginia	1,300,647	742,872	360,761	119,237	447,944	109,831	1,230,731	437,546	376,158	124,219	49,717	1,062,648	168,900	39,098
Wisconsin	3,310,232	2,140,836	510,379	873,723	792,038	377,358	3,406,685	1,212,248	290,400	653,805	128,160	1,009,601	75,000	49,165
Wyoming	336,743	154,268	73,235	—	130,407	52,068	300,645	97,554	89,164	17,543	9,933	77,285	3,230	1,250
TOTAL	134,611,410	80,154,888	24,780,056	18,818,789	37,827,222	16,629,300	138,303,990	54,012,300	17,482,945	25,558,918	7,094,587	72,127,377	8,391,869	2,920,287

Fiscal year ending June 30, 1975, except Alabama, September 30; New York, March 31; and Texas, August 31. *Long term only.
Source: U.S. Department of Commerce, Bureau of the Census, *State Government Finances in 1975.*

Education

Public elementary and secondary schools

Fall 1975 estimates

State	ENROLLMENT		INSTRUCTIONAL STAFF				TEACHERS' AVERAGE ANNUAL SALARIES		STUDENT-TEACHER RATIO		Expenditure per pupil
	Elementary	Secondary	Total*	Principals and supervisors	Teachers, elementary	Teachers, secondary	Elementary	Secondary	Elementary	Secondary	
Alabama	383,386	372,995	38,853	2,178	17,878	18,797	$10,495	$10,702	21.4	19.8	$1,027
Alaska	50,874	38,004	4,884	240	2,112	2,182	19,899	19,857	24.1	17.4	2,026
Arizona	346,380	146,615	25,903	1,132	16,249	6,685	11,548	12,710	21.3	21.9	1,330
Arkansas	242,794	213,909	24,370	1,760	10,395	10,861	9,401	9,983	23.4	19.7	978
California	2,645,000	1,758,000	206,550	9,850	111,500	75,800	14,700	16,000	23.7	23.2	1,267
Colorado	303,020	259,980	31,500	1,750	13,000	13,750	11,580	12,400	23.3	18.9	1,361
Connecticut	453,129	203,875	40,210	1,900	19,290	15,700	12,261	13,098	23.5	13.0	1,601
Delaware	64,512	62,964	7,218	385	2,633	3,702	12,346	12,686	24.5	17.0	1,491
District of Columbia	72,019	57,950	7,873	522	3,762	2,936	...	...	19.1	19.7	1,780
Florida	881,325	813,524	84,488	4,748	37,003	35,847	10,328	10,670	23.8	22.7	1,254
Georgia	656,392	419,650	54,791	2,407	31,447	20,937	10,681	11,091	20.9	20.0	996
Hawaii	92,100	84,600	9,262	615	4,404	3,456	15,209	15,209	20.9	24.5	1,089
Idaho	99,922	96,694	10,109	572	4,301	4,708	10,054	10,345	23.2	20.5	...
Illinois	1,360,000	910,000	126,646	8,100	63,457	47,289	13,567	14,834	21.4	19.2	1,322
Indiana	601,600	564,100	58,360	3,630	26,130	26,200	11,660	12,320	23.0	21.5	1,132
Iowa	314,947	288,972	38,167	1,341	16,069	16,907	10,587	11,847	19.6	17.1	1,373
Kansas	239,337	202,163	28,596	1,400	13,660	11,895	10,166	10,581	17.5	17.0	1,304
Kentucky	432,000	266,000	35,700	1,910	19,640	12,160	9,505	10,210	22.0	21.9	917
Louisiana	507,969	336,432	44,366	2,230	23,619	18,517	9,885	10,352	21.5	18.2	992
Maine	172,000	71,900	12,995	1,100	7,000	4,765	9,942	10,837	24.6	15.1	1,120
Maryland	456,440	429,084	49,682	3,317	21,446	22,258	13,440	13,959	21.3	19.3	1,529
Massachusetts	615,340	571,310	76,400	5,000	30,700	33,400	11,800	12,000	20.0	17.1	1,331
Michigan	1,064,800	1,073,850	103,178	6,950	44,903	43,900	14,200	14,780	23.7	24.5	...
Minnesota	436,100	452,750	49,270	2,920	19,500	24,250	12,663	13,906	22.4	18.7	1,410
Mississippi	286,645	225,222	26,430	1,610	12,995	10,595	9,114	9,573	22.1	21.3	943
Missouri	645,886	319,474	55,208	3,312	24,666	23,599	10,349	10,638	26.2	13.5	...
Montana	114,696	57,137	10,495	530	5,260	4,185	10,121	11,189	21.8	13.6	1,525
Nebraska	168,032	145,542	19,697	1,225	9,362	8,880	9,403	10,664	17.9	16.4	1,274
Nevada	73,434	66,234	6,560	370	2,960	2,790	13,300	13,500	24.8	23.7	1,160
New Hampshire	103,392	71,196	10,095	700	4,825	3,950	10,310	10,720	21.4	18.0	1,000
New Jersey	920,000	534,000	96,000	6,200	47,700	32,400	13,195	13,683	19.3	16.5	1,718
New Mexico	133,681	140,931	14,522	1,100	6,512	6,340	11,000	11,010	20.5	22.2	1,200
New York	1,753,293	1,647,921	217,470	14,654	90,607	98,523	15,615	16,258	19.4	16.7	1,962
North Carolina	817,540	365,164	59,415	2,582	36,104	18,158	10,693	11,582	22.6	20.1	998
North Dakota	83,747	47,584	8,281	338	4,475	3,110	9,322	11,725	18.7	15.3	1,167
Ohio	1,337,060	946,584	120,600	6,800	53,100	51,200	11,150	11,750	25.2	18.5	1,176
Oklahoma	315,000	274,000	32,577	1,650	15,112	14,650	9,400	9,850	20.8	18.7	1,079
Oregon	278,615	198,385	27,284	1,585	11,680	10,489	11,602	12,210	23.8	18.9	1,404
Pennsylvania	1,127,800	1,113,300	129,200	5,400	57,400	58,200	12,200	12,500	19.6	19.1	1,532
Rhode Island	101,491	74,826	10,560	551	5,171	4,025	12,508	13,637	19.6	18.6	1,494
South Carolina	380,057	238,123	32,012	2,192	16,603	11,297	9,658	10,306	22.9	21.1	1,007
South Dakota	99,699	51,182	8,953	450	5,222	2,861	9,030	9,345	19.1	17.9	1,050
Tennessee	525,952	352,833	44,496	2,177	24,568	15,287	10,062	10,681	21.4	23.1	915
Texas	1,522,833	1,277,367	160,000	7,510	75,925	67,465	11,206	11,529	20.1	18.9	1,016
Utah	163,453	146,255	14,167	800	6,392	6,265	11,150	11,570	25.6	23.3	1,020
Vermont	63,160	41,170	7,320	770	2,910	3,165	9,575	10,250	21.7	13.0	1,342
Virginia	685,782	417,887	62,475	4,125	33,700	24,650	10,750	11,900	20.3	16.9	1,153
Washington	398,825	386,624	40,450	3,215	18,300	15,250	13,270	14,035	21.8	25.3	1,350
West Virginia	229,919	173,728	22,500	1,597	10,995	9,143	10,456	10,780	20.9	19.0	1,015
Wisconsin	539,731	424,488	52,689	2,430	26,480	23,779	12,005	12,736	20.4	17.8	1,450
Wyoming	44,140	44,044	5,858	389	2,573	2,611	11,000	11,250	17.2	16.9	1,482
TOTAL U.S.	25,405,249	19,476,522	2,464,685	140,219	1,171,695	1,009,769	$12,130	$12,844	21.7	19.3	$1,295

Kindergartens included in elementary schools; junior high schools, in secondary schools.
*Includes librarians, guidance and psychological personnel, and related educational workers.
Source: National Education Association, Research Division, *Estimates of School Statistics, 1975-76* (Copyright 1976. All rights reserved. Used by permission).

Universities and colleges

state statistics

State	NUMBER OF INSTITUTIONS 1975–1976		Enrollment*† fall, 1975	EARNED DEGREES CONFERRED 1973–1974		
	Total	Public		Bachelor's and first professional	Master's except first professional	Doctor's
Alabama	56	34	136,000	15,085	4,262	273
Alaska	9	7	14,000	638	211	9
Arizona	22	17	132,000	9,015	3,678	421
Arkansas	29	16	56,000	7,287	1,269	116
California	247	131	1,312,000	91,845	24,549	3,699
Colorado	39	27	130,000	14,698	4,262	715
Connecticut	46	22	150,000	14,831	5,999	577
Delaware	10	6	29,000	2,551	464	68
District of Columbia	18	3	84,000	9,153	5,027	559
Florida	74	37	277,000	28,049	6,530	762
Georgia	66	33	152,000	17,954	6,819	545
Hawaii	12	9	37,000	3,860	1,423	109
Idaho	9	6	34,000	3,115	567	69
Illinois	147	60	468,000	50,904	16,040	2,165
Indiana	64	23	199,000	27,007	10,155	1,298
Iowa	63	24	104,000	15,378	2,413	565
Kansas	52	29	111,000	13,230	3,133	447
Kentucky	38	9	108,000	13,705	4,231	259
Louisiana	30	19	141,000	17,031	4,235	406
Maine	25	10	34,000	4,841	728	29
Maryland	52	30	167,000	16,969	4,337	584
Massachusetts	119	34	343,000	39,367	12,797	2,022
Michigan	93	45	383,000	40,412	13,817	1,582
Minnesota	66	31	165,000	20,377	2,786	575
Mississippi	45	27	78,000	10,234	2,465	241
Missouri	81	27	192,000	23,787	6,229	706
Montana	12	9	28,000	3,924	672	103
Nebraska	30	17	64,000	9,803	1,521	237
Nevada	6	5	20,000	1,393	461	11
New Hampshire	24	10	32,000	5,279	751	51
New Jersey	64	30	263,000	26,056	7,666	597
New Mexico	17	14	50,000	5,361	1,577	218
New York	285	84	962,000	88,665	36,654	3,680
North Carolina	114	72	182,000	24,063	4,530	824
North Dakota	15	11	26,000	4,068	580	82
Ohio	129	59	370,000	50,564	11,262	1,491
Oklahoma	44	29	128,000	14,444	3,758	474
Oregon	43	21	110,000	11,517	3,006	481
Pennsylvania	175	62	423,000	60,221	14,405	1,663
Rhode Island	13	3	59,000	6,307	1,758	220
South Carolina	55	31	110,000	10,849	2,402	134
South Dakota	17	7	27,000	4,935	738	51
Tennessee	67	23	164,000	19,363	4,586	570
Texas	145	90	507,000	52,565	12,712	1,486
Utah	14	9	75,000	9,694	2,371	442
Vermont	23	6	28,000	3,884	1,014	38
Virginia	73	39	205,000	19,365	4,303	501
Washington	47	33	164,000	17,726	3,536	538
West Virginia	28	16	67,000	9,184	1,775	109
Wisconsin	58	30	180,000	24,358	5,319	911
Wyoming	8	8	18,000	1,521	348	85
TOTAL U.S.	3,018	1,434	9,298,000	996,432	276,131	33,798

Excludes service academies. *Excludes non-degree-credit students. †Estimated.
Source: U.S. Department of Health, Education, and Welfare, National Center for Education Statistics, *Digest of Education Statistics*, *Education Directory*, and *Earned Degrees Conferred*.

Level of school completed

25 years old and over, by race

Level of school completed	April 1950	April 1960	March 1970	March 1974	March 1975
Less than 5 years elementary school, percent:					
White	8.7	6.7	4.2	3.5	3.3
Nonwhite	31.4	23.5	14.7	12.2	11.8
4 years of high school or more, percent:					
White	35.5	43.2	57.4	63.3	64.6
Nonwhite	13.4	21.7	36.1	44.3	46.4
4 years of college or more, percent:					
White	6.4	8.1	11.6	14.0	14.5
Nonwhite	2.2	3.5	6.1	8.0	9.1
Median school years completed:					
White	9.7	10.8	12.2	12.4	12.4
Nonwhite	6.9	8.2	10.1	11.1	11.4

Source: U.S. Department of Health, Education, and Welfare, National Center for Education Statistics, *Digest of Education Statistics*, 1975 edition.

Cost of attending college

in current dollars

Expenditure	1965–66		1970–71		1975–76	
	Public	Private	Public	Private	Public	Private
Tuition and required fees						
Universities	327	1,369	478	1,981	731	3,013
Other 4-year institutions	240	1,086	333	1,603	574	2,444
2-year institutions	109	768	186	1,110	322	1,667
Board rates						
Universities	473	529	568	640	746	860
Other 4-year institutions	408	482	500	562	689	730
2-year institutions	367	473	492	560	727	744
Charges for dormitory rooms						
Universities	305	418	432	542	627	771
Other 4-year institutions	254	329	376	433	600	615
2-year institutions	194	316	339	434	540	601

Data are estimated for the entire academic year and are average charges per full-time resident degree-credit student.
Source: U.S. Department of Health, Education, and Welfare, National Center for Education Statistics, *Digest of Education Statistics*, 1975 edition.

Universities and colleges, 1975–76*

Selected four-year schools

Institution	Location	Year founded	Total students†	Total faculty‡	Bound library volumes
ALABAMA					
Alabama A. & M. U.	Normal	1875	4,046	234	182,100
Alabama State U.	Montgomery	1874	3,158	179	133,800
Auburn U.	Auburn	1856	17,044	896	784,000
Birmingham-Southern	Birmingham	1856	872	76	107,400
Jacksonville State U.	Jacksonville	1883	5,606	240	241,200
Troy State U.	Troy	1887	3,483	143	250,000
Tuskegee Institute	Tuskegee Institute	1881	3,262	316	...
U. of Alabama	University	1831	13,819	756	861,500
U. of South Alabama	Mobile	1963	6,146	366	202,000
ALASKA					
U. of Alaska	Fairbanks	1917	3,401	220	303,500
ARIZONA					
Arizona State U.	Tempe	1885	36,441	1,262	1,227,600
Northern Arizona U.	Flagstaff	1899	12,000	500§	500,000
U. of Arizona	Tucson	1885	29,123	1,768	898,400
ARKANSAS					
Arkansas State U.	State University	1909	7,979	664	279,800
U. of Arkansas	Fayetteville	1871	11,448	676	737,300
U. of A. at Little Rock	Little Rock	1927	8,104	364	205,300
U. of A. at Monticello	Monticello	1909	1,563	112	70,000
U. of Central Arkansas	Conway	1907	4,685	265	200,000
CALIFORNIA					
California Inst. of Tech.	Pasadena	1891	1,544	458	285,000
Cal. Polytech. State U.	San Luis Obispo	1901	15,158	939	486,300
Cal. State, Bakersfield	Bakersfield	1965	3,115	165	166,400
Cal. State, Dominguez Hills	Dominguez Hills	1960	7,000	300	175,000
Cal. State, San Bernardino	San Bernardino	1962	3,500	205	200,000
Cal. State, Sonoma	Rohnert Park	1960	6,004	474	200,000
Cal. State, Stanislaus	Turlock	1957	3,180	185	160,000
Cal. State Polytech. U.	Pomona	1938	12,651	640	302,400
Cal. State U., Chico	Chico	1887	13,010	920	424,100
Cal. State U., Fresno	Fresno	1911	15,218	1,132	510,200
Cal. State U., Fullerton	Fullerton	1957	21,700	1,387	386,200
Cal. State U., Hayward	Hayward	1957	11,771	550	440,000
Cal. State U., Long Beach	Long Beach	1949	31,785	1,819	614,000
Cal. State U., Los Angeles	Los Angeles	1947	27,300	1,100	650,000
Cal. State U., Northridge	Northridge	1958	27,778	1,496	500,000
Cal. State U., Sacramento	Sacramento	1947	21,000	935§	500,000
Golden Gate U.	San Francisco	1901	8,350	588	150,000
Humboldt State U.	Arcata	1913	7,500	506	179,500
Loma Linda U.	Riverside	1905	3,873	1,285	264,900
Loyola Marymount U.	Los Angeles	1911	5,250	311	316,000
Occidental	Los Angeles	1887	1,750	120	270,000
Pepperdine U.	Los Angeles	1937	3,830§	311	159,500
San Francisco State U.	San Francisco	1899	22,983	1,300	488,100
San Jose State U.	San Jose	1857	27,221	1,500	700,000
Stanford U.	Stanford	1885	12,469	1,327	3,982,000
U. of C., Berkeley	Berkeley	1868	28,106	1,832	4,000,000
U. of C., Davis	Davis	1905	17,648	1,266	1,359,900
U. of C., Irvine	Irvine	1960	9,547	724	716,500
U. of C., Los Angeles	Los Angeles	1919	28,638	2,527	3,500,000
U. of C., Riverside	Riverside	1868	4,732	352	800,000
U. of C., San Diego	La Jolla	1912	9,000	450	1,200,000
U. of C., Santa Barbara	Santa Barbara	1944	14,584	862	1,200,000
U. of C., Santa Cruz	Santa Cruz	1965	6,158	430	514,700
U. of the Pacific	Stockton	1851	4,200	272§	301,900
U. of Redlands	Redlands	1907	2,498	111	193,500
U. of San Francisco	San Francisco	1855	6,236	229	441,700
U. of Santa Clara	Santa Clara	1851	7,010	289	396,000
U. of Southern California	Los Angeles	1880	24,174	1,426	1,650,000
COLORADO					
Colorado	Colorado Springs	1874	1,925	160	300,000
Colorado School of Mines	Golden	1874	1,687	174	158,000
Colorado State U.	Fort Collins	1870	16,809	1,110§	1,000,000
Metropolitan State	Denver	1963	10,256	331	150,000
‖U.S. Air Force Academy	USAF Academy	1954	4,500	560	263,000
U. of Colorado	Boulder	1876	22,420	1,102§	1,525,800
U. of Denver	Denver	1864	7,708	368§	1,000,000
U. of Northern Colorado	Greeley	1889	10,829	798	250,000
U. of Southern Colorado	Pueblo	1933	5,458	607	165,000
CONNECTICUT					
Central Connecticut State	New Britain	1849	13,432	455	300,000
Fairfield U.	Fairfield	1942	4,865	273	245,000
Southern Connecticut State	New Haven	1893	12,798	457	500,000
Trinity	Hartford	1823	2,002	154	536,000
‖U.S. Coast Guard Acad.	New London	1876	1,088	130	90,000
U. of Bridgeport	Bridgeport	1927	7,200	345	240,300
U. of Connecticut	Storrs	1881	20,946	1,915§	1,325,000
U. of Hartford	West Hartford	1877	8,939	355	246,500
U. of New Haven	West Haven	1920	5,835	400	100,000
Wesleyan U.	Middletown	1831	2,499	313	784,500
Western Connecticut State	Danbury	1903	5,123	180	106,300
Yale U.	New Haven	1701	9,900	1,516	6,500,000
DELAWARE					
Delaware State	Dover	1891	2,219	114	61,000
U. of Delaware	Newark	1833	18,511	1,166	945,400
DISTRICT OF COLUMBIA					
American U.	Washington	1893	13,881	784	430,100
Catholic U. of America	Washington	1887	7,061	543	900,000
George Washington U.	Washington	1821	21,529	2,384	632,200
Georgetown U.	Washington	1789	11,043	1,284	868,300
Howard U.	Washington	1867	9,228	997§	843,700
FLORIDA					
Florida A. & M. U.	Tallahassee	1887	5,130	250	243,000
Florida State U.	Tallahassee	1857	20,589	1,233	1,017,100
Florida Tech. U.	Orlando	1963	8,500	453	200,000
Rollins	Winter Park	1885	3,535	170	172,000
U. of Florida	Gainesville	1853	28,184	2,603	1,800,000
U. of Miami	Coral Gables	1925	18,034	1,388	1,178,200
U. of South Florida	Tampa	1960	19,300	900	407,800
U. of West Florida	Pensacola	1963	4,906	258	229,900
GEORGIA					
Atlanta U.	Atlanta	1865	1,090	166	300,000
Augusta	Augusta	1925	4,100	157	183,500
Emory U.	Atlanta	1836	6,746	1,024	1,051,700
Georgia	Milledgeville	1889	3,490	173	117,000
Georgia Inst. of Tech.	Atlanta	1885	8,300	700	800,000
Georgia Southern	Statesboro	1906	6,125	346	168,900
Georgia State U.	Atlanta	1913	20,283	950	512,900
Mercer U.	Macon	1833	2,205	130	180,000
‖Morehouse	Atlanta	1867	1,275	100	30,000
Oglethorpe U.	Atlanta	1835	834	45	58,400
¶Spelman	Atlanta	1881	1,155	100	38,600
U. of Georgia	Athens	1785	21,442	2,140	1,522,700
HAWAII					
Brigham Young U.-Hawaii	Laie	1955	1,104	77	60,000
U. of Hawaii	Honolulu	1907	20,961	1,392	1,379,900
IDAHO					
Boise State U.	Boise	1932	10,049	450	280,000
Idaho State U.	Pocatello	1901	8,500	400	200,000
U. of Idaho	Moscow	1889	7,138	528	815,100
ILLINOIS					
Augustana	Rock Island	1860	2,200	149	191,100
Bradley U.	Peoria	1897	5,025	320	325,000
Chicago State U.	Chicago	1869	6,615	347	178,700
Concordia Teachers	River Forest	1864	1,272	101	111,000
De Paul U.	Chicago	1898	10,010	552	356,400
Eastern Illinois U.	Charleston	1895	8,994	500	337,000
Illinois Inst. of Tech.	Chicago	1892	6,317	735	1,338,000
Illinois State U.	Normal	1857	19,048	988	650,000
Knox	Galesburg	1837	1,220	95	158,800
Lake Forest	Lake Forest	1857	1,050	90	152,000
Loyola U.	Chicago	1870	14,000	610	654,000
Northeastern Ill. State U.	Chicago	1869	9,945	420	259,900
Northern Illinois U.	DeKalb	1895	19,971	1,355	648,000
Northwestern U.	Evanston	1851	15,500	1,653	2,300,000
Southern Illinois U.	Carbondale	1869	22,119	1,431	1,450,700
SIU at Edwardsville	Edwardsville	1957	13,607	829	606,000
U. of Chicago	Chicago	1891	9,037	1,045	3,762,100

Universities and colleges (continued)

Selected four-year schools

Institution	Location	Year founded	Total students†	Total faculty‡	Bound library volumes
U. of Illinois	Urbana	1867	35,117	1,882	5,368,700
Chicago Circle Campus	Chicago	1965	25,230	1,690	885,821
Western Illinois U.	Macomb	1899	14,218	729	321,200
Wheaton	Wheaton	1860	2,234	163	156,000
INDIANA					
Ball State U.	Muncie	1918	17,400	895	729,900
Butler U.	Indianapolis	1855	4,200	225	360,000
De Pauw U.	Greencastle	1837	2,396	186	318,100
Indiana State U.	Terre Haute	1865	11,012	...	670,000
Indiana U.	Bloomington	1820	30,623	1,682	2,823,700
Purdue U.	West Lafayette	1869	28,923	2,013	1,231,700
U. of Evansville	Evansville	1854	5,075	418	200,000
U. of Notre Dame	Notre Dame	1842	8,808	651	1,115,000
Valparaiso U.	Valparaiso	1859	4,319	305	250,000
IOWA					
Coe	Cedar Rapids	1851	1,162	125	140,000
Drake U.	Des Moines	1881	6,802	433	441,900
Grinnell	Grinnell	1846	1,174	97	228,500
Iowa State U.	Ames	1858	21,205	1,543	1,125,800
U. of Iowa	Iowa City	1847	22,512	1,529	1,956,000
U. of Northern Iowa	Cedar Falls	1876	9,287	575	426,800
KANSAS					
Emporia Kansas State	Emporia	1863	6,511	295	552,000
Kan. State C. of Pittsburg	Pittsburg	1903	5,688	209§	300,000
Kansas State U.	Manhattan	1863	19,650	879	730,000
U. of Kansas	Lawrence	1866	20,395	1,147§	1,684,300
Wichita State U.	Wichita	1895	15,714	818	524,800
KENTUCKY					
Berea	Berea	1855	1,411	133	200,000
Eastern Kentucky U.	Richmond	1906	13,430	581	522,000
Kentucky State U.	Frankfort	1886	2,000	150	105,500
Morehead State U.	Morehead	1922	6,765	350	300,000
Murray State U.	Murray	1922	7,349	349	295,000
U. of Kentucky	Lexington	1865	20,000	1,500	1,200,000
U. of Louisville	Louisville	1798	15,781	1,718	1,000,000
Western Kentucky U.	Bowling Green	1907	13,040	785	431,100
LOUISIANA					
Grambling	Grambling	1901	3,627	252	110,000
Louisiana State U.	Baton Rouge	1860	24,791	1,019	1,529,700
Louisiana Tech. U.	Ruston	1894	8,811	382	206,400
Northeast Louisiana U.	Monroe	1931	9,143	406	225,000
Northwestern State U.	Natchitoches	1884	6,290	320	190,000
Southern U.	Baton Rouge	1880	8,685	397	260,000
Tulane U.	New Orleans	1834	9,048	787	1,192,100
U. of Southwestern La.	Lafayette	1898	13,078	570	387,100
MAINE					
Bates	Lewiston	1864	1,250	100	200,000
Bowdoin	Brunswick	1794	1,348	121	515,000
Colby	Waterville	1813	1,648	132	330,000
U. of Maine, Farmington	Farmington	1864	2,100	120	60,000
U. of Maine, Orono	Orono	1865	8,978	600	500,000
U. of Maine, Portland-Gorham	Portland	1957	9,169	325	231,000
MARYLAND					
¶Goucher	Towson	1885	1,038	119	181,600
Johns Hopkins U.	Baltimore	1876	9,799	1,524	2,049,700
Morgan State U.	Baltimore	1867	6,397	310	164,400
Towson State U.	Baltimore	1866	14,500	450§	257,800
‖U.S. Naval Academy	Annapolis	1845	4,000	545	324,000
U. of Maryland	College Park	1807	35,890	2,255§	1,465,100
MASSACHUSETTS					
Amherst	Amherst	1821	1,334	162	507,000
Boston	Chestnut Hill	1863	15,738	805	933,500
Boston U.	Boston	1869	24,622	1,582	1,820,300
Brandeis U.	Waltham	1948	3,400	360	658,000
Clark U.	Worcester	1887	3,237	256	330,000
Harvard U.	Cambridge	1636	20,498	3,860	8,500,000
¶Radcliffe	Cambridge	1879	1,673	♀	♂
Holy Cross	Worcester	1843	2,694	183	310,000
Mass. Inst. of Tech.	Cambridge	1861	8,482	1,155	1,600,000
¶Mt. Holyoke	South Hadley	1837	1,850	175	380,000
Northeastern U.	Boston	1898	42,709	1,800	375,000
Salem State	Salem	1854	4,373	292	100,000
¶Simmons	Boston	1899	2,804	150	170,000
Smith	Northampton	1871	2,404	240	803,000
Tufts U.	Medford	1852	5,126	486	452,800
U. of Lowell	Lowell	1895	10,000	300	145,000
U. of Massachusetts	Amherst	1863	24,128	1,000	850,000
¶Wellesley	Wellesley	1870	2,026	245	500,000
¶Wheaton	Norton	1834	1,275	121	184,000
Williams	Williamstown	1793	1,962	185	400,000
MICHIGAN					
Albion	Albion	1835	1,757	122	190,000
Central Michigan U.	Mt. Pleasant	1892	15,708	740	549,800
Eastern Michigan U.	Ypsilanti	1849	18,568	746	456,700
Ferris State	Big Rapids	1884	9,934	515	167,700
Hope	Holland	1866	2,198	150	153,600
Michigan State U.	East Lansing	1855	40,624	2,311	2,000,000
Michigan Tech. U.	Houghton	1885	5,366	402	293,200
Northern Michigan U.	Marquette	1899	8,187	312	281,200
Oakland U.	Rochester	1957	9,704	400	250,000
U. of Detroit	Detroit	1877	8,268	526	479,000
U. of Michigan	Ann Arbor	1817	37,505	4,487	4,790,800
Wayne State U.	Detroit	1868	38,073	2,182	1,663,300
Western Michigan U.	Kalamazoo	1903	21,361	942	879,000
MINNESOTA					
Carleton	Northfield	1866	1,636	150	242,900
Concordia	Moorhead	1891	2,402	168	198,000
Gustavus Adolphus	St. Peter	1862	1,959	132	130,400
Hamline U.	St. Paul	1854	1,327	100	138,600
Macalester	St. Paul	1874	1,748	166	255,000
Mankato State U.	Mankato	1867	13,130	629	400,000

Institution	Location	Year founded	Total students†	Total faculty‡	Bound library volumes
Moorhead State U.	Moorhead	1885	6,103	320	210,000
¶St. Catherine	St. Paul	1905	1,688	105	195,000
St. Cloud State U.	St. Cloud	1869	11,198	466	466,400
‖St. John's U.	Collegeville	1857	1,888	101	250,000
St. Olaf	Northfield	1874	2,760	251	268,700
‖St. Thomas	St. Paul	1885	2,707	149	169,000
U. of Minnesota	Minneapolis	1851	42,970	5,055	3,071,600
Winona State U.	Winona	1858	4,533	231	172,000
MISSISSIPPI					
Alcorn State U.	Lorman	1871	2,568	106	65,000
Jackson State U.	Jackson	1877	5,205	350	200,900
Mississippi	Clinton	1826	3,000	130	150,000
Mississippi U. for Women	Columbus	1884	2,700	164	350,000
Mississippi State U.	Mississippi State	1878	11,709	664	545,900
U. of Mississippi	University	1848	8,434	442	548,800
U. of Southern Mississippi	Hattiesburg	1910	9,200	600	525,500
MISSOURI					
Central Missouri State U.	Warrensburg	1871	7,346	425	352,500
Northeast Missouri State U.	Kirksville	1867	5,231	295	238,000
Northwest Missouri State U.	Maryville	1905	4,503	244	166,900
St. Louis U.	St. Louis	1818	10,329	1,759	911,400
Southeast Missouri State U.	Cape Girardeau	1873	7,632	376	225,000
Southwest Missouri State U.	Springfield	1906	12,153	644	305,000
U. of Missouri-Columbia	Columbia	1839	23,524	3,515	1,571,800
U. of Missouri-Kansas City	Kansas City	1933	11,387	1,552	402,800
U. of Missouri-Rolla	Rolla	1870	4,451	670	245,200
U. of Missouri-St. Louis	St. Louis	1963	11,843	562	352,400
Washington U.	St. Louis	1853	10,917	2,085	1,500,000
MONTANA					
Montana State U.	Bozeman	1893	9,063	634	639,200
U. of Montana	Missoula	1893	8,566	466	500,000
NEBRASKA					
Creighton U.	Omaha	1878	4,745	749	423,800
Kearney State	Kearney	1905	5,119	200	228,600
U. of Nebraska	Lincoln	1869	20,892	990	1,160,300
U. of Nebraska at Omaha	Omaha	1908	13,575	542	368,000
Wayne State	Wayne	1910	2,032	94	138,100
NEVADA					
U. of Nevada-Las Vegas	Las Vegas	1951	8,916	347§	314,200
U. of Nevada-Reno	Reno	1874	8,326	617	513,000
NEW HAMPSHIRE					
Dartmouth	Hanover	1769	3,849	383	1,009,200
U. of New Hampshire	Durham	1866	11,987	658	698,800
NEW JERSEY					
Fairleigh Dickinson U.	Rutherford	1941	4,845	340	196,800
Glassboro State	Glassboro	1923	12,000	...	225,000
Jersey City State	Jersey City	1927	10,965	440	160,400
Kean Col. of N.J.	Union	1855	12,462	681	190,000
Monmouth	West Long Branch	1933	3,957	203	185,000
Montclair State	Upper Montclair	1908	14,790	585§	209,400
Princeton U.	Princeton	1746	5,735	725	3,000,000
Rider	Lawrenceville	1865	5,700	248	180,000
Rutgers State U.	New Brunswick	1766	46,305	3,465	1,839,900
Seton Hall U.	South Orange	1856	8,289	550	300,000
Stevens Inst. of Tech.	Hoboken	1870	2,075	189	97,500
Trenton State	Trenton	1855	10,613	524	300,000
Upsala	East Orange	1893	1,703	97	132,300
William Patterson	Wayne	1855	12,981	443	235,000
NEW MEXICO					
New Mexico State U.	Las Cruces	1888	11,649	527	500,000
U. of New Mexico	Albuquerque	1889	21,529	936	800,000
NEW YORK					
Adelphi U.	Garden City	1896	10,250	718	300,000
Alfred U.	Alfred	1836	2,088	183	190,600
Canisius	Buffalo	1870	3,827	249	195,000
City U. of New York					
Bernard M. Baruch	New York	1919	17,746	1,250	200,000
Brooklyn	Brooklyn	1930	33,882	2,505	541,000
City	New York	1847	20,388	1,438	900,000
Herbert H. Lehman	Bronx	1931	13,693	1,250	286,000
Hunter	New York	1870	24,000	2,500	400,000
Queens	Flushing	1937	30,077	2,007	439,500
Richmond	Staten Island	1965	4,011	280	165,000
York	Jamaica	1966	6,017	371	120,000
Colgate U.	Hamilton	1819	2,500§	205§	320,000
Columbia U.	New York	1754	15,432	3,500	4,474,000
¶Barnard	New York	1889	2,005	141	135,000
Teachers	New York	1887	6,107	222	450,000
Cooper Union	New York	1859	893	156	100,000
Cornell U.	Ithaca	1865	16,208§	1,460	4,000,000
Elmira	Elmira	1855	3,750	104	125,000
Fordham U.	Bronx	1841	6,081	359	1,075,300
Hofstra U.	Hempstead	1935	10,793	419	575,400
Ithaca	Ithaca	1892	4,000	350	220,000
Juilliard School	New York	1905	1,233	186	42,000
Long Island U.	Greenvale	1926	18,788	1,000	400,000
‖Manhattan	Bronx	1853	4,229	282	204,500
‖Marymount	Tarrytown	1907	1,038	102	96,000
New School for Soc. Res.	New York	1919	3,639	500	135,000
New York U.	New York	1831	40,834	1,900	2,456,000
Niagara U.	Niagara University	1856	3,750	199	175,000
Pace U.	New York	1906	8,700	460	216,500
Polytechnic Inst. of N.Y.	Brooklyn	1854	4,500	235	222,000
Pratt Inst.	Brooklyn	1887	4,551	488	216,060
Rensselaer Polytech. Inst.	Troy	1824	5,087	324	245,100
Rochester Inst. of Tech.	Rochester	1829	10,247	729	142,100
St. Bonaventure U.	St. Bonaventure	1859	2,347	160	211,000
St. John's U.	Jamaica	1870	13,450	688	790,000
St. Lawrence U.	Canton	1856	2,330	146	241,000
State U. of N.Y. at Albany	Albany	1844	15,450	934	850,000
SUNY at Binghamton	Binghamton	1946	9,107	538	546,100
SUNY at Buffalo	Buffalo	1846	26,000	1,900	1,678,400
SUNY at Stony Brook	Stony Brook	1957	14,849	732	905,500

Institution	Location	Year founded	Total students†	Total faculty‡	Bound library volumes
State U. Colleges					
Brockport	Brockport	1867	11,696	593	260,600
Buffalo	Buffalo	1867	12,383	560	280,000
Cortland	Cortland	1868	6,075	356	200,000
Fredonia	Fredonia	1867	5,232	279	237,100
Geneseo	Geneseo	1867	6,374	341	290,000
New Paltz	New Paltz	1828	8,497	450	300,000
Oneonta	Oneonta	1889	6,806	396	256,000
Oswego	Oswego	1861	9,143	468	305,400
Plattsburgh	Plattsburgh	1889	6,709	336§	260,000
Potsdam	Potsdam	1816	5,045	301	232,900
Syracuse U.	Syracuse	1870	19,356	1,303	1,637,400
‖U.S. Merchant Marine Acad.	Kings Point	1938	1,000	92	74,900
‖U.S. Military Academy	West Point	1802	4,000	500	400,000
U. of Rochester	Rochester	1850	8,380	2,287	2,250,000
Vassar	Poughkeepsie	1861	2,190	221	444,000
Wagner	Staten Island	1883	2,500	195	250,000
Yeshiva U.	New York	1886	3,328	2,425	605,100
NORTH CAROLINA					
Appalachian State U.	Boone	1899	8,541	448	309,200
Catawba	Salisbury	1851	1,147	82	100,000
‖Davidson	Davidson	1837	1,350	100	215,000
Duke U.	Durham	1838	8,513	794	2,764,300
East Carolina U.	Greenville	1907	11,725	685	458,200
Lenoir Rhyne	Hickory	1891	1,333	101	93,100
N. Carolina A. & T. St. U.	Greensboro	1891	4,937	288	262,500
N. Carolina Central U.	Durham	1910	4,062	262	272,200
N. Carolina State U.	Raleigh	1887	17,420	1,200	700,000
U. of N.C. at Chapel Hill	Chapel Hill	1789	20,536	1,632	2,900,000
U. of N.C. at Charlotte	Charlotte	1946	7,570	474	207,500
U. of N.C. at Greensboro	Greensboro	1891	9,733	610	850,000
U. of N.C. at Wilmington	Wilmington	1947	3,309	183	134,800
Wake Forest U.	Winston-Salem	1834	4,442	467	603,700
Western Carolina U.	Cullowhee	1889	5,934	300	215,000
NORTH DAKOTA					
North Dakota State U.	Fargo	1890	6,957	328	300,000
U. of North Dakota	Grand Forks	1883	8,632	869	368,100
OHIO					
Antioch	Yellow Springs	1852	1,330	98	218,700
Bowling Green State U.	Bowling Green	1910	16,263	718	550,000
Case Western Reserve U.	Cleveland	1826	8,843	1,400	1,556,400
Cleveland State U.	Cleveland	1964	16,261	674	427,500
Denison U.	Granville	1831	2,129	167	219,500
John Carroll U.	Cleveland	1886	3,600	200	340,000
Kent State U.	Kent	1910	20,060	1,000§	1,125,000
Kenyon	Gambier	1824	1,406	108	238,000
Marietta	Marietta	1835	1,795	119	200,000
Miami U.	Oxford	1809	14,655	632	826,000
Oberlin	Oberlin	1833	2,757	187§	860,000
Ohio State U.	Columbus	1870	49,275	3,428□	2,911,800□
Ohio U.	Athens	1804	13,144	745	848,300
U. of Akron	Akron	1870	21,757	982	833,000
U. of Cincinnati	Cincinnati	1819	33,946	3,046	1,152,500
U. of Dayton	Dayton	1850	8,700	560	430,000
U. of Toledo	Toledo	1872	15,742	670	306,400
Wooster	Wooster	1866	1,850	150	200,000
Xavier U.	Cincinnati	1831	6,267	277	170,000
Youngstown State U.	Youngstown	1908	15,573	720	363,000
OKLAHOMA					
Central State U.	Edmond	1890	11,953	341	322,400
Oklahoma State U.	Stillwater	1890	19,281	1,475	1,132,000
U. of Oklahoma	Norman	1890	23,995	1,521	1,544,100
U. of Tulsa	Tulsa	1894	6,540	362	580,700
OREGON					
Lewis and Clark	Portland	1867	2,333	145	164,900
Oregon State U.	Corvallis	1868	16,601	1,095	758,000
Portland State U.	Portland	1946	15,320	665	496,000
Reed	Portland	1909	1,183	105	238,000
U. of Oregon	Eugene	1872	17,384	1,082§	1,200,000
PENNSYLVANIA					
Allegheny	Meadville	1815	1,804	120	300,000
¶Bryn Mawr	Bryn Mawr	1885	1,615	194	450,000
Bucknell U.	Lewisburg	1846	3,248	250	372,000
Carnegie-Mellon U.	Pittsburgh	1900	4,842	522	510,800
Dickinson	Carlisle	1773	1,683	110	240,000
Drexel U.	Philadelphia	1891	9,275	520	300,000
Duquesne U.	Pittsburgh	1878	7,221	484	360,000
Edinboro State	Edinboro	1857	7,041	434	312,200
Franklin and Marshall	Lancaster	1787	2,190	146	250,000
Gettysburg	Gettysburg	1832	1,915	169	220,000
Indiana U. of Pa.	Indiana	1875	11,200	630	475,000
Juniata	Huntingdon	1876	1,173	100	165,000
Lafayette	Easton	1826	2,231	163	300,000
La Salle	Philadelphia	1863	5,522	348	190,900
Lehigh U.	Bethlehem	1865	6,284	367	630,000
Moravian	Bethlehem	1742	1,672	80	125,000
Muhlenberg	Allentown	1848	1,617	121	164,800
Pennsylvania State U.	University Park	1855	39,077	1,739	1,332,500
St. Joseph's	Philadelphia	1851	5,911	229	160,300
Slippery Rock State	Slippery Rock	1889	6,299	374	327,600
Susquehanna U.	Selinsgrove	1858	1,433	126	105,000
Swarthmore	Swarthmore	1864	1,254	146	378,300
Temple U.	Philadelphia	1884	34,950	1,990	1,000,000
U. of Pennsylvania	Philadelphia	1740	19,435	4,635	2,500,000
U. of Pittsburgh	Pittsburgh	1787	29,888	2,451	1,643,600
Ursinus	Collegeville	1869	1,799	135	110,000
Villanova U.	Villanova	1842	9,910	474	530,000
West Chester State	West Chester	1812	7,200	463	331,400
PUERTO RICO					
Catholic U.	Ponce	1948	8,101	438	124,000
Inter American U.	San Germán	1912	16,952	774	78,000
U. of Puerto Rico	Río Piedras	1903	26,357	...	879,000

Institution	Location	Year founded	Total students†	Total faculty‡	Bound library volumes
RHODE ISLAND					
Brown U.	Providence	1764	6,766	492	1,531,000
Rhode Island	Providence	1854	8,385	362	170,000
U. of Rhode Island	Kingston	1892	10,585	900	527,800
SOUTH CAROLINA					
‖The Citadel	Charleston	1842	2,964	154	123,100
Clemson U.	Clemson	1889	10,112	689	507,000
Furman U.	Greenville	1826	2,563	139	214,400
U. of South Carolina	Columbia	1801	20,278	712	1,140,000
SOUTH DAKOTA					
South Dakota State U.	Brookings	1881	6,412	382	275,000
U. of South Dakota	Vermillion	1882	5,190	391	361,600
TENNESSEE					
Austin Peay State U.	Clarksville	1929	4,124	175	150,000
East Tennessee State U.	Johnson City	1911	9,285	641	370,000
Fisk U.	Nashville	1867	1,559	110	170,300
Memphis State U.	Memphis	1909	22,349	799	700,000
Middle Tennessee State U.	Murfreesboro	1911	9,706	432	264,200
Tennessee State U.	Nashville	1909	4,670	319	221,400
Tennessee Tech. U.	Cookeville	1911	7,062	300	361,000
U. of Tennessee	Knoxville	1794	29,804	1,420	1,239,000
Vanderbilt U.	Nashville	1873	7,034	1,488	1,301,600
TEXAS					
Austin	Sherman	1849	1,216	92	142,200
Baylor U.	Waco	1845	8,628	459§	752,000
East Texas State U.	Commerce	1889	9,981	647	530,000
Hardin-Simmons U.	Abilene	1891	1,630	110	139,500
Lamar U.	Beaumont	1923	11,852	507	259,800
North Texas State U.	Denton	1890	15,875	1,084	1,034,700
Prairie View A. & M.	Prairie View	1876	4,573	292	90,000
Rice U.	Houston	1891	3,587	408	915,000
Sam Houston State U.	Huntsville	1879	10,460	342	491,500
Southern Methodist U.	Dallas	1911	9,643	662	1,363,000
Southwest Texas State U.	San Marcos	1899	12,894	532	365,000
Stephen F. Austin State U.	Nacogdoches	1923	11,414	810	274,000
Sul Ross State U.	Alpine	1917	2,871	130	173,000
Texas A. & I. U.	Kingsville	1925	6,896	297	325,000
Texas A. & M. U.	College Station	1876	21,245	1,276	858,800
Texas Christian U.	Fort Worth	1873	6,018	444	809,800
Texas Southern U.	Houston	1947	7,367	348	228,600
Texas Tech. U.	Lubbock	1923	22,580	1,410	1,501,000
U. of Houston	Houston	1927	29,812	1,646	986,100
U. of Texas at Arlington	Arlington	1895	16,309	844	505,400
U. of Texas at Austin	Austin	1881	42,598	2,727	3,726,100
U. of Texas at El Paso	El Paso	1913	13,614	609	454,300
West Texas State U.	Canyon	1910	6,645	264	203,100
UTAH					
Brigham Young U.	Provo	1875	26,500	1,587	1,300,000
U. of Utah	Salt Lake City	1850	22,575	1,700	1,500,000
Utah State U.	Logan	1888	8,049§	403§	400,000
Weber State	Ogden	1889	9,640	342	230,800
VERMONT					
Bennington	Bennington	1925	600	75	67,600
Middlebury	Middlebury	1800	1,867§	143§	310,800
U. of Vermont	Burlington	1791	10,716	1,000	599,000
VIRGINIA					
Madison	Harrisonburg	1908	6,841	403	209,400
Old Dominion U.	Norfolk	1930	13,192	561	448,400
U. of Richmond	Richmond	1830	3,520	300	321,000
U. of Virginia	Charlottesville	1819	14,382	1,393	1,951,000
Virginia Commonwealth U.	Richmond	1838	18,700	1,463	396,900
‖Virginia Military Inst.	Lexington	1839	1,297	132	243,300
Va. Polytech. Inst. & State U.	Blacksburg	1872	18,816	1,000	627,000
‖Washington & Lee U.	Lexington	1749	1,670	152	260,000
William & Mary	Williamsburg	1693	4,492	414	1,500,000
WASHINGTON					
Central Washington State	Ellensburg	1890	8,677	352	216,500
Eastern Washington State	Cheney	1882	6,200	366	250,000
Gonzaga U.	Spokane	1887	3,046	223	194,800
U. of Washington	Seattle	1861	34,524§	2,085§	2,012,000
Washington State U.	Pullman	1890	16,184	945	975,000
Western Washington State	Bellingham	1893	10,500	450	400,000
Whitman	Walla Walla	1859	1,126	81§	173,000
WEST VIRGINIA					
Bethany	Bethany	1840	1,190	85	126,000
Marshall U.	Huntington	1837	9,774	369	240,000
West Virginia U.	Morgantown	1867	19,258	868	721,100
WISCONSIN					
Beloit	Beloit	1846	1,551	91	236,100
Lawrence U.	Appleton	1847	1,350	127	198,000
Marquette U.	Milwaukee	1881	12,000	710	600,000
St. Norbert	De Pere	1898	1,384	108	92,800
U. of W.-Eau Claire	Eau Claire	1916	9,920	460	479,500
U. of W.-Green Bay	Green Bay	1965	3,874	179	225,000
U. of W.-La Crosse	La Crosse	1908	7,734	325	438,000
U. of W.-Madison	Madison	1848	38,545	2,173	3,000,000
U. of W.-Milwaukee	Milwaukee	1956	24,961	1,642	300,000
U. of W.-Oshkosh	Oshkosh	1871	10,624	448§	443,000
U. of W.-Parkside	Kenosha	1965	5,404	175	240,000
U. of W.-Platteville	Platteville	1866	4,300	273	285,000
U. of W.-River Falls	River Falls	1874	4,433	212§	175,200
U. of W.-Stevens Point	Stevens Point	1894	9,000	450	500,000
U. of W.-Stout	Menomonie	1893	6,000	367§	140,000
U. of W.-Superior	Superior	1893	2,610	165	200,000
U. of W.-Whitewater	Whitewater	1868	8,727	493	262,800
WYOMING					
U. of Wyoming	Laramie	1886	8,500	858	500,000

*Latest data available; coeducational unless otherwise indicated. †Total includes part-time students. ‡Total includes part-time or full-time equivalent faculty. §Total includes full-time equivalent only. ‖Men's school. ¶Women's school. ♀Students taught by faculty of Harvard U. δIncluded with Harvard U. □Includes main campus and other regional campuses.

Living Conditions

Public expenditure for social welfare programs

in millions of dollars

Program	1929	1950	1955	1960	1965	1970	1972	1973	1974	1975
Social insurance	342.4	4,946.6	9,834.9	19,306.7	28,122.8	54,691.2	74,810.2	86,152.7	98,952.1	123,444.1
Old-age, survivors, disability, and health insurance	—	784.1	4,436.3	11,032.3	16,997.5	36,835.4	48,229.1	57,766.6	66,286.6	78,456.3
Health insurance (Medicare)	—	—	—	—	—	7,149.2	8,819.2	9,478.8	11,347.5	14,781.4
Railroad retirement	—	306.4	556.0	934.7	1,128.1	1,609.9	2,141.2	2,477.5	2,692.6	3,085.1
Public employee retirement	113.1	817.9	1,388.5	2,569.9	4,528.5	8,658.7	11,921.3	14,010.8	16,692.1	20,000.0
Unemployment insurance and employment service	—	2,190.1	2,080.6	2,829.6	3,002.6	3,819.5	7,651.0	6,065.9	6,660.7	14,396.5
Railroad unemployment insurance	—	119.6	158.7	215.2	76.7	38.5	86.0	45.2	25.6	41.5
Railroad temporary disability insurance	—	31.1	54.2	68.5	46.5	61.1	42.1	34.9	31.5	33.0
State temporary disability insurance	—	72.1	217.5	347.9	483.5	717.7	783.7	848.2	915.4	994.2
Hospital and medical benefits	—	2.2	20.0	40.2	50.9	62.6	68.3	69.8	70.7	73.3
Workmen's compensation	229.3	625.1	943.0	1,308.5	1,859.4	2,950.4	3,955.7	4,903.6	5,647.6	6,437.5
Hospital and medical benefits	75.0	193.0	315.0	420.0	580.0	985.0	1,185.0	1,335.0	1,560.0	1,830.0
Public aid	60.0	2,496.2	3,003.0	4,101.1	6,283.4	16,487.7	26,077.0	28,696.5	31,997.0	40,536.3
Public assistance	59.9	2,490.2	2,941.1	4,041.7	5,874.9	14,433.5	21,895.0	24,002.6	23,827.4	26,610.6
Vendor medical payments	—	51.3	211.9	492.7	1,367.1	5,212.8	7,751.6	9,208.6	10,371.9	12,968.0
Social services	—	—	—	—	—	712.6	2,160.5	2,306.2	2,155.0	2,522.5
Supplemental security income	—	—	—	—	—	—	—	45.7	2,799.9	6,036.4
Food stamps	—	—	—	—	35.6	576.9	1,865.6	2,218.1	2,818.4	4,677.4
Other	.1	6.0	61.9	59.4	373.0	1,477.3	2,316.4	2,430.2	2,551.3	3,211.2
Health and medical programs	351.1	2,063.5	3,103.1	4,463.8	6,246.4	9,752.8	12,681.6	13,187.5	14,359.7	16,635.7
Hospital and medical care	146.3	1,222.3	2,042.4	2,853.3	3,452.3	5,176.4	6,634.2	7,180.5	7,802.0	8,502.7
Civilian programs	117.1	886.1	1,297.6	1,973.2	2,515.5	3,416.8	4,293.2	4,712.5	5,061.0	5,491.7
Defense Department	29.2	336.2	744.8	880.1	936.8	1,759.6	2,341.0	2,468.0	2,741.0	3,011.0
Maternal and child health programs	6.2	29.8	92.9	141.3	227.3	431.4	495.3	455.3	493.4	540.0
Medical research	—	—	.2	.6	4.3	—	—	—	—	—
Medical research	—	69.2	132.8	448.9	1,165.2	1,561.4	1,772.0	2,001.0	2,092.0	2,424.0
School health (education agencies)	9.4	30.6	65.9	101.0	142.2	246.6	281.3	300.0	—	—
Other public health activities	88.8	350.8	383.7	401.2	671.0	1,405.0	2,075.3	2,151.7	2,625.3	3,457.0
Medical-facilities construction	100.4	360.8	385.4	518.1	588.3	932.1	1,423.5	1,099.0	1,347.0	1,712.0
Defense Department	—	1.1	33.0	40.0	31.1	52.5	100.0	76.0	86.0	157.0
Other	100.4	359.8	352.4	478.1	557.2	879.6	1,323.5	1,023.0	1,261.0	1,555.0
Veterans' programs	657.9	6,865.7	4,833.5	5,479.2	6,031.0	9,078.0	11,522.4	13,026.4	14,112.4	16,660.8
Pensions and compensation	434.7	2,092.1	2,689.7	3,402.7	4,141.4	5,393.8	6,209.3	6,605.8	6,777.4	7,578.3
Health and medical programs	50.9	748.0	761.1	954.0	1,228.7	1,784.0	2,431.4	2,766.1	2,983.6	3,468.9
Hospital and medical care	46.7	582.8	721.5	879.4	1,114.8	1,651.4	2,255.6	2,587.3	2,786.6	3,242.3
Hospital construction	4.2	161.5	34.1	59.6	77.0	70.9	109.8	104.8	118.9	135.7
Medical and prosthetic research	—	3.7	5.6	15.1	36.9	61.8	66.0	74.0	78.0	91.0
Education	—	2,691.6	706.1	409.6	40.9	1,018.5	1,924.6	2,647.9	3,206.8	4,420.6
Life insurance	136.4	475.7	490.2	494.1	434.3	502.3	523.7	532.2	538.5	556.1
Welfare and other	35.8	858.3	186.5	218.8	185.8	379.4	433.3	474.4	606.1	637.0
Education	2,433.7	6,674.1	11,157.2	17,626.2	28,107.9	50,905.0	59,626.2	65,379.1	70,149.5	78,438.5
Elementary and secondary	2,216.2	5,596.2	9,734.3	15,109.0	22,357.7	38,632.3	44,524.0	48,376.9	52,083.5	57,905.4
Construction	377.0	1,019.4	2,231.9	2,661.8	3,267.0	4,659.1	4,458.9	5,008.4	5,259.3	5,487.0
Higher	182.1	914.7	1,214.4	2,190.7	4,826.4	9,970.3	11,850.8	13,259.2	13,893.6	15,972.5
Construction	.2	310.3	198.6	357.9	1,081.4	1,629.1	1,736.7	1,793.4	1,758.7	1,942.0
Vocational and adult	34.9	160.8	204.9	298.0	853.9	2,145.9	3,034.8	3,496.4	3,900.3	4,295.6
Housing	—	14.6	89.3	176.8	318.1	701.2	1,332.4	2,179.6	2,553.8	2,954.0
Public housing	—	14.5	74.7	143.5	234.5	459.9	731.1	1,101.9	1,232.9	1,456.0
Other	—	.1	14.6	33.2	83.6	241.3	601.3	1,077.7	1,320.9	1,498.1
Other social welfare	76.2	447.7	619.0	1,139.4	2,065.7	4,145.2	5,363.9	5,768.2	7,178.1	7,877.5
Vocational rehabilitation	1.6	30.0	42.4	96.3	210.5	703.8	875.5	911.7	926.8	950.0
Medical services	.1	7.4	9.1	17.7	34.2	133.8	179.2	175.0	185.2	190.0
Medical research	—	—	.3	6.6	22.4	29.6	17.0	15.0	—	—
Institutional care	74.7	145.5	195.3	420.5	789.5	201.7	251.1	263.5	284.8	301.8
Child nutrition	—	160.2	239.6	398.7	617.4	896.0	1,502.3	1,707.0	2,023.0	2,517.7
Child welfare	—	104.9	135.1	211.5	354.3	585.3	532.0	526.0	510.0	480.0
Special OEO and Action programs	—	—	—	—	51.7	752.8	782.7	894.9	766.7	602.3
Social welfare, not elsewhere classified	—	7.1	6.5	12.4	42.3	1,005.6	1,420.2	1,465.1	2,666.8	3,025.7
TOTAL	3,921.2	23,508.4	32,639.9	52,293.3	77,175.3	145,761.1	191,413.6	214,389.9	239,302.6	286.547.0

Source: U.S. Department of Health, Education, and Welfare, Social Security Administration, *Social Security Bulletin.*

Health personnel and facilities

State	Physicians 1974*	Dentists 1976	Registered Nurses 1972†	Hospital facilities 1975		Nursing homes 1973	
				Hospitals	Beds	Facilities	Beds
Alabama	3,509	1,221	10,235	147	25,397	197	14,844
Alaska	302	147	2,030	25	1,593	8	606
Arizona	3,772	1,146	12,383	78	10,917	88	6,430
Arkansas	2,039	759	5,033	96	11,696	211	17,952
California	44,093	14,343	103,385	638	123,090	4,145	150,956
Colorado	4,488	1,520	15,515	101	14,612	214	16,670
Connecticut	6,646	2,153	23,612	69	20,063	365	23,294
Delaware	850	262	4,389	15	4,635	36	2,213
District of Columbia	3,249	627	5,545	20	11,050	72	3,147
Florida	14,275	4,772	38,398	239	55,023	360	34,956
Georgia	5,916	1,937	17,423	182	31,284	306	25,936
Hawaii	1,412	568	4,117	29	4,726	142	2,726
Idaho	802	422	3,755	52	3,661	64	4,190
Illinois	17,594	6,053	60,806	289	78,395	1,039	80,151
Indiana	5,919	2,277	21,481	138	35,169	495	34,247
Iowa	3,122	1,447	17,812	144	21,891	678	35,152
Kansas	2,969	1,089	12,655	166	18,531	468	22,889
Kentucky	3,879	1,359	11,734	127	19,696	312	18,177
Louisiana	4,806	1,487	11,524	156	24,632	212	17,004
Maine	1,342	486	7,440	55	7,629	341	9,227
Maryland	8,567	2,144	22,462	82	28,635	204	17,755
Massachusetts	13,226	4,140	56,567	195	49,825	945	53,858
Michigan	12,608	4,827	46,681	254	54,158	577	48,567
Minnesota	6,522	2,639	23,638	192	31,860	589	44,661
Mississippi	2,112	685	6,288	115	17,423	143	7,886
Missouri	6,741	2,336	18,823	171	35,149	502	33,644
Montana	814	404	4,429	65	4,358	105	4,759
Nebraska	1,971	940	9,798	109	11,483	251	17,396
Nevada	695	311	2,564	23	3,156	41	1,482
New Hampshire	1,247	449	7,044	34	6,083	130	5,873
New Jersey	12,102	4,724	51,061	146	49,073	549	34,430
New Mexico	1,401	431	4,077	54	6,484	66	3,345
New York	45,026	13,913	125,794	407	159,381	1,083	92,888
North Carolina	6,614	1,980	21,366	161	34,441	838	22,145
North Dakota	632	291	3,653	60	5,792	107	6,631
Ohio	15,383	5,118	57,052	251	72,921	1,163	65,134
Oklahoma	2,892	1,110	8,698	147	17,506	417	29,512
Oregon	3,736	1,630	11,382	87	11,888	312	18,306
Pennsylvania	19,349	6,570	96,414	320	94,698	768	65,963
Rhode Island	1,733	497	6,638	22	7,672	159	6,493
South Carolina	2,981	946	10,187	88	18,253	123	8,131
South Dakota	566	302	3,852	70	5,943	160	7,795
Tennessee	5,480	1,897	12,051	158	30,341	244	14,827
Texas	15,440	5,137	40,372	571	78,609	967	80,510
Utah	1,789	803	4,531	39	4,843	120	4,556
Vermont	931	272	4,521	21	3,839	101	3,902
Virginia	6,846	2,234	23,935	129	32,314	348	16,732
Washington	5,694	2,506	21,953	127	16,308	382	31,147
West Virginia	2,128	685	7,314	86	15,984	137	4,753
Wisconsin	6,026	2,642	23,318	176	31,076	516	51,960
Wyoming	375	179	1,922	30	2,642	34	1,896
TOTAL U.S.	342,611	124,659‡	1,127,657	7,156	1,465,828	21,834	1,327,704

*Non-federal only. †Preliminary. ‡Including 7,842 federally employed dentists who are not distributed by state.

Sources: American Medical Association, *Physician Distribution and Medical Licensure in the U.S., 1974;* American Hospital Association, *Hospital Statistics*, 1976 Edition; American Dental Association; American Nurses' Association; U.S. Department of Health, Education, and Welfare, Public Health Service.

Crime rates per 100,000 population

State or metropolitan area	VIOLENT CRIME Total 1970	Total 1975	Murder 1970	Murder 1975	Rape 1970	Rape 1975	Robbery 1970	Robbery 1975	Assault 1970	Assault 1975	PROPERTY CRIME Total 1970	Total 1975	Burglary 1970	Burglary 1975	Larceny 1970	Larceny 1975	Auto theft 1970	Auto theft 1975
Alabama	295.7	392.9	11.7	**16.0**	18.5	20.4	50.3	123.0	215.2	233.5	1,569.7	3,079.6	763.1	1,163.8	583.2	1,645.5	223.5	270.3
Alaska	278.0	539.8	12.2	12.2	26.1	44.6	71.8	129.5	167.8	353.4	2,412.5	5,656.8	789.9	1,214.5	1,071.2	3,522.4	551.3	919.9
Arizona	370.3	547.8	9.5	8.6	27.0	35.5	120.2	170.0	213.7	333.8	3,074.9	**7,793.7**	1,493.0	**2,529.9**	1,080.7	**4,747.7**	501.2	516.1
Arkansas	222.3	348.3	10.1	10.1	17.1	25.9	45.6	87.6	149.5	224.7	1,381.4	3,191.9	685.1	1,077.1	587.4	1,947.0	109.0	167.8
California	474.8	655.4	6.9	10.4	35.1	41.6	206.9	282.4	225.9	321.0	**3,832.1**	6,549.2	**1,753.0**	2,217.3	**1,389.9**	3,703.7	689.2	628.2
Colorado	356.7	463.1	6.2	7.4	**36.0**	41.5	129.1	174.1	185.4	240.1	3,305.5	6,212.4	1,380.9	2,001.2	1,336.1	3,744.0	588.4	467.2
Connecticut	170.4	268.4	3.5	3.9	9.1	12.4	70.4	131.5	87.4	120.6	2,404.5	4,688.6	1,084.2	1,512.6	836.1	2,603.6	484.2	572.4
Delaware	256.0	392.1	6.9	7.3	16.8	18.1	102.0	157.2	130.3	209.5	2,460.1	6,276.2	979.0	1,826.3	936.5	3,926.9	544.6	523.0
Florida	498.2	688.5	12.7	13.5	22.2	35.7	186.1	239.7	227.2	**399.6**	3,101.5	7,032.7	1,561.8	2,349.6	1,143.1	4,240.4	396.6	442.6
Georgia	304.5	459.0	**15.3**	14.4	16.1	25.4	95.8	166.5	177.3	252.6	1,902.2	4,167.0	899.9	1,580.7	693.7	2,248.5	308.6	337.7
Hawaii	121.8	218.4	3.6	7.7	11.8	24.7	63.3	127.6	43.1	58.3	3,274.4	5,808.2	1,456.1	1,826.8	1,237.2	3,457.7	581.1	523.7
Idaho	123.3	203.7	4.6	5.2	12.3	16.1	20.5	42.0	85.8	140.4	1,661.8	3,937.4	673.6	1,063.0	844.0	2,651.3	144.2	223.0
Illinois	467.9	549.7	9.6	10.6	20.4	25.7	251.1	276.2	186.8	237.2	1,879.2	4,832.3	765.4	1,291.1	596.0	3,030.0	517.8	511.1
Indiana	225.5	332.8	4.8	8.5	17.9	24.3	107.5	156.8	95.3	143.3	2,045.0	4,578.6	860.0	1,376.4	756.1	2,813.9	428.9	388.3
Iowa	79.3	140.7	1.9	2.5	6.2	10.3	28.5	53.5	42.8	74.4	1,356.0	3,768.0	507.3	818.5	673.7	2,719.8	175.0	229.7
Kansas	202.8	278.2	4.8	5.4	14.5	17.2	75.1	92.8	108.5	162.8	1,941.0	4,468.8	881.7	1,369.5	802.7	2,862.8	256.6	236.4
Kentucky	222.3	264.0	11.1	10.2	13.7	15.4	72.8	103.2	124.7	135.3	1,702.2	3,000.3	703.9	962.8	651.9	1,774.2	346.3	263.4
Louisiana	413.5	478.4	11.7	12.6	23.1	23.7	140.8	153.1	237.8	289.0	1,991.2	3,645.0	890.0	1,114.6	716.4	2,191.8	384.7	338.5
Maine	82.8	219.5	1.5	2.8	7.0	10.4	12.6	36.4	61.7	169.8	1,058.8	3,740.1	562.4	1,361.5	350.3	2,167.9	146.1	210.8
Maryland	624.9	709.8	9.2	10.7	23.9	31.5	338.6	344.2	253.3	323.4	2,722.1	5,197.7	1,051.2	1,413.2	1,123.3	3,267.6	547.6	516.9
Massachusetts	202.9	442.6	3.5	4.2	12.0	19.2	99.5	227.0	87.9	192.2	2,801.1	5,635.3	1,134.1	1,712.5	788.9	2,351.7	**878.1**	**1,571.1**
Michigan	562.8	685.7	8.9	11.9	22.9	38.1	348.4	353.1	182.6	282.7	3,096.3	6,114.6	1,493.5	1,891.8	1,143.8	3,572.9	459.0	649.9
Minnesota	152.0	207.0	2.0	3.3	9.7	18.6	89.1	103.6	51.2	81.4	1,951.4	4,091.7	801.7	1,193.1	804.0	2,516.1	345.7	382.5
Mississippi	179.3	315.9	11.5	13.9	8.9	16.5	19.0	54.6	139.8	230.9	684.1	2,094.8	351.2	784.2	254.6	1,181.3	78.4	129.3
Missouri	405.9	493.8	10.7	10.6	27.4	25.2	200.8	244.7	167.0	213.3	2,359.1	4,904.0	1,137.0	1,512.6	684.2	2,924.7	537.8	466.7
Montana	111.5	189.6	3.2	5.2	10.5	14.3	22.3	41.4	75.5	128.6	1,525.3	3,999.3	593.7	875.1	709.8	2,814.8	221.8	309.4
Nebraska	184.1	257.8	3.0	4.3	9.3	19.2	57.3	90.4	114.5	143.9	1,333.1	3,356.2	504.5	760.2	536.7	2,365.0	291.9	231.0
Nevada	398.6	678.7	8.8	13.0	19.6	**47.1**	188.4	302.5	181.7	316.0	3,597.6	7,474.2	1,660.6	2,447.1	1,276.3	4,517.1	660.7	510.0
New Hampshire	56.0	99.8	2.0	2.9	6.0	8.7	12.1	28.9	35.9	59.3	1,136.7	3,246.8	565.6	853.1	399.1	2,135.7	172.0	258.1
New Jersey	287.1	413.0	5.7	6.8	12.9	18.9	169.4	222.6	99.0	164.6	2,457.1	4,731.3	1,041.4	1,521.2	858.2	2,672.5	557.4	537.7
New Mexico	292.8	534.8	9.4	13.3	21.7	41.0	66.1	126.7	195.7	353.8	2,572.6	5,304.6	1,141.5	1,728.7	1,039.1	3,258.8	392.0	317.2
New York	**676.0**	**856.4**	7.9	11.0	15.5	28.1	**443.3**	**516.0**	209.3	301.3	3,246.0	4,779.3	1,414.2	1,666.6	1,149.6	2,471.0	682.2	641.7
North Carolina	362.5	436.5	11.1	12.4	12.6	16.2	49.2	82.2	**289.6**	325.6	1,498.9	3,380.3	708.6	1,285.1	639.7	1,909.2	150.6	186.0
North Dakota	34.2	53.1	0.5	0.8	6.2	5.8	6.5	14.3	21.0	32.1	812.0	2,284.1	286.4	539.2	434.6	1,614.3	91.0	130.6
Ohio	284.3	408.0	6.6	8.1	16.0	25.3	145.9	220.0	115.9	154.6	2,092.4	4,506.4	853.9	1,271.4	745.8	2,808.6	492.8	426.4
Oklahoma	197.8	303.3	5.9	9.4	15.6	27.2	53.8	90.2	122.4	176.5	1,753.2	4,274.8	793.3	1,551.8	684.4	2,375.0	275.4	348.0
Oregon	256.9	438.5	4.6	6.2	18.0	32.6	102.5	130.3	131.7	269.4	2,730.4	6,313.7	1,273.4	1,911.6	1,124.1	3,935.9	332.8	466.2
Pennsylvania	212.2	329.2	5.3	6.8	11.3	17.4	106.0	168.6	89.6	136.5	1,329.1	3,020.3	594.3	983.3	394.7	1,670.0	340.1	367.0
Rhode Island	204.7	302.3	3.2	3.0	3.6	10.9	78.3	95.9	119.6	192.4	2,721.1	5,341.5	1,018.9	1,446.3	843.2	2,878.4	859.0	1,016.8
South Carolina	285.2	511.4	14.6	14.7	17.1	26.5	60.0	110.9	193.4	359.3	1,781.6	4,130.1	905.8	1,714.2	629.3	2,156.3	246.5	259.6
South Dakota	92.5	205.3	3.8	3.7	11.1	16.5	17.1	31.0	60.5	154.0	1,059.7	2,533.7	471.3	667.8	494.7	1,698.0	93.7	167.9
Tennessee	274.9	397.0	8.8	11.4	15.5	26.1	82.0	166.8	168.6	192.6	1,613.4	3,873.5	806.7	1,379.3	517.4	2,129.5	289.3	364.7
Texas	361.5	390.6	11.6	13.4	21.0	28.0	134.1	164.1	194.8	185.2	2,344.3	5,016.5	1,151.3	1,665.6	798.7	2,963.7	394.3	387.2
Utah	137.7	231.8	3.4	2.7	10.9	20.9	53.1	79.0	70.3	129.2	2,235.0	4,880.8	915.0	1,187.8	1,003.8	3,372.6	316.3	320.5
Vermont	74.0	95.1	1.3	2.1	10.3	14.6	7.6	15.7	54.6	62.6	1,195.1	3,386.0	730.6	1,100.0	340.7	2,112.1	123.9	173.9
Virginia	259.0	380.9	8.4	11.5	15.4	24.0	92.0	138.5	143.2	206.9	1,890.2	4,165.6	805.6	1,165.7	787.2	2,730.7	297.4	269.2
Washington	221.3	390.8	3.5	5.7	18.0	32.7	93.5	124.0	106.3	228.4	2,935.2	5,750.1	1,444.5	1,723.1	1,129.0	3,641.6	361.8	385.4
West Virginia	123.7	161.7	6.2	7.4	6.7	9.3	27.3	45.5	83.5	99.5	835.0	1,946.1	388.5	591.0	354.0	1,228.7	92.4	126.4
Wisconsin	85.8	151.8	2.0	3.3	6.7	10.6	33.1	73.4	44.0	64.5	1,428.6	3,823.9	538.5	918.5	672.5	2,665.4	217.6	239.9
Wyoming	113.1	204.3	5.7	10.2	12.3	17.1	22.0	49.5	73.1	127.5	1,632.0	3,951.6	645.9	863.4	821.6	2,810.7	164.6	277.5
Baltimore	**1,008.3**	965.2	13.2	14.8	34.9	36.1	564.4	492.1	**395.9**	422.2	3,361.5	5,641.2	1,351.4	1,542.4	1,309.1	3,474.8	701.0	624.0
Boston	250.3	544.5	4.4	5.3	14.8	22.9	136.2	308.0	95.0	208.4	2,847.7	5,910.7	1,053.9	1,693.3	809.9	2,315.8	983.9	**1,901.6**
Chicago	633.6	693.7	12.9	13.9	25.4	31.2	362.5	374.7	232.7	273.8	2,155.1	5,449.0	829.6	1,359.9	617.2	3,406.5	708.4	682.7
Cleveland	453.2	687.7	14.5	17.0	18.7	31.6	287.9	429.5	132.1	209.6	2,629.5	4,690.7	826.1	1,152.7	595.2	2,493.4	**1,208.1**	1,044.6
Detroit	916.8	993.7	14.7	17.9	31.1	48.7	648.5	604.2	222.5	323.0	4,232.1	6,922.1	1,986.3	2,095.1	1,488.2	3,728.2	757.6	1,098.8
Houston	562.4	508.7	**16.9**	**19.1**	27.1	34.0	335.3	326.7	183.2	128.8	3,030.3	5,634.4	1,532.1	1,947.5	757.6	2,947.3	740.6	739.6
Los Angeles	737.5	927.1	9.4	14.3	**50.0**	**51.2**	307.3	421.2	370.8	440.3	4,326.4	6,274.4	1,980.5	**2,332.9**	1,401.3	3,078.6	944.6	863.0
Minneapolis	286.5	337.8	2.6	4.8	16.8	27.7	178.6	180.3	88.6	125.1	2,959.2	5,350.0	1,198.4	1,571.2	1,146.1	3,202.1	614.7	576.7
Newark	545.1	613.7	9.5	9.1	20.5	26.1	333.1	349.6	182.1	228.8	2,934.8	4,808.0	1,315.4	1,545.9	952.6	2,610.1	666.8	651.9
New York	980.7	**1,423.2**	10.5	18.0	19.9	41.9	**664.8**	**889.4**	285.6	**473.9**	4,239.3	5,544.1	1,821.0	2,081.0	1,471.2	2,514.0	947.1	949.1
Philadelphia	321.1	508.7	9.3	12.0	15.2	26.1	173.3	284.7	123.4	185.9	1,758.1	3,781.1	754.0	1,240.2	470.0	1,959.4	534.1	581.5
Pittsburgh	271.6	356.5	4.4	5.6	14.0	17.4	145.1	182.4	108.1	151.0	1,758.5	2,933.1	695.5	900.5	526.1	1,552.1	537.0	480.6
St. Louis	531.4	719.7	14.8	16.1	34.4	35.6	279.5	385.2	202.7	282.8	3,034.6	6,383.3	1,458.2	2,019.0	736.2	3,612.1	840.2	752.2
San Francisco	625.1	758.9	8.3	12.4	42.9	48.5	347.7	396.5	226.1	301.5	**4,704.2**	**7,293.3**	**2,163.7**	2,315.7	**1,583.4**	**4,283.7**	957.0	693.9
Washington, D.C.	769.9	749.3	11.4	12.0	23.0	41.4	503.5	473.6	232.0	222.2	3,340.7	5,527.9	1,432.5	1,431.2	1,141.4	3,608.2	766.8	488.5

Boldface: highest rate among states or listed metropolitan areas. Source: U.S. Department of Justice, Federal Bureau of Investigation, *Uniform Crime Reports*.

Transport, Communication, and Trade

Transportation

State	Road and street mi* 1975	Motor vehicles in 000s, 1975† Total	Auto-mobiles	Trucks and buses	Railroad mileage 1975	Airports 1976	Pipeline mileage 1974‡
Ala.	86,474	2,493	1,900	592	4,543	129	1,759
Alaska	9,941	226	143	83	20	769	124
Ariz.	51,602	1,459	1,064	395	2,034	196	1,352
Ark.	77,836	1,283	865	418	3,559	165	2,997
Calif.	171,100	13,891	11,226	2,664	7,317	781	10,183
Colo.	85,545	1,925	1,440	485	3,457	230	2,180
Conn.	18,946	1,949	1,793	156	656	91	92
Del.	5,194	351	289	62	291	32	6
D.C.	1,102	255	236	19	30	16	§
Fla.	101,538	5,395	4,499	896	4,107	355	273
Ga.	101,466	3,211	2,509	701	5,408	248	1,886
Hawaii	3,750	462	395	67	—	47	—
Idaho	57,489	647	407	241	2,633	181	633
Ill.	131,531	6,344	5,350	993	10,572	831	11,405
Ind.	91,232	3,315	2,565	750	6,374	237	4,629
Iowa	112,354	2,099	1,543	556	7,587	241	3,951
Kan.	134,691	1,805	1,241	564	7,616	318	15,907
Ky.	70,131	2,245	1,676	569	3,516	87	2,326
La.	54,697	2,187	1,661	526	3,683	281	8,791
Maine	21,580	648	499	149	1,665	161	354
Md.	25,949	2,423	2,072	350	1,091	128	220
Mass.	32,829	3,107	2,776	331	1,405	139	347
Mich.	118,790	5,545	4,628	918	5,963	400	3,929
Minn.	128,383	2,524	1,952	572	7,366	301	3,099
Miss.	67,488	1,376	990	387	3,644	145	3,389
Mo.	117,007	2,866	2,177	689	6,062	343	6,928
Mont.	78,177	602	370	232	4,898	167	2,806
Neb.	97,108	1,178	824	354	5,415	296	3,283
Nev.	49,742	464	346	118	1,573	113	198
N.H.	15,257	485	405	81	752	58	108
N.J.	33,036	4,154	3,736	419	1,687	222	472
N.M.	70,621	827	555	272	2,057	134	5,927
N.Y.	108,635	7,591	6,735	856	5,310	488	1,939
N.C.	90,810	3,690	2,860	829	4,115	237	900
N.D.	105,972	551	331	220	5,070	198	1,741
Ohio	110,620	7,179	6,288	891	7,727	548	6,965
Okla.	109,399	2,113	1,432	680	4,944	277	20,547
Ore.	104,477	1,628	1,320	307	3,043	277	673
Pa.	115,187	7,659	6,589	1,070	8,020	609	8,038
R.I.	5,528	563	499	64	139	18	17
S.C.	60,945	1,772	1,400	372	3,034	116	669
S.D.	82,293	521	336	185	3,351	125	642
Tenn.	81,272	2,726	2,093	633	3,184	128	707
Texas	255,887	8,396	6,217	2,179	13,306	1,213	65,472
Utah	48,854	845	587	258	1,726	90	1,341
Vt.	13,886	287	233	54	716	62	177
Va.	62,767	3,251	2,709	541	3,875	230	834
Wash.	84,315	2,540	1,883	656	4,767	307	760
W.Va.	36,984	966	735	231	3,494	51	3,540
Wis.	105,171	2,591	2,126	464	5,808	303	942
Wyo.	32,558	337	202	135	1,779	88	6,897
TOTAL	3,838,146	132,950	106,712	26,238	200,389	13,207	222,355

*Includes federally controlled rural roads. †Registrations, excluding military. Detail may not add to totals because of rounding. ‡Petroleum and products only.
§Included with Maryland. Sources: Interstate Commerce Commission; Department of Transportation, Federal Aviation Administration, Federal Highway Administration.

Communications facilities

State	Post Offices July 1, 1975	TELEPHONES January 1, 1975		COMMERCIAL BROADCAST STATIONS, 1974			Public TV stations 1974	NEWSPAPERS					
				Radio				Daily		Weekly April 1, 1976*		Sunday	
		Total	Residential	AM	FM	TV		Number Feb. 1, 1976	Circulation Sept. 30, 1975	Number	Circulation	Number Feb. 1, 1976	Circulation Sept. 30, 1975
Alabama	635	1,965,000	1,494,600	136	60	17	9	24	736,995	109	458,010	17	666,398
Alaska	193	167,000	95,200	18	3	7	3	7	87,040	12	21,665	1	39,458
Arizona	212	1,372,400	978,000	54	19	11	2	14	514,448	55	372,532	4	429,572
Arkansas	645	1,139,800	855,800	87	47	8	1	34	458,706	119	327,726	13	388,838
California	1,126	15,755,300	11,237,300	226	162	53	12	122	5,687,649	450	5,940,617	41	4,894,314
Colorado	409	1,746,700	1,221,800	67	32	11	2	27	733,370	114	430,062	10	749,756
Connecticut	249	2,332,600	1,719,400	38	21	5	4	28	912,761	57	438,993	8	673,903
Delaware	56	447,600	326,800	10	6	—	—	3	157,607	13	110,812	2	151,228
District of Columbia	1	984,600	488,000	7	7	6	1	2	887,568	...	...	2	1,072,614
Florida	464	6,017,000	4,385,300	194	96	27	10	51	2,197,085	139	713,556	34	2,156,057
Georgia	646	3,225,300	2,378,900	173	77	18	10	37	1,009,563	165	596,673	15	985,700
Hawaii	76	545,000	343,300	25	4	10	2	4	210,868	3	101,304	2	196,347
Idaho	265	488,600	356,700	43	10	6	3	16	208,965	60	131,743	5	151,361
Illinois	1,273	8,294,200	6,063,600	123	118	24	6	88	3,522,713	549	2,705,881	20	2,542,523
Indiana	758	3,476,800	2,658,500	86	84	17	7	80	1,663,271	198	647,101	17	1,126,735
Iowa	954	1,912,700	1,462,800	74	54	13	6	42	937,172	335	736,371	9	788,436
Kansas	694	1,554,000	1,167,200	60	32	12	2	52	651,850	241	491,710	14	448,799
Kentucky	1,267	1,832,100	1,382,000	110	76	12	14	27	768,731	132	540,732	12	586,456
Louisiana	535	2,170,300	1,633,800	92	45	17	2	26	823,765	95	486,519	14	751,254
Maine	497	619,100	473,600	36	18	7	5	9	269,983	40	163,989	1	108,694
Maryland	427	2,937,400	2,160,500	51	33	7	4	13	732,390	67	592,535	4	676,009
Massachusetts	435	3,969,900	2,785,500	64	38	10	3	46	2,060,570	138	993,089	8	1,450,280
Michigan	863	6,064,800	4,577,200	124	92	21	7	54	2,459,805	262	1,482,668	14	2,262,862
Minnesota	858	2,708,900	2,024,100	89	53	11	5	31	1,085,333	327	900,911	9	1,001,994
Mississippi	470	1,166,600	895,400	102	53	11	8	23	378,273	95	269,685	10	282,414
Missouri	968	3,207,500	2,381,000	108	57	23	3	57	1,723,791	254	860,607	17	1,404,017
Montana	377	450,200	326,100	41	13	12	—	11	190,610	70	139,480	8	189,792
Nebraska	553	1,082,800	813,300	48	21	15	9	19	489,718	205	456,390	4	362,370
Nevada	92	477,900	308,700	21	11	7	1	9	179,464	15	43,881	4	154,532
New Hampshire	243	537,600	408,100	27	15	4	5	9	180,716	30	202,873	2	69,745
New Jersey	520	5,542,000	4,100,500	37	27	4	4	29	1,701,328	208	1,625,356	13	1,363,065
New Mexico	330	637,400	436,600	57	19	8	3	20	242,411	25	136,969	12	212,609
New York	1,634	12,902,300	8,971,300	161	113	29	11	77	7,009,256	396	2,038,157	24	6,647,900
North Carolina	780	3,144,700	2,384,000	203	78	18	9	52	1,291,379	134	552,848	22	1,015,583
North Dakota	453	409,500	305,400	26	9	12	2	10	193,524	87	168,765	2	102,145
Ohio	1,083	7,125,700	5,364,900	121	120	27	12	95	3,348,364	256	1,637,960	23	2,338,383
Oklahoma	635	1,820,300	1,331,700	67	39	9	3	53	843,033	198	378,520	42	843,771
Oregon	352	1,494,300	1,084,300	80	24	13	3	22	638,591	91	548,895	5	533,228
Pennsylvania	1,794	8,508,900	6,433,800	173	118	23	8	105	3,867,394	226	1,462,672	12	2,976,364
Rhode Island	56	611,800	454,000	15	7	2	1	7	310,935	14	101,243	2	217,024
South Carolina	392	1,593,800	1,191,100	104	47	12	7	19	561,897	72	253,456	7	446,973
South Dakota	413	416,800	323,300	30	14	10	6	13	176,831	148	186,827	4	121,656
Tennessee	576	2,530,900	1,907,600	154	66	17	5	34	1,102,140	118	471,746	14	961,842
Texas	1,520	8,000,600	5,774,100	284	140	57	7	114	3,230,489	517	1,276,889	87	3,309,308
Utah	220	786,700	573,200	32	12	3	2	5	251,753	54	168,640	4	250,382
Vermont	288	288,600	206,300	18	6	2	4	8	113,387	19	61,383	1	6,742
Virginia	908	3,120,100	2,277,600	128	64	15	7	33	1,014,617	99	546,684	13	699,041
Washington	473	2,384,100	1,739,500	93	40	15	6	22	1,041,717	133	1,130,929	13	1,001,201
West Virginia	1,030	893,400	679,400	60	27	9	3	29	483,293	77	252,873	9	395,100
Wisconsin	781	2,857,900	2,103,400	99	83	18	7	35	1,229,717	237	742,656	6	835,275
Wyoming	169	252,000	178,400	29	3	3	—	9	82,595	28	74,547	3	56,273
TOTAL U.S.	30,649	143,971,500	105,222,900	4,305	2,413	708	256	1,756	60,655,431	7,486	35,176,130	639	51,096,323

*Excluding District of Columbia. Sources: U.S. Postal Service; Federal Communications Commission; American Telephone and Telegraph Co.; The Editor & Publisher Co., Inc., *International Year Book, 1976* (Copyright 1976. All rights reserved. Used by permission); National Newspaper Association, *1976 National Directory of Weekly Newspapers;* Corporation for Public Broadcasting.

Major trading partners, by value

in millions of dollars

Country	EXPORTS		IMPORTS	
	1970	1975	1970	1975
North America	12,367	30,058	13,970	30,577
Canada	9,079*	21,759	11,092	21,747
Mexico	1,704	5,144	1,218	3,059
South America	3,244	8,814	2,958	7,220
Argentina	441	628	172	215
Brazil	840	3,056	670	1,464
Chile	300	533	157	138
Colombia	395	643	269	590
Peru	214	904	340	399
Venezuela	759	2,243	1,082	3,624
Europe	14,817	32,726	11,395	21,466
Belgium and Luxembourg	1,195	2,427	696	1,190
France	1,483	3,031	942	2,137
Germany, West	2,741	5,194	3,127	5,382
Italy	1,353	2,867	1,316	2,397
Netherlands, The	1,651	4,183	528	1,083
Spain	712	2,161	353	831
Sweden	543	925	399	877
Switzerland	700	1,153	459	867
United Kingdom	2,536	4,525	2,194	3,784
U.S.S.R.	119	1,836	72	254
Asia	10,105	28,942	9,644	27,083
Hong Kong	406	808	944	1,575
India	574	1,290	298	548
Indonesia	266	810	182	2,221
Iran	326	3,242	67	1,400
Israel	592	1,551	150	313
Japan	4,652	9,565	5,875	11,268
Korea, South	643	1,761	370	1,416
Malaysia	67	395	270	766
Philippines	373	832	472	754
Saudi Arabia	141	1,502	20	2,625
Singapore	240	994	81	532
Taiwan	527	1,660	549	1,938
Oceania	1,189	2,339	871	1,508
Australia	986	1,816	611	1,147
Africa	1,502	4,267	1,090	8,277
Algeria	62	632	10	1,359
Nigeria	129	536	71	3,282
South Africa†	563	1,302	290	841
Total	43,224*	107,652*	39,952	96,140*

*Includes shipments to or from unidentified countries. †Includes South West Africa.
Source: U.S. Department of Commerce, Domestic and International Business Administration, *Overseas Business Reports.*

Major commodities traded, 1975

in millions of dollars

Item	Total*	Canada	American Republics	Western Europe	Far East†
TOTAL EXPORTS	107,652	21,759‡	15,670	29,939	19,660
Agricultural commodities					
Grains and preparations	11,643	148	1,307	3,098	3,545
Soybeans	2,865	85	28	1,654	869
Cotton, including linters, wastes	1,011	40	6	121	722
Nonagricultural commodities					
Ores and scrap metals	1,355	157	178	555	436
Coal, coke, and briquettes	3,343	711	239	924	1,435
Chemicals	8,705	1,223	2,135	2,699	1,579
Machinery	29,101	6,140	5,052	8,085	3,936
Agricultural machines, tractors, parts	2,832	989	611	465	128
Electrical apparatus	7,587	1,330	1,349	2,211	1,482
Transport equipment§	15,005	6,220	2,011	2,364	1,310
Civilian aircraft and parts	4,864	370	475	1,725	934
Paper manufactures	1,448	390	292	412	99
Metal manufactures	1,891	575	315	348	224
Iron and steel mill products‖	2,382	553	563	258	228
Yarn, fabrics, and clothing	1,464	291	307	526	98
Other exports	27,439	5,226	3,237	8,895	5,179
TOTAL IMPORTS	96,140	21,747	11,840	20,735	21,492
Agricultural commodities					
Meat and preparations	1,141	47	209	291	4
Fish, including shellfish	1,356	291	370	246	257
Coffee	1,561	¶	1,095	7	60
Sugar	1,870	14	982	¶	423
Nonagricultural commodities					
Ores and scrap metal	1,977	720	599	50	54
Petroleum, crude	19,293	3,067	2,741	101	1,851
Petroleum products	5,521	346	1,391	335	235
Chemicals	3,696	870	144	1,710	429
Machinery	11,970	2,244	900	4,540	4,156
Transport equipment	11,495	4,988	127	3,373	2,978
Automobiles, new	7,130	2,809	¶	2,560	1,761
Iron and steel mill products	4,037	351	38	1,484	2,107
Nonferrous metals	2,063	866	177	405	364
Textiles other than clothing	1,219	27	125	388	603
Other imports	28,941	7,916	2,942	7,805	7,971

*Includes areas not shown separately. †Includes Japan, East and South Asia.
‡Excludes grains and oilseeds valued at $505 million transshipped through Canada to unidentified overseas countries. §Excludes parts for tractors.
‖Excludes pig iron. ¶Less than $500,000. Source: U.S. Dept. of Commerce, Domestic and International Business Administration, *Overseas Business Reports.*

Upper Volta

A republic of West Africa, Upper Volta is bordered by Mali, Niger, Benin, Togo, Ghana, and Ivory Coast. Area: 105,869 sq mi (274,200 sq km). Pop. (1975 census): 6,144,000. Cap. and largest city: Ouagadougou (pop., 1970 est., 110,000). Language: French (official). Religion: animist; Muslim and Christian minorities. President and premier in 1976, Gen. Sangoulé Lamizana.

On Jan. 29, 1976, after several weeks of tension resulting from a crisis in the relations between the labour unions and the military government, President Lamizana dissolved his ministry and on February 9 formed a new Cabinet comprising a civilian majority. On July 23 there was another reshuffle, as a result of which the finance minister was changed for the second time in less than six months.

A special 32-member constitutional commission, announced by the president in January and set up in April, completed its work on October 5. Among its recommendations for constitutional civilian government, it proposed the holding of a referendum in March 1977, a maximum of three political parties, and presidential elections in May.

Speaking on the 16th anniversary of Upper Volta's independence, President Lamizana said that pessimism about national finances was unwarranted and that the country was well able to honour its commitments. He also condemned tendencies toward regionalism and sectarianism within the nation.

(PHILIPPE DECRAENE)

[978.E.4.a.i]

UPPER VOLTA

Education. (1973–74) Primary, pupils 124,966, teachers 2,775; secondary, pupils 11,953, teachers 445; vocational, pupils 2,101, teachers c. 140; teacher training, students 362, teachers c. 30; higher, students 436, teaching staff 40.

Finance. Monetary unit: CFA franc, with (Sept. 20, 1976) a parity of CFA Fr 50 to the French franc (free rate of CFA Fr 245.90 = U.S. $1; CFA Fr. 423.62 = £1 sterling). Budget (1973 actual) balanced at CFA Fr 11,726,000,000 (includes capital expenditure of CFA Fr 961 million).

Foreign Trade. (1974) Imports CFA Fr 34,660,000,000; exports CFA Fr 8.7 billion. Import sources (1973): France 49%; Ivory Coast 17%; West Germany 5%. Export destinations (1973): Ivory Coast 41%; France 26%; Italy 7%; Ghana 7%. Main exports (1972): livestock 41%; cotton 20%; peanuts 7%; sesame seed 5%.

Uruguay

A republic of South America, Uruguay is on the Atlantic Ocean and is bounded by Brazil and Argentina. Area: 68,536 sq mi (177,508 sq km). Pop. (1975 census): 2,764,000, including (1961) white 89%; mestizo 10%. Cap. and largest city: Montevideo (pop., 1975 census, 1,229,700). Language: Spanish. Religion: mainly Roman Catholic. Presidents in 1976, Juan María Bordaberry, Alberto Demicheli (interim) from June 12, and, from September 1, Aparicio Méndez.

The chief political event of 1976 was the removal of President Bordaberry from office on June 12 by the Army following disagreements on future policy between the president and the generals. A joint civilian-military National Council was established on June 27 to draft a new constitution. A new permanent president, Aparicio Méndez, took office for a five-year term

PAUL HARRISON

This man from Upper Volta is one of thousands of migrants who labour on the plantations of neighbouring Ivory Coast. The migration has caused a dispute between impoverished Volta and its more prosperous neighbour. Volta wants a greater share of the wealth created by its migrants.

URUGUAY

Education. (1975) Primary, pupils 355,328, teachers 13,935; secondary, pupils 143,852, teachers (1969) 9,668; vocational, pupils 38,343, teachers (1973) 3,953; teacher training, students 3,997, teachers (1973) 341; higher, students 33,664, teaching staff 2,545.

Finance. Monetary unit: new peso, with (Sept. 20, 1976) a free commercial rate of 3.62 new pesos to U.S. $1 (6.23 new pesos = £1 sterling). Gold, SDR's, and foreign exchange (May 1976) U.S. $235 million. Budget (1974 actual): revenue 587.9 billion pesos; expenditure 786.9 billion pesos. Gross national product (1974) 4,443,300,000 new pesos. Cost of living (Montevideo; 1970 = 100; June 1976) 1,933.

Foreign Trade. (1975) Imports U.S. $546.5 million; exports U.S. $383.8 million. Import sources: Kuwait 16%; Brazil 13%; U.S. 10%; Argentina 9%; West Germany 8%; U.K. 5%. Export destinations: West Germany 22%; The Netherlands 13%; U.S. 12%; Italy 10%; U.K. 8%; Greece 6%; Spain 5%. Main exports: wool 23%; meat 19%.

Transport and Communications. Roads (1973) 49,634 km. Motor vehicles in use (1974): passenger c. 151,600; commercial (including buses) c. 85,700. Railways (1974): 2,975 km; traffic 353 million passenger-km; freight 239 million net ton-km. Air traffic (1974): 80 million passenger-km; freight 100,000 net ton-km. Shipping (1975): merchant vessels 100 gross tons and over 38; gross tonnage 130,998. Telephones (Dec. 1974) 247,900. Radio receivers (Dec. 1973) 1.5 million. Television receivers (Dec. 1973) 305,000.

Agriculture. Production (in 000; metric tons; 1975): wheat 497; oats 58; corn 157; rice 189; potatoes (1974) 129; sweet potatoes (1974) c. 88; sorghum 77; linseed 39; sunflower seed 51; sugar, raw value (1974) 105; oranges (1974) c. 56; wine (1974) c. 92; wool 37; beef and veal (1974) c. 353. Livestock (in 000; May 1975): sheep c. 16,000; pigs c. 450; cattle c. 11,200; horses (1974) c. 410; chickens (1974) c. 7,200.

Industry. Production (in 000; metric tons; 1974): crude steel 14; cement (1973) 526; petroleum products c. 1,570; electricity (excluding most industrial production; kw-hr) c. 2,458,000.

Universities: *see* Education

Urban Mass Transit: *see* Transportation

U.S.S.R.: *see* Union of Soviet Socialist Republics

on September 1. Among the first acts of the new government was the withdrawal of political rights from many Uruguayans previously active in politics. The government stated that it would continue current economic policies, which had brought about some improvement in the economic situation. In 1975 gross domestic product grew by 3.6%, compared with 1.6% in 1974, and inflation was 66.8%, compared with 107.3%.

With its new regime Uruguay was more in tune with its military-ruled neighbours. However, revelations by Amnesty International over the treatment of political prisoners, a diplomatic dispute with Venezuela, and the withdrawal of political rights from some Uruguayans damaged the country's reputation. Indeed, the U.S. Congress deprived Uruguay of U.S. military aid. (JOHN HALE)

[974.F.2]

Vatican City State

This independent sovereignty is surrounded by but is not part of Rome. As a state with territorial limits, it is properly distinguished from the Holy See, which constitutes the worldwide administrative and legislative body for the Roman Catholic Church. The area of Vatican City is 108.7 ac (44 ha). Pop. (1976 est.): 700. As sovereign pontiff, Paul VI is the chief of state. Vatican City is administered by a pontifical commission of five cardinals, of which the secretary of state, Jean Cardinal Villot, is president.

In October 1976 the Vatican approved the statute of the East German episcopal conference, under which the dioceses of West Germany were separated from those of East Germany. Thereby, the Vatican acknowledged the existence of two German states, which it had never recognized de jure. In November, Msgr. Agostino Casaroli, Vatican "foreign minister," held talks in Bulgaria with Pres. Todor Zhivkov.

In October and November, Msgr. Luigi Poggi, itinerant nuncio of the State Secretariat, visited Romania but could not settle the question of Romania's 1.7 million Uniate Catholics, who had been forcibly incorporated into the Orthodox Church in 1948. The establishment of diplomatic relations with Greece was under negotiation. Relations with Spain became more normal, progressing to revision of the 1953 concordat, and agreement on major revisions of the 1929 concordat was reached with the Italian government. In April Pres. Anwar as-Sadat's visit confirmed the Vatican's excellent relations with Egypt.

In May the pope conferred the scarlet hat on the archbishop of Hanoi among 21 new cardinals, but he reserved one hat *in petto* (in his breast, secretly), probably for the archbishop of Prague, since relations with Czechoslovakia were strained. (MAX BERGERRE)

See also Religion.

Egypt's President Anwar as-Sadat presents a 2,000-year-old alabaster bowl to Pope Paul VI. Sadat called on the pope at the end of his three-day official visit to Italy in April. At left is Sadat's wife, Jehan.

KEYSTONE

Venezuela

A republic of northern South America, Venezuela is bounded by Colombia, Brazil, Guyana, and the Caribbean Sea. Area: 352,144 sq mi (912,050 sq km). Pop. (1976 est.): 12,493,000, including mestizo 69%; white 20%; Negro 9%; Indian 2%. Cap. and largest city: Caracas (metro. area pop., 1976 est., 2,576,000). Language: Spanish. Religion: predominantly Roman Catholic. President in 1976, Carlos Andrés Pérez.

VENEZUELA

Education. (1973–74) Primary, pupils 1,924,040, teachers 58,457; secondary, pupils 543,104; vocational, pupils 31,617; teacher training, students 9,490; secondary, vocational, and teacher training, teachers 30,913; higher, students 161,054, teaching staff 11,228.

Finance. Monetary unit: bolívar, with (Sept. 20, 1976) a par value of 4.29 bolivares to U.S. $1 (free rate of 7.35 bolivares = £1 sterling). Gold, SDR's, and foreign exchange (June 1976) U.S. $6,727,000,000. Budget (1975 est.): revenue 40,542,000,000 bolivares; expenditure 31,629,000,000 bolivares. Gross national product (1974) 108,450,000,000 bolivares. Money supply (May 1976) 24,158,000,000 bolivares. Cost of living (Caracas; 1970 = 100; May 1976) 141.

Foreign Trade. (1975) Imports 20,662,000,000 bolivares; exports 43,426,000,000 bolivares. Import sources (1974): U.S. *c.* 47%; Japan *c.* 11%; West Germany *c.* 9%; Italy *c.* 6%. Export destinations (1974): U.S. *c.* 43%; Canada *c.* 12%; Netherlands Antilles 12%. Main exports: crude oil 58%; petroleum products 37%.

Transport and Communications. Roads (1974) 65,718 km. Motor vehicles in use (1973): passenger 820,000; commercial 295,000. Railways: (1974) 175 km; traffic (1971) 42 million passenger-km, freight 15 million net ton-km. Air traffic (1975): 2,269,000,000 passenger-km; freight 73,061,000 net ton-km. Shipping (1975): merchant vessels 100 gross tons and over 152; gross tonnage 515,661. Telephones (Dec. 1974) 554,000. Radio receivers (Dec. 1973) 2 million. Television receivers (Dec. 1973) 995,000.

Agriculture. Production (in 000; metric tons; 1975): corn 686; rice *c.* 369; potatoes (1974) 125; cassava (1974) 325; sesame seed *c.* 60; sugar, raw value 515; cocoa *c.* 21; bananas *c.* 1,000; oranges (1974) *c.* 220; coffee *c.* 64; tobacco *c.* 16; cotton, lint *c.* 43; beef and veal (1974) *c.* 251. Livestock (in 000; 1975): cattle 9,089; pigs 1,795; sheep 101; goats (1974) 1,419; horses (1974) 450; asses (1974) *c.* 528; poultry 28,217.

Industry. Production (in 000; metric tons; 1975): crude oil 122,736; natural gas (cu m; 1974) 11,633,000; petroleum products (1974) 61,283; iron ore (64% metal content) 24,104; cement (1972) 2,765; gold (troy oz; 1974) 17; diamonds (metric carats; 1974) 819; electricity (kw-hr; 1974) 18,396,000.

The oil industry was nationalized on Jan. 1, 1976. Production decreased toward the 2.2 million-bbl-a-day target. The iron-ore industry (taken over in 1975) dropped production to about 18 million tons in 1976, as against the 22 million tons planned, because of reduced world demand. Lack of qualified manpower to run these newly nationalized industries, except in the oil industry, was a brake on long-term development plans. Many of the nonskilled workers were illegal immigrants from Colombia, Peru, and Chile.

President Pérez was halfway through his five-year term in office, and his Acción Democrática party had a majority in both houses of the Congress. The principal mandate of the party was the attainment of a more equitable society; the administration chose to do this by taking a more active role in the economy, as well as by fiscal and social means. The five-year development plan (1976–80) called for public sector investments of $27.6 billion, or 53.1% of the total investment under the plan. Annual gross domestic product growth rates were expected to average 8.3% over the duration of the plan. Major investments would be channeled to the petroleum and mining ($5.5 billion), agricultural ($1.9 billion), electrical ($4.1 billion), and manufacturing ($5.3 billion) sectors. Agricultural production was projected to rise at 9.2% a year, so that by 1980 only 8% of the nation's food would have to be imported. Petroleum exploration and drilling offshore and on the Orinoco tar belt were provided for, and local refining patterns were restructured toward the export of more expensive oil products; $700 million was to be invested in the petrochemicals industry. Large-scale hydroelectric projects on the Guri, Uribante-Doradas, and Caroní rivers would be developed, while projects in education, housing, and communications were to receive $5.9 billion. The Sider steel plant at Ciudad Guayana, with an annual capacity of 1.2 million tons, was being enlarged with the aim of quadrupling production.

Other projects included shipbuilding and a restructuring of the automobile industry. Over 10% of expenditure was to be financed through the normal budget between 1976 and 1980 with 38.8% from state agencies and 11.2% from local government; the investment fund was to lend $2,960,000,000, and the remainder, $5.5 billion, was to be raised from abroad. The government recognized the inflationary consequences of such heavy expenditure, and through monetary and food subsidies restrained the rate of inflation; in 1974 and 1975, the Caracas cost-of-living index increased respectively by 11.6 and 8%; however, restrictions in the money supply restrained the rate to a 3.9% increase in the first eight months of 1976, representing an annual rate of increase of 5.9%.

To aid countries affected by the rise in oil prices Venezuela contributed 600 million Special Drawing Rights to the World Bank's petrodollar-recycling facility, and also set up a $500 million fund within the Inter-American Development Bank to promote regional integration and industrial and energy projects. Venezuela was active, as a leading member, in the Andean Group and the Sistema Económico Latino Americano, or SELA. (*See* LATIN-AMERICAN AFFAIRS.)

Guerrillas kidnapped William Niehous, vice-president of a U.S. company, from his home near Caracas on February 27, and he had not been released by the end of the year. The alleged murder by police agents of Jorge Rodríguez, leader of the (Trotskyist) Socialist League, on July 25, supposedly in connection with the kidnapping, caused a public outcry, and steps were taken to bring the agents to justice. Two parliamentary deputies were brought to trial for alleged involvement in the Niehous kidnapping. In June, Occidental Petroleum was named in connection with bribery, denied by the company. Venezuela broke off diplomatic relations with Uruguay on July 6, after a woman seeking asylum in the Venezuelan embassy in Montevideo was seized by Uruguayan police.

(MICHAEL WOOLLER)

[974.C.1]

WIDE WORLD

Venezuelan Pres. Carlos Andrés Pérez (arm raised) led ceremonies marking the nationalization of the country's oil industry on New Year's Day. Venezuela is the world's third largest exporter of oil. The government took control of 38 companies, including subsidiaries of Exxon, Shell, Gulf, and Mobil.

Veterinary Science

There were about 29,000 active veterinarians in the United States in 1976. The Senate Committee on Government Operations recommended that this number be increased to 40,075 by 1980. Twenty-one colleges in the United States were offering the doctor of veterinary medicine degree. Student enrollment for the 1975–76 academic year was 6,274, an increase of 269 over the previous year. Females made up 29% of the entering classes in 1975 and 16% of the graduating classes. Because of the limited capacity of U.S. colleges, some U.S. citizens applied for admission to foreign colleges of veterinary medicine. Many graduates of foreign veterinary colleges sought employment in the U.S. Most state licensing boards and the U.S. Civil Service Commission required that an applicant be a graduate of a college accredited by the American Veterinary Medical Association (AVMA) or have a certificate from the AVMA. The steps required for certification of foreign graduates were (1) proof of graduation from a college of veterinary medicine; (2) proof of comprehension and ability to communicate in English; (3) a passing score on the AVMA's examination in veterinary medicine; and (4) proof of successful completion of a year of evaluated clinical experience at a site approved by the AVMA.

In 1976 the United States continued to be among the few countries in the world where cloven-hoofed animals were free of foot-and-mouth disease. The last case was in 1929. Veterinarians administered control programs to prevent entry of the dreaded virus. Completion of the Pan-American Highway was dependent on the development of adequate controls to prevent the spread of the virus from Colombia.

The Animal and Plant Health Inspection Service of the U.S. Department of Agriculture had a data bank on 13 exotic animal diseases containing over

13,000 articles. Using a combination of computer and microfilm, 1,000 articles per minute could be reviewed. Its Emergency Programs Information Center (EPIC) could now respond almost immediately should a disease strike. It had more than 30,000 geologic survey maps of various parts of the United States and 3,600 county maps on 35-mm aperture cards. There were also maps of other parts of the world. The maps could be printed from the aperture cards and sent via telecopier to wherever they were needed in the field.

The production and release of sterile screwworms in the southwestern states and in Mexico continued to hold down screwworm infestation of livestock and wildlife west of the Mississippi River. The sterile screwworms mate with fertile ones, but produce no offspring. A new screwworm production plant, the largest in the world, was opened on the Isthmus of Tehuantepec, Mexico, in 1976 and the first sterile flies were released in Baja California in September. The plan was to push the barrier zone south to the Isthmus of Panama. Screwworms had already been eradicated from Puerto Rico and the Virgin Islands.

Swine vesicular disease (SVD) was found to be spreading throughout Europe and Asia. This disease cannot be distinguished from other vesicular diseases without laboratory confirmation. The U.S. established veterinary controls over the importation of meat and animals to guard against entry of the virus.

The rapid, indirect enzyme-labeled antibody (ELA) microplate test was developed as a diagnostic and surveillance tool to aid in the control of animal disease. The ELA test showed great promise in the rapid and accurate diagnosis of such diseases as hog cholera, trichinosis, and brucellosis.

The Animal Welfare Act was amended by the U.S. Congress "(1) to insure that animals intended for use in research facilities or for exhibition purposes or for use as pets are provided humane care and treatment; (2) to assure humane treatment of animals during transportation in commerce; and (3) to protect the owners of animals from the theft of their animals by preventing the sale or use of animals which have been stolen." The act required that dogs, cats, and other animals shipped by common carrier have a health certificate signed by a veterinarian and that care and treatment of laboratory animals be under the supervision of a doctor of veterinary medicine at all facilities where animals are used for biomedical research. This meant an added responsibility for veterinarians.

Biologists at the Ames, Iowa, National Animal Disease Center are studying adenoviruses that produce weak calf syndrome in newborn calves. Microphoto below shows adenovirus growing in a cell nucleus. At bottom, researcher takes a blood sample from a heifer that has been injected with adenoviruses.

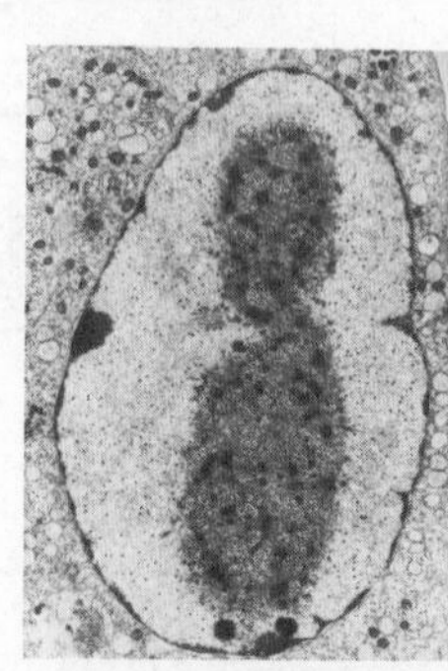

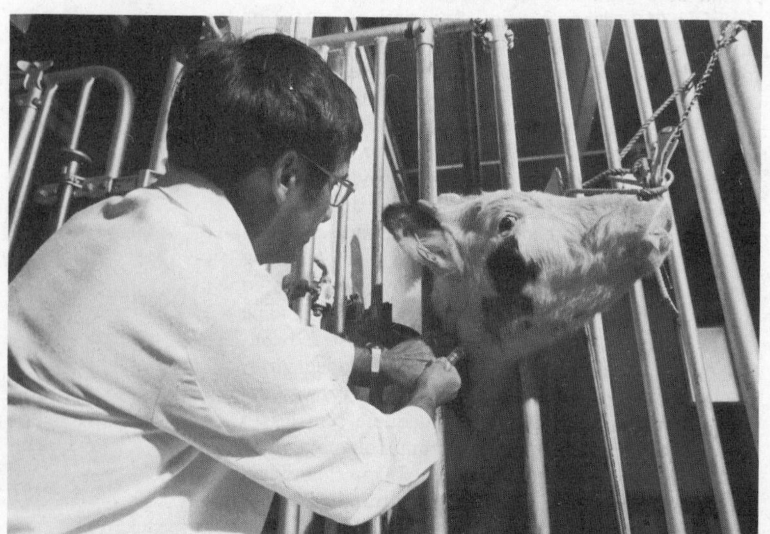

PHOTOS, AGRICULTURAL RESEARCH MAGAZINE

AGIP/PICTORIAL PARADE

French veterinarians remove an ovary from a zebra using the "Ysop bubble," a kind of inflatable balloon with gloves built in.

The incidence of animal rabies in the United States continued to decline in 1976. Worldwide, however, the number of cases was increasing. The animals most commonly found positive for rabies were dogs and vampire bats in Latin America, foxes in Europe, stray dogs in Asia, dogs, jackals, and mongooses in Africa, and foxes and skunks in Canada. (*See* HEALTH AND DISEASE.) (CLARENCE H. PALS)

[353.C]

ENCYCLOPÆDIA BRITANNICA FILMS. *Country Vet* (1972).

Vietnam

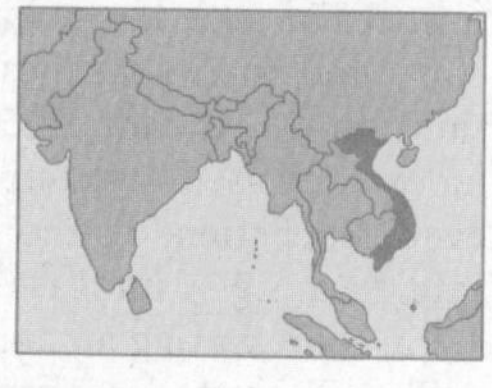

The Socialist Republic of Vietnam (S.R.V.N.) was named after reunification of North and South Vietnam under Communist rule. It is bordered in the north by China, in the west by Laos and Cambodia, and in the south and east by the South China Sea. Area: 130,654 sq mi (338,392 sq km). Pop. (1976 est.): over 50 million. Capital: Hanoi (pop., 1976 est., 1,443,500). Largest city: Saigon, former capital of South Vietnam, renamed Ho Chi Minh City (pop., 1976 est., 3,460,500). Languages: Vietnamese, French, English. Religion: Buddhist, animist, Confucian, Christian (Roman Catholic), Hoa Hao and Cao Dai religious sects. Secretary of the Vietnamese Workers' (Communist) Party in 1976, Le Duan; president, Ton Duc Thang; premier, Pham Van Dong.

The conquest of South Vietnam by North Vietnamese troops on April 30, 1975, after a long, frustrating war, ended 21 years of partition and resulted in one Vietnam. The new nation emerged as Southeast Asia's paramount military power. Its economic and political potential was also considerable, but a long and painful period of consolidation and assimilation lay ahead. While Vietnam had considerable success in winning international acceptance, its Southeast Asian neighbours remained suspicious of its intentions. A major foreign policy goal, diplomatic relations with the U.S., continued to elude Hanoi.

Rebuilding and modernizing the country's economy, in a low state of development and devastated by nearly 30 years of war, was and would continue to be the country's primary task for many years, but harsh economic realities were not allowed to dim the hard-won glory of unification. Formal reunification was declared July 2, 1976, when a newly elected National Assembly met in Hanoi. The Assembly's 492 members were chosen on April 25 in an all-Vietnam election in which opposition candidates were not allowed.

Some observers had difficulty distinguishing the new government from that of the old Democratic Republic of (North) Vietnam. The hardened leaders who had steered North Vietnam through nearly three decades of war remained in place. Only six South Vietnamese were absorbed into the new government, and they were given honorary or technical positions. Pres. Ton Duc Thang, who had succeeded the late Ho Chi Minh in 1969 and who, at 88, might have been expected to retire, stayed on for the sake of continuity. The new nation adopted the North Vietnamese flag, national anthem, and national emblem. Hanoi remained the capital. The new constitution was little different from that of North Vietnam.

Not everyone liked the new regime. In South Vietnam, in both the Mekong Delta and the Central Highlands, armed bands of former South Vietnamese soldiers continued to hold out against the Communists, but this resistance had no long-term significance. More than 3,000 refugees escaped from South Vietnam by boat in 1976. Most would eventually join the 140,000 Vietnamese who had been granted refuge in the U.S. before the fall of South Vietnam. On the other hand, the Communist regime and the Roman Catholic Church, once considered irreconcilable enemies, appeared to have come to terms. The archbishop of Hanoi was made a cardinal by Pope Paul VI.

TERZIANO TERZANI—SYGMA

Hanoi billboard shows the distribution of seats in the new National Assembly and lists the leaders of the government of unified Vietnam.

With the shooting war won, the economy became the new battlefield. In Hanoi a high-ranking party official told a visitor: "It [the economy] is our third resistance. We fought the first one against the French, the second against the Americans, now we have to fight a new war against our own underdevelopment." As if to act out the military metaphor, the North Vietnamese Army was thrown into the economic campaign. According to Defense Minister Vo Nguyen Giap, "We can only have a solid defense if the country is prosperous."

A new five-year plan to merge the agricultural resources of the South with the more industrialized North was approved at the (Communist) Vietnamese Workers' Party's fourth congress, the first to be held in 16 years, in mid-December. North Vietnam was far better prepared to fight the economic war than the South. After so many years of war and sacrifice, the North was no stranger to austerity or adversity. By contrast, under the stimulus of a false prosperity generated by billions of U.S. dollars, the South was accustomed to luxuries it could no longer afford. The North also had another advantage in that it had a two-year head start. Made safe from U.S. bombers by the January 1973 cease-fire, North Vietnam had immediately begun the reconstruction of its economy. The South, by contrast, had been totally unprepared for its final collapse.

Hoang Tung, editor of the official party newspaper *Nhan Dan,* summed up the problems of the South in terms of three "armies." First, there was the problem of finding jobs for South Vietnam's vanquished mil-

VIETNAM

Education. (1974–75 est.) Primary, secondary, and vocational, pupils *c.* 9.6 million, teachers *c.* 250,000; higher, students *c.* 130,000, teaching staff *c.* 7,000.

Finance. Monetary units: dong (North Vietnam), with (Sept. 20, 1976) an official rate of 2.93 dong to U.S. $1 (nominal rate of 5.05 dong = £1 sterling); new piastre (South Vietnam), with (Sept. 20, 1976) a nominal rate of 1.85 new piastre to U.S. $1 (3.20 new piastres = £1 sterling). Budgets: (North; 1975) balanced at *c.* 6.5 billion dong; (South; 1974) revenue 908 million new piastres, expenditure 1.1 billion new piastres.

Foreign Trade. (1974) Imports *c.* U.S. $2 billion; exports U.S. $400 million. Import sources: U.S. *c.* 35%; U.S.S.R. 13%; China *c.* 12%; Singapore *c.* 12%; Japan *c.* 6%. Export destinations: U.S.S.R. *c.* 14%; China *c.* 12%; East Germany *c.* 10%; Japan *c.* 7%. Main exports: clothing *c.* 10%; fish *c.* 10%; rubber *c.* 10%; coal *c.* 5%.

Transport and Communications. Roads (1972) *c.* 34,400 km. Railways (1973): *c.* 1,500 km; traffic (South only) 170 million passenger-km, freight 1.3 million net ton-km. Air traffic (South only; 1974): 377.5 million passenger-km; freight 3,570,000 net ton-km. Navigable waterways (1973) *c.* 4,500 km. Telephones (South only; Dec. 1973) 47,000. Radio receivers (Dec. 1973) *c.* 2,075,000. Television receivers (Dec. 1973) 500,000.

Agriculture. Production (in 000; metric tons; 1974): rice *c.* 11,400; sweet potatoes *c.* 1,200; cassava *c.* 1,080; rubber *c.* 28; tea *c.* 8; coffee *c.* 7; pork *c.* 440; timber (cu m) 18,400; fish catch *c.* 1,010. Livestock (in 000; 1974): cattle *c.* 1,800; buffalo *c.* 1,800; pigs *c.* 12,300; chickens *c.* 55,000; ducks *c.* 39,000.

Industry. Production (in 000; metric tons; 1974): coal *c.* 2,000; cement *c.* 800; salt *c.* 300; electricity (kw-hr) *c.* 2,300,000.

lion-man army; South Vietnam had an estimated five million unemployed at the time of surrender. The second "army" was the "army of beauty," a reference to the Saigon prostitutes who, in Tung's words, were "attacking our People's army." The third was the "army of intellectuals" who could be useful in science and technology but were poor at farming—the skill Vietnam now needed most. Moving South Vietnam's army of unemployed from the war-swollen urban areas to gainful employment in the countryside was a continuing process. According to one estimate, 600,000 people from Saigon alone were transferred to "new economic zones."

Hanoi again failed to win admission to the UN. On November 15 its application was vetoed in the Security Council by the U.S. because of Hanoi's refusal to account for about 800 Americans missing in action in Vietnam. Earlier, Hanoi had supplied the names of 12 Americans—all had died—but the U.S. dismissed this as "tokenism." For their part, the Vietnamese insisted that the U.S. pay the $3.2 billion to "heal the wounds of war" that had been promised by former president Richard Nixon. The stalemate was evident when, on November 12, representatives of the U.S. and Vietnam met in the Parisian suburb of Neuilly. It was indicated that the talks, the first formal contact between the two countries since the fall of Saigon, were aimed at determining whether conditions were ripe for full-scale negotiations. The U.S. State Department announced that nothing in the talks warranted any change in the U.S. intention to veto Vietnam's UN membership, and no date for renewed talks was set. No further developments in U.S.-Vietnam relations were expected until after President-elect Jimmy Carter took office in January 1977.

Vietnam managed to gain admission to three international financial bodies: the World Bank, the International Monetary Fund, and the Asian Development Bank—all over U.S. objections. This made Vietnam eligible for indirect U.S. aid, since loans by all three organizations were in part financed by U.S. funds.

After branding the Association of Southeast Asian Nations (ASEAN) as a "neocolonialist" tool of "American imperialism," Hanoi underwent a change of mind and dispatched a goodwill mission to all five member countries—the Philippines, Malaysia, Singapore, Indonesia, and Thailand. This conciliatory approach was apparently more a change of tactics than of heart, however, because Vietnam subsequently renewed its propaganda attacks on the ASEAN countries, all of which were plagued by Communist insurgencies of varying importance. Matters were further complicated when Thailand's placatory democratic government was replaced by a strongly anti-Communist military junta that took a hard line toward Hanoi. Contrary to earlier fears, there was no flood of arms from Hanoi to Communist insurgents in other Southeast Asian countries. Nevertheless, Hanoi made plain its support for "the common revolutionary cause of the peoples of Southeast Asia." (KEYES BEECH)

[976.B.4.a–d]

Virgin Islands: *see* Dependent States

Vital Statistics: *see* Demography

Volleyball: *see* Court Games

Wages and Hours: *see* Economy, World; Industrial Relations

Wales: *see* United Kingdom

Warsaw Treaty Organization: *see* Defense

Water Resources: *see* Earth Sciences; Environment

Water Sports

Motorboating. The Bicentennial Gold Cup race, highlight of the unlimited hydroplane circuit and worth more than $76,000 in prize money, was appropriately won by "Miss U.S." driven by Tom D'Eath. But while the Detroit thunderboat delighted the local audience with its winning performance on the Detroit River, the rest of the circuit was dominated by another driver. Bill Muncey, the long-time veteran of unlimited racing, won five of nine regattas to earn the national championship. It was Muncey's fifth title since his first championship in 1960. His five race victories boosted his career total to 38, more than any other man in the sport.

A major factor in his triumph was Muncey's preseason acquisition of the most successful boat in the history of unlimited competition. It was "Pay 'N Pak," owned by Dave Heerensperger. Built of honeycomb aluminum and fitted with a novel tail wing, it had won 16 regattas and 3 national championships in 1973–75. Muncey renamed it the "Atlas Van Lines" (he was a vice-president of the moving firm) and ended a three-year dry spell by winning the season opener at Miami, Fla., in May. Demonstrating the blazing speed of the boat, he drove it at a record qualifying speed of 128.023 mph at San Diego, Calif., the fastest single lap ever recorded in the sport, even in competition. Along with his Miami victory Muncey won at Madison, Ind., Owensboro, Ky., Dayton, Ohio, and the Tri-Cities event in Washington. As mentioned above, D'Eath won in Detroit, while Mickey Remund in "Miss Budweiser" was victorious at Seattle. The 1975 unlimited national champion, Billy Schumacher, won at Washington, D.C., and San Diego to rank second in the standings. He drove "Olympia Beer."

In ocean racing, Honolulu contractor Tom Gentry won the world Union of International Motorboating (UIM) championship after an arduous and expensive campaign. He began the year by winning in Brazil and Uruguay and placing second in Argentina. In two South African races he earned nothing, because he failed to finish one and because the other was not recognized by the UIM. He went on, however, to win in Italy and Sweden, and to finish third at Poole and Cowes-Torquay, both in the U.K. He also won the Bahamas 500. Gentry drove a 35-ft Cigarette with Kiekhaefer Aeromarine engines.

Joel Halpern of New York won the U.S. national offshore championship. He won at Key West, Fla., and Marina del Rey, Calif.; finished second in the Bacardi Trophy Race at Miami; placed third in the Grand Prix del Rey and Bushmills races, both in California; fourth in the Benihana race in New Jersey; fifth in the Bahamas 500; out of the money in Ohio; and blew an engine at the final race of the year in San Francisco. Halpern decided to go after the world title halfway through the year and began commuting to Europe. Despite a late start with his 38-ft Cobra and dual MerCruiser power, he won at Poole, England, and finished third in Sweden's Gettingloppet and in the French Dauphin d'Or. He was fourth in Naples, and with the points earned in the Bahamas 500, Bacardi, and Benihana races in the U.S. finished the year second to Gentry.

(JAMES E. MARTENHOFF)

Canoeing. The big news of the year in 1976 was, of course, the 1976 Olympic Games in Montreal. East Germany and the Soviet Union were the most successful teams. Although the U.S. competitors were outstroked by their opponents, they improved some of their personal best times by as much as six seconds. White-water canoeing was not represented at the 1976 Olympics as it had been in Munich in 1972. To include it or not is left up to the host country. (*See* TRACK AND FIELD SPORTS: *Special Report.*)

White-water canoeing and kayaking continued to enjoy a surge of popularity in the U.S. Increasing effort was being made to save the nation's free-flowing rivers in order to accommodate the growing number of river running enthusiasts. Restoring urban rivers was becoming more widespread so that people could enjoy the sport closer to home.

A remarkable record was set in white-water kayaking in the U.S. by Eric Evans. At the 1976 national championships in California, he retained his title as the national K1 (singles) men's champion for the seventh consecutive year. During this time Evans also ranked among the top ten slalom paddlers of the world.

With the continued growth of canoeing and of the number of persons actively involved in it, safety considerations became more and more important. The American Canoe Association, the U.S. Coast Guard, and the American Red Cross continued to work closely together to put out the most helpful information to the public in order to keep the sport as safe as possible. (JOAN L. MASON)

Water Skiing. A short, wiry Venezuelan with the muscle control of a ballet artist strengthened his hold on his title as the men's world water ski champion during 1976. In the off-year for the official biennial world water ski championships, 17-year-old Carlos Suárez of Maracay, Venezuela, won overall titles in the major international invitational tournaments and proved even to the most skeptical that his narrow 1975 victory over the world's best was only the beginning of his reign as king of water skiing. Establishing new trick records in nearly every appearance, Suárez won the Moomba Masters in Australia in March, took the Western Hemisphere title in Mexico a month later, and captured the Masters Trophy at Callaway Gardens, Ga., in July.

In women's competition, Cindy Todd of Pierson, Fla., moved out front in the chase to determine the successor to the perennial world champion, Liz Allan Shetter, who decided to retire after the 1975 season. Todd won the overall title in the Western Hemisphere competition, took the measure of the women's field in the Masters, and wrapped up a successful season with an overall victory in the U.S. National Championships at Miami, Fla., in August.

Chris Redmond of Canton, Ohio, won the men's U.S. open overall title, while individual event honours went to Bob LaPoint of Castro Valley, Calif., who became the national open champion in both slalom and jumping, and Tony Krupa of Jackson, Mich., who won tricks. In women's jumping Linda Giddens of Eastman, Ga., set a new world record with a leap of 129 ft, two feet better than the mark established by Shetter in 1975.

(THOMAS C. HARDMAN)

Surfing. Professionals, with the Australians and South Africans in the forefront, continued to dominate competitive surfing. The north shore of Oahu, Hawaii, was the scene of five major professional contests during the year. Mark Richards of Australia projected his slashing, aggressive style from his customary 4-ft Australian waves to the 20-ft Hawaiian giants. He so impressed the judges that he won both the Smirnoff and the Men's Cup, taking home an impressive $10,000. His teammate Ian Cairns captured the Duke Classic, with South Africa's Shaun Tomson taking first in the Pipeline Masters. Smooth-surfing Hawaiian Rory Russell saved the occasion for the Islands by winning The Bolt, the only professional contest that used the objective scoring system of awarding fixed points for each maneuver. Back in his homeland, Richards won the Australian Coke Contest. It became evident during these tournaments that the distinctive mode of surfing was changing, from flowing with the waves to attacking them.

Surfing continued to suffer from a shortage of surfing areas and more participants. The consequent crowds led to short tempers and resistance to organized activities.

(J. C. FLANAGAN)

Water Polo. The world's top 12 teams competed in the premier water polo event of 1976, the Olympic Games. After preliminary contests the Hungarians won their first four final-round games to take the gold medal. Italy took home the silver, finishing with a record of two wins, one loss, and two ties; The Netherlands, with an identical record, placed third. Close behind, in order, were Romania, Yugoslavia, and West Germany. The competition among these teams was extremely close, as 6 of their final 15 games were ties and the margin of victory never exceeded two goals.

One of the major Olympic surprises was the failure of the Soviet team, winner of the world championships in 1975 and the Olympic gold medal in 1972, to advance out of the preliminary round; there they were tied by Romania and beaten by The Netherlands. Cuba gained seventh place after being awarded a 5–0 forfeit victory over the Soviet team when the latter failed to attend a scheduled game. The U.S.S.R. played its remaining games to finish eighth. Canada finished ninth, followed by Mexico, Australia, and Iran. Absent from the Olympics after a third-place finish in 1972 was the United States, which failed to qualify at the Pan American Games.

In competition within the U.S., coach Pete Cutino led his University of California Bears to the 1975 National Collegiate Athletic Association championships. The University of California at Irvine finished second and the University of California at Los Angeles third. In the 1976 Amateur Athletic Union championships Cutino's Concord (Calif.) squad took home the honours, followed by Stanford and the Southern California All Stars.

(WILLIAM ENSIGN FRADY)

See also Track and Field Sports: *Special Report*.)

Skin and Scuba Diving. One of the world's finest facilities related to undersea phenomena opened during the year in Miami. Planet Ocean Museum, the brainchild of F. G. Walton-Smith and the International Oceanographic Foundation, was expected to cost

The Embassy-Daily Express International Offshore Powerboat Race at Cowes-Torquay in August was won by Englishman Charles Gill. Photo shows start of the race along Britain's south coast, with third-place winner Tom Gentry of Honolulu in foreground.

LONDON DAILY EXPRESS/PICTORIAL PARADE

ADN-ZB/EASTFOTO

Bernd Olbricht (left) and Joachim Mattern of East Germany won the 500-metre kayak pairs at the Olympic Games in July.

$7 million when finally completed. Half-finished in 1976, it contained such exhibits as the original deep-diving craft, designed by Ed Link and built by John Perry; a replica of the submersible craft "Alvin," donated by the U.S. Navy; an 11-ton oil rig; a real, if small, iceberg; and an immense array of films, slide shows, ship models, diving equipment, and demonstrations. *Planet Ocean,* the motion picture that introduced the exhibit, was nominated for an Academy Award in 1975. When complete, Planet Ocean was expected to become a mecca for divers everywhere.

In other developments, a major step was taken to enhance safety under the sea. Authorities have known that about one-third of all scuba-diving fatalities are related to exhausting the air supply in the tank. Therefore, the leading associations of instructors in 1976 began requiring the use of submersible pressure gauges in training classes. Employment of such gauges, which provide an accurate and constant means of checking on the remaining air supply, should reduce the number of fatalities caused by running out of air. (JAMES E. MARTENHOFF)

See also **Rowing; Sailing; Swimming.**

[452.B.4.a]

Western Samoa

A constitutional monarchy and member of the Commonwealth of Nations, Western Samoa is an island group in the South Pacific Ocean, about 1,600 mi. E of New Zealand and 2,200 mi. S of Hawaii. Area: 1,075 sq mi (2,784 sq km), with two major islands, Savai'i (662 sq mi) and Upolu (435 sq mi), and seven smaller islands. Pop. (1976 est.): 152,200. Cap. and largest city: Apia (pop., 1971, 30,300). Language: Samoan and English. Religion (1971): Congregational 51%, Roman Catholic 22%, Methodist 16%, others 11%. Head of state (*O le Ao o le Malo*) in 1976, Malietoa Tanumafili II; prime ministers, Tupua Tamasese Lealofi IV and, from March 24, Tupuola Taisi Tufuga Efi.

In elections held in March 1976 about half of the 36 members who sought reelection for the Legislative Assembly were successful; there were 28 new members, younger and well educated. An issue was the deterioration of living standards caused by a minor economic recession. The new prime minister, Tupuola Taisi Tufuga Efi, replaced his cousin, Tupua Tamasese Lealofi IV, and was the first non-*Tama Aiga* ("royal son") to hold the office.

In 1975 the Tamasese government had recognized China and reached preliminary agreement on diplomatic links with the U.S.S.R. In 1976 this latter decision was confirmed and followed by discussions on "mutual cooperation" with particular reference to fisheries. Similar discussions took place with Chinese diplomats, and during a visit to Peking by Malietoa Tanumafili II an agreement under which China would provide technical assistance was signed. During the year Western Samoa and the other South Pacific Forum countries agreed not to make any fisheries agreements final until after the conclusion of the Law of the Sea Conference. (*See* LAW: *Special Report.*) On December 15 Western Samoa became the 147th member of the UN. (BARRIE MACDONALD)

[977.A.3]

WESTERN SAMOA

Education. (1975) Primary, pupils 32,642, teachers 968; secondary, pupils 15,098, teachers 773; vocational, pupils 131, teachers 10; teacher training, students 490, teachers 30; higher, students 249, teaching staff 9.

Finance and Trade. Monetary unit: tala (dollar), with (Sept. 20, 1976) a free rate of 0.87 tala to U.S. $1 (1.50 tala = £1 sterling). Budget (1973 actual): revenue 9,174,000 tala; expenditure 10,569,000 tala. Foreign trade (1975): imports 20,482,000 tala; exports 4,541,000 tala. Import sources: New Zealand 27%; Australia 24%; U.S. 13%; Japan 11%; U.K. 7%; Singapore 5%. Export destinations: The Netherlands 33%; New Zealand 20%; West Germany 20%; Sweden 9%. Main exports: copra 58%; cocoa 26%.

Winter Sports

The worldwide coverage of sports on snow and ice in the Winter Olympics did much in 1976 to further public awareness of these recreations. (See *Special Report.*)

Ice Skating. A survey of recreational skating in Canada estimated that at least two million people participated on some 2,000 rinks of all kinds. It was believed that the sport attracted nearly ten million in the U.S. and approximately half that number in Western Europe. By the end of May, the Canadian Figure Skating Association, the largest organization of its kind in the world, had increased its membership to 152,475 in 1,015 clubs. Following a period of marking time in Australia, a national resurgence of ice skating was sparked by government grants, enabling improvements to be made at the main Sydney rink.

Singles events provided new titleholders in the world ice figure and dance championships, held in Göteborg, Sweden, on March 2–6; 22 nations were represented by 110 skaters, including the first entry from New Zealand.

FIGURE SKATING. John Curry (*see* BIOGRAPHY) enterprisingly blended athleticism with advanced artistic grace to become Britain's first men's world champion in 37 years, after winning the Olympic and European titles during the preceding 50 days. This third leg of the rarely achieved triple crown was an exacting trial of character and temperament as well as technique. Curry owed his world title to a well-nigh perfect performance in the final free skating. It enabled him to turn a deficit into victory by the narrowest of margins. Two earlier errors by Curry had enabled Vladimir

Kovalev of the Soviet Union to begin the last round ahead on points, and Kovalev almost made it, the judges ultimately splitting 5–4 in the Englishman's favour. Curry included his usual three triple jumps, but Kovalev attempted four—and it proved one too many. The Moscow skater fell from an almost desperate triple toe loop jump, and this undoubtedly cost him the title. Third was Jan Hoffmann, the 1974 champion from East Germany.

An unprecedented back somersault by Terry Kubicka of the U.S., who placed sixth, was cheered by the crowd, but at the annual meeting of the International Skating Union (ISU) council, in Rome, Italy, on May 21–24, it was decided that somersault-type jumps as elements of free skating in competitions henceforth would be forbidden and penalized by the judges.

Dorothy Hamill (*see* BIOGRAPHY) of the U.S. enhanced her Olympic victory by dethroning The Netherlands' U.S.-based Dianne de Leeuw to become the women's champion. Hamill paced her free skating shrewdly, taking no undue risks and attempting no triple jumps. Her highlights were two good double axels and her own special spin, the "Hamill camel." The victory was clear-cut, but there was a mighty duel for the silver medal between de Leeuw and Christine Errath, the East German gaining second place by a hairline decision.

Irina Rodnina won the pairs title for a record-shattering eighth successive time, and the fourth with Aleksandr Zaitsev as partner. With powerful overhead lifts and neatly matched jumps and spins, the Soviet duo once more outclassed their East German "shadows," Rolf Österreich and Romy Kermer. Third place was taken by another Soviet partnership, Aleksandr Vlasov and Irina Vorobieva.

ICE DANCING. Aleksandr Gorshkov and his wife, Ludmila Pakhomova, recaptured the ice dance title. Watched by a capacity crowd of 11,500, the elegant Soviet couple scored seven sixes for artistic impression and three more for technical merit—the highest marks in any world championship—to gain their sixth win in seven years. They were never seriously challenged by their compatriots, Andrey Minenkov and Irina Moiseyeva, who had won the previous year when Gorshkov was unable to compete because of illness. But "Min and Mo" did manage to resist constant pressure from the third-place Americans, Jim Millns and Colleen O'Connor.

The number of international figure and dance competitions increased at all levels. Augmenting the successful continuance in Geneva, Switz., of the senior European championships, which date from 1891, the first ISU junior championships were held at Mégève, France, as an experiment likely to lead to official world junior championships. A third international Skate Canada senior tournament was well supported at Edmonton, Alta.; the Richmond Trophy women's senior international had its 28th event in London, England; and 18 other international meets were staged in Austria, Belgium, Bulgaria, Czechoslovakia, France, East Germany, Italy, Poland, Romania, Switzerland, West Germany and Yugoslavia.

SPEED SKATING. Piet Kleine maintained Dutch superiority when he became the new overall winner in the men's world ice speed championship on his home track at Heerenveen on February 28–29. Sten Stensen of Norway was runner-up without winning any of the four races, and another Dutchman, Hans van Helden, finished third. The versatile Kleine was first in both the 1,500 m and the 10,000 m; van Helden won the 5,000 m; and Eric Heiden of the U.S. took the 500 m.

WIDE WORLD

Galina Stepanskaya of the Soviet Union skates to victory in the women's 1,500-metre speed skating event at the Winter Olympics in Innsbruck in February.

The women's world speed championship at Gjøvik, Norway, on February 21–22, produced the first Canadian overall winner, Sylvia Burka, since the institution of the title in 1936. For the second straight year Tatyana Averina (U.S.S.R.) and Sheila Young (U.S.) finished runner-up and third, respectively. Young won both the shorter distances, 500 m and 1,000 m. Burka, first in the 1,500 m, recorded the first victory in any event for Canada. Karin Kessow, the deposed East German overall champion, won the 3,000 m.

Separate world sprint titles for men and women, in West Berlin on March 6–7, were won, respectively, by Johan Granath (the first victory for a Swede) and Sheila Young (her third triumph in four seasons).

World records were broken over four men's and two women's distances. At Medeo, U.S.S.R., Stensen lowered the 10,000 m to 14 min 38.08 sec and Yevgeni Kulikov of the Soviet Union reduced the 1,000 m to 1 min 15.70 sec. At Inzell, West Germany, van Helden clocked the 1,500 m in 1 min 55.61 sec, and Kleine covered the 5,000 m in 7 min 2.38 sec. Young closed a personally gratifying season with a new time of 40.68 sec for the 500-m sprint at Inzell, and the Soviet long-distance racer, Galina Stepanskaya, brought the 3,000-m figures down to 4 min 31.00 sec at Medeo. Eighty-two nonchampionship international speed meets were held during the season in Austria, East Germany, Italy, The Netherlands, Norway, Sweden, Switzerland, West Germany, and the U.S.S.R.

The status of indoor speed skating was raised significantly by the appointment of a new ISU technical committee for short-track racing. The sequel was expected to be the institution of indoor world ice speed championships, probably starting in 1978, to satisfy a demand from many nations without outdoor circuits.

Skiing. The continuing spread and advancing standards of skiing throughout the world were underlined by Olympic entries from 33 of the 48 member nations of the International Ski Federation (FIS). Both governmental and private investments to develop new skiing areas were supported by the manufacturers of a growing variety of improved, more sophisticated equipment. A new era of South American skiing was

Weather:
see Earth Sciences

Weight Lifting:
see Gymnastics and Weight Lifting

Welfare:
see Social and Welfare Services

West Indies:
see Bahamas, The; Barbados; Cuba; Dependent States; Dominican Republic; Grenada; Haiti; Jamaica; Latin-American Affairs; Trinidad and Tobago

apparent, particularly in the Argentine and Chilean Andes, respectively spearheaded by increased investment and participation at Bariloche and Portillo.

The Soviet Skiing Federation exceeded the four million-membership mark and had 51,519 paid trainers at 9,088 centres. Sigge Bergman, the FIS secretary-general, made an official visit to the Far East and reported considerable expansion in Asia, notably at Ho-huan in Taiwan, which claimed to have 30,000 skiers. In Japan the number of skiers exceeded six million, with more than 300 clubs in Tokyo alone. The country had 34 ski manufacturers with an annual output of more than one million pairs of skis, 140,000 pairs of which were exported. Japan's newest alpine racing centre, Kitanomine, was preparing to rival Sapporo as host to international events. An impressive new resort opened at Gulmarg in Kashmir, India.

Nordic disciplines gained more active following outside their traditional north European strongholds, especially in Switzerland and the U.S. Dual or parallel slaloming, previously well supported in North America, attracted more interest in Europe. Freestyle skiing, stressing spectacular acrobatic and ballet movements, also gained a firmer foothold. Grass skiing, while providing wider facilities for off-snow practice, thrived also as a sport in its own right.

ALPINE SKIING. In alpine racing, the biennial world championships were, as usual in an Olympic year, decided concurrently with the Winter Games results, from which alpine combination titles were calculated on an overall points basis. The men's world champion was Gustav Thöni of Italy, repeating his 1972 combination success. The runner-up was Willy Frommelt of Liechtenstein, with Greg Jones of the U.S. third. Rosi Mittermaier (*see* BIOGRAPHY) of West Germany, the season's outstanding racer, was an easy women's winner, with Daniele Debernard of France trailing in second. Another Liechtenstein skier, Hanny Wenzel, was third in a memorable season for the principality, whose competitors also secured fifth place in both the men's and women's overall ratings.

Despite the glamour of the Olympics the tenth annual World Cup series was generally regarded as the season's major test, and it produced new winners. Ingemar Stenmark of Sweden, the previous year's runner-up, went one better in 1976 to become the first victor from a non-Alpine nation. Second was Piero Gros of Italy, the 1974 winner, and third was Thöni, the title defender, with a great record of four wins in five years halted. Stenmark was first in both slalom and giant slalom, but failed to take a point in downhill, which was once more gained decisively by the Austrian specialist, Franz Klammer (*see* BIOGRAPHY).

Karl Schnabl of Austria won the 90-metre ski jump at the Winter Olympics in Innsbruck.

GERRY CRANHAM

Mittermaier, a convincing winner of the women's World Cup, proved a rightful successor to Annemarie Proell-Moser, who did not compete. After struggling through nine seasons with only modest achievements, Mittermaier owed her eventual triumph to all-round consistency, finishing first in slalom, third in giant slalom, and ninth in downhill. Overall second was Lise-Marie Morerod of Switzerland, who won the giant slalom. In third place was Monika Kaserer of Austria. Although another Austrian, Brigitte Totschnig, led in the downhill, she only finished sixth because of relatively weak performances in the slalom races.

The World Cup series was contested over 26 men's and 27 women's events spread through four months of meetings in Austria, Canada, France, Italy, Switzerland, the U.S., West Germany, and Yugoslavia. For the second year, dual slaloms provided crowd-pulling final events, although less hinged on these than in 1975 because the trophy winners had scored enough points earlier to ensure their victories. The Nations' Cup was won by Austria for the fourth consecutive year, with Switzerland and Italy second and third. Italians topped the men's standings, but Austria emerged ahead because of its women's superiority.

The sixth Can-Am Trophy series, at ten North American venues, was won by Eric Wilson and Viki Fleckenstein, both of the U.S. Ten nations contested the third international parallel slalom tournament for citadin racers, won by the Swiss at Val d'Isère, France, on April 10–11. The idea of citadin racing had been inspired a decade earlier by the winter sports pioneer Sir Arnold Lunn to establish an intermediate "league" barring full-time racers and thereby to encourage the part-timers. The objective remained sensible, but the definition of a citadin racer (one not domiciled in a mountain resort) seemed outmoded. Changing conditions appeared to justify a revised definition, perhaps to restrict eligibility to racers having earned fewer than a stipulated number of FIS points.

Henri Duvillard of France won 15 of 21 races, including seven in succession, to become world professional champion on the North American circuit, comfortably ahead of the Swiss runner-up, Josef Odermatt. Third place was shared by two Americans, Tyler Palmer and Bobby Cochran. The professional world was jolted by the shooting death on March 21 of the flamboyant U.S. alpine racer Vladimir "Spider" Sabich, 31, world professional champion in 1971 and 1972 and probably the biggest reason, through his inspiring performances, for the professional circuit's rapid success after a tentative start in 1970.

NORDIC SKIING. In Nordic skiing the giant Finn Juha Mieto, after a disappointing effort at the Innsbruck Olympics, had a string of successes late in the season and won the unofficial cross-country World Cup, decided over 14 selected races. His teammate Arto Koivisto was a close second, with Ivar Formo of Norway third. The prestigious Holmenkollen 50 km in Norway was taken by Sven-Åke Lundbäck of Sweden, followed by Mieto and Koivisto.

As usual, the Norwegian Birkebeiner Ski Race, covering the 55-km distance from Rena to Lillehammer, attracted one of the largest fields in any race—3,500 entrants. The grueling contest was won on March 21 by Audun Kolstad, a Norwegian army lieutenant.

Reidar Hjermstad, also of Norway, was second, followed by John Downey, the first U.S. skier ever to gain a place. For the first time a women's section was included, and the winner among the 75 competitors was Berit Mørdre Lammedal of Norway.

A new world record ski jump was achieved by Toni Innauer of Austria when he cleared 176 m (577.42 ft) at Oberstdorf, West Germany, on March 7. The most successful jumper during the season was Karl Schnabl, an Austrian Olympic gold medalist, who was ranked first in a series of selected tournaments, followed by Innauer and Jochen Danneberg of East Germany. The FIS council, meeting at Innsbruck in February, decided to establish a commission to standardize equipment.

OTHER SKIING EVENTS. In the most lucrative North American professional freestyle season so far, the men's and women's World Trophy titles were won by Scott Brooksbank and Marion Post, both of the U.S. John Eaves, a Canadian, was second to Brooksbank, and Manfred Kastner of Austria finished third. Joannie Teorey was runner-up in the overall standings for women, followed by fellow American Sandra Poulson. Officials of leading professional freestyle skiers' organizations from the U.S., Canada, and Europe met at Heavenly Valley, Calif., on April 19 to form a joint committee to develop international safety guidelines and standards for this daring branch of the sport.

There was a trend toward the use of lighter weight machines by skibobbers of all grades. The men's and women's combination titles in the European skibob championships, at Spindleruv Mlyn, Czech., from February 29 to March 6, were won by Moulis Jirf of the host nation and Gudrun Müller of West Germany.

Bobsledding. Senior bobsled racing during the season was limited to six tracks: at Königssee, West Germany; Igls, Austria (used in the Winter Olympics); St.-Moritz, Switz.; Cervinia, Italy; Oberhof, East Germany; and Lake Placid, N.Y. Early training was hampered by rain at Königssee during January and the restricted use of the Igls track, which handicapped the Japanese, whose course at Sapporo had not opened. Plans were agreed to begin the full refrigeration of the Lake Placid run, which would make it the world's first wholly artificially frozen course designed exclusively for bobsledding.

Next to the Winter Olympics, the major international meet was the European championships, at Saint-Moritz from February 17 to March 1. The Swiss course was regarded as more challenging than the shorter one at Igls, and so many enthusiasts took the European contests more seriously than the Olympics. The East Germans, who had won both Olympic events after simulating the conditions at Igls during training at Oberhof, this time were unplaced. Erich Schärer drove his Swiss sled to victory in the two-man event, more than two seconds ahead of Stefan Gaisreiter's West German entry. Gaisreiter, who had not been in the Olympics, won the four-man event, outpacing his more experienced compatriot, Wolfgang Zimmerer, by 0.18 sec. Schärer finished third. Zimmerer, one of the sport's most successful drivers, afterward announced his retirement.

Tobogganing. Favourable weather enabled an exceptionally successful season of skeleton tobogganing on the Cresta Run at Saint-Moritz. (A skeleton toboggan is a sled consisting of steel runners fastened to a platform chassis with a sliding seat; it is ridden in a headfirst, prone position.) A record number of 7,832 descents beat by 83 the previous best figure set the year before. The season's fastest times were 54.80 sec from Top by Ulie Burgerstein and 43.30 sec from Junction by Reto Gansser. The track's major event, the 67th Grand National, was won by Gansser, with Burgerstein the runner-up and Franco Gansser completing a Swiss grand slam. The 53rd Curzon Cup Race from Junction also went to Reto Gansser, setting a new aggregate record of 260.72 sec for the six descents, followed by his brother Franco and yet another Swiss rider, Bruno Bischofberger. The Italian veteran Nino Bibbia, 53, remained remarkably sharp and competitive, winning the Johannes Badrutt Trophy and finishing respectably high in most other events.

WIDE WORLD

East Germany's team won the four-man bobsled competition at the Winter Olympics.

The number of serious participants, worldwide, in luge tobogganing rose above 40,000, the majority in Europe but with increased interest evident in North America. Seventeen nations took part in the 22nd world championships, decided concurrently with the Winter Olympics. (*See* Special Report.)

Curling. The 18th world championship for the Air Canada Silver Broom was won by the U.S., defeating Scotland 6–5 in the final, at Duluth, Minn., on March 22–28. This was the third victory for the Americans since the event began in 1959; they had previously held the title in 1965 and 1974. The winning rink, from Hibbing, Minn., was skipped by Bruce Roberts and included his younger brother Joe Roberts, Gary Kleffman, and Jerry Scott. Scotland was represented by a rink from Perth, comprising Bill Muirhead (skip), Derek Scott, Len Dudman, and Roy Sinclair. In the semifinals Switzerland, the title defender, lost 5–3 to Scotland, and the U.S. beat Sweden 9–3. The other six nations competing were Italy, Norway, France, West Germany, Canada, and Denmark.

In the European championships, held in January at Mégève, Norway and Scotland won the men's and women's contests, respectively, with Sweden the runner-up in each. An indication of the game's growth was the sponsoring by the British firm Uniroyal Ltd. of a second annual world junior championship. At the meet the title defended by the first winner, Sweden, was captured by Canada at Aviemore, Scotland.

Ice Boating. Speeds of 80 kph were achieved by ice boats on a frozen lake at La Valle, Switz. The main activity, however, was in North America, near the New Jersey and New Hampshire coasts and in the Great Lakes Basin, where the most popular craft remained the bow-steered Skeeter class, limited to 75 sq ft of sail.

(HOWARD BASS)

See also Ice Hockey.

[452.B.4.g–h]

Wood Products: *see* Industrial Review

World Bank: *see* Economy, World

Wrestling: *see* Combat Sports

Yachting: *see* Sailing

INNSBRUCK: THE XII WINTER OLYMPIC GAMES

By Howard Bass

The Olympic future for sports on snow and ice was largely reassured by the experienced organization of the XII Winter Olympic Games, declared open on Feb. 4, 1976, by Pres. Rudolf Kirchschläger of Austria. The 37 events on skis, skates, or sleds —two more than in 1972—were held on seven sites compactly within a 15-mi radius of Innsbruck, the Austrian Alpine resort which, because of its successful staging of the 1964 Games, was entrusted sooner than expected with its second presentation. Denver, Colo., the venue originally selected, withdrew owing to financial and environmental difficulties.

Thirty-seven nations were represented by 1,036 competitors (788 men and 248 women). Because the majority of the 1964 sites could be adapted for use again and most facilities could be put to subsequent community use, the budget was markedly modest compared with the two previous meets (Sapporo, Japan, and Grenoble, France). Administration ran smoothly, with only minor sensations when a Soviet Nordic skier was deprived of a bronze medal and the Czechoslovak ice-hockey team was penalized, in both cases for dope-taking infringements. Favourable weather conditions enabled every event to be held as and when it had been scheduled. Contestants from 12 nations shared the gold medals, the U.S.S.R. gaining 13; East Germany 7; Norway and the U.S. 3 each; Austria, Finland, and West Germany 2 each; and Canada, Great Britain, Italy, The Netherlands, and Switzerland 1 apiece.

The opening alpine skiing event brought local glory in the men's downhill for Austria's Franz Klammer (*see* BIOGRAPHY). On a hard, icy course down the lofty Patscherkofel Mountain, he resisted the pressure of being the favourite to outpace Bernhard Russi, the veteran Swiss runner-up, at a speed averaging 66.5 mph. The other five alpine events were held at Axamer-Lizum, where there was a double Swiss success on a difficult giant slalom course when Heini Hemmi beat his compatriot Ernst Good, both surprisingly ahead of Sweden's Ingemar Stenmark and the World Cup holder, Gustav Thöni of Italy. In the slalom, Thöni was narrowly defeated by his teammate Piero Gros, who rallied magnificently in his second descent after having previously placed only fifth.

Rosi Mittermaier (*see* BIOGRAPHY), a West German who reached her career peak at exactly the right moment, became the first woman to gain two golds and a silver in alpine skiing. Amazingly, the downhill victory was her first senior international triumph, more than half a second ahead of Austria's Brigitte Totschnig. Mittermaier's slalom win was helped when the favoured Swiss racer, Lise-Marie Morerod, fell during her second run. In the giant slalom, Mittermaier was denied a grand slam by Kathy Kreiner of Canada, only 0.12 sec separating them. The alpine skiing was also notable for the only two medals gained by Liechtenstein competitors in any Olympic winter or summer event: bronzes for Willy Frommelt in the men's slalom and Hanny Wenzel in the women's.

Skiers from five nations took the 12 gold medals in Nordic skiing. In the cross-country racing, contested over well-devised courses at Seefeld, Nikolay Bajukov and Yevgeni Beliaev finished first and second for the U.S.S.R. in the 15 km. Their fellow countryman, Sergey Saveliev, won the 30 km, in which second-place William Koch became the first U.S. skier ever to gain a Nordic event medal. In the supreme test of stamina, the 50 km, Ivar Formo gained Norway's third successive victory with a strategically brilliant performance in a blinding snowstorm, 0.83 sec faster than the veteran East German Gert-Dietmar Klause.

Raisa Smetanina (U.S.S.R.) was the most successful woman racer, achieving two golds and a silver. She won the 10 km and was in the victorious Soviet relay team, but in the 5 km was unexpectedly defeated by Helena Takalo of Finland. Galina Kulakova, also in the Soviet relay team, became the first woman to win a fourth Olympic gold medal in Nordic skiing, having earned the others at Sapporo in 1972.

The Soviets took both team and individual biathlon honours. In the latter, Nikolay Kruglov outpointed Heikki Ikola of Finland, after the favourite, three-time world champion Aleksandr Tikhonov, ruined an early lead with six faults in a tricky wind at the final firing range.

OLYMPIC CHAMPIONS, 1976 WINTER GAMES, INNSBRUCK

Event	Winner	Result
Alpine Skiing		
Men		
Downhill	F. Klammer (Austria)	1 min 45.73 sec
Slalom	P. Gros (Italy)	2 min 03.29 sec
Giant slalom	H. Hemmi (Switz.)	3 min 26.97 sec
Women		
Downhill	R. Mittermaier (West Germany)	1 min 46.16 sec
Slalom	R. Mittermaier (West Germany)	1 min 30.54 sec
Giant slalom	K. Kreiner (Canada)	1 min 29.13 sec
Nordic Skiing		
Men		
15-km cross-country	N. Bajukov (U.S.S.R.)	43 min 58.47 sec
30-km cross-country	S. Saveliev (U.S.S.R.)	1 hr 30 min 29.38 sec
50-km cross-country	I. Formo (Norway)	2 hr 37 min 30.05 sec
40-km ski relay	Finland	2 hr 7 min 59.72 sec
70-m ski jump	H.-G. Aschenbach (East Germany)	252.0 pt
90-m ski jump	K. Schnabl (Austria)	234.8 pt
Nordic combined	U. Wehling (East Germany)	423.39 pt
Women		
5-km cross-country	H. Takalo (Finland)	15 min 48.69 sec
10-km cross-country	R. Smetanina (U.S.S.R.)	30 min 13.41 sec
20-km ski relay	U.S.S.R.	1 hr 7 min 49.75 sec
Biathlon		
Individual	N. Kruglov (U.S.S.R.)	1 hr 14 min 12.26 sec
Relay	U.S.S.R.	1 hr 57 min 55.64 sec
Figure Skating		
Men	J. Curry (U.K.)	192.74 pt
Women	D. Hamill (U S.)	193.80 pt
Pairs	I. Rodnina and A. Zaitsev (U.S.S.R.)	140.54 pt
Ice dancing	L. Pakhomova and A. Gorshkov (U.S.S.R.)	209.92 pt
Speed Skating		
Men		
500 m	Y. Kulikov (U.S.S.R.)	39.17 sec*
1,000 m	P. Mueller (U.S.)	1 min 19.32 sec
1,500 m	J. Storholt (Norway)	1 min 59.38 sec*
5,000 m	S. Stensen (Norway)	7 min 24.48 sec
10,000 m	P. Kleine (Neth.)	14 min 50.59 sec*
Women		
500 m	S. Young (U.S.)	42.76 sec*
1,000 m	T. Averina (U.S.S.R.)	1 min 28.43 sec*
1,500 m	G. Stepanskaya (U.S.S.R.)	2 min 16.58 sec*
3,000 m	T. Averina (U.S.S.R.)	4 min 45.19 sec*
Ice Hockey		
Winning team	U.S.S.R. (beat Czechoslovakia 4–3 in final)	
Bobsledding		
Two man	East Germany	3 min 44.42 sec
Four man	East Germany	3 min 40.43 sec
Tobogganing (Luge)		
Single (men)	D. Günther (East Germany)	3 min 27.69 sec
Two man	East Germany	1 min 25.60 sec
Single (women)	M. Schumann (East Germany)	2 min 50.62 sec

*Olympic record.

Howard Bass is winter sports correspondent for the Daily Telegraph, *London, and other newspapers and periodicals, and for the BBC. His publications include* This Skating Age, The Magic of Skiing, International Encyclopaedia of Winter Sports, *and* Let's Go Skating.

LEFT, UPI COMPIX; RIGHT, CAMERA PRESS

Lighting the twin flames to open the XII Winter Olympics in February. Thirty-seven nations were represented. Ski jumpers on the 90-metre slope had a breathtaking view of the main streets of Innsbruck, nestled in the Austrian Alps.

In the ski jumping on the 70-m hill at Seefeld, Hans-Georg Aschenbach and Jochen Danneberg, both East Germans, finished first and second with Austria's Karl Schnabl in third place. But Schnabl took his revenge in the spectacular final event of the Games, winning the 90-m jump on Bergisel Hill, which towered majestically above and in sight of Innsbruck's main streets. Another Austrian, Toni Innauer, at 17 a great prospect, placed second after recording the best single leap. An East German, Ulrich Wehling, defeated his West German rival, Urban Hettich, in the Nordic combined event.

The figure skating will be best remembered for a new dimension of stylish technique by the men's victor, John Curry (*see* BIOGRAPHY), the first Briton to win the title. He followed meticulously executed figures with all-round competence in free skating that was unprecedented. His brilliantly prepared program was a masterly combination of great jumps, including three triples, versatile spins, and artistic linking steps, all smoothly molded with admirably timed continuity. Among the vanquished were the 1975 and 1974 world champions.

Although not including a triple jump in her always graceful repertoire, Dorothy Hamill (*see* BIOGRAPHY) became the fourth American to take the women's figure-skating title, avenging her defeat in the world games during the previous season by Dianne de Leeuw of The Netherlands, this time a close runner-up. The Italian coach Carlo Fassi gained the distinction of being the first to train both singles winners the same year.

Irina Rodnina, this time partnered by Aleksandr Zaitsev, retained the pairs title she had won at Sapporo with Aleksey Ulanov. The Soviet pair was outstanding in overhead lifts and well-synchronized jumps, despite a faulty double axel by Zaitsev. Ice dancing was included for the first time in an Olympic program and the victors, Aleksandr Gorshkov and Ludmila Pakhomova of the U.S.S.R., endorsed previous general assessments of their world superiority and contributed appreciably by their elegant performance toward justification of the event's inclusion.

Norwegian supporters equipped with bells, horns, flags, and even kites added colourfully to the atmosphere at the speed skating, held in the heart of Innsbruck on a renovated 400-m outdoor circuit, adjacent to the architecturally impressive indoor stadium used for the figure skating and ice hockey events. The Norwegian fans did not cheer in vain. Their idol, Sten Stensen, defeated the Dutch racer Piet Kleine in the 5,000 m, though Kleine reversed the order in the arduous 10,000 m. Another Norwegian, Jan Egil Storholt, won the 1,500 m on his 27th birthday. Peter Mueller of the U.S. won the newly introduced 1,000 m, and the 500-m sprint went to Yevgeni Kulikov (U.S.S.R.). The victories of Kulikov, Storholt, and Kleine were all achieved in new Olympic record times.

Conditions were calmer and sunnier for the four women's events, in which previous Olympic records were bettered no fewer than 36 times. The most prominent racer, Tatyana Averina of the U.S.S.R., won the 1,000 m and 3,000 m on consecutive days and finished third in each of the other two events. Next best was Sheila Young of the U.S., who gained three medals, one of each colour, her gold for the 500 m confirming her world sprinting superiority. The middle-distance 1,500 m was won by the Soviet racer Galina Stepanskaya.

Ice-hockey enthusiasts were not disappointed with a fitting climax, the destiny of gold and silver medals resting on the final game between the Soviet title defenders and the Czechoslovak challengers. The latter led 3–2 with only five minutes left, but two late Soviet goals denied Czechoslovakia its first Olympic victory in the event and clinched the Soviets' fifth. The U.S.S.R. looked more vulnerable than in previous years yet still managed to pull through. The U.S., fielding the youngest team in the tournament, lost 4–1 to West Germany in its final match, a defeat that cost it what had earlier looked like a likely bronze medal. In the 15-match series Vladimir Shadrin of the U.S.S.R. was highest scorer, with six, and Jiri Holecek of Czechoslovakia was a persistently safe netminder.

For the first time, mainly for reasons of economy, the bobsledding and luge tobogganing were held on the same course, the world's largest artificially frozen track—4,000 ft long with 14 bends and 50 mi of cooling pipes—built at Igls, the mini-resort 1,000 ft above Innsbruck. Meinhard Nehmer, the East German driver, mastered the winding, steeply banked ice chute to gain his country both the two-man and four-man bobsled titles. Practice seemed more important than experience on a track shorter, slower, and simpler than most bobsledders would have wished. East Germans also won all three luge titles, Detlef Günther and Margit Schumann taking the men's and women's singles. The winning men's double-seater sled was ridden by Hans Rinn and Norbert Hahn.

The politically trouble-free meet closed on February 15 with a new confidence that the Winter Olympics could be maintained as a viable undertaking—but perhaps only if restricted to a handful of the world's most suitably equipped locations, which might include Lake Placid, N.Y., the chosen site for 1980.

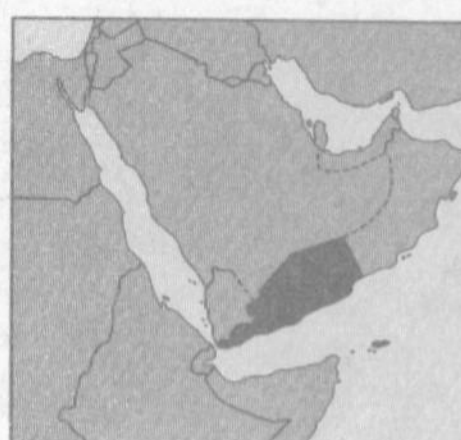

Yemen, People's Democratic Republic of

A people's republic in the southern coastal region of the Arabian Peninsula, Yemen (Aden) is bordered by Yemen (San'a'), Saudi Arabia, and Oman. Area: 111,074 sq mi (287,680 sq km). Pop. (1975 est.): 1,690,000. Cap. and largest city: Aden (pop., 1973, 132,500). Language: Arabic. Religion: Muslim. Chairman of the Presidential Council in 1976, Salem Ali Rubayyi; prime minister, Ali Nasir Muhammad Husani.

For the People's Democratic Republic of Yemen (South Yemen) 1976 was marked by the establishment on March 9 of diplomatic relations with Saudi Arabia, which had boycotted its Marxist-oriented regime. Saudi Arabia provided South Yemen with a reported $100 million in aid. The government attempted to improve its relations with other Arab states, and the foreign minister toured most of them during the spring. The rapprochement with the Saudis led on March 11 to a cease-fire with Oman, whose Dhofari rebels South Yemen had been supporting, but there were additional border incidents later in the year. South Yemen criticized Iraq for ratifying its agreement with Iran that effectively ended Iraq's support for the Dhofari rebels.

The new relationship with Saudi Arabia raised doubts about South Yemen's close ties with the U.S.S.R. However, the U.S.S.R. continued to supply economic aid, on which South Yemen remained dependent. Reports that the government had closed the office of the Eritrean Liberation Front in Aden at the request of Ethiopia were denied, but South Yemen clearly reduced its support for the Eritrean rebels.

The country relied on outside aid for development. Hopes for a 500% increase in shipping calling at Aden after the Suez Canal's reopening in 1975 were not fulfilled; the increase was still less than 50% early in 1976. (PETER MANSFIELD)

[978.B.4.b]

YEMEN, PEOPLE'S DEMOCRATIC REPUBLIC OF

Education. (1973–74) Primary, pupils 183,744, teachers 6,355; secondary, pupils 30,808, teachers 1,445; vocational (1970–71), pupils 952, teachers 142; teacher training, students 408, teachers 35; higher, students 383, teaching staff 75.

Finance and Trade. Monetary unit: Yemen dinar, with (Sept. 20, 1976) a par value of 0.345 dinar to U.S. $1 (free rate of 0.62 dinar = £1 sterling). Budget (1974–75 actual): revenue 18,130,000 dinars; expenditure 27,450,000 dinars. Foreign trade: imports (1974) 64.7 million dinars; exports (1973) 39,490,000 dinars. Import sources (1973): Japan *c.* 8%; Kuwait *c.* 8%; Iraq *c.* 8%; U.K. *c.* 7%. Export destinations (1973): Canada *c.* 21%; Yemen (San'a') *c.* 7%; U.K. *c.* 7%; Australia *c.* 6%; Angola *c.* 6%; United Arab Emirates 5%. Main export petroleum products 72%.

Transport. Roads (1972) *c.* 4,500 km (mainly tracks; including *c.* 1,000 km with improved surface). Motor vehicles in use (1973): passenger 10,600; commercial (including buses) 7,900. There are no railways. Ships entered (1974): vessels totaling 5,160,000 net registered tons; goods loaded 2,308,000 metric tons, unloaded 3,780,000 metric tons.

Agriculture. Production (in 000; metric tons; 1974): millet and sorghum *c.* 76; wheat *c.* 15; watermelons *c.* 30; dates *c.* 8; cotton, lint *c.* 5; fish catch 133. Livestock (in 000; 1974): cattle *c.* 99; sheep *c.* 230; goats *c.* 915; camels *c.* 40; chickens *c.* 1,350.

Industry. Production (in 000; metric tons; 1974): petroleum products *c.* 2,600; salt *c.* 75; electricity (kw-hr) *c.* 174,000.

Yemen Arab Republic

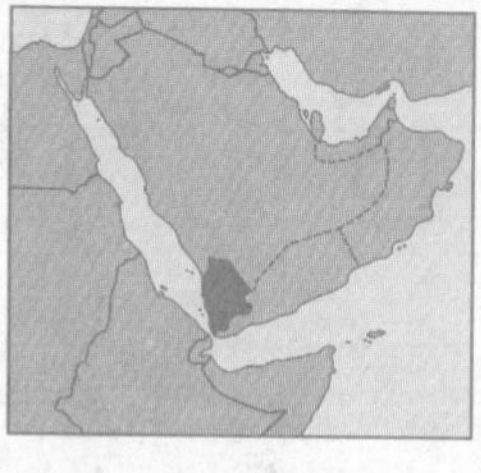

A republic situated in the southwestern coastal region of the Arabian Peninsula, Yemen (San'a') is bounded by Yemen (Aden), Saudi Arabia, and the Rea Sea. Area: 77,200 sq mi (200,000 sq km). Pop. (1975): 5,237,900. Cap. and largest city: San'a' (pop., 1975, 134,600). Language: Arabic. Religion: Muslim. Chairman of the Command Council in 1976, Col. Ibrahim al-Hamdi; premier, Abdel-Aziz Abdel-Ghani.

In 1976 the Yemen Arab Republic (North Yemen) continued to move closer to Saudi Arabia, which supplied it with budgetary and development aid, and the possibility of a full union between the two countries was raised. In April there were reports that North Yemen would buy $139 million worth of U.S. arms to reduce dependence on Soviet arms and to establish a triangular U.S.-Saudi-North Yemen defense relationship, but Colonel Hamdi said that the country wished to maintain friendly relations with the U.S.S.R. After a visit to Paris of the armed forces chief of staff in June, it was reported that North Yemen would buy arms from France. Premier Abdel-Ghani said he hoped Shell Oil would succeed in discovering offshore oil.

There were a few reports of border incidents with the People's Democratic Republic of Yemen (South Yemen), but the two governments continued to declare that their objective was unification. Relations were helped by the establishment of diplomatic ties between Saudi Arabia and South Yemen in March, and North Yemen offered to help mediate in the dispute between South Yemen and Oman.

Internally, Colonel Hamdi maintained a firm hold on the country, although there were reports early in the year of disagreement with the leader of the most powerful tribal confederation and former head of the Consultative Council, suspended by Hamdi when he took power in 1974. On the second anniversary of his "corrective revolution" on June 13, Hamdi said that elections would be held and representative institutions introduced. (PETER MANSFIELD)

[978.B.4.b]

YEMEN ARAB REPUBLIC

Education. (1973–74) Primary, pupils 178,755, teachers (1972–73) 4,053; secondary, pupils 12,460, teachers (1972–73) 544; vocational, pupils 466, teachers (1972–73) 50; teacher training, students 1,349; higher, students 950, teaching staff 42.

Finance and Trade. Monetary unit: riyal, with (Sept. 20, 1976) a par value of 4.56 riyals to U.S. $1 (free rate of 7.86 riyals = £1 sterling). Budget (1974–75 est.): revenue 380.5 million riyals; expenditure 541.3 million riyals. Foreign trade (1975): imports 1,341,400,000 riyals; exports 49.7 million riyals. Import sources (1974): Japan 15%; China 7%; West Germany 6%; Saudi Arabia 5%; Australia 5%; Yemen (Aden) 5%; France 5%; Ethiopia 5%; U.S.S.R. 5%; The Netherlands 5%. Export destinations (1974): Japan 42%; China 20%; Yemen (Aden) 10%; Somalia 8%; Italy 6%. Main exports (1973): cotton 49%; coffee 17%; hides and skins 15%; cottonseed 6%.

Agriculture. Production (in 000; metric tons; 1974): barley 230; corn 84; wheat 71; sorghum (1975) *c.* 1,570; dates *c.* 60; coffee *c.* 5; tobacco *c.* 5; cotton, lint *c.* 5. Livestock (in 000; 1974): cattle *c.* 1,250; sheep *c.* 3,500; goats *c.* 8,100; camels *c.* 61; asses *c.* 706.

Yugoslavia

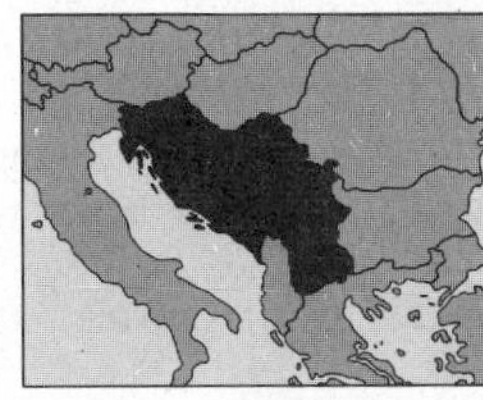

A federal socialist republic, Yugoslavia is bordered by Italy, Austria, Hungary, Romania, Bulgaria, Greece, Albania, and the Adriatic Sea. Area: 98,766 sq mi (255,804 sq km). Pop. (1976 est.): 21,520,000. Cap. and largest city: Belgrade (pop., 1975 UN est., 870,000). Language: Serbo-Croatian, Slovenian, and Macedonian. Religion (1953): Orthodox 41%; Roman Catholic 32%; Muslim 12%. President of the republic for life and president of the League of Communists in 1976, Marshal Tito (Josip Broz); president of the Federal Executive Council (premier), Dzemal Bijedic.

Defense preparations and the clampdown on dissent were intensified in 1976. Relations with the U.S.S.R. improved late in the year, while those with Austria deteriorated, but the main thrust of Yugoslavia's diplomatic activity was in the third world.

In January Yugoslavia and 26 other nonaligned nations agreed to pool their newsgathering agencies into a central information unit. Yugoslavia played a key role in the preparation of the conference of nonaligned nations in Colombo, Sri Lanka, in August, which President Tito attended personally. Tito paid visits, many concerned with the conference, to Mexico, Panama, Venezuela, Sweden, and Portugal in March, to Greece in May, and to Turkey in June. In March and April nonaligned leaders visiting Yugoslavia included the presidents of Somalia, Uganda, and Egypt and the prime ministers of Sri Lanka and Cuba. Yugoslavia took part in the Balkan economic ministers' conference, held in Athens from January 26 to February 5. When Austria decided to hold a language census on November 14 to implement a new law for the protection of national minorities, Yugoslavia attacked the plan as a capitulation to German-speaking nationalists seeking to destroy Austria's Slav minorities.

Tito represented Yugoslavia at the conference of 29 European Communist parties held in East Berlin on June 29 and 30, and met the Soviet party leader, Leonid I. Brezhnev, on the eve of the conference. Brezhnev visited Yugoslavia from November 15 to 17 and used the visit to proclaim the U.S.S.R.'s peaceful intentions toward Yugoslavia. By this time Tito, who had suffered a severe liver ailment in September, had fully recovered. The Soviet Navy commander, Adm. Sergey G. Gorshkov, visited Yugoslavia in August, reportedly to seek more facilities for the Soviet Navy in Yugoslav ports. The question of whether the U.S. would defend Yugoslavia from a Soviet attack became a topic in the U.S. presidential election campaign.

In March the U.S. company Dow Chemical signed an agreement with Yugoslavia's largest oil company for the joint construction and operation of a $700 million petrochemical complex on the Adriatic coastal island of Krk. In November the European Economic Community announced that it was seeking a closer institutional link with Yugoslavia.

Late in 1975 the federal minister of the interior, Gen. Franjo Herljevic, stated that the security organs had broken up 13 illegal organizations and arrested 237 of their members in the past two years. In February, 31 Albanians were given prison sentences for alleged irredentist activity, and in June, 11 Croatian nationalists were tried and convicted in Zagreb on charges of planning sabotage and assassination. About 30 pro-Moscow conservatives, mainly Serbs, were tried and sentenced in the first three months of the year. On September 10 four Croatian-born men and

KEYSTONE

Every year the town of Arandjelovac, near Belgrade, Yugoslavia, holds a sculpture festival. Guest artists are supplied with white marble from the local quarries, and their productions are exhibited in the town park.

Yiddish Literature: *see* Literature

Yugoslavian Literature: *see* Literature

YUGOSLAVIA

Education. (1973–74) Primary, pupils 2,869,344, teachers 126,327; secondary, pupils 203,296, teachers 10,164; vocational, pupils 545,629, teachers 33,458; teacher training, students 9,096, teachers 624; higher (including 15 universities), students 328,536, teaching staff 19,197.

Finance. Monetary unit: dinar, with (Sept. 20, 1976) a free rate of 18.74 dinars to U.S. $1 (32.29 dinars = £1 sterling). Gold, SDR's, and foreign exchange (June 1976) U.S. $1,650,000,000. Budget (1974 actual): revenue 63,394,000,000 dinars; expenditure 62,584,000,000 dinars. Gross material product (1974) 407 billion dinars. Money supply (May 1976) 160.3 billion dinars. Cost of living (1970 = 100; June 1976) 279.

Foreign Trade. (1975) Imports 134,510,000,000 dinars; exports 70,870,000,000 dinars. Import sources: West Germany 19%; Italy 11%; U.S.S.R. 10%; U.S. 5%; Iraq 5%; France 5%. Export destinations: U.S.S.R. 25%; Italy 9%; West Germany 8%; Czechoslovakia 6%; East Germany 5%. Main exports: machinery 15%; transport equipment 13%; chemicals 9%; food 9%; nonferrous metals 9%; iron and steel 5%; clothing 5%. Tourism (1974): visitors 5,458,000; gross receipts U.S. $701 million.

Transport and Communications. Roads (1974) 110,290 km. Motor vehicles in use (1974): passenger 1,332,972; commercial 136,110. Railways: (1974) 10,319 km; traffic (1975) 10,243,000,000 passenger-km, freight 21,606,000,000 net ton-km. Air traffic (1975): 1,697,000,000 passenger-km; freight 14,569,000 net ton-km. Shipping (1975): merchant vessels 100 gross tons and over 414; gross tonnage 1,873,482. Telephones (Jan. 1975) 1,142,880. Radio licenses (Dec. 1974) 4,081,000. Television licenses (Dec. 1974) 2,784,000.

Agriculture. Production (in 000; metric tons; 1975): wheat 4,396; barley 703; oats 368; rye 98; corn 9,390; potatoes 2,394; sunflower seed *c.* 273; sugar, raw value *c.* 482; dry beans 166; onions *c.* 305; tomatoes *c.* 418; cabbages (1974) 673; watermelons (1974) *c.* 491; plums (1974) *c.* 900; apples (1974) 370; pears (1974) 93; wine (1974) 588; tobacco *c.* 59; beef and veal (1974) *c.* 295; pork (1974) *c.* 323; timber (cu m; 1974) 13,915; fish catch (1974) 54. Livestock (in 000; Jan. 1975): cattle 5,872; sheep *c.* 8,000; pigs 7,683; horses (1974) 945; chickens 50,785.

Industry. Fuel and power (in 000; metric tons; 1975): coal 599; lignite 34,939; crude oil 3,691; natural gas (cu m) 1,554,000; manufactured gas (cu m) 145,000; electricity (kw-hr) 39,880,000. Production (in 000; metric tons; 1975): cement 7,065; iron ore (35% metal content) 5,237; pig iron 2,197; crude steel 2,858; bauxite 2,252; antimony ore (metal content; 1974) 2.2; chrome ore (oxide content; 1974) 0.3; magnesite (1974) 463; manganese ore (metal content) 4.2; aluminum 168; copper 138; zinc 98; gold (troy oz; 1974) 170; silver (troy oz; 1974) 4,690; petroleum products (1974) 9,813; sulfuric acid 936; cotton yarn 107; wool yarn 42; rayon, etc., filament yarns and fibres (1974) 71; nylon, etc., filament yarns and fibres (1974) 19; wood pulp (1974) 595; newsprint 85; other paper (1974) 660.

an American-born woman hijacked a TWA Boeing 727 on a New York–Chicago flight and forced it to fly to Europe; the hijackers, who demanded that leaflets containing Croatian nationalist propaganda be dropped over major U.S. and European cities and that similar material be published in selected U.S. newspapers, eventually surrendered in Paris. (*See* CRIME AND LAW ENFORCEMENT.)

The grain harvest of 5.9 million tons was the best in many years. Exports in the first nine months of 1976 were 22% higher than in the corresponding period of 1975, while imports were down 9%. Inflation dropped to below 12% in March. Prices of bread, oil, and some other basic foods went up by an average of 15–30% on October 16. By September Yugoslavia had wiped out its balance of payments deficit with the West. On September 10 the worst midair collision to that time occurred over Zagreb. (*See* DISASTERS.)

(K. F. CVIIC)

[973.B.3]

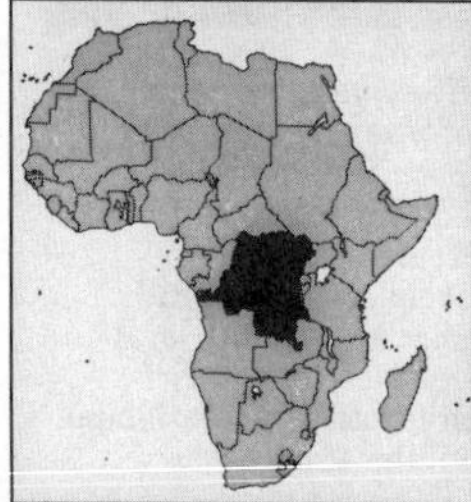

Zaire

A republic of equatorial Africa, Zaire is bounded by the Central African Empire, Sudan, Uganda, Rwanda, Burundi, Tanzania, Zambia, Angola, Congo, and the Atlantic Ocean. Area: 905,365 sq mi (2,344,885 sq km). Pop. (1975 est.): 24,902,000. Cap. and largest city: Kinshasa (pop., 1974, 1,733,800). Language: French; Bantu dialects. Religion: animist approximately 50%; Christian 43%. President in 1976, Mobutu Sese Seko.

The defeat in the Angolan civil war of the forces of the National Front for the Liberation of Angola, led by Holden Roberto, President Mobutu's brother-in-law, was a setback to Zaire, which had to recognize (Feb. 28, 1976) the victorious Popular Movement for the Liberation of Angola, which it had previously opposed. Zaire had relied upon railways passing through Angola for the export of Katanga's copper. The Benguela Railway, however, was temporarily closed because of war damage. Tanzania offered to transport some of the copper to Dar es Salaam, but that port was said to be operating to the limit of its capacity. South Africa provided another outlet, via East London, but Zaire was still threatened with strangulation. Moreover, prices offered for copper on the world market were low, and production of palm oil had fallen because the government's policy of keeping as much as possible for domestic consumption at a low price discouraged producers.

Relations with Belgium improved when an agreement in March provided for compensation for Belgians dispossessed by Mobutu's nationalization policy of 1974. In return Belgium offered assistance and trained personnel in education, public health, and agriculture. The government also decided to restore to their former owners more than half the foreign-owned companies nationalized during the previous two years.

(KENNETH INGHAM)

[978.E.7.a.i]

ZAIRE

Education. (1972–73) Primary, pupils 3,292,020, teachers 80,481; secondary, pupils 229,473, teachers 13,792; vocational, pupils 34,687, teachers (1969–70) 3,515; teacher training, students 52,687, teachers (1969–70) 2,643; higher (1973–74), students 19,294, teaching staff 2,550.

Finance. Monetary unit: zaire, with (Sept. 20, 1976) a free rate of 0.88 zaire to U.S. $1 (1.51 zaire = £1 sterling). Gold, SDR's, and foreign exchange (June 1976) U.S. $111,690,000. Budget (1974 est.): revenue 539 million zaires; expenditure 545 million zaires. Gross national product (1974) 1,663,800,000 zaires. Money supply (April 1976) 545,040,000 zaires. Cost of living (Kinshasa; 1970 = 100; April 1976) 422.

Foreign Trade. (1974) Imports 494.7 million zaires; exports 686.7 million zaires. Import sources: Belgium-Luxembourg *c.* 18%; U.S. *c.* 14%; West Germany *c.* 14%; France *c.* 10%; Italy *c.* 7%; Japan *c.* 7%; U.K. *c.* 5%. Export destinations: Belgium-Luxembourg *c.* 45%; Italy *c.* 14%; France *c.* 7%; Japan *c.* 6%; West Germany *c.* 6%; U.K. *c.* 5%. Main exports: copper 63%; cobalt 5%.

Transport and Communications. Roads (1973) *c.* 140,000 km (including 69,347 km main regional roads). Motor vehicles in use (1974): passenger 84,800; commercial (including buses) 76,400. Railways: (1974) 5,280 km; traffic (1973) 447 million passenger-km, freight 3,017,000,000 net ton-km. Air traffic (1974): 655 million passenger-km; freight 35.4 million net ton-km. Shipping (1975): merchant vessels 100 gross tons and over 28; gross tonnage 85,232. Inland waterways (including Zaire River; 1974) *c.* 16,000 km. Telephones (Jan. 1975) 26,000. Radio receivers (Dec. 1973) 100,000. Television receivers (Dec. 1973) 7,000.

Agriculture. Production (in 000; metric tons; 1975): rice *c.* 250; corn *c.* 577; sweet potatoes (1974) 294; cassava (1974) *c.* 12,000; peanuts 268; dry peas *c.* 219; palm kernels *c.* 75; palm oil *c.* 165; sugar, raw value (1974) *c.* 67; bananas (1974) *c.* 76; oranges (1974) *c.* 95; coffee *c.* 61; rubber *c.* 39; cotton, lint *c.* 27; timber (cu m; 1974) *c.* 14,680; fish catch (1974) *c.* 124. Livestock (in 000; Dec. 1973): cattle 1,111; sheep 730; goats 2,237; pigs 606; poultry 10,474.

Industry. Production (in 000; metric tons; 1974): coal 88; copper 255; tin 0.6; zinc 66; manganese ore (metal content) 118; gold (troy oz) 129; silver (troy oz) 1,700; diamonds (metric carats) 13,611; petroleum products *c.* 640; electricity (kw-hr) 4,000,000.

Zambia

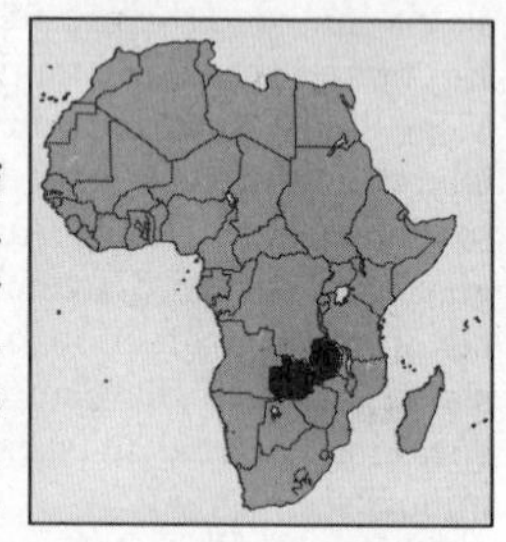

A republic and a member of the Commonwealth of Nations, Zambia is bounded by Tanzania, Malawi, Mozambique, Rhodesia, South West Africa, Angola, and Zaire. Area: 290,586 sq mi (752,614 sq km). Pop. (1976 est.): 5,138,000, about 99% of whom are Africans. Cap. and largest city: Lusaka (pop., 1976 est., 483,000). Language: English and Bantu. Religion: predominantly animist. President in 1976, Kenneth Kaunda; prime minister, Elijah Mudenda.

On Jan. 28, 1976, President Kaunda invoked full emergency powers to deal with the deterioration in security arising mainly from the economic crisis the country was facing. Twelve days later the University of Zambia was closed in response to action by students demonstrating for and against the government, but it was reopened in May. Zambia had supported the idea of a government of national unity in Angola and had looked askance at the dependence of the Popular Movement for the Liberation of Angola (MPLA) upon Cuban troops. In April, however, Zambia recognized the MPLA government, but damage to the Benguela Railway through Angola still blocked an important outlet for Zambia's copper. With the railway through Rhodesia to Beira also closed for political reasons, the port of Dar es Salaam, outlet for the Tanzam railway—handed over to Tanzania and Zambia by the Chinese on July 14—was inadequate by itself to handle Zambia's exports. Added to these difficulties was that of the low price offered for copper, while Zambia's observance of sanctions

ZAMBIA

Education. (1973–74) Primary, pupils 810,234, teachers 16,916; secondary, pupils 61,354, teachers 2,880; vocational, pupils 4,609; teacher training, students 2,588, teachers 210; higher, students 2,324, teaching staff (1970) 189.

Finance. Monetary unit: kwacha, with (Sept. 20, 1976) a free rate of 0.80 kwacha to U.S. $1 (free rate of 1.38 kwacha = £1 sterling). Gold, SDR's, and foreign exchange (June 1976) U.S. $81.3 million. Budget (1975 est.): revenue 644 million kwachas; expenditure 755 million kwachas. Gross national product (1974) 1,764,000,000 kwachas. Cost of living (1970 = 100; Aug. 1975) 146.

Foreign Trade. (1974) Imports 585.7 million kwachas; exports 905.1 million kwachas. Import sources: U.K. 17%; Japan 8%; Iran *c.* 8%; West Germany 7%; U.S. 7%; South Africa 7%; Italy *c.* 6%. Export destinations: U.K. 22%; Japan 19%; Italy 14%; West Germany 13%; France *c.* 12%. Main export copper 93%.

Transport and Communications. Roads (1972) 34,963 km. Motor vehicles in use (1974): passenger 86,000; commercial (including buses) 62,000. Railways (1975) *c.* 2,197 km (including *c.* 900 km of the 1,870-km Tanzam railway linking Kapiri Mposhi in Zambia with Dar es Salaam in Tanzania, completed in 1975). Air traffic (1974): 362 million passenger-km; freight 20.8 million net ton-km. Telephones (Jan. 1975) 68,000. Radio receivers (Dec. 1973) *c.* 100,000. Television receivers (Dec. 1973) *c.* 21,000.

Agriculture. Production (in 000; metric tons; 1975): corn 450; cassava (1974) *c.* 146; millet *c.* 63; sorghum *c.* 188; peanuts *c.* 100; sugar, raw value (1974) *c.* 97; tobacco *c.* 7; cotton, lint *c.* 4. Livestock (in 000; 1974): cattle *c.* 1,748; sheep *c.* 29; goats *c.* 194; pigs *c.* 121; chickens *c.* 7,950.

Industry. Production (in 000; metric tons; 1975): copper 619; coal 813; lead 19; zinc 47; electricity (kw-hr) 6,258,000.

against Rhodesia made the country's economic plight still more serious.

Kaunda played an important part, particularly from September onward, in discussions about African majority rule in Rhodesia. He attempted to induce the African Rhodesian leaders to reach agreement among themselves, but he allowed guerrillas to establish bases in Zambia. (KENNETH INGHAM)

[978.E.8.b.iii]

Zoos and Botanical Gardens

Zoos. Because of the economic situation prevailing in the Western world through much of 1976, zoos in general succeeded only in maintaining their attendance figures and some experienced considerable declines. In some ways this proved advantageous, as many of the smaller sideshow-type zoos, where animals were possibly less well cared for, were forced out of business because of lack of visitors and escalating food costs. Many of the larger zoos were forced to cut back on expansion and to concentrate on improvements to existing facilities. Latest trends, however, indicated an upsurge in zoo visitors, and most large zoos were concentrating on providing improved educational facilities.

In the U.K., London Zoo celebrated its 150th anniversary and opened a completely new Big Cat exhibit. The new building made use of modern construction techniques; fewer species were exhibited than in the old house, but they were kept in breeding groups. Krefeld Zoo, West Germany, opened a new ape house after receiving a gift of DM 2 million. This spacious building provided artificial sunlight and rain for the inmates, and there were facilities for 700 people to sit while observing the animals. Barcelona Zoo in Spain opened a new ape nursery isolated from the public by glass; it incorporated a bedroom with cots, a kitchen area, and a solarium located outside the building.

Most countries now had legislation restricting the import and export of animals, designed to protect indigenous cattle from disease and also to preserve endangered species in their natural environment. (*See* ENVIRONMENT: *Wildlife.*) It was very rare and, in most cases, virtually impossible for zoos to import any of the larger animals. These were bred in captivity and used as exchange specimens. Chester Zoo, England, exported chimpanzees and zebras to Australia, receiving in return various kangaroos, wallabies, and cockatoos. Another English zoo, Blackpool, sent a pair of lions to Kano, Nigeria. Import restrictions had helped to reduce the pressure on some endangered species, but the major threat was from habitat destruction in the wild. It was hoped that current legislation would lead to a reduction in the number of animals imported from the wild to be sold as pets and for research purposes, practices that for many years had caused a greater drain on natural resources than had the requirements of zoological collections. The extermination of yet another animal had to be recorded. The Lesser Swan Island hutia had almost certainly been exterminated by domestic cats abandoned on the island when a radar station was closed on an adjoining island.

In the past zoos had saved several species from extinction. Tigers had become very rare throughout much of their range, and zoos had concentrated on captive breeding. This had led to a surplus of tigers in captivity, and Marwell Zoo, Winchester, England, offered breeding pairs of the rare Siberian tiger on permanent loan to accredited zoos. The World Wildlife Fund suggested that zoos should concentrate on breeding rare subspecies such as the Sumatran tiger,

WIDE WORLD

Audrey and her baby Gum Drop arrived at the San Diego Zoo in July, along with five other koalas.

Zanzibar: *see* Tanzania

Zoology: *see* Life Sciences

KEYSTONE

The great drought that hit Britain in the summer of 1976 endangered many rare plants in the Royal Botanic Gardens near London. Visitors were excluded from some areas because of falling branches.

which had a total population of 800, approximately 100 of which were killed illegally each year.

Notable first breedings in captivity included a plate-billed mountain toucan at Los Angeles Zoo and a manatee, the first to be actually conceived in captivity, at the Miami Seaquarium in Florida. An interesting experiment was being undertaken at Rabat, Morocco. The wild Barbary lion had been extinct for 50 years, but specimens at Rabat Zoo showed features found only in this subspecies. By selecting various characteristics and cross-breeding certain individuals, an attempt was being made to breed the true Barbary lion.

Zoo animals were enjoying increased longevity. The Philadelphia Zoo lost a female orangutan which had reached the age of 56 years. Smokey Bear, for years the symbol of the U.S. Forest Service's anti-forest fire campaign, died at the National Zoo in Washington, D.C., at the age of 26. He had been found as a cub by forest rangers after a fire in a national forest in New Mexico and sent to Washington, where he became one of the National Zoo's most popular attractions. Smokey the symbol, wearing a forest ranger's hat and with the slogan "Only You Can Prevent Forest Fires," appeared widely in posters and ads. The actual bear, suffering from arthritis, was retired in 1975 and replaced by a new official "Smokey," also an orphaned cub from New Mexico.

Throughout the world many zoological meetings were held in order to disseminate information to zoo personnel. An exhibition entitled "Animals and Man" took place at the Swiss Industries Fair in Basel; the Association of British Wild Animal Keepers held a symposium on general management; at Paignton Zoo, England, a second International Symposium of Zoo Design and Construction was attended by delegates from many leading zoos; over 300 delegates from 67 countries attended a meeting of the International Union for Conservation of Nature and Natural Resources in Switzerland; and the fourth international congress of the World Wildlife Fund was held in San Francisco. *International Zoo News*, an invaluable journal for zoo administrations, celebrated 25 years of publication in 1976.

(G. S. MOTTERSHEAD)

Botanical Gardens. During much of 1976 Western Europe suffered severe drought and exceptionally high air temperatures, resulting in the loss of shallow-rooted trees in many botanical gardens. At the Royal Botanic Gardens, Kew, England, birches died and old trees were found to be seasoning on the roots, causing stresses that led to dangerous fissures. Dutch elm disease coupled with drought accounted for further losses, but at Kew wild-collected elm cuttings were being stocked as a genetic resource in the interests of conservation. Subsequent to the 1975 International Association of Botanical Gardens conference on plant conservation, moves were being made to integrate European gardens with a view to propagating all threatened European plant species.

Continuing inflation restricted development of some gardens, and many were concentrating their resources on certain aspects of research, such as the potato relatives at Birmingham University Botanical Gardens, England. A step toward the rationalization of collections at the Royal Botanic Garden, Edinburgh, was taken with the transfer to Kew of their *Aeonium* plants. In Copenhagen the University Botanic Garden was devoting new greenhouses to experimental work and to the cultivation of alpine species, while the hothouses were used for succulent asclepiads and plants from Madagascar and for a taxonomic study of aquatic *Cryptocoryne*.

Despite the economic difficulties, restoration of the 19th-century palm house in Belfast Botanic Garden, Northern Ireland, was being undertaken at a cost of more than £200,000; the first stage of sandblasting the metalwork, spraying, and reglazing was completed in August. At Kew construction was begun on a remarkable pyramidal alpine house surrounded by a moat over which cool, moist air would be drawn. Work was also proceeding on science-support greenhouses and tropical and micropropagation units, as well as on the landscaping of parts of the palm house and ferneries.

At the University Botanic Garden, Cambridge, England, the educational value of the garden was improved by the addition of several demonstrations. Although some of these were temporary exhibits in the greenhouses, others were more permanent displays on a number of themes, including a European collection of *Saxifraga*, ecotypes of native British *Juniperus communis*, and a taxonomic demonstration collection of *Geranium*. A special section for the documentation and propagation of all nationally rare species occurring in the eastern region of England was financed by the Nature Conservancy Council. Only a few years after its foundation, the Ventnor Botanic Garden, Isle of Wight, reported it probably had the largest outdoor collection of tender species in Britain.

Reconstruction of the Khorogsk Botanical Garden in the Pamirs area of southern U.S.S.R. was scheduled for the period 1976–80. At this high-altitude (over 2,000 m) garden, conditions were being created for plants of the Hindu Kush and Himalayan regions, as well as for the introduction of foreign plants. Irrigation was made possible by lifting Dhakhder River water 140 m by an electric pump.

A new botanical garden was being prepared at Kuala Lumpur for the University of Malaya. The 100-ac site, with outcrops of limestone and granite, a permanent stream, and some altitudinal diversity, was being laid out with examples of vegetation types and demonstrations of plant families. One of the objectives was to gather and preserve many of the spices and medicinal plants, as well as the wild progenitors of tropical plants, occurring in the Malaysian region. At the Singapore Botanic Gardens public interest was encouraged by a new aviary and a bandstand.

In October the Pukeiti Rhododendron Trust of New Zealand celebrated its silver jubilee. Its first 25 years had seen the realization, to a large extent, of its founding concept: the gathering together of a collection of rhododendrons and their cultivation in a natural environment. The 900-ac garden, clothed in a forest of indigenous evergreen vegetation, was supporting over 850 species, varieties, and hybrids of rhododendron.

The dedication of Totten Center, the first permanent building in the North Carolina Botanical Garden, took place on April 11. The start of the U.S. bicentennial project—"The Thirteen Colonies Trail"—coincided with the dedication ceremony, which took place ten years after the opening of the first nature trail in the garden. At South Coast Botanic Garden, Los Angeles, the new administration centre was dedicated on May 7, climaxing years of effort. The Education Center at the Chicago Botanic Garden was opened on June 26. (FRANK N. HEPPER)

[355.C.6]

ENCYCLOPÆDIA BRITANNICA FILMS. *A Zoo's-Eye View: Dawn to Dark* (1973); *Pandas: A Gift from China* (1974).

CONTRIBUTORS

Names of contributors to the Britannica Book of the Year *with the articles written by them. The arrangement is alphabetical by last name.*

AARSDAL, STENER. Economic Editor, *Børsen,* Copenhagen.
Denmark

ADAMS, ANDREW M. Correspondent, CBS Radio; *Daily Mail,* London; *San Francisco Chronicle; Black Belt* magazine. Editor and Publisher, *Sumo World.*
Combat Sports: *Judo; Karate; Kendo; Sumo*

AGRELLA, JOSEPH C. Turf Editor, *Chicago Sun-Times.* Co-author of *Ten Commandments for Professional Handicapping; American Race Horses.*
Equestrian Sports: *Thoroughbred Racing and Steeplechasing (in part)*

ALEXIOU, CHRISTOS. Lecturer in Modern Greek, School of Hellenic and Roman Studies, University of Birmingham, England.
Literature: *Greek*

ALLABY, MICHAEL. Free-lance Writer and Lecturer. Author of *The Eco-Activists; Who Will Eat? ; Robots Behind the Plow; A Blueprint for Survival.* Editor of *The Survival Handbook.*
Environment *(in part)*

ALLAN, J. A. Lecturer in Geography, School of Oriental and African Studies, University of London.
Libya

ALSTON, REX. Broadcaster and Journalist; retired BBC Commentator. Author of *Taking the Air; Over to Rex Alston; Test Commentary; Watching Cricket.*
Cricket

ANTONINI, GUSTAVO. Research Associate Professor, Center for Latin American Studies, University of Florida. Author of *Population and Energy: A Systems Analysis of Resource Utilization in the Dominican Republic.*
Dominican Republic

ARCHIBALD, JOHN J. Feature Writer, *St. Louis Post-Dispatch.* Author of *Bowling for Boys and Girls.*
Bowling: *Tenpin Bowling (in part); Duckpins*

ARNOLD, BRUCE. Free-lance Journalist and Writer, Dublin. Parliamentary Correspondent, *Irish Independent.*
Ireland; United Kingdom: *Special Report*

ARRINGTON, LEONARD JAMES. Church Historian, Church of Jesus Christ of Latter-day Saints. Author of *Great Basin Kingdom: An Economic History of the Latter-day Saints; Charles C. Rich: Mormon General and Western Frontiersman.*
Religion: *Church of Jesus Christ of Latter-day Saints*

ASHBY, PHILIP H. William H. Danforth Professor of Religion, Princeton University. Author of *Modern Trends in Hinduism; The Conflict of Religions.*
Religion: *Hinduism*

AYTON, CYRIL J. Editor, *Motorcycle Sport,* London.
Motor Sports: *Motorcycles*

BALLARD, MARTIN. Director, Book Development Council, London.
Publishing: *Books (in part)*

BASS, HOWARD. Journalist and Broadcaster. Editor, *Winter Sports,* 1948–69. Winter Sports Correspondent, *Daily Telegraph* and *Sunday Telegraph,* London; *Christian Science Monitor,* Boston; *Canadian Skater,* Ottawa; *Skate,* London; *Skating,* Boston; *Ski Racing,* Denver; *Sports Review,* London. Author of *The Sense in Sport; This Skating Age; The Magic of Skiing; International Encyclopaedia of Winter Sports; Let's Go Skating.*
Ice Hockey *(in part)*; **Winter Sports; Winter Sports:** *Special Report*

BATE, JOHN M. Director, Salvation Army International Information Services, London.
Religion: *Salvation Army*

BEALL, JOHN V. Business Development Engineer, Fluor Utah, Inc. Author of sections 1 and 34, *Mining Engineering Handbook.* Frequent Contributor to *Mining Engineering,* New York.
Mining and Quarrying *(in part)*

BEATTY, J. R. Senior Research Associate, B. F. Goodrich Research and Development Center, Brecksville, Ohio. Co-author of *Concepts in Compounding.*
Industrial Review: *Rubber*

BECKWITH, DAVID C. Correspondent, *Time* magazine, Washington, D.C.
United States Statistical Supplement: *Developments in the states in 1976*

BEECH, KEYES. Far East Correspondent, *Chicago Daily News.* Author of *Tokyo and Points East; Not Without the Americans.*
Vietnam

BENTON, CHARLES. President, Films Incorporated; Member of the Board of Encyclopædia Britannica Educational Corp.
United States: *Special Report*

BERGERRE, MAX. Correspondent ANSA for Vatican Affairs, Rome.
Vatican City State

BICKELHAUPT, DAVID L. Professor of Insurance and Finance, College of Administrative Science, Ohio State University. Author of *Transition to Multiple-Line Insurance Companies; General Insurance* (9th ed.).
Industrial Review: *Insurance*

BILEFIELD, LIONEL. Technical Journalist.
Industrial Review: *Paints and Varnishes*

BINSTED, ARTHUR T. E. Chairman, British Bottlers' Institute, London.
Industrial Review: *Alcoholic Beverages (in part)*

BLYTH, ALAN. Music Critic, *The Times,* London; Assistant Editor, *Opera;* Broadcaster.
Biography *(in part)*; **Music:** *Introduction; Opera; Symphonic*

BODDY, WILLIAM C. Editor, *Motor Sport.* Full Member, Guild of Motoring Writers. Author of *The 200 Mile Race; The World's Land Speed Record; Continental Sports Cars; The Bugatti Story; History of Montlhéry; Vintage Years of the Morgan Threewheeler.*
Biography *(in part)*; **Motor Sports:** *Grand Prix Racing; International Rallying*

BÖDVARSSON, HAUKUR B. Co-editor and Text Supervisor, *Iceland Review,* Reykjavik.
Literature: *Icelandic*

BOLT, PETER H. Secretary, British Committee, World Methodist Council. Author of *A Way of Loving.*
Religion: *Methodist Churches*

BOONSTRA, DICK. Assistant Professor, Department of Political Science, Free University, Amsterdam.
Netherlands, The; Surinam

BOOTH, JOHN NICHOLLS. Lecturer and Writer; Co-founder, Japan Free Religious Association; Senior Pastor of a number of U.S. churches. Author of *The Quest for Preaching Power; Introducing Unitarian Universalism.*
Religion: *Unitarian Churches*

BOSWALL, JEFFERY. Producer of Sound and Television Programs, British Broadcasting Corporation Natural History Unit, Bristol, Eng.
Life Sciences: *Ornithology*

BOYLE, C. L. Lieutenant Colonel, R.A. (retd.). Chairman, Survival Service Commission, International Union for Conservation of Nature and Natural Resources, 1958–63; Secretary, Fauna Preservation Society, London, 1950–63.
Environment *(in part)*

BRACKMAN, ARNOLD C. Asian Affairs Specialist. Author of *Indonesian Communism: A History; Southeast Asia's Second Front: The Power Struggle in the Malay Archipelago; The Communist Collapse in Indonesia; The Last Emperor.*
Indonesia

BRADSHER, HENRY S. Foreign Affairs Writer, *Washington* (D.C.) *Star.*
Philippines

BRAIDWOOD, ROBERT J. Professor of Old World Prehistory, the Oriental Institute, and Professor of Anthropology, the University of Chicago. Author of *Prehistoric Men* (8th ed.); *Archaeology of the Plain of Antioch.*
Archaeology *(in part)*

BRANCH, MICHAEL ARTHUR. Lecturer in Finnish, University of London. Author of *A. J. Sjögren: Studies of the North.* Co-editor of *An Anthology of Finnish Folk Poetry.*
Literature: *Finnish*

BRASHER, CHRISTOPHER. Sports Correspondent, *The Observer;* Reporter and Producer, BBC Television. Past Olympic Gold Medalist. Author of *Tokyo 1964; Mexico 1968; Munich 72.*
Track and Field Sports: *Special Report*

BRAZEE, RUTLAGE J. Geophysicist, EDS/NOAA, U.S. Dept. of Commerce, Boulder, Colo.
Earth Sciences: *Geophysics*

BRECHER, KENNETH. Assistant Professor of Physics, Massachusetts Institute of Technology. Co-author and Co-editor of *High Energy Astrophysics and Its Relation to Elementary Particle Physics.*
Astronomy

BRIERRE, ANNIE. Literary Critic, *La Croix; Histoire Pour Tous; France-Culture; France-U.S.A.* Author of *Ninon de Lenclos.*
Literature: *French (in part)*

BRUNO, HAL. Chief Political Correspondent, *Newsweek* magazine.
Biography *(in part)*

BURDIN, JOEL L. Associate Director, American Association of Colleges for Teacher Education; Executive Secretary, Associated Organizations for Teacher Education; Editor, *Journal of Teacher Education,* Washington, D.C. Author of *A Reader's Guide to the Comprehensive Models for Preparing Elementary Teachers.* Co-author of *Elementary School Curriculum and Instruction.*
Education (*in part*)

BURKE, DONALD P. Executive Editor, *Chemical Week.*
Industrial Review: *Chemicals*

BURKS, ARDATH W. Professor of Political Science and Associate Vice-President for Academic Affairs, Rutgers University, New Brunswick, N.J. Author of *The Government of Japan; East Asia: China, Korea, Japan.*
Japan

BURNETT, LEE. Director, Department of Hematology, National Institute of Cardiology, Mexico City; Bullfight Columnist, *El Redondel.* Translator into English of *El Toreo* by Rafael Vilar.
Arena Sports: *Bullfighting* (*in part*)

BUTLER, DAVID RICHARD. Information Manager, British Gas Corporation, London.
Energy: *Gas*

BUTLER, FRANK. Sports Editor, *News of the World,* London. Author of *A History of Boxing in Britain.*
Combat Sports: *Boxing*

CALHOUN, DAVID R. Editor, *Encyclopædia Britannica,* Yearbooks.
Biography (*in part*); **Gambling**

CAMPBELL, H. C. Chief Librarian, Toronto Public Library, Toronto. Author of *Public Libraries in the Urban Metropolitan Setting.*
Literature: *English* (*in part*)

CAMPOS DE ESPAÑA, RAFAÉL. Journalist; Chief, Bullfighting Division, Radiotelevisión Española. Director, International Press Club, Madrid. Author of *Joselito; Filosofía del toreo; Los toros y la radio.*
Arena Sports: *Bullfighting* (*in part*)

CASEMENT, RICHARD. Transport Correspondent, *The Economist,* London. Author of *Urban Traffic: Policies in Congestion.*
Transportation (*in part*)

CASSIDY, VICTOR M. Writer and Editor, currently at work on a biography of Wyndham Lewis.
Biography (*in part*)

CEGIELSKI, CHARLES M. Assistant Editor, *Encyclopædia Britannica,* Yearbooks.
Biography (*in part*)

CHALMEY, LUCIEN. Honorary Secretary-General, Union Internationale des Producteurs et Distributeurs d'Énergie Électrique, Paris.
Energy: *Electricity*

CHANCE, PAUL. President, Science Interface, Monmouth Junction, N.J.
Behavioural Sciences

CHAPMAN, KENNETH F. Editor, *Stamp Collecting;* Philatelic Correspondent, *The Times,* London. Author of *Good Stamp Collecting; Commonwealth Stamp Collecting.*
Philately and Numismatics (*in part*)

CHAPMAN, ROBIN. Senior Economic Research Officer, Lloyds Bank International, Ltd., London.
Cuba; Haiti

CHAPPELL, DUNCAN. Director, Law and Justice Study Center, Battelle Memorial Institute, Seattle, Washington. Co-author of *The Police and the Public in Australia and New Zealand.* Co-editor of *The Australian Criminal Justice System; Violence and Criminal Justice.*
Crime and Law Enforcement

CHOATE, ROGER NYE. Stockholm Correspondent, *The Times,* London.
Biography (*in part*); **Sweden**

CHU, HUNG-TI. Expert in Far Eastern Affairs; Former International Civil Servant and University Professor.
China; Taiwan

CLARKE, R. O. Principal Administrator, Social Affairs and Industrial Relations Division, Organization for Economic Cooperation and Development, Paris. Co-author of *Workers' Participation in Management in Britain.*
Industrial Relations

CLEGG, JERRY S. Professor of Philosophy, Mills College, Oakland, Calif. Author of *The Structure of Plato's Philosophy.*
Philosophy

CLEVELAND, WILLIAM A. Geography Editor, *Encyclopædia Britannica.*
Mining and Quarrying (*in part*)

CLIFTON, DONALD F. Professor of Metallurgy, University of Idaho.
Materials Sciences: *Metallurgy*

CLOUD, STANLEY W. Political Correspondent, *Time* magazine.
United States: *Special Report*

COCKSEDGE, DAVID. Features Writer, *Athletics Weekly.*
Track and Field Sports (*in part*)

COGLE, T. C. J. Editor, *Electrical Review,* London.
Industrial Review: *Electrical*

COLLINS, L. J. D. Lecturer in Bulgarian History, University of London.
Cyprus

COPELAND, JAMES C. Associate Professor of Microbiology, Ohio State University; Editor, *Microbial Genetics Bulletin.*
Life Sciences: *Genetics*

COPPOCK, CHARLES DENNIS. President, English Lacrosse Union. Author of "Men's Lacrosse" in *The Oxford Companion to Sports and Games.*
Field Hockey and Lacrosse (*in part*)

COSTIN, STANLEY H. British Correspondent, *Australian Tailor and Menswear* and *Herrenjournal International.* Former President, Men's Fashion Writers International.
Fashion and Dress (*in part*)

CRATER, RUFUS W. Chief Correspondent, *Broadcasting,* New York City.
Television and Radio (*in part*)

CROSSLAND, NORMAN. Bonn Correspondent, *The Guardian* and *The Economist,* London.
German Democratic Republic; Germany, Federal Republic of

CVIIC, K. F. Leader Writer and East European Specialist, *The Economist,* London.
Yugoslavia

CZERWINSKI, EDWARD J. Professor of Slavic Literature, State University of New York, Stony Brook; Artistic Director, Slavic Cultural Center, Inc. Author of *The Soviet Invasion of Czechoslovakia; The Polish Theatre of the Absurd.*
Literature: *Polish*

DAIFUKU, HIROSHI. Chief, Sites and Monuments Division, UNESCO, Paris.
Historic Preservation

DAVID, TUDOR. Managing Editor, *Education,* London.
Education (*in part*)

DAVIDSON, BASIL. Historian and Writer on African affairs. Author of *Africa in History: Themes and Outlines; The African Genius; In the Eye of the Storm: Angola's People.*
Feature Article: *The Aftermath of Angola*

DAVIS, DONALD A. Editor, *Drug & Cosmetic Industry,* New York. Contributor to *The Science and Technology of Aerosol Packaging.*
Industrial Review: *Pharmaceuticals*

DAVIS, J. E. London Editor, *Britannica Book of the Year.*
Biography (*in part*)

DAVIS, RUTH M. Director, Institute for Computer Sciences and Technology, U.S. National Bureau of Standards.
Computers

DAWBER, ALFRED. Textile consultant in all aspects of textile production. Specialized writer on textile, engineering, and electrical subjects.
Industrial Review: *Textiles* (*in part*)

d'EÇA, RAUL. Retired from foreign service with U.S. Information Service. Corresponding member of the Brazilian Historical and Geographical Institute. Co-author of *Latin American History.*
Brazil

DECRAENE, PHILIPPE. Member of editorial staff, *Le Monde,* Paris. Editor in Chief, *Revue française d'Études politiques africaines.* Author of *Le Panafricanisme; Tableau des Partis Politiques Africains; Lettres de l'Afrique Atlantique.*
Benin; Cameroon; Central African Empire; Chad; Comoro Islands; Congo; Dahomey; Dependent States (*in part*); **Gabon; Guinea; Ivory Coast; Madagascar; Mali; Mauritania; Niger; Senegal; Togo; Tunisia; Upper Volta**

de la BARRE, KENNETH. Director, Montreal Office, Arctic Institute of North America.
Arctic Regions

DE PUY, NORMAN R. Executive Minister, First Baptist Church of Dearborn, Mich. Author of *The Bible Alive.*
Religion: *Baptist Churches*

DESAUTELS, PAUL ERNEST. Curator, Department of Mineral Sciences, National Museum of Natural History, Smithsonian Institution, Washington, D.C. Author of *The Mineral Kingdom; The Gem Kingdom.*
Industrial Review: *Gemstones*

DIRNBACHER, ELFRIEDE. Austrian Civil Servant.
Austria

DUHART, JAIME R. Research Officer, Economics Department, Lloyds Bank International Ltd., London.
Argentina; Latin-American Affairs; Peru

DUNICAN, PETER. Senior Partner, Ove Arup Partnership, London.
Engineering Projects: *Buildings*

EAGLE, HERBERT J. Chairman for Slavic Languages and Literatures, Purdue University, Lafayette, Ind.
Literature: *Czechoslovakian*

EDLIN, HERBERT L. Publications Officer, Forestry Commission of Great Britain. Author of *Wayside and Woodland Trees; What Wood Is That?; Guide to Tree Planting and Cultivation; Observer's Book of Trees.* Co-author *of Atlas of Plant Life.*
Environment *(in part)*

EISENBERG, WARREN W. Administrative Assistant to Rep. H. John Heinz III, Washington, D.C.
Populations and Areas

EIU. The Economist Intelligence Unit, London.
Economy, World *(in part)*

EMOTO, YOSHINOBU. Staff Writer, *Yomiuri Shimbun,* Tokyo.
Biography *(in part)*

ENGELS, JAN R. Editor, *Vooruitgang* (Quarterly of the Belgian Party for Freedom and Progress), Brussels.
Belgium; Biography *(in part)*

EWART, W. D. Editor and Director, *Fairplay International Shipping Weekly,* London. Author of *Marine Engines; Atomic Submarines; Hydrofoils and Hovercraft; Building a Ship.* Editor of *World Atlas of Shipping.*
Industrial Review: *Shipbuilding;* Transportation *(in part)*

FABINYI, ANDREW. Director, Pergamon Press, Australia.
Publishing: *Books (in part)*

FARR, D. M. L. Professor of History, Carleton University, Ottawa. Author of *Two Democracies; The Canadian Experience.*
Canada

FENDELL, ROBERT J. New York Editor, *Automotive News.* Author of *The New Era Car Book and Auto Survival Guide.* Co-author of *Encyclopedia of Motor Racing Greats.*
Motor Sports: *U.S. Racing*

FERRIER, R. W. Group Historian, British Petroleum Company Ltd., London.
Energy: *Petroleum*

FIDDICK, PETER. Specialist Writer, *The Guardian,* London.
Publishing: *Introduction; Newspapers (in part); Magazines (in part)*

FIELDS, DONALD. Helsinki Correspondent, *The Guardian,* London.
Finland

FIRTH, DAVID. Editor, *The Friend,* London; formerly Editor, *Quaker Monthly,* London.
Religion: *Religious Society of Friends*

FISHER, DAVID. Civil Engineer, Freeman Fox & Partners, London; formerly Executive Editor, *Engineering,* London.
Engineering Projects: *Bridges*

FLANAGAN, J. C. Newspaper Columnist.
Water Sports: *Surfing*

FOWELL, R. J. Lecturer, Department of Mining Engineering, University of Newcastle upon Tyne, England.
Energy: *Coal*

FRADY, WILLIAM ENSIGN, III. Editor, *Water Polo Scoreboard,* Newport Beach, Calif.
Water Sports: *Water Polo*

FRANCO, JEAN. Chairperson, Department of Spanish and Portuguese, Stanford University. Author of *The Modern Culture of Latin America; An Introduction to Spanish-American Literature.*
Literature: *Spanish (in part)*

FRANKLIN, HAROLD. Editor, *English Bridge Quarterly.* Bridge Correspondent, *Yorkshire Post; Yorkshire Evening Post.* Broadcaster. Author of *Best of Bridge on the Air.*
Contract Bridge

FRAWLEY, MARGARET-LOUISE. Press Officer, All-England Women's Lacrosse Association.
Field Hockey and Lacrosse *(in part)*

FREDRICKSON, DAVID A. Professor of Anthropology, California State College, Sonoma, Rohnert Park.
Archaeology *(in part)*

FRIDOVICH, IRWIN. James B. Duke Professor of Biochemistry, Duke University Medical Center, Durham, N.C. Contributor to *Oxidase and Redox Systems; Molecular Mechanisms of Oxygen Activation.*
Life Sciences: *Biochemistry*

FRIEDLY, ROBERT L. Executive Director, Office of Communication, Christian Church (Disciples of Christ), Indianapolis, Ind.
Religion: *Disciples of Christ*

FROST, DAVID. Rugby Union Correspondent, *The Guardian,* London.
Football: *Rugby*

GADDUM, PETER W. Chairman, H. T. Gaddum and Company Ltd., Silk Merchants, Macclesfield, Cheshire, Eng. President, International Silk Association, Lyons. Author of *Silk—How and Where It Is Produced.*
Industrial Review: *Textiles (in part)*

GALVANO, FABIO. Foreign Editor, *Stampa Sera,* Turin, Italy. Author of *Jimmy Carter.*
Biography *(in part)*; Italy

GANADO, ALBERT. Lawyer, Malta.
Malta

GEORGE, T. J. S. Editor, *Asiaweek,* Hong Kong. Author of *Krishna Menon: A Biography; Lee Kuan Yew's Singapore.*
Biography *(in part)*; Cambodia; Korea; Laos; Southeast Asian Affairs; Thailand

GIBBS, JERRY. Angling Editor, *Outdoor Life.* Contributor to *Experts' Book of Freshwater Fishing; American Fisherman's Fresh and Salt Water Guide.*
Hunting and Fishing: *Angling (in part)*

GJESTER, FAY. Oslo Correspondent, *Financial Times,* London.
Norway

GOLDSMITH, ARTHUR. Editorial Director, *Popular Photography,* New York City. Author of *The Photography Game; The Nude in Photography.* Co-author of *The Eye of Eisenstaedt.*
Photography

GOLOMBEK, HARRY. British Chess Champion, 1947, 1949, and 1955. Chess Correspondent, *The Times* and *Observer,* London. Author of *Penguin Handbook on the Game of Chess; Modern Opening Chess Strategy.*
Board Games: *Chess*

GOODWIN, R. M. Free-lance Writer, London.
Equestrian Sports: *Thoroughbred Racing and Steeplechasing (in part)*

GOODWIN, ROBERT E. Managing Director, Billiard Congress of America, Chicago. Publisher-Editor of various trade magazines.
Billiard Games

GOULD, DONALD W. Medical Correspondent, *New Statesman,* London.
Drug Abuse; Health and Disease: *General Overview (in part); Medical-Social Policy (in part); Mental Health (in part)*

GREEN, BENNY. Jazz Critic, *Observer,* London; Record Reviewer, British Broadcasting Corporation. Author of *The Reluctant Art; Blame It on My Youth; 58 Minutes to London; Jazz Decade; Drums in My Ears.* Contributor to *Encyclopedia of Jazz.*
Music: *Jazz*

GREENBERG, HERBERT. Professor and Past Chairman, Department of Mathematics, University of Denver.
Feature Article: *The Coming of Metricated Man*

GREENE, FREDERICK D. Professor of Chemistry, Massachusetts Institute of Technology. Editor, *Journal of Organic Chemistry.*
Chemistry: *Organic*

GRIFFITHS, A. R. G. Senior Lecturer in History, Flinders University of South Australia.
Australia; Biography *(in part)*; Nauru; Papua New Guinea

GROSSBERG, ROBERT H. Executive Director, U.S. Jai Alai Players Association, Miami, Fla.; Vice-President, Shearson Hayden Stone Inc.
Court Games: *Jai Alai*

GROVE, ROBERT D. Former Director, Division of Vital Statistics, U.S. Public Health Service. Co-author of *Vital Statistics Rates in the United States, 1900–1940; Vital Statistics Rates in the United States, 1940–1960.*
Demography

GUNDLACH, RICHARD GERARD. Communications Editor, *Electronics* magazine.
Industrial Review: *Communications*

GUTELLE, PIERRE. Naval Architect and Journalist, *Bateaux,* Paris.
Biography *(in part)*

HADY, EDMUND CARL. Executive Secretary, American Dart Association. Author and Publisher of *American and English Dart Game Including Tournament Rules.*
Target Sports: *Darts*

HALE, JOHN. Research Officer, Economics Department, Lloyds Bank International Ltd., London.
Bolivia; Guatemala; Uruguay

HARDMAN, THOMAS C. Editor and Publisher, *The Water Skier,* American Water Ski Association. Co-author of *Let's Go Water Skiing.*
Water Sports: *Water Skiing*

HARRIES, DAVID A. Director, Kinnear Moodie (1973) Ltd., Peterborough, Eng.
Engineering Projects: *Tunnels*

HARTER, DONALD H. Charles L. Mix Professor of Neurology and Chairman, Department of Neurology, Northwestern University Medical School, Chicago. Member of Editorial Board, *Neurology.* Contributor to *Harrison's Principles of Internal Medicine; Merritt's Textbook of Neurology.*
Health and Disease: *Neurological Diseases*

HASEGAWA, RYUSAKU. Editor, TBS-Britannica Co., Ltd., Tokyo.
Baseball *(in part)*

HAWKLAND, WILLIAM D. Professor of Law, University of Illinois. Author of *Sales Under Uniform Commercial Code; Cases on Bills and Notes; Commercial Paper; Transactional Guide of the Uniform Commercial Code; Cases on Sales and Security.*
Law: *Court Decisions*

HAWLEY, H. B. Specialist, Human Nutrition and Food Science, Switzerland.
Food Processing

HEBBLETHWAITE, PETER. Lecturer, Wadham College, Oxford, England. Author of *Bernanos; The Council Fathers and Atheism; Understanding the Synod; The Runaway Church.*
Biography (*in part*); Religion: *Roman Catholic Church*

HEINDL, L. A. Executive Secretary, U.S. National Committee on Scientific Hydrology, U.S. Geological Survey National Center, Reston, Va. Author of *The Water We Live By.*
Earth Sciences (*in part*)

HENDERSHOTT, MYRL C. Associate Professor of Oceanography, Scripps Institution of Oceanography, La Jolla, Calif.
Earth Sciences: *Oceanography*

HENDERSON, DONALD. Physician; Director, World Health Organization's Smallpox Eradication Program.
Health and Disease: *Special Report*

HEPPER, FRANK N. Principal Scientific Officer, Herbarium, Royal Botanic Gardens, Kew, England. Author of *West African Herbaria* of *Isert and Thonning.* Co-author of *Plant Collectors in West Africa.* Editor of *Flora of West Tropical Africa* (vol. ii and iii).
Zoos and Botanical Gardens (*in part*)

HERMAN, ROBIN CATHY. Reporter, *The New York Times.*
Ice Hockey (*in part*)

HESS, MARVIN G. Executive Vice-President, National Wrestling Coaches Association, Salt Lake City, Utah.
Combat Sports: *Wrestling*

HOLLANDS, R. L. Hockey Correspondent, *Daily Telegraph,* London; Chairman, Hockey Writers Club. Co-author of *Hockey.*
Field Hockey and Lacrosse (*in part*)

HOPE, THOMAS W. President and Publisher, Hope Reports, Inc., Rochester, N.Y. Author of *Hope Reports AV-USA; Hope Reports Education & Media; Hope Reports Perspective.*
Motion Pictures (*in part*)

HORRY, JOHN H. Formerly Squash Editor, *British Lawn Tennis and Squash.* Contributor to *The Oxford Companion to Sports and Games.*
Racket Games: *Squash Rackets*

HORSBRUGH-PORTER, SIR ANDREW. Former Polo Correspondent, *The Times,* London.
Equestrian Sports: *Polo*

HOTZ, LOUIS. Former Editorial Writer, the *Johannesburg* (S.Af.) *Star.* Co-author and contributor to *The Jews in South Africa: A History.*
South Africa; Transkei

HOWKINS, JOHN ANTHONY. Editor, *InterMedia,* International Broadcast Institute, London. Author of *Understanding Television.*
Television and Radio (*in part*)

HUNNINGS, NEVILLE MARCH. General Editor, Common Law Reports Ltd., London. Editor of *Common Market Law Reports, European Law Digest,* and *Eurolaw Commercial Intelligence.* Author of *Film Censors and the Law.* Co-editor of *Legal Problems of an Enlarged European Community.*
Law: *International Law*

INGHAM, KENNETH. Professor of History, University of Bristol, Eng. Author of *Reformers in India; A History of East Africa.*
Angola; Cape Verde Islands; Guinea-Bissau; Kenya; Malawi; Mozambique; Rhodesia; São Tomé and Príncipe; Tanzania; Uganda; Zaire; Zambia

IRF. International Road Federation, Geneva.
Engineering Projects: *Roads*

ISSA. International Social Security Association, Geneva.
Social and Welfare Services (*in part*)

JARDINE, ADRIAN. Company Director and Public Relations Consultant. Member, Guild of Yachting Writers.
Sailing

JASPERT, W. PINCUS. Technical Editorial Consultant. European Editor, North American Publishing Company, Philadelphia, Pa. Member, Comprint International Planning Committee. Editor of *Encyclopaedia of Type Faces.*
Industrial Review: *Printing*

JOHNSON, D. GALE. Eliakim Hastings Moore Distinguished Service Professor of Economics and Provost, University of Chicago. Author of *World Agriculture in Disarray; World Food Problems and Prospects.*
Agriculture and Food Supplies: *Special Report*

JONES, C. M. Editor, *World Bowls; Lawn Tennis.* Member, British Association of National Coaches. Author of *Winning Bowls; How to Become a Champion;* numerous books on tennis. Co-author of *Tackle Bowls My Way; Bryant on Bowls*
Bowling: *Lawn Bowls*

JONES, D. A. N. Assistant Editor, *The Listener,* London. Author of *Parade in Paris; Never Had It So Good.*
Biography (*in part*)

JONES, W. GLYN. Professor of Scandinavian Studies, University of Newcastle upon Tyne, Eng. Author of *Johannes Jørgensens modne år; Johannes Jørgensen; Denmark; William Heinesen; Færø og kosmos.*
Literature: *Danish*

JOSEPH, LOU. Manager of Media Relations, Bureau of Public Information, American Dental Association. Author of *A Doctor Discusses Allergy: Facts and Fiction.*
Health and Disease: *Dentistry*

KAAN, FREDERIK H. Secretary of the Department of Cooperation and Witness, World Alliance of Reformed Churches (Presbyterian and Congregational), Geneva. Author of *Pilgrim Praise; Break Not the Circle* (hymnals).
Religion: *Presbyterian and Reformed Churches*

KATZ, WILLIAM A. Professor, School of Library Science, State University of New York, Albany. Author of *Magazines for Libraries* (2nd ed. and supplement).
Publishing: *Magazines* (*in part*)

KELLEHER, JOHN A. Editor, *The Dominion,* Wellington, N.Z.
Biography (*in part*); New Zealand

KENNEDY, RICHARD M. Agricultural Economist, Economic Research Service, U.S. Department of Agriculture.
Agriculture and Food Supplies

KERRIGAN, ANTHONY. Visiting Professor, State University of New York, Buffalo. Editor and Translator of *Selected Works* of Miguel de Unamuno (10 vol.) and of works of Jorge Luis Borges. Author of *At the Front Door of the Atlantic.*
Literature: *Spanish* (*in part*)

KIDD, BRUCE. Championship Runner and Assistant Professor of Physical Education, University of Toronto. Co-author of *The Death of Hockey.*
Canada: *Special Report*

KILIAN, MICHAEL D. Columnist and Editorial Writer, *Chicago Tribune;* News Commentator, WTTW Television and WBBM Radio, Chicago.
Aerial Sports

KILNER, PETER. Editor, *Arab Report and Record,* London.
Algeria; Morocco; Sudan

KIMCHE, JON. Editor, *Afro-Asian Affairs,* London. Author of *There Could Have Been Peace: The Untold Story of Why We Failed with Palestine and Again with Israel; Seven Fallen Pillars.*
Biography (*in part*); Israel

KIND, JOSHUA B. Associate Professor of Art History, Northern Illinois University, De Kalb. Author of *Rouault; Naive Art in Illinois 1830–1976.*
Museums (*in part*)

KITAGAWA, JOSEPH M. Professor of History of Religions and Dean of the Divinity School, the University of Chicago. Author of *Religions of the East; Religion in Japanese History.*
Religion: *Buddhism*

KLARE, HUGH J. Chairman, Gloucestershire Probation Training Committee, England. Secretary, Howard League for Penal Reform 1950–71. Author of *People in Prison.* Regular Contributor to *Justice of the Peace.*
Prisons and Penology

KNECHT, JEAN. Formerly Assistant Foreign Editor, *Le Monde,* Paris; Formerly Permanent Correspondent in Washington and Vice-President of the Association de la Presse Diplomatique Française.
France

KNORR, N. H. President, Watch Tower Bible and Tract Society of Pennsylvania.
Religion: *Jehovah's Witnesses*

KOPPER, PHILIP. Free-lance Writer, Washington, D.C.
Biography (*in part*); Nobel Prizes

KOUTCHOUMOW, JOSEPH A. Secretary General, International Publishers Association, Geneva. Author of art and children's books.
Publishing: *Books* (*in part*)

KOVAN, RICHARD W. Deputy Editor, *Nuclear Engineering International,* London.
Industrial Review: *Nuclear Industry*

KRADER, BARBARA. Past President, Society for Ethnomusicology; Executive Secretary, International Folk Music Council, London, 1965–66.
Music: *Folk*

KUBITSCHEK, H. E. Senior Biophysicist, Division of Biological and Medical Research, Argonne National Laboratory. Author of *Introduction to Research with Continuous Cultures.*
Life Sciences: *Biophysics*

KWAN-TERRY, JOHN. Senior Lecturer, Department of English Language and Literature, University of Singapore. Editor of *The Teaching of Languages in Institutions of Higher Learning in Southeast Asia.*
Literature: *Chinese*

LAMB, KEVIN M. Sports Writer, *Chicago Daily News.*
Biography (*in part*); Football: *U.S. Football; Canadian Football*

LATHAM, ARTHUR. Associate Editor, *Encyclopædia Britannica,* Yearbooks.
Biography (*in part*)

LEGUM, COLIN. Associate Editor, *The Observer,* and Editor, *Africa Contemporary Record,* London. Author of *Must We Lose Africa?; Congo Disaster; Pan-Africanism: A Political Guide; South Africa: Crisis for the West.*
African Affairs; Biography (*in part*)

LEIFER, MICHAEL. Reader in International Relations, London School of Economics and Political Science. Author of *Dilemmas of Statehood in Southeast Asia.*
Biography (*in part*); Malaysia; Singapore

LENNOX-KERR, PETER. European Editor, *Textile Industries.* Author of *Index to Man-Made Fibres of the World; The World Fibres Book.* Editor of *Nonwovens '71;* Publisher of *OE-Report,* New Mills, England.
Industrial Review: *Textiles* (*in part*)

LEVE, MORTON. Executive Director, United States Handball Association, Skokie, Ill.; Founder and Executive Director, National Court Clubs Association. Co-author of *Inside Handball.*
Court Games: *Handball*

LITTELL, FRANKLIN H. Professor of Religion, Temple University, Philadelphia, Pa. Co-editor of *Weltkirchenlexikon.*
Religion: *World Church Membership*

LOEFFLER, EDWARD J. Technical Director, National Machine Tool Builders' Association, McLean, Va.
Industrial Review: *Machinery and Machine Tools*

LOESCHER, ROBERT J. Associate Professor and Chairman, Department of Art History and Aesthetics, School of the Art Institute of Chicago. Former Senior Editor, *Encyclopædia Britannica.*
Art and Art Exhibitions (*in part*)

LOFTAS, TONY. Editor, *Marine Policy;* Marine Consultant, *New Scientist.* Author of *Wealth from the Oceans; The Last Resource: Man's Exploitation of the Oceans.*
Law: *Special Report*

LÓPEZ PORTILLO, JOSÉ. President of Mexico; Lawyer and former Professor of Political Science.
Feature Article: *Mexican Mythology and Modern Society*

LOTERY, FRANÇOISE. Research Officer, Economics Department, Lloyds Bank International Ltd., London.
Biography (*in part*); Costa Rica; Paraguay; Spain

LULING, VIRGINIA R. Social Anthropologist.
Somalia

MACDONALD, BARRIE. Lecturer in History, Massey University, Palmerston North, N.Z. Author of several articles on the history and politics of Pacific islands.
Dependent States (*in part*); Fiji; Tonga; Western Samoa

MacDONALD, M. C. Director, Econtel Research Ltd., London. Editor, *World Series; Business Cycle Series.*
Agriculture and Food Supplies: *grain table;* Transportation: *table*

MACDONALD, TREVOR J. Manager, International Affairs, British Steel Corporation.
Industrial Review: *Iron and Steel*

MACGREGOR-MORRIS, PAMELA. Equestrian Correspondent, *The Times* and *Horse and Hound,* London. Author of books on equestrian topics.
Equestrian Sports: *Show Jumping*

McINNES, NEIL. Specialist in Communist affairs; Associate Editor, *Barron's.* Author of *The Western Marxists; The Communist Parties of Europe.*
Communist Movement: *Special Report*

MALLETT, H. M. F. Editor, *Weekly Wool Chart,* Bradford, England.
Industrial Review: *Textiles* (*in part*)

MANGO, ANDREW. Orientalist and Broadcaster.
Turkey

MANSFIELD, PETER. Formerly Middle East Correspondent, *Sunday Times,* London. Free-lance Writer on Middle East affairs.
Bahrain; Biography (*in part*); Egypt; Iraq; Jordan; Kuwait; Lebanon; Middle Eastern Affairs; Oman; Qatar; Saudi Arabia; Syria; United Arab Emirates; Yemen, People's Democratic Republic of; Yemen Arab Republic

MARSHALL, J. G. SCOTT. Horticultural Consultant.
Gardening (*in part*)

MARTENHOFF, JAMES E. Boating Writer, *Miami* (Fla.) *Herald.* Author of *Handbook of Skin and Scuba Diving; The Powerboat Handbook.*
Water Sports: *Motorboating; Skin and Scuba Diving*

MARTY, MARTIN E. Professor of the History of Modern Christianity, University of Chicago; Associate Editor, *The Christian Century.*
Religion: *Introduction*

MARYLES, DAISY G. Associate Editor, Bookselling and Marketing, *Publishers Weekly,* New York City.
Publishing: *Books* (*in part*)

MASI, ALFONSE T. Professor of Medicine and Director, Division of Connective Tissue Diseases, Department of Medicine, University of Tennessee, Memphis.
Health and Disease: *Rheumatic Diseases*

MASON, JOAN L. Executive Secretary, American Canoe Association, Denver, Colo.; Book Editor, *Canoe* magazine.
Water Sports: *Canoeing*

MATEJA, JAMES L. Automobile Writer and Financial Reporter, *Chicago Tribune.*
Industrial Review: *Automobiles*

MATTHÍASSON, BJÖRN. Iceland Correspondent, *Financial Times,* London.
Iceland

MAURON, PAUL. Director, International Vine and Wine Office, Paris.
Industrial Review: *Alcoholic Beverages* (*in part*)

MAY, YOLANTA. Foreign Editor, *New Review,* London.
Biography (*in part*)

MAZIE, DAVID M. Associate of Carl T. Rowan, syndicated columnist. Free-lance Writer.
Social and Welfare Services (*in part*)

MAZZE, EDWARD MARK. Dean and Professor of Marketing, W. Paul Stillman School of Business, Seton Hall University, South Orange, N.J. Author of *Personal Selling: Choice Against Chance; Introduction to Marketing: Readings in the Discipline.*
Consumerism (*in part*); Industrial Review: *Advertising*

MEIJER, REINDER PIETER. Professor of Dutch Language and Literature, University of London. Author of *Literature of the Low Countries; Dutch Grammar and Reader.*
Literature: *Dutch*

MEYENDORFF, JOHN. Professor of Church History and Patristics, St. Vladimir's Seminary; Professor of Byzantine History, Fordham University, New York City. Author of *Christ in Eastern Christian Thought; Byzantine Theology.*
Religion: *Eastern Churches*

MIHAILOVICH, VASA D. Professor of Slavic Languages and Literatures, University of North Carolina, Chapel Hill.
Literature: *Yugoslavian*

MILES, PETER W. Chairman, Department of Entomology, University of Adelaide, Australia.
Life Sciences: *Entomology*

MILLIKIN, SANDRA. Architectural Historian.
Architecture; Art and Art Exhibitions (*in part*); Museums (*in part*)

MITCHELL, K. K. Lecturer, Department of Physical Education, University of Leeds, England. Hon. General Secretary, English Basket Ball Association.
Basketball (*in part*)

MODEAN, ERIK W. Director, News Bureau, Lutheran Council in the U.S.A., New York City.
Religion: *Lutheran Churches*

MODIANO, MARIO. Athens Correspondent, *The Times,* London.
Greece

MOERS, ELLEN. University Professor, Department of English, University of Connecticut. Author of *Literary Women.*
Literature: *Special Report*

MONACO, ALBERT M., JR. Executive Director, United States Volleyball Association, San Francisco, Calif.
Court Games: *Volleyball*

MORGAN, HAZEL. Production Assistant (Sleevenotes and Covers), E.M.I. Records Ltd., London.
Music: *Popular*

MORRISON, DONALD M. Staff Writer, *Time* magazine.
Publishing: *Newspapers* (*in part*)

MORTIMER, MOLLY. Commonwealth Correspondent, *The Spectator,* London. Author of *Trusteeship in Practice; Kenya.*
Botswana; Burundi; Commonwealth of Nations; Dependent States (*in part*); Equatorial Guinea; Gambia, The; Ghana; Lesotho; Liberia; Maldives; Mauritius; Nigeria; Rwanda; Seychelles; Sierra Leone; Swaziland

MOSS, ROBERT V. (d. 1976). President, United Church of Christ, New York City. Author of *The Life of Paul; We Believe; As Paul Sees Christ.*
Religion: *United Church of Christ*

MOTTERSHEAD, G. S. Director-Secretary, Chester Zoo, Chester, England.
Zoos and Botanical Gardens (*in part*)

MULLINS, STEPHANIE. Historian, London.
Biography (*in part*)

NATOLI, SALVATORE J. Educational Affairs Director, Association of American Geographers. Co-author of *Dictionary of Basic Geography; Experiences in Inquiry.*
Geography

NAYLOR, ERNEST. Professor of Marine Biology, University of Liverpool; Director, Marine Biological Laboratory, Port Erin, Isle of Man. Author of *British Marine Isopods.*
Life Sciences: *Marine Biology*

NEILL, JOHN. Chief Chemical Engineer, Submerged Combustion Ltd. Author of Climbers' Club Guides; *Cwm Silyn and Tremadoc, Snowdon South;* Alpine Club Guide: *Selected Climbs in the Pennine Alps.*
Mountaineering

NELSON, BERT D. Editor and Publisher, *Track and Field News.* Author of *Little Red Book; The Decathlon Book; Olympic Track and Field.*
Track and Field Sports (*in part*)

NEMOIANU, VIRGIL P. Literary Critic; Professor of Literature, University of Bucharest, Romania. Author of several volumes on English, German, and Romanian literature.
Literature: *Romanian*

NETSCHERT, BRUCE C. Vice-President, National Economic Research Associates, Inc., Washington, D.C. Author of *The Future Supply of Oil and Gas.* Co-author of *Energy in the American Economy: 1850–1975.*
Energy: *World Summary*

NEUSNER, JACOB. Professor of Religious Studies and The Ungerleider Distinguished Scholar of Judaic Studies, Brown University, Providence, R.I. Author of *Invitation to the Talmud; A History of the Mishnaic Law of Purities.*
Religion: *Judaism*

NOEL, H. S. Free-lance Journalist; formerly Managing Editor, *World Fishing,* London.
Fisheries

NORMAN, GERALDINE. Saleroom Correspondent, *The Times,* London. Author of *The Sale of Works of Art.*
Art Sales

NOVALES, RONALD R. Professor of Biological Sciences, Northwestern University, Evanston, Ill. Contributor to *Handbook of Physiology; Comparative Animal Physiology.*
Life Sciences: *Zoology Overview*

NOVICK, JULIUS. Associate Professor of Literature, State University of New York at Purchase; Theater Critic, *The Village Voice* and *The Humanist.* Author of *Beyond Broadway: The Quest for Permanent Theatres.*
Theatre (*in part*)

NOVOSTI. Novosti Press Agency, Moscow.
Literature: *Russian* (*in part*)

OBOLENSKY, PRINCE ALEXIS. President, World Backgammon Club, Inc. Co-author of *Backgammon: The Action Game.*
Board Games: *Backgammon*

O'LEARY, JEREMIAH A., JR. Diplomatic Correspondent, *Washington Star.* Author of *Dominican Action—1965; Panama: Canal Issues and Treaty Talks—1967.*
Biography (*in part*); Chile

OSBORNE, KEITH. Editor, *Rowing,* 1961–63; Hon. Editor, *British Rowing Almanack,* 1961– . Author of *Boat Racing in Britain, 1715–1975.*
Rowing

OSTERBIND, CARTER C. Director, Bureau of Economic and Business Research, University of Florida. Editor of *Income in Retirement; Migration, Mobility, and Aging.*
Industrial Review: *Building and Construction*

PAGE, SHEILA A. B. Research Officer, National Institute of Economic and Social Research, London.
Economy, World (*in part*)

PALMER, S. B. Lecturer, Department of Applied Physics, University of Hull, England.
Physics

PALS, CLARENCE H. Former Executive Vice-President, U.S. National Association of Federal Veterinarians; former Director, Federal Meat Inspection Service, U.S. Department of Agriculture.
Veterinary Science

PARKER, SANDY. Fur and Ready-to-Wear News Editor, *Women's Wear Daily.*
Industrial Review: *Furs*

PARNELL, COLIN. Editor, *Wine and Spirit,* London. Publisher, *Decanter Magazine,* London.
Industrial Review: *Alcoholic Beverages* (*in part*)

PATTERSON, SHEILA. Research Associate, Department of Anthropology, University College, London. Author of *Colour and Culture in South Africa; Dark Strangers; Immigrants in Industry.* Co-editor of *Studies in African Social Anthropology.*
Bahamas, The; Barbados; Dependent States (*in part*); Grenada; Guyana; Jamaica; Migration, International; Race Relations (*in part*); Trinidad and Tobago.

PAUL, CHARLES ROBERT, JR. Staff Member, U.S. Olympic Committee, New York City; Senior Editor, *The Olympian.* Author of *The Olympic Games, 1968.*
Gymnastics and Weight Lifting

PAUL, OGLESBY. J. Roscoe Miller Professor of Medicine, Northwestern University Medical School, Chicago.
Health and Disease: *Heart Disease and High Blood Pressure*

PEARCE, JOAN. Research Officer, Economics Department, Lloyds Bank International Ltd., London. Editor of *Latin America: A Broader World Role.*
Colombia

PENFOLD, ROBIN C. Free-lance Writer specializing in industrial topics. Author of *A Journalist's Guide to Plastics.*
Industrial Review: *Plastics*

PERTILE, LINO. Lecturer in Italian, University of Sussex, England.
Literature: *Italian*

PETHERICK, KARIN. Crown Princess Louise Lecturer in Swedish, University College, London.
Literature: *Swedish*

PETTIGREW, THOMAS FRASER. Professor of Social Psychology and Sociology, Harvard University. Author of *Racially Separate or Together?; Racial Discrimination in the United States.*
Race Relations (*in part*)

PFEFFER, IRVING. Professor of Insurance and Finance, Virginia Polytechnic Institute and State University. Author of *Insurance and Economic Theory; The Financing of Small Business; Perspectives on Insurance.*
Stock Exchanges (*in part*)

PICK, OTTO. Professor of International Relations, University of Surrey, Guildford, England. Co-author of *Collective Security.*
Union of Soviet Socialist Republics

PIERCE, FRANCIS S. Editor, *Encyclopædia Britannica,* Yearbooks.
Economics

PINDER, JOHN. Director, PEP (Political and Economic Planning), London. Author of *Britain and the Common Market.* Co-author of *Europe After de Gaulle; The Economies of Europe.*
European Unity

PLOTKIN, FREDERICK S. Professor of English Literature and Chairman, Division of Humanities, Stern College, Yeshiva University, New York. Author of *Milton's Inward Jerusalem; Faith and Reason; Judaism and Tragic Theology.*
Literature: *United States*

PRASAD, H. Y. SHARADA. Information Adviser, Prime Minister's Secretariat, New Delhi, India.
India

PREIL, GABRIEL. Free-lance Writer; Hebrew and Yiddish Poet. Author of *Israeli Poetry in Peace and War; Ner Mul Kokhavim* ("Candle Against the Stars"); *Lieder* ("Poems"); *Haesh Vehadmama* ("The Fire and the Silence"); *Mitoch Zeman Venof* ("Of Time and Place"); *Shirim Mishnai Hakezavot* ("Poems from Both Ends").
Literature: *Hebrew*

PRICE, FREDERICK C. World News Correspondent for the chemical and oil industries, McGraw-Hill. Formerly Managing Editor, *Chemical Engineering.* Editor of McGraw-Hill's *1972 Report on Business & the Environment.*
Chemistry: *Applied*

PROSSNITZ, ERNEST PAUL. President, Safaris International, division of Special Tours & Travel Inc. Contributor to books on safaris.
Hunting and Fishing: *Safaris*

RANGER, ROBIN J. Associate Professor, Department of Political Science, St. Francis Xavier University, Antigonish, Nova Scotia. Author of *Arms and Politics.*
Defense

RAY, G. F. Senior Research Fellow, National Institute of Economic and Social Research, London; Visiting Professor, University of Surrey, Guildford, England.
Industrial Review: *Introduction*

RECKERT, STEPHEN. Camoens Professor of Portuguese, King's College, University of London. Author of *Do cancioneiro de amigo; Gil Vicente: espíritu y letra.*
Literature: *Portuguese* (*in part*)

REIBSTEIN, JOAN NATALIE. Associate Editor, Wesleyan University Press, Middletown, Conn. Former Staff Writer, *Encyclopædia Britannica.*
Biography (*in part*)

REICHELDERFER, F. W. Consultant on Atmospheric Sciences; Retired Director, Weather Bureau, U.S. Department of Commerce, Washington, D.C.
Earth Sciences: *Meteorology*

REID, J. H. Senior Lecturer in German, University of Nottingham, England. Author of *Heinrich Böll: Withdrawal and Re-emergence.* Co-author of *Critical Strategies: German Fiction in the 20th Century.*
Literature: *German*

REYNOLDS, ARTHUR GUY. Formerly Registrar and Professor of Church History, Emmanuel College, Toronto.
Religion: *United Church of Canada*

ROBINSON, DAVID. Film Critic, *The Times,* London. Author of *Buster Keaton; Hollywood in the Twenties; The Great Funnies—A History of Screen Comedy; A History of World Cinema.*
Biography (*in part*); Motion Pictures (*in part*)

ROONEY, WILLIAM R. Managing Editor, *Outdoor Life* magazine. Contributing Editor to *Complete Outdoors Encyclopedia; Guns.*
Hunting and Fishing: *Game Shooting* (*in part*)

ROSEVEARE, J. C. A. Partner, Freeman Fox & Partners, London.
Engineering Projects: *Dams*

RUDNICK, DAVID. Research Fellow, Royal Institute of International Affairs, London.
Spain: *Special Report*

RUTFORD, ROBERT H. Director, Division of Polar Programs, U.S. National Science Foundation.
Antarctica

SAEKI, SHOICHI. Professor, College of General Education, University of Tokyo. Author of *In Search of Japanese Ego.*
Literature: *Japanese*

SAINT-AMOUR, ROBERT. Professor, Department of Literary Studies, University of Quebec at Montreal.
Literature: *French* (*in part*)

SAMBUELLI, LUIGI. President, International Bocce Federation, Turin, Italy.
Bowling: *Boccie*

SANDERS, IVAN. Associate Professor of English, Suffolk County (N.Y.) Community College.
Literature: *Hungarian*

SANDON, HAROLD. Former Professor of Zoology, University of Khartoum, Sudan. Author of *The Protozoan Fauna of the Soil; The Food of Protozoa; An Illustrated Guide to the Fresh-Water Fishes of the Sudan; Essays on Protozoology.*
Life Sciences: *Introduction*

SARAHETE, YRJÖ. Secretary, Fédération Internationale des Quilleurs, Helsinki, Fin.
Bowling: *Tenpin Bowling* (*in part*)

SAWER, GEOFFREY. Professor Emeritus of the Faculty of Law, Australian National University. Author of *Law in Society; Modern Federalism.*
Australia: *Special Report*

SCHOENFIELD, ALBERT. Publisher, *Swimming World.* Contributor to *The Technique of Water Polo; The History of Swimming; Competitive Swimming as I See It.*
Swimming

SCHÖPFLIN, GEORGE. Lecturer in East European Political Institutions, London School of Economics and School of Slavonic and East European Studies, University of London.
Czechoslovakia

SCHULIAN, JOHN. Sportswriter, *Washington* (D.C.) *Post.*
Basketball (*in part*)

SCHULMAN, ELIAS. Associate Professor, Queens College, City University of New York; Professor, Graduate School, Jewish Teachers Seminary. Author of *Israel Tsinberg, His Life and Works; Young Wilno; Soviet-Yiddish Literature.* Co-editor of *A Biographical Dictionary of Yiddish Literature* (vol. vii–ix).
Literature: *Yiddish*

SEARS, ROBERT N. Associate Technical Editor, *The American Rifleman.*
Target Sports: *Shooting*

SERGEANT, HOWARD. Lecturer and Writer. Editor of *Outposts,* Walton-on-Thames, England. Author of *The Cumberland Wordsworth; Tradition in the Making of Modern Poetry.*
Literature: *United Kingdom* (*in part*)

SHACKLEFORD, PETER. Director, International Tourism Consultants.
Industrial Review: *Tourism*

SHARPE, MITCHELL R. Science Writer; Historian, Alabama Space and Rocket Center, Huntsville. Author of *Living in Space: The Environment of the Astronaut; Yuri Gagarin, First Man in Space; "It Is I, Seagull": Valentina Tereshkova, First Woman in Space.* Co-author of *Applied Astronautics; Basic Astronautics.*
Space Exploration

SHAW, T. R. Commander, Royal Navy. Member, British Cave Research Association.
Speleology

SHENK, CLAYTON B. Executive Secretary, U.S. National Archery Association.
Target Sports: *Archery*

SIMPSON, NOEL. Managing Director, Sydney Bloodstock Proprietary Ltd., Sydney, Australia.
Equestrian Sports: *Harness Racing*

SMEDLEY, GLENN B. Member of Board of Governors, American Numismatic Association.
Philately and Numismatics (*in part*)

SMITH, NICOLA. Research Assistant, *Africa Contemporary Record.*
Biography (*in part*)

SMITH, R. W. Dean, Graduate School, University of the Pacific, Stockton, Calif. Editor of *Venture of Islam* by M. G. S. Hodgson.
Religion: *Islam*

SMOGORZEWSKI, K. M. Writer on contemporary history. Founder and Editor, *Free Europe,* London. Author of *The United States and Great Britain; Poland's Access to the Sea.*
Albania; Andorra; Biography (*in part*); Bulgaria; Economy, World (*in part*); Hungary; Liechtenstein; Luxembourg; Monaco; Mongolia; Poland; Political Parties; Romania; San Marino

SNIDER, ARTHUR J. Science Editor, *Chicago Daily News.* Author of *Learning How to Live with Heart Trouble; Learning How to Live with Nervous Tension.*
Health and Disease: *General Overview* (*in part*); *Medical-Social Policy* (*in part*)

SPELMAN, ROBERT A. Administrative Vice-President, National Association of Furniture Manufacturers, Washington, D.C.
Industrial Review: *Furniture* (*in part*)

STACKS, JOHN F. Correspondent, *Time* magazine, Washington, D.C. Author of *Stripping: The Surface Mining of America.*
Biography (*in part*)

STAERK, MELANIE. Member, Swiss National Commission for UNESCO (Information).
Switzerland

STEEN, LYNN ARTHUR. Professor of Mathematics, St. Olaf College, Northfield, Minn. Editor, *Mathematics Magazine.* Author of *Counterexamples in Topology.*
Mathematics

STEPHENS, WILSON. Editor, *The Field,* London. Editor of *The Field Bedside Book* series; Co-editor of *In Praise of Hunting; Nymphs & the Trout.*
Hunting and Fishing: *Game Shooting* (*in part*); *Fox Hunting; Angling* (*in part*)

STERN, IRWIN. Assistant Professor of Portuguese and Spanish, City College of New York, and Ph.D. Program in Comparative Literature, City University of New York. Author of *Júlio Dinis e o romance português (1860–1870).*
Literature: *Portuguese* (*in part*)

STEVENSON, TOM. Garden Columnist, *Baltimore News American; Washington Post;* Washington Post-Los Angeles Times News Service. Author of *Pruning Guide for Trees, Shrubs and Vines; Lawn Guide; Gardening for the Beginner.*
Gardening (*in part*)

STOKES, J. BUROUGHS. Manager, Committees on Publication, The First Church of Christ, Scientist, Boston.
Religion: *Church of Christ, Scientist*

STØVERUD, TORBJØRN. W. P. Ker Senior Lecturer in Norwegian, University College, London.
Literature: *Norwegian*

STRAUSS, MICHAEL. Sports Reporter, Ski Editor, and Horse Racing Feature Writer, *New York Times.* Author of *The New York Times Ski Guide to the United States.*
Combat Sports: *Fencing*

SWEETINBURGH, THELMA. Paris Fashion Correspondent for *International Textiles* (Amsterdam) and the British Wool Textile Industry.
Fashion and Dress (*in part*)

SWIFT, RICHARD N. Professor of Politics, New York University, New York City. Author of *International Law: Current and Classic; World Affairs and the College Curriculum.*
United Nations

SYNAN, VINSON. General Secretary, Pentecostal Holiness Church; Chairman, History Department, Oklahoma City Southwestern College. Author of *The Holiness-Pentecostal Movement; The Old Time Power.*
Religion: *Pentecostal Churches*

TAISHOFF, SOL J. Chairman and Editor, *Broadcasting,* Washington, D.C.
Television and Radio (*in part*)

TALLAN, NORMAN N. Acting Chief, Processing and High Temperature Materials Branch, Air Force Materials Laboratory, Wright-Patterson Air Force Base, Dayton, Ohio. Editor of *Electrical Properties, Ceramics and Glass.*
Materials Sciences: *Ceramics*

TATTERSALL, ARTHUR. Textile Trade Statistician, Manchester, England.
Industrial Review: *Textiles* (*in part*)

TAUBERT, SIGFRED. Chairman, International Book Committee, UNESCO; formerly Director, Frankfurt Book Fair.
Publishing: *Books* (*in part*)

TERRY, WALTER, JR. Dance Critic and Dance Editor, *Saturday Review* magazine, New York. Author of *The Dance in America; The Ballet Companion; Miss Ruth: The "More Living Life" of Ruth St. Denis.*
Dance (*in part*); Dance: *Special Report*

THAINE, MARINA. Editor, *Tobacco,* London.
Industrial Review: *Tobacco*

THOMAS, HARFORD. Retired City and Financial Editor, *The Guardian,* London.
Biography *(in part)*; Environment: *Special Report*; United Kingdom

THOMPSON, ANTHONY. European Linguist Research Fellow, CLW, Aberystwyth, Wales. General Secretary, International Federation of Library Associations, 1962–70. Author of *Vocabularium Bibliothecarii; Library Buildings of Britain and Europe.*
Libraries

TINGAY, LANCE. Lawn Tennis Correspondent, the *Daily Telegraph,* London.
Tennis

TRIGG, ROBERT H. Senior Economic Adviser and Manager, Institutional Research, New York Stock Exchange.
Stock Exchanges *(in part)*

TRILLING, OSSIA. Vice-President, International Association of Theatre Critics. Co-editor and contributor, *International Theatre.* Contributor, BBC, the *Financial Times,* London.
Biography *(in part)*; Theatre *(in part)*

TRUSSELL, TAIT. Administrative Vice-President, American Forest Institute.
Industrial Review: *Wood Products*

TSUJIMOTO, ICHIRO. Public Relations Officer, Nippon Hoso Kyokai (Japan Broadcasting Corp.), Tokyo.
Television and Radio *(in part)*

TURKEVICH, JOHN. Eugene Higgins Professor of Chemistry, Department of Chemistry, Princeton University. Author of *Chemistry in the Soviet Union; Soviet Men of Science.*
Chemistry: *Physical and Inorganic*

TYPE, MICHAEL. Head of Permanent Secretariat, European Broadcasting Union, Geneva.
Television and Radio *(in part)*

UNHCR. The Office of the United Nations High Commissioner for Refugees, Geneva.
Refugees

UNNY, GOVINDAN. Agence France-Presse Special Correspondent for India, Nepal, and Sri Lanka.
Bangladesh; Bhutan; Biography *(in part)*; Burma; Dependent States *(in part)*; Nepal; Sri Lanka

VALCKE, HENRY MAURICE. Secretary General, European Furniture Industries Federation, Brussels.
Industrial Review: *Furniture (in part)*

van den HOVEN, ISOLA. Writer on Consumer Affairs, The Hague, Neth.
Consumerism *(in part)*

van PRAAG, JACK H. Chairman, National Badminton News Committee, American Badminton Association, Pasadena, Calif.
Racket Games: *Badminton*

VERDI, ROBERT WILLIAM. Sportswriter, *Chicago Tribune.*
Baseball *(in part)*

VIANSSON-PONTÉ, PIERRE. Editorial Adviser and Leader Writer, *Le Monde,* Paris. Author of *Les Gaullistes; The King and His Court; Les Politiques; Histoire de la République Gaullienne.*
Biography *(in part)*

VINT, ARTHUR KINGSLEY. Honorary General Secretary, International Table Tennis Federation, Sussex, England.
Table Tennis

WADLEY, J. B. Writer and Broadcaster on cycling. Author of *Tour de France 1970, 1971,* and *1973; Old Roads and New; Cycling* (Leisureguides series).
Cycling

WARD-THOMAS, P. A. Golf Correspondent, *The Guardian,* London.
Golf

WAY, DIANE LOIS. Researcher, University of Toronto, Ont., Sesquicentennial History Project.
Biography *(in part)*

WEBB, GORDON A. Editor, *Toys International,* London.
Games and Toys

WEBB, HENRY, JR. Retired from U.S. Foreign Service.
El Salvador; Honduras; Nicaragua

WEBB, W. L. Literary Editor, *The Guardian,* London and Manchester.
Literature: *United Kingdom (in part); Russian (in part)*

WEBER, GEORGE. Associate Director, Council for Basic Education; Editor, *Council for Basic Education Bulletin.* Co-author of *Consumer's Guide to Educational Innovations.*
Education: *Special Report*

WEBSTER, PETER L. Associate Professor, Department of Botany, University of Massachusetts, Amherst.
Life Sciences: *Botany*

WEEDEN, CYRIL. Assistant Director, Glass Manufacturers' Federation, London.
Industrial Review: *Glass*

WEIGEL, J. TIMOTHY. Sportscaster, NBC Television. Author of *The Buckeyes: Ohio State Football.*
Biography *(in part)*

WETTSTEIN, KURT ERICH. Secretary, Swiss Booksellers and Publishers Association, Zurich.
Publishing: *Books (in part)*

WHITTEN, NORMAN E., JR. Professor of Anthropology, University of Illinois, Urbana. Author of *Black Frontiersmen: A South American Case; Sacha Runa: Ethnicity and Adaptation of Ecuadorian Jungle Quichua.*
Anthropology

WIJNGAARD, BARBARA. Research Officer, Economics Department, Lloyds Bank International Ltd., London.
Ecuador; Mexico

WILLIAMS, BRIAN. Free-lance Writer, London.
Biography *(in part)*; Television and Radio *(in part)*

WILLIAMS, DAVID L. Associate Professor of Government, Ohio University.
Communist Movement

WILLIAMS, L. F. RUSHBROOK. Fellow of All Souls College, Oxford University, 1914–21; Professor of Modern Indian History, Allahabad, India, 1914–19. Honorary Adviser, *Keesing's Contemporary Archives.* Author of *The State of Pakistan; Kutch in History and Legend.* Editor of *Handbook to India, Pakistan, Bangladesh, Nepal, and Sri Lanka; Sufi Studies East and West; Pakistan Under Challenge.*
Afghanistan; Iran; Pakistan

WILLIAMS, PETER. Editor, *Dance and Dancers,* London. Chairman, Arts Council, Great Britain's Dance Theatre Committee; Chairman, British Council's Drama Advisory Committee.
Biography *(in part)*; Dance *(in part)*

WILLIAMSON, TREVOR. Chief Sports Subeditor, the *Daily Telegraph,* London.
Football: *Association Football*

WILSON, MICHAEL. Technical Editor, *Flight International,* London.
Industrial Review: *Aerospace*

WISWELL, TOM. Author; Freestyle World Checkers Champion, 1951–1976. Author of *The Science of Checkers; Complete Guide to Checkers.*
Board Games: *Checkers*

WITTE, RANDALL E. News Bureau Director, Professional Rodeo Cowboys Association. Author of annual rodeo reference book.
Arena Sports: *Rodeo*

WOOD, CHRISTINA MARGARET. Free-lance Sportswriter.
Racket Games: *Rackets; Real Tennis*

WOOD, KENNETH H. Editor, *The Advent Review and Sabbath Herald.* Author of *Meditations for Moderns; Relevant Religions.* Co-author of *His Initials Were F. D. N.*
Religion: *Seventh-day Adventist Church*

WOOLLER, MICHAEL. Economic Research Officer, Lloyds Bank International Ltd., London.
Biography *(in part)*; Portugal; Venezuela

WOOLLEY, DAVID. Editor, *Airports International,* London.
Transportation *(in part)*

WORSNOP, RICHARD L. Associate Editor, Editorial Research Reports, Washington, D.C.
United States

WRIGHT, ALMON R. Retired Senior Historian, U.S. Department of State.
Panama

WYLLIE, PETER JOHN. Professor of Petrology and Geochemistry, University of Chicago. Author of *The Dynamic Earth; The Way the Earth Works.*
Earth Sciences: *Geology and Geochemistry*

YAGHI, ABDUL RAHMAN. Professor of Modern Arabic Literature, Department of Arabic, University of Jordan. Author of works on modern Arabic literature.
Literature: *Arabic*

YOUNG, M. NORVEL. Chancellor, Pepperdine University, Malibu, Calif. Editor of *Twentieth Century Christian; Power for Today.* Author of *Preachers of Today; History of Colleges Connected with Churches of Christ.*
Religion: *Churches of Christ*

YOUNG, SUSAN. News Editor, *Church Times,* London.
Religion: *Anglican Communion*

YUFIT, ROBERT I. Coordinator, Suicide Assessment Team, Illinois Masonic Medical Center; Project Director, Drug Abuse Program, Department of Psychiatry, University of Chicago.
Health and Disease: *Mental Health (in part)*

Index

The black type entries are article headings in the *Book of the Year*. These black type article entries do not show page notations because they are to be found in their alphabetical position in the body of the book. They show the dates of the issues of the *Book of the Year* in which the articles appear. For example "Archaeology 77, 76, 75" indicates that the article "Archaeology" is to be found in the 1977, 1976, and 1975 ***Book of the Year.***

The light type headings that are indented under black type article headings refer to material elsewhere in the text related to the subject under which they are listed. The light type headings that are not indented refer to information in the text not given a special article. Biographies and obituaries are listed as cross references to the sections "Biography" and "Obituaries" within the article "*People of the Year.*" References to illustrations are preceded by the abbreviation "il."

All headings, whether consisting of a single word or more, are treated for the purpose of alphabetization as single complete headings. Names beginning with "Mc" and "Mac" are alphabetized as "Mac"; "St." is treated as "Saint." All references below show the exact quarter of the page by means of the letters *a, b, c* and *d,* signifying, respectively, the upper and lower halves of the first column and the upper and lower halves of the second column. Exceptions to this rule are tables, illustrations, and references from the articles "*Energy*" and "*Industrial Review.*"

A

D

G

H

I

P

V

W

Z